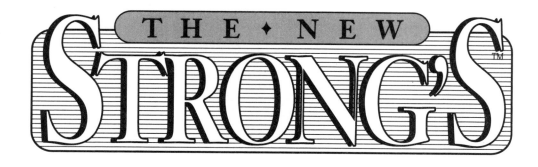

THE · NEW
STRONG'S
C·O·N·C·I·S·E
DICTIONARY
OF
BIBLE WORDS

James Strong, LL.D., S.T.D.

THOMAS NELSON PUBLISHERS
Nashville

Published in Nashville, Tennessee, by Thomas Nelson, Inc.

The publisher wishes to acknowledge the editorial and composition services of John R. Kohlenberger III and Multnomah Graphics.

Library of Congress Cataloging-in-Publication Data

Strong, James, 1822–1894.
    The new Strong's concise dictionary of Bible words / James Strong.
      p. cm.
    ISBN 0-7852-4537-5
    1. Bible—Concordances, English. 2. Hebrew language—Dictionaries—English. 3. Aramaic language—Dictionaries—English. 4. Greek language, Biblical—Dictionaries—English. 5. Bible. O.T.—Dictionaries—Hebrew. 6. Bible. O.T.—Dictionaries—Aramaic. 7. Bible, N.T.—Dictionaries—Greek. I. Strong, James, 1822–1894. New exhaustive concordance of the Bible. II. Strong, James, 1822–1894. New Strong's complete dictionary of Bible words. III. Strong, James, 1822–1894. New Strong's Hebrew and Aramaic dictionary. IV. Strong, James, 1822–1894. New Strong's Greek dictionary. V. Title.
BS425.S85   1997
220.5′2033—dc20   96–36197
                                                 CIP

1519+1096 ĕis (1), to or into
1519+5318 ĕis (2), to or into
1632 ĕkchĕō (1), to pour forth; to bestow
1831 ĕxĕrchōmai (4), to issue; to leave
4496 rhiptō (1), to fling, toss; to lay out
4650 skŏrpizō (2), to dissipate, be liberal

ABSALOM
53 'Ăbîyshâlôwm (102), friendly

ABSALOM'S
53 'Ăbîyshâlôwm (5), friendly

ABSENCE
666 apŏusia (1), being away, absence
817 atĕr (1), apart from, without

ABSENT
5641 çâthar (1), to hide by covering
548 apĕimi (7), to be away, be absent
553 apĕkdĕchŏmai (3), to expect fully, await

ABSTAIN
567 apĕchŏmai (6), to hold oneself off

ABSTINENCE
776 asitia (1), state of food fasting

ABUNDANCE
369+4557 'ayin (1), there is no, none
1995 hâmôwn (3), noise, tumult; many, crowd
2123 zîyz (1), fulness of the breast
3502 yithrâh (1), wealth, abundance
4342 makbîyr (1), plenty
6109 'otsmâh (1), numerousness
6283 'ăthereth (1), copiousness
7227 rab (1), great
7230 rôb (35), abundance
7235 râbâh (2), to increase
7647 sâbâ' (1), copiousness
7962 shalvâh (1), security, ease
8228 shepha' (1), abundance
8229 shiph'âh (3), copiousness
8317 shârats (1), to swarm, or abound
100 hadrŏtēs (1), liberality
1411 dunamis (1), force, power, miracle
4050 pĕrissĕia (2), superabundance
4051 pĕrissĕuma (4), superabundance
4052 pĕrissĕuō (5), to superabound
5236 hupĕrbŏlē (1), supereminence

ABUNDANT
1419 gâdôwl (1), great
7227 rab (2), great
4052 pĕrissĕuō (2), to superabound
4055 pĕrissŏtĕrŏs (3), more superabundant
4056 pĕrissŏtĕrōs (2), more superabundantly
4121 plĕŏnazō (1), o superabound
4183 pŏlus (1), much
5250 hupĕrplĕŏnazō (1), to superabound

ABUNDANTLY
1288 bârak (1), to bless
3381 yârad (1), to descend
5042 nâba' (1), to gush forth; to utter
6524 pârach (1), to break forth; to flourish
7227 rab (2), great
7230 rôb (4), abundance
7235 râbâh (1), to increase
7301 râvâh (2), to slake thirst or appetites
7937 shâkar (1), to become tipsy, to satiate
8317 shârats (6), to swarm, or abound
1519+4050 ĕis (1), to or into
1537+4053 ĕk (1), out of
4053 pĕrissŏs (1), superabundant
4054 pĕrissŏtĕrŏn (2), superabundant way
4056 pĕrissŏtĕrōs (4), more superabundantly
4146 plŏusiōs (2), copiously, abundantly

ABUSE
5953 'âlal (2), to glean; to overdo
2710 katachraŏmai (1), to overuse

ABUSED
5953 'âlal (1), to glean; to overdo

ABUSERS
733 arsĕnŏkŏitēs (1), sodomite

ABUSING
2710 katachraŏmai (1), to overuse

ACCAD
390 'Akkad (1), Accad

ACCEPT
1878 dâshên (1), to be fat, thrive; to satisfy
3947 lâqach (1), to take
5375 nâsâ' (8), to lift up
7306 rûwach (1), to smell or perceive
7521 râtsâh (13), to be pleased with; to satisfy
588 apŏdĕchŏmai (1), welcome persons

ACCEPTABLE
977 bâchar (1), select, chose, prefer
2656 chêphets (1), pleasure; desire
7522 râtsôwn (9), delight

8232 sh°phar (Ch.) (1), to be beautiful
587 apŏdĕktŏs (2), agreeable, pleasant
1184 dĕktŏs (2), approved, favorable
2101 ĕuarĕstŏs (4), fully agreeable, pleasing
2144 ĕuprŏsdĕktŏs (2), approved, favorable
5285 hupŏpnĕō (1), to breathe gently

ACCEPTABLY
2102 ĕuarĕstōs (1), quite agreeably

ACCEPTANCE
7522 râtsôwn (1), delight

ACCEPTATION
594 apŏdŏchē (2), acceptance, approval

ACCEPTED
3190 yâtab (2), to be, make well
5307 nâphal (2), to fall
5375 nâsâ' (3), to lift up
7521 râtsâh (7), to be pleased with; to satisfy
7522 râtsôwn (4), delight
7613 s°'êth (1), elevation; swelling leprous scab
1184 dĕktŏs (3), approved, favorable
1209 dĕchŏmai (2), to receive, welcome
2101 ĕuarĕstŏs (1), fully agreeable, pleasing
2144 ĕuprŏsdĕktŏs (3), approved, favorable
5487 charitŏō (1), one highly favored

ACCEPTEST
2983 lambanō (1), to take, receive

ACCEPTETH
5375 nâsâ' (1), to lift up
7521 râtsâh (1), to be pleased with; to satisfy
2983 lambanō (1), to take, receive

ACCEPTING
4327 prŏsdĕchŏmai (1), to receive; to await for

ACCESS
4318 prŏsagōgē (3), admission, access

ACCHO
5910 'Akkôw (1), to hem in

ACCOMPANIED
2064+4862 ĕrchŏmai (1), to go or come
4311 prŏpĕmpō (1), to escort or aid in travel
4902 sunĕpŏmai (1), travel in company with
4905 sunĕrchŏmai (1), to go with

ACCOMPANY
2192 ĕchō (1), to have; hold; keep

ACCOMPANYING
5973 'îm (1), with

ACCOMPLISH
3615 kâlâh (5), to complete, prepare

4390 mâlê' (1), to fill
6213 'âsâh (2), to do or make
6381 pâlâ' (1), to be, make great, difficult
6965 qûwm (1), to rise
7521 râtsâh (1), to be pleased with; to satisfy
8552 tâmam (1), to complete, finish
4137 plērŏō (1), to fill, make complete

ACCOMPLISHED
1961 hâyâh (1), to exist, i.e. be or become
3615 kâlâh (7), to complete, prepare
4390 mâlê' (6), to fill
8552 tâmam (1), to complete, finish
1822 ĕxartizō (1), to finish out; to equip fully
2005 ĕpitĕlĕō (1), to terminate; to undergo
4130 plēthō (4), to fulfill, complete
5055 tĕlĕō (4), to end, i.e. complete, execute

ACCOMPLISHING
2005 ĕpitĕlĕō (1), to terminate; to undergo

ACCOMPLISHMENT
1604 ĕkplērōsis (1), completion, end

ACCORD
5599 çâphîyach (1), self-sown crop; freshet
6310 peh (1), mouth; opening
830 authairĕtŏs (1), self-chosen
844 autŏmatŏs (1), spontaneous, by itself
3661 hŏmŏthumadŏn (11), in togetherness
4861 sumpsuchŏs (1), united in spirit

ACCORDING
413 'êl (2), to, toward
834 'âsher (1), because, in order that
1767 day (1), enough, sufficient
3605 kôl (1), all, any
3644 k°môw (2), like, as
3651 kên (1), just; right, correct
4481 min (Ch.) (1), from or out of
5921 'al (39), above, over, upon, or against
6310 peh (21), mouth; opening
6903 q°bêl (Ch.) (1), on account of, so as, since
7272 regel (1), foot; step
2526 kathŏ (2), precisely as, in proportion as
2530 kathŏti (1), as far or inasmuch as
2531 kathōs (5), just or inasmuch as, that
2596 kata (109), down; according to
4314 prŏs (3), for; on, at; to, toward; against
5613 hōs (2), which, how

ACCORDINGLY
5922 'al (Ch.) (1), *above, over, upon,* or *against*

ACCOUNT
2803 châshab (1), to *think, regard;* to *value*
2808 cheshbôwn (1), *contrivance; plan*
4557 miçpâr (1), *number*
6030 'ânâh (1), to *respond, answer*
6486 pᵉquddâh (1), *visitation; punishment*
1677 ĕllŏgĕŏ (1), to *charge to one's account*
2233 hēgĕŏmai (1), to *deem,* i.e. *consider*
3049 lŏgizŏmai (1), to *credit;* to *think, regard*
3056 lŏgŏs (8), *word, matter, thing; Word*

ACCOUNTED
2803 châshab (5), to *think, regard;* to *value*
5608 çâphar (1), to *enumerate;* to *recount*
1380 dŏkĕŏ (2), to *think, regard, seem good*
2661 kataxiŏō (2), to *deem entirely deserving*
3049 lŏgizŏmai (2), to *credit;* to *think, regard*

ACCOUNTING
3049 lŏgizŏmai (1), to *credit;* to *think, regard*

ACCOUNTS
2941 ṭa'am (Ch.) (1), *sentence, command*

ACCURSED
2763 charam (1), to *devote to destruction*
2764 chêrem (13), *doomed object*
7043 qâlal (1), to *be easy, trifling, vile*
7045 qᵉlâlâh (1), *vilification*
331 anathĕma (4), *excommunicated*

ACCUSATION
7855 siṭnâh (1), *opposition*
156 aitia (3), *logical reason;* legal *crime*
2724 katēgŏria (3), legal criminal *charge*
2920 krisis (2), *decision; tribunal; justice*
4811 sukŏphantĕŏ (1), to *exact unlawfully, extort*

ACCUSE
3960 lâshan (1), to *calumniate, malign*
1908 ĕpērĕazō (1), to *insult, slander*
2722 katĕchŏ (11), to *hold down fast*
2723 katēgŏrĕō (2), to *bring a charge*
4811 sukŏphantĕŏ (1), to *exact unlawfully, extort*

ACCUSED
399+7170 'ăkal (Ch.) (2), to *eat*
1225 diaballō (1), to *malign by accusation*

1458 ĕgkalĕŏ (4), to *charge, criminate*
1722+2724 ĕn (1), *in; during; because of*
2722 katĕchŏ (4), to *hold down fast*
2723 katēgŏrĕō (2), to *bring a charge*

ACCUSER
2723 katēgŏrĕō (1), to *bring a charge*

ACCUSERS
1228 diabŏlŏs (2), *traducer,* i.e. *Satan*
2723 katēgŏrĕō (6), to *bring a charge*

ACCUSETH
2723 katēgŏrĕō (1), to *bring a charge*

ACCUSING
2722 katĕchŏ (1), to *hold down fast*

ACCUSTOMED
3928 limmûwd (1), *instructed* one

ACELDAMA
184 Akeldama (1), *field of blood*

ACHAIA
882 Achaïa (11), *Greece*

ACHAICUS
883 Achaïkŏs (1), *Achaïan*

ACHAN
5912 'Âkân (6), *troublesome*

ACHAR
5917 'Âkâr (1), *troublesome*

ACHAZ
881 Achaz (2), *possessor*

ACHBOR
5907 'Akbôwr (7), *Akbor*

ACHIM
885 Achĕim (2), cf. *Jehovah will raise*

ACHISH
397 'Âkîysh (21), *Akish*

ACHMETHA
307 'Achmᵉthâ' (1), *Ecbatana*

ACHOR
5911 'Âlôwr (5), *troubled*

ACHSA
5915 'Akçâh (1), *anklet*

ACHSAH
5915 'Akçâh (2), *anklet*
5919 'akshûwb (2), *asp,* coiling *serpent*

ACHSHAPH
407 'Akshâph (3), *fascination*

ACHZIB
392 'Akzîyb (4), *deceitful*

ACKNOWLEDGE
3045 yâda' (5), to *know*
5234 nâkar (6), to *acknowledge*
1921 ĕpiginōskō (4), to *acknowledge*

ACKNOWLEDGED
3045 yâda' (1), to *know*

5234 nâkar (1), to *acknowledge*
1922 ĕpignōsis (1), *acknowledgement*

ACKNOWLEDGEMENT
1922 ĕpignōsis (1), *acknowledgement*

ACKNOWLEDGING
1922 ĕpignōsis (3), *acknowledgement*

ACQUAINT
5532 çâkan (1), to *be familiar with*

ACQUAINTANCE
3045 yâda (6), to *know*
4378 makkâr (2), *acquaintance*
1110 gnōstŏs (2), *well-known*
2398 idiŏs (1), *private* or *separate*

ACQUAINTED
3045 yâda' (1), to *know*
5532 çâkan (1), to *be familiar with*

ACQUAINTING
5090 nâhag (1), to *drive forth;* to *lead*

ACQUIT
5352 nâqâh (2), to *be, make clean*

ACRE
4618 ma'ănâh (1), *furrow, plow path*

ACRES
6776 tsemed (1), *acre* (i.e. a day's plowing)

ACT
5556 çol'âm (1), *destructive locust* kind
6467 pô'al (1), *act* or *work, deed*
1888 ĕpautŏphōrŏᵢ (1), *in actual crime*

ACTIONS
5949 'ălîylâh (1), *opportunity, action*

ACTIVITY
2428 chayil (1), *wealth; virtue; valor; strength*

ACTS
1697 dâbâr (51), *word; matter; thing*
4640 Ma'say (4), *operative*
5949 'ălîylâh (1), *opportunity, action*
6467 pô'al (2), *act* or *work, deed*

ADADAH
5735 'Ăd'âdâh (1), *festival*

ADAH
5711 'Âdâh (8), *ornament*

ADAIAH
5718 'Ădâyâh (9), *Jehovah has adorned*

ADALIA
118 'Ădalyâ' (1), *Adalja*

ADAM
120 'âdâm (14), *human being; mankind*
121 'Âdâm (8), *Adam*

76 *Adam* (8), first *man*

ADAM'S
76 *Adam* (1), first *man*

ADAMAH
128 'Ădâmâh (1), *soil; land*

ADAMANT
8068 shâmîyr (2), *thorn;* (poss.) *diamond*

ADAMI
129 'Ădâmîy (1), *earthy*

ADAR
143 'Ădâr (8), (poss.) *fire; Adar*
144 'Ădâr (Ch.) (1), (poss.) *fire; Adar*
146 'Addâr (1), *ample*

ADBEEL
110 'Adbᵉ'êl (2), *chastised of God*

ADD
3254 yâçaph (22), to *add* or *augment*
5414 nâthan (2), to *give*
5595 çâphâh (3), to *accumulate;* to *remove*
2007 ĕpitithēmi (2), to *impose*
2018 ĕpiphĕrō (1), to *inflict, bring upon*
2023 ĕpichŏrēgĕō (1), to *fully supply*
4369 prŏstithēmi (2), to *lay beside, annex*

ADDAN
135 'Addân (1), *firm*

ADDAR
146 'Addâr (1), *ample*

ADDED
3254 yâçaph (4), to *add* or *augment*
3255 yᵉçaph (Ch.) (1), to *add* or *augment*
4323 prŏsanatithēmi (1), to *add;* to *impart*
4369 prŏstithēmi (9), to *lay beside, annex, repeat*

ADDER
6620 pethen (2), *asp*
6848 tsepha' (1), *viper*
8207 shᵉphîyphôn (1), *cerastes* or *adder*

ADDERS'
5919 'akshûwb (1), *asp,* coiling *serpent*

ADDETH
3254 yâçaph (3), to *add* or *augment*
1928 ĕpidiatassŏmai (1), to *supplement*

ADDI
78 Addi (1), *finery*

ADDICTED
5021 tassō (1), to *arrange*

ADDITION
3914 lôyâh (1), *wreath*

ADDITIONS
3914 lôyâh (2), *wreath*

ADDON
114 'Addôwn (1), *powerful*

ADER
5738 'Eder (1),
arrangement

ADIEL
5717 'Ădîy'êl (3),
ornament of God

ADIN
5720 'Âdîyn (4),
voluptuous

ADINA
5721 'Ădîynâ' (1),
effeminacy

ADINO
5722 'ădîynôw (1), his
spear

ADITHAIM
5723 'Ădîythayim (1),
double prey

ADJURE
7650 shâba' (2), to swear
1844 ĕxŏrkizō (1), to
charge under oath
3726 hŏrkizō (2), to
solemnly enjoin

ADJURED
422 'âlâh (1), imprecate,
utter a curse
7650 shâba' (1), to swear

ADLAI
5724 'Adlay (1), Adlai

ADMAH
126 'Admâh (5), earthy

ADMATHA
133 'Admâthâ' (1),
Admatha

ADMINISTERED
1247 diakŏnĕō (2), to act
as a deacon

ADMINISTRATION
1248 diakŏnia (1),
attendance, aid, service

ADMINISTRATIONS
1248 diakŏnia (1),
attendance, aid, service

ADMIRATION
2295 thauma (1),
wonder, marvel
2296 thaumazō (1), to
wonder; to admire

ADMIRED
2296 thaumazō (1), to
wonder; to admire

ADMONISH
3560 nŏuthĕtĕō (3), to
caution or reprove

ADMONISHED
2094 zâhar (2), to
enlighten
5749 'ûwd (1), to protest,
testify; to restore
3867 parainĕō (1), to
recommend or advise
5537 chrēmatizō (1), to
utter an oracle

ADMONISHING
3560 nŏuthĕtĕō (1), to
caution or reprove

ADMONITION
3559 nŏuthĕsia (3), mild
rebuke or warning

ADNA
5733 'Adnâ' (2), pleasure

ADNAH
5734 'Adnâh (2), pleasure

ADO
2350 thŏrubĕō (1), to
disturb; clamor

ADONI-BEZEK
137 'Ădônîy-Bezeq (3),
lord of Bezek

ADONI-ZEDEK
139 'Ădônîy-Tsedeq (2),
lord of justice

ADONIJAH
138 'Ădônîyâh (25),
worshipper of Jehovah

ADONIKAM
140 'Ădônîyqâm (3),
high, lofty

ADONIRAM
141 'Ădônîyrâm (2), lord
of height

ADOPTION
5206 huiŏthĕsia (5),
adoption

ADORAIM
115 'Ădôwrayim (1),
double mound

ADORAM
151 'Ădôrâm (2), Adoram

ADORN
2885 kŏsmĕō (2), to
decorate; to snuff

ADORNED
5710 'âdâh (1), to
remove; to bedeck
2885 kŏsmĕō (3), to
decorate; to snuff

ADORNETH
5710 'âdâh (1), to
remove; to bedeck

ADORNING
2889 kŏsmŏs (2), world

ADRAMMELECH
152 'Adrammelek (3),
splendor of (the) king

ADRAMYTTIUM
98 Adramuttēnŏs (1),
Adramyttene

ADRIA
99 Adrias (1), Adriatic
Sea

ADRIEL
5741 'Adrîy'êl (2), flock
of God

ADULLAM
5725 'Ădullâm (8),
Adullam

ADULLAMITE
5726 'Ădullâmîy (3),
Adullamite

ADULTERER
5003 nâ'aph (3), to
commit adultery

ADULTERERS
5003 nâ'aph (5), to
commit adultery
3432 mŏichŏs (4), male
paramour

ADULTERESS
802+376 'ishshâh (1),
woman, wife
5003 nâ'aph (2), to
commit adultery

3428 mŏichalis (2),
adulteress

ADULTERESSES
5003 nâ'aph (2), to
commit adultery
3428 mŏichalis (1),
adulteress

ADULTERIES
5004 nî'ûph (2), adultery
5005 na'ăphûwph (1),
adultery
3430 mŏichĕia (2),
adultery

ADULTEROUS
5003 nâ'aph (1), to
commit adultery
3428 mŏichalis (3),
adulteress

ADULTERY
5003 nâ'aph (17), to
commit adultery
3428 mŏichalis (1),
adulteress
3429 mŏichaō (6), to
commit adultery
3430 mŏichĕia (2),
adultery
3431 mŏichĕuō (14), to
commit adultery

ADUMMIM
131 'Ădummîym (2), red
spots

ADVANCED
1431 gâdal (1), to be
great, make great
5375 nâsâ' (2), to lift up
6213 'âsâh (1), to do or
make

ADVANTAGE
5532 çâkan (1), to be
serviceable to
4053 pĕrissŏs (1),
superabundant
4122 plĕŏnĕktĕō (1), to
be covetous
5622 ŏphĕlĕia (1), value,
advantage

ADVANTAGED
5623 ŏphĕlĕō (1), to
benefit, be of use

ADVANTAGETH
3786 ŏphĕlŏs (1),
accumulate or benefit

ADVENTURE
5254 nâçâh (1), to test,
attempt
1325 didōmi (1), to give

ADVENTURED
7993 shâlak (1), to throw
out, down or away

ADVERSARIES
6696 tsûwr (1), to cramp,
i.e. confine; to harass
6862 tsar (21), trouble;
opponent
6887 tsârar (2), to cramp
7378 rîyb (1), to hold a
controversy; to defend
7853 sâṭan (5), to attack
by accusation
7854 sâṭân (1), opponent
480 antikĕimai (4), be
adverse to
5227 hupĕnantiŏs (1),
opposed; opponent

ADVERSARY
376+7379 'îysh (1), man;
male; someone
1166+4941 bâ'al (1), to be
master; to marry
6862 tsar (6), trouble;
opponent
6869 tsârâh (1), trouble;
rival-wife
6887 tsârar (1), to cramp
7854 sâṭân (6), opponent
476 antidikŏs (5),
opponent
480 antikĕimai (1), be
adverse to

ADVERSITIES
6869 tsârâh (1), trouble;
rival-wife
7451 ra' (1), bad; evil

ADVERSITY
6761 tsela' (1), limping
6862 tsar (1), trouble;
opponent
6869 tsârâh (4), trouble;
rival-wife
7451 ra' (3), bad; evil
2558 kakŏuchĕō (1), to
maltreat; to torment

ADVERTISE
1540+241 gâlâh (1), to
denude; to reveal
3289 yâ'ats (1), to advise

ADVICE
1697 dâbâr (2), word;
matter; thing
2940 ṭa'am (1),
intelligence; mandate
3289 yâ'ats (2), to advise
5779 'ûwts (1), to consult
6098 'êtsâh (1), advice;
plan; prudence
8458 tachbûlâh (1),
guidance; plan
1106 gnōmē (1),
cognition, opinion

ADVISE
3045 yâda' (1), to know
3289 yâ'ats (1), to advise
7200 râ'âh (1), to see

ADVISED
3289 yâ'ats (1), to advise
1012+5087 bŏulē (1),
purpose, plan, decision

ADVISEMENT
6098 'êtsâh (1), advice;
plan; prudence

ADVOCATE
3875 paraklētŏs (1),
intercessor, consoler

AENEAS
132 Ainĕas (2), (poss.)
praise

AENON
137 Ainōn (1), springs

AFAR
4801 merchâq (3),
distant place; from afar
7350 râchôwq (29),
remote, far
7368 râchaq (1), to
recede; remove
3112 makran (2), at a
distance, far away
3113 makrŏthĕn (13),
from a distance or afar

3467 muŏpazō (1), to *see
indistinctly, be myopic*
4207 pŏrrhŏthĕn (2),
distantly, at a distance

AFFAIRS
1697 dâbâr (2), *word;
matter; thing*
5673 'ăbîydâh (Ch.) (2),
labor or business
2596 kata (1), *down;
according to*
4012 pĕri (2), *about;
around*
4230 pragmatĕia (1),
transaction

AFFECT
2206 zēlŏō (2), to *have
warmth* of feeling for

AFFECTED
2206 zēlŏō (1), to *have
warmth* of feeling for
2559 kakŏō (1), to *injure;
to oppress; to embitter*

AFFECTETH
5953 'âlal (1), to *glean;* to
overdo

AFFECTION
7521 râtsâh (1), to *be
pleased with; to satisfy*
794 astŏrgŏs (2),
hard-hearted
3806 pathŏs (1), *passion,
concupiscence*
4698 splagchnŏn (1),
intestine; affection, pity
5426 phrŏnĕō (1), to *be
mentally disposed*

AFFECTIONATELY
2442 himĕirŏmai (1), to
long for, desire

AFFECTIONED
5387 philŏstŏrgŏs (1),
lovingly devoted

AFFECTIONS
3804 pathēma (1),
passion; suffering
3806 pathŏs (1), *passion,
concupiscence*

AFFINITY
2859 châthan (3), to
become related

AFFIRM
1226 diabĕbaiŏŏmai (2),
to *confirm thoroughly*
5346 phēmi (1), to *speak
or say*

AFFIRMED
1340 diïschurizŏmai (2),
to *asseverate*
5335 phaskō (1), to
assert a claim

AFFLICT
3013 yâgâh (1), to *grieve;
to torment*
3513 kâbad (1), to *be
heavy, severe, dull*
3905 lâchats (1), to *press;
to distress*
6031 'ânâh (28), to *afflict,
be afflicted*
6887 tsârar (2), to *cramp*
7489 râ'a' (2), to *break to
pieces*

AFFLICTED
1790 dak (1), *injured,
oppressed*
3013 yâgâh (3), to *grieve;
to torment*
4523 mâç (1),
disconsolate
6031 'ânâh (21), to *afflict,
be afflicted*
6040 'ŏnîy (1),
depression, i.e. *misery*
6041 'ânîy (15), *depressed*
6862 tsar (1), *trouble;
opponent*
6887 tsârar (2), to *cramp*
7043 qâlal (1), to *be easy,
trifling, vile*
7489 râ'a' (3), to *break to
pieces*
2346 thlibō (3), to *crowd,
press, trouble*
2347 thlipsis (1),
pressure, trouble
2553 kakŏpathĕō (1), to
undergo hardship
5003 talaipōrĕō (1), to *be
wretched*

AFFLICTEST
6031 'ânâh (1), to *afflict,
be afflicted*

AFFLICTION
205 'âven (3), *trouble,
vanity, wickedness*
3905 lâchats (3), to *press;
to distress*
4157 mûw'âqâh (1),
pressure; distress
6039 'ênûwth (1),
affliction
6040 'ŏnîy (33),
depression, i.e. *misery*
6862 tsar (3), *trouble;
opponent*
6869 tsârâh (7), *trouble;
rival-wife*
6887 tsârar (1), to *cramp*
7451 ra' (5), *bad; evil*
7667 sheber (2), *fracture;
ruin*
2347 thlipsis (11),
pressure, trouble
2552 kakŏpathĕia (1),
hardship, suffering
2561 kakōsis (1),
maltreatment
4797 sugchĕō (1), to
throw into disorder

AFFLICTIONS
6031 'ânâh (1), to *afflict,
be afflicted*
7451 ra' (1), *bad; evil*
2347 thlipsis (6),
pressure, trouble
2553 kakŏpathĕō (1), to
undergo hardship
3804 pathēma (3),
passion; suffering
4777 sugkakŏpathĕō (1),
to *suffer hardship*

AFFORDING
6329 pûwq (1), to *issue;
to furnish; to secure*

AFFRIGHT
3372 yârê' (1), to *fear; to
revere*

AFFRIGHTED
270+8178 'âchaz (1), to
seize, grasp; possess
926 bâhal (1), to *tremble;
be, make agitated*
1204 bâ'ath (1), to *fear*
2865 châthath (1), to
break down
6206 'ârats (1), to *awe; to
dread; to harass*
1568 ĕkthambĕō (2), to
astonish utterly
1719 ĕmphŏbŏs (2),
alarmed, terrified

AFOOT
3978 pĕzĕuŏ (1), to *travel
by land,* i.e. *on foot*
3979 pĕzē, (1), *on foot*

AFORE
3808 lô' (1), *no, not*
6440 pânîym (2), *face;
front*
6924 qedem (1), *before,
anciently*
4270 prŏgraphō (1), to
write previously
4279 prŏĕpaggĕllŏmai
(1), to *promise from
before*
4282 prŏĕtŏimazō (1), to
fit up in advance

AFOREHAND
4301 prŏlambanō (1), to
take before

AFORETIME
4481+6928+1836 min
(Ch.) (1), *from or out of*
6440 pânîym (2), *face;
front*
6924 qedem (1), *before,
anciently*
7223 rî'shôwn (1), *first, in
place, time or rank*
4218 pŏtĕ (1), *at some
time, ever*
4270 prŏgraphō (1), to
write previously

AFRAID
926 bâhal (3), to *tremble;
be, make agitated;
hasten, hurry anxiously*
1204 bâ'ath (10), to *fear*
1481 gûwr (6), to *sojourn,
live as an alien*
1672 dâ'ag (3), *be
anxious, be afraid*
1763 d^echal (Ch.) (1), to
fear; be formidable
2119 zâchal (1), to *crawl,
glide*
2296 châgar (1), to *gird
on a belt; put on armor*
2342 chûwl (1), to *dance,
whirl; to writhe*
2727 chârag (1), to *be
dismayed, tremble*
2729 chârad (20), to
shudder with terror
2730 chârêd (1), *fearful*
2865 châthath (6), to
*break down, either by
violence, or by fear*
3025 yâgôr (5), to *fear*
3372 yârê' (78), to *fear; to
revere*
3373 yârê' (3), *fearing;
reverent*

6206 'ârats (3), to *awe; to
dread; to harass*
6342 pâchad (9), to *be
startled; to fear*
7264 râgaz (1), to *quiver*
7297 râhâh (1), to *fear*
7493 râ'ash (1), to
undulate, quake
8175 sâ'ar (3), to *storm;
to shiver,* i.e. *fear*
1168 dĕiliaō (1), to *be
timid, cowardly*
1630 ĕkphŏbŏs (1),
frightened out of one's
wits
1719 ĕmphŏbŏs (3),
alarmed, terrified
5141 trĕmō (1), to
tremble or fear
5399 phŏbĕō (29), to *fear,
be frightened*

AFRESH
388 anastaurŏō (1), to
re-crucify

AFTER
167 'âhal (1), to *pitch a
tent*
310 'achar (492), *after*
311 'achar (Ch.) (3), *after*
314 'achărôwn (5), *late
or last; behind; western*
413 'êl (4), *to, toward*
834 'ăsher (2), *because,
in order that*
870 'âthar (Ch.) (3), *after*
1767 day (2), *enough,
sufficient*
1863 dardar (1), *thorn*
3602 kâkâh (4), *just so*
4480 min (1), *from, out of*
4481 min (Ch.) (1), *from
or out of*
5921 'al (18), *above, over,
upon, or against*
6256 'êth (1), *time*
6310 peh (1), *mouth;
opening*
7093 qêts (10), *extremity;
after*
7097 qâtseh (1), *extremity*
7272 regel (4), *foot; step*
516 axiōs (1),
appropriately, suitable
1207 dĕutĕrŏprōtŏs (1),
second-first
1223 dia (3), *through, by
means of; because of*
1230 diaginŏmai (1), to
have time elapse
1377 diōkō (1), to *pursue;
to persecute*
1534 ĕita (3), *then,
moreover*
1567 ĕkzētĕō (2), to *seek
out*
1722 ĕn (1), *in; during;
because of*
1836 hĕxēs (1),
successive, next
1872 ĕpakŏlŏuthĕō (1), to
accompany, follow
1887 ĕpauriŏn (1),
to-morrow
1894 ĕpĕidē (1), *when,
whereas*
1899 ĕpĕita (3),
thereafter, afterward
1905 ĕpĕrōtaō (1), to
inquire, seek

1909 ĕpi (3), *on, upon*
1934 ĕpizētĕō (4), *to search (inquire) for*
1938 ĕpithumētēs (1), *craver*
1971 ĕpipŏthĕō (3), *intensely crave*
2089 ĕti (1), *yet, still*
2517 kathĕxēs (1), *in a sequence*
2569 kalŏpŏiĕō (3), *to do well*
2596 kata (58), *down; according to*
2614 katadiōkō (1), *to search for, look for*
2628 katakŏlŏuthĕō (1), *to accompany closely*
3195 mĕllō (2), *to intend,* i.e. *be about to be*
3326 mĕta (96), *with, among; after, later*
3693 ŏpisthĕn (2), *at the back; after*
3694 ŏpisō (22), *behind, after, following*
3753 hŏtĕ (3), *when; as*
3765 ŏukĕti (1), *not yet, no longer*
3779 hŏutō (2), *in this way; likewise*
4023 pĕriĕchō (1), *to clasp; to encircle*
4137 plērŏō (1), *to fill, make complete*
4329 prŏsdŏkia (1), *apprehension*
4459 pōs (1), *in what way?; how?; how much!*
5225 huparchō (1), *to come into existence*
5613 hōs (3), *which, how,* i.e. *in that manner*
5615 hōsautōs (1), *in the same way*
5618 hōspĕr (1), *exactly like*

AFTERNOON
5186+3117 nâṭâh (1), *to stretch* or spread out

AFTERWARD
310 'achar (21), *after*
314 'achărôwn (2), *late* or *last; behind; western*
1208 dĕutĕrŏs (1), *second; secondly*
1534 ĕita (1), *then, moreover*
1899 ĕpĕita (2), *thereafter, afterward*
2517 kathĕxēs (1), *in a sequence*
2547 kakĕithĕn (1), *from that place* (or *time)*
3347 mĕtĕpĕita (1), *thereafter*
5305 hustĕrŏn (7), *more lately,* i.e. *eventually*

AFTERWARDS
268 'âchôwr (1), *behind, backward; west*
310 'achar (5), *after*
310+3651 'achar (2), *after*
314 'achărôwn (1), *late* or *last; behind; western*
1899 ĕpĕita (1), *thereafter, afterward*

5305 hustĕrŏn (1), *more lately,* i.e. *eventually*

AGABUS
13 Agabŏs (2), *locust*

AGAG
90 'Ăgag (8), *flame*

AGAGITE
91 'Ăgâgîy (5), *Agagite*

AGAIN
310 'achar (1), *after*
322 'ăchôrannîyth (1), *by turning around*
1571 gam (2), *also; even*
1906 hêd (1), *shout of joy*
1946 hûwk (Ch.) (1), *to go, come*
3138 yôwreh (2), *autumn rain showers*
3254 yâçaph (49), *to add* or *augment*
3284 ya'ănâh (1), *ostrich*
5437 câbab (1), *to surround*
5750 'ôwd (51), *again; repeatedly; still; more*
7725 shûwb (246), *to turn back; to return*
7999 shâlam (3), *to reciprocate*
8138 shânâh (1), *to fold;* to *transmute*
8145 shênîy (7), *second; again*
8579 tinyânûwth (Ch.) (1), *second time*
313 anagĕnnaŏ (2), *to beget or bear again*
321 anagō (2), *to lead up; to bring out*
326 anazaō (3), *to recover life, live again*
330 anathallō (1), *to flourish;* to *revive*
344 anakamptō (1), *to turn back, come back*
364 anamnēsis (1), *recollection*
375 anapĕmpō (2), *to send up or back*
386 anastasis (2), *resurrection from death*
450 anistēmi (15), *to come back to life*
456 anŏikŏdŏmĕō (2), *to rebuild*
467 antapŏdidōmi (2), *to requite good or evil*
470 antapŏkrinŏmai (1), *to contradict or dispute*
479 antikalĕō (1), *to reciprocate*
483 antilĕgō (1), *to dispute, refuse*
486 antilŏidŏrĕō (1), *to rail in reply, retaliate*
488 antimĕtrĕō (2), *to measure in return*
509 anōthĕn (2), *from the first; anew*
518 apaggĕllō (2), *to announce, proclaim*
523 apaitĕō (1), *to demand back*
560 apĕlpizō (1), *to fully expect in return*
591 apŏdidōmi (2), *to give away*

5305 hustĕrŏn (1), *more lately,* i.e. *eventually*

AGABUS
13 Agabŏs (2), *locust*

600 apŏkathistēmi (1), *to reconstitute*
618 apŏlambanō (1), *to receive; be repaid*
654 apŏstrĕphō (2), *to turn away or back*
1208 dĕutĕrŏs (3), *second; secondly*
1364 dis (2), *twice*
1453 ĕgĕirō (8), *to waken,* i.e. *rouse*
1458 ĕgkalĕō (1), *to charge*
1515 ĕirēnē (1), *peace; health; prosperity*
1880 ĕpanĕrchŏmai (1), *return home*
1994 ĕpistrĕphō (5), *to revert, turn back to*
3326 mĕta (1), *with, among; after, later*
3825 palin (141), *anew,* i.e. *back; once more*
4388 prŏtithĕmai (2), *to place before*
4762 strĕphō (2), *to turn around or reverse*
5290 hupŏstrĕphō (6), *to return*

AGAINST
413 'êl (144), *to, toward*
431 'ălûw (Ch.) (1), *lo!*
834 'âsher (1), *because, in order that*
4136 mûwl (19), *in front of, opposite*
4775 mârad (1), *to rebel*
5048 neged (33), *over against or before*
5227 nôkach (11), *opposite, in front of*
5704 'ad (3), *as far (long) as; during; while; until*
5921 'al (525), *above, over, upon, or against*
5922 'al (Ch.) (7), *above, over, upon, or against*
5971 'am (1), *people; tribe; troops*
5973 'îm (35), *with*
5978 'immâd (1), *along with*
5980 'ummâh (26), *near, beside, along with*
6440 pânîym (11), *face; front*
6640 tsᵉbûw (Ch.) (1), *affair; matter of determination*
6655 tsad (Ch.) (1), *at or upon the side of; against*
6903 qᵉbêl (Ch.) (1), *in front of, before*
6965 qûwm (1), *to rise*
7125 qîr'âh (41), *to encounter, to happen*
210 akōn (1), *unwilling*
368 anantirrhētŏs (1), *indisputable*
470 antapŏkrinŏmai (1), *to contradict or dispute*
471 antĕpō (1), *to refute*
481 antikru (1), *opposite*
483 antilĕgō (5), *to dispute, refuse*
495 antipĕran (1), *on the opposite side*

497 antistratĕuŏmai (1), *to wage war against*
561 apĕnanti (2), *before or against*
1519 ĕis (24), *to or into*
1690 ĕmbrimaŏmai (1), *to blame, warn sternly*
1693 ĕmmainŏmai (1), *to rage at*
1715 ĕmprŏsthĕn (1), *in front of*
1722 ĕn (1), *in; during*
1727 ĕnantiŏs (1), *opposite*
1909 ĕpi (38), *on, upon*
2018 ĕpiphĕrō (1), *to inflict, bring upon*
2019 ĕpiphōnĕō (1), *to exclaim, shout*
2596 kata (59), *down; according to*
2620 katakauchaŏmai (2), *to exult against*
2649 katamarturĕō (1), *to testify against*
2691 katastrēniaō (1), *to be voluptuous against*
2702 kataphĕrō (1), *to bear down*
2713 katĕnanti (4), *directly opposite*
2729 katischuō (1), *to overpower, prevail*
3326 mĕta (4), *with, among; after, later*
3844 para (2), *from; with; besides; on account of*
4012 pĕri (2), *around*
4314 prŏs (23), *for; on, at; to, toward; against*
4366 prŏsrĕgnumi (1), *to burst upon*
5396 phluarĕō (1), *to berate*

AGAR
28 Agar (2), *Hagar*

AGATE
3539 kadkôd (1), (poss.) *sparkling ruby*
7618 shᵉbûw (2), *agate*

AGATES
3539 kadkôd (1), (poss.) *sparkling ruby*

AGE
582 'ĕnôwsh (1), *man; person, human*
1121 bên (3), *son, descendant; people*
1755 dôwr (2), *dwelling*
2207 zôqen (1), *old age*
2209 ziqnâh (1), *old age*
2465 cheled (2), *fleeting time; this world*
3117 yôwm (6), *day; time period*
3485 Yissâˢkâr (1), *he will bring a reward*
3624 kelach (2), *maturity*
7869 sêyb (1), *old age*
7872 sêybâh (6), *old age*
2244 hēlikia (4), *maturity*
2250 hēmĕra (1), *day; period of time*
5046 tĕlĕiŏs (1), *complete; mature*
5230 hupĕrakmŏs (1), *past the prime of youth*

AGED
2204 zâqên (1), to *be old*
2205 zâqên (4), *old*
3453 yâshîysh (1), *old*
man
4246 prĕsbutĕs (2), *old*
man
4247 prĕsbutis (1), *old*
woman

AGEE
89 'Âgê' (1), *Agee*

AGES
165 aiŏn (2), *perpetuity,*
ever; world
1074 gĕnĕa (2),
generation; age

AGO
3117 yôwm (1), *day; time*
period
6928 qadmâh (Ch.) (1),
former time; formerly
7350 râchôwq (3),
remote, far
575 apŏ (4), *from, away*
3819 palai (2), *formerly;*
sometime since
4253 prŏ (1), *before in*
time or *space*

AGONY
74 agōnia (1), *anguish,*
anxiety

AGREE
1526 ĕisi (1), *they are*
2132 ĕunŏĕŏ (1), *to*
reconcile
2470 isŏs (1), *similar*
4160+3391+1106 pŏiĕō
(1), to *make* or *do*
4856 sumphōnĕŏ (3), *to*
be harmonious

AGREED
3259 yâ'ad (1), to *meet;*
to *summon;* to *direct*
800 asumphōnŏs (1),
disagreeable
2470 isŏs (1), *similar*
3982 pĕithō (1), to *pacify*
or *conciliate*
4856 sumphōnĕŏ (2), *to*
be harmonious
4934 suntithĕmai (2), *to*
consent, concur, agree

AGREEMENT
2374 chôzeh (1),
beholder in vision
2380 châzûwth (1),
revelation; compact
4339 mêyshâr (1),
straightness; rectitude
4783 sugkatathĕsis (1),
accord with

AGREETH
3662 hŏmŏiazō (1), to
resemble, be like
4856 sumphōnĕŏ (1), to
be harmonious

AGRIPPA
67 Agrippas (12),
wild-horse tamer

AGROUND
2027 ĕpŏkĕllō (1), to
beach a ship vessel

AGUE
6920 qaddachath (1),
inflammation

AGUR
94 'Âgûwr (1), one
received

AH
162 'ăhâhh (8), *Oh!,*
Alas!, Woe!
253 'âch (2), *Oh!; Alas!*
1945 hôwy (7), *oh!, woe!*
3758 ŏua (1), *ah!; so!*

AHA
253 'âch (7), *Oh!; Alas!*

AHAB
256 'Ach'âb (90), *friend*
of (his) *father*

AHAB'S
256 'Ach'âb (2), *friend of*
(his) *father*

AHARAH
315 'Achrach (1), *after*
(his) *brother*

AHARHEL
316 'Ächarchêl (1), *safe*

AHASAI
273 'Achzay (1), *seizer*

AHASBAI
308 'Ächaçbay (1),
Achasbai

AHASUERUS
325 'Ächashvêrôwsh
(30), *Xerxes*

AHASUERUS'
325 'Ächashvêrôwsh (1),
Xerxes

AHAVA
163 'Ahăvâ' (3), *Ahava*

AHAZ
271 'Âchâz (41),
possessor

AHAZIAH
274 'Ächazyâh (37),
Jehovah has seized

AHBAN
257 'Achbân (1), *one who*
understands

AHER
313 'Achêr (1), *Acher*

AHI
277 'Ächîy (2), *brotherly*

AHIAH
281 'Ächîyâh (4),
worshipper of Jehovah

AHIAM
279 'Ächîy'âm (2), *uncle*

AHIAN
291 'Achyân (1), *brotherly*

AHIEZER
295 'Ächîy'ezer (6),
brother of help

AHIHUD
282 'Ächîyhûwd (1),
possessor of renown
284 'Ächîychûd (1),
mysterious

AHIJAH
281 'Ächiyâh (20),
worshipper of Jehovah

AHIKAM
296 'Ächîyqâm (20),
high, exalted

AHILUD
286 'Ächîylûwd (5),
brother of one born

AHIMAAZ
290 'Ächîyma'ats (15),
brother of anger

AHIMAN
289 'Ächîyman (4), *gift*

AHIMELECH
288 'Ächîymelek (16),
brother of (the) *king*

AHIMELECH'S
288 'Ächîymelek (1),
brother of (the) *king*

AHIMOTH
287 'Ächîymôwth (1),
brother of death

AHINADAB
292 'Ächîynâdâb (1),
brother of liberality

AHINOAM
293 'Ächîynô'am (7),
brother of pleasantness

AHIO
283 'Achyôw (6),
brotherly

AHIRA
299 'Ächîyra' (5), *brother*
of wrong

AHIRAM
297 'Ächîyrâm (1), *high,*
exalted

AHIRAMITES
298 'Ächîyrâmîy (1),
Achiramite

AHISAMACH
294 'Ächîyçâmâk (3),
brother of support

AHISHAHAR
300 'Achîyshachar (1),
brother of (the) *dawn*

AHISHAR
301 'Ächîyshâr (1),
brother of (the) *singer*

AHITHOPHEL
302 'Ächîythôphel (20),
brother of folly

AHITUB
285 'Ächîyṭûwb (15),
brother of goodness

AHLAB
303 'Achlâb (1), *fertile*

AHLAI
304 'Achlay (2), *wishful*

AHOAH
265 'Ächôwach (1),
brotherly

AHOHITE
266 'Ächôwchîy (4),
Achochite
1121+266 bên (1), *son,*
descendant; people

AHOLAH
170 'Ohŏlâh (5), *her tent*
(idolatrous *sanctuary*)

AHOLIAB
171 'Ohŏlîy'âb (5), *tent of*
(his) *father*

AHOLIBAH
172 'Ohŏlîybâh (6), *my*
tent (is) *in her*

AHOLIBAMAH
173 'Ohŏlîybâmâh (8),
tent of (the) *height*

AHUMAI
267 'Ächûwmay (1),
neighbor of water

AHUZAM
275 'Ächuzzâm (1),
seizure

AHUZZATH
276 'Ächuzzath (1),
possession

AI
5857 'Ay (34), *ruin*
5892 'îyr (1), *city, town,*
unwalled-*village*

AIAH
345 'Ayâh (5), *hawk*

AIATH
5857 'Ay (1), *ruin*

AIDED
2388+3027 châzaq (1), to
be strong; courageous

AIJA
5857 'Ay (1), *ruin*

AIJALON
357 'Ayâlôwn (7),
deer-field

AIJELETH
365 'ayeleth (1), *doe* deer

AIN
5871 'Ayin (5), *fountain*

AIR
7307 rûwach (1), *breath;*
wind; life-spirit
8064 shâmayim (21), *sky;*
unseen celestial places
109 aēr (7), *air, sky*
3772 ŏuranŏs (10), *sky;*
air; heaven

AJAH
345 'Ayâh (1), *hawk*

AJALON
357 'Ayâlôwn (3),
deer-field

AKAN
6130 'Äqân (1), *crooked*

AKKUB
6126 'Aqqûwb (8),
insidious

AKRABBIM
6137 'aqrâb (2), *scorpion*

ALABASTER
211 alabastrŏn (3),
alabaster

ALAMETH
5964 'Âlemeth (1),
covering

ALAMMELECH
487 'Allammelek (1),
oak of (the) *king*

ALAMOTH
5961 'Âlâmôwth (2),
soprano

ALARM
7321 rûwa' (4), to *shout*
for alarm or joy
8643 tᵉrûw'âh (6),
battle-cry; clangor

ALAS
160 'ahăbâh (7),
affection, love
188 'ôwy (1), Oh!, Woe!
253 'âch (1), Oh!; Alas!
994 bîy (1), Oh that!
1930 hôw (1), oh! ah!
1945 hôwy (2), oh!, woe!
3758 ŏua (5), ah!; so!

ALBEIT
2443 hina (1), in order
that

ALEMETH
5964 'Âlemeth (3),
covering

ALEXANDER
223 Alĕxandrŏs (5),
man-defender

ALEXANDRIA
221 Alĕxandrĕus (3), of
Alexandria

ALEXANDRIANS
221 Alĕxandrĕus (1), of
Alexandria

ALGUM
418 'algûwmmîym (3),
Algum-wood

ALIAH
5933 'Alvâh (1), moral
perverseness

ALIAN
5935 'Alvân (1), lofty

ALIEN
1616 gêr (1), foreigner
5236 nêkâr (1), foreigner
5237 nokrîy (3), foreign;
non-relative

ALIENATE
5674 'âbar (1), to cross
over; to transition

ALIENATED
3363 yâqa' (2), to be
dislocated
5361 nâqa' (3), to feel
aversion
526 apallŏtriŏō (2), to be
excluded

ALIENS
5237 nokrîy (1), foreign;
non-relative
245 allŏtriŏs (1), not
one's own
526 apallŏtriŏō (1), to be
excluded

ALIKE
259 'echâd (1), first
834 'ăsher (1), who,
which, what, that
1571 gam (1), also; even
3162 yachad (5), unitedly
7737 shâvâh (1), to
equalize; to resemble

ALIVE
2416 chay (30), alive;
raw; fresh; life
2418 chăyaʼ (Ch.) (1), to
live
2421 châyâh (34), to live;
to revive
8300 sârîyd (1), survivor;
remainder
326 anazaō (2), to
recover life, live again
2198 zaō (15), to live

2227 zōŏpŏiĕō (1), to (re-)
vitalize, give life

ALL
622 'âçaph (1), to gather,
collect
1571 gam (1), also; even
3162 yachad (1), unitedly
3605 kôl (4194), all, any
3606 kôl (Ch.) (50), all,
any or every
3632 kâlîyl (2), whole,
entire; complete; whole
3885 lûwn (14), to be
obstinate with
4393 mᵉlô' (9), fulness
4557 miçpâr (3), number
5973 'îm (2), with
7230 rôb (1), abundance
8552 tâmam (2), to
complete, finish
537 hapas (39), all, every
one, whole
1273 dianuktĕrĕuō (1), to
pass, spend the night
2178 ĕphapax (1), once
for all
2527 kathŏlŏu (1),
entirely, completely
3122 malista (1), in the
greatest degree
3364 ŏu mē (7), not at all,
absolutely not
3367 mēdĕis (1), not even
one
3650 hŏlŏs (62), whole or
all, i.e. complete
3654 hŏlōs (2), completely
3745 hŏsŏs (6), as much
as
3762 ŏudĕis (4), none,
nobody, nothing
3779 hŏutō (1), in this
way; likewise
3829 pandŏchĕiŏn (1),
public lodging-place
3832 panŏiki (1), with
the whole family
3833 panŏplia (1), full
armor
3837 pantachŏu (1),
universally, everywhere
3843 pantōs (2), entirely;
at all events
3956 pas (947), all, any,
every, whole
4219 pŏtĕ (1), at what
time?
4561 sarx (1), flesh

ALLEGING
3908 paratithēmi (1), to
present something

ALLEGORY
238 allēgŏrĕō (1), to
allegorize

ALLELUIA
239 allēlŏuïa (4), praise
Jehovah!

ALLIED
7138 qârôwb (1), near,
close

ALLON
438 'Allôwn (2), oak

ALLON-BACHUTH
439 'Allôwn Bâkûwth (1),
oak of weeping

ALLOW
1097 ginōskō (1), to know
4327 prŏsdĕchŏmai (1),
to receive; to await for
4909 sunĕudŏkĕō (1), to
assent to, feel gratified

ALLOWANCE
737 'ărûchâh (1), ration,
portion of food

ALLOWED
1381 dŏkimazō (1), to
test; to approve

ALLOWETH
1381 dŏkimazō (1), to
test; to approve

ALLURE
6601 pâthâh (1), to be,
make simple; to delude
1185 dĕlĕazō (1), to
delude, seduce

ALMIGHTY
7706 Shadday (48), the
Almighty God
3841 pantŏkratōr (9),
Absolute sovereign

ALMODAD
486 'Almôwdâd (2),
Almodad

ALMON
5960 'Almôwn (1), hidden

ALMON-DIBLATHAIM
5963 'Almôn
Diblâthâyᵉmâh (2),
Almon toward
Diblathajim

ALMOND
8247 shâqêd (2), almond
tree or nut

ALMONDS
8246 shâqad (6), to be,
almond-shaped
8247 shâqêd (2), almond
tree or nut

ALMOST
4592 mᵉʻaṭ (5), little or
few
3195 mĕllō (1), to intend,
i.e. be about to be
4975 schĕdŏn (3), nigh,
i.e. nearly

ALMS
1654 ĕlĕĕmŏsunē (13),
benefaction

ALMSDEEDS
1654 ĕlĕĕmŏsunē (1),
benefaction

ALMUG
484 'almuggiym (3),
Almug-wood

ALOES
174 'ăhâlîym (4),
aloe-wood sticks
250 alŏē (1), aloes

ALONE
259 'echâd (4), first
905 bad (42), apart, only,
besides
909 bâdad (9), to be
solitary, be alone
2308 châdal (2), to desist,
stop; be fat
4422 mâlaṭ (1), to escape
as if by slipperiness

7503 râphâh (4), to
slacken
7662 shᵉbaq (Ch.) (1), to
allow to remain
7896 shîyth (1), to place,
put
863 aphiēmi (6), to leave;
to pardon, forgive
1439 ĕaō (3), to let be, i.e.
permit or leave alone
2651 katamŏnas (2),
separately, alone
3440 mŏnŏn (3), merely,
just
3441 mŏnŏs (21), single,
only; by oneself

ALONG
1980 hâlak (3), to walk;
live a certain way

ALOOF
5048 neged (1), over
against or before

ALOTH
1175 Bᵉʻâlôwth (1),
mistresses

ALOUD
1419+3605 gâdôwl (1),
great
1627 gârôwn (1), throat
1993 hâmâh (1), to be in
great commotion
2429 chayil (Ch.) (3),
strength; loud sound
5414+854+6963 nâthan
(1), to give
6670 tsâhal (2), to be
cheerful; to sound
6963+1419 qôwl (1), voice
or sound
7311+1419 rûwm (1), to
be high; to rise or raise
7321 rûwa' (1), to shout
for alarm or joy
7442 rânan (5), to shout
for joy
7452 rêaʼ (1), crash;
noise; shout
7768 shâvaʼ (1), to
halloo, call for help
310 anabŏaō (1), to cry
out

ALPHA
1 A (4), first

ALPHAEUS
256 Alphaiŏs (5),
Alphæus

ALREADY
3528 kᵉbâr (5), long ago,
formerly, hitherto
2235 ēdē (18), even now
4258 prŏamartanō (1), to
sin previously
5348 phthanō (1), to be
beforehand

ALTAR
741 'ărîʼêyl (3), altar
4056 madbach (Ch.) (1),
sacrificial altar
4196 mizbêach (347),
altar
1041 bōmŏs (1), altar
2379 thusiastēriŏn (21),
altar

ALTARS
4196 mizbêach (52), altar

2379 thusiastēriŏn (1), *altar*

ALTASCHITH
516 'Al tashchêth (4), "Thou must not destroy"

ALTER
2498 châlaph (1), to *hasten* away; to *pass*
8133 shᵉnâ' (Ch.) (2), to *alter, change*
8138 shânâh (1), to *transmute*

ALTERED
5674 'âbar (1), to *cross over*; to *transition*
1096+2087 ginŏmai (1), to be, *become*

ALTERETH
5709 'ădâ' (Ch.) (2), to *pass on* or *continue*

ALTOGETHER
259 'echâd (1), *first*
1571 gam (1), *also; even*
3162 yachad (5), *unitedly*
3605 kôl (4), *all, any*
3617 kâlâh (3), *complete destruction*
3650 hŏlŏs (1), *whole or all*, i.e. *complete*
3843 pantōs (2), *entirely; at all events*

ALUSH
442 'Âlûwsh (2), *Alush*

ALVAH
5933 'Alvâh (1), *moral perverseness*

ALVAN
5935 'Alvân (1), *lofty*

ALWAY
3605+3117 kôl (4), *all, any* or *every*
5331 netsach (1), *splendor; lasting*
5769 'ôwlâm (2), *eternity; ancient; always*
8548 tâmîyd (4), *constantly, regularly*
104 aĕi (8), *ever, always*
1275 diapantŏs (2), *constantly, continually*
3842 pantŏtĕ (1), *at all times*
3956+2250 pas (1), *all, any, every, whole*

ALWAYS
3605+3117 kôl (4), *all, any* or *every*
3605+6256 kôl (4), *all, any* or *every*
5331 netsach (2), *splendor; lasting*
5769 'ôwlâm (3), *eternity; ancient; always*
8548 tâmîyd (8), *constantly, regularly*
104 aĕi (3), *ever, always*

1223+3956 dia (3), *through*, by means of
1275 diapantŏs (3), *constantly, continually*
1539 hĕkastŏtĕ (1), *at every time*
1722+3956+2540 ĕn (2), *in; during; because of*
3839 pantĕ (1), *wholly*
3842 pantŏtĕ (29), *at all times*

AMAD
6008 'Am'âd (1), *people of time*

AMAL
6000 'Âmâl (1), *wearing effort; worry*

AMALEK
6002 'Ămâlêq (24), *Amalek*

AMALEKITE
6003 'Ămâlêqîy (3), *Amalekite*

AMALEKITES
6003 'Ămâlêqîy (24), *Amalekite*

AMAM
538 'Ămâm (1), *gathering*-spot

AMANA
549 'Ămânâh (1), *covenant*

AMARIAH
568 'Ămaryâh (14), *Jehovah has promised*

AMASA
6021 'Ămâsâ' (16), *burden*

AMASAI
6022 'Ămâsay (5), *burdensome*

AMASHAI
6023 'Ămashçay (1), *burdensome*

AMASIAH
6007 'Ămaçyâh (1), *Jehovah has loaded*

AMAZED
926 bâhal (2), to *tremble; be, make agitated*
2865 châthath (1), to *break down*
8074 shâmêm (1), to *devastate; to stupefy*
8539 tâmahh (1), to *be astounded*
1096+2285 ginŏmai (1), to be, *become*
1568 ĕkthambĕō (2), to *astonish* utterly
1605 ĕkplēssō (3), to *astonish*
1611 ĕkstasis (1), *astonishment*
1611+2983 ĕkstasis (1), *astonishment*
1839 ĕxistēmi (6), to *become astounded*
2284 thambĕō (2), to *astound, be amazed*

AMAZEMENT
1611 ĕkstasis (1), *astonishment*

4423 ptŏēsis (1), something *alarm*

AMAZIAH
558 'Ămatsyâh (40), *strength of Jehovah*

AMBASSADOR
6735 tsîyr (3), *hinge; herald* or *errand-doer*
4243 prĕsbĕuō (1), to *act as a representative*

AMBASSADORS
3887 lûwts (1), to *scoff*; to *interpret*; to *intercede*
4397 mal'âk (4), *messenger*
6735 tsîyr (2), *hinge; herald* or *errand-doer*
4243 prĕsbĕuō (1), to *act as a representative*

AMBASSAGE
4242 prĕsbĕia (1), *ambassadors*

AMBER
2830 chashmal (3), *bronze*

AMBUSH
693 'ârab (7), to *ambush, lie in wait*

AMBUSHES
693 'ârab (1), to *ambush, lie in wait*

AMBUSHMENT
3993 ma'ărâb (2), *ambuscade, ambush*

AMBUSHMENTS
693 'ârab (1), to *ambush, lie in wait*

AMEN
543 'âmên (22), *truly, "may it be so!"*
281 amēn (51), *surely; so be it*

AMEND
2388 châzaq (1), to *fasten* upon; to *seize*
3190 yâţab (4), to *be, make well*
2192+2866 ĕchō (1), to *have; hold; keep*

AMENDS
7999 shâlam (1), to *be friendly*; to *reciprocate*

AMERCE
6064 'ânash (1), to *inflict a penalty*, to *fine*

AMETHYST
306 'achlâmâh (2), *amethyst*
271 amĕthustŏs (1), *amethyst*

AMI
532 'Âmîy (1), *skilled craftsman*

AMIABLE
3039 yᵉdîyd (1), *loved*

AMINADAB
284 Aminadab (3), *people of liberality*

AMISS
5753 'âvâh (1), to *be crooked*
7955 shâlâh (Ch.) (1), *wrong*

824 atŏpŏs (1), *improper; injurious; wicked*
2560 kakōs (1), *badly; wrongly; ill*

AMITTAI
573 'Ămittay (2), *veracious*

AMMAH
522 'Ammâh (1), *cubit*

AMMI
5971 'am (1), *people*

AMMI-NADIB
5993 'Ammîy Nâdîyb (1), *my people (are) liberal*

AMMIEL
5988 'Ammîy'êl (6), *people of God*

AMMIHUD
5989 'Ammîyhûwd (10), *people of splendor*

AMMINADAB
5992 'Ammîynâdâb (13), *people of liberality*

AMMISHADDAI
5996 'Ammîyshadday (5), *people of* (the) *Almighty*

AMMIZABAD
5990 'Ammîyzâbâd (1), *people of endowment*

AMMON
5983 'Ammôwn (91), *inbred*

AMMONITE
5984 'Ammôwnîy (9), *Ammonite*

AMMONITES
1121+5984 bên (7), *son, descendant; people*
5984 'Ammôwnîy (16), *Ammonite*

AMMONITESS
5984 'Ammôwnîy (4), *Ammonite*

AMNON
550 'Amnôwn (25), *faithful*

AMNON'S
550 'Amnôwn (3), *faithful*

AMOK
5987 'Âmôwq (2), *deep*

AMON
526 'Âmôwn (17), *skilled craftsman*
300 Amŏn (2), *skilled craftsman*

AMONG
413 'êl (7), *to, toward*
854 'êth (8), *with; among*
996 bêyn (33), *between*
997 bêyn (Ch.) (1), *between; "either...or"*
1460 gêv (1), *middle, inside, in, on*, etc.
1767 day (1), *enough, sufficient*
4480 min (4), *from, out of*
5921 'al (7), *above, over, upon*, or *against*
5973 'îm (8), *with*
7130 qereb (74), *nearest part*, i.e. the *center*

7310 rᵉvâyâh (1),
satisfaction
8432 tâvek (142), center,
middle
575 apŏ (1), from, away
1223 dia (1), through, by
means of; because of
1519 ĕis (18), to or into
1537 ĕk (5), out, out of
1722 ĕn (115), in; during;
because of
1909 ĕpi (4), on, upon
2596 kata (2), down;
according to
3319 mĕsŏs (7), middle
3326 mĕta (5), with,
among; after, later
3844 para (2), from; with;
besides; on account of
4045 pĕripiptō (1), to fall
into the hands of
4314 prŏs (19), for; on, at;
to, toward; against
4315 prŏsabbatŏn (1),
Sabbath-eve
5259 hupŏ (1), under; by
means of; at

AMONGST
8432 tâvek (2), center,
middle

AMORITE
567 'Ĕmôrîy (14),
mountaineer

AMORITES
567 'Ĕmôrîy (73),
mountaineer

AMOS
5986 'Âmôwç (7),
burdensome
301 Amŏs (1), strong

AMOZ
531 'Âmôwts (13), strong

AMPHIPOLIS
295 Amphipŏlis (1), city
surrounded by a river

AMPLIAS
291 Amplias (1), enlarged

AMRAM
2566 Chamrân (1), red
6019 'Amrâm (13), high
people

AMRAM'S
6019 'Amrâm (1), high
people

AMRAMITES
6020 'Amrâmîy (2),
Amramite

AMRAPHEL
569 'Amrâphel (2),
Amraphel

AMZI
557 'Amtsîy (2), strong

ANAB
6024 'Ănâb (2), fruit

ANAH
6034 'Ănâh (12), answer

ANAHARATH
588 'Ănâchărâth (1),
gorge or narrow pass

ANAIAH
6043 'Ănâyâh (2),
Jehovah has answered

ANAK
6061 'Ânâq (9), necklace
chain

ANAKIMS
6062 'Ănâqîy (9), Anakite

ANAMIM
6047 'Ănâmîm (2),
Anamim

ANAMMELECH
6048 'Ănammelek (1),
Anammelek

ANAN
6052 'Ânân (1), cloud

ANANI
6054 'Ănânîy (1), cloudy

ANANIAH
6055 'Ănanyâh (2),
Jehovah has covered

ANANIAS
367 Ananias (11),
Jehovah has favored

ANATH
6067 'Ănâth (2), answer

ANATHEMA
331 anathĕma (1),
excommunicated

ANATHOTH
6068 'Ănâthôwth (16),
answers

ANCESTORS
7223 rî'shôwn (1), first, in
place, time or rank

ANCHOR
45 agkura (1), anchor

ANCHORS
45 agkura (2), anchor

ANCIENT
2204 zâqên (6), to be old,
venerated
3453 yâshîysh (1), old
man
5769 'ôwlâm (6), eternity;
ancient; always
6267 'attîyq (1), weaned;
antique
6268 'attîyq (Ch.) (3),
venerable, old
6917 qâdûwm (1),
pristine hero
6924 qedem (8), East,
eastern; antiquity;
before, anciently

ANCIENTS
2204 zâqên (9), to be old,
venerated
6931 qadmôwnîy (1),
anterior time; oriental

ANCLE
4974 sphurŏn (1), ankle

ANCLES
657 'epheç (1), end; no
further

ANDREW
406 Andrĕas (13), manly

ANDRONICUS
408 Andrŏnikŏs (1), man
of victory

ANEM
6046 'Ânêm (1), two
fountains

ANER
6063 'Ânêr (3), Aner

ANETHOTHITE
6069 'Anthôthîy (1),
Antothite

ANETOTHITE
6069 'Anthôthîy (1),
Antothite

ANGEL
4397 mal'âk (100),
messenger
4398 mal'ak (Ch.) (2),
messenger
32 aggĕlŏs (95),
messenger; angel

ANGEL'S
32 aggĕlŏs (2),
messenger; angel

ANGELS
430 'ĕlôhîym (1), the true
God; gods; great ones
4397 mal'âk (10),
messenger
8136 shin'ân (1), change,
i.e. repetition
32 aggĕlŏs (80),
messenger; angel
2465 isaggĕlŏs (1),
angelic, like an angel

ANGELS'
47 'abbîyr (1), mighty

ANGER
639 'aph (173), nose or
nostril; face; person
2195 za'am (1), fury,
anger
2534 chêmâh (1), heat;
anger; poison
3707 kâ'aç (42), to grieve,
rage, be indignant
3708 ka'aç (2), vexation,
grief
5006 nâ'ats (1), to scorn
5674 'âbar (1), to cross
over; to transition
5678 'ebrâh (1), outburst
of passion
6440 pânîym (3), face;
front
7307 rûwach (1), breath;
wind; life-spirit
3709 ŏrgē (3), ire;
punishment
3949 parŏrgizō (1), to
enrage, exasperate

ANGERED
7107 qâtsaph (1), to burst
out in rage

ANGLE
2443 chakkâh (2), fish
hook

ANGRY
599 'ânaph (13), be
enraged, be angry
639 'aph (4), nose or
nostril; face; person
1149 bᵉnaç (Ch.) (1), to
be enraged, be angry
2194 zâ'am (2), to be
enraged
2734 chârâh (10), to
blaze up
3707 kâ'aç (2), to grieve,
rage, be indignant
3708 ka'aç (1), vexation,
grief
4751+5315 mar (1), bitter;
bitterness; bitterly

6225 'âshan (1), to
envelope in smoke
7107 qâtsaph (2), to burst
out in rage
3710 ŏrgizō (5), to
become exasperated,
enraged
3711 ŏrgilŏs (1),
irascible, hot-tempered
5520 chŏlaŏ (1), irritable,
enraged

ANGUISH
2342 chûwl (1), to dance,
whirl; to writhe in pain
4689 mâtsôwq (1),
confinement; disability
4691 mᵉtsûwqâh (1),
trouble, anguish
6695 tsôwq (3), distress
6862 tsar (1), trouble;
opponent
6869 tsârâh (5), trouble;
rival-wife
7115 qôtser (1),
shortness (of spirit)
7661 shâbâts (1),
intanglement
2347 thlipsis (1),
pressure, trouble
4730 stĕnŏchôria (1),
calamity, distress
4928 sunŏchē (1),
anxiety, distress

ANIAM
593 'Ănîy'âm (1),
groaning of (the) people

ANIM
6044 'Ănîym (1),
fountains

ANISE
432 anēthŏn (1), dill
seed for seasoning

ANNA
451 Anna (1), favored

ANNAS
452 Annas (4), Jehovah
has favored

ANOINT
4886 mâshach (25), to
rub or smear
5480 çûwk (5), to smear
218 alĕiphō (3), to oil
with perfume, anoint
1472 ĕgchriō (1), to
besmear, anoint
3462 murizō (1), to apply
perfumed unguent to

ANOINTED
1101 bâlal (1), to mix
1121+3323 bên (1), son,
descendant; people
4473 mimshach (1), with
outstretched wings
4886 mâshach (43), to
rub or smear with oil
4888 mishchâh (1),
unction; gift
4899 mâshîyach (37),
consecrated person;
Messiah
5480 çûwk (2), to smear
218 alĕiphō (5), to oil
with perfume, anoint
2025 ĕpichriō (1), to
smear over, anoint

2025+1909 ĕpichriō (1), to *smear over, anoint*
5548 chriō (5), to *smear* or *rub* with oil

ANOINTEDST
4886 mâshach (1), to *rub* or *smear* with oil

ANOINTEST
1878 dâshên (1), to *anoint; to satisfy*

ANOINTING
4888 mishchâh (24), *unction; gift*
8081 shemen (1), *olive*
218 alĕiphō (1), to *oil* with perfume, *anoint*
5545 chrisma (2), special *endowment*

ANON
2112 ĕuthĕōs (1), *at once* or *soon*
2117 ĕuthus (1), *at once, immediately*

ANOTHER
250 'Ezrâchîy (22), *Ezrachite*
251 'âch (1), *brother; relative*
259 'echâd (35), *first*
269 'achôwth (6), *sister*
312 'achêr (58), *other, another, different; next*
317 'ochŏrîy (Ch.) (5), *other, another*
321 'ochŏrân (Ch.) (1), *other, another*
376 'îysh (5), *man; male; someone*
1668 dâ' (Ch.) (2), *this*
1836 dên (Ch.) (1), *this*
2088 zeh (10), *this* or *that*
2090 zôh (1), *this* or *that*
2114 zûwr (3), to *be foreign, strange*
3671 kânâph (1), *edge* or *extremity; wing*
5234 nâkar (2), to *treat as a foreigner*
5997 'âmîyth (2), *comrade* or *kindred*
7453 rêa' (20), *associate*
7468 re'ûwth (2), *female associate*
8145 shênîy (7), *second; again*
8264 shâqaq (1), to *seek greedily*
240 allêlôn (70), *one another*
243 allŏs (60), *different, other*
245 allŏtriŏs (4), *not one's own*
246 allŏphulŏs (1), *Gentile, foreigner*
1438 hĕautŏu (7), *himself, herself, itself*
1520 hĕis (2), *one*
2087 hĕtĕrŏs (44), *other* or *different*
3588 hŏ (1), *"the,"* i.e. the definite article
3739 hŏs (6), *who, which*
4299 prŏkrima (1), *prejudgment*
4835 sumpathēs (1), *commiserative*

ANOTHER'S
7453 rêa' (2), *associate; one close*
240 allêlôn (2), *one another*
2087 hĕtĕrŏs (1), *other* or *different*

ANSWER
559 'âmar (9), to *say, speak*
1696 dâbar (1), to *speak, say; to subdue*
1697 dâbâr (7), *word; matter; thing*
3045 yâda' (1), to *know*
4405 millâh (1), *word; discourse; speech*
4617 ma'ăneh (7), *reply, answer*
6030 'ânâh (60), to *respond, answer;*
6600 pithgâm (Ch.) (2), *decree; report*
7725 shûwb (12), to *turn back; to return*
8421 tûwb (Ch.) (2), to *reply, answer*
470 antapŏkrinŏmai (1), to *contradict* or *dispute*
611 apŏkrinŏmai (12), to *respond*
612 apŏkrisis (3), *response*
626 apŏlŏgĕŏmai (4), to give an *account* of self
627 apŏlŏgia (4), *plea* or verbal *defense*
1906 ĕpĕrōtēma (1), *inquiry*
2036 ĕpō (1), to *speak*
5538 chrēmatismŏs (1), divine *response*

ANSWERABLE
5980 'ummâh (1), *near, beside, along with*

ANSWERED
559 'âmar (90), to *say, speak*
1697 dâbâr (4), *word; matter; thing*
6030 'ânâh (175), to *respond, answer*
6032 'ănâh (Ch.) (16), to *respond, answer*
6039 'ĕnûwth (1), *affliction*
7725 shûwb (2), to *turn back; to return*
8421 tûwb (Ch.) (1), to *reply, answer*
611 apŏkrinŏmai (201), to *respond*
626 apŏlŏgĕŏmai (2), to give an *account* of self

ANSWEREDST
6030 'ânâh (2), to *respond, answer*

ANSWEREST
6030 'ânâh (2), to *respond, answer*
611 apŏkrinŏmai (4), to *respond*

ANSWERETH
6030 'ânâh (6), to *respond, answer*
7725 shûwb (1), to *turn back; to return*

611 apŏkrinŏmai (4), to *respond*
4960 sustŏichĕō (1), to *correspond* to

ANSWERING
488 antimĕtrĕō (1), to *measure in return*
611 apŏkrinŏmai (29), to *respond*
5274 hupŏlambanō (1), to *take up,* i.e. *continue*

ANSWERS
8666 tᵉshûwbâh (2), *reply*
612 apŏkrisis (1), *response*

ANT
5244 nᵉmâlâh (1), *ant*

ANTICHRIST
500 antichristŏs (4), *opponent of Messiah*

ANTICHRISTS
500 antichristŏs (1), *opponent of Messiah*

ANTIOCH
490 Antiŏchĕia (18), *Antiochia*
491 Antiŏchĕus (1), *inhabitant of Antiochia*

ANTIPAS
493 Antipas (1), *instead of father*

ANTIPATRIS
494 Antipatris (1), *Antipatris*

ANTIQUITY
6927 qadmâh (1), *priority in time; before; past*

ANTOTHIJAH
6070 'Anthôthîyâh (1), *answers of Jehovah*

ANTOTHITE
6069 'Anthôthîy (2), *Antothite*

ANTS
5244 nᵉmâlâh (1), *ant*

ANUB
6036 'Ânûwb (1), *borne*

ANVIL
6471 pa'am (1), *time; step; occurence*

ANY
259 'echâd (18), *first*
376 'îysh (25), *man*
1697 dâbâr (2), *thing*
1991 hêm (1), *wealth*
3254 yâçaph (2), to *add*
3605 kôl (175), *all, any*
3606 kôl (Ch.) (8), *all, any* or *every*
3792 kᵉthâb (Ch.) (1), *writing, record* or *book*
3972 mᵉ'ûwmâh (12), *something; anything*
4310 mîy (1), *who?*
5315 nephesh (3), *life; breath; soul; wind*
5750 'ôwd (9), *again; repeatedly; still; more*
5769 'ôwlâm (1), *eternity; ancient; always*
1520 hĕis (2), *one*
1535 ĕitĕ (1), *if too*
1536 ĕi tis (52), *if any*
1538 hĕkastŏs (1), *each*

2089 ĕti (10), *yet, still*
3361 mē (1), *not; lest*
3362 ĕan mē (2), *if not*
3364 ŏu mē (2), *not at all*
3367 mēdĕis (5), *not even one*
3370 Mēdŏs (2), *inhabitant of Media*
3379 mēpŏtĕ (7), *not ever; if,* or *lest ever*
3381 mēpōs (4), *lest somehow*
3387 mētis (6), *whether any*
3588 hŏ (1), *"the,"* i.e. the definite article
3762 ŏudĕis (12), *none, nobody, nothing*
3763 ŏudĕpŏtĕ (2), *never at all*
3765 ŏukĕti (4), *not yet, no longer*
3956 pas (9), *all, any, every, whole*
4218 pŏtĕ (4), *at some time, ever*
4455 pōpŏtĕ (3), *at no time*
4458 -pōs (4), particle used in composition
5100 tis (122), *some* or *any* person or object
5150 trimēnŏn (1), *three months' space*

APART
905 bad (6), *apart, only, besides*
5079 niddâh (3), *time of menstrual impurity*
5674 'âbar (1), to *cross over; to transition*
6395 pâlâh (1), to *distinguish*
659 apŏtithēmi (1), to *put away; get rid of*
2596 kata (7), *down; according to*

APELLES
559 Apĕllēs (1), *Apelles*

APES
6971 qôwph (2), *ape* or *monkey*

APHARSACHITES
671 'Ăpharçᵉkay (Ch.) (2), *Apharsekite*

APHARSATHCHITES
671 'Ăpharçᵉkay (Ch.) (1), *Apharsekite*

APHARSITES
670 'Ăphârᵉçay (Ch.) (1), *Apharesite*

APHEK
663 'Ăphêq (8), *fortress*

APHEKAH
664 'Ăphêqâh (1), *fortress*

APHIAH
647 'Ăphîyach (1), *breeze*

APHIK
663 'Ăphêq (1), *fortress*

APHRAH
1036 Bêyth lᵉ-'Aphrâh (1), *house of dust*

APHSES
6483 Pitstsêts (1), *dispersive*

APIECE
259 'echâd (1), *first*
5982+259 'ammûwd (1), *column, pillar*
303 ana (2), *each; in turn; among*

APOLLONIA
624 Apŏllōnia (1), *sun*

APOLLOS
625 Apŏllōs (10), *sun*

APOLLYON
623 Apŏlluŏn (1), *Destroyer*

APOSTLE
652 apŏstŏlŏs (19), *commissioner* of Christ

APOSTLES
652 apŏstŏlŏs (53), *commissioner* of Christ
5570 psĕudapŏstŏlŏs (1), *pretended preacher*

APOSTLES'
652 apŏstŏlŏs (5), *commissioner* of Christ

APOSTLESHIP
651 apŏstŏlē (4), office of *apostle*

APOTHECARIES
7543 râqach (1), to *perfume, blend spice*

APOTHECARIES'
4842 mirqachath (1), *unguent; unguent-pot*

APOTHECARY
7543 râqach (4), to *perfume, blend spice*

APPAIM
649 'Appayim (2), *two nostrils*

APPAREL
899 beged (4), *clothing; treachery* or *pillage*
1264 berôwm (1), *damask*
3830 lᵉbûwsh (8), *garment; wife*
3847 lâbash (1), to *clothe*
4254 machălâtsâh (1), *mantle, garment*
4403 malbûwsh (4), *garment, clothing*
8071 simlâh (2), *dress, mantle*
2066 ĕsthēs (3), to *clothe; dress*
2440 himatiŏn (1), to *put on clothes*
2441 himatismŏs (1), *clothing*
2689 katastŏlē (1), *costume* or *apparel*

APPARELLED
3847 lâbash (1), to *clothe*
2441 himatismŏs (1), *clothing*

APPARENTLY
4758 mar'eh (1), *appearance; vision*

APPEAL
1941 ĕpikalĕŏmai (2), to *invoke*

APPEALED
1941 ĕpikalĕŏmai (4), to *invoke*

APPEAR
1540 gâlâh (1), to *denude; uncover*
1570 gâlash (2), to *caper*
4286 machsôph (1), *peeling, baring*
6524 pârach (1), to *break forth*; to *bloom*; to *fly*
7200 râ'âh (24), to *see*
82 adēlŏs (1), *indistinct, not clear*
398 anaphainō (1), to *appear*
1718 ĕmphanizō (1), to *show forth*
2064 ĕrchŏmai (1), to *go or come*
3700 ŏptanŏmai (2), to *appear*
5316 phainō (9), to *show; to appear, be visible*
5318+5600 phanĕrŏs (1), *apparent, visible, clear*
5319 phanĕrŏō (9), to *render apparent*

APPEARANCE
4758 mar'eh (30), *appearance; vision*
5869 'ayin (1), *eye; sight; fountain*
1491 ĕidŏs (1), *form, appearance, sight*
3799 ŏpsis (1), *face; appearance*
4383 prŏsōpŏn (2), *face, presence*

APPEARANCES
4758 mar'eh (2), *appearance; vision*

APPEARED
1540 gâlâh (1), to *denude; uncover*
3318 yâtsâ' (1), to *go, bring out*
6437 pânâh (1), to *turn, to face*
7200 râ'âh (39), to *see*
1718 ĕmphanizō (1), to *show forth*
2014 ĕpiphainō (3), to *become visible*
3700 ŏptanŏmai (15), to *appear*
5316 phainō (5), to *show; to appear, be visible*
5319 phanĕrŏō (3), to *render apparent*

APPEARETH
1540 gâlâh (1), to *denude; uncover*
4758 mar'eh (1), *appearance; vision*
7200 râ'âh (3), to *see*
8259 shâqaph (1), to *peep or gaze*
5316 phainō (3), to *show; to appear, be visible*

APPEARING
602 apŏkalupsis (1), *disclosure, revelation*
2015 ĕpiphanĕia (5), *manisfestation*

APPEASE
3722+6440 kâphar (1), to *cover*; to *expiate*

APPEASED
7918 shâkak (1), to *lay a trap*; to *allay*
2687 katastĕllō (1), to *quell, quiet*

APPEASETH
8252 shâqaṭ (1), to *repose*

APPERTAIN
2969 yâ'âh (1), to *be suitable, proper*

APPETITE
2416 chay (1), *alive; raw; fresh; life*
5315 nephesh (2), *life; breath; soul; wind*
8264 shâqaq (1), to *seek greedily*

APPHIA
682 Apphia (1), *Apphia*

APPII
675 'Appiŏs (1), *Appius*

APPLE
380 'îyshôwn (2), *pupil, eyeball*
380+1323 'îyshôwn (1), *pupil, eyeball*
892 bâbâh (1), *pupil of the eye*
1323 bath (1), *daughter, descendant, woman*
8598 tappûwach (3), *apple*

APPLES
8598 tappûwach (3), *apple*

APPLIED
5414 nâthan (2), to *give*
5437 çâbab (1), to *surround*

APPLY
935 bôw' (2), to *go, come*
5186 nâṭâh (1), to *stretch or spread out*
7896 shîyth (1), to *place, put*

APPOINT
559 'âmar (1), to *say, speak*
977 bâchar (1), *select, chose, prefer*
3259 yâ'ad (2), to *meet; to summon; to direct*
5344 nâqab (1), to *specify, designate, libel*
5414 nâthan (4), to *give*
5975 'âmad (2), to *stand*
6485 pâqad (10), to *visit, care for, count*
6680 tsâvâh (1), to *constitute, enjoin*
7136 qârâh (1), to *bring about; to impose*
7760 sûwm (11), to *put*
7896 shîyth (2), to *place*
7971 shâlach (1), to *send away*
1303 diatithĕmai (1), to *put apart*, i.e. *dispose*
2525 kathistēmi (1), to *designate, constitute*
5087 tithēmi (2), to *place, put*

APPOINTED
559 'âmar (2), to *say*

561 'êmer (1), *something said*
1121 bên (3), *son, people* of a class or kind
1696 dâbar (1), to *speak, say*; to *subdue*
2163 zâman (3), to *fix a time*
2296 châgar (3), to *gird* on a belt; *put on* armor
2706 chôq (1), *appointment; allotment*
2708 chuqqâh (1), to *delineate*
2710 châqaq (1), to *enact laws*; to *prescribe*
2764 chêrem (1), *doomed object*
3045 yâda' (1), to *know*
3198 yâkach (2), to *decide, justify*
3245 yâçad (1), *settle, consult, establish*
3259 yâ'ad (3), to *meet; to summon*; to *direct*
3677 keçe' (2), *full moon*
4150 môw'êd (20), *assembly, congregation*
4151 môw'âd (1), *ranking of troop*
4152 môw'âdâh (1), *appointed* place
4487 mânâh (4), to *allot; to enumerate or enroll*
4662 miphqâd (1), *designated spot; census*
5324 nâtsab (1), to *station*
5414 nâthan (7), to *give*
5567 çâman (1), to *designate*
5975 'âmad (10), to *stand*
6213 'âsâh (2), to *do or make*
6485 pâqad (4), to *visit, care for, count*
6635 tsâbâ' (3), *army, military host*
6680 tsâvâh (1), to *constitute, enjoin*
6942 qâdâsh (1), to *be, make clean*
7760 sûwm (8), to *put*
7896 shîyth (1), to *place*
322 anadĕiknumi (1), to *indicate, appoint*
606 apŏkĕimai (1), to *be reserved; to await*
1299 diatassō (4), to *institute, prescribe*
1303 diatithĕmai (1), to *put apart*, i.e. *dispose*
1476 hĕdraiŏs (1), *immovable; steadfast*
1935 ĕpithanatiŏs (1), *doomed to death*
2476 histēmi (1), to *stand, establish*
2749 kĕimai (1), to *lie outstretched*
4160 pŏiĕō (1), to *do*
4287 prŏthĕsmiŏs (1), *designated* day or time
4384 prŏtassō (1), to *prescribe beforehand*
4929 suntassō (2), to *direct, instruct*
5021 tassō (3), to *assign or dispose*

5081 tēlaugōs (1), in a far-shining manner
5087 tithēmi (3), to *put*

APPOINTETH
6966 qûwm (Ch.) (1), to rise

APPOINTMENT
3259 yâ'ad (1), to *meet;* to *summon;* to *direct*
3883 lûwl (1), *spiral* step
6310 peh (2), *mouth; opening*

APPREHEND
2638 katalambanō (1), to seize; to *understand*
4084 piazō (1), to *seize, arrest,* or *capture*

APPREHENDED
2638 katalambanō (2), to seize; to *possess;* to *understand*
4084 piazō (1), to *seize, arrest,* or *capture*

APPROACH
5066 nâgash (5), to *be, come, bring near*
7126 qârab (12), to *approach, bring near*
7138 qârôwb (1), *near, close*
676 aprŏsitŏs (1), *unapproachable*

APPROACHED
5066 nâgash (1), to *be, come, bring near*
7126 qârab (1), to *approach, bring near*

APPROACHETH
1448 ĕggizō (1), to *approach*

APPROACHING
7132 qᵉrâbâh (1), *approach*
1448 ĕggizō (1), to *approach*

APPROVE
7520 râtsad (1), to *look askant;* to *be jealous*
1381 dŏkimazō (2), to *test;* to *approve*

APPROVED
584 apŏdĕiknumi (1), to *accredit*
1384 dŏkimŏs (6), *acceptable, approved*
4921 sunistaō (1), to *introduce* (favorably)

APPROVEST
1381 dŏkimazō (1), to *test;* to *approve*

APPROVETH
7200 râ'âh (1), to *see*

APPROVING
4921 sunistaō (1), to *introduce* (favorably)

APRONS
2290 chăgôwr (1), *belt* for the waist
4612 simikinthiŏn (1), narrow *apron*

APT
6213 'âsâh (1), to *do*
1317 didaktikŏs (2), *instructive*

AQUILA
207 Akulas (6), *eagle*

AR
6144 'Âr (6), *city*

ARA
690 'Ărâ' (1), *lion*

ARAB
694 'Ărâb (1), *ambush*

ARABAH
6160 'ărâbâh (2), *desert, wasteland*

ARABIA
6152 'Ărâb (6), *Arabia*
688 Arabia (2), *Arabia*

ARABIAN
6153 'ereb (1), *dusk*
6163 'Ărâbîy (3), *Arabian*

ARABIANS
6163 'Ărâbîy (5), *Arabian*
690 'Araps (1), *native of Arabia*

ARAD
6166 'Ărâd (5), *fugitive*

ARAH
733 'Ărach (4), *way-faring*

ARAM
758 'Ărâm (7), *highland*
689 Aram (3), *high*

ARAM-NAHARAIM
763 'Ăram Nahărayim (1), *Aram of* (the) *two rivers*

ARAM-ZOBAH
760 'Ăram Tsôwbâh (1), *Aram of* Coele-Syria

ARAMITESS
761 'Ărammîy (1), *Aramite*

ARAN
765 'Ărân (2), *stridulous*

ARARAT
780 'Ărâraṭ (2), *Ararat*

ARAUNAH
728 'Ăravnâh (9), *Aravnah* or *Ornah*

ARBA
704 'Arba' (2), *four*

ARBAH
704 'Arba' (1), *four*

ARBATHITE
6164 'Arbâthîy (2), *Arbathite*

ARBITE
701 'Arbîy (1), *Arbite*

ARCHANGEL
743 archaggĕlŏs (2), *chief angel*

ARCHELAUS
745 Archĕlaŏs (1), *people-ruling*

ARCHER
1869 dârak (1), to *walk, lead;* to *string* a bow
7198 qesheth (1), *bow; rainbow*

ARCHERS
1167+2671 ba'al (1), *master; husband*
1869+7198 dârak (1), to *walk;* to *string* a bow

ARCHES
361 'êylâm (15), *portico, porch*

ARCHEVITES
756 'Arkᵉvay (Ch.) (1), *Arkevite*

ARCHI
757 'Arkîy (1), *Arkite*

ARCHIPPUS
751 Archippŏs (2), *horse-ruler*

ARCHITE
757 'Arkîy (5), *Arkite*

ARCTURUS
5906 'Ayish (2), Great *Bear* constellation

ARD
714 'Ard (3), *fugitive*

ARDITES
716 'Ardîy (1), *Ardite*

ARDON
715 'Ardôwn (1), *roaming*

ARELI
692 'Ar'êlîy (2), *heroic*

ARELITES
692 'Ar'êlîy (1), *heroic*

AREOPAGITE
698 Arĕŏpagitēs (1), *Areopagite*

AREOPAGUS
697 Arĕiŏs Pagŏs (1), *rock of Ares*

ARETAS
702 Arĕtas (1), *Aretas*

ARGOB
709 'Argôb (5), *stony*

ARGUING
3198 yâkach (1), to *be correct;* to *argue*

ARGUMENTS
8433 tôwkêchâh (1), *correction, refutation*

ARIDAI
742 'Ărîyday (1), *Aridai*

ARIDATHA
743 'Ărîydâthâ' (1), *Aridatha*

ARIEH
745 'Aryêh (1), *lion*

ARIEL
740 'Ărî'êl (5), *Lion of God*

ARIGHT
3190 yâṭab (1), to *be, make well*
3559 kûwn (1), to *render sure, proper*
3651 kên (1), *just; right, correct*

ARIMATHAEA
707 Arimathaia (4), *height*

ARIOCH
746 'Ăryôwk (7), *Arjok*

ARISAI
747 'Ăriyçay (1), *Arisai*

ARISE
2224 zârach (3), to *rise;* to *be bright*
5782 'ûwr (1), to *awake*
5927 'âlâh (2), to *ascend, be high, mount*
5975 'âmad (1), to *stand*
6965 qûwm (106), to *rise*
6966 qûwm (Ch.) (3), to *rise*
6974 qûwts (1), to *awake*
7721 sôw' (1), *rising*
305 anabainō (1), to *go up, rise*
393 anatĕllō (1), to *cause to arise*
450 anistēmi (14), to *stand up;* to *come back to life*
1453 ĕgĕirō (13), to *waken,* i.e. *rouse*

ARISETH
2224 zârach (4), to *rise;* to *be bright*
5927 'âlâh (1), to *ascend, be high, mount*
6965 qûwm (2), to *rise*
450 anistēmi (1), to *stand up;* to *come back to life*
1096 ginŏmai (2), to *be, become*
1453 ĕgĕirō (1), to *waken,* i.e. *rouse*

ARISING
6965 qûwm (1), to *rise*

ARISTARCHUS
708 Aristarchŏs (5), *best ruling*

ARISTOBULUS'
711 Aristŏbŏulŏs (1), *best counselling*

ARK
727 'ârôwn (194), *box*
8392 têbâh (28), *box, basket*
2787 kibōtŏs (6), *ark; chest* or *box*

ARKITE
6208 'Arqîy (2), *tush*

ARM
248 'ezrôwa (2), *arm*
2220 zᵉrôwa (59), *arm; foreleg; force, power*
2502 châlats (1), to *depart;* to *equip*
3802 kâthêph (1), *side-piece*
1023 brachiōn (3), *arm*
3695 hŏplizō (1), to *equip*

ARMAGEDDON
717 Armagĕddōn (1), *hill* of the *rendezvous*

ARMED
2502 châlats (16), to *equip;* to *present*

2571 châmûsh (3), able-bodied *soldiers*
3847 lâbash (3), to *clothe*
4043 mâgên (2), small *shield* (*buckler*)
5401 nâshaq (3), to *kiss; to equip with weapons*
5402 nesheq (1), military *arms, arsenal*
7324 rûwq (1), to *pour out, i.e. empty*
2528 kathŏplizō (1), to *equip fully with armor*

ARMENIA
780 'Ărâraṭ (2), *Ararat*

ARMHOLES
679+3027 'atstsîyl (2), *joint of the hand*

ARMIES
1416 gᵉdûwd (1), *band of soldiers*
2428 chayil (4), *army; wealth; virtue; valor*
4264 machăneh (4), *encampment*
4630 ma'ărâh (1), *open spot*
4634 ma'ărâkâh (6), *row; pile; military array*
6635 tsâbâ' (22), *army, military host*
3925 parĕmbŏlē (1), *battle-array*
4753 stratĕuma (3), body *of troops*
4760 stratŏpĕdŏn (1), *body of troops*

ARMONI
764 'Armônîy (1), *palatial*

ARMOUR
2185 zônôwth (1), *harlots*
2290 chăgôwr (1), *belt for the waist*
2488 chălîytsâh (1), *spoil, booty of the dead*
3627 kᵉlîy (11), *implement, thing*
4055 mad (2), *vesture, garment; carpet*
5402 nesheq (1), military *arms, arsenal*
3696 hŏplŏn (2), *implement, or utensil or tool*
3833 panŏplia (3), *full armor*

ARMOURBEARER
5375+3627 nâsâ' (18), to *lift up*

ARMOURY
214 'ôwtsâr (1), *depository*
5402 nesheq (1), military *arms, arsenal*
8530 talpîyâh (1), *something tall*

ARMS
1672 dâ'ag (1), *be anxious, be afraid*
2220 zᵉrôwa' (24), *arm; foreleg; force, power*
2684 chôtsen (1), *bosom*
43 agkalē (1), *arm*
1723 ĕnagkalizŏmai (2), *to take into one's arms*

ARMY
1416 gᵉdûwd (4), *band of soldiers*
2426 chêyl (1), *rampart, battlement*
2426+6635 chêyl (1), *rampart, battlement*
2428 chayil (52), *army; wealth; virtue; valor*
2429 chayil (Ch.) (2), *army; strength*
2502 châlats (1), to *deliver, equip*
4634 ma'ărâkâh (7), *row; pile; military array*
4675 matstsâbâh (1), *military guard*
6635 tsâbâ' (7), *army, military host*
4753 stratĕuma (3), body *of troops*

ARNAN
770 'Arnân (1), *noisy*

ARNON
769 'Arnôwn (25), *brawling stream*

AROD
720 'Ărôwd (1), *fugitive*

ARODI
722 'Ărôwdîy (1), *Arodite*

ARODITES
722 'Ărôwdîy (1), *Arodite*

AROER
6177 'Ărôw'êr (16), *nudity of situation*

AROERITE
6200 'Ărô'êrîy (1), *Aroërite*

AROSE
2224 zârach (2), to *rise; to be bright*
5927 'âlâh (2), to *ascend, be high, mount*
5975 'âmad (1), to *stand*
6965 qûwm (107), to *rise*
6966 qûwm (Ch.) (1), to *rise*
7925 shâkam (7), to *start early in the morning*
305 anabainō (1), to *go up, rise*
450 anistēmi (24), to *stand up; to come back to life*
906 ballō (1), to *throw*
1096 ginŏmai (11), to *be, become*
1326 diĕgĕirō (2), to *arouse, stimulate*
1453 ĕgĕirō (13), to *waken, i.e. rouse*
1525 ĕisĕrchŏmai (1), to *enter*

ARPAD
774 'Arpâd (4), *spread out*

ARPHAD
774 'Arpâd (2), *spread out*

ARPHAXAD
775 'Arpakshad (9), *Arpakshad*
742 Arphaxad (1), *Arphaxad*

ARRAY
631 'âçar (1), to *fasten; to join* battle
3847 lâbash (2), to *clothe*
5844 'âṭâh (1), to *wrap, i.e. cover, veil, clothe*
6186 'ârak (26), to set in a *row, i.e. arrange,*
7896 shîyth (1), to *place*
2441 himatismŏs (1), *clothing*

ARRAYED
3847 lâbash (4), to *clothe*
1746 ĕnduō (1), to *invest with clothing*
4016 pĕriballō (6), to *wrap around, clothe*

ARRIVED
2668 kataplĕō (1), to *sail down*
3846 paraballō (1), to *reach a place; to liken*

ARROGANCY
1347 gâ'ôwn (3), *ascending; majesty*
6277 'âthâq (1), *impudent*

ARROW
1121+7198 bên (1), *people of a class or kind*
2671 chêts (11), *arrow; shaft of a spear*
2678 chitstsîy (4), *arrow*

ARROWS
1121 bên (1), *people of a class or kind*
2671 chêts (36), *arrow; wound; shaft of a spear*
2678 chitstsîy (1), *arrow*
2687 châtsâts (1), *gravel, grit*
7565 resheph (1), *flame*

ARTAXERXES
783 'Artachshastâ' (Ch.) (14), *Artaxerxes*

ARTAXERXES'
783 'Artachshastâ' (Ch.) (1), *Artaxerxes*

ARTEMAS
734 Artĕmas (1), *gift of Artemis*

ARTIFICER
2794 chôrêsh (1), *skilled fabricator* worker
2796 chârâsh (1), *skilled fabricator or worker*

ARTIFICERS
2796 chârâsh (2), *skilled fabricator or worker*

ARTILLERY
3627 kᵉlîy (1), *implement, thing*

ARTS
4021 pĕriĕrgŏs (1), *magic, sorcery*

ARUBOTH
700 'Ărubbôwth (1), *Arubboth*

ARUMAH
725 'Ărûwmâh (1), *height*

ARVAD
719 'Arvad (2), *refuge for the roving*

ARVADITE
721 'Arvâdîy (2), *Arvadite*

ARZA
777 'artsâ' (1), *earthiness*

ASA
609 'Âçâ' (57), *Asa*
760 Asa (2), *Asa*

ASA'S
609 'Âçâ' (1), *Asa*

ASAHEL
760 'Ăram Tsôwbâh (1), *Aram of* Coele-Syria
6214 'Ăsâh'êl (17), *God has made*

ASAHIAH
6222 'Ăsâyâh (2), *Jehovah has made*

ASAIAH
6222 'Ăsâyâh (6), *Jehovah has made*

ASAPH
623 'Âçâph (44), *collector*

ASAPH'S
623 'Âçâph (1), *collector*

ASAREEL
840 'Ăsar'êl (1), *right of God*

ASARELAH
841 'Ăsar'êlâh (1), *right toward God*

ASCEND
5927 'âlâh (9), to *ascend, be high, mount*
305 anabainō (4), to *go up, rise*

ASCENDED
5927 'âlâh (10), to *ascend, be high, mount*
305 anabainō (9), to *go up, rise*

ASCENDETH
305 anabainō (2), to *go up, rise*

ASCENDING
5927 'âlâh (2), to *ascend, be high, mount*
305 anabainō (3), to *go up, rise*

ASCENT
4608 ma'ăleh (2), *elevation; platform*
5930 'ôlâh (1), *sacrifice wholly consumed in fire*
5944 'ălîyâh (1), *upper things; second-story*

ASCRIBE
3051 yâhab (1), to *give*
5414 nâthan (2), to *give*

ASCRIBED
5414 nâthan (2), to *give*

ASENATH
621 'Âçᵉnath (3), *Asenath*

ASER
768 Asēr (2), *happy*

ASH
766 'ôren (1), *ash* tree

ASHAMED
954 bûwsh (79), to be *ashamed; disappointed*
1322 bôsheth (1), *shame*
2659 châphêr (4), to *be ashamed, disappointed*
3637 kâlam (12), to *taunt or insult*

153 aischunŏmai (5), *to feel shame* for oneself
422 anĕpaischuntŏs (1), *unashamed*
1788 ĕntrĕpŏ (2), *to respect; to confound*
1870 ĕpaischunŏmai (11), *to feel shame*
2617 kataischunŏ (7), *to disgrace or shame*

ASHAN
6228 'Âshân (4), *smoke*

ASHBEA
791 'Ashbêa' (1), *adjurer*

ASHBEL
788 'Ashbêl (3), *flowing*

ASHBELITES
789 'Ashbêlîy (1), *Ashbelite*

ASHCHENAZ
813 'Ashkᵉnaz (2), *Ashkenaz*

ASHDOD
795 'Ashdôwd (21), *ravager*

ASHDODITES
796 'Ashdôwdîy (1), *Ashdodite*

ASHDOTH-PISGAH
798+6449 'Ashdôwth hap-Piçgâh (3), *ravines of the Pisgah*

ASHDOTHITES
796 'Ashdôwdîy (1), *Ashdodite*

ASHER
836 'Âshêr (42), *happy*

ASHERITES
843 'Âshêrîy (1), *Asherite*

ASHES
665 'êpher (24), *ashes*
1878 dâshên (2), *to be fat, thrive; to fatten*
1880 deshen (8), *fat; fatness, ashes*
6083 'âphâr (2), *dust, earth, mud; clay,*
6368 pîyach (2), *powder dust or ashes*
4700 spŏdŏs (3), *ashes*
5077 tĕphrŏŏ (1), *to incinerate*

ASHIMA
807 'Ăshîymâ' (1), *Ashima*

ASHKELON
831 'Ashqᵉlôwn (9), *Ashkelon*

ASHKENAZ
813 'Ashkᵉnaz (1), *Ashkenaz*

ASHNAH
823 'Ashnâh (2), *Ashnah*

ASHPENAZ
828 'Ashpᵉnaz (1), *Ashpenaz*

ASHRIEL
845 'Asrî'êlîy (1), *Asrielite*

ASHTAROTH
6252 'Ashtârôwth (11), *increases*

ASHTERATHITE
6254 'Ashtᵉrâthîy (1), *Ashterathite*

ASHTEROTH
6255 'Ashtᵉrôth Qarnayim (1), *Ashtaroth of* (the) *double horns*

ASHTORETH
6252 'Ashtârôwth (3), *increases*

ASHUR
804 'Ashshûwr (2), *successful*

ASHURITES
843 'Âshêrîy (2), *Asherite*

ASHVATH
6220 'Ashvâth (1), *bright*

ASIA
773 Asia (20), *Asia Minor*
775 Asiarchēs (1), *ruler in Asia*

ASIDE
2015 hâphak (1), *to turn about or over*
3943 lâphath (1), *to clasp; to turn aside*
5186 nâtâh (16), *to stretch or spread out*
5265 nâça' (1), *start* on a journey
5437 çâbab (2), *to surround*
5493 çûwr (4), *to turn off*
5844 'âtâh (1), *to wrap, i.e. cover, veil, clothe*
6437 pânâh (1), *to turn, to face*
7750 sûwt (1), *become derelict*
7847 sâtâh (5), *to deviate from duty, go astray*
402 anachŏrĕŏ (2), *to retire, withdraw*
565 apĕrchŏmai* (1), *to go off, i.e. depart*
659 apŏtithĕmi* (2), *to put away; get rid of*
863 aphiēmi (1), *to leave; to pardon, forgive*
1824 ĕxautēs (2), *instantly, at once*
2596 kata (1), *down; according to*
5087 tithēmi (1), *to place, put*
5298 hupŏchōrĕŏ* (1), *to vacate down, i.e. retire*

ASIEL
6221 'Ăsîy'êl (1), *made of God*

ASK
1156 bᵉ'â' (Ch.) (2), *to seek or ask*
1245 bâqash (1), *to search* out
1875 dârash (1), *to pursue or search*
7592 shâ'al (41), *to ask*
154 aitĕŏ (38), *to ask for*
523 apaitĕŏ (1), *to demand back*
1833 ĕxĕtazŏ* (1), *to ascertain or interrogate*
1905 ĕpĕrōtaŏ* (8), *to inquire, seek*

2065 ĕrōtaŏ* (11), *to interrogate; to request*
4441 punthanŏmai* (2), *to ask for information*

ASKED
1156 bᵉ'â' (Ch.) (1), *to seek or ask*
1245 bâqash (1), *to search* out
7592 shâ'al (49), *to ask*
7593 shᵉ'êl (Ch.) (3), *to ask*
154 aitĕŏ (4), *to ask for*
1905 ĕpĕrōtaŏ* (45), *to inquire, seek*
2065 ĕrōtaŏ* (11), *to interrogate; to request*
3004 lĕgŏ (1), *to say*
4441 punthanŏmai* (4), *to ask for information*

ASKELON
831 'Ashqᵉlôwn (3), *Ashkelon*

ASKEST
7592 shâ'al (1), *to ask*
154 aitĕŏ (1), *to ask for*
1905 ĕpĕrōtaŏ* (1), *to inquire, seek*

ASKETH
7592 shâ'al (5), *to ask*
154 aitĕŏ (5), *to ask for*
2065 ĕrōtaŏ* (1), *to interrogate; to request*

ASKING
7592 shâ'al (3), *to ask*
350 anakrinŏ (2), *to interrogate, determine*
1905 ĕpĕrōtaŏ* (1), *to inquire, seek*
2065 ĕrōtaŏ* (1), *to interrogate; to request*

ASLEEP
3463 yâshên (2), *sleepy*
7290 râdam (2), *to stupefy*
879 aphupnŏŏ (1), *to drop* (off) *in slumber*
2518 kathĕudŏ* (5), *to fall asleep*
2837 kŏimaŏ* (6), *to slumber; to decease*

ASNAH
619 'Açnâh (1), *Asnah*

ASNAPPER
620 'Oçnappar (Ch.) (1), *Osnappar*

ASP
6620 pethen (1), *asp*

ASPATHA
630 'Açpâthâ' (1), *Aspatha*

ASPS
6620 pethen (3), *asp*
785 aspis (1), *serpent,* (poss.) *asp*

ASRIEL
844 'Asrîy'êl (2), *right of God*

ASRIELITES
845 'Asrîy'êl (1), *Asrielite*

ASS
860 'âthôwn (16), *female donkey, ass*

2543 châmôwr (55), *male donkey or ass*
5601 çappîyr (1), *sapphire*
5895 'ayîr (2), *young robust donkey or ass*
6171 'ârôwd (1), *onager or wild donkey*
6501 pere' (3), *onager, wild* donkey
3678 ŏnariŏn (1), *little donkey*
3688 ŏnŏs (5), *donkey*
5268 hupŏzugiŏn (2), *donkey*

ASS'S
860 'âthôwn (1), *female donkey, ass*
2543 châmôwr (1), *male donkey or ass*
6501 pere' (1), *onager, wild* donkey
3688 ŏnŏs (1), *donkey*

ASSAULT
6696 tsûwr (1), *to cramp, i.e. confine; to harass*
3730 hŏrmē (1), *violent impulse, i.e. onset*

ASSAULTED
2186 ĕphistēmi (1), *to be present; to approach*

ASSAY
5254 nâçâh (1), *to test, attempt*

ASSAYED
2974 yâ'al (1), *to assent; to undertake, begin*
5254 nâçâh (1), *to test, attempt*
3985 pĕirazŏ (1), *to endeavor, scrutinize, entice, discipline*
3987 pĕiraŏ (1), *to attempt, try*

ASSAYING
3984+2983 pĕira (1), *attempt, experience*

ASSEMBLE
622 'âçaph (10), *to gather, collect*
1481 gûwr (1), *to sojourn, live as an alien*
2199 zâ'aq (2), *to call out, convene publicly*
3259 yâ'ad (1), *to meet; to summon; to direct*
5789 'ûwsh (1), *to hasten*
6908 qâbats (1), *to collect, assemble*

ASSEMBLED
622 'âçaph (4), *to gather, collect*
662 'âphaq (1), *to abstain*
1413 gâdad (1), *to gash, slash oneself*
2199 zâ'aq (1), *to call out, convene publicly*
3259 yâ'ad (3), *to meet; to summon; to direct*
6633 tsâbâ' (1), *to mass an army or servants*
6638 tsâbâh (1), *to array an army against*
6908 qâbats (1), *to collect, assemble*

ASSEMBLIES
6950 qâhal (11), to convoke, gather
7284 rᵉgash (Ch.) (3), to gather tumultuously
1096 ginŏmai (1), to be, become
4863 sunagŏ (6), to gather together
4871 sunalizŏ (1), to accumulate
4905 sunĕrchŏmai (1), to gather together

ASSEMBLIES
627 'ăçuppâh (1), collection of sayings
4150 môw'êd (1), assembly, congregation
4744 miqrâ' (2), public meeting
5712 'êdâh (1), assemblage; family
6116 'ătsârâh (1), assembly

ASSEMBLING
6633 tsâbâ' (1), to mass an army or servants
1997 ĕpisunagŏgē (1), meeting, gathering

ASSEMBLY
4150 môw'êd (3), assembly, congregation
4186 môwshâb (1), seat; site; abode
5475 çôwd (5), intimacy; consultation; secret
5712 'êdâh (8), assemblage; family
6116 'ătsârâh (9), assembly
6951 qâhâl (17), assemblage
6952 qᵉhillâh (1), assemblage
1577 ĕkklēsia (3), congregation
3831 panēguris (1), mass-meeting
4864 sunagŏgē (1), assemblage

ASSENT
6310 peh (1), mouth; opening

ASSENTED
4934 suntithĕmai (1), to place jointly

ASSES
860 'âthôwn (17), female donkey, ass
2543 chămôwr (40), male donkey or ass
5895 'ayîr (2), young robust donkey or ass
6167 'ărâd (Ch.) (1), onager or wild donkey
6501 pere' (4), onager, wild donkey

ASSHUR
804 'Ashshûwr (8), successful

ASSHURIM
805 'Ăshûwrîy (1), Ashurite

ASSIGNED
5414 nâthan (2), to give

ASSIR
617 'Aççîyr (5), prisoner

ASSIST
3936 paristēmi (1), to stand beside, present

ASSOCIATE
7489 râ'a' (1), to break to pieces; to make

ASSOS
789 Assŏs (2), Assus

ASSUR
804 'Ashshûwr (2), successful

ASSURANCE
539 'âman (1), to be firm, faithful, true; to trust
983 beṭach (1), safety, security, trust
4102 pistis (1), faithfulness; faith, belief
4136 plērŏphŏria (4), full assurance

ASSURE
3983 pĕinaō (1), to famish; to crave

ASSURED
571 'emeth (1), certainty, truth, trustworthiness
6966 qûwm (Ch.) (1), to rise
4104 pistŏō (1), to assure

ASSUREDLY
571 'emeth (1), certainty, truth, trustworthiness
3045 yâda' (1), to know
3318 yâtsâ' (1), to go, bring out
3588 kîy (3), for, that because
8354 shâthâh (1), to drink, imbibe
806 asphalŏs (1), securely
4822 sumbibazŏ (1), to unite; to infer, show

ASSWAGE
2820 châsak (1), to refuse, spare, preserve

ASSWAGED
2820 châsak (1), to refuse, spare, preserve
7918 shâkak (1), to lay a trap; to allay

ASSYRIA
804 'Ashshûwr (118), successful

ASSYRIAN
804 'Ashshûwr (13), successful

ASSYRIANS
804 'Ashshûwr (10), successful

ASTAROTH
6252 'Ashtârôwth (1), increases

ASTONIED
1724 dâham (1), to be astounded
7672 shᵉbash (Ch.) (1), to perplex, be baffled
8074 shâmêm (6), to devastate; to stupefy
8075 shᵉmam (Ch.) (1), to devastate; to stupefy
8429 tᵉvahh (Ch.) (1), to amaze, take alarm

ASTONISHED
8074 shâmêm (14), to devastate; to stupefy
8539 tâmahh (1), to be astounded
1605 ĕkplēssō (10), to astonish
1839 ĕxistēmi (6), to become astounded
2284 thambĕō (2), to astound, be amazed
4023+2285 pĕriĕchō (1), to clasp; to encircle

ASTONISHMENT
8047 shammâh (14), ruin; consternation
8074 shâmêm (1), to devastate; to stupefy
8078 shimmâmôwn (2), stupefaction, despair
8541 timmâhôwn (2), consternation, panic
8653 tar'êlâh (1), reeling, staggering
1611 ĕkstasis (1), bewilderment, ecstasy, astonishment

ASTRAY
5080 nâdach (1), to push off, scattered
7683 shâgag (1), to stray
7686 shâgâh (2), to stray
8582 tâ'âh (13), to vacillate, stray
4105 planaō (5), to roam, wander from safety

ASTROLOGER
826 'ashshâph (Ch.) (1), conjurer, enchanter

ASTROLOGERS
825 'ashshâph (2), conjurer, enchanter
826 'ashshâph (Ch.) (5), conjurer, enchanter
1895+8064 hâbar (1), to be a horoscopist

ASUNDER
996 bêyn (1), between
673 apŏchōrizŏ (1), to rend apart; to separate
1288 diaspaō (1), to sever or dismember
1371 dichŏtŏmĕō (1), to flog severely
2997 laschō (1), to crack open
4249 prizō (1), to saw in two
5563 chōrizō (2), to place room between

ASUPPIM
624 'ăçuph (2), stores of goods

ASYNCRITUS
799 Asugkritŏs (1), incomparable

ATAD
329 'âṭâd (2), buckthorn tree

ATARAH
5851 'Ăṭârâh (1), crown

ATAROTH
5852 'Ăṭârôwth (5), crowns

ATAROTH-ADAR
5853 'Aṭrôwth 'Addâr (1), crowns of Addar

ATAROTH-ADDAR
5853 'Aṭrôwth 'Addâr (1), crowns of Addar

ATE
398 'âkal (2), to eat
2719 katĕsthiō (1), to devour

ATER
333 'Âṭêr (5), maimed

ATHACH
6269 'Ăthâk (1), lodging

ATHAIAH
6265 'Ăthâyâh (1), Jehovah has helped

ATHALIAH
6271 'Ăthalyâh (17), Jehovah has constrained

ATHENIANS
117 Athēnaiŏs (1), inhabitant of Athenæ

ATHENS
116 Athēnai (6), city Athenæ
117 Athēnaiŏs (1), inhabitant of Athenæ

ATHIRST
6770 tsâmê' (2), to thirst
1372 dipsaō (3), to thirst for

ATHLAI
6270 'Athlay (1), compressed

ATONEMENT
3722 kâphar (73), to cover; to expiate
3725 kippûr (7), expiation
2643 katallagē (1), restoration

ATONEMENTS
3725 kippûr (1), expiation

ATROTH
5855 'Aṭrôwth Shôwphân (1), crowns of Shophan

ATTAI
6262 'Attay (4), timely

ATTAIN
3201 yâkôl (1), to be able
5381 nâsag (1), to reach
7069 qânâh (1), to create; to procure
2658 katantaō (2), to attain or reach

ATTAINED
935 bôw' (4), to go or come
5381 nâsag (1), to reach
2638 katalambanō (1), to seize; to possess
2983 lambanō (1), to take, receive
3877 parakŏlŏuthĕō (1), to attend; trace out
5348 phthanō (2), to anticipate or precede

ATTALIA
825 Attalĕia (1), Attaleia

ATTEND
6440 pânîym (1), *face; front*
7181 qashab (9), to *prick up the ears*
2145 ĕuprŏsĕdrŏs (1), *diligent service*

ATTENDANCE
4612 ma'ămâd (2), *position; attendant*
4337 prŏsĕchō (2), to *pay attention to*

ATTENDED
995 bîyn (1), to *understand; discern*
7181 qashab (1), to *prick up the ears*
4337 prŏsĕchō (1), to *pay attention to*

ATTENDING
4343 prŏskartĕrĕsis (1), *persistency*

ATTENT
7183 qashshâb (2), *hearkening*

ATTENTIVE
7183 qashshâb (3), *hearkening*
1582 ĕkkrĕmamai (1), to *listen closely*

ATTENTIVELY
8085 shâma' (1), to *hear intelligently*

ATTIRE
2871 ṭâbûwl (1), *turban*
7196 qishshûr (1), *girdle or sash for women*
7897 shîyth (1), *garment*

ATTIRED
6801 tsânaph (1), to *wrap, i.e. roll or dress*

AUDIENCE
241 'ôzen (7), *ear*
189 akŏē (1), *hearing; thing heard*
191 akŏuō (4), to *hear; obey*

AUGMENT
5595 çâphâh (1), to *scrape; to accumulate*

AUGUSTUS
828 Augŏustŏs (3), *revered one*

AUGUSTUS'
828 Augŏustŏs (1), *revered one*

AUL
4836 martsêa' (2), *awl for piercing*

AUNT
1733 dôwdâh (1), *aunt*

AUSTERE
840 austĕrŏs (2), *severe, harsh; exacting*

AUTHOR
159 aitiŏs (1), *causer*
747 archēgŏs (1), *chief leader; founder*

AUTHORITIES
1849 ĕxŏusia (1), *authority, power, right*

AUTHORITY
7235 râbâh (1), to *increase*
8633 tôqeph (1), *might*
831 authĕntĕō (1), to *have authority*
1413 dunastēs (1), *ruler or officer*
1849 ĕxŏusia (28), *authority, power, right*
1850 ĕxŏusiazō (1), to *control, master another*
2003 ĕpitagē (1), *injunction or decree*
2715 katĕxŏusiazō (2), to *wield full privilege over*
5247 hupĕrŏchē (1), *superiority*

AVA
5755 'Ivvâh (1), *overthrow, ruin*

AVAILETH
7737 shâvâh (1), to *level; to resemble; to adjust*
2480 ischuō (3), to *have or exercise force*

AVEN
206 'Âven (3), *idolatry*

AVENGE
5358 nâqam (8), to *avenge or punish*
5358+5360 nâqam (1), to *avenge or punish*
5414+5360 nâthan (1), to *give*
6485 pâqad (1), to *visit, care for, count*
1556 ĕkdikĕō (4), to *vindicate; retaliate*
4160+3588+1557 pŏiĕō (2), to *make or do*

AVENGED
3467 yâsha' (1), to make *safe, free*
5358 nâqam (9), to *avenge or punish*
5414+5360 nâthan (1), to *give*
8199 shâphaṭ (2), to *judge*
1556 ĕkdikĕō (1), to *vindicate; retaliate*
2919+3588+2917 krinō (1), to *decide; to try*

AVENGER
1350 gâ'al (6), to *redeem; to be the next of kin*
5358 nâqam (2), to *avenge or punish*
1558 ĕkdikŏs (1), *punisher, avenger*

AVENGETH
5414+5360 nâthan (2), to *give*

AVENGING
3467 yâsha' (2), to make *safe, free*
6544+6546 pâra' (1), to *absolve, begin*

AVERSE
7725 shûwb (1), to *turn back; to return*

AVIM
5761 'Avvîym (1), *Avvim*

AVIMS
5757 'Avvîy (1), *Avvite*

AVITES
5757 'Avvîy (2), *Avvite*

AVITH
5762 'Ăvîyth (2), *ruin*

AVOID
6544 pâra' (1), to *loosen; to expose, dismiss*
1223 dia (1), *through,* by *means of; because of*
1578 ĕkklinō (1), to *shun; to decline*
3868 paraitĕŏmai (1), to *deprecate, decline*
4026 pĕriistēmi (1), to *stand around; to avoid*

AVOIDED
5437 çâbab (1), to *surround*

AVOIDING
1624 ĕktrĕpō (1), to *turn away*
4724 stĕllō (1), to *repress, abstain* from

AVOUCHED
559 'âmar (2), to *say, speak*

AWAIT
1917 ĕpibŏulē (1), *plot, plan*

AWAKE
5782 'ûwr (20), to *awake*
6974 qûwts (11), to *awake*
1235 diagrēgŏrĕō (1), to *waken thoroughly*
1326 diĕgĕirō (1), to *arouse, stimulate*
1453 ĕgĕirō (2), to *waken, i.e. rouse*
1594 ĕknēphō (1), to *rouse (oneself) out*
1852 ĕxupnizō (1), to *waken, rouse*

AWAKED
3364 yâqats (4), to *awake*
6974 qûwts (4), to *awake*

AWAKEST
5782 'ûwr (1), to *awake*
6974 qûwts (1), to *awake*

AWAKETH
6974 qûwts (3), to *awake*

AWAKING
1096+1853 ginŏmai (1), to *be, become*

AWARE
3045 yâda' (2), to *know*
1097 ginōskō (2), to *know*
1492 ĕidō (1), to *know.*

AWAY
310 'achar (1), *after*
1197 bâ'ar (16), to *be brutish, be senseless*
1272 bârach (1), to *flee suddenly*
1473 gôwlâh (7), *exile; captive*
1497 gâzal (4), to *rob*
1540 gâlâh (17), to *denude; uncover*
1541 gᵉlâh (Ch.) (1), to *reveal mysteries*
1546 gâlûwth (4), *captivity; exiles*
1589 gânab (1), to *thieve; to deceive*

1639 gâra' (1), to *shave, remove, lessen*
1870 derek (1), *road; course of life*
1898 hâgâh (2), to *remove, expel*
1920 hâdaph (1), to *push away or down; drive out*
2219 zârâh (1), to *toss about; to diffuse*
2763 charam (1), to *devote to destruction*
2846 châthâh (1), to *lay hold of; to take away*
2862 châthaph (1), to *clutch, snatch*
3212 yâlak (4), to *walk; to live; to carry*
3318 yâtsâ' (4), to *go, bring out*
3988 mâ'aç (1), to *spurn; to disappear*
4422 mâlaṭ (1), to *escape as if by slipperiness*
5074 nâdad (1), to *rove, flee; to drive away*
5077 nâdâh (1), to *exclude, i.e. banish*
5111 nûwd (Ch.) (1), to *flee*
5186 nâṭâh (1), to *stretch or spread out*
5265 nâça' (3), *start on a journey*
5493 çûwr (70), to *turn off*
5496 çûwth (1), to *stimulate; to seduce*
5674 'âbar (7), to *cross over; to transition*
5709 'ădâ' (Ch.) (3), to *remove; to bedeck*
5710 'âdâh (1), to *pass on or continue; to remove*
7311 rûwm (2), to *be high; to rise or raise*
7368 râchaq (3), to *recede; remove*
7617 shâbâh (7), to *transport into captivity*
7628 shᵉbîy (1), *exile; booty*
7673 shâbath (1), to *repose; to desist* from
7726 shôwbâb (1), *apostate, i.e. idolatrous*
7953 shâlâh (1), to *draw out or off, i.e. remove*
115 athĕtēsis (1), *cancellation*
142 airō (12), to *lift, to take up*
337 anairĕō (1), to *take away, i.e. abolish*
343 anakaluptō (1), to *unveil*
520 apagō (12), to *take away*
522 apairō (1), to *remove, take away*
565 apĕrchŏmai (15), to *go off, i.e. depart*
577 apŏballō (2), to *throw off; fig. to lose*
580 apŏbŏlē (1), *rejection, loss*
595 apŏthĕsis (1), *laying aside*
617 apŏkuliō (3), to *roll away, roll back*

628 apŏlŏuō (1), to *wash fully*
630 apŏluō (27), to *relieve, release*
645 apŏspaō (1), to *withdraw* with force
646 apŏstasia (1), *defection* from truth
649 apŏstĕllō (4), to *send out* on a mission
654 apŏstrĕphō (6), to *turn away or back*
657 apŏtassŏmai (1), to *say adieu; to renounce*
659 apŏtithēmi (1), to *put away; get rid of*
665 apŏtrĕpō (1), to *deflect, avoid*
667 apŏhĕrō (3), to *bear off, carry away*
683 apŏthĕŏmai (4), to *push off; to reject*
726 harpazō (2), to *seize*
851 aphairĕō (8), to *remove, cut off*
863 aphiĕmi (4), to *leave; to pardon, forgive*
868 aphistēmi (2), *instigate* to revolt
1294 diastrĕphō (1), to *distort*
1544 ĕkballō (1), to *throw out*
1593 ĕknĕuō (1), to *quietly withdraw*
1599 ĕkpĕmpō (1), to *despatch, send out*
1601 ĕkpiptō (1), to *drop away*
1602 ĕkplĕō (1), to *depart* by ship
1808 ĕxairō (1), to *remove, drive away*
1813 ĕxalĕiphō (2), to *obliterate*
1821 ĕxapŏstĕllō (4), to *despatch,* or to *dismiss*
1831 ĕxĕrchŏmai (1), to *issue; to leave*
1854 ĕxō (1), *out, outside*
2210 zēmiŏō (1), to *experience detriment*
2673 katargĕō (6), to *be, render entirely useless*
3179 mĕthistēmi (1), to *move*
3334 mĕtakinĕō (1), to *be removed, shifted from*
3350 mĕtŏikĕsia (3), *expatriation, exile*
3351 mĕtŏikizō (1), to *transfer* as a *settler* or *captive*
3895 parapiptō (1), to *apostatize, fall away*
3911 paraphĕrō (1), to *carry off; to avert*
3928 parĕrchŏmai (5), to *go by; to perish*
4014 pĕriairĕō (3), to *cast off anchor; to expiate*
4879 sunapagō (2), to *take off together*
5217 hupagō (3), to *withdraw or retire*

AWE
1481 gûwr (1), to *sojourn, live as an alien*

6342 pâchad (1), to *be startled; to fear*
7264 râgaz (1), to *quiver*

AWOKE
3364 yâqats (6), to *awake*
1326 diĕgĕirō (1), to *arouse, stimulate*
1453 ĕgĕirō (1), to *waken,* i.e. *rouse*

AX
1270 barzel (1), *iron; iron implement*
1631 garzen (2), *axe*
4601 Ma'ăkâh (1), *depression*
4621 ma'ătsâd (1), *axe*
7134 qardôm (1), *axe*
513 axinē (1), *axe*

AXE
1631 garzen (2), *axe*
7134 qardôm (1), *axe*
513 axinē (1), *axe*

AXES
2719 chereb (1), *knife, sword*
3781 kashshîyl (1), *axe*
4037 magzêrâh (1), *cutting blade, ax*
4050 mᵉgêrâh (1), *stone cutting saw*
7134 qardôm (3), *axe*

AXLETREES
3027 yâd (2), *hand; power*

AZAL
682 'Âtsêl (1), *noble*

AZALIAH
683 'Ătsalyâhûw (2), *Jehovah has reserved*

AZANIAH
245 'Ăzanyâh (1), *heard by Jehovah*

AZARAEL
5832 'Ăzar'êl (1), *God has helped*

AZAREEL
5832 'Ăzar'êl (5), *God has helped*

AZARIAH
5838 'Ăzaryâh (47), *Jehovah has helped*
5839 'Ăzaryâh (Ch.) (1), *Jehovah has helped*

AZAZ
5811 'Âzâz (1), *strong*

AZAZIAH
5812 'Ăzazyâhûw (3), *Jehovah has strengthened*

AZBUK
5802 'Azbûwq (1), *stern depopulator*

AZEKAH
5825 'Ăzêqâh (7), *tilled*

AZEL
682 'Âtsêl (6), *noble*

AZEM
6107 'Etsem (2), *bone*

AZGAD
5803 'Azgâd (4), *stern troop*

AZIEL
5815 'Ăzîy'êl (1), *strengthened of God*

AZIZA
5819 'Ăzîyzâ' (1), *strengthfulness*

AZMAVETH
5820 'Azmâveth (8), *strong (one) of death*

AZMON
6111 'Atsmôwn (3), *bone-like*

AZNOTH-TABOR
243 'Aznôwth Tâbôwr (1), *flats of Tabor*

AZOR
107 Azōr (2), *helpful*

AZOTUS
108 Azōtŏs (1), *Azotus,* i.e. *Ashdod*

AZRIEL
5837 'Azrîy'êl (3), *help of God*

AZRIKAM
5840 'Azrîyqâm (6), *help of an enemy*

AZUBAH
5806 'Ăzûwbâh (4), *forsaking*

AZUR
5809 'Azzûwr (2), *helpful*

AZZAH
5804 'Azzâh (3), *strong*

AZZAN
5821 'Azzân (1), *strong one*

AZZUR
5809 'Azzûwr (1), *helpful*

BAAL
1168 Ba'al (61), *master*
896 Baal (1), *master*

BAAL'S
1168 Ba'al (1), *master*

BAAL-BERITH
1170 Ba'al Bᵉrîyth (2), *Baal of (the) covenant*

BAAL-GAD
1171 Ba'al Gâd (3), *Baal of Fortune*

BAAL-HAMON
1174 Ba'al Hâmôwn (1), *possessor of a multitude*

BAAL-HANAN
1177 Ba'al Chânân (5), *possessor of grace*

BAAL-HAZOR
1178 Ba'al Châtsôwr (1), *possessor of a village*

BAAL-HERMON
1179 Ba'al Chermôwn (2), *possessor of Hermon*

BAAL-MEON
1186 Ba'al Mᵉ'ôwn (3), *Baal of (the) habitation*

BAAL-PEOR
1187 Ba'al Pᵉ'ôwr (6), *Baal of Peor*

BAAL-PERAZIM
1188 Ba'al Pᵉ'râtsîym (4), *possessor of breaches*

BAAL-SHALISHA
1190 Ba'al Shâlîshâh (1), *Baal of Shalishah*

BAAL-TAMAR
1193 Ba'al Tâmâr (1), *possessor of (the) palm-tree*

BAAL-ZEBUB
1176 Ba'al Zᵉbûwb (4), *Baal of (the) Fly*

BAAL-ZEPHON
1189 Ba'al Tsᵉphôwn (3), *Baal of winter*

BAALAH
1173 Ba'ălâh (5), *mistress*

BAALATH
1191 Ba'ălâth (3), office of *mistress*

BAALATH-BEER
1192 Ba'ălath Bᵉ'êr (1), *mistress of a well*

BAALE
1184 Ba'ălêy Yᵉhûwdâh (1), *masters of Judah*

BAALI
1180 Ba'ălîy (1), *my master*

BAALIM
1168 Ba'al (18), *master*

BAALIS
1185 Ba'ălîç (1), *in exultation*

BAANA
1195 Ba'ănâ' (2), *in affliction*

BAANAH
1195 Ba'ănâ' (10), *in affliction*

BAARA
1199 Bâ'ărâ' (1), *brutish*

BAASEIAH
1202 Ba'ăsêyâh (1), *in (the) work of Jehovah*

BAASHA
1201 Ba'shâ' (28), *offensiveness*

BABBLER
1167+3956 ba'al (1), *master; husband*
4691 spĕrmŏlŏgŏs (1), *gossip or trifler in talk*

BABBLING
7879 sîyach (1), uttered *contemplation*

BABBLINGS
2757 kĕnŏphōnia (2), *fruitless discussion*

BABE
5288 na'ar (1), male *child; servant*
1025 brĕphŏs (4), *infant*
3516 nēpiŏs (1), *infant; simple-minded person*

BABEL
894 Bâbel (2), *confusion*

BABES
5768 'ôwlêl (2), *suckling child*
8586 ta'ălûwl (1), *caprice* (as a fit *coming on*)
1025 brĕphŏs (1), *infant*

3516 něpiŏs (5), *infant; simple-minded* person

BABYLON
894 Bâbel (247), *confusion*
895 Bâbel (Ch.) (25), *confusion*
897 Babulōn (12), *Babylon*

BABYLON'S
894 Bâbel (8), *confusion*

BABYLONIANS
896 Bablîy (Ch.) (1), *Babylonian*
1121+894 bên (3), *people* of a class or kind

BABYLONISH
8152 Shin'âr (1), *Shinar*

BACA
1056 Bâkâ' (1), *Baca*

BACHRITES
1076 Bakrîy (1), *Bakrite*

BACK
268 'âchôwr (16), *behind, backward; west*
310 'achar (1), *after*
322 'ăchôrannîyth (1), *backwardly, by turning*
1354 gab (1), *mounded* or *rounded: top* or *rim*
1355 gab (Ch.) (1), *back*
1458 gav (7), *back*
1639 gâra' (1), to *shave, remove, lessen*
1973 hâlě'âh (1), *far away; thus far*
2015 hâphak (2), to *turn* about or over
2820 châsak (4), to *restrain* or *refrain*
3607 kâlâ' (1), to *hold* back or in; to *prohibit*
4185 mûwsh (1), to *withdraw*
4513 mâna' (4), to *deny, refuse*
5253 nâçag (1), to *retreat*
5437 çâbab (1), to *surround*
5472 çûwg (3), to *go back,* to *retreat*
5493 çûwr (2), to *turn* off
5637 çârar (1), to be *refractory, stubborn*
6203 'ôreph (4), *nape* or *back* of the neck
6437 pânâh (6), to *turn,* to *face*
6544 pâra' (1), to *loosen;* to *expose, dismiss*
7725 shûwb (70), to *turn* back; to *return*
7926 shěkem (2), *neck; spur* of a hill
617 apŏkuliō (2), to *roll away, roll back*
650 apŏstěrěō (1), to *deprive;* to *despoil*
3557 nŏsphizŏmai (2), to *sequestrate*
3577 nōtŏs (1), *back*
3694 ŏpisō (5), *behind, after, following*
4762 strěphō (1), to *turn* quite around or *reverse*
5288 hupŏstěllō (2), to *cower* or *shrink*

5289 hupŏstŏlē (1), *shrinkage, timidity*
5290 hupŏstrěphō (3), to *turn under, behind*

BACKBITERS
2637 katalalŏs (1), *slanderer*

BACKBITETH
7270 râgal (1), to *reconnoiter;* to *slander*

BACKBITING
5643 çěther (1), *cover, shelter*

BACKBITINGS
2636 katalalia (1), *defamation, slander*

BACKBONE
6096 'âtseh (1), *spine*

BACKS
268 'âchôwr (1), *behind, backward; west*
1354 gab (1), *mounded* or *rounded: top* or *rim*
1458 gav (1), *back*
6203 'ôreph (4), *nape* of the neck

BACKSIDE
268 'âchôwr (1), *behind, backward; west*
310 'achar (1), *after*
3693 ŏpisthěn (1), *at the back; after*

BACKSLIDER
5472 çûwg (1), to *go back,* to *apostatize*

BACKSLIDING
4878 měshûwbâh (7), *apostasy*
5637 çârar (1), to be *refractory, stubborn*
7726 shôwbâb (2), *apostate,* i.e. *idolatrous*
7728 shôwbêb (2), *apostate, heathenish*

BACKSLIDINGS
4878 měshûwbâh (4), *apostasy*

BACKWARD
268 'âchôwr (11), *behind, backward; west*
322 'ăchôrannîyth (6), *backwardly, by turning*
1519+3588+3694 ěis (1), *to* or *into*

BAD
873 bî'ûwsh (Ch.) (1), *wicked, evil*
7451 ra' (13), *bad; evil*
2556 kakŏs (1), *bad, evil*
4190 pŏnērŏs (1), *malice, wicked, bad; crime*
4550 saprŏs (1), *rotten,* i.e. *worthless*

BADE
559 'âmar (6), to *say, speak*
1696 dâbar (1), to *speak, say;* to *subdue*
6680 tsâvâh (1), to *constitute, enjoin*
657 apŏtassŏmai (1), to *say adieu;* to *renounce*
2036 ěpō (3), to *speak*
2564 kalěō (4), to *call*

BADEST
1696 dâbar (1), to *speak, say;* to *subdue*

BADGERS'
8476 tachash (14), (poss.) *antelope*

BADNESS
7455 rôa' (1), *badness*

BAG
3599 kîyç (4), *cup;* utility *bag*
3627 kělîy (2), *implement, thing*
6872 tsěrôwr (3), *parcel; kernel* or *particle*
1101 glōssŏkŏmŏn (2), *money purse*

BAGS
2754 chârîyt (1), *pocket*
6696 tsûwr (1), to *cramp,* i.e. *confine;* to *harass*
905 balantiŏn (1), *money pouch*

BAHARUMITE
978 Bachărûwmîy (1), *Bacharumite*

BAHURIM
980 Bachûrîym (5), *young men*

BAJITH
1006 Bayith (1), *house; temple; family, tribe*

BAKBAKKAR
1230 Baqbaqqar (1), *searcher*

BAKBUK
1227 Baqbûwq (2), *bottle*

BAKBUKIAH
1229 Baqbuqyâh (3), *wasting of Jehovah*

BAKE
644 'âphâh (6), to *bake*
1310 bâshal (1), to *boil* up, cook; to *ripen*
5746 'ûwg (1), to *bake*

BAKED
644 'âphâh (2), to *bake*
1310 bâshal (1), to *boil* up, cook; to *ripen*

BAKEMEATS
3978+4639+644 ma'ăkâl (1), *food*

BAKEN
644 'âphâh (4), to *bake*
7246 râbak (1), to *soak* bread in oil
8601 tûphîyn (1), *baked cake*

BAKER
644 'âphâh (8), to *bake*

BAKERS
644 'âphâh (2), to *bake*

BAKERS'
644 'âphâh (1), to *bake*

BAKETH
644 'âphâh (1), to *bake*

BALAAM
1109 Bil'âm (57), *foreigner*
903 Balaam (3), *foreigner*

BALAAM'S
1109 Bil'âm (3), *foreigner*

BALAC
904 Balak (1), *waster*

BALADAN
1081 Bal'ădân (2), *Bel* (is his) *lord*

BALAH
1088 Bâlâh (1), *failure*

BALAK
1111 Bâlâq (42), *waster*

BALAK'S
1111 Bâlâq (1), *waster*

BALANCE
3976 mô'zên (7), pair of balance *scales*
7070 qâneh (1), *reed*

BALANCES
3976 mô'zên (8), pair of balance *scales*
3977 mô'zên (Ch.) (1), pair of balance *scales*

BALANCINGS
4657 miphlâs (1), *poising*

BALD
1371 gibbêach (1), *bald forehead*
1372 gabbachath (3), *baldness* on forehead
5556 çol'âm (1), *destructive locust* kind
7139 qârach (4), to *depilate, shave*
7142 qêrêach (3), *bald* on the back of the head
7144 qorchâh (1), *baldness*
7146 qârachath (1), *bald spot; threadbare* spot

BALDNESS
7144 qorchâh (9), *baldness*

BALL
1754 dûwr (1), *circle; ball*

BALM
6875 tsěrîy (6), *balsam*

BAMAH
1117 Bâmâh (1), *elevation, high place*

BAMOTH
1120 Bâmôwth (2), *heights*

BAMOTH-BAAL
1120 Bâmôwth (1), *heights of Baal*

BAND
613 'ěçûwr (Ch.) (2), *manacles, chains*
1416 gědûwd (5), *band of soldiers*
2428 chayil (2), *army; wealth; virtue; valor*
5688 'ăbôth (1), *entwined things: a string, wreath*
8193 sâphâh (1), *lip, language, speech*
4686 spěira (7), *tenth of a Roman Legion*

BANDED
4160+4963 pŏiěō (1), to *make* or *do*

BANDS
102 'aggâph (7), *crowds* of troops

BANI

612 'êçûwr (2), *manacles, chains*
631 'âçar (1), to *fasten*; to *join* battle
1416 gᵉdûwd (8), *band* of soldiers
2256 chebel (3), *company, band*
2683 chêtsen (1), *bosom*
2784 chartsubbâh (2), *fetter; pain*
4133 môwţâh (2), *pole; ox-bow; yoke*
4147 môwçêr (6), *halter; restraint*
4189 môwshᵉkâh (1), *cord, band*
4264 machăneh (2), *encampment*
5688 'ăbôth (3), *entwined* things: a *string, wreath*
7218 rô'sh (2), *head*
1199 dĕsmŏn (3), *shackle; impediment*
2202 zĕuktēria (1), *tiller-rope, band*
4886 sundĕsmŏs (1), *ligament; control*

BANI

1137 Bânîy (15), *built*

BANISHED

5080 nâdach (2), to *push* off, *scattered*

BANISHMENT

4065 maddûwach (1), *seduction, misleading*
8331 sharshâh (1), *chain*

BANK

5550 çôlᵉlâh (3), *siege* mound, i.e. *rampart*
8193 sâphâh (10), *lip; edge, margin*
5132 trapĕza (1), *table* or *stool*

BANKS

1415 gâdâh (3), *border, bank* of a river
1428 gidyâh (1), *border, bank* of a river

BANNER

1714 degel (1), *flag, standard, banner*
5251 nêç (2), *flag; signal; token*

BANNERS

1713 dâgal (3), to *be conspicuous*

BANQUET

3738 kârâh (1), to *dig*; to *plot*; to *bore, hew*
4797 mirzach (1), *cry* of joy; *revel* or *feast*
4960 mishteh (10), *drink; banquet* or *feast*
4961 mishteh (Ch.) (1), *drink; banquet* or feast
8354 shâthâh (1), to *drink, imbibe*

BANQUETING

3196 yayin (1), *wine; intoxication*

BANQUETINGS

4224 pŏtŏs (1), *drinking-bout*

BAPTISM

908 baptisma (22), *baptism*

BAPTISMS

909 baptismŏs (1), *baptism*

BAPTIST

907 baptizō (1), *baptize*
910 Baptistēs (13), *baptizer*

BAPTIST'S

910 Baptistēs (1), *baptizer*

BAPTIZE

907 baptizō (9), *baptize*

BAPTIZED

907 baptizō (57), *baptize*

BAPTIZEST

907 baptizō (1), *baptize*

BAPTIZETH

907 baptizō (2), *baptize*

BAPTIZING

907 baptizō (4), *baptize*

BAR

270 'âchaz (1), to *seize, grasp; possess*
1280 bᵉrîyach (4), *bolt; cross-bar* of a door
4132 môwţ (2), *pole; yoke*

BAR-JESUS

919 Bariēsŏus (1), *son of Joshua*

BAR-JONA

920 Bariōnas (1), *son of Jonah*

BARABBAS

912 Barabbas (11), *son of Abba*

BARACHEL

1292 Bârak'êl (2), *God has blessed*

BARACHIAS

914 Barachias (1), *blessing* of Jehovah

BARAK

1301 Bârâq (13), *(flash of) lightning*
913 Barak (1), *(flash of) lightning*

BARBARIAN

915 barbarŏs (3), *foreigner, non-Greek*

BARBARIANS

915 barbarŏs (2), *foreigner, non-Greek*

BARBAROUS

915 barbarŏs (1), *foreigner, non-Greek*

BARBED

7905 sukkâh (1), *dart, harpoon*

BARBER'S

1532 gallâb (1), *barber*

BARE

2029 hârâh (1), to *conceive, be pregnant*
2308 châdal (1), to *desist, stop; be fat*
2342 chûwl (1), to *dance, whirl*; to *writhe* in pain
2554 châmaç (1), to *be violent; to maltreat*

BASE

2834 châsaph (4), to *drain* away or *bail* up
3205 yâlad (110), to *bear* young; to *father a child*
4910 mâshal (1), to *rule*
5190 nâţal (1), to *lift*; to *impose*
5375 nâsâ' (34), to *lift up*
6181 'eryâh (4), *nudity*
6209 'ârar (1), to *bare*; to *demolish*
6544 pâra' (1), to *loosen*; to *expose, dismiss*
7146 qârachath (1), *bald* spot; *threadbare* spot
7287 râdâh (2), to *subjugate*; to *crumble*
7980 shâlaţ (1), to *dominate*, i.e. *govern*
399 anaphĕrō (1), to *take* up; to *lead up*
941 bastazō (4), to *lift, bear*
1080 gĕnnaō (1), to *procreate, regenerate*
1131 gumnŏs (1), *nude* or *not well clothed*
3140 marturĕō (9), to *testify*; to *commend*
4160 pŏiĕō (2), to *make* or do
5342 phĕrō (1), to *bear* or *carry*
5576 psĕudŏmarturĕō (2), to *offer false evidence*

BAREFOOT

3182 yâchêph (4), *not wearing sandals*

BAREST

4910 mâshal (1), to *rule*
5375 nâsâ' (1), to *lift up*
3140 marturĕō (1), to *testify*; to *commend*

BARHUMITE

1273 Barchûmîy (1), *Barchumite*

BARIAH

1282 Bârîyach (1), *Bariach*

BARK

5024 nâbach (1), to *bark*

BARKED

7111 qᵉtsâphâh (1), *fragment*

BARKOS

1302 Barqôwç (2), *Barkos*

BARLEY

8184 sᵉ'ôrâh (33), *barley*
2915 krithē (1), *barley*
2916 krithinŏs (2), *consisting of barley*

BARN

1637 gôren (1), *open area*
4035 mᵉgûwrâh (1), *fright; granary*
596 apŏthēkē (2), *granary, grain barn*

BARNABAS

921 Barnabas (29), *son of prophecy*

BARNFLOOR

1637 gôren (1), *open area*

BARNS

618 'âçâm (1), *barn*

BASES — BASES 21 column

4460 mammᵉgûrâh (1), *granary, grain pit*
596 apŏthēkē (2), *granary, grain barn*

BARREL

3537 kad (3), *jar, pitcher*

BARRELS

3537 kad (1), *jar, pitcher*

BARREN

4420 mᵉlêchâh (1), *salted* land, i.e. a *desert*
6115 'ôtser (1), *closure; constraint*
6135 'âqâr (11), *sterile, barren*
6723 tsîyâh (1), *arid desert*
7909 shakkuwl (2), *bereaved*
7921 shâkôl (2), to *miscarry*
692 argŏs (1), *lazy; useless*
4722 stĕgō (4), to *endure* patiently

BARRENNESS

4420 mᵉlêchâh (1), *salted* land, i.e. a *desert*

BARS

905 bad (1), *limb, member; bar; chief*
1280 bᵉrîyach (35), *bolt; cross-bar* of a door
4800 merchâb (1), *open space; liberty*

BARSABAS

923 Barsabas (2), *son of Sabas*

BARTHOLOMEW

918 Barthŏlŏmaiŏs (4), *son of Tolmai*

BARTIMAEUS

924 Bartimaiŏs (1), *son* of the *unclean*

BARUCH

1263 Bârûwk (26), *blessed*

BARZILLAI

1271 Barzillay (12), *iron-hearted*

BASE

1097+8034 bᵉlîy (1), *without, not yet*
3653 kên (2), *pedestal* or *station* of a basin
4350 mᵉkôwnâh (7), *pedestal; spot* or *place*
4369 mᵉkûnâh (1), *spot*
7034 qâlâh (1), to *be light*
8217 shâphâl (4), *depressed, low*
36 agĕnēs (1), *ignoble, lowly*
5011 tapĕinŏs (1), *humiliated, lowly*

BASER

60 agŏraiŏs (1), *people* of the *market place*

BASES

4350 mᵉkôwnâh (13), *pedestal; spot* or *place*
4369 mᵉkûnâh (1), *spot*

BASEST
8215 shᵉphal (Ch.) (1), *low*
8217 shâphâl (1), *depressed, low*

BASHAN
1316 Bâshân (59), *Bashan*

BASHAN-HAVOTH-JAIR
1316+2334 Bâshân (1), *Bashan*

BASHEMATH
1315 Bosmath (6), *fragrance*

BASKET
1731 dûwd (2), *pot, kettle; basket*
2935 ṭene' (4), *basket*
3619 kᵉlûwb (2), *bird-trap; basket*
5536 çal (12), *basket*
4553 sarganê (1), *wicker basket*
4711 spuris (1), *hamper or lunch-receptacle*

BASKETS
1731 dûwd (1), *pot, kettle; basket*
1736 dûwday (1), *basket*
5536 çal (2), *basket*
5552 çalçillâh (1), *twig*
2894 kŏphinŏs (6), *small basket*
4711 spuris (4), *hamper or lunch-receptacle*

BASMATH
1315 Bosmath (1), *fragrance*

BASON
3713 kᵉphôwr (2), *bowl; white frost*
5592 çaph (2), *dish*
3537 niptēr (1), *basin for washing*

BASONS
101 'aggân (1), *bowl*
3713 kᵉphôwr (3), *bowl; white frost*
4219 mîzrâq (11), *bowl for sprinkling*
5592 çaph (2), *dish*

BASTARD
4464 mamzêr (2), *mongrel*

BASTARDS
3541 nôthŏs (1), *spurious or illegitimate son*

BAT
5847 'ăṭallêph (2), *mammal, bat*

BATH
1324 bath (6), *liquid measure*

BATH-RABBIM
1337 Bath Rabbîym (1), *city of Rabbah*

BATH-SHEBA
1339 Bath-Sheba' (11), *daughter of an oath*

BATH-SHUA
1340 Bath-Shûwa' (1), *daughter of wealth*

BATHE
7364 râchats (18), to *lave, bathe*

BATHED
7301 râvâh (1), to *slake thirst or appetites*

BATHS
1324 bath (8), *liquid measure*
1325 bath (Ch.) (1), *liquid measure*

BATS
5847 'ăṭallêph (1), *bat*

BATTERED
7843 shâchath (1), to *decay; to ruin*

BATTLE
3593 kîydôwr (1), (poss.) *tumult, battle*
4221 môach (1), *bone marrow*
4264 machăneh (1), *encampment*
4421 milchâmâh (143), *battle; war; fighting*
4661 mappêts (1), *war-club*
5402 nesheq (1), *military arms, arsenal*
5430 çe'ôwn (1), *military boot*
6635 tsâbâ' (5), *army, military host*
6635+4421 tsâbâ' (1), *army, military host*
7128 qᵉrâb (5), *hostile encounter*
4171 pŏlĕmŏs (5), *warfare; battle; fight*

BATTLEMENT
4624 ma'ăqeh (1), *parapet*

BATTLEMENTS
5189 nᵉṭîyshâh (1), *tendril plant shoot*

BATTLES
4421 milchâmâh (6), *battle; war; fighting*

BAVAI
942 Bavvay (1), *Bavvai*

BAY
249 'ezrâch (1), *native born*
554 'âmôts (2), *red*
3956 lâshôwn (3), *tongue; tongue-shaped*

BAZLITH
1213 Batslûwth (1), *peeling*

BAZLUTH
1213 Batslûwth (1), *peeling*

BDELLIUM
916 bᵉdôlach (2), *bdellium, amber; pearl*

BEACON
8650 tôren (1), *mast pole; flag-staff pole*

BEALIAH
1183 Bᵉ'alyâh (1), *Jehovah (is) master*

BEALOTH
1175 Bᵉ'âlôwth (1), *mistresses*

BEAM
708 'ereg (1), *weaving; braid; also shuttle*

3714 kâphîyç (1), *girder, beam*
4500 mânôwr (4), *frame of a loom*
5646 'âb (1), *architrave*
6982 qôwrâh (2), *rafter; roof*
1385 dŏkŏs (6), *stick or plank*

BEAMS
1356 gêb (1), *well, cistern*
3773 kârûthâh (3), *hewn timber beams*
6763 tsêlâ' (1), *side of a person or thing*
6982 qôwrâh (2), *rafter; roof*
7136 qârâh (4), to *bring about; to impose*

BEANS
6321 pôwl (2), *beans*

BEAR
1319 bâsar (4), to *announce (good news)*
1677 dôb (10), *bear*
1678 dôb (Ch.) (1), *bear*
2398 châṭâ' (2), to *sin*
3205 yâlad (16), to *bear young; to father a child*
3212 yâlak (1), to *walk; to live; to carry*
3318 yâtsâ' (1), to *go, bring out*
3557 kûwl (1), to *keep in; to measure*
4910 mâshal (1), to *rule*
5187 nᵉṭîyl (1), *laden*
5201 nâṭar (1), to *guard; to cherish anger*
5375 nâsâ' (100), to *lift up*
5445 çâbal (3), to *carry*
5749 'ûwd (1), to *protest, testify; to encompass*
6030 'ânâh (2), to *respond, answer*
6213 'âsâh (4), to *do*
7287 râdâh (1), to *subjugate; to crumble*
7981 shᵉlêṭ (Ch.) (1), to *dominate, i.e. govern*
8323 sârar (1), to *have, exercise, get dominion*
8382 tâ'am (1), to *be twinned, i.e. duplicate*
8505 tâkan (1), to *balance, i.e. measure*
142 airō (4), to *lift, to take up*
399 anaphërō (1), to *take up; to lead up*
430 anĕchŏmai (4), *put up with, endure*
503 antŏphthalmĕō (1), to *face into the wind*
715 arktŏs (1), *bear (animal)*
941 bastazō (11), to *lift, bear*
1080 gĕnnaō (1), to *procreate, regenerate*
3114 makrŏthumĕō (1), to *be forbearing, patient*
3140 marturĕō (21), to *testify; to commend*
4160 pŏiĕō (2), to *do*
5041 tĕknŏgŏnĕō (1), to *be a child bearer*

5297 hupŏphĕrō (1), to *bear from underneath*
5342 phĕrō (4), to *bear*
5409 phŏrĕō (1), to *wear*
5576 psĕudŏmarturĕō (4), to offer *falsehood in evidence*

BEARD
2206 zâqân (14), *beard*
8222 sâphâm (1), *beard*

BEARDS
2206 zâqân (4), *beard*

BEARERS
5449 çabbâl (3), *porter, carrier*

BEAREST
3205 yâlad (1), to *bear young; to father a child*
941 bastazō (1), to *lift, bear*
3140 marturĕō (1), to *testify; to commend*
5088 tiktō (1), to *produce from seed*

BEARETH
3205 yâlad (2), to *bear young; to father a child*
4910 mâshal (1), to *rule*
5375 nâsâ' (7), to *lift up*
6030 'ânâh (2), to *respond, answer*
6509 pârâh (1), to *bear fruit*
6779 tsâmach (1), to *sprout*
8382 tâ'am (1), to *be twinned, i.e. duplicate*
1627 ĕkphĕrō (1), to *bear out; to produce*
2592 karpŏphŏrĕō (1), to *be fertile*
3140 marturĕō (3), to *testify; to commend*
4722 stĕgō (1), to *endure patiently*
4828 summarturĕō (1), to *testify jointly*
5342 phĕrō (2), to *bear or carry*
5409 phŏrĕō (1), to *wear*

BEARING
2232 zâra' (1), to *sow seed; to disseminate*
3205 yâlad (3), to *bear young; to father a child*
5375 nâsâ' (10), to *lift up*
941 bastazō (3), to *lift, bear*
4064 pĕriphĕrō (1), to *transport*
4828 summarturĕō (2), to *testify jointly*
4901 sunĕpimarturĕō (1), to *testify further jointly*
5342 phĕrō (1), to *bear or carry*

BEARS
1677 dôb (2), *bear*

BEAST
929 bᵉhêmâh (83), *animal, beast*
1165 bᵉ'îyr (1), *cattle, livestock*
2123 zîyz (1), *moving creature*

BERODACH-BALADAN
1255 Bᵉrô'dak Bal'ădân (1), *Berodak-Baladan*

BEROTHAH
1268 Bĕrôwthâh (1), *cypress-like*

BEROTHAI
1268 Bĕrôwthâh (1), *cypress-like*

BEROTHITE
1307 Bêrôthîy (1), *Berothite*

BERRIES
1620 gargar (1), *berry*
1636 ĕlaia (1), *olive*

BERYL
8658 tarshîysh (7), (poss.) *topaz*
969 bĕrullŏs (1), *beryl*

BESAI
1153 Bᵉçay (2), *domineering*

BESEECH
577 'ânnâ' (8), *I ask you!*
2470+6440 châlâh (1), to *be weak, sick, afflicted*
4994 nâ' (26), *I pray!, please!, I beg you!*
1189 dĕŏmai (6), to *beg, petition, ask*
2065 ĕrōtaō (4), to *interrogate; to request*
3870 parakalĕō (20), to *call, invite*

BESEECHING
2065 ĕrōtaō (1), to *interrogate; to request*
3870 parakalĕō (2), to *call, invite*

BESET
3803 kâthar (1), to *enclose, besiege; to wait*
5437 çâbab (3), to *surround*
6696 tsûwr (1), to *cramp, i.e. confine; to harass*
2139 ĕupĕristatŏs (1), *entangling, obstructing*

BESIDE
310 'achar (1), *after*
413 'êl (2), *to, toward*
657 'epheç (3), *end; no further*
681 'êtsel (12), *side; near*
854 'êth (2), *with; by; at; among*
905 bad (45), *apart, only, besides*
1107 bil'ădêy (7), *except, without, besides*
1115 biltîy (3), *except, without, unless, besides*
2108 zûwlâh (6), *except; apart from; besides*
3027 yâd (1), *hand; power*
5921 'al (17), *above, over, upon, or against*
5973 'îm (4), *with*
5980 'ummâh (2), *near, beside, along with*
6654 tsad (3), *side; adversary*
846 autŏs (1), *he, she, it*
1839 ĕxistēmi (2), to *astound*
1909 ĕpi (3), *on, upon*

3105 mainŏmai (1), to *rave as a maniac*
4862 sun (1), *with or together*
5565 chōris (3), *separately, apart* from

BESIDES
905 bad (1), *apart, only, besides*
2108 zûwlâh (1), *except; apart from; besides*
5750 'ôwd (4), *again; repeatedly; still; more*
5921 'al (1), *above, over, upon, or against*
3063 lŏipŏn (1), *something remaining; finally*
4359 prŏsŏphĕilō (1), to *be indebted*

BESIEGE
6696 tsûwr (8), to *cramp, i.e. confine; to harass*
6887 tsârar (3), to *cramp*

BESIEGED
935+4692 bôw' (3), to *go or come*
4692 mâtsôwr (1), *siege-mound; distress*
4693 mâtsôwr (2), *limit, border*
5341 nâtsar (2), to *guard, protect, maintain*
5437 çâbab (1), to *surround*
6696 tsûwr (14), to *cramp, i.e. confine*

BESODEIAH
1152 Bᵉçôwdᵉyâh (1), *in* (the) *counsel of Jehovah*

BESOM
4292 maṭ'ăṭê' (1), *broom*

BESOR
1308 Bᵉsôwr (3), *cheerful*

BESOUGHT
1245 bâqash (2), to *search* out
2470 châlâh (5), to *be weak, sick, afflicted*
2603 chânan (4), to *implore*
1189 dĕŏmai (3), to *beg, petition, ask*
2065 ĕrōtaō (9), to *interrogate; to request*
3870 parakalĕō (21), to *call, invite*

BEST
2173 zimrâh (1), *choice*
2459 cheleb (5), *fat; choice part*
2896 ṭôwb (8), *good; well*
3190 yâṭab (1), to *be, make well*
4315 mêyṭâb (6), *best*
5324 nâtsab (1), to *station*
6338 pâzaz (1), to *refine gold*
2909 krĕittōn (1), *stronger, i.e. nobler*
4413 prōtŏs (1), *foremost*

BESTIR
2782 chârats (1), to *be alert, to decide*

BESTOW
5414 nâthan (2), to *give*

5415 nᵉthan (Ch.) (2), to *give*
6213 'âsâh (1), to *do or make*
4060 pĕritithēmi (1), to *present*
4863 sunagō (2), to *gather together*
5595 psōmizō (1), to *nourish, feed*

BESTOWED
1580 gâmal (2), to *benefit or requite; to wean*
3240 yânach (2), to *allow to stay*
5414 nâthan (2), to *give*
6485 pâqad (1), to *visit, care for, count*
1325 didōmi (2), to *give*
2872 kŏpiaō (3), to *feel fatigue; to work hard*

BETAH
984 Beṭach (1), *safety, security, trust*

BETEN
991 Beṭen (1), *belly; womb; body*

BETH-ANATH
1043 Bêyth 'Ănâth (3), *house of replies*

BETH-ANOTH
1042 Bêyth 'Ănôwth (1), *house of replies*

BETH-ARABAH
1026 Bêyth hâ-'Ărâbâh (3), *house of the desert*

BETH-ARAM
1027 Bêyth hâ-Râm (1), *house of the height*

BETH-ARBEL
1009 Bêyth 'Arbê'l (1), *house of God's ambush*

BETH-AVEN
1007 Bêyth 'Âven (7), *house of vanity*

BETH-AZMAVETH
1041 Bêyth 'Azmâveth (1), *house of Azmaveth*

BETH-BAAL-MEON
1010 Bêyth Ba'al Mᵉ'ôwn (1), *house of Baal of* (the) *habitation*

BETH-BARAH
1012 Bêyth Bârâh (2), *house of* (the) *river ford*

BETH-BIREI
1011 Bêyth Bir'îy (1), *house of a creative one*

BETH-CAR
1033 Bêyth Kar (1), *house of pasture*

BETH-DAGON
1016 Bêyth-Dâgôwn (2), *house of Dagon*

BETH-DIBLATHAIM
1015 Bêyth Diblâthayim (1), *house of* (the) *two figcakes*

BETH-EL
1008 Bêyth-'Êl (66), *house of God*

BETH-ELITE
1017 Bêyth hâ-'Êlîy (1), *Beth-elite*

BETH-EMEK
1025 Bêyth hâ-'Êmeq (1), *house of the valley*

BETH-EZEL
1018 Bêyth hâ-'Êtsel (1), *house of the side*

BETH-GADER
1013 Bêyth-Gâdêr (1), *house of* (the) *wall*

BETH-GAMUL
1014 Bêyth Gâmûwl (1), *house of* (the) *weaned*

BETH-HACCEREM
1021 Bêyth hak-Kerem (2), *house of the vineyard*

BETH-HARAN
1028 Bêyth hâ-Rân (1), *house of the height*

BETH-HOGLA
1031 Bêyth Choglâh (1), *house of a partridge*

BETH-HOGLAH
1031 Bêyth Choglâh (2), *house of a partridge*

BETH-HORON
1032 Bêyth Chôwrôwn (14), *house of hollowness*

BETH-JESHIMOTH
1020 Bêyth ha-Yᵉshîy-môwth (3), *house of the deserts*

BETH-JESIMOTH
1020 Bêyth ha-Yᵉshîy-môwth (1), *house of the deserts*

BETH-LEBAOTH
1034 Bêyth Lᵉbâ'ôwth (1), *house of lionesses*

BETH-LEHEM
1035 Bêyth Lechem (30), *house of bread*

BETH-LEHEM-JUDAH
1035 Bêyth Lechem (10), *house of bread*

BETH-LEHEMITE
1022 Bêyth hal-Lachmîy (4), *Beth-lechemite*

BETH-MAACHAH
1038 Bêyth Ma'âkâh (2), *house of Maakah*

BETH-MARCABOTH
1024 Bêyth ham-Markâbôwth (2), *place of* (the) *chariots*

BETH-MEON
1010 Bêyth Ba'al Mᵉ'ôwn (1), *house of Baal of* (the) *habitation*

BETH-NIMRAH
1039 Bêyth Nimrâh (2), *house of* (the) *leopard*

BETH-PALET
1046 Bêyth Peleṭ (1), *house of escape*

BETH-PAZZEZ
1048 Bêyth Patstsêts (1), *house of dispersion*

BETH-PEOR
1047 Bêyth Pᵉ'ôwr (4), *house of Peor*

BETH-PHELET
1046 Bêyth Peleṭ (1), *house of escape*

BETH-RAPHA
1051 Bêyth Râphâ' (1), *house of (the) giant*

BETH-REHOB
1050 Bêyth Rᵉchôwb (2), *house of (the) street*

BETH-SHAN
1052 Bêyth Shᵉ'ân (3), *house of ease*

BETH-SHEAN
1052 Bêyth Shᵉ'ân (6), *house of ease*

BETH-SHEMESH
1053 Bêyth Shemesh (21), *house of (the) sun*

BETH-SHEMITE
1030 Bêyth hash-Shimshîy (2), *Beth-shimshite*

BETH-SHITTAH
1029 Bêyth hash-Shiṭṭâh (1), *house of the acacia*

BETH-TAPPUAH
1054 Bêyth Tappûwach (1), *house of (the) apple*

BETH-ZUR
1049 Bêyth Tsûwr (4), *house of (the) rock*

BETHABARA
962 Bēthabara (1), *ferry-house*

BETHANY
963 Bēthania (11), *date-house*

BETHER
1336 Bether (1), *section*

BETHESDA
964 Bēthĕsda (1), *house of kindness*

BETHINK
7725+413+3820 shûwb (2), *to turn back*

BETHLEHEM
1035 Bêyth Lechem (1), *house of bread*
965 Bēthlĕĕm (8), *house of bread*

BETHPHAGE
967 Bēthphagē (3), *fig-house*

BETHSAIDA
966 Bēthsaïda (7), *fishing-house*

BETHUEL
1328 Bᵉthûw'êl (10), *destroyed of God*

BETHUL
1329 Bᵉthûwl (1), *Bethuel*

BETIMES
7836 shâchar (3), *to search for*
7925 shâkam (2), *to load up, i.e. to start early*

BETONIM
993 Bᵉṭônîym (1), *hollows*

BETRAY
7411 râmâh (1), *to hurl; to shoot; to delude*
3860 paradidōmi (17), *to hand over*

BETRAYED
3860 paradidōmi (18), *to hand over*

BETRAYERS
4273 prŏdŏtēs (1), *betraying*

BETRAYEST
3860 paradidōmi (1), *to hand over*

BETRAYETH
3860 paradidōmi (3), *to hand over*

BETROTH
781 'âras (4), *to engage for matrimony, betroth*

BETROTHED
781 'âras (6), *to engage for matrimony, betroth*
2778 châraph (1), *to spend the winter*
3259 yâ'ad (2), *to engage for marriage*

BETTER
2896 ṭôwb (75), *good; well*
3027 yâd (1), *hand; power*
3148 yôwthêr (1), *moreover; rest; gain*
3190 yâṭab (4), *to be, make well*
3504 yithrôwn (1), *preeminence, gain*
1308 diaphĕrō (3), *to differ; to surpass*
2570 kalŏs (5), *good; beautiful; valuable*
2573 kalŏs (1), *well*
2909 krĕittōn (18), *stronger, i.e. nobler*
3081 lusitĕlĕi (1), *it is advantageous*
4052 pĕrissĕuō (1), *to superabound*
4284 prŏĕchŏmai (1), *to excel*
4851 sumphĕrō (1), *to collect; advantage*
5242 hupĕrĕchō (1), *to excel; superior*
5543 chrēstŏs (1), *employed, i.e. useful*

BETTERED
5623 ōphĕlĕō (1), *to benefit, be of use*

BETWEEN
996 bêyn (190), *between*
997 bêyn (Ch.) (1), *between; "either...or"*
5921 'al (1), *upon, against*
5973 'îm (2), *with*
8432 tâvek (3), *center, middle*
1722 ĕn (1), *in; during; because of*
3307 mĕrizō (1), *to apportion, bestow*
3342 mĕtaxu (6), *betwixt*
4314 prŏs (2), *for; on, at; to, toward; against*

BETWIXT
996 bêyn (13), *between*
6293 pâga' (1), *to impinge*

1537 ĕk (1), out, out of

BEULAH
1166 bâ'al (1), *to be master; to marry*

BEWAIL
1058 bâkâh (4), *to weep, moan*
2799 klaiō (1), *to sob, wail*
3996 pĕnthĕō (1), *to grieve*

BEWAILED
1058 bâkâh (1), *to weep, moan*
2875 kŏptō (2), *to beat the breast*

BEWAILETH
3306 yâphach (1), *to breathe hard, gasp*

BEWARE
6191 'âram (1), *to be cunning; be prudent*
8104 shâmar (9), *to watch*
991 blĕpō (6), *to look at*
4337 prŏsĕchō (7), *to pay attention to*
5442 phulassō (2), *to watch, i.e. be on guard*

BEWITCHED
940 baskainō (1), *to fascinate, bewitch*
1839 ĕxistēmi (2), *to astound; to be insane*

BEWRAY
1540 gâlâh (1), *to denude; uncover*

BEWRAYETH
5046 nâgad (1), *to announce*
7121 qârâ' (1), *to call out*
1212+4160 dēlŏs (1), *clear, plain, evident*

BEYOND
1973 hâlᵉâh (5), *far away; thus far*
5674 'âbar (4), *to cross over; to transition*
5675 'âbar (Ch.) (7), *region across*
5676 'êber (21), *opposite side; east*
5921 'al (2), *above, over*
1900 ĕpĕkĕina (1), *on the further side of, beyond*
4008 pĕran (7), *across, beyond*
5228 hupĕr (1), *over; above; beyond*
5233 hupĕrbainō (1), *to transcend*
5238 hupĕrĕkĕina (1), *beyond, still farther*
5239 hupĕrĕktĕinō (1), *to overreach*
5249 hupĕrpĕrissōs (1), *exceedingly*

BEZAI
1209 Bêtsay (3), *Betsai*

BEZALEEL
1212 Bᵉtsal'êl (9), *in (the) protection of God*

BEZEK
966 Bezeq (3), *lightning*

BEZER
1221 Betser (5), *inaccessible spot*

BICHRI
1075 Bikrîy (8), *youthful*

BID
559 'âmar (6), *to say*
1696 dâbar (2), *to speak, say; to subdue*
6942 qâdâsh (1), *to be, make clean*
479 antikalĕō (1), *to invite in return*
657 apŏtassŏmai (1), *to say adieu; to renounce*
2036 ĕpō (2), *to speak*
2564 kalĕō (2), *to call*
2753 kĕlĕuō (1), *to order*
3004 lĕgō (1), *to say*

BIDDEN
559 'âmar (1), *to say*
7121 qârâ' (2), *to call out*
2564 kalĕō (10), *to call*
4367 prŏstassō (1), *to arrange towards*

BIDDETH
3004 lĕgō (1), *to say*

BIDDING
4928 mishma'ath (1), *royal court; obedience*

BIDKAR
920 Bidqar (1), *stabbing assassin*

BIER
4296 miṭṭâh (1), *bed; sofa, litter or bier*
4673 sŏrŏs (1), *funeral bier*

BIGTHA
903 Bigthâ' (1), *Bigtha*

BIGTHAN
904 Bigthân (1), *Bigthan*

BIGTHANA
904 Bigthân (1), *Bigthana*

BIGVAI
902 Bigvay (6), *Bigvai*

BILDAD
1085 Bildad (5), *Bildad*

BILEAM
1109 Bil'âm (1), *foreigner*

BILGAH
1083 Bilgâh (3), *desistance*

BILGAI
1084 Bilgay (1), *desistant*

BILHAH
1090 Bilhâh (11), *timid*

BILHAN
1092 Bilhân (4), *timid*

BILL
5612 çêpher (4), *writing*
975 bibliŏn (1), *scroll; certificate*
1121 gramma (2), *writing; education*

BILLOWS
1530 gal (1), *heap; ruins*
4867 mishbâr (1), *breaker*

BILSHAN
1114 Bilshân (2), *Bilshan*

BIMHAL
1118 Bimhâl (1), *with pruning*

BIND
631 'âçar (13), to *fasten*; to *join* battle
2280 châbash (6), to *wrap* firmly, *bind*
3729 kephath (Ch.) (1), to *fetter, bind*
6029 'ânad (1), to *lace* fast, *bind*
6887 tsârar (3), to *cramp*
7164 qâraç (1), to *hunch*
7194 qâshar (10), to *tie, bind*
7405 râkaç (2), to *tie, bind*
7573 râtham (1), to *yoke*
1195 děsměuō (1), to *enchain, tie on*
1210 děō (9), to *bind*
5265 hupŏděō (1), to *put on* shoes or sandals

BINDETH
247 'âzar (1), to *belt*
631 'âçar (1), to *fasten*; to *join* battle
2280 châbash (4), to *wrap* firmly, *bind*
6014 'âmar (1), to *gather* grain into sheaves
6887 tsârar (2), to *cramp*

BINDING
481 'âlam (1), to be *tongue-tied, be silent*
632 'ěçâr (1), *obligation, vow, pledge*
681 'êtsel (1), *side; near*
8193 sâphâh (1), *lip, edge, margin*
1195 děsměuō (1), to *enchain, tie on*

BINEA
1150 Bin'â' (2), *Bina*

BINNUI
1131 Binnûwy (7), *built*

BIRD
1167+3671 ba'al (1), *master; owner; citizen*
5775 'ôwph (3), *bird*
5861 'ayiṭ (2), bird of prey (poss.) *hawk*
6833 tsippôwr (21), little *hopping bird*
3732 ŏrněŏn (1), *bird*

BIRD'S
6833 tsippôwr (1), little *hopping bird*

BIRDS
5775 'ôwph (6), *winged bird*
5861 'ayiṭ (1), bird of prey (poss.) *hawk*
6833 tsippôwr (10), little *hopping bird*
4071 pětěinŏn (5), *bird* which *flies*
4421 ptěnŏn (1), *bird*

BIRDS'
6853 tsephar (Ch.) (1), *bird*

BIRSHA
1306 Birsha' (1), *with wickedness*

BIRTH
3205 yâlad (2), to *bear young*; to *father a child*
4351 mekûwrâh (1), *origin*
4866 mishbêr (2), vaginal *opening*
5309 nephel (3), *abortive miscarriage*
7665 shâbar (1), to *burst*
8435 tôwledâh (1), family *descent,* family *record*
1079 gěnětě (1), *birth*
1083 gěnněsis (2), *nativity*
5605 ōdinō (2), to *experience labor pains*

BIRTHDAY
3117+3205 yôwm (1), *day; time period*
1077 gěněsia (2), *birthday* ceremonies

BIRTHRIGHT
1062 bekôwrâh (9), *state of, rights of first born*
4415 prōtŏtŏkia (1), *primogeniture* rights

BIRZAVITH
1269 Birzôwth (1), *holes*

BISHLAM
1312 Bishlâm (1), *Bishlam*

BISHOP
1984 ěpiskŏpě (1), *episcopate*
1985 ěpiskŏpŏs (5), *overseer, supervisor*

BISHOPRICK
1984 ěpiskŏpě (1), *episcopate*

BISHOPS
1985 ěpiskŏpŏs (1), *overseer, supervisor*

BIT
4964 metheg (1), *bit*
5391 nâshak (2), to *strike;* to *oppress*

BITE
5391 nâshak (6), to *strike;* to *oppress*
1143 daknō (1), to *bite*

BITETH
5391 nâshak (2), to *strike;* to *oppress*

BITHIAH
1332 Bithyâh (1), *worshipper of Jehovah*

BITHRON
1338 Bithrôwn (1), *craggy* spot

BITHYNIA
978 Bithunia (2), *Bithynia*

BITS
5469 chalinŏs (1), *curb* or *head-stall,* i.e. *bit*

BITTEN
5391 nâshak (2), to *strike;* to *oppress*

BITTER
4751 mar (20), *bitter; bitterness; bitterly*
4784 mârâh (1), to *rebel* or *resist;* to *provoke*

BITTER
4805 meriy (1), *rebellion, rebellious*
4815 meriyriy (1), *bitter,* i.e. *poisonous*
4843 mârar (2), to *be, make bitter*
4844 merôr (2), *bitter* herb
4846 merôrâh (1), bitter *bile; venom* of a serpent
8563 tamrûwr (2), *bitterness*
4087 pikrainō (4), to *embitter, turn sour*
4089 pikrŏs (2), *sharp, pungent,* i.e. *bitter*

BITTERLY
779 'ârar (1), to *execrate,* place a *curse*
4751 mar (3), *bitter; bitterness; bitterly*
4843 mârar (2), to *be, make bitter*
8563 tamrûwr (1), *bitterness*
4090 pikrŏs (2), *bitterly,* i.e. *violently*

BITTERN
7090 qippôwd (3), *bittern*

BITTERNESS
4470 memer (1), *sorrow*
4472 mamrôr (1), *bitterness, misery*
4751 mar (10), *bitter; bitterness; bitterly*
4814 meriyrûwth (1), *bitterness*
4843 mârar (4), to *be, make bitter*
4844 merôr (1), *bitter* herb
4088 pikria (4), *acridity, bitterness*

BIZJOTHJAH
964 bizyôwtheyâh (1), *contempts of Jehovah*

BIZTHA
968 Bizthâ' (1), *Biztha*

BLACK
380 'îyshôwn (1), *pupil, eyeball; middle*
3648 kâmar (1), to *shrivel* with heat
5508 çôchereth (1), (poss.) black *tile*
6937 qâdar (4), to be *dark-colored*
7835 shâchar (1), to *be dim* or *dark* in color
7838 shâchôr (6), *dusky, jet black*
7840 shecharchôreth (1), *swarthy, dark*
3189 mělas (3), *black*

BLACKER
2821 châshak (1), to *be dark;* to *darken*

BLACKISH
6937 qâdar (1), to be *dark-colored*

BLACKNESS
3650 kimrîyr (1), *obscuration, eclipse*
6289 pâ'rûwr (2), *flush* of anxiety

BLADE
3851 lahab (2), *flame* of fire; *flash* of a *blade*
7929 shikmâh (1), *shoulder*-bone
5528 chŏrtŏs (2), *pasture, herbage* or *vegetation*

BLAINS
76 'ăba'bû'âh (2), *pustule, skin eruption*

BLAME
2398 châṭâ' (2), to *sin*
299 amōmŏs (1), *unblemished, blameless*
3469 mōmaŏmai (1), to *carp at,* i.e. to *censure*

BLAMED
2607 kataginŏskō (1), to *find fault with*
3469 mōmaŏmai (1), to *carp at,* i.e. to *censure*

BLAMELESS
5352 nâqâh (1), to *be, make clean;* to *be bare*
5355 nâqîy (2), *innocent*
273 aměmptŏs (3), *irreproachable*
274 aměmptŏs (1), *faultlessly*
298 amōmětŏs (1), *unblamable*
338 anaitiŏs (1), *innocent*
410 aněgklētŏs (4), *irreproachable*
423 aněpilěptŏs (2), *not open to blame*

BLASPHEME
1288 bârak (2), to *bless*
5006 nâ'ats (2), to *scorn*
987 blasphěměō (6), to *speak impiously*

BLASPHEMED
1442 gâdaph (5), to *revile, blaspheme*
2778 châraph (1), to *spend the winter*
5006 nâ'ats (2), to *scorn*
5344 nâqab (1), to *specify, designate, libel*
987 blasphěměō (7), to *speak impiously*

BLASPHEMER
989 blasphěmŏs (1), *slanderous*

BLASPHEMERS
987 blasphěměō (1), to *speak impiously*
989 blasphěmŏs (1), *slanderous*

BLASPHEMEST
987 blasphěměō (1), to *speak impiously*

BLASPHEMETH
1442 gâdaph (1), to *revile, blaspheme*
5344 nâqab (2), to *specify, designate, libel*
987 blasphěměō (2), to *speak impiously*

BLASPHEMETH
6940 qadrûwth (1), *duskiness*
1105 gnŏphŏs (1), *gloom* as of a storm, *darkness*
2217 zŏphŏs (1), *gloom*

BLADE
3851 lahab (2), *flame* of fire; *flash* of a *blade*
7929 shikmâh (1), *shoulder*-bone
5528 chŏrtŏs (2), *pasture, herbage* or *vegetation*

BLASPHEMIES
5007 nĕ'âtsâh (1), *scorn;*
to bloom
988 blasphēmia (5),
impious speech

BLASPHEMING
987 blasphēmĕō (1), to
speak impiously

BLASPHEMOUS
989 blasphēmŏs (2),
slanderous

BLASPHEMOUSLY
987 blasphēmĕō (1), to
speak impiously

BLASPHEMY
5007 nĕ'âtsâh (2), *scorn;*
to bloom
987 blasphēmĕō (1), to
speak impiously
988 blasphēmia (11),
impious speech

BLAST
5397 nĕshâmâh (3),
breath, life
7307 rûwach (4), *breath;*
wind; life-spirit

BLASTED
7709 shĕdêmâh (1),
cultivated field
7710 shâdaph (3), to
scorch
7711 shĕdêphâh (1),
blight; scorching

BLASTING
7711 shĕdêphâh (5),
blight; scorching

BLASTUS
986 Blastŏs (1), (poss.) to
yield fruit

BLAZE
1310 diaphēmizō (1), to
spread news

BLEATING
6963 qôwl (1), *voice or*
sound

BLEATINGS
8292 shĕrûwqâh (1),
whistling; scorn

BLEMISH
3971 m'ûwm (15),
blemish; fault
8400 tĕballûl (1),
cataract in the eye
8549 tâmîym (44), *entire,*
complete; integrity
299 amōmŏs (2),
unblemished, blameless

BLEMISHES
3971 m'ûwm (1),
blemish; fault
3470 mōmŏs* (1), *flaw or*
blot

BLESS
1288 bârak (115), to *bless*
2127 ĕulŏgĕō* (10), to
invoke a benediction

BLESSED
833 'âshar (7), to *be*
honest, prosper
835 'esher (27), *how*
happy!
1288 bârak (175), to *bless*
1289 bĕrak (Ch.) (4), to
bless

1293 bĕrâkâh (3),
benediction, blessing
1757 ĕnĕulŏgĕō (2), to
confer a benefit, bless
2127 ĕulŏgĕō* (30), to
invoke a benediction
2128 ĕulŏgētŏs* (8),
adorable, praised
3106 makarizō* (1), to
pronounce fortunate
3107 makariŏs* (43),
fortunate, well off

BLESSEDNESS
3108 makarismŏs* (3),
fortunate

BLESSEST
1288 bârak (3), to *bless*

BLESSETH
1288 bârak (8), to *bless*

BLESSING
1288 bârak (1), to *bless*
1293 bĕrâkâh (51),
benediction, blessing
2127 ĕulŏgĕō* (1), to
invoke a benediction
2129 ĕulŏgia* (12),
benediction

BLESSINGS
1293 bĕrâkâh (11),
benediction, blessing
2129 ĕulŏgia* (1),
benediction

BLEW
8628 tâqa' (18), to *clatter,*
slap, drive, clasp
1920 ĕpiginŏmai (1), to
come up, happen
4154 pnĕō* (3), to *breeze*
5285 hupŏpnĕō* (1), to
breathe gently

BLIND
5786 'âvar (1), to *blind*
5787 'ivvêr (26), *blind*
5788 'ivvârôwn (1),
blindness
5956 'âlam (1), to *veil*
from sight, i.e. *conceal*
5185 tuphlŏs* (52),
blindness; blind person

BLINDED
4456 pōrŏō* (2), to *render*
stupid or callous
5186 tuphlŏō* (3), to
cause blindness

BLINDETH
5786 'âvar (1), to *blind*

BLINDFOLDED
4028 pĕrikaluptō* (1), to
cover eyes

BLINDNESS
5575 çanvêr (3),
blindness
5788 'ivvârôwn (2),
blindness
4457 pōrōsis* (2),
stupidity or callousness

BLOOD
1818 dâm (337), *blood;*
juice; life
5332 nêtsach (1), blood
(as if *red juice*)
129 haima (97), *blood*
130 haimatĕkchusia (1),
pouring of blood

131 haimŏrrhĕŏ (1), to
have a hemorrhage

BLOODGUILTINESS
1818 dâm (1), *blood;*
juice; life

BLOODTHIRSTY
582+1818 'ĕnôwsh (1),
man; person, human

BLOODY
1818 dâm (15), *blood;*
juice; life
1420 dusĕntĕria (1),
dysentery

BLOOMED
6692 tsûwts (1), to
blossom, flourish

BLOSSOM
6524 pârach (4), to
bloom; to fly; to flourish
6525 perach (1), *calyx*
flower; bloom
6692 tsûwts (1), to
blossom, flourish

BLOSSOMED
6692 tsûwts (1), to
blossom, flourish

BLOSSOMS
5322 nêts (1), *flower*
6731 tsîyts (1), burnished
plate; bright flower

BLOT
3971 m'ûwm (2),
blemish; fault
4229 mâchâh (10), to
erase; to grease
1813 ĕxalĕiphō* (1), to
obliterate

BLOTTED
4229 mâchâh (5), to
erase; to grease
1813 ĕxalĕiphō* (1), to
obliterate

BLOTTETH
4229 mâchâh (1), to
erase; to grease

BLOTTING
1813 ĕxalĕiphō* (1), to
obliterate

BLOW
2690 châtsar (1), to blow
the *trumpet*
4347 makkâh (1), *blow;*
wound; pestilence
5265 nâça' (1), *start* on a
journey
5301 nâphach (3), to
inflate, blow hard
5380 nâshab (1), to *blow;*
to *disperse*
5398 nâshaph (2), to
breeze as the wind
6315 pûwach (2), to *blow,*
to *fan, kindle;* to *utter*
7321 rûwa' (1), to *shout*
8409 tigrâh (1), *strife,* i.e.
infliction
8628 tâqa' (23), to *clatter,*
slap, drive, clasp
8643 tĕrûw'âh (1),
battle-cry; clangor
4154 pnĕō* (2), to *breeze*

BLOWETH
5301 nâphach (1), to
inflate, blow hard

5380 nâshab (1), to *blow;*
to *disperse*
8628 tâqa' (1), to *clatter,*
slap, drive, clasp
4154 pnĕō* (1), to *breeze*

BLOWING
8628 tâqa' (2), to *clatter,*
slap, drive, clasp
8643 tĕrûw'âh (2),
battle-cry; clangor

BLOWN
5301 nâphach (1), to
inflate, blow hard
8628 tâqa' (3), to *clatter,*
slap, drive, clasp

BLUE
8504 tĕkêleth (50), color
violet

BLUENESS
2250 chabbûwrâh (1),
weal, bruise

BLUNT
6949 qâhâh (1), to *be*
dull; be blunt

BLUSH
3637 kâlam (3), to *taunt*
or *insult*

BOANERGES
993 Bŏanĕrgĕs (1), *sons*
of commotion

BOAR
2386 chăzîyr (1), *hog,*
boar

BOARD
7175 qeresh (17), *slab or*
plank; deck of a ship

BOARDS
3871 lûwach (4), *tablet*
6763 tsêlâ' (2), *side*
7175 qeresh (33), *slab*
7713 sĕdêrâh (1), *row,* i.e.
rank of soldiers
4548 sanis (1), *planked*
timber, board

BOAST
559 'âmar (1), to *say*
1984 hâlal (6), to *boast*
3235 yâmar (1), to
exchange
3513 kâbad (1), to *be*
heavy, severe, dull
6286 pâ'ar (1), to *shake a*
tree
2620 katakauchaŏmai
(1), to *exult against*
2744 kauchaŏmai (8), to
glory in; to boast

BOASTED
1431 gâdal (1), to *be*
great, make great
2744 kauchaŏmai (1), to
glory in; to boast

BOASTERS
213 alazōn (2), *braggart*

BOASTEST
1984 hâlal (1), to *boast*

BOASTETH
1984 hâlal (3), to boast
3166 mĕgalauchĕō* (1), to
be arrogant, egotistic

BOASTING
2744 kauchaŏmai (1), to
glory in; to boast

BRIGHTNESS

1305 bârar (1), to
brighten; purify
2385 chăzîyz (1), flash of
lightning
3851 lahab (1), flame of
fire; flash of a blade
3974 mâ'ôwr (1),
luminary, light source
4803 mâraṭ (1), to polish;
to make bald
4838 mâraq (1), to polish;
to sharpen; to rinse
5051 nôgahh (1),
brilliancy
6219 'âshôwth (1),
polished
6247 'esheth (1), fabric
7043 qâlal (1), to be,
make light
796 astrapē (1),
lightning; light's glare
2986 lamprŏs (2),
radiant; clear
5460 phōtĕinŏs (1),
well-illuminated

BRIGHTNESS

2096 zôhar (2),
brilliancy, shining
2122 zîyv (Ch.) (2),
cheerfulness
3314 yiph'âh (2),
splendor, beauty
3368 yâqâr (1), valuable
5051 nôgahh (11),
brilliancy
5054 nᵉgôhâh (1),
splendor, luster
541 apaugasma (1),
effulgence, radiance
2015 ĕpiphanĕia (1),
manisfestation
2987 lamprŏtēs (1),
brilliancy

BRIM

7097 qâtseh (1), extremity
8193 sâphâh (7), lip;
edge, margin
507 anō (1), upward or
on the top, heavenward

BRIMSTONE

1614 gophrîyth (7),
sulphur
2303 thĕiŏn (7), sulphur
2306 thĕiōdēs (1),
sulphurous yellow

BRING

338 'îy (1), solitary wild
creature that howls
503 'âlaph (1), increase
by thousands
622 'âçaph (2), to gather,
collect
858 'âthâh (Ch.) (2), to
arrive; go
935 bôw' (248), to go or
come
1069 bâkar (1), to give
the birthright
1431 gâdal (1), to be
great, make great
1518 gîyach (1), to issue
forth; to burst forth
1876 dâshâ' (1), to sprout
new plants
1980 hâlak (1), to walk;
live a certain way
2142 zâkar (2), to
remember; to mention

2342 chûwl (1), to dance,
whirl; to writhe in pain
2381 Chăzîy'êl (1), seen
of God
2986 yâbal (5), to bring
3051 yâhab (2), to give
3205 yâlad (17), to bear
young; to father a child
3212 yâlak (3), to walk;
to live; to carry
3254 yâçaph (1), to add
or augment
3318 yâtsâ' (73), to go,
bring out
3381 yârad (24), to
descend
3513 kâbad (1), to be
heavy, severe, dull
3533 kâbash (1), to
conquer, subjugate
3665 kâna' (3), to
humiliate, vanquish
3947 lâqach (17), to take
4608 ma'âleh (1),
elevation; platform
4672 mâtsâ' (2), to find
or acquire; to occur
5060 nâga' (3), to strike
5066 nâgash (14), to be,
come, bring near
5080 nâdach (1), to push
off, scattered
5107 nûwb (1), to (make)
flourish; to utter
5375 nâsâ' (10), to lift up
5381 nâsag (1), to reach
5414 nâthan (11), to give
5437 çâbab (2), to
surround
5647 'âbad (1), to do,
work, serve
5674 'âbar (1), to cross
over; to transition
5924 'êllâ (Ch.) (3), above
5927 'âlâh (35), to
ascend, be high, mount
6049 'ânan (1), to cover,
becloud; to act covertly
6213 'âsâh (9), to do or
make
6315 pûwach (1), to blow,
to fan, kindle; to utter
6398 pâlach (1), to slice;
to break open; to pierce
6509 pârâh (2), to bear
fruit
6779 tsâmach (1), to
sprout
6805 tsâ'ad (1), to pace,
step regularly
7034 qâlâh (1), to hold in
contempt
7126 qârab (36), to
approach, bring near
7311 rûwm (1), to be
high; to rise or raise
7392 râkab (1), to ride
7665 shâbar (1), to burst
7725 shûwb (72), to turn
back; to return
7760 sûwm (1), to put,
place
7817 shâchach (1), to
sink or depress
7896 shîyth (1), to place
7971 shâlach (1), to send
away
8045 shâmad (1), to
desolate

8074 shâmêm (2), to
devastate; to stupefy
8213 shâphêl (4), to
humiliate
8317 shârats (3), to
wriggle, swarm
71 agō (14), to lead; to
bring, drive; to weigh
114 athĕtĕō (1), to
disesteem, neutralize
321 anagō (2), to lead
up; to bring out; to sail
363 anamimnēskō (1), to
remind; to recollect
518 apaggĕllō (2), to
announce, proclaim
520 apagō (1), to take
away
667 apŏhĕrō (1), to bear
off, carry away
1295 diasōzō (1), to cure,
preserve, rescue
1396 dŏulagōgĕō (1), to
enslave, subdue
1402 dŏulŏō (1), to
enslave
1521 ĕisagō (1), to lead
into
1533 ĕisphĕrō (2), to
carry inward
1625 ĕktrĕphō (1), to
cherish or train
1627 ĕkphĕrō (1), to bear
out; to produce
1863 ĕpagō (2), inflict;
charge
2018 ĕpiphĕrō (1), to
inflict, bring upon
2036 ĕpō (1), to speak or
say
2097 ĕuaggĕlizō (2), to
announce good news
2592 karpŏphŏrĕō (4), to
be fertile
2609 katagō (3), to lead
down; to moor a vessel
2615 katadŏulŏō (2), to
enslave utterly
2673 katargĕō (1), to be,
render entirely useless
3919 parĕisagō (1), to
lead in aside
4160 pŏiĕō (6), to do
4311 prŏpĕmpō (3), to
send forward
4317 prŏsagō (2), to
bring near
4374 prŏsphĕrō (2), to
present to; to treat as
5062 tĕssarakŏnta (1),
forty
5088 tiktō (3), to produce
from seed
5179 tupŏs (1), shape, i.e.
statue or resemblance
5342 phĕrō (17), to bear
or carry
5461 phōtizō (1), to shine
or to brighten up

BRINGERS

539 'âman (1), to be firm,
faithful, true; to trust

BRINGEST

935 bôw' (1), to go, come
1319 bâsar (3), to
announce (good news)
1533 ĕisphĕrō (1), to
carry inward

BRINGETH

935 bôw' (6), to go or
come
1069 bâkar (1), to give
the birthright
1319 bâsar (5), to
announce (good news)
2142 zâkar (1), to
remember
2659 châphêr (1), to
shame, reproach
3318 yâtsâ' (18), to go,
bring out
3381 yârad (2), to
descend
3615 kâlâh (1), to
complete, prepare
5060 nâga' (1), to strike
5107 nûwb (1), to (make)
flourish; to utter
5148 nâchâh (2), to guide
5414 nâthan (3), to give
5927 'âlâh (3), to ascend,
be high, mount
6213 'âsâh (1), to do or
make
6331 pûwr (1), to crush
6445 pânaq (1), to
enervate, reduce vigor
6779 tsâmach (1), to
sprout
7725 shûwb (3), to turn
back; to return
7737 shâvâh (1), to level,
equalize; to resemble
7817 shâchach (1), to
sink or depress
8213 shâphêl (1), to
humiliate
399 anaphĕrō (1), to take
up; to lead up
616 apŏkuĕō (1), to bring
into being
1521 ĕisagō (1), to lead
into
1544 ĕkballō (3), to
throw out
2592 karpŏphŏrĕō (2), to
be fertile
4160 pŏiĕō (7), to do
4393 prŏphĕrō (2), to
bear forward
4992 sōtēriŏn (1),
defender or defence
5088 tiktō (2), to produce
from seed
5342 phĕrō (2), to bear or
carry

BRINGING

935 bôw' (6), to go, come
2142 zâkar (1), to
remember; to mention
3318 yâtsâ' (3), to go,
bring out
5375 nâsâ' (3), to lift up
7725 shûwb (2), to turn
back; to return
71 agō (1), to lead; to
bring, drive; to weigh
163 aichmalōtizō (2), to
make captive
1863 ĕpagō (1), inflict;
charge
1898 ĕpĕisagōgē (1),
introduction
4160 pŏiĕō (1), to do
5342 phĕrō (3), to bear or
carry

BRINK
7097 qâtseh (1), *extremity*
8193 sâphâh (5), *lip; edge, margin*

BROAD
7338 rachab (1), *width, expanse*
7338+3027 rachab (1), *width, expanse*
7339 rᵉchôb (3), *myriad*
7341 rôchab (21), *width*
7342 râchâb (5), *roomy, spacious*
7554 râqa' (1), to *pound*
7555 riqqûa' (1), *thin* metallic *plate*
2149 ĕuruchōrŏs (1), *spacious, wide*
4115 platunō (1), to *widen*

BROADER
7342 râchâb (1), *roomy, spacious*

BROIDED
4117 plĕgma (1), *plait* or *braid* of hair

BROIDERED
7553 riqmâh (7), *embroidery*
8665 tashbêts (1), *checkered* stuff

BROILED
3702 ŏptŏs (1), *roasted, broiled*

BROKEN
6 'âbad (1), *perish; destroy*
1234 bâqa' (6), to *cleave, break, tear open*
1638 gâraç (1), to *crush, break; to dissolve*
1792 dâkâ' (3), to *pulverize; be contrite*
1794 dâkâh (3), to *collapse; contrite*
1854 dâqaq (1), to *crush; crumble*
1986 hâlam (2), to *strike, beat, stamp, conquer*
2040 hâraç (4), to *pull* down; *break, destroy*
2490 châlal (1), to *profane, defile*
2844 chath (6), *terror*
2865 châthath (6), to *break* down
3807 kâthath (1), to *bruise* or *strike*
4535 maççâch (1), *cordon; barrier; in turn*
4790 mᵉrôwach (1), *bruised, pounded*
5181 nâchath (2), to *sink, descend; to press*
5218 nâkê' (3), *smitten; afflicted*
5310 nâphats (1), to *dash* to pieces; to *scatter*
5421 nâtha' (1), to *tear* out
5422 nâthats (5), to *tear* down
5423 nâthaq (7), to *tear* off
5927 'âlâh (1), to *ascend, be high, mount*

6105 'âtsam (1), to *be, make powerful*
6209 'ârar (1), to *bare; to demolish*
6331 pûwr (1), to *crush*
6480 pâtsam (1), to *rend, tear* by earthquake
6524 pârach (2), to *break* forth; to *bloom*
6531 perek (1), *severity*
6555 pârats (12), to *break* out
6565 pârar (9), to *break* up; to *violate, frustrate*
7280 râga' (1), to *stir up*
7462 râ'âh (1), to *tend* a flock, i.e. *pasture* it
7465 rô'âh (1), *breakage*
7489 râ'a' (2), to *break* to pieces
7533 râtsats (4), to *crack* in pieces, *smash*
7616 shâbâb (1), *fragment*, i.e. *ruin*
7665 shâbar (65), to *burst*
8406 tᵉbar (Ch.) (1), to *be fragile*
1358 diŏrussō (2), to *penetrate* burglariously
1575 ĕkklaō (3), to *exscind, cut off*
1846 ĕxŏrussō (1), to *dig* out
2608 katagnumi (1), to *crack apart*
2801 klasma (2), *piece, bit*
2806 klaō (3), to *break* bread
3089 luō (6), to *loosen*
4917 sunthlaō (2), to *dash together, shatter*
4937 suntribō (3), to *crush completely*
4977 schizō (1), to *split* or *sever*

BROKENFOOTED
7667+7272 sheber (1), *fracture; ruin*

BROKENHANDED
7667+3027 sheber (1), *fracture; ruin*

BROKENHEARTED
7665+3820 shâbar (1), to *burst*
4937+2588 suntribō (1), to *crush completely*

BROOD
3555 nŏssia (1), hen's *brood*

BROOK
4323 mîykâl (1), *brook*
5158 nachal (37), *valley, ravine*; mine *shaft*
5493 chĕimarrhŏs (1), *winter-torrent*

BROOKS
650 'âphîyq (1), *valley; stream; mighty, strong*
2975 yᵉ'ôr (4), Nile *River*; Tigris *River*
5158 nachal (9), *valley, ravine*; mine *shaft*

BROTH
4839 mârâq (2), *soup*-broth

6564 pârâq (1), *fragments* in soup

BROTHER
251 'âch (244), *brother; relative; member*
1730 dôwd (1), *beloved, friend; relative*
2992 yâbam (2), to *marry* a brother's widow
2993 yâbâm (2), *husband's brother*
7453 rêa' (1), *associate; one close*
80 adĕlphŏs (109), *brother*

BROTHER'S
251 'âch (25), *brother; relative; member*
2994 yᵉbêmeth (3), dead brother's widow, i.e. *sister-in-law*
80 adĕlphŏs (7), *brother*

BROTHERHOOD
264 'achăvâh (1), *fraternity; brotherhood*
81 adĕlphŏtēs (1), *fraternity, brotherhood*

BROTHERLY
251 'âch (1), *brother; relative; member*
5360 philadĕlphia (5), *fraternal affection*

BROTHERS'
1730 dôwd (1), *beloved, friend; relative*

BROUGHT
539 'âman (5), to *be firm, faithful, true; to trust*
622 'âçaph (3), to *gather, collect*
656 'âphêç (1), to *cease*
857 'âthâh (1), to *arrive; go*
858 'âthâh (Ch.) (7), to *arrive; go*
935 bôw' (264), to *go* or *come*
1197 bâ'ar (1), to *be brutish, be senseless*
1310 bâshal (1), to *boil* up, cook; to *ripen*
1319 bâsar (2), to *announce* (good news)
1431 gâdal (6), to *be great, make great*
1468 gûwz (1), to *pass* rapidly
1540 gâlâh (1), to *denude; uncover*
1541 gᵉlâh (Ch.) (1), to *reveal mysteries*
1589 gânab (1), to *thieve; to deceive*
1809 dâlal (3), to *slacken, dangle*
1820 dâmâh (2), to *be silent; to fail, cease*
1946 hûwk (Ch.) (1), to *go, come*
1961 hâyâh (2), to *exist*, i.e. *be* or *become*
2254 châbal (2), to *bind* by a *pledge; to pervert*
2342 chûwl (3), to *dance, whirl; to writhe* in pain
2659 châphêr (3), to *be ashamed, disappointed*

2986 yâbal (7), to *bring*
2987 yᵉbal (Ch.) (2), to *bring*
3205 yâlad (12), to *bear* young; to *father a child*
3212 yâlak (8), to *walk; to live; to carry*
3218 yekeq (1), young *locust*
3318 yâtsâ' (127), to *go, bring out*
3381 yârad (17), to *descend*
3467 yâsha' (2), to *make safe, free*
3474 yâshar (1), to *be straight; to make right*
3533 kâbash (3), to *conquer, subjugate*
3665 kâna' (4), to *humiliate, vanquish*
3766 kâra' (2), to *make miserable*
3947 lâqach (8), to *take*
4161 môwtsâ' (2), *going forth*
4355 mâkak (2), to *tumble; to perish*
4551 maççâ' (1), stone *quarry; projectile*
5060 nâga' (1), to *strike*
5066 nâgash (13), to *be, come, bring near*
5090 nâhag (4), to *drive* forth; to *carry away*
5148 nâchâh (2), to *guide*
5265 nâça' (3), *start* on a journey
5375 nâsâ' (13), to *lift up*
5414 nâthan (3), to *give*
5437 çâbab (1), to *surround*
5493 çûwr (1), to *turn* off
5674 'âbar (6), to *cross* over; to *transition*
5927 'âlâh (65), to *ascend, be high, mount*
5954 'ălal (Ch.) (4), to *go in; to lead in*
6030 'ânâh (1), to *respond, answer*
6213 'âsâh (3), to *do* or *make*
6565 pârar (1), to *break* up; to *violate, frustrate*
6819 tsâ'ar (1), to *be small; be trivial*
6908 qâbats (1), to *collect, assemble*
7126 qârab (27), to *approach, bring near*
7127 qᵉrêb (Ch.) (1), to *approach, bring near*
7136 qârâh (1), to *bring about; to impose*
7235 râbâh (1), to *increase*
7311 rûwm (1), to *be high; to rise* or *raise*
7323 rûwts (1), to *run*
7392 râkab (3), to *ride*
7617 shâbâh (1), to *transport* into captivity
7725 shûwb (39), to *turn* back; to *return*
7760 sûwm (4), to *put, place*
7817 shâchach (3), to *sink* or *depress*

7971 shâlach (1), to *send away*
8213 shâphêl (3), to *humiliate*.
8239 shâphath (1), to *place* or *put*
8317 shârats (2), to *swarm*, or *abound*
71 agō (32), to *lead*; to *bring, drive*; to *weigh*
321 anagō (4), to *lead up*; to *bring out*; to *sail*
397 anatrĕphō (1), to *rear, care* for
654 apŏstrĕphō (1), to *turn away* or *back*
985 blastanō (1), to *yield* fruit
1080 gĕnnaō (1), to *procreate, regenerate*
1096 ginŏmai (2), to *be, become*
1325 didōmi (1), to *give*
1402 dŏulŏō (1), to *enslave*
1521 ĕisagō (7), to *lead into*
1533 ĕisphĕrō (2), to *carry inward*
1627 ĕkphĕrō (1), to *bear out*; to *produce*
1806 ĕxagō (6), to *lead forth, escort*
1850 ĕxŏusiazō (1), to *control, master another*
2018 ĕpiphĕrō (2), to *inflict, bring upon*
2049 ĕrēmŏō (2), to *lay waste*
2064 ĕrchŏmai (1), to *go*
2097 ĕuaggĕlizō (1), to *announce good news*
2164 ĕuphŏrĕō (1), to *be fertile, produce a crop*
2476 histēmi (1), to *stand, establish*
2601 katabibazō (1), to *cause to bring down*
2609 katagō (4), to *lead down*; to *moor a vessel*
2865 kŏmizō (1), to *provide* for
2989 lampō (1), to *radiate brilliancy*
3350 mĕtŏikĕsia (1), *exile, deportation*
3860 paradidōmi (1), to *hand over*
3920 parĕisaktŏs (1), *smuggled in, infiltrated*
3930 parĕchō (2), to *hold near*, i.e. to *present*
3936 paristēmi (2), to *stand beside, present*
4160 pŏiĕō (1), to *make*
4254 prŏagō (3), to *lead forward*; to *precede*
4311 prŏpĕmpō (4), to *send forward*
4317 prŏsagō (1), to *bring near*
4374 prŏsphĕrō (15), to *present to*; to *treat as*
4851 sumphĕrō (1), to *collect*; to *conduce*
4939 suntrŏphŏs (1), *one brought up with*
5013 tapĕinŏō (1), to *depress*; to *humiliate*

5044 tĕknŏtrŏphĕō (1), to *be a child-rearer*
5088 tiktō (4), to *produce from seed*
5142 trĕphō (1), to *nurse, feed, care for*
5342 phĕrō (17), to *bear* or *carry*
5461 phōtizō (1), to *shine* or to *brighten* up

BROUGHTEST
935 bôw' (4), to *go* or *come*
3318 yâtsâ' (7), to *go, bring out*
5927 'âlâh (2), to *ascend, be high, mount*

BROW
4696 mêtsach (1), *forehead*
3790 ŏphrus (1), eye-*brow*

BROWN
2345 chûwm (4), *sunburnt* or *swarthy*

BRUISE
1792 dâkâ' (1), to *pulverize*; be *contrite*
1854 dâqaq (1), to *crush; crumble*
7490 rᵉ'a' (Ch.) (1), to *shatter, dash to pieces*
7667 sheber (2), *fracture; ruin*
7779 shûwph (2), to *gape*, i.e. *snap* at
4937 suntribō (1), to *crush completely*

BRUISED
1792 dâkâ' (1), to *pulverize*; be *contrite*
1854 dâqaq (1), to *crush; crumble*
4600 mâ'ak (1), to *press*, to *pierce, emasculate*
6213 'âsâh (2), to *do* or *make*
7533 râtsats (2), to *crack in pieces, smash*
2352 thrauō (1), to *crush*
4937 suntribō (1), to *crush completely*

BRUISES
2250 chabbûwrâh (1), *weal, bruise*

BRUISING
6213 'âsâh (1), to *do* or *make*
4937 suntribō (1), to *crush completely*

BRUIT
8052 shᵉmûw'âh (1), *announcement*
8088 shêma' (1), *something heard*

BRUTE
249 alŏgŏs (2), *irrational, not reasonable*

BRUTISH
1197 bâ'ar (11), to *be brutish, be senseless*

BUCKET
1805 dᵉlîy (1), *pail, bucket*

BUCKETS
1805 dᵉlîy (1), *pail, bucket*

BUCKLER
4043 mâgên (6), *small shield (buckler); skin*
5507 çôchêrâh (1), *surrounding shield*
6793 tsinnâh (3), *large shield; piercing cold*
7420 rômach (1), *iron pointed spear*

BUCKLERS
4043 mâgên (3), *small shield (buckler); skin*
6793 tsinnâh (2), *large shield; piercing cold*

BUD
4161 môwtsâ' (1), *going forth*
5132 nûwts (1), to *fly away, leave*
6524 pârach (2), to *break forth*; to *bloom*
6525 perach (1), *calyx flower; bloom*
6779 tsâmach (6), to *sprout*

BUDDED
5132 nûwts (1), to *fly away, leave*
6524 pârach (3), to *break forth*; to *bloom*
985 blastanō (1), to *yield* fruit

BUDS
6525 perach (1), *calyx flower; bloom*

BUFFET
2852 kŏlaphizō (2), to *strike*

BUFFETED
2852 kŏlaphizō (3), to *strike*

BUILD
1124 bᵉnâ' (Ch.) (6), to *build*
1129 bânâh (140), to *build; to establish*
456 anŏikŏdŏmĕō (2), to *rebuild*
2026 ĕpŏikŏdŏmĕō (2), to *rear up, build up*
3618 ŏikŏdŏmĕō (12), *construct; edification*

BUILDED
1124 bᵉnâ' (Ch.) (10), to *build*
1129 bânâh (36), to *build; to establish*
2680 kataskĕuazō (2), to *construct; to arrange*
3618 ŏikŏdŏmĕō (1), *construct; edification*
4925 sunŏikŏdŏmĕō (1), to *construct*

BUILDEDST
1129 bânâh (1), to *build; to establish*

BUILDER
5079 tĕchnitēs (1), *artisan, craftsman*

BUILDERS
1129 bânâh (9), to *build; to establish*
3618 ŏikŏdŏmĕō (5), *construct; edification*

BUILDEST
1129 bânâh (3), to *build; to establish*
3618 ŏikŏdŏmĕō (2), *construct; edification*

BUILDETH
1129 bânâh (7), to *build; to establish*
2026 ĕpŏikŏdŏmĕō (2), to *rear up, build up*

BUILDING
1124 bᵉnâ' (Ch.) (3), to *build*
1129 bânâh (15), to *build; to establish*
1140 binyâh (1), *structure*
1146 binyân (7), *edifice, building*
1147 binyân (Ch.) (1), *edifice, building*
4746 mᵉqâreh (1), *frame of timbers*
1739 ĕndōmēsis (1), *structure*
2026 ĕpŏikŏdŏmĕō (1), to *rear up, build up*
2937 ktisis (1), *formation*
3618 ŏikŏdŏmĕō (1), *construct; edification*
3619 ŏikŏdŏmē (3), *structure; edification*

BUILDINGS
3619 ŏikŏdŏmē (3), *structure; edification*

BUILT
1124 bᵉnâ' (Ch.) (1), to *build*
1129 bânâh (155), to *build; to establish*
2026 ĕpŏikŏdŏmĕō (3), to *rear up, build up*
2680 kataskĕuazō (1), to *construct; to arrange*
3618 ŏikŏdŏmĕō (10), *construct; edification*

BUKKI
1231 Buqqîy (5), *wasteful*

BUKKIAH
1232 Buqqîyâh (2), *wasting of Jehovah*

BUL
945 Bûwl (1), *rain*

BULL
7794 shôwr (1), *bullock*
8377 tᵉ'ôw (1), *antelope*

BULLOCK
1121+1241 bên (3), *son, descendant*
1241 bâqâr (1), *plowing ox; herd*
5695 'êgel (1), bull-*calf*
6499 par (89), *bullock*
7794 shôwr (10), *bullock*

BULLOCK'S
6499 par (3), *bullock*

BULLOCKS
1241 bâqâr (4), *plowing ox; herd*
5695 'êgel (1), bull-*calf*
6499 par (36), *bullock*
7794 shôwr (1), *bullock*
8450 tôwr (Ch.) (3), *bull*

BULLS
47 'abbîyr (4), *mighty*

1241 bâqâr (1), *plowing ox; herd*
6499 par (2), *bullock*
5022 taurŏs (2), *bullock, ox*

BULRUSH
100 'agmôwn (1), *rush; rope of rushes*

BULRUSHES
1573 gôme' (2), *papyrus plant*

BULWARKS
2426 chêyl (1), *entrenchment, rampart*
2430 chêylâh (1), *entrenchment, rampart*
4685 mâtsôwd (1), *net or snare; besieging tower*
4692 mâtsôwr (1), *siege-mound; distress*
6438 pinnâh (1), *pinnacle; chieftain*

BUNAH
946 Bûwnâh (1), *discretion*

BUNCH
92 'ăguddâh (1), *band; bundle; knot; arch*

BUNCHES
1707 dabbesheth (1), *hump of a camel*
6778 tsammûwq (2), *lump of dried grapes*

BUNDLE
6872 tsᵉrôwr (3), *parcel; kernel or particle*
4128 plêthŏs (1), *large number, throng*

BUNDLES
6872 tsᵉrôwr (1), *parcel; kernel or particle*
1197 dĕsmē (1), *bundle*

BUNNI
1137 Bânîy (3), *built*

BURDEN
3053 yᵉhâb (1), *lot given*
4853 massâ' (52), *burden, utterance*
4858 massâ'âh (1), *conflagration from the rising of smoke*
4864 mas'êth (1), *raising; beacon; present*
5445 çâbal (1), *to carry*
5448 çôbel (3), *load, burden*
5449 çabbâl (1), *porter, carrier*
6006 'âmaç (1), *to impose a burden*
922 barŏs (3), *load, abundance, authority*
1117 gŏmŏs (1), *cargo, wares or freight*
2599 katabarĕŏ (1), *to be a burden*
5413 phŏrtĭŏn (2), *burden, task or service*

BURDENED
916 barĕŏ (1), *to weigh down, cause pressure*
2347 thlipsis (1), *pressure, trouble*

BURDENS
92 'ăguddâh (1), *band; bundle; knot; arch*
4853 massâ' (5), *burden, utterance*
4864 mas'êth (2), *raising; beacon; present*
4942 mishpâth (1), *pair of stalls for cattle*
5447 çêbel (1), *load; forced labor*
5449 çabbâl (5), *porter, carrier*
5450 çᵉbâlâh (6), *porterage; forced labor*
922 barŏs (1), *load, abundance, authority*
5413 phŏrtĭŏn (3), *burden, task or service*

BURDENSOME
4614 ma'ămâçâh (1), *burdensomeness*
4 abarēs (1), *not burdensome*
1722+922 ĕn (1), *in; during; because of*
2655 katanarkaŏ (2), *to be a burden*

BURIAL
6900 qᵉbûwrâh (4), *sepulchre*
1779 ĕntaphiazŏ (1), *to enswathe for burial*

BURIED
6912 qâbar (96), *to inter, pile up*
2290 thaptŏ (7), *to celebrate funeral rites*
4916 sunthaptŏ (2), *to be buried with*

BURIERS
6912 qâbar (1), *to inter, pile up*

BURN
1197 bâ'ar (19), *to be brutish, be senseless*
1754 dûwr (1), *circle; ball; pile*
2734 chârâh (1), *to blaze*
2787 chârar (1), *to melt, burn, dry up*
3344 yâqad (3), *to burn*
3857 lâhaṭ (1), *to blaze*
4729 miqtâr (1), *hearth*
5400 nâsaq (1), *to catch fire*
5927 'âlâh (2), *to ascend, be high, mount*
6702 tsûwth (1), *to blaze, set on fire*
6999 qâṭar (59), *to turn into fragrance by fire*
8313 sâraph (40), *to be, set on fire*
2370 thumiaŏ (1), *to offer aromatic fumes*
2545 kaiŏ (1), *to set on fire*
2618 katakaiŏ (4), *to consume wholly by burning*
4448 purŏŏ (2), *to be ignited, glow; inflamed*

BURNED
1197 bâ'ar (8), *to be brutish, be senseless*

2787 chârar (7), *to melt, burn, dry up*
3341 yâtsath (9), *to burn or set on fire*
3554 kâvâh (2), *to blister, be scorched*
3857 lâhaṭ (2), *to blaze*
5375 nâsâ' (2), *to lift up*
6866 tsârab (1), *to burn*
6999 qâṭar (19), *to turn into fragrance by fire*
8313 sâraph (33), *to be, set on fire*
8314 sârâph (1), *poisonous serpent*
8316 sᵉrêphâh (1), *cremation*
1572 ĕkkaiŏ (1), *to inflame deeply*
1714 ĕmprēthŏ (1), *to burn, set on fire*
2545 kaiŏ (3), *to set on fire*
2618 katakaiŏ (6), *to consume wholly by burning*
2740 kausis (1), *act of burning*
4448 purŏŏ (1), *to be ignited, glow; inflamed*

BURNETH
1197 bâ'ar (4), *to be brutish, be senseless*
2142 zâkar (1), *to remember; to mention*
3344 yâqad (1), *to burn*
3857 lâhaṭ (2), *to blaze*
4348 mikvâh (1), *burn*
5635 çâraph (1), *to cremate*
6919 qâdach (1), *to inflame*
6999 qâṭar (2), *to turn into fragrance by fire*
8313 sâraph (4), *to be, set on fire*
2545 kaiŏ (1), *to set on fire*

BURNING
784 'êsh (3), *fire*
1197 bâ'ar (6), *to be brutish, be senseless*
1513 gechel (1), *ember, hot coal*
1814 dâlaq (1), *to flame; to pursue*
1815 dᵉlaq (Ch.) (1), *to flame, burn*
2746 charchûr (1), *hot fever*
3344 yâqad (3), *to burn*
3345 yᵉqad (Ch.) (10), *to burn*
3346 yᵉqêdâ' (Ch.) (1), *consuming fire*
3350 yᵉqôwd (1), *burning, blazing*
3555 kᵉvîyâh (1), *branding, scar*
3587 kîy (1), *brand or scar*
3940 lappîyd (1), *flaming torch, lamp or flame*
4169 môwqᵉdâh (1), *fuel*
4348 mikvâh (4), *burn*
6867 tsârebeth (2), *conflagration*
6920 qaddachath (1), *inflammation*

6999 qâṭar (1), *to turn into fragrance by fire*
7565 resheph (1), *flame*
8316 sᵉrêphâh (9), *cremation*
2545 kaiŏ (6), *to set on fire*
2742 kausōn (1), *burning heat, hot day*
4451 purōsis (2), *ignition; conflagration, calamity*

BURNINGS
4168 môwqêd (1), *conflagration, burning*
4955 misrâphâh (2), *cremation*

BURNISHED
7044 qâlâl (1), *brightened, polished*

BURNT
398 'âkal (1), *to eat*
1197 bâ'ar (6), *to be brutish, be senseless*
3632 kâlîyl (1), *whole, entire; complete; whole*
4198 mâzeh (1), *exhausted, empty*
5927 'âlâh (1), *to ascend, be high, mount*
5928 'ălâh (Ch.) (1), *wholly consumed in fire*
5930 'ôlâh (284), *sacrifice wholly consumed in fire*
6999 qâṭar (24), *to turn into fragrance by fire*
8313 sâraph (36), *to be, set on fire*
8316 sᵉrêphâh (2), *cremation*
2618 katakaiŏ (2), *to consume wholly by burning*
3646 hŏlŏkautōma (3), *wholly-consumed*

BURST
1234 bâqa' (1), *to cleave, break, tear open*
5423 nâthaq (4), *to tear off*
6555 pârats (1), *to break out*
2997 laschŏ (1), *to crack open*
4486 rhēgnumi (2), *to break, burst forth*

BURSTING
4386 mᵉkittâh (1), *fracture*

BURY
6912 qâbar (33), *to inter, pile up*
1779 ĕntaphiazŏ (1), *to enswathe for burial*
2290 thaptŏ (4), *to celebrate funeral rites*
5027 taphē (1), *burial*

BURYING
6912 qâbar (2), *to inter, pile up*
1780 ĕntaphiasmŏs (2), *preparation for burial*

BURYINGPLACE
6913 qeber (7), *sepulchre*

BUSH
5572 çᵉneh (6), *bramble*
942 batŏs (5), *brier*

BUSHEL
3426 mŏdiŏs (3), dry measure of volume

BUSHES
5097 nahălôl (1), pasture
7880 sîyach (2), shrubbery

BUSHY
8534 taltal (1), wavy

BUSINESS
1697 dâbâr (8), word; matter; thing
4399 mᵉlâ'kâh (12), work; property
4639 ma'ăseh (1), action; labor
6045 'inyân (2), employment, labor
2398 idiŏs (1), private or separate
4229 pragma (1), matter, deed, affair
4710 spŏudē (1), despatch; eagerness
5532 chrěia (1), affair; occasion, demand

BUSY
6213 'âsâh (1), to do or make

BUSYBODIES
4020 pěriěrgazŏmai (1), to meddle
4021 pěriěrgŏs (1), busybody; magic

BUSYBODY
244 allotriěpiskŏpŏs (1), meddler, busybody

BUTLER
4945 mashqeh (8), butler; drink; well-watered

BUTLERS
4945 mashqeh (1), butler; drink; well-watered

BUTLERSHIP
4945 mashqeh (1), butler; drink; well-watered

BUTTER
2529 chem'âh (10), curds, milk or cheese
4260 machămâ'âh (1), buttery; flattery

BUTTOCKS
4667 miphsâ'âh (1), crotch area
8357 shêthâh (2), seat i.e. buttock

BUY
3739 kârâh (1), to purchase by bargaining
3947 lâqach (3), to take
7066 qᵉnâ' (Ch.) (1), to purchase
7069 qânâh (24), to create; to procure
7666 shâbar (14), to deal in cereal grain
59 agŏrazō (13), to purchase; to redeem
1710 ěmpŏrěuŏmai (1), to trade, do business

BUYER
7069 qânâh (3), to create; to procure

BUYEST
7069 qânâh (2), to create; to procure

BUYETH
3947 lâqach (1), to take
59 agŏrazō (2), to purchase; to redeem

BUZ
938 Bûwz (3), disrespect, scorn

BUZI
941 Bûwzîy (1), Buzi

BUZITE
940 Bûwzîy (2), Buzite

BYWAYS
734+6128 'ôrach (1), well-traveled road

BYWORD
4405 millâh (1), word; discourse; speech
4912 mâshâl (1), pithy maxim; taunt
4914 mᵉshôl (1), satire
8148 shᵉnîynâh (3), gibe, verbal taunt

CAB
6894 qab (1), dry measure of volume

CABBON
3522 Kabbôwn (1), hilly

CABINS
2588 chânûwth (1), vault or cell

CABUL
3521 Kâbûwl (2), sterile

CAESAR
2541 Kaisar (21), Cæsar

CAESAR'S
2541 Kaisar (9), Cæsar

CAESAREA
2542 Kaisarěia (17), of Cæsar

CAGE
3619 kᵉlûwb (1), bird-trap; basket
5438 phulakē (1), guarding or guard

CAIAPHAS
2533 Kaïaphas (9), dell

CAIN
7014 Qayin (17), lance
2535 Kaïn (3), lance

CAINAN
7018 Qêynân (5), fixed
2536 Kaïnan (2), fixed

CAKE
1690 dᵉbêlâh (1), cake of pressed figs
2471 challâh (7), cake shaped as a ring
4580 mâ'ôwg (1), cake of bread, provision
5692 'uggâh (3), round-cake
6742 tsᵉlûwl (1), round or flattened cake

CAKES
1690 dᵉbêlâh (2), cake of pressed figs
2471 challâh (8), cake shaped as a ring
3561 kavvân (2), sacrificial wafer

3823 lâbab (1), to make cakes
3834 lâbîybâh (3), fried or turned cake
4682 matstsâh (4), unfermented cake
5692 'uggâh (4), round-cake
7550 râqîyq (1), thin cake, wafer

CALAH
3625 Kelach (2), maturity

CALAMITIES
343 'êyd (3), misfortune, ruin, disaster
1942 havvâh (1), desire; craving
7451 ra' (1), bad; evil

CALAMITY
343 'êyd (16), misfortune, ruin, disaster
1942 havvâh (3), desire; craving

CALAMUS
7070 qâneh (3), reed

CALCOL
3633 Kalkôl (1), sustenance

CALDRON
100 'agmôwn (1), rush; rope of rushes
5518 çîyr (3), thorn; hook
7037 qallachath (2), kettle

CALDRONS
1731 dûwd (1), pot, kettle; basket
5518 çîyr (2), thorn; hook

CALEB
3612 Kâlêb (32), forcible

CALEB'S
3612 Kâlêb (4), forcible

CALEB-EPHRATAH
3613 Kâlêb 'Ephrâthâh (1), Caleb-Ephrathah

CALF
1121+1241 bên (2), son, descendant
5695 'êgel (21), calf
3447 mŏschŏpŏiěō (1), to fabricate a bullock-idol
3448 mŏschŏs (4), young bullock

CALF'S
5695 'êgel (1), calf

CALKERS
2388+919 châzaq (2), to fasten upon; to seize

CALL
559 'âmar (2), to say, speak
833 'âshar (5), to go forward; guide
2142 zâkar (3), to remember; to mention
5493 çûwr (1), to turn off
5749 'ûwd (3), to duplicate or repeat
7121 qârâ' (131), to call out
7725 shûwb (1), to turn back; to return
8085 shâma' (2), to hear intelligently

363 anamimnēskō (1), to remind; to recollect
1941 ěpikalěŏmai (9), to invoke
2564 kalěō (17), to call
2840 kŏinŏō (2), to make profane
2983 lambanō (1), to take, receive
3004 lěgō (4), to say
3106 makarizō (1), to pronounce fortunate
3333 mětakalěō (2), to summon for, call for
3343 mětapěmpō (2), to summon or invite
3687 ŏnŏmazō (1), to give a name
4341 prŏskalěŏmai (2), to call toward oneself
4779 sugkalěō (1), to convoke, call together
5455 phōněō (4), to emit a sound

CALLED
559 'âmar (4), to say, speak
935 bôw' (1), to go or come
2199 zâ'aq (3), to call out, announce
6817 tsâ'aq (2), to shriek; to proclaim
7121 qârâ' (380), to call out
7123 qᵉrâ' (Ch.) (1), to call out
7760 sûwm (1), to put, place
8085 shâma' (1), to hear intelligently
154 aitěō (1), to ask for
363 anamimnēskō (1), to remind; to recollect
1458 ěgkalěō (1), to charge, criminate
1528 ěiskalěō (1), to invite in
1941 ěpikalěŏmai (4), to invoke
1951 ěpilěgŏmai (1), to surname, select
2028 ěpŏnŏmazō (1), to be called, denominate
2036 ěpō (1), to speak
2046 ěrěō (1), to utter
2564 kalěō (103), to call
2822 klētŏs (11), appointed, invited
2919 krinō (2), to decide; to try, condemn, punish
3004 lěgō (36), to say
3044 Linŏs (1), (poss.) flax linen
3333 mětakalěō (2), to summon for, call for
3686 ŏnŏma (4), name
3687 ŏnŏmazō (1), to give a name
3739+2076 hŏs (1), who, which, what, that
3870 parakalěō (1), to call, invite
4316 prŏsagŏrěuō (1), to designate a name
4341 prŏskalěŏmai (25), to call toward oneself
4377 prŏsphōněō (2), to address, exclaim

4779 *sugkalĕō* (5), to
convoke, call together
4867 *sunathrŏizō* (1), to
convene
5455 *phōnĕō* (16), to emit
a *sound*
5537 *chrēmatizō* (2), to
utter an oracle
5581 *psĕudōnumŏs* (1),
untruly named

CALLEDST
6485 *pâqad* (1), to *visit,*
care for, count
7121 *qârâ'* (3), to *call* out

CALLEST
3004 *lĕgō* (3), to *say*

CALLETH
7121 *qârâ'* (13), to *call*
out
2564 *kalĕō* (6), to *call*
3004 *lĕgō* (4), to *say*
4341 *prŏskalĕŏmai* (1),
to *call toward oneself*
4779 *sugkalĕō* (2), to
convoke, call together
5455 *phōnĕō* (4), to emit
a *sound*

CALLING
2142 *zâkar* (1), to
remember; to *mention*
4744 *miqrâ'* (1), public
meeting
7121 *qârâ'* (3), to *call* out
363 *anamimnēskō* (1), to
remind; to recollect
1941 *ĕpikalĕŏmai* (2), to
invoke
2564 *kalĕō* (1), to *call*
2821 *klēsis* (10),
invitation; station in life
4341 *prŏskalĕŏmai* (2),
to *call toward oneself*
4377 *prŏsphōnĕō* (2), to
address, exclaim
5455 *phōnĕō* (1), to emit
a *sound*

CALM
1827 *dᵉmâmâh* (1), *quiet*
8367 *shâthaq* (2), to
subside
1055 *galēnē* (3),
tranquillity, *calm*

CALNEH
3641 Kalneh (2), *Calneh*
or *Calno*

CALNO
3641 Kalneh (1), *Calneh*
or *Calno*

CALVARY
2898 *kraniŏn* (1), *skull*

CALVE
2342 *chûwl* (2), to *dance,*
whirl; to *writhe* in pain

CALVED
3205 *yâlad* (1), to *bear*
young; to *father a child*

CALVES
1121 *bên* (2), *son,*
descendant
1121+1241 *bên* (1), *son,*
descendant
5695 *'êgel* (10), bull *calf*
5697 *'eglâh* (2), cow *calf*
6499 *par* (1), *bullock*

3448 *mŏschŏs* (2), young
bullock

CALVETH
6403 *pâlaṭ* (1), to *slip* out,
i.e. *escape;* to *deliver*

CAME
857 *'âthâh* (4), to *arrive;*
go
858 *'âthâh* (Ch.) (3), to
arrive; go
935 *bôw'* (668), to *go* or
come
1061 *bikkûwr* (1),
first-fruits of the crop
1518 *gîyach* (1), to *issue*
forth; to *burst forth*
1691 Diblayim (1), *two*
cakes
1916 *hădôm* (2),
foot-stool
1946 *hûwk* (Ch.) (1), to
go, come
1961 *hâyâh* (527), to
exist, i.e. *be* or *become*
1980 *hâlak* (7), to *walk;*
live a certain way
2015 *hâphak* (1), to *turn*
about or over
3212 *yâlak* (6), to *walk;*
to *live;* to *carry*
3318 *yâtsâ'* (106), to *go,*
bring out
3329 *yâtsîy'* (1), *issue*
forth, i.e. offspring
3381 *yârad* (42), to
descend
3847 *lâbash* (3), to *clothe*
3996 *mâbôw'* (1),
entrance; sunset; west
4161 *môwtsâ'* (1), *going*
forth
4291 *mᵉṭâ'* (Ch.) (4), to
arrive, to extend
4672 *mâtsâ'* (2), to *find*
or *acquire;* to *occur*
5060 *nâga'* (5), to *strike*
5066 *nâgash* (27), to *be,*
come, bring near
5182 *nᵉchath* (Ch.) (1), to
descend; to depose
5312 *nᵉphaq* (Ch.) (3), to
issue forth; to bring out
5437 *çâbab* (1), to
surround
5559 *çᵉlîq* (Ch.) (5), to
ascend, go up
5674 *'âbar* (4), to *cross*
over; to transition
5927 *'âlâh* (82), to
ascend, be high, mount
5954 *'ălal* (Ch.) (4), to *go*
in; to *lead in*
5957 *'âlam* (Ch.) (1),
forever
6293 *pâga'* (1), to *impinge*
6473 *pâ'ar* (1), to *open*
wide
6555 *pârats* (1), to *break*
out
6743 *tsâlach* (5), to *push*
forward
7122 *qârâ'* (1), to
encounter, to *happen*
7126 *qârab* (20), to
approach, bring near
7127 *qᵉrêb* (Ch.) (5), to
approach, bring near
7131 *qârêb* (1), *near*

7725 *shûwb* (16), to *turn*
back; to *return*
191 *akŏuō* (1), to *hear;*
obey
305 *anabainō* (3), to *go*
up, rise
565 *apĕrchŏmai* (1), to
go off, i.e. depart
1096 *ginŏmai* (88), to *be,*
become
1237 *diadĕchŏmai* (1),
succeed, receive in turn
1448 *ĕggizō* (3), to
approach
1525 *ĕisĕrchŏmai* (10), to
enter
1531 *ĕispŏrĕuŏmai* (1), to
enter
1607 *ĕkpŏrĕuŏmai* (1), to
depart, be discharged
1831 *ĕxĕrchŏmai* (38), to
issue; to leave
1904 *ĕpĕrchŏmai* (1), to
supervene
1910 *ĕpibainō* (1), to
mount, ascend
1994 *ĕpistrĕphō* (1), to
revert, turn back to
1998 *ĕpisuntrĕchō* (1), to
hasten together upon
2064 *ĕrchŏmai* (199), to
go or come
2113 *ĕuthudrŏmĕō* (1), to
sail direct
2186 *ĕphistēmi* (7), to be
present; to approach
2240 *hēkō* (3), to *arrive,*
i.e. be present
2597 *katabainō* (16), to
descend
2658 *katantaō* (8), to
arrive at; to *attain*
2718 *katĕrchŏmai* (6), to
go, come down
2944 *kuklŏō* (1), to
surround, encircle
2983 *lambanō* (1), to
take, receive
3415 *mnaŏmai* (1), to
bear in mind
3719 *ŏrthrizō* (1), to *get*
up early in the morning
3854 *paraginŏmai* (16),
to *arrive;* to appear
3918 *parĕimi* (1), to be
present; to have come
3922 *parĕisĕrchŏmai* (1),
to supervene
3928 *parĕrchŏmai* (1), to
go by; to perish
4130 *plēthō* (1), to *fulfill,*
complete
4334 *prŏsĕrchŏmai* (65),
to come near, visit
4370 *prŏstrĕchō* (1), to
hasten by running
4836 *sumparaginŏmai*
(1), to convene
4863 *sunagō* (6), to
gather together
4872 *sunanabainō* (2), to
ascend in company
4905 *sunĕrchŏmai* (8), to
gather together
5342 *phĕrō* (3), to *bear* or
carry

CAMEL
1581 *gâmâl* (5), *camel*
2574 *kamēlŏs* (4), *camel*

CAMEL'S
1581 *gâmâl* (1), *camel*
2574 *kamēlŏs* (2), *camel*

CAMELS
327 *'ăchastârân* (2), *mule*
1581 *gâmâl* (44), *camel*

CAMELS'
1581 *gâmâl* (3), *camel*

CAMEST
935 *bôw'* (8), to *go, come*
1518 *gîyach* (1), to *issue*
forth; to *burst forth*
1980 *hâlak* (3), to *walk;*
live a certain way
3318 *yâtsâ'* (7), to *go,*
bring out
3381 *yârad* (3), to
descend
7126 *qârab* (1), to
approach, bring near
7725 *shûwb* (1), to *turn*
back; to *return*
1096 *ginŏmai* (1), to *be,*
become
1525 *ĕisĕrchŏmai* (1), to
enter
1831 *ĕxĕrchŏmai* (1), to
issue; to leave
2064 *ĕrchŏmai* (1), to *go*
or *come*

CAMON
7056 Qâmôwn (1),
elevation

CAMP
2583 *chânâh* (3), to
encamp
4264 *machăneh* (127),
encampment
8466 *tachănâh* (1),
encampment
3925 *parĕmbŏlē* (3),
encampment

CAMPED
2583 *chânâh* (1), to
encamp

CAMPHIRE
3724 *kôpher* (2), *village;*
bitumen; henna

CAMPS
4264 *machăneh* (7),
encampment

CAN
3045 *yâda'* (1), to *know*
3201 *yâkôl* (18), to be able
3202 *yᵉkêl* (Ch.) (2), to be
able
1097 *ginōskō* (1), to *know*
1410 *dunamai* (65), to be
able or possible
1492 *ĕidō* (2), to *know*
2480 *ischuō* (1), to *have*
or *exercise force*

CANA
2580 Kana (4), *Cana*

CANAAN
3667 Kᵉna'an (90),
humiliated
5478 Chanaanaiŏs (1),
Kenaanite

CANAANITE
3669 Kᵉna'ănîy (12),
Kenaanite; merchant
2581 Kananitēs (2),
zealous

CANAANITES
3669 Kᵉna'ănîy (55), *Kenaanite; merchant*

CANAANITESS
3669 Kᵉna'ănîy (1), *Kenaanite; merchant*

CANAANITISH
3669 Kᵉna'ănîy (2), *Kenaanite; merchant*

CANDACE
2582 Kandakē (1), *Candacë*

CANDLE
5216 nîyr (8), *lamp; lamplight*
3088 luchnŏs (8), *portable lamp*

CANDLES
5216 nîyr (1), *lamp; lamplight*

CANDLESTICK
4501 mᵉnôwrâh (34), *chandelier, lamp-stand*
5043 nebrᵉshâ' (Ch.) (1), *lamp-stand*
3087 luchnia (6), *lamp-stand*

CANDLESTICKS
4501 mᵉnôwrâh (6), *chandelier, lamp-stand*
3087 luchnia (6), *lamp-stand*

CANE
7070 qâneh (2), *reed*

CANKER
1044 gaggraina (1), *ulcer*, i.e. gangrene

CANKERED
2728 katiŏō (1), to *corrode, tarnish*

CANKERWORM
3218 yekeq (6), *young locust*

CANNEH
3656 Kanneh (1), *Canneh*

CANNOT
369 'ayin (1), *there is no, i.e., not exist, none*
408 'al (2), *not; nothing*
518 'îm (1), *whether?; if, although; Oh that!*
1077 bal (2), *nothing; not at all; lest*
1097 bᵉlîy (1), *without, not yet; lacking*;
1115 biltîy (1), *not, except, without, unless*
3201 yâkôl (3), to *be able*
3308 yŏphîy (2), *beauty*
3808 lô' (57), *no, not*
176 akatagnōstŏs (1), *unblamable*
180 akatapaustŏs (1), *unrefraining, unceasing*
215 alalētŏs (1), *unspeakable*
368 anantirrhētŏs (1), *indisputable*
551 apēirastŏs (1), *not temptable*
761 asalĕutŏs (1), *immovable, fixed*
893 apsĕudēs (1), *veracious, free of deceit*
1492 ĕidō (2), to *know*

3361 mē (2), *not; lest*
3467 muōpazō (1), to *see indistinctly, be myopic*
3756 ŏu (3), *no or not*

CANST
3201 yâkôl (6), to *be able*
3202 yᵉkêl (Ch.) (2), to *be able*
1097 ginōskō (1), to *know*
1410 dunamai (9), to *be able or possible*
1492 ĕidō (1), to *know*

CAPERNAUM
2584 Kapĕrnaŏum (16), *walled village which is comfortable*

CAPHTHORIM
3732 Kaphtôrîy (1), *Caphtorite*

CAPHTOR
3731 Kaphtôr (3), *wreath-shaped island*

CAPHTORIM
3732 Kaphtôrîy (1), *Caphtorite*

CAPHTORIMS
3732 Kaphtôrîy (1), *Caphtorite*

CAPPADOCIA
2587 Kappadŏkia (2), *Cappadocia*

CAPTAIN
1167 ba'al (1), *master; husband; owner; citizen*
2951 ṭiphçar (1), *military governor*
5057 nâgîyd (5), *commander, official*
5387 nâsîy' (12), *leader; rising mist, fog*
5921 'al (1), *above, over, upon, or against*
6346 pechâh (2), *prefect, officer*
7101 qâtsîyn (2), *magistrate*
7218 rô'sh (4), *head*
7227 rab (23), *great*
7229 rab (Ch.) (1), *great*
7990 shallîyṭ (Ch.) (1), *premier, sovereign*
7991 shâlîysh (2), *officer; of the third rank*
8269 sar (51), *head person, ruler*
747 archēgŏs (1), *chief leader; founder*
4755 stratēgŏs (3), *military governor*
4759 stratŏpĕdarchēs (1), *military commander*
5506 chiliarchŏs (18), *colonel*

CAPTAINS
441 'allûwph (1), *friend, one familiar; chieftain*
2951 ṭiphçar (1), *military governor*
3733 kar (1), *ram sheep; battering ram*
3746 kârîy (2), *life-guardsman*
5057 nâgîyd (1), *commander, official*
6346 pechâh (7), *prefect, officer*

6347 pechâh (Ch.) (4), *prefect, officer*
7101 qâtsîyn (1), *magistrate*
7218 rô'sh (6), *head*
7991 shâlîysh (9), *officer; of the third rank*
8269 sar (80), *head person, ruler*
4755 stratēgŏs (2), *military governor*
5506 chiliarchŏs (4), *colonel*

CAPTIVE
1473 gôwlâh (4), *exile; captive*
1540 gâlâh (24), to *denude; uncover*
1546 gâlûwth (2), *captivity; exiles*
6808 tsâ'âh (1), to *depopulate; imprison*
7617 shâbâh (21), to *transport into captivity*
7628 shᵉbîy (3), *exile; booty*
162 aichmalōtĕuō (2), to *capture*
163 aichmalōtizō (1), to *make captive*
2221 zōgrĕō (1), to *capture or ensnare*

CAPTIVES
1123+1547 bên (Ch.) (1), *son*
1473 gôwlâh (3), *exile; captive*
1540 gâlâh (3), to *denude; uncover*
1546 gâlûwth (3), *captivity; exiles*
7617 shâbâh (16), to *transport into captivity*
7628 shᵉbîy (8), *exile; booty*
7633 shibyâh (8), *exile; captive*
164 aichmalōtŏs (1), *captive*

CAPTIVITY
1473 gôwlâh (28), *exile; captive*
1540 gâlâh (9), to *denude; uncover*
1546 gâlûwth (11), *captivity; exiles*
1547 gâlûwth (Ch.) (3), *captivity; exiles*
2925 ṭalṭêlâh (1), *overthrow or rejection*
7622 shᵉbûwth (31), *exile; prisoners*
7628 shᵉbîy (30), *exile; booty*
7633 shibyâh (6), *exile; captive*
161 aichmalōsia (2), *captivity*
163 aichmalōtizō (2), to *make captive*

CARBUNCLE
1304 bârᵉqath (3), *flashing gem* (poss.) *emerald*

CARBUNCLES
68+688 'eben (1), *stone*

CARCAS
3752 Karkaç (1), *Karkas*

CARCASE
1472 gᵉvîyâh (2), *dead body*
4658 mappeleth (1), *down-fall; ruin; carcase*
5038 nᵉbêlâh (29), *carcase or carrion*
6297 peger (1), *carcase; corpse*
4430 ptōma (1), *corpse, carrion*

CARCASES
5038 nᵉbêlâh (7), *carcase or carrion*
6297 peger (13), *carcase; corpse*
2966 kōlŏn (1), *corpse*

CARCHEMISH
3751 Karkᵉmîysh (2), *Karkemish*

CARE
983 beṭach (1), *safety, security, trust*
1674 dᵉ'âgâh (1), *anxiety*
1697 dâbâr (1), *word; matter; thing*
2731 chărâdâh (1), *fear, anxiety*
7760+3820 sûwm (2), to *put, place*
1959 ĕpimĕlĕŏmai (3), to *care for*
3199 mĕlō (3), *it is a care or concern*
3308 mĕrimna (3), *solicitude; worry*
3309 mĕrimnaō (2), to *be anxious about*
4710 spŏudē (2), *despatch; eagerness*
5426 phrŏnĕō (1), to *be mentally disposed*

CAREAH
7143 Qârêach (1), *bald*

CARED
1875 dârash (1), to *pursue or search*
3199 mĕlō (2), *it is a care or concern*

CAREFUL
1672 dâ'ag (1), *be anxious, be afraid*
2729 chârad (1), to *hasten with anxiety*
2818 chăshach (Ch.) (1), to *need*
3309 mĕrimnaō (2), to *be anxious about*
5426 phrŏnĕō (1), to *be mentally disposed*
5431 phrŏntizō (1), *be anxious; to be careful*

CAREFULLY
2470 châlâh (1), to *be weak, sick, afflicted*
8085 shâma' (1), to *hear intelligently*
1567 ĕkzētĕō (1), to *seek out*
4708 spŏudaiŏtĕrōs (1), *more speedily*

CAREFULNESS
1674 dᵉ'âgâh (2), *anxiety*

275 amĕrimnŏs (1), *not anxious, free of care*
4710 spŏudē (1), *despatch; eagerness*

CARELESS
982 bâṭach (3), to *trust, be confident or sure*
983 beṭach (2), *safety, security, trust*

CARELESSLY
983 beṭach (3), *safety, security, trust*

CARES
3303 mĕn (3), not translated

CAREST
3199 mēlō (3), *it is a care or concern*

CARETH
1875 dârash (1), to *pursue or search*
3199 mēlō (2), *it is a care or concern*
3309 mĕrimnaō (4), to *be anxious* about

CARMEL
3760 Karmel (26), planted *field; garden*

CARMELITE
3761 Karmᵉlîy (5), *Karmelite*

CARMELITESS
3762 Karmᵉlîyth (2), *Karmelitess*

CARMI
3756 Karmîy (8), *gardener*

CARMITES
3757 Karmîy (1), *Karmite*

CARNAL
4559 sarkikŏs (9), *pertaining to flesh*
4561 sarx (2), *flesh*

CARNALLY
7902+2233 shᵉkâbâh (2), *lying* down
7903+2233 shᵉkôbeth (1), sexual *lying* down with
4561 sarx (1), *flesh*

CARPENTER
2796 chârâsh (1), skilled *fabricator* or worker
2796+6086 chârâsh (1), skilled *fabricator*
5045 tĕktōn (1), *craftsman* in wood

CARPENTER'S
5045 tĕktōn (1), *craftsman* in wood

CARPENTERS
2796 chârâsh (6), skilled *fabricator* or worker
2796+6086 chârâsh (2), skilled *fabricator*
6086 'êts (1), *wood*, things made of *wood*

CARPUS
2591 Karpŏs (1), (poss.) *fruit*

CARRIAGE
3520 kᵉbûwddâh (1), *magnificence, wealth*

3627 kᵉlîy (2), *implement, thing*

CARRIAGES
3627 kᵉlîy (1), *implement, thing*
5385 nᵉsûw'âh (1), *load, burden*
643 apŏskĕuazō (1), to *pack up baggage*

CARRIED
935 bôw' (10), to *go, come*
1473 gôwlâh (10), *exile; captive*
1540 gâlâh (35), to *denude; uncover*
1541 gᵉlâh (Ch.) (1), to *reveal mysteries*
1546 gâlûwth (3), *captivity; exiles*
1980 hâlak (1), to *walk; live a certain way*
2986 yâbal (3), to *bring*
3212 yâlak (2), to *walk; to live; to carry*
3318 yâtsâ' (3), to *go, bring out*
3947 lâqach (3), to *take*
4116 mâhar (1), to *hurry; promptly*
4131 môwṭ (1), to *slip, shake, fall*
5090 nâhag (3), to *drive; to lead, carry away*
5095 nâhal (1), to *conduct; to protect*
5186 nâṭâh (2), to *stretch or spread out*
5375 nâsâ' (15), to *lift up*
5376 nᵉsâ' (Ch.) (1), to *lift up*
5437 çâbab (3), to *surround*
5445 çâbal (1), to *carry*
5674 'âbar (1), to *cross over; to transition*
5927 'âlâh (3), to *ascend, be high, mount*
7392 râkab (3), to *ride*
7617 shâbâh (18), to *transport into captivity*
7725 shûwb (2), to *turn back; to return*
71 agō (1), to *lead; to bring, drive; to weigh*
339 anakathizō (1), to *sit up*
520 apagō (1), to *take away*
667 apŏhĕrō (4), to *bear off, carry away*
941 bastazō (1), to *lift, bear*
1580 ĕkkŏmizō (1), to *bear forth* to burial
1627 ĕkphĕrō (1), to *bear out; to produce*
1643 ĕlaunō (1), to *push*
3346 mĕtatithēmi (1), to *transport; to exchange*
3350 mĕtŏikĕsia (1), *exile, deportation*
4064 pĕriphĕrō (3), to *transport*
4216 pŏtamŏphŏrētŏs (1), *overwhelmed by a stream*
4792 sugkŏmizō (1), to *convey together*

4879 sunapagō (1), to *take off together*

CARRIEST
2229 zâram (1), to *gush water, pour forth*

CARRIETH
1589 gânab (1), to *thieve; to deceive*
5375 nâsâ' (1), to *lift up*
941 bastazō (1), to *lift, bear*

CARRY
935 bôw' (7), to *go or come*
1319 bâsar (1), to *announce* (good news)
1540 gâlâh (5), to *denude; uncover*
1980 hâlak (1), to *walk; live a certain way*
2904 ṭûwl (1), to *cast down or out, hurl*
2986 yâbal (1), to *bring*
2987 yᵉbal (Ch.) (1), to *bring*
3212 yâlak (3), to *walk; to live; to carry*
3318 yâtsâ' (18), to *go, bring out*
3381 yârad (2), to *descend*
3947 lâqach (2), to *take*
4853 massâ' (1), *burden, utterance*
5182 nᵉchath (Ch.) (1), to *descend; to depose*
5375 nâsâ' (18), to *lift up*
5445 çâbal (3), to *carry*
5674 'âbar (2), to *cross over; to transition*
5927 'âlâh (4), to *ascend, be high, mount*
6403 pâlaṭ (1), to *slip* out, i.e. *escape; to deliver*
7400 râkîyl (1), *scandal-monger*
7617 shâbâh (5), to *transport* into captivity
7725 shûwb (4), to *turn back; to return*
142 airō (1), to *lift, to take up*
941 bastazō (1), to *lift, bear*
1308 diaphĕrō (1), to *bear, carry; to differ*
1627 ĕkphĕrō (2), to *bear out; to produce*
3351 mĕtŏikizō (1), to *transfer* as a *captive*
4046 pĕripŏiĕŏmai (1), to *acquire; to gain*
5342 phĕrō (1), to *bear or carry*

CARRYING
1540 gâlâh (1), to *denude; uncover*
5375 nâsâ' (3), to *lift up*
7411 râmâh (1), to *hurl; to shoot; to delude*
1627 ĕkphĕrō (1), to *bear out; to produce*
3350 mĕtŏikĕsia (2), *exile, deportation*

CARSHENA
3771 Karshᵉnâ' (1), *Karshena*

CART
5699 'ăgâlâh (15), wheeled *vehicle*

CARVED
2405 chăṭûbâh (1), *tapestry*
2707 châqaq (1), to *carve; to delineate*
4734 miqla'ath (1), bas-relief *sculpture*
6456 pᵉçîyl (3), *idol*
6459 peçel (2), *idol*
6603 pittûwach (2), *sculpture; engraving*
7049 qâla' (3), to *sling* a stone; to *carve*

CARVING
2799 chărôsheth (2), skilled *work*

CARVINGS
4734 miqla'ath (1), bas-relief *sculpture*

CASE
1697 dâbâr (1), *word; matter; thing*
3602 kâkâh (1), *just so*
7725 shûwb (2), to *turn back; to return*
156 aitia (1), logical *reason; legal crime*
3364 ŏu mē (1), *not* at all, absolutely *not*

CASEMENT
822 'eshnâb (1), latticed *window*

CASIPHIA
3703 Kâçiphyâ' (2), *silvery*

CASLUHIM
3695 Kaçlûchîym (2), *Casluchim*

CASSIA
6916 qiddâh (2), *cassia*
7102 qᵉtsîy'âh (1), *cassia*

CAST
1299 bâraq (1), to *flash* lightning
1457 gâhar (1), to *prostrate* oneself
1602 gâ'al (1), to *detest; to reject; to fail*
1644 gârash (1), to *drive* out; to *expatriate*
1740 dûwach (1), to *rinse clean, wash*
1760 dâchâh (1), to *push* down; to *totter*
1920 hâdaph (2), to *push* away or down; *drive out*
1972 hâlâ' (1), to *remove* or be *remote*
2186 zânach (17), to *reject, forsake, fail*
2219 zârâh (1), to *toss* about; to *diffuse*
2490 châlal (1), to *profane, defile*
2904 ṭûwl (12), to *cast* down or out, *hurl*
3032 yâdad (2), to *throw* lots
3034 yâdâh (2), to *throw; to revere or worship*
3240 yânach (1), to *allow to stay*

3332 yâtsaq (10), to *pour out*

3333 yᵉtsûqâh (1), *poured out into a mold*

3381 yârad (3), to *descend*

3384 yârâh (4), to *throw, shoot an arrow*

3423 yârash (10), to *inherit; to impoverish*

3766 kâra' (1), to *prostrate*

3782 kâshal (3), to *totter, waver; to falter*

3874 lûwt (1), to *wrap up*

3988 mâ'aç (10), to *spurn; to disappear*

4048 mâgar (1), to *yield up, be thrown*

4054 migrâsh (1), *open country*

4131 môwṭ (1), to *slip, shake, fall*

4166 mûwtsâqâh (1), *casting of metal; tube*

4788 mârûwd (1), *outcast; destitution*

5060 nâga' (1), to *strike*

5077 nâdâh (1), to *exclude*, i.e. *banish*

5080 nâdach (4), to *push off, scattered*

5203 nâṭash (1), to *disperse; to thrust* off

5221 nâkâh (1), to *strike, kill*

5307 nâphal (24), to *fall*

5375 nâsâ' (1), to *lift up*

5390 nᵉshîyqâh (1), *kiss*

5394 nâshal (1), to *divest, eject, or drop*

5414 nâthan (5), to *give*

5422 nâthats (3), to *tear down*

5437 çâbab (1), to *surround*

5499 çᵉchâbâh (2), *rag*

5549 çâlal (4), to *mound up; to exalt; to oppose*

5619 çâqal (1), to *throw large stones*

5927 'âlâh (2), to *ascend, be high, mount*

6080 'âphar (1), to *be dust*

6327 pûwts (2), to *dash in pieces; to disperse*

6437 pânâh (1), to *turn, to face*

6696 tsûwr (1), to *cramp*, i.e. *confine; to harass*

7290 râdam (1), to *stupefy*

7324 rûwq (1), to *pour out*, i.e. *empty*

7368 râchaq (1), to *recede; remove*

7412 rᵉmâh (Ch.) (11), to *throw; to set; to assess*

7760 sûwm (1), to *put, place*

7817 shâchach (4), to *sink or depress*

7843 shâchath (1), to *decay; to ruin*

7921 shâkôl (3), to *miscarry*

7933 sheken (4), *residence*

7971 shâlach (14), to *send away*

7993 shâlak (113), to *throw out, down*

7995 shalleketh (1), *felling of trees*

7998 shâlâl (1), *booty*

8210 shâphak (8), to *spill forth; to expend*

8213 shâphêl (1), to *humiliate*

8628 tâqa' (1), to *clatter, slap, drive, clasp*

114 athĕtĕō (1), to *disesteem, neutralize*

577 apŏballō (1), to *throw off;* fig. *to lose*

641 apŏrrhiptō (1), to *throw oneself into*

656 apŏsunagōgŏs (1), *excommunicated*

683 apōthĕŏmai (2), to *push off; to reject*

906 ballō (81), to *throw*

1000 bŏlē (1), *throw as a measure*

1260 dialŏgizŏmai (1), to *deliberate*

1544 ĕkballō (51), to *throw out*

1601 ĕkpiptō (1), to *drop away*

1614 ĕktĕinō (1), to *stretch*

1620 ĕktithĕmi (1), to *expose; to declare*

1685 ĕmballō (1), to *throw in*

1911 ĕpiballō (2), to *throw upon*

1977 ĕpirrhiptō (1), to *throw upon*

2210 zēmiŏō (1), to *experience detriment*

2598 kataballō (2), to *throw down*

2630 katakrēmnizō (1), to *precipitate down*

2975 lagchanō (1), to *determine by lot*

3036 lithŏbŏlĕō (1), to *throw stones*

3679 ŏnĕidizō (1), to *rail at, chide, taunt*

3860 paradidōmi (1), to *hand over*

4016 pĕriballō (3), to *wrap around, clothe*

4406 prŏïmŏs (1), *autumnal showering*

4496 rhiptō (5), to *fling, toss; to lay out*

5011 tapĕinŏs (1), *humiliated, lowly*

5020 tartarŏō (1), to *incarcerate in Tartaros*

CASTAWAY

96 adŏkimŏs (1), *failing the test, worthless*

CASTEDST

5307 nâphal (1), to *fall*

CASTEST

2186 zânach (1), to *reject, forsake, fail*

6565 mâtsâ' (1), to *break up; to violate, frustrate*

7993 shâlak (1), to *throw out, down or away*

CASTETH

1920 hâdaph (1), to *push away or down; drive out*

3381 yârad (1), to *descend*

3384 yârâh (1), to *throw, shoot an arrow*

5307 nâphal (1), to *fall*

6884 tsâraph (1), to *fuse metal; to refine*

6979 qûwr (2), to *throw forth; to wall up*

7921 shâkôl (1), to *miscarry*

7993 shâlak (1), to *throw out, down or away*

8213 shâphêl (1), to *humiliate*

906 ballō (2), to *throw*

1544 ĕkballō (4), to *throw out*

CASTING

2866 chăthath (1), *dismay*

3445 yeshach (1), *hunger*

4165 mûwtsâq (1), *casting of metal*

5307 nâphal (1), to *fall*

7901 shâkab (1), to *lie down*

8210 shâphak (1), to *spill forth; to expend*

577 apŏballō (1), to *throw off;* fig. *to lose*

580 apŏbŏlē (1), *rejection, loss*

906 ballō (6), to *throw*

1544 ĕkballō (3), to *throw out*

1977 ĕpirrhiptō (1), to *throw upon*

2507 kathairĕō (1), to *lower, or demolish*

CASTLE

759 'armôwn (1), *citadel, high fortress*

4679 mᵉtsad (1), *stronghold*

4686 mâtsûwd (1), *net or capture; fastness*

3925 parĕmbŏlē (6), *encampment*

CASTLES

1003 bîyrânîyth (2), *fortress, citadel*

2918 ṭîyrâh (3), *fortress; hamlet*

4026 migdâl (1), *tower; rostrum*

CASTOR

1359 Diŏskŏurŏi (1), *twins of Zeus*

CATCH

1641 gârar (1), to *drag off roughly*

2414 châṭaph (3), to *seize as a prisoner*

2480 châlaṭ (1), to *snatch at, seizing*

2963 ṭâraph (2), to *pluck off or pull to pieces*

3920 lâkad (2), to *catch; to capture*

4672 mâtsâ' (1), to *find or acquire; to occur*

5367 nâqash (1), to *entrap with a noose*

8610 tâphas (1), to *manipulate*, i.e. *seize*

64 agrĕuō (1), to *entrap, catch*

2221 zōgrĕō (1), to *capture or ensnare*

2340 thērĕuō (1), to *carp at*

CATCHETH

6679 tsûwd (1), to *lie in wait; to catch*

726 harpazō (2), to *seize*

CATERPILLER

2625 chaçîyl (5), *locust*

CATERPILLERS

2625 chaçîyl (1), *locust*

3218 yekeq (3), *young locust*

CATTLE

926 bâhal (1), to *tremble; be, make agitated*

929 bᵉhêmâh (56), *animal, beast*

1165 bᵉ'îyr (2), *cattle, livestock*

1241 bâqâr (1), *plowing ox; herd*

4399 mᵉlâ'kâh (1), *work; property*

4734 miqla'ath (1), *bas-relief sculpture*

4735 miqneh (57), *live-stock*

4806 mᵉrîy' (3), *stall-fed animal*

6629 tsŏ'n (13), *flock of sheep or goats*

7069 qânâh (1), to *create; to procure*

7716 seh (7), *sheep or goat*

2353 thrĕmma (1), *stock*

4165 pŏimainō (1), to *tend as a shepherd*

CAUGHT

270 'âchaz (4), to *seize, grasp; possess*

962 bâzaz (1), to *plunder, take booty*

1497 gâzal (1), to *rob*

2388 châzaq (8), to *fasten upon; to seize*

3920 lâkad (3), to *catch; to capture*

8610 tâphas (3), to *manipulate*, i.e. *seize*

726 harpazō (5), to *seize*

1949 ĕpilambanŏmai (2), to *seize*

2983 lambanō (3), to *take, receive*

4084 piazō (2), to *seize, arrest, or capture*

4815 sullambanō (1), to *seize (arrest, capture)*

4884 sunarpazō (4), to *snatch together*

CAUL

3508 yôthereth (11), *lobe or flap of the liver*

5458 çᵉgôwr (1), *breast*

CAULS

7636 shâbîyç (1), *netting*

CAUSE

657 'epheç (1), *end; no further*

834 'ăsher (1), *because, in order that*
1697 dâbâr (6), *word; matter; thing*
1700 dibrâh (1), *because, on account of*
1779 dîyn (7), *judge; judgment; law suit*
1961 hâyâh (1), *to exist, i.e. be or become*
2600 chinnâm (15), *gratis, free*
3651 kên (1), *just; right, correct*
4616 ma'an (1), *on account of*
4941 mishpâṭ (12), *verdict; formal decree*
5252 n°çibbâh (1), *turn of affairs*
5414 nâthan (5), *to give*
5438 çibbâh (1), *turn of affairs*
5668 'âbûwr (1), *on account of*
7379 rîyb (23), *contest, personal or legal*
7387 rêyqâm (2), *emptily; ineffectually*
7945 shel (1), *on account of; whatsoever*
8267 sheqer (1), *untruth; sham*
156 aitia (9), *logical reason; legal crime*
158 aitiŏn (2), *reason, basis; crime*
846 autŏs (1), *he, she, it*
873 aphŏrizŏ (1), *to limit, exclude, appoint*
1223 dia (13), *because of, for the sake of*
1352 diŏ (2), *consequently, therefore*
1432 dŏrĕan (1), *gratuitously, freely*
1500 ĕikĕ (1), *idly, i.e. without reason or effect*
1752 hĕnĕka (4), *on account of*
2289 thanatŏŏ (3), *to kill*
3056 lŏgŏs (1), *word, matter, thing*
4160 pŏiĕŏ (3), *to do*
5484 charin (3), *on account of, because of*

CAUSED
1961 hâyâh (1), *to exist, i.e. be or become*
5414 nâthan (7), *to give*
3076 lupĕŏ (1), *to distress; to be sad*
4160 pŏiĕŏ (2), *to do*

CAUSELESS
2600 chinnâm (2), *gratis, free*

CAUSES
182 'ôwdôwth (1), *on account of; because*
1697 dâbâr (2), *word; matter; thing*
7379 rîyb (1), *contest, personal or legal*
1752 hĕnĕka (1), *on account of*

CAUSETH
5414 nâthan (1), *to give*

2358 thriambĕuŏ (1), *to lead in triumphal procession*
2716 katĕrgazŏmai (1), *to finish; to accomplish*
4160 pŏiĕŏ (3), *to do*

CAUSEWAY
4546 m°çillâh (2), *main thoroughfare; viaduct*

CAVE
4631 m°'ârâh (32), *dark cavern*
4693 spĕlaiŏn (1), *cavern; hiding-place*

CAVE'S
4631 m°'ârâh (1), *dark cavern*

CAVES
2356 chôwr (1), *cavity, socket, den*
4247 m°chillâh (1), *cavern, hole*
4631 m°'ârâh (3), *dark cavern*
3692 ŏpĕ (1), *hole, i.e. cavern; spring of water*

CEASE
988 bâṭêl (1), *to desist from labor, cease*
989 b°ṭêl (Ch.) (3), *to stop*
1820 dâmâh (1), *to be silent; to fail, cease*
1826 dâmam (1), *to stop, cease; to perish*
2308 châdal (12), *to desist, stop; be fat*
2790 chârash (1), *to be silent; to be deaf*
3254 yâçaph (1), *to add or augment*
3615 kâlâh (1), *to complete, consume*
4185 mûwsh (1), *to withdraw*
6565 pârar (1), *to break up; to violate, frustrate*
7503 râphâh (1), *to slacken*
7647 sâbâ' (1), *copiousness*
7673 shâbath (37), *to repose; to desist*
7725 shûwb (1), *to turn back; to return*
7918 shâkak (1), *to lay a trap; to allay*
8552 tâmam (1), *to complete, finish*
180 akatapaustŏs (1), *unrefraining, unceasing*
3973 pauŏ (4), *to stop, i.e. restrain, quit*

CEASED
989 b°ṭêl (Ch.) (1), *to stop*
1826 dâmam (1), *to stop, cease; to perish*
1934+989 hăvâ' (Ch.) (1), *to be, to exist*
2308 châdal (6), *to desist, stop; be fat*
5117 nûwach (1), *to rest; to settle down*
5307 nâphal (1), *to fall*
5975 'âmad (1), *to stand*
6313 pûwg (1), *to be sluggish; be numb*

7673 shâbath (6), *to repose; to desist*
1257 dialĕipŏ (1), *to intermit, stop*
2270 hēsuchazŏ (1), *to refrain*
2664 katapauŏ (1), *to cause to desist*
2673 katargĕŏ (1), *to be, render entirely useless*
2869 kŏpazŏ (3), *to tire, i.e. to relax*
3973 pauŏ (7), *to stop, i.e. restrain, quit*

CEASETH
1584 gâmar (1), *to end; to complete; to fail*
1820 dâmâh (1), *to be silent; to fail, cease*
2308 châdal (1), *to desist, stop; be fat*
3615 kâlâh (1), *to cease, be finished, perish*
7673 shâbath (4), *to repose; to desist*
8367 shâthaq (1), *to subside*
3973 pauŏ (1), *to stop, i.e. restrain, quit*

CEASING
2308 châdal (1), *to desist, stop; be fat*
83 adĕlŏtēs (1), *uncertainty*
89 adialĕiptŏs (4), *without omission*
1618 ĕktĕnēs (1), *intent, earnest*

CEDAR
729 'âraz (1), *of cedar*
730 'erez (49), *cedar tree*
731 'arzâh (1), *cedar paneling*

CEDARS
730 'erez (24), *cedar tree*

CEDRON
2748 Kĕdrŏn (1), *dusky place*

CELEBRATE
1984 hâlal (1), *to speak words of thankfulness*
2278 chăbereth (1), *consort, companion*
7673 shâbath (1), *to repose*

CELESTIAL
2032 ĕpŏuraniŏs (2), *above the sky, celestial*

CELLARS
214 'ôwtsâr (2), *depository*

CENCHREA
2747 Kĕgchrĕai (2), *millet*

CENSER
4289 machtâh (7), *pan for live coals*
4730 miqṭereth (2), *incense coal-pan*
2369 thumiastēriŏn (1), *altar of incense*
3031 libanŏtŏs (1), *censer for incense*

CENSERS
4289 machtâh (8), *pan for live coals*

CENTURION
1543 hĕkatŏntarchēs (17), *captain of a hundred*
2760 kĕnturiŏn (3), *captain of a hundred*

CENTURION'S
1543 hĕkatŏntarchēs (1), *captain of a hundred*

CENTURIONS
1543 hĕkatŏntarchēs (3), *captain of a hundred*

CEPHAS
2786 Kēphas (6), *rock*

CEREMONIES
4941 mishpâṭ (1), *verdict; formal decree; justice*

CERTAIN
259 'echâd (9), *first*
376 'îysh (4), *man; male; someone*
582 'ĕnôwsh (8), *man; person, human*
592 'ănîyâh (2), *groaning*
1400 g°bar (Ch.) (2), *person; someone*
1697 dâbâr (2), *word; matter; thing*
3045 yâda' (3), *to know*
3330 yatstsìyb (Ch.) (1), *fixed, sure*
3559 kûwn (2), *to render sure, proper*
6256 'êth (1), *time*
6422 palmôwnîy (1), *a certain one*
444 anthrōpŏs (2), *human being; mankind*
444+5100 anthrōpŏs (1), *human being; mankind*
790 astatĕŏ (1), *homeless, vagabond*
804 asphalēs (1), *secure; certain*
1212 dēlŏs (1), *clear, plain, evident*
1520 hĕis (5), *one*
4225 pŏu (2), *somewhere, i.e. nearly*
5100 tis (112), *some or any person or object*

CERTAINLY
389 'ak (1), *surely; only, however*
403 'âkên (1), *surely!, truly!; but*
3588 kìy (1), *for, that because*
3689 ŏntōs (1), *really, certainly*

CERTAINTY
3330 yatstsìyb (Ch.) (1), *fixed, sure*
3559 kûwn (1), *to render sure, proper*
7189 qôsheṭ (1), *reality*
803 asphalĕia (1), *security; certainty*
804 asphalēs (2), *secure; certain*

CERTIFIED
559 'âmar (1), *to say*
3064 Y°hûwdîy (1), *Jehudite*

CERTIFY

CERTIFY
3046 y°da' (Ch.) (3), to *know*
5046 nâgad (1), to *announce*
1107 gnōrizō (1), to *make known, reveal*

CHAFED
4751 mar (1), *bitter; bitterness; bitterly*

CHAFF
2842 châshash (2), dry *grass, chaff*
4671 môts (8), *chaff*
5784 'ûwr (Ch.) (1), *chaff*
8401 teben (1), *threshed stalks* of cereal grain
892 achurŏn (2), *chaff* of grain

CHAIN
2002 hamnîyk (Ch.) (3), *necklace*
5178 n°chôsheth (1), *copper; bronze*
6059 'ânaq (1), to *collar; to fit out*
6060 'ânâq (1), *necklace chain*
7242 râbîyd (2), *collar spread* around the neck
7659 shib'âthayim (1), *seven-fold*
8333 sharsh°râh (1), *chain*
254 halusis (3), *fetter or manacle*

CHAINS
246 'ăziqqîym (2), *manacles, chains*
685 'ets'âdâh (1), *bracelet*
2131 zîyqâh (3), *burning arrow; bond, fetter*
2397 chách (2), *ring* for the nose or lips
2737 chârûwz (1), strung *beads*
3574 kôwshârâh (1), *prosperity*
5178 n°chôsheth (2), *copper; bronze*
5188 n°ṭîyphâh (1), *pendant* for the ears
5688 'ăbôth (3), *entwined* things: *string, wreath*
6060 'ânâq (2), *necklace chain*
7569 rattôwq (2), *chain*
8333 sharsh°râh (6), *chain*
8337 shêsh (1), *six; sixth*
254 halusis (7), *fetter or manacle*
1199 dĕsmŏn (1), *shackle; impediment*
4577 sĕira (1), *chain*, as *binding or drawing*

CHALCEDONY
5472 chalkĕdōn (1), *copper-like, chalcedony*

CHALCOL
3633 Kalkôl (1), *sustenance*

CHALDAEANS
5466 Chaldaiŏs (1), *native or the region of the lower Euphrates*

CHALDEA

CHALDEA
3778 Kasdîy (7), *astrologer*

CHALDEAN
3777 Kesed (2), *Kesed*

CHALDEANS
3778 Kasdîy (48), *astrologer*
3779 Kasday (Ch.) (17), *magian or astrologer*

CHALDEANS'
3778 Kasdîy (1), *astrologer*

CHALDEES
3778 Kasdîy (13), *astrologer*

CHALDEES'
3778 Kasdîy (1), *astrologer*

CHALKSTONES
68+1615 'eben (1), *stone*

CHALLENGETH
559 'âmar (1), to *say*

CHAMBER
2315 cheder (15), *apartment, chamber*
2646 chuppâh (1), *canopy*
3326 yâtsûwa' (1), *bed; wing or lean-to*
3957 lishkâh (14), *room*
5393 nishkâh (2), *room, cell*
5944 'ălîyâh (6), *second-story* room
5952 'allîyth (Ch.) (1), *second-story* room
6763 tsêlâ' (3), *side* of a person or thing
8372 tâ' (4), *room*
5253 hupĕrō¡ŏn (3), *third story* apartment

CHAMBERING
2845 kŏitē (1), *couch; conception*

CHAMBERLAIN
5631 çârîyç (4), *eunuch; official* of state
1909+3588+2846 ĕpi (1), *on, upon*
3623 ŏikŏnŏmŏs (1), *overseer, manager*

CHAMBERLAINS
5631 çârîyç (9), *eunuch; official* of state

CHAMBERS
2315 cheder (8), *apartment, chamber*
3326 yâtsûwa' (2), *bed; wing or lean-to* of a building
3957 lishkâh (31), *room* in a building
5393 nishkâh (1), *room, cell*
5944 'ălîyâh (6), *upper* things; *second-story* room
6763 tsêlâ' (8), *side* of a person or thing
8372 tâ' (9), *room*
5009 tamĕiŏn (1), *room*

CHAMELEON
3581 kôach (1), large *lizard*

CHAMOIS

CHAMOIS
2169 zemer (1), *gazelle*

CHAMPAIGN
6160 'ărâbâh (1), *desert, wasteland*

CHAMPION
376+1143 'îysh (2), *man; male; someone*
1368 gibbôwr (1), *powerful;* great *warrior*

CHANAAN
5477 Chanaan (2), *humiliated*

CHANCE
4745 miqreh (1), *accident or fortune*
6294 pega' (1), casual *impact*
7122 qârâ' (2), to *encounter*, to *happen*
4795 sugkuria (1), *chance occurrence*
5177 tugchanō (1), to *happen; perhaps*

CHANCELLOR
1169+2942 b°'êl (Ch.) (3), *master*

CHANCETH
4745 miqreh (1), *accident or fortune*

CHANGE
2015 hâphak (1), to *change, overturn*
2487 chălîyphâh (4), *alternation, change*
2498 châlaph (1), to *pierce; to change*
4171 mûwr (5), to *alter; to barter, to dispose of*
4254 machălâtsâh (1), *mantle, garment*
7760 sûwm (1), to *put, place*
8133 sh°nâ' (Ch.) (1), to *alter, change*
8138 shânâh (3), to *fold,* i.e. *duplicate;* to *transmute*
8545 t°mûwrâh (1), *barter, compensation*
236 allassō (2), to *make different, change*
3331 mĕtathĕsis (1), *transferral, disestablishment*
3337 mĕtallassō (1), to *exchange*
3345 mĕtaschēmatizō (1), to *transfigure or disguise;* to *apply*

CHANGEABLE
4254 machălâtsâh (1), *mantle, garment*

CHANGED
2015 hâphak (2), to *change, overturn*
2498 châlaph (6), to *pass on;* to *change*
2664 châphas (1), to *seek;* to *mask*
4171 mûwr (6), to *alter; to barter, to dispose of*
5437 çâbab (2), to *surround*
8132 shânâ' (3), to *alter, change*

CHARGE

8133 sh°nâ' (Ch.) (12), to *alter, change*
8138 shânâh (3), to *fold, to transmute*
236 allassō (4), to *make different, change*
3328 mĕtaballō (1), to *turn about* in opinion
3337 mĕtallassō (1), to *exchange*
3339 mĕtamŏrphŏō (1), to *transform,* i.e. metamorphose
3346 mĕtatithēmi (1), to *transport;* to *exchange*

CHANGERS
2773 kĕrmatistēs (1), *money-broker*

CHANGERS'
2855 kŏllubistēs (1), *coin-dealer*

CHANGES
2487 chălîyphâh (7), *alternation, change*

CHANGEST
8138 shânâh (1), to *fold,* to *transmute*

CHANGETH
4171 mûwr (1), to *alter; to barter, to dispose of*
8133 sh°nâ' (Ch.) (1), to *alter, change*

CHANGING
8545 t°mûwrâh (1), *barter, compensation*

CHANNEL
7641 shibbôl (1), *stream; ear of grain*

CHANNELS
650 'âphîyq (3), *valley; stream; mighty, strong*

CHANT
6527 pâraṭ (1), to *scatter* words, i.e. *prate*

CHAPEL
4720 miqdâsh (1), *sanctuary of deity*

CHAPITER
3805 kôthereth (12), *capital* of a column
6858 tsepheth (1), *capital* of a column

CHAPITERS
3805 kôthereth (12), *capital* of a column
7218 rô'sh (4), *head*

CHAPMEN
582+8846 'ĕnôwsh (1), *man; person, human*

CHAPT
2865 châthath (1), to *break* down

CHARASHIM
2798 Chărâshîym (1), *skilled worker*

CHARCHEMISH
3751 Kark°mîysh (1), *Karkemish*

CHARGE
3027 yâd (1), *hand; power*
4931 mishmereth (46), *watch, sentry, post*

4941 mishpâṭ (1), *verdict; formal decree; justice*
5414 nâthan (1), *to give*
5447 çêbel (1), *load; forced labor*
5749 'ûwd (1), *to protest, testify*
5921 'al (3), *above, over, upon, or against*
6213 'âsâh (1), *to do or make*
6485 pâqad (1), *to visit, care for, count*
6486 pᵉquddâh (2), *visitation; punishment*
6496 pâqîyd (1), *superintendent, officer*
6680 tsâvâh (16), *to constitute, enjoin*
7130 qereb (1), *nearest part, i.e. the center*
7592 shâ'al (1), *to ask*
7650 shâba' (7), *to swear*
77 adapanŏs (1), *free of charge*
1263 diamarturŏmai (2), *to attest or protest*
1458+2596 ĕgkalĕŏ (1), *to charge, criminate*
1462 ĕgklēma (1), *accusation*
1781 ĕntĕllŏmai (2), *to enjoin, give orders*
1909 ĕpi (1), *on, upon*
2004 ĕpitassŏ (1), *to order, command*
2476 histēmi (1), *to stand, establish*
3049 lŏgizŏmai (1), *to take an inventory*
3726 hŏrkizŏ (1), *solemnly enjoin*
3852 paraggĕlia (2), *mandate, order*
3853 paraggĕllŏ (4), *to enjoin; to instruct*

CHARGEABLE
3513 kâbad (2), *to be rich, glorious*
1912 ĕpibarĕŏ (2), *to be severe toward*
2655 katanarkaŏ (1), *to be a burden*

CHARGED
559 'âmar (1), *to say*
5414 nâthan (1), *to give*
5674+5921 'âbar (1), *to cross over; to transition*
6485 pâqad (3), *to visit, care for, count*
6680 tsâvâh (23), *to constitute, enjoin*
7650 shâba' (2), *to swear*
7760 sûwm (1), *to put, place*
916 barĕŏ (1), *to weigh down, cause pressure*
1291 diastĕllŏmai (6), *to distinguish*
1690 ĕmbrimaŏmai (2), *to blame, warn sternly*
1781 ĕntĕllŏmai (1), *to enjoin, give orders*
2008 ĕpitimaŏ (5), *to rebuke, warn, forbid*
3146 mastigŏŏ (1), *to punish by flogging*
3853 paraggĕllŏ (3), *to enjoin; to instruct*

CHARGEDST
5749 'ûwd (1), *to protest, testify; to encompass*

CHARGER
7086 qᵉ'ârâh (13), *bowl*
4094 pinax (4), *plate, platter, dish*

CHARGERS
105 ăgarṭâl (2), *basin*
7086 qᵉ'ârâh (1), *bowl*

CHARGES
4931 mishmereth (4), *watch, sentry, post*
1159 dapanaŏ (1), *to incur cost; to waste*
3800 ŏpsōniŏn (1), *rations, stipend or pay*

CHARGEST
6485 pâqad (1), *to visit, care for, count*

CHARGING
1263 diamarturŏmai (1), *to attest or protest*
3853 paraggĕllŏ (1), *to enjoin; to instruct*

CHARIOT
668 'appiryôwn (1), *palanquin, carriage*
4818 merkâbâh (23), *chariot*
5699 'ăgâlâh (1), *wheeled vehicle*
7393 rekeb (28), *vehicle for riding*
7395 rakkâb (2), *charioteer*
7398 rᵉkûwb (1), *vehicle ridden on*
716 harma (3), *chariot, carriage*

CHARIOTS
2021 hôtsen (1), *weapon*
4817 merkâb (1), *chariot; seat in chariot*
4818 merkâbâh (20), *chariot*
7393 rekeb (87), *vehicle for riding*
7396 rikbâh (1), *chariot*
716 harma (1), *chariot, carriage*
4480 rhĕda (1), *wagon for riding*

CHARITABLY
2596+26 kata (1), *down; according to*

CHARITY
26 agapē (28), *love; love-feast*

CHARMED
3908 lachash (1), *incantation; amulet*

CHARMER
2266+2267 châbar (1), *to fascinate by spells*

CHARMERS
328 'aṭ (1), *gently, softly*
3907 lâchash (1), *to whisper a magic spell*

CHARMING
2266+2267 châbar (1), *to fascinate by spells*

CHARRAN
5488 Charrhan (2), *parched*

CHASE
1760 dâchâh (1), *to push down; to totter*
7291 râdaph (5), *to run after with hostility*

CHASED
1272 bârach (1), *to flee suddenly*
5074 nâdad (2), *to rove, flee; to drive away*
5080 nâdach (1), *to push off, scattered*
6679 tsûwd (1), *to lie in wait; to catch*
7291 râdaph (8), *to run after with hostility*

CHASETH
1272 bârach (1), *to flee suddenly*

CHASING
1814 dâlaq (1), *to flame; to pursue*

CHASTE
53 hagnŏs (3), *innocent, modest, perfect, pure*

CHASTEN
3198 yâkach (1), *to decide, justify, convict*
3256 yâçar (3), *to chastise; to instruct*
6031 'ânâh (1), *to afflict, be afflicted*
3811 paidĕuŏ (1), *to educate or discipline*

CHASTENED
3198 yâkach (1), *to decide, justify, convict*
3256 yâçar (2), *to chastise; to instruct*
8433 tôwkêchâh (1), *chastisement*
3811 paidĕuŏ (3), *to educate or discipline*

CHASTENEST
3256 yâçar (1), *to chastise; to instruct*

CHASTENETH
3256 yâçar (2), *to chastise; to instruct*
4148 mûwçâr (1), *reproof, warning*
3811 paidĕuŏ (1), *to educate or discipline*

CHASTENING
4148 mûwçâr (3), *reproof, warning*
3809 paidĕia (1), *disciplinary correction*

CHASTISE
3256 yâçar (6), *to chastise; to instruct*
3811 paidĕuŏ (2), *to educate or discipline*

CHASTISED
3256 yâçar (5), *to chastise; to instruct*

CHASTISEMENT
4148 mûwçâr (3), *reproof, warning*
3809 paidĕia (1), *disciplinary correction*

CHASTISETH
3256 yâçar (1), *to chastise; to instruct*

CHATTER
6850 tsâphaph (1), *to coo or chirp as a bird*

CHEBAR
3529 Kᵉbâr (8), *length*

CHECK
4148 mûwçâr (1), *reproof, warning*

CHECKER
7639 sᵉbâkâh (1), *net-work balustrade*

CHEDORLAOMER
3540 Kᵉdorlâ'ômer (5), *Kedorlaomer*

CHEEK
3895 lᵉchîy (6), *jaw; area of the jaw*
4973 mᵉthallᵉ'âh (1), *tooth*
4600 siagŏn (2), *cheek*

CHEEKS
3895 lᵉchîy (5), *jaw; area of the jaw*

CHEER
3190 yâṭab (1), *to be, make well*
8055 sâmach (1), *to be, make gleesome*
2114 ĕuthumĕŏ (3), *to be cheerful*
2293 tharsĕŏ (5), *to have courage; take heart!*

CHEERETH
8055 sâmach (1), *to be, make gleesome*

CHEERFUL
2896 ṭôwb (1), *good; well*
3190 yâṭab (1), *to be, make well*
5107 nûwb (1), *to (make) flourish; to utter*
2431 hilarŏs (1), *prompt or willing*

CHEERFULLY
2115 ĕuthumŏs (1), *cheerful, encouraged*

CHEERFULNESS
2432 hilarŏtēs (1), *cheerful readiness*

CHEESE
1385 gᵉbînah (1), *curdled milk*
8194 shâphâh (1), *cheese*

CHEESES
2757+2461 chârîyts (1), *slice, portion*

CHELAL
3636 Kᵉlâl (1), *complete*

CHELLUH
3622 Kᵉlûwhay (1), *completed*

CHELUB
3620 Kᵉlûwb (2), *bird-trap; basket*

CHELUBAI
3621 Kᵉlûwbay (1), *forcible*

CHEMARIMS
3649 kâmâr (1), *pagan priest*

CHEMOSH
3645 Kᵉmôwsh (8), *powerful*

CHENAANAH
3668 Kᵉna'ănâh (5), *humiliated*

CHENANI
3662 Kᵉnânîy (1), *planted*

CHENANIAH
3663 Kᵉnanyâh (3), *Jehovah has planted*

CHEPHAR-HAAMMONAI
3726 Kᵉphar hâ-'Ammôwnîy (1), *village of the Ammonite*

CHEPHIRAH
3716 Kᵉphîyrâh (4), *village*

CHERAN
3763 Kᵉrân (2), *Keran*

CHERETHIMS
3774 Kᵉrêthîy (1), *executioner*

CHERETHITES
3746 kârîy (1), *life-guardsman*
3774 Kᵉrêthîy (8), *executioner*

CHERISH
5532 çâkan (1), to *be familiar* with

CHERISHED
5532 çâkan (1), to *be familiar* with

CHERISHETH
2282 thalpō (2), to *foster, care for*

CHERITH
3747 Kᵉrîyth (2), *cut*

CHERUB
3742 kᵉrûwb (26), *cherub*
3743 Kᵉrûwb (2), *cherub*

CHERUBIM
3742 kᵉrûwb (2), *cherub*

CHERUBIMS
3742 kᵉrûwb (61), *cherub*
5502 chĕrŏubim (1), *cherubs or kerubim*

CHERUBIMS'
3742 kᵉrûwb (1), *cherub*

CHESALON
3693 Kᵉçâlôwn (1), *fertile*

CHESED
3777 Kesed (1), *Kesed*

CHESIL
3686 Kᵉçîyl (1), *stupid or silly*

CHESNUT
6196 'armôwn (2), *plane tree*

CHEST
727 'ârôwn (6), *box*

CHESTS
1595 genez (1), *treasury coffer*

CHESULLOTH
3694 Kᵉçullôwth (1), *fattened*

CHEW
5927 'âlâh (3), to *ascend, be high, mount*

CHEWED
3772 kârath (1), to *cut* (off, down or asunder)

CHEWETH
1641 gârar (1), to *chew*
5927 'âlâh (6), to *ascend, be high, mount*

CHEZIB
3580 Kᵉzîyb (1), *falsified*

CHICKENS
3556 nŏssîôn (1), *birdling, chick-bird*

CHIDE
7378 rîyb (4), to *hold a controversy; to defend*

CHIDING
7379 rîyb (1), *contest, personal or legal*

CHIDON
3592 Kîydôwn (1), *dart, javelin*

CHIEF
1 'âb (3), *father*
441 'allûwph (1), *friend, chieftain, leader*
678 'âtsîyl (1), *extremity; noble*
1167 ba'al (1), *master; husband; owner; citizen*
1368 gibbôwr (1), *powerful; great warrior*
3548 kôhên (2), one *officiating as a priest*
5051 nôgahh (1), *brilliancy*
5057 nâgîyd (1), *commander, official*
5059 nâgan (1), to *play; to make music*
5329 nâtsach (55), i.e. to *be eminent*
5387 nâsîy' (8), *leader; rising mist, fog*
6260 'attûwd (1), *he-goats; leaders* of the people
6438 pinnâh (2), *pinnacle; chieftain*
7217 rê'sh (Ch.) (1), *head*
7218 rô'sh (97), *head*
7223 ri'shôwn (3), *first*
7225 rê'shîyth (5), *first*
7229 rab (Ch.) (1), *great*
7725 shûwb (3), to *turn back; to return*
8269 sar (33), *head person, ruler*
204 akrŏgōniaiŏs (2), *corner, cornerstone*
749 archiĕrĕus (65), *high-priest, chief priest*
750 archipŏimēn (1), *head shepherd*
752 archisunagōgŏs (2), *director of the synagogue services*
754 architĕlōnēs (1), *chief tax-gatherer*
758 archōn (3), *first in rank or power*
775 Asiarchēs (1), *ruler in Asia*
2233 hēgĕŏmai (3), to *lead, i.e. command*
4410 prōtŏkathĕdria (2), *place of pre-eminence*

4411 prōtŏklisia (2), *pre-eminence at meals*
4413 prōtŏs (10), *foremost*
5506 chiliarchŏs (19), *colonel*

CHIEFEST
47 'abbîyr (1), *mighty*
1713 dâgal (1), to *be conspicuous*
4608 ma'ăleh (1), *elevation; platform*
7218 rô'sh (1), *head*
7225 rê'shîyth (1), *first*
3390 mētrŏpŏlis (1), *main city*
4413 prōtŏs (1), *foremost*
5228+3029 hupĕr (2), *over; above; beyond*

CHIEFLY
3122 malista (2), *in the greatest degree*
4412 prōtŏn (1), *firstly*

CHILD
1121 bên (10), *son, descendant*
2029 hârâh (2), to *conceive, be pregnant*
2030 hâreh (12), *pregnant*
2056 vâlâd (1), *boy*
2233 zera' (2), *seed; fruit*
3173 yâchîyd (1), *only son; alone; beloved*
3205 yâlad (5), to *bear young; to father a child*
3206 yeled (39), *young male*
4392 mâlê' (1), *full; filling; fulness; fully*
5288 na'ar (44), *male child; servant*
5290 nô'ar (1), *boyhood*
5768 'ôwlêl (1), *suckling child*
1025 brĕphŏs (1), *infant*
1471 ĕgkuŏs (1), *pregnant*
1722+1064+2192 ĕn (7), *in; during; because of*
3439 mŏnŏgĕnēs (1), *sole, one and only*
3516 nēpiŏs (1), *infant; simple-minded* person
3812 paidiŏthĕn (1), *from infancy*
3813 paidiŏn (28), *child: immature*
3816 pais (5), *child; slave or servant*
5043 tĕknŏn (5), *child*
5088 tiktō (1), to *produce from seed*
5207 huiŏs (3), *son*

CHILD'S
3206 yeled (2), *young male*
5290 nô'ar (1), *boyhood*
3813 paidiŏn (1), *child: immature*

CHILDBEARING
5042 tĕknŏgŏnia (1), *maternity, childbearing*

CHILDHOOD
3208 yaldûwth (1), *boyhood or girlhood*
5271 nâ'ûwr (1), *youth; juvenility; young* people

CHILDISH
3516 nēpiŏs (1), *infant; simple-minded* person

CHILDLESS
6185 'ărîyrîy (4), *barren of child*
7921 shâkôl (2), to *miscarry*
815 atĕknŏs (1), *childless*

C

CHILDREN
1121 bên (1523), *son, descendant*
1123 bên (Ch.) (4), *son*
1129 bânâh (2), to *build; to establish*
2945 ṭaph (12), *family of children and women*
3205 yâlad (1), to *bear young; to father a child*
3206 yeled (31), *young male*
3211 yâlîyd (4), *born; descendants*
5288 na'ar (7), *male child; servant*
5768 'ôwlêl (12), *suckling child*
6768 Tseleq (1), *fissure*
815 atĕknŏs (2), *childless*
1025 brĕphŏs (1), *infant*
3515 nēpiazō (1), to *act as a baby*
3516 nēpiŏs (2), *infant; simple-minded* person
3808 paidariŏn (1), *little boy*
3813 paidiŏn (17), *child: immature*
3816 pais (2), *child; slave or servant*
5027 taphē (2), *act of burial*
5040 tĕkniŏn (9), *infant, i.e. a darling*
5041 tĕknŏgŏnĕō (1), to *be a child bearer*
5043 tĕknŏn (70), *child*
5044 tĕknŏtrŏphĕō (1), to *be a child-rearer*
5206 huiŏthĕsia (1), *adoption*
5207 huiŏs (44), *son*
5388 philŏtĕknŏs (1), *loving one's child(ren)*

CHILDREN'S
1121 bên (16), *son, descendant*
3813 paidiŏn (1), *child: immature* Christian
5043 tĕknŏn (2), *child*

CHILEAB
3609 Kil'âb (1), *restraint of* (his) *father*

CHILION
3630 Kilyôwn (2), *pining, destruction*

CHILION'S
3630 Kilyôwn (1), *pining, destruction*

CHILMAD
3638 Kilmâd (1), *Kilmad*

CHIMHAM
3643 Kimhâm (4), *pining*

CHIMNEY
699 'ărubbâh (1), *window; chimney*

CHINNERETH
3672 Kinnᵉrôwth (4),
(poss.) *harp*-shaped

CHINNEROTH
3672 Kinnᵉrôwth (2),
(poss.) *harp*-shaped

CHIOS
5508 Chiŏs (1), *Chios*

CHISLEU
3691 Kiçlêv (2), *Hebrew month*

CHISLON
3692 Kiçlôwn (1), *hopeful*

CHISLOTH-TABOR
3696 Kiçlôth Tâbôr (1),
flanks of Tabor

CHITTIM
3794 Kittîy (6), *islander*

CHIUN
3594 Kîyûwn (1), *deity*
(poss.) *Priapus or Baal-peor*

CHLOE
5514 Chlŏē (1), *green*

CHODE
7378 rîyb (2), to *hold a controversy; to defend*

CHOICE
970 bâchûwr (3), *male youth; bridegroom*
977 bâchar (4), *select, chose, prefer*
1249 bar (1), *beloved; pure; empty*
1305 bârar (2), to *examine; select*
4005 mibchâr (9), *select*
8321 sôrêq (1), choice *vine stock*
1586 ĕklĕgŏmai (1), *select, choose, pick out*

CHOICEST
4055 mad (1), *vesture, garment; carpet*
8321 sôrêq (1), choice *vine stock*

CHOKE
4846 sumpnigō (2), to *drown; to crowd*

CHOKED
638 apŏpnigō (3), to *stifle or choke*
4155 pnigō (1), to *throttle or strangle; to drown*
4846 sumpnigō (2), to *drown; to crowd*

CHOLER
4843 mârar (2), to *be, make bitter*

CHOOSE
972 bâchîyr (1), *selected one*
977 bâchar (53), *select, chose, prefer*
1254 bârâ' (2), to *create; fashion*
1262 bârâh (1), to *feed*
6901 qâbal (1), to *take*
138 hairĕŏmai (1), to *prefer, choose*

CHOOSEST
977 bâchar (2), *select, chose, prefer*

CHOOSETH
977 bâchar (3), *select, chose, prefer*

CHOOSING
138 hairĕŏmai (1), to *prefer, choose*

CHOP
6566 pâras (1), to *break apart, disperse, scatter*

CHOR-ASHAN
3565 Kôwr 'Âshân (1),
furnace of smoke

CHORAZIN
5523 Chŏrazin (2),
Chorazin

CHOSE
977 bâchar (24), *select, chose, prefer*
1586 ĕklĕgŏmai (4), to *select, choose, pick out*
1951 ĕpilĕgŏmai (1), to *surname, select*

CHOSEN
970 bâchûwr (21), *male youth; bridegroom*
972 bâchîyr (8), *selected one*
977 bâchar (58), *select, chose, prefer*
1305 bârar (2), to *examine; select*
4005 mibchâr (4), *select*
138 hairĕŏmai (1), to *prefer, choose*
140 hairĕtizō (1), to *make a choice*
1586 ĕklĕgŏmai (15), to *select, choose, pick out*
1588 ĕklĕktŏs (7),
selected; chosen
1589 ĕklŏgē (1),
selection, choice
4400 prŏchĕirizŏmai (1),
to *purpose*
4401 prŏchĕirŏtŏnĕō (1),
to *elect in advance*
4758 stratŏlŏgĕō (1), to *enlist in the army*
5500 chĕirŏtŏnĕō (1), to *select or appoint*

CHOZEBA
3578 Kôzᵉbâ' (1),
fallacious

CHRIST
5477 Chanaan (1),
humiliated
5547 Christŏs (551),
Anointed One

CHRIST'S
5547 Christŏs (15),
Anointed One

CHRISTIAN
5546 Christianŏs (2),
follower of Christ

CHRISTIANS
5546 Christianŏs (1),
follower of Christ

CHRISTS
5580 psĕudŏchristŏs (2),
spurious Messiah

CHRONICLES
1697+3117 dâbâr (38),
word; matter; thing

CHRYSOLITE
5555 chrusŏlithŏs (1),
yellow chrysolite

CHRYSOPRASUS
5556 chrusŏprasŏs (1),
greenish-yellow chrysoprase

CHUB
3552 Kûwb (1), *Kub*

CHUN
3560 Kûwn (1),
established

CHURCH
1577 ĕkklēsia (80),
congregation

CHURCHES
1577 ĕkklēsia (36),
congregation
2417 hiĕrŏsulŏs (1),
temple-despoiler

CHURL
3596 kîylay (2),
begrudging

CHURLISH
7186 qâsheh (1), *severe*

CHURNING
4330 mîyts (1), *pressure*

CHUSHAN-RISHATHAIM
3573 Kûwshan
Rish'âthayim (4),
Cushan of double wickedness

CHUZA
5529 Chŏuzas (1),
Chuzas

CIELED
2645 châphâh (1), to *cover; to veil, to encase*
5603 çâphan (2), to *hide by covering; to roof*
7824 shâchîyph (1),
board, panel

CIELING
5604 çippûn (1),
wainscot, paneling

CILICIA
2791 Kilikia (8), *Cilicia*

CINNAMON
7076 qinnâmôwn (3),
cinnamon spice
2792 kinamŏmŏn (1),
cinnamon

CINNEROTH
3672 Kinnᵉrôwth (1),
(poss.) *harp*-shaped

CIRCLE
2329 chûwg (1), *circle*

CIRCUIT
2329 chûwg (1), *circle*
5437 çâbab (1), to *surround*
8622 tᵉqûwphâh (1),
revolution, course

CIRCUITS
5439 çâbîyb (1), *circle; neighbor; environs*

CIRCUMCISE
4135 mûwl (5), to *circumcise*
5243 nâmal (1), to *be circumcised*
4059 pĕritĕmnō (4), to *circumcise*

CIRCUMCISED
4135 mûwl (23), to *circumcise*
203 akrŏbustia (1),
uncircumcised
4059 pĕritĕmnō (13), to *circumcise*
4061 pĕritŏmē (1),
circumcision; Jews

CIRCUMCISING
4135 mûwl (1), to *circumcise*
4059 pĕritĕmnō (1), to *circumcise*

CIRCUMCISION
4139 mûwlâh (1),
circumcision
4061 pĕritŏmē (35),
circumcision; Jews

CIRCUMSPECT
8104 shâmar (1), to *watch*

CIRCUMSPECTLY
199 akribōs (1), *exactly, carefully*

CIS
2797 Kis (1), *bow*

CISTERN
953 bôwr (4), pit *hole, cistern, well*

CISTERNS
877 bô'r (1), *well, cistern*

CITIES
5892 'îyr (419), *city, town, unwalled-village*
7141 Qôrach (1), *ice*
8179 sha'ar (2), *opening, i.e. door or gate*
4172 pŏlis (19), *town*

CITIZEN
4177 pŏlitēs (2), *citizen*

CITIZENS
4177 pŏlitēs (1), *citizen*

CITY
4062 madhêbâh (1), *gold making*
5892 'îyr (650), *city, town, unwalled-village*
5982 'ammûwd (1),
column, pillar
7149 qiryâ' (Ch.) (6), *city*
7151 qiryâh (32), *city*
7176 qereth (5), *city*
7179 qash (1), *dry straw*
8179 sha'ar (1), *opening, i.e. door or gate*
3390 mĕtrŏpŏlis (1),
main city
4172 pŏlis (143), *town*
4173 pŏlitarchēs (2),
magistrate, city official

CLAD
3680 kâçâh (1), to *cover*
5844 'âţâh (1), to *wrap, i.e. cover, veil, clothe*

CLAMOROUS
1993 hâmâh (1), to *be in great commotion*

CLAMOUR
2906 kraugē (1), *outcry*

CLAP
4222 mâchâ' (2), to *strike the hands together*

5606 çâphaq (2), to *clap the hands*
8628 tâqa' (2), to *clatter, slap, drive, clasp*

CLAPPED
4222 mâchâ' (1), to *strike the hands together*
5221 nâkâh (1), to *strike, kill*

CLAPPETH
5606 çâphaq (1), to *clap the hands*

CLAUDA
2802 Klaudē (1), *Claude*

CLAUDIA
2803 Klaudia (1), *Claudia*

CLAUDIUS
2804 Klaudiŏs (3), *Claudius*

CLAVE
1234 bâqa' (6), to *cleave, break, tear open*
1692 dâbaq (6), to *cling or adhere*
2388 châzaq (1), to *fasten upon; to seize; to be strong; courageous*
2853 kŏllaō (1), to *glue together*

CLAWS
6541 parçâh (2), split *hoof*

CLAY
2563 chômer (11), *clay; dry measure*
2635 chăçaph (Ch.) (9), *clay*
2916 ţîyţ (3), *mud or clay*
4423 meleţ (1), *smooth clay cement floor*
4568 ma'ăbeh (2), *compact part of soil*
5671 'abţîyţ (1), *something pledged, i.e. (collect.) pawned goods*
4081 pēlŏs (6), *lump of clay*

CLEAN
656 'âphêç (1), to *cease*
1249 bar (3), *beloved; pure; empty*
1305 bârar (1), to *brighten; purify*
2134 zak (2), *pure; clear*
2135 zâkâh (4), to *be translucent*
2141 zâkak (2), to *be transparent; clean, pure*
2548 châmîyts (1), *salted provender or fodder*
2889 ţâhôwr (49), *pure, clean, flawless*
2891 ţâhêr (41), to *be pure, unadulterated*
5355 nâqîy (1), *innocent*
6565 pârar (1), to *break up; to violate, frustrate*
8552 tâmam (3), to *complete, finish*
2511 katharizō (5), to *cleanse*
2513 katharŏs (10), *clean, pure*
2889 kŏsmŏs (3), *world*
3689 ŏntōs (1), *really, certainly*

CLEANNESS
1252 bôr (4), *purity, cleanness*
5356 niqqâyôwn (1), *clearness; cleanness*

CLEANSE
1305 bârar (1), to *brighten; purify*
2135 zâkâh (1), to *be translucent*
2398 châţâ' (7), to *sin*
2891 ţâhêr (15), to *be pure, unadulterated*
5352 nâqâh (3), to *be, make clean; to be bare*
2511 katharizō (6), to *cleanse*

CLEANSED
2135 zâkâh (1), to *be translucent*
2891 ţâhêr (23), to *be pure, unadulterated*
2893 ţohŏrâh (1), *purification; purity*
3722 kâphar (1), to *cover; to expiate*
5352 nâqâh (1), to *be, make clean; to be bare*
6663 tsâdaq (1), to *be, make right*
2511 katharizō (9), to *cleanse*

CLEANSETH
2891 ţâhêr (1), to *be pure, unadulterated*
8562 tamrûwq (1), *scouring, i.e. soap*
2511 katharizō (1), to *cleanse*

CLEANSING
2893 ţohŏrâh (8), *purification; purity*
2512 katharismŏs (2), *ablution; expiation*

CLEAR
216 'ôwr (1), *luminary; lightning; happiness*
1249 bar (1), *beloved; pure; empty*
2135 zâkâh (1), to *be translucent*
3368 yâqâr (1), *valuable*
5352 nâqâh (3), to *be, make clean; to be bare*
5355 nâqîy (1), *innocent*
6663 tsâdaq (1), to *be, make right*
6703 tsach (1), *dazzling, i.e. sunny, bright*
53 hagnŏs (1), *innocent, modest, perfect, pure*
2513 katharŏs (1), *clean, pure*
2929 krustallizō (1), to *appear as ice*
2986 lamprŏs (1), *radiant; clear*

CLEARER
6965 qûwm (1), to *rise*

CLEARING
5352 nâqâh (1), to *be, make clean; to be bare*
627 apŏlŏgia (1), *plea or verbal defense*

CLEARLY
1305 bârar (1), to *brighten; purify*
1227 diablĕpō (2), see *clearly*
2529 kathŏraō (1), to *distinctly apprehend*
5081 tēlaugŏs (1), *plainly*

CLEARNESS
2892 ţôhar (1), *brightness; purification*

CLEAVE
1234 bâqa' (3), to *cleave, break, tear open*
1692 dâbaq (18), to *cling or adhere; to catch*
1693 dᵉbaq (Ch.) (1), to *stick; to be united*
1695 dâbêq (1), *adhering, sticking to*
3867 lâvâh (1), to *unite*
5596 çâphach (1), to *associate; be united*
8156 shâça' (1), to *split or tear; to upbraid*
2853 kŏllaō (1), to *glue together*
4347 prŏskŏllaō (3), to *glue to, i.e. to adhere*

CLEAVED
1692 dâbaq (3), to *cling or adhere; to catch*

CLEAVETH
1234 bâqa' (2), to *cleave, break, tear open*
1692 dâbaq (6), to *cling or adhere; to catch*
3332 yâtsaq (1), to *pour out*
6398 pâlach (1), to *slice; to break open; to pierce*
6821 tsâphad (1), to *adhere, join*
8157 sheça' (1), *fissure, split*
2853 kŏllaō (1), to *glue together*

CLEFT
1234 bâqa' (1), to *cleave, break, tear open*
8156 shâça' (1), to *split or tear; to upbraid*

CLEFTS
1233 bᵉqîya' (1), *fissure, breach*
2288 chăgâv (3), *rift, cleft in rocks*
5366 nᵉqârâh (1), *fissure*

CLEMENCY
1932 ĕpiĕikĕia (1), *mildness, gentleness*

CLEMENT
2815 Klēmēs (1), *merciful*

CLEOPAS
2810 Klĕŏpas (1), *renown father*

CLEOPHAS
2832 Klōpas (1), cf. *friend of (his) father*

CLIFF
4608 ma'ăleh (1), *elevation; platform*

CLIFFS
6178 'ârûwts (1), *feared; horrible place or chasm*

CLIFT
5366 nᵉqârâh (1), *fissure*

CLIFTS
5585 çâ'îyph (1), *fissure of rocks; bough*

CLIMB
5927 'âlâh (4), to *ascend, be high, mount*

CLIMBED
5927 'âlâh (1), to *ascend, be high, mount*
305 anabainō (1), to *go up, rise*

CLIMBETH
305 anabainō (1), to *go up, rise*

CLIPPED
1639 gâra' (1), to *shave, remove, lessen*

CLODS
1487 gûwsh (1), *mass of earth, dirt clod*
4053 migrâphâh (1), *clod of cultivated dirt*
7263 regeb (2), *lump of clay*
7702 sâdad (2), to *harrow a field*

CLOKE
4598 mᵉ'îyl (1), *outer garment or robe*
1942 ĕpikaluma (1), *pretext, covering*
2440 himation (2), to *put on clothes*
4392 prŏphasis (2), *pretext, excuse*
5341 phĕlŏnēs (1), *outer garment, mantle, cloak*

CLOSE
681 'êtsel (1), *side; near*
1443 gâdar (1), to *build a stone wall*
1692 dâbaq (1), to *cling or adhere; to catch*
4526 miçgereth (2), *margin; stronghold*
5641 çâthar (1), to *hide by covering*
5956 'âlam (1), to *veil from sight, i.e. conceal*
6113 'âtsar (1), to *hold back; to maintain*
6862 tsar (1), *trouble; opponent*
788 assŏn (1), *more nearly, i.e. very near*
4601 sigaō (1), to *keep silent*

CLOSED
2115 zûwr (1), to *press together, tighten*
3680 kâçâh (1), to *cover*
5437 çâbab (1), to *surround*
5462 çâgar (2), to *shut up; to surrender*
5640 çâtham (1), to *stop up; to keep secret*
6105 'âtsam (1), to *be, make powerful*
6113 'âtsar (1), to *hold back; to maintain*
2576 kammuō (2), to *close or shut the eyes*

4428 ptussō (1), to *fold,*
i.e. *furl* or *roll* a scroll

CLOSEST
8474 tachârâh (1), to *vie*
with a rival

CLOSET
2646 chuppâh (1), *canopy*
5009 tamĕiŏn (1), *room*

CLOSETS
5009 tamĕiŏn (1), *room*

CLOTH
899 beged (9), *clothing;*
treachery or *pillage*
4346 makbâr (1),
netted-cloth
8071 simlâh (2), *dress,*
mantle
4470 rhakŏs (2), *piece of*
cloth
4616 sindōn (3), *byssos,*
i.e. bleached *linen*

CLOTHE
3847 lâbash (12), to
clothe
294 amphiĕnnumi (2), to
enrobe, clothe

CLOTHED
3680 kâçâh (1), to *cover*
3736 karbêl (1), to *gird*
or *clothe*
3830 lᵉbûwsh (1),
garment; wife
3847 lâbash (39), to
clothe
3848 lᵉbash (Ch.) (3), to
clothe
294 amphiĕnnumi (2), to
enrobe, clothe
1463 ĕgkŏmbŏŏmai (1),
to *wear*, be clothed
1737 ĕndiduskō (1), to
clothe
1746 ĕnduō (6), to *invest*
with clothing, i.e. to
dress
1902 ĕpĕnduŏmai (2), to
clothe
2439 himatizō (2), to
dress, clothe
4016 pĕriballō (14), to
wrap around, clothe

CLOTHES
899 beged (69), *clothing;*
treachery or *pillage*
1545 gᵉlôwm (1),
clothing, fabric
4055 mad (1), *vesture,*
garment; carpet
5497 çûwth (1), *clothing*
8008 salmâh (3), *clothing*
8071 simlâh (6), *dress,*
mantle
2440 himatiŏn (12), to
put on clothes
3608 ŏthŏniŏn (5), strips
of linen *bandage*
4683 sparganŏō (2), to
wrap with cloth
5509 chitōn (1), *tunic* or
shirt

CLOTHEST
3847 lâbash (1), to *clothe*

CLOTHING
899 beged (1), *clothing;*
treachery or *pillage*

3830 lᵉbûwsh (9),
garment; wife
4374 mᵉkaççeh (1),
covering
8071 simlâh (2), *dress,*
mantle
8516 talbôsheth (1),
garment
1742 ĕnduma (1),
apparel, outer *robe*
2066 ĕsthēs (2), to *clothe*
4749 stŏlē (1),
long-fitting *gown*

CLOTHS
899 beged (4), *clothing;*
treachery or *pillage*

CLOUD
5645 'âb (9), *thick*
clouds; thicket
5743 'ûwb (1), to darkly
becloud
6051 'ânân (75), *nimbus*
cloud
6053 'ănânâh (1),
cloudiness
6205 'ărâphel (1), *gloom,*
darkness
3507 nĕphĕlē (18), *cloud*
3509 nĕphŏs (1), *cloud*

CLOUDS
2385 chăzîyz (1), *flash* of
lightning
3709 kaph (1), hollow of
hand; paw; sole of foot
5387 nâsîy' (1), *leader;*
rising *mist, fog*
5645 'âb (20), *thick*
clouds; thicket
6050 'ănan (Ch.) (1),
nimbus cloud
6051 'ânân (5), *nimbus*
cloud
6053 'ănânâh (1),
cloudiness
7834 shachaq (11),
firmament, clouds
3507 nĕphĕlē (8), *cloud*

CLOUDY
6051 'ânân (6), *nimbus*
cloud

CLOUTED
2921 tâlâ' (1), to be
spotted or *variegated*

CLOUTS
5499 çᵉchâbâh (2), *rag*

CLOVEN
8156 shâça' (1), to *split*
or *tear;* to *upbraid*
1266 diamĕrizō (1), to
distribute

CLOVENFOOTED
8156+8157 shâça' (1), to
split or *tear;* to *upbraid*
8156+8157+6541 shâça'
(2), to *split* or *tear*

CLUSTER
811 'eshkôwl (5), *bunch*
of grapes

CLUSTERS
811 'eshkôwl (4), *bunch*
of grapes
6778 tsammûwq (2),
lump of *dried* grapes
1009 bŏtrus (1), *bunch,*
cluster of grapes

CNIDUS
2834 Knidŏs (1), *Cnidus*

COAL
1513 gechel (2), *ember,*
hot coal
7531 ritspâh (1), *hot*
stone; pavement
7815 shᵉchôwr (1), *soot*

COALS
1513 gechel (16), *ember,*
hot coal
6352 pechâm (3), *black*
coal, charcoal
7529 retseph (1), *red-hot*
stone for baking
7565 resheph (2), *flame*
439 anthrakia (2), *fire*
bed of burning *coals*
440 anthrax (1), live *coal*

COAST
1366 gᵉbûwl (47),
boundary, border
2256 chebel (4),
company, band
2348 chôwph (1), *cove,*
sheltered bay
3027 yâd (5), *hand; power*
5299 nâphâh (1), *height;*
sieve
7097 qâtseh (1), *extremity*
3864 parathalassiŏs (1),
by the lake
3882 paraliŏs (1),
maritime; seacoast

COASTS
1366 gᵉbûwl (23),
boundary, border
1367 gᵉbûwlâh (5), *region*
1552 gᵉlîylâh (1), *circuit*
or *region*
2348 chôwph (1), *cove,*
sheltered bay
3027 yâd (1), *hand; power*
3411 yᵉrêkâh (3), *far*
away places
7097 qâtseh (1), *extremity*
7098 qâtsâh (1),
termination; fringe
3313 mĕrŏs (3), *division*
or *share*
3725 hŏriŏn (10), *region,*
area, vicinity
5117 tŏpŏs (1), *place*
5561 chōra (1), *territory*

COAT
3801 kᵉthôneth (16),
garment that *covers*
4598 mᵉ'îyl (1), *outer*
garment or *robe*
8302 shiryôwn (3),
corslet, coat of mail
1903 ĕpĕndutēs (1), *outer*
garment, coat
5509 chitōn (4), *tunic* or
shirt

COATS
3801 kᵉthôneth (7),
garment that *covers*
5622 çarbal (Ch.) (2),
cloak
5509 chitōn (5), *tunic* or
shirt

COCK
220 alĕktōr (12), *rooster*

COCKATRICE
6848 tsepha' (1), *hissing*
viper

COCKATRICES
6848 tsepha' (1), *hissing*
viper

COCKCROWING
219 alektŏrŏphōnia (1),
rooster-crowing

COCKLE
890 bo'shâh (1), *weed*

COFFER
712 'argâz (3), *box, chest*

COFFIN
727 'ârôwn (1), *box*

COGITATIONS
7476 ra'yôwn (Ch.) (1),
mental conception

COLD
2779 chôreph (1),
autumn (and winter)
6793 tsinnâh (1), *large*
shield; piercing cold
7119 qar (2), *cool; quiet;*
cool-headed
7120 qôr (1), *cold*
7135 qârâh (5), *coolness,*
cold
5592 psuchŏs (3),
coolness, cold
5593 psuchrŏs (4), *chilly,*
cold
5594 psuchō (1), to *chill,*
grow cold

COLHOZEH
3626 Kol-Chôzeh (2),
every seer

COLLAR
6310 peh (1), *mouth;*
opening

COLLARS
5188 nᵉṭîyphâh (1),
pendant for the ears

COLLECTION
4864 mas'êth (2), *raising;*
beacon; present
3048 lŏgia (1),
contribution, collection

COLLEGE
4932 mishneh (2),
duplicate copy; double

COLLOPS
6371 pîymâh (1), *obesity*

COLONY
2862 kŏlōnia (1), *colony*

COLORS
6320 pûwk (1), *stibium*

COLOSSE
2857 Kŏlŏssai (1),
colossal

COLOSSIANS
2858 Kŏlŏssaĕus (1),
inhabitant of Colossæ

COLOUR
5869 'ayin (11), *eye;*
sight; fountain
4392 prŏphasis (1),
pretext, excuse

COLOURS
2921 ṭâlâ' (1), to be
spotted or *variegated*
6446 paç (5), *long*
-sleeved tunic

6648 tseba' (3), *dye*
7553 riqmâh (2), *variegation* of color

COLT

1121 bên (1), *son, descendant*
5895 'ayîr (2), *young robust donkey* or *ass*
4454 pōlŏs (12), *young donkey*

COLTS

1121 bên (1), *son, descendant*
5895 'ayîr (2), *young robust donkey* or *ass*

COME

270 'âchaz (1), to *seize, grasp; possess*
314 'achărôwn (8), *late* or *last; behind; western*
635 'Eçtêr (1), *Esther*
835 'esher (3), *how happy!*
857 'âthâh (12), to *arrive*
858 'âthâh (Ch.) (3), to *arrive; go*
935 bôw' (681), to *go, come*
1869 dârak (1), to *walk, lead;* to *string* a bow
1934 hăvâ' (Ch.) (3), to *be,* to *exist*
1961 hâyâh (131), to *exist,* i.e. *be* or *become*
1980 hâlak (7), to *walk; live a certain way*
3045 yâda' (3), to *know*
3051 yâhab (1), to *give*
3205 yâlad (1), to *bear young;* to *father a child*
3212 yâlak (72), to *walk;* to *live;* to *carry*
3318 yâtsâ' (84), to *go, bring out*
3381 yârad (57), to *descend*
4279 mâchar (8), *tomorrow; hereafter*
4291 mᵉțâ' (Ch.) (1), to *arrive,* to *extend*
4609 ma'ălâh (1), *thought arising*
4672 mâtsâ' (8), to *find* or *acquire;* to *occur*
5060 nâga' (13), to *strike*
5066 nâgash (28), to *be, come, bring near*
5181 nâchath (2), to *sink, descend*
5185 nâchêth (1), *descending*
5312 nᵉphaq (Ch.) (1), to *issue forth;* to *bring out*
5506 çᵉchôrâh (1), *traffic*
5674 'âbar (14), to *cross over;* to *transition*
5927 'âlâh (104), to *ascend, be high, mount*
6213 'âsâh (1), to *do* or *make*
6264 'âthîyd (1), *prepared; treasure*
6631 tse'ĕtsâ' (1), *produce, children*
6743 tsâlach (1), to *push forward*
6923 qâdam (5), to *anticipate, hasten*

7122 qârâ' (4), to *encounter,* to *happen*
7125 qîr'âh (1), to *encounter,* to *happen*
7126 qârab (33), to *approach, bring near*
7131 qârêb (2), *near*
7136 qârâh (2), to *bring about;* to *impose*
7138 qârôwb (1), *near, close*
7725 shûwb (30), to *turn back;* to *return*
8175 sâ'ar (1), to *storm;* to *shiver,* i.e. *fear*
8622 tᵉqûwphâh (1), *revolution, course*
191 akŏuō (1), to *hear; obey*
305 anabainō (7), to *go up, rise*
565 apérchŏmai (3), to *go off,* i.e. *depart*
576 apŏbainō (1), to *eventuate, become*
864 aphiknĕŏmai (1), to *go forth* by rumor
1096 ginŏmai (43), to *be, become*
1204 dĕurŏ (8), *hither!; hitherto*
1205 dĕutĕ (12), *come hither!*
1224 diabainō (1), to *pass by, over, across*
1330 diĕrchŏmai (1), to *traverse, travel through*
1448 ĕggizō (9), to *approach*
1511 ĕinai (8), to *exist*
1525 ĕisérchŏmai (18), to *enter*
1531 ĕispŏrĕuŏmai (1), to *enter*
1607 ĕkpŏrĕuŏmai (3), to *depart, be discharged*
1684 ĕmbainō (2), to *embark;* to *reach*
1764 ĕnistēmi (1), to *be present*
1831 ĕxérchŏmai (24), to *issue;* to *leave*
1834 ĕxēgĕŏmai (1), to *tell, relate again*
1880 ĕpanérchŏmai (1), *return home*
1904 ĕpérchŏmai (8), to *supervene*
1910 ĕpibainō (1), to *ascend, embark, arrive*
1975 ĕpipŏrĕuŏmai (1), to *go, come to*
2049 ĕrēmŏō (1), to *lay waste*
2064 ĕrchŏmai (290), to *go* or *come*
2186 ĕphistēmi (2), to *be present;* to *approach*
2240 hēkō (24), to *arrive,* i.e. *be present*
2597 katabainō (20), to *descend*
2638 katalambanō (1), to *seize;* to *possess*
2647 kataluō (1), to *halt* for the night
2658 katantaō (3), to *arrive at;* to *attain*

2673 katargĕō (1), to *be, render entirely useless*
2718 katérchŏmai (2), to *go, come down*
3195 méllō (16), to *intend,* i.e. *be about to*
3854 paraginŏmai (15), to *arrive;* to *appear*
3918 parĕimi (6), to *be present;* to *have come*
3928 parérchŏmai (1), to *go by;* to *perish*
3936 paristēmi (1), to *stand beside, present*
4137 plērŏō (1), to *fill, make complete*
4301 prŏlambanō (1), to *take before*
4331 prŏsĕggizō (1), to *approach near*
4334 prŏsérchŏmai (6), to *come near, visit*
4365 prŏspŏrĕuŏmai (1), to *come towards*
4845 sumplērŏō (2), to *be complete, fulfill*
4905 sunérchŏmai (14), to *go with*
4940 suntugchanō (1), to *come together*
5290 hupŏstrĕphō (1), to *turn under, behind*
5302 hustĕrĕō (3), to *be inferior;* to *fall short*
5348 phthanō (4), to *be anticipate* or *precede*
5562 chōrĕō (1), to *pass, enter;* to *hold, admit*

COMELINESS

1926 hâdâr (3), *magnificence*
1935 hôwd (1), *grandeur, majesty*
2157 ĕuschēmŏsunē (1), *decorousness*

COMELY

2433 chîyn (1), *graceful beauty*
3190 yâṭab (1), to *be, make well*
3303 yâpheh (1), *beautiful; handsome*
4998 nâ'âh (1), to *be pleasant* or *suitable*
5000 nâ'veh (7), *suitable* or *beautiful*
8389 tô'ar (1), *outline, figure* or *appearance*
8597 tiph'ârâh (1), *ornament*
2158 ĕuschēmōn (2), *decorous, proper; noble*
4241 prĕpō (1), to *be suitable* or *proper*

COMERS

4334 prŏsérchŏmai (1), to *come near, visit*

COMEST

935 bôw' (22), to *go* or *come*
2199 zâ'aq (1), to *call out, announce*
7126 qârab (2), to *approach, bring near*
2064 ĕrchŏmai (3), to *go* or *come*

COMETH

857 'âthâh (3), to *arrive*
935 bôw' (89), to *go, come*
1961 hâyâh (1), to *exist,* i.e. *be* or *become*
1980 hâlak (2), to *walk; live a certain way*
3318 yâtsâ' (19), to *go, bring out*
3381 yârad (1), to *descend*
4672 mâtsâ' (1), to *occur, meet* or *be present*
5034 nâbêl (1), to *wilt;* to *fall away*
5060 nâga' (1), to *strike*
5414 nâthan (1), to *give*
5674 'âbar (1), to *cross over;* to *transition*
5927 'âlâh (10), to *ascend, be high, mount*
6293 pâga' (1), to *impinge*
6437 pânâh (1), to *turn,* to *face*
6627 tsâ'âh (2), human *excrement*
6631 tse'ĕtsâ' (1), *produce, children*
7131 qârêb (5), *near*
7698 sheger (1), *what comes forth*
7725 shûwb (3), to *turn back;* to *return*
305 anabainō (1), to *go up, rise*
1096 ginŏmai (2), to *be, become*
1511 ĕinai (1), to *exist*
1607 ĕkpŏrĕuŏmai (2), to *depart, be discharged*
1831 ĕxérchŏmai (1), to *issue;* to *leave*
1999 ĕpisustasis (1), *insurrection*
2064 ĕrchŏmai (97), to *go* or *come*
2186 ĕphistēmi (1), to *be present;* to *approach*
2591 Karpŏs (1), (poss.) *fruit*
2597 katabainō (3), to *descend*
3854 paraginŏmai (3), to *arrive;* to *appear*
4334 prŏsérchŏmai (1), to *come near, visit*
4905 sunérchŏmai (1), to *gather together*

COMFORT

1082 bâlag (2), to *be comforted*
4010 mablîygîyth (1), *desolation*
5162 nâcham (33), to *be sorry;* to *pity, console*
5165 nechâmâh (1), *consolation*
5582 çâ'ad (3), to *support*
7502 râphad (1), to *spread a bed;* to *refresh*
2174 ĕupsuchĕō (1), to *feel encouraged*
2293 tharsĕō (3), to *have courage; take heart!*
3870 parakalĕō (9), to *call, invite*
3874 paraklēsis (6), *imploring, exhortation*

3888 paramuthĕŏmai (2), to *console*
3889 paramuthia (1), *consolation*
3890 paramuthiŏn (1), *consolation*
3931 parēgŏria (1), *consolation, comfort*

COMFORTABLE
4496 mᵉnûwchâh (1), *peacefully; consolation*
5150 nichûwm (1), *consoled; solace*

COMFORTABLY
5921+3820 'al (4), *above, over, upon, or against*
5921+3824 'al (1), *above, over, upon, or against*

COMFORTED
5162 nâcham (20), to *be sorry; to pity, console*
3870 parakalĕō (13), to *call, invite*
3888 paramuthĕŏmai (2), to *console*
4837 sumparakalĕō (1), to *console jointly*

COMFORTEDST
5162 nâcham (1), to *be sorry; to pity, console*

COMFORTER
5162 nâcham (3), to *be sorry; to pity, console*
3875 paraklētŏs (4), *intercessor, consoler*

COMFORTERS
5162 nâcham (5), to *be sorry; to pity, console*

COMFORTETH
5162 nâcham (3), to *be sorry; to pity, console*
3870 parakalĕō (2), to *call, invite*

COMFORTLESS
3737 ŏrphanŏs (1), *parentless, orphaned*

COMFORTS
5150 nichûwm (1), *consoled; solace*
8575 tanchûwm (1), *compassion, solace*

COMING
857 'âthâh (1), to *arrive*
935 bôw' (19), to *go, come*
1980 hâlak (1), to *walk; live a certain way*
3318 yâtsâ' (2), to *go, bring out*
3381 yârad (2), to *descend*
3996 mâbôw' (1), *entrance; sunset; west*
4126 môwbâ' (1), *entrance*
5182 nᵉchath (Ch.) (1), to *descend; to depose*
5674 'âbar (1), to *cross over; to transition*
7122 qârâ' (1), to *encounter, to happen*
7272 regel (1), *foot; step*
305 anabainō (2), to *go up, rise*
602 apŏkalupsis (1), *disclosure, revelation*

1525 ĕisĕrchŏmai (3), to *enter*
1529 ĕisŏdŏs (1), *entrance*
1531 ĕispŏrĕuŏmai (1), to *enter*
1660 ĕlĕusis (1), *advent, coming*
1831 ĕxĕrchŏmai (1), to *issue; to leave*
1904 ĕpĕrchŏmai (1), to *supervene*
2064 ĕrchŏmai (27), to *go or come*
2186 ĕphistēmi (1), to *be present; to approach*
2597 katabainō (1), to *descend*
3854 paraginŏmai (1), to *arrive; to appear*
3952 parŏusia (22), *advent, coming*
4334 prŏsĕrchŏmai (3), to *come near, visit*

COMINGS
4126 môwbâ' (1), *entrance*

COMMAND
559 'âmar (2), to *say*
6310 peh (1), *mouth; opening*
6680 tsâvâh (84), to *constitute, enjoin*
1781 ĕntĕllŏmai (4), to *enjoin, give orders*
2004 ĕpitassō (1), to *order, command*
2036 ĕpō (3), to *speak*
2753 kĕlĕuō (1), to *order, direct*
3853 paraggĕllō (8), to *enjoin; to instruct*

COMMANDED
559 'âmar (25), to *say*
560 'ămar (Ch.) (12), to *say, speak*
1696 dâbar (4), to *speak, say; to subdue*
4480+2941 min (1), *from or out of*
4687 mitsvâh (2), *command*
6680 tsâvâh (333), to *constitute, enjoin*
7761+2942 sûwm (Ch.) (3), to *put, place*
1291 diastĕllŏmai (1), to *enjoin*
1299 diatassō (6), to *institute, prescribe*
1781 ĕntĕllŏmai (6), to *enjoin, give orders*
2004 ĕpitassō (4), to *order, command*
2036 ĕpō (5), to *speak*
2750 kĕiria (1), *swathe of cloth*
2753 kĕlĕuō (20), to *order, direct*
3853 paraggĕllō (11), to *enjoin; to give instruction*
4367 prŏstassō (6), to *enjoin*
4483 rhĕō (1), to *utter, i.e. speak or say*

COMMANDEDST
6680 tsâvâh (4), to *constitute, enjoin*

COMMANDER
6680 tsâvâh (1), to *constitute, enjoin*

COMMANDEST
6680 tsâvâh (2), to *constitute, enjoin*
2753 kĕlĕuō (1), to *order, direct*

COMMANDETH
559 'âmar (3), to *say, speak*
6680 tsâvâh (6), to *constitute, enjoin*
2004 ĕpitassō (3), to *order, command*
3853 paraggĕllō (1), to *enjoin; to instruct*

COMMANDING
6680 tsâvâh (1), to *constitute, enjoin*
1299 diatassō (1), to *institute, prescribe*
2753 kĕlĕuō (1), to *order, direct*

COMMANDMENT
559 'âmar (2), to *say*
565 'imrâh (1), *something said*
1697 dâbâr (15), *word; matter; thing*
1881 dâth (2), *royal edict or statute*
2941 ṭa'am (Ch.) (2), *sentence, command*
2942 ṭᵉ'êm (Ch.) (2), *judgment; account*
3318 yâtsâ' (1), to *go, bring out*
3982 ma'ămar (2), *edict, command*
4406 millâh (Ch.) (1), *word, command*
4662 miphqâd (1), *appointment*
4687 mitsvâh (43), *command*
6310 peh (37), *mouth; opening*
6673 tsav (1), *injunction*
6680 tsâvâh (9), to *constitute, enjoin*
1291 diastĕllŏmai (1), to *enjoin*
1297 diatagma (1), *authoritative edict*
1781 ĕntĕllŏmai (2), to *enjoin, give orders*
1785 ĕntŏlē (42), *prescription, regulation*
2003 ĕpitagē (6), *injunction or decree*
2753 kĕlĕuō (2), to *order, direct*
3852 paraggĕlia (1), *mandate, order*
3853 paraggĕllō (1), to *enjoin; to instruct*

COMMANDMENTS
1697 dâbâr (5), *word; matter; thing*
2706 chôq (1), *appointment; allotment*
4687 mitsvâh (130), *command*

COMMANDEDST
6680 tsâvâh (4), to *constitute, enjoin*

COMMANDER
6680 tsâvâh (1), to *constitute, enjoin*

COMMANDEST
6680 tsâvâh (2), to *constitute, enjoin*
2753 kĕlĕuō (1), to *order, direct*

COMMANDETH
559 'âmar (3), to *say, speak*
6680 tsâvâh (6), to *constitute, enjoin*
2004 ĕpitassō (3), to *order, command*
3853 paraggĕllō (1), to *enjoin; to instruct*

COMMENDATION
4956 sustatikŏs (2), *recommendatory*

COMMENDED
1984 hâlal (2), to *speak words of thankfulness*
7623 shâbach (1), to *address in a loud tone*
1867 ĕpainĕō (1), to *applaud, commend*
3908 paratithēmi (1), to *present something*
4921 sunistaō (1), to *set together*

COMMENDETH
3936 paristēmi (1), to *stand beside, present*
4921 sunistaō (3), to *set together*

COMMENDING
4921 sunistaō (1), to *set together*

COMMISSION
2011 ĕpitrŏpē (1), *permission*

COMMISSIONS
1881 dâth (1), *royal edict or statute*

COMMIT
1556 gâlal (2), to *roll; to commit*
2181 zânâh (11), to *commit adultery*
4560 mâçar (1), to *set apart; apostatize*
4603 mâ'al (4), to *act treacherously*
5003 nâ'aph (6), to *commit adultery*
5414 nâthan (1), to *give*
5753 'âvâh (2), to *be crooked*
6213 'âsâh (14), to *do or make*
6313 pûwg (1), to *be sluggish; be numb*
6466 pâ'al (1), to *do, make or practice*
6485 pâqad (2), to *visit, care for, count*
7760 sûwm (1), to *put, place*
2038 ĕrgazŏmai (1), to *toil*
2416 hiĕrŏsulĕō (1), to *be a temple-robber*
3429 mŏichaō (2), to *commit adultery*
3431 mŏichĕuō (10), to *commit adultery*

3908 paratithēmi (3), to
present something
4100 pisteuō (2), to have
faith, to entrust
4160 poieō (2), to make
4203 porneuō (3), to
indulge unlawful lust
4238 prassō (2), to
execute, accomplish

COMMITTED
1961 hâyâh (2), to exist,
i.e. be or become
2181 zânâh (5), to
commit adultery
2398 châţâ' (6), to sin
4600 mâ'ak (6), to pierce,
emasculate, handle
5003 nâ'aph (5), to
commit adultery
5414 nâthan (5), to give
5753 'âvâh (2), to be
crooked
6213 'âsâh (28), to do or
make
6485 pâqad (4), to visit,
care for, count
7561 râsha' (1), to be, do,
declare wrong
8581 tâ'ab (1), to loathe,
i.e. detest
764 asebēō (1), to be, act
impious or wicked
1325 didōmi (1), to give
1439 eaō (1), to let be, i.e.
permit or leave alone
3431 moicheuō (1), to
commit adultery
3860 paradidōmi (2), to
hand over
3866 parathēkē (1), trust,
deposit entrusted
3872 parakatathekē (2),
deposit, trust
3908 paratithēmi (1), to
present something
4100 pisteuō (5), to have
faith; to entrust
4160 poieō (4), to make
4203 porneuō (4), to
indulge unlawful lust
4238 prassō (3), to
execute, accomplish
5087 tithēmi (1), to place

COMMITTEST
2181 zânâh (1), to
commit adultery

COMMITTETH
5003 nâ'aph (4), to
commit adultery
5800 'âzab (1), to loosen;
relinquish; permit
6213 'âsâh (4), to do or
make
3429 moichaō (4), to
commit adultery
3431 moicheuō (2), to
commit adultery
4160 poieō (3), to make
or do
4203 porneuō (1), to
indulge unlawful lust

COMMITTING
5003 nâ'aph (1), to
commit adultery
6213 'âsâh (1), to do or
make

COMMODIOUS
428 aneuthetŏs (1),
inconvenient

COMMON
776 'erets (1), earth,
land, soil; country
1121 bên (1), people of a
class or kind
2455 chôl (2), profane,
common, not holy
2490 châlal (1), to
profane, defile
7227 rab (1), great
7230 rôb (1), abundance
442 anthrōpinŏs (1),
human
1219 dēmŏsiŏs (1),
public; in public
2839 koinŏs (8),
common, i.e. profane
2840 koinŏō (1), to make
profane
4183 pŏlus (1), much,
many
4232 praitōriŏn (1),
governor's court-room

COMMONLY
1310 diaphēmizō (1), to
spread news
3654 hŏlōs (1), altogether

COMMONWEALTH
4174 pŏliteia (1),
citizenship

COMMOTION
7494 ra'ash (1),
bounding, uproar

COMMOTIONS
181 akatastasia (1),
disorder, riot

COMMUNE
559 'âmar (1), to say
1696 dâbar (4), to speak,
say; to subdue
1697 dâbâr (1), word;
matter; thing
5608 çâphar (1), to
enumerate; to recount
7878 sîyach (1), to
ponder, muse aloud

COMMUNED
1696 dâbar (14), to
speak, say; to subdue
1255 dialalĕō (1), to
converse, discuss
3656 hŏmilĕō (2), to
converse, talk
4814 sullalĕō (1), to talk
together, i.e. converse

COMMUNICATE
2841 koinōnĕō (1), to
share or participate
2842 koinōnia (1),
benefaction; sharing
2843 koinōnikŏs (1),
liberal
4790 sugkoinōnĕō (1), to
co-participate in

COMMUNICATED
394 anatithĕmai (1),
propound, set forth
2841 koinōnĕō (1), to
share or participate

COMMUNICATION
1697 dâbâr (1), word;
matter; thing

7879 sîyach (1), uttered
contemplation
148 aischrŏlŏgia (1), vile
conversation
2842 koinōnia (1),
benefaction; sharing
3056 lŏgŏs (2), word,
matter, thing; Word

COMMUNICATIONS
3056 lŏgŏs (1), word,
matter, thing
3657 hŏmilia (1),
associations

COMMUNING
1696 dâbar (2), to speak,
say; to subdue

COMMUNION
2842 koinōnia (4),
benefaction; sharing

COMPACT
2266 châbar (1), to
fascinate by spells

COMPACTED
4822 sumbibazō (1), to
drive together

COMPANIED
4905 sunĕrchŏmai (1), to
gather together

COMPANIES
736 'ôrechâh (1), caravan
1416 gedûwd (1), band of
soldiers
1979 hălîykâh (1),
walking; procession
4256 machălŏqeth (1),
section or division
4264 machăneh (1),
encampment
6951 qâhâl (1),
assemblage
7218 rô'sh (7), head
4849 sumpŏsiŏn (1),
group

COMPANION
2270 châbêr (2),
associate, friend
2278 châbereth (1),
consort, companion
4828 mêrêa' (3), close
friend
7453 rêa' (3), associate;
one close
7462 râ'âh (2), to
associate as a friend
4791 sugkoinōnŏs (1),
co-participant
4904 sunĕrgŏs (1),
fellow-worker

COMPANIONS
2269 châber (Ch.) (1),
associate, friend
2270 châbêr (5),
associate, friend
2271 chabbâr (1), partner
3675 kenâth (Ch.) (8),
colleague
4828 mêrêa' (1), close
friend
7453 rêa' (1), associate;
one close
7464 rê'âh (2), female
associate
2844 koinōnŏs (1),
associate, partner
4898 sunĕkdēmŏs (1),
fellow-traveller

COMPANIONS'
7453 rêa' (1), associate;
one close

COMPANY
736 'ôrechâh (1), caravan
1323 bath (1), daughter,
descendant, woman
1416 gedûwd (3), band of
soldiers
1995 hâmôwn (1), noise,
tumult; many, crowd
2199 zâ'aq (1), to
convene publicly
2256 chebel (2),
company, band
2267 cheber (1), society,
group; magic spell;
2274 chebrâh (1),
association
2416 chay (1), alive; raw;
fresh; life
2428 chayil (1), army;
wealth; virtue; valor;
strength
3862 lahăqâh (1),
assembly
4246 mechôwlâh (1),
round-dance
4264 machăneh (5),
encampment
5712 'êdâh (13),
assemblage; crowd
6635 tsâbâ' (1), army,
military host
6951 qâhâl (16),
assemblage
7218 rô'sh (5), head
7285 regesh (1),
tumultuous crowd
7462 râ'âh (1), to
associate as a friend
8229 shiph'âh (2),
copiousness
2398 idiŏs (1), private or
separate
2828 klisia (1), party or
group
2853 kŏllaō (1), to glue
together
3461 murias (1),
ten-thousand
3588+4012 hŏ (1), "the"
3658 hŏmilŏs (1),
multitude
3792 ŏchlŏpŏieō (1), to
raise a disturbance
3793 ŏchlŏs (7), throng
4012 peri (1), about;
around
4128 plēthŏs (1), large
number, throng
4874 sunanamignumi
(3), to associate with
4923 sunŏdia (1),
traveling company

COMPARABLE
5577 çançîn (1), twig

COMPARE
4911 mâshal (1), to use
figurative language
6186 'ârak (1), to set in a
row, i.e. arrange,
3846 paraballō (1), to
reach a place; to liken
4793 sugkrinō (1), to
combine

COMPARED
1819 dâmâh (1), *to resemble, liken*
6186 'ârak (1), *to set in a row,* i.e. *arrange,*
7737 shâvâh (2), *to resemble; to adjust*

COMPARING
4793 sugkrinō (2), *to combine*

COMPARISON
3644 kᵉmôw (1), *like, as; for; with*
3850 parabŏlē (1), *fictitious narrative*

COMPASS
247 'âzar (1), *to belt*
2329 chûwg (1), *circle*
3749 karkôb (2), *rim, ledge, or top margin*
3803 kâthar (2), *to enclose, besiege; to wait*
4230 mᵉchûwgâh (1), *compass*
4524 mêçab (1), *around, surround*
5362 nâqaph (3), *to surround or circulate*
5437 çâbab (22), *to surround*
5439 çâbîyb (2), *circle; environs; around*
5849 'âṭar (1), *to encircle, enclose in; to crown*
4013 pĕriagō (1), *to walk around*
4022 pĕriĕrchŏmai (1), *to stroll, vacillate, veer*
4033 pĕrikuklŏō (1), *to blockade completely*

COMPASSED
661 'âphaph (5), *to surround*
2328 chûwg (1), *to describe a circle*
5362 nâqaph (4), *to surround or circulate*
5437 çâbab (28), *to surround*
5849 'âṭar (1), *to encircle, enclose in; to crown*
2944 kuklŏō (3), *to surround, encircle*
4029 pĕrikĕimai (2), *to enclose, encircle*

COMPASSEST
2219 zârâh (1), *to toss about; to diffuse*

COMPASSETH
5437 çâbab (4), *to surround*
6059 'ânaq (1), *to collar; to fit out*

COMPASSING
5362 nâqaph (2), *to surround or circulate*
5437 çâbab (1), *to surround*

COMPASSION
2550 châmal (5), *to spare, have pity on*
7349 rachûwm (5), *compassionate*
7355 râcham (8), *to be compassionate*

7356 racham (2), *compassion; womb*
1653 ĕlĕĕŏ (3), *to give out compassion*
3356 mĕtriŏpathĕō (1), *to deal gently*
3627 ŏiktĕirō (1), *to exercise pity*
4697 splagchnizŏmai (12), *to feel sympathy*
4834 sumpathĕō (1), *to commiserate*
4835 sumpathēs (1), *commiserative*

COMPASSIONS
7355 râcham (1), *to be compassionate*
7356 racham (1), *compassion; womb*

COMPEL
597 'ânaç (1), *to insist, compel*
5647 'âbad (1), *to do, work, serve*
29 aggarĕuō (2), *to press into public service*
315 anagkazō (1), *to necessitate, compel*

COMPELLED
5080 nâdach (1), *to push off, scattered*
6555 pârats (1), *to break out*
29 aggarĕuō (1), *to press into public service*
315 anagkazō (3), *to necessitate, compel*

COMPELLEST
315 anagkazō (1), *to necessitate, compel*

COMPLAIN
596 'ânan (1), *complain*
1058 bâkâh (1), *to weep, moan*
7378 rîyb (1), *to hold a controversy; to defend*
7878 sîyach (1), *to ponder, muse aloud*

COMPLAINED
596 'ânan (1), *complain*
7878 sîyach (1), *to ponder, muse aloud*

COMPLAINERS
3202 mĕmpsimŏirŏs (1), *discontented*

COMPLAINING
6682 tsᵉvâchâh (1), *screech of anguish*

COMPLAINT
7878 sîyach (9), *to ponder, muse aloud*

COMPLAINTS
157 aitiama (1), *thing charged*

COMPLETE
8549 tâmîym (1), *entire, complete; integrity*
4137 plērŏō (2), *to fill, make complete*

COMPOSITION
4971 mathkôneth (2), *proportion*

COMPOUND
4842 mirqachath (1), *unguent; unguent-pot*

COMPOUNDETH
7543 râqach (1), *to perfume, blend spice*

COMPREHEND
3045 yâda' (1), *to know*
2638 katalambanō (1), *to possess; to understand*

COMPREHENDED
3557 kûwl (1), *to measure; to maintain*
346 anakĕphalaiŏmai (1), *to sum up*
2638 katalambanō (1), *to possess; to understand*

CONANIAH
3562 Kôwnanyâhûw (1), *Jehovah has sustained*

CONCEAL
2790 chârash (1), *to be silent; to be deaf*
3582 kâchad (2), *to destroy; to hide*
3680 kâçâh (2), *to cover*
5641 çâthar (1), *to hide*

CONCEALED
3582 kâchad (2), *to destroy; to hide*

CONCEALETH
3680 kâçâh (2), *to cover*

CONCEIT
4906 maskîyth (1), *carved figure*
5869 'ayin (4), *eye; sight; fountain*

CONCEITS
3844+1438 para (2), *from; with; besides*

CONCEIVE
2029 hârâh (3), *to conceive, be pregnant*
2030 hâreh (4), *pregnant*
2232 zâra' (1), *to sow seed; to disseminate*
3179 yâcham (4), *to conceive*
2602 katabŏlē (1), *conception, beginning*
4815 sullambanō (1), *to conceive; to aid*

CONCEIVED
2029 hârâh (1), *to conceive, be pregnant*
2030 hâreh (33), *pregnant*
2232 zâra' (1), *to sow seed; to disseminate*
2803 châshab (1), *to plot; to think, regard*
3179 yâcham (2), *to conceive*
3254 yâçaph (1), *to add or augment*
1080 gĕnnaō (1), *to procreate, regenerate*
2845+2192 kŏitē (1), *couch; conception*
4815 sullambanō (4), *to conceive; to aid*
5087 tithēmi (1), *to place*

CONCEIVING
2030 hâreh (1), *pregnant*

CONCEPTION
2032 hêrôwn (3), *pregnancy*

CONCERN
4012 pĕri (2), *about; around*

CONCERNETH
1157 bᵉ'ad (1), *at, beside, among, behind, for*

CONCERNING
413 'êl (15), *to, toward*
854 'êth (1), *with; by; at; among*
5921 'al (78), *above, over, upon, or against*
5922 'al (Ch.) (6), *above, over, upon, or against*
6655 tsad (Ch.) (1), *at the side of; against*
1519 ĕis (5), *to or into*
2596 kata (5), *down; according to*
3754 hŏti (1), *that; because; since*
4012 pĕri (44), *about; around*
4314 prŏs (1), *for; on, at; to, toward; against*
5228 hupĕr (1), *over; above; beyond*

CONCISION
2699 katatŏmē (1), *mutilation, cutting*

CONCLUDE
3049 lŏgizŏmai (1), *to credit; to think, regard*

CONCLUDED
2919 krinō (1), *to decide; to try, condemn, punish*
4788 sugklĕiō (2), *to net fish; to lock up persons*

CONCLUSION
5490 çôwph (1), *termination; end*

CONCORD
4857 sumphōnēsis (1), *accordance, agreement*

CONCOURSE
1993 hâmâh (1), *to be in great commotion*
4963 sustrŏphē (1), *riotous crowd*

CONCUBINE
6370 pîylegesh (22), *concubine*

CONCUBINES
3904 lᵉchênâh (Ch.) (3), *concubine*
6370 pîylegesh (14), *concubine*

CONCUPISCENCE
1939 ĕpithumia (3), *longing*

CONDEMN
7561 râsha' (11), *to be, do, declare wrong*
8199 shâphaṭ (1), *to judge*
2607 kataginōskō (2), *to condemn*
2618 katakaiō (1), *to consume wholly by burning*
2632 katakrinō (7), *to judge against*
2633 katakrisis (1), *act of sentencing adversely*
2919 krinō (1), *to decide; to try, condemn, punish*

CONDEMNATION
2631 katakrima (3), *adverse sentence*
2633 katakrisis (1), act of *sentencing adversely*
2917 krima (5), *decision*
2920 krisis (2), *decision; tribunal; justice*
5272 hupŏkrisis (1), *deceit, hypocrisy*

CONDEMNED
3318+7563 yâtsâ' (1), to *go, bring out*
6064 'ânash (2), to *inflict a penalty, to fine*
7561 râsha' (1), to *be, do, declare wrong*
176 akatagnōstŏs (1), *unblamable*
843 autŏkatakritŏs (1), *self-condemned*
1519+2917 ĕis (1), *to or into*
2613 katadikazō (4), to *condemn*
2632 katakrinō (8), to *judge against*
2919 krinō (2), to *decide; to try, condemn, punish*

CONDEMNEST
2632 katakrinō (1), to *judge against*

CONDEMNETH
7561 râsha' (2), to *be, do, declare wrong*
2632 katakrinō (1), to *judge against*
4314 prŏs (1), *for; on, at; to, toward; against*

CONDEMNING
7561 râsha' (1), to *be, do, declare wrong*
2919 krinō (1), to *decide; to try, condemn, punish*

CONDESCEND
4879 sunapagō (1), to *take off together*

CONDITIONS
4314 prŏs (1), *for; on, at; to, toward; against*

CONDUCT
5674 'âbar (1), to *cross over; to transition*
7971 shâlach (1), to *send away*
4311 prŏpĕmpō (1), to *send forward*

CONDUCTED
5674 'âbar (1), to *cross over; to transition*
2525 kathistēmi (1), to *designate, constitute*

CONDUIT
8585 tᵉ'âlâh (4), *irrigation channel; bandage or plaster*

CONEY
8227 shâphân (2), *rock-rabbit, (poss.) hyrax*

CONFECTION
7545 rôqach (1), *aromatic, fragrance*

CONFECTIONARIES
7543 râqach (1), to *perfume, blend spice*

CONFEDERACY
1285 bᵉrîyth (1), *compact, agreement*
7195 qesher (2), *unlawful alliance*

CONFEDERATE
1167+1285 ba'al (1), *master; owner; citizen*
1285+3772 bᵉrîyth (1), *compact, agreement*
5117 nûwach (1), to *rest; to settle down*

CONFERENCE
4323 prŏsanatithēmi (1), to *add; to consult*

CONFERRED
1961+1697 hâyâh (1), to *exist, i.e. be or become*
4323 prŏsanatithēmi (1), to *add; to consult*
4814 sullalĕō (1), to *talk together, i.e. converse*
4820 sumballō (1), to *converse, consult*

CONFESS
3034 yâdâh (11), to *revere or worship*
1843 ĕxŏmŏlŏgĕō (5), to *acknowledge or agree*
3670 hŏmŏlŏgĕō (12), to *acknowledge, agree*

CONFESSED
3034 yâdâh (3), to *throw; to revere or worship*
1843 ĕxŏmŏlŏgĕō (1), to *acknowledge or agree*
3670 hŏmŏlŏgĕō (3), to *acknowledge, agree*

CONFESSETH
3034 yâdâh (1), to *throw; to revere or worship*
3670 hŏmŏlŏgĕō (2), to *acknowledge, agree*

CONFESSING
3034 yâdâh (1), to *throw; to revere or worship*
1843 ĕxŏmŏlŏgĕō (2), to *acknowledge or agree*

CONFESSION
3034 yâdâh (2), to *throw; to revere or worship*
8426 tôwdâh (2), *expressions of thanks*
3670 hŏmŏlŏgĕō (1), to *acknowledge, agree*
3671 hŏmŏlŏgia (1), *confession*

CONFIDENCE
982 bâṭach (4), to *trust, be confident or sure*
983 beṭach (1), *safety, security, trust*
985 biṭchâh (1), *trust*
986 biṭṭâchôwn (2), *trust*
3689 keçel (1), *loin; back; viscera; trust*
3690 kiçlâh (1), *trust*
4009 mibṭâch (8), *security; assurance*
2292 tharrhĕō (1), to *exercise courage*
3954 parrhēsia (6), *frankness, boldness*
3982 pĕithō (6), to *rely*
4006 pĕpŏithēsis (5), *reliance, trust*

CONFIDENCES
5287 hupŏstasis (2), *essence; assurance*

CONFIDENCES
4009 mibṭâch (1), *security; assurance*

CONFIDENT
982 bâṭach (2), to *trust, be confident or sure*
2292 tharrhĕō (2), to *exercise courage*
3982 pĕithō (3), to *rely*
5287 hupŏstasis (1), *essence; assurance*

CONFIDENTLY
1340 diïschurizŏmai (1), to *asseverate*

CONFIRM
553 'âmats (1), to *be strong; be courageous*
1396 gâbar (1), to *be strong; to prevail*
2388 châzaq (2), to *bind, restrain, conquer*
3559 kûwn (1), to *set up: establish, fix, prepare*
4390 mâlê' (1), to *fill; be full*
6965 qûwm (4), to *rise*
950 bĕbaiŏō (2), to *stabilitate, keep strong*
2964 kurŏō (1), to *ratify, validate a treaty*

CONFIRMATION
951 bĕbaiōsis (2), *confirmation*

CONFIRMED
2388 châzaq (1), to *bind, restrain, conquer*
3559 kûwn (2), to *render sure, proper or prosperous*
5975 'âmad (2), to *stand*
6965 qûwm (2), to *rise*
950 bĕbaiŏō (2), to *stabilitate, keep strong*
1991 ĕpistērizō (1), to *re-establish, strengthen*
2964 kurŏō (1), to *ratify, validate a treaty*
3315 mĕsitĕuō (1), to *ratify as surety, confirm*
4300 prŏkurŏō (1), to *ratify previously*

CONFIRMETH
6965 qûwm (3), to *rise*

CONFIRMING
950 bĕbaiŏō (1), to *stabilitate, keep strong*
1991 ĕpistērizō (2), to *re-establish, strengthen*

CONFISCATION
6065 'ănash (Ch.) (1), *fine, penalty, mulct*

CONFLICT
73 agōn (2), *contest, struggle*

CONFORMABLE
4832 summŏrphŏs (1), *similar, conformed to*

CONFORMED
4832 summŏrphŏs (1), *similar, conformed to*
4964 suschēmatizō (1), to *conform*

CONFOUND
1101 bâlal (2), to *mix; confuse*
2865 châthath (1), to *break down*
2617 kataischunō (2), to *disgrace or shame*

CONFOUNDED
954 bûwsh (21), be *ashamed; disappointed*
2659 châphêr (6), to *be ashamed, disappointed*
3001 yâbêsh (9), to *dry up; to wither*
3637 kâlam (11), to *taunt or insult*
2617 kataischunō (1), to *disgrace or shame*
4797 sugchĕō (2), to *throw into disorder*

CONFUSED
7494 ra'ash (1), *bounding, uproar*
4797 sugchĕō (1), to *throw into disorder*

CONFUSION
954 bûwsh (1), be *ashamed, disappointed*
1322 bôsheth (7), *shame*
2659 châphêr (2), to *be ashamed, disappointed*
3637 kâlam (1), to *taunt or insult*
3639 kᵉlimmâh (6), *disgrace, scorn*
7036 qâlôwn (1), *disgrace*
8397 tebel (2), *confused mixture*
8414 tôhûw (3), *waste, desolation, formless*
181 akatastasia (2), *disorder, riot*
4799 sugchusis (1), *riotous disturbance*

CONGEALED
7087 qâphâ' (1), to *thicken, congeal*

CONGRATULATE
1288 bârak (1), to *bless*

CONGREGATION
482 'êlem (1), *silence*
2416 chay (2), *alive; raw; fresh; life*
4150 môw'êd (147), *assembly, congregation*
5712 'êdâh (123), *assemblage; crowd*
6951 qâhâl (85), *assemblage*
6952 qᵉhillâh (1), *assemblage*
4865 sunagōnizŏmai (1), to *be a partner*

CONGREGATIONS
4150 môw'êd (1), *assembly, congregation*
4721 maqhêl (2), *assembly*

CONIAH
3659 Konyâhûw (3), *Jehovah will establish*

CONIES
8226 sâphan (2), to *conceal*

CONONIAH
3562 Kôwnanyâhûw (2),
Jehovah has sustained

CONQUER
3528 nikaō (1), to
subdue, conquer

CONQUERING
3528 nikaō (1), to
subdue, conquer

CONQUERORS
5245 hupĕrnikaō (1), to
gain a decisive victory

CONSCIENCE
4893 sunĕidĕsis (31),
moral *consciousness*

CONSCIENCES
4893 sunĕidĕsis (1),
moral *consciousness*

CONSECRATE
2763 charam (1), to
devote to destruction
4390+3027 mâlê' (10), to
fill; be full
5144 nâzar (1), to *devote*
6942 qâdâsh (2), to *be,
make clean*

CONSECRATED
4390+3027 mâlê' (7), to
fill; be full
6942 qâdâsh (4), to *be,
make clean*
6944 qôdesh (1), *sacred*
place or thing
1457 ĕgkainizō (1), to
inaugurate
5048 tĕlĕiŏō (1), to
perfect, complete

CONSECRATION
4394 millû' (7), *fulfilling;
setting; consecration*
5145 nezer (2), *set apart;
dedication*

CONSECRATIONS
4394 millû' (4), *fulfilling;
setting; consecration*

CONSENT
14 'âbâh (4), to *be
acquiescent*
225 'ûwth (3), to *assent*
376 'îysh (1), *man; male*
3820 lêb (1), *heart*
7926 shĕkem (2), *neck;
spur of a hill*
4334 prŏsĕrchŏmai (1),
to *assent to*
4852 sumphĕmi (1), to
assent to
4859 sumphōnŏs (1),
agreeing; agreement

CONSENTED
225 'ûwth (1), to *assent;
agree*
8085 shâma' (1), to *hear*
1962 ĕpinĕuō (1), to
assent, give consent
4784 sugkatatithĕmai
(1), to *accord with*

CONSENTEDST
7521 râtsâh (1), to *be
pleased with; to satisfy*

CONSENTING
4909 sunĕudŏkĕō (2), to
assent to, feel gratified

CONSIDER
559 'âmar (1), to *say*
995 bîyn (20), to
understand; discern
3045 yâda' (4), to *know*
5027 nâbaṭ (5), to *scan;
to regard with favor*
6448 pâçag (1), to
contemplate
7200 râ'âh (15), to *see*
7725 shûwb (1), to *turn
back; to return*
7760 sûwm (2), to *put*
7760+3820 sûwm (4), to
put, place
7760+3820+5921 sûwm
(2), to *put, place*
7919 sâkal (2), to *be or
act circumspect*
357 analŏgizŏmai (1), to
contemplate
1260 dialŏgizŏmai (1), to
deliberate
1492 ĕidō (1), to *know*
2334 thĕōrĕō (1), to *see;
to discern*
2648 katamanthanō (1),
to *note carefully*
2657 katanŏĕō (4), to
observe fully
3539 nŏiĕō (1), to
exercise the mind

CONSIDERED
995 bîyn (1), to
understand; discern
2803 châshab (1), to
think, regard; to value
5414 nâthan (1), to *give*
7200 râ'âh (4), to *see*
7760+3820 sûwm (2), to
put, place
7896+3820 shîyth (1), to
place, put
7920 sĕkal (Ch.) (1), to *be
or act circumspect*
8085 shâma' (1), to *hear*
2657 katanŏĕō (2), to
observe fully
4894 sunĕidō (1), to
understand
4920 suniĕmi (1), to
comprehend

CONSIDEREST
7200 râ'âh (1), to *see*
2657 katanŏĕō (1), to
observe fully

CONSIDERETH
995 bîyn (1), to
understand; discern
2161 zâmam (1), to *plan*
3045 yâda' (2), to *know*
7200 râ'âh (2), to *see*
7725 shûwb (1), to *turn
back; to return*
7919 sâkal (2), to *be or
act circumspect*

CONSIDERING
995 bîyn (2), to
understand; discern
333 anathĕōrĕō (1), to
look again
4648 skŏpĕō (1), to *watch
out for, i.e. to regard*

CONSIST
4921 sunistaō (1), to *set
together*

CONSISTETH
2076 ĕsti (1), he (she or
it) *is; they are*

CONSOLATION
8575 tanchûwm (1),
compassion, solace
3874 paraklēsis (14),
imploring, solace

CONSOLATIONS
8575 tanchûwm (3),
compassion, solace

CONSORTED
4845 sumplĕrŏō (1), to *be
complete, fulfill*

CONSPIRACY
7195 qesher (9), unlawful
alliance
4945 sunōmŏsia (1), *plot,
conspiracy*

CONSPIRATORS
7194 qâshar (1), to *tie,
bind*

CONSPIRED
5320 Naphtûchîym (1),
Naphtuchim
7194 qâshar (18), to *tie,
bind*

CONSTANT
2388 châzaq (1), to
fasten upon; to seize

CONSTANTLY
5331 netsach (1),
splendor; lasting
1226 diabĕbaiŏŏmai (1),
to *confirm thoroughly*
1340 diïschurizŏmai (1),
to *asseverate*

CONSTELLATIONS
3685 Kĕçîyl (1),
constellation Orion

CONSTRAIN
315 anagkazō (1), to
necessitate, compel

CONSTRAINED
2388 châzaq (1), to
fasten upon; to seize
315 anagkazō (3), to
necessitate, compel
3849 parabiazŏmai (2),
to *compel by entreaty*

CONSTRAINETH
6693 tsûwq (1), to
oppress, distress
4912 sunĕchō (1), to *hold
together*

CONSTRAINT
317 anagkastōs (1),
compulsorily

CONSULT
3289 yâ'ats (1), to *advise*

CONSULTATION
4824 sumbŏuliŏn (1),
advisement

CONSULTED
3272 yĕ'aṭ (Ch.) (1), to
counsel
3289 yâ'ats (8), to *advise*
4427 mâlak (1), to *reign
as king*
7592 shâ'al (1), to *ask*
1011 bŏuleuō (1), to
deliberate; to resolve
4823 sumbŏuleuō (1), to
recommend, deliberate

CONSULTER
7592 shâ'al (1), to *ask*

CONSULTETH
1011 bŏuleuō (1), to
deliberate; to resolve

CONSUME
398 'âkal (9), to *eat*
402 'oklâh (1), *food*
1086 bâlâh (1), to *wear
out, decay; consume*
1497 gâzal (1), to *rob*
2000 hâmam (1), to
disturb, drive, destroy
2628 châçal (1), to *eat
off, consume*
3423 yârash (1), to
inherit; to impoverish
3615 kâlâh (23), to
complete, consume
4529 mâçâh (1), to
dissolve, melt
4743 mâqaq (4), to *melt;
to flow, dwindle, vanish*
5486 çûwph (4), to
terminate
5487 çûwph (Ch.) (1), to
come to an end
5595 çâphâh (1), to
scrape; to accumulate
8046 shĕmad (Ch.) (1), to
desolate
8552 tâmam (2), to
complete, finish
355 analiskō (2), *destroy*
1159 dapanaō (1), to
incur cost; to waste

CONSUMED
398 'âkal (21), to *eat*
622 'âçaph (1), to *gather*
1846 dâ'ak (1), to *be
extinguished; to expire*
3615 kâlâh (37), to
complete, consume
4127 mûwg (1), to *soften,
flow down, disappear*
5486 çûwph (1), to
terminate
5595 çâphâh (5), to
scrape; to accumulate
6244 'âshêsh (3), to *fail*
6789 tsâmath (1), to
extirpate, root out
8552 tâmam (24), to
complete, finish
355 analiskō (1), *destroy*

CONSUMETH
398 'âkal (2), to *eat*
1086 bâlâh (1), to *wear
out, decay; consume*
7503 râphâh (1), to
slacken

CONSUMING
398 'âkal (2), to *eat*
2654 katanaliskō (1), to
consume utterly

CONSUMMATION
3617 kâlâh (1), *complete
destruction*

CONSUMPTION
3617 kâlâh (2), *complete
destruction*
3631 killâyôwn (1),
pining, destruction
7829 shachepheth (2),
wasting disease

CONTAIN
1004 bayith (1), *house; temple; family, tribe*
3557 kûwl (3), *to keep in; to maintain*
5375 nâsâ' (1), *to lift up*
1467 ĕgkratĕuŏmai (1), *to exercise self-restraint*
5562 chōrĕō (1), *to pass, enter; to hold, admit*

CONTAINED
3557 kûwl (2), *to keep in; to maintain*
4023 pĕriĕchō (1), *to encircle; to contain*

CONTAINETH
3557 kûwl (1), *to keep in; to maintain*

CONTAINING
5562 chōrĕō (1), *to pass, enter; to hold, admit*

CONTEMN
3988 mâ'aç (1), *to spurn; to disappear*
5006 nâ'ats (1), *to scorn*

CONTEMNED
936 bûwz (1), *to disrespect, scorn*
959 bâzâh (1), *to disesteem, ridicule*
5006 nâ'ats (1), *to scorn*
7034 qâlâh (1), *to hold in contempt*

CONTEMNETH
3988 mâ'aç (1), *to spurn; to disappear*

CONTEMPT
937 bûwz (7), *disrespect, scorn*
963 bizzâyôwn (1), *disesteem, disrespect*
1860 dᵉrâ'ôwn (1), *object of loathing*
7043 qâlal (1), *to be easy, trifling, vile*

CONTEMPTIBLE
959 bâzâh (3), *to disesteem, ridicule*
1848 ĕxŏuthĕnĕō (1), *to treat with contempt*

CONTEMPTUOUSLY
937 bûwz (1), *disrespect*

CONTEND
1624 gârâh (3), *to provoke to anger*
1777 dîyn (1), *to judge; to strive or contend for*
3401 yârîyb (1), *contentious; adversary*
7378 rîyb (7), *to hold a controversy; to defend*
8474 tachârâh (1), *to vie with a rival*
1864 ĕpagōnizŏmai (1), *to struggle for, fight for*

CONTENDED
4695 matstsûwth (1), *quarrel, contention*
7378 rîyb (4), *to hold a controversy; to defend*
1252 diakrinō (1), *to decide; to hesitate*

CONTENDEST
7378 rîyb (1), *to hold a controversy; to defend*

CONTENDETH
3401 yârîyb (1), *contentious; adversary*
7378 rîyb (1), *to hold a controversy; to defend*
8199 shâphaṭ (1), *to judge*

CONTENDING
1252 diakrinō (1), *to decide; to hesitate*

CONTENT
14 'âbâh (1), *to be acquiescent*
2974 yâ'al (7), *to assent; to undertake, begin*
3190+5869 yâṭab (1), *to be, make well*
8085 shâma' (1), *to hear intelligently*
714 'arkĕō (4), *to avail; be satisfactory*
842 autarkĕs (1), *contented*
2425+3588+4160 hikanŏs (1), *ample; fit*

CONTENTION
4066 mâdôwn (3), *contest or quarrel*
4683 matstsâh (1), *quarrel*
7379 rîyb (2), *contest, personal or legal*
73 agōn (1), *contest, struggle*
2052 ĕrithĕia (1), *faction, strife, selfish ambition*
3948 parŏxusmŏs (1), *incitement; dispute*

CONTENTIONS
4079 midyân (4), *contest or quarrel*
2054 ĕris (2), *quarrel, i.e. wrangling*

CONTENTIOUS
4066 mâdôwn (3), *contest or quarrel*
1537+2052 ĕk (1), *out of*
5380 philŏnĕikŏs (1), *disputatious*

CONTENTMENT
841 autarkeia (1), *contentedness*

CONTINUAL
1115+5627 biltîy (1), *not, except, without, unless*
2956 ṭârad (1), *to drive on*
8548 tâmîyd (27), *constantly, regularly*
88 adialĕiptŏs (1), *permanent, constant*
1519+5056 ĕis (1), *to or into*

CONTINUALLY
1980 hâlak (3), *to walk; live a certain way*
1980+7725 hâlak (1), *to walk; live a certain way*
3605+3117 kôl (10), *all, any or every*
6256 'êth (1), *time*
8411 tᵉdîyrâ' (Ch.) (2), *constantly, faithfully*
8544 tᵉmûwnâh (1), *something fashioned*
8548 tâmîyd (52), *constantly, regularly*

CONTINUALLY
1275 diapantŏs (1), *constantly, continually*
1519+1336 ĕis (2), *to or into*
1725 ĕnanti (1), *before, in presence of*
4342 prŏskartĕrĕō (3), *to be constantly diligent*

CONTINUANCE
539 'âman (2), *to be firm; to be permanent*
3117 yôwm (1), *day; time period*
5769 'ôwlâm (1), *eternity; ancient; always*
5281 hupŏmŏnē (1), *endurance, constancy*

CONTINUE
309 'âchar (1), *to remain; to delay*
1961 hâyâh (2), *to exist, i.e. be or become*
3427 yâshab (2), *to dwell, to remain; to settle*
3885 lûwn (1), *to be obstinate*
4900 mâshak (1), *to draw out; to be tall*
5975 'âmad (4), *to stand*
6965 qûwm (3), *to rise*
7931 shâkan (1), *to reside*
1265 diamĕnō (2), *to stay constantly*
1696 ĕmmĕnō (1), *to remain; to persevere*
1961 ĕpimĕnō (5), *to remain; to persevere*
2476 histēmi (1), *to stand, establish*
3306 mĕnō (7), *to stay, remain*
3887 paramĕnō (1), *to be permanent, persevere*
4160 pŏiĕō (2), *to do*
4342 prŏskartĕrĕō (1), *to persevere*
4357 prŏsmĕnō (1), *to remain; to adhere to*
4839 sumparamĕnō (1), *to remain in company*

CONTINUED
1961 hâyâh (3), *to exist, i.e. be or become*
2388 châzaq (1), *to fasten upon; to seize*
3254 yâçaph (2), *to add or augment*
3427 yâshab (3), *to dwell, to remain; to settle*
5125 nûwn (1), *to be perpetual*
5975 'âmad (1), *to stand*
7235 râbâh (1), *to increase*
1096 ginŏmai (1), *to be, become*
1265 diamĕnō (1), *to stay constantly*
1273 dianuktĕrĕuō (1), *to pass, spend the night*
1300 diatĕlĕō (1), *to persist, continue*
1304 diatribō (2), *to remain, stay*
1696 ĕmmĕnō (1), *to remain; to persevere*
1961 ĕpimĕnō (1), *to remain; to persevere*

CONTINUETH
5975 'âmad (1), *to stand*
1696 ĕmmĕnō (1), *to remain; to persevere*
3306 mĕnō (1), *to stay, remain*
3887 paramĕnō (1), *to be permanent, persevere*
4357 prŏsmĕnō (1), *to remain; to adhere to*

CONTINUING
1641 gârar (1), *to ruminate; to saw*
3306 mĕnō (1), *to stay, remain*
4342 prŏskartĕrĕō (2), *to persevere; to adhere*

CONTRADICTING
483 antilĕgō (1), *to dispute, refuse*

CONTRADICTION
485 antilŏgia (2), *dispute, disobedience*

CONTRARIWISE
5121 tŏunantiŏn (3), *on the contrary*

CONTRARY
2016 hephek (2), *reverse, perversion*
7147 qᵉrîy (7), *hostile encounter*
480 antikĕimai (2), *be adverse to*
561 apĕnanti (1), *opposite, against*
1727 ĕnantiŏs (6), *opposite*
3844 para (3), *from; with; besides; on account of*
3891 paranŏmĕō (1), *to transgress, violate law*
5227 hupĕnantiŏs (1), *opposed; opponent*

CONTRIBUTION
2842 kŏinōnia (1), *benefaction; sharing*

CONTRITE
1792 dâkâ' (1), *to be contrite, be humbled*
1793 dakkâ' (2), *contrite, humbled*
1794 dâkâh (1), *to collapse; contrite*
5223 nâkeh (1), *maimed; dejected*

CONTROVERSIES
7379 rîyb (1), *contest, personal or legal*

CONTROVERSY
7379 rîyb (12), *contest, personal or legal*
3672 hŏmŏlŏgŏumĕnōs (1), *confessedly*

CONVENIENT
2706 chôq (1), *appointment; allotment*
3477 yâshâr (2), *straight*

433 anēkō (2), *be proper, fitting*
2119 ĕukairēō (1), *to have opportunity*
2121 ĕukairōs (1), *opportune, suitable*
2520 kathēkō (1), *becoming, proper*
2540 kairōs (1), *occasion, set or proper*

CONVENIENTLY
2122 ĕukairōs (1), *opportunely*

CONVERSANT
1980 hâlak (2), *to walk; live a certain way*

CONVERSATION
1870 derek (2), *road; course* of life
390 anastrĕphō (2), *to remain, to live*
391 anastrŏphē (13), *behavior*
4175 pŏlitĕuma (1), *citizenship*
4176 pŏlitĕuŏmai (1), *to behave as a citizen*
5158 trŏpŏs (1), *deportment, character*

CONVERSION
1995 ĕpistrŏphē (1), *moral revolution*

CONVERT
7725 shûwb (1), *to turn back; to return*
1994 ĕpistrĕphō (1), *revert, turn back to*

CONVERTED
2015 hâphak (1), *to turn about or over*
7725 shûwb (1), *to turn back; to return*
1994 ĕpistrĕphō (6), *revert, turn back to*
4762 strĕphō (1), *to turn around or reverse*

CONVERTETH
1994 ĕpistrĕphō (1), *to revert, turn back to*

CONVERTING
7725 shûwb (1), *to turn back; to return*

CONVERTS
7725 shûwb (1), *to turn back; to return*

CONVEY
5674 'âbar (1), *to cross over; to transition*
7760 sûwm (1), *to put*

CONVEYED
1593 ĕknĕuō (1), *to quietly withdraw*

CONVICTED
1651 ĕlĕgchō (1), *to confute, admonish*

CONVINCE
1651 ĕlĕgchō (1), *to confute, admonish*
1827 ĕxĕlĕgchō (1), *to punish*

CONVINCED
3198 yâkach (1), *to be correct; to argue*

1246 diakatĕlĕgchŏmai (1), *to prove downright*
1651 ĕlĕgchō (2), *to confute, admonish, rebuke*

CONVINCETH
1651 ĕlĕgchō (1), *to confute, admonish*

CONVOCATION
4744 miqrâ' (15), *public meeting*

CONVOCATIONS
4744 miqrâ' (3), *public meeting*

COOK
2876 ṭabbâch (2), *butcher, cook*

COOKS
2876 ṭabbâch (1), *butcher, cook*

COOL
7307 rûwach (1), *breath; wind; life-*spirit
2711 katapsuchō (1), *to refresh, cool off*

COOS
2972 Kōs (1), *Cos*

COPIED
6275 'âthaq (1), *to grow old; to transcribe*

COPING
2947 ṭêphach (1), *palm-breadth*

COPPER
5178 nᵉchôsheth (1), *copper; bronze*

COPPERSMITH
5471 chalkĕus (1), *copper-worker*

COPULATION
7902 shᵉkâbâh (3), *lying down*

COPY
4932 mishneh (2), *duplicate copy; double*
6572 parshegen (3), *transcript*
6573 parshegen (Ch.) (4), *transcript*

COR
3734 kôr (1), *dry measure*

CORAL
7215 râ'mâh (2), *high* in value, (poss.) *coral*

CORBAN
2878 kŏrban (1), *votive offering or gift*

CORD
2256 chebel (4), *company, band*
2339 chûwṭ (1), *string; measuring tape; line*
3499 yether (1), *remainder; small rope*

CORDS
2256 chebel (12), *company, band*
4340 mêythâr (8), *tent-cord; bow-string*
5688 'ăbôth (5), *entwined things*
4979 schŏiniŏn (1), *rushlet, i.e. grass-withe*

CORE
2879 Kŏrĕ (1), *ice*

CORIANDER
1407 gad (2), *coriander*

CORINTH
2882 Kŏrinthŏs (6), *Corinthus*

CORINTHIANS
2881 Kŏrinthiŏs (4), *inhabitant of Corinth*

CORINTHUS
2882 Kŏrinthŏs (1), *Corinthus*

CORMORANT
6893 qâ'ath (2), *pelican*
7994 shâlâk (2), *bird of prey* (poss.) *pelican*

CORN
1098 bᵉlîyl (1), *feed, fodder*
1121 bên (1), *son, descendant*
1250 bâr (9), *cereal grain*
1637 gôren (1), *open area*
1643 geres (2), *grain*
1715 dâgân (37), *grain*
3759 karmel (1), *planted field; garden produce*
5669 'âbûwr (2), *kept over; stored grain*
6194 'ârêm (1), *heap, mound; sheaf*
7054 qâmâh (7), *stalk of cereal grain*
7383 rîyphâh (1), *grits cereal*
7668 sheber (7), *grain*
7688 shâgach (1), *to glance sharply at*
2848 kŏkkŏs (1), *kernel*
4621 sitŏs (2), *grain, especially wheat*
4702 spŏrimŏs (3), *field planted with seed*
4719 stachus (3), *head of grain*

CORNELIUS
2883 Kŏrnĕliŏs (10), *Cornelius*

CORNER
2106 zâvîyth (1), *angle, corner* (as projecting)
3671 kânâph (1), *edge or extremity; wing*
3802 kâthêph (2), *shoulder-piece; wall*
4742 mᵉquts'âh (1), *angle*
6285 pê'âh (5), *direction; region; extremity*
6434 pên (1), *angle*
6437 pânâh (1), *to turn, to face*
6438 pinnâh (17), *pinnacle; chieftain*
204 akrŏgōniaiŏs (2), *corner, cornerstone*
1137 gōnia (6), *angle; cornerstone*

CORNERS
2106 zâvîyth (1), *angle, corner* (as projecting)
3671 kânâph (2), *edge or extremity; wing*
4740 maqtsôwa' (1), *angle*
4742 mᵉquts'âh (6), *angle*

CORE
6284 pâ'âh (1), *to blow away*
6285 pê'âh (11), *region; extremity*
6438 pinnâh (6), *pinnacle; chieftain*
6471 pa'am (3), *time; step; occurence*
6763 tsêlâ' (2), *side*
7098 qâtsâh (1), *termination; fringe*
7106 qâtsa' (1), *to strip off, i.e.* (partially) *scrape*
746 archē (2), *first in rank; first in time*
1137 gōnia (2), *angle; cornerstone*

CORNET
7162 qeren (Ch.) (4), *horn*
7782 shôwphâr (3), *curved ram's horn*

CORNETS
4517 mᵉna'na' (1), *rattling* instrument
7782 shôwphâr (1), *curved ram's horn*

CORNFLOOR
1637+1715 gôren (1), *open area*

CORPSE
4430 ptōma (1), *corpse, carrion*

CORPSES
1472 gᵉvîyâh (2), *dead body*
6297 peger (2), *carcase; corpse*

CORRECT
3198 yâkach (1), *to be correct; to argue*
3256 yâçar (6), *to chastise; to instruct*

CORRECTED
3256 yâçar (1), *to chastise; to instruct*
3810 paidĕutēs (1), *teacher or discipliner*

CORRECTETH
3198 yâkach (2), *to be correct; to argue*

CORRECTION
3198 yâkach (1), *to be correct; to argue*
4148 mûwçâr (8), *reproof, warning*
7626 shêbeṭ (1), *stick; clan, family*
8433 tôwkêchâh (1), *correction*
1882 ĕpanŏrthōsis (1), *rectification, correction*

CORRUPT
1605 gâ'ar (1), *to chide, reprimand*
2254 châbal (1), *to bind by a pledge; to pervert*
2610 chânêph (1), *to soil, be defiled*
4167 mûwq (1), *to blaspheme, scoff*
4743 mâqaq (1), *to melt; to flow, dwindle, vanish*
7843 shâchath (11), *to decay; to ruin*
7844 shᵉchath (Ch.) (1), *to decay; to ruin*

853 *aphanizō* (2), to *consume* (*becloud*)
1311 *diaphthēirō* (1), to *ruin*, to *pervert*
2585 *kapēlĕuō* (1), to *retail*, i.e. to *adulterate*
2704 *kataphthēirō* (1), to *spoil entirely*
4550 *saprŏs* (6), *rotten*, i.e. *worthless*
5351 *phthĕirō* (4), to *spoil*; to *deprave*

CORRUPTED
7843 shâchath (11), to *decay*; to *ruin*
4595 *sēpō* (1), to *putrefy*, *rot*
5351 *phthĕirō* (2), to *spoil*; to *deprave*

CORRUPTERS
7843 shâchath (2), to *decay*; to *ruin*

CORRUPTETH
1311 *diaphthĕirō* (1), to *ruin*, to *pervert*

CORRUPTIBLE
862 *aphthartŏs* (1), *undecaying, immortal*
5349 *phthartŏs* (6), *perishable, not lasting*

CORRUPTING
7843 shâchath (1), to *decay*; to *ruin*

CORRUPTION
1097 *bᵉlîy* (1), *without, not yet; lacking;*
4889 mashchîyth (2), *destruction; corruption*
4893 mishchâth (1), *disfigurement*
7845 shachath (4), *pit; destruction*
1312 *diaphthŏra* (6), *decay, corruption*
5356 *phthŏra* (7), *ruin; depravity, corruption*

CORRUPTLY
2254 châbal (1), to *bind* by a *pledge*; to *pervert*
7843 shâchath (1), to *decay*; to *ruin*

COSAM
2973 *Kōsam* (1), *Cosam*

COST
2600 chinnâm (2), *free*
1160 *dapanē* (1), *expense, cost*

COSTLINESS
5094 *timiŏtēs* (1), *expensiveness*

COSTLY
3368 yâqâr (4), *valuable*
4185 *pŏlutĕlēs* (1), *extremely expensive*
4186 *pŏlutimŏs* (1), *extremely valuable*

COTES
220 'ăvêrâh (1), *stall, pen*

COTTAGE
4412 mᵉlûwnâh (1), *hut*
5521 çukkâh (1), *tabernacle; shelter*

COTTAGES
3741 kârâh (1), *meadow*

COUCH
3326 yâtsûwa' (1), *bed; wing or lean-to*
4904 mishkâb (1), *bed; sleep*
6210 'eres (2), *canopy couch*
7742 sûwach (1), to *muse pensively*
2826 *klinidiŏn* (2), *pallet or little couch*

COUCHED
3766 kâra' (1), to *prostrate*
7257 râbats (1), to *recline, repose, brood*

COUCHES
6210 'eres (1), *canopy couch*
2895 *krabbatŏs* (1), *sleeping mat*

COUCHETH
7257 râbats (1), to *recline, repose, brood*

COUCHING
7257 râbats (1), to *recline, repose, brood*

COUCHINGPLACE
4769 marbêts (1), *resting place*

COULD
3045 yâda' (2), to *know*
3201 yâkôl (46), to *be able*
3202 yᵉkêl (Ch.) (1), to *be able*
3546 kᵉhal (Ch.) (1), to *be able*
5074 nâdad (1), to *rove, flee*; to *drive* away
5234 nâkar (1), to *acknowledge*
5346 Neqeb (1), *dell*
102 *adunatŏs* (1), *weak; impossible*
1410 *dunamai* (29), to *be able or possible*
1415 *dunatŏs* (1), *powerful or capable*
2192 *ĕchō* (3), to *have; hold; keep*
2480 *ischuō* (7), to *have or exercise force*
2489 *Iōanna* (1), *Jehovah-favored*
5342 *phĕrō* (1), to *bear or carry*

COULDEST
3201 yâkôl (1), to *be able*
2480 *ischuō* (1), to *have or exercise force*

COULDST
3202 yᵉkêl (Ch.) (1), to *be able*

COULTER
855 'êth (1), *digging implement*

COULTERS
855 'êth (1), *digging implement*

COUNCIL
7277 rigmâh (1), *throng*
4824 *sumbŏuliŏn* (2), *deliberative body*
4892 *sunĕdriŏn* (20), *tribunal*

COUNCILS
4891 *sunĕgĕirō* (2), to *raise up with*

COUNSEL
1697 dâbâr (1), *word; matter; thing*
3245 yâçad (2), *settle, consult*
3289 yâ'ats (21), to *advise*
4431 mᵉlak (Ch.) (1), *counsel, advice*
5475 çôwd (6), *intimacy; consultation; secret*
5843 'êţâ' (Ch.) (1), *prudence*
6098 'êtsâh (80), *advice; plan; prudence*
8458 tachbûlâh (2), *guidance; plan*
1011 *bŏulĕuō* (1), to *deliberate*; to *resolve*
1012 *bŏulē* (9), *purpose, plan, decision*
4823 *sumbŏulĕuō* (4), to *recommend, deliberate*
4824 *sumbŏuliŏn* (5), *deliberative body*

COUNSELED
3289 yâ'ats (1), to *advise*

COUNSELLED
3289 yâ'ats (3), to *advise*

COUNSELLOR
3289 yâ'ats (10), to *advise*
6098 'êtsâh (1), *advice; plan; prudence*
1010 *bŏulĕutēs* (2), *adviser, councillor*
4825 *sumbŏulŏs* (1), *adviser*

COUNSELLORS
1884 dᵉthâbâr (Ch.) (2), *skilled in law; judge*
1907 haddâbâr (Ch.) (4), *vizier, high official*
3272 yᵉ'aţ (Ch.) (2), to *counsel*
3289 yâ'ats (12), to *advise*
6098 'êtsâh (1), *advice; plan; prudence*

COUNSELS
4156 môw'êtsâh (6), *purpose, plan*
6098 'êtsâh (2), *advice; plan; prudence*
8458 tachbûlâh (3), *guidance; plan*
1012 *bŏulē* (1), *purpose, plan, decision*

COUNT
1961 hâyâh (1), to *exist*, i.e. *be or become*
2803 châshab (3), to *think*; to *compute*
3699 kâçaç (1), to *estimate, determine*
4487 mânâh (1), to *allot*; to *enumerate* or *enroll*
5414 nâthan (1), to *give*
5608 çâphar (4), to *inscribe*; to *enumerate*
515 axiŏō (1), to *deem entitled or fit, worthy*
2192 *ĕchō* (2), to *have; hold; keep*
2233 *hēgĕŏmai* (7), to *deem*, i.e. *consider*

3049 *lŏgizŏmai* (1), to *credit*; to *think, regard*
3106 *makarizō* (1), to *esteem fortunate*
5585 *psēphizō* (1), to *compute, estimate*

COUNTED
2803 châshab (18), to *think*; to *compute*
5608 çâphar (2), to *inscribe*; to *enumerate*
6485 pâqad (3), to *visit, care for, count*
515 axiŏō (2), to *deem entitled or fit, worthy*
1075 *gĕnĕalŏgĕō* (1), *trace in genealogy*
2192 *ĕchō* (2), to *have; hold; keep*
2233 *hēgĕŏmai* (3), to *deem*, i.e. *consider*
2661 *kataxiŏō* (2), to *deem entirely deserving*
3049 *lŏgizŏmai* (4), to *credit*; to *think, regard*
4860 *sumpsēphizō* (1), to *compute jointly*

COUNTENANCE
639 'aph (1), *nose or nostril; face; person*
1921 hâdar (1), to *favor or honor*; to *be proud*
2122 zîyv (Ch.) (4), *cheerfulness*
4758 mar'eh (8), *appearance; vision*
5869 'ayin (1), *eye; sight; fountain*
6440 pânîym (30), *face*
8389 tô'ar (1), *outline, figure or appearance*
2397 *idĕa* (1), *sight*
3799 *ŏpsis* (1), *face; appearance*
4383 *prŏsōpŏn* (3), *face, presence*
4659 *skuthrōpŏs* (1), *gloomy or mournful*

COUNTENANCES
4758 mar'eh (2), *appearance; vision*

COUNTERVAIL
7737 shâvâh (1), to *resemble*; to *adjust*

COUNTETH
2803 châshab (2), to *think*; to *compute*
5585 *psēphizō* (1), to *compute, estimate*

COUNTRIES
776 'erets (48), *earth, land, soil; country*
5316 nepheth (1), *height*
5561 *chōra* (1), *space of territory*

COUNTRY
127 'ădâmâh (1), *soil; land*
249 'ezrâch (5), *native born*
339 'îy (1), *dry land; coast; island*
776 'erets (91), *earth, land, soil; country*
1552 gᵉlîylâh (1), *circuit or region*

2256 chebel (1), *company, band*

4725 mâqôwm (1), *general locality, place*

6521 pᵉrâzîy (1), *rustic*

7704 sâdeh (17), *field*

68 agrŏs (8), *farm*land, *countryside*

589 apŏdēmĕō (4), *visit a foreign land*

1085 gĕnŏs (1), *kin, offspring in kind*

1093 gē (2), *soil, region, whole earth*

3968 patris (8), *hometown*

4066 pĕrichōrŏs (4), *surrounding country*

5561 chōra (15), space of territory

COUNTRYMEN

1085 gĕnŏs (1), *kin, offspring in kind*

4853 sumphulĕtēs (1), *of the same country*

COUPLE

2266 châbar (5), to *fascinate* by spells

6776 tsemed (4), *paired yoke*

8147 shᵉnayim (1), *two*-fold

COUPLED

2266 châbar (7), to *fascinate* by spells

8382 tâ'am (2), to *be twinned*, i.e. *duplicate*

8535 tâm (2), morally *pious; gentle, dear*

COUPLETH

2279 chôbereth (2), *joint*

COUPLING

2279 chôbereth (2), *joint*

4225 machbereth (8), *junction*

COUPLINGS

4226 mᵉchabbᵉrâh (1), *joiner*

COURAGE

553 'âmats (9), to *be strong; be courageous*

2388 châzaq (8), to *be strong; courageous*

3824 lêbâb (1), *heart*

7307 rûwach (1), *breath; wind; life*-spirit

2294 tharsŏs (1), *boldness, courage*

COURAGEOUS

533+3820 'ammîyts (1), *strong; mighty; brave*

553 'âmats (2), to *be strong; be courageous*

2388 châzaq (2), to *be strong; courageous*

COURAGEOUSLY

2388 châzaq (1), to *be strong; courageous*

COURSE

4131 môwṭ (1), to *slip, shake, fall*

4256 machălôqeth (19), *section or division*

4794 mᵉrûwtsâh (2), *race*

165 aiōn (1), *perpetuity, ever; world*

1408 drŏmŏs (3), *career, course of life*

2113 ĕuthudrŏmĕō (1), to *sail direct*

2183 ĕphēmĕria (2), *rotation or class*

3313 mĕrŏs (1), *division or share*

4144 plŏŏs (2), *navigation, voyage*

5143 trĕchō (1), to *run or walk hastily; to strive*

5164 trŏchŏs (1), *wheel; circuitous course of life*

COURSES

2487 chălîyphâh (1), *alternation, change*

2988 yâbâl (1), *stream*

4255 machlᵉqâh (Ch.) (1), *section or division*

4256 machălôqeth (14), *section or division*

4546 mᵉçillâh (1), *main thoroughfare; viaduct*

COURT

1004 bayith (1), *house; temple; family, tribe*

2681 châtsîyr (1), *court or abode*

2691 châtsêr (114), *enclosed yard*

5835 'ăzârâh (2), *enclosure; border*

5892 'îyr (1), *city, town, unwalled-village*

833 aulē (1), *palace; house; courtyard*

COURTEOUS

5391 philŏphrōn (1), *kind, well-disposed*

COURTEOUSLY

5364 philanthrōpōs (1), *fondly to mankind*

5390 philŏphrŏnōs (1), *friendliness of mind*

COURTS

2691 châtsêr (24), *enclosed yard*

COUSIN

4773 suggĕnēs (1), *relative; countryman*

COUSINS

4773 suggĕnēs (1), *relative; countryman*

COVENANT

1285 bᵉrîyth (264), *compact, agreement*

1242 diathēkē (17), *contract;* devisory *will*

COVENANTBREAKERS

802 asunthĕtŏs (1), *untrustworthy*

COVENANTED

3772 kârath (2), to *make an agreement*

2476 histēmi (1), to *stand, establish*

4934 suntithĕmai (1), to *consent, concur, agree*

COVENANTS

1242 diathēkē (3), *contract;* devisory *will*

COVER

2645 châphâh (1), to *cover; to veil, to encase*

3680 kâçâh (50), to *cover*

4374 mᵉkaççeh (1), *covering*

5258 nâçak (4), to *pour a libation; to anoint*

5526 çâkak (5), to *fence in; cover over; protect*

5844 'âṭâh (5), to *wrap,* i.e. *cover, veil, clothe*

7159 qâram (1), to *cover*

7779 shûwph (1), to *gape, to overwhelm*

2572 kaluptō (2), to *cover*

2619 katakaluptō (1), *cover with a veil*

4028 pĕrikaluptō (1), to *cover eyes*

COVERED

1104 bâla' (1), to *swallow; to destroy*

2645 châphâh (7), to *cover; to veil, to encase*

2926 ṭâlal (1), to *cover, roof*

3271 yâ'aṭ (1), to *clothe, cover*

3680 kâçâh (61), to *cover*

3728 kâphash (1), to *tread down*

3780 kâsâh (1), to *grow fat*

3813 lâ'aṭ (1), to *muffle, cover*

4374 mᵉkaççeh (1), *covering*

5526 çâkak (8), to *fence in; cover over; protect*

5603 çâphan (3), to *hide by covering; to roof*

5743 'ûwb (1), to *darkly becloud*

5844 'âṭâh (3), to *wrap,* i.e. *cover, veil, clothe*

5848 'âṭaph (1), to *shroud, clothe*

6632 tsâb (1), covered *cart*

6823 tsâphâh (5), to *sheet over with metal*

7159 qâram (1), to *cover*

1943 ĕpikaluptō (1), to *forgive*

2572 kaluptō (2), to *cover*

2596 kata (1), *down*

2619 katakaluptō (2), *cover with a veil*

4780 sugkaluptō (1), to *conceal altogether*

COVEREDST

3680 kâçâh (1), to *cover*

COVEREST

3680 kâçâh (1), to *cover*

5844 'âṭâh (1), to *wrap,* i.e. *cover, veil, clothe*

COVERETH

3680 kâçâh (20), to *cover*

4374 mᵉkaççeh (2), *covering*

5526 çâkak (2), to *fence in; cover over; protect*

5844 'âṭâh (1), to *wrap,* i.e. *cover, veil, clothe*

5848 'âṭaph (1), to *shroud,* i.e. *clothe*

2572 kaluptō (2), to *cover*

COVERING

168 'ôhel (1), *tent*

3680 kâçâh (2), to *cover*

3681 kâçûwy (2), *covering*

3682 kᵉçûwth (6), *cover; veiling*

3875 lôwṭ (1), *veil*

4372 mikçeh (16), *covering*

4539 mâçâk (7), *veil; shield*

4540 mᵉçukkâh (1), *covering*

4541 maççêkâh (2), *cast image); woven coverlet*

4817 merkâb (1), *chariot; seat in chariot*

5526 çâkak (2), to *fence in; cover over; protect*

5643 çêther (1), *cover, shelter*

5844 'âṭâh (1), to *wrap,* i.e. *cover, veil, clothe*

6781 tsâmîyd (1), *bracelet; lid*

6826 tsippûwy (3), *encasement* with metal

4018 pĕribŏlaiŏn (1), *mantle, veil*

COVERINGS

4765 marbad (2), *coverlet, covering*

COVERS

7184 qâsâh (3), *jug*

COVERT

4329 mêyçâk (1), covered *portico*

4563 miçtôwr (1), *refuge, hiding place*

5520 çôk (1), *hut of entwined boughs; lair*

5521 çukkâh (1), *tabernacle; shelter*

5643 çêther (5), *cover, shelter*

COVET

183 'âvâh (1), to *wish* for, *desire*

2530 châmad (3), to *delight* in; *lust for*

1937 ĕpithumĕō (2), to *long for*

2206 zēlŏō (2), to *have warmth* of feeling for

COVETED

2530 châmad (1), to *delight* in; *lust for*

1937 ĕpithumĕō (1), to *long for*

3713 ŏrĕgŏmai (1), to *reach* out after, *long* for

COVETETH

183 'âvâh (1), to *wish* for, *desire*

1214 bâtsa' (1), to *plunder; to finish*

COVETOUS

1214 bâtsa' (1), to *plunder; to finish*

866 aphilargurŏs (1), *not greedy*

4123 plĕŏnĕktēs (4), *eager for gain, greedy*

4124 plĕŏnĕxia (1), *fraudulence, extortion*

5366 philargurŏs (2), *avaricious*

C

COVETOUSNESS
1215 betsa' (10), *plunder; unjust gain*
866 aphilargurŏs (1), *not greedy*
4124 plĕŏnĕxia (8), *fraudulence, avarice*

COVOCATION
4744 miqrâ' (1), *public meeting*

COW
5697 'eglâh (1), *cow calf*
6510 pârâh (2), *heifer*
7794 shôwr (2), *bullock*

COW'S
1241 bâqâr (1), *plowing ox; herd*

COZ
6976 Qôwts (1), *thorns*

COZBI
3579 Kozbîy (2), *false*

CRACKLING
6963 qôwl (1), *voice or sound*

CRACKNELS
5350 niqqud (1), *crumb, morsel; biscuit*

CRAFT
4820 mirmâh (1), *fraud*
1388 dŏlŏs (1), *wile, deceit, trickery*
2039 ĕrgasia (1), *occupation; profit*
3313 mĕrŏs (1), *division or share*
3673 hŏmŏtĕchnŏs (1), *fellow-artificer*
5078 tĕchnĕ (1), *trade, craft; skill*

CRAFTINESS
6193 'ôrem (1), *stratagem, craftiness*
3834 panŏurgia (4), *trickery or sophistry*

CRAFTSMAN
2976 yâ'ash (1), *to despond, despair*
5079 tĕchnitĕs (1), *skilled craftsman*

CRAFTSMEN
2796 chârâsh (5), *skilled fabricator or worker*
5079 tĕchnitĕs (2), *skilled craftsman*

CRAFTY
6175 'ârûwm (2), *cunning; clever*
6191 'âram (1), *to be cunning; be prudent*
3835 panŏurgŏs (1), *shrewd, clever*

CRAG
8127 shên (1), *tooth; ivory; cliff*

CRANE
5483 çûwç (2), *horse; bird swallow*

CRASHING
7667 sheber (1), *fracture; ruin*

CRAVED
154 aitĕŏ (1), *to ask for*

CRAVETH
404 'âkaph (1), *to urge*

CREATE
1254 bârâ' (8), *to create; fashion*

CREATED
1254 bârâ' (33), *to create; fashion*
2936 ktizō (12), *to fabricate, create*

CREATETH
1254 bârâ' (1), *to create; fashion*

CREATION
2937 ktisis (6), *formation*

CREATOR
1254 bârâ' (3), *to create; fashion*
2936 ktizō (1), *to fabricate, create*
2939 ktistĕs (1), *founder*

CREATURE
2416 chay (6), *alive; raw; fresh; life*
5315 nephesh (9), *life; breath; soul; wind*
8318 sherets (1), *swarm, teeming mass*
2937 ktisis (11), *formation*
2938 ktisma (2), *created product*

CREATURES
255 'ôach (1), *creature that howls;*
2416 chay (9), *alive; raw; fresh; life*
2938 ktisma (2), *created product*

CREDITOR
1167+4874+3027 ba'al (1), *master; owner; citizen*
5383 nâshâh (1), *to lend or borrow*
1157 danĕistĕs (1), *money lender*

CREDITORS
5383 nâshâh (1), *to lend or borrow*

CREEK
2859 kŏlpŏs (1), *lap area; bay*

CREEP
7430 râmas (2), *to glide swiftly, i.e. crawl*
8317 shârats (2), *to wriggle, swarm*
8318 sherets (2), *swarm, teeming mass*
1744+1519 ĕndunō (1), *to sneak in, creep in*

CREEPETH
7430 râmas (9), *to glide swiftly, i.e. crawl*
7431 remes (1), *any rapidly moving animal*
8317 shârats (4), *to wriggle, swarm*

CREEPING
7431 remes (15), *any rapidly moving animal*
8318 sherets (11), *swarm, teeming mass*
2062 hĕrpĕtŏn (3), *reptile*

CREPT
3921 parĕisdunō (1), *to slip in secretly*

CRESCENS
2913 Krĕskĕs (1), *growing*

CRETE
2914 Krĕtĕ (5), *Cretë*

CRETES
2912 Krēs (1), *inhabitant of Crete*

CRETIANS
2912 Krēs (2), *inhabitant of Crete*

CREW
5455 phōnĕō (5), *to emit a sound*

CRIB
18 'êbûwç (3), *manger or stall*

CRIED
2199 zâ'aq (31), *to call out, announce*
2200 z^e'îq (Ch.) (1), *to make an outcry, shout*
2980 yâbab (1), *to bawl, cry out*
5414 nâthan (1), *to give*
6817 tsâ'aq (29), *to shriek; to proclaim*
7121 qârâ' (54), *to call out*
7123 q^erâ' (Ch.) (3), *to call out*
7321 rûwa' (2), *to shout for alarm or joy*
7768 shâva' (10), *to halloo, call for help*
310 anabŏaō (2), *to cry out*
349 anakrazō (5), *to scream aloud*
863 aphiēmi (1), *to leave; to pardon, forgive*
994 bŏaō (3), *to shout for help*
2019 ĕpiphōnĕō (2), *to exclaim, shout*
2896 krazō (43), *to call aloud*
2905 kraugazō (6), *to clamor, shout*
5455 phōnĕō (5), *to emit a sound*

CRIES
995 bŏē (1), *to call for aid*

CRIEST
2199 zâ'aq (2), *to call out, announce*
6817 tsâ'aq (1), *to shriek; to proclaim*
7121 qârâ' (2), *to call out*

CRIETH
2199 zâ'aq (1), *to call out, announce*
5414+6963 nâthan (1), *to give*
6817 tsâ'aq (2), *to shriek; to proclaim*
7121 qârâ' (4), *to call out*
7442 rânan (3), *to shout for joy*
7768 shâva' (2), *to halloo, call for help*
2896 krazō (4), *to call aloud*

CRIME
2154 zimmâh (1), *bad plan*
1462 ĕgklēma (1), *accusation*

CRIMES
4941 mishpâṭ (1), *verdict; formal decree; justice*
156 aitia (1), *logical reason; legal crime*

CRIMSON
3758 karmîyl (3), *carmine, deep red*
8144 shânîy (1), *crimson dyed stuffs*
8438 tôwlâ' (1), *maggot worm; crimson-grub*

CRIPPLE
5560 chŏlŏs (1), *limping, crippled*

CRISPING
2754 chârîyṭ (1), *pocket*

CRISPUS
2921 Krispŏs (2), *crisp*

CROOKBACKT
1384 gibbên (1), *hunch-backed*

CROOKED
1281 bârîyach (1), *fleeing, gliding serpent*
1921 hâdar (1), *to favor or honor; to be high*
4625 ma'ăqâsh (1), *crook in a road*
5753 'âvâh (1), *to be crooked*
5791 'âvath (2), *to wrest, twist*
6121 'âqôb (1), *fraudulent; tracked*
6128 'ăqalqal (1), *crooked*
6129 'ăqallâthôwn (1), *crooked*
6140 'âqash (1), *to knot or distort; to pervert*
6141 'iqqêsh (1), *distorted, warped, false*
6618 p^ethaltôl (1), *tortuous, perverse*
4646 skŏliŏs (2), *crooked; perverse*

CROP
4760 mur'âh (1), *craw or crop of a bird*
6998 qâṭaph (1), *to strip off, pick off*

CROPPED
6998 qâṭaph (1), *to strip off, pick off*

CROSS
4716 staurŏs (28), *pole or cross*

CROSSWAY
6563 pereq (1), *rapine; fork in roads*

CROUCH
7812 shâchâh (1), *to prostrate in homage*

CROUCHETH
1794 dâkâh (1), *to collapse; contrite*

CROW
5455 phōnĕō (7), *to emit a sound*

CROWN
2213 zêr (10), border
  molding on a building
3804 kether (3), *royal
  headdress*
5145 nezer (11), royal
  chaplet
5850 'ăṭârâh (20), *crown*
6936 qodqôd (7), *crown*
  of the head
4735 stěphanŏs (15),
  chaplet, wreath

CROWNED
3803 kâthar (1), to
  enclose, besiege; *to wait*
4502 minnᵉzâr (1), *prince*
5849 'âṭar (2), to *encircle,
  enclose in; to crown*
4737 stephanŏō (2), to
  adorn with a wreath

CROWNEDST
4737 stephanŏō (1), to
  adorn with a wreath

CROWNEST
5849 'âṭar (1), to *encircle,
  enclose in; to crown*

CROWNETH
5849 'âṭar (1), to *encircle,
  enclose in; to crown*

CROWNING
5849 'âṭar (1), to *encircle,
  enclose in; to crown*

CROWNS
5850 'ăṭârâh (3), *crown*
1238 diadēma (3), crown
  or *diadem*
4735 stěphanŏs (3),
  chaplet, wreath

CRUCIFIED
4362 prŏspēgnumi (1), to
  fasten to a cross
4717 staurŏō (31), to
  crucify
4957 sustaurŏō (5), to
  crucify with

CRUCIFY
388 anastaurŏō (1), to
  re-crucify
4717 staurŏō (13), to
  crucify

CRUEL
393 'akzâr (3), *violent,
  deadly; brave*
394 'akzârîy (8), *terrible,
  cruel*
395 'akzᵉrîyûwth (1),
  fierceness, cruelty
2555 châmâç (1),
  violence; malice
2556 châmêts (1), to *be
  fermented; be soured*
7185 qâshâh (2), to *be
  tough or severe*
7186 qâsheh (1), *severe*

CRUELLY
6233 'ôsheq (1), *injury;
  fraud; distress*

CRUELTY
2555 châmâç (4),
  violence; malice
6531 perek (1), *severity*

CRUMBS
5589 psichiŏn (3), *little
  bit or morsel*

CRUSE
1228 baqbûk (1), *bottle*
6746 tsᵉlôchîyth (1), *vial*
  or salt-*cellar*
6835 tsappachath (7),
  flat saucer

CRUSH
1792 dâkâ' (1), to
  pulverize; be *contrite*
2115 zûwr (1), to *press
  together, tighten*
7533 râtsats (1), to *crack*
  in pieces, *smash*
7665 shâbar (1), to *burst*

CRUSHED
1792 dâkâ' (2), to
  pulverize; be *contrite*
2000 hâmam (1), to
  disturb, drive, destroy
2116 zûwreh (1), *trodden*
  on
3807 kâthath (1), to
  bruise, strike, beat
3905 lâchats (1), to *press;*
  to *distress*
7533 râtsats (1), to *crack*
  in pieces, *smash*

CRY
602 'ânaq (3), to *shriek,
  cry out in groaning*
1993 hâmâh (1), to *be in
  great commotion*
2199 zâ'aq (25), to *call
  out, announce*
2201 za'aq (18), *shriek,
  outcry, lament*
5414+6963 nâthan (1), to
  give
6030 'ânâh (2), to
  respond, answer
6165 'ârag (1), to *long
  for, pant* for
6463 pâ'âh (1), to *scream*
  in childbirth
6670 tsâhal (3), to *be
  cheerful;* to *sound*
6682 tsᵉvâchâh (2),
  screech of anguish
6817 tsâ'aq (15), to
  shriek; to *proclaim*
6818 tsa'ăqâh (19),
  shriek, wail
6873 tsârach (1), to
  whoop
6963 qôwl (1), *voice* or
  sound
7121 qârâ' (37), to *call*
  out
7321 rûwa' (5), to *shout*
  for alarm or joy
7440 rinnâh (12), *shout*
7442 rânan (1), to *shout*
  for joy
7768 shâva' (8), to *call*
  for help
7769 shûwa' (1), *call*
7773 sheva' (1), *call*
7775 shav'âh (11), *call*
8173 shâ'a' (1), to *fondle,
  please* or *amuse* (self)
994 bŏaō (2), to *shout* for
  help
2896 krazō (3), to *call*
2905 kraugazō (1), to
  clamor, shout
2906 kraugē (3), *outcry*

CRYING
603 'ănâqâh (1),
  shrieking, groaning
2201 za'aq (2), *shriek,
  outcry, lament*
4191 mûwth (1), to *die;* to
  kill
6682 tsᵉvâchâh (1),
  screech of anguish
6818 tsa'ăqâh (2), *shriek,
  wail*
7121 qârâ' (1), to *call* out
7771 shôwa' (1), *call*
8663 tᵉshu'âh (1),
  crashing or clamor
310 anabŏaō (1), to *cry
  out*
994 bŏaō (6), to *shout* for
  help
1916 ĕpibŏaō (1), to *cry
  out loudly*
2896 krazō (9), to *call*
2906 kraugē (2), *outcry*

CRYSTAL
2137 zᵉkûwkîyth (1),
  transparent glass
7140 qerach (1), *ice; hail;*
  rock *crystal*
2929 krustallizō (1), to
  appear as ice
2930 krustallŏs (2), rock
  crystal

CUBIT
520 'ammâh (35), *cubit*
1574 gômed (1),
  measurement of length
4083 pēchus (2), *measure*
  of time or length

CUBITS
520 'ammâh (197), *cubit*
521 'ammâh (Ch.) (4),
  cubit
4088 pikria (2), *acridity,
  bitterness*

CUCKOW
7828 shachaph (2), *gull*

CUCUMBERS
4750 miqshâh (1),
  cucumber field
7180 qishshu' (1),
  cucumber

CUD
1625 gêrâh (11), *cud*

CUMBERED
4049 pĕrispaō (1), to *be
  distracted*

CUMBERETH
2673 katargĕō (1), to *be,
  render entirely useless*

CUMBRANCE
2960 ṭôrach (1), *burden*

CUMI
2891 kŏumi (1), *rise!*

CUMMIN
3646 kammôn (3),
  cummin
2951 kuminŏn (1), dill or
  fennel

CUNNING
542 'âman (1), *expert
  artisan, craftsman*
995 bîyn (1), to
  understand; discern
1847 da'ath (1),
  understanding

2450 châkâm (10), *wise,
  intelligent, skillful*
2803 châshab (11), to
  plot; to *think, regard*
3045 yâda' (4), to *know*
4284 machăshâbâh (3),
  contrivance; plan

CUP
1375 gᵉbîya' (4), *goblet;
  bowl*
3563 kôwç (29), *cup;*
  (poss.) *owl*
3599 kîyç (1), *cup;* utility
  bag
5592 çaph (1), *dish*
4221 pŏtēriŏn (31),
  drinking-vessel

CUPBEARER
4945 mashqeh (1), *butler;
  drink; well-watered*

CUPBEARERS
4945 mashqeh (2), *butler;
  drink; well-watered*

CUPS
101 'aggân (1), *bowl*
3563 kôwç (1), *cup*
4518 mᵉnaqqîyth (1),
  sacrificial basin
7184 qâsâh (1), *jug*
4221 pŏtēriŏn (2),
  drinking-vessel

CURDLED
7087 qâphâ' (1), to
  thicken, congeal

CURE
1455 gâhâh (1), to *heal*
7495 râphâ' (1), to *cure,
  heal*
2323 thĕrapĕuō (2), to
  relieve disease

CURED
8585 tᵉ'âlâh (1), *bandage*
  or *plaster*
2323 thĕrapĕuō (3), to
  relieve disease

CURES
2392 iasis (1), *curing*

CURIOUS
4284 machăshâbâh (1),
  contrivance; plan
4021 pĕriĕrgŏs (1),
  meddlesome, busybody

CURIOUSLY
7551 râqam (1),
  variegation; embroider

CURRENT
5674 'âbar (1), to *cross*
  over; to *transition*

CURSE
423 'âlâh (9),
  imprecation: curse
779 'ârar (15), to
  execrate, place a curse
1288 bârak (3), to *bless*
2764 chêrem (4),
  doomed object
3994 mᵉ'êrâh (4),
  execration, curse
5344 nâqab (4), to
  specify, designate, libel
6895 qâbab (7), to *stab*
  with words
7043 qâlal (17), to *be
  easy, trifling, vile*

DECLINE
5186 nâṭâh (3), to *stretch*
or *spread out*
5493 çûwr (1), to *turn off*
7847 sâṭâh (1), to *deviate*
from duty, *go astray*

DECLINED
5186 nâṭâh (3), to *stretch*
or *spread out*
5493 çûwr (1), to *turn off*

DECLINETH
5186 nâṭâh (2), to *stretch*
or *spread out*

DECREASE
4591 mâ'aṭ (1), to *be,
make small or few*
1642 ĕlattŏō (1), to *lessen*

DECREASED
2637 châçêr (1), to *lack;*
to *fail, want, make less*

DECREE
633 'ĕçâr (Ch.) (7), *edict,
decree*
1504 gâzar (1), to
exclude; decide
1510 gᵉzêrâh (Ch.) (2),
decree, decision
1697 dâbâr (1), *word;
matter; thing*
1881 dâth (9), *royal edict
or statute*
1882 dâth (Ch.) (3), *Law;
royal edict or statute*
2706 chôq (7),
appointment; allotment
2710 châqaq (2), to
engrave; to *enact laws*
2940 ṭa'am (1), *taste;
intelligence; mandate*
2942 ṭᵉ'êm (Ch.) (13),
judgment; account
3982 ma'ămar (1), *edict,
command*
6599 pithgâm (1),
judicial sentence; edict
1378 dŏgma (1), *law*

DECREED
1504 gâzar (1), to
destroy, exclude; decide
2706 chôq (1),
appointment; allotment
2782 chârats (1), to *be
alert,* to *decide*
6965 qûwm (1), to *rise*
2919 krinō (1), to *decide;*
to *try, condemn, punish*

DECREES
2711 chêqeq (1),
enactment, resolution
1378 dŏgma (2), *law*

DEDAN
1719 Dᵉdân (11), *Dedan*

DEDANIM
1720 Dᵉdânîym (1),
Dedanites

DEDICATE
2596 chânak (1), to
initiate or discipline
6942 qâdâsh (3), to *be,
make clean*

DEDICATED
2596 chânak (3), to
initiate or discipline
2764 chêrem (1),
doomed object

6942 qâdâsh (7), to *be,
make clean*
6944 qôdesh (12), *sacred
place or thing*
1457 ĕgkainizō (1), to
inaugurate

DEDICATING
2598 chănukkâh (2),
dedication

DEDICATION
2597 chănukkâ' (Ch.) (4),
dedication
2598 chănukkâh (6),
dedication
1456 ĕgkainia (1), Feast
of *Dedication*

DEED
199 'ûwlâm (2), *however
or on the contrary*
1697 dâbâr (3), *word;
matter; thing*
3559 kûwn (1), to *set up:
establish, fix, prepare*
4639 ma'ăseh (1), *action;
labor*
2041 ĕrgŏn (6), *work*
2108 ĕuĕrgĕsia (1),
beneficence
4162 pŏiēsis (1), *action,*
i.e. *performance*
4334 prŏsĕrchŏmai (1),
to *come near, visit*

DEEDS
1578 gᵉmûwlâh (1), *act;
service; reward*
1697 dâbâr (2), *word;
matter; thing*
4639 ma'ăseh (2), *action;
labor*
5949 'ălîylâh (2),
opportunity, action
6467 pô'al (2), *act or
work, deed*
1411 dunamis (1), *force,
power, miracle*
2041 ĕrgŏn (16), *work*
2735 katŏrthōma (1),
made fully upright
3739+4238 hŏs (1), *who,
which, what, that*
4234 praxis (3), *act;
function*

DEEMED
5282 hupŏnŏĕō (1), to
think; to *expect*

DEEP
4113 mahămôrâh (1),
(poss.) *abyss, pits*
4278 mechqâr (1), *recess,
unexplored place*
4615 ma'ămâq (2), *deep
place*
4688 mᵉtsôwlâh (5), *deep
place*
4950 mishqâ' (1), *clear
pond with settled water*
5994 'ămîyq (Ch.) (1),
profound, unsearchable
6009 'âmaq (5), to *be,
make deep*
6013 'âmôq (8), *deep,
profound*
6683 tsûwlâh (1), *watery
abyss*
7290 râdam (2), to
stupefy

8257 shâqa' (1), to *be
overflowed;* to *cease*
8328 sheresh (1), *root*
8415 tᵉhôwm (20), *abyss
of the sea,* i.e. the *deep*
8639 tardêmâh (7),
trance, deep sleep
12 abussŏs (2), *deep
place, abyss*
899 bathŏs (3), *extent;
mystery,* i.e. *deep*
901 bathus (2), *deep,
profound*
1037 buthŏs (1), *deep sea*
2532+900 kai (1), *and; or;
even; also*

DEEPER
6012 'âmêq (1), *deep,
obscure*
6013 'âmôq (8), *deep,
profound*

DEEPLY
6009 'âmaq (2), to *be,
make deep*
389 anastĕnazō (1), to
sigh deeply

DEEPNESS
899 bathŏs (1), *extent;
mystery,* i.e. *deep*

DEEPS
4688 mᵉtsôwlâh (3), *deep
place*
8415 tᵉhôwm (1), *abyss
of the sea,* i.e. the *deep*

DEER
3180 yachmûwr (1), *deer*

DEFAMED
987 blasphēmĕō (1), to
speak impiously

DEFAMING
1681 dibbâh (1), *slander,
bad report*

DEFEAT
6565 pârar (2), to *break
up;* to *violate, frustrate*

DEFENCE
1220 betser (1), *gold*
2646 chuppâh (1), *canopy*
4043 mâgên (2), *small
shield (buckler); animal
skin*
4686 mâtsûwd (1), *net or
capture; fastness*
4692 mâtsôwr (2),
siege-mound; distress
4869 misgâb (7), *refuge*
5526 çâkak (1), to *fence
in; cover over; protect*
6738 tsêl (3), *shade;
protection*
626 apŏlŏgĕŏmai (1), to
give an account
627 apŏlŏgia (3), *plea or
verbal defense*

DEFENCED
1219 bâtsar (5), to *be
inaccessible*
4013 mibtsâr (4),
fortification; defender

DEFEND
1598 gânan (7), to *protect*
3467 yâsha' (1), to *make
safe, free*
7682 sâgab (2), to *be,
make lofty; be safe*

8199 shâphaṭ (1), to *judge*

DEFENDED
5337 nâtsal (1), to *deliver*
292 amunŏmai (1), to
protect, help

DEFENDEST
5526 çâkak (1), to *fence
in; cover over; protect*

DEFENDING
1598 gânan (1), to *protect*

DEFER
309 'âchar (2), to *remain;*
to *delay*
748 'ârak (1), to *be,
make long*

DEFERRED
309 'âchar (1), to *remain;*
to *delay*
4900 mâshak (1), to *draw
out;* to *be tall*
306 anaballŏmai (1), to
put off, adjourn

DEFERRETH
748 'ârak (1), to *be,
make long*

DEFIED
2194 zâ'am (1), to *be
enraged*
2778 châraph (5), to
spend the winter

DEFILE
1351 gâ'al (2), to *soil,
stain; desecrate*
2490 châlal (2), to
profane, defile
2930 ṭâmê' (25), to *be
morally contaminated*
2936 ṭânaph (1), to *soil,
make dirty*
733 arsĕnŏkŏitēs (1),
sodomite
2840 kŏinŏō (6), to *make
profane*
3392 miainō (1), to
contaminate
5351 phthĕirō (1), to
spoil, ruin; to *deprave*

DEFILED
1351 gâ'al (2), to *soil,
stain; desecrate*
2490 châlal (5), to
profane, defile
2610 chânêph (3), to *soil,
be defiled*
2930 ṭâmê' (44), to *be
morally contaminated*
2931 ṭâmê' (5), *foul;
ceremonially impure*
2933 ṭâmâh (1), to *be
ceremonially impure*
5953 'âlal (1), to *glean;* to
overdo
6031 'ânâh (1), to *afflict,
be afflicted*
6942 qâdâsh (1), to *be,
make clean*
2839 kŏinŏs (1),
common, i.e. *profane*
3392 miainō (4), to
contaminate
3435 mŏlunō (3), to *soil,
make impure*

DEFILEDST
2490 châlal (1), to
profane, defile

DEFILETH
2490 châlal (1), to *profane, defile*
2610 chânêph (1), to *soil, be defiled*
2930 ṭâmê' (1), to *be foul; be morally contaminated*
2840 *kŏinŏŏ* (5), to *make profane*
4695 *spilŏŏ* (1), to *stain or soil*

DEFRAUD
6231 'âshaq (1), to *oppress; to defraud*
650 *apŏstĕrĕŏ* (3), to *despoil or defraud*
4122 *plĕŏnĕktĕŏ* (1), to *be covetous*

DEFRAUDED
6231 'âshaq (2), to *oppress; to defraud*
650 *apŏstĕrĕŏ* (1), to *despoil or defraud*
4122 *plĕŏnĕktĕŏ* (1), to *be covetous*

DEFY
2194 zâ'am (2), to *be enraged*
2778 châraph (3), to *spend the winter*

DEGENERATE
5494 çûwr (1), *turned* off; *deteriorated*

DEGREE
898 bathmŏs (1), *grade* of dignity
5011 tapĕinŏs (2), *humiliated, lowly*

DEGREES
4609 ma'ălâh (24), *thought* arising

DEHAVITES
1723 Dahăvâ' (Ch.) (1), *Dahava*

DEKAR
1857 Deqer (1), *stab*

DELAIAH
1806 D[e]lâyâh (6), *Jehovah has delivered*

DELAY
309 'âchar (1), to *remain; to delay; to procrastinate*
311 anabŏlē (1), *putting off, delay*
3635 ŏknĕŏ (1), to *be slow, delay*

DELAYED
954 bûwsh (1), to *be disappointed; delayed*
4102 mâhahh (1), to *be reluctant*

DELAYETH
5549 chrŏnizŏ (2), to *take time, i.e. linger*

DELECTABLE
2530 châmad (1), to *delight in; lust for*

DELICACIES
4764 strēnŏs (1), *luxury, sensuality*

DELICATE
6026 'ânag (1), to *be soft or pliable*
6028 'ânŏg (3), *luxurious*
8588 ta'ănûwg (1), *luxury; delight*

DELICATELY
4574 ma'ădân (2), *delicacy; pleasure*
6445 pânaq (1), to *enervate, reduce vigor*
5172 truphē (1), *luxury or debauchery*

DELICATENESS
6026 'ânag (1), to *be soft or pliable*

DELICATES
5730 'êden (1), *pleasure*

DELICIOUSLY
4763 strēniaŏ (2), to *be luxurious, live sensually*

DELIGHT
1523 gîyl (1), *rejoice*
2530 châmad (1), to *delight in; lust for*
2531 chemed (1), *delight*
2654 châphêts (17), to *be pleased with, desire*
2655 châphêts (1), *pleased with*
2656 chêphets (3), *pleasure; desire*
2836 châshaq (1), to *join; to love, delight*
4574 ma'ădân (1), *delicacy; pleasure*
5276 nâ'êm (1), to *be agreeable*
6026 'ânag (6), to *be soft or pliable*
6027 'ôneg (1), *luxury*
7521 râtsâh (2), to *be pleased with*
7522 râtsôwn (5), *delight*
8173 shâ'a' (4), to *fondle, please or amuse* (self) *dismay, i.e. stare*
8191 sha'shûa' (4), *enjoyment*
8588 ta'ănûwg (1), *luxury; delight*
4913 sunēdŏmai (1), to *rejoice in with oneself*

DELIGHTED
2654 châphêts (10), to *be pleased with, desire*
5727 'âdan (1), to *be soft or pleasant*
6026 'ânag (1), to *be soft or pliable*

DELIGHTEST
7521 râtsâh (1), to *be pleased with*

DELIGHTETH
2654 châphêts (12), to *be pleased with, desire*
7521 râtsâh (2), to *be pleased with*

DELIGHTS
5730 'êden (1), *pleasure*
8191 sha'shûa' (3), *enjoyment*
8588 ta'ănûwg (2), *luxury; delight*

DELIGHTSOME
2656 chêphets (1), *pleasure; desire*

DELILAH
1807 D[e]lîylâh (6), *languishing*

DELIVER
579 'ânâh (1), to *meet, to happen*
1350 gâ'al (1), to *redeem; to be the next of kin*
2502 châlats (5), to *depart; to deliver*
3467 yâsha' (3), to *make safe, free*
4042 mâgan (2), to *rescue, to surrender*
4422 mâlaṭ (17), to *be delivered; be smooth*
4672 mâtsâ' (1), to *find or acquire; to occur*
5186 nâṭâh (1), to *stretch or spread out*
5337 nâtsal (115), to *deliver*
5338 n[e]tsal (Ch.) (2), to *extricate, deliver*
5414 nâthan (78), to *give*
5462 çâgar (10), to *shut up; to surrender*
6299 pâdâh (3), to *ransom; to release*
6308 pâda' (1), to *retrieve*
6403 pâlaṭ (11), to *escape; to deliver*
6561 pâraq (1), to *break off or crunch; to deliver*
7725 shûwb (5), to *turn back; to return*
7804 sh[e]zab (Ch.) (6), to *leave; to free*
8000 sh[e]lam (Ch.) (1), to *restore; be safe*
8199 shâphaṭ (1), to *judge*
525 apallassŏ (1), to *release; be reconciled*
1325 didŏmi (1), to *give*
1807 ĕxairĕŏ (2), to *tear out; to select; to release*
3860 paradidŏmi (15), to *hand over*
4506 rhuŏmai (8), to *rescue*
5483 charizŏmai (2), to *grant as a favor, rescue*

DELIVERANCE
2020 hatstsâlâh (1), *rescue, deliverance*
3444 y[e]shûw'âh (2), *deliverance; aid*
6405 pallêṭ (1), *escape*
6413 p[e]lêyṭâh (5), *escaped portion*
8668 t[e]shûw'âh (5), *rescue, deliverance*
629 apŏlutrōsis (1), *ransom in full*
859 aphĕsis (1), *pardon, freedom*

DELIVERANCES
3444 y[e]shûw'âh (1), *deliverance; aid*

DELIVERED
2502 châlats (9), to *depart; to deliver*
3052 y[e]hab (Ch.) (1), to *give*

3205 yâlad (6), to *bear young; to father a child*
3467 yâsha' (8), to *make safe, free*
4042 mâgan (1), to *rescue, to surrender*
4422 mâlaṭ (16), to *be delivered; be smooth*
4560 mâçar (1), to *set apart; apostatize*
4672 mâtsâ' (1), to *find or acquire; to occur*
5234 nâkar (1), to *acknowledge, care for*
5337 nâtsal (58), to *deliver*
5414 nâthan (98), to *give*
5462 çâgar (6), to *shut up; to surrender*
5674 'âbar (1), to *cross over; to transition*
6299 pâdâh (2), to *ransom; to release*
6403 pâlaṭ (3), to *slip out, i.e. escape; to deliver*
6487 piqqâdôwn (2), *deposit*
7804 sh[e]zab (Ch.) (2), to *leave; to free*
325 anadidŏmi (1), to *hand over, deliver*
525 apallassŏ (1), to *release; be reconciled*
591 apŏdidŏmi (2), to *give away*
1080 gĕnnaō (1), to *procreate, regenerate*
1325 didŏmi (2), to *give*
1560 ĕkdŏtŏs (1), *surrendered*
1659 ĕlĕuthĕrŏŏ (1), to *exempt, liberate*
1807 ĕxairĕŏ (2), to *tear out; to select; to release*
1825 ĕxĕgĕirō (1), to *resuscitate; release*
1929 ĕpididŏmi (2), to *give over*
2673 katargĕŏ (1), to *be, render entirely useless*
3860 paradidŏmi (44), to *hand over*
4506 rhuŏmai (9), to *rescue*
5088 tiktō (5), to *produce from seed*

DELIVEREDST
5414 nâthan (1), to *give*
3860 paradidŏmi (2), to *hand over*

DELIVERER
3467 yâsha' (2), to *make safe, free*
5337 nâtsal (1), to *deliver*
6403 pâlaṭ (5), to *slip out, i.e. escape; to deliver*
3086 lutrōtēs (1), *redeemer, deliverer*
4506 rhuŏmai (1), to *rescue*

DELIVEREST
5337 nâtsal (1), to *deliver*
6403 pâlaṭ (1), to *slip out, i.e. escape; to deliver*

DELIVERETH
2502 châlats (2), to *depart; to deliver*
5337 nâtsal (7), to *deliver*

DELIVERING
5414 nâthan (1), to *give*
6403 pâlaṭ (1), to *slip* out,
i.e. *escape;* to *deliver*
6475 pâtsaĥ (1), to *rend,*
i.e. *open*
7804 sheᶻzab (Ch.) (1), to
leave; to *free*

DELIVERING
1807 ĕxairĕō (1), to *tear
out;* to *select;* to *release*
3860 paradidōmi (2), to
hand over

DELIVERY
3205 yâlad (1), to *bear
young;* to *father a child*

DELUSION
4106 planē (1),
fraudulence; straying

DELUSIONS
8586 ta'ălûwl (1), *caprice*
(as a fit *coming on*)

DEMAND
7592 shâ'al (3), to *ask*
7595 sheᵉêlâ' (Ch.) (1),
judicial *decision*

DEMANDED
559 'âmar (1), to *say*
7592 shâ'al (1), to *ask*
7593 sheᵉêl (Ch.) (1), to
ask
1905 ĕpĕrōtaō (2), to
inquire, seek
4441 punthanōmai (2), to
ask for information

DEMAS
1214 Dēmas (3), *Demas*

DEMETRIUS
1216 Dēmētriŏs (3),
Demetrius

DEMONSTRATION
585 apŏdĕixis (1),
manifestation, proof

DEN
1358 gôb (Ch.) (10), lion
pit
3975 meᵉûwrâh (1),
serpent's *hole* or *den*
4583 mâ'ôwn (2), *retreat*
or asylum *dwelling*
4585 meᵉôwnâh (1), *abode*
4631 meᵉârâh (1), dark
cavern
5520 çôk (1), *hut* of
entwined boughs
4693 spēlaiŏn (3),
cavern; hiding-place

DENIED
3584 kâchash (2), to *lie,
disown;* to *disappoint*
4513 mâna' (1), to *deny,
refuse*
533 aparnĕŏmai (2),
disown, deny
720 arnĕŏmai (14), to
disavow, reject

DENIETH
720 arnĕŏmai (4), to
disavow, reject

DENOUNCE
5046 nâgad (1), to
announce

DENS
695 'ereb (1), *hiding
place; lair*

DEPARTED
4492 minhârâh (1),
cavern, fissure
4585 meᵉôwnâh (4), *abode*
4631 meᵉârâh (1), dark
cavern
4693 spēlaiŏn (2),
cavern; hiding-place

DENY
3584 kâchash (3), to *lie,
disown;* to *disappoint,
cringe*
4513 mâna' (1), to *deny,
refuse*
7725 shûwb (1), to *turn
back;* to *return*
483 antilĕgō (1), to
dispute, refuse
533 aparnĕŏmai (11),
disown, deny
720 arnĕŏmai (7), to
disavow, reject

DENYING
720 arnĕŏmai (4), to
disavow, reject

DEPART
1540 gâlâh (1), to
denude; uncover
1980 hâlak (3), to *walk;
live a certain way*
3212 yâlak (15), to *walk;
to live; to carry*
3249 yâçûwr (1),
departing
3318 yâtsâ' (3), to *go,
bring out*
3363 yâqa' (1), to *be
dislocated*
3868 lûwz (2), to *depart;
to be perverse*
4185 mûwsh (8), to
withdraw
5493 çûwr (42), to *turn* off
5927 'âlâh (2), to *ascend,
be high, mount*
6852 tsâphar (1), to
return
7971 shâlach (4), to *send
away*
8159 shâ'âh (1), to *be
nonplussed, bewildered*
321 anagō (1), to *lead
up;* to *bring out;* to *sail*
360 analuō (1), to *depart*
565 apĕrchōmai (4), to
go off, i.e. *depart*
630 apŏluō (2), to *relieve,
release*
672 apŏchōrĕō (1), to *go
away, leave*
868 aphistēmi (4), to
desist, desert
1607 ĕkpŏrĕuŏmai (2), to
depart, be discharged
1633 ĕkchōrĕō (1), to
depart, go away
1826 ĕxĕimi (1), *leave;
escape*
1831 ĕxĕrchōmai (7), to
issue; to *leave*
3327 mĕtabainō (3), to
depart, move from
4198 pŏrĕuŏmai (5), to
go, come; to *travel*
5217 hupagō (1), to
withdraw or *retire*
5562 chōrĕō (6), to *pass,
enter;* to *hold, admit*

DEPARTED
935 bôw' (1), to *go, come*
1540 gâlâh (3), to
denude; uncover
1980 hâlak (3), to *walk;
live a certain way*
3212 yâlak (47), to *walk;
to live;* to *carry*
3318 yâtsâ' (10), to *go,
bring out*
4185 mûwsh (2), to
withdraw
5074 nâdad (1), to *rove,
flee;* to *drive away*
5265 nâça' (30), *start* on
a journey
5493 çûwr (31), to *turn* off
5709 'ădâ' (Ch.) (1), to
pass on or *continue*
5927 'âlâh (1), to *ascend,
be high, mount*
321 anagō (2), to *lead
up;* to *bring out;* to *sail*
402 anachōrĕō (8), to
retire, withdraw
525 apallassō (1), to
release; be reconciled
565 apĕrchōmai (24), to
go off, i.e. *depart*
630 apŏluō (1), to *relieve,
release;* to *let die,
pardon* or *divorce*
673 apŏchōrizō (2), to
rend apart; to *separate*
868 aphistēmi (6), to
desist, desert
1316 diachōrizŏmai (1),
to *remove* (oneself)
1330 diĕrchōmai (1), to
traverse, travel through
1607 ĕkpŏrĕuŏmai (1), to
depart, be discharged
1826 ĕxĕimi (1), *leave;
escape*
1831 ĕxĕrchōmai (22), to
issue; to *leave*
2718 katĕrchōmai (1), to
go, come down
3327 mĕtabainō (3), to
depart, move from
3332 mĕtairō (2), to
move on, leave
3855 paragō (1), to *go
along* or *away*
4198 pŏrĕuŏmai (6), to
go, come; to *travel*
5562 chōrĕō (1), to *pass,
enter;* to *hold, admit*
5563 chōrizō (1), to *part;
to go away*

DEPARTETH
3212 yâlak (2), to *walk;
to live;* to *carry*
4185 mûwsh (1), to
withdraw
5493 çûwr (3), to *turn* off
672 apŏchōrĕō (1), to *go
away, leave*

DEPARTING
3318 yâtsâ' (2), to *go,
bring out*
5253 nâçag (1), to *retreat*
5493 çûwr (2), to *turn* off
672 apŏchōrĕō (1), to *go
away, leave*
867 aphixis (1),
departure, leaving
868 aphistēmi (1), to
desist, desert

1831 ĕxĕrchōmai (1), to
issue; to *leave*
1841 ĕxŏdŏs (1), *exit,* i.e.
death
5217 hupagō (1), to
withdraw or *retire*

DEPARTURE
3318 yâtsâ' (1), to *go,
bring out*
359 analusis (1),
departure

DEPOSED
5182 neᶜchath (Ch.) (1), to
descend; to *depose*

DEPRIVED
5382 nâshâh (1), to *forget*
6485 pâqad (1), to *visit,
care for, count*
7921 shâkôl (1), to
miscarry

DEPTH
6009 'âmaq (1), to *be,
make deep*
6012 'âmêq (1), *deep,
obscure*
8415 teᵉhôwm (5), *abyss*
of the sea, i.e. the *deep*
899 bathŏs (4), *extent;
mystery,* i.e. *deep*
3989 pĕlagŏs (1), deep or
open sea

DEPTHS
4615 ma'ămâq (3), *deep
place*
4688 metsôwlâh (2), *deep
place*
6010 'êmeq (1), broad
depression or valley
8415 teᵉhôwm (10), *abyss*
of the sea, i.e. the *deep*
899 bathŏs (1), *extent;
mystery,* i.e. *deep*

DEPUTIES
6346 pechâh (2), *prefect,
officer*
446 anthupatŏs (1),
Roman *proconsul*

DEPUTY
5324 nâtsab (1), to *station*
446 anthupatŏs (4),
Roman *proconsul*

DERBE
1191 Dĕrbē (4), *Derbe*

DERIDE
7832 sâchaq (1), to
laugh; to *scorn;* to *play*

DERIDED
1592 ĕkmuktĕrizō (2), to
sneer at, ridicule

DERISION
3887 lûwts (1), to *scoff;* to
interpret; to *intercede*
3932 lâ'ag (5), to *deride;
to speak unintelligibly*
7047 qeleç (3),
laughing-stock
7814 seᶜchôwq (5),
laughter; scorn
7832 sâchaq (1), to
laugh; to *scorn;* to *play*

DESCEND
3381 yârad (6), to
descend
2597 katabainō (4), to
descend

DESCENDED
3381 yârad (12), to *descend*
2597 katabainō (7), to *descend*

DESCENDETH
2718 katĕrchŏmai (1), to go, *come down*

DESCENDING
3381 yârad (1), to *descend*
2597 katabainō (7), to *descend*

DESCENT
35 agĕnĕalŏgētŏs (1), *unregistered* as to birth
1075 gĕnĕalŏgĕŏ (1), *trace in genealogy*
2600 katabasis (1), *declivity, slope*

DESCRIBE
3789 kâthab (4), to *write*

DESCRIBED
3789 kâthab (2), to *write*

DESCRIBETH
1125 graphō (1), to *write*
3004 lĕgō (1), to *say*

DESCRY
8446 tûwr (1), to *wander, meander* for trade

DESERT
1576 gᵉmûwl (1), *act; service; reward*
2723 chorbâh (1), *desolation, dry* desert
3452 yᵉshîymôwn (4), *desolation*
4057 midbâr (13), *desert; also speech; mouth*
6160 'ărâbâh (8), *desert, wasteland*
6728 tsîyîy (3), *desert-dweller; beast*
2048 ĕrēmŏs (12), *remote place, deserted place*

DESERTS
2723 chorbâh (2), *desolation, dry* desert
4941 mishpât (1), *verdict; formal decree; justice*
6160 'ărâbâh (1), *desert, wasteland*
2047 ĕrēmia (1), *place of solitude, remoteness*
2048 ĕrēmŏs (1), *remote place, deserted place*

DESERVING
1576 gᵉmûwl (1), *act; service; reward*

DESIRABLE
2531 chemed (3), *delight*

DESIRE
15 'âbeh (1), *longing*
35 'abîyôwnâh (1), *caper*-berry
183 'âvâh (7), to *wish for, desire*
1156 bᵉ'â' (Ch.) (1), to *seek or ask*
1245 bâqash (1), to *search* out; to *strive*
2530 châmad (4), to *delight in; lust for*
2532 chemdâh (3), *delight*

2654 châphêts (6), to *be pleased* with, *desire*
2655 châphêts (2), *pleased* with
2656 chêphets (9), *pleasure; desire*
2836 châshaq (1), to *join; to love, delight*
2837 chêsheq (1), *delight, desired* thing
3700 kâçaph (1), to *pine* after; to *fear*
4261 machmâd (3), *object of desire*
5315 nephesh (3), *life; breath; soul; wind*
5375+5315 nâsâ' (2), to *lift up*
7522 râtsôwn (3), *delight*
7592 shâ'al (3), to *ask*
7602 shâ'aph (1), to *be angry; to hasten*
8378 ta'ăvâh (14), *longing; delight*
8420 tâv (1), *mark, signature*
8669 tᵉshûwqâh (3), *longing*
154 aitĕō (5), to *ask* for
515 axiŏō (1), to *deem entitled* or *fit, worthy*
1934 ĕpizētĕō (2), to *demand, to crave*
1937 ĕpithumĕō (4), to *long* for
1939 ĕpithumia (3), *longing*
1971 ĕpipŏthĕō (1), *intensely crave*
1972 ĕpipŏthēsis (2), *longing for*
1974 ĕpipŏthia (1), *intense longing*
2065 ĕrōtaō (1), to *interrogate; to request*
2107 ĕudŏkia (1), *delight, kindness, wish*
2206 zēlŏō (2), to *have warmth* of feeling for
2309 thĕlō (9), to *will; to desire; to choose*
3713 ŏrĕgŏmai (2), to *reach* out after, *long* for

DESIRED
183 'âvâh (5), to *wish* for, *desire*
559 'âmar (1), to *say, speak*
1156 bᵉ'â' (Ch.) (2), to *seek or ask*
2530 châmad (5), to *delight in; lust for*
2532 chemdâh (1), *delight*
2654 châphêts (1), to *be pleased* with, *desire*
2656 chêphets (2), *pleasure; desire*
2836 châshaq (2), to *join; to love, delight*
3700 kâçaph (1), to *pine* after; to *fear*
7592 shâ'al (4), to *ask*
154 aitĕō (10), to *ask* for
1809 ĕxaitĕŏmai (1), to *demand*
1905 ĕpĕrōtaō (1), to *inquire, seek*

1934 ĕpizētĕō (1), to *demand, to crave*
1937 ĕpithumĕō (1), to *long* for
1939 ĕpithumia (1), *longing*
2065 ĕrōtaō (4), to *interrogate; to request*
2212 zētĕō (1), to *seek*
2309 thĕlō (1), to *will; to desire; to choose*
3870 parakalĕō (5), to *call, invite*

DESIREDST
7592 shâ'al (1), to *ask*
3870 parakalĕō (1), to *call, invite*

DESIRES
3970 ma'ăvay (1), *desire*
4862 mish'âlâh (1), *request*
2307 thĕlēma (1), *purpose; inclination*

DESIREST
2654 châphêts (2), to *be pleased* with, *desire*

DESIRETH
183 'âvâh (4), to *wish for, desire*
559 'âmar (1), to *say, speak*
2530 châmad (2), to *delight in; lust for*
2655 châphêts (1), *pleased* with
2656 chêphets (1), *pleasure; desire*
7592 shâ'al (1), to *ask*
7602 shâ'aph (1), to *be angry; to hasten*
8378 ta'ăvâh (3), *longing; delight*
1937 ĕpithumĕō (1), to *long* for
2065 ĕrōtaō (1), to *interrogate; to request*
2309 thĕlō (1), to *will; to desire; to choose*

DESIRING
154 aitĕō (2), to *ask* for
1937 ĕpithumĕō (1), to *long* for
1971 ĕpipŏthĕō (3), *intensely crave*
2212 zētĕō (2), to *seek*
2309 thĕlō (2), to *will; to desire; to choose*
3870 parakalĕō (2), to *call, invite*

DESIROUS
183 'âvâh (1), to *wish for, desire*
2309 thĕlō (3), to *will; to desire; to choose*
2442 himĕirŏmai (1), to *long for, desire*
2755 kĕnŏdŏxŏs (1), *self-conceited*

DESOLATE
490 'almânâh (2), *widow*
816 'âsham (6), to *be guilty; to be punished*
820 'ashmân (1), *uninhabited places*
910 bâdâd (1), *separate, alone*

1327 battâh (1), *area of desolation*
1565 galmûwd (2), *sterile, barren, desolate*
2717 chârab (5), to *parch through drought; desolate, destroy*
2723 chorbâh (7), *desolation, dry* desert
3173 yâchîyd (1), *only son; alone; beloved*
3341 yâtsath (1), to *burn or set on fire*
3456 yâsham (4), to *lie waste*
3582 kâchad (1), to *destroy; to hide*
4923 mᵉshammâh (2), *waste; object of horror*
5352 nâqâh (1), to *be, make clean; to be bare*
7722 shôw' (2), *tempest; devastation*
8047 shammâh (11), *ruin; consternation*
8074 shâmêm (43), to *devastate; to stupefy*
8076 shâmêm (8), *ruined, deserted*
8077 shᵉmâmâh (42), *devastation*
2048 ĕrēmŏs (4), *remote place, deserted place*
2049 ĕrēmŏō (2), to *lay waste*
3443 mŏnŏō (1), to *isolate, i.e. bereave*

DESOLATION
2721 chôreb (1), *ruined; desolate*
2723 chorbâh (5), *desolation, dry* desert
4875 mᵉshôw'âh (1), *ruin*
7584 sha'ăvâh (1), *rushing tempest*
7612 shê'th (1), *devastation*
7701 shôd (2), *violence, ravage, destruction*
7722 shôw' (4), *tempest; devastation*
8047 shammâh (12), *ruin; consternation*
8074 shâmêm (3), to *devastate; to stupefy*
8077 shᵉmâmâh (11), *devastation*
2049 ĕrēmŏō (2), to *lay waste*
2050 ĕrēmōsis (3), *despoliation, desolation*

DESOLATIONS
2723 chorbâh (3), *desolation, dry* desert
4876 mashshûw'âh (1), *ruin*
8047 shammâh (1), *ruin; consternation*
8074 shâmêm (4), to *devastate; to stupefy*
8077 shᵉmâmâh (2), *devastation*

DESPAIR
2976 yâ'ash (2), to *despond, despair*
1820 ĕxapŏrĕŏmai (1), to *be utterly at a loss*

DESPAIRED
1820 ĕxapŏrĕŏmai (1), to *be utterly at a loss*

DESPERATE
605 'ânash (1), to *be frail, feeble*
2976 yâ'ash (1), to *despond, despair*

DESPERATELY
605 'ânash (1), to *be frail, feeble*

DESPISE
936 bûwz (4), to *disrespect, scorn*
959 bâzâh (6), to *ridicule, scorn*
2107 zûwl (1), to *treat lightly*
3988 mâ'aç (9), to *spurn; to disappear*
5006 nâ'ats (1), to *scorn*
7043 qâlal (1), to *be easy, trifling, vile*
7590 shâ'ṭ (2), *reject by maligning*
114 athĕtĕō (1), to *disesteem, neutralize*
1848 ĕxŏuthĕnĕō (3), to *treat with contempt*
2706 kataphrŏnĕō (7), to *disesteem, despise*
3643 ŏligōrĕō (1), to *disesteem, despise*
4065 pĕriphrŏnĕō (1), to *depreciate, contemn*

DESPISED
937 bûwz (4), *disrespect, scorn*
939 bûwzâh (1), *something scorned*
959 bâzâh (26), to *ridicule, scorn*
3988 mâ'aç (12), to *spurn; to disappear*
5006 nâ'ats (6), to *scorn*
7034 qâlâh (1), to *be, hold in contempt*
7043 qâlal (2), to *be easy, trifling, vile*
7590 shâ'ṭ (1), *reject by maligning*
114 athĕtĕō (1), to *disesteem, set aside*
818 atimazō (1), to *maltreat, dishonor*
820 atimŏs (1), *without honor*
1519+3762+3049 ĕis (1), *to or into*
1848 ĕxŏuthĕnĕō (3), to *treat with contempt*

DESPISERS
865 aphilagathŏs (1), *hostile to virtue*
2707 kataphrŏntēs (1), *contemner, scoffer*

DESPISEST
2706 kataphrŏnĕō (1), to *disesteem, despise*

DESPISETH
936 bûwz (4), to *disrespect, scorn*
959 bâzâh (4), to *ridicule, scorn*
960 bâzôh (1), *scorned*
3988 mâ'aç (3), to *spurn; to disappear*

DESPISING
2706 kataphrŏnĕō (1), to *disesteem, despise*

DESPITE
7589 she'âṭ (1), *contempt*
1796 ĕnubrizō (1), to *insult*

DESPITEFUL
7589 she'âṭ (2), *contempt*
5197 hubristēs (1), *maltreater*

DESPITEFULLY
1908 ĕpērĕazō (2), to *insult, slander*
5195 hubrizō (1), to *exercise violence*

DESTITUTE
2638 châçer (1), *lacking*
5800 'âzab (1), to *loosen; relinquish; permit*
6168 'ârâh (1), to *empty, pour out; demolish*
6199 'ar'âr (1), *naked; poor*
8047 shammâh (1), *ruin; consternation*
650 apŏstĕrĕō (1), to *deprive; to despoil*
3007 lĕipō (1), to *fail or be absent*
5302 hustĕrĕō (1), to *be inferior; to fall short*

DESTROY
6 'âbad (38), *perish; destroy*
7 'âbad (Ch.) (4), *perish; destroy*
9 'ăbêdâh (1), *destruction*
622 'âçaph (1), to *gather, collect*
816 'âsham (1), to *be guilty; to be punished*
1104 bâla' (7), to *swallow; to destroy*
1641 gârar (1), to *ruminate; to saw*
1792 dâkâ' (1), to *be contrite, be humbled*
1820 dâmâh (1), to *be silent; to fail, cease*
1949 hûwm (1), to *make an uproar; agitate*
2000 hâmam (3), to *disturb, drive, destroy*
2040 hâraç (1), to *pull down; break, destroy*
2254 châbal (5), to *pervert, destroy*
2255 chăbal (Ch.) (2), to *ruin, destroy*
2763 charam (14), to *devote to destruction*
3238 yânâh (1), to *rage or be violent*
3423 yârash (1), to *inherit; to impoverish*
3615 kâlâh (1), to *complete, consume*
3772 kârath (2), to *cut (off, down or asunder)*
4049 me'gar (Ch.) (1), to *overthrow, depose*
4135 mûwl (3), to *circumcise*

4191 mûwth (1), to *die; to kill*
4229 mâchâh (2), to *erase; to grease*
4889 mashchîyth (4), *destruction; corruption*
5255 nâçach (1), to *tear away*
5362 nâqaph (1), to *strike; to surround*
5395 nâsham (1), to *destroy*
5422 nâthats (4), to *tear down*
5595 çâphâh (3), to *scrape; to remove*
6789 tsâmath (4), to *extirpate, destroy*
6979 qûwr (1), to *throw forth; to wall up*
7665 shâbar (2), to *burst*
7703 shâdad (1), to *ravage*
7722 shōw' (1), *tempest; devastation*
7843 shâchath (68), to *decay; to ruin*
7921 shâkôl (1), to *miscarry*
8045 shâmad (40), to *desolate*
8074 shâmêm (2), to *devastate; to stupefy*
622 apŏllumi (19), to *destroy fully; to perish*
1311 diaphthĕirō (1), to *ruin, to decay*
2647 kataluō (6), to *demolish; to halt*
2673 katargĕō (3), to *be, render entirely useless*
3089 luō (2), to *loosen*
5351 phthĕirō (1), to *spoil, ruin; to deprave*

DESTROYED
6 'âbad (17), *perish; destroy*
7 'âbad (Ch.) (1), *perish; destroy*
1104 bâla' (1), to *swallow; to destroy*
1696 dâbar (1), to *speak, say; to subdue*
1792 dâkâ' (1), to *pulverize; be contrite*
1820 dâmâh (1), to *be silent; to fail, cease*
1822 dummâh (1), *desolation*
2026 hârag (1), to *kill, slaughter*
2040 hâraç (3), to *pull down; break, destroy*
2254 châbal (2), to *pervert, destroy*
2255 chăbal (Ch.) (3), to *ruin, destroy*
2717 chârab (1), to *desolate, destroy*
2718 chărab (Ch.) (1), to *demolish*
2763 charam (23), to *devote to destruction*
2764 chêrem (1), *extermination*
3615 kâlâh (1), to *cease, be finished, perish*
3772 kârath (2), to *cut (off, down or asunder)*

3807 kâthath (3), to *bruise, strike, beat*
4229 mâchâh (3), to *erase; to grease*
5422 nâthats (1), to *tear down*
5428 nâthash (1), to *tear away, be uprooted*
5595 çâphâh (2), to *scrape; to remove*
5642 çe'thar (Ch.) (1), to *demolish*
6658 tsâdâh (1), to *desolate*
6789 tsâmath (1), to *extirpate, destroy*
7321 rûwa' (1), to *shout*
7665 shâbar (7), to *burst*
7703 shâdad (1), to *ravage*
7843 shâchath (21), to *decay; to ruin*
8045 shâmad (43), to *desolate*
8074 shâmêm (1), to *devastate; to stupefy*
622 apŏllumi (7), to *destroy fully; to perish*
1311 diaphthĕirō (1), to *ruin, to pervert*
1842 ĕxŏlŏthrĕuō (1), to *extirpate*
2507 kathairĕō (2), to *lower, or demolish*
2647 kataluō (1), to *demolish; to halt*
2673 katargĕō (2), to *be, render entirely useless*
3645 ŏlŏthrĕuō (1), to *slay, destroy*
4199 pŏrthĕō (2), to *ravage, pillage*
5356 phthŏra (1), *ruin; depravity, corruption*

DESTROYER
2717 chârab (1), to *desolate, destroy*
6530 pe'rîyts (1), *violent, i.e. a tyrant*
7703 shâdad (1), to *ravage*
7843 shâchath (3), to *decay; to ruin*
3644 ŏlŏthrĕutēs (1), *serpent which destroys*

DESTROYERS
2040 hâraç (1), to *pull down; break, destroy*
4191 mûwth (1), to *die; to kill*
7843 shâchath (1), to *decay; to ruin*
8154 shâçâh (1), to *plunder*

DESTROYEST
6 'âbad (1), *perish; destroy*
7843 shâchath (1), to *decay; to ruin*
2647 kataluō (2), to *demolish; to halt*

DESTROYETH
6 'âbad (4), *perish; destroy*
3615 kâlâh (1), to *complete, consume*
4229 mâchâh (1), to *erase; to grease*

7843 shâchath (2), to *decay;* to *ruin*

DESTROYING
1104 bâla' (1), to *swallow;* to *destroy*
2763 charam (5), to *devote* to destruction
4889 mashchîyth (1), *destruction; corruption*
4892 mashchêth (1), *destruction*
6986 qeṭeb (1), *ruin*
7843 shâchath (5), to *decay;* to *ruin*

DESTRUCTION
6 'âbad (1), *perish; destroy*
10 'ăbaddôh (1), *perishing*
11 'ăbaddôwn (5), *perishing*
12 'abdân (1), *perishing*
13 'obdân (1), *perishing*
343 'êyd (7), *misfortune, ruin, disaster*
1793 dakkâ' (1), *crushed, destroyed; contrite*
2035 hărîyçûwth (1), *demolition, destruction*
2041 hereç (1), *demolition, destruction*
2256 chebel (1), *company, band*
2475 chălôwph (1), *destitute orphans*
2764 chêrem (2), *extermination*
3589 kîyd (1), *calamity, destruction*
4103 mᵉhûwmâh (3), *confusion* or uproar
4288 mᵉchittâh (7), *ruin; consternation*
4876 mashshûw'âh (1), *ruin*
4889 mashchîyth (2), *destruction; corruption*
6365 pîyd (2), *misfortune*
6986 qeṭeb (2), *ruin*
6987 qôṭeb (1), *extermination*
7089 qᵉphâdâh (1), *terror*
7171 qerets (1), *extirpation*
7591 shᵉ'îyâh (1), *desolation*
7667 sheber (20), *fracture; ruin*
7670 shibrôwn (1), *ruin*
7701 shôd (7), *violence, ravage, destruction*
7722 shôw' (2), *tempest; devastation*
7843 shâchath (1), to *decay;* to *ruin*
7845 shachath (2), *pit; destruction*
8045 shâmad (1), to *desolate*
8395 tᵉbûwçâh (1), *ruin*
8399 tablîyth (1), *consumption*
684 apôlĕia (5), *ruin* or *loss*
2506 kathairĕsis (2), *demolition*
3639 ŏlĕthrŏs (4), *death, punishment*

4938 suntrimma (1), complete *ruin*

DESTRUCTIONS
2723 chorbâh (1), *desolation, dry desert*
7722 shôw' (1), *tempest; devastation*
7825 shᵉchîyth (1), *pit*-fall

DETAIN
6113 'âtsar (2), to *hold back;* to *maintain*

DETAINED
6113 'âtsar (1), to *hold back;* to *maintain*

DETERMINATE
3724 hŏrizō (1), to *appoint, decree, specify*

DETERMINATION
4941 mishpâṭ (1), *verdict; formal decree; justice*

DETERMINED
559 'âmar (1), to *say*
2782 chârats (6), to *be alert, to decide*
2852 châthak (1), to *decree*
3289 yâ'ats (2), to *advise*
3615 kâlâh (5), to *cease, be finished, perish*
7760 sûwm (1), to *put, place*
1011 bŏulĕuō (1), to *deliberate;* to *resolve*
1956 ĕpiluō (1), to *explain;* to *decide*
2919 krinō (7), to *decide; to try, condemn, punish*
3724 hŏrizō (3), to *appoint, decree, specify*
4309 prŏŏrizō (1), to *predetermine*
5021 tassō (1), to *assign* or *dispose*

DETEST
8262 shâqats (1), to *loathe, pollute*

DETESTABLE
8251 shiqqûwts (6), *disgusting idol*

DEUEL
1845 Dᵉ'ûw'êl (4), *known of God*

DEVICE
1902 higgâyôwn (1), *musical notation*
2808 cheshbôwn (1), *contrivance; plan*
4209 mᵉzimmâh (1), *plan; sagacity*
4284 machăshâbâh (4), *contrivance; plan*
1761 ĕnthumēsis (1), *deliberation; idea*

DEVICES
2154 zimmâh (1), bad *plan*
4156 môw'êtsâh (1), *purpose, plan*
4209 mᵉzimmâh (5), *plan; sagacity*
4284 machăshâbâh (8), *contrivance; plan*
3540 nŏēma (1), *perception, purpose*

DEVIL
1139 daimŏnizŏmai (7), to *be demonized*
1140 daimŏniŏn (18), *demonic being*
1142 daimōn (1), evil *supernatural spirit*
1228 diabŏlŏs (35), *traducer,* i.e. *Satan*

DEVILISH
1141 daimŏniōdēs (1), *demon-like, of the devil*

DEVILS
7700 shêd (2), *demon*
8163 sâ'îyr (2), *shaggy; he-goat; goat idol*
1139 daimŏnizŏmai (6), to *be demonized*
1140 daimŏniŏn (40), *demonic being*
1142 daimōn (4), evil *supernatural spirit*

DEVISE
2790 chârash (3), to *engrave;* to *plow*
2803 châshab (13), to *weave, fabricate*

DEVISED
908 bâdâ' (1), to *invent;* to *choose*
1819 dâmâh (1), to *resemble, liken*
2161 zâmam (3), to *plan*
2803 châshab (5), to *plot; to think, regard*
4284 machăshâbâh (1), *contrivance; plan*
4679 sŏphizō (1), to *make wise*

DEVISETH
2790 chârash (2), to *engrave;* to *plow*
2803 châshab (4), to *plot; to think, regard*
3289 yâ'ats (2), to *advise*

DEVOTE
2763 charam (1), to *devote* to destruction

DEVOTED
2763 charam (1), to *devote* to destruction
2764 chêrem (5), *doomed* object

DEVOTIONS
4574 sĕbasma (1), *object of worship*

DEVOUR
398 'âkal (57), to *eat*
399 'ăkal (Ch.) (2), to *eat*
402 'oklâh (2), *food*
7462 râ'âh (1), to *tend* a *flock,* i.e. *pasture* it
7602 shâ'aph (1), to *be angry;* to *hasten*
2068 ĕsthiō (1), to *eat*
2666 katapinō (1), to *devour by swallowing*
2719 katĕsthiō (6), to *devour*

DEVOURED
398 'âkal (42), to *eat*
399 'ăkal (Ch.) (2), to *eat*
402 'oklâh (1), *food*
1104 bâla' (2), to *swallow;* to *destroy*

3898 lâcham (1), to *fight* a *battle,* i.e. *consume*
2719 katĕsthiō (5), to *devour*

DEVOURER
398 'âkal (1), to *eat*

DEVOUREST
398 'âkal (1), to *eat*

DEVOURETH
398 'âkal (6), to *eat*
1104 bâla' (2), to *swallow;* to *destroy*
3216 yâla' (1), to *blurt* or *utter inconsiderately*
2719 katĕsthiō (1), to *devour*

DEVOURING
398 'âkal (5), to *eat*
1105 bela' (1), *gulp; destruction*

DEVOUT
2126 ĕulabēs (3), *circumspect, pious*
2152 ĕusĕbēs (3), *pious*
4576 sĕbŏmai (3), to *revere,* i.e. *adore*

DEW
2919 ṭal (30), *dew, morning mist*
2920 ṭal (Ch.) (5), *dew, morning mist*

DIADEM
4701 mitsnepheth (1), *turban*
6797 tsânîyph (2), *head-dress, turban*
6843 tsᵉphîyrâh (1), *encircling crown*

DIAL
4609 ma'ălâh (2), *thought arising*

DIAMOND
3095 yahălôm (3), (poss.) *onyx*
8068 shâmîyr (1), *thorn;* (poss.) *diamond*

DIANA
735 Artĕmis (5), *prompt*

DIBLAIM
1691 Diblayim (1), *two cakes*

DIBLATH
1689 Diblâh (1), *Diblah*

DIBON
1769 Dîybôwn (9), *pining*

DIBON-GAD
1769 Dîybôwn (2), *pining*

DIBRI
1704 Dibrîy (1), *wordy*

DID
1580 gâmal (2), to *benefit* or *requite;* to *wean*
1961 hâyâh (1), to *exist,* i.e. *be* or *become*
2052 Vâhêb (1), *Vaheb*
5648 'ăbad (Ch.) (1), to *do, work, serve*
6213 'âsâh (327), to *do* or *make*
6313 pûwg (1), to *be sluggish; be numb*
7965 shâlôwm (2), *safe; well; health, prosperity*

15 agathŏpŏiĕō (1), to be
a well-doer
91 adikĕō (1), to do
wrong
1731 ĕndĕiknumi (1), to
show, display
3000 latrĕuō (1), to
minister to God
4160 pŏiĕō (54), to make
or do
4238 prassō (1), to
execute, accomplish

DIDDEST
387 anastatŏō (1), to
disturb, cause trouble

DIDST
6213 'âsâh (14), to do or
make
6466 pâ'al (1), to do,
make or practice

DIDYMUS
1324 Didumŏs (3), twin

DIE
1478 gâva' (8), to expire,
die
4191 mûwth (255), to die;
to kill
4194 mâveth (7), death;
dead
8546 tᵉmûwthâh (1),
execution, death
599 apŏthnēskō (40), to
die off
622 apŏllumi (1), to
destroy fully; to perish
684 apŏlĕia (1), ruin or
loss
4880 sunapŏthnēskō (2),
to decease with
5053 tĕlĕutaō (3), to
finish life, i.e. expire

DIED
1478 gâva' (3), to expire,
die
4191 mûwth (154), to die;
to kill
4194 mâveth (7), death;
dead
5038 nᵉbêlâh (1), carcase
or carrion
5307 nâphal (1), to fall
599 apŏthnēskō (32), to
die off
5053 tĕlĕutaō (2), to
finish life, i.e. expire

DIEST
4191 mûwth (1), to die; to
kill

DIET
737 'ărûchâh (2), ration,
portion of food

DIETH
4191 mûwth (16), to die;
to kill
4194 mâveth (4), death;
dead
5038 nᵉbêlâh (4), carcase
or carrion
599 apŏthnēskō (2), to
die off
5053 tĕlĕutaō (3), to
finish life, i.e. expire

DIFFER
1252 diakrinō (1), to
decide; to hesitate

DIFFERENCE
914 bâdal (3), to divide,
separate, distinguish
6395 pâlâh (1), to
distinguish
1252 diakrinō (2), to
decide; to hesitate
1293 diastŏlē (2),
variation, distinction
3307 mĕrizō (1), to
disunite, differ

DIFFERENCES
1243 diairĕsis (1),
distinction or variety

DIFFERETH
1308 diaphĕrō (2), to
bear, carry; to differ

DIFFERING
1313 diaphŏrŏs (1),
varying; surpassing

DIG
2658 châphar (3), to
delve, to explore
2672 châtsab (1), to cut
stone or carve wood
2864 châthar (5), to
break or dig into
3738 kârâh (2), to dig; to
plot; to bore, hew
4626 skaptō (2), to dig

DIGGED
2658 châphar (13), to
delve, to explore
2672 châtsab (3), to cut
stone or carve wood
2864 châthar (2), to
break or dig into
3738 kârâh (8), to dig; to
plot; to bore, hew
5365 nâqar (3), to bore;
to gouge
5737 'âdar (2), to hoe a
vineyard
6131 'âqar (1), to pluck
up; to hamstring
2679 kataskaptō (1), to
destroy, be ruined
3736 ŏrussō (3), to
burrow, i.e. dig out
4626 skaptō (1), to dig

DIGGEDST
2672 châtsab (1), to cut
stone or carve wood

DIGGETH
2658 châphar (1), to
delve, to explore
3738 kârâh (2), to dig; to
plot; to bore, hew

DIGNITIES
1891 Ĕpaphrŏditŏs (2),
devoted to Venus

DIGNITY
1420 gᵉdûwlâh (1),
greatness, grandeur
4791 mârôwm (1),
elevation; haughtiness
7613 sᵉ'êth (2), elevation;
swelling scab

DIKLAH
1853 Diqlâh (2), Diklah

DILEAN
1810 Dil'ân (1), Dilan

DILIGENCE
4929 mishmâr (1), guard;
deposit; usage; example

2039 ĕrgasia (1),
occupation; profit
4704 spŏudazō (2), to
make effort
4710 spŏudē (6),
despatch; eagerness

DILIGENT
2742 chârûwts (5),
diligent, earnest
3190 yâṭab (1), to be,
make well
3966 mᵉ'ôd (1), very,
utterly
4106 mâhîyr (1), skillful
4704 spŏudazō (2), to
make effort
4705 spŏudaiŏs (1),
prompt, energetic
4707 spŏudaiŏtĕrŏs (1),
more earnest

DILIGENTLY
149 'adrazdâ' (Ch.) (1),
carefully, diligently
995 bîyn (1), to
understand; discern
3190 yâṭab (2), to be,
make well
3966 mᵉ'ôd (4), very,
utterly
5172 nâchash (1), to
prognosticate
7182 qesheb (1),
hearkening
7836 shâchar (2), to
search for
8150 shânan (1), to
pierce; to inculcate
199 akribōs (2), exactly,
carefully
1567 ĕkzētĕō (1), to seek
out
1960 ĕpimĕlōs (1),
carefully, diligently
4706 spŏudaiŏtĕrŏn (1),
more earnestly
4709 spŏudaiŏs (1),
earnestly, promptly

DIM
2821 châshak (1), to be
dark; to darken
3513 kâbad (1), to be
heavy, severe, dull
3543 kâhâh (3), to grow
dull, fade; to be faint
3544 kêheh (1), feeble;
obscure
6004 'âmam (1), to
overshadow
6965 qûwm (1), to rise
8159 shâ'âh (1), to
inspect, consider

DIMINISH
1639 gâra' (6), to shave,
remove, lessen
4591 mâ'aṭ (2), to be,
make small or few

DIMINISHED
1639 gâra' (2), to shave,
remove, lessen
4591 mâ'aṭ (3), to be,
make small or few

DIMINISHING
2275 hĕttēma (1), failure
or loss

DIMNAH
1829 Dimnâh (1),
dung-heap

DIMNESS
4155 mûw'âph (1),
obscurity; distress
4588 mâ'ûwph (1),
darkness, gloom

DIMON
1775 Dîymôwn (2),
Dimon

DIMONAH
1776 Dîymôwnâh (1),
Dimonah

DINAH
1783 Dîynâh (7), justice

DINAH'S
1783 Dîynâh (1), justice

DINAITES
1784 Dîynay (Ch.) (1),
Dinaite

DINE
398 'âkal (1), to eat
709 aristaō (2), to eat a
meal

DINED
709 aristaō (1), to eat a
meal

DINHABAH
1838 Dinhâbâh (2),
Dinhabah

DINNER
737 'ărûchâh (1), ration,
portion of food
712 aristŏn (3), breakfast
or lunch; feast

DIONYSIUS
1354 Diŏnusiŏs (1),
reveller

DIOTREPHES
1361 Diŏtrĕphēs (1),
Zeus-nourished

DIP
2881 ṭâbal (9), to dip
911 baptō (1), to
overwhelm, cover

DIPPED
2881 ṭâbal (6), to dip
4272 mâchats (1), to
crush; to subdue
911 baptō (2), to
overwhelm, cover
1686 ĕmbaptō (1), to wet

DIPPETH
1686 ĕmbaptō (2), to wet

DIRECT
3384 yârâh (1), to point;
to teach
3474 yâshar (3), to be
straight; to make right
3559 kûwn (1), to set up:
establish, fix, prepare
3787 kâshêr (1), to be
straight or right
5414 nâthan (1), to give
6186 'ârak (1), to set in a
row, i.e. arrange
2720 katĕuthunō (2), to
direct, lead, direct

DIRECTED
3559 kûwn (1), to set up:
establish, fix, prepare
6186 'ârak (1), to set in a
row, i.e. arrange
8505 tâkan (1), to
balance, i.e. measure

D

DIRECTETH
3474 yâshar (1), to be straight; to make right
3559 kûwn (2), to set up: establish, fix, prepare

DIRECTLY
413+5227 'êl (1), to, toward
1903 hâgîyn (1), (poss.) suitable or turning

DIRT
2916 țîyț (2), mud or clay
6574 parshedôn (1), crotch or anus

DISALLOW
5106 nûw' (1), to refuse, forbid, dissuade

DISALLOWED
5106 nûw' (3), to refuse, forbid, dissuade
593 apŏdŏkimazō (2), to repudiate, reject

DISANNUL
6565 pârar (2), to break up; to violate, frustrate
208 akurŏō (1), to invalidate, nullify

DISANNULLED
3722 kâphar (1), to placate or cancel

DISANNULLETH
114 athĕtĕō (1), to neutralize or set aside

DISANNULLING
115 athĕtĕsis (1), cancellation

DISAPPOINT
6923 qâdam (1), to anticipate, hasten

DISAPPOINTED
6565 pârar (1), to break up; to violate, frustrate

DISAPPOINTETH
6565 pârar (1), to break up; to violate, frustrate

DISCERN
995 bîyn (2), to understand; discern
3045 yâda' (3), to know
5234 nâkar (4), to acknowledge
7200 râ'âh (1), to see
8085 shâma' (2), to hear intelligently
1252 diakrinō (1), to decide; to hesitate
1253 diakrisis (1), estimation
1381 dŏkimazō (1), to test; to approve

DISCERNED
995 bîyn (1), to understand; discern
5234 nâkar (2), to acknowledge
350 anakrinō (1), to interrogate, determine

DISCERNER
2924 kritikŏs (1), discriminative

DISCERNETH
3045 yâda' (1), to know

DISCERNING
1252 diakrinō (1), to decide; to hesitate
1253 diakrisis (1), estimation

DISCHARGE
4917 mishlachath (1), mission; release; army

DISCHARGED
5310 nâphats (1), to dash to pieces; to scatter

DISCIPLE
3100 mathĕtĕuō (1), to become a student
3101 mathĕtēs (27), pupil, student
3102 mathētria (1), female pupil, student

DISCIPLES
3928 limmûwd (1), instructed one
3101 mathĕtēs (240), pupil, student

DISCIPLES'
3101 mathĕtēs (1), pupil, student

DISCIPLINE
4148 mûwçâr (1), reproof, warning

DISCLOSE
1540 gâlâh (1), to denude; uncover

DISCOMFITED
1949 hûwm (3), to make an uproar; agitate
2000 hâmam (2), to put in commotion
2522 châlash (1), to prostrate, lay low
2729 chârad (1), to shudder with terror
3807 kâthath (1), to bruise, strike, beat
4522 maç (1), forced labor

DISCOMFITURE
4103 mehûwmâh (1), confusion or uproar

DISCONTENTED
4751+5315 mar (1), bitter; bitterness; bitterly

DISCONTINUE
8058 shâmaț (1), to let alone, desist, remit

DISCORD
4066 mâdôwn (1), contest or quarrel
4090 medân (1), contest or quarrel

DISCOURAGE
5106 nûw' (1), to refuse, forbid, dissuade

DISCOURAGED
2865 châthath (1), to break down
4549 mâçaç (1), to waste; to faint
5106 nûw' (1), to refuse, forbid, dissuade
7114 qâtsar (1), to curtail, cut short
7533 râtsats (1), to crack in pieces, smash

DISCERNING
120 athumĕō (1), to be disheartened

DISCOVER
1540 gâlâh (10), to denude; uncover
2834 châsaph (1), to drain away or bail up
6168 'ârâh (1), to be, make bare; to empty

DISCOVERED
1540 gâlâh (18), to denude; uncover
3045 yâda' (1), to know
6168 'ârâh (1), to be, make bare; to empty
398 anaphainō (1), to appear
2657 katanŏĕō (1), to observe fully

DISCOVERETH
1540 gâlâh (1), to denude; uncover
2834 châsaph (1), to drain away or bail up

DISCOVERING
6168 'ârâh (1), to be, make bare; to empty

DISCREET
995 bîyn (2), to understand; discern
4998 sōphrōn (1), self-controlled

DISCREETLY
3562 nŏunĕchōs (1), prudently

DISCRETION
2940 ța'am (1), taste; intelligence; mandate
4209 mezimmâh (4), plan; sagacity
4941 mishpâț (2), verdict; formal decree; justice
7922 sekel (1), intelligence; success
8394 tâbûwn (1), intelligence; argument

DISDAINED
959 bâzâh (1), to ridicule, scorn
3988 mâ'aç (1), to spurn; to disappear

DISEASE
1697 dâbâr (1), word; matter; thing
2483 chŏlîy (7), malady; anxiety; calamity
4245 machăleh (1), sickness
3119 malakia (3), enervation, debility
3553 nŏsēma (1), ailment, disease

DISEASED
2456 châlâ' (2), to be sick
2470 châlâh (2), to be weak, sick, afflicted
770 asthĕnĕō (1), to be feeble
2560+2192 kakōs (2), badly; wrongly; ill

DISEASES
4064 madveh (2), sickness
4245 machăleh (1), sickness

DISMAYED
4251 machlûy (1), disease
8463 tachălûw' (2), malady, disease
769 asthĕnĕia (1), feebleness of body
3554 nŏsŏs (6), malady, disease

DISFIGURE
853 aphanizō (1), to consume (becloud)

DISGRACE
5034 nâbêl (1), to be foolish or wicked

DISGUISE
2664 châphas (2), to let be sought; to mask
8138 shânâh (1), to transmute

DISGUISED
2664 châphas (5), to let be sought; to mask

DISGUISETH
5643 çêther (1), cover, shelter

DISH
5602 çêphel (1), basin, bowl
6747 tsallachath (1), bowl
5165 trubliŏn (2), bowl

DISHAN
1789 Dîyshân (5), antelope

DISHES
7086 qe'ârâh (3), bowl

DISHON
1788 dîyshôn (7), antelope

DISHONEST
1215 betsa' (2), plunder; unjust gain

DISHONESTY
152 aischunē (1), shame or disgrace

DISHONOUR
3639 kelimmâh (3), disgrace, scorn
6173 'arvâh (Ch.) (1), nakedness
7036 qâlôwn (1), disgrace
818 atimazō (2), to maltreat, dishonor
819 atimia (4), disgrace

DISHONOUREST
818 atimazō (1), to maltreat, dishonor

DISHONOURETH
5034 nâbêl (1), to wilt; to be foolish or wicked
2617 kataischunō (2), to disgrace or shame

DISINHERIT
3423 yârash (1), to inherit; to impoverish

DISMAYED
926 bâhal (1), to tremble; hurry anxiously
2844 chath (1), terror
2865 châthath (26), to break down
8159 shâ'âh (2), to be bewildered

DISMAYING
4288 mᵉchittâh (1), *ruin; consternation*

DISMISSED
6362 pâṭar (1), to *burst through;* to *emit*
630 apŏluō (2), to *relieve, release;* to *divorce*

DISOBEDIENCE
543 apĕithĕia (3), *disbelief*
3876 parakŏĕ (3), *disobedience*

DISOBEDIENT
4784 mârâh (2), to *rebel* or *resist;* to *provoke*
506 anupŏtaktŏs (1), *insubordinate*
544 apĕithĕō (4), to *disbelieve*
545 apĕithēs (6), *willful disobedience*

DISOBEYED
4784 mârâh (1), to *rebel* or *resist;* to *provoke*

DISORDERLY
812 ataktĕō (1), to *be, act irregular*
814 ataktŏs (2), *morally irregularly*

DISPATCH
1254 bârâ' (1), to *create; fashion*

DISPENSATION
3622 ŏikŏnŏmia (4), *administration*

DISPERSE
2219 zârâh (7), to *toss about;* to *diffuse*
6327 pûwts (1), to *dash* in pieces; to *disperse*

DISPERSED
2219 zârâh (1), to *toss about;* to *diffuse*
5310 nâphats (1), to *dash* to pieces; to *scatter*
6327 pûwts (2), to *dash* in pieces; to *disperse*
6340 pâzar (1), to *scatter*
6504 pârad (1), to *spread* or *separate*
6555 pârats (1), to *break* out
1287 diaskŏrpizō (1), to *scatter;* to *squander*
1290 diaspŏra (1), *dispersion*
4650 skŏrpizō (1), to *dissipate*

DISPERSIONS
8600 tᵉphôwtsâh (1), *dispersal*

DISPLAYED
5127 nûwç (1), to *vanish* away, *flee*

DISPLEASE
2734 chârâh (1), to *blaze* up
6213+7451+5869 'âsâh (1), to *do* or *make*
7489+5869 râ'a' (3), to *be* good for nothing

DISPLEASED
599 'ânaph (1), *be enraged, be angry*

888 bᵉ'êsh (Ch.) (1), to *be* displeased
2198 zâ'êph (2), *angry, raging*
2734 chârâh (3), to *blaze* up
3415+5869 yâra' (1), to *fear*
6087 'âtsab (1), to *worry, have pain* or *anger*
7107 qâtsaph (3), to *burst* out in rage
7451+241 ra' (1), *bad; evil*
7489+5869 râ'a' (7), to *be* good for nothing
23 aganaktĕō (3), to *be* indignant
2371 thumŏmachĕō (1), to *be exasperated*

DISPLEASURE
2534 chêmâh (3), *heat; anger; poison*
2740 chârôwn (1), *burning* of anger
7451 ra' (1), *bad; evil*

DISPOSED
7760 sûwm (2), to *put, place*
1014 bŏulŏmai (1), to *be willing, desire*
2309 thĕlō (1), to *will;* to *desire;* to *choose*

DISPOSING
4941 mishpâṭ (1), *verdict;* formal *decree; justice*

DISPOSITION
1296 diatagē (1), *putting into effect*

DISPOSSESS
3423 yârash (2), to *inherit;* to *impoverish*

DISPOSSESSED
3423 yârash (2), to *inherit;* to *impoverish*

DISPUTATION
4803 suzētēsis (1), *discussion, dispute*

DISPUTATIONS
1253 diakrisis (1), *estimation*

DISPUTE
3198 yâkach (1), to *be* correct; to *argue*

DISPUTED
1256 dialĕgŏmai (3), to *discuss*
1260 dialŏgizŏmai (1), to *deliberate*
4802 suzētĕō (1), to *discuss, controvert*

DISPUTER
4804 suzētētēs (1), *sophist*

DISPUTING
1256 dialĕgŏmai (3), to *discuss*
4802 suzētĕō (1), to *discuss, controvert*
4803 suzētēsis (1), *discussion, dispute*

DISPUTINGS
1261 dialŏgismŏs (1), *consideration; debate*
3859 paradiatribē (1), *meddlesomeness*

DISQUIET
7264 râgaz (1), to *quiver*

DISQUIETED
1993 hâmâh (4), to *be in* great *commotion*
7264 râgaz (2), to *quiver*

DISQUIETNESS
5100 nᵉhâmâh (1), *snarling, growling*

DISSEMBLED
3584 kâchash (1), to *lie, disown;* to *disappoint*
8582 tâ'âh (1), to *vacillate, reel* or *stray*
4942 sunupŏkrinŏmai (1), to *act hypocritically*

DISSEMBLERS
5956 'âlam (1), to *veil* from sight, i.e. *conceal*

DISSEMBLETH
5234 nâkar (1), to *treat* as a *foreigner*

DISSENSION
4714 stasis (3), one leading an *uprising*

DISSIMULATION
505 anupŏkritŏs (1), *sincere, genuine*
5272 hupŏkrisis (1), *deceit, hypocrisy*

DISSOLVE
8271 shᵉrê' (Ch.) (1), to *unravel, commence*

DISSOLVED
4127 mûwg (3), to *soften, flow down, disappear*
4743 mâqaq (1), to *melt;* to *flow, dwindle, vanish*
6565 pârar (1), to *break* up; to *violate, frustrate*
2647 kataluō (1), to *demolish;* to *halt*
3089 luō (2), to *loosen*

DISSOLVEST
4127 mûwg (1), to *soften, flow down, disappear*

DISSOLVING
8271 shᵉrê' (Ch.) (1), to *free, separate*

DISTAFF
6418 pelek (1), *spindle-whorl; crutch*

DISTANT
7947 shâlab (1), to *make equidistant*

DISTIL
5140 nâzal (1), to *drip,* or *shed* by trickling
7491 râ'aph (1), to *drip*

DISTINCTION
1293 diastŏlē (1), *variation, distinction*

DISTINCTLY
6567 pârash (1), to *separate;* to *specify*

DISTRACTED
6323 pûwn (1), to *be* perplexed

DISTRACTION
563 apĕrispastŏs (1), *undistractedly*

DISTRESS
4689 mâtsôwq (1), *confinement; disability*
4691 mᵉtsûwqâh (1), *trouble, anguish*
4712 mêtsar (1), *trouble*
6693 tsûwq (5), to *oppress, distress*
6696 tsûwr (2), to *cramp,* i.e. *confine;* to *harass*
6862 tsar (4), *trouble; opponent*
6869 tsârâh (8), *trouble; rival-wife*
6887 tsârar (5), to *cramp*
7451 ra' (1), *bad; evil*
318 anagkē (3), *constraint; distress*
4730 stĕnŏchōria (1), *calamity, distress*
4928 sunŏchē (1), *anxiety, distress*

DISTRESSED
3334 yâtsar (4), to *be in* distress
5065 nâgas (2), to *exploit;* to *tax, harass*
6696 tsûwr (1), to *cramp,* i.e. *confine;* to *harass*
6887 tsârar (2), to *cramp*
6973 qûwts (1), to *be, make disgusted*
4729 stĕnŏchōrĕō (1), to *hem in* closely

DISTRESSES
4691 mᵉtsûwqâh (5), *trouble, anguish*
6862 tsar (1), *trouble; opponent*
4730 stĕnŏchōria (2), *calamity, distress*

DISTRIBUTE
2505 châlaq (1), to *be smooth; be slippery*
5157 nâchal (1), to *inherit*
5414 nâthan (1), to *give*
1239 diadidōmi (1), to *divide up, distribute*
2130 ĕumĕtadŏtŏs (1), *liberal, generous*

DISTRIBUTED
2505 châlaq (2), to *be smooth; be slippery*
5157 nâchal (1), to *inherit*
1239 diadidōmi (1), to *divide up, distribute*
3307 mĕrizō (2), to *apportion, bestow*

DISTRIBUTETH
2505 châlaq (1), to *be smooth; be slippery*

DISTRIBUTING
2841 kŏinōnĕō (1), to *share* or *participate*

DISTRIBUTION
1239 diadidōmi (1), to *divide up, distribute*
2842 kŏinōnia (1), *benefaction; sharing*

DITCH
4724 miqvâh (1), *water reservoir*
7745 shûwchâh (1), *chasm*
7845 shachath (2), *pit; destruction*

999 bŏthunŏs (2), *cistern, pit-hole*

DITCHES
1356 gêb (1), *well, cistern; pit*

DIVERS
582 'ĕnôwsh (1), *man; person, human*
2921 țâlâ' (1), *to be spotted or variegated*
3610 kil'ayim (1), *two different kinds of thing*
6446 paç (2), *long -sleeved tunic*
6648 tseba' (3), *dye*
7553 riqmâh (2), *variegation of color*
8162 sha'ațnêz (1), *linen and woolen*
1313 diaphŏrŏs (1), *varying; surpassing*
4164 pŏikilŏs (8), *various in character or kind*
4187 pŏlutrŏpŏs (1), *in many ways*
5100 tis (2), *some or any*

DIVERSE
3610 kil'ayim (1), *two different kinds of thing*
8133 shᵉnâ' (Ch.) (5), *to alter, change*
8138 shânâh (2), *to duplicate; to transmute*

DIVERSITIES
1085 gĕnŏs (1), *kin, offspring in kind*
1243 diairĕsis (2), *distinction or variety*

DIVIDE
914 bâdal (5), *to divide, separate, distinguish*
1234 bâqa' (2), *to cleave, break, tear open*
1504 gâzar (2), *to destroy, divide*
2505 châlaq (17), *to be smooth; be slippery*
2673 châtsâh (3), *to cut or split in two; to halve*
5157 nâchal (3), *to inherit*
5307 nâphal (4), *to fall*
5312 nᵉphaq (Ch.) (2), *to issue forth; to bring out*
6385 pâlag (1), *to split*
6536 pâraç (4), *to break in pieces; to split*
6565 pârar (1), *to break up; to violate, frustrate*
1266 diamĕrizō (1), *to distribute*
3307 mĕrizō (1), *to apportion, bestow*

DIVIDED
914 bâdal (2), *to divide, separate, distinguish*
1234 bâqa' (2), *to cleave, break, tear open*
1334 bâthar (1), *to chop up, cut up*
1504 gâzar (1), *to destroy, divide*
2505 châlaq (21), *to be smooth; be slippery*
2673 châtsâh (3), *to cut or split in two; to halve*
5307 nâphal (2), *to fall*

5408 nâthach (1), *to dismember, cut up*
5504 çachar (1), *profit from trade*
6385 pâlag (3), *to split*
6386 pᵉlag (Ch.) (1), *dis-united*
6504 pârad (2), *to spread or separate*
6537 pᵉraç (Ch.) (1), *to split up*
7280 râga' (1), *to settle, to stir up*
7323 rûwts (1), *to run*
1096 ginŏmai (1), *to be, become*
1244 diairĕō (1), *distribute, apportion*
1266 diamĕrizō (4), *to distribute*
2624 kataklērŏdŏtĕō (1), *to apportion an estate*
3307 mĕrizō (8), *to apportion, bestow*
4977 schizō (2), *to split or sever*

DIVIDER
3312 mĕristēs (1), *apportioner*

DIVIDETH
2672 châtsab (1), *to cut stone or carve wood*
6536 pâraç (5), *to break; to split, distribute*
7280 râga' (2), *to settle, to stir up*
873 aphŏrizō (1), *to limit, exclude, appoint*
1239 diadidōmi (1), *to divide up, distribute*

DIVIDING
1234 bâqa' (1), *to cleave, break, tear open*
2505 châlaq (1), *to be smooth; be slippery*
6387 pᵉlag (Ch.) (1), *half-time unit*
1244 diairĕō (1), *distribute, apportion*
3311 mĕrismŏs (1), *separation, distribution*
3718 ŏrthŏtŏmĕō (1), *to expound correctly*

DIVINATION
4738 miqçâm (2), *augury, divination*
7080 qâçam (1), *to divine magic*
7081 qeçem (8), *divination*
4436 Puthōn (1), *inspiration in soothsaying*

DIVINATIONS
7081 qeçem (1), *divination*

DIVINE
5172 nâchash (1), *to prognosticate*
7080 qâçam (5), *to divine magic*
7081 qeçem (1), *divination*
7181 qâshab (1), *to prick up the ears*
2304 thĕiŏs (2), *divinity*
2999 latrĕia (1), *worship, ministry service*

DIVINERS
7080 qâçam (7), *to divine magic*

DIVINETH
5172 nâchash (1), *to prognosticate*

DIVINING
7080 qâçam (1), *to divine magic*

DIVISION
2515 chăluqqâh (1), *distribution, portion*
6304 pᵉdûwth (1), *distinction; deliverance*
1267 diamĕrismŏs (1), *disunion*
4978 schisma (3), *dissension, i.e. schism*

DIVISIONS
4256 machălŏqeth (8), *section or division*
4653 miphlaggâh (1), *classification, division*
6391 pᵉluggâh (3), *section*
6392 pᵉluggâh (Ch.) (1), *section*
1370 dichŏstasia (2), *dissension*
4978 schisma (2), *dissension, i.e. schism*

DIVORCE
3748 kᵉrîythûwth (1), *divorce*

DIVORCED
1644 gârash (3), *to drive out; to divorce*
630 apŏluō (1), *to relieve, release; to divorce*

DIVORCEMENT
3748 kᵉrîythûwth (3), *divorce*
647 apŏstasiŏn (3), *marriage divorce*

DIZAHAB
1774 Dîy zâhâb (1), *of gold*

DO
1167 ba'al (1), *master; husband; owner; citizen*
1580 gâmal (1), *to benefit or requite; to wean*
3190 yâțab (2), *to be, make well*
3318 yâtsâ' (1), *to go, bring out*
4640 Ma'say (1), *operative*
5647 'âbad (17), *to do, work, serve*
5648 'âbad (Ch.) (5), *to do, work, serve*
5674 'âbar (1), *to cross over; to transition*
5953 'âlal (2), *to glean; to overdo*
6213 'âsâh (617), *to do*
6466 pâ'al (6), *to do*
6467 pô'al (1), *act or work, deed*
14 agathŏĕrgĕō (1), *to do good work*
15 agathŏpŏiĕō (6), *to be a well-doer*
17 agathŏpŏiŏs (1), *virtuous one*

91 adikĕō (2), *to do wrong*
1107 gnōrizō (1), *to make known, reveal*
1286 diasĕiō (1), *to intimidate*
1398 dŏulĕuō (1), *to serve as a slave*
1754 ĕnĕrgĕō (1), *to be active, efficient, work*
2005 ĕpitĕlĕō (1), *to terminate; to undergo*
2038 ĕrgazŏmai (2), *to toil*
2140 ĕupŏiïa (1), *beneficence, doing good*
2192 ĕchō (1), *to have; hold; keep*
2480 ischuō (1), *to have or exercise force*
2554 kakŏpŏiĕō (2), *to injure; to sin, do wrong*
2698 katatithēmi (1), *to place down*
2716 katĕrgazŏmai (3), *to finish; to accomplish*
3930 parĕchō (1), *to hold near, i.e. to present*
4160 pŏiĕō (199), *to do*
4238 prassō (15), *to execute, accomplish*
4704 spŏudazō (2), *to make effort*
4982 sōzō (1), *to deliver; to protect*

DOCTOR
3547 nŏmŏdidaskalŏs (1), *Rabbi*

DOCTORS
1320 didaskalŏs (1), *instructor*
3547 nŏmŏdidaskalŏs (1), *Rabbi*

DOCTRINE
3948 leqach (4), *instruction*
4148 mûwçâr (1), *reproof, warning*
8052 shᵉmûw'âh (1), *announcement*
1319 didaskalia (15), *instruction*
1322 didachē (28), *instruction*
3056 lŏgŏs (1), *word, matter, thing*

DOCTRINES
1319 didaskalia (4), *instruction*
1322 didachē (1), *instruction*

DODAI
1739 dâveh (1), *menstrual; fainting*

DODANIM
1721 Dôdânîym (2), *Dodanites*

DODAVAH
1735 Dôwdâvâhûw (1), *love of Jehovah*

DODO
1734 Dôwdôw (5), *loving*

DOEG
1673 Dô'êg (6), *anxious*

DOER
6218 'âsôwr (3), group of ten
2557 kakŏurgŏs (1), criminal, evildoer
4163 pŏiĕtēs (3), performer; poet

DOERS
6213 'âsâh (2), to do or make
6466 pâ'al (1), to do, make or practice
4163 pŏiĕtēs (2), performer; poet

DOEST
5648 'âbad (Ch.) (1), to do, work, serve
6213 'âsâh (18), to do or make
6466 pâ'al (1), to do, make or practice
7965 shâlôwm (1), safe; well; health, prosperity
4160 pŏiĕō (14), to do
4238 prassō (1), to execute, accomplish

DOETH
1580 gâmal (1), to benefit or requite; to wean
5648 'âbad (Ch.) (1), to do, work, serve
6213 'âsâh (44), to do
7760 sûwm (1), to put, place
15 agathŏpŏiĕō (1), to be a well-doer
91 adikĕō (1), to do wrong
2554 kakŏpŏiĕō (1), to injure; to sin, do wrong
4160 pŏiĕō (34), to do
4238 prassō (2), to execute, accomplish
4374 prŏsphĕrō (1), to present to; to treat as

DOG
3611 keleb (14), dog; male prostitute
2965 kuōn (1), dog

DOG'S
3611 keleb (2), dog; male prostitute

DOGS
3611 keleb (16), dog; male prostitute
2952 kunariŏn (4), small dog
2965 kuōn (4), dog

DOING
854 'êth (1), with; by; at; among
4640 Ma'say (1), operative
5949 'ălîylâh (1), opportunity, action
6213 'âsâh (14), to do or make
15 agathŏpŏiĕō (2), to be a well-doer
16 agathŏpŏiïa (1), virtue, doing good
92 adikĕma (1), wrong done
1096 ginŏmai (2), to be, become
1398 dŏulĕuō (1), to serve as a slave

DOINGS
4611 ma'ălâl (35), act, deed
4640 Ma'say (3), operative
5949 'ălîylâh (13), opportunity, action

DOLEFUL
255 'ôach (1), creature that howls;
5093 nihyâh (1), lamentation

DOMINION
1166 bâ'al (1), to be master; to marry
1196 Ba'ănâh (1), in affliction
3027 yâd (2), hand; power
4474 mimshâl (2), ruler; dominion, rule
4475 memshâlâh (10), rule; realm or a ruler
4896 mishṭâr (1), jurisdiction, rule
4910 mâshal (7), to rule
4915 môshel (2), empire; parallel
7287 râdâh (9), to subjugate
7300 rûwd (1), to ramble free or disconsolate
7980 shâlaṭ (1), to dominate, i.e. govern
7985 sholṭân (Ch.) (11), official
2634 katakuriĕuō (1), to control, subjugate
2904 kratŏs (4), vigor, strength
2961 kuriĕuō (4), to rule, be master of
2963 kuriŏtēs (2), rulers, masters

DOMINIONS
7985 sholṭân (Ch.) (1), official
2963 kuriŏtēs (1), rulers, masters

DONE
466 'Ĕlîyphᵉlêhûw (1), God of his distinction
1254 bârâ' (1), to create; fashion
1580 gâmal (1), to benefit or requite; to wean
1639 gâra' (1), to shave, remove, lessen
1697 dâbâr (1), word; matter; thing
1961 hâyâh (2), to exist, i.e. be or become
3254 yâçaph (1), to add or augment
3615 kâlâh (9), to complete, prepare
5414 nâthan (1), to give
5647 'âbad (1), to do, work, serve

DOING *(continued right column)*
2041 ĕrgŏn (1), work
2109 ĕuĕrgĕtĕō (1), to be philanthropic
2554 kakŏpŏiĕō (1), to injure; to sin, do wrong
2569 kalŏpŏiĕō (1), to do well
4160 pŏiĕō (8), to do

5648 'âbad (Ch.) (4), to do, work, serve
5953 'âlal (3), to glean; to overdo
6213 'âsâh (318), to do or make
6466 pâ'al (21), to do, make or practice
7760 sûwm (1), to put, place
8552 tâmam (2), to complete, finish
91 adikĕō (3), to do wrong
1096 ginŏmai (61), to be, become
1796 ĕnubrizō (1), to insult
2673 katargĕō (4), to be, render entirely useless
2716 katĕrgazŏmai (2), to finish; to accomplish
4160 pŏiĕō (52), to do
4238 prassō (6), to execute, accomplish

DOOR
1004 bayith (1), house; temple; family, tribe
1817 deleth (21), door; gate
4201 mᵉzûwzâh (2), door-post
4947 mashqôwph (1), lintel
5592 çaph (11), dish
6607 pethach (114), opening; door
6907 qubba'ath (2), goblet, cup
8179 sha'ar (1), opening, i.e. door or gate
2374 thura (28), entrance, i.e. door, gate
2377 thurŏrŏs (2), doorkeeper

DOORKEEPER
5605 çâphaph (1), to wait at (the) threshold

DOORKEEPERS
7778 shôw'êr (2), janitor, door-keeper

DOORS
1817 deleth (48), door; gate
5592 çaph (2), dish
6607 pethach (11), opening; door
8179 sha'ar (1), opening, i.e. door or gate
2374 thura (9), entrance, i.e. door, gate

DOPHKAH
1850 Dophqâh (2), knock

DOR
1756 Dôwr (6), dwelling

DORCAS
1393 Dŏrkas (2), gazelle

DOTE
2973 yâ'al (1), to be or act foolish

DOTED
5689 'âgab (6), to lust sensually

DOTHAN
1886 Dôthân (3), Dothan

DOTING
3552 nŏsĕō (1), to be sick, be ill

DOUBLE
3717 kâphal (2), to fold together; to repeat
3718 kephel (3), duplicate, double
4932 mishneh (8), duplicate copy; double
8147 shᵉnayim (5), two-fold
1362 diplŏus (2), two-fold
1374 dipsuchŏs (2), vacillating
3588+1362 hŏ (1), "the," i.e. the definite article

DOUBLED
3717 kâphal (3), to fold together; to repeat
8138 shânâh (1), to fold, i.e. duplicate

DOUBLETONGUED
1351 dilŏgŏs (1), insincere

DOUBT
551 'omnâm (1), verily, indeed, truly
142+5590 airō (1), to lift, to take up
639 apŏrĕō (1), be at a mental loss, be puzzled
686 ara (1), then, so, therefore
1063 gar (1), for, indeed, but, because
1252 diakrinō (2), to decide; to hesitate
1280 diapŏrĕō (1), to be thoroughly puzzled
1365 distazō (1), to waver in opinion
3843 pantōs (1), at all events; in no event

DOUBTED
639 apŏrĕō (1), be at a mental loss, be puzzled
1280 diapŏrĕō (2), to be thoroughly puzzled
1365 distazō (1), to waver in opinion

DOUBTETH
1252 diakrinō (1), to decide; to hesitate

DOUBTFUL
1261 dialŏgismŏs (1), consideration; debate
3349 mĕtĕōrizō (1), to be anxious

DOUBTING
639 apŏrĕō (1), be at a mental loss, be puzzled
1252 diakrinō (2), to decide; to hesitate
1261 dialŏgismŏs (1), consideration; debate

DOUBTLESS
518 'îm (1), whether?; if, although; Oh that!
3588 kîy (1), for, that because
1065 gĕ (1), particle of emphasis
1211 dē (1), now, then; indeed, therefore

3304 měnŏungě (1), *so then at least*

DOUBTS
7001 qᵉṭar (Ch.) (2), *riddle*

DOUGH
1217 bâtsêq (4), fermenting *dough*
6182 'ărîyçâh (4), *ground-up meal*

DOVE
3123 yôwnâh (14), *dove*
4058 pěristěra (4), *pigeon, dove*

DOVE'S
1686 dibyôwn (1), (poss.) *vegetable or root*

DOVES
3123 yôwnâh (5), *dove*
4058 pěristěra (5), *pigeon, dove*

DOVES'
3123 yôwnâh (2), *dove*

DOWN
935 bôw' (11), to *go or come*
1288 bârak (1), to *bless*
1438 gâda' (9), to *fell a tree; to destroy*
1457 gâhar (1), to *prostrate, bow down*
1760 dâchâh (1), to *push down; to totter*
2040 hâraç (22), to *pull down; break, destroy*
2904 ṭûwl (2), to *cast down or out, hurl*
3212 yâlak (1), to *walk; to live; to carry*
3281 Ya'lâm (1), *occult*
3332 yâtsaq (1), to *pour out*
3381 yârad (339), to *descend*
3665 kâna' (3), to *humiliate, vanquish*
3766 kâra' (9), to *prostrate*
3782 kâshal (4), to *totter, waver, stumble*
3996 mâbôw' (2), *entrance; sunset; west; towards*
4174 môwrâd (3), *descent, slope*
4295 maṭṭâh (1), *below or beneath*
4535 maççâch (1), *cordon; military barrier*
4606 mê'al (Ch.) (1), *setting of the sun*
4769 marbêts (2), *resting place*
5117 nûwach (1), to *rest; to settle down*
5128 nûwa' (1), to *waver*
5181 nâchath (4), to *sink, descend; to lead down*
5182 nᵉchath (Ch.) (2), to *descend; to depose*
5183 nachath (1), *descent; quiet*
5186 nâṭâh (8), to *stretch or spread out*
5242 Nᵉmûw'êlîy (2), *Nemuelite*

5243 nâmal (1), to *be circumcised*
5307 nâphal (9), to *fall*
5422 nâthats (29), to *tear down*
5456 çâgad (4), to *prostrate oneself*
5493 çûwr (1), to *turn off*
6131 'âqar (1), to *pluck up; to hamstring*
6201 'âraph (1), to *drip*
6915 qâdad (5), to *bend*
7250 râba' (2), to *lay down*
7252 reba' (1), *prostration for sleep*
7257 râbats (13), to *recline, repose, brood*
7323 rûwts (1), to *run*
7491 râ'aph (1), to *drip*
7503 râphâh (2), to *slacken*
7665 shâbar (1), to *burst*
7673 shâbath (1), to *repose; to desist*
7743 shûwach (1), to *sink*
7812 shâchâh (20), to *prostrate in homage*
7817 shâchach (12), to *sink or depress*
7821 shᵉchîyṭâh (1), *slaughter*
7901 shâkab (40), to *lie down*
7971 shâlach (2), to *send away*
8045 shâmad (2), to *desolate*
8058 shâmaṭ (2), to *jostle; to let alone*
8213 shâphêl (7), to *humiliate*
8214 shᵉphal (Ch.) (1), to *humiliate*
8231 shâphar (1), to *be, make fair*
8257 shâqa' (1), to *be overflowed; to cease*
8497 tâkâh (1), to *strew, i.e. encamp*
345 anakěimai (2), to *recline at a meal*
347 anaklinō (7), to *lean back, recline*
377 anapiptō (10), *lie down, lean back*
387 anastatóō (1), to *disturb, cause trouble*
1308 diaphěrō (1), to *bear, carry; to differ*
1581 ěkkŏptō (5), to *cut off; to frustrate*
1931 ěpiduō (1), to *set*
2504 kagō (1), *and also*
2506 kathairěsis (1), *demolition*
2507 kathairěō (6), to *lower, or demolish*
2521 kathēmai (4), to *sit down; to remain, reside*
2523 kathizō (14), to *seat down, dwell*
2524 kathiēmi (4), to *lower, let down*
2596 kata (3), *down; according to*
2597 katabainō (64), to *descend*

2598 kataballō (2), to *throw down*
2601 katabibazō (2), to *cause to bring down*
2609 katagō (5), to *lead down; to moor a vessel*
2621 katakěimai (1), to *lie down; to recline*
2625 kataklinō (2), to *take a place at table*
2630 katakrēmnizō (1), to *precipitate down*
2647 kataluō (3), to *halt for the night*
2662 katapatěō (1), to *trample down; to reject*
2667 katapiptō (1), to *fall down*
2673 katargěō (1), to *be, render entirely useless*
2679 kataskaptō (1), to *destroy, be ruined*
2701 katatrěchō (1), to *hasten, run*
2718 katěrchŏmai (6), to *go, come down*
2736 katō (5), *downwards*
2778 kēnsŏs (1), *enrollment*
2875 kŏptō (2), to *beat the breast*
3879 parakuptō (3), to *lean over*
3935 pariēmi (1), to *neglect; to be weakened*
4098 piptō (2), to *fall*
4496 rhiptō (2), to *fling, toss; to lay out*
4776 sugkathizō (1), to *give, take a seat with*
4781 sugkamptō (1), to *afflict*
4782 sugkatabainō (1), to *descend with*
5011 tapěinŏs (1), *humiliated, lowly*
5294 hupŏtithēmi (1), to *hazard; to suggest*
5465 chalaō (5), to *lower as into a void*

DOWNSITTING
3427 yâshab (1), to *dwell, to remain; to settle*

DOWNWARD
4295 maṭṭâh (5), *below or beneath*

DOWRY
2065 zebed (1), *gift*
4119 môhar (3), *wife-price*

DRAG
4365 mikmereth (2), fishing-*net*

DRAGGING
4951 surō (1), to *trail, drag, sweep*

DRAGON
8577 tannîyn (6), *sea-serpent; jackal*
1404 drakōn (13), *fabulous kind of serpent*

DRAGONS
8568 tannâh (1), female *jackal*
8577 tannîyn (15), *sea-serpent; jackal*

DRAMS
150 'ădarkôn (2), *daric*
1871 darkᵉmôwn (4), *coin*

DRANK
4960 mishteh (2), *drink; banquet or feast*
8354 shâthâh (8), to *drink, imbibe*
8355 shᵉthâh (Ch.) (3), to *drink, imbibe*
4095 pinō (5), to *imbibe, drink*

DRAUGHT
4280 machără'âh (1), privy *sink, latrine*
61 agra (2), *haul of fish in a net*
856 aphědrōn (2), *privy or latrine*

DRAVE
1644 gârash (3), to *drive out; to expatriate*
3423 yârash (2), to *impoverish; to ruin*
5071 nᵉdâbâh (1), *abundant gift*
5090 nâhag (4), to *drive forth; to lead*
5394 nâshal (1), to *divest, eject, or drop*
556 apělaunō (1), to *dismiss, eject*
1856 ěxōthěō (1), to *expel; to propel*

DRAW
748 'ârak (1), to *be, make long*
1518 gîyach (1), to *issue forth; to burst forth*
1802 dâlâh (1), to *draw out water); to deliver*
2502 châlats (1), to *pull off; to strip; to depart*
2834 châsaph (1), to *drain away or bail up*
3318 yâtsâ' (1), to *go, bring out*
4900 mâshak (11), to *draw out; to be tall*
5423 nâthaq (1), to *tear off*
5498 çâchab (3), to *trail along*
6329 pûwq (1), to *issue; to furnish; to secure*
7324 rûwq (8), to *pour out, i.e. empty*
7579 shâ'ab (9), to *bale up water*
8025 shâlaph (4), to *pull out, up or off*
501 antlěō (3), *dip water*
502 antlēma (1), *bucket for drawing water*
645 apŏspaō (1), *unsheathe a sword*
1670 hělkuō (4), to *drag, draw, pull in*
4334 prŏsěrchŏmai (1), to *come near, visit*
5288 hupŏstěllō (1), to *cower or shrink*
5289 hupŏstŏlē (1), *shrinkage, timidity*

DRAWER
7579 shâ'ab (1), to *bale up water*

DRAWERS
7579 shâ'ab (3), to *bale up water*

DRAWETH
4900 mâshak (2), to *draw out; to be tall*
7503 râphâh (1), to *slacken*

DRAWING
4857 mash'âb (1), *water trough for cattle*
1096 ginŏmai (1), to *be, become*

DRAWN
3318 yâtsâ' (1), to *go, bring out*
3947 lâqach (1), to *take*
4900 mâshak (2), to *draw out; to be tall*
5080 nâdach (1), to *push off, scattered*
5203 nâṭash (1), to *disperse; to thrust* off
5423 nâthaq (3), to *tear* off
5498 çâchab (1), to *trail along*
6267 'attîyq (1), *weaned; antique*
6605 pâthach (2), to *open wide; to loosen, begin*
6609 pᵉthîchâh (1), *drawn sword*
7579 shâ'ab (1), to *bale up water*
7725 shûwb (1), to *turn back; to return*
8025 shâlaph (5), to *pull out, up or off*
8388 tâ'ar (5), to *delineate; to extend*
385 anaspaŏ (1), to *take up or extricate*
1828 ĕxĕlkō (1), to *drag away, i.e. entice*

DREAD
367 'êymâh (1), *fright*
2844 chath (1), *terror*
3372 yârê' (1), to *fear; to revere*
4172 môwrâ' (1), *fearful*
6206 'ârats (2), to *awe; to dread; to harass*
6343 pachad (3), *sudden alarm, fear*

DREADFUL
1763 dᵉchal (Ch.) (2), to *fear; be formidable, awesome*
3372 yârê' (5), to *fear; to revere*
3374 yir'âh (1), *fear; reverence*
6343 pachad (1), *sudden alarm, fear*

DREAM
2472 chălôwm (44), *dream; dreamer*
2492 châlam (1), to *dream*
2493 chêlem (Ch.) (21), *dream*
1798 ĕnupniŏn (1), *dream, vision*
3677 ŏnar (6), *dream*

DREAMED
2492 châlam (19), to *dream*

DREAMER
1167+2472 ba'al (1), *master; owner; citizen*
2492 châlam (3), to *dream*

DREAMERS
2492 châlam (1), to *dream*
1797 ĕnupniazŏmai (1), to *dream*

DREAMETH
2492 châlam (2), to *dream*

DREAMS
2472 chălôwm (19), *dream; dreamer*
2493 chêlem (Ch.) (1), *dream*
1797 ĕnupniazŏmai (1), to *dream*

DREGS
6907 qubba'ath (2), *goblet, cup*
8105 shemer (1), *settlings of wine, dregs*

DRESS
5647 'âbad (2), to *do, work, serve*
6213 'âsâh (7), to *do or make*

DRESSED
6213 'âsâh (6), to *do or make*
1090 gĕōrgĕō (1), to *till the soil*

DRESSER
289 ampĕlŏurgŏs (1), *vineyard caretaker*

DRESSERS
3755 kôrêm (1), *vinedresser*

DRESSETH
3190 yâṭab (1), to *be, make well*

DREW
748 'ârak (2), to *be, make long*
1802 dâlâh (2), to *draw out water); to deliver*
1869 dârak (1), to *walk, lead; to string a bow*
3318 yâtsâ' (1), to *go, bring out*
4871 mâshâh (3), to *pull out*
4900 mâshak (6), to *draw out; to be tall*
7579 shá'ab (4), to *bale up water*
7725 shûwb (2), to *turn back; to return*
8025 shâlaph (15), to *pull out, up or off*
307 anabibazō (1), *haul up a net*
501 antlĕō (1), *dip water*
645 apŏspaō (1), *unsheathe a sword*
868 aphistēmi (1), to *desist, desert*
1670 hĕlkuō (4), to *drag, draw, pull in*

2020 ĕpiphōskō (1), to *grow light*
4264 prŏbibazō (1), to *bring to the front*
4317 prŏsagō (1), to *bring near*
4334 prŏsĕrchŏmai (1), to *come near, visit*
4358 prŏsŏrmizō (1), to *moor to, i.e. land at*
4685 spaō (2), to *draw a sword*
4951 surō (3), to *trail, drag, sweep*

DRIED
1809 dâlal (1), to *slacken, dangle*
2717 chârab (9), to *parch; desolate, destroy*
2787 chârar (1), to *melt, burn, dry up*
3001 yâbêsh (22), to *dry up; to wither*
3002 yâbêsh (1), *dry*
6704 tsîcheh (1), *parched*
7033 qâlâh (1), to *toast, scorch*
3583 xērainō (3), to *shrivel, to mature*

DRIEDST
3001 yâbêsh (1), to *dry up; to wither*

DRIETH
3001 yâbêsh (3), to *dry up; to wither*

DRINK
1572 gâmâ' (1), to *swallow*
4469 mamçâk (1), *mixed-wine*
4945 mashqeh (2), *butler; drink; well-watered*
4960 mishteh (3), *drink; banquet or feast*
5257 nᵉçîyk (1), *libation; molten image; prince*
5261 nᵉçak (Ch.) (1), *libation*
5262 neçek (59), *libation; cast idol*
5435 çôbe' (1), *wine*
7937 shâkar (2), to *become tipsy, to satiate*
7941 shêkâr (21), *liquor*
8248 shâqâh (42), to *quaff, i.e. to irrigate*
8249 shiqqûv (1), *draught, drink*
8250 shiqqûwy (1), *beverage; refreshment*
8353 shêth (Ch.) (1), *six; sixth*
8354 shâthâh (161), to *drink, imbibe*
8355 shᵉthâh (Ch.) (1), to *drink, imbibe*
4095 pinō (50), to *imbibe, drink*
4188 pŏma (1), *beverage, drink*
4213 pŏsis (3), *draught, drink*
4222 pŏtizō (9), to *furnish drink, irrigate*
4608 sikĕra (1), *intoxicant*
4844 sumpinō (1), to *partake a beverage*

DRINKERS
8354 shâthâh (1), to *drink, imbibe*

DRINKETH
6231 'âshaq (1), to *overflow*
8354 shâthâh (8), to *drink, imbibe*
4095 pinō (7), to *imbibe, drink*

DRINKING
4945 mashqeh (2), *butler; drink; well-watered*
8354 shâthâh (12), to *drink, imbibe*
8360 shᵉthîyâh (1), *manner of drinking*
4095 pinō (6), to *imbibe, drink*

DRINKS
4188 pŏma (1), *beverage, drink*

DRIVE
1644 gârash (12), to *drive out; to divorce*
1920 hâdaph (2), to *push away or down; drive out*
2957 ṭᵉrad (Ch.) (2), to *expel, drive on*
3423 yârash (30), to *impoverish; to ruin*
5080 nâdach (5), to *push off, scattered*
5086 nâdaph (1), to *disperse, be windblown*
5090 nâhag (2), to *drive forth; to carry away*
6327 pûwts (1), to *dash in pieces; to disperse*
1929 ĕpididōmi (1), to *give over*

DRIVEN
1644 gârash (5), to *drive out; to divorce*
1760 dâchâh (2), to *push down; to totter*
1920 hâdaph (1), to *push away or down; drive out*
2957 ṭᵉrad (Ch.) (2), to *expel, drive on*
3423 yârash (2), to *impoverish; to ruin*
5080 nâdach (23), to *push off, scattered*
5086 nâdaph (4), to *disperse, be windblown*
5437 çâbab (2), to *surround*
5472 çûwg (1), to *go back, to retreat*
5590 çâ'ar (1), to *rush upon; to toss about*
7617 shâbâh (1), to *transport into captivity*
416 anemizō (1), to *toss with the wind*
1308 diaphĕrō (1), to *bear, carry; to differ*
1643 ĕlaunō (2), to *push*
5342 phĕrō (1), to *bear or carry*

DRIVER
5065 nâgas (1), to *exploit; to tax, harass*

7395 rakkâb (1), *charioteer*

DRIVETH
2342 chûwl (1), to *dance, whirl;* to *writhe*
5086 nâdaph (1), to *disperse, be windblown*
5090 nâhag (1), to *drive forth;* to *carry away*
1544 ĕkballō (1), to *throw out*

DRIVING
1644 gârash (1), to *drive out;* to *divorce*
3423 yârash (1), to *impoverish;* to *ruin*
4491 minhâg (2), *chariot-driving*

DROMEDARIES
1070 beker (1), *young bull camel*
7409 rekesh (1), *relay of animals on a post-route*
7424 rammâk (1), *brood mare*

DROMEDARY
1072 bikrâh (1), *young she-camel*

DROP
4752 mar (1), *drop* in a bucket
5140 nâzal (1), to *drip,* or *shed* by trickling
5197 nâṭaph (7), to *fall in drops*
6201 'âraph (2), to *drip*
7491 râ'aph (4), to *drip*

DROPPED
1982 hêlek (1), *wayfarer, visitor; flowing*
5197 nâṭaph (5), to *fall in drops*
5413 nâthak (1), to *flow forth, pour out*

DROPPETH
1811 dâlaph (1), to *drip*

DROPPING
1812 deleph (2), *dripping*
5197 nâṭaph (1), to *fall in drops*

DROPS
96 'egel (1), *reservoir*
5197 nâṭaph (1), to *fall in drops*
7447 râçîyç (1), *ruin; dew-drop*
2361 thrŏmbŏs (1), *clot of blood*

DROPSY
5203 hudrōpikŏs (1), to *suffer edema*

DROSS
5509 çîyg (8), *refuse, scoria*

DROUGHT
1226 batstsôreth (1), *drought*
2721 chôreb (3), *parched; ruined*
2725 chărâbôwn (1), *parching heat*
6710 tsachtsâchâh (1), *dry desert place*
6723 tsîyâh (2), *arid desert*

6774 tsimmâ'ôwn (1), *desert*
8514 tal'ûwbâh (1), *dehydration*

DROVE
1272 bârach (1), to *flee suddenly*
1644 gârash (3), to *drive out;* to *divorce*
3423 yârash (2), to *impoverish;* to *ruin*
4264 machăneh (1), *encampment*
5380 nâshab (1), to *blow;* to *disperse*
5425 nâthar (1), to *jump;* to *terrify; shake off*
5739 'êder (3), *muster, flock*
1544 ĕkballō (1), to *throw out*

DROVES
5739 'êder (1), *muster, flock*

DROWN
7857 shâṭaph (1), to *gush;* to *inundate*
1036 buthizō (1), to *sink;* to *plunge*

DROWNED
2823 châshôk (1), *obscure*
8248 shâqâh (2), to *quaff,* i.e. to *irrigate*
2666 katapinō (1), to *devour by swallowing*
2670 katapŏntizō (1), to *submerge, be drowned*

DROWSINESS
5124 nûwmâh (1), *sleepiness*

DRUNK
7301 râvâh (1), to *slake thirst or appetites*
7910 shikkôwr (2), *intoxicated*
7937 shâkar (4), to *become tipsy, to satiate*
8354 shâthâh (15), to *drink, imbibe*
8355 shᵉthâh (Ch.) (1), to *drink, imbibe*
3182 mĕthuskō (2), to *become drunk*
3184 mĕthuō (1), to *get drunk*
4095 pinō (2), to *imbibe, drink*

DRUNKARD
5435 çôbe' (2), *wine*
7910 shikkôwr (2), *intoxicated*
3183 mĕthusŏs (1), *drunkard*

DRUNKARDS
5435 çôbe' (1), *wine*
7910 shikkôwr (3), *intoxicated*
8354+7941 shâthâh (1), to *drink, imbibe*
3183 mĕthusŏs (1), *drunkard*

DRUNKEN
5435 çôbe' (1), *wine*
7301 râvâh (1), to *slake thirst or appetites*

7910 shikkôwr (6), *intoxicated*
7937 shâkar (13), to *become tipsy, to satiate*
7943 shikkârôwn (2), *intoxication*
8354 shâthâh (3), to *drink, imbibe*
3182 mĕthuskō (1), to *become drunk*
3184 mĕthuō (5), to *get drunk*
4095 pinō (1), to *imbibe, drink*

DRUNKENNESS
7302 râveh (1), *sated, full with drink*
7943 shikkârôwn (2), *intoxication*
8358 shᵉthîy (1), *intoxication*
3178 mĕthē (3), *intoxication*

DRUSILLA
1409 Drŏusilla (1), *Drusilla*

DRY
954 bûwsh (1), be *ashamed; disappointed*
2717 chârab (3), to *parch, desolate, destroy*
2720 chârêb (3), *parched; ruined*
2721 chôreb (3), *parched; ruined*
2724 chârâbâh (8), *desert, dry land*
3001 yâbêsh (9), to *dry up;* to *wither*
3002 yâbêsh (7), *dry*
3004 yabbâshâh (14), *dry ground*
3006 yabbesheth (2), *dry ground*
5424 netheq (1), *scurf,* i.e. *diseased skin*
6703 tsach (1), *dazzling,* i.e. *sunny, bright*
6707 tsᵉchîychâh (1), *parched desert region*
6723 tsîyâh (10), *arid desert*
6724 tsîyôwn (2), *desert*
6774 tsimmâ'ôwn (1), *desert*
6784 tsâmaq (1), to *dry up, shrivel up*
504 anudrŏs (2), *dry, arid*
3584 xērŏs (2), *scorched; arid; withered*

DRYSHOD
5275 na'al (1), *sandal*

DUE
1167 ba'al (1), *master; husband; owner; citizen*
1697 dâbâr (1), *word; matter; thing*
2706 chôq (2), *appointment; allotment*
4941 mishpâṭ (1), *verdict; formal decree; justice*
514 axiŏs (1), *deserving, comparable or suitable*
2398 idiŏs (3), *private or separate*
3784 ŏphĕilō (2), to *owe;* to *be under obligation*

DUES
3782 ŏphĕilē (1), *sum owed; obligation*

DUKE
441 'allûwph (20), *friend, one familiar; chieftain*

DUKES
441 'allûwph (13), *friend, one familiar; chieftain*
5257 nᵉçîyk (1), *libation; molten image; prince*

DULCIMER
5481 çûwmpôwnᵉyâh (Ch.) (3), *bagpipe*

DULL
917 barĕŏs (2), *heavily, with difficulty*
3576 nōthrŏs (1), *lazy; stupid*

DUMAH
1746 Dûwmâh (4), *silence; death*

DUMB
481 'âlam (7), to *be tongue-tied, be silent*
483 'illêm (6), *speechless*
1748 dûwmâm (1), *silently*
216 alalŏs (3), *mute, not able to speak*
880 aphōnŏs (3), *mute, silent; unmeaning*
2974 kōphŏs (8), *deaf or silent*
4623 siōpaō (1), to *be quiet*

DUNG
830 'ashpôth (4), *heap of rubbish; Dung gate*
1557 gâlâl (1), *dung pellets*
1561 gêlel (4), *dung; dung pellets*
1828 dômen (6), *manure, dung*
2716+(6675) chere' (2), *excrement*
2755 chărêy-yôwnîym (1), *excrements of doves or a vegetable*
6569 peresh (7), *excrement*
6832 tsᵉphûwa' (1), *excrement*
906+2874 ballō (1), to *throw*
4657 skubalŏn (1), *what is thrown to the dogs*

DUNGEON
953 bôwr (13), *pit hole, cistern, well; prison*

DUNGHILL
830 'ashpôth (2), *heap of rubbish; Dung gate*
4087 madmênâh (1), *dunghill*
5122 nᵉvâlûw (Ch.) (3), to *be foul; sink*
2874 kŏpria (1), *manure or rubbish pile*

DUNGHILLS
830 'ashpôth (1), *heap of rubbish; Dung gate*

DURA
1757 Dûwrâ' (Ch.) (1), *circle* or *dwelling*

DURABLE
6266 'âthîyq (1), *venerable* or *splendid*
6276 'âthêq (1), *enduring value*

DURETH
2076 ĕstí (1), he (she or it) *is;* they *are*

DURST
3372 yârê' (1), to *fear;* to *revere*
5111 tôlmaō (7), to be *bold;* to *dare*

DUST
80 'âbâq (5), *fine dust; cosmetic powder*
1854 dâqaq (1), to *crush; crumble*
6083 'âphâr (91), *dust, earth, mud; clay,*
7834 shachaq (1), *firmament, clouds*
2868 kŏniŏrtŏs (5), *blown dust*
5522 chŏŏs (2), loose *dirt*

DUTY
1697 dâbâr (2), *word; matter; thing*
3784 ŏphĕilō (2), to *owe;* to *fail* in duty

DWARF
1851 daq (1), *crushed; small* or *thin*

DWELL
1481 gûwr (11), to *sojourn, live as an alien*
1752 dûwr (1), *remain*
1753 dûwr (Ch.) (3), to *reside, live in*
2073 zᵉbûwl (1), *residence, dwelling*
2082 zâbal (1), to *reside*
3427 yâshab (210), to *dwell,* to *remain*
3488 yᵉthîb (Ch.) (1), to *sit* or *dwell*
3885 lûwn (1), to be *obstinate*
4186 môwshâb (1), *seat; site; abode*
5975 'âmad (1), to *stand*
7931 shâkan (69), to *reside*
7932 shᵉkan (Ch.) (1), to *reside*
1774 ĕnŏikĕō (2), to *inhabit, live with*
2521 kathēmai (1), to *sit down;* to *remain, reside*
2730 katŏikĕō (19), to *reside, live in*
3306 mĕnō (2), to *stay, remain*
3611 ŏikĕō (4), to *reside, inhabit, remain*
4637 skēnŏō (4), to *occupy;* to *reside*
4924 sunŏikĕō (1), to *reside together* as a family

DWELLED
3427 yâshab (6), to *dwell,* to *remain;* to *settle*

DWELLERS
7931 shâkan (1), to *reside*
2730 katŏikĕō (2), to *reside, live in*

DWELLEST
3427 yâshab (14), to *dwell,* to *remain*
7931 shâkan (3), to *reside*
2730 katŏikĕō (1), to *reside, live in*
3306 mĕnō (1), to *stay, remain*

DWELLETH
1481 gûwr (1), to *sojourn, live as an alien*
3427 yâshab (20), to *dwell,* to *remain*
4908 mishkân (1), *residence*
7931 shâkan (9), to *reside*
8271 shᵉrê' (Ch.) (1), to *free, separate;* to *reside*
1774 ĕnŏikĕō (2), to *inhabit, live with*
2730 katŏikĕō (7), to *reside, live in*
3306 mĕnō (9), to *stay, remain*
3611 ŏikĕō (4), to *reside, inhabit, remain*

DWELLING
168 'ôhel (3), *tent*
2073 zᵉbûwl (1), *residence, dwelling*
3427 yâshab (17), to *dwell,* to *remain*
4070 mᵉdôwr (Ch.) (4), *dwelling*
4186 môwshâb (5), *seat; site; abode*
4349 mâkôwn (2), *basis; place*
4583 mâ'ôwn (6), *retreat* or *asylum dwelling*
4585 mᵉ'ôwnâh (1), *abode*
4908 mishkân (4), *residence*
5116 nâveh (3), *at home; lovely; home*
7931 shâkan (1), to *reside*
1460 ĕgkatŏikĕō (1), *reside, live among*
2730 katŏikĕō (3), to *reside, live in*
2731 katŏikēsis (1), *residence*
3611 ŏikĕō (1), to *reside, inhabit, remain*

DWELLINGPLACE
4186 môwshâb (1), *seat; site; abode*
790 astatĕō (1), *homeless, vagabond*

DWELLINGPLACES
4186 môwshâb (2), *seat; site; abode*
4908 mishkân (3), *residence*

DWELLINGS
4033 mâgûwr (2), *abode*
4186 môwshâb (8), *seat; site; abode*
4908 mishkân (6), *residence*
5116 nâveh (1), *at home; lovely; home*

DWELT
1753 dûwr (Ch.) (2), to *reside, live in*
2583 chânâh (2), to *encamp*
3427 yâshab (189), to *dwell,* to *remain*
4186 môwshâb (2), *seat; site; abode*
7931 shâkan (11), to *reside*
1774 ĕnŏikĕō (1), to *inhabit, live with*
2730 katŏikĕō (12), to *reside, live in*
3306 mĕnō (2), to *stay, remain*
3940 parŏikia (1), *foreign residence*
4039 pĕriŏikĕō (1), to be a *neighbor*
4637 skēnŏō (1), to *occupy;* to *reside*

DYED
2556 châmêts (1), to be *fermented; be soured*
2871 ţâbûwl (1), *turban*

DYING
1478 gâva' (1), to *expire, die*
599 apŏthnēskō (4), to *die off*
3500 nĕkrōsis (1), *death, deadness*

EACH
259 'echâd (10), *first*
376 'îysh (5), *man; male; someone*
802 'ishshâh (2), *woman, wife; women, wives*
905 bad (1), *limb, member; bar; chief*
240 allēlōn (2), *one another*
303 ana (1), *each; in turn; among*
1538 hĕkastŏs (2), *each* or *every*

EAGLE
5404 nesher (19), *large bird of prey*
7360 râchâm (2), *kind of vulture*
105 aĕtŏs (2), *eagle, vulture*

EAGLE'S
5403 nᵉshar (Ch.) (1), *large bird of prey*
5404 nesher (1), *large bird of prey*

EAGLES
5404 nesher (5), *large bird of prey*
105 aĕtŏs (2), *eagle, vulture*

EAGLES'
5403 nᵉshar (Ch.) (1), *large bird of prey*
5404 nesher (1), *large bird of prey*

EAR
24 'âbîyb (1), *head of grain; month of Abib*
238 'âzan (33), to *listen*
241 'ôzen (63), *ear*

2790 chârash (1), to be *silent;* to be *deaf*
5647 'âbad (1), to *do, work, serve*
8085 shâma' (1), to *hear intelligently*
3775 ŏus (13), *ear; listening*
4719 stachus (2), *head of grain*
5621 ōtiŏn (5), *earlet, ear (-lobe)*

EARED
5647 'âbad (1), to *do, work, serve*

EARING
2758 chârîysh (2), *plowing; plowing season*

EARLY
1242 bôqer (3), *morning*
6852 tsâphar (1), to *return*
7836 shâchar (6), to *search for*
7837 shachar (2), *dawn*
7925 shâkam (62), to *start early*
8238 shᵉpharphar (Ch.) (1), *dawn*
260+4404 hama (1), *at the same time, together*
3719 ŏrthrizō (1), to *get up early in the morning*
3721 ŏrthriŏs (1), *up at day-break*
3722 ŏrthrŏs (3), *dawn, daybreak*
4404 prōï (3), *at dawn; day-break* watch
4405 prōïa (1), *day-dawn, early morn*
4406 prōïmŏs (1), *autumnal showering*

EARNEST
603 apŏkaradŏkia (2), *intense anticipation*
728 arrhabōn (3), *pledge, security*
1972 ĕpipŏthēsis (1), *longing for*
4056 pĕrissŏtĕrōs (1), *more superabundantly*
4710 spŏudē (1), *eagerness, earnestness*

EARNESTLY
2734 chârâh (1), to *blaze up*
3190 yâţab (1), to be, *make well*
816 atĕnizō (3), to *gaze intently*
1617 ĕktĕnĕstĕrŏn (1), *more earnest*
1864 ĕpagōnizŏmai (1), to *struggle for, fight for*
1971 ĕpipŏthĕō (1), *intensely crave*
2206 zēlŏō (1), to *have warmth of feeling for*
4335 prŏsĕuchē (1), *prayer; prayer chapel*

EARNETH
7936 sâkar (1), to *hire*

EARRING
5141 nezem (5), *nose-ring*

EARRINGS
3908 lachash (1),
incantation; amulet
5141 nezem (9),
nose-ring
5694 'âgîyl (2), *ear-ring*

EARS
24 'âbîyb (1), *head of
grain; month of Abib*
241 'ôzen (100), *ear*
3759 karmel (3), *planted
field; garden produce*
4425 mᵉlîylâh (1), *cut-off
head* of cereal grain
7641 shibbôl (13),
stream; ear of grain
189 akŏē (4), *hearing;
thing heard*
191 akŏuō (1), to *hear;
obey*
3775 ŏus (24), *ear;
listening*
4719 stachus (3), *head of
grain*

EARTH
127 'ădâmâh (52), *soil;
land*
772 'ăra' (Ch.) (20),
earth, ground, land
776 'erets (710), *earth,
land, soil; country*
778 'ăraq (Ch.) (1), *earth*
2789 cheres (1), *piece of
earthenware pottery*
3007 yabbesheth (Ch.)
(1), *dry land*
6083 'âphâr (7), *dust,
earth, mud; clay,*
1093 gē (186), *soil,
region, whole earth*
1919 ĕpigĕiŏs (1),
worldly, earthly
2709 katachthŏniŏs (1),
infernal
3625 ŏikŏumĕnē (1),
Roman empire
3749 ŏstrakinŏs (1),
made of clay

EARTHEN
2789 cheres (8), *piece of
earthenware pottery*
3335 yâtsar (1), to *form;
potter; to determine*
3749 ŏstrakinŏs (1),
made of clay

EARTHLY
1537+3588+1093 ĕk (1),
out, out of
1919 ĕpigĕiŏs (4),
worldly, earthly

EARTHQUAKE
7494 ra'ash (6),
vibration, uproar
4578 sĕismŏs (10), *gale
storm; earthquake*

EARTHQUAKES
4578 sĕismŏs (3), *gale
storm; earthquake*

EARTHY
5517 chŏïkŏs (4), *dusty,
dirty, i.e. terrene*

EASE
2896 tôwb (1), *good; well*
3427 yâshab (1), to *dwell,
to remain; to settle*

4496 mᵉnûwchâh (1),
peacefully; consolation
5162 nâcham (1), to *be
sorry; to pity, console*
5375 nâsâ' (1), to *lift up*
7043 qâlal (2), to *be easy,
trifling, vile*
7280 râga' (1), to *settle,
i.e. quiet; to wink*
7599 shâ'an (2), to *loll,
i.e. be peaceful*
7600 sha'ănân (6),
secure; haughty
7946 shal'ănân (1),
tranquil
7961 shâlêv (2), *carefree;
security, at ease*
373 anapauō (1), to
repose; to refresh

EASED
1980 hâlak (1), to *walk;
live a certain way*
425 anĕsis (1),
relaxation; relief

EASIER
7043 qâlal (1), to *be easy,
trifling, vile*
2123 ĕukŏpōtĕrŏs (7),
better for toil

EAST
2777 charçûwth (1),
pottery
4161 môwtsâ' (1), *going
forth*
4217 mizrâch (33), *place
of sunrise; east*
4217+8121 mizrâch (2),
place of sunrise; east
6921 qâdîym (61), *east;
eastward; east wind*
6924 qedem (42), *east,
eastern; antiquity*
6926 qidmâh (3), *east; on
the east, in front*
6930 qadmôwn (1),
eastern
6931 qadmôwnîy (4),
oriental, eastern
395 anatŏlē (9), *dawn of
sun; east*

EASTER
3957 pascha (1),
Passover events

EASTWARD
1870+6921 derek (1),
road; course of life
4217 mizrâch (19), *place
of sunrise; east*
4217+8121 mizrâch (1),
place of sunrise; east
6921 qâdîym (7), *East;
eastward; east wind*
6924 qedem (11), *east,
eastern; antiquity*
6926 qidmâh (1), *east; on
the east, in front*

EASY
7043 qâlal (1), to *be easy,
trifling, vile*
2138 ĕupĕithēs (1),
compliant, submissive
2154 ĕusēmŏs (1),
significant
5543 chrēstŏs (1),
employed, i.e. useful

EAT
398 'âkal (497), to *eat*

399 'ăkal (Ch.) (1), to *eat*
402 'oklâh (2), *food*
1262 bârâh (4), to *feed*
2490 châlal (1), to
profane, defile
2939 tᵉ'am (Ch.) (2), to
feed
3898 lâcham (5), to *fight
a battle, i.e. consume*
3899 lechem (1), *food,
bread*
6310 peh (1), *mouth;
opening*
7462 râ'âh (2), to *tend a
flock, i.e. pasture it*
1089 gĕuŏmai (1), to
taste; to eat
2068 ĕsthiō (39), to *eat*
2719 katĕsthiō (1), to
devour
3335 mĕtalambanō (1),
to *participate*
3542+2192 nŏmē (1),
pasture, feeding
4906 sunĕsthiō (4), to
take food with
5315 phagō (88), to *eat*

EATEN
398 'âkal (86), to *eat*
935+413+7130 bôw' (2), to
go or come
1197 bâ'ar (2), to *be
brutish, be senseless*
2490 châlal (1), to
profane, defile
7462 râ'âh (1), to *tend a
flock, i.e. pasture it*
977 bibrōskō (1), to *eat*
1089 gĕuŏmai (2), to
taste; to eat
2068 ĕsthiō (1), to *eat*
2719 katĕsthiō (1), to
devour
2880 kŏrĕnnumi (1), to
cram, i.e. glut or sate
4662 skōlēkŏbrōtŏs (1),
diseased with maggots
5315 phagō (5), to *eat*

EATER
398 'âkal (3), to *eat*

EATERS
2151 zâlal (1), to *be loose
morally, worthless*

EATEST
398 'âkal (3), to *eat*

EATETH
398 'âkal (31), to *eat*
1104 bâla' (1), to
swallow; to destroy
2068 ĕsthiō (13), to *eat*
4906 sunĕsthiō (1), to
take food with
5176 trōgō (5), to *gnaw
or chew, i.e. to eat*

EATING
398 'âkal (13), to *eat*
400 'ôkel (4), *food*
3894 lâchûwm (1), *flesh
as food*
1035 brōsis (1), *food;
rusting corrosion*
2068 ĕsthiō (6), to *eat*
5176 trōgō (1), to *gnaw
or chew, i.e. to eat*
5315 phagō (1), to *eat*

EBAL
5858 'Êybâl (8), *bare, bald*

EBED
5651 'Ebed (6), *servant*

EBED-MELECH
5663 'Ebed Melek (6),
servant of a king

EBEN-EZER
72 'Eben hâ-'êzer (3),
stone of the help

EBER
5677 'Êber (13), *regions
beyond*

EBIASAPH
43 'Ebyâçâph (3),
Ebjasaph

EBONY
1894 hôben (1), *ebony*

EBRONAH
5684 'Ebrônâh (2),
Ebronah

EDAR
5740 'Êder (1), *flock*

EDEN
5731 'Êden (20), *pleasure*

EDER
5740 'Êder (3), *flock*

EDGE
5310 nâphats (1), to *dash
to pieces; to scatter*
6310 peh (34), *mouth;
opening*
6440 pânîym (1), *face;
front*
6697 tsûwr (1), *rock*
6949 qâhâh (3), to *be
dull; be blunt*
7097 qâtseh (8), *extremity*
8193 sâphâh (5), *lip;
edge, margin*
4750 stŏma (2), *mouth;
edge*

EDGES
6366 pêyâh (1), *edge*
7098 qâtsâh (1),
termination; fringe
7099 qetsev (1), *limit,
borders*
1366 distŏmŏs (1),
double-edged

EDIFICATION
3619 ŏikŏdŏmē (4),
edification

EDIFIED
3618 ŏikŏdŏmĕō (2), to
construct, edify

EDIFIETH
3618 ŏikŏdŏmĕō (3), to
construct, edify

EDIFY
3618 ŏikŏdŏmĕō (2), to
construct, edify
3619 ŏikŏdŏmē (1),
edification

EDIFYING
3618 ŏikŏdŏmĕō (1), to
construct, edify
3619 ŏikŏdŏmē (7),
edification

EDOM
123 'Êdôm (87), *red*

EDOMITE
130 'Êdômîy (6), *Edomite*

EDOMITES
130 'Ĕdômîy (12), Edomite

EDREI
154 'edre'îy (8), mighty

EFFECT
1697 dâbâr (1), word; matter; thing
5106 nûw' (1), to refuse, forbid, dissuade
5656 'ăbôdâh (1), work of any kind
6213 'âsâh (1), to do or make
6565 pârar (1), to break up; to violate, frustrate
208 akuróŏ (2), to invalidate, nullify
1601 ĕkpiptō (1), to drop away
2673 katargĕŏ (4), to be, render entirely useless
2758 kĕnŏŏ (1), to make empty

EFFECTED
6743 tsâlach (1), to push forward

EFFECTUAL
1753 ĕnĕrgĕia (2), efficiency, energy
1754 ĕnĕrgĕŏ (2), to be active, efficient, work
1756 ĕnĕrgēs (2), active, operative

EFFECTUALLY
1754 ĕnĕrgĕŏ (2). to be active, efficient, work

EFFEMINATE
3120 malakŏs (1), soft; catamite homosexual

EGG
2495 challâmûwth (1), (poss.) purslain plant
5609 ŏŏn (1), egg

EGGS
1000 bêytsâh (6), egg

EGLAH
5698 'Eglâh (2), heifer

EGLAIM
97 'Eglayim (1), double pond

EGLON
5700 'Eglôwn (13), vituline

EGYPT
4713 Mitsrîy (1), Mitsrite
4714 Mitsrayim (585), double border
125 Aiguptŏs (24), Ægyptus

EGYPTIAN
4713 Mitsrîy (18), Mitsrite
4714 Mitsrayim (2), double border
124 Aiguptiŏs (3), inhabitant of Ægyptus

EGYPTIAN'S
4713 Mitsrîy (4), Mitsrite

EGYPTIANS
4713 Mitsrîy (7), Mitsrite
4714 Mitsrayim (88), double border
124 Aiguptiŏs (2), inhabitant of Ægyptus

EHI
278 'Êchîy (1), Echi

EHUD
261 'Êchûwd (10), united

EIGHT
8083 shᵉmôneh (74), eight; eighth
3638 ŏktō (6), eight

EIGHTEEN
7239+8083 ribbôw (1), myriad
8083+6240 shᵉmôneh (18), eight; eighth
1176+2532+3638 dĕka (3), ten

EIGHTEENTH
8083+6240 shᵉmôneh (11), eight; eighth

EIGHTH
8066 shᵉmîynîy (28), eight, eighth
8083 shᵉmôneh (4), eight; eighth
3590 ŏgdŏŏs (5), eighth
3637 ŏktaēmĕrŏs (1), eighth-day

EIGHTIETH
8084 shᵉmônîym (1), eighty; eightieth

EIGHTY
8084 shᵉmônîym (3), eighty; eightieth

EITHER
176 'ôw (7), or, whether; desire
376 'îysh (3), man; male; someone
518 'îm (1), whether?; if, although; Oh that!
1571 gam (1), also; even; "both...and"
3588 kîy (1), for, that because
8145 shênîy (1), second; again
2228 ē (9), or; than

EKER
6134 'Êqer (1), naturalized citizen

EKRON
6138 'Eqrôwn (22), eradication

EKRONITES
6139 'Eqrôwnîy (2), Ekronite

EL-BETH-EL
416 'Êl Bêyth-'Êl (1), God of Bethel

EL-ELOHE-ISRAEL
415 'Êl 'ĕlôhêy Yisrâ'êl (1), mighty God of Israel

EL-PARAN
364 'Êyl Pâ'rân (1), oak of Paran

ELADAH
497 'El'âdâh (1), God has decked

ELAH
425 'Êlâh (17), oak

ELAM
5867 'Êylâm (28), distant

ELAMITES
5962 'Almîy (Ch.) (1), Elamite
1639 'Êlamitēs (1), distant ones

ELASAH
501 'El'âsâh (2), God has made

ELATH
359 'Êylôwth (5), grove (of palms)

ELDAAH
420 'Elda'âh (2), God of knowledge

ELDAD
419 'Eldâd (2), God has loved

ELDER
1419 gâdôwl (8), great
2205+3117 zâqên (1), old, venerated
7227 rab (1), great
3187 mĕizōn (1), larger, greater
4245 prĕsbutĕrŏs (7), elderly; older; presbyter
4850 sumprĕsbutĕrŏs (1), co-presbyter

ELDERS
2205 zâqên (113), old, venerated
7868 sîyb (Ch.) (5), to become aged
4244 prĕsbutĕriŏn (2), order of elders
4245 prĕsbutĕrŏs (58), elderly; older; presbyter

ELDEST
1060 bᵉkôwr (5), firstborn, i.e. oldest son
1419 gâdôwl (6), great
2205 zâqên (1), old, venerated
7223 rî'shôwn (1), first, in place, time or rank
4245 prĕsbutĕrŏs (1), elderly; older; presbyter

ELEAD
496 'El'âd (1), God has testified

ELEALEH
500 'El'âlê' (5), God (is) going up

ELEASAH
501 'El'âsâh (4), God has made

ELEAZAR
499 'El'âzâr (71), God (is) helper
1648 Elĕazar (2), God (is) helper

ELECT
972 bâchîyr (4), selected one
1588 ĕklĕktŏs (13), selected; chosen

ELECT'S
1588 ĕklĕktŏs (3), selected; chosen

ELECTED
4899 sunĕklĕktŏs (1), co-elected

ELECTION
1589 ĕklŏgē (6), selection, choice

ELEMENTS
4747 stŏichĕiŏn (4), elements, elementary

ELEPH
507 'Eleph (1), thousand

ELEVEN
259+6240 'echâd (9), first
505+3967 eleph (3), thousand
6249+6240 'ashtêy (6), eleven; eleventh
1733 hĕndĕka (6), eleven

ELEVENTH
259+6240 'echâd (4), first
6249+6240 'ashtêy (12), eleven; eleventh
1734 hĕndĕkatŏs (3), eleventh

ELHANAN
445 'Elchânân (4), God (is) gracious

ELI
5941 'Êlîy (32), lofty
2241 ēli (1), my God

ELI'S
5941 'Êlîy (1), lofty

ELIAB
446 'Êlîy'âb (20), God of (his) father

ELIAB'S
446 'Êlîy'âb (1), God of (his) father

ELIADA
450 'Elyâdâ' (3), God (is) knowing

ELIADAH
450 'Elyâdâ' (1), God (is) knowing

ELIAH
452 'Êlîyâh (2), God of Jehovah

ELIAHBA
455 'Elyachbâ' (2), God will hide

ELIAKIM
471 'Elyâqîym (12), God of raising
1662 Ĕliakĕim (3), God of raising

ELIAM
463 'Êlîy'âm (2), God of (the) people

ELIAS
2243 Hēlias (30), God of Jehovah

ELIASAPH
460 'Elyâçâph (6), God (is) gatherer

ELIASHIB
475 'Elyâshîyb (17), God will restore

ELIATHAH
448 'Êlîy'âthâh (2), God of (his) consent

ELIDAD
449 'Êlîydâd (1), God of (his) love

E

ELIEL
447 'Ĕlîy'êl (10), *God of* (his) *God*

ELIENAI
462 'Ĕlîy'êynay (1), *Elienai*

ELIEZER
461 'Ĕlîy'ezer (14), *God of help*
1663 Ĕliĕzĕr (1), *God of help*

ELIHOENAI
454 'Elyᵉhôw'êynay (1), *toward Jehovah* (are) *my eyes*

ELIHOREPH
456 'Ĕlîychôreph (1), *God of autumn*

ELIHU
453 'Ĕlîyhûw (11), *God of him*

ELIJAH
452 'Ĕlîyâh (69), *God of Jehovah*

ELIKA
470 'Ĕlîyqâ' (1), *God of rejection*

ELIM
362 'Êylîm (6), palm-*trees*

ELIMELECH
458 'Ĕlîymelek (4), *God of* (the) *king*

ELIMELECH'S
458 'Ĕlîymelek (2), *God of* (the) *king*

ELIOENAI
454 'Elyᵉhôw'êynay (8), *toward Jehovah* (are) *my eyes*

ELIPHAL
465 'Ĕlîyphâl (1), *God of judgment*

ELIPHALET
467 'Ĕlîypheleṭ (2), *God of deliverance*

ELIPHAZ
464 'Ĕlîyphaz (15), *God of gold*

ELIPHELEH
466 'Ĕlîyphᵉlêhûw (2), *God of his distinction*

ELIPHELET
467 'Ĕlîypheleṭ (6), *God of deliverance*

ELISABETH
1665 Ĕlisabĕt (8), *God of* (the) *oath*

ELISABETH'S
1665 Ĕlisabĕt (1), *God of* (the) *oath*

ELISEUS
1666 Ĕlissaiŏs (1), *Elisha*

ELISHA
477 'Ĕlîyshâ' (58), *Elisha*

ELISHAH
473 'Ĕlîyshâh (3), *Elishah*

ELISHAMA
476 'Ĕlîyshâmâ' (17), *God of hearing*

ELISHAPHAT
478 'Ĕlîyshâphâṭ (1), *God of judgment*

ELISHEBA
472 'Ĕlîysheba' (1), *God of* (the) *oath*

ELISHUA
474 'Ĕlîyshûwa' (2), *God of supplication* (or *of riches*)

ELIUD
1664 Ĕliŏud (2), *God of majesty*

ELIZAPHAN
469 'Ĕlîytsâphân (4), *God of treasure*

ELIZUR
468 'Ĕlîytsûwr (5), *God of* (the) *rock*

ELKANAH
511 'Elqânâh (20), *God has obtained*

ELKOSHITE
512 'Elqôshîy (1), *Elkoshite*

ELLASAR
495 'Ellâçâr (2), *Ellasar*

ELMODAM
1678 Ĕlmŏdam (1), *Elmodam*

ELMS
424 'êlâh (1), *oak*

ELNAAM
493 'Elna'am (1), *God* (is) his) *delight*

ELNATHAN
494 'Elnâthân (7), *God* (is the) *giver*

ELOI
1682 ĕlōï (1), *my God*

ELON
356 'Êylôwn (7), *oak-grove*

ELON-BETH-HANAN
358 'Êylôwn Bêyth Chânân (1), *oak-grove of* (the) *house of favor*

ELONITES
440 'Êlôwnîy (1), *Elonite*

ELOQUENT
376+1697 'îysh (1), *man; male; someone*
995 bîyn (1), *to understand; discern*
3052 lŏgiŏs (1), *fluent,* i.e. an *orator*

ELOTH
359 'Êylôwth (3), *grove* (*of palms*)

ELPAAL
508 'Elpa'al (3), *God* (is) *act*

ELPALET
467 'Ĕlîypheleṭ (1), *God of deliverance*

ELSE
369 'ayin (1), *there is no,* i.e., *not exist, none*
518 'îm (1), *whether?; if, although; Oh that!*
3588 kîy (3), *for, that because*

5750 'ôwd (13), *again; repeatedly; still; more*
1490 ĕi dĕ mĕ(gĕ) (8), *but if not*
1893 ĕpĕi (2), *since*
2087 hĕtĕrŏs (1), *other or different*
2532 kai (1), *and; or; even; also*

ELTEKEH
514 'Eltᵉqê' (2), *Eltekeh*

ELTEKON
515 'Eltᵉqôn (1), *God* (is) *straight*

ELTOLAD
513 'Eltôwlad (2), *God* (is) *generator*

ELUL
435 'Ĕlûwl (1), *Elul*

ELUZAI
498 'El'ûwzay (1), *God* (is) *defensive*

ELYMAS
1681 Ĕlumas (1), *Elymas*

ELZABAD
443 'Elzâbâd (2), *God has bestowed*

ELZAPHAN
469 'Ĕlîytsâphân (2), *God of treasure*

EMBALM
2590 chânaṭ (1), *to embalm; to ripen*

EMBALMED
2590 chânaṭ (3), *to embalm; to ripen*

EMBOLDENED
3618 ŏikŏdŏmĕō (1), *to construct, edify*

EMBOLDENETH
4834 mârats (1), *to be pungent or vehement*

EMBRACE
2263 châbaq (8), *to clasp the hands, embrace*

EMBRACED
2263 châbaq (3), *to clasp the hands, embrace*
782 aspazŏmai (2), *to salute, welcome*

EMBRACING
2263 châbaq (1), *to clasp the hands, embrace*
4843 sumpĕrilambanō (1), *to embrace*

EMBROIDER
7660 shâbats (1), *to interweave*

EMBROIDERER
7551 râqam (1), *variegation; embroider*

EMERALD
5306 nôphek (3), (poss.) *garnet*
4664 smaragdinŏs (1), *of emerald*
4665 smaragdŏs (1), *green emerald*

EMERALDS
5306 nôphek (1), (poss.) *garnet*

EMERODS
2914 ṭᵉchôr (2), *piles, tumor*
6076 'ôphel (6), *tumor; fortress*

EMIMS
368 'Êymîym (3), *terrors*

EMINENT
1354 gab (3), *mounded or rounded: top or rim*
8524 tâlal (1), *to elevate*

EMMANUEL
1694 Ĕmmanŏuĕl (1), *God with us*

EMMAUS
1695 Ĕmmaŏus (1), *Emmaüs*

EMMOR
1697 Ĕmmŏr (1), *male donkey or ass*

EMPIRE
4438 malkûwth (1), *rule; dominion*

EMPLOY
935+6440 bôw' (1), *to go or come*

EMPLOYED
5921 'al (1), *above, over, upon, or against*
5975 'âmad (1), *to stand*

EMPTIED
1238 bâqaq (2), *to depopulate, ruin*
1809 dâlal (1), *to slacken, dangle*
6168 'ârâh (2), *to be, make bare; to empty*
7324 rûwq (2), *to pour out, i.e. empty*
7386 rêyq (1), *empty; worthless*

EMPTIERS
1238 bâqaq (1), *to depopulate, ruin*

EMPTINESS
922 bôhûw (1), *ruin, desolation*

EMPTY
950 bûwqâh (1), *empty, pillaged*
1238 bâqaq (3), *to depopulate, ruin*
6437 pânâh (1), *to turn, to face*
6485 pâqad (3), *to visit, care for, count*
7324 rûwq (5), *to pour out, i.e. empty*
7385 rîyq (5), *emptiness; worthless* thing; *in vain*
7386 rêyq (2), *empty; worthless*
7387 rêyqâm (12), *emptily; ineffectually*
8414 tôhûw (1), *waste, desolation, formless*
2756 kĕnŏs (4), *empty; vain; useless*
4980 schŏlazō (1), *to take a holiday*

EMULATION
3863 parazēlŏō (1), *to excite to rivalry*

EMULATIONS
2205 zēlŏs (1), *zeal,
ardor; jealousy, malice*

EN-DOR
5874 'Êyn-Dô'r (3),
fountain of dwelling

EN-EGLAIM
5882 'Êyn 'Eglayim (1),
fountain of two calves

EN-GANNIM
5873 'Êyn Gannîym (3),
fountain of gardens

EN-GEDI
5872 'Êyn Gedîy (6),
fountain of a kid

EN-HADDAH
5876 'Êyn Chaddâh (1),
fountain of sharpness

EN-HAKKORE
5875 'Êyn haq-Qôwrê'
(1), *fountain of One
calling*

EN-HAZOR
5877 'Êyn Châtsôwr (1),
fountain of a village

EN-MISHPAT
5880 'Êyn Mishpâṭ (1),
fountain of judgment

EN-RIMMON
5884 'Êyn Rimmôwn (1),
*fountain of a
pomegranate*

EN-ROGEL
5883 'Êyn Rôgêl (4),
fountain of a traveller

EN-SHEMESH
5885 'Êyn Shemesh (2),
fountain of (the) sun

EN-TAPPUAH
5887 'Êyn Tappûwach
(1), *fountain of an
apple tree*

ENABLED
1743 ĕndunamŏō (1), to
empower, strengthen

ENAM
5879 'Êynayim (1),
double fountain

ENAN
5881 'Êynân (5), *having
eyes*

ENCAMP
2583 chânâh (11), to
*encamp for abode or
siege*

ENCAMPED
2583 chânâh (33), to
encamp

ENCAMPETH
2583 chânâh (2), to
encamp

ENCAMPING
2583 chânâh (1), to
encamp

ENCHANTER
5172 nâchash (1), to
prognosticate

ENCHANTERS
6049 'ânan (1), to *cover,
becloud; to act covertly*

ENCHANTMENT
3908 lachash (1),
incantation; amulet
5172 nâchash (2), to
prognosticate

ENCHANTMENTS
2267 cheber (2), *society,
group; magic spell*
3858 lahaṭ (1), *blaze;
magic*
3909 lâṭ (3), *incantation;
secrecy; covertly*
5172 nâchash (4), to
prognosticate

ENCOUNTERED
4820 sumballō (1), to
consider; to aid; to join

ENCOURAGE
2388 châzaq (4), to *be
strong; couraqeousd,
restrain, conquer*

ENCOURAGED
2388 châzaq (5), to *be
strong; courageous*

END
319 'achărîyth (21),
future; posterity
657 'epheç (1), *end; no
further*
1104 bâla' (1), to
swallow; to destroy
1584 gâmar (1), to *end;
to complete; to fail*
1700 dibrâh (1), *reason,
suit or style; because*
2583 chânâh (1), to
encamp
2856 châtham (1), to
close up; to affix a seal
3318 yâtsâ' (1), to *go,
bring out*
3615 kâlâh (56), to
complete, prepare
4390 mâlê' (1), to *fill; be
full*
4616 ma'an (8), *in order
that*
5239 nâlâh (1), to
complete, attain
5331 netsach (2),
splendor; lasting
5486 çûwph (1), to
terminate
5490 çôwph (3),
termination; end
5491 çôwph (Ch.) (5), *end*
5704+5769+5703 'ad (1),
during; while; until
6118 'êqeb (2), on
account of
6285 pê'âh (1), *direction;
region; extremity*
6310 peh (3), *mouth;
opening*
7078 qenets (1),
perversion
7093 qêts (51), *extremity;
after*
7097 qâtseh (48),
extremity
7098 qâtsâh (4),
termination; fringe
7117 qᵉtsâth (3),
termination; portion
7118 qᵉtsâth (Ch.) (2),
termination; portion

7999 shâlam (2), to *be
safe; complete*
8503 taklîyth (2),
extremity
8537 tôm (1),
completeness
8552 tâmam (2), to
complete, finish
8622 tᵉqûwphâh (2),
revolution, course
165+3588+165 aiōn (1),
perpetuity, ever; world
206 akrŏn (1), *extremity:
end, top*
1519 ĕis (4), *to or into*
1545 ĕkbasis (1), *exit,
way out*
2078 ĕschatŏs (1),
farthest, final
3796 ŏpsĕ (1), *late in the
day*
4009 pĕras (1), *extremity,
end, limit*
4930 suntĕlĕia (6), *entire
completion*
5049 tĕlĕiŏs (1),
completely
5055 tĕlĕō (1), to *end, i.e.
complete, conclude*
5056 tĕlŏs (34),
conclusion

ENDAMAGE
5142 nᵉzaq (Ch.) (1), to
suffer, inflict loss

ENDANGER
2325 chûwb (1), to *tie, to
owe, to forfeit*

ENDANGERED
5533 çâkan (1), to
damage; to grow

ENDEAVOUR
4704 spŏudazō (1), to
make effort

ENDEAVOURED
2212 zētĕō (1), to *seek*
4704 spŏudazō (1), to
make effort

ENDEAVOURING
4704 spŏudazō (1), to
make effort

ENDEAVOURS
4611 ma'ălâl (1), *act,
deed*

ENDED
3615 kâlâh (7), to *cease,
be finished, perish*
7999 shâlam (2), to *be
safe; be complete*
8552 tâmam (5), to
complete, finish
1096 ginŏmai (1), to *be,
become*
4137 plērŏō (2), to *fill,
make complete*
4931 suntĕlĕō (4), to
complete entirely

ENDETH
2308 châdal (1), to *desist,
stop; be fat*

ENDING
5056 tĕlŏs (1), *conclusion
of an act or state*

ENDLESS
179 akatalutŏs (1),
permanent

562 apĕrantŏs (1),
without a finish

ENDOW
4117 mâhar (1), to *wed a
wife by bargaining*

ENDS
657 'epheç (13), *end; no
further*
1383 gablûth (2), *twisted
chain or lace*
3671 kânâph (2), *edge or
extremity; wing*
4020 migbâlâh (1),
border on garb
7097 qâtseh (7), *extremity*
7098 qâtsâh (17),
termination; fringe
7099 qetsev (4), *limit,
borders*
7218 rô'sh (2), *head*
2078 ĕschatŏs (1),
farthest, final
4009 pĕras (1), *extremity,
end, limit*
5056 tĕlŏs (1), *conclusion
of an act or state*

ENDUED
2064 zâbad (1), to *confer,
bestow a gift*
3045 yâda' (2), to *know*
1746 ĕnduō (1), to *dress*
1990 ĕpistēmōn (1),
intelligent, learned

ENDURE
1961 hâyâh (3), to *exist,
i.e. be or become*
3201 yâkôl (2), to *be able*
3427 yâshab (2), to *dwell,
to remain; to settle*
3885 lûwn (1), to *be
obstinate*
5975 'âmad (3), to *stand*
6440 pânîym (1), *face;
front*
6965 qûwm (1), to *rise*
7272 regel (1), *foot; step*
430 anĕchŏmai (2), *put
up with, endure*
2076 ĕsti (1), *he (she or
it) is; they are*
2553 kakŏpathĕō (2), to
undergo hardship
5278 hupŏmĕnō (5), to
undergo (trials)
5297 hupŏphĕrō (1), to
undergo hardship
5342 phĕrō (1), to *bear or
carry*

ENDURED
1961 hâyâh (1), to *exist,
i.e. be or become*
2594 kartĕrĕō (1), to *be
steadfast or patient*
3114 makrŏthumĕō (1),
to *be forbearing, patient*
5278 hupŏmĕnō (3), to
undergo (trials)
5297 hupŏphĕrō (1), to
undergo hardship
5342 phĕrō (1), to *bear or
carry*

ENDURETH
1097 bᵉlîy (1), *without,
not yet; lacking*;
5975 'âmad (4), to *stand*
3306 mĕnō (2), to *stay,
remain*

5278 hupŏmĕnō (3), to undergo (trials)

ENDURING
5975 'âmad (1), to stand
3306 mĕnō (1), to stay, remain
5281 hupŏmŏnē (1), endurance, constancy

ENEMIES
341 'ôyêb (199), adversary, enemy
6145 'âr (1), foe
6146 'âr (Ch.) (1), foe
6862 tsar (26), trouble; opponent
6887 tsârar (9), to cramp
6965 qûwm (1), to rise
7790 shûwr (1), foe as lying in wait
8130 sânê' (3), to hate
8324 shârar (5), opponent
2190 ĕchthrŏs (19), adversary

ENEMIES'
341 'ôyêb (3), adversary, enemy

ENEMY
340 'âyab (1), to be hostile, be an enemy
341 'ôyêb (78), adversary, enemy
6145 'âr (1), foe
6862 tsar (9), trouble; opponent
6887 tsârar (5), to cramp
8130 sânê' (2), to hate
2190 ĕchthrŏs (11), adversary

ENEMY'S
341 'ôyêb (1), adversary, enemy
6862 tsar (2), trouble; opponent

ENFLAMING
2552 châmam (1), to be hot; to be in a rage

ENGAGED
6148 'ârab (1), to intermix

ENGINES
2810 chishshâbôwn (1), machination, scheme
4239 mᵉchîy (1), stroke of a battering-ram

ENGRAFTED
1721 ĕmphutŏs (1), implanted

ENGRAVE
6605 pâthach (2), to open wide; to plow, carve

ENGRAVEN
1795 ĕntupŏō (1), to engrave, carve

ENGRAVER
2796 chârâsh (3), skilled fabricator or worker

ENGRAVINGS
6603 pittûwach (5), sculpture; engraving

ENJOIN
2004 ĕpitassō (1), to order, command

ENJOINED
6485 pâqad (1), to visit, care for, count

6965 qûwm (1), to rise
1781 ĕntĕllŏmai (1), to enjoin, give orders

ENJOY
1086 bâlâh (1), to wear out; consume, spend
1961 hâyâh (1), to exist, i.e. be or become
3423 yârash (2), to inherit; to impoverish
7200 râ'âh (4), to see
7521 râtsâh (3), to be pleased with; to satisfy
619 apŏlausis (1), full enjoyment, pleasure
2192+619 ĕchō (1), to have; hold; keep
5177 tugchanō (1), to take part in; to obtain

ENJOYED
7521 râtsâh (1), to be pleased with; to satisfy

ENLARGE
6601 pâthâh (1), to be, make simple; to delude
7235 râbâh (1), to increase
7337 râchab (7), to broaden
3170 mĕgalunō (1), to increase or extol

ENLARGED
7337 râchab (8), to broaden
3170 mĕgalunō (1), to increase or extol
4115 platunō (2), to widen

ENLARGEMENT
7305 revach (1), room; deliverance

ENLARGETH
7337 râchab (2), to broaden
7849 shâṭach (1), to expand

ENLARGING
7337 râchab (1), to broaden

ENLIGHTEN
5050 nâgahh (1), to illuminate

ENLIGHTENED
215 'ôwr (4), to be luminous
5461 phōtizō (2), to shine or to brighten up

ENLIGHTENING
215 'ôwr (1), to be luminous

ENMITY
342 'êybâh (2), hostility
2189 ĕchthra (5), hostility; opposition

ENOCH
2585 Chănôwk (9), initiated
1802 Ĕnôch (3), initiated

ENOS
583 'Ĕnôwsh (6), man; person, human
1800 Ĕnôs (1), man

ENOSH
583 'Ĕnôwsh (1), man; person, human

ENOUGH
1767 day (6), enough, sufficient
1952 hôwn (2), wealth
3027 yâd (1), hand; power
3605 kôl (1), all, any or every
4672 mâtsâ' (1), to find or acquire; to occur
7227 rab (7), great
7654 sob'âh (2), satiety
566 apĕchĕi (1), it is sufficient
713 arkĕtŏs (1), satisfactory, enough
714 arkĕō (1), to avail; be satisfactory
2425 hikanŏs (1), ample; fit
2880 kŏrĕnnumi (1), to cram, i.e. glut or sate
4052 pĕrissĕuō (1), to superabound

ENQUIRE
1158 bâ'âh (2), to ask; be bulging, swelling
1239 bâqar (2), to inspect, admire, care for, consider
1240 bᵉqar (Ch.) (1), to inspect, admire, care for, consider
1875 dârash (32), to pursue or search; to seek or ask; to worship
7592 shâ'al (7), to ask
1231 diaginōskŏ (1), ascertain exactly
1833 ĕxĕtazō (1), to ascertain or interrogate
1934 ĕpizētĕō (1), to search (inquire) for
2212 zētĕō (2), to seek
4441 punthanŏmai (1), to ask for information
4802 suzētĕō (1), to discuss, controvert

ENQUIRED
1245 bâqash (2), to search; to strive after
1875 dârash (10), to pursue or search
7592 shâ'al (15), to ask
7836 shâchar (1), to search for
198 akribŏō (2), to ascertain, find out
1567 ĕkzētĕō (1), to seek
4441 punthanŏmai (1), to ask for information

ENQUIREST
1245 bâqash (1), to search; to strive after

ENQUIRY
1239 bâqar (1), to inspect, admire, care
1331 diĕrōtaō (1), to question throughout

ENRICH
6238 'âshar (2), to grow, make rich

ENRICHED
4148 plŏutizō (2), to make wealthy

ENRICHEST
6238 'âshar (1), to grow, make rich

ENSAMPLE
5179 tupŏs (1), shape or resemblance; "type"
5262 hupŏdĕigma (1), exhibit, specimen

ENSAMPLES
5179 tupŏs (3), shape or resemblance; "type"

ENSIGN
226 'ôwth (1), signal, sign
5251 nêç (6), flag; signal
5264 nâçaç (1), to gleam; to flutter a flag

ENSIGNS
226 'ôwth (1), signal, sign

ENSNARED
4170 môwqêsh (1), noose for catching animals

ENSUE
1377 diōkō (1), to pursue; to persecute

ENTANGLE
3802 pagidĕuō (1), to ensnare, entrap

ENTANGLED
943 bûwk (1), to be confused
1707 ĕmplĕkō (1), to involve with
1758 ĕnĕchō (1), to keep a grudge

ENTANGLETH
1707 ĕmplĕkō (1), to involve with

ENTER
935 bôw' (81), to go or come
1980 hâlak (1), to walk; live a certain way
5674 'âbar (1), to cross over; to transition
1525 ĕisĕrchŏmai (63), to enter
1529 ĕisŏdŏs (1), entrance
1531 ĕispŏrĕuŏmai (1), to enter

ENTERED
935 bôw' (38), to go or come
305 anabainō (2), to go up, rise
1524 ĕisĕimi (1), to enter
1525 ĕisĕrchŏmai (53), to enter
1531 ĕispŏrĕuŏmai (3), to enter
1684 ĕmbainō (7), to embark; to reach
2064 ĕrchŏmai (2), to go or come
3922 parĕisĕrchŏmai (1), to supervene

ENTERETH
935 bôw' (9), to go or come
5181 nâchath (1), to sink, descend; to press down
1531 ĕispŏrĕuŏmai (5), to enter
1535 ĕitĕ (4), if too

ENTERING
935 bôw' (15), to go, come
3996 mâbôw' (3), entrance; sunset; west
6607 pethach (17), opening; entrance way
1525 ĕisĕrchŏmai (4), to enter
1529 ĕisŏdŏs (1), entrance
1531 ĕispŏrĕuŏmai (4), to enter
1684 ĕmbainō (1), to embark; to reach
1910 ĕpibainō (1), to mount, arrive

ENTERPRISE
8454 tûwshîyâh (1), ability, undertaking

ENTERTAIN
5381 philŏnĕxia (1), hospitableness

ENTERTAINED
3579 xĕnizō (1), to be a host; to be a guest

ENTICE
5496 çûwth (1), to stimulate; to seduce
6601 pâthâh (7), to be, make simple; to delude

ENTICED
6601 pâthâh (2), to be, make simple; to delude
1185 dĕlĕazō (1), to delude, seduce

ENTICETH
6601 pâthâh (1), to be, make simple; to delude

ENTICING
3981 pĕithŏs (1), persuasive
4086 pithanŏlŏgia (1), persuasive language

ENTIRE
3648 hŏlŏklērŏs (1), entirely sound in body

ENTRANCE
935 bôw' (2), to go or come
2978 y^{e}'îthôwn (1), entry
3996 mâbôw' (3), entrance; sunset; west
6607 pethach (2), opening; entrance way
6608 pêthach (1), opening
1529 ĕisŏdŏs (2), entrance

ENTRANCES
6607 pethach (1), opening; entrance way

ENTREAT
6293 pâga' (1), to impinge
2559 kakŏō (1), to injure; to oppress; to embitter

ENTREATED
818 atimazō (1), to maltreat, dishonor
2559 kakŏō (1), to injure; to oppress; to embitter
5195 hubrizō (3), to exercise violence
5530 chraŏmai (1), to employ or to act toward

ENTRIES
6607 pethach (1), opening; entrance way

ENTRY
872 b^{e}'âh (1), entrance
3996 mâbôw' (6), entrance; sunset; west
6310 peh (1), mouth; opening
6607 pethach (7), opening; entrance way

ENVIED
7065 qânâ' (5), to be, make jealous, envious
7068 qin'âh (1), jealousy or envy

ENVIES
5355 phthŏnŏs (1), spiteful jealousy, envy

ENVIEST
7065 qânâ' (1), to be, make jealous, envious

ENVIETH
2206 zēlŏō (1), to have warmth of feeling for

ENVIOUS
7065 qânâ' (4), to be, make jealous, envious

ENVIRON
5437 çâbab (1), to surround

ENVY
7065 qânâ' (3), to be, make zealous, jealous or envious
7068 qin'âh (7), jealousy or envy
2205 zēlŏs (1), zeal, ardor; jealousy, malice
2206 zēlŏō (2), to have warmth of feeling for
5355 phthŏnŏs (7), spiteful jealousy, envy

ENVYING
2205 zēlŏs (4), zeal, ardor; jealousy, malice
5354 phthŏnĕō (1), to be jealous of

ENVYINGS
2205 zēlŏs (1), zeal, ardor; jealousy, malice
5355 phthŏnŏs (1), spiteful jealousy, envy

EPAENETUS
1866 Ĕpainĕtŏs (1), praised

EPAPHRAS
1889 Ĕpaphras (3), devoted to Venus

EPAPHRODITUS
1891 Ĕpaphrŏditŏs (3), devoted to Venus

EPHAH
374 'êyphâh (34), dry grain measure
5891 'Êyphâh (5), obscurity

EPHAI
5778 'Ôwphay (1), birdlike

EPHER
6081 'Êpher (4), gazelle

EPHES-DAMMIM
658 'Epheç Dammîym (1), boundary of blood

EPHESIAN
2180 Ĕphĕsiŏs (1), Ephesian

EPHESIANS
2180 Ĕphĕsiŏs (5), Ephesian

EPHESUS
2181 Ĕphĕsŏs (17), Ephesus

EPHLAL
654 'Ephlâl (2), judge

EPHOD
641 'Êphôd (1), Ephod
642 'êphuddâh (2), plating
646 'êphôwd (49), ephod

EPHPHATHA
2188 ĕphphatha (1), be opened!

EPHRAIM
669 'Ephrayim (171), double fruit
2187 Ĕphraïm (1), double fruit

EPHRAIM'S
669 'Ephrayim (4), double fruit

EPHRAIMITE
673 'Ephrâthîy (1), Ephrathite or Ephraimite

EPHRAIMITES
669 'Ephrayim (5), double fruit

EPHRAIN
6085 'Ephrôwn (1), fawn-like

EPHRATAH
672 'Ephrâth (5), fruitfulness

EPHRATH
672 'Ephrâth (5), fruitfulness

EPHRATHITE
673 'Ephrâthîy (3), Ephrathite or Ephraimite

EPHRATHITES
673 'Ephrâthîy (1), Ephrathite or Ephraimite

EPHRON
6085 'Ephrôwn (13), fawn-like

EPICUREANS
1946 Ĕpikŏurĕiŏs (1), servant

EPISTLE
1992 ĕpistŏlē (13), written message

EPISTLES
1992 ĕpistŏlē (2), written message

EQUAL
1809 dâlal (1), to slacken, dangle
4339 mêyshâr (1), straightness; rectitude
6186 'ârak (2), to set in a row, i.e. arrange,
6187 'êrek (1), pile, equipment, estimate
7737 shâvâh (3), to level, i.e. equalize
8505 tâkan (7), to balance, i.e. measure
2465 isaggĕlŏs (1), angelic, like an angel
2470 isŏs (4), similar
2471 isŏtēs (1), likeness; fairness

EQUALITY
2471 isŏtēs (2), likeness; fairness

EQUALLY
7947 shâlab (1), to make equidistant

EQUALS
4915 sunēlikiōtēs (1), alike, contemporary

EQUITY
3476 yôsher (1), right
3477 yâshâr (1), straight
3788 kishrôwn (1), success; advantage
4334 mîyshôwr (2), plain; justice
4339 mêyshâr (4), straightness; rectitude
5229 n^{e}kôchâh (1), integrity; truth

ER
6147 'Êr (10), watchful
2262 Ēr (1), watchful

ERAN
6197 'Êrân (1), watchful

ERANITES
6198 'Êrânîy (1), Eranite

ERASTUS
2037 Ĕrastŏs (3), beloved

ERE
2962 ṭerem (4), not yet or before
3808 lô' (4), no, not
4250 prin (1), prior, sooner, before

ERECH
751 'Erek (1), length

ERECTED
5324 nâtsab (1), to station

ERI
6179 'Êrîy (2), watchful

ERITES
6180 'Êrîy (1), Erite

ERR
7686 shâgâh (4), to stray, wander; to transgress
8582 tâ'âh (14), to vacillate, i.e. stray
4105 planaō (6), to roam, wander; to deceive

ERRAND
1697 dâbâr (3), word; matter; thing

ERRED
7683 shâgag (5), to stray; to sin
7686 shâgâh (2), to stray, wander; to transgress
8582 tâ'âh (2), to vacillate, i.e. stray

635 apŏplanaō (1), *to lead astray; to wander*
795 astŏchĕō (2), *deviate or wander* from truth

ERRETH
7686 shâgâh (1), *to stray, wander; to transgress*
8582 tâ'âh (1), *to vacillate*, i.e. *stray*

ERROR
4879 mᵉshûwgâh (1), *mistake*
7684 shᵉgâgâh (2), *mistake*
7944 shal (1), *fault*
7960 shâlûw (Ch.) (1), *fault, error*
8432 tâvek (1), *center, middle*
4106 planē (7), *fraudulence; straying*

ERRORS
7691 shᵉgîy'âh (1), *moral mistake*
8595 ta'tûa' (2), *fraud*
51 agnŏēma (1), *sin committed in ignorance*

ESAIAS
2268 Hēsaïas (21), *Jehovah has saved*

ESAR-HADDON
634 'Êçar-Chaddôwn (3), *Esar-chaddon*

ESAU
6215 'Êsâv (84), *rough*
2269 Ēsau (3), *rough*

ESAU'S
6215 'Êsâv (12), *rough*

ESCAPE
3318 yâtsâ' (1), *to go, bring out*
4422 mâlaṭ (22), *to escape; be delivered*
4498+6 mânôwç (1), *fleeing; place of refuge*
4655 miphlâṭ (1), *escape, shelter*
5337 nâtsal (1), *to deliver; to be snatched*
5674 'âbar (1), *to cross over; to transition*
6403 pâlaṭ (2), *to slip out, i.e. escape; to deliver*
6405 pallêṭ (1), *escape*
6412 pâlîyṭ (2), *refugee*
6413 pᵉlêyṭâh (9), *escaped* portion
1309 diapheúgō (1), *to escape, flee*
1545 ĕkbasis (1), *exit, way out*
1628 ĕkpheúgō (4), *to flee out, escape*
5343 pheúgō (1), *to run away; to vanish*
5343+575 pheúgō (1), *to run away; to vanish*

ESCAPED
3318 yâtsâ' (1), *to go, bring out*
4422 mâlaṭ (25), *to escape; be delivered*
5337 nâtsal (1), *to deliver; to be snatched*
6412 pâlîyṭ (8), *refugee*

6413 pᵉlêyṭâh (11), *escaped* portion
7611 shᵉ'êrîyth (1), *remainder* or *residual*
668 apŏpheúgō (3), *to escape* from
1295 diasōzō (3), *to cure, preserve, rescue*
1628 ĕkpheúgō (1), *to flee out, escape*
1831 ĕxĕrchŏmai (1), *to issue; to leave*
5343 pheúgō (2), *to run away; to vanish*

ESCAPETH
4422 mâlaṭ (3), *to escape; be delivered; be smooth*
6412 pâlîyṭ (2), *refugee*
6413 pᵉlêyṭâh (1), *escaped* portion

ESCAPING
6413 pᵉlêyṭâh (1), *escaped* portion

ESCHEW
1578 ĕkklinō (1), *to shun; to decline*

ESCHEWED
5493 çûwr (1), *to turn off*

ESCHEWETH
5493 çûwr (2), *to turn off*

ESEK
6230 'Êseq (1), *strife*

ESH-BAAL
792 'Eshba'al (2), *man of Baal*

ESHBAN
790 'Eshbân (2), *vigorous*

ESHCOL
812 'Eshkôl (6), *bunch of grapes*

ESHEAN
824 'Esh'ân (1), *support*

ESHEK
6232 'Êsheq (1), *oppression*

ESHKALONITES
832 'Eshqᵉlôwnîy (1), *Ashkelonite*

ESHTAOL
847 'Eshtâ'ôl (7), *entreaty*

ESHTAULITES
848 'Eshtâ'ûlîy (1), *Eshtaolite*

ESHTEMOA
851 'Eshtᵉmôa' (5), *Eshtemoa* or *Eshtemoh*

ESHTEMOH
851 'Eshtᵉmôa' (1), *Eshtemoa* or *Eshtemoh*

ESHTON
850 'Eshtôwn (2), *restful*

ESLI
2069 Ĕsli (1), *Esli*

ESPECIALLY
3966 mᵉ'ôd (1), *very, utterly*
3122 malista (4), *in the greatest degree*

ESPIED
7200 râ'âh (1), *to see*
8446 tûwr (1), *to wander, meander*

ESPOUSALS
2861 chăthunnâh (1), *wedding*
3623 kᵉlûwlâh (1), *bridehood*

ESPOUSED
781 'âras (1), *to engage for matrimony, betroth*
718 harmŏzō (1), *to betroth for marriage*
3423 mnēstĕuō (3), *to betroth, be engaged*

ESPY
6822 tsâphâh (1), *to peer; to observe, await*
7270 râgal (1), *to reconnoiter; to slander*

ESROM
2074 Ēsrōm (3), *court-yard*

ESTABLISH
3322 yâtsag (1), *to place permanently*
3427 yâshab (1), *to dwell, to remain; to settle*
3559 kûwn (14), *to set up: establish, fix, prepare*
5324 nâtsab (1), *to station*
5582 çâ'ad (1), *to support*
5975 'âmad (3), *to stand*
6965 qûwm (17), *to rise*
6966 qûwm (Ch.) (2), *to rise*
2476 histēmi (3), *to stand, establish*
4741 stērizō (1), *to turn resolutely; to confirm*

ESTABLISHED
539 'âman (7), *to be firm, faithful, true; to trust*
553 'âmats (1), *to be strong; be courageous*
2388 châzaq (1), *to fasten upon; to seize*
3245 yâçad (2), *settle, establish a foundation*
3559 kûwn (44), *to set up: establish, fix, prepare*
5564 çâmak (1), *to lean upon; take hold of*
5975 'âmad (1), *to stand*
6965 qûwm (9), *to rise*
8627 tᵉqan (Ch.) (1), *to straighten up, confirm*
950 bĕbaiŏō (1), *to stabilitate, keep strong*
2476 histēmi (2), *to stand, establish*
3549 nŏmŏthĕtĕō (1), *to be founded, enacted*
4732 stĕrĕŏō (1), *to be, become strong*
4741 stērizō (2), *to turn resolutely; to confirm*

ESTABLISHETH
5975 'âmad (1), *to stand*
6965 qûwm (1), *to rise*
6966 qûwm (Ch.) (1), *to rise*

ESTABLISHMENT
571 'emeth (1), *certainty, truth, trustworthiness*

ESTATE
1700 dibrâh (1), *reason, suit* or *style; because*

3653 kên (5), *pedestal* or *station* of a basin
8448 tôwr (1), *manner*
3588+4012 hŏ (1), *"the,"* i.e. the definite article

ESTEEM
2803 châshab (1), *to plot; to think, regard*
6186 'ârak (1), *to set in a row,* i.e. *arrange,*
2233 hēgĕŏmai (2), *to deem,* i.e. *consider*

ESTEEMED
2803 châshab (3), *to plot; to think, regard*
5034 nâbêl (1), *to wilt; to fall away; to be foolish*
6845 tsâphan (1), *to deny; to protect; to lurk*
7043 qâlal (2), *to be, make light*
1848 ĕxŏuthĕnĕō (1), *to treat with contempt*

ESTEEMETH
2803 châshab (1), *to plot; to think, regard*
2919 krinō (2), *to decide; to try, condemn, punish*
3049 lŏgizŏmai (1), *to credit; to think, regard*

ESTEEMING
2233 hēgĕŏmai (1), *to lead; to deem, consider*

ESTHER
635 'Eçtêr (52), *Esther*

ESTHER'S
635 'Eçtêr (3), *Esther*

ESTIMATE
6186 'ârak (2), *to set in a row,* i.e. *arrange,*

ESTIMATION
6187 'êrek (23), *pile, equipment, estimate*

ESTIMATIONS
6187 'êrek (1), *pile, equipment, estimate*

ESTRANGED
2114 zûwr (4), *to be foreign, strange*
5234 nâkar (1), *to treat as a foreigner*

ETAM
5862 'Êyṭâm (5), *hawk-ground*

ETERNAL
5769 'ôwlâm (1), *eternity; ancient; always*
6924 qedem (1), *eastern; antiquity; before*
126 aïdiŏs (1), *everduring, eternal*
165 aiōn (2), *perpetuity; ever; world*
166 aiōniŏs (42), *perpetual, long ago*

ETERNITY
5703 'ad (1), *perpetuity; ancient*

ETHAM
864 'Êthâm (4), *Etham*

ETHAN
387 'Êythân (8), *permanent*

ETHANIM
388 Êythânîym (1), *permanent* brooks

ETHBAAL
856 'Ethba'al (1), *with Baal*

ETHER
6281 'Ether (2), *abundance*

ETHIOPIA
3568 Kûwsh (19), *Cush*
128 Aithiŏps (1), *inhabitant of Æthiop*

ETHIOPIAN
3569 Kûwshîy (8), *Cushite*

ETHIOPIANS
3569 Kûwshîy (12), *Cushite*
128 Aithiŏps (1), *inhabitant of Æthiop*

ETHNAN
869 'Ethnan (1), *gift price of harlotry*

ETHNI
867 'Ethnîy (1), *munificence, lavishness*

EUBULUS
2103 Êubŏulŏs (1), *good-willer*

EUNICE
2131 Êunikē (1), *victorious*

EUNUCH
5631 çârîyç (2), *eunuch; official of state*
2135 ĕunŏuchŏs (5), *castrated; impotent*

EUNUCHS
5631 çârîyç (15), *eunuch; official of state*
2134 ĕunŏuchizō (3), *to castrate*
2135 ĕunŏuchŏs (2), *castrated; impotent*

EUODIAS
2136 Êuŏdia (1), *fine travelling*

EUPHRATES
6578 Pᵉrâth (19), *rushing*
2166 Êuphratēs (2), *Euphrates*

EUROCLYDON
2148 Êurŏkludōn (1), *wind from the east*

EUTYCHUS
2161 Êutuchŏs (1), *fortunate*

EVANGELIST
2099 ĕuaggĕlistēs (2), *preacher of the gospel*

EVANGELISTS
2099 ĕuaggĕlistēs (1), *preacher of the gospel*

EVE
2332 Chavvâh (2), *life-giver*
2096 Êua (2), *life-giver*

EVEN
227 'âz (1), *at that time or place; therefore*
389 'ak (2), *surely; only, however*

518 'îm (1), *whether?; if, although; Oh that!*
637 'aph (7), *also or yea; though*
853 'êth (25), *not translated*
1571 gam (50), *also; even; yea; though*
1887 hê' (1), *Lo!, Look!*
3588 kîy (7), *for, that because*
3602 kâkâh (5), *just so*
3651 kên (3), *just; right, correct*
4334 mîyshôwr (1), *plain; justice*
5704 'ad (3), *as far (long) as; during; while; until*
5705 'ad (Ch.) (2), *as far (long) as; during*
6153 'ereb (71), *dusk*
6664 tsedeq (1), *right*
7535 raq (1), *merely; although*
737 arti (1), *just now; at once*
891 achri (1), *until or up to*
1063 gar (1), *for, indeed, but, because*
1161 dĕ (3), *but, yet; and then*
2089 ĕti (1), *yet, still*
2193 hĕōs (2), *until*
2504 kagō (7), *and also, even*
2509 kathapĕr (2), *exactly as*
2531 kathōs (24), *just or inasmuch as, that*
2532 kai (108), *and; or; even; also*
2548 kakĕinŏs (2), *likewise that or those*
3303 mĕn (1), *not translated*
3483 nai (4), *yes*
3676 hŏmōs (1), *at the same time, yet still*
3761 ŏudĕ (3), *neither, nor, not even*
3779 hŏutō (3), *in this way; likewise*
3796 ŏpsĕ (2), *late in the day*
3798 ŏpsiŏs (8), *late; early eve; later eve*
5037 tĕ (1), *both or also*
5613 hōs (3), *which, how, i.e. in that manner*
5615 hōsautōs (1), *in the same way*
5618 hōspĕr (2), *exactly like*

EVENING
6150 'ârab (2), *to grow dusky at sundown*
6153 'ereb (49), *dusk*
2073 hĕspĕra (2), *evening*
3798 ŏpsiŏs (5), *late; early eve; later eve*

EVENINGS
6160 'ărâbâh (1), *desert, wasteland*

EVENINGTIDE
6256+6153 'êth (2), *time*

EVENT
4745 miqreh (3), *accident or fortune*

EVENTIDE
6153 'ereb (1), *dusk*
6256+6153 'êth (2), *time*
2073 hĕspĕra (1), *evening*

EVER
753+3117 'ôrek (2), *length*
3605+3117 kôl (18), *all, any or every*
3808 lô' (1), *no, not*
3809 lâ' (Ch.) (1), *as nothing*
5331 netsach (23), *splendor; lasting*
5703 'ad (40), *perpetuity; ancient*
5704+5769 'ad (1), *as far (long) as; during; while*
5750 'ôwd (1), *again; repeatedly; still; more*
5757 'Avvîy (1), *Avvite*
5769 'ôwlâm (266), *ancient; always*
5769+5703 'ôwlâm (1), *ancient; always*
5865 'êylôwm (1), *forever*
5957 'âlam (Ch.) (11), *forever*
6783 tsᵉmîythûth (2), *perpetually*
6924 qedem (1), *eastern; antiquity; before*
8548 tâmîyd (3), *constantly, regularly*
104 aĕi (1), *ever, always*
165 aiōn (49), *perpetuity; ever; world*
166 aiōniŏs (1), *perpetual, long ago*
1336 diēnĕkĕs (2), *perpetually, endless*
2250+165 hēmĕra (1), *day; period of time*
3364 ŏu mē (1), *not at all, absolutely not*
3745 hŏsŏs (2), *as much as*
3842 pantŏtĕ (6), *at all times*
3956+165 pas (1), *all, any, every, whole*
4218 pŏtĕ (1), *at some time, ever*
4253 prŏ (1), *before in time or space*

EVERLASTING
5703 'ad (2), *perpetuity; ancient*
5769 'ôwlâm (60), *ancient; always*
5957 'âlam (Ch.) (4), *forever*
6924 qedem (1), *eastern; antiquity; before*
126 aïdiŏs (1), *everduring, eternal*
166 aiōniŏs (25), *perpetual, long ago*

EVERMORE
1755 dôwr (1), *dwelling*
3605+3117 kôl (2), *all, any or every*
5331 netsach (1), *splendor; lasting*
5703 'ad (1), *perpetuity; ancient*

5769 'ôwlâm (15), *ancient; always*
8548 tâmîyd (1), *constantly, regularly*
3588+165 hŏ (3), *"the,"* i.e. the definite article
3842 pantŏtĕ (2), *at all times*

EVERY
259 'echâd (5), *first*
376 'îysh (125), *man; male; someone*
802 'ishshâh (4), *woman, wife; women, wives*
1397 geber (1), *person, man*
3605 kôl (451), *all, any or every*
3606 kôl (Ch.) (4), *all, any or every*
3632 kâlîyl (1), *whole, entire; complete; whole*
5437 çâbab (26), *to surround*
7218 rô'sh (1), *head*
303 ana (3), *each; in turn; among*
376 anapērŏs (1), *maimed; crippled*
537 hapas (2), *all, every one, whole*
1330 diĕrchŏmai (1), *to traverse, travel through*
1538 hĕkastŏs (73), *each or every*
2596 kata (15), *down; according to*
3596 hŏdŏipŏrĕō (2), *to travel*
3650 hŏlŏs (2), *whole or all, i.e. complete*
3836 pantachŏthĕn (1), *from all directions*
3837 pantachŏu (6), *universally, everywhere*
3840 pantŏthĕn (1), *from, on all sides*
3956 pas (162), *all, any, every, whole*
5100 tis (2), *some or any person or object*
5101 tis (1), *who?, which? or what?*

EVI
189 'Ĕvîy (2), *desirous*

EVIDENCE
5612 çêpher (6), *writing*
1650 ĕlĕgchŏs (1), *proof, conviction*

EVIDENCES
5612 çêpher (2), *writing*

EVIDENT
5921+6440 'al (1), *above, over, upon, or against*
1212 dēlŏs (1), *clear, plain, evident*
1732 ĕndĕixis (1), *demonstration*
2612 katadēlŏs (1), *manifest, clear*
4271 prŏdēlŏs (1), *obvious, evident*

EVIDENTLY
4270 prŏgraphō (1), *to announce, prescribe*
5320 phanĕrŏs (1), *plainly, i.e. clearly*

EVIL
205 'âven (1), *trouble, vanity, wickedness*
1100 bᵉlîya'al (1), *wickedness, trouble*
1681 dibbâh (1), *slander, bad report*
7451 ra' (434), *bad; evil*
7455 rôa' (11), *badness, evil*
7462 râ'âh (1), *to associate* with
7489 râ'a' (24), *to be good for nothing*
92 adikēma (1), *wrong done*
987 blasphēmēō (9), *to speak impiously*
988 blasphēmia (1), *impious speech*
1426 dusphēmia (1), *defamation, slander*
2549 kakia (1), *depravity; malignity*
2551 kakŏlŏgēō (1), *to revile, curse*
2554 kakŏpŏiĕō (4), *to injure; to sin, do wrong*
2556 kakŏs (44), *bad, evil, wrong*
2557 kakŏurgŏs (1), *criminal, evildoer*
2559 kakŏō (3), *to injure; to oppress; to embitter*
2560 kakŏs (2), *badly; wrongly; ill*
2635 katalalĕŏ (4), *to speak slander*
2636 katalalia (1), *defamation, slander*
4190 pŏnērŏs (49), *malice, wicked, bad*
4190+4487 pŏnērŏs (1), *malice, wicked, bad*
5337 phaulŏs (4), *foul or flawed, i.e. wicked*

EVIL-MERODACH
192 'Ĕvîyl Mᵉrôdak (2), *Evil-Merodak*

EVILDOER
7489 râ'a' (1), *to be good for nothing*
2555 kakŏpŏiŏs (1), *bad-doer; criminal*

EVILDOERS
7489 râ'a' (9), *to be good for nothing*
2555 kakŏpŏiŏs (3), *bad-doer; criminal*

EVILFAVOUREDNESS
1697+7451 dâbâr (1), *word; matter; thing*

EVILS
7451 ra' (8), *bad; evil*
4190 pŏnērŏs (1), *malice, wicked, bad; crime*

EWE
3535 kibsâh (6), *ewe sheep*
7716 seh (1), *sheep or goat*

EWES
5763 'ûwl (1), *to suckle, i.e. give milk*
7353 râchêl (2), *ewe*

EXACT
5065 nâgas (3), *to exploit; to tax, harass*
5378 nâshâ' (2), *to lend on interest*
5383 nâshâh (2), *to lend or borrow*
4238 prassō (1), *to execute, accomplish*

EXACTED
3318 yâtsâ' (1), *to go, bring out*
5065 nâgas (1), *to exploit; to tax, harass*

EXACTETH
5382 nâshâh (1), *to forget*

EXACTION
4855 mashshâ' (1), *loan; interest on a debt*

EXACTIONS
1646 gᵉrûshâh (1), *dispossession*

EXACTORS
5065 nâgas (1), *to exploit; to tax, harass*

EXALT
1361 gâbahh (3), *to be lofty; to be haughty*
5375 nâsâ' (2), *to lift up*
5549 çâlal (1), *to mound up; to exalt; to oppose*
7311 rûwm (17), *to be high; to rise or raise*
1869 ĕpairō (1), *to raise up, look up*
5312 hupsŏō (2), *to elevate; to exalt*

EXALTED
1361 gâbahh (5), *to be lofty; to be haughty*
5375 nâsâ' (8), *to lift up*
5927 'âlâh (2), *to ascend, be high, mount*
7311 rûwm (28), *to be high; to rise or raise*
7426 râmam (2), *to rise*
7682 sâgab (5), *to be, make lofty; be safe*
5229 hupĕrairŏmai (2), *to raise oneself over*
5251 hupĕrupsŏō (1), *to raise to the highest*
5311 hupsŏs (1), *altitude; sky; dignity*
5312 hupsŏō (10), *to elevate; to exalt*

EXALTEST
5549 çâlal (1), *to mound up; to exalt; to oppose*

EXALTETH
1361 gâbahh (1), *to be lofty; to be haughty*
7311 rûwm (3), *to be high; to rise or raise*
7682 sâgab (1), *to be, make lofty; be safe*
1869 ĕpairō (1), *to raise up, look up*
5229 hupĕrairŏmai (1), *to raise oneself over*
5312 hupsŏō (2), *to elevate; to exalt*

EXAMINATION
351 anakrisis (1), *judicial investigation*

EXAMINE
974 bâchan (1), *to test; to investigate*
1875 dârash (1), *to seek or ask; to worship*
350 anakrinō (1), *to interrogate, determine*
1381 dŏkimazō (1), *to test; to approve*
3985 pĕirazō (1), *to endeavor, scrutinize*

EXAMINED
350 anakrinō (4), *to interrogate, determine*
426 anĕtazō (2), *to investigate; to question*

EXAMINING
350 anakrinō (1), *to interrogate, determine*

EXAMPLE
1164 dĕigma (1), *specimen, example*
3856 paradĕigmatizō (1), *to expose to infamy*
5179 tupŏs (1), *shape, resemblance; "type"*
5261 hupŏgrammŏs (1), *copy, example, model*
5262 hupŏdĕigma (4), *exhibit; specimen*

EXAMPLES
5179 tupŏs (1), *shape, resemblance; "type"*

EXCEED
3254 yâçaph (2), *to add or augment*
4052 pĕrissĕuō (2), *to superabound*

EXCEEDED
1396 gâbar (1), *to be strong; to prevail*
1431 gâdal (1), *to be great, make great*

EXCEEDEST
3254 yâçaph (1), *to add or augment*

EXCEEDETH
3254 yâçaph (1), *to add or augment*

EXCEEDING
430 'ĕlôhîym (1), the true *God; gods; great ones*
1419 gâdôwl (1), *great*
2302 châdâh (1), *to rejoice, be glad*
2493 chêlem (Ch.) (1), *dream*
3493 yattîyr (Ch.) (1), *preeminent; very*
3499 yether (1), *remainder; small rope*
3966 mᵉôd (18), *very, utterly*
4605 ma'al (2), *upward, above, overhead*
5628 çârach (1), *to extend even to excess*
7235 râbâh (1), *to increase*
7235+3966 râbâh (1), *to increase*
7689 saggîy' (1), *mighty*
8057 simchâh (1), *blithesomeness or glee*
1519+5236 ĕis (1), *to or into*

EXCELLENCY
1346 ga'ăvâh (3), *arrogance; majesty*
1347 gâ'ôwn (10), *ascending; majesty*
1363 gôbahh (1), *height; grandeur; arrogance*
1926 hâdâr (2), *magnificence*
3499 yether (2), *remainder; small rope*
3504 yithrôwn (1), *preeminence, gain*

EXCELLENCY
2596+5236 kata (1), *down; according to*
3029 lian (5), *very much*
3588+2316 hŏ (1), *"the," i.e. the definite article*
4036 pĕrilupŏs (3), *intensely sad*
4970 sphŏdra (4), *vehemently, much*
5228 hupĕr (1), *over; above; beyond*
5235 hupĕrballō (3), *to surpass*
5248 hupĕrpĕrissĕuō (1), *to superabound*
5250 hupĕrplĕŏnazō (1), *to superabound*

EXCEEDINGLY
413+1524 'êl (1), *to, toward*
1419 gâdôwl (5), *great*
1419+3966 gâdôwl (1), *great*
3493 yattîyr (Ch.) (1), *preeminent; very*
3966 mᵉôd (9), *very, utterly*
4605 ma'al (4), *upward, above, overhead*
7227 rab (2), *great*
7235 râbâh (1), *to increase*
7235+3966 râbâh (1), *to increase*
8057 simchâh (1), *blithesomeness or glee*
1613 ĕktarassō (1), *to disturb wholly*
1630 ĕkphŏbŏs (1), *frightened out of one's wits*
4056 pĕrissŏtĕrŏs (3), *more superabundantly*
4057 pĕrissōs (1), *superabundantly*
4970 sphŏdra (1), *vehemently, much*
4971 sphŏdrōs (1), *very much*
5228+1537+4053 hupĕr (1), *over; above; beyond*
5401+3173 phŏbŏs (1), *alarm, or fright*

EXCEL
1368 gibbôwr (1), *powerful; great warrior*
3498 yâthar (1), *to remain or be left*
5329 nâtsach (1), i.e. *to be eminent*
4052 pĕrissĕuō (1), *to superabound*

EXCELLED
7227 rab (1), *great*

EXCELLENCY
1346 ga'ăvâh (3), *arrogance; majesty*
1347 gâ'ôwn (10), *ascending; majesty*
1363 gôbahh (1), *height; grandeur; arrogance*
1926 hâdâr (2), *magnificence*
3499 yether (2), *remainder; small rope*
3504 yithrôwn (1), *preeminence, gain*

7613 s^e'êth (2), *elevation; swelling* scab
7863 sîy' (1), *elevation*
5236 hupĕrbŏlē (1), *super-eminence*
5242 hupĕrĕchō (1), to *excel; be superior*
5247 hupĕrŏchē (1), *superiority*

EXCELLENT
117 'addîyr (4), *powerful; majestic*
977 bâchar (1), *select, chose, prefer*
1347 gâ'ôwn (1), *ascending; majesty*
1348 gê'ûwth (1), *ascending; majesty*
1420 g^edûwlâh (1), *greatness, grandeur*
1431 gâdal (1), to *be great, make great*
3368 yâqâr (1), *valuable*
3493 yattîyr (Ch.) (5), *preeminent; very*
3499 yether (1), *remainder; small rope*
5057 nâgîyd (1), *commander, official*
5716 'ădîy (1), *finery; outfit; headstall*
7119 qar (1), *cool; quiet; cool*-headed
7218 rô'sh (1), *head*
7230 rôb (1), *abundance*
7682 sâgab (1), to *be, make lofty; be safe*
7689 saggîy' (1), *mighty*
7991 shâlîysh (1), *officer; of the third rank*
8446 tûwr (1), to *wander, meander*
1308 diaphĕrō (2), to *differ; to surpass*
1313 diaphŏrŏs (2), *varying; surpassing*
2596+5236 kata (1), *down; according to*
2903 kratistŏs (2), *very honorable*
3169 mĕgalŏprĕpēs (1), *befitting greatness*
4119 plĕiōn (1), *more*

EXCELLEST
5927 'âlâh (1), to *ascend, be high, mount*

EXCELLETH
3504 yithrôwn (2), *preeminence, gain*
5235 hupĕrballō (1), to *surpass*

EXCEPT
369 'ayin (1), *there is no, i.e., not exist, none*
905 bad (1), *chief; apart, only, besides*
1115 biltîy (3), *not, except, without, unless*
3588 kîy (2), *for, that because*
3861 lâhên (Ch.) (3), *therefore; except*
3884 lûwlê' (3), *if not*
7535 raq (1), *merely; although*
1508 ĕi mē (7), *if not*
1509 ĕi mē ti (3), *if not somewhat*

2228 ē (1), *or; than*
3362 ĕan mē (33), *if not, i.e. unless*
3923 parĕisphĕrō (1), to *bear in alongside*
4133 plēn (1), *albeit, save that, rather, yet*

EXCEPTED
1622 ĕktŏs (1), *aside from, besides; except*

EXCESS
192 akrasia (1), *lack of control of self*
401 anachusis (1), *excessively pour out*
810 asōtia (1), *profligacy, debauchery*
3632 ŏinŏphlugia (1), *drunkenness*

EXCHANGE
4171 mûwr (1), to *alter; to barter, to dispose of*
8545 t^emûwrâh (2), *barter, compensation*
465 antallagma (2), *equivalent* exchange

EXCHANGERS
5133 trapĕzitēs (1), *money-broker*

EXCLUDE
1576 ĕkklĕiō (1), to *shut out, exclude*

EXCLUDED
1576 ĕkklĕiō (1), to *shut out, exclude*

EXCUSE
379 anapŏlŏgētŏs (1), *without excuse*
626 apŏlŏgĕŏmai (1), to *give an account*
3868 paraitĕŏmai (1), to *deprecate, decline*

EXCUSED
3868 paraitĕŏmai (2), to *deprecate, decline*

EXCUSING
626 apŏlŏgĕŏmai (1), to *give an account*

EXECRATION
423 'âlâh (2), *curse, oath, public agreement*

EXECUTE
1777 dîyn (1), to *judge; to strive or contend for*
5647 'âbad (1), to *do, work, serve*
6213 'âsâh (25), to *do or make*
8199 shâphaṭ (2), to *judge*
4160 pŏiĕō (2), to *do*

EXECUTED
5648 'ăbad (Ch.) (1), to *do, work, serve*
6213 'âsâh (15), to *do or make*
2407 hiĕratĕuō (1), to *be a priest*

EXECUTEDST
6213 'âsâh (1), to *do*

EXECUTEST
6213 'âsâh (1), to *do*

EXECUTETH
6213 'âsâh (5), to *do*

EXECUTING
6213 'âsâh (1), to *do*

EXECUTION
6213 'âsâh (1), to *do*

EXECUTIONER
4688 spĕkŏulatōr (1), *life-guardsman*

EXEMPTED
5355 nâqîy (1), *innocent*

EXERCISE
1980 hâlak (1), to *walk; live a certain way*
6213 'âsâh (1), to *do or make*
778 askĕō (1), to *strive for one's best*
1128 gumnazō (1), to *train by exercise*
1129 gumnasia (1), *training of the body*
1850 ĕxŏusiazō (1), to *control, master another*
2634 katakuriĕuō (2), to *control, subjugate*
2715 katĕxŏusiazō (2), to *wield full privilege over*
2961 kuriĕuō (1), to *rule, be master of*

EXERCISED
6031 'ânâh (2), to *afflict, be afflicted*
1128 gumnazō (3), to *train by exercise*

EXERCISETH
4160 pŏiĕō (1), to *do*

EXHORT
3867 parainĕō (1), to *recommend or advise*
3870 parakalĕō (14), to *call, invite*

EXHORTATION
3870 parakalĕō (2), to *call, invite*
3874 paraklēsis (8), *imploring, exhortation*

EXHORTED
3870 parakalĕō (3), to *call, invite*

EXHORTETH
3870 parakalĕō (1), to *call, invite*

EXHORTING
3870 parakalĕō (3), to *call, invite*
4389 prŏtrĕpŏmai (1), to *encourage*

EXILE
1540 gâlâh (1), to *denude; uncover*
6808 tsâ'âh (1), to *tip over; to depopulate*

EXORCISTS
1845 ĕxŏrkistēs (1), *exorcist, i.e. conjurer*

EXPECTATION
4007 mabbâṭ (3), *expectation, hope*
8615 tiqvâh (7), *cord; expectancy*
603 apŏkaradŏkia (2), *intense anticipation*
4328 prŏsdŏkaō (1), to *anticipate; to await*

4329 prŏsdŏkia (1), *apprehension* of evil

EXPECTED
8615 tiqvâh (1), *cord; expectancy*

EXPECTING
1551 ĕkdĕchŏmai (1), to *await, expect*
4328 prŏsdŏkaō (1), to *anticipate; to await*

EXPEDIENT
4851 sumphĕrō (7), to *collect; to conduce*

EXPEL
1644 gârash (1), to *drive out; to expatriate*
1920 hâdaph (1), to *push away or down; drive out*

EXPELLED
3423 yârash (2), to *inherit; to impoverish*
5080 nâdach (1), to *push off, scattered*
1544 ĕkballō (1), to *throw out*

EXPENCES
5313 niphqâ' (Ch.) (2), *outgo, i.e. expense*

EXPERIENCE
5172 nâchash (1), to *prognosticate*
7200 râ'âh (1), to *see*
1382 dŏkimē (2), *test, i.e. trustiness*

EXPERIMENT
1382 dŏkimē (1), *test, i.e. trustiness*

EXPERT
3925 lâmad (1), to *teach, train*
6186 'ârak (3), to set in a *row, i.e. arrange*
7919 sâkal (1), to *be or act circumspect*
1109 gnōstēs (1), *knower, expert*

EXPIRED
3615 kâlâh (1), to *cease, be finished, perish*
4390 mâlê' (3), to *fill; be full*
8666 t^eshûwbâh (3), *recurrence; reply*
4137 plērŏō (1), to *fill, make complete*
5055 tĕlĕō (1), to *end, i.e. complete, execute*

EXPOUND
5046 nâgad (1), to *announce*

EXPOUNDED
5046 nâgad (1), to *announce*
1329 diĕrmēnĕuō (1), to *explain thoroughly*
1620 ĕktithēmi (1), to *expose; to declare*
1956 ĕpiluō (1), to *explain; to decide*

EXPRESS
5481 charaktĕr (1), *exact copy or representation*

EXPRESSED
5344 nâqab (5), to
specify, designate, libel

EXPRESSLY
559 'âmar (1), to say
4490 rhētŏs (1),
out-spoken, distinctly

EXTEND
4900 mâshak (1), to draw
out; to be tall
5186 nâṭâh (1), to stretch
or spread out

EXTENDED
5186 nâṭâh (2), to stretch
or spread out

EXTINCT
1846 dâ'ak (1), to be
extinguished; to expire
2193 zâ'ak (1), to
extinguish

EXTOL
5549 çâlal (1), to mound
up; to exalt; to oppose
7311 rûwm (2), to be
high; to rise or raise
7313 rûwm (Ch.) (1),
elation, arrogance

EXTOLLED
5375 nâsâ' (1), to lift up
7318 rôwmâm (1),
exaltation, praise

EXTORTION
6233 'ôsheq (1), fraud;
distress; unjust gain
724 harpagē (1), pillage;
greediness; robbery

EXTORTIONER
4160 mûwts (1), to
oppress
5383 nâshâh (1), to lend
or borrow
727 harpax (1),
rapacious; robbing

EXTORTIONERS
727 harpax (3),
rapacious; robbing

EXTREME
2746 charchûr (1), hot
fever

EXTREMITY
6580 pash (1), stupidity
as a result of grossness

EYE
5869 'ayin (73), eye;
sight; fountain
5870 'ayin (Ch.) (1), eye;
sight
3442 mŏnŏphthalmŏs
(2), one-eyed
3788 ŏphthalmŏs (29),
eye
5168 trumalia (2),
needle's eye
5169 trupēma (1),
needle's eye

EYE'S
5869 'ayin (1), eye; sight;
fountain

EYEBROWS
1354+5869 gab (1),
rounded: top or rim;
arch

EYED
5770 'âvan (1), to watch
with jealousy
5869 'ayin (1), eye; sight;
fountain

EYELIDS
6079 'aph'aph (9),
fluttering eyelash

EYES
5869 'ayin (417), eye;
sight; fountain
5870 'ayin (Ch.) (5), eye;
sight
3659 ŏmma (1), eye
3788 ŏphthalmŏs (70),
eye

EYESALVE
2854 kŏllŏuriŏn (1),
poultice

EYESERVICE
3787 ŏphthalmŏdŏulĕia
(2), service that needs
watching

EYESIGHT
5869 'ayin (1), eye; sight;
fountain

EYEWITNESSES
845 autŏptēs (1),
eyewitness
2030 ĕpŏptēs (1),
looker-on

EZAR
687 'Etser (1), treasure

EZBAI
229 'Ezbay (1),
hyssop-like

EZBON
675 'Etsbôwn (2), Etsbon

EZEKIAS
1478 Ēzĕkias (2),
strengthened of
Jehovah

EZEKIEL
3168 Yᵉchezqê'l (2), God
will strengthen

EZEL
237 'ezel (1), departure

EZEM
6107 'Etsem (1), bone

EZER
687 'Etser (4), treasure
5827 'Ezer (1), help
5829 'Êzer (4), aid

EZION-GABER
6100 'Etsyôwn (short (4),
backbone-like of a man

EZION-GEBER
6100 'Etsyôwn (short (3),
backbone-like of a man

EZNITE
6112 'Êtsen (1), spear

EZRA
5830 'Ezrâ' (26), aid

EZRAHITE
250 'Ezrâchîy (3),
Ezrachite

EZRI
5836 'Ezrîy (1), helpful

FABLES
3454 muthŏs (5), tale,
fiction, myth

FACE
600 'ănaph (Ch.) (1), face
639 'aph (19), nose or
nostril; face; person
5869 'ayin (9), eye; sight;
fountain
6440 pânîym (313), face;
front
1799 ĕnōpiŏn (1), in the
face of, before
3799 ŏpsis (1), face;
appearance
4383 prŏsōpŏn (48), face,
presence
4750 stŏma (4), mouth;
edge

FACES
639 'aph (3), nose or
nostril; face; person
6440 pânîym (62), face;
front
4383 prŏsōpŏn (5), face,
presence

FADE
5034 nâbêl (5), to wilt; to
fall away; to be foolish
3133 marainō (1), to pass
away, fade away

FADETH
5034 nâbêl (5), to wilt; to
fall away; to be foolish
262 amarantinŏs (1),
fadeless
263 amarantŏs (1),
perpetual, never fading

FADING
5034 nâbêl (2), to wilt; to
fall away; to be foolish

FAIL
235 'âzal (1), to disappear
656 'âphêç (1), to cease
1238 bâqaq (1), to
depopulate, ruin
1584 gâmar (1), to end;
to complete; to fail
1809 dâlal (1), to
slacken, dangle
2637 châçêr (3), to lack;
to fail, want, make less
2638 châçêr (1), lacking
3543 kâhâh (1), to grow
dull, fade; to be faint
3576 kâzab (1), to lie,
deceive
3584 kâchash (2), to lie,
disown; to disappoint
3615 kâlâh (14), to cease,
be finished, perish
3772 kârath (6), to cut
(off, down or asunder)
3808+539 lô' (1), no, not
5307 nâphal (2), to fall
5405 nâshath (1), to dry
up
5674 'âbar (2), to cross
over; to transition
5737 'âdar (3), to
arrange as a battle
5848 'âṭaph (1), to
shroud, to languish
6461 paçaç (1), to
disappear
6565 pârar (1), to break
up; to violate, frustrate
7503 râphâh (4), to
slacken

FAILED
6 'âbad (1), perish;
destroy
2308 châdal (1), to desist,
stop; be fat
3318 yâtsâ' (2), to go,
bring out
3615 kâlâh (1), to cease,
be finished, perish
5307 nâphal (4), to fall
5405 nâshath (1), to dry
up
8552 tâmam (2), to
complete, finish

FAILETH
6 'âbad (1), perish;
destroy
369 'ayin (1), there is no,
i.e., not exist, none
656 'âphêç (1), to cease
1602 gâ'al (1), to detest;
to reject; to fail
2638 châçêr (1), lacking
3584 kâchash (1), to lie,
disown; to disappoint
3615 kâlâh (4), to cease,
be finished, perish
3782 kâshal (1), to totter,
waver; to falter
5405 nâshath (1), to dry
up
5737 'âdar (3), to
arrange as a battle
5800 'âzab (2), to loosen;
relinquish; permit
413 anĕklĕiptŏs (1), not
failing
1601 ĕkpiptō (1), to drop
away

FAILING
3631 killâyôwn (1),
pining, destruction
674 apŏpsuchō (1), to
faint

FAIN
1272 bârach (1), to flee
suddenly
1937 ĕpithumĕō (1), to
long for

FAINT
1738 dâvâh (1), to be in
menstruation cycle
1739 dâveh (1),
menstrual; fainting
1742 davvây (3), sick;
troubled, afflicted
3286 yâ'aph (3), to tire
3287 yâ'êph (2),
exhausted
3543 kâhâh (1), to grow
dull, fade; to be faint

4127 mûwg (3), to *soften, flow down, disappear*
4549 mâçaç (1), to *waste*; to *faint*
5774 'ûwph (3), to *cover, to fly*; to *faint*
5848 'âṭaph (1), to *shroud, to languish*
5889 'âyêph (6), *languid*
5968 'âlaph (1), to *be languid, faint*
6296 pâgar (2), to *become exhausted*
7401 râkak (2), to *soften*
7503 râphâh (2), to *slacken*
1573 ĕkkakĕō (4), to *be weak, fail*
1590 ĕkluō (5), to *lose heart*

FAINTED
1961 hâyâh (1), to *exist,* i.e. *be or become*
3021 yâga' (1), to *be exhausted, to tire,*
3856 lâhahh (1), to *languish*
5848 'âṭaph (2), to *shroud, to languish*
5968 'âlaph (2), to *be languid, faint*
5969 'ulpeh (1), *mourning*
6313 pûwg (1), to *be sluggish; be numb*
1590 ĕkluō (1), to *lose heart*
2577 kamnō (1), to *tire; to faint, sicken*

FAINTEST
3811 lâ'âh (1), to *tire;* to *be, make disgusted*

FAINTETH
3286 yâ'aph (1), to *tire*
3615 kâlâh (2), to *cease, be finished, perish*
4549 mâçaç (1), to *waste*; to *faint*

FAINTHEARTED
3824+7401 lêbâb (1), *heart*
4127 mûwg (1), to *soften;* to *fear, faint*
7390+3824 rak (1), *tender; weak*

FAINTNESS
4816 môrek (1), *despondent fear*

FAIR
2091 zâhâb (1), *gold, golden colored*
2603 chânan (1), to *implore*
2889 ṭâhôwr (2), *pure, clean, flawless*
2896 ṭôwb (6), *good; well*
2896+4758 ṭôwb (1), *good; well*
2897+4758 Ṭôwb (1), *good*
2898 ṭûwb (1), *good; goodness; beauty*
3302 yâphâh (12), to *be beautiful*
3303 yâpheh (14), *beautiful; handsome*
3303+8389 yâpheh (1), *beautiful; handsome*

3304 yᵉphêh-phîyâh (1), *very beautiful*
3948 leqach (1), *instruction*
6320 pûwk (1), *stibium*
8209 sappîyr (Ch.) (2), *beautiful*
8597 tiph'ârâh (3), *ornament*
791 astĕiŏs (1), *handsome*
2105 ĕudia (1), *clear sky,* i.e. *fine weather*
2129 ĕulŏgia (1), *benediction*
2146 ĕuprŏsōpĕō (1), to *make a good display*
2568 Kalŏi Limĕnĕs (1), *Good Harbors*

FAIRER
2896 ṭôwb (2), *good; well*
3302 yâphâh (1), to *be beautiful*

FAIREST
3303 yâpheh (3), *beautiful; handsome*

FAIRS
5801 'izzâbôwn (6), *trade, merchandise*

FAITH
529 'êmûwn (1), *trustworthiness; faithful*
530 'ĕmûwnâh (1), *fidelity; steadiness*
1680 ĕlpis (1), *expectation; hope*
3640 ŏligŏpistŏs (5), *lacking full confidence*
4102 pistis (238), *faithfulness; faith, belief*

FAITHFUL
529 'êmûwn (3), *trustworthiness; faithful*
530 'ĕmûwnâh (3), *fidelity; steadiness*
539 'âman (20), to *be firm, faithful, true*
540 'âman (Ch.) (1), to *be firm, faithful, true*
571 'emeth (1), *certainty, truth, trustworthiness*
4103 pistŏs (53), *trustworthy; reliable*

FAITHFULLY
530 'ĕmûwnâh (5), *fidelity; steadiness*
571 'emeth (2), *certainty, truth, trustworthiness*
4103 pistŏs (1), *trustworthy; reliable*

FAITHFULNESS
530 'ĕmûwnâh (18), *fidelity; steadiness*
3559 kûwn (1), to *render sure, proper*

FAITHLESS
571 apistŏs (4), *without faith; untrustworthy*

FALL
2342 chûwl (2), to *dance, whirl;* to *writhe* in pain
3318 yâtsâ' (1), to *go, bring out*
3381 yârad (1), to *descend*

3782 kâshal (22), to *totter, waver;* to *falter*
3783 kishshâlôwn (1), *ruin*
3832 lâbaṭ (3), to *overthrow;* to *fall*
3872 Lûwchîyth (1), *floored*
4131 môwṭ (1), to *slip, shake, fall*
4383 mikshôwl (1), *stumbling-block*
4658 mappeleth (7), *down-fall; ruin; carcase*
5034 nâbêl (1), to *wilt;* to *fall away;* to *be foolish*
5064 nâgar (1), to *pour out;* to *deliver* over
5203 nâṭash (1), to *disperse;* to *thrust* off
5307 nâphal (149), to *fall*
5308 nᵉphal (Ch.) (3), to *fall*
5456 çâgad (2), to *prostrate* oneself
6293 pâga' (8), to *impinge*
7264 râgaz (1), to *quiver*
7812 shâchâh (2), to *prostrate* in homage
7997 shâlal (1), to *drop* or *strip;* to *plunder*
868 aphistēmi (1), to *desist, desert*
1601 ĕkpiptō (4), to *drop away*
1706 ĕmpiptō (3), to *be entrapped by*
3895 parapiptō (1), to *apostatize, fall away*
3900 paraptōma (2), *error; transgression*
4045 pĕripiptō (1), to *fall into the hands of*
4098 piptō (22), to *fall*
4417 ptaiō (1), to *trip up, stumble* morally
4431 ptōsis (2), *downfall, crash*
4625 skandalŏn (1), *snare*

FALLEN
935 bôw' (1), to *go or come*
3782 kâshal (2), to *totter, waver;* to *falter*
4131+3027 môwṭ (1), to *slip, shake, fall*
4803 mâraṭ (2), to *polish;* to *make bald*
5307 nâphal (55), to *fall*
1601 ĕkpiptō (3), to *drop away*
1706 ĕmpiptō (1), to *be entrapped by*
1968 ĕpipiptō (1), to *embrace;* to *seize*
2064 ĕrchŏmai (1), to *go or come*
2667 katapiptō (2), to *fall down*
2702 kataphĕrō (1), to *bear down*
2837 kŏimaō (2), to *slumber;* to *decease*
4098 piptō (4), to *fall*

FALLEST
5307 nâphal (1), to *fall*

FALLETH
3918 layish (1), *lion*
5034 nâbêl (1), to *wilt;* to *fall* away; to *be foolish*
5307 nâphal (15), to *fall*
5308 nᵉphal (Ch.) (2), to *fall*
5456 çâgad (2), to *prostrate* oneself
7122 qârâ' (1), to *encounter,* to *happen*
1601 ĕkpiptō (2), to *drop away*
1911 ĕpiballō (1), to *throw upon*
4098 piptō (3), to *fall*

FALLING
1762 dᵉchîy (2), *stumbling fall*
3782 kâshal (1), to *totter, waver;* to *falter*
4131 môwṭ (1), to *slip, shake, fall*
5034 nâbêl (1), to *wilt;* to *fall* away; to *be foolish*
5307 nâphal (3), to *fall*
646 apŏstasia (1), *defection, rebellion*
679 aptaistŏs (1), *not stumbling, without sin*
2597 katabainō (1), to *descend*
4045 pĕripiptō (1), to *fall into the hands of*
4098 piptō (1), to *fall*
4248+1096 prēnēs (1), *headlong*
4363 prŏspiptō (1), to *prostrate* oneself

FALLOW
3180 yachmûwr (1), *kind of deer*
5215 nîyr (2), *freshly plowed land*

FALLOWDEER
3180 yachmûwr (1), *kind of deer*

FALSE
205 'âven (1), *trouble, vanity, wickedness*
2555 châmâç (2), *violence; malice*
3577 kâzâb (1), *falsehood; idol*
4820 mirmâh (2), *fraud*
7423 rᵉmîyâh (1), *remissness; treachery*
7723 shâv' (5), *ruin; guile; idolatry*
8267 sheqer (20), *untruth; sham*
1228 diabŏlŏs (2), *traducer,* i.e. *Satan*
4811 sukŏphantĕō (1), to *defraud, extort*
5569 psĕudadĕlphŏs (2), *pretended associate*
5570 psĕudapŏstŏlŏs (1), *pretended preacher*
5571 psĕudēs (2), *erroneous, deceitful*
5572 psĕudŏdidaskalŏs (1), *propagator of erroneous doctrine*
5573 psĕudŏlŏgŏs (4), *promulgating erroneous doctrine*

F

5575 pseŭdŏmartur (3),
bearer of untrue
testimony
5576 pseŭdŏmartureŏ
(6), to offer *falsehood*
5577 pseŭdŏmarturia (1),
untrue testimony
5578 pseŭdŏprŏphētēs
(6), pretended foreteller
5580 pseŭdŏchristŏs (2),
spurious Messiah

FALSEHOOD
4604 ma'al (1), sinful
treachery
8267 sheqer (13),
untruth; sham

FALSELY
3584 kâchash (1), to *lie,
disown*; to *disappoint*
5921+8267 'al (1), *above,
over, upon,* or *against*
7723 shâv' (1), *ruin;
guile; idolatry*
8266 shâqar (2), to *cheat,*
i.e. *be untrue* in words
8267 sheqer (12),
untruth; sham
5574 pseŭdŏmai (1), to
utter an untruth
5581 pseŭdŏnumŏs (1),
untruly named

FALSIFYING
5791 'âvath (1), to *wrest,*
twist

FAME
6963 qôwl (1), *voice* or
sound
8034 shêm (4),
appellation, i.e. name
8052 shᵉmûw'âh (2),
announcement
8088 shêma' (5),
something *heard*
8089 shôma' (4), *report;
reputation*
189 akŏē (3), *hearing;*
thing *heard*
1310 diaphēmizō (1), to
spread news
2279 ēchŏs (1), *roar;
rumor*
3056 lŏgŏs (1), *word,
matter, thing; Word*
5345 phēmē (2), *news,
report*

FAMILIAR
3045 yâda' (1), to *know*
7965 shâlôwm (1), *safe;
well; health, prosperity*

FAMILIARS
7965 shâlôwm (1), *safe;
well; health, prosperity*

FAMILIES
1004 bayith (2), *house;
temple; family, tribe*
1004+1 bayith (2), *house;
temple; family, tribe*
2945 taph (1), *family* of
children and women
4940 mishpâchâh (169),
family, clan, people

FAMILY
504 'eleph (1), *ox; cow* or
cattle
1004 bayith (1), *house;
temple; family, tribe*

4940 mishpâchâh (120),
family, clan, people
3965 patria (1), *family,
race, nation*

FAMINE
3720 kâphân (2), *hunger*
7458 râ'âb (86), *hunger*
7459 rᵉ'âbôwn (3), *famine*
3042 limŏs (4), *scarcity*
of food, *famine*

FAMINES
3042 limŏs (3), *scarcity*
of food, *famine*

FAMISH
7329 râzâh (1), to *make,
become thin*
7456 râ'êb (1), to *hunger*

FAMISHED
7456 râ'êb (1), to *hunger*
7458 râ'âb (1), *hunger*

FAMOUS
117 'addîyr (2), *powerful;
majestic*
3045 yâda' (1), to *know*
7121 qârâ' (2), to *call* out
7148 qârîy' (1), *called,*
i.e. *select*
8034 shêm (4),
appellation, i.e. name

FAN
2219 zârâh (4), to *toss
about*; to *winnow*
4214 mizreh (1),
winnowing *shovel*
4425 ptuŏn (2),
winnowing-fork

FANNERS
2114 zûwr (1), to *be
foreign, strange*

FAR
1419 gâdôwl (1), *great*
2008 hênnâh (2), *from
here; from there*
2186 zânach (1), to
reject, forsake, fail
2486 châlîylâh (9), *far be
it!, forbid!*
3966 mᵉ'ôd (3), *very,
utterly*
4801 merchâq (15),
distant place; *from afar*
5048 neged (3), *over
against* or *before*
5079 niddâh (1), time of
menstrual *impurity*
7350 râchôwq (59),
remote, far
7352 rachîyq (Ch.) (1),
far away; aloof
7368 râchaq (39), to
recede; remove
7369 râchêq (2), *remote,
far*
891 achri (2), *until* or up
to
1519 eis (1), *to* or *into*
2193 heŏs (4), *until*
2436 hileŏs (1), God be
gracious!, far be it!
3112 makran (6), *at a
distance, far away*
3113 makrŏthĕn (1),
from a distance or *afar*
3117 makrŏs (2), *long,* in
place or time

4054 pĕrissŏtĕrŏn (1), in
a *superabundant* way
4183 pŏlus (3), *much,
many*
4206 pŏrrhō (2),
forwards, at a distance
5231 hupĕranō (2),
above, upward

FARE
7939 sâkâr (1), *payment,
salary; compensation*
7965 shâlôwm (1), *safe;
well; health, prosperity*
4517 rhŏnnumi (1), to
strengthen

FARED
2165 ĕuphrainō (1), to
rejoice, be glad

FAREWELL
657 apŏtassŏmai (2), to
say adieu; to renounce
4517 rhŏnnumi (1), to
strengthen
5463 chairō (1), to *be
cheerful*

FARM
68 agrŏs (1), *farmland,
countryside*

FARTHER
4008 pĕran (1), *across,
beyond*
4260 prŏbainō (1), to
advance
4281 prŏĕrchŏmai (1), to
go onward, precede

FARTHING
787 assariŏn (1), *assarius*
2835 kŏdrantēs (2),
quadrans

FARTHINGS
787 assariŏn (1), *assarius*

FASHION
1823 dᵉmûwth (1),
resemblance, likeness
3559 kûwn (1), to *set up:
establish, fix, prepare*
4941 mishpât (2), *verdict;
formal decree; justice*
8498 tᵉkûwnâh (1),
structure; equipage
1491 eidŏs (1), *form,
appearance, sight*
3778 hŏutŏs (1), *this* or
that
4383 prŏsōpŏn (1), *face,
presence*
4976 schēma (2), *form* or
appearance
5179 tupŏs (1), *shape,
resemblance; "type"*

FASHIONED
3335 yâtsar (3), to *form;
potter; to determine*
3559 kûwn (2), to *set up:
establish, fix, prepare*
6213 'âsâh (1), to *do* or
make
4832 summŏrphŏs (1),
similar, conformed to

FASHIONETH
3335 yâtsar (3), to *form;
potter; to determine*

FASHIONING
4964 suschēmatizō (1),
to *conform* to the same

4941 mishpât (1), *verdict;
formal decree; justice*

FAST
629 'ŏçparnâ' (Ch.) (1),
diligently
3966 mᵉ'ôd (1), *very,
utterly*
6684 tsûwm (8), to *fast*
from food
6685 tsôwm (16), *fast*
from food
472 antĕchŏmai (1), to
adhere to; to care for
805 asphalizō (1), to
render secure
2722 katĕchō (3), to *hold
down fast*
3521 nēstĕia (1),
abstinence
3522 nēstĕuō (16), to
abstain from food

FASTED
6684 tsûwm (12), to *fast*
from food
3522 nēstĕuō (3), to
abstain from food

FASTEN
2388 châzaq (1), to
fasten upon; to seize
5414 nâthan (3), to *give*
8628 tâqᵃ' (1), to *clatter,
slap, drive, clasp*

FASTENED
270 'âchaz (3), to *seize,
grasp; possess*
2388 châzaq (1), to
fasten upon; to seize
2883 tâba' (1), to *sink;* to
be drowned
3559 kûwn (1), to *set up:
establish, fix, prepare*
5193 nâta' (1), to *plant*
5414 nâthan (2), to *give*
6775 tsâmad (1), to *link,*
i.e. *gird*
6795 tsânach (1), to
descend, i.e. *drive* down
8628 tâqa' (4), to *clatter,
slap, drive, clasp*
816 atĕnizō (2), to *gaze
intently*
2510 kathaptō (1), to
seize upon

FASTENING
816 atĕnizō (1), to *gaze
intently*

FASTEST
2522 kathēmĕrinŏs (1),
quotidian, i.e. *daily*

FASTING
2908 tᵉvâth (Ch.) (1),
hunger
6685 tsôwm (8), *fast*
777 asitŏs (1), *without*
taking food
3521 nēstĕia (4),
abstinence
3522 nēstĕuō (1), to
abstain from food
3523 nēstis (2), *abstinent*
from food

FASTINGS
6685 tsôwm (1), *fast*
3521 nēstĕia (3),
abstinence

FAT
1254 bârâ' (1), to *create;
fashion*
1277 bârîy' (6), *fatted* or
plump; healthy
1878 dâshên (7), to *be
fat, thrive; to fatten*
1879 dâshên (3), *fat; rich,
fertile*
2459 cheleb (79), *fat;
choice* part
2502 châlats (1), to *pull
off; to strip; to depart*
2954 țâphash (1), to *be
stupid*
3368 yâqâr (1), *valuable*
4220 mêach (1), *fat; rich*
4770 marbêq (1), *stall*
4806 mᵉrîy' (4), *stall-fed*
animal
4924 mashmân (2),
*fatness; rich dish;
fertile* field; *robust* man
4945 mashqeh (1), *butler;
drink; well-watered*
6309 peder (3), *suet*
6335 pûwsh (1), to
spread; to act proudly
6371 pîymâh (1), *obesity*
8080 shâman (3), to *be,
make oily or gross*
8081 shemen (4), *olive
oil, wood, lotions*
8082 shâmên (10), *rich;
fertile*

FATFLESHED
1277 bârîy' (2), *fatted* or
plump; healthy

FATHER
1 'âb (504), *father*
2 'ab (Ch.) (13), *father*
25 'Ăbîy Gib'ôwn (67),
founder of Gibon
1121 bên (1), *son,
descendant; people*
2524 châm (4),
father-in-law
2589 channôwth (1),
supplication
2859 châthan (20), to
become related
540 apatōr (1), *of
unrecorded paternity*
3962 patēr (344), *father*
3995 pēnthĕrŏs (1), *wife's
father*

FATHER'S
1 'âb (126), *father*
1730 dôwd (2), *beloved,
friend; relative*
1733 dôwdâh (1), *aunt*
3962 patēr (17), *father*

FATHERLESS
369+1 'ayin (1), *there is
no, i.e., not exist, none*
3490 yâthôwm (41), *child
alone, fatherless child*
3737 ŏrphanŏs (1),
parentless, orphaned

FATHERS
1 'âb (475), *father*
2 'ab (Ch.) (3), *father*
3962 patēr (52), *father*
3964 patralŏₗas (1),
killing of father
3967 patrikŏs (1),
ancestral, paternal

3970 patrŏparadŏtŏs (1),
traditionary
3971 patrŏₗōs (3), *from
forefathers*

FATHERS'
1 'âb (10), *father*
3962 patēr (1), *father*

FATHOMS
3712 ŏrguia (2), *measure
of about six feet*

FATLING
4806 mᵉrîy' (1), *stall-fed*
animal

FATLINGS
4220 mêach (1), *fat; rich*
4806 mᵉrîy' (2), *stall-fed*
animal
4932 mishneh (1),
duplicate copy; double
4619 sitistŏs (1), *grained,
i.e. fatted*

FATNESS
1880 deshen (7), *fat;
fatness, abundance*
2459 cheleb (4), *fat;
choice* part
4924 mashmân (3),
fatness; fertile; robust
8081 shemen (1), *olive
oil, wood, lotions*
4096 piŏtēs (1), *oiliness,
i.e. nourishing* sap

FATS
3342 yeqeb (2), wine-*vat,*
wine-*press*

FATTED
75 'âbaç (1), to *feed; be
fattened with feed*
4770 marbêq (1), *stall*
4618 sitĕutŏs (3),
fattened, i.e. stall-fed

FATTER
1277 bârîy' (1), *fatted* or
plump; healthy

FATTEST
4924 mashmân (2),
fatness; fertile; robust

FAULT
2398 châțâ' (1), to *sin*
3972 mᵉ'ûwmâh (1),
something; anything
5771 'âvôn (2), *moral evil*
7564 rish'âh (1), *moral
wrong*
7844 shᵉchath (Ch.) (2),
to *decay; to ruin*
156 aitia (3), *logical
reason; legal crime*
158 aitiŏn (2), *reason,
basis; crime*
299 amōmŏs (1),
unblemished, blameless
1651 ĕlĕgchō (1), to
confute, admonish
2275 hēttēma (1), *failure
or loss*
3201 mĕmphŏmai (3), to
blame
3900 paraptōma (1),
error; transgression

FAULTLESS
278 amĕtamĕlētŏs (1),
irrevocable
299 amōmŏs (1),
unblemished, blameless

FAULTS
2399 chêț' (1), *crime* or
its *penalty*
264 hamartanō (1), to
miss the mark, to *err*
3900 paraptōma (1),
error; transgression

FAULTY
816 'âsham (1), to *be
guilty; to be punished*
818 'âshêm (1), *bearing
guilt, guilty*

FAVOUR
2580 chên (26),
graciousness; beauty
2594 chănîynâh (1),
graciousness, kindness
2603 chânan (8), to
implore
2617 cheçed (3),
kindness, favor
2655 châphêts (1),
pleased with
2896 țôwb (2), *good; well*
3190 yâțab (1), to *be,
make well*
6440 pânîym (4), *face;
front*
7520 râtsad (1), to *look
askant; to be jealous*
7522 râtsôwn (15), *delight*
7965 shâlôwm (1), *safe;
well; health, prosperity*
8467 tᵉchinnâh (1),
gracious entreaty
5485 charis (6),
gratitude; benefit given

FAVOURABLE
2603 chânan (1), to
implore
7520 râtsad (3), to *look
askant; to be jealous*

FAVOURED
2603 chânan (1), to
implore
4758 mar'eh (7),
appearance; vision
8389 tô'ar (2), *outline,
i.e. figure or
appearance*
5487 charitŏō (1), to *give
special honor; one
highly favored*

FAVOUREST
2654 châphêts (1), to *be
pleased* with, *desire*

FAVOURETH
2654 châphêts (1), to *be
pleased* with, *desire*

FEAR
367 'êymâh (5), *fright*
1481 gûwr (2), to *sojourn,
live as an alien*
1674 dᵉ'âgâh (1), *anxiety*
1763 dᵉchal (Ch.) (1), to
*fear; be formidable,
awesome*
2342 chûwl (2), to *dance,
whirl; to writhe* in pain;
to *wait; to pervert*
2731 chărâdâh (2), *fear,
anxiety*
2844 chath (1), *terror*
3025 yâgôr (1), to *fear*
3372 yârê' (148), to *fear;
to revere*

3373 yârê' (35), *fearing;
reverent*
3374 yir'âh (41), *fear;
reverence*
4032 mâgôwr (6), *fright,
horror*
4034 mᵉgôwrâh (1),
affright, dread
4172 môwrâ' (6), *fearful*
6206 'ârats (2), to *awe; to
dread; to harass*
6342 pâchad (9), to *be
startled; to fear*
6343 pachad (41),
sudden alarm, fear
6345 pachdâh (1), *awe*
6440 pânîym (8), *face;
front*
7267 rôgez (1), *disquiet;
anger*
7374 rețeț (1), *terror,
panic*
7461 ra'ad (1), *shudder*
820 atimŏs (1),
*dishonoured; without
honor*
870 aphŏbŏs (3),
fearlessly
1167 dĕilia (1), *timidity,
cowardice*
1630+1510 ĕkphŏbŏs (1),
*frightened out of one's
wits*
2124 ĕulabĕia (1),
reverence; submission
2125 ĕulabĕŏmai (1), to
have reverence
5399 phŏbĕō (35), to *fear,
be frightened; to revere*
5401 phŏbŏs (40), *alarm,
or fright; reverence*
5401+2192 phŏbŏs (1),
fright; reverence

FEARED
1481 gûwr (1), to *sojourn,
live as an alien*
1763 dᵉchal (Ch.) (1), to
fear; be formidable
3372 yârê' (38), to *fear; to
revere*
3373 yârê' (8), *fearing;
reverent*
4172 môwrâ' (1), *fearful*
6206 'ârats (1), to *awe; to
dread; to harass*
6342 pâchad (3), to *be
startled; to fear*
8175 sâ'ar (1), to *storm;
to shiver, i.e. fear*
2124 ĕulabĕia (1),
reverence; submission
5399 phŏbĕō (17), to *fear,
to be in awe of, revere*
5399+5401 phŏbĕō (1), to
fear, be in awe of

FEAREST
1481 gûwr (1), to *sojourn,
live as an alien*
3372 yârê' (1), to *fear; to
revere*
3373 yârê' (1), *fearing;
reverent*

FEARETH
3372 yârê' (2), to *fear; to
revere*
3373 yârê' (13), *fearing;
reverent*

6342 pâchad (1), to *be startled; to fear*
5399 phŏbĕŏ (4), to *fear, be in awe of, revere*

FEARFUL
3372 yârê' (2), to *fear; to revere*
3373 yârê' (2), *fearing; reverent*
4116 mâhar (1), to *hurry; promptly*
1169 dĕilŏs (3), *timid, i.e. faithless*
5398 phŏbĕrŏs (2), *frightful, i.e. formidable*
5400 phŏbĕtrŏn (1), *frightening* thing

FEARFULLY
3372 yârê' (1), to *fear; to revere*

FEARFULNESS
3374 yir'âh (1), *fear; reverence*
6427 pallâtsûwth (1), *affright, trembling fear*
7461 ra'ad (1), *shudder*

FEARING
3372 yârê' (1), to *fear; to revere*
2125 ĕulabĕŏmai (1), to *have reverence*
5399 phŏbĕŏ (6), to *fear, be in awe of, revere*

FEARS
2849 chathchath (1), *terror, horror*
4035 mᵉgûwrâh (2), *fright; granary*
5401 phŏbŏs (1), *alarm, or fright; reverence*

FEAST
2282 chag (53), *solemn festival*
2287 châgag (4), to *observe a festival*
3899 lechem (1), *food, bread*
3900 lᵉchem (Ch.) (1), *food, bread*
4150 môw'êd (3), *assembly, congregation*
4960 mishteh (21), *drink; banquet or feast*
755 architriklinŏs (3), *director of the entertainment*
1408 drŏmŏs (2), *career, course of life*
1456 ĕgkainia (1), Feast of *Dedication*
1858 hĕŏrtazŏ (1), to *observe a festival*
1859 hĕŏrtē (26), *festival*
4910 sunĕuōchĕŏ (2), to *feast together*

FEASTED
6213+4960 'âsâh (1), to *do or make*

FEASTING
4960 mishteh (7), *drink; banquet or feast*

FEASTS
2282 chag (5), *solemn festival*
4150 môw'êd (19), *assembly, congregation*

4580 mâ'ôwg (1), *cake* of bread, *provision*
4960 mishteh (2), *drink; banquet* or feast
1173 dĕipnŏn (3), *principal meal*

FEATHERED
3671 kânâph (2), *edge* or *extremity; wing*

FEATHERS
84 'ebrâh (2), *pinion*
2624 chăçîydâh (1), *stork*
5133 nôwtsâh (3), *plumage*

FED
398 'âkal (5), to *eat*
1277 bârîy' (1), *fatted* or *plump; healthy*
2109 zûwn (1), to *nourish; feed*
2110 zûwn (Ch.) (1), to *nourish; feed*
2939 ṭᵉ'am (Ch.) (1), to *feed*
3557 kûwl (3), to *keep in; to measure*
4806 mᵉrîy' (1), *stall-fed* animal
5095 nâhal (1), to *flow; to protect, sustain*
7462 râ'âh (10), to *tend a flock, i.e. pasture* a flock
1006 bŏskō (2), to *pasture* a flock
4222 pŏtizō (1), to *furnish drink, irrigate*
5142 trĕphō (1), to *nurse, feed, care for*
5526 chŏrtazō (1), to *supply food*

FEEBLE
535 'âmal (1), to *be weak; to be sick*
537 'ămêlâl (1), *languid, feeble*
2826 châshal (1), to *make unsteady*
3766 kâra' (1), to *make miserable*
3782 kâshal (4), to *totter, waver; to falter*
3808+3524 lô' (1), *no, not*
3808+6099 lô' (1), *no, not*
5848 'âṭaph (1), to *shroud; to languish*
6313 pûwg (1), to *be sluggish; be numb*
7503 râphâh (6), to *slacken*
772 asthĕnēs (1), *strengthless, weak*
3886 paraluō (1), to *be paralyzed or enfeebled*

FEEBLEMINDED
3642 ŏligŏpsuchŏs (1), *timid, faint-hearted*

FEEBLENESS
7510 riphyôwn (1), *slackness*

FEEBLER
5848 'âṭaph (1), to *shroud, to languish*

FEED
398 'âkal (8), to *eat*
1197 bâ'ar (1), to *be brutish, be senseless*

2963 ṭâraph (1), to *supply, provide* food
3557 kûwl (3), to *keep in; to measure*
3938 lâ'aṭ (1), to *swallow greedily, gulp*
7462 râ'âh (55), to *tend a flock, i.e. pasture* it
1006 bŏskō (3), to *pasture* a flock
4165 pŏimainō (4), to *tend* as a shepherd
5142 trĕphō (1), to *nurse, feed, care for*
5595 psōmizō (2), to *nourish, feed*

FEEDEST
398 'âkal (1), to *eat*
7462 râ'âh (1), to *tend a flock, i.e. pasture* it

FEEDETH
7462 râ'âh (5), to *tend a flock, i.e. pasture* it
4165 pŏimainō (1), to *tend* as a shepherd
5142 trĕphō (2), to *nurse, feed, care for*

FEEDING
7462 râ'âh (4), to *tend a flock, i.e. pasture* it
1006 bŏskō (3), to *pasture* a flock
4165 pŏimainō (2), to *tend* as a shepherd

FEEL
995 bîyn (1), to *understand; discern*
3045 yâda' (2), to *know*
4184 mûwsh (2), to *touch, feel*
4959 mâshash (1), to *feel* of; to *grope*
5584 psēlaphaō (1), to *verify* by contac

FEELING
524 apalgĕō (1), *become apathetic, callous*
4834 sumpathĕō (1), to *commiserate*

FEET
4772 margᵉlâh (5), *at the foot*
6471 pa'am (6), *time; step; occurence*
7166 qarçôl (2), *ankles*
7271 rᵉgal (Ch.) (7), *pair of feet*
7272 regel (151), *foot; step*
939 basis (1), *foot*
4228 pŏus (76), *foot*

FEIGN
5234 nâkar (1), to *treat as a foreigner*
5271 hupŏkrinŏmai (1), to *pretend*

FEIGNED
4820 mirmâh (1), *fraud*
4112 plastŏs (1), *artificial, fabricated*

FEIGNEDLY
8267 sheqer (1), *untruth; sham*

FEIGNEST
908 bâdâ' (1), to *invent; to choose*

FELIX
5344 Phēlix (8), *happy*

FELIX'
5344 Phēlix (1), *happy*

FELL
1961 hâyâh (7), to *exist, i.e. be or become*
3318 yâtsâ' (2), to *go, bring out*
3381 yârad (2), to *descend*
3766 kâra' (2), to *prostrate*
3782 kâshal (2), to *totter, waver; to falter*
5307 nâphal (122), to *fall*
5308 nᵉphal (Ch.) (5), to *fall*
5927 'âlâh (2), to *ascend, be high, mount*
6293 pâga' (4), to *impinge*
6298 pâgash (2), to *come in contact with*
6584 pâshaṭ (2), to *strip, i.e. unclothe, plunder*
7257 râbats (1), to *recline, repose, brood*
7812 shâchâh (2), to *prostrate*
634 apŏpiptō (1), to *fall off, drop off*
1096 ginŏmai (1), to *be, become*
1356 diŏpĕtēs (1), *sky-fallen*
1601 ĕkpiptō (1), to *drop away*
1706 ĕmpiptō (1), to *be entrapped by*
1968 ĕpipiptō (10), to *embrace; to seize*
2597 katabainō (1), to *descend*
4045 pĕripiptō (1), to *fall into the hands of*
4098 piptō (56), to *fall*
4363 prŏspiptō (6), to *prostrate oneself*

FELLED
5307 nâphal (1), to *fall*

FELLER
3772 kârath (1), to *cut (off, down or asunder)*

FELLEST
5307 nâphal (1), to *fall*

FELLING
5307 nâphal (1), to *fall*

FELLOES
2839 chishshûq (1), *wheel-spoke*

FELLOW
376 'îysh (1), *man; male; someone*
2270 châbêr (1), *associate, friend*
5997 'âmîyth (1), *comrade or kindred*
7453 rêa' (9), *associate; one close*

FELLOW'S
7453 rêa' (1), *associate; one close*

FELLOWCITIZENS
4847 sumpŏlitēs (1), *fellow citizen*

FELLOWDISCIPLES
4827 summathētēs (1), co-learner

FELLOWHEIRS
4789 sugklērŏnŏmŏs (1), participant in common

FELLOWHELPER
4904 sunĕrgŏs (1), fellow-worker

FELLOWHELPERS
4904 sunĕrgŏs (1), fellow-worker

FELLOWLABOURER
4904 sunĕrgŏs (2), fellow-worker

FELLOWLABOURERS
4904 sunĕrgŏs (2), fellow-worker

FELLOWPRISONER
4869 sunaichmalōtŏs (2), co-captive

FELLOWPRISONERS
4869 sunaichmalōtŏs (1), co-captive

FELLOWS
582 'ĕnôwsh (1), *man; person, human*
2269 chăbar (Ch.) (2), *associate, friend*
2270 chábêr (3), *associate, friend*
2273 chabrâh (Ch.) (1), *similar, associated*
7453 rêa' (1), *associate; one close*
7464 rê'âh (1), *female associate*
435 anēr (1), *man; male*
2083 hĕtairŏs (1), *comrade, friend*
3353 mĕtŏchŏs (1), *sharer, associate*

FELLOWSERVANT
4889 sundŏulŏs (6), servitor of the same master

FELLOWSERVANTS
4889 sundŏulŏs (4), servitor of the same master

FELLOWSHIP
2266 chábar (1), to *fascinate* by spells
8667+3027 t^esûwmeth (1), deposit, *i.e. pledging*
2842 kŏinōnia (12), benefaction; sharing
2844 kŏinōnŏs (1), *associate, partner*
3352 mĕtŏchē (1), *something in common*
4790 sugkŏinōnĕō (1), to co-participate

FELLOWSOLDIER
4961 sustratiōtēs (1), soldier together with

FELT
3045 yâda' (1), to *know*
4959 mâshash (2), to *feel of; to grope*
1097 ginōskō (1), to *know*
3958 paschō (1), to *experience* pain

FEMALE
802 'ishshâh (2), *woman, wife; women, wives*
5347 n^eqêbâh (19), *female, woman*
2338 thēlus (3), *female*

FENCE
1447 gâdêr (1), *enclosure, wall or fence*

FENCED
1211 betsel (1), *onion*
1219 bâtsar (15), to *be inaccessible*
1443 gâdar (1), to *build a stone wall*
4013 mibtsâr (12), *fortification; defender*
4390 mâlê' (1), to *fill; be full*
4692 mâtsôwr (1), siege-*mound; distress*
4694 m^etsûwrâh (5), *rampart, fortification*
5823 'âzaq (1), to *grub over, dig*
7753 sûwk (1), to *shut in with hedges*

FENS
1207 bitstsâh (1), *swamp, marsh*

FERRET
604 'ănâqâh (1), *gecko*

FERRY
5679 'âbârâh (1), *crossing*-place

FERVENT
1618 ĕktĕnēs (1), *intent, earnest*
2204 zĕō (2), to *be fervid or earnest*
2205 zēlŏs (1), *zeal, ardor; jealousy, malice*

FERVENTLY
1619 ĕktĕnōs (1), *intently, earnestly*

FESTUS
5347 Phēstŏs (12), *festal*

FESTUS'
5347 Phēstŏs (1), *festal*

FETCH
935 bôw' (1), to *go or come*
3318 yâtsâ' (1), to *go, bring out*
3947 lâqach (20), to *take*
5375 nâsâ' (1), to *lift up*
5437 çâbab (1), to *surround*
5670 'âbat (1), to *pawn; to lend; to entangle*
5927 'âlâh (1), to *ascend, be high, mount*
7725 shûwb (1), to *turn back; to return*
1806 ĕxagō (1), to *lead forth, escort*

FETCHED
622 'âçaph (1), to *gather, collect*
3318 yâtsâ' (1), to *go, bring out*
3947 lâqach (10), to *take*
5375 nâsâ' (1), to *lift up*
5927 'âlâh (1), to *ascend, be high, mount*

FETCHETH
5080 nâdach (1), to *push off, scattered*

FETCHT
3947 lâqach (1), to *take*

FETTERS
2131 zîyqâh (1), *arrow; bond, fetter*
3525 kebel (2), *fetter, shackles*
5178 n^echôsheth (5), *copper; bronze*
3976 pĕdē (3), *shackle for the feet*

FEVER
6920 qaddachath (1), *inflammation*
4445 purĕssō (2), to *burn with a fever*
4446 purĕtŏs (6), *fever*

FEW
259 'echâd (3), *first*
4213 miz'âr (1), *fewness, smallness*
4557 miçpâr (5), *number*
4591 mâ'at (4), to *be, make small or few*
4592 m^e'at (24), *little or few*
4962 math (4), *men*
7116 qâtsêr (1), *short*
1024 brachus (1), *little, short*
3641 ŏligŏs (20), *puny, small*
4935 suntŏmōs (1), *briefly*

FEWER
4592 m^e'at (1), *little or few*

FEWEST
4592 m^e'at (1), *little or few*

FEWNESS
4591 mâ'at (1), to *be, make small or few*

FIDELITY
4102 pistis (1), *faithfulness; faith, belief*

FIELD
776 'erets (1), *earth, land, soil; country*
1251 bar (Ch.) (8), *field*
2513 chelqâh (3), *flattery; allotment*
7704 sâdeh (246), *field*
68 agrŏs (22), *farmland, countryside*
5564 chōriŏn (3), *spot or plot of ground*

FIELDS
2351 chûwts (2), *outside, outdoors; countryside*
3010 yâgêb (1), *plowed field*
7704 sâdeh (46), *field*
7709 sh^edêmâh (4), *cultivated field*
8309 sh^erêmâh (1), *common*
68 agrŏs (1), *farmland, countryside*
5561 chōra (2), *space of territory*

FIERCE
393 'akzâr (1), *violent, deadly; brave*
2300 châdad (1), to *be, make sharp; fierce*
2740 chârôwn (23), *burning* of anger
2750 chŏrîy (3), *burning* anger
3267 yâ'az (1), to *be obstinate, be arrogant*
5794 'az (4), *strong, vehement, harsh*
7826 shachal (3), *lion*
434 anēmĕrŏs (1), *brutal, savage*
2001 ĕpischuō (1), to *insist stoutly*
4642 sklērŏs (1), *hard or tough; harsh, severe*
5467 chalĕpŏs (1), *difficult, furious*

FIERCENESS
2740 chârôwn (9), *burning* of anger
7494 ra'ash (1), *bounding, uproar*
2372 thumŏs (2), *passion, anger*

FIERCER
7185 qâshâh (1), to *be tough or severe*

FIERY
784 'êsh (1), *fire*
799 'eshdâth (1), *fire-law*
5135 nûwr (Ch.) (10), *fire*
8314 sârâph (5), *poisonous* serpent
4442 pur (1), *fire*
4448 purŏō (1), to *be ignited, glow*
4451 purōsis (1), *ignition, conflagration, calamity*

FIFTEEN
2568+6240 châmêsh (16), *five*
6235+2568 'eser (1), *ten*
7657+2568 shib'îym (3), *seventy*
1178 děkapěntě (3), *fifteen*
1440+4002 hěbdŏ-mēkŏnta (1), *seventy*

FIFTEENTH
2568+6240 châmêsh (17), *five*
4003 pěntěkaiděkatŏs (1), *five and tenth*

FIFTH
2549 chămîyshîy (44), *fifth; fifth part*
2567 châmash (1), to *tax a fifth*
2568 châmêsh (6), *five*
2569 chômesh (1), *fifth tax*
2570 chômesh (4), *abdomen, belly*
3991 pěmptŏs (4), *fifth*

FIFTIES
2572 chămishshîym (5), *fifty*
4004 pěntěkŏnta (2), *fifty*

FIFTIETH
2572 chămishshîym (4), *fifty*

FIFTY
2572 chămishshîym (148), *fifty*
4002+3461 pĕntĕ (1), *five*
4004 pĕntēkŏnta (5), *fifty*

FIG
8384 tᵉ'ên (24), *fig tree or fruit*
4808 sukē (16), *fig-tree*

FIGHT
3898 lâcham (85), to *fight a battle*, i.e. *consume*
4421 milchâmâh (5), *battle; war; fighting*
4634 ma'ărâkâh (1), *row; pile; military array*
6633 tsâbâ' (4), to *mass an army or servants*
73 agŏn (1), *contest, struggle*
75 agŏnizŏmai (2), to *struggle; to contend*
119 athlēsis (1), *struggle, contest*
2313 thĕŏmachĕŏ (1), to *resist deity*
2314 thĕŏmachŏs (1), *opponent of deity*
3164 machŏmai (1), to *war*, i.e. to *quarrel*
4170 pŏlĕmĕŏ (1), to *battle, make war*
4171 pŏlĕmŏs (1), *warfare; battle; fight*
4438 puktĕŏ (1), to *box as a sporting event*

FIGHTETH
3898 lâcham (3), to *fight a battle*, i.e. *consume*

FIGHTING
3898 lâcham (2), to *fight a battle*, i.e. *consume*
6213+4421 'âsah (1), to *do or make*

FIGHTINGS
3163 machē (2), *controversy, conflict*

FIGS
6291 pag (1), *unripe fig*
8384 tᵉ'ên (15), *fig tree or fruit*
3653 ŏlunthŏs (1), *unripe fig*
4810 sukŏn (4), *fig*

FIGURE
5566 çemel (1), *likeness*
8403 tabnîyth (1), *model, resemblance*
499 antitupŏn (1), *representative*
3345 mĕtaschĕmatizŏ (1), to *transfigure*
3850 parabŏlē (2), *fictitious narrative*
5179 tupŏs (1), *shape, resemblance; "type"*

FIGURES
4734 miqla'ath (1), *bas-relief sculpture*
499 antitupŏn (1), *representative*
5179 tupŏs (1), *shape, resemblance; "type"*

FILE
6477+6310 pᵉtsîyrâh (1), *bluntness*

FILL
4390 mâlê' (33), to *fill; be full*
4393 mᵉlô' (2), *fulness*
5433 çâbâ' (1), to *quaff* to *satiety*
7301 râvâh (1), to *slake thirst or appetites*
7646 sâba' (1), *fill to satiety*
7648 sôba' (2), *satisfaction*
466 antanaplērŏŏ (1), to *fill up*
878 aphrŏn (1), *ignorant; egotistic; unbelieving*
1072 gĕmizŏ (1), to *fill entirely*
2767 kĕrannumi (1), to *mingle*, i.e. to *pour*
4137 plērŏŏ (3), to *fill, make complete*
4138 plērŏma (1), what *fills*; what is *filled*
5526 chŏrtazŏ (1), to *supply food*

FILLED
4390 mâlê' (74), to *fill; be full*
4391 mᵉlâ' (Ch.) (1), to *fill; be full*
7059 qâmaṭ (1), to *pluck*, i.e. *destroy*
7301 râvâh (1), to *slake thirst or appetites*
7646 sâba' (22), *fill to satiety*
1072 gĕmizŏ (7), to *fill entirely*
1705 ĕmpiplēmi (3), to *satisfy*
2767 kĕrannumi (1), to *mingle*, i.e. to *pour*
4130 plēthŏ (17), to *fulfill, complete*
4137 plērŏŏ (17), to *fill, make complete*
4138 plērŏma (1), what *fills*; what is *filled*
4845 sumplērŏŏ (1), to be *complete, fulfill*
5055 tĕlĕŏ (1), to *end*, i.e. *complete, execute*
5526 chŏrtazŏ (11), to *supply food*

FILLEDST
4390 mâlê' (1), to *fill; be full*
7646 sâba' (1), *fill to satiety*

FILLEST
4390 mâlê' (1), to *fill; be full*

FILLET
2339 chûwṭ (1), *string; measuring tape; line*

FILLETED
2836 châshaq (3), to *join; to love, delight*

FILLETH
4390 mâlê' (2), to *fill; be full*
5844 'âṭâh (1), to *wrap*, i.e. *cover, veil, clothe*
7646 sâba' (2), *fill to satiety*

4131 plēktēs (1), *pugnacious*

FILLETS
2838 châshûq (8), *fence-rail or rod*

FILLING
1705 ĕmpiplēmi (1), to *satisfy*

FILTH
6675 tsôw'âh (1), *pollution*
4027 pĕrikatharma (1), *refuse, scum*
4509 rhupŏs (1), *dirt*, i.e. moral *depravity*

FILTHINESS
2932 ṭum'âh (7), ceremonial *impurity*
5079 niddâh (2), time of menstrual *impurity*
5178 nᵉchôsheth (1), *copper; bronze*
6675 tsôw'âh (2), *pollution*
151 aischrŏtēs (1), *obscenity*
168 akathartēs (1), state of *impurity*
3436 mŏlusmŏs (1), *contamination*
4507 rhuparia (1), moral *dirtiness*

FILTHY
444 'âlach (3), to *be or turn morally corrupt*
4754 mârâ' (1), to *rebel; to lash with whip; flap*
5708 'êd (1), periodical *menstrual flux*
6674 tsôw' (2), *excrementitious, soiled*
147 aischrŏkĕrdŏs (1), *sordidly, greedily*
148 aischrŏlŏgia (1), *filthy speech*
150 aischrŏs (2), *shameful thing, base*
766 asĕlgĕia (1), *debauchery, lewdness*
4510 rhupŏŏ (2), to *become morally dirty*

FINALLY
3063 lŏipŏn (5), *finally*
5056 tĕlŏs (1), *conclusion*

FIND
2803 châshab (1), to *think, regard; to value*
4672 mâtsâ' (100), to *find or acquire; to occur*
7912 shᵉkach (Ch.) (6), to *discover, find out*
2147 hĕuriskŏ (46), to *find*

FINDEST
4672 mâtsâ' (2), to *find or acquire; to occur*

FINDETH
4672 mâtsâ' (11), to *find or acquire; to occur*
2147 hĕuriskŏ (12), to *find*

FINDING
2714 chêqer (1), *examination*
4672 mâtsâ' (2), to *find or acquire; to occur*

421 anĕxichniastŏs (1), *unsearchable*
429 anĕuriskŏ (1), to *find out*
2147 hĕuriskŏ (4), to *find*

FINE
2212 zâqaq (1), to *strain, refine; extract, clarify*
2869 ṭâb (Ch.) (1), *good*
2896 tôwb (2), *good; well*
6668 tsâhab (1), to *be golden in color*
8305 sᵉrîyqâh (1), *linen cloth*
4585 sĕmidalis (1), fine wheat *flour*

FINER
6884 tsâraph (1), to *fuse metal; to refine*

FINEST
2459 cheleb (2), *fat; choice part*

FINGER
676 'etsba' (19), *finger; toe*
1147 daktulŏs (5), *finger*

FINGERS
676 'etsba' (11), *finger; toe*
677 'etsba' (Ch.) (1), *finger; toe*
1147 daktulŏs (3), *finger*

FINING
4715 mitsrêph (2), *crucible*

FINISH
1214 bâtsa' (1), to *plunder; to finish*
3607 kâlâ' (1), to *hold back or in; to prohibit*
3615 kâlah (1), to *cease, be finished, perish*
535 apartismŏs (1), *completion*
1615 ĕktĕlĕŏ (2), to *complete fully, finish*
2005 ĕpitĕlĕŏ (1), to *terminate; to undergo*
4931 suntĕlĕŏ (1), to *complete entirely*
5048 tĕlĕiŏŏ (3), to *perfect, complete*

FINISHED
3319 yᵉtsâ' (Ch.) (1), to *complete*
3615 kâlah (19), to *cease, be finished, perish*
3635 kᵉlal (Ch.) (1), to *complete*
7999 shâlam (3), to *be safe; be complete*
8000 shᵉlam (Ch.) (2), to *complete, to restore*
8552 tâmam (4), to *complete, finish*
658 apŏtĕlĕŏ (1), to *bring to completion*
1096 ginŏmai (1), to *be, become*
1274 dianuŏ (1), to *accomplish thoroughly*
5048 tĕlĕiŏŏ (1), to *perfect, complete*
5055 tĕlĕŏ (8), to *end, complete, conclude*

FINISHER
5047 tĕlĕiŏtēs (1),
completeness; maturity

FINS
5579 çᵉnappîyr (5), *fin*

FIR
1265 bᵉrôwsh (20), (poss.)
cypress
1266 bᵉrôwth (1), (poss.)
cypress

FIRE
215 'ôwr (1), to *be
luminous*
217 'ûwr (4), *flame; East*
784 'êsh (375), *fire*
1200 bᵉ'êrâh (1), *burning*
3857 lâhaṭ (4), to *blaze*
5135 nûwr (Ch.) (8), *fire*
4442 pur (73), *fire*
4443 pura (1), *fire*
4447 purinŏs (1), *fiery,*
i.e. *flaming*
4448 purŏŏ (1), to *be
ignited, glow*
5394 phlŏgizō (2), to
cause a blaze
5457 phôs (2),
luminousness, light

FIREBRAND
181 'ûwd (1), *poker stick
for a fire*
3940 lappîyd (1), *flaming
torch, lamp* or *flame*

FIREBRANDS
181 'ûwd (1), *poker stick
for a fire*
2131 zîyqâh (1), *flash of
fire*
3940 lappîyd (1), *flaming
torch, lamp* or *flame*

FIREPANS
4289 machtâh (4), *pan
for live coals*

FIRES
217 'ûwr (1), *flame; East*

FIRKINS
3355 mĕtrētēs (1), *liquid
measure:* 8-10 gallons

FIRM
1277 bârîy' (1), *fatted* or
plump; healthy
3332 yâtsaq (2), to *pour
out*
3559 kûwn (2), to *set up:
establish, fix, prepare*
8631 tᵉqêph (Ch.) (1), to
become, make mighty
949 bĕbaiŏs (1), *stable,
certain, binding*

FIRMAMENT
7549 râqîya' (17), *expanse*

FIRST
259 'echâd (34), *first*
1061 bikkûwr (1),
first-fruits of the crop
1069 bâkar (1), *bear the
first born*
1073 bakkûrâh (1),
first-ripe fruit of a fig
1121 bên (51), *son,
descendant*
1323 bath (3), *daughter,
descendant, woman*
2298 chad (Ch.) (4), *one;
single; first; at once*

2490 châlal (1), to
profane, defile
3138 yôwreh (1), *autumn
rain showers*
4395 mᵉlê'âh (1),
fulfilled; abundance
6440 pânîym (1), *face;
front*
6933 qadmay (Ch.) (3),
first
7218 rô'sh (6), *head*
7223 ri'shôwn (130), *first,
in place, time* or *rank*
7224 ri'shônîy (1), *first*
7225 rê'shîyth (11), *first*
8462 tᵉchillâh (7),
original; originally
509 anŏthĕn (1), *from
above; from the first*
746 archē (4), *first in
rank; first in time*
1207 dĕutĕrŏprōtŏs (1),
second-first
1722+4413 ĕn (1), *in;
during; because of*
3391 mia (7), *one* or *first*
3891 paranŏmĕŏ (1), to
transgress, violate law
4272 prŏdidōmi (1), to
give before
4276 prŏĕlpizō (1), to
hope in advance of
4295 prŏkĕimai (1), to *be
present* to the mind
4386 prŏtĕrŏn (3),
previously
4412 prōtŏn (58), *firstly*
4413 prōtŏs (84), *foremost*
4416 prōtŏtŏkŏs (1),
first-born

FIRSTBEGOTTEN
4416 prōtŏtŏkŏs (1),
first-born

FIRSTBORN
1060 bᵉkôwr (101),
firstborn
1062 bᵉkôwrâh (1), *state
of, rights of first born*
1067 bᵉkîyrâh (6), *first
born, eldest* daughter
1069 bâkar (1), *bear the
first born*
4416 prōtŏtŏkŏs (7),
first-born

FIRSTFRUIT
7225 rê'shîyth (1), *first*
536 aparchē (1), *first-fruit*

FIRSTFRUITS
1061 bikkûwr (13),
first-fruits of the crop
7225 rê'shîyth (11), *first*
536 aparchē (7), *first-fruit*

FIRSTLING
1060 bᵉkôwr (8),
firstborn, i.e. oldest son
1069 bâkar (1), *bear the
first born*
6363 peṭer (4), *firstling,
first born*

FIRSTLINGS
1060 bᵉkôwr (1),
firstborn, i.e. oldest son
1062 bᵉkôwrâh (5), *state
of, rights of first born*

FIRSTRIPE
1061 bikkûwr (1),
first-fruits of the crop

1063 bikkûwrâh (3),
early fig

FISH
1709 dâg (11), *fish; fishes*
1710 dâgâh (14), *fish;
fishes*
1770 dîyg (1), to *catch
fish*
5315 nephesh (1), *life;
breath; soul; wind*
2486 ichthus (5), *fish*
3795 ŏpsariŏn (3), *small
fish*

FISH'S
1710 dâgâh (1), *fish;
fishes*

FISHER'S
1903 ĕpĕndutēs (1), *outer
garment, coat*

FISHERMEN
231 haliĕus (1), one who
fishes for a living

FISHERS
1728 davvâg (2),
fisherman
1771 dayâg (1), *fisherman*
231 haliĕus (4), one who
fishes for a living

FISHES
1709 dâg (8), *fish; fishes*
2485 ichthudiŏn (2), *little
fish*
2486 ichthus (15), *fish*
3795 ŏpsariŏn (2), *small
fish*

FISHHOOKS
5518+1729 çîyr (1), *thorn;
hook*

FISHING
232 haliĕuō (1), to *catch
fish*

FISHPOOLS
1295 bᵉrêkâh (1),
reservoir, pool

FIST
106 'egrôph (2), *clenched
hand*

FISTS
2651 chôphen (1), *pair of
fists*

FIT
6257 'âthad (1), to
prepare
6261 'ittîy (1), *timely*
433 anēkō (1), *be proper,
fitting*
2111 ĕuthĕtŏs (2),
appropriate, suitable
2520 kathēkō (1),
becoming, proper

FITCHES
3698 kuçςemeth (1), *spelt*
7100 qetsach (3),
fennel-flower

FITLY
5921+655 'al (1), *above,
over, upon,* or *against*
5921+4402 'al (1), *above,
over, upon,* or *against*
4883 sunarmŏlŏgĕŏ (2),
to *render close-jointed*

FITTED
3474 yâshar (1), to *be
straight;* to *make right*

FISH
3559 kûwn (1), to *render
sure, proper*
2675 katartizō (1), to
repair; to *prepare*

FITTETH
6213 'âsâh (1), to *do* or
make

FIVE
2568 châmêsh (271), *five*
3999 pĕntakis (1), *five
times*
4000 pĕntakischiliŏi (16),
five times a thousand
4001 pĕntakŏsiŏi (2), *five
hundred*
4002 pĕntĕ (25), *five*

FIXED
3559 kûwn (4), to *render
sure, proper*
4741 stērizō (1), to *turn
resolutely;* to *confirm*

FLAG
260 'âchûw (1), *bulrush*
or any marshy grass

FLAGON
809 'ăshîyshâh (2), *cake*
of raisins

FLAGONS
809 'ăshîyshâh (2), *cake*
of raisins
5035 nebel (1), skin-*bag*
for liquids; *vase; lyre*

FLAGS
5488 çûwph (3), *papyrus
reed; reed*

FLAKES
4651 mappâl (1), *chaff;
flap* or *fold* of skin

FLAME
785 'êsh (Ch.) (1), *fire*
3632 kâlîyl (1), *whole,
entire; complete; whole*
3827 labbâh (1), *flame*
3851 lahab (6), *flame* of
fire; *flash of a blade*
3852 lehâbâh (12), *flame;
flash*
4864 mas'êth (2), *raising;
beacon; present*
7631 sᵉbîyb (Ch.) (2),
flame tongue
7957 shalhebeth (3),
flare, flame of fire
5395 phlŏx (6), *flame;
blaze*

FLAMES
3851 lahab (2), *flame* of
fire; *flash of a blade*
3852 lehâbâh (1), *flame;
flash*

FLAMING
784 'êsh (1), *fire*
3852 lehâbâh (5), *flame;
flash*
3857 lâhaṭ (1), to *blaze*
3858 lahaṭ (1), *blaze;
magic*
5395 phlŏx (1), *flame;
blaze*

FLANKS
3689 keçel (6), *loin;
back; viscera*

FLASH
965 bâzâq (1), *flash* of
lightning

F

FLAT
2763 charam (1), to *devote* to destruction
8478 tachath (2), *bottom; underneath;* in *lieu of*

FLATTER
2505 châlaq (1), to *be smooth; be slippery*
6601 pâthâh (1), to *be, make simple;* to *delude*

FLATTERETH
2505 châlaq (5), to *be smooth; be slippery*
6601 pâthâh (1), to *be, make simple;* to *delude*

FLATTERIES
2514 châlaqqâh (1), *smoothness; flattery*
2519 châlaqlaqqâh (2), *smooth; treacherous*

FLATTERING
2506 chêleq (1), *smoothness* of tongue
2509 châlâq (2), *smooth, slippery* of tongue
2513 chelqâh (2), *smoothness; flattery*
3665 kâna' (2), to *humiliate, vanquish*
2850 kŏlakĕia (1), *flattery*

FLATTERY
2506 chêleq (1), *smoothness* of tongue
2513 chelqâh (1), *smoothness; flattery*

FLAX
6593 pishteh (7), linen, made of *carded* thread
6594 pishtâh (3), *flax; flax wick*
3043 linŏn (1), flax *linen*

FLAY
6584 pâshaṭ (3), to *strip,* i.e. *unclothe, flay*

FLAYED
6584 pâshaṭ (1), to *strip,* i.e. *unclothe, flay*

FLEA
6550 par'ôsh (2), *flea*

FLED
1272 bârach (40), to *flee* suddenly
5074 nâdad (8), to *rove, flee;* to *drive* away
5127 nûwç (83), to *vanish* away, *flee*
5132 nûwts (1), to *fly* away, *leave*
1628 ĕkphĕugō (2), to *flee out, escape*
2703 kataphĕugō (2), to *flee down*
5343 phĕugō (11), to *run* away; to *shun*

FLEDDEST
1272 bârach (1), to *flee* suddenly
5127 nûwç (1), to *vanish* away, *flee*

FLEE
1227 Baqbûwq (1), *gurgling bottle*
1272 bârach (14), to *flee* suddenly
3680 kâçâh (1), to *cover*

FLIETH
1675 dâ'âh (1), to *fly* rapidly, *soar*
5774 'ûwph (2), to *cover,* to *fly;* to *faint*
5775 'ôwph (1), *bird*

FLIGHT
1272 bârach (1), to *flee* suddenly
4498 mânôwç (1), *fleeing; place* of *refuge*
4499 mᵉnuwçâh (1), *retreat, fleeing*
5127 nûwç (1), to *vanish* away, *flee*
7291 râdaph (1), to *run after* with hostility
5437 phugē (2), *escape, flight, fleeing*

FLINT
2496 challâmîysh (3), *flint, flinty rock*
6864 tsôr (2), flint-*stone knife*

FLINTY
2496 challâmîysh (1), *flint, flinty rock*

FLOATS
1702 dôbᵉrâh (1), *raft, collection of logs*

FLOCK
5739 'êder (16), *muster, flock*
6629 tsô'n (83), *flock*
4167 pŏimnē (4), *flock*
4168 pŏimniŏn (5), flock

FLOCKS
2835 châsîph (1), small *company, flock*
4735 miqneh (3), *stock*
4830 mir'îyth (1), *pasturage; flock*
5739 'êder (16), *muster, flock*
6251 'ashtᵉrâh (4), *flock of ewes*
6629 tsô'n (54), *flock*

FLOOD
2229 zâram (1), to *gush* water, *pour forth*
2230 zerem (1), *gush* of water, *flood*
2975 yᵉ'ôr (6), Nile *River;* Tigris *River*
3999 mabbûwl (13), *deluge*
5104 nâhâr (8), *stream;* Nile; Euphrates; Tigris
5158 nachal (3), *valley, ravine;* mine *shaft*
7858 sheṭeph (3), *deluge, torrent*
2627 kataklusmŏs (4), *inundation, flood*
4182 pŏlupŏikilŏs (1), *many-sided*
4215 pŏtamŏs (2), *current, brook*
4216 pŏtamŏphŏrētŏs (1), *overwhelmed by a stream*

FLOODS
5104 nâhâr (10), *stream;* Nile; Euphrates; Tigris
5140 nâzal (3), to *drip,* or *shed* by trickling

FLIES
2070 zᵉbûwb (1), stinging *fly*
6157 'ârôb (2), swarming *mosquitoes*

FLEW
5774 'ûwph (1), to *cover,* to *fly;* to *faint*
6213 'âsâh (1), to *do* or *make*

FLESHY
4560 sarkinŏs (1), *similar to flesh*

FLESHLY
4559 sarkikŏs (2), *pertaining to flesh*

FLESHHOOKS
4207 mazlêg (5), three-tined meat *fork*

FLESHHOOK
4207 mazlêg (2), three-tined meat *fork*

FLESH
829 'eshpâr (2), measured *portion*
1320 bâsâr (253), *flesh; body; person*
1321 bᵉsar (Ch.) (3), *flesh; body; person*
2878 ṭibehâh (1), *butchery*
3894 lâchûwm (1), *flesh*
7607 shᵉ'êr (7), *flesh, meat; kindred* by blood
2907 krĕas (2), butcher's *meat*
4561 sarx (143), *flesh*

FLEETH
1272 bârach (1), to *flee* suddenly
5127 nûwç (4), to *vanish* away, *flee*
5211 niyç (1), *fugitive*
5775 'ôwph (1), *bird*
5343 phĕugō (2), to *run* away; to *shun*

FLEEING
4499 mᵉnuwçâh (1), *retreat, fleeing*
5127 nûwç (1), to *vanish* away, *flee*
6207 'âraq (1), to *gnaw;* a *pain*

FLEECE
1488 gêz (2), shorn *fleece;* mown *grass*
1492 gazzâh (7), wool *fleece*

FLEE (continued from col 2 top)
4498 mânôwç (1), *fleeing; place* of *refuge*
5074 nâdad (4), to *rove, flee;* to *drive* away
5110 nûwd (1), to *waver;* to *wander, flee*
5127 nûwç (62), to *vanish* away, *flee*
5323 nâtsâ' (1), to *go* away
5756 'ûwz (1), to *save* by fleeing
7368 râchaq (1), to *recede; remove*
5343 phĕugō (15), to *run* away; to *shun*

FLOOR
1637 gôren (10), open *area*
7136 qârâh (1), to *bring about;* to *impose*
7172 qarqa' (6), *floor* of a building or the sea
257 halôn (2), threshing-*floor*

FLOORS
1637 gôren (1), open *area*

FLOTES
7513 raphçôdâh (1), log *raft*

FLOUR
1217 bâtsêq (1), fermenting *dough*
5560 çôleth (52), *fine flour*
7058 qemach (4), *flour*
4585 sĕmidalis (1), fine wheat *flour*

FLOURISH
5006 nâ'ats (1), to *scorn*
6524 pârach (9), to *break forth;* to *bloom, flourish*
6692 tsûwts (3), to *blossom, flourish*

FLOURISHED
6524 pârach (1), to *break forth;* to *bloom, flourish*
330 anathallō (1), to *flourish;* to *revive*

FLOURISHETH
6692 tsûwts (2), to *blossom, flourish*

FLOURISHING
7487 ra'ânan (Ch.) (1), *prosperous*
7488 ra'ănân (1), *verdant; prosperous*

FLOW
2151 zâlal (1), to *be loose* morally, *worthless*
3212 yâlak (2), to *walk;* to *live;* to *carry*
5064 nâgar (1), to *pour* out; to *deliver* over
5102 nâhar (5), to *sparkle;* to *flow*
5140 nâzal (3), to *drip,* or *shed* by trickling
4482 rhĕō (1), to *flow* water

FLOWED
2151 zâlal (1), to *be loose* morally, *worthless*
3212 yâlak (1), to *walk;* to *live;* to *carry*
6687 tsûwph (1), to *overflow*

FLOWER
582 'ĕnôwsh (1), *man; person, human*
5328 nitstsâh (2), *blossom*
6525 perach (5), *calyx flower; bloom*

FLOWERS

6731 tsîyts (6), burnished
plate; bright *flower*
6733 tsîytsâh (1), *flower*
438 anthŏs (4), flower
blossom
5230 hupĕrakmŏs (1),
past the *bloom* of youth

FLOWERS

4026 migdâl (1), *tower;*
rostrum
5079 niddâh (2), time of
menstrual *impurity;*
idolatry
5339 nitstsân (1), *blossom*
6525 perach (9), *calyx*
flower; bloom
6731 tsîyts (4), burnished
plate; bright *flower*

FLOWETH

2100 zûwb (12), to *flow*
freely, *gush*

FLOWING

2100 zûwb (9), to *flow*
freely, *gush*
5042 nâba' (1), to *gush*
forth; to *utter*
5140 nâzal (1), to *drip*, or
shed by trickling
7857 shâṭaph (1), to
gush; to *inundate*

FLUTE

4953 mashrôwqîy (Ch.)
(4), musical *pipe*

FLUTTERETH

7363 râchaph (1), to
brood; to *be relaxed*

FLUX

1420 dusĕntĕria (1),
dysentery

FLY

82 'âbar (1), to *soar*
1675 dâ'âh (3), to *fly*
rapidly, *soar*
2070 zᵉbûwb (1), *fly*
3286 yâ'aph (1), to *tire*
5774 'ûwph (13), to *cover*,
to *fly;* to *faint*
5860 'îyṭ (1), to *swoop*
down upon; to *insult*
6524 pârach (2), to *break*
forth; to *bloom;* to *fly*
4072 pĕtŏmai (3), to *fly*

FLYING

3671 kânâph (1), *edge* or
extremity; wing
5774 'ûwph (6), to *cover*,
to *fly;* to *faint*
5775 'ôwph (2), *bird*
4072 pĕtŏmai (2), to *fly*

FOAL

1121 bên (1), *son*,
descendant
5895 'ayir (1), young
donkey or *ass*
5207 huiŏs (1), *son*

FOALS

5895 'ayir (1), young
donkey or *ass*

FOAM

7110 qetseph (1), *rage* or
strife

FOAMETH

875 aphrizō (1), to *froth*
at the mouth

876 aphrŏs (1), *froth*,
foam

FOAMING

875 aphrizō (1), to *froth*
at the mouth
1890 ĕpaphrizō (1), to
foam upon

FODDER

1098 bᵉlîyl (1), *feed*,
fodder

FOES

341 'ôyêb (2), *adversary*,
enemy
6862 tsar (2), *trouble;*
opponent
8130 sânê' (1), to *hate*
2190 ĕchthrŏs (2),
adversary

FOLD

1699 dôber (1), grazing
pasture
4356 miklâ'âh (1), sheep
or goat *pen*
5116 nâveh (3), *at home;*
lovely; home
7257 râbats (1), to
recline, repose, brood
833 aulē (1), *palace;*
house; sheepfold
1667 hĕlissō (1), to *coil,*
roll up, or *wrap*
4167 pŏimnē (1), *flock*

FOLDEN

5440 çâbak (1), to
entwine

FOLDETH

2263 châbaq (1), to *clasp*
the hands, *embrace*

FOLDING

1550 gâlîyl (2), *valve* of a
folding door
2264 chibbûq (2), *folding*

FOLDS

1448 gᵉdêrâh (3),
enclosure for flocks
4356 miklâ'âh (1), sheep
or goat *pen*
5116 nâveh (1), *at home;*
lovely; home

FOLK

3816 lᵉ'ôm (1),
community, nation
5971 'am (2), *people;*
tribe; flock

FOLLOW

310 'achar (5), *after*
935+310 bôw' (1), to *go or*
come
1692 dâbaq (1), to *cling*
or *adhere;* to *catch*
1961 hâyâh (3), to *exist*,
i.e. *be or become*
1961+310 hâyâh (1), to
exist, i.e. *be or become*
1980+310 hâlak (1), to
walk; live a certain way
1980+7272 hâlak (1), to
walk; live a certain way
3212+310 yâlak (8), to
walk; to *live;* to *carry*
7272 regel (3), *foot; step*
7291 râdaph (1), to *run*
after with hostility
190 akŏlŏuthĕō (30), to
accompany, follow

1205+3694 dĕutĕ (1),
come hither!
1377 diōkō (8), to *pursue;*
to *persecute*
1811 ĕxakŏlŏuthĕō (1), to
imitate, obey
1872 ĕpakŏlŏuthĕō (2), to
accompany, follow
2071 ĕsŏmai (1), *will be*
2517 kathĕxēs (1), *in a*
sequence
3326+5023 mĕta (1), *with*,
among; after, later
3401 mimĕŏmai (4), to
imitate, i.e. *model*
3877 parakŏlŏuthĕō (1),
to *attend; trace out*
4870 sunakŏlŏuthĕō (1),
to *follow, accompany*

FOLLOWED

310 'achar (16), *after*
1692 dâbaq (4), to *cling*
or *adhere;* to *catch*
1961+310 hâyâh (2), to
exist, i.e. *be or become*
1980+310 hâlak (7), to
walk; live a certain way
3112+310 Yôwyâkîyn (1),
Jehovah will establish
3212+310 yâlak (9), to
walk; to *live;* to *carry*
3318+310 yâtsâ' (1), to
go, bring out
6213 'âsâh (1), to *do or*
make
7272 regel (1), *foot; step*
7291 râdaph (2), to *run*
after with hostility
190 akŏlŏuthĕō (53), to
accompany, follow
1096 ginŏmai (1), to *be,*
become
1377 diōkō (2), to *pursue;*
to *persecute*
1811 ĕxakŏlŏuthĕō (1), to
imitate, obey
1872 ĕpakŏlŏuthĕō (1), to
accompany, follow
2076+3326 ĕsti (1), he
(she or it) *is*
2614 katadiōkō (1), to
search for, look for
2628 katakŏlŏuthĕō (2),
to *accompany closely*
4870 sunakŏlŏuthĕō (1),
to *follow, accompany*

FOLLOWEDST

3212+310 yâlak (1), to
walk; to *live;* to *carry*

FOLLOWERS

3402 mimētēs (7),
imitator, example
4831 summimētēs (1),
co-imitator

FOLLOWETH

310 'achar (1), *after*
935+310 bôw' (2), to *go or*
come
1692 dâbaq (1), to *cling*
or *adhere;* to *catch*
7291 râdaph (6), to *run*
after with hostility
190 akŏlŏuthĕō (5), to
accompany, follow

FOLLOWING

310 'achar (26), *after*
310+3651 'achar (1), *after*

312 'achêr (1), *other*,
another, different; next
314 'achârôwn (1), *late*
or *last; behind; western*
3212+310 yâlak (2), to
walk; to *live;* to *carry*
190 akŏlŏuthĕō (3), to
accompany, follow
1811 ĕxakŏlŏuthĕō (1), to
imitate, obey
1836 hĕxēs (1),
successive, next
1872 ĕpakŏlŏuthĕō (1), to
accompany, follow
1887 ĕpauriŏn (2),
to-morrow
1966 ĕpiŏusa (1), *ensuing*
2192 ĕchō (1), to *have;*
hold; keep

FOLLY

200 'ivveleth (13),
silliness, foolishness
3689 keçel (2), *loin;*
back; viscera; silliness
3690 kiçlâh (1), *trust;*
silliness
5039 nᵉbâlâh (10), moral
wickedness; crime
5529 çekel (1), *silliness;*
dolts
5531 çiklûwth (5),
silliness
8417 tohŏlâh (1), *bluster*,
braggadocio, i.e. *fatuity*
8604 tiphlâh (2), *frivolity*,
foolishness
454 anŏia (1), *stupidity;*
rage
877 aphrŏsunē (1),
senselessness

FOOD

398 'âkal (1), to *eat*
400 'ôkel (16), *food*
402 'oklâh (1), *food*
944 bûwl (1), *produce*
3899 lechem (21), *food*,
bread
3978 ma'ăkâl (5), *food*,
something to *eat*
4361 makkôleth (1),
nourishment
6718 tsayid (1), hunting
game; lunch, food
7607 shᵉ'êr (1), *flesh*,
meat; kindred by blood
1035 brōsis (1), *food;*
rusting corrosion
1304 diatribō (1), to
remain, stay
5160 trŏphē (2),
nourishment; rations

FOOL

191 'ĕvîyl (11), *silly; fool*
3684 kᵉçîyl (34), *stupid*
or *silly*
5030 nâbîy' (1), *prophet;*
inspired man
5036 nâbâl (6), *stupid;*
impious
5528 çâkal (1), to *be silly*
5530 çâkâl (3), *silly*
5536 çal (1), *basket*
876 aphrŏs (6), *froth*,
foam
3474 mōrŏs (2), *heedless*,
moral *blockhead*
3912 paraphrŏnĕō (1), to
be insane

FOOL'S
191 'ĕvîyl (2), *silly; fool*
3684 keçîyl (5), *stupid or silly*

FOOLISH
191 'ĕvîyl (6), *silly; fool*
196 'ĕvîlîy (1), *silly, foolish*
200 'ivveleth (1), *silliness, foolishness*
1198 ba'ar (1), *brutishness; stupidity*
1984 hâlal (2), to *boast*
2973 yâ'al (1), to *be or act foolish*
3684 keçîyl (9), *stupid or silly*
3687 keçîylûwth (1), *silliness, stupidity*
3688 kâçal (1), *silly, stupid*
5036 nâbâl (6), *stupid; impious*
5039 nebâlâh (1), moral *wickedness; crime*
5528 çâkal (1), to *be silly*
5530 çâkâl (2), *silly*
6612 pethîy (1), *silly, i.e. seducible*
8602 tâphêl (1), to *plaster; frivolity*
453 anŏētŏs (4), *unintelligent, senseless*
801 asunĕtŏs (2), *senseless, dull; wicked*
878 aphrōn (2), *ignorant; egotistic; unbelieving*
3471 mōrainō (1), to *become insipid*
3473 mōrŏlŏgia (1), *buffoonery, foolish talk*
3474 mōrŏs (7), *heedless, moral blockhead*

FOOLISHLY
200 'ivveleth (1), *silliness, foolishness*
1984 hâlal (1), to *boast*
2973 yâ'al (1), to *be or act foolish*
5034 nâbêl (1), to *wilt; to fall away; to be foolish or wicked*
5528 çâkal (5), to *be silly*
8604 tiphlâh (1), *frivolity, foolishness*
1722+877 ĕn (2), *in; during; because of*

FOOLISHNESS
200 'ivveleth (10), *silliness, foolishness*
5528 çâkal (1), to *be silly*
5531 çiklûwth (2), *silliness*
877 aphrŏsunē (1), *senselessness*
3472 mōria (5), *absurdity, foolishness*
3474 mōrŏs (1), *heedless, moral blockhead*

FOOLS
191 'ĕvîyl (7), *silly; fool*
1984 hâlal (2), to *boast*
2973 yâ'al (1), to *be or act foolish*
3684 keçîyl (22), *stupid or silly*
5036 nâbâl (2), *stupid; impious*

453 anŏētŏs (1), *unintelligent, senseless*
781 asŏphŏs (1), *unwise, foolish*
878 aphrōn (2), *ignorant; egotistic; unbelieving*
3471 mōrainō (1), to *become insipid*
3474 mōrŏs (3), *heedless, moral blockhead*

FOOT
947 bûwç (2), to *trample down; oppress*
3653 kên (8), *pedestal or station of a basin*
4001 mebûwçâh (1), *trampling, oppression*
4823 mirmâç (1), *abasement*
5541 çâlâh (1), to *contemn, reject*
7272 regel (61), *foot; step*
7273 raglîy (1), *footman soldier*
2662 katapatĕō (2), to *trample down; to reject*
3979 pĕzēi (1), *on foot*
4158 pŏdērēs (1), *robe reaching the ankles*
4228 pŏus (9), *foot*

FOOTBREADTH
3709+4096+7272 kaph (1), *sole of foot*

FOOTMEN
376+7273 'îysh (4), *man; male; someone*
7273 raglîy (7), *footman soldier*
7328 râz (Ch.) (1), *mystery*

FOOTSTEPS
6119 'âqêb (3), *track, footprint; rear position*
6471 pa'am (1), *time; step; occurence*

FOOTSTOOL
1916+7272 hădôm (6), *foot-stool*
3534 kebesh (1), *footstool*
5286 hupŏpŏdiŏn (1), *under the feet*
5286+3588+4228 hupŏpŏdiŏn (8), *under the feet, i.e. a foot-rest*

FORASMUCH
310 'achar (1), *after*
310+834 'achar (2), *after*
854+834 'êth (1), *with; by; at; among*
3282 ya'an (1), *because, for this reason*
3282+365 ya'an (2), *because, for this reason*
3282+834 ya'an (5), *because, for this reason*
3588 kîy (1), *for, that because*
3588+5921+3651 kîy (1), *for, that because*
3606+6903+1768 kôl (Ch.) (8), *all, any or every*
5704 'ad (1), *as far (long) as; during; while; until*
1487 ĕi (1), *if, whether, that*
1893 ĕpĕi (2), *since*

1894 ĕpĕidē (1), *when, whereas*
1895 ĕpĕidēpĕr (1), *since indeed*
5607 ōn (1), *being, existence*

FORBAD
6680 tsâvâh (1), to *constitute, enjoin*
1254 diakōluō (1), *utterly prohibit or prevent*
2967 kōluō (3), to *stop*

FORBARE
2308 châdal (3), to *desist, stop; be fat*

FORBEAR
1826 dâmam (1), to *stop, cease; to perish*
2308 châdal (15), to *desist, stop; be fat*
2820 châsak (1), to *restrain or refrain*
4900 mâshak (1), to *draw out; to be tall*
3361 mē (1), *not; lest*
4722 stĕgō (2), to *endure patiently*
5339 phĕidŏmai (1), to *abstain; treat leniently*

FORBEARANCE
463 anŏchē (2), *tolerance, clemency*

FORBEARETH
2308 châdal (1), to *desist, stop; be fat*
2310 châdêl (1), *ceasing or destitute*

FORBEARING
639 'aph (1), *nose or nostril; face; person*
3557 kûwl (1), to *maintain*
430 anĕchŏmai (2), *put up with, endure*
447 aniēmi (1), to *slacken, loosen*

FORBID
2486 châlîylâh (12), *far be it!, forbid!*
3607 kâlâ' (1), to *hold back or in; to prohibit*
2967 kōluō (9), to *stop*
3361+1096 mē (14), *not; lest*

FORBIDDEN
3808 lô' (1), *no, not*
6680 tsâvâh (1), to *constitute, enjoin*
2967 kōluō (1), to *stop*

FORBIDDETH
2967 kōluō (1), to *stop*

FORBIDDING
209 akōlutōs (1), *in an unhindered manner*
2967 kōluō (3), to *stop*

FORBORN
2308 châdal (1), to *desist, stop; be fat*

FORCE
153 'edra' (Ch.) (1), *power*
202 'ôwn (1), *ability, power; wealth*
1369 gebûwrâh (1), *force; valor; victory*
1497 gâzal (1), to *rob*

2388 châzaq (1), to *fasten upon; to seize*
2394 chozqâh (2), *vehemence, harshness*
3027 yâd (2), *hand; power*
3533 kâbash (1), to *conquer, subjugate*
3581 kôach (3), *force, might; strength*
3893 lêach (1), *fresh strength, vigor*
6031 'ânâh (1), to *afflict, be afflicted*
726 harpazō (3), to *seize*
949 bĕbaiŏs (1), *stable, certain, binding*

FORCED
662 'âphaq (1), to *abstain*
3905 lâchats (1), to *press; to distress*
5080 nâdach (1), to *push off, scattered*
6031 'ânâh (4), to *afflict, be afflicted*

FORCES
2428 chayil (14), *army; wealth; virtue; valor*
3981 ma'ămâts (1), *strength; resources*
4581 mâ'ôwz (1), *fortified place; defense*

FORCIBLE
4834 mârats (1), to *be pungent or vehement*

FORCING
4330 mîyts (1), *pressure*
5080 nâdach (1), to *push off, scattered*

FORD
4569 ma'ăbâr (1), *crossing-place*

FORDS
4569 ma'ăbâr (3), *crossing-place*

FORECAST
2803 châshab (2), to *plot; to think, regard*

FOREFATHERS
4269 prŏgŏnŏs (1), *ancestor*

FOREFRONT
4136+6440 mûwl (1), *in front of, opposite*
4136+6440 mûwl (3), *in front of, opposite*
6440 pânîym (4), *face; front*
7218 rô'sh (1), *head*
8127 shên (1), *tooth; ivory; cliff*

FOREHEAD
639 'aph (1), *nose or nostril; face; person*
1371 gibbêach (1), *bald forehead*
1372 gabbachath (3), *baldness on forehead*
4696 mêtsach (9), *forehead*
3359 mĕtōpŏn (2), *forehead*

FOREHEADS
4696 mêtsach (2), *forehead*

3359 mĕtŏpŏn (6),
forehead

FOREIGNER
5237 nokrîy (1), foreign;
non-relative; different
8453 tôwshâb (1),
temporary dweller

FOREIGNERS
5237 nokrîy (1), foreign;
non-relative; different
3941 parŏikŏs (1),
strange; stranger

FOREKNEW
4267 prŏginōskō (1), to
know beforehand

FOREKNOW
4267 prŏginōskō (1), to
know beforehand

FOREKNOWLEDGE
4268 prŏgnōsis (2),
forethought

FOREMOST
7223 rî'shôwn (3), first

FOREORDAINED
4267 prŏginōskō (1), to
know beforehand

FOREPART
6440 pânîym (4), face;
front
4408 prōra (1), prow, i.e.
forward part of a vessel

FORERUNNER
4274 prŏdrŏmŏs (1),
runner ahead

FORESAW
4308 prŏŏraō (1), to
notice previously

FORESEEING
4375 prŏsphilĕs (1),
acceptable, pleasing

FORESEETH
7200 râ'âh (2), to see

FORESHIP
4408 prōra (1), prow, i.e.
forward part of a vessel

FORESKIN
6188 'ârêl (1), to refrain
from using
6190 'orlâh (8), prepuce
or penile foreskin

FORESKINS
6190 'orlâh (5), prepuce
or penile foreskin

FOREST
3293 ya'ar (37), honey in
the comb
6508 pardêç (1), park,
cultivated garden area

FORESTS
2793 chôresh (1),
wooded forest
3293 ya'ar (1), honey in
the comb
3295 ya'ărâh (1), honey
in the comb

FORETELL
4302 prŏlĕgō (1), to
predict, forewarn

FORETOLD
4280 prŏĕrĕō (1), to say
already, predict
4293 prŏkataggĕllō (1),
to predict, foretell

FOREWARN
5263 hupŏdĕiknumi (1),
to exemplify, instruct

FOREWARNED
4277 prŏĕpō (1), to say
already, to predict

FORFEITED
2763 charam (1), to
devote to destruction

FORGAT
5382 nâshâh (1), to forget
7911 shâkach (7), to be
oblivious of, forget

FORGAVE
3722 kâphar (1), to
cover; to expiate
863 aphiēmi (2), to leave;
to pardon, forgive
5483 charizŏmai (4), to
grant as a favor, pardon

FORGAVEST
5375 nâsâ' (2), to lift up

FORGED
2950 ţâphal (1), to
impute falsely

FORGERS
2950 ţâphal (1), to
impute falsely

FORGET
5382 nâshâh (2), to forget
7911 shâkach (48), to be
oblivious of, forget
7913 shâkêach (1),
oblivious, forgetting
1950 ĕpilanthanŏmai (2),
to lose out of mind

FORGETFUL
1950 ĕpilanthanŏmai (1),
to lose out of mind
1953 ĕpilĕsmŏnē (1),
negligence

FORGETFULNESS
5388 nᵉshîyâh (1),
oblivion

FORGETTEST
7911 shâkach (2), to be
oblivious of, forget

FORGETTETH
7911 shâkach (2), to be
oblivious of, forget
7913 shâkêach (1),
oblivious, forgetting
1950 ĕpilanthanŏmai (1),
to lose out of mind

FORGETTING
1950 ĕpilanthanŏmai (1),
to lose out of mind

FORGIVE
3722 kâphar (1), to
cover; to expiate
5375 nâsâ' (8), to lift up
5545 çâlach (18), to
forgive
5546 çallâch (1),
placable, tolerant
630 apŏluō (1), to relieve,
release; to pardon
863 aphiēmi (22), to
leave; to pardon, forgive
5483 charizŏmai (3), to
grant as a favor, pardon

FORGIVEN
3722 kâphar (1), to
cover; to expiate

5375 nâsâ' (4), to lift up
5545 çâlach (13), to
forgive
630 apŏluō (1), to relieve,
release; to pardon
863 aphiēmi (21), to
leave; to pardon, forgive
5483 charizŏmai (2), to
grant as a favor, pardon

FORGIVENESS
5547 çᵉlîychâh (1),
pardon
859 aphĕsis (6), pardon,
freedom

FORGIVENESSES
5547 çᵉlîychâh (1),
pardon

FORGIVETH
5545 çâlach (1), to forgive
863 aphiēmi (1), to leave;
to pardon, forgive

FORGIVING
5375 nâsâ' (2), to lift up
5483 charizŏmai (2), to
grant as a favor, pardon

FORGOT
7911 shâkach (1), to be
oblivious of, forget

FORGOTTEN
5382 nâshâh (1), to forget
7911 shâkach (39), to be
oblivious of, forget
7913 shâkêach (1),
oblivious, forgetting
1585 ĕklanthanŏmai (1),
to forget
1950 ĕpilanthanŏmai (3),
to lose out of mind
3024+2983 lēthē (1),
forgetfulness

FORKS
7969+7053 shâlôwsh (1),
three; third; thrice

FORM
3335 yâtsar (1), to form;
potter; to determine
4758 mar'eh (1),
appearance; vision
4941 mishpâţ (1), verdict;
formal decree; justice
6440 pânîym (1), face;
front
6699 tsûwrâh (2), rock;
form as if pressed out
6755 tselem (Ch.) (1),
idolatrous figure
7299 rêv (Ch.) (2), aspect,
appearance
8389 tô'ar (3), outline,
i.e. figure, appearance
8403 tabnîyth (3), model,
resemblance
8414 tôhûw (2), waste,
desolation, formless
3444 mŏrphē (3), shape,
form; nature, character
3446 mŏrphōsis (2),
appearance; semblance
5179 tupŏs (1), shape
resemblance; "type"
5296 hupŏtupōsis (1),
example, pattern

FORMED
2342 chûwl (5), to dance,
whirl; to writhe in pain

3335 yâtsar (23), to form;
potter; to determine
7169 qârats (1), to bite
the lips, blink the eyes
3445 mŏrphŏō (1), to
fashion, take on a form
4110 plasma (2), molded,
what is formed
4111 plassō (1), to mold,
i.e. shape or fabricate

FORMER
570 'emesh (1), last night
3138 yôwreh (2), autumn
rain showers
3335 yâtsar (2), to form;
potter; to determine
4175 môwreh (2), archer;
teaching; early rain
6440 pânîym (1), face;
front
6927 qadmâh (3), priority
in time; before; past
6931 qadmôwnîy (2),
anterior time; eastern
7223 rî'shôwn (32), first
4386 prŏtĕrŏn (2),
previously
4387 prŏtĕrŏs (1), prior
or previous
4413 prōtŏs (2), foremost

FORMETH
3335 yâtsar (2), to form;
potter; to determine

FORMS
6699 tsûwrâh (2), rock;
form as if pressed out

FORNICATION
2181 zânâh (3), to
commit adultery
8457 taznûwth (1),
harlotry
1608 ĕkpŏrnĕuō (1), to
fornicate
4202 pŏrnĕia (24), sexual
immorality
4203 pŏrnĕuō (7), to
indulge unlawful lust

FORNICATIONS
8457 taznûwth (1),
harlotry
4202 pŏrnĕia (2), sexual
immorality

FORNICATOR
4205 pŏrnŏs (2), sexually
immoral person

FORNICATORS
4205 pŏrnŏs (3), sexually
immoral person

FORSAKE
2308 châdal (1), to desist,
stop; be fat
5203 nâţash (7), to
disperse; to abandon
5800 'âzab (45), to
loosen; relinquish
7503 râphâh (2), to
slacken
646+575 apŏstasia (1),
defection, rebellion
1459 ĕgkatalĕipō (1), to
desert, abandon

FORSAKEN
488 'almân (1),
discarded, forsaken
5203 nâţash (6), to
disperse; to abandon

5428 nâthash (1), to *tear away, be uprooted*
5800 'âzab (60), to *loosen; relinquish*
7971 shâlach (1), to *send away*
863 aphiêmi (2), to *leave; to pardon, forgive*
1459 ĕgkatalĕipō (4), to *desert, abandon*
2641 katalĕipō (1), to *abandon*

FORSAKETH
5800 'âzab (5), to *loosen; relinquish; permit*
657 apŏtassŏmai (1), to *say adieu; to renounce*

FORSAKING
5805 'ăzûwbâh (1), *desertion, forsaking*
1459 ĕgkatalĕipō (1), to *desert, abandon*

FORSOMUCH
2530 kathŏti (1), *as far or inasmuch as*

FORSOOK
5203 nâṭash (2), to *disperse; to abandon*
5800 'âzab (16), to *loosen; relinquish*
863 aphiêmi (4), to *leave; to pardon, forgive*
1459 ĕgkatalĕipō (1), to *desert, abandon*
2641 katalĕipō (1), to *abandon*

FORSOOKEST
5800 'âzab (2), to *loosen; relinquish; permit*

FORSWEAR
1964 ĕpiŏrkĕō (1), to *commit perjury*

FORT
1785 dâyêq (3), *battering-tower*
4581 mâ'ôwz (1), *fortified place; defense*
4686 mâtsûwd (1), *net or capture; fastness*
4869 misgâb (1), *high refuge*

FORTH
935 bôw' (1), to *go or come*
1310 bâshal (1), to *boil up, cook; to ripen*
1319 bâsar (1), to *announce* (good news)
1518 gîyach (4), to *issue forth; to burst forth*
1645 geresh (1), *produce, yield*
1876 dâshâ' (1), to *sprout new plants*
1921 hâdar (1), to *favor or honor; to be high*
2254 châbal (2), to *writhe in labor pain*
2315 cheder (1), *apartment, chamber*
2330 chûwd (4), to *propound a riddle*
2342 chûwl (4), to *dance, whirl; to writhe in pain*
2590 chânaṭ (1), to *embalm; to ripen*

2904 ṭûwl (3), to *cast down or out, hurl*
2986 yâbal (1), to *bring*
3205 yâlad (26), to *bear young; to father a child*
3209 yillôwd (1), *born*
3318 yâtsâ' (403), to *go, bring out*
3329 yâtsîy' (1), *issue forth, i.e. offspring*
4161 môwtsâ' (11), *going forth*
4163 môwtsâ'âh (3), *family descent*
4866 mishbêr (1), *vaginal opening*
5066 nâgash (2), to *be, come, bring near*
5107 nûwb (2), to (*make*) *flourish; to utter*
5132 nûwts (1), to *fly away, leave*
5221 nâkâh (1), to *strike, kill*
5265 nâça' (5), *start on a journey*
5312 nᵉphaq (Ch.) (7), to *issue forth; to bring out*
5375 nâsâ' (2), to *lift up*
5414 nâthan (1), to *give*
5608 çâphar (1), to *inscribe; to enumerate*
5674 'âbar (2), to *cross over; to transition*
5975 'âmad (1), to *stand*
6213 'âsâh (10), to *do or make*
6398 pâlach (1), to *slice; to break open; to pierce*
6440 pânîym (1), *face; front*
6509 pârâh (1), to *bear fruit*
6556 perets (1), *break, gap*
6566 pâras (1), to *break apart, disperse, scatter*
6605 pâthach (1), to *open wide; to loosen, begin*
6631 tse'ĕtsâ' (1), *produce, children*
6779 tsâmach (4), to *sprout*
7126 qârab (1), to *approach, bring near*
7737 shâvâh (1), to *level, i.e. equalize*
7971 shâlach (27), to *send away*
8317 shârats (5), to *swarm, or abound*
8444 tôwtsâ'âh (2), *exit, boundary; deliverance*
321 anagō (3), to *lead up; to bring out; to sail*
392 anatassŏmai (1), to *arrange*
584 apŏdĕiknumi (1), to *demonstrate*
616 apŏkuĕō (1), to *bring into being*
649 apŏstĕllō (11), to *send out on a mission*
669 apŏphthĕggŏmai (1), *declare, address*
985 blastanō (1), to *yield fruit*
1032 bruō (1), to *gush, pour forth*

1080 gĕnnaō (1), to *procreate, regenerate*
1544 ĕkballō (7), to *throw out*
1554 ĕkdidōmi (2), to *lease, rent*
1584 ĕklampō (1), to *be resplendent, shine*
1599 ĕkpĕmpō (1), to *despatch, send out*
1600 ĕkpĕtannumi (1), to *extend, spread out*
1607 ĕkpŏrĕuŏmai (4), to *depart, be discharged*
1614 ĕktĕinō (17), to *stretch*
1627 ĕkphĕrō (3), to *bear out; to produce*
1631 ĕkphuō (2), to *sprout up, put forth*
1632 ĕkchĕō (1), to *pour forth; to bestow*
1731 ĕndĕiknumi (1), to *show, display*
1754 ĕnĕrgĕō (2), to *be active, efficient, work*
1804 ĕxaggĕllō (1), to *declare, proclaim*
1806 ĕxagō (1), to *lead forth, escort*
1821 ĕxapŏstĕllō (4), to *despatch, or to dismiss*
1831 ĕxĕrchŏmai (32), to *issue; to leave*
1854 ĕxō (8), *out, outside*
1901 ĕpĕktĕinŏmai (1), to *stretch oneself forward*
1907 ĕpĕchō (1), to *retain; to detain*
1911 ĕpiballō (1), to *throw upon*
2164 ĕuphŏrĕō (1), to *be fertile, produce a crop*
2564 kalĕō (1), to *call*
2592 karpŏphŏrĕō (2), to *be fertile*
2604 kataggĕlĕus (1), *proclaimer*
2609 katagō (1), to *lead down; to moor a vessel*
3004 lĕgō (1), to *say*
3318 Mĕsŏpŏtamia (2), *between the Rivers*
3855 paragō (1), to *go along or away*
3860 paradidōmi (1), to *hand over*
3908 paratithēmi (1), to *present something*
3928 parĕrchŏmai (1), to *go by; to perish*
4160 pŏiĕō (14), to *do*
4198 pŏrĕuŏmai (1), to *go, come; to travel*
4254 prŏagō (2), to *lead forward; to precede*
4261 prŏballō (1), to *push to the front, germinate*
4270 prŏgraphō (1), to *announce, prescribe*
4295 prŏkĕimai (1), to *stand forth*
4311 prŏpĕmpō (1), to *send forward*
4388 prŏtithĕmai (1), to *place before, exhibit*
4393 prŏphĕrō (3), to *bear forward*

4486 rhĕgnumi (1), to *break, burst forth*
5087 tithēmi (1), to *place*
5088 tiktō (9), to *produce from seed*
5319 phanĕrŏō (1), to *render apparent*
5348 phthanō (1), to *be beforehand, precede*

FORTHWITH
629 oçparnâ' (Ch.) (1), *with diligence*
2112 ĕuthĕŏs (7), *at once or soon*
2117 ĕuthus (1), *at once, immediately*
3916 parachrēma (1), *instantly, immediately*

FORTIETH
705 arbâ'îym (4), *forty*

FORTIFIED
2388 châzaq (2), to *fasten upon; be strong*
4692 mâtsôwr (1), *siege-mound; distress*
5800 'âzab (1), to *loosen; relinquish; permit*

FORTIFY
553 'âmats (1), to *be strong; be courageous*
1219 bâtsar (2), to *be inaccessible*
2388 châzaq (1), to *fasten upon; be strong*
5800 'âzab (1), to *loosen; relinquish; permit*
6696 tsûwr (1), to *cramp, i.e. confine; to harass*

FORTRESS
4013 mibtsâr (4), *fortification; defender*
4581 mâ'ôwz (3), *fortified place; defense*
4686 mâtsûwd (6), *net or capture; fastness*
4693 mâtsôwr (2), *limit, border*

FORTRESSES
4013 mibtsâr (2), *fortification; defender*

FORTS
1785 dâyêq (3), *battering-tower*
4679 mᵉtsad (1), *stronghold*
4694 mᵉtsûwrâh (1), *rampart, fortification*
6076 'ôphel (1), *tumor; fortress*

FORTUNATUS
5415 Phŏrtŏunatŏs (2), *fortunate*

FORTY
702+7239 'arba' (2), *four*
705 'arbâ'îym (126), *forty*
5062 tĕssarakŏnta (22), *forty*
5063 tĕssarakŏntaĕtēs (2), *of forty years of age*

FORTY'S
705 'arbâ'îym (1), *forty*

FORUM
675 'Appiŏs (1), *Appius*

FORWARD
1973 hâl°âh (5), *far away; thus far*
1980 hâlak (1), to *walk; live a certain way*
3276 yâ'al (1), to *be valuable*
4605 ma'al (2), *upward, above, overhead*
5265 nâça' (18), *start on a journey*
5921 'al (3), *above, over, upon,* or *against*
6440 pânîym (4), *face; front*
6584 pâshaṭ (1), to *strip,* i.e. *unclothe, plunder*
6924 qedem (1), *eastern; antiquity; before*
2309 thĕlō (1), to *will;* to *desire;* to *choose*
4261 prŏballō (1), to *push to the front, germinate*
4281 prŏĕrchŏmai (1), to *go onward, precede*
4311 prŏpĕmpō (1), to *send forward*
4704 spŏudazō (1), to *make effort*
4707 spŏudaiŏtĕrŏs (1), *more earnest*

FORWARDNESS
4288 prŏthumia (1), *alacrity, eagerness*
4710 spŏudē (1), *despatch; eagerness*

FOUGHT
3898 lâcham (58), to *fight a battle,* i.e. *consume*
6633 tsâbâ' (1), to *mass an army or servants*
75 agōnizŏmai (1), to *struggle;* to *contend*
2341 thēriŏmachĕō (1), to *be a beast fighter*
4170 pŏlĕmĕō (2), to *battle, make war*

FOUL
2560 châmar (1), to *ferment, foam;* to *glow*
7515 râphas (1), to *trample,* i.e. *roil* water
169 akathartŏs (2), *impure; evil*
5494 chĕimōn (1), *winter season; stormy weather*

FOULED
4833 mirpâs (1), *muddied* water

FOULEDST
7515 râphas (1), to *trample,* i.e. *roil* water

FOUND
2713 châqar (2), to *examine, search*
4672 mâtsâ' (267), to *find* or *acquire;* to *occur*
7912 sh°kach (Ch.) (11), to *discover, find out*
429 anĕuriskō (1), to *find out*
1096 ginŏmai (1), to *be, become*
2147 hĕuriskō (111), to *find*
2638 katalambanō (1), to *seize;* to *possess*

FOUNDATION
787 'ôsh (Ch.) (1), *foundation*
3245 yâçad (15), *settle, establish a foundation*
3247 y°çôwd (7), *foundation*
3248 y°çûwdâh (5), *foundation*
4143 mûwçâd (2), *foundation*
4527 maççad (1), *foundation*
2310 thĕmĕliŏs (12), *substruction*
2311 thĕmĕliŏō (1), to *erect;* to *consolidate*
2602 katabŏlē (10), *conception, beginning*

FOUNDATIONS
134 'eden (1), *base, footing*
787 'ôsh (Ch.) (2), *foundation*
803 'ăshûwyâh (1), *foundation*
808 'âshîysh (1), (ruined) *foundation*
3245 yâçad (4), *settle, establish a foundation*
3247 y°çôwd (3), *foundation*
4146 môwçâdâh (13), *foundation*
4328 m°yuççâdâh (1), *foundation*
4349 mâkôwn (1), *basis; place*
8356 shâthâh (1), *basis*
2310 thĕmĕliŏs (4), *substruction*

FOUNDED
3245 yâçad (8), *settle, establish a foundation*
2311 thĕmĕliŏō (2), to *erect;* to *consolidate*

FOUNDER
6884 tsâraph (5), to *fuse* metal; to *refine*

FOUNDEST
4672 mâtsâ' (1), to *find* or *acquire;* to *occur*

FOUNTAIN
953 bôwr (1), pit *hole, cistern, well*
4002 mabbûwa' (1), *fountain, water spring*
4599 ma'yân (9), *fountain; source*
4726 mâqôwr (11), *flow*
5869 'ayin (7), *eye; sight; fountain*
4077 pēgē (4), *source or supply*

FOUNTAINS
4599 ma'yân (7), *fountain; source*
5869 'ayin (4), *eye; sight; fountain*
4077 pēgē (4), *source or supply*

FOUR
702 'arba' (258), *four*
703 'arba' (Ch.) (8), *four*
5064 tĕssarēs (43), *four*
5066 tĕtartaiŏs (1), *of the fourth* day

5067 tĕtartŏs (1), *fourth*
5070 tĕtrakischiliŏi (5), *four times a thousand*
5071 tĕtrakŏsiŏi (2), *four hundred*
5072 tĕtramĕnŏn (1), *four months'* time

FOURFOLD
706 'arba'tayim (1), *fourfold*
5073 tĕtraplŏŏs (1), *quadruple,* i.e. *four-fold*

FOURFOOTED
5074 tĕtrapŏus (3), *quadruped*

FOURSCORE
8084 sh°mônîym (34), *eighty; eightieth*
3589 ŏgdŏĕkŏnta (2), *ten times eight*

FOURSQUARE
7243 r°bîy'îy (1), *fourth; fourth*
7251 râba' (8), to *be four sided,* to *be quadrate*
5068 tĕtragōnŏs (1), *four-cornered*

FOURTEEN
702+6240 'arba' (2), *four*
702+6246 'arba' (4), *four*
702+7657 'arba' (3), *four*
1180 dĕkatĕssarēs (5), *fourteen*

FOURTEENTH
702+6240 'arba' (23), *four*
5065 tĕssarĕskaidĕkatŏs (2), *fourteenth*

FOURTH
702 'arba' (5), *four*
7243 r°bîy'îy (55), *fourth; fourth*
7244 r°bîy'ay (Ch.) (5), *fourth; fourth*
7253 reba' (2), *fourth part or side*
7255 rôba' (2), *quarter*
7256 ribbêa' (4), *fourth; fourth* generation
5067 tĕtartŏs (9), *fourth*

FOWL
1257 barbûr (1), *fowl*
5775 'ôwph (23), *bird*
5776 'ôwph (Ch.) (1), *bird*
5861 'ayiṭ (1), *bird of prey* (poss.) *hawk*
6833 tsippôwr (5), *little hopping bird*

FOWLER
3353 yâqûwsh (3), *snarer, trapper of fowl*

FOWLERS
3369 yâqôsh (1), to *ensnare, trap*

FOWLS
5775 'ôwph (36), *winged bird*
5776 'ôwph (Ch.) (1), *winged bird*
5861 'ayiṭ (3), *bird of prey* (poss.) *hawk*
6833 tsippôwr (1), *little hopping bird*
6853 ts°phar (Ch.) (3), *bird*
3732 ŏrnĕŏn (2), *bird*

4071 pĕtĕinŏn (9), *bird* which *flies*

FOX
7776 shûw'âl (1), *jackal*
258 alōpēx (1), *fox*

FOXES
7776 shûw'âl (6), *jackal*
258 alōpēx (2), *fox*

FRAGMENTS
2801 klasma (7), *piece, bit*

FRAIL
2310 châdêl (1), *ceasing* or *destitute*

FRAME
3335 yâtsar (1), to *form; potter;* to *determine*
3336 yêtser (1), *form*
3559 kûwn (1), to *set up: establish, fix, prepare*
4011 mibneh (1), *building*
5414 nâthan (1), to *give*

FRAMED
3335 yâtsar (1), to *form; potter;* to *determine*
3336 yêtser (1), *form*
2675 katartizō (1), to *repair;* to *prepare*
4883 sunarmŏlŏgĕō (1), to *render close-jointed*

FRAMETH
3335 yâtsar (1), to *form; potter;* to *determine*
6775 tsâmad (1), to *link,* i.e. *gird*

FRANKINCENSE
3828 l°bôwnâh (15), *frankincense*
3030 libanŏs (2), *fragrant incense* resin or gum

FRANKLY
5435 Phrugia (1), *Phrygia*

FRAUD
8496 tôk (1), *oppression*
650 apŏstĕrĕō (1), to *deprive;* to *despoil*

FRAY
2729 chârad (3), to *shudder;* to *hasten*

FRECKLED
933 bôhaq (1), *white scurf, rash*

FREE
2600 chinnâm (1), *gratis, free*
2666 châphash (1), to *loose; free from* slavery
2670 chophshîy (16), *exempt, free*
5071 n°dâbâh (2), *abundant* gift
5081 nâdîyb (1), *magnanimous*
5082 n°dîybâh (1), *nobility,* i.e. *reputation*
5352 nâqâh (2), to *be, make clean;* to *be bare*
5355 nâqîy (1), *innocent*
6362 pâṭar (1), to *burst through;* to *emit*
6605 pâthach (1), to *open wide;* to *loosen, begin*
1658 ĕlĕuthĕrŏs (20), *not a slave*

1659 ĕlĕuthĕrŏō (6), to *exempt, liberate*
5486 charisma (2), spiritual *endowment*

FREED
3772 kârath (1), to *cut* (off, down or asunder)
1344 dikaiŏō (1), *show* or *regard* as *innocent*

FREEDOM
2668 chuphshâh (1), *liberty* from slavery
4174 pŏlitĕia (1), *citizenship*

FREELY
2600 chinnâm (1), *gratis, free*
5071 nedâbâh (2), *abundant gift*
1432 dōrĕan (6), *gratuitously, freely*
3326+3954 mĕta (1), *with, among; after, later*
3955 parrhēsiazŏmai (1), to *be confident*

FREEMAN
558 apĕlĕuthĕrŏs (1), *freedman*

FREEWILL
5069 nedab (Ch.) (2), *be, give without coercion*
5071 nedâbâh (15), *abundant gift*

FREEWOMAN
1658 ĕlĕuthĕrŏs (2), *not a slave*

FREQUENT
4056 pĕrissŏtĕrŏs (1), *more superabundantly*

FRESH
2319 châdâsh (1), *new, recent*
3955 leshad (1), *juice; vigor; sweet* or *fat cake*
7488 ra'ănân (1), *new; prosperous*
1099 glukus (1), *sweet, fresh*

FRESHER
7375 rûwṭăphash (1), to *be rejuvenated*

FRET
2734 chârâh (4), to *blaze up*
6356 pechetheth (1), *mildewed garment hole*
7107 qâtsaph (1), to *burst out in rage*
7481 râ'am (1), to *crash thunder; to irritate*

FRETTED
7264 râgaz (1), to *quiver*

FRETTETH
2196 zâ'aph (1), to *be angry*

FRETTING
3992 mâ'ar (3), to *be painful; destructive*

FRIED
7246 râbak (2), to *soak bread in oil*

FRIEND
157 'âhab (4), to *have affection, love*

7451 ra' (1), *bad; evil*
7453 rêa' (27), *associate; one close*
7462 râ'âh (1), to *associate* as a friend
7463 rê'eh (3), *male advisor*
2083 hĕtairŏs (3), *comrade, friend*
3982 pĕithō (1), to *pacify* or *conciliate*
5384 philŏs (12), *friend; friendly*

FRIENDLY
3820 lêb (2), *heart*
7489 râ'a' (1), to *make, be good for nothing*

FRIENDS
157 'âhab (8), to *have affection, love*
441 'allûwph (2), *friend, one familiar; chieftain*
605+7965 'ânash (1), to *be frail, feeble*
4828 mêrêa' (3), close *friend*
4962 math (1), *men*
7453 rêa' (14), *associate; one close*
3588+3844 hŏ (1), "*the,*" i.e. the definite article
4674 sŏs (1), *things that are yours*
5384 philŏs (17), *friend; friendly*

FRIENDSHIP
7462 râ'âh (1), to *associate* as a friend
5373 philia (1), *fondness*

FRINGE
6734 tsîytsîth (2), *fore-lock* of hair; *tassel*

FRINGES
1434 gedîl (1), *tassel; festoon*
6734 tsîytsîth (1), *fore-lock* of hair; *tassel*

FRO
235 'âzal (1), to *disappear*
7725 shûwb (1), to *turn back; to return*
7751 shûwṭ (8), to *travel, roam*
8264 shâqaq (1), to *seek greedily*
2831 kludōnizŏmai (1), to *fluctuate back and forth on the waves*

FROGS
6854 tsephardêa' (13), *frog, leaper*
944 batrachŏs (1), *frog*

FRONT
6440 pânîym (2), *face; front*

FRONTIERS
7097 qâtseh (1), *extremity*

FRONTLETS
2903 ṭôwphâphâh (3), *sign* or *symbolic box*

FROST
2602 chănâmâl (1), *aphis* or *plant-louse*
3713 kephôwr (3), *bowl; white frost*

7140 qerach (3), *ice; hail; rock crystal*

FROWARD
2019 hăphakpak (1), *very perverse, crooked*
3868 lûwz (2), to *depart; to be perverse*
6141 'iqqêsh (6), *distorted, warped, false*
6143 'iqqeshûwth (2), *perversity*
6617 pâthal (3), to *struggle; to be tortuous*
8419 tahpûkâh (3), *perversity* or *fraud*
4646 skŏliŏs (1), *crooked; perverse*

FROWARDLY
7726 shôwbâb (1), *apostate*, i.e. *idolatrous*

FROWARDNESS
8419 tahpûkâh (3), *perversity* or *fraud*

FROZEN
3920 lâkad (1), to *catch; to capture*

FRUIT
4 'êb (Ch.) (3), *green plant*
1061 bikkûwr (2), *first-fruits* of the crop
2981 yebûwl (3), *produce, crop; harvest*
3206 yeled (1), *young male*
3899 lechem (1), *food, bread*
3978 ma'ăkâl (1), *food, something to eat*
4395 melê'âh (1), *fulfilled; abundance*
5107 nûwb (1), to (*make*) *flourish; to utter*
5108 nôwb (2), *agricultural produce*
6509 pârâh (1), to *bear fruit*
6529 perîy (106), *fruit*
7920 sekal (Ch.) (1), to *be* or *act circumspect*
8270 shôr (1), *umbilical cord; strength*
8393 tebûw'âh (7), *income*, i.e. *produce*
8570 tenûwbâh (1), *crop, produce*
175 akarpŏs (1), *barren, unfruitful*
1081 gĕnnēma (3), *offspring; produce*
2590 karpŏs (54), *fruit; crop*
2592 karpŏphŏrĕō (7), to *be fertile*
5052 tĕlĕsphŏrĕō (1), to *ripen fruit*
5352 phthinŏpōrinŏs (1), *autumnal*

FRUITFUL
1121+8081 bên (1), *people of a class or kind*
2233 zera' (1), *seed; fruit, plant, sowing-time*
3759 karmel (7), *planted field; garden produce*
6500 pârâ (1), to *bear fruit*

6509 pârâh (21), to *bear fruit*
6529 perîy (2), *fruit*
2592 karpŏphŏrĕō (1), to *be fertile*
2593 karpŏphŏrŏs (1), *fruitbearing*

FRUITS
3 'êb (1), *green* plant
1061 bikkûwr (1), *first-fruits* of the crop
2173 zimrâh (1), *choice fruit*
3581 kôach (1), *force, might; strength*
4395 melê'âh (1), *fulfilled; abundance*
6529 perîy (7), *fruit*
8393 tebûw'âh (6), *income*, i.e. *produce*
8570 tenûwbâh (1), *crop, produce*
1081 gĕnnēma (2), *offspring; produce*
2590 karpŏs (12), *fruit; crop*
3703 ŏpōra (1), *ripe* fruit

FRUSTRATE
656 'âphêç (1), to *cease*
114 athĕtĕō (1), to *disesteem, neutralize*

FRUSTRATETH
6565 pârar (1), to *break up; to violate, frustrate*

FRYING
4802 marchesheth (1), *stew-*pan

FRYINGPAN
4802 marchesheth (1), *stew-*pan

FUEL
402 'oklâh (3), *food*
3980 ma'ăkôleth (2), *fuel* for fire

FUGITIVE
5128 nûwa' (2), to *waver*

FUGITIVES
1280 berîyach (1), *bolt; cross-bar* of a door
4015 mibrâch (1), *refugee*
5307 nâphal (1), to *fall*
6412 pâlîyṭ (1), *refugee*

FULFIL
3615 kâlâh (1), to *complete, consume*
4390 mâlê' (7), to *fill; be full*
6213 'âsâh (2), to *do* or *make*
378 anaplērŏō (1), to *complete; to occupy*
4137 plērŏō (6), to *fill, make complete*
4160 pŏiĕō (2), to *make* or *do*
5055 tĕlĕō (3), to *end*, i.e. *complete, execute*

FULFILLED
1214 bâtsa' (1), to *finish; to stop*
3615 kâlâh (2), to *complete, consume*
4390 mâlê' (20), to *fill; be full*
5487 çûwph (Ch.) (1), to *come to an end*

6213 'âsâh (1), to *do*
378 anaplērŏō (1), to
complete; accomplish
1096 ginŏmai (3), to be,
become
1603 ekplērŏō (1), to
accomplish, fulfill
4137 plērŏō (45), to *fill,
make complete*
4931 suntĕlĕō (1), to
complete entirely
5048 tĕlĕiŏō (2), to
perfect, complete
5055 tĕlĕō (4), to *end*, i.e.
complete, execute

FULFILLING
6213 'âsâh (1), to *do or
make*
4138 plērōma (1), what
fills; what is filled
4160 pŏiĕō (1), to *do*

FULL
3117 yôwm (10), *day;
time period*
3624 kelach (1), *maturity*
3759 karmel (1), *planted
field; garden produce*
4390 mâlê' (50), to *fill; be
full*
4391 mᵉlâ' (Ch.) (1), to
fill; be full
4392 mâlê' (58), *full;
filling; fulness; fully*
4393 mᵉlô' (11), *fulness*
7227 rab (1), *great*
7235 râbâh (1), to
increase
7646 sâba' (20), *fill to
satiety*
7648 sôba' (3),
satisfaction
7649 sâbêa' (2), *satiated*
7654 sob'âh (3), *satiety*
7999 shâlam (1), to *be
safe; be, make complete*
8003 shâlêm (2),
complete; friendly; safe
8537 tôm (1),
completeness
8549 tâmîym (1), *entire,
complete; integrity*
8552 tâmam (1), to
complete, finish
1072 gĕmizŏ (1), to *fill
entirely*
1073 gĕmō (11), to *swell
out*, i.e. *be full*
1705 ĕmpiplēmi (1), to
satisfy
2880 kŏrĕnnumi (1), to
cram, i.e. *glut or sate*
3324 mĕstŏs (8), *replete,
full*
3325 mĕstŏō (1), to
intoxicate
4130 plēthō (1), to *fulfill,
complete*
4134 plērēs (17), *replete,
full, complete*
4135 plērŏphŏrĕō (1), to
fill completely
4136 plērŏphŏria (3), *full
assurance*
4137 plērŏō (9), to *fill,
make complete*
4138 plērōma (1), what
fills; what is filled
5046 tĕlĕiŏs (1),
complete; mature

5460 phōtĕinŏs (4),
well-illuminated
5526 chŏrtazŏ (1), to
supply food until full

FULLER
1102 gnaphĕus (1),
cloth-*dresser*

FULLER'S
3526 kâbaç (3), to *wash*

FULLERS'
3526 kâbaç (1), to *wash*

FULLY
3615 kâlâh (1), to
complete, consume
4390 mâlê' (3), to *fill; be
full*
4392 mâlê' (1), *full;
filling; fulness; fully*
5046 nâgad (1), to
announce
3877 parakŏlŏuthĕō (1),
to *attend; trace out*
4135 plērŏphŏrĕō (3), to
fill completely
4137 plērŏō (1), to *fill,
make complete*
4845 sumplērŏō (1), to be
complete, fulfill

FULNESS
4390 mâlê' (1), to *fill; be
full*
4393 mᵉlô' (8), *fulness*
4395 mᵉlê'âh (1),
fulfilled; abundance
7648 sôba' (1),
satisfaction
7653 sib'âh (1), *satiety*
4138 plērōma (13), what
fills; what is filled

FURBISH
4838 mâraq (1), to *polish;
to sharpen; to rinse*

FURBISHED
4803 mârat (5), to *polish;
to sharpen*

FURIOUS
1167+2534 ba'al (1),
master; owner; citizen
2534 chêmâh (4), *heat;
anger; poison*
7108 qᵉtsaph (Ch.) (1), to
become enraged

FURIOUSLY
2534 chêmâh (1), *heat;
anger; poison*
7697 shiggâ'ôwn (1),
craziness

FURLONGS
4712 stadiŏn (5), *length
of about 200 yards*

FURNACE
861 'attûwn (Ch.) (10),
fire *furnace*
3536 kibshân (4),
smelting *furnace*
3564 kûwr (9), smelting
furnace
5948 'ăliyl (1), (poss.)
crucible
8574 tannûwr (2), *fire-pot*
2575 kaminŏs (4),
furnace

FURNACES
8574 tannûwr (2), *fire-pot*

FURNISH
4390 mâlê' (1), to *fill; be
full*
6059 'ânaq (1), to *collar;
to fit out*
6186 'ârak (1), to set in a
row, i.e. *arrange,*
6213+3627 'âsâh (1), to
do or make

FURNISHED
5375 nâsâ' (1), to *lift up*
6186 'ârak (1), to set in a
row, i.e. *arrange,*
1822 ĕxartizŏ (1), to
finish out; to equip fully
4130 plēthō (1), to *fulfill,
complete*
4766 strŏnnumi (2),
strew, spread a carpet

FURNITURE
3627 kᵉlîy (7),
implement, thing
3733 kar (1), *saddle bag*

FURROW
8525 telem (1), *bank or
terrace*

FURROWS
1417 gᵉdûwd (1), *furrow
ridge*
4618 ma'ănâh (1),
furrow, plow path
5869 'ayin (1), *eye; sight;
fountain*
6170 'ărûwgâh (2),
parterre, kind of garden
8525 telem (3), *bank or
terrace*

FURTHER
3148 yôwthêr (1),
moreover; rest; gain
3254 yâçaph (4), to *add
or augment*
5750 'ôwd (2), *again;
repeatedly; still; more*
6329 pûwq (1), to *issue;
to furnish; to secure*
1339 diïstēmi (1), to
remove, intervene
2089 ĕti (6), *yet, still*
4206 pŏrrhō (1),
forwards, at a distance

FURTHERANCE
4297 prŏkŏpē (2),
progress, advancement

FURTHERED
5375 nâsâ' (1), to *lift up*

FURTHERMORE
637 'aph (1), *also or yea;
though*
5750 'ôwd (1), *again;
repeatedly; still; more*
1161 dĕ (1), *but, yet; and
then*
1534 ĕita (1), *succession,
then, moreover*
3063 lŏipŏn (1),
remaining; finally

FURY
2528 chĕmâ' (Ch.) (2),
anger
2534 chêmâh (67), *heat;
anger; poison*
2740 chârôwn (1),
burning of anger

GAAL
1603 Ga'al (9), *loathing*

GAASH
1608 Ga'ash (4), *quaking*

GABA
1387 Geba' (3), *Geba*

GABBAI
1373 Gabbay (1),
collective

GABBATHA
1042 gabbatha (1), *knoll*

GABRIEL
1403 Gabrîy'êl (2), *man
of God*
1043 Gabriēl (2), *man of
God*

GAD
1410 Gâd (71), *Gad*
1045 Gad (1), *Gad*

GADARENES
1046 Gadarēnŏs (3),
inhabitant of Gadara

GADDEST
235 'âzal (1), to *disappear*

GADDI
1426 Gaddîy (1), *Gaddi*

GADDIEL
1427 Gaddîy'êl (1),
fortune of God

GADI
1424 Gâdîy (2), *fortunate*

GADITE
1425 Gâdîy (1), *Gadite*

GADITES
1425 Gâdîy (14), *Gadite*

GAHAM
1514 Gacham (1), *flame*

GAHAR
1515 Gachar (2), *lurker*

GAIN
1214 bâtsa' (9), to
*plunder; to finish; to
stop*
2084 zᵉban (Ch.) (1), to
acquire by purchase
4242 mᵉchîyr (1), *price,
payment, wages*
8393 tᵉbûw'âh (1),
income, i.e. *produce*
8636 tarbîyth (1),
percentage or bonus
2039 ĕrgasia (2),
occupation; profit
2770 kĕrdainŏ (9), to
gain; to spare
2771 kĕrdŏs (2), *gain,
profit*
4122 plĕŏnĕktĕō (2), to
be covetous
4200 pŏrismŏs (2),
money-getting

GAINED
1214 bâtsa' (2), to
plunder; to finish
1281 diapragmatĕuŏmai
(1), to *earn, make gain*
2770 kĕrdainŏ (5), to
gain; to spare
4160 pŏiĕō (1), to *make
or do*
4333 prŏsĕrgazŏmai (1),
to *acquire besides*

GAINS
2039 ĕrgasia (1),
occupation; profit

GAINSAY
471 antĕpō (1), to *refute* or *deny*

GAINSAYERS
483 antilĕgō (1), to *dispute, refuse*

GAINSAYING
369 anantirrhētōs (1), *without raising objection*
483 antilĕgō (1), to *dispute, refuse*
485 antilŏgia (1), *dispute, disobedience*

GAIUS
1050 Gaïŏs (5), *Gaïus*

GALAL
1559 Gâlâl (3), *great*

GALATIA
1053 Galatia (4), *Galatia*
1054 Galatikŏs (2), relating to *Galatia*

GALATIANS
1052 Galatēs (2), *inhabitant of Galatia*

GALBANUM
2464 chelbᵉnâh (1), *fragrant resin gum*

GALEED
1567 Gal'êd (2), *heap of testimony*

GALILAEAN
1057 Galilaiŏs (3), belonging to *Galilæa*

GALILAEANS
1057 Galilaiŏs (5), belonging to *Galilæa*

GALILEE
1551 Gâlîyl (6), *circle* as a special *circuit*
1056 Galilaia (66), heathen *circle*

GALL
4845 mᵉrêrâh (1), bitter *bile* of the gall bladder
4846 mᵉrôrâh (2), bitter *bile*; venom of a serpent
7219 rô'sh (9), *poisonous plant; poison*
5521 chŏlē (2), *gall* or *bile; bitterness*

GALLANT
117 'addîyr (1), *powerful; majestic*

GALLERIES
862 'attûwq (3), *ledge* or offset
7298 rahaṭ (1), *ringlet* of hair

GALLERY
862 'attûwq (1), *ledge* or offset

GALLEY
590 'ŏnîy (1), *ship; fleet of ships*

GALLIM
1554 Gallîym (2), *springs*

GALLIO
1058 Galliōn (3), *Gallion,* i.e. *Gallio*

GALLOWS
6086 'êts (8), *wood,* things made of *wood*

GAMALIEL
1583 Gamliy'êl (5), *reward of God*
1059 Gamaliēl (2), *reward of God*

GAMMADIMS
1575 Gammâd (1), *warrior*

GAMUL
1577 Gâmûwl (1), *rewarded*

GAP
6556 perets (1), *break, gap*

GAPED
6473 pâ'ar (1), to *open* wide
6475 pâtsâh (1), to *rend,* i.e. *open*

GAPS
6556 perets (1), *break, gap*

GARDEN
1588 gan (39), *garden*
1593 gannâh (3), *garden, grove*
1594 ginnâh (4), *garden, grove*
2779 kēpŏs (5), *garden, grove*

GARDENER
2780 kēpŏurŏs (1), *gardener*

GARDENS
1588 gan (3), *garden*
1593 gannâh (9), *garden, grove*

GAREB
1619 Gârêb (3), *scabby*

GARLANDS
4725 stĕmma (1), *wreath*

GARLICK
7762 shûwm (1), *garlic*

GARMENT
155 'addereth (4), *large; splendid*
899 beged (36), *clothing; treachery or pillage*
3801 kᵉthôneth (2), garment that *covers*
3830 lᵉbûwsh (7), *garment; wife*
3831 lᵉbûwsh (Ch.) (1), *garment*
4055 mad (3), *vesture, garment; carpet*
4594 ma'ăṭeh (1), *vestment, garment*
7897 shîyth (1), *garment*
8008 salmâh (4), *clothing*
8071 simlâh (4), *dress, mantle*
8162 sha'aṭnêz (1), *linen and woolen*
8509 takrîyk (1), *wrapper or robe*
1742 ĕnduma (2), *apparel,* outer *robe*
2440 himatiŏn (15), to *put on clothes*
4158 pŏdērēs (1), robe reaching the *ankles*
4749 stŏlē (1), long-fitting *gown* as a mark of dignity

GAMALIEL

GARMENTS
899 beged (69), *clothing; treachery or pillage*
3801 kᵉthôneth (3), garment that *covers*
3830 lᵉbûwsh (2), *garment; wife*
3831 lᵉbûwsh (Ch.) (1), *garment*
4055 mad (1), *vesture, garment; carpet*
4060 middâh (1), *portion; vestment; tribute*
4063 medev (2), *dress, garment*
8008 salmâh (4), *clothing*
8071 simlâh (2), *dress, mantle*
2067 ĕsthēsis (1), *clothing*
2440 himatiŏn (15), to *put on clothes*

GARMITE
1636 Garmîy (1), *strong*

GARNER
596 apŏthēkē (2), *granary, grain barn*

GARNERS
214 'ôwtsâr (1), *depository*
4200 mezev (1), *granary*

GARNISH
2885 kŏsmĕō (1), to *decorate; to snuff*

GARNISHED
6823 tsâphâh (1), to *sheet* over with metal
8235 shiphrâh (1), *brightness of skies*
2885 kŏsmĕō (3), to *decorate; to snuff*

GARRISON
4673 matstsâb (7), *spot; office; military post*
4675 matstsâbâh (1), military *guard*
5333 nᵉtsîyb (4), military *post; statue*
5432 phrŏurĕō (1), to *post spies at gates*

GARRISONS
4676 matstsêbâh (1), *column or stone*
5333 nᵉtsîyb (5), military *post; statue*

GASHMU
1654 Geshem (1), *rain downpour*

GAT
622 'âçaph (1), to *gather, collect*
935 bôw' (2), to *go or come*
3212 yâlak (4), to *walk; to live; to carry*
5927 'âlâh (7), to *ascend, be high, mount*
6213 'âsâh (2), to *do or make*
7392 râkab (1), to *ride*

GATAM
1609 Ga'tâm (3), *Gatam*

GATE
6607 pethach (4), *opening; door; entrance*
8179 sha'ar (240), *opening, door or gate*
8651 tᵉra' (Ch.) (1), *door*
2374 thura (1), *entrance,* i.e. *door, gate*
4439 pulē (8), *gate*
4440 pulōn (5), *gate-way, door-way*

GATES
1817 deleth (14), *door; gate*
5592 çaph (2), *dish*
6607 pethach (3), *opening; door; entrance*
8179 sha'ar (112), *opening, door or gate*
4439 pulē (2), *gate*
4440 pulōn (11), *gate-way, door-way*

GATH
1661 Gath (33), *wine-press or vat*

GATH-HEPHER
1662 Gath-ha-Chêpher (1), *wine-press of* (the) *well*

GATH-RIMMON
1667 Gath-Rimmôwn (4), *wine-press of* (the) *pomegranate*

GATHER
103 'âgar (1), to *harvest*
622 'âçaph (36), to *gather, collect*
1219 bâtsar (2), to *gather grapes*
1413 gâdad (2), to *gash, slash oneself*
1481 gûwr (3), to *sojourn, live as an alien*
1716 dâgar (1), to *brood over; to care for young*
2490 châlal (1), to *profane, defile*
3259 yâ'ad (1), to *meet; to summon; to direct*
3664 kânaç (5), to *collect; to enfold*
3673 kânash (Ch.) (1), to *assemble*
3950 lâqaṭ (13), to *pick up, gather; to glean*
3953 lâqash (1), to *gather the after crop*
4390 mâlê' (2), to *fill; be full*
5619 çâqal (1), to *throw large stones*
5756 'ûwz (3), to *strengthen*
6908 qâbats (56), to *collect, assemble*
6910 qᵉbûtsâh (1), *hoard, gathering*
6950 qâhal (8), to *convoke, gather*
7197 qâshash (4), to *assemble*
346 anakĕphalaiŏmai (1), to *sum up*
1996 ĕpisunagō (2), to *collect upon*
4816 sullĕgō (6), to *collect, gather*

4863 sunagō (11), to gather together
5166 trugaō (2), to collect the vintage

GATHERED
622 'âçaph (97), to gather, collect
626 'ăçêphâh (1), (collect) *together*
717 'ârâh (1), to pluck, pick *fruit*
1219 bâtsar (1), to *gather* grapes
1481 gûwr (2), to *sojourn, live as an alien*
2199 zâ'aq (4), to *call out, announce*
3254 yâçaph (1), to *add* or *augment*
3259 yâ'ad (3), to *meet; to summon*; to *direct*
3664 kânaç (2), to collect; to *enfold*
3673 kânash (Ch.) (2), to *assemble*
3950 lâqaṭ (11), to pick up, *gather*; to *glean*
4390 mâlê' (1), to *fill; be full*
5413 nâthak (2), to *flow* forth, *pour* out
5596 çâphach (1), to *associate; be united*
6192 'âram (2), to *pile* up
6213 'âsâh (1), to *do or make*
6651 tsâbar (2), to *aggregate, gather*
6817 tsâ'aq (5), to *shriek; to* proclaim
6908 qâbats (57), to collect, *assemble*
6950 qâhal (19), to *convoke, gather*
6960 qâvâh (2), to *collect; to expect*
7035 qâlahh (1), to *assemble*
7197 qâshash (1, to *assemble*
7408 râkash (1), to *lay up*, i.e. *collect*
8085 shâma' (1), to *hear* intelligently
1865 ĕpathrŏïzō (1), to *accumulate, increase*
1996 ĕpisunagō (4), to *collect upon*
3792 ŏchlŏpŏïĕō (1), to *raise a disturbance*
4816 sullĕgō (2), to *collect, gather*
4863 sunagō (29), to *gather together*
4867 sunathrŏïzō (1), to *convene*
4896 sunĕimi (1), to *assemble, gather*
4962 sustrĕphō (1), to *collect a bundle, crowd*
5166 trugaō (1), to *collect* the vintage

GATHERER
1103 bâlaç (1), to pinch sycamore figs

GATHEREST
1219 bâtsar (1), to *gather* grapes

GATHERETH
103 'âgar (2), to *harvest*
622 'âçaph (4), to *gather, collect*
3664 kânaç (2), to collect; to *enfold*
3950 lâqaṭ (1), to *pick* up, *gather*; to *glean*
6908 qâbats (4), to collect, *assemble*
1996 ĕpisunagō (1), to *collect upon*
4863 sunagō (3), to *gather together*

GATHERING
625 'ôçeph (2), fruit *harvest collection*
962 bâzaz (1), to *plunder, take boot̤y*
3349 yiqqâhâh (1), *obedience*
4723 miqveh (1), *confidence; collection*
7197 qâshash (3), to *assemble*
1997 ĕpisunagōgē (1), *meeting, gathering*
4822 sumbibazō (1), to *drive together*
4863 sunagō (1), to *gather together*

GATHERINGS
3048 lŏgia (1), *contribution, collection*

GAVE
935 bôw' (1), to *go, come*
1696 dâbar (3), to *speak, say; to subdue*
3052 yᵉhab (Ch.) (4), to *give*
3254 yâçaph (1), to *add* or *augment*
3289 yâ'ats (2), to *advise*
5414 nâthan (252), to *give*
5462 çâgar (3), to *shut* up; to *surrender*
7121 qârâ' (3), to *call* out
7311 rûwm (4), to be *high; to rise or raise*
7725 shûwb (1), to *turn* back; to *return*
7760 sûwm (4), to *put, place*
7971 shâlach (1), to *send* away
437 anthŏmŏlŏgĕŏmai (1), to *give thanks*
591 apŏdidōmi (2), to *give away*
1291 diastĕllŏmai (1), to *distinguish*
1325 didōmi (77), to *give*
1433 dōrĕŏmai (1), to *bestow* gratuitously
1502 ĕikō (1), to be *weak*, i.e. *yield*
1781 ĕntĕllŏmai (1), to *enjoin, give orders*
1788 ĕntrĕpō (1), to *respect; to confound*
1907 ĕpĕchō (1), to *retain; to detain*
1929 ĕpididōmi (2), to *give over*
2010 ĕpitrĕpō (3), to *allow, permit*
2702 kataphĕrō (1), to *bear down*

2753 kĕlĕuō (1), to *order, direct*
3140 marturĕō (3), to *testify; to commend*
3860 paradidōmi (7), to *hand over*
4160 pŏiĕō (2), to *make or do*
4222 pŏtizō (5), to *furnish drink, irrigate*
4337 prŏsĕchō (3), to *pay attention to*
4823 sumbŏulĕuō (1), to *recommend, deliberate*
5483 charizŏmai (2), to *grant as a favor, pardon*

GAVEST
5414 nâthan (21), to *give*
7760 sûwm (1), to *put, place*
1325 didōmi (11), to *give*

GAY
2986 lamprŏs (1), *clear; magnificent*

GAZA
5804 'Azzâh (18), *strong*
1048 Gaza (1), *strong*

GAZATHITES
5841 'Azzâthîy (1), *Azzathite*

GAZE
7200 râ'âh (1), to *see*

GAZER
1507 Gezer (2), *portion, piece*

GAZEZ
1495 Gâzêz (2), *shearer*

GAZING
1689 ĕmblĕpō (1), to *observe; to discern*

GAZINGSTOCK
7210 rô'îy (1), *sight; spectacle*
2301 thĕatrizō (1), to *expose as a spectacle*

GAZITES
5841 'Azzâthîy (1), *Azzathite*

GAZZAM
1502 Gazzâm (2), *devourer*

GEBA
1387 Geba' (12), *Geba*

GEBAL
1381 Gᵉbâl (2), *mountain*

GEBER
1398 Geber (2), *(valiant) man*

GEBIM
1374 Gêbîym (1), *cisterns*

GEDALIAH
1436 Gᵉdalyâh (32), *Jehovah has become great*

GEDEON
1066 Gĕdĕōn (1), *warrior*

GEDER
1445 Geder (1), *wall or fence*

GEDERAH
1449 Gᵉdêrâh (1), *enclosure* for flocks

GEDERATHITE
1452 Gᵉdêrâthîy (1), *Gederathite*

GEDERITE
1451 Gᵉdêrîy (1), *Gederite*

GEDEROTH
1450 Gᵉdêrôwth (2), *walls*

GEDEROTHAIM
1453 Gᵉdêrôthayim (1), *double wall*

GEDOR
1446 Gᵉdôr (7), *enclosure*

GEHAZI
1522 Gêychăzîy (12), *valley of a visionary*

GELILOTH
1553 Gᵉlîylôwth (1), *circles*

GEMALLI
1582 Gᵉmalliy (1), *camel-driver*

GEMARIAH
1587 Gᵉmaryâh (5), *Jehovah has perfected*

GENDER
7250 râba' (1), to *lay down*; have sex
1080 gĕnnaō (1), to *procreate, regenerate*

GENDERED
3205 yâlad (1), to *bear young*; to *father a child*

GENDERETH
5674 'âbar (1), to *cross over; to transition*
1080 gĕnnaō (1), to *procreate, regenerate*

GENEALOGIES
3187 yâchas (6), to *enroll* by *family list*
1076 gĕnĕalŏgia (2), *genealogy, lineage*

GENEALOGY
3188 yachas (15), *family list*

GENERAL
8269 sar (1), *head person, ruler*
3831 panēguris (1), *mass-meeting*

GENERALLY
3605 kôl (1), *all, any* or *every*

GENERATION
1755 dôwr (50), *dwelling*
1859 dâr (Ch.) (2), *age; generation*
1074 gĕnĕa (30), *generation; age*
1078 genesis (1), *nativity, nature*
1081 gĕnnēma (4), *offspring; produce*
1085 gĕnŏs (1), *kin, offspring in kind*

GENERATIONS
1755 dôwr (73), *dwelling*
8435 tôwlᵉdâh (39), *family descent*, family *record*

1074 gĕnĕa (6),
generation; age

GENNESARET
1082 Gĕnnēsarĕt (3),
(poss.) *harp*-shaped

GENTILE
1672 Hĕllēn (2), *Greek*
(*-speaking*)

GENTILES
1471 gôwy (30), foreign
nation; Gentiles
1483 ĕthnikōs (1), *as a
Gentile*
1484 ĕthnŏs (93), *race;
tribe; pagan*
1672 Hĕllēn (5), *Greek*
(*-speaking*)

GENTLE
1933 ĕpiĕikēs (3), *mild,
gentle*
2261 ēpiŏs (2), *affable,*
i.e. *mild or kind*

GENTLENESS
6031 'ănâh (1), to *afflict,
be afflicted*
6038 'ănâváh (1),
modesty, clemency
1932 ĕpiĕikĕia (1),
mildness, gentleness
5544 chrēstŏtēs (1),
moral *excellence*

GENTLY
3814 lâ'ṭ (1), *silently*

GENUBATH
1592 Gᵉnûbath (2), *theft*

GERA
1617 Gêrâ' (9), *cereal
grain*

GERAHS
1626 gêrâh (5), *measure*

GERAR
1642 Gᵉrâr (10), *rolling*
country

GERGESENES
1086 Gĕrgĕsēnŏs (1),
Gergesene

GERIZIM
1630 Gᵉrîzîym (4), *rocky*

GERSHOM
1648 Gêrᵉshôwn (14),
refugee

GERSHON
1647 Gêrᵉshôm (17),
refugee

GERSHONITE
1649 Gerᵉshunnîy (3),
Gereshonite

GERSHONITES
1649 Gerᵉshunnîy (9),
Gereshonite

GESHAM
1529 Gêyshân (1),
lumpish

GESHEM
1654 Geshem (3), *rain
downpour*

GESHUR
1650 Gᵉshûwr (8), *bridge*

GESHURI
1651 Gᵉshûwrîy (2),
Geshurite

GESHURITES
1651 Gᵉshûwrîy (5),
Geshurite

GET
776 'erets (1), *earth,
land, soil; country*
935 bôw' (8), to *go or
come*
1214 bâtsa' (1), to
plunder; to finish
1245 bâqash (1), to
search; to strive after
1980 hâlak (1), to *walk;
live a certain way*
3212 yâlak (17), to *walk;
to live; to carry*
3318 yâtsâ' (7), to *go,
bring out*
3381 yârad (9), to
descend
3513 kâbad (1), to *be
heavy, severe, dull*
3947 lâqach (5), to *take*
4422 mâlaṭ (1), to *escape
as if by slipperiness*
4672 mâtsâ' (2), to *find
or acquire; to occur*
5110 nûwd (1), to *waver;
to wander, flee*
5111 nûwd (Ch.) (1), to
flee
5265 nâça' (1), *start on a
journey*
5381 nâsag (6), to *reach*
5674 'âbar (1), to *cross
over; to transition*
5927 'âlâh (18), to
ascend, be high, mount
6213 'âsâh (2), to *do or
make*
6965 qûwm (1), to *rise*
7069 qânâh (8), to *create;
to procure*
7426 râmam (1), to *rise*
7725 shûwb (1), to *turn
back; to return*
1684 ĕmbainō (2), to
embark; to reach
1826 ĕxĕimi (1), *leave;
escape*
1831 ĕxĕrchŏmai (3), to
issue; to leave
2147 hĕuriskō (1), to *find*
2597 katabainō (1), to
descend
4122 plĕŏnĕktĕō (1), to
be covetous
5217 hupagō (4), to
withdraw or retire

GETHER
1666 Gether (2), *Gether*

GETHSEMANE
1068 Gĕthsĕmanē (2),
oil-press

GETTETH
3947 lâqach (1), to *take*
5060 nâga' (1), to *strike*
5927 'âlâh (1), to *ascend,
be high, mount*
6213 'âsâh (1), to *do or
make*
6329 pûwq (1), to *issue;
to furnish; to secure*
7069 qânâh (3), to *create;
to procure*

GETTING
6467 pô'al (1), *act or
work, deed*
7069 qânâh (1), to *create;
to procure*
7075 qinyân (1),
acquisition, purchase

GEUEL
1345 Gᵉ'ûw'êl (1),
majesty of God

GEZER
1507 Gezer (13), *portion,
piece*

GEZRITES
1511 Gizrîy (1), *Gezerite;
Girzite*

GHOST
1478 gâva' (9), to *expire,
die*
5315 nephesh (2), *life;
breath; soul; wind*
1606 ĕkpnĕō (3), to *expire*
1634 ĕkpsuchō (3), to
expire, die
4151 pnĕuma (92), *spirit*

GIAH
1520 Gîyach (1), *fountain*

GIANT
1368 gibbôwr (1),
powerful; great warrior
7497 râphâ' (7), *giant*

GIANTS
1368 gibbôwr (1),
powerful; great warrior
5303 nᵉphîyl (2), *bully or
tyrant*
7497 râphâ' (10), *giant*

GIBBAR
1402 Gibbâr (1), *Gibbar*

GIBBETHON
1405 Gibbᵉthôwn (6),
hilly spot

GIBEA
1388 Gib'â' (1), *hill*

GIBEAH
1390 Gib'âh (48), *hillock*

GIBEATH
1394 Gib'ath (1), *hilliness*

GIBEATHITE
1395 Gib'âthîy (1),
Gibathite

GIBEON
1391 Gib'ôwn (35), *hilly*

GIBEONITE
1393 Gib'ônîy (2),
Gibonite

GIBEONITES
1393 Gib'ônîy (6),
Gibonite

GIBLITES
1382 Gibliy (1), *Gebalite*

GIDDALTI
1437 Giddaltîy (2), *I have
made great*

GIDDEL
1435 Giddêl (4), *stout*

GIDEON
1439 Gîd'ôwn (39),
warrior

GIDEONI
1441 Gid'ônîy (5), *warlike*

GIDOM
1440 Gid'ôm (1),
desolation

GIER
7360 râchâm (2), kind of
vulture

GIFT
4503 minchâh (1),
tribute; offering
4976 mattân (4), *present,
gift*
4979 mâttânâh (5),
present; offering; bribe
4991 mattâth (3), *present*
5379 nissê'th (1), *present*
7810 shachad (6), to
bribe; gift
1390 dŏma (1), *present,
gift*
1394 dŏsis (1), *gift*
1431 dōrĕa (11), *gratuity,
gift*
1434 dōrēma (1),
bestowment, gift
1435 dōrŏn (10),
sacrificial present
5485 charis (1),
gratitude; benefit given
5486 charisma (10),
spiritual *endowment*

GIFTS
814 'eshkâr (1), *gratuity,
gift; payment*
4503 minchâh (6),
tribute; offering
4864 mas'êth (1), *tribute;
reproach*
4976 mattân (1), *present,
gift*
4978 mattᵉnâ' (Ch.) (3),
present, gift
4979 mâttânâh (11),
present; offering; bribe
5078 nêdeh (1), *bounty,
reward for prostitution*
5083 nâdân (1), *present
for prostitution*
7810 shachad (4), to
bribe; gift
8641 tᵉrûwmâh (1),
tribute, present
334 anathēma (1), *votive
offering to God*
1390 dŏma (2), *present,
gift*
1435 dōrŏn (9),
sacrificial present
3311 mĕrismŏs (1),
distribution
5486 charisma (7),
spiritual *endowment*

GIHON
1521 Gîychôwn (6),
stream

GILALAI
1562 Gîlălay (1), *dungy*

GILBOA
1533 Gilbôa' (8),
bubbling fountain

GILEAD
1568 Gil'âd (100), *Gilad*

GILEAD'S
1568 Gil'âd (1), *Gilad*

GILEADITE
1569 Gil'âdîy (9), *Gileadite*

GILEADITES
1569 Gil'âdîy (4), *Giladite*

GILGAL
1537 Gilgâl (39), *wheel*

GILOH
1542 Gîlôh (2), *open*

GILONITE
1526 Gîylônîy (2), *Gilonite*

GIMZO
1579 Gimzôw (1), Gimzo

GIN
4170 môwqêsh (1), *noose*
6341 pach (2), thin metallic *sheet; net*

GINATH
1527 Gîynath (2), *Ginath*

GINNETHO
1599 Ginn^ethôwn (1), *gardener*

GINNETHON
1599 Ginn^ethôwn (2), *gardener*

GINS
4170 môwqêsh (2), *noose*

GIRD
247 'âzar (4), to *belt*
640 'âphad (1), to *fasten, gird*
2290 chăgôwr (1), *belt for the waist*
2296 chăgar (16), to *gird on a belt; put on* armor
328 anazōnnumi (1), to *gird, bind afresh*
2224 zōnnumi (2), to *bind about*
4024 pĕrizōnnumi (2), to *fasten on one's belt*

GIRDED
247 'âzar (7), to *belt*
631 'âçar (1), to *fasten; to join* battle
2280 châbash (1), to *wrap* firmly, *bind*
2289 chăgôwr (1), *belted around waist*
2296 chăgar (18), to *gird on a belt; put on* armor
8151 shânaç (1), to *compress*
1241 diazōnnumi (2), to *gird tightly, wrap*
4024 pĕrizōnnumi (2), to *fasten on one's belt*

GIRDEDST
2224 zōnnumi (1), to *bind about*

GIRDETH
247 'âzar (1), to *belt*
631 'âçar (1), to *fasten; to join* battle
2296 chăgar (2), to *gird on a belt; put on* armor

GIRDING
2296 chăgar (1), to *gird on a belt; put on* armor
4228 machăgôreth (1), *girdle* of sackcloth

GIRDLE
73 'abnêṭ (6), *belt*
232 'êzôwr (13), *belt; band around waist*

GIRDLES
73 'abnêṭ (3), *belt*
232 'êzôwr (1), *belt; band around waist*
2289 chăgôwr (1), *belted around waist*
2223 zōnē (1), *belt, sash*

GIRGASHITE
1622 Girgâshîy (1), *Girgashite*

GIRGASHITES
1622 Girgâshîy (5), *Girgashite*

GIRGASITE
1622 Girgâshîy (1), *Girgashite*

GIRL
3207 yaldâh (1), *young female*

GIRLS
3207 yaldâh (1), *young female*

GIRT
247 'âzar (1), to *belt*
1241 diazōnnumi (1), to *gird tightly, wrap*
4024 pĕrizōnnumi (2), to *fasten on one's belt*

GISPA
1658 Gishpâ' (1), *Gishpa*

GITTAH-HEPHER
1662 Gath-ha-Chêpher (1), *wine-press of* (the) *well*

GITTAIM
1664 Gittayim (2), *double wine-press*

GITTITE
1663 Gittîy (8), *Gittite*

GITTITES
1663 Gittîy (2), *Gittite*

GITTITH
1665 Gittîyth (3), *harp*

GIVE
1262 bârâh (1), to *feed*
1478 gâva' (3), to *expire, die*
1696 dâbar (1), to *speak, say; to subdue*
1961+413 hâyâh (1), to *exist,* i.e. *be or become*
3051 yâhab (24), to *give*
3052 y^ehab (Ch.) (2), to *give*
3190 yâṭab (1), to *be, make well*
4900 mâshak (1), to *draw out; to be tall*
4991 mattâth (2), *present*
5066 nâgash (1), to *be, come, bring near*
5414 nâthan (482), to *give*
5415 n^ethan (Ch.) (2), to *give*
5441 çôbek (1), *copse or thicket*

GIVEN
1167 ba'al (2), *master; husband; owner; citizen*
1478 gâva' (1), to *expire, die*
1576 g^emûwl (1), *act; reward, recompense*
2505 châlaq (1), to *be smooth; be slippery*
2603 chânan (1), to *implore*
3052 y^ehab (Ch.) (16), to *give*
3254 yâçaph (1), to *add or augment*
3289 yâ'ats (2), to *advise*
5221 nâkâh (3), to *strike, kill*
5301 nâphach (1), to *inflate, blow, scatter*
5375 nâsâ' (1), to *lift up*
5414 nâthan (253), to *give*
5462 çâgar (1), to *shut up; to surrender*
6213 'âsâh (1), to *do or make*
7760 sûwm (1), to *put, place*
7761 sûwm (Ch.) (1), to *put, place*

GIVEN
5534 çâkar (1), to *shut up; to surrender*
6213 'âsâh (1), to *do or make*
7311 rûwm (1), to *be high; to rise or raise*
7725 shûwb (3), to *turn back; to return or restore*
7760 sûwm (5), to *put, place*
7761 sûwm (Ch.) (1), to *put, place*
7999 shâlam (1), to *be safe; be, make complete*
402 anachōrĕō (1), to *retire, withdraw*
591 apŏdidōmi (8), to *give away*
1096 ginŏmai (1), to *be, become*
1239 diadidōmi (1), to *divide up, distribute*
1325 didōmi (139), to *give*
1929 ĕpididōmi (5), to *give over*
2014 ĕpiphainō (1), to *become known*
2468 isthi (1), *be thou*
3330 mĕtadidōmi (1), to *share, distribute*
3844 para (1), *from; with; besides; on account of*
3860 paradidōmi (1), to *hand over*
3930 parĕchō (1), to *hold near,* i.e. *to present*
3936 paristēmi (1), to *stand beside, present*
4222 pŏtizō (3), to *furnish drink, irrigate*
4342 prŏskartĕrĕō (1), to *attend; to adhere*
4980 schŏlazō (1), to *devote oneself* wholly to
5461 phōtizō (1), to *shine or to brighten up*
5483 charizŏmai (1), to *grant as a favor*

GIVER
1167 ba'al (2), *master; husband; owner; citizen*
1478 gâva' (1), to *expire, die*
1576 g^emûwl (1), *act; reward, recompense*
2505 châlaq (1), to *be smooth; be slippery*
2603 chânan (1), to *implore*
3052 y^ehab (Ch.) (16), to *give*
3254 yâçaph (1), to *add or augment*
3289 yâ'ats (2), to *advise*
5221 nâkâh (3), to *strike, kill*
5301 nâphach (1), to *inflate, blow, scatter*
5375 nâsâ' (1), to *lift up*
5414 nâthan (253), to *give*
5462 çâgar (1), to *shut up; to surrender*
6213 'âsâh (1), to *do or make*
7760 sûwm (1), to *put, place*
7761 sûwm (Ch.) (1), to *put, place*

GIVE
1325 didōmi (123), to *give*
1377 diōkō (1), to *pursue; to persecute*
1402 dŏulŏō (1), to *enslave*
1433 dōrĕŏmai (2), to *bestow gratuitously*
1547 ĕkgamizō (1), to *marry off* a daughter
2227 zōŏpŏiĕō (1), to (re-) *vitalize, give life*
3860 paradidōmi (2), to *hand over*
3930 parĕchō (1), to *present, afford, exhibit*
3943 parŏinŏs (2), *tippling*
4272 prŏdidōmi (1), to *give before*
4337 prŏsĕchō (1), to *pay attention to*
4369 prŏstithēmi (1), to *lay beside, repeat*
5483 charizŏmai (5), to *grant as a favor*

GIVER
1395 dŏtēs (1), *giver*

GIVEST
5414 nâthan (7), to *give*
7971 shâlach (1), to *send away*

GIVETH
1478 gâva' (1), to *expire, die*
3052 y^ehab (Ch.) (1), to *give*
5414 nâthan (77), to *give*
5415 n^ethan (Ch.) (3), to *give*
1325 didōmi (13), to *give*
3330 mĕtadidōmi (1), to *share, distribute*
3930 parĕchō (1), to *present, afford, exhibit*
5087 tithēmi (1), to *place*
5524 chŏrēgĕō (1), to *furnish, supply, provide*

GIVING
4646 mappâch (1), *expiring, dying*
5414 nâthan (5), to *give*
632 apŏnĕmō (1), *bestow, treat with respect*
1325 didōmi (3), to *give*
1394 dŏsis (1), *gift*
3004 lĕgō (1), to *say*
3548 nŏmŏthĕsia (1), *legislation, law*
3923 parĕisphĕrō (1), to *bear in alongside*

GIZONITE
1493 Gizôwnîy (1), *Gizonite*

GLAD
1523 gîyl (6), *rejoice*
1528 gîyr (Ch.) (4), *lime for plaster*
2302 châdâh (1), to *rejoice, be glad*
2868 ṭ^eêb (Ch.) (1), to *rejoice, be pleased*
2896 ṭôwb (2), *good; well*
7796 Sôwrêq (2), *vine*
7797 sûws (1), to *be bright; to be cheerful*
7996 Shalleketh (1), *felling* of trees

8056 sâmêach (49), blithe or gleeful
8190 Sha'ashgaz (1), Shaashgaz
21 agalliaō (2), to exult
2097 ĕuaggĕlizō (4), to announce good news
2165 ĕuphrainō (1), to rejoice, be glad
5463 chairō (14), to be cheerful

GLADLY
780 asmĕnōs (2), with pleasure, gladly
2234 hĕdĕōs (3), with pleasure, with delight
2236 hĕdista (2), with great pleasure

GLADNESS
1524 gîyl (1), age, stage in life
2304 chedvâh (1), rejoicing, joy
2898 ţûwb (1), good; goodness; gladness
7440 rinnâh (1), shout
8057 simchâh (34), blithesomeness or glee
8342 sâsôwn (2), cheerfulness; welcome
20 agalliasis (3), exultation, delight
2167 ĕuphrŏsunē (1), joyfulness, cheerfulness
5479 chara (3), calm delight, joy

GLASS
7209 rᵉ'îy (1), mirror
2072 ĕsŏptrŏn (2), mirror for looking into
2734 katŏptrizŏmai (1), to see reflected
5193 hualinŏs (3), pertaining to glass
5194 hualŏs (2), glass, crystal

GLASSES
1549 gillâyôwn (1), tablet for writing; mirror

GLEAN
3950 lâqaţ (7), to pick up, gather; to glean
5953 'âlal (3), to glean; to overdo

GLEANED
3950 lâqaţ (5), to pick up, gather; to glean
5953 'âlal (1), to glean; to overdo

GLEANING
3951 leqeţ (1), gleaning after a harvest
5955 'ôlêlâh (4), gleaning; gleaning-time

GLEANINGS
3951 leqeţ (1), gleaning

GLEDE
7201 râ'âh (1), bird of prey (poss. vulture)

GLISTERING
6320 pûwk (1), stibium
1823 ĕxastraptō (1), to be radiant

GLITTER
1300 bârâq (1), lightning; flash of lightning

GLITTERING
1300 bârâq (5), lightning; flash of lightning
3851 lahab (1), flame of fire; flash of a blade

GLOOMINESS
653 'ăphêlâh (2), duskiness, darkness

GLORIEST
1984 hâlal (1), to shine, flash, radiate

GLORIETH
1984 hâlal (1), to shine, flash, radiate
2744 kauchaŏmai (2), to glory in, rejoice in

GLORIFIED
1922 hădar (Ch.) (1), to magnify, glorify
3513 kâbad (6), to be heavy, severe, dull; to be rich, glorious
6286 pâ'ar (6), to shake a tree
1392 dŏxazō (34), to render, esteem glorious
1740 ĕndŏxazō (2), to glorify
4888 sundŏxazō (1), to share glory with

GLORIFIETH
3513 kâbad (1), to be rich, glorious

GLORIFY
3513 kâbad (7), to be rich, glorious
6286 pâ'ar (1), to shake a tree
1392 dŏxazō (17), to render, esteem glorious

GLORIFYING
1392 dŏxazō (3), to render, esteem glorious

GLORIOUS
117 'addîyr (1), powerful; majestic
142 'âdar (2), magnificent; glorious
215 'ôwr (1), to be luminous
1921 hâdar (1), to favor or honor; to be high or proud
1926 hâdâr (1), magnificence
1935 hôwd (1), grandeur, majesty
3513 kâbad (5), to be rich, glorious
3519 kâbôwd (11), splendor, wealth
3520 kᵉbûwddâh (1), magnificence, wealth
6643 tsᵉbîy (5), conspicuous splendor
8597 tiph'ârâh (3), ornament
1223+1391 dia (1), through, by means of
1391 dŏxa (6), glory; brilliance
1392 dŏxazō (1), to render, esteem glorious

1722+1391 ĕn (3), in; during; because of
1741 ĕndŏxŏs (2), splendid; noble

GLORIOUSLY
3519 kâbôwd (1), splendor, copiousness

GLORY
155 'adderETH (1), large; splendid
1925 heder (1), honor
1926 hâdâr (7), magnificence
1935 hôwd (9), grandeur, majesty
1984 hâlal (12), to shine, flash, radiate
2892 ţôhar (1), brightness; purification
3367 yᵉqâr (Ch.) (5), glory, honor
3513 kâbad (1), to be rich, glorious
3519 kâbôwd (155), splendor, wealth
6286 pâ'ar (1), to shake a tree
6643 tsᵉbîy (7), conspicuous splendor
7623 shâbach (1), to address; to pacify
8597 tiph'ârâh (22), ornament
1391 dŏxa (146), glory; brilliance
1392 dŏxazō (3), to render, esteem glorious
2620 katakauchaŏmai (1), to exult against
2744 kauchaŏmai (18), to glory in, rejoice in
2745 kauchēma (3), boast; brag
2746 kauchēsis (1), boasting; bragging
2755 kĕnŏdŏxŏs (1), self-conceited
2811 klĕŏs (1), renown, credited honor

GLORYING
2744 kauchaŏmai (1), to glory in, rejoice in
2745 kauchēma (2), boast; brag
2746 kauchēsis (1), boasting; bragging

GLUTTON
2151 zâlal (2), to be loose morally, worthless

GLUTTONOUS
5314 phagŏs (2), glutton

GNASH
2786 châraq (2), to grate, grind the teeth

GNASHED
2786 châraq (1), to grate, grind the teeth
1031 bruchō (1), to grate, grind teeth

GNASHETH
2786 châraq (2), to grate, grind the teeth
5149 trizō (1), to grate the teeth in frenzy

GNASHING
1030 brugmŏs (7), grinding of teeth

GNAT
2971 kōnōps (1), stinging mosquito

GNAW
1633 gâram (1), to crunch the bones

GNAWED
3145 massaŏmai (1), to chew, gnaw

GO
236 'ăzal (Ch.) (1), to depart
258 'âchad (1), to unify, i.e. collect
833 'âshar (2), to go forward; guide
935 bôw' (154), to go, come
1718 dâdâh (1), to walk gently; lead
1869 dârak (2), to tread, trample; to walk, lead
1946 hûwk (Ch.) (1), to go, come
1961 hâyâh (2), to exist, i.e. be or become
1980 hâlak (83), to walk; live a certain way
1982 hêlek (1), wayfarer, visitor; flowing
2498 châlaph (1), to hasten away; to pass on
2559 châmaq (1), to depart, i.e. turn about
3051 yâhab (4), to give
3212 yâlak (351), to walk; to live; to carry
3312 Yᵉphunneh (1), he will be prepared
3318 yâtsâ' (185), to go, bring out
3381 yârad (73), to descend
3518 kâbâh (1), to extinguish
4161 môwtsâ' (1), going forth
4609 ma'ălâh (1), thought arising
4994 nâ' (2), I pray!, please!, I beg you!
5066 nâgash (2), to be, come, bring near
5181 nâchath (1), to sink, descend; to press down
5186 nâţâh (1), to stretch or spread out
5265 nâça' (7), start on a journey
5362 nâqaph (2), to strike; to surround
5437 çâbab (7), to surround
5472 çûwg (1), to go back, to retreat
5493 çûwr (4), to turn off
5503 çâchar (1), to travel round; to palpitate
5674 'âbar (51), to cross over; to transition
5927 'âlâh (129), to ascend, be high, mount
5930 'ôlâh (1), sacrifice wholly consumed in fire
6213 'âsâh (1), to do

6310 peh (1), *mouth; opening*
6485 pâqad (1), *to visit, care for, count*
6544 pâra' (1), *to absolve, begin*
6585 pâsa' (1), *to stride*
6805 tsâ'ad (1), *to pace, step regularly*
6806 tsa'ad (1), *pace or regular step*
6923 qâdam (1), *to hasten, meet*
7126 qârab (3), *to approach, bring near*
7368 râchaq (3), *to recede; remove*
7503 râphâh (4), *to slacken*
7686 shâgâh (2), *to stray, wander; to transgress*
7725 shûwb (15), *to turn back; to return*
7751 shûwṭ (1), *to travel, roam*
7847 sâṭâh (1), *to deviate from duty, go astray*
7971 shâlach (76), *to send away*
8582 tâ'âh (4), *to vacillate, reel or stray*
8637 tirgal (1), *to cause to walk*
33 agĕ (2), *to come on*
71 agō (6), *to lead; to bring, drive; to weigh*
305 anabainō (9), *to go up, rise*
565 apĕrchŏmai (25), *to go off, i.e. depart, withdraw*
630 apŏluō (13), *to relieve, release*
863 aphiĕmi (1), *to leave; to pardon, forgive*
1330 diĕrchŏmai (4), *to traverse, travel through*
1524 ĕisĕimi (1), *to enter*
1525 ĕisĕrchŏmai (11), *to enter*
1607 ĕkpŏrĕuŏmai (1), *depart, proceed, project*
1830 ĕxĕrĕunaō (1), *to explore*
1831 ĕxĕrchŏmai (14), *to issue; to leave*
1881 ĕpanistamai (2), *to stand up on, to attack*
1931 ĕpiduō (1), *to set*
1994 ĕpistrĕphō (1), *to revert, turn back to*
2064 ĕrchŏmai (2), *to go or come*
2212 zētĕō (1), *to seek*
2597 katabainō (2), *to descend*
3327 mĕtabainō (1), *to depart, move from*
3928 parĕrchŏmai (1), *to go by; to perish*
4043 pĕripatĕō (1), *to walk; to live a life*
4198 pŏrĕuŏmai (74), *to go, come; to travel*
4254 prŏagō (5), *to lead forward; to precede*
4281 prŏĕrchŏmai (2), *to go onward, precede*

4313 prŏpŏrĕuŏmai (2), *to precede*
4320 prŏsanabainō (1), *to be promoted*
4334 prŏsĕrchŏmai (1), *to come near, visit*
4782 sugkatabainō (1), *to descend with*
4905 sunĕrchŏmai (1), *to go with*
5217 hupagō (54), *to withdraw or retire*
5233 hupĕrbainō (1), *to transcend, to overreach*
5342 phĕrō (1), *to bear or carry*

GOAD
4451 malmâd (1), *ox-goad*

GOADS
1861 dorbôwn (2), *iron goad stick*

GOAT
689 'aqqôw (1), *ibex*
5795 'êz (9), *she-goat; goat's hair*
6842 tsâphîyr (3), *male goat*
8163 sâ'îyr (21), *shaggy; he-goat; goat idol*
8495 tayish (1), *buck or he-goat*

GOATH
1601 Gô'âh (1), *lowing, bellowing*

GOATS
3277 yâ'êl (3), *ibex animal*
5795 'êz (45), *she-goat; goat's hair*
6260 'attûwd (26), *he-goats; leaders*
6842 tsâphîyr (1), *he-goat*
8163 sâ'îyr (1), *shaggy; he-goat; goat idol*
8495 tayish (3), *he-goat*
2055 ĕriphiŏn (1), *goat*
2056 ĕriphŏs (1), *kid or goat*
5131 tragŏs (4), *he-goat*

GOATS'
5795 'êz (10), *she-goat; goat's hair*

GOATSKINS
122+1192 aigĕiŏs (1), *belonging to a goat*

GOB
1359 Gôb (2), *pit*

GOBLET
101 'aggân (1), *bowl*

GOD
136 'Ădônây (1), *the Lord*
401 'Ûkâl (1), *devoured*
410 'êl (217), *mighty; the Almighty*
426 'ĕlâhh (Ch.) (79), *God*
430 'ĕlôhîym (2340), *God; gods; great ones*
433 'ĕlôwahh (55), *the true God; god*
1008 Bêyth-'Êl (5), *house of God*
3068 Yᵉhôvâh (4), *Jehovah, the self-Existent or Eternal*

3069 Yᵉhôvîh (301), *Jehovah, (the) self-Existent or Eternal*
3609 Kil'âb (1), *restraint of (his) father*
4010 mablîygîyth (1), *desolation*
6697 tsûwr (2), *rock*
112 athĕŏs (1), *godless*
2312 thĕŏdidaktŏs (1), *divinely instructed*
2313 thĕŏmachĕō (1), *to resist deity*
2314 thĕŏmachŏs (1), *opponent of deity*
2315 thĕŏpnĕustŏs (1), *divinely breathed in*
2316 thĕŏs (1292), *deity; the Supreme Deity*
2318 thĕŏsĕbēs (1), *pious, devout, God-fearing*
2319 thĕŏstugēs (1), *impious, God-hating*
2962 kuriŏs (1), *supreme, controller, Mr.*
3361+1096 mē (15), *not; lest*
5377 philŏthĕŏs (1), *pious, i.e. loving God*
5537 chrēmatizō (1), *to utter an oracle*

GOD'S
410 'êl (2), *mighty; the Almighty*
430 'ĕlôhîym (7), *the true God; gods; great ones*
433 'ĕlôwahh (1), *the true God; god*
2316 thĕŏs (15), *deity; the Supreme Deity*

GOD-WARD
4136+430 mûwl (1), *in front of, opposite*
4314+2316 prŏs (2), *for; on, at; to, toward*

GODDESS
430 'ĕlôhîym (2), *god; gods; great ones*
2299 thĕa (3), *female deity, goddess*

GODHEAD
2304 thĕiŏs (1), *divinity*
2305 thĕiŏtēs (1), *divinity*
2320 thĕŏtēs (1), *divinity*

GODLINESS
2150 ĕusĕbĕia (14), *piety, religious*
2317 thĕŏsĕbĕia (1), *piety, worship of deity*

GODLY
430 'ĕlôhîym (1), *the true God; gods; great ones*
2623 châçiyd (3), *religiously pious, godly*
516+2316 axiŏs (1), *appropriately, suitable*
2152 ĕusĕbēs (1), *pious*
2153 ĕusĕbōs (2), *piously*
2316 thĕŏs (3), *deity; the Supreme Deity*
2596+2316 kata (3), *down; according to*

GODS
410 'êl (2), *mighty; the Almighty*
426 'ĕlâhh (Ch.) (14), *God*

430 'ĕlôhîym (214), *God; gods; judges, great ones*
1140 daimŏniŏn (1), *demonic being; god*
2316 thĕŏs (8), *deity; the Supreme Deity*

GOEST
935 bôw' (13), *to go or come*
1980 hâlak (5), *to walk; live a certain way*
3212 yâlak (13), *to walk; to live; to carry*
3318 yâtsâ' (7), *to go, bring out*
5927 'âlâh (1), *to ascend, be high, mount*
565 apĕrchŏmai (1), *to go off, i.e. depart*
5217 hupagō (5), *to withdraw or retire*

GOETH
732 'ârach (1), *to travel, wander*
925 bâhîyr (1), *shining, bright*
935 bôw' (14), *to go or come*
1869 dârak (1), *to tread, trample; to walk, lead*
1980 hâlak (19), *to walk; live a certain way*
3212 yâlak (2), *to walk; to live; to carry*
3318 yâtsâ' (31), *to go, bring out*
3381 yârad (5), *to descend*
3518 kâbâh (2), *to extinguish*
3996 mâbôw' (1), *entrance; sunset; west*
4609 ma'ălâh (1), *thought arising*
5186 nâṭâh (1), *to stretch or spread out*
5493 çûwr (1), *to turn off*
5648 'ăbad (Ch.) (1), *to do, work, serve*
5674 'âbar (6), *to cross over; to transition*
5927 'âlâh (10), *to ascend, be high, mount*
6437 pânâh (1), *to turn, to face*
7126 qârab (1), *to approach, bring near*
7847 sâṭâh (1), *to deviate from duty, go astray*
305 anabainō (1), *to go up, rise*
565 apĕrchŏmai (1), *to go off, i.e. depart*
1525 ĕisĕrchŏmai (1), *to enter*
1607 ĕkpŏrĕuŏmai (3), *to depart, be discharged*
2212 zētĕō (1), *to seek*
3597 hŏdŏipŏria (1), *traveling*
4198 pŏrĕuŏmai (7), *to go/come; to travel*
4254 prŏagō (2), *to lead forward; to precede*
4334 prŏsĕrchŏmai (1), *to come near, visit*
5217 hupagō (9), *to withdraw or retire*

5562 chôrĕŏ (1), to pass, enter; to hold, admit

GOG
1463 Gôwg (10), Gog
1136 Gŏg (1), Gog

GOING
235 'âzal (1), to disappear
838 'âshshûwr (1), step; track
935 bôw' (7), to go or come
1980 hâlak (8), to walk; live a certain way
3212 yâlak (5), to walk; to live; to carry
3318 yâtsâ' (13), to go, bring out
3381 yârad (3), to descend
3996 mâbôw' (5), entrance; sunset; west
4161 môwtsâ' (5), going forth
4174 môwrâd (3), descent, slope
4606 mê'al (Ch.) (1), setting of the sun
4608 ma'ăleh (9), elevation; platform
5362 nâqaph (1), to strike; to surround
5674 'âbar (2), to cross over; to transition
5927 'âlâh (4), to ascend, be high, mount
5944 'ălîyâh (2), upper things; second-story
6807 tse'âdâh (2), stepping march
7751 shûwṭ (2), to travel, roam
8444 tôwtsâ'âh (1), exit, boundary; deliverance
8582 tâ'âh (1), to vacillate, reel or stray
71 agō (1), to lead; to bring, drive; to weigh
305 anabainō (2), to go up, rise
565 apérchŏmai (1), to go off, i.e. depart
1330 diérchŏmai (1), to traverse, travel through
1607 ĕkpŏrĕuŏmai (1), to depart, be discharged
2212 zētĕō (1), to seek
2597 katabainō (1), to descend
4105 planaō (1), to roam, wander; to deceive
4108 planŏs (1), roving, impostor or misleader
4198 pŏrĕuŏmai (1), to go/come; to travel
4254 prŏagō (2), to lead forward; to precede
4260 prŏbainō (1), to advance
4281 prŏĕrchŏmai (1), to go onward, precede
5217 hupagō (1), to withdraw or retire

GOINGS
838 'âshshûwr (2), step; track
1979 hălîykâh (2), walking; procession

4161 môwtsâ' (4), going forth
4163 môwtsâ'âh (1), family descent
4570 ma'gâl (2), circular track or camp rampart
4703 mits'âd (1), step; companionship
6471 pa'am (1), time; step; occurence
6806 tsa'ad (1), pace or regular step
8444 tôwtsâ'âh (12), exit, boundary; deliverance

GOLAN
1474 Gôwlân (4), captive

GOLD
1220 betser (2), gold
1222 bᵉtsar (1), gold
1722 dᵉhab (Ch.) (14), gold
2091 zâhâb (340), gold, golden colored
2742 chârûwts (6), mined gold; trench
3800 kethem (7), pure gold
5458 çᵉgôwr (1), breast; gold
6337 pâz (9), pure gold
5552 chrusĕŏs (3), made of gold
5553 chrusiŏn (9), golden thing
5554 chrusŏdaktuliŏs (1), gold-ringed
5557 chrusŏs (13), gold; golden article

GOLDEN
1722 dᵉhab (Ch.) (9), gold
2091 zâhâb (38), gold, golden colored
3800 kethem (1), pure gold
4062 madhêbâh (1), gold making
5552 chrusĕŏs (15), made of gold

GOLDSMITH
6884 tsâraph (3), to fuse metal; to refine

GOLDSMITH'S
6885 Tsôrᵉphîy (1), refiner

GOLDSMITHS
6884 tsâraph (2), to fuse metal; to refine

GOLGOTHA
1115 Golgŏtha (3), skull knoll

GOLIATH
1555 Golyath (6), exile

GOMER
1586 Gômer (6), completion

GOMORRAH
6017 'Ämôrâh (19), (ruined) heap
1116 Gŏmŏrrha (1), ruined heap

GOMORRHA
1116 Gŏmŏrrha (4), ruined heap

GONE
230 'âzad (Ch.) (2), firm, assured

235 'âzal (2), to disappear
369 'ayin (4), there is no, i.e., not exist, none
656 'âphêç (1), to cease
935 bôw' (10), to go or come
1540 gâlâh (1), to denude; uncover
1961 hâyâh (1), to exist, i.e. be or become
1980 hâlak (22), to walk; live a certain way
2114 zûwr (1), to be foreign, strange
3212 yâlak (17), to walk; to live; to carry
3318 yâtsâ' (31), to go, bring out
3381 yârad (14), to descend
4059 middad (1), flight
4161 môwtsâ' (2), going forth
4185 mûwsh (1), to withdraw
5128 nûwa' (1), to waver
5186 nâṭâh (1), to stretch or spread out
5312 nᵉphaq (Ch.) (1), to issue forth; to bring out
5362 nâqaph (2), to surround or circulate
5437 çâbab (1), to surround
5472 çûwg (1), to go back, to retreat
5493 çûwr (2), to turn off
5674 'âbar (16), to cross over; to transition
5927 'âlâh (22), to ascend, be high, mount
6805 tsâ'ad (1), to pace, step regularly
7725 shûwb (2), to turn back; to return
7751 shûwṭ (1), to travel, roam
7847 sâṭâh (2), to deviate from duty, go astray
8582 tâ'âh (2), to vacillate, reel or stray
305 anabainō (2), to go up, rise
402 anachŏrĕō (1), to retire, withdraw
565 apérchŏmai (4), to go off, i.e. depart
576 apŏbainō (1), to disembark
1276 diapĕraō (1), to cross over
1330 diérchŏmai (4), to traverse, travel through
1339 diïstēmi (1), to remove, intervene
1525 ĕisérchŏmai (1), to enter
1578 ĕkklinō (1), to shun; to decline
1607 ĕkpŏrĕuŏmai (1), to depart, proceed, project
1826 ĕxĕimi (1), leave; escape
1831 ĕxérchŏmai (11), to issue; to leave
3985 pĕirazō (1), to endeavor, scrutinize
4105 planaō (2), to roam, wander

4198 pŏrĕuŏmai (3), to go, come; to travel
4260 prŏbainō (1), to advance
4570 sbĕnnumi (1), to extinguish, snuff out
5055 tĕlĕō (1), to end, i.e. complete, execute

GOOD
1319 bâsar (7), to announce (good news)
1390 Gib'âh (1), hillock
1580 gâmal (1), to benefit or requite; to wean
2492 châlam (1), to be, make plump; to dream
2617 cheçed (1), kindness, favor
2623 châçîyd (1), religiously pious, godly
2869 ṭâb (Ch.) (1), good
2895 ṭowb (6), to be good
2896 ṭôwb (363), good; well
2898 ṭûwb (11), good; goodness; beauty, gladness, welfare
3190 yâṭab (20), to be, make well
3191 yᵉṭab (Ch.) (1), to be, make well
3276 yâ'al (1), to be valuable
3474 yâshar (1), to be straight; to make right
3788 kishrôwn (1), success; advantage
3966 mᵉ'ôd (3), very, utterly
5750 'ôwd (1), again; repeatedly; still; more
6743 tsâlach (1), to push forward
7368 râchaq (2), to recede; remove
7522 râtsôwn (2), delight
7965 shâlôwm (1), safe; well; health, prosperity
7999 shâlam (6), to be safe; be, make complete
8232 shᵉphar (Ch.) (1), to be beautiful
14 agathŏĕrgĕō (1), to do good work
15 agathŏpŏiĕō (6), to be a well-doer
18 agathŏs (98), good
515 axiŏō (1), to deem entitled or fit, worthy
865 aphilagathŏs (1), hostile to virtue
979 biŏs (1), livelihood; property
2095 ĕu (1), well
2097 ĕuaggĕlizō (2), to announce good news
2106 ĕudŏkĕō (1), to think well, i.e. approve
2107 ĕudŏkia (3), delight, kindness, wish
2108 ĕuĕrgĕsia (1), beneficence
2109 ĕuĕrgĕtĕō (1), to be philanthropic
2133 ĕunŏia (1), eagerly, with a whole heart
2140 ĕupŏïïa (1), beneficence, doing good

2162 ĕuphēmia (1), good
repute
2163 ĕuphēmŏs (1),
reputable
2425 hikanŏs (1), ample;
fit
2480 ischuō (1), to have
or exercise force
2565 kalliĕlaiŏs (1),
cultivated olive
2567 kalŏdidaskalŏs (1),
teacher of the right
2570 kalŏs (78), good;
beautiful; valuable
2573 kalŏs (3), well, i.e.
rightly
2750 kĕiria (2), swathe of
cloth
3112 makran (1), at a
distance, far away
4851 sumphĕrō (1), to
collect; to conduce
5358 philagathŏs (1),
promoter of virtue
5542 chrēstŏlŏgia (1),
fair speech, plausibility
5543 chrēstŏs (1),
employed, i.e. useful
5544 chrēstŏtēs (1),
moral excellence

GOODLIER
2896 ṭôwb (1), good; well

GOODLIEST
2896 ṭôwb (2), good; well

GOODLINESS
2617 cheçed (1),
kindness, favor

GOODLY
117 'addîyr (1), powerful;
majestic
145 'eder (1), mantle;
splendor
155 'addereth (1), large;
splendid
410 'êl (1), mighty; the
Almighty
1926 hâdâr (1),
magnificence
1935 hôwd (1), grandeur,
majesty
2530 châmad (1), to
delight in; lust for
2532 chemdâh (1),
delight
2896 ṭôwb (11), good; well
4261 machmâd (1),
delightful
4758 mar'eh (1),
appearance; vision
6287 pe'êr (1), fancy
head-dress
6643 tsebîy (1),
conspicuous splendor
7443 renen (1), female
ostrich
8231 shâphar (1), to be,
make fair
8233 shepher (1), beauty
2573 kalŏs (2), well, i.e.
rightly
2986 lamprŏs (2),
radiant; magnificent

GOODMAN
376 'îysh (1), man; male;
someone
3611 ŏikĕŏ (5), to reside,
inhabit, remain

GOODNESS
2617 cheçed (12),
kindness, favor
2896 ṭôwb (16), good; well
2898 ṭûwb (13), good;
goodness; beauty
19 agathōsunē (4), virtue
or beneficence
5543 chrēstŏs (1),
employed, i.e. useful
5544 chrēstŏtēs (4),
moral excellence

GOODNESS'
2898 ṭûwb (1), good;
goodness; beauty

GOODS
202 'ôwn (1), ability,
power; wealth
2428 chayil (2), army;
wealth; virtue; valor
2896 ṭôwb (2), good; well
2898 ṭûwb (3), good;
goodness; beauty
4399 melâ'kâh (2), work;
property
5232 nekaç (Ch.) (2),
treasure, riches
7075 qinyân (2),
purchase, wealth
7399 rekûwsh (12),
property
18 agathŏs (2), good
3776 ŏusia (1), wealth,
property, possessions
4147 plŏutĕŏ (1), to be,
become wealthy
4632 skĕuŏs (2), vessel,
implement, equipment
4674 sŏs (1), things that
are yours
5223 huparxis (1),
property, wealth
5224 huparchŏnta (7),
property or possessions

GOPHER
1613 gôpher (1), (poss.)
cypress

GORE
5055 nâgach (1), to butt
with bull's horns

GORED
5055 nâgach (2), to butt
with bull's horns

GORGEOUS
2986 lamprŏs (1),
radiant; magnificent

GORGEOUSLY
4358 miklôwl (1),
perfection; splendidly
1741 ĕndŏxŏs (1),
splendid; noble

GOSHEN
1657 Gôshen (15),
Goshen

GOSPEL
2097 ĕuaggĕlizō (24), to
announce good news
2098 ĕuaggĕliŏn (73),
good message
4283 prŏĕuaggĕlizŏmai
(1), to announce glad
news in advance

GOSPEL'S
2098 ĕuaggĕliŏn (3),
good message

GOT
3318 yâtsâ' (2), to go,
bring out
3423 yârash (1), to
inherit; to impoverish
7069 qânâh (3), to create;
to procure
7408 râkash (1), to lay
up, i.e. collect

GOTTEN
622 'âçaph (1), to gather,
collect
3254 yâçaph (1), to add
or augment
4069 maddûwa' (1),
why?, what?
4672 mâtsâ' (2), to find
or acquire; to occur
5414 nâthan (1), to give
6213 'âsâh (8), to do or
make
7069 qânâh (1), to create;
to procure
7408 râkash (3), to lay
up, i.e. collect
645 apŏspaŏ (1),
unsheathe; withdraw

GOURD
7021 qîyqâyôwn (5),
gourd plant

GOURDS
6498 paqqû'âh (1), wild
cucumber

GOVERN
2280 châbash (1), to
wrap firmly, bind
5148 nâchâh (1), to guide
6213 'âsâh (1), to do

GOVERNMENT
4475 memshâlâh (1),
rule; realm or a ruler
4951 misrâh (2), empire
2963 kuriŏtēs (1), rulers,
masters

GOVERNMENTS
2941 kubĕrnēsis (1),
directorship

GOVERNOR
441 'allûwph (1), friend,
one familiar; chieftain
4910 mâshal (3), to rule
5057 nâgîyd (3),
commander, official
5387 nâsîy' (1), leader;
rising mist, fog
5921 'al (1), above, over,
upon, or against
6346 pechâh (10),
prefect, officer
6347 pechâh (Ch.) (6),
prefect, officer
6485 pâqad (5), to visit,
care for, count
7989 shallîyṭ (1), prince
or warrior
8269 sar (4), head
person, ruler
755 architriklinŏs (2),
director of the
entertainment
1481 ĕthnarchēs (1),
governor of a district
2116 ĕuthunŏ (1), to
straighten or level
2230 hēgĕmŏnĕuŏ (3), to
act as ruler

GOVERNOR'S
2232 hēgĕmōn (1), chief
person

GOVERNORS
441 'allûwph (2), friend,
one familiar; chieftain
2710 châqaq (2), to
engrave; to enact laws
4910 mâshal (1), to rule
5461 çâgân (5), prfect of
a province
6346 pechâh (7), prefect,
officer
8269 sar (2), head
person, ruler
2232 hēgĕmōn (2), chief
person
3623 ŏikŏnŏmŏs (1),
overseer, manager

GOZAN
1470 Gôwzân (5), quarry

GRACE
2580 chên (37),
graciousness; beauty
8467 techinnâh (1),
gracious entreaty,
supplication
2143 ĕuprĕpĕia (1),
gracefulness
5485 charis (127),
gratitude; benefit given

GRACIOUS
2580 chên (2),
graciousness; beauty
2587 channûwn (14),
gracious
2589 channôwth (1),
supplication
2603 chânan (11), to
implore
5485 charis (1),
gratitude; benefit given
5543 chrēstŏs (1),
employed, i.e. useful

GRACIOUSLY
2603 chânan (3), to
implore
2896 ṭôwb (1), good; well

GRAFF
1461 ĕgkĕntrizō (1), to
engraft

GRAFFED
1461 ĕgkĕntrizō (5), to
engraft

GRAIN
6872 tserôwr (1), parcel;
kernel or particle
2848 kŏkkŏs (6), kernel

GRANDMOTHER
3125 mammē (1),
grandmother

GRANT
5414 nâthan (12), to give
7558 rîshyôwn (1), permit
1325 didŏmi (7), to give
2036 ĕpō (1), to speak or
say

GRANTED
935 bôw' (1), to go or
come
5414 nâthan (9), to give

GOODLIER

6213 'âsâh (1), to *do* or
make
1325 didômi (3), to *give*
5483 charizŏmai (1), to
grant as a *favor*

GRAPE
1154 beçer (1),
immature, sour grapes
1155 bôçer (3),
immature, sour grapes
5563 çᵉmâdar (2), vine
blossom
6025 'ênâb (1), *grape*
cluster
6528 peret (1), *stray* or
single berry

GRAPEGATHERER
1219 bâtsar (1), to *gather*
grapes

GRAPEGATHERERS
1219 bâtsar (2), to *gather*
grapes

GRAPEGLEANINGS
5955 'ôlêlâh (1),
gleaning; gleaning-time

GRAPES
891 bᵉ'ûshîym (2), *rotten
fruit*
1154 beçer (1),
immature, sour grapes
5563 çᵉmâdar (1), vine
blossom
6025 'ênâb (15), *grape*
cluster
4718 staphulē (3), *cluster*
of grapes

GRASS
1758 dûwsh (1), to
trample or *thresh*
1877 deshe' (7), *sprout;*
green *grass*
1883 dethe' (Ch.) (2),
sprout; green *grass*
2682 châtsîyr (17), *grass;*
leek plant
3418 yereq (1), *green*
grass or vegetation
6211 'âsh (5), *moth*
6212 'eseb (16), *grass,* or
any green, tender shoot
5528 chŏrtŏs (12),
pasture, herbage

GRASSHOPPER
697 'arbeh (1), *locust*
2284 châgâb (2), *locust*

GRASSHOPPERS
697 'arbeh (3), *locust*
1462 gôwb (2), *locust*
2284 châgâb (2), *locust*

GRATE
4345 makbêr (6), *grate,
lattice*

GRAVE
1164 bᵉ'îy (1), *prayer*
6603 pittûwach (1),
sculpture; engraving
6605 pâthach (3), to *open*
wide; to *loosen, begin*
6900 qᵉbûwrâh (4),
sepulchre
6913 qeber (19),
sepulchre
7585 shᵉ'ôwl (30), abode
of the *dead*
7845 shachath (1), *pit;
destruction*

86 ha¡dēs (1), *Hades,* i.e.
place of the dead
3419 mnēmĕiŏn (4),
place of interment
4586 sĕmnŏs (3),
honorable, noble

GRAVE'S
7585 shᵉ'ôwl (1), abode
of the *dead*

GRAVECLOTHES
2750 kĕiria (1), *swathe* of
cloth

GRAVED
6605 pâthach (2), to
loosen, plow, carve

GRAVEL
2687 châtsâts (2), *gravel,
grit*
4579 mê'âh (1), *belly*

GRAVEN
2672 châtsab (1), to *cut*
stone or *carve* wood
2710 châqaq (1), to
engrave; to *enact* laws
2790 chârash (1), to
engrave; to *plow*
2801 chârath (1), to
engrave
6456 pᵉçîyl (18), *idol*
6458 pâçal (1), to *carve,*
to *chisel*
6459 peçel (29), *idol*
6605 pâthach (2), to
loosen, plow, carve
5480 charagma (1),
mark, sculptured figure

GRAVES
6913 qeber (16),
sepulchre
3418 mnēma (1),
sepulchral *monument*
3419 mnēmĕiŏn (4),
place of interment

GRAVETH
2710 châqaq (1), to
engrave; to *enact* laws

GRAVING
2747 cheret (1), *chisel;
style* for writing
6603 pittûwach (2),
sculpture; engraving

GRAVINGS
4734 miqla'ath (1),
bas-relief *sculpture*

GRAVITY
4587 sĕmnŏtēs (2),
venerableness

GRAY
7872 sêybâh (5), old *age*

GRAYHEADED
7867 sîyb (2), to *become*
aged, i.e. to *grow gray*

GREASE
2459 cheleb (1), *fat;
choice* part

GREAT
410 'êl (1), *mighty;* the
Almighty
417 'elgâbîysh (3), *hail*
430 'ĕlôhîym (2), the true
God; gods; great ones
679 'atstsîyl (1), *joint* of
the hand

1004 bayith (1), *house;
temple; family, tribe*
1167 ba'al (1), *master;
husband; owner; citizen*
1241 bâqâr (1), *plowing*
ox; *herd*
1396 gâbar (2), to *be
strong;* to *prevail;* to
act insolently
1419 gâdôwl (413), *great*
1420 gᵉdûwlâh (3),
greatness, grandeur
1431 gâdal (33), to *be
great, make great*
1432 gâdêl (2), *large,
powerful*
1462 gôwb (1), *locust*
1560 gᵉlâl (Ch.) (2), *large*
stones
2030 hâreh (1), *pregnant*
2342 chûwl (1), to *dance,
whirl;* to *writhe* in pain
2750 chŏrîy (2), *burning*
anger
3244 yanshûwph (2), *bird*
3514 kôbed (1), *weight,
multitude, vehemence*
3515 kâbêd (8),
numerous; severe
3699 kâçaç (1), to
estimate, determine
3833 lâbîy' (3), *lion,
lioness*
3966 mᵉ'ôd (11), *very,
utterly*
4306 mâtâr (1), *rain,
shower of rain*
4459 maltâ'âh (1),
grinder, molar *tooth*
4766 marbeh (1),
increasing; greatness
5006 nâ'ats (1), to *scorn*
6099 'âtsûwm (1),
powerful; numerous
6105 'âtsam (1), to *be,
make powerful*
6343 pachad (1), *sudden
alarm, fear*
7091 qippôwz (1),
arrow-snake
7227 rab (125), *great*
7229 rab (Ch.) (7), *great*
7230 rôb (7), *abundance*
7235 râbâh (9), to
increase
7236 rᵉbâh (Ch.) (1), to
increase
7239 ribbôw (1), *myriad,*
indefinite *large number*
7260 rabrab (Ch.) (8),
huge; domineering
7350 râchôwq (2),
remote, far
7451 ra' (1), *bad; evil*
7689 saggîy' (1), *mighty*
7690 saggîy' (Ch.) (3),
large
7991 shâlîysh (2), *officer;*
of the *third* rank
8514 tal'ûwbâh (1),
desiccation
1974 ĕpipŏthia (1),
intense longing
2245 hēlikŏs (2), *how
much, how great*
2425 hikanŏs (2), *ample;
fit*
3029 lian (1), *very much*

3112 makran (1), *at a
distance, far away*
3123 mallŏn (1), *in a
greater degree*
3166 mĕgalauchĕŏ (1), to
be arrogant, egotistic
3167 mĕgalĕiŏs (1), *great
things, wonderful works*
3170 mĕgalunō (1), to
increase or *extol*
3171 mĕgalōs (1), *much,
greatly*
3173 mĕgas (149), *great,
many*
3175 mĕgistanĕs (2),
great person
3176 mĕgistŏs (1),
greatest or *very great*
3745 hŏsŏs (6), *as much
as*
3819 palai (1), *formerly;
sometime since*
3827 pampŏlus (1), *full
many,* i.e. *immense*
4080 pēlikŏs (1), *how
much, how great*
4118 plĕistŏs (1), *largest
number* or *very large*
4183 pŏlus (60), *much,
many*
4185 pŏlutĕlēs (2),
extremely expensive
4186 pŏlutimŏs (1),
extremely valuable
4214 pŏsŏs (1), *how
much?; how much!*
5082 tēlikŏutŏs (3), *so
vast*
5118 tŏsŏutŏs (5), *such
great*
5246 hupĕrŏgkŏs (2),
insolent, boastful

GREATER
1419 gâdôwl (20), *great*
1431 gâdal (3), to *be
great, make great*
1980 hâlak (1), to *walk;
live a certain way*
7227 rab (4), *great*
7235 râbâh (2), to
increase
3186 mĕizŏtĕrŏs (1), *still
larger, greater*
3187 mĕizōn (34), *larger,
greater*
4055 pĕrissŏtĕrŏs (3),
more superabundant
4119 plĕiŏn (6), *more*

GREATEST
1419 gâdôwl (9), *great*
4768 marbîyth (1),
multitude; offspring
3173 mĕgas (2), *great,
many*
3187 mĕizōn (9), *larger,
greater*

GREATLY
3966 mᵉ'ôd (49), *very,
utterly*
7227 rab (3), *great*
7230 rôb (1), *abundance*
7690 saggîy' (Ch.) (1),
large
1568 ĕkthambĕō (1), to
astonish utterly
1569 ĕkthambŏs (1),
utterly astounded

GREATNESS

1971 ĕpipŏthĕō (3), *intensely crave*
3029 lian (4), very *much*
3171 mĕgalōs (1), *much, greatly*
4183 pŏlus (4), *much, many*
4970 sphŏdra (2), *high degree, much*
5479 chara (1), *calm delight, joy*

GREATNESS

1419 gâdôwl (1), *great*
1420 gᵉdûwlâh (7), *greatness, grandeur*
1433 gôdel (11), *magnitude, majesty*
4768 marbîyth (1), *multitude; offspring*
7230 rôb (9), *abundance*
7238 rᵉbûw (Ch.) (2), *increase*
3174 mĕgĕthŏs (1), *greatness*

GREAVES

4697 mitschâh (1), *shin-piece* of armor

GRECIA

3120 Yâvân (3), *effervescent*

GRECIANS

3125 Yᵉvânîy (1), *Jevanite*
1675 Hĕllēnistēs (3), *Hellenist* or Greek-speaking Jew

GREECE

3120 Yâvân (1), *effervescent*
1671 Hĕllas (1), *Hellas*

GREEDILY

8378 ta'ăvâh (1), *longing; delight*
1632 ĕkchĕō (1), to *pour forth;* to *bestow*

GREEDINESS

4124 plĕŏnĕxia (1), *extortion, avarice*

GREEDY

1214 bâtsa' (2), to *plunder;* to *finish*
3700 kâçaph (1), to *pine after;* to *fear*
5794+5315 'az (1), *strong, vehement, harsh*
146 aischrŏkĕrdēs (1), *sordid, greedy*
866 aphilargurŏs (1), *unavaricious*

GREEK

1672 Hĕllēn (7), *Greek (-speaking)*
1673 Hĕllēnikŏs (2), *Grecian* language
1674 Hĕllēnis (1), *Grecian* woman
1676 Hĕllēnisti (2), *Hellenistically,* i.e. in the *Grecian language*

GREEKS

1672 Hĕllēn (13), *Greek (-speaking)*
1674 Hĕllēnis (1), *Grecian* woman

GREEN

1877 deshe' (1), *sprout;* green *grass*
3387 yârôwq (1), *green* plant
3410 yarkâ' (Ch.) (1), *thigh*
3418 yereq (5), *green* grass or vegetation
3419 yârâq (1), *vegetable greens*
3768 karpaç (1), *byssus* linen
3892 lach (5), *fresh cut*
6291 pag (1), *unripe* fig
7373 râṭôb (1), *moist* with sap
7488 ra'ănân (18), *verdant; new*
5200 hugrŏs (1), *fresh and moist*
5515 chlōrŏs (3), *greenish,* i.e. *verdant*

GREENISH

3422 yᵉraqraq (2), *yellowishness*

GREENNESS

3 'êb (1), *green* plant

GREET

7592+7965 shâ'al (1), to *ask*
782 aspazŏmai (14), to *salute, welcome*

GREETETH

782 aspazŏmai (1), to *salute, welcome*

GREETING

5463 chairō (3), *salutation, "be well"*

GREETINGS

783 aspasmŏs (3), *greeting*

GREW

1431 gâdal (9), to *be great, make great*
1432 gâdêl (2), *large, powerful*
6509 pârâh (1), to *bear fruit*
6555 pârats (1), to *break out*
6779 tsâmach (2), to *sprout*
6780 tsemach (2), *sprout, branch*
7236 rᵉbâh (Ch.) (2), to *increase*
305 anabainō (1), to *go up, rise*
837 auxanō (6), to *grow,* i.e. *enlarge*
2064 ĕrchŏmai (1), to *go* or *come*

GREY

7872 sêybâh (1), old *age*

GREYHEADED

7872 sêybâh (1), old *age*

GREYHOUND

2223+4975 zarzîyr (1), fleet animal (*slender*)

GRIEF

2470 châlâh (2), to *be weak, sick, afflicted*
2483 chŏlîy (3), *malady; anxiety; calamity*

3013 yâgâh (1), to *grieve;* to *torment*
3015 yâgôwn (2), *affliction, sorrow*
3511 kᵉ'êb (2), *suffering; adversity*
3708 ka'aç (7), *vexation, grief*
4341 mak'ôb (2), *anguish; affliction*
4786 môrâh (1), *bitterness; trouble*
6330 pûwqâh (1), *stumbling-block*
7451 ra' (1), *bad; evil*
3076 lupĕō (1), to *distress;* to *be sad*
3077 lupē (1), *sadness, grief*
4727 stĕnazō (1), to *sigh, murmur, pray* inaudibly

GRIEFS

2483 chŏlîy (1), *malady; anxiety; calamity*

GRIEVANCE

5999 'âmâl (1), *wearing effort; worry*

GRIEVE

109 'âdab (1), to *languish, grieve*
3013 yâgâh (1), to *grieve;* to *torment*
6087 'âtsab (2), to *worry, have pain* or *anger*
3076 lupĕō (1), to *distress;* to *be sad*

GRIEVED

2342 chûwl (2), to *dance, whirl;* to *writhe* in pain
2470 châlâh (2), to *be weak, sick, afflicted*
2556 châmêts (1), to *be fermented; be soured*
2734 chârâh (1), to *blaze up*
3512 kâ'âh (1), to *despond;* to *deject*
3707 kâ'aç (1), to *grieve, rage, be indignant*
3735 kârâ' (Ch.) (1), to *grieve, be anxious*
3811 lâ'âh (1), to *tire;* to *be, make disgusted*
4784 mârâh (1), to *rebel* or *resist;* to *provoke*
4843 mârar (1), to *be, make bitter*
5701 'âgam (1), to *be sad*
6087 'âtsab (8), to *worry, have pain* or *anger*
6962 qûwṭ (3), to *detest*
6973 qûwts (1), to *be, make disgusted*
7114 qâtsar (1), to *curtail, cut short*
7489 râ'a' (4), to *break;* to *be good for nothing*
1278 diapŏnĕō (2), to *be worried*
3076 lupĕō (5), to *distress;* to *be sad*
4360 prŏsŏchthizō (2), to *be vexed* with
4818 sullupĕō (1), to *afflict jointly, sorrow* at

GRIEVETH

3811 lâ'âh (1), to *tire;* to *be, make disgusted*
4843 mârar (1), to *be, make bitter*

GRIEVING

3510 kâ'ab (1), to *feel pain;* to *grieve;* to *spoil*

GRIEVOUS

2342 chûwl (2), to *dance, whirl;* to *writhe* in pain
2470 châlâh (4), to *be weak, sick, afflicted*
3415 yâra' (1), to *fear*
3513 kâbad (1), to *be heavy, severe, dull*
3515 kâbêd (8), *severe, difficult, stupid*
4834 mârats (1), to *be vehement;* to *irritate*
5493 çûwr (1), to *turn* off
6089 'etseb (1), *earthen vessel;* painful *toil*
6277 'âthâq (1), *impudent*
7185 qâshâh (2), to *be tough* or *severe*
7186 qâsheh (3), *severe*
7451 ra' (2), *bad; evil*
7489 râ'a' (2), to *break;* to *be good for nothing*
8463 tachălûw' (1), *malady, disease*
926 barus (3), *weighty*
1418 dus- (2), *hard,* i.e. with *difficulty*
3077 lupē (1), *sadness, grief*
3636 ŏknērŏs (1), *irksome; lazy*
4190 pŏnērŏs (1), *malice, wicked, bad; crime*

GRIEVOUSLY

2342 chûwl (1), to *dance, whirl;* to *writhe* in pain
2399 chêṭ' (1), *crime* or its *penalty*
3513 kâbad (1), to *be heavy, severe, dull*
4604 ma'al (1), *sinful treachery*
4784 mârâh (1), to *rebel* or *resist;* to *provoke*
1171 dĕinōs (1), *terribly,* i.e. *excessively, fiercely*
2560 kakōs (1), *badly; wrongly; ill*

GRIEVOUSNESS

3514 kôbed (1), *weight, multitude, vehemence*
5999 'âmâl (1), *wearing effort; worry*

GRIND

2911 ṭᵉchôwn (1), hand *mill; millstone*
2912 ṭâchan (4), to *grind* flour meal
3039 likmaō (2), to *grind* to *powder*

GRINDERS

2912 ṭâchan (1), to *grind* flour meal

GRINDING

2913 ṭachănâh (1), *chewing, grinding*
229 alēthō (2), to *grind* grain

GRISLED
1261 bârôd (4), *spotted, dappled*

GROAN
584 'ânach (1), *to sigh, moan*
602 'ânaq (1), *to shriek, cry out in groaning*
5008 nâ'aq (2), *to groan*
4727 stĕnazō (3), *to sigh, murmur, pray inaudibly*

GROANED
1690 ĕmbrimaŏmai (1), *to blame, to sigh*

GROANETH
4959 sustĕnazō (1), *to moan jointly*

GROANING
585 'ănâchâh (4), *sighing, moaning*
603 'ănâqâh (1), *shrieking, groaning*
5009 nᵉ'âqâh (2), *groaning*
1690 ĕmbrimaŏmai (1), *to blame, to sigh*
4726 stĕnagmŏs (1), *sigh, groan*

GROANINGS
5009 nᵉ'âqâh (2), *groaning*
4726 stĕnagmŏs (1), *sigh, groan*

GROPE
1659 gâshash (2), *to feel about, grope around*
4959 mâshash (3), *to feel of; to grope*

GROPETH
4959 mâshash (1), *to feel of; to grope*

GROSS
6205 'ărâphel (2), *gloom, darkness*
3975 pachunō (2), *to fatten; to render callous*

GROUND
127 'ădâmâh (44), *soil; land*
776 'erets (97), *earth, land, soil; country*
2513 chelqâh (1), *smoothness; allotment*
2758 chârîysh (1), *plowing (season)*
2912 ṭâchan (3), *to grind flour meal*
6083 'âphâr (1), *dust, earth, mud; clay,*
7383 rîyphâh (1), *grits cereal*
7704 sâdeh (4), *field*
68 agrŏs (1), *farmland, countryside*
1093 gē (18), *soil, region, whole earth*
1474 ĕdaphizō (1), *to raze, dash to the ground*
1475 ĕdaphŏs (1), *soil, ground*
1477 hĕdraiŏma (1), *basis, foundation*
5476 chamai (2), *toward the ground*
5561 chōra (1), *space of territory*

GROUNDED
4145 mûwçâdâh (1), *foundation*
2311 thĕmĕliŏō (2), *to erect; to consolidate*

GROVE
815 'êshel (1), *tamarisk tree*
842 'ăshêrâh (16), *happy; Astarte (goddess)*

GROVES
842 'ăshêrâh (24), *happy; Astarte (goddess)*

GROW
1342 gâ'âh (1), *to rise; to grow tall; be majestic*
1431 gâdal (2), *to be great, make great*
1711 dâgâh (1), *to become numerous*
3212 yâlak (1), *to walk; to live; to carry*
3318 yâtsâ' (1), *to go, bring out*
5599 çâphîyach (2), *self-sown crop; freshet*
5927 'âlâh (2), *to ascend, be high, mount*
6335 pûwsh (1), *to spread; to act proudly*
6509 pârâh (1), *to bear fruit*
6524 pârach (2), *to break forth; to bloom; flourish*
6779 tsâmach (9), *to sprout*
7235 râbâh (1), *to increase*
7680 sᵉgâ' (Ch.) (1), *to increase*
7685 sâgâh (1), *to enlarge, be prosperous*
7735 sûwg (1), *to hedge in, make grow*
7971 shâlach (1), *to send away*
837 auxanō (5), *to grow, i.e. enlarge*
1096 ginŏmai (2), *to be, become*
3373 mēkunō (1), *to enlarge, grow long*
4886 sundĕsmŏs (1), *ligament; control*

GROWETH
2498 châlaph (2), *to spring up; to change*
2583 chânâh (1), *to encamp*
3332 yâtsaq (1), *to pour out*
5599 çâphîyach (3), *self-sown crop; freshet*
5927 'âlâh (1), *to ascend, be high, mount*
6524 pârach (1), *to break forth; to bloom; flourish*
6779 tsâmach (1), *to sprout*
8025 shâlaph (1), *to pull out, up or off*
305 anabainō (1), *to go up, rise*
837 auxanō (1), *to grow, i.e. enlarge*

GROUND (cont.) 5564 chōriŏn (1), *spot or plot of ground*

GROWN
648 'âphîyl (1), *unripe*
1431 gâdal (9), *to be great, make great*
5927 'âlâh (1), *to ascend, be high, mount*
6335 pûwsh (1), *to spread; to act proudly*
6779 tsâmach (4), *to sprout*
6965 qûwm (2), *to rise*
7236 rᵉbâh (Ch.) (3), *to increase*
837 auxanō (1), *to grow, i.e. enlarge*

GROWTH
3954 leqesh (2), *after crop, second crop*

GRUDGE
3885 lûwn (1), *to be obstinate*
5201 nâṭar (1), *to guard; to cherish anger*
4727 stĕnazō (1), *to sigh, murmur, pray inaudibly*

GRUDGING
1112 gŏggusmŏs (1), *grumbling*

GRUDGINGLY
1537+3077 ĕk (1), *out, out of*

GUARD
2876 ṭabbâch (29), *king's guard, executioner*
2877 ṭabbâch (Ch.) (1), *king's guard, executioner*
4928 mishma'ath (2), *royal court; subject*
4929 mishmâr (2), *guard; deposit; usage; example*
7323 rûwts (14), *to run*
4759 stratŏpĕdarchēs (1), *military commander*

GUARD'S
2876 ṭabbâch (1), *king's guard, executioner*

GUDGODAH
1412 Gudgôdâh (2), *cleft*

GUEST
2647 kataluō (1), *to halt for the night*

GUESTCHAMBER
2646 kataluma (2), *lodging-place*

GUESTS
7121 qârâ' (4), *to call out*
345 anakĕimai (2), *to recline at a meal*

GUIDE
441 'allûwph (4), *friend, one familiar; leader*
833 'âshar (1), *to go forward; guide*
1869 dârak (1), *to tread, trample; to walk, lead*
3289 yâ'ats (1), *to advise*
3557 kûwl (1), *to keep in; to measure*
5090 nâhag (1), *to drive forth; to lead*
5095 nâhal (3), *to flow; to conduct; to protect*

GUIDE (cont.)
5148 nâchâh (4), *to guide*
7101 qâtsîyn (1), *magistrate, leader*
2720 katĕuthunō (1), *to direct, lead, direct*
3594 hŏdēgĕō (2), *to show the way, guide*
3595 hŏdēgŏs (2), *conductor, guide*
3616 ŏikŏdĕspŏtĕō (1), *to be the head of a family*

GUIDED
5090 nâhag (1), *to drive forth; to lead*
5095 nâhal (2), *to flow; to conduct; to protect*
5148 nâchâh (2), *to guide*

GUIDES
3595 hŏdēgŏs (2), *conductor, guide*

GUILE
4820 mirmâh (2), *fraud*
6195 'ormâh (1), *trickery; discretion*
7423 rᵉmîyâh (1), *remissness; treachery*
1388 dŏlŏs (7), *wile, deceit, trickery*

GUILTINESS
817 'âshâm (1), *guilt; fault; sin-offering*

GUILTLESS
5352 nâqâh (5), *to be, make clean; to be bare*
5355 nâqîy (4), *innocent*
338 anaitiŏs (1), *innocent*

GUILTY
816 'âsham (16), *to be guilty; to be punished*
7563 râshâ' (1), *morally wrong; bad person*
1777 ĕnŏchŏs (4), *liable*
3784 ŏphĕilō (1), *to owe; to be under obligation*
5267 hupŏdikŏs (1), *under sentence*

GULF
5490 chasma (1), *chasm or vacancy*

GUNI
1476 Gûwnîy (4), *protected*

GUNITES
1477 Gûwnîy (1), *Gunite*

GUR
1483 Gûwr (1), *cub*

GUR-BAAL
1485 Gûwr-Ba'al (1), *dwelling of Baal*

GUSH
5140 nâzal (1), *to drip, or shed by trickling*

GUSHED
2100 zûwb (3), *to flow freely, gush*
8210 shâphak (1), *to spill forth; to expend*
1632 ĕkchĕō (1), *to pour forth; to bestow*

GUTTER
6794 tsinnûwr (1), *culvert, water-shaft*

GUTTERS
7298 raḥaṭ (2), *ringlet* of
hair

HA
1889 he'âch (1), *aha!*

HAAHASHTARI
326 'ăchashtârîy (1),
courier

HABAIAH
2252 Chăbayâh (2),
Jehovah has hidden

HABAKKUK
2265 Chăbaqqûwq (2),
embrace

HABAZINIAH
2262 Chăbatstsanyâh (1),
Chabatstsanjah

HABERGEON
8302 shiryôwn (1),
corslet, coat of mail
8473 tachărâ' (2), *linen
corslet*

HABERGEONS
8302 shiryôwn (2),
corslet, coat of mail

HABITABLE
8398 têbêl (1), *earth;
world; inhabitants*

HABITATION
1628 gêrûwth (1),
(temporary) *residence*
2073 z°bûwl (3),
residence, dwelling
2918 ṭîyrâh (1), *fortress;
hamlet*
3427 yâshab (3), to *dwell,*
to *remain;* to *settle*
4186 môwshâb (4), *seat;
site; abode*
4349 mâkôwn (2), *basis;
place*
4351 m°kûwrâh (1),
origin
4583 mâ'ôwn (9), *retreat*
or asylum *dwelling*
4907 mishkan (Ch.) (1),
residence
4908 mishkân (3),
residence
5115 nâvâh (1), to *rest* as
at home
5116 nâveh (21), *at
home; lovely; home*
7931 shâkan (1), to *reside*
7932 sh°kan (Ch.) (1), to
reside
7933 sheken (1),
residence
1886 ĕpaulis (1),
dwelling,residence
2732 katŏikĕtĕriŏn (2),
dwelling-place, home
2733 katŏikia (1),
residence, dwelling
3613 ŏikĕtĕriŏn (1),
residence, home

HABITATIONS
4186 môwshâb (8), *seat;
site; abode*
4380 m°kêrâh (1),
stabbing-sword
4583 mâ'ôwn (1), *retreat*
or asylum *dwelling*
4585 m°'ôwnâh (1), *abode*
4908 mishkân (2),
residence

HA... (second column)

4999 nâ'âh (5), *home,
dwelling; pasture*
5116 nâveh (1), *at home;
lovely; home*
4638 skēnōma (1),
dwelling: the *Temple*

HABOR
2249 Châbôwr (3), *united*

HACHALIAH
2446 Chăkalyâh (2),
darkness (of) *Jehovah*

HACHILAH
2444 Chakîylâh (3), *dark*

HACHMONI
2453 Chakmôwnîy (1),
skillful

HACHMONITE
2453 Chakmôwnîy (1),
skillful

HAD
935 bôw' (1), to *go, come*
1961 hâyâh (104), to
exist, i.e. *be* or *become*
2370 chăzâ' (Ch.) (1), to
gaze upon; to *dream*
3426 yêsh (5), there *is*
3884 lûwlê' (1), *if not*
7760 sûwm (1), to *put*
1096 ginŏmai (1), to *be,
become*
1510 ĕimi (8), I *exist,* I *am*
1746 ĕnduŏ (1), to *dress*
2192 ĕchō (106), to *have*
2722 katĕchō (1), to *hold
down fast*
2983 lambanō (2), to
take, receive
3844 para (1), *from; with;
besides; on account of*
5607 ŏn (1), *being,
existence*

HADAD
1908 Hădad (13), *Hadad*
2301 Chădad (1), *fierce*

HADADEZER
1909 Hădad'ezer (9),
Hadad (is his) *help*

HADADRIMMON
1910 Hădadrimmôwn
(1), *Hadad-Rimmon*

HADAR
1924 Hădar (2),
magnificence

HADAREZER
1928 Hădar'ezer (12),
Hadad is his help

HADASHAH
2322 Chădâshâh (1), *new*

HADASSAH
1919 Hădaççâh (1),
Esther

HADATTAH
2675 Châtsôwr
Chădattâh (1), *new
village*

HADID
2307 Châdîyd (3), *peak*

HADLAI
2311 Chadlay (1), *idle*

HADORAM
1913 Hădôwrâm (4),
Hadoram

HADRACH (third column)
2317 Chadrâk (1), *Syrian
deity*

HAFT
5325 nitstsâb (1), *handle*
of a sword or dagger

HAGAB
2285 Châgâb (1), *locust*

HAGABA
2286 Chăgâbâ' (1), *locust*

HAGABAH
2286 Chăgâbâ' (1), *locust*

HAGAR
1904 Hâgâr (12), *Hagar*

HAGARENES
1905 Hagrîy (1), *Hagrite*

HAGARITES
1905 Hagrîy (3), *Hagrite*

HAGERITE
1905 Hagrîy (1), *Hagrite*

HAGGAI
2292 Chaggay (11),
festive

HAGGERI
1905 Hagrîy (1), *Hagrite*

HAGGI
2291 Chaggîy (2), *festive*

HAGGIAH
2293 Chaggîyâh (1),
festival of Jehovah

HAGGITES
2291 Chaggîy (1), *festive*

HAGGITH
2294 Chaggiyîth (5),
festive

HAI
5857 'Ay (2), *ruin*

HAIL
1258 bârad (1), to *rain
hail*
1259 bârâd (26), *hail,
hailstones*
5463 chairō (6),
salutation, *"be well"*
5464 chalaza (4), *frozen
ice crystals,* i.e. *hail*

HAILSTONES
68+417 'eben (3), *stone*
68+1259 'eben (2), *stone*

HAIR
1803 dallâh (1), *loose
thread;* loose *hair*
4748 miqsheh (1), *curl* of
beautiful tresses
4803 mâraṭ (2), to *polish;*
to *make bald*
5145 nezer (1), *set apart;*
royal chaplet
8177 s°'ar (Ch.) (2), *hair*
8181 sê'âr (23), *tossed
hair*
8185 sa'ărâh (5),
hairiness
2359 thrix (9), *hair;*
single *hair*
2863 kŏmaō (2), to *wear
long* hair
2864 kŏmē (1), long *hair*
4117 plĕgma (1), *plait* or
braid of hair
5155 trichinŏs (1), made
of *hair*

HAIRS (fourth column)
8177 s°'ar (Ch.) (1), *hair*
8181 sê'âr (1), tossed *hair*
8185 sa'ărâh (2),
hairiness
2359 thrix (5), *hair*

HAIRY
1167+8181 ba'al (1),
master; owner; citizen
8163 sâ'îyr (2), *shaggy;
he-goat; goat idol*
8181 sê'âr (2), tossed *hair*

HAKKATAN
6997 Qâṭân (1), *small*

HAKKOZ
6976 Qôwts (1), *thorns*

HAKUPHA
2709 Chăqûwphâ' (2), to
bend, crooked

HALAH
2477 Chălach (3),
Chalach

HALAK
2510 Châlâq (2), *bare*

HALE
2694 katasurō (1), to
arrest judicially

HALF
1235 beqa' (1), *half
shekel*
2673 châtsâh (1), to *cut*
or *split* in two; to *halve*
2677 chêtsîy (106), *half*
or *middle, midst*
4275 mechĕtsâh (2),
halving, half
4276 machătsîyth (14),
halving or the *middle*
8432 tâvek (1), *center,
middle*
2253 hēmithanēs (1),
entirely exhausted
2255 hēmisu (5), *half*
2256 hēmiōriŏn (1),
half-hour

HALHUL
2478 Chalchûwl (1),
contorted

HALI
2482 Chălîy (1), *polished
trinket, ornament*

HALING
4951 surō (1), to *trail,
drag, sweep*

HALL
833 aulē (2), *palace;
house; courtyard*
4232 praitōriŏn (6),
governor's court-room

HALLOHESH
3873 Lôwchêsh (1),
enchanter

HALLOW
6942 qâdâsh (15), to *be,
make clean*

HALLOWED
4720 miqdâsh (1),
sanctuary of deity
6942 qâdâsh (10), to *be,
make clean*
6944 qôdesh (9), *sacred*
place or thing
37 hagiazō (2), to *purify*
or *consecrate*

HALOHESH
3873 Lôwchêsh (1), *enchanter*

HALT
6452 pâçach (1), to *hop, skip* over; to *hesitate*
6761 tsela' (1), *limping*
5560 chôlŏs (4), *limping, crippled*

HALTED
6761 tsela' (2), *limping*

HALTETH
6761 tsela' (2), *limping*

HALTING
6761 tsela' (1), *limping*

HAM
1990 Hâm (1), *Ham*
2526 Châm (16), *hot*

HAMAN
2001 Hâmân (50), *Haman*

HAMAN'S
2001 Hâmân (3), *Haman*

HAMATH
2574 Chămâth (33), *walled*
2579 Chămath Rabbâh (1), *walled of Rabbah*

HAMATH-ZOBAH
2578 Chămath Tsôwbâh (1), *walled of Tsobah*

HAMATHITE
2577 Chămâthîy (2), *Chamathite*

HAMMATH
2575 Chammath (1), *hot springs*

HAMMEDATHA
4099 Mᵉdâthâ (5), *Medatha*

HAMMELECH
4429 Melek (2), *king*

HAMMER
1989 halmûwth (1), *hammer* or *mallet*
4717 maqqâbâh (1), *hammer*
4718 maqqebeth (1), *hammer*
6360 paṭṭîysh (3), *hammer* which *pounds*

HAMMERS
3597 kêylaph (1), *club* or *sledge-hammer*
4717 maqqâbâh (2), *hammer*

HAMMOLEKETH
4447 Môleketh (1), *queen*

HAMMON
2540 Chammôwn (2), *warm* spring

HAMMOTH-DOR
2576 Chammôth Dô'r (1), *hot springs of Dor*

HAMON-GOG
1996 Hămôwn Gôwg (2), *multitude of Gog*

HAMONAH
1997 Hămôwnâh (1), *multitude*

HAMOR
2544 Chămôwr (12), male donkey or *ass*

HAMOR'S
2544 Chămôwr (1), male donkey or *ass*

HAMUEL
2536 Chammûw'êl (1), *anger of God*

HAMUL
2538 Châmûwl (3), *pitied*

HAMULITES
2539 Châmûwlîy (1), *Chamulite*

HAMUTAL
2537 Chămûwṭal (3), *father-in-law of dew*

HANAMEEL
2601 Chănam'êl (4), *God has favored*

HANAN
2605 Chânân (12), *favor*

HANANEEL
2606 Chănan'êl (4), *God has favored*

HANANI
2607 Chănânîy (11), *gracious*

HANANIAH
2608 Chănanyâh (29), *Jehovah has favored*

HAND
405 'ekeph (1), *stroke, blow*
854 'êth (1), *with; by; at; among*
2026 hârag (1), to *kill, slaughter*
2651 chôphen (1), *pair of fists*
2947 ṭêphach (1), *palm-breadth*
2948 ṭôphach (4), *palm-breadth*
3027 yâd (1086), *hand; power*
3028 yad (Ch.) (12), *hand; power*
3079 Yᵉhôwyâqîym (2), *Jehovah will raise*
3221 yâm (Ch.) (1), *sea; basin; west*
3225 yâmîyn (87), *right; south*
3227 yᵉmîynîy (1), *right*
3235 yâmar (1), to *exchange*
3325 Yitshârîy (1), *Jitsharite*
3709 kaph (52), *hollow* of *hand; paw; sole* of foot
4672 mâtsâ' (1), to *find* or *acquire; to occur*
7126 qârab (4), to *approach, bring near*
7138 qârôwb (5), *near, close*
8040 sᵉmô'wl (14), *north; left* hand
8041 sâma'l (1), to *use* the *left* hand or go *left*
8042 sᵉmâ'lîy (2), on the *left* side; *northern*
1448 ĕggizō (9), to *approach*
1451 ĕggus (6), *near, close*
1764 ĕnistēmi (1), to be *present*

2021 ĕpichĕirĕō (1), to *undertake, try*
2186 ĕphistēmi (1), to be *present; to approach*
5495 chĕir (87), *hand*
5496 chĕiragōgĕō (2), to *guide* a blind person by the hand
5497 chĕiragōgŏs (1), *conductor* of a blind person by the hand

HANDBREADTH
2947 ṭêphach (2), *palm-breadth*
2948 ṭôphach (1), *palm-breadth*

HANDED
3027 yâd (1), *hand; power*

HANDFUL
4390+3709 mâlê' (3), to *fill; be full*
4393+7062 mᵉlô' (2), *fulness*
5995 'âmîyr (1), *bunch of* cereal new-cut grain
6451 piççâh (1), *abundance*
7061 qâmats (1), to *grasp* a handful
7062 qômets (1), *handful; abundance*

HANDFULS
4393+2651 mᵉlô' (1), *fulness*
6653 tsebeth (1), *lock of* stalks, *bundle* of grain
7062 qômets (1), *handful; abundance*
8168 shô'al (2), *palm* of hand; *handful*

HANDKERCHIEFS
4676 sŏudariŏn (1), *towel*

HANDLE
270 'âchaz (1), to *seize, grasp; possess*
4184 mûwsh (1), to *touch, feel*
4900 mâshak (1), to *draw out; to be tall*
6186 'ârak (1), to *set in a row, i.e. arrange,*
8610 tâphas (5), to *manipulate, i.e. seize*
2345 thigganō (1), to *touch*
5584 psēlaphaō (1), to *manipulate*

HANDLED
8610+3709 tâphas (1), to *manipulate, i.e. seize*
821 atimŏō (1), to *maltreat, disgrace*
5584 psēlaphaō (1), to *manipulate*

HANDLES
3709 kaph (1), *hollow* of *hand; paw; sole* of foot

HANDLETH
5921 'al (1), *above, over, upon,* or *against*
8610 tâphas (2), to *manipulate, i.e. seize*

HANDLING
8610 tâphas (1), to *manipulate, i.e. seize*

1389 dŏlŏō (1), to *adulterate, falsify*

HANDMAID
519 'âmâh (22), *female servant* or *slave*
8198 shiphchâh (22), *household female slave*
1399 dŏulē (1), *female slave*

HANDMAIDEN
1399 dŏulē (1), *female slave*

HANDMAIDENS
8198 shiphchâh (2), *household female slave*
1399 dŏulē (1), *female slave*

HANDMAIDS
519 'âmâh (1), *female servant* or *slave*
8198 shiphchâh (7), *household female slave*

HANDS
2651 chôphen (3), *pair of fists*
3027 yâd (274), *hand; power*
3028 yad (Ch.) (4), *hand; power*
3709 kaph (67), *hollow* of *hand; paw; sole* of foot
849 autŏchĕir (1), *self-handed, personally*
886 achĕirŏpŏiētŏs (3), *unmanufactured*
2902 kratĕō (2), to *seize*
4084 piazō (1), to *seize, arrest,* or *capture*
4475 rhapisma (1), *slap, strike*
5495 chĕir (90), *hand*
5499 chĕirŏpŏiētŏs (6), of *human construction*

HANDSTAVES
4731+3027 maqqêl (1), *shoot; stick; staff*

HANDWRITING
5498 chĕirŏgraphŏn (1), *document* or *bond*

HANDYWORK
4639+3027 ma'ăseh (1), *action; labor*

HANES
2609 Chânêç (1), *Chanes*

HANG
3363 yâqa' (2), to be *dislocated; to impale*
3381 yârad (1), to *descend*
5414 nâthan (3), to *give*
5628 çârach (2), to *extend* even to *excess*
8511 tâlâ' (1), to *suspend; to be uncertain*
8518 tâlâh (7), to *suspend, hang*
2910 krĕmannumi (2), to *hang*
3935 pariēmi (1), to *neglect; to be weakened*

HANGED
2614 chânaq (1), to *choke oneself*
3363 yâqa' (2), to be *dislocated; to impale*

4223 mᵉchâ' (Ch.) (1), to *strike; to impale*
8511 tâlâ' (1), to *suspend; to be uncertain*
8518 tâlâh (18), to *suspend, hang*
519 apagchŏmai (1), to *strangle oneself*
2910 krĕmannumi (4), to *hang*
4029 pĕrikĕimai (2), to *enclose, encircle*

HANGETH
8518 tâlâh (1), to *suspend, hang*
2910 krĕmannumi (1), to *hang*

HANGING
4539 mâçâk (17), *veil; shield*
8518 tâlâh (1), to *suspend, hang*

HANGINGS
1004 bayith (1), *house; temple; family, tribe*
7050 qela' (15), *slinging weapon; door screen*

HANIEL
2592 Chănnîy'êl (1), *favor of God*

HANNAH
2584 Channâh (13), *favored*

HANNATHON
2615 Channâthôn (1), *favored*

HANNIEL
2592 Chănnîy'êl (1), *favor of God*

HANOCH
2585 Chănôwk (5), *initiated*

HANOCHITES
2599 Chănôkîy (1), *Chanokite*

HANUN
2586 Chânûwn (11), *favored*

HAP
4745 miqreh (1), *accident or fortune*

HAPHRAIM
2663 Chăphârayîm (1), *double pit*

HAPLY
3863 lûw' (1), *if; would that!*
686 ara (2), *then, so, therefore*
3379 mēpŏtĕ (2), *not ever; if, or lest ever*
3381 mēpōs (1), *lest somehow*

HAPPEN
579 'ânâh (1), to *meet, to happen*
7136 qârâh (2), to *bring about; to impose*
4819 sumbainō (1), to *concur, happen*

HAPPENED
1961 hâyâh (1), to *exist, i.e. be or become*

7122 qârâ' (2), to *encounter, to happen*
7136 qârâh (2), to *bring about; to impose*
1096 ginŏmai (1), to be, *become*
4819 sumbainō (5), to *concur, happen*

HAPPENETH
4745 miqreh (1), *accident or fortune*
5060 nâga' (2), to *strike*
7136 qârâh (3), to *bring about; to impose*

HAPPIER
3107 makariŏs (1), *fortunate, well off*

HAPPY
833 'âshar (2), to be *honest, prosper*
835 'esher (16), *how happy!*
837 'ôsher (1), *happiness, blessedness*
7951 shâlah (1), to be *tranquil, i.e. secure*
3106 makarizō (1), to *esteem fortunate*
3107 makariŏs (5), *fortunate, well off*

HARA
2024 Hârâ' (1), *mountainousness*

HARADAH
2732 Chărâdâh (2), *fear, anxiety*

HARAN
2039 Hârân (1), *mountaineer*
2309 chedel (6), *state of the dead, deceased*
2771 Chârân (12), *parched*

HARARITE
2043 Hărârîy (5), *mountaineer*

HARBONA
2726 Charbôwnâ' (1), *Charbona, Charbonah*

HARBONAH
2726 Charbôwnâ' (1), *Charbona, Charbonah*

HARD
280 'ăchîydâh (Ch.) (1), *enigma*
386 'êythân (1), *never-failing; eternal*
681 'êtsel (1), *side; near*
1692 dâbaq (4), to *cling or adhere; to catch*
2420 chîydâh (2), *puzzle; conundrum; maxim*
3332 yâtsaq (1), to *pour out*
3515 kâbêd (2), *severe, difficult, stupid*
5066 nâgash (1), to be, *come, bring near*
5221 nâkâh (1), to *strike, kill*
5564 çâmak (1), to *lean upon; take hold of*
5980 'ummâh (1), *near, beside, along with*
6277 'âthâq (1), *impudent*

6381 pâlâ' (5), to be, *make great, difficult*
7185 qâshâh (5), to be *tough or severe*
7186 qâsheh (6), *severe*
1421 dusĕrmēnĕutŏs (1), *difficult to explain*
1422 duskŏlōs (1), *impracticable, difficult*
1425 dusnŏētŏs (1), *difficult of perception*
4642 sklērŏs (5), *hard or tough; harsh, severe*
4927 sunŏmŏrĕŏ (1), to *border together*

HARDEN
533 'ammîyts (1), *strong; mighty; brave*
2388 châzaq (4), to be *obstinate; to bind*
5513 Çîynîy (1), *Sinite*
5539 çâlad (1), to *leap with joy*
7185 qâshâh (2), to be *tough or severe*
4645 sklērunō (3), to *indurate, be stubborn*

HARDENED
553 'âmats (1), to be *strong; be courageous*
2388 châzaq (9), to be *obstinate; to bind*
3513 kâbad (4), to be *heavy, severe, dull*
3515 kâbêd (3), *severe, difficult, stupid*
7185 qâshâh (8), to be *tough or severe*
7188 qâshach (2), to be, *make unfeeling*
8631 tᵉqêph (Ch.) (1), to *be obstinate*
4456 pōrŏō (3), to *render stupid or callous*
4645 sklērunō (2), to *indurate, be stubborn*

HARDENETH
5810 'âzaz (1), to be *stout; be bold*
7185 qâshâh (2), to be *tough or severe*
4645 sklērunō (1), to *indurate, be stubborn*

HARDER
2388 châzaq (1), to be *obstinate; to bind*
2389 châzâq (1), *strong; severe, hard, violent*

HARDHEARTED
7186+3820 qâsheh (1), *severe*

HARDLY
6031 'ânâh (1), to *afflict, be afflicted*
7185 qâshâh (2), to be *tough or severe*
1423 duskŏlōs (3), *impracticably, with difficulty*
3425 mŏgis (1), *with difficulty*
3433 mŏlis (1), *with difficulty*

HARDNESS
4165 mûwtsâq (1), *casting of metal*

6381 pâlâ' ...

6381 pâlâ'

2553 kakŏpathĕō (1), to *undergo hardship*
4457 pōrōsis (1), *stupidity or callousness*
4641 sklērŏkardia (3), *hard-heartedness*
4643 sklērŏtēs (1), *stubbornness*

HARE
768 'arnebeth (2), *hare, rabbit*

HAREPH
2780 Chârêph (1), *reproachful*

HARETH
2802 Chereth (1), *forest*

HARHAIAH
2736 Charhăyâh (1), *fearing Jehovah*

HARHAS
2745 Charchaç (1), *sun*

HARHUR
2744 Charchûwr (2), *inflammation*

HARIM
2766 Chârîm (11), *snub-nosed*

HARIPH
2756 Chârîyph (2), *autumnal*

HARLOT
2181 zânâh (33), to *commit adultery*
6948 qᵉdêshâh (3), *sacred female prostitute*
4204 pŏrnē (4), *strumpet, i.e. prostitute; idolater*

HARLOT'S
2181 zânâh (2), to *commit adultery*

HARLOTS
2181 zânâh (2), to *commit adultery*
6948 qᵉdêshâh (1), *sacred female prostitute*
4204 pŏrnē (4), *strumpet, i.e. prostitute; idolater*

HARLOTS'
2181 zânâh (1), to *commit adultery*

HARM
1697+7451 dâbâr (1), *word; matter; thing*
2398 châţâ' (1), to *sin*
3415 yâra' (1), to *fear*
7451 ra' (4), *bad; evil*
7489 râ'a' (3), to *make, be good for nothing*
824 atŏpŏs (1), *improper; injurious; wicked*
2556 kakŏs (2), *bad, evil, wrong*
2559 kakŏō (1), to *injure; to oppress; to embitter*
4190 pŏnērŏs (1), *malice, wicked, bad; crime*
5196 hubris (1), *insult; injury*

HARMLESS
172 akakŏs (1), *innocent, blameless*

185 akĕraiŏs (2), innocent

HARNEPHER
2774 Charnepher (1), *Charnepher*

HARNESS
631 'âçar (1), to *fasten*; to *join* battle
5402 nesheq (1), military *arms, arsenal*
8302 shiryôwn (2), *corslet, coat of mail*

HARNESSED
2571 châmûsh (1), able-bodied *soldiers*

HAROD
5878 'Êyn Chărôd (1), *fountain of trembling*

HARODITE
2733 Chărôdîy (1), *Charodite*

HAROEH
7204 Rô'êh (1), *seer*

HARORITE
2033 Hărôwrîy (1), *mountaineer*

HAROSHETH
2800 Chărôsheth (3), skilled *worker*

HARP
3658 kinnôwr (25), *harp*
7030 qîythârôç (Ch.) (4), *lyre*
2788 kithara (1), *lyre*

HARPED
2789 *kitharizō* (1), to *play a lyre*

HARPERS
2790 *kitharōįdŏs* (2), one who *plays a lyre*

HARPING
2789 *kitharizō* (1), to *play a lyre*

HARPS
3658 kinnôwr (17), *harp*
2788 *kithara* (3), *lyre*

HARROW
7702 sâdad (1), to *harrow* a field

HARROWS
2757 chârîyts (2), *threshing-sledge; slice*

HARSHA
2797 Charshâ' (2), *magician*

HART
354 'ayâl (9), *stag* deer

HARTS
354 'ayâl (2), *stag* deer

HARUM
2037 Hârûm (1), *high, exalted*

HARUMAPH
2739 Chărûwmaph (1), *snub-nosed*

HARUPHITE
2741 Chărûwphîy (1), *Charuphite*

HARUZ
2743 Chârûwts (1), *earnest*

HARVEST
7105 qâtsîyr (47), *harvest; limb* of a tree
2326 thĕrismŏs (13), *harvest, crop*

HARVESTMAN
7105 qâtsîyr (1), *harvest; limb* of a tree
7114 qâtsar (1), to *curtail, cut short*

HASADIAH
2619 Chăçadyâh (1), *Jehovah has favored*

HASENUAH
5574 Çᵉnûw'âh (1), *pointed*

HASHABIAH
2811 Chăshabyâh (15), *Jehovah has regarded*

HASHABNAH
2812 Chăshabnâh (1), *inventiveness*

HASHABNIAH
2813 Chăshabnᵉyâh (2), *thought of Jehovah*

HASHBADANA
2806 Chashbaddânâh (1), *considerate judge*

HASHEM
2044 Hâshêm (1), *wealthy*

HASHMONAH
2832 Chashmônâh (2), *fertile*

HASHUB
2815 Chashshûwb (4), *intelligent*

HASHUBAH
2807 Chăshûbâh (1), *estimation*

HASHUM
2828 Châshûm (5), *enriched*

HASHUPHA
2817 Chăsûwphâ' (1), *nakedness*

HASRAH
2641 Chaçrâh (1), *want*

HASSENAAH
5570 Çᵉnâ'âh (1), *thorny*

HASSHUB
2815 Chashshûwb (1), *intelligent*

HAST
1961 hâyâh (2), to *exist*, i.e. *be* or *become*
3426 yêsh (3), there *is* or *are*
2076 ĕsti (1), he (she or it) *is*; they *are*
2192 ĕchō (28), to *have*; *hold; keep*
5224 huparchŏnta (1), *property* or *possessions*

HASTE
213 'ûwts (1), to *be close, hurry, withdraw*
924 bᵉhîylûw (Ch.) (1), *hastily, at once*
926 bâhal (1), to *hasten, hurry anxiously*
927 bᵉhal (Ch.) (3), to *terrify; hasten*

1272 bârach (1), to *flee suddenly*
2363 chûwsh (11), to *hurry; to be eager*
2439 chîysh (1), to *hurry, hasten*
2648 châphaz (5), to *hasten* away, to *fear*
2649 chîppâzôwn (3), *hasty flight*
4116 mâhar (20), to *hurry; promptly*
5169 nâchats (1), to *be urgent*
4692 spĕudō (4), to *urge* on diligently
4710 spŏudē (2), *despatch; eagerness*

HASTED
213 'ûwts (2), to *be close, hurry, withdraw*
926 bâhal (1), to *hasten, hurry anxiously*
1765 dâchaph (2), to *urge; to hasten*
2363 chûwsh (2), to *hurry; to be eager*
2648 châphaz (2), to *hasten* away, to *fear*
4116 mâhar (14), to *hurry; promptly*
4692 spĕudō (1), to *urge* on diligently

HASTEN
2363 chûwsh (4), to *hurry; to be eager*
4116 mâhar (3), to *hurry; promptly*
8245 shâqad (1), to *be alert, i.e. sleepless*

HASTENED
213 'ûwts (2), to *be close, hurry, withdraw*
926 bâhal (1), to *hasten, hurry anxiously*
1765 dâchaph (1), to *urge; to hasten*
4116 mâhar (2), to *hurry; promptly*

HASTENETH
4116 mâhar (1), to *hurry; promptly*

HASTETH
213 'ûwts (1), to *be close, hurry, withdraw*
926 bâhal (1), to *hasten, hurry anxiously*
2363 chûwsh (1), to *hurry; to be eager*
2648 châphaz (1), to *hasten* away, to *fear*
2907 tûws (1), to *pounce* or *swoop upon*
4116 mâhar (3), to *hurry; promptly*
7602 shâ'aph (1), to be *angry; to hasten*

HASTILY
926 bâhal (1), to *hasten, hurry anxiously*
4116 mâhar (2), to *hurry; promptly*
4118 mahêr (2), *in a hurry*
4120 mᵉhêrâh (1), *hurry; promptly*
7323 rûwts (1), to *run*

5030 tachĕŏs (1), *speedily, rapidly*

HASTING
4106 mâhîyr (1), *skillful*
4692 spĕudō (1), to *urge* on diligently

HASTY
213 'ûwts (2), to *be close, hurry, withdraw*
926 bâhal (2), to *hasten, hurry anxiously*
1061 bikkûwr (1), *first-fruits* of the crop
2685 chătsaph (Ch.) (1), to *be severe*
4116 mâhar (2), to *hurry; promptly*
7116 qâtsêr (1), *short*

HASUPHA
2817 Chăsûwphâ' (1), *nakedness*

HATACH
2047 Hăthâk (4), *Hathak*

HATCH
1234 bâqa' (2), to *cleave, break, tear open*

HATCHETH
3205 yâlad (1), to *bear young; to father a child*

HATE
7852 sâtam (2), to *persecute*
8130 sânê (67), to *hate*
8131 sᵉnê (Ch.) (1), *enemy*
3404 misĕō (16), to *detest, to love less*

HATED
7852 sâtam (2), to *persecute*
8130 sânê (42), to *hate*
8135 sin'âh (2), *hate, malice*
8146 sânîy' (1), *hated*
3404 misĕō (12), to *detest; to love less*

HATEFUL
8130 sânê (1), to *hate*
3404 misĕō (1), to *detest, persecute; to love less*
4767 stugnētŏs (1), *hated, i.e. odious*

HATEFULLY
8135 sin'âh (1), *hate, malice*

HATERS
8130 sânê (1), to *hate*
2319 thĕŏstugēs (1), *impious, God-hating*

HATEST
8130 sânê (5), to *hate*
3404 misĕō (1), to *detest, persecute; to love less*

HATETH
7852 sâtam (1), to *persecute*
8130 sânê (20), to *hate*
3404 misĕō (9), to *detest, persecute; to love less*

HATH
413 'êl (1), *to, toward*
1167 ba'al (3), *master; husband; owner; citizen*

1172 ba'ălâh (2), *mistress; female owner*
1933 hăvâ' (1), to *be*, to *exist*
1961 hâyâh (6), to *exist*, i.e. *be* or *become*
3426 yêsh (3), *there is* or *are*
4672 mâtsâ' (1), to *find* or *acquire*; to *occur, meet* or *be present*
2192 ĕchō (128), to *have; hold; keep*
5220 hupandrŏs (1), *married* woman
5224 huparchŏnta (2), *property* or *possessions*

HATHATH
2867 Chăthath (1), *dismay*

HATING
8130 sânê' (1), to *hate*
3404 misĕŏ (2), to *detest, persecute*; to *love less*

HATIPHA
2412 Chătîyphâ' (2), *robber*

HATITA
2410 Chătîyţa' (2), *explorer*

HATRED
342 'êybâh (2), *hostility*
4895 masţêmâh (2), *enmity*
8135 sin'âh (13), *hate, malice*
2189 ĕchthra (1), *hostility; opposition*

HATS
3737 karbᵉlâ' (Ch.) (1), *mantle*

HATTIL
2411 Chaţţîyl (2), *fluctuating*

HATTUSH
2407 Chaţţûwsh (5), *Chattush*

HAUGHTILY
7317 rôwmâh (1), *proudly*

HAUGHTINESS
1346 ga'ăvâh (2), *arrogance; majesty*
7312 rûwm (3), *elevation; elation*

HAUGHTY
1361 gâbahh (5), to *be lofty*; to *be haughty*
1363 gôbahh (1), *height; grandeur; arrogance*
1364 gâbôahh (1), *high; powerful; arrogant*
3093 yâhîyr (2), *arrogant*
4791 mârôwm (1), *elevation; haughtiness*
7311 rûwm (1), to *be high*; to *rise* or *raise*

HAUNT
1980 hâlak (1), to *walk; live a certain way*
3427 yâshab (1), to *dwell*, to *remain*; to *settle*
7272 regel (1), *foot; step*

HAURAN
2362 Chavrân (2), *cavernous*

HAVE
270 'âchaz (1), to *seize, grasp; possess*
383 'îythay (Ch.) (3), *there is*
935 bôw' (1), to *go, come*
1167 ba'al (1), *master; husband; owner; citizen*
1934 hăvâ' (Ch.) (2), to *be*, to *exist*
1961 hâyâh (87), to *exist*, i.e. *be* or *become*
3045 yâda' (2), to *know*
3318 yâtsâ' (3), to *go, bring out*
3426 yêsh (12), *there is*
3947 lâqach (1), to *take*
4672 mâtsâ' (1), to *find* or *acquire*; to *occur*
5307 nâphal (1), to *fall*
5375 nâsâ' (1), to *lift up*
5674 'âbar (1), to *cross over; to transition*
5921 'al (1), *above, over, upon,* or *against*
474 antiballō (1), to *exchange words*
568 apĕchō (4), to *be distant*
1096 ginŏmai (1), to *be, become*
1099 glukus (1), *sweet, fresh*
1526 ĕisi (1), *they are*
1699 ĕmŏs (1), *my*
1751 ĕnĕimi (1), to *be within*
2070 ĕsmĕn (1), *we are*
2071 ĕsŏmai (6), *will be*
2076 ĕsti (11), *he (she or it) is; they are*
2192 ĕchō (266), to *have; hold; keep*
2701 katatrĕchō (1), to *hasten, run*
2983 lambanō (1), to *take, receive*
3335 mĕtalambanō (1), to *accept and use*
3918 parĕimi (1), to *be present; to have come*
5224 huparchŏnta (1), *property* or *possessions*
5225 huparchō (1), to *come into existence*

HAVEN
2348 chôwph (2), *cove, sheltered bay*
4231 mâchôwz (1), *harbor*
3040 limēn (2), *harbor*

HAVENS
2568 Kalŏi Limĕnĕs (1), *Good Harbors*

HAVILAH
2341 Chăvîylâh (7), *circular*

HAVING
1167 ba'al (2), *master; husband; owner; citizen*
5414 nâthan (1), to *give*
1746 ĕnduŏ (1), to *dress*
2192 ĕchō (85), to *have; hold; keep*

HAVOCK
3075 lumainŏmai (1), to *insult, maltreat*

HAVOTH-JAIR
2334 Chavvôwth Yâ'îyr (2), *hamlets of Jair*

HAWK
5322 nêts (3), *flower; hawk*
8464 tachmâç (2), *unclean bird* (poss.) *owl*

HAY
2682 châtsîyr (2), *grass; leek* plant
5528 chŏrtŏs (1), *pasture, herbage* or *vegetation*

HAZAEL
2371 Chăzâ'êl (23), *God has seen*

HAZAIAH
2382 Chăzâyâh (1), *Jehovah has seen*

HAZAR-ADDAR
2692 Chătsar 'Addâr (1), *village of Addar*

HAZAR-ENAN
2703 Chătsar 'Êynôwn (1), *village of springs*
2704 Chătsar 'Êynân (3), *village of springs*

HAZAR-GADDAH
2693 Chătsar Gaddâh (1), *village of Fortune*

HAZAR-HATTICON
2694 Chătsar hat-Tîykôwn (1), *village of the middle*

HAZAR-SHUAL
2705 Chătsar Shûw'âl (4), *village of* (the) *fox*

HAZAR-SUSAH
2701 Chătsar Çûwçâh (1), *village of cavalry*

HAZAR-SUSIM
2702 Chătsar Çûwçîym (1), *village of horses*

HAZARDED
3860 paradidōmi (1), to *hand over*

HAZARMAVETH
2700 Chătsarmâveth (2), *village of death*

HAZAZON-TAMAR
2688 Chatsᵉtsôwn Tâmâr (1), *row of* (the) *palm-tree*

HAZEL
3869 lûwz (1), *nut*-tree, (poss.) *almond*

HAZELELPONI
6753 Tsᵉlelpôwnîy (1), *shade-facing*

HAZERIM
2699 Chătsêrîym (1), *yards*

HAZEROTH
2698 Chătsêrowth (6), *yards*

HAZEZON-TAMAR
2688 Chatsᵉtsôwn Tâmâr (1), *row of* (the) *palm-tree*

HAZIEL
2381 Chăzîy'êl (1), *seen of God*

HAZO
2375 Chăzow (1), *seer*

HAZOR
2674 Châtsôwr (18), *village*
2675 Châtsôwr Chădattâh (1), *new village*

HEAD
1270 barzel (2), *iron; iron implement*
1538 gulgôleth (1), *skull*
3852 lehâbâh (1), *flame; flash*
4763 mᵉra'ăshâh (1), *headpiece; head-rest*
6936 qodqôd (8), *crown of the head*
7217 rê'sh (Ch.) (11), *head*
7218 rô'sh (262), *head*
2775 kĕphalaiŏō (1), to *strike on the head*
2776 kĕphalē (55), *head*

HEADBANDS
7196 qishshûr (1), *girdle* or *sash for women*

HEADLONG
2630 katakrēmnizō (1), to *precipitate down*
4248 prēnēs (1), *head foremost, headlong*

HEADS
7217 rê'sh (Ch.) (1), *head*
7218 rô'sh (83), *head*
2776 kĕphalē (19), *head*

HEADSTONE
68+7222 'eben (1), *stone*

HEADY
4312 prŏpĕtēs (1), *falling forward headlong*

HEAL
7495 râphâ' (21), to *cure, heal*
1295 diasōzō (1), to *cure, preserve, rescue*
2323 thĕrapĕuō (10), to *relieve disease*
2390 iaŏmai (6), to *cure, heal*
2392 iasis (2), *curing*

HEALED
5414+7499 nâthan (1), to *give*
7495 râphâ' (31), to *cure, heal*
2323 thĕrapĕuō (25), to *relieve disease*
2390 iaŏmai (18), to *cure, heal*
4982 sōzō (3), to *deliver*; to *protect*

HEALER
2280 châbash (1), to *wrap firmly, bind*

HEALETH
7495 râphâ' (4), to *cure, heal*

HEALING
3545 kêhâh (1), *alleviation,* i.e. a *cure*
4832 marpê' (3), *cure; deliverance; placidity*
8585 tᵉ'âlâh (1), *bandage* or *plaster*

2322 thĕrapĕia (2), *cure,*
healing; domestics
2323 thĕrapĕuō (3), *to*
relieve disease
2386 iama (2), *cure*
2390 iaŏmai (1), *to cure,*
heal
2392 iasis (1), *curing*

HEALINGS
2386 iama (1), *cure*

HEALTH
724 'ărûwkâh (4),
wholeness, health
3444 yᵉshûw'âh (2), *aid;*
victory; prosperity
4832 marpê' (5), *cure;*
deliverance; placidity
7500 riph'ûwth (1), *cure,*
healing
7965 shâlôwm (2), *safe;*
well; health, prosperity
4491 rhiza (1), *root*
5198 hugiainō (1), *to*
have sound health

HEAP
1530 gal (12), *heap; ruins*
2266 châbar (1), *to*
fascinate by spells
2563 chômer (1), *clay;*
dry measure
2846 châthâh (1), *to lay*
hold of; to pick up fire
3664 kânaç (1), *to*
collect; to enfold
4596 mᵉ'îy (1), *pile of*
rubbish, ruin
5067 nêd (6), *mound,*
heap, dam
5595 çâphâh (1), *to*
scrape; to accumulate
5856 'îy (1), *ruin; rubble*
6194 'ârêm (3), *heap,*
mound; sheaf
6651 tsâbar (2), *to*
aggregate, gather
7235 râbâh (1), *to*
increase
7760 sûwm (1), *to put,*
place
8510 têl (4), *mound*
2002 ĕpisōrĕuō (1), *to*
accumulate further
4987 sōrĕuō (1), *to pile*
up, load up

HEAPED
6651 tsâbar (1), *to*
aggregate, gather
2343 thēsaurizō (1), *to*
amass or reserve, store

HEAPETH
6651 tsâbar (1), *to*
aggregate, gather
6908 qâbats (1), *to*
collect, assemble

HEAPS
1530 gal (6), *heap; ruins*
2563 chômer (1), *clay;*
dry measure
2565 chămôrâh (1), *heap*
5856 'îy (3), *ruin; rubble*
6194 'ârêm (6), *heap,*
mound; sheaf
6632 tsâb (1), *lizard;*
covered cart
8564 tamrûwr (1),
erection, i.e. pillar

HEAR
238 'âzan (2), *to listen*
2045 hâshmâ'ûwth (1),
communication
6030 'ânâh (28), *to*
respond, answer
7181 qâshab (1), *to prick*
up the ears
8085 shâma' (364), *to*
hear
8086 shᵉma' (Ch.) (4), *to*
hear
191 akŏuō (131), *to hear;*
obey
1251 diakŏuŏmai (1), *to*
patiently listen
1522 ĕisakŏuō (1), *to*
listen to
3878 parakŏuō (2), *to*
disobey

HEARD
6030 'ânâh (11), *to*
respond, answer
7181 qâshab (1), *to prick*
up the ears
8085 shâma' (376), *to*
hear
8086 shᵉma' (Ch.) (4), *to*
hear
189 akŏē (1), *hearing;*
thing heard
191 akŏuō (239), *to hear;*
obey
1522 ĕisakŏuō (4), *to*
listen to
1873 ĕpakŏuō (1), *to*
hearken favorably to
1874 ĕpakrŏaŏmai (1), *to*
listen intently to
4257 prŏakŏuō (1), *to*
hear beforehand

HEARDEST
6030 'ânâh (1), *to*
respond, answer
8085 shâma' (11), *to hear*

HEARER
202 akrŏatēs (2), *hearer*

HEARERS
191 akŏuō (2), *to hear;*
obey
202 akrŏatēs (2), *hearer*

HEAREST
6030 'ânâh (1), *to*
respond, answer
8085 shâma' (6), *to hear*
191 akŏuō (4), *to hear;*
obey

HEARETH
8085 shâma' (29), *to hear*
191 akŏuō (22), *to hear;*
obey

HEARING
241 'ôzen (5), *ear*
4926 mishmâ' (1), *report*
7182 qesheb (1),
hearkening
8085 shâma' (6), *to hear*
8088 shēma' (1),
something heard
189 akŏē (10), *hearing;*
thing heard
191 akŏuō (13), *to hear;*
obey
201 akrŏatēriŏn (1),
audience-room

1233 diagnōsis (1),
magisterial
examination

HEARKEN
238 'âzan (5), *to listen*
7181 qâshab (21), *to*
prick up the ears
8085 shâma' (119), *to*
hear
191 akŏuō (6), *to hear;*
obey
1801 ĕnōtizŏmai (1), *to*
take in one's ear
5219 hupakŏuō (1), *to*
listen attentively

HEARKENED
238 'âzan (1), *to listen*
7181 qâshab (5), *to prick*
up the ears
8085 shâma' (74), *to hear*
3980 pĕitharchĕō (1), *to*
submit to authority

HEARKENEDST
8085 shâma' (1), *to hear*

HEARKENETH
8085 shâma' (2), *to hear*

HEARKENING
8085 shâma' (1), *to hear*

HEART
1079 bâl (Ch.) (1), *heart,*
mind
3820 lêb (479), *heart*
3821 lêb (Ch.) (1), *heart*
3823 lâbab (2), *to*
transport with love
3824 lêbâb (207), *heart*
3825 lᵉbab (Ch.) (7), *heart*
3826 libbâh (2), *heart*
4578 mê'âh (1), *viscera;*
anguish, tenderness
5315 nephesh (12), *life;*
breath; soul; wind
7130 qereb (1), *nearest*
part, i.e. the center
7907 sekvîy (1), *mind*
2588 kardia (101), *heart,*
i.e. thoughts or feelings
4641 sklērŏkardia (2),
hard-heartedness
5590 psuchē (1), *soul,*
vitality; heart, mind

HEART'S
3820 lêb (1), *heart*
5315 nephesh (1), *life;*
breath; soul; wind
2588 kardia (1), *heart,*
i.e. thoughts or feelings

HEARTED
3820 lêb (8), *heart*

HEARTH
254 'âch (3), *fire-pot*
3344 yâqad (1), *to burn*
3595 kîyôwr (1), *dish;*
caldron; washbowl
4168 môwqêd (1),
conflagration, burning

HEARTILY
1537+5590 ĕk (1), *out, out*
of

HEARTS
3820 lêb (21), *heart*
3824 lêbâb (22), *heart*
3826 libbâh (6), *heart*
5315 nephesh (2), *life;*
breath; soul; wind

674 apŏpsuchō (1), *to*
faint
2588 kardia (57), *heart,*
i.e. thoughts or feelings
2589 kardiŏgnōstēs (2),
heart-knower
4641 sklērŏkardia (1),
hard-heartedness

HEARTS'
3820 lêb (1), *heart*

HEARTY
5315 nephesh (1), *life;*
breath; soul; wind

HEAT
228 'ăzâ' (Ch.) (1), *to heat*
2527 chôm (9), *heat*
2534 chêmâh (1), *heat;*
anger; poison
2535 chammâh (1), *heat*
of sun
2552 châmam (2), *to be*
hot; to be in a rage
2721 chôreb (6),
parched; ruined
2750 chŏrîy (1), *burning*
anger
3179 yâcham (1), *to*
conceive
7565 resheph (1), *flame*
8273 shârâb (1), *glow of*
the hot air; mirage
2329 thĕrmē (1), *warmth,*
heat
2738 kauma (2),
scorching heat
2741 kausŏō (2), *to set*
on fire
2742 kausōn (3), *burning*
heat, hot day

HEATED
228 'ăzâ' (Ch.) (1), *to heat*
1197 bâ'ar (1), *to be*
brutish, be senseless

HEATH
6176 'ărôw'êr (2), *juniper*
bush

HEATHEN
1471 gôwy (143), *foreign*
nation; Gentiles
1482 ĕthnikŏs (2), *Gentile*
1484 ĕthnŏs (5), *race;*
tribe; pagan

HEAVE
7311 rûwm (1), *to be*
high; to rise or raise
8641 tᵉrûwmâh (28),
sacrifice, tribute

HEAVED
7311 rûwm (3), *to be*
high; to rise or raise

HEAVEN
1534 galgal (1), *wheel;*
something round
7834 shachaq (2),
firmament, clouds
8064 shâmayim (285),
sky; unseen celestial
places
8065 shâmayin (Ch.) (35),
sky; unseen celestial
places
2032 ĕpŏuraniŏs (1),
above the sky, celestial
3321 mĕsŏuranēma (3),
mid-sky, mid-heaven

3771 ŏuranŏthĕn (2), from the *sky* or *heaven*
3772 ŏuranŏs (248), *sky; air; heaven*

HEAVEN'S
3772 ŏuranŏs (1), *sky; air; heaven*

HEAVENLY
1537+3772 ĕk (1), *out, out of*
2032 ĕpŏuraniŏs (16), *above the sky, celestial*
3770 ŏuraniŏs (6), *belonging to or coming from the sky or heaven*

HEAVENS
6160 'ărâbâh (1), *desert, wasteland*
6183 'ărîyph (1), *sky*
8064 shâmayim (107), *sky; unseen celestial places*
8065 shâmayin (Ch.) (3), *sky; unseen celestial places*
3772 ŏuranŏs (19), *sky; air; heaven*

HEAVIER
3513 kâbad (3), to be *heavy, severe, dull*

HEAVILY
3513 kâbad (1), to be *heavy, severe, dull*
3517 kᵉbêdûth (1), *difficulty*
6957 qav (1), *rule* for measuring; *rim*

HEAVINESS
1674 dᵉ'âgâh (1), *anxiety*
3544 kêheh (1), *feeble; obscure*
5136 nûwsh (1), to be *sick*
6440 pânîym (1), *face; front*
8386 ta'ănîyâh (1), *lamentation*
8424 tûwgâh (3), *depression; grief*
8589 ta'ănîyth (1), *affliction* of self, *fasting*
85 adēmŏnĕō (1), to be in mental *distress*
2726 katēphĕia (1), *sadness, dejection*
3076 lupĕō (1), to *distress; to be sad*
3077 lupē (2), *sadness, grief*

HEAVY
3513 kâbad (16), to be *heavy, severe, dull*
3514 kôbed (2), *weight, multitude, vehemence*
3515 kâbêd (3), *severe, difficult, stupid*
4133 môwṭâh (1), *pole; ox-bow; yoke*
4751 mar (1), *bitter; bitterness; bitterly*
5620 çar (2), *peevish, sullen*
7186 qâsheh (1), *severe*
7451 ra' (1), *bad; evil*
85 adēmŏnĕō (2), to be in mental *distress*
916 barĕō (3), to *weigh down, cause pressure*

926 barus (1), *weighty*

HEBER
2268 Cheber (10), *community*
5677 'Êber (2), *regions beyond*
1443 Ēbĕr (1), *regions beyond*

HEBER'S
2268 Cheber (1), *community*

HEBERITES
2277 Chebrîy (1), *Chebrite*

HEBREW
5680 'Ibrîy (14), *Eberite* (i.e. Hebrew)
1444 Hĕbraïkŏs (1), *Hebraïc* or the *Jewish* language
1446 Hĕbraïs (4), *Hebrew* or *Jewish* language
1447 Hĕbraïsti (1), *Hebraistically* or in the *Jewish* language

HEBREWESS
5680 'Ibrîy (1), *Eberite* (i.e. Hebrew)

HEBREWS
5680 'Ibrîy (17), *Eberite* (i.e. Hebrew)
1445 Hĕbraiŏs (3), *Hebrew* or *Jew*

HEBREWS'
5680 'Ibrîy (1), *Eberite* (i.e. Hebrew)

HEBRON
2275 Chebrôwn (72), *seat of association*

HEBRONITES
2276 Chebrôwnîy (6), *Chebronite*

HEDGE
1447 gâdêr (3), *enclosure, wall* or *fence*
4534 mᵉçûwkâh (1), *thorn-hedge*
4881 mᵉsûwkâh (2), *thorn hedge*
7753 sûwk (2), to *shut* in with hedges
5418 phragmŏs (1), *fence* or enclosing *barrier*

HEDGED
1443 gâdar (1), to *build a* stone *wall*
5526 çâkak (1), to *entwine; to fence* in
5418+4060 phragmŏs (1), *fence* or *barrier*

HEDGES
1447 gâdêr (1), *enclosure, wall* or *fence*
1448 gᵉdêrâh (4), *enclosure* for flocks
5418 phragmŏs (1), *fence* or enclosing *barrier*

HEED
238 'âzan (1), to *listen*
2095 zᵉhar (Ch.) (1), *be admonished, be careful*
5414+3820 nâthan (1), to *give*
5535 çâkath (1), to be *silent*

7181 qâshab (3), to *prick up* the ears
7182 qesheb (1), *hearkening*
7200 râ'âh (2), to *see*
8104 shâmar (35), to *watch*
433 anēkō (1), *be proper, fitting*
991 blĕpō (14), to *look at*
1907 ĕpĕchō (2), to *detain; to pay attention*
3708 hŏraō (5), to *stare, see clearly; to discern*
4337 prŏsĕchō (11), to *pay attention to*
4648 skŏpĕō (1), to *watch out for,* i.e. to *regard*

HEEL
6117 'âqab (1), to *seize by the heel; to circumvent*
6119 'âqêb (4), *track, footprint; rear* position
4418 ptērna (1), *heel*

HEELS
6119 'âqêb (2), *track, footprint; rear* position
6120 'âqêb (1), *one who lies in wait*
8328 sheresh (1), *root*

HEGAI
1896 Hêgê' (3), *Hege* or *Hegai*

HEGE
1896 Hêgê' (1), *Hege* or *Hegai*

HEIFER
5697 'eglâh (11), *cow calf*
6510 pârâh (6), *heifer*
1151 damalis (1), *heifer*

HEIFER'S
5697 'eglâh (1), *cow calf*

HEIGHT
1361 gâbahh (2), to be *lofty; to be haughty*
1363 gôbahh (8), *height; grandeur; arrogance*
1364 gâbôahh (2), *high; powerful; arrogant*
4791 mârôwm (9), *elevation; elation*
6967 qôwmâh (30), *height*
7218 rô'sh (1), *head*
7312 rûwm (2), *elevation; elation*
7314 rûwm (Ch.) (4), *altitude, tallness*
7419 râmûwth (1), *heap* of carcases
5311 hupsŏs (2), *altitude; sky; dignity*
5313 hupsōma (1), *altitude; barrier*

HEIGHTS
1116 bâmâh (1), *elevation, high place*
4791 mârôwm (1), *elevation; elation*

HEINOUS
2154 zimmâh (1), *bad plan*

HEIR
3423 yârash (9), to *inherit; to impoverish*
2816 klērŏnŏmĕō (1), to *be an heir* to, *inherit*

2818 klērŏnŏmŏs (8), *possessor by inheritance*

HEIRS
3423 yârash (1), to *inherit; to impoverish*
2816 klērŏnŏmĕō (1), to *be an heir* to, *inherit*
2818 klērŏnŏmŏs (7), *possessor by inheritance*
4789 sugklērŏnŏmŏs (2), *participant in common*

HELAH
2458 Chel'âh (2), *rust*

HELAM
2431 Chêylâm (2), *fortress*

HELBAH
2462 Chelbâh (1), *fertility*

HELBON
2463 Chelbôwn (1), *fruitful*

HELD
270 'âchaz (3), to *seize, grasp; possess*
631 'âçar (1), to *fasten; to join* battle
1102 bâlam (1), to *muzzle, control*
1826 dâmam (1), to be *silent; to be astonished*
2244 châbâ' (1), to *secrete*
2388 châzaq (6), to *fasten* upon; to *seize*
2790 chârash (10), to *engrave; to plow*
2814 châshâh (2), to *hush* or *keep quiet*
2820 châsak (1), to *restrain or refrain*
3447 yâshaṭ (2), to *extend*
3557 kûwl (1), to *keep in; to measure*
5582 çâ'ad (1), to *support*
6213 'âsâh (1), to *do*
6901 qâbal (1), to *admit; to take*
7311 rûwm (2), to be *high; to rise or raise*
8557 temeç (1), *melting disappearance*
2192 ĕchō (1), to *have; hold; keep*
2258 ēn (1), I *was*
2270 hēsuchazō (2), to *refrain*
2722 katĕchō (1), to *hold down fast*
2902 kratĕō (2), to *seize*
2983 lambanō (1), to *take, receive*
4160 pŏiĕō (1), to *make*
4601 sigaō (2), to *keep silent*
4623 siōpaō (4), to be *quiet*
4912 sunĕchō (1), to *hold together*

HELDAI
2469 Chelday (2), *worldliness*

HELEB
2460 Chêleb (1), *fatness*

HELED
2466 Chêled (1), *fleeting time; this world*

HELEK
2507 Chêleq (2), *portion*

HELEKITES
2516 Chelqîy (1), *Chelkite*

HELEM
2494 Chêlem (2), *dream*

HELEPH
2501 Cheleph (1), *change*

HELEZ
2503 Chelets (5), *strength*

HELI
2242 Hêli (1), *lofty*

HELKAI
2517 Chelqay (1), *apportioned*

HELKATH
2520 Chelqath (2), *smoothness*

HELKATH-HAZZURIM
2521 Chelqath hats-Tsûrîym (1), *smoothness of the rocks*

HELL
7585 sheʼôwl (31), *abode of the dead*
86 haₗdēs (10), *Hades, i.e. place of the dead*
1067 gěěnna (12), *valley of (the son of) Hinnom,* fig. *hell*
5020 tartaróō (1), *to incarcerate in Tartaros*

HELM
4079 pēdalión (1), *blade of an oar which steers*

HELMET
3553 kôwbaʼ (4), *helmet*
6959 qôwbaʼ (2), *helmet*
4030 pěrikěphalaia (2), *helmet*

HELMETS
3553 kôwbaʼ (2), *helmet*

HELON
2497 Chêlôn (5), *strong*

HELP
2388 châzaq (2), *to fasten upon; to seize*
3444 yeshûwʼâh (2), *deliverance; aid*
3447 yâshaṭ (1), *to extend*
3467 yâshaʼ (9), *to make safe, free*
5375 nâsâʼ (1), *to lift up*
5800 ʼâzab (2), *to loosen; relinquish; permit*
5826 ʼâzar (44), *to protect or aid*
5828 ʼêzer (21), *aid*
5833 ʼezrâh (24), *aid*
6965 qûwm (2), *to rise*
7125 qîrʼâh (1), *to encounter, to happen*
8668 teshûwʼâh (5), *rescue, deliverance*
996 bŏēthĕia (1), *aid*
997 bŏēthĕō (5), *to aid or relieve*
1947 ĕpikŏuria (1), *assistance, aid*
4815 sullambanō (2), *to conceive; to aid*

HELPED
3467 yâshaʼ (2), *to make safe, free*
5375 nâsâʼ (1), *to lift up*
5826 ʼâzar (18), *to protect or aid*
5833 ʼezrâh (1), *aid*
997 bŏēthĕō (1), *to aid or relieve*
4820 sumballō (1), *to aid; to join, attack*

HELPER
5826 ʼâzar (7), *to protect or aid*
998 bŏēthŏs (1), *succorer, helper*
4904 sunĕrgŏs (1), *fellow-worker*

HELPERS
5826 ʼâzar (4), *to protect or aid*
5833 ʼezrâh (1), *aid*
4904 sunĕrgŏs (2), *fellow-worker*

HELPETH
5826 ʼâzar (2), *to protect or aid*
4878 sunantilambanŏmai (1), *co-operate, assist*
4903 sunĕrgĕō (1), *to be a fellow-worker*

HELPING
3467 yâshaʼ (1), *to make safe, free*
5582 çâʼad (1), *to support*
4943 sunupŏurgĕō (1), *assist, join to help*

HELPS
484 antilēpsis (1), *relief, aid*
996 bŏēthĕia (1), *aid*

HELVE
6086 ʼêts (1), *wood, things made of wood*

HEM
7757 shûwl (5), *skirt; bottom edge*
2899 kraspĕdŏn (2), *margin*

HEMAM
1967 Hêymâm (1), *raging*

HEMAN
1968 Hêymân (16), *faithful*

HEMATH
2574 Chămâth (3), *walled*

HEMDAN
2533 Chemdân (1), *pleasant*

HEMLOCK
3939 laʼănâh (1), *poisonous wormwood*
7219 rôʼsh (1), *poisonous plant; poison*

HEMS
7757 shûwl (1), *skirt; bottom edge*

HEN
2581 Chên (1), *grace*
3733 ŏrnis (2), *hen*

HENA
2012 Hênaʼ (3), *Hena*

HENADAD
2582 Chênâdâd (4), *favor of Hadad*

HENCE
2088 zeh (14), *this or that*
3212 yâlak (1), *to walk; to live; to carry*
3318 yâtsâʼ (1), *to go, bring out*
1782 ĕntĕuthĕn (9), *hence, from here*
1821 ĕxapŏstĕllō (1), *to despatch,* or *to dismiss*
3326+5025 mĕta (1), *with, among; after, later*
5217 hupagō (1), *to withdraw or retire*

HENCEFORTH
3254 yâçaph (5), *to add or augment*
5750 ʼôwd (2), *again; repeatedly; still; more*
6258 ʼattâh (5), *at this time, now*
534 aparti (1), *henceforth, from now*
575+737 apŏ (2), *from, away*
575+3588+3568 apŏ (1), *from, away*
737 arti (1), *just now; at once*
2089 ĕti (1), *yet, still*
3063 lŏipŏn (4), *remaining; finally*
3371 mĕkĕti (4), *no further*
3568 nun (4), *now; the present or immediate*
3765 ŏukĕti (1), *not yet, no longer*

HENCEFORWARD
1973 hâlʼâh (1), *far away; thus far*
3371 mĕkĕti (1), *no further*

HENOCH
2585 Chănôwk (2), *initiated*

HEPHER
2660 Chêpher (9), *pit or shame*

HEPHERITES
2662 Chephrîy (1), *Chephrite*

HEPHZI-BAH
2657 Chephtsîy bâhh (2), *my delight* (is) *in her*

HERALD
3744 kârôwz (Ch.) (1), *herald*

HERB
1877 desheʼ (6), *sprout; green grass*
2682 châtsîyr (1), *grass; leek plant*
6212 ʼeseb (12), *grass, or any green, tender shoot*

HERBS
216 ʼôwr (1), *luminary; lightning; happiness*
219 ʼôwrâh (2), *luminousness, light*
3419 yârâq (3), *vegetable greens*

HEREIN
6212 ʼeseb (5), *grass, or any green, tender shoot*
1008 bŏtanĕ (1), *grazing herbage, vegetation*
3001 lachanŏn (4), *vegetable*

HERD
1241 bâqâr (14), *plowing ox; herd*
34 agĕlĕ (8), *drove, herd*

HERDMAN
951 bôwkêr (1), *herder, cattle-tender*

HERDMEN
5349 nôqêd (1), *owner or tender of sheep*
7462 râʼâh (6), *to tend a flock, i.e. pasture it*

HERDS
1241 bâqâr (30), *plowing ox; herd*
4735 miqneh (1), *live-stock*
5739 ʼêder (2), *muster, flock*

HERE
645 ʼêphôw (1), *then*
1988 hălôm (2), *hither, to here*
2005 hên (5), *lo!; if!*
2008 hênnâh (2), *from here; from there*
2009 hinnêh (12), *lo!; Look!*
2088 zeh (12), *this or that*
2236 zâraq (1), *to sprinkle, scatter*
3541 kôh (4), *thus*
4672 mâtsâʼ (1), *to find or acquire; to occur,*
6311 pôh (43), *here or hence*
8033 shâm (2), *where, there*
8552 tâmam (1), *to complete, finish*
848 hautŏu (1), *self*
1759 ĕnthadĕ (3), *here, hither*
3918 parĕimi (2), *to be present; to have come*
3936 paristĕmi (1), *to stand beside, present*
4840 sumparĕimi (1), *to be at hand together*
5602 hŏdĕ (44), *here or hither*

HEREAFTER
268 ʼâchôwr (1), *behind, backward; west*
310 ʼachar (1), *after*
737 arti (1), *just now; at once*
2089 ĕti (1), *yet, still*
3195 mĕllō (1), *to intend, i.e. be about to*
3370 Mēdŏs (1), *inhabitant of Media*

HEREBY
2063 zôʼth (4), *this*
1537+5124 ĕk (1), *out, out of*
1722+5129 ĕn (8), *in; during; because of*

HEREIN
2063 zôʼth (1), *this*

5921+2063 'al (1), *above, over, upon,* or *against*
1722+5129 ĕn (7), *in; during; because of*

HEREOF
3778 hŏutŏs (1), *this* or *that*
5026 tautē̦ (1), *(toward* or *of) this*

HERES
2776 Chereç (1), *shining*

HERESH
2792 Cheresh (1), *magical craft; silence*

HERESIES
139 hairĕsis (3), *party, sect; disunion* or *heresy*

HERESY
139 hairĕsis (1), *party, sect; disunion* or *heresy*

HERETICK
141 hairĕtikŏs (1), *schismatic, division*

HERETOFORE
865 'ethmôwl (1), *heretofore, formerly*
8543 tᵉmôwl (6), *yesterday*
4258 prŏamartanō (1), *to sin previously*

HEREUNTO
1519+5124 ĕis (1), *to* or *into*

HEREWITH
2063 zō'th (2), *this*

HERITAGE
3425 yᵉrushâh (1), *conquest*
4181 môwrâshâh (1), *possession*
5157 nâchal (1), *to inherit*
5159 nachălâh (26), *occupancy*
2819 klērŏs (1), *lot, portion*

HERITAGES
5159 nachălâh (1), *occupancy*

HERMAS
2057 Hĕrmas (1), *born of god Hermes*

HERMES
2060 Hĕrmēs (1), *born of god Hermes*

HERMOGENES
2061 Hĕrmŏgĕnēs (1), *born of god Hermes*

HERMON
2768 Chermôwn (13), *abrupt*

HERMONITES
2769 Chermôwnîym (1), *peaks of Hermon*

HEROD
2264 Hērōdēs (40), *heroic*

HEROD'S
2264 Hērōdēs (4), *heroic*

HERODIANS
2265 Hērōdianŏi (3), *Herodians*

HERODIAS
2266 Hērōdias (4), *heroic*

HERODIAS'
2266 Hērōdias (2), *heroic*

HERODION
2267 Hērōdiōn (1), *heroic*

HERON
601 'ănâphâh (2), *(poss.) parrot*

HESED
2618 Cheçed (1), *favor*

HESHBON
2809 Cheshbôwn (38), *contrivance; plan*

HESHMON
2829 Cheshmôwn (1), *opulent*

HETH
2845 Chêth (14), *terror*

HETHLON
2855 Chethlôn (2), *enswathed*

HEW
1414 gᵉdad (Ch.) (2), *to cut* down
1438 gâda' (1), *to fell* a tree; *to destroy*
2404 châṭab (1), *to chop* or *carve* wood
2672 châtsab (2), *to cut* stone or *carve* wood
3772 kârath (3), *to cut* (off, down or asunder)
6458 pâçal (3), *to carve, to chisel*

HEWED
1496 gâzîyth (5), *dressed* stone
2672 châtsab (3), *to cut* stone or *carve* wood
4274 machtsêb (1), *quarry* stone
5408 nâthach (1), *to dismember, cut up*
6458 pâçal (2), *to carve, to chisel*
8158 shâçaph (1), *to hack* in pieces, i.e. *kill*

HEWER
2404 châṭab (1), *to chop* or *carve* wood

HEWERS
2404 châṭab (5), *to chop* or *carve* wood
2672 châtsab (4), *to cut* stone or *carve* wood

HEWETH
2672 châtsab (2), *to cut* stone or *carve* wood
3772 kârath (1), *to cut* (off, down or asunder)

HEWN
1438 gâda' (1), *to fell* a tree; *to destroy*
1496 gâzîyth (5), *dressed* stone
2672 châtsab (2), *to cut* stone or *carve* wood
4274 machtsêb (2), *quarry* stone
7060 qâmal (1), *to wither*
1581 ĕkkŏptō (3), *to cut off; to frustrate*
2991 laxĕutŏs (1), *rock-quarried*
2998 latŏmĕō (2), *to quarry*

HEZEKI
2395 Chizqîy (1), *strong*

HEZEKIAH
2396 Chizqîyâh (128), *strengthened of Jehovah*

HEZION
2383 Chezyôwn (1), *vision*

HEZIR
2387 Chêzîyr (2), *protected*

HEZRAI
2695 Chetsrôw (1), *enclosure*

HEZRO
2695 Chetsrôw (1), *enclosure*

HEZRON
2696 Chetsrôwn (17), *court-yard*

HEZRON'S
2696 Chetsrôwn (1), *court-yard*

HEZRONITES
2697 Chetsrôwnîy (2), *Chetsronite*

HID
2244 châbâ' (25), *to secrete*
2934 ṭâman (16), *to hide*
3582 kâchad (6), *to destroy; to hide*
3680 kâçâh (2), *to cover*
4301 maṭmôwn (2), *secret* storehouse
5641 çâthar (30), *to hide* by covering
5956 'âlam (11), *to veil* from sight, i.e. *conceal*
6845 tsâphan (8), *to hide; to hoard* or *reserve*
8587 ta'ălummâh (1), *secret*
613 apŏkruptō (5), *to keep secret, conceal*
614 apŏkruphŏs (2), *secret, hidden* things
1470 ĕgkruptō (2), *incorporate with, mix in*
2572 kaluptō (1), *to cover* up
2927 kruptŏs (3), *private, unseen*
2928 kruptō (10), *to conceal*
2990 lanthanō (2), *to lie hid; unwittingly*
3871 parakaluptō (1), *veil, be hidden*
4032 pĕrikruptō (1), *to conceal all around*

HIDDAI
1914 Hidday (1), *Hiddai*

HIDDEKEL
2313 Chiddeqel (2), *Tigris river*

HIDDEN
2664 châphas (1), *to seek; to mask*
2934 ṭâman (1), *to hide*
4301 maṭmôwn (1), *secret* storehouse
4710 mitspûn (1), *secret*

5341 nâtsar (1), *to guard; to conceal, hide*
5640 çâtham (1), *to stop* up; *to keep secret*
5956 'âlam (1), *to veil* from sight, i.e. *conceal*
6381 pâlâ' (1), *to be, make great, difficult*
6845 tsâphan (3), *to hide; to hoard* or *reserve*
613 apŏkruptō (1), *to keep secret, conceal*
2927 kruptŏs (3), *private, unseen*
2928 kruptō (1), *to conceal*
2990 lanthanō (1), *to lie hid; unwittingly*

HIDE
2244 châbâ' (6), *to secrete*
2247 châbah (5), *to hide*
2934 ṭâman (5), *to hide*
3582 kâchad (10), *to destroy; to hide*
3680 kâçâh (3), *to cover*
5127 nûwç (1), *to vanish* away, *flee*
5641 çâthar (33), *to hide* by covering
5785 'ôwr (2), *skin, leather*
5956 'âlam (8), *to veil* from sight, i.e. *conceal*
6004 'âmam (2), *to overshadow* by *huddling* together
6845 tsâphan (5), *to hide; to hoard* or *reserve*
2572 kaluptō (1), *to cover*
2928 kruptō (2), *to conceal*

HIDEST
5641 çâthar (5), *to hide* by covering
5956 'âlam (1), *to veil* from sight, i.e. *conceal*

HIDETH
2244 châbâ' (1), *to secrete*
2821 châshak (1), *to be dark; to darken*
2934 ṭâman (2), *to hide*
3680 kâçâh (1), *to cover*
5641 çâthar (5), *to hide* by covering
5848 'âṭaph (1), *to shroud, i.e. clothe*
5956 'âlam (2), *to veil* from sight, i.e. *conceal*
6845 tsâphan (1), *to hide; to hoard* or *reserve*
2928 kruptō (1), *to conceal*

HIDING
2253 chebyôwn (1), *concealment, hiding*
2934 ṭâman (1), *to hide*
4224 machăbê' (1), *refuge, shelter*
5643 çêther (3), *cover, shelter*

HIEL
2419 Chîy'êl (1), *living of God*

HIERAPOLIS
2404 Hiĕrapŏlis (1), *holy city*

HIGGAION
1902 higgâyôwn (1), *musical notation*

HIGH
376 'îysh (2), *man; male; someone*
753 'ôrek (1), *length*
1111 Bâlâq (1), *waster*
1116 bâmâh (99), *elevation, high place*
1361 gâbahh (4), *to be lofty; to be haughty*
1362 gâbâhh (3), *high; lofty*
1363 gôbahh (2), *height; grandeur; arrogance*
1364 gâbôahh (25), *high; powerful; arrogant*
1386 gabnôn (2), *peak of hills*
1419 gâdôwl (22), *great*
1870 derek (1), *road; course of life*
4546 meçillâh (1), *main thoroughfare; viaduct*
4605 ma'al (7), *upward, above, overhead*
4608 ma'ăleh (1), *elevation; platform*
4791 mârôwm (33), *elevation; elation*
4796 Mârôwth (1), *bitter springs*
4869 misgâb (4), high *refuge*
5375 nâsâ' (1), *to lift up*
5920 'al (3), *the Highest God*
5943 'illay (Ch.) (9), *the supreme God*
5945 'elyôwn (37), *loftier, higher; Supreme God*
5946 'elyôwn (Ch.) (4), *the Supreme God*
6381 pâlâ' (1), *to be, make great, difficult*
6877 tserîyach (1), *citadel*
6967 qôwmâh (5), *height*
7218 rô'sh (3), *head*
7311 rûwm (2), *to be high; to rise or raise*
7312 rûwm (3), *elevation; elation*
7315 rôwm (1), *aloft, on high*
7319 rôwmemâh (1), *exaltation, i.e. praise*
7413 râmâh (4), *height; high seat of idolatry*
7682 sâgab (6), *to be, make lofty; be safe*
8192 shâphâh (1), *to bare*
8203 Shephaṭyâh (2), *Jehovah has judged*
8205 shephîy (7), *bare hill or plain*
8564 tamrûwr (1), *erection, i.e. pillar*
8643 terûw'âh (1), *battle-cry; clangor*
507 anō (1), *upward or on the top, heavenward*
749 archiĕrĕus (59), *high-priest, chief priest*
2032 ĕpŏuraniŏs (1), *above the sky, celestial*
2409 hiĕrĕus (1), *priest*
3173 mĕgas (2), *great, many*

5308 hupsēlŏs (9), *lofty* in place or character
5310 hupsistŏs (5), the *Supreme God*
5311 hupsŏs (3), *altitude; sky; dignity*
5313 hupsōma (1), *altitude; barrier*

HIGHER
1354 gab (1), *mounded or rounded: top or rim*
1361 gâbahh (4), *to be lofty; to be haughty*
1364 gâbôahh (5), *high; powerful; arrogant*
3201 yâkôl (1), *to be able*
5945 'elyôwn (4), *loftier, higher; Supreme God*
6706 tsechîyach (1), *glaring*
7311 rûwm (2), *to be high; to rise or raise*
511 anōtĕrŏs (1), *upper part; former part*
5242 hupĕrĕchō (1), *to excel; superior*
5308 hupsēlŏs (1), *lofty*

HIGHEST
1364 gâbôahh (1), *high; powerful; arrogant*
4791 mârôwm (3), *elevation; elation*
5945 'elyôwn (3), *loftier, higher; Supreme God*
6788 tsammereth (2), *foliage*
7218 rô'sh (1), *head*
4410 prōtŏkathĕdria (1), *pre-eminence in council*
4411 prōtŏklisia (1), *pre-eminence at meals*
5310 hupsistŏs (8), the *Supreme God*

HIGHLY
1537+4053 ĕk (1), *out of*
2371 thumŏmachĕō (1), *to be exasperated*
5251 hupĕrupsŏō (1), *to raise to the highest*
5252 hupĕrphrŏnĕō (1), *to esteem oneself overmuch*
5308 hupsēlŏs (1), *lofty* in place or character

HIGHMINDED
5187 tuphŏō (1), *to inflate with self-conceit*
5309 hupsēlŏphrŏnĕō (2), *to be lofty in mind*

HIGHNESS
1346 ga'ăvâh (1), *arrogance; majesty*
7613 se'êth (1), *elevation; swelling leprous scab*

HIGHWAY
4546 meçillâh (13), main *thoroughfare; viaduct*
4547 maçlûwl (1), main *thoroughfare*
3598 hŏdŏs (1), *road*

HIGHWAYS
734 'ôrach (1), *well-traveled road; manner of life*
2351 chûwts (1), *outside, outdoors; open market*

4546 meçillâh (6), main *thoroughfare; viaduct*
1327+3598 diĕxŏdŏs (1), *open square*
3598 hŏdŏs (2), *road*

HILEN
2432 Chîylên (1), *fortress*

HILKIAH
2518 Chilqîyâh (33), *portion (of) Jehovah*

HILKIAH'S
2518 Chilqîyâh (1), *portion (of) Jehovah*

HILL
1389 gib'âh (30), *hillock*
2022 har (34), *mountain or range of hills*
4608 ma'ăleh (1), *elevation; platform*
7161 qeren (1), *horn*
697 Arĕiŏs Pagŏs (1), *rock of Ares*
1015 bŏunŏs (1), *small hill*
3714 ŏrĕinŏs (2), *Highlands of Judæa*
3735 ŏrŏs (3), *hill, mountain*

HILL'S
2022 har (1), *mountain or range of hills*

HILLEL
1985 Hillêl (2), *praising (God)*

HILLS
1389 gib'âh (39), *hillock*
2022 har (23), *mountain or range of hills*
2042 hârâr (2), *mountain*
1015 bŏunŏs (1), *small hill*

HIN
1969 hîyn (22), *liquid measure*

HIND
355 'ayâlâh (1), *doe deer*
365 'ayeleth (2), *doe deer*

HINDER
268 'âchôwr (3), *behind, backward; west*
309 'âchar (1), *to remain; to delay*
310 'achar (1), *after*
314 'achărôwn (1), *late or last; behind; western*
4513 mâna' (1), *to deny, refuse*
5490 çôwph (1), *termination; end*
6213+8442 'âsâh (1), *to do or make*
7725 shûwb (2), *to turn back; to return*
348 anakŏptō (1), *to beat back, i.e. check*
2967 kōluō (1), *to stop*
4403 prumna (2), *stern of a ship*
5100+1464+1325 tis (1), *some or any person*

HINDERED
989 beṭêl (Ch.) (1), *to stop*
1465 ĕgkŏptō (2), *to impede, detain*

1581 ĕkkŏptō (1), *to cut off; to frustrate*
2967 kōluō (1), *to stop*

HINDERETH
2820 châsak (1), *to restrain or refrain*

HINDERMOST
314 'achărôwn (1), *late or last; behind; western*
319 'achărîyth (1), *future; posterity*

HINDMOST
314 'achărôwn (1), *late or last; behind; western*
2179 zânab (2), *militarily attack the rear position*

HINDS
355 'ayâlâh (4), *doe deer*

HINDS'
355 'ayâlâh (3), *doe deer*

HINGES
6596 pôth (1), *hole; hinge; female genitals*
6735 tsîyr (1), *hinge*

HINNOM
2011 Hinnôm (13), *Hinnom*

HIP
7785 shôwq (1), lower *leg*

HIRAH
2437 Chîyrâh (2), *splendor*

HIRAM
2438 Chîyrâm (22), *noble*

HIRAM'S
2438 Chîyrâm (1), *noble*

HIRE
868 'ethnan (7), *gift* price of harlotry
4242 mechîyr (1), *price, payment, wages*
7936 sâkar (2), *to hire*
7939 sâkâr (8), *payment, salary; compensation*
3408 misthŏs (3), *pay* for services
3409 misthŏō (1), *to hire*

HIRED
7916 sâkîyr (11), man *at wages, hired hand*
7917 sekîyrâh (1), *hiring*
7936 sâkar (14), *to hire*
8566 tânâh (2), *to bargain with a harlot*
3407 misthiŏs (2), *hired-worker*
3409 misthŏō (1), *to hire*
3410 misthōma (1), *rented building*
3411 misthōtŏs (1), *wage-worker*

HIRELING
7916 sâkîyr (6), man *at wages, hired hand*
3411 misthōtŏs (2), *wage-worker*

HIRES
868 'ethnan (1), *gift* price of harlotry

HIREST
7806 shâzar (1), *to twist a thread of straw*

HISS
8319 shâraq (12), to whistle or *hiss*

HISSING
8292 sh^{e}rûwqâh (1), *whistling; scorn*
8322 sh^{e}rêqâh (7), *derision*

HIT
4672 mâtsâ' (2), to *find* or *acquire;* to *occur*

HITHER
1988 hălôm (6), *hither, to here*
2008 hênnâh (2), *from here; from there*
5066 nâgash (7), to *be, come, bring near*
6311 pôh (1), *here* or *hence*
1204 *dĕurŏ* (2), *hither!; hitherto*
1759 *ĕnthadĕ* (4), *here, hither*
3333 *mĕtakalĕō* (1), to *summon for, call for*
5602 *hōdĕ* (14), *here* or *hither*

HITHERTO
227 'âz (1), *at that time* or *place; therefore*
1973 hâl^{e}âh (2), *far away; thus far*
1988 hălôm (2), *hither, to here*
5704+2008 'ad (6), *as far (long) as; during*
5704+3541 'ad (2), *as far (long) as; during*
5704+6311 'ad (1), *as far (long) as; during*
5705+3542 'ad (Ch.) (1), *as far (long) as; during*
891+1204 *achri* (1), *until* or *up to*
2193+737 *hĕōs* (2), *until*
3768 *ŏupō* (1), *not yet*

HITTITE
2850 Chittîy (26), *Chittite*

HITTITES
2850 Chittîy (22), *Chittite*

HIVITE
2340 Chivvîy (9), *villager*

HIVITES
2340 Chivvîy (16), *villager*

HIZKIAH
2396 Chizqîyâh (1), *strengthened of Jehovah*

HIZKIJAH
2396 Chizqîyâh (1), *strengthened of Jehovah*

HO
1945 hôwy (3), *oh!, woe!*

HOAR
3713 k^{e}phôwr (2), *bowl;* white *frost*
7872 sêybâh (3), old *age*

HOARY
3713 k^{e}phôwr (1), *bowl;* white *frost*
7872 sêybâh (3), old *age*

HOBAB
2246 Chôbâb (2), *cherished*

HOBAH
2327 chôwbâh (1), *hiding* place

HOD
1963 hêyk (1), *how?*

HODAIAH
1939 Howday^{e}vâhûw (1), *majesty of Jehovah*

HODAVIAH
1938 Hôwdavyâh (3), *majesty of Jehovah*

HODESH
2321 Chôdesh (1), *new moon*

HODEVAH
1937 Hôwd^{e}vâh (1), *majesty of Jehovah*

HODIAH
1940 Hôwdîyâh (1), *Jewess*

HODIJAH
1940 Hôwdîyâh (5), *Jewess*

HOGLAH
2295 Choglâh (4), *partridge*

HOHAM
1944 Hôwhâm (1), *Hoham*

HOISED
1869 *ĕpairō* (1), to *raise up, look up*

HOLD
270 'âchaz (26), to *seize, grasp; possess*
816 'âsham (1), to *be guilty;* to *be punished*
1225 bitstsârôwn (1), *fortress*
2013 hâçâh (2), to *hush, be quiet*
2388 châzaq (35), to *fasten* upon; to *seize*
2790 chârash (16), to *engrave;* to *plow*
2814 châshâh (6), to *hush* or *keep quiet*
3447 yâshaṭ (1), to *extend*
3557 kûwl (1), to *keep in;* to *maintain*
3905 lâchats (1), to *press;* to *distress*
3943 lâphath (1), to *clasp;* to *turn* around
4013 mibtsâr (2), *fortification; defender*
4581 mâ'ôwz (1), *fortified* place; *defense*
4672 mâtsâ' (2), to *find* or *acquire;* to *occur*
4679 m^{e}tsad (2), *stronghold*
4686 mâtsûwd (7), *net* or *capture; fastness*
4692 mâtsôwr (1), *distress; fastness*
5253 nâçag (1), to *retreat*
5375 nâsâ' (1), to *lift up*
5381 nâsag (5), to *reach*
5553 çela' (1), craggy *rock; fortress*
5582 çâ'ad (1), to *support*
6076 'ôphel (1), *tumor; fortress*
6877 ts^{e}rîyach (3), *citadel*
6901 qâbal (1), to *admit;* to *take*
6965 qûwm (1), to *rise*
8551 tâmak (4), to *obtain, keep fast*
8610 tâphas (7), to *manipulate,* i.e. *seize*
472 *antĕchŏmai* (2), to *adhere to;* to *care for*
1949 *ĕpilambanŏmai* (5), to *seize*
2192 *ĕchō* (3), to *have; hold; keep*
2722 *katĕchō* (5), to *hold down fast*
2902 *kratĕō* (19), to *seize*
4601 *sigaō* (2), to *keep silent*
4623 *siōpaō* (5), to *be quiet*
5083 *tērĕō* (1), to *keep, guard, obey*
5084 *tērēsis* (1), *observance; prison*
5392 *phimŏō* (2), to *restrain to silence*
5438 *phulakē* (1), *guarding* or *guard*

HOLDEN
270 'âchaz (1), to *seize, grasp; possess*
2388 châzaq (1), to *fasten* upon; to *seize*
2814 châshâh (1), to *hush* or *keep quiet*
3920 lâkad (1), to *catch;* to *capture*
5564 çâmak (1), to *lean* upon; *take hold* of
5582 çâ'ad (1), to *support*
6213 'âsâh (2), to *do* or *make*
8551 tâmak (1), to *obtain, keep fast*
2902 *kratĕō* (2), to *seize*

HOLDEST
270 'âchaz (1), to *seize, grasp; possess*
2790 chârash (2), to *engrave;* to *plow*
2803 châshab (1), to *weave, fabricate*
8610 tâphas (1), to *manipulate,* i.e. *seize*
2902 *kratĕō* (1), to *seize*

HOLDETH
270 'âchaz (1), to *seize, grasp; possess*
2388 châzaq (2), to *fasten* upon; to *seize*
2790 chârash (2), to *engrave;* to *plow*
7760 sûwm (1), to *put, place*
8551 tâmak (2), to *obtain, keep fast*
2902 *kratĕō* (1), to *seize*

HOLDING
3557 kûwl (1), to *keep in;* to *measure*
8551 tâmak (1), to *obtain, keep fast*
472 *antĕchŏmai* (1), to *adhere to;* to *care for*
1907 *ĕpĕchō* (1), to *retain;* to *pay attention*
2192 *ĕchō* (2), to *have; hold; keep*
2902 *kratĕō* (3), to *seize*

HOLDS
4013 mibtsâr (11), *fortification; defender*
4581 mâ'ôwz (1), *fortified* place; *defense*
4679 m^{e}tsad (6), *stronghold*
4686 mâtsûwd (1), *net* or *capture; fastness*
4694 m^{e}tsûwrâh (1), *rampart, fortification*

HOLE
2356 chôwr (4), *cavity, socket, den*
4718 maqqebeth (1), *hammer*
5357 nâqîyq (1), *cleft, crevice*
6310 peh (6), *mouth; opening*

HOLE'S
6354 pachath (1), *pit*

HOLES
2356 chôwr (4), *cavity, socket, den*
4526 miçgereth (1), *margin; stronghold*
4631 m^e'ârâh (1), dark *cavern*
5344 nâqab (1), to *puncture, perforate*
5357 nâqîyq (2), *cleft, crevice*
5454 *phōlĕŏs* (2), *burrow, den hole*

HOLIER
6942 qâdâsh (1), to *be, make clean*

HOLIEST
39 *hagiŏn* (3), *sacred* thing, place or person

HOLILY
3743 *hŏsiōs* (1), *piously*

HOLINESS
6944 qôdesh (30), *sacred* place or thing
38 *hagiasmŏs* (5), state of *purity*
41 *hagiŏtēs* (1), state of *holiness*
42 *hagiōsunē* (3), quality of *holiness*
2150 *ĕusĕbĕia* (1), *piety, religious*
2412 *hiĕrŏprĕpēs* (1), *reverent*
3742 *hŏsiŏtēs* (2), *piety*

HOLLOW
3709 kaph (4), hollow of *hand; paw; sole* of foot
4388 maktêsh (1), *mortar; socket*
5014 nâbab (3), to *be hollow; be foolish*
8168 shô'al (1), *palm* of hand; *handful*
8258 sh^{e}qa'rûwrâh (1), *depression*

HOLON
2473 Chôlôwn (3), *sandy*

HOLPEN
2220 zᵉrôwa' (1), *arm;*
foreleg; force, power
5826 'âzar (3), to *protect*
or *aid*
482 antilambanŏmai (1),
to *come to the aid*

HOLY
2623 châçîyd (5),
religiously *pious, godly*
4720 miqdâsh (3),
sanctuary of deity
6918 qâdôwsh (100),
sacred
6922 qaddîysh (Ch.) (7),
sacred
6942 qâdâsh (7), to *be,*
make clean
6944 qôdesh (297),
sacred place or thing
37 hagiazŏ (1), to *purify*
or *consecrate*
39 hagiŏn (3), *sacred*
thing, place or person
40 hagiŏs (162), *sacred,*
holy
2413 hiĕrŏs (2), *sacred,*
set apart for God
3741 hŏsiŏs (6),
hallowed, pious, sacred

HOLYDAY
2287 châgag (1), to
observe a festival
1859 hĕŏrtē (1), *festival*

HOMAM
1950 Hôwmâm (1), *raging*

HOME
168 'ôhel (1), *tent*
1004 bayith (26), *house;*
temple; family, tribe
4725 mâqôwm (3),
general *locality, place*
5115 nâvâh (1), to *rest* as
at home
7725 shûwb (5), to *turn*
back; to *return*
8432 tâvek (1), *center,*
middle
1438 hĕautŏu (1),
himself, herself, itself
1736 ĕndĕmĕŏ (1), to be
at home
2398 idiŏs (2), *private* or
separate
3614 ŏikia (1), *abode;*
family
3624 ŏikŏs (4), *dwelling;*
family
3626 ŏikŏurŏs (1),
domestically inclined

HOMEBORN
249 'ezrâch (1), *native*
born
1004 bayith (1), *house;*
temple; family, tribe

HOMER
2563 chômer (10), *clay;*
dry *measure*

HOMERS
2563 chômer (1), *clay;*
dry *measure*

HONEST
2570 kalŏs (5), *good;*
valuable; virtuous
4586 sĕmnŏs (1),
honorable, noble

HONESTLY
2156 ĕuschēmŏnōs (2),
fittingly, properly
2573 kalōs (1), *well,* i.e.
rightly

HONESTY
4587 sĕmnŏtēs (1),
venerableness

HONEY
1706 dᵉbash (52), *honey*
3192 mĕli (4), *honey*

HONEYCOMB
3293 ya'ar (1), *honey* in
the *comb*
3295+1706 ya'ărâh (1),
honey in the *comb*
5317 nôpheth (4), *honey*
from the comb
5317+6688 nôpheth (1),
honey from the comb
6688+1706 tsûwph (1),
comb of *dripping* honey
3193+2781 mĕlissiŏs (1),
honeybee comb

HONOUR
1921 hâdar (2), to *favor*
or *honor;* to *be high*
1922 hădar (Ch.) (1), to
magnify, glorify
1923 hădâr (Ch.) (2),
magnificence, glory
1926 hâdâr (5),
magnificence
1927 hădârâh (1),
ornament; splendor
1935 hôwd (6), *grandeur,*
majesty
3366 yᵉqâr (12), *wealth;*
costliness; dignity
3367 yᵉqâr (Ch.) (2),
glory, honor
3513 kâbad (22), to *be*
rich, glorious
3515 kâbêd (1), *severe,*
difficult, stupid
3519 kâbôwd (32),
splendor, wealth
8597 tiph'ârâh (4),
ornament
820 atimŏs (2),
dishonoured
1391 dŏxa (6), *glory;*
brilliance
5091 timaŏ (14), to
revere, honor
5092 timē (31), *esteem;*
nobility; money

HONOURABLE
142 'âdar (1),
magnificent; glorious
1935 hôwd (2), *grandeur,*
majesty
3368 yâqâr (1), *valuable*
3513 kâbad (13), to *be*
rich, glorious
3519 kâbôwd (2),
splendor, wealth
5375+6440 nâsâ' (4), to
lift up
820 atimŏs (1),
dishonoured
1741 ĕndŏxŏs (1), *noble;*
honored
1784 ĕntimŏs (1), *valued,*
considered *precious*
2158 ĕuschēmŏn (3),
decorous, proper; noble

HONESTLY
5093 timiŏs (1), *costly;*
honored, esteemed

HONOURED
1921 hâdar (1), to *favor*
or *honor;* to *be high*
1922 hădar (Ch.) (1), to
magnify, glorify
3513 kâbad (5), to *be*
rich, glorious
1392 dŏxazŏ (1), to
render, esteem glorious
5092 timē (1), *esteem;*
nobility; money

HONOUREST
3513 kâbad (1), to *be*
rich, glorious

HONOURETH
3513 kâbad (4), to *be*
rich, glorious
1392 dŏxazŏ (1), to
render, esteem glorious
5091 timaŏ (3), to *revere,*
honor, show respect

HONOURS
5091 timaŏ (1), to *revere,*
honor, show respect

HOODS
6797 tsânîyph (1),
head-dress, turban

HOOF
6541 parçâh (12), *split*
hoof

HOOFS
6536 pâraç (1), to *break*
in pieces; to *split*
6541 parçâh (5), split
hoof

HOOK
100 'agmôwn (1), *rush;*
rope of rushes
2397 châch (2), *ring* for
the nose or lips
2443 chakkâh (1), fish
hook
44 agkistrŏn (1), fish
hook

HOOKS
2053 vâv (13), *hook*
2397 châch (2), *ring* for
the nose or lips
6793 tsinnâh (1), large
shield; piercing cold
8240 shâphâth (1),
two-pronged hook

HOPE
982 bâṭach (1), to *trust,*
be confident or *sure*
983 beṭach (1), *safety,*
security, trust
986 biṭṭâchôwn (1), *trust*
2342 chûwl (1), to *dance,*
whirl; to *wait;* to *pervert*
2620 châçâh (1), to *flee*
to; to *confide* in
2976 yâ'ash (3), to
despond, despair
3176 yâchal (19), to *wait;*
to *be patient, hope*
3689 keçel (3), *loin;*
back; viscera; trust
4009 mibṭâch (1),
security; assurance
4268 machâçeh (2),
shelter; refuge
4723 miqveh (4),
confidence; collection

HOPE *(cont.)*
7663 sâbar (1), to *expect*
with hope
7664 sêber (2),
expectation
8431 tôwcheleth (6),
hope, expectation
8615 tiqvâh (23), *cord;*
expectancy
1679 ĕlpizō (7), to *expect*
or *confide, hope* for
1680 ĕlpis (51), *hope;*
confidence

HOPE'S
1679 ĕlpizō (1), to *expect*
or *confide, hope* for

HOPED
982 bâṭach (1), to *trust,*
be confident or *sure*
3176 yâchal (3), to *wait;*
to *be patient, hope*
7663 sâbar (2), to *expect*
with hope
1679 ĕlpizō (4), to *expect*
or *confide, hope* for

HOPETH
1679 ĕlpizō (1), to *expect*
or *confide, hope* for

HOPHNI
2652 Chophnîy (5), pair
of *fists*

HOPING
560 apĕlpizō (1), to *fully*
expect in return
1679 ĕlpizō (1), to *expect*
or *confide, hope* for

HOR
2023 Hôr (12), *mountain*

HOR-HAGIDGAD
2735 Chôr hag-Gidgâd
(2), *hole of the cleft*

HORAM
2036 Hôrâm (1), *high,*
exalted

HOREB
2722 Chôrêb (17),
desolate

HOREM
2765 Chŏrêm (1), *devoted*

HORI
2753 Chôrîy (4),
cave-dweller

HORIMS
2752 Chôrîy (2),
cave-dweller

HORITE
2752 Chôrîy (1),
cave-dweller

HORITES
2752 Chôrîy (3),
cave-dweller

HORMAH
2767 Chormâh (9),
devoted

HORN
7161 qeren (28), *horn*
7162 qeren (Ch.) (5), *horn*
2768 kĕras (1), *horn*

HORNET
6880 tsir'âh (2), *wasp*

HORNETS
6880 tsir'âh (1), *wasp*

HORNS
3104 yôwbêl (3), *blast of a ram's horn*
7160 qâran (1), *to protrude out horns*
7161 qeren (46), *horn*
7162 qeren (Ch.) (5), *horn*
2768 kĕras (10), *horn*

HORONAIM
2773 Chôrônayim (4), *double cave-town*

HORONITE
2772 Chôrônîy (3), *Choronite*

HORRIBLE
2152 zal'âphâh (1), *glow; famine*
7588 shâ'ôwn (1), *uproar; destruction*
8186 sha'ărûwrâh (4), *something fearful*

HORRIBLY
8175 sâ'ar (1), *to storm; to shiver*, i.e. *fear*
8178 sa'ar (1), *tempest; terror*

HORROR
367 'êymâh (1), *fright*
2152 zal'âphâh (1), *glow; famine*
6427 pallâtsûwth (2), *affright, trembling fear*

HORSE
5483 çûwç (35), *horse*
2462 hippŏs (8), *horse*

HORSEBACK
5483 çûwç (1), *horse*
7392 râkab (2), *to ride*
7392+5483 râkab (2), *to ride*

HORSEHOOFS
6119+5483 'âqêb (1), *track, footprint*

HORSELEACH
5936 'ălûwqâh (1), *leech*

HORSEMAN
6571 pârâsh (1), *horse; chariot driver*
7395 rakkâb (1), *charioteer*

HORSEMEN
6571 pârâsh (56), *horse; chariot driver*
2460 hippĕus (2), *member of a cavalry*
2461 hippikŏn (1), *cavalry force*

HORSES
5483 çûwç (96), *horse*
5484 çûwçâh (1), *mare*
2462 hippŏs (7), *horse*

HORSES'
5483 çûwç (1), *horse*
2462 hippŏs (1), *horse*

HOSAH
2621 Chôçâh (5), *hopeful*

HOSANNA
5614 hōsanna (6), *"oh save!"*

HOSEA
1954 Hôwshêä' (3), *deliverer*

HOSEN
6361 paṭṭîysh (Ch.) (1), *garment*

HOSHAIAH
1955 Hôwshi'yâh (3), *Jehovah has saved*

HOSHAMA
1953 Hôwshâmâ' (1), *Jehovah has heard*

HOSHEA
1954 Hôwshêä' (11), *deliverer*

HOSPITALITY
5381 philŏnĕxia (1), *hospitableness*
5382 philŏxĕnŏs (3), *hospitable*

HOST
2426 chêyl (2), *rampart, battlement*
2428 chayil (28), *army; wealth; virtue; valor*
4264 machăneh (54), *encampment*
6635 tsâbâ' (100), *army, military host*
3581 xĕnŏs (1), *alien; guest or host*
3830 pandŏchĕus (1), *innkeeper*
4756 stratia (2), *army; celestial luminaries*

HOSTAGES
1121+8594 bên (2), *son, descendant; people*

HOSTS
2428 chayil (1), *army; wealth; virtue; valor*
4264 machăneh (4), *encampment*
6635 tsâbâ' (293), *army, military host*

HOT
228 'ăzâ' (Ch.) (1), *to heat*
784 'êsh (1), *fire*
2525 châm (1), *hot, sweltering*
2527 chôm (4), *heat*
2534 chêmâh (3), *heat; anger; poison*
2552 châmam (3), *to be hot; to be in a rage*
2734 chârâh (10), *to blaze up*
3179 yâcham (2), *to conceive*
7565 resheph (1), *flame*
2200 zĕstŏs (3), *hot*, i.e. *fervent*
2743 kautēriazō (1), *to brand or cauterize*

HOTHAM
2369 Chôwthâm (1), *seal*

HOTHAN
2369 Chôwthâm (1), *seal*

HOTHIR
1956 Hôwthîyr (2), *he has caused to remain*

HOTLY
1814 dâlaq (1), *to flame; to pursue*

HOTTEST
2389 châzâq (1), *strong; severe, hard, violent*

HOUGH
6131 'âqar (1), *to pluck up roots; to hamstring*

HOUGHED
6131 'âqar (3), *to pluck up roots; to hamstring*

HOUR
8160 shâ'âh (Ch.) (5), *immediately*
734 Artĕmas (1), *gift of Artemis*
2256 hēmiōriŏn (1), *half-hour*
5610 hōra (85), *hour*, i.e. *a unit of time*

HOURS
5610 hōra (3), *hour*, i.e. *a unit of time*

HOUSE
1004 bayith (1745), *house; temple; family*
1005 bayith (Ch.) (41), *house; temple; family*
1008 Bêyth-'Êl (5), *house of God*
1035 Bêyth Lechem (1), *house of bread*
5854 'Aṭrôwth Bêyth Yôw'âb (1), *crowns of* (the) *house of Joäb*
3609 ŏikĕiŏs (1), *of the household*
3613 ŏikētēriŏn (1), *residence, home*
3614 ŏikia (84), *abode; family*
3616 ŏikŏdĕspŏtĕō (1), *to be the head of a family*
3617 ŏikŏdĕspŏtēs (7), *head of a family*
3624 ŏikŏs (96), *dwelling; family*
3832 panŏiki (1), *with the whole family*

HOUSEHOLD
1004 bayith (47), *house; temple; family, tribe*
5657 'ăbuddâh (1), *service*
2322 thĕrapĕia (2), *cure, healing; domestics*
3609 ŏikĕiŏs (2), *of the household*
3610 ŏikĕtēs (1), *menial domestic servant*
3614 ŏikia (1), *abode; family*
3615 ŏikiakŏs (2), *relatives*
3624 ŏikŏs (3), *dwelling; family*

HOUSEHOLDER
3617 ŏikŏdĕspŏtēs (4), *head of a family*

HOUSEHOLDS
1004 bayith (7), *house; temple; family, tribe*

HOUSES
490 'almânâh (1), *widow*
1004 bayith (116), *house; temple; family, tribe*
1005 bayith (Ch.) (2), *house; temple; family*
4999 nâ'âh (1), *home, dwelling; pasture*

HOUSETOP
1406 gâg (2), *roof; top*
1430 dōma (5), *roof, housetop*

HOUSETOPS
1406 gâg (5), *roof; top*
1430 dōma (2), *roof, housetop*

HOW
335 'ay (1), *where?*
346 'ayêh (2), *where?*
349 'êyk (75), *how? or how!; where?*
434 'ĕlûwl (1), *good for nothing*
637 'aph (18), *also or yea; though*
834 'ăsher (26), *how, because, in order that*
1963 hêyk (2), *how?*
3588 kîy (11), *for, that because*
4069 maddûwa' (1), *why?, what?*
4100 mâh (59), *how?, how!; what, whatever*
4101 mâh (Ch.) (3), *how?, how!; what, whatever*
5704 'ad (47), *as far* (long) *as; during*
2193 hĕōs (6), *until*
2245 hēlikŏs (1), *how much, how great*
2531 kathōs (1), *just or inasmuch as, that*
3386 mētigĕ (1), *not to say* (the rather still)
3704 hŏpōs (4), *in the manner that*
3745 hŏsŏs (7), *as much as*
3754 hŏti (14), *that; because; since*
4012 pĕri (1), *about; around*
4080 pēlikŏs (2), *how much, how great*
4212 pŏsakis (2), *how many times*
4214 pŏsŏs (26), *how much?; how much!*
4219 pŏtĕ (1), *at what time?*
4459 pōs (96), *in what way?; how?; how much!*
4559 sarkikŏs (2), *pertaining to flesh*
5101 tis (11), *who?, which? or what?*
5613 hōs (19), *which, how*, i.e. *in that manner*

HOWBEIT
199 'ûwlâm (1), *however or on the contrary*
389 'ak (1), *surely; only, however*
657 'epheç (1), *end; no further*
3651 kên (1), *just; right, correct*
7535 raq (1), *merely; although*
235 alla (8), *but, yet, except, instead*

1161 dĕ (1), *but, yet*
3305 mĕntŏi (1), *however*

HOWL
3213 yâlal (27), to *howl,*
wail, yell
3649 ŏlŏluzō (1), to *howl,*
i.e. *shriek or wail*

HOWLED
3213 yâlal (1), to *howl,*
wail, yell

HOWLING
3213 yâlal (5), to *howl,*
wail, yell
3214 yᵉlêl (1), *howl, wail*

HOWLINGS
3213 yâlal (1), to *howl,*
wail, yell

HOWSOEVER
1961+4101 hâyâh (1), to
exist, i.e. *be or become*
3605+834 kôl (1), *all, any*
or *every*
7535 raq (1), *merely;*
although

HUGE
7230 rôb (1), *abundance*

HUKKOK
2712 Chuqqôq (1),
appointed

HUKOK
2712 Chuqqôq (1),
appointed

HUL
2343 Chûwl (2), *circle*

HULDAH
2468 Chuldâh (2), *weasel*

HUMBLE
3665 kâna' (2), to
humiliate, vanquish,
subdue
6031 'ânâh (4), to *afflict,*
be afflicted
6041 'ânîy (5), *depressed*
7511 râphaç (1), to
trample; to prostrate
7807+5869 shach (1),
sunk, i.e. *downcast*
8213 shâphêl (2), to
humiliate
8217 shâphâl (3),
depressed, low
5011 tapĕinŏs (2),
humiliated, lowly
5013 tapĕinŏō (5), to
depress; to humiliate

HUMBLED
1792 dâkâ' (1), to be
contrite, be humbled
3665 kâna' (13), to
humiliate, vanquish
6031 'ânâh (7), to *afflict,*
be afflicted
7743 shûwach (1), to *sink*
8213 shâphêl (4), to
humiliate
8214 shᵉphal (Ch.) (1), to
humiliate
5013 tapĕinŏō (1), to
depress; to humiliate

HUMBLEDST
3665 kâna' (1), to
humiliate, vanquish

HUMBLENESS
5012 tapĕinŏphrŏsunē
(1), *modesty, humility*

HUMBLETH
3665 kâna' (2), to
humiliate, vanquish
7817 shâchach (1), to
sink or depress
8213 shâphêl (2), to
humiliate
5013 tapĕinŏō (2), to
depress; to humiliate

HUMBLY
6800 tsâna' (1), to
humiliate
7812 shâchâh (1), to
prostrate in homage

HUMILIATION
5014 tapĕinōsis (1),
humbleness, lowliness

HUMILITY
6038 'ănâvâh (3),
condescension
5012 tapĕinŏphrŏsunē
(4), *modesty, humility*

HUMTAH
2457 chel'âh (1), *rust*

HUNDRED
520 'ammâh (1), *cubit*
3967 mê'âh (545),
hundred
3969 mᵉ'âh (Ch.) (7),
hundred
1250 diakŏsiŏi (8), *two*
hundred
1540 hĕkatŏn (14),
hundred
1541 hĕkatŏntaĕtēs (1),
centenarian
3461 murias (1),
ten-thousand
4001 pĕntakŏsiŏi (2), *five*
hundred
5071 tĕtrakŏsiŏi (4), *four*
hundred
5145 triakŏsiŏi (2), *three*
hundred
5516 chi xi stigma (2), *666*

HUNDREDFOLD
3967+8180 mê'âh (1),
hundred
1540 hĕkatŏn (2),
hundred
1542 hĕkatŏntaplasiōn
(3), *hundred times*

HUNDREDS
3967 mê'âh (27), *hundred*
1540 hĕkatŏn (1),
hundred

HUNDREDTH
3967 mê'âh (3), *hundred*

HUNGER
7456 râ'êb (5), to *hunger*
7457 râ'êb (8), *hungry*
3042 limŏs (3), *scarcity,*
famine
3983 pĕinaō (8), to
famish; to crave

HUNGERBITTEN
7457 râ'êb (1), *hungry*

HUNGERED
3983 pĕinaō (2), to
famish; to crave

HUNGRED
3983 pĕinaō (9), to
famish; to crave

HUNGRY
7456 râ'êb (25), to *hunger*
3983 pĕinaō (4), to
famish; to crave
4361 prŏspĕinŏs (1),
intensely hungry

HUNT
6679 tsûwd (11), to *lie in*
wait; to *catch*
7291 râdaph (1), to *run*
after with hostility

HUNTED
4686 mâtsûwd (1), *net or*
capture; fastness

HUNTER
6718 tsayid (4), *hunting*
game; lunch, food

HUNTERS
6719 tsayâd (1),
huntsman

HUNTEST
6658 tsâdâh (1), to
desolate
6679 tsûwd (1), to *lie in*
wait; to *catch*

HUNTETH
6679 tsûwd (1), to *lie in*
wait; to *catch*

HUNTING
6718 tsayid (2), *hunting*
game; lunch, food

HUPHAM
2349 Chûwphâm (1),
protection

HUPHAMITES
2350 Chûwphâmîy (1),
Chuphamite

HUPPAH
2647 Chuppâh (1),
canopy

HUPPIM
2650 Chuppîym (3),
canopies

HUR
2354 Chûwr (16), *cell of a*
prison or white linen

HURAI
2360 Chûwray (1),
linen-worker

HURAM
2361 Chûwrâm (6), *noble*
2438 Chîyrâm (6), *noble*

HURI
2359 Chûwrîy (1),
linen-worker

HURL
7993 shâlak (1), to *throw*
out, down or away

HURLETH
8175 sâ'ar (1), to *storm;*
to *shiver,* i.e. *fear*

HURT
1697 dâbâr (1), *word;*
matter; thing
2248 chăbûwlâh (Ch.)
(1), *crime, wrong*
2250 chabbûwrâh (1),
weal, bruise
2255 chăbal (Ch.) (1), to
ruin, destroy

HUNGRED
2257 chăbal (Ch.) (2),
harm, wound
3637 kâlam (2), to *taunt*
or *insult*
5062 nâgaph (2), to
inflict a disease
5142 nᵉzaq (Ch.) (1), to
suffer, inflict loss
6031 'ânâh (1), to *afflict,*
be afflicted
6087 'âtsab (1), to *worry,*
have pain or anger
6485 pâqad (1), to *visit,*
care for, count
7451 ra' (20), *bad; evil*
7489 râ'a' (7), to *break to*
pieces
7665 shâbar (3), to *burst*
7667 sheber (4), *fracture;*
ruin
91 adikĕō (10), to *do*
wrong
984 blaptō (2), to *hinder,*
i.e. *to injure*
2559 kakŏō (1), to *injure;*
to oppress; to embitter
5196 hubris (1), *insult;*
injury

HURTFUL
5142 nᵉzaq (Ch.) (1), to
suffer, inflict loss
7451 ra' (1), *bad; evil*
983 blabĕrŏs (1),
injurious, harmful

HURTING
7489 râ'a' (1), to *break to*
pieces

HUSBAND
376 'îysh (66), *man;*
male; someone
1167 ba'al (13), *master;*
husband; owner; citizen
2860 châthân (2),
bridegroom
435 anēr (38), *man; male*
5220 hupandrŏs (1),
married woman

HUSBAND'S
376 'îysh (2), *man; male;*
someone
2992 yâbam (2), to *marry*
a dead brother's widow
2993 yâbâm (2),
husband's brother

HUSBANDMAN
376+127 'îysh (1), *man;*
male; someone
406 'ikkâr (2), *farmer*
5647 'âbad (1), to *do,*
work, serve
1092 gĕōrgŏs (3), *farmer;*
tenant farmer

HUSBANDMEN
406 'ikkâr (3), *farmer*
1461 gûwb (1), to *dig*
3009 yâgab (1), to *dig or*
plow
1092 gĕōrgŏs (16),
farmer; tenant farmer

HUSBANDRY
127 'ădâmâh (1), *soil;*
land
1091 gĕōrgiŏn (1),
cultivable, i.e. *farm*

HUSBANDS
376 'îysh (1), *man; male*

582 'ĕnôwsh (3), *man;*
person, human
1167 ba'al (2), *master;*
husband; owner; citizen
435 anêr (12), *man; male*
5362 philandrŏs (1),
affectionate as a wife
to her *husband*

HUSHAH
2364 Chûwshâh (1), *haste*

HUSHAI
2365 Chûwshay (14),
hasty

HUSHAM
2367 Chûwshâm (4),
hastily

HUSHATHITE
2843 Chûshâthîy (5),
Chushathite

HUSHIM
2366 Chûwshîym (4),
those who *hasten*

HUSK
2085 zâg (1), grape *skin*
6861 tsiqlôn (1), tied up
sack

HUSKS
2769 kĕratiŏn (1), *pod*

HUZ
5780 'Ûwts (1),
consultation

HUZZAB
5324 nâtsab (1), to *station*

HYMENAEUS
5211 Humĕnaiŏs (2), one
dedicated to the god of
weddings

HYMN
5214 humnĕō (1), to
celebrate God in song

HYMNS
5215 humnŏs (2), *hymn*
or religious *ode*

HYPOCRISIES
5272 hupŏkrisis (1),
deceit, hypocrisy

HYPOCRISY
2612 chôneph (1), moral
filth, i.e. *wickedness*
505 anupŏkritŏs (1),
sincere, genuine
5272 hupŏkrisis (4),
deceit, hypocrisy

HYPOCRITE
120+2611 'âdâm (1),
human being; mankind
2611 chânêph (6), *soiled*
(i.e. with sin), *impious*
5273 hupŏkritĕs (3),
dissembler, hypocrite

HYPOCRITE'S
2611 chânêph (1), *soiled*
(i.e. with sin), *impious*

HYPOCRITES
120+2611 'âdâm (1),
human being; mankind
2611 chânêph (2), *soiled*
(i.e. with sin), *impious*
5273 hupŏkritĕs (17),
dissembler, hypocrite

HYPOCRITICAL
2611 chânêph (2), *soiled*
(i.e. with sin), *impious*

HYSSOP
231 'êzôwb (10), *hyssop*
5301 hussōpŏs (2),
hyssop plant

I-CHABOD
350 Îy-kâbôwd (1),
inglorious

I-CHABOD'S
350 Îy-kâbôwd (1),
inglorious

IBHAR
2984 Yibchar (3), *choice*

IBLEAM
2991 Yibleʿâm (3),
devouring people

IBNEIAH
2997 Yibnᵉyâh (1), *built*
of Jehovah

IBNIJAH
2998 Yibnîyâh (1),
building of Jehovah

IBRI
5681 'Ibrîy (1), *Eberite*
(i.e. Hebrew)

IBZAN
78 'Ibtsân (2), *splendid*

ICE
7140 qerach (3), *ice; hail;*
rock *crystal*

ICONIUM
2430 Ikŏniŏn (6),
image-like

IDALAH
3030 Yid'ălâh (1), *Jidalah*

IDBASH
3031 Yidbâsh (1),
honeyed

IDDO
112 'Iddôw (2), *Iddo*
3035 Yiddôw (1), *praised*
3260 Yᵉʿdîy (1), *appointed*
5714 'Iddôw (10), *timely*

IDLE
7423 rᵉmîyâh (1),
remissness; treachery
7504 râpheh (2), *slack*
692 argŏs (6), *lazy;*
useless
3026 lērŏs (1), *twaddle,*
i.e. an *incredible* story

IDLENESS
6104 'atslûwth (1),
indolence
8220 shiphlûwth (1),
remissness, idleness
8252 shâqaṭ (1), to *repose*

IDOL
205 'âven (1), *trouble,*
vanity, wickedness
457 'ĕlîyl (1), *vain idol*
4656 miphletseth (4),
terror idol
5566 çemel (2), *likeness*
6089 'etseb (1), earthen
vessel; painful *toil*
6090 'ôtseb (1),
fashioned *idol;* pain
1494 ĕidōlŏthutŏn (1),
idolatrous offering
1497 ĕidōlŏn (4), *idol,* or
the *worship* of such

IDOL'S
1493 ĕidōlĕiŏn (1), *idol*
temple

IDOLATER
1496 ĕidōlŏlatrĕs (2),
image-worshipper

IDOLATERS
1496 ĕidōlŏlatrĕs (5),
image-worshipper

IDOLATRIES
1495 ĕidōlŏlatrĕia (1),
image-worship

IDOLATROUS
3649 kâmâr (1), pagan
priest

IDOLATRY
8655 tᵉrâphîym (1),
healer
1495 ĕidōlŏlatrĕia (3),
image-worship
2712 katĕidōlŏs (1),
utterly idolatrous

IDOLS
367 'êymâh (1), *fright*
410 'êl (1), *mighty;* the
Almighty
457 'ĕlîyl (16), *vain idol*
1544 gillûwl (47), *idol*
2553 chammân (1),
*sun-*pillar
6091 'âtsâb (16), *image,*
idol
6736 tsîyr (1), *carved*
idolatrous *image*
8251 shiqqûwts (1),
disgusting; idol
8655 tᵉrâphîym (1),
healer
1494 ĕidōlŏthutŏn (9),
idolatrous offering
1497 ĕidōlŏn (7), *idol,* or
the *worship* of such

IDUMAEA
2401 Idŏumaia (1),
Idumæa, i.e. *Edom*

IDUMEA
123 'Ĕdôm (4), *red*

IF
176 'ôw (3), *or, whether*
194 'ûwlay (9), *if not*
432 'illûw (1), *if*
518 'îm (557), *whether?; if*
834 'âsher (19), *who,*
which, what, that
2005 hên (3), *lo!; if!*
2006 hên (Ch.) (11), *lo;*
whether, but, if
3588 kîy (159), *for, that*
because
3808 lô' (1), *no, not*
3863 lûw' (7), *if; would*
that!
3883 lûwl (1), *spiral* step
3884 lûwlê' (2), *if not*
6112 'Êtsen (1), *spear*
148 aischrŏlŏgia (3), *vile*
conversation
1437 ĕan (216), *in case*
that, provided
1477 hĕdraiŏma (5),
basis, foundation
1487 ĕi (305), *if, whether*
1489 ĕigĕ (5), *if indeed*
1490 ĕi dĕ mē(gĕ) (4), *but*
if not
1499 ĕi kai (6), *if also*

1512 ĕi pĕr (4), *if perhaps*
1513 ĕi pōs (4), *if*
somehow
1535 ĕitĕ (1), *if too*
2579 kan (5), *and if*
3379 mēpŏtĕ (1), *not*
ever; if, or *lest ever*

IGAL
3008 Yig'âl (2), *avenger*

IGDALIAH
3012 Yigdalyâhûw (1),
magnified of Jehovah

IGEAL
3008 Yig'âl (1), *avenger*

IGNOMINY
7036 qâlôwn (1), *disgrace*

IGNORANCE
7684 shᵉgâgâh (12),
mistake, transgression
7686 shâgâh (1), to
transgress by mistake
52 agnŏia (4), *ignorance*
56 agnŏsia (1), state of
ignorance

IGNORANT
3808+3045 lô' (3), no, *not*
know; not understand
50 agnŏĕō (10), to *not*
know; not understand
2399 idiŏtĕs (1), *not*
initiated; untrained
2990 lanthanō (2), to *lie*
hid; unwittingly

IGNORANTLY
1097+1847 bᵉlîy (1), *not*
yet; lacking
7683 shâgag (1), to *sin*
through oversight
50 agnŏĕō (2), to *not*
know; not *understand*

IIM
5864 'Iyîym (2), *ruins*

IJE-ABARIM
5863 'Iyêy hâ-'Ăbârîym
(2), *ruins of the passers*

IJON
5859 'Iyôwn (3), *ruin*

IKKESH
6142 'Iqqêsh (3), *perverse*

ILAI
5866 'Îylay (1), *elevated*

ILL
3415 yâra' (2), to *fear*
6709 tsachănâh (1),
stench
7451 ra' (8), *bad; evil*
7489 râ'a' (3), to be *good*
for nothing
2556 kakŏs (1), *bad, evil,*
wrong

ILLUMINATED
5461 phōtizō (1), to *shine*
or to *brighten* up

ILLYRICUM
2437 Illurikŏn (1),
Illyricum

IMAGE
4676 matstsêbâh (3),
column or *stone*
4906 maskîyth (1),
carved *figure*
5566 çemel (2), *likeness*
6459 peçel (2), *idol*
6676 tsavva'r (Ch.) (1),
back of the *neck*

6754 tselem (6),
phantom; idol
6755 tselem (Ch.) (16),
idolatrous figure
6816 tsa'tsûa' (1),
sculpture work
8544 tᵉmûwnâh (1),
something *fashioned*
8655 tᵉrâphîym (2),
healer
1504 ĕikōn (22), *likeness*
5481 charaktēr (1), exact
copy or *representation*

IMAGE'S
6755 tselem (Ch.) (1),
idolatrous figure

IMAGERY
4906 maskîyth (1),
carved *figure*

IMAGES
457 'ĕlîyl (1), *vain idol*
1544 gillûwl (1), *idol*
2553 chammân (6),
sun-pillar
4676 matstsêbâh (14),
column or *stone*
6091 'âtsâb (1), *image,*
idol
6456 pᵉçîyl (2), *idol*
6754 tselem (9),
phantom; idol
8655 tᵉrâphîym (5),
healer

IMAGINATION
3336 yêtser (4), *form*
8307 shᵉrîyrûwth (9),
obstinacy
1271 dianŏia (1), *mind*
or *thought*

IMAGINATIONS
3336 yêtser (1), *form*
4284 machăshâbâh (3),
contrivance; plan
1261 dialŏgismŏs (1),
consideration; debate
3053 lŏgismŏs (1),
reasoning; conscience

IMAGINE
1897 hâgâh (2), to
murmur, ponder
2050 hâthath (1), to
assail, verbally attack
2554 châmaç (1), to be
violent; to maltreat
2790 chârash (1), to be
silent; to be deaf
2803 châshab (5), to *plot;*
to *think, regard*
3191 mĕlĕtaŏ (1), to *plot,*
think about

IMAGINED
2161 zâmam (1), to *plan*
2803 châshab (2), to *plot;*
to *think, regard*

IMAGINETH
2803 châshab (1), to *plot;*
to *think, regard*

IMLA
3229 Yimlâ' (2), *full*

IMLAH
3229 Yimlâ' (2), *full*

IMMANUEL
6005 'Immânûw'êl (2),
with us (is) *God*

IMMEDIATELY
1824 ĕxautēs (3),
instantly, at once
2112 ĕuthĕōs (35), *at*
once or soon
2117 ĕuthus (3), *at once,*
immediately
3916 parachrēma (13),
instantly, immediately

IMMER
564 'Immêr (10),
talkative

IMMORTAL
862 aphthartŏs (1),
undecaying, immortal

IMMORTALITY
110 athanasia (3),
deathlessness
861 aphtharsia (2),
unending existence

IMMUTABILITY
276 amĕtathĕtŏs (1),
unchangeable

IMMUTABLE
276 amĕtathĕtŏs (1),
unchangeable

IMNA
3234 Yimnâ' (1), *he will*
restrain

IMNAH
3232 Yimnâh (2),
prosperity

IMPART
3330 mĕtadidōmi (2), to
share, distribute

IMPARTED
2505 châlaq (1), to be
smooth; be slippery
3330 mĕtadidōmi (1), to
share, distribute

IMPEDIMENT
3424 mŏgilalŏs (1),
hardly talking

IMPENITENT
279 amĕtanŏĕtŏs (1),
unrepentant

IMPERIOUS
7986 shalleṭeth (1),
dominant woman

IMPLACABLE
786 aspŏndŏs (1), *not*
reconcilable

IMPLEAD
1458 ĕgkalĕō (1), to
charge, criminate

IMPORTUNITY
335 anaidĕia (1),
importunity, boldness

IMPOSE
7412 rᵉmâh (Ch.) (1), to
throw; to *set;* to *assess*

IMPOSED
1942 ĕpikaluma (1),
pretext, covering

IMPOSSIBLE
101 adunatĕō (2), to be
impossible
102 adunatŏs (6), *weak;*
impossible
418 anĕndĕktŏs (1),
impossible

IMPOTENT
102 adunatŏs (1), *weak;*
impossible
770 asthĕnĕō (2), to be
feeble
772 asthĕnēs (1),
strengthless, weak

IMPOVERISH
7567 râshash (1), to
demolish

IMPOVERISHED
1809 dâlal (1), to be
feeble; to be *oppressed*
5533 çâkan (1), to *grow,*
make poor
7567 râshash (1), to
demolish

IMPRISONED
5439 phulakizō (1), to
incarcerate, imprison

IMPRISONMENT
613 'ĕçûwr (Ch.) (1),
manacles, chains
5438 phulakē (1), *watch;*
prison; haunt

IMPRISONMENTS
5438 phulakē (1), *watch;*
prison; haunt

IMPUDENT
2389+4696 châzâq (1),
severe, hard, violent
5810 'âzaz (1), to be
stout; be bold
7186+6440 qâsheh (1),
severe

IMPUTE
2803 châshab (1), to
regard; to *compute*
7760 sûwm (1), to *put,*
place
3049 lŏgizŏmai (1), to
credit; to *think, regard*

IMPUTED
2803 châshab (2), to
think, regard; compute
1677 ĕllŏgĕō (1), to
charge to one's account
3049 lŏgizŏmai (5), to
credit; to *think, regard*

IMPUTETH
2803 châshab (1), to
think, regard; compute
3049 lŏgizŏmai (1), to
credit; to *think, regard*

IMPUTING
3049 lŏgizŏmai (1), to
credit; to *think, regard*

IMRAH
3236 Yimrâh (1),
interchange

IMRI
556 'amtsâh (2),
strength, force

INASMUCH
1115 biltiy (1), *except,*
without, unless, besides
3588 kîy (1), *for, that*
because
2526 kathŏ (1), *precisely*
as, in proportion as

INCENSE
3828 lᵉbôwnâh (6),
frankincense

6999 qâṭar (58), to *turn*
into fragrance by fire
7002 qiṭṭêr (1), *perfume*
7004 qᵉṭôreth (57),
fumigation
2368 thumiama (4),
incense offering
2370 thumiaŏ (1), to
offer aromatic *fumes*

INCENSED
2734 chârâh (2), to *blaze*

INCLINE
5186 nâṭâh (15), to
stretch or spread out
7181 qâshab (1), to *prick*
up the ears

INCLINED
5186 nâṭâh (13), to
stretch or spread out

INCLINETH
7743 shûwach (1), to *sink*

INCLOSE
6696 tsûwr (1), to *cramp,*
i.e. *confine;* to *harass*

INCLOSED
1443 gâdar (1), to *build a*
stone wall
3803 kâthar (1), to
enclose, besiege; to *wait*
4142 mûwçabbâh (2),
backside; fold
5274 nâ'al (1), to *fasten*
up, lock
5362 nâqaph (1), to
surround or *circulate*
5462 çâgar (1), to *shut*
up; to *surrender*
4788 suglĕiŏ (1), to *net*
fish; to *lock up* persons

INCLOSINGS
4396 millû'âh (2), *setting*

INCONTINENCY
192 akrasia (1), *lack of*
control of self

INCONTINENT
193 akratēs (1), *without*
self-control

INCORRUPTIBLE
862 aphthartŏs (4),
undecaying, immortal

INCORRUPTION
861 aphtharsia (4),
unending existence

INCREASE
2981 yᵉbûwl (10),
produce, crop; harvest
3254 yâçaph (6), to *add*
or *augment*
4768 marbîyth (3),
interest on money
5107 nûwb (1), to *(make)*
flourish; to *utter*
6555 pârats (1), to *break*
out
7235 râbâh (18), to
increase
7239 ribbôw (1), *myriad,*
indefinite *large number*
7685 sâgâh (2), to
enlarge, be prosperous
7698 sheger (4), what
comes forth
8393 tᵉbûw'âh (23),
income, i.e. *produce*

8570 tᵉnûwbâh (2), *crop,*
produce
8635 tarbûwth (6),
progeny, brood
837 auxanō (4), to *grow,*
i.e. *enlarge*
838 auxēsis (2), *growth,*
increase
4052 pĕrissĕuō (1), to
superabound
4121 plĕŏnazō (1), to
increase; superabound
4298 prŏkŏptō (1), to *go*
ahead, advance
4369 prŏstithēmi (1), to
lay beside, annex

INCREASED
1431 gâdal (1), to *be*
great, make great
3254 yâçaph (5), to *add*
or *augment*
5927 'âlâh (3), to *ascend,*
be high, mount
6105 'âtsam (4), to *be,*
make numerous
6509 pârâh (3), to *bear*
fruit
6555 pârats (4), to *break*
out
7227 rab (2), *great*
7230 rôb (1), *abundance*
7231 râbab (3), to
increase; to multiply
7235 râbâh (15), to
increase
8317 shârats (1), to
swarm, or abound
837 auxanō (3), to *grow,*
i.e. *enlarge*
1743 ĕndunamŏō (1), to
empower, strengthen
4052 pĕrissĕuō (1), to
superabound
4147 plŏutĕō (1), to *be,*
become wealthy
4298 prŏkŏptō (1), to *go*
ahead, advance

INCREASEST
7235 râbâh (1), to
increase

INCREASETH
553 'âmats (1), to *be*
strong; be courageous
1342 gâ'âh (1), to *rise; to*
grow tall; be majestic
3254 yâçaph (4), to *add*
or *augment*
5927 'âlâh (1), to *ascend,*
be high, mount
7235 râbâh (5), to
increase
7679 sâgâ' (1), to *laud,*
extol
837 auxanō (1), to *grow,*
i.e. *enlarge*

INCREASING
837 auxanō (1), to *grow,*
i.e. *enlarge*

INCREDIBLE
571 apistŏs (1), *without*
faith; incredible

INCURABLE
369+4832 'ayin (1), *there*
is no, i.e., not exist
605 'ânash (5), to *be frail,*
feeble

INDEBTED
3784 ŏphĕilō (1), to *owe;*
to *be under obligation*

INDEED
61 'ăbâl (2), *truly, surely;*
yet, but
389 'ak (1), *surely; only,*
however
546 'omnâh (2), *surely*
551 'omnâm (2), *verily,*
indeed, truly
552 'umnâm (3), *verily,*
indeed, truly
1571 gam (1), *also; even;*
yea; though
230 alēthōs (6), *truly,*
surely
235 alla (1), *but, yet,*
except, instead
1063 gar (2), *for, indeed,*
but, because
2532 kai (2), *and; or;*
even; also
3303 mĕn (22), *indeed*
3689 ŏntōs (6), *really,*
certainly

INDIA
1912 Hôdûw (2), *India*

INDIGNATION
2194 zâ'am (4), to *be*
enraged
2195 za'am (20), *fury,*
anger
2197 za'aph (2), *anger,*
rage
2534 chêmâh (1), *heat;*
anger; poison
3707 kâ'aç (1), to *grieve,*
rage, be indignant
3708 ka'aç (1), *vexation,*
grief
7110 qetseph (3), *rage* or
strife
23 aganaktĕō (4), to *be*
indignant
24 aganaktēsis (1),
indignation
2205 zēlŏs (2), *zeal,*
ardor; jealousy, malice
2372 thumŏs (1),
passion, anger
3709 ŏrgē (1), *ire;*
punishment

INDITING
7370 râchash (1), to *gush*

INDUSTRIOUS
6213+4399 'âsâh (1), to
do or *make*

INEXCUSABLE
379 anapŏlŏgētŏs (1),
without excuse

INFAMOUS
2931+8034 tâmê' (1), *foul;*
ceremonially impure

INFAMY
1681 dibbâh (2), *slander,*
bad report

INFANT
5764 'ûwl (1), nursing
babe
5768 'ôwlêl (1), *suckling*
child

INFANTS
5768 'ôwlêl (2), *suckling*
child
1025 brĕphŏs (1), *infant*

INFERIOR
772 'ăra' (Ch.) (1), *earth,*
ground, land; inferior
5307 nâphal (2), to *fall*
2274 hēttaō (1), to *rate*
lower, be inferior

INFIDEL
571 apistŏs (2), *without*
faith; untrustworthy

INFINITE
369+4557 'ayin (1), *there*
is no, i.e., not exist
369+7093 'ayin (2), *there*
is no, i.e., not exist

INFIRMITIES
769 asthĕnĕia (10),
feebleness; malady
771 asthĕnĕma (1),
failing, weakness
3554 nŏsŏs (1), *malady,*
disease

INFIRMITY
1738 dâvâh (1), to *be in*
menstruation cycle
2470 châlâh (1), to *be*
weak, sick, afflicted
4245 machăleh (1),
sickness
769 asthĕnĕia (7),
feebleness; malady

INFLAME
1814 dâlaq (1), to *flame;*
to *pursue*

INFLAMMATION
1816 dalleqeth (1),
burning fever
6867 tsârebeth (1),
conflagration

INFLUENCES
4575 ma'ădannâh (1),
bond, i.e. *group*

INFOLDING
3947 lâqach (1), to *take*

INFORM
3384 yârâh (1), to *point;*
to *teach*

INFORMED
995 bîyn (1), to
understand; discern
1718 ĕmphanizō (3), to
show forth
2727 katēchĕō (2), to
indoctrinate

INGATHERING
614 'âçîyph (2), *harvest,*
gathering in of crops

INHABIT
3427 yâshab (8), to *dwell,*
to *remain; to settle*
7931 shâkan (2), to *reside*

INHABITANT
1481 gûwr (1), to *sojourn,*
live as an alien
3427 yâshab (31), to
dwell, to remain
7934 shâkên (1),
resident; fellow-citizen

INHABITANTS
1753 dûwr (Ch.) (2), to
reside, live in
3427 yâshab (190), to
dwell, to remain
7934 shâkên (2),
resident; fellow-citizen

8453 tôwshâb (1),
temporary dweller
2730 katŏikĕō (1), to
reside, live in

INHABITED
1509 gᵉzêrâh (1), *desert,*
unfertile place
3427 yâshab (29), to
dwell, to remain
4186 môwshâb (1), *seat;*
site; abode
7931 shâkan (1), to *reside*

INHABITERS
2730 katŏikĕō (2), to
reside, live in

INHABITEST
3427 yâshab (1), to *dwell,*
to *remain; to settle*

INHABITETH
3427 yâshab (1), to *dwell,*
to *remain; to settle*
7931 shâkan (1), to *reside*

INHABITING
6728 tsîyîy (1), *desert-*
dweller; wild beast

INHERIT
3423 yârash (21), to
inherit; to impoverish
5157 nâchal (25), to
inherit
5159 nachălâh (2),
occupancy
2816 klĕrŏnŏmĕō (14), to
be an heir to, inherit

INHERITANCE
2490 châlal (1), to
profane, defile
2506 chêleq (1),
allotment
3423 yârash (1), to
inherit; to impoverish
3425 yᵉrushâh (2),
conquest
4181 môwrâshâh (2),
possession
5157 nâchal (18), to
inherit
5159 nachălâh (189),
occupancy
2817 klĕrŏnŏmia (14),
inherited possession
2819 klĕrŏs (2), *lot,*
portion
2820 klĕrŏō (2), to *allot*

INHERITANCES
5159 nachălâh (1),
occupancy

INHERITED
3423 yârash (2), to
inherit; to impoverish
5157 nâchal (3), to *inherit*
2816 klĕrŏnŏmĕō (1), to
be an heir to, inherit

INHERITETH
5157 nâchal (1), to *inherit*

INHERITOR
3423 yârash (1), to
inherit; to impoverish

INIQUITIES
1647+5771 Gêrᵉshôm (1),
refugee
5758 'ivyâ' (Ch.) (1),
perverseness
5766 'evel (1), moral *evil*
5771 'âvôn (47), *evil*

92 adikēma (1), *wrong done*
458 anŏmia (3), *violation of law, wickedness*
4189 pŏnēria (1), *malice, evil, wickedness*

INIQUITY
205 'âven (47), *trouble, vanity, wickedness*
1942 havvâh (1), *desire; craving*
5753 'âvâh (4), to *be crooked*
5766 'evel (35), moral *evil*
5771 'âvôn (170), moral *evil*
5932 'alvâh (1), *moral perverseness*
5999 'âmâl (1), *wearing effort; worry*
7562 resha' (1), moral *wrong*
93 adikia (6), *wrongfulness*
458 anŏmia (8), *violation of law, wickedness*
3892 paranŏmia (1), *transgression*

INJURED
91 adikĕō (1), to *do wrong*

INJURIOUS
5197 hubristēs (1), *maltreater, violent*

INJUSTICE
2555 châmâç (1), *violence; malice*

INK
1773 dᵉyôw (1), *ink*
3188 mᵉlan (3), *black ink*

INKHORN
7083 qeçeth (3), *ink-stand*

INN
4411 mâlôwn (3), *lodgment* for night
2646 kataluma (1), *lodging-place*
3829 pandŏchĕiŏn (1), public *lodging*-place

INNER
2315 cheder (4), *apartment, chamber*
6441 pᵉnîymâh (1), *indoors, inside*
6442 pᵉnîymîy (30), *interior, inner*
2080 ĕsō (1), *inside, inner, in*
2082 ĕsōtĕrŏs (1), *interior, inner*

INNERMOST
2315 cheder (2), *apartment, chamber*

INNOCENCY
2136 zâkûw (Ch.) (1), *purity; justice*
5356 niqqâyôwn (4), *clearness; cleanness*

INNOCENT
2600 chinnâm (1), *gratis, free*
2643 chaph (1), *pure, clean*

5352 nâqâh (5), to *be, make clean;* to *be bare*
5355 nâqîy (29), *innocent*
121 athŏŏs (2), *not guilty*

INNOCENTS
5355 nâqîy (2), *innocent*

INNUMERABLE
369+4557 'ayin (4), *there is no, i.e., not exist*
382 anarithmētŏs (1), *without number*
3461 murias (2), *ten-thousand*

INORDINATE
5691 'ăgâbâh (1), *love, amorousness*
3806 pathŏs (1), *passion, concupiscence*

INQUISITION
1245 bâqash (1), to *search;* to *strive after*
1875 dârash (2), to *pursue or search*

INSCRIPTION
1924 ĕpigraphō (1), to *inscribe, write upon*

INSIDE
1004 bayith (1), *house; temple; family, tribe*

INSOMUCH
1519 ĕis (1), to *or into*
5620 hōstĕ (17), *thus, therefore*

INSPIRATION
5397 nᵉshâmâh (1), *breath, life*
2315 thĕŏpnĕustŏs (1), *divinely breathed* in

INSTANT
6621 petha' (2), *wink, i.e. moment; quickly*
7281 rega' (2), very *short space* of time
1945 ĕpikĕimai (1), to *rest upon; press upon*
2186 ĕphistēmi (1), to *be present;* to *approach*
4342 prŏskartĕrĕō (1), to *attend;* to *adhere*
5610 hōra (1), *hour, i.e. a unit of time*

INSTANTLY
1722+1616 ĕn (1), *in; during; because of*
4705 spŏudaiōs (1), *prompt, energetic*

INSTEAD
8478 tachath (35), *underneath;* in *lieu of*

INSTRUCT
995 bîyn (1), to *understand; discern*
3250 yiççôwr (1), *reprover, corrector*
3256 yâçar (3), to *chastise;* to *instruct*
3925 lâmad (1), to *teach, train*
7919 sâkal (2), to *be or act circumspect*
4822 sumbibazō (1), to *unite; to show, teach*

INSTRUCTED
995 bîyn (2), to *understand; discern*

3045 yâda' (1), to *know*
3245 yâçad (1), *settle, consult, establish*
3256 yâçar (5), to *chastise;* to *instruct*
3384 yârâh (1), to *point;* to *teach*
3925 lâmad (2), to *teach, train*
7919 sâkal (1), to *be or act circumspect*
2727 katēchĕō (3), to *indoctrinate*
3100 mathētĕuō (1), to *become a student*
3453 muĕō (1), to *initiate*
4264 prŏbibazō (1), to *bring to the front*

INSTRUCTER
3913 lâṭash (1), to *sharpen;* to *pierce*

INSTRUCTERS
3807 paidagōgŏs (1), *tutor,* cf. *pedagogue*

INSTRUCTING
3811 paidĕuō (1), to *educate or discipline*

INSTRUCTION
4148 mûwçâr (30), *reproof, warning*
4561 môçâr (1), *admonition*
3809 paidĕia (1), *disciplinary correction*

INSTRUCTOR
3810 paidĕutēs (1), *teacher or discipliner*

INSTRUMENT
3627 kᵉlîy (2), *implement, thing*

INSTRUMENTS
1761 dachăvâh (Ch.) (1), *musical instrument*
3627 kᵉlîy (37), *implement, thing*
4482 mên (1), *part; musical chord*
7991 shâlîysh (1), *triangle* instrument
3696 hŏplŏn (2), *implement, or utensil*

INSURRECTION
5376 nᵉsâ' (Ch.) (1), to *lift up*
7285 regesh (1), *tumultuous crowd*
2721 katĕphistēmi (1), to *rush upon* in an *assault*
4714 stasis (2), one *leading an uprising*
4955 sustasiastēs (1), *fellow-insurgent*

INTEGRITY
8537 tôm (11), *prosperity; innocence*
8538 tummâh (5), *innocence*

INTELLIGENCE
995 bîyn (1), to *understand; discern*

INTEND
559 'âmar (2), to *say*
1014 bŏulŏmai (1), to *be willing, desire; choose*

3195 mĕllō (1), to *intend, i.e. be about* to

INTENDED
5186 nâṭâh (1), to *stretch or spread out*

INTENDEST
559 'âmar (1), to *say*

INTENDING
1011 bŏulĕuō (1), to *deliberate;* to *resolve*
2309 thĕlō (1), to *will;* to *desire; choose*
3195 mĕllō (1), to *intend, i.e. be about* to

INTENT
1701 dibrâh (Ch.) (1), *because, on account of*
4616 ma'an (2), on *account of; in order*
5668 'âbûwr (1), on *account of; in order*
2443 hina (2), in *order that*
3056 lŏgŏs (1), *word, matter, thing*

INTENTS
4209 mᵉzimmâh (1), *plan; sagacity*
1771 ĕnnŏia (1), moral *understanding*

INTERCESSION
6293 pâga' (4), to *impinge*
1793 ĕntugchanō (4), to *entreat, petition*
5241 hupĕrĕntugchanō (1), to *intercede*

INTERCESSIONS
1783 ĕntĕuxis (1), *intercession*

INTERCESSOR
6293 pâga' (1), to *impinge*

INTERMEDDLE
6148 'ârab (1), to *intermix*

INTERMEDDLETH
1566 gâla' (1), to *be obstinate;* to *burst forth*

INTERMISSION
2014 hăphûgâh (1), *relaxation*

INTERPRET
6622 pâthar (4), to *interpret* a dream
1329 diĕrmĕnĕuō (4), to *explain thoroughly*

INTERPRETATION
4426 mᵉlîytsâh (1), *aphorism, saying*
6591 pᵉshar (Ch.) (30), *interpretation*
6592 pêsher (1), *interpretation*
6623 pithrôwn (5), *interpretation*
7667 sheber (1), *solution* of a dream
1329 diĕrmĕnĕuō (1), to *explain thoroughly*
1955 ĕpilusis (1), *interpretation*
2058 hĕrmēnĕia (2), *translation*
2059 hĕrmēnĕuō (3), to *translate*
3177 mĕthĕrmēnĕuō (1), to *translate*

INTERPRETATIONS
6591 pᵉshar (Ch.) (1),
interpretation
6623 pithrôwn (1),
interpretation

INTERPRETED
6622 pâthar (3), to
interpret a dream
8638 tirgam (1), to
translate, interpret
2059 hĕrmĕnĕuŏ (1), to
translate
3177 mĕthĕrmĕnĕuŏ (6),
to *translate*

INTERPRETER
3887 lûwts (2), to *scoff; to*
interpret; to intercede
6622 pâthar (1), to
interpret a dream
1328 diĕrmĕnĕutēs (1),
explainer, translator

INTERPRETING
6591 pᵉshar (Ch.) (1),
interpretation

INTREAT
2470 châlâh (3), to *be*
weak, sick, afflicted
6279 'âthar (6), *intercede*
6293 pâga' (2), to *impinge*
6419 pâlal (1), to
intercede, pray
2065 ĕrŏtaŏ (1), to
interrogate; to request
3870 parakalĕŏ (2), to
call, invite

INTREATED
2470 châlâh (1), to *be*
weak, sick, afflicted
2589 channôwth (1),
supplication
2603 chânan (1), to
implore
6279 'âthar (12),
intercede in prayer
2138 ĕupĕithēs (1),
compliant, submissive
3862 paradŏsis (1),
precept; tradition
3870 parakalĕŏ (1), to
call, invite

INTREATIES
8469 tachănûwn (1),
earnest *prayer, plea*

INTREATY
3874 paraklēsis (1),
imploring, exhortation

INTRUDING
1687 ĕmbatĕuŏ (1), to
intrude on

INVADE
935 bôw' (1), to *go or*
come
1464 gûwd (1), to *attack*

INVADED
935 bôw' (1), to *go or*
come
6584 pâshaṭ (4), to *strip,*
i.e. *unclothe, plunder*

INVASION
6584 pâshaṭ (1), to *strip,*
i.e. *unclothe, plunder,*
flay

INVENT
2803 châshab (1), to
weave, fabricate

INVENTED
2803 châshab (1), to
weave, fabricate

INVENTIONS
2810 chishshâbôwn (1),
machination, scheme
4209 mᵉzimmâh (1),
plan; sagacity
4611 ma'ălâl (2), *act,*
deed
5949 'ălîylâh (1),
opportunity, action

INVENTORS
2182 ĕphĕurĕtēs (1),
contriver, inventor

INVISIBLE
517 aŏratŏs (5), *invisible,*
not seen

INVITED
7121 qârâ' (3), to *call* out

INWARD
1004 bayith (7), *house;*
temple; family, tribe
2315 cheder (2),
apartment, chamber
2910 ṭûwchâh (2), inmost
thought
5475 çôwd (1), *intimacy;*
consultation; secret
6441 pᵉnîymâh (2),
indoors, inside
6442 pᵉnîymîy (1),
interior, inner
7130 qereb (5), *nearest*
part, i.e. *the center*
2080 ĕsŏ (1), *inside,*
inner, in
2081 ĕsŏthĕn (2), *from*
inside; inside
4698 splagchnŏn (1),
intestine; affection, pity
or sympathy

INWARDLY
7130 qereb (1), *nearest*
part, i.e. *the center*
1722+2927 ĕn (1), *in;*
during; because of
2081 ĕsŏthĕn (1), *from*
inside; inside

INWARDS
7130 qereb (19), *nearest*
part, i.e. *the center*

IPHEDEIAH
3301 Yiphdᵉyâh (1),
Jehovah will liberate

IR
5893 'Îyr (1), *city, town,*
unwalled-village

IR-NAHASH
5904 'Îyr Nâchâsh (1),
city of a serpent

IR-SHEMESH
5905 'Îyr Shemesh (1),
city of (the) *sun*

IRA
5896 'Îyrâ' (6),
wakefulness

IRAD
5897 'Îyrâd (2), *fugitive*

IRAM
5902 'Îyrâm (2), *city-wise*

IRI
5901 'Îyrîy (1), *urbane*

IRIJAH
3376 Yir'îyâyh (2), *fearful*
of Jehovah

IRON
1270 barzel (72), *iron;*
iron implement
3375 Yir'ôwn (1),
fearfulness
6523 parzel (Ch.) (19),
iron
4603 sidĕrĕŏs (5), made
of iron
4604 sidĕrŏs (1), *iron*

IRONS
7905 sukkâh (1), *dart,*
harpoon

IRPEEL
3416 Yirpᵉ'êl (1), *God*
will heal

IRU
5902 'Îyrâm (1), *city-wise*

ISAAC
3327 Yitschâq (104),
laughter
3446 Yischâq (4), *he will*
laugh
2464 Isaak (20), *he will*
laugh

ISAAC'S
3327 Yitschâq (4),
laughter

ISAIAH
3470 Yᵉsha'yâh (32),
Jehovah has saved

ISCAH
3252 Yiçkâh (1),
observant

ISCARIOT
2469 Iskariŏtēs (11),
inhabitant of Kerioth

ISH-BOSHETH
378 'Îysh-Bôsheth (11),
man of shame

ISH-TOB
382 'Îysh-Ṭôwb (2), *man*
of Tob

ISHBAH
3431 Yishbach (1), *he*
will praise

ISHBAK
3435 Yishbâq (2), *he will*
leave

ISHBI-BENOB
3430 Yishbôw bᵉ-Nôb (1),
his dwelling (is) *in Nob*

ISHI
376 'îysh (1), *man; male;*
someone
3469 Yish'îy (5), *saving*

ISHIAH
3449 Yishshîyâh (1),
Jehovah will lend

ISHIJAH
3449 Yishshîyâh (1),
Jehovah will lend

ISHMA
3457 Yishmâ' (1),
desolate

ISHMAEL
3458 Yishmâ'ê'l (47),
God will hear

ISHMAEL'S
3458 Yishmâ'ê'l (1), *God*
will hear

ISHMAELITE
3458 Yishmâ'ê'l (1), *God*
will hear

ISHMAELITES
3459 Yishmâ'ê'lîy (2),
Jishmaëlite

ISHMAIAH
3460 Yishma'yâh (1),
Jehovah will hear

ISHMEELITE
3459 Yishmâ'ê'lîy (1),
Jishmaëlite

ISHMEELITES
3459 Yishmâ'ê'lîy (4),
Jishmaëlite

ISHMERAI
3461 Yishmᵉray (1),
preservative

ISHOD
379 'Îyshhôwd (1), *man*
of renown

ISHPAN
3473 Yishpân (1), *he will*
hide

ISHUAH
3438 Yishvâh (1), *he will*
level

ISHUAI
3440 Yishvîy (1), *level*

ISHUI
3440 Yishvîy (1), *level*

ISLAND
336 'îy (1), *not*
338 'îy (1), solitary wild
creature that howls
3519 nēsiŏn (1), small
island
3520 nēsŏs (6), *island*

ISLANDS
338 'îy (1), solitary wild
creature that howls
339 'îy (6), dry *land;*
coast; island

ISLE
339 'îy (3), *coast; island*
3520 nēsŏs (3), *island*

ISLES
339 'îy (27), dry *land;*
coast; island

ISMACHIAH
3253 Yiçmakyâhûw (1),
Jehovah will sustain

ISMAIAH
3460 Yishma'yâh (1),
Jehovah will hear

ISPAH
3472 Yishpâh (1), *he will*
scratch

ISRAEL
3478 Yisrâ'êl (2477), *he*
will rule (as) *God*
3479 Yisrâ'êl (Ch.) (8), *he*
will rule (as) *God*
3481 Yisrᵉ'êlîy (1),
Jisreëlite
2474 Israēl (70), *he will*
rule (as) *God*
2475 Israēlitēs (5),
descendants of Israel

ISRAEL'S
3478 Yisrâ'êl (10), *he will rule* (as) *God*

ISRAELITE
1121+3478 bên (1), *son, descendant; people*
3481 Yisrᵉ'êlîy (1), *Jisreëlite*
2475 Israēlitēs (2), *descendants of Israel*

ISRAELITES
3478 Yisrâ'êl (16), *he will rule* (as) *God*
2475 Israēlitēs (2), *descendants of Israel*

ISRAELITISH
3482 Yisrᵉ'êlîyth (3), *Jisreëlitess*

ISSACHAR
3485 Yissâˢkâr (43), *he will bring a reward*
2466 Isachar (1), *he will bring a reward*

ISSHIAH
3449 Yishshîyâh (2), *Jehovah will lend*

ISSUE
2100 zûwb (16), *to flow freely, gush*
2101 zôwb (11), *flux or discharge*
2231 zirmâh (1), *emission* of semen
3318 yâtsâ' (3), *to go, bring out*
4138 môwledeth (1), *offspring, family*
4726 mâqôwr (1), *flow*
6849 tsᵉphî'âh (1), *outcast* thing, *offshoots*
131 haimŏrrhĕō (1), to *have a hemorrhage*
4511 rhusis (3), *flux*
4690 spĕrma (1), *seed, offspring*

ISSUED
3318 yâtsâ' (4), *to go, bring out*
5047 nᵉgad (Ch.) (1), *to flow*
1607 ĕkpŏrĕuŏmai (2), *to depart, be discharged*

ISSUES
8444 tôwtsâ'âh (2), *exit, boundary; source*

ISUAH
3440 Yishvîy (1), *level*

ISUI
3440 Yishvîy (1), *level*

ITALIAN
2483 Italikŏs (1), *belonging to Italia*

ITALY
2482 Italia (4), *Italia*

ITCH
2775 chereç (1), *itch; sun*

ITCHING
2833 knēthō (1), *to tickle, feel an itch*

ITHAI
863 'Ittay (1), *near*

ITHAMAR
385 'Îythâmâr (21), *coast of the palm-tree*

ITHIEL
384 'Îythîy'êl (3), *God has arrived*

ITHMAH
3495 Yithmâh (1), *orphanage*

ITHNAN
3497 Yithnân (1), *extensive*

ITHRA
3501 Yithrâ' (1), *wealth*

ITHRAN
3506 Yithrân (3), *excellent*

ITHREAM
3507 Yithrᵉ'âm (2), *excellence of people*

ITHRITE
3505 Yithrîy (4), *Jithrite*

ITHRITES
3505 Yithrîy (1), *Jithrite*

ITTAH-KAZIN
6278 'Êth Qâtsîyn (1), *time of a judge*

ITTAI
863 'Ittay (8), *near*

ITURAEA
2434 hilasmŏs (1), *atonement, expiator*

IVAH
5755 'Ivvâh (3), *overthrow, ruin*

IVORY
8127 shên (10), *tooth; ivory; cliff*
8143 shenhabbîym (2), *elephant's ivory tusk*
1661 ĕlĕphantinŏs (1), *of ivory*

IZEHAR
3324 Yitshâr (1), *olive oil; anointing*

IZEHARITES
3325 Yitshârîy (1), *Jitsharite*

IZHAR
3324 Yitshâr (8), *olive oil; anointing*

IZHARITES
3325 Yitshârîy (3), *Jitsharite*

IZRAHIAH
3156 Yizrachyâh (2), *Jehovah will shine*

IZRAHITE
3155 Yizrâch (1), *Ezrachite or Zarchite*

IZRI
3342 yeqeb (1), *wine-vat, wine-press*

JAAKAN
3292 Ya'ăqân (1), *Jaakan*

JAAKOBAH
3291 Ya'ăqôbâh (1), *heel-catcher*

JAALA
3279 Ya'ălâ' (1), *to be valuable*

JAALAH
3279 Ya'ălâ' (1), *to be valuable*

JAALAM
3281 Ya'lâm (4), *occult*

JAANAI
3285 Ya'ănay (1), *responsive*

JAARE-OREGIM
3296 Ya'ărêy 'Orᵉgîym (1), *woods of weavers*

JAASAU
3299 Ya'ăsûw (1), *they will do*

JAASIEL
3300 Ya'ăsîy'êl (1), *made of God*

JAAZANIAH
2970 Ya'ăzanyâh (4), *heard of Jehovah*

JAAZER
3270 Ya'ăzêyr (2), *helpful*

JAAZIAH
3269 Ya'ăzîyâhûw (2), *emboldened of Jehovah*

JAAZIEL
3268 Ya'ăzîy'êl (1), *emboldened of God*

JABAL
2989 Yâbâl (1), *stream*

JABBOK
2999 Yabbôq (7), *pouring forth*

JABESH
3003 Yâbêsh (12), *dry*

JABESH-GILEAD
3003+1568 Yâbêsh (12), *dry*

JABEZ
3258 Ya'bêts (4), *sorrowful*

JABIN
2985 Yâbîyn (7), *intelligent*

JABIN'S
2985 Yâbîyn (1), *intelligent*

JABNEEL
2995 Yabnᵉ'êl (2), *built of God*

JABNEH
2996 Yabneh (1), *building*

JACHAN
3275 Ya'kân (1), *troublesome*

JACHIN
3199 Yâkîyn (8), *he* (or *it*) *will establish*

JACHINITES
3200 Yâkîynîy (1), *Jakinite*

JACINTH
5191 huakinthinŏs (1), *deep blue color*
5192 huakinthŏs (1), *blue gem,* (poss.) *zircon*

JACOB
3290 Ya'ăqôb (331), *heel-catcher*
2384 Iakōb (26), *heel-catcher*

JACOB'S
3290 Ya'ăqôb (17), *heel-catcher*

JAALAM
2384 Iakōb (1), *heel-catcher*

JADA
3047 Yâdâ' (2), *knowing*

JADAU
3035 Yiddôw (1), *praised*

JADDUA
3037 Yaddûwa' (3), *knowing*

JADON
3036 Yâdôwn (1), *thankful*

JAEL
3278 Yâ'êl (6), *ibex animal*

JAGUR
3017 Yâgûwr (1), *lodging*

JAH
3050 Yâhh (1), *Jehovah,* (the) *self-Existent or Eternal One*

JAHATH
3189 Yachath (8), *unity*

JAHAZ
3096 Yahats (5), *threshing-floor*

JAHAZA
3096 Yahats (1), *threshing-floor*

JAHAZAH
3096 Yahats (2), *threshing-floor*

JAHAZIAH
3167 Yachzᵉyâh (1), *Jehovah will behold*

JAHAZIEL
3166 Yachăzîy'êl (6), *beheld of God*

JAHDAI
3056 Yehday (1), *Judaistic*

JAHDIEL
3164 Yachdîy'êl (1), *unity of God*

JAHDO
3163 Yachdôw (1), *his unity*

JAHLEEL
3177 Yachlᵉ'êl (2), *expectant of God*

JAHLEELITES
3178 Yachlᵉ'êlîy (1), *Jachleëlite*

JAHMAI
3181 Yachmay (1), *hot*

JAHZAH
3096 Yahats (1), *threshing-floor*

JAHZEEL
3183 Yachtsᵉ'êl (2), *God will allot*

JAHZEELITES
3184 Yachtsᵉ'êlîy (1), *Jachtseëlite*

JAHZERAH
3170 Yachzêrâh (1), *protection*

JAHZIEL
3185 Yachtsîy'êl (1), *allotted of God*

JAILER
1200 dĕsmŏphulax (1), jailer

JAIR
2971 Yâ'îyr (10), enlightener

JAIRITE
2972 Yâ'îrîy (1), Jaïrite

JAIRUS
2383 Iaĕirŏs (3), enlightener

JAKAN
3292 Ya'ăqân (1), Jaakan

JAKEH
3348 Yâqeh (1), obedient

JAKIM
3356 Yâqîym (2), he will raise

JALON
3210 Yâlôwn (1), lodging

JAMBRES
2387 Iambrēs (1), Jambres

JAMES
2385 Iakŏbŏs (41), heel-catcher

JAMIN
3226 Yâmîyn (6), right; south

JAMINITES
3228 Yᵉmîynîy (1), Jeminite

JAMLECH
3230 Yamlêk (1), he will make king

JANGLING
3150 mataiŏlŏgia (1), babble, meaningless talk

JANNA
2388 Ianna (1), Janna

JANNES
2389 Iannēs (1), Jannes

JANOAH
3239 Yânôwach (1), quiet

JANOHAH
3239 Yânôwach (2), quiet

JANUM
3241 Yânîym (1), asleep

JAPHETH
3315 Yepheth (11), expansion

JAPHIA
3309 Yâphîya' (5), bright

JAPHLET
3310 Yaphlêṭ (3), he will deliver

JAPHLETI
3311 Yaphlêṭîy (1), Japhletite

JAPHO
3305 Yâphôw (1), beautiful

JARAH
3294 Ya'râh (2), honey in the comb

JAREB
3377 Yârêb (2), he will contend

JARED
3382 Yered (5), descent
2391 Iarĕd (1), descent

JARESIAH
3298 Ya'ăreshyâh (1), Jaareshjah

JARHA
3398 Yarchâ' (2), Jarcha

JARIB
3402 Yârîyb (3), contentious; adversary

JARMUTH
3412 Yarmûwth (7), elevation

JAROAH
3386 Yârôwach (1), (born at the) new moon

JASHEN
3464 Yâshên (1), sleepy

JASHER
3477 yâshâr (2), straight

JASHOBEAM
3434 Yâshob'âm (3), people will return

JASHUB
3437 Yâshûwb (3), he will return

JASHUBI-LEHEM
3433 Yâshûbîy Lechem (1), returner of bread

JASHUBITES
3432 Yâshûbîy (1), Jashubite

JASIEL
3300 Ya'ăsîy'êl (1), made of God

JASON
2394 Iasōn (5), about to cure

JASPER
3471 yâshᵉphêh (3), jasper stone
2393 iaspis (4), jasper

JATHNIEL
3496 Yathnîy'êl (1), continued of God

JATTIR
3492 Yattîyr (4), redundant

JAVAN
3120 Yâvân (7), effervescent

JAVELIN
2595 chănîyth (6), lance, spear
7420 rômach (1), iron pointed spear

JAW
3895 lᵉchîy (3), jaw; jaw-bone
4973 mᵉthallᵉ'âh (1), tooth

JAWBONE
3895 lᵉchîy (3), jaw; jaw-bone

JAWS
3895 lᵉchîy (4), jaw; jaw-bone
4455 malqôwach (1), spoil, plunder
4973 mᵉthallᵉ'âh (1), tooth

JAZER
3270 Ya'ăzêyr (11), helpful

JAZIZ
3151 Yâzîyz (1), he will make prominent

JEALOUS
7065 qânâ' (11), to be, make zealous, jealous
7067 qannâ' (4), jealous
7072 qannôw' (2), jealous
2206 zēlŏō (1), to have warmth of feeling for

JEALOUSIES
7068 qin'âh (1), jealousy or envy

JEALOUSY
7065 qânâ' (5), to be, make zealous, jealous
7068 qin'âh (23), jealousy
7069 qânâh (1), to create; to procure
2205 zēlŏs (1), zeal, ardor; jealousy, malice

JEARIM
3297 Yᵉ'ârîym (1), forests

JEATERAI
2979 Yᵉ'âthᵉray (1), stepping

JEBERECHIAH
3000 Yᵉberekyâhûw (1), blessed of Jehovah

JEBUS
2982 Yᵉbûwç (4), trodden

JEBUSI
2983 Yᵉbûwçîy (2), Jebusite

JEBUSITE
2983 Yᵉbûwçîy (14), Jebusite

JEBUSITES
2983 Yᵉbûwçîy (25), Jebusite

JECAMIAH
3359 Yᵉqamyâh (1), Jehovah will rise

JECHOLIAH
3203 Yᵉkolyâh (1), Jehovah will enable

JECHONIAS
2423 Iĕchŏnias (2), Jehovah will establish

JECOLIAH
3203 Yᵉkolyâh (1), Jehovah will enable

JECONIAH
3204 Yᵉkonyâh (7), Jehovah will establish

JEDAIAH
3042 Yᵉdâyâh (2), praised of Jehovah
3048 Yᵉda'yâh (11), Jehovah has known

JEDIAEL
3043 Yᵉdîy'ă'êl (6), knowing God

JEDIDAH
3040 Yᵉdîydâh (1), beloved

JEDIDIAH
3041 Yᵉdîydᵉyâh (1), beloved of Jehovah

JEDUTHUN
3038 Yᵉdûwthûwn (16), laudatory

JEEZER
372 'Îy'ezer (1), helpless

JEEZERITES
373 'Îy'ezrîy (1), Iezrite

JEGAR-SAHADUTHA
3026 Yᵉgar Sahădûwthâ' (Ch.) (1), heap of the testimony

JEHALELEEL
3094 Yᵉhallel'êl (1), praising God

JEHALELEL
3094 Yᵉhallel'êl (1), praising God

JEHDEIAH
3165 Yechdîyâhûw (2), unity of Jehovah

JEHEZEKEL
3168 Yᵉchezqê'l (1), God will strengthen

JEHIAH
3174 Yᵉchîyâh (1), Jehovah will live

JEHIEL
3171 Yᵉchîy'êl (14), God will live
3273 Yᵉ'îy'êl (2), carried away of God

JEHIELI
3172 Yᵉchîy'êlîy (2), Jechiëlite

JEHIZKIAH
3169 Yᵉchizqîyâh (1), strengthened of Jehovah

JEHOADAH
3085 Yᵉhôw'addâh (2), Jehovah-adorned

JEHOADDAN
3086 Yᵉhôw'addîyn (2), Jehovah-pleased

JEHOAHAZ
3059 Yᵉhôw'âchâz (21), Jehovah-seized
3099 Yôw'âchâz (1), Jehovah-seized

JEHOASH
3060 Yᵉhôw'âsh (17), Jehovah-fired

JEHOHANAN
3076 Yᵉhôwchânân (6), Jehovah-favored

JEHOIACHIN
3078 Yᵉhôwyâkîyn (10), Jehovah will establish

JEHOIACHIN'S
3112 Yôwyâkîyn (1), Jehovah will establish

JEHOIADA
3111 Yᵉhôwyâdâ' (52), Jehovah-known

JEHOIAKIM
3079 Yᵉhôwyâqîym (37), Jehovah will raise

JEHOIARIB
3080 Yᵉhôwyârîyb (2), Jehovah will contend

JEHONADAB
3082 Yᵉhôwnâdâb (3), *Jehovah-largessed*

JEHONATHAN
3083 Yᵉhôwnâthân (3), *Jehovah-given*

JEHORAM
3088 Yᵉhôwrâm (23), *Jehovah-raised*

JEHOSHABEATH
3090 Yᵉhôwshab'ath (2), *Jehovah-sworn*

JEHOSHAPHAT
3046 yᵉda' (Ch.) (1), *to know*
3092 Yᵉhôwshâphâṭ (84), *Jehovah-judged*

JEHOSHEBA
3089 Yᵉhôwsheba' (1), *Jehovah-sworn*

JEHOSHUA
3091 Yᵉhôwshûw'a (1), *Jehovah-saved*

JEHOSHUAH
3091 Yᵉhôwshûw'a (1), *Jehovah-saved*

JEHOVAH
3068 Yᵉhôvâh (4), (the) *self-Existent or Eternal*

JEHOVAH-JIREH
3070 Yᵉhôvâh Yir'eh (1), *Jehovah will see* (to it)

JEHOVAH-NISSI
3071 Yᵉhôvâh Niççîy (1), *Jehovah* (is) *my banner*

JEHOVAH-SHALOM
3073 Yᵉhôvâh Shâlôwm (1), *Jehovah* (is) *peace*

JEHOZABAD
3075 Yᵉhôwzâbâd (4), *Jehovah-endowed*

JEHOZADAK
3087 Yᵉhôwtsâdâq (2), *Jehovah-righted*

JEHU
3058 Yêhûw' (57), *Jehovah* (is) *He*

JEHUBBAH
3160 Yᵉchubbâh (1), *hidden*

JEHUCAL
3081 Yᵉhûwkal (1), *potent*

JEHUD
3055 Yᵉhûd (1), *celebrated*

JEHUDI
3065 Yᵉhûwdîy (4), *Jehudite*

JEHUDIJAH
3057 Yᵉhûdîyâh (1), *celebrated*

JEHUSH
3266 Yᵉ'ûwsh (1), *hasty*

JEIEL
3273 Yᵉ'îy'êl (11), *carried away of God*

JEKABZEEL
3343 Yᵉqabtsᵉ'êl (1), *God will gather*

JEKAMEAM
3360 Yᵉqam'âm (2), *people will rise*

JEKAMIAH
3359 Yᵉqamyâh (2), *Jehovah will rise*

JEKUTHIEL
3354 Yᵉqûwthîy'êl (1), *obedience of God*

JEMIMA
3224 Yᵉmîymâh (1), *dove*

JEMUEL
3223 Yᵉmûw'êl (2), *day of God*

JEOPARDED
2778 châraph (1), *to spend the winter*

JEOPARDY
2793 kinduněuō (2), *to undergo peril*

JEPHTHAE
2422 Iĕphthaě (1), *he will open*

JEPHTHAH
3316 Yiphtâch (29), *he will open*

JEPHUNNEH
3312 Yᵉphunneh (16), *he will be prepared*

JERAH
3392 Yerach (2), *lunar month*

JERAHMEEL
3396 Yᵉrachmᵉ'êl (8), *God will be compassionate*

JERAHMEELITES
3397 Yᵉrachmᵉ'êlîy (2), *Jerachmeëlite*

JERED
3382 Yered (2), *descent*

JEREMAI
3413 Yᵉrêmay (1), *elevated*

JEREMIAH
3414 Yirmᵉyâh (146), *Jehovah will rise*

JEREMIAH'S
3414 Yirmᵉyâh (1), *Jehovah will rise*

JEREMIAS
2408 Hiĕrĕmias (1), *Jehovah will rise*

JEREMOTH
3406 Yᵉrîymôwth (5), *elevations*

JEREMY
2408 Hiĕrĕmias (2), *Jehovah will rise*

JERIAH
3404 Yᵉrîyâh (2), *Jehovah will throw*

JERIBAI
3403 Yᵉrîybay (1), *contentious*

JERICHO
3405 Yᵉrîychôw (57), *its month, or fragrant*
2410 Hiĕrichô (7), *its month or fragrant*

JERIEL
3400 Yᵉrîy'êl (1), *thrown of God*

JERIJAH
3404 Yᵉrîyâh (1), *Jehovah will throw*

JERIMOTH
3406 Yᵉrîymôwth (8), *elevations*

JERIOTH
3408 Yᵉrîy'ôwth (1), *curtains*

JEROBOAM
3379 Yârob'âm (102), *people will contend*

JEROBOAM'S
3379 Yârob'âm (2), *people will contend*

JEROHAM
3395 Yᵉrôchâm (10), *compassionate*

JERUBBAAL
3378 Yᵉrubba'al (14), *Baal will contend*

JERUBBESHETH
3380 Yᵉrubbesheth (1), *the idol will contend*

JERUEL
3385 Yᵉrûw'êl (1), *founded of God*

JERUSALEM
3389 Yᵉrûwshâlaim (640), *founded peaceful*
3390 Yᵉrûwshâlêm (Ch.) (26), *founded peaceful*
2414 Hiĕrŏsŏluma (61), *founded peaceful*
2419 Hiĕrŏusalēm (81), *founded peaceful*

JERUSALEM'S
3389 Yᵉrûwshâlaim (3), *founded peaceful*

JERUSHA
3388 Yᵉrûwshâ' (1), *possessed*

JERUSHAH
3388 Yᵉrûwshâ' (1), *possessed*

JESAIAH
3470 Yᵉsha'yâh (2), *Jehovah has saved*

JESHAIAH
3740 kêrâh (5), *purchase*

JESHANAH
3466 Yᵉshânâh (1), *old*

JESHARELAH
3480 Yᵉsar'êlâh (1), *right towards God*

JESHEBEAB
3434 Yâshob'âm (1), *people will return*

JESHER
3475 Yêsher (1), *right*

JESHIMON
3452 yᵉshîymôwn (5), *desolation*

JESHISHAI
3454 Yᵉshîyshay (1), *aged*

JESHOHAIAH
3439 Yᵉshôwchâyâh (1), *Jehovah will empty*

JESHUA
3442 Yêshûwa' (28), *he will save*
3443 Yêshûwa' (Ch.) (2), *he will save*

JESHURUN
3484 Yᵉshûrûwn (3), *upright*

JESIAH
3449 Yishshîyâh (2), *Jehovah will lend*

JESIMIEL
3450 Yᵉsîymâ'êl (1), *God will place*

JESSE
3448 Yîshay (41), *extant*
2421 Iĕssai (5), *extant*

JESTING
2160 ĕutrapĕlia (1), *ribaldry*

JESUI
3440 Yishvîy (1), *level*

JESUITES
3441 Yishvîy (1), *Jishvite*

JESURUN
3484 Yᵉshûrûwn (1), *upright*

JESUS
846 autŏs (1), *he, she, it*
2424 Iēsŏus (967), *Jehovah-saved*

JESUS'
2424 Iēsŏus (10), *Jehovah-saved*

JETHER
3500 Yether (8), *remainder*

JETHETH
3509 Yᵉthêyth (2), *Jetheth*

JETHLAH
3494 Yithlâh (1), *be high*

JETHRO
3503 Yithrôw (10), *his excellence*

JETUR
3195 Yᵉṭûwr (3), *enclosed*

JEUEL
3262 Yᵉ'ûw'êl (1), *carried away of God*

JEUSH
3266 Yᵉ'ûwsh (8), *hasty*

JEUZ
3263 Yᵉ'ûwts (1), *counselor*

JEW
3064 Yᵉhûwdîy (10), *Jehudite*
2453 Iŏudaiŏs (22), *belonging to Jehudah*

JEWEL
3627 kᵉlîy (1), *implement, thing*
5141 nezem (2), *nose-ring*

JEWELS
2484 chelyâh (2), *trinket, ornament*
3627 kᵉlîy (18), *implement, thing*
5141 nezem (1), *nose-ring*
5459 çᵉgullâh (1), *wealth*

JEWESS
2453 Iŏudaiŏs (2),
belonging to Jehudah

JEWISH
2451 Iŏudaïkŏs (1),
resembling a Judæan

JEWRY
3061 Yᵉhûwd (Ch.) (1),
celebrated
2449 Iŏudaia (2),
Judæan land

JEWS
3054 yâhad (1), to
become Jewish
3062 Yᵉhûwdâ'îy (Ch.)
(8), Jew
3064 Yᵉhûwdîy (65),
Jehudite
2450 Iŏudaïzō (1), to
Judaize, live as a Jew
2452 Iŏudaïkōs (1), in a
Judæan manner
2453 Iŏudaïŏs (167),
belonging to Jehudah

JEWS'
3064 Yᵉhûwdîy (4),
Jehudite
3066 Yᵉhûwdîyth (4), in
the Jewish language
2453 Iŏudaïŏs (4),
belonging to Jehudah
2454 Iŏudaismŏs (2),
Jewish faith

JEZANIAH
3153 Yᵉzanyâh (2), heard
of Jehovah

JEZEBEL
348 'Îyzebel (21), chaste
2403 Iĕzabēl (1), chaste

JEZEBEL'S
348 'Îyzebel (1), chaste

JEZER
3337 Yêtser (3), form

JEZERITES
3339 Yitsrîy (1),
formative

JEZIAH
3150 Yizzîyâh (1),
sprinkled of Jehovah

JEZIEL
3149 Yᵉzav'êl (1),
sprinkled of God

JEZLIAH
3152 Yizlîy'ah (1), he will
draw out

JEZOAR
3328 Yitschar (1), he will
shine

JEZRAHIAH
3156 Yizrachyâh (1),
Jehovah will shine

JEZREEL
3157 Yizrᵉ'ê'l (36), God
will sow

JEZREELITE
3158 Yizrᵉ'ê'lîy (8),
Jizreëlite

JEZREELITESS
3159 Yizrᵉ'ê'lîyth (5),
Jezreëlitess

JIBSAM
3005 Yibsâm (1), fragrant

JIDLAPH
3044 Yidlâph (1), tearful

JIMNA
3232 Yimnâh (1),
prosperity

JIMNAH
3232 Yimnâh (1),
prosperity

JIMNITES
3232 Yimnâh (1),
prosperity

JIPHTAH
3316 Yiphtâch (1), he
will open

JIPHTAH-EL
3317 Yiphtach-'êl (2),
God will open

JOAB
3097 Yôw'âb (137),
Jehovah-fathered
5854 'Aṭrôwth Bêyth
Yôw'âb (1), crowns of
(the) house of Joäb

JOAB'S
3097 Yôw'âb (8),
Jehovah-fathered

JOAH
3098 Yôw'âch (11),
Jehovah-brothered

JOAHAZ
3098 Yôw'âch (1),
Jehovah-brothered

JOANNA
2489 Iōanna (3),
Jehovah-favored

JOASH
3101 Yôw'âsh (47),
Jehovah-fired
3135 Yôw'âsh (2),
Jehovah-hastened

JOATHAM
2488 Iōatham (2),
Jehovah (is) perfect

JOB
347 'Îyôwb (57),
persecuted
3102 Yôwb (1), Job
2492 Iōb (1), persecuted

JOB'S
347 'Îyôwb (1), persecuted

JOBAB
3103 Yôwbâb (9), howler

JOCHEBED
3115 Yôwkebed (2),
Jehovah-gloried

JOED
3133 Yôw'êd (1),
appointer

JOEL
3100 Yôw'êl (19),
Jehovah (is his) God
2493 Iōēl (1), Jehovah (is
his) God

JOELAH
3132 Yôw'ê'lâh (1),
furthermore

JOEZER
3134 Yôw'ezer (1),
Jehovah (is his) help

JOGBEHAH
3011 Yogbᵉhâh (2),
hillock

JOGLI
3020 Yoglîy (1), exiled

JOHA
3109 Yôwchâ' (2),
Jehovah-revived

JOHANAN
3076 Yᵉhôwchânân (3),
Jehovah-favored
3110 Yôwchânân (24),
Jehovah-favored

JOHN
2491 Iōannēs (131),
Jehovah-favored

JOHN'S
2491 Iōannēs (2),
Jehovah-favored

JOIADA
3111 Yôwyâdâ' (4),
Jehovah-known

JOIAKIM
3113 Yôwyâqîym (4),
Jehovah will raise

JOIARIB
3114 Yôwyârîyb (5),
Jehovah will contend

JOIN
2266 châbar (2), to
fascinate by spells
2859 châthan (1), to
become related
3254 yâçaph (1), to add
or augment
3867 lâvâh (2), to unite;
to remain; to borrow
5060 nâga' (1), to strike
5526 çâkak (1), to
entwine; to fence in
7126 qârab (1), to
approach, bring near
2853 kŏllaō (3), to glue
together

JOINED
977 bâchar (1), select,
chose, prefer
1692 dâbaq (2), to cling
or adhere; to catch
2266 châbar (8), to
fascinate by spells
2302 châdâh (1), to
rejoice, be glad
2338 chûwṭ (Ch.) (1), to
repair; lay a foundation
2859 châthan (1), to
become related
3161 yâchad (1), to be,
become one
3867 lâvâh (8), to unite;
to remain; to borrow
5208 nîychôwach (Ch.)
(1), pleasure
5595 çâphâh (1), to
scrape; to accumulate
6186 'ârak (1), to set in a
row, i.e. arrange,
6775 tsâmad (3), to link,
i.e. gird
7000 qâṭar (1), to enclose
7126 qârab (1), to
approach, bring near
7194 qâshar (1), to tie,
bind
2675 katartizō (1), to
repair; to prepare
2853 kŏllaō (3), to glue
together

JOGLI (column 4)

4347 prŏskŏllaō (2), to
glue to, i.e. to adhere
4801 suzĕugnumi (2), to
conjoin in marriage
4883 sunarmŏlŏgĕō (1),
to render close-jointed
4927 sunŏmŏrĕō (1), to
border together

JOINING
1692 dâbaq (1), to cling
or adhere; to catch

JOININGS
4226 mᵉchabbᵉrâh (1),
joiner, brace or cramp

JOINT
3363 yâqa' (1), to be
dislocated
4154 mûw'edeth (1),
dislocated
6504 pârad (1), to spread
or separate
860 haphē (1), fastening
ligament, joint

JOINT-HEIRS
4789 sugklērŏnŏmŏs (1),
participant in common

JOINTS
1694 debeq (2), joint
2542 chammûwq (1),
wrapping, i.e. drawers
7001 qᵉṭar (Ch.) (1),
riddle; vertebra
719 harmŏs (1),
articulation, body-joint
860 haphē (1), fastening
ligament, joint

JOKDEAM
3347 Yoqdᵉ'âm (1),
burning of (the) people

JOKIM
3137 Yôwqîym (1),
Jehovah will raise

JOKMEAM
3361 Yoqmᵉ'âm (1),
people will be raised

JOKNEAM
3362 Yoqnᵉ'âm (4),
people will be lamented

JOKSHAN
3370 Yoqshân (4),
insidious

JOKTAN
3355 Yoqṭân (6), he will
be made little

JOKTHEEL
3371 Yoqthᵉ'êl (2),
veneration of God

JONA
2495 Iōnas (1), dove

JONADAB
3082 Yᵉhôwnâdâb (4),
Jehovah-largessed
3122 Yôwnâdâb (8),
Jehovah-largessed

JONAH
3124 Yôwnâh (19), dove

JONAN
2494 Iōnan (1), Jehovah-
favored or a dove

JONAS
2495 Iōnas (12), dove

JONATH-ELEM-RECHOKIM
3128 Yôwnath 'êlem rᵉchôqîym (1), *dove of* (the) *silence*

JONATHAN
3083 Yᵉhôwnâthân (81), *Jehovah-given*
3129 Yôwnâthân (37), *Jehovah-given*

JONATHAN'S
3129 Yôwnâthân (3), *Jehovah-given*

JOPPA
3305 Yâphôw (3), *beautiful*
2445 Iŏppē (10), *beautiful*

JORAH
3139 Yôwrâh (1), *rainy*

JORAI
3140 Yôwray (1), *rainy*

JORAM
3141 Yôwrâm (19), *Jehovah-raised*
3088 Yᵉhôwrâm (7), *Jehovah-raised*
2496 Iōram (2), *Jehovah-raised*

JORDAN
3383 Yardên (182), *descender*
2446 Iŏrdanēs (15), *descender*

JORIM
2497 Iōrĕim (1), (poss.) *Jehovah-raised*

JORKOAM
3421 Yorqᵉ'âm (1), *people will be poured forth*

JOSABAD
3107 Yôwzâbâd (1), *Jehovah-endowed*

JOSAPHAT
2498 Iōsaphat (2), *Jehovah-judged*

JOSE
2499 Iōsē (1), (poss.) *let him add*

JOSEDECH
3087 Yᵉhôwtsâdâq (6), *Jehovah-righted*

JOSEPH
3084 Yᵉhôwçêph (1), *let him add* or *adding*
3130 Yôwçêph (193), *let him add* or *adding*
2501 Iōsēph (33), *let him add* or *adding*

JOSEPH'S
3130 Yôwçêph (20), *let him add* or *adding*
2501 Iōsēph (2), *let him add* or *adding*

JOSES
2500 Iōsēs (6), (poss.) *let him add*

JOSHAH
3144 Yôwshâh (1), *Joshah*

JOSHAPHAT
3146 Yôwshâphâṭ (1), *Jehovah-judged*

JOSHAVIAH
3145 Yôwshavyâh (1), *Jehovah-set*

JOSHBEKASHAH
3436 Yoshbᵉqâshâh (2), *hard seat*

JOSHUA
3091 Yᵉhôwshûw'a (215), *Jehovah-saved*

JOSIAH
2977 Yô'shîyâh (53), *founded of Jehovah*

JOSIAS
2502 Iōsias (2), *founded of Jehovah*

JOSIBIAH
3143 Yôwshîbyâh (1), *Jehovah will cause to dwell*

JOSIPHIAH
3131 Yôwçiphyâh (1), *Jehovah* (is) *adding*

JOT
2503 iōta (1), *iota*

JOTBAH
3192 Yoṭbâh (1), *pleasantness*

JOTBATH
3193 Yoṭbâthâh (1), *pleasantness*

JOTBATHAH
3193 Yoṭbâthâh (2), *pleasantness*

JOTHAM
3147 Yôwthâm (24), *Jehovah* (is) *perfect*

JOURNEY
1870 derek (23), *road; course* of life; *mode of action*
4109 mahălâk (3), *passage* or a *distance*
4550 maçça' (1), *departure*
5265 nâça' (12), *start on a journey*
5575+7272 çanvêr (1), *blindness*
589 apŏdēmĕō (2), *visit a foreign land*
590 apŏdēmŏs (1), *foreign traveller*
1279 diapŏrĕuŏmai (1), *to travel through*
2137 ĕuŏdŏō (1), *to succeeʋ' in business*
3596 hŏdŏipŏrĕō (1), *to travel*
3597 hŏdŏipŏria (1), *traveling*
3598 hŏdŏs (6), *road*
4198 pŏrĕuŏmai (2), *to go, come; to travel*

JOURNEYED
5265 nâça' (28), *start on a journey*
6213+1870 'âsâh (1), *to do or make*
3593 hŏdĕuō (1), *to travel*
4198 pŏrĕuŏmai (2), *to go/come; to travel*
4922 sunŏdĕuō (1), *to travel* in company *with*

JOURNEYING
4550 maçça' (1), *departure*
5265 nâça' (1), *start* on a journey
4197+4160 pŏrĕia (1), *journey; life's conduct*

JOURNEYINGS
4550 maçça' (1), *departure*
3597 hŏdŏipŏria (1), *traveling*

JOURNEYS
4550 maçça' (9), *departure*

JOY
1523 gîyl (2), *rejoice*
1524 gîyl (3), *age, stage in life*
1525 gîylâh (1), *joy, delight*
2304 chedvâh (1), *rejoicing, joy*
2305 chedvâh (Ch.) (1), *rejoicing, joy*
2898 ṭûwb (1), *good; beauty, gladness*
4885 mâsôws (12), *delight*
7440 rinnâh (3), *shout*
7442 rânan (3), *to shout for joy*
7796 Sôwrêq (1), *vine*
8055 sâmach (4), *to be, make gleesome*
8056 sâmêach (2), *blithe or gleeful*
8057 simchâh (43), *blithesomeness or glee*
8342 sâsôwn (14), *cheerfulness; welcome*
8643 tᵉrûw'âh (2), *battle-cry; clangor*
20 agalliasis (2), *exultation, delight*
21 agalliaō (1), *to exult*
2167 ĕuphrŏsunē (1), *joyfulness, cheerfulness*
2744 kauchaŏmai (1), *to glory in, rejoice in; to boast*
3685 ŏninēmi (1), *to gratify, derive pleasure*
5468 chalinagōgĕō (3), *to curb, hold in check*
5479 chara (51), *calm delight, joy*
5485 charis (1), *gratitude; benefit given*

JOYED
5463 chairō (1), *to be cheerful*

JOYFUL
1523 gîyl (4), *rejoice*
2896 ṭôwb (1), *good; well*
5937 'âlaz (2), *to jump for joy*
5970 'âlats (1), *to jump for joy*
7442 rânan (1), *to shout for joy*
7445 rᵉnânâh (2), *shout for joy*
8055 sâmach (2), *to be, make gleesome*
8056 sâmêach (3), *blithe or gleeful*

JOURNEY (cont.)
4550 maçça' (1), *departure*
5265 nâça' (12), *start* on a journey

JOYFULLY
2416 chay (1), *alive; raw; fresh; life*
3326+5479 mĕta (1), *with, among; after, later*
5463 chairō (1), *to be cheerful*

JOYFULNESS
8057 simchâh (1), *blithesomeness or glee*
5479 chara (1), *calm delight, joy*

JOYING
5463 chairō (1), *to be cheerful*

JOYOUS
5947 'allîyz (3), *exultant; reveling*
5479 chara (1), *calm delight, joy*

JOZABAD
3107 Yôwzâbâd (9), *Jehovah-endowed*

JOZACHAR
3108 Yôwzâkâr (1), *Jehovah-remembered*

JOZADAK
3136 Yôwtsâdâq (5), *Jehovah-righted*

JUBAL
3106 Yûwbâl (1), *stream*

JUBILE
3104 yôwbêl (21), *blast of a ram's horn*
8643 tᵉrûw'âh (1), *battle-cry; clangor*

JUCAL
3116 Yûwkal (1), *potent*

JUDA
2448 Iŏuda (1), *celebrated*
2455 Iŏudas (7), *celebrated*

JUDAEA
2449 Iŏudaia (41), *Judæan land*
2453 Iŏudaiŏs (1), *belonging to Jehudah*
2499 Iōsē (1), (poss.) *let him add*

JUDAH
3061 Yᵉhûwd (Ch.) (5), *celebrated*
3063 Yᵉhûwdâh (806), *celebrated*
3064 Yᵉhûwdîy (1), *Jehudite*
2455 Iŏudas (1), *celebrated*

JUDAH'S
3063 Yᵉhûwdâh (4), *celebrated*

JUDAS
2455 Iŏudas (33), *celebrated*

JUDE
2455 Iŏudas (1), *celebrated*

JUDE *(right header)*

JUDEA
3061 Yᵉhûwd (Ch.) (1), celebrated

JUDGE
430 'ĕlôhîym (1), God; magistrates, judges
1777 dîyn (14), to judge; to strive or contend for
1781 dayân (1), judge; advocate
1784 Dîynay (Ch.) (1), Dinaite
3198 yâkach (1), to decide, justify, convict
6416 pᵉlîylîy (1), judicial
8199 shâphaṭ (102), to judge
350 anakrinō (1), to interrogate, determine
1252 diakrinō (3), to decide; to hesitate
1348 dikastēs (3), one who judges
2919 krinō (45), to decide; to try
2922 kritēriŏn (1), rule; tribunal; lawsuit
2923 kritēs (13), judge

JUDGED
1777 dîyn (2), to judge; to strive or contend for
4941 mishpâṭ (1), verdict; formal decree; justice
5307 nâphal (1), to fall
6419 pâlal (1), to intercede, pray
8199 shâphaṭ (28), to judge
350 anakrinō (3), to interrogate, determine
2233 hēgĕŏmai (1), to deem, i.e. consider
2919 krinō (26), to decide; to try, condemn, punish

JUDGES
148 'ădargâzêr (Ch.) (2), chief diviner
430 'ĕlôhîym (4), God; magistrates, judges
1782 dayân (Ch.) (1), judge
6414 pâlîyl (3), magistrate
8199 shâphaṭ (38), to judge
2923 kritēs (4), judge

JUDGEST
8199 shâphaṭ (2), to judge
2919 krinō (6), to decide; to try, condemn, punish

JUDGETH
1777 dîyn (1), to judge; to strive or contend for
8199 shâphaṭ (5), to judge
350 anakrinō (1), to interrogate, determine
2919 krinō (10), to try, condemn, punish

JUDGING
8199 shâphaṭ (4), to judge
2919 krinō (2), to decide; to try, condemn, punish

JUDGMENT
1777 dîyn (1), to judge; to strive or contend for

1779 dîyn (9), judge; judgment; law suit
1780 dîyn (Ch.) (5), judge; judgment
2940 ṭa'am (1), perception; mandate
4055 mad (1), vesture, garment; carpet
4941 mishpâṭ (187), verdict; decree; justice
6415 pᵉlîylâh (1), justice
6417 pᵉlîylîyâh (1), judgment
6419 pâlal (1), to intercede, pray
6485 pâqad (2), to visit, care for, count
8196 shᵉphôwṭ (2), sentence, punishment
8199 shâphaṭ (2), to judge
8201 shepheṭ (2), criminal sentence
144 aisthēsis (1), discernment
968 bēma (10), tribunal platform; judging place
1106 gnōmē (3), cognition, opinion
1341 dikaiŏkrisia (1), just sentence
1345 dikaiōma (1), statute or decision
1349 dikē (1), justice
2250 hēmĕra (1), day; period of time
2917 krima (12), decision
2920 krisis (39), decision; tribunal; justice
2922 kritēriŏn (1), rule; tribunal; lawsuit
4232 praitōriŏn (5), governor's court-room

JUDGMENTS
4941 mishpâṭ (108), verdict; decree; justice
8201 shepheṭ (14), criminal sentence
1345 dikaiōma (1), deed; statute or decision
2917 krima (1), decision
2920 krisis (2), decision; tribunal; justice
2922 kritēriŏn (1), rule; tribunal; lawsuit

JUDITH
3067 Yᵉhûwdîyth (1), Jewess

JUICE
6071 'âçîyç (1), expressed fresh grape-juice

JULIA
2456 Iŏulia (1), Julia

JULIUS
2457 Iŏuliŏs (2), Julius

JUMPING
7540 râqad (1), to spring about wildly or for joy

JUNIA
2458 Iŏunias (1), Junias

JUNIPER
7574 rethem (4), broom tree

JUPITER
1356 diŏpĕtēs (1), sky-fallen

2203 Zĕus (2), Jupiter or Jove

JURISDICTION
1849 ĕxŏusia (1), authority, dominion

JUSHAB-HESED
3142 Yûwshab Cheçed (1), kindness will be returned

JUST
3477 yâshâr (1), straight
4941 mishpâṭ (1), verdict; formal decree; justice
6662 tsaddîyq (42), just
6663 tsâdaq (3), to be, make right
6664 tsedeq (8), right
8003 shâlêm (1), complete; friendly; safe
1342 dikaiŏs (33), equitable, holy
1738 ĕndikŏs (2), equitable, deserved, just

JUSTICE
4941 mishpâṭ (1), verdict; formal decree; justice
6663 tsâdaq (2), to be, make right
6664 tsedeq (10), right
6666 tsᵉdâqâh (15), rightness

JUSTIFICATION
1345 dikaiōma (1), deed; statute or decision
1347 dikaiōsis (2), acquittal, vindication

JUSTIFIED
6663 tsâdaq (12), to be, make right
1344 dikaiŏō (31), show or regard as just

JUSTIFIER
1344 dikaiŏō (1), show or regard as just

JUSTIFIETH
6663 tsâdaq (2), to be, make right
1344 dikaiŏō (2), show or regard as just

JUSTIFY
6663 tsâdaq (7), to be, make right
1344 dikaiŏō (4), show or regard as just

JUSTIFYING
6663 tsâdaq (2), to be, make right

JUSTLE
8264 shâqaq (1), to seek greedily

JUSTLY
4941 mishpâṭ (1), verdict; formal decree; justice
1346 dikaiōs (2), equitably

JUSTUS
2459 Iŏustŏs (3), just

JUTTAH
3194 Yuṭṭâh (2), extended

KABZEEL
6909 Qabtsᵉ'êl (3), God has gathered

KADESH
6946 Qâdêsh (17), sanctuary

KADESH-BARNEA
6947 Qâdêsh Barnêa' (10), Kadesh of (the) Wilderness of Wandering

KADMIEL
6934 Qadmîy'êl (8), presence of God

KADMONITES
6935 Qadmônîy (1), ancient

KALLAI
7040 Qallay (1), frivolous

KANAH
7071 Qânâh (3), reediness

KAREAH
7143 Qârêach (13), bald

KARKAA
7173 Qarqa' (1), ground-floor

KARKOR
7174 Qarqôr (1), foundation

KARTAH
7177 Qartâh (1), city

KARTAN
7178 Qartân (1), city-plot

KATTATH
7005 Qaṭṭâth (1), littleness

KEDAR
6938 Qêdâr (12), dusky

KEDEMAH
6929 Qêdᵉmâh (2), precedence

KEDEMOTH
6932 Qᵉdêmôwth (4), beginnings

KEDESH
6943 Qedesh (11), sanctum

KEDESH-NAPHTALI
6943+5321 Qedesh (1), sanctum

KEEP
1692 dâbaq (3), to cling or adhere; to catch
1961 hâyâh (1), to exist, i.e. be or become
2287 châgag (12), to observe a festival
2820 châsak (1), to refuse, spare, preserve
3533 kâbash (1), to conquer, subjugate
3607 kâlâ' (1), to hold back or in; to prohibit
4513 mâna' (2), to deny, refuse
4931 mishmereth (1), watch, sentry, post
5201 nâṭar (3), to guard; to cherish anger
5341 nâtsar (26), to guard, protect
5647 'âbad (1), to do, work, serve
5737 'âdar (2), to arrange as a battle

6113 'âtsar (1), to *hold back*; to *maintain, rule*
6213 'âsâh (30), to *do or make*
6485 pâqad (1), to *visit, care for, count*
6942 qâdâsh (1), to *be, make clean*
7069 qânâh (1), to *create*; to *procure*
7368 râchaq (1), to *recede; remove*
8104 shâmar (186), to *watch*
1301 diatērĕō (1), to *observe* strictly
1314 diaphulassō (1), to *protect, guard carefully*
1858 hĕŏrtazō (1), to *observe a festival*
2722 katĕchō (3), to *hold down fast*
2853 kŏllaō (1), to *glue together*
3557 nŏsphizŏmai (1), to *sequestrate, embezzle*
4160 pŏiĕō (2), to *do*
4238 prassō (1), to *execute, accomplish*
4601 sigaō (2), to *keep silent*
4874 sunanamignumi (1), to *associate with*
4912 sunĕchō (1), to *hold together*
5083 tērĕō (32), to *keep, guard, obey*
5299 hupōpiazō (1), to *beat up*; to *wear out*
5432 phrŏurĕō (1), to *hem in, protect*
5442 phulassō (13), to *watch*, i.e. *be on guard*

KEEPER
5201 nâţar (1), to *guard*; to *cherish* anger
5341 nâtsar (1), to *guard, protect, maintain*
7462 râ'âh (1), to *tend* a flock, i.e. *pasture* it
8104 shâmar (13), to *watch*
8269 sar (3), *head person, ruler*
1200 dĕsmŏphulax (2), *jailer*

KEEPERS
5201 nâţar (1), to *guard*; to *cherish* anger
8104 shâmar (15), to *watch*
3626 ŏikŏurŏs (1), *domestically inclined*
5083 tērĕō (1), to *keep, guard, obey*
5441 phulax (3), *watcher or sentry*

KEEPEST
8104 shâmar (3), to *watch*
5442 phulassō (1), to *watch*, i.e. *be on guard*

KEEPETH
2820 châsak (1), to *refuse, spare, preserve*
4513 mâna' (1), to *deny, refuse*
5307 nâphal (1), to *fall*

5341 nâtsar (7), to *guard, protect, maintain*
7462 râ'âh (1), to *tend* a flock, i.e. *pasture* it
7623 shâbach (1), to *address*; to *pacify*
8104 shâmar (18), to *watch*
4160 pŏiĕō (1), to *do*
5083 tērĕō (10), to *keep, guard, obey*
5442 phulassō (1), to *watch*, i.e. *be on guard*

KEEPING
5341 nâtsar (1), to *guard, protect, maintain*
7462 râ'âh (1), to *tend* a flock, i.e. *pasture* it
8104 shâmar (7), to *watch*
5084 tērēsis (1), *observance; prison*
5442 phulassō (1), to *watch*, i.e. *be on guard*

KEHELATHAH
6954 Qᵉhêlâthâh (2), *convocation*

KEILAH
7084 Qᵉ'îylâh (18), *citadel*

KELAIAH
7041 Qêlâyâh (1), *insignificance*

KELITA
7042 Qᵉlîyţâ' (3), *maiming*

KEMUEL
7055 Qᵉmûw'êl (3), *raised of God*

KENAN
7018 Qêynân (1), *fixed*

KENATH
7079 Qᵉnâth (2), *possession*

KENAZ
7073 Qᵉnaz (11), *hunter*

KENEZITE
7074 Qᵉnizzîy (3), *Kenizzite*

KENITE
7014 Qayin (2), *lance*
7017 Qêynîy (4), *Kenite*

KENITES
7017 Qêynîy (8), *Kenite*

KENIZZITES
7074 Qᵉnizzîy (1), *Kenizzite*

KEPT
631 'âçar (1), to *fasten*; to *join* battle
680 'âtsal (1), to *select; refuse; narrow*
1639 gâra' (1), to *shave, remove,* or *withhold*
1692 dâbaq (1), to *cling* or *adhere*; to *catch*
2287 châgag (1), to *observe* a festival
2790 chârash (2), to *engrave*; to *plow*
2820 châsak (2), to *refuse, spare, preserve*
3607 kâlâ' (1), to *hold back or in*; to *prohibit*

4513 mâna' (2), to *deny, refuse*
4931 mishmereth (6), *watch, sentry, post*
5201 nâţar (1), to *guard*; to *cherish* anger
5202 nᵉţar (Ch.) (1), to *retain*
5341 nâtsar (4), to *guard, protect, maintain*
5641 çâthar (2), to *hide by covering*
5648 'ăbad (Ch.) (1), to *do, work, serve*
6113 'âtsar (2), to *hold back*; to *maintain, rule*
6213 'âsâh (18), to *do or make*
6942 qâdâsh (1), to *be, make clean*
7462 râ'âh (3), to *tend* a flock, i.e. *pasture* it
7673 shâbath (1), to *repose; to desist*
8104 shâmar (70), to *watch*
71 agō (1), to *lead*; to *bring, drive*; to *weigh*
650 apŏstĕrĕō (1), to *deprive*; to *despoil*
1006 bŏskō (1), to *pasture* a flock
1096 ginŏmai (1), to *be, become*
1301 diatērĕō (1), to *observe* strictly
2192 ĕchō (1), to *have; hold; keep*
2343 thēsaurizō (1), to *amass* or *reserve, store*
2377 thurōrŏs (2), *doorkeeper*
2621 katakĕimai (1), to *lie down in bed*
2902 kratĕō (1), to *seize*
2967 kōluō (1), to *stop*
3557 nŏsphizŏmai (1), to *sequestrate, embezzle*
3930 parĕchō (1), to *hold near*, i.e. *to present*
4160 pŏiĕō (1), to *do*
4601 sigaō (2), to *keep silent*
4933 suntērĕō (1), to *protect*
5083 tērĕō (15), to *keep, guard, obey*
5288 hupŏstĕllō (1), to *conceal (reserve)*
5432 phrŏurĕō (3), to *hem in, protect*
5442 phulassō (8), to *watch*, i.e. *be on guard*

KERCHIEFS
4556 miçpachath (2), *scurf, rash*

KEREN-HAPPUCH
7163 Qeren Hap-pûwk (1), *horn of cosmetic*

KERIOTH
7152 Qᵉrîyôwth (3), *buildings*

KERNELS
2785 chartsan (1), *sour, tart grape*

KEROS
7026 Qêyrôç (2), *ankled*

KETTLE
1731 dûwd (1), *pot, kettle; basket*

KETURAH
6989 Qᵉţûwrâh (4), *perfumed*

KEY
4668 maphtêach (2), *opening; key*
2807 klĕis (4), *key*

KEYS
2807 klĕis (2), *key*

KEZIA
7103 Qᵉtsîy'âh (1), *cassia*

KEZIZ
7104 Qᵉtsîyts (1), *abrupt*

KIBROTH-HATTAAVAH
6914 Qibrôwth hat-Ta'ăvâh (5), *graves of the longing*

KIBZAIM
6911 Qibtsayim (1), *double heap*

KICK
1163 bâ'aţ (1), *kick*
2979 laktizō (2), to *recalcitrate, kick back*

KICKED
1163 bâ'aţ (1), *kick*

KID
1423 gᵉdîy (8), *young male goat*
1423+5795 gᵉdîy (5), *young male goat*
5795 'êz (1), *she-goat; goat's hair*
8163 sâ'îyr (26), *shaggy; he-goat; goat idol*
8166 sᵉ'îyrâh (2), *she-goat*
2056 ĕriphŏs (1), *kid or goat*

KIDNEYS
3629 kilyâh (18), *kidney; mind, heart, spirit*

KIDRON
6939 Qidrôwn (11), *dusky place*

KIDS
1423 gᵉdîy (4), *young male goat*
5795 'êz (1), *she-goat; goat's hair*
8163 sâ'îyr (2), *shaggy; he-goat; goat idol*

KILL
2026 hârag (17), to *kill, slaughter*
2076 zâbach (3), to *(sacrificially) slaughter*
2491 châlâl (2), *pierced to death, one slain*
2873 ţâbach (1), to *kill, butcher*
4191 mûwth (24), to *die; to kill*
5221 nâkâh (4), to *strike, kill*
5362 nâqaph (1), to *strike; to surround*
7523 râtsach (4), to *murder*
7819 shâchaţ (22), to *slaughter; butcher*

KILLED
337 anairĕŏ (6), *to abolish, murder*
615 apŏktĕinō (28), *to kill outright; to destroy*
1315 diachĕirizŏmai (1), *to lay hands upon*
2380 thuō (3), *to kill; to butcher; to sacrifice*
4969 sphazō (1), *to slaughter or to maim*
5407 phŏnĕuō (8), *to commit murder*

KILLED
2026 hârag (3), *to kill, slaughter*
2076 zâbach (1), *to (sacrificially) slaughter*
2873 ţâbach (3), *to kill, butcher*
3076 Yᵉhôwchânân (1), *Jehovah-favored*
4191 mûwth (6), *to die; to kill*
5221 nâkâh (3), *to strike, kill*
7523 râtsach (1), *to murder*
7819 shâchaţ (15), *to slaughter; butcher*
337 anairĕŏ (3), *to take away, murder*
615 apŏktĕinō (22), *to kill outright; to destroy*
2289 thanatŏō (2), *to kill*
2380 thuō (5), *to kill; to butcher; to sacrifice*
5407 phŏnĕuō (2), *to commit murder*

KILLEDST
2026 hârag (2), *to kill, slaughter*

KILLEST
615 apŏktĕinō (2), *to kill outright; to destroy*

KILLETH
2026 hârag (1), *to kill, slaughter*
4191 mûwth (2), *to die; to kill*
5221 nâkâh (13), *to strike, kill*
6991 qâţal (1), *to put to death*
7819 shâchaţ (3), *to slaughter; butcher*
615 apŏktĕinō (3), *to kill outright; to destroy*

KILLING
2026 hârag (1), *to kill, slaughter*
7523 râtsach (1), *to murder*
7819 shâchaţ (1), *to slaughter; butcher*
7821 shᵉchîyţâh (1), *slaughter*
615 apŏktĕinō (1), *to kill outright; to destroy*

KIN
1320 bâsâr (2), *flesh; body; person*
7138 qârôwb (1), *near, close*
7607 shᵉʼêr (2), *flesh, meat; kindred by blood*
4773 suggĕnēs (1), *blood relative; countryman*

KINAH
7016 Qîynâh (1), *dirge*

KIND
2896 ţôwb (1), *good; well*
4327 mîyn (29), *sort, i.e. species*
1085 gĕnŏs (3), *kin, offspring in kind*
5100 tis (1), *some or any person or object*
5449 phusis (1), *genus or sort*
5541 chrēstĕuŏmai (1), *to show oneself useful*
5543 chrēstŏs (2), *employed, i.e. useful*

KINDLE
215 ʼôwr (1), *to be luminous*
1197 bâʽar (4), *to be brutish, be senseless*
1814 dâlaq (2), *to flame; to pursue*
2787 chârar (1), *to melt, burn, dry up*
3341 yâtsath (8), *to burn or set on fire*
3344 yâqad (1), *to burn*
6919 qâdach (1), *to inflame*
6999 qâţar (1), *to turn into fragrance by fire*

KINDLED
1197 bâʽar (9), *to be brutish, be senseless*
2734 chârâh (43), *to blaze up*
3341 yâtsath (4), *to burn or set on fire*
3648 kâmar (1), *to shrivel with heat*
5400 nâsaq (1), *to catch fire*
6919 qâdach (3), *to inflame*
8313 sâraph (1), *to be, set on fire*
381 anaptō (2), *to kindle, set on fire*
681 haptō (1), *to set on fire*

KINDLETH
3857 lâhaţ (1), *to blaze*
5400 nâsaq (1), *to catch fire*
381 anaptō (1), *to kindle, set on fire*

KINDLY
2617 cheçed (5), *kindness, favor*
2896 ţôwb (2), *good; well*
5921+3820 ʽal (2), *above, over, upon, or against*
5387 philŏstŏrgŏs (1), *fraternal, devoted*

KINDNESS
2617 cheçed (40), *kindness, favor*
2896 ţôwb (1), *good; well*
5360 philadĕlphia (2), *fraternal affection*
5363 philanthrōpia (1), *benevolence*
5544 chrēstŏtēs (4), *moral excellence*

KINDRED
250 ʼEzrâchîy (1), *Ezrachite*
1353 gᵉullâh (1), *blood relationship*
4130 môwdaʽath (1), *distant relative*
4138 môwledeth (11), *lineage, family*
4940 mishpâchâh (6), *family, clan, people*
1085 gĕnŏs (3), *kin*
4772 suggĕnĕia (3), *relatives; one's people*
5443 phulē (2), *race or clan*

KINDREDS
4940 mishpâchâh (3), *family, clan, people*
3965 patria (1), *family, group, race, i.e. nation*
5443 phulē (4), *race or clan*

KINDS
2177 zan (5), *form or sort*
4327 mîyn (1), *sort, i.e. species*
4940 mishpâchâh (2), *family, clan, people*
1085 gĕnŏs (2), *kin, offspring in kind*

KINE
504 ʼeleph (4), *ox; cow or cattle*
1241 bâqâr (2), *plowing ox; herd*
6510 pârâh (18), *heifer*

KING
4427 mâlak (43), *to reign as king*
4428 melek (1957), *king*
4430 melek (Ch.) (140), *king*
935 basilĕus (86), *sovereign*

KING'S
4410 mᵉlûwkâh (2), *realm, rulership*
4428 melek (259), *king*
4430 melek (Ch.) (18), *king*
4467 mamlâkâh (1), *royal dominion*
935 basilĕus (2), *sovereign*
937 basilikŏs (1), *befitting the sovereign*

KINGDOM
4410 mᵉlûwkâh (18), *realm, rulership*
4437 malkûw (Ch.) (45), *dominion*
4438 malkûwth (47), *rule; dominion*
4467 mamlâkâh (61), *royal dominion*
4468 mamlâkûwth (8), *royal dominion*
932 basilĕia (155), *rule; realm*

KINGDOMS
4437 malkûw (Ch.) (2), *dominion*
4438 malkûwth (1), *rule; dominion*
4467 mamlâkâh (49), *royal dominion*

KINDRED
932 basilĕia (5), *rule; realm*

KINGLY
4437 malkûw (Ch.) (1), *dominion*

KINGS
4428 melek (283), *king*
4430 melek (Ch.) (13), *king*
935 basilĕus (29), *sovereign*
936 basilĕuō (1), *to rule*

KINGS'
4428 melek (3), *king*
933 basilĕiŏn (1), *royal palace*
935 basilĕus (1), *sovereign*

KINSFOLK
7138 qârôwb (1), *near, close*
4773 suggĕnēs (1), *blood relative; countryman*

KINSFOLKS
1350 gâʼal (1), *to redeem; to be the next of kin*
3045 yâdaʽ (1), *to know*
4773 suggĕnēs (1), *blood relative; countryman*

KINSMAN
1350 gâʼal (12), *to be the next of kin*
3045 yâdaʽ (1), *to know*
7607 shᵉʼêr (1), *flesh, meat; kindred by blood*
4773 suggĕnēs (2), *blood relative; countryman*

KINSMAN'S
1350 gâʼal (1), *to redeem; to be the next of kin*

KINSMEN
1350 gâʼal (1), *to redeem; to be the next of kin*
7138 qârôwb (1), *near, close*
4773 suggĕnēs (5), *blood relative; countryman*

KINSWOMAN
4129 môwdaʽ (1), *distant relative*
7607 shᵉʼêr (2), *flesh, meat; kindred by blood*

KINSWOMEN
7608 shaʼârâh (1), *female kindred by blood*

KIR
7024 Qîyr (5), *fortress*

KIR-HARASETH
7025 Qîyr Cheres (1), *fortress of earthenware*

KIR-HARESETH
7025 Qîyr Cheres (1), *fortress of earthenware*

KIR-HARESH
7025 Qîyr Cheres (1), *fortress of earthenware*

KIR-HERES
7025 Qîyr Cheres (2), *fortress of earthenware*

KIRIATHAIM
7156 Qiryâthayim (3), *double city*

7741 Shâvêh
Qiryâthayim (1), *plain
of a double city*

KIRIOTH
7152 Qᵉrîyôwth (1),
buildings

KIRJATH
7157 Qiryath Yᵉ'ârîym
(1), *city of forests*

KIRJATH-ARBA
7153 Qiryath 'Arba' (6),
*city of Arba or of the
four* (giants)

KIRJATH-ARIM
7157 Qiryath Yᵉ'ârîym
(1), *city of forests or of
towns*

KIRJATH-BAAL
7154 Qiryath Ba'al (2),
city of Baal

KIRJATH-HUZOTH
7155 Qiryath Chûtsôwth
(1), *city of streets*

KIRJATH-JEARIM
7157 Qiryath Yᵉ'ârîym
(18), *city of forests*

KIRJATH-SANNAH
7158 Qiryath Çannâh
(1), *city of branches or
of a book*

KIRJATH-SEPHER
7158 Qiryath Çannâh
(4), *city of branches or
of a book*

KIRJATHAIM
7156 Qiryâthayim (3),
double city

KISH
7027 Qîysh (20), *bow*

KISHI
7029 Qîyshîy (1), *bowed*

KISHION
7191 Qishyôwn (1), *hard
ground*

KISHON
7028 Qîyshôwn (5),
winding
7191 Qishyôwn (1), *hard
ground*

KISON
7028 Qîyshôwn (1),
winding

KISS
5401 nâshaq (9), to *kiss*
2705 kataphilĕŏ (1), to
kiss earnestly
5368 philĕŏ (3), to *be a
friend, to kiss*
5379 philēma (7), *kiss*

KISSED
5401 nâshaq (21), to *kiss*
2705 kataphilĕŏ (5), to
kiss earnestly

KISSES
5390 nᵉshîyqâh (2), *kiss*

KITE
344 'ayâh (2), *hawk*

KITHLISH
3798 Kithlîysh (1), *wall of
a man*

KITRON
7003 Qiṭrôwn (1),
fumigative

KITTIM
3794 Kittîy (2), *islander*

KNEAD
3888 lûwsh (2), to *knead*

KNEADED
3888 lûwsh (3), to *knead*

KNEADINGTROUGHS
4863 mish'ereth (2),
kneading-trough

KNEE
1290 berek (1), *knee*
1119 gŏnu (3), *knee*

KNEEL
1288 bârak (2), to *bless*

KNEELED
1288 bârak (1), to *bless*
1289 bᵉrak (Ch.) (1), to
bless
1120 gŏnupĕtĕŏ (1), to
fall on the knee, kneel
5087+1119 tithēmi (5), to
place, put

KNEELING
3766 kâra' (1), to
prostrate
1120 gŏnupĕtĕŏ (2), to
fall on the knee, kneel

KNEES
755 'arkûbâh (Ch.) (1),
knees
1290 berek (24), *knee*
1291 berek (Ch.) (1), *knee*
1119 gŏnu (4), *knee joint*

KNEW
1847 da'ath (1),
knowledge
3045 yâda' (83), to *know*
3046 yᵉda' (Ch.) (2), to
know
5234 nâkar (9), to
acknowledge
50 agnŏĕŏ (1), to *not
know; understand*
1097 ginōskō (30), to
know
1492 ĕidō (27), to *know*
1912 ĕpibarĕŏ (1), to *be
severe toward*
1921 ĕpiginōskō (13), to
acknowledge
4267 prŏginōskō (1), to
know beforehand

KNEWEST
3045 yâda' (5), to *know*
3046 yᵉda' (Ch.) (1), to
know
1097 ginōskō (1), to *know*
1492 ĕidō (3), to *know*

KNIFE
2719 chereb (2), *knife,
sword*
3979 ma'ăkeleth (3),
knife
7915 sakkîyn (1), *knife*

KNIT
2270 châber (1),
associate, friend
3162 yachad (1), *unitedly*
7194 qâshar (1), to *tie,
bind*
1210 dĕŏ (1), to *bind*

4822 sumbibazō (2), to
drive together

KNIVES
2719 chereb (3), *knife,
sword*
3979 ma'ăkeleth (1),
knife
4252 machălâph (1),
butcher knife

KNOCK
2925 krŏuŏ (4), to *rap,
knock*

KNOCKED
2925 krŏuŏ (1), to *rap,
knock*

KNOCKETH
1849 dâphaq (1), to
knock; to press severely
2925 krŏuŏ (3), to *rap,
knock*

KNOCKING
2925 krŏuŏ (1), to *rap,
knock*

KNOP
3730 kaphtôr (10),
capital; button or disk

KNOPS
3730 kaphtôr (6), *capital;
button or disk*
6497 peqa' (3),
ornamental semi-globe

KNOW
995 bîyn (1), to
understand; discern
1847 da'ath (4),
knowledge
3045 yâda' (429), to *know*
3046 yᵉda' (Ch.) (15), to
know
5234 nâkar (9), to
acknowledge
50 agnŏĕŏ (2), to *not
know; not understand*
1097 ginōskō (92), to
know
1110 gnōstŏs (1),
well-known
1231 diaginōskō (1),
ascertain exactly
1492 ĕidō (176), to *know*
1921 ĕpiginōskō (8), to
acknowledge
1987 ĕpistamai (9), to *be
acquainted with*
2467 isēmi (2), to *know*
4267 prŏginōskō (1), to
know beforehand
4892 sunĕdriŏn (1), head
Jewish *tribunal*

KNOWEST
1847 da'ath (1),
knowledge
3045 yâda' (66), to *know*
1097 ginōskō (5), to *know*
1492 ĕidō (15), to *know*
1921 ĕpiginōskō (1), to
acknowledge
2589 kardiŏgnōstēs (1),
heart-knower

KNOWETH
854 'êth (1), *with; by; at;
among*
3045 yâda' (59), to *know*
3046 yᵉda' (Ch.) (1), to
know

5234 nâkar (1), to
acknowledge
1097 ginōskō (16), to
know
1492 ĕidō (22), to *know*
1921 ĕpiginōskō (2), to
acknowledge
1987 ĕpistamai (1), to
comprehend
2589 kardiŏgnōstēs (1),
heart-knower

KNOWING
3045 yâda' (2), to *know*
50 agnŏĕŏ (1), to *not
know; not understand*
1097 ginōskō (5), to *know*
1492 ĕidō (38), to *know*
1921 ĕpiginōskō (2), to
acknowledge
1987 ĕpistamai (3), to
comprehend

KNOWLEDGE
998 bîynâh (3),
understanding
1843 dêa' (2), *knowledge*
1844 dê'âh (6),
knowledge
1847 da'ath (82),
knowledge
3045 yâda' (19), to *know*
4093 maddâ' (4),
intelligence
5234 nâkar (2), to *treat
as a foreigner*
5869 'ayin (1), *eye; sight;
fountain*
7922 sekel (1),
intelligence; success
56 agnōsia (1), state of
ignorance
1097 ginōskō (1), to *know*
1108 gnōsis (28),
knowledge
1492 ĕidō (1), to *know*
1921 ĕpiginōskō (3), to
acknowledge
1922 ĕpignōsis (16), *full
discernment*
1990 ĕpistēmōn (1),
intelligent, learned
4907 sunĕsis (1),
intelligence, intellect

KNOWN
3045 yâda' (105), to *know*
3046 yᵉda' (Ch.) (24), to
know
5234 nâkar (2), to
acknowledge
319 anagnōrizŏmai (1),
to make oneself known
1097 ginōskō (46), to
know
1107 gnōrizō (16), to
make known, reveal
1110 gnōstŏs (11),
well-known
1232 diagnōrizō (1), to
tell abroad
1492 ĕidō (6), to *know*
1921 ĕpiginōskō (4), to
acknowledge
3877 parakŏlouthĕŏ (1),
to *attend; trace out*
4135 plērŏphŏrĕŏ (1), to
assure or convince
5318 phanĕrŏs (3),
apparent, visible, clear

KOA
KOA
6970 Qôwa' (1),
curtailment

KOHATH
6955 Qᵉhâth (32), *allied*

KOHATHITES
6956 Qŏhâthîy (15),
Kohathite

KOLAIAH
6964 Qôwlâyâh (2), *voice
of Jehovah*

KORAH
7141 Qôrach (37), *ice*

KORAHITE
7145 Qorchîy (1),
Korchite

KORAHITES
7145 Qorchîy (1),
Korchite

KORATHITES
7145 Qorchîy (1),
Korchite

KORE
6981 Qôwrê' (3), *crier*
7145 Qorchîy (1),
Korchite

KORHITES
7145 Qorchîy (4),
Korchite

KOZ
6976 Qôwts (4), *thorns*

KUSHAIAH
6984 Qûwshâyâhûw (1),
entrapped of Jehovah

LAADAH
3935 La'dâh (1), *Ladah*

LAADAN
3936 La'dân (7), *Ladan*

LABAN
3837 Lâbân (51), *white*

LABAN'S
3837 Lâbân (4), *white*

LABOUR
213 'ûwts (1), *to be close,
hurry, withdraw*
1518 gîyach (1), *to issue
forth; to burst forth*
3018 yᵉgîya' (12), *toil,
work; produce, property*
3021 yâga' (8), *to be
exhausted, to tire,*
3023 yâgêa' (1), *tiresome*
3027 yâd (1), *hand; power*
3205 yâlad (2), *to bear
young; to father a child*
4399 mᵉlâ'kâh (1), *work;
property*
4639 ma'ăseh (1), *action;
labor*
5445 çâbal (1), *to carry*
5647 'âbad (2), *to do,
work, serve*
5656 'ăbôdâh (1), *work of
any kind*
5998 'âmal (2), *to work
severely, put forth effort*
5999 'âmâl (25), *wearing
effort; worry*
6001 'âmêl (1), *toiling;
laborer; sorrowful*
6089 'etseb (1), *earthen
vessel; painful toil*
6213 'âsâh (2), *to do*

6468 pᵉ'ullâh (2), *work,
deed*
2038 ĕrgazŏmai (1), *to
toil*
2041 ĕrgŏn (1), *work*
2872 kŏpiaō (11), *to feel
fatigue; to work hard*
2873 kŏpŏs (8), *toil; pains*
4704 spŏudazō (1), *to
make effort*
4904 sunĕrgŏs (1),
fellow-worker
5389 philŏtimĕŏmai (1),
to be eager or earnest

LABOURED
3021 yâga' (4), *to be
exhausted, to tire,*
3022 yâgâ' (1), *earnings,
i.e. the product of toil*
5998 'âmal (5), *to work
severely, put forth effort*
6001 'âmêl (1), *toiling;
laborer; sorrowful*
6213 'âsâh (1), *to do or
make*
7712 shᵉdar (Ch.) (1), *to
endeavor, strive*
2872 kŏpiaō (5), *to feel
fatigue; to work hard*
4866 sunathlĕō (1), *to
wrestle with*

LABOURER
2040 ĕrgatēs (2), *toiler,
worker*

LABOURERS
2040 ĕrgatēs (8), *toiler,
worker*
4904 sunĕrgŏs (1),
fellow-worker

LABOURETH
5998 'âmal (1), *to work
severely, put forth effort*
6001 'âmêl (2), *toiling;
laborer; sorrowful*
2872 kŏpiaō (2), *to feel
fatigue; to work hard*

LABOURING
5647 'âbad (1), *to do,
work, serve*
75 agōnizŏmai (1), *to
struggle; to contend*
2872 kŏpiaō (1), *to feel
fatigue; to work hard*
2873 kŏpŏs (1), *toil; pains*

LABOURS
3018 yᵉgîya' (3), *toil,
work; produce, property*
4639 ma'ăseh (3), *action;
labor*
6089 'etseb (1), *earthen
vessel; painful toil;
mental pang*
6092 'âtsêb (1), *hired
workman*
2873 kŏpŏs (5), *toil; pains*

LACE
6616 pâthîyl (4), *twine,
cord*

LACHISH
3923 Lâchîysh (24),
Lakish

LACK
1097 bᵉlîy (3), *without,
not yet; lacking;*
2637 châçêr (4), *to lack;
to fail, want, make less*

4270 machçôwr (1),
impoverishment
7326 rûwsh (1), *to be
destitute*
1641 ĕlattŏnĕō (1), *to fall
short, have too little*
3007 lĕipō (1), *to fail or
be absent*
5302 hustĕrĕō (1), *to be
inferior; to fall short*
5303 hustĕrēma (1),
deficit; poverty; lacking
5332 pharmakĕus (1),
magician, sorcerer

LACKED
2637 châçêr (2), *to lack;
to fail, want, make less*
2638 châçêr (1), *lacking*
5737 'âdar (2), *to
arrange as a battle*
6485 pâqad (1), *to visit,
care for, count*
170 akairĕŏmai (1), *to
fail of a proper occasion*
1729 ĕndĕēs (1), *lacking;
deficient in; needy*
3361+2192 mē (1), *not;
lest*
5302 hustĕrĕō (2), *to be
inferior; to fall short*

LACKEST
3007 lĕipō (1), *to fail or
be absent*
5302 hustĕrĕō (1), *to be
inferior; to fall short*

LACKETH
2638 châçêr (3), *lacking*
6485 pâqad (1), *to visit,
care for, count*
3361+3918 mē (1), *not;
lest*

LACKING
5737 'âdar (1), *to
arrange as a battle*
6485 pâqad (2), *to visit,
care for, count*
7038 qâlaṭ (1), *to be
maim*
7673 shâbath (1), *to
repose; to desist*
5303 hustĕrēma (3),
deficit; poverty; lacking

LAD
5288 na'ar (32), *male
child; servant*
3808 paidariŏn (1), *little
boy*

LAD'S
5288 na'ar (1), *male
child; servant*

LADDER
5551 çullâm (1),
stair-case

LADE
2943 ṭâ'an (1), *to load a
beast*
6006 'âmaç (1), *to impose
a burden*
5412 phŏrtizō (1), *to
overburden*

LADED
5375 nâsâ' (1), *to lift up*
6006 'âmaç (2), *to impose
a burden*
2007 ĕpitithēmi (1), *to
impose*

LADEN
3515 kâbêd (1), *severe,
difficult, stupid*
5375 nâsâ' (2), *to lift up*
4987 sōrĕuō (1), *to pile
up, load up*
5412 phŏrtizō (1), *to
overburden*

LADETH
3515 kâbêd (1), *severe,
difficult, stupid*

LADIES
8282 sârâh (2), *female
noble*

LADING
6006 'âmaç (1), *to impose
a burden*
5414 phŏrtŏs (1), *cargo of
a ship*

LADS
5288 na'ar (1), *male
child; servant*

LADY
1404 gᵉbereth (2),
mistress, noblewoman
2959 Kuria (2), *Lady*

LAEL
3815 Lâ'êl (1), *belonging
to God*

LAHAD
3854 lahag (1), *mental
application*

LAHAI-ROI
883 Bᵉ'êr la-Chay Rô'îy
(2), *well of a living
(One) my seer*

LAHMAM
3903 Lachmâç (1),
food-like

LAHMI
3902 Lachmîy (1), *foodful*

LAID
935 bôw' (1), *to go or
come*
2470 châlâh (1), *to be
weak, sick, afflicted*
2630 châçan (1), *to
hoard, store up*
2934 ṭâman (2), *to hide*
3052 yᵉhab (Ch.) (1), *to
give*
3240 yânach (1), *to allow
to stay*
3241 Yânîym (8), *asleep*
3318 yâtsâ' (2), *to go,
bring out*
3332 yâtsaq (1), *to pour
out*
3369 yâqôsh (1), *to
ensnare, trap*
3384 yârâh (1), *to point;
to teach*
3515 kâbêd (1),
numerous; severe
3647 kâmaç (1), *to store
away*
5060 nâga' (1), *to strike*
5182 nᵉchath (Ch.) (1), *to
descend; to depose*
5186 nâṭâh (1), *to stretch
or spread out*
5324 nâtsab (1), *to station*
5375 nâsâ' (4), *to lift up*
5414 nâthan (13), *to give*

5446 çᵉbal (Ch.) (1), to *raise*
5493 çûwr (1), to *turn* off
5564 çâmak (6), to *lean* upon; *take hold* of
5674 'âbar (1), to *cross* over; to *transition*
5927 'âlâh (1), to *ascend, be high, mount*
6293 pâga' (1), to *impinge*
6485 pâqad (2), to *visit, care for, count*
6486 pᵉquddâh (1), *visitation; punishment*
6845 tsâphan (3), to *hide; to hoard or reserve; to deny; to protect; to lurk*
7737 shâvâh (3), to *level,* i.e. *equalize*
7760 sûwm (38), to *put, place*
7896 shîyth (8), to *place, put*
7901 shâkab (17), to *lie down*
7971 shâlach (6), to *send away*
8371 shâthath (1), to *place,* i.e. *array; to lie*
8610 tâphas (1), to *manipulate,* i.e. *seize*
347 anaklinō (1), to *lean back, recline*
606 apŏkĕimai (3), to be *reserved; to await*
659 apŏtithēmi (1), to *put away; get rid of*
906 ballō (3), to *throw*
1096 ginŏmai (1), to be, *become*
1462 ĕgklēma (2), *accusation*
1911 ĕpiballō (7), to *throw upon*
1945 ĕpikĕimai (2), to *rest upon; press upon*
2007 ĕpitithēmi (13), to *impose*
2071 ĕsŏmai (1), *will be*
2698 katatithēmi (1), to *place down*
2749 kĕimai (6), to *lie outstretched*
3049 lŏgizŏmai (1), to *credit; to think, regard*
4369 prŏstithēmi (1), to *lay beside, annex*
5087 tithēmi (29), to *place, put*
5294 hupŏtithēmi (1), to *hazard; to suggest*
5342 phĕrō (1), to *bear*

LAIDST
7760 sûwm (1), to *put*

LAIN
3045+4904 yâda' (1), to *know*
5414+7903 nâthan (1), to *give*
7901 shâkab (2), to *lie down*
2749 kĕimai (1), to *lie outstretched*

LAISH
3919 Layish (7), *lion*

LAKE
3041 limnē (10), *pond; lake*

LAKUM
3946 Laqqûwm (1), (poss.) *fortification*

LAMA
2982 lama (2), *why?*

LAMB
2924 țâleh (2), *lamb*
3532 kebes (44), *young ram*
3535 kibsâh (5), *ewe sheep*
3733 kar (1), *ram sheep; battering ram*
3775 keseb (3), *young ram sheep*
3776 kisbâh (1), *young ewe sheep*
6629 tsô'n (1), *flock of sheep or goats*
7716 seh (17), *sheep or goat*
286 amnŏs (4), *lamb*
721 arniŏn (27), *lamb, sheep*

LAMB'S
721 arniŏn (2), *lamb, sheep*

LAMBS
563 'immar (Ch.) (3), *lamb*
1121+6629 bên (2), *son, descendant; people*
2922 țᵉlâ' (1), *lamb*
3532 kebes (60), *young ram*
3535 kibsâh (3), *ewe sheep*
3733 kar (9), *ram sheep; battering ram*
3775 keseb (1), *young ram sheep*
704 arēn (1), *male lamb*
721 arniŏn (1), *lamb, sheep*

LAME
5223 nâkeh (2), *maimed; dejected*
6452 pâçach (1), to *hop, skip* over; to *hesitate*
6455 piççêach (14), *lame*
5560 chōlŏs (10), *limping, crippled*

LAMECH
3929 Lemek (11), *Lemek*
2984 Lamĕch (1), *Lemek*

LAMENT
56 'âbal (2), to *bewail*
421 'âlâh (1), to *bewail, mourn*
578 'ânâh (1), to *groan, lament*
5091 nâhâh (1), to *bewail; to assemble*
5594 çâphad (9), to *tear the hair, wail*
6969 qûwn (4), to *chant or wail at a funeral*
8567 tânâh (1), to *ascribe praise,* i.e. *celebrate*
2354 thrēnĕō (1), to *bewail, lament*
2875 kŏptō (1), to *beat the breast*

LAMENTABLE
6088 'ătsab (Ch.) (1), to *afflict; be afflicted*

LAMENTATION
592 'ănîyâh (1), *groaning*
1058 bâkâh (1), to *weep, moan*
4553 miçpêd (3), *lamentation, howling*
5092 nᵉhîy (3), *elegy*
7015 qîynâh (14), *dirge*
2355 thrēnŏs (1), *wailing, funeral song*
2870 kŏpĕtŏs (1), *mourning*

LAMENTATIONS
7015 qîynâh (3), *dirge*

LAMENTED
56 'âbal (1), to *bewail*
5091 nâhâh (1), to *bewail; to assemble*
5594 çâphad (4), to *tear the hair, wail*
6969 qûwn (3), to *chant or wail at a funeral*
2354 thrēnĕō (1), to *bewail, lament*
2875 kŏptō (1), to *beat the breast*

LAMP
3940 lappîyd (3), *flaming torch, lamp or flame*
5216 nîyr (9), *lamp; lamplight*
2985 lampas (1), *lamp, lantern, torch*

LAMPS
3940 lappîyd (5), *flaming torch, lamp or flame*
5216 nîyr (26), *lamp; lamplight*
2985 lampas (6), *lamp, lantern, torch*

LANCE
3591 kîydôwn (1), *dart, javelin*

LANCETS
7420 rômach (1), *iron pointed spear*

LAND
127 'ădâmâh (123), *soil; land*
249 'ezrâch (2), *native born*
776 'erets (1505), *earth, land, soil; country*
3004 yabbâshâh (1), *dry ground*
7704 sâdeh (7), *field*
68 agrŏs (1), *farmland, countryside*
1093 gē (42), *soil, region, whole earth*
3584 xērŏs (1), *scorched; arid; withered*
5561 chōra (3), *space of territory*
5564 chōriŏn (2), *spot or plot* of ground

LANDED
2609 katagō (1), to *lead down; to moor a vessel*
2718 katĕrchŏmai (1), to *go/come down*

LANDING
2609 katagō (1), to *lead down; to moor a vessel*

LANDMARK
1366 gᵉbûwl (4), *boundary, border*

LANDMARKS
1367 gᵉbûwlâh (1), *boundary marker*

LANDS
127 'ădâmâh (3), *soil; land*
776 'erets (34), *earth, land, soil; country, nation*
7704 sâdeh (4), *field*
68 agrŏs (3), *farmland, countryside*
5564 chōriŏn (1), *spot or plot* of ground

LANES
4505 rhumē (1), *alley or crowded avenue*

LANGUAGE
1697 dâbâr (1), *word; matter; thing*
3937 lâ'az (1), to *speak in a foreign tongue*
3956 lâshôwn (9), *tongue; tongue-shaped*
3961 lishshân (Ch.) (1), *nation*
8193 sâphâh (7), *lip, language, speech*
1258 dialĕktŏs (1), *known language*

LANGUAGES
3956 lâshôwn (1), *tongue; tongue-shaped*
3961 lishshân (Ch.) (6), *nation*

LANGUISH
535 'âmal (5), to be *weak; to be sick*

LANGUISHED
535 'âmal (1), to be *weak; to be sick*

LANGUISHETH
535 'âmal (8), to be *weak; to be sick*

LANGUISHING
1741 dᵉvay (1), *sickness*

LANTERNS
5322 phanŏs (1), *light; lantern,* i.e. *torch*

LAODICEA
2993 Laŏdikĕia (5), *Laodicea*

LAODICEANS
2994 Laŏdikĕus (2), *inhabitant of Laodicea*

LAP
899 beged (1), *clothing; treachery or pillage*
2436 chêyq (1), *bosom, heart*
2684 chôtsen (1), *bosom*

LAPIDOTH
3941 Lappîydôwth (1), *flaming torch, lamp*

LAPPED
3952 lâqaq (2), to *lick or lap*

LAPPETH
3952 lâqaq (2), to *lick or lap*

LAPWING
1744 dûwkîyphath (2), hoopoe; (poss.) grouse

LARGE
4800 merchâb (5), open space; liberty
7304 râvach (1), to revive; to have ample room
7337 râchab (2), to broaden
7342 râchâb (5), roomy, spacious
2425 hikanŏs (1), ample; fit
3173 mĕgas (2), great, many
4080 pēlikŏs (1), how much, how great
5118 tŏsŏutŏs (1), such great

LARGENESS
7341 rôchab (1), width

LASCIVIOUSNESS
766 asĕlgĕia (6), licentiousness

LASEA
2996 Lasaia (1), Lasæa

LASHA
3962 Lesha' (1), boiling spring

LASHARON
8289 Shârôwn (1), plain

LAST
314 'achărôwn (20), late or last; behind; western
318 'ochŏrêyn (Ch.) (1), at last, finally
319 'achărîyth (10), future; posterity
6119 'âqêb (1), track, footprint; rear position
2078 ĕschatŏs (48), farthest, final
4218 pŏtĕ (1), at some time, ever
5305 hustĕrŏn (4), more lately, i.e. eventually

LASTED
1961 hâyâh (1), to exist, i.e. be or become

LASTING
5769 'ôwlâm (1), eternity; ancient; always

LATCHET
8288 sĕrôwk (1), sandal thong
2438 himas (3), strap; lash

LATE
309 'âchar (1), to delay; to procrastinate
865 'ethmôwl (1), formerly; yesterday
3568 nun (1), now; the present or immediate

LATELY
4373 prŏsphatŏs (1), recently

LATIN
4513 Rhōmaïkŏs (2), Latin

LATTER
314 'achărôwn (8), late or last; behind; western
319 'achărîyth (20), future; posterity
320 'achărîyth (Ch.) (1), later, end
3954 leqesh (2), after crop, second crop
4456 malqôwsh (8), spring rain
2078 ĕschatŏs (1), farthest, final
3797 ŏpsimŏs (1), later, i.e. vernal showering
5305 hustĕrŏn (1), more lately, i.e. eventually

LATTICE
822 'eshnâb (1), latticed window
2762 cherek (1), window lattice
7639 sĕbâkâh (1), net-work balustrade

LAUD
1867 ĕpainĕō (1), to applaud, commend

LAUGH
3932 lâ'ag (4), to deride; to speak unintelligibly
6711 tsâchaq (3), to laugh; to scorn
6712 tsĕchôq (1), laughter; scorn
7832 sâchaq (8), to laugh; to scorn; to play
1070 gĕlaō (2), to laugh

LAUGHED
3932 lâ'ag (3), to deride; to speak unintelligibly
6711 tsâchaq (3), to laugh; to scorn
6712 tsĕchôq (1), laughter; scorn
7832 sâchaq (3), to laugh; to scorn; to play
2606 katagĕlaō (3), to laugh down, i.e. deride

LAUGHETH
7832 sâchaq (1), to laugh; to scorn; to play

LAUGHING
7814 sĕchôwq (1), laughter; scorn

LAUGHTER
7814 sĕchôwq (6), laughter; scorn
1071 gĕlōs (1), laughter

LAUNCH
1877 ĕpanagō (1), to put out to sea; to return

LAUNCHED
321 anagō (4), to bring out; to sail away

LAVER
3595 kîyôwr (15), caldron; washbowl

LAVERS
3595 kîyôwr (5), caldron; washbowl

LAVISH
2107 zûwl (1), to treat lightly

LAW
1881 dâth (6), royal edict or statute
1882 dâth (Ch.) (9), Law; royal edict or statute
2524 châm (4), father-in-law
2545 chămôwth (11), mother-in-law
2706 chôq (4), appointment; allotment
2710 châqaq (1), to engrave; to enact laws; to prescribe
2859 châthan (32), to become related
2860 châthân (5), relative by marriage
2994 yĕbêmeth (2), sister-in-law
3618 kallâh (17), bride; son's wife
4687 mitsvâh (1), command
4941 mishpâṭ (2), verdict; formal decree; justice
8451 tôwrâh (206), precept or statute
60 agŏraiŏs (1), people of the market place
458 anŏmia (1), violation of law, wickedness
459 anŏmŏs (3), without Jewish law
460 anŏmŏs (1), lawlessly
1772 ĕnnŏmŏs (1), legal, or subject to law
2917 krima (1), decision
2919 krinō (2), to decide; to try, condemn, punish
3544 nŏmikŏs (1), expert in the (Mosaic) law
3547 nŏmŏdidaskalŏs (3), a Rabbi
3548 nŏmŏthĕsia (1), legislation, law
3549 nŏmŏthĕtĕō (1), to be given law
3551 nŏmŏs (192), law
3565 numphē (3), young married woman
3891 paranŏmĕō (1), to transgress, violate law
3994 pĕnthĕra (3), wife's mother, mother-in-law
3995 pĕnthĕrŏs (1), wife's father
4160+458 pŏiĕō (1), to make or do

LAWFUL
4941 mishpâṭ (7), verdict; formal decree; justice
6662 tsaddîyq (1), just
7990 shallîyṭ (Ch.) (1), premier, sovereign
1772 ĕnnŏmŏs (1), legal, or subject to law
1832 ĕxĕsti (12), it is right, it is proper
1833 ĕxĕtazō (17), to ascertain or interrogate

LAWFULLY
3545 nŏmimŏs (2), agreeably to the rules

LAWGIVER
2710 châqaq (6), to engrave; to enact laws

3550 nŏmŏthĕtēs (1), legislator, lawgiver

LAWLESS
459 anŏmŏs (1), without Jewish law

LAWS
1881 dâth (3), royal edict or statute
1882 dâth (Ch.) (2), Law; royal edict or statute
8451 tôwrâh (12), precept or codified statute
8541 timmâhôwn (1), consternation, panic
3551 nŏmŏs (2), law

LAWYER
3544 nŏmikŏs (3), expert in the (Mosaic) law

LAWYERS
3544 nŏmikŏs (5), expert in the (Mosaic) law

LAY
3241 Yânîym (10), asleep
3331 yâtsa' (1), to strew as a surface
3885 lûwn (1), to be obstinate
4422 mâlaṭ (1), to be delivered; be smooth
5117 nûwach (1), to rest; to settle down
5186 nâṭâh (1), to stretch or spread out
5307 nâphal (4), to fall
5414 nâthan (20), to give
5493 çûwr (1), to turn off
5564 çâmak (12), to lean upon; take hold of
6651 tsâbar (1), to aggregate, gather
6845 tsâphan (2), to hide; to hoard or reserve
7126 qârab (1), to approach, bring near
7257 râbats (3), to recline, repose, brood
7258 rebets (1), place of repose
7760 sûwm (26), to put, place
7871 shîybâh (1), residence
7896 shîyth (5), to place, put
7901 shâkab (45), to lie down
7902 shĕkâbâh (2), lying down
7931 shâkan (1), to reside
7971 shâlach (8), to send away
659 apŏtithēmi (2), to put away; get rid of
1458 ĕgkalĕō (1), to charge, criminate
1474 ĕdaphizō (1), to dash to the ground
1911 ĕpiballō (2), to throw upon
1945 ĕpikĕimai (2), to rest upon; press upon
1949 ĕpilambanŏmai (2), to seize
2007 ĕpitithēmi (7), to impose
2343 thēsaurizō (1), to amass or reserve, store

2476 histēmi (1), to stand, establish
2621 katakĕimai (5), to lie down; to recline
2749 kĕimai (1), to lie outstretched
2827 klinō (2), to slant or slope
5087 tithēmi (13), to place

LAYEDST
5087 tithēmi (1), to place

LAYEST
7760 sûwm (1), to put

LAYETH
5381 nâsag (1), to reach
5414 nâthan (1), to give
6845 tsâphan (2), to hide; to hoard or reserve
7760 sûwm (5), to place
7896 shîyth (1), to place
7971 shâlach (1), to send away
2007 ĕpitithēmi (1), to impose

LAYING
2934 ṭâman (1), to hide
597 apŏthēsaurizō (1), to store treasure away
659 apŏtithēmi (1), to put away; get rid of
863 aphiēmi (1), to leave; to pardon, forgive
1748 ĕnĕdrĕuō (1), to lurk
1917 ĕpibŏulē (1), plot, plan
1936 ĕpithĕsis (3), imposition
2598 kataballō (1), to throw down
4160 pŏiĕō (1), to make or do

LAZARUS
2976 Lazarŏs (15), God (is) helper

LEAD
833 'âshar (1), to go forward; guide
1869 dârak (2), to tread, trample; to walk, lead
1980 hâlak (1), to walk; live a certain way
2986 yâbal (1), to bring
3212 yâlak (2), to walk; to live; to carry
3318 yâtsâ' (1), to go, bring out
5090 nâhag (9), to drive forth; to lead, carry
5095 nâhal (2), to flow; to conduct; to protect
5148 nâchâh (16), to guide
5777 'ôwphereth (9), mineral lead
7218 rô'sh (1), head
71 agō (1), to lead; to bring, drive; to weigh
162 aichmalōtĕuō (1), to capture
520 apagō (2), to take away
1236 diagō (1), to pass time, conduct one's life
1533 ĕisphĕrō (2), to carry inward
1806 ĕxagō (1), to lead forth, escort

3594 hŏdēgĕō (3), to show the way, i.e. lead
4013 pĕriagō (1), to take around as a companion
5497 chĕiragōgŏs (1), conductor of the blind

LEADER
5057 nâgîyd (3), commander, official

LEADERS
833 'âshar (1), to go forward; guide
5057 nâgîyd (1), commander, official
3595 hŏdēgŏs (1), conductor, guide

LEADEST
5090 nâhag (1), to drive forth; to lead away

LEADETH
1869 dârak (1), to tread, trample; to walk, lead
3212 yâlak (3), to walk; to live; to carry
5090 nâhag (1), to drive forth; to lead away
5095 nâhal (1), to flow; to conduct; to protect
71 agō (1), to lead; to bring, drive; to weigh
399 anaphĕrō (1), to take up; to lead up
520 apagō (1), to take away
1806 ĕxagō (1), to lead forth, escort
4863 sunagō (1), to gather together
5342 phĕrō (1), to bear or carry

LEAF
5929 'âleh (11), leaf; foliage

LEAGUE
1285 bᵉrîyth (17), compact, agreement
2266 châbar (1), to fascinate by spells
3772 kârath (1), to cut (off, down or asunder)

LEAH
3812 Lê'âh (29), weary

LEAH'S
3812 Lê'âh (5), weary

LEAN
1800 dal (1), weak, thin; humble, needy
5564 çâmak (2), to lean upon; take hold of
7329 râzâh (1), to make, become thin
7330 râzeh (2), thin, lean
7534 raq (1), emaciated, lank
8172 shâ'an (4), to support, rely on

LEANED
5564 çâmak (1), to lean upon; take hold of
8172 shâ'an (4), to support, rely on
377 anapiptō (1), lie down, lean back

LEANETH
2388 châzaq (1), to fasten upon; to seize
8127 shên (1), tooth; ivory; cliff

LEANFLESHED
1851+1320 daq (2), crushed; small or thin
7534 raq (1), emaciated, lank

LEANING
7514 râphaq (1), to recline
345 anakĕimai (1), to recline at a meal

LEANNESS
3585 kachash (1), emaciation; hypocrisy
7332 râzôwn (2), thinness
7334 râzîy (1), thinness

LEANNOTH
6030 'ânâh (1), to sing, shout

LEAP
1801 dâlag (2), to spring up, ascend
2178 zan (Ch.) (1), sort, kind
4422 mâlaṭ (1), to escape as if by slipperiness
5425 nâthar (1), to jump; to be agitated
5927 'âlâh (1), to ascend, be high, mount
7520 râtsad (1), to look askant; to be jealous
7540 râqad (1), to spring about wildly or for joy
4640 skirtaō (1), to jump

LEAPED
1801 dâlag (2), to spring up, ascend
5927 'âlâh (1), to ascend, be high, mount
6452 pâçach (1), to hop, skip over; to limp
242 hallŏmai (1), to jump up; to gush up
2177 ĕphallŏmai (1), to spring upon, leap upon
4640 skirtaō (2), to jump

LEAPING
1801 dâlag (1), to spring up, ascend
6339 pâzaz (1), to solidify by refining; to spring
242 hallŏmai (1), to jump up; to gush up
1814 ĕxallŏmai (1), to spring forth

LEARN
502 'âlaph (1), to learn; to teach
3925 lâmad (17), to teach, train
3129 manthanō (13), to learn
3811 paidĕuō (1), to educate or discipline

LEARNED
3045+5612 yâda' (3), to know
3925 lâmad (5), to teach, train
3928 limmûwd (2), instructed one

5172 nâchash (1), to prognosticate
3129 manthanō (10), to learn
3811 paidĕuō (1), to educate or discipline

LEARNING
3948 leqach (4), instruction
5612 çêpher (2), writing
1121 gramma (1), writing; education
1319 didaskalia (1), instruction
3129 manthanō (1), to learn

LEASING
3577 kâzâb (2), falsehood; idol

LEAST
176 'ôw (1), or, whether; desire
389 'ak (1), surely; only, however
4591 mâ'aṭ (1), to be, make small or few
6810 tsâ'îyr (4), little in number; few in age
6994 qâṭôn (1), to be, make diminutive
6996 qâṭân (10), small, least, youngest
7535 raq (1), merely; although
1646 ĕlachistŏs (9), least
1647 ĕlachistŏtĕrŏs (1), far less
1848 ĕxŏuthĕnĕō (1), to treat with contempt
2534 kaigĕ (1), and at least (or even, indeed)
2579 kan (1), and if
3398 mikrŏs (6), small, little

LEATHER
5785 'ôwr (1), skin, leather

LEATHERN
1193 dĕrmatinŏs (1), made of leather hide

LEAVE
2308 châdal (3), to desist, stop; be fat
3241 Yânîym (14), asleep
3322 yâtsag (1), to place
3498 yâthar (7), to remain or be left
3499 yether (1), remainder; small rope
5157 nâchal (1), to inherit
5203 nâṭash (6), to disperse; to thrust off
5414 nâthan (2), to give
5800 'âzab (30), to loosen; relinquish
6168 'ârâh (1), to be, make bare; to empty
7503 râphâh (1), to slacken
7592 shâ'al (1), to ask
7604 shâ'ar (13), to leave, remain
7662 shᵉbaq (Ch.) (3), to allow to remain
8338 shâwshâw (1), (poss.) to annihilate

LEAVED

447 aniĕmi (1), to *desert, desist* from

657 apŏtassŏmai (2), to *say adieu*; to *renounce*

782 aspazŏmai (1), to *give salutation*

863 aphiĕmi (11), to *leave*; to *pardon, forgive*

1459 ĕgkataleĭpō (1), to *desert, abandon*

1544 ĕkballō (1), to *throw out*

2010 ĕpitrĕpō (2), *allow, permit*

2641 kataleĭpō (6), to *abandon*

LEAVED

1817 deleth (1), *door; gate*

LEAVEN

2557 châmêts (5), *ferment, yeasted*

4682 matstsâh (1), *unfermented cake*

7603 se'ôr (4), yeast-cake for *fermentation*

2219 zumē (13), *ferment*

LEAVENED

2557 châmêts (11), *ferment, yeasted*

7603 se'ôr (1), yeast-cake for *fermentation*

2220 zumŏō (2), to *cause to ferment*

LEAVENETH

2220 zumŏō (2), to *cause to ferment*

LEAVES

1817 deleth (3), *door; gate*

2529 chem'âh (1), *curds, milk* or *cheese*

2964 ţereph (1), *fresh torn prey*

6074 'ŏphîy (Ch.) (3), *foliage*

6763 tsêlâ' (1), *side*

7050 qela' (1), *slinging* weapon; door *screen*

5444 phullŏn (6), *leaf*

LEAVETH

5800 'âzab (2), to *loosen; relinquish; permit*

863 aphiĕmi (2), to *leave*; to *pardon, forgive*

LEAVING

863 aphiĕmi (3), to *leave*; to *pardon, forgive*

2641 kataleĭpō (1), to *abandon*

5277 hupŏlimpanō (1), to *leave behind*

LEBANA

3848 lebash (Ch.) (1), to *clothe*

LEBANAH

3848 lebash (Ch.) (1), to *clothe*

LEBANON

3844 Lebânôwn (71), *white snow* mountain

LEBAOTH

3822 Lebâ'ôwth (1), *lionesses*

LEBBAEUS

3002 Lĕbbaiŏs (1), *Lebbæus*

LEBONAH

3829 Lebôwnâh (1), *frankincense*

LECAH

3922 Lêkâh (1), *journey*

LED

833 'âshar (1), to *go forward; guide*

935 bôw' (1), to *go*

1869 dârak (2), to *tread, trample*; to *walk, lead*

2986 yâbal (1), to *bring*

3212 yâlak (13), to *walk; to live*; to *carry*

5090 nâhag (4), to *drive forth*; to *lead away*

5148 nâchâh (6), to *guide*

5437 çâbab (3), to *surround*

71 agō (11), to *lead; to bring, drive*; to *weigh*

162 aichmalōtĕuō (1), to *capture*

163 aichmalōtizō (1), to *make captive*

321 anagō (2), to *lead up*; to *bring out*

520 apagō (8), to *take away*

1521 eisagō (1), to *lead into*

1806 ĕxagō (3), to *lead forth, escort*

4879 sunapagō (1), to *take off together*

5496 cheiragōgĕō (2), to *guide* a blind person

LEDDEST

3318 yâtsâ' (2), to *go, bring out*

5148 nâchâh (2), to *guide*

1806 ĕxagō (1), to *lead forth, escort*

LEDGES

3027 yâd (2), *hand; power*

7948 shâlâb (3), *interval*

LEEKS

2682 châtsîyr (1), *grass; leek* plant

LEES

8105 shemer (4), *settlings* of wine, *dregs*

LEFT

2308 châdal (7), to *desist, stop; be fat*

2790 chârash (1), to *be silent*; to *be deaf*

3240 yânach (8), to *allow to stay*

3241 Yânîym (3), *asleep*

3498 yâthar (47), to *remain* or *be left*

3499 yether (3), *remainder*; small *rope*

3615 kâlâh (3), to *cease, be finished, perish*

3885 lûwn (1), to *be obstinate with*

4672 mâtsâ' (1), to *find* or *acquire*; to *occur*

5203 nâţash (7), to *disperse*; to *thrust* off

5414 nâthan (1), to *give*

LEBBAEUS continued

5493 çûwr (1), to *turn* off

5800 'âzab (43), to *loosen; relinquish*

5975 'âmad (2), to *stand*

6275 'âthaq (1), to *remove*; to *grow old*

7604 shâ'ar (65), to *leave, remain*

7611 she'êrîyth (1), *remainder* or residual

7662 shebaq (Ch.) (1), to *allow to remain*

7673 shâbath (1), to *repose*; to *desist*

7971 shâlach (1), to *send away*

8040 semô'wl (55), *north; left* hand

8041 sâma'l (4), to *use* the *left* hand or go *left*

8042 semâ'lîy (9), on the *left* side; *northern*

8300 sârîyd (3), *survivor; remainder*

620 apŏleĭpō (3), to *leave behind*; to *forsake*

710 aristĕrŏs (3), *left* hand

863 aphiĕmi (36), to *leave*; to *pardon, forgive*

1439 eaō (1), to *let be*, i.e. *permit* or *leave alone*

1459 ĕgkataleĭpō (1), to *desert, abandon*

2176 ĕuŏnumŏs (10), *left; at the left* hand; *south*

2641 kataleĭpō (15), to *abandon*

3973 pauō (2), to *stop,* i.e. *restrain, quit*

4051 pĕrissĕuma (1), *superabundance*

4052 pĕrissĕuō (1), to *superabound*

5275 hupŏleĭpō (1), to *remain, survive*

LEFTEST

5800 'âzab (1), to *loosen; relinquish; permit*

LEFTHANDED

334+3027+3225 'iţţêr (2), *impeded* (as to the right hand), *left-handed*

LEG

7640 shôbel (1), lady's garment *train*

LEGION

3003 lĕgĕōn (3), *legion*

LEGIONS

3003 lĕgĕōn (1), *legion*

LEGS

3767 kârâ' (9), *leg*

6807 tse'âdâh (1), *march; ankle-chain*

7272 regel (1), *foot; step*

7785 shôwq (4), lower *leg*

8243 shâq (Ch.) (1), *shank,* or whole *leg*

4628 skĕlŏs (3), *leg*

LEHABIM

3853 Lehâbîym (2), *flames*

LEHI

3896 Lechîy (3), *jaw-bone*

LEISURE

2119 ĕukairĕō (1), to *have leisure*

LEMUEL

3927 Lemûw'êl (2), (belonging) *to God*

LEND

3867 lâvâh (4), to *unite; to remain; to lend*

5383 nâshâh (2), to *lend* or *borrow*

5391 nâshak (3), to *strike; to oppress*

5414 nâthan (1), to *give*

5670 'âbaţ (2), to *pawn; to lend; to entangle*

1155 danĕizō (3), to *loan* on interest; to *borrow*

5531 chraō (1), to *loan, lend*

LENDER

3867 lâvâh (2), to *unite; to borrow; to lend*

LENDETH

3867 lâvâh (3), to *unite; to borrow; to lend*

5383 nâshâh (1), to *lend* or *borrow*

LENGTH

319 'achârîyth (1), *future; posterity*

753 'ôrek (70), *length*

3372 mêkôs (3), *length*

4218 pŏtĕ (1), at *some time, ever*

LENGTHEN

748 'ârak (2), to *be, make long*

LENGTHENED

748 'ârak (1), to *be, make long*

LENGTHENING

754 'arkâ' (Ch.) (1), *length*

LENT

5383 nâshâh (2), to *lend* or *borrow*

5391 nâshak (1), to *strike; to oppress*

7592 shâ'al (4), to *ask*

LENTILES

5742 'âdâsh (4), *lentil* bean

LEOPARD

5245 nemar (Ch.) (1), *leopard*

5246 nâmêr (4), *leopard*

3917 pardalis (1), *leopard, panther*

LEOPARDS

5246 nâmêr (2), *leopard*

LEPER

6879 tsâra' (13), to *be stricken with leprosy*

3015 lĕprŏs (4), *leper*

LEPERS

6879 tsâra' (1), to *be stricken with leprosy*

3015 lĕprŏs (5), *leper*

LEPROSY

6883 tsâra'ath (35), *leprosy*

3014 lĕpra (4), *leprosy*

LEPROUS

6879 tsâra' (6), to *be stricken with leprosy*

LESHEM
3959 Leshem (2), *jacinth*
stone

LESS
657 'epheç (1), *end; no*
further
4295 maţţâh (1), *below*
or beneath
4591 mâ'aţ (4), *to be,*
make small or few
6996 qâţân (3), *small,*
least, youngest
253 alupŏtĕrŏs (1), *more*
without grief
820 atimŏs (1), *without*
honor
1640 ĕlassŏn (1), *smaller*
1647 ĕlachistŏtĕrŏs (1),
far less
2276 hēttŏn (1), *worse;*
less
3398 mikrŏs (2), *small,*
little

LESSER
6996 qâţân (2), *small,*
least, youngest
7716 seh (1), *sheep or*
goat

LEST
1077 bal (1), *nothing; not*
at all; lest
1115 biltîy (3), *not,*
except, without, unless
3808 lô' (12), no, *not*
6435 pên (120), *lest, not*
3361 mē (13), *not; lest*
3379 mēpŏtĕ (20), *not*
ever; if, or lest ever
3381 mēpŏs (12), *lest*
somehow

LET
3212 yâlak (1), *to walk;*
to live; to carry
3240 yânach (3), *to allow*
to stay
3381 yârad (7), *to*
descend
5117 nûwach (1), *to rest;*
to settle down
5186 nâţâh (1), *to stretch*
or spread out
5414 nâthan (3), *to give*
6544 pâra' (1), *to loosen*
7503 râphâh (2), *to*
slacken
7725 shûwb (1), *to turn*
back; to return
7971 shâlach (2), *to send*
away
630 apŏluō (10), *to*
relieve, release
863 aphiēmi (16), *to*
leave; to pardon, forgive
1439 ĕaō (4), *to let be, i.e.*
permit or leave alone
1554 ĕkdidōmi (4), *to*
lease, rent
1832 ĕxĕsti (1), *it is right,*
it is proper
1929 ĕpididōmi (1), *to*
give over
2010 ĕpitrĕpō (1), *allow,*
permit
2524 kathiĕmi (1), *to*
lower, let down
2722 katĕchō (2), *to hold*
down fast
2967 kōluō (1), *to stop*

5465 chalaō (5), *to lower*
as into a void

LETTER
104 'iggᵉrâ' (Ch.) (3),
epistle, letter
107 'iggereth (4), *epistle,*
letter
5406 nishtᵉvân (2),
written epistle
5407 nishtᵉvân (Ch.) (3),
written epistle
5612 çêpher (13), *writing*
6600 pithgâm (Ch.) (1),
decree; report
1121 gramma (6),
writing; education
1989 ĕpistĕllō (1), *to*
communicate by letter
1992 ĕpistŏlē (3), *written*
message

LETTERS
107 'iggereth (6), *epistle,*
letter
5612 çêpher (16), *writing*
1121 gramma (3),
writing; education
1992 ĕpistŏlē (6), *written*
message

LETTEST
8257 shâqa' (1), *to be*
overflowed; to cease
630 apŏluō (1), *to relieve,*
release

LETTETH
6362 pâţar (1), *to burst*
through; to emit
2722 katĕchō (1), *to hold*
down fast

LETUSHIM
3912 Lᵉţûwshîm (1),
oppressed ones

LEUMMIM
3817 Lᵉ'ummîym (1),
communities

LEVI
3878 Lêvîy (64), *attached*
3017 Lĕuï (5), *attached*
3018 Lĕuïs (3), *attached*

LEVIATHAN
3882 livyâthân (5),
serpent (crocodile)

LEVITE
3881 Lêvîyîy (26), *Levite*
3019 Lĕuïtēs (2),
descendants of Levi

LEVITES
3878 Lêvîy (1), *attached*
3879 Lêvîy (Ch.) (4),
attached
3881 Lêvîyîy (259), *Levite*
3019 Lĕuïtēs (1),
descendants of Levi

LEVITICAL
3020 Lĕuïtikŏs (1),
relating to the Levites

LEVY
4522 maç (4), *forced*
labor
5927 'âlâh (1), *to ascend,*
be high, mount
7311 rûwm (1), *to be*
high; to rise or raise

LEWD
2154 zimmâh (2), *bad*
plan

4190 pŏnērŏs (1), *malice,*
wicked, bad; crime

LEWDLY
2154 zimmâh (1), *bad*
plan

LEWDNESS
2154 zimmâh (14), *bad*
plan
4209 mᵉzimmâh (1),
plan; sagacity
5040 nablûwth (1),
female genitals
4467 rha₁diŏurgēma (1),
crime, legal fraction

LIAR
376+3576 'îysh (1), *man;*
male; someone
391 'akzâb (1), *deceit;*
treachery
3576 kâzab (2), *to lie,*
deceive
8267 sheqer (1), *untruth;*
sham
5583 psĕustēs (8), *falsifier*

LIARS
907 bad (2), *brag or lie;*
liar, boaster
3576 kâzab (1), *to lie,*
deceive
3584 kâchash (1), *to lie,*
disown; to disappoint
5571 psĕudēs (2),
erroneous, deceitful
5583 psĕustēs (2), *falsifier*

LIBERAL
1293 bᵉrâkâh (1),
benediction, blessing
5081 nâdîyb (3), *generous*
572 haplŏtēs (1),
sincerity; generosity

LIBERALITY
572 haplŏtēs (1),
sincerity; generosity
5485 charis (1),
graciousness

LIBERALLY
6059 'ânaq (1), *to collar;*
to fit out
574 haplōs (1),
bountifully, generously

LIBERTINES
3032 Libĕrtinŏs (1),
Freedman

LIBERTY
1865 dᵉrôwr (7),
freedom; clear, pure
2670 chophshîy (1),
exempt from bondage
7342 râchâb (1), *roomy,*
spacious
425 anĕsis (1),
relaxation; relief
630 apŏluō (2), *to relieve,*
release; to pardon
859 aphĕsis (1), *pardon,*
freedom
1657 ĕlĕuthĕria (11),
freedom
1658 ĕlĕuthĕrŏs (1),
unrestrained
1849 ĕxŏusia (1),
authority, power, right
2010 ĕpitrĕpō (1), *to allow*

LIBNAH
3841 Libnâh (18),
storax-tree

LIBNI
3845 Libnîy (5), *white*

LIBNITES
3864 Lûwbîy (2), *dry*
region

LIBYA
6316 Pûwţ (2), *Put,*
person
3033 Libuĕ (1), *south*
region

LIBYANS
3864 Lûwbîy (1), *dry*
region
6316 Pûwţ (1), *Put,*
person

LICE
3654 kên (6), *stinging bug*

LICENCE
2010 ĕpitrĕpō (1), *allow,*
permit
5117 tŏpŏs (1), *place*

LICK
3897 lâchak (4), *to lick*
3952 lâqaq (1), *to lick*

LICKED
3897 lâchak (1), *to lick*
3952 lâqaq (2), *to lick*
621 apŏlĕichō (1), *to lick*
off clean

LICKETH
3897 lâchak (1), *to lick*

LID
1817 deleth (1), *door;*
gate

LIE
391 'akzâb (1), *deceit;*
treachery
693 'ârab (2), *to ambush,*
lie in wait
2583 chânâh (2), *to*
encamp
3576 kâzab (12), *to lie,*
deceive
3584 kâchash (1), *to lie,*
disown; to disappoint
3885 lûwn (2), *to be*
obstinate
4769 marbêts (1),
reclining or resting
place
5203 nâţash (1), *to*
disperse; to abandon
5307 nâphal (1), *to fall*
5414+7903 nâthan (3), *to*
give
6658 tsâdâh (1), *to*
desolate
7250 râba' (2), *to lay*
down; have sex
7257 râbats (15), *to*
recline, repose, brood
7258 rebets (1), *place of*
repose
7693 shâgal (1), *to*
copulate
7901 shâkab (59), *to lie*
down
8266 shâqar (5), *to cheat,*
i.e. be untrue in words
8267 sheqer (8), *untruth;*
sham
893 apsĕudēs (1),
veracious, free of deceit
2621 katakĕimai (1), *to*
lie down; to recline

2749 kĕimai (1), to *lie*
outstretched
3180 mĕthŏdĕia (1),
trickery, scheming
3582 xĕstēs (1), *vessel*
5574 psĕudŏmai (11), to
utter an untruth
5579 psĕudŏs (7),
falsehood

LIED
3576 kâzab (2), to *lie,
deceive*
3584 kâchash (1), to *lie,
disown;* to *disappoint*
5574 psĕudŏmai (1), to
utter an untruth

LIEN
7693 shâgal (1), to
copulate with
7901 shâkab (2), to *lie*
down

LIES
907 bad (3), *brag* or *lie;
liar, boaster*
1697+3576 dâbâr (1),
word; matter; thing
1697+8267 dâbâr (1),
word; matter; thing
3576 kâzab (22), to *lie,
deceive*
3585 kachash (4),
emaciation; hypocrisy
7723 shâv' (1), *ruin;
guile; idolatry*
8267 sheqer (17),
untruth; sham
8383 tᵉʾûn (1), *toil*
5573 psĕudŏlŏgŏs (1),
*promulgating
erroneous doctrine*

LIEST
5307 nâphal (1), to *fall*
7901 shâkab (4), to *lie*
down

LIETH
3318 yâtsâ' (3), to *go,
bring out*
3584 kâchash (1), to *lie,
disown;* to *disappoint*
4904 mishkâb (1), *bed;
sleep; intercourse*
5564 çâmak (1), to *lean*
upon; *take hold of*
6437 pânâh (1), to *turn,*
to *face*
7257 râbats (2), to
recline, repose, brood
7901 shâkab (20), to *lie*
down
8172 shâ'an (1), to
support, rely on
906 ballō (1), to *throw*
991 blĕpō (1), to *look at*
2192 ĕchō (1), to *have;
hold; keep*
2749 kĕimai (2), to *lie*
outstretched

LIEUTENANTS
323 'ăchashdarpan (4),
satrap

LIFE
2416 chay (143), *alive;
raw; fresh; life*
2417 chay (Ch.) (1), *alive;
life*
2421 châyâh (10), to *live;*
to *revive*

2425 châyay (1), to *live;*
to *revive*
3117 yôwm (3), *day; time
period*
3117+5921 yôwm (1),
day; time period
5315 nephesh (90), *life;
breath; soul; wind*
6106 'etsem (1), *bone;
body; substance*
72 agŏgē (1), *mode of
living, way of life*
895 apsuchŏs (1), *lifeless,*
i.e. *inanimate*
979 biŏs (5), *present
state of existence*
981 biŏsis (1), *mode of
living*
982 biŏtikŏs (3), *relating*
to the present *existence*
2198 zaō (1), to *live*
2222 zōē (132), *life*
2227 zōŏpŏiĕō (2), to (re-)
vitalize, give life
4151 pnĕuma (1), *spirit*
5590 psuchē (36), *soul,
vitality; heart, mind*

LIFETIME
2416 chay (1), *alive; raw;
fresh; life*
2198 zaō (1), to *live*
2222 zōē (1), *life*

LIFT
5127 nûwç (1), to *vanish
away, flee*
5130 nûwph (3), to
quiver, vibrate, rock
5375 nâsâ' (66), to *lift up*
5414 nâthan (1), to *give*
6030 'ânâh (1), to
respond, answer
6670 tsâhal (1), to *be
cheerful;* to *sound*
6965 qûwm (3), to *rise*
7311 rûwm (18), to *be
high;* to *rise or raise*
352 anakuptō (1), to
straighten up
461 anŏrthŏō (1), to
straighten up
1458 ĕgkalĕō (1), to
charge, criminate
1869 ĕpairō (4), to *raise
up, look up*
5312 hupsŏō (1), to
elevate; to *exalt*

LIFTED
935 bôw' (1), to *go or
come*
1361 gâbahh (7), to *be
lofty;* to *be haughty*
1431 gâdal (1), to *be
great, make great*
1802 dâlâh (1), to *draw
out water);* to *deliver*
5130 nûwph (1), to
quiver, vibrate, rock
5191 nᵉṭal (Ch.) (2), to
raise; to *repent*
5264 nâçaç (1), to *gleam;*
to *flutter a flag*
5375 nâsâ' (92), to *lift up*
5423 nâthaq (1), to *tear
off*
5782 'ûwr (3), to *awake*
5927 'âlâh (1), to *ascend,
be high, mount*

6075 'âphal (1), to *swell;
be elated*
7213 râ'am (1), to *rise*
7311 rûwm (15), to *be
high;* to *rise or raise*
7313 rûwm (Ch.) (2),
elation, arrogance
7426 râmam (2), to *rise*
142 airō (4), to *lift,* to
take up
352 anakuptō (2), to
straighten up
450 anistēmi (1), to
stand up; to *come back*
to *life*
1453 ĕgĕirō (3), to
waken, i.e. *rouse*
1869 ĕpairō (10), to *raise
up, look up*
5188 tuphō (1), to make
a *smoke*
5312 hupsŏō (5), to
elevate; to *exalt*

LIFTER
7311 rûwm (1), to *be
high;* to *rise or raise*

LIFTEST
5375 nâsâ' (1), to *lift up*
5414 nâthan (1), to *give*
7311 rûwm (2), to *be
high;* to *rise or raise*

LIFTETH
4754 mârâ' (1), to *rebel;*
to *lash* with whip; *flap*
5375 nâsâ' (2), to *lift up*
5749 'ûwd (1), to
duplicate or repeat
5927 'âlâh (2), to *ascend,
be high, mount*
7311 rûwm (4), to *be
high;* to *rise or raise*

LIFTING
1348 gê'ûwth (1),
ascending; majesty
1466 gêvâh (1),
exaltation; arrogance
4607 mô'al (1), *raising* of
the hands
4864 mas'êth (1), *raising;
beacon; present*
5375 nâsâ' (1), to *lift up*
5782 'ûwr (1), to *awake*
7311 rûwm (1), to *be
high;* to *rise or raise*
7427 rômêmûth (1),
exaltation
1869 ĕpairō (2), to *raise
up, look up*

LIGHT
215 'ôwr (1), to *be
luminous*
216 'ôwr (126), *luminary;
lightning; happiness*
217 'ûwr (1), *flame; East*
219 'ôwrâh (2),
luminousness, light
3313 yâpha' (1), to *shine*
3974 mâ'ôwr (15),
luminary, light source
4237 mechĕzâh (2),
window
5051 nôgahh (1),
brilliancy
5094 nᵉhîyr (Ch.) (3),
illumination
5105 nᵉhârâh (1),
daylight

5117 nûwach (1), to *rest;*
to *settle* down
5216 nîyr (4), *lamp;
lamplight*
5927 'âlâh (2), to *ascend,
be high, mount*
6348 pâchaz (2), to *be
unimportant*
7031 qal (1), *rapid, swift*
7034 qâlâh (1), to *be light*
7043 qâlal (7), to *be,
make light*
7052 qᵉlôqêl (1),
insubstantial food
7136 qârâh (1), to *bring
about;* to *impose*
7837 shachar (1), *dawn*
272 amĕlĕō (1), to *be
careless* of, *neglect*
681 haptō (1), to *set* on
fire
1645 ĕlaphrŏs (2), *light,*
i.e. *easy*
2014 ĕpiphainō (1), to
become visible
2017 ĕpiphauō (1), to
illuminate, shine on
2545 kaiō (1), to *set* on
fire
2989 lampō (1), to
radiate brilliancy
3088 luchnŏs (5), lamp
or other *illuminator*
4098 piptō (1), to *fall*
5338 phĕggŏs (3),
brilliancy, radiance
5457 phōs (65),
luminousness, light
5458 phōstēr (1),
celestial *luminary*
5460 phōtĕinŏs (4),
well-illuminated
5461 phōtizō (4), to *shine*
or to *brighten* up
5462 phōtismŏs (2), *light;
illumination*

LIGHTED
3381 yârad (2), to
descend
4672 mâtsâ' (1), to *find
or acquire;* to *occur*
5307 nâphal (3), to *fall*
5927 'âlâh (2), to *ascend,
be high, mount*
6293 pâga' (1), to *impinge*
6795 tsânach (2), to
descend, i.e. *drive* down
681 haptō (2), to *set* on
fire

LIGHTEN
215 'ôwr (2), to *be
luminous*
5050 nâgahh (1), to
illuminate
7043 qâlal (2), to *be,
make light*
602 apŏkalupsis (1),
disclosure, revelation
5461 phōtizō (1), to *shine*
or to *brighten* up

LIGHTENED
215 'ôwr (1), to *be
luminous*
5102 nâhar (1), to
sparkle; to *be cheerful*
1546+4160 ĕkbŏlē (1),
jettison of cargo

2893 kŏuphizō (1), to unload, make lighter
5461 phōtizō (1), to shine or to brighten up

LIGHTENETH
215 'ôwr (1), to be luminous
797 astraptō (1), to flash as lightning

LIGHTER
7043 qâlal (4), to be, make light

LIGHTEST
5927 'âlâh (1), to ascend, be high, mount

LIGHTETH
4672 mâtsâ' (1), to find or acquire; to occur
5927 'âlâh (1), to ascend, be high, mount
5461 phōtizō (1), to shine or to brighten up

LIGHTING
5183 nachath (1), descent; quiet
2064 ĕrchŏmai (1), to go or come

LIGHTLY
4592 mᵉ'aṭ (1), little or few
5034 nâbêl (1), to wilt; to fall away; to be foolish
7034 qâlâh (1), to be light
7043 qâlal (3), to be, make light
5035 tachu (1), without delay, soon, suddenly

LIGHTNESS
6350 pachăzûwth (1), frivolity
6963 qôwl (1), voice or sound
1644 ĕlaphria (1), fickleness

LIGHTNING
216 'ôwr (1), luminary; lightning; happiness
965 bâzâq (1), flash of lightning
1300 bârâq (5), lightning; flash of lightning
2385 chăzîyz (2), flash of lightning
796 astrapē (4), lightning; light's glare

LIGHTNINGS
1300 bârâq (9), lightning; flash of lightning
3940 lappîyd (1), flaming torch, lamp or flame
796 astrapē (4), lightning; light's glare

LIGHTS
216 'ôwr (1), luminary; lightning; happiness
3974 mâ'ôwr (4), luminary, light source
8261 shâqŭph (1), opening
2985 lampas (1), lamp, lantern, torch
3088 luchnŏs (1), lamp or other illuminator
5457 phōs (1), luminousness, light

5458 phōstēr (1), celestial luminary

LIGURE
3958 leshem (2), (poss.) jacinth

LIKE
251 'âch (1), brother; relative; member
1571 gam (2), also; even
1819 dâmâh (16), to resemble, liken
1821 dᵉmâh (Ch.) (2), to resemble; be like
1823 dᵉmûwth (2), resemblance, likeness
1825 dimyôwn (1), resemblance, likeness
1922 hădar (Ch.) (1), to magnify, glorify
2088 zeh (1), this or that
2421 châyah (1), to live; to revive
2654 châphêts (2), to be pleased with, desire
2803 châshab (1), to think, regard; to value
3541 kôh (1), thus
3644 kᵉmôw (61), like, as; for; with
3651 kên (7), just; right, correct
4711 mâtsats (1), to suck
4911 mâshal (5), to use figurative language
4915 môshel (1), empire; parallel
5973 'îm (2), with
5974 'îm (Ch.) (1), with
7737 shâvâh (2), to resemble; to adjust
407 andrizŏmai (1), to act manly
499 antitupŏn (1), representative
871 aphŏmŏiŏō (1), to be like
1381 dŏkimazō (1), to test; to approve
1503 ĕikō (2), to resemble, be like
2470 isŏs (1), similar
2472 isŏtimŏs (1), of equal value or honor
2504 kagō (1), and also
2532 kai (1), and; or
3663 hŏmŏiŏpathēs (2), similarly affected
3664 hŏmŏiŏs (47), similar
3665 hŏmŏiŏtēs (1), resemblance, similarity
3666 hŏmŏiŏō (4), to become like
3667 hŏmŏiōma (1), form; resemblance
3779 hŏutō (2), in this way; likewise
3945 parŏmŏiazō (2), to resemble, be like
3946 parŏmŏiŏs (2), similar, like
4832 summŏrphŏs (1), similar, conformed to
5024 tauta (1), in the same way
5108 tŏiŏutŏs (1), truly this, i.e. of this sort
5613 hōs (10), which, how, i.e. in that manner

5615 hōsautōs (2), in the same way
5616 hōsĕi (6), as if
5618 hōspĕr (1), exactly like

LIKED
7521 râtsâh (1), to be pleased with; to satisfy

LIKEMINDED
2473 isŏpsuchŏs (1), of similar spirit
3588+846+5426 hŏ (2), "the," definite article

LIKEN
1819 dâmâh (4), to resemble, liken
3666 hŏmŏiŏō (5), to become like

LIKENED
1819 dâmâh (2), to resemble, liken
3666 hŏmŏiŏō (4), to become like

LIKENESS
1823 dᵉmûwth (19), resemblance, likeness
8403 tabnîyth (5), resemblance
8544 tᵉmûwnâh (5), something fashioned
3666 hŏmŏiŏō (1), to become like
3667 hŏmŏiōma (3), form; resemblance

LIKETH
157 'âhab (1), to have affection, love
2896 ṭôwb (2), good; well

LIKEWISE
1571 gam (15), also; even; yea; though
2063 zō'th (2), this
3162 yachad (1), unitedly
3651 kên (14), just; right
36 agĕnēs (1), ignoble, lowly
437 anthŏmŏlŏgĕŏmai (1), respond in praise
2532 kai (11), and; or
3668 hŏmŏiŏs (29), in the same way
3779 hŏutō (5), in this way; likewise
3898 paraplēsiŏs (1), in a manner near by
5615 hōsautōs (13), in the same way

LIKHI
3949 Liqchîy (1), learned

LIKING
2492 châlam (1), to be, make plump; to dream

LILIES
7799 shûwshan (8), white lily; straight trumpet
2918 krinŏn (2), lily

LILY
7799 shûwshan (5), white lily; straight trumpet

LIME
7875 sîyd (2), lime

LIMIT
1366 gᵉbûwl (1), boundary, border

LIMITED
8428 tâvâh (1), to grieve, bring pain

LIMITETH
3724 hŏrizō (1), to appoint, decree, specify

LINE
2256 chebel (5), company, band
2339 chûwṭ (2), string; line
6616 pâthîyl (1), twine, cord
6957 qav (14), rule; musical string
8279 sered (1), scribing-awl
8515 Tᵉla'ssar (1), Telassar
8615 tiqvâh (1), cord; expectancy
2583 kanōn (1), rule, standard

LINEAGE
3965 patria (1), family, group, race, i.e. nation

LINEN
906 bad (23), linen garment
948 bûwts (9), Byssus, (poss.) cotton
4723 miqveh (4), confidence; collection
5466 çâdîyn (2), shirt
6593 pishteh (9), linen, from carded thread
8162 sha'aṭnêz (1), linen and woolen
8336 shêsh (37), white linen; white marble
1039 bussinŏs (4), linen
1040 bussŏs (2), white linen
3043 linŏn (1), flax linen
3608 ŏthŏniŏn (5), strips of linen bandage
4616 sindōn (6), byssos, i.e. bleached linen

LINES
2256 chebel (2), company, band

LINGERED
4102 mâhahh (2), to be reluctant

LINGERETH
691 argĕō (1), to delay, grow weary

LINTEL
352 'ayîl (1), chief; ram; oak tree
3730 kaphtôr (1), capital; wreath-like button
4947 mashqôwph (2), lintel

LINTELS
3730 kaphtôr (1), capital; wreath-like button

LINUS
3044 Linŏs (1), (poss.) flax linen

LION
738 'ărîy (56), lion
739 'ărîy'êl (2), Lion of God

3715 kᵉphîyr (16), walled *village; young lion*
3833 lâbîy' (9), *lion, lioness*
3918 layish (3), *lion*
7826 shachal (6), *lion*
3023 lĕôn (6), *lion*

LION'S
738 'ărîy (4), *lion*
3833 lâbîy' (1), *lion, lioness*
7830 shachats (1), *haughtiness; dignity*

LIONESS
3833 lâbîy' (1), *lion, lioness*

LIONESSES
3833 lâbîy' (1), *lion, lioness*

LIONLIKE
739 'ărîy'êl (2), *Lion of God*

LIONS
738 'ărîy (17), *lion*
744 'aryêh (Ch.) (8), *lion*
3715 kᵉphîyr (14), walled *village; young lion*
3833 lâbîy' (1), *lion, lioness*
3023 lĕôn (3), *lion*

LIONS'
738 'ărîy (2), *lion*
744 'aryêh (Ch.) (1), *lion*

LIP
822 'eshnâb (1), *latticed window*
8193 sâphâh (2), *lip, language, speech*

LIPS
2193 zâ'ak (1), to *extinguish*
8193 sâphâh (109), *lip, language, speech*
8222 sâphâm (3), *beard*
5491 chĕilŏs (6), *lip*

LIQUOR
4197 mezeg (1), *tempered wine*
4952 mishrâh (1), steeped *juice*

LIQUORS
1831 dema' (1), *juice*

LISTED
2309 thĕlō (2), to *will*; to *desire*; to *choose*

LISTEN
8085 shâma' (1), to *hear* intelligently

LISTETH
2309 thĕlō (1), to *will*; to *desire*; to *choose*
3730+1014 hŏrmē (1), *impulse*, i.e. *onset*

LITTERS
6632 tsâb (1), *lizard; covered* cart

LITTLE
1851 daq (1), *crushed; small or thin*
2191 zᵉ'êyr (3), *small, little*
2192 zᵉ'êyr (Ch.) (1), *small, little*

2835 châsîph (1), *small company, flock*
2945 ṭaph (32), *family* of children and women
3530 kibrâh (3), *measure of length*
3563 kôwç (2), *cup*; (poss.) *owl*
4591 mâ'aṭ (3), to *be, make small or few*
4592 mᵉ'aṭ (52), *little or few*
4704 mitstsᵉ'îyrâh (1), *diminutive*
4705 mits'âr (3), *little; short time*
5759 'ăvîyl (1), *infant, young child*
5768 'ôwlêl (1), *suckling child*
6810 tsâ'îyr (4), *little* in number; *few* in age
6819 tsâ'ar (1), to *be small; be trivial*
6966 qûwm (Ch.) (1), to *rise*
6995 qôṭen (2), *little finger*
6996 qâṭân (20), *small, least, youngest*
8102 shemets (2), *inkling*
8241 shetseph (1), *outburst* of anger
8585 tᵉ'âlâh (1), *channel; bandage or plaster*
974 bibliaridiŏn (4), *little scroll*
1024 brachus (6), *little, short*
1646 ĕlachistŏs (1), *least*
2365 thugatriŏn (1), *little daughter*
2485 ichthudiŏn (1), *little fish*
3357 mĕtriŏs (1), *moderately*, i.e. *slightly*
3397 mikrŏn (14), *small* space of *time or degree*
3398 mikrŏs (16), *small, little*
3640 ŏligŏpistŏs (5), *little confidence*
3641 ŏligŏs (9), *puny, small*
3813 paidiŏn (12), *child: immature*
4142 plŏiariŏn (2), *small boat*
5040 tĕkniŏn (9), *infant,* i.e. a *darling* Christian
5177 tugchanō (1), to *take part in*; to *obtain*

LIVE
2414 châṭaph (3), to *seize* as a prisoner
2416 chay (44), *alive; raw; fresh; life*
2418 chăyâ' (Ch.) (2), to *live*
2421 châyâh (110), to *live*; to *revive*
2425 châyay (15), to *live*; to *revive*
3117 yôwm (2), *day; time period*
7531 ritspâh (1), *hot stone; pavement*
390 anastrĕphō (2), to *remain*, to *live*

980 biŏō (1), to *live life*
1514 ĕirēnĕuō (2), to *be, act peaceful*
2068 ĕsthiō (1), to *eat*
2071+3118 ĕsŏmai (1), *will be*
2198 zaō (53), to *live*
2225 zōŏgŏnĕō (1), to *rescue; be saved*
4800 suzaō (3), to *live in common with*
5225 huparchō (1), to *come into existence*

LIVED
2416 chay (5), *alive; raw; fresh; life*
2421 châyâh (39), to *live*; to *revive*
2425 châyay (5), to *live*; to *revive*
326 anazaō (1), to *recover life, live again*
2198 zaō (4), to *live*
4176 pŏlitĕuŏmai (1), to *behave as a citizen*
5171 truphaō (1), to *live indulgently*

LIVELY
2416 chay (1), *alive; raw; fresh; life*
2422 châyeh (1), *vigorous*
2198 zaō (3), to *live*

LIVER
3516 kâbêd (14), *liver*

LIVES
2416 chay (2), *alive; raw; fresh; life*
2417 chay (Ch.) (1), *alive; life*
2421 châyâh (2), to *live*; to *revive*
5315 nephesh (18), *life; breath; soul; wind*
5590 psuchē (5), *soul, vitality; heart, mind*

LIVEST
2416 chay (1), *alive; raw; fresh; life*
3117 yôwm (1), *day; time period*
2198 zaō (2), to *live*

LIVETH
2416 chay (61), *alive; raw; fresh; life*
2421 châyâh (2), to *live*; to *revive*
2425 châyay (2), to *live*; to *revive*
3117 yôwm (1), *day; time period*
2198 zaō (24), to *live*

LIVING
2416 chay (98), *alive; raw; fresh; life*
2417 chay (Ch.) (4), *alive; life*
2424 chayûwth (1), *life; lifetime*
979 biŏs (5), *present state of existence*
1236 diagō (1), to *pass* time or life
2198 zaō (34), to *live*

LIZARD
3911 lᵉṭâ'âh (1), *kind of lizard*

LO
718 'ărûw (Ch.) (1), *lo!, behold!*
1883 dethe' (Ch.) (1), *sprout; green grass*
1888 hê' (Ch.) (1), *Lo!, Look!*
2005 hên (13), *lo!; if!*
2009 hinnêh (103), *lo!; Look!*
2114 zûwr (1), to *be foreign, strange*
7200 râ'âh (3), to *see*
2395 iatrŏs (1), *physician*
2396 idĕ (2), *surprise!, lo!, look!*
2400 idŏu (29), *lo!, note!, see!*

LO-AMMI
3818 Lô' 'Ammîy (1), *not my people*

LO-DEBAR
3810 Lô' Dᵉbar (3), *pastureless*

LO-RUHAMAH
3819 Lô' Rûchâmâh (2), *not pitied*

LOADEN
6006 'âmaç (1), to *impose* a burden

LOADETH
6006 'âmaç (1), to *impose* a burden

LOAF
3603 kikkâr (2), round *loaf; talent*
740 artos (1), *loaf of bread*

LOAN
7596 shᵉ'êlâh (1), *petition*

LOATHE
3988 mâ'aç (1), to *spurn*; to *disappear*

LOATHETH
947 bûwç (1), to *trample down; oppress*
6973 qûwts (1), to *be, make disgusted*

LOATHSOME
887 bâ'ash (1), to *be a moral stench*
2214 zârâ' (1), *disgusting, loathing*
3988 mâ'aç (1), to *spurn*; to *disappear*
7033 qâlâh (1), to *toast, scorch*

LOAVES
3603 kikkâr (2), round *loaf; talent*
3899 lechem (5), *food, bread*
740 artos (22), *loaf of bread*

LOCK
4514 man'ûwl (1), *bolt on door*
6734 tsîytsîth (1), *fore-lock* of hair; *tassel*

LOCKED
5274 nâ'al (2), to *fasten up, lock*

LOCKS
4253 machlâphâh (2), *ringlet* or *braid,* of hair
4514 man'ûwl (5), *bolt* on door
6545 pera' (2), *hair* as *dishevelled*
6777 tsammâh (4), *veil*
6977 qᵉvutstsâh (2), *forelock* of hair

LOCUST
697 'arbeh (9), *locust*
5556 çol'âm (1), destructive *locust* kind
6767 tsᵉlâtsal (1), *cricket*

LOCUSTS
697 'arbeh (11), *locust*
1357 gêb (1), *locust* swarm
2284 châgâb (1), *locust*
200 akris (4), *locust*

LOD
3850 Lôd (4), *Lod*

LODGE
3885 lûwn (22), to *be obstinate*
4412 mᵉlûwnâh (1), *hut*
2647 kataluō (1), to *halt* for the night
2681 kataskēnŏō (2), to *remain, live*
3579 xĕnizō (1), to *be a host;* to *be a guest*

LODGED
3885 lûwn (12), to *be obstinate*
4411 mâlôwn (1), *lodging* for night
7901 shâkab (1), to *lie down*
835 aulizŏmai (1), to *pass the night*
2681 kataskēnŏō (1), to *remain, live*
3579 xĕnizō (4), to *be a host;* to *be a guest*
3580 xĕnŏdŏchĕō (1), to *be hospitable*

LODGEST
3885 lûwn (1), to *be obstinate*

LODGETH
3579 xĕnizō (1), to *be a host;* to *be a guest*

LODGING
3885 lûwn (1), to *be obstinate*
4411 mâlôwn (3), *lodgment* for night
3578 xĕnia (2), *place of entertainment*

LODGINGS
4411 mâlôwn (1), *lodgment* for night

LOFT
5944 'ălîyâh (1), *upper things; second-story*

LOFTILY
4791 mârôwm (1), *elevation; elation*

LOFTINESS
1363 gôbahh (1), *height; grandeur; arrogance*
1365 gabhûwth (1), *pride, arrogance*

LOFTY
1364 gâbôahh (2), *high; powerful; arrogant*
1365 gabhûwth (1), *pride, arrogance*
5375 nâsâ' (1), to *lift up*
7311 rûwm (3), to *be high;* to *rise* or *raise*
7682 sâgab (1), to *be, make lofty;* be *safe*

LOG
3849 lôg (5), liquid *measure*

LOINS
2504 châlâts (9), *loins,* areas of the *waist*
2788 chârêr (1), *arid, parched*
3409 yârêk (2), *leg* or *shank, flank; side*
3689 keçel (1), *loin; back; viscera*
4975 môthen (42), *loins*
3751 ŏsphus (8), *loin; belt*

LOIS
3090 Lŏïs (1), *Lŏïs*

LONG
748 'ârak (4), to *be, make long*
752 'ârôk (2), *long*
753 'ôrek (23), *length*
954 bûwsh (1), to *be delayed*
1419 gâdôwl (1), *great*
2442 châkâh (1), to *await; hope for*
3117 yôwm (16), *day; time period*
4101 mâh (Ch.) (1), *what?, how?, why?*
4900 mâshak (2), to *draw out;* to *be tall*
4970 mâthay (1), *when; when?, how long?*
5704 'ad (51), *as far (long) as; during*
5750 'ôwd (1), *again; repeatedly; still; more*
5769 'ôwlâm (3), *eternity; ancient; always*
5973 'im (1), *with*
6256 'êth (1), *time*
6440 pânîym (1), *face; front*
7221 rî'shâh (1), *beginning*
7227 rab (11), *great*
7230 rôb (2), *abundance*
7235 râbâh (3), to *increase*
7350 râchôwq (3), *remote, far*
8615 tiqvâh (1), *cord; expectancy*
1909 ĕpi (1), *on, upon*
1909+4119 ĕpi (1), *on, upon*
1971 ĕpipŏthĕō (3), *intensely crave*
2118 ĕuthutēs (1), *rectitude, uprightness*
2193 hĕōs (7), *until*
2425 hikanŏs (6), *ample; fit*
2863 kŏmaō (2), to *wear long hair*
3114 makrŏthumĕō (3), to *be forbearing, patient*

3117 makrŏs (3), *long,* in place or time
3752 hŏtan (1), *inasmuch as, at once*
3756+3641 ŏu (1), *no* or *not*
3819 palai (1), *formerly; sometime since*
4183 pŏlus (4), *much, many*
4214 pŏsŏs (1), *how much?; how much!*
5118 tŏsŏutŏs (2), *such great*
5550 chrŏnŏs (4), *space of time, period*

LONGED
183 'âvâh (2), to *wish for, desire*
2968 yâ'ab (1), to *desire, long for*
3615 kâlâh (1), to *cease, be finished, perish*
8373 tâ'ab (2), to *desire*
1971 ĕpipŏthĕō (1), *intensely crave*
1973 ĕpipŏthētŏs (1), *yearned upon*

LONGEDST
3700 kâçaph (1), to *pine after;* to *fear*

LONGER
752 'ârôk (1), *long*
3254 yâçaph (1), to *add* or *augment*
5750 'ôwd (4), *again; repeatedly; still; more*
2089 ĕti (4), *yet, still*
3370 Mēdŏs (5), inhabitant of Media
4119 plĕiŏn (1), *more*

LONGETH
183 'âvâh (1), to *wish for, desire*
2836 châshaq (1), to *join;* to *love, delight*
3642 kâmahh (1), to *pine after, long for*
3700 kâçaph (1), to *pine after;* to *fear*

LONGING
8264 shâqaq (1), to *seek greedily*
8375 ta'ăbâh (1), *desire*

LONGSUFFERING
750+639 'ârêk (4), *patient*
3114 makrŏthumĕō (1), to *be forbearing, patient*
3115 makrŏthumia (12), *forbearance; fortitude*

LONGWINGED
750+83 'ârêk (1), *patient*

LOOK
2342 chûwl (1), to *wait;* to *pervert*
2372 châzâh (3), to *gaze at;* to *perceive*
2376 chêzev (Ch.) (1), *sight, revelation*
4758 mar'eh (6), *appearance; vision*
5027 nâbaţ (24), to *scan;* to *regard* with favor
5869 'ayin (3), *eye; sight*
6437 pânâh (13), to *turn,* to *face*

6440 pânîym (1), *face; front*
6485 pâqad (1), to *visit, care for, count*
6822 tsâphâh (2), to *peer into the distance*
6960 qâvâh (4), to *collect;* to *expect*
7200 râ'âh (53), to *see*
7210 rô'iy (1), *sight; spectacle*
7688 shâgach (1), to *glance sharply at*
7760 sûwm (2), to *put, place*
7789 shûwr (1), to *spy out, survey*
7896 shîyth (1), to *place, put*
8159 shâ'âh (4), to *inspect, consider*
8259 shâqaph (3), to *peep* or *gaze*
308 anablĕpō (1), to *look up;* to *recover sight*
352 anakuptō (1), to *straighten up*
553 apĕkdĕchŏmai (2), to *expect fully*
816 atĕnizō (2), to *gaze intently*
991 blĕpō (5), to *look at*
1492 ĕidō (1), to *know*
1551 ĕkdĕchŏmai (1), to *await, expect*
1914 ĕpiblĕpō (1), to *gaze at*
1980 ĕpiskĕptŏmai (1), to *inspect;* to *go to see*
2300 thĕaŏmai (1), to *look closely at*
3700 ŏptanŏmai (2), to *appear*
3706 hŏrasis (1), *vision*
3879 parakuptō (1), to *lean over* to *peer within*
4328 prŏsdŏkaō (5), to *anticipate;* to *await*
4648 skŏpĕō (2), to *watch out for,* i.e. to *regard*

LOOKED
5027 nâbaţ (12), to *scan;* to *regard* with favor
6437 pânâh (18), to *turn,* to *face*
6440 pânîym (1), *face; front*
6960 qâvâh (8), to *collect;* to *expect*
6970 Qôwa' (1), *curtailment*
7200 râ'âh (55), to *see*
7805 shâzaph (1), to *scan*
8159 shâ'âh (1), to *inspect, consider*
8259 shâqaph (12), to *peep* or *gaze*
8559 Tâmâr (1), *palm tree*
308 anablĕpō (6), to *look up;* to *recover sight*
816 atĕnizō (4), to *gaze intently*
991 blĕpō (1), to *look at*
1492 ĕidō (7), to *know*
1551 ĕkdĕchŏmai (1), to *await, expect*
1689 ĕmblĕpō (2), to *observe;* to *discern*

1869 ĕpairō (1), to *raise up, look up*
2300 thĕaŏmai (1), to *look* closely at
4017 pĕriblĕpō (6), to *look* all *around*
4327 prŏsdĕchŏmai (1), to *receive; to await for*
4328 prŏsdŏkaō (2), to *anticipate; to await*

LOOKEST
5027 nâbaṭ (1), to *scan; to regard* with favor
8104 shâmar (1), to *watch*

LOOKETH
995 bîyn (1), to *understand; discern*
4758+5869 mar'eh (1), *appearance; vision*
5027 nâbaṭ (3), to *scan; to regard* with favor
6437 pânâh (8), to *turn, to face*
6440 pânîym (2), *face; front*
6822 tsâphâh (2), to *peer* into the distance
6960 qâvâh (1), to *collect; to expect*
7200 râ'âh (4), to *see*
7688 shâgach (2), to *glance* sharply at
7789 shûwr (1), to *spy* out, *survey*
8259 shâqaph (4), to *peep* or *gaze*
991 blĕpō (1), to *look* at
3879 parakuptō (1), to *lean over to peer within*
4328 prŏsdŏkaō (2), to *anticipate; to await*

LOOKING
6437 pânâh (9), to *turn, to face*
7209 r'eîy (1), *mirror*
8259 shâqaph (1), to *peep* or *gaze*
308 anablĕpō (3), to *look up; to recover sight*
816 atĕnizō (1), to *gaze* intently
872 aphŏraō (1), to *consider* attentively
991 blĕpō (1), to *look* at
1561 ĕkdŏchē (1), *expectation*
1689 ĕmblĕpō (2), to *observe; to discern*
1983 ĕpiskŏpĕō (1), to *oversee; to beware*
2334 thĕōrĕō (1), to *see; to discern*
4017 pĕriblĕpō (1), to *look* all *around*
4327 prŏsdĕchŏmai (3), to *receive; to await for*
4328 prŏsdŏkaō (1), to *anticipate; to await*
4329 prŏsdŏkia (1), *apprehension* of evil

LOOKINGGLASSES
4759 mar'âh (1), *vision; mirror*

LOOKS
5869 'ayin (3), *eye; sight; fountain*

6400 pelach (2), *slice*

LOOPS
3924 lûlâ'âh (13), curtain *loop*

LOOSE
2502 châlats (1), to *pull* off; to *strip; to depart*
5394 nâshal (1), to *divest, eject*, or *drop*
5425 nâthar (1), to *terrify; shake* off; *untie*
6605 pâthach (7), to *open* wide; to *loosen, begin*
7971 shâlach (3), to *send away*
8271 sh'erê' (Ch.) (1), to *free, separate; unravel*
3089 luō (15), to *loosen*

LOOSED
2118 zâchach (2), to *shove* or *displace*
2502 châlats (1), to *pull* off; to *strip; to depart*
4549 mâçaç (1), to *waste* with disease; to *faint*
5203 nâṭash (1), to *disperse; to thrust* off
5425 nâthar (1), to *terrify; shake* off; *untie*
6605 pâthach (5), to *open* wide; to *loosen, begin*
7368 râchaq (1), to *recede; remove*
8271 sh'erê' (Ch.) (1), to *free, separate; unravel*
321 anagō (2), to *lead up; to bring out; to sail*
447 aniēmi (2), to *slacken, loosen*
630 apŏluō (2), to *relieve, release; to pardon*
2673 katargĕō (1), to *be, render entirely useless*
3080 lusis (1), *divorce*
3089 luō (10), to *loosen*

LOOSETH
5425 nâthar (1), to *terrify; shake* off; *untie*
6605 pâthach (1), to *open* wide; to *loosen, begin*

LOOSING
142 airō (1), to *lift*, to *take up*
321 anagō (1), to *lead up; to bring out; to sail*
3089 luō (2), to *loosen*

LOP
5586 çâ'aph (1), to *dis-branch* a tree

LORD
113 'âdôwn (201), *sovereign*, i.e. *controller*
136 'Ădônây (430), the *Lord*
1376 g'ebîyr (2), *master*
3050 Yâhh (50), *Jehovah, self-Existent* or *Eternal*
3068 Y'ehôvâh (6394), *Jehovah, self-Existent*
4756 mârê' (Ch.) (4), *master*
7229 rab (Ch.) (1), *great*
7991 shâlîysh (3), *officer;* of the *third* rank
1203 dĕspŏtēs (4), *absolute ruler*

2961 kuriĕuō (1), to *rule, be master of*
2962 kuriŏs (694), *supreme, controller, Mr.*
4462 rhabbŏni (1), *my master*

LORD'S
113 'âdôwn (8), *sovereign*, i.e. *controller*
136 'Ădônây (1), the *Lord*
3068 Y'ehôvâh (108), *Jehovah, self-Existent*
2960 kuriakŏs (2), *belonging* to the *Lord*
2962 kuriŏs (15), *supreme, controller, Mr.*

LORDLY
117 'addîyr (1), *powerful; majestic*

LORDS
113 'âdôwn (4), *sovereign*, i.e. *controller*
1167 ba'al (2), *master; husband; owner; citizen*
5633 çeren (21), *axle; peer*
7261 rab'ebân (Ch.) (6), *magnate, noble*
7300 rûwd (1), to *ramble* free or disconsolate
7991 shâlîysh (1), *officer;* of the *third* rank
8269 sar (1), *head person, ruler*
2634 katakuriĕuō (1), to *control, subjugate, lord*
2961 kuriĕuō (1), to *rule, be master of*
2962 kuriŏs (3), *supreme, controller, Mr.*
3175 mĕgistanĕs (1), *great person*

LORDSHIP
2634 katakuriĕuō (1), to *subjugate, lord over*
2961 kuriĕuō (1), to *rule, be master of*

LOSE
6 'âbad (1), *perish; destroy*
622 'âçaph (1), to *gather, collect*
3772 kârath (1), to *cut* (off, down or asunder)
5307 nâphal (1), to *fall*
7843 shâchath (1), to *decay; to ruin*
622 apŏllumi (17), to *perish or lose*
2210 zēmiŏō (2), to *suffer loss*

LOSETH
622 apŏllumi (1), to *perish or lose*

LOSS
2398 châṭâ' (1), to *sin*
7674 shebeth (1), *rest, interruption, cessation*
7921 shâkôl (2), to *miscarry*
580 apŏbŏlē (1), *rejection, loss*
2209 zēmia (3), *detriment; loss*
2210 zēmiŏō (2), to *suffer loss*

LOST
6 'âbad (9), to *perish*
9 'âbêdâh (4), *destruction*
5307 nâphal (2), to *fall*
7908 sh'ekôwl (1), *bereavement*
7923 shikkûlîym (1), *childlessness*
358+1096 analŏs (1), *saltless*, i.e. *insipid*
622 apŏllumi (13), to *perish or lose*
3471 môrainō (2), to *become insipid*

LOT
1486 gôwrâl (60), *lot, allotment*
2256 chebel (3), *company, band*
3876 Lôwṭ (32), *veil*
2624 kataklērŏdŏtĕō (1), to *apportion an estate*
2819 klērŏs (2), *lot, portion*
2975 lagchanō (1), to *determine* by *lot*
3091 Lôt (3), *veil*

LOT'S
3876 Lôwṭ (1), *veil*

LOTAN
3877 Lôwṭân (5), *covering*

LOTAN'S
3877 Lôwṭân (2), *covering*

LOTHE
3811 lâ'âh (1), to *tire;* to *be, make disgusted*
6962 qûwṭ (3), to *detest*

LOTHED
1602 gâ'al (2), to *detest; to reject; to fail*
7114 qâtsar (1), to *curtail, cut short*

LOTHETH
1602 gâ'al (1), to *detest; to reject; to fail*

LOTHING
1604 gô'al (1), *abhorrence*

LOTS
1486 gôwrâl (16), *lot, allotment*
2819 klērŏs (6), *lot, portion*
2975 lagchanō (1), to *determine* by *lot*

LOUD
1419 gâdôwl (19), *great*
1993 hâmâh (1), to *be in great commotion*
2389 châzâq (1), *strong; severe, hard, violent*
5797 'ôz (1), *strength*
7311 rûwm (1), to *be high; to rise or raise*
8085 shâma' (2), to *hear*
3173 mĕgas (33), *great, many*

LOUDER
3966 m'eôd (1), *very, utterly*

LOVE
157 'âhab (73), to *have affection, love*
160 'ahăbâh (34), *affection, love*

L

1730 dôwd (7), *beloved, friend; uncle, relative*
2836 châshaq (3), *to join; to love, delight*
5690 'egeb (1), *amative words, words of love*
5691 'âgâbâh (1), *love, amorousness*
7355 râcham (1), *to be compassionate*
7474 ra'yâh (9), *female associate*
25 agapaō (70), *to love*
26 agapē (85), *love; love-feast*
2309 thělō (1), *to will; to desire; to choose*
5360 philadĕlphia (4), *fraternal affection*
5361 philadĕlphŏs (1), *fraternal*
5362 philandrŏs (1), *affectionate as a wife to her husband*
5363 philanthrōpia (1), *benevolence*
5365 philarguria (1), *avarice, greedy love of possessions*
5368 philĕō (10), *to be a friend, have affection*
5388 philŏtĕknŏs (1), *loving one's child(ren)*

LOVE'S
26 agapē (1), *love*

LOVED
157 'âhab (48), *to have affection, love*
160 'ahăbâh (7), *affection, love*
2245 châbab (1), *to cherish*
25 agapaō (37), *to love*
26 agapē (1), *love*
5368 philĕō (3), *to be a friend, have affection*

LOVEDST
157 'âhab (1), *to have affection, love*
25 agapaō (1), *to love*

LOVELY
157 'âhab (1), *to have affection, love*
4261 machmâd (1), *object of affection*
5690 'egeb (1), *amative words, words of love*
4375 prŏsphilēs (1), *acceptable, pleasing*

LOVER
157 'âhab (2), *to have affection, love*
5358 philagathŏs (1), *promoter of virtue*
5382 philŏxĕnŏs (1), *hospitable*

LOVERS
157 'âhab (17), *to have affection, love*
158 'ahab (1), *affection, love*
5689 'âgab (1), *to lust sensually*
7453 rêa' (1), *associate; one close*
5367 philautŏs (1), *selfish*

5369 philēdŏnŏs (1), *loving pleasure*
5377 philŏthĕŏs (1), *pious, i.e. loving God*

LOVES
159 'ôhab (1), *affection, love*
1730 dôwd (1), *beloved, friend; uncle, relative*
3039 yᵉdîyd (1), *loved*

LOVEST
157 'âhab (7), *to have affection, love*
25 agapaō (2), *to love*
5368 philĕō (3), *to be a friend, have affection*

LOVETH
157 'âhab (37), *to have affection, love*
25 agapaō (19), *to love*
5368 philĕō (6), *to be a friend, have affection*
5383 philŏprōtĕuō (1), *loving to be first*

LOVING
157 'âhab (1), *to have affection, love*
158 'ahab (1), *affection, love*
2896 ţôwb (1), *good; well*

LOVINGKINDNESS
2617 cheçed (26), *kindness, favor*

LOVINGKINDNESSES
2617 cheçed (4), *kindness, favor*

LOW
120 'âdâm (1), *human being; mankind*
1809 dâlal (3), *to slacken, dangle*
3665 kâna' (2), *to humiliate, subdue*
3766 kâra' (1), *to prostrate*
4295 maţţâh (1), *below or beneath*
4355 mâkak (2), *to tumble in ruins*
6030 'ânâh (1), *to respond, answer*
6819 tsâ'ar (1), *to be small; be trivial*
7817 shâchach (3), *to sink or depress*
8213 shâphêl (11), *to humiliate*
8216 shêphel (1), *humble state or rank*
8217 shâphâl (5), *depressed, low*
8219 shᵉphêlâh (5), *lowland,*
8482 tachtîy (2), *lowermost; depths*
5011 tapĕinŏs (3), *humiliated, lowly*
5013 tapĕinŏō (1), *to depress; to humiliate*
5014 tapĕinōsis (1), *humbleness, lowliness*

LOWER
2637 châçêr (1), *to lack; to fail, want, make less*
8213 shâphêl (1), *to humiliate*

8217 shâphâl (4), *depressed, low*
8481 tachtôwn (5), *bottommost*
8482 tachtîy (4), *lowermost; depths*
1642 ĕlattŏō (2), *to lessen*
2737 katōtĕrŏs (2), *inferior, lower*

LOWEST
7098 qâtsâh (3), *termination; fringe*
8481 tachtôwn (2), *bottommost*
8482 tachtîy (4), *lowermost; depths*
2078 ĕschatŏs (2), *farthest, final*

LOWETH
1600 gâ'âh (1), *to bellow, i.e. low of a cow*

LOWING
1600 gâ'âh (1), *to bellow, i.e. low of a cow*
6963 qôwl (1), *voice or sound*

LOWLINESS
5012 tapĕinŏphrŏsunē (2), *modesty, humility*

LOWLY
6041 'ânîy (3), *depressed*
6800 tsâna' (1), *to humiliate*
8217 shâphâl (1), *depressed, low*
5011 tapĕinŏs (1), *humiliated, lowly*

LOWRING
4768 stugnazō (1), *to be overcast, somber*

LUBIM
3864 Lûwbîy (2), *dry region*

LUBIMS
3864 Lûwbîy (1), *dry region*

LUCAS
3065 Lŏukas (2), *Lucanus*

LUCIFER
1966 hêylêl (1), *Venus (i.e. morning star)*

LUCIUS
3066 Lŏukiŏs (2), *illuminative*

LUCRE
1215 betsa' (1), *plunder; unjust gain*
146 aischrŏkĕrdēs (2), *shamefully greedy*
147 aischrŏkĕrdōs (1), *sordidly, greedily*
866 aphilargurŏs (1), *unavaricious*

LUCRE'S
2771 kĕrdŏs (1), *gain, profit*

LUD
3865 Lûwd (4), *Lud*

LUDIM
3866 Lûwdîy (2), *Ludite*

LUHITH
3872 Lûwchîyth (2), *floored*

LUKE
3065 Lŏukas (2), *Lucanus*

LUKEWARM
5513 chliarŏs (1), *tepid*

LUMP
1690 dᵉbêlâh (2), *cake of pressed figs*
5445 phurama (5), *lump of clay; mass of dough*

LUNATICK
4583 sĕlēniazŏmai (2), *to be moon-struck*

LURK
6845 tsâphan (2), *to hide; to hoard; to lurk*

LURKING
3427 yâshab (1), *to dwell, to remain; to settle*
3993 ma'ărâb (1), *ambuscade, ambush*
4224 machăbê' (1), *refuge, shelter*

LUST
2530 châmad (1), *to delight in; lust for*
5315 nephesh (2), *life; breath; soul; wind*
8307 shᵉrîyrûwth (1), *obstinacy*
8378 ta'ăvâh (1), *longing; delight*
1511+1938 ĕinai (1), *to exist*
1937 ĕpithumĕō (2), *to long for*
1939 ĕpithumia (9), *longing*
3715 ŏrĕxis (1), *longing after, lust, desire*
3806 pathŏs (1), *passion, especially concupiscence*

LUSTED
183 'âvâh (2), *to wish for, desire*
1937 ĕpithumĕō (2), *to long for*

LUSTETH
183 'âvâh (4), *to wish for, desire*
1937 ĕpithumĕō (1), *to long for*
1971 ĕpipŏthĕō (1), *intensely crave*

LUSTING
8378 ta'ăvâh (1), *longing; delight*

LUSTS
1939 ĕpithumia (22), *longing*
2237 hēdŏnē (2), *delight; desire*

LUSTY
8082 shâmên (1), *rich; fertile*

LUZ
3870 Lûwz (7), *Luz*

LYCAONIA
3071 Lukaŏnia (2), *Lycaonia*

LYCIA
3073 Lukia (1), *Lycia*

LYDDA
3069 Ludda (3), *Lod*

LYDIA
3865 Lûwd (1), *Lud*
3070 *Ludia* (2), *Lydian* in Asia Minor

LYDIANS
3866 Lûwdîy (1), *Ludite*

LYING
3538 kᵉdab (Ch.) (1), *false, misleading*
3576 kâzab (1), to *lie, deceive*
3577 kâzâb (2), *falsehood; idol*
3584 kâchash (2), to *lie, disown;* to *disappoint*
3585 kachash (1), *emaciation; hypocrisy*
3586 kechâsh (1), *faithless*
4904 mishkâb (4), *bed; sleep; intercourse*
5307 nâphal (1), to *fall*
7252 reba' (1), *prostration* for sleep
7257 râbats (2), to *recline, repose, brood*
7723 shâv' (2), *ruin; guile; idolatry*
7901 shâkab (3), to *lie down*
8267 sheqer (21), *untruth; sham*
345 anakĕimai (1), to *recline* at a meal
906 ballō (1), to *throw*
1968 ĕpipiptō (1), to *embrace;* to *seize*
2749 kĕimai (4), to *lie outstretched*
5579 psĕudŏs (2), *falsehood*

LYSANIAS
3078 *Lusanias* (1), *grief-dispelling*

LYSIAS
3079 *Lusias* (3), *Lysias*

LYSTRA
3082 *Lustra* (6), *Lystra*

MAACAH
4601 Ma'ăkâh (3), *depression*

MAACHAH
4601 Ma'ăkâh (18), *depression*

MAACHATHI
4602 Ma'ăkâthîy (1), *Maakathite*

MAACHATHITE
4602 Ma'ăkâthîy (4), *Maakathite*

MAACHATHITES
4602 Ma'ăkâthîy (4), *Maakathite*

MAADAI
4572 Ma'ăday (1), *ornamental*

MAADIAH
4573 Ma'adyâh (1), *ornament of Jehovah*

MAAI
4597 Mâ'ay (1), *sympathetic*

MAALEH-ACRABBIM
4610 Ma'ălêh 'Aqrabbîym (1), *Steep of Scorpions*

MAARATH
4638 Ma'ărâth (1), *waste*

MAASEIAH
4271 Machçêyâh (2), *refuge in Jehovah*
4641 Ma'ăsêyâh (23), *work of Jehovah*

MAASIAI
4640 Ma'say (1), *operative*

MAATH
3092 *Maath* (1), *Maath*

MAAZ
4619 Ma'ats (1), *closure*

MAAZIAH
4590 Ma'azyâh (2), *rescue of Jehovah*

MACEDONIA
3109 Makĕdŏnia (24), *Macedonia*
3110 Makĕdōn (4), of *Macedonia*

MACEDONIAN
3110 Makĕdōn (1), of *Macedonia*

MACHBANAI
4344 Makbannay (1), *Macbannai*

MACHBENAH
4343 Makbênâ' (1), *knoll*

MACHI
4352 Mâkîy (1), *pining*

MACHIR
4353 Mâkîyr (22), *salesman*

MACHIRITES
4354 Mâkîyrîy (1), *Makirite*

MACHNADEBAI
4367 Maknadbay (1), *what* (is) *like* (a) *liberal* (man)?

MACHPELAH
4375 Makpêlâh (6), *fold*

MAD
1984 hâlal (8), to *shine, flash, radiate; boast*
3856 lâhahh (1), to *languish*
7696 shâga' (7), to *rave* through insanity
1519+3130 ĕis (1), to or *into*
1693 ĕmmainŏmai (1), to *rage at*
3105 mainŏmai (4), to *rave;* to *act insane*

MADAI
4074 Mâday (2), *Madai*

MADE
1129 bânâh (3), to *build;* to *establish*
1443 gâdar (1), to *build a stone wall*
1961 hâyâh (1), to *exist,* i.e. *be* or *become*
2342 chûwl (1), to *dance, whirl;* to *writhe* in pain

2672 châtsab (1), to *cut stone* or *carve wood*
3322 yâtsag (2), to *place permanently*
3335 yâtsar (2), to *form; potter;* to *determine*
3627 kᵉlîy (1), *implement, thing*
3738 kârâh (2), to *dig;* to *plot;* to *bore, hew*
3772 kârath (50), to *cut* (off, down or asunder)
3835 lâban (1), to *make bricks*
4399 mᵉlâ'kâh (1), *work; property*
4639 ma'ăseh (2), *action; labor*
5221 nâkâh (1), to *strike, kill*
5414 nâthan (42), to *give*
5648 'ăbad (Ch.) (7), to *do, work, serve*
5975 'âmad (1), to *stand*
6087 'âtsab (1), to *fabricate* or *fashion*
6213 'âsâh (394), to *make*
6235 'eser (1), *ten*
6466 pâ'al (3), to *do, make* or *practice*
6555 pârats (1), to *break out*
6743 tsâlach (1), to *push forward*
7194 qâshar (1), to *tie, bind*
7236 rᵉbâh (Ch.) (1), to *increase*
7495 râphâ' (1), to *cure, heal*
7502 râphad (1), to *spread* a bed; to *refresh*
7543 râqach (1), to *perfume, blend spice*
7737 shâvâh (1), to *level;* to *resemble;* to *adjust*
7739 shᵉvâh (Ch.) (1), to *resemble*
7760 sûwm (50), to *put, place*
7761 sûwm (Ch.) (10), to *put, place*
7896 shîyth (5), to *place*
208 akurŏō (1), to *invalidate, nullify*
272 amĕlĕō (1), to *be careless* of, *neglect*
319 anagnŏrizŏmai (1), to *make* oneself *known*
347 anaklinō (1), to *lean back, recline*
461 anŏrthŏō (1), to *strengthen, build*
591 apŏdidōmi (2), to *give away*
626 apŏlŏgĕŏmai (1), to *give an account*
770 asthĕnĕō (1), to *be feeble*
805 asphalizō (3), to *render secure*
871 aphŏmŏiŏō (1), to *assimilate closely*
886 achĕirŏpŏiĕtŏs (2), *unmanufactured*
1080 gĕnnaō (1), to *procreate, regenerate*
1096 ginŏmai (72), to *be, become*

1107 gnōrizō (9), to *make known, reveal*
1165 dĕigmatizō (1), to *expose to spectacle*
1215 dēmēgŏrĕō (1), to *address an assembly*
1232 diagnōrizō (1), to *tell abroad*
1239 diadidōmi (2), to *divide up, distribute*
1295 diasōzō (1), to *cure, preserve, rescue*
1303 diatithĕmai (1), to *put apart,* i.e. *dispose*
1392 dŏxazō (1), to *render, esteem glorious*
1402 dŏulŏō (1), to *enslave*
1511 ĕinai (1), to *exist*
1517 ĕirēnŏpŏiĕō (1), to *harmonize, make peace*
1519 ĕis (2), to or *into*
1586 ĕklĕgŏmai (1), to *select, choose, pick out*
1642 ĕlattŏō (1), to *lessen*
1659 ĕlĕuthĕrŏō (4), to *exempt, liberate*
1743 ĕndunamŏō (1), to *empower, strengthen*
1770 ĕnnĕuō (1), to *gesture,* i.e. *signal*
1839 ĕxistēmi (1), to *astound;* to *be insane*
1861 ĕpaggĕllō (2), to *engage to do*
2005 ĕpitĕlĕō (1), to *terminate;* to *undergo*
2049 ĕrēmŏō (1), to *lay waste*
2090 hĕtŏimazō (4), to *prepare*
2092 hĕtŏimŏs (1), *ready, prepared*
2134 ĕunŏuchizō (2), to *castrate;* to *live unmarried*
2227 zōŏpŏiĕō (1), to (re-) *vitalize, give life*
2301 thĕatrizō (1), to *expose as a spectacle*
2390 iaŏmai (1), to *cure, heal*
2427 hikanŏō (2), to *make competent*
2525 kathistēmi (7), to *designate, constitute*
2559 kakŏō (1), to *injure;* to *oppress;* to *embitter*
2673 katargĕō (1), to *be, render entirely useless*
2680 kataskĕuazō (1), to *prepare thoroughly*
2721 katĕphistēmi (1), to *rush upon* in an *assault*
2722 katĕchō (1), to *hold down fast*
2749 kĕimai (1), to *lie outstretched*
2758 kĕnŏō (2), to *make empty*
2841 kŏinōnĕō (1), to *share* or *participate*
3021 lĕukainō (1), to *whiten*
3076 lupĕō (5), to *distress;* to *be sad*
3182 mĕthuskō (1), to *become drunk*

3421 mnēmŏnĕuō (1), to exercise memory
3447 mŏschŏpŏiĕō (1), to fabricate a bull image
3471 mōrainō (1), to become insipid
3489 nauagĕō (1), to be shipwrecked
3666 hŏmŏiŏō (2), to become like
3670 hŏmŏlŏgĕō (1), to acknowledge, agree
3822 palaiŏō (1), to make, become worn out
3903 paraskĕuazō (1), to get ready, prepare
3982 pĕithō (1), to pacify or conciliate
4087 pikrainō (1), to embitter, turn sour
4147 plŏutĕō (2), to be, become wealthy
4160 pŏiĕō (51), to make
4161 pŏiēma (1), what is made, product
4198 pŏrĕuŏmai (1), to go, come; to travel
4222 pŏtizō (2), to furnish drink, irrigate
4364 prŏspŏiĕŏmai (1), to pretend as if about to
4483 rhĕō (1), to utter, i.e. speak or say
4692 spĕudō (1), to urge; to await eagerly
4732 stĕrĕŏō (1), to be, become strong
4776 sugkathizō (1), to give, take a seat in company with
4832 summŏrphŏs (1), similar, conformed to
4955 sustasiastēs (1), fellow-insurgent
4982 sōzō (9), to deliver; to protect
5014 tapĕinōsis (1), humbleness, lowliness
5048 tĕlĕiŏō (9), to perfect, complete
5055 tĕlĕō (1), to end, i.e. complete, execute
5087 tithēmi (3), to place
5293 hupŏtassō (2), to subordinate; to obey
5319 phanĕrŏō (13), to render apparent
5487 charitŏō (1), to give special honor
5499 chĕirŏpŏiētŏs (6), of human construction

MADEST
3045 yâda' (1), to know
3772 kârath (1), to cut (off, down or asunder)
6213 'âsâh (1), to make
387 anastatŏō (1), to disturb, cause trouble
1642 ĕlattŏō (1), to lessen

MADIAN
3099 Madian (1), contest or quarrel

MADMANNAH
4089 Madmannâh (2), dunghill

MADMEN
4086 Madmên (1), dunghill

MADMENAH
4088 Madmênâh (1), dunghill

MADNESS
1947 hôwlêlâh (4), folly, delusion
1948 hôwlêlûwth (1), folly, delusion
7697 shiggâ'ôwn (2), craziness
454 anŏia (1), stupidity; rage
3913 paraphrŏnia (1), foolhardiness, insanity

MADON
4068 Mâdôwn (2), height

MAGBISH
4019 Magbîysh (1), stiffening

MAGDALA
3093 Magdala (1), tower

MAGDALENE
3094 Magdalēnē (12), of Magdala

MAGDIEL
4025 Magdîy'êl (2), preciousness of God

MAGICIAN
2749 charṭôm (Ch.) (1), horoscopist, magician

MAGICIANS
2748 charṭôm (11), horoscopist, magician
2749 charṭôm (Ch.) (4), horoscopist, magician

MAGISTRATE
3423+6114 yârash (1), to inherit; to impoverish
758 archōn (1), first

MAGISTRATES
8200 sh^{e}phaṭ (Ch.) (1), to judge
746 archē (1), first in rank; first in time
3980 pĕitharchĕō (1), to submit to authority
4755 stratēgŏs (5), military governor

MAGNIFICAL
1431 gâdal (1), to be great, make great

MAGNIFICENCE
3168 mĕgalĕiŏtēs (1), grandeur or splendor

MAGNIFIED
1431 gâdal (17), to be great, make great
5375 nâsâ' (1), to lift up
3170 mĕgalunō (3), to increase or extol

MAGNIFY
1431 gâdal (15), to be great, make great
7679 sâgâ' (1), to laud, extol
1392 dŏxazō (1), to render, esteem glorious
3170 mĕgalunō (2), to increase or extol

MAGOG
4031 Mâgôwg (4), Magog
3098 Magōg (1), Magog

MAGOR-MISSABIB
4036 Mâgôwr miç-Çâbîyb (1), affright from around

MAGPIASH
4047 Magpîy'âsh (1), exterminator of (the) moth

MAHALAH
4244 Machlâh (1), sickness

MAHALALEEL
4111 Mahălal'êl (7), praise of God

MAHALATH
4257 Machălath (2), sickness
4258 Machălath (2), sickness

MAHALI
4249 Machlîy (1), sick

MAHANAIM
4266 Machănayim (13), double camp

MAHANEH-DAN
4265 Machănêh-Dân (1), camp of Dan

MAHARAI
4121 Mahăray (3), hasty

MAHATH
4287 Machath (3), erasure

MAHAVITE
4233 Machăvîym (1), Machavite

MAHAZIOTH
4238 Machăzîy'ôwth (2), visions

MAHER-SHALAL-HASH-BAZ
4122 Mahêr Shâlâl Châsh Baz (2), hasting is he to the booty, swift to the prey

MAHLAH
4244 Machlâh (4), sickness

MAHLI
4249 Machlîy (10), sick

MAHLITES
4250 Machlîy (2), Machlite

MAHLON
4248 Machlôwn (3), sick

MAHLON'S
4248 Machlôwn (1), sick

MAHOL
4235 Mâchôwl (1), (round) dance

MAID
519 'âmâh (5), female servant or slave
1330 b^{e}thûwlâh (4), virgin maiden
1331 b^{e}thûwlîym (2), virginity
5291 na'ărâh (4), female child; servant
5347 n^{e}qêbâh (1), female, woman
5959 'almâh (2), lass, young woman
8198 shiphchâh (12), household female slave
2877 kŏrasiŏn (2), little girl
3814 paidiskē (2), female slave or servant
3816 pais (1), child; slave or servant

MAID'S
5291 na'ărâh (1), female child; servant

MAIDEN
1330 b^{e}thûwlâh (2), virgin maiden
5291 na'ărâh (3), female child; servant
8198 shiphchâh (2), household female slave
3816 pais (1), child; slave or servant

MAIDENS
1330 b^{e}thûwlâh (3), virgin maiden
5291 na'ărâh (13), female child; servant
8198 shiphchâh (1), household female slave
3814 paidiskē (1), female slave or servant

MAIDS
519 'âmâh (3), female servant or slave
1330 b^{e}thûwlâh (3), virgin maiden
5291 na'ărâh (2), female child; servant
3814 paidiskē (1), female slave or servant

MAIDSERVANT
519 'âmâh (13), female servant or slave
8198 shiphchâh (3), household female slave

MAIDSERVANT'S
519 'âmâh (1), female servant or slave

MAIDSERVANTS
519 'âmâh (4), female servant or slave
8198 shiphchâh (5), household female slave

MAIDSERVANTS'
519 'âmâh (1), female servant or slave

MAIL
7193 qasqeseth (2), fish scales; coat of mail

MAIMED
2782 chârats (1), to be alert, to decide
376 anapērŏs (2), maimed; crippled
2948 kullŏs (4), crippled, i.e. maimed

MAINSAIL
736 artĕmōn (1), foresail or jib

MAINTAIN
2388 châzaq (1), to bind, restrain, conquer
3198 yâkach (1), to be correct; to argue
6213 'âsâh (6), to do or make

MAINTAINED
4291 prŏĭstēmi (2), to preside; to practice

MAINTAINED
6213 'âsâh (1), to do or make

MAINTAINEST
8551 tâmak (1), to obtain, keep fast

MAINTENANCE
2416 chay (1), alive; raw; fresh; life
4415 melach (Ch.) (1), to eat salt

MAJESTY
1347 gâ'ôwn (7), ascending; majesty
1348 gê'ûwth (2), ascending; majesty
1420 gedûwlâh (1), greatness, grandeur
1923 hâdar (Ch.) (1), magnificence, glory
1926 hâdâr (7), magnificence
1935 hôwd (4), grandeur, majesty
7238 rebûw (Ch.) (3), increase
3168 mĕgalĕĭŏtēs (1), grandeur or splendor
3172 mĕgalōsunē (3), divinity, majesty

MAKAZ
4739 Mâqats (1), end

MAKE
1124 benâ' (Ch.) (1), to build
1254 bârâ' (1), to create; fashion
1443 gâdar (2), to build a stone wall
2015 hâphak (1), to change, overturn
3331 yâtsa' (1), to strew as a surface
3335 yâtsar (1), to form; potter; to determine
3635 kelal (Ch.) (2), to complete
3772 kârath (31), to cut (off, down or asunder)
3823 lâbab (1), transport with love; to stultify
5414 nâthan (64), to give
5674 'âbar (2), to cross over; to transition
6014 'âmar (1), to gather grain into sheaves
6213 'âsâh (238), to make
6381 pâlâ' (1), to be, make great, wonderful
7760 sûwm (65), to put, place
7761 sûwm (Ch.) (5), to put, place
7896 shîyth (9), to place
8074 shâmêm (1), to devastate; to stupefy
142 airō (1), to lift, to take up
347 anaklinō (2), to lean back, recline
805 asphalizō (1), to render secure
1107 gnōrizō (6), to make known, reveal

1303 diatithĕmai (2), to put apart, i.e. dispose
1325 didōmi (2), to give
1510 eimi (1), I exist, I am
1519 eis (1), to or into
1659 elĕuthĕrŏō (2), to exempt, liberate
1710 empŏrĕuŏmai (1), to trade, do business
1793 entugchanō (1), to entreat, petition
2005 epitĕlĕō (1), to terminate; to undergo
2090 hĕtŏimazō (6), to prepare
2116 euthunō (1), to straighten or level
2146 euprŏsōpĕō (1), to make a good display
2165 euphrainō (3), to rejoice, be glad
2350 thŏrubĕō (1), to disturb; clamor
2433 hilaskŏmai (1), to conciliate, to atone for
2476 histēmi (1), to stand, establish
2511 katharizō (5), to cleanse
2525 kathistēmi (6), to designate, constitute
2625 kataklinō (2), to recline, take a place
2673 katargĕō (3), to be, render entirely useless
2675 katartizō (2), to repair; to prepare
2758 kĕnŏō (1), to make empty
2936 ktizō (1), to fabricate, create
3076 lupĕō (1), to distress; to be sad
3753 hŏtĕ (1), when; as
3856 paradĕigmatizō (1), to expose to infamy
3868 paraitĕŏmai (1), to deprecate, decline
4052 pĕrissĕuō (1), to superabound
4062 pĕritrĕpō (1), to drive crazy
4087 pikrainō (1), to embitter, turn sour
4115 platunō (1), to widen
4121 plĕŏnazō (1), to increase; superabound
4122 plĕŏnĕktĕō (2), to be covetous
4135 plērŏphŏrĕō (1), to fill completely; assure
4137 plērŏō (1), to fill, make complete
4160 pŏiĕō (48), to make
4170 pŏlĕmĕō (3), to battle, make war
4294 prŏkatartizō (1), to prepare in advance
4336 prŏsĕuchŏmai (3), to supplicate, pray
4400 prŏchĕirizŏmai (1), to purpose
4624 skandalizō (2), to entrap, i.e. trip up
4679 sŏphizō (1), to be cleverly invented
4692 spĕudō (2), to urge on

4766 strōnnumi (1), strew, i.e. spread
4820 sumballō (1), to aid; to join, attack
4921 sunistaō (1), to set together, to introduce
4931 suntĕlĕō (1), to complete entirely
5055 tĕlĕō (3), to end, i.e. complete, execute
5087 tithēmi (6), to place
5319 phanĕrŏō (2), to render apparent
5461 phōtizō (1), to shine or to brighten up

MAKER
3335 yâtsar (4), to form; potter; to determine
6213 'âsâh (13), to make
6466 pâ'al (1), to make
6467 pô'al (1), act or work, deed
1217 dēmiŏurgŏs (1), worker, mechanic

MAKERS
2796 chârâsh (1), skilled fabricator or worker

MAKEST
6213 'âsâh (6), to make
7760 sûwm (1), to place
7896 shîyth (1), to place
2744 kauchaŏmai (2), to glory in, rejoice in
4160 pŏiĕō (4), to make

MAKETH
3772 kârath (1), to cut (off, down or asunder)
5414 nâthan (2), to give
6213 'âsâh (23), to make
6466 pâ'al (1), to make
7706 Shadday (1), the Almighty God
7737 shâvâh (2), to level, i.e. equalize
7760 sûwm (6), to place
393 anatĕllō (1), to cause to arise
1252 diakrinō (1), to decide; to hesitate
1308 diaphĕrō (1), to bear, carry; to differ
1793 entugchanō (3), to entreat, petition
2165 euphrainō (1), to rejoice, be glad
2390 iaŏmai (1), to cure, heal
2525 kathistēmi (1), to designate, constitute
2617 kataischunō (1), to disgrace or shame
4160 pŏiĕō (6), to make
4977 schizō (1), to split or sever
5241 hupĕrĕntugchanō (1), to intercede in behalf of
5319 phanĕrŏō (1), to render apparent

MAKHELOTH
4721 maqhêl (2), assembly

MAKING
3772 kârath (1), to cut (off, down or asunder)
4639 ma'ăseh (2), action; labor

MALICIOUSNESS
2549 kakia (2), depravity; malignity

6213 'âsâh (1), to make
208 akurŏō (1), to invalidate, nullify
1189 dĕŏmai (1), to beg, petition, ask
1252 diakrinō (1), to decide; to hesitate
2350 thŏrubĕō (1), to disturb; clamor
4148 plŏutizō (1), to make wealthy
4160 pŏiĕō (7), to make
5567 psallō (1), to play a stringed instrument

MAKKEDAH
4719 Maqqêdâh (9), herding-fold

MAKTESH
4389 Maktêsh (1), dell

MALACHI
4401 Mal'âkîy (1), ministrative

MALCHAM
4445 Malkâm (2), Malcam or Milcom

MALCHI-SHUA
4444 Malkîyshûwa' (3), king of wealth

MALCHIAH
4441 Malkîyâh (9), appointed by Jehovah

MALCHIEL
4439 Malkîy'êl (3), appointed by God

MALCHIELITES
4440 Malkîy'êlîy (1), Malkiëlite

MALCHIJAH
4441 Malkîyâh (6), appointed by Jehovah

MALCHIRAM
4443 Malkîyrâm (1), king of a high one

MALCHUS
3124 Malchŏs (1), king

MALE
376 'îysh (2), man; male
2138 zâkûwr (1), male
2142 zâkar (1), to be male
2145 zâkâr (37), male
730 arrhĕn (4), male

MALEFACTOR
2555 kakŏpŏiŏs (1), bad-doer; criminal

MALEFACTORS
2557 kakŏurgŏs (3), criminal, evildoer

MALELEEL
3121 Malĕlĕēl (1), praise of God

MALES
2138 zâkûwr (2), male
2145 zâkâr (30), male

MALICE
2549 kakia (6), depravity; malignity

MALICIOUS
4190 pŏnērŏs (1), malice, wicked, bad; crime

MALICIOUSNESS
2549 kakia (2), depravity; malignity

MALIGNITY
2550 kakŏĕthĕia (1), mischievousness

MALLOTHI
4413 Mallôwthîy (2), loquacious

MALLOWS
4408 mallûwach (1), salt-purslain

MALLUCH
4409 Mallûwk (6), regnant

MAMMON
3126 mammônas (4), wealth, riches

MAMRE
4471 Mamrê' (10), lusty

MAN
120 'âdâm (388), human being; mankind
375 'êyphôh (1), where?; when?; how?
376 'îysh (967), man; male; someone
376+2145 'îysh (1), man; male; someone
582 'ĕnôwsh (32), man; person, human
606 'ĕnâsh (Ch.) (8), man
935 bôw' (1), to go, come
1121 bên (3), son, descendant; people
1121+120 bên (1), son, descendant; people
1167 ba'al (5), master; husband; owner; citizen
1201 Ba'shà' (1), offensiveness
1396 gâbar (1), to be strong; to prevail
1397 geber (54), person, man
1400 gᵉbar (Ch.) (2), person; someone
1538 gulgôleth (2), skull
2145 zâkâr (11), male
5315 nephesh (3), life; breath; soul; wind
5958 'elem (1), lad, young man
435 anêr (75), man; male
442 anthrōpinŏs (2), human
444 anthrōpŏs (347), human being; mankind
730 arrhēn (2), male
1520 hěis (3), one
1538 hěkastŏs (3), each or every
2478 ischurŏs (1), forcible, powerful
3367 mēděis (33), not even one
3494 nĕanias (4), youth
3495 nĕaniskŏs (5), youth
3762 ŏuděis (96), none, nobody, nothing
3956 pas (3), all, any, every, whole
5100 tis (40), some or any

MAN'S
120 'âdâm (17), human being; mankind
312 'achêr (1), other, another, different
376 'îysh (42), man; male; someone

582 'ĕnôwsh (3), man; person, human
606 'ĕnâsh (Ch.) (3), man
1167 ba'al (1), master; husband; owner; citizen
1397 geber (2), person, man
245 allŏtriŏs (4), not one's own
435 anêr (1), man; male
442 anthrōpinŏs (3), human
444 anthrōpŏs (10), human being; mankind
3494 nĕanias (1), youth
3762 ŏuděis (1), none, nobody, nothing
5100 tis (3), some or any

MANAEN
3127 Manaēn (1), Manaën

MANAHATH
4506 Mânachath (3), rest

MANAHETHITES
2679 Chătsîy ham-Mᵉnûchôwth (1), midst of the resting-places
2680 Chătsîy ham-Mᵉnachtîy (1), Chatsi-ham-Menachtite

MANASSEH
4519 Mᵉnashsheh (141), causing to forget
4520 Mᵉnashshîy (2), Menashshite

MANASSEH'S
4519 Mᵉnashsheh (4), causing to forget

MANASSES
3128 Manassēs (3), causing to forget

MANASSITES
4519 Mᵉnashsheh (1), causing to forget
4520 Mᵉnashshîy (2), Menashshite

MANDRAKES
1736 dûwday (6), mandrake

MANEH
4488 mâneh (1), weight

MANGER
5336 phatnē (3), crib; stall

MANIFEST
1305 bârar (1), to examine; select
852 aphanēs (1), non-apparent, invisible
1212 dēlŏs (1), clear, plain, evident
1552 ĕkdēlŏs (1), wholly evident, clear
1717 ĕmphanēs (1), apparent, seen, visible
1718 ĕmphanizō (2), to show forth
4271 prŏdēlŏs (1), obvious, evident
5318 phanĕrŏs (7), apparent, visible, clear
5319 phanĕrŏō (23), to render apparent

MANIFESTATION
602 apŏkalupsis (1), disclosure, revelation
5321 phanĕrōsis (2), manifestation

MANIFESTED
5319 phanĕrŏō (10), to render apparent

MANIFESTLY
5319 phanĕrŏō (1), to render apparent

MANIFOLD
7227 rab (3), great
7231 râbab (1), to increase
4164 pŏikilŏs (2), various
4179 pŏllaplasiōn (1), very much more
4182 pŏlupŏikilŏs (1), multifarious

MANKIND
1320+376 bâsâr (1), flesh; body; person
2145 zâkâr (2), male
733 arsĕnŏkŏitēs (2), sodomite
5449+442 phusis (1), genus or sort

MANNA
4478 mân (14), manna, i.e. a "whatness?"
3131 manna (5), edible gum-like food

MANNER
734 'ôrach (1), road; manner of life
1571 gam (1), also; even; yea; though
1697 dâbâr (15), word; matter; thing
1699 dôber (1), grazing pasture
1823 dᵉmûwth (1), resemblance, likeness
1870 derek (8), road; course of life
1881 dâth (1), royal edict or statute
2177 zan (1), form or sort
3541 kôh (6), thus
3605 kôl (1), all, any or every
3651 kên (3), just; right, correct
3654 kên (1), stinging bug
4941 mishpâṭ (36), verdict; decree; justice
8452 tôwrâh (1), custom
72 agōgē (1), mode of living, way of life
195 akribĕia (1), thoroughness
442 anthrōpinŏs (1), human
686 ara (3), then, so, therefore
981 biōsis (1), mode of living
1483 ĕthnikōs (1), as a Gentile
1485 ĕthŏs (5), usage prescribed
1486 ĕthō (1), to be used by habit or convention
3592 hŏdĕ (1), this or that; these or those

MANIFESTATION (continued not shown)

3634 hŏiŏs (2), such or what sort of
3697 hŏpŏiŏs (2), what kind of, what sort of
3779 hŏutō (5), in this way; likewise
4012 pĕri (1), about; around
4169 pŏiŏs (1), what sort of?; which one?
4217 pŏtapŏs (6), of what possible sort?
4458 -pōs (1), particle used in composition
5158 trŏpŏs (2), deportment, character
5179 tupŏs (1), shape, resemblance; "type"
5615 hōsautōs (2), in the same way

MANNERS
2708 chuqqâh (1), to delineate
4941 mishpâṭ (2), verdict; formal decree; justice
2239 ēthŏs (1), usage, i.e. moral habits
4187 pŏlutrŏpŏs (1), in many ways
5159 trŏpŏphŏrĕō (1), to endure one's habits

MANOAH
4495 Mânôwach (18), rest

MANSERVANT
5650 'ebed (12), servant

MANSERVANT'S
5650 'ebed (1), servant

MANSERVANTS
5650 'ebed (1), servant

MANSIONS
3438 mŏnē (1), residence, dwelling place

MANSLAYER
7523 râtsach (2), to murder

MANSLAYERS
409 andrŏphŏnŏs (1), murderer

MANTLE
155 'addereth (5), large; splendid
4598 mᵉ'îyl (7), outer garment or robe
8063 sᵉmîykâh (1), rug

MANTLES
4595 ma'ăṭâphâh (1), cloak

MANY
1995 hâmôwn (3), noise, tumult; many, crowd
3513 kâbad (2), to be heavy, severe, dull
3605 kôl (1), all, any or every
7227 rab (196), great
7230 rôb (4), abundance
7231 râbab (6), to increase; to multiply
7233 rᵉbâbâh (1), myriad
7235 râbâh (27), to increase
7690 saggîy' (Ch.) (2), large
2425 hikanŏs (11), ample; fit

3745 hŏsŏs (31), *as much as*
4119 plĕiŏn (14), *more*
4183 pŏlus (207), *much, many*
4214 pŏsŏs (11), *how much?; how much!*
5118 tŏsŏutŏs (6), *such great*

MAOCH
4582 Mâ'ôwk (1), *oppressed*

MAON
4584 Mâ'ôwn (7), *residence*

MAONITES
4584 Mâ'ôwn (1), *residence*

MAR
3510 kâ'ab (1), to *feel pain; to grieve; to spoil*
5420 nâthaç (1), to *tear up*
7843 shâchath (4), to *decay; to ruin*

MARA
4755 Mârâ' (1), *bitter*

MARAH
4785 Mârâh (5), *bitter*

MARALAH
4831 Mar'ălâh (1), (poss.) *earthquake*

MARANATHA
3134 maran atha (1), *Come, Lord!*

MARBLE
7898 shayith (1), *wild growth of weeds*
8336 shêsh (2), *white linen; white marble*
8338 shâwshâw (1), (poss.) to *annihilate*
3139 marmarŏs (1), *sparkling white marble*

MARCH
1980 hâlak (1), to *walk; live a certain way*
3212 yâlak (2), to *walk; to live; to carry*
6805 tsâ'ad (2), to *pace, step regularly*

MARCHED
5265 nâça' (1), *start on a journey*

MARCHEDST
6805 tsâ'ad (1), to *pace, step regularly*

MARCUS
3138 Markŏs (3), *Marcus*

MARESHAH
4762 Mar'êshâh (8), *summit*

MARINERS
4419 mallâch (4), *salt-water sailor*
7751 shûwt (1), to *travel, roam*

MARISHES
1360 gebe' (1), *reservoir; marsh*

MARK
226 'ôwth (1), *signal, sign*

995 bîyn (1), to *understand; discern*
3045 yâda' (3), to *know*
4307 mattârâ' (3), *jail (guard-house); aim*
4645 miphgâ' (1), *object of attack, target*
6437 pânâh (1), to *turn, to face*
7181 qâshab (1), to *prick up the ears*
7200 râ'âh (1), to *see*
7760 sûwm (2), to *place*
7896 shîyth (1), to *place*
8104 shâmar (4), to *watch*
8420 tâv (2), *mark; signature*
3138 Markŏs (5), *Marcus*
4648 skŏpĕŏ (2), to *watch out for, i.e. to regard*
4649 skŏpŏs (1), *goal*
5480 charagma (8), *mark, stamp*

MARKED
2856 châtham (1), to *close up; to affix a seal*
3799 kâtham (1), to *inscribe indelibly*
7181 qâshab (1), to *prick up the ears*
8104 shâmar (2), to *watch*
1907 ĕpĕchō (1), to *pay attention to*

MARKEST
8104 shâmar (1), to *watch*

MARKET
4627 ma'ărâb (4), *mercantile goods*
58 agŏra (2), *town-square, market*

MARKETH
8104 shâmar (1), to *watch*
8388 tâ'ar (2), to *delineate; to extend*

MARKETPLACE
58 agŏra (3), *town-square, market*

MARKETPLACES
58 agŏra (1), *town-square, market*

MARKETS
58 agŏra (4), *town-square, market*

MARKS
7085 qa'ăqa' (1), *incision or gash*
4742 stigma (1), *mark, scar of service*

MAROTH
4796 Mârôwth (1), *bitter springs*

MARRED
4893 mishchâth (1), *disfigurement*
7843 shâchath (3), to *decay; to ruin*
622 apŏllumi (1), to *destroy fully*

MARRIAGE
1984 hâlal (1), to *shine, flash, radiate*

5772 'ôwnâh (1), *marital cohabitation*
1061 gamiskō (1), to *espouse*
1062 gamŏs (9), *nuptials*
1547 ĕkgamizō (3), to *marry off a daughter*
1548 ĕkgamiskō (4), to *marry off a daughter*

MARRIAGES
2859 châthan (3), to *be related by marriage*

MARRIED
802 'ishshâh (3), *woman, wife; women, wives*
1166 bâ'al (7), to *be master; to marry*
1166+802 bâ'al (1), to *be master; to marry*
3427 yâshab (1), to *dwell, to remain; to settle*
3947 lâqach (4), to *take*
5375 nâsâ' (1), to *lift up*
1060 gamĕō (9), to *wed*
1096 ginŏmai (3), to *be, become*

MARRIETH
1166 bâ'al (1), to *be master; to marry*
1060 gamĕō (3), to *wed*

MARROW
2459 cheleb (1), *fat; choice part*
4221 môach (1), *bone marrow*
4229 mâchâh (1), to *erase; to grease*
8250 shiqqûwy (1), *beverage; refreshment*
3452 muĕlŏs (1), *marrow*

MARRY
802 'ishshâh (2), *woman, wife; women, wives*
1166 bâ'al (1), to *be master; to marry*
1961+376 hâyâh (1), to *exist, i.e. be or become*
2992 yâbam (1), to *marry a dead brother's widow*
1060 gamĕō (16), to *wed*
1918 ĕpigambrĕuō (1), to *form an affinity with*

MARRYING
3427 yâshab (1), to *dwell, to remain; to settle*
1060 gamĕō (1), to *wed*

MARS'
697 Arĕiŏs Pagŏs (1), *rock of Ares*

MARSENA
4826 Marçᵉnâ' (1), *Marsena*

MART
5505 çâchar (1), *profit from trade*

MARTHA
3136 Martha (12), *mistress, i.e. lady lord*

MARTYR
3144 martus (2), *witness*

MARTYRS
3144 martus (1), *witness*

MARVEL
8539 tâmahh (1), to *be astounded*

2296 thaumazō (9), to *wonder; to admire*
2298 thaumastŏs (1), *wonderful, marvelous*

MARVELLED
8539 tâmahh (2), to *be astounded*
2296 thaumazō (21), to *wonder; to admire*

MARVELLOUS
6381 pâlâ' (16), to *be, make great, wonderful*
6382 pele' (1), *miracle*
6395 pâlâh (1), to *distinguish*
2298 thaumastŏs (6), *wonderful, marvelous*

MARVELLOUSLY
6381 pâlâ' (2), to *be, make great, wonderful*
8539 tâmahh (1), to *be astounded*

MARVELS
6381 pâlâ' (1), to *be, make great, wonderful*

MARY
3137 Maria (54), *rebelliously*

MASCHIL
4905 maskîyl (13), *instructional poem*

MASH
4851 Mash (1), *Mash*

MASHAL
4913 Mâshâl (1), *request*

MASONS
1443 gâdar (2), to *build a stone wall*
2672 châtsab (3), to *cut stone or carve wood*

MASREKAH
4957 Masrêqâh (2), *vineyard*

MASSA
4854 Massâ' (2), *burden*

MASSAH
4532 Maççâh (4), *testing*

MAST
2260 chibbêl (1), *ship's mast*
8650 tôren (1), *mast ship pole; flag-staff pole*

MASTER
113 'âdôwn (75), *sovereign, i.e. controller*
729 'âraz (2), *of cedar*
1167 ba'al (3), *master; husband; owner; citizen*
5782 'ûwr (1), to *awake*
7227 rab (1), *great*
8269 sar (1), *head person, ruler*
1320 didaskalŏs (47), *instructor*
1988 ĕpistatēs (6), *commander*
2519 kathēgētēs (2), *teacher*
2942 kubĕrnētēs (1), *helmsman, captain*
2962 kuriŏs (4), *supreme, controller, Mr.*
3617 ŏikŏdĕspŏtēs (2), *head of a family*

M

4461 rhabbi (8), *my master*

MASTER'S
113 'âdôwn (22), *sovereign*, i.e. *controller*
1167 ba'al (1), *master; husband; owner; citizen*
1203 děspótēs (1), absolute *ruler*

MASTERBUILDER
753 architěktōn (1), *architect, expert builder*

MASTERS
113 'âdôwn (5), *sovereign*, i.e. *controller*
1167 ba'al (1), *master; husband; owner; citizen*
1203 děspótēs (4), absolute *ruler*
1320 didaskalŏs (1), *instructor*
2519 kathēgētēs (1), *teacher*
2962 kuriŏs (8), *supreme, controller, Mr.*

MASTERS'
113 'âdôwn (1), *sovereign*, i.e. *controller*
2962 kuriŏs (1), *supreme, controller, Mr.*

MASTERY
1369 gᵉbûwrâh (1), *force; valor; victory*
6981 Qôwrê' (1), *crier*

MASTS
8650 tôren (1), mast ship *pole;* flag-staff *pole*

MATE
7468 rᵉ'ûwth (2), female *associate*

MATHUSALA
3103 Mathŏusala (1), *man of a dart*

MATRED
4308 Maṭrêd (2), *propulsive*

MATRI
4309 Maṭrîy (1), *rainy*

MATRIX
7358 rechem (5), *womb*

MATTAN
4977 Mattân (3), *present, gift*

MATTANAH
4980 Mattânâh (2), *present; sacrificial offering; bribe*

MATTANIAH
4983 Mattanyâh (16), *gift of Jehovah*

MATTATHA
3160 Mattatha (1), *gift of Jehovah*

MATTATHAH
4992 Mattattâh (1), *gift of Jehovah*

MATTATHIAS
3161 Mattathias (2), *gift of Jehovah*

MATTENAI
4982 Mattᵉnay (3), *liberal*

MATTER
1697 dâbâr (48), *word; matter; thing*
1836 dên (Ch.) (1), *this*
2659 châphêr (1), to *shame, reproach*
2941 ṭa'am (Ch.) (1), *sentence, command*
3602 kâkâh (1), *just so*
4405 millâh (1), *word; discourse; speech*
4406 millâh (Ch.) (4), *command, discourse*
6600 pithgâm (Ch.) (2), *decree; report*
1308 diaphěrō (1), to *bear, carry;* to *differ*
2596 kata (1), *down; according to*
3056 lŏgŏs (4), *word, matter, thing*
4229 pragma (3), *matter, deed, affair*
5208 hulē (1), *forest*, i.e. wood *fuel*

MATTERS
1419 gâdôwl (1), *great*
1697 dâbâr (15), *word; matter; thing*
4406 millâh (Ch.) (1), *word, command*

MATTHAN
3157 Matthan (2), *present, gift*

MATTHAT
3158 Matthat (2), *gift of Jehovah*

MATTHEW
3156 Matthaiŏs (5), *gift of Jehovah*

MATTHIAS
3159 Matthias (2), *gift of Jehovah*

MATTITHIAH
4993 Mattithyâh (8), *gift of Jehovah*

MATTOCK
4281 machărêshâh (1), (poss.) *pick-axe*
4576 ma'dêr (1), *hoe*

MATTOCKS
2719 chereb (1), *knife, sword*
4281 machărêshâh (1), (poss.) *pick-axe*

MAUL
4650 mêphîyts (1), *mallet-club*

MAW
6896 qêbâh (1), *paunch cavity; stomach*

MAY
194 'ûwlay (4), *if not; perhaps*
3201 yâkôl (11), to *be able*
1410 dunamai (9), to be *able or possible*
1832 ĕxĕsti (1), *it is right, it is proper*
2481 isŏs (1), *perhaps*

MAYEST
3201 yâkôl (5), to *be able*
1410 dunamai (2), to be *able or possible*

1832 ĕxĕsti (1), *it is right, it is proper*

MAZZAROTH
4216 Mazzârâh (1), *constellation*

ME-JARKON
4313 Mêy hay-Yarqôwn (1), *water of the yellowness*

MEADOW
260 'âchûw (2), *bulrush* or any marshy grass

MEADOWS
4629 ma'ăreh (1), *nude place*, i.e. a *common*

MEAH
3968 Mê'âh (2), *hundred*

MEAL
7058 qemach (9), *flour*
7058+5560 qemach (1), *flour*
224 alĕurŏn (2), *flour*

MEALTIME
6256+400 'êth (1), *time*

MEAN
120 'âdâm (3), *human being; mankind*
2823 châshôk (1), *obscure*
5704+3541 'ad (1), *as far (long) as; during*
767 asēmŏs (1), *ignoble,* i.e. *ordinary*
1498 ĕiēn (1), *might could, would*
2076 ĕsti (1), *he (she or it) is;* they *are*
2309+1511 thĕlō (1), to *will;* to *desire;* to *choose*
3342 mĕtaxu (2), *betwixt; meanwhile*
4160 pŏiĕō (1), to *make*

MEANETH
1819 dâmâh (1), to *resemble, liken*
2076 ĕsti (2), *he (she or it) is;* they *are*
2309+1511 thĕlō (1), to *will;* to *desire;* to *choose*

MEANING
998 bîynâh (1), *understanding*
1411 dunamis (1), *force, power, miracle*
3195 mĕllō (1), to *intend,* i.e. *be about to*

MEANS
1157 bᵉ'ad (1), *at, beside, among, behind, for*
3027 yâd (4), *hand; power*
4284 machăshâbâh (1), *contrivance; plan*
6903 qᵉbêl (Ch.) (1), *on account of, so as, since*
1096 ginŏmai (1), to *be, become*
3361 mĕ (1), *not; lest*
3364 ŏu mĕ (1), *not at all, absolutely not*
3843 pantŏs (2), *entirely; at all events*
4458 -pŏs (9), *particle used in composition*
4459 pōs (2), *in what way?; how?; how much!*

5158 trŏpŏs (2), *deportment, character*

MEANT
2803 châshab (1), to *think, regard;* to *value*
1498 ĕiēn (2), *might could, would be*

MEARAH
4632 Mᵉ'ârâh (1), *cave*

MEASURE
374 'êyphâh (2), dry grain *measure*
520 'ammâh (1), *cubit*
2706 chôq (1), *appointment; allotment*
4055 mad (1), *vesture, garment; carpet*
4058 mâdad (7), to *measure*
4060 middâh (15), *measure; portion*
4884 mᵉsûwrâh (4), liquid *measure*
4941 mishpâṭ (2), *verdict; formal decree; justice*
4971 mathkôneth (1), *proportion*
5429 çᵉ'âh (3), volume *measure* for grain
5432 ça'çᵉ'âh (1), *moderation*
7991 shâlîysh (2), *three-fold measure*
8506 tôken (1), fixed *quantity*
280 amĕtrŏs (2), *immoderate*
3354 mĕtrĕō (3), to *admeasure*
3358 mĕtrŏn (13), *what is apportioned*
4053 pĕrissŏs (1), *superabundant*
4057 pĕrissōs (1), *superabundantly*
5234 hupĕrballŏntōs (1), *to a greater degree*
5236 hupĕrbŏlē (2), *super-eminence*
5249 hupĕrpĕrissōs (1), *beyond all measure*
5518 chŏinix (1), *about a dry quart measure*

MEASURED
4058 mâdad (40), to *measure*
4128 mûwd (1), to *shake*
488 antimĕtrĕō (2), to *measure in return*
3354 mĕtrĕō (3), to *admeasure*

MEASURES
374 'êyphâh (2), dry grain *measure*
3734 kôr (8), dry *measure*
4055 mad (1), *vesture, garment; carpet*
4060 middâh (12), *measure; portion*
4461 mêmad (1), *measurement*
5429 çᵉ'âh (6), volume *measure* for grain
943 batŏs (1), *measure* for liquids
2884 kŏrŏs (1), dry *bushel* measure

4568 satŏn (2), *measure of about 12 dry quarts*
5518 chŏinix (1), *about a dry quart measure*

MEASURING
4060 middâh (10), *measure; portion*
3354 mĕtrĕō (1), *to admeasure*

MEAT
396 'ăkîylâh (1), *food*
398 'âkal (5), *to eat*
400 'ôkel (18), *food*
402 'oklâh (8), *food*
1262 bârâh (1), *to feed*
1267 bârûwth (1), *food*
1279 biryâh (3), *food*
2964 ţereph (3), *fresh torn prey*
3899 lechem (18), *food, bread*
3978 ma'ăkâl (22), *food, something to eat*
4202 mâzôwn (1), *food, provisions*
4203 mâzôwn (Ch.) (2), *food, provisions*
6595 path (1), *bit, morsel*
6598 pathbag (6), *dainty food*
6720 tsêydâh (1), *food, supplies*
1033 brōma (10), *food*
1034 brōsimŏs (1), *eatable*
1035 brōsis (7), *food; rusting corrosion*
4371 prŏsphagiŏn (1), *little fish*
4620 sitŏmĕtrŏn (1), *allowance or ration*
5132 trapĕza (1), *four-legged table*
5160 trŏphē (13), *nourishment; rations*
5315 phagō (3), *outer garment, i.e. a mantle*

MEATS
1033 brōma (6), *food*

MEBUNNAI
4012 Mᵉbunnay (1), *built up*

MECHERATHITE
4382 Mᵉkêrâthîy (1), *Mekerathite*

MEDAD
4312 Mêydâd (2), *affectionate*

MEDAN
4091 Mᵉdân (2), *contest or quarrel*

MEDDLE
1624 gârâh (4), *to provoke to anger*
6148 'ârab (2), *to intermix*

MEDDLED
1566 gâla' (1), *to be obstinate; to burst forth*

MEDDLETH
5674 'âbar (1), *to cross over; to transition*

MEDDLING
1566 gâla' (1), *to be obstinate; to burst forth*

MEDE
4075 Mâday (1), *Madian*

MEDEBA
4311 Mêydᵉbâ' (5), *water of quiet*

MEDES
4074 Mâday (9), *Madai*
4076 Mâday (Ch.) (4), *Madai*
3370 Mēdŏs (1), *inhabitant of Media*

MEDIA
4074 Mâday (6), *Madai*

MEDIAN
4077 Mâday (Ch.) (1), *Madian*

MEDIATOR
3316 mĕsitēs (6), *reconciler, intercessor*

MEDICINE
1456 gêhâh (1), *medicinal cure*
8644 tᵉrûwphâh (1), *remedy, healing*

MEDICINES
7499 rᵉphû'âh (2), *medicament, healing*

MEDITATE
1897 hâgâh (6), *to murmur, ponder*
7742 sûwach (1), *to muse pensively*
7878 sîyach (5), *to ponder, muse aloud*
3191 mĕlĕtaō (1), *to plot, think about*
4304 prŏmĕlĕtaō (1), *to premeditate*

MEDITATION
1900 hâgûwth (1), *musing, meditation*
1901 hâgîyg (1), *complaint, sighing*
1902 higgâyôwn (1), *musical notation*
7879 sîyach (1), *uttered contemplation*
7881 sîychâh (2), *reflection; devotion*

MEEK
6035 'ânâv (13), *needy; oppressed*
4235 pra¡ŏs (1), *gentle, i.e. humble*
4239 praüs (3), *mild, humble, gentle*

MEEKNESS
6037 'anvâh (1), *mildness; oppressed*
6038 'ănâvâh (1), *modesty, clemency*
4236 pra¡ŏtēs (9), *gentleness, humility*
4240 praütēs (3), *humility, meekness*

MEET
749 'ărak (Ch.) (1), *to suit*
1121 bên (1), *son, descendant; people*
3259 yâ'ad (8), *to meet; to summon; to direct*
3474 yâshar (1), *to be straight; to make right*
3476 yôsher (1), *right*
3477 yâshâr (1), *straight*

3559 kûwn (1), *to set up; establish, fix, prepare*
4672 mâtsâ' (2), *to find or acquire; to occur*
5828 'êzer (2), *aid*
6213 'âsâh (2), *to make*
6293 pâga' (5), *to impinge*
6298 pâgash (6), *to come in contact with*
6440 pânîym (3), *face; front*
6743 tsâlach (1), *to push forward*
7125 qîr'âh (70), *to encounter, to happen*
7136 qârâh (1), *to bring about; to impose*
7200 râ'âh (1), *to see*
514 axiŏs (4), *deserving, comparable or suitable*
528 apantaō (2), *encounter, meet*
529 apantēsis (2), *friendly encounter*
1163 děi (2), *it is (was) necessary*
1342 dikaiŏs (2), *equitable, holy*
2111 ĕuthĕtŏs (1), *appropriate, suitable*
2173 ĕuchrēstŏs (1), *useful, serviceable*
2425 hikanŏs (1), *ample; fit*
2427 hikanŏō (1), *to make competent*
2570 kalŏs (2), *good; beautiful; valuable*
4876 sunantaō (1), *to meet with; to occur*
4877 sunantēsis (1), *meeting with*
5222 hupantēsis (1), *encounter; concurrence*

MEETEST
3477 yâshâr (1), *straight*
6293 pâga' (1), *to impinge*

MEETETH
6293 pâga' (2), *to impinge*
6298 pâgash (1), *to come in contact with*

MEETING
6116 'ătsârâh (1), *assembly*
7125 qîr'âh (1), *to encounter, to happen*

MEGIDDO
4023 Mᵉgiddôwn (11), *rendezvous*

MEGIDDON
4023 Mᵉgiddôwn (1), *rendezvous*

MEHETABEEL
4105 Mᵉhêyţab'êl (1), *bettered of God*

MEHETABEL
4105 Mᵉhêyţab'êl (2), *bettered of God*

MEHIDA
4240 Mᵉchîydâ' (2), *junction*

MEHIR
4243 Mᵉchîyr (1), *price*

MEHOLATHITE
4259 Mᵉchôlâthîy (2), *Mecholathite*

MEHUJAEL
4232 Mᵉchûwyâ'êl (2), *smitten of God*

MEHUMAN
4104 Mᵉhûwmân (1), *Mehuman*

MEHUNIM
4586 Mᵉ'ûwnîy (1), *Menite*

MEHUNIMS
4586 Mᵉ'ûwnîy (1), *Menite*

MEKONAH
4368 Mᵉkônâh (1), *base*

MELATIAH
4424 Mᵉlaţyâh (1), *Jehovah has delivered*

MELCHI
3197 Mĕlchi (2), *king*

MELCHI-SHUA
4444 Malkîyshûwa' (2), *king of wealth*

MELCHIAH
4441 Malkîyâh (1), *appointed by Jehovah*

MELCHISEDEC
3198 Mĕlchisĕdĕk (9), *king of right*

MELCHIZEDEK
4442 Malkîy-Tsedeq (2), *king of right*

MELEA
3190 Mĕlĕas (1), *Meleas*

MELECH
4429 Melek (2), *king*

MELICU
4409 Mallûwk (1), *regnant*

MELITA
3194 Mĕlitē (1), *Melita*

MELODY
2172 zimrâh (2), *song*
5059 nâgan (1), *to play; to make music*
5567 psallō (1), *to play a stringed instrument*

MELONS
20 'ăbaţţiyach (1), *melon*

MELT
3988 mâ'aç (1), *to spurn; to disappear*
4127 mûwg (4), *to soften, flow down, disappear*
4529 mâçâh (1), *to dissolve, melt*
4549 mâçaç (6), *to waste; to faint*
5413 nâthak (2), *to pour out; to liquefy, melt*
6884 tsâraph (1), *to fuse metal; to refine*
3089 luō (1), *to loosen*
5080 tēkō (1), *to liquefy, melt*

MELTED
2046 hittûwk (1), *melting*
4127 mûwg (3), *to soften, flow down, disappear*
4549 mâçaç (6), *to waste; to faint fear or grief*
5140 nâzal (1), *to drip, or shed by trickling*
5413 nâthak (2), *to pour out; to liquefy, melt*

MELTETH
1811 dâlaph (1), to *drip*
4549 mâçaç (3), to *waste*;
to *faint*
5258 nâçak (1), to *pour* a
libation
6884 tsâraph (1), to *fuse*
metal; to *refine*
8557 temeç (1), *melting
disappearance*

MELTING
2003 hâmâç (1), dry *twig*
or *brushwood*

MELZAR
4453 Meltsâr (2), court
officer (poss.) *butler*

MEMBER
3196 mĕlŏs (5), *limb* or
part of the body

MEMBERS
3338 yâtsûr (1),
structure, human frame
3196 mĕlŏs (29), *limb* or
part of the body

MEMORIAL
234 'azkârâh (7),
remembrance-offering
2143 zêker (5),
*recollection;
commemoration*
2146 zikrôwn (17),
commemoration
3422 mnēmŏsunŏn (3),
memorandum

MEMORY
2143 zêker (5),
commemoration

MEMPHIS
4644 Môph (1), *Moph*

MEMUCAN
4462 Mᵉmûwkân (3),
Memucan or *Momucan*

MEN
120 'âdâm (107), *human
being; mankind*
376 'îysh (211), *man;
male; someone*
582 'ĕnôwsh (491), *man;
person, human*
606 'ĕnâsh (Ch.) (12),
man
1121 bên (16), *son,
descendant; people*
1167 ba'al (20), *master;
husband; owner; citizen*
1368 gibbôwr (1),
powerful; great warrior
1397 geber (6), *person,
man*
1400 gᵉbar (Ch.) (18),
person; someone
2145 zâkâr (1), *male*
2388 châzaq (1), to *be
strong; courageous*
4962 math (14), *men*
4974 mᵉthôm (1),
completely
407 andrizŏmai (1), to
act manly
435 anēr (79), *man; male*
442 anthrōpinŏs (1),
human
444 anthrōpŏs (192),
human being; mankind
730 arrhēn (3), *male*
3495 nĕaniskŏs (5), *youth*

MEN'S
120 'âdâm (10), *human
being; mankind*
582 'ĕnôwsh (2), *man;
person, human*
444 anthrōpŏs (4),
human being; mankind
4283 prŏĕuaggĕlizŏmai
(1), to *announce* glad
news *in advance*

MENAHEM
4505 Mᵉnachêm (8),
comforter

MENAN
3104 Maïnan (1), *Maïnan*

MEND
2388 châzaq (1), to
fasten upon; to *bind*

MENDING
2675 katartizō (2), to
repair; to *prepare*

MENE
4484 menê' (Ch.) (2),
numbered

MENPLEASERS
441 anthrōparĕskŏs (2),
man-courting, fawning

MENSERVANTS
5650 'ebed (9), *servant*
3816 pais (1), *child; slave
or servant*

MENSTEALERS
405 andrapŏdistēs (1),
enslaver, kidnapper

MENSTRUOUS
1739 dâveh (1),
menstrual; fainting
5079 niddâh (2), time of
menstrual *impurity*

MENTION
2142 zâkar (18), to
remember; to *mention*
3417 mnĕia (4),
recollection; recital
3421 mnēmŏnĕuō (1), to
exercise memory

MENTIONED
935 bôw' (1), to *go, come*
2142 zâkar (3), to
remember; to *mention*
5927 'âlâh (1), to *ascend,
be high, mount*
7121 qârâ' (1), to *call* out
8052 shᵉmûw'âh (1),
announcement

MEONENIM
6049 'ânan (1), to *cover,
becloud;* to *act covertly*

MEONOTHAI
4587 Mᵉ'ôwnôthay (1),
habitative

MEPHAATH
4158 Môwpha'ath (4),
illuminative

MEPHIBOSHETH
4648 Mᵉphîybôsheth
(15), *dispeller of Shame*

MERAB
4764 Mêrâb (3), *increase*

MERAIAH
4811 Mᵉrâyâh (1),
rebellion

MERAIOTH
4812 Mᵉrâyôwth (7),
rebellious

MERARI
4847 Mᵉrârîy (39), *bitter*

MERARITES
4848 Mᵉrârîy (1),
Merarite

MERATHAIM
4850 Mᵉrâthayim (1),
double bitterness

MERCHANDISE
4267 machănaq (1),
choking, strangling
4627 ma'ărâb (4),
mercantile goods
4819 markôleth (1),
mart, market
5504 çachar (4), *profit*
from trade
5505 çâchar (2), *profit*
from trade
5506 çᵉchôrâh (1), *traffic*
6014 'âmar (2), to *gather*
grain into sheaves
7404 rᵉkullâh (2),
peddled trade
1117 gŏmŏs (2), *cargo,
wares or freight*
1711 ĕmpŏria (1), *traffic,
business trade*
1712 ĕmpŏriŏn (1),
emporium marketplace

MERCHANT
3667 Kᵉna'an (3),
humiliated
5503 çâchar (4), to *travel*
round; to *palpitate*
7402 râkal (3), to *travel*
for trading
1713 ĕmpŏrŏs (1),
tradesman, merchant

MERCHANTMEN
5503 çâchar (1), to *travel*
round; to *palpitate*
8446 tûwr (1), to wander,
meander for trade

MERCHANTS
3669 Kᵉna'ănîy (1),
Kenaanite; merchant
5503 çâchar (9), to *travel*
round; to *palpitate*
7402 râkal (14), to *travel*
for trading
1713 ĕmpŏrŏs (4),
tradesman, merchant

MERCHANTS'
5503 çâchar (1), to *travel*
round; to *palpitate*

MERCIES
2617 cheçed (9),
kindness, favor
7356 racham (25),
compassion; womb
7359 rᵉchêm (Ch.) (1),
pity
3628 ŏiktirmŏs (4), *pity,
compassion*
3741 hŏsiŏs (1),
hallowed, pious, sacred

MERCIES'
2617 cheçed (3),
kindness, favor
7356 racham (1),
compassion; womb

MERCIFUL
2551 chemlâh (1),
commiseration, pity
2603 chânan (11), to
implore
2616 châçad (2), to
reprove, shame
2617 cheçed (5),
kindness, favor
2623 châçîyd (3),
religiously *pious, godly*
3722 kâphar (2), to
cover; to *expiate*
7349 rachûwm (8),
compassionate
7355 râcham (1), to *be
compassionate*
1655 ĕlĕēmōn (2),
compassion
2433 hilaskŏmai (1), to
conciliate, to *atone* for
2436 hilĕōs (1), God be
gracious!, far be it!
3629 ŏiktirmōn (2),
compassionate

MERCURIUS
2060 Hĕrmēs (1), *born of
god Hermes*

MERCY
2603 chânan (16), to
implore
2604 chănan (Ch.) (1), to
favor
2617 cheçed (137),
kindness, favor
3727 kappôreth (27), *lid,
cover*
7355 râcham (31), to *be
compassionate*
7356 racham (4),
compassion; womb
448 anilĕōs (1),
inexorable, merciless
1653 ĕlĕĕō (27), to give
out *compassion*
1656 ĕlĕŏs (28),
compassion
3628 ŏiktirmŏs (1), *pity,
compassion*
3629 ŏiktirmōn (1),
compassionate

MERCYSEAT
2435 hilastēriŏn (1),
expiatory place

MERED
4778 Mered (2), *rebellion*

MEREMOTH
4822 Mᵉrêmôwth (6),
heights

MERES
4825 Mereç (1), *Meres*

MERIB-BAAL
4807 Mᵉrîyb Ba'al (3),
quarreller of Baal
4810 Mᵉrîy Ba'al (1),
rebellion against Baal

MERIBAH
4809 Mᵉrîybâh (6),
quarrel

MIDNIGHT
2676+3915 châtsôwth (3), *middle* of the night
2677+3915 chêtsîy (3), *half* or *middle, midst*
8432+3915 tâvek (1), *center, middle*
3317 mĕsŏnuktiŏn (4), *midnight* watch
3319+3571 mĕsŏs (2), *middle*

MIDST
1459 gav (Ch.) (10), *middle*
2436 chêyq (1), *bosom, heart*
2673 châtsâh (1), to *cut* or *split* in two; to *halve*
2677 chêtsîy (8), *half* or *middle, midst*
2686 châtsats (1), to *curtail;* to *distribute*
2872 ṭabbûwr (1), *summit*
3820 lêb (12), *heart*
3824 lêbâb (1), *heart*
7130 qereb (73), *nearest* part, i.e. the *center*
8432 tâvek (209), *center, middle*
8484 tîykôwn (1), *central, middle*
3319 mĕsŏs (41), *middle*
3321 mĕsŏuranĕma (3), *mid-sky, mid-heaven*
3322 mĕsŏŏ (1), to *be at midpoint*

MIDWIFE
3205 yâlad (3), to *bear young;* to *father a child*

MIDWIVES
3205 yâlad (7), to *bear young;* to *father a child*

MIGDAL-EL
4027 Migdal-'Êl (1), *tower of God*

MIGDAL-GAD
4028 Migdal-Gâd (1), *tower of Fortune*

MIGDOL
4024 Migdôwl (4), *tower*

MIGHT
202 'ôwn (2), *ability, power; wealth*
410 'êl (1), *mighty;* the *Almighty*
1369 gᵉbûwrâh (27), *force; valor; victory*
1370 gᵉbûwrâh (Ch.) (2), *power, strength*
2428 chayil (6), *army; wealth; virtue; strength*
3201 yâkôl (2), to *be able*
3581 kôach (7), *force, might; strength*
3966 mᵉ'ôd (2), *very, utterly*
5797 'ôz (2), *strength*
5807 'ĕzûwz (1), *forcibleness*
6108 'ôtsem (1), *power; framework of the body*
8632 tᵉqôph (Ch.) (1), *power*
1410 dunamai (6), to *be able* or *possible*
1411 dunamis (4), *force, power, miracle*

2479 ischus (2), *forcefulness, power*
2480 ischuŏ (1), to *have* or *exercise force*

MIGHTIER
117 'addîyr (1), *powerful; majestic*
6099 'âtsûwm (7), *powerful; numerous*
6105 'âtsam (1), to *be, make powerful*
8623 taqqîyph (1), *powerful*
2478 ischurŏs (3), *forcible, powerful*

MIGHTIES
1368 gibbôwr (2), *powerful; great warrior*

MIGHTIEST
1368 gibbôwr (1), *powerful; great warrior*

MIGHTILY
2393 chezqâh (2), *prevailing power*
3966 mᵉ'ôd (2), *very, utterly*
1722+1411 ĕn (1), *in; during; because of*
1722+2479 ĕn (1), *in; during; because of*
2159 ĕutŏnŏs (1), *intensely, cogently*
2596+2904 kata (1), *down; according to*

MIGHTY
46 'âbîyr (6), *mighty*
47 'abbîyr (4), *mighty*
117 'addîyr (5), *powerful; majestic*
193 'ûwl (1), *powerful; mighty*
352 'ayîl (2), *chief; ram; oak tree*
376 'îysh (2), *man; male; someone*
386 'êythân (4), *never-failing; eternal*
410 'êl (5), *mighty;* the *Almighty*
430 'ĕlôhîym (2), the true *God; great ones*
533 'ammîyts (1), *strong; mighty; brave*
650 'âphîyq (1), *valley; stream; mighty, strong*
1121+410 bên (1), *son, descendant; people*
1219 bâtsar (1), to *be inaccessible*
1368 gibbôwr (135), *powerful; great warrior*
1369 gᵉbûwrâh (7), *force; valor; victory*
1396 gâbar (1), to *be strong; to prevail*
1397 geber (2), *person, man*
1401 gibbâr (Ch.) (1), *valiant man,* or *warrior*
1419 gâdôwl (7), *great*
2220 zᵉrôwa' (1), *arm; foreleg; force, power*
2388 châzaq (2), to *be strong; courageous*
2389 châzâq (20), *strong; severe, hard, violent*

2428 chayil (1), *army; wealth; virtue; strength*
3524 kabbîyr (5), *mighty; aged; mighty*
3966 mᵉ'ôd (1), *very, utterly*
5794 'az (3), *strong, vehement, harsh*
5797 'ôz (1), *strength*
5868 'ăyâm (1), (poss.) *strength*
6099 'âtsûwm (8), *powerful; numerous*
6105 'âtsam (4), to *be, make powerful*
6184 'ârîyts (1), *powerful* or *tyrannical*
6697 tsûwr (2), *rock*
7227 rab (5), *great*
7989 shallîyṭ (1), *prince* or *warrior*
8624 taqqîyph (Ch.) (2), *powerful*
972 biaiŏs (1), *violent*
1411 dunamis (14), *force, power, miracle*
1413 dunastēs (1), *ruler* or *officer*
1414 dunatĕŏ (1), to *be efficient, able, strong*
1415 dunatŏs (7), *powerful* or *capable*
1754 ĕnĕrgĕŏ (1), to *be active, efficient, work*
2478 ischurŏs (7), *forcible, powerful*
2479 ischus (1), *forcefulness, power*
2900 krataiŏs (1), *powerful, mighty*
3168 mĕgalĕiŏtēs (1), *grandeur* or *splendor*
3173 mĕgas (3), *great, many*
5082 tēlikŏutŏs (1), *so vast*

MIGRON
4051 Migrôwn (2), *precipice*

MIJAMIN
4326 Mîyâmîn (2), *from* (the) *right hand*

MIKLOTH
4732 Miqlôwth (4), *rods*

MIKNEIAH
4737 Miqnêyâhûw (2), *possession of Jehovah*

MILALAI
4450 Mîlălay (1), *talkative*

MILCAH
4435 Milkâh (11), *queen*

MILCH
3243 yânaq (1), to *suck; to give milk*
5763 'ûwl (2), to *suckle,* i.e. *give milk*

MILCOM
4445 Malkâm (3), *Malcam* or *Milcom*

MILDEW
3420 yêrâqôwn (5), *paleness; mildew*

MILE
3400 miliŏn (1), *about* 4,850 feet, Roman *mile*

MILETUM
3399 Milētŏs (1), *Miletus*

MILETUS
3399 Milētŏs (2), *Miletus*

MILK
2461 châlâb (42), *milk*
4711 mâtsats (1), to *suck*
1051 gala (5), *milk*

MILL
7347 rêcheh (1), *mill-*stone
3459 mulŏn (1), *mill-house*

MILLET
1764 dôchan (1), *millet cereal grain*

MILLIONS
7233 rᵉbâbâh (1), *myriad number*

MILLO
4407 millôw' (10), *citadel*

MILLS
7347 rêcheh (1), *mill-*stone

MILLSTONE
7347 rêcheh (1), *mill-*stone
7393 rekeb (2), *upper millstone*
3037+3457 lithŏs (1), *stone*
3458 mulŏs (2), *grinder millstone*
3458+3684 mulŏs (2), *grinder millstone*

MILLSTONES
7347 rêcheh (2), *mill-*stone

MINCING
2952 ṭâphaph (1), to *trip* or *step*

MIND
3336 yêtser (1), *form*
3820 lêb (12), *heart*
3824 lêbâb (4), *heart*
5315 nephesh (11), *life; breath; soul; wind*
5973 'îm (1), *with*
6310 peh (1), *mouth; opening*
7307 rûwach (6), *breath; wind; life-*spirit
363 anamimnĕskŏ (1), to *remind; to recollect*
1106 gnŏmē (2), *cognition, opinion*
1271 dianŏia (7), *mind* or *thought*
1771 ĕnnŏia (1), *moral understanding*
1878 ĕpanamimnēskŏ (1), to *remind* again of
3563 nŏus (15), *intellect, mind; understanding*
3661 hŏmŏthumadŏn (1), *unanimously*
3675 hŏmŏphrŏn (1), *like-minded*
4288 prŏthumia (4), *alacrity, eagerness*
4290 prŏthumŏs (1), *with alacrity, with eagerness*
4993 sŏphrŏnĕŏ (2), to *be in a right state of mind*

4995 sŏphrŏnismŏs (1),
self-discipline
5012 tapĕinŏphrŏsunē
(1), *modesty, humility*
5279 hupŏmimnēskō (1),
to *suggest* to *memory*
5426 phrŏnĕō (9), to *be*
mentally *disposed*
5427 phrŏnēma (2),
inclination or *purpose*
5590 psuchē (1), *soul,*
vitality; heart, mind

MINDED
5973+3820 'îm (1), *with*
1011 bŏulĕuō (1), to
deliberate; to *resolve*
1014 bŏulŏmai (3), to *be*
willing, desire
1374 dipsuchŏs (2),
vacillating
4993 sōphrŏnĕō (1), to *be*
in a right *state of mind*
5426 phrŏnĕō (3), to *be*
mentally *disposed*
5427 phrŏnēma (2),
mental *inclination*

MINDFUL
2142 zâkar (6), to
remember; to *mention*
3403 mimnēskō (3), to
remind or to *recall*
3421 mnēmŏnĕuō (1), to
exercise memory

MINDING
3195 mĕllō (1), to *intend,*
i.e. *be about* to

MINDS
5315 nephesh (4), *life;*
breath; soul; wind
1271 dianŏia (2), *mind*
or *thought*
3540 nŏēma (4),
perception, i.e. *purpose*
3563 nŏus (2), *intellect,*
mind; understanding
5590 psuchē (2), *soul,*
vitality; heart, mind

MINGLE
4537 mâçak (1), to *mix*
6151 'ărab (Ch.) (1), to
co-mingle, mix

MINGLED
1101 bâlal (37), to *mix;*
confuse; to *feed*
3610 kil'ayim (2), *two*
different kinds of thing
3947 lâqach (1), to *take*
4537 mâçak (4), to *mix*
6148 'ărab (2), to *intermix*
6154 'êreb (4), *mixed* or
woven things
3396 mignumi (4), to
mix, mingle

MINIAMIN
4509 Minyâmîyn (3),
from (the) *right hand*

MINISH
1639 gâra' (1), to *shave,*
remove, lessen

MINISHED
4591 mâ'aṭ (1), to *be,*
make small or *few*

MINISTER
1777 dîyn (1), to *judge;* to
strive or *contend for*

8334 shârath (50), to
attend as a menial
8335 shârêth (1), *service*
1247 diakŏnĕō (8), to *act*
as a *deacon*
1248 diakŏnia (1),
attendance, aid, service
1249 diakŏnŏs (14),
waiter; deacon (-*ess*)
1325 didōmi (1), to *give*
2038 ĕrgazŏmai (1), to
toil
3008 lĕitŏurgĕō (1), to
perform religious or
charitable *functions*
3011 lĕitŏurgŏs (1),
functionary in the
Temple or Gospel
3930 parĕchō (1), to *hold*
near, i.e. to *present*
5256 hupĕrĕtĕō (1), to *be*
a *subordinate*
5257 aulētēs (3),
servant, attendant
5524 chŏrēgĕō (1), to
furnish, supply, provide

MINISTERED
8120 sh^emash (Ch.) (1),
to *serve*
8334 shârath (15), to
attend as a menial
1247 diakŏnĕō (14), to
wait upon, serve
2023 ĕpichŏrēgĕō (2), to
fully *supply;* to *aid*
3008 lĕitŏurgĕō (1), to
perform religious or
charitable *functions*
3011 lĕitŏurgŏs (1),
functionary in the
Temple or Gospel
5256 hupĕrĕtĕō (1), to *be*
a *subordinate*

MINISTERETH
2023 ĕpichŏrēgĕō (2), to
fully *supply;* to *aid*

MINISTERING
5656 'ăbôdâh (1), *work* of
any kind
8334 shârath (1), to
attend as a menial
1247 diakŏnĕō (1), to
wait upon, serve
1248 diakŏnia (3),
attendance, aid, service
2418 hiĕrŏurgĕō (1),
officiate as a priest
3008 lĕitŏurgĕō (1), to
perform religious or
charitable *functions*
3010 lĕitŏurgikŏs (1),
engaged in holy service

MINISTERS
6399 p^elach (Ch.) (1), to
serve or worship
8334 shârath (15), to
attend as a menial
1249 diakŏnŏs (6),
attendant, deacon
3011 lĕitŏurgŏs (2),
functionary in the
Temple or Gospel
5257 hupĕrĕtēs (2),
servant, attendant

MINISTRATION
1248 diakŏnia (6),
attendance, aid, service

3009 lĕitŏurgia (1),
service, ministry

MINISTRY
3027 yâd (2), *hand; power*
5656 'ăbôdâh (1), *work*
8335 shârêth (1), *service*
in the Temple
1248 diakŏnia (16),
attendance, aid, service
3009 lĕitŏurgia (2),
service, ministry

MINNI
4508 Minnîy (1), *Minni*

MINNITH
4511 Minnîyth (2),
enumeration

MINSTREL
5059 nâgan (2), to *play;*
to *make music*

MINSTRELS
834 aulētēs (1),
flute-player

MINT
2238 hēduŏsmŏn (2),
sweet-scented, mint

MIPHKAD
4663 Miphqâd (1),
assignment

MIRACLE
4159 môwphêth (1),
miracle; token or *omen*
1411 dunamis (1), *force,*
power, miracle
4592 sēmĕiŏn (7),
indication, sign, signal

MIRACLES
226 'ôwth (2), *signal, sign*
4159 môwphêth (1),
miracle; token or *omen*
6381 pâlâ' (1), to *be,*
make great, wonderful
1411 dunamis (8), *force,*
power, miracle
4592 sēmĕiŏn (15),
indication, sign, signal

MIRE
1206 bôts (1), *mud*
1207 bitstsâh (1), *swamp,*
marsh
2563 chômer (2), *clay;*
dry measure
2916 ṭîyṭ (8), *mud* or *clay*
3121 yâvên (1), *mud,*
sediment
7516 rephesh (1), *mud* of
the sea
1004 bŏrbŏrŏs (1), *mud*

MIRIAM
4813 Miryâm (15),
rebelliously

MIRMA
4821 Mirmâh (1), *fraud*

MIRTH
4885 mâsôws (3), *delight*
7797 sûws (1), to *be*
bright, i.e. *cheerful*
8057 simchâh (8),
blithesomeness or *glee*
8342 sâsôwn (3),
cheerfulness; welcome

MIRY
1207 bitstsâh (1), *swamp,*
marsh

2917 ṭîyn (Ch.) (2), *wet*
clay
3121 yâvên (1), *mud,*
sediment

MISCARRYING
7921 shâkôl (1), to
miscarry

MISCHIEF
205 'âven (4), *trouble,*
vanity, wickedness
611 'âçôwn (5), *hurt,*
injury
1943 hôvâh (2), *ruin,*
disaster
2154 zimmâh (3), bad
plan
4827 mêra' (1),
wickedness
5771 'âvôn (1), moral *evil*
5999 'âmâl (9), *wearing*
effort; worry
7451 ra' (19), *bad; evil*
7489 râ'a' (1), to *be good*
for nothing
4468 rha₁diŏurgia (1),
malignity, trickery

MISCHIEFS
1942 havvâh (1), *desire;*
craving
7451 ra' (2), *bad; evil*

MISCHIEVOUS
1942 havvâh (2), *desire;*
craving
4209 m^ezimmâh (2),
plan; sagacity
7451 ra' (1), *bad; evil*

MISERABLE
5999 'âmâl (1), *wearing*
effort; worry
1652 ĕlĕĕinŏs (2), *worthy*
of *mercy*

MISERABLY
2560 kakōs (1), *badly;*
wrongly; ill

MISERIES
4788 mârûwd (1),
outcast; destitution
5004 talaipōria (1),
calamity, distress

MISERY
4788 mârûwd (1),
outcast; destitution
5999 'âmâl (3), *wearing*
effort; worry
6001 'âmêl (1), *toiling;*
laborer; sorrowful
7451 ra' (1), *bad; evil*
5004 talaipōria (1),
calamity, distress

MISGAB
4869 misgâb (1), high
refuge

MISHAEL
4332 Mîyshâ'êl (8), *who*
(is) *what God* (is)?

MISHAL
4861 Mish'âl (1), *request*

MISHAM
4936 Mish'âm (1),
inspection

MISHEAL
4861 Mish'âl (1), *request*

MISHMA
4927 Mishmâ' (4), *report*

MISHMANNAH
4925 Mishmannâh (1), *fatness*

MISHRAITES
4954 Mishrâ'îy (1), *extension*

MISPERETH
4559 Miçpereth (1), *enumeration*

MISREPHOTH-MAIM
4956 Misrᵉphôwth Mayim (2), *burnings of water*

MISS
2398 châṭâ' (1), to *sin*
6485 pâqad (1), to *visit, care for, count*

MISSED
6485 pâqad (3), to *visit, care for, count*

MISSING
6485 pâqad (2), to *visit, care for, count*

MIST
108 'êd (1), *fog*
887 achlus (1), *dimness of sight*, i.e. *cataract*
2217 zŏphŏs (1), *gloom*

MISTRESS
1172 ba'ălâh (2), *mistress; female owner*
1404 gᵉbereth (7), *mistress, noblewoman*

MISUSED
8591 tâ'a' (1), to *cheat*; to *maltreat*

MITE
3016 lĕptŏn (1), small *coin*

MITES
3016 lĕptŏn (2), small *coin*

MITHCAH
4989 Mithqâh (2), *sweetness*

MITHNITE
4981 Mithnîy (1), *slenderness*

MITHREDATH
4990 Mithrᵉdâth (2), *Mithredath*

MITRE
4701 mitsnepheth (11), *royal/priestly turban*
6797 tsânîyph (2), *head-dress, turban*

MITYLENE
3412 Mitulēnē (1), *abounding in shell-fish*

MIXED
1101 bâlal (1), to *mix; confuse*; to *feed*
4107 mâhal (1), to *dilute* a mixture
4469 mamçâk (1), *mixed-wine*
6151 'ărab (Ch.) (3), to *co-mingle, mix*
6154 'êreb (2), *mixed* or *woven things*
4786 sugkĕrannumi (1), to *combine; assimilate*

MIXTURE
4538 meçek (1), wine *mixture* with spices
194 akratŏs (1), *undiluted*
3395 migma (1), *compound, mixture*

MIZAR
4706 Mits'âr (1), *little*

MIZPAH
4708 Mitspeh (5), *observatory*
4709 Mitspah (18), *observatory*

MIZPAR
4558 Miçpâr (1), *number*

MIZPEH
4708 Mitspeh (9), *observatory*
4709 Mitspah (14), *observatory*

MIZRAIM
4714 Mitsrayim (4), double *border*

MIZZAH
4199 Mizzâh (3), *terror*

MNASON
3416 Mnasŏn (1), *Mnason*

MOAB
4124 Môw'âb (165), *from mother's father*
4125 Môw'âbîy (2), *Moäbite* or *Moäbitess*

MOABITE
4125 Môw'âbîy (3), *Moäbite* or *Moäbitess*

MOABITES
4124 Môw'âb (16), *from mother's father*
4125 Môw'âbîy (3), *Moäbite* or *Moäbitess*

MOABITESS
4125 Môw'âbîy (6), *Moäbite* or *Moäbitess*

MOABITISH
4125 Môw'âbîy (1), *Moäbite* or *Moäbitess*

MOADIAH
4153 Môw'adyâh (1), *assembly of Jehovah*

MOCK
2048 hâthal (1), to *deride, mock*
3887 lûwts (1), to *scoff*; to *interpret*; to *intercede*
3932 lâ'ag (2), to *deride*; to *speak unintelligibly*
5953 'âlal (1), to *glean*; to *overdo*
6711 tsâchaq (2), to *scorn*; to make *sport of*
7046 qâlaç (1), to *disparage*, i.e. *ridicule*
7832 sâchaq (1), to *laugh*; to *scorn*; to *play*
1702 ĕmpaizō (3), *deride, ridicule*

MOCKED
2048 hâthal (4), to *deride, mock*
3931 lâ'ab (1), to *deride, mock*
3932 lâ'ag (2), to *deride*; to *speak unintelligibly*

5953 'âlal (1), to *glean*; to *overdo*
6711 tsâchaq (1), to *scorn*; to make *sport of*
7046 qâlaç (1), to *disparage*, i.e. *ridicule*
7832 sâchaq (1), to *laugh*; to *scorn*; to *play*
1702 ĕmpaizō (8), *deride, ridicule*
3456 muktērizō (1), to *ridicule*
5512 chlĕuazō (1), *jeer at, sneer at*

MOCKER
3887 lûwts (1), to *scoff*; to *interpret*; to *intercede*

MOCKERS
2049 hâthôl (1), *derision, mockery*
3887 lûwts (1), to *scoff*; to *interpret*; to *intercede*
3934 lâ'êg (1), *buffoon; foreigner*
7832 sâchaq (1), to *laugh*; to *scorn*; to *play*
1703 ĕmpaiktēs (1), *derider; false teacher*

MOCKEST
3932 lâ'ag (1), to *deride*; to *speak unintelligibly*

MOCKETH
2048 hâthal (1), to *deride, mock*
3932 lâ'ag (3), to *deride*; to *speak unintelligibly*
7832 sâchaq (1), to *laugh*; to *scorn*; to *play*

MOCKING
6711 tsâchaq (1), to *scorn*; to make *sport of*
7048 qallâçâh (1), *ridicule*
1702 ĕmpaizō (2), to *deride, ridicule*
5512 chlĕuazō (1), *jeer at, sneer at*

MOCKINGS
1701 ĕmpaigmŏs (1), *derision, jeering*

MODERATELY
6666 tsᵉdâqâh (1), *rightness*

MODERATION
1933 ĕpiĕikēs (1), *mild, gentle*

MODEST
2887 kŏsmiŏs (1), *orderly*

MOIST
3892 lach (1), *fresh* cut, i.e. *unused* or *undried*

MOISTENED
8248 shâqâh (1), to *quaff*, i.e. to *irrigate*

MOISTURE
3955 lᵉshad (1), *juice; vigor*; sweet or fat *cake*
2429 hikmas (1), *dampness, dampness*

MOLADAH
4137 Môwlâdâh (4), *birth*

MOLE
8580 tanshemeth (1), (poss.) *tree-toad*

MOLECH
4432 Môlek (8), *king*

MOLES
2661 chăphôr (1), *hole*, i.e. a *burrowing rat*

MOLID
4140 Môwlîyd (1), *genitor*

MOLLIFIED
7401 râkak (1), to *soften*

MOLOCH
4432 Môlek (1), *king*
3434 Mŏlŏch (1), *king*

MOLTEN
3332 yâtsaq (6), to *pour out*
4541 maççêkâh (25), *cast image); libation*
4549 mâçaç (1), to *waste*; to *faint*
5258 nâçak (1), to *pour a libation*
5262 neçek (4), *libation; cast idol*
5413 nâthak (1), to *flow forth, pour out*
6694 tsûwq (1), to *pour out; melt*

MOMENT
7281 rega' (19), very *short space* of time
823 atŏmŏs (1), *indivisible* unit of time
3901 pararrhuĕō (1), to *flow by*
4743 stigmē (1), *point* of time, i.e. an *instant*

MONEY
3701 keçeph (112), *silver money*
3702 kᵉçaph (Ch.) (1), *silver money*
7192 qᵉsîyṭah (2), *coin* of unknown weight
694 arguriŏn (11), *silver; silver money*
2772 kĕrma (1), *coin*
2773 kĕrmatistēs (1), *money-broker*
3546 nŏmisma (1), *coin*
4715 statēr (1), *coin* worth four day's wage
5365 philarguria (1), *avarice*
5475 chalkŏs (2), *copper*
5536 chrēma (4), *wealth, price*

MONEYCHANGERS
2855 kŏllubistēs (2), *coin-dealer*

MONSTERS
8577 tannîyn (1), *sea-serpent; jackal*

MONTH
2320 chôdesh (215), *new moon; month*
3391 yerach (6), *lunar month*
3393 yᵉrach (Ch.) (1), *lunar* month
3376 mēn (4), *month; month's time*

MONTHLY
2320 chôdesh (1), *new moon; month*

MONTHS

2320 chôdesh (37), *new moon; month*
3391 yerach (5), *lunar month*
3393 yᵉrach (Ch.) (1), *lunar month*
3376 mên (14), *month; month's time*
5072 tĕtramēnŏn (1), *four months' time*
5150 trimēnŏn (1), *three months' space*

MONUMENTS

5341 nâtsar (1), to *guard, protect, maintain*

MOON

2320 chôdesh (9), *new moon; month*
3391 yerach (2), *lunar month*
3394 yârêach (26), *moon*
3842 lᵉbânâh (3), *white moon*
3561 nŏumēnia (1), festival of *new moon*
4582 sĕlēnē (9), *moon*

MOONS

2320 chôdesh (11), *new moon; month*

MORASTHITE

4183 Mowrashtîy (2), *Morashtite*

MORDECAI

4782 Mordᵉkay (58), *Mordecai*

MORDECAI'S

4782 Mordᵉkay (2), *Mordecai*

MORE

637 'aph (1), *also or yea; though*
1058 bâkâh (1), to *weep, moan*
1490 gizbâr (Ch.) (3), *treasurer*
1980 hâlak (1), to *walk; live a certain way*
2351 chûwts (1), *outside, outdoors; open market; countryside*
3148 yôwthêr (3), *moreover; rest; gain*
3254 yâçaph (59), to *add or augment*
3499 yether (1), *remainder;* small *rope*
3513 kâbad (1), to *be heavy, severe, dull*
3651 kên (2), *just; right, correct*
4480 min (4), *from, out of*
4481 min (Ch.) (1), *from or out of*
5674 'âbar (1), to *cross over;* to *transition*
5720 'Âdîyn (1), *voluptuous*
5736 'âdaph (1), to *be redundant, have surplus*
5750 'ôwd (196), *again; repeatedly; still; more*
5922 'al (Ch.) (1), *above, over, upon,* or *against*
5973 'îm (1), *with*

6105 'âtsam (2), to *be, make numerous*
6440 pânîym (1), *face; front*
7138 qârôwb (1), *near, close*
7227 rab (14), *great*
7230 rôb (1), *abundance*
7231 râbab (2), to *increase*
7235 râbâh (11), to *increase*
7608 sha'ărâh (1), female *kindred* by blood
7725 shûwb (1), to *turn back;* to *return*
8145 shênîy (3), *second; again*
197 akribĕstŏrŏn (4), *more exactly*
243 allŏs (1), *different, other*
316 anagkaiŏs (1), *necessary*
414 anĕktŏtĕrŏs (6), *more bearable*
1065 gĕ (1), particle of *emphasis*
1308 diaphĕrō (2), to *differ;* to *surpass*
1508 ĕi mē (1), *if not*
1617 ĕktĕnĕstĕrŏn (1), *more intently*
1833 ĕxĕtazō (1), to *ascertain or interrogate*
2001 ĕpischuŏ (7), to *insist stoutly*
2089 ĕti (39), *yet, still*
2115 ĕuthumŏs (1), *cheerful, encouraged*
3122 malista (1), *in the greatest degree*
3123 mallŏn (47), *in a greater degree*
3185 mĕizŏn (1), *in greater degree*
3187 mĕizōn (1), *larger, greater*
3370 Mēdŏs (3), *inhabitant of Media*
3745 hŏsŏs (1), *as much as*
3761 ŏudĕ (1), *neither, nor, not even*
3765 ŏukĕti (17), *not yet, no longer*
3844 para (2), *from; with; besides; on account of*
4053 pĕrissŏs (2), *superabundant*
4054 pĕrissŏtĕrŏn (1), *more superabundant*
4055 pĕrissŏtĕrŏs (10), *more superabundant*
4056 pĕrissŏtĕrōs (10), *more superabundantly*
4057 pĕrissŏs (1), *superabundantly*
4065 pĕriphrŏnĕō (1), to *depreciate, contemn*
4119 plĕiōn (25), *more*
4179 pŏllaplasiōn (1), *very much more*
4325 prŏsdapanaō (1), to *expend additionally*
4369 prŏstithĕmi (2), to *lay beside, repeat*
4707 spŏudaiŏtĕrŏs (2), *more prompt*

5112 tŏlmĕrŏtĕrŏn (1), *more daringly*
5228 hupĕr (4), *over; above; beyond*
5245 hupĕrnikaō (1), to *gain* a decisive *victory*

MOREH

4176 Môwreh (3), *archer; teaching; early rain*

MOREOVER

518 'îm (1), *whether?; if, although; Oh that!*
637 'aph (2), *also or yea; though*
1571 gam (25), *also; even; yea; though*
3148 yôwthêr (1), *moreover; rest; gain*
3254 yâçaph (1), to *add or augment*
5750 'ôwd (6), *again; repeatedly; still; more*
1161 dĕ (12), *but, yet; and then*
2089 ĕti (1), *yet, still*
2532 kai (1), *and; or; even; also*

MORESHETH-GATH

4182 Môwresheth Gath (1), *possession of Gath*

MORIAH

4179 Môwrîyâh (2), *seen of Jehovah*

MORNING

216 'ôwr (1), *luminary; lightning; happiness*
1242 bôqer (187), *morning*
4891 mishchâr (1), *dawn*
5053 nôgahh (Ch.) (1), *dawn*
6843 tsᵉphîyrâh (2), *mishap*
7836 shâchar (1), to *search for*
7837 shachar (12), *dawn*
7904 shâkâh (1), to *roam* because of lust
7925 shâkam (1), to *start early* in the morning
3720 ŏrthrinŏs (1), *matutinal, i.e. early*
4404 prōï (6), *at dawn; day-break* watch
4405 prōïa (3), *day-dawn, early morn*
4407 prōïnŏs (1), *matutinal, i.e. early*

MORROW

1242 bôqer (7), *morning*
4279 mâchar (45), *tomorrow; hereafter*
4283 mochŏrâth (28), *tomorrow, next day*
839 auriŏn (14), *to-morrow*
1836 hĕxēs (1), *successive, next*
1887 ĕpauriŏn (8), *to-morrow*

MORSEL

3603 kikkâr (1), *round loaf; talent*
6595 path (8), *bit, morsel*
1035 brōsis (1), *food; rusting corrosion*

MORSELS

6595 path (1), *bit, morsel*

MORTAL

582 'ĕnôwsh (1), *man; person, human*
2349 thnētŏs (5), *liable to die,* i.e. *mortal*

MORTALITY

2349 thnētŏs (1), *liable to die,* i.e. *mortal*

MORTALLY

5315 nephesh (1), *life; breath; soul; wind*

MORTAR

4085 mᵉdôkâh (1), *mortar for bricks*
4388 maktêsh (1), *mortar; socket*

MORTER

2563 chômer (4), *clay; dry measure*
6083 'âphâr (2), *dust, earth, mud; clay,*

MORTGAGED

6148 'ârab (1), to *intermix;* to *give or be security*

MORTIFY

2289 thanatŏō (1), to *kill*
3499 nĕkrŏō (1), to *deaden,* i.e. to *subdue*

MOSERA

4149 Môwçêrâh (1), *corrections*

MOSEROTH

4149 Môwçêrâh (2), *corrections*

MOSES

4872 Môsheh (749), *drawing* out of the water
4873 Môsheh (Ch.) (1), *drawing* out of the water
3475 Môsĕus (77), *drawing* out of the water

MOSES'

4872 Môsheh (16), *drawing* out of the water
3475 Môsĕus (3), *drawing* out of the water

MOST

2429 chayil (Ch.) (1), *army; strength*
2896 ţôwb (1), *good; well*
3524 kabbîyr (1), *mighty; aged; mighty*
3800 kethem (1), *pure gold*
4581 mâ'ôwz (1), *fortified place; defense*
4971 mathkôneth (1), *proportion*
5920 'al (2), the *Highest God*
5943 'illay (Ch.) (9), the *supreme God*
5945 'elyôwn (25), *loftier, higher; Supreme God*
5946 'elyôwn (Ch.) (3), the *Supreme God*

6579 partam (1), *grandee, noble*
6944 qôdesh (48), *sacred* place or thing
7230 rôb (1), *abundance*
8077 sh°mâmâh (1), *devastation*
8563 tamrûwr (1), *bitterness*
40 hagiŏs (1), *sacred, holy*
2236 hēdista (1), *with great pleasure*
2903 kratistŏs (4), *very honorable*
3122 malista (1), *in the greatest degree*
4118 plĕistŏs (1), *very large, i.e. the most*
4119 plēiŏn (3), *more*
5310 hupsistŏs (5), *highest; the Supreme* God

MOTE
2595 karphŏs (6), *dry twig or straw*

MOTH
6211 'âsh (7), *moth*
4597 sēs (3), *moth* insect

MOTHEATEN
4598 sētŏbrōtŏs (1), *moth-eaten*

MOTHER
517 'êm (143), *mother*
2545 chămôwth (11), *mother-in-law*
2859 châthan (1), *to become related* by marriage,
282 amētōr (1), *of unknown maternity*
3384 mētēr (76), *mother*
3994 pĕnthĕra (6), *wife's mother*

MOTHER'S
517 'êm (67), *mother*
3384 mētēr (7), *mother*

MOTHERS
517 'êm (3), *mother*
3384 mētēr (2), *mother*
3389 mētralō₁as (1), *matricide*

MOTHERS'
517 'êm (1), *mother*

MOTIONS
3804 pathēma (1), *passion; suffering*

MOULDY
5350 niqqud (2), *crumb, morsel; biscuit*

MOUNT
55 'âbak (1), *to coil* upward
1361 gâbahh (1), *to be lofty; to be haughty*
2022 har (222), *mountain* or *range* of hills
2042 hârâr (1), *mountain*
4674 mutstsâb (1), *station*, military *post*
5550 çôl°lâh (5), military siege *mound, rampart*
5927 'âlâh (4), *to ascend, be high, mount*
7311 rûwm (1), *to be high; to rise* or *raise*

3735 ŏrŏs (21), *hill, mountain*

MOUNTAIN
2022 har (104), *mountain* or *range* of hills
2042 hârâr (2), *mountain*
2906 ţûwr (Ch.) (2), *rock* or *hill*
3735 ŏrŏs (28), *hill, mountain*

MOUNTAINS
2022 har (155), *mountain* or *range* of hills
2042 hârâr (8), *mountain*
3735 ŏrŏs (13), *hill, mountain*

MOUNTED
7426 râmam (1), *to rise*

MOUNTING
4608 ma'ăleh (1), *elevation; platform*

MOUNTS
5550 çôl°lâh (3), military siege *mound, rampart*

MOURN
56 'âbal (15), *to bewail*
57 'âbêl (3), *lamenting*
578 'ânâh (1), *to groan, lament*
584 'ânach (1), *to sigh, moan*
1897 hâgâh (4), *to murmur, utter a sound*
5098 nâham (2), *to growl, groan*
5110 nûwd (1), *to deplore; to taunt*
5594 çâphad (9), *to tear* the hair, *wail*
6937 qâdar (2), *to mourn* in *dark* garments
7300 rûwd (1), *to ramble*
2875 kŏptō (1), *to beat* the breast
3996 pĕnthĕō (5), *to grieve*

MOURNED
56 'âbal (10), *to bewail*
1058 bâkâh (2), *to weep, moan*
5594 çâphad (6), *to tear* the hair, *wail*
2354 thrēnĕō (2), *to bewail, lament*
3996 pĕnthĕō (2), *to grieve*

MOURNER
56 'âbal (1), *to bewail*

MOURNERS
57 'âbêl (2), *lamenting*
205 'âven (1), *trouble, vanity, wickedness*
5594 çâphad (2), *to tear* the hair, *wail*

MOURNETH
56 'âbal (8), *to bewail*
57 'âbêl (1), *lamenting*
1669 dâ'ab (1), *to pine, feel sorrow*
5594 çâphad (1), *to tear* the hair, *wail*

MOURNFULLY
6941 q°dôranniyth (1), *in sackcloth*

MOURNING
56 'âbal (2), *to bewail*
57 'âbêl (2), *lamenting*
60 'êbel (24), *lamentation*
205 'âven (1), *trouble, vanity, wickedness*
585 'ănâchâh (1), *sighing, moaning*
1086 bâlâh (1), *to wear out, decay; consume*
1899 hegeh (1), *muttering; mourning*
1993 hâmâh (1), *to be in great commotion*
3382 Yered (1), *descent*
4553 miçpêd (6), *lamentation, howling*
4798 marzêach (1), *cry of lamentation*
6937 qâdar (4), *to mourn* in *dark* garments
6969 qûwn (1), *to chant* or *wail* at a funeral
8386 ta'ăniyâh (1), *lamentation*
3602 ŏdurmŏs (2), *lamentation*
3997 pĕnthŏs (2), *grief, mourning, sadness*

MOUSE
5909 'akbâr (2), *mouse*

MOUTH
1627 gârôwn (1), *throat*
2441 chêk (14), *area of mouth*
5716 'ădîy (2), *finery; outfit; headstall*
6310 peh (326), *mouth; opening*
6433 pûm (Ch.) (5), *mouth*
8651 t°ra' (Ch.) (1), *door; palace*
3056 lŏgŏs (1), *word, matter, thing*
4750 stŏma (69), *mouth; edge*

MOUTHS
6310 peh (12), *mouth; opening*
6433 pûm (Ch.) (1), *mouth*
1993 ĕpistŏmizō (1), *to silence*
4750 stŏma (4), *mouth; edge*

MOVE
2782 chârats (1), *to be alert, to decide*
5110 nûwd (1), *to waver; to wander, flee*
5128 nûwa' (1), *to waver*
5130 nûwph (1), *to quiver, vibrate, rock*
6328 pûwq (1), *to waver*
6470 pâ'am (1), *to tap; to impel* or *agitate*
7264 râgaz (2), *to quiver*
8318 sherets (1), *swarm, teeming* mass
2795 kinĕō (2), *to stir, move, remove*
3056+4160 lŏgŏs (1), *word, matter, thing*

MOVEABLE
5128 nûwa' (1), *to waver*

MOVED
1607 gâ'ash (3), *to agitate* violently, *shake*
1949 hûwm (1), *to make an uproar; agitate*
1993 hâmâh (1), *to be in great commotion*
2111 zûwâ' (1), *to shake* with fear, *tremble*
2782 chârats (1), *to be alert, to decide*
4131 môwţ (19), *to slip, shake, fall*
4132 môwţ (3), *pole; yoke*
5074 nâdad (1), *to rove, flee; to drive* away
5120 nûwţ (1), *to quake*
5128 nûwa' (5), *to waver*
5425 nâthar (1), *to jump; to be agitated*
5496 çûwth (4), *to stimulate; to seduce*
5648 'ăbad (Ch.) (1), *to do, work, serve*
7043 qâlal (1), *to be, make light, swift*
7264 râgaz (5), *to quiver*
7363 râchaph (1), *to brood; to be relaxed*
7430 râmas (1), *to glide* swiftly, *move, swarm*
7493 râ'ash (2), *to undulate, quake*
23 aganaktĕō (1), *to be indignant*
383 anasĕiō (1), *to excite, stir up*
761 asalĕutŏs (1), *immovable, fixed*
2125 ĕulabĕŏmai (1), *to have reverence*
2206 zēlŏō (2), *to have* warmth of feeling for
2795 kinĕō (2), *to stir, move, remove*
3334 mĕtakinĕō (1), *to be removed, shifted from*
4525 sainō (1), *to shake; to disturb*
4531 salĕuō (1), *to waver, i.e. agitate, rock, topple*
4579 sĕiō (1), *to vibrate; to agitate*
4697 splagchnizŏmai (5), *to feel sympathy, to pity*
5342 phĕrō (1), *to bear or carry*

MOVEDST
5496 çûwth (1), *to stimulate; to seduce*

MOVER
2795 kinĕō (1), *to stir, move, remove*

MOVETH
1980 hâlak (1), *to walk; live a certain way*
2654 châphêts (1), *to be pleased with, desire*
7430 râmas (5), *to glide* swiftly, i.e. *crawl, move, swarm*
8317 shârats (1), *to wriggle, swarm*

MOVING
5205 nîyd (1), *motion of* the lips in speech
7169 qârats (1), *to bite* the lips, *blink* the eyes

7430 râmas (1), to *glide swiftly, crawl, move*
8318 sherets (1), *swarm, teeming* mass
2796 kinēsis (1), *stirring, motion*

MOWER
7114 qâtsar (1), to *curtail, cut short*

MOWINGS
1488 gêz (1), shorn *fleece;* mown *grass*

MOWN
1488 gêz (1), shorn *fleece;* mown *grass*

MOZA
4162 Môwtsâ' (5), *going forth*

MOZAH
4681 Môtsâh (1), *drained*

MUCH
634 'Êçar-Chaddôwn (1), *Esar-chaddon*
637 'aph (15), *also or yea; though*
834 'âsher (2), *how, because, in order that*
1431 gâdal (2), to *be great, make great*
1571 gam (2), *also; even; yea; though*
1767 day (2), *enough, sufficient*
1931 hûw' (1), *he, she, it; this or that*
2479 chalchâlâh (1), *writhing* in childbirth
3254 yâçaph (1), to *add or augment*
3498 yâthar (1), to *remain or be left*
3515 kâbêd (2), *numerous; severe*
3524 kabbîyr (2), *mighty; aged; mighty*
3605 kôl (1), *all, any*
3966 m e'ôd (9), *very, utterly*
4276 machătsîyth (1), *halving* or the *middle*
4767 mirbâh (1), *great* quantity
5704 'ad (2), *as far (long) as; during; while; until*
6079 'aph'aph (1), *fluttering eyelash*
6581 pâsâh (4), to *spread*
7114 qâtsar (1), to *curtail, cut short*
7225 rê'shîyth (1), *first*
7227 rab (38), *great*
7230 rôb (7), *abundance*
7235 râbâh (31), to *increase*
7335 râzam (1), to *twinkle* the *eye*
7690 saggîy' (Ch.) (4), *large*
23 aganaktĕō (2), to be *indignant*
1280 diapŏrĕō (1), to be *thoroughly puzzled*
2425 hikanŏs (6), *ample*
2470 isŏs (1), *similar*
2579 kan (1), *and (or even) if*

3123 mallŏn (3), *in a greater degree*
3366 mēdĕ (1), *but not, not even; nor*
3383 mētĕ (1), *neither or nor; not even*
3386 mētigĕ (1), *not to say (the rather still)*
3433 mŏlis (1), *with difficulty*
3588 hŏ (2), *"the,"* i.e. the definite article
3745 hŏsŏs (4), *as much as*
3761 ŏudĕ (4), *neither, nor, not even*
4055 pĕrissŏtĕrŏs (1), *more superabundant*
4056 pĕrissŏtĕrŏs (1), *more superabundantly*
4124 plĕŏnĕxia (2), *extortion, avarice*
4180 pŏlulŏgia (1), *prolixity, wordiness*
4183 pŏlus (73), *much, many*
4214 pŏsŏs (11), *how much?; how much!*
5118 tŏsŏutŏs (7), *such great*
5248 hupĕrpĕrissĕuō (2), to *super-abound*

MUFFLERS
7479 ra'ălâh (1), long *veil*

MULBERRY
1057 bâkâ' (4), (poss.) *balsam* tree

MULE
6505 pered (6), *mule*
6506 pirdâh (3), *she-mule*

MULES
3222 yêm (1), *warm* spring
6505 pered (8), *mule*
7409 rekesh (2), *relay of* animals on a post-route

MULES'
6505 pered (1), *mule*

MULTIPLIED
1995 hâmôwn (1), *noise, tumult; many, crowd*
6280 'âthar (1), to *be, make abundant*
7231 râbab (3), to *increase*
7235 râbâh (29), to *increase*
7680 s e gâ' (Ch.) (2), to *increase*
4129 plēthunō (8), to *increase*

MULTIPLIEDST
7235 râbâh (1), to *increase*

MULTIPLIETH
3527 kâbar (1), to *augment; accumulate*
7235 râbâh (2), to *increase*

MULTIPLY
7227 rab (1), *great*
7231 râbab (1), to *increase*
7233 r e bâbâh (1), *myriad number*

7235 râbâh (41), to *increase*
4129 plēthunō (2), to *increase*

MULTIPLYING
7235 râbâh (1), to *increase*
4129 plēthunō (1), to *increase*

MULTITUDE
527 'âmôwn (4), *throng* of people, *crowd*
582 'ĕnôwsh (1), *man; person, human*
628 'açp e çûph (1), *assemblage*
1995 hâmôwn (55), *noise, tumult; many, crowd*
2416 chay (1), *alive; raw; fresh; life*
4392 mâlê' (1), *full; filling; fulness; fully*
4393 m e lô' (2), *fulness*
4768 marbîyth (1), *multitude; offspring*
5519 çâk (1), *crowd*
5712 'êdâh (1), *assemblage; crowd*
6154 'êreb (1), *mixed or woven things*
6951 qâhâl (3), *assemblage*
7227 rab (7), *great*
7230 rôb (68), *abundance*
7379 rîyb (1), *contest*
7393 rekeb (1), *upper millstone*
8229 shiph'âh (1), *copiousness*
3461 murias (1), *ten-thousand*
3793 ŏchlŏs (59), *throng*
4128 plēthŏs (29), *large number, throng*

MULTITUDES
1995 hâmôwn (2), *noise, tumult; many, crowd*
3793 ŏchlŏs (20), *throng*
4128 plēthŏs (1), *large number, throng*

MUNITION
4685 mâtsôwd (1), *net or snare; besieging tower*
4694 m e tsûwrâh (1), *rampart; fortification*

MUNITIONS
4679 m e tsad (1), *stronghold*

MUPPIM
4649 Muppîym (1), *wavings*

MURDER
2026 hârag (1), to *kill, slaughter*
7523 râtsach (3), to *murder*
5407 phŏnĕuō (1), to *commit murder*
5408 phŏnŏs (3), *slaying; murder*

MURDERER
2026 hârag (1), to *kill, slaughter*
7523 râtsach (13), to *murder*

7235 râbâh (41), to *increase*
4129 plēthunō (2), to *increase*

443 anthrŏpŏktŏnŏs (3), *killer of humans*
5406 phŏnĕus (3), *murderer*

MURDERERS
2026 hârag (1), to *kill, slaughter*
5221 nâkâh (1), to *strike, kill*
7523 râtsach (1), to *murder*
3389 mētralō i as (1), *matricide*
3964 patralō i as (1), *parricide*
4607 sikariŏs (1), *dagger-man*
5406 phŏnĕus (4), *murderer*

MURDERS
5408 phŏnŏs (4), *slaying; murder*

MURMUR
3885 lûwn (7), to *be obstinate with* words
1111 gŏgguzō (2), to *grumble, mutter*

MURMURED
3885 lûwn (7), to *be obstinate with* words
7279 râgan (3), to *grumbling* rebel
1111 gŏgguzō (6), to *grumble, mutter*
1234 diagŏgguzō (2), to *complain throughout*
1690 ĕmbrimaŏmai (1), to *blame, warn sternly*

MURMURERS
1113 gŏggustēs (1), *grumbler*

MURMURING
1112 gŏggusmŏs (2), *grumbling*

MURMURINGS
8519 t e lûwnâh (8), *grumbling*
1112 gŏggusmŏs (1), *grumbling*

MURRAIN
1698 deber (1), *pestilence, plague*

MUSE
7878 sîyach (1), to *ponder, muse aloud*

MUSED
1260 dialŏgizŏmai (1), to *deliberate*

MUSHI
4187 Mûwshîy (8), *sensitive*

MUSHITES
4188 Mûwshîy (2), *Mushite*

MUSICAL
7705 shiddâh (1), *wife (as mistress of the house)*
7892 shîyr (2), *song; singing*

MUSICIAN
5329 nâtsach (55), i.e. to *be eminent*

MUSICIANS
3451 mŏusikŏs (1), *minstrel, musician*

MUSICK
2170 z^emâr (Ch.) (4), instrumental *music*
4485 mangîynâh (1), *satire, mocking*
5058 n^egîynâh (1), stringed *instrument*
7892 shîyr (7), *song; singing*
4858 sumphōnia (1), *concert* of instruments

MUSING
1901 hâgîyg (1), *complaint, sighing*

MUST
318 anagkē (1), *constraint; distress*
1163 dĕi (63), *it is (was) necessary*
2192 ĕchō (1), to *have; hold; keep*
2443 hina (1), in order that
3784 ŏphĕilō (1), to *owe; to be under obligation*

MUSTARD
4615 sinapi (5), *mustard*

MUSTERED
6633 tsâbâ' (2), to *mass* an army or servants

MUSTERETH
6485 pâqad (1), to *visit, care for, count*

MUTH-LABBEN
4192 Mûwth (1), *"To die for the son"*

MUTTER
1897 hâgâh (1), to *murmur, utter a sound*

MUTTERED
1897 hâgâh (1), to *murmur, utter a sound*

MUTUAL
1722+240 ĕn (1), *in; during; because of*

MUZZLE
2629 châçam (1), to *muzzle; block*
5392 phimŏŏ (2), to *muzzle; silence*

MYRA
3460 Mura (1), *Myra*

MYRRH
3910 lôt (2), *sticky gum resin* (poss.) *ladanum*
4753 môr (12), *myrrh*
4666 smurna (2), *myrrh*
4669 smurnizō (1), to *mix with myrrh*

MYRTLE
1918 hădaç (6), *myrtle*

MYSIA
3463 muriŏi (2), *ten thousand*

MYSTERIES
3466 mustēriŏn (5), *secret*

MYSTERY
3466 mustēriŏn (22), *secret*

NAAM
5277 Na'am (1), *pleasure*

NAAMAH
5279 Na'ămâh (5), *pleasantness*

NAAMAN
5283 Na'ămân (15), *pleasantness*
3497 Nĕĕman (1), *pleasantness*

NAAMAN'S
5283 Na'ămân (1), *pleasantness*

NAAMATHITE
5284 Na'ămâthîy (4), *Naamathite*

NAAMITES
5280 Na'ămîy (1), *Naamanite*

NAARAH
5292 Na'ărâh (3), *female child; servant*

NAARAI
5293 Na'ăray (1), *youthful*

NAARAN
5295 Na'ărân (1), *juvenile*

NAARATH
5292 Na'ărâh (1), *female child; servant*

NAASHON
5177 Nachshôwn (1), *enchanter*

NAASSON
3476 Naassōn (3), *enchanter*

NABAL
5037 Nâbâl (18), *dolt*

NABAL'S
5037 Nâbâl (4), *dolt*

NABOTH
5022 Nâbôwth (22), *fruits*

NACHON'S
5225 Nâkôwn (1), *prepared*

NACHOR
5152 Nâchôwr (1), *snorer*
3493 Nachōr (1), *snorer*

NADAB
5070 Nâdâb (20), *liberal*

NAGGE
3477 Naggai (1), (poss.) *brilliancy*

NAHALAL
5096 Nahălâl (1), *pasture*

NAHALIEL
5160 Nachălîy'êl (2), *valley of God*

NAHALLAL
5096 Nahălâl (1), *pasture*

NAHALOL
5096 Nahălâl (1), *pasture*

NAHAM
5163 Nacham (1), *consolation*

NAHAMANI
5167 Nachămânîy (1), *consolatory*

NAHARAI
5171 Nachăray (1), *snorer*

NAHARI
5171 Nachăray (1), *snorer*

NAHASH
5176 Nâchâsh (9), *snake*

NAHATH
5184 Nachath (5), *quiet*

NAHBI
5147 Nachbîy (1), *occult*

NAHOR
5152 Nâchôwr (15), *snorer*

NAHOR'S
5152 Nâchôwr (2), *snorer*

NAHSHON
5177 Nachshôwn (9), *enchanter*

NAHUM
5151 Nachûwm (1), *comfortable*

NAIL
3489 yâthêd (8), tent *peg*

NAILING
4338 prŏsēlŏō (1), to *nail* to something

NAILS
2953 t^ephar (Ch.) (2), finger-*nail; claw*
4548 maçmêr (4), *peg*
4930 masm^erâh (1), *pin* on the end of a goad
6856 tsippôren (1), *nail; point of a pen*
2247 hēlŏs (2), *stud,* i.e. *spike or nail*

NAIN
3484 Naïn (1), cf. a *home, dwelling; pasture*

NAIOTH
5121 Nâvîyth (6), *residence*

NAKED
4636 ma'ărôm (1), *bare, stripped*
5783 'ûwr (1), to (*be) bare*
5903 'êyrôm (9), *naked; nudity*
6168 'ârâh (1), to *be, make bare; to empty*
6174 'ârôwm (16), *nude; partially stripped*
6181 'eryâh (1), *nudity*
6544 pâra' (3), to *loosen; to expose, dismiss*
1130 gumnētĕuō (1), *go poorly clad, be in rags*
1131 gumnŏs (14), *nude or poorly clothed*

NAKEDNESS
4589 mâ'ôwr (1), *nakedness; exposed*
4626 ma'ar (1), *bare place; nakedness*
5903 'êyrôm (1), *naked; nudity*
6172 'ervâh (50), *nudity; disgrace; blemish*
1132 gumnŏtēs (3), *nudity or poorly clothed*

NAME
559 'âmar (2), to *say*
8034 shêm (735), *appellation*
8036 shum (Ch.) (8), *name*

2564 kalĕō (1), to *call*
3686 ŏnŏma (170), *name*

NAME'S
8034 shêm (19), *appellation,* i.e. name
3686 ŏnŏma (11), *name*

NAMED
559 'âmar (1), to *say*
1696 dâbar (1), to *speak, say; to subdue*
5344 nâqab (1), to *specify, designate, libel*
7121 qârâ' (5), to *call* out
7121+8034 qârâ' (1), to *call out*
8034 shêm (4), *appellation,* i.e. name
8034+7121 shêm (1), *appellation,* i.e. name
8036 shum (Ch.) (1), *name*
2564 kalĕō (2), to *call*
3004 lĕgō (2), to *say*
3686 ŏnŏma (28), *name*
3687 ŏnŏmazō (7), to *give a name*

NAMELY
1722 ĕn (1), *in; during; because of*

NAMES
8034 shêm (82), *appellation,* i.e. name
8036 shum (Ch.) (3), *name*
3686 ŏnŏma (11), *name*

NAMETH
3687 ŏnŏmazō (1), to *give a name*

NAOMI
5281 No'ŏmîy (20), *pleasant*

NAOMI'S
5281 No'ŏmîy (1), *pleasant*

NAPHISH
5305 Nâphîysh (2), *refreshed*

NAPHTALI
5321 Naphtâlîy (49), *my wrestling*

NAPHTUHIM
5320 Naphtûchîym (1), *Naphtuchim*

NAPKIN
4676 sŏudariŏn (3), *towel*

NAPTHTUHIM
5320 Naphtûchîym (1), *Naphtuchim*

NARCISSUS
3488 Narkissŏs (1), *stupefaction*

NARROW
213 'ûwts (1), to *be close, hurry, withdraw*
331 'âtam (4), to *close*
3334 yâtsar (1), to *be in distress*
6862 tsar (2), *trouble; opponent*
2346 thlibō (1), to *crowd, press, trouble*

NARROWED
4052 migrâ'âh (1), *ledge or offset*

NARROWER
6887 tsârar (1), to *cramp*

NARROWLY
8104 shâmar (1), to
watch

NATHAN
5416 Nâthân (42), *given*
3481 Nathan (1), *given*

NATHAN-MELECH
5419 Nᵉthan-Melek (1),
given of (the) *king*

NATHANAEL
3482 Nathanaël (6),
given of God

NATION
249 'ezrâch (1), *native
born*
524 'ummâh (Ch.) (1),
community, clan, tribe
1471 gôwy (105), *foreign
nation; Gentiles*
3816 lᵉ'ôm (1),
community, nation
5971 'am (2), *people;
tribe; troops*
246 allŏphulŏs (1),
Gentile, foreigner
1074 gĕnĕa (1),
generation; age
1085 gĕnŏs (2), *kin,
offspring in kind*
1484 ĕthnŏs (24), *race;
tribe; pagan*

NATIONS
523 'ummâh (1),
community, clan, tribe
524 'ummâh (Ch.) (7),
community, clan, tribe
776 'erets (1), *earth,
land, soil; nation*
1471 gôwy (266), *foreign
nation; Gentiles*
3816 lᵉ'ôm (9),
community, nation
5971 'am (14), *people;
tribe; troops*
1484 ĕthnŏs (37), *race;
tribe; pagan*

NATIVE
4138 môwledeth (1),
lineage, native country

NATIVITY
4138 môwledeth (6),
lineage, native country
4351 mᵉkûwrâh (1),
origin

NATURAL
3893 lêach (1), *fresh
strength, vigor*
1083 gĕnnĕsis (1),
nativity
2596+6449 kata (2),
down; according to
5446 phusikŏs (3),
instinctive, natural
5591 psuchikŏs (4),
physical and *brutish*

NATURALLY
1103 gnēsiŏs (1),
genuine, true
5447 phusikōs (1),
instinctively, naturally

NATURE
1078 genesis (1), *nativity,
nature*

5449 phusis (10), *genus
or sort; disposition*

NAUGHT
7451 ra' (2), *bad; evil*

NAUGHTINESS
1942 havvâh (1), *desire;
craving*
7455 rôa' (1), *badness,
evil*
2549 kakia (1),
*depravity; malignity;
trouble*

NAUGHTY
1100 bᵉlîya'al (1),
wickedness, trouble
1942 havvâh (1), *desire;
craving*
7451 ra' (1), *bad; evil*

NAUM
3486 Naŏum (1),
comfortable

NAVEL
8270 shôr (2), umbilical
cord; strength
8306 shârîyr (1), *sinew*
8326 shôrer (1),
umbilical *cord*

NAVES
1354 gab (1), *mounded:
top, rim; arch, bulwarks*

NAVY
590 'ŏnîy (6), *ship; fleet of
ships*

NAY
408 'al (8), *not; nothing*
1571 gam (2), *also; even*
3808 lô' (17), *no, not*
6440 pânîym (1), *face;
front*
235 alla (4), *but, yet*
3304 mĕnŏungĕ (1), *so
then at least*
3756 ŏu (8), *no or not*
3780 ŏuchi (5), *not indeed*

NAZARENE
3480 Nazōraiŏs (1),
inhabitant of Nazareth

NAZARENES
3480 Nazōraiŏs (1),
inhabitant of Nazareth

NAZARETH
3478 Nazarĕth (29),
Nazareth or Nazaret

NAZARITE
5139 nâzîyr (9), *prince;
separated Nazirite*

NAZARITES
5139 nâzîyr (3), *prince;
separated Nazirite*

NEAH
5269 Nê'âh (1), *motion*

NEAPOLIS
3496 Nĕapŏlis (1), *new
town*

NEAR
413 'êl (1), *to, toward*
681 'êtsel (3), *side; near*
3027 yâd (2), *hand; power*
5060 nâga' (4), to *strike*
5066 nâgash (58), to *be,
come, bring near*
5921 'al (1), *above, over,
upon, or against*
5973 'îm (1), *with*

7126 qârab (54), to
approach, bring near
7127 qᵉrêb (Ch.) (5), to
approach, bring near
7131 qârêb (2), *near*
7132 qᵉrâbâh (1),
approach
7138 qârôwb (42), *near,
close*
7200 râ'âh (1), to *see*
7607 shᵉ'êr (4), *flesh,
meat; kindred* by blood
7608 sha'ărâh (1), female
kindred by blood
316 anagkaiŏs (1),
necessary
1448 ĕggizō (10), to
approach
1451 ĕggus (4), *near,
close*
4139 plēsiŏn (1),
neighbor, fellow
4317 prŏsagō (1), to
bring near
4334 prŏsĕrchŏmai (3),
to *come near, visit*

NEARER
7138 qârôwb (1), *near,
close*
1452 ĕggutĕrŏn (1),
nearer, closer

NEARIAH
5294 Nᵉ'aryâh (3),
servant of Jehovah

NEBAI
5109 Nôwbay (1), *fruitful*

NEBAIOTH
5032 Nᵉbâyôwth (2),
fruitfulnesses

NEBAJOTH
5032 Nᵉbâyôwth (3),
fruitfulnesses

NEBALLAT
5041 Nᵉballâṭ (1), *foolish
secrecy*

NEBAT
5028 Nᵉbâṭ (25), *regard*

NEBO
5015 Nᵉbôw (13), *Nebo*

NEBUCHADNEZZAR
5019 Nᵉbûwkadne'tstsar
(29), *Nebukadnetstsar*
5020 Nᵉbûwkadnetstsar
(Ch.) (31),
Nebukadnetstsar

NEBUCHADREZZAR
5019 Nᵉbûwkadne'tstsar
(31), *Nebukadnetstsar*

NEBUSHASBAN
5021 Nᵉbûwshazbân (1),
Nebushazban

NEBUZAR-ADAN
5018 Nᵉbûwzar'ădân
(15), *Nebuzaradan*

NECESSARY
2706 chôq (1),
appointment; allotment
316 anagkaiŏs (5),
necessary
318 anagkē (1),
constraint; distress
1876 ĕpanagkĕs (1),
necessarily
4314+3588+5532 prŏs (1),
for; on, at; to, toward

NECESSITIES
318 anagkē (2),
constraint; distress
5532 chrĕia (1), *demand,
requirement*

NECESSITY
316 anagkaiŏs (1),
necessary
318 anagkē (6),
constraint; distress
2192+318 ĕchō (1), to
have; hold; keep
5532 chrĕia (2), *demand,
requirement*

NECHO
5224 Nᵉkôw (3), *Neko*

NECK
1621 gargᵉrôwth (4),
throat
1627 gârôwn (1), *throat*
4665 miphreketh (1),
vertebra of the neck
6202 'âraph (3), to *break
the neck,* to *destroy*
6203 'ôreph (12), *nape* or
back of the neck
6676 tsavva'r (Ch.) (5),
back of the neck
6677 tsavva'r (30), *back
of the neck*
5137 trachēlŏs (6), *throat
or neck; life*

NEARER *(see above)*

NECKS
1627 gârôwn (1), *throat*
6203 'ôreph (6), *nape* or
back of the neck
6677 tsavva'r (10), *back
of the neck*
5137 trachēlŏs (1), *throat
or neck; life*

NECROMANCER
1875+4191 dârash (1), to
seek or ask; to *worship*

NEDABIAH
5072 Nᵉdabyâh (1),
largess of Jehovah

NEED
2637 châcêr (1), to *lack;
to fail, want, make less*
2638 châcêr (1), *lacking*
2818 chăshach (Ch.) (1),
to *need*
4270 machçôwr (1),
impoverishment
6878 tsôrek (1), *need*
1163 dĕi (1), *it is* (was)
necessary
2121 ĕukairŏs (1),
opportune, suitable
2192+5532 ĕchō (8), to
have; hold; keep
3784 ŏphĕilō (1), to *owe;
to be under obligation*
5532 chrĕia (26),
demand, requirement
5535 chrĕizō (4), to *have
necessity, be in want of*

NEEDED
2192+5532 ĕchō (1), to
have; hold; keep
4326 prŏsdĕŏmai (1), to
require additionally

NEEDEST
2192+5532 ĕchō (1), to
have; hold; keep

NEEDETH
422 anĕpaischuntŏs (1), *unashamed*
2192+318 ĕchō (1), to *have; hold; keep*
2192+5532 ĕchō (1), to *have; hold; keep*
5532 chrĕia (1), *demand, requirement*
5535 chrē₁zō (1), to *have necessity, be in want* of

NEEDFUL
2819 chashchûwth (1), *necessity*
316 anagkaiŏs (1), *necessary*
318 anagkē (1), *constraint; distress*
1163 dĕi (1), *it is (was) necessary*
2006 ĕpitēdĕiŏs (1), *requisite, needful*
5532 chrĕia (1), *demand, requirement*

NEEDLE
4476 rhaphis (2), *sewing needle*

NEEDLE'S
4476 rhaphis (1), *sewing needle*

NEEDLEWORK
4639+7551 ma'ăseh (1), *action; labor*
7551 râqam (5), *variegation; embroider*
7553 riqmâh (3), *variegation* of color; *embroidery*

NEEDS
318 anagkē (3), *constraint; distress*
3843 pantōs (1), *entirely; at all events*

NEEDY
34 'ebyôwn (35), *destitute; poor*
1800 dal (2), *weak, thin; humble, needy*
7326 rûwsh (1), to *be destitute*

NEESINGS
5846 'ăṭîyshâh (1), *sneezing*

NEGINAH
5058 nᵉgîynâh (1), *stringed instrument*

NEGINOTH
5058 nᵉgîynâh (6), *stringed instrument*

NEGLECT
272 amĕlĕŏ (2), to *be careless* of, *neglect*
3878 parakŏuŏ (2), to *disobey*

NEGLECTED
3865 parathĕŏrĕŏ (1), to *overlook* or *disregard*

NEGLECTING
857 aphĕidia (1), *austerity, asceticism*

NEGLIGENT
7952 shâlâh (1), to *mislead*
272 amĕlĕŏ (1), to *be careless* of, *neglect*

NEHELAMITE
5161 Nechĕlâmîy (3), *dreamed*

NEHEMIAH
5166 Nᵉchemyâh (8), *consolation of Jehovah*

NEHILOTH
5155 Nᵉchîylâh (1), *flute*

NEHUM
5149 Nᵉchûwm (1), *comforted*

NEHUSHTA
5179 Nᵉchushtâ' (1), *copper*

NEHUSHTAN
5180 Nᵉchushtân (1), *copper serpent*

NEIEL
5272 Nᵉʿîyʾêl (1), *moved of God*

NEIGHBOUR
5997 'âmîyth (7), *comrade* or *kindred*
7138 qârôwb (2), *near, close*
7453 rêa' (74), *associate; one close*
7468 rᵉʿûwth (2), female *associate*
7934 shâkên (6), *resident; fellow-citizen*
4139 plēsiŏn (16), *neighbor, fellow*

NEIGHBOUR'S
5997 'âmîyth (2), *comrade* or *kindred*
7453 rêa' (26), *associate; one close*

NEIGHBOURS
7138 qârôwb (3), *near, close*
7453 rêa' (2), *associate; one close*
7934 shâkên (11), *resident; fellow-citizen*
1069 gĕitōn (4), *neighbour*
4040 pĕriŏikŏs (1), *neighbor*

NEIGHBOURS'
7453 rêa' (1), *associate; one close*

NEIGHED
6670 tsâhal (1), to *be cheerful; to sound*

NEIGHING
4684 matshâlâh (1), *whinnying*

NEIGHINGS
4684 matshâlâh (1), *whinnying*

NEITHER
369 'ayin (40), *there is no, i.e., not exist, none*
408 'al (66), *not; nothing*
518 'îm (5), *whether?; if, although; Oh that!*
1077 bal (3), *nothing; not at all; lest*
1115 biltîy (4), *not, except, without, unless*
1571 gam (5), *also; even*
3608 kele' (2), *prison*

3804 kether (1), *royal headdress*
3808 lô' (475), no, *not*
3809 lâ' (Ch.) (3), *as nothing*
4480 min (2), *from, out of*
2228 ē (4), *or; than*
3361 mē (5), *not; lest*
3366 mĕdĕ (34), *but not, not even; nor*
3383 mĕtĕ (19), *neither or nor; not even*
3756 ŏu (12), *no or not*
3761 ŏudĕ (67), *neither, nor, not even*
3763 ŏudĕpŏtĕ (1), *never at all*
3777 ŏutĕ (39), *not even*

NEKEB
5346 Neqeb (1), *dell*

NEKODA
5353 Nᵉqôwdâ' (4), *distinction*

NEMUEL
5241 Nᵉmûwʾêl (3), *day of God*

NEMUELITES
5242 Nᵉmûwʾêlîy (1), *Nemuelite*

NEPHEG
5298 Nepheg (4), *sprout*

NEPHEW
5220 neked (2), *offspring*

NEPHEWS
1121 bên (1), *son, descendant; people*
1549 ĕkgŏnŏn (1), *grandchild*

NEPHISH
5305 Nâphîysh (1), *refreshed*

NEPHISHESIM
5300 Nᵉphûwshᵉçîym (1), *expansions*

NEPHTHALIM
3508 Nĕphthalĕim (2), *my wrestling*

NEPHTOAH
5318 Nephtôwach (2), *spring*

NEPHUSIM
5304 Nᵉphîyçîym (1), *expansions*

NEPTHALIM
3508 Nĕphthalĕim (1), *my wrestling*

NER
5369 Nêr (16), *lamp*

NEREUS
3517 Nērĕus (1), *wet*

NERGAL
5370 Nêrgal (1), *Nergal*

NERGAL-SHAREZER
5371 Nêrgal Shar'etser (3), *Nergal-Sharetser*

NERI
3518 Nēri (1), *light of Jehovah*

NERIAH
5374 Nêrîyâh (10), *light of Jehovah*

NERO
3505 Nĕrōn (1), *Nero*

NEST
7064 qên (12), *nest; nestlings; chamber*
7077 qânan (3), to *nestle*

NESTS
7077 qânan (2), to *nestle*
2682 kataskēnōsis (2), *perch* or *nest*

NET
2764 chêrem (5), *doomed object*
4364 makmâr (1), *hunter's snare-net*
4685 mâtsôwd (2), *net* or *snare; besieging tower*
4686 mâtsûwd (2), *net* or *capture; fastness*
7568 resheth (20), *hunting net; network*
293 amphiblēstrŏn (2), *fishing net which is cast*
1350 diktuŏn (6), *drag net*
4522 sagēnē (1), *seine*

NETHANEEL
5417 Nᵉthanʾêl (14), *given of God*

NETHANIAH
5418 Nᵉthanyâh (20), *given of Jehovah*

NETHER
7347 rêcheh (1), *mill-stone*
8481 tachtôwn (5), *bottommost*
8482 tachtîy (9), *lowermost; depths*

NETHERMOST
8481 tachtôwn (1), *bottommost*

NETHINIMS
5411 Nâthîyn (17), *ones given to duty*
5412 Nᵉthîyn (Ch.) (1), *ones given to duty*

NETOPHAH
5199 Nᵉṭôphâh (2), *distillation*

NETOPHATHI
5200 Nᵉṭôphâthîy (1), *Netophathite*

NETOPHATHITE
5200 Nᵉṭôphâthîy (8), *Netophathite*

NETOPHATHITES
5200 Nᵉṭôphâthîy (2), *Netophathite*

NETS
2764 chêrem (4), *doomed object*
4364 makmâr (1), *hunter's snare-net*
4365 mikmereth (1), *fishing-net*
7638 sâbâk (1), *netting*
1350 diktuŏn (6), *drag net*

NETTLES
2738 chârûwl (3), *bramble, thorny weed*
7057 qimmôwsh (1), *prickly plant*

NETWORK
4640+7568 Ma'say (2), operative
7639 sᵉbâkâh (5), net-work balustrade

NETWORKS
2355 chôwr (1), white linen
7639 sᵉbâkâh (2), net-work balustrade

NEVER
369 'ayin (2), there is no, i.e., not exist, none
408 'al (1), not; nothing
1253 bôr (1), vegetable lye as soap; flux
1755 dôwr (1), dwelling
3808 lô' (17), no, not
165 aiŏn (1), perpetuity, ever; world
3361 mē (1), not; lest
3364 ŏu mē (1), not at all, absolutely not
3368 mēdĕpŏtĕ (1), not even ever
3756 ŏu (5), no or not
3762 ŏudĕis (1), none, nobody, nothing
3763 ŏudĕpŏtĕ (14), never at all
3764 ŏudĕpō (2), not even yet

NEVERTHELESS
61 'âbâl (2), truly, surely; yet, but
389 'ak (11), surely; only, however
403 'âkên (1), surely!, truly!; but
657 'epheç (1), end; no further
1297 bᵉram (Ch.) (1), however, but
1571 gam (3), also; even
3588 kîy (4), for, that because
7535 raq (5), merely; although
235 alla (10), but, yet, except, instead
1161 dĕ (11), but, yet; and then
2544 kaitŏigĕ (1), although really
3305 mĕntŏi (1), however
4133 plēn (8), albeit, save that, rather, yet

NEW
1069 bâkar (1), bear the first born
1278 bᵉrîy'âh (1), creation
2319 châdâsh (50), new, recent
2320 chôdesh (20), new moon; month
2323 chădath (Ch.) (1), new
2961 ṭârîy (1), fresh
8492 tîyrôwsh (11), fresh squeezed grape-juice
46 agnaphŏs (2), new, unshrunk cloth
1098 glĕukŏs (1), sweet wine
2537 kainŏs (44), freshness, i.e. new
3501 nĕŏs (11), new

3561 nŏumēnia (1), festival of new moon
4372 prŏsphatŏs (1), lately made, i.e. new

NEWBORN
738 artigĕnnētŏs (1), new born; young convert

NEWLY
6965 qûwm (1), to rise
7138 qârôwb (1), near, close

NEWNESS
2538 kainŏtēs (2), renewal, newness

NEWS
8052 shᵉmûw'âh (1), announcement

NEXT
312 'achêr (2), other, another, different; next
4283 mochŏrâth (3), tomorrow, next day
4932 mishneh (7), duplicate copy; double
7138 qârôwb (5), near, close
839 auriŏn (1), to-morrow
1206 dĕutĕraiŏs (1), on the second day
1836 hĕxēs (2), successive, next
1887 ĕpauriŏn (7), to-morrow
1966 ĕpiŏusa (3), ensuing
2064 ĕrchŏmai (1), to go or come
2087 hĕtĕrŏs (2), other or different
2192 ĕchō (3), to have; hold; keep
3342 mĕtaxu (1), betwixt; meanwhile

NEZIAH
5335 Nᵉtsîyach (2), conspicuous

NEZIB
5334 Nᵉtsîyb (1), station

NIBHAZ
5026 Nibchaz (1), Nibchaz

NIBSHAN
5044 Nibshân (1), Nibshan

NICANOR
3527 Nikanŏr (1), victorious

NICODEMUS
3530 Nikŏdēmŏs (5), victorious among his people

NICOLAITANES
3531 Nikŏlaïtēs (2), adherent of Nicolaüs

NICOLAS
3532 Nikŏlaŏs (1), victorious over the people

NICOPOLIS
3533 Nikŏpŏlis (2), victorious city

NIGER
3526 Nigĕr (1), black

NIGH
4952 mishrâh (1), steeped juice
5060 nâga' (3), to strike
5066 nâgash (12), to be, come, bring near
7126 qârab (32), to approach, bring near
7138 qârôwb (4), near, close
7607 shᵉ'êr (1), flesh, meat; kindred by blood
7934 shâkên (1), resident; fellow-citizen
1448 ĕggizō (21), to approach
1451 ĕggus (18), near, close
3844 para (2), from; with; besides; on account of
3897 paraplēsiŏn (1), almost
4314 prŏs (1), for; on, at; to, toward; against

NIGHT
956 bûwth (Ch.) (1), to lodge over night
2822 chôshek (1), darkness; misery
3915 layil (208), night; adversity
3916 leylᵉyâ' (Ch.) (4), night
5399 nesheph (3), dusk, dawn
6153 'ereb (4), dusk
6916 qiddâh (1), cassia bark
8464 tachmâç (2), unclean bird (poss.) owl
1273 dianuktĕrĕuō (1), to pass, spend the night
3571 nux (60), night
3574 nuchthēmĕrŏn (1), full day

NIGHTS
3915 layil (15), night; adversity
3571 nux (3), night

NIMRAH
5247 Nimrâh (1), clear water

NIMRIM
5249 Nimrîym (2), clear waters

NIMROD
5248 Nimrôwd (4), Nimrod

NIMSHI
5250 Nimshîy (5), extricated

NINE
8672 têsha' (44), nine; ninth
1767 ĕnnĕa (1), nine
1768 ĕnnĕnĕkŏntaĕnnĕa (4), ninety-nine

NINETEEN
8672+6240 têsha' (3), nine; ninth

NINETEENTH
8672+6240 têsha' (4), nine; ninth

NINETY
8673 tish'îym (20), ninety

1768 ĕnnĕnĕkŏntaĕnnĕa (4), ninety-nine

NINEVE
3535 Ninĕuï (1), Nineveh

NINEVEH
5210 Nîynᵉvêh (17), Nineveh
3536 Ninĕuïtēs (1), inhabitant of Nineveh

NINEVITES
3536 Ninĕuïtēs (1), inhabitant of Nineveh

NINTH
8671 tᵉshîy'îy (18), ninth
8672 têsha' (6), nine; ninth
1766 ĕnnatŏs (10), ninth

NISAN
5212 Nîyçân (2), Nisan

NISROCH
5268 Niçrôk (2), Nisrok

NITRE
5427 nether (2), mineral potash for washing

NOADIAH
5129 Nôw'adyâh (2), convened of Jehovah

NOAH
5146 Nôach (44), rest
5270 Nô'âh (4), movement
3575 Nŏĕ (3), rest

NOAH'S
5146 Nôach (2), rest

NOB
5011 Nôb (6), fruit

NOBAH
5025 Nôbach (3), bark

NOBLE
3358 yaqqîyr (Ch.) (1), precious
6579 partam (1), grandee, noble
2104 ĕugĕnēs (2), high in rank; generous
2908 krĕissŏn (2), better, i.e. greater advantage

NOBLEMAN
937 basilikŏs (2), befitting the sovereign
2104+444 ĕugĕnēs (1), high in rank; generous

NOBLES
117 'addîyr (7), powerful; majestic
678 'âtsîyl (1), extremity; noble
1281 bârîyach (1), fleeing, gliding serpent
1419 gâdôwl (1), great
2715 chôr (13), noble, i.e. in high rank
3513 kâbad (1), to be rich, glorious
5057 nâgîyd (1), commander, official
5081 nâdîyb (4), magnanimous
6579 partam (1), grandee, noble

NOD
5113 Nôwd (1), vagrancy

NODAB
5114 Nôwdâb (1), *noble*

NOE
3575 Nôĕ (5), *rest*

NOGAH
5052 Nôgahh (2), *brilliancy*

NOHAH
5119 Nôwchâh (1), *quietude*

NOISE
1949 hûwm (2), to *make an uproar; agitate*
1993 hâmâh (4), to *be in great commotion*
1995 hâmôwn (4), *noise, tumult; many, crowd*
1998 hemyâh (1), *sound, tone*
6476 pâtsach (1), to *break out in sound*
6963 qôwl (48), *voice or sound*
7267 rôgez (1), *disquiet; anger*
7452 rêa' (1), *crash; noise; shout*
7588 shâ'ôwn (8), *uproar; destruction*
8085 shâma' (2), to *hear intelligently*
8643 teʳûw'âh (1), *battle-cry; clangor*
8663 teʳshû'âh (1), *crashing or clamor*
2350 thôrubĕô (1), to *disturb; clamor*
4500 rhŏizĕdŏn (1), *with a crash, with a roar*
5456 phônē (1), *voice, sound*

NOISED
191 akŏuō (1), to *hear; obey*
1096+5408 ginŏmai (1), to *be, become*
1255 dialalĕō (1), to *converse, discuss*

NOISOME
1942 havvâh (1), *desire; craving*
7451 ra' (2), *bad; evil*
2556 kakŏs (1), *bad, evil, wrong*

NON
5126 Nûwn (1), *perpetuity*

NOON
6672 tsôhar (11), *window: noon time*
3314 mĕsēmbria (1), *midday; south*

NOONDAY
6672 tsôhar (10), *window: noon time*

NOONTIDE
6256+6672 'êth (1), *time*

NOPH
5297 Nôph (7), *Noph*

NOPHAH
5302 Nôphach (1), *gust*

NORTH
4215 meʳzâreh (1), north wind
6828 tsâphôwn (128), *north, northern*

1005 borrhas (2), *north*
5566 chōrŏs (1), *north-west* wind

NORTHERN
6828 tsâphôwn (1), *north, northern*
6830 tseʳphôwnîy (1), *northern*

NORTHWARD
6828 tsâphôwn (24), *north, northern*

NOSE
639 'aph (11), *nose or nostril; face; person*
2763 charam (1), to *devote to destruction*

NOSES
639 'aph (1), *nose or nostril; face; person*

NOSTRILS
639 'aph (13), *nose or nostril; face; person*
5156 neʳchîyr (1), pair of nostrils
5170 nachar (1), *snorting*

NOTABLE
2380 châzûwth (2), striking *appearance*
1110 gnōstŏs (1), *well-known*
1978 ĕpisēmŏs (1), *eminent, prominent*
2016 ĕpiphanēs (1), *conspicuous*

NOTE
2710 châqaq (1), to *engrave; to enact laws*
1978 ĕpisēmŏs (1), *eminent, prominent*
4593 sēmĕiŏō (1), to *mark for avoidance*

NOTED
7559 râsham (1), to *record*

NOTHING
369 'ayin (23), *there is no, i.e., not exist, none*
408 'al (3), *not; nothing*
657 'epheç (2), *end; no further*
1099 beʳlîymâh (1), *nothing whatever*
1115 biltîy (3), *not, except, without, unless*
1697 dâbâr (2), *word; matter; thing*
2600 chinnâm (2), *gratis, free*
3605 kôl (1), *all, any or every*
3808 lô' (25), no, *not*
3809 lâ' (Ch.) (1), *as nothing*
4591 mâ'aṭ (1), to *be, make small or few*
7535 raq (1), *merely; although*
8414 tôhûw (1), *waste, desolation, formless*
114 athĕtĕō (1), to *disesteem, neutralize*
3361 mē (1), *not; lest*
3367 mēdeis (27), *not even one*
3385 mēti (2), *whether at all*

3756 ŏu (4), *no or not*
3762 ŏudĕis (66), *none, nobody, nothing*
3777 ŏutĕ (1), *not even*

NOTICE
5234 nâkar (1), to *acknowledge*
4293 prŏkataggĕllō (1), to *predict, promise*

NOTWITHSTANDING
389 'ak (6), *surely; only, however*
657 'epheç (1), *end; no further*
7535 raq (2), *merely; although*
235 alla (1), *but, yet, except, instead*
4133 plēn (4), *albeit, save that, rather, yet*

NOUGHT
205 'âven (1), *trouble, vanity, wickedness*
369 'ayin (1), *there is no, i.e., not exist, none*
408+3972 'al (1), *not; nothing*
434 'ĕlûwl (1), good for *nothing*
656 'âpheç (1), to *cease*
657 'epheç (1), *end; no further*
659 'êpha' (1), *nothing*
2600 chinnâm (6), *gratis, free*
3808 lô' (1), no, *not*
3808+1697 lô' (1), no, *not*
3808+1952 lô' (1), no, *not*
5034 nâbêl (1), to *wilt; to fall away; to be foolish*
6331 pûwr (1), to *crush*
6544 pâra' (1), to *loosen; to expose, dismiss*
6565 pârar (2), to *break up; to violate, frustrate*
8045 shâmad (1), to *desolate*
8414 tôhûw (2), *waste, desolation, formless*
557 apĕlĕgmŏs (1), *refutation, discrediting*
1432 dōrĕan (1), *gratuitously, freely*
1847 ĕxŏudĕnŏō (1), to *be treated with contempt*
1848 ĕxŏuthĕnĕō (3), to *treat with contempt*
2049 ĕrēmŏō (1), to *lay waste*
2647 kataluō (3), to *demolish*
2673 katargĕō (2), to *be, render entirely useless*
3762 ŏudĕis (1), *none, nobody, nothing*

NOURISH
1431 gâdal (2), to *be great, make great*
2421 châyâh (1), to *live; to revive*
3557 kûwl (2), to *keep in; to maintain*

NOURISHED
1431 gâdal (1), to *be great, make great*

2421 châyâh (1), to *live; to revive*
3557 kûwl (1), to *keep in; to measure*
7235 râbâh (1), to *increase*
397 anatrĕphō (2), to *rear, care for*
1789 ĕntrĕphō (1), to *educate; to be trained*
5142 trĕphō (3), to *nurse, feed, care for*

NOURISHER
3557 kûwl (1), to *keep in; to measure*

NOURISHETH
1625 ĕktrĕphō (1), to *cherish or train*

NOURISHING
1431 gâdal (1), to *be great, make great*

NOURISHMENT
2023 ĕpichŏrēgĕō (1), to *fully supply; to aid*

NOVICE
3504 nĕŏphutŏs (1), *young convert*

NOW
116 ĕdayin (Ch.) (2), *then*
227 'âz (2), *at that time or place; therefore*
645 'êphôw (10), *then*
1768 dîy (Ch.) (1), *that; of*
2008 hênnâh (1), *from here; from there*
2088 zeh (3), *this or that*
3117 yôwm (4), *day; time period*
3528 keʳbâr (4), *long ago, formerly, hitherto*
3588 kîy (2), *for, that because*
3705 keʳan (Ch.) (14), *now*
4994 nâ' (172), *I pray!, please!, I beg you!*
6254 'Ashteʳrâthîy (1), *Ashterathite*
6258 'attâh (401), *at this time, now*
6288 peʳôrâh (3), *foliage, branches*
6471 pa'am (5), *time; step; occurence*
737 arti (25), *just now; at once*
1160 dapanē (2), *expense, cost*
1161 dĕ (160), *but, yet; and then*
1211 dē (1), *now, then; indeed, therefore*
2235 ēdē (3), *even now*
2236 hēdista (38), *with great pleasure*
2532 kai (5), *and; or; even; also*
3063 lŏipŏn (2), *remaining; finally*
3568 nun (127), *now; the present or immediate*
3570 nuni (20), *just now, indeed, in fact*
3765 ŏukĕti (5), *not yet, no longer*
3767 ŏun (12), *certainly, accordingly*

5927 'âlâh (9), to *ascend, be high, mount*
5930 'ôlâh (1), *sacrifice wholly consumed in fire*
6213 'âsâh (2), to *make*
7126 qârab (1), to *approach, bring near*
7133 qorbân (66), sacrificial *present*
8573 tᵉnûwphâh (6), *undulation* of offerings
8641 tᵉrûwmâh (40), *sacrifice, tribute*
4374 prŏsphĕrō (2), to *present to; to treat as*
4376 prŏsphŏra (8), *presentation; oblation*

OFFERINGS
1890 habhâb (1), *gift given as a sacrifice*
2077 zebach (5), *animal flesh; sacrifice*
4503 minchâh (16), *tribute; offering*
5262 neçek (1), *libation; cast idol*
7133 qorbân (1), sacrificial *present*
8641 tᵉrûwmâh (10), *sacrifice, tribute*
1435 dōrŏn (1), *sacrificial present*
3646 hŏlŏkautōma (3), *wholly-consumed sacrifice*
4376 prŏsphŏra (1), *presentation; oblation*

OFFICE
3653 kên (1), *pedestal* or *station* of a basin
4612 ma'ămâd (1), *position; attendant*
5656 'ăbôdâh (3), *work*
6486 pᵉquddâh (1), *visitation; punishment*
1247 diakŏnĕō (2), to *wait upon, serve*
1248 diakŏnia (1), *attendance, aid, service*
1984 ĕpiskŏpē (1), *episcopate*
2405 hiĕratĕia (2), *priestly office*
2407 hiĕratĕuō (1), to *be a priest*
4234 praxis (1), *act; function*

OFFICER
5324 nâtsab (1), to *station*
5333 nᵉtsîyb (1), *military post; statue*
5631 çârîyç (5), *eunuch; official* of state
6496 pâqîyd (2), *superintendent, officer*
4233 praktōr (2), *official collector*
5257 hupĕrĕtēs (1), *servant, attendant*

OFFICERS
5324 nâtsab (6), to *station*
5631 çârîyç (7), *eunuch; official* of state
6213 'âsâh (1), to *do*
6485 pâqad (3), to *visit, care for, count*
6486 pᵉquddâh (3), *visitation; punishment*

6496 pâqîyd (3), *superintendent, officer*
7227 rab (1), *great*
7860 shôṭêr (23), to *write; official who is a scribe*
5257 hupĕrĕtēs (10), *servant, attendant*

OFFICES
4929 mishmâr (1), *guard; deposit; usage; example*
4931 mishmereth (1), *watch, sentry, post*
6486 pᵉquddâh (2), *visitation; punishment*

OFFSCOURING
5501 çᵉchîy (1), *refuse*
4067 pĕripsōma (1), *scum, garbage*

OFFSPRING
6631 tse'ĕtsâ' (9), *produce, children*
1085 gĕnŏs (3), *kin*

OFT
1767 day (1), *enough, sufficient*
3740 hŏsakis (1), *as often as, when*
4178 pŏllakis (5), *many times, i.e. frequently*
4183 pŏlus (1), *much, many*
4212 pŏsakis (1), *how many times*
4435 pugmē (1), *with the fist*

OFTEN
3740 hŏsakis (6), *as often as, when*
4178 pŏllakis (3), *many times, i.e. frequently*
4212 pŏsakis (2), *how many times*
4437 puknŏs (2), *frequent; frequently*

OFTENER
4437 puknŏs (1), *frequent; frequently*

OFTENTIMES
6471+7227 pa'am (1), *time; step; occurence*
6471+7969 pa'am (1), *time; step; occurence*
4178 pŏllakis (3), *many times, i.e. frequently*
4183+5550 pŏlus (1), *much, many*

OFTTIMES
4178 pŏllakis (3), *many times, i.e. frequently*

OG
5747 'Ôwg (22), *round*

OH
518 'îm (1), *whether?; if, although; Oh that!*
577 'ânnâ' (1), *oh now!, I ask you!*
994 bîy (7), *Oh that!*
3863 lûw' (2), *if; would that!*
4994 nâ' (6), *I pray!, please!, I beg you!*

OHAD
161 'Ôhad (2), *unity*

OHEL
169 'Ôhel (1), *Ohel*

OIL
3323 yitshâr (21), *olive oil; anointing*
4887 mᵉshach (Ch.) (2), *olive oil*
6671 tsâhar (1), to *press out olive oil*
8081 shemen (163), *olive oil, wood, lotions*
1637 ĕlaiŏn (11), *olive oil*

OILED
8081 shemen (2), *olive oil, wood, lotions*

OINTMENT
4841 merqâchâh (1), *unguent-kettle*
4842 mirqachath (1), *aromatic unguent*
4888 mishchâh (1), *unction; gift*
7545 rôqach (1), *aromatic, fragrance*
8081 shemen (11), *olive oil, wood, lotions*
3464 murŏn (12), *perfumed oil*

OINTMENTS
8081 shemen (3), *olive oil, wood, lotions*
3464 murŏn (2), *perfumed oil*

OLD
227 'âz (2), *at that time* or *place; therefore*
865 'ethmôwl (1), *heretofore, formerly*
1086 bâlâh (11), to *wear out, decay; consume*
1087 bâleh (5), *worn out*
1094 bᵉlôw' (3), *rags, worn out fabric*
1121 bên (132), *son, descendant; people*
1247 bar (Ch.) (1), *son, child; descendant*
1323 bath (1), *daughter, descendant, woman*
2204 zâqên (26), to *be old, venerated*
2205 zâqên (41), *old, venerated*
2208 zâqûn (4), *old age*
2209 ziqnâh (6), *old age*
2416 chay (1), *alive; raw; fresh; life*
3117 yôwm (1), *day; time period*
3117+8140+3117 yôwm (1), *day; time period*
3453 yâshîysh (1), *old man*
3462 yâshên (2), to *sleep; to grow old, stale*
3465 yâshân (7), *old*
3833 lâbîy' (1), *lion, lioness*
3918 layish (1), *lion*
5288 na'ar (1), *male child; servant*
5669 'âbûwr (2), *kept over; stored grain*
5703 'ad (1), *perpetuity; ancient*
5769 'ôwlâm (26), *eternity; ancient*
5957 'âlam (Ch.) (2), *forever*

6275 'âthaq (2), to *remove; to grow old*
6440 pânîym (3), *face; front*
6924 qedem (17), *East, eastern; antiquity*
6927 qadmâh (1), *priority in time; before; past*
6931 qadmôwnîy (2), *anterior time; oriental*
7223 rî'shôwn (2), *first*
7350 râchôwq (2), *remote, far*
7872 sêybâh (6), *old age*
7992 shᵉlîyshîy (2), *third*
8027 shâlash (3), to *be, triplicate*
744 archaiŏs (11), *original* or *primeval*
1088 gĕrŏn (1), *aged, old person*
1094 gĕras (1), *senility, old age*
1095 gĕraskō (2), to *be senescent, grow old*
1126 graŏdēs (1), *old lady-like, i.e. silly*
1332 diĕtēs (1), *of two years* in age
1541 hĕkatŏntaĕtēs (1), *centenarian*
1597 ĕkpalai (1), *long ago, for a long while*
3819 palai (2), *formerly; sometime since*
3820 palaiŏs (19), *not recent, worn out, old*
3822 palaiŏō (3), to *become worn out*
4218 pŏtĕ (2), *at some time, ever*
4245 prĕsbutĕrŏs (1), *elderly; older; presbyter*
4246 prĕsbutēs (1), *old man*
5550 chrŏnŏs (1), *space of time, period*

OLDNESS
3821 palaiŏtēs (1), *antiquatedness*

OLIVE
2132 zayith (27), *olive*
8081 shemen (4), *olive oil, wood, lotions*
65 agriĕlaiŏs (2), *wild olive tree*
1636 ĕlaia (4), *olive*
2565 kalliĕlaiŏs (1), *cultivated olive*

OLIVES
2132 zayith (4), *olive*
1636 ĕlaia (11), *olive*

OLIVET
2132 zayith (1), *olive*
1638 ĕlaiŏn (1), *Mt. of Olives*

OLIVEYARD
2132 zayith (1), *olive*

OLIVEYARDS
2132 zayith (5), *olive*

OLYMPAS
3632 ŏinŏphlugia (1), *drunkenness*

OMAR
201 'Ôwmâr (3), *talkative*

OMEGA
5598 Ō (4), last letter of the Greek alphabet

OMER
6016 'ômer (5), *sheaf* of grain; dry *measure*

OMERS
6016 'ômer (1), *sheaf* of grain; dry *measure*

OMITTED
863 aphiēmi (1), to *leave*; to *pardon, forgive*

OMNIPOTENT
3841 pantŏkratŏr (1), Absolute *sovereign*

OMRI
6018 'Omrîy (18), *heaping*

ONAM
208 'Ôwnâm (4), *strong*

ONAN
209 'Ôwnân (8), *strong*

ONCE
227 'âz (1), *at that time* or *place; therefore*
259 'echâd (15), *first*
996 bêyn (1), *between; "either...or"*
3162 yachad (1), *unitedly*
4118 mahêr (1), *in a hurry*
5750 'ôwd (1), *again; repeatedly; still; more*
6471 pa'am (10), *time; step; occurence*
6471+259 pa'am (1), *time; step; occurence*
530 hapax (15), *once for all*
2178 ĕphapax (5), *upon one occasion*
3366 mĕdĕ (1), *but not, not even; nor*
3826 pamplēthĕi (1), *in full multitude*
4218 pŏtĕ (2), at *some time, ever*

ONE
259 'echâd (658), *first*
376 'îysh (173), *man; male; someone*
428 'êl-leh (2), *these* or *those*
492 'almônîy (1), certain *so and so, whoever*
802 'ishshâh (8), *woman, wife; women, wives*
1397 geber (1), *person, man*
1571 gam (1), *also; even*
1668 dâ' (Ch.) (2), *this*
1836 dên (Ch.) (1), *this*
2063 zô'th (1), *this*
2088 zeh (10), *this* or *that*
2297 chad (1), *one*
2298 chad (Ch.) (5), *one; single; first; at once*
3605 kôl (1), *all, any*
3627 kᵉlîy (1), *implement, thing*
3671 kânâph (1), *edge* or *extremity; wing*
5315 nephesh (1), *life; breath; soul; wind*
6918 qâdôwsh (2), *sacred*
240 allēlōn (77), *one another*

243 allŏs (4), *different, other*
1438 hĕautŏu (6), *himself, herself, itself*
1515 ĕirēnē (1), *peace; health; prosperity*
1520 hēis (231), *one*
2087 hĕtĕrŏs (1), *other* or *different*
3303 mĕn (2), *not translated*
3391 mia (56), *one* or *first*
3442 mŏnŏphthalmŏs (2), *one-eyed*
3661 hŏmŏthumadŏn (12), *unanimously*
3675 hŏmŏphrōn (1), *like-minded*
3739 hŏs (1), *who, which, what, that*
3956 pas (2), *all, any, every, whole*
4861 sumpsuchŏs (1), *similar in sentiment*
5100 tis (35), *some* or *any* person or object
5129 tŏutōᵢ (1), *in this* person or thing

ONES
1121 bên (1), *son, descendant; people*

ONESIMUS
3682 Ŏnēsimŏs (4), *profitable*

ONESIPHORUS
3683 Ŏnēsiphŏrŏs (2), *profit-bearer*

ONIONS
1211 betsel (1), *onion*

ONLY
259 'echâd (2), *first*
389 'ak (33), *surely; only, however*
905 bad (35), *apart, only, besides*
910 bâdâd (1), *separate, alone*
2108 zûwlâh (1), *except; apart from; besides*
3162 yachad (2), *unitedly*
3173 yâchîyd (7), *only son; alone; beloved*
3535 kibsâh (1), *ewe sheep*
3697 kâçam (1), to *shear, clip*
7535 raq (52), *merely; although*
1520 hēis (1), *one*
3439 mŏnŏgĕnēs (9), *sole, one and only*
3440 mŏnŏn (62), *merely, just*
3441 mŏnŏs (24), *single, only; by oneself*

ONO
207 'Ôwnôw (5), *strong*

ONYCHA
7827 shᵉchêleth (1), *scale* or shell, *mussel*

ONYX
7718 shôham (11), (poss.) pale green *beryl* stone

OPEN
1540 gâlâh (6), to *denude; uncover*

3605 kôl (1), *all, any* or *every*
4725 mâqôwm (1), general *locality, place*
5869 'ayin (1), *eye; sight; fountain*
6358 pât̂ûwr (4), *opened; bud*
6363 peter (1), *firstling, first born*
6440 pânîym (13), *face; front*
6475 pâtsâh (3), to *rend, i.e. open*
6491 pâqach (10), to *open* the eyes
6555 pârats (1), to *break out*
6566 pâras (1), to *break apart, disperse, scatter*
6605 pâthach (49), to *open* wide; to *loosen*
6606 pᵉthach (Ch.) (1), to *open*
6610 pithchôwn (1), act of *opening* the mouth
8365 shâtham (2), to *unveil, i.e. open*
71 agō (1), to *lead*; to *bring, drive; to weigh*
343 anakaluptō (1), to *unveil*
455 anŏigō (21), to *open up*
1722+457 ĕn (1), *in; during; because of*
3856 paradĕigmatizō (1), to *expose to infamy*
4271 prŏdēlŏs (1), *obvious, evident*

OPENED
1540 gâlâh (3), to *denude; uncover*
3738 kârâh (1), to *dig*; to *plot; to bore, hew*
6473 pâ'ar (3), to *open wide*
6475 pâtsâh (7), to *rend, i.e. open*
6491 pâqach (7), to *open* the eyes
6589 pâsaq (1), to *dispart, i.e., spread*
6605 pâthach (51), to *open* wide; to *loosen*
6606 pᵉthach (Ch.) (1), to *open*
380 anaptussō (1), to *unroll* a scroll
455 anŏigō (53), to *open up*
1272 dianŏigō (6), to *open thoroughly*
4977 schizō (1), to *split* or *sever*
5136 trachēlizō (1), to *lay bare*

OPENEST
6605 pâthach (2), to *open* wide; to *loosen, begin*

OPENETH
1540 gâlâh (3), to *denude; uncover*
6363 peter (7), *firstling, first born*
6491 pâqach (2), to *open* the eyes

6589 pâsaq (1), to *dispart, i.e., spread*
6605 pâthach (4), to *open* wide; to *loosen, begin*
455 anŏigō (3), to *open up*
1272 dianŏigō (1), to *open thoroughly*

OPENING
4668 maphtêach (1), *opening; key*
4669 miphtâch (1), *utterance of lips*
6491 pâqach (1), to *open* the eyes
6495 pᵉqach-qôwach (1), *jail-delivery; salvation*
6605 pâthach (1), to *open* wide; to *loosen, begin*
6610 pithchôwn (1), act of *opening* the mouth
1272 dianŏigō (1), to *open thoroughly*

OPENINGS
6607 pethach (1), *opening; door, entrance*

OPENLY
5879 'Êynayim (1), *double fountain*
1219 dēmŏsiŏs (1), *public; in public*
1717 ĕmphanēs (1), *apparent in self, seen*
1722+3588+5318 ĕn (3), *in; during; because of*
1722+3954 ĕn (2), *in; during; because of*
3954 parrhēsia (4), *frankness, boldness*
5320 phanĕrŏs (2), *plainly, i.e. clearly*

OPERATION
4639 ma'ăseh (2), *action; labor*
1753 ĕnĕrgĕia (1), *efficiency, energy*

OPERATIONS
1755 ĕnĕrgēma (1), *effect, activity*

OPHEL
6077 'Ôphel (5), *fortress*

OPHIR
211 'Ôwphîyr (13), *Ophir*

OPHNI
6078 'Ophnîy (1), *Ophnite*

OPHRAH
6084 'Ophrâh (8), *female fawn*

OPINION
1843 dêa' (3), *knowledge*

OPINIONS
5587 çâ'îph (1), *divided in mind; sentiment*

OPPORTUNITY
170 akairĕŏmai (1), to *fail of a proper occasion*
2120 ĕukairia (2), *favorable occasion*
2540 kairŏs (2), *occasion, set time*

OPPOSE
475 antidiatithĕmai (1), *be disputatious*

OPPOSED
498 antitassŏmai (1),
oppose, resist

OPPOSEST
7852 sâṭam (1), *to*
persecute

OPPOSETH
480 antikĕimai (1), *to be*
an opponent

OPPOSITIONS
477 antithĕsis (1),
opposition

OPPRESS
1792 dâkâʾ (1), *to*
pulverize; be contrite
3238 yânâh (5), *to*
suppress; to maltreat
3905 lâchats (5), *to press;*
to distress
6206 ʾârats (1), *to awe; to*
dread; to harass
6231 ʾâshaq (9), *to*
oppress; to defraud
7703 shâdad (1), *to*
ravage
2616 katadunastĕuō (1),
to oppress, exploit

OPPRESSED
1790 dak (3), *injured,*
oppressed
2541 châmôwts (1),
violent
3238 yânâh (3), *to*
suppress; to maltreat
3905 lâchats (7), *to press;*
to distress
5065 nâgas (2), *to*
exploit; to tax, harass
6217 ʾâshûwq (1), *used*
tyranny
6231 ʾâshaq (11), *to*
oppress; to defraud
6234 ʾoshqâh (1),
anguish, trouble
7533 râtsats (6), *to crack*
in pieces, smash
2616 katadunastĕuō (1),
to oppress, exploit
2669 katapŏnĕō (1), *to*
harass, oppress

OPPRESSETH
3905 lâchats (1), *to press;*
to distress
6231 ʾâshaq (3), *to*
oppress; to defraud
6887 tsârar (1), *to cramp*

OPPRESSING
3238 yânâh (3), *to*
suppress; to maltreat

OPPRESSION
3238 yânâh (1), *to*
suppress; to maltreat
3906 lachats (7), *distress*
4939 mispâch (1),
slaughter
6115 ʾôtser (1), *closure;*
constraint
6125 ʾâqâh (1), *constraint*
6233 ʾôsheq (12), *injury;*
fraud; distress
7701 shôd (1), *violence,*
ravage, destruction

OPPRESSIONS
4642 maʾăshaqqâh (1),
oppression

6217 ʾâshûwq (2), *used*
tyranny

OPPRESSOR
376+2555 ʾîysh (1), *man;*
male; someone
3238 yânâh (1), *to*
suppress; to maltreat
4642 maʾăshaqqâh (1),
oppression
5065 nâgas (5), *to*
exploit; to tax, harass
6184 ʾârîyts (1), *powerful*
or tyrannical
6216 ʾâshôwq (1), *tyrant*
6231 ʾâshaq (2), *to*
oppress; to defraud
6693 tsûwq (2), *to*
oppress, distress

OPPRESSORS
3905 lâchats (1), *to press;*
to distress
5065 nâgas (2), *to*
exploit; to tax, harass
6184 ʾârîyts (2), *powerful*
or tyrannical
6231 ʾâshaq (2), *to*
oppress; to defraud
7429 râmaç (1), *to tread*
upon

ORACLE
1687 dᵉbîyr (16), *inmost*
part of the sanctuary
1697 dâbâr (1), *word;*
matter; thing

ORACLES
3051 lŏgiŏn (4),
utterance of God

ORATION
1215 dēmēgŏrĕō (1), *to*
address an assembly

ORATOR
3908 lachash (1),
incantation; amulet
4489 rhētōr (1), *legal*
advocate

ORCHARD
6508 pardêç (1), *park,*
cultivated garden area

ORCHARDS
6508 pardêç (1), *park,*
cultivated garden area

ORDAIN
3245 yâçad (1), *settle,*
establish a foundation
7760 sûwm (1), *to put,*
place
8239 shâphath (1), *to*
place or put
1299 diatassō (1), *to*
institute, prescribe
2525 kathistēmi (1), *to*
designate, constitute

ORDAINED
3245 yâçad (1), *settle,*
establish a foundation
3559 kûwn (1), *to set up:*
establish, fix, prepare
4483 mᵉnâʾ (Ch.) (1), *to*
count, appoint
5414 nâthan (2), *to give*
5975 ʾâmad (1), *to stand*
6186 ʾârak (2), *to set in a*
row, i.e. arrange,
6213 ʾâsâh (3), *to do or*
make
6965 qûwm (1), *to rise*

7760 sûwm (2), *to put,*
place
1096 ginŏmai (1), *to be,*
become
1299 diatassō (2), *to*
institute, prescribe
2525 kathistēmi (2), *to*
designate, constitute
2680 kataskĕuazō (1), *to*
prepare thoroughly
2919 krinō (1), *to decide;*
to try, condemn, punish
3724 hŏrizō (2), *to*
appoint, decree, specify
4160 pŏiĕō (1), *to make*
or do
4270 prŏgraphō (1), *to*
announce, prescribe
4282 prŏĕtŏimazō (1), *to*
fit up in advance
4304 prŏmĕlĕtaō (1), *to*
premeditate
5021 tassō (2), *to*
arrange, assign
5087 tithēmi (2), *to place*
5500 chĕirŏtŏnĕō (3), *to*
select or appoint

ORDAINETH
6466 pâʾal (1), *to do,*
make or practice

ORDER
631 ʾâçar (1), *to fasten; to*
join battle
1700 dibrâh (1), *reason,*
suit or style; because
3027 yâd (2), *hand; power*
3559 kûwn (3), *to set up:*
establish, fix, prepare
4634 maʾărâkâh (1),
arrangement, row; pile
4941 mishpâṭ (5), *verdict;*
formal decree; justice
5468 çeder (1), *to*
arrange, order
6186 ʾârak (19), *to set in*
a row, i.e. arrange,
6187 ʾêrek (1), *pile,*
equipment, estimate
6471 paʾam (1), *time;*
step; occurence
6680 tsâvâh (3), *to*
constitute, enjoin
7947 shâlab (1), *to make*
equidistant
8626 tâqan (1), *to*
straighten; to compose
1299 diatassō (3), *to*
institute, prescribe
1930 ĕpidiŏrthŏō (1), *to*
arrange additionally
2517 kathĕxēs (3), *in a*
sequence, subsequent
5001 tagma (1), *series or*
succession
5010 taxis (10),
succession; kind

ORDERED
3559 kûwn (1), *to set up:*
establish, fix, prepare
4634 maʾărâkâh (1),
arrangement, row; pile
6186 ʾârak (2), *to set in a*
row, i.e. arrange,

ORDERETH
7760 sûwm (1), *to put,*
place

ORDERINGS
6486 pᵉquddâh (1),
visitation; punishment

ORDERLY
4748 stŏichĕō (1), *to*
follow, walk; to conform

ORDINANCE
2706 chôq (6),
appointment; allotment
2708 chuqqâh (12), *to*
delineate
3027 yâd (1), *hand; power*
4931 mishmereth (3),
watch, sentry, post
4941 mishpâṭ (5), *verdict;*
formal decree; justice
1296 diatagē (1),
institution
2937 ktisis (1), *formation*

ORDINANCES
2706 chôq (3),
appointment; allotment
2708 chuqqâh (10), *to*
delineate
4687 mitsvâh (1),
command
4941 mishpâṭ (6), *verdict;*
formal decree; justice
1345 dikaiōma (3),
statute or decision
1378 dŏgma (3), *law*
1379 dŏgmatizō (1), *to*
submit to a certain rule
3862 paradŏsis (1),
precept; tradition

ORDINARY
2706 chôq (1),
appointment; allotment

OREB
6157 ʾârôb (6), *swarming*
mosquitoes

OREN
767 ʾÔren (1), *ash tree*

ORGAN
5748 ʾûwgâb (3),
reed-instrument

ORGANS
5748 ʾûwgâb (1),
reed-instrument

ORION
3685 Kᵉçîyl (3),
constellation Orion

ORNAMENT
642 ʾêphuddâh (1),
plating
2481 châlîy (1), *polished*
trinket, ornament
3880 livyâh (2), *wreath*
5716 ʾădîy (2), *finery;*
outfit; headstall

ORNAMENTS
5716 ʾădîy (9), *finery;*
outfit; headstall
5914 ʾekeç (1), *anklet,*
bangle
6287 pᵉʾêr (1), *fancy*
head-dress
6807 tsᵉʾâdâh (1), *march;*
ankle-chain
7720 sahărôn (2), *round*
pendant or crescent

ORNAN
771 ʾÔrnân (11), *strong*

ORPAH
6204 ʾOrpâh (2), *mane*

G

ORPHANS
3490 yâthôwm (1), child alone, fatherless child

OSEE
5617 Hōsēĕ (1), deliverer

OSHEA
1954 Hôwshêä' (2), deliverer

OSPRAY
5822 'oznîyâh (2), (poss.) sea-eagle

OSSIFRAGE
6538 pereç (2), kind of eagle

OSTRICH
5133 nôwtsâh (1), plumage

OSTRICHES
3283 yâ'ên (1), ostrich

OTHER
251 'âch (1), brother; relative; member
259 'echâd (32), first
269 'achôwth (1), sister
312 'achêr (99), other, another, different; next, more
317 'ochŏrîy (Ch.) (1), other, another
321 'ochŏrân (Ch.) (3), other, another
428 'êl-leh (3), these or those
2063 zô'th (2), this
2088 zeh (16), this or that
3541 kôh (1), thus
3671 kânâph (1), edge or extremity; wing
5048 neged (2), over against or before
5676 'êber (25), opposite side; east
6311 pôh (5), here or hence
7453 rêa' (2), associate; one close
7605 shᵉ'âr (1), remainder
8145 shênîy (36), second; again
237 allachŏthĕn (1), from elsewhere
240 allēlôn (5), one another
243 allŏs (51), different, other
244 allotriĕpiskŏpŏs (1), meddler, busybody
245 allŏtriŏs (2), not one's own
492 antiparĕrchŏmai (2), to go along opposite
846 autŏs (1), he, she, it
1520 hĕis (7), one
1565 ĕkĕinŏs (2), that one
1622 ĕktŏs (1), aside from, besides; except
2084 hĕtĕrŏglŏssŏs (1), foreigner
2085 hĕtĕrŏdidaskalĕō (1), to instruct differently
2087 hĕtĕrŏs (34), other or different
2548 kakĕinŏs (2), likewise that or those

3062 lŏipŏi (16), remaining ones
3739 hŏs (2), who, which, what, that
4008 pĕran (12), across, beyond

OTHERS
312 'achêr (9), other, another, different; next
428 'êl-leh (1), these
243 allŏs (29), different, other
245 allŏtriŏs (1), not one's own
2087 hĕtĕrŏs (11), other or different
3062 lŏipŏi (9), remaining ones
3588 hŏ (2), "the," i.e. the definite article
3739 hŏs (1), who, which

OTHERWISE
176 'ôw (1), or, whether
3808 lô' (1), no, not
243 allŏs (5), different, other
247 allŏs (1), differently
1490 ĕi dĕ mē(gĕ) (3), but if not
1893 ĕpĕi (4), since
2085 hĕtĕrŏdidaskalĕō (1), to instruct differently
2088 hĕtĕrŏs (1), differently, otherly

OTHNI
6273 'Otnîy (1), forcible

OTHNIEL
6274 'Othnîy'êl (7), force of God

OUCHES
4865 mishbᵉtsâh (8), reticulated setting

OUGHT
1697 dâbâr (2), word; matter; thing
3972 mᵉ'ûwmâh (6), something; anything
4465 mimkâr (1), merchandise
1163 dĕi (29), it is (was) necessary
3762 ŏudĕis (1), none, nobody, nothing
3784 ŏphĕilō (15), to owe; to be under obligation
5100 tis (8), some or any
5534 chrē (1), it needs (must or should) be

OUGHTEST
1163 dĕi (3), it is (was) necessary

OUTCAST
5080 nâdach (1), to push off, scattered

OUTCASTS
1760 dâchâh (3), to push down; to totter
5080 nâdach (4), to push off, scattered

OUTER
2435 chîytsôwn (1), outer wall side; exterior; secular
1857 ĕxōtĕrŏs (3), exterior, outer

OUTGOINGS
4161 môwtsâ' (1), going forth
8444 tôwtsâ'âh (7), exit, boundary; deliverance

OUTLANDISH
5237 nokrîy (1), foreign; non-relative

OUTLIVED
748+3117+310 'ârak (1), to be, make long

OUTMOST
7020 qîytsôwn (1), terminal, end
7097 qâtseh (2), extremity

OUTRAGEOUS
7858 sheṭeph (1), deluge, torrent

OUTRUN
4370+5032 prŏstrĕchō (1), to hasten by running

OUTSIDE
2351 chûwts (2), outside, outdoors; open market
7097 qâtseh (3), extremity
1623 hĕktŏs (1), sixth
1855 ĕxōthĕn (2), outside, external (-ly)

OUTSTRETCHED
5186 nâṭâh (3), to stretch or spread out

OUTWARD
2435 chîytsôwn (8), outer wall side; exterior
5869 'ayin (1), eye; sight; fountain
1722+3588+5318 ĕn (1), in; during; because of
1854 ĕxō (1), out, outside
1855 ĕxōthĕn (2), outside, external (-ly)
4383 prŏsōpŏn (1), face, presence

OUTWARDLY
1722+5318 ĕn (1), in; during; because of
1855 ĕxōthĕn (1), outside, external (-ly)

OUTWENT
4281 prŏĕrchŏmai (1), to go onward, precede

OVEN
8574 tannûwr (10), fire-pot
2823 klibanŏs (2), earthen pot

OVENS
8574 tannûwr (1), fire-pot

OVER
413 'êl (19), to, toward
1157 bᵉ'ad (1), up to or over against
1541 gᵉlâh (Ch.) (1), to reveal mysteries
1591 gᵉnêbâh (1), something stolen
1869 dârak (1), to tread, trample; to walk, lead
2498 châlaph (1), to hasten away; to pass on
3148 yôwthêr (1), moreover; rest; gain
4136 mûwl (14), in front of, opposite
4480 min (1), from, out of

4605 ma'al (3), upward, above, overhead
5048 neged (27), over against or before
5226 nêkach (1), opposite
5227 nôkach (9), opposite, in front of
5414 nâthan (1), to give
5462 çâgar (2), to shut up; to surrender
5534 çâkar (1), to shut up; to surrender
5674 'âbar (171), to cross over; to transition
5736 'âdaph (3), to have surplus
5764 'ûwl (2), nursing babe
5848 'âṭaph (1), to shroud, i.e. clothe
5921 'al (406), above, over, upon, or against
5922 'al (Ch.) (12), above, over, upon, or against
5924 'êllâ' (Ch.) (1), above
5927 'âlâh (1), to ascend, be high, mount
5975 'âmad (3), to stand
5980 'ummâh (23), near, beside, along with
6440 pânîym (2), face; front
6743 tsâlach (1), to push forward
6903 qᵉbêl (Ch.) (1), in front of, before
7235 râbâh (2), to increase
481 antikru (1), opposite of
495 antipĕran (1), on the opposite side
561 apĕnanti (2), opposite, before
1224 diabainō (1), to pass by, over, across
1276 diapĕraō (5), to cross over
1277 diaplĕō (1), to sail through, across
1330 diĕrchŏmai (4), to traverse, travel through
1537 ĕk (3), out, out of
1608 ĕkpŏrnĕuō (1), to be utterly unchaste
1722 ĕn (1), in; during; because of
1883 ĕpanō (6), over or on
1909 ĕpi (49), on, upon
1924 ĕpigraphō (1), to inscribe, write upon
2596 kata (2), down; according to
2634 katakuriĕuō (1), to control, lord over
2713 katĕnanti (4), directly opposite
3346 mĕtatithēmi (1), to transport; to exchange
3860 paradidōmi (2), to hand over
3928 parĕrchŏmai (1), to go by; to perish
4008 pĕran (3), across, beyond
4012 pĕri (2), about; around
4052 pĕrissĕuō (1), to superabound

4121 plĕŏnazō (1), to
superabound
4291 prŏistēmi (1), to
preside; to practice
5055 tĕlĕō (1), to end, i.e.
complete, execute
5228 hupĕr (1), over;
above; beyond
5231 hupĕranō (1),
above, upward
5240 hupĕrĕkchunō (1),
to overflow

OVERCAME
2634 katakuriĕuō (1), to
control, lord over
3528 nikaō (2), to
subdue, conquer

OVERCHARGE
1912 ĕpibarĕō (1), to be
severe toward

OVERCHARGED
925 barunō (1), to
burden; to grieve

OVERCOME
1464 gûwd (2), to attack
1986 hâlam (1), to strike,
beat, stamp, conquer
2476 chălûwshâh (1),
defeat
3201 yâkôl (1), to be able
3898 lâcham (2), to fight
a battle
5674 'âbar (1), to cross
over; to transition
7292 râhab (1), to urge
severely, i.e. importune
2274 hēttaō (2), to rate
lower, be inferior
3528 nikaō (10), to
subdue, conquer

OVERCOMETH
3528 nikaō (11), to
subdue, conquer

OVERDRIVE
1849 dâphaq (1), to
knock; to press severely

OVERFLOW
6687 tsûwph (1), to
overflow
7783 shûwq (2), to
overflow
7857 shâṭaph (10), to
gush; to inundate

OVERFLOWED
7857 shâṭaph (1), to
gush; to inundate
2626 katakluzō (1), to
deluge, flood

OVERFLOWETH
4390 mâlê' (1), to fill; be
full

OVERFLOWING
1065 bᵉkîy (1), weeping
2230 zerem (1), gush of
water, flood
7857 shâṭaph (8), to
gush; to inundate
7858 sheṭeph (1), deluge,
torrent

OVERFLOWN
3332 yâtsaq (1), to pour
out
4390 mâlê' (1), to fill; be
full

7857 shâṭaph (1), to
gush; to inundate
OVERLAID
2645 châphâh (4), to
cover; to veil, to encase
5968 'âlaph (1), to be
languid, faint
6823 tsâphâh (28), to
sheet over with metal
7901 shâkab (1), to lie
down
4028 pĕrikaluptō (1), to
cover eyes; to plait

OVERLAY
2902 ṭûwach (1), to
whitewash
6823 tsâphâh (12), to
sheet over with metal

OVERLAYING
6826 tsippûwy (2),
encasement with metal

OVERLIVED
748+3117+310 'ârak (1),
to be, make long

OVERMUCH
4055 pĕrissŏtĕrŏs (1),
more superabundant

OVERPASS
5674 'âbar (1), to cross
over; to transition

OVERPAST
5674 'âbar (2), to cross
over; to transition

OVERPLUS
5736 'âdaph (1), to have
surplus

OVERRAN
5674 'âbar (1), to cross
over; to transition

OVERRUNNING
5674 'âbar (1), to cross
over; to transition

OVERSEE
5329 nâtsach (1), i.e. to
be eminent

OVERSEER
6485 pâqad (2), to visit,
care for, count
6496 pâqîyd (4),
superintendent, officer
7860 shôṭêr (1), to write;
official who is a scribe

OVERSEERS
5329 nâtsach (2), i.e. to
be eminent
6485 pâqad (2), to visit,
care for, count
6496 pâqîyd (1),
superintendent, officer
1985 ĕpiskŏpŏs (1),
overseer, supervisor

OVERSHADOW
1982 ĕpiskiazō (2), to
cast a shade upon

OVERSHADOWED
1982 ĕpiskiazō (3), to
cast a shade upon

OVERSIGHT
4870 mishgeh (1), error
5414 nâthan (1), to give
5921 'al (2), above, over,
upon, or against
6485 pâqad (4), to visit,
care for, count

6486 pᵉquddâh (2),
visitation; punishment
1983 ĕpiskŏpĕō (1), to
oversee; to beware

OVERSPREAD
5310 nâphats (1), to dash
to pieces; to scatter

OVERSPREADING
3671 kânâph (1), edge or
extremity; wing

OVERTAKE
5066 nâgash (2), to be,
come, bring near
5381 nâsag (14), to reach
2638 katalambanō (1), to
seize; to possess

OVERTAKEN
5381 nâsag (1), to reach
4301 prŏlambanō (1), to
take before

OVERTAKETH
5381 nâsag (1), to reach

OVERTHREW
2015 hâphak (4), to
change, overturn
4114 mahpêkâh (3),
destruction
5286 nâ'ar (1), to growl
5287 nâ'ar (1), to tumble
about
390 anastrĕphō (1), to
remain, to live
2690 katastrĕphō (2), to
upset, overturn

OVERTHROW
1760 dâchâh (1), to push
down; to totter
2015 hâphak (5), to
change, overturn
2018 hâphêkâh (1),
destruction, demolition
2040 hâraç (2), to pull
down; break, destroy
4073 mᵉdachphâh (1),
ruin
4114 mahpêkâh (2),
destruction
5186 nâṭâh (1), to stretch
or spread out
5307 nâphal (2), to fall
5422 nâthats (1), to tear
down
396 anatrĕpō (1), to
overturn, destroy
2647 kataluō (1), to
demolish
2692 katastrŏphē (1),
catastrophical ruin

OVERTHROWETH
2040 hâraç (1), to pull
down; break, destroy
5557 çâlaph (4), to
wrench; to subvert

OVERTHROWN
2015 hâphak (4), to
change, overturn
2040 hâraç (2), to pull
down; break, destroy
3782 kâshal (2), to totter,
waver; to falter
4114 mahpêkâh (1),
destruction
5307 nâphal (3), to fall
5791 'âvath (1), to wrest,
twist

8045 shâmad (1), to
desolate
8058 shâmaṭ (1), to
jostle; to let alone
2693 katastrōnnumi (1),
to prostrate, i.e. slay

OVERTOOK
1692 dâbaq (3), to cling
or adhere; to catch
5381 nâsag (7), to reach

OVERTURN
2015 hâphak (1), to
change, overturn
5754 'avvâh (1),
overthrow, ruin

OVERTURNED
2015 hâphak (1), to
change, overturn

OVERTURNETH
2015 hâphak (3), to
change, overturn

OVERWHELM
5307 nâphal (1), to fall

OVERWHELMED
3680 kâçâh (2), to cover
5848 'âṭaph (5), to
shroud, i.e. clothe
7857 shâṭaph (1), to
gush; to inundate

OWE
3784 ŏphĕilō (1), to owe;
to be under obligation

OWED
3781 ŏphĕilĕtēs (1),
person indebted
3784 ŏphĕilō (2), to owe;
to be under obligation

OWEST
3784 ŏphĕilō (3), to owe;
to be under obligation
4359 prŏsŏphĕilō (1), to
be indebted

OWETH
3784 ŏphĕilō (1), to owe;
to be under obligation

OWL
1323+3284 bath (2),
daughter, descendant
3244 yanshûwph (3), bird
3563 kôwç (3), cup;
(poss.) owl
3917 lîylîyth (1), night
spectre (spirit)
7091 qippôwz (1),
arrow-snake

OWLS
1323+3284 bath (6),
daughter, descendant

OWN
249 'ezrâch (15), native
born
3548 kôhên (2), one
officiating as a priest
5315 nephesh (1), life;
breath; soul; wind
7522 râtsôwn (1), delight
830 authairĕtŏs (1),
self-chosen
846 autŏs (1), he, she, it
848 hautŏu (15), self
849 autŏchĕir (1),
self-handed, personally
1103 gnēsiŏs (2),
genuine, true

1438 hĕautŏu (24),
himself, herself, itself
1683 ĕmautŏu (2), *myself*
1699 ĕmŏs (2), *my*
2398 idiŏs (76), *private or
separate*
2596 kata (1), *down;
according to*
4572 sĕautŏu (2), *of
yourself*

OWNER
113 'âdôwn (1),
sovereign, i.e. *controller*
1167 ba'al (10), *master;
husband; owner; citizen*
7069 qânâh (1), *to create;
to procure*
3490 nauklĕrŏs (1), ship
captain

OWNERS
1167 ba'al (4), *master;
husband; owner; citizen*
2962 kuriŏs (1), *supreme,
controller, Mr.*

OWNETH
2076 ĕsti (1), he (she or
it) *is;* they *are*

OX
441 'allûwph (1), *friend,
one familiar; chieftain,
leader*
1241 bâqâr (3), *plowing
ox; herd*
7794 shôwr (53), *bullock*
8377 t͏eʹôw (1), *antelope*
1016 bŏus (4), *ox, cattle*

OXEN
441 'allûwph (1), *friend,
one familiar; chieftain*
504 'eleph (2), *ox; cow or
cattle*
1241 bâqâr (74), *plowing
ox; herd*
5091 nâhâh (1), *to
bewail; to assemble*
6499 par (2), *bullock*
7794 shôwr (8), *bullock*
8450 tôwr (Ch.) (4), *bull*
1016 bŏus (4), *ox, cattle*
5022 taurŏs (2), *bullock,
ox*

OZEM
684 'Ôtsem (2), *strong*

OZIAS
3604 Ŏzias (2), *strength
of Jehovah*

OZNI
244 'Oznîy (1), *having
(quick) ears*

OZNITES
244 'Oznîy (1), *having
(quick) ears*

PAARAI
6474 Pa'ăray (1), *yawning*

PACATIANA
3818 Pakatianē (1),
Pacatianian

PACES
6806 tsa'ad (1), *pace* or
regular *step*

PACIFIED
3722 kâphar (1), *to
placate* or *cancel*
7918 shâkak (1), *to lay* a
trap; *to allay*

PACIFIETH
3240 yânach (1), *to allow
to stay*
3711 kâphâh (1), *to tame*
or *subdue*

PACIFY
3722 kâphar (1), *to
cover;* to *placate*

PADAN
6307 Paddân (1),
table-land of Aram

PADAN-ARAM
6307 Paddân (10),
table-land of Aram

PADDLE
3489 yâthêd (1), tent peg

PADON
6303 Pâdôwn (2), *ransom*

PAGIEL
6295 Pag'îy'êl (5),
accident of God

PAHATH-MOAB
6355 Pachath Môw'âb
(6), *pit of Moăb*

PAI
6464 Pâ'ûw (1),
screaming

PAID
3052 yᵉhab (Ch.) (1), to
give
5414 nâthan (1), to *give*
591 apŏdidōmi (2), to
give away

PAIN
2256 chebel (1),
company, band
2342 chûwl (6), to *dance,
whirl; to writhe* in pain
2427 chîyl (3), *throe* of
painful childbirth
2470 châlâh (1), to be
weak, sick, afflicted
2479 chalchâlâh (4),
writhing in childbirth
3510 kâ'ab (1), to feel
pain; to *grieve;* to *spoil*
3511 kᵉʹêb (1), *suffering;
adversity*
4341 mak'ôb (2),
anguish; affliction
5999 'âmâl (1), *wearing
effort; worry*
4192 pŏnŏs (2), *toil,* i.e.
anguish

PAINED
2342 chûwl (3), to *dance,
whirl; to writhe* in pain
3176 yâchal (1), to *wait;
to be patient, hope*
928 basanizō (1), to
torture, torment

PAINFUL
5999 'âmâl (1), *wearing
effort; worry*

PAINFULNESS
3449 mŏchthŏs (1),
sadness

PAINS
4712 mêtsar (1), *trouble*
6735 tsîyr (1), *hinge;
trouble*
4192 pŏnŏs (1), *toil,* i.e.
anguish

5604 ōdin (1), *pang* of
childbirth; *agony*

PAINTED
4886 mâshach (1), to *rub
or smear* with oil
7760+6320 sûwm (1), to
put, place

PAINTEDST
3583 kâchal (1), to *paint*
the eyes with stibnite

PAINTING
6320 pûwk (1), *stibium*

PAIR
2201 zĕugŏs (1), *team,
pair*
2218 zugŏs (1), *coupling,
yoke*

PALACE
643 'appeden (1),
pavilion or palace-tent
759 'armôwn (4), *citadel,
high fortress*
1002 bîyrâh (17), *palace,
citadel*
1004 bayith (1), *house;
temple; family, tribe*
1055 bîythân (3), *large
house*
1964 hêykâl (8), *palace;
temple; hall*
1965 hêykal (Ch.) (4),
palace; temple
2038 harmôwn (1), *high
castle* or fortress
2918 ţîyrâh (1), *fortress;
hamlet*
833 aulē (7), *palace;
house; courtyard*
4232 praitōriŏn (1),
court-room or palace

PALACES
759 'armôwn (27),
citadel, high fortress
1964 hêykâl (3), *palace;
temple; hall*
2918 ţîyrâh (2), *fortress;
hamlet*

PALAL
6420 Pâlâl (1), *judge*

PALE
2357 châvar (1), to
blanch with shame
5515 chlōrŏs (1),
greenish, verdant

PALENESS
3420 yêrâqôwn (1),
paleness; mildew

PALESTINA
6429 Pᵉlesheth (3),
migratory

PALESTINE
6429 Pᵉlesheth (1),
migratory

PALLU
6396 Pallûw' (4),
distinguished

PALLUITES
6384 Pallû'îy (1), *Palluïte*

PALM
3709 kaph (2), hollow of
hand; *paw;* sole of foot
8558 tâmâr (12), *palm
tree*

8560 tômer (2), *palm
trunk*
8561 timmôr (17),
palm-like pilaster
4475 rhapisma (1), *slap,
strike*
5404 phŏinix (1),
palm-tree

PALMERWORM
1501 gâzâm (3), kind of
locust

PALMS
3709 kaph (4), hollow of
hand; *paw;* sole of foot
4474 rhapizō (1), to *slap,
rap, strike*
4475 rhapisma (1), *slap,
strike*
5404 phŏinix (1),
palm-tree

PALSIES
3886 paraluō (1), to be
paralyzed or enfeebled

PALSY
3885 paralutikŏs (10),
lame person
3886 paraluō (3), to be
paralyzed or enfeebled

PALTI
6406 Palţîy (1), *delivered*

PALTIEL
6409 Palţîy'êl (1),
deliverance of God

PALTITE
6407 Palţîy (1), *Paltite*

PAMPHYLIA
3828 Pamphulia (5),
every-tribal, i.e.
heterogeneous

PAN
3595 kîyôwr (1), *caldron;
washbowl*
4227 machăbath (6),
metal *pan* for baking in
4958 masrêth (1), *pan*

PANGS
2256 chebel (2),
company, band
2427 chîyl (2), *throe* of
painful childbirth
6735 tsîyr (3), *hinge;
herald, trouble*
6887 tsârar (2), to *cramp*

PANNAG
6436 Pannag (1), *food,*
(poss.) *pastry*

PANS
2281 châbêth (1),
griddle-*cake*
5518 çîyr (1), *thorn; hook*
6517 pârûwr (1), *skillet*
6745 tsêlâchâh (1),
flattened out *platter*

PANT
7602 shâ'aph (1), to be
angry; to *hasten*

PANTED
7602 shâ'aph (1), to be
angry; to *hasten*
8582 tâ'âh (1), to
vacillate, i.e. *reel*

PANTETH
5503 çâchar (1), to *travel*
round; to *palpitate*

6165 'ârag (2), to *long for*, *pant for*

PAPER
6169 'ârâh (1), *bulrushes, reeds*
5489 chartēs (1), *sheet of papyrus paper*

PAPHOS
3974 Paphŏs (2), *Paphus*

PAPS
7699 shad (1), female *breast*
3149 mastŏs (3), female *breast; chest* area

PARABLE
4912 mâshâl (17), pithy *maxim; taunt*
3850 parabŏlē (31), *fictitious narrative*
3942 parŏimia (1), *illustration; adage*

PARABLES
4912 mâshâl (1), pithy *maxim; taunt*
3850 parabŏlē (15), *fictitious narrative*

PARADISE
3857 paradĕisŏs (3), *park*

PARAH
6511 Pârâh (1), *heifer*

PARAMOURS
6370 pîylegesh (1), *concubine; paramour*

PARAN
6290 Pâ'rân (11), *ornamental*

PARBAR
6503 Parbâr (2), *Parbar or Parvar*

PARCEL
2513 chelqâh (5), *allotment*
5564 chōriŏn (1), *spot or plot* of ground

PARCHED
2788 chârêr (1), *arid, parched*
7039 qâlîy (6), *roasted ears of cereal grain*
8273 shârâb (1), *glow of the hot air; mirage*

PARCHMENTS
3200 mĕmbrana (1), *sheep-skin for writing*

PARDON
3722 kâphar (1), to *cover; to expiate*
5375 nâsâ' (3), to *lift up*
5545 çâlach (11), to *forgive*
5547 çᵉlîychâh (1), *pardon*

PARDONED
5545 çâlach (2), to *forgive*
7521 râtsâh (1), to *be pleased with; to satisfy*

PARDONETH
5375 nâsâ' (1), to *lift up*

PARE
6213 'âsâh (1), to *do or make*

PARENTS
1118 gŏnĕus (19), *parents*

3962 patēr (1), *father*
4269 prŏgŏnŏs (1), *ancestor*

PARLOUR
3957 lishkâh (1), *room*
5944 'ălîyâh (4), *upper things; second-story*

PARLOURS
2315 cheder (1), *apartment, chamber*

PARMASHTA
6534 Parmashtâ' (1), *Parmashta*

PARMENAS
3937 Parmĕnas (1), *constant*

PARNACH
6535 Parnak (1), *Parnak*

PAROSH
6551 Par'ôsh (5), *flea*

PARSHANDATHA
6577 Parshandâthâ' (1), *Parshandatha*

PART
2505 châlaq (3), to *be smooth; be slippery*
2506 chêleq (19), *allotment*
2513 chelqâh (1), *flattery; allotment*
2673 châtsâh (1), to *cut or split* in two; to *halve*
2677 chêtsîy (3), *half or middle, midst*
4481 min (Ch.) (5), *from or out of*
4490 mânâh (1), *ration; lot or portion*
4940 mishpâchâh (2), *family, clan, people*
5337 nâtsal (1), to *deliver; snatched* away
6418 pelek (7), *spindle-whorl; crutch*
6447 paç (Ch.) (2), *palm of the hand*
6504 pârad (1), to *spread or separate*
6626 pâthath (1), to *break, crumble*
7117 qᵉtsâth (1), *termination; portion*
2819 klērŏs (2), *lot, portion*
3307 mĕrizō (1), to *apportion, share*
3310 meris (5), *portion, share, participation*
3313 mĕrŏs (17), *division or share*
3348 mĕtĕchō (1), to *share or participate*
4119 plĕiŏn (1), *more*
4403 prumna (1), *stern* of a ship

PARTAKER
2506 chêleq (1), *smoothness; allotment*
2841 kŏinōnĕō (2), to *share or participate*
2844 kŏinōnŏs (1), *associate, partner*
3335 mĕtalambanō (1), to *participate*
3348 mĕtĕchō (2), *share or participate*

3962 *(see above)*

4777 sugkakŏpathĕō (1), to *suffer hardship with*
4791 sugkŏinōnŏs (1), *co-participant*

PARTAKERS
482 antilambanŏmai (1), to *succor; aid*
2841 kŏinōnĕō (3), to *share or participate*
2844 kŏinōnŏs (4), *associate, partner*
3310 meris (1), *portion, share, participation*
3335 mĕtalambanō (1), to *participate*
3348 mĕtĕchō (3), to *share or participate*
3353 mĕtŏchŏs (4), *sharer, associate*
4790 sugkŏinōnĕō (1), to *co-participate in*
4791 sugkŏinōnŏs (1), *co-participant*
4829 summĕrizŏmai (1), to *share jointly*
4830 summĕtŏchŏs (2), *co-participant*

PARTAKEST
1096+4791 Bêlţᵉsha'tstsar (Ch.) (1), *Belteshatstsar*

PARTED
2505 châlaq (2), to *be smooth; be slippery*
2673 châtsâh (1), to *cut or split* in two; to *halve*
6504 pârad (2), to *spread or separate*
1266 diamĕrizō (6), to *have dissension*
1339 diïstēmi (1), to *remove, intervene*

PARTETH
6504 pârad (1), to *spread or separate*
6536 pâraç (2), to *break in pieces; to split*

PARTHIANS
3934 Parthŏs (1), *inhabitant of Parthia*

PARTIAL
5375+6440 nâsâ' (1), to *lift up*
1252 diakrinō (1), to *decide; to hesitate*

PARTIALITY
87 adiakritŏs (1), *impartial*
4346 prŏsklisis (1), *favoritism*

PARTICULAR
3313 mĕrŏs (1), *division or share*
3588+1520 hŏ (1), *"the,"* i.e. the definite article

PARTICULARLY
1520+1538+2596 hĕis (1), *one*
2596+3313 kata (1), *down; according to*

PARTING
517 'êm (1), *mother*

PARTITION
5674 'âbar (1), to *cross over; to transition*

5418 phragmŏs (1), *fence or enclosing barrier*

PARTLY
7118 qᵉtsâth (Ch.) (1), *termination; portion*
1161 dĕ (1), *but, yet*
3313+5100 mĕrŏs (1), *division or share*
5124+3303 tŏutŏ (1), *that thing*

PARTNER
2505 châlaq (1), to *be smooth; be slippery*
2844 kŏinōnŏs (2), *associate, partner*

PARTNERS
2844 kŏinōnŏs (1), *associate, partner*
3353 mĕtŏchŏs (1), *sharer, associate*

PARTRIDGE
7124 qôrê' (2), *calling partridge*

PARTS
905 bad (1), *limb, member; bar*
1335 bether (2), *section, piece*
1506 gezer (1), *portion, piece*
1697 dâbâr (1), *word; matter; thing*
2506 chêleq (6), *smoothness; allotment*
2677 chêtsîy (1), *half or middle, midst*
3027 yâd (3), *hand; power*
3411 yᵉrêkâh (2), *recesses, far places*
5409 nêthach (1), *fragment*
6310 peh (1), *mouth; opening*
7098 qâtsâh (1), *termination; fringe*
2825 klinē (1), *couch*
3313 mĕrŏs (6), *division or share*

PARUAH
6515 Pârûwach (1), *blossomed*

PARVAIM
6516 Parvayim (1), *Parvajim*

PAS-DAMMIM
6450 Paç Dammîym (1), *dell of bloodshed*

PASACH
6457 Pâçak (1), *divider*

PASEAH
6454 Pâçêach (3), *limping*

PASHUR
6583 Pashchûwr (14), *liberation*

PASS
935 bôw' (3), to *go or come*
1980 hâlak (1), to *walk; live a certain way*
2498 châlaph (2), to *hasten away; to pass on*
2499 châlaph (Ch.) (4), to *have time pass by*
3615 kâlâh (1), to *cease, be finished, perish*

4569 ma'ăbâr (1), *crossing*-place
5674 'âbar (153), to *cross over*; to *transition*
5709 'ădâ' (Ch.) (1), to *pass on* or *continue*
6213 'âsâh (5), to *do* or *make*
6452 pâçach (2), to *hop, skip over*; to *hesitate*
390 anastrĕphŏ (1), to *remain*, to *live*
1224 diabainŏ (1), to *pass by, over, across*
1276 diapĕraŏ (1), to *cross over*
1279 diapŏrĕuŏmai (1), to *travel through*
1330 diĕrchŏmai (7), to *traverse, travel through*
3928 parĕrchŏmai (19), to *go by*; to *perish*
5230 hupĕrakmŏs (1), *past the bloom* of youth

PASSAGE
1552 gᵉlîylâh (1), *circuit* or *region*
4569 ma'ăbâr (2), *crossing*-place
5674 'âbar (1), to *cross over*; to *transition*

PASSAGES
4569 ma'ăbâr (4), *crossing*-place
5676 'êber (1), *opposite side*; *east*

PASSED
1431 gâdal (1), to *be great, make great*
2498 châlaph (2), to *hasten* away; to *pass on*
5674 'âbar (117), to *cross over*; to *transition*
5709 'ădâ' (Ch.) (1), to *pass on* or *continue*
5710 'âdâh (1), to *pass on* or *continue*; to *remove*
6437 pânâh (1), to *turn*, to *face*
6452 pâçach (1), to *hop, skip over*; to *hesitate*
492 antiparĕrchŏmai (2), to *go along opposite*
565 apĕrchŏmai (1), to *go off*, i.e. *depart*
1224 diabainŏ (1), to *pass by, over, across*
1276 diapĕraŏ (3), to *cross over*
1330 diĕrchŏmai (11), to *traverse, travel through*
1353 diŏdĕuŏ (1), to *travel through*
3327 mĕtabainŏ (2), to *depart, move from*
3855 paragŏ (6), to *go along* or *away*
3899 parapŏrĕuŏmai (4), to *travel near*
3928 parĕrchŏmai (3), to *go by*; to *perish, neglect*
4281 prŏĕrchŏmai (1), to *go onward, precede*

PASSEDST
5674 'âbar (1), to *cross over*; to *transition*

PASSENGERS
5674 'âbar (4), to *cross over*; to *transition*
5674+1870 'âbar (1), to *cross over*; to *transition*

PASSEST
5674 'âbar (5), to *cross over*; to *transition*

PASSETH
1980 hâlak (4), to *walk*; *live a certain way*
2498 châlaph (1), to *hasten* away; to *pass on*
5674 'âbar (28), to *cross over*; to *transition*
3855 paragŏ (2), to *go along* or *away*
3928 parĕrchŏmai (1), to *go by*; to *perish*
5235 hupĕrballŏ (1), to *surpass*
5242 hupĕrĕchŏ (1), to *excel; superior*

PASSING
5674 'âbar (7), to *cross over*; to *transition*
1330 diĕrchŏmai (2), to *traverse, travel through*
2064 ĕrchŏmai (1), to *go, come*
3881 paralĕgŏmai (1), to *sail past*
3928 parĕrchŏmai (2), to *go by*; to *perish*

PASSION
3958 paschŏ (1), to *experience* pain

PASSIONS
3663 hŏmŏiŏpathēs (2), *similarly affected*

PASSOVER
6453 Peçach (48), *Passover*
3957 pascha (28), *Passover* events

PASSOVERS
6453 Peçach (1), *Passover*

PAST
369 'ayin (1), *there is no, i.e., not exist, none*
5493 çûwr (2), to *turn off*
5674 'âbar (8), to *cross over*; to *transition*
6924 qedem (1), *eastern; antiquity; before*
7223 rî'shôwn (1), *first*
7291 râdaph (1), to *run after* with hostility
7725 shûwb (1), to *turn back*; to *return*
8032 shilshôwm (9), *day before yesterday*
421 anĕxichniastŏs (1), *untraceable*
524 apalgĕŏ (1), *become apathetic*
565 apĕrchŏmai (2), to *go off*, i.e. *depart*
1096 ginŏmai (2), to *be, become*
1230 diaginŏmai (1), to *have time elapse*
1330 diĕrchŏmai (1), to *traverse, travel through*
3819 palai (1), *formerly; sometime since*

3844 para (1), *from; with; besides; on account of*
3855 paragŏ (1), to *go along* or *away*
3928 parĕrchŏmai (3), to *go by*; to *perish*
3944 parŏichŏmai (1), to *escape along*
4266 prŏginŏmai (1), to *have previously transpired*
4302 prŏlĕgŏ (1), to *predict, forewarn*

PASTOR
7462 râ'âh (1), to *tend* a flock, i.e. *pasture* it

PASTORS
7462 râ'âh (7), to *tend* a flock, i.e. *pasture* it
4166 pŏimēn (1), *shepherd*

PASTURE
4829 mir'eh (11), *pasture; haunt*
4830 mir'îyth (1), *pasturage; flock*
3542 nŏmē (1), *pasture, i.e. the act of feeding*

PASTURES
3733 kar (2), *ram sheep*
4829 mir'eh (1), *pasture; haunt*
4830 mir'îyth (1), *pasturage; flock*
4945 mashqeh (1), *butler; drink; well-watered*
4999 nâ'âh (5), *home, dwelling; pasture*
7471 rᵉ'îy (1), *pasture*

PATARA
3959 Patara (1), *Patara*

PATE
6936 qodqôd (1), *crown of the head*

PATH
734 'ôrach (9), *road; manner of life*
4546 mᵉçillâh (1), main *thoroughfare; viaduct*
4570 ma'gâl (3), *circular track* or *camp rampart*
4934 mish'ôwl (1), *narrow passage*
5410 nâthîyb (8), (*beaten*) *track, path*
7635 shâbîyl (1), *track* or *passage-way*

PATHROS
6624 Pathrôwç (5), *Pathros*

PATHRUSIM
6625 Pathrûçîy (2), *Pathrusite*

PATHS
734 'ôrach (16), *road; manner of life*
4546 mᵉçillâh (1), main *thoroughfare; viaduct*
4570 ma'gâl (6), *circular track* or *camp rampart*
5410 nâthîyb (14), (*beaten*) *track, path*
7635 shâbîyl (1), *track* or *passage-way*
5147 tribŏs (3), *rut*, or *worn track*

5163 trŏchia (1), *course* of conduct, *path* of life

PATHWAY
1870+5410 derek (1), *road; course* of life

PATIENCE
3114 makrŏthumĕŏ (3), to *be forbearing, patient*
3115 makrŏthumia (2), *forbearance; fortitude*
5281 hupŏmŏnē (29), *endurance, constancy*

PATIENT
750 'ârêk (1), *patient*
420 anĕxikakŏs (1), *forbearing*
1933 ĕpiĕikēs (1), *mild, gentle*
3114 makrŏthumĕŏ (3), to *be forbearing, patient*
5278 hupŏmĕnŏ (1), to *undergo, bear* (trials)
5281 hupŏmŏnē (2), *perseverance*

PATIENTLY
2342 chûwl (1), to *dance, whirl*; to *wait*; to *pervert*
6960 qâvâh (1), to *collect*; to *expect*
3114 makrŏthumĕŏ (1), to *be forbearing, patient*
3116 makrŏthumŏs (1), *with long, enduring temper, i.e. leniently*
5278 hupŏmĕnŏ (2), to *undergo, bear* (trials)

PATMOS
3963 Patmŏs (1), *Patmus*

PATRIARCH
3966 patriarchēs (2), *progenitor* or patriarch

PATRIARCHS
3966 patriarchēs (2), *progenitor* or patriarch

PATRIMONY
1+5921 'âb (1), *father*

PATROBAS
3969 Patrŏbas (1), *father's life*

PATTERN
4758 mar'eh (1), *appearance; vision*
8403 tabnîyth (9), *structure; model*
8508 toknîyth (1), *admeasurement*
5179 tupŏs (2), *shape, resemblance; "type"*
5296 hupŏtupŏsis (1), *example, pattern*

PATTERNS
5262 hupŏdĕigma (1), *exhibit; specimen*

PAU
6464 Pâ'ûw (1), *screaming*

PAUL
3972 Paulŏs (157), *little*

PAUL'S
3972 Paulŏs (6), *little*

PAULUS
3972 Paulŏs (1), *little*

PAVED
3840 libnâh (1), *transparency*
7528 râtsaph (1), to *tessellate, embroider*

PAVEMENT
4837 martsepheth (1), *pavement, stone base*
7531 ritspâh (7), *hot stone; pavement*
3037 lithŏs (1), *stone*

PAVILION
5520 çôk (1), *hut of entwined boughs*
5521 çukkâh (2), *tabernacle; shelter*
8237 shaphrûwr (1), *tapestry or canopy*

PAVILIONS
5521 çukkâh (3), *tabernacle; shelter*

PAW
3027 yâd (2), *hand; power*

PAWETH
2658 châphar (1), to *delve, to explore*

PAWS
3709 kaph (1), *hollow of hand; paw; sole of foot*

PAY
5414 nâthan (2), to *give*
5414+4377 nâthan (1), to *give*
5415 nᵉthan (Ch.) (1), to *give*
5927 'âlâh (1), to *ascend, be high, mount*
7725 shûwb (1), to *turn back; to return*
7999 shâlam (19), to be *safe; be, make complete*
8254 shâqal (4), to *suspend in trade*
586 apŏdĕkatŏŏ (1), to *tithe, give a tenth*
591 apŏdidōmi (7), to *give away*
5055 tĕlĕŏ (2), to *end, discharge* (a debt)

PAYED
7999 shâlam (1), to be *safe; be, make complete*
1183 dĕkatŏŏ (1), to *give or take a tenth*

PAYETH
7999 shâlam (1), to be *safe; be, make complete*

PAYMENT
591 apŏdidōmi (1), to *give away*

PEACE
1826 dâmam (1), to be *silent; to be astonished*
2013 hâçâh (2), to *hush, be quiet*
2790 chârash (26), to be *silent; to be deaf*
2814 châshâh (9), to *hush or keep quiet*
6963 qôwl (1), *voice or sound*
7962 shalvâh (1), *security, ease*
7965 shâlôwm (169), *safe; well; health, peace*

7999 shâlam (11), to be *safe; be, make complete*
8001 shᵉlâm (Ch.) (4), *prosperity*
8002 shelem (87), *thank offering*
1515 ĕirēnē (87), *peace; health; prosperity*
1517 ĕirēnŏpŏiĕŏ (1), to *harmonize, make peace*
1518 ĕirēnŏpŏiŏs (3), *peaceable*
2270 hēsuchazŏ (2), to *refrain*
4263 prŏbatŏn (1), *sheep*
4601 sigaŏ (4), to *keep silent*
4623 siōpaŏ (9), to be *quiet*
5392 phimŏŏ (2), to *muzzle; restrain to silence*

PEACEABLE
7961 shâlêv (1), *careless, carefree; security*
7965 shâlôwm (2), *safe; well; health, peace*
7999 shâlam (1), to be *safe; be, make complete*
8003 shâlêm (1), *complete; friendly; safe*
1516 ĕirēnikŏs (2), *pacific, peaceful*
2272 hēsuchiŏs (1), *still, undisturbed*

PEACEABLY
7962 shalvâh (2), *security, ease*
7965 shâlôwm (9), *safe; well; health, peace*
1518 ĕirēnŏpŏiŏs (1), *peaceable*

PEACEMAKERS
1518 ĕirēnŏpŏiŏs (1), *peaceable*

PEACOCKS
7443 renen (1), *female ostrich*
8500 tukkîy (2), (poss.) *peacock*

PEARL
3135 margaritēs (2), *pearl*

PEARLS
1378 gâbîysh (1), *crystal*
3135 margaritēs (7), *pearl*

PECULIAR
5459 çᵉgullâh (5), *wealth*
1519+4047 ĕis (1), to or *into*
4041 pĕriŏusiŏs (1), *special, one's very own*

PEDAHEL
6300 Pᵉdah'êl (1), *God has ransomed*

PEDAHZUR
6301 Pᵉdâhtsûwr (5), *Rock has ransomed*

PEDAIAH
6305 Pᵉdâyâh (8), *Jehovah has ransomed*

PEDIGREES
3205 yâlad (1), to *bear young; to father a child*

PEELED
4178 môwrâṭ (2), *obstinate*, independent
4803 mâraṭ (1), to *polish; to make bald*

PEEP
6850 tsâphaph (1), to *coo or chirp as a bird*

PEEPED
6850 tsâphaph (1), to *coo or chirp as a bird*

PEKAH
6492 Peqach (11), *watch*

PEKAHIAH
6494 Pᵉqachyâh (3), *Jehovah has observed*

PEKOD
6489 Pᵉqôwd (2), *punishment*

PELAIAH
6411 Pᵉlâyâh (3), *Jehovah has distinguished*

PELALIAH
6421 Pᵉlalyâh (1), *Jehovah has judged*

PELATIAH
6410 Pᵉlaṭyâh (5), *Jehovah has delivered*

PELEG
6389 Peleg (7), *earthquake*

PELET
6404 Peleṭ (2), *escape*

PELETH
6431 Peleth (2), *swiftness*

PELETHITES
6432 Pᵉlêthîy (7), *courier or official messenger*

PELICAN
6893 qâ'ath (3), *pelican*

PELONITE
6397 Pᵉlôwnîy (3), *separate*

PEN
2747 chereṭ (1), *chisel; style for writing*
5842 'êṭ (4), *stylus; reed pen*
7626 shêbeṭ (1), *stick; clan, family*
2563 kalamŏs (1), *reed; pen*

PENCE
1220 dēnariŏn (5), *denarius*

PENIEL
6439 Pᵉnûw'êl (1), *face of God*

PENINNAH
6444 Pᵉninnâh (3), *round pearl*

PENKNIFE
8593 ta'ar (1), *knife; razor; scabbard*

PENNY
1220 dēnariŏn (9), *denarius*

PENNYWORTH
1220 dēnariŏn (2), *denarius*

PENTECOST
4005 pĕntēkŏstē (3), the festival of *Pentecost*

PENUEL
6439 Pᵉnûw'êl (7), *face of God*

PENURY
4270 machçôwr (1), *impoverishment*
5303 hustĕrēma (1), *deficit; poverty; lacking*

PEOPLE
376 'îysh (1), *man; male; someone*
523 'ummâh (1), *community, clan, tribe*
528 'Âmôwn (1), *Amon*
582 'ĕnôwsh (1), *man; person, human*
1121 bên (1), *son, descendant; people*
1471 gôwy (11), *foreign nation; Gentiles*
3816 lᵉ'ôm (24), *community, nation*
5712 'êdâh (1), *assemblage; family*
5971 'am (1827), *people; tribe; troops*
5972 'am (Ch.) (15), *people, nation*
1218 dēmŏs (4), *public, crowd*
1484 ĕthnŏs (2), *race; tribe; pagan*
2992 laŏs (138), *people; public*
3793 ŏchlŏs (83), *throng*

PEOPLE'S
5971 'am (2), *people; tribe; troops*
2992 laŏs (2), *people; public*

PEOPLES
2992 laŏs (2), *people; public*

PEOR
6465 Pᵉ'ôwr (4), *gap*

PEOR'S
6465 Pᵉ'ôwr (1), *gap*

PERADVENTURE
194 'ûwlay (23), *if not; perhaps*
3863 lûw' (1), *if; would that!*
6435 pên (1), *lest, not*
3379 mēpŏtĕ (1), *not ever; if, or lest ever*
5029 tacha (1), *shortly, i.e. possibly*

PERAZIM
6559 Pᵉrâtsîym (1), *breaks*

PERCEIVE
995 bîyn (1), to *understand; discern*
3045 yâda' (7), to *know*
7200 râ'âh (1), to *see*
8085 shâma' (1), to *hear intelligently*
991 blĕpŏ (1), to *look at*
1097 ginōskŏ (2), to *know*
1492 ĕidŏ (3), to *know*
2334 thĕōrĕŏ (4), to *see; to discern*

P

2638 *katalambanō* (1), to *seize; to possess*
3539 *nŏiĕŏ* (2), to *exercise the mind*
3708 *hŏraō* (1), to *stare, see clearly; to discern*

PERCEIVED
238 *'āzan* (1), to *listen*
995 *bîyn* (3), to *understand; discern*
3045 *yâda'* (11), to *know*
5234 *nâkar* (1), to *acknowledge*
7200 *râ'âh* (4), to *see*
8085 *shâma'* (1), to *hear intelligently*
143 *aisthanŏmai* (1), to *apprehend*
1097 *ginōskō* (7), to *know*
1921 *ĕpiginōskō* (3), to *become fully acquainted with*
2147 *hĕuriskō* (1), to *find*
2638 *katalambanō* (1), to *possess; to understand*
2657 *katanŏĕō* (1), to *observe fully*

PERCEIVEST
3045 *yâda'* (1), to *know*
2657 *katanŏĕō* (1), to *observe fully*

PERCEIVETH
995 *bîyn* (1), to *understand; discern*
2938 *ţâ'am* (1), to *taste; to perceive, experience*
7789 *shûwr* (1), to *spy out, survey*

PERCEIVING
1492 *ĕidō* (3), to *know*

PERDITION
684 *apŏlĕia* (8), *ruin or loss*

PERES
6537 *pᵉraç* (Ch.) (1), to *split up*

PERESH
6570 Peresh (1), *excrement*

PEREZ
6557 Perets (3), *breech*

PEREZ-UZZA
6560 Perets 'Uzzâ' (1), *break of Uzza*

PEREZ-UZZAH
6560 Perets 'Uzzâ' (1), *break of Uzza*

PERFECT
1584 *gâmar* (1), to *end; to complete; to fail*
1585 *gᵉmar* (Ch.) (1), to *complete*
3559 *kûwn* (1), to *render sure, proper*
3632 *kâlîyl* (3), *whole, entire; complete; whole*
3634 *kâlal* (1), to *complete*
4357 *miklâh* (1), *wholly, solidly*
7999 *shâlam* (1), to *be safe; be, make complete*
8003 *shâlêm* (15), *complete; friendly; safe*

8503 *taklîyth* (1), *extremity*
8535 *tâm* (9), *morally pious; gentle, dear*
8537 *tôm* (1), *prosperity*
8549 *tâmîym* (18), *entire, complete; integrity*
8552 *tâmam* (2), to *complete, finish*
195 *akribĕia* (1), *exactness*
197 *akribĕstĕrŏn* (1), *more exactly*
199 *akribōs* (1), *exactly, carefully*
739 *artiŏs* (1), *complete, thorough, capable*
2005 *ĕpitĕlĕō* (2), to *terminate; to undergo*
2675 *katartizō* (5), to *repair; to prepare*
3647 *hŏlŏklēria* (1), *wholeness*
4137 *plērŏō* (1), to *fill, make complete*
5046 *tĕlĕiŏs* (17), *complete; mature*
5048 *tĕlĕiŏō* (13), to *perfect, complete*

PERFECTED
3634 *kâlal* (1), to *complete*
5927+724 *'âlâh* (1), to *ascend, be high, mount*
8003 *shâlêm* (1), *complete; friendly; safe*
2675 *katartizō* (1), to *repair; to prepare*
5048 *tĕlĕiŏō* (4), to *perfect, complete*

PERFECTING
2005 *ĕpitĕlĕō* (1), to *terminate; to undergo*
2677 *katartismŏs* (1), *complete furnishing*

PERFECTION
3632 *kâlîyl* (1), *whole, entire; complete; whole*
4359 *miklâl* (1), *perfection of beauty*
4512 *minleh* (1), *wealth*
8502 *tiklâh* (1), *completeness*
8503 *taklîyth* (2), *extremity*
8537 *tôm* (1), *completeness*
2676 *katartisis* (1), *thorough equipment*
5050 *tĕlĕiōsis* (1), *completion; verification*
5051 *tĕlĕiōtēs* (1), *consummator, perfecter*
5052 *tĕlĕsphŏrĕō* (1), to *ripen fruit*

PERFECTLY
998 *bîynâh* (1), *discernment*
197 *akribĕstĕrŏn* (3), *more exactly*
199 *akribōs* (1), *exactly, carefully*
1295 *diasōzō* (1), to *cure, preserve, rescue*
2675 *katartizō* (1), to *repair; to prepare*

PERFECTNESS
5047 *tĕlĕiŏtēs* (1), *completeness; maturity*

PERFORM
5414 *nâthan* (1), to *give*
6213 *'âsâh* (12), to *do or make*
6633 *tsâbâ'* (1), to *mass an army or servants*
6965 *qûwm* (13), to *rise*
7999 *shâlam* (4), to *be safe; be, make complete*
591 *apŏdidōmi* (1), to *give away*
2005 *ĕpitĕlĕō* (2), to *terminate; to undergo*
2716 *katĕrgazŏmai* (1), to *finish; to accomplish*
4160 *pŏiĕō* (2), to *do*

PERFORMANCE
2005 *ĕpitĕlĕō* (1), to *terminate; to undergo*
5050 *tĕlĕiōsis* (1), *completion; verification*

PERFORMED
1214 *bâtsa'* (1), to *plunder; to finish*
6213 *'âsâh* (5), to *do or make*
6965 *qûwm* (11), to *rise*
7999 *shâlam* (1), to *be safe; be, make complete*
1096 *ginŏmai* (1), to *be, become*
2005 *ĕpitĕlĕō* (1), to *terminate; to undergo*
5055 *tĕlĕō* (1), to *end, i.e. complete, execute*

PERFORMETH
1584 *gâmar* (1), to *end; to complete; to fail*
6965 *qûwm* (1), to *rise*
7999 *shâlam* (2), to *be safe; be, make complete*

PERFORMING
6381 *pâlâ'* (2), to *be, make great, wonderful*

PERFUME
7004 *qᵉţôreth* (3), *fumigation*

PERFUMED
5130 *nûwph* (1), to *quiver, vibrate, rock*
6999 *qâţar* (1), to *turn into fragrance* by fire

PERFUMES
7547 *raqqûach* (1), *scented ointment*

PERGA
4011 *Pĕrgē* (3), *tower*

PERGAMOS
4010 *Pĕrgamŏs* (2), *fortified*

PERHAPS
686 *ara* (1), *then, so, therefore*
3381 *mēpōs* (1), *lest somehow*
5029 *tacha* (1), *shortly, i.e. possibly*

PERIDA
6514 *Pᵉrûwdâ'* (1), *dispersion*

PERIL
2794 *kindunŏs* (1), *danger, risk*

PERILOUS
5467 *chalĕpŏs* (1), *difficult, i.e. dangerous*

PERILS
2794 *kindunŏs* (8), *danger, risk*

PERISH
6 *'âbad* (73), *perish; destroy*
7 *'âbad* (Ch.) (2), *perish; destroy*
8 *'ôbêd* (2), *wretched; destruction*
1478 *gâva'* (1), to *expire, die*
1820 *dâmâh* (2), to *be silent; to fail, cease*
3772 *kârath* (1), to *cut (off, down or asunder)*
5307 *nâphal* (1), to *fall*
5486 *çûwph* (1), to *terminate*
5595 *çâphâh* (2), to *scrape; to remove*
5674 *'âbar* (1), to *cross over; to transition*
6544 *pâra'* (1), to *loosen; to expose, dismiss*
7843 *shâchath* (1), to *decay; to ruin*
622 *apŏllumi* (25), to *destroy fully; to perish*
853 *aphanizō* (1), to *disappear, be destroyed*
1311 *diaphthĕirō* (1), to *ruin, to decay*
1510+1519+604 *ĕimi* (1), I *exist, I am*
2704 *kataphthĕirō* (1), to *spoil entirely*
5356 *phthŏra* (1), *ruin; depravity, corruption*

PERISHED
6 *'âbad* (17), *perish; destroy*
1478 *gâva'* (1), to *expire, die*
8045 *shâmad* (1), to *desolate*
599 *apŏthnēskō* (1), to *die off*
622 *apŏllumi* (5), to *destroy fully; to perish*
4881 *sunapŏllumi* (1), to *destroy, be slain with*

PERISHETH
6 *'âbad* (6), *perish; destroy*
622 *apŏllumi* (3), to *destroy fully; to perish*

PERISHING
5674 *'âbar* (1), to *cross over; to transition*

PERIZZITE
6522 *Pᵉrîzzîy* (5), *of the open country*

PERIZZITES
6522 *Pᵉrîzzîy* (18), *of the open country*

PERJURED
1965 *ĕpiŏrkŏs* (1), *forswearer, perjurer*

PERMISSION
4774 suggnōmē (1), concession

PERMIT
2010 ĕpitrĕpō (2), allow, permit

PERMITTED
2010 ĕpitrĕpō (2), allow, permit

PERNICIOUS
684 apōlĕia (1), ruin or loss

PERPETUAL
5331 netsach (4), splendor; lasting
5769 'ôwlâm (22), eternity; always
8548 tâmîyd (2), constantly, regularly

PERPETUALLY
3605+3711 kôl (2), all, any or every
5703 'ad (1), perpetuity

PERPLEXED
943 bûwk (2), to be confused
639 apŏrĕō (1), be at a mental loss, be puzzled
1280 diapŏrĕō (2), to be thoroughly puzzled

PERPLEXITY
3998 m^{e}bûwkâh (2), perplexity, confusion
640 apŏria (1), state of quandary, perplexity

PERSECUTE
1814 dâlaq (1), to flame; to pursue
7291 râdaph (14), to run after with hostility
7921+310 shâkôl (1), to miscarry
1377 diōkō (8), to pursue; to persecute
1559 ĕkdiōkō (1), to expel or persecute

PERSECUTED
4783 murdâph (1), persecuted
7291 râdaph (5), to run after with hostility
1377 diōkō (13), to pursue; to persecute
1559 ĕkdiōkō (1), to expel or persecute

PERSECUTEST
1377 diōkō (6), to pursue; to persecute

PERSECUTING
1377 diōkō (1), to pursue; to persecute

PERSECUTION
7291 râdaph (1), to run after with hostility
1375 diōgmŏs (5), persecution
1377 diōkō (3), to pursue; to persecute
2347 thlipsis (1), pressure, trouble

PERSECUTIONS
1375 diōgmŏs (5), persecution

PERSECUTOR
1376 diōktēs (1), persecutor

PERSECUTORS
1814 dâlaq (1), to flame; to pursue
7291 râdaph (7), to run after with hostility

PERSEVERANCE
4343 prŏskartĕrēsis (1), perseverance

PERSIA
6539 Pâraç (27), Paras
6540 Pâraç (Ch.) (2), Paras

PERSIAN
6523 parzel (Ch.) (1), iron
6542 Parçîy (1), Parsite

PERSIANS
6539 Pâraç (1), Paras
6540 Pâraç (Ch.) (4), Paras

PERSIS
4069 Pĕrsis (1), Persis

PERSON
120 'âdâm (2), human being; mankind
376 'îysh (3), man; male; someone
376+120 'îysh (1), man; male; someone
1167 ba'al (1), master; husband; owner; citizen
5315 nephesh (14), life; breath; soul; wind
6440 pânîym (10), face; front
4383 prŏsōpŏn (5), face, presence
5287 hupŏstasis (1), essence; assurance

PERSONS
120 'âdâm (3), human being; mankind
376 'îysh (8), man; male; someone
582 'ĕnôwsh (2), man; person, human
4962 math (1), men
5315 nephesh (12), life; breath; soul; wind
5315+120 nephesh (4), life; breath; soul; wind
6440 pânîym (11), face; front
678 aprŏsōpŏlēptōs (2), without prejudice
4380 prŏsōpŏlēptĕō (1), to show partiality
4381 prŏsōpŏlēptēs (1), exhibiting partiality
4382 prŏsōpŏlēpsia (4), favoritism
4383 prŏsōpŏn (2), face, presence

PERSUADE
5496 çûwth (3), to stimulate; to seduce
6601 pâthâh (3), to be, make simple; to delude
3982 pĕithō (3), to assent to evidence

PERSUADED
5496 çûwth (1), to stimulate; to seduce
6601 pâthâh (1), to be, make simple; to delude
3982 pĕithō (16), to assent to evidence
4135 plērŏphŏrĕō (2), to assure or convince

PERSUADEST
3982 pĕithō (1), to assent to evidence

PERSUADETH
5496 çûwth (1), to stimulate; to seduce
374 anapĕithō (1), to incite, persuade

PERSUADING
3982 pĕithō (2), to assent to evidence

PERSUASION
3988 pĕismŏnē (1), persuadableness

PERTAINED
1961 hâyâh (1), to exist

PERTAINETH
1961 hâyâh (1), to exist
3627 k^{e}lîy (1), implement, thing
3348 mĕtĕchō (1), to share or participate

PERTAINING
4012 pĕri (1), about

PERUDA
6514 P^{e}rûwdâ' (1), dispersion

PERVERSE
1942 havvâh (1), desire; craving
2015 hâphak (1), to change, pervert
3399 yâraṭ (1), to be rash
3868 lûwz (1), to depart; to be perverse
3891 l^{e}zûwth (1), perverseness
5753 'âvâh (2), to be crooked
5773 'av'eh (1), perversity
6140 'âqash (2), to knot or distort; to pervert
6141 'iqqêsh (4), distorted, warped, false
8419 tahpûkâh (1), perversity or fraud
1294 diastrĕphō (4), to be morally corrupt
3859 paradiatribē (1), meddlesomeness

PERVERSELY
5753 'âvâh (2), to be crooked
5791 'âvath (1), to wrest, twist

PERVERSENESS
3868 lûwz (1), to depart; to be perverse
4297 muṭṭeh (1), distortion; iniquity
5558 çeleph (2), distortion; viciousness
5766 'evel (1), moral evil
5999 'âmâl (1), wearing effort; worry

PERVERT
5186 nâṭâh (2), to stretch or spread out
5557 çâlaph (1), to wrench; to subvert
5791 'âvath (3), to wrest, twist
6140 'âqash (1), to knot or distort; to pervert
8138 shânâh (1), to fold, to transmute
1294 diastrĕphō (1), to be morally corrupt
3344 mĕtastrĕphō (1), to transmute; corrupt

PERVERTED
2015 hâphak (1), to change, pervert
5186 nâṭâh (1), to stretch or spread out
5753 'âvâh (2), to be crooked
7725 shûwb (1), to turn back; to return

PERVERTETH
5186 nâṭâh (1), to stretch or spread out
5557 çâlaph (2), to wrench; to subvert
6140 'âqash (1), to knot or distort; to pervert
654 apŏstrĕphō (1), to turn away or back

PERVERTING
1294 diastrĕphō (1), to be morally corrupt

PESTILENCE
1698 deber (47), pestilence, plague

PESTILENCES
3061 lŏimŏs (2), plague; disease; pest

PESTILENT
3061 lŏimŏs (1), plague; disease; pest

PESTLE
5940 'ĕlîy (1), mortar pestle

PETER
4074 Pĕtrŏs (157), piece of rock

PETER'S
4074 Pĕtrŏs (4), piece of rock

PETHAHIAH
6611 P^{e}thachyâh (4), Jehovah has opened

PETHOR
6604 P^{e}thôwr (2), Pethor

PETHUEL
6602 P^{e}thûw'êl (1), enlarged of God

PETITION
1159 bâ'ûw (Ch.) (2), request; prayer
7596 sh^{e}'êlâh (10), petition

PETITIONS
4862 mish'âlâh (1), request
155 aitēma (1), thing asked, request

PEULTHAI
6469 P^{e}'ull'thay (1), laborious

PHALEC
5317 Phalĕk (1), earthquake

PHALLU
6396 Pallûw' (1), distinguished

PHALTI
6406 Palṭiy (1), delivered

PHALTIEL
6409 Palṭiy'êl (1), deliverance of God

PHANUEL
5323 Phanûêl (1), face of God

PHARAOH
6547 Par'ôh (221), Paroh
5328 Pharaō (3), Pharaoh

PHARAOH'S
6547 Par'ôh (46), Paroh
5328 Pharaō (2), Pharaoh

PHARAOH-HOPHRA
6548 Par'ôh Chophra' (1), Paroh-Chophra

PHARAOH-NECHO
6549 Par'ôh Nᵉkôh (1), Paroh-Nekoh (or -Neko)

PHARAOH-NECHOH
6549 Par'ôh Nᵉkôh (4), Paroh-Nekoh (or -Neko)

PHARES
5329 Pharĕs (3), breech

PHAREZ
6557 Perets (12), breech

PHARISEE
5330 Pharisaiŏs (10), separatist

PHARISEE'S
5330 Pharisaiŏs (2), separatist

PHARISEES
5330 Pharisaiŏs (86), separatist

PHARISEES'
5330 Pharisaiŏs (1), separatist

PHAROSH
6551 Par'ôsh (1), flea

PHARPAR
6554 Parpar (1), rapid

PHARZITES
6558 Partsîy (1), Partsite

PHASEAH
6454 Pâçeach (1), limping

PHEBE
5402 Phŏibē (2), bright

PHENICE
5403 Phŏinikē (2), palm-country
5405 Phŏinix (1), palm-tree

PHENICIA
5403 Phŏinikē (1), palm-country

PHICHOL
6369 Pîykôl (3), mouth of all

PHILADELPHIA
5359 Philadĕlphĕia (2), fraternal

PHILEMON
5371 Philēmōn (2), friendly

PHILETUS
5372 Philētŏs (1), amiable

PHILIP
5376 Philippŏs (33), fond of horses

PHILIP'S
5376 Philippŏs (3), fond of horses

PHILIPPI
5375 Philippŏi (8), Philippi

PHILIPPIANS
5374 Philippēsiŏs (1), native of Philippi

PHILISTIA
6429 Pᵉlesheth (3), migratory

PHILISTIM
6430 Pᵉlishtîy (1), Pelishtite

PHILISTINE
6430 Pᵉlishtîy (33), Pelishtite

PHILISTINES
6430 Pᵉlishtîy (250), Pelishtite

PHILISTINES'
6430 Pᵉlishtîy (4), Pelishtite

PHILOLOGUS
5378 Philŏlŏgŏs (1), argumentative, learned

PHILOSOPHERS
5386 philŏsŏphŏs (1), one fond of wise things, i.e. philosopher

PHILOSOPHY
5385 philŏsŏphia (1), wise things

PHINEHAS
6372 Pîynᵉchâç (24), mouth of a serpent

PHINEHAS'
6372 Pîynᵉchâç (1), mouth of a serpent

PHLEGON
5393 Phlĕgōn (1), blazing

PHRYGIA
5435 Phrugia (4), Phrygia

PHURAH
6513 Pûrâh (2), foliage

PHUT
6316 Pûwṭ (2), Put

PHUVAH
6312 Pûw'âh (1), blast

PHYGELLUS
5436 Phugĕllŏs (1), fugitive

PHYLACTERIES
5440 phulaktēriŏn (1), guard-case

PHYSICIAN
7495 râphâ' (1), to cure, heal
2395 iatrŏs (5), physician

PHYSICIANS
7495 râphâ' (4), to cure, heal

2395 iatrŏs (2), physician

PI-BESETH
6364 Pîy-Beçeth (1), Pi-Beseth

PI-HAHIROTH
6367 Piy ha-Chîrôth (4), mouth of the gorges

PICK
5365 nâqar (1), to bore; to gouge

PICTURES
4906 maskîyth (2), carved figure
7914 sᵉkîyâh (1), conspicuous object

PIECE
95 'ăgôwrâh (1), coin
829 'eshpâr (2), portion
915 bâdâl (1), part
1335 bether (1), piece
2513 chelqâh (3), flattery; allotment
3603 kikkâr (2), round loaf; talent
4060 middâh (7), measure; portion
4749 miqshâh (1), work molded by hammering
5409 nêthach (2), fragment
6400 peiach (6), slice
6595 path (2), bit, morsel
1406 drachmē (2), coin
1915 ĕpiblēma (4), patch
3313 mĕrŏs (1), division or share
4138 plērōma (1), what fills; what is filled

PIECES
1506 gezer (1), portion, piece
1917 haddâm (Ch.) (2), bit, piece
5409 nêthach (9), fragment
6595 path (3), bit, morsel
7168 qera' (3), rag, torn pieces
7518 rats (1), fragment
1288 diaspaō (1), to sever or dismember
1406 drachmē (1), coin

PIERCE
4272 mâchats (1), to crush; to subdue
5344 nâqab (2), to puncture, perforate
1330 diĕrchŏmai (1), to traverse, travel through

PIERCED
738 'ărîy (1), lion
1856 dâqar (1), to stab, pierce
4272 mâchats (1), to crush; to subdue
5365 nâqar (1), to bore; to gouge
1574 ĕkkĕntĕō (2), to pierce or impale
3572 nussŏ (1), to pierce, stab
4044 pĕripĕirō (1), to penetrate entirely

PIERCETH
5344 nâqab (1), to puncture, perforate

PIERCING
1281 bârîyach (1), fleeing, gliding serpent
1338 diiknĕŏmai (1), penetrate, pierce

PIERCINGS
4094 madqârâh (1), wound

PIETY
2151 ĕusĕbĕō (1), to put show piety toward

PIGEON
1469 gôwzâl (1), young of a bird
3123 yôwnâh (1), dove

PIGEONS
3123 yôwnâh (9), dove
4058 pĕristĕra (1), pigeon, dove

PILATE
4091 Pilatŏs (55), firm

PILDASH
6394 Pildâsh (1), Pildash

PILE
4071 mᵉdûwrâh (2), pile

PILEHA
6401 Pilchâ' (1), slicing

PILGRIMAGE
4033 mâgûwr (4), abode

PILGRIMS
3927 parepidēmŏs (2), resident foreigner

PILLAR
4676 matstsêbâh (10), column or stone
4678 matstsebeth (4), stock of a tree
5324 nâtsab (1), to station
5333 nᵉtsîyb (1), military post; statue
5982 'ammûwd (29), column, pillar
4769 stulŏs (2), supporting pillar; leader

PILLARS
547 'ômᵉnâh (1), column
4552 miç'âd (1), balustrade for stairs
4676 matstsêbâh (2), column or stone
4690 mâtsûwq (1), column; hilltop
5982 'ammûwd (79), column, pillar
8490 tîymârâh (2), column, i.e. cloud
4769 stulŏs (2), supporting pillar; leader

PILLED
6478 pâtsal (2), to peel

PILLOW
3523 kᵉbîyr (2), matrass, quilt of animal hair
4344 prŏskĕphalaiŏn (1), cushion pillow

PILLOWS
3704 keçeth (2), cushion or pillow
4763 mᵉra'ăshâh (2), headpiece; head-rest

PILOTS
2259 chôbêl (4), sailor

PILTAI
6408 Piltay (1), *Piltai*

PIN
3489 yâthêd (3), tent *peg*

PINE
2100 zûwb (1), to *waste away*
4743 mâqaq (4), to *melt; to flow, dwindle, vanish*
6086+8081 'êts (1), *wood*
8410 tidhâr (2), *lasting tree* (poss.) *oak*

PINETH
3583 xĕrainŏ (1), to *shrivel*, to *mature*

PINING
1803 dallâh (1), *loose hair; indigent, needy*

PINNACLE
4419 ptĕrugiŏn (2), *winglet*, i.e. *extremity*

PINON
6373 Pîynôn (2), *Pinon*

PINS
3489 yâthêd (10), tent *peg*

PIPE
2485 châlîyl (3), *flute*
836 aulŏs (1), *flute*

PIPED
2490 châlal (1), to *play the flute*
832 aulĕŏ (3), to play the *flute*

PIPERS
834 aulētēs (1), *flute-player*

PIPES
2485 châlîyl (3), *flute instrument*
4166 mûwtsâqâh (1), *tube*
5345 neqeb (1), *bezel, gem mounting*
6804 tsantârâh (1), *tube, pipe*

PIRAM
6502 Pir'âm (1), *wildly*

PIRATHON
6552 Pir'âthôwn (1), *chieftaincy*

PIRATHONITE
6553 Pir'âthôwnîy (5), *Pirathonite*

PISGAH
6449 Piçgâh (5), *cleft*

PISIDIA
4099 Pisidia (2), *Pisidia*

PISON
6376 Pîyshôwn (1), *dispersive*

PISPAH
6462 Piçpâh (1), *dispersion*

PISS
7890 shayin (2), *urine*

PISSETH
8366 shâthan (6), to *urinate* as a male

PIT
875 be'êr (3), *well, cistern*
953 bôwr (41), pit *hole, cistern, well; prison*
1360 gebe' (1), *reservoir*

1475 gûwmmâts (1), *pit*
6354 pachath (8), *pit* for catching animals
7585 she'ôwl (3), abode of the *dead*
7743+7882 shûwach (1), to *sink*
7745 shûwchâh (2), *chasm*
7816 shechûwth (1), *pit*
7845 shachath (14), *pit; destruction*
7882 shîychâh (1), *pit-fall*
999 bôthunŏs (1), *cistern, pit-hole*
5421 phrĕar (5), *cistern or water well; abyss*

PITCH
167 'âhal (1), to pitch a *tent*
2203 zepheth (3), *asphalt*
2583 chânâh (11), to *encamp*
3724 kôpher (1), *village; bitumen; henna*
6965 qûwm (1), to *rise*
8628 tâqa' (1), to *clatter, slap, drive, clasp*

PITCHED
167 'âhal (1), to pitch a *tent*
2583 chânâh (70), to *encamp*
5186 nâtâh (8), to *stretch or spread out*
8628 tâqa' (2), to *clatter, slap, drive, clasp*
4078 pēgnumi (1), to *set up a tent*

PITCHER
3537 kad (10), *jar, pitcher*
2765 kĕramiŏn (2), *earthenware* vessel

PITCHERS
3537 kad (4), *jar, pitcher*
5035 nebel (1), skin-*bag for liquids; vase; lyre*

PITHOM
6619 Pîthôm (1), *Pithom*

PITHON
6377 Pîythôwn (2), *expansive*

PITIED
2347 chûwç (1), to be *compassionate*
2550 châmal (4), to *spare, have pity on*
7356 racham (1), *compassion; womb*

PITIETH
4263 machmâl (1), *delight*
7355 râcham (2), to be *compassionate*

PITIFUL
7362 rachmânîy (1), *compassionate*
2155 ĕusplagchnŏs (1), *compassionate*
4184 pŏlusplagchnŏs (1), *extremely compassionate*

PITS
953 bôwr (1), pit *hole, cistern, well; prison*

1356 gêb (1), *well, cistern; pit*
7745 shûwchâh (1), *chasm*
7825 shechîyth (1), *pit-fall*
7882 shîychâh (1), *pit-fall*

PITY
2347 chûwç (6), to be *compassionate*
2550 châmal (14), to *spare, have pity on*
2551 chemlâh (1), *commiseration, pity*
2603 chânan (3), to *implore*
2617 cheçed (1), *kindness, favor*
5110 nûwd (1), to *console, deplore; to taunt*
7355 râcham (1), to be *compassionate*
7356 racham (1), *compassion; womb*
1653 ĕlĕĕŏ (1), to give out *compassion*

PLACE
870 'âthar (Ch.) (5), *after*
1004 bayith (7), *house; temple; family, tribe*
1367 gebûwlâh (1), *region*
3027 yâd (7), *hand; power*
3241 Yânîym (1), *asleep*
3427 yâshab (2), to *dwell, to remain; to settle*
3653 kên (1), *pedestal or station* of a basin
4349 mâkôwn (11), *basis; place*
4612 ma'ămâd (1), *position; attendant*
4634 ma'ărâkâh (1), *arrangement, row; pile*
4724 miqvâh (1), *water reservoir*
4725 mâqôwm (373), general *locality, place*
4800 merchâb (1), *open space; liberty*
5182 nechath (Ch.) (1), to *descend; to depose*
5414 nâthan (3), to *give*
5977 'ômed (6), fixed *spot*
6607 pethach (1), *opening; door*
7675 shebeth (1), *abode or locality*
7760 sûwm (1), to *place*
7931 shâkan (5), to *reside*
8414 tôhûw (1), *waste, desolation, formless*
8478 tachath (17), *bottom; underneath*
201 akrŏatēriŏn (1), *audience-room*
402 anachŏrĕŏ (1), to *retire, withdraw*
1502 ĕikŏ (1), to *be weak*, i.e. *yield*
1564 ĕkĕithĕn (1), *from there*
1786 ĕntŏpiŏs (1), local *resident*
3692 ŏpē (1), *hole*, i.e. *cavern; spring* of water
3699 hŏpŏu (1), *at whichever* spot
4042 pĕriŏchē (1), *passage* of Scripture

5117 tŏpŏs (74), *place*
5562 chōrĕŏ (1), to *pass, enter; to hold, admit*
5564 chōriŏn (2), *spot* or *plot* of ground
5602 hōdĕ (2), *here*

PLACED
776 'erets (1), *earth, land, soil; country*
3240 yânach (2), to *allow to stay*
3427 yâshab (5), to *dwell, to remain; to settle*
3947 lâqach (1), to *take*
5414 nâthan (1), to *give*
5975 'âmad (1), to *stand*
7760 sûwm (1), to *place*
7931 shâkan (2), to *reside*

PLACES
168 'ôhel (1), *tent*
1004 bayith (9), *house; temple; family, tribe*
2723 chorbâh (1), *desolation, dry* desert
3027 yâd (1), *hand; power*
4585 me'ôwnâh (1), *abode*
4725 mâqôwm (20), general *locality, place*
5439 çâbîyb (1), *circle; environs; around*
8478 tachath (1), *bottom; underneath; in lieu of*
3837 pantachŏu (1), *universally, everywhere*
5117 tŏpŏs (7), *place*

PLAGUE
4046 maggêphâh (20), *pestilence; defeat*
4347 makkâh (2), *blow; wound; pestilence*
5061 nega' (64), *infliction, affliction; leprous spot*
5063 negeph (7), *infliction* of disease
3148 mastix (2), *flogging* device
4127 plēgē (1), *stroke; wound; calamity*

PLAGUED
4046 maggêphâh (1), *pestilence; defeat*
5060 nâga' (3), to *strike*
5062 nâgaph (2), to *inflict* a disease

PLAGUES
1698 deber (1), *pestilence, plague*
4046 maggêphâh (1), *pestilence; defeat*
4347 makkâh (8), *blow; wound; pestilence*
5061 nega' (1), *infliction, affliction; leprous spot*
3148 mastix (2), *flogging* device
4127 plēgē (10), *stroke; wound; calamity*

PLAIN
58 'âbêl (1), *meadow*
436 'êlôwn (7), *oak*
874 bâ'ar (1), to *explain*
1236 biq'â (Ch.) (1), wide level *valley*
1237 biq'âh (7), wide level *valley*

3603 kikkâr (13), *tract or region*; round *loaf*
4334 mîyshôwr (14), *plain; justice*
5228 nâkôach (1), *equitable, correct*
5549 çâlal (1), to *mound up*; to *exalt*; to *oppose*
6160 'ărâbâh (22), *desert, wasteland*
7737 shâvâh (1), to *level*, i.e. *equalize*
8219 sh^ephêlâh (3), *lowland*,
8535 tâm (1), morally *pious; gentle, dear*
3723 ŏrthōs (1), *correctly, rightly*
5117+3977 tŏpŏs (1), *place*

PLAINLY
559 'âmar (1), to *say*
874 bâ'ar (1), to *explain*
1540 gâlâh (1), to *denude; uncover*
5046 nâgad (1), to *announce*
6568 p^erash (Ch.) (1), to *specify, translate*
6703 tsach (1), *dazzling*, i.e. *sunny, bright*
1718 ĕmphanizō (1), to *show forth*
3954 parrhēsia (4), *frankness, boldness*

PLAINNESS
3954 parrhēsia (1), *frankness, boldness*

PLAINS
436 'êlôwn (2), *oak*
4334 mîyshôwr (1), *plain; justice*
6160 'ărâbâh (20), *desert, wasteland*
8219 sh^ephêlâh (2), *lowland*,

PLAISTER
1528 gîyr (Ch.) (1), *lime for plaster*
2902 ţûwach (1), to *whitewash*
4799 mârach (1), to *apply by rubbing*
7874 sîyd (2), to *plaster, whitewash* with lime

PLAISTERED
2902 ţûwach (2), to *whitewash*

PLAITING
1708 ĕmplŏkē (1), *braiding* of the hair

PLANES
4741 maqtsû'âh (1), wood-carving *chisel*

PLANETS
4208 mazzâlâh (1), *constellations*

PLANKS
5646 'âb (1), *architrave*
6086 'êts (1), *wood*, things made of *wood*
6763 tsêlâ' (1), *side*

PLANT
4302 maţţâ' (1), something *planted*
5193 nâţa' (31), to *plant*

5194 neţa' (3), *plant; plantation; planting*
5414 nâthan (1), to *give*
7880 sîyach (1), *shrubbery*
8362 shâthal (2), to *transplant*
5451 phuţĕia (1), *shrub or vegetable*

PLANTATION
4302 maţţâ' (1), something *planted*

PLANTED
5193 nâţa' (21), to *plant*
8362 shâthal (8), to *transplant*
4854 sumphutŏs (1), closely *united* to
5452 phutĕuō (8), to *implant*, i.e. to *instill* doctrine

PLANTEDST
5193 nâţa' (2), to *plant*

PLANTERS
5193 nâţa' (1), to *plant*

PLANTETH
5192 nêţel (2), *burden*
5452 phutĕuō (3), to *implant*, i.e. to *instill*

PLANTING
4302 maţţâ' (2), something *planted*

PLANTINGS
4302 maţţâ' (1), something *planted*

PLANTS
4302 maţţâ' (1), something *planted*
5189 n^eţîyshâh (1), *tendril* plant shoot
5194 neţa' (2), *plant; plantation; planting*
5195 nâţîya' (1), *plant*
7973 shelach (1), *spear; shoot* of growth
8291 sarûwq (1), choice *grapevine*
8363 sh^ethîyl (1), *sucker plant*

PLAT
2513 chelqâh (2), *smoothness; flattery*

PLATE
6731 tsîyts (3), burnished *plate; bright flower*

PLATES
3871 lûwach (1), *tablet*
5633 çeren (1), *axle; peer*
6341 pach (2), thin metallic *sheet; net*

PLATTED
4120 plĕkō (3), to *twine or braid*

PLATTER
3953 parŏpsis (2), *side-dish receptacle*
4094 pinax (1), *plate, platter, dish*

PLAY
5059 nâgan (4), to *play; to make music*
6711 tsâchaq (1), to *laugh; to make sport of*

7832 sâchaq (5), to *laugh; to scorn; to play*
8173 shâ'a' (1), to *fondle, please or amuse* (self)
3815 paizō (1), to *indulge in (sexual) revelry*

PLAYED
5059 nâgan (4), to *play; to make music*
7832 sâchaq (3), to *laugh; to scorn; to play*

PLAYER
5059 nâgan (1), to *play; to make music*

PLAYERS
2490 châlal (1), to *play* the flute
5059 nâgan (1), to *play; to make music*

PLAYING
5059 nâgan (1), to *play; to make music*
7832 sâchaq (2), to *laugh; to scorn; to play*

PLEA
1779 dîyn (1), *judge; judgment; law suit*

PLEAD
1777 dîyn (2), to *judge*; to *strive or contend for*
3198 yâkach (3), to *be correct*; to *argue*
7378 rîyb (23), to *hold a controversy; to defend*
8199 shâphaţ (9), to *judge*

PLEADED
7378 rîyb (2), to *hold a controversy; to defend*
8199 shâphaţ (1), to *judge*

PLEADETH
7378 rîyb (1), to *hold a controversy; to defend*
8199 shâphaţ (1), to *judge*

PLEADINGS
7379 rîyb (1), *contest*, personal or legal

PLEASANT
2530 châmad (3), to *delight in; lust for*
2531 chemed (2), *delight*
2532 chemdâh (11), *delight*
2580 chên (1), *graciousness; beauty*
2656 chêphets (1), *pleasure; desire*
2896 ţôwb (2), *good; well*
3303 yâpheh (1), *beautiful; handsome*
4022 meged (3), *valuable*
4261 machmâd (5), *delightful*
4262 machmûd (3), *desired; valuable*
4999 nâ'âh (1), *home, dwelling; pasture*
5116 nâveh (1), *at home; lovely; home*
5273 nâ'îym (8), *delightful; sweet*
5276 nâ'êm (5), to *be agreeable*
5278 no'am (2), *agreeableness, delight*
6027 'ōneg (1), *luxury*
6148 'ârab (1), to *intermix*

7832 sâchaq (5), to *laugh; to scorn; to play*
6643 ts^ebîy (1), *conspicuous splendor*
8191 sha'shûa' (2), *enjoyment*
8378 ta'ăvâh (1), *longing; delight*
8588 ta'ănûwg (1), *luxury; delight*

PLEASANTNESS
5278 no'am (1), *agreeableness*

PLEASE
2654 châphêts (5), to *be pleased with, desire*
2655 châphêts (1), *pleased with*
2894 ţûw' (3), to *sweep away*
2895 ţowb (6), to *be good*
2896 ţôwb (2), *good; well*
3190 yâţab (2), to *be, make well*
3477+5869 yâshâr (1), *straight*
5606 çâphaq (1), to *be enough; to vomit*
7451+5869 ra' (1), *bad; evil*
7521 râtsâh (3), to *be pleased with; to satisfy*
700 arĕskō (11), to *seek to please*
701 arĕstŏs (1), *agreeable; desirable; fit*
2001+1511 ĕpischuō (1), to *insist stoutly*
2100 ĕuarĕstĕō (1), to *gratify entirely, please*

PLEASED
2654 châphêts (8), to *be pleased with, desire*
2895 ţowb (1), to *be good*
2896+5869 ţôwb (1), *good; well*
2974 yâ'al (1), to *assent; to undertake, begin*
3190 yâţab (2), to *be, make well*
3190+5869 yâţab (10), to *be, make well*
3477+5869 yâshâr (7), *straight*
7451+5869 ra' (1), *bad; evil*
7521 râtsâh (4), to *be pleased with; to satisfy*
8232 sh^ephar (Ch.) (1), to *be beautiful*
700 arĕskō (5), to *seek to please*
701 arĕstŏs (1), *agreeable; desirable; fit*
1380 dŏkĕō (2), to *think, regard, seem good*
2100 ĕuarĕstĕō (2), to *gratify entirely, please*
2106 ĕudŏkĕō (12), to *think well*, i.e. *approve*
2309 thĕlō (2), to *will; to desire; to choose*
4909 sunĕudŏkĕō (2), to *assent to, feel gratified*

PLEASETH
2654 châphêts (1), to *be pleased with, desire*
2896+5869 ţôwb (2), *good; well*

PLEASING

2896+6440 ṭôwb (1), *good; well*
3190+5869 yâṭab (1), to *be, make well*
3477+5869 yâshâr (1), *straight*

PLEASING

2896 ṭôwb (1), *good; well*
6148 'ârab (1), to *give or be security*
699 arĕskĕia (1), *complaisance, amiable*
700 arĕskŏ (2), to *seek to please*
701 arĕstŏs (1), *agreeable; desirable; fit*

PLEASURE

185+5315 'avvâh (1), *longing*
2654 châphêts (3), to *be pleased with, desire*
2655 châphêts (2), *pleased with*
2656 chêphets (16), *pleasure; desire*
2837 chêsheq (1), *delight, desired thing*
2896 ṭôwb (2), *good; well*
5315 nephesh (2), *life; breath; soul; wind*
5730 'êden (1), *pleasure*
6148 'ârab (1), to *give or be security*
7470 rᵉ'ûwth (Ch.) (1), *desire*
7521 râtsâh (6), to *be pleased with; to satisfy a debt*
7522 râtsôwn (5), *delight*
8057 simchâh (1), *blithesomeness or glee*
2106 ĕudŏkĕŏ (6), to *think well, i.e. approve*
2107 ĕudŏkia (4), *delight, kindness, wish*
2237 hēdŏnē (1), *delight; desire*
2307 thĕlēma (1), *decree; inclination*
3588+1380 hŏ (1), *"the,"* i.e. the definite article
4684 spatalaŏ (1), to *live in luxury*
4909 sunĕudŏkĕŏ (1), to *assent to, feel gratified*
5171 truphaŏ (1), to *indulge in luxury*
5485 charis (2), *gratitude; benefit given*

PLEASURES

5273 nâ'îym (2), *delightful; sweet*
5719 'âdîyn (1), *voluptuous*
5730 'êden (1), *pleasure*
2237 hēdŏnē (2), *delight; desire*
5569 psĕudadĕlphŏs (1), *pretended associate*

PLEDGE

2254 châbal (10), to *bind by a pledge; to pervert*
2258 chăbôl (4), *pawn, pledge as security*
5667 'ăbôwṭ (4), *pledged item*
6161 'ărubbâh (1), as *security; bondsman*

6162 'ărâbôwn (3), *pawn, security pledge*

PLEDGES

6148 'ârab (2), to *give or be security*

PLEIADES

3598 Kîymâh (2), *cluster of stars, Pleiades*

PLENTEOUS

1277 bârîy' (1), *fatted or plump; healthy*
3498 yâthar (2), to *remain or be left*
7227 rab (3), *great*
7235 râbâh (1), to *increase*
7647 sâbâ' (2), *copiousness*
8082 shâmên (1), *rich; fertile*
4180 pŏlulŏgia (1), *prolixity, wordiness*

PLENTEOUSNESS

4195 môwthar (1), *gain; superiority*
7647 sâbâ' (1), *copiousness*

PLENTIFUL

3759 karmel (3), *planted field; garden produce*
5071 nᵉdâbâh (1), *abundant gift*

PLENTIFULLY

3499 yether (1), *remainder; small rope*
7230 rôb (1), *abundance*
2164 ĕuphŏrĕŏ (1), to *be fertile, produce a crop*

PLENTY

398 'âkal (1), to *eat*
4723 miqveh (1), *confidence; collection*
7230 rôb (3), *abundance*
7235 râbâh (1), to *increase*
7646 sâba' (2), *fill to satiety*
7647 sâbâ' (4), *copiousness*
8443 tôw'âphâh (1), *treasure; speed*

PLOTTETH

2161 zâmam (1), to *plan*

PLOUGH

723 arŏtrŏn (1), *plow*

PLOW

2790 chârash (6), to *engrave; to plow*
722 arŏtriŏŏ (1), to *plough, make furrows*

PLOWED

2790 chârash (5), to *engrave; to plow*

PLOWERS

2790 chârash (1), to *engrave; to plow*

PLOWETH

722 arŏtriŏŏ (1), to *plough, make furrows*

PLOWING

2790 chârash (2), to *engrave; to plow*
5215 nîyr (1), *freshly plowed land*

722 arŏtriŏŏ (1), to *plough, make furrows*

PLOWMAN

2790 chârash (2), to *engrave; to plow*

PLOWMEN

406 'ikkâr (2), *farmer*

PLOWSHARES

855 'êth (3), *digging implement*

PLUCK

717 'ârâh (1), to *pluck, pick fruit*
1497 gâzal (2), to *rob*
3318 yâtsâ' (1), to *go, bring out*
3615 kâlâh (1), to *cease, be finished, perish*
5255 nâçach (1), to *tear away*
5375 nâsâ' (1), to *lift up*
5423 nâthaq (2), to *tear off*
5428 nâthash (10), to *tear away, be uprooted*
5493 çûwr (1), to *turn off*
6131 'âqar (1), to *pluck up roots; to hamstring*
6998 qâṭaph (1), to *strip off, pick off*
8045 shâmad (1), to *desolate*
726 harpazŏ (2), to *seize*
1544 ĕkballŏ (1), to *throw out*
1807 ĕxairĕŏ (1), to *tear out; to select; to release*
1808 ĕxairŏ (1), to *remove, drive away*
5089 tillŏ (2), to *pull off grain heads*

PLUCKED

1497 gâzal (2), to *rob*
3318 yâtsâ' (1), to *go, bring out*
4803 mâraṭ (3), to *polish; to make bald*
4804 mᵉraṭ (Ch.) (1), to *pull off, tear off*
5255 nâçach (1), to *tear away*
5337 nâtsal (2), to *be snatched away*
5423 nâthaq (1), to *tear off*
5428 nâthash (4), to *tear away, be uprooted*
6132 'âqar (Ch.) (1), to *pluck up roots*
7993 shâlak (1), to *throw out, down or away*
8025 shâlaph (1), to *pull out, up or off*
1288 diaspaŏ (1), to *sever or dismember*
1610 ĕkrizoŏ (2), to *uproot*
1846 ĕxŏrussŏ (1), to *dig out*
5089 tillŏ (1), to *pull off grain heads*

PLUCKETH

2040 hâraç (1), to *pull down; break, destroy*

PLUCKT

2965 ṭârâph (1), *freshly picked vegetation*

PLUMBLINE

594 'ănâk (4), *plumb-line, plummet*

PLUMMET

68+913 'eben (1), *stone*
4949 mishqeleth (2), *plummet weight*

PLUNGE

2881 ṭâbal (1), to *dip*

POCHERETH

6380 Pôkereth Tsᵉbâyîym (2), *trap of gazelles*

POETS

4163 pŏiētēs (1), *performer; poet*

POINT

19 'ibchâh (1), *brandishing of a sword*
184 'âvâh (1), to *extend or mark out*
1980 hâlak (1), to *walk; live a certain way*
6856 tsippôren (1), *nail; point of a style or pen*
8376 tâ'âh (2), to *mark off, i.e. designate*
2079 ĕschatŏs (1), *finally, i.e. at the extremity*
3195 mĕllŏ (1), to *intend, i.e. be about to*

POINTED

2742 chârûwts (1), *threshing-sledge*

POINTS

5980 'ummâh (1), *near, beside, along with*

POISON

2534 chêmâh (5), *heat; anger; poison*
7219 rô'sh (1), *poisonous plant; poison*
2447 iŏs (2), *corrosion; venom*

POLE

5251 nêç (2), *flag; signal; token*

POLICY

7922 sekel (1), *intelligence; success*

POLISHED

1305 bârar (1), to *brighten; purify*
2404 châṭab (1), to *chop or carve wood*
7044 qâlâl (1), *brightened, polished*

POLISHING

1508 gizrâh (1), *figure, appearance; enclosure*

POLL

1494 gâzaz (1), to *shear; shave; destroy*
1538 gulgôleth (1), *skull*
3697 kâçam (1), to *shear, clip*

POLLED

1548 gâlach (3), to *shave; to lay waste*

POLLS

1538 gulgôleth (6), *skull*

POLLUTE

2490 châlal (8), to *profane, defile*

2610 chânêph (1), to *soil, be defiled*
2930 ṭâmê' (2), to *be morally contaminated*

POLLUTED
947 bûwç (2), to *trample down; oppress*
1351 gâ'al (7), to *soil, stain; desecrate*
2490 châlal (13), to *profane, defile*
2610 chânêph (3), to *soil, be defiled*
2930 ṭâmê' (12), to *be morally contaminated*
2931 ṭâmê' (1), *foul; ceremonially impure*
6121 'âqôb (1), *fraudulent; tracked*
2840 kŏinŏŏ (1), to *make profane*

POLLUTING
2490 châlal (2), to *profane, defile*

POLLUTION
2931 ṭâmê' (1), *foul; ceremonially impure*

POLLUTIONS
234 alisgĕma (1), *ceremonially polluted*
3393 miasma (1), *foulness, corruption*

POLLUX
1359 Diŏskŏurŏi (1), *twins of Zeus*

POMEGRANATE
7416 rimmôwn (10), *pomegranate*

POMEGRANATES
7416 rimmôwn (22), *pomegranate*

POMMELS
1543 gullâh (3), *fountain; bowl or globe*

POMP
1347 gâ'ôwn (5), *ascending; majesty*
7588 shâ'ôwn (1), *uproar; destruction*
5325 phantasia (1), vain *show, i.e. pomp*

PONDER
6424 pâlaç (2), to *weigh mentally*

PONDERED
4820 sumballō (1), to *consider; to aid; to join, attack*

PONDERETH
6424 pâlaç (1), to *weigh mentally*
8505 tâkan (2), to *balance, i.e. measure*

PONDS
98 'ăgam (2), *marsh; pond; pool*
99 'âgêm (1), *sad*

PONTIUS
4194 Pŏntiŏs (4), *bridged*

PONTUS
4195 Pŏntŏs (3), *sea*

POOL
98 'ăgam (2), *marsh; pond; pool*

1295 bᵉrêkâh (15), *reservoir, pool*
2861 kŏlumbēthra (5), *pond*

POOLS
98 'ăgam (2), *marsh; pond; pool*
1293 bᵉrâkâh (1), *benediction, blessing*
1295 bᵉrêkâh (1), *reservoir, pool*
4723 miqveh (1), *confidence; collection*

POOR
34 'ebyôwn (25), *destitute; poor*
1800 dal (44), *weak, thin; humble, needy*
1803 dallâh (4), *indigent, needy*
2489 chêlᵉkâ' (3), *unhappy wretch*
3423 yârash (2), to *impoverish; to ruin*
4134 mûwk (4), to *be impoverished*
4270 machçôwr (1), *impoverishment*
4542 miçkên (4), *indigent, needy*
6033 'ănâh (Ch.) (1), to *afflict, be afflicted*
6035 'ânâv (1), *needy; oppressed*
6035+6041 'ânâv (3), *needy; oppressed*
6041 'ănîy (56), *depressed*
7326 rûwsh (21), to *be destitute*
3993 pĕnēs (1), *poor*
3998 pĕnichrŏs (1), *needy, impoverished*
4433 ptōchĕuō (1), to *become indigent, poor*
4434 ptōchŏs (31), *pauper, beggar*

POORER
4134 mûwk (1), to *be impoverished*

POOREST
1803 dallâh (1), *indigent, needy*

POPLAR
3839 libneh (1), *whitish tree, (poss.) storax*

POPLARS
3839 libneh (1), *whitish tree, (poss.) storax*

POPULOUS
527 'âmôwn (1), *crowd*
7227 rab (1), *great*

PORATHA
6334 Pôwrâthâ' (1), *Poratha*

PORCH
197 'ûwlâm (33), *vestibule, portico*
4528 miçdᵉrôwn (1), *colonnade or portico*
4259 prŏauliŏn (1), *vestibule, i.e. alley-way*
4440 pulōn (1), *gate-way, door-way*
4745 stŏa (3), *colonnade or interior piazza*

PORCHES
197 'ûwlâm (1), *vestibule, portico*
4745 stŏa (1), *colonnade or interior piazza*

PORCIUS
4201 Pŏrkiŏs (1), *swinish*

PORT
8179 sha'ar (1), *opening, i.e. door or gate*

PORTER
7778 shôw'êr (4), *janitor, door-keeper*
2377 thurŏrŏs (2), *gate-warden, doorkeeper*

PORTERS
7778 shôw'êr (31), *janitor, door-keeper*
8179 sha'ar (1), *opening, i.e. door or gate*
8652 târâ' (Ch.) (1), *doorkeeper*

PORTION
270 'âchaz (2), to *seize, grasp; possess*
1697 dâbâr (4), *word; matter; thing*
2256 chebel (2), *company, band*
2505 châlaq (1), to *be smooth; be slippery*
2506 chêleq (36), *allotment*
2508 chălâq (Ch.) (3), *part, portion*
2513 chelqâh (6), *allotment*
2706 chôq (3), *appointment; allotment*
4490 mânâh (4), *ration; lot or portion*
4521 mᵉnâth (4), *allotment*
6310 peh (2), *mouth; opening*
6598 pathbag (5), *dainty food*
7926 shᵉkem (1), *neck; spur of a hill*
3313 mĕrŏs (3), *division or share*
4620 sitŏmĕtrŏn (1), *allowance or ration*

PORTIONS
2256 chebel (2), *company, band*
2506 chêleq (4), *allotment*
4256 machălôqeth (1), *section or division*
4490 mânâh (6), *ration; lot or portion*
4521 mᵉnâth (3), *allotment*

POSSESS
423 'âlâh (2), *public agreement*
2631 chăçan (Ch.) (1), to *take possession*
3423 yârash (93), to *inherit; to impoverish*
5157 nâchal (5), to *inherit*
2932 ktaŏmai (3), to *get*

POSSESSED
270 'âchaz (1), to *seize, grasp; possess*

2631 chăçan (Ch.) (1), to *take possession*
3423 yârash (19), to *inherit; to impoverish*
7069 qânâh (3), to *create; to procure*
1139 daimŏnizŏmai (11), to *be demon-possessed*
2192 ĕchō (2), to *have; hold; keep*
2722 katĕchō (1), to *hold down fast*
5224 huparchŏnta (1), *property or possessions*

POSSESSEST
3423 yârash (1), to *inherit; to impoverish*

POSSESSETH
3423 yârash (1), to *inherit; to impoverish*
5224 huparchŏnta (1), *property or possessions*

POSSESSING
2722 katĕchō (1), to *hold down fast*

POSSESSION
270 'âchaz (1), to *seize, grasp; possess*
272 'ăchuzzâh (64), *possession*
3423 yârash (6), to *inherit; to impoverish*
3424 yᵉrêshâh (2), *occupancy*
3425 yᵉrushâh (11), *conquest*
4180 môwrâsh (1), *possession*
4181 môwrâshâh (6), *possession*
4735 miqneh (3), *live-stock*
4736 miqnâh (1), *acquisition*
5157 nâchal (1), to *inherit*
5159 nachălâh (1), *occupancy*
7272 regel (1), *foot; step*
2697 kataschĕsis (2), *occupancy, possession*
2933 ktēma (1), *estate; wealth, possessions*
4047 pĕripŏiĕsis (1), *acquisition*

POSSESSIONS
270 'âchaz (3), to *seize, grasp; possess*
272 'ăchuzzâh (2), *possession*
4180 môwrâsh (1), *possession*
4639 ma'ăseh (1), *action; labor*
4735 miqneh (2), *live-stock*
2933 ktēma (3), *estate; wealth, possessions*
5564 chōriŏn (1), *spot or plot of ground*

POSSESSOR
7069 qânâh (2), to *create; to procure*

POSSESSORS
7069 qânâh (1), to *create; to procure*
2935 ktētōr (1), land *owner*

POSSIBLE
102 adunatŏs (1), *weak; impossible*
1410 dunamai (1), *to be able* or *possible*
1415 dunatŏs (13), *capable; possible*

POST
352 'ayîl (4), *chief; ram; oak* tree
4201 mᵉzûwzâh (4), *door-post*
4947 mashqôwph (1), *lintel*
7323 rûwts (2), to *run*

POSTERITY
310 'achar (4), *after*
319 'achărîyth (3), *future; posterity*
1755 dôwr (1), *dwelling*
7611 shᵉ'êrîyth (1), *remainder* or *residual*

POSTS
352 'ayîl (17), *chief; ram; oak* tree
520 'ammâh (1), *cubit*
4201 mᵉzûwzâh (15), *door-post*
5592 çaph (3), *dish*
7323 rûwts (6), to *run*

POT
610 'âçûwk (1), oil-*flask*
1731 dûwd (1), *pot, kettle; basket*
3627 kᵉlîy (1), *implement, thing*
4715 mitsrêph (2), *crucible*
5518 çîyr (12), *thorn; hook*
6517 pârûwr (2), *skillet*
6803 tsintseneth (1), *vase, receptacle*
4713 stamnŏs (1), *jar* or earthen *tank*

POTENTATE
1413 dunastēs (1), *ruler* or *officer*

POTI-PHERAH
6319 Pôwṭîy Phera' (3), *Poti-Phera*

POTIPHAR
6318 Pôwṭîyphar (2), *Potiphar*

POTS
1375 gᵉbîya' (1), *goblet; bowl*
1731 dûwd (1), *pot, kettle; basket*
5518 çîyr (9), *thorn; hook*
8240 shâphâth (1), *hook; hearth*
3582 xĕstēs (2), *vessel; measure*

POTSHERD
2789 cheres (4), piece of earthenware *pottery*

POTSHERDS
2789 cheres (1), piece of earthenware *pottery*

POTTAGE
5138 nâzîyd (6), *boiled* soup or stew

POTTER
3335 yâtsar (8), to *form; potter;* to *determine*
2763 kĕramĕus (1), *potter*
2764 kĕramikŏs (1), *made of clay*

POTTER'S
3335 yâtsar (7), to *form; potter;* to *determine*
2763 kĕramĕus (2), *potter*

POTTERS
3335 yâtsar (1), to *form; potter;* to *determine*

POTTERS'
3335 yâtsar (1), to *form; potter;* to *determine*
6353 pechâr (Ch.) (1), *potter*

POUND
4488 mâneh (2), fixed *weight*
3046 litra (2), 12 oz. measure, i.e. a *pound*
3414 mna (4), certain *weight*

POUNDS
4488 mâneh (2), fixed *weight*
3414 mna (5), certain *weight*

POUR
2212 zâqaq (1), to *strain, refine; extract, clarify*
3332 yâtsaq (13), to *pour* out
5042 nâba' (1), to *gush* forth; to *utter*
5064 nâgar (2), to *pour* out; to *deliver* over
5140 nâzal (2), to *drip,* or *shed* by trickling
5258 nâçak (6), to *pour* a libation; to *anoint*
5414 nâthan (1), to *give*
7324 rûwq (1), to *pour* out, i.e. *empty*
8210 shâphak (33), to *spill* forth; to *expend*
1632 ĕkchĕŏ (3), to *pour forth;* to *bestow*

POURED
2229 zâram (1), to *gush* water, pour forth
3251 yâçak (1), to *pour*
3332 yâtsaq (13), to *pour* out; to *deliver* over
5064 nâgar (1), to *pour* out; to *deliver* over
5258 nâçak (10), to *pour* a libation; to *anoint*
5413 nâthak (13), to *flow* forth, pour out
6168 'ârâh (2), to *empty, pour* out; *demolish*
6694 tsûwq (2), to *pour* out; *melt*
7324 rûwq (1), to *pour* out, i.e. *empty*
8210 shâphak (25), to *spill* forth
8211 shephek (2), ash-*heap, dump*
906 ballō (1), to *throw*
1632 ĕkchĕŏ (9), to *pour forth;* to *bestow*
2708 katachĕŏ (2), to *pour down* or *out*

POTTER
2767 kĕrannumi (1), to *mingle,* i.e. to *pour*

POUREDST
8210 shâphak (1), to *spill* forth; to *expend*

POURETH
1811 dâlaph (1), to *drip*
5042 nâba' (2), to *gush* forth; to *utter*
5064 nâgar (1), to *pour* out; to *deliver* over
8210 shâphak (6), to *spill* forth; to *expend*
906 ballō (1), to *throw*

POURING
8210 shâphak (1), to *spill* forth; to *expend*

POURTRAY
2710 châqaq (1), to *engrave;* to *enact* laws

POURTRAYED
2707 châqah (2), to *carve;* to *delineate*
2710 châqaq (1), to *engrave;* to *enact* laws

POVERTY
2639 cheçer (1), *lack; destitution*
3423 yârash (3), to *impoverish;* to *ruin*
4270 machçôwr (1), *impoverishment*
7389 rêysh (7), *poverty*
4432 ptōchĕia (3), *indigence, poverty*

POWDER
80 'âbâq (1), *fine dust; cosmetic powder*
1854 dâqaq (2), to *crush; crumble*
6083 'âphâr (3), *dust, earth, mud; clay,*
3039 likmaō (2), to *grind* to *powder*

POWDERS
81 'ăbâqâh (1), *cosmetic powder*

POWER
410 'êl (3), *mighty;* the *Almighty*
1369 gᵉbûwrâh (9), *force; valor; victory*
2220 zᵉrôwa' (3), *arm; foreleg; force, power*
2428 chayil (9), *army; wealth; virtue; strength*
2429 chayil (Ch.) (1), *army; strength; loud sound*
2632 chêçen (Ch.) (2), *strength, powerful rule*
3027 yâd (13), *hand; power*
3028 yad (Ch.) (1), *hand; power*
3201 yâkôl (1), to *be able*
3581 kôach (47), *force, might; strength*
3709 kaph (1), hollow of *hand; paw; sole* of *foot*
4475 memshâlâh (1), *rule; realm* or a *ruler*
4910 mâshal (2), to *rule*
5794 'az (1), *strong, vehement, harsh*
5797 'ôz (11), *strength*

5808 'izzûwz (1), *forcible; army*
6184 'ârîyts (1), *powerful* or *tyrannical*
7786 sûwr (1), to *rule, crown*
7980 shâlaṭ (3), to *dominate,* i.e. *govern*
7981 shᵉlêṭ (Ch.) (1), to *dominate,* i.e. *govern*
7983 shilṭôwn (2), *potentate*
7989 shallîyṭ (1), *prince* or *warrior*
8280 sârâh (2), to *prevail, contend*
8592 ta'ătsûmâh (1), *might*
8617 tᵉqûwmâh (1), *resistfulness*
8633 tôqeph (1), *might*
746 archē (1), *first in rank; first in time*
1325 didōmi (2), to *give*
1410 dunamai (1), to *be able* or *possible*
1411 dunamis (71), *force, power, miracle*
1415 dunatŏs (1), *powerful* or *capable; possible*
1849 ĕxŏusia (61), *authority, power, right*
1850 ĕxŏusiazō (3), to *control, master another*
2479 ischus (2), *forcefulness, power*
2904 kratŏs (6), *vigor, strength*
3168 mĕgalĕiŏtēs (1), *grandeur* or *splendor*

POWERFUL
3581 kôach (1), *force, might; strength*
1756 ĕnĕrgēs (1), *active, operative*
2478 ischurŏs (1), *forcible, powerful*

POWERS
1411 dunamis (6), *force, power, miracle*
1849 ĕxŏusia (8), *authority, power, right*

PRACTISE
5953 'âlal (1), to *glean;* to *overdo*
6213 'âsâh (3), to *do* or *make*

PRACTISED
2790 chârash (1), to *engrave;* to *plow*
6213 'âsâh (1), to *do*

PRAETORIUM
4232 praitōriŏn (1), *governor's court-room*

PRAISE
1288 bârak (1), to *bless*
1974 hillûwl (1), *harvest celebration*
1984 hâlal (92), to *praise; thank; boast*
2167 zâmar (4), to *play music*
3034 yâdâh (52), to *revere* or *worship*
4110 mahălâl (1), *fame, good reputation*

7623 shâbach (4), to
address; to pacify
7624 sh°bach (Ch.) (2), to
adulate, i.e. adore
8416 t°hillâh (52),
laudation; hymn
8426 tôwdâh (5),
expressions of thanks
133 ainĕsis (1),
thank-offering. praise
134 ainĕō (3), to praise
136 ainŏs (2), praise
1391 dŏxa (4), glory;
brilliance
1867 ĕpainĕō (3), to
applaud, commend
1868 ĕpainŏs (12),
laudation
5214 humnĕō (1), to
celebrate in song

PRAISED
1288 bârak (1), to bless
1984 hâlal (19), to praise;
thank; boast
3034 yâdâh (1), to throw;
to revere or worship
7623 shâbach (1), to
address
7624 sh°bach (Ch.) (3), to
adulate, i.e. adore
2127 ĕulŏgĕō (1), to
invoke a benediction

PRAISES
1984 hâlal (1), to praise;
thank; boast
8416 t°hillâh (5),
laudation; hymn
8426 tôwdâh (1),
expressions of thanks
703 arĕtĕ (1), excellence,
virtue

PRAISETH
1984 hâlal (1), to praise;
thank; boast

PRAISING
1984 hâlal (4), to praise;
thank; boast
134 ainĕō (6), to praise

PRANSING
1725 dâhar (1), to prance

PRANSINGS
1726 dahăhar (2), gallop

PRATING
8193 sâphâh (2), lip,
language, speech
5396 phluarĕō (1), to
berate

PRAY
577 'ânnâ' (2), oh now!, I
ask you!
2470 châlâh (3), to be
weak, sick, afflicted
2603 chânan (1), to
implore
3863 lûw' (1), if; would
that!
4994 nâ' (195), I pray!,
please!, I beg you!
6279 'âthar (1), intercede
6293 pâga' (1), to impinge
6419 pâlal (34), to
intercede, pray
6739 ts°lâ' (Ch.) (1), pray
7592 shâ'al (1), to ask
7878 sîyach (1), to
ponder, muse aloud

1189 dĕŏmai (7), to beg,
petition, ask
2065 ĕrōtaō (10), to
interrogate; to request
2172 ĕuchŏmai (2), to
wish for; to pray
3870 parakalĕō (4), to
call, invite
4336 prŏsĕuchŏmai (42),
to supplicate, pray

PRAYED
6419 pâlal (30), to
intercede, pray
6739 ts°lâ' (Ch.) (1), pray
1189 dĕŏmai (3), to beg,
petition, ask
2065 ĕrōtaō (4), to
interrogate; to request
3870 parakalĕō (2), to
call, invite
4336 prŏsĕuchŏmai (25),
to supplicate, pray

PRAYER
2470 châlâh (1), to be
weak, sick, afflicted
3908 lachash (1),
incantation; amulet
6279 'âthar (1), intercede
in prayer
6419 pâlal (2), to
intercede, pray
7878 sîyach (1), to
ponder, muse aloud
7879 sîyach (1), uttered
contemplation
8605 t°phillâh (75),
intercession
1162 dĕĕsis (7), petition,
request
1783 ĕntĕuxis (1),
intercession
2171 ĕuchĕ (1), wish,
petition
4335 prŏsĕuchĕ (21),
prayer; prayer chapel
4336 prŏsĕuchŏmai (1),
to supplicate, pray

PRAYERS
8605 t°phillâh (2),
intercession
1162 dĕĕsis (5), petition,
request
4335 prŏsĕuchĕ (15),
prayer; prayer chapel
4336 prŏsĕuchŏmai (2),
to supplicate, pray

PRAYEST
4336 prŏsĕuchŏmai (2),
to supplicate, pray

PRAYETH
6419 pâlal (4), to
intercede, pray
4336 prŏsĕuchŏmai (3),
to supplicate, pray

PRAYING
1156 b°'â' (Ch.) (1), to
seek or ask
6419 pâlal (5), to
intercede, pray
1189 dĕŏmai (2), to beg,
petition, ask
4336 prŏsĕuchŏmai (12),
to supplicate, pray

PREACH
1319 bâsar (1), to
announce (good news)
7121 qârâ' (2), to call out

1229 diaggĕllō (1), to
herald thoroughly
2097 ĕuaggĕlizō (18), to
announce good news
2605 kataggĕllō (4), to
proclaim, promulgate
2784 kĕrussō (22), to
herald
2980 lalĕō (1), to talk

PREACHED
1319 bâsar (1), to
announce (good news)
189 akŏĕ (1), hearing;
thing heard
1256 dialĕgŏmai (1), to
discuss
2097 ĕuaggĕlizō (22), to
announce good news
2605 kataggĕllō (6), to
proclaim, promulgate
2784 kĕrussō (20), to
herald
2907 krĕas (1), meat
2980 lalĕō (4), to talk
3954 parrhĕsia (1),
frankness, boldness
4137 plĕrŏō (1), to fill,
make complete
4283 prŏĕuaggĕlizŏmai
(1), to announce glad
news in advance
4296 prŏkĕrussō (2), to
proclaim in advance

PREACHER
6953 qôheleth (7),
assembler i.e. lecturer
2783 kĕrux (3), herald
2784 kĕrussō (1), to
herald

PREACHEST
2784 kĕrussō (1), to
herald

PREACHETH
2097 ĕuaggĕlizō (1), to
announce good news
2784 kĕrussō (2), to
herald

PREACHING
7150 q°rîy'âh (1),
proclamation
1256 dialĕgŏmai (1), to
discuss
2097 ĕuaggĕlizō (6), to
announce good news
2782 kĕrugma (8),
proclamation
2784 kĕrussō (8), to
herald
2980 lalĕō (1), to talk
3056 lŏgŏs (1), word,
matter, thing; Word

PRECEPT
4687 mitsvâh (1),
command
6673 tsav (4), injunction
1785 ĕntŏlĕ (2),
prescription, regulation

PRECEPTS
4687 mitsvâh (3),
command
6490 piqqûwd (21),
mandate of God, Law

PRECIOUS
2530 châmad (3), to
delight in; lust for

2532 chemdâh (1),
delight
2580 chên (1),
graciousness; beauty
2667 chôphesh (1), carpet
2896 tôwb (4), good; well
3365 yâqar (8), to be
valuable; to make rare
3366 y°qâr (4), wealth;
costliness; dignity
3368 yâqâr (25), valuable
4022 meged (5), valuable
4030 migdânâh (3),
preciousness, i.e. a gem
4901 meshek (1), sowing;
possession
5238 n°kôth (2),
valuables
927 barutimŏs (1), highly
valuable
1784 ĕntimŏs (2), valued,
considered precious
2472 isŏtimŏs (1), of
equal value or honor
4185 pŏlutĕlĕs (1),
extremely expensive
5092 timĕ (1), esteem;
nobility; money
5093 timiŏs (11), costly;
honored, esteemed

PREDESTINATE
4309 prŏŏrizō (2), to
predetermine

PREDESTINATED
4309 prŏŏrizō (2), to
predetermine

PREEMINENCE
4195 môwthar (1), gain;
superiority
4409 prōtĕuō (1), to be
first
5383 philŏprōtĕuō (1),
loving to be first

PREFER
5927 'âlâh (1), to ascend,
be high, mount

PREFERRED
5330 n°tsach (Ch.) (1), to
become chief
8138 shânâh (1), to fold,
to transmute
1096 ginŏmai (3), to be,
become

PREFERRING
4285 prŏĕgĕŏmai (1), to
show deference
4299 prŏkrima (1),
prejudgment, partiality

PREMEDITATE
3191 mĕlĕtaō (1), to plot,
think about

PREPARATION
3559 kûwn (2), to set up:
establish, fix, prepare
2091 hĕtŏimasia (1),
preparation
3904 paraskĕuĕ (6),
readiness

PREPARATIONS
4633 ma'ărâk (1), mental
disposition, plan

PREPARE
631 'âçar (1), to fasten; to
join battle
3559 kûwn (41), to set up:
establish, fix, prepare

4487 mânâh (1), to *allot;* to *enumerate* or enroll
6186 'ârak (2), to set in a row, i.e. *arrange,*
6213 'âsâh (9), to *do* or *make*
6437 pânâh (4), to *turn,* to *face*
6942 qâdâsh (7), to *be, make clean*
2090 hĕtŏimazō (11), to *prepare*
2680 kataskĕuazō (3), to *prepare thoroughly*
3903 paraskĕuazō (1), to *get ready, prepare*

PREPARED
2164 z°man (Ch.) (1), to *agree, conspire*
2502 châlats (2), to *deliver, equip*
3559 kûwn (53), to *set up: establish, fix, prepare*
3739 kârâh (1), to *purchase* by bargaining
4487 mânâh (4), to *allot;* to *enumerate* or enroll
6186 'ârak (2), to set in a row, i.e. *arrange,*
6213 'âsâh (13), to *do* or *make*
6437 pânâh (1), to *turn,* to *face*
7543 râqach (1), to *perfume, blend spice*
2090 hĕtŏimazō (18), to *prepare*
2092 hĕtŏimŏs (1), *ready, prepared*
2675 katartizō (1), to *repair;* to *prepare*
2680 kataskĕuazō (2), to *prepare thoroughly*
4282 prŏĕtŏimazō (1), to *fit up in advance*

PREPAREDST
6437 pânâh (1), to *turn,* to *face*

PREPAREST
3559 kûwn (1), to *set up: establish, fix, prepare*
6186 'ârak (1), to set in a row, i.e. *arrange,*
6213 'âsâh (1), to *do* or *make*

PREPARETH
3559 kûwn (3), to *set up: establish, fix, prepare*

PREPARING
6213 'âsâh (1), to *do* or *make*
2680 kataskĕuazō (1), to *prepare thoroughly*

PRESBYTERY
4244 prĕsbutĕriŏn (1), *order of elders*

PRESCRIBED
3789 kâthab (1), to *write*

PRESCRIBING
3792 k°thâb (Ch.) (1), *writing, record* or *book*

PRESENCE
5048 neged (8), *over against* or *before*
5869 'ayin (9), *eye; sight; fountain*

5921 'al (1), *above, over, upon,* or *against*
6440 pânîym (76), *face; front*
6925 qŏdâm (Ch.) (1), *before*
561 apĕnanti (1), *before* or *against*
1715 ĕmprŏsthĕn (1), *in front of*
1799 ĕnōpiŏn (9), *in the face* of, *before*
2714 katĕnōpiŏn (1), *directly in front of*
3952 parŏusia (2), *coming; presence*
4383 prŏsōpŏn (7), *face, presence*

PRESENT
814 'eshkâr (1), *gratuity, gift; payment*
1293 b°râkâh (3), *benediction, blessing*
3320 yâtsab (5), to *station, offer, continue*
3557 kûwl (1), to *keep in;* to *measure*
4503 minchâh (22), *tribute; offering*
4672 mâtsâ' (17), to *find* or *acquire;* to *occur*
5307 nâphal (3), to *fall*
5324 nâtsab (1), to *station*
5975 'âmad (6), to *stand*
7810 shachad (2), to *bribe; gift*
7862 shay (1), *gift*
7964 shillûwach (1), *daughter's dower*
8670 t°shûwrâh (1), *gift*
737 arti (2), just *now;* at *once*
1736 ĕndēmĕō (2), to *be at home*
1764 ĕnistēmi (5), to *be present*
2186 ĕphistēmi (1), to *be present;* to *approach*
2476 histēmi (1), to *stand, establish*
3306 mĕnō (1), to *stay, remain*
3568 nun (4), *now;* the *present* or *immediate*
3854 paraginŏmai (1), to *arrive;* to *appear*
3873 parakĕimai (2), to *be at hand*
3918 parĕimi (14), to *be present;* to *have come*
3936 paristēmi (7), to *stand beside, present*
4840 sumparĕimi (1), to *be now present*

PRESENTED
3320 yâtsab (4), to *station, offer, continue*
3322 yâtsag (1), to *place*
4672 mâtsâ' (3), to *find meet* or *be present*
5066 nâgash (1), to *be, come, bring near*
5307 nâphal (1), to *fall*
5414 nâthan (1), to *give*
5975 'âmad (1), to *stand*
7126 qârab (2), to *approach, bring near*
7200 râ'âh (1), to *see*

3936 paristēmi (2), to *stand beside, present*
4374 prŏsphĕrō (1), to *present to;* to *treat as*

PRESENTING
5307 nâphal (1), to *fall*

PRESENTLY
3117 yôwm (2), *day; time period*
1824 ĕxautēs (1), *instantly, at once*
3916 parachrēma (1), *instantly, immediately*
3936 paristēmi (1), to *stand beside, present*

PRESENTS
4030 migdânâh (1), *preciousness,* i.e. a *gem*
4503 minchâh (6), *tribute; offering*
7862 shay (2), *gift*
7964 shillûwach (1), *daughter's dower*

PRESERVE
2421 châyâh (4), to *live;* to *revive*
3498 yâthar (1), to *remain* or *be left*
4241 michyâh (1), *preservation of life*
4422 mâlaṭ (1), to *escape* as if by *slipperiness*
5341 nâtsar (11), to *guard, protect*
7760 sûwm (1), to *put*
8104 shâmar (9), to *watch*
2225 zōŏgŏnĕō (1), to *rescue; be saved*
4982 sōzō (1), to *deliver;* to *protect*

PRESERVED
3467 yâsha' (4), to *make safe, free*
5336 nâtsîyr (1), *delivered*
5337 nâtsal (1), to *deliver;* to *be snatched*
8104 shâmar (6), to *watch*
4933 suntērĕō (2), to *preserve in memory*
5083 tērĕō (2), to *keep, guard, obey*

PRESERVER
5314 nâphash (1), to *be refreshed*

PRESERVEST
2421 châyâh (1), to *live;* to *revive*
3467 yâsha' (1), to *make safe, free*

PRESERVETH
2421 châyâh (1), to *live;* to *revive*
5341 nâtsar (1), to *guard, protect, maintain*
8104 shâmar (6), to *watch*

PRESIDENTS
5632 çârêk (Ch.) (5), *emir, high official*

PRESS
1660 gath (1), wine-*press* or *vat*
6333 pûwrâh (1), *wine-press trough*

598 apŏthlibō (1), to *crowd, press up* against
1377 diōkō (1), to *pursue;* to *persecute*
3793 ŏchlŏs (5), *throng,* i.e. *crowd* or *mob*

PRESSED
1765 dâchaph (1), to *urge;* to *hasten*
4600 mâ'ak (1), to *press*
5781 'ûwq (2), to *pack, be pressed*
6484 pâtsar (2), to *stun* or *dull*
6555 pârats (2), to *break out*
6693 tsûwq (1), to *oppress, distress*
7818 sâchaṭ (1), to *tread out,* i.e. *squeeze* grapes
916 barĕō (1), to *weigh down, cause pressure*
1945 ĕpikĕimai (1), to *rest upon; press upon*
1968 ĕpipiptō (1), to *embrace;* to *seize*
4085 piĕzō (1), to *pack down firm*
4912 sunĕchō (1), to *hold together, compress*

PRESSES
3342 yeqeb (2), wine-*vat,* wine-*press*

PRESSETH
5181 nâchath (1), to *sink, descend;* to *press* down
971 biazō (1), to *crowd oneself* into

PRESSFAT
3342 yeqeb (1), wine-*vat.* wine-*press*

PRESUME
2102 zûwd (1), to *be insolent*
4390 mâlê' (1), to *fill; be full*

PRESUMED
6075 'âphal (1), to *swell; be elated*

PRESUMPTUOUS
2086 zêd (1), *arrogant, proud*
5113 tŏlmētēs (1), *daring (audacious) man*

PRESUMPTUOUSLY
2087 zâdôwn (2), *arrogance, pride*
2102 zûwd (3), to *be insolent*
3027 yâd (1), *hand; power*

PRETENCE
4392 prŏphasis (3), *pretext, excuse*

PREVAIL
1396 gâbar (5), to *act insolently*
2388 châzaq (2), to *bind, restrain, conquer*
3201 yâkôl (13), to *be able*
3898 lâcham (1), to *fight a battle*
5810 'âzaz (1), to *be stout; be bold*
6113 'âtsar (1), to *hold back;* to *maintain, rule*

6206 'ârats (1), to *awe;* to *dread;* to *harass*
8630 tâqaph (2), to *overpower*
2729 katischuŏ (1), to *overpower, prevail*
5623 ōphĕlĕō (2), to *benefit, be of use*

PREVAILED
553 'âmats (1), to *be strong; be courageous*
1396 gâbar (9), to *be strong; to prevail*
2388 châzaq (8), to *bind, restrain, conquer*
3201 yâkôl (9), to *be able*
3202 yᵉkêl (Ch.) (1), to *be able*
3513 kâbad (1), to *be heavy, severe, dull*
5810 'âzaz (2), to *be stout; be bold*
7186 qâsheh (1), *severe*
2480 ischuŏ (3), to *have or exercise force*
2729 katischuŏ (1), to *overpower, prevail*
3528 nikaō (1), to *subdue, conquer*

PREVAILEST
8630 tâqaph (1), to *overpower*

PREVAILETH
7287 râdâh (1), to *subjugate; to crumble*

PREVENT
6923 qâdam (6), to *anticipate, hasten*
5348 phthanō (1), to *anticipate or precede*

PREVENTED
6923 qâdam (8), to *anticipate, hasten*
4399 prŏphthanō (1), to *anticipate*

PREVENTEST
6923 qâdam (1), to *anticipate, hasten*

PREY
400 'ôkel (2), *food*
957 baz (17), *plunder, loot*
961 bizzâh (4), *booty, plunder*
962 bâzaz (9), to *plunder, take booty*
2863 chetheph (1), *robber or robbery*
2963 ṭâraph (1), to *pluck off or pull to pieces*
2964 ṭereph (18), *fresh torn prey*
4455 malqôwach (6), *spoil, plunder*
5706 'ad (3), *booty*
7997 shâlal (1), to *drop or strip; to plunder*
7998 shâlâl (11), *booty*

PRICE
3365 yâqar (1), to *be valuable; to make rare*
3701 keçeph (3), *silver money*
4242 mᵉchîyr (11), *price, payment, wages*
4377 meker (1), *merchandise; value*

4736 miqnâh (2), *acquisition*
4901 meshek (1), *sowing; possession*
6187 'êrek (1), *pile, equipment, estimate*
7939 sâkâr (2), *payment, salary; compensation*
4185 pŏlutĕlēs (1), *extremely expensive*
4186 pŏlutimŏs (1), *extremely valuable*
5092 timē (7), *esteem; nobility; money*

PRICES
5092 timē (1), *esteem; nobility; money*

PRICKED
8150 shânan (1), to *pierce; to inculcate*
2669 katapŏnĕō (1), to *harass, oppress*

PRICKING
3992 mâ'ar (1), to *be painful; destructive*

PRICKS
7899 sêk (1), *brier of a hedge*
2759 kĕntrŏn (2), *sting; goad*

PRIDE
1344 gê'âh (1), *arrogance, pride*
1346 ga'ăvâh (9), *arrogance; majesty*
1347 gâ'ôwn (20), *ascending; majesty*
1348 gê'ûwth (2), *ascending; majesty*
1363 gôbahh (2), *height; grandeur; arrogance*
1466 gêvâh (3), *arrogance, pride*
2087 zâdôwn (6), *arrogance, pride*
2103 zûwd (Ch.) (1), to *be proud*
7407 rôkeç (1), *snare as of tied meshes*
7830 shachats (1), *haughtiness; dignity*
212 alazŏnĕia (1), *boasting*
5187 tuphŏō (1), to *inflate with self-conceit*
5243 hupĕrēphania (1), *haughtiness, arrogance*

PRIEST
3547 kâhan (2), to *officiate as a priest*
3548 kôhên (423), one *officiating as a priest*
3549 kâhên (Ch.) (1), one *officiating as a priest*
748 archiĕratikŏs (1), *high-priestly*
749 archiĕrĕus (53), *high-priest, chief priest*
2409 hiĕrĕus (16), *priest*

PRIEST'S
3547 kâhan (20), to *officiate as a priest*
3548 kôhên (17), one *officiating as a priest*
3550 kᵉhunnâh (4), *priesthood*

749 archiĕrĕus (4), *high-priest, chief priest*
2405 hiĕratĕia (1), *priestly office*
2407 hiĕratĕuō (1), to *be a priest*

PRIESTHOOD
3550 kᵉhunnâh (9), *priesthood*
2405 hiĕratĕia (1), *priestly office*
2406 hiĕratĕuma (2), *priestly order*
2420 hiĕrōsunē (4), *priestly office*

PRIESTS
3548 kôhên (300), one *officiating as a priest*
3549 kâhên (Ch.) (6), one *officiating as a priest*
3649 kâmâr (1), *pagan priest*
749 archiĕrĕus (67), *high-priest, chief priest*
2409 hiĕrĕus (15), *priest*

PRIESTS'
3548 kôhên (8), one *officiating as a priest*

PRINCE
5057 nâgîyd (8), *commander, official*
5081 nâdîyb (4), *grandee or tyrant*
5387 nâsîy' (56), *leader; rising mist, fog*
7101 qâtsîyn (2), *magistrate; leader*
7333 râzôwn (1), *dignitary*
8269 sar (19), *head person, ruler*
8323 sârar (1), to *have, exercise, get dominion*
747 archēgŏs (2), *chief leader; founder*
758 archōn (8), *first*

PRINCE'S
5081 nâdîyb (1), *grandee or tyrant*
5387 nâsîy' (2), *leader; rising mist, fog*

PRINCES
324 ăchashdarpan (Ch.) (9), *satrap*
2831 chashmân (1), *(poss.) wealthy*
3548 kôhên (1), one *officiating as a priest*
5057 nâgîyd (1), *commander, official*
5081 nâdîyb (10), *grandee or tyrant*
5257 nᵉçîyk (3), *libation; molten image; prince*
5387 nâsîy' (40), *leader; rising mist, fog*
5461 çâgân (1), *prefect of a province*
6579 partam (1), *grandee, noble*
7101 qâtsîyn (2), *magistrate; leader*
7227 rab (2), *great*
7261 rabrᵉbân (Ch.) (2), *magnate, noble*
7336 râzan (5), *honorable*

7991 shâlîysh (1), *officer; of the third rank*
8269 sar (190), *head person, ruler*
758 archōn (3), *first*
2232 hēgĕmōn (1), *chief*

PRINCESS
8282 sârâh (1), *female noble*

PRINCESSES
8282 sârâh (1), *female noble*

PRINCIPAL
1 'âb (1), *father*
117 'addîyr (3), *powerful; majestic*
3548 kôhên (1), one *officiating as a priest*
5257 nᵉçîyk (1), *libation; molten image; prince*
7218 rô'sh (5), *head*
7225 rê'shîyth (1), *first*
7795 sôwrâh (1), *row*
8269 sar (2), *head person, ruler*
8291 sarûwq (1), *choice grapevine*

PRINCIPALITIES
4761 mar'âshâh (1), *headship, dominion*
746 archē (6), *first in rank; first in time*

PRINCIPALITY
746 archē (2), *first in rank; first in time*

PRINCIPLES
746 archē (1), *first in rank; first in time*
4747 stŏichĕiŏn (1), *basic principles*

PRINT
2707 châqah (1), to *carve; to delineate*
5414 nâthan (1), to *give*
5179 tupŏs (2), *shape, resemblance; "type"*

PRINTED
2710 châqaq (1), to *engrave; to enact laws*

PRISCA
4251 Priska (1), *ancient*

PRISCILLA
4252 Priskilla (5), *little Prisca*

PRISED
3365 yâqar (1), to *be valuable; to make rare*

PRISON
631 'âçar (2), to *fasten; to join battle*
1004+612 bayith (3), *house; temple; family*
1004+3608 bayith (7), *house; temple; family*
1004+5470 bayith (8), *house; temple; family*
1004+6486 bayith (1), *house; temple; family*
3608 kele' (4), *prison*
4115 mahpeketh (2), *stocks for punishment*
4307 maṭṭârâ' (13), *jail (guard-house); aim*
4525 maçgêr (3), *prison; craftsman*

4929 mishmâr (1), *guard; deposit; usage; example*
6115 'ôtser (1), *closure; constraint*
6495 peqach-qôwach (1), *jail-delivery; salvation*
1200 dĕsmŏphulax (2), *jailer*
1201 dĕsmôtḗriŏn (4), *dungeon, jail*
3612 ŏikḗma (1), *jail cell*
3860 paradidŏmi (2), to *hand over*
5084 tḗrēsis (1), *observance; prison*
5438 phulakḗ (33), *night watch; prison; haunt*

PRISONER
615 'âçîyr (1), *captive, prisoner*
616 'aççîyr (1), *captive, prisoner*
1198 dĕsmiŏs (11), *bound captive; one arrested*

PRISONERS
615 'âçîyr (8), *captive, prisoner*
616 'aççîyr (3), *captive, prisoner*
631 'âçar (2), to *fasten; to join* battle
7628 shebîy (2), *exile; booty*
1198 dĕsmiŏs (3), *bound captive; one arrested*
1202 dĕsmôtēs (2), *captive*

PRISONS
5438 phulakḗ (3), *night watch; prison; haunt*

PRIVATE
2398 idiŏs (1), *private or separate*

PRIVATELY
2596+2398 kata (8), *down; according to*

PRIVILY
652 'ôphel (1), *dusk, darkness*
2934 ţâman (3), to *hide*
3909 lât (1), *incantation; secrecy; covertly*
5643 çĕther (1), *cover, shelter*
6845 tsâphan (1), to *hide; to protect; to lurk*
8649 tormâh (1), *fraud*
2977 lathra (3), *privately, secretly*
3918 parĕimi (1), to *be present; to have come*
3922 parĕisĕrchŏmai (1), to *supervene stealthily*

PRIVY
2314 châdar (1), to *enclose; to beset*
3045 yâda' (1), to *know*
8212 shophkâh (1), *penis*
4894 sunĕidŏ (1), to *understand*

PRIZE
1017 brabĕiŏn (2), *prize in the public games*

PROCEED
3254 yâçaph (2), to *add or augment*

3318 yâtsâ' (8), to *go, bring out*
1607 ĕkpŏrĕuŏmai (3), to *proceed, project*
1831 ĕxĕrchŏmai (1), to *issue; to leave*
4298 prŏkŏptŏ (1), to *go ahead, advance*

PROCEEDED
3254 yâçaph (1), to *add or augment*
3318 yâtsâ' (2), to *go, bring out*
4161 môwtsâ' (1), *going forth*
1607 ĕkpŏrĕuŏmai (3), to *proceed, project*
1831 ĕxĕrchŏmai (1), to *issue; to leave*
4369 prŏstithḗmi (1), to *annex, repeat*

PROCEEDETH
3318 yâtsâ' (6), to *go, bring out*
4161 môwtsâ' (1), *going forth*
1607 ĕkpŏrĕuŏmai (3), to *proceed, project*
1831 ĕxĕrchŏmai (1), to *issue; to leave*

PROCEEDING
1607 ĕkpŏrĕuŏmai (1), to *proceed, project*

PROCESS
7093 qêts (1), *extremity; after*
7227 rab (1), *great*
7235 râbâh (1), to *increase*

PROCHORUS
4402 Prŏchŏrŏs (1), *before the dance*

PROCLAIM
5674 'âbar (1), to *cross over; to transition*
6942 qâdâsh (1), to *be, make clean*
7121 qârâ' (21), to *call out*

PROCLAIMED
2199 zâ'aq (1), to *call out, announce*
5674 'âbar (1), to *cross over; to transition*
7121 qârâ' (11), to *call out*
8085 shâma' (1), to *hear*
2784 kĕrussŏ (1), to *herald*

PROCLAIMETH
7121 qârâ' (1), to *call out*

PROCLAIMING
7121 qârâ' (2), to *call out*
2784 kĕrussŏ (1), to *herald*

PROCLAMATION
3745 keraz (Ch.) (1), to *proclaim*
5674+6963 'âbar (4), to *cross over; to transition*
6963 qôwl (1), *voice or sound*
7121 qârâ' (1), to *call out*
7440 rinnâh (1), *shout*
8085 shâma' (1), to *hear*

PROCURE
6213 'âsâh (2), to *make*

PROCURED
6213 'âsâh (2), to *make*

PROCURETH
1245 bâqash (1), to *search out*

PRODUCE
7126 qârab (1), to *approach, bring near*

PROFANE
2455 chôl (4), *profane, common, not holy*
2490 châlal (18), to *profane, defile*
2491 châlâl (3), *pierced to death, one slain*
2610 chânêph (1), to *soil, be defiled*
952 bĕbēlŏs (5), *irreligious, profane*
953 bĕbēlŏŏ (2), to *desecrate, profane*

PROFANED
2490 châlal (15), to *profane, defile*

PROFANENESS
2613 chănûphâh (1), *impiety, ungodliness*

PROFANETH
2490 châlal (1), to *profane, defile*

PROFANING
2490 châlal (2), to *profane, defile*

PROFESS
5046 nâgad (1), to *announce*
3670 hŏmŏlŏgĕŏ (2), to *acknowledge, declare*

PROFESSED
3670 hŏmŏlŏgĕŏ (1), to *acknowledge, declare*
3671 hŏmŏlŏgia (1), *acknowledgment*

PROFESSING
1861 ĕpaggĕllŏ (2), to *assert*
5335 phaskŏ (1), to *assert a claim*

PROFESSION
3671 hŏmŏlŏgia (4), *acknowledgment*

PROFIT
1215 betsa' (3), *plunder; unjust gain*
3148 yôwthêr (1), *moreover; rest; gain*
3276 yâ'al (18), to *be valuable*
3504 yithrôwn (5), *preeminence, gain*
4195 môwthar (1), *gain; superiority*
7737 shâvâh (1), to *resemble; to adjust*
3786 ŏphĕlŏs (2), *accumulate or benefit*
4851 sumphĕrŏ (4), to *collect; advantage*
5539 chrĕsimŏs (1), *useful, valued*
5622 ŏphĕlĕia (1), *value, advantage*

5623 ŏphĕlĕŏ (4), to *benefit, be of use*

PROFITABLE
3276 yâ'al (1), to *be valuable*
3504 yithrôwn (1), *preeminence, gain*
5532 çâkan (2), to *be serviceable to*
6743 tsâlach (1), to *push forward*
2173 ĕuchrēstŏs (2), *useful, serviceable*
4851 sumphĕrŏ (3), to *conduce; advantage*
5624 ŏphĕlimŏs (3), *advantageous, useful*

PROFITED
7737 shâvâh (1), to *resemble; to adjust*
4298 prŏkŏptŏ (1), to *go ahead, advance*
5623 ŏphĕlĕŏ (4), to *benefit, be of use*

PROFITETH
3276 yâ'al (1), to *be valuable*
5532 çâkan (1), to *be serviceable to*
5623 ŏphĕlĕŏ (3), to *benefit, be of use*
5624+2076 ŏphĕlimŏs (1), *useful, valuable*

PROFITING
4297 prŏkŏpē (1), *progress, advancement*

PROFOUND
6009 'âmaq (1), to *be, make deep*

PROGENITORS
2029 hârâh (1), to *conceive, be pregnant*

PROGNOSTICATORS
3045 yâda' (1), to *know*

PROLONG
748 'ârak (12), to *be, make long*
3254 yâçaph (1), to *add or augment*
5186 nâţâh (1), to *stretch or spread out*

PROLONGED
748 'ârak (5), to *be, make long*
754+3052 'arkâ' (Ch.) (1), *length*
4900 mâshak (3), to *draw out; to be tall*

PROLONGETH
748 'ârak (1), to *be, make long*
3254 yâçaph (1), to *add or augment*

PROMISE
562 'ômer (1), *something said*
1697 dâbâr (6), *word; matter; thing*
1860 ĕpaggĕlia (40), *divine assurance*
1861 ĕpaggĕllŏ (3), to *assert*
1862 ĕpaggĕlma (1), *self-committal*

PROMISED
559 'âmar (5), to *say*
1696 dâbar (29), to
speak, say; to *subdue*
1843 ĕxŏmŏlŏgĕō (1), to
acknowledge or *agree*
1861 ĕpaggĕllō (10), to
assert
3670 hŏmŏlŏgĕō (1), to
acknowledge, agree
4279 prŏĕpaggĕllŏmai
(1), to *promise before*

PROMISEDST
559 'âmar (1), to *say*
1696 dâbar (2), to *speak*

PROMISES
1860 ĕpaggĕlia (12),
divine assurance
1862 ĕpaggĕlma (1),
self-committal

PROMISING
2421 châyâh (1), to *live*;
to *revive*

PROMOTE
1431 gâdal (1), to *make
great, enlarge*
3513 kâbad (3), to *be
rich, glorious*
7311 rûwm (1), to *be
high*; to *rise* or *raise*

PROMOTED
1431 gâdal (1), to *make
great, enlarge*
5128 nûwa' (3), to *waver*
6744 tsᵉlach (Ch.) (1), to
advance; *promote*

PROMOTION
7311 rûwm (2), to *be
high*; to *rise* or *raise*

PRONOUNCE
981 bâṭâ' (1), to *babble,
speak rashly*
1696 dâbar (1), to *speak*

PRONOUNCED
1691 Diblayim (2), *two
cakes*
1696 dâbar (11), to *speak*
7126 qârab (1), to
approach, bring near

PRONOUNCING
981 bâṭâ' (1), to *babble,
speak rashly*

PROOF
1382 dŏkimē (3), *test,* i.e.
trustiness
1732 ĕndĕixis (1),
demonstration
4135 plērŏphŏrĕō (1), to
assure or *convince*

PROOFS
5039 tĕkmēriŏn (1),
criterion of certainty

PROPER
5459 çᵉgullâh (1), *wealth*
791 astĕiŏs (1),
handsome
2398 idiŏs (2), *private* or
separate

PROPHECIES
4394 prŏphētĕia (2),
prediction

PROPHECY
4853 massâ' (2), *burden,
utterance*

5016 nᵉbûw'âh (3),
prediction
5030 nâbîy' (1), *prophet;
inspired* man
4394 prŏphētĕia (14),
prediction
4397 prŏphētikŏs (1),
prophetic

PROPHESIED
5012 nâbâ' (40), to *speak*
as a *prophet*
5013 nᵉbâ' (Ch.) (1), to
speak as a *prophet*
4395 prŏphētĕuō (9), to
foretell events, *divine*

PROPHESIETH
5012 nâbâ' (3), to *speak*
as a *prophet*
4395 prŏphētĕuō (4), to
foretell events, *divine*

PROPHESY
2372 châzâh (2), to *gaze
at; have a vision*
5012 nâbâ' (66), to *speak*
as a *prophet*
5197 nâṭaph (5), to *speak*
by inspiration
4395 prŏphētĕuō (14), to
foretell events, *divine*

PROPHESYING
5012 nâbâ' (2), to *speak*
as a *prophet*
5017 nᵉbûw'âh (Ch.) (1),
inspired teaching
4394 prŏphētĕia (2),
prediction
4395 prŏphētĕuō (1), to
foretell events, *divine*

PROPHESYINGS
4394 prŏphētĕia (1),
prediction

PROPHET
5012 nâbâ' (2), to *speak*
as a *prophet*
5029 nᵉbîy' (Ch.) (2),
prophet
5030 nâbîy' (164),
prophet; inspired man
5197 nâṭaph (1), to *speak*
by inspiration
4396 prŏphētēs (67),
foreteller
5578 pseudŏprŏphētēs
(4), *pretended foreteller*

PROPHET'S
5030 nâbîy' (1), *prophet;
inspired* man
4396 prŏphētēs (1),
foreteller

PROPHETESS
5031 nᵉbîy'âh (6),
prophetess
4398 prŏphētis (2),
female foreteller

PROPHETS
2374 chôzeh (1),
beholder in vision
5029 nᵉbîy' (Ch.) (2),
prophet
5030 nâbîy' (147),
prophet; inspired man
4396 prŏphētēs (80),
foreteller
4397 prŏphētikŏs (1),
prophetic

5578 pseudŏprŏphētēs
(7), *pretended foreteller*

PROPITIATION
2434 hilasmŏs (2),
atonement
2435 hilastēriŏn (1),
expiatory place

PROPORTION
4626 ma'ar (1), *vacant
space*
6187 'êrek (1), *pile,
equipment, estimate*
356 analŏgia (1),
proportion

PROSELYTE
4339 prŏsēlutŏs (2),
convert, i.e. *proselyte*

PROSELYTES
4339 prŏsēlutŏs (2),
convert, i.e. *proselyte*

PROSPECT
6440 pânîym (6), *face;
front*

PROSPER
3787 kâshêr (1), to *be
straight* or *right*
6743 tsâlach (37), to *push
forward*
7919 sâkal (7), to *be* or
act circumspect
7951 shâlâh (3), to *be
secure* or *successful*
2137 ĕuŏdŏō (1), to
succeed in business

PROSPERED
1980 hâlak (1), to *walk;
live a certain way*
6743 tsâlach (6), to *push
forward*
6744 tsᵉlach (Ch.) (2), to
advance; *promote*
7919 sâkal (1), to *be* or
act circumspect
7965 shâlôwm (1), *safe;
well; health, prosperity*
7999 shâlam (1), to *be
safe; be, make complete*
2137 ĕuŏdŏō (1), to
succeed in business

PROSPERETH
6743 tsâlach (1), to *push
forward*
6744 tsᵉlach (Ch.) (1), to
advance; promote
7919 sâkal (1), to *be* or
act circumspect
2137 ĕuŏdŏō (1), to
succeed in business

PROSPERITY
2896 tôwb (6), *good; well*
6743 tsâlach (1), to *push
forward*
7961 shâlêv (2), *careless,
carefree; security*
7962 shalvâh (3),
security, ease
7965 shâlôwm (4), *safe;
well; health, prosperity*

PROSPEROUS
6743 tsâlach (5), to *push
forward*
7965 shâlôwm (1), *safe;
well; health, prosperity*
7999 shâlam (1), to *be
safe; be, make complete*

2137 ĕuŏdŏō (1), to
succeed in business

PROSPEROUSLY
6743 tsâlach (2), to *push
forward*

PROSTITUTE
2490 châlal (1), to
profane, defile

PROTECTION
5643 çêther (1), *cover,
shelter*

PROTEST
5749 'ûwd (2), to *protest*
3513 nê (1), *as sure as*

PROTESTED
5749 'ûwd (3), to *protest*

PROTESTING
5749 'ûwd (1), to *protest*

PROUD
1341 gê' (2), *haughty,
proud*
1343 gê'eh (8), *arrogant,
haughty*
1346 ga'ăvâh (1),
arrogance; majesty
1347 gâ'ôwn (1),
ascending; majesty
1349 ga'ăyôwn (1),
haughty, arrogant
1362 gâbâhh (2), *high;
lofty*
1364 gâbôahh (1), *high;
powerful; arrogant*
1419 gâdôwl (1), *great*
2086 zêd (12), *arrogant,
proud*
2087 zâdôwn (3),
arrogance, pride
2102 zûwd (1), to *seethe,
to be insolent*
2121 zêydôwn (1),
boiling, raging wave
3093 yâhîyr (1), *arrogant*
7293 rahab (2), *bluster*
7295 râhâb (1), *insolent*
7311 rûwm (1), to *be
high*; to *rise* or *raise*
7342 râchâb (3), *roomy,
spacious*
5187 tuphŏō (1), to
inflate with *self-conceit*
5244 hupĕrēphanŏs (5),
haughty, arrogant

PROUDLY
1346 ga'ăvâh (1),
arrogance; majesty
1348 gê'ûwth (1),
ascending; majesty
1364 gâbôahh (1), *high;
powerful; arrogant*
1431 gâdal (1), to *be
great, make great*
2102 zûwd (4), to *seethe;
to be insolent*
7292 râhab (1), to *urge,
embolden*

PROVE
974 bâchan (1), to *test; to
investigate*
5254 nâçâh (14), to *test,
attempt*
584 apŏdĕiknumi (1), to
demonstrate
1381 dŏkimazō (6), to
test; to approve

3936 paristēmi (1), to
stand beside, present
3985 pĕirazō (1), to
endeavor, scrutinize

PROVED
974 bâchan (6), to *test;* to
investigate
5254 nâçâh (5), to *test,*
attempt
1381 dŏkimazō (3), to
test; to *approve*
4256 prŏaitiaŏmai (1), to
previously charge

PROVENDER
1098 bᵉlîyl (1), *feed,*
fodder
1101 bâlal (1), to *mix;*
confuse; to *feed*
4554 miçpôw' (5), *fodder,*
animal feed

PROVERB
2420 chîydâh (1), *puzzle;*
conundrum; maxim
4911 mâshal (4), to *use*
figurative language
4912 mâshâl (12), pithy
maxim; taunt
3850 parabŏlē (1),
fictitious narrative
3942 parŏimia (2),
illustration; adage

PROVERBS
4911 mâshal (2), to *use*
figurative language
4912 mâshâl (5), pithy
maxim; taunt
3942 parŏimia (2),
illustration; adage

PROVETH
5254 nâçâh (1), to *test,*
attempt

PROVIDE
2372 châzâh (1), to *gaze*
at; to *perceive*
3559 kûwn (2), to *set up:*
establish, fix, prepare
6213 'âsâh (1), to *do*
7200 râ'âh (2), to *see*
2532 kai (1), *and; or*
3936 paristēmi (1), to
stand beside, present
4160 pŏiĕō (1), to *do*
4306 prŏnŏĕō (2), to *look*
out for *beforehand*

PROVIDED
3559 kûwn (1), to *set up:*
establish, fix, prepare
6213 'âsâh (1), to *do*
7200 râ'âh (2), to *see*
2090 hĕtŏimazō (1), to
prepare
4265 prŏblĕpō (1), to
furnish in advance

PROVIDENCE
4307 prŏnŏia (1),
provident *care, supply*

PROVIDETH
3559 kûwn (2), to *set up:*
establish, fix, prepare

PROVIDING
4306 prŏnŏĕō (1), to *look*
out for *beforehand*

PROVINCE
4082 mᵉdîynâh (20),
governmental *region*

4083 mᵉdîynâh (Ch.) (5),
governmental *region*
1885 ĕparchia (2),
Roman *præfecture*

PROVINCES
4082 mᵉdîynâh (29),
governmental *region*
4083 mᵉdîynâh (Ch.) (1),
governmental *region*

PROVING
1381 dŏkimazō (1), to
test; to *approve*
4822 sumbibazō (1), to
infer, show, teach

PROVISION
1697 dâbâr (1), *word;*
matter; thing
3557 kûwl (1), to
measure; to *maintain*
3559 kûwn (1), to *set up:*
establish, fix, prepare
3740 kêrâh (1), *purchase*
3899 lechem (1), *food,*
bread
6679 tsûwd (1), to *lie in*
wait; to *catch*
6718 tsayid (2), hunting
game; lunch, food
6720 tsêydâh (2), *food,*
supplies
4307 prŏnŏia (1),
provident *care, supply*

PROVOCATION
3708 ka'aç (4), *vexation,*
grief
4784 mârâh (1), to *rebel*
or *resist;* to *provoke*
4808 mᵉrîybâh (1),
quarrel
3894 parapikrasmŏs (2),
irritation

PROVOCATIONS
3708 ka'aç (1), *vexation,*
grief
5007 nᵉ'âtsâh (2), *scorn;*
to *bloom*

PROVOKE
4784 mârâh (2), to *rebel*
or *resist;* to *provoke*
4843 mârar (1), to *be,*
make bitter
5006 nâ'ats (2), to *scorn*
7264 râgaz (1), to *quiver*
653 apŏstŏmatizō (1), to
question carefully
2042 ĕrĕthizō (1), to
stimulate, provoke
3863 parazēlŏō (4), to
excite to rivalry
3893 parapikrainō (1), to
embitter alongside
3948 parŏxusmŏs (1),
incitement to good
3949 parŏrgizō (1), to
enrage, exasperate

PROVOKED
3707 kâ'aç (4), to *grieve,*
rage, be indignant
4784 mârâh (4), to *rebel*
or *resist;* to *provoke*
5006 nâ'ats (3), to *scorn*
5496 çûwth (1), to
stimulate; to *seduce*
7265 rᵉgaz (Ch.) (1), to
quiver
2042 ĕrĕthizō (1), to
stimulate, provoke

3947 parŏxunō (1), to
exasperate

PROVOKETH
5674 'âbar (1), to *cross*
over; to *transition*

PROVOKING
3707 kâ'aç (1), to *grieve,*
rage, be indignant
4784 mârâh (1), to *rebel*
or *resist;* to *provoke*
4292 prŏkalĕŏmai (1), to
irritate

PRUDENCE
6195 'ormâh (1), *trickery;*
discretion
7922 sekel (1),
intelligence; success
5428 phrŏnēsis (1), moral
insight, understanding

PRUDENT
995 bîyn (8), to
understand; discern
6175 'ârûwm (8),
cunning; clever
6191 'âram (1), to *be*
cunning; be prudent
7080 qâçam (1), to *divine*
magic
7919 sâkal (2), to *be or*
act circumspect
4908 sunĕtŏs (4),
sagacious, learned

PRUDENTLY
7919 sâkal (1), to *be or*
act circumspect

PRUNE
2168 zâmar (2), to *trim*
or a *vine*

PRUNED
2167 zâmar (1), to *play*
music

PRUNINGHOOKS
4211 mazmêrâh (4),
pruning-knife

PSALM
2172 zimrâh (2), *song*
4210 mizmôwr (58),
poem set to music
5568 psalmŏs (2), *psalm;*
book of the *Psalms*

PSALMIST
2158 zâmîyr (1), *song*

PSALMS
2158 zâmîyr (1), *song*
2167 zâmar (2), to *play*
music
5567 psallō (1), to *play* a
stringed instrument
5568 psalmŏs (5), *psalm;*
book of the *Psalms*

PSALTERIES
3627 kᵉlîy (1),
implement, thing
5035 nebel (13), skin-*bag*
for liquids; *vase; lyre*

PSALTERY
3627 kᵉlîy (1),
implement, thing
5035 nebel (8), skin-*bag*
for liquids; *vase; lyre*
6460 pᵉçantêrîyn (Ch.)
(4), *lyre instrument*

PTOLEMAIS
4424 Ptŏlĕmaïs (1), of
Ptolemy

PUA
6312 Pûw'âh (1), *blast*

PUAH
6312 Pûw'âh (2), *blast*
6326 Pûw'âh (1),
brilliancy

PUBLICAN
5057 tĕlōnēs (6),
collector of *revenue*

PUBLICANS
754 architĕlōnēs (1),
chief *tax-gatherer*
5057 tĕlōnēs (16),
collector of *revenue*

PUBLICK
3856 paradĕigmatizō (1),
to *expose to infamy*

PUBLICKLY
1219 dēmŏsiŏs (2),
public; in public

PUBLISH
1319 bâsar (2), to
announce (good news)
7121 qârâ' (1), to *call* out
8085 shâma' (11), to *hear*
2784 kērussō (2), to
herald

PUBLISHED
559 'âmar (1), to *say*
1319 bâsar (1), to
announce (good news)
1540 gâlâh (2), to *reveal*
1696 dâbar (1), to *speak*
8085 shâma' (1), to *hear*
1096 ginŏmai (1), to *be,*
become
1308 diaphĕrō (1), to
bear, carry; to *differ*
2784 kērussō (3), to
herald

PUBLISHETH
8085 shâma' (4), to *hear*

PUBLIUS
4196 Pŏpliŏs (2), *popular*

PUDENS
4227 Pŏudēs (1), *modest*

PUFFED
5448 phusiŏō (6), to
inflate, i.e. *make proud*

PUFFETH
6315 pûwach (2), to *blow,*
to *fan, kindle;* to *utter*
5448 phusiŏō (1), to
inflate, i.e. *make proud*

PUHITES
6336 Pûwthîy (1), *hinge*

PUL
6322 Pûwl (4), *Pul,* i.e. a
person or tribe

PULL
2040 hâraç (3), to *pull*
down; *break, destroy*
3318 yâtsâ' (1), to *go,*
bring out
5422 nâthats (2), to *tear*
down
5423 nâthaq (2), to *tear*
off
6584 pâshaṭ (1), to *strip,*
i.e. *unclothe, plunder*

F

7725 shûwb (1), to *turn* back; to *return*
385 anaspaō (1), to *take up* or *extricate*
1544 ĕkballō (3), to *throw out*
2507 kathairĕō (1), to *lower*, or *demolish*

PULLED
935 bôw' (1), to *go, come*
4026 migdâl (1), *tower; rostrum*
5256 nᵉçach (Ch.) (1), to *tear away*
5414 nâthan (1), to *give*
5428 nâthash (1), to *tear away, be uprooted*
6582 pâshach (1), to *tear in pieces*
1288 diaspaō (1), to *sever* or *dismember*

PULLING
726 harpazō (1), to *seize*
2506 kathairĕsis (1), *demolition*

PULPIT
4026 migdâl (1), *tower; rostrum*

PULSE
2235 zêrôa' (2), *vegetable*

PUNISH
3256 yâçar (1), to *chastise; to instruct*
5221 nâkâh (1), to *strike, kill*
6064 'ânash (1), to *inflict a penalty, to fine*
6485 pâqad (27), to *visit, care for, count*
7489 râ'a' (1), to *break to pieces*
2849 kŏlazō (1), to *chastise, punish*

PUNISHED
2820 châsak (1), to *restrain or refrain*
5358 nâqam (2), to *avenge or punish*
6064 'ânash (4), to *inflict a penalty, to fine*
6485 pâqad (4), to *visit, care for, count*
1349+5099 dikē (1), *justice*
2849 kŏlazō (1), to *chastise, punish*
5097 timōrĕō (2), to *avenge*

PUNISHMENT
2399 chêṭ' (1), *crime or its penalty*
2403 chaṭṭâ'âh (3), *offence; sin offering*
5771 'âvôn (9), moral *evil*
6066 'ônesh (1), *fine*
1557 ĕkdikēsis (1), *retaliation, punishment*
2009 ĕpitimia (1), *penalty*
2851 kŏlasis (1), *infliction, punishment*
5098 timōria (1), *penalty, punishment*

PUNISHMENTS
5771 'âvôn (2), moral *evil*

PUNITES
6324 Pûwnîy (1), *turn*

PUNON
6325 Pûwnôn (2), *perplexity*

PUR
6332 Pûwr (3), *lot* cast

PURCHASE
1350 gâ'al (1), to *redeem;* to *be the next of kin*
4736 miqnâh (6), *acquisition*
4046 pĕripŏiĕŏmai (1), to *acquire;* to *gain*

PURCHASED
7069 qânâh (5), to *create;* to *procure*
2932 ktaŏmai (2), to *get,* i.e. *acquire*
4046 pĕripŏiĕŏmai (1), to *acquire;* to *gain*
4047 pĕripŏiēsis (1), *acquisition*

PURE
1249 bar (2), *beloved; pure; empty*
1305 bârar (3), to *brighten; purify*
1865 dᵉrôwr (1), *freedom; clear, pure*
2134 zak (9), *pure; clear*
2135 zâkâh (1), to *be innocent*
2141 zâkak (1), to *be transparent; clean, pure*
2561 chemer (1), *fermenting wine*
2888 Ṭabbath (2), *Tabbath*
2889 ṭâhôwr (40), *pure, clean, flawless*
2891 ṭâhêr (2), to *be pure, unadulterated*
3795 kâthîyth (1), pure oil from *beaten* olives
5343 nᵉqê' (Ch.) (1), *clean, pure*
5462 çâgar (8), to *shut up;* to *surrender*
6337 pâz (1), *pure* gold
6884 tsâraph (2), to *fuse* metal; to *refine*
53 hagnŏs (4), *innocent, modest, perfect, pure*
1506 ĕilikrinēs (1), tested as *genuine*, i.e. *pure*
2513 katharŏs (16), *clean, pure*

PURELY
1252 bôr (1), *purity, cleanness*

PURENESS
1252 bôr (1), *purity, cleanness*
2890 ṭᵉhôwr (1), *purity*
54 hagnŏtēs (1), *blamelessness, purity*

PURER
2141 zâkak (1), to *be transparent; clean, pure*
2889 ṭâhôwr (1), *pure, clean, flawless*

PURGE
1305 bârar (2), to *brighten; purify*
2212 zâqaq (1), to *strain, refine; extract, clarify*
2398 châṭâ' (1), to *sin*

2891 ṭâhêr (1), to *be pure, unadulterated*
3722 kâphar (4), to *cover;* to *expiate*
6884 tsâraph (1), to *fuse* metal; to *refine*
1245 diakatharizō (2), to *cleanse perfectly*
1571 ĕkkathairō (2), to *cleanse thoroughly*
2511 katharizō (1), to *cleanse*

PURGED
1740 dûwach (1), to *rinse clean, wash*
2891 ṭâhêr (4), to *be pure, unadulterated*
3722 kâphar (5), to *cover;* to *expiate*
2508 kathairō (1), to *prune dead* wood
2511 katharizō (1), to *cleanse*
2512 katharismŏs (1), *ablution; expiation*
4160+2512 pŏiĕō (1), to *make* or *do*

PURGETH
2508 kathairō (1), to *prune dead* wood

PURGING
2511 katharizō (1), to *cleanse*

PURIFICATION
2403 chaṭṭâ'âh (2), *offence; sin offering*
2893 ṭohŏrâh (2), *ceremonial purification*
8562 tamrûwq (2), *scouring, perfumery*
49 hagnismŏs (1), *purification*
2512 katharismŏs (1), *ablution; expiation*

PURIFICATIONS
4795 mârûwq (1), *rubbing*

PURIFIED
1305 bârar (1), to *brighten; purify*
2212 zâqaq (1), to *strain, refine; extract, clarify*
2398 châṭâ' (3), to *sin*
2891 ṭâhêr (1), to *be pure, unadulterated*
6942 qâdâsh (1), to *be, make clean*
48 hagnizō (2), *sanctify;* to *cleanse in ritual*
2511 katharizō (1), to *cleanse*

PURIFIER
2891 ṭâhêr (1), to *be pure, unadulterated*

PURIFIETH
2398 châṭâ' (1), to *sin*
48 hagnizō (1), *sanctify;* to *cleanse in ritual*

PURIFY
2398 châṭâ' (7), to *sin*
2891 ṭâhêr (3), to *be pure, unadulterated*
48 hagnizō (3), *sanctify;* to *cleanse in ritual*
2511 katharizō (1), to *cleanse*

PURIFYING
2403 chaṭṭâ'âh (1), *offence; sin* offering
2892 ṭôhar (1), *ceremonial purification*
2893 ṭohŏrâh (3), *ceremonial purification*
8562 tamrûwq (1), *scouring, perfumery*
48 hagnizō (1), *sanctify;* to *cleanse in ritual*
2511 katharizō (1), to *cleanse*
2512 katharismŏs (2), *ablution; expiation*
2514 katharŏtēs (1), *cleanness*

PURIM
6332 Pûwr (5), *lot* cast

PURITY
47 hagnĕia (2), moral *chastity, purity*

PURLOINING
3557 nŏsphizŏmai (1), to *embezzle*

PURPLE
710 'argᵉvân (1), *purple*
713 'argâmân (38), *purple*
4209 pŏrphura (5), *red-blue color*
4210 pŏrphurŏus (3), *bluish-red*
4211 pŏrphurŏpōlis (1), *trader in bluish-red cloth*

PURPOSE
559 'âmar (2), to *say*
1697 dâbâr (1), *word; matter; thing*
2656 chêphets (3), *pleasure; desire*
2803 châshab (2), to *plot;* to *think, regard*
4284 machăshâbâh (3), *contrivance; plan*
4639 ma'ăseh (1), *action; labor*
6098 'êtsâh (2), *advice; plan; prudence*
6640 tsᵉbûw (Ch.) (1), *determination*
7385 rîyq (1), *emptiness; worthless* thing; *in vain*
7997 shâlal (1), to *drop* or *strip;* to *plunder*
1011 bŏulĕuō (2), to *deliberate;* to *resolve*
1013 bŏulēma (1), *resolve, willful choice*
4286 prŏthĕsis (8), *setting forth*

PURPOSED
2161 zâmam (2), to *plan*
2803 châshab (4), to *plot;* to *think, regard*
3289 yâ'ats (5), to *advise*
3335 yâtsar (1), to *form; potter;* to *determine*
6440 pânîym (1), *face; front*
7760 sûwm (1), to *put, place*
1096+1106 ginŏmai (1), to *be, become*
4160 pŏiĕō (1), to *do*
4388 prŏtithĕmai (2), to *propose, determine*

5087 tithēmi (1), to *place*

PURPOSES
2154 zimmâh (1), *plan*
4284 machăshâbâh (3), *contrivance; plan*
8356 shâthâh (1), *basis*

PURPOSETH
4255 prŏairĕŏmai (1), to *propose, intend, decide*

PURSE
3599 kîyç (1), *cup;* utility *bag*
905 balantiŏn (3), money *pouch*
2223 zōnē (1), *belt, sash*

PURSES
2223 zōnē (1), *belt, sash*

PURSUE
3212 yâlak (1), to *walk;* to *live;* to *carry*
7291 râdaph (28), to *run after* with hostility

PURSUED
1692 dâbaq (1), to *cling* or *adhere;* to *catch*
1814 dâlaq (2), to *flame;* to *pursue*
7291 râdaph (35), to *run after* with hostility

PURSUER
7291 râdaph (1), to *run after* with hostility

PURSUERS
7291 râdaph (5), to *run after* with hostility

PURSUETH
7291 râdaph (7), to *run after* with hostility

PURSUING
310 'achar (2), *after*
7291 râdaph (4), to *run after* with hostility
7873 sîyg (1), *withdrawal* into a private place

PURTENANCE
7130 qereb (1), *nearest* part, i.e. the *center*

PUSH
5055 nâgach (6), to *butt*
5056 naggâch (2), act of *butting*
7971 shâlach (1), to *send* away

PUSHED
5055 nâgach (1), to *butt*

PUSHING
5055 nâgach (1), to *butt*

PUT
622 'âçaph (2), to *gather, collect*
935 bôw' (10), to *go, come*
1197 bâ'ar (13), to *be brutish, be senseless*
1396 gâbar (1), to *be strong;* to *prevail*
1644 gârash (2), to *drive* out; to *divorce*
1645 geresh (1), *produce, yield*
1846 dâ'ak (6), to *be extinguished;* to *expire*
1911 hâdâh (1), to *stretch forth* the hand

1921 hâdar (1), to *favor* or *honor;* to *be high*
2026 hârag (1), to *kill, slaughter*
2280 châbash (2), to *wrap* firmly, *bind*
2296 châgar (1), to *gird* on a belt; *put on* armor
2330 chûwd (4), to *propound* a riddle
2502 châlats (1), to *pull* off; to *strip;* to *depart*
3240 yânach (5), to *allow* to *stay*
3254 yâçaph (5), to *add* or *augment*
3318 yâtsâ' (2), to *go, bring out*
3322 yâtsag (2), to *place*
3381 yârad (2), to *descend*
3455 yâsam (1), to *put*
3518 kâbâh (3), to *extinguish*
3637 kâlam (1), to *taunt* or *insult*
3722 kâphar (1), to *cover;* to *expiate*
3847 lâbash (41), to *clothe*
3947 lâqach (1), to *take*
4191 mûwth (3), to *die;* to *kill*
4229 mâchâh (3), to *touch,* i.e. reach to
4916 mishlôwach (1), *sending* out
5056 naggâch (1), act of *butting*
5079 niddâh (2), time of menstrual *impurity*
5114 Nôwdâb (3), *noble*
5148 nâchâh (1), to *guide*
5186 nâţâh (1), to *stretch* or spread out
5365 nâqar (2), to *bore;* to *gouge*
5381 nâsag (1), to *reach*
5394 nâshal (2), to *divest, eject,* or *drop*
5411 Nâthîyn (1), ones given to duty
5414 nâthan (187), to *give*
5493 çûwr (19), to *turn off*
5564 çâmak (5), to *lean* upon; *take hold* of
5595 çâphâh (1), to *scrape;* to *remove*
5596 çâphach (1), to *associate; be united*
5674 'âbar (4), to *cross* over; to *transition*
5786 'âvar (3), to *blind*
5927 'âlâh (3), to *ascend, be high, mount*
6006 'âmaç (1), to *impose* a burden
6186 'ârak (1), to *set in a* row, i.e. *arrange,*
6213 'âsâh (1), to *do*
6316 Pûwţ (2), *Put*
6319 Pôwţîy Phera' (2), *Poti-Phera*
6584 pâshaţ (6), to *strip,* i.e. *unclothe, plunder*
6605 pâthach (1), to *open* wide; to *loosen, begin*
6695 tsôwq (1), *distress*

7368 râchaq (4), to *recede; remove*
7392 râkab (2), to *ride*
7673 shâbath (2), to *repose;* to *desist*
7725 shûwb (7), to *turn* back; to *return*
7760 sûwm (150), to *put*
7896 shîyth (11), to *put*
7971 shâlach (45), to *send away*
7972 shᵉlach (Ch.) (1), to *send away*
7973 shelach (1), *spear; shoot* of growth
8214 shᵉphal (Ch.) (1), to *humiliate*
115 athĕtēsis (1), *cancellation*
142 airō (1), to *lift,* to *take up*
337 anairĕō (2), to *take away,* i.e. *abolish*
363 anamimnēskō (1), to *remind;* to *recollect*
506 anupŏtaktŏs (1), *independent*
520 apagō (1), to *take away*
554 apĕkduŏmai (1), to *divest wholly* oneself
595 apŏthĕsis (1), *laying aside*
615 apŏktĕinō (6), to *kill* outright; to *destroy*
630 apŏluō (13), to *relieve, release*
654 apŏstrĕphō (1), to *turn away* or *back*
659 apŏtithēmi (2), to *put away; get rid of*
683 apōthĕŏmai (2), to *push off;* to *reject*
863 aphiēmi (2), to *leave;* to *pardon, forgive*
906 ballō (14), to *throw*
1096 ginŏmai (1), to *be, become*
1252 diakrinō (1), to *decide;* to *hesitate*
1325 didōmi (5), to *give*
1544 ĕkballō (4), to *throw out*
1614 ĕktĕinō (3), to *stretch*
1677 ĕllŏgĕō (1), *attribute*
1688 ĕmbibazō (1), to *transfer*
1746 ĕnduō (16), to *dress*
1749 ĕnĕdrŏn (1), *ambush*
1808 ĕxairō (1), to *remove, drive away*
1911 ĕpiballō (1), to *throw upon*
2007 ĕpitithēmi (9), to *impose*
2289 thanatŏō (7), to *kill*
2507 kathairĕō (1), to *lower,* or *demolish*
2673 katargĕō (2), to *be, render entirely useless*
3004 lĕgō (1), to *say*
3089 luō (1), to *loosen*
3179 mĕthistēmi (1), to *move*
3856 paradĕigmatizō (1), to *expose to infamy*

3860 paradidōmi (1), to *hand over*
3908 paratithēmi (2), to *present*
3982 pĕithō (1), to *pacify* or *conciliate*
4016 pĕriballō (1), to *wrap around, clothe*
4060 pĕritithēmi (5), to *present*
4160 pŏiĕō (3), to *do*
4374 prŏsphĕrō (1), to *present to;* to *treat as*
5087 tithēmi (15), to *place, put*
5279 hupŏmimnēskō (4), to *suggest to memory*
5293 hupŏtassō (9), to *subordinate;* to *obey*
5294 hupŏtithēmi (1), to *hazard;* to *suggest*
5392 phimŏō (1), to *restrain to silence*
5562 chōrĕō (2), to *pass, enter;* to *hold, admit*

PUTEOLI
4223 Pŏtiŏlŏi (1), *little wells*

PUTIEL
6317 Pûwţîy'êl (1), *contempt of God*

PUTRIFYING
2961 ţârîy (1), *fresh*

PUTTEST
4916 mishlôwach (2), *presentation; seizure*
5414 nâthan (1), to *give*
5596 çâphach (1), to *associate; be united*
7673 shâbath (1), to *repose;* to *desist*
7760 sûwm (2), to *put, place*

PUTTETH
2590 chânaţ (1), to *embalm;* to *ripen*
5414 nâthan (4), to *give*
5844 'âţâh (1), to *wrap,* i.e. *cover, veil, clothe*
6605 pâthach (1), to *open* wide; to *loosen, begin*
7760 sûwm (5), to *put*
7971 shâlach (2), to *send away*
8213 shâphêl (1), to *humiliate*
630 apŏluō (1), to *relieve, release;* divorce
649 apŏstĕllō (1), to *send out* on a mission
906 ballō (2), to *throw*
1544 ĕkballō (1), to *throw out*
1631 ĕkphuō (2), to *sprout up, put forth*
1911 ĕpiballō (2), to *throw upon*
5087 tithēmi (2), to *place, put*

PUTTING
5414 nâthan (1), to *give*
7760 sûwm (1), to *put, place*
7971 shâlach (2), to *send away*
555 apĕkdusis (1), *divestment, removal*

595 apŏthĕsis (1), *laying aside*
659 apŏtithēmi (1), to *put away; get rid of*
1745 ĕndusis (1), *investment*
1746 ĕnduō (1), to *dress*
1878 ĕpanamimnēskō (1), to *remind* again *of*
1936 ĕpithĕsis (1), *imposition*
2007 ĕpitithēmi (2), to *impose*
4261 prŏballō (1), to *push to the front, germinate*
5087 tithēmi (1), to *place, put*
5279 hupŏmimnēskō (1), to *suggest to memory*

PYGARG
1787 Dîyshôwn, (1), *antelope*

QUAILS
7958 sᵉlâv (4), *quail* bird

QUAKE
7264 râgaz (1), to *quiver*
7493 râ'ash (1), to *undulate, quake*
1790 ĕntrŏmŏs (1), *terrified*
4579 sĕiō (1), to *vibrate; to agitate*

QUAKED
2729 chârad (1), to *shudder*
7264 râgaz (1), to *quiver*

QUAKING
2731 chărâdâh (1), *fear, anxiety*
7494 ra'ash (1), *vibration, uproar*

QUARREL
579 'ânâh (1), to *meet,* to *happen*
5359 nâqâm (1), *revenge*
1758 ĕnĕchō (1), to *keep a grudge*
3437 mŏmphē (1), *blame*

QUARRIES
6456 pᵉçîyl (2), *idol*

QUARTER
5676 'êber (1), *opposite side; east*
6285 pê'âh (4), *region; extremity*
7098 qâtsâh (2), *termination; fringe*
3836 pantachŏthĕn (1), *from all* directions

QUARTERS
1366 gᵉbûwl (1), *boundary, border*
3411 yᵉrêkâh (1), *far away places*
3671 kânâph (1), *edge* or *extremity; wing*
7098 qâtsâh (1), *termination; fringe*
7307 rûwach (1), *breath; wind; life-*spirit
1137 gōnia (1), *angle; cornerstone*
5117 tŏpŏs (2), *place*

QUARTUS
2890 Kŏuartŏs (1), *fourth*

QUATERNIONS
5069 tĕtradiŏn (1), *squad of four Roman soldiers*

QUEEN
1377 gᵉbîyrâh (6), *mistress*
4427 mâlak (2), to *reign as king*
4433 malkâ' (Ch.) (2), *queen*
4436 malkâh (33), *queen*
4446 mᵉleketh (5), *queen*
7694 shêgâl (2), *queen*
938 basilissa (4), *queen*

QUEENS
4436 malkâh (2), *queen*
8282 sârâh (1), *female noble*

QUENCH
3518 kâbâh (8), to *extinguish*
7665 shâbar (1), to *burst*
4570 sbĕnnumi (3), to *extinguish, snuff out*

QUENCHED
1846 dâ'ak (1), to *be extinguished;* to *expire*
3518 kâbâh (9), to *extinguish*
8257 shâqa' (1), to *be overflowed;* to *cease*
762 asbĕstŏs (2), *not extinguished*
4570 sbĕnnumi (4), to *extinguish, snuff out*

QUESTION
1458 ĕgkaleō (1), to *bring crimination*
2213 zētēma (2), *debate, dispute*
2214 zētēsis (1), *dispute* or its *theme*
2919 krinō (2), to *decide;* to *try, condemn, punish*
3056 lŏgŏs (1), *word, matter, thing; Word*
4802 suzētĕō (2), to *discuss, controvert*

QUESTIONED
1875 dârash (1), to *seek* or *ask;* to *worship*
1905 ĕpĕrōtaō (1), to *inquire, seek*
4802 suzētĕō (1), to *discuss, controvert*

QUESTIONING
4802 suzētĕō (2), to *discuss, controvert*

QUESTIONS
1697 dâbâr (2), *word; matter; thing*
2420 chîydâh (2), *puzzle; conundrum; maxim*
1905 ĕpĕrōtaō (1), to *inquire, seek*
2213 zētēma (3), *debate, dispute*
2214 zētēsis (5), *dispute*

QUICK
2416 chay (3), *alive; raw; fresh; life*
4241 michyâh (2), *preservation of life*
2198 zaō (4), to *live*

QUICKEN
2421 châyâh (12), to *live*

2227 zōŏpŏiĕō (1), to (re-) *vitalize, give life*

QUICKENED
2421 châyâh (2), to *live*
2227 zōŏpŏiĕō (2), to (re-) *vitalize, give life*
4806 suzōŏpŏiĕō (2), to *reanimate conjointly*

QUICKENETH
2227 zōŏpŏiĕō (5), to (re-) *vitalize, give life*

QUICKENING
2227 zōŏpŏiĕō (1), to (re-) *vitalize, give life*

QUICKLY
3966 mᵉ'ôd (1), *very*
4116 mâhar (3), to *hurry*
4118 mahêr (8), *in a hurry*
4120 mᵉhêrâh (10), *hurry; promptly*
1722+5034 ĕn (2), *in; during; because of*
5030 tachĕŏs (2), *speedily, rapidly*
5032 tachiŏn (1), *more rapidly, more speedily*
5035 tachu (12), *without delay, soon, suddenly*

QUICKSANDS
4950 surtis (1), *sand drawn by the waves*

QUIET
2790 chârash (1), to *be silent;* to *be deaf*
4496 mᵉnûwchâh (1), *peacefully; consolation*
5117 nûwach (1), to *rest;* to *settle down*
5183 nachath (1), *descent; quiet*
7282 râgêa' (1), *restful, i.e. peaceable*
7599 shâ'an (2), to *loll, i.e. be peaceful*
7600 sha'ănân (2), *secure; haughty*
7961 shâlêv (2), *carefree; security, at ease*
8003 shâlêm (1), *complete; friendly; safe*
8252 shâqat (15), to *repose*
8367 shâthaq (1), to *subside*
2263 ĕrĕmŏs (1), *tranquil, peaceful*
2270 hēsuchazō (1), to *refrain*
2272 hēsuchiŏs (1), *still, undisturbed*
2687 katastĕllō (1), to *quell, quiet*

QUIETED
1826 dâmam (1), to *be silent;* to *stop, cease*
5117 nûwach (1), to *rest;* to *settle down*

QUIETETH
8252 shâqat (1), to *repose*

QUIETLY
7987 shᵉlîy (1), *privacy*

QUIETNESS
5183 nachath (1), *quiet*
7961 shâlêv (1), *carefree; security, at ease*

2227 zōŏpŏiĕō (1), to (re-) *vitalize, give life*

QUICKENED [duplicate]

7962 shalvâh (1), *security, ease*
8252 shâqat (4), to *repose*
8253 sheqet (1), *tranquillity*
1515 ĕirēnē (1), *peace; health; prosperity*
2271 hēsuchia (1), *stillness*

QUIT
1961 hâyâh (1), to *exist, i.e. be or become*
5352 nâqâh (1), to *be bare, i.e. extirpated*
5355 nâqîy (2), *innocent*
407 andrizŏmai (1), to *act manly*

QUITE
3615 kâlâh (1), to *cease, be finished, perish*
5080 nâdach (1), to *push off, scattered*
6181 'eryâh (1), *nudity*

QUIVER
827 'ashpâh (6), *quiver*
8522 tᵉlîy (1), *quiver*

QUIVERED
6750 tsâlal (1), to *tinkle,* to *rattle* together

RAAMAH
7484 Ra'mâh (5), horse's *mane*

RAAMIAH
7485 Ra'amyâh (1), *Jehovah has shaken*

RAAMSES
7486 Ra'mᵉçêç (1), *Rameses* or *Raamses*

RAB-MAG
7248 Rab-Mâg (2), *chief Magian*

RAB-SARIS
7249 Rab-Çârîyç (3), *chief chamberlain*

RAB-SHAKEH
7262 Rabshâqêh (8), *chief butler*

RABBAH
7237 Rabbâh (13), *great*

RABBATH
7237 Rabbâh (2), *great*

RABBI
4461 rhabbi (7), *my master*

RABBITH
7245 Rabbîyth (1), *multitude*

RABBONI
4462 rhabbŏni (1), *my master*

RABSHAKEH
7262 Rabshâqêh (8), *chief butler*

RACA
4469 rhaka (1), *O empty one, i.e. worthless*

RACE
734 'ôrach (1), *road; manner of life*
4793 mêrôwts (1), *running foot-race*
73 agŏn (1), *contest, struggle*

4712 stadiŏn (1), *length of about 200 yards*

RACHAB
4477 *Rhachab* (1), *proud*

RACHAL
7403 *Râkâl* (1), *merchant*

RACHEL
7354 *Râchêl* (41), *ewe*
4478 *Rhachêl* (1), *ewe*

RACHEL'S
7354 *Râchêl* (5), *ewe*

RADDAI
7288 *Radday* (1), *domineering*

RAFTERS
7351 rᵉchîyṭ (1), *panel*

RAGAU
4466 *Rhagau* (1), *friend*

RAGE
1984 hâlal (2), *to boast*
2195 za'am (1), *fury*
2197 za'aph (2), *anger*
2534 chêmâh (2), *heat; anger; poison*
5678 'ebrâh (2), *outburst*
7264 râgaz (5), *to quiver*
7266 rᵉgaz (Ch.) (1), *violent anger*
7267 rôgez (1), *disquiet; anger*
7283 râgash (1), *to be tumultuous*
5433 phruassō (1), *to make a tumult*

RAGED
1993 hâmâh (1), *to be in great commotion*

RAGETH
5674 'âbar (1), *to cross over; to transition*

RAGING
1348 gê'ûwth (1), *ascending; majesty*
1993 hâmâh (1), *to be in great commotion*
2197 za'aph (1), *anger, rage*
66 agriŏs (1), *wild (country)*
2830 kludōn (1), *surge, raging*

RAGS
899 beged (1), *clothing; treachery or pillage*
4418 mâlâch (2), *rag or old garment*
7168 qera' (1), *rag, torn pieces*

RAGUEL
7467 Rᵉ'ûw'êl (1), *friend of God*

RAHAB
7294 Rahab (3), *boaster*
7343 Râchâb (5), *proud*
4460 Rhaab (2), *proud*

RAHAM
7357 Racham (1), *pity*

RAHEL
7354 Râchêl (1), *ewe*

RAIL
2778 châraph (1), *to spend the winter*

RAILED
5860 'îyṭ (1), *to swoop down upon; to insult*
987 blasphēmĕō (2), *to speak impiously*

RAILER
3060 lŏidŏrŏs (1), *verbal abuser*

RAILING
988 blasphēmia (1), *impious speech*
989 blasphēmŏs (1), *slanderous*
3059 lŏidŏria (1), *slander*

RAILINGS
988 blasphēmia (1), *impious speech*

RAIMENT
899 beged (12), *clothing; treachery or pillage*
3682 kᵉçûwth (1), *cover; veiling*
3830 lᵉbûwsh (1), *garment; wife*
4055 mad (1), *vesture, garment; carpet*
4254 machălâtsâh (1), *mantle, garment*
4403 malbûwsh (3), *garment, clothing*
7553 riqmâh (1), *variegation of color*
8008 salmâh (5), *clothing*
8071 simlâh (11), *dress*
1742 ĕnduma (5), *apparel, outer robe*
2066 ĕsthēs (1), *to clothe*
2440 himation (12), *to put on clothes*
2441 himatismŏs (2), *clothing*
4629 skĕpasma (1), *clothing; covering*

RAIN
1653 geshem (30), *rain*
3138 yôwreh (1), *autumn rain showers*
3384 yârâh (2), *to throw, shoot an arrow*
4175 môwreh (3), *archer; teaching; early rain*
4305 mâṭar (11), *to rain*
4306 mâṭâr (37), *rain, shower of rain*
4456 malqôwsh (6), *spring rain*
8164 sâ'îyr (1), *shower*
1026 brĕchō (2), *to make wet; to rain*
1026+5205 brĕchō (1), *to make wet; to rain*
1028 brŏchē (1), *rain*
5205 huĕtŏs (5), *rain; rain shower*

RAINBOW
2463 iris (2), *rainbow*

RAINED
1656 gôshem (1), *rain downpour*
4305 mâṭar (6), *to rain*
1026 brĕchō (2), *to make wet; to rain*

RAINY
5464 çagrîyd (1), *pouring rain*

RAISE
5375 nâsâ' (2), *to lift up*
5549 çâlal (2), *to mound up; to exalt*
5782 'ûwr (6), *to awake*
6965 qûwm (30), *to rise*
450 anistēmi (8), *to rise; to come to life*
1453 ĕgĕirō (8), *to waken, i.e. rouse*
1817 ĕxanistēmi (2), *to beget, raise up*
1825 ĕxĕgĕirō (1), *to resuscitate; release*

RAISED
1361 gâbahh (1), *to be lofty; to be haughty*
5782 'ûwr (12), *to awake*
5927 'âlâh (3), *to ascend, be high, mount*
5975 'âmad (1), *to stand*
6209 'ârar (1), *to bare; to demolish*
6965 qûwm (10), *to rise*
6966 qûwm (Ch.) (1), *to rise*
386 anastasis (1), *resurrection from death*
450 anistēmi (6), *to rise; to come to life*
1326 diĕgĕirō (1), *to arouse, stimulate*
1453 ĕgĕirō (45), *to waken, i.e. rouse*
1825 ĕxĕgĕirō (1), *to resuscitate; release*
1892 ĕpĕgĕirō (1), *to excite against, stir up*
4891 sunĕgĕirō (1), *to raise up with*

RAISER
5674 'âbar (1), *to cross over; to transition*

RAISETH
2210 zâqaph (2), *to lift up, comfort*
5975 'âmad (1), *to stand*
6965 qûwm (2), *to rise*
7613 sᵉ'êth (1), *elevation; swelling leprous scab*
1453 ĕgĕirō (2), *to waken, i.e. rouse*

RAISING
5872 'Êyn Gedîy (1), *fountain of a kid*
4160+1999 pŏiĕō (1), *to do*

RAISINS
6778 tsammûwq (4), *lump of dried grapes*

RAKEM
7552 Reqem (1), *versi-color*

RAKKATH
7557 Raqqath (1), *beach (as expanded shingle)*

RAKKON
7542 Raqqôwn (1), *thinness*

RAM
352 'ayîl (89), *chief; ram*
7410 Râm (7), *high*

RAM'S
3104 yôwbêl (1), *blast of a ram's horn*

RAMA
4471 Rhama (1), *height*

RAMAH
7414 Râmâh (36), *height*

RAMATH
7418 Râmôwth-Negeb (1), *heights of (the) South*

RAMATH-LEHI
7437 Râmath Lechîy (1), *height of (a) jaw-bone*

RAMATH-MIZPEH
7434 Râmath ham-Mitspeh (1), *height of the watch-tower*

RAMATHAIM-ZOPHIM
7436 Râmâthayim Tsôwphîym (1), *double height of watchers*

RAMATHITE
7435 Râmâthîy (1), *Ramathite*

RAMESES
7486 Ra'mᵉçêç (4), *Rameses or Raamses*

RAMIAH
7422 Ramyâh (1), *Jehovah has raised*

RAMOTH
3406 Yᵉrîymôwth (1), *elevations*
7216 Râ'môwth (6), *heights*
7418 Râmôwth-Negeb (1), *heights of (the) South*

RAMOTH-GILEAD
7433 Râmôth Gil'âd (19), *heights of Gilad*

RAMPART
2426 chêyl (2), *rampart, battlement*

RAMS
352 'ayîl (61), *chief; ram*
1798 dᵉkar (Ch.) (3), *male sheep*
3733 kar (2), *ram sheep; battering ram*
6260 'attûwd (2), *he-goats; leaders*

RAMS'
352 'ayîl (5), *chief; ram*
3104 yôwbêl (4), *blast of a ram's horn*

RAN
1272 bârach (1), *to flee suddenly*
1980 hâlak (2), *to walk; live a certain way*
3331 yâtsa' (1), *to strew as a surface*
3332 yâtsaq (1), *to pour out*
5064 nâgar (1), *to pour out; to deliver over*
6379 pâkâh (1), *to pour, trickle*
6584 pâshaṭ (1), *to strip, i.e. unclothe, plunder*
7323 rûwts (30), *to run*
7519 râtsâ' (1), *to run; to delight in*
7857 shâṭaph (1), *to gush; to inundate*

R

1530 ĕispēdaŏ (1), to *rush in*
1532 ĕistrĕchō (1), to *hasten inward*
1632 ĕkchĕō (1), to *pour forth; to bestow*
2027 ĕpŏkĕllō (1), to *beach a ship vessel*
2701 katatrĕchō (1), to *hasten, run*
3729 hŏrmaŏ (4), to *dash or plunge, stampede*
4063 pĕritrĕchō (1), to *traverse, run about*
4370 prŏstrĕchō (1), to *hasten by running*
4390 prŏtrĕchō (1), to *run ahead, i.e. to precede*
4890 sundrŏmē (1), *(riotous) concourse*
4936 suntrĕchō (2), to *rush together*
5143 trĕchō (6), to *run or walk hastily; to strive*

RANG
1949 hûwm (2), to *make an uproar; agitate*

RANGE
3491 yâthûwr (1), *gleaning*

RANGES
3600 kîyr (1), portable cooking *range*
7713 sᵉdêrâh (3), *row*, i.e. *rank* of soldiers; *story*

RANGING
8264 shâqaq (1), to *seek*

RANK
1277 bârîy' (2), *fatted or plump; healthy*
4634 ma'ărâkâh (1), *row; pile; military array*
5737 'âdar (1), to *arrange; hoe a vineyard*

RANKS
734 'ôrach (1), *road; manner of life*
6471 pa'am (2), *time; step; occurence*
4237 prasia (1), *arranged group*

RANSOM
3724 kôpher (8), *village; redemption-price*
6299 pâdâh (1), to *ransom; to release*
6306 pidyôwm (1), *ransom; payment*
487 antilutrŏn (1), *redemption-price*
3083 lutrŏn (2), *redemption-price*

RANSOMED
1350 gâ'al (2), to *redeem; to be the next of kin*
6299 pâdâh (1), to *ransom; to release*

RAPHA
7498 Râphâ' (2), *giant*

RAPHU
7505 Râphûw' (1), *cured*

RARE
3358 yaqqîyr (Ch.) (1), *precious*

RASE
6168 'ârâh (1), to *be, make bare; demolish*

RASH
926 bâhal (1), to *tremble; hasten, hurry anxiously*
4116 mâhar (1), to *hurry; promptly*

RASHLY
4312 prŏpĕtēs (1), *falling forward headlong*

RASOR
8593 ta'ar (1), *knife; razor; scabbard*

RATE
1697 dâbâr (5), *word; matter; thing*

RATHER
408 'al (2), *not; nothing*
977 bâchar (1), *select, chose, prefer*
2228 ē (3), *or; than*
2309 thĕlō (1), to *will; to desire; to choose*
3123 mallŏn (34), *in a greater degree*
3304 mĕnŏungĕ (1), *so then at least*
4056 pĕrissŏtĕrōs (1), *more superabundantly*
4133 plēn (2), *rather, yet*

RATTLETH
7439 rânâh (1), to *whiz, rattle*

RATTLING
7494 ra'ash (1), *vibration, bounding*

RAVEN
6158 'ôrêb (6), *dusky*-hue *raven*

RAVENING
2963 ţâraph (3), to *pluck off or pull to pieces*
724 harpagē (1), *pillage; greediness; robbery*
727 harpax (1), *rapacious; robbing*

RAVENOUS
5861 'ayiţ (2), bird of prey (poss.) *hawk*
6530 pᵉrîyts (1), *violent*

RAVENS
6158 'ôrêb (4), *dusky*-hue *raven*
2876 kŏrax (1), *crow or raven*

RAVIN
2963 ţâraph (1), to *pluck off or pull to pieces*
2966 ţᵉrêphâh (1), *torn prey*

RAVISHED
3823 lâbab (2), *transport with love; to stultify*
6031 'ânâh (1), to *afflict, be afflicted*
7686 shâgâh (2), to *stray, wander; to transgress*
7693 shâgal (2), to *copulate with*

RAW
2416 chay (6), *alive; raw; fresh; life*
4995 nâ' (1), *uncooked*

RAZOR
4177 môwrâh (3), *razor*
8593 ta'ar (2), *knife; razor; scabbard*

REACH
1272 bârach (1), to *flee suddenly*
1961 hâyâh (1), to *exist, i.e. be or become*
4229 mâchâh (1), to *touch, i.e. reach to*
5060 nâga' (5), to *strike*
5381 nâsag (2), to *reach*
2185 ĕphiknĕōmai (1), to *extend to, reach to*
5342 phĕrō (2), to *bear or carry*

REACHED
4291 mᵉţâ' (Ch.) (2), to *arrive, to extend*
5060 nâga' (1), to *strike*
6293 pâga' (1), to *impinge*
6642 tsâbaţ (1), to *hand out food*
190 akŏlŏuthĕō (1), to *accompany, follow*
2185 ĕphiknĕōmai (1), to *extend to, reach to*

REACHETH
4291 mᵉţâ' (Ch.) (1), to *arrive, to extend*
5060 nâga' (4), to *strike*
6293 pâga' (5), to *impinge*
7971 shâlach (1), to *send away*

REACHING
5060 nâga' (3), to *strike*
1901 ĕpĕktĕinŏmai (1), to *stretch oneself forward*

READ
7121 qârâ' (35), to *call out*
7123 qᵉrâ' (Ch.) (7), to *call out*
314 anaginōskō (28), to *read aloud in public*

READEST
314 anaginōskō (2), to *read aloud in public*

READETH
7121 qârâ' (1), to *call out*
314 anaginōskō (3), to *read aloud in public*

READINESS
2092 hĕtŏimŏs (1), *ready, prepared*
4288 prŏthumia (2), *alacrity, eagerness*

READING
4744 miqrâ' (1), *public meeting*
7121 qârâ' (2), to *call out*
320 anagnōsis (3), act of *public reading*

READY
631 'âçar (4), to *fasten; to join battle*
1951 hûwn (1), to *be, act light*
2363 chûwsh (1), to *hurry; to be eager*
2896 ţôwb (1), *good; well*
3559 kûwn (17), to *set up; establish, fix, prepare*
4106 mâhîyr (2), *skillful*

4116 mâhar (2), to *hurry; promptly*
4131 môwţ (1), to *slip, shake, fall*
4672 mâtsâ' (1), to *find or acquire; to occur*
5750 'ôwd (1), *again; repeatedly; still; more*
6257 'âthad (1), to *prepare*
6263 'ăthîyd (Ch.) (1), *prepared*
6264 'ăthîyd (4), *prepared; treasure*
7126 qârab (1), to *approach, bring near*
7138 qârôwb (1), *near, close*
8003 shâlêm (1), *complete; friendly; safe*
1451 ĕggus (1), *near, close*
2090 hĕtŏimazō (10), to *prepare*
2092 hĕtŏimŏs (15), *ready, prepared*
2093 hĕtŏimōs (3), *in readiness*
2130 ĕumĕtadŏtŏs (1), *liberal, generous*
3195 mĕllō (4), to *intend, i.e. be about to*
3903 paraskĕuazō (3), to *get ready, prepare*
4288 prŏthumia (1), *alacrity, eagerness*
4289 prŏthumŏs (3), *alacrity, eagerness*
4689 spĕndō (1), to *pour out as a libation*

REAIA
7211 Rᵉ'âyâh (1), *Jehovah has seen*

REAIAH
7211 Rᵉ'âyâh (3), *Jehovah has seen*

REALM
4437 malkûw (Ch.) (3), *dominion*
4438 malkûwth (4), *rule; dominion*

REAP
7114 qâtsar (18), to *curtail, cut short*
2325 thĕrizō (13), to *harvest, reap a crop*

REAPED
7114 qâtsar (1), to *curtail, cut short*
270 amaŏ (1), *reap, mow down grain*
2325 thĕrizō (2), to *harvest, reap a crop*

REAPER
7114 qâtsar (1), to *curtail, cut short*

REAPERS
7114 qâtsar (7), to *curtail, cut short*
2327 thĕristēs (2), *harvester, reaper*

REAPEST
7114 qâtsar (1), to *curtail, cut short*
2325 thĕrizō (1), to *harvest, reap a crop*

REAPETH
7114 qâtsar (1), to curtail, cut short
2325 thĕrizō (3), to harvest, reap a crop

REAPING
7114 qâtsar (1), to curtail, cut short
2325 thĕrizō (2), to harvest, reap a crop

REAR
6965 qûwm (3), to rise
1453 ĕgĕirō (1), to waken, i.e. rouse

REARED
5324 nâtsab (1), to station
6965 qûwm (9), to rise

REASON
413 'êl (1), to, toward
1697 dâbâr (1), word; matter; thing
2808 cheshbôwn (1), intelligent plan
2940 ṭa'am (1), taste; intelligence; mandate
3198 yâkach (3), to be correct; to argue
4480 min (5), from, out of
4486 manda' (Ch.) (1), wisdom or intelligence
5921 'al (2), above, over, upon, or against
5973 'îm (1), with
6440 pânîym (9), face; front
6903 qᵉbêl (Ch.) (1), on account of, so as, since
8199 shâphaṭ (1), to judge
701 arĕstŏs (1), agreeable; desirable; fit
1223 dia (5), through, by means of; because of
1260 dialŏgizŏmai (5), to deliberate
1537 ĕk (3), out, out of
1752 hĕnĕka (1), on account of
3056 lŏgŏs (2), word, matter, thing; Word

REASONABLE
3050 lŏgikŏs (1), rational, logical

REASONED
1256 dialĕgŏmai (4), to discuss
1260 dialŏgizŏmai (5), to deliberate
3049 lŏgizŏmai (1), to credit; to think, regard
4802 suzĕtĕō (1), to discuss, controvert
4817 sullŏgizŏmai (1), to reckon together

REASONING
8433 tôwkêchâh (1), correction, refutation
1260 dialŏgizŏmai (1), to deliberate
1261 dialŏgismŏs (1), consideration; debate
4802 suzĕtĕō (1), to discuss, controvert
4803 suzĕtēsis (1), discussion, dispute

REASONS
8394 tâbûwn (1), intelligence; argument

REBA
7254 Reba' (2), fourth

REBECCA
4479 Rhĕbĕkka (1), fettering (by beauty)

REBEKAH
7259 Ribqâh (28), fettering (by beauty)

REBEKAH'S
7259 Ribqâh (2), fettering (by beauty)

REBEL
4775 mârad (9), to rebel
4784 mârâh (4), to rebel or resist; to provoke
5493 çûwr (1), to turn off

REBELLED
4775 mârad (12), to rebel
4784 mârâh (16), to rebel or resist; to provoke
6586 pâsha' (5), to break away from authority
6856 tsippôren (1), nail; point of a style or pen

REBELLEST
4775 mârad (2), to rebel

REBELLION
4776 mᵉrad (Ch.) (1), rebellion
4779 mârâd (Ch.) (1), rebellious
4805 mᵉrîy (4), rebellion, rebellious
5627 çârâh (2), apostasy; crime; remission
6588 pesha' (1), revolt

REBELLIOUS
4775 mârad (1), to rebel
4779 mârâd (Ch.) (2), rebellious
4780 mardûwth (1), rebelliousness
4784 mârâh (9), to rebel or resist; to provoke
4805 mᵉrîy (17), rebellion, rebellious
5637 çârar (6), to be refractory, stubborn

REBELS
4775 mârad (1), to rebel
4784 mârâh (1), to rebel or resist; to provoke
4805 mᵉrîy (1), rebellion, rebellious

REBUKE
1605 gâ'ar (7), to chide, reprimand
1606 gᵉ'ârâh (12), chiding, rebuke
2781 cherpâh (2), contumely, disgrace
3198 yâkach (3), to be correct; to argue
4045 mig'ereth (1), reproof (i.e. a curse)
8433 tôwkêchâh (4), refutation, proof
298 amōmētŏs (1), unblemished
1651 ĕlĕgchō (4), to admonish, rebuke

REASONS (center col top)
1969 ĕpiplēssō (1), to upbraid, rebuke
2008 ĕpitimaō (6), to rebuke, warn, forbid

REBUKED
1605 gâ'ar (4), to chide, reprimand
3198 yâkach (1), to be correct; to argue
7378 rîyb (1), to hold a controversy; to defend
1651 ĕlĕgchō (1), to admonish, rebuke
2008 ĕpitimaō (17), to rebuke, warn, forbid
2192+1649 ĕchō (1), to have; hold; keep

REBUKER
4148 mûwçâr (1), reproof, warning

REBUKES
8433 tôwkêchâh (3), correction, refutation

REBUKETH
1605 gâ'ar (1), to chide, reprimand
3198 yâkach (3), to be correct; to argue

REBUKING
1606 gᵉ'ârâh (1), chiding, rebuke
2008 ĕpitimaō (1), to rebuke, warn, forbid

RECALL
7725 shûwb (1), to turn back; to return

RECEIPT
5058 tĕlōniŏn (3), tax-gatherer's booth

RECEIVE
1878 dâshên (1), to fatten; to satisfy
3557 kûwl (2), to keep in; to measure
3947 lâqach (35), to take
5162 nâcham (1), to be sorry; to pity, console
5375 nâsâ' (3), to lift up
6901 qâbal (3), to admit; to take
6902 qᵉbal (Ch.) (1), to acquire
8254 shâqal (1), to suspend in trade
308 anablĕpō (7), to look up; to recover sight
568 apĕchō (1), to be distant
588 apŏdĕchŏmai (1), to welcome; approve
618 apŏlambanō (8), to receive; be repaid
1209 dĕchŏmai (24), to receive, welcome
1325 didōmi (1), to give
1523 ĕisdĕchŏmai (1), to take into one's favor
1926 ĕpidĕchŏmai (1), to admit, welcome
2210 zēmiŏō (1), to experience detriment
2865 kŏmizō (6), to provide for
2983 lambanō (61), to take, receive

RECEIVETH (right col top)
3858 paradĕchŏmai (4), to accept, receive
3880 paralambanō (1), to assume an office
4327 prŏsdĕchŏmai (2), to receive; to await for
4355 prŏslambanō (4), to welcome, receive
5562 chōrĕō (5), to pass, enter; to hold, admit

RECEIVED
622 'âçaph (1), to gather, collect
1961 hâyâh (2), to exist, i.e. be or become
2388 châzaq (1), to fasten upon; to seize
2505 châlaq (1), to be smooth; be slippery
3947 lâqach (22), to take
4672 mâtsâ' (1), to find or acquire; to occur
6901 qâbal (3), to admit; to take
308 anablĕpō (8), to look up; to recover sight
324 anadĕchŏmai (2), to entertain as a guest
353 analambanō (3), to take up, bring up
354 analēpsis (1), ascension
568 apĕchō (1), to be distant
588 apŏdĕchŏmai (4), welcome; approve
618 apŏlambanō (1), to receive; be repaid
1183 dĕkatŏō (1), to give or take a tenth
1209 dĕchŏmai (16), to receive, welcome
1653 ĕlĕĕō (1), to give out compassion
2865 kŏmizō (3), to provide for, to carry off
2983 lambanō (56), to take, receive
3336 mĕtalēmpsis (1), participation, sharing
3549 nŏmŏthĕtĕō (1), to be given law
3880 paralambanō (13), to assume an office
4355 prŏslambanō (3), to welcome, receive
4687 spĕirō (4), to scatter, i.e. sow seed
4732 stĕrĕŏō (1), to be, become strong
5264 hupŏdĕchŏmai (4), to entertain hospitably
5274 hupŏlambanō (1), to take up, i.e. continue

RECEIVEDST
618 apŏlambanō (1), to receive; be repaid

RECEIVER
8254 shâqal (1), to suspend in trade

RECEIVETH
622 'âçaph (1), to gather, collect
3947 lâqach (4), to take
1209 dĕchŏmai (8), to receive, welcome
1926 ĕpidĕchŏmai (1), to admit, welcome

2983 lambanō (14), to take, receive
3335 mĕtalambanō (1), to participate
3858 paradĕchŏmai (1), to accept, receive
4327 prŏsdĕchŏmai (1), to receive; to await for

RECEIVING
3947 lâqach (1), to take
618 apŏlambanō (1), to receive; be repaid
2865 kŏmizō (1), to provide for, to carry off
2983 lambanō (1), to take, receive
3028 lēmpsis (1), act of receipt
3880 paralambanō (1), to assume an office
4356 prŏslēpsis (1), admission, acceptance

RECHAB
7394 Rêkâb (13), rider

RECHABITES
7397 Rêkâh (4), softness

RECHAH
7397 Rêkâh (1), softness

RECKON
2803 châshab (3), to think, regard; to value
5608 çâphar (1), to inscribe; to enumerate
6485 pâqad (1), to visit, care for, count
3049 lŏgizŏmai (2), to credit; to think, regard
4868 sunairō (1), to compute an account

RECKONED
2803 châshab (4), to think, regard; to value
3187 yâchas (12), to enroll by family list
7737 shâvâh (1), to resemble; to adjust
3049 lŏgizŏmai (4), to credit; to think, regard

RECKONETH
4868+3056 sunairō (1), to compute an account

RECKONING
2803 châshab (1), to think, regard; to value
6486 pᵉquddâh (1), visitation; punishment

RECOMMENDED
3860 paradidōmi (2), to hand over

RECOMPENCE
1576 gᵉmûwl (9), act; reward, recompense
7966 shillûwm (1), requital; retribution; fee
8005 shillêm (1), requital
8545 tᵉmûwrâh (1), ʟarter, compensation
468 antapŏdŏma (2), requital, recompense
489 antimisthia (2), correspondence
3405 misthapŏdŏsia (3), requital, good or bad

RECOMPENCES
1578 gᵉmûwlâh (1), act; reward, recompense
7966 shillûwm (1), requital; retribution; fee

RECOMPENSE
1580 gâmal (2), to benefit or requite; to wean
5414 nâthan (9), to give
7725 shûwb (3), to return or restore
7999 shâlam (7), to be safe; to reciprocate
467 antapŏdidōmi (3), to requite good or evil
591 apŏdidōmi (1), to give away

RECOMPENSED
5414 nâthan (1), to give
7725 shûwb (5), to return or restore
7999 shâlam (2), to be safe; to reciprocate
467 antapŏdidōmi (2), to requite good or evil

RECOMPENSEST
7999 shâlam (1), to be safe; to reciprocate

RECOMPENSING
5414 nâthan (1), to give

RECONCILE
3722 kâphar (2), to placate or cancel
7521 râtsâh (1), to be pleased with; to satisfy
604 apŏkatallassō (2), to reconcile fully, reunite

RECONCILED
604 apŏkatallassō (1), to reconcile fully, reunite
1259 diallassō (1), to be reconciled
2644 katallassō (5), to change mutually

RECONCILIATION
2398 châṭâ' (1), to sin
3722 kâphar (4), to placate or cancel
2433 hilaskŏmai (1), to conciliate, to atone for
2643 katallagē (2), restoration

RECONCILING
3722 kâphar (1), to cover; to expiate
2643 katallagē (1), restoration
2644 katallassō (1), to change mutually

RECORD
1799 dikrôwn (Ch.) (1), official register
2142 zâkar (2), to remember; to mention
5749 'ûwd (3), to duplicate or repeat
7717 sâhêd (1), witness
3140 marturĕō (13), to testify; to commend
3141 marturia (7), evidence given
3143 marturŏmai (1), to witness
3144 martus (2), witness

RECORDED
3789 kâthab (1), to write

RECORDER
2142 zâkar (9), to remember; to mention

RECORDS
1799 dikrôwn (Ch.) (2), official register
2146 zikrôwn (1), commemoration

RECOUNT
2142 zâkar (1), to remember; to mention

RECOVER
622 'âçaph (4), to gather, collect
1082 bâlag (1), to be comforted
2421 châyâh (6), to live; to revive
2492 châlam (1), to be, make plump; to dream
4241 michyâh (1), preservation of life; sustenance
5337 nâtsal (3), to deliver; to be snatched
6113 'âtsar (1), to hold back; to maintain, rule
7069 qânâh (1), to create; to procure
7725 shûwb (1), to turn back; to return
366 ananēphō (1), to regain one's senses
2192+2573 ĕchō (1), to have; hold; keep

RECOVERED
2388 châzaq (1), to fasten upon; to seize
2421 châyâh (2), to live; to revive
5337 nâtsal (2), to deliver; to be snatched
5927 'âlâh (1), to ascend, be high, mount
7725 shûwb (5), to turn back; to return

RECOVERING
309 anablĕpsis (1), restoration of sight

RED
119 'âdam (9), to be red in the face
122 'âdôm (7), rosy, red
132 'admônîy (1), reddish, ruddy
923 bahaṭ (1), white marble
2447 chaklîyl (1), darkly flashing eyes; brilliant
2560 châmar (1), to ferment, foam; to glow
2561 chemer (1), fermenting wine
5488 çûwph (24), papyrus reed; reed
5489 Çûwph (1), reed
5492 çûwphâh (1), hurricane wind
2281 thalassa (2), sea or lake
4449 purrhazō (2), to redden
4450 purrhŏs (2), fire-like, flame-colored

REDDISH
125 'ădamdâm (6), reddish

REDEEM
1350 gâ'al (23), to redeem; be next of kin
1353 gᵉullâh (5), redemption
6299 pâdâh (24), to ransom; to release
6304 pᵉdûwth (2), distinction; deliverance
1805 ĕxagŏrazō (1), to buy up, ransom
3084 lutrŏō (1), to free by paying a ransom

REDEEMED
1350 gâ'al (24), to redeem; be next of kin
1353 gᵉullâh (2), redemption
6299 pâdâh (23), to ransom; to release
6302 pâdûwy (2), ransom
6306 pidyôwm (2), ransom payment
6561 pâraq (1), to break off or crunch; to deliver
7069 qânâh (1), to create; to procure
59 agŏrazō (3), to purchase; to redeem
1805 ĕxagŏrazō (1), to buy up, ransom
3084 lutrŏō (2), to free by paying a ransom
4160+3085 pŏiĕō (1), to make or do

REDEEMEDST
6299 pâdâh (1), to ransom; to release

REDEEMER
1350 gâ'al (18), to redeem; be next of kin

REDEEMETH
1350 gâ'al (1), to redeem; to be the next of kin
6299 pâdâh (1), to ransom; to release

REDEEMING
1353 gᵉullâh (1), redemption
1805 ĕxagŏrazō (2), to buy up, ransom

REDEMPTION
1353 gᵉullâh (5), redemption
6304 pᵉdûwth (2), distinction; deliverance
6306 pidyôwm (2), ransom payment
629 apŏlutrōsis (9), ransom in full
3085 lutrōsis (2), ransoming

REDNESS
2498 châlaph (1), to hasten away; to pass on

REDOUND
4052 pĕrissĕuō (1), to superabound

REED
7070 qâneh (21), reed
2563 kalamŏs (11), reed

REEDS
98 'âgam (1), marsh; pond; pool
7070 qâneh (6), reed

REEL
2287 châgag (1), to
observe a festival
5128 nûwa' (1), to waver

REELAIAH
7480 Rᵉ'êlâyâh (1),
fearful of Jehovah

REFINE
6884 tsâraph (1), to fuse
metal; to refine

REFINED
2212 zâqaq (3), to strain,
refine; extract, clarify
6884 tsâraph (2), to fuse
metal; to refine

REFINER
6884 tsâraph (1), to fuse
metal; to refine

REFINER'S
6884 tsâraph (1), to fuse
metal; to refine

REFORMATION
1357 diŏrthōsis (1),
Messianic restoration

REFORMED
3256 yâçar (1), to
chastise; to instruct

REFRAIN
662 'âphaq (2), to abstain
2413 châṭam (1), to stop,
restrain
2820 châsak (1), to
restrain or refrain
4513 mâna' (2), to deny
7368 râchaq (1), to
recede; remove
868 aphistēmi (1), to
desist, desert
3973 pauō (1), to stop

REFRAINED
662 'âphaq (3), to abstain
2820 châsak (1), to
restrain or refrain
3601 kîyshôwr (1),
spindle
3607 kâlâ' (1), to hold
back; to prohibit, stop
6113 'âtsar (1), to hold
back; to maintain, rule

REFRAINETH
2820 châsak (1), to
restrain or refrain

REFRESH
5582 çâ'ad (1), to support
373 anapauō (1), to
repose; to refresh
1958+5177 ĕpimĕlĕia (1),
carefulness

REFRESHED
5314 nâphash (3), to be
refreshed
7304 râvach (2), to
revive; to have room
373 anapauō (3), to
repose; to refresh
404 anapsuchō (1), to
relieve
4875 sunanapauŏmai
(1), to recruit oneself

REFRESHETH
7725 shûwb (1), to return
or restore

REFRESHING
4774 margê'âh (1), place
of rest
403 anapsuxis (1),
revival, relief

REFUGE
2620 châçâh (1), to flee
to; to confide in
4268 machăçeh (15),
shelter; refuge
4498 mânôwç (4), fleeing;
place of refuge
4585 mᵉ'ôwnâh (1), abode
4733 miqlâṭ (20), asylum,
place of protection
4869 misgâb (5), high
refuge
2703 kataphĕugō (1), to
flee down

REFUSE
3973 mâ'ôwç (1), refuse
3985 mâ'ên (10), to
refuse, reject
3986 mâ'ên (4),
unwilling, refusing
3987 mê'ên (1),
refractory, stubborn
3988 mâ'aç (3), to spurn;
to disappear
4549 mâçaç (1), to waste;
to faint
4651 mappâl (1), chaff;
flap or fold of skin
6544 pâra' (1), to loosen;
to expose, dismiss
3868 paraitĕŏmai (4), to
deprecate, decline

REFUSED
3985 mâ'ên (24), to
refuse, reject
3988 mâ'aç (5), to spurn;
to disappear
579 apŏblētŏs (1),
rejected
720 arnĕŏmai (2), to
disavow, reject
3868 paraitĕŏmai (1), to
deprecate, decline

REFUSEDST
3985 mâ'ên (1), to refuse,
reject

REFUSETH
3985 mâ'ên (5), to refuse,
reject
3988 mâ'aç (1), to spurn;
to disappear
5800 'âzab (1), to loosen;
relinquish; permit
6544 pâra' (2), to loosen;
to expose, dismiss

REGARD
995 bîyn (4), to
understand; discern
1875 dârash (1), to
pursue or search
2803 châshab (1), to
think, regard; to value
3820 lêb (3), heart
5027 nâbaṭ (4), to scan;
to regard with favor
5375 nâsâ' (3), to lift up
5375+6440 nâsâ' (1), to
lift up
5869+2437+5921 'ayin (1),
eye; sight; fountain
5921+1700 'al (1), above,
over, upon, or against

6437 pânâh (3), to turn,
to face
7200 râ'âh (1), to see
7789 shûwr (1), to spy
out, survey
8104 shâmar (2), to
watch
8159 shâ'âh (1), to
inspect, consider
1788 ĕntrĕpō (1), to
respect; to confound
4337 prŏsĕchō (1), to pay
attention to
5426 phrŏnĕō (1), to be
mentally disposed

REGARDED
3820 lêb (1), heart
7181 qâshab (1), to prick
up the ears
7182 qesheb (1),
hearkening
7200 râ'âh (2), to see
7761+2942 sûwm (Ch.)
(1), to put, place
272 amĕlĕō (1), to be
careless of, neglect
1788 ĕntrĕpō (1), to
respect; to confound
1914 ĕpiblĕpō (1), to gaze
at

REGARDEST
995 bîyn (1), to
understand; discern
991 blĕpō (2), to look at

REGARDETH
995 bîyn (1), to
understand; discern
2803 châshab (1), to
think, regard; to value
3045 yâda' (1), to know
5234 nâkar (1), to
respect, revere
5375 nâsâ' (1), to lift up
6437 pânâh (1), to turn,
to face
7200 râ'âh (1), to see
7761+2942 sûwm (Ch.)
(1), to put, place
8085 shâma' (1), to hear
8104 shâmar (3), to
watch
5426 phrŏnĕō (2), to be
mentally disposed

REGARDING
7760 sûwm (1), to put,
place
3851 parabŏulĕuŏmai
(1), to misconsult, i.e.
disregard

REGEM
7276 Regem (1),
stone-heap

REGEM-MELECH
7278 Regem Melek (1),
king's heap

REGENERATION
3824 paliggĕnĕsia (2),
renovation; restoration

REGION
2256 chebel (3),
company, band
5299 nâphâh (1), height;
sieve
4066 pĕrichōrŏs (6),
surrounding country
5561 chōra (4), territory

REGIONS
2825 klinē (2), couch
5561 chōra (1), territory

REGISTER
3791 kâthâb (2), writing,
record or book
5612 çêpher (1), writing

REHABIAH
7345 Rᵉchabyâh (5),
Jehovah has enlarged

REHEARSE
7760 sûwm (1), to put,
place
8567 tânâh (1), to
commemorate

REHEARSED
1696 dâbar (1), to speak,
say; to subdue
5046 nâgad (1), to
announce
312 anaggĕllō (1), to
announce in detail
756 archŏmai (1), to
begin

REHOB
7340 Rᵉchôb (10), myriad

REHOBOAM
7346 Rᵉchab'âm (50),
people has enlarged

REHOBOTH
7344 Rᵉchôbôwth (4),
streets

REHUM
7348 Rᵉchûwm (8),
compassionate

REI
7472 Rê'îy (1), social

REIGN
4427 mâlak (117), to
reign as king
4437 malkûw (Ch.) (4),
dominion
4438 malkûwth (21),
rule; dominion
4467 mamlâkâh (2),
royal dominion
4468 mamlâkûwth (1),
royal dominion
4910 mâshal (3), to rule
6113 'âtsar (1), to hold
back; to rule, assemble
7287 râdâh (1), to
subjugate
757 archō (1), to rule, be
first in rank
936 basilĕuō (13), to rule
2231 hēgĕmŏnia (1),
rulership, leadership
4821 sumbasilĕuō (2), to
be co-regent

REIGNED
4427 mâlak (159), to
reign as king
4910 mâshal (3), to rule
7786 sûwr (1), to rule,
crown
936 basilĕuō (6), to rule

REIGNEST
4910 mâshal (1), to rule

REIGNETH
4427 mâlak (11), to reign
as king
936 basilĕuō (1), to rule
2192+932 ĕchō (1), to
have; hold; keep

REIGNING
4427 mâlak (1), to *reign as king*

REINS
2504 châlâts (1), *loins, areas of the waist*
3629 kilyâh (13), *kidney; mind, heart, spirit*
3510 nĕphrŏs (1), inmost mind

REJECT
3988 mâˈaç (1), to *spurn; to disappear*
114 athĕtĕō (2), to *disesteem, neutralize*
3868 paraitĕŏmai (1), to *deprecate, decline*

REJECTED
2310 châdêl (1), *ceasing or destitute*
3988 mâˈaç (17), to *spurn; to disappear*
96 adŏkimŏs (1), *failing the test, worthless*
114 athĕtĕō (1), to *disesteem, neutralize*
593 apŏdŏkimazŏ (7), to *repudiate, reject*
1609 ĕkptuō (1), to *spurn, scorn*

REJECTETH
14 agathŏĕrgĕō (1), to do *good work*

REJOICE
1523 gîyl (23), *rejoice*
1524 gîyl (2), *age, stage in life*
4885 mâsôws (1), *delight*
5937 'âlaz (8), to *jump for joy*
5947 'allîyz (3), *exultant; reveling*
5965 'âlaç (1), to *leap for joy, i.e. exult, wave*
5970 'âlats (4), to *jump for joy*
7442 rânan (11), to *shout for joy*
7797 sûws (14), to be *bright, i.e. cheerful*
7832 sâchaq (1), to *laugh; to scorn; to play*
8055 sâmach (70), to be, *make gleesome*
8056 sâmêach (5), *blithe or gleeful*
8057 simchâh (4), *blithesomeness or glee*
21 agalliaō (4), to *exult*
2165 ĕuphrainō (5), to *rejoice, be glad*
2744 kauchaŏmai (4), to *glory in, rejoice in*
2745 kauchēma (1), *boast; brag*
4796 sugchairō (5), to *sympathize in gladness*
5463 chairō (24), to be *cheerful*

REJOICED
1523 gîyl (2), *rejoice*
2302 châdâh (1), to *rejoice, be glad*
5937 'âlaz (2), to *jump for joy*
6670 tsâhal (1), to be *cheerful*

7797 sûws (3), to be *bright, i.e. cheerful*
8055 sâmach (20), to be, *make gleesome*
8056 sâmêach (3), *blithe or gleeful*
8057 simchâh (1), *blithesomeness or glee*
21 agalliaō (4), to *exult*
2165 ĕuphrainō (1), to *rejoice, be glad*
4796 sugchairō (1), to *sympathize in gladness*
5463 chairō (8), to be *cheerful*

REJOICEST
5937 'âlaz (1), to *jump for joy*

REJOICETH
1523 gîyl (1), *rejoice*
4885 mâsôws (1), *delight*
5937 'âlaz (1), to *jump for joy*
5938 'âlêz (1), *exultant*
5970 'âlats (2), to *jump for joy*
7797 sûws (3), to be *bright, i.e. cheerful*
8055 sâmach (4), to be, *make gleesome*
2620 katakauchaŏmai (1), to *exult over*
4796 sugchairō (1), to *sympathize in gladness*
5463 chairō (3), to be *cheerful*

REJOICING
1524 gîyl (1), *age, stage in life*
1525 gîylâh (1), *joy, delight*
5947 'allîyz (1), *exultant; reveling*
5951 'ălîytsûwth (1), *exultation*
7440 rinnâh (3), *shout*
7832 sâchaq (2), to *laugh; to scorn; to play*
8055 sâmach (1), to be, *make gleesome*
8056 sâmêach (1), *blithe or gleeful*
8057 simchâh (2), *blithesomeness or glee*
8342 sâsôwn (1), *cheerfulness; welcome*
8643 tᵉrûwˈâh (1), *battle-cry; clangor*
2745 kauchēma (4), *boast; brag*
2746 kauchēsis (4), *boasting; bragging*
5463 chairō (5), to be *cheerful*

REKEM
7552 Reqem (5), *versi-color*

RELEASE
2010 hănâchâh (1), *quiet*
8058 shâmaṭ (2), to *let alone, desist, remit*
8059 shᵉmiṭṭâh (5), *remission of debt*
630 apŏluō (13), to *relieve, release*

RELEASED
630 apŏluō (4), to *relieve, release; to divorce*

RELIED
8172 shâˈan (3), to *support, rely on*

RELIEF
1248 diakŏnia (1), *attendance, aid, service*

RELIEVE
833 'âshar (1), to go *forward; guide; prosper*
2388 châzaq (1), to *bind, restrain, conquer*
7725 shûwb (3), to *turn back; to return*
1884 ĕparkĕō (2), to *help*

RELIEVED
1884 ĕparkĕō (1), to *help*

RELIEVETH
5749 'ûwd (1), to *protest, testify; to restore*

RELIGION
2356 thrēskĕia (3), *observance, religion*
2454 Iŏudaismŏs (2), *Jewish faith*

RELIGIOUS
2357 thrēskŏs (1), *ceremonious, pious*
4576 sĕbŏmai (1), to *revere, i.e. adore*

RELY
8172 shâˈan (1), to *support, rely on*

REMAIN
1481 gûwr (1), to *sojourn, live as an alien*
1961 hâyâh (1), to *exist, i.e. be or become*
3241 Yânîym (1), *asleep*
3427 yâshab (11), to *dwell, to remain*
3498 yâthar (13), to *remain or be left*
3885 lûwn (5), to be *obstinate with*
5117 nûwach (1), to *rest; to settle down*
5975 'âmad (3), to *stand*
6965 qûwm (1), to *rise*
7604 shâˈar (15), to *leave, remain*
7611 sheˈêrîyth (1), *remainder or residual*
7931 shâkan (3), to *reside*
8245 shâqad (1), to be *alert, i.e. sleepless*
8300 sârîyd (8), *survivor; remainder*
3062 lŏipŏi (1), *remaining ones*
3306 mĕnō (8), to *remain*
4035 pĕrilĕipō (2), to *survive, be left, remain*
4052 pĕrissĕuō (1), to *superabound*

REMAINDER
3498 yâthar (4), to *remain or be left*
7611 sheˈêrîyth (2), *remainder or residual*

REMAINED
1961 hâyâh (1), to *exist, i.e. be or become*

3427 yâshab (10), to *dwell, to remain*
3462 yâshên (1), to *sleep; to grow old, stale*
3498 yâthar (5), to *remain or be left*
5975 'âmad (4), to *stand*
7604 shâˈar (23), to *leave, remain*
8277 sârad (1), to *escape or survive*
8300 sârîyd (1), *survivor; remainder*
1265 diamĕnō (1), to *stay constantly*
3306 mĕnō (3), to *remain*
4052 pĕrissĕuō (3), to *superabound*

REMAINEST
3427 yâshab (1), to *dwell, to remain; to settle*
1265 diamĕnō (1), to *stay constantly*

REMAINETH
3117 yôwm (1), *day; time period*
3427 yâshab (1), to *dwell, to remain; to settle*
3498 yâthar (4), to *remain or be left*
3885 lûwn (2), to be *obstinate with*
5736 'âdaph (4), to be *redundant*
5975 'âmad (1), to *stand*
7604 shâˈar (8), to *leave, remain*
7931 shâkan (1), to *reside*
8300 sârîyd (3), *survivor; remainder*
620 apŏlĕipō (3), to *leave behind; to forsake*
3306 mĕnō (5), to *stay, remain*
3588+3063 hŏ (1), "the," i.e. the definite article

REMAINING
3320 yâtsab (1), to *station, offer, continue*
3498 yâthar (1), to *remain or be left*
7931 shâkan (1), to *reside*
8300 sârîyd (9), *survivor; remainder*
3306 mĕnō (1), to *remain*

REMALIAH
7425 Rᵉmalyâhûw (11), *Jehovah has bedecked*

REMALIAH'S
7425 Rᵉmalyâhûw (2), *Jehovah has bedecked*

REMEDY
4832 marpê' (3), *cure; deliverance; placidity*

REMEMBER
2142 zâkar (120), to *remember; to mention*
6485 pâqad (1), to *visit, care for, count*
3403 mimnēskō (1), to *remind or to recall*
3415 mnaŏmai (9), to *bear in mind*
3421 mnēmŏnĕuō (16), to *exercise memory*
5279 hupŏmimnēskō (1), to *suggest to memory*

REMEMBERED
2142 zâkar (48), to *remember;* to *mention*
2143 zêker (1), *commemoration*
3415 mnaŏmai (6), to *recollect*
3421 mnēmŏnĕuō (1), to *recall*
5279 hupŏmimnēskō (1), to *remind oneself*

REMEMBEREST
2142 zâkar (1), to *remember;* to *mention*
3415 mnaŏmai (1), to *recollect*

REMEMBERETH
2142 zâkar (3), to *remember;* to *mention*
363 anamimnēskō (1), to *remind;* to *recollect*
3421 mnēmŏnĕuō (1), to *recall*

REMEMBERING
2142 zâkar (1), to *remember;* to *mention*
3421 mnēmŏnĕuō (1), to *recall*

REMEMBRANCE
2142 zâkar (13), to *remember;* to *mention*
2143 zêker (11), *recollection*
2146 zikrôwn (5), *commemoration*
6485 pâqad (1), to *visit, care for, count*
363 anamimnēskō (3), to *remind;* to *recollect*
364 anamnēsis (5), *recollection*
3415 mnaŏmai (3), to *recollect*
3417 mnēia (3), *recollection; recital*
3418 mnēma (1), sepulchral *monument*
5179 tupŏs (2), *shape, resemblance;* "*type*"
5279 hupŏmimnēskō (2), to *remind oneself*
5280 hupŏmnēsis (3), *reminding*
5294 hupŏtithēmi (1), to *hazard;* to *suggest*

REMEMBRANCES
2146 zikrôwn (1), *commemoration*

REMETH
7432 Remeth (1), *height*

REMISSION
859 aphĕsis (9), *pardon, freedom*
3929 parĕsis (1), *toleration, passing over*

REMIT
863 aphiĕmi (1), to *leave;* to *pardon, forgive*

REMITTED
863 aphiĕmi (1), to *leave;* to *pardon, forgive*

REMMON
7417 Rimmôwn (1), *pomegranate*

REMMON-METHOAR
7417 Rimmôwn (1), *pomegranate*

REMNANT
310 'achar (1), *after*
319 'achărîyth (1), *future; posterity*
3498 yâthar (4), to *remain* or *be left*
3499 yether (14), *remainder;* small *rope*
5629 çerach (1), *redundancy*
6413 pᵉlêyţâh (1), *escaped* portion
7604 shâ'ar (4), to *leave, remain*
7605 shᵉᵉâr (11), *remainder*
7611 shᵉᵉêrîyth (44), *remainder* or *residual*
8293 shêrûwth (1), *freedom*
8300 sârîyd (2), *survivor; remainder*
2640 katalĕimma (1), *few, remnant*
3005 lĕimma (1), *remainder, remnant*
3062 lŏipŏi (4), *remaining* ones

REMOVE
1540 gâlâh (2), to *denude; uncover*
1556 gâlal (1), to *roll;* to *commit*
4185 mûwsh (4), to *withdraw*
5110 nûwd (4), to *waver;* to *wander, flee*
5253 nâçag (4), to *retreat*
5265 nâça' (1), *start*
5437 çâbab (2), to *surround*
5472 çûwg (1), to *go back,* to *retreat*
5493 çûwr (15), to *turn* off
7368 râchaq (5), to *recede; remove*
7493 râ'ash (1), to *undulate, quake*
2795 kinĕō (1), to *stir, move, remove*
3179 mĕthistēmi (1), to *move*
3327 mĕtabainō (2), to *depart, move from*
3911 paraphĕrō (1), to *carry off;* to *avert*

REMOVED
167 'âhal (1), to *pitch a tent*
1540 gâlâh (3), to *denude; uncover*
1556 gâlal (1), to *roll;* to *commit*
2186 zânach (1), to *reject, forsake, fail*
2189 za'ăvâh (6), *agitation, maltreatment*
3014 yâgâh (1), to *push away, be removed*
3670 kânaph (1), to *withdraw*
4131 môwţ (5), to *slip, shake, fall*

REMMON
4171 mûwr (1), to *alter;* to *barter,* to *dispose* of
4185 mûwsh (2), to *withdraw*
5074 nâdad (1), to *rove, flee;* to *drive* away
5079 niddâh (2), time of menstrual *impurity*
5110 nûwd (1), to *waver;* to *wander, flee*
5128 nûwa' (1), to *waver*
5206 nîydâh (1), *removal*
5265 nâça' (26), *start*
5437 çâbab (1), to *surround*
5493 çûwr (21), to *turn* off
5674 'âbar (1), to *cross* over; to *transition*
6275 'âthaq (4), to *remove*
7368 râchaq (4), to *recede*
142 airō (2), to *lift,* to *take up*
3179 mĕthistēmi (1), to *move*
3346 mĕtatithēmi (1), to *transport;* to *exchange*
3351 mĕtŏikizō (1), to *transfer* as a *settler*

REMOVETH
5253 nâçag (1), to *retreat*
5265 nâça' (1), *start*
5493 çûwr (1), to *turn* off
5709 'ădâ' (Ch.) (1), to *pass* on or *continue*
6275 'âthaq (1), to *remove*

REMOVING
1473 gôwlâh (2), *exile; captive*
5493 çûwr (2), to *turn* off
3331 mĕtathĕsis (1), *transferral* to heaven

REMPHAN
4481 Rhĕmphan (1), *Kijun* (a pagan god)

REND
1234 bâqa' (3), to *cleave, break, tear open*
6533 pâram (2), to *tear, be torn*
7167 qâra' (11), to *rend*
4486 rhēgnumi (1), to *tear to pieces*
4977 schizō (1), to *split* or *sever*

RENDER
5415 nᵉthan (Ch.) (1), to *give*
7725 shûwb (16), to *turn back;* to *return*
7999 shâlam (7), to *be safe; be, make complete*
467 antapŏdidōmi (1), to *requite* good or evil
591 apŏdidōmi (8), to *give away*

RENDERED
7725 shûwb (4), to *turn back;* to *return*

RENDEREST
7999 shâlam (1), to *be safe; be, make complete*

RENDERETH
7999 shâlam (1), to *be safe; be, make complete*

RENDERING
591 apŏdidōmi (1), to *give away*

RENDING
6561 pâraq (1), to *break* off or *crunch;* to *deliver*

RENEW
2318 châdash (3), to *be new, renew;* to *rebuild*
2498 châlaph (2), to *spring up;* to *change*
340 anakainizō (1), to *restore, bring back*

RENEWED
2318 châdash (2), to *be new, renew;* to *rebuild*
2498 châlaph (1), to *spring up;* to *change*
341 anakainŏō (2), to *renovate, renew*
365 ananĕŏō (1), to *renovate, i.e. reform*

RENEWEST
2318 châdash (2), to *be new, renew;* to *rebuild*

RENEWING
342 anakainōsis (2), *renovation, renewal*

RENOUNCED
550 apĕipŏmēn (1), to *disown*

RENOWN
8034 shêm (7), *name, appellation*

RENOWNED
1984 hâlal (1), to *boast*
7121 qârâ' (3), to *call* out

RENT
1234 bâqa' (5), to *cleave, break, tear open*
2963 ţâraph (1), to *pluck* off or *pull* to pieces
5364 niqpâh (1), *rope*
6533 pâram (1), to *tear, be torn*
6561 pâraq (1), to *break* off or *crunch;* to *deliver*
7167 qâra' (43), to *rend*
8156 shâça' (2), to *split* or *tear;* to *upbraid*
1284 diarrhēssō (3), to *tear asunder*
4048 pĕrirrhēgnumi (1), to *tear all around*
4682 sparassō (1), to *convulse* with epilepsy
4977 schizō (5), to *split* or *sever*
4978 schisma (2), *divisive dissension*

RENTEST
7167 qâra' (1), to *rend*

REPAID
7999 shâlam (1), to *be safe;* to *reciprocate*

REPAIR
918 bâdaq (1), to *mend a breach*
2318 châdash (3), to *be new, renew;* to *rebuild*
2388 châzaq (8), to *fasten* upon; to *seize*
2393 chezqâh (1), prevailing *power*
5975 'âmad (1), to *stand*

R

REPAIRED
1129 bânâh (2), to *build*; to *establish*
2388 châzaq (39), to *fasten* upon; to *seize*
2421 châyâh (1), to *live*; to *revive*
5462 çâgar (1), to *shut* up; to *surrender*
7495 râphâ' (1), to *cure*, *heal*

REPAIRER
1443 gâdar (1), to *build a* stone *wall*

REPAIRING
3247 yᵉçôwd (1), *foundation*

REPAY
7999 shâlam (5), to be *complete*; to *reciprocate*
457 anöixis (1), act of *opening*
591 apŏdidōmi (1), to *give away*
661 apŏtinō (1), to *pay in* full, *make restitution*

REPAYETH
7999 shâlam (1), to be *complete*; to *reciprocate*

REPEATETH
8138 shânâh (1), to *fold*, i.e. *duplicate*

REPENT
5162 nâcham (19), to be *sorry*; to *pity*, *rue*
7725 shûwb (3), to *turn* back; to *return*
3338 mĕtamĕllŏmai (2), to *regret*
3340 mĕtanŏĕō (21), to *reconsider*

REPENTANCE
5164 nôcham (1), *ruefulness*
278 amĕtamĕlētŏs (1), *irrevocable*
3341 mĕtanŏia (24), *reversal*

REPENTED
5162 nâcham (17), to be *sorry*; to *pity*, *rue*
278 amĕtamĕlētŏs (1), *irrevocable*
3338 mĕtamĕllŏmai (3), to *regret*
3340 mĕtanŏĕō (11), to *reconsider*

REPENTEST
5162 nâcham (1), to be *sorry*; to *pity*, *rue*

REPENTETH
5162 nâcham (3), to be *sorry*; to *pity*, *rue*
3340 mĕtanŏĕō (2), to *reconsider*

REPENTING
5162 nâcham (1), to be *sorry*; to *pity*, *rue*

REPENTINGS
5150 nichûwm (1), *consoled*; *solace*

REPETITIONS
945 battŏlŏgĕō (1), to *prate* tediously, *babble*

REPHAEL
7501 Rᵉphâ'êl (1), *God has cured*

REPHAH
7506 Rephach (1), *support*

REPHAIAH
7509 Rᵉphâyâh (5), *Jehovah has cured*

REPHAIM
7497 râphâ' (6), *giant*

REPHAIMS
7497 râphâ' (2), *giant*

REPHIDIM
7508 Rᵉphîydîym (5), *balusters*

REPLENISH
4390 mâlê' (2), to *fill*; be *full*

REPLENISHED
4390 mâlê' (5), to *fill*; be *full*

REPLIEST
470 antapŏkrinŏmai (1), to *contradict* or *dispute*

REPORT
1681 dibbâh (3), *slander*, *bad report*
1697 dâbâr (2), *word*; *matter*; *thing*
5046 nâgad (1), to *announce*
8034 shêm (1), *name*, *appellation*
8052 shᵉmûw'âh (4), *announcement*
8088 shêma' (5), something *heard*
189 akŏē (2), *hearing*; thing *heard*
518 apaggĕllō (1), to *announce*, *proclaim*
1426 dusphēmia (1), *defamation*, *slander*
2162 ĕuphēmia (1), good *repute*
2163 ĕuphēmŏs (1), *reputable*
3140 marturĕō (6), to *testify*; to *commend*
3141 marturia (1), *evidence* given

REPORTED
559 'âmar (2), 'to *say*
7725 shûwb (1), to *turn* back; to *return*
8085 shâma' (2), to *hear*
191 akŏuō (1), to *hear*
312 anaggĕllō (1), to *announce*, *report*
518 apaggĕllō (1), to *announce*, *proclaim*
987 blasphēmĕō (1), to *speak impiously*
1310 diaphēmizō (1), to *spread news*
3140 marturĕō (2), to *testify*; to *commend*

REPROACH
2617 cheçed (1), *kindness*, *favor*
2659 châphêr (1), to *shame*, *reproach*
2778 châraph (10), to *spend the winter*

2781 cherpâh (65), *contumely*, *disgrace*
3637 kâlam (1), to *taunt* or *insult*
3639 kᵉlimmâh (1), *disgrace*, *scorn*
7036 qâlôwn (1), *disgrace*
819 atimia (1), *disgrace*
3679 ŏnĕidizō (2), to *rail at*, *chide*, *taunt*
3680 ŏnĕidismŏs (3), *with insult*
3681 ŏnĕidŏs (1), *notoriety*, i.e. a *taunt*

REPROACHED
2778 châraph (12), to *spend the winter*
3637 kâlam (1), to *taunt* or *insult*
3679 ŏnĕidizō (2), to *rail at*, *chide*, *taunt*

REPROACHES
1421 giddûwph (1), *vilification*, *scorn*
2781 cherpâh (1), *contumely*, *disgrace*
3679 ŏnĕidizō (1), to *rail at*, *chide*, *taunt*
3680 ŏnĕidismŏs (1), *with insult*
5196 hubris (1), *insult*

REPROACHEST
5195 hubrizō (1), to *exercise violence*, *abuse*

REPROACHETH
1442 gâdaph (1), to *revile*, *blaspheme*
2778 châraph (5), to *spend the winter*
2781 cherpâh (1), *contumely*, *disgrace*

REPROACHFULLY
2781 cherpâh (1), *contumely*, *disgrace*
5484+3059 charin (1), on account of, *because* of

REPROBATE
3988 mâ'aç (1), to *spurn*; to *disappear*
96 adŏkimŏs (3), *failing the test*, *worthless*

REPROBATES
96 adŏkimŏs (3), *failing the test*, *worthless*

REPROOF
1606 gᵉ'ârâh (2), *chiding*, *rebuke*
8433 tôwkêchâh (12), *correction*, *refutation*
1650 ĕlĕgchŏs (1), *proof*, *conviction*

REPROOFS
8433 tôwkêchâh (2), *correction*, *refutation*

REPROVE
3198 yâkach (16), to be *correct*; to *argue*
1651 ĕlĕgchō (3), to *confute*, *admonish*

REPROVED
1605 gâ'ar (1), to *chide*, *reprimand*
3198 yâkach (4), to be *correct*; to *argue*

8433 tôwkêchâh (2), *correction*, *refutation*
1651 ĕlĕgchō (3), to *confute*, *admonish*

REPROVER
3198 yâkach (2), to be *correct*; to *argue*

REPROVETH
3198 yâkach (3), to be *correct*; to *argue*
3256 yâçar (1), to *chastise*; to *instruct*

REPUTATION
3368 yâqâr (1), *valuable*
1380 dŏkĕō (1), to *think*, *regard*, seem good
1784 ĕntimŏs (1), *valued*, considered *precious*
2758 kĕnŏō (1), to *make empty*
5093 timiŏs (1), *costly*; *honored*, *esteemed*

REPUTED
2804 chăshab (Ch.) (2), to *regard*

REQUEST
782 'ăresheth (1), *longing for*
1245 bâqash (3), to *search*; to *strive after*
1246 baqqâshâh (8), *petition*, *request*
1697 dâbâr (2), *word*; *matter*; *thing*
7596 shᵉ'êlâh (3), *petition*
1162 dĕēsis (1), *petition*, *request*
1189 dĕŏmai (1), to *beg*, *petition*, *ask*

REQUESTED
1156 bᵉ'â' (Ch.) (1), to *seek* or *ask*
1245 bâqash (1), to *search*; to *strive after*
7592 shâ'al (3), to *ask*

REQUESTS
155 aitēma (1), *thing asked*, *request*

REQUIRE
977 bâchar (1), *select*, *chose*, *prefer*
1245 bâqash (10), to *search*; to *strive after*
1875 dârash (11), to *pursue* or *search*
3117 yôwm (1), *day*; *time period*
7592 shâ'al (3), to *ask*
7593 shᵉ'êl (Ch.) (1), to *ask*
154 aitĕō (1), to *ask* for
1096 ginŏmai (1), to *be*, *become*

REQUIRED
1245 bâqash (3), to *search*; to *strive after*
1875 dârash (2), to *pursue* or *search*
1961 hâyâh (1), to *exist*, i.e. *be* or *become*
3117 yôwm (3), *day*; *time period*
7592 shâ'al (4), to *ask*
155 aitēma (1), *thing asked*, *request*

523 apaitĕō (1), to
demand back
1567 ĕkzētĕō (2), to seek
out
2212 zētĕō (2), to seek
4238 prassō (1), to
execute, accomplish

REQUIREST
559 'âmar (1), to say

REQUIRETH
1245 bâqash (1), to
search; to strive after
7593 sheʾêl (Ch.) (1), to
ask

REQUIRING
154 aitĕō (1), to ask for

REQUITE
1580 gâmal (1), to benefit
or requite; to wean
5414 nâthan (1), to give
6213 'âsâh (1), to do or
make
7725 shûwb (2), to turn
back; to return
7999 shâlam (3), to be
safe; to reciprocate
287+591 amŏibē (1),
requital, recompense

REQUITED
7725 shûwb (1), to turn
back; to return
7999 shâlam (1), to be
safe; to reciprocate

REQUITING
7725 shûwb (1), to turn
back; to return

REREWARD
314 'achărôwn (1), late
or last; behind; western
622 'âçaph (5), to gather,
collect

RESCUE
3467 yâsha' (1), to make
safe, free
5337 nâtsal (1), to
deliver; to be snatched
7725 shûwb (1), to turn
back; to return

RESCUED
5337 nâtsal (1), to
deliver; to be snatched
6299 pâdâh (1), to
ransom; to release
1807 ĕxairĕō (1), to tear
out; to select; to release

RESCUETH
5338 neʾtsal (Ch.) (1), to
extricate, deliver

RESEMBLANCE
5869 'ayin (1), eye; sight;
fountain

RESEMBLE
3666 hŏmŏiŏō (1), to
become similar

RESEMBLED
8389 tô'ar (1), outline,
figure or appearance

RESEN
7449 Reçen (1), bridle

RESERVE
5201 nâtar (1), to guard;
to cherish anger
7604 shâ'ar (1), to be,
make redundant

5083 tērĕō (1), to keep,
guard, obey

RESERVED
680 'âtsal (1), to select;
refuse; narrow
2820 châsak (2), to
restrain or refrain
3498 yâthar (3), to
remain or be left
3947 lâqach (1), to take
2641 katalĕipō (1), to
have remaining
5083 tērĕō (7), to keep,
guard, obey

RESERVETH
5201 nâtar (1), to guard;
to cherish anger
8104 shâmar (1), to
watch

RESHEPH
7566 Resheph (1), flame

RESIDUE
319 'achărîyth (1), future;
posterity
3498 yâthar (3), to
remain or be left
3499 yether (8),
remainder; small rope
7605 sheʾâr (4),
remainder
7606 sheʾâr (Ch.) (2),
remainder
7611 sheʾêrîyth (13),
remainder or residual
2645 katalŏipŏs (1),
remaining; rest
3062 lŏipŏi (1),
remaining ones

RESIST
7853 sâtan (1), to attack
by accusation
436 anthistēmi (7),
oppose, rebel
496 antipiptō (1), to
oppose, resist
498 antitassŏmai (1),
oppose, resist

RESISTED
436 anthistēmi (1),
oppose, rebel
478 antikathistēmi (1),
withstand, contest

RESISTETH
436 anthistēmi (1),
oppose, rebel
498 antitassŏmai (3),
oppose, resist

RESOLVED
1097 ginōskō (1), to know

RESORT
935 bôw' (1), to go, come
6908 qâbats (1), to
collect, assemble
4848 sumpŏrĕuŏmai (1),
to journey together
4905 sunĕrchŏmai (1), to
gather together

RESORTED
3320 yâtsab (1), to
station, offer, continue
2064 ĕrchŏmai (2), to go
4863 sunagō (1), to
gather together
4905 sunĕrchŏmai (1), to
gather together

RESPECT
3045 yâda' (1), to know
4856 massô' (1), partiality
5027 nâbat (3), to scan;
to regard with favor
5234 nâkar (3), to
respect, revere
5375 nâsâ' (2), to lift up
6437 pânâh (6), to turn,
to face
7200 râ'âh (4), to see
8159 shâ'âh (3), to
inspect, consider
578 apŏblĕpō (1), to
intently regard, pay
attention
678 aprŏsŏpŏlēptōs (1),
without prejudice
1914 ĕpiblĕpō (1), to gaze
at
2596 kata (1), down;
according to
3313 mĕros (2), division
or share
3382 mĕros (1), thigh
4380 prŏsŏpŏlĕptĕō (1),
to show partiality
4382 prŏsŏpŏlēpsia (3),
favoritism

RESPECTED
5375 nâsâ' (1), to lift up

RESPECTER
4381 prŏsŏpŏlēptēs (1),
exhibiting partiality

RESPECTETH
6437 pânâh (1), to turn,
to face
7200 râ'âh (1), to see

RESPITE
7309 reʾvâchâh (1), relief
7503 râphâh (1), to
slacken

REST
1824 deʾmîy (1), quiet,
peacefulness
1826 dâmam (1), to be
silent; to be astonished;
to stop, cease; to perish
2308 châdal (1), to desist,
stop; be fat
2342 chûwl (1), to wait;
to pervert
2790 chârash (1), to be
silent; to be deaf
3498 yâthar (12), to
remain or be left
3499 yether (65),
remainder; small rope
4494 mânôwach (6),
quiet spot, home
4496 meʾnûwchâh (16),
peacefully; consolation
4771 margôwa' (1),
resting place
5117 nûwach (44), to
rest; to settle down
5118 nûwach (1), quiet
5183 nachath (4),
descent; quiet
6314 pûwgâh (1),
intermission, relief
7257 râbats (1), to
recline, repose, brood
7280 râga' (5), to settle,
i.e. quiet; to wink
7599 shâ'an (1), to loll,
i.e. be peaceful

7604 shâ'ar (2), to be,
make redundant
7605 sheʾâr (10),
remainder
7606 sheʾâr (Ch.) (9),
remainder
7611 sheʾêrîyth (3),
remainder or residual
7673 shâbath (7), to
repose; to desist
7677 shabbâthôwn (8),
special holiday
7901 shâkab (2), to lie
down
7931 shâkan (2), to reside
7954 sheʾlâh (Ch.) (1), to
be secure, at rest
7965 shâlôwm (1), safe;
well; health, prosperity
8058 shâmat (1), to let
alone, desist, remit
8172 shâ'an (2), to
support, rely on
8252 shâqat (15), to
repose
8300 sârîyd (1), survivor;
remainder
372 anapausis (4),
recreation, rest
373 anapauō (6), to
repose; to refresh
425 anĕsis (3),
relaxation; relief
1515 ĕirēnē (1), peace;
health; prosperity
1879 ĕpanapauŏmai (1),
to settle on, rely on
1954 ĕpilŏipŏs (1),
remaining, rest
1981 ĕpiskēnŏō (1), to
abide with
2192+372 ĕchō (1), to
have; hold; keep
2663 katapausis (9),
abode for resting
2664 katapauō (2), to
settle down
2681 kataskēnŏō (1), to
remain, live
3062 lŏipŏi (13),
remaining ones
4520 sabbatismŏs (1),
sabbatism

RESTED
270 'âchaz (1), to seize,
grasp; possess
1826 dâmam (1), to stop,
cease; to perish
2583 chânâh (2), to
encamp
5117 nûwach (7), to rest;
to settle down
5118 nûwach (2), quiet
5564 çâmak (1), to lean
upon; take hold of
7673 shâbath (4), to
repose; to desist
7931 shâkan (1), to reside
8252 shâqat (1), to repose
2270 hēsuchazō (1), to
refrain

RESTEST
1879 ĕpanapauŏmai (1),
to settle on, rely on

RESTETH
5117 nûwach (2), to rest
8172 shâ'an (1), to
support, rely on

373 anapauō (1), to *repose*; to *refresh*

RESTING
4496 mᵉnûwchâh (2), *peacefully; consolation*
5118 nûwach (1), *quiet*
7258 rebets (1), place of *repose*

RESTINGPLACE
7258 rebets (1), place of *repose*

RESTITUTION
7999 shâlam (4), to *make complete; to reciprocate*
8545 tᵉmûwrâh (1), *barter, compensation*
605 apŏkatastasis (1), *reconstitution*

RESTORE
5927 'âlâh (1), to *ascend, be high, mount*
7725 shûwb (27), to *return* or restore
7999 shâlam (8), to *make complete; to reciprocate*
591 apŏdidōmi (1), to *give away*
600 apŏkathistēmi (2), to *reconstitute*
2675 katartizō (1), to *repair; to prepare*

RESTORED
2421 châyâh (4), to *live; to revive*
5414 nâthan (1), to *give*
7725 shûwb (16), to *return* or restore
8421 tûwb (Ch.) (1), to *come back with answer*
600 apŏkathistēmi (5), to *reconstitute*

RESTORER
7725 shûwb (2), to *return* or restore

RESTORETH
7725 shûwb (1), to *return* or restore
600 apŏkathistēmi (1), to *reconstitute*

RESTRAIN
1639 gâra' (1), to *shave, remove, lessen*
2296 châgar (1), to *gird on a belt; put on* armor

RESTRAINED
662 'âphaq (1), to *abstain*
1219 bâtsar (1), to *be inaccessible*
3543 kâhâh (1), to *grow dull, fade; to be faint*
3607 kâlâ' (2), to *hold back or in; to prohibit*
4513 mâna' (1), to *deny, refuse*
6113 'âtsar (1), to *hold back; to maintain, rule*
2664 katapauō (1), to *cause to desist*

RESTRAINEST
1639 gâra' (1), to *remove, lessen, or withhold*

RESTRAINT
4622 ma'tsôwr (1), *hindrance*

RESURRECTION
386 anastasis (39), *resurrection* from death
1454 ĕgĕrsis (1), *resurgence* from death
1815 ĕxanastasis (1), *rising from* death

RETAIN
2388 châzaq (1), to *fasten* upon; to *seize*;
3607 kâlâ' (1), to *hold back or in; to prohibit*
6113 'âtsar (1), to *hold back; to maintain, rule*
8551 tâmak (2), to *obtain, keep fast*
2192 ĕchō (1), to *have; hold; keep*
2902 kratĕō (1), to *seize*

RETAINED
2388 châzaq (2), to *fasten* upon; to *seize*
6113 'âtsar (2), to *hold back; to maintain, rule*
2722 katĕchō (1), to *hold down fast*
2902 kratĕō (1), to *seize*

RETAINETH
2388 châzaq (1), to *fasten* upon; to *seize*
8551 tâmak (2), to *obtain, keep fast*

RETIRE
5756 'ûwz (1), to *strengthen; to save*
7725 shûwb (1), to *return* or restore

RETIRED
2015 hâphak (1), to *return, pervert*
6327 pûwts (1), to *dash in pieces; to disperse*

RETURN
3427 yâshab (1), to *dwell, to remain; to settle*
6437 pânâh (1), to *turn, to face*
7725 shûwb (242), to *turn back; to return*
8666 tᵉshûwbâh (3), *recurrence; reply*
344 anakamptō (1), to *turn back, come back*
360 analuō (1), to *depart*
390 anastrĕphō (1), to *remain; to return*
844 autŏmatŏs (1), *spontaneous, by itself*
1994 ĕpistrĕphō (4), to *revert, turn back to*
5290 hupŏstrĕphō (5), to *turn under, to return*

RETURNED
5437 çâbab (2), to *surround*
7725 shûwb (151), to *turn back; to return*
8421 tûwb (Ch.) (2), to *reply*
344 anakamptō (1), to *turn back, come back*
390 anastrĕphō (1), to *remain, to return*
1877 ĕpanagō (1), to *put out to sea; to return*
1880 ĕpanĕrchŏmai (1), *return home*

RESURRECTION *[continued]*
1994 ĕpistrĕphō (2), to *revert, turn back to*
5290 hupŏstrĕphō (24), to *turn under, to return*

RETURNETH
7725 shûwb (6), to *turn back; to return*
8138 shânâh (1), to *fold, to transmute*

RETURNING
7729 shûwbâh (1), *return, i.e. repentance*
5290 hupŏstrĕphō (3), to *turn under, to return*

REU
7466 Rᵉ'ûw (5), *friend*

REUBEN
7205 Rᵉ'ûwbên (72), *see ye a son*
7206 Rᵉ'ûwbênîy (1), *Rebenite*
4502 Rhŏubēn (1), *see ye a son*

REUBENITE
7206 Rᵉ'ûwbênîy (1), *Rebenite*

REUBENITES
7206 Rᵉ'ûwbênîy (16), *Rebenite*

REUEL
7467 Rᵉ'ûw'êl (10), *friend of God*

REUMAH
7208 Rᵉ'ûwmâh (1), *raised*

REVEAL
1540 gâlâh (2), to *denude; to reveal*
1541 gᵉlâh (Ch.) (1), to *reveal mysteries*
601 apŏkaluptō (4), *disclose, reveal*

REVEALED
1540 gâlâh (11), to *denude; to reveal*
1541 gᵉlâh (Ch.) (2), to *reveal mysteries*
601 apŏkaluptō (22), *disclose, reveal*
602 apŏkalupsis (2), *disclosure, revelation*
5537 chrēmatizō (1), to *utter an oracle*

REVEALER
1541 gᵉlâh (Ch.) (1), to *reveal mysteries*

REVEALETH
1540 gâlâh (3), to *denude; to reveal*
1541 gᵉlâh (Ch.) (3), to *reveal mysteries*

REVELATION
602 apŏkalupsis (10), *disclosure, revelation*

REVELATIONS
602 apŏkalupsis (2), *disclosure, revelation*

REVELLINGS
2970 kōmŏs (2), *carousal, reveling, orgy*

REVENGE
5358 nâqam (1), to *avenge or punish*

REVENGED
5360 nᵉqâmâh (2), *avengement*
1556 ĕkdikĕō (1), to *vindicate; retaliate*
1557 ĕkdikēsis (1), *vindication; retaliation*

REVENGED
5358 nâqam (1), to *avenge or punish*

REVENGER
1350 gâ'al (6), to *redeem; to be the next of kin*
1558 ĕkdikŏs (1), *punisher, avenger*

REVENGERS
1350 gâ'al (1), to *redeem; to be the next of kin*

REVENGES
6546 par'âh (1), *leadership*

REVENGETH
5358 nâqam (2), to *avenge or punish*

REVENGING
5360 nᵉqâmâh (1), *avengement*

REVENUE
674 'appᵉthôm (Ch.) (1), *revenue*
8393 tᵉbûw'âh (2), *income, i.e. produce*

REVENUES
8393 tᵉbûw'âh (3), *income, i.e. produce*

REVERENCE
3372 yârê' (2), to *fear; to revere*
7812 shâchâh (5), to *prostrate* in homage
127 aidōs (1), *modesty; awe*
1788 ĕntrĕpō (4), to *respect; to confound*
5399 phŏbĕō (1), to *be in awe* of, i.e. *revere*

REVERENCED
7812 shâchâh (1), to *prostrate* in homage

REVEREND
3372 yârê' (1), to *fear; to revere*

REVERSE
7725 shûwb (3), to *turn back; to return*

REVILE
7043 qâlal (1), to *be easy, trifling, vile*
3679 ŏnĕidizō (1), to *rail at, chide, taunt*

REVILED
486 antilŏidŏrĕō (1), to *rail in reply, retaliate*
937 basilikŏs (1), *befitting the sovereign*
3058 lŏidŏrĕō (2), *vilify, insult*
3679 ŏnĕidizō (1), to *rail at, chide, taunt*

REVILERS
3060 lŏidŏrŏs (1), *verbal abuser*

REVILEST
3058 lŏidŏrĕō (1), *vilify, insult*

REVILINGS
1421 giddûwph (2), *vilification, scorn*

REVIVE
2421 châyâh (8), to *live; to revive*

REVIVED
2421 châyâh (4), to *live; to revive*
326 anazaō (2), to *recover life, live again*

REVIVING
4241 michyâh (2), *preservation of life*

REVOLT
5627 çârâh (2), *apostasy; crime; remission*
6586 pâsha' (1), to *break away from authority*

REVOLTED
5498 çâchab (1), to *trail along*
5627 çârâh (1), *apostasy; crime; remission*
6586 pâsha' (5), to *break away from authority*

REVOLTERS
5637 çârar (2), to *be refractory, stubborn*
7846 sêṭ (1), *departure*

REVOLTING
5637 çârar (1), to *be refractory, stubborn*

REWARD
319 'achărîyth (2), *future; posterity*
868 'ethnan (3), *gift price of harlotry*
1309 bᵉsôwrâh (1), glad *tidings, good news*
1576 gᵉmûwl (3), *reward, recompense*
1578 gᵉmûwlâh (1), *reward, recompense*
1580 gâmal (1), to *benefit or requite; to wean*
4864 mas'êth (1), *tribute; reproach*
4909 maskôreth (1), *wages; reward*
4991 mattâth (1), *present*
6118 'êqeb (3), unto *the end; for ever*
6468 pᵉ'ullâh (1), *work, deed*
6529 pᵉrîy (1), *fruit*
7725 shûwb (2), to *turn back; to return*
7809 shâchad (1), to *bribe; gift*
7810 shachad (7), to *bribe; gift*
7938 seker (1), *wages, reward*
7939 sâkâr (5), *payment, salary; compensation*
7966 shillûwm (1), *requital; retribution; fee*
7999 shâlam (6), to *make complete; to reciprocate*
8011 shillumâh (1), *retribution*
469 antapŏdŏsis (1), *requital, reward*
514 axiŏs (1), *deserving, comparable or suitable*

591 apŏdidōmi (6), to *give away*
2603 katabrabĕuō (1), to *award the price*
3405 misthapŏdŏsia (3), *requital, good or bad*
3408 misthŏs (24), *pay*

REWARDED
1580 gâmal (7), to *benefit or requite; to wean*
7760 sûwm (1), to *place*
7939 sâkâr (2), *payment, salary; compensation*
7999 shâlam (3), to *make complete; to reciprocate*
591 apŏdidōmi (1), to *give away*

REWARDER
3406 misthapŏdŏtēs (1), *rewarder*

REWARDETH
7725 shûwb (1), to *turn back; to return*
7936 sâkar (2), to *hire*
7999 shâlam (3), to *make complete; to reciprocate*

REWARDS
866 'êthnâh (1), *gift price of harlotry*
5023 nᵉbizbâh (Ch.) (2), *largess, gift*
8021 shalmôn (1), *bribe, gift*

REZEPH
7530 Retseph (2), hot *stone for baking*

REZIA
7525 Ritsyâ' (1), *delight*

REZIN
7526 Rᵉtsîyn (10), *delight*

REZON
7331 Rᵉzôwn (1), *prince*

RHEGIUM
4484 Rhēgiŏn (1), *Rhegium*

RHESA
4488 Rhēsa (1), (poss.) *Jehovah has cured*

RHODA
4498 Rhŏdē (1), *rose*

RHODES
4499 Rhŏdŏs (1), *rose*

RIB
6763 tsêlâ' (1), *side*

RIBAI
7380 Rîybay (2), *contentious*

RIBBAND
6616 pâthîyl (1), *twine, cord*

RIBLAH
7247 Riblâh (11), *fertile*

RIBS
6763 tsêlâ' (2), *side*

RICH
1952 hôwn (1), *wealth*
3513 kâbad (1), to *be rich, glorious*
5381 nâsag (1), to *reach*
6223 'âshîyr (23), *rich; rich person*
6238 'âshar (13), to *grow, make rich*

7771 shôwa' (1), *noble, i.e. liberal; opulent*
4145 plŏusiŏs (28), *wealthy; abounding*
4147 plŏutĕō (11), to *be, become wealthy*
4148 plŏutizō (1), to *make wealthy*

RICHER
6238 'âshar (1), to *grow, make rich*

RICHES
1952 hôwn (9), *wealth*
1995 hâmôwn (1), *noise, tumult; many, crowd*
2428 chayil (11), *army; wealth; virtue; valor*
2633 chôçen (1), *wealth, stored riches*
3502 yithrâh (1), *wealth, abundance*
4301 maṭmôwn (1), *secret storehouse*
5233 nekeç (1), *treasure*
6239 'ôsher (37), *wealth*
7075 qinyân (1), *purchase, wealth*
7399 rᵉkûwsh (5), *property*
7769 shûwa' (1), *call*
4149 plŏutŏs (22), *abundant riches*
5536 chrēma (3), *wealth*

RICHLY
4146 plŏusiŏs (2), *copiously, abundantly*

RID
5337 nâtsal (3), to *deliver; to be snatched*
6475 pâtsâh (2), to *rend*
7673 shâbath (1), to *repose; to desist*

RIDDANCE
3615 kâlâh (1), to *cease, be finished, perish*
3617 kâlâh (1), *complete destruction*

RIDDEN
7392 râkab (1), to *ride*

RIDDLE
2420 chîydâh (9), *puzzle; conundrum; maxim*

RIDE
7392 râkab (20), to *ride*

RIDER
7392 râkab (7), to *ride*

RIDERS
7392 râkab (5), to *ride*

RIDETH
7392 râkab (7), to *ride*

RIDGES
8525 telem (1), *bank or terrace*

RIDING
7392 râkab (10), to *ride*

RIE
3698 kuççemeth (2), *spelt*

RIFLED
8155 shâçaç (1), to *plunder, ransack*

RIGHT
541 'âman (1), to take *the right hand road*

571 'emeth (3), *certainty, truth, trustworthiness*
1353 gᵉullâh (1), *blood relationship*
3225 yâmîyn (136), *right; south*
3227 yᵉmîynîy (1), *right*
3231 yâman (4), to *be right-handed*
3233 yᵉmânîy (31), *right*
3474 yâshar (2), to *be straight; to make right*
3476 yôsher (2), *right*
3477 yâshâr (52), *straight*
3559 kûwn (4), to *render sure, proper*
3651 kên (3), *just; right*
3787 kâshêr (1), to *be straight or right*
3788 kishrôwn (1), *success; advantage*
4334 mîyshôwr (1), *plain; justice*
4339 mêyshâr (3), *straightness; rectitude*
4941 mishpât (19), *verdict; decree; justice*
5227 nôkach (2), *forward, in behalf of*
5228 nâkôach (2), *equitable, correct*
5229 nᵉkôchâh (2), *integrity; truth*
6227 'âshân (1), *smoke*
6437 pânâh (1), to *turn, to face*
6440 pânîym (1), *face; front*
6664 tsedeq (3), *right*
6666 tsᵉdâqâh (9), *rightness*
1188 dĕxiŏs (53), *right*
1342 dikaiŏs (5), *equitable, holy*
1849 ĕxŏusia (2), *authority, power, right*
2117 ĕuthus (3), *at once, immediately*
3723 ŏrthōs (1), *rightly*
4993 sōphrŏnĕō (2), to *be in a right state of mind*

RIGHTEOUS
3477 yâshâr (8), *straight*
6662 tsaddîyq (166), *just*
6663 tsâdaq (8), to *be, make right*
6664 tsedeq (9), *right*
6666 tsᵉdâqâh (3), *rightness*
1341 dikaiŏkrisia (1), *proper judgment*
1342 dikaiŏs (39), *equitable, holy*
1343 dikaiŏsunē (1), *equity, justification*

RIGHTEOUSLY
4334 mîyshôwr (1), *plain; justice*
4339 mêyshâr (1), *straightness; rectitude*
6664 tsedeq (3), *right*
6666 tsᵉdâqâh (1), *rightness*
1346 dikaiŏs (2), *equitably*

RIGHTEOUSNESS
6663 tsâdaq (1), to *be, make right*

R

6782 tsammîym (2), *noose, snare*
3027 lē₁stēs (2), *brigand*

ROBBERS
962 bâzaz (1), to *plunder, take booty*
6530 pᵉrîyts (3), *violent*
7703 shâdad (2), to *ravage*
2417 hiĕrŏsulŏs (1), *temple-despoiler*
3027 lē₁stēs (2), *brigand*

ROBBERY
1498 gâzêl (3), *robbery, stealing*
6503 Parbâr (1), *Parbar* or *Parvar*
7701 shôd (2), *violence, ravage, destruction*
725 harpagmŏs (1), *plunder*

ROBBETH
1497 gâzal (1), to *rob*

ROBE
145 'eder (1), *mantle; splendor*
155 'addereth (1), *large; splendid*
3301 Yiphdᵉyâh (1), *Jehovah will liberate*
4598 mᵉˁîyl (17), *outer garment or robe*
2066 ĕsthēs (1), to *clothe*
2440 himatiŏn (2), to *put on clothes*
4749 stŏlē (1), *long-fitting gown*
5511 chlamus (2), *military cloak*

ROBES
899 beged (4), *clothing; treachery or pillage*
4598 mᵉˁîyl (2), *outer garment or robe*
4749 stŏlē (5), *long-fitting gown*

ROBOAM
4497 Rhŏbŏam (2), *people has enlarged*

ROCK
2496 challâmîysh (1), *flint, flinty rock*
4581 mâˁôwz (1), *fortified place; defense*
5553 çela' (44), *craggy rock; fortress*
5558 çeleph (2), *distortion; viciousness*
6697 tsûwr (56), *rock*
4073 pĕtra (13), *mass of rock*

ROCKS
3710 kêph (2), *hollow rock*
5553 çela' (10), *craggy rock; fortress*
6697 tsûwr (7), *rock*
4073 pĕtra (3), *mass of rock*
5138+5117 trachus (1), *uneven, jagged, rocky*

ROD
2415 chôṭer (2), *twig; shoot of a plant*
4294 maṭṭeh (42), *tribe; rod, scepter; club*

4731 maqqêl (2), *shoot; stick; staff*
7626 shêbeṭ (34), *stick; clan, family*
4464 rhabdŏs (6), *stick, rod*

RODE
7392 râkab (15), to *ride*

RODS
4294 maṭṭeh (8), *tribe; rod, scepter; club*
4731 maqqêl (6), *shoot; stick; staff*
4463 rhabdizō (1), to *strike with a stick*

ROE
3280 ya'ălâh (1), *ibex*
6643 tsᵉbîy (6), *gazelle*

ROEBUCK
6643 tsᵉbîy (4), *gazelle*

ROEBUCKS
6643 tsᵉbîy (1), *gazelle*

ROES
6643 tsᵉbîy (3), *gazelle*
6646 tsᵉbîyâh (2), *gazelle*

ROGELIM
7274 Rôgᵉlîym (2), *fullers* as *tramping* the cloth

ROHGAH
7303 Rôwhăgâh (1), *outcry*

ROLL
1549 gîllâyôwn (1), *tablet* for writing; *mirror*
1556 gâlal (4), to *roll;* to *commit*
4039 mᵉgillâh (14), *roll, scroll*
4040 mᵉgillâh (Ch.) (7), *roll, scroll*
6428 pâlash (1), to *roll in dust*
617 apŏkuliō (1), to *roll away, roll back*

ROLLED
1556 gâlal (6), to *roll;* to *commit*
617 apŏkuliō (3), to *roll away, roll back*
1507 hĕilissō (1), to *roll, coil or wrap*
4351 prŏskuliō (2), to *roll towards*

ROLLER
2848 chittûwl (1), *bandage* for a wound

ROLLETH
1556 gâlal (1), to *roll*

ROLLING
1534 galgal (1), *wheel; something round*

ROLLS
5609 çᵉphar (Ch.) (1), *book*

ROMAMTI-EZER
7320 Rôwmamtîy 'Ezer (2), *I have raised* up a *help*

ROMAN
4514 Rhōmaiŏs (5), *Roman; of Rome*

ROMANS
4514 Rhōmaiŏs (7), *Roman; of Rome*

ROME
4516 Rhōmē (15), *strength*

ROOF
1406 gâg (11), *roof; top*
2441 chêk (5), *area of mouth*
6982 qôwrâh (1), *rafter; roof*
4721 stĕgē (3), *roof*

ROOFS
1406 gâg (2), *roof; top*

ROOM
4725 mâqôwm (3), *general locality, place*
4800 merchâb (1), *open space; liberty*
7337 râchab (2), to *broaden*
8478 tachath (11), *bottom; underneath*
473 anti (1), *instead of , because of*
508 anŏgĕŏn (1), *dome* or a *balcony*
1240 diadŏchŏs (1), *successor* in office
4411 prŏtŏklisia (1), *pre-eminence* at meals
5117 tŏpŏs (5), *place*
5253 hupĕrŏ₁ŏn (1), *upper room*
5362 philandrŏs (1), *affectionate* as a wife to her *husband*

ROOMS
7064 qên (1), *nest; nestlings; chamber*
8478 tachath (2), *bottom; underneath;* in *lieu of*
4411 prŏtŏklisia (4), *pre-eminence* at meals

ROOT
5428 nâthash (2), to *tear away, be uprooted*
8327 shârash (7), to *root, insert;* to *uproot*
8328 sheresh (17), *root*
1610 ĕkrizŏō (2), to *uproot*
4491 rhiza (15), *root*

ROOTED
5255 nâçach (1), to *tear away*
5423 nâthaq (1), to *tear off*
5428 nâthash (1), to *tear away, be uprooted*
6131 'âqar (1), to *pluck* up roots; to *hamstring*
8327 shârash (1), to *root, insert;* to *uproot*
1610 ĕkrizŏō (1), to *uproot*
4492 rhizŏō (2), to *root;* to *become stable*

ROOTS
5428 nâthash (1), to *tear away, be uprooted*
6132 'âqar (Ch.) (1), to *pluck* up roots
8328 sheresh (13), *root*

8330 shôresh (Ch.) (3), *root*
1610 ĕkrizŏō (1), to *uproot*
4491 rhiza (1), *root*

ROPE
5688 'ăbôth (1), *entwined things: a string, wreath*

ROPES
2256 chebel (3), *band*
5688 'ăbôth (2), *entwined things: a string, wreath*
4979 schŏiniŏn (1), *withe* or *tie or rope*

ROSE
2224 zârach (3), to *rise;* to *be bright*
2261 chăbatstseleth (2), *meadow-saffron*
5927 'âlâh (2), to *ascend, be high, mount*
6965 qûwm (71), to *rise*
7925 shâkam (29), to *load up,* to *start early*
305 anabainō (1), to *go up, rise*
450 anistēmi (18), to *rise;* to *come back to life*
1453 ĕgĕirō (3), to *waken, i.e. rouse*
1817 ĕxanistēmi (1), to *beget, raise up*
4911 sunĕphistēmi (1), to *resist or assault jointly*

ROSH
7220 Rô'sh (1), *head*

ROT
5307 nâphal (3), to *fall*
7537 râqab (2), to *decay* by worm-eating

ROTTEN
4418 mâlâch (2), *rag* or *old garment*
5685 'âbash (1), to *dry* up
7538 râqâb (1), *decay* by *caries*
7539 riqqâbôwn (1), *decay* by *caries*

ROTTENNESS
4716 maq (1), *putridity, stench*
7538 râqâb (4), *decay* by *caries*

ROUGH
386 'êythân (1), *never-failing; eternal*
5569 çâmâr (1), *shaggy*
7186 qâsheh (1), *severe*
7406 rekeç (1), *ridge*
8163 sâˁîyr (1), *shaggy; he-goat; goat idol*
8181 sêˁâr (1), *tossed hair*
5138 trachus (1), *uneven, jagged, rocky, reefy*

ROUGHLY
5794 'az (1), *strong, vehement, harsh*
7186 qâsheh (5), *severe*

ROUND
1754 dûwr (1), *circle; ball; pile*
2636 chaçpaç (1), to *peel;* to *be scale-like*
3803 kâthar (2), to *enclose, besiege;* to *wait*

R

4524 mêçab (3), *divan couch; around*
5362 nâqaph (4), to *strike; to surround*
5437 çâbab (7), to *surround*
5439 çâbîyb (254), *circle; environs; around*
5469 çahar (1), *roundness*
5696 'âgôl (6), *circular*
5921 'al (2), *above, over*
7720 sahărôn (1), round *pendant* or *crescent*
2943 kuklŏthěn (10), *from the circle*
2944 kuklŏō (2), to *surround, encircle*
3840 pantŏthěn (1), *from, on all* sides
4015 pěriastraptō (2), *to shine around*
4017 pěriblěpō (5), to *look all around*
4026 pěriistěmi (1), to *stand around; to avoid*
4033 pěrikuklŏō (1), to *blockade completely*
4034 pěrilampō (2), to *shine all around*
4038 pěrix (1), all *around*
4039 pěriŏikěō (1), to *be a neighbor*
4066 pěrichōrŏs (9), *surrounding country*

ROUSE
6965 qûwm (1), to *rise*

ROW
2905 tûwr (14), *row, course* built into a *wall*
4635 ma'ăreketh (2), *pile* of loaves, *arrangement*
5073 nidbâk (Ch.) (1), *layer, row*

ROWED
2864 châthar (1), to *row*
1643 ĕlaunō (1), to *push*

ROWERS
7751 shûwt (1), to *travel, roam*

ROWING
1643 ĕlaunō (1), to *push*

ROWS
2905 tûwr (12), *row, course* built into a *wall*
2918 tîyrâh (1), *fortress; hamlet*
4634 ma'ărâkâh (1), *arrangement, row; pile*
5073 nidbâk (Ch.) (1), *layer, row*
8447 tôwr (1), *succession*

ROYAL
4410 mᵉlûwkâh (4), *realm, rulership*
4428 melek (2), *king*
4430 melek (Ch.) (1), *king*
4438 malkûwth (13), *rule; dominion*
4467 mamlâkâh (4), royal *dominion*
8237 shaphrûwr (1), *tapestry* or *canopy*
934 basilĕiŏs (1), *royal, kingly* in nature
937 basilikŏs (2), *befitting the sovereign*

RUBBING
5597 psōchō (1), to *rub* out grain kernels

RUBBISH
6083 'âphâr (2), *dust, earth, mud; clay,*

RUBIES
6443 pânîyn (6), (poss.) *round pearl*

RUDDER
4079 pēdaliŏn (1), *blade*

RUDDY
119 'âdam (1), to *red* in the face
132 'admônîy (3), *reddish, ruddy*

RUDE
2399 idiōtēs (1), not *initiated; untrained*

RUDIMENTS
4747 stŏichěiŏn (2), *elementary* truths

RUE
4076 pēganŏn (1), *rue*

RUFUS
4504 Rhŏuphŏs (2), *red*

RUHAMAH
7355 râcham (1), to *be compassionate*

RUIN
4072 midcheh (1), *overthrow, downfall*
4288 mᵉchittâh (1), *ruin; consternation*
4383 mikshôwl (1), *obstacle; enticement*
4384 makshêlâh (1), *enticement*
4654 mappâlâh (2), *ruin*
4658 mappeleth (2), *down-fall; ruin; carcase*
6365 pîyd (1), *misfortune*
4485 rhēgma (1), *ruin*

RUINED
2040 hâraç (2), to *pull* down; *break, destroy*
3782 kâshal (1), to *totter, waver;* to *falter*

RUINOUS
4654 mappâlâh (1), *ruin*
5327 nâtsâh (2), to *be desolate,* to *lay waste*

RUINS
2034 hărîyçâh (1), *demolished, ruins*
4383 mikshôwl (1), *obstacle; enticement*
2679 kataskaptō (1), to *destroy, be ruined*

RULE
4427 mâlak (1), to *reign as king*
4475 memshâlâh (4), *rule; realm* or a *ruler*
4623 ma'tsâr (1), *self-control*
4910 mâshal (25), to *rule*
7287 râdâh (10), to *subjugate; to crumble*
7980 shâlat (3), to *dominate,* i.e. *govern*
7981 shᵉlêt (Ch.) (1), to *dominate,* i.e. *govern*

7990 shallîyt (Ch.) (1), *premier, sovereign*
8323 sârar (3), to *have, exercise, get dominion*
746 archē (1), *first*
757 archō (1), to *rule, be first in rank*
1018 braběuō (1), to *govern;* to *prevail*
2233 hēgěŏmai (3), to *lead,* i.e. *command*
2583 kanōn (4), *rule, standard*
4165 pŏimainō (4), to *tend* as a shepherd
4291 prŏïstēmi (2), to *preside; to practice*

RULED
4474 mimshâl (1), *ruler; dominion, rule*
4910 mâshal (5), to *rule*
5401 nâshaq (1), to *kiss;* to *equip* with weapons
7287 râdâh (3), to *subjugate; to crumble*
7990 shallîyt (Ch.) (2), *premier, sovereign*
8199 shâphat (1), to *judge*

RULER
834+5921 'ăsher (1), *who, which, what, that*
4910 mâshal (13), to *rule*
5057 nâgîyd (19), *commander, official*
5387 nâsîy' (3), *leader; rising mist, fog*
6485 pâqad (2), to *visit, care for, count*
7101 qâtsîyn (2), *magistrate; leader*
7287 râdâh (1), to *subjugate; to crumble*
7860 shôtêr (1), to *write;* official who is a *scribe*
7981 shᵉlêt (Ch.) (1), to *dominate,* i.e. *govern*
7989 shallîyt (1), *prince* or *warrior*
7990 shallîyt (Ch.) (2), *premier, sovereign*
8269 sar (10), *head person, ruler*
752 archisunagōgŏs (6), *director of* the *synagogue* services
755 architriklinŏs (1), *director of* the *entertainment*
758 archōn (9), *first*
2525 kathistēmi (6), to *designate, constitute*

RULER'S
4910 mâshal (1), to *rule*
758 archōn (1), *first*

RULERS
4043 mâgên (1), small *shield (buckler)*
4910 mâshal (4), to *rule*
5057 nâgîyd (1), *commander, official*
5387 nâsîy' (3), *leader; rising mist, fog*
5461 çâgan (16), *prefect*
6485 pâqad (2), to *visit, care for, count*
7101 qâtsîyn (2), *magistrate; leader*
7218 rô'sh (2), *head*

7336 râzan (1), *honorable*
7984 shiltôwn (Ch.) (2), *official*
8269 sar (21), *ruler*
752 archisunagōgŏs (2), *director of* the *synagogue* services
758 archōn (14), *first*
2232 hēgěmōn (2), *chief*
2888 kŏsmŏkratōr (1), *world-ruler*
4178 pŏllakis (2), *many times,* i.e. *frequently*

RULEST
4910 mâshal (2), to *rule*

RULETH
4910 mâshal (7), to *rule*
7300 rûwd (1), to *ramble*
7980 shâlat (4), to *dominate,* i.e. *govern*
4291 prŏïstēmi (2), to *preside; to practice*

RULING
4910 mâshal (2), to *rule*
4291 prŏïstēmi (1), to *preside; to practice*

RUMAH
7316 Rûwmâh (1), *height*

RUMBLING
1995 hâmôwn (1), *noise, tumult; many, crowd*

RUMOUR
8052 shᵉmûw'âh (8), *announcement*
3056 lŏgŏs (1), *word, matter, thing*

RUMOURS
189 akŏē (2), *hearing; thing heard*

RUMP
451 'alyâh (5), fat *tail*

RUN
935 bôw' (1), to *go, come*
1556 gâlal (1), to *roll;* to *commit*
1980 hâlak (3), to *walk; live a certain way*
2100 zûwb (1), to *flow freely, gush*
3212 yâlak (1), to *walk;* to *live;* to *carry*
3381 yârad (6), to *descend*
6293 pâga' (1), to *impinge*
6805 tsâ'ad (1), to *pace*
7323 rûwts (36), to *run*
7325 rûwr (1), to *emit a fluid*
7751 shûwt (6), to *travel, roam*
8264 shâqaq (2), to *seek*
4936 suntrĕchō (1), to *rush together*
5143 trĕchō (8), to *run* or *walk hastily;* to *strive*

RUNNEST
7323 rûwts (1), to *run*

RUNNETH
935 bôw' (1), to *go, come*
3381 yârad (2), to *descend*
7310 rᵉvâyâh (1), *satisfaction*
7323 rûwts (4), to *run*

1632 ĕkchĕō (1), to *pour forth; to bestow*
5143 trĕchō (2), to *run*

RUNNING
1980 hâlak (1), to *walk*
2100 zûwb (2), to *discharge; waste away*
2416 chay (7), *alive; raw*
4794 mᵉrûwtsâh (2), *race*
4944 mashshâq (1), rapid *traversing motion*
5140 nâzal (1), to *drip*
7323 rûwts (6), to *run*
1998 ĕpisuntrĕchō (1), to *hasten together upon*
4370 prŏstrĕchō (2), to *hasten by running*
5143 trĕchō (1), to *run*
5240 hupĕrĕkchunō (1), to *overflow*
5295 hupŏtrĕchō (1), to *run under*

RUSH
100 'agmôwn (2), *rush*
1573 gôme' (1), *papyrus*
7582 shâ'âh (1), to *moan*

RUSHED
6584 pâshaṭ (2), to *strip*
3729 hŏrmaō (1), to *dash*

RUSHES
1573 gôme' (1), *papyrus*

RUSHETH
7857 shâṭaph (1), to *gush*

RUSHING
7494 ra'ash (3), *uproar*
7582 shâ'âh (1), to *moan*
7588 shâ'ôwn (2), *uproar*
5342 phĕrō (1), to *bear*

RUST
1035 brōsis (2), *food; rust*
2447 iŏs (1), *corrosion*

RUTH
7327 Rûwth (12), *friend*
4503 Rhŏuth (1), *friend*

SABACHTHANI
4518 sabachthani (2), *thou hast left me*

SABAOTH
4519 sabaōth (2), *armies*

SABBATH
7673 shâbath (1), to *repose; to desist*
7676 shabbâth (73), *day of rest*
7677 shabbâthôwn (3), *special holiday*
4315 prŏsabbatŏn (1), *Sabbath-eve*
4521 sabbatŏn (59), *day of repose*

SABBATHS
4868 mishbâth (1), *cessation; destruction*
7676 shabbâth (34), *day of rest*

SABEANS
5433 çâbâ' (1), to *quaff*
5436 Çᵉbâ'îy (1), *Sebaite*
7614 Shᵉbâ' (1), *Sheba*
7615 Shᵉbâ'îy (1), *Shebaïte*

SABTA
5454 Çabtâ' (1), *Sabta or Sabtah*

SABTAH
5454 Çabtâ' (1), *Sabta or Sabtah*

SABTECHA
5455 Çabtᵉkâ' (1), *Sabteca*

SABTECHAH
5455 Çabtᵉkâ' (1), *Sabteca*

SACAR
7940 Sâkar (2), *recompense*

SACK
572 'amtêchath (5), *sack*
8242 saq (4), *bag*

SACK'S
572 'amtêchath (3), *sack*

SACKBUT
5443 çabbᵉkâ' (Ch.) (4), *lyre musical instrument*

SACKCLOTH
8242 saq (41), coarse cloth or *sacking; bag*
4526 sakkŏs (4), *sack-cloth*

SACKCLOTHES
8242 saq (1), coarse cloth or *sacking; bag*

SACKS
572 'amtêchath (6), *sack*
3672 Kinnᵉrôwth (1), (poss.) *harp-shaped*
8242 saq (2), *bag*

SACKS'
572 'amtêchath (1), *sack*

SACRIFICE
2076 zâbach (48), to (sacrificially) *slaughter*
2077 zebach (102), animal *flesh; sacrifice*
2282 chag (2), solemn *festival*
4503 minchâh (5), *tribute; offering*
6213 'âsâh (1), to *make*
7133 qorbân (1), sacrificial *present*
1494 ĕidōlŏthutŏn (3), idolatrous *offering*
2378 thusia (17), *sacrifice*
2380 thuō (4), to *sacrifice*

SACRIFICED
2076 zâbach (29), to (sacrificially) *slaughter*
6213 'âsâh (1), to *make*
1494 ĕidōlŏthutŏn (2), idolatrous *offering*
2380 thuō (1), to *kill; to butcher; to sacrifice*

SACRIFICEDST
2076 zâbach (1), to (sacrificially) *slaughter*

SACRIFICES
1685 dᵉbach (Ch.) (1), animal *sacrifice*
2077 zebach (53), animal *flesh; sacrifice*
2282 chag (1), solemn *festival*
2378 thusia (12), *sacrifice, offering*

SACRIFICETH
2076 zâbach (6), to (sacrificially) *slaughter*

SACRIFICING
2076 zâbach (2), to (sacrificially) *slaughter*

SACRILEGE
2416 hiĕrŏsulĕō (1), to *be a temple-robber*

SAD
2196 zâ'aph (1), to *be angry*
3510 kâ'ab (1), to feel *pain; to grieve; to spoil*
3512 kâ'âh (1), to *despond; to deject*
5620 çar (1), *sullen*
7451 ra' (2), *bad; evil*
7489 râ'a' (1), to *be good for nothing*
4659 skuthrōpŏs (2), *gloomy, mournful*
4768 stugnazō (1), to *be overcast; somber*

SADDLE
2280 châbash (3), to *wrap firmly, bind*
4817 merkâb (1), *chariot; seat in chariot*

SADDLED
2280 châbash (10), to *wrap firmly, bind*

SADDUCEES
4523 Saddŏukaiŏs (14), *of Tsadok*

SADLY
7451 ra' (1), *bad; evil*

SADNESS
7455 rôa' (1), *badness*

SADOC
4524 Sadōk (1), *just*

SAFE
983 beṭach (2), *safety*
3467 yâsha' (1), to *make safe, free*
6403 pâlaṭ (1), to *slip out, i.e. escape; to deliver*
7682 sâgab (2), to *be safe*
7965 shâlôwm (3), *safe*
809 aschēmōn (1), *inelegant, indecent*
1295 diasōzō (2), to *cure, preserve, rescue*
5198 hugiainō (1), to *have sound health*

SAFEGUARD
4931 mishmereth (1), *watch, sentry, post*

SAFELY
983 beṭach (17), *safety*
7965 shâlôwm (1), *safe*
806 asphalōs (2), *securely*

SAFETY
983 beṭach (9), *safety*
3468 yesha' (3), *liberty, deliverance, prosperity*
7951 shâlâh (1), to *be secure or successful*
8668 tᵉshûw'âh (4), *rescue, deliverance*
803 asphalĕia (2), *security; certainty*

SAFFRON
3750 karkôm (1), *crocus*

SAID
559 'âmar (2772), to *say*

SAID (cont.)
560 'âmar (Ch.) (41), to *say*
1696 dâbar (85), to *say*
1697 dâbâr (8), *word; matter; thing*
4448 mâlal (1), to *speak*
4449 mᵉlal (Ch.) (1), to *speak, say*
5002 nᵉ'ûm (9), *oracle*
6030 'ânâh (1), to *respond*
7121 qârâ' (1), to *call out*
669 apŏphthĕggŏmai (1), *declare, address*
2036 ĕpō (756), to *speak*
2046 ĕrĕō (21), to *utter*
2063 ĕruthrŏs (3), *red*
2980 lalĕō (7), to *talk*
3004 lĕgō (200), to *say*
4280 prŏĕrĕō (4), to *say already, predict*
4483 rhĕō (15), to *utter*
5346 phēmi (48), to *make known one's thoughts*

SAIDST
559 'âmar (20), to *say*
1696 dâbar (1), to *speak*
2046 ĕrĕō (1), to *utter*

SAIL
5251 nêç (2), *flag; signal*
321 anagō (1), to *sail*
636 apŏplĕō (1), to *set sail, sail away*
3896 paraplĕō (1), to *sail near*
4126 plĕō (2), to *travel in a ship*
4632 skĕuŏs (1), *vessel, implement, equipment*

SAILED
321 anagō (2), to *lead up; to sail away*
636 apŏplĕō (3), to *set sail, sail away*
1020 braduplŏĕō (1), to *sail slowly*
1277 diaplĕō (1), to *sail through, across*
1602 ĕkplĕō (3), to *depart by ship*
3881 paralĕgŏmai (1), to *sail past*
4126 plĕō (2), to *travel in a ship*
5284 hupŏplĕō (2), to *sail under the lee of*

SAILING
1276 diapĕraō (1), to *cross over*
4126 plĕō (1), to *travel in a ship*
4144 plŏŏs (1), *navigation, voyage*

SAILORS
3492 nautēs (1), *sailor*

SAINT
6918 qâdôwsh (3), *sacred*
40 hagiŏs (1), *holy*

SAINTS
2623 châçîyd (19), religiously *pious, godly*
6918 qâdôwsh (9), *sacred*
6922 qaddîysh (Ch.) (6), *sacred*
6944 qôdesh (1), *sacred*
40 hagiŏs (60), *holy*

S

SAINTS'
40 hagiŏs (1), *holy*

SAITH
559 'âmar (581), to *say*
1696 dâbar (7), to *speak*
5001 nâ'am (10), to *utter as an oracle*
5002 nᵉ'ûm (353), *oracle*
6310 peh (1), *mouth*
2036 ĕpŏ (1), to *speak*
2980 lalĕō (2), to *talk*
3004 lĕgō (297), to *say*
5346 phēmi (5), to *make known* one's thoughts

SAKE
182 'ôwdôwth (1), on *account of; because*
1558 gâlâl (3), on *account of, because of*
1697 dâbâr (2), *word; matter; thing*
4616 ma'an (45), *on account of*
5668 'âbûwr (15), on *account of*
7068 qin'âh (1), *jealousy*
7945 shel (1), on *account of; whatsoever*
8478 tachath (2), *bottom; underneath; in lieu of*
1722 ĕn (1), *because of*
1752 hĕnĕka (14), *on account of*

SAKES
1558 gâlâl (1), on *account of, because of*
1697 dâbâr (1), *matter*
1701 dibrâh (Ch.) (1), *because, on account of*
5668 'âbûwr (1), on *account of*
5921 'al (3), *above, over*
6616 pâthîyl (6), *twine*

SALA
4527 Sala (1), *spear*

SALAH
7974 Shelach (6), *spear*

SALAMIS
4529 Salamis (1), *surge*

SALATHIEL
7597 Shᵉ'altîy'êl (1), *I have asked God*
4528 Salathiēl (3), *I have asked God*

SALCAH
5548 Çalkâh (2), *walking*

SALCHAH
5548 Çalkâh (2), *walking*

SALE
4465 mimkâr (3), *merchandise*

SALEM
8004 Shâlêm (2), *peaceful*
4532 Salēm (2), *peaceful*

SALIM
4530 Salĕim (1), (poss.) *waver*

SALLAI
5543 Çallûw (2), *weighed*

SALLU
5543 Çallûw (3), *weighed*

SALMA
8007 Salmâ' (4), *clothing*

SALMON
6756 Tsalmôwn (1), *shady*
8009 Salmâh (1), *clothing*
8012 Salmôwn (1), *investiture*
4533 Salmōn (3), *investiture*

SALMONE
4534 Salmōnē (1), (poss.) *surge* on the shore

SALOME
4539 Salōmē (2), *peace*

SALT
4416 mᵉlach (Ch.) (2), *salt*
4417 melach (27), *salt*
4420 mᵉlêchâh (1), *salted* land, i.e. a *desert*
5898 'Îyr ham-Melach (1), *city of* (the) *salt*
217 halas (8), *salt*
251 hals (1), *salt*
252 halukŏs (1), *salty*

SALTED
4414 mâlach (1), to *salt*
233 halizō (3), to *salt*

SALTNESS
1096+358 ginŏmai (1), to *be, become*

SALTPITS
4417 melach (1), *salt*

SALU
5543 Çallûw (1), *weighed*

SALUTATION
783 aspasmŏs (6), *greeting*

SALUTATIONS
783 aspasmŏs (1), *greeting*

SALUTE
1288 bârak (4), to *bless*
7592+7965 shâ'al (1), to *ask*
7965 shâlôwm (2), *safe; well; health, prosperity*
782 aspazŏmai (32), to *give salutation*

SALUTED
1288 bârak (1), to *bless*
7592+7965 shâ'al (3), to *ask*
782 aspazŏmai (5), to *give salutation*

SALUTETH
782 aspazŏmai (5), to *give salutation*

SALVATION
3444 yᵉshûw'âh (65), *deliverance; aid*
3467 yâsha' (3), to make *safe, free*
3468 yesha' (32), *liberty, deliverance, prosperity*
4190 môwshâ'âh (1), *deliverance*
8668 tᵉshûw'âh (17), *rescue, deliverance*
4991 sōtēria (40), *rescue*
4992 sōtēriŏn (5), *defender* or *defence*

SAMARIA
8111 Shômᵉrown (109), *watch-station*

8115 Shomrayin (Ch.) (2), *watch-station*
4540 Samarĕia (13), *watch-station*

SAMARITAN
4541 Samarĕitēs (3), *inhabitant of Samaria*

SAMARITANS
8118 Shômᵉrônîy (1), *Shomeronite*
4541 Samarĕitēs (6), *inhabitant of Samaria*

SAME
428 'êl-leh (1), *these*
1459 gav (Ch.) (1), *middle*
1791 dêk (Ch.) (1), *this*
1797 dikkên (Ch.) (1), *this*
1931 hûw' (73), *this*
1933 hâvâ' (1), to *be*
1992 hêm (4), *they*
2063 zô'th (1), *this*
2088 zeh (9), *this or that*
6106 'etsem (6), *selfsame*
8478 tachath (1), *bottom*
846 autŏs (87), *he, she, it*
1565 ĕkĕinŏs (24), *that*
2532 kai (1), *even; also*
3673 hŏmŏtĕchnŏs (1), *of the same trade*
3748 hŏstis (1), *whoever*
3761 ŏudĕ (1), *neither*
3778 hŏutŏs (37), *this*
4954 sussōmŏs (1), *fellow-member*
5023 tauta (2), *these*
5026 tautē₁ (5), (*toward or of*) *this*
5126 tŏutŏn (2), to *this*
5129 tŏutŏ₁ (1), in *this*
5615 hōsautōs (1), *in the same way*

SAMGAR-NEBO
5562 Çamgar Nᵉbôw (1), *Samgar-Nebo*

SAMLAH
8072 Samlâh (4), *mantle*

SAMOS
4544 Samŏs (1), *Samus*

SAMOTHRACIA
4543 Samŏthra₁kē (1), *Samos of Thrace*

SAMSON
8123 Shimshôwn (35), *sunlight*
4546 Sampsōn (1), *sunlight*

SAMSON'S
8123 Shimshôwn (3), *sunlight*

SAMUEL
8050 Shᵉmûw'êl (135), *heard of God*
4545 Samŏuēl (3), *heard of God*

SANBALLAT
5571 Çanballaṭ (10), *Sanballat*

SANCTIFICATION
38 hagiasmŏs (5), state of *purity*

SANCTIFIED
6942 qâdâsh (46), to *be, make clean*
37 hagiazō (16), to *purify*

SANCTIFIETH
37 hagiazō (4), to *purify*

SANCTIFY
6942 qâdâsh (63), to *be, make clean*
37 hagiazō (6), to *purify*

SANCTUARIES
4720 miqdâsh (5), *sanctuary of deity*

SANCTUARY
4720 miqdâsh (64), *sanctuary of deity*
6944 qôdesh (68), *sacred*
39 hagiŏn (4), *sacred*

SAND
2344 chôwl (23), *sand*
285 ammŏs (5), *sand*

SANDALS
4547 sandaliŏn (2), *sandal*

SANG
6030 'ânâh (2), to *sing*
7442 rânan (1), to *shout for joy*
7891 shîyr (7), to *sing*
5214 humnĕō (1), to *celebrate* God in song

SANK
3381 yârad (1), to *descend*
6749 tsâlal (1), to *settle*

SANSANNAH
5578 Çancannâh (1), *bough*

SAPH
5593 Çaph (1), *dish*

SAPHIR
8208 Shâphîyr (1), *beautiful*

SAPPHIRA
4551 Sapphĕirē (1), *sapphire* or *lapis-lazuli*

SAPPHIRE
5601 çappîyr (8), *sapphire*
4552 sapphĕirŏs (1), *sapphire* or *lapis-lazuli*

SAPPHIRES
5601 çappîyr (3), *sapphire*

SARA
4564 Sarrha (1), *princess*

SARAH
8283 Sârâh (36), *princess*
8294 Serach (1), *superfluity*
4564 Sarrha (2), *princess*

SARAH'S
8283 Sârâh (2), *princess*
4564 Sarrha (1), *princess*

SARAI
8297 Sâray (16), *dominative*

SARAI'S
8297 Sâray (1), *dominative*

SARAPH
8315 Sâraph (1), *burning one, serpent*

SARDINE
4555 sardinŏs (1), *sard*

SARDIS
4554 Sardĕis (3), Sardis

SARDITES
5625 Çardîy (1), Seredite

SARDIUS
124 'ôdem (3), ruby
4556 sardiŏs (1), sardian

SARDONYX
4557 sardŏnux (1),
  sard-onyx

SAREPTA
4558 Sarĕpta (1),
  refinement

SARGON
5623 Çargôwn (1),
  Sargon

SARID
8301 Sârîyd (2), survivor

SARON
4565 Sarōn (1), plain

SARSECHIM
8310 Sarçᵉkîym (1),
  Sarsekim

SARUCH
4562 Sarŏuch (1), tendril

SAT
3427 yâshab (94), to dwell
8497 tâkâh (1), to camp
339 anakathizō (2), to sit
  up
345 anakĕimai (6), to
  recline at a meal
347 anaklinō (1), to lean
  back, recline
377 anapiptō (4), lie
  down, lean back
2516 kathĕzŏmai (4), to
  sit down, be seated
2521 kathēmai (43), to
  sit down; to remain
2523 kathizō (21), to seat
  down, dwell
2621 katakĕimai (3), to
  lie down; recline
2625 kataklinō (1), to
  recline, take a place
3869 parakathizō (1), to
  sit down near, beside
4775 sugkathēmai (2), to
  seat oneself with
4873 sunanakĕimai (8),
  to recline with

SATAN
7854 sâţân (18), opponent
4567 Satanas (34),
  accuser, i.e. the Devil

SATAN'S
4567 Satanas (1),
  accuser, i.e. the Devil

SATEST
3427 yâshab (2), to settle

SATIATE
7301 râvâh (1), to slake
7646 sâba' (1), to fill

SATIATED
7301 râvâh (1), to slake

SATISFACTION
3724 kôpher (2),
  redemption-price

SATISFIED
4390 mâlê' (1), to fill
7301 râvâh (1), to slake
7646 sâba' (36), fill

SATISFIEST
7646 sâba' (1), to fill

SATISFIETH
7646 sâba' (2), to fill
7654 sob'âh (1), satiety

SATISFY
4390 mâlê' (1), to fill
7301 râvâh (1), to slake
7646 sâba' (7), to fill
5526 chŏrtazō (1), to
  supply food

SATISFYING
7648 sôba' (1),
  satisfaction
4140 plēsmŏnē (1),
  gratification

SATISIFED
7649 sâbêa' (1), satiated

SATYR
8163 sâ'îyr (1), shaggy;
  he-goat; goat idol

SATYRS
8163 sâ'îyr (1), shaggy;
  he-goat; goat idol

SAUL
7586 Shâ'ûwl (367), asked
4569 Saulŏs (23), asked

SAUL'S
7586 Shâ'ûwl (31), asked

SAVE
389 'ak (1), surely; only
518 'îm (1), Oh that!
657 'epheç (1), end; no
  further
1107 bil'ădêy (4), except
1115 biltîy (2), except
1115+518 biltîy (1), not,
  except, without, unless
2108 zûwlâh (6), except
2421 châyâh (21), to live;
  to revive
2425 châyay (1), to live;
  to revive
3444 yᵉshûw'âh (1),
  deliverance; aid
3467 yâsha' (106), to
  make safe, free
3588+518 kîy (12), for,
  that because
3861 lâhên (Ch.) (2),
  therefore; except
4422 mâlaţ (4), to escape
7535 raq (3), although
8104 shâmar (1), to
  watch
235 alla (2), except
1295 diasōzō (1), to cure,
  preserve, rescue
1508 ĕi mē (18), if not
2228 ē (1), or; than
3844 para (1), besides
4133 plēn (1), save that
4982 sōzō (41), to deliver

SAVED
2421 châyâh (8), to live;
  to revive
3467 yâsha' (35), to make
  safe, free
4422 mâlaţ (1), to escape
5337 nâtsal (1), to deliver
8104 shâmar (1), to
  watch
1295 diasōzō (1), to cure,
  preserve, rescue

SAW
7649 sâbêa' (3), satiated

4982 sōzō (53), to deliver
4991 sōtēria (2), rescue
5442 phulassō (1), to
  watch, i.e. be on guard

SAVEST
3467 yâsha' (3), to make
  safe, free

SAVETH
3467 yâsha' (7), to make
  safe, free

SAVING
518 'îm (1), Oh that!
657 'epheç (1), end; no
  further
2421 châyâh (1), to live;
  to revive
3444 yᵉshûw'âh (2),
  deliverance; aid
3468 yesha' (1), liberty,
  deliverance, prosperity
1508 ĕi mē (2), if not
3924 parĕktŏs (1), besides
4047 pĕripŏiēsis (1),
  preservation
4991 sōtēria (1), rescue

SAVIOUR
3467 yâsha' (13), to make
  safe, free
4990 sōtēr (24), Deliverer

SAVIOURS
3467 yâsha' (2), to make
  safe, free

SAVOUR
6709 tsachănâh (1),
  stench
7381 rêyach (46), odor
2175 ĕuŏdia (1), aroma
3471 mōrainō (2), to
  become insipid
3744 ŏsmē (4), fragrance

SAVOUREST
5426 phrŏnĕō (2), to be
  mentally disposed

SAVOURS
5208 nîychôwach (Ch.)
  (1), pleasure

SAVOURY
4303 maţ'am (6), delicacy

SAW
2370 châzâ' (Ch.) (9), to
  gaze upon; to dream
2372 châzâh (8), to gaze
  at; to perceive
4883 massôwr (1), saw
7200 râ'âh (306), to see
7805 shâzaph (1), to scan
991 blĕpō (9), to look at
1492 ĕidō (188), to know
1689 ĕmblĕpō (1), to
  observe; to discern
2147 hĕuriskō (1), to find
2300 thĕaŏmai (8), to
  look closely at
2334 thĕŏrĕō (9), to see
3708 hŏraō (4), to stare,
  see clearly; to discern

SAWED
1641 gârar (1), to saw

SAWEST
2370 châzâ' (Ch.) (7), to
  gaze upon; to dream
2372 châzâh (1), to gaze
  at; to perceive
7200 râ'âh (6), to see
1492 ĕidō (7), to know

SAWN
4249 prizō (1), to saw in
  two

SAWS
4050 mᵉgêrâh (3), saw

SAY
559 'âmar (573), to say
560 'ămar (Ch.) (2), to say
1696 dâbar (28), to speak
1697 dâbâr (1), word
4405 millâh (2), word
471 antĕpō (1), to refute
2036 ĕpō (66), to speak
2046 ĕrĕō (39), to utter
2980 lalĕō (6), to talk
3004 lĕgō (293), to say
3056 lŏgŏs (1), word
5335 phaskō (1), to
  assert a claim
5346 phēmi (6), to make
  known one's thoughts

SAYEST
559 'âmar (18), to say
2036 ĕpō (1), to speak
3004 lĕgō (20), to say

SAYING
559 'âmar (916), to say
560 'ămar (Ch.) (2), to say
1697 dâbâr (20), word
2420 chîydâh (1), puzzle;
  conundrum; maxim
2036 ĕpō (18), to speak
2981 lalia (1), talk
3004 lĕgō (380), to say
3007 lĕipō (5), to fail
3056 lŏgŏs (33), word
3058 lŏidŏrĕō (1), to
  vilify, insult
4487 rhēma (6),
  utterance; matter
5335 phaskō (1), to assert

SAYINGS
561 'êmer (2), saying
1697 dâbâr (5), word
2420 chîydâh (2), puzzle;
  conundrum; maxim
6310 peh (1), mouth
3004 lĕgō (1), to say
3056 lŏgŏs (16), word
4487 rhēma (3),
  utterance; matter

SCAB
1618 gârâb (1), itching
4556 miçpachath (3),
  scurf, rash
5597 çappachath (3),
  skin mange

SCABBARD
8593 ta'ar (1), scabbard

SCABBED
3217 yallepheth (2), scurf

SCAFFOLD
3595 kîyôwr (1), caldron

SCALES
650+4043 'âphîyq (1),
  valley; stream; mighty
6425 peleç (1), balance
7193 qasqeseth (7), fish
  scales; coat of mail
3013 lĕpis (1), flake, scale

SCALETH
5927 'âlâh (1), to ascend,
  be high, mount

SCALL
5424 netheq (14), scurf

S

SCALP
6936 qodqôd (1), *crown* of the head

SCANT
7332 râzôwn (1), *thinness*

SCAPEGOAT
5799 'ăză'zêl (4), *goat of departure; scapegoat*

SCARCE
3433 mŏlis (2), *with difficulty*

SCARCELY
3433 mŏlis (2), *with difficulty*

SCARCENESS
4544 miçkênûth (1), *indigence, poverty*

SCAREST
2865 châthath (1), to *break down*

SCARLET
711 'argᵉvân (Ch.) (3), *purple*
8144 shânîy (9), *crimson*
8144+8438 shânîy (33), *crimson dyed stuffs*
8529 tâla' (1), to *dye crimson*
2847 kŏkkinŏs (6), *crimson*

SCATTER
921 bᵉdar (Ch.) (1), to *scatter*
967 bâzar (2), to *scatter*
2210 zâqaph (1), to *lift up*
2219 zârâh (11), to *diffuse*
2236 zâraq (2), to *sprinkle, scatter*
5128 nûwa' (1), to *waver*
5310 nâphats (1), to *dash*
6284 pâ'âh (1), to *blow away*
6327 pûwts (18), to *dash*

SCATTERED
2219 zârâh (6), to *diffuse*
4900 mâshak (2), to *draw out; to be tall*
5310 nâphats (1), to *dash*
6327 pûwts (34), to *dash*
6340 pâzar (7), to *scatter*
6504 pârad (2), to *spread*
6555 pârats (1), to *break out*
6566 pâras (3), to *scatter*
1262 dialuō (1), to *break up*
1287 diaskŏrpizō (4), to *scatter; to squander*
1289 diaspĕirō (3), to *scatter like seed*
1290 diaspŏra (2), *dispersion*
4496 rhiptō (1), to *fling*
4650 skŏrpizō (1), to *dissipate*

SCATTERETH
2219 zârâh (2), to *diffuse*
6327 pûwts (3), to *dash in pieces; to disperse*
6340 pâzar (2), to *scatter*
4650 skŏrpizō (3), to *dissipate*

SCATTERING
5311 nephets (1), *storm which disperses*

SCENT
2143 zêker (1), *commemoration*
7381 rêyach (2), *odor*

SCEPTRE
7626 shêbeṭ (9), *stick*
8275 sharbîyṭ (4), *ruler's rod*
4464 rhabdŏs (2), *stick*

SCEPTRES
7626 shêbeṭ (1), *stick*

SCEVA
4630 Skĕuas (1), *left-handed*

SCHISM
4978 schisma (1), *divisive dissension*

SCHOLAR
6030 'ânâh (1), to *respond*
8527 talmîyd (1), *pupil*

SCHOOL
4981 schŏlē (1), *lecture hall, i.e. school*

SCHOOLMASTER
3807 paidagōgŏs (2), *tutor, cf. pedagogue*

SCIENCE
4093 maddâ' (1), *intelligence*
1108 gnōsis (1), *knowledge*

SCOFF
7046 qâlaç (1), to *disparage, i.e. ridicule*

SCOFFERS
1703 ĕmpaiktēs (1), *derider; false teacher*

SCORCH
2739 kaumatizō (1), to *burn, scorch, sear*

SCORCHED
2739 kaumatizō (3), to *burn, scorch, sear*

SCORN
959 bâzah (1), to *scorn*
3887 lûwts (1), to *scoff*
3933 la'ag (2), *scoffing*
4890 mischâq (1), *laughing-stock*
2606 katagĕlaō (3), to *laugh down, i.e. deride*

SCORNER
3887 lûwts (11), to *scoff*

SCORNERS
3887 lûwts (3), to *scoff*
3945 lâtsats (1), to *scoff*

SCORNEST
3887 lûwts (1), to *scoff*
7046 qâlaç (1), to *disparage, i.e. ridicule*

SCORNETH
3887 lûwts (2), to *scoff; to interpret; to intercede*
7832 sâchaq (1), to *scorn*

SCORNFUL
3887 lûwts (1), to *scoff*
3944 lâtsôwn (2), *scoffing*

SCORNING
3933 la'ag (2), *scoffing*
3944 lâtsôwn (1), *scoffing*

SCORPION
4651 skŏrpiŏs (2), *scorpion*

SCORPIONS
6137 'aqrâb (6), *scorpion*
4651 skŏrpiŏs (3), *scorpion*

SCOURED
4838 mâraq (1), to *polish*

SCOURGE
7752 shôwṭ (4), *lash*
7885 shayiṭ (1), *oar*
3147 mastizō (1), to *whip*
3164 machŏmai (5), to *war, i.e. to quarrel*
5416 phragĕlliŏn (1), *lash*

SCOURGED
1244 biqqôreth (1), *due punishment*
3146 mastigŏō (1), to *punish by flogging*
5417 phragĕllŏō (2), to *whip, i.e. to lash*

SCOURGES
7850 shôṭêṭ (1), *goad, flogging device*

SCOURGETH
3146 mastigŏō (1), to *punish by flogging*

SCOURGING
3148 mastix (1), *flogging device*

SCOURGINGS
3148 mastix (1), *flogging device*

SCRABBLED
8427 tâvâh (1), to *mark*

SCRAPE
1623 gârad (1), to *rub off*
5500 çâchâh (1), to *sweep away*
7096 qâtsâh (1), to *cut off*

SCRAPED
7096 qâtsâh (1), to *cut off*
7106 qâtsa' (1), to *scrape*

SCREECH
3917 lîylîyth (1), *night spectre (spirit)*

SCRIBE
5608 çâphar (42), to *inscribe; to enumerate*
5613 çâphêr (Ch.) (6), *scribe, recorder*
1122 grammatĕus (4), *secretary, scholar*

SCRIBE'S
5608 çâphar (2), to *inscribe; to enumerate*

SCRIBES
5608 çâphar (6), to *inscribe; to enumerate*
1122 grammatĕus (62), *secretary, scholar*

SCRIP
3219 yalqûwṭ (1), *pouch*
4082 pēra (6), *wallet*

SCRIPTURE
3791 kâthâb (1), *writing*
1124 graphē (31), *document, i.e. holy Writ*

SCRIPTURES
1121 gramma (1), *writing*

1124 graphē (20), *document, i.e. holy Writ*

SCROLL
5612 çêpher (1), *writing*
975 bibliŏn (1), *scroll*

SCUM
2457 chel'âh (5), *rust*

SCURVY
1618 gârâb (2), *itching*

SCYTHIAN
4658 Skuthēs (1), *Scythene*

SEA
3220 yâm (291), *sea*
3221 yâm (Ch.) (2), *sea*
1724 ĕnaliŏs (1), *marine*
2281 thalassa (93), *sea*
3864 parathalassiŏs (1), *by the lake*
3882 paraliŏs (1), *maritime; seacoast*
3989 pĕlagŏs (1), *open sea*

SEAFARING
3220 yâm (1), *sea; basin*

SEAL
2368 chôwthâm (5), *seal*
2856 châtham (6), to *close up; to affix a seal*
4972 sphragizō (4), to *stamp with a signet*
4973 sphragis (11), *stamp impressed*

SEALED
2856 châtham (14), to *close up; to affix a seal*
2857 châtham (Ch.) (1), to *affix a seal*
2696 katasphragizō (1), to *seal closely*
4972 sphragizō (20), to *stamp with a signet*

SEALEST
2856 châtham (1), to *close up; to affix a seal*

SEALETH
2856 châtham (3), to *close up; to affix a seal*

SEALING
4972 sphragizō (1), to *stamp with a signet*

SEALS
4973 sphragis (5), *stamp*

SEAM
729 arrhaphŏs (1), *without seam*

SEARCH
1239 bâqar (1), to *inspect, admire*
1240 bᵉqar (Ch.) (4), to *inspect, admire*
1875 dârash (4), to *pursue or search*
2658 châphar (3), to *delve, to explore*
2664 châphas (8), to *seek; to let be sought*
2665 chêphes (1), *secret trick, plot*
2713 châqar (11), to *examine, search*
2714 chêqer (3), *examination*

4290 machtereth (1), burglary
8446 tûwr (9), to meander
1833 ĕxĕtazō (1), to ascertain or interrogate
2045 ĕrĕunaō (2), to seek, i.e. to investigate

SEARCHED
2664 châphas (3), to seek
2713 châqar (7), to examine intimately
2714 chêqer (1), examination
4959 mâshash (2), to feel
7270 râgal (1), to reconnoiter; to slander
8446 tûwr (4), to meander
350 anakrinō (1), interrogate, determine
1830 ĕxĕrĕunaō (1), to explore

SEARCHEST
1875 dârash (1), to search
2664 châphas (1), to seek

SEARCHETH
1875 dârash (2), to search
2713 châqar (3), to search
2045 ĕrĕunaō (3), to seek

SEARCHING
2664 châphas (1), to seek
2714 chêqer (2), examination
8446 tûwr (1), to meander
2045 ĕrĕunaō (1), to seek

SEARCHINGS
2714 chêqer (1), examination

SEARED
2743 kautēriazō (1), to brand or cauterize

SEAS
3220 yâm (24), sea
1337 dithalassŏs (1), having two seas

SEASON
2165 zᵉmân (1), time
2166 zᵉmân (Ch.) (1), time, appointed
3117 yôwm (3), day; time
4150 môw'êd (10), place of meeting
4414 mâlach (1), to disappear as dust
6256 'êth (14), time
171 akairōs (1), inopportunely
741 artuō (1), to spice
2121 ĕukairōs (1), opportune, suitable
2540 kairōs (11), set or proper time
3641 ŏligŏs (1), puny
4340 prŏskairŏs (1), temporary
5550 chrŏnŏs (3), time
5610 hōra (3), hour

SEASONED
741 artuō (2), to spice

SEASONS
2166 zᵉmân (Ch.) (1), time, appointed
4150 môw'êd (3), place of meeting; assembly
6256 'êth (2), time
2540 kairōs (4), set or proper time

5550 chrŏnŏs (1), time
SEAT
3678 kiççê' (7), throne
4186 môwshâb (7), seat
7674 shebeth (1), rest
7675 shebeth (2), abode
8499 tᵉkûwnâh (1), something arranged
968 bēma (10), tribunal platform; judging place
2362 thrŏnŏs (3), throne
2515 kathĕdra (1), bench

SEATED
5603 çâphan (1), to roof

SEATS
2362 thrŏnŏs (4), throne
2515 kathĕdra (2), bench
4410 prōtŏkathĕdria (4), pre-eminence in council

SEBA
5434 Çᵉbâ' (4), Seba

SEBAT
7627 Shᵉbâṭ (1), Shebat

SECACAH
5527 Çᵉkâkâh (1), enclosure

SECHU
7906 Sêkûw (1), Seku

SECOND
4932 mishneh (12), double; second
8138 shânâh (3), to fold, i.e. duplicate
8145 shênîy (99), second
8147 shᵉnayim (10), two-fold
8578 tinyân (Ch.) (1), second
8648 tᵉrêyn (Ch.) (1), two
1207 dĕutĕrŏprōtŏs (1), second-first
1208 dĕutĕrŏs (42), second; secondly

SECONDARILY
1208 dĕutĕrŏs (1), second; secondly

SECRET
328 'aṭ (1), gently, softly
2934 ṭâman (1), to hide
4565 miçtâr (8), covert hiding place
5475 çôwd (8), secret
5640 çâtham (1), to repair; to keep secret
5641 çâthar (4), to hide
5642 çᵉthar (Ch.) (1), to demolish
5643 çêther (15), cover
5956 'âlam (2), to conceal
6383 pil'îy (1), remarkable
6596 pôth (1), hole; hinge
6845 tsâphan (2), to hide
7328 râz (Ch.) (6), mystery
8368 sâthar (1), to break out as an eruption
614 apŏkruphŏs (1), secret, hidden things
2926 kruptē (1), hidden
2927 kruptŏs (10), private
2928 kruptō (1), to conceal
2931 kruphē (1), in secret
4601 sigaō (1), to keep silent

5009 tamĕiŏn (1), room

SECRETLY
1589 gânab (1), to deceive
2244 châbâ' (1), to secrete
2644 châphâ' (1), to act covertly
2790 chârash (1), to engrave; to plow
2791 cheresh (1), magical craft; silence
3909 lâṭ (1), secrecy
4565 miçtâr (2), covert hiding place
5643 çêther (9), cover
6845 tsâphan (1), to hide
2928 kruptō (1), to conceal
2977 lathra (1), secretly

SECRETS
4016 mâbûsh (1), male genitals
5475 çôwd (2), secret
7328 râz (Ch.) (3), mystery
8587 ta'ălummâh (2), secret
2927 kruptŏs (2), private

SECT
139 hairĕsis (5), sect

SECUNDUS
4580 Sĕkŏundŏs (1), second

SECURE
982 bâṭach (4), to trust
983 beṭach (1), security
987 baṭṭûchôwth (1), security
4160+275 mûwts (1), to oppress

SECURELY
983 beṭach (2), safety, security, trust

SECURITY
2425 hikanŏs (1), ample

SEDITION
849 'eshtaddûwr (Ch.) (2), rebellion
4714 stasis (3), one leading an uprising

SEDITIONS
1370 dichŏstasia (1), dissension

SEDUCE
635 apŏplanaō (1), to lead astray; to wander
4105 planaō (2), to deceive

SEDUCED
2937 ṭâ'âh (1), to lead astray
8582 tâ'âh (2), to stray

SEDUCERS
1114 gŏēs (1), imposter

SEDUCETH
8582 tâ'âh (1), to stray

SEDUCING
4108 planŏs (1), roving

SEE
2009 hinnêh (2), Look!
2370 châzâ' (Ch.) (4), to gaze upon; to dream
2372 châzâh (15), to gaze at; to perceive

2374 chôzeh (2), beholder in vision
4758 mar'eh (1), appearance; vision
5027 nâbaṭ (4), to scan; to regard with favor
7200 râ'âh (346), to see
7789 shûwr (4), to spy out, survey
308 anablēpō (1), to look up; to recover sight
542 apĕidō (1), to see fully
991 blĕpō (46), to look at
1227 diablĕpō (2), to see clearly, recover vision
1492 ĕidō (79), to know
1689 ĕmblĕpō (1), to observe; to discern
2300 thĕaŏmai (4), to look closely at
2334 thĕōrĕō (17), to see
2396 idĕ (1), lo!, look!
2400 idŏu (3), lo!, see!
2477 histŏrĕō (1), to visit
3467 muōpazō (1), to see indistinctly, be myopic
3700 ŏptanŏmai (29), to appear
3708 hŏraō (11), to stare, see clearly; to discern
5461 phōtizō (1), to shine or to brighten up

SEED
2233 zera' (218), seed
2234 zᵉra' (Ch.) (1), posterity, progeny
6507 pᵉrûdâh (1), kernel
4687 spĕirō (4), to scatter, i.e. sow seed
4690 spĕrma (41), seed
4701 spŏra (1), sowing
4703 spŏrŏs (5), seed

SEED'S
2233 zera' (1), seed; fruit

SEEDS
4690 spĕrma (3), seed

SEEDTIME
2233 zera' (1), seed; fruit

SEEING
310 'achar (1), after
518 'îm (1), whether?; if
1768 dîy (Ch.) (1), that; of
3282 ya'an (1), because
3588 kîy (9), for, that
6493 piqqêach (1), clear-sighted
7200 râ'âh (16), to see
990 blemma (1), vision
991 blĕpō (8), to look at
1063 gar (1), for, indeed, but, because
1492 ĕidō (8), to know
1512 ĕi pĕr (1), if perhaps
1893 ĕpĕi (4), since
1894 ĕpĕidē (2), whereas
1897 ĕpĕipĕr (1), since
2334 thĕōrĕō (1), to see
3708 hŏraō (1), to stare, see clearly; to discern
3754 hŏti (1), that; since
4275 prŏĕidō (1), to foresee

SEEK
1239 bâqar (3), to inspect, admire

S

1245 bâqash (112), to
search out; to strive
1556 gâlal (1), to roll
1875 dârash (56), to seek
2713 châqar (1), to search
7125 qîr'âh (1), to
encounter, to happen
7836 shâchar (8), to
search for
8446 tûwr (1), to wander
327 anazētĕō (1), to
search out
1567 ĕkzĕtĕō (2), to seek
out
1934 ĕpizētĕō (6), to
search (inquire) for
2212 zētĕō (48), to seek

SEEKEST
1245 bâqash (7), to
search out; to strive
2212 zētĕō (2), to seek

SEEKETH
579 'ânâh (1), to meet
1243 baqqârâh (1),
looking after
1245 bâqash (19), to
search out; to strive
1875 dârash (6), to seek
2658 châphar (1), to delve
7836 shâchar (1), to
search for
1567 ĕkzĕtĕō (1), to seek
out
1934 ĕpizētĕō (3), to
search (inquire) for
2212 zētĕō (9), to seek

SEEKING
1875 dârash (2), to seek
2212 zētĕō (12), to seek

SEEM
3191 yᵉṭab (Ch.) (1), to
be, make well
4591 mâ'aṭ (1), to be,
make small or few
4758 mar'eh (1),
appearance; vision
5869 'ayin (2), eye; sight
7034 qâlâh (1), to be light
7185 qâshâh (1), to be
tough or severe
1380 dŏkĕō (5), to seem

SEEMED
5869 'ayin (4), eye; sight
1380 dŏkĕō (6), to think,
regard, seem good
5316 phainō (1), to
lighten; to appear

SEEMETH
5869 'ayin (18), eye; sight
6440 pânîym (2), face
7200 râ'âh (1), to see
1380 dŏkĕō (5), to seem

SEEMLY
5000 nâ'veh (2), suitable

SEEN
2370 chăzâ' (Ch.) (3), to
gaze upon; to dream
2372 châzâh (9), to gaze
at; to perceive
7200 râ'âh (162), to see
7210 rô'îy (2), sight
7805 shâzaph (1), to scan
991 blĕpō (9), to look at
1492 ĕidō (33), to know
2300 thĕaŏmai (8), to
look closely at

2334 thĕōrĕō (2), to see
2529 kathŏraō (1), to see
clearly
3700 ŏptanŏmai (8), to
appear
3708 hŏraō (32), to stare,
see clearly; to discern
3780 ŏuchi (1), not indeed
4308 prŏŏraō (1), to
notice previously
5316 phainō (2), to
lighten; be visible

SEER
2374 chôzeh (11),
beholder in vision
7200 râ'âh (10), to see

SEER'S
7200 râ'âh (1), to see

SEERS
2374 chôzeh (5),
beholder in vision
7200 râ'âh (1), to see

SEEST
2372 châzâh (2), to gaze
at; to perceive
7200 râ'âh (27), to see
7210 rô'îy (1), sight;
spectacle
991 blĕpō (5), to look at
2334 thĕōrĕō (1), to see

SEETH
2372 châzâh (3), to gaze
at; to perceive
7200 râ'âh (27), to see
7210 rô'îy (1), sight;
spectacle
991 blĕpō (11), to look at
2334 thĕōrĕō (9), to see
3708 hŏraō (1), to stare

SEETHE
1310 bâshal (8), to boil

SEETHING
1310 bâshal (1), to boil
5301 nâphach (2), to
inflate, blow, kindle

SEGUB
7687 Sᵉgûwb (3), aloft

SEIR
8165 Sê'îyr (39), rough

SEIRATH
8167 Sᵉ'îyrâh (1),
roughness

SEIZE
3423 yârash (1), to
inherit; to impoverish
3451 yᵉshîymâh (1),
desolation
3947 lâqach (1), to take
2722 katĕchō (1), to hold
down fast

SEIZED
2388 châzaq (1), to seize

SELA
5554 Çela' (1), craggy
rock; fortress

SELA-HAMMAHLEKOTH
5555 Çela' ham-
machlᵉqôwth (1), rock
of the divisions

SELAH
5542 Çelâh (74),
suspension of music
5554 Çela' (1), craggy
rock; fortress

SELED
5540 Çeled (1),
exultation

SELEUCIA
4581 Sĕlĕukĕia (1), of
Seleucus

SELFWILL
7522 râtsôwn (1), delight

SELFWILLED
829 authadēs (2),
self-pleasing, arrogant

SELL
4376 mâkar (24), to sell
7666 shâbar (3), to deal
1710 ĕmpŏrĕuŏmai (1),
to trade, do business
4453 pōlĕō (7), to barter

SELLER
4376 mâkar (3), to sell
4211 pŏrphurŏpōlis (1),
female trader in
bluish-red cloth

SELLERS
4376 mâkar (1), to sell

SELLEST
4376 mâkar (1), to sell

SELLETH
4376 mâkar (5), to sell
7666 shâbar (1), to deal
4453 pōlĕō (1), to barter

SELVEDGE
7098 qâtsâh (2),
termination; fringe

SEM
4590 Sēm (1), name

SEMACHIAH
5565 Çᵉmakyâhûw (1),
supported of Jehovah

SEMEI
4584 Sĕmĕï (1), famous

SENAAH
5570 Çᵉnâ'âh (2), thorny

SENATE
1087 gĕrŏusia (1), Jewish
Sanhedrin

SENATORS
2205 zâqên (1), old,
venerated

SEND
935 bôw' (1), to go, come
5042 nâba' (1), to gush
5130 nûwph (1), to rock
5414 nâthan (6), to give
7136 qârâh (1), to bring
about; to impose
7971 shâlach (157), to
send away
7972 shᵉlach (Ch.) (1), to
send away
630 apŏluō (6), to relieve,
release; divorce
649 apŏstĕllō (23), to
send out on a mission
906 ballō (3), to throw
1032 bruō (1), to gush
1544 ĕkballō (3), to
throw out
1821 ĕxapŏstĕllō (1), to
despatch, or to dismiss
3343 mĕtapĕmpō (2), to
summon or invite
3992 pĕmpō (25), to send

SENDEST
7971 shâlach (6), to send
away

SENDETH
5414 nâthan (2), to give
7971 shâlach (8), to send
away
649 apŏstĕllō (4), to send
out on a mission
1026 brĕchō (1), to make
wet; to rain

SENDING
4916 mishlôwach (3),
sending out
4917 mishlachath (1),
mission; release; army
7971 shâlach (9), to send
away
3992 pĕmpō (1), to send

SENEH
5573 Çeneh (1), thorn

SENIR
8149 Shᵉnîyr (2), peak

SENNACHERIB
5576 Çanchêrîyb (13),
Sancherib

SENSE
7922 sekel (1),
intelligence; success

SENSES
145 aisthētēriŏn (1),
judgment, sense

SENSUAL
5591 psuchikŏs (2),
physical and brutish

SENT
1980 hâlak (1), to walk
2904 ṭûwl (1), to cast
down or out, hurl
3947 lâqach (1), to take
5414 nâthan (5), to give
5674 'âbar (2), to cross
over; to transition
6680 tsâvâh (1), to
constitute, enjoin
7725 shûwb (1), to return
7964 shillûwach (1),
divorce; dower
7971 shâlach (459), to
send away
7972 shᵉlach (Ch.) (12),
to send away
375 anapĕmpō (4), to
send up or back
628 apŏlŏuō (2), to wash
fully
630 apŏluō (6), to
release; divorce
640 apŏria (1), state of
quandary, perplexity
649 apŏstĕllō (104), to
send out on a mission
652 apŏstŏlŏs (2),
commissioner of Christ
657 apŏtassŏmai (1), to
say adieu; to renounce
863 aphiēmi (2), to leave
1524 ĕisĕimi (1), to enter
1544 ĕkballō (1), to
throw out
1599 ĕkpĕmpō (2), to
despatch, send out
1821 ĕxapŏstĕllō (10), to
despatch, or to dismiss
3343 mĕtapĕmpō (4), to
summon or invite

SENTENCE
3992 pĕmpō (49), to *send*
4842 sumpĕmpō (2), to
dispatch with
4882 sunapŏstĕllō (1), to
despatch with

SENTENCE
1697 dâbâr (3), *word*
4941 mishpât (2), *verdict;*
formal decree; justice
6310 peh (1), *mouth*
6599 pithgâm (1),
judicial sentence; edict
7081 qeçem (1),
divination
610 apŏkrima (1),
decision or sentence
1948 ĕpikrinō (1), to
adjudge, decide
2919 krinō (1), to *decide*

SENTENCES
280 'ǎchîydâh (Ch.) (1),
enigma
2420 chîydâh (1), *puzzle*

SENTEST
7971 shâlach (4), to *send*
away

SENUAH
5574 Çᵉnûw'âh (1),
pointed

SEORIM
8188 Sᵉ'ôrîym (1), *barley*

SEPARATE
914 bâdal (7), to *divide*
1508 gizrâh (7), *figure,*
appearance; enclosure
2505 châlaq (1), to *be*
smooth; be slippery
3995 mibdâlâh (1),
separation; separate
5139 nâzîyr (1), *prince;*
separated Nazirite
5144 nâzar (4), to *set*
apart, devote
6381 pâlâ' (1), to *be,*
make great, difficult
6504 pârad (2), to *spread*
873 aphŏrizō (5), to *limit,*
exclude, appoint
5562 chôrĕō (3), to *pass,*
enter; to hold, admit

SEPARATED
914 bâdal (17), to *divide*
5139 nâzîyr (1), *prince;*
separated Nazirite
5144 nâzar (1), to *set*
apart, devote
6395 pâlâh (2), to
distinguish
6504 pârad (8), to *spread*
873 aphŏrizō (4), to *limit,*
exclude, appoint

SEPARATETH
5144 nâzar (3), to *set*
apart, devote
6504 pârad (2), to *spread*

SEPARATING
5144 nâzar (1), to *set*
apart, devote

SEPARATION
914 bâdal (1), to *divide*
5079 niddâh (14), time of
menstrual impurity
5145 nezer (11), *set*
apart; dedication

SEPHAR
5611 Çᵉphâr (1), *census*

SEPHARAD
5614 Çᵉphârâd (1),
Sepharad

SEPHARVAIM
5617 Çᵉpharvayim (6),
Sepharvajim

SEPHARVITES
5616 Çᵉpharvîy (1),
Sepharvite

SEPULCHRE
6900 qᵉbûwrâh (5),
sepulchre
6913 qeber (14),
sepulchre
3418 mnēma (4),
sepulchral monument
3419 mnēmĕiŏn (26),
place of interment
5028 taphŏs (5), *grave*

SEPULCHRES
6913 qeber (12),
sepulchre
3419 mnēmĕiŏn (3),
place of interment
5028 taphŏs (1), *grave*

SERAH
8294 Serach (2),
superfluity

SERAIAH
8304 Sᵉrâyâh (20),
Jehovah has prevailed

SERAPHIMS
8314 sârâph (2), *saraph*

SERED
5624 Çered (2), *trembling*

SERGIUS
4588 Sĕrgiŏs (1), *Sergius*

SERJEANTS
4465 rhabdŏuchŏs (2),
constable

SERPENT
5175 nâchâsh (25), *snake*
8314 sârâph (3),
poisonous serpent
8577 tannîyn (2),
sea-serpent; jackal
3789 ŏphis (8), *snake*

SERPENT'S
5175 nâchâsh (2), *snake*

SERPENTS
2119 zâchal (1), to *crawl*
5175 nâchâsh (4), *snake*
8577 tannîyn (1),
sea-serpent; jackal
2062 hĕrpĕtŏn (1), *reptile*
3789 ŏphis (6), *snake*

SERUG
8286 Sᵉrûwg (5), *tendril*

SERVANT
5288 na'ar (30), *servant*
5647 'âbad (1), to *serve*
5649 'ǎbad (Ch.) (1),
servant
5650 'ebed (363), *servant*
7916 sâkîyr (8), man *at*
wages, hired hand
8334 shârath (4), to
attend
1248 diakŏnia (2),
attendance, aid, service
1249 diakŏnŏs (3),
attendant, deacon

SERVANT
1401 dŏulŏs (66), *servant*
1402 dŏulŏō (1), to
enslave
2324 thĕrapōn (1),
menial attendant
3610 ŏikĕtēs (3), menial
domestic servant
3816 pais (8), *servant*

SERVANT'S
5650 'ebed (8), *servant*
1401 dŏulŏs (1), *servant*

SERVANTS
582 'ĕnôwsh (1), *man*
5288 na'ar (21), *servant*
5647 'âbad (4), to *serve*
5649 'ǎbad (Ch.) (6),
servant
5650 'ebed (367), *servant*
5657 'ǎbuddâh (1),
service
8334 shârath (1), to
attend as a menial
341 anakainŏō (1), to
renovate, renew
1249 diakŏnŏs (2),
attendant, deacon
1401 dŏulŏs (55), *servant*
1402 dŏulŏō (2), to
enslave
3407 misthiŏs (2),
hired-worker
3610 ŏikĕtēs (1), menial
domestic servant
3816 pais (1), *servant*
5257 hupĕrētēs (4),
servant, attendant

SERVANTS'
5650 'ebed (4), *servant*

SERVE
5647 'âbad (162), to *serve*
5656 'ǎbôdâh (1), *work*
5975+6440 'âmad (1), to
stand
6399 pᵉlach (Ch.) (7), to
serve or worship
8334 shârath (4), to
attend as a menial
1247 diakŏnĕō (7), to
wait upon, serve
1398 dŏulĕuō (13), to
serve as a slave
3000 latrĕuō (13), to
minister to God

SERVED
1580 gâmal (1), to *benefit*
or requite; to wean
5647 'âbad (61), to *serve*
5975+6440 'âmad (1), to
stand
6213 'âsâh (1), to *do*
8334 shârath (4), to
attend as a menial
1247 diakŏnĕō (1), to
wait upon, serve
1398 dŏulĕuō (1), to
serve as a slave
3000 latrĕuō (2), to
minister to God
5256 hupĕrĕtĕō (1), to *be*
a subordinate

SERVEDST
5647 'âbad (1), to *serve*

SERVEST
6399 pᵉlach (Ch.) (2), to
serve or worship

SERVETH
5647 'âbad (2), to *serve*
5656 'ǎbôdâh (1), *work*
1247 diakŏnĕō (2), to
wait upon, serve
1398 dŏulĕuō (1), to
serve as a slave

SERVICE
3027 yâd (2), *hand; power*
5647 'âbad (4), to *serve*
5656 'ǎbôdâh (98), *work*
5673 'ǎbîydâh (Ch.) (1),
labor or business
6402 polchân (Ch.) (1),
worship
6635 tsâbâ' (4), *army,*
military host
8278 sᵉrâd (4), *stitching*
8334 shârath (3), to
attend as a menial
1248 diakŏnia (3),
attendance, aid, servic
1398 dŏulĕuō (3), to
serve as a slave
2999 latrĕia (5), *worship,*
ministry service
3000 latrĕuō (1), to
minister to God
3009 lĕitŏurgia (3),
service, ministry

SERVILE
5656 'ǎbôdâh (12), *work*

SERVING
5647 'âbad (2), to *serve*
1248 diakŏnia (1),
attendance, aid, service
1398 dŏulĕuō (3), to
serve as a slave
3000 latrĕuō (1), to
minister to God

SERVITOR
8334 shârath (1), to
attend as a menial

SERVITUDE
5656 'ǎbôdâh (2), *work*

SET
530 'ĕmûwnâh (5),
fidelity; steadiness
631 'âçar (1), to *fasten*
935 bôw' (1), to *go, come*
1129 bânâh (2), to *build*
1197 bâ'ar (1), to *be*
brutish, be senseless
1379 gâbal (1), to set a
boundary line, limit
1431 gâdal (2), to *be*
great, make great
2211 zᵉqaph (Ch.) (1), to
impale by hanging
2232 zâra' (1), to *sow*
seed; to disseminate
2706 chôq (1),
appointment; allotment
2710 châqaq (1), to
engrave; to enact laws
3051 yâhab (1), to *give*
3240 yânach (8), to *allow*
to stay
3245 yâçad (1), *settle,*
consult, establish
3259 yâ'ad (3), to *meet;*
to summon; to direct
3320 yâtsab (5), to
station, offer, continue
3322 yâtsag (8), to *place*
3332 yâtsaq (1), to *pour*
out

S

3335 yâtsar (1), to *form*
3341 yâtsath (1), to *burn*
3427 yâshab (13), to *settle*
3488 yᵉthîb (Ch.) (2), to *sit*
3559 kûwn (6), to *set up*
3635 kᵉlal (Ch.) (4), to *complete*
3966 mᵉʿôd (2), *very*
4142 mûwçabbâh (1), *backside; fold*
4150 môwʿêd (10), *place of meeting*
4390 mâlê' (5), to *fill*
4394 millû' (4), *fulfilling; setting; consecration*
4427 mâlak (1), to *reign as king*
4483 mᵉnâ' (Ch.) (3), to *count, appoint*
4487 mânâh (1), to *allot*
4853 massâ' (1), *burden*
5079 niddâh (1), time of menstrual *impurity*
5117 nûwach (2), to *rest; to settle* down
5128 nûwa' (1), to *waver*
5183 nachath (1), *descent; quiet*
5258 nâçak (2), to *pour*
5265 nâça' (16), *start*
5324 nâtsab (18), to *station*
5329 nâtsach (4), to be *eminent*
5375 nâsâ' (9), to *lift up*
5414 nâthan (103), to *give*
5473 çûwg (1), to *hem in*
5496 çûwth (1), to *stimulate; to seduce*
5526 çâkak (1), to *entwine; to fence in*
5564 çâmak (1), to *lean upon; take hold of*
5774 'ûwph (1), to *cover, to fly; to faint*
5927 'âlâh (2), to *ascend, be high, mount*
5975 'âmad (44), to *stand*
6186 'ârak (1), to set in a *row*, i.e. *arrange,*
6187 'êrek (1), *pile, equipment, estimate*
6213 'âsâh (3), to *do*
6395 pâlâh (1), to *distinguish*
6485 pâqad (7), to *care*
6496 pâqîyd (1), *superintendent, officer*
6584 pâshaṭ (1), to *strip*
6605 pâthach (1), to *open*
6845 tsâphan (1), to *hide*
6965 qûwm (28), to *rise*
6966 qûwm (Ch.) (11), to *rise*
7311 rûwm (7), to *rise*
7313 rûwm (Ch.) (1), *elation, arrogance*
7392 râkab (2), to *ride*
7660 shâbats (1), to *interweave*
7682 sâgab (1), to be, *make lofty; be safe*
7725 shûwb (1), to *return*
7737 shâvâh (1), to *level*
7760 sûwm (129), to *put*
7761 sûwm (Ch.) (2), to *put, place*
7896 shîyth (22), to *place*
7931 shâkan (3), to *reside*

7947 shâlab (1), to *make equidistant*
7971 shâlach (5), to *send away*
8239 shâphath (2), to *put*
8371 shâthath (1), to *place*, i.e. *array; to lie*
8427 tâvâh (1), to *mark out; imprint*
321 anagō (1), to *lead up; to bring out*
345 anakĕimai (1), to *recline at a meal*
377 anapiptō (1), *lie down, lean back*
392 anatassŏmai (1), to *arrange*
461 anŏrthŏō (1), to *strengthen, build*
584 apŏdĕiknumi (1), to *demonstrate*
630 apŏluō (2), to *relieve, release; divorce*
649 apŏstĕllō (1), to *send out* on a mission
816 atĕnizō (1), to *gaze*
968 bēma (1), *tribunal platform; judging place*
1299 diatassō (1), to *institute, prescribe*
1325 didōmi (1), to *give*
1369 dichazō (1), to *sunder*, i.e. *alienate*
1416 dunō (1), to *have the sun set*
1847 ĕxŏudĕnŏō (1), to *be treated with contempt*
1848 ĕxŏuthĕnĕō (3), to *treat with contempt*
1913 ĕpibibazō (3), to *cause to mount*
1930 ĕpidiŏrthŏō (1), to *set in order*
1940 ĕpikathizō (1), to *seat upon*
2007 ĕpitithēmi (3), to *impose*
2064 ĕrchŏmai (1), to *go*
2350 thŏrubĕō (1), to *clamor; start a riot*
2476 histēmi (11), to *stand, establish*
2521 kathēmai (1), to *sit down; to remain, reside*
2523 kathizō (6), to *seat down, dwell*
2525 kathistēmi (1), to *designate, constitute*
2749 kĕimai (6), to *lie outstretched*
3908 paratithēmi (9), to *present something*
4060 pĕritithēmi (1), to *present*
4270 prŏgraphō (1), to *announce, prescribe*
4295 prŏkĕimai (4), to be *present* to the mind
4388 prŏtithēmi (1), to *place before*
4741 stĕrizō (1), to *turn resolutely; to confirm*
4776 sugkathizō (1), to *give, take a seat with*
4900 sunĕlaunō (1), to *drive together*
4972 sphragizō (2), to *stamp* with a signet

5002 taktŏs (1), *appointed* or *stated*
5021 tassō (1), to *arrange, assign*
5087 tithēmi (5), to *place*
5394 phlŏgizō (1), to *cause a blaze, ignite*
5426 phrŏnĕō (1), to be *mentally disposed*

SETH
8352 Shêth (7), *put*
4589 Sêth (1), *put*

SETHUR
5639 Çᵉthûwr (1), *hidden*

SETTER
2604 kataggĕlĕus (1), *proclaimer*

SETTEST
4916 mishlôwach (3), *sending out*
5324 nâtsab (1), to *station*
7760 sûwm (1), to *put*
7896 shîyth (1), to *place*

SETTETH
3320 yâtsab (1), to *station, offer, continue*
3427 yâshab (1), to *dwell, to remain; to settle*
3559 kûwn (1), to *set up: establish, fix, prepare*
3857 lâhaṭ (1), to *blaze*
5265 nâça' (2), *start*
5375 nâsâ' (1), to *lift up*
5496 çûwth (1), to *stimulate; to seduce*
5927 'âlâh (1), to *ascend, be high, mount*
5975 'âmad (2), to *stand*
6966 qûwm (Ch.) (2), to *rise*
7034 qâlâh (1), to be *light*
7311 rûwm (1), to *raise*
7760 sûwm (1), to *put*
7918 shâkak (1), to *lay a trap; to allay*
2007 ĕpitithēmi (1), to *impose*
2476 histēmi (1), to *stand*
5394 phlŏgizō (1), to *cause a blaze*, i.e. *ignite*

SETTING
5414 nâthan (1), to *give*
1416 dunō (1), to *have the sun set*
3326 mĕta (1), *with*

SETTINGS
4396 millû'âh (1), *setting*

SETTLE
3427 yâshab (1), to *settle*
5835 'ăzârâh (6), *enclosure; border*
5975 'âmad (1), to *stand*
2311 thĕmĕliŏō (1), to *erect; to consolidate*
5087 tithēmi (1), to *place*

SETTLED
2883 ṭâba' (1), to *sink*
4349 mâkôwn (1), *place*
5324 nâtsab (1), to *station*
5975 'âmad (1), to *stand*
7087 qâphâ' (1), to *thicken, congeal*
8252 shâqaṭ (1), to *repose*
1476 hĕdraiŏs (1), *immovable; steadfast*

SETTLEST
5181 nâchath (1), to *sink*

SEVEN
3598 Kîymâh (1), *cluster of stars, the Pleiades*
7651 sheba' (346), *seven*
7655 shib'âh (Ch.) (6), *satiety*
7658 shib'ânâh (1), *seven*
7659 shib'âthayim (1), *seven-fold*
2033 hĕpta (80), *seven*
2034 hĕptakis (4), *seven times*
2035 hĕptakischiliŏi (1), *seven times a thousand*

SEVENFOLD
7659 shib'âthayim (6), *seven-fold*

SEVENS
7651 sheba' (2), *seven*

SEVENTEEN
7651+6240 sheba' (9), *seven*
7657+7651 shib'îym (1), *seventy*

SEVENTEENTH
7651+6240 sheba' (6), *seven*

SEVENTH
7637 shᵉbîy'îy (96), *seventh*
7651 sheba' (13), *seven*
1442 hĕbdŏmŏs (9), *seventh*
2035 hĕptakischiliŏi (1), *seven times a thousand*

SEVENTY
7657 shib'îym (58), *seventy*
1440 hĕbdŏmēkŏnta (2), *seventy*
1441 hĕbdŏmēkŏntakis (1), *seventy times*

SEVER
914 bâdal (1), to *divide, separate, distinguish*
6395 pâlâh (2), to *distinguish*
873 aphŏrizō (1), to *limit, exclude, appoint*

SEVERAL
2669 chôphshûwth (2), *prostration by sickness*
2398 idiŏs (1), *private*

SEVERALLY
2398 idiŏs (1), *private*

SEVERED
914 bâdal (2), to *divide*
6504 pârad (1), to *spread*

SEVERITY
663 apŏtŏmia (2), *rigor, severity*

SEW
8609 tâphar (2), to *sew*

SEWED
8609 tâphar (2), to *sew*

SEWEST
2950 ṭâphal (1), to *impute falsely*

SEWETH
1976 ĕpirrhaptō (1), to *stitch upon*

SHAALABBIN
8169 Sha'albîym (1),
fox-holes

SHAALBIM
8169 Sha'albîym (2),
fox-holes

SHAALBONITE
8170 Sha'albônîy (2),
Shaalbonite

SHAAPH
8174 Sha'aph (2),
fluctuation

SHAARAIM
8189 Sha'ărayim (2),
double gates

SHAASHGAZ
8190 Sha'ashgaz (1),
Shaashgaz

SHABBETHAI
7678 Shabbᵉthay (3),
restful

SHACHIA
7634 Shobyâh (1),
captivation

SHADE
6783 tsᵉmîythûth (1),
perpetually

SHADOW
2927 ţᵉlal (Ch.) (1), to
cover with shade
6738 tsêl (47), *shade*
6752 tsêlêl (1), *shade*
6757 tsalmâveth (16),
shade of death
644 apóskiasma (1),
shading off
4639 skia (7), *shade*

SHADOWING
6751 tsâlal (1), to *shade;*
to *grow dark*
6767 tsᵉlâtsal (1),
whirring of wings
2683 kataskiazō (1), to
cover, overshadow

SHADOWS
6752 tsêlel (3), *shade*

SHADRACH
7714 Shadrak (1),
Shadrak
7715 Shadrak (Ch.) (14),
Shadrak

SHADY
6628 tse'el (2), *lotus* tree

SHAFT
2671 chêts (1), *shaft*
3409 yârêk (3), *shank*

SHAGE
7681 Shâgê' (1), *erring*

SHAHAR
7837 shachar (1), *dawn*

SHAHARAIM
7842 Shachărayim (1),
double dawn

SHAHAZIMAH
7831 Shachatsôwm (1),
proudly

SHAKE
2554 châmaç (1), to *be
violent;* to *maltreat*
4571 mâ'ad (1), to *waver*
5128 nûwa' (2), to *waver*
5130 nûwph (5), to
quiver, vibrate, rock

5287 nâ'ar (4), to *tumble*
5426 nᵉthar (Ch.) (1), to
tear off; to *shake off*
6206 'ârats (2), to *dread*
6342 pâchad (1), to *fear*
7264 râgaz (1), to *quiver*
7363 râchaph (1), to
brood; to *be relaxed*
7493 râ'ash (14), to *quake*
660 apótinassō (1), to
brush off, shake off
1621 ĕktinassō (2), to
shake violently
4531 saleúō (1), to *waver*
4579 sĕiō (2), to *agitate*

SHAKED
5128 nûwa' (1), to *waver*

SHAKEN
1607 gâ'ash (1), to *agitate*
5086 nâdaph (1), to
disperse, be windblown
5110 nûwd (1), to *waver*
5128 nûwa' (3), to *waver*
5287 nâ'ar (2), to *tumble*
6327 pûwts (1), to *dash*
7477 râ'al (1), to *reel*
4531 saleúō (11), to *waver*
4579 sĕiō (1), to *agitate*

SHAKETH
2342 chûwl (2), to *writhe*
4131 môwţ (1), to *shake*
5130 nûwph (2), to *rock*
5287 nâ'ar (1), to *tumble*
7264 râgaz (1), to *quiver*

SHAKING
4493 mânôwd (1), *nod*
5363 nôqeph (2),
threshing of olives
7494 ra'ash (3),
vibration, bounding
8573 tᵉnûwphâh (2),
undulation of offerings

SHALEM
8003 shâlêm (1),
complete; friendly; safe

SHALIM
8171 Sha'ălîym (1), *foxes*

SHALISHA
8031 Shâlîshâh (1),
trebled land

SHALLECHETH
7996 Shalleketh (1),
felling of trees

SHALLUM
7967 Shallûwm (27),
retribution

SHALLUN
7968 Shallûwn (1),
retribution

SHALMAI
8014 Salmay (1), *clothed*
8073 Shamlay (1), *clothed*

SHALMAN
8020 Shalman (1),
Shalman

SHALMANESER
8022 Shalman'eçer (2),
Shalmaneser

SHAMA
8091 Shâmâ' (1), *obedient*

SHAMBLES
3111 makĕllŏn (1),
butcher's stall

SHAME
954 bûwsh (9), be
ashamed
955 bûwshâh (4), *shame*
1317 boshnâh (1),
shamefulness
1322 bôsheth (20), *shame*
2616 châçad (1), to
reprove, shame
2659 châphêr (4), to *be
ashamed*
2781 cherpâh (3),
contumely, disgrace
3637 kâlam (6), to *taunt*
3639 kᵉlimmâh (20),
disgrace, scorn
3640 kᵉlimmûwth (1),
disgrace, scorn
6172 'ervâh (1), *disgrace*
7036 qâlôwn (13),
disgrace
8103 shimtsâh (1),
scornful whispering
149 aischrŏn (3),
shameful thing
152 aischunē (5), *shame*
808 aschēmósunē (1),
indecency; shame
818 atimazō (1), to
maltreat, dishonor
819 atimia (1), *disgrace*
1788 ĕntrĕpō (1), to
respect; to *confound*
1791 ĕntrŏpē (2), *shame*
2617 kataischunō (1), to
disgrace or shame
3856 paradĕigmatizō (1),
to *expose to infamy*

SHAMED
937 bûwz (1), *disrespect*
954 bûwsh (1), to be
ashamed
3001 yâbêsh (1), to *dry
up;* to *wither*
8106 Shemer (1),
settlings of wine, *dregs*

SHAMEFACEDNESS
127 aidōs (1), *modesty*

SHAMEFUL
1322 bôsheth (1), *shame*
7022 qîyqâlôwn (1),
disgrace

SHAMEFULLY
3001 yâbêsh (1), to *dry
up;* to *wither*
818 atimazō (1), to
maltreat, dishonor
821 atimŏō (1), to
maltreat, disgrace
5195 hubrizō (1), to
exercise violence, abuse

SHAMELESSLY
1540 gâlâh (1), to *denude*

SHAMER
8106 Shemer (2),
settlings of wine, *dregs*

SHAMETH
3637 kâlam (1), to *taunt*

SHAMGAR
8044 Shamgar (2),
Shamgar

SHAMHUTH
8049 Shamhûwth (1),
desolation

SHAMIR
8053 Shâmûwr (1),
observed
8069 Shâmîyr (3), *thorn*
or (poss.) *diamond*

SHAMMA
8037 Shammâ' (1),
desolation

SHAMMAH
8048 Shammâh (8),
desolation

SHAMMAI
8060 Shammay (6),
destructive

SHAMMOTH
8054 Shammôwth (1),
ruins

SHAMMUA
8051 Shammûwa' (4),
renowned

SHAMMUAH
8051 Shammûwa' (1),
renowned

SHAMSHERAI
8125 Shamshᵉray (1),
sun-like

SHAPE
1491 ĕidŏs (2), *form,
appearance, sight*

SHAPEN
2342 chûwl (1), to *dance,
whirl;* to *writhe* in pain

SHAPES
3667 hŏmŏiōma (1), *form*

SHAPHAM
8223 Shâphâm (1), *baldly*

SHAPHAN
8227 shâphân (30), *hyrax*

SHAPHAT
8202 Shâphâţ (8), *judge*

SHAPHER
8234 Shepher (2), *beauty*

SHARAI
8298 Shâray (1), *hostile*

SHARAIM
8189 Sha'ărayim (1),
double gates

SHARAR
8325 Shârâr (1), *hostile*

SHARE
4282 machăresheth (1),
(poss.) *hoe*

SHAREZER
8272 Shar'etser (2),
Sharetser

SHARON
8289 Shârôwn (6), *plain*

SHARONITE
8290 Shârôwnîy (1),
Sharonite

SHARP
2299 chad (4), *sharp
sword*
2303 chaddûwd (1),
pointed, jagged
2742 chârûwts (2),
threshing-sledge
3913 lâţash (1), to
sharpen; to *pierce*
6697 tsûwr (2), *rock*
6864 tsôr (1), flint-*stone
knife*

SHARPEN

8127 shên (2), *tooth*
8150 shânan (4), to *pierce*
3691 ŏxus (7), *sharp*

SHARPEN
3913 lâṭash (1), to *sharpen; to pierce*
5324 nâtsab (1), to *station*

SHARPENED
2300 châdad (3), to *be, make sharp; severe*
8150 shânan (1), to *pierce; to inculcate*

SHARPENETH
2300 châdad (2), to *be, make sharp; severe*
3913 lâṭash (1), to *sharpen; to pierce*

SHARPER
5114 tŏmŏtĕrŏs (1), *more keen*

SHARPLY
2394 chozqâh (1), *vehemence, harshness*
664 apŏtŏmŏs (1), *abruptly, peremptorily*

SHARPNESS
664 apŏtŏmŏs (1), *abruptly, peremptorily*

SHARUHEN
8287 Shârûwchen (1), *abode of pleasure*

SHASHAI
8343 Shâshay (1), *whitish*

SHASHAK
8349 Shâshaq (2), *pedestrian*

SHAUL
7586 Shâ'ûwl (7), *asked*

SHAULITES
7587 Shâ'ûwlîy (1), *Shalite*

SHAVE
1548 gâlach (12), to *shave*
5674+8593 'âbar (1), to *cross over; to transition*
3587 xuraŏ (1), to *shave*

SHAVED
1494 gâzaz (1), to *shave*
1548 gâlach (3), to *shave*

SHAVEH
7740 Shâvêh (1), *plain*
7741 Shâvêh Qiryâthayim (1), *plain of a double city*

SHAVEN
1548 gâlach (5), to *shave*
3587 xuraŏ (2), to *shave*

SHAVSHA
7798 Shavshâ' (1), *joyful*

SHEAF
485 'ălummâh (2), *sheaf*
5995 'âmîyr (1), *bunch*
6016 'ômer (6), *measure*

SHEAL
7594 She'âl (1), *request*

SHEALTIEL
7597 She'altîy'êl (9), *I have asked God*

SHEAR
1494 gâzaz (4), to *shear*

SHEAR-JASHUB
7610 She'âr Yâshûwb (1), *remnant will return*

SHEARER
2751 kĕirŏ (1), to *shear*

SHEARERS
1494 gâzaz (3), to *shear*

SHEARIAH
8187 She'aryâh (2), *Jehovah has stormed*

SHEARING
1044 Bêyth 'Êqed (1), *house of (the) binding*
1044+7462 Bêyth 'Êqed (1), *house of (the) binding*
1494 gâzaz (1), to *shear*

SHEATH
5084 nâdân (1), *sheath*
8593 ta'ar (6), *scabbard*
2336 thēkē (1), *scabbard*

SHEAVES
485 'ălummâh (3), *sheaf*
5995 'âmîyr (2), *bunch*
6016 'ômer (2), *measure*
6194 'ârêm (1), *sheaf*

SHEBA
7614 She'bâ' (22), *Sheba*
7652 Sheba' (10), *seven*

SHEBAH
7656 Shib'âh (1), *seventh*

SHEBAM
7643 Se'bâm (1), *spice*

SHEBANIAH
7645 She'banyâh (7), *Jehovah has prospered*

SHEBARIM
7671 She'bârîym (1), *ruins*

SHEBER
7669 Sheber (1), *crushing*

SHEBNA
7644 Shebnâ' (9), *growth*

SHEBUEL
7619 She'bûw'êl (3), *captive (or returned) of God*

SHECANIAH
7935 She'kanyâh (2), *Jehovah has dwelt*

SHECHANIAH
7935 She'kanyâh (8), *Jehovah has dwelt*

SHECHEM
7927 She'kem (45), *ridge*
7928 Shekem (17), *shoulder*

SHECHEM'S
7927 She'kem (2), *ridge*

SHECHEMITES
7930 Shikmîy (1), *Shikmite*

SHED
5064 nâgar (1), to *pour*
7760 sûwm (1), to *put*
8210 shâphak (35), to *spill forth; to expend;*
1632 ĕkchĕŏ (11), to *pour*

SHEDDER
8210 shâphak (1), to *spill forth; to expend*

SHEDDETH
8210 shâphak (2), to *spill*

SHEDDING
130 haimatĕkchusia (1), *pouring of blood*

SHEDEUR
7707 She'dêy'ûwr (5), *spreader of light*

SHEEP
3532 kebes (2), *young ram*
3775 keseb (9), *young ram sheep*
6629 tsô'n (111), *flock of sheep or goats*
6792 tsônê' (2), *flock*
7353 râchêl (2), *ewe*
7716 seh (16), *sheep*
4262 prŏbatikŏs (1), *Sheep Gate*
4263 prŏbatŏn (39), *sheep*

SHEEP'S
4263 prŏbatŏn (1), *sheep*

SHEEPCOTE
5116 nâveh (2), *at home; lovely; home*

SHEEPCOTES
1448+6629 ge'dêrâh (1), *enclosure for flocks*

SHEEPFOLD
833+4263 aulē (1), *house; courtyard; sheepfold*

SHEEPFOLDS
1488+6629 gêz (1), *shorn fleece; mown grass*
4356+6629 miklâ'âh (1), *sheep or goat pen*
4942 mishpâth (1), *pair of stalls for cattle*

SHEEPMASTER
5349 nôqêd (1), *owner or tender of sheep*

SHEEPSHEARERS
1494 gâzaz (2), to *shear; shave; destroy*
1494+6629 gâzaz (2), to *shear; shave; destroy*

SHEEPSKINS
3374 mēlōtē (1), *sheep-skin*

SHEET
3607 ŏthŏnē (2), *linen sail cloth*

SHEETS
5466 çâdîyn (2), *shirt*

SHEHARIAH
7841 She'charyâh (1), *Jehovah has sought*

SHEKEL
1235 beqa' (1), *half shekel*
8255 sheqel (41), *standard weight*

SHEKELS
8255 sheqel (45), *standard weight*

SHELAH
7956 Shêlâh (10), *request*
7974 Shelach (1), *spear*

SHELANITES
8024 Shêlânîy (1), *Shelanite*

SHELEMIAH
8018 Shelemyâh (10), *thank-offering of Jehovah*

SHELEPH
8026 Sheleph (2), *extract*

SHELESH
8028 Shelesh (1), *triplet*

SHELOMI
8015 She'lômîy (1), *peaceable*

SHELOMITH
8013 She'lômôwth (4), *pacifications*
8019 She'lômîyth (5), *peaceableness*

SHELOMOTH
8013 She'lômôwth (1), *pacifications*

SHELTER
4268 machăçeh (2), *shelter; refuge*

SHELUMIEL
8017 She'lûmîy'êl (5), *peace of God*

SHEM
8035 Shêm (17), *name*

SHEMA
8087 Shema' (6), *heard*

SHEMAAH
8094 She'mâ'âh (1), *annunciation*

SHEMAIAH
8098 She'ma'yâh (40), *Jehovah has heard*

SHEMARIAH
8114 She'maryâh (4), *Jehovah has guarded*

SHEMEBER
8038 Shem'êber (1), *illustrious*

SHEMER
8106 Shemer (2), *settlings of wine, dregs*

SHEMIDA
8061 She'mîydâ' (2), *name of knowing*

SHEMIDAH
8061 She'mîydâ' (1), *name of knowing*

SHEMIDAITES
8062 She'mîydâ'îy (1), *Shemidaite*

SHEMINITH
8067 she'mîynîyth (3), (poss.) *eight-stringed lyre*

SHEMIRAMOTH
8070 She'mîyrâmôwth (4), *name of heights*

SHEMUEL
8050 She'mûw'êl (3), *heard of God*

SHEN
8129 Shên (1), *crag*

SHENAZAR
8137 Shen'atstsar (1), *Shenatstsar*

SHENIR
8149 She'nîyr (2), *peak*

SHEPHAM
8221 Shephâm (2), *bare*

SHEPHATIAH
8203 Shephatyâh (13), *Jehovah has judged*

SHEPHERD
7462 râ'âh (27), to *tend* a flock, i.e. *pasture* it
7462+6629 râ'âh (1), to *tend* a flock
7473 rô'îy (1), *shepherd*
750 archipŏimēn (1), *head shepherd*
4166 pŏimēn (13), *shepherd*

SHEPHERD'S
7462 râ'âh (1), to *tend* a flock, i.e. *pasture* it
7473 rô'îy (1), *shepherd*

SHEPHERDS
7462 râ'âh (31), to *tend* a flock, i.e. *pasture* it
7462+6629 râ'âh (2), to *tend* a flock
4166 pŏimēn (4), *shepherd*

SHEPHERDS'
7462 râ'âh (1), to *tend* a flock, i.e. *pasture* it

SHEPHI
8195 Shephôw (1), *baldness*

SHEPHO
8195 Shephôw (1), *baldness*

SHEPHUPHAN
8197 Shephûwphâm (1), *serpent-like*

SHERAH
7609 She'ĕrâh (1), *kindred* by blood

SHERD
2789 cheres (1), *pottery*

SHERDS
2789 cheres (1), *pottery*

SHEREBIAH
8274 Shêrêbyâh (8), *Jehovah has brought heat*

SHERESH
8329 Sheresh (1), *root*

SHEREZER
8272 Shar'etser (1), *Sharetser*

SHERIFFS
8614 tiphtay (Ch.) (2), *lawyer, officer*

SHESHACH
8347 Shêshak (2), *Sheshak*

SHESHAI
8344 Shêshay (3), *whitish*

SHESHAN
8348 Shêshân (4), *lily*

SHESHBAZZAR
8339 Shêshbatstsar (4), *Sheshbatstsar*

SHETH
8352 Shêth (2), *put*, i.e. *substituted*

SHETHAR
8369 Shêthâr (1), *Shethar*

SHETHAR-BOZNAI
8370 Shethar Bôwze'nay (4), *Shethar-Bozenai*

SHEVA
7724 Shevâ' (2), *false*

SHEW
1319 bâsar (3), to *announce* (good news)
1540 gâlâh (5), to *reveal*
1971 hakkârâh (1), *respect*, i.e. *partiality*
2324 chăvâ' (Ch.) (13), to *show*
2331 châvâh (5), to *show*
3045 yâda' (12), to *know*
3313 yâpha' (1), to *shine*
5046 nâgad (37), to *announce*
5608 çâphar (5), to *inscribe*; to *enumerate*
6213 'âsâh (21), to *do*
6754 tselem (1), *phantom; idol*
7200 râ'âh (27), to *see*
7760 sûwm (1), to *put*
7896 shîyth (1), to *place*
8085 shâma' (3), to *hear*
312 anaggĕllō (4), to *announce* in detail
322 anadĕiknumi (1), to *indicate, appoint*
518 apaggĕllō (5), to *announce, proclaim*
1165 dĕigmatizō (1), to *exhibit, expose*
1166 dĕiknuō (20), to *show, make known*
1325 didōmi (3), to *give*
1334 diēgĕŏmai (1), to *relate fully, describe*
1731 ĕndĕiknumi (7), to *show, display*
1754 ĕnĕrgĕō (2), to be *active, efficient, work*
1804 ĕxaggĕllō (1), to *declare, proclaim*
1925 ĕpidĕiknumi (6), to *exhibit, call attention to*
2097 ĕuaggĕlizō (1), to *announce good news*
2146 ĕuprŏsōpĕō (1), to *make a good display*
2151 ĕusĕbĕō (1), to *put religion into practice*
2605 kataggĕllō (3), to *proclaim, promulgate*
2698 katatithēmi (1), to *place down, to deposit*
3004 lĕgō (1), to *say*
3056 lŏgŏs (1), *word, matter, thing; Word*
3377 mēnuō (1), to *report, declare*
3936 paristēmi (1), to *stand beside, present*
4392 prŏphasis (1), *pretext, excuse*
5263 hupŏdĕiknumi (2), to *exemplify*
5319 phanĕrŏō (1), to *render apparent*

SHEWBREAD
3899+4635 lechem (4), *food, bread*
3899+6440 lechem (6), *food, bread*

4635 ma'ăreketh (3), *pile of loaves, arrangement*
6440 pânîym (1), *face*
740+4286 artos (3), *loaf of bread*
4286+740 prŏthĕsis (1), *setting forth*

SHEWED
1540 gâlâh (2), to *reveal*
3045 yâda' (5), to *know*
3190 yâṭab (1), to be, *make well*
3384 yârâh (1), to *throw*
5046 nâgad (18), to *announce*
5186 nâṭâh (1), to *stretch*
5414 nâthan (1), to *give*
6213 'âsâh (17), to *do*
6567 pârash (1), to *separate; to disperse*
7200 râ'âh (37), to *see*
7760 sûwm (1), to *put*
8085 shâma' (4), to *hear*
312 anaggĕllō (2), to *announce* in detail
518 apaggĕllō (6), to *announce, proclaim*
1096 ginŏmai (1), to be
1166 dĕiknuō (8), to *show, make known*
1213 dēlŏō (1), to *make plain* by words
1325+1717+1096 didōmi (1), to *give*
1718 ĕmphanizō (1), to *show forth*
1731 ĕndĕiknumi (1), to *show, display*
1925 ĕpidĕiknumi (1), to *exhibit, call attention to*
3170 mĕgalunō (1), to *increase* or *extol*
3377 mēnuō (1), to *report, declare*
3700 ŏptanŏmai (1), to *appear*
3930 parĕchō (1), to *hold near*, i.e. to *present*
3936 paristēmi (1), to *stand beside, present*
4160 pŏiĕō (4), to *make*
4293 prŏkataggĕllō (2), to *predict, promise*
5268 hupŏzugiŏn (1), *donkey*
5319 phanĕrŏō (4), to *render apparent*

SHEWEDST
5414 nâthan (1), to *give*
7200 râ'âh (1), to *see*

SHEWEST
6213 'âsâh (1), to *do*
1166 dĕiknuō (1), to *show*
4160 pŏiĕō (1), to *make*

SHEWETH
1540+241 gâlâh (2), to *denude; uncover*
2331 châvâh (1), to *show*
5046 nâgad (6), to *announce*
6213 'âsâh (2), to *do*
7200 râ'âh (3), to *see*
1166 dĕiknuō (2), to *show*
1658 ĕlĕuthĕrŏs (2), *unrestrained*

SHEWING
263 'achăvâh (Ch.) (1), *solution*
5608 çâphar (1), to *inscribe*; to *enumerate*
6213 'âsâh (2), to *do*
6692 tsûwts (1), to *twinkle*, i.e. *glance*
323 anadĕixis (1), act of public *exhibition*
584 apŏdĕiknumi (1), to *demonstrate*
1731 ĕndĕiknumi (2), to *show, display*
1925 ĕpidĕiknumi (2), to *exhibit, call attention to*
3930 parĕchō (1), to *hold near*, i.e. to *present*

SHIBBOLETH
7641 shibbôl (1), *stream; ear* of grain

SHIBMAH
7643 Sebâm (1), *spice*

SHICRON
7942 Shikkerôwn (1), *drunkenness*

SHIELD
3591 kîydôwn (2), *dart*
4043 mâgên (33), small *shield (buckler)*
6793 tsinnâh (9), large *shield; piercing cold*
2375 thurĕŏs (1), large *door-shaped shield*

SHIELDS
4043 mâgên (15), small *shield (buckler)*
6793 tsinnâh (1), large *shield; piercing cold*
7982 sheleṭ (7), *shield*

SHIGGAION
7692 Shiggâyôwn (1), *dithyramb* or poem

SHIGIONOTH
7692 Shiggâyôwn (1), *dithyramb* or poem

SHIHON
7866 Shî'yôwn (1), *ruin*

SHIHOR
7883 Shîychôwr (1), *dark*, i.e. *turbid*

SHIHOR-LIBNATH
7884 Shîychôwr Libnâth (1), *darkish whiteness*

SHILHI
7977 Shilchîy (2), *armed*

SHILHIM
7978 Shilchîym (1), *javelins* or *sprouts*

SHILLEM
8006 Shillêm (2), *requital*

SHILLEMITES
8016 Shillêmîy (1), *Shilemite*

SHILOAH
7975 Shilôach (1), *small stream*

SHILOH
7886 Shîylôh (1), *tranquil*
7887 Shîylôh (32), *tranquil*

SHILONI
8023 Shîlônîy (1), *Shiloni*

SHILONITE
7888 Shiylôwnîy (5), *Shilonite*

SHILONITES
7888 Shiylôwnîy (1), *Shilonite*

SHILSHAH
8030 Shilshâh (1), *triplication*

SHIMEA
8092 Shim'â' (4), *annunciation*

SHIMEAH
8039 Shim'âh (1), *obedient*
8092 Shim'â' (1), *annunciation*
8093 Shim'âh (2), *annunciation*

SHIMEAM
8043 Shim'âm (1), *obedient*

SHIMEATH
8100 Shim'âth (2), *annunciation*

SHIMEATHITES
8101 Shim'âthiy (1), *Shimathite*

SHIMEI
8096 Shim'iy (41), *famous*
8097 Shim'iy (1), *Shimite*

SHIMEON
8095 Shim'ôwn (1), *hearing*

SHIMHI
8096 Shim'iy (1), *famous*

SHIMI
8096 Shim'iy (1), *famous*

SHIMITES
8097 Shim'iy (1), *Shimite*

SHIMMA
8092 Shim'â' (1), *annunciation*

SHIMON
7889 Shîymôwn (1), *desert*

SHIMRATH
8119 Shimrâth (1), *guardship*

SHIMRI
8113 Shimriy (3), *watchful*

SHIMRITH
8116 Shimrîyth (1), *female guard*

SHIMROM
8110 Shimrôwn (1), *guardianship*

SHIMRON
8110 Shimrôwn (4), *guardianship*

SHIMRON-MERON
8112 Shimrôwn Mᵉr'ôwn (1), *guard of lashing*

SHIMRONITES
8117 Shimrônîy (1), *Shimronite*

SHIMSHAI
8124 Shimshay (Ch.) (4), *sunny*

SHINAB
8134 Shin'âb (1), *father has turned*

SHINAR
8152 Shin'âr (7), *Shinar*

SHINE
215 'ôwr (11), to *be luminous*
1984 hâlal (1), to *shine*
2094 zâhar (1), to *enlighten*
3313 yâpha' (4), to *shine*
5050 nâgahh (3), to *illuminate*
5774 'ûwph (1), to *cover*
6245 'âshath (1), to *be sleek; to excogitate*
6670 tsâhal (1), to *be cheerful; to sound*
826 augazō (1), to *beam forth*
1584 ĕklampō (1), to *be resplendent, shine*
2989 lampō (3), to *radiate brilliancy*
5316 phainō (3), to *shine*

SHINED
215 'ôwr (1), to *be luminous*
1984 hâlal (2), to *shine*
3313 yâpha' (2), to *shine*
5050 nâgahh (1), to *illuminate*
2989 lampō (2), to *radiate brilliancy*
4015 pĕriastraptō (1), *to envelop in light, shine*

SHINETH
166 'âhal (1), to *be bright*
215 'ôwr (2), to *be luminous*
2989 lampō (1), to *radiate*
5316 phainō (5), to *shine*

SHINING
5051 nôgahh (6), *brilliancy*
796 astrapē (1), *lightning; light's glare*
797 astraptō (1), to *flash*
4034 pĕrilampō (1), to *shine all around*
4744 stilbō (1), to *gleam*
5316 phainō (1), to *shine*

SHIP
591 'ŏnîyâh (4), *ship*
5600 çᵉphîynâh (1), *sea-going vessel*
6716 tsîy (1), *ship*
3490 nauklērŏs (1), *ship captain*
3491 naus (1), *boat*
4142 plŏiariŏn (2), *small boat*
4143 plŏiŏn (58), *ship*

SHIPHI
8230 Shiph'îy (1), *copious*

SHIPHMITE
8225 Shiphmîy (1), *Shiphmite*

SHIPHRAH
8236 Shiphrâh (1), *brightness of skies*

SHIPHTAN
8204 Shiphṭân (1), *judge-like*

SHIPMASTER
7227+2259 rab (1), *great*
2942 kubĕrnētēs (1), *helmsman, captain*

SHIPMEN
582+591 'ĕnôwsh (1), *man; person, human*
3492 nautēs (2), *sailor*

SHIPPING
4143 plŏiŏn (1), *ship*

SHIPS
591 'ŏnîyâh (26), *ship*
6716 tsîy (3), *ship*
4142 plŏiariŏn (1), *small boat*
4143 plŏiŏn (8), *boat*

SHIPWRECK
3489 nauagĕō (2), to *be shipwrecked*

SHISHA
7894 Shîyshâ' (1), *whiteness*

SHISHAK
7895 Shîyshaq (7), *Shishak*

SHITRAI
7861 Shiṭray (1), *magisterial*

SHITTAH
7848 shiṭṭâh (1), *acacia*

SHITTIM
7848 shiṭṭâh (27), *acacia*
7851 Shiṭṭîym (5), *acacia*

SHIVERS
4937 suntribō (1), to *crush completely*

SHIZA
7877 Shîyzâ' (1), *Shiza*

SHOA
7772 Shôwa' (1), *rich*

SHOBAB
7727 Shôwbâb (4), *rebellious*

SHOBACH
7731 Shôwbâk (2), (poss.) *thicket*

SHOBAI
7630 Shôbay (2), *captor*

SHOBAL
7732 Shôwbâl (9), *overflowing*

SHOBEK
7733 Shôwbêq (1), *forsaking*

SHOBI
7629 Shôbîy (1), *captor*

SHOCHO
7755 Sôwkôh (1), *hedged*

SHOCHOH
7755 Sôwkôh (2), *hedged*

SHOCK
1430 gâdîysh (1), *stack of sheaves, shock of grain*

SHOCKS
1430 gâdîysh (1), *stack of sheaves, shock of grain*

SHOCO
7755 Sôwkôh (1), *hedged*

SHOD
5274 nâ'al (2), to *fasten up, to put on sandals*

5265 hupŏdĕō (2), to *put on shoes or sandals*

SHOE
5275 na'al (9), *sandal*

SHOE'S
5266 hupŏdĕma (1), *sandal*

SHOELATCHET
8288+5275 sᵉrôwk (1), *sandal thong*

SHOES
4515 man'âl (1), *bolt on gate*
5275 na'al (11), *sandal*
5266 hupŏdĕma (9), *sandal*

SHOHAM
7719 Shôham (1), *beryl*

SHOMER
7763 Shôwmêr (2), *keeper*

SHONE
2224 zârach (1), to *rise; to be bright*
7160 qâran (3), to *shine*
4015 pĕriastraptō (1), to *envelop in light, shine*
4034 pĕrilampō (1), to *shine all around*
5316 phainō (1), to *shine*

SHOOK
1607 gâ'ash (3), to *agitate violently, shake*
5287 nâ'ar (1), to *tumble*
7264 râgaz (1), to *quiver*
7493 râ'ash (2), to *quake*
8058 shâmaṭ (1), to *jostle*
660 apŏtinassō (1), to *brush off, shake off*
1621 ĕktinassō (2), to *shake violently*
4531 salĕuō (1), to *waver*

SHOOT
1272 bârach (1), to *flee*
1869 dârak (1), to *tread; to string a bow*
3034 yâdâh (1), to *throw*
3384 yârâh (10), to *throw, shoot an arrow*
5414 nâthan (2), to *give*
6362 pâṭar (1), to *burst through; to emit*
7971 shâlach (1), to *send away*
4261 prŏballō (1), to *push to the front, germinate*

SHOOTERS
3384 yârâh (1), to *throw, shoot an arrow*

SHOOTETH
3318 yâtsâ' (1), to *go, bring out*
7971 shâlach (1), to *send away*
4160 pŏiĕō (1), to *do*

SHOOTING
5927 'âlâh (1), to *ascend, be high, mount*

SHOPHACH
7780 Shôwphâk (2), *poured*

SHOPHAN
5855 'Åţrôwth
Shôwphân (1), *crowns
of Shophan*

SHORE
2348 chôwph (2), *cove*
7097 qâtseh (1), *extremity*
8193 sâphâh (6), *edge*
123 aigialŏs (6), *beach*
4358 prŏsŏrmizō (1), to
moor to, i.e. *land at*
5491 chĕilŏs (1), *lip*

SHORN
7094 qâtsab (1), to *clip*
2751 kĕirō (3), to *shear*

SHORT
2465 cheled (1), *fleeting*
7114 qâtsar (1), to *curtail*
7138 qârôwb (2), *near*
3641 ŏligŏs (2), *small*
4932 suntĕmnō (2), to *cut
short*, i.e. *do speedily*
4958 sustĕllō (1), to *draw
together*, i.e. *enwrap*
5302 hustĕrĕō (2), to *be
inferior*; to *fall short*
5610 hōra (1), *hour*

SHORTENED
7114 qâtsar (5), to *curtail*
2856 kŏlŏbŏō (4), *shorten*

SHORTER
7114 qâtsar (2), to *curtail*

SHORTLY
4116 mâhar (1), to *hurry*
4120 mᵉhêrâh (1), *hurry*
7138 qârôwb (1), *near*
1722+5034 ĕn (4), *in;
during; because of*
2112 ĕuthĕōs (1), *at once*
5030 tachĕōs (4), *speedily*
5031 tachinŏs (1), *soon*
5032 tachiŏn (2), *more
rapidly, more speedily*

SHOSHANNIM
7799 shûwshan (2), *white
lily; straight trumpet*

SHOSHANNIM-EDUTH
7802 Shûwshan 'Êdûwth
(1), *lily (or trumpet) of
assemblage*

SHOT
3384 yârâh (7), to *shoot*
5927 'âlâh (1), to *ascend,
be high, mount*
7232 râbab (2), to *shoot*
7819 shâchaţ (1), to
slaughter; butcher
7971 shâlach (5), to *send
away*

SHOULD
1163 dĕi (3), *it is (was)
necessary*
3195 mĕllō (25), to
intend, i.e. *be about to*
3784 ŏphĕilō (1), to *owe*

SHOULDER
2220 zᵉrôwa' (2), *arm*
3802 kâthêph (9),
shoulder-piece; wall
7785 shôwq (13), *lower
leg*
7926 shᵉkem (12), *neck*
7929 shikmâh (1),
shoulder-bone

SHOULDERPIECES
3802 kâthêph (4),
shoulder-piece; wall

SHOULDERS
3802 kâthêph (13),
shoulder-piece; wall
7926 shᵉkem (5), *neck*
5606 ōmŏs (2), *shoulder*

SHOUT
1959 hêydâd (1),
acclamation, shout
6030 'ânâh (1), to *shout*
6670 tsâhal (1), to *be
cheerful; to sound*
6681 tsâvach (1), to
screech exultingly
7321 rûwa' (12), to *shout*
7442 rânan (6), to *shout*
7768 shâva' (1), to
halloo, call for help
8643 tᵉrûw'âh (9),
battle-cry; clangor
2019 ĕpiphōnĕō (1), to
exclaim, shout
2752 kĕleuma (1), *cry of
incitement*

SHOUTED
7321 rûwa' (11), to *shout*
7442 rânan (1), to *shout*
7452 rêa' (1), *shout*
8643 tᵉrûw'âh (1),
battle-cry; clangor

SHOUTETH
7442 rânan (1), to *shout*

SHOUTING
1959 hêydâd (4), *shout of
joy*
7321 rûwa' (1), to *shout*
7440 rinnâh (1), *shout*
8643 tᵉrûw'âh (8),
battle-cry; clangor

SHOUTINGS
8663 tᵉshû'âh (1),
crashing or clamor

SHOVEL
7371 rachath (1),
winnowing-fork

SHOVELS
3257 yâ' (9), *shove*

SHOWER
1653 geshem (3), *rain*
3655 ŏmbrŏs (1), *storm*

SHOWERS
1653 geshem (2), *rain*
2230 zerem (1), *flood*
7241 râbîyb (6), *rain*

SHRANK
5384 nâsheh (2),
rheumatic or crippled

SHRED
6398 pâlach (1), to *slice*

SHRINES
3485 naŏs (1), *shrine*

SHROUD
2793 chôresh (1), *forest*

SHRUBS
7880 sîyach (1),
shrubbery

SHUA
7770 Shûwa' (1), *halloo*
7774 Shûw'â' (1), *wealth*

SHUAH
7744 Shûwach (2), *dell*

SHUCHAH
7746 Shûwchâh (1),
chasm
7770 Shûwa' (2), *halloo*

SHUAL
7777 Shûw'âl (2), *jackal*

SHUBAEL
2619 Chăçadyâh (3),
Jehovah has favored

SHUHAM
7748 Shûwchâm (1),
humbly

SHUHAMITES
7749 Shûwchâmîy (2),
Shuchamite

SHUHITE
7747 Shuchîy (5),
Shuchite

SHULAMITE
7759 Shûwlammîyth (2),
peaceful

SHUMATHITES
8126 Shûmâthîy (1),
Shumathite

SHUN
4026 pĕriistēmi (1), to
avoid, shun

SHUNAMMITE
7767 Shûwnammîyth (8),
Shunammitess

SHUNEM
7766 Shûwnêm (3),
quietly

SHUNI
7764 Shûwnîy (2), *quiet*

SHUNITES
7765 Shûwnîy (1),
Shunite

SHUNNED
5288 hupŏstĕllō (1), to
cower or shrink

SHUPHAM
8197 Shᵉphûwphâm (1),
serpent-like

SHUPHAMITES
7781 Shûwphâmîy (1),
Shuphamite

SHUPPIM
8206 Shuppîym (3),
serpents

SHUR
7793 Shûwr (6), *wall*

SHUSHAN
7800 Shûwshan (21), *lily*

SHUSHAN-EDUTH
7802 Shûwshan 'Êdûwth
(1), *lily (or trumpet) of
assemblage*

SHUT
332 'âţar (1), to *close* up
1479 gûwph (1), to *shut*
2902 ţûwach (1), to
whitewash
3607 kâlâ' (4), to *stop*
5274 nâ'al (1), to *lock*
5462 çâgar (55), to *shut*
5463 çᵉgar (Ch.) (1), to
close up
5526 çâkak (1), to
entwine; to fence in
5640 çâtham (2), to *stop*
6113 'âtsar (16), to *hold*
6887 tsârar (1), to *cramp*

SHUTTETH
331 'âţam (1), to *close*
5462 çâgar (1), to *shut*
5640 çâtham (1), to *stop*
6095 'âtsâh (1), to *close*
6105 'âtsam (1), to *be,
make powerful*
2808 klĕiō (3), to *shut*

SHUTTING
5462 çâgar (1), to *shut*

SHUTTLE
708 'ereg (1), *shuttle*

SIA
5517 Çîy'â' (1),
congregation

SIAHA
5517 Çîy'â' (1),
congregation

SIBBECAI
5444 Çibbᵉkay (2),
thicket-like

SIBBECHAI
5444 Çibbᵉkay (2),
thicket-like

SIBBOLETH
5451 Çibbôleth (1), *ear of
grain*

SIBMAH
7643 Sᵉbâm (4), *spice*

SIBRAIM
5453 Çibrayim (1),
double hope

SICHEM
7927 Shᵉkem (1), *ridge*

SICK
605 'ânash (1), to *be frail*
1739 dâveh (1),
menstrual; fainting
2470 châlâh (34), to *be
weak, sick, afflicted*
2483 chŏlîy (1), *malady*
8463 tachălûw' (1),
malady, disease
732 arrhōstŏs (4),
infirmed, ill
770 asthĕnĕō (17), to *be
feeble*
772 asthĕnēs (6), *weak*
2192+2560 ĕchō (8), to
have; hold; keep
2577 kamnō (1), to *sicken*
3885 paralutikŏs (11),
lame person
4445 purĕssō (2), to *burn
with a fever*

SICKLE
2770 chermêsh (2), *sickle*
4038 maggâl (2), *sickle*

SHUTHALHITES
8364 Shûthalchîy (1),
Shuthalchite

SHUTHELAH
7803 Shûwthelach (4),
crash of breakage

SHOPHAN
7092 qâphats (3), to *draw
together, to leap; to die*
8173 shâ'a' (1), to *fondle,
please* or *amuse* (self)
608 apŏklĕiō (1), to *close*
2623 kataklĕiō (2), to
incarcerate, lock up
2808 klĕiō (13), to *close*
4788 sugklĕiō (1), to *net
fish; to lock up* persons

S

1407 drĕpanŏn (8), gathering *hook*

SICKLY
732 arrhôstŏs (1), *infirmed, ill*

SICKNESS
1739 dâveh (1), *menstrual; fainting*
2483 chŏlîy (11), *malady*
4245 machăleh (3), *sickness*
769 asthĕnĕia (1), *feebleness* of body
3554 nŏsŏs (3), *malady*

SICKNESSES
2483 chŏlîy (1), *malady*
8463 tachălûw' (1), *malady, disease*
3554 nŏsŏs (2), *malady*

SIDDIM
7708 Siddîym (3), *flats*

SIDE
2296 châgar (1), to *gird*
2348 chôwph (1), *cove*
3027 yâd (5), *hand; power*
3225 yâmîyn (4), *right*
3409 yârêk (7), *side*
3411 yᵉrêkâh (2), *far away places*
3541 kôh (2), *thus*
3802 kâthêph (29), *side-piece*
4217 mizrâch (2), *east*
4975 môthen (4), *loins*
5048 neged (2), *beside*
5437 çâbab (1), to *surround*
5439 çâbîyb (26), *circle*
5675 'âbar (Ch.) (7), region *across*
5676 'êber (56), *opposite*
6285 pê'âh (50), *direction*
6311 pôh (2), *here*
6654 tsad (20), *side*
6753 Tsᵉlelpôwnîy (2), *shade-facing*
6763 tsêlâ' (22), *side*
6921 qâdîym (1), *East; eastward; east wind*
6924 qedem (3), *East, eastern; antiquity*
6954 Qᵉhêlâthâh (1), *convocation*
7023 qîyr (2), *side-wall*
7097 qâtseh (1), *extremity*
7307 rûwach (5), *breath; wind; life-spirit*
7859 sᵉṭar (Ch.) (1), *side*
8040 sᵉmô'wl (1), *left*
8193 sâphâh (3), *edge*
492 antiparĕrchŏmai (2), to *go along opposite*
1188 dĕxiŏs (2), *right*
1782 ĕntĕuthĕn (2), on *both sides*
3313 mĕrŏs (1), *division*
3840 pantŏthĕn (1), *from, on all* sides
3844 para (15), *besides*
4008 pĕran (13), *across*
4125 plĕura (5), *side*

SIDES
3411 yᵉrêkâh (19), *far away places*
3802 kâthêph (4), *shoulder-piece; wall*
5676 'êber (4), *opposite*

6285 pê'âh (1), *direction*
6654 tsad (9), *side*
6763 tsêlâ' (4), *side*
7023 qîyr (2), *side-wall*
7253 reba' (3), *fourth*
7307 rûwach (1), *breath; wind; life*-spirit

SIDON
6721 Tsîydôwn (2), *fishery*
4605 Sidôn (12), *fishery*

SIDONIANS
6722 Tsîydônîy (5), *Tsidonian*

SIEGE
4692 mâtsôwr (13), *siege-mound; distress*
6696 tsûwr (3), to *cramp*

SIEVE
3531 kᵉbârâh (1), *sieve*
5299 nâphâh (1), *sieve*

SIFT
5128 nûwa' (1), to *waver*
5130 nûwph (1), to *quiver, vibrate, rock*
4617 siniazō (1), to *shake in a sieve*

SIFTED
5128 nûwa' (1), to *waver*

SIGH
584 'ânach (7), to *sigh*

SIGHED
584 'ânach (1), to *sigh*
389 anastĕnazō (1), to *sigh deeply*
4727 stĕnazō (1), to *sigh*

SIGHEST
584 'ânach (1), to *sigh*

SIGHETH
584 'ânach (1), to *sigh*

SIGHING
585 'ânâchâh (5), *sighing*
603 ănâqâh (2), *shrieking, groaning*

SIGHS
585 'ânâchâh (1), *sighing*

SIGHT
2379 chăzôwth (Ch.) (2), *view, visible sight*
4758 mar'eh (18), *appearance; vision*
5048 neged (2), *before*
5869 'ayin (218), *sight*
6440 pânîym (39), *face*
7200 râ'âh (5), to *see*
308 anablĕpō (15), to *look up; to recover sight*
309 anablĕpsis (1), *restoration of sight*
991 blĕpō (2), to *look* at
1491 ĕidŏs (2), *sight*
1715 ĕmprŏsthĕn (3), *in front of*
1726 ĕnantiŏn (1), *in the presence of*
1799 ĕnōpiŏn (21), *before*
2335 thĕōria (1), *sight*
2714 katĕnōpiŏn (2), *directly in front of*
3705 hŏrama (1), supernatural *spectacle*
3706 hŏrasis (1), *appearance, vision*
3788 ŏphthalmŏs (1), *eye*
3844 para (1), *from; with; besides; on account of*

5324 phantazō (1), to *appear; spectacle, sight*

SIGHTS
5400 phŏbĕtrŏn (1), *frightening* thing

SIGN
226 'ôwth (33), *sign*
4159 môwphêth (8), *miracle; token* or *omen*
4864 mas'êth (1), *beacon*
5251 nêç (1), *flag; signal*
6725 tsîyûwn (1), *guiding pillar, monument*
7560 rᵉsham (Ch.) (1), to *record*
3902 parasēmŏs (1), *labeled, marked*
4592 sēmĕiŏn (29), *sign*

SIGNED
7560 rᵉsham (Ch.) (4), to *record*

SIGNET
2368 chôwthâm (8), *signature*-ring, *seal*
2858 chôthemeth (1), *signet ring seal*
5824 'izqâ' (Ch.) (2), *signet* or *signet*-ring

SIGNETS
2368 chôwthâm (1), *signature*-ring, *seal*

SIGNIFICATION
880 aphōnŏs (1), *mute, silent; unmeaning*

SIGNIFIED
4591 sēmainō (2), to *indicate, make known*

SIGNIFIETH
1213 dēlŏō (1), to *make plain* by words

SIGNIFY
1213 dēlŏō (1), to *make plain* by words
1229 diaggĕllō (1), to *herald thoroughly*
1718 ĕmphanizō (1), to *show forth*
4591 sēmainō (1), to *indicate, make known*

SIGNIFYING
1213 dēlŏō (1), to *make plain* by words
4591 sēmainō (3), to *indicate, make known*

SIGNS
226 'ôwth (27), *sign*
852 'âth (3), *sign*
1770 ĕnnĕuō (1), to *signal*
4591 sēmainō (17), to *indicate, make known*
4592 sēmĕiŏn (5), *sign*

SIHON
5511 Çîychôwn (37), *tempestuous*

SIHOR
7883 Shîychôwr (3), *dark*, i.e. *turbid*

SILAS
4609 Silas (13), *sylvan*

SILENCE
481 'âlam (1), to *be silent*
1745 dûwmâh (2), *silence*
1747 dûwmîyâh (1), *silently; quiet, trust*

1820 dâmâh (1), to *be silent; to fail, cease*
1824 dᵉmîy (2), *quiet*
1826 dâmam (6), to *be silent; to be astonished*
1827 dᵉmâmâh (1), *quiet*
2013 hâçâh (3), to *hush*
2790 chârash (5), to *be silent; to be deaf*
2814 châshâh (2), to *hush*
2271 hēsuchia (3), *stillness*
4601 sigaō (3), to *keep silent*
4602 sigē (2), *silence*
5392 phimŏō (2), to *restrain to silence*

SILENT
1748 dûwmâm (1), *silently*
1826 dâmam (4), to *be silent; to be astonished*
1947 hôwlêlâh (1), *folly*
2013 hâçâh (1), to *hush*
2790 chârash (2), to *be silent; to be deaf*

SILK
4897 meshîy (2), *silk*
8336 shêsh (1), *white linen; white marble*
2596 kata (1), *down; according to*

SILLA
5538 Çillâ' (1), *embankment*

SILLY
6601 pâthâh (2), to *be, make simple; to delude*
1133 gunaikariŏn (1), *little*, i.e. *foolish woman*

SILOAH
7975 Shilôach (1), *rill*

SILOAM
4611 Silōam (3), *rill*

SILVANUS
4610 Silŏuanŏs (4), *sylvan*

SILVER
3701 keçeph (280), *silver*
3702 kᵉçaph (Ch.) (12), *silver money*
7192 qᵉsîytah (1), *coin*
693 argurĕŏs (3), *made of silver*
694 arguriŏn (9), *silver*
696 argurŏs (5), *silver*
1406 drachmē (1), *silver coin*

SILVERLINGS
3701 keçeph (1), *silver*

SILVERSMITH
695 argurŏkŏpŏs (1), *worker of silver*

SIMEON
8095 Shim'ôwn (43), *hearing*
8099 Shim'ôniy (1), *Shimonite*
4826 Sumĕōn (6), *hearing*

SIMEONITES
8099 Shim'ôniy (3), *Shimonite*

SIMILITUDE
1823 dᵉmûwth (2), *resemblance, likeness*

8403 tabnîyth (2), *model, resemblance*
8544 tᵉmûwnâh (4), something *fashioned*
3665 hŏmŏiŏtēs (1), *resemblance, similarity*
3667 hŏmŏiōma (1), *form; resemblance*
3669 hŏmŏiōsis (1), *resemblance, likeness*

SIMILITUDES
1819 dâmâh (1), to *liken*

SIMON
4613 Simōn (67), *hearing*

SIMON'S
4613 Simōn (7), *hearing*

SIMPLE
6612 pᵉthîy (17), *silly*
6615 pᵉthayûwth (1), *silliness, i.e. seducible*
172 akakŏs (1), *innocent*
185 akĕraiŏs (1), *innocent*

SIMPLICITY
6612 pᵉthîy (1), *silly*
8537 tôm (1), *innocence*
572 haplŏtēs (3), *sincerity*

SIMRI
8113 Shimriy (1), *watchful*

SIN
817 'âshâm (3), *guilt*
819 'ashmâh (2), *guiltiness*
2398 châṭâ' (68), to *sin*
2399 chêṭ' (22), *crime*
2401 chăṭâ'âh (8), *offence*
2402 chaṭṭâ'âh (Ch.) (2), *offence, and penalty*
2403 chaṭṭâ'âh (215), *offence; sin offering*
2409 chaṭṭâyâ' (Ch.) (1), *expiation, sin offering*
5512 Çîyn (6), *Sin*
5771 'âvôn (1), *moral evil*
6588 pesha' (1), *revolt*
7686 shâgâh (1), to *stray*
264 hamartanō (15), to *miss the mark, to err*
265 hamartēma (1), *sin*
266 hamartia (91), *sin*
361 anamartētŏs (1), *sinless*

SINA
4614 Sina (2), *Sinai*

SINAI
5514 Çîynay (35), *Sinai*
4614 Sina (2), *Sinai*

SINCE
227 'âz (3), *therefore*
310 'achar (2), *after*
518 'îm (1), *whether?; if, although; Oh that!*
1767 day (3), *enough, sufficient*
2008 hênnâh (1), *from here; from there*
3588 kîy (1), *for, that*
4480 min (12), *from*
4480+227 min (1), *from*
4481 min (Ch.) (1), *from*
5750 'ôwd (2), *more*
575 apŏ (9), *from, away*
575+3739 apŏ (3), *from*
1537 ĕk (1), *out, out of*
1893 ĕpĕi (1), *since*

1894 ĕpĕidē (1), *when*
3326 mĕta (1), *after, later*
5613 hōs (1), *which, how*

SINCERE
97 adŏlŏs (1), *pure*
1506 ĕilikrinēs (1), *pure*

SINCERELY
8549 tâmîym (2), *entire*
55 hagnōs (1), *purely*

SINCERITY
8549 tâmîym (1), *integrity*
861 aphtharsia (2), *genuineness*
1103 gnēsiŏs (1), *genuine*
1505 ĕilikrinĕia (3), *purity, sincerity*

SINEW
1517 gîyd (3), *tendon*

SINEWS
1517 gîyd (4), *tendon*
6207 'âraq (1), to *gnaw*

SINFUL
2398 châṭâ' (1), to *sin*
2400 chaṭṭâ' (1), *guilty*
2401 chăṭâ'âh (1), *offence or sacrifice*
266 hamartia (1), *sin*
268 hamartōlŏs (4), *sinner; sinful*

SING
1984 hâlal (2), to *speak praise; thank*
2167 zâmar (33), to *play music*
5414+6963 nâthan (1), to *give*
6030 'ânâh (4), to *sing*
6031 'ânâh (2), to *afflict*
7440 rinnâh (1), *shout*
7442 rânan (25), to *shout*
7788 shûwr (1), to *travel*
7891 shîyr (32), to *sing*
7892 shîyr (1), *singing*
103 a₁dō (1), to *sing*
5214 humnĕō (1), to *celebrate* God in song
5567 psallō (4), to *play a stringed instrument*

SINGED
2761 chărak (Ch.) (1), to *scorch, singe*

SINGER
5329 nâtsach (1), i.e. to *be eminent*
7891 shîyr (1), to *sing*

SINGERS
2171 zammâr (Ch.) (1), *musician*
7891 shîyr (35), to *sing*
7892 shîyr (1), *singing*

SINGETH
7891 shîyr (1), to *sing*

SINGING
2158 zâmîyr (1), *song*
7440 rinnâh (9), *shout*
7442 rânan (2), to *shout for joy*
7445 rᵉnânâh (1), *shout for joy*
7891 shîyr (5), to *sing*
7892 shîyr (4), *singing*
103 a₁dō (2), to *sing*

SINGLE
573 haplŏus (2), *single*

SINGLENESS
572 haplŏtēs (2), *sincerity*
858 aphĕlŏtēs (1), *simplicity; sincerity*

SINGULAR
6381 pâlâ' (1), to *be, make great, difficult*

SINIM
5515 Çîynîym (1), *Sinim*

SINITE
5513 Çîynîy (2), *Sinite*

SINK
2883 ṭâba' (2), to *sink*
8257 shâqa' (1), to *be overflowed; to abate*
1036 buthizō (1), to *sink*
2670 katapŏntizō (1), to *submerge, be drowned*
5087 tithēmi (1), to *place*

SINNED
2398 châṭâ' (102), to *sin*
264 hamartanō (15), to *miss the mark, to sin*
4258 prŏamartanō (2), to *sin previously*

SINNER
2398 châṭâ' (8), to *sin*
2403 chaṭṭâ'âh (1), *offence; sin offering*
268 hamartōlŏs (12), *sinner; sinful*

SINNERS
2400 chaṭṭâ' (16), *guilty*
268 hamartōlŏs (30), *sinner; sinful*
3781 ŏphĕilĕtēs (1), *person indebted*

SINNEST
2398 châṭâ' (1), to *sin*

SINNETH
2398 châṭâ' (13), to *sin*
6213 'âsâh (1), to *do*
7683 shâgag (1), to *sin*
264 hamartanō (7), to *sin*

SINNING
2398 châṭâ' (2), to *sin*

SINS
819 'ashmâh (2), *guiltiness*
2399 chêṭ' (8), *crime*
2403 chaṭṭâ'âh (71), *offence; sin offering*
2408 chăṭîy (Ch.) (1), *sin*
6588 pesha' (2), *revolt*
265 hamartēma (3), *sin*
266 hamartia (78), *sin*
3900 paraptōma (3), *error; transgression*

SION
6726 Tsîyôwn (1), *capital*
7865 Sîy'ôn (1), *peak*
4622 Siōn (7), *capital*

SIPHMOTH
8224 Siphmôwth (1), *Siphmoth*

SIPPAI
5598 Çippay (1), *bason-like*

SIR
113 'âdôwn (1), *sovereign, i.e. controller*
2962 kuriŏs (11), *supreme, controller, Mr.*

SIRAH
5626 Çîrâh (1), *departure*

SIRION
8304 Sᵉrâyâh (2), *Jehovah has prevailed*

SIRS
435 anēr (6), *man; male*
2962 kuriŏs (1), *supreme, controller, Mr.*

SISAMAI
5581 Çiçmay (2), *Sismai*

SISERA
5516 Çîyçᵉrâ' (21), *Sisera*

SISTER
269 'achôwth (91), *sister*
1733 dôwdâh (1), *aunt*
2994 yᵉbêmeth (2), *sister-in-law*
79 adĕlphē (15), *sister*

SISTER'S
269 'achôwth (5), *sister*
79 adĕlphē (1), *sister*
431 anĕpsiŏs (1), *cousin*

SISTERS
269 'achôwth (11), *sister*
79 adĕlphē (8), *sister*

SIT
3427 yâshab (65), to *dwell, to settle*
3488 yᵉthîb (Ch.) (2), to *sit*
5414 nâthan (1), to *give*
5437 çâbab (1), to *surround*
7674 shebeth (1), *rest*
347 anaklinō (6), to *recline*
377 anapiptō (5), *lie down, lean back*
2521 kathēmai (12), to *sit down; to remain*
2523 kathizō (15), to *seat down, dwell*
2621 katakĕimai (1), to *lie down*
2625 kataklinō (2), to *recline, take a place*
4776 sugkathizō (1), to *give, take a seat with*
4873 sunanakĕimai (1), to *recline with at meal*

SITH
518 'îm (1), *whether?; if, although; Oh that!*

SITNAH
7856 Siṭnâh (1), *opposition*

SITTEST
3427 yâshab (6), to *settle*
2521 kathēmai (1), to *sit*

SITTETH
1716 dâgar (1), to *brood over; to care for young*
3427 yâshab (25), to *settle*
345 anakĕimai (2), to *recline at a meal*
2521 kathēmai (10), to *sit down; to reside*
2523 kathizō (3), to *seat down, dwell*

SITTING
3427 yâshab (15), to *settle*
4186 môwshâb (2), *seat*
7257 râbats (1), to *recline*
1910 ĕpibainō (1), to *mount, ascend*

2516 kathĕzŏmai (2), *to sit down, be seated*
2521 kathēmai (21), *to sit down; to reside*
2523 kathizŏ (1), *to seat down, dwell*

SITUATE
3427 yâshab (2), *to settle*
4690 mâtsûwq (1), *column; hilltop*

SITUATION
4186 môwshâb (1), *site*
5131 nôwph (1), *elevation*

SIVAN
5510 Çîyvân (1), *Sivan*

SIX
8337 shêsh (185), *six; sixth*
8353 shêth (Ch.) (1), *six; sixth*
1803 hĕx (11), *six*
1812 hĕxakŏsiŏi (1), *six hundred*
5516 chi xi stigma (1), 666

SIXSCORE
3967+6242 mê'âh (1), *hundred*
8147+6240+7239 shᵉnayim (1), *two-fold*

SIXTEEN
8337+6240 shêsh (22), *six; sixth*
1440+1803 hĕbdŏmĕkŏnta (1), *seventy*

SIXTEENTH
8337+6240 shêsh (3), *six; sixth*

SIXTH
8337 shêsh (2), *six; sixth*
8338 shâwshâw (1), (poss.) *to annihilate*
8341 shâshâh (1), *to divide into sixths*
8345 shishshîy (26), *sixth*
8353 shêth (Ch.) (1), *six; sixth*
1623 hĕktŏs (14), *sixth*

SIXTY
8346 shishshîym (11), *sixty*
1835 hĕxĕkŏnta (3), *sixty*

SIXTYFOLD
1835 hĕxĕkŏnta (1), *sixty*

SIZE
4060 middâh (3), *measure; portion*
7095 qetseb (2), *shape*

SKIES
7834 shachaq (5), *clouds*

SKILFUL
995 bîyn (1), *to discern*
2451 chokmâh (1), *wisdom*
2796 chârâsh (1), *skilled fabricator or worker*
3045 yâda' (2), *to know*
3925 lâmad (1), *to teach*
7919 sâkal (1), *to be or act circumspect*

SKILFULLY
3190 yâṭab (1), *to be, make well*

SKILFULNESS
8394 tâbûwn (1), *intelligence; argument*

SKILL
995 bîyn (1), *to discern*
3045 yâda' (4), *to know*
7919 sâkal (2), *to be or act circumspect*

SKIN
1320 bâsâr (1), *flesh*
1539 geled (1), *skin*
5785 'ôwr (71), *skin*
1193 dĕrmatinŏs (1), made of leather *hide*

SKINS
5785 'ôwr (20), *skin*

SKIP
7540 râqad (1), *to spring*

SKIPPED
7540 râqad (2), *to spring*

SKIPPEDST
5110 nûwd (1), *to waver*

SKIPPING
7092 qâphats (1), *to leap*

SKIRT
3671 kânâph (12), *wing*

SKIRTS
3671 kânâph (2), *wing*
6310 peh (1), *mouth*
7757 shûwl (4), *skirt*

SKULL
1538 gulgôleth (2), *skull*
2898 kraniŏn (3), *skull*

SKY
7834 shachaq (2), *clouds*
3772 ŏuranŏs (5), *sky*

SLACK
309 'âchar (2), *to delay*
6113 'âtsar (1), *to hold back; to maintain, rule*
7423 rᵉmîyâh (1), *remissness; treachery*
7503 râphâh (3), *to slacken*
1019 bradunŏ (1), *to delay, hesitate*

SLACKED
6313 pûwg (1), *to be sluggish; be numb*

SLACKNESS
1022 bradutēs (1), *tardiness, slowness*

SLAIN
2026 hârag (31), *to kill*
2027 hereg (1), *kill*
2076 zâbach (2), *to (sacrificially) slaughter*
2490 châlal (1), *to profane, defile*
2491 châlâl (75), *slain*
2717 chârab (1), *to desolate, destroy*
2873 ṭâbach (1), *to kill*
4191 mûwth (18), *to kill*
5062 nâgaph (2), *to strike*
5221 nâkâh (20), *to kill*
6992 qᵉṭal (Ch.) (4), *to kill*
7523 râtsach (3), *to murder*
7819 shâchaṭ (5), *to slaughter; butcher*
337 anairĕŏ (3), *to take away, murder*
615 apŏktĕinŏ (7), *to kill*

1722+5408+599 ĕn (1), *in; during; because of*
4968 sphagiŏn (1), *offering for slaughter*
4969 sphazŏ (6), *to slaughter or to maim*

SLANDER
1681 dibbâh (3), *slander*

SLANDERED
7270 râgal (1), *to slander*

SLANDERERS
1228 diabŏlŏs (1), *traducer, i.e. Satan*

SLANDEREST
5414+1848 nâthan (1), *to give*

SLANDERETH
3960 lâshan (1), *to calumniate, malign*

SLANDEROUSLY
987 blasphēmĕŏ (1), *to speak impiously*

SLANDERS
7400 râkîyl (2), *scandal-monger*

SLANG
7049 qâla' (1), *to sling*

SLAUGHTER
2027 hereg (4), *kill*
2028 hărêgâh (5), *kill*
2873 ṭâbach (5), *to kill*
2875 Ṭebach (9), *massacre*
2878 ṭibehâh (1), *butchery*
4046 maggêphâh (3), *pestilence; defeat*
4293 maṭbêach (1), *slaughter place*
4347 makkâh (14), *blow; wound; pestilence*
4660 mappâts (1), *striking to pieces*
5221 nâkâh (5), *to kill*
6993 qeṭel (1), *death*
7524 retsach (1), *crushing; murder-cry*
7819 shâchaṭ (5), *to slaughter; butcher*
2871 kŏpĕ (1), *carnage*
4967 sphagē (3), *butchery*
5408 phŏnŏs (1), *slaying*

SLAVES
4983 sōma (1), *body*

SLAY
1194 Bᵉ'ôn (1), *Beon*
2026 hârag (38), *to kill*
2717 chârab (1), *to desolate, destroy*
2763 charam (1), *to devote to destruction*
2873 ṭâbach (1), *to kill, butcher*
2875 Ṭebach (1), *massacre*
4191 mûwth (43), *to kill*
5221 nâkâh (11), *to kill*
5221+5315 nâkâh (1), *to strike, kill*
6991 qâṭal (2), *to put to death*
6992 qᵉṭal (Ch.) (1), *to kill*
7819 shâchaṭ (9), *to slaughter; butcher*

337 anairĕŏ (2), *to take away, murder*
615 apŏktĕinŏ (3), *to kill*
2380 thuŏ (1), *to kill*
2695 katasphattŏ (1), *to slaughter, strike down*

SLAYER
2026 hârag (1), *to kill*
5221 nâkâh (1), *to kill*
7523 râtsach (17), *to murder*

SLAYETH
2026 hârag (2), *to kill*
2490 châlal (1), *to profane, defile*
4191 mûwth (1), *to kill*
7523+5315 râtsach (1), *to murder*

SLAYING
2026 hârag (3), *to kill*
4191 mûwth (1), *to kill*
5221 nâkâh (2), *to kill*
7819 shâchaṭ (1), *to slaughter; butcher*

SLEEP
3462 yâshên (11), *to sleep; to grow old*
3463 yâshên (4), *sleepy*
7290 râdam (3), *to stupefy*
7901 shâkab (11), *to lie*
8139 shᵉnâh (Ch.) (1), *sleep*
8142 shênâh (24), *sleep*
8639 tardêmâh (4), *trance, deep sleep*
1852 ĕxupnizŏ (1), *to waken, rouse*
1853 ĕxupnŏs (1), *awake*
2518 kathĕudō (7), *to fall asleep*
2837 kŏimaŏ (5), *to slumber; to decease*
5258 hupnŏs (6), *sleep*

SLEEPER
7290 râdam (1), *to stupefy*

SLEEPEST
3462 yâshên (1), *to sleep*
7901 shâkab (1), *to lie*
2518 kathĕudō (2), *to fall asleep*

SLEEPETH
3463 yâshên (1), *sleepy*
7290 râdam (1), *to stupefy*
2518 kathĕudō (3), *to fall asleep*
2837 kŏimaŏ (1), *to slumber; to decease*

SLEEPING
1957 hâzâh (1), *to dream*
3463 yâshên (1), *sleepy*
2518 kathĕudō (2), *to fall asleep*
2837 kŏimaŏ (2), *to slumber; to decease*

SLEIGHT
2940 kubĕia (1), *artifice or fraud, deceit*

SLEPT
3462 yâshên (5), *to sleep*
3463 yâshên (1), *sleepy*
5123 nûwm (1), *to slumber*
7901 shâkab (37), *to lie*

2518 kathĕudō (2), to *fall asleep*
2837 kŏimaō (3), to *slumber; to decease*

SLEW
2026 hârag (55), to *kill*
2076 zâbach (3), to (sacrificially) *slaughter*
2126 Zïynâ' (1), well-*fed*
2490 châlal (1), to *profane, defile*
2491 châlâl (3), *slain*
4191 mûwth (40), to *kill*
5221 nâkâh (57), to *kill*
5307 nâphal (1), to *fall*
6992 qᵉtal (Ch.) (2), to *kill*
7819 shâchat (21), to *slaughter; butcher*
337 anairĕō (3), to *take away, murder*
615 apŏktĕinō (4), to *kill*
1315 diachĕirizŏmai (1), to *lay hands* upon
4969 sphazō (2), to *slaughter* or to *maim*
5407 phŏnĕuō (1), to *commit murder*

SLEWEST
5221 nâkâh (1), to *kill*

SLIDDEN
7725 shûwb (1), to *return*

SLIDE
4131 môwt (1), to *slip*
4571 mâ'ad (2), to *waver*

SLIDETH
5637 çârar (1), to *be refractory, stubborn*

SLIGHTLY
7043 qâlal (2), to *be, make light*

SLIME
2564 chêmâr (2), *bitumen*

SLIMEPITS
2564 chêmâr (1), *bitumen*

SLING
4773 margêmâh (1), *sling* for *stones*
7049 qâla' (3), to *sling*
7050 qela' (4), *sling*

SLINGERS
7051 qallâ' (1), *slinger*

SLINGS
7050 qela' (1), *sling*

SLINGSTONES
68+7050 'eben (1), *stone*

SLIP
4131 môwt (1), to *slip*
4571 mâ'ad (3), to *waver*
3901 pararrhuĕō (1), to *flow by,* to pass (*miss*)

SLIPPED
6362 pâtar (1), to *burst through;* to *emit*
8210 shâphak (1), to *spill* forth; to *expend*

SLIPPERY
2513 chelqâh (1), *smoothness; flattery*
2519 chălaqlaqqâh (2), *smooth; treacherous*

SLIPPETH
4131 môwt (2), to *slip*
5394 nâshal (1), to *drop*

SLIPS
2156 zᵉmôwrâh (1), *twig, vine branch*

SLOTHFUL
6101 'âtsal (1), to *be slack*
6102 'âtsêl (8), *indolent*
7423 rᵉmîyâh (2), *remissness; treachery*
7503 râphâh (1), to *slacken*
3576 nôthrŏs (1), *lazy*
3636 ŏknĕrŏs (2), *lazy*

SLOTHFULNESS
6103 'atslâh (2), *indolence*

SLOW
750 'ârêk (10), *patient*
3515 kâbêd (1), *stupid*
692 argŏs (1), *lazy*
1021 bradus (2), *slow*

SLOWLY
1020 braduplŏĕō (1), to *sail slowly*

SLUGGARD
6102 'âtsêl (6), *indolent*

SLUICES
7938 seker (1), *wages*

SLUMBER
5123 nûwm (5), to *slumber*
8572 tᵉnûwmâh (4), *drowsiness, i.e. sleep*
2659 katanuxis (1), *stupor, bewilderment*

SLUMBERED
3573 nustazō (1), to *fall asleep; to delay*

SLUMBERETH
3573 nustazō (1), to *fall asleep; to delay*

SLUMBERINGS
8572 tᵉnûwmâh (1), *drowsiness, i.e. sleep*

SMALL
1571 gam (1), *also; even*
1639 gâra' (1), to *lessen*
1851 daq (5), *small*
1854 dâqaq (5), to *crush*
3190 yâtab (1), to *be, make well*
4213 miz'âr (1), *fewness*
4592 mᵉ'at (9), *little*
4705 mits'âr (2), *little; short* time
4962 math (1), *men*
6694 tsûwq (1), to *pour* out; *melt*
6810 tsâ'îyr (2), *small*
6819 tsâ'ar (1), to *be small; be trivial*
6862 tsar (1), *trouble; opponent*
6994 qâtôn (2), to *be, make diminutive*
6996 qâtân (34), *small*
7116 qâtsêr (2), *short*
1646 ĕlachistŏs (1), *least*
2485 ichthudiŏn (1), *little fish*
3398 mikrŏs (6), *small*
3641 ŏligŏs (5), *small*
3795 ŏpsariŏn (1), *small fish*
4142 plŏiariŏn (1), small *boat*

4979 schŏiniŏn (1), *rope*

SMALLEST
6996 qâtân (1), *small*
1646 ĕlachistŏs (1), *least*

SMART
7321+7451 rûwa' (1), to *shout* for alarm or joy

SMELL
1314 besem (1), *spice*
7306 rûwach (5), to *smell*
7381 rêyach (10), *odor*
7382 rêyach (Ch.) (1), *odor*
2175 ĕuŏdia (1), *fragrance, aroma*

SMELLED
7306 rûwach (2), to *smell*

SMELLETH
7306 rûwach (1), to *smell*

SMELLING
5674 'âbar (2), to *cross over; to transition*
3750 ŏsphrĕsis (1), *smell*

SMITE
1986 hâlam (1), to *strike*
3807 kâthath (1), to *strike*
4272 mâchats (2), to *crush; to subdue*
5062 nâgaph (9), to *strike*
5221 nâkâh (94), to *strike*
5307 nâphal (1), to *fall*
5596 çâphach (1), to *associate; be united*
5606 çâphaq (1), to *clap*
6221 'Ăsîy'êl (2), *made of God*
6375 pîyq (1), *tottering*
1194 dĕrō (1), to *flay*
3960 patassō (5), to *strike*
4474 rhapizō (1), to *slap*
5180 tuptō (3), to *strike*

SMITERS
5221 nâkâh (1), to *strike*

SMITEST
5221 nâkâh (1), to *strike*
1194 dĕrō (1), to *flay*

SMITETH
4272 mâchats (1), to *crush; to subdue*
5221 nâkâh (11), to *strike*
5180 tuptō (1), to *strike*

SMITH
2796 chârâsh (2), skilled *fabricator* or worker
2796+1270 chârâsh (1), skilled *fabricator*

SMITHS
4525 maçgêr (4), *prison; craftsman*

SMITING
5221 nâkâh (5), to *strike*

SMITTEN
1792 dâkâ' (1), to *pulverize; be contrite*
3807 kâthath (1), to *strike*
5060 nâga' (1), to *strike*
5062 nâgaph (15), to *inflict; to strike*
5221 nâkâh (43), to *strike*
4141 plēssō (1), to *pound*
5180 tuptō (1), to *strike*

SMOKE
6225 'âshan (5), to *envelope in smoke*

4979 schŏiniŏn (1), *rope*

6227 'âshân (24), *smoke*
7008 qîytôwr (3), *fume*
2586 kapnŏs (13), *smoke*

SMOKING
3544 kêheh (1), *feeble; obscure*
6226 'âshên (2), *smoky*
6227 'âshân (1), *smoke*
5187 tuphŏō (1), to *inflate* with self-conceit

SMOOTH
2509 châlâq (1), *smooth*
2511 challâq (1), *smooth*
2512 challûq (1), *smooth*
2513 chelqâh (2), *smoothness; flattery*
3006 lĕiŏs (1), *smooth*

SMOOTHER
2505 châlaq (1), to *be smooth; be slippery*
2513 chelqâh (1), *smoothness; flattery*

SMOOTHETH
2505 châlaq (1), to *be smooth; be slippery*

SMOTE
1986 hâlam (2), to *strike*
3766 kâra' (1), to *prostrate*
4223 mᵉchâ' (Ch.) (2), to *strike; to impale*
4277 mâchaq (1), to *crush*
4347 makkâh (1), *blow*
5060 nâga' (2), to *strike*
5062 nâgaph (6), to *strike*
5221 nâkâh (194), to *strike*
5368 nᵉqash (Ch.) (1), to *knock; to be frightened*
5606 çâphaq (2), to *clap*
8628 tâqa' (1), to *slap*
851 aphairĕō (1), to *remove, cut off*
1194 dĕrō (1), to *flay, i.e.* to *scourge* or *thrash*
1325+4475 didōmi (1), to *give*
3817 paiō (4), to *hit*
3960 patassō (4), to *strike*
4474 rhapizō (1), to *strike*
5180 tuptō (4), to *strike*

SMOTEST
5221 nâkâh (1), to *strike*

SMYRNA
4667 Smurna (1), *myrrh*
4668 Smurnaiŏs (1), *inhabitant of Smyrna*

SNAIL
2546 chômet (1), *lizard*
7642 shablûwl (1), *snail*

SNARE
2256 chebel (1), *band*
3369 yâqôsh (1), to *trap*
4170 môwqêsh (14), *noose*
4686 mâtsûwd (2), *net*
5367 nâqash (1), to *entrap* with a noose
6315 pûwach (1), to *blow, to fan, kindle;* to *utter*
6341 pach (17), *net*
6354 pachath (1), *pit for catching animals*
6983 qôwsh (1), to *set a trap*
7639 sᵉbâkâh (1), *snare*

1029 brŏchŏs (1), *noose*
3803 pagis (5), *trap; trick*

SNARED
3369 yâqôsh (5), to *trap*
4170 môwqêsh (1), *noose*
5367 nâqash (2), to *entrap* with a noose
6351 pâchach (1), to *spread a net*

SNARES
3353 yâqûwsh (1), *snarer*
4170 môwqêsh (6), *noose*
4685 mâtsôwd (1), *snare*
5367 nâqash (1), to *entrap* with a noose
6341 pach (6), *net*

SNATCH
1504 gâzar (1), to *destroy*

SNEEZED
2237 zârar (1), to *sneeze*

SNORTING
5170 nachar (1), *snorting*

SNOUT
639 'aph (1), *nose, nostril*

SNOW
7949 shâlag (1), to *be snow-white*
7950 sheleg (19), *white snow*
8517 tᵉlag (Ch.) (1), *snow*
5510 chiŏn (3), *snow*

SNOWY
7950 sheleg (1), *white snow*

SNUFFDISHES
4289 machtâh (3), *pan for live coals*

SNUFFED
5301 nâphach (1), to *inflate, blow, expire*
7602 shâ'aph (1), to *be angry; to hasten*

SNUFFERS
4212 mᵉzammᵉrâh (5), *tweezer, trimmer*
4457 melqâch (1), *pair of tweezers or tongs*

SNUFFETH
7602 shâ'aph (1), to *be angry; to hasten*

SOAKED
7301 râvâh (1), to *slake*

SOBER
3524 nēphalĕŏs (2), *circumspect, temperate*
3525 nēphō (4), to *abstain* from wine
4993 sōphrŏnĕō (3), to *be in a right state of mind*
4994 sōphrŏnizō (1), to *discipline or correct*
4998 sōphrōn (2), *self-controlled*

SOBERLY
1519+4993 ĕis (1), to
4996 sōphrŏnōs (1), *with sound mind*

SOBERNESS
4997 sōphrŏsunē (1), *self-control, propriety*

SOBRIETY
4997 sōphrŏsunē (2), *self-control, propriety*

SOCHO
7755 Sôwkôh (1), *hedged*

SOCHOH
7755 Sôwkôh (1), *hedged*

SOCKET
134 'eden (1), *footing*

SOCKETS
134 'eden (52), *footing*

SOCOH
7755 Sôwkôh (2), *hedged*

SOD
1310 bâshal (1), to *boil*
2102 zûwd (1), to *seethe*

SODDEN
1310 bâshal (5), to *boil*
1311 bâshêl (1), *boiled*

SODERING
1694 debeq (1), *solder*

SODI
5476 Çôwdîy (1), *confidant*

SODOM
5467 Çᵉdôm (39), *volcanic or bituminous*
4670 Sŏdŏma (9), *volcanic or bituminous*

SODOMA
4670 Sŏdŏma (1), *volcanic or bituminous*

SODOMITE
6945 qâdêsh (1), *sacred male prostitute*

SODOMITES
6945 qâdêsh (3), *sacred male prostitute*

SOFT
4127 mûwg (1), to *soften*
7390 rak (3), *tender*
7401 râkak (1), to *soften*
3120 malakŏs (3), *soft*

SOFTER
7401 râkak (1), to *soften*

SOFTLY
328 'aṭ (3), *gently, softly*
3814 lâ'ṭ (1), *silently*
3909 lâṭ (1), *covertly*
5285 hupŏpnĕō (1), to *breathe gently*

SOIL
7704 sâdeh (1), *field*

SOJOURN
1481 gûwr (30), to *sojourn*
4033 mâgûwr (1), *abode*
1510+3941 ĕimi (1), I *exist, I am*

SOJOURNED
1481 gûwr (11), to *sojourn*
3939 parŏikĕō (1), to *reside* as a foreigner

SOJOURNER
1616 gêr (1), *foreigner*
8453 tôwshâb (7), *temporary dweller*

SOJOURNERS
1481 gûwr (1), to *sojourn*
8453 tôwshâb (2), *temporary dweller*

SOJOURNETH
1481 gûwr (15), to *sojourn*

SOJOURNING
1481 gûwr (1), to *sojourn*
4186 môwshâb (1), *seat*

3940 parŏikia (1), *foreign residence*

SOLACE
5965 'âlaç (1), to *leap for joy*, i.e. *exult, wave*

SOLD
935+4242 bôw' (1), to *go*
4376 mâkar (45), to *sell*
4465 mimkâr (5), *merchandise*
7666 shâbar (2), to *deal*
591 apŏdidōmi (3), to *give away*
4097 pipraskō (9), to *sell*
4453 pōlĕō (14), to *barter*

SOLDIER
4757 stratiōtēs (4), *common warrior*
4758 stratŏlŏgĕō (1), to *enlist* in the army

SOLDIERS
1121 bên (1), *son, descendant; people*
2428 chayil (1), *army*
2502 châlats (1), to *equip*
6635 tsâbâ' (1), *army*
4753 stratĕuma (1), *body of troops*
4754 stratĕuŏmai (1), to *serve* in military
4757 stratiōtēs (21), *common warrior*

SOLDIERS'
4757 stratiōtēs (1), *common warrior*

SOLE
3709 kaph (12), *sole*

SOLEMN
2282 chag (3), *solemn festival*
2287 châgag (1), to *observe* a festival
4150 môw'êd (14), *assembly*
6116 'ătsârâh (10), *assembly*

SOLEMNITIES
4150 môw'êd (3), *assembly*

SOLEMNITY
2282 chag (3), *solemn festival*
4150 môw'êd (1), *assembly*

SOLEMNLY
5749 'ûwd (2), to *protest, testify; to encompass*

SOLES
3709 kaph (7), *sole* of foot

SOLITARILY
910 bâdâd (1), *separate*

SOLITARY
910 bâdâd (1), *separate*
1565 galmûwd (2), *sterile, barren, desolate*
3173 yâchîyd (1), *only son*
3452 yᵉshîymôwn (1), *desolation*
6723 tsîyâh (1), *desert*
2048 ĕrēmŏs (1), *remote place, deserted place*

SOLOMON
8010 Shᵉlômôh (271), *peaceful*

4672 Sŏlŏmōn (9), *peaceful*

SOLOMON'S
8010 Shᵉlômôh (22), *peaceful*
4672 Sŏlŏmōn (3), *peaceful*

SOME
259 'echâd (7), *first*
428 'êl-leh (3), *these*
582 'ĕnôwsh (2), *person*
1697 dâbâr (1), *thing*
4592 mᵉ'aṭ (2), *little*
7097 qâtseh (2), *extremity*
243 allŏs (9), *other*
1520 hĕis (2), *one*
2087 hĕtĕrŏs (2), *other*
3381 mēpōs (1), *lest somehow*
3588 hŏ (7), "*the,*" i.e. the definite article
4218 pŏtĕ (1), *some* time
5100 tis (79), *some*

SOMEBODY
5100 tis (2), *some* or *any*

SOMETHING
4745 miqreh (1), *accident or fortune*
5100 tis (5), *some* or *any*

SOMETIME
4218 pŏtĕ (2), *some* time

SOMETIMES
4218 pŏtĕ (3), *some* time

SOMEWHAT
3544 kêheh (5), *feeble*
3972 mᵉ'ûwmâh (1), *something; anything*
3313 mĕrŏs (1), *division*
5100 tis (6), *some* or *any*

SON
1121 bên (1798), *son, descendant; people*
1125 Ben-'Ăbîynâdâb (1), (the) *son of Abinadab*
1127 Ben-Geber (1), *son of* (the) *hero*
1128 Ben-Deqer (1), *son of piercing*
1133 Ben-Chûwr (1), *son of Chur*
1136 Ben-Cheçed (1), *son of kindness*
1247 bar (Ch.) (7), *son*
1248 bar (4), *son, heir*
2859 châthan (5), to *become related*
2860 châthân (7), *relative; bridegroom*
3025 yâgôr (1), to *fear*
3173 yâchîyd (1), *only son*
4497 mânôwn (1), *heir*
5209 nîyn (2), *progeny*
5220 neked (1), *offspring*
431 anĕpsiŏs (1), *cousin*
3816 pais (3), *child; slave*
5043 tĕknŏn (14), *child*
5048 tĕlĕiŏō (1), to *perfect, complete*
5207 huiŏs (304), *son*

SON'S
1121 bên (21), *son*
5220 neked (1), *offspring*

SONG
2176 zimrâth (3), *song*
4853 massâ' (3), *burden, utterance*

SONGS (cont.)
5058 negîynâh (4), *instrument, poem*
7892 shîyr (62), *song*
5603 ōidē (5), *religious chant or ode*

SONGS
2158 zâmîyr (3), *song*
5058 negîynâh (1), *instrument; poem*
7438 rôn (1), *shout of deliverance*
7440 rinnâh (1), *shout*
7892 shîyr (12), *song*
5603 ōidē (2), *religious chant or ode*

SONS
1121 bên (1024), *son*
1123 bên (Ch.) (3), *son*
2860 châthân (2), *relative; bridegroom*
3206 yeled (3), *young male*
3211 yâlîyd (2), *born; descendants*
5043 tĕknŏn (6), *child*
5206 huiŏthĕsia (1), *placing as a son*
5207 huiŏs (24), *son*

SONS'
1121 bên (26), *son*

SOON
834 'âsher (6), *because, in order that*
1571 gam (1), *also; even*
2440 chîysh (1), *hurry*
4116 mâhar (3), to *hurry*
4120 mehêrâh (1), *hurry*
4592 me'aṭ (2), *little*
4758 mar'eh (1), *appearance; vision*
7116 qâtsêr (1), *short*
7323 rûwts (1), to *run*
1096 ginŏmai (1), to be
2112 ĕuthĕŏs (2), *soon*
3711 ŏrgilŏs (1), *irascible, hot-tempered*
3752 hŏtan (2), *inasmuch as, at once*
3753 hŏtĕ (2), *when; as*
3916 parachrēma (1), *instantly, immediately*
5030 tachĕŏs (2), *speedily, rapidly*

SOONER
5032 tachiŏn (1), *more rapidly, more speedily*

SOOTHSAYER
7080 qâçam (1), to *divine magic*

SOOTHSAYERS
1505 gezar (Ch.) (4), to *determine by divination*
6049 'ânan (2), to *cover, becloud; to act covertly*

SOOTHSAYING
3132 mantĕuŏmai (1), to *utter spells, fortune-tell*

SOP
5596 psōmiŏn (4), *morsel*

SOPATER
4986 Sōpatrŏs (1), *of a safe father*

SOPE
1287 bôrîyth (2), *alkali soap*

SOPHERETH
5618 Çôphereth (2), *female scribe*

SORCERER
3097 magŏs (2), *Oriental scientist, i.e. magician*

SORCERERS
3784 kâshaph (3), to *enchant*
3786 kashshâph (1), *magician, sorcerer*
5332 pharmakĕus (1), *magician, sorcerer*
5333 pharmakŏs (1), *magician, sorcerer*

SORCERESS
6049 'ânan (1), to *cover, becloud; to act covertly*

SORCERIES
3785 kesheph (2), *sorcery*
3095 magĕia (1), *sorcery*
5331 pharmakĕia (2), *magic, witchcraft*

SORCERY
3096 magĕuŏ (1), to *practice magic, sorcery*

SORE
1419 gâdôwl (3), *great*
2388 châzaq (4), to *fasten upon; to seize*
2389 châzâq (3), *severe*
2470 châlâh (2), to be *weak, sick, afflicted*
3027 yâd (1), *hand; power*
3510 kâ'ab (2), to feel *pain; to grieve; to spoil*
3513 kâbad (3), to be *heavy, severe, dull*
3515 kâbêd (4), *severe*
3708 ka'aç (1), *vexation*
3966 me'ôd (22), *very*
4834 mârats (1), to be *pungent or vehement*
5061 nega' (5), *inflliction; affliction; leprous spot*
5704+3966 'ad (1), *as far (long) as; during*
7185 qâshâh (1), to be *tough or severe*
7186 qâsheh (1), *severe*
7188 qâshach (1), to be, *make unfeeling*
7235 râbâh (1), to *increase*
7451 ra' (9), *bad; evil*
7690 saggîy' (Ch.) (1), *large*
8178 sa'ar (1), *tempest; terror*
23 aganaktĕŏ (1), to be *indignant*
1568 ĕkthambĕŏ (1), to *astonish utterly*
1630 ĕkphŏbŏs (1), *frightened out*
1668 hĕlkŏs (1), *sore*
2425 hikanŏs (1), *ample*
2560 kakŏs (1), *badly; wrongly; ill*
3029 lian (1), *very much*
3173 mĕgas (1), *great*
4183 pŏlus (1), *much*
4970 sphŏdra (1), *much*

SOREK
7796 Sôwrêq (1), *vine*

SORELY
4843 mârar (1), to *embitter*

SORER
5501 chĕirōn (1), *more evil or aggravated*

SORES
4347 makkâh (1), *wound*
1668 hĕlkŏs (2), *sore*
1669 hĕlkŏō (1), to be *ulcerous*

SORROW
17 'ăbôwy (1), *want*
205 'âven (1), *trouble, vanity, wickedness*
592 'ănîyâh (1), *groaning*
1669 dâ'ab (1), to *pine*
1670 de'âbâh (1), *pining*
1671 de'âbôwn (1), *pining*
1674 de'âgâh (1), *anxiety*
1727 dûwb (1), to *pine*
2342 chûwl (1), to *dance, whirl;* to *writhe* in pain
2427 chîyl (2), *throe*
2490 châlal (1), to *profane, defile*
3015 yâgôwn (12), *sorrow*
3511 ke'êb (3), *suffering*
3708 ka'aç (4), *vexation*
4044 meginnâh (1), *covering, veil*
4341 mak'ôb (6), *anguish*
4620 ma'ătsêbâh (1), *anguish* place
5999 'âmâl (2), *worry*
6089 'etseb (2), *painful toil; mental pang*
6090 'ôtseb (1), *pain*
6093 'itstsâbôwn (2), *labor or pain*
6094 'atstsebeth (2), *pain or wound, sorrow*
6862 tsar (1), *trouble; opponent*
7451 ra' (1), *bad; evil*
7455 rôa' (1), *badness*
8424 tûwgâh (1), *grief*
3076 lupĕŏ (1), to be sad
3077 lupē (10), *sadness*
3601 ŏdunē (1), *grief*
3997 pĕnthŏs (3), *grief*

SORROWED
3076 lupĕŏ (2), to be sad

SORROWETH
1672 dâ'ag (1), be *anxious, be afraid*

SORROWFUL
1669 dâ'ab (1), to *pine*
1741 devay (1), *sickness*
2342 chûwl (1), to *dance, whirl;* to *writhe* in pain
3013 yâgâh (1), to *grieve*
3510 kâ'ab (2), to feel *pain; to grieve; to spoil*
7186 qâsheh (1), *severe*
253 alupŏtĕrŏs (1), *more without grief*
3076 lupĕŏ (6), to be sad
4036 pĕrilupŏs (4), *intensely sad*

SORROWING
3600 ŏdunaŏ (2), to *grieve*

SORROWS
2256 chebel (10), *company, band*
4341 mak'ôb (5), *anguish*

6089 'etseb (1), *pang*
6094 'atstsebeth (2), *pain*
6735 tsîyr (1), *trouble*
3601 ŏdunē (1), *grief*
5604 ōdin (2), *pang*

SORRY
1672 dâ'ag (1), be *anxious, be afraid*
2470 châlâh (1), to be *weak, sick, afflicted*
5110 nûwd (1), to *console*
6087 'âtsab (1), to *worry*
3076 lupĕŏ (9), to be sad
4036 pĕrilupŏs (1), *intensely sad*

SORT
1524 gîyl (1), *age, stage*
1697 dâbâr (1), *thing*
3660 kenêmâ' (Ch.) (1), *so or thus*
3671 kânâph (2), *edge*
516 axiōs (1), *suitable*
3313 mĕrŏs (1), *division*
3697 hŏpŏiŏs (1), *what kind of, what sort of*

SORTS
4358 miklôwl (1), *perfection; splendidly*
4360 miklûl (1), *perfectly splendid garment*

SOSIPATER
4989 Sōsipatrŏs (1), *of a safe father*

SOSTHENES
4988 Sōsthĕnēs (2), *of safe strength*

SOTAI
5479 Çôwṭay (2), *roving*

SOTTISH
5530 çâkâl (1), *silly*

SOUGHT
1156 be'â' (Ch.) (1), to *seek or ask*
1158 bâ'âh (3), to *ask*
1245 bâqash (55), to *search; to strive after*
1875 dârash (25), to *seek or ask; to worship*
2713 châqar (1), to *examine, search*
8446 tûwr (1), to *wander*
327 anazētĕŏ (1), to *search out*
1567 ĕkzētĕŏ (1), to *seek*
1934 ĕpizētĕŏ (1), to *search (inquire) for*
2212 zētĕŏ (36), to *seek*

SOUL
5082 nedîybâh (1), *nobility, i.e. reputation*
5315 nephesh (416), *soul*
5590 psuchē (39), *soul*

SOUL'S
5315 nephesh (1), *soul*

SOULS
5315 nephesh (58), *soul*
5397 neshâmâh (1), *breath, life*
5590 psuchē (19), *soul*

SOUND
1899 hegeh (1), *muttering; rumbling*
1902 higgâyôwn (1), *musical notation*

1993 hâmâh (3), to *be in great commotion*
4832 marpê' (1), *cure; deliverance; placidity*
5674 'âbar (2), to *cross over; to transition*
6310 peh (1), *mouth*
6963 qôwl (39), *sound*
7032 qâl (Ch.) (4), *sound*
7321 rûwa' (2), to *shout*
8085 shâma' (3), to *hear*
8454 tûwshîyâh (3), *ability, help*
8549 tâmîym (1), *entire, complete; integrity*
8629 têqa' (1), *blast of a trumpet*
8643 t⁽ᵉ⁾rûw'âh (1), *battle-cry; clangor*
2279 êchôs (2), *roar*
4537 salpizō (5), to *sound a trumpet blast*
4995 sōphrŏnismŏs (1), *self-control*
5198 hugiainō (8), to *have sound health*
5199 hugiēs (1), *well*
5353 phthŏggŏs (1), *utterance; musical*
5456 phōnē (8), *sound*

SOUNDED
2690 châtsar (3), to *blow the trumpet*
2713 châqar (1), to *search*
8628 tâqa' (2), to *clatter, slap, drive, clasp*
1001 bŏlizō (2), to *heave a weight*
1096 ginŏmai (1), to *be*
1837 ĕxĕchĕŏmai (1), to *echo forth*, i.e. *resound*
4537 salpizō (7), to *sound a trumpet blast*

SOUNDING
1906 hêd (1), *shout of joy*
1995 hâmôwn (1), *noise*
2690 châtsar (3), to *blow the trumpet*
8085 shâma' (1), to *hear*
8643 t⁽ᵉ⁾rûw'âh (2), *battle-cry; clangor*
2278 êchĕō (1), to *reverberate, ring out*

SOUNDNESS
4974 m⁽ᵉ⁾thôm (3), *wholesomeness*
3647 hŏlŏklēria (1), *wholeness*

SOUNDS
5353 phthŏggŏs (1), *utterance; musical*

SOUR
1155 bôçer (4), *immature, sour grapes*
5493 çûwr (1), to *turn off*

SOUTH
1864 dârôwm (17), *south; south wind*
2315 cheder (1), *apartment, chamber*
3220 yâm (1), *sea; west*
3225 yâmîyn (3), *south*
4057 midbâr (1), *desert*
5045 negeb (97), *South*
8486 têymân (14), *south; southward; south wind*
3047 lips (1), *southwest*

3314 mĕsēmbria (1), *midday; south*
3558 nŏtŏs (7), *south*

SOUTHWARD
5045 negeb (17), *south*
8486 têymân (7), *south*

SOW
2232 zâra' (28), to *sow seed; to disseminate*
4687 spĕirō (8), to *scatter*, i.e. *sow seed*
5300 hus (1), *swine*

SOWED
2232 zâra' (2), to *sow seed; to disseminate*
4687 spĕirō (8), to *scatter*, i.e. *sow seed*

SOWEDST
2232 zâra' (1), to *sow seed; to disseminate*

SOWER
2232 zâra' (2), to *sow seed; to disseminate*
4687 spĕirō (6), to *scatter*, i.e. *sow seed*

SOWEST
4687 spĕirō (3), to *scatter*, i.e. *sow seed*

SOWETH
2232 zâra' (2), to *sow seed; to disseminate*
4900 mâshak (1), to *draw out; to be tall*
7971 shâlach (3), to *send away*
4687 spĕirō (9), to *scatter*, i.e. *sow seed*

SOWING
2221 zêrûwa' (1), *plant*
2233 zera' (1), *seed; fruit, plant, sowing-time*

SOWN
2221 zêrûwa' (1), *plant*
2232 zâra' (14), to *sow seed; to disseminate*
4218 mizrâ' (1), *planted field*
4687 spĕirō (15), to *scatter*, i.e. *sow seed*

SPACE
1366 g⁽ᵉ⁾bûwl (2), *border*
3117 yôwm (3), *day; time*
4390 mâlê' (1), to *fill*
4725 mâqôwm (1), *place*
5750 'ôwd (1), *again*
7281 rega' (1), *very short space of time*
7305 revach (1), *room*
7350 râchôwq (1), *remote*
575 apŏ (1), *from, away*
1024 brachus (1), *short*
1292 diastēma (1), *interval* of *time*
1339 diïstēmi (1), to *remove, intervene*
1909 ĕpi (3), *on, upon*
4158 pŏdērēs (1), *robe reaching the ankles*
5550 chrŏnŏs (2), *space of time, period*

SPAIN
4681 Spania (2), *Spania*

SPAKE
559 'âmar (109), to *say*
560 'ămar (Ch.) (1), to *say*

981 bâṭâ' (1), to *babble*
1696 dâbar (318), to *say*
4449 m⁽ᵉ⁾lal (Ch.) (2), to *speak, say*
5002 n⁽ᵉ⁾ûm (1), *oracle*
6030 'ânâh (3), to *respond*
6032 'ănâh (Ch.) (14), to *respond, answer*
400 anaphōnĕō (1), to *exclaim*
483 antilĕgō (2), to *dispute, refuse*
626 apŏlŏgĕŏmai (1), to *give an account*
2036 ĕpō (30), to *speak*
2046 ĕrĕō (3), to *utter*
2551 kakŏlŏgĕō (1), to *revile, curse*
2980 lalĕō (72), to *talk*
3004 lĕgō (17), to *say*
4227 Pŏudēs (1), *modest*
4377 prŏsphōnĕō (3), to *address, exclaim*
4814 sullalĕō (1), to *talk together*, i.e. *converse*
5537 chrēmatizō (1), to *utter an oracle*

SPAKEST
559 'âmar (1), to *say*
1696 dâbar (8), to *speak*
1697 dâbâr (1), *word*

SPAN
2239 zereth (7), *span*
2949 ṭippûch (1), *nursing, caring for*

SPANNED
2946 ṭâphach (1), to *extend, spread out*

SPARE
2347 chûwç (14), to *be compassionate*
2550 châmal (13), to *spare, have pity on*
2820 châsak (3), to *refuse, spare, preserve*
5375 nâsâ' (3), to *lift up*
5545 çâlach (1), to *forgive*
8159 shâ'âh (1), to *inspect, consider*
4052 pĕrissĕuō (1), to *superabound*
5339 phĕidŏmai (4), to *treat leniently*

SPARED
2347 chûwç (2), to *be compassionate*
2550 châmal (4), to *spare, have pity on*
2820 châsak (2), to *refuse, spare, preserve*
5339 phĕidŏmai (4), to *treat leniently*

SPARETH
2550 châmal (1), to *spare, have pity on*
2820 châsak (3), to *refuse, spare, preserve*

SPARING
5339 phĕidŏmai (1), to *treat leniently*

SPARINGLY
5340 phĕidŏmĕnōs (2), *stingily, sparingly*

SPARK
5213 nîytsôwts (1), *spark*
7632 shâbîyb (1), *flame*

SPARKLED
5340 nâtsats (1), to *be bright-colored*

SPARKS
1121+7565 bên (1), *son, descendant; people*
2131 zîyqâh (2), *flash*
3590 kîydôwd (1), *spark*

SPARROW
6833 tsippôwr (2), *little hopping bird*

SPARROWS
4765 strŏuthiŏn (4), *little sparrow*

SPAT
4429 ptuō (1), to *spit*

SPEAK
559 'âmar (47), to *say*
560 'ămar (Ch.) (2), to *say*
1680 dâbab (1), to *move slowly*, i.e. *glide*
1696 dâbar (276), to *speak*
1897 hâgâh (3), to *murmur, utter a sound*
2790 chârash (1), to *engrave; to plow*
4405 millâh (1), *word; discourse; speech*
4448 mâlal (1), to *speak*
4449 m⁽ᵉ⁾lal (Ch.) (1), to *speak, say*
4911 mâshal (2), to *use figurative language*
5608 çâphar (1), to *recount an event*
5790 'ûwth (1), to *succor*
6030 'ânâh (5), to *answer*
6315 pûwach (1), to *utter*
7878 sîyach (4), to *ponder, muse aloud*
653 apŏstŏmatizō (1), to *question carefully*
669 apŏphthĕggŏmai (1), *declare, address*
987 blasphēmĕō (5), to *speak impiously*
1097 ginōskō (1), to *know*
2036 ĕpō (6), to *speak*
2046 ĕrĕō (2), to *utter*
2551 kakŏlŏgĕō (1), to *revile, curse*
2635 katalalĕō (3), to *speak slander*
2980 lalĕō (101), to *talk*
3004 lĕgō (30), to *say*
4354 prŏslalĕō (1), to *converse with*
5350 phthĕggŏmai (2), to *utter a clear sound*

SPEAKER
376+3956 'îysh (1), *man*
3056 lŏgŏs (1), *word*

SPEAKEST
1696 dâbar (11), to *speak*
2980 lalĕō (4), to *talk*
3004 lĕgō (2), to *say*

SPEAKETH
559 'âmar (7), to *say*
981 bâṭâ' (1), to *babble*
1696 dâbar (22), to *say*
1897 hâgâh (1), to *murmur, utter a sound*
4448 mâlal (1), to *speak*
5046 nâgad (1), to *announce*

6315 pûwach (5), to *utter*
6963 qôwl (1), *voice*
483 antilĕgō (1), to *dispute, refuse*
1256 dialĕgŏmai (1), to *discuss*
2036 ĕpō (2), to *speak*
2635 katalalĕō (2), to speak *slander*
2980 lalĕō (22), to *talk*
3004 lĕgō (4), to *say*

SPEAKING
1696 dâbar (37), to *speak*
2790 chârash (1), to *engrave; to plow*
4405 millâh (2), *word; discourse; speech*
4449 m^elal (Ch.) (1), to *speak, say*
226 alēthĕuō (1), to *be true*
987 blasphēmĕō (1), to speak *impiously*
988 blasphēmia (1), *impious speech*
2980 lalĕō (11), to *talk*
3004 lĕgō (1), to *say*
4180 pŏlulŏgia (1), *prolixity, wordiness*
4354 prŏslalĕō (1), to *converse with*
5350 phthĕggŏmai (1), to utter a clear sound
5573 psĕudŏlŏgŏs (1), *promulgating erroneous doctrine*

SPEAKINGS
2636 katalalia (1), *defamation, slander*

SPEAR
2595 chănîyth (34), *lance, spear*
3591 kîydôwn (5), *dart, javelin*
7013 qayin (1), *lance*
7420 rômach (3), iron pointed spear
3057 lŏgchē (1), *lance, spear*

SPEAR'S
2595 chănîyth (1), *lance, spear*

SPEARMEN
7070 qâneh (1), *reed*
1187 dĕxiŏlabŏs (1), *guardsman*

SPEARS
2595 chănîyth (6), *lance, spear*
6767 ts^elâtsal (1), *whirring* of wings
7420 rômach (9), iron pointed spear

SPECIAL
5459 ç^egullâh (1), *wealth*
3756+3858+5177 ŏu (1), *no* or *not*

SPECIALLY
3122 malista (5), *particularly*

SPECKLED
5348 náqôd (9), *spotted*
6641 tsâbûwa' (1), *hyena*
8320 sâruq (1), *bright red, bay* colored

SPECTACLE
2302 thĕatrŏn (1), *audience-room*

SPED
4672 mâtsâ' (1), to *find* or *acquire;* to *occur*

SPEECH
562 'ômer (2), something *said*
565 'imrâh (7), something *said*
1697 dâbâr (7), *word*
1999 hămullâh (1), *sound, roar, noise*
3066 Y^ehûwdîyth (2), in the *Jewish language*
3948 leqach (1), *instruction*
4057 midbâr (1), *desert;* also *speech; mouth*
4405 millâh (4), *word; discourse; speech*
6310 peh (1), *mouth; opening*
8088 shêma' (1), something *heard*
8193 sâphâh (6), *lip, language, speech*
2981 lalia (3), *talk, speech*
3056 lŏgŏs (8), *word*
3072 Lukaŏnisti (1), in *Lycaonian language*
3424 mŏgilalŏs (1), *hardly talking*

SPEECHES
561 'êmer (2), something *said*
2420 chîydâh (1), *puzzle; conundrum; maxim*
4405 millâh (2), *word; discourse; speech*
2129 ĕulŏgia (1), *benediction*

SPEECHLESS
1769 ĕnnĕŏs (1), *speechless, silent*
2974 kōphŏs (1), *silent*
5392 phimŏō (1), to *restrain to silence*

SPEED
553 'âmats (2), to *be strong; be courageous*
629 'ŏçparnâ' (Ch.) (1), *with diligence*
4116 mâhar (2), to *hurry*
4120 m^ehêrâh (2), *hurry*
7136 qârâh (1), to *bring about;* to *impose*
5463 chairō (2), *salutation, "be well"*
5613+5033 hōs (1), *which, how,* i.e. *in that manner*

SPEEDILY
629 'ŏçparnâ' (Ch.) (4), *with diligence*
926 bâhal (1), to *hasten, hurry anxiously*
1980 hâlak (1), to *walk; live a certain way*
4116 mâhar (1), to *hurry; promptly*
4118 mahêr (4), *in a hurry*
4120 m^ehêrâh (4), *hurry; promptly*

4422 mâlaṭ (1), to *escape* as if by *slipperiness*
5674 'âbar (1), to *cross over;* to *transition*
1722+5034 ĕn (1), *in; during; because of*

SPEEDY
926 bâhal (1), to *hasten, hurry anxiously*

SPEND
3615 kâlâh (4), to *cease, be finished, perish*
8254 shâqal (1), to *suspend* in trade
1159 dapanaō (1), to *incur cost;* to *waste*
5551 chrŏnŏtribĕō (1), to *procrastinate, linger*

SPENDEST
4325 prŏsdapanaō (1), to *expend additionally*

SPENDETH
6 'âbad (1), *perish; destroy*
1104 bâla' (1), to *swallow;* to *destroy*
6213 'âsâh (1), to *do*

SPENT
235 'âzal (1), to *disappear*
3615 kâlâh (4), to *complete, consume*
7286 râdad (1), to *conquer;* to *overlay*
8552 tâmam (3), to *complete, finish*
1159 dapanaō (2), to *incur cost;* to *waste*
1230 diaginŏmai (1), to have time *elapse*
1550 ĕkdapanaō (1), to *exhaust, be exhausted*
2119 ĕukairĕō (1), to *have opportunity*
2827 klinō (1), to *slant*
4160 pŏiĕō (1), to *do*
4298 prŏkŏptō (1), to *go ahead, advance*
4321 prŏsanaliskō (1), to *expend further*

SPEWING
7022 qîyqâlôwn (1), *disgrace*

SPICE
1313 bâsâm (1), *balsam*
1314 besem (2), *spice; fragrance; balsam*
7402 râkal (1), to *travel*
7543 râqach (1), to *perfume, blend spice*

SPICED
7544 reqach (1), *spice*

SPICERY
5219 n^ekô'th (1), *gum,* (poss.) *styrax*

SPICES
1314 besem (22), *spice; fragrance; balsam*
5219 n^ekô'th (1), *gum,* (poss.) *styrax*
5561 çam (3), *aroma*
759 arōma (4), *scented oils, perfumes, spices*

SPIDER
8079 s^emâmîyth (1), *lizard*

SPIDER'S
5908 'akkâbîysh (2), *web*-making *spider*

SPIED
7200 râ'âh (5), to *see*
7270 râgal (1), to *reconnoiter;* to *slander*

SPIES
871 'Äthârîym (1), *places to step*
7270 râgal (10), to *reconnoiter;* to *slander*
8104 shâmar (1), to *watch*
1455 ĕgkathĕtŏs (1), *spy*
2685 kataskŏpŏs (1), *reconnoiterer,* i.e. a *spy*

SPIKENARD
5373 nêrd (3), *nard*
3487+4101 nardŏs (2), oil from spike-*nard* root

SPILLED
7843 shâchath (1), to *decay;* to *ruin*
1632 ĕkchĕō (2), to *pour forth;* to *bestow*

SPILT
5064 nâgar (1), to *pour* out; to *deliver* over

SPIN
2901 ṭâvâh (1), to *spin* yarn
3514 nēthō (2), to *spin* yarn

SPINDLE
3601 kîyshôwr (1), *spindle* or shank

SPIRIT
178 'ôwb (7), *wineskin; necromancer, medium*
5397 n^eshâmâh (2), *breath, life*
7307 rûwach (226), *breath; wind; life*-spirit
7308 rûwach (Ch.) (8), *breath; wind; life*-spirit
4151 pnĕuma (255), *spirit*
5326 phantasma (2), *spectre, apparition*

SPIRITS
178 'ôwb (9), *wineskin; necromancer, medium*
7307 rûwach (5), *breath; wind; life*-spirit
4151 pnĕuma (32), *spirit*

SPIRITUAL
7307 rûwach (1), *breath; wind; life*-spirit
4151 pnĕuma (1), *spirit*
4152 pnĕumatikŏs (25), *spiritual*

SPIRITUALLY
3588+4151 hŏ (1), *"the,"* i.e. the definite article
4153 pnĕumatikŏs (2), *non-physical*

SPIT
3417 yâraq (2), to *spit*
7536 rôq (1), *spittle, saliva*
7556 râqaq (1), to *spit*
1716 ĕmptuō (5), to *spit at*
4429 ptuō (2), to *spit*

SPITE
3708 ka'aç (1), *vexation*

SPITEFULLY
5195 hubrizō (2), *to exercise violence, abuse*

SPITTED
1716 ĕmptuō (1), *to spit at*

SPITTING
7536 rôq (1), *spittle*

SPITTLE
7388 rîyr (1), *saliva; broth*
7536 rôq (1), *spittle*
4427 ptusma (1), *saliva*

SPOIL
957 baz (4), *plunder, loot*
961 bizzâh (6), *plunder*
962 bâzaz (8), *to plunder*
1500 gᵉzêlâh (1), *robbery, stealing; things stolen*
2254 châbal (1), *to pervert, destroy*
2488 chălîytsâh (1), *spoil, booty* of the dead
2964 ṭereph (1), *fresh torn prey*
4882 mᵉshûwçâh (1), *spoilation, loot*
4933 mᵉshiççâh (3), *plunder*
5337 nâtsal (1), *to deliver; to be snatched*
6584 pâshaṭ (1), *to strip*
6906 qâba' (1), *to defraud, rob*
7701 shôd (5), *violence, ravage, destruction*
7703 shâdad (8), *to ravage*
7921 shâkôl (1), *to miscarry*
7997 shâlal (4), *to drop or strip; to plunder*
7998 shâlâl (62), *booty*
8154 shâçâh (3), *to plunder*
8155 shâçaç (1), *to plunder, ransack*
1283 diarpazō (4), *plunder, rob*
4812 sulagōgĕō (1), *to take captive as booty*

SPOILED
957 baz (2), *plunder, loot*
958 bâzâ' (2), *to divide*
962 bâzaz (6), *to plunder*
1497 gâzal (7), *to rob*
5337 nâtsal (1), *to deliver; to be snatched*
6906 qâba' (1), *to defraud*
7701 shôd (3), *violence, ravage, destruction*
7703 shâdad (20), *to ravage*
7758 shôwlâl (2), *stripped; captive*
7997 shâlal (4), *to drop or strip; to plunder*
8154 shâçâh (3), *to plunder*
8155 ⌐hâçaç (3), *to plunder, ransack*
554 apĕkduōmai (1), *to despoil*

SPOILER
7701 shôd (1), *violence, ravage, destruction*

SPOILERS
7703 shâdad (3), *to ravage*
7843 shâchath (2), *to decay; to ruin*
8154 shâçâh (2), *to plunder*

SPOILEST
7703 shâdad (1), *to ravage*

SPOILETH
1497 gâzal (1), *to rob*
6584 pâshaṭ (2), *to strip*
7703 shâdad (1), *to ravage*

SPOILING
7701 shôd (3), *violence, ravage, destruction*
7908 shᵉkôwl (1), *bereavement*
724 harpagē (1), *pillage*

SPOILS
698 'orŏbâh (1), *ambuscades*
7998 shâlâl (2), *booty*
205 akrŏthiniŏn (1), *best of the booty*
4661 skulŏn (1), *plunder*

SPOKEN
559 'âmar (15), *to say*
560 'ămar (Ch.) (1), *to say*
1696 dâbar (174), *to speak, say*
1697 dâbâr (2), *word*
6310 peh (1), *mouth*
312 anaggĕllō (1), *to announce, report*
369 anantirrhētŏs (1), *without objection*
483 antilĕgō (2), *to dispute, refuse*
987 blasphēmĕō (5), *to speak impiously*
2036 ĕpō (19), *to speak*
2046 ĕrĕō (4), *to utter*
2605 kataggĕllō (1), *to proclaim, promulgate*
2980 lalĕō (33), *to talk*
3004 lĕgō (7), *to say*
4280 prŏĕrĕō (2), *to say already, predict*
4369 prŏstithēmi (1), *to repeat*
4483 rhĕō (15), *to utter*

SPOKES
2840 chishshûr (1), *hub*

SPOKESMAN
1696 dâbar (1), *to speak*

SPOON
3709 kaph (12), *bowl; handle*

SPOONS
3709 kaph (12), *bowl; handle*

SPORT
6026 'ânag (1), *to be soft or pliable*
6711 tsâchaq (1), *to laugh; to make sport of*
7814 sᵉchôwq (1), *laughter; scorn*
7832 sâchaq (3), *to laugh; to scorn; to play*

SPORTING
6711 tsâchaq (1), *to laugh; to make sport of*
1792 ĕntruphaō (1), *to revel in, carouse*

SPOT
933 bôhaq (1), *white scurf, rash*
934 bôhereth (9), *whitish, bright spot*
3971 m'ûwm (3), *blemish; fault*
8549 tâmîym (6), *entire, complete; integrity*
299 amōmŏs (1), *unblemished, blameless*
784 aspilŏs (3), *unblemished*
4696 spilŏs (1), *stain or blemish, i.e. defect*

SPOTS
934 bôhereth (2), *whitish, bright spot*
2272 chăbarbûrâh (1), *streak, stripe*
4694 spilas (1), *ledge or reef of rock in the sea*
4696 spilŏs (1), *stain or blemish, i.e. defect*

SPOTTED
2921 ṭâlâ' (6), *to be spotted or variegated*
4695 spilŏō (1), *to soil*

SPOUSE
3618 kallâh (6), *bride; son's wife*

SPOUSES
3618 kallâh (2), *bride; son's wife*

SPRANG
305 anabainō (1), *to go up, rise*
393 anatĕllō (1), *to cause to arise*
1080 gĕnnaō (1), *to procreate, regenerate*
1530 ĕispēdaō (1), *to rush in*
1816 ĕxanatĕllō (1), *to germinate, spring forth*
4855 sumphuō (1), *to grow jointly*
5453 phuō (1), *to germinate or grow*

SPREAD
2219 zârâh (2), *to toss about; to diffuse*
3212 yâlak (2), *to walk; to live; to carry*
3318 yâtsâ' (1), *to go, bring out*
3331 yâtsa' (2), *to strew*
4894 mishṭôwach (2), *spreading-place*
5186 nâṭâh (6), *to stretch or spread out*
5203 nâṭash (4), *to disperse; to thrust off*
5259 nâçak (1), *to interweave*
6327 pûwts (2), *to dash in pieces; to disperse*
6335 pûwsh (1), *to spread; to act proudly*
6555 pârats (1), *to break out*

SPORTING (continued column)
6566 pâras (49), *to break apart, disperse, scatter*
6581 pâsâh (17), *to spread*
6584 pâshaṭ (2), *to strip*
6605 pâthach (1), *to open wide; to loosen, begin*
7286 râdad (1), *to conquer; to overlay*
7554 râqa' (4), *to pound*
7849 shâṭach (3), *to expand*
1268 dianĕmō (1), *to spread information*
1310 diaphēmizō (1), *to spread news*
1831 ĕxĕrchŏmai (2), *to issue; to leave*
4766 strŏnnumi (3), *strew, i.e. spread*
5291 hupŏstrŏnnumi (1), *to strew underneath*

SPREADEST
4666 miphrâs (1), *expansion*

SPREADETH
4969 mâthach (1), *to stretch out*
5186 nâṭâh (1), *to stretch or spread out*
6566 pâras (6), *to break apart, disperse, scatter*
6576 parshêz (1), *to expand*
6581 pâsâh (1), *to spread*
7502 râphad (1), *to spread a bed; to refresh*
7554 râqa' (2), *to pound*
7971 shâlach (1), *to send away*

SPREADING
4894 mishṭôwach (1), *spreading-place*
5628 çârach (1), *to extend even to excess*
6168 'ârâh (1), *to pour out; demolish*
6524 pârach (1), *to break forth; to bloom; to fly*

SPREADINGS
4666 miphrâs (1), *expansion*

SPRIGS
2150 zalzal (1), *twig, shoot*
6288 pᵉ'ôrâh (1), *foliage, branches*

SPRING
1530 gal (1), *heap; ruins*
1876 dâshâ' (1), *to sprout new plants*
3318 yâtsâ' (1), *to go, bring out*
4161 môwtsâ' (2), *going forth*
4726 mâqôwr (2), *flow of liquids, or ideas*
5927 'âlâh (3), *to ascend, be high, mount*
6524 pârach (1), *to break forth; to bloom; to fly*
6779 tsâmach (10), *to sprout*
6780 tsemach (1), *sprout, branch*
985 blastanō (1), *to yield fruit*

SPRINGETH
3318 yâtsâ' (1), to go,
bring out
6524 pârach (1), to break
forth; to bloom; to fly
7823 shâchîyç (2),
after-growth

SPRINGING
2416 chay (1), alive; raw;
fresh; life
6780 tsemach (1), sprout,
branch
242 hallŏmai (1), to jump
up; to gush up
5453 phuŏ (1), to
germinate or grow

SPRINGS
794 'ăshêdâh (3), ravine
1543 gullâh (4), fountain;
bowl or globe
4002 mabbûwa' (2),
fountain, water spring
4161 môwtsâ' (1), going
forth
4599 ma'yân (2),
fountain; source
4726 mâqôwr (1), flow
5033 nêbek (1), fountain

SPRINKLE
2236 zâraq (14), to
sprinkle, scatter
5137 nâzâh (17), to
splash or sprinkle

SPRINKLED
2236 zâraq (16), to
sprinkle, scatter
5137 nâzâh (6), to splash
or sprinkle
4472 rhantizō (3), to
asperse, sprinkle

SPRINKLETH
2236 zâraq (1), to
sprinkle, scatter
5137 nâzâh (1), to splash
or sprinkle

SPRINKLING
4378 prŏschusis (1),
affusion, sprinkling
4472 rhantizō (1), to
asperse, sprinkle
4473 rhantismŏs (2),
aspersion, sprinkling

SPROUT
2498 châlaph (1), to
spring up; to pierce

SPRUNG
6524 pârach (1), to break
forth; to bloom; to fly
6779 tsâmach (2), to
sprout
305 anabainō (1), to go
up, rise
393 anatĕllō (1), to cause
to arise
985 blastanō (1), to yield
fruit
1816 ĕxanatĕllō (1), to
germinate, spring forth
5453 phuŏ (1), to
germinate or grow

SPUE
6958 qôw' (2), to vomit
7006 qâyâh (1), to vomit
1692 ĕmĕŏ (1), to vomit

SPUED
6958 qôw' (1), to vomit

SPUN
2901 ṭâvâh (1), to spin
yarn
4299 maṭveh (1),
something spun

SPUNGE
4699 spŏggŏs (3), sponge

SPY
7200 râ'âh (2), to see
7270 râgal (7), to
reconnoiter; to slander
8446 tûwr (2), to wander,
meander
2684 kataskŏpĕŏ (1), to
inspect, spy on

SQUARE
7251 râba' (3), to be four
sided, to be quadrate

SQUARED
7251 râba' (1), to be four
sided, to be quadrate

SQUARES
7253 reba' (2), fourth

STABILITY
530 'ĕmûwnâh (1),
fidelity; steadiness

STABLE
3559 kûwn (1), to set up:
establish, fix, prepare
5116 nâveh (1), at home;
lovely; home

STABLISH
3559 kûwn (2), to set up:
establish, fix, prepare
5324 nâtsab (1), to station
6965 qûwm (3), to rise
4741 stĕrizō (6), to
confirm

STABLISHED
3559 kûwn (2), to set up:
establish, fix, prepare
5975 'âmad (1), to stand
950 bĕbaiŏŏ (1), to
stabilitate, keep strong

STABLISHETH
3559 kûwn (1), to set up:
establish, fix, prepare
950 bĕbaiŏŏ (1), to
stabilitate, keep strong

STACHYS
4720 Stachus (1), head of
grain

STACKS
1430 gâdîysh (1), stack of
sheaves, shock of grain

STACTE
5198 nâṭâph (1), drop;
aromatic gum resin

STAFF
2671 chêts (1), arrow;
shaft of a spear
4132 môwṭ (1), pole; yoke
4294 maṭṭeh (15), tribe;
rod, scepter; club
4731 maqqêl (7), shoot;
stick; staff
4938 mish'ênâh (11),
walking-stick
6086 'êts (3), wood
6418 pelek (1),
spindle-whorl; crutch
7626 shêbeṭ (2), stick
4464 rhabdŏs (2), stick,
rod

STAGGER
5128 nûwa' (2), to waver
8582 tâ'âh (1), to
vacillate, i.e. reel

STAGGERED
1252 diakrinō (1), to
decide; to hesitate

STAGGERETH
8582 tâ'âh (1), to
vacillate, i.e. reel

STAIN
1350 gâ'al (1), to redeem;
to be the next of kin
1351 gâ'al (1), to soil,
stain; desecrate
2490 châlal (1), to
profane, defile

STAIRS
3883 lûwl (1), spiral step
4095 madrêgâh (1), steep
or inaccessible place
4608 ma'âleh (1),
platform; stairs
4609 ma'ălâh (5),
thought arising
304 anabathmŏs (2),
stairway step

STAKES
3489 yâthêd (2), tent peg

STALK
7054 qâmâh (1), stalk of
grain
7070 qâneh (2), reed

STALKS
6086 'êts (1), wood

STALL
4770 marbêq (2), stall
5336 phatnē (1), stall

STALLED
75 'âbaç (1), to feed

STALLS
723 'urvâh (3),
herding-place
7517 repheth (1), stall
for cattle

STAMMERERS
5926 'illêg (1), stuttering,
stammering

STAMMERING
3932 lâ'ag (1), to deride;
to speak unintelligibly
3934 lâ'êg (1), buffoon;
foreigner

STAMP
1854 dâqaq (1), to crush
7554 râqa' (1), to pound

STAMPED
1854 dâqaq (3), to crush
3807 kâthath (1), to
bruise, strike, beat
7429 râmaç (2), to tread
7512 rᵉphaç (Ch.) (2), to
trample; to ruin
7554 râqa' (1), to pound

STAMPING
8161 sha'ăṭâh (1), clatter
of hoofs

STANCHED
2476 histēmi (1), to
stand, establish

STAND
539 'âman (1), to be firm,
faithful, true; to trust

1481 gûwr (1), to sojourn
1826 dâmam (1), to stop,
cease; to perish
3318 yâtsâ' (1), to go,
bring out
3320 yâtsab (22), to
station, offer, continue
5066 nâgash (1), to be,
come, bring near
5324 nâtsab (9), to station
5564 çâmak (1), to lean
upon; take hold of
5749 'ûwd (1), to protest,
testify; to restore
5975 'âmad (144), to
stand
5976 'âmad (1), to shake
6965 qûwm (31), to rise
6966 qûwm (Ch.) (2), to
rise
7126 qârab (1), to
approach, bring near
8617 tᵉqûwmâh (1),
resistfulness
450 anistēmi (2), to rise;
to come back to life
639 apŏrĕŏ (1), be at a
mental loss, be puzzled
1453 ĕgĕirō (1), to
waken, i.e. rouse
1510 ĕimi (1), I exist, I am
2476 histēmi (36), to
stand, establish
3306 mĕnō (1), to stay
3936 paristēmi (3), to
stand beside, present
4026 pĕriistēmi (1), to
stand around; to avoid
4739 stĕkō (7), to
persevere, be steadfast

STANDARD
1714 degel (10), flag,
standard, banner
5127 nûwç (1), to vanish
5251 nêç (7), flag; signal

STANDARD-BEARER
5264 nâçaç (1), to gleam;
to flutter a flag

STANDARDS
1714 degel (3), flag,
standard, banner

STANDEST
5975 'âmad (4), to stand
2476 histēmi (2), to stand

STANDETH
3559 kûwn (1), to set up
5324 nâtsab (4), to station
5975 'âmad (14), to stand
2476 histēmi (8), to stand
4739 stĕkō (1), to
persevere, be steadfast

STANDING
98 'ăgam (2), marsh;
pond; pool
3320 yâtsab (1), to
station, offer, continue
4613 mo'ŏmâd (1),
foothold
4676 matstsêbâh (2),
column or stone
5324 nâtsab (4), to station
5975 'âmad (12), to stand
5979 'emdâh (1), station
7054 qâmâh (5), stalk
2186 ĕphistēmi (1), to be
present; to approach

2192+4174 ĕchŏ (1), to
have; hold; keep
2476 histēmi (23), to
stand, establish
3936 paristēmi (1), to
stand beside, present
4921 sunistaō (1), to *set
together; to stand near*

STANK
887 bâ'ash (4), to *smell
bad*

STAR
3556 kôwkâb (2), *star*
792 astēr (11), *star*
798 astrŏn (1),
constellation; star
5459 phōsphŏrŏs (1),
morning-star

STARE
7200 râ'âh (1), to *see*

STARGAZERS
2374+3556 chôzeh (1),
beholder in vision

STARS
3556 kôwkâb (34), *star*
3598 Kîymâh (1), *cluster*
of stars, the *Pleiades*
792 astēr (13), *star*
798 astrŏn (3),
constellation; star

STATE
3027 yâd (2), *hand; power*
3651 kên (1), *just; right,
correct*
4612 ma'ămâd (1),
position; attendant
4971 mathkôneth (1),
proportion
5324 nâtsab (1), to *station*
6440 pânîym (1), *face;
front*
3588+2596 hŏ (1), "*the*,"
i.e. the definite article
3588+4012 hŏ (2), "*the*,"
i.e. the definite article

STATELY
3520 kᵉbûwddâh (1),
magnificence, wealth

STATION
4673 matstsâb (1), fixed
spot; office; post

STATURE
4055 mad (1), *vesture,
garment; carpet*
4060 middâh (4),
measure; portion
6967 qôwmâh (7), *height*
2244 hēlikia (5), *maturity*

STATUTE
2706 chôq (13),
appointment; allotment
2708 chuqqâh (20), to
delineate
7010 qᵉyâm (Ch.) (2),
edict arising in law

STATUTES
2706 chôq (73),
appointment; allotment
2708 chuqqâh (58), to
delineate
6490 piqqûwd (1),
mandate of God, *Law*

STAVES
905 bad (37), *limb,
member; bar; chief*

4133 môwṭâh (1), *pole;
ox-bow; yoke*
4294 maṭṭeh (1), *tribe;
rod, scepter; club*
4731 maqqêl (2), *shoot;
stick; staff*
4938 mish'ênâh (1),
walking-stick
3586 xulŏn (5), *timber,*
i.e. a *stick, club*
4464 rhabdŏs (2), *stick,
rod*

STAY
4102 mâhahh (1), to *be
reluctant*
4223 mᵉchâ' (Ch.) (1), to
strike; to arrest
4937 mish'ên (5),
support; protector
5564 çâmak (2), to *lean
upon; take hold* of
5702 'âgan (1), to *debar,
withdraw*
5975 'âmad (10), to *stand*
6117 'âqab (1), to *seize by
the heel; to circumvent*
6438 pinnâh (1),
pinnacle; chieftain
7503 râphâh (3), to
slacken
7901 shâkab (1), to *lie
down*
8172 shâ'an (5), to
support, rely on
8551 tâmak (1), to
obtain, keep fast

STAYED
309 'âchar (1), to *remain*
2342 chûwl (2), to *wait;
to pervert*
3176 yâchal (1), to *wait;
to be patient, hope*
3322 yâtsag (1), to *place*
3607 kâlâ' (3), to *hold
back or in; to prohibit*
5564 çâmak (1), to *lean
upon; take hold* of
5975 'âmad (9), to *stand*
6113 'âtsar (7), to *hold
back; to maintain*
7896 shîyth (1), to *place*
8156 shâça' (1), to *split
or tear; to upbraid*
8551 tâmak (1), to
obtain, keep fast
1907 ĕpĕchō (1), to
retain; to detain
2722 katĕchō (1), to *hold
down fast*

STAYETH
1898 hâgâh (1), to *remove*

STAYS
3027 yâd (4), *hand; power*

STEAD
8478 tachath (91), in *lieu
of*
5228 hupĕr (2), *in behalf
of*

STEADS
8478 tachath (1), in *lieu
of*

STEADY
530 'ĕmûwnâh (1),
fidelity; steadiness

STEAL
1589 gânab (11), to
thieve; to deceive
2813 klĕptō (10), to *steal*

STEALETH
1589 gânab (3), to *thieve*

STEALING
1589 gânab (2), to *thieve*

STEALTH
1589 gânab (1), to *thieve*

STEDFAST
539 'âman (2), to *be firm,
faithful, true; to trust*
3332 yâtsaq (1), to *pour
out*
7011 qayâm (Ch.) (1),
permanent
949 bĕbaiŏs (4), *stable,
certain, binding*
1476 hĕdraiŏs (2),
immovable; steadfast
4731 stĕrĕŏs (1), *solid,
stable*

STEDFASTLY
553 'âmats (1), to *be
strong; be courageous*
7760 sûwm (1), to *put*
816 atĕnizō (6), to *gaze
intently*
4342 prŏskartĕrĕō (1), to
be constantly diligent
4741 stērizō (1), to *turn
resolutely; to confirm*

STEDFASTNESS
4733 stĕrĕōma (1),
stability, firmness
4740 stērigmŏs (1),
stability; firmness

STEEL
5154 nᵉchûwshâh (3),
copper; bronze
5178 nᵉchôsheth (1),
copper; bronze

STEEP
4095 madrêgâh (1), *steep
or inaccessible* place
4174 môwrâd (1),
descent, slope
2911 krĕmnŏs (3),
precipice, steep cliff

STEM
1503 geza' (1), *stump*

STEP
838 'âshshûwr (1), *step*
6587 pesa' (1), *stride, step*

STEPHANAS
4734 Stĕphanas (3),
crowned

STEPHANUS
4734 Stĕphanas (1),
crowned

STEPHEN
4736 Stĕphanŏs (7),
wreath

STEPPED
1684 ĕmbainō (1), to
embark; to reach

STEPPETH
2597 katabainō (1), to
descend

STEPS
838 'âshshûwr (5), *step*
1978 hâlîyk (1), *step*

4609 ma'ălâh (11),
thought arising
4703 mits'âd (2), *step*
6119 'âqêb (1), *track,
footprint; rear* position
6471 pa'am (4), *step*
6806 tsa'ad (11), *step*
2487 ichnŏs (3), *track*

STERN
4403 prumna (1), *stern*

STEWARD
376+834+5921 'îysh (1),
man; male; someone
834+5921 'âsher (3), *who*
1121+4943 bên (1), *son,
descendant; people*
2012 ĕpitrŏpŏs (2),
manager, guardian
3621 ŏikŏnŏmĕō (1), to
manage a household
3622 ŏikŏnŏmia (3),
administration
3623 ŏikŏnŏmŏs (2),
overseer, manager

STEWARDS
8269 sar (1), *head, ruler*
3623 ŏikŏnŏmŏs (3),
overseer, manager

STEWARDSHIP
3622 ŏikŏnŏmia (3),
administration

STICK
1692 dâbaq (2), to *cling
or adhere; to catch*
3920 lâkad (1), to *catch;
to capture*
5181 nâchath (1), to *sink,
descend; to press* down
6086 'êts (9), *wood*
8205 shᵉphîy (1), *bare*
hill or plain

STICKETH
1695 dâbêq (1),
adhering, sticking to

STICKS
6086 'êts (5), *wood*
5484 charin (1), *on
account of, because* of

STIFF
6277 'âthâq (1), *impudent*
7185 qâshâh (1), to *be
tough or severe*
7186 qâsheh (1), *severe*

STIFFENED
7185 qâshâh (1), to *be
tough or severe*

STIFFHEARTED
2389+3820 châzâq (1),
strong; severe, hard

STIFFNECKED
7185+6203 qâshâh (2), to
be tough or severe
7186+6203 qâsheh (6),
severe
4644 sklērŏtrachēlŏs (1),
obstinate

STILL
1826 dâmam (6), to *be
silent; to be astonished*
1827 dᵉmâmâh (1), *quiet*
2790 chârash (1), to *be
silent; to be deaf*
2814 châshâh (2), to
hush or keep quiet

4496 mᵉnûwchâh (1), *peacefully; consolation*
5265 nâça' (1), to *start*
5750 'ôwd (19), *still; more*
5975 'âmad (3), to *stand*
7503 râphâh (1), to *slacken*
7673 shâbath (2), to *repose; to desist*
8252 shâqaṭ (2), to *repose*
2089 ěti (4), *yet, still*
2476 histēmi (4), to *stand, establish*
4357 prŏsměnō (1), to *remain* in a place
5392 phimŏō (1), to *restrain to silence*

STILLED
2013 hâçâh (1), to *hush*
2814 châshâh (1), to *hush* or *keep quiet*

STILLEST
7623 shâbach (1), to *pacify*

STILLETH
7623 shâbach (1), to *pacify*

STING
2759 kěntrŏn (2), *sting*

STINGETH
6567 pârash (1), to *wound*

STINGS
2759 kěntrŏn (1), *sting*

STINK
887 bâ'ash (4), to *smell bad*
889 bᵉ'ôsh (3), *stench*
4716 maq (1), *putridity, stench*

STINKETH
887 bâ'ash (1), to *smell bad*
3605 ŏzō (1), to *stink*

STINKING
887 bâ'ash (1), to *smell bad*

STIR
5782 'ûwr (13), to *awake*
5927 'âlâh (1), to *ascend, be high, mount*
6965 qûwm (1), to *rise*
329 anazōpurěō (1), to re-enkindle, fan a flame
1326 diěgěirō (2), to *arouse, stimulate*
5017 tarachŏs (2), *disturbance, tumult*

STIRRED
1624 gârâh (3), to *provoke to anger*
5375 nâsâ' (3), to *lift up*
5496 çûwth (2), to *stimulate; to seduce*
5782 'ûwr (5), to *awake*
5916 'âkar (1), to *disturb* or *afflict*
6965 qûwm (3), to *rise*
1892 ěpěgěirō (1), to *excite against, stir up*
3947 parŏxunō (1), to *exasperate*
3951 parŏtrunō (1), to *stimulate* to hostility

4531 salěuō (1), to *waver*, i.e. *agitate, rock, topple*
4787 sugkiněō (1), to *excite* to sedition
4797 sugchěō (1), to *throw into disorder*

STIRRETH
1624 gârâh (3), to *provoke to anger*
5782 'ûwr (4), to *awake*
383 anasěiō (1), to *excite, stir up*

STIRS
8663 tᵉshû'âh (1), *crashing* or *clamor*

STOCK
944 bûwl (1), *produce*
1503 geza' (2), *stump*
6086 'êts (2), *wood*
6133 'êqer (1), *naturalized* citizen
1085 gěnŏs (2), *kin*

STOCKS
4115 mahpeketh (2), *stocks* for punishment
5465 çad (2), *stocks*
5914 'ekeç (1), *anklet*
6086 'êts (2), (of) *wood*
6729 tsîynôq (1), *pillory*
3586 xulŏn (1), (of) *timber*

STOICKS
4770 Stŏïkŏs (1), *porch*

STOLE
1589 gânab (4), to *thieve*
2813 klěptō (2), to *steal*

STOLEN
1589 gânab (14), to *thieve*

STOMACH'S
4751 stŏmachŏs (1), *stomach*

STOMACHER
6614 pᵉthîygîyl (1), *fine mantle* for holidays

STONE
68 'eben (104), *stone*
69 'eben (Ch.) (6), *stone*
1496 gâzîyth (3), *dressed stone*
5619 çâqal (7), to *throw large stones*
6697 tsûwr (1), *rock*
6872 tsᵉrôwr (1), *parcel; kernel* or *particle*
7275 râgam (10), to *cast stones*
8068 shâmîyr (1), *thorn;* (poss.) *diamond*
2642 katalithazō (1), to *stone to death*
2991 laxěutŏs (1), *rock-quarried*
3034 lithazō (4), to *lapidate, to stone*
3035 lithinŏs (3), made of *stone*
3036 lithŏbŏlěō (1), to *throw stones*
3037 lithŏs (36), *stone*
4074 Pětrŏs (1), piece of *rock*
5586 psēphŏs (2), *pebble stone*

STONE'S
3037 lithŏs (1), *stone*

STONED
5619 çâqal (8), to *throw large stones*
7275 râgam (5), to *cast stones*
3034 lithazō (4), to *lapidate, to stone*
3036 lithŏbŏlěō (5), to *throw stones*

STONES
68 'eben (136), *stone*
69 'eben (Ch.) (2), *stone*
810 'eshek (1), *testicle*
1496 gâzîyth (4), *dressed stone*
2106 zâvîyth (1), *angle, corner* (as *projecting*)
2687 châtsâts (1), *gravel*
2789 cheres (1), piece of earthenware *pottery*
5553 çela' (1), *craggy rock; fortress*
5619 çâqal (1), to *throw large stones*
6344 pachad (1), *male testicle*
6697 tsûwr (1), *rock*
3036 lithŏbŏlěō (1), to *throw stones*
3037 lithŏs (16), *stone*

STONESQUARERS
1382 Gibliy (1), *Gebalite*

STONEST
3036 lithŏbŏlěō (2), to *throw stones*

STONING
5619 çâqal (1), to *throw large stones*

STONY
68 'eben (2), *stone*
5553 çela' (1), *craggy rock; fortress*
4075 pětrōdēs (4), *rocky*

STOOD
1826 dâmam (1), to *stop, cease; to perish*
3320 yâtsab (7), to *station, offer, continue*
3559 kûwn (1), to *set up*
4673 matstsâb (2), *fixed spot; office; post*
5324 nâtsab (19), to *station*
5568 çâmar (1), to *bristle*
5975 'âmad (189), to *stand*
5977 'ômed (1), fixed *spot*
6965 qûwm (15), to *rise*
6966 qûwm (Ch.) (4), to *rise*
450 anistēmi (7), to *rise; to come back to life*
2186 ěphistēmi (5), to *be present; to approach*
2476 histēmi (60), to *stand, establish*
2944 kuklŏō (1), to *surround, encircle*
3936 paristēmi (14), to *stand beside, present*
4026 pěriistēmi (1), to *stand around; to avoid*
4836 sumparaginŏmai (1), to *convene; to appear in aid*
4921 sunistaō (1), to *set together*

STOODEST
5324 nâtsab (1), to *station*
5975 'âmad (2), to *stand*

STOOL
3678 kiççê' (1), *throne*

STOOLS
70 'ôben (1), potter's *wheel;* midwife's *stool*

STOOP
7164 qâraç (1), to *hunch*
7812 shâchâh (1), to *prostrate* in homage
7817 shâchach (1), to *sink* or *depress*
2955 kuptō (1), to *bend forward, stoop down*

STOOPED
3486 yâshêsh (1), *gray-haired, aged*
3766 kâra' (1), to *prostrate*
6915 qâdad (2), to *bend*
2955 kuptō (2), to *bend forward, stoop down*
3879 parakuptō (1), to *lean over to peer within*

STOOPETH
7164 qâraç (1), to *hunch*

STOOPING
3879 parakuptō (2), to *lean overto peer within*

STOP
2629 châçam (1), to *muzzle; block*
5462 çâgar (1), to *shut* up
5640 çâtham (2), to *stop* up; to *repair*
6113 'âtsar (1), to *hold back; to maintain, rule*
7092 qâphats (1), to *draw together, to leap; to die*
5420 phrassō (1), to *fence* or *enclose, to block* up

STOPPED
2856 châtham (1), to *close* up; to *affix a seal*
3513 kâbad (1), to *be heavy, severe, dull*
5534 çâkar (2), to *shut* up
5640 çâtham (6), to *stop* up; to *repair*
8610 tâphas (1), to *manipulate,* i.e. *seize*
1998 ěpisuntrěchō (1), to *hasten together upon*
4912 suněchō (1), to *hold together*
5420 phrassō (2), to *fence* or *enclose, to block* up

STOPPETH
331 'âṭam (3), to *close*
7092 qâphats (1), to *draw together, to leap; to die*

STORE
214 'ôwtsâr (1), *depository*
686 'âtsar (3), to *store* up
1995 hâmôwn (2), *noise, tumult; many, crowd*
3462 yâshên (1), to *sleep; to grow old, stale*
4543 miçkᵉnâh (5), *storage-magazine*
4863 mish'ereth (2), *kneading-trough*

6487 piqqâdôwn (1), *deposit*

7235 râbâh (1), to *increase*

8498 tᵉkûwnâh (1), *structure; equipage*

597 apŏthēsaurizō (1), to store *treasure away*

2343 thēsaurizō (2), to *amass, reserve, store up*

STOREHOUSE
214 'ôwtsâr (1), *depository*
5009 tamêïŏn (1), *room*

STOREHOUSES
214 'ôwtsâr (2), *depository*
618 'âçâm (1), *storehouse, barn*
834 'âsher (1), *who, which, what, that*
3965 ma'ăbûwç (1), *granary, barn*
4543 miçkᵉnâh (1), *storage-magazine*

STORIES
4609 ma'ălâh (1), *thought arising*

STORK
2624 chăçîydâh (5), *stork*

STORM
2230 zerem (3), *flood*
5492 çûwphâh (3), *hurricane wind*
5584 çâ'âh (1), to *rush*
5591 ça'ar (1), *hurricane*
7722 shôw' (1), *tempest; devastation*
8178 sa'ar (1), *tempest*
8183 sᵉ'ârâh (1), *hurricane wind*
2978 lailaps (2), *whirlwind; hurricane*

STORMY
5591 ça'ar (4), *hurricane*

STORY
4097 midrâsh (2), *treatise*

STOUT
1433 gôdel (1), *magnitude, majesty*
2388 châzaq (1), to *be strong; courageous*
7229 rab (Ch.) (1), *great*

STOUTHEARTED
47+3820 'abbîyr (2), *mighty*

STOUTNESS
1433 gôdel (1), *magnitude, majesty*

STRAIGHT
3474 yâshar (9), to *be straight; to make right*
4334 mîyshôwr (2), *plain; justice*
5676 'êber (3), *opposite*
8626 tâqan (2), to *straighten; to compose*
461 anŏrthŏō (1), to *straighten up*
2113 ĕuthudrŏmĕō (2), to *sail direct*
2116 ĕuthunō (1), to *straighten or level*
2117 ĕuthus (5), *at once, immediately*

3717 ŏrthŏs (1), *straight*

STRAIGHTWAY
3651 kên (1), *just; right*
4116 mâhar (1), to *hurry*
6258 'attâh (1), *now*
6597 pith'ôwm (1), *instantly, suddenly*
1824 ĕxautēs (1), *instantly, at once*
2112 ĕuthĕŏs (32), *at once or soon*
2117 ĕuthus (2), *at once*
3916 parachrēma (3), *instantly, immediately*

STRAIN
1368 diulizō (1), to *strain out*

STRAIT
6862 tsar (3), *trouble*
6887 tsârar (3), to *cramp*
4728 stĕnŏs (3), *narrow*
4912 sunĕchō (1), to *hold together*

STRAITEN
6693 tsûwq (1), to *oppress*

STRAITENED
680 'âtsal (1), to *select; refuse; narrow*
3334 yâtsar (2), to *be in distress*
4164 mûwtsaq (1), *distress*
7114 qâtsar (1), to *curtail, cut short*
4729 stĕnŏchŏrĕō (2), to *hem in closely*
4912 sunĕchō (1), to *hold together*

STRAITENETH
5148 nâchâh (1), to *guide*

STRAITEST
196 akribĕstatŏs (1), *most exact, very strict*

STRAITLY
547 apĕilē (1), *menace, threat*
4183 pŏlus (2), *much*

STRAITNESS
4164 mûwtsaq (1), *distress*
4689 mâtsôwq (4), *confinement; disability*

STRAITS
3334 yâtsar (1), to *be in distress*
4712 mêtsar (1), *trouble*

STRAKE
5465 chalaō (1), to *lower as into a void*

STRAKES
6479 pᵉtsâlâh (1), *peeling*
8258 shᵉqa'rûwrâh (1), *depression*

STRANGE
312 'achêr (1), *different*
1970 hâkar (1), (poss.) to *injure*
2114 zûwr (22), to *be foreign, strange*
3937 lâ'az (1), to *speak in a foreign tongue*
5234 nâkar (1), to *treat as a foreigner*
5235 neker (1), *calamity*

5236 nêkâr (16), *foreigner; heathendom*
5237 nokrîy (20), *foreign; non-relative; different*
6012 'âmêq (2), *obscure*
245 allŏtriŏs (2), *not one's own*
1854 ĕxŏ (1), *out, outside*
2087 hĕtĕrŏs (1), *different*
3579 xĕnizō (3), to *be a guest; to be strange*
3581 xĕnŏs (3), *alien*
3861 paradŏxŏs (1), *extraordinary*

STRANGELY
5234 nâkar (1), to *treat as a foreigner*

STRANGER
376+1616 'îysh (1), *man; male; someone*
376+2114 'îysh (3), *man; male; someone*
376+5237 'îysh (2), *man; male; someone*
1121+5235 bên (3), *son, descendant; people*
1121+5236 bên (2), *son, descendant; people*
1616 gêr (69), *foreigner*
2114 zûwr (18), to *be foreign, strange*
4033 mâgûwr (3), *abode*
5235 neker (1), *calamity*
5236 nêkâr (3), *foreigner*
5237 nokrîy (14), *foreign*
8453 tôwshâb (2), *temporary dweller*
241 allŏgĕnēs (1), *foreign, i.e. not a Jew*
245 allŏtriŏs (1), *not one's own*
3581 xĕnŏs (4), *alien*
3939 parŏikĕō (1), to *reside as a foreigner*
3941 parŏikŏs (1), *strange; stranger*

STRANGER'S
1121+5236 bên (1), *son, descendant; people*
1616 gêr (1), *foreigner*

STRANGERS
582+1616 'ĕnôwsh (1), *man; person, human*
1121+5236 bên (6), *son, descendant; people*
1481 gûwr (6), to *sojourn*
1616 gêr (18), *stranger*
2114 zûwr (26), to *be foreign, strange*
4033 mâgûwr (1), *abode*
5236 nêkâr (3), *foreigner*
5237 nokrîy (2), *foreign*
8453 tôwshâb (1), *temporary dweller*
245 allŏtriŏs (3), *not one's own*
1722+3940 ĕn (1), *in; during; because of*
1927 ĕpidĕmĕō (1), to *make oneself at home*
3580 xĕnŏdŏchĕō (1), to *be hospitable*
3581 xĕnŏs (6), *alien*
3927 parepidēmŏs (1), *resident foreigner*
3941 parŏikŏs (1), *strange; stranger*

5381 philŏnĕxia (1), *hospitableness to strangers*

STRANGERS'
2114 zûwr (1), to *be foreign, strange*

STRANGLED
2614 chânaq (1), to *choke*
4156 pniktŏs (3), *animal choked to death*

STRANGLING
4267 machănaq (1), *choking, strangling*

STRAW
4963 mathbên (1), *straw*
8401 teben (15), *threshed stalks of grain*

STRAWED
2219 zârâh (1), to *toss about; to winnow*
1287 diaskŏrpizō (2), to *scatter; to squander*
4766 strŏnnumi (2), *strew, i.e. spread*

STREAM
650 'âphîyq (1), *valley; stream; mighty, strong*
793 'eshed (1), *stream*
5103 nᵉhar (Ch.) (1), *river; Euphrates River*
5158 nachal (7), *valley*
4215 pŏtamŏs (2), *current, brook*

STREAMS
650 'âphîyq (1), *valley; stream; mighty, strong*
2975 yᵉ'ôr (1), *Nile River; Tigris River*
2988 yâbâl (1), *stream*
5104 nâhâr (2), *stream*
5140 nâzal (2), to *drip*
5158 nachal (4), *valley*
6388 peleg (1), *small irrigation channel*

STREET
2351 chûwts (8), *outside, outdoors; open market*
2351+6440 chûwts (1), *outside, outdoors*
7339 rᵉchôb (22), *myriad*
7784 shûwq (1), *street*
4113 platĕia (3), *wide, open square*
4505 rhumē (2), *alley or crowded avenue*

STREETS
2351 chûwts (34), *outside, outdoors*
7339 rᵉchôb (19), *myriad*
7784 shûwq (3), *street*
58 agŏra (3), *town-square, market*
4113 platĕia (6), *wide, open square*
4505 rhumē (1), *alley or crowded avenue*

STRENGTH
193 'ûwl (1), *powerful; mighty*
202 'ôwn (7), *ability, power; wealth*
353 'ĕyâl (1), *strength*
360 'ĕyâlûwth (1), *power*
386 'êythân (2), *never-failing; eternal*

556 'amtsâh (1),
strength, force
905 bad (2), *limb,
member; bar; chief*
1082 bâlag (1), to *be
strengthened; invade*
1369 gᵉbûwrâh (17),
force; valor; victory
1679 dôbe' (1), *leisurely*
2220 zᵉrôwa' (1), *arm;
foreleg; force, power*
2388 châzaq (1), to *be
strong; courageous*
2391 chêzeq (1), *help*
2392 chôzeq (5), *power*
2394 chozqâh (1),
vehemence, harshness
2428 chayil (1), *army;
wealth; virtue; strength*
2633 chôçen (2), *wealth,
stored riches*
3027 yâd (1), *hand; power*
3581 kôach (57), *force,
might; strength*
4206 mâzîyach (2), *belt*
4581 mâ'ôwz (24),
fortified place; *defense*
5326 nitsbâh (Ch.) (1),
firmness, hardness
5331 netsach (2),
splendor; lasting
5332 nêtsach (1), blood
(as if *red juice*)
5797 'ôz (60), *strength*
5807 'ĕzûwz (2),
forcibleness
6106 'etsem (1), *bone;
body; substance*
6109 'otsmâh (2),
powerfulness
6697 tsûwr (5), *rock*
7293 rahab (1), *bluster*
7296 rôhab (1), *pride*
8443 tôw'âphâh (3),
treasure; speed
8510 têl (1), *mound*
8632 tᵉqôph (Ch.) (1),
power
8633 tôqeph (1), *might*
772 asthĕnĕs (1),
strengthless, weak
1411 dunamis (7), *force,
power, miracle*
1743 ĕndunamŏŏ (1), to
empower, strengthen
1849 ĕxŏusia (1),
authority, power, right
2479 ischus (4),
forcefulness, power
2480 ischuŏ (1), to *have
or exercise force*
2904 kratŏs (1), *vigor,
strength*
4732 stĕrĕŏŏ (1), to *be,
become strong*

STRENGTHEN
553 'âmats (7), to *be
strong; be courageous*
1396 gâbar (2), to *be
strong; to prevail*
2388 châzaq (14), to *be
strong; courageous*
4581 mâ'ôwz (1), *fortified*
place; *defense*
5582 çâ'ad (2), to *support*
5810 'âzaz (2), to *be
stout; be bold*
6965 qûwm (1), to *rise*

4599 sthĕnŏŏ (1), to
strengthen
4741 stĕrizŏ (2), to *turn
resolutely;* to *confirm*

STRENGTHENED
553 'âmats (3), to *be
strong; be courageous*
2388 châzaq (28), to *be
strong; courageous*
2394 chozqâh (1),
vehemence, harshness
5810 'âzaz (3), to *be
stout; be bold*
1412 dunamŏŏ (1), to
enable, strengthen
1743 ĕndunamŏŏ (1), to
empower, strengthen
1765 ĕnischuŏ (1), to
invigorate oneself
2901 krataiŏŏ (1),
increase in vigor

STRENGTHENEDST
7292 râhab (1), to *urge,
importune, embolden*

STRENGTHENETH
553 'âmats (2), to *be
strong; be courageous*
1082 bâlag (1), to *be
strengthened*
1396 gâbar (1), to *be
strong; to prevail*
5582 çâ'ad (1), to *support*
5810 'âzaz (1), to *be
stout; be bold*
1743 ĕndunamŏŏ (1), to
empower, strengthen

STRENGTHENING
1765 ĕnischuŏ (1), to
invigorate oneself
1991 ĕpistērizŏ (1), to
re-establish, strengthen

STRETCH
5186 nâţâh (28), to
stretch or *spread out*
5628 çârach (1), to
extend even to *excess*
6566 pâras (4), to *break
apart, disperse, scatter*
7323 rûwts (1), to *run*
7971 shâlach (10), to
send away
8311 sâra' (1), to *be
deformed*
1614 ĕktĕinŏ (4), to
stretch
5239 hupĕrĕktĕinŏ (1), to
extend inordinately

STRETCHED
1457 gâhar (2), to
prostrate, bow down
4058 mâdad (1), to *be
extended*
4900 mâshak (1), to *draw
out;* to *be tall*
5186 nâţâh (47), to
stretch or *spread out*
5203 nâţash (1), to
disperse; to *thrust* off
5628 çârach (1), to
extend even to *excess*
6504 pârad (1), to *spread
or separate*
6566 pâras (2), to *break
apart, disperse, scatter*
7554 râqa' (1), to *pound*
7849 shâţach (1), to
expand

7971 shâlach (4), to *send
away*
1600 ĕkpĕtannumi (1), to
extend, spread out
1614 ĕktĕinŏ (7), to
stretch
1911 ĕpiballŏ (1), to
throw upon

STRETCHEDST
5186 nâţâh (1), to *stretch*

STRETCHEST
5186 nâţâh (1), to *stretch*

STRETCHETH
5186 nâţâh (6), to *stretch*
6566 pâras (1), to *break
apart, disperse, scatter*

STRETCHING
4298 muţţâh (1),
expansion, extending
1614 ĕktĕinŏ (1), to
stretch

STRICKEN
935 bôw' (7), to *go, come*
1856 dâqar (1), to *stab,
pierce;* to *starve*
2498 châlaph (1), to
pierce; to *change*
5060 nâga' (1), to *strike*
5061 nega' (1), *infliction,
affliction; leprous spot*
5218 nâkê' (1), *smitten*
5221 nâkâh (3), to *strike,
kill*
8628 tâqa' (1), to *slap*
4260 prŏbainŏ (2), to
advance

STRIFE
1777 dîyn (1), to *judge;* to
strive or contend for
1779 dîyn (1), *judge;
judgment; law suit*
4066 mâdôwn (7),
contest or quarrel
4683 matstsâh (1),
quarrel
4808 mᵉrîybâh (5),
quarrel
7379 rîyb (14), *contest*
485 antilŏgia (1),
dispute, disobedience
2052 ĕrithĕia (4), *faction,
strife, selfish ambition*
2054 ĕris (4), *quarrel,* i.e.
wrangling
5379 philŏnĕikia (1),
dispute, strife

STRIFES
4090 mᵉdân (1), *contest
or quarrel*
2052 ĕrithĕia (1), *faction,
strife, selfish ambition*
3055 lŏgŏmachia (1),
disputation
3163 machē (1),
controversy, conflict

STRIKE
2498 châlaph (1), *too
pierce;* to *change*
4272 mâchats (1), to
crush; to *subdue*
5060 nâga' (1), to *strike*
5130 nûwph (1), to
quiver, vibrate, rock
5221 nâkâh (1), to *strike,
kill*

5344 nâqab (1), to
puncture, perforate
5414 nâthan (1), to *give*
6398 pâlach (1), to *pierce*
8628 tâqa' (2), to *slap*
906 ballŏ (1), to *throw*

STRIKER
4131 plēktēs (2),
pugnacious

STRIKETH
5606 çâphaq (1), to *clap*
the hands
8628 tâqa' (1), to *clatter,
slap, drive, clasp*
3817 paiŏ (1), to *hit*

STRING
3499 yether (1),
remainder; small rope
1199 dĕsmŏn (1),
shackle; impediment

STRINGED
4482 mên (1), *part;*
musical *chord*
5058 nᵉgîynâh (2),
stringed *instrument*

STRINGS
4340 mêythâr (1),
tent-*cord;* bow-*string*

STRIP
6584 pâshaţ (7), to *strip*

STRIPE
2250 chabbûwrâh (1),
weal, bruise

STRIPES
2250 chabbûwrâh (1),
weal, bruise
4112 mahălummâh (1),
blow
4347 makkâh (2), *blow;
wound; pestilence*
5061 nega' (2), *infliction,
affliction; leprous spot*
5221 nâkâh (2), to *strike,
kill*
3468 mōlōps (1), *black
eye or blow-mark, welt*
4127 plēgē (7), *stroke;
wound; calamity*

STRIPLING
5958 'elem (1), *lad,
young man*

STRIPPED
5337 nâtsal (2), to
deliver; to *be snatched*
6584 pâshaţ (6), to *strip*
7758 shôwlâl (1),
bare-foot; stripped
1562 ĕkduŏ (2), to *divest*

STRIPT
6584 pâshaţ (1), to *strip*

STRIVE
1777 dîyn (1), to *judge;* to
strive or contend for
3401 yârîyb (1),
contentious; adversary
5327 nâtsâh (2), to
quarrel, fight
7378 rîyb (9), to *hold a
controversy;* to *defend*
7379 rîyb (1), *contest*
75 agŏnizŏmai (1), to
struggle; to *contend*
118 athlĕŏ (2), to
contend in games

2051 ĕrizō (1), to *wrangle, quarrel*
3054 lŏgŏmachĕō (1), to *be disputatious*
3164 machŏmai (1), to *quarrel, dispute*
4865 sunagōnizŏmai (1), to *struggle with*

STRIVED
5389 philŏtimĕŏmai (1), *eager* or *earnest* to do

STRIVEN
1624 gârâh (1), to *provoke to anger*

STRIVETH
7378 rîyb (1), to *hold a controversy; to defend*
75 agōnizŏmai (1), to *struggle; to contend*

STRIVING
75 agōnizŏmai (1), to *struggle; to contend*
464 antagōnizŏmai (1), to *struggle against*
4866 sunathlĕō (1), to *wrestle with*

STRIVINGS
7379 rîyb (2), *contest*
3163 machĕ (1), *controversy, conflict*

STROKE
3027 yâd (1), *hand; power*
4046 maggêphâh (1), *pestilence; defeat*
4273 machats (1), *contusion*
4347 makkâh (2), *blow; wound; pestilence*
5061 nega' (3), *infliction, affliction; leprous spot*
5607 çêpheq (1), *satiety*

STROKES
4112 mahălummâh (1), *blow*

STRONG
47 'abbîyr (3), *mighty*
386 'êythân (5), *never-failing; eternal*
410 'êl (1), *mighty*
533 'ammîyts (4), *strong; mighty; brave*
553 'âmats (4), to *be strong; be courageous*
559 'âmar (1), to *say*
650 'âphîyq (1), *valley; stream; mighty, strong*
1219 bâtsar (1), to *be inaccessible*
1225 bitstsârôwn (1), *fortress*
1368 gibbôwr (5), *powerful; great warrior*
1634 gerem (1), *bone; self*
2364 Chûwshâh (1), *haste*
2388 châzaq (47), to *be strong; courageous*
2389 châzâq (26), *strong; severe, hard, violent*
2393 chezqâh (1), *power*
2394 chozqâh (1), *vehemence, harshness*
2428 chayil (5), *army; wealth; virtue; strength*
2626 chăçîyn (1), *mighty*
2634 châçôn (1), *strong*

3524 kabbîyr (1), *mighty; aged; mighty*
4013 mibtsâr (14), *fortification; defender*
4581 mâ'ôwz (5), *fortified place; defense*
4679 mᵉtsad (5), *stronghold*
4686 mâtsûwd (2), *net or capture; fastness*
4692 mâtsôwr (3), *siege-mound; distress*
4694 mᵉtsûwrâh (1), *rampart, fortification*
5553 çela' (1), *craggy rock; fortress*
5794 'az (12), *strong, vehement, harsh*
5797 'ôz (17), *strength*
5808 'izzûwz (1), *forcible; army*
5810 'âzaz (1), to *be stout; be bold*
6076 'ôphel (1), *tumor; fortress*
6099 'âtsûwm (13), *powerful; numerous*
6105 'âtsam (4), to *be, make powerful*
6108 'ôtsem (1), *power; framework of the body*
6110 'atstsûmâh (1), *defensive argument*
6184 'ârîyts (1), *powerful or tyrannical*
6339 pâzaz (1), to *solidify by refining; to spring*
6697 tsûwr (1), *rock*
7682 sâgab (1), to *be safe, strong*
7941 shêkâr (1), *liquor*
8624 taqqîyph (Ch.) (3), *powerful*
8631 tᵉqêph (Ch.) (3), to *become, make mighty*
1415 dunatŏs (3), *powerful or capable*
1743 ĕndunamŏō (4), to *empower, strengthen*
1753 ĕnĕrgĕia (1), *energy, power*
2478 ischurŏs (11), *forcible, powerful*
2901 krataiŏō (3), *increase in vigor*
3173 mĕgas (1), *great*
3794 ŏchurōma (1), *fortress, stronghold*
4608 sikĕra (1), *intoxicant*
4731 stĕrĕŏs (2), *solid*
4732 stĕrĕŏō (1), to *be, become strong*

STRONGER
553 'âmats (2), to *be strong; be courageous*
555 'ômets (1), *strength*
1396 gâbar (1), to *be strong; to prevail*
2388 châzaq (6), to *be strong; courageous*
2389 châzâq (1), *strong*
2390 châzêq (1), *powerful; loud*
5794 'az (1), *strong*
6105 'âtsam (1), to *be, make powerful*
7194 qâshar (2), to *tie, bind*

2478 ischurŏs (3), *forcible, powerful*

STRONGEST
1368 gibbôwr (1), *powerful; great warrior*

STROVE
1519 gîyach (Ch.) (1), to *rush forth*
5327 nâtsâh (6), to *quarrel, fight*
6229 'âsaq (1), to *quarrel*
7378 rîyb (3), to *hold a controversy; to defend*
1264 diamachŏmai (1), to *fight fiercely*
3164 machŏmai (2), to *war, quarrel, dispute*

STROWED
2236 zâraq (1), to *scatter*

STRUCK
5062 nâgaph (2), to *inflict a disease; strike*
5221 nâkâh (1), to *strike*
8138 shânâh (1), to *fold*
1325+4475 didōmi (1), to *give*
3960 patassō (1), to *strike*
5180 tuptō (1), to *strike*

STRUGGLED
7533 râtsats (1), to *crack in pieces, smash*

STUBBLE
7179 qash (16), *dry straw*
8401 teben (1), *threshed stalks of grain*
2562 kalamē (1), *stubble*

STUBBORN
5637 çârar (4), to *be refractory, stubborn*
7186 qâsheh (1), *severe*

STUBBORNNESS
6484 pâtsar (1), to *stun or dull*
7190 qᵉshîy (1), *obstinacy*

STUCK
1692 dâbaq (1), to *cling or adhere; to catch*
4600 mâ'ak (1), to *press*
2043 ĕrĕidō (1), to *make immovable*

STUDIETH
1897 hâgâh (2), to *murmur, ponder*

STUDS
5351 nᵉquddâh (1), *ornamental boss*

STUDY
3854 lahag (1), *mental application*
4704 spŏudazō (1), to *make effort*
5389 philŏtimĕŏmai (1), *eager* or *earnest* to do

STUFF
3627 kᵉlîy (14), *thing*
4399 mᵉlâ'kâh (1), *work*
4632 skĕuŏs (1), *vessel*

STUMBLE
3782 kâshal (15), to *stumble*
5062 nâgaph (2), to *inflict a disease; strike*
6328 pûwq (1), to *waver*

4350 prŏskŏptō (1), to *trip up; to strike*

STUMBLED
3782 kâshal (3), to *totter*
8058 shâmaţ (1), to *jostle; to let alone*
4350 prŏskŏptō (1), to *trip up; to strike*
4417 ptaiō (1), to *trip up*

STUMBLETH
3782 kâshal (1), to *totter*
4350 prŏskŏptō (3), to *trip up; to strike*

STUMBLING
5063 negeph (1), *trip*
4625 skandalŏn (1), *snare*

STUMBLINGBLOCK
4383 mikshôwl (7), *stumbling-block*
4348 prŏskŏmma (2), *occasion of apostasy*
4625 skandalŏn (3), *snare*

STUMBLINGBLOCKS
4383 mikshôwl (1), *stumbling-block*
4384 makshêlâh (1), *stumbling-block*

STUMBLINGSTONE
3037+4348 lithŏs (2), *stone*

STUMP
6136 'iqqar (Ch.) (3), *stock*

SUAH
5477 Çûwach (1), *sweeping*

SUBDUE
1696 dâbar (1), to *subdue*
3533 kâbash (3), to *conquer, subjugate*
3665 kâna' (1), to *humiliate, subdue*
7286 râdad (1), to *conquer; to overlay*
8214 shᵉphal (Ch.) (1), to *humiliate*
5293 hupŏtassō (1), to *subordinate; to obey*

SUBDUED
3381 yârad (1), to *descend*
3533 kâbash (5), to *conquer, subjugate*
3665 kâna' (9), to *humiliate, subdue*
3766 kâra' (2), to *prostrate*
2610 katagōnizŏmai (1), to *overcome, defeat*
5293 hupŏtassō (1), to *subordinate; to obey*

SUBDUEDST
3665 kâna' (1), to *humiliate, subdue*

SUBDUETH
1696 dâbar (1), to *subdue*
2827 chăshal (Ch.) (1), to *crush, pulverize*
7286 râdad (1), to *conquer; to overlay*

SUBJECT
1379 dŏgmatizō (1), to *submit* to a certain *rule*

1777 ĕnŏchŏs (1), *liable*
3663 hŏmŏiŏpathēs (1),
  similarly affected
5293 hupŏtassō (14), *to*
  subordinate; to obey

SUBJECTED
5293 hupŏtassō (1), *to*
  subordinate; to obey

SUBJECTION
3533 kâbash (2), *to*
  conquer, subjugate
3665 kâna' (1), *to*
  humiliate, subdue
1396 dŏulagōgĕō (1), *to*
  enslave, subdue
5292 hupŏtagē (4),
  subordination
5293 hupŏtassō (6), *to*
  subordinate; to obey

SUBMIT
3584 kâchash (3), *to lie,*
  disown; to cringe
6031 'ânâh (1), *to afflict,*
  be afflicted
7511 râphaç (1), *to*
  trample; to prostrate
5226 hupĕikō (1), *to*
  surrender, yield
5293 hupŏtassō (6), *to*
  subordinate; to obey

SUBMITTED
3584 kâchash (1), *to lie,*
  disown; to cringe
5414+3027 nâthan (1), *to*
  give
5293 hupŏtassō (1), *to*
  subordinate; to obey

SUBMITTING
5293 hupŏtassō (1), *to*
  subordinate; to obey

SUBORNED
5260 hupŏballō (1), *to*
  throw in stealthily

SUBSCRIBE
3789 kâthab (2), *to write*

SUBSCRIBED
3789 kâthab (2), *to write*

SUBSTANCE
202 'ôwn (1), *ability,*
  power; wealth
1564 gôlem (1), *embryo*
1942 havvâh (1), *desire;*
  craving
1952 hôwn (7), *wealth*
2428 chayil (7), *wealth;*
  virtue; valor; strength
3351 yᵉqûwm (3), *living*
  thing
3426 yêsh (1), *there is*
3428 Yesheb'âb (1), *seat*
  of (his) *father*
3581 kôach (1), *force,*
  might; strength
4678 matstsebeth (2),
  stock of a tree
4735 miqneh (1), *stock*
6108 'ôtsem (1), *power;*
  framework of the body
7009 qîym (1), *opponent*
7075 qinyân (4),
  acquisition, purchase
7399 rᵉkûwsh (11),
  property
7738 shâvâh (1), *to*
  destroy

3776 ŏusia (1), *wealth,*
  property, possessions
5223 huparxis (1),
  property, possessions
5224 huparchŏnta (1),
  property or possessions
5287 hupŏstasis (1),
  essence; assurance

SUBTIL
2450 châkâm (1), *wise,*
  intelligent, skillful
5341 nâtsar (1), *to*
  conceal, hide
6175 'ârûwm (1),
  cunning; clever

SUBTILLY
5230 nâkal (1), *to act*
  treacherously
6191 'âram (1), *to be*
  cunning; be prudent
2686 katasŏphizŏmai*
  (1), *to be crafty against*

SUBTILTY
4820 mirmâh (1), *fraud*
6122 'oqbâh (1), *trickery*
6195 'ormâh (1), *trickery;*
  discretion
1388 dŏlŏs (2), *wile,*
  deceit, trickery
3834 panŏurgia (1),
  trickery or sophistry

SUBURBS
4054 migrâsh (110), *open*
  country
6503 Parbâr (1), *Parbar*

SUBVERT
5791 'âvath (1), *to wrest,*
  twist
396 anatrĕpō (1), *to*
  overturn, destroy

SUBVERTED
1612 ĕkstrĕphō (1), *to*
  pervert, be warped

SUBVERTING
384 anaskĕuazō (1), *to*
  upset, trouble
2692 katastrŏphē (1),
  catastrophical ruin

SUCCEED
6965 qûwm (1), *to rise*

SUCCEEDED
3423 yârash (3), *to*
  impoverish; to ruin

SUCCEEDEST
3423 yârash (2), *to*
  impoverish; to ruin

SUCCESS
7919 sâkal (1), *to be or*
  act circumspect

SUCCOTH
5523 Çukkôwth (18),
  booths

SUCCOTH-BENOTH
5524 Çukkôwth Bᵉnôwth
  (1), *brothels*

SUCCOUR
5826 'âzar (2), *to aid*
997 bŏēthĕō (1), *to aid*

SUCCOURED
5826 'âzar (1), *to aid*
997 bŏēthĕō (1), *to aid*

SUCCOURER
4368 prŏstatis (1),
  assistant, helper

SUCHATHITES
7756 Sûwkâthîy (1),
  Sukathite

SUCK
3243 yânaq (13), *to suck*
4680 mâtsâh (1), *to*
  drain; to squeeze out
5966 'âla' (1), *to sip up*
2337 thēlazō (4), *to suck*

SUCKED
3243 yânaq (1), *to suck*
2337 thēlazō (1), *to suck*

SUCKING
2461 châlâb (1), *milk*
3243 yânaq (3), *to suck*
5764 'ûwl (1), *babe*

SUCKLING
3243 yânaq (3), *to suck*

SUCKLINGS
3243 yânaq (3), *to suck*
2337 thēlazō (1), *to suck*

SUDDEN
6597 pith'ôwm (2),
  instantly, suddenly
160 aiphnidiŏs (1),
  suddenly

SUDDENLY
4116 mâhar (1), *to hurry*
4118 mahêr (1), *in a*
  hurry
6597 pith'ôwm (22),
  instantly, suddenly
6621 petha' (4), *wink, i.e.*
  moment; quickly
7280 râga' (2), *to settle,*
  i.e. quiet; to wink
7281 rega' (1), *very short*
  space of time
869 aphnō (3), *suddenly*
1810 ĕxaiphnēs (5),
  suddenly, unexpectedly
1819 ĕxapina (1),
  unexpectedly
5030 tachĕōs (1), *rapidly*

SUE
2919 krinō (1), *to decide;*
  to try, condemn, punish

SUFFER
3201 yâkôl (1), *to be able*
3240 yânach (3), *to allow*
  to stay
3803 kâthar (1), *to*
  enclose, besiege; to wait
5375 nâsâ' (5), *to lift up*
5414 nâthan (11), *to give*
430 anĕchŏmai (7), *put*
  up with, endure
818 atimazō (1), *to*
  maltreat, dishonor
863 aphiēmi (8), *to leave;*
  to pardon, forgive
1325 didōmi (2), *to give*
1377 diōkō (3), *to pursue;*
  to persecute
1439 ĕaō (2), *to let be, i.e.*
  permit or leave alone
2010 ĕpitrĕpō (6), *allow*
2210 zēmiŏō (1), *to*
  experience detriment
2553 kakŏpathĕō (1), *to*
  undergo suffering
2558 kakŏuchĕō (1), *to*
  maltreat; to torment
3805 pathētŏs (1),
  doomed to pain

3958 paschō (20), *to*
  experience pain
4722 stĕgō (1), *to endure*
  patiently
4778 sugkakŏuchĕō (1),
  to endure persecution
4841 sumpaschō (2), *to*
  experience pain jointly
5278 hupŏmĕnō (1), *to*
  undergo, bear (trials)
5302 hustĕrĕō (1), *to be*
  inferior; to fall short

SUFFERED
3240 yânach (2), *to allow*
  to stay
5203 nâţash (1), *to*
  disperse; to thrust off
5375 nâsâ' (1), *to lift up*
5414 nâthan (7), *to give*
863 aphiēmi (6), *to leave;*
  to pardon, forgive
1439 ĕaō (5), *to let be, i.e.*
  permit or leave alone
2010 ĕpitrĕpō (4), *allow*
2210 zēmiŏō (1), *to suffer*
  loss
2967 kōluō (1), *to stop*
3958 paschō (17), *to*
  experience pain
4310 prŏpaschō (1), *to*
  undergo hardship
5159 trŏpŏphŏrĕō (1), *to*
  endure one's habits

SUFFEREST
1439 ĕaō (1), *to let be*

SUFFERETH
5414 nâthan (1), *to give*
971 biazō (1), *to crowd*
  oneself into
1439 ĕaō (1), *to let be*
3114 makrŏthumĕō (1),
  to be forbearing, patient

SUFFERING
2552 kakŏpathĕia (1),
  hardship, suffering
3804 pathēma (1),
  passion; suffering
3958 paschō (1), *to*
  experience pain
4330 prŏsĕaō (1), *to*
  permit further progress
5254 hupĕchō (1), *to*
  endure with patience

SUFFERINGS
3804 pathēma (10),
  passion; suffering

SUFFICE
4672 mâtsâ' (2), *to find*
  or acquire; to occur
5606 çâphaq (1), *to be*
  enough; to vomit
7227 rab (3), *great*
713 arkĕtŏs (1), *enough*

SUFFICED
4672 mâtsâ' (1), *to find*
  or acquire; to occur
7646 sâba' (1), *fill to*
  satiety
7648 sôba' (1),
  satisfaction

SUFFICETH
714 arkĕō (1), *to avail; be*
  satisfactory

SUFFICIENCY
5607 çêpheq (1), *satiety*

841 autarkeia (1),
contentedness
2426 hikanŏtēs (1),
ability, competence

SUFFICIENT
1767 day (5), *enough*
7227 rab (1), *great*
713 arkĕtŏs (1), enough
714 arkĕō (2), to *avail; be satisfactory*
2425 hikanŏs (3), *ample*

SUFFICIENTLY
4078 madday (1),
sufficiently
7654 sob'âh (1), *satiety*

SUIT
2470 châlâh (1), to *be weak, sick, afflicted*
6187 'êrek (1), *pile, equipment, estimate*
7379 rîyb (1), *contest*

SUKKIIMS
5525 Çukkĭy (1),
hut-dwellers

SUM
3724 kôpher (1),
redemption-price
4557 miçpâr (2), *number*
6485 pâqad (1), to *visit, care for, count*
6575 pârâshâh (1),
exposition
7217 rê'sh (Ch.) (1), *head*
7218 rô'sh (9), *head*
8508 toknîyth (1),
consummation
8552 tâmam (1), to *complete, finish*
2774 kĕphalaiŏn (2),
principal; amount
5092 timē (1), *esteem; nobility; money*

SUMMER
4747 mᵉqêrâh (2),
cooling off, *coolness*
6972 qûwts (1), to *spend the harvest season*
7007 qâyit (Ch.) (1),
harvest season
7019 qayits (20), *harvest*
2330 thĕrŏs (3), *summer*

SUMPTUOUSLY
2983 lambanŏ (1), to *take, receive*

SUN
216 'ôwr (1), *luminary*
2535 chammâh (4), *heat of sun*
2775 chereç (3), *itch; sun*
8121 shemesh (120), *sun*
8122 shemesh (Ch.) (1), *sun*
2246 hēliŏs (30), *sun*

SUNDERED
6504 pârad (1), to *spread or separate*

SUNDRY
4181 pŏlumĕrŏs (1), *in many portions*

SUNG
7891 shîyr (1), to *sing*
103 aᵢdō (2), to *sing*
5214 humnĕō (2), to *celebrate* God in song

SUNK
2883 ţâba' (5), to *sink*
3766 kâra' (1), to *prostrate*
2702 kataphĕrō (1), to *bear down*

SUNRISING
4217 mizrâch (1), place of *sunrise; east*
4217+8121 mizrâch (9), place of *sunrise; east*

SUP
4041 mᵉgammâh (1),
accumulation
1172 dĕipnĕō (2), to *eat the principal meal*

SUPERFLUITY
4050 pĕrissĕia (1),
superabundance

SUPERFLUOUS
8311 sâra' (2), to *be deformed*
4053 pĕrissŏs (1),
superabundant

SUPERSCRIPTION
1923 ĕpigraphē (5),
superscription

SUPERSTITION
1175 dĕisidaimŏnia (1),
religion

SUPERSTITIOUS
1174 dĕisidaimŏnĕstĕrŏs (1), *more religious*

SUPPED
1172 dĕipnĕō (1), to *eat the principal meal*

SUPPER
1172 dĕipnĕō (1), to *eat the principal meal*
1173 dĕipnŏn (13),
principal *meal*

SUPPLANT
6117 'âqab (1), to *seize by the heel; to circumvent*

SUPPLANTED
6117 'âqab (1), to *seize by the heel; to circumvent*

SUPPLE
4935 mish'îy (1),
inspection

SUPPLIANTS
6282 'âthâr (1), *incense; worshipper*

SUPPLICATION
2420 chîydâh (1), *puzzle; conundrum; maxim*
2603 chânan (10), to *implore*
2604 chănan (Ch.) (1), to *favor*
6419 pâlal (1), to *intercede, pray*
8467 tᵉchinnâh (22),
supplication
1162 dĕĕsis (4), petition

SUPPLICATIONS
8467 tᵉchinnâh (1),
supplication
8469 tachănûwn (17),
earnest *prayer, plea*
1162 dĕĕsis (2), petition
2428 hikĕtēria (1),
entreaty, supplication

SUPPLIED
378 anaplĕrŏō (1), to *complete; to supply*
4322 prŏsanaplĕrŏō (1), to *furnish fully*

SUPPLIETH
2024 ĕpichŏrēgia (1),
contribution, aid
4322 prŏsanaplĕrŏō (1), to *furnish fully*

SUPPLY
378 anaplĕrŏō (1), to *complete; to supply*
2024 ĕpichŏrēgia (1),
contribution, aid
4137 plĕrŏō (1), to *fill, make complete*

SUPPORT
472 antĕchŏmai (1), to *adhere to; to care for*
482 antilambanŏmai (1), to *succor; aid*

SUPPOSE
559 'âmar (1), to *say*
1380 dŏkĕō (3), to *think, regard, seem* good
3049 lŏgizŏmai (2), to *credit; to think, regard*
3543 nŏmizō (1), to *deem*
3633 ŏiŏmai (1), to *imagine, opine*
5274 hupŏlambanō (2), to *assume, presume*

SUPPOSED
1380 dŏkĕō (2), to *think*
2233 hēgĕŏmai (1), to *deem*, i.e. *consider*
3543 nŏmizō (4), to *deem*
5282 hupŏnŏĕō (1), to *think; to expect*

SUPPOSING
1380 dŏkĕō (2), to *think*
3543 nŏmizō (2), to *deem*
3633 ŏiŏmai (1), to *imagine, opine*

SUPREME
5242 hupĕrĕchō (1), to *excel; be superior*

SUR
5495 Çûwr (1),
deteriorated

SURE
539 'âman (11), to *be firm, faithful, true*
546 'omnâh (1), *surely*
548 'ămânâh (1),
covenant
571 'emeth (1), *certainty, truth, trustworthiness*
982 bâţach (1), to *trust, be confident* or *sure*
2388 châzaq (1), to *bind*
3045 yâda' (1), to *know*
3245 yâçad (1), *settle, consult, establish*
4009 mibţâch (1),
security; assurance
6965 qûwm (2), to *rise*
7011 qayâm (Ch.) (1),
permanent
7292 râhab (1), to *urge, embolden, capture*
8104 shâmar (1), to *watch*
804 asphalēs (1), *secure*

SUPPLIED ... 805 asphalizō (3), to *render secure*
949 bĕbaiŏs (3), *stable, certain, binding*
1097 ginŏskŏ (2), to *know*
1492 ĕidō (3), to *know*
4103 pistŏs (1),
trustworthy; reliable
4731 stĕrĕŏs (1), *solid*

SURETIES
6148 'ârab (1), to *give or be security*

SURETISHIP
8628 tâqa' (1), to *clatter, slap, drive, clasp*

SURETY
389 'ak (1), *surely*
552 'umnâm (1), *verily*
3045 yâda' (1), to *know*
6148 'ârab (8), to *give or be security*
6161 'ărubbâh (1), as *security; bondsman*
230 alēthŏs (1), *surely*
1450 ĕgguŏs (1),
bondsman, guarantor

SURFEITING
2897 kraipalē (1),
debauch

SURMISINGS
5283 hupŏnŏia (1),
suspicion

SURNAME
3655 kânâh (1), to *address, give title*
1941 ĕpikalĕŏmai (6), to *invoke*
2564 kalĕō (1), to *call*

SURNAMED
3655 kânâh (1), to *address, give title*
1941 ĕpikalĕŏmai (5), to *invoke*
2007+3686 ĕpitithēmi (2), to *impose*

SURPRISED
270 'âchaz (1), to *seize*
8610 tâphas (2), to *seize*

SUSANCHITES
7801 Shûwshankîy (Ch.) (1), *Shushankite*

SUSANNA
4677 Sŏusanna (1), *lily*

SUSI
5485 Çûwçîy (1),
horse-like

SUSTAIN
3557 kûwl (4), to *maintain*

SUSTAINED
5564 çâmak (3), to *lean* upon; *take hold* of

SUSTENANCE
3557 kûwl (1), to *maintain*
4241 michyâh (1),
sustenance
5527 chŏrtasma (1), *food*

SWADDLED
2853 châthal (1), to *swathe, wrap in cloth*
2946 ţâphach (1), to *nurse*

SWADDLING
4683 *sparganŏō* (2), to *wrap* with cloth

SWADDLINGBAND
2854 chăthullâh (1), *swathing* cloth to wrap

SWALLOW
1104 bâla' (13), to *swallow; to destroy*
1866 dᵉrôwr (2), *swallow*
3886 lûwa' (1), to *be rash*
5693 'âgûwr (2), *swallow*
7602 shâ'aph (4), to *be angry; to hasten*
2666 katapinō (1), to *devour by swallowing*

SWALLOWED
1104 bâla' (19), to *swallow; to destroy*
1105 bela' (1), *gulp*
3886 lûwa' (1), to *be rash*
7602 shâ'aph (1), to *be angry; to hasten*
2666 katapinō (4), to *devour by swallowing*

SWALLOWETH
1572 gâmâ' (1), to *swallow*
7602 shâ'aph (1), to *be angry; to hasten*

SWAN
8580 tanshemeth (2), (poss.) *water-hen*

SWARE
5375 nâsâ' (1), to *lift up*
7650 shâba' (70), to *swear*
3660 ŏmnuō (7), to *swear, declare on oath*

SWAREST
7650 shâba' (5), to *swear*

SWARM
5712 'êdâh (1), *assemblage; family*
6157 'ârôb (2), swarming *mosquitoes*

SWARMS
6157 'ârôb (5), swarming *mosquitoes*

SWEAR
422 'âlâh (2), *imprecate, utter a curse*
5375 nâsâ' (2), to *lift up*
7650 shâba' (43), to *swear*
3660 ŏmnuō (13), to *swear, declare on oath*

SWEARERS
7650 shâba' (1), to *swear*

SWEARETH
7650 shâba' (7), to *swear*
3660 ŏmnuō (4), to *swear, declare on oath*

SWEARING
422 'âlâh (2), *imprecate, utter a curse*
423 'âlâh (2), *imprecation: curse*

SWEAT
2188 zê'âh (1), *sweat*
3154 yeza' (1), *sweat*
2402 hidrōs (1), *sweat*

SWEEP
2894 ṭûw' (1), to *sweep away*

3261 yâ'âh (1), to *brush aside*
4563 sarŏō (1), to *sweep clean*

SWEEPING
5502 çâchaph (1), to *scrape off, sweep off*

SWEET
1314 besem (5), *spice; fragrance; balsam*
2896 ṭôwb (1), *good; well*
3190 yâṭab (1), to *be, make well*
4452 mâlats (1), to *be smooth; to be pleasant*
4477 mamtaq (2), *sweet*
4575 ma'ădannâh (1), *bond,* i.e. *group*
4840 merqâch (1), *spicy*
4966 mâthôwq (7), *sweet*
4985 mâthaq (5), to *relish; to be sweet*
5207 nîchôwach (43), *pleasant; delight*
5208 nîychôwach (Ch.) (2), *pleasure*
5273 nâ'îym (2), *delightful; sweet*
5276 nâ'êm (1), to *be agreeable*
5561 çam (16), *aroma*
5674 'âbar (2), to *cross over; to transition*
6071 'âçîyç (2), *expressed fresh* grape-juice
6148 'ârab (5), to *intermix*
6149 'ârêb (2), *agreeable*
8492 tîyrôwsh (1), *wine; squeezed* grape-juice
1099 glukus (3), *sweet*
2175 ĕuōdia (2), *fragrance, aroma*

SWEETER
4966 mâthôwq (2), *sweet*

SWEETLY
4339 mêyshâr (1), *straightness; rectitude*
4988 mâthâq (1), sweet *food*

SWEETNESS
4966 mâthôwq (2), *sweet*
4986 metheq (2), *pleasantness*
4987 môtheq (1), *sweetness*

SWEETSMELLING
2175 ĕuōdia (1), *fragrance, aroma*

SWELL
1216 bâtsêq (1), to *blister*
6638 tsâbâh (2), to *array* an army against
6639 tsâbeh (1), *swollen*

SWELLED
1216 bâtsêq (1), to *blister*

SWELLING
1158 bâ'âh (1), to *ask; be bulging, swelling*
1346 ga'ăvâh (1), *arrogance; majesty*
1347 gâ'ôwn (3), *ascending; majesty*
5246 hupĕrŏgkŏs (2), *insolent, boastful*

SWELLINGS
5450 phusiōsis (1), *haughtiness, arrogance*

SWEPT
1640 gâraph (1), to *sweep away*
5502 çâchaph (1), to *scrape off, sweep off*
4563 sarŏō (2), to *sweep clean*

SWERVED
795 astŏchĕō (1), *deviate*

SWIFT
16 'êbeh (1), *papyrus*
3753 karkârâh (1), cow-*camel*
4116 mâhar (3), to *hurry*
7031 qal (9), *rapid, swift*
7043 qâlal (1), to *be, make light (swift)*
7409 rekesh (1), *relay*
3691 ŏxus (1), *rapid, fast*
5031 tachinŏs (1), *soon, immanent*
5036 tachus (1), *prompt*

SWIFTER
7031 qal (1), *rapid, swift*
7043 qâlal (5), to *be, make light (swift)*

SWIFTLY
3288 yᵉ'âph (1), utterly *exhausted*
4120 mᵉhêrâh (1), *hurry*
7031 qal (2), *rapid, swift*

SWIM
6687 tsûwph (1), to *overflow*
7811 sâchâh (2), to *swim*
7813 sâchûw (1), *pond* for *swimming*
1579 ĕkkŏlumbaō (1), to *escape by swimming*
2860 kŏlumbaō (1), to *plunge into water*

SWIMMEST
6824 tsâphâh (1), *inundation*

SWIMMETH
7811 sâchâh (1), to *swim*

SWINE
2386 chăzîyr (2), *hog*
5519 chŏirŏs (14), *pig*

SWINE'S
2386 chăzîyr (4), *hog*

SWOLLEN
4092 pimprēmi (1), to *become inflamed*

SWOON
5848 'âṭaph (1), to *languish*

SWOONED
5848 'âṭaph (1), to *languish*

SWORD
1300 bârâq (1), *lightning; flash of lightning*
2719 chereb (380), *sword*
7524 retsach (1), *crushing; murder-cry*
7973 shelach (3), *spear*
3162 machaira (22), short *sword*
4501 rhŏmphaia (7), *sabre, cutlass*

SWORDS
2719 chereb (17), *sword*
6609 pᵉthîchâh (1), *drawn* sword
3162 machaira (6), short *sword*

SWORN
1167+7621 ba'al (1), *master; husband*
3027+5920+3676 yâd (1), *hand; power*
5375 nâsâ' (1), to *lift up*
7650 shâba' (42), to *swear*
3660 ŏmnuō (3), to *swear*

SYCAMINE
4807 sukaminŏs (1), *sycamore-*fig tree

SYCHAR
4965 Suchar (1), *liquor*

SYCHEM
4966 Suchĕm (2), *ridge*

SYCOMORE
8256 shâqâm (6), *sycamore* tree
4809 sukŏmōraia (1), *sycamore-*fig tree

SYCOMORES
8256 shâqâm (1), *sycamore* tree

SYENE
5482 Çᵉvênêh (2), the local *Seven*

SYNAGOGUE
656 apŏsunagōgŏs (2), *excommunicated*
752 archisunagōgŏs (7), *director of* the *synagogue* services
4864 sunagōgē (34), *assemblage*

SYNAGOGUE'S
752 archisunagōgŏs (2), *director of* the *synagogue* services

SYNAGOGUES
4150 môw'êd (1), *place of meeting; congregation*
656 apŏsunagōgŏs (1), *excommunicated*
4864 sunagōgē (22), *assemblage*

SYNTYCHE
4941 Suntuchē (1), *accident*

SYRACUSE
4946 Surakŏusai (1), *Syracuse*

SYRIA
758 'Arâm (66), *highland*
4947 Suria (8), (poss.) *rock*

SYRIA-DAMASCUS
758+1834 'Arâm (1), *highland*

SYRIA-MAACHAH
758 'Arâm (1), *highland*

SYRIACK
762 'Ărâmîyth (1), *in Araman*

SYRIAN
761 'Ărammîy (7), *Aramite*

762 'Ărâmîyth (4), *in Araman*

4948 Surŏs (1), *native of Syria*

SYRIANS
758 'Arâm (57), *highland*
761 'Ărammîy (4), *Aramite*

SYROPHENICIAN
4949 Surŏphŏinissa (1), *native of Phœnicia*

TAANACH
8590 Ta'ănâk (6), *Taanak or Tanak*

TAANATH-SHILOH
8387 Ta'ănath Shîlôh (1), *approach of Shiloh*

TABBAOTH
2884 Ṭabbâ'ôwth (2), *rings*

TABBATH
2888 Ṭabbath (1), *Tabbath*

TABEAL
2870 Ṭâbᵉ'êl (1), *pleasing* (to) *God*

TABEEL
2870 Ṭâbᵉ'êl (1), *pleasing* (to) *God*

TABERAH
8404 Tab'êrâh (2), *burning*

TABERING
8608 tâphaph (1), to *drum* on a tambourine

TABERNACLE
168 'ôhel (187), *tent*
4908 mishkân (114), *residence*
5520 çôk (1), *hut of entwined boughs*
5521 çukkâh (3), *tabernacle; shelter*
5522 çikkûwth (1), *idolatrous booth*
7900 sôk (1), *booth*
4633 skĕnē (15), *tent*
4636 skĕnŏs (2), *tent*
4638 skĕnōma (3), *dwelling: the Temple*

TABERNACLES
168 'ôhel (11), *tent*
4908 mishkân (5), *residence*
5521 çukkâh (9), *tabernacle; shelter*
4633 skĕnē (4), *tent*
4634 skĕnŏpēgia (1), *tabernacles, i.e.* booths

TABITHA
5000 Tabitha (2), *gazelle*

TABLE
3871 lûwach (4), *tablet*
4524 mêçab (1), *divan couch; around*
7979 shulchân (56), *table*
345 anakĕimai (1), to *recline at a meal*
4093 pinakidiŏn (1), *wooden writing tablet*
5132 trapĕza (9), four-legged *table or stool*

TABLES
3871 lûwach (34), *tablet*

7979 shulchân (14), *table*
2825 klinē (1), *couch*
4109 plax (3), *tablet*
5132 trapĕza (4), four-legged *table or stool*

TABLETS
1004+5315 bayith (1), *house; temple; family*
3558 kûwmâz (2), *jewel*

TABOR
8396 Tâbôwr (10), *broken*

TABRET
8596 tôph (3), *tambourine*
8611 tôpheth (1), *smiting*

TABRETS
8596 tôph (5), *tambourine*

TABRIMON
2886 Tabrimmôwn (1), *pleasing* (to) *Rimmon*

TACHES
7165 qereç (10), *knob*

TACHMONITE
8461 Tachkᵉmônîy (1), *sagacious*

TACKLING
4631 skĕuē (1), *tackle*

TACKLINGS
2256 chebel (1), *company*

TADMOR
8412 Tadmôr (2), *palm*

TAHAN
8465 Tachan (2), *station*

TAHANITES
8470 Tachănîy (1), *Tachanite*

TAHAPANES
8471 Tachpanchêç (1), *Tachpanches*

TAHATH
8480 Tachath (6), *bottom*

TAHPANHES
8471 Tachpanchêç (5), *Tachpanches*

TAHPENES
8472 Tachpᵉnêyç (3), *Tachpenes*

TAHREA
8475 Tachrêa' (1), (poss.) *earth, ground; low*

TAHTIM-HODSHI
8483 Tachtîym Chodshîy (1), *lower* (ones) *monthly*

TAIL
2180 zânâb (8), *tail*
3769 ŏura (1), *tail*

TAILS
2180 zânâb (2), *tail*
3769 ŏura (4), *tail*

TAKE
6 'âbad (1), to *perish*
270 'âchaz (12), to *seize*
622 'âçaph (7), to *gather*
680 'âtsal (1), to *select*
935 bôw' (1), to *go, come*
962 bâzaz (9), to *plunder*
1197 bâ'ar (4), to *be brutish, be senseless*
1497 gâzal (3), to *rob*

1692 dâbaq (1), to *cling* or *adhere;* to *catch*
1898 hâgâh (2), to *remove, expel*
1961 hâyâh (1), to *exist*
2095 zᵉhar (Ch.) (1), *be admonished, be careful*
2254 châbal (7), to *bind* by a *pledge;* to *pervert*
2388 châzaq (9), to *fasten* upon; to *seize*
2502 châlats (1), to *present, strengthen*
2834 châsaph (1), to *drain* away or *bail* up
2846 châthâh (3), to *lay hold* of; to *take away*
3051 yâhab (1), to *give*
3212 yâlak (1), to *carry*
3318 yâtsâ' (2), to *go, bring out*
3381 yârad (3), to *descend*
3423 yârash (3), to *inherit*
3615 kâlâh (1), to *complete, prepare*
3920 lâkad (19), to *catch*
3947 lâqach (367), to *take*
5253 nâçag (2), to *retreat*
5267 nᵉçaq (Ch.) (1), to *go up*
5312 nᵉphaq (Ch.) (1), to *issue forth;* to *bring out*
5337 nâtsal (1), to *deliver;* to *be snatched*
5375 nâsâ' (60), to *lift up*
5376 nᵉsâ' (Ch.) (1), to *lift up*
5381 nâsag (5), to *reach*
5414 nâthan (1), to *give*
5493 çûwr (45), to *turn off*
5496 çûwth (1), to *stimulate;* to *seduce*
5535 çâkath (1), to *be silent;* to *observe*
5674 'âbar (2), to *cross over;* to *transition*
5709 'ădâ' (Ch.) (1), to *pass on* or *continue*
5749 'ûwd (2), to *encompass, restore*
5927 'âlâh (4), to *ascend*
5978 'immâd (1), *with*
6213 'âsâh (1), to *do*
6331 pûwr (1), to *crush*
6679 tsûwd (1), to *catch*
6901 qâbal (1), to *admit*
6902 qᵉbal (Ch.) (1), to *acquire*
7061 qâmats (3), to *grasp*
7126 qârab (1), to *approach, bring near*
7200 râ'âh (2), to *see*
7311 rûwm (11), to *be high;* to *rise or raise*
7760 sûwm (2), to *put*
7896 shîyth (1), to *place*
7901 shâkab (2), to *lie*
7997 shâlal (4), to *drop* or *strip;* to *plunder*
8175 sâ'ar (1), to *storm;* to *shiver, i.e. fear*
8551 tâmak (2), to *obtain*
8610 tâphas (10), to *manipulate, i.e. seize*
142 airō (35), to *lift up*
353 analambanō (3), to *take up, bring up*
726 harpazō (3), to *seize*

851 aphairĕō (5), to *remove, cut off*
1209 dĕchŏmai (3), to *receive, accept*
1949 ĕpilambanŏmai (2), to *seize*
2507 kathairĕō (1), to *lower,* or *demolish*
2722 katĕchō (1), to *hold down fast*
2902 kratĕō (4), to *seize*
2983 lambanō (31), to *take, receive*
3335 mĕtalambanō (1), to *accept and use*
3880 paralambanō (5), to *associate with oneself*
3911 paraphĕrō (1), to *carry off;* to *avert*
4014 pĕriairĕō (1), to *unveil;* to *cast off*
4084 piazō (4), to *seize*
4355 prŏslambanō (1), to *take along, receive*
4648 skŏpĕō (1), to *watch out for, i.e. to regard*
4815 sullambanō (3), to *seize (arrest, capture)*
4838 sumparalambanō (2), to *take along*
4868 sunairō (1), to *compute an account*

TAKEN
247 'âzar (1), to *belt*
270 'âchaz (7), to *seize*
622 'âçaph (7), to *gather*
935 bôw' (1), to *go, come*
1197 bâ'ar (2), to *be brutish, be senseless*
1497 gâzal (5), to *rob*
1639 gâra' (4), to *remove, lessen,* or *withhold*
2254 châbal (1), to *bind* by a *pledge;* to *pervert*
2388 châzaq (5), to *fasten* upon; to *seize*
2502 châlats (1), to *pull off;* to *strip;* to *depart*
2974 yâ'al (2), to *assent;* to *undertake, begin*
3289 yâ'ats (2), to *advise*
3381 yârad (1), to *descend*
3427 yâshab (5), to *dwell*
3885 lûwn (1), to *be obstinate with*
3920 lâkad (42), to *catch*
3921 leked (1), *noose*
3947 lâqach (84), to *take*
4672 mâtsâ' (1), to *find*
5267 nᵉçaq (Ch.) (1), to *go up*
5312 nᵉphaq (Ch.) (2), to *issue forth;* to *bring out*
5337 nâtsal (3), to *deliver;* to *be snatched*
5375 nâsâ' (10), to *lift up*
5381 nâsag (1), to *reach*
5414 nâthan (1), to *give*
5493 çûwr (19), to *turn off*
5674 'âbar (1), to *cross over;* to *transition*
5709 'ădâ' (Ch.) (1), to *remove;* to *bedeck*
5927 'âlâh (9), to *ascend*
6001 'âmêl (1), *laborer*
6213 'âsâh (1), to *make*
6679 tsûwd (1), to *catch*
6813 tsâ'an (1), to *load*

7092 qâphats (1), to *draw together*, to *leap*; to *die*
7287 râdâh (1), to *subjugate*; to *crumble*
7311 rûwm (4), to *be high*; to *rise or raise*
7628 sh^ebîy (2), *booty*
7725 shûwb (1), to *turn back*; to *return*
8610 tâphas (12), to *manipulate*, i.e. *seize*
142 airō (16), to *lift up*
259 halōsis (1), *capture*
353 analambanō (3), to *take up, bring up*
522 apairō (3), to *remove, take away*
642 apŏrphanizō (1), to *separate*
782 aspazŏmai (1), to give *salutation*
851 aphairĕō (1), to *remove*
1096 ginŏmai (1), to be
1723 ĕnagkalizŏmai (1), *take into one's arms*
1808 ĕxairō (1), to *remove, drive away*
1869 ĕpairō (1), to *raise*
2021 ĕpichĕirĕō (1), to *undertake, try*
2221 zōgrĕō (1), to *capture or ensnare*
2638 katalambanō (2), to *seize; to possess*
2639 katalĕgō (1), to *enroll, put on a list*
2983 lambanō (12), to *take, receive*
3880 paralambanō (5), to *associate with* oneself
4014 pĕriairĕō (3), to *unveil; to cast off*
4084 piazō (2), to *seize*
4355 prŏslambanō (1), to *take along; receive*
4815 sullambanō (2), to *seize (arrest, capture)*
4912 sunĕchō (3), to *hold together*

TAKEST
622 'âçaph (1), to *gather*
1980 hâlak (1), to *walk*
3947 lâqach (2), to *take*
5375 nâsâ' (1), to *lift up*
6001 'âmêl (1), *laborer*
8104 shâmar (1), to *watch*
142 airō (1), to *lift up*

TAKETH
270 'âchaz (2), to *seize*
1197 bâ'ar (1), to *be brutish, be senseless*
2254 châbal (1), to *bind by a pledge; to pervert*
2388 châzaq (4), to *fasten upon; to seize*
2862 châthaph (1), to *clutch, snatch*
3920 lâkad (5), to *catch*
3947 lâqach (11), to *take*
5190 nâṭal (1), to *lift; to impose*
5337 nâtsal (1), to *deliver; to be snatched*
5375 nâsâ' (3), to *lift up*
5493 çûwr (2), to *turn* off
5710 'âdâh (1), to *pass on or continue; to remove*

5998 'âmal (2), to *work severely, put forth effort*
6908 qâbats (1), to *collect, assemble*
7953 shâlâh (1), to *draw out or off*, i.e. *remove*
8610 tâphas (1), to *manipulate*, i.e. *seize*
142 airō (11), to *lift up*
337 anairĕō (1), to *take away*, i.e. *abolish*
851 aphairĕō (1), to *remove, cut off*
1405 drassŏmai (1), to *grasp*, i.e. *entrap*
2018 ĕpiphĕrō (1), to *inflict, bring upon*
2638 katalambanō (1), to *seize; to possess*
2983 lambanō (4), to *take, receive*
3880 paralambanō (8), to *associate with* oneself
4301 prŏlambanō (1), to *take before; be caught*

TAKING
3947 lâqach (1), to *take*
4727 miqqâch (1), *reception*
8610 tâphas (1), to *manipulate*, i.e. *seize*
142 airō (1), to *lift up*
321 anagō (1), to *lead up; to bring out*
353 analambanō (1), to *take up, bring up*
1325 didōmi (1), to *give*
2983 lambanō (4), to *take*

TALE
1899 hegeh (1), *muttering*
4557 miçpâr (1), *number*
4971 mathkôneth (1), *proportion*
8506 tôken (1), *quantity*

TALEBEARER
1980+7400 hâlak (1), to *walk; live a certain way*
5372 nirgân (3), *slanderer*
7400 râkîyl (2), *scandal-monger*

TALENT
3603 kikkâr (10), *talent*
5006 talantiaiŏs (1), *weight of 57-80 lbs.*
5007 talantŏn (3), *weight*

TALENTS
3603 kikkâr (38), *talent*
3604 kikkêr (Ch.) (1), *talent weight*
5007 talantŏn (12), *weight of 57-80 lbs.*

TALES
7400 râkîyl (1), *scandal-monger*
3026 lērŏs (1), *twaddle*

TALITHA
5008 talitha (1), *young girl*

TALK
1696 dâbar (11), to *speak*
1697 dâbâr (2), *word*
1897 hâgâh (1), to *murmur, utter a sound*
5608 çâphar (1), to *recount an event*
6310 peh (1), *mouth*

7878 sîyach (5), to *ponder, muse aloud*
8193 sâphâh (1), *lip, language, speech*
2980 lalĕō (1), to *talk*
3056 lŏgŏs (1), *word, matter, thing*

TALKED
559 'âmar (1), to *say*
1696 dâbar (29), to *speak*
2980 lalĕō (8), to *talk*
3656 hŏmilĕō (1), to *talk*
4814 sullalĕō (1), to *talk*
4926 sunŏmilĕō (1), to *converse* mutually

TALKERS
3956 lâshôwn (1), *tongue*
3151 mataiŏlŏgŏs (1), *senseless talker*

TALKEST
1696 dâbar (2), to *speak*
2980 lalĕō (1), to *talk*

TALKETH
1696 dâbar (1), to *speak*
2980 lalĕō (1), to *talk*

TALKING
1696 dâbar (3), to *speak*
4405 millâh (1), *word; discourse; speech*
7879 sîyach (1), uttered *contemplation*
2980 lalĕō (1), to *talk*
3473 mōrŏlŏgia (1), *buffoonery, foolish talk*
4814 sullalĕō (2), to *talk together*, i.e. *converse*

TALL
6967 qôwmâh (2), *height*
7311 rûwm (3), to *be high*

TALLER
7311 rûwm (1), to *be high*

TALMAI
8526 Talmay (6), *ridged*

TALMON
2929 Ṭalmôwn (5), *oppressive*

TAMAH
8547 Temach (1), *Temach*

TAMAR
8559 Tâmâr (24), *palm*

TAME
1150 damazō (2), to *tame*

TAMED
1150 damazō (2), to *tame*

TAMMUZ
8542 Tammûwz (1), *Tammuz*

TANACH
8590 Ta'ănâk (1), *Taanak or Tanak*

TANHUMETH
8576 Tanchûmeth (2), *compassion, solace*

TANNER
1033 brōma (3), *food*

TAPHATH
2955 Ṭâphath (1), *dropping* (of ointment)

TAPPUAH
8599 Tappûwach (6), *apple*

TARAH
8646 Terach (2), *Terach*

TARALAH
8634 Tar'ălâh (1), *reeling*

TARE
1234 bâqa' (1), to *cleave, break, tear open*
7167 qâra' (1), to *rend*
4682 sparassō (1), to *convulse* with epilepsy
4952 susparassō (1), to *convulse* violently

TAREA
8390 Ta'ărêa' (1), (poss.) *earth, ground; low*

TARES
2215 zizaniŏn (8), *darnel*

TARGET
3591 kîydôwn (1), *dart*
6793 tsinnâh (2), large *shield; piercing cold*

TARGETS
6793 tsinnâh (3), large *shield; piercing cold*

TARPELITES
2967 Ṭarpelay (Ch.) (1), *Tarpelite*

TARRIED
748 'ârak (2), to *be long*
2342 chûwl (1), to *wait*
3176 yâchal (1), to *wait*
3186 yâchar (1), to *delay*
3427 yâshab (6), to *dwell, to remain; to settle*
3885 lûwn (3), to *be obstinate with*
4102 mâhahh (2), to *be reluctant*
5116 nâveh (1), *at home*
5975 'âmad (1), to *stand*
1304 diatribō (2), to *stay*
1961 ĕpimĕnō (3), to *remain; to persevere*
3306 mĕnō (3), to *stay*
4160 pŏiĕō (1), to *do*
4328 prŏsdŏkaō (1), to *anticipate; to await*
4357 prŏsmĕnō (1), to *remain in a place*
5278 hupŏmĕnō (1), to *undergo, (trials)*
5549 chrŏnizō (2), to *take time*, i.e. *linger*

TARRIEST
3195 mĕllō (1), to *intend*, i.e. *be about* to

TARRIETH
3427 yâshab (1), to *dwell, to remain; to settle*
6960 qâvâh (1), to *expect*

TARRY
309 'âchar (4), to *remain; to delay*
1826 dâmam (1), to *stop, cease; to perish*
2442 châkâh (2), to *await; hope for*
3176 yâchal (2), to *wait*
3427 yâshab (3), to *dwell, to remain*
3559 kûwn (1), to *set up: establish, fix, prepare*
3885 lûwn (7), to *be obstinate with*

4102 mâhahh (3), to *be reluctant*
5975 'âmad (1), to *stand*
7663 sâbar (1), to *scrutinize; to expect*
1019 bradunō (1), to *delay, hesitate*
1551 ĕkdĕchŏmai (1), to *await, expect*
1961 ĕpimĕnō (4), to *remain; to persevere*
2523 kathizō (1), to *seat down, dwell*
3306 mĕnō (7), to *stay*
5549 chrŏnizō (1), to *take time*, i.e. *linger*

TARRYING
309 'âchar (2), to *remain*

TARSHISH
8659 Tarshîysh (24), *merchant* vessel

TARSUS
5018 Tarsĕus (2), *native of Tarsus*
5019 Tarsŏs (3), *flat*

TARTAK
8662 Tartâq (1), *Tartak*

TARTAN
8661 Tartân (2), *Tartan*

TASK
1697 dâbâr (1), *word; matter; thing*
2706 chôq (1), *appointment; allotment*

TASKMASTERS
5065 nâgas (5), to *exploit; to tax, harass*

TASKS
1697 dâbâr (1), *word; matter; thing*

TASTE
2441 chêk (4), area of *mouth*
2938 ţâ'am (6), to *taste*
2940 ţa'am (5), *taste*
1089 gĕuŏmai (7), to *taste*

TASTED
2938 ţâ'am (2), to *taste*
2942 ţe'êm (Ch.) (1), *judgment; account*
1089 gĕuŏmai (5), to *taste; to eat*

TASTETH
2938 ţâ'am (1), to *taste*

TATNAI
8674 Tattenay (4), *Tattenai*

TATTLERS
5397 phluarŏs (1), *pratery*

TAUGHT
995 bîyn (1), to *understand; discern*
1696 dâbar (2), to *speak*
3045 yâda' (3), to *know*
3256 yâçar (2), to *instruct*
3384 yârâh (5), to *teach*
3925 lâmad (17), to *teach*
3928 limmûwd (1), *instructed* one
4000 mâbôwn (1), *instructing*
7919 sâkal (1), to *be or act circumspect*

8637 tirgal (1), to *cause to walk*
1318 didaktŏs (1), *instructed, taught*
1321 didaskō (36), to *teach*
1322 didachē (1), *instruction*
2258+1321 ēn (4), I *was*
2312 thĕŏdidaktŏs (1), *divinely instructed*
2727 katēchĕō (1), to *indoctrinate*
3100 mathētĕuō (1), to *become a student*
3811 paidĕuō (1), to *educate* or *discipline*

TAUNT
1422 gedûwphâh (1), *revilement, taunt*
8148 shenîynâh (1), *gibe, verbal taunt*

TAUNTING
4426 melîytsâh (1), *aphorism, saying*

TAVERNS
4999 Tabĕrnai (1), *huts*

TAXATION
6187 'êrek (1), *estimate*

TAXED
6186 'ârak (1), to *arrange*
582 apŏgraphē (3), *census registration*

TAXES
5065 nâgas (1), to *exploit; to tax, harass*

TAXING
583 apŏgraphō (2), *enroll, take a census*

TEACH
502 'âlaph (1), to *teach*
2094 zâhar (1), to *enlighten*
3045 yâda' (5), to *know*
3046 yeda' (Ch.) (1), to *know*
3384 yârâh (33), to *teach*
3925 lâmad (32), to *teach*
8150 shânan (1), to *pierce; to inculcate*
1317 didaktikŏs (2), *instructive*
1321 didaskō (26), to *teach*
2085 hĕtĕrŏdidaskalĕō (2), to *instruct differently*
2605 kataggĕllō (1), to *proclaim, promulgate*
2727 katēchĕō (1), to *indoctrinate*
3100 mathētĕuō (1), to *become a student*
4994 sōphrŏnizō (1), to *train up*

TEACHER
995 bîyn (1), to *understand; discern*
3384 yârâh (1), to *teach*
1320 didaskalŏs (4), *instructor*

TEACHERS
3384 yârâh (3), to *teach*
3887 lûwts (1), to *scoff; to interpret; to intercede*
3925 lâmad (1), to *teach*

1320 didaskalŏs (6), *instructor*
2567 kalŏdidaskalŏs (1), *teacher* of *the right*
3547 nŏmŏdidaskalŏs (1), *Rabbi*
5572 psĕudŏdidaskalŏs (1), *propagator of erroneous doctrine*

TEACHEST
3925 lâmad (1), to *teach*
1321 didaskō (7), to *teach*

TEACHETH
502 'âlaph (1), to *teach*
3384 yârâh (3), to *teach*
3925 lâmad (4), to *teach*
7919 sâkal (1), to *be or act circumspect*
1318 didaktŏs (2), *taught*
1321 didaskō (3), to *teach*
2727 katēchĕō (1), to *indoctrinate*

TEACHING
3384 yârâh (1), to *teach*
3925 lâmad (1), to *teach*
1319 didaskalia (1), *instruction*
1321 didaskō (21), to *teach*
3811 paidĕuō (1), to *educate* or *discipline*

TEAR
1234 bâqa' (1), to *cleave, break, tear open*
1758 dûwsh (1), to *trample* or *thresh*
2963 ţâraph (5), to *pluck off* or *pull* to pieces
5498 çâchab (1), to *trail along*
6536 pâraç (1), to *break in pieces; to split*
6561 pâraq (1), to *break off* or *crunch; to deliver*
7167 qâra' (3), to *rend*

TEARETH
2963 ţâraph (4), to *pluck off* or *pull* to pieces
4486 rhēgnumi (1), to *tear to pieces*
4682 sparassō (1), to *convulse* with epilepsy

TEARS
1058 bâkâh (1), to *weep*
1832 dim'âh (23), *tears*
1144 dakru (11), *teardrop*

TEATS
1717 dad (2), female *breast* or *bosom*
7699 shad (1), *breast*

TEBAH
2875 Ţebach (1), *massacre*

TEBALIAH
2882 Ţebalyâhûw (1), *Jehovah has dipped*

TEBETH
2887 Ţêbeth (1), a month

TEDIOUS
1465 ĕgkŏptō (1), to *impede, detain*

TEETH
4973 methalle'âh (3), *tooth*
6374 pîyphîyâh (1), *tooth*

8127 shên (31), *tooth*
8128 shên (Ch.) (3), *tooth*
3599 ŏdŏus (10), *tooth*
3679 ŏnĕidizō (1), to *rail at, chide, taunt*

TEHAPHNEHES
8471 Tachpanchêç (1), *Tachpanches*

TEHINNAH
8468 Techinnâh (1), *supplication*

TEIL
424 'êlâh (1), *oak*

TEKEL
8625 teqal (Ch.) (2), to *weigh in a scale*

TEKOA
8620 Teqôwa' (6), *trumpet*

TEKOAH
8620 Teqôwa' (1), *trumpet*
8621 Teqôw'îy (2), *Tekoite*

TEKOITE
8621 Teqôw'îy (3), *Tekoite*

TEKOITES
8621 Teqôw'îy (2), *Tekoite*

TEL-ABIB
8512 Têl 'Âbîyb (1), *mound* of *green* growth

TEL-HARESHA
8521 Têl Charshâ' (1), *mound of workmanship*

TEL-HARSA
8521 Têl Charshâ' (1), *mound of workmanship*

TEL-MELAH
8528 Têl Melach (2), *mound of salt*

TELAH
8520 Telach (1), *breach*

TELAIM
2923 Ţelâ'îym (1), *lambs*

TELASSAR
8515 Tela'ssar (1), *Telassar*

TELEM
2928 Ţelem (2), *oppression*

TELL
559 'âmar (29), to *say*
560 'ămar (Ch.) (5), to *say*
1696 dâbar (7), to *speak*
3045 yâda' (7), to *know*
5046 nâgad (69), to *announce*
5608 çâphar (12), to *recount an event*
8085 shâma' (2), to *hear*
226 alēthĕuō (1), to *be true*
312 anaggĕllō (2), to *announce, report*
518 apaggĕllō (6), to *announce, proclaim*
1334 diēgĕŏmai (2), to *relate fully, describe*
1492 ĕidō (9), to *know*
1583 ĕklalĕō (1), to *tell*
1650 ĕlĕgchŏs (1), *proof*
2036 ĕpō (28), to *speak*
2046 ĕrĕō (28), to *utter*
2980 lalĕō (2), to *talk*
3004 lĕgō (28), to *say*

4302 prŏlĕgō (1), to
predict, forewarn

TELLEST
5608 çâphar (1), to
recount an event

TELLETH
1696 dâbar (2), to speak
4487 mânâh (2), to allot;
to enumerate or enroll
5046 nâgad (2), to
announce
3004 lĕgō (1), to say

TELLING
1696 dâbar (1), to speak
4557 miçpâr (1), number
5608 çâphar (1), to
recount an event

TEMA
8485 Têymâ' (5), Tema

TEMAN
8487 Têymân (11), south

TEMANI
8489 Têymânîy (1),
Temanite

TEMANITE
8489 Têymânîy (6),
Temanite

TEMANITES
8489 Têymânîy (1),
Temanite

TEMENI
8488 Têymᵉnîy (1),
Temeni

TEMPER
7450 râçaç (1), to
moisten with drops

TEMPERANCE
1466 ĕgkratĕia (4),
self-control

TEMPERATE
1467 ĕgkratĕuŏmai (1),
to exercise self-restraint
1468 ĕgkratēs (1),
self-controlled
4998 sōphrōn (1),
self-controlled

TEMPERED
1101 bâlal (1), to mix
4414 mâlach (1), to salt
4786 sugkĕrannumi (1),
to combine, assimilate

TEMPEST
2230 zerem (3), flood
5492 çûwphâh (1),
hurricane wind
5590 çâ'ar (1), to rush
upon; to toss about
5591 ça'ar (6), hurricane
7307 rûwach (1), breath;
wind; life-spirit
8183 sᵉ'ârâh (1),
hurricane wind
2366 thuĕlla (1), blowing
2978 lailaps (1),
whirlwind; hurricane
4578 sĕismŏs (1), gale
storm; earthquake
5492 chĕimazō (1), to be
battered in a storm
5494 chĕimōn (1), winter
season; stormy weather

TEMPESTUOUS
5490 çôwph (2),
termination; end

8175 sâ'ar (1), to storm
5189 tuphōnikŏs (1),
stormy

TEMPLE
1004 bayith (11), house;
temple; family, tribe
1964 hêykâl (68), temple
1965 hêykal (Ch.) (8),
palace; temple
2411 hiĕrŏn (71), sacred
place; sanctuary
3485 naŏs (43), temple
3624 ŏikŏs (1), dwelling

TEMPLES
1964 hêykâl (2), temple
7451 ra' (5), bad; evil
3485 naŏs (2), temple

TEMPORAL
4340 prŏskairŏs (1),
temporary

TEMPT
974 bâchan (1), to test
5254 nâçâh (4), to test
1598 ĕkpĕirazō (3), to
test thoroughly
3985 pĕirazō (6), to
endeavor, scrutinize

TEMPTATION
4531 maççâh (1), testing
3986 pĕirasmŏs (15), test

TEMPTATIONS
4531 maççâh (3), testing
3986 pĕirasmŏs (5), test

TEMPTED
5254 nâçâh (8), to test
551 apĕirastŏs (1), not
temptable
1598 ĕkpĕirazō (1), to
test thoroughly
3985 pĕirazō (14), to
endeavor, scrutinize

TEMPTER
3985 pĕirazō (2), to
endeavor, scrutinize

TEMPTETH
3985 pĕirazō (1), to
endeavor, scrutinize

TEMPTING
3985 pĕirazō (7), to
endeavor, scrutinize

TEN
6218 'âsôwr (4), ten
6235 'eser (164), ten
6236 'ăsar (Ch.) (4), ten
7231 râbab (1), to
multiply by the myriad
7233 rᵉbâbâh (13),
myriad
7239 ribbôw (2), myriad
7240 ribbôw (Ch.) (2),
myriad
1176 dĕka (24), ten
3461 murias (3), ten
thousand
3463 muriŏi (3), ten
thousand; innumerably

TEN'S
6235 'eser (1), ten

TENDER
3126 yôwnêq (1), sucker
plant; nursing infant
3127 yôwneqeth (1),
sprout, new shoot
7390 rak (10), tender
7401 râkak (2), to soften

527 hapalŏs (2), tender
3629 ŏiktirmōn (1),
compassionate
4698 splagchnŏn (1),
intestine; affection, pity

TENDERHEARTED
7390+3824 rak (1),
tender; weak
2155 ĕusplagchnŏs (1),
compassionate

TENDERNESS
7391 rôk (1), softness

TENONS
3027 yâd (6), hand; power

TENOR
6310 peh (2), mouth

TENS
6235 'eser (3), ten

TENT
167 'âhal (3), to pitch a
tent
168 'ôhel (89), tent
6898 qubbâh (1), pavilion

TENTH
4643 ma'ăsêr (4), tithe,
one-tenth
6218 'âsôwr (13), ten
6224 'ăsîyrîy (26), tenth
6237 'âsar (3), to tithe
6241 'issârôwn (28), tenth
1181 dĕkatē (2), tenth
1182 dĕkatŏs (3), tenth

TENTMAKERS
4635 skēnŏpŏiŏs (1),
manufacturer of tents

TENTS
168 'ôhel (50), tent
2583 chânâh (1), to
encamp
4264 machăneh (5),
encampment
4908 mishkân (1),
residence
5521 çukkâh (1),
tabernacle; shelter

TERAH
8646 Terach (11), Terach

TERAPHIM
8655 tᵉrâphîym (6),
healer

TERESH
8657 Teresh (2), Teresh

TERMED
559 'âmar (2), to say

TERRACES
4546 mᵉçillâh (1),
viaduct; staircase

TERRESTRIAL
1919 ĕpigĕiŏs (2),
worldly, earthly

TERRIBLE
366 'âyôm (3), frightful
367 'êymâh (2), fright
574 'emtânîy (Ch.) (1),
burly or mighty
1763 dᵉchal (Ch.) (1), to
fear; be formidable
2152 zal'âphâh (1), glow
3372 yârê' (30), to fear
6184 'ârîyts (13),
powerful or tyrannical
5398 phŏbĕrŏs (1),
frightful, i.e. formidable

TERRIBLENESS
3372 yârê' (1), to fear
4172 môwrâ' (1), fearful
8606 tiphletseth (1),
fearfulness

TERRIBLY
6206 'ârats (2), to dread

TERRIFIED
6206 'ârats (1), to dread
4422 ptŏĕō (2), to be
scared
4426 pturō (1), to be
frightened

TERRIFIEST
1204 bâ'ath (1), to fear

TERRIFY
1204 bâ'ath (2), to fear
2865 châthath (1), to
break down
1629 ĕkphŏbĕō (1), to
frighten utterly

TERROR
367 'êymâh (4), fright
928 behâlâh (1), sudden
panic, destruction
1091 ballâhâh (3),
sudden destruction
2283 châgâ' (1), terror
2847 chittâh (1), terror
2851 chittîyth (8), terror
4032 mâgôwr (1), fright
4172 môwrâ' (2), fearful
4288 mᵉchittâh (2), ruin;
consternation
4637 ma'ărâtsâh (1),
terrifying violent power
6343 pachad (2), fear
5401 phŏbŏs (3), alarm,
or fright; reverence

TERRORS
367 'êymâh (3), fright
928 behâlâh (1), sudden
panic, destruction
1091 ballâhâh (6),
sudden destruction
1161 bî'ûwthîym (2),
alarms, startling things
4032 mâgôwr (1), fright
4048 mâgar (1), to yield
up, be thrown
4172 môwrâ' (1), fearful

TERTIUS
5060 Tĕrtiŏs (1), third

TERTULLUS
5061 Tĕrtullŏs (2),
Tertullus

TESTAMENT
1242 diathēkē (11),
contract; devisory will
1248 diakŏnia (2),
attendance, aid, service

TESTATOR
1303 diatithĕmai (2), to
put apart, i.e. dispose

TESTIFIED
5749 'ûwd (7), to protest,
testify; to encompass
6030 'ânâh (3), to
respond, answer
1263 diamarturŏmai (6),
to attest earnestly
3140 marturĕō (6), to
testify; to commend
3142 marturiŏn (1),
something evidential

4303 prŏmarturŏmai (1), to *predict beforehand*

TESTIFIEDST
5749 'ûwd (2), to *protest, testify;* to *encompass*

TESTIFIETH
6030 'ânâh (1), to *respond, answer*
3140 marturĕō (4), to *testify;* to *commend*

TESTIFY
5749 'ûwd (6), to *protest, testify;* to *encompass*
6030 'ânâh (8), to *respond, answer*
1263 diamarturŏmai (4), to *attest earnestly*
3140 marturĕō (8), to *testify;* to *commend*
3143 marturŏmai (2), to *be witness,* i.e. to *obtest*
4828 summarturĕō (1), to *testify jointly*

TESTIFYING
1263 diamarturŏmai (1), to *attest earnestly*
1957 ĕpimarturĕō (1), to *corroborate*
3140 marturĕō (1), to *testify;* to *commend*

TESTIMONIES
5713 'êdâh (21), *testimony*
5715 'êdûwth (15), *testimony*

TESTIMONY
5713 'êdâh (1), *testimony*
5715 'êdûwth (40), *testimony*
8584 tᵉ'ûwdâh (3), *attestation, precept*
3140 marturĕō (3), to *testify;* to *commend*
3141 marturia (14), *evidence* given
3142 marturiŏn (15), something *evidential*

TETRARCH
5075 tĕtrarchĕō (3), to *be a tetrarch*
5076 tĕtrarchēs (4), *ruler of a fourth* part

THADDAEUS
2280 Thaddaiŏs (2), *Thaddæus*

THAHASH
8477 Tachash (1), (poss.) *antelope*

THAMAH
8547 Temach (1), *Temach*

THAMAR
2283 Thamar (1), *palm*

THANK
2192+5485 zᵉ'êyr (Ch.) (3), *small, little*
3029 yᵉdâ' (Ch.) (1), to *praise*
3034 yâdâh (4), to *throw;* to *revere or worship*
8426 tôwdâh (3), *thanks*
1843 ĕxŏmŏlŏgĕō (2), to *acknowledge*
2168 ĕucharistĕō (11), to *express gratitude*

5485 charis (3), *gratitude; benefit given*

THANKED
1288 bârak (1), to *bless*
2168 ĕucharistĕō (1), to *express gratitude*
5485 charis (1), *gratitude; benefit given*

THANKFUL
3034 yâdâh (1), to *throw;* to *revere or worship*
2168 ĕucharistĕō (1), to *express gratitude*
2170 ĕucharistŏs (1), *grateful, thankful*

THANKFULNESS
2169 ĕucharistia (1), *gratitude*

THANKING
3034 yâdâh (1), to *throw;* to *revere or worship*

THANKS
3029 yᵉdâ' (Ch.) (1), to *praise*
3034 yâdâh (32), to *throw;* to *revere, worship*
8426 tôwdâh (3), *thanks*
437 anthŏmŏlŏgĕŏmai (1), to *give thanks*
2168 ĕucharistĕō (26), to *express gratitude*
2169 ĕucharistia (5), *gratitude*
3670 hŏmŏlŏgĕō (1), to *acknowledge, agree*
5485 charis (4), *gratitude; benefit given*

THANKSGIVING
1960 huyᵉdâh (1), *choir*
3034 yâdâh (2), to *throw;* to *revere or worship*
8426 tôwdâh (16), *thanks*
2169 ĕucharistia (8), *gratitude; grateful*

THANKSGIVINGS
8426 tôwdâh (1), *thanks*
2169 ĕucharistia (1), *gratitude; grateful*

THANKWORTHY
5485 charis (1), *gratitude; benefit given*

THARA
2291 Thara (1), *Thara*

THARSHISH
8659 Tarshîysh (4), *merchant vessel*

THEATRE
2302 thĕatrŏn (2), *audience-room; show*

THEBEZ
8405 Têbêts (3), *whiteness*

THEFT
1591 gᵉnêbâh (2), something *stolen*

THEFTS
2804 Klaudiŏs (1), *Claudius*
2829 klŏpē (2), *theft*

THELASAR
8515 Tᵉla'ssar (1), *Telassar*

THEOPHILUS
2321 Thĕŏphilŏs (2), *friend of God*

THERE
2008 hênnâh (1), *from here; from there*
8033 shâm (440), *there*
8536 tâm (Ch.) (2), *there*
847 autŏu (3), *in this*
1563 ĕkĕi (98), *there*
1564 ĕkĕithĕn (1), *from there*
1566 ĕkĕisĕ (2), *there*
1759 ĕnthadĕ (1), *here*
1927 ĕpidēmĕō (1), to *make oneself at home*
5602 hōdĕ (1), *here*

THEREABOUT
4012+5127 pĕri (1), *about*

THEREAT
1223+846 dia (1), *through,* by means of

THEREBY
2004 hên (2), *they*
5921 'al (2), *above, over*

THEREFORE
1571 gam (5), *also; even*
2006 hên (Ch.) (2), *lo; therefore, unless*
2063 zô'th (1), *this*
3588 kîy (2), *for, that*
3651 kên (170), *just; right, correct*
235 alla (3), *but, yet*
686 ara (6), *therefore*
1063 gar (1), *for, indeed*
1160 dapanē (1), *expense, cost*
1211 dē (1), *therefore*
1352 diŏ (9), *therefore*
1360 diŏti (1), *inasmuch as*
2532 kai (1), *and; or*
3747 ŏstĕŏn (1), *bone*
3757 hŏu (1), *at which*
3767 ŏun (255), *certainly*
5105 tŏigarŏun (1), *then*
5106 tŏinun (3), *then*
5124 tŏutŏ (1), *that* thing
5620 hōstĕ (9), *thus*

THEREIN
413 'êl (2), *to, toward*
1459 gav (Ch.) (1), *middle*
2004 hên (4), *they*
2007 hênnâh (1), *themselves*
4393 mᵉlô' (7), *fulness*
5921 'al (9), *above, over*
7130 qereb (2), *nearest*
8033 shâm (10), *there*
8432 tâvek (3), *center*
5125 tŏutŏis (1), *in these*

THEREINTO
1519+846 ĕis (1), *to*

THEREOF
8033 shâm (1), *there*
846 autŏs (26), *he, she, it*

THEREON
5921 'al (48), *above, over*
846 autŏs (2), *he, she, it*
1911 ĕpiballō (1), to *throw upon*
1913 ĕpibibazō (1), to *cause to mount*
1924 ĕpigraphō (1), to *inscribe, write upon*

1945 ĕpikĕimai (1), to *rest upon; press upon*
2026 ĕpŏikŏdŏmĕō (1), to *rear up, build up*

THEREOUT
8033 shâm (1), *where, there*

THERETO
5921 'al (8), *above, over*
1928 ĕpidiatassŏmai (1), to *appoint besides*

THEREUNTO
1519+846+5124 ĕis (1), to
1519+5124 ĕis (2), to
4334 prŏsĕrchŏmai (1), to *come near, visit*

THEREUPON
2026 ĕpŏikŏdŏmĕō (2), to *rear up, build up*

THEREWITH
854 'êth (1), *with; by; at*
5921 'al (2), *above, over*
1722+846 ĕn (2), *in*
1909+5125 ĕpi (1), *on*
5125 tŏutŏis (1), *in these*

THESSALONIANS
2331 Thĕssalŏnikĕus (5), *of Thessalonice*

THESSALONICA
2331 Thĕssalŏnikĕus (1), *of Thessalonice*
2332 Thĕssalŏnikē (5), *Thessalonice*

THEUDAS
2333 Thĕudas (1), *Theudas*

THICK
653 'ăphêlâh (1), *duskiness, darkness*
3515 kâbêd (1), *numerous; severe*
5441 çôbek (1), *thicket*
5645 'âb (2), *thick clouds*
5666 'âbâh (1), to *be dense*
5672 'ăbîy (2), *density*
5687 'âbôth (4), *dense*
5688 'ăbôth (4), *entwined*
6282 'âthâr (1), *incense; worshipper*
7341 rôchab (1), *width*

THICKER
5666 'âbâh (2), to *be dense*

THICKET
5441 çôbek (1), *thicket*
5442 çᵉbâk (1), *thicket*

THICKETS
2337 châvach (1), *dell* or *crevice* of rock
5442 çᵉbâk (2), *thicket*
5645 'âb (1), *thick clouds; thicket*

THICKNESS
5672 'ăbîy (2), *density*
7341 rôchab (2), *width*

THIEF
1590 gannâb (13), *stealer*
2812 klĕptēs (12), *stealer*
3027 lēᵢstēs (3), *brigand*

THIEVES
1590 gannâb (4), *stealer*
2812 klĕptēs (4), *stealer*
3027 lēᵢstēs (8), *brigand*

THIGH
3409 yârêk (19), leg or
shank, flank; side
7785 shôwq (1), lower leg
3382 mёrŏs (1), thigh

THIGHS
3409 yârêk (2), leg or
shank, flank; side
3410 yarkâ' (Ch.) (1),
thigh

THIMNATHAH
8553 Timnâh (1), portion

THIN
1809 dâlal (1), to
slacken, dangle
1851 daq (5), thin
4174 môwrâd (1),
descent, slope
7534 raq (1), emaciated

THING
562 'ômer (1), something
said
1697 dâbâr (182), thing
3627 kᵉlîy (11), thing
3651 kên (2), just; right
3972 mᵉ'ûwmâh (3),
something; anything
4399 mᵉlâ'kâh (2), work;
property
4406 millâh (Ch.) (9),
word, command
4859 mashshâ'âh (1),
secured loan
5315 nephesh (2), life;
breath; soul; wind
1520 hĕis (1), one
3056 lŏgŏs (2), word,
matter, thing
4110 plasma (1), molded
4229 pragma (2), matter
4487 rhēma (1), matter
5313 hupsōma (1), barrier

THINGS
1697 dâbâr (47), thing
4406 millâh (Ch.) (1),
word or subject
18 agathŏs (1), good
846 autŏs (1), he, she, it
3056 lŏgŏs (3), thing
4229 pragma (4), matter
4487 rhēma (2), thing
5023 tauta (1), these

THINK
559 'âmar (3), to say
995 bîyn (1), to
understand; discern
1819 dâmâh (1), to
consider, think
2142 zâkar (3), to
remember; to mention
2803 châshab (6), to
think, regard; to value
5452 çᵉbar (Ch.) (1), to
bear in mind, i.e. hope
5869 'ayin (2), eye; sight
6245 'âshath (1), to be
sleek; to excogitate
1380 dŏkĕŏ (22), to think
1760 ĕnthumĕŏmai (1),
ponder, reflect on
2233 hēgĕŏmai (2), to
deem, i.e. consider
3049 lŏgizŏmai (7), to
credit; to think, regard
3539 nŏiĕŏ (1), to
exercise the mind

3543 nŏmizō (4), to deem
or regard
3633 ŏiŏmai (1), to
imagine, opine
5252 hupĕrphrŏnĕō (1),
to esteem oneself
5282 hupŏnŏĕō (1), to
think; to expect
5316 phainō (1), to
lighten (shine)
5426 phrŏnĕō (4), to be
mentally disposed

THINKEST
2803 châshab (1), to
think, regard; to value
5869 'ayin (2), eye; sight
1380 dŏkĕŏ (4), to think
3049 lŏgizŏmai (1), to
think, regard
5426 phrŏnĕō (1), to be
mentally disposed

THINKETH
2803 châshab (1), to
think, regard; to value
7200 râ'âh (1), to see
8176 shâ'ar (1), to
estimate
1380 dŏkĕŏ (2), to think
3049 lŏgizŏmai (1), to
think, regard

THINKING
559 'âmar (1), to say
1931+1961 hûw' (1), this

THIRD
7969 shâlôwsh (9), three;
third; thrice
7992 shᵉlîyshîy (104),
third
8027 shâlash (2), to be
triplicate
8029 shillêsh (5), great
grandchild
8523 tᵉlîythay (Ch.) (2),
third
8531 tᵉlath (Ch.) (3),
tertiary, i.e. third rank
5152 tristĕgŏn (1), third
story place
5154 tritŏs (56), third
part; third time, thirdly

THIRDLY
5154 tritŏs (1), third part

THIRST
6770 tsâmê' (2), to thirst
6771 tsâmê' (1), thirsty
6772 tsâmâ' (16), thirst
6773 tsim'âh (1), thirst
1372 dipsaō (10), to thirst
1373 dipsŏs (1), thirst

THIRSTED
6770 tsâmê' (2), to thirst

THIRSTETH
6770 tsâmê' (2), to thirst
6771 tsâmê' (1), thirsty

THIRSTY
6770 tsâmê' (2), to thirst
6771 tsâmê' (7), thirsty
6772 tsâmâ' (1), thirst
6774 tsimmâ'ôwn (1),
desert
1372 dipsaō (3), to thirst

THIRTEEN
7969 shâlôwsh (2), three
7969+6240 shâlôwsh (13),
three; third; thrice

THIRTEENTH
7969+6240 shâlôwsh (11),
three; third; thrice

THIRTIETH
7970 shᵉlôwshîym (9),
thirty; thirtieth

THIRTY
7970 shᵉlôwshîym (161),
thirty; thirtieth
8533 tᵉlâthîyn (Ch.) (2),
thirty
5144 triakŏnta (9), thirty

THIRTYFOLD
5144 triakŏnta (2), thirty

THISTLE
1863 dardar (1), thorn
2336 chôwach (4), thorn

THISTLES
1863 dardar (1), thorn
2336 chôwach (1), thorn
5146 tribŏlŏs (1), thorny
caltrop plant

THITHER
1988 hălôm (1), hither
2008 hênnâh (3), from
here; from there
5704 'ad (1), until
8033 shâm (63), there
1563 ĕkĕi (8), thither
1904 ĕpĕrchŏmai (1), to
supervene
3854 paraginŏmai (1), to
arrive; to appear
4370 prŏstrĕchō (1), to
hasten by running

THITHERWARD
2008 hênnâh (1), from
here; from there
8033 shâm (1), there
1563 ĕkĕi (1), thither

THOMAS
2381 Thōmas (12), twin

THONGS
2438 himas (1), strap

THORN
2336 chôwach (2), thorn
4534 mᵉçûwkâh (1),
thorn-hedge
5285 na'ătsûwts (1),
brier; thicket
6975 qôwts (2), thorns
4647 skŏlŏps (1), thorn

THORNS
329 'âţâd (1), buckthorn
2312 chêdeq (1), prickly
2336 chôwach (3), thorn
5285 na'ătsûwts (1),
brier; thicket
5518 çîyr (4), thorn; hook
5544 çillôwn (1), prickle
6791 tsên (2), thorn
6975 qôwts (12), thorns
7063 qimmâshôwn (1),
prickly plant
7898 shayith (7), wild
growth of briers
173 akantha (14), thorn
174 akanthinŏs (2),
thorny

THOROUGHLY
3190 yâţab (1), to be,
make well
7495 râphâ' (1), to cure

THOUGHT
559 'âmar (9), to say

1672 dâ'ag (1), be
anxious, be afraid
1696 dâbar (1), to speak
1697 dâbâr (1), word;
matter; thing
1819 dâmâh (4), to think
2154 zimmâh (1), plan
2161 zâmam (5), to plan
2803 châshab (10), to
think, regard; to value
4093 maddâ' (1),
intelligence
4209 mᵉzimmâh (1), plan
4284 machăshâbâh (1),
contrivance; plan
5869 'ayin (3), eye; sight
6246 'ăshîth (Ch.) (1), to
purpose, plan
6248 'ashtûwth (1),
cogitation, thinking
6419 pâlal (1), to
intercede, pray
7454 rêa' (1), thought
7807 shach (1), sunk
8232+6925 shᵉphar (Ch.)
(1), to be beautiful
1260 dialŏgizŏmai (1), to
deliberate
1261 dialŏgismŏs (1),
consideration; debate
1380 dŏkĕŏ (5), to think
1760 ĕnthumĕŏmai (2),
ponder, reflect on
1911 ĕpiballō (1), to
throw upon
1963 ĕpinŏia (1),
thought, intention
2106 ĕudŏkĕŏ (1), to
think well, i.e. approve
2233 hēgĕŏmai (2), to
deem, i.e. consider
2919 krinō (1), to decide;
to try, condemn, punish
3049 lŏgizŏmai (1), to
credit; to think, regard
3309 mĕrimnaō (11), to
be anxious about
3540 nŏĕma (1),
perception, i.e. purpose
3543 nŏmizō (1), to deem
4305 prŏmĕrimnaō (1), to
care in advance

THOUGHTEST
1819 dâmâh (1), to
consider, think

THOUGHTS
2031 harhôr (Ch.) (1),
mental conception
2711 chêqeq (1),
enactment, resolution
4180 môwrâsh (1),
possession
4209 mᵉzimmâh (2),
plan; sagacity
4284 machăshâbâh (24),
contrivance; plan
5587 çâ'îph (2), divided
in mind; sentiment
5588 çê'êph (1), divided
in mind; skeptic
6250 'eshtônâh (1),
thinking
7454 rêa' (1), thought
7476 ra'yôwn (Ch.) (5),
mental conception
8312 sar'aph (2),
cogitation
1261 dialŏgismŏs (8),
consideration; debate

T

1270 dianŏēma (1), sentiment, thought
1761 ĕnthumēsis (3), deliberation; idea
3053 lŏgismŏs (1), reasoning; conscience

THOUSAND
505 'eleph (436), thousand
506 'ălaph (Ch.) (3), thousand
7233 rᵉbâbâh (4), myriad
7239 ribbôw (5), myriad
7239+505 ribbôw (1), myriad, large number
7240 ribbôw (Ch.) (1), myriad, large number
1367 dischiliŏi (1), two thousand
2035 hĕptakischiliŏi (1), seven times a thousand
3461 murias (3), ten thousand
3463 muriŏi (3), ten thousand
4000 pĕntakischiliŏi (6), five times a thousand
5070 tĕtrakischiliŏi (5), four times a thousand
5153 trischiliŏi (1), three times a thousand
5505 chilias (21), one thousand
5507 chiliŏi (11), thousand

THOUSANDS
503 'âlaph (1), increase by thousands
505 'eleph (46), thousand
506 'ălaph (Ch.) (1), thousand
7232 râbab (1), to shoot
7233 rᵉbâbâh (7), myriad
7239 ribbôw (1), myriad
3461 murias (2), ten thousand
5505 chilias (1), one thousand

THREAD
2339 chûwṭ (4), string
6616 pâthîyl (1), twine

THREATEN
546 apĕilĕō (1), to menace; to forbid

THREATENED
546 apĕilĕō (1), to menace; to forbid
4324 prŏsapĕilĕō (1), to menace additionally

THREATENING
547 apĕilē (1), menace

THREATENINGS
547 apĕilē (2), menace

THREE
7969 shâlôwsh (377), three; third; thrice
7991 shâlîysh (1), triangle, three
7992 shᵉlîyshîy (4), third
8027 shâlash (6), to be triplicate
8032 shilshôwm (1), day before yesterday
8532 tᵉlâth (Ch.) (10), three or third
5140 trĕis (69), three

5145 triakŏsiŏi (2), three hundred
5148 triĕtia (1), three years' period
5150 trimēnŏn (1), three months' space
5151 tris (1), three times
5153 trischiliŏi (1), three times a thousand

THREEFOLD
8027 shâlash (1), to be triplicate

THREESCORE
7239 ribbôw (1), myriad
7657 shib'îym (38), seventy
8346 shishshîym (42), sixty
8361 shittîyn (Ch.) (4), sixty
1440 hĕbdŏmēkŏnta (3), seventy
1835 hĕxēkŏnta (4), sixty
5516 chi xi stigma (1), 666

THRESH
1758 dûwsh (3), to thresh
1869 dârak (1), to tread

THRESHED
1758 dûwsh (2), to thresh
2251 châbaṭ (1), to thresh

THRESHETH
248 alŏaō (1), to tread

THRESHING
1758 dûwsh (3), to thresh
1786 dayîsh (1), threshing-time
2742 chârûwts (2), threshing-sledge
4098 mᵉdushshâh (1), down-trodden people
4173 môwrag (3), threshing sledge

THRESHINGFLOOR
1637 gôren (17), open area

THRESHINGFLOORS
147 'iddar (Ch.) (1), threshing-floor
1637 gôren (1), open area

THRESHINGPLACE
1637 gôren (1), open area

THRESHOLD
4670 miphtân (8), sill
5592 çaph (6), dish

THRESHOLDS
624 'âçûph (1), collection, stores
5592 çaph (2), dish

THREW
5422 nâthats (1), to tear down
5619 çâqal (1), to throw large stones
8058 shâmaṭ (1), to jostle
906 ballō (2), to throw
4952 susparassō (1), to convulse violently

THREWEST
7993 shâlak (1), to throw

THRICE
7969+6471 shâlôwsh (4), three; third; thrice
5151 tris (11), three times

THROAT
1627 gârôwn (4), throat
3930 lôa' (1), throat
2995 larugx (1), throat
4155 pnigŏ (1), to throttle

THRONE
3678 kiççê' (120), throne
3764 korçê' (Ch.) (2), throne
968 bēma (1), tribunal platform; judging place
2362 thrŏnŏs (50), throne

THRONES
3678 kiççê' (4), throne
3764 korçê' (Ch.) (1), throne
2362 thrŏnŏs (4), throne

THRONG
2346 thlibō (1), to crowd
4912 sunĕchō (1), to hold together

THRONGED
4846 sumpnigō (1), to drown; to crowd
4918 sunthlibō (1), to compress, i.e. to crowd

THRONGING
4918 sunthlibō (1), to compress, i.e. to crowd

THROUGH
413 'êl (2), to, toward
1119 bᵉmôw (1), in, with
1157 bᵉ'ad (5), through
1234 bâqa' (3), to cleave
1811 dâlaph (1), to drip
1856 dâqar (2), to pierce
1870 derek (1), road
2864 châthar (1), to break or dig into
2944 ṭâ'an (1), to stab
3027 yâd (1), hand; power
4480 min (2), from, out of
5674 'âbar (10), to cross
5921 'al (5), over, upon
6440 pânîym (1), face
7130 qereb (5), nearest part, i.e. the center
7751 shûwt (1), to travel
8432 tâvek (7), center
303 ana (1), through
1223 dia (93), through
1224 diabainō (1), to pass by, over, across
1279 diapŏrĕuŏmai (1), to travel through
1330 diĕrchŏmai (8), to traverse, travel through
1350 diktuŏn (1), drag net
1358 diŏrussō (3), to penetrate burglariously
1537 ĕk (3), out, out of
1653 ĕlĕĕō (1), to give out compassion
1722 ĕn (37), in; during
1909 ĕpi (2), on, upon
2569 kalŏpŏiĕō (1), to do well
2596 kata (4), down; according to
2700 katatŏxĕuō (1), to shoot down
4044 pĕripĕirō (1), to penetrate entirely
4063 pĕritrĕchō (1), to traverse, run about

THROUGHLY
7235 râbâh (1), to increase
1245 diakatharizō (2), to cleanse perfectly
1722+3956 ĕn (1), in
1822 ĕxartizō (1), to finish out; to equip fully

THROUGHOUT
5921 'al (2), above, over
1223 dia (3), through
1330 diĕrchŏmai (2), to traverse, travel through
1519 ĕis (6), to or into
1722 ĕn (5), in; during
1909 ĕpi (2), on, upon
2596 kata (8), down; according to

THROW
2040 hâraç (6), to pull down; break, destroy
5307 nâphal (1), to fall
5422 nâthats (1), to tear down
8058 shâmaṭ (1), to jostle

THROWING
3027 yâd (1), hand; power

THROWN
2040 hâraç (7), to pull down; break, destroy
5422 nâthats (3), to tear down
7411 râmâh (1), to hurl
7993 shâlak (1), to throw
906 ballō (1), to throw
2647 kataluō (3), to demolish; to halt
4496 rhiptō (1), to toss

THRUST
926 bâhal (1), to be, make agitated; hasten
1333 bâthaq (1), to cut in pieces, hack up
1644 gârash (6), to drive out; to expatriate
1760 dâchâh (1), to push down; to totter
1766 dâchaq (1), to oppress
1856 dâqar (2), to stab
1920 hâdaph (4), to push away or down; drive out
2115 zûwr (1), to press
2944 ṭâ'an (1), to stab
3238 yânâh (1), to suppress; to maltreat
3905 lâchats (1), to press
5074 nâdad (1), to rove, flee; to drive away
5080 nâdach (2), to push off, scattered
5365 nâqar (1), to bore
5414 nâthan (1), to give
8628 tâqa' (2), to clatter, slap, drive, clasp
683 apōthĕŏmai (2), to push off; to reject
906 ballō (5), to throw
1544 ĕkballō (3), to throw out
1856 ĕxōthĕō (1), to expel; to propel
1877 ĕpanagō (1), to put out to sea; to return
2601 katabibazō (1), to cause to bring down

THRUSTETH
2700 katatŏxĕuō (1), to
 shoot down
3992 pĕmpō (2), to send

THRUSTETH
5086 nâdaph (1), to
 disperse, be windblown

THUMB
931 bôhen (6), thumb

THUMBS
931 bôhen (1), thumb
931+3027 bôhen (2),
 thumb; big toe

THUMMIM
8550 Tummîym (5),
 perfections

THUNDER
6963 qôwl (7), sound
7481 râ'am (3), to crash
 thunder; to irritate
7482 ra'am (6), peal of
 thunder
7483 ra'mâh (1), horse's
 mane
1027 brŏntē (3), thunder

THUNDERBOLTS
7565 resheph (1), flame

THUNDERED
7481 râ'am (3), to crash
 thunder; to irritate
1027+1096 brŏntē (1),
 thunder

THUNDERETH
7481 râ'am (3), to crash
 thunder; to irritate

THUNDERINGS
6963 qôwl (2), sound
1027 brŏntē (4), thunder

THUNDERS
6963 qôwl (3), sound
1027 brŏntē (4), thunder

THYATIRA
2363 Thuatĕira (4),
 Thyatira

THYINE
2367 thuïnŏs (1), of citron

TIBERIAS
5085 Tibĕrias (3), Tiberius

TIBERIUS
5086 Tibĕriŏs (1), (poss.)
 pertaining to the river
 Tiberis or Tiber

TIBHATH
2880 Ṭibchath (1),
 slaughter

TIBNI
8402 Tibnîy (3), strawy

TIDAL
8413 Tid'âl (2),
 fearfulness

TIDINGS
1309 bᵉsôwrâh (6), glad
 tidings, good news
1319 bâsar (16), to
 announce (good news)
1697 dâbâr (4), word
8052 shᵉmûw'âh (8),
 announcement
8088 shêma' (2),
 something heard
2097 ĕuaggĕlizō (6), to
 announce good news
3056 lŏgŏs (1), word
5334 phasis (1), news

TIE
631 'âçar (1), to fasten
6029 'ânad (1), to bind

TIED
631 'âçar (3), to fasten
5414 nâthan (1), to give
1210 dĕō (4), to bind

TIGLATH-PILESER
8407 Tiglath Pil'eçer (3),
 Tiglath-Pileser

TIKVAH
8616 Tiqvâh (2), hope

TIKVATH
8616 Tiqvâh (1), hope

TILE
3843 lᵉbênâh (1), brick

TILGATH-PILNESER
8407 Tiglath Pil'eçer (3),
 Tiglath-Pileser

TILING
2766 kĕramŏs (1), clay
 roof tile

TILL
5647 'âbad (4), to work
5704 'ad (90), until
5705 'ad (Ch.) (1), until
6440 pânîym (1), face;
 front
891 achri (5), until, up to
1519 ĕis (1), to or into
2193 hĕōs (41), until
3360 mĕchri (2), until

TILLAGE
5215 nîyr (1), plowed land
5656 'ăbôdâh (2), work

TILLED
5647 'âbad (2), to work

TILLER
5647 'âbad (1), to work

TILLEST
5647 'âbad (1), to work

TILLETH
5647 'âbad (2), to work

TILON
8436 Tûwlôn (1),
 suspension

TIMAEUS
5090 Timaiŏs (1), (poss.)
 foul; impure

TIMBER
636 'â' (Ch.) (3), wood
6086 'êts (23), wood

TIMBREL
8596 tôph (5),
 tambourine

TIMBRELS
8596 tôph (4),
 tambourine
8608 tâphaph (1), to
 drum on a tambourine

TIME
116 'êdayin (Ch.) (1), then
227 'âz (5), at that time
268 'âchôwr (1), behind,
 backward; west
570 'emesh (1),
 yesterday evening
1767 day (1), enough
2165 zᵉmân (2), time
2166 zᵉmân (Ch.) (6),
 time, appointed
3117 yôwm (55), day
3118 yôwm (Ch.) (2), day

4150 môw'êd (3),
 assembly
4279 mâchar (7),
 tomorrow; hereafter
5732 'iddân (Ch.) (7), set
 time; year
5769 'ôwlâm (1), eternity
6256 'êth (220), time
6258 'attâh (3), now
6440 pânîym (2), front
6471 pa'am (14), time
6635 tsâbâ' (2), army
7225 rê'shîyth (1), first
7227 rab (2), great
7674 shebeth (1), rest
8032 shilshôwm (1), day
 before yesterday
8462 tᵉchillâh (2),
 original; originally
8543 tᵉmôwl (1),
 yesterday
744 archaiŏs (3), original
1074 gĕnĕa (1), age
1208 dĕutĕrŏs (1), second
1597 ĕkpalai (1), long ago
1909 ĕpi (2), on, upon
2119 ĕukairĕō (2), to
 have opportunity
2121 ĕukairŏs (1),
 opportune, suitable
2235 ēdĕ (1), even now
2250 hēmĕra (4), day
2540 kairŏs (54), set time
3195 mĕllō (1), to intend
3379 mēpŏtĕ (6), never
3568 nun (2), now
3598 hŏdŏs (1), road
3819 palai (1), formerly
4218 pŏtĕ (12), ever
4287 prŏthĕsmiŏs (1),
 designated day or time
4340 prŏskairŏs (1),
 temporary
4455 pôpŏtĕ (3), at no
 time
5119 tŏtĕ (4), at the time
5550 chrŏnŏs (28), time
5551 chrŏnŏtribĕō (1), to
 procrastinate, linger
5610 hōra (12), hour

TIMES
2165 zᵉmân (1), time
2166 zᵉmân (Ch.) (3),
 time, appointed
3027 yâd (1), hand; power
3117 yôwm (5), day; time
4150 môw'êd (1),
 assembly
4151 môw'âd (1), troop
4489 môneh (2), instance
5732 'iddân (Ch.) (6), set
 time; year
6256 'êth (22), time
6471 pa'am (42), time
8543 tᵉmôwl (2),
 yesterday
1074 gĕnĕa (1), age
1441 hĕbdŏmēkŏntakis
 (1), seventy times
2034 hĕptakis (4), seven
 times
2540 kairŏs (8), set time
3999 pĕntakis (1), five
 times
4218 pŏtĕ (3), ever
5151 tris (3), three times
5550 chrŏnŏs (8), time

TIMNA
8555 Timnâ' (4), restraint

TIMNAH
8553 Timnâh (3), portion
8555 Timnâ' (2), restraint

TIMNATH
8553 Timnâh (8), portion

TIMNATH-HERES
8556 Timnath Chereç
 (1), portion of (the) sun

TIMNATH-SERAH
8556 Timnath Chereç
 (2), portion of (the) sun

TIMNITE
8554 Timnîy (1), Timnite

TIMON
5096 Timōn (1), valuable

TIMOTHEOUS
5095 Timŏthĕŏs (1), dear
 to God

TIMOTHEUS
5095 Timŏthĕŏs (18),
 dear to God

TIMOTHY
5095 Timŏthĕŏs (9), dear
 to God

TIN
913 bᵉdîyl (5), tin

TINGLE
6750 tsâlal (3), to tinkle

TINKLING
5913 'âkaç (1), to put on
 anklets
214 alalazō (1), to clang

TIP
8571 tᵉnûwk (8),
 pinnacle, i.e. extremity
206 akrŏn (1), extremity

TIPHSAH
8607 Tiphçach (2), ford

TIRAS
8493 Tîyrᵉyâ' (2), fearful

TIRATHITES
8654 Tir'âthîy (1), gate

TIRE
6287 pᵉ'êr (1), head-dress

TIRED
3190 yâṭab (1), to be,
 make well; successful

TIRES
6287 pᵉ'êr (1), fancy
 head-dress
7720 sahărôn (1), round
 pendant or crescent

TIRHAKAH
8640 Tirhâqâh (2),
 Tirhakah

TIRHANAH
8647 Tirchănâh (1),
 Tirchanah

TIRIA
8493 Tîyrᵉyâ' (1), fearful

TIRSHATHA
8660 Tirshâthâ' (5),
 deputy or governor

TIRZAH
8656 Tirtsâh (18),
 delightsomeness

TISHBITE
8664 Tishbîy (6), Tishbite

TITHE
4643 ma'ăsêr (11), tithe
6237 'âsar (1), to tithe

586 apŏdĕkatŏō (2), to
tithe

TITHES
4643 ma'ăsêr (16), *tithe*
6237 'âsar (2), to *tithe*
586 apŏdĕkatŏō (2), to
tithe, give a tenth
1181 dĕkatē (1), *tithe*
1183 dĕkatŏō (3), to *give*
or *take a tenth*

TITHING
4643 ma'ăsêr (1), *tithe*
6237 'âsar (1), to *tithe*

TITLE
6725 tsîyûwn (1), guiding
pillar, monument
5102 titlŏs (2), *title*

TITTLE
2762 kĕraia (2), *horn-like*

TITUS
5103 Titŏs (15), *Titus*

TIZITE
8491 Tîytsîy (1), *Titsite*

TOAH
8430 Tôwach (1), *humble*

TOB
2897 Ţôwb (2), *good*

TOB-ADONIJAH
2899 Ţôwb Ădônîyâhûw
(1), *pleasing* (to)
Adonijah

TOBIAH
2900 Ţôwbîyâh (15),
goodness of Jehovah

TOBIJAH
2900 Ţôwbîyâh (3),
goodness of Jehovah

TOCHEN
8507 Tôken (1), *quantity*

TOE
931 bôhen (6), *big toe*

TOES
676 'etsba' (2), *finger; toe*
677 'etsba' (Ch.) (2), *toe*
931 bôhen (1), *big toe*
931+7272 bôhen (2),
thumb; big toe

TOGARMAH
8425 Tôwgarmâh (4),
Togarmah

TOGETHER
259 'echâd (5), *first*
2298 chad (Ch.) (1), *one*
3162 yachad (125),
unitedly
6776 tsemed (1), *yoke*
240 allēlōn (1), *one*
another
260 hama (3), *together*
346 anakĕphalaiŏmai
(1), to *sum up*
1794 ĕntulissō (1), *wind*
up in, *enwrap*
1865 ĕpathrŏizō (1), to
accumulate, increase
1996 ĕpisunagō (6), to
collect upon
1997 ĕpisunagōgē (2),
meeting, gathering
1998 ĕpisuntrĕchō (1), to
hasten together upon
2086 hĕtĕrŏzugĕō (1), to
associate discordantly

2675 katartizō (1), to
prepare, equip
3674 hŏmŏu (3), *at the*
same place or time
4776 sugkathizō (2), to
give, take a seat with
4779 sugkalĕō (8), to
convoke, call together
4786 sugkĕrannumi (1),
to combine, assimilate
4789 sugklērŏnŏmŏs (1),
participant in common
4794 sugkuptō (1), to be
completely overcome
4801 suzĕugnumi (2), to
conjoin in marriage
4802 suzētĕō (1), to
discuss, controvert
4806 suzōŏpŏiĕō (2), to
reanimate conjointly
4811 sukŏphantĕō (1), to
defraud, i.e. exact
4816 sullĕgō (1), to gather
4822 sumbibazō (2), to
drive together, unite
4831 summimētēs (1),
co-imitator
4836 sumparaginŏmai
(1), to convene
4837 sumparakalĕō (1),
to console jointly
4851 sumphĕrō (1), to
collect; to conduce
4853 sumphulĕtēs (1),
native of the same
country
4854 sumphutŏs (1),
closely united to
4856 sumphōnĕō (1), to
be harmonious
4863 sunagō (31), to
gather together
4865 sunagōnizŏmai (1),
to struggle with
4866 sunathlĕō (1), to
wrestle with
4867 sunathrŏizō (3), to
convene
4873 sunanakĕimai (1),
to recline with
4883 sunarmŏlŏgĕō (2),
to render close-jointed
4886 sundĕsmŏs (1),
ligament; uniting
4888 sundŏxazō (1), to
share glory with
4890 sundrŏmē (1),
(riotous) concourse
4891 sunĕgĕirō (1), to
raise up with
4896 sunĕimi (1), to
assemble, gather
4897 sunĕisĕrchŏmai (1),
to enter with
4899 sunĕklĕktŏs (1),
chosen together with
4903 sunĕrgĕō (2), to be
a fellow-worker
4904 sunĕrgŏs (1),
fellow-worker
4905 sunĕrchŏmai (16),
to gather together
4911 sunĕphistēmi (1), to
resist or assault jointly
4925 sunŏikŏdŏmĕō (1),
to construct
4943 sunupŏurgĕō (1),
assist, join to help

4944 sunōdinō (1), to
sympathize

TOHU
8459 Tôchûw (1),
abasement

TOI
8583 Tô'ûw (3), *error*

TOIL
5999 'âmâl (1), *effort*
6093 'itstsâbôwn (1),
labor or pain
2872 kŏpiaō (2), to feel
fatigue; to work hard

TOILED
2872 kŏpiaō (1), to feel
fatigue; to work hard

TOILING
928 basanizō (1), to
torture, torment

TOKEN
226 'ôwth (10), *sign*
1730 ĕndĕigma (1), plain
indication
1732 ĕndĕixis (1),
indication
4592 sēmĕiŏn (1), *sign*
4953 sussēmŏn (1), *sign*
in common

TOKENS
226 'ôwth (4), *signal, sign*

TOLA
8439 Tôwlâ' (6), *worm*

TOLAD
8434 Tôwlâd (1), *posterity*

TOLAITES
8440 Tôwlâ'îy (1), *Tolaite*

TOLD
559 'âmar (13), to *say*
560 'âmar (Ch.) (5), to *say*
1540 gâlâh (2), to *reveal*
1696 dâbar (15), to *speak*
4487 mânâh (1), to *allot;*
to enumerate or enroll
5046 nâgad (152), to
announce
5608 çâphar (27), to
recount an event
8085 shâma' (2), to *hear*
8505 tâkan (1), to
balance, i.e. measure
312 anaggĕllō (4), to
announce, report
513 axinē (3), *axe*
518 apaggĕllō (17), to
announce, proclaim
1285 diasaphĕō (1), to
declare, tell
1334 diēgĕŏmai (2), to
relate fully, describe
1834 ĕxēgĕŏmai (1), to
tell, relate again
2036 ĕpō (13), to *speak*
2046 ĕrĕō (1), to *utter*
2980 lalĕō (10), to *talk*
3004 lĕgō (4), to *say*
3377 mēnuō (1), to *report*
4277 prŏĕpō (1), to *say*
already; to predict
4280 prŏĕrĕō (2), to *say*
already, predict
4302 prŏlĕgō (1), to
predict, forewarn

TOLERABLE
414 anĕktŏtĕrŏs (6),
more endurable

TOLL
4061 middâh (Ch.) (3),
tribute, tax money

TOMB
1430 gâdîysh (1), *stack*
3419 mnēmĕiŏn (2),
place of interment

TOMBS
3418 mnēma (2),
monument
3419 mnēmĕiŏn (3),
place of interment
5028 taphŏs (1), *grave*

TONGS
4457 melqâch (5), *tongs*
4621 ma'ătsâd (1), *axe*

TONGUE
762 'Ărâmîyth (2), *in*
Aramean
2013 hâçâh (1), to *hush*
2790 chârash (4), to *be*
silent; to be deaf
3956 lâshôwn (89),
tongue; tongue-shaped
1100 glōssa (24), *tongue*
1258 dialĕktŏs (5),
language
1447 Hĕbraïsti (3), *in the*
Jewish language

TONGUES
3956 lâshôwn (9), *tongue*
1100 glōssa (26), *tongue*
2084 hĕtĕrŏglōssŏs (1),
foreigner

TOOK
270 'âchaz (6), to *seize*
622 'âçaph (2), to *gather*
680 'âtsal (1), to *select*
935 bôw' (1), to *go, come*
1197 bâ'ar (1), to *be*
brutish, be senseless
1491 gâzâh (1), to *cut off*
1497 gâzal (1), to *rob*
1518 gîyach (1), to *issue*
forth; to burst forth
2388 châzaq (4), to
fasten upon; to seize
3318 yâtsâ' (1), to *bring*
out
3381 yârad (4), to
descend
3920 lâkad (43), to *catch*
3947 lâqach (359), to *take*
4185 mûwsh (1), to
withdraw
5265 nâça' (2), to *start*
5267 n°çaq (Ch.) (1), to
go up
5312 n°phaq (Ch.) (2), to
issue forth; to bring out
5375 nâsâ' (45), to *lift up*
5384 nâsheh (1),
rheumatic or crippled
5414 nâthan (1), to *give*
5493 çûwr (11), to *turn off*
5674 'âbar (2), to *cross*
over; to transition
5709 'ădâ' (Ch.) (1), to
remove
5927 'âlâh (3), to *ascend*
6901 qâbal (3), to *take*
6902 q°bal (Ch.) (1), to
acquire
7287 râdâh (1), to
subjugate; to crumble
7311 rûwm (2), to *be*
high; to rise or raise

7673 shâbath (1), to *repose; to desist*
7760 sûwm (1), to *put*
8610 tâphas (18), to *manipulate,* i.e. *seize*
142 airō (18), to *take up*
337 anairĕō (1), to *take away,* i.e. *abolish*
353 analambanō (3), to *take up, bring up*
520 apagō (1), to *take away*
589 apŏdēmĕō (2), *visit a foreign land*
618 apŏlambanō (1), to *receive; be repaid*
643 apŏskĕuazō (1), to *pack up baggage*
657 apŏtassŏmai (1), to *say adieu;* to *renounce*
941 bastazō (1), to *lift*
1011 bŏulĕuō (1), to *deliberate;* to *resolve*
1209 dĕchŏmai (2), to *receive, welcome*
1453 ĕgĕirō (1), to *waken*
1544 ĕkballō (1), to *throw out*
1562 ĕkduō (2), to *divest*
1723 ĕnagkalizŏmai (1), *take into one's arms*
1921 ĕpiginōskō (1), to *acknowledge*
1949 ĕpilambanŏmai (12), to *seize*
1959 ĕpimĕlĕŏmai (1), to *care for*
2021 ĕpichĕirĕō (1), *undertake, try*
2192 ĕchō (1), to *have*
2507 kathairĕō (3), to *lower,* or *demolish*
2902 kratĕō (11), to *seize*
2983 lambanō (57), to *take, receive*
3348 mĕtĕchō (1), to *share or participate*
3830 pandŏchĕus (1), *innkeeper*
3880 paralambanō (16), to *associate with*
4084 piazō (1), to *seize*
4160 pŏiĕō (1), to *make*
4327 prŏsdĕchŏmai (1), to *receive;* to *await for*
4355 prŏslambanō (5), to *take along*
4815 sullambanō (3), to *seize (arrest, capture)*
4823 sumbŏulĕuō (2), to *recommend, deliberate*
4838 sumparalambanō (2), to *take along with*
4863 sunagō (3), to *gather together*

TOOKEST
3947 lâqach (1), to *take*

TOOL
2719 chereb (1), *knife*
3627 kᵉlîy (1), *thing*

TOOTH
8127 shên (6), *tooth*
3599 ŏdŏus (1), *tooth*

TOOTH'S
8127 shên (1), *tooth*

TOP
1406 gâg (8), *roof; top*

1634 gerem (1), *bone; self*
5585 çâ'îyph (2), *bough*
6706 tsᵉchîyach (4), *exposed* to the sun
6788 tsammereth (3), *foliage*
6936 qodqôd (2), *crown*
7218 rô'sh (67), *head*
206 akrŏn (1), *extremity*
509 anōthĕn (3), *from above; from the first*

TOPAZ
6357 piṭdâh (4), *topaz*
5116 tŏpazion (1), *topaz*

TOPHEL
8603 Tôphel (1), *quagmire*

TOPHET
8612 Tôpheth (8), *smiting*
8613 Tophteh (1), place of *cremation*

TOPHETH
8612 Tôpheth (1), *smiting*

TOPS
1406 gâg (2), *roof; top*
5585 çâ'îyph (1), *bough*
7218 rô'sh (8), *head*

TORCH
3940 lappîyd (1), *torch*

TORCHES
3940 lappîyd (1), *torch*
6393 pᵉlâdâh (1), iron *armature*
2985 lampas (1), *torch*

TORMENT
928 basanizō (3), to *torture, torment*
929 basanismŏs (6), *torture, agony*
931 basanŏs (1), *torture*
2851 kŏlasis (1), *infliction, punishment*

TORMENTED
928 basanizō (5), to *torture, torment*
2558 kakŏuchĕō (1), to *maltreat;* to *torment*
3600 ŏdunaō (2), to *grieve*

TORMENTORS
930 basanistēs (1), *torturer*

TORMENTS
931 basanŏs (2), *torture*

TORN
1497 gâzal (1), to *rob*
2963 ṭâraph (4), to *pluck*
2966 ṭᵉrêphâh (8), *torn prey*
5478 çûwchâh (1), *filth*
7665 shâbar (2), to *burst*
4682 sparassō (1), to *convulse* with epilepsy

TORTOISE
6632 tsâb (1), *lizard*

TORTURED
5178 tumpanizō (1), to *beat* to death

TOSS
1607 gâ'ash (1), to *agitate* violently, *shake*
6802 tsᵉnêphâh (1), *ball*

TOSSED
5086 nâdaph (1), to *disperse, be windblown*

5287 nâ'ar (1), to *tumble*
928 basanizō (1), to *torture, torment*
2831 kludōnizŏmai (1), to *fluctuate on waves*
4494 rhipizō (1), to *be tossed about*
5492 chĕimazō (1), to *be battered in a storm*

TOSSINGS
5076 nâdûd (1), *tossing* and *rolling* on the bed

TOTTERING
1760 dâchâh (1), to *totter*

TOU
8583 Tô'ûw (2), *error*

TOUCH
5060 nâga' (31), to *strike*
680 haptŏmai (13), to *touch*
2345 thigganō (2), to *touch*
4379 prŏspsauō (1), to *lay a finger on*

TOUCHED
5060 nâga' (24), to *strike*
5401 nâshaq (1), to *touch*
680 haptŏmai (21), to *touch*
2609 katagō (1), to *lead down;* to *moor* a vessel
4834 sumpathĕō (1), to *commiserate*
5584 psēlaphaō (1), to *manipulate*

TOUCHETH
5060 nâga' (37), to *strike*
7306 rûwach (1), to *smell*
680 haptŏmai (2), to *touch*

TOUCHING
413 'êl (3), *to, toward*
5921 'al (1), *against*
1909 ĕpi (2), *on, upon*
2596 kata (3), *down; according to*
4012 pĕri (11), *about*

TOW
5296 nᵉ'ôreth (2), *tow*
6594 pishtâh (1), *flax*

TOWEL
3012 lĕntiŏn (2), *linen*

TOWER
969 bâchôwn (1), *assayer*
1431 gâdal (1), to *be great, make great*
4024 Migdôwl (2), *tower*
4026 migdâl (34), *tower*
4692 mâtsôwr (1), *siege-mound; distress*
4869 misgâb (3), *refuge*
6076 'ôphel (1), *fortress*
4444 purgŏs (4), *tower*

TOWERS
971 bachîyn (1), *siege-tower*
975 bachan (1), *watch-tower*
4026 migdâl (13), *tower*
6438 pinnâh (2), *pinnacle*

TOWN
5892 'îyr (3), *city, town*
7023 qîyr (2), *wall*
2968 kōmē (8), *town*

TOWNCLERK
1122 grammatĕus (1), *secretary, scholar*

TOWNS
1323 bath (27), *outlying village*
2333 chavvâh (4), *village*
2691 châtsêr (1), *village*
5892 'îyr (3), *city, town*
6519 pᵉrâzâh (1), *rural*
2968 kōmē (3), *town*
2969 kōmŏpŏlis (1), *unwalled city*

TRACHONITIS
5139 Trachōnitis (1), *rough* district

TRADE
582 'ĕnôwsh (2), *man; person, human*
5503 çâchar (2), to *travel*
2038 ĕrgazŏmai (1), to *toil*

TRADED
5414 nâthan (4), to *give*
2038 ĕrgazŏmai (1), to *toil*

TRADING
1281 diapragmatĕuŏmai (1), to *earn, make gain*

TRADITION
3862 paradŏsis (11), Jewish *traditionary law*

TRADITIONS
3862 paradŏsis (2), Jewish *traditionary law*

TRAFFICK
3667 Kᵉna'an (1), *humiliated*
4536 miççhâr (1), *trade*
5503 çâchar (1), to *travel round;* to *palpitate*
7404 rᵉkullâh (2), *peddled trade*

TRAFFICKERS
3669 Kᵉna'ănîy (1), *Kenaanite; pedlar*

TRAIN
2428 chayil (1), *army; wealth; virtue; valor*
2596 chânak (1), to *initiate* or *discipline*
7757 shûwl (1), *skirt*

TRAINED
2593 chânîyk (1), *trained*

TRAITOR
4273 prŏdŏtēs (1), *betraying*

TRAITORS
4273 prŏdŏtēs (1), *betraying*

TRAMPLE
7429 râmaç (2), to *tread*
2662 katapatĕō (1), to *trample down;* to *reject*

TRANCE
1611 ĕkstasis (3), *bewilderment, ecstasy*

TRANQUILITY
7963 shᵉlêvâh (Ch.) (1), *safety*

TRANSFERRED
3345 mĕtaschēmatizō (1), to *transfigure*

TRANSFIGURED
3339 mĕtamŏrphŏō (2), to *transform*

TRANSFORMED
3339 mĕtamŏrphŏō (1), to *transform*
3345 mĕtaschēmatizō (2), to *transfigure*

TRANSFORMING
3345 mĕtaschēmatizō (1), to *transfigure*

TRANSGRESS
898 bâgad (1), to *act treacherously*
4603 mâ'al (2), to *act treacherously*
5647 'âbad (1), to *do*
5674 'âbar (4), to *cross*
6586 pâsha' (3), to *break away from authority*
3845 parabainō (2), to *violate* a command
3848 parabatēs (1), *violator, lawbreaker*

TRANSGRESSED
898 bâgad (1), to *act treacherously*
4603 mâ'al (7), to *act treacherously*
5674 'âbar (12), to *cross*
6586 pâsha' (13), to *break* from authority
3928 parĕrchŏmai (1), to *go by*; to *perish*

TRANSGRESSEST
5674 'âbar (1), to *cross*

TRANSGRESSETH
898 bâgad (1), to *act treacherously*
4603 mâ'al (1), to *act treacherously*
458+4160 anŏmia (1), *violation of law*
3845 parabainō (1), to *violate* a command

TRANSGRESSING
5674 'âbar (1), to *cross*
6586 pâsha' (1), to *break away from authority*

TRANSGRESSION
4604 ma'al (6), *treachery*
6586 pâsha' (1), to *break away from authority*
6588 pesha' (38), *revolt*
458 anŏmia (1), *violation of law, wickedness*
3845 parabainō (1), to *violate* a command
3847 parabasis (4), *violation, breaking*

TRANSGRESSIONS
6588 pesha' (46), *revolt*
3847 parabasis (2), *violation, breaking*

TRANSGRESSOR
898 bâgad (2), to *act treacherously*
6586 pâsha' (1), to *break away from authority*
3848 parabatēs (2), *violator, lawbreaker*

TRANSGRESSORS
898 bâgad (8), to *act treacherously*
5674 'âbar (1), to *cross*

6586 pâsha' (8), to *break away from authority*
459 anŏmŏs (2), *without* Jewish *law*
3848 parabatēs (1), *violator, lawbreaker*

TRANSLATE
5674 'âbar (1), to *cross*

TRANSLATED
3179 mĕthistēmi (1), to *move*
3346 mĕtatithēmi (2), to *transport*; to *exchange*

TRANSLATION
3331 mĕtathĕsis (1), *transferral to heaven*

TRANSPARENT
1307 diaphanēs (1), *appearing through*

TRAP
4170 môwqêsh (1), *noose*
4434 malkôdeth (1), *snare*
4889 mashchîyth (1), *bird snare; corruption*
2339 thēra (1), *hunting*

TRAPS
4170 môwqêsh (1), *noose*

TRAVAIL
2342 chûwl (2), to *dance, whirl*; to *writhe* in pain
2470 châlâh (1), to *be weak, sick, afflicted*
3205 yâlad (11), to *bear young*; to *father a child*
5999 'âmâl (3), *worry*
6045 'inyân (6), *labor; affair, care*
8513 t͏eʹlâ'âh (1), *distress*
3449 mŏchthŏs (2), *sadness*
5088 tiktō (1), to *produce from seed*
5604 ōdin (1), *pang*
5605 ōdinō (1), to *experience labor pains*

TRAVAILED
2342 chûwl (2), to *dance, whirl*; to *writhe* in pain
3205 yâlad (3), to *bear young*; to *father a child*

TRAVAILEST
5605 ōdinō (1), to *experience labor pains*

TRAVAILETH
2254 châbal (1), to *writhe in labor pain*
2342 chûwl (1), to *writhe in pain*; to *wait*
3205 yâlad (4), to *bear young*; to *father a child*
4944 sunōdinō (1), to *sympathize*

TRAVAILING
3205 yâlad (2), to *bear young*; to *father a child*
5605 ōdinō (1), to *experience labor pains*

TRAVEL
8513 t͏eʹlâ'âh (2), *distress*
4898 sunĕkdēmŏs (2), *fellow-traveller*

TRAVELERS
1980+5410 hâlak (1), to *walk*

TRAVELLED
1330 diĕrchŏmai (1), to *traverse, travel through*

TRAVELLER
734 'ôrach (1), *road*
1982 hêlek (1), *wayfarer*

TRAVELLETH
1980 hâlak (2), to *walk*

TRAVELLING
736 'ôr͏eʹchâh (1), *caravan*
6808 tsâ'âh (1), to *tip over*; to *depopulate*
589 apŏdēmĕō (1), *visit a foreign land*

TRAVERSING
8308 sârak (1), to *interlace*

TREACHEROUS
898 bâgad (6), to *act treacherously*
900 bôg͏eʹdôwth (1), *treachery*
901 bâgôwd (2), *treacherous*

TREACHEROUSLY
898 bâgad (23), to *act treacherously*

TREACHERY
4820 mirmâh (1), *fraud*

TREAD
947 bûwç (6), to *trample*
1758 dûwsh (1), to *trample or thresh*
1759 dûwsh (Ch.) (1), to *trample; destroy*
1869 dârak (14), to *tread*
1915 hâdak (1), to *crush*
6072 'âçaç (1), to *trample*
7429 râmaç (6), to *tread*
7760+4823 sûwm (1), to *put, place*
3961 patĕō (2), to *trample*

TREADER
1869 dârak (1), to *tread*

TREADERS
1869 dârak (1), to *tread*

TREADETH
1758 dûwsh (1), to *trample or thresh*
1869 dârak (4), to *tread*
7429 râmaç (2), to *tread*
248 alŏaō (2), to *tread out grain*
3961 patĕō (1), to *trample*

TREADING
1318 bâshaç (1), to *trample down*
1869 dârak (1), to *tread*
4001 m͏eʹbûwçâh (1), *trampling, oppression*
4823 mirmâç (1), *abasement*

TREASON
7195 qesher (5), *unlawful alliance*

TREASURE
214 'ôwtsâr (11), *depository*
1596 g͏eʹnaz (Ch.) (2), *treasury storeroom*
2633 chôçen (2), *wealth*
4301 maṭmôwn (1), *secret storehouse*

4543 miçk͏eʹnâh (1), *storage-magazine*
1047 gaza (1), *treasure*
2343 thēsaurizō (2), to *amass or reserve*
2344 thēsaurŏs (13), *wealth, what is stored*

TREASURED
686 'âtsar (1), to *store up*

TREASURER
1489 gizbâr (1), *treasurer*
5532 çâkan (1), to *minister to*

TREASURERS
686 'âtsar (1), to *store up*
1411 g͏eʹdâbâr (Ch.) (2), *treasurer*
1490 gizbâr (Ch.) (1), *treasurer*

TREASURES
214 'ôwtsâr (50), *depository*
1596 g͏eʹnaz (Ch.) (1), *treasury storeroom*
4301 maṭmôwn (3), *secret storehouse*
4362 mikman (1), *hidden-treasure*
6259 'âthûwd (1), *prepared*
8226 sâphan (1), to *conceal*
2344 thēsaurŏs (5), *wealth, what is stored*

TREASUREST
2343 thēsaurizō (1), to *amass or reserve*

TREASURIES
214 'ôwtsâr (7), *depository*
1595 genez (2), *treasury coffer*
1597 ginzak (1), *treasury storeroom*

TREASURY
214 'ôwtsâr (3), *depository*
1049 gazŏphulakiŏn (5), *treasure-house*
2878 kŏrban (1), *votive offering or gift*

TREATISE
3056 lŏgŏs (1), *word*

TREE
363 'îylân (Ch.) (6), *tree*
815 'êshel (2), *tamarisk*
6086 'êts (88), *wood*
65 agriĕlaiŏs (2), *wild olive* tree
1186 dĕndrŏn (17), *tree*
2565 kalliĕlaiŏs (1), *cultivated olive*
3586 xulŏn (10), *timber*
4808 sukē (16), *fig-tree*
4809 sukŏmōraia (1), *sycamore-fig tree*

TREES
352 'ayîl (2), *oak tree*
6086 'êts (77), *wood*
6097 'êtsâh (1), *timber*
1186 dĕndrŏn (9), *tree*

TREMBLE
2111 zûwâ' (1), to *tremble*
2112 zûwa' (Ch.) (1), to *shake* with fear

2342 chûwl (2), to *writhe*
2648 châphaz (1), to
hasten away, to fear
2729 charad (6), to
shudder with terror
2730 chârêd (2), *fearful*
6426 pâlats (1), to *quiver*
7264 râgaz (9), to *quiver*
7322 rûwph (1), to *quake*
7493 râ'ash (4), to *quake*
5425 phrissō (1), to
shudder in *fear*

TREMBLED
2112 zûwa' (Ch.) (1), to
shake with fear
2342 chûwl (2), to *writhe*
2729 chârad (5), to
shudder with terror
2730 chârêd (2), *fearful*
7264 râgaz (2), to *quiver*
7364 râchats (1), to *bathe*
7493 râ'ash (5), to *quake*
*1719+1096 ĕmphŏbŏs (1),
alarmed, terrified*
*1790+1096 ĕntrŏmŏs (1),
terrified*
*2192+5156 ĕchō (1), to
have; hold; keep*

TREMBLETH
2729 chârad (1), to
shudder with terror
2730 chârêd (1), *fearful*
5568 çâmar (1), to *bristle*
7460 râ'ad (1), to *shudder*

TREMBLING
2729 chârad (1), to
shudder with terror
2731 chârâdâh (4), *fear*
6427 pallâtsûwth (1),
trembling fear
7268 raggâz (1), *timid*
7269 rogzâh (1),
trepidation
7460 râ'ad (6), to
shudder violently
7478 ra'al (1), *reeling*
7578 rᵉthêth (1), *terror*
8653 tar'êlâh (2), *reeling*
*1096+1790 ginŏmai (1),
to be, become*
5141 trĕmō (3), to tremble
*5156 trŏmŏs (4), quaking
with fear*

TRENCH
2426 chêyl (1),
entrenchment
4570 ma'gâl (3), *circular
track or camp rampart*
8565 tan (2), *jackal*
8585 tᵉ'âlâh (1),
irrigation channel
5482 charax (1), *rampart*

TRESPASS
816 'âsham (2), to *be
guilty; to be punished*
817 'âshâm (41), *guilt*
819 'ashmâh (11),
guiltiness
2398 châṭâ' (1), to *sin*
4603 mâ'al (1), to *act
treacherously*
4604 ma'al (18), *sinful
treachery*
6588 pesha' (5), *revolt*
264 hamartanō (3), to sin

TRESPASSED
816 'âsham (2), to *be
guilty; to be punished*
819 'ashmâh (1),
guiltiness
4603 mâ'al (8), to *act
treacherously*
4604 ma'al (3), *sinful
treachery*

TRESPASSES
817 'âshâm (1), *guilt*
819 'ashmâh (1),
guiltiness
4604 ma'al (1), *sinful
treachery*
*3900 paraptōma (9),
error; transgression*

TRESPASSING
819 'ashmâh (1),
guiltiness
4603 mâ'al (1), to *act
treacherously*

TRIAL
974 bâchan (1), to *test*
4531 maççâh (1), *testing*
1382 dŏkimē (1), test
*1383 dŏkimiŏn (1),
testing; trustworthiness*
3984 pĕira (1), attempt

TRIBE
4294 maṭṭeh (160), *tribe*
7626 shêbeṭ (57), *clan*
5443 phulē (19), clan

TRIBES
4294 maṭṭeh (20), *tribe*
7625 shᵉbaṭ (Ch.) (1), *clan*
7626 shêbeṭ (84), *clan*
*1429 dōdĕkaphulŏn (1),
twelve tribes*
5443 phulē (6), clan

TRIBULATION
6862 tsar (1), *trouble*
6869 tsârâh (2), *trouble*
2346 thlibō (1), to trouble
2347 thlipsis (18), trouble

TRIBULATIONS
6869 tsârâh (1), *trouble*
2347 thlipsis (3), trouble

TRIBUTARIES
4522 maç (4), *labor*

TRIBUTARY
4522 maç (1), *labor*

TRIBUTE
1093 bᵉlôw (Ch.) (3), *tax*
4060 middâh (1), *tribute*
4061 middâh (Ch.) (1),
tribute
4371 mekeç (6),
assessment, census-tax
4522 maç (12), *labor*
4530 miççâh (1), *liberally*
4853 massâ' (1), *burden*
6066 'ônesh (1), *fine*
*1323 didrachmŏn (2),
double drachma*
*2778 kēnsŏs (4),
enrollment*
5411 phŏrŏs (4), tax, toll

TRICKLETH
5064 nâgar (1), to *pour
out; to deliver* over

TRIED
974 bâchan (4), to *test; to
investigate*
976 bôchan (1), *trial*

6884 tsâraph (7), to *refine*
*1381 dŏkimazō (1), to
test; to approve*
*1384 dŏkimŏs (1),
acceptable, approved*
*3985 pĕirazō (3), to
endeavor, scrutinize*
*4448 purŏō (1), to be
ignited, glow*

TRIEST
974 bâchan (3), to *test*

TRIETH
974 bâchan (4), to *test; to
investigate*
*1381 dŏkimazō (1), to
test; to approve*

TRIMMED
6213 'âsâh (1), to *do*
2885 kŏsmĕō (1), to *snuff*

TRIMMEST
3190 yâṭab (1), to *be,
make well*

TRIUMPH
5937 'âlaz (2), to *jump for
joy*
5970 'âlats (1), to *jump
for joy*
7321 rûwa' (3), to *shout*
7440 rinnâh (1), *shout*
7442 rânan (1), to *shout
for joy*
7623 shâbach (1), to
*address in a loud tone;
to pacify*
*2358 thriambĕuō (1), to
give victory, lead in
triumphal procession*

TRIUMPHED
1342 gâ'âh (2), to *be
exalted*

TRIUMPHING
7445 rᵉnânâh (1), *shout
for joy*
*2358 thriambĕuō (1), to
give victory, lead in
triumphal procession*

TROAS
*5174 Trōas (6), plain of
Troy*

TRODDEN
947 bûwç (3), to *trample*
1758 dûwsh (2), to
trample or thresh
1869 dârak (7), to *tread*
4001 mᵉbûwçâh (2),
trampling, oppression
4823 mirmâç (4),
abasement
5541 çâlâh (2), to
contemn, reject
7429 râmaç (2), to *tread*
*2662 katapatĕō (3), to
trample down; to reject*
3961 patĕō (2), to trample

TRODE
1869 dârak (2), to *tread*
7429 râmaç (5), to *tread*
*2662 katapatĕō (1), to
trample down; to reject*

TROGYLLIUM
*5175 Trōgulliŏn (1),
Trogyllium*

TROOP
92 'ăguddâh (2), *band*
1409 gâd (2), *fortune*

1416 gᵉdûwd (7), *band*
2416 chay (2), *alive; raw*

TROOPS
734 'ôrach (1), *road*
1416 gᵉdûwd (3), *band*

TROPHIMUS
*5161 Trŏphimŏs (3),
nutritive*

TROUBLE
926 bâhal (2), to *tremble*
927 bᵉhal (Ch.) (2), to
terrify; hasten
928 behâlâh (2), *sudden
panic, destruction*
1091 ballâhâh (1),
sudden destruction
1205 bᵉ'âthâh (2), *fear*
1804 dâlach (1), to *roil
water, churn up*
2189 za'ăvâh (1),
agitation
2960 ṭôrach (1), *burden*
4103 mᵉhûwmâh (4),
confusion or uproar
5916 'âkar (4), to *disturb*
5999 'âmâl (3), *worry*
6040 'ŏnîy (3), *misery*
6862 tsar (17), *trouble*
6869 tsârâh (34), *trouble*
6887 tsârar (2), to *cramp*
*7186+3117 qâsheh (1),
severe*
7267 rôgez (2), *disquiet*
7451 ra' (9), *bad; evil*
7561 râsha' (1), to *be, do,
declare wrong*
8513 tᵉlâ'âh (1), *distress*
*387 anastatŏō (1), to
disturb, cause trouble*
*1613 ĕktarassō (1), to
disturb wholly*
*1776 ĕnŏchlĕō (1), to
annoy, cause trouble*
2346 thlibō (1), to trouble
2347 thlipsis (3), trouble
*2350 thŏrubĕō (1), to
disturb; clamor*
*2553 kakŏpathĕō (1), to
undergo hardship*
2873 kŏpŏs (1), toil; pains
2873+3930 kŏpŏs (2), toil
*3926 parĕnŏchlĕō (1), to
annoy, make trouble*
*3930 parĕchō (1), to hold
near, i.e. to present*
4660 skullō (2), to harass
*5015 tarassō (1), to
trouble, disturb*

TROUBLED
926 bâhal (12), to *tremble*
927 bᵉhal (Ch.) (6), to
terrify; hasten
1089 bâlahh (1), to *terrify*
1204 bâ'ath (1), to *fear,
be afraid*
1607 gâ'ash (1), to
agitate violently, shake
1644 gârash (1), to *drive
out; to divorce*
1993 hâmâh (2), to *be in
great commotion*
2000 hâmam (1), to *put
in commotion*
2560 châmar (3), to
ferment, foam
5590 çâ'ar (1), to *rush
upon; to toss about*

5753 'âvâh (1), *to be crooked*
5916 'âkar (4), *to disturb*
6031 'ânâh (1), *to afflict*
6470 pâ'am (4), *to impel or agitate*
7114 qâtsar (1), *to curtail, cut short*
7264 râgaz (3), *to quiver*
7481 râ'am (1), *to crash thunder; to irritate*
7515 râphas (1), *to trample, i.e. roil water*
1298 diatarassō (1), *to disturb wholly*
2346 thlibō (3), *to crowd, press, trouble*
2360 throĕō (3), *to frighten, be alarmed*
5015 tarassō (14), *to trouble, disturb*
5015+1438 tarassō (1), *to trouble, disturb*
5182 turbazō (1), *to make turbid*

TROUBLEDST
1804 dâlach (1), *to roil water, churn up*

TROUBLER
5916 'âkar (1), *to disturb or afflict*

TROUBLES
6869 tsârâh (10), *trouble*
7451 ra' (1), *bad; evil*
5016 tarachē (1), *mob disturbance; roiling*

TROUBLEST
4660 skullō (1), *to harass*

TROUBLETH
598 'ănaç (Ch.) (1), *to distress*
926 bâhal (2), *to tremble*
1204 bâ'ath (1), *to fear, be afraid*
5916 'âkar (4), *to disturb*
3930+2873 parĕchō (1), *to hold near*
5015 tarassō (1), *to trouble, disturb*

TROUBLING
7267 rôgez (1), *disquiet; anger*
5015 tarassō (1), *to trouble, disturb*

TROUBLOUS
5916 'âkar (1), *to disturb or afflict*

TROUGH
8268 shôqeth (1), *watering-trough*

TROUGHS
7298 rahaṭ (1), *ringlet of hair*
8268 shôqeth (1), *watering-trough*

TROW
1380 dŏkĕō (1), *to think, regard, seem good*

TRUCEBREAKERS
786 aspŏndŏs (1), *not reconcilable*

TRUE
551 'omnâm (1), *verily, indeed, truly*

571 'emeth (18), *truth, trustworthiness*
3330 yatstsîyb (Ch.) (2), *fixed, sure*
3651 kên (5), *just; right*
6656 tseʰdâ' (Ch.) (1), *(sinister) design*
227 alēthēs (22), *true; genuine*
228 alēthinŏs (27), *truthful*
1103 gnēsiŏs (1), *genuine, true*
2227 zōŏpŏiĕō (1), *to (re-) vitalize, give life*
3588+225 hŏ (1), *"the," i.e. the definite article*
4103 pistŏs (2), *trustworthy; reliable*

TRULY
199 'ûwlâm (4), *however*
389 'ak (3), *surely; only*
403 'âkên (2), *truly!*
530 'ĕmûwnâh (1), *fidelity; steadiness*
551 'omnâm (1), *truly*
571 'emeth (8), *certainty, truth, trustworthiness*
577 'ânnâ' (1), *oh now!*
3588 kîy (1), *for, that*
227 alēthēs (1), *true*
230 alēthōs (2), *truly*
686 ara (1), *then, so*
1161 dĕ (1), *but, yet*
1909+225 ĕpi (1), *on, upon*
3303 mĕn (12), *truly*

TRUMP
2689 chătsôtseʰrâh (1), *trumpet*
7782 shôwphâr (1), *curved ram's horn*
4536 salpigx (2), *trumpet*

TRUMPET
3104 yôwbêl (1), *blast of a ram's horn*
7782 shôwphâr (47), *curved ram's horn*
8628 tâqa' (1), *to clatter, slap, drive, clasp*
4536 salpigx (7), *trumpet*
4537 salpizō (1), *to sound a trumpet blast*

TRUMPETERS
2689 chătsôtseʰrâh (2), *trumpet*
2690 châtsar (1), *to blow the trumpet*
4538 salpistēs (1), *trumpeter*

TRUMPETS
2689 chătsôtseʰrâh (24), *trumpet*
7782 shôwphâr (20), *curved ram's horn*
4536 salpigx (2), *trumpet*

TRUST
539 'âman (4), *to be firm, faithful, true; to trust*
982 bâṭach (61), *to trust, be confident or sure*
2342 chûwl (1), *to wait; to pervert*
2620 châçâh (32), *to confide in*
2622 châçûwth (1), *confidence*

3176 yâchal (2), *to wait; to be patient, hope*
4004 mibchôwr (1), *select, i.e. well fortified*
4009 mibṭâch (3), *security; assurance*
4268 machăçeh (1), *shelter; refuge*
1679 ĕlpizō (15), *to confide, hope for*
3892 paranŏmia (1), *wrongdoing*
3982 pĕithō (6), *to rely by inward certainty*
4006 pĕpŏithēsis (1), *reliance, trust*
4100 pistĕuō (3), *to have faith, credit; to entrust*

TRUSTED
539 'âman (1), *to trust, to be permanent*
982 bâṭach (18), *to trust, be confident or sure*
1556 gâlal (1), *to roll; to commit*
2620 châçâh (1), *to confide in*
7365 reʰchats (Ch.) (1), *to attend upon, trust*
1679 ĕlpizō (2), *to expect or confide, hope for*
3982 pĕithō (3), *to rely by inward certainty*
4276 prŏĕlpizō (1), *to hope in advance*

TRUSTEDST
982 bâṭach (3), *to trust, be confident or sure*

TRUSTEST
982 bâṭach (6), *to trust, be confident or sure*

TRUSTETH
982 bâṭach (14), *to trust, be confident or sure*
2620 châçâh (2), *to confide in*
1679 ĕlpizō (1), *to expect or confide, hope for*

TRUSTING
982 bâṭach (1), *to trust, be confident or sure*

TRUSTY
539 'âman (1), *to be firm, faithful, true; to trust*

TRUTH
518+3808 'îm (1), *if, although; Oh that!*
529 'êmûwn (1), *trustworthiness; faithful*
530 'ĕmûwnâh (13), *fidelity; steadiness*
544 'ômen (1), *verity, faithfulness*
548 'ămânâh (2), *covenant*
551 'omnâm (3), *verily, indeed, truly*
571 'emeth (90), *certainty, truth*
3321 yeʰtsêb (Ch.) (1), *to speak surely*
3330 yatstsîyb (Ch.) (1), *fixed, sure*
3588+518 kîy (1), *for, that because*
7187 qeʰshôwṭ (Ch.) (2), *fidelity, truth*

7189 qôsheṭ (1), *reality*
225 alēthĕia (99), *truth, truthfulness*
226 alēthĕuō (8), *to be true*
227 alēthēs (1), *true; genuine*
230 alēthōs (7), *truly, surely*
3483 nai (1), *yes*
3689 ŏntōs (1), *really, certainly*

TRUTH'S
571 'emeth (1), *certainty, truth, trustworthiness*
225 alēthĕia (1), *truth, truthfulness*

TRY
974 bâchan (8), *to test; to investigate*
2713 châqar (1), *to examine, search*
5254 nâçâh (1), *to test, attempt*
6884 tsâraph (3), *to fuse metal; to refine*
1381 dŏkimazō (2), *to test; to approve*
3985 pĕirazō (1), *to endeavor, scrutinize*
4314+3986 prŏs (1), *to, toward; against*

TRYING
1383 dŏkimiŏn (1), *testing; trustworthiness*

TRYPHENA
5170 Truphaina (1), *luxurious*

TRYPHOSA
5173 Truphōsa (1), *luxuriating*

TUBAL
8422 Tûwbal (8), *Tubal*

TUBAL-CAIN
8423 Tûwbal Qayin (2), *offspring of Cain*

TUMBLED
2015 hâphak (1), *to change, overturn*

TUMULT
1993 hâmâh (1), *to be in great commotion*
1995 hâmôwn (4), *noise, tumult; many, crowd*
1999 hămullâh (1), *sound, roar, noise*
4103 meʰhûwmâh (1), *confusion or uproar*
7588 shâ'ôwn (3), *uproar; destruction*
7600 sha'ănân (2), *secure; haughty*
2351 thŏrubŏs (4), *disturbance*

TUMULTS
4103 meʰhûwmâh (1), *confusion or uproar*
181 akatastasia (2), *disorder, riot*

TUMULTUOUS
1121+7588 bên (1), *son, descendant; people*
1993 hâmâh (1), *to be in great commotion*

3920 parĕisaktŏs (1),
smuggled in, infiltrated
3921 parĕisdunō (1), to
slip in secretly

UNBELIEF
543 apĕithĕia (4),
disbelief
570 apistia (12),
disbelief; disobedience

UNBELIEVERS
571 apistŏs (4), without
faith; untrustworthy

UNBELIEVING
544 apĕithĕō (1), to
disbelieve
571 apistŏs (5), without
faith; untrustworthy

UNBLAMEABLE
299 amōmŏs (2),
unblemished, blameless

UNBLAMEABLY
274 amĕmptŏs (1),
faultlessly

UNCERTAIN
82 adēlŏs (1), indistinct,
not clear
83 adēlŏtēs (1),
uncertainty

UNCERTAINLY
82 adēlŏs (1), indistinct,
not clear

UNCHANGEABLE
531 aparabatŏs (1),
untransferable

UNCIRCUMCISED
6189 'ârêl (34), to be
uncircumcised
6190 'orlâh (2), prepuce
or penile foreskin
203+2192 akrŏbustia (1),
uncircumcised
564 apĕritmētŏs (1),
uncircumcised
1722+3588+203 ĕn (2), in;
during; because of
1986 ĕpispaŏmai (1), to
efface the mark of
circumcision

UNCIRCUMCISION
203 akrŏbustia (16),
uncircumcised

UNCLE
1730 dôwd (10), beloved,
friend; uncle, cousin

UNCLE'S
1730 dôwd (1), beloved,
friend; uncle, cousin
1733 dôwdâh (6), aunt

UNCLEAN
2930 ţâmê' (74), to be
morally contaminated
2931 ţâmê' (78), foul;
ceremonially impure
2932 ţum'âh (4),
ceremonial impurity
5079 niddâh (2), time of
menstrual impurity
6172 'ervâh (1), nudity;
disgrace; blemish
6945 qâdêsh (1), sacred
male prostitute
169 akathartŏs (28),
impure; evil
2839 kŏinŏs (3),
common, i.e. profane

2840 kŏinŏō (1), to make
profane

UNCLEANNESS
2930 ţâmê' (1), to be
morally contaminated
2932 ţum'âh (25),
ceremonial impurity
5079 niddâh (1), time of
menstrual impurity
6172 'ervâh (1), nudity;
disgrace; blemish
7137 qâreh (1),
accidental occurrence
167 akatharsia (10),
quality of impurity
3394 miasmŏs (1), act of
moral contamination

UNCLEANNESSES
2932 ţum'âh (1),
ceremonial impurity

UNCLOTHED
1562 ĕkduō (1), to divest

UNCOMELY
807 aschēmŏnĕō (1), to
be, act unbecoming
809 aschēmōn (1),
inelegant, indecent

UNCONDEMNED
178 akatakritŏs (2),
without legal trial

UNCORRUPTIBLE
862 aphthartŏs (1),
undecaying, immortal

UNCORRUPTNESS
90 adiaphthŏria (1),
purity of doctrine

UNCOVER
1540 gâlâh (22), to
denude; uncover
6168 'ârâh (1), to be,
make bare; to empty
6544 pâra (3), to loosen;
to expose, dismiss

UNCOVERED
1540 gâlâh (10), to
denude; uncover
2834 châsaph (2), to
drain away or bail up
6168 'ârâh (1), to be,
make bare; to empty
177 akatakaluptŏs (2),
unveiled
648 apŏstĕgazō (1), to
unroof, make a hole in
a roof

UNCOVERETH
1540 gâlâh (2), to
denude; uncover
6168 'ârâh (1), to be,
make bare; to empty

UNCTION
5545 chrisma (1), special
endowment of the Holy
Spirit

UNDEFILED
8535 tâm (2), morally
pious; gentle, dear
8549 tâmîym (1), entire,
complete; integrity
283 amiantŏs (4), pure

UNDER
413 'êl (2), to, toward
4295 maţţâh (1), below
or beneath

5921 'al (9), above, over,
upon, or against
8460 tᵉchôwth (Ch.) (4),
beneath, under
8478 tachath (231),
bottom; underneath
332 anathĕmatizō (2), to
declare or vow an oath
506 anupŏtaktŏs (1),
independent
1640 ĕlassōn (1), smaller
1722 ĕn (2), in; during;
because of
1772 ĕnnŏmŏs (1), legal,
or subject to law
1909 ĕpi (3), on, upon
2662 katapatĕō (2), to
trample down; to reject
2709 katachthŏniŏs (1),
infernal
2736 katō (1), downwards
5259 hupŏ (47), under; by
means of; at
5270 hupŏkatō (8), down
under, i.e. beneath
5273 hupŏkritēs (1),
dissembler, hypocrite
5284 hupŏplĕō (2), to sail
under the lee of
5293 hupŏtassō (4), to
subordinate; to obey
5295 hupŏtrĕchō (1), to
run under
5299 hupōpiazō (1), to
beat up; to wear out

UNDERGIRDING
5269 hupŏzōnnumi (1),
to gird under

UNDERNEATH
4295 maţţâh (2), below
or beneath
8478 tachath (1), bottom;
underneath; in lieu of

UNDERSETTERS
3802 kâthêph (4),
shoulder-piece; wall

UNDERSTAND
995 bîyn (44), to
understand; discern
998 bîynâh (1),
understanding
3045 yâda' (3), to know
7919 sâkal (9), to be or
act circumspect
8085 shâma' (6), to hear
intelligently
50 agnŏĕō (1), to not
know; not understand
1097 ginōskō (3), to know
1107 gnōrizō (1), to
make known, reveal
1492 ĕidō (1), to know
1987 ĕpistamai (1), to
comprehend
3539 nŏiĕō (8), to
exercise the mind
4920 suniēmi (13), to
comprehend

UNDERSTANDEST
995 bîyn (2), to
understand; discern
8085 shâma' (1), to hear
intelligently
1097 ginōskō (1), to know

UNDERSTANDETH
995 bîyn (5), to
understand; discern

7919 sâkal (1), to be or
act circumspect
191 akŏuō (1), to hear;
obey
1492 ĕidō (1), to know
4920 suniēmi (3), to
comprehend

UNDERSTANDING
995 bîyn (33), to
understand; discern
998 bîynâh (32),
understanding
999 bîynâh (Ch.) (1),
understanding
2940 ţa'am (1), taste;
intelligence; mandate
3820 lêb (10), heart
3824 lêbâb (3), heart
4486 manda' (Ch.) (1),
wisdom or intelligence
7306 rûwach (1), to smell
or perceive
7919 sâkal (5), to be or
act circumspect
7922 sekel (7),
intelligence; success
7924 soklᵉthânûw (Ch.)
(3), intelligence
8085 shâma' (1), to hear
intelligently
8394 tâbûwn (38),
intelligence; argument
801 asunĕtŏs (3),
senseless, dull; wicked
1271 dianŏia (3), mind
or thought
3563 nŏus (7), intellect,
mind; understanding
3877 parakŏlŏuthĕō (1),
to attend; trace out
4907 sunĕsis (6),
understanding
4920 suniēmi (2), to
understand
5424 phrēn (2), mind or
cognitive faculties

UNDERSTOOD
995 bîyn (11), to
understand; discern
3045 yâda' (4), to know
7919 sâkal (1), to be or
act circumspect
8085 shâma' (1), to hear
intelligently
50 agnŏĕō (2), to not
know; not understand
1097 ginōskō (4), to know
1425 dusnŏĕtŏs (1),
difficult of perception
2154 ĕusēmŏs (1),
significant
3129 manthanō (1), to
learn
3539 nŏiĕō (1), to
exercise the mind
4441 punthanŏmai (1), to
ask for information
4920 suniēmi (7), to
understand
5426 phrŏnĕō (1), to be
mentally disposed

UNDERTAKE
6148 'ârab (1), to
intermix; to give or be
security

UNDERTOOK
6901 qâbal (1), to admit;
to take

UNDO
5425 nâthar (1), to
terrify; shake off; untie
6213 'âsâh (1), to do or
make

UNDONE
6 'âbad (1), to perish;
destroy
1820 dâmâh (1), to be
silent; to fail, cease
5493 çûwr (1), to turn off

UNDRESSED
5139 nâzîyr (2), prince;
separated Nazirite

UNEQUAL
3808+8505 lô' (2), no, not

UNEQUALLY
2086 hĕtĕrŏzugĕŏ (1), to
associate discordantly

UNFAITHFUL
898 bâgad (1), to act
treacherously

UNFAITHFULLY
898 bâgad (1), to act
treacherously

UNFEIGNED
505 anupŏkritŏs (4),
sincere, genuine

UNFRUITFUL
175 akarpŏs (6), barren,
unfruitful

UNGIRDED
6605 pâthach (1), to open
wide; to loosen, begin

UNGODLINESS
763 asĕbĕia (4),
wickedness, impiety

UNGODLY
1100 bᵉlîya'al (4),
wickedness, trouble
3808+2623 lô' (1), no, not
5760 'âvîyl (1), morally
perverse
7563 râshâ' (8), morally
wrong; bad person
763 asĕbĕia (3),
wickedness, impiety
764 asĕbĕŏ (2), to be, act
impious or wicked
765 asĕbĕs (8), impious
or wicked

UNHOLY
2455 chôl (1), profane,
common, not holy
462 anŏsiŏs (2), wicked,
unholy
2839 kŏinŏs (1),
common, i.e. profane

UNICORN
7214 rᵉ'êm (6), wild bull

UNICORNS
7214 rᵉ'êm (3), wild bull

UNITE
3161 yâchad (1), to be,
become one

UNITED
3161 yâchad (1), to be,
become one

UNITY
3162 yachad (1), unitedly
1775 hĕnŏtēs (2),
unanimity, unity

UNJUST
205 'âven (1), trouble,
vanity, wickedness
5766 'evel (2), moral evil
5767 'avvâl (1), morally
evil
8636 tarbîyth (1),
percentage or bonus
91 adikĕŏ (1), to do
wrong
93 adikia (2),
wrongfulness
94 adikŏs (8), unjust,
wicked

UNJUSTLY
5765 'âval (1), to morally
distort
5766 'evel (1), moral evil

UNKNOWN
50 agnŏĕŏ (2), to not
know; not understand
57 agnŏstŏs (1), unknown

UNLADE
670 ȧpŏphŏrtizŏmai (1),
to unload

UNLAWFUL
111 athĕmitŏs (1),
illegal; detestable
459 anŏmŏs (1), without
Jewish law

UNLEARNED
62 agrammatŏs (1),
illiterate, unschooled
261 amathēs (1),
ignorant
521 apaidĕutŏs (1),
stupid, uneducated
2399 idiŏtēs (3), not
initiated; untrained

UNLEAVENED
4682 matstsâh (51),
unfermented cake
106 azumŏs (9), made
without yeast; Passover

UNLESS
194 'ûwlay (1), if not;
perhaps
3884 lûwlê' (3), if not

UNLOOSE
3089 luŏ (3), to loosen

UNMARRIED
22 agamŏs (4),
unmarried

UNMERCIFUL
415 anĕlĕĕmōn (1),
merciless, ruthless

UNMINDFUL
7876 shâyâh (1), to keep
in memory

UNMOVABLE
277 amĕtakinētŏs (1),
immovable

UNMOVEABLE
761 asalĕutŏs (1),
immovable, fixed

UNNI
6042 'Unnîy (3), afflicted

UNOCCUPIED
2308 châdal (1), to desist,
stop; be fat

UNPREPARED
532 aparaskĕuastŏs (1),
unready

UNPROFITABLE
5532 çâkan (1), to be
serviceable to
255 alusitĕlēs (1),
gainless, pernicious
512 anŏphĕlĕs (1), useless
888 achrĕiŏs (2), useless,
i.e. unmeritorious
889 achrĕiŏō (1), render
useless, i.e. spoil
890 achrēstŏs (1),
inefficient, detrimental

UNPROFITABLENESS
512 anŏphĕlĕs (1), useless

UNPUNISHED
5352 nâqâh (11), to be,
make clean; to be bare

UNQUENCHABLE
762 asbĕstŏs (2), not
extinguished

UNREASONABLE
249 alŏgŏs (1), irrational,
not reasonable
824 atŏpŏs (1), improper;
injurious; wicked

UNREBUKEABLE
423 anĕpilēptŏs (1), not
open to blame

UNREPROVEABLE
410 anĕgklētŏs (1),
irreproachable

UNRIGHTEOUS
205 'âven (2), trouble,
vanity, wickedness
2555 châmâç (1),
violence; malice
5765 'âval (1), to morally
distort
5767 'avvâl (1), morally
evil
94 adikŏs (4), unjust,
wicked

UNRIGHTEOUSLY
5766 'evel (1), moral evil

UNRIGHTEOUSNESS
3808+6664 lô' (1), no, not
5766 'evel (3), moral evil
93 adikia (16),
wrongfulness
458 anŏmia (1), violation
of law, wickedness

UNRIPE
1154 beçer (1),
immature, sour grapes

UNRULY
183 akataschĕtŏs (1),
unrestrainable
506 anupŏtaktŏs (2),
insubordinate
813 ataktŏs (1),
insubordinate

UNSATIABLE
1115+7654 biltîy (1), not,
except, without, unless

UNSAVOURY
6617 pâthal (1), to
struggle; to be tortuous
8602 tâphêl (1), to
plaster; be tasteless

UNSEARCHABLE
369+2714 'ayin (3), there
is no, i.e., not exist
419 anĕxĕrĕunētŏs (1),
inscrutable

421 anĕxichniastŏs (1),
unsearchable

UNSEEMLY
808 aschēmŏsunē (1),
indecency; shame

UNSHOD
3182 mĕthuskŏ (1), to
intoxicate, become
drunk

UNSKILFUL
552 apĕirŏs (1), ignorant,
not acquainted with

UNSPEAKABLE
411 anĕkdiĕgētŏs (1),
indescribable
412 anĕklalētŏs (1),
unutterable
731 arrhētŏs (1),
inexpressible

UNSPOTTED
784 aspilŏs (1),
unblemished

UNSTABLE
6349 pachaz (1),
ebullition, turbulence
182 akatastatŏs (1),
inconstant, restless
793 astēriktŏs (2),
vacillating, unstable

UNSTOPPED
6605 pâthach (1), to open
wide; to loosen, begin

UNTAKEN
3361+348 mē (1), not; lest

UNTEMPERED
8602 tâphêl (5), to be
tasteless; frivolity

UNTHANKFUL
884 acharistŏs (2),
ungrateful

UNTIL
5704 'ad (288), as far
(long) as; during; until
891 achri (16), until or
up to
1519 ĕis (1), to or into
2193 hĕōs (35), until
3360 mĕchri (7), until, to
the point of

UNTIMELY
5309 nephel (3), abortive
miscarriage
3653 ŏlunthŏs (1), unripe
fig

UNTOWARD
4646 skŏliŏs (1), crooked;
perverse

UNWALLED
6519 pᵉrâzâh (1), rural,
open country
6521 pᵉrâzîy (1), rustic

UNWASHEN
449 aniptŏs (3), without
ablution, unwashed

UNWISE
3808+2450 lô' (2), no, not
453 anŏētŏs (1),
unintelligent, senseless
878 aphrōn (1), ignorant;
egotistic; unbelieving

UNWITTINGLY
1097+1847 bᵉlîy (2),
without, not yet

7684 sh°gâgâh (1), *mistake,* inadvertent *transgression*

UNWORTHILY
371 anaxiŏs (2), in a manner *unworthy*

UNWORTHY
370 anaxiŏs (1), *unfit, unworthy*
3756+514 ŏu (1), *no or not*

UPBRAID
2778 châraph (1), to spend the *winter*
3679 ŏnĕidizō (1), to *rail at, chide, taunt*

UPBRAIDED
3679 ŏnĕidizō (1), to *rail at, chide, taunt*

UPBRAIDETH
3679 ŏnĕidizō (1), to *rail at, chide, taunt*

UPHARSIN
6537 p°raç (Ch.) (1), to *split* up

UPHAZ
210 'Ûwphâz (2), *Uphaz*

UPHELD
5564 çâmak (1), to *lean* upon; *take hold* of

UPHOLD
5564 çâmak (5), to *lean* upon; *take hold* of
8551 tâmak (3), to *obtain, keep fast*

UPHOLDEN
5582 çâ'ad (1), to *support*
6965 qûwm (1), to *rise*

UPHOLDEST
8551 tâmak (1), to *obtain, keep fast*

UPHOLDETH
5564 çâmak (3), to *lean* upon; *take hold* of
8551 tâmak (1), to *obtain, keep fast*

UPHOLDING
5342 phĕrō (1), to *bear* or *carry*

UPPER
3730 kaphtôr (1), *capital; wreath-like button*
4947 mashqôwph (1), *lintel*
5942 'illîy (2), *higher*
5944 'ălîyâh (4), *upper* things; *second-story*
5945 'elyôwn (8), *loftier, higher; Supreme* God
7393 rekeb (1), *upper millstone*
8222 sâphâm (1), *beard*
508 anŏgĕŏn (2), *dome* or a *balcony*
510 anōtĕrikŏs (1), *more remote regions*
5250 hupĕrplĕŏnazō (1), to *superabound*
5253 hupĕrō̧ŏn (3), *room* in the *third story*

UPPERMOST
5945 'elyôwn (1), *loftier, higher; Supreme* God
4410 prōtŏkathĕdria (1), *pre-eminence* in council

4411 prōtŏklisia (2), *pre-eminence* at meals

UPRIGHT
3474 yâshar (1), to *be straight;* to *make right*
3476 yôsher (1), *right*
3477 yâshâr (43), *straight*
4339 mêyshâr (1), *straightness; rectitude*
4749 miqshâh (1), *work molded by hammering*
5977 'ômed (2), *fixed spot*
6968 qôwm°mîyûwth (1), *erectly,* with head high
8535 tâm (1), *morally pious; gentle, dear*
8537 tôm (2), *prosperity; innocence*
8549 tâmîym (8), *entire, complete; integrity*
8549+8552 tâmîym (1), *complete; integrity*
8552 tâmam (2), to *complete, finish*
3717 ŏrthŏs (1), *straight, level*

UPRIGHTLY
3474 yâshar (1), to *be straight;* to *make right*
3477 yâshâr (1), *straight*
4339 mêyshâr (3), *straightness; rectitude*
8537 tôm (2), *prosperity; innocence*
8549 tâmîym (4), *entire, complete; integrity*
3716 ŏrthŏpŏdĕō (1), to act *rightly*

UPRIGHTNESS
3476 yôsher (9), *right*
3477 yâshâr (1), *straight*
3483 yishrâh (1), *moral integrity*
4334 mîyshôwr (1), *plain; justice*
4339 mêyshâr (3), *straightness; rectitude*
5228 nâkôach (1), *equitable, correct*
5229 n°kôchâh (1), *integrity; truth*
8537 tôm (2), *prosperity; innocence*

UPRISING
6965 qûwm (1), to *rise*

UPROAR
1993 hâmâh (1), to *be in great commotion*
387 anastatŏō (1), to *disturb, cause trouble*
2350 thŏrubĕō (1), to *clamor; start a riot*
2351 thŏrubŏs (3), *commotion*
4714 stasis (1), one leading an *uprising*
4797 sugchĕō (1), to *throw into disorder*

UPSIDE
5921+6440 'al (2), *above, over, upon,* or *against*
389 anastĕnazō (1), to *sigh deeply*

UPWARD
1361 gâbahh (1), to *be lofty;* to *be haughty*

4605 ma'al (59), *upward, above, overhead*
4791 mârôwm (1), *elevation; elation*

UR
218 'Ûwr (5), *Ur*

URBANE
3779 hŏutō (1), *in this way; likewise*

URGE
1758 ĕnĕchō (1), to *keep a grudge*

URGED
509 'âlats (1), to *press, urge*
6484 pâtsar (4), to *stun or dull*
6555 pârats (1), to *break out*

URGENT
2388 châzaq (1), to *fasten upon;* to *seize*
2685 châtsaph (Ch.) (1), to *be severe*

URI
221 'Ûwrîy (8), *fiery*

URIAH
223 'Ûwrîyâh (27), *flame of Jehovah*

URIAH'S
223 'Ûwrîyâh (1), *flame of Jehovah*

URIAS
3774 Ôurias (1), *flame of Jehovah*

URIEL
222 'Ûwrîy'êl (4), *flame of God*

URIJAH
223 'Ûwrîyâh (11), *flame of Jehovah*

URIM
224 'Ûwrîym (7), *lights*

US-WARD
413 'êl (1), *to, toward*
1519+2248 ĕis (2), *to or into*

USE
559 'âmar (1), to *say*
3231 yâman (1), to *be right-handed*
3947 lâqach (1), to *take*
4399 m°lâ'kâh (1), *work; property*
4911 mâshal (3), to *use figurative language*
4912 mâshâl (1), *pithy maxim; taunt*
5172 nâchash (1), to *prognosticate*
5656 'ăbôdâh (1), *work*
7080 qâçam (1), to *divine magic*
1838 hĕxis (1), *practice, constant use*
1908 ĕpĕrĕazō (2), to *insult* with threats
5195 hubrizō (1), to *exercise violence, abuse*
5382 philŏxĕnŏs (1), *hospitable*
5530 chraŏmai (7), to *furnish* what is needed

5532 chrĕia (1), *affair; occasion, demand*
5540 chrēsis (2), *employment*

USED
3928 limmûwd (1), *instructed* one
6213 'âsâh (2), to *do or make*
390 anastrĕphō (1), to *remain, to live*
1247 diakŏnĕō (1), to *wait upon, serve*
1387 dŏliŏō (1), to *practice deceit*
1510 ĕimi (1), I *exist,* I *am*
3096 magĕuó (1), to *practice magic, sorcery*
4238 prassō (1), to *execute, accomplish*
5530 chraŏmai (3), to *furnish* what is needed

USES
5532 chrĕia (1), *affair; occasion, demand*

USEST
4941 mishpât̤ (1), *verdict; formal decree; justice*

USETH
1696 dâbar (1), to *speak, say;* to *subdue*
3348 mĕtĕchō (1), to *share or participate*

USING
671 apŏchrēsis (1), *consumption, using up*
2192 ĕchō (1), to *have; hold; keep*

USURER
5383 nâshâh (1), to *lend or borrow*

USURP
831 authĕntĕō (1), to *dominate*

USURY
5378 nâsha' (1), to *lend* on interest
5383 nâshâh (5), to *lend or borrow*
5391 nâshak (4), to *oppress* through finance
5392 neshek (11), *interest*
5110 tŏkŏs (2), *interest* on money loaned

UTHAI
5793 'Ûwthay (2), *succoring*

UTMOST
314 'achărôwn (2), *late or last; behind; western*
7093 qêts (1), *extremity; after*
7097 qâtseh (3), *extremity*
7112 qâtsats (3), to *chop* off; to *separate*
4009 pĕras (1), *extremity, end, limit*

UTTER
1696 dâbar (5), to *speak, say;* to *subdue*
1897 hâgâh (1), to *murmur, utter a sound; ponder*

2435 chîytsôwn (12), outer *wall side; exterior*
2531 chemed (1), *delight*
3318 yâtsâ' (3), to *go, bring out*
3617 kâlâh (2), *complete destruction*
4448 mâlal (2), to *speak, say*
4911 mâshal (1), to *use figurative language*
5042 nâba' (4), to *gush forth; to utter*
5046 nâgad (3), to *announce*
5414 nâthan (4), to *give*
6030 'ânâh (1), to *respond, answer*
6315 pûwach (1), to *blow, to fan, kindle; to utter*
1325 didōmi (1), to *give*
2044 ĕrĕugŏmai (1), to *speak out*
2980 lalĕō (1), to *talk*

UTTERANCE
669 apŏphthĕggŏmai (1), *declare, address*
3056 lŏgŏs (4), *word, matter, thing*

UTTERED
1696 dâbar (1), to *speak, say; to subdue*
3318 yâtsâ' (1), to *go, bring out*
4008 mibṭâ' (2), *rash utterance*
5046 nâgad (2), to *announce*
5414 nâthan (5), to *give*
6475 pâtsâh (1), to *rend, i.e. open*
215 alalĕtŏs (1), *unspeakable*
2980 lalĕō (3), to *talk*
3004 lĕgō (1), to *say*

UTTERETH
502 'âlaph (1), to *learn; to teach*
559 'âmar (1), to *say*
1696 dâbar (1), to *speak, say; to subdue*
3318 yâtsâ' (2), to *go, bring out*
5042 nâba' (1), to *gush forth; to utter*
5414 nâthan (3), to *give*

UTTERING
1897 hâgâh (1), to *murmur, utter a sound*

UTTERLY
3605 kôl (1), *all, any or every*
3615 kâlâh (1), to *complete, prepare*
3632 kâlîyl (1), *whole, entire; complete; whole*
3966 me'ôd (2), *very, utterly*
7703 shâdad (1), to *ravage*
2618 katakaiō (1), to *consume wholly by burning*
2704 kataphthĕirō (1), to *spoil entirely*
3654 hŏlŏs (1), *completely, altogether*

UTTERMOST
314 'achărôwn (1), *late or last; behind; western*
319 'achărîyth (1), *future; posterity*
657 'ephеç (1), *end; no further*
3671 kânâph (1), *edge or extremity; wing*
7020 qîytsôwn (3), *terminal, end*
7097 qâtseh (10), *extremity*
7098 qâtsâh (3), *termination; fringe*
206 akrŏn (2), *extremity: end, top*
1231 diaginōskō (1), *ascertain exactly*
2078 ĕschatŏs (2), *farthest, final*
3838 pantĕlēs (1), *entire; completion*
4009 pĕras (1), *extremity, end, limit*
5056 tĕlŏs (1), *conclusion*

UZ
5780 'Ûwts (7), *consultation*

UZAI
186 'Ûwzay (1), *Uzai*

UZAL
187 'Ûwzâl (2), *Uzal*

UZZA
5798 'Uzzâ' (10), *strength*

UZZAH
5798 'Uzzâ' (4), *strength*

UZZEN-SHERAH
242 'Uzzên She'ĕrâh (1), *land of Sheerah*

UZZI
5813 'Uzzîy (11), *forceful*

UZZIA
5814 'Uzzîyâ' (1), *strength of Jehovah*

UZZIAH
5818 'Uzzîyâh (27), *strength of Jehovah*

UZZIEL
5816 'Uzzîy'êl (16), *strength of God*

UZZIELITES
5817 'Ozzîy'êlîy (2), *Uzziëlite*

VAGABOND
5110 nûwd (2), to *waver; to wander, flee*
4022 pĕriĕrchŏmai (1), to *stroll, vacillate, veer*

VAGABONDS
5128 nûwa' (1), to *waver*

VAIL
4304 miṭpachath (1), *cloak, woman's shawl*
4533 maçveh (1), *veil, cover*
4541 maççêkâh (1), *woven coverlet*
6532 pôreketh (25), *sacred screen, curtain*
6809 tsâ'îyph (3), *veil*
2571 kaluma (4), *veil, covering*

VAILS
7289 râdîyd (1), *veil*

VAIN
205 'âven (1), *trouble, vanity, wickedness*
1891 hâbal (5), to *be vain, be worthless*
1892 hebel (11), *emptiness or vanity*
2600 chinnâm (2), *gratis, free*
3576 kâzab (1), to *lie, deceive*
5014 nâbab (1), to *be hollow; be foolish*
7307 rûwach (2), *breath; wind; life-spirit*
7385 rîyq (8), *emptiness; worthless thing; in vain*
7386 rêyq (7), *empty; worthless*
7387 rêyqâm (1), *emptily; ineffectually*
7723 shâv' (22), *ruin; guile; idolatry*
8193 sâphâh (2), *lip, language, speech*
8267 sheqer (6), *untruth; sham*
8414 tôhûw (4), *waste, formless; in vain*
1432 dōrĕan (1), *gratuitously, freely*
1500 ĕikē (5), *idly, i.e. without reason or effect*
2755 kĕnŏdŏxŏs (1), *self-conceited*
2756 kĕnŏs (14), *empty; vain; useless*
2757 kĕnŏphōnia (2), *fruitless discussion*
2761 kĕnŏs (2), *vainly, i.e. to no purpose*
3150 mataiŏlŏgia (1), *meaningless talk*
3151 mataiŏlŏgŏs (1), *mischievous talker*
3152 mataiŏs (5), *profitless, futile; idol*
3154 mataiŏō (1), *wicked; idolatrous*
3155 matēn (2), *to no purpose, in vain*

VAINGLORY
2754 kĕnŏdŏxia (1), *self-conceit, vanity*

VAINLY
1500 ĕikē (1), *idly, i.e. without reason or effect*

VAJEZATHA
2055 Vaye͏zâthâ' (1), *Vajezatha*

VALE
6010 'êmeq (4), broad *depression or valley*
8219 she͏phêlâh (5), *lowland,*

VALIANT
47 'abbîyr (1), *mighty*
691 'er'êl (1), *hero, brave person*
1121+2428 bên (4), *son, descendant; people*
1368 gibbôwr (6), *powerful; great warrior*
1396 gâbar (1), to *be strong; to prevail*

VANISHED
2428 chayil (16), *army; wealth; virtue; valor*
3524 kabbîyr (1), *mighty; aged; mighty*
2478 ischurŏs (1), *forcible, powerful*

VALIANTEST
1121+2428 bên (1), *son, descendant; people*

VALIANTLY
2388 châzaq (1), to *be strong; courageous*
2428 chayil (5), *army; wealth; virtue; valor*

VALLEY
1237 biq'âh (9), *wide level valley*
1516 gay' (52), *gorge, valley*
5158 nachal (18), *valley, ravine; mine shaft*
6010 'êmeq (54), broad *depression or valley*
8219 she͏phêlâh (6), *lowland,*
5327 pharagx (1), *wadi ravine; valley*

VALLEYS
1237 biq'âh (4), *wide level valley*
1516 gay' (8), *gorge, valley*
5158 nachal (5), *valley, ravine; mine shaft*
6010 'êmeq (9), broad *depression or valley*
8219 she͏phêlâh (2), *lowland,*

VALOUR
2428 chayil (37), *army; wealth; virtue; valor*

VALUE
457 'ĕlîyl (1), *vain idol*
6186 'ârak (3), to *set in a row; to arrange*
1308 diaphĕrō (2), to *bear, carry; to differ*
5091 timaŏ (1), to *revere, honor, show respect*

VALUED
5541 çâlâh (2), to *contemn, reject*
5091 timaŏ (1), to *revere, honor, show respect*

VALUEST
6187 'êrek (1), *pile, equipment, estimate*

VANIAH
2057 Vanyâh (1), *Vanjah*

VANISH
4414 mâlach (1), to *disappear as dust*
6789 tsâmath (1), to *extirpate, root out*
854 aphanismŏs (1), *disappearance*
2673 katargĕō (1), to *be, render entirely useless*

VANISHED
5628 çârach (1), to *extend even to excess*
1096+855 ginŏmai (1), to *be, become*

VANISHETH
3212 yâlak (1), to *walk*;
to *live*; to *carry*
853 aphanizō (1), to
disappear, be destroyed

VANITIES
1892 hebel (12),
emptiness or *vanity*
3152 mataiŏs (1),
profitless, futile; *idol*

VANITY
205 'âven (6), *trouble,
vanity, wickedness*
1892 hebel (49),
emptiness or *vanity*
7385 rîyq (2), *emptiness;
worthless* thing; *in vain*
7723 shâv' (22), *ruin;
guile; idolatry*
8414 tôhûw (4), *waste,
formless; in vain*
3153 mataiŏtēs (3),
transientness; depravity

VAPORS
5387 nâsîy' (2), *leader;
rising mist, fog*

VAPOUR
108 'êd (1), *fog*
5927 'âlâh (1), to *ascend,
be high, mount*
822 atmis (2), *mist,
vapor; billows of smoke*

VAPOURS
5387 nâsîy' (1), *leader;
rising mist, fog*
7008 qîyṭôwr (1), *fume,
i.e. smoke cloud*

VARIABLENESS
3883 parallagē (1),
change or variation

VARIANCE
1369 dichazō (1), to
sunder, i.e. alienate
2054 ĕris (1), *quarrel*, i.e.
wrangling

VASHNI
2059 Vashnîy (1), *weak*

VASHTI
2060 Vashtîy (10), *Vashti*

VAUNT
6286 pâ'ar (1), to *shake a
tree*

VAUNTETH
4068 pĕrpĕrĕuŏmai (1),
to *boast, brag*

VEHEMENT
2759 chărîyshîy (1),
sultry, searing
3050 Yâhh (1), *Jehovah,
(the) self-Existent or
Eternal One*
1972 ĕpipŏthēsis (1),
longing for

VEHEMENTLY
1171 dĕinōs (1), *terribly,
i.e. excessively, fiercely*
1722+4 ĕn (1), *in; during;
because of*
2159 ĕutŏnōs (1),
intensely, cogently
4366 prŏsrēgnumi (2), to
burst upon

VEIL
7289 râdîyd (1), *veil*

2665 katapĕtasma (6),
door screen

VEIN
4161 môwtsâ' (1), *going
forth*

VENGEANCE
5358 nâqam (4), to
avenge or punish
5359 nâqâm (15), *revenge*
5360 nᵉqâmâh (19),
avengement
1349 dikē (2), *justice*
1557 ĕkdikēsis (4),
retaliation, punishment
3709 ŏrgē (1), *ire;
punishment*

VENISON
6718 tsayid (7), *hunting
game; lunch, food*
6720 tsêydâh (1), *food,
supplies*

VENOM
7219 rô'sh (1), *poisonous
plant; poison*

VENT
6605 pâthach (1), to *open
wide; to loosen, begin*

VENTURE
8537 tôm (2), *prosperity;
innocence*

VERIFIED
539 'âman (3), to *be firm,
faithful, true; to trust*

VERILY
61 'ăbâl (3), *truly, surely;
yet, but*
389 'ak (6), *surely; only,
however*
403 'âkên (2), *surely!,
truly!; but*
518 'îm (1), *whether?; if,
although; Oh that!*
518+3808 'îm (1), *Oh that!*
530 'ĕmûwnâh (1),
fidelity; steadiness
559 'âmar (1), to *say*
7069 qânâh (1), to *create;
to procure*
230 alēthōs (1), *truly,
surely*
281 amēn (76), *surely; so
be it*
1063 gar (2), *for, indeed,
but, because*
1222 dēpŏu (1), *indeed
doubtless*
2532 kai (1), *and; or;
even; also*
3303 mĕn (13), *verily*
3303+3767 mĕn (1), *verily*
3304 mĕnŏungĕ (1), *so
then at least*
3483 nai (1), *yes*
3689 ŏntōs (1), *really,
certainly*

VERITY
571 'emeth (1), *certainty,
truth, trustworthiness*
225 alēthĕia (1), *truth,
truthfulness*

VERMILION
8350 shâshar (2), *red*

VERY
199 'ûwlâm (2), *however
or on the contrary*

430 'ĕlôhîym (1), *the true
God; great ones*
552 'umnâm (1), *verily,
indeed, truly*
651 'âphêl (1), *dusky,
dark*
898 bâgad (1), to *act
covertly*
899 beged (2), *clothing;
treachery or pillage*
1419 gâdôwl (1), *great*
1767 day (2), *enough,
sufficient*
1851 daq (1), *crushed;
small or thin*
1854 dâqaq (1), to *crush;
crumble*
1942 havvâh (1), *desire;
craving*
2088 zeh (2), *this or that*
3190 yâṭab (2), to *be,
make well; be
successful*
3304 yᵉphêh-phîyâh (1),
very beautiful
3453 yâshîysh (2), *old
man*
3559 kûwn (1), to *render
sure, proper*
3966 mᵉ'ôd (136), *very,
utterly*
4213 miz'âr (3), *fewness,
smallness*
4295 maṭṭâh (1), *below
or beneath*
4592 mᵉ'aṭ (1), *little or
few*
4605 ma'al (2), *upward,
above, overhead*
4801 merchâq (1),
distant place; from afar
5464 çagrîyd (1), *pouring
rain*
5690 'egeb (1), *amative
words, words of love*
5704 'ad (2), *as far (long)
as; during; while; until*
6106 'etsem (2), *bone;
substance; selfsame*
6621 petha' (1), *wink, i.e.
moment; quickly*
6985 qaṭ (1), *little, i.e.
merely*
7023 qîyr (1), *wall,
side-wall*
7230 rôb (1), *abundance*
7260 rabrab (Ch.) (1),
huge, domineering
7690 saggîy' (Ch.) (1),
large
85 adĕmŏnĕō (2), to *be in
mental distress*
230 alēthōs (1), *truly,
surely*
662 apŏtŏlmaō (1), to
venture plainly
846 autŏs (5), *he, she, it*
927 barutimōs (1), *highly
valuable*
957 bĕltiŏn (1), *better*
1565 ĕkĕinŏs (2), *that one*
1582 ĕkkrĕmamai (1), to
listen closely
1646 ĕlachistŏs (3), *least*
1888 ĕpautŏphōrōi (1), *in
actual crime*
2236 hēdista (1), *with
great pleasure*

2532 kai (4), *and; or;
even; also*
2566 kalliŏn (1), *better*
2735 katŏrthōma (2),
made fully upright
3029 lian (2), *very much*
3827 pampŏlus (1), *full
many*, i.e. *immense*
4036 pĕrilupŏs (1),
intensely sad
4118 plĕistŏs (1), *very
large*, i.e. *the most*
4119 plĕiōn (1), *more*
4184 pŏlusplagchnŏs (1),
*extremely
compassionate*
4185 pŏlutĕlēs (1),
extremely expensive
4186 pŏlutimŏs (1),
extremely valuable
4361 prŏspĕinŏs (1),
intensely hungry
4708 spŏudaiŏtĕrōs (1),
more speedily
4970 sphŏdra (4), *high
degree, much*
5228 hupĕr (2), *over;
above; beyond*

VESSEL
3627 kᵉlîy (33),
implement, thing
5035 nebel (1), *skin-bag
for liquids; vase; lyre*
4632 skĕuŏs (11), *vessel,
implement, equipment*

VESSELS
3627 kᵉlîy (129),
implement, thing
3984 mâ'n (Ch.) (7),
utensil, vessel
30 aggĕiŏn (2),
receptacle, vessel
4632 skĕuŏs (8), *vessel,
implement, equipment*

VESTMENTS
3830 lᵉbûwsh (1),
garment; wife
4403 malbûwsh (1),
garment, clothing

VESTRY
4458 meltâchâh (1),
wardrobe

VESTURE
3682 kᵉçûwth (1), *cover;
veiling*
3830 lᵉbûwsh (2),
garment; wife
2440 himatiŏn (2), to *put
on clothes*
2441 himatismŏs (2),
clothing
4018 pĕribŏlaiŏn (1),
thrown around

VESTURES
899 beged (1), *clothing;
treachery or pillage*

VEX
926 bâhal (1), to *tremble;
be, make agitated*
2000 hâmam (1), to *put
in commotion*
2111 zûwâ' (1), to *shake
with fear, tremble*
3013 yâgâh (1), to *grieve;
to torment*
3238 yânâh (2), to *rage
or be violent*

3707 kâ'aç (1), *to grieve, rage, be indignant*
6213+7451 'âsâh (1), *to do or make*
6887 tsârar (5), *to cramp*
6973 qûwts (1), *to be, make anxious*
2559 kakŏō (1), *to injure; to oppress; to embitter*

VEXATION
2113 z°vâ'âh (1), *agitation, fear*
4103 m°hûwmâh (1), *confusion or uproar*
4164 mûwtsaq (1), *distress*
7469 r°'ûwth (7), *grasping after*
7475 ra'yôwn (3), *desire, chasing after*
7667 sheber (1), *fracture; ruin*

VEXATIONS
4103 m°hûwmâh (1), *confusion or uproar*

VEXED
926 bâhal (3), *to tremble; be, make agitated*
1766 dâchaq (1), *to oppress*
3238 yânâh (2), *to rage or be violent*
3334 yâtsar (1), *to be in distress*
4103 m°hûwmâh (1), *confusion or uproar*
4843 mârar (2), *to be, make bitter*
6087 'âtsab (1), *to worry, have pain or anger*
6887 tsârar (1), *to cramp*
7114 qâtsar (1), *to curtail, cut short*
7489 râ'a' (1), *to be good for nothing*
7492 râ'ats (1), *to break in pieces; to harass*
7561 râsha' (1), *to be, do, declare wrong*
928 basanizō (1), *to torture, torment*
1139 daimŏnizŏmai (1), *to be exercised by a demon*
2669 katapŏnĕō (1), *to harass, oppress*
3791 ŏchlĕō (2), *to harass, be tormented*
3958 paschō (1), *to experience pain*

VIAL
6378 pak (1), *flask, small jug*
5357 phialē (7), *broad shallow cup*, i.e. a *phial*

VIALS
5357 phialē (5), *broad shallow cup*, i.e. a *phial*

VICTORY
3467 yâsha' (1), *to make safe, free*
5331 netsach (2), *splendor; lasting*
8668 t°shûw'âh (3), *rescue, deliverance*
3528 nikaō (1), *to subdue, conquer*

3529 nikē (1), *conquest, victory, success*
3534 nikŏs (4), *triumph, victory*

VICTUAL
3557 kûwl (1), *to measure; to maintain*
3978 ma'ăkâl (1), *food, something to eat*
4202 mâzôwn (1), *food, provisions*
6720 tsêydâh (2), *food, supplies*

VICTUALS
400 'ôkel (3), *food*
737 'ărûchâh (1), *ration, portion of food*
3557 kûwl (1), *to measure; to maintain*
3899 lechem (2), *food, bread*
4241 michyâh (1), *sustenance; quick*
6718 tsayid (2), *hunting game; lunch, food*
6720 tsêydâh (4), *food, supplies*
7668 sheber (1), *grain*
1033 brōma (1), *food*
1979 ĕpisitismŏs (1), *food*

VIEW
5048 neged (2), *in front of*
7200 râ'âh (1), *to see*
7270 râgal (1), *to reconnoiter; to slander*

VIEWED
995 bîyn (1), *to understand; discern*
7370 râchash (1), *to gush*
7663 sâbar (2), *to scrutinize; to expect*

VIGILANT
1127 grēgŏrĕuō (1), *to watch, guard*
3524 nēphalĕŏs (1), *circumspect, temperate*

VILE
959 bâzâh (2), *to disesteem, ridicule*
2151 zâlal (2), *to be loose morally, worthless*
2933 ţâmâh (1), *to be ceremonially impure*
5034 nâbêl (1), *to wilt; to fall away; to be foolish*
5036 nâbâl (2), *stupid; impious*
5039 n°bâlâh (1), *moral wickedness; crime*
5240 n°mibzeh (1), *despised*
7034 qâlâh (1), *to be, hold in contempt*
7043 qâlal (4), *to be easy, trifling, vile*
8182 shô'âr (1), *harsh or horrid*, i.e. *offensive*
819 atimia (1), *disgrace*
4508 rhuparŏs (1), *shabby, dirty; wicked*
5014 tapĕinōsis (1), *humbleness, lowliness*

VILELY
1602 gâ'al (1), *to detest; to reject; to fail*

VILER
5217 nâkâ' (1), *to smite*, i.e. *drive away*

VILEST
2149 zullûwth (1), (poss.) *tempest*

VILLAGE
2968 kōmē (10), *hamlet, town*

VILLAGES
1323 bath (12), *daughter, outlying village*
2691 châtsêr (47), *yard; walled village*
3715 k°phîyr (1), *walled village; young lion*
3723 kâphâr (2), *walled village*
3724 kôpher (1), *village; bitumen; henna*
6518 pârâz (1), *chieftain*
6519 p°râzâh (1), *rural, open country*
6520 p°râzôwn (2), *magistracy, leadership*
6521 p°râzîy (1), *rustic*
2968 kōmē (7), *hamlet, town*

VILLANY
5039 n°bâlâh (2), *moral wickedness; crime*

VINE
1612 gephen (44), *grape vine*
2156 z°môwrâh (1), *pruned twig, branch*
3196 yayin (1), *wine; intoxication*
3755 kôrêm (1), *vinedresser*
5139 nâzîyr (2), *prince; unpruned vine*
8321 sôrêq (3), *choice vine stock*
288 ampĕlŏs (9), *grape vine*

VINEDRESSERS
3755 kôrêm (4), *vinedresser*

VINEGAR
2558 chômets (6), *vinegar*
3690 ŏxŏs (7), *sour wine*

VINES
1612 gephen (9), *grape vine*
3754 kerem (3), *garden or vineyard*

VINEYARD
3657 kannâh (1), *plant*
3754 kerem (44), *garden or vineyard*
289 ampĕlŏurgŏs (1), *vineyard caretaker*
290 ampĕlōn (23), *vineyard*

VINEYARDS
3754 kerem (45), *garden or vineyard*

VINTAGE
1208 bâtsôwr (1), *inaccessible*
1210 bâtsîyr (7), *grape crop, harvest*
3754 kerem (1), *garden or vineyard*

VIOL
5035 nebel (2), *skin-bag for liquids; vase; lyre*

VIOLATED
2554 châmaç (1), *to be violent; to maltreat*

VIOLENCE
1497 gâzal (1), *to rob*
1498 gâzêl (1), *robbery, stealing*
1499 gêzel (1), *violence*
1500 g°zêlâh (3), *robbery, stealing; things stolen*
2554 châmaç (2), *to be violent; to maltreat*
2555 châmâç (39), *violence; malice*
4835 m°rûtsâh (1), *oppression*
6231 'âshaq (1), *to violate; to overflow*
970 bia (4), *force, pounding violence*
971 biazō (1), *to crowd oneself into*
1286 diasĕiō (1), *to intimidate, extort*
1411 dunamis (1), *force, power, miracle*
3731 hŏrmēma (1), *sudden attack*

VIOLENT
1499 gêzel (1), *violence*
2555 châmâç (7), *violence; malice*
6184 'ârîyts (1), *powerful or tyrannical*
973 biastēs (1), *energetic, forceful one*

VIOLENTLY
1497 gâzal (4), *to rob*
1500 g°zêlâh (1), *robbery, stealing; things stolen*
2554 châmaç (1), *to be violent; to maltreat*

VIOLS
5035 nebel (2), *skin-bag for liquids; vase; lyre*

VIPER
660 'eph'eh (2), *asp*
2191 ĕchidna (1), *adder*

VIPER'S
660 'eph'eh (1), *asp*

VIPERS
2191 ĕchidna (4), *adder*

VIRGIN
1330 b°thûwlâh (24), *virgin*
5959 'almâh (2), *lass, young woman*
3933 parthĕnŏs (7), *virgin*

VIRGIN'S
3933 parthĕnŏs (1), *virgin*

VIRGINITY
1331 b°thûwlîym (8), *virginity; proof of female virginity*
3932 parthĕnia (1), *maidenhood, virginity*

VIRGINS
1330 b°thûwlâh (14), *virgin*
5959 'almâh (2), *lass, young woman*
3933 parthĕnŏs (6), *virgin*

VIRTUE
703 arětē (4), *excellence, virtue*
1411 dunamis (3), *force, power, miracle*

VIRTUOUS
2428 chayil (3), *army; wealth; virtue; valor*

VIRTUOUSLY
2428 chayil (1), *army; wealth; virtue; valor*

VISAGE
600 'ănaph (Ch.) (1), *face*
4758 mar'eh (1), *appearance; vision*
8389 tô'ar (1), *outline, appearance*

VISIBLE
3707 hŏratŏs (1), *capable of being seen*

VISION
2376 chêzev (Ch.) (2), *sight, revelation*
2377 cházôwn (32), *sight; revelation*
2380 cházûwth (2), *striking appearance*
2384 chizzâyôwn (6), *dream; vision*
4236 machăzeh (4), *vision*
4758 mar'eh (14), *appearance; vision*
4759 mar'âh (3), *vision; mirror*
7203 rô'eh (1), *seer; vision*
3701 ŏptasia (2), *supernatural vision*
3705 hŏrama (12), *supernatural spectacle*
3706 hŏrasis (1), *appearance, vision*

VISIONS
2376 chêzev (Ch.) (9), *sight, revelation*
2377 cházôwn (3), *sight; revelation*
2378 cházôwth (1), *revelation*
2384 chizzâyôwn (3), *dream; vision*
4759 mar'âh (5), *vision; mirror*
7200 râ'âh (1), *to see*
3701 ŏptasia (1), *supernatural vision*
3706 hŏrasis (1), *appearance, vision*

VISIT
6485 pâqad (33), *to visit, care for, count*
1980 ĕpiskĕptŏmai (4), *inspect, to go to see*

VISITATION
6486 pᵉquddâh (13), *visitation; punishment*
1984 ĕpiskŏpē (2), *episcopate*

VISITED
6485 pâqad (18), *to visit, care for, count*
1980 ĕpiskĕptŏmai (5), *to inspect; to go to see*

VISITEST
6485 pâqad (2), *to visit, care for, count*
1980 ĕpiskĕptŏmai (1), *to inspect; to go to see*

VISITETH
6485 pâqad (1), *to visit, care for, count*

VISITING
6485 pâqad (4), *to visit, care for, count*

VOCATION
2821 klēsis (1), *invitation; station in life*

VOICE
6963 qôwl (379), *voice or sound*
7032 qâl (Ch.) (3), *sound, music*
5456 phōnē (116), *voice, sound*
5586 psēphŏs (1), *pebble stone*

VOICES
6963 qôwl (2), *voice or sound*
5456 phōnē (15), *voice, sound*

VOID
6 'âbad (1), *perish; destroy*
922 bôhûw (2), *ruin, desolation*
1238 bâqaq (1), *to depopulate, ruin*
1637 gôren (2), open *area*
2638 châçêr (6), *lacking*
4003 mᵉbûwqâh (1), *emptiness, devastation*
5010 nâ'ar (1), *to reject*
6565 pârar (5), *to break up; to violate, frustrate*
7387 rêyqâm (1), *emptily; ineffectually*
677 aprŏskŏpŏs (1), *not led into sin*
2673 katargĕō (1), *to be, render entirely useless*
2758 kĕnŏō (2), *to make empty*

VOLUME
4039 mᵉgillâh (1), *roll, scroll*
2777 kĕphalis (1), *roll, scroll*

VOLUNTARILY
5071 nᵉdâbâh (1), *abundant* gift

VOLUNTARY
5071 nᵉdâbâh (2), *abundant* gift
7522 râtsôwn (1), *delight*
2309 thĕlō (1), *to will; to desire; to choose*

VOMIT
6892 qê' (4), *vomit*
6958 qôw' (3), *to vomit*
1829 ĕxĕrama (1), *vomit*

VOMITED
6958 qôw' (1), *to vomit*

VOMITETH
6958 qôw' (1), *to vomit*

VOPHSI
2058 Vophçîy (1), *additional*

VOW
5087 nâdar (9), *to promise, vow*
5088 neder (30), *promise to God; thing promised*
2171 ĕuchē (2), *wish, petition*

VOWED
5087 nâdar (16), *to promise, vow*
5088 neder (2), *promise to God; thing promised*

VOWEDST
5087 nâdar (1), *to promise, vow*

VOWEST
5087 nâdar (2), *to promise, vow*

VOWETH
5087 nâdar (1), *to promise, vow*

VOWS
5088 neder (30), *promise to God; thing promised*

VOYAGE
4144 plŏŏs (1), *navigation, voyage*

VULTURE
1676 dâ'âh (1), *kite*
1772 dayâh (1), *falcon*

VULTURE'S
344 'ayâh (1), *hawk*

VULTURES
1772 dayâh (1), *falcon*

WAFER
7550 râqîyq (3), *thin cake, wafer*

WAFERS
6838 tsappîychîth (1), *flat thin cake*
7550 râqîyq (4), *thin cake, wafer*

WAG
5110 nûwd (1), *to waver; to wander, flee*
5128 nûwa' (2), *to waver*

WAGES
2600 chinnâm (1), *gratis, free*
4909 maskôreth (3), *wages; reward*
6468 pᵉ'ullâh (1), *work, deed*
7936 sâkar (1), *to hire*
7939 sâkâr (6), *payment, salary; compensation*
3408 misthŏs (2), *pay for services, good or bad*
3800 ŏpsōniŏn (3), *rations, stipend or pay*

WAGGING
2795 kinĕō (2), *to stir, move, remove*

WAGON
5699 'ăgâlâh (1), *wheeled vehicle*

WAGONS
5699 'ăgâlâh (8), *wheeled vehicle*
7393 rekeb (1), *vehicle for riding*

WAIL
5091 nâhâh (1), *to bewail; to assemble*
5594 çâphad (1), *to tear the hair, wail*
2875 kŏptō (1), *to beat the breast*

WAILED
214 alalazō (1), *to wail; to clang*

WAILING
4553 miçpêd (6), *lamentation, howling*
5089 nôahh (1), *lamentation*
5092 nᵉhîy (4), *elegy*
5204 nîy (1), *lamentation*
2805 klauthmŏs (2), *lamentation, weeping*
3996 pĕnthĕō (2), *to grieve*

WAIT
693 'ârab (34), *to ambush, lie in wait*
695 'ereb (1), *hiding place; lair*
696 'ôreb (1), *hiding place; lair*
1748 dûwmâm (1), *silently*
1826 dâmam (1), *to stop, cease; to perish*
2342 chûwl (1), *to wait; to pervert*
2442 châkâh (6), *to await; hope for*
3027 yâd (1), *hand; power*
3176 yâchal (5), *to wait; to be patient, hope*
3993 ma'ărâb (1), *ambuscade, ambush*
6119 'âqêb (1), *track, footprint; rear position*
6633 tsâbâ' (1), *to mass an army or servants*
6658 tsâdâh (1), *to desolate*
6660 tsᵉdîyâh (2), *design, lying in wait*
6960 qâvâh (22), *to collect; to expect*
7663 sâbar (2), *to scrutinize; to expect*
7789 shûwr (1), *to spy out, survey*
8104 shâmar (4), *to watch*
362 anamĕnō (1), *to await in expectation*
553 apĕkdĕchŏmai (2), *to expect fully, await*
1096+1917 ginŏmai (1), *to be, become*
1747 ĕnĕdra (1), *ambush*
1748 ĕnĕdrĕuō (2), *to lurk*
1917 ĕpibŏulē (2), *plot, plan*
3180 mĕthŏdĕia (1), *trickery, scheming*
4037 pĕrimĕnō (1), *to await*
4160+1747 pŏiĕō (1), *to make or do*
4327 prŏsdĕchŏmai (1), *to receive; to await for*
4332 prŏsĕdrĕuō (1), *to attend as a servant*

4342 prŏskartĕrĕŏ (1), to
persevere

WAITED
1961+6440 hâyâh (1), to
exist, i.e. be or become
2342 chûwl (1), to wait;
to pervert
2442 châkâh (2), to
await; hope for
3176 yâchal (6), to wait;
to be patient, hope
5975 'âmad (5), to stand
6822 tsâphâh (1), to
observe, await
6960 qâvâh (8), to collect;
to expect
8104 shâmar (1), to
watch
8334 shârath (1), to
attend as a menial
1551 ĕkdĕchŏmai (2), to
await, expect
4327 prŏsdĕchŏmai (2),
to receive; to await for
4328 prŏsdŏkaō (2), to
anticipate; to await
4342 prŏskartĕrĕŏ (1), to
persevere, be constant

WAITETH
1747 dûwmîyâh (2),
silently; quiet, trust
2442 châkâh (3), to
await; hope for
3176 yâchal (1), to wait;
to be patient, hope
8104 shâmar (1), to
watch
553 apĕkdĕchŏmai (2),
to expect fully, await
1551 ĕkdĕchŏmai (1), to
await, expect

WAITING
6635 tsâbâ' (1), army,
military host
8104 shâmar (1), to
watch
553 apĕkdĕchŏmai (2),
to expect fully, await
1551 ĕkdĕchŏmai (1), to
await, expect
4327 prŏsdĕchŏmai (1),
to receive; to await for
4328 prŏsdŏkaō (1), to
anticipate; to await

WAKE
5782 'ûwr (1), to awake
6974 qûwts (2), to awake
1127 grĕgŏrĕuō (1), to
watch, guard

WAKED
5782 'ûwr (1), to awake

WAKENED
5782 'ûwr (2), to awake

WAKENETH
5782 'ûwr (2), to awake

WAKETH
5782 'ûwr (1), to awake
8245 shâqad (1), to be
alert, i.e. sleepless

WAKING
8109 shᵉmûrâh (1),
eye-lid

WALK
1869 dârak (2), to tread;
trample; to walk

1979 hălîykâh (1),
walking; procession
1980 hâlak (61), to walk;
live a certain way
1981 hălak (Ch.) (1), to
walk; live a certain way
3212 yâlak (79), to walk;
to live; to carry
4108 mahlêk (1), access;
journey
4109 mahălâk (1),
passage or a distance
5437 çâbab (1), to
surround
1704 ĕmpĕripatĕō (1), to
be occupied among
4043 pĕripatĕō (55), to
walk; to live a life
4198 pŏrĕuŏmai (4), to
go, come; to travel
4748 stŏichĕō (4), to
follow, walk; to conform

WALKED
1980 hâlak (67), to walk;
live a certain way
1981 hălak (Ch.) (1), to
walk; live a certain way
3212 yâlak (32), to walk;
to live; to carry
3716 ŏrthŏpŏdĕō (1), to
act rightly
4043 pĕripatĕō (19), to
walk; to live a life
4198 pŏrĕuŏmai (1), to
go, come; to travel

WALKEDST
4043 pĕripatĕō (1), to
walk; to live a life

WALKEST
1980 hâlak (1), to walk;
live a certain way
3212 yâlak (3), to walk;
to live; to carry
4043 pĕripatĕō (2), to
walk; to live a life
4748 stŏichĕō (1), to
follow, walk; to conform

WALKETH
1980 hâlak (31), to walk;
live a certain way
3212 yâlak (2), to walk;
to live; to carry
1330 diĕrchŏmai (2), to
traverse, travel through
4043 pĕripatĕō (5), to
walk; to live a life

WALKING
1980 hâlak (10), to walk;
live a certain way
1981 hălak (Ch.) (1), to
walk; live a certain way
3212 yâlak (3), to walk;
to live; to carry
4043 pĕripatĕō (12), to
walk; to live a life
4198 pŏrĕuŏmai (4), to
go, come; to travel

WALL
846 'ushsharnâ' (Ch.) (1),
wall
1444 geder (2), wall or
fence
1447 gâdêr (5),
enclosure, i.e. wall
1448 gᵉdêrâh (1),
enclosure for flocks
2346 chôwmâh (92), wall

2426 chêyl (1),
entrenchment
2434 chayits (1), wall
2742 chârûwts (1),
mined gold; trench
3796 kôthel (1), house
wall
3797 kᵉthal (Ch.) (1),
house wall
7023 qîyr (50), wall,
side-wall
7791 shûwr (3), wall
7794 shôwr (1), bullock
5038 tĕichŏs (8), house
wall
5109 tŏichŏs (1), wall

WALLED
1219 bâtsar (2), to be
inaccessible
2346 chôwmâh (2), wall

WALLOW
5606 çâphaq (1), to be
enough; to vomit
6428 pâlash (3), to roll in
dust

WALLOWED
1556 gâlal (1), to roll; to
commit
2947 kuliŏō (1), to roll
about

WALLOWING
2946 kulisma (1),
wallowing in filth

WALLS
846 'ushsharnâ' (Ch.) (1),
wall
1447 gâdêr (1),
enclosure, i.e. wall
2346 chôwmâh (39), wall
2426 chêyl (1), rampart,
battlement
3797 kᵉthal (Ch.) (1),
house wall
7023 qîyr (16), wall,
side-wall
7791 shûwr (4), wall
8284 shârâh (1),
fortification
5038 tĕichŏs (1), house
wall

WANDER
5074 nâdad (1), to rove,
flee; to drive away
5128 nûwa' (4), to waver
6808 tsâ'âh (1), to tip
over; to depopulate
7462 râ'âh (1), to tend a
flock, i.e. pasture it
7686 shâgâh (2), to stray,
wander; to transgress
8582 tâ'âh (5), to
vacillate, i.e. reel, stray

WANDERED
1980 hâlak (1), to walk;
live a certain way
5128 nûwa' (3), to waver
7686 shâgâh (1), to stray,
wander; to transgress
8582 tâ'âh (1), to
vacillate, i.e. reel, stray
4022 pĕriĕrchŏmai (1), to
stroll, vacillate, veer
4105 planaō (1), to roam,
wander from safety

WANDERERS
5074 nâdad (1), to rove,
flee; to drive away
6808 tsâ'âh (1), to tip
over; to depopulate

WANDEREST
6808 tsâ'âh (1), to tip
over; to depopulate; to
imprison; to lay down

WANDERETH
5074 nâdad (5), to rove,
flee; to drive away
8582 tâ'âh (1), to
vacillate, i.e. reel, stray

WANDERING
1981 hălak (Ch.) (1), to
walk; live a certain way
5074 nâdad (1), to rove,
flee; to drive away
5110 nûwd (1), to waver;
to wander, flee
8582 tâ'âh (1), to
vacillate, i.e. reel, stray
4022 pĕriĕrchŏmai (1), to
stroll, vacillate, veer
4107 planētēs (1), roving,
erratic teacher

WANDERINGS
5112 nôwd (1), exile

WANT
657 'epheç (1), end; no
further
1097 bᵉlîy (2), without,
not yet; lacking;
2637 châçêr (4), to lack;
to fail, want, make less
2638 châçêr (1), lacking
2639 checer (1), lack;
destitution
2640 chôcer (3), poverty
3772 kârath (3), to cut
(off, down or asunder)
3808 lô' (1), no, not
4270 machçôwr (7),
impoverishment
6485 pâqad (1), to visit,
care for, count
5302 hustĕrĕō (1), to be
inferior; to fall short (be
deficient)
5303 hustĕrēma (3),
deficit; poverty; lacking
5304 hustĕrēsis (2),
penury, lack, need

WANTED
2637 châçêr (1), to lack;
to fail, want, make less
5302 hustĕrĕō (2), to be
inferior; to fall short

WANTETH
2308 châdal (1), to desist,
stop; be fat
2637 châçêr (2), to lack;
to fail, want, make less
2638 châçêr (4), lacking

WANTING
2627 chaççîyr (Ch.) (1),
deficient, wanting
2642 checrôwn (1),
deficiency
3808 lô' (1), no, not
6485 pâqad (2), to visit,
care for, count
3007 lĕipō (3), to fail or
be absent

W

WANTON
8265 sâqar (1), to *ogle*,
i.e. *blink* coquettishly
2691 katastrēniaō (1), to
be *voluptuous against*
4684 spatalaō (1), to *live*
in *luxury*

WANTONNESS
766 asĕlgĕia (2),
debauchery, *lewdness*

WANTS
4270 machçôwr (1),
impoverishment
5532 chrěia (1), *affair*;
requirement

WAR
2428 chayil (1), *army*;
wealth; virtue; *valor*
2438 Chîyrâm (1), *noble*
3898 lâcham (9), to *fight*
a *battle*
3901 lâchem (1), *battle*,
war
4421 milchâmâh (151),
battle; war; *fighting*
4421+7128 milchâmâh
(1), battle; war; *fighting*
6635 tsâbâ' (41), *army*,
military host
6904 qôbel (1),
battering-ram
7128 qᵉrâb (3), hostile
encounter
7129 qᵉrâb (Ch.) (1),
hostile *encounter*
4170 pŏlĕmĕō (4), to
battle, make *war*
4171 pŏlĕmŏs (6),
warfare; battle; *fight*
4753 stratĕuma (1), body
of *troops*
4754 stratĕuŏmai (4), to
serve in *military*

WARD
4929 mishmâr (11),
guard; deposit; *usage*
4931 mishmereth (6),
watch, sentry, *post*
5474 çûwgar (1), animal
cage
6488 pᵉqîdûth (1),
supervision
5438 phulakē (1),
guarding or *guard*

WARDROBE
899 beged (2), *clothing*;
treachery or *pillage*

WARDS
4931 mishmereth (3),
watch, sentry, *post*

WARE
4377 meker (1),
merchandise; *value*
4465 mimkâr (1),
merchandise
4728 maqqâchâh (1),
merchandise, wares
1737 ĕndiduskō (1), to
clothe
4894 ʒunĕidō (1), to
understand or be *aware*
5442 phulassō (1), to
watch, i.e. be on *guard*

WARES
3627 kᵉlîy (1),
implement, thing

3666 kin'âh (1), *package*,
bundle
4639 ma'ăseh (2), *action*;
labor
5801 'izzâbôwn (1),
trade, *merchandise*

WARFARE
6635 tsâbâ' (2), *army*,
military host
4752 stratĕia (2),
warfare; *fight*
4754 stratĕuŏmai (1), to
serve in *military*

WARM
2215 zârab (1), to *flow*
away, be *dry*
2525 châm (1), *hot*,
sweltering
2527 chôm (1), *heat*
2552 châmam (4), to *be*
hot; to be in a *rage*
3179 yâcham (1), to
conceive

WARMED
2552 châmam (1), to *be*
hot; to be in a *rage*
2328 thĕrmainō (5), to
heat *oneself*

WARMETH
2552 châmam (2), to *be*
hot; to be in a *rage*

WARMING
2328 thĕrmainō (1), to
heat *oneself*

WARN
2094 zâhar (8), to
enlighten
3560 nŏuthĕtĕō (3), to
caution or *reprove*

WARNED
2094 zâhar (4), to
enlighten
5263 hupŏdĕiknumi (2),
to *exemplify*
5537 chrēmatizō (4), to
utter an *oracle*

WARNING
2094 zâhar (6), to
enlighten
5749 'ûwd (1), to
duplicate or *repeat*
3560 nŏuthĕtĕō (1), to
caution or *reprove*

WARP
8359 shᵉthîy (9), *warp* in
weaving

WARRED
3898 lâcham (7), to *fight*
a *battle*
6633 tsâbâ' (2), to *mass*
an army or *servants*

WARRETH
4754 stratĕuŏmai (1), to
serve in *military*

WARRING
3898 lâcham (2), to *fight*
a *battle*
497 antistratĕuŏmai (1),
destroy, wage *war*

WARRIOR
5431 çâ'an (1), *soldier*
wearing boots

WARRIORS
6213+4421 'âsâh (2), to
do or *make*

WARS
4421 milchâmâh (9),
battle; war; *fighting*
4171 pŏlĕmŏs (4),
warfare; battle; *fight*

WASH
3526 kâbaç (39), to *wash*
7364 râchats (36), to
lave, bathe
628 apŏlŏuō (1), to *wash*
fully
907 baptizō (1), *baptize*
1026 brĕchō (1), to *make*
wet; to *rain*
3538 niptō (11), to *wash*,
bathe

WASHED
1740 dûwach (2), to rinse
clean, *wash*
3526 kâbaç (7), to *wash*
7364 râchats (17), to
lave, bathe
7857 shâṭaph (2), to
inundate, *cleanse*
628 apŏlŏuō (1), to *wash*
fully
633 apŏniptō (1), to *wash*
off *hands*
907 baptizō (1), *baptize*
1026 brĕchō (1), to *make*
wet; to *rain*
3068 lŏuō (6), to *bathe*; to
wash
3538 niptō (6), to *wash*,
bathe
4150 plunō (1), to *wash*
or *launder* clothing

WASHEST
7857 shâṭaph (1), to
inundate, *cleanse*

WASHING
3526 kâbaç (1), to *wash*
4325 mayim (1), *water*
7364 râchats (1), to *lave*,
bathe
7367 rachtsâh (2),
bathing *place*
637 apŏplunō (1), to
rinse off, wash *out*
909 baptismŏs (2),
baptism
3067 lŏutrŏn (2),
washing, *baptism*

WASHINGS
909 baptismŏs (1),
baptism

WASHPOT
5518+7366 çîyr (2), *thorn*;
hook

WAST
1961 hâyâh (13), to *exist*,
i.e. be or *become*
2258 ēn (5), I *was*
5607 ŏn (1), *being*,
existence

WASTE
1086 bâlâh (1), to *wear*
out, decay; *consume*
1110 bâlaq (2), to
annihilate, *devastate*
1326 bâthâh (1), area of
desolation

2717 chârab (13), to
desolate, *destroy*
2720 chârêb (6), *ruined*;
desolate
2721 chôreb (2),
parched; *ruined*
2723 chorbâh (14),
desolation, dry desert
3615 kâlâh (1), to
complete, *prepare*
3765 kirçêm (1), to *lay*
waste, ravage
4875 mᵉshôw'âh (2), *ruin*
5327 nâtsâh (1), to *be*
desolate, to lay *waste*
7489 râ'a' (1), to be *good*
for nothing
7582 shâ'âh (2), to *moan*;
to *desolate*
7703 shâdad (5), to
ravage
8047 shammâh (3), *ruin*;
consternation
8074 shâmêm (5), to
devastate; to *stupefy*
8077 shᵉmâmâh (1),
devastation
8414 tôhûw (1), *waste*,
desolation, formless
684 apŏlĕia (2), *ruin* or
loss

WASTED
1197 bâ'ar (1), to *be*
brutish, be *senseless*
2717 chârab (1), to
parch; desolate, *destroy*
2723 chorbâh (1),
desolation, dry desert
3615 kâlâh (1), to
complete, *consume*
7582 shâ'âh (1), to *moan*;
to *desolate*
7703 shâdad (2), to
ravage
7843 shâchath (1), to
decay; to *ruin*
8437 tôwlâl (1), *oppressor*
8552 tâmam (2), to
complete, *finish*
1287 diaskŏrpizō (2), to
scatter; to *squander*
4199 pŏrthĕō (1), to
ravage, *pillage*

WASTENESS
7722 shôw' (1), *tempest*;
devastation

WASTER
7843 shâchath (2), to
decay; to *ruin*

WASTES
2723 chorbâh (7),
desolation, dry desert

WASTETH
2522 châlash (1), to
prostrate, lay *low*
7703 shâdad (1), to
ravage
7736 shûwd (1), to
devastate

WASTING
7701 shôd (2), *violence*,
ravage, *destruction*

WATCH
821 'ashmûrâh (4), night
watch
4707 mitspeh (1),
military *observatory*

WATCHED
4929 mishmâr (4), *guard; deposit; usage; example*
4931 mishmereth (5), *watch, sentry, post*
6822 tsâphâh (5), to *observe, await*
8104 shâmar (5), to *watch*
8108 shomrâh (1), *watchfulness*
8245 shâqad (6), to *be on the lookout*
69 agrupněŏ (3), to *be sleepless, keep awake*
1127 grěgŏrěuŏ (16), to *watch, guard*
2892 kŏustŏdia (3), *sentry*
3525 nêphŏ (2), to *abstain from wine*
5438 phulakē (6), *night watch; prison; haunt*

WATCHED
6822 tsâphâh (1), to *observe, await*
8104 shâmar (2), to *watch*
8245 shâqad (2), to *be on the lookout*
1127 grěgŏrěuŏ (2), to *watch, guard*
3906 paratěrěŏ (5), to *note insidiously*
5083 těrěŏ (1), to *keep, guard, obey*

WATCHER
5894 'îyr (Ch.) (2), *watcher-angel*

WATCHERS
5341 nâtsar (1), to *guard, protect, maintain*
5894 'îyr (Ch.) (1), *watcher-angel*

WATCHES
821 'ashmûrâh (3), *night watch*
4931 mishmereth (2), *watch, sentry, post*

WATCHETH
6822 tsâphâh (1), to *observe, await*
6974 qûwts (1), to *awake*
1127 grěgŏrěuŏ (1), to *watch, guard*

WATCHFUL
1127 grěgŏrěuŏ (1), to *watch, guard*

WATCHING
6822 tsâphâh (2), to *observe, await*
8245 shâqad (1), to *be on the lookout*
69 agrupněŏ (1), to *be sleepless, keep awake*
1127 grěgŏrěuŏ (1), to *watch, guard*
5083 těrěŏ (1), to *keep, guard, obey*

WATCHINGS
70 agrupnia (2), *keeping awake*

WATCHMAN
6822 tsâphâh (14), to *peer into the distance*
8104 shâmar (4), to *watch*

WATCHMAN'S
6822 tsâphâh (1), to *peer into the distance*

WATCHMEN
5341 nâtsar (3), to *guard, protect, maintain*
6822 tsâphâh (5), to *peer into the distance*
8104 shâmar (4), to *watch*

WATCHTOWER
4707 mitspeh (1), *military observatory*
6844 tsâphîyth (1), *sentry*

WATER
1119 bᵉmôw (1), *in, with, by*
2222 zarzîyph (1), *pouring rain*
4325 mayim (308), *water*
4529 mâçâh (1), to *dissolve, melt*
7301 râvâh (1), to *slake thirst or appetites*
8248 shâqâh (9), to *quaff, i.e. to irrigate*
504 anudrŏs (2), *dry, arid*
5202 hudrŏpŏtěŏ (1), to *drink water exclusively*
5204 hudŏr (62), *water*

WATERCOURSE
4161+4325 môwtsâ' (1), *going forth*
8585 tᵉ'âlâh (1), *irrigation channel*

WATERED
3384 yârâh (1), to *point; to teach*
4945 mashqeh (1), *butler; drink; well-watered*
7302 râveh (2), *sated, full with drink*
8248 shâqâh (6), to *quaff, i.e. to irrigate*
4222 pŏtizŏ (1), to *furnish drink, irrigate*

WATEREDST
8248 shâqâh (1), to *quaff, i.e. to irrigate*

WATEREST
7301 râvâh (1), to *slake thirst or appetites*
7783 shûwq (1), to *overflow*

WATERETH
7301 râvâh (2), to *slake thirst or appetites*
8248 shâqâh (1), to *quaff, i.e. to irrigate*
4222 pŏtizŏ (2), to *furnish drink, irrigate*

WATERFLOOD
7641+4325 shibbôl (1), *stream; ear of grain*

WATERING
4325 mayim (1), *water*
7377 rîy (1), *irrigation*
4222 pŏtizŏ (2), to *furnish drink, irrigate*

WATERPOT
5201 hudria (1), *water jar, i.e. receptacle*

WATERPOTS
5201 hudria (2), *water jar, i.e. receptacle*

WATERS
4325 mayim (265), *water*
4215 pŏtamŏs (1), *current, brook, running water*
5204 hudŏr (15), *water*

WATERSPOUTS
6794 tsinnûwr (1), *culvert, water-shaft*

WATERSPRINGS
4161+4325 môwtsâ' (2), *going forth*

WAVE
5130 nûwph (11), to *quiver, vibrate, rock*
8573 tᵉnûwphâh (19), *official undulation of sacrificial offerings*
2830 kludŏn (1), *surge, raging*

WAVED
5130 nûwph (5), to *quiver, vibrate, rock*
8573 tᵉnûwphâh (1), *official undulation of sacrificial offerings*

WAVERETH
1252 diakrinŏ (1), to *decide; to hesitate*

WAVERING
186 aklinēs (1), *firm, unswerving*
1252 diakrinŏ (1), to *decide; to hesitate*

WAVES
1116 bâmâh (1), *elevation, high place*
1530 gal (14), *heap; ruins*
1796 dŏkîy (1), *dashing, pounding of surf*
4867 mishbâr (4), *breaker sea-waves*
2949 kuma (5), *bursting or toppling*
4535 salŏs (1), *billow, i.e. rolling motion of waves*

WAX
1749 dôwnag (4), *bees-wax*
2691 katastrēniaŏ (1), to *be voluptuous against*
3822 palaiŏŏ (2), to *make, become worn out*
4298 prŏkŏptŏ (1), to *go ahead, advance*
5594 psuchŏ (1), to *chill, grow cold*

WAXED
1980 hâlak (5), to *walk; live a certain way*
1096 ginŏmai (2), to *be, become*
2901 krataiŏŏ (2), *increase in vigor*
3955 parrhēsiazŏmai (1), to *be frank in utterance*
3975 pachunŏ (2), to *fatten; to render callous*
4147 plŏutěŏ (1), to *be, become wealthy*

WAXETH
1095 gēraskŏ (1), to *be senescent, grow old*

WAXING
3982 pěithŏ (1), to *pacify or conciliate; to assent*

WAY
734 'ôrach (18), *road; manner of life*
776 'erets (3), *earth, land, soil; country*
935 bôw' (1), to *go, come*
1870 derek (466), *road; course of life; mode*
2008 hênnâh (1), *from here; from there*
2088 zeh (1), *this or that*
3212 yâlak (6), to *walk; to live; to carry*
3541 kôh (1), *thus*
4498 mânôwç (1), *fleeing; place of refuge*
5265 nâça' (1), *start on a journey*
5410 nâthîyb (2), (*beaten*) *track, path*
7125 qîr'âh (1), to *encounter, to happen*
7971 shâlach (1), to *send away*
8582 tâ'âh (2), to *vacillate, i.e. reel*
1545 ěkbasis (1), *exit, way out*
1624 ěktrěpŏ (1), to *turn away*
1722 ěn (1), *in; during; because of*
3112 makran (2), *at a distance, far away*
3319 měsŏs (2), *middle*
3598 hŏdŏs (81), *road*
3938 parŏdŏs (1), *by-road, i.e. a route*
4105 planaŏ (1), to *roam, wander from safety*
4206 pŏrrhŏ (1), *forwards*
4311 prŏpěmpŏ (5), to *send forward*
5158 trŏpŏs (2), *deportment, character*

WAYFARING
732 'ârach (4), to *travel, wander*
1980+1870 hâlak (1), to *walk; live a certain way*
5674+734 'âbar (1), to *cross over; to transition*

WAYMARKS
6725 tsîyûwn (1), *guiding pillar, monument*

WAYS
734 'ôrach (8), *road; manner of life*
735 'ôrach (Ch.) (2), *road*
1870 derek (161), *road; course of life; mode of action*
1979 hălîykâh (2), *walking; procession or march; caravan*
4546 mᵉcillâh (1), *main thoroughfare; viaduct*
4570 ma'gâl (1), *circular track or camp rampart*
7339 rᵉchôb (1), *myriad*
296 amphŏdŏn (1), *fork in the road*
684 apŏlěia (1), *ruin or loss*
3598 hŏdŏs (11), *road*

4197 pŏrĕia (1), journey; life's daily conduct

WAYSIDE
3027+4570 yâd (1), hand; power
3197+1870 yak (1), hand or side

WEAK
535 'âmal (1), to be weak; to be sick
536 'umlal (1), sick, faint
2470 châlâh (4), to be weak, sick, afflicted
2523 challâsh (1), frail, weak
3212 yâlak (2), to walk; to live; to carry
3782 kâshal (1), to totter, waver; to falter
7390 rak (1), tender; weak
7503 râphâh (1), to slacken
7504 râpheh (4), slack
102 adunatŏs (1), weak; impossible
770 asthĕnĕō (19), to be feeble
772 asthĕnēs (8), strengthless, weak

WEAKEN
2522 châlash (1), to prostrate, lay low

WEAKENED
6031 'ânâh (1), to afflict, be afflicted
7503 râphâh (2), to slacken

WEAKENETH
7503 râphâh (2), to slacken

WEAKER
1800 dal (1), weak, thin; humble, needy
772 asthĕnēs (1), strengthless, weak

WEAKNESS
769 asthĕnĕia (5), feebleness; frailty
772 asthĕnēs (2), strengthless, weak

WEALTH
1952 hôwn (5), wealth
2428 chayil (10), army; wealth; virtue; valor
2896 ṭôwb (3), good; well
3581 kôach (1), force, might; strength
5233 nekeç (4), treasure, riches
2142 ĕupŏria (1), resources, prosperity

WEALTHY
7310 rᵉvâyâh (1), satisfaction
7961 shâlêv (1), careless, carefree; security

WEANED
1580 gâmal (12), to benefit or requite

WEAPON
240 'âzên (1), spade; paddle
3627 kᵉlîy (4), implement, thing

5402 nesheq (1), military arms, arsenal
7973 shelach (2), spear; shoot of growth

WEAPONS
3627 kᵉlîy (17), implement, thing
5402 nesheq (2), military arms, arsenal
3696 hŏplŏn (2), implement, or utensil

WEAR
1080 bᵉlâ' (Ch.) (1), to afflict, torment
1961 hâyâh (1), to exist, i.e. be or become
3847 lâbash (4), to clothe
5034 nâbêl (1), to wilt; to fall away; to be foolish
5375 nâsâ' (2), to lift up
7833 shâchaq (1), to grind or wear away
2827 klinō (1), to slant or slope
5409 phŏrĕō (1), to wear

WEARETH
5409 phŏrĕō (1), to wear

WEARIED
3021 yâga' (5), to be exhausted, to tire,
3811 lâ'âh (5), to tire; to be, make disgusted
5888 'âyêph (1), to languish
2577 kamnō (1), to tire; to faint, sicken
2872 kŏpiaō (1), to feel fatigue; to work hard

WEARIETH
2959 ṭârach (1), to overburden
3021 yâga' (1), to be exhausted, to tire,

WEARINESS
3024 yᵉgî'âh (1), fatigue
4972 mattᵉlâ'âh (1), what a trouble!
2873 kŏpŏs (1), toil; pains

WEARING
5375 nâsâ' (1), to lift up
4025 pĕrithĕsis (1), putting all around, i.e. decorating oneself with
5409 phŏrĕō (1), to wear

WEARISOME
5999 'âmâl (1), wearing effort; worry

WEARY
3019 yâgîya' (1), tired, exhausted
3021 yâga' (7), to be exhausted, to tire,
3023 yâgêa' (2), tiresome
3286 yâ'aph (5), to tire
3287 yâ'êph (1), exhausted
3811 lâ'âh (10), to tire; to be, make disgusted
5354 nâqaṭ (1), to loathe
5774 'ûwph (1), to cover, to fly; to faint
5889 'âyêph (8), languid
6973 qûwts (2), to be, make disgusted
7646 sâba' (1), fill to satiety

1573 ĕkkakĕō (2), to be weak, fail
5299 hupōpiazō (1), to beat up; to wear out

WEASEL
2467 chôled (1), weasel

WEATHER
2091 zâhâb (1), gold, piece of gold
3117 yôwm (1), day; time period
2105 ĕudia (1), clear sky, i.e. fine weather
5494 chĕimōn (1), winter season; stormy weather

WEAVE
707 'ârag (2), to plait or weave

WEAVER
707 'ârag (2), to plait or weave

WEAVER'S
707 'ârag (4), to plait or weave

WEAVEST
707 'ârag (1), to plait or weave

WEB
1004 bayith (1), house; temple; family, tribe
4545 maççeketh (2), length-wise threads
6980 qûwr (1), spider web

WEBS
6980 qûwr (1), spider web

WEDDING
1062 gamŏs (7), nuptials

WEDGE
3956 lâshôwn (2), tongue; tongue-shaped

WEDLOCK
5003 nâ'aph (1), to commit adultery

WEEDS
5488 çûwph (1), papyrus reed; reed

WEEK
7620 shâbûwa' (4), seven-day week
4521 sabbatŏn (9), day of weekly repose

WEEKS
7620 shâbûwa' (15), seven-day week

WEEP
1058 bâkâh (29), to weep, moan
1065 bᵉkîy (2), weeping
1830 dâma' (1), to weep
2799 klaiō (15), to sob, wail

WEEPEST
1058 bâkâh (1), to weep, moan
2799 klaiō (2), to sob, wail

WEEPETH
1058 bâkâh (4), to weep, moan

WEEPING
1058 bâkâh (8), to weep, moan
1065 bᵉkîy (21), weeping

2799 klaiō (9), to sob, wail
2805 klauthmŏs (6), lamentation, weeping

WEIGH
4948 mishqâl (2), weight, weighing
6424 pâlaç (2), to weigh mentally
8254 shâqal (2), to suspend in trade

WEIGHED
8254 shâqal (12), to suspend in trade
8505 tâkan (1), to balance, i.e. measure
8625 tᵉqal (Ch.) (1), to weigh in a balance

WEIGHETH
8505 tâkan (2), to balance, i.e. measure

WEIGHT
68 'eben (4), stone
4946 mishqôwl (1), weight
4948 mishqâl (44), weight, weighing
6425 peleç (1), balance, scale
922 barŏs (1), load, abundance, authority
3591 ŏgkŏs (1), burden, hindrance
5006 talantiaiŏs (1), weight of 57-80 lbs.

WEIGHTIER
926 barus (1), weighty

WEIGHTS
68 'eben (6), stone

WEIGHTY
5192 nêṭel (1), burden
926 barus (1), weighty

WELFARE
2896 ṭôwb (1), good; well
3444 yᵉshûw'âh (1), victory; prosperity
7965 shâlôwm (5), safe; well; health, prosperity

WELL
71 'Âbânâh (1), stony
369 'ayin (1), there is no, i.e., not exist, none
375 'êyphôh (2), where?; when?; how?
875 bᵉ'êr (21), well, cistern
883 Bᵉ'êr la-Chay Rô'îy (1), well of a living (One) my seer
953 bôwr (6), pit hole, cistern, well; prison
995 bîyn (1), to understand; discern
2090 zôh (1), this or that
2654 châphêts (1), to be pleased with, desire
2895 ṭowb (9), to be good
2896 ṭôwb (20), good; well
2898 ṭûwb (1), good; goodness; beauty, gladness, welfare
3190 yâṭab (35), to be, make well
3303 yâpheh (5), beautiful; handsome

3651 kên (4), *just; right, correct*

3966 mᵉʾôd (1), *very, utterly*

4599 ma'yân (2), *fountain; source*

4639 ma'ăseh (1), *action; labor*

4726 mâqôwr (1), *flow of liquids, or ideas*

5869 'ayin (9), *eye; sight; fountain*

5878 'Êyn Chărôd (1), *fountain of trembling*

6822 tsâphâh (1), *to peer into the distance*

7181 qâshab (1), *to prick up the ears*

7571 rethach (1), *boiling*

7965 shâlôwm (14), *safe; well; health, prosperity*

15 agathŏpŏiĕŏ (4), *to be a well-doer*

16 agathŏpŏiïa (1), *virtue, doing good*

17 agathŏpŏiŏs (1), *virtuous one*

18 agathŏs (1), *good*

957 bĕltiŏn (1), *better*

1510+2101 ĕimi (1), *I exist, I am*

1921 ĕpiginōskō (1), *to acknowledge*

2095 ĕu (6), *well*

2100 ĕuarĕstĕō (1), *to gratify entirely, please*

2101 ĕuarĕstŏs (1), *fully agreeable, pleasing*

2106 ĕudŏkĕō (7), *to think well, i.e. approve*

2509 kathapĕr (1), *exactly as*

2532 kai (2), *and; or*

2569 kalŏpŏiĕō (1), *to do well*

2570 kalŏs (1), *good; beautiful; valuable*

2573 kalōs (33), *well, i.e. rightly*

3140 marturĕō (2), *to testify; to commend*

3184 mĕthuō (1), *to get drunk*

4077 pēgē (3), *source or supply*

4260 prŏbainō (2), *to advance*

4982 sōzō (1), *to deliver; to protect*

5421 phrĕar (2), *cistern or water well; abyss*

WELL'S

875 bᵉʾêr (6), *well, cistern*

WELLBELOVED

1730 dôwd (1), *beloved, friend; uncle, relative*

3039 yᵉdîyd (2), *loved*

27 agapētŏs (3), *beloved*

WELLFAVOURED

2896+2580 ṭôwb (1), *good; well*

WELLPLEASING

2101 ĕuarĕstŏs (2), *fully agreeable, pleasing*

WELLS

875 bᵉʾêr (3), *well, cistern*

---

953 bôwr (3), *pit hole, cistern, well; prison*

4599 ma'yân (3), *fountain; source*

5869 'ayin (1), *eye; sight; fountain*

4077 pēgē (1), *source or supply*

WELLSPRING

4726 mâqôwr (2), *flow*

WEN

2990 yabbêl (1), *having running sores*

WENCH

8198 shiphchâh (1), *household female slave*

WENT

236 'ăzal (Ch.) (6), *to depart*

935 bôw' (115), *to go*

980 Bachûrîym (1), *young men*

1718 dâdâh (1), *to walk gently; lead*

1961 hâyâh (4), *to exist, i.e. be or become*

1980 hâlak (93), *to walk; live a certain way*

3212 yâlak (281), *to walk; to live; to carry*

3318 yâtsâ' (216), *to go*

3381 yârad (64), *to descend*

3518 kâbâh (1), *to extinguish*

5066 nâgash (4), *to be, come, bring near*

5075 nᵉdad (Ch.) (1), *to depart*

5221 nâkâh (1), *to strike, kill*

5265 nâça' (13), *start on a journey*

5312 nᵉphaq (Ch.) (1), *to issue forth; to bring out*

5437 çâbab (6), *to surround*

5493 çûwr (1), *to turn off*

5674 'âbar (38), *to cross over; to transition*

5927 'âlâh (160), *to ascend, be high, mount*

5954 'ălal (Ch.) (3), *to go in; to lead in*

5974 'im (Ch.) (1), *with*

6743 tsâlach (1), *to push*

6805 tsâ'ad (1), *to pace, step regularly*

6923 qâdam (2), *to anticipate, hasten*

7121 qârâ' (1), *to call out*

7126 qârab (2), *to approach, bring near*

7311 rûwm (1), *to be high; to rise or raise*

7683 shâgag (1), *to stray; to sin*

7725 shûwb (6), *to turn back; to return*

7751 shûwṭ (1), *to travel, roam*

8582 tâ'âh (6), *to vacillate, i.e. reel, stray*

305 anabainō (24), *to go up, rise*

402 anachōrĕō (1), *retire, withdraw*

---

424 anĕrchŏmai (3), *to ascend*

549 apĕimi (1), *to go away*

565 apĕrchŏmai (54), *to go off, i.e. depart*

589 apŏdēmĕō (3), *visit a foreign land*

1279 diapŏrĕuŏmai (3), *to travel through*

1330 diĕrchŏmai (6), *to traverse, travel through*

1353 diŏdĕuō (1), *to travel through*

1524 ĕisĕimi (2), *to enter*

1525 ĕisĕrchŏmai (25), *to enter*

1531 ĕispŏrĕuŏmai (1), *to enter*

1607 ĕkpŏrĕuŏmai (7), *to depart, be discharged, proceed, project*

1681 Ĕlumas (1), *Elymas*

1684 ĕmbainō (2), *to embark; to reach*

1821 ĕxapŏstĕllō (2), *to despatch, or to dismiss*

1831 ĕxĕrchŏmai (86), *to issue; to leave*

1910 ĕpibainō (1), *to embark, arrive*

2021 ĕpichĕirĕō (1), *to undertake, try*

2064 ĕrchŏmai (11), *to go, come*

2212 zētĕō (1), *to seek*

2597 katabainō (13), *to descend*

2718 katĕrchŏmai (2), *to go, come down*

3596 hŏdŏipŏrĕō (1), *to travel*

3854 paraginŏmai (1), *to arrive; to appear*

3899 parapŏrĕuŏmai (1), *to travel near*

3987 pĕiraō (1), *to attempt, try*

4013 pĕriagō (4), *to walk around*

4105 planaō (1), *to roam, wander from safety*

4198 pŏrĕuŏmai (44), *to go, come; to travel*

4254 prŏagō (6), *to lead forward; to precede*

4281 prŏĕrchŏmai (4), *to go onward, precede*

4334 prŏsĕrchŏmai (3), *to come near, visit*

4344 prŏskĕphalaiŏn (2), *cushion pillow*

4848 sumpŏrĕuŏmai (3), *to journey together*

4897 sunĕisĕrchŏmai (2), *to enter with*

4905 sunĕrchŏmai (3), *to gather together*

5217 hupagō (5), *to withdraw or retire*

5221 hupantaō (1), *to meet, encounter*

5298 hupŏchōrĕō (1), *vacate down, i.e. retire*

WENTEST

1980 hâlak (6), *to walk; live a certain way*

3212 yâlak (1), *to walk; to live; to carry*

3318 yâtsâ' (3), *to go, bring out*

5927 'âlâh (2), *to ascend, be high, mount*

7788 shûwr (1), *i.e. travel about*

1525 ĕisĕrchŏmai (1), *to enter*

WEPT

1058 bâkâh (57), *to weep, moan*

1145 dakruō (1), *to shed tears*

2799 klaiō (11), *to sob, wail*

WERT

1498 ĕiēn (1), *might could, would, or should*

WEST

3220 yâm (51), *sea; basin; west*

3996+8121 mâbôw' (1), *entrance; sunset; west*

4628 ma'ărâb (10), *west*

1424 dusmē (5), *western*

3047 lips (1), *southwest*

5566 chōrŏs (1), *north-west wind*

WESTERN

3220 yâm (1), *sea; basin; west*

WESTWARD

3220 yâm (21), *sea; basin; west*

3996+8121 mâbôw' (1), *entrance; sunset; west*

4628 ma'ărâb (4), *west*

WET

6647 tsᵉba' (Ch.) (5), *to dip, be wet*

7372 râṭab (1), *to be moist*

WHALE

8565 tan (1), *jackal*

8577 tannîyn (1), *sea-serpent; jackal*

WHALE'S

2785 kētŏs (1), *huge fish*

WHALES

8577 tannîyn (1), *sea-serpent; jackal*

WHEAT

1250 bâr (5), *grain*

1715 dâgân (2), *grain*

2406 chiṭṭâh (29), *wheat*

2591 chinṭâ' (Ch.) (2), *wheat*

7383 rîyphâh (1), *grits cereal*

4621 sitŏs (12), *grain, especially wheat*

WHEATEN

2406 chiṭṭâh (1), *wheat*

WHEEL

212 'ôwphân (10), *wheel*

1534 galgal (3), *wheel; something round*

1536 gilgâl (1), *wheel*

WHEELS

70 'ôben (1), *potter's wheel; midwife's stool*

212 'ôwphân (24), *wheel*

1534 galgal (6), *wheel; something round*

1535 galgal (Ch.) (1), *wheel*

6471 pa'am (1), *time; step; occurence*

WHELP
1482 gûwr (3), *cub*

WHELPS
1121 bên (2), *son, descendant; people*
1482 gûwr (3), *cub*
1484 gôwr (2), lion *cub*

WHEN
310 'achar (1), *after*
518 'îm (19), *whether?*
834 'ăsher (83), *who, what, that; when*
1767 day (3), *enough, sufficient*
1768 dîy (Ch.) (4), *that; of*
1961 hâyâh (4), *to exist*
3117 yôwm (7), *day; time*
3588 kîy (280), *for, that*
3644 kemôw (1), *like, as*
4970 mâthay (14), *when; when?, how long?*
5704 'ad (3), *as far (long) as; during; while; until*
5750 'ôwd (2), *again; repeatedly; still; more*
5921 'al (1), *above, over, upon, or against*
6256 'êth (7), *time*
6310 peh (2), *mouth; opening*
1437 ĕan (2), *indefiniteness*
1875 ĕpan (3), *whenever*
1893 ĕpĕi (1), *since*
2259 hēnika (2), *at which time, whenever*
2531 kathōs (1), *just or inasmuch as, that*
3326 mĕta (2), *with, among; after, later*
3698 hŏpŏtĕ (1), *as soon as, when*
3704 hŏpŏs (1), *in the manner that*
3752 hŏtan (123), *inasmuch as, at once*
3753 hŏtĕ (99), *when; as*
3756 ŏu (1), *no or not*
4218 pŏtĕ (13), *at some time, ever*
5613 hŏs (40), *which, how, i.e. in that manner*
5618 hŏspĕr (2), *exactly like*

WHENCE
335 'ay (1), *where?*
370 'ayin (19), *where from?, whence?*
1992 hêm (1), *they*
3606 hŏthĕn (4), *from which place or source*
3739 hŏs (2), *who, which, what, that*
4159 pŏthĕn (28), *from which; what*

WHENSOEVER
3605 kôl (1), *all, any or every*
3752 hŏtan (1), *inasmuch as, at once*
5613+1437 hŏs (1), *which, how, i.e. in that manner*

WHERE
335 'ay (16), *where?*
346 'ayêh (45), *where?*
349 'êyk (1), *where?*
351 'êykôh (1), *where*
370 'ayin (2), *where from?, whence?*
375 'êyphôh (9), *where?*
413 'êl (2), *to, toward*
575 'ân (2), *where from?*
645 'êphôw (5), *then*
657 'epheç (1), *end; no further*
834 'ăsher (58), *where*
1768 dîy (Ch.) (1), *that; of*
3027 yâd (1), *hand; power*
5921 'al (2), *above, over, upon, or against*
8033 shâm (20), *where*
8478 tachath (1), *bottom; underneath; in lieu of*
8536 tâm (Ch.) (1), *there*
296 amphŏdŏn (1), *fork in the road*
1330 diĕrchŏmai (1), *to traverse, travel through*
1337 dithalassŏs (1), *having two seas*
2596 kata (1), *down; according to*
3606 hŏthĕn (2), *from which place or source*
3699 hŏpŏu (58), *at whichever spot*
3757 hŏu (21), *at which place, i.e. where*
3837 pantachŏu (5), *universally, everywhere*
3838 pantĕlēs (1), *entire; completion*
4226 pŏu (37), *at what locality?*
5101 tis (1), *who?, which? or what?*

WHEREABOUT
834 'ăsher (1), *where, how, because*

WHEREAS
518 'îm (1), *whether?; if, although; Oh that!*
834 'ăsher (2), *because, in order that*
1768 dîy (Ch.) (4), *that; of*
3588 kîy (5), *for, that because*
6258 'attâh (2), *at this time, now*
8478 tachath (1), *bottom; underneath; in lieu of*
3699 hŏpŏu (2), *at whichever spot*
3748 hŏstis (1), *whoever*

WHEREBY
834 'ăsher (17), *because, in order that*
4100 mâh (1), *whatever; that which*
4482 mên (1), *part; musical chord*
3588 hŏ (1), *"the," i.e. the definite article*
3739 hŏs (1), *who, which, what, that*

WHEREFORE
199 'ûwlâm (1), *however or on the contrary*
3651 kên (18), *just; right, correct*

3861 lâhên (Ch.) (1), *therefore; except*
4069 maddûwa' (28), *why?, what?*
4100 mâh (86), *what?, how?, why?, when?*
686 ara (1), *therefore*
1161 dĕ (2), *but, yet*
1302 diati (4), *why?*
1352 diŏ (41), *consequently, therefore*
1355 diŏpĕr (3), *on which very account*
3606 hŏthĕn (4), *from which place or source*
3767 ŏun (7), *certainly; accordingly*
5101 tis (3), *who?, which? or what?*
5105 tŏigarŏun (1), *consequently, then*
5620 hŏstĕ (17), *thus, therefore*

WHEREIN
834 'ăsher (70), *when, where, how, because*
1459 gav (Ch.) (1), *middle*
2098 zûw (2), *this or that*
4100 mâh (15), *what?, how?, why?, when?*
8033 shâm (1), *where*
3739 hŏs (1), *what, that*
3757 hŏu (3), *where*

WHEREINSOEVER
1722+3739+302 ĕn (1), *in; during; because of*

WHEREINTO
824+8432 'Esh'ân (1), *support*
834+413+8432 'ăsher (1), *when, where, how*
1519+3739 ĕis (1), *to or into*

WHEREOF
834 'ăsher (24), *where*
3739 hŏs (11), *who, which, what, that*

WHEREON
834 'ăsher (2), *where, how, because*
834+5921 'ăsher (13), *where, how, because*
5921 'al (2), *above, over, upon, or against*
5921+4100 'al (1), *above, over, upon, or against*
1909+3739 ĕpi (4), *on, upon*
3739 hŏs (1), *who, which, what, that*

WHERESOEVER
834 'ăsher (1), *where, how, because*
3605 kôl (1), *all, any*
3699 hŏpŏu (1), *at whichever spot*

WHERETO
834 'ăsher (1), *where, how, because*
4100 mâh (1), *what?, how?, why?, when?*
1519+3739 ĕis (1), *to or into*

WHEREUNTO
834 'ăsher (6), *where, how, because*

3739 hŏs (6), *who, which, what, that*
5101 tis (5), *who?, which? or what?*

WHEREUPON
413 'êl (2), *to, toward*
5921 'al (1), *above, over, upon, or against*
3606 hŏthĕn (3), *from which place or source*

WHEREWITH
834 'ăsher (68), *when, where, how, because*
1697 dâbâr (1), *word; matter; thing*
4100 mâh (9), *what?, how?, why?, when?*
1722+3739 ĕn (2), *in; during; because of*
1722+5101 ĕn (3), *in; during; because of*
3739 hŏs (9), *who, which*
3745 hŏsŏs (1), *as much as*
5101 tis (1), *who?, which? or what?*

WHEREWITHAL
5101 tis (1), *who?, which? or what?*

WHET
3913 lâţash (1), *to sharpen; to pierce*
7043 qâlal (1), *to be, make light (sharp)*
8150 shânan (2), *to pierce; to inculcate*

WHETHER
176 'ôw (8), *or, whether*
335 'ay (1), *where?*
518 'îm (27), *whether?*
996 bêyn (4), *"either...or"*
2006 hên (Ch.) (2), *whether, but, if*
3588 kîy (1), *for, that because*
4100 mâh (1), *what?, how?, why?, when?*
4480 min (3), *from, out of*
5704 'ad (1), *as far (long) as; during; while; until*
5750 'ôwd (2), *again; repeatedly; still; more*
1487 ĕi (22), *if, whether*
1535 ĕitĕ (31), *if too*
2273 ētŏi (1), *either...or*
3379 mēpŏtĕ (1), *not ever; if, or lest ever*
4220 pŏtĕrŏn (1), *which*
5037 tĕ (1), *both or also*
5101 tis (8), *who?, which? or what?*

WHILE
518 'îm (1), *whether?; if, although; Oh that!*
834 'ăsher (1), *when, where, how, because*
3117 yôwm (7), *day; time*
3541 kôh (1), *thus*
3588 kîy (3), *for, that because*
4705 mits'âr (1), *little; short time*
5704 'ad (9), *during; while*
5750 'ôwd (7), *again; repeatedly; still; more*
5751 'ôwd (Ch.) (1), *again; repeatedly; still*

7350 râchôwq (1),
remote, far
2193 *hĕŏs* (8), *until*
2250 *hēmĕra* (2), *day;*
period of time
2540 *kairŏs* (1),
occasion, i.e. *set time*
3153 *mataiŏtēs* (1),
transientness; depravity
3397 *mikrŏn* (2), *small*
space of time or degree
3641 *ŏligŏs* (2), *puny,*
small
3752 *hŏtan* (1),
inasmuch as, at once
3753 *hŏtĕ* (1), *when; as*
3819 *palai* (1), *formerly;*
sometime since
4340 *prŏskairŏs* (1),
temporary
5550 *chrŏnŏs* (3), *time*
5613 *hōs* (4), *which, how,*
i.e. *in that manner*

WHILES
5750 'ôwd (1), *again;*
repeatedly; still; more
2193+3755 *hĕŏs* (1), *until*

WHILST
834 'âsher (1), *when,*
where, how, because
5704 'ad (4), *as far (long)*
as; during; while; until

WHIP
7752 shôwṭ (2), *lash*

WHIPS
7752 shôwṭ (4), *lash*

WHIRLETH
1980 hâlak (1), to *walk;*
live a certain way

WHIRLWIND
5492 çûwphâh (10),
hurricane wind
5590 çâ'ar (3), to *rush*
upon; to *toss* about
5591 ça'ar (11),
hurricane wind
7307+5591 rûwach (1),
breath; wind; life-spirit
8175 sâ'ar (2), to *storm;*
to *shiver*, i.e. *fear*

WHIRLWINDS
5492 çûwphâh (1),
hurricane wind
5591 ça'ar (1), *hurricane*

WHISPER
3907 lâchash (1), to
whisper a magic spell
6850 tsâphaph (1), to *coo*
or *chirp* as a bird

WHISPERED
3907 lâchash (1), to
whisper a magic spell

WHISPERER
5372 nirgân (1),
slanderer, gossip

WHISPERERS
5588 psithuristēs (1),
maligning gossip

WHISPERINGS
5587 psithurismŏs (1),
whispering, detraction

WHIT
1697 dâbâr (1), *word;*
matter; thing

3632 kâlîyl (1), *whole,*
entire; complete; whole
3367 *mĕdĕis* (1), *not even*
3650 *hŏlŏs* (2), *whole* or
all, i.e. *complete*

WHITE
1858 dar (1),
mother-of-pearl or
alabaster
2353 chûwr (2), *white*
linen
2751 chôrîy (1), *white*
bread
3835 lâban (4), to *be,*
become white
3836 lâbân (29), *white*
6703 tsach (1), *dazzling*
6713 tsachar (1),
whiteness
6715 tsâchôr (1), *white*
7388 rîyr (1), *saliva; broth*
2986 lamprŏs (1),
radiant; clear
3021 lĕukainō (2), to
whiten
3022 lĕukŏs (24), *bright*
white

WHITED
2867 kŏniaō (2), to
whitewash

WHITER
3835 lâban (1), to *be,*
become white
6705 tsâchach (1), to *be*
dazzling white

WHITHER
413 'êl (2), *to, toward*
575 'ân (20), *where*
from?, when?
834 'âsher (6), *when,*
where, how, because
8033 shâm (3), *where*
3699 hŏpŏu (9), *at*
whichever spot
3757 hŏu (2), *where*
4226 pŏu (10), *at what?*

WHITHERSOEVER
413+3605+834 'êl (1), *to,*
toward
413+3605+834+8033 'êl
(1), *to, toward*
575 'ân (1), *where from?*
834 'âsher (2), *where,*
how, because
1870+834 derek (1),
road; course of life
3605+834 kôl (13), *all,*
any or every
3605+834+8033 kôl (1),
all, any or every
4725+834 mâqôwm (1),
general locality, place
5921+834+8033 'al (1),
above, over, upon
5921+3605+834 'al (1),
above, over, upon
3699+302 hŏpŏu (4), *at*
whichever spot
3699+1437 hŏpŏu (1), *at*
whichever spot
3757+1437 hŏu (1), *at*
which place, i.e. *where*

WHOLE
854+3605 'êth (13), *with;*
by; at; among
2421 châyâh (1), to *live;*
to *revive*

3117 yôwm (4), *day; time*
3605 kôl (115), *all, any*
3606 kôl (Ch.) (6), *all, any*
3632 kâlîyl (2), *whole*
4749 miqshâh (1), *work*
molded by hammering
7495 râphâ' (2), to *heal*
8003 shâlêm (4),
complete; friendly; safe
8549 tâmîym (4), *entire*
8552 tâmam (1), to
complete, finish
537 hapas (3), *whole*
1295 diasōzō (1), to *cure*
2390 iaŏmai (1), to *heal*
2480 ischuŏ (2), to *have*
or *exercise force*
3390 mētrŏpŏlis (1),
main city, metropolis
3646 hŏlŏkautōma (1),
wholly-consumed
3648 hŏlŏklērŏs (1),
sound in the *entire*
body
3650 hŏlŏs (43), *whole*
3956 pas (10), *all, any*
3958 paschō (2), to
experience pain
4982 sōzō (11), to *deliver;*
to *protect*
5198 hugiainō (2), to
have sound health
5199 hugiēs (13), *well,*
healthy; true

WHOLESOME
4832 marpê' (1), *cure;*
deliverance; placidity
5198 hugiainō (1), to
have sound health

WHOLLY
3605 kôl (9), *all, any*
3615 kâlâh (1), to
complete, prepare
3632 kâlîyl (4), *whole*
4390 mâlê' (6), to *fill*
5352 nâqâh (1), to *be,*
make clean; to be bare
6942 qâdâsh (1), to *be,*
make clean
7760 sûwm (1), to *put*
7965 shâlôwm (1), *safe;*
well; health, prosperity
1510+1722 ĕimi (1), I
exist, I *am*
3651 hŏlŏtĕlēs (1),
absolutely perfect

WHORE
2181 zânâh (9), to
commit adultery
6948 qᵉdêshâh (1),
sacred female
prostitute
4204 pŏrnē (4), *prostitute*

WHORE'S
2181 zânâh (1), to
commit adultery

WHOREDOM
2181 zânâh (11), to
commit adultery
2183 zânûwn (1),
adultery; idolatry
2184 zᵉnûwth (7),
adultery, infidelity
8457 taznûwth (3),
harlotry

WHOREDOMS
2181 zânâh (2), to
commit adultery
2183 zânûwn (11),
adultery; idolatry
2184 zᵉnûwth (2),
adultery, infidelity
8457 taznûwth (15),
harlotry, physical or
spiritual

WHOREMONGER
4205 pŏrnŏs (1),
debauchee, immoral

WHOREMONGERS
4205 pŏrnŏs (4),
debauchee, immoral

WHORES
2181 zânâh (2), to
commit adultery

WHORING
2181 zânâh (19), to
commit adultery

WHORISH
2181 zânâh (3), to
commit adultery

WHY
4060 middâh (1),
measure
4069 maddûwa' (41),
why?, what?
4100 mâh (119), *what?,*
how?, why?, when?
4101 mâh (Ch.) (2),
what?, how?, why?
1063 gar (4), *for, indeed,*
but, because
1302 diati (23), *why?*
2444 hinati (4), *why?*
3754 hŏti (2), *that;*
because; since
5101 tis (66), *who?,*
which? or what?

WICKED
205 'âven (6), *trouble,*
vanity, wickedness
605 'ânash (1), to *be frail,*
feeble
1100 bᵉlîya'al (5),
wickedness, trouble
2154 zimmâh (2), *bad*
plan
2162 zâmâm (1), *plot*
2617 cheçed (1),
kindness, favor
4209 mᵉzimmâh (3),
plan; sagacity
4849 mirsha'ath (1),
female *wicked-doer*
5766 'evel (1), *evil*
5767 'avvâl (3), *evil*
6001 'âmêl (1), *toiling;*
laborer; sorrowful
6090 'ôtseb (1), *idol; pain*
7451 ra' (26), *bad; evil*
7489 râ'a' (5), to *be good*
for nothing
7561 râsha' (4), to *be, do,*
declare wrong
7562 resha' (4), *wrong*
7563 râshâ' (252), *wrong;*
bad person
113 athĕsmŏs (2),
criminal
459 anŏmŏs (2), *without*
Jewish law
2556 kakŏs (1), *wrong*

W

4190 pŏnērŏs (17),
malice, wicked, bad
4191 pŏnērŏtĕrŏs (2),
more evil

WICKEDLY
4209 mᵉzimmâh (1),
plan; sagacity
5753 'âvâh (1), to be
crooked
5766 'evel (1), moral evil
7451 ra' (1), bad; evil
7489 râ'a' (5), to be good
for nothing
7561 râsha' (13), to be,
do, declare wrong
7564 rish'âh (1), moral
wrong

WICKEDNESS
205 'âven (2), trouble,
vanity, wickedness
1942 havvâh (3), desire;
craving
2154 zimmâh (4), bad
plan
5766 'evel (7), moral evil
5999 'âmâl (1), wearing
effort; worry
7451 ra' (59), bad; evil
7455 rôa' (3), badness
7561 râsha' (1), to be, do,
declare wrong
7562 resha' (25), wrong
7564 rish'âh (13), wrong
2549 kakia (1),
depravity; malignity;
trouble
4189 pŏnēria (6), malice,
evil, wickedness
4190 pŏnērŏs (1), malice,
wicked, bad; crime
5129+824 tŏutŏᵢ (1), in
this person or thing

WIDE
2267 cheber (2), society,
group; magic spell;
4060 middâh (1),
measure; portion
6605 pâthach (3), to open
wide; to loosen, begin
7337 râchab (3), to
broaden
7342 râchâb (1), roomy
7342+3027 râchâb (2),
roomy, spacious
4116 platus (1), wide

WIDENESS
7341 rôchab (1), width

WIDOW
490 'almânâh (37), widow
5503 chêra (13), widow

WIDOW'S
490 'almânâh (4), widow
491 'almânûwth (1),
widow; widowhood

WIDOWHOOD
489 'almôn (1),
widowhood
491 'almânûwth (3),
widow; widowhood

WIDOWS
490 'almânâh (12), widow
5503 chêra (10), widow

WIDOWS'
5503 chêra (3), widow

WIFE
802 'ishshâh (301),
woman, wife
1166 bâ'al (1), to be
master; to marry
1753 dûwr (Ch.) (1), to
reside, live in
2994 yᵉbêmeth (3),
sister-in-law
1134 gunaikĕiŏs (1),
feminine
1135 gunē (80), wife

WIFE'S
802 'ishshâh (8), woman,
wife; women, wives
3994 pĕnthĕra (3), wife's
mother

WILD
338 'îy (3), solitary wild
creature that howls
689 'aqqôw (1), ibex
891 bᵉ'ûshîym (2), rotten
fruit
2123 zîyz (2), fulness
2416 chay (1), alive; raw
3277 yâ'êl (3), ibex
6167 'ărâd (Ch.) (1),
onager or wild donkey
6171 'ârôwd (1), onager
or wild donkey
6501 pere' (10), onager,
wild donkey
6728 tsîyîy (3), wild beast
7704 sâdeh (8), field
8377 tᵉ'ôw (2), antelope
65 agriĕlaiŏs (2), wild
olive tree
66 agriŏs (2), wild
2342 thēriŏn (3),
dangerous animal

WILDERNESS
3452 yᵉshîymôwn (2),
desolation
4057 midbâr (255),
desert; also speech
6160 'ărâbâh (4), desert,
wasteland
6166 'Arâd (1), fugitive
6723 tsîyâh (2), desert
6728 tsîyîy (3), wild beast
8414 tôhûw (2), waste,
desolation, formless
2047 ĕrēmia (3), place of
solitude, remoteness
2048 ĕrēmŏs (32), remote
place, deserted place

WILES
5231 nêkel (1), deceit
3180 mĕthŏdĕia (1),
trickery, scheming

WILFULLY
1596 hĕkŏusiŏs (1),
voluntarily, willingly

WILILY
6195 'ormâh (1), trickery;
discretion

WILL
14 'âbâh (5), to be
acquiescent
165 'êhîy (3), Where?
2654 châphêts (2), to be
pleased with, desire
3045 yâda' (1), to know
5314 nâphash (1), to be
refreshed
5315 nephesh (3), life;
breath; soul; wind

6634 tsᵉbâ' (Ch.) (5), to
please
7470 rᵉ'ûwth (Ch.) (1),
desire
7522 râtsôwn (15), delight
210 akôn (1), unwilling
1012 bŏulē (1), purpose,
plan, decision
1013 bŏulēma (1),
resolve, willful choice
1014 bŏulŏmai (12), to be
willing, desire
1106 gnōmē (1), opinion,
resolve
1479 ĕthĕlŏthrēskĕia (1),
voluntary piety
2107 ĕudŏkia (2),
delight, kindness, wish
2133 ĕunŏia (1), eagerly,
with a whole heart
2307 thĕlēma (62),
purpose; decree
2308 thĕlēsis (1),
determination
2309 thĕlō (70), to will; to
desire; to choose
3195 mĕllō (6), to intend,
i.e. be about to

WILLETH
2309 thĕlō (1), to will; to
desire; to choose

WILLING
14 'âbâh (4), to be
acquiescent
2655 châphêts (1),
pleased with
5068 nâdab (3), to
volunteer
5071 nᵉdâbâh (2),
spontaneous gift
5081 nâdîyb (3),
magnanimous
830 authairĕtŏs (1),
self-chosen,voluntary
1014 bŏulŏmai (5), to be
willing, desire
2106 ĕudŏkĕō (2), to
think well, i.e. approve
2309 thĕlō (8), to will; to
desire; to choose
2843 kŏinōnikŏs (1),
liberal
4288 prŏthumia (1),
alacrity, eagerness
4289 prŏthumŏs (1),
alacrity, eagerness

WILLINGLY
2656 chêphets (1),
pleasure; desire
2974 yâ'al (1), to assent;
to undertake, begin
3820 lêb (1), heart
5068 nâdab (13), to
volunteer
5071 nᵉdâbâh (1),
spontaneous gift
5414 nâthan (1), to give
1596 hĕkŏusiŏs (1),
voluntarily, willingly
1635 hĕkōn (2), voluntary
2309 thĕlō (2), to will

WILLOW
6851 tsaphtsâphâh (1),
willow tree

WILLOWS
6155 'ârâb (5), willow

WILT
2309 thĕlō (21), to will

WIMPLES
4304 mitpachath (1),
cloak, shawl

WIN
1234 bâqa' (1), to cleave
2770 kĕrdainō (1), to
gain; to spare

WIND
7307 rûwach (82),
breath; wind; life-spirit
7308 rûwach (Ch.) (1),
breath; wind; life-spirit
416 anemizō (1), to toss
with the wind
417 anĕmŏs (20), wind
4151 pnĕuma (1), spirit
4154 pnĕō (1), to breeze
4157 pnŏē (1), breeze;
breath

WINDING
3583 kâchal (1), to paint
4141 mûwçâb (1), circuit
5437 çâbab (1), to
surround

WINDOW
2474 challôwn (13),
window; opening
6672 tsŏhar (1), window
2376 thuris (2), window

WINDOWS
699 'ărubbâh (8),
window; chimney
2474 challôwn (18),
window; opening
3551 kav (Ch.) (1),
window
8121 shemesh (1), sun
8260 sheqeph (1),
loophole
8261 shâqûph (1),
opening

WINDS
7307 rûwach (11),
breath; wind; life-spirit
7308 rûwach (Ch.) (1),
breath; wind; life-spirit
417 anĕmŏs (11), wind

WINDY
7307 rûwach (1), breath;
wind; life-spirit

WINE
2561 chemer (1),
fermenting wine
2562 chămar (Ch.) (6),
wine
3196 yayin (135), wine
3342 yeqeb (1), wine-vat
4469 mamçâk (1),
mixed-wine
5435 çôbe' (1), wine
6025 'ênâb (1), grape
6071 'âçîyç (4), expressed
fresh grape-juice
7491 râ'aph (1), to drip
8492 tîyrôwsh (40), wine,
squeezed grape-juice
1098 glĕukŏs (1), sweet
wine
3631 ŏinŏs (32), wine
3632 ŏinŏphlugia (1),
drunkenness
3943 parŏinŏs (2),
tippling

WINEBIBBER
3630 ŏinŏpŏtēs (1), *tippler*

WINEBIBBERS
5433+3196 çâbâ' (1), to *become tipsy*

WINEFAT
1660 gath (1), wine-*press* or *vat*
5276 hupŏlēniŏn (1), lower *wine vat*

WINEPRESS
1660 gath (2), wine-*press* or *vat*
3342 yeqeb (7), wine-*vat*, wine-*press*
6333 pûwrâh (1), *wine-press* trough
3025 lēnŏs (4), *trough*, i.e. wine-*vat*
3025+3631 lēnŏs (1), *trough*, i.e. wine-*vat*

WINEPRESSES
1660 gath (1), wine-*press*
3342 yeqeb (3), wine-*press*

WINES
8105 shemer (2), *settlings* of wine, *dregs*

WING
3671 kânâph (13), *edge* or *extremity; wing*

WINGED
3671 kânâph (2), *edge* or *extremity; wing*

WINGS
34 'ebyôwn (1), *destitute; poor*
83 'êber (2), *pinion*
84 'ebrâh (1), *pinion*
1611 gaph (Ch.) (3), *wing*
3671 kânâph (60), *edge* or *extremity; wing*
6731 tsîyts (1), *wing*
4420 ptĕrux (5), *wing*

WINK
7169 qârats (1), to *blink*
7335 râzam (1), to *twinkle* the eye

WINKED
5237 hupĕrĕidŏ (1), to *not punish*

WINKETH
7169 qârats (2), to *blink*

WINNETH
3947 lâqach (1), to *take*

WINNOWED
2219 zârâh (1), to *winnow*

WINNOWETH
2219 zârâh (1), to *winnow*

WINTER
2778 châraph (2), to spend the *winter*
2779 chôreph (3), *autumn, ripeness* of age
5638 çᵉthâv (1), *winter*
3914 parachĕimazŏ (3), to *spend the winter*
3915 parachĕimasia (1), *wintering* over
5494 chĕimōn (4), *winter*

WINTERED
3916 parachrēma (1), *instantly, immediately*

WINTERHOUSE
2779 chôreph (1), *autumn* (and winter)

WIPE
4229 mâchâh (3), to *erase;* to *grease*
631 apŏmassŏmai (1), to *scrape away, wipe off*
1591 ĕkmassŏ (2), to *wipe dry*
1813 ĕxalĕiphō (2), to *obliterate*

WIPED
4229 mâchâh (1), to *erase;* to *grease*
1591 ĕkmassŏ (3), to *wipe dry*

WIPETH
4229 mâchâh (2), to *erase;* to *grease*

WIPING
4229 mâchâh (1), to *erase;* to *grease*

WIRES
6616 pâthîyl (1), *twine, cord*

WISDOM
998 bîynâh (2), *understanding*
2449 châkam (1), to *be wise*
2451 chokmâh (144), *wisdom*
2452 chokmâh (Ch.) (8), *wisdom*
2454 chokmôwth (4), *wisdom*
2942 tᵉ'êm (Ch.) (1), *judgment; account*
3820 lêb (6), *heart*
6195 'ormâh (1), *trickery; discretion*
7919 sâkal (2), to *be* or *act circumspect*
7922 sekel (3), *intelligence; success*
8394 tâbûwn (1), *intelligence; argument*
8454 tûwshîyâh (7), *undertaking*
4678 sŏphia (51), *wisdom*
5428 phrŏnēsis (1), moral *insight, understanding*

WISE
995 bîyn (3), to *understand; discern*
2445 chakkîym (Ch.) (14), *wise one*
2449 châkam (19), to *be wise*
2450 châkâm (122), *wise, intelligent, skillful*
2454 chokmôwth (1), *wisdom*
3198 yâkach (1), to *be correct;* to *argue*
3823 lâbab (1), *transport* with love; to *stultify*
6031 'ânâh (1), to *afflict, be afflicted*
6493 piqqêach (1), *clear-sighted*
7919 sâkal (12), to *be* or *act circumspect*
7922 sekel (1), *intelligence; success*

WINTERHOUSE
3097 magŏs (4), Oriental *scientist,* i.e. *magician*
3364 ŏu mē (1), *not* at all, absolutely *not*
3588+3838 hŏ (1), *"the,"* i.e. the definite article
3779 hŏutō (6), *in this way; likewise*
3843 pantŏs (1), *entirely; at all events*
4679 sŏphizō (1), to *make wise*
4680 sŏphŏs (21), *wise*
4920 suniēmi (1), to *comprehend*
5429 phrŏnimŏs (13), *sagacious* or *discreet*

WISELY
995 bîyn (1), to *understand; discern*
2449 châkam (2), to *be wise*
2451 chokmâh (2), *wisdom*
7919 sâkal (8), to *be* or *act circumspect*
5430 phrŏnimŏs (1), *prudently, shrewdly*

WISER
2449 châkam (4), to *be wise*
2450 châkâm (2), *wise, intelligent, skillful*
4680 sŏphŏs (1), *wise*
5429 phrŏnimŏs (1), *sagacious* or *discreet*

WISH
2655 châphêts (1), *pleased* with
4906 maskîyth (1), carved *figure*
6310 peh (1), *mouth*
2172 ĕuchŏmai (3), to *wish for;* to *pray*

WISHED
7592 shâ'al (1), to *ask*
2172 ĕuchŏmai (1), to *wish for;* to *pray*

WISHING
7592 shâ'al (1), to *ask*

WIST
3045 yâda' (7), to *know*
1492 ĕidō (6), to *know*

WIT
3045 yâda' (2), to *know*
1107 gnōrizō (1), to *make known, reveal*
5613 hōs (1), *which, how*

WIT'S
2451 chokmâh (1), *wisdom*

WITCH
3784 kâshaph (2), to *enchant*

WITCHCRAFT
3784 kâshaph (1), to *enchant*
7081 qeçem (1), *divination*
5331 pharmakĕia (1), *magic, witchcraft*

WITCHCRAFTS
3785 kesheph (4), *magic, sorcery*

WITHAL
834+3605 'ăsher (1), *who, which, what, that*
1992 hêm (1), *they*
2004 hên (3), *they*
3162 yachad (2), *unitedly*
5973 'îm (1), *with*
260 hama (3), *at the same time, together*

WITHDRAW
622 'âçaph (4), to *gather, collect*
3240 yânach (1), to *allow to stay*
3365 yâqar (1), to *be valuable;* to *make rare*
5493 çûwr (1), to *turn off*
7368 râchaq (1), to *recede*
7725 shûwb (1), to *turn back;* to *return*
868 aphistēmi (1), to *desist, desert*
4724 stĕllō (1), to *repress*

WITHDRAWEST
7725 shûwb (1), to *turn back;* to *return*

WITHDRAWETH
1639 gâra' (1), to *shave, remove, lessen*

WITHDRAWN
2502 châlats (1), to *pull off;* to *strip;* to *depart*
2559 châmaq (1), to *depart,* i.e. turn about
5080 nâdach (1), to *push off, scattered*
7725 shûwb (2), to *turn back;* to *return*
645 apŏspaŏ (1), *withdraw* with force

WITHDREW
5414+5437 nâthan (1), to *give*
7725 shûwb (1), to *turn back;* to *return*
402 anachōrĕō (2), to *retire, withdraw*
5288 hupŏstĕllō (1), to *cower* or *shrink*
5298 hupŏchōrĕō (1), to *vacate down,* i.e. *retire*

WITHER
3001 yâbêsh (8), to *wither*
5034 nâbêl (2), to *wilt*
7060 qâmal (1), to *wither*

WITHERED
3001 yâbêsh (11), to *wither*
6798 tsânam (1), to *blast*
3583 xērainō (9), to *shrivel,* to *mature*
3584 xērŏs (4), *withered*

WITHERETH
3001 yâbêsh (5), to *wither*
3583 xērainō (2), to *shrivel,* to *mature*
5352 phthinŏpōrinŏs (1), *autumnal*

WITHHELD
2820 châsak (3), to *restrain* or *refrain*
4513 mâna' (3), to *deny, refuse*

WITHHELDEST
4513 mâna' (1), to *deny, refuse*

WITHHOLD
3240 yânach (1), to *allow to stay*
3607 kâlâ' (2), to *hold*
4513 mâna' (5), to *deny*
6113 'âtsar (1), to *hold*

WITHHOLDEN
1219 bâtsar (1), to *be inaccessible*
2254 châbal (1), to *bind by a pledge; to pervert*
4513 mâna' (8), to *deny, refuse*

WITHHOLDETH
2820 châsak (1), to *restrain or refrain*
4513 mâna' (1), to *deny, refuse*
6113 'âtsar (1), to *hold back; to maintain*
2722 katĕchō (1), to *hold down fast*

WITHIN
413 'êl (2), *to, toward*
990 beṭen (2), *belly; womb; body*
996 bêyn (1), *between*
1004 bayith (23), *house; temple; family, tribe*
1157 bᵉ'ad (3), *up to or over against*
2315 cheder (1), *apartment, chamber*
2436 chêyq (1), *bosom, heart*
4481 min (Ch.) (1), *from or out of*
5704 'ad (2), *as far (long) as; during; while; until*
5705 'ad (Ch.) (1), *as far (long) as; during*
5750 'ôwd (4), *again; repeatedly; still; more*
5921 'al (8), *above, over, upon, or against*
5978 'immâd (1), *along with*
6440 pânîym (1), *face; front*
6441 pᵉnîymâh (10), *indoors, inside*
6442 pᵉnîymîy (1), *interior, inner*
7130 qereb (26), *nearest part, i.e. the center*
7146 qârachath (1), *bald spot; threadbare spot*
8432 tâvek (20), *center, middle*
8537 tôm (1), *completeness*
1223 dia (1), *through*, by means of; *because of*
1722 ĕn (13), *in; during; because of*
1737 ĕndiduskō (1), to *clothe*
1787 ĕntŏs (1), *inside, within*
2080 ĕsō (3), *inside, inner, in*
2081 ĕsōthĕn (10), *from inside; inside*
2082 ĕsōtĕrŏs (1), *interior, inner*
4314 prŏs (1), *for; on, at; to, toward; against*

WITHOUT
268 'âchôwr (1), *behind, backward; west*
369 'ayin (42), *there is no, i.e., not exist, none*
657 'ephes (3), *end; no further*
1097 bᵉlîy (16), *without, not yet; lacking;*
1107 bil'ădêy (4), *except, without, besides*
1115 biltîy (4), *not, except, without, unless*
1372 gabbachath (1), *baldness on forehead*
2351 chûwts (71), *outside, outdoors*
2435 chîytsôwn (5), outer *wall side; exterior*
2600 chinnâm (17), *gratis, free*
2963 ṭâraph (1), to *pluck off* or *pull to pieces*
3808 lô' (29), no, *not*
3809 lâ' (Ch.) (1), *as nothing*
4682 matstsâh (1), *unfermented cake*
5493 çûwr (1), to *turn* off
7387 rêyqâm (2), *emptily; ineffectually*
8267 sheqer (1), *untruth; sham*
8414 tôhûw (2), *waste, desolation, formless*
8549 tâmîym (50), *entire, complete; integrity*
35 agĕnĕalŏgētŏs (1), *unregistered* as to birth
77 adapanŏs (1), *free of charge*
87 adiakritŏs (1), *impartial*
88 adialĕiptŏs (1), *permanent, constant*
89 adialĕiptŏs (4), *without omission*
112 athĕŏs (1), *godless*
175 akarpŏs (1), *barren, unfruitful*
186 aklinēs (1), *firm, unswerving*
194 akratŏs (1), *undiluted*
267 amarturŏs (1), *without witness*
275 amĕrimnŏs (1), *not anxious, free of care*
278 amĕtamĕlētŏs (1), *irrevocable*
280 amĕtrŏs (2), *immoderate*
282 amĕtōr (1), *of unknown maternity*
298 amōmētŏs (1), *unblemished*
299 amōmŏs (5), *unblemished, blameless*
361 anamartētŏs (1), *sinless*
369 anantirrhētŏs (1), *without raising objection*
379 anapŏlŏgētŏs (1), *without excuse*
427 anĕu (3), *without, apart from*
448 anilĕŏs (1), *inexorable, merciless*
459 anŏmŏs (4), *without* Jewish *law*
460 anŏmŏs (2), *lawlessly*, i.e. apart from Jewish Law
504 anudrŏs (2), *dry, arid*
505 anupŏkritŏs (2), *sincere, genuine*
540 apatōr (1), *of unrecorded paternity*
563 apĕrispastŏs (1), *undistractedly*
677 aprŏskŏpŏs (1), *faultless*
678 aprŏsōpŏlēptŏs (1), *without prejudice*
729 arrhaphŏs (1), *of a single piece, without seam*
772 asthĕnēs (1), *strengthless, weak*
784 aspilŏs (3), *unblemished*
794 astŏrgŏs (2), *hard-hearted*
801 asunĕtŏs (3), *senseless, dull; wicked*
815 atĕknŏs (2), *childless*
817 atĕr (1), *apart from, without*
820 atimŏs (2), *without honor*
866 aphilargurŏs (1), *not greedy*
870 aphŏbŏs (4), *fearlessly*
880 aphōnŏs (1), *mute, silent; unmeaning*
886 achĕirŏpŏiētŏs (2), *unmanufactured*
895 apsuchŏs (1), *lifeless, i.e. inanimate*
1432 dōrĕan (1), *gratuitously, freely*
1500 ĕikē (1), *idly, i.e. without reason or effect*
1618 ĕktĕnēs (1), *intent, earnest*
1622 ĕktŏs (1), *aside from, besides; except*
1854 ĕxō (23), *out, outside*
1855 ĕxōthĕn (6), *outside, external (-ly)*
2673 katargĕō (1), to *be, render entirely useless*
3361 mē (1), *not; lest*
3672 hŏmŏlŏgŏumĕnōs (1), *confessedly*
3924 parĕktŏs (1), *besides; apart from*
5565 chōris (36), *at a space, i.e. separately*

WITHS
3499 yether (3), *remainder; small rope*

WITHSTAND
2388 châzaq (2), to *bind, restrain, conquer*
3320 yâtsab (1), to *station, offer, continue*
5975 'âmad (4), to *stand*
7854 sâṭân (1), *opponent*
436 anthistēmi (1), *oppose, rebel*
2967 kōluō (1), to *stop*

WITHSTOOD
5975 'âmad (2), to *stand*

436 anthistēmi (4), *oppose, rebel*

WITNESS
5707 'êd (45), *witness; testimony*
5711 'Âdâh (1), *ornament*
5713 'êdâh (3), *testimony*
5715 'êdûwth (4), *testimony*
5749 'ûwd (5), to *protest, testify; to encompass*
6030 'ânâh (2), to *respond, answer*
8085 shâma' (1), to *hear* intelligently
267 amarturŏs (1), *without witness*
2649 katamarturĕō (4), to *testify against*
3140 marturĕō (28), to *testify; to commend*
3141 marturia (15), *evidence* given
3142 marturiŏn (4), something *evidential;* the *Decalogue*
3144 martus (8), *witness*
4828 summarturĕō (3), to *testify jointly*
4901 sunĕpimarturĕō (1), to *testify further jointly*
5576 psĕudŏmarturĕō (6), to *be an untrue testifier*
5577 psĕudŏmarturia (2), *untrue testimony*

WITNESSED
5749 'ûwd (1), to *protest, testify; to encompass*
3140 marturĕō (3), to *testify; to commend*

WITNESSES
5707 'êd (23), *witness; testimony*
3140 marturĕō (1), to *testify; to commend*
3144 martus (21), *witness*
5575 psĕudŏmartur (3), *bearer of untrue testimony*

WITNESSETH
1263 diamarturŏmai (1), to *attest or protest*
3140 marturĕō (1), to *testify; to commend*

WITNESSING
3140 marturĕō (1), to *testify; to commend*

WITTINGLY
7919 sâkal (1), to *be or act circumspect*

WIVES
802 'ishshâh (115), *woman, wife*
5389 nâshîyn (Ch.) (1), *women, wives*
7695 shêgâl (Ch.) (3), *queen*
1135 gunē (12), *woman; wife*

WIVES'
1126 graōdēs (1), *old lady-like, i.e. silly*

WIZARD
3049 yiddᵉ'ônîy (2), *conjurer; ghost*

W

WORK'S
2716 katĕrgazomai (1),
to *finish*; to *accomplish*
3056 lŏgŏs (2), *word,*
matter, thing; Word
3433+2480 mŏlis (1), *with*
difficulty
4229 pragma (1), *matter,*
deed, affair
4903 sunĕrgĕŏ (1), to *be*
a fellow-worker

WORK'S
2041 ĕrgŏn (1), *work*

WORKER
2790 chârash (1), to
engrave; to *plow*

WORKERS
2796 chârâsh (1), *skilled*
fabricator or worker
6213 'âsâh (1), to *do*
6466 pâ'al (19), to *do,*
make or practice
1411 dunamis (1), *force,*
power, miracle
2040 ĕrgatēs (3), *toiler,*
worker
4903 sunĕrgĕŏ (1), to *be*
a fellow-worker

WORKETH
5648 'ăbad (Ch.) (1), to
work, serve
6213 'âsâh (6), to *do or*
make
6466 pâ'al (4), to *do,*
make or practice
1754 ĕnĕrgĕō (11), to *be*
active, efficient, work
2038 ĕrgazŏmai (7), to
toil
2716 katĕrgazŏmai (7),
to *finish*; to *accomplish*
4160 pŏiĕō (1), to *make*
or do

WORKFELLOW
4904 sunĕrgŏs (1),
fellow-worker

WORKING
4639 ma'ăseh (1), *action;*
labor
6213 'âsâh (1), to *do or*
make
6466 pâ'al (1), to *do,*
make or practice
8454 tûwshîyâh (1),
ability, i.e. direct *help*
1753 ĕnĕrgĕia (6),
efficiency, energy
1755 ĕnĕrgĕma (1),
effect, activity
2038 ĕrgazŏmai (4), to
toil
2716 katĕrgazŏmai (2),
to *finish*; to *accomplish*
4160 pŏiĕō (2), to *make*
or do
4903 sunĕrgĕŏ (1), to *be*
a fellow-worker

WORKMAN
542 'âmân (1), *expert*
artisan, craftsman
2796 chârâsh (5), *skilled*
fabricator or worker
2803 châshab (2), to
weave, fabricate
2040 ĕrgatēs (2), *toiler,*
worker

WORKMANSHIP
4399 mᵉlâ'kâh (5), *work;*
property
4639 ma'ăseh (1), *action;*
labor
4161 pŏiĕma (1), *what is*
made, product

WORKMEN
582+4399 'ĕnôwsh (1),*
man; person, human
2796 chârâsh (1), *skilled*
fabricator or worker
6213+4399 'âsâh (7), to
do or make
2040 ĕrgatēs (1), *toiler,*
worker

WORKMEN'S
6001 'âmêl (1), *toiling;*
laborer; sorrowful

WORKS
1697 dâbâr (1), *word;*
matter; thing
4399 mᵉlâ'kâh (3), *work;*
property
4566 ma'bâd (1), *act,*
deed
4567 ma'bâd (Ch.) (1),
act, deed
4611 ma'ălâl (3), *act,*
deed
4639 ma'ăseh (70),
action; labor
4640 Ma'say (2),
operative
4659 miph'âl (3),
performance, deed
5652 'ăbâd (1), *deed*
5949 'ălîylâh (3),
opportunity, action
6467 pô'al (2), *act or*
work, deed
6468 pᵉ'ullâh (1), *work,*
deed
2041 ĕrgŏn (104), *work*
4234 praxis (1), *act;*
function

WORKS'
2041 ĕrgŏn (1), *work*

WORLD
776 'erets (4), *earth,*
land, soil; country
2309 chedel (1), *state of*
the dead, deceased
2465 cheled (2), *fleeting*
time; this world
5769 'ôwlâm (4), *eternity;*
ancient; always
8398 têbêl (35), *earth;*
world; inhabitants
165 aiōn (37), *perpetuity,*
ever; world
166 aiōniŏs (3),
perpetual, long ago
1093 gē (1), *soil, region,*
whole earth
2889 kŏsmŏs (183), *world*
3625 ŏikŏumĕnē (14),
Roman empire

WORLD'S
2889 kŏsmŏs (1), *world*

WORLDLY
2886 kŏsmikŏs (2),
earthly, worldly

WORLDS
165 aiōn (2), *perpetuity,*
ever; world

WORM
5580 çâç (1), *garment*
moth
7415 rimmâh (5), *maggot*
8438 tôwlâ' (5), *maggot*
worm; crimson-grub
4663 skōlēx (3), *grub,*
maggot or earth-worm

WORMS
2119 zâchal (1), to *crawl;*
glide
7415 rimmâh (2), *maggot*
8438 tôwlâ' (3), *maggot*
worm; crimson-grub
4662 skōlēkŏbrōtŏs (1),
diseased with maggots

WORMWOOD
3939 la'ănâh (7),
poisonous wormwood
894 apsinthŏs (2),
wormwood, bitterness

WORSE
2196 zâ'aph (1), to *be*
angry
5062 nâgaph (5), to
inflict a disease
7451 ra' (1), *bad; evil*
7489 râ'a' (5), to *be good*
for nothing
1640 ĕlassŏn (1), *smaller*
2276 hĕttŏn (1), *worse*
5302 hustĕrĕō (1), to *be*
inferior; to fall short
5501 chĕirōn (10), *more*
evil or aggravated

WORSHIP
5457 çᵉgîd (Ch.) (8), to
prostrate oneself
6087 'âtsab (1), to
fabricate or fashion
7812 shâchâh (54), to
prostrate in homage
1391 dŏxa (1), *glory;*
brilliance
1479 ĕthĕlŏthrĕskĕia (1),
voluntary piety
2151 ĕusĕbĕŏ (1), to *put*
religion into practice
3000 latrĕuŏ (3), to
minister to God
4352 prŏskunĕō (34), to
prostrate oneself
4352+1799 prŏskunĕō (1),
to *prostrate oneself*
4576 sĕbŏmai (3), to
revere, i.e. *adore*

WORSHIPPED
5457 çᵉgîd (Ch.) (2), to
prostrate oneself
7812 shâchâh (39), to
prostrate in homage
2323 thĕrapĕuō (1), to
adore God
4352 prŏskunĕō (24), to
prostrate oneself
4573 sĕbazŏmai (1), to
venerate, worship
4574 sĕbasma (1), *object*
of worship
4576 sĕbŏmai (2), to
revere, i.e. *adore*

WORSHIPPER
2318 thĕŏsĕbēs (1), *pious,*
devout, God-fearing
3511 nĕŏkŏrŏs (1),
temple servant

WORSHIPPERS
5647 'âbad (5), to *serve*
3000 latrĕuŏ (1), to
minister to God
4353 prŏskunētēs (1),
adorer

WORSHIPPETH
5457 çᵉgîd (Ch.) (2), to
prostrate oneself
7812 shâchâh (3), to
prostrate in homage
4576 sĕbŏmai (1), to
revere, i.e. *adore*

WORSHIPPING
7812 shâchâh (3), to
prostrate in homage
2356 thrĕskĕia (1),
observance, religion
4352 prŏskunĕō (1), to
prostrate oneself

WORST
7451 ra' (1), *bad; evil*

WORTH
3644 kᵉmôw (1), *like, as;*
for; with
4242 mᵉchîyr (1), *price,*
payment, wages
4373 mikçâh (1),
valuation of a thing
4392 mâlê' (1), *full;*
filling; fulness; fully
7939 sâkâr (1), *payment,*
salary; compensation

WORTHIES
117 'addîyr (1), *powerful;*
majestic

WORTHILY
2428 chayil (1), *army;*
wealth; virtue; valor

WORTHY
376 'îysh (1), *man; male;*
someone
639 'aph (1), *nose or*
nostril; face; person
1121 bên (2), *son,*
descendant; people
2428 chayil (1), *army;*
wealth; virtue; valor
6994 qâţŏn (1), to *be,*
make diminutive
514 axiŏs (35), *deserving,*
comparable or suitable
515 axiŏō (5), to *deem*
entitled or fit, worthy
516 axiŏs (3),
appropriately, suitable
2425 hikanŏs (5), *ample;*
fit
2570 kalŏs (1), *good;*
beautiful; valuable
2661 kataxiŏō (4), to
deem entirely deserving
2735 katŏrthōma (1),
made fully upright

WOT
3045 yâda' (6), to *know*
1107 gnōrizō (1), to
make known, reveal
1492 ĕidō (3), to *know*

WOTTETH
3045 yâda' (1), to *know*

WOULD
14 'âbâh (41), to *be*
acquiescent
305 'achălay (1), *would*
that!, Oh that!, If Only!

2654 châphêts (1), to be
pleased with, desire
2655 châphêts (1),
pleased with
2974 yâ'al (3), to assent;
to undertake, begin
3863 lûw' (6), would that!
5315 nephesh (1), life;
breath; soul; wind
6634 tseba' (Ch.) (5), to
please
1096 ginŏmai (1), to be,
become
2172 ĕuchŏmai (1), to
wish for; to pray
2309 thĕlō (73), to will; to
desire; to choose
3195 mĕllō (9), to intend,
i.e. be about to
3785 ŏphĕlŏn (4), I wish

WOULDEST
3426 yêsh (1), there is
2309 thĕlō (4), to will; to
desire; to choose

WOUND
2671 chêts (1), arrow;
wound; thunder-bolt
4204 mâzôwr (1), ambush
4205 mâzôwr (2), sore
4272 mâchats (3), to
crush; to subdue
4347 makkâh (8), blow;
wound; pestilence
5061 nega' (1), infliction;
affliction; leprous spot
6482 petsa' (2), wound
1210 dĕō (1), to bind
4127 plēgē (3), stroke;
wound; calamity
4958 sustĕllō (1), to draw
together, i.e. enwrap or
enshroud a corpse
5180 tuptō (1), to strike,
beat, wound

WOUNDED
1214 bâtsa' (1), to
plunder; to finish
1795 dakkâh (1),
mutilated by crushing
1856 dâqar (1), to stab,
pierce; to starve
2342 chûwl (2), to dance,
whirl; to writhe in pain
2470 châlâh (3), to be
weak, sick, afflicted
2490 châlal (3), to
profane, defile
2491 châlâl (10), pierced
to death, one slain
4272 mâchats (2), to
crush; to subdue
4347 makkâh (1), blow;
wound; pestilence
5218 nâkê' (1), smitten;
afflicted
5221 nâkâh (3), to strike,
kill
6481 pâtsa' (2), to wound
4127+2007 plēgē (1),
stroke; wound
4969 sphazō (1), to
slaughter or to maim
5135 traumatizō (2), to
inflict a wound

WOUNDEDST
4272 mâchats (1), to
crush; to subdue

WOUNDETH
4272 mâchats (1), to
crush; to subdue

WOUNDING
6482 petsa' (1), wound

WOUNDS
2250 chabbûwrâh (1),
weal, bruise
3859 lâham (2), to rankle
4347 makkâh (6), blow;
wound; pestilence
6094 'atstsebeth (1), pain
or wound, sorrow
6482 petsa' (4), wound
5134 trauma (1), wound

WOVE
707 'ârag (1), to plait or
weave

WOVEN
707 'ârag (3), to plait or
weave
5307 huphantŏs (1),
knitted, woven

WRAP
3664 kânaç (1), to
collect; to enfold
5686 'âbath (1), to pervert

WRAPPED
1563 gâlam (1), to fold
2280 châbash (1), to
wrap firmly, bind
3874 lûwṭ (2), to wrap up
4593 mâ'ôṭ (1), sharp,
thin-edged
5440 çâbak (1), to
entwine
5968 'âlaph (1), to be
languid, faint
8276 sârag (1), to entwine
1750 ĕnĕilĕō (1), to
enwrap
1794 ĕntulissō (3), wind
up in, enwrap
4683 sparganŏō (2), to
strap or wrap

WRATH
639 'aph (42), nose or
nostril; face; person
2197 za'aph (1), anger,
rage
2534 chêmâh (34), heat;
anger; poison
2740 chârôwn (6),
burning of anger
3707 kâ'aç (1), to grieve,
rage, be indignant
3708 ka'aç (4), vexation,
grief
5678 'ebrâh (31),
outburst of passion
7107 qâtsaph (5), to burst
out in rage
7109 qetsaph (Ch.) (1),
rage
7110 qetseph (23), rage
or strife
7265 regaz (Ch.) (1),
quiver
7267 rôgez (1), disquiet;
anger
2372 thumŏs (14),
passion, anger
3709 ŏrgē (31), ire;
punishment
3949 parŏrgizō (1), to
enrage, exasperate

3950 parŏrgismŏs (1),
rage

WRATHFUL
2534 chêmâh (1), heat;
anger; poison
2740 chârôwn (1),
burning of anger

WRATHS
2372 thumŏs (1),
passion, anger

WREATH
7639 sebâkâh (1),
reticulated ornament

WREATHED
8276 sârag (1), to entwine

WREATHEN
5688 'ăbôth (8), entwined
things: a string, wreath
7639 sebâkâh (2),
reticulated ornament

WREATHS
1434 gedîl (1), tassel;
festoon
7639 sebâkâh (2),
reticulated ornament

WREST
5186 nâṭâh (3), to stretch
or spread out
6087 'âtsab (1), to
fabricate or fashion
4761 strĕblŏō (1), to
pervert, twist

WRESTLE
2076+3823 ĕsti (1), he
(she or it) is; they are

WRESTLED
79 'âbaq (2), grapple,
wrestle
6617 pâthal (1), to
struggle; to be tortuous

WRESTLINGS
5319 naphtûwl (1),
struggle

WRETCHED
5005 talaipōrŏs (2),
miserable, wretched

WRETCHEDNESS
7451 ra' (1), bad; evil

WRING
4454 mâlaq (2), to wring
a bird's neck
4680 mâtsâh (1), to
drain; to squeeze out

WRINGED
4680 mâtsâh (1), to
drain; to squeeze out

WRINGING
4330 mîyts (1), pressure

WRINKLE
4512 rhutis (1), face
wrinkle

WRINKLES
7059 qâmaṭ (1), to pluck,
i.e. destroy

WRITE
3789 kâthab (35), to write
3790 kethab (Ch.) (1), to
write
1125 graphō (50), to write
1924 ĕpigraphō (2), to
inscribe, write upon
1989 ĕpistĕllō (1), to
communicate by letter

WRITER
5608 çâphar (2), to
inscribe; to enumerate

WRITER'S
5608 çâphar (2), to
inscribe; to enumerate

WRITEST
3789 kâthab (2), to write

WRITETH
3789 kâthab (1), to write

WRITING
3789 kâthab (1), to write
3791 kâthâb (14),
writing, record or book
3792 kethâb (Ch.) (10),
writing, record or book
4385 miktâb (8), written
thing
975 bibliŏn (1), scroll;
certificate
1125 graphō (1), to write
4093 pinakidiŏn (1),
wooden writing tablet

WRITINGS
1121 gramma (1),
writing; education

WRITTEN
3789 kâthab (138), to
write
3790 kethab (Ch.) (2), to
write
3792 kethâb (Ch.) (1),
writing, record or book
7560 resham (Ch.) (2), to
record
583 apŏgraphō (1),
enroll, take a census
1123 graptŏs (1),
inscribed, written
1125 graphō (134), to
write
1449 ĕggraphō (2),
inscribe, write
1722+1121 ĕn (1), in;
during; because of
1924 ĕpigraphō (2), to
inscribe, write upon
1989 ĕpistĕllō (2), to
communicate by letter
4270 prŏgraphō (2), to
write previously; to
announce, prescribe

WRONG
2555 châmâç (3),
violence; malice
3238 yânâh (1), to
suppress; to maltreat
3808+4941 lô' (1), no, not
5627 çârâh (1), apostasy;
crime; remission
5753 'âvâh (1), to be
crooked
5792 'avvâthâh (1),
oppression
6127 'âqal (1), to wrest,
be crooked
6231 'âshaq (2), to
violate; to overflow
7451 ra' (1), bad; evil
7563 râshâ' (1), morally
wrong; bad person
91 adikĕō (11), to do
wrong
92 adikĕma (1), wrong
93 adikia (1),
wrongfulness

W

WRONGED
91 adikĕŏ (2), to *do wrong*

WRONGETH
2554 châmaç (1), to *be violent; to maltreat*

WRONGFULLY
2554 châmaç (1), to *be violent; to maltreat*
3808+4941 lô' (1), *no, not*
8267 sheqer (4), *untruth; sham*
95 adikŏs (1), *unjustly*

WROTE
3789 kâthab (34), to *write*
3790 kᵉthab (Ch.) (5), to *write*
1125 graphō (21), to *write*
4270 prŏgraphō (1), to *write previously; to announce, prescribe*

WROTH
2196 zâ'aph (2), to *be angry*
2534 chêmâh (1), *heat; anger; poison*
2734 chârâh (13), to *blaze up*
3707 kâ'aç (1), to *grieve, rage, be indignant*
5674 'âbar (5), to *cross over; to transition*
7107 qâtsaph (22), to *burst in rage*
7264 râgaz (1), to *quiver*
2373 thumŏŏ (1), to *enrage*
3710 ŏrgizō (3), to *become exasperated*

WROUGHT
1496 gâzîyth (1), *dressed stone*
1980 hâlak (2), to *walk; live a certain way*
2790 chârash (1), to *engrave; to plow*
4639 ma'ăseh (3), *action; labor*
4865 mishbᵉtsâh (1), *reticulated setting*
5647 'âbad (1), to *do, work, serve*
5648 'ăbad (Ch.) (1), to *work, serve*
5656 'ăbôdâh (1), *work*
5927 'âlâh (1), to *ascend, be high, mount*
5953 'âlal (2), to *glean; to overdo*
6213 'âsâh (52), to *do*
6466 pâ'al (7), to *do, make or practice*
7194 qâshar (1), to *tie, bind*
7551 râqam (1), *variegation; embroider*
7760 sûwm (1), to *put, place*
1096 ginŏmai (2), to *be, become*
1754 ĕnĕrgĕŏ (2), to *be active, efficient, work*
2038 ĕrgazŏmai (7), to *toil*
2716 katĕrgazŏmai (6), to *finish; to accomplish*

4160 pŏiĕŏ (5), to *make or do*
4903 sunĕrgĕŏ (1), to *be a fellow-worker*

WROUGHTEST
6213 'âsâh (1), to *make*

WRUNG
4680 mâtsâh (4), to *drain; to squeeze out*

YARN
4723 miqveh (4), *confidence; collection*

YEA
432 'illûw (1), *if*
637 'aph (39), *also or yea; though*
834 'âsher (1), *who, which, what, that*
1571 gam (66), *also; even; yea; though*
3588 kîy (7), *for, that because*
235 alla (15), *but, yet, except, instead*
1161 dĕ (13), *but, yet; and then*
2089 ĕti (1), *yet, still*
2228 ē (1), *or; than*
2532 kai (5), *and; or; even; also*
3304 mĕnŏungĕ (1), *so then at least*
3483 nai (22), *yes*

YEAR
3117 yôwm (6), *day; time period*
8140 shᵉnâh (Ch.) (5), *year*
8141 shâneh (323), *year*
1763 ĕniautŏs (13), *year*
2094 ĕtŏs (3), *year*
4070 pĕrusi (2), *last year; from last year*

YEAR'S
3117 yôwm (1), *day; time period*
8141 shâneh (1), *year*

YEARLY
3117 yôwm (6), *day; time period*
8141 shâneh (3), *year*

YEARN
3648 kâmar (1), to *shrivel with heat*

YEARNED
3648 kâmar (1), to *shrivel with heat*

YEARS
3027 yâd (1), *hand; power*
3117 yôwm (3), *day; time period*
8027 shâlash (2), to *be, triplicate*
8140 shᵉnâh (Ch.) (2), *year*
8141 shâneh (466), *year*
1096+3173 ginŏmai (1), to *be, become*
1332 diĕtēs (1), *of two years in age*
1333 diĕtia (2), *interval of two years*
1541 hĕkatŏntaĕtēs (1), *centenarian*
1763 ĕniautŏs (2), *year*
2094 ĕtŏs (46), *year*

2250 hēmĕra (2), *day; period of time*
5063 tĕssarakŏntaĕtēs (2), *of forty years of age*
5148 triĕtia (1), *triennium, three years*

YEARS'
8141 shâneh (2), *year*

YELL
5286 nâ'ar (1), to *growl*

YELLED
5414+6963 nâthan (1), to *give*

YELLOW
3422 yᵉraqraq (1), *yellowishness*
6669 tsâhôb (3), *golden in color*

YES
3304 mĕnŏungĕ (1), *so then at least*
3483 nai (3), *yes*

YESTERDAY
570 'emesh (1), *yesterday evening*
865 'ethmôwl (1), *heretofore, formerly*
8543 tᵉmôwl (4), *yesterday*
5504 chthĕs (3), *yesterday; in time past*

YESTERNIGHT
570 'emesh (3), *yesterday evening*

YET
227 'âz (1), *at that time or place; therefore*
389 'ak (13), *surely; only, however*
559 'âmar (1), to *say*
637 'aph (1), *also or yea*
1297 bᵉram (Ch.) (2), *however, but*
1571 gam (14), *also; even; yea; though*
2962 ţerem (4), *not yet or before*
3588 kîy (14), *for, that because*
5704 'ad (4), *as far (long) as; during; while; until*
5728 'ăden (2), *till now, yet*
5750 'ôwd (142), *again; repeatedly; still; more*
7535 raq (2), *merely; although*
188 akmēn (1), *just now, still*
235 alla (11), *but, yet, except, instead*
1063 gar (3), *for, indeed, but, because*
1065 gĕ (3), *particle of emphasis*
1161 dĕ (19), *but, yet; and then*
2089 ĕti (54), *yet, still*
2236 hēdista (2), *with great pleasure*
2532 kai (7), *and; or; even; also*
2539 kaipĕr (1), *nevertheless*
2579 kan (1), *and (or even) if*

2596 kata (2), *down; according to*
3195 mĕllō (1), to *intend, i.e. be about to*
3305 mĕntŏi (2), *however*
3364 ŏu mē (1), *not at all, absolutely not*
3369 mĕdĕpō (1), *not even yet*
3380 mēpō (1), *not yet*
3764 ŏudĕpō (4), *not even yet*
3765 ŏukĕti (3), *not yet, no longer*
3768 ŏupō (21), *not yet*

YIELD
3254 yâçaph (1), to *add or augment*
5186 nâţâh (1), to *stretch or spread out*
5375 nâsâ' (1), to *lift up*
5414 nâthan (13), to *give*
5414+3027 nâthan (1), to *give*
6213 'âsâh (6), to *do or make*
1325 didōmi (1), to *give*
3936 paristēmi (4), to *stand beside, present*
3982 pĕithō (1), to *assent to authority*
4160 pŏiĕŏ (1), to *make or do*

YIELDED
1478 gâva' (1), to *expire, die*
1580 gâmal (1), to *benefit or requite; to wean*
3052 yᵉhab (Ch.) (1), to *give*
591 apŏdidōmi (1), to *give away*
863 aphiēmi (1), to *leave; to pardon, forgive*
1325 didōmi (1), to *give*
1634 ĕkpsuchō (1), to *expire, die*
3936 paristēmi (1), to *stand beside, present*

YIELDETH
5414 nâthan (1), to *give*
7235 râbâh (1), to *increase*
591 apŏdidōmi (1), to *give away*

YIELDING
2232 zâra' (3), to *sow seed; to disseminate*
4832 marpê' (1), *cure; deliverance; placidity*
6213 'âsâh (3), to *do or make*

YOKE
4132 môwţ (1), *pole; yoke*
4133 môwţâh (4), *pole; ox-bow; yoke*
5923 'ôl (39), *neck yoke*
6776 tsemed (7), *paired yoke*
2201 zĕugŏs (1), *team*
2218 zugŏs (5), *coupling, yoke*

YOKED
2086 hĕtĕrŏzugĕō (1), to *associate discordantly*

YOKEFELLOW
4805 suzugŏs (1), *colleague*

YOKES
4133 môwṭâh (4), *pole; ox-bow; yoke*

YONDER
1973 hâlᵉâh (1), *far away; thus far*
3541 kôh (2), *thus*
5676 'êber (1), *opposite side; east*
5704+3541 'ad (1), *as far (long) as; during; while; until*
1563 ĕkĕi (2), *there, thither*

YOUNG
667 'ephrôach (4), *brood of a bird*
970 bâchûwr (42), *male youth; bridegroom*
979 bᵉchûrôwth (1), *youth*
1121 bên (20), *son, descendant; people*
1121+1241 bên (34), *son, descendant; people*
1123 bên (Ch.) (1), *son*
1241 bâqâr (1), *plowing ox; herd*
1469 gôwzâl (2), *young of a bird*
1482 gûwr (1), *cub*
3127 yôwneqeth (1), *sprout, new shoot*
3206 yeled (10), *young male*
3242 yᵉnîqâh (1), *sucker or sapling*
3715 kᵉphîyr (25), *walled village; young lion*
3833 lâbîy' (1), *lion, lioness*
5288 na'ar (92), *male child; servant*
5288+970 na'ar (1), *male child; servant*
5291 na'ărâh (6), *female child; servant*
5763 'ûwl (3), *to suckle, i.e. give milk*
5958 'elem (1), *lad, young man*
6082 'ôpher (5), *dusty-colored fawn*
6499 par (1), *bullock*
6810+3117 tsâ'îyr (1), *young in value*
6996 qâṭân (1), *small, least, youngest*
7988 shilyâh (1), *fetus or infant baby*
1025 brĕphŏs (1), *infant*
2365 thugatriŏn (1), *little daughter*
3494 nĕanias (5), *youth, up to about forty years*
3495 nĕaniskŏs (10), *youth under forty*
3501 nĕŏs (4), *new*
3502 nĕŏssŏs (1), *young*
3678 ŏnariŏn (1), *little donkey*
3813 paidiŏn (10), *child; immature*
3816 pais (1), *child; slave or servant*

YOUNGER
6810 tsâ'îyr (7), *little, young*
6810+3117 tsâ'îyr (1), *little, young*
6996 qâṭân (14), *small, least, youngest*
1640 ĕlassŏn (1), *smaller*
3501 nĕŏs (8), *new*

YOUNGEST
6810 tsâ'îyr (3), *little, young*
6996 qâṭân (15), *small, least, youngest*

YOUTH
979 bᵉchûrôwth (2), *youth*
2779 chôreph (1), *autumn (and winter)*
3208 yaldûwth (2), *boyhood or girlhood*
5271 nâ'ûwr (46), *youth; juvenility; young people*
5288 na'ar (5), *male child; servant*
5290 nô'ar (2), *boyhood*
5934 'âlûwm (4), *adolescence; vigor*
6526 pirchach (1), *progeny, i.e. a brood*
6812 tsᵉ'îyrâh (1), *juvenility*
7839 shachărûwth (1), *juvenescence, youth*
3503 nĕŏtēs (5), *youthfulness*

YOUTHFUL
3512 nĕŏtĕrikŏs (1), *juvenile, youthful*

YOUTHS
1121 bên (1), *son, descendant; people*
5288 na'ar (1), *male child; servant*

ZAANAIM
6815 Tsa'ănannîym (1), *removals*

ZAANAN
6630 Tsa'ănân (1), *sheep pasture*

ZAANANNIM
6815 Tsa'ănannîym (1), *removals*

ZAAVAN
2190 Za'ăvân (1), *disquiet*

ZABAD
2066 Zâbâd (8), *giver*

ZABBAI
2079 Zabbay (2), *Zabbai*

ZABBUD
2072 Zabbûwd (1), *given*

ZABDI
2067 Zabdîy (6), *giving*

ZABDIEL
2068 Zabdîy'êl (2), *gift of God*

ZABUD
2071 Zâbûwd (1), *given*

ZABULON
2194 Zaboûlŏn (3), *habitation*

ZACCAI
2140 Zakkay (2), *pure*

ZACCHAEUS
2195 Zakchaiŏs (3), *Zacchæus*

ZACCHUR
2139 Zakkûwr (1), *mindful*

ZACCUR
2139 Zakkûwr (8), *mindful*

ZACHARIAH
2148 Zᵉkaryâh (4), *Jehovah has remembered*

ZACHARIAS
2197 Zacharias (11), *Jehovah has remembered*

ZACHER
2144 Zeker (1), *recollection; commemoration*

ZADOK
6659 Tsâdôwq (52), *just*

ZADOK'S
6659 Tsâdôwq (1), *just*

ZAHAM
2093 Zaham (1), *loathing*

ZAIR
6811 Tsâ'îyr (1), *little*

ZALAPH
6764 Tsâlâph (1), *Tsalaph*

ZALMON
6756 Tsalmôwn (2), *shady*

ZALMONAH
6758 Tsalmônâh (2), *shadiness*

ZALMUNNA
6759 Tsalmunnâ' (12), *shade has been denied*

ZAMZUMMIMS
2157 Zamzôm (1), *intriguing*

ZANOAH
2182 Zânôwach (5), *rejected*

ZAPHNATH-PAANEAH
6847 Tsophnath Pa'nêach (1), *Tsophnath-Paneäch*

ZAPHON
6829 Tsâphôwn (1), *boreal, northern*

ZARA
2196 Zara (1), *rising of light, dawning*

ZARAH
2226 Zerach (2), *rising of light, dawning*

ZAREAH
6881 Tsor'âh (1), *stinging wasp*

ZAREATHITES
6882 Tsor'îy (1), *Tsorite or Tsorathite*

ZARED
2218 Zered (1), *lined with shrubbery*

ZAREPHATH
6886 Tsârᵉphath (3), *refinement*

ZARETAN
6891 Tsârᵉthân (1), *Tsarethan*

ZARETH-SHAHAR
6890 Tsereth hash-Shachar (1), *splendor of the dawn*

ZARHITES
2227 Zarchîy (6), *Zarchite*

ZARTANAH
6891 Tsârᵉthân (1), *Tsarethan*

ZARTHAN
6891 Tsârᵉthân (1), *Tsarethan*

ZATTHU
2240 Zattûw' (1), *Zattu*

ZATTU
2240 Zattûw' (3), *Zattu*

ZAVAN
2190 Za'ăvân (1), *disquiet*

ZAZA
2117 Zâzâ' (1), *prominent*

ZEAL
7065 qânâ' (1), *to be, make zealous, jealous or envious*
7068 qin'âh (9), *jealousy or envy*
2205 zēlŏs (6), *zeal, ardor; jealousy, malice*

ZEALOUS
7065 qânâ' (2), *to be, make zealous*
2206 zēlŏŏ (1), *to have warmth of feeling for*
2207 zēlōtēs (5), *zealot*

ZEALOUSLY
2206 zēlŏŏ (2), *to have warmth of feeling for*

ZEBADIAH
2069 Zᵉbadyâh (9), *Jehovah has given*

ZEBAH
2078 Zebach (12), *sacrifice*

ZEBAIM
6380 Pôkereth Tsᵉbâyîym (2), *trap of gazelles*

ZEBEDEE
2199 Zĕbĕdaiŏs (10), *Zebedæus*

ZEBEDEE'S
2199 Zĕbĕdaiŏs (2), *Zebedæus*

ZEBINA
2081 Zᵉbîynâ' (1), *gainfulness*

ZEBOIIM
6636 Tsᵉbô'iym (2), *gazelles*

ZEBOIM
6636 Tsᵉbô'iym (3), *gazelles*
6650 Tsᵉbô'îym (2), *hyenas*

ZEBUDAH
2081 Zᵉbîynâ' (1), *gainfulness*

ZEBUL
2083 Zᵉbûl (6), *dwelling*

Z

ZEBULONITE
2075 Zᵉbûwlônîy (2),
Zebulonite

ZEBULUN
2074 Zᵉbûwlûwn (44),
habitation

ZEBULUNITES
2075 Zᵉbûwlônîy (1),
Zebulonite

ZECHARIAH
2148 Zᵉkaryâh (39),
Jehovah has
remembered

ZEDAD
6657 Tsᵉdâd (2), siding

ZEDEKIAH
6667 Tsidqîyâh (61), right
of Jehovah

ZEDEKIAH'S
6667 Tsidqîyâh (1), right
of Jehovah

ZEEB
2062 Zᵉ'êb (6), wolf

ZELAH
6762 Tsela' (2), limping

ZELEK
6768 Tseleq (2), fissure

ZELOPHEHAD
6765 Tsᵉlophchâd (11),
Tselophchad

ZELOTES
2208 Zēlōtēs (2), Zealot,
partisan

ZELZAH
6766 Tseltsach (1), clear
shade

ZEMARAIM
6787 Tsᵉmârayim (2),
double fleece

ZEMARITE
6786 Tsᵉmârîy (2),
Tsemarite

ZEMIRA
2160 Zᵉmîyrâh (1), song

ZENAN
6799 Tsᵉnân (1), Tsenan

ZENAS
2211 Zēnas (1),
Jove-given

ZEPHANIAH
6846 Tsᵉphanyâh (10),
Jehovah has secreted

ZEPHATH
6857 Tsᵉphath (1),
watch-tower

ZEPHATHAH
6859 Tsᵉphâthâh (1),
watch-tower

ZEPHI
6825 Tsᵉphôw (1),
observant

ZEPHO
6825 Tsᵉphôw (2),
observant

ZEPHON
6827 Tsᵉphôwn (1),
watch-tower

ZEPHONITES
6831 Tsᵉphôwnîy (1),
Tsephonite

ZER
6863 Tsêr (1), rock

ZERAH
2226 Zerach (19), rising
of light, dawning

ZERAHIAH
2228 Zᵉrachyâh (5),
Jehovah has risen

ZERED
2218 Zered (3), lined
with shrubbery

ZEREDA
6868 Tsᵉrêdâh (1),
puncture

ZEREDATHAH
6868 Tsᵉrêdâh (1),
puncture

ZERERATH
6888 Tsᵉrêrâh (1),
puncture

ZERESH
2238 Zeresh (4), Zeresh

ZERETH
6889 Tsereth (1),
splendor

ZERI
6874 Tsᵉrîy (1), balsam

ZEROR
6872 tsᵉrôwr (1), parcel;
kernel or particle

ZERUAH
6871 Tsᵉrûw'âh (1),
leprous

ZERUBBABEL
2216 Zᵉrubbâbel (21),
from Babylon
2217 Zᵉrubbâbel (Ch.)
(1), from Babylon

ZERUIAH
6870 Tsᵉrûwyâh (26),
wounded

ZETHAM
2241 Zêthâm (2), seed

ZETHAN
2133 Zêythân (1), olive
grove

ZETHAR
2242 Zêthar (1), Zethar

ZIA
2127 Zîya' (1), agitation

ZIBA
6717 Tsîybâ' (16), station

ZIBEON
6649 Tsib'ôwn (8),
variegated

ZIBIA
6644 Tsibyâ' (1), female
gazelle

ZIBIAH
6645 Tsibyâh (2), female
gazelle

ZICHRI
2147 Zikrîy (12),
memorable

ZIDDIM
6661 Tsiddîym (1), sides

ZIDKIJAH
6667 Tsidqîyâh (1), right
of Jehovah

ZIDON
6721 Tsîydôwn (20),
fishery
6722 Tsîydônîy (1),
Tsidonian

ZIDONIANS
6722 Tsîydônîy (10),
Tsidonian

ZIF
2099 Zìv (2), flowers

ZIHA
6727 Tsîychâ' (3), drought

ZIKLAG
6860 Tsiqlâg (14),
Tsiklag or Tsikelag

ZILLAH
6741 Tsillâh (3), Tsillah

ZILPAH
2153 Zilpâh (7), fragrant
dropping as myrrh

ZILTHAI
6769 Tsillᵉthay (2), shady

ZIMMAH
2155 Zimmâh (3), bad
plan

ZIMRAN
2175 Zimrân (2), musical

ZIMRI
2174 Zimrîy (15), musical

ZIN
6790 Tsîn (10), crag

ZINA
2126 Zîynâ' (1), well-fed

ZION
6726 Tsîyôwn (152),
permanent capital or
monument

ZION'S
6726 Tsîyôwn (1),
permanent capital or
monument

ZIOR
6730 Tsîy'ôr (1), small

ZIPH
2128 Zîyph (10), flowing

ZIPHAH
2129 Zîyphâh (1), flowing

ZIPHIMS
2130 Zîyphîy (1), Ziphite

ZIPHION
6837 Tsiphyôwn (1),
watch-tower

ZIPHITES
2130 Zîyphîy (2), Ziphite

ZIPHRON
2202 Ziphrôn (1),
fragrant

ZIPPOR
6834 Tsippôwr (7), little
hopping bird

ZIPPORAH
6855 Tsippôrâh (3), bird

ZITHRI
5644 Çithrîy (1),
protective

ZIZ
6732 Tsîyts (1), bloom

ZIZA
2124 Zîyzâ' (2),
prominence

ZIZAH
2125 Zîyzâh (1),
prominence

ZOAN
6814 Tsô'an (7), Tsoän

ZOAR
6820 Tsô'ar (10), little

ZOBA
6678 Tsôwbâ' (2), station

ZOBAH
6678 Tsôwbâ' (11), station

ZOBEBAH
6637 Tsôbêbâh (1),
canopier

ZOHAR
6714 Tsôchar (4),
whiteness

ZOHELETH
2120 Zôcheleth (1),
serpent

ZOHETH
2105 Zôwchêth (1),
Zocheth

ZOPHAH
6690 Tsôwphach (2),
breath

ZOPHAI
6689 Tsûwph (1),
honey-comb

ZOPHAR
6691 Tsôwphar (4),
departing

ZOPHIM
6839 Tsôphîym (1),
watchers

ZORAH
6681 tsâvach (8), to
screech exultingly

ZORATHITES
6882 Tsor'îy (1), Tsorite
or Tsorathite

ZOREAH
6881 Tsor'âh (1), stinging
wasp

ZORITES
6882 Tsor'îy (1), Tsorite
or Tsorathite

ZOROBABEL
2216 Zŏrŏbabĕl (3), from
Babylon

ZUAR
6686 Tsûw'âr (5), small

ZUPH
6689 Tsûwph (3),
honey-comb

ZUR
6698 Tsûwr (5), rock

ZURIEL
6700 Tsûwrîy'êl (1), rock
of God

ZURISHADDAI
6701 Tsûwrîyshadday
(5), rock of (the)
Almighty

ZUZIMS
2104 Zûwzîym (1),
prominent

New Strong's™
Concise Dictionary

of the Words in the

Hebrew Bible

with their Renderings in the
King James Version

Read this first!

How to Use the Hebrew and Aramaic Dictionary

For many people Strong's unique system of numbers continues to be *the* bridge between the original languages of the Bible and the English of the *King James Version* (AV). In order to enhance the strategic importance of *Strong's Hebrew and Aramaic Dictionary* for Bible students, it has been significantly improved in this brand-new, up-to-date edition. It is now completely re-typeset with modern, larger typefaces that are kind to the eye, and all known errors in the original typesetting have been corrected, bringing this pivotal work to a new level of usefulness and accuracy.

1. What the Dictionary Is

Strong's Hebrew and Aramaic Dictionary is a fully integrated companion to the main concordance. Its compact entries contain a wealth of information about the words of the Bible in their original language. You can enrich your study of the Bible enormously if you will invest the time to understand the various elements included in each entry and their significance. The example that follows identifies many of these entry elements; and the following sections on the transliteration, abbreviations, and special symbols used offer fuller explanations. While no dictionary designed for readers who do not know biblical Hebrew can explain all that a faithful student of the language would know, this *Dictionary* gives the serious student of the English Bible the basic information needed to pursue infinitely deeper and broader studies of God's Word. Vast amounts of biblical insight can be gained by using this *Concordance* alone or in conjunction with other time-proven biblical reference works, such as Thomas Nelson's *Vine's Complete Expository Dictionary of Old and New Testament Words* and *Nelson's New Illustrated Bible Dictionary.*

2. Using the Dictionary with the Main Concordance

To use this *Dictionary*, locate the number given next to the biblical reference for any particular entry in the main concordance. For example, under "SHADY," you find *Strong's* number 6628 next to the first Bible reference shown, "Job 40:21." Since the reference is in the Old Testament (and since this numeral is set in regular type [and not in italic type]), you know that it refers to the *Hebrew and Aramaic Dictionary.* You may view that enlarged entry, here, or on page 118 in this *Dictionary.* The enlarged example that follows, together with the following sections of explanation, identify the kinds of information such entries provide.

3. Using the Dictionary to Do Word Studies

Careful Bible students do word studies, and *The New Strong's™ Exhaustive Concordance* with this revised, newly-typeset *Hebrew and Aramaic Dictionary* offers unique assistance. Consider the word "love" as found the King James Bible. By skimming the main concordance, you find these numbers for Hebrew (and Aramaic) words that the King James Bible translates with the English word "love": 157, 160, 2836, 7355, 1730, 7474, 5691, 5690. Now for any one Bible reference in this entry there is only one Hebrew word cited, and you may be interested only in establishing the precise meaning for just that word in that occurrence. If so, it will be very helpful for you to observe that same Hebrew word in *each* of its occurrences in the Bible. In that way, you develop an idea of its possible range of meanings, and you help clarify what it probably meant precisely in the specific Bible reference you are studying.

But don't overlook exploring each Hebrew (and Aramaic) word translated as "love." You may wish to take notes as you look up each occurrence of the word that goes with 157, and then each occurrence of the word that goes with 160, and so forth. This method gives you an excellent basis for understanding all that the Hebrew Bible (the Old Testament) signifies with the King James Version's word "love."

Now see the *Dictionary* entry 157 itself, and notice that after the symbol :— all the words and word prefixes and suffixes are listed. These show you that this one Hebrew word, *'ahab*, is translated into several different, but related words in the King James Bible: beloved, love, loved, lovely, lover, like, befriend. This list tells you the range of uses of the one Hebrew word in the King James Bible. This information can help you distinguish between the nuances of meaning found where this and the other Hebrew words are translated by these same words and similar ones in the King James Bible.

These three ways of using the *Dictionary* in conjunction with the main concordance show you only a sampling of the many ways *The New Strong's™ Exhaustive Concordance* can enrich your study of the Bible. And they show you why it is important that you take the time to become familiar with each feature in the *Dictionary* as illustrated in the example on the following page.

An Example
from the
Hebrew and Aramaic Dictionary

Strong's number, corresponding to the numbers at the ends of the context lines in the main concordance.

An unnumbered cross-reference entry.

The word as it appears in the original Hebrew (or Aramaic) spelling.

The degree symbol denotes the presence of a textual variation. (See "Special Symbols")

The Hebrew (or Aramaic) word represented in English letters in **bold** type (the transliteration).

Strong's syllable-by-syllable pronunciation in *italics*, with the emphasized syllable marked by the accent.

Information regarding relationship to other Hebrew (or Aramaic) words, usually cited by Strong's numbers. Sometimes a word may refer to a Greek entry (shown by *italic* numbers) or it may come from another language.

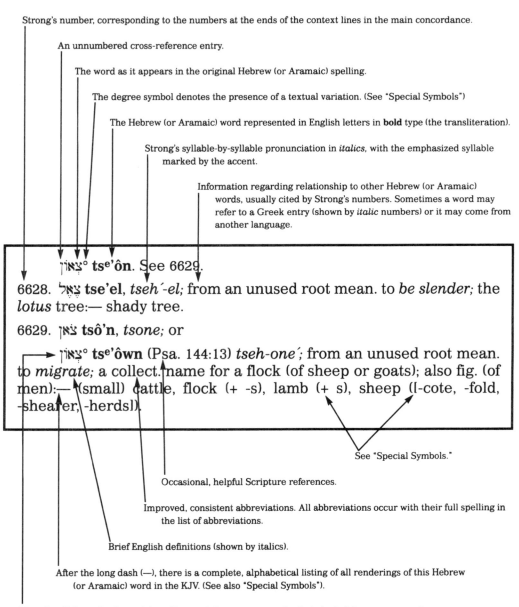

צֹאוֹן° **tseʾôn**. See 6629.

6628. צֶאֱל **tseʾel**, *tseh´-el*; from an unused root mean. to *be slender*; the *lotus* tree:— shady tree.

6629. צֹאן **tsôʾn**, *tsone*; or

צֹאוֹן° **tseʾôwn** (Psa. 144:13) *tseh-oneʹ*; from an unused root mean. to *migrate*; a collect. name for a flock (of sheep or goats); also fig. (of men):— (small) cattle, flock (+ -s), lamb (+ s), sheep ([-cote, -fold, -shearer, -herds]).

See "Special Symbols."

Occasional, helpful Scripture references.

Improved, consistent abbreviations. All abbreviations occur with their full spelling in the list of abbreviations.

Brief English definitions (shown by italics).

After the long dash (—), there is a complete, alphabetical listing of all renderings of this Hebrew (or Aramaic) word in the KJV. (See also "Special Symbols").

Note that Hebrew (or Aramaic) spelling variations are conveniently indented for easy comparison.

Plan of the Hebrew and Aramaic Dictionary

1. All the original words are presented in their alphabetical order (according to Hebrew and Aramaic). They are numbered for easy matching between this Dictionary and the main part of the Concordance. Many reference books also use these same numbers created by Dr. Strong.

2. Immediately after each word, the exact equivalent of each sound (phoneme) is given in English characters, according to the transliteration system given below.

3. Next follows the precise pronunciation, with the proper stress mark.

4. Then comes the etymology, root meaning, and common uses of the word, along with any other important related details.

5. In the case of proper names, the normal English spelling is given, accompanied by a few words of explanation.

6. Finally, after the colon and the dash (:—), all the different ways that the word appears in the Authorized Version (KJV) are listed in alphabetical order. When the Hebrew or Aramaic word appears in English as a phrase, the main word of the phrase is used to alphabetize it.

By looking up these words in the main concordance and by noting the passages which display the same number in the right-hand column, the reader also possesses a complete *Hebrew Concordance*, expressed in the words of the Authorized Version.

Transliteration and Pronunciation of the Hebrew and Aramaic

The following shows how the Hebrew words are transliterated into English in this Dictionary.

1. The Hebrew and Aramaic read *from right to left*. Both alphabets consist of 22 letters (and their variations), which are all regarded as *consonants*, although four consonants (א ה ו י) sometimes indicate vowel sounds. To help enunciation, vowels are primarily indicated by certain "points" or marks, mostly beneath the letters. Hebrew and Aramaic do not use *capitals, italics*, etc.

2. The Hebrew and Aramaic characters are as follows:

No.	Form	Name	Transliteration and Pronunciation
1.	א	'Aleph (*aw´-lef*)	', silent
2.	ב	Bêyth (*bayth*)	**b**
3.	ג	Gîymel (*ghee´-mel*)	**g** hard = γ
4.	ד	Dâleth (*daw´-leth*)	**d**
5.	ה	Hê' (*hay*)	**h**, often quiescent
6.	ו	Vâv (*vawv*) or Wâw (*waw*)	**v** or **w**, quiescent
7.	ז	Zayin (*zah´-yin*)	**z**, as in *zeal*
8.	ח	Chêyth (*khayth*)	German **ch** = χ (nearly *kh*)
9.	ט	Têyth (*tayth*)	**ṭ** = T
10.	י	Yôwd (*yode*)	**y**, often quiescent
11.	כ final ך	Kaph (*caf*)	**k** = כ
12.	ל	Lâmed (*law´-med*)	**l**
13.	מ final ם	Mêm (*mame*)	**m**
14.	נ final ן	Nûwn (*noon*)	**n**
15.	ס	Çâmek (*saw´-mek*)	**ç** = *s* sharp = ש
16.	ע	'Ayin (*ah´-yin*)	' peculiar [1]
17.	פ final ף	Phê' (*fay*)	**ph** = *f* = φ
	ב	Pê' (*pay*)	**p**
18.	צ, final ץ	Tsâdêy (*tsaw-day´*)	**ts**
19.	ק	Qôwph (*cofe*)	**q** = *k* = כ
20.	ר	Rêysh (*raysh*)	**r**
21.	שׂ	Sîyn (*seen*)	**s** sharp = ס = σ
	שׁ	Shîyn (*sheen*)	**sh**
22.	ת	Thâv (*thawv*)	**th**, as in *THin* = θ
	ת	Tâv (*tawv*)	**t** = ט = τ

---

[1] The letter *'Ayin*, because Westerners find it difficult to pronounce accurately (it is a deep guttural sound, like that made in *gargling*), is generally passed over silently in reading. We have represented it to the eye (but not exactly to the ear) by the Greek *rough breathing* mark (') in order to distinguish it from *'Aleph*, which is likewise treated as silent, being similarly represented by the Greek *smooth breathing* (').

3. The vowel points are as follows:

Form [2] Name	Transliteration and Pronunciation
בָ Qâmêts (*caw-mates*)	â, as in *All*
בַ Pattach (*pat´-takh*)	a, as in *mAn*
בֲ Shevâ'-Pattach (*she-vaw´ pat´-takh*)	ă, as in *hAt*
בֵ Tsêrêy (*tsay-ray*)	ê, as in *thEy* = η
בֶ Çegôwl (*seg-ole*)	e, as in *thEir*
	e, as in *mEn* = ε
בֱ Shevâ'-Çegôwl (*she-vaw´ seg-ole*)	ĕ, as in *mEt*
בְ Shevâ' (*she-vaw*) [3]	obscure, as in *avErage*
	silent, as *e* in *madE*
בִ Chîyriq (*khee´-rik*)	î, as in *machIne* [4]
	i, as in *supplIant* (*misery, hit*)
בֹ Chôwlem (*kho´-lem*) [5]	ô, as in *no* = ω
בָ Short Qâmêts (*caw-mates*) [6]	o, as in *nor* = o
בֳ Shevâ -Qâmêts (*she-vaw´ caw-mates*)	ŏ, as in *not*
וּ Shûwrêq * (*shoo-rake*) [7]	û, as in *crUel*
בֻ Qîbbûts * (*kib´-boots*) [7]	u, as in *fUll, rude*

4. A point in the heart of a letter is called *Dâgêsh´*, and is of two kinds, which must be carefully distinguished.

    a. Dâgêsh *lenè* occurs only in the letters ב, ג, ד, כ, פ, ת (technically vocalized *Begad´-Kephath*), when they *begin* a clause or sentence, or are preceded by a consonant *sound;* and simply has the effect of removing their aspiration. [8]

    b. Dâgêsh *fortè* may occur in any letter except א, ה, ח, ע or ר ; it is equivalent to *doubling* the letter, and at the same time it removes the aspiration of a Begad-Kephath letter. [9]

5. The *Maqqêph´* (-), like a *hyphen*, unites words only for purposes of pronunciation (by removing the primary accent from all except the last word), but it does not affect their meaning or grammatical construction.

Special Symbols

+ (*addition*) denotes a rendering in the A.V. of one or more Hebrew or Aramaic words in connection with the one under consideration. For example, in 2 Kgs. 4:41, No. 1697, דָּבָר (**dâbâr**) is translated as "harm," in connection with No. 7451. Literally, it is "bad thing."

× (*multiplication*) denotes a rendering in the A.V. that results from an idiom peculiar to the Hebrew or Aramaic. For example, in Psa. 132:15, the whole Hebrew phrase in which בָּרַךְ, **bârak** (1288) appears is a means of expressing a verb root emphatically, i. e. "blessing, I will bless" = "I will abundantly bless."

° (*degree*), attached to a Hebrew word, denotes a corrected vowel pointing which is different from the Biblical text. (This mark is set in Hebrew Bibles over syllables in which the vowels of the margin have been inserted instead of those which properly belong to the text.)

For example, see the difference between the Hebrew text and the scribes' marginal note in Ezek. 40:15 for No. 2978, translated "entrance."

( ) (*parentheses*), in the renderings from the A.V., denote a word or syllable which is sometimes given in connection with the principal word to which it is attached. In Num. 34:6, the only occurrence of "western" in the A. V., the underlying Hebrew word is יָם (**yâm**, No. 3220), which is usually translated "sea."

[ ] (*brackets*), in the rendering from the A.V., denote the inclusion of an additional word in the Hebrew or Aramaic. For example, No. 3117, יוֹם (**yôwm**), is translated as "birthday" in Gen. 40:20, along with No. 3205. So, two Hebrew words are translated by one English word.

Italics, at the end of a rendering from the A.V., denote an explanation of the variations from the usual form.

---

[2] The same Hebrew/Aramaic consonant (ב) is shown here in order to show the position of the vowel points, whether below, above, or in the middle of Hebrew or Aramaic consonants.

[3] *Silent Shevâ'* is not represented by any mark in our method of transliteration, since it is understood whenever there is no other vowel point.

[4] *Chîyriq* is long only when it is followed by a quiescent *yôwd* (either expressed or implied).

[5] *Chôwlem* is written *fully* only over *Vâv* or *Wâw* (ו), which is then quiescent (*w*); but when used "defectively" (without the *Vâv* or *Wâw*) it may be written either over the left-hand corner of the letter to which it belongs, or over the right-hand corner of the following one.

[6] Short *Qâmêts* is found only in *unaccented syllables ending with a consonant sound.*

[7] *Shûwrêq* is written only in the heart of *Vâv* or *Wâw*. Sometimes it is said to be "defectively" written (without the *Vâv* or *Wâw*), and then takes the form of *Qibbûts*, which in such cases is called *vicarious.*

[8] In our system of transliteration Dâgêsh *lenè* is represented only in the letters פ and ת, because elsewhere it does not affect the pronunciation.

[9] A point in the heart of ה is called *Mappîyq* (*map-peek*). It occurs only in the final vowel-less letter of a few words, and we have represented it by hh. A Dâgêsh *fortè* in the heart of ו may easily be distinguished from the vowel *Shûwrêq* by noticing that in the former case the letter has a proper vowel point accompanying it.

It should be noted that both kinds of Dâgêsh are often omitted in writing (being *implied*), but (in the case at least of Dâgêsh *fortè*) the word is usually pronounced the same as if it were present.

Abbreviations

abb. = abbreviated
    abbreviation
abstr. = abstract
    abstractly
act. = active (voice)
    actively
acc. = accusative (case) [1]
adj. = adjective
    adjectivally
adv. = adverb
    adverbial
    adverbially
aff. = affix [2]
    affixed
affin. = affinity
alt. = alternate
    alternately
anal. = analogy
appar. = apparent
    apparently
arch. = architecture
    architectural
    architecturally
art. = article [3]
artif. = artificial
    artificially
Ass. = Assyrian
A.V. = Authorized Version
    (King James Version)
Bab. = Babylon
    Babylonia
    Babylonian
caus. = causative [4]
    causatively
cerem. = ceremony
    ceremonial
    ceremonially
Chald. = Chaldee (Aramaic)
    Chaldaism
    (Aramaism)
Chr. = Christian
collat. = collateral
    collaterally
collect. = collective
    collectively
comp. = compare [5]
    comparison
    comparative
    comparatively
concr. = concrete
    concretely
conjec. = conjecture
    conjectural
    conjecturally
conjug. = conjugation [6]
    conjugational
    conjugationally
conjunc. = conjunction
    conjunctional
    conjunctionally
constr. = construct [7]
    construction
    constructive
    constructively

contr. = contracted [8]
    contraction
correl. = correlated
    correlation
    correlative
    correlatively
corresp. = corresponding
    correspondingly
dat. = dative (case) [9]
def. = definite [10]
    definitely
demonstr. = demonstrative [11]
denom. = denominative [12]
    denominatively
der. = derived
    derivation
    derivative
    derivatively
desc. = descended
    descendant
    descendants
dimin. = diminutive [13]
dir. = direct
    directly
E. = East
    Eastern
eccl. = ecclesiastical
    ecclesiastically
e.g. = for example
Eg. = Egypt
    Egyptian
    Egyptians
ellip. = ellipsis [14]
    elliptical
    elliptically
emphat. = emphatic
    emphatically
equiv. = equivalent
    equivalently
err. = error
    erroneous
    erroneously
espec. = especially
etym. = etymology [15]
    etymological
    etymologically
euphem. = euphemism [16]
    euphemistic
    euphemistically
euphon. = euphonious [17]
    euphonically
extens. = extension [18]
    extensive
extern. = external
    externally
fem. = feminine (gender)
fig. = figurative
    figuratively
for. = foreign
    foreigner
freq. = frequentative
    frequentatively
fut. = future

gen. = general
    generally
    generic
    generical
    generically
Gr. = Greek
    Graecism
gut. = guttural [19]
Heb. = Hebrew
    Hebraism
i.e. = that is
ident. = identical
    identically
immed. = immediate
    immediately
imper. = imperative [20]
    imperatively
imperf. = imperfect [21]
impers. = impersonal
    impersonally
impl. = implied
    impliedly
    implication
incept. = inceptive [22]
    inceptively
incl. = including
    inclusive
    inclusively
indef. = indefinite
    indefinitely
ind. = indicative [23]
    indicatively
indiv. = individual
    individually
infer. = inference
    inferential
    inferentially
infin. = infinitive
inhab. = inhabitant
    inhabitants
ins. = inserted
intens. = intensive
    intensively
interch. = interchangeable
intern. = internal
    internally
interj. = interjection [24]
    interjectional
    interjectionally
interrog. = interrogative [25]
    interrogatively
intr. = intransitive [26]
    intransitively
invol. = involuntary
    involuntarily
irreg. = irregular
    irregularly
Isr. = Israelite
    Israelites
    Israelitish
Lat. = Latin
Levit. = Levital
    Levitically

lit. = literal
    literally
marg. = margin
    marginal reading
masc. = masculine (gender)
mean. = meaning
ment. = mental
    mentally
metaph. = metaphorical
    metaphorically
mid. = middle (voice) [27]
modif. = modified
    modification
mor. = moral
    morally
mult. = multiplicative [28]
nat. = natural
    naturally
neg. = negative
    negatively
neut. = neuter (gender)
obj. = object
    objective
    objectively
obs. = obsolete
ord. = ordinal [29]
or. = origin
orig. = original
    originally
orth. = orthography [30]
    orthographical
    orthographically
Pal. = Palestine
part. = participle
pass. = passive (voice)
    passively
patron. = patronymic [31]
    patronymical
    patronymically
perh. = perhaps
perm. = permutation [32] (of
    adjacent letters)
pers. = person
    personal
    personally
Pers. = Persia
    Persian
    Persians
phys. = physical
    physically
plur. = plural
poet. = poetry
    poetical
    poetically
pos. = positive
    positively
pref. = prefix
    prefixed
prep. = preposition
    prepositional
    prepositionally
prim. = primitive
prob. = probable
    probably

prol. = prolonged [33]
    prolongation
pron. = pronoun
    pronominal
    pronominally
prop. = properly
prox. = proximate
    proximately
recip. = reciprocal
    reciprocally
redupl. = reduplicated [34]
    reduplication
refl. = reflexive [35]
    reflexively
reg. = regular
rel. = relative
    relatively
relig. = religion
    religious
    religiously
Rom. = Roman
second. = secondary
    secondarily
signif. = signification
    signifying
short. = shorter
    shortened
sing. = singular
spec. = specific
    specifically
streng. = strengthening
subdiv. = subdivision
    subdivisional
    subdivisionally
subj. = subjectively
    subjective
    subject
substit. = substituted
suff. = suffix
superl. = superlative [36]
    superlatively
symb. = symbolic
    symbolical
    symbolically
tech. = technical
    technically
term. = termination
tran. = transitive [37]
    transitively
transc. = transcription
transm. = transmutation [38]
transp. = transposed [39]
    transposition
typ. = typical
    typically
uncert. = uncertain
    uncertainly
var. = various
    variation
voc. = vocative (case) [40]
vol. = voluntary
    voluntarily

---

[1] often indicating the direct object of an action verb

[2] part of a word which, when attached to the beginning of the word is called a prefix; if attaching within a word, an infix; and if at the end, a suffix

[3] "the" is the definite article; "a" and "an" are indefinite articles

[4] expressing or denoting causation

[5] the comparative of an adjective or adverb expresses a greater degree of an attribute, e.g. "higher"; "more slowly"

[6] a systematic array of various verbal forms

[7] the condition in Hebrew and Aramaic when two adjacent nouns are combined semantically as follows, e.g."sword" + "king" = "(the) sword of (the) king" or "(the) king's sword". These languages tend to throw the stress of the entire noun phrase toward the end of the whole expression.

[8] a shortened form of a word. It is made by omitting or combining some elements or by reducing vowels or syllables, e.g. "is not" becomes "isn't".

[9] often the indirect object of an action verb

[10] the definite article ("the")

[11] demonstrative pronouns which point (show), e.g. "this," "that"

[12] derived from a noun

[13] a grammatical form which expresses smallness and/or endearment

[14] a construction which leaves out understood words

[15] the historical origin of a word

[16] the use of a pleasant, polite, or harmless-sounding word or phrase to hide harsh, rude, or infamous truths, e.g. "to pass away" = "to die"

[17] a linguistic mechanism to make pronunciation easier, e.g. "an" before "hour" instead of "a"

[18] when a general term can denote an entire class of things

[19] speech sounds which are produced deep in the throat

[20] the mood which expresses a command

[21] used of a tense which expresses a continuous but unfinished action or state

[22] used of a verbal aspect which denotes the beginning of an action

[23] used of the mood which expresses a verbal action as actually occurring (not hypothetical)

[24] an exclamation which expresses emotion

[25] indicating a question

[26] referring to verbs which do not govern direct objects

[27] reflexive

[28] capable of multiplying or tending to multiply

[29] This shows the position or the order within a series, e.g. "second"; the corresponding cardinal number is "two".

[30] the written system of spelling in a given language

[31] a name derived from that of a paternal ancestor, often created by an affix in various languages

[32] a rearrangement

[33] lengthening a pronunciation

[34] the repetition of a letter or syllable to form a new, inflected word

[35] denoting an action by the subject upon itself

[36] expressing the highest degree of comparison of the quality indicated by an adjective or an adverb, e.g. "highest"; "most timely"

[37] expressing an action directed toward a person or a thing (the direct object)

[38] the change of one grammatical element to another

[39] switching word order

[40] an inflection which is used when one is addressing a person or a thing directly, e.g. "John, come here!"

HEBREW AND ARAMAIC DICTIONARY OF THE OLD TESTAMENT

א

1. אָב **'âb**, awb; a prim. word; father in a lit. and immed., or fig. and remote application:— chief, (fore-) father (l-less)l, × patrimony, principal. Comp. names in "Abi-".

2. אַב **'ab** (Chald.), ab; corresp. to 1:— father.

3. אֵב **'êb**, abe; from the same as 24; a green plant:— greenness, fruit.

4. אֵב **'êb** (Chald.), abe; corresp. to 3:— fruit.

אֹב **'ôb**. See 178.

5. אֲבַגְתָא **'Ăbagthâ'**, ab-ag-thaw'; of for. or.; Abagtha, a eunuch of Xerxes:— Abagtha.

6. אָבַד **'âbad**, aw-bad'; a prim. root; prop. to wander away, i.e. lose oneself; by impl. to perish (caus. destroy):— break, destroy (-uction), + not escape, fail, lose, (cause to, make) perish, spend, × and surely, take, be undone, × utterly, be void of, have no way to flee.

7. אֲבַד **'ăbad** (Chald.), ab-ad'; corresp. to 6:— destroy, perish.

8. אֹבֵד **'ôbêd**, o-bade'; act. of part. of 6; (concr.) wretched or (abstr.) destruction:— perish.

9. אֲבֵדָה **'ăbêdâh**, ab-ay-daw'; from 6; concr. something lost; abstr. destruction, i.e. Hades:— lost. Comp. 10.

10. אֲבֵדֹה **'ăbaddôh**, ab-ad-do'; the same as 9, miswritten for 11; a perishing:— destruction.

11. אֲבַדּוֹן **'ăbaddôwn**, ab-ad-done'; intens. from 6; abstr. a perishing; concr. Hades:— destruction.

12. אַבְדָן **'abdân**, ab-dawn'; from 6; a perishing:— destruction.

13. אָבְדָן **'obdân**, ob-dawn'; from 6; a perishing:— destruction.

14. אָבָה **'âbâh**, aw-baw'; a prim. root; to breathe after, i.e. (fig.) to be acquiescent:— consent, rest content, will, be willing.

15. אָבֶה **'âbeh**, aw-beh'; from 14; longing:— desire.

16. אֵבֶה **'êbeh**, ay-beh'; from 14 (in the sense of bending toward); the papyrus:— swift.

17. אֲבוֹי **'ăbôwy**, ab-o'ee; from 14 (in the sense of desiring); want:— sorrow.

18. אֵבוּס **'êbûwç**, ay-booce'; from 75; a manger or stall:— crib.

19. אִבְחָה **'ibchâh**, ib-khaw'; from an unused root (appar. mean. to turn); brandishing of a sword:— point.

20. אֲבַטִּיחַ **'ăbaṭṭîyach**, ab-at-tee'-akh; of uncert. der.; a melon (only plur.):— melon.

21. אֲבִי **'Ăbîy**, ab-ee'; from 1; fatherly; Abi, Hezekiah's mother:— Abi.

22. אֲבִיאֵל **'Ăbîy'êl**, ab-ee-ale'; from 1 and 410; father (i.e. possessor) of God; Abiel, the name of two Isr.:— Abiel.

23. אֲבִיאָסָף **'Ăbîy'âçâph**, ab-ee-aw-sawf'; from 1 and 622; father of gathering (i.e. gatherer); Abiasaph, an Isr.:— Abiasaph.

24. אָבִיב **'âbîyb**, aw-beeb'; from an unused root (mean. to be tender); green, i.e. a young ear of grain; hence, the name of the month Abib or Nisan:— Abib, ear, green ears of corn.

25. אֲבִי גִבְעוֹן **'Ăbîy Gib'ôwn**, ab-ee' ghib-one'; from 1 and 1391; father (i.e. founder) of Gibon; Abi-Gibon, perh. an Isr.:— father of Gibeon.

26. אֲבִיגַיִל **'Ăbîygayil**, ab-ee-gah'-yil, or short.

אֲבִיגַל **'Ăbîygal**, ab-ee-gal'; from 1 and 1524; father (i.e. source) of joy; Abigail or Abigal, the name of two Israelitesses:— Abigail.

27. אֲבִידָן **'Ăbîydân**, ab-ee-dawn'; from 1 and 1777; father of judgment (i.e. judge); Abidan, an Isr.:— Abidan.

28. אֲבִידָע **'Ăbîydâ'**, ab-ee-daw'; from 1 and 3045; father of knowledge (i.e. knowing); Abida, a son of Abraham by Keturah:— Abida, Abidah.

29. אֲבִיָּה **'Ăbîyâh**, ab-ee-yaw'; or prol.

אֲבִיָּהוּ **'Ăbîyâhûw**, ab-ee-yaw'-hoo; from 1 and 3050; father (i.e. worshipper) of Jah; Abijah, the name of several Isr. men and two Israelitesses:— Abiah, Abijah.

30. אֲבִיהוּא **'Ăbîyhûw'**, ab-ee-hoo'; from 1 and 1931; father (i.e. worshipper) of Him (i.e. God); Abihu, a son of Aaron:— Abihu.

31. אֲבִיהוּד **'Ăbîyhûwd**, ab-ee-hood'; from 1 and 1935; father (i.e. possessor) of renown; Abihud, the name of two Isr.:— Abihud.

32. אֲבִיחַיִל **'Ăbîyhayil**, ab-ee-hah'-yil; or (more correctly)

אֲבִיחַיִל **'Ăbîychayil**, ab-ee-khah'-yil; from 1 and 2428; father (i.e. possessor) of might; Abihail or Abichail, the name of three Isr. and two Israelitesses:— Abihail.

33. אֲבִי הָעֶזְרִי **'Ăbîy hâ-'Ezrîy**, ab-ee'-haw-ez-ree'; from 44 with the art. ins.; father of the Ezrite; an Abiezrite or desc. of Abiezer:— Abiezrite.

34. אֶבְיוֹן **'ebyôwn**, eb-yone'; from 14, in the sense of want (espec. in feeling); destitute:— beggar, needy, poor (man).

35. אֲבִיוֹנָה **'abîyôwnâh**, ab-ee-yo-naw'; from 14; provocative of desire; the caper berry (from its stimulative taste):— desire.

אֲבִיחַיִל **'Ăbîychayil**. See 32.

36. אֲבִיטוּב **'Ăbîyṭûwb**, ab-ee-toob'; from 1 and 2898; father of goodness (i.e. good); Abitub, an Isr.:— Abitub.

37. אֲבִיטַל **'Ăbîyṭal**, ab-ee-tal'; from 1 and 2919; father of dew (i.e. fresh); Abital, a wife of King David:— Abital.

38. אֲבִיָּם **'Ăbîyâm**, ab-ee-yawm'; from 1 and 3220; father of (the) sea (i.e. seaman); Abijam (or Abijah), a king of Judah:— Abijam.

39. אֲבִימָאֵל **'Ăbîymâ'êl**, ab-ee-maw-ale'; from 1 and an elsewhere unused (prob. for.) word; father of Mael (appar. some Arab tribe); Abimael, a son of Joktan:— Abimael.

40. אֲבִימֶלֶךְ **'Ăbîymelek**, ab-ee-mel'-ek; from 1 and 4428; father of (the) king; Abimelek, the name of two Philistine kings and of two Isr.:— Abimelech.

41. אֲבִינָדָב **'Ăbîynâdâb**, ab-ee-naw-dawb'; from 1 and 5068; father of generosity (i.e. liberal); Abinadab, the name of four Isr.:— Abinadab.

42. אֲבִינֹעַם **'Ăbîynô'am**, ab-ee-no'-am; from 1 and 5278; father of pleasantness (i.e. gracious); Abinoam, an Isr.:— Abinoam.

אֲבִינֵר **'Ăbîynêr**. See 74.

43. אֶבְיָסָף **'Ebyâçâph**, eb-yaw-sawf'; contr. from 23; Ebjasaph, an Isr.:— Ebiasaph.

44. אֲבִיעֶזֶר **'Ăbîy'ezer**, ab-ee-ay'-zer; from 1 and 5829; father of help (i.e. helpful); Abiezer, the name of two Isr.:— Abiezer.

45. אֲבִי־עַלְבוֹן **'Ăbîy-'albôwn**, ab-ee-al-bone'; from 1 and an unused root of uncert. der.; prob. father of strength (i.e. valiant); Abialbon, an Isr.:— Abialbon.

46. אָבִיר **'âbîyr**, aw-beer'; from 82; mighty (spoken of God):— mighty (one).

47. אַבִּיר **'abbîyr**, ab-beer'; from 46:— angel, bull, chiefest, mighty (one), stout l-heartedl, strong (one), valiant.

48. אֲבִירָם **'Ăbîyrâm**, ab-ee-rawm'; from 1 and 7311; father of height (i.e. lofty); Abiram, the name of two Isr.:— Abiram.

49. אֲבִישַׁג **'Ăbîyshag**, ab-ee-shag'; from 1 and 7686; father of error (i.e. blundering); Abishag, a concubine of David:— Abishag.

50. אֲבִישׁוּעַ **'Ăbîyshûwa'**, ab-ee-shoo'-ah; from 1 and 7771; father of plenty (i.e. prosperous); Abishua, the name of two Isr.:— Abishua.

51. אֲבִישׁוּר **'Ăbîyshûwr**, ab-ee-shoor'; from 1 and 7791; father of (the) wall (i.e. perh. mason); Abishur, an Isr.:— Abishur.

52. אֲבִישַׁי **'Ăbîyshay**, ab-ee-shah'ee; or (short.)

אַבְשַׁי **'Abshay**, ab-shah'ee; from 1 and 7862; father of a gift (i.e. prob. generous); Abishai, an Isr.:— Abishai.

53. אֲבִישָׁלוֹם **'Ăbîyshâlôwm**, ab-ee-shaw-lome'; or (short.)

אַבְשָׁלוֹם **'Abshâlôwm**, ab-shaw-lome'; from 1 and 7965; father of peace (i.e. friendly); Absalom, a son of David; also (the fuller form) a later Isr.:— Abishalom, Absalom.

54. אֶבְיָתָר **'Ebyâthâr**, ab-yaw-thawr'; contr. from 1 and 3498; father of abundance (i.e. liberal); Ebjathar, an Isr.:— Abiathar.

1

55. אָבַק **'âbak**, *aw-bak´*; a prim. root; prob. to *coil* upward:— mount up.

56. אָבַל **'âbal**, *aw-bal´*; a prim. root; to *bewail*:— lament, mourn.

57. אָבֵל **'âbêl**, *aw-bale´*; from 56; *lamenting*:— mourn (-er, -ing).

58. אָבֵל **'âbêl**; from an unused root (mean. to *be grassy*); a *meadow*:— plain. Comp. also the prop. names beginning with Abel-.

59. אָבֵל **'Âbêl**, *aw-bale´*; from 58; a *meadow*; *Abel*, the name of two places in Pal.:— Abel.

60. אֵבֶל **'êbel**, *ay´-bel*; from 56; *lamentation*:— mourning.

61. אֲבָל **'âbâl**, *ab-awl´*; appar. from 56 through the idea of *negation*; *nay* (i.e. *truly* or *yet*):— but, indeed, nevertheless, verily.

62. אָבֵל בֵּית־מַעֲכָה **'Âbêl Bêyth-Mä'akâh**, *aw-bale´ bayth ma-a-kaw´*; from 58 and 1004 and 4601; *meadow of Beth-Maakah*; *Abel of Beth-maakah*, a place in Pal.:— Abel-beth-maachah, Abel of Beth-maachah.

63. אָבֵל הַשִּׁטִּים **'Âbêl hash-Shiṭṭîym**, *aw-bale´ hash-shit-teem´*; from 58 and the plur. of 7848, with the art. ins.; *meadow of the acacias*; *Abel hash-Shittim*, a place in Pal.:— Abel-shittim.

64. אָבֵל כְּרָמִים **'Âbêl Kᵉrâmîym**, *aw-bale´ ker-aw-meem´*; from 58 and the plur. of 3754; *meadow of vineyards*; *Abel-Keramim*, a place in Pal.:— plain of the vineyards.

65. אָבֵל מְחוֹלָה **'Âbêl Mᵉchôwlâh**, *aw-bale´ mekh-o-law´*; from 58 and 4246; *meadow of dancing*; *Abel-Mecholah*, a place in Pal.:— Abel-meholah.

66. אָבֵל מַיִם **'Âbêl Mayim**, *aw-bale´ mah´-yim*; from 58 and 4325; *meadow of water*; *Abel-Majim*, a place in Pal.:— Abel-maim.

67. אָבֵל מִצְרַיִם **'Âbêl Mitsrayim**, *aw-bale´ mits-rah´-yim*; from 58 and 4714; *meadow of Egypt*; *Abel-Mitsrajim*, a place in Pal.:— Abel-mizraim.

68. אֶבֶן **'eben**, *eh´-ben*; from the root of 1129 through the mean. to *build*; a *stone*:— + carbuncle, + mason, + plummet, (chalk-, hail-, head-, sling-) stone (-ny), (divers) weight (-s).

69. אֶבֶן **'eben** (Chald.), *eh´-ben*; corresp. to 68:— stone.

70. אֹבֶן **'ôben**, *o´-ben*; from the same as 68; a *pair of stones* (only dual) or a potter's *wheel* or a midwife's *stool* (consisting alike of two horizontal disks with a support between):— wheel, stool.

71. אֲבָנָה **'Âbânâh**, *ab-aw-naw´*; perh. fem. of 68; *stony*; *Abanah*, a river near Damascus:— Abana. Comp. 549.

72. אֶבֶן הָעֵזֶר **'Eben hâ-'êzer**, *eh´-ben haw-e´-zer*; from 68 and 5828 with the art. ins.; *stone of the help*; *Eben-ha-Ezer*, a place in Pal.:— Ebenezer.

73. אַבְנֵט **'abnêṭ**, *ab-nate´*; of uncert. der.; a *belt*:— girdle.

74. אַבְנֵר **'Abnêr**, *ab-nare´*; or (fully)

אֲבִינֵר **'Ăbîynêr**; from 1

and 5216; *father of light* (i.e. *enlightening*); *Abner*, an Isr.:— Abner.

75. אָבָס **'âbaç**, *aw-bas´*; a prim. root; to *fodder*:— fatted, stalled.

76. אַבְעֲבֻעָה **'aba'bû'âh**, *ab-ah-boo-aw´*; (by redupl.) from an unused root (mean. to *belch* forth); an inflammatory *pustule* (as *eruption*):— blains.

77. אָבֵץ **'Ebets**, *eh´-bets*; from an unused root prob. mean. to *gleam*; *conspicuous*; *Ebets*, a place in Pal.:— Abez.

78. אִבְצָן **'Ibtsân**, *ib-tsawn´*; from the same as 76; *splendid*; *Ibtsan*, an Isr.:— Ibzan.

79. אָבַק **'âbaq**, *aw-bak´*; a prim. root, prob. to *float* away (as vapor), but used only as denom. from 80; to *bedust*, i.e. *grapple*:— wrestle.

80. אָבָק **'âbâq**, *aw-bawk´*; from root of 79; light *particles* (as *volatile*):— (small) dust, powder.

81. אֲבָקָה **'âbâqâh**, *ab-aw-kaw´*; fem. of 80:— powder.

82. אָבַר **'âbar**, *aw-bar´*; a prim. root; to *soar*:— fly.

83. אֵבֶר **'êber**, *ay-ber´*; from 82; a *pinion*:— (long-) wing (-ed).

84. אֶבְרָה **'ebrâh**, *eb-raw´*; fem. of 83:— feather, wing.

85. אַבְרָהָם **'Abrâhâm**, *ab-raw-hawm´*; contr. from 1 and an unused root (prob. mean. to *be populous*); *father of a multitude*; *Abraham*, the later name of Abram:— Abraham.

86. אַבְרֵךְ **'abrêk**, *ab-rake´*; prob. an Eg. word mean. *kneel*:— bow the knee.

87. אַבְרָם **'Abrâm**, *ab-rawm´*; contr. from 48; *high father*; *Abram*, the original name of Abraham:— Abram.

אַבְשַׁי **'Abshay**. See 52.

אַבְשָׁלוֹם **'Abshâlôwm**. See 53.

88. אֹבֹה **'Ôbôth**, *o-both´*; plur. of 178; *water-skins*; *Oboth*, a place in the Desert:— Oboth.

89. אָגֵא **'Âgê**, *aw-gay´*; of uncert. der. [comp. 90]; *Agê*, an Isr.:— Agee.

90. אֲגַג **'Agag**, *ag-ag´*; or

אֲגָג **'Âgâg**, *ag-awg´*; of uncert. der. [comp. 89]; *flame*; *Agag*, a title of Amalekitish kings:— Agag.

91. אֲגָגִי **'Ăgâgîy**, *ag-aw-ghee´*; patrial or patron. from 90; an *Agagite* or descendent (subject) of Agag:— Agagite.

92. אֲגֻדָּה **'ăguddâh**, *ag-ood-daw´*; fem. pass. part. of an unused root (mean. to *bind*); a *band*, *bundle*, *knot*, or *arch*:— bunch, burden, troop.

93. אֱגוֹז **'ĕgôwz**, *eg-oze´*; prob of Pers. or.; a *nut*:— nut.

94. אָגוּר **'Âgûwr**, *aw-goor´*; pass. part. of 103; *gathered* (i.e. *received* among the sages); *Agur*, a fanciful name for Solomon:— Agur.

95. אֲגוֹרָה **'ăgôwrâh**, *ag-o-raw´*; from the same as 94; prop. something *gathered*, i.e. perh. a *grain* or *berry*; used only of a small (silver) *coin*:— piece [of] silver.

96. אֵגֶל **'egel**, *eh´-ghel*; from an unused root (mean. to *flow* down or together as drops); a *reservoir*:— drop.

97. אֶגְלַיִם **'Eglayim**, *eg-lah´-yim*; dual of 96; a *double pond*; *Eglajim*, a place in Moab:— Eglaim.

98. אֲגַם **'ăgam**, *ag-am´*; from an unused root (mean. to *collect* as water); a *marsh*; hence, a *rush* (as growing in swamps); hence, a *stockade* of reeds:— pond, pool, standing [water].

99. אָגֵם **'âgêm**, *aw-game´*; prob. from the same as 98 (in the sense of *stagnant* water); fig. *sad*:— pond.

100. אַגְמוֹן **'agmôwn**, *ag-mone´*; from the same as 98; a marshy *pool* [others from a different root, a *kettle*]; by impl. a *rush* (as growing there); collect. a rope of rushes:— bulrush, caldron, hook, rush.

101. אַגָּן **'aggân**, *ag-gawn´*; prob. from 5059; a *bowl* (as *pounded* out hollow):— basin, cup, goblet.

102. אַגָּף **'aggâph**, *ag-gawf´*; prob. from 5062 (through the idea of *impending*); a *cover* or *heap*; i.e. (only plur.) *wings* of an army, or *crowds* of troops:— bands.

103. אָגַר **'âgar**, *aw-gar´*; a prim. root; to *harvest*:— gather.

104. אִגְּרָא **'iggᵉrâ** (Chald.), *ig-er-aw´*; of Pers. or.; an *epistle* (as carried by a state courier or postman):— letter.

105. אַגַרְטָל **'ăgarṭâl**, *ag-ar-tawl´*; of uncert. der.; a *basin*:— charger.

106. אֶגְרֹף **'egrôph**, *eg-rofe´*; from 1640 (in the sense of *grasping*); the *clenched* hand:— fist.

107. אִגֶּרֶת **'iggereth**, *ig-eh´-reth*; fem. of 104; an *epistle*:— letter.

108. אֵד **'êd**, *ade* from the same as 181 (in the sense of *enveloping*); a *fog*:— mist, vapor.

109. אָדַב **'âdab**, *aw-dab´*; a prim. root; to *languish*:— grieve.

110. אַדְבְּאֵל **'Adbᵉ'êl**, *ad-beh-ale´*; prob. from 109 (in the sense of *chastisement*) and 410; *disciplined of God*; *Adbeël*, a son of Ishmael:— Adbeel.

111. אֲדַד **'Ădad**, *ad-ad´*; prob. an orth. var. for 2301; *Adad* (or Hadad), an Edomite:— Hadad.

112. אִדּוֹ **'Iddôw**, *id-do´*; of uncert. der.; *Iddo*, an Isr.:— Iddo.

אֱדוֹם **'Ĕdôwm**. See 123.

אֱדוֹמִי **'Ĕdôwmîy**. See 30.

113. אָדוֹן **'âdôwn**, *aw-done´*; or (short.)

אָדֹן **'âdôn**, *aw-done´*; from an unused root (mean. to *rule*); *sovereign*, i.e. *controller* (human or divine):— lord, master, owner. Comp. also names beginning with "Adoni-".

114. אַדּוֹן **'Addôwn**, *ad-done´*; prob. intens. for 113; *powerful*; *Addon*, appar. an Isr.:— Addon.

115. אֲדוֹרַיִם **'Ădôwrayim**, *ad-o-rah´-yim*; dual from 142 (in the sense of *eminence*); *double mound*; *Adorajim*, a place in Pal.:— Adoraim.

116. אֱדַיִן **'ĕdayin** (Chald.), *ed-ah´-yin*; of uncert. der.; *then* (of time):— now, that time, then.

117. אַדִּיר **'addîyr**, *ad-deer´*; from 142; *wide* or (gen.) *large*; fig. *powerful*:— excellent, famous, gallant, glorious,

goodly, lordly, mighty (-ier, one), noble, principal, worthy.

118. אֲדַלְיָא **'Ădalyâ**, ad-al-yaw'; of Pers. der.; *Adalja*, a son of Haman:— Adalia.

119. אָדַם **'âdam**, aw-dam'; to *show blood* (in the face), i.e. *flush* or turn rosy:— be (dyed, made) red (ruddy).

120. אָדָם **'âdâm**, aw-dawm'; from 119; *ruddy*, i.e. *a human being* (an individual or the species, *mankind*, etc.):— × another, + hypocrite, + common sort, × low, man (mean, of low degree), person.

121. אָדָם **'Âdâm**, aw-dawm'; the same as 120; *Adam* the name of the first man, also of a place in Pal.:— Adam.

122. אָדֹם **'âdôm**, aw-dome'; from 119; *rosy:*— red, ruddy.

123. אֱדֹם **'Ĕdôm**, ed-ome'; or (fully)

אֱדוֹם **'Ĕdôwm**, ed-ome'; from 122; *red* [see Gen. 25:25]; *Edom*, the elder twin-brother of Jacob; hence, the region (*Idumæa*) occupied by him:— Edom, Edomites, Idumea.

124. אֹדֶם **'ôdem**, o'-dem; from 119; *redness*, i.e. the *ruby, garnet*, or some other red gem:— sardius.

125. אֲדַמְדָּם **'ădamdâm**, ad-am-dawm'; redupl. from 119; *reddish:*— (somewhat) reddish.

126. אַדְמָה **'Admâh**, ad-maw'; contr. for 127; *earthy; Admah*, a place near the Dead Sea:— Admah.

127. אֲדָמָה **'ădâmâh**, ad-aw-maw'; from 119; *soil* (from its gen. *redness*):— country, earth, ground, husband [-man] (-ry), land.

128. אֲדָמָה **'Ădâmâh**, ad-aw-maw'; the same as 127; *Adamah*, a place in Pal.:— Adamah.

אַדְמֹנִי **'admôwniy**. See 132.

129. אֲדָמִי **'Ădâmîy**, ad-aw-mee'; from 127; *earthy; Adami*, a place in Pal.:— Adami.

130. אֱדֹמִי **'Ĕdômîy**, ed-o-mee'; or (fully)

אֱדוֹמִי **'Ĕdôwmîy**, ed-o-mee'; patron. from 123; an *Edomite*, or desc. from (or inhab. of) Edom:— Edomite. See 726.

131. אֲדֻמִּים **'Ădummîym**, ad-oom-meem'; plur. of 121; *red* spots; *Adummim*, a pass in Pal.:— Adummim.

132. אַדְמֹנִי **'admônîy**, ad-mo-nee'; or (fully)

אַדְמוֹנִי **'admôwniy**, ad-mo-nee'; from 119; *reddish* (of the hair or the complexion):— red, ruddy.

133. אַדְמָתָא **'Admâthâ**, ad-maw-thaw'; prob. of Pers. der.; *Admatha*, a Pers. nobleman:— Admatha.

134. אֶדֶן **'eden**, eh'-den; from the same as 113 (in the sense of *strength*); a *basis* (of a building, a column, etc.):— foundation, socket.

אָדֹן **'âdôn**. See 113.

135. אַדָּן **'Addân**, ad-dawn'; intens. from the same as 134; *firm; Addan*, an Isr.:— Addan.

136. אֲדֹנָי **'Ădônây**, ad-o-noy'; am em-

phat. form of 113; the *Lord* (used as a proper name of God only):— (my) Lord.

137. אֲדֹנִי־בֶזֶק **'Ădônîy-Bezeq**, ad-o''-nee-beh'-zek; from 113 and 966; *lord of Bezek; Adoni-Bezek;* a Canaanitish king:— Adoni-bezek.

138. אֲדֹנִיָּה **'Ădônîyâh**, ad-o-nee-yaw'; or (prol.)

אֲדֹנִיָּהוּ **'Ădônîyâhûw**, ad-o-nee-yaw'-hoo; from 113 and 3050; *lord* (i.e. worshipper) of Jah; *Adonijah*, the name of three Isr.:— Adonijah.

139. אֲדֹנִי־צֶדֶק **'Ădônîy-Tsedeq**, ad-o''-nee-tseh'-dek; from 113 and 6664; *lord of justice; Adoni-Tsedek*, a Canaanitish king:— Adonizedec.

140. אֲדֹנִיקָם **'Ădônîyqâm**, ad-o-nee-kawm'; from 113 and 6965; *lord of rising* (i.e. *high*); *Adonikam*, the name of one or two Isr.:— Adonikam.

141. אֲדֹנִירָם **'Ădônîyrâm**, ad-o-nee-rawm'; from 113 and 7311; *lord of height; Adoniram*, an Isr.:— Adoniram.

142. אָדַר **'âdar**, aw-dar'; a prim. root; to *expand*, i.e. *be great* or (fig.) *magnificent:*— (become) glorious, honourable.

143. אֲדָר **'Ădâr**, ad-awr'; prob. of for. der.; perh. mean. *fire; Adar*, the 12th Heb. month:— Adar.

144. אֲדָר **'Ădâr** (Chald.), ad-awr'; corresp. to 143:— Adar.

145. אֶדֶר **'eder**, eh'-der; from 142; *amplitude*, i.e. (concr.) a *mantle*; also (fig.) *splendor:*— goodly, robe.

146. אַדָּר **'Addâr**, ad-dawr'; intens. from 142; *ample; Addar*, a place in Pal.; also an Isr.:— Addar.

147. אִדַּר **'iddar** (Chald.), id-dar'; intens. from a root corresp. to 142; *ample*, i.e. a threshing- *floor:*— threshing-floor.

148. אַדַּרְגָּזַר **'ădargâzêr** (Chald.), ad-ar''-gaw-zare'; from the same as 147 and 1505; a *chief diviner*, or *astrologer:*— judge.

149. אַדְרַזְדָּא **'adrazdâ** (Chald.), ad-raz-daw'; prob. of Pers. or.; *quickly* or *carefully:*— diligently.

150. אֲדַרְכֹּן **'ădarkôn**, ad-ar-kone'; of Pers. or.; a *daric* or Pers. coin:— dram.

151. אֲדֹרָם **'Ădôrâm**, ad-o-rawm'; contr. for 141; *Adoram* (or Adoniram), an Isr.:— Adoram.

152. אַדְרַמֶּלֶךְ **'Adrammelek**, ad-ram-meh'-lek; from 142 and 4428; *splendor of* (the) *king; Adrammelek*, the name of an Ass. idol, also of a son of Sennacherib:— Adrammelech.

153. אֶדְרַע **'edra'** (Chald.), ed-raw'; an orth. var. for 1872; an *arm*, i.e. (fig.) *power:*— force.

154. אֶדְרֶעִי **'edre'îy**, ed-reh'-ee; from the equiv. of 153; *mighty; Edrei*, the name of two places in Pal.:— Edrei.

155. אַדֶּרֶת **'addereth**, ad-deh'-reth; fem. of 117; something *ample* (as a *large* vine, a *wide* dress); also the same as 145:— garment, glory, goodly, mantle, robe.

156. אָדַשׁ **'âdash**, aw-dash'; a prim. root; to *tread* out (grain):— thresh.

157. אָהַב **'âhab**, aw-hab'; or

אָהֵב **'âhêb**, aw-habe'; a prim. root; to *have affection* for (sexually or otherwise):— (be-) love (-d, -ly, -r), like, friend.

158. אַהַב **'ahab**, ah'-hab; from 157; *affection* (in a good or a bad sense):— love (-r).

159. אֹהַב **'ôhab**, o'-hab; from 156; *mean.* the same as 158:— love.

160. אַהֲבָה **'ahăbâh**, ă-hab-aw'; fem. of 158 and mean. the same:— love.

161. אֹהַד **'Ôhad**, o'-had; from an unused root mean. to *be united; unity; Ohad*, an Isr.:— Ohad.

162. אֲהָהּ **'ăhâhh**, ă-haw'; appar. a prim. word expressing *pain* exclamatorily: *Oh!*:— ah, alas.

163. אֲהָוָא **'Ăhăvâ'**, ă-hav-aw'; prob. of for. or.; *Ahava*, a river of Bab.:— Ahava.

164. אֵהוּד **'Êhûwd**, ay-hood'; from the same as 161; *united; Ehud*, the name of two or three Isr.:— Ehud.

165. אֱהִי **'ĕhîy**, e-hee'; appar. an orth. var. for 346; *where:*— I will be (Hos. 13:10, 14) [which is often the rendering of the same Heb. form from 1961].

166. אָהַל **'âhal**, aw-hal'; a prim. root; to *be clear:*— shine.

167. אָהַל **'âhal**, aw-hal'; a denom. from 168; to *tent:*— pitch (remove) a tent.

168. אֹהֶל **'ôhel**, o'-hel; from 166; a *tent* (as *clearly* conspicuous from a distance):— covering, (dwelling) (place), home, tabernacle, tent.

169. אֹהֶל **'Ôhel**, o'-hel; the same as 168; *Ohel*, an Isr.:— Ohel.

170. אָהֳלָה **'Ohŏlâh**, ŏ-hol-aw'; in form a fem. of 168, but in fact for

אָהֳלָה **'Ohŏlâh**, ŏ-hol-aw'; from 168; *her tent* (i.e. idolatrous *sanctuary*); *Oholah*, a symbol. name for Samaria:— Aholah.

171. אָהֳלִיאָב **'Ohŏlîy'âb**, ŏ''-hol-e-awb'; from 168 and 1; *tent of* (his) *father; Oholiab*, an Isr.:— Aholiab.

172. אָהֳלִיבָה **'Ohŏlîybâh**, ŏ''-hol-ee-baw'; (similarly with 170) for

אָהֳלִיבָה **'Ohŏlîybâhh**, ŏ''-hol-e-baw'; from 168; *my tent* (is) *in her; Oholibah*, a symb. name for Judah:— Aholibah.

173. אָהֳלִיבָמָה **'Ohŏlîybâmâh**, ŏ''-hol-ee-baw-maw'; from 168 and 1116; *tent of* (the) *height; Oholibamah*, a wife of Esau:— Aholibamah.

174. אֲהָלִים **'ăhâlîym**, ă-haw-leem'; or (fem.)

אֲהָלוֹת **'ăhâlôwth**, ă-haw-loth' (only used thus in the plur.); of for. or.; *aloe* wood (i.e. sticks):— (tree of lign-) aloes.

175. אַהֲרֹן **'Ahărôwn**, ă-har-one'; of uncert. der.; *Aharon*, the brother of Moses:— Aaron.

176. או **'ôw**, o; presumed to be the "constr." or genitival form of

או **'av**, av; short. for 185; *desire* (and so prob. in Prov. 31:4); hence, (by way of alternative) *or*, also *if:*— also, and, either, if, at the least, × nor, or, otherwise, then, whether.

177. אֲרְאֵל **'Ûw'êl,** *oo-ale´;* from 176 and 410; *wish of God; Uel,* an Isr.:— Uel.

178. אוֹב **'ôwb,** *obe;* from the same as 1 (appar. through the idea of *prattling* a father's name); prop. a *mumble,* i.e. a water- *skin* (from its hollow sound); hence, a *necromancer* (ventriloquist, as from a jar):— bottle, familiar spirit.

179. אוֹבִיל **'Ôwbîyl,** *o-beel´;* prob. from 56; *mournful; Obil,* an Ishmaelite:— Obil.

180. אוֹבָל **'ûwbâl,** *oo-bawl´;* or (short.)

אֻבָל **'ubâl,** *oo-bawl´;* from 2986 (in the sense of 2988); a *stream:*— river.

181. אוּד **'ûwd,** *ood;* from an unused root mean. to *rake* together; a *poker* (for *turning* or *gathering* embers):— (fire-) brand.

182. אוֹדוֹת **'ôwdôwth,** *o-dōth´;* or (short.)

אֹדוֹת **'ôdôwth,** *o-dōth´* (only thus in the plur.); from the same as 181; *turnings* (i.e. *occasions);* (adv.) on *account of:*— (be-) cause, concerning, sake.

183. אָוָה **'âvâh,** *aw-vaw´;* a prim. root; to *wish* for:— covet, (greatly) desire, be desirous, long, lust (after).

184. אָוָה **'âvâh,** *aw-vaw´;* a prim. root; to *extend* or *mark* out:— point out.

185. אַוָּה **'avvâh,** *av-vaw´;* from 183; *longing:*— desire, lust after, pleasure.

186. אוּזַי **'Ûwzay,** *oo-zah´-ee;* perh. by perm. for 5813, *strong; Uzai,* an Isr.:— Uzai.

187. אוּזָל **'Ûwzâl,** *oo-zawl´;* of uncert. der.; *Uzal,* a son of Joktan:— Uzal.

188. אוֹי **'ôwy,** *ō´-ee;* prob. from 183 (in the sense of *crying* out after); *lamentation;* also interj. *Oh!*:— alas, woe.

189. אֱוִי **'Ĕvîy,** *ev-ee´;* prob. from 183; *desirous; Evi,* a Midianitish chief:— Evi.

אוֹיֵב **'ôwyêb.** See 341.

190. אוֹיָה **'ôwyâh,** *o-yaw´;* fem. of 188:— woe.

191. אֱוִיל **'ĕvîyl,** *ev-eel´;* from an unused root (mean. to *be perverse);* (fig.) *silly:*— fool (-ish) (man).

192. אֱוִיל מְרֹדַךְ **'Ĕvîyl Merôdak,** *ev-eel´ mer-o-dak´;* of Chald. der. and prob. mean. *soldier of Merodak; Evil-Merodak,* a Bab. king:— Evil-merodach.

193. אוּל **'ûwl,** *ool;* from an unused root mean. to *twist,* i.e. (by impl.) *be strong;* the *body* (as being *rolled* together); also *powerful:*— mighty, strength.

194. אוּלַי **'ûwlay,** *oo-lah´ee;* or (short.)

אֻלַי **'ulay,** *oo-lah´ee;* from 176; *if not;* hence, *perhaps:*— if so be, may be, peradventure, unless.

195. אוּלַי **'Ûwlay,** *oo-lah´ee;* of Pers. der.; the *Ulai* (or Eulæus), a river of Pers.:— Ulai.

196. אֱוִילִי **'ĕvîlîy,** *ev-ee-lee´;* from 191; *silly, foolish;* hence, (mor.) *impious:*— foolish.

197. אוּלָם **'ûwlâm,** *oo-lawm´;* or (short.)

אֻלָם **'ulâm,** *oo-lawm´;* from 481 (in the sense of *tying);* a *vestibule* (as *bound* to the building):— porch.

198. אוּלָם **'Ûwlâm,** *oo-lawm´;* appar. from 481 (in the sense of *dumbness);* solitary; *Ulam,* the name of two Isr.:— Ulam.

199. אוּלָם **'ûwlâm,** *oo-lawm´;* appar. a var. of 194; *however* or *on the contrary:*— as for, but, howbeit, in very deed, surely, truly, wherefore.

200. אֱוֶלֶת **'ivveleth,** *iv-veh´-leth;* from the same as 191; *silliness:*— folly, foolishly (-ness).

201. אוֹמָר **'Ôwmâr,** *o-mawr´;* from 559; *talkative; Omar,* a grandson of Esau:— Omar.

202. אוֹן **'ôwn,** *ōne;* prob. from the same as 205 (in the sense of *effort,* but successful); *ability, power,* (fig.) *wealth:*— force, goods, might, strength, substance.

203. אוֹן **'Ôwn,** *ōne;* the same as 202; *On,* an Isr.:— On.

204. אוֹן **'Ôwn,** *ōne;* or (short.);

אֹן **'Ôn,** *ōne;* of Eg. der.; *On,* a city of Egypt:— On.

205. אָוֶן **'âven,** *aw-ven´;* from an unused root perh. mean. prop. to *pant* (hence, to *exert* oneself, usually in vain; to *come* to *naught);* strictly *nothingness;* also *trouble, vanity, wickedness;* spec. an *idol:*— affliction, evil, false, idol, iniquity, mischief, mourners (-ing), naught, sorrow, unjust, unrighteous, vain ,vanity, wicked (-ness). Comp. 369.

206. אָוֶן **'Âven,** *aw´-ven;* the same as 205; *idolatry; Aven,* the contemptuous synonym of three places, one in Cæle-Syria, one in Egypt (On), and one in Pal. (Bethel):— Aven. See also 204, 1007.

207. אוֹנוֹ **'Ôwnôw,** *o-no´;* or (short.)

אֹנוֹ **'Ônôw,** *o-no´;* prol. from 202; *strong; Ono,* a place in Pal.:— Ono.

208. אוֹנָם **'Ôwnâm,** *o-nawm´;* a var. of 209; *strong; Onam,* the name of an Edomite and of an Isr.:— Onam.

209. אוֹנָן **'Ôwnân,** *o-nawn´;* a var. of 207; *strong; Onan,* a son of Judah:— Onan.

210. אוּפָז **'Ûwphâz,** *oo-fawz´;* perh. a corruption of 211; *Uphaz,* a famous gold region:— Uphaz.

211. אוֹפִיר **'Ôwphîyr,** *o-feer´;* or (short.)

אֹפִיר **'Ôphîyr,** *o-feer´;* and

אוֹפִר **'Ôwphir,** *o-feer´;* of uncert. der.; *Ophir,* the name of a son of Joktan, and of a gold region in the East:— Ophir.

212. אוֹפָן **'ôwphân,** *o-fawn´;* or (short.)

אֹפָן **'ôphân,** *o-fawn´;* from an unused root mean. to *revolve;* a *wheel:*— wheel.

אוֹפִר **'Ôwphîr.** See 211.

213. אוּץ **'ûwts,** *oots;* a prim. root; to *press;* (by impl.) to *be close, hurry, withdraw:*— (make) haste (-n, -y), labor, be narrow.

214. אוֹצָר **'ôwtsâr,** *o-tsawr´;* from 686; a *depository:*— armory, cellar, garner, store (-house), treasure (-house) (-y).

215. אוֹר **'ôwr,** *ore;* a prim. root; to *be* (caus. *make) luminous* (lit. and metaph.):— × break of day, glorious, kindle, (be, en-, give, show) light (-en, -ened), set on fire, shine.

216. אוֹר **'ôwr,** *ore;* from 215; *illumination* or (concr.) *luminary* (in every sense, incl. *lightning, happiness,* etc.):— bright, clear, + day, light (-ning), morning, sun.

217. אוּר **'ûwr,** *oor;* from 215; *flame,* hence, (in the plur.) the *East* (as being the region of light):— fire, light. See also 224.

218. אוּר **'Ûwr,** *oor;* the same as 217; *Ur,* a place in Chaldæa; also an Isr.:— Ur.

219. אוֹרָה **'ôwrâh,** *o-raw´;* fem. of 216; *luminousness,* i.e. (fig.) *prosperity;* also a plant (as being *bright):*— herb, light.

220. אֻרָה **'ăvêrâh,** *av-ay-raw´;* by transp. for 723; a *stall:*— cote.

221. אוּרִי **'Ûwrîy,** *oo-ree´;* from 217; *fiery; Uri,* the name of three Isr.:— Uri.

222. אוּרִיאֵל **'Ûwrîy'êl,** *oo-ree-ale´;* from 217 and 410; *flame of God; Uriel,* the name of two Isr.:— Uriel.

223. אוּרִיָּה **'Ûwrîyâh,** *oo-ree-yaw´;* or (prol.)

אוּרִיָּהוּ **'Ûwrîyâhûw,** *oo-ree-yaw´-hoo;* from 217 and 3050; *flame of Jah; Urijah,* the name of one Hittite and five Isr.:— Uriah, Urijah.

224. אוּרִים **'Ûwrîym,** *oo-reem´;* plur. of 217; *lights; Urim,* the oracular brilliancy of the figures in the high-priest's breastplate:— Urim.

אוֹרְנָה **'Ôwrenâh.** See 728.

225. אוּת **'ûwth,** *ooth;* a prim. root; prop. to *come,* i.e. (impl.) to *assent:*— consent.

226. אוֹת **'ôwth,** *ōth;* prob. from 225 (in the sense of *appearing);* a *signal* (lit. or fig.), as a *flag, beacon, monument, omen, prodigy, evidence,* etc.:— mark, miracle, (en-) sign, token.

227. אָז **'âz,** *awz;* a demonstr. adv.; *at that time* or *place;* also a conjunc., *therefore:*— beginning, for, from, hitherto, now, of old, once, since, then, at which time, yet.

228. אֱזָא **'ăzâ'** (Chald.), *az-zaw´;* or

אֱזָה **'ăzâh** (Chald.), *az-aw´;* to *kindle;* (by impl.) to *heat:*— heat, hot.

229. אֶזְבַּי **'Ezbay,** *ez-bah´ee;* prob. from 231; *hyssop-like; Ezbai,* an Isr.:— Ezbai.

230. אֲזַד **'ăzad** (Chald.), *az-zawd´;* of uncert. der.; *firm:*— be gone.

231. אֵזוֹב **'êzôwb,** *ay-zobe´;* prob. of for. der.; *hyssop:*— hyssop.

232. אֵזוֹר **'êzôwr,** *ay-zore´;* from 246; something *girt;* a *belt,* also a *band:*— girdle.

233. אֲזַי **'ăzay,** *az-ah´ee;* prob. from 227; *at that time:*— then.

234. אַזְכָּרָה **'azkârâh,** *az-kaw-raw´;* from 2142; a *reminder;* spec. *remembrance-offering:*— memorial.

235. אָזַל **'âzal,** *aw-zal´;* a prim. root; to *go away,* hence, to *disappear:*— fail, gad about, go to and fro [but in Ezek. 27:19 the word is rendered by many "from Uzal," by others "yarn"], be gone (spent).

236. אֲזַל **'ăzal** (Chald.), *az-al´;* the same as 235; to *depart:*— go (up).

237. אֵזֶל **'ezel,** *eh´-zel;* from 235; *depar-*

ture; *Ezel*, a memorial stone in Pal.:— Ezel.

238. אָזַן **'âzan**, *aw-zan´*; a prim. root; prob. to *expand*; but used only as a denom. from 241; to *broaden out the ear* (with the hand), i.e. (by impl.) to *listen*:— give (perceive by the) ear, hear (-ken). See 239.

239. אָזַן **'âzan**, *aw-zan´*; a prim. root [rather ident. with 238 through the idea of *scales* as if two ears]; to *weigh*, i.e. (fig.) *ponder*:— give good head.

240. אָזֵן **'âzên**, *aw-zane´*; from 238; a *spade* or *paddle* (as having a *broad* end):— weapon.

241. אֹזֶן **'ôzen**, *o´-zen*; from 238; *broadness*, i.e. (concr.) the *ear* (from its form in man):— + advertise, audience, + displease, ear, hearing, + show.

242. אֹזֶן שֶׁאֱרָה **'Uzzên She'ĕrâh**, *ooz-zane´ sheh-er-aw´*; from 238 and 7609; *plat of Sheerah* (i.e. settled by him); *Uzzen-Sheërah*, a place in Pal.:— Uzzen-sherah.

243. אַזְנוֹת תָּבוֹר **'Aznôwth Tâbôwr**, *az-nôth´ taw-bore´*; from 238 and 8396; *flats* (i.e. *tops*) *of Tabor* (i.e. situated on it); *Aznoth-Tabor*, a place in Pal.:— Aznoth-tabor.

244. אָזְנִי **'Oznîy**, *oz-nee´*; from 241; *having* (quick) *ears*; *Ozni*, an Isr.; also an *Oznite* (collect.), his desc.:— Ozni, Oznites.

245. אֲזַנְיָה **'Azanyâh**, *az-an-yaw´*; from 238 and 3050; *heard* by *Jah*; *Azanjah*, an Isr.:— Azaniah.

246. אֲזִקִּים **'ăziqqîym**, *az-ik-keem´*; a var. for 2131; *manacles*:— chains.

247. אָזַר **'âzar**, *aw-zar´*; a prim. root; to *belt*:— bind (compass) about, gird (up, with).

248. אֶזְרוֹעַ **'ezrôwa'**, *ez-ro´-ă*; a var. for 2220; the *arm*:— arm.

249. אֶזְרָח **'ezrâch**, *ez-rawkh´*; from 2224 (in the sense of *springing up*); a spontaneous *growth*, i.e. *native* (tree or persons):— bay tree, (home-) born (in the land), of the (one's own) country (nation).

250. אֶזְרָחִי **'Ezrâchîy**, *ez-raw-khee´*; patron. from 2246; an *Ezrachite* or desc. of Zerach:— Ezrahite.

251. אָח **'âch**, *awkh*; a prim. word; a *brother* (used in the widest sense of lit. relationship and metaph. affinity or resemblance [like 1]):— another, brother (-ly), kindred, like, other. Compare also the proper names beginning with "Ah-" or "Ahi-".

252. אָח **'ach** (Chald.), *akh*; corresp. to 251:— brother.

253. אָח **'âch**, *awkh*; a var. for 162; *Oh!* (expressive of grief or surprise):— ah, alas.

254. אָח **'âch**, *awkh*; of uncert. der.; a fire-*pot* or chafing-dish:— hearth.

255. אֹחַ **'ôach**, *o´-akh*; prob. from 253; a *howler* or lonesome wild animal:— doleful creature.

256. אַחְאָב **'Ach'âb**, *akh-awb´*; once (by contr.)

אֶחָב **'Echâb** (Jer. 29:22), *ekh-awb´*;

from 251 and 1; *brother* [i.e. *friend*] *of* (his) *father*; *Achab*, the name of a king of Israel and of a prophet at Bab.:— Ahab.

257. אַחְבָּן **'Achbân**, *akh-bawn´*; from 251 and 995; *brother* (i.e. *possessor*) of *understanding*; *Achban*, an Isr.:— Ahban.

258. אָחַד **'âchad**, *aw-khad´*; perh. a prim. root; to *unify*, i.e. (fig.) *collect* (one's thoughts):— go one way or other.

259. אֶחָד **'echâd**, *ekh-awd´*; a numeral from 258; prop. *united*, i.e. *one*; or (as an ord.) *first*:— a, alike, alone, altogether, and, any (-thing), apiece, a certain, [dai-]ly, each (one), + eleven, every, few, first, + highway, a man, once, one, only, other, some, together.

260. אָחוּ **'âchûw**, *aw´-khoo*; of uncert. (perh. Eg.) der.; a *bulrush* or any marshy grass (particularly that along the Nile):— flag, meadow.

261. אֵחוּד **'Êchûwd**, *ay-khood´*; from 258; *united*; *Echud*, the name of three Isr.:— Ehud.

262. אַחְוָה **'achvâh**, *akh-vaw´*; from 2331 (in the sense of 2324); an *utterance*:— declaration.

263. אַחֲוָה **'achăvâh** (Chald.), *akh-av-aw´*; corresp. to 262; *solution* (of riddles):— showing.

264. אַחֲוָה **'achăvâh**, *akh-av-aw´*; from 251; *fraternity*:— brotherhood.

265. אֲחוֹחַ **'Achôwach**, *akh-o´-akh*; by redupl. from 251; *brotherly*; *Achoach*, an Isr.:— Ahoah.

266. אֲחוֹחִי **'Achôwchîy**, *akh-o-khee´*; patron. from 264; an *Achochite* or desc. of Achoach:— Ahohite.

267. אֲחוּמַי **'Achûwmay**, *akh-oo-mah´-ee*; perh. from 251 and 4325; *brother* (i.e. *neighbour*) *of water*; *Achumai*, an Isr.:— Ahumai.

268. אָחוֹר **'âchôwr**, *aw-khore´*; or

אָחֹר **'âchôr**, *aw-khore´*; from 299; the *hinder* part; hence, (adv.) *behind*, *backward*; also (as facing north) the *West*:— after (-ward), back (part, -side, -ward), hereafter, (be-) hind (-er part), time to come, without.

269. אָחוֹת **'achôwth**, *aw-khôth´*; irreg. fem. of 251; a *sister* (used very widely [like 250], lit. and fig.):— (an-) other, sister, together.

270. אָחַז **'âchaz**, *aw-khaz´*; a prim. root; to *seize* (often with the accessory idea of holding in possession):— + be affrighted, bar, (catch, lay, take) hold (back), come upon, fasten, handle, portion, (get, have or take) possess (-ion).

271. אָחָז **'Âchâz**, *aw-khawz´*; from 270; *possessor*; *Achaz*, the name of a Jewish king and of an Isr.:— Ahaz.

272. אֲחֻזָּה **'ăchuzzâh**, *akh-ooz-zaw´*; fem. pass. part. from 270; something *seized*, i.e. a *possession* (espec. of land):— possession.

273. אַחְזַי **'Achzay**, *akh-zah´ee*; from 270; *seizer*; *Achzai*, an Isr.:— Ahasai.

274. אֲחַזְיָה **'Ăchazyâh**, *akh-az-yaw´*; or (prol.)

אֲחַזְיָהוּ **'Ăchazyâhûw**, *akh-az-yaw´-hoo*; from 270 and 3050; *Jah has seized*; *Achazjah*, the name of a Jewish and an Isr. king:— Ahaziah.

275. אֲחֻזָּם **'Ăchuzzâm**, *akh-ooz-zawm´*; from 270; *seizure*; *Achuzzam*, an Isr.:— Ahuzam.

276. אֲחֻזַּת **'Ăchuzzath**, *akh-ooz-zath´*; a var. of 272; *possession*; *Achuzzath*, a Philistine:— Ahuzzath.

277. אָחִי **'Âchîy**, *akh-ee´*; from 251; *brotherly*; *Achi*, the name of two Isr.:— Ahi.

278. אֵחִי **'Êchîy**, *ay-khee´*; prob. the same as 277; *Echi*, an Isr.:— Ehi.

279. אֲחִיאָם **'Ăchîy'âm**, *akh-ee-awm´*; from 251 and 517; *brother of* (the) *mother* (i.e. *uncle*); *Achiam*, an Isr.:— Ahiam.

280. אֲחִידָה **'ăchîydâh** (Chald.), *akh-ee-daw´*; corresp. to 2420, an *enigma*:— hard sentence.

281. אֲחִיָּה **'Ăchiyâh**, *akh-ee-yaw*; or (prol.)

אֲחִיָּהוּ **'Ăchiyâhûw**, *akh-ee-yaw´-hoo*; from 251 and 3050; *brother* (i.e. *worshipper*) *of Jah*; *Achijah*, the name of nine Isr.:— Ahiah, Ahijah.

282. אֲחִיהוּד **'Ăchîyhûwd**, *akh-ee-hood´*; from 251 and 1935; *brother* (i.e. *possessor*) *of renown*; *Achihud*, an Isr.:— Ahihud.

283. אַחְיוֹ **'Achyôw**, *akh-yo´*; prol. from 251; *brotherly*; *Achio*, the name of three Isr.:— Ahio.

284. אֲחִיחֻד **'Ăchîychûd**, *akh-ee-khood´*; from 251 and 2330; *brother of a riddle* (i.e. *mysterious*); *Achichud*, an Isr.:— Ahihud.

285. אֲחִיטוּב **'Ăchîyṭûwb**, *akh-ee-toob´*; from 251 and 2898; *brother of goodness*; *Achitub*, the name of several priests:— Ahitub.

286. אֲחִילוּד **'Ăchîylûwd**, *akh-ee-lood´*; from 251 and 3205; *brother of* one *born*; *Achilud*, an Isr.:— Ahilud.

287. אֲחִימוֹת **'Ăchîymôwth**, *akh-ee-môth´*; from 251 and 4191; *brother of death*; *Achimoth*, an Isr.:— Achimoth.

288. אֲחִימֶלֶךְ **'Ăchîymelek**, *akh-ee-meh´-lek*; from 251 and 4428; *brother of* (the) *king*; *Achimelek*, the name of an Isr. and of a Hittite:— Ahimelech.

289. אֲחִימַן **'Ăchîyman**, *akh-ee-man´*; or

אֲחִימָן **'Ăchîymân**, *akh-ee-mawn´*; from 251 and 4480; *brother of a portion* (i.e. *gift*); *Achiman*, the name of an Anakite and of an Isr.:— Ahiman.

290. אֲחִימַעַץ **'Ăchîyma'ats**, *akh-ee-mah´-ats*; from 251 and the equiv. of 4619; *brother of anger*; *Achimaats*, the name of three Isr.:— Ahimaaz.

291. אַחְיָן **'Achyân**, *akh-yawn´*; from 251; *brotherly*; *Achjan*, an Isr.:— Ahian.

292. אֲחִינָדָב **'Ăchîynâdâb**, *akh-ee-naw-dawb´*; from 251 and 5068; *brother of liberality*; *Achinadab*, an Isr.:— Ahinadab.

293. אֲחִינֹעַם **'Ăchîynô'am**, *akh-ee-no´-am*; from 251 and 5278; *brother of pleasantness*; *Achinoam*, the name of two Israelitesses:— Ahinoam.

294. אֲחִיסָמָךְ **'Ăchîyçâmâk**, *akh-ee-saw-mawk'*; from 251 and 5564; *brother of support; Achisamak*, an Isr.:— Ahisamach.

295. אֲחִיעֶזֶר **'Ăchîy'ezer**, *akh-ee-eh'-zer*; from 251 and 5828; *brother of help; Achiezer*, the name of two Isr.:— Ahiezer.

296. אֲחִיקָם **'Ăchîyqâm**, *akh-ee-kawm'*; from 251 and 6965; *brother of rising* (i.e. *high); Achikam*, an Isr.:— Ahikam.

297. אֲחִירָם **'Ăchîyrâm**, *akh-ee-rawm'*; from 251 and 7311; *brother of height* (i.e. *high); Achiram*, an Isr.:— Ahiram.

298. אֲחִירָמִי **'Ăchîyrâmîy**, *akh-ee-raw-mee'*; patron. from 297; an *Achiramite* or desc. (collect.) of Achiram:— Ahiramites.

299. אֲחִירַע **'Ăchîyra'**, *akh-ee-rah'*; from 251 and 7451; *brother of wrong; Achira*, an Isr.:— Ahira.

300. אֲחִישַׁחַר **'Ăchîyshachar**, *akh-ee-shakh'-ar*; from 251 and 7837; *brother of* (the) *dawn; Achishachar*, an Isr.:— Ahishar.

301. אֲחִישָׁר **'Ăchîyshâr**, *akh-ee-shawr'*; from 251 and 7891; *brother of* (the) *singer; Achishar*, an Isr.:— Ahishar.

302. אֲחִיתֹפֶל **'Ăchîythôphel**, *akh-ee-tho'-fel*; from 251 and 8602; *brother of folly; Achithophel*, an Isr.:— Ahithophel.

303. אַחְלָב **'Achlâb**, *akh-lawb'*; from the same root as 2459; *fatness* (i.e. *fertile); Achlab*, a place in Pal.:— Ahlab.

304. אַחְלַי **'Achlay**, *akh-lah'ee*; the same as 305; *wishful; Achlai*, the name of an Israelitess and of an Isr.:— Ahlai.

305. אַחְלַי **'achălay**, *akh-al-ah'ee*; or

אַחְלַי **'achăley**, *akh-al-ay'*; prob. from 253 and a var. of 3863; *would that!*:— O that, would God.

306. אַחְלָמָה **'achlâmâh**, *akh-law'-maw*; perh. from 2492 (and thus *dream-stone*); a gem. prob. the *amethyst*:— amethyst.

307. אַחְמְתָא **'Achmᵉthâ'**, *akh-me-thaw'*; of Pers. der.; *Achmetha* (i.e. *Ecbatana*), the summer capital of Persia:— Achmetha.

308. אֲחַזְבַּי **'Ăchaçbay**, *akh-as-bah'ee*; of uncert. der.; *Achasbai*, an Isr.:— Ahasbai.

309. אָחַר **'âchar**, *aw-khar'*; a prim. root; to *loiter* (i.e. *be behind*) by impl. to *procrastinate*:— continue, defer, delay, hinder, be late (slack), stay (there), tarry (longer).

310. אַחַר **'achar**, *akh-ar'*; from 309; prop. the *hind* part; gen. used as an adv. or conjunc., *after* (in various senses):— after (that, -ward), again, at, away from, back (from, -side), behind, beside, by, follow (after, -ing), forasmuch, from, hereafter, hinder end, + out (over) live, + persecute, posterity, pursuing, remnant, seeing, since, thence (-forth), when, with.

311. אַחַר **'achar** (Chald.), *akh-ar'*; corresp. to 310; *after*:— [here-] after.

312. אָחֵר **'achêr**, *akh-air'*; from 309; prop. *hinder*; gen. next, other, etc.:—

(an-) other man, following, next, strange.

313. אַחֵר **'Achêr**, *akh-air'*; the same as 312; *Acher*, an Isr.:— Aher.

314. אַחֲרוֹן **'achărôwn**, *akh-ar-one'*; or (short.)

אַחֲרֹן **'achărôn**, *akh-ar-one'*; from 309; *hinder*; gen. *late* or *last*; spec. (as facing the east) *western*:— after (-ward), to come, following, hind (-er, -ermost, -most), last, latter, rereward, ut(ter)most.

315. אַחְרַח **'Achrach**, *akh-rakh'*; from 310 and 251; *after* (his) *brother; Achrach*, an Isr.:— Aharah.

316. אַחְרְחֵל **'Acharchêl**, *akh-ar-kale'*; from 310 and 2426; *behind* (the) *intrenchment* (i.e. *safe); Acharchel*, an Isr.:— Aharhel.

317. אָחֳרִי **'ochŏrîy** (Chald.), *okh-or-ee'*; from 311; *other*:— (an-) other.

318. אָחֳרֵין **'ochŏrêyn** (Chald.), *okh-or-ane'*; or (short.)

אָחֳרֵן **'ochŏrên** (Chald.), *okh-or-ane'*; from 317; *last*:— at last.

319. אַחֲרִית **'achărîyth**, *akh-ar-eeth'*; from 310; the *last* or *end*, hence, the *future*; also *posterity*:— (last, latter) end (time), hinder (utter) -most, length, posterity, remnant, residue, reward.

320. אַחֲרִית **'achărîyth** (Chald.), *akh-ar-eeth'*; from 311; the same as 319; *later*:— latter.

321. אָחֳרָן **'ochŏrân** (Chald.), *okh-or-awn'*; from 311; the same as 317; *other*:— (an-) other.

אָחֳרֵן **'ochŏrên**. See 318.

322. אֲחֹרַנִּית **'ăchôrannîyth**, *akh-o-ran-neeth'*; prol. from 268; *backwards*:— back (-ward, again).

323. אֲחַשְׁדַּרְפָּן **'ăchashdarpan**, *akh-ash-dar-pan'*; of Pers. der.; a *satrap* or governor of a main province (of Persia):— lieutenant.

324. אֲחַשְׁדַּרְפָּן **ăchashdarpan** (Chald.), *akh-ash-dar-pan'*; corresp. to 323:— prince.

325. אֲחַשְׁוֵרוֹשׁ **'Ăchashvêrôwsh**, *akh-ash-vay-rōsh'*; or (short.)

אֲחַשְׁרֹשׁ **'Achashrôsh**, *akh-ash-rôsh'* (Esth. 10:1); of Pers. or.; *Achashverosh* (i.e. Ahasuerus or Artaxerxes, but in this case Xerxes), the title (rather than name) of a Pers. king:— Ahasuerus.

326. אֲחַשְׁתָּרִי **'ăchashtârîy**, *akh-ash-taw-ree'*; prob. of Pers. der.; an *achastarite* (i.e. *courier*); the designation (rather than name) of an Isr.:— Haakashtari [includ. the art.].

327. אֲחַשְׁתָּרָן **'ăchastârân**, *akh-ash-taw-rawn'*; of Pers. or.; a *mule*:— camel.

328. אַט **'aţ**, *at*; from an unused root perh. mean. to *move softly*; (as a noun) a *necromancer* (from their soft incantations), (as an adv.) *gently*:— charmer, gently, secret, softly.

329. אָטָד **'âţâd**, *aw-tawd'*; from an unused root prob. mean. to *pierce* or *make fast*; a *thorn*-tree (espec. the *buckthorn*):— Atad, bramble, thorn.

330. אֵטוּן **'êţûwn**, *ay-toon'*; from an unused root (prob. mean. to *bind*); prop. *twisted* (yarn), i.e. *tapestry*:— fine linen.

331. אָטַם **'âţam**, *aw-tam'*; a prim. root; to *close* (the lips or ears); by anal. to *contract* (a window by bevelled jambs):— narrow, shut, stop.

332. אָטַר **'âţar**, *aw-tar'*; a prim. root; to *close* up:— shut.

333. אָטֵר **'Âţêr**, *aw-tare'*; from 332; *maimed; Ater*, the name of three Isr.:— Ater.

334. אִטֵּר **'iţţêr**, *it-tare'*; from 332; *shut up*, i.e. *impeded* (as to the use of the right hand):— + left-handed.

335. אַי **'ay**, *ah'ee*; perh. from 370; *where?* hence, *how?*:— how, what, whence, where, whether, which (way).

336. אִי **'îy**, *ee*; prob. ident. with 335 (through the idea of a *query*); *not*:— island (Job 22:30).

337. אִי **'îy**, *ee*; short. from 188; *alas!*:— woe.

338. אִי **'îy**, *ee*; prob. ident. with 337 (through the idea of a *doleful* sound); a *howler* (used only in the plur.), i.e. any solitary wild creature:— wild beast of the islands.

339. אִי **'îy**, *ee*; from 183; prop. a *habitable* spot (as *desirable*); dry *land*, a *coast*, an *island*:— country, isle, island.

340. אָיַב **'âyab**, *aw-yab'*; a prim. root; to *hate* (as one of an opposite tribe or party); hence, to *be hostile*:— be an enemy.

341. אֹיֵב **'ôyêb**, *o-yabe'*; or (fully)

אוֹיֵב **'ôwyêb**, *o-yabe'*; act. part. of 340; *hating*; an *adversary*:— enemy, foe.

342. אֵיבָה **'êybâh**, *ay-baw'*; from 340; *hostility*:— enmity, hatred.

343. אֵיד **'êyd**, *ade*; from the same as 181 (in the sense of *bending* down); *oppression*; by impl. *misfortune, ruin*:— calamity, destruction.

344. אַיָּה **'ayâh**, *ah-yaw'*; perh. from 337; the *screamer*, i.e. a *hawk*:— kite, vulture.

345. אַיָּה **'Ayâh**, *ah-yaw'*; the same as 344; *Ajah*, the name of two Isr.:— Aiah, Ajah.

346. אַיֵּה **'ayêh**, *ah-yay'*; prol. from 335; *where?*:— where.

347. אִיּוֹב **'Îyôwb**, *ee-yobe'*; from 340; *hated* (i.e. *persecuted); Ijob*, the patriarch famous for his patience:— Job.

348. אִיזֶבֶל **'Îyzebel**, *ee-zeh'-bel*; from 336 and 2083; *chaste; Izebel*, the wife of king Ahab:— Jezebel.

349. אֵיךְ **'êyk**, *ake*; also

אֵיכָה **'êykâh**, *ay-kaw'*; and

אֵיכָכָה **'êykâkâh**, *ay-kaw'-kah*; prol. from 335; *how?* or *how!*; also *where*:— how, what.

350. אִי־כָבוֹד **Îy-kâbôwd**, *ee-kaw-bode'*; from 336 and 3519; (there is) *no glory*, i.e. *inglorious; Ikabod*, a son of Phineas:— I-chabod.

351. אֵיכֹה **'êykôh**, *ay-kō*; prob. a var. for

349, but not as an interrogative; *where*:— where.

אִיכָה **'êykâh**;

אֵיכָכָה **'êykâkâh**. See 349.

352. אַיִל **'ayil**, *ah´-yil*; from the same as 193; prop. *strength*; hence, anything *strong*; spec. a *chief* (politically); also a *ram* (from his strength); a *pilaster* (as a strong support); an *oak* or other strong tree:— mighty (man), lintel, oak, post, ram, tree.

353. אֱיָל **'ĕyâl**, *eh-yawl´*; a var. of 352; *strength*:— strength.

354. אַיָּל **'ayâl**, *ah-yawl´*; an intens. form of 352 (in the sense of *ram*); a *stag* or male deer:— hart.

355. אַיָּלָה **'ayâlâh**, *ah-yaw-law´*; fem. of 354; a *doe* or female deer:— hind.

356. אֵילוֹן **'Êylôwn**, *ay-lone´*; or (short.)

אֵלוֹן **'Êlôwn**, *ay-lone´*; or

אֵילֹן **'Êylôn**, *ay-lone´*; from 352; *oak-grove; Elon*, the name of a place in Pal., and also of one Hittite, two Isr.:— Elon.

357. אַיָּלוֹן **'Ayâlôwn**, *ah-yaw-lone´*; from 354; *deer-field; Ajalon*, the name of five places in Pal.:— Aijalon, Ajalon.

358. אֵילוֹן בֵּית חָנָן **'Êylôwn Bêyth Chânân**, *ay-lone´ bayth chaw-nawn´*; from 356, 1004, and 2603; *oak-grove of* (the) *house of favor; Elon of Beth-chanan*, a place in Pal.:— Elon-beth-hanan.

359. אֵילוֹת **'Êylôwth**, *ay-lôth´*; or

אֵילַת **'Êylath**, *ay-lath´*; from 352; *trees* or a *grove* (i.e. palms); *Eloth* or *Elath*, a place on the Red Sea:— Elath, Eloth.

360. אֱיָלוּת **'ĕyâlûwth**, *eh-yaw-looth´*; fem. of 353; *power*; by impl. *protection*:— strength.

361. אֵילָם **'êylâm**, *ay-lawm´*; or (short.)

אֵלָם **'êlâm**, *ay-lawm´*; or (fem.)

אֵלַמָּה **'êlammâh**, *ay-lam-maw´*; prob. from 352; a *pillar-space* (or colonnade), i.e. a *pale* (or portico):— arch.

362. אֵילִם **'Êylim**, *ay-leem´*; plur. of 352; *palm-trees; Elim*, a place in the Desert:— Elim.

363. אִילָן **'îylân** (Chald.), *ee-lawn´*; corresp. to 356; a *tree*:— tree.

364. אֵיל פָּארָן **'Êyl Pâ'rân**, *ale paw-rawn´*; from 352 and 6290; *oak of Paran; El-Paran*, a portion of the district of Paran:— El-paran.

אֵילֹן **'Êylôn**. See 356.

365. אַיֶּלֶת **'ayeleth**, *ah-yeh´-leth*; the same as 355; a *doe*:— hind, Aijeleth.

אַיִם **'ayim**. See 368.

366. אָיֹם **'âyôm**, *aw-yome´*; from an unused root (mean. to *frighten*); *frightful*:— terrible.

367. אֵימָה **'êymâh**, *ay-maw´*; or (short.)

אֵמָה **'êmah**, *ay-maw´*; from the same as 366; *fright*; concr. an *idol* (as a bugbear):— dread, fear, horror, idol, terrible, terror.

368. אֵימִים **'Êymîym**, *ay-meem´*; plur. of 367; *terrors; Emim*, an early Canaanitish (or Moabitish) tribe:— Emims.

369. אַיִן **'ayin**, *ah´-yin*; as if from a prim.

root mean. to *be nothing* or *not exist*; a *non-entity*; gen. used as a neg. particle:— else, except, fail, [father-]less, be gone, in[-curable], neither, never, no (where), none, nor, (any, thing), not, nothing, to nought, past, un[-searchable], well-nigh, without. Comp. 370.

370. אַיִן **'ayin**, *ah´-yin*; prob. ident. with 369 in the sense of *query* (comp. 336); *where?* (only in connection with prep. pref., *whence?*):— whence, where.

371. אַיִן **'îyn**, *een*; appar. a short. form of 369; but (like 370) interrog.; is it *not?*:— not.

372. אִיעֶזֶר **'Îy'ezer**, *ee-eh´-zer*; from 336 and 5828; *helpless; Iezer*, an Isr.:— Jeezer.

373. אִיעֶזְרִי **'Îy'ezrîy**, *ee-ez-ree´*; patron. from 372; an *Iezrite* or desc. of Iezer:— Jezerite.

374. אֵיפָה **'êyphâh**, *ay-faw´*; or (short.)

אֵפָה **'êphâh**, *ay-faw´*; of Eg. der.; an *ephah* or measure for grain; hence, a *measure* in gen.:— ephah, (divers) measure (-s).

375. אֵיפֹה **'êyphôh**, *ay-fō´*; from 335 and 6311; *what place?*; also (of time) *when?*; or (of means) *how?*:— what manner, where.

376. אִישׁ **'îysh**, *eesh*; contr. for 582 [or perh. rather from an unused root mean. to *be extant*]; a *man* as an individual or a male person; often used as an adjunct to a more def. term (and in such cases frequently not expressed in translation):— also, another, any (man), a certain, + champion, consent, each, every (one), fellow, [foot-, husband-] man, (good-, great, mighty) man, he, high (degree), him (that is), husband, man [-kind], + none, one, people, person, + steward, what (man) soever, whoso (-ever), worthy. Comp. 802.

377. אִישׁ **'îysh**, *eesh*; denom. from 376; to *be a man*, i.e. act in a manly way:— show (one) self a man.

378. אִישׁ־בֹּשֶׁת **'Îysh-Bôsheth**, *eesh-bō´-sheth*; from 376 and 1322; *man of shame; Ish-Bosheth*, a son of King Saul:— Ish-bosheth.

379. אִישְׁהוֹד **'Îyshhôwd**, *eesh-hode´*; from 376 and 1935; *man of renown; Ishod*, an Isr.:— Ishod.

380. אִישׁוֹן **'îyshôwn**, *ee-shone´*; dimin. from 376; the *little man* of the eye; the *pupil* or *ball*; hence, the *middle* (of night):— apple [of the eye], black, obscure.

אִישׁ־חַי **'Îysh-Chay**. See 381.

381. אִישׁ־חַיִל **'Îysh-Chayil**, *eesh-khah´-yil*; from 376 and 2428; *man of might*; by defect. transc. (2 Sam. 23:20)

אִישׁ־חַי **'Îysh-Chay**, *eesh-khah´ee*; as if from 376 and 2416; *living man; Ish-chail* (or *Ish-chai*), an Isr.:— a valiant man.

382. אִישׁ־טוֹב **'Îysh-Ṭôwb**, *eesh-tobe´*; from 376 and 2897; *man of Tob; Ish-Tob*, a place in Pal.:— Ish-tob.

אִישַׁי **'Îshay**. See 3448.

אִיתוֹן **'îthôwn**. See 2978.

383. אִיתַי **'îythay** (Chald.), *ee-thah´ee*; corresp. to 3426; prop. *entity*; used only as a particle of affirmation, there *is*:— art thou, can, do ye, have, it be, there is (are), × we will not.

384. אִיתִיאֵל **'Îythîy'êl**, *eeth-ee-ale´*; perh. from 837 and 410; *God has arrived; Ithiel*, the name of an Isr., also of a symb. person:— Ithiel.

385. אִיתָמָר **'Îythâmâr**, *eeth-aw-mawr´*; from 339 and 8558; *coast of* the *palmtree; Ithamar*, a son of Aaron:— Ithamar.

386. אֵיתָן **'êythân**, *ay-thawn´*; or (short.)

אֵתָן **'êthân**, *ay-thawn´*; from an unused root (mean. to *continue*); *permanence*; hence, (concr.) *permanent*; spec. a *chieftain*:— hard, mighty, rough, strength, strong.

387. אֵיתָן **'Êythân**, *ay-thawn´*; the same as 386; *permanent; Ethan*, the name of four Isr.:— Ethan.

388. אֵיתָנִים **'Êythânîym**, *ay-thaw-neem´*; plur. of 386; always with the art.; the *permanent* brooks; *Ethanim*, the name of a month:— Ethanim.

389. אַךְ **'ak**, *ak*; akin to 403; a particle of affirmation, *surely*; hence, (by limitation) *only*:— also, in any wise, at least, but, certainly, even, howbeit, nevertheless, notwithstanding, only, save, surely, of a surety, truly, verily, + wherefore, yet (but).

390. אַכַּד **'Akkad**, *ak-kad´*; from an unused root prob. mean. to *strengthen*; a *fortress; Accad*, a place in Bab.:— Accad.

391. אַכְזָב **'akzâb**, *ak-zawb´*; from 3576; *falsehood*; by impl. *treachery*:— liar, lie.

392. אַכְזִיב **'Akzîyb**, *ak-zeeb´*; from 391; *deceitful* (in the sense of a winter-torrent which *fails* in summer); *Akzib*, the name of two places in Pal.:— Achzib.

393. אַכְזָר **'akzâr**, *ak-zawr´*; from an unused root (appar. mean. to *act harshly*); *violent*; by impl. *deadly*; also (in a good sense) *brave*:— cruel, fierce.

394. אַכְזָרִי **'akzârîy**, *ak-zaw-ree´*; from 393; *terrible*:— cruel (one).

395. אַכְזְרִיוּת **'akzᵉrîyûwth**, *ak-ze-ree-ooth´*; from 394; *fierceness*:— cruel.

396. אֲכִילָה **'ăkîylâh**, *ak-ee-law´*; fem. from 398; something *eatable*, i.e. *food*:— meat.

397. אָכִישׁ **'Âkîysh**, *aw-keesh´*; of uncert. der.; *Akish*, a Philistine king:— Achish.

398. אָכַל **'âkal**, *aw-kal´*; a prim. root; to *eat* (lit. or fig.):— × at all, burn up, consume, devour (-er, up), dine, eat (-er, up), feed (with), food, × freely, × in ... wise (-deed, plenty), (lay) meat, × quite.

399. אֲכַל **'ăkal** (Chald.), *ak-al´*; corresp. to 398:— + accuse, devour, eat.

400. אֹכֶל **'ôkel**, *o´-kel*; from 398; *food*:— eating, food, meal [-time], meat, prey, victuals.

401. אֻכָל **'Ûkâl**, *oo-kawl´*; or

אֻכָּל **'Ukkâl**, *ook-kawl´*; appar. from 398; *devoured; Ucal*, a fancy name:— Ucal.

402. אָכְלָה **'oklâh**, *ok-law´*; fem. of 401;

food:— consume, devour, eat, food, meat.

403. אָכֵן **'âkên**, *aw-kane'*; from 3559 [comp. 3651]; *firmly;* fig. *surely;* also (advers.) *but:*— but, certainly, nevertheless, surely, truly, verily.

404. אָכַף **'âkaph**, *aw-kaf'*; a prim. root; appar. mean. to *curve* (as with a burden): to *urge:*— crave.

405. אֶכֶף **'ekeph**, *eh'-kef*; from 404; a *load;* by impl. a *stroke* (others *dignity*):— hand.

406. אִכָּר **'ikkâr**, *ik-kawr'*; from an unused root mean. to *dig;* a *farmer:*— husbandman, ploughman.

407. אַכְשָׁף **'Akshâph**, *ak-shawf'*; from 3784; *fascination; Acshaph,* a place in Pal.:— Achshaph.

408. אַל **'al**, *al;* a neg. particle [akin to 3808]; *not* (the qualified negation, used as a deprecative); once (Job 24:25) as a noun, *nothing:*— nay, neither, + never, no, nor, not, nothing [worth], rather than.

409. אַל **'al** (Chald.), *al;* corresp. to 408:— not.

410. אֵל **'êl**, *ale;* short. from 352; *strength;* as adj. *mighty;* espec. the *Almighty* (but used also of any *deity*):— God (god), × goodly, × great, idol, might (-y one), power, strong. Comp. names in "-el."

411. אֵל **'êl**, *ale;* a demonstr. particle (but only in a plur. sense) *these* or *those:*— these, those. Comp. 428.

412. אֵל **'êl** (Chald.), *ale;* corresp. to 411:— these.

413. אֵל **'êl**, *ale;* (but only used in the short. constr. form

אֶל **'el**, *el*); a prim. particle; prop. denoting motion *towards,* but occasionally used of a quiescent position, i.e. *near, with* or *among;* often in general, *to:*— about, according to, after, against, among, as for, at, because (-fore, -side), both ... and, by, concerning, for, from, × hath, in (-to), near, (out) of, over, through, to (-ward), under, unto, upon, whether, with (-in).

414. אֵלָא **'Êlâ'**, *ay-law';* a var. of 424; *oak; Ela,* an Isr.:— Elah.

415. אֵל אֱלֹהֵי יִשְׂרָאֵל **'Êl 'ĕlôhêy Yisrâ'êl**, *ale el-o-hay' yis-raw-ale';* from 410 and 430 and 3478; the *mighty God of Jisrael; El-Elohi-Jisrael,* the title given to a consecrated spot by Jacob:— El-elohe-israel.

416. אֵל בֵּית־אֵל **'Êl Bêyth-'Êl**, *ale bayth-ale';* from 410 and 1008; the *God of Bethel; El-Bethel,* the title given to a consecrated spot by Jacob:— El-beth-el.

417. אֶלְגָּבִישׁ **'elgâbîysh**, *el-gaw-beesh';* from 410 and 1378; *hail* (as if a great *pearl*):— great hail [-stones].

418. אַלְגּוּמִּים **'algûwmmîym**, *al-goom-meem';* by transp. for 484; sticks of *algum* wood:— algum [trees].

419. אֶלְדָּד **'Eldâd**, *el-dâd';* from 410 and 1730; *God has loved; Eldad,* an Isr.:— Eldad.

420. אֶלְדָּעָה **'Eldâ'âh**, *el-daw-aw';* from 410 and 3045; *God of knowledge; Eldaah,* a son of Midian:— Eldaah.

421. אָלָה **'âlâh**, *aw-law';* a prim. root [rather ident. with 422 through the idea of *invocation*]; to *bewail:*— lament.

422. אָלָה **'âlâh**, *aw-law';* a prim. root; prop. to *adjure,* i.e. (usually in a bad sense) *imprecate:*— adjure, curse, swear.

423. אָלָה **'âlâh**, *aw-law';* from 422; an *imprecation:*— curse, cursing, execration, oath, swearing.

424. אֵלָה **'êlâh**, *ay-law';* fem. of 352; an *oak* or other strong tree:— elm, oak, teil tree.

425. אֵלָה **'Êlâh**, *ay-law';* the same as 424; *Elah,* the name of an Edomite, of four Isr., and also of a place in Pal.:— Elah.

426. אֱלָהּ **'ĕlâhh** (Chald.), *el-aw';* corresp. to 433; *God:*— God, god.

427. אַלָּה **'allâh**, *al-law';* a var. of 424:— oak.

428. אֵל־לֶה **'êl-leh**, *ale'-leh;* prol. from 411; *these* or *those:*— an(the) other; one sort, so, some, such, them, these (same), they, this, those, thus, which, who (-m).

429. אֵלֶּה **'êlleh** (Chald.), *ale'-leh;* corresp. to 428:— these.

אֱלָהּ **'ĕlôahh**. See 433.

430. אֱלֹהִים **'ĕlôhîym**, *el-o-heem';* plur. of 433; *gods* in the ordinary sense; but spec. used (in the plur. thus, espec. with the art.) of the supreme *God;* occasionally applied by way of deference to *magistrates;* and sometimes as a superlative:— angels, × exceeding, God (gods) (-dess, -ly), × (very) great, judges, × mighty.

431. אֲלוּ **'ălûw** (Chald.), *al-oo';* prob. prol. from 412; *lo!:*— behold.

432. אִלּוּ **'illûw**, *il-loo';* prob. from 408; *nay,* i.e. (softened) *if:*— but if, yea though.

433. אֱלוֹהַּ **'ĕlôwahh**, *el-o'-ah;* rarely (short.)

אֱלֹהַּ **'ĕlôahh**, *el-o'-ah;* prob. prol. (emphat.) from 410; a *deity* or the *Deity:*— God, god. See 430.

434. אֱלוּל **'ĕlûwl**, *el-ool';* for 457; good for *nothing:*— thing of nought.

435. אֱלוּל **'Ĕlûwl**, *el-ool';* prob. of for. der.; *Elul,* the sixth Jewish month:— Elul.

436. אֵלוֹן **'êlôwn**, *ay-lone';* prol. from 352; an *oak* or other strong tree:— plain. See also 356.

437. אַלּוֹן **'allôwn**, *al-lone';* a var. of 436:— oak.

438. אַלּוֹן **'Allôwn**, *al-lone';* the same as 437; *Allon,* an Isr., also a place in Pal.:— Allon.

439. אַלּוֹן בָּכוּת **'Allôwn Bâkûwth**, *al-lone' baw-kooth';* from 437 and a var. of 1068; *oak of weeping; Allon-Bakuth,* a monumental tree:— Allon-bachuth.

440. אֵלֹנִי **'Êlôwnîy**, *ay-lo-nee';* or rather (short.)

אֵלֹנִי **'Êlônîy**, *ay-lo-nee';* patron. from 438; an *Elonite* or desc. (collect.) of Elon:— Elonites.

441. אַלּוּף **'allûwph**, *al-loof';* or (short.)

אַלֻּף **'allûph**, *al-loof';* from 502; *familiar;* a *friend,* also *gentle;* hence, a *bullock* (as being tame; applied, although masc., to a *cow*); and so, a *chieftain* (as notable, like neat cattle):— captain, duke, (chief) friend, governor, guide, ox.

442. אָלוּשׁ **'Âlûwsh**, *aw-loosh';* of uncert. der.; *Alush,* a place in the Desert:— Alush.

443. אֶלְזָבָד **'Elzâbâd**, *el-zaw-bawd';* from 410 and 2064; *God has bestowed; Elzabad,* the name of two Isr.:— Elzabad.

444. אָלַח **'âlach**, *aw-lakh';* a prim. root; to *muddle,* i.e. (fig. and intr.) to *turn* (morally) *corrupt:*— become filthy.

445. אֶלְחָנָן **'Elchânân**, *el-khaw-nawn';* from 410 and 2603; *God (is) gracious; Elchanan,* an Isr.:— Elkanan.

אֵלִי **'Êlîy**. See 1017.

446. אֱלִיאָב **'Ĕlîy'âb**, *el-ee-awb';* from 410 and 1; *God of* (his) *father; Eliab,* the name of six Isr.:— Eliab.

447. אֱלִיאֵל **'Ĕlîy'êl**, *el-ee-ale';* from 410 repeated; *God of* (his) *God; Eliel,* the name of nine Isr.:— Eliel.

448. אֱלִיאָתָה **'Ĕlîy'âthâh**, *el-ee-aw-thaw';* or (contr.)

אֱלִיָתָה **'Ĕlîyâthâh**, *el-ee-yaw-thaw';* from 410 and 225; *God of* (his) *consent; Eliathah,* an Isr.:— Eliathah.

449. אֱלִידָד **'Ĕlîydâd**, *el-ee-dawd';* from the same as 419; *God of* (his) *love; Elidad,* an Isr.:— Elidad.

450. אֶלְיָדָע **'Elyâdâ'**, *el-yaw-daw';* from 410 and 3045; *God (is) knowing; Eljada,* the name of two Isr. and of an Aramaean leader:— Eliada.

451. אַלְיָה **'alyâh**, *al-yaw';* from 422 (in the orig. sense of *strength*); the *stout* part, i.e. the fat *tail* of the Oriental sheep:— rump.

452. אֵלִיָּה **'Êlîyâh**, *ay-lee-yaw';* or prol.

אֵלִיָּהוּ **'Êlîyâhûw**, *ay-lee-yaw'-hoo;* from 410 and 3050; *God of Jehovah; Elijah,* the name of the famous prophet and of two other Isr.:— Elijah, Eliah.

453. אֱלִיהוּ **'Ĕlîyhûw**, *el-ee-hoo';* or (fully)

אֱלִיהוּא **'Ĕlîyhûw'**, *el-ee-hoo';* from 410 and 1931; *God of him; Elihu,* the name of one of Job's friends, and of three Isr.:— Elihu.

454. אֶלְיְהוֹעֵינַי **'Elyehôw'êynay**, *el-ye-ho-ay-nah'ee;* or (short.)

אֶלְיוֹעֵינַי **'Elyôw'êynay**, *el-yo-ay-nah'ee;* from 413 and 3068 and 5869; *toward Jehovah (are) my eyes; Eljehoenai* or *Eljoenai,* the name of seven Isr.:— Elihoenai, Elionai.

455. אֶלְיַחְבָּא **'Elyachbâ'**, *el-yakh-baw';* from 410 and 2244; *God will hide; Eljachba,* an Isr.:— Eliahbah.

456. אֱלִיחֹרֶף **'Ĕlîychôreph**, *el-ee-kho'-ref;* from 410 and 2779; *God of autumn; Elichoreph,* an Isr.:— Elihoreph.

457. אֱלִיל **'ĕlîyl**, *el-eel';* appar. from 408; good for *nothing,* by anal. *vain* or *vanity;* spec. an *idol:*— idol, no value, thing of nought.

458. אֱלִימֶלֶךְ 'Ĕlîymelek, el-ee-meh´-lek; from 410 and 4428; God of (the) king; Elimelek, an Isr.:— Elimelech.

459. אִלֵּין 'illêyn (Chald.), il-lane´; or short.

אִלֵּן 'illên, il-lane´; prol. from 412; these:— the, these.

460. אֶלְיָקֻף 'Ĕlyâçâph, el-yaw-sawf´; from 410 and 3254; God (is) gatherer; Eljasaph, the name of two Isr.:— Eliasaph.

461. אֱלִיעֶזֶר 'Ĕlîy'ezer, el-ee-eh´-zer; from 410 and 5828; God of help; Eliezer, the name of a Damascene and of ten Isr.:— Eliezer.

462. אֱלִיעֵינַי 'Ĕlîy'êynay, el-ee-ay-nah´ee; prob. contr. for 454; Elienai, an Isr.:— Elienai.

463. אֱלִיעָם 'Ĕlîy'âm, el-ee-awm´; from 410 and 5971; God of (the) people; Eliam, an Isr.:— Eliam.

464. אֱלִיפַז 'Ĕlîyphaz, el-ee-faz´; from 410 and 6337; God of gold; Eliphaz, the name of one of Job's friends, and of a son of Esau:— Eliphaz.

465. אֱלִיפָל 'Ĕlîyphâl, el-ee-fawl´; from 410 and 6419; God of judgment; Eliphal, an Isr.:— Eliphal.

466. אֱלִיפְלֵהוּ 'Ĕlîyphᵉlêhûw, el-ee-fe-lay´-hoo; from 410 and 6395; God of his distinction; Eliphelehu, an Isr.:— Elipheleh.

467. אֱלִיפֶלֶט 'Ĕlîypheleṭ, el-ee-feh´-let; or (short.)

אֶלְפֶלֶט 'Elpeleṭ, el-peh´-let; from 410 and 6405; God of deliverance; Eliphelet or Elpelet, the name of six Isr.:— Eliphalet, Eliphelet, Elpalet.

468. אֱלִיצוּר 'Ĕlîyṣûwr, el-ee-tsoor´; from 410 and 6697; God of (the) rock; Elitsur, an Isr.:— Elizur.

469. אֱלִיצָפָן 'Ĕlîyṣâphân, el-ee-tsaw-fawn´; or (short.)

אֶלְצָפָן 'Elṣâphân, el-tsaw-fawn´; from 410 and 6845; God of treasure; Elitsaphan or Eltsaphan, an Isr.:— Elizaphan, Elzaphan.

470. אֱלִיקָא 'Ĕlîyqâ, el-ee-kaw´; from 410 and 6958; God of rejection; Elika, an Isr.:— Elika.

471. אֶלְיָקִים 'Ĕlyâqîym, el-yaw-keem´; from 410 and 6965; God of raising; Eljakim, the name of four Isr.:— Eliakim.

472. אֱלִישֶׁבַע 'Ĕlîysheba', el-ee-sheh´-bah; from 410 and 7651 (in the sense of 7650); God of (the) oath; Elisheba, the wife of Aaron:— Elisheba.

473. אֱלִישָׁה 'Ĕlîyshâh, el-ee-shaw´; prob. of for. der.; Elishah, a son of Javan:— Elishah.

474. אֱלִישׁוּעַ 'Ĕlîyshûwa', el-ee-shoo´-ah; from 410 and 7769; God of supplication (or of riches); Elishua, a son of King David:— Elishua.

475. אֱלְיָשִׁיב 'Ĕlyâshîyb, el-yaw-sheeb´; from 410 and 7725; God will restore; Eljashib, the name of six Isr.:— Eliashib.

476. אֱלִישָׁמָע 'Ĕlîyshâmâ', el-ee-shaw-maw´; from 410 and 8085; God of hear-

ing; Elishama, the name of seven Isr.:— Elishama.

477. אֱלִישָׁע 'Ĕlîyshâ', el-ee-shaw´; contr. for 474; Elisha, the famous prophet:— Elisha.

478. אֱלִישָׁפָט 'Ĕlîyshâphâṭ, el-ee-shaw-fawt´; from 410 and 8199; God of judgment; Elishaphat, an Isr.:— Elishaphat.

אֱלִיָּתָה 'Ĕlîyâthâh. See 448.

479. אִלֵּךְ 'illêk (Chald.), il-lake´; prol. from 412; these:— these, those.

480. אַלְלַי 'al'lay, al-le-lah´ee; by redupl. from 421; alas!:— woe.

481. אָלַם 'âlam, aw-lam´; a prim. root; to tie fast; hence, (of the mouth) to be tongue-tied:— bind, be dumb, put to silence.

482. אֶלֶם 'êlem, ay´-lem; from 481; silence (i.e. mute justice):— congregation. Comp. 3128.

אֵלָם 'êlâm. See 361.

אֻלָּם 'âlum. See 485.

483. אִלֵּם 'illêm, il-lame´; from 481; speechless:— dumb (man).

484. אַלְמֻגִּים 'almuggiym, al-moog-gheem´; prob. of for. der. (used thus only in the plur.); almug (i.e. prob. sandal-wood) sticks:— almug trees. Comp. 418.

485. אֲלֻמָּה 'ălummâh, al-oom-maw´; or (masc.)

אָלֻם 'âlum, aw-loom´; pass. part. of 481; something bound; a sheaf:— sheaf.

486. אַלְמוֹדָד 'Almôwdâd, al-mo-dawd´; prob. of for. der.; Almodad, a son of Joktan:— Almodad.

487. אַלַמֶּלֶךְ 'Allammelek, al-lam-meh´-lek; from 427 and 4428; oak of (the) king; Allammelek, a place in Pal.:— Alammelech.

488. אַלְמָן 'almân, al-mawn´; prol. from 481 in the sense of bereavement; discarded (as a divorced person):— forsaken.

489. אַלְמֹן 'almôn, al-mone´; from 481 as in 488; bereavement:— widowhood.

490. אַלְמָנָה 'almânâh, al-maw-naw´; fem. of 488; a widow; also a desolate place:— desolate house (palace), widow.

491. אַלְמָנוּת 'almânûwth, al-maw-nooth´; fem. of 488; concr. a widow; abstr. widowhood:— widow, widowhood.

492. אַלְמֹנִי 'almônîy, al-mo-nee´; from 489 in the sense of concealment; some one (i.e. so and so, without giving the name of the person or place):— one, and such.

אִלֵּן 'illên. See 459.

אֱלֹנִי 'Ĕlônîy. See 440.

493. אֶלְנַעַם 'Elna'am, el-nah´-am; from 410 and 5276; God (is his) delight; Elnaam, an Isr.:— Elnaam.

494. אֶלְנָתָן 'Elnâthân, el-naw-thawn´; from 410 and 5414; God (is the) giver; Elnathan, the name of four Isr.:— Elnathan.

495. אֶלָּסָר 'Ellâçâr, el-law-sawr´; prob. of for. der.; Ellasar, an early country of Asia:— Ellasar.

496. אֶלְעָד 'El'âd, el-awd´; from 410 and 5749; God has testified; Elad, an Isr.:— Elead.

497. אֶלְעָדָה 'El'âdâh, el-aw-daw´; from 410 and 5710; God has decked; Eladah, an Isr.:— Eladah.

498. אֶלְעוּזַי 'El'ûwzay, el-oo-zah´ee; from 410 and 5756 (in the sense of 5797); God (is) defensive; Eluzai, an Isr.:— Eluzai.

499. אֶלְעָזָר 'El'âzâr, el-aw-zawr´; from 410 and 5826; God (is) helper; Elazar, the name of seven Isr.:— Eleazar.

500. אֶלְעָלֵא 'El'âlê', el-aw-lay´; or (more prop.)

אֶלְעָלֵה 'El'âlêh, el-aw´-lay´; from 410 and 5927; God (is) going up; Elale or Elaleh, a place east of the Jordan:— Elealeh.

501. אֶלְעָשָׂה 'El'âsâh, el-aw-saw´; from 410 and 6213; God has made; Elasah, the name of four Isr.:— Elasah, Eleasah.

502. אָלַף 'âlaph, aw-laf´; a prim. root, to associate with; hence, to learn (and caus. to teach):— learn, teach, utter.

503. אָלַף 'âlaph, aw-laf´; denom. from 505; caus. to make a thousandfold:— bring forth thousands.

504. אֶלֶף 'eleph, eh´-lef; from 502; a family; also (from the sense of yoking or taming) an ox or cow:— family, kine, oxen.

505. אֶלֶף 'eleph, eh´-lef; prop. the same as 504; hence, (the ox's head being the first letter of the alphabet, and this eventually used as a numeral) a thousand:— thousand.

506. אֲלַף 'ălaph (Chald.), al-af´; or

אֶלֶף 'eleph (Chald.), eh´-lef; corresp. to 505:— thousand.

507. אֶלֶף 'Eleph, eh´-lef; the same as 505; Eleph, a place in Pal.:— Eleph.

אַלּוּף 'allûph. See 441.

אֶלְפֶלֶט 'Elpeleṭ. See 467.

508. אֶלְפַּעַל 'Elpa'al, el-pah´-al; from 410 and 6466; God (is) act; Elpaal, an Isr.:— Elpaal.

509. אָלַץ 'âlats, aw-lats´; a prim. root; to press:— urge.

אֶלְצָפָן 'Elṣâphân. See 469.

510. אַלְקוּם 'alqûwm, al-koom´; prob. from 408 and 6965; a non-rising (i.e. resistlessness):— no rising up.

511. אֶלְקָנָה 'Elqânâh, el-kaw-naw´; from 410 and 7069; God has obtained; Elkanah, the name of several Isr.:— Elkanah.

512. אֶלְקֹשִׁי 'Elqôshîy, el-ko-shee´; patrial from a name of uncert. der.; an Elkoshite or native of Elkosh:— Elkoshite.

513. אֶלְתּוֹלַד 'Eltôwlad, el-to-lad´; prob. from 410 and a masc. form of 8435 [comp. 8434]; God (is) generator; Eltolad, a place in Pal.:— Eltolad.

514. אֶלְתְּקֵא 'Eltᵉqê, el-te-kay´; or (more prop.)

אֶלְתְּקֵה 'Eltᵉqêh, el-te-kay´; of uncert. der.; Eltekeh or Eteke, a place in Pal.:— Eltekeh.

515. אֶלְתְּקֹן **'Elteqôn**, *el-te-kone'*; from 410 and 8626; *God* (is) *straight; Eltekon*, a place in Pal.:— Eltekon.

516. אַל תַּשְׁחֵת **'Al tashchêth**, *al tash-kayth'*; from 408 and 7843; *Thou must not destroy*; prob. the opening words of a popular song:— Al-taschith.

517. אֵם **'êm**, *ame*; a prim. word; a *mother* (as the *bond* of the family); in a wide sense (both lit. and fig. llike 1l:— dam, mother, × parting.

518. אִם **'îm**, *eem*; a prim. particle; used very widely as demonstr., *lo!*; interrog., *whether?*; or conditional, *if, although*; also *Oh that!, when*; hence, as a neg., *not*:— (and, can-, doubtless, if, that) (not), + but, either, + except, + more (-over if, than), neither, nevertheless, nor, oh that, or, + save (only, -ing), seeing, since, sith, + surely (no more, none, not), though, + of a truth, + unless, + verily, when, whereas, whether, while, + yet.

519. אָמָה **'âmâh**, *aw-maw'*; appar. a prim. word; a *maid-servant* or female *slave*:— (hand-) bondmaid (-woman), maid (-servant).

אֵמָה **'êmâh**. See 367.

520. אַמָּה **'ammâh**, *am-maw'*; prol. from 517; prop. a *mother* (i.e. *unit* of measure, or the *fore-arm* (below the elbow), i.e. a *cubit*; also a door-*base* (as a *bond* of the entrance):— cubit, + hundred lby exchange for 3967l, measure, post.

521. אַמָּה **'ammâh** (Chald.), *am-maw'*; corresp. to 520:— cubit.

522. אַמָּה **'Ammâh**, *am-maw'*; the same as 520; *Ammah*, a hill in Pal.:— Ammah.

523. אֻמָּה **'ummâh**, *oom-maw'*; from the same as 517; a *collection*, i.e. community of persons:— nation, people.

524. אֻמָּה **'ummâh** (Chald.), *oom-maw'*; corresp. to 523:— nation.

525. אָמוֹן **'âmôwn**, *aw-mone'*; from 539, prob. in the sense of *training; skilled*, i.e. an architect llike 542l:— one brought up.

526. אָמוֹן **'Âmôwn**, *aw-mone'*; the same as 525; *Amon*, the name of three Isr.:— Amon.

527. אָמוֹן **'âmôwn**, *aw-mone'*; a var. for 1995; a *throng* of people:— multitude.

528. אָמוֹן **'Âmôwn**, *aw-mone'*; of Eg. der.; *Amon* (i.e. Ammon or Amn), a deity of Egypt (used only as an adjunct of 4996):— multitude, populous.

529. אֵמוּן **'êmûwn**, *ay-moon'*; from 539; *established*, i.e. (fig.) *trusty*; also (abstr.) *trustworthiness*:— faith (-ful), truth.

530. אֱמוּנָה **'ĕmûwnâh**, *em-oo-naw'*; or (short.)

אֱמֻנָה **'ĕmûnâh**, *em-oo-naw'*; fem. of 529; lit. *firmness*; fig. *security*; mor. *fidelity*:— faith (-ful, -ly, -ness, lmanl), set office, stability, steady, truly, truth, verily.

531. אָמוֹץ **'Âmôwts**, *aw-mohts'*; from 553; *strong; Amots*, an Isr.:— Amoz.

532. אָמִי **'Âmîy**, *aw-mee'*; an abbrev. for 526; *Ami*, an Isr.:— Ami.

אֱמוּן **'Âmîynôwn**. See 550.

533. אָמִיץ **'ammîyts**, *am-meets'*; or (short.)

אַמִּץ **'ammîts**, *am-meets'*; from 553; *strong* or (abstr.) *strength*:— courageous, mighty, strong (one).

534. אָמִיר **'âmîyr**, *aw-meer'*; appar. from 559 (in the sense of *self-exaltation*); a *summit* (of a tree or mountain:— bough, branch.

535. אָמַל **'âmal**, *aw-mal'*; a prim. root; to *droop*; by impl. to *be sick*, to *mourn*:— languish, be weak, wax feeble.

536. אֻמְלַל **'umlal**, *oom-lal'*; from 535; *sick*:— weak.

537. אֲמֵלָל **'ămêlâl**, *am-ay-lawl'*; from 535; *languid*:— feeble.

538. אָמָם **'Âmâm**, *am-awm'*; from 517; *gathering*-spot; *Amam*, a place in Pal.:— Amam.

539. אָמַן **'âman**, *aw-man'*; a prim. root; prop. to *build up* or *support*; to *foster* as a parent or nurse; fig. to *render* (or be) *firm* or *faithful*, to *trust* or believe, to be *permanent* or quiet; mor. to be *true* or *certain*; once (Isa. 30:21; interch. for 541) to *go to the right hand*:— hence, assurance, believe, bring up, establish, + fail, be faithful (of long continuance, stedfast, sure, surely, trusty, verified), nurse, (-ing father), (put), trust, turn to the right.

540. אֲמַן **'ăman** (Chald.), *am-an'*; corresp. to 539:— believe, faithful, sure.

541. אָמַן **'âman**, *aw-man'*; denom. from 3225; to take the *right hand* road:— turn to the right. See 539.

542. אָמָן **'âmân**, *aw-mawn'*; from 539 (in the sense of *training*); an *expert*:— cunning workman.

543. אָמֵן **'âmên**, *aw-mane'*; from 539; *sure*; abstr. *faithfulness*; adv. *truly*:— Amen, so be it, truth.

544. אֹמֶן **'ômen**, *oh-men'*; from 539; *verity*:— truth.

545. אָמְנָה **'omnâh**, *om-naw'*; fem. of 544 (in the spec. sense of *training*); *tutelage*:— brought up.

546. אָמְנָה **'omnâh**, *om-naw'*; fem. of 544 (in its usual sense); adv. *surely*:— indeed.

547. אֹמְנָה **'ômenâh**, *om-me-naw'*; fem. act. part. of 544 (in the orig. sense of *supporting*); a *column*:— pillar.

548. אֲמָנָה **'ămânâh**, *am-aw-naw'*; fem. of 543; something *fixed*, i.e. a *covenant*, an *allowance*:— certain portion, sure.

549. אֲמָנָה **'Ămânâh**, *am-aw-naw'*; the same as 548; *Amanah*, a mountain near Damascus:— Amana.

אֱמֻנָה **'ĕmûnâh**. See 530.

550. אַמְנוֹן **'Amnôwn**, *am-nohn'*; or

אֲמִינוֹן **'Amîynôwn**, *am-ee-nohn'*; from 539; *faithful; Amnon* (or Aminon), a son of David:— Amnon.

551. אָמְנָם **'omnâm**, *om-nawm'*; adv. from 544; *verily*:— indeed, no doubt, surely, (it is, of a) true (-ly, -th).

552. אֻמְנָם **'umnâm**, *oom-nawm'*; an

orth. var. of 551:— in (very) deed; of a surety.

553. אָמַץ **'âmats**, *aw-mats'*; a prim. root; to *be alert*, phys. (on foot) or ment. (in courage):— confirm, be courageous (of good courage, stedfastly minded, strong, stronger), establish, fortify, harden, increase, prevail, strengthen (self), make strong (obstinate, speed).

554. אָמֹץ **'âmôts**, *aw-mohts'*; prob. from 553; of a *strong* color, i.e. *red* (others *fleet*):— bay.

555. אֹמֶץ **'ômets**, *o'-mets*; from 553; *strength*:— stronger.

אַמִּץ **'ammîts**. See 533.

556. אַמְצָה **'amtsâh**, *am-tsaw'*; from 553; *force*:— strength.

557. אַמְצִי **'Amtsîy**, *am-tsee'*; from 553; *strong; Amtsi*, an Isr.:— Amzi.

558. אֲמַצְיָה **'Ămatsyâh**, *am-ats-yaw'*; or

אֲמַצְיָהוּ **'Ămatsyâhûw**, *am-ats-yaw'-hoo*; from 553 and 3050; *strength of Jah; Amatsjah*, the name of four Isr.:— Amaziah.

559. אָמַר **'âmar**, *aw-mar'*; a prim. root; to *say* (used with great latitude):— answer, appoint, avouch, bid, boast self, call, certify, challenge, charge, + (at the, give) command (-ment), commune, consider, declare, demand, × desire, determine, × expressly, × indeed, × intend, name, × plainly, promise, publish, report, require, say, speak (against, of), × still, × suppose, talk, tell, term, × that is, × think, use lspeechl, utter, × verily, × yet.

560. אֲמַר **'ămar** (Chald.), *am-ar'*; corresp. to 559:— command, declare, say, speak, tell.

561. אֵמֶר **'êmer**, *ay'-mer*; from 559; something *said*:— answer, × appointed unto him, saying, speech, word.

562. אֹמֶר **'ômer**, *o'-mer*; the same as 561:— promise, speech, thing, word.

563. אִמַּר **'immar** (Chald.), *im-mar'*; perh. from 560 (in the sense of *bringing forth*); a *lamb*:— lamb.

564. אִמֵּר **'Immêr**, *im-mare'*; from 559; *talkative; Immer*, the name of five Isr.:— Immer.

565. אִמְרָה **'imrâh**, *im-raw'*; or

אֶמְרָה **'emrâh**, *em-raw'*; fem. of 561, and mean. the same:— commandment, speech, word.

566. אִמְרִי **'Imrîy**, *im-ree'*; from 564; *wordy; Imri*, the name of two Isr.:— Imri.

567. אֱמֹרִי **'Ĕmôrîy**, *em-o-ree'*; prob. a patron. from an unused name derived from 559 in the sense of *publicity*, i.e. prominence; thus, a *mountaineer*; an *Emorite*, one of the Canaanitish tribes:— Amorite.

568. אֲמַרְיָה **'Ămaryâh**, *am-ar-yaw'*; or prol.

אֲמַרְיָהוּ **'Ămaryâhûw**, *am-ar-yaw'-hoo*; from 559 and 3050; *Jah has said* (i.e. promised); *Amarjah*, the name of nine Isr.:— Amariah.

569. אַמְרָפֶל **'Amrâphel**, *am-raw-fel'*; of uncert. (perh. for.) der.; *Amraphel*, a king of Shinar:— Amraphel.

Hebrew

570. אֶמֶשׁ **'emesh**, *eh´-mesh*; time *past*, i.e. *yesterday* or *last night*:— former time, yesterday (-night).

571. אֶמֶת **'emeth**, *eh´-meth*; contr. from 539; *stability*; fig. *certainty, truth, trustworthiness*:— assured (-ly), establishment, faithful, right, sure, true (-ly, -th), verity.

572. אַמְתַּחַת **'amtêchath**, *am-takh´-ath*; from 4969; prop. something *expansive*, i.e. a *bag*:— sack.

573. אֲמִתַּי **'Ămittay**, *am-it-tah´ee*; from 571; *veracious*; *Amittai*, an Isr.:— Amittai.

574. אֱמְתָּנִי **'emtâniy** (Chald.), *em-taw-nee´*; from a root corresp. to that of 4975; well-*loined* (i.e. burly) or *mighty*:— terrible.

575. אָן **'ân**, *awn*; or

אָנָה **'ânâh**, *aw-naw´*; contr. from 370; *where?*; hence, *whither?, when?*; also *hither* and *thither*:— + any (no) whither, now, where, whither (-soever).

אֹן **'Ôn**. See 204.

576. אֲנָא **'ănâ** (Chald.), *an-aw´*; or

אֲנָה **'ănâh** (Chald.), *an-aw´*; corresp. to 589; *I*:— I, as for me.

577. אָנָּא **'ânnâ'**, *awn-naw´*; or

אָנָּה **'ânnâh**, *awn-naw´*; appar. contr. from 160 and 4994; *oh now!*:— I (me) beseech (pray) thee, O.

אֲנָה **'ănâh**. See 576.

אָנָּה **'ânâh**. See 575.

578. אָנָה **'ânâh**, *aw-naw´*; a prim. root; to *groan*:— lament, mourn.

579. אָנָה **'ânâh**, *aw-naw´*; a prim. root [perh. rather ident. with 578 through the idea of *contraction* in anguish]; to *approach*; hence, to *meet* in various senses:— befall, deliver, happen, seek a quarrel.

אָנָּה **'ânnâh**. See 577.

580. אָנוּ **'ănûw**, *an-oo´*; contr. for 587; *we*:— we.

אֹנוֹ **'Ônôw**. See 207.

581. אִנּוּן **'innûwn** (Chald.), *in-noon´*; or (fem.)

אִנִּין **'inniyn** (Chald.), *in-neen´*; corresp. to 1992; *they*:— × are, them, these.

582. אֱנוֹשׁ **'ĕnôwsh**, *en-oshe´*; from 605; prop. a *mortal* (and thus differing from the more dignified 120); hence, a *man* in gen. (singly or collect.):— another, × [blood-] thirsty, certain, chap [-man]; divers, fellow, × in the flower of their age, husband, (certain, mortal) man, people, person, servant, some (× of them), + stranger, those, + their trade. It is often unexpressed in the English Version, espec. when used in apposition with another word. Comp. 376.

583. אֱנוֹשׁ **'Ĕnôwsh**, *en-ohsh´*; the same as 582; *Enosh*, a son of Seth:— Enos.

584. אָנַח **'ânach**, *aw-nakh´*; a prim. root; to *sigh*:— groan, mourn, sigh.

585. אֲנָחָה **'ănâchâh**, *an-aw-khaw´*; from 584; *sighing*:— groaning, mourn, sigh.

586. אֲנַחְנָא **'ănachnâ'** (Chald.), *an-akh´-naw*; or

אֲנַחְנָה **'ănachnâh** (Chald.), *an-akh-naw´*; corresp. to 587; *we*:— we.

587. אֲנַחְנוּ **'ănachnûw**, *an-akh´-noo*; appar. from 595; *we*:— ourselves, us, we.

588. אֲנָחֲרָת **'Ănâchărâth**, *an-aw-khaw-rawth´*; prob. from the same root as 5170; a *gorge* or *narrow pass*; *Anacharath*, a place in Pal.:— Anaharath.

589. אֲנִי **'ăniy**, *an-ee´*; contr. from 595; *I*:— I, (as for) me, mine, myself, we, × which, × who.

590. אֳנִי **'ŏniy**, *on-ee´*; prob. from 579 (in the sense of *conveyance*); a *ship* or (collect.) a *fleet*:— galley, navy (of ships).

591. אֳנִיָּה **'ŏnîyâh**, *on-ee-yaw´*; fem. of 590; a *ship*:— ship (I-men]).

592. אֲנִיָּה **'ăniyâh**, *an-ee-yaw´*; from 578; *groaning*:— lamentation, sorrow.

אֲנִין **'inniyn**. See 581.

593. אֲנִיעָם **'Ănîy'âm**, *an-ee-awm´*; from 578 and 5971; *groaning of* (the) *people*; *Aniam*, an Isr.:— Aniam.

594. אֲנָךְ **'ânâk**, *an-awk´*; prob. from an unused root mean. to *be narrow*; according to most a plumb-*line*, and to others a *hook*:— plumb-line.

595. אָנֹכִי **'ânôkiy**, *aw-no-kee´* (sometimes *aw-no´-kee*); a prim. pron.; *I*:— I, me, × which.

596. אָנַן **'ânan**, *aw-nan´*; a prim. root; to *mourn*, i.e. *complain*:— complain.

597. אָנַס **'ânaç**, *aw-nas´*; to *insist*:— compel.

598. אֲנַס **'ănaç** (Chald.), *an-as´*; corresp. to 597; fig. to *distress*:— trouble.

599. אָנַף **'ânaph**, *aw-naf´*; a prim. root; to *breathe* hard, i.e. *be enraged*:— be angry (displeased).

600. אֲנַף **'ănaph** (Chald.), *an-af´*; corresp. to 639 (only in the plur. as a sing.); the *face*:— face, visage.

601. אֲנָפָה **'ănâphâh**, *an-aw-faw´*; from 599; an unclean bird, perh. the *parrot* (from its *irascibility*):— heron.

602. אָנַק **'ânaq**, *aw-nak´*; a prim. root; to *shriek*:— cry, groan.

603. אֲנָקָה **'ănâqâh**, *an-aw-kaw´*; from 602; *shrieking*:— crying out, groaning, sighing.

604. אֲנָקָה **'ănâqâh**, *an-aw-kaw´*; the same as 603; some kind of lizard, prob. the *gecko* (from its *wail*):— ferret.

605. אָנַשׁ **'ânash**, *aw-nash´*; a prim. root; to *be frail, feeble*, or (fig.) *melancholy*:— desperate (-ly wicked), incurable, sick, woeful.

606. אֱנָשׁ **'ĕnâsh** (Chald.), *en-awsh´*; or

אֱנָשׁ **'ĕnash** (Chald.), *en-ash´*; corresp. to 582; a *man*:— man, + whosoever.

אֲנָת **'ant**. See 859.

607. אַנְתָּה **'antâh** (Chald.), *an-taw´*; corresp. to 859; *thou*:— as for thee, thou.

608. אַנְתּוּן **'antûwn** (Chald.), *an-toon´*; plur. of 607; *ye*:— ye.

609. אָסָא **'Âçâ'**, *aw-saw´*; of uncert. der.; *Asa*, the name of a king and of a Levite:— Asa.

610. אָסוּךְ **'âçûwk**, *aw-sook´*; from 5480; *anointed*, i.e. an oil-*flask*:— pot.

611. אָסוֹן **'âçôwn**, *aw-sone´*; of uncert. der.; *hurt*:— mischief.

612. אֵסוּר **'êçûwr**, *ay-soor´*; from 631; a *bond* (espec. *manacles* of a prisoner):— band, + prison.

613. אֱסוּר **'ĕçûwr** (Chald.), *es-oor´*; corresp. to 612:— band, imprisonment.

614. אָסִיף **'âçîyph**. See 622;

615. אָסִיר **'âçîyr**, *aw-sere´*; from 631; *bound*, i.e. a *captive*:— (those which are) bound, prisoner.

616. אַסִּיר **'açcîyr**, *as-sere´*; for 615:— prisoner.

617. אַסִּיר **'Açcîyr**, *as-sere´*; the same as 616; *prisoner*; *Assir*, the name of two Isr.:— Assir.

618. אָסָם **'âçâm**, *aw-sawm´*; from an unused root mean. to *heap* together; a *storehouse* (only in the plur.):— barn, storehouse.

619. אַסְנָה **'Açnâh**, *as-naw´*; of uncert. der.; *Asnah*, one of the Nethinim:— Asnah.

620. אָסְנַפַּר **'Oçnappar** (Chald.), *os-nap-par´*; of for. der.; *Osnappar*, an Ass. king:— Asnapper.

621. אָסְנַת **'Âç°nath**, *aw-se-nath´*; of Eg. der.; *Asenath*, the wife of Joseph:— Asenath.

622. אָסַף **'âçaph**, *aw-saf´*; a prim. root; to *gather* for any purpose; hence, to *receive, take away*, i.e. remove (destroy, leave behind, put up, restore, etc.):— assemble, bring, consume, destroy, fetch, gather (in, together, up again), × generally, get (him), lose, put all together, receive, recover [another from leprosy], (be) rereward, × surely, take (away, into, up), × utterly, withdraw.

623. אָסָף **'Âçâph**, *aw-sawf´*; from 622; *collector*; *Asaph*, the name of three Isr., and of the family of the first:— Asaph.

אָסִיף **'âçîph**. See 614.

624. אָסֻף **'âçuph**, *aw-soof´*; pass. part. of 622; *collected* (only in the plur.), i.e. a *collection* (of offerings):— threshold, Asuppim.

625. אֹסֶף **'ôçeph**, *o´-sef*; from 622; a *collection* (of fruits):— gathering.

626. אֲסֵפָה **'ăçêphâh**, *as-ay-faw´*; from 622; a *collection* of people (only adv.):— × together.

627. אֲסֻפָּה **'ăçuppâh**, *as-up-paw´*; fem. of 624.; a *collection* of (learned) men (only in the plur.):— assembly.

628. אֲסַפְסֻף **'açp°çuph**, *as-pes-oof´*; by redupl. from 624; *gathered up together*, i.e. a promiscuous *assemblage* (of people):— mixt multitude.

629. אָסְפַּרְנָא **'oçparnâ'** (Chald.), *os-par-naw´*; of Pers. der.; *diligently*:— fast, forthwith, speed (-ily).

630. אַסְפָּתָא **'Açpâthâ'**, *as-paw-thaw´*; of Pers. der.; *Aspatha*, a son of Haman:— Aspatha.

631. אָסַר **'âçar**, aw-sar´; a prim. root; to yoke or hitch; by anal. to fasten in any sense, to join battle:— bind, fast, gird, harness, hold, keep, make ready, order, prepare, prison (-er), put in bonds, set in array, tie.

632. אֵסָר **'êçâr**, es-sawr´; or

אִסָּר **'içâr**, is-sawr´; from 631; an obligation or vow (of abstinence):— binding, bond.

633. אֱסָר **'êçâr** (Chald.), es-sawr´; corresp. to 632 in a legal sense; an interdict:— decree.

634. אֵסַר־חַדּוֹן **'Êçar-Chaddôwn**, ay-sar´chad-dohn´; of for. der.; Esar-chaddon, an Ass. king:— Esar-haddon.

635. אֶסְתֵּר **'Eçtêr**, es-tare´; of Pers. der.; Ester, the Jewish heroine:— Esther.

636. אָע **'â** (Chald.), aw; corresp. to 6086; a tree or wood:— timber, wood.

637. אַף **'aph**, af; a prim. particle; mean. accession (used as an adv. or conjunc.); also or yea; adversatively though:— also, + although, and (furthermore, yet), but, even, + how much less (more, rather than), moreover, with, yea.

638. אַף **'aph** (Chald.), af; corresp. to 637:— also.

639. אַף **'aph**, af; from 599; prop. the nose or nostril; hence, the face, and occasionally a person; also (from the rapid breathing in passion) ire:— anger (-gry), + before, countenance, face, + forebearing, forehead, + (long-) suffering, nose, nostril, snout, × worthy, wrath.

640. אָפַד **'âphad**, aw-fad´; a prim. root (rather a denom. from 646); to gird on (the ephod):— bind, gird.

אֵפֹד **'êphôd**. See 646.

641. אֵפֹד **'Êphôd**, ay-fode´; the same as 646 short.; Ephod, an Isr.:— Ephod.

642. אֲפֻדָּה **'êphuddâh**, ay-food-daw´; fem. of 646; a girding on (of the ephod); hence, gen. a plating (of metal):— ephod, ornament.

643. אַפֶּדֶן **'appeden**, ap-peh´-den; appar. of for. der.; a pavilion or palacetent:— palace.

644. אָפָה **'âphâh**, aw-faw´; a prim. root; to cook, espec. to bake:— bake (-r, (-meats)).

אֵפֹה **'êphâh**. See 374.

645. אֵפוֹ **'êphôw**, ay-fo´; or

אֵפוֹא **'êphôw**, ay-fo´; from 6311; strictly a demonstr. particle, here; but used of time, now or then:— here, now, where?

646. אֵפוֹד **'êphôwd**, ay-fode´; rarely

אֵפֹד **'êphôd**, ay-fode´; prob. of for. der.; a girdle; spec. the ephod or highpriest's shoulder-piece; also gen. an image:— ephod.

647. אֲפִיחַ **'Âphîyach**, af-ee´-akh; perh. from 6315; breeze; Aphiach, an Isr.:— Aphiah.

648. אָפִיל **'âphîyl**, aw-feel´; from the same as 651 (in the sense of weakness); unripe:— not grown up.

649. אַפַּיִם **'Appayim**, ap-pah´-yim; dual

of 639; two nostrils; Appajim, an Isr.:— Appaim.

650. אָפִיק **'âphîyq**, aw-feek´; from 622; prop. containing, i.e. a tube; also a bed or valley of a stream; also a strong thing or a hero:— brook, channel, mighty, river, + scale, stream, strong piece.

אֹפִיר **'Ôphîyr**. See 211.

651. אָפֵל **'âphêl**, aw-fale´; from an unused root mean. to set as the sun; dusky:— very dark.

652. אֹפֶל **'ôphel**, o´fel; from the same as 651; dusk:— darkness, obscurity, privily.

653. אֲפֵלָה **'ăphêlâh**, af-ay-law´; fem. of 651; duskiness, fig. misfortune; concr. concealment:— dark, darkness, gloominess, × thick.

654. אֶפְלָל **'Ephlâl**, ef-lawl´; from 6419; judge; Ephlal, an Isr.:— Ephlal.

655. אֹפֶן **'ôphen**, o´-fen; from an unused root mean. to revolve; a turn, i.e. a season:— + fitly.

אוֹפָן **'ôphân**. See 212.

656. אָפֵס **'âphêç**, aw-face´; a prim. root; to disappear, i.e. cease:— be clean gone (at an end, brought to nought), fail.

657. אֶפֶס **'epheç**, eh´-fes; from 656; cessation, i.e. an end (espec. of the earth); often used adv. no further; also (like 6466) the ankle (in the dual), as being the extremity of the leg or foot:— ankle, but (only), end, howbeit, less than nothing, nevertheless (where), no, none (beside), not (any, -withstanding), thing of nought, save (-ing), there, uttermost part, want, without (cause).

658. אֶפֶס דַּמִּים **'Epheç Dammîym**, eh´-fes dam-meem´; from 657 and the plur. of 1818; boundary of blood-drops; Ephes-Dammim, a place in Pal.:— Ephes-dammim.

659. אֶפַע **'êpha**, eh´-fah; from an unused root prob. mean. to breathe; prop. a breath, i.e. nothing:— of nought.

660. אֶפְעֶה **'eph'eh**, ef-eh´; from 659 (in the sense of hissing); an asp or other venomous serpent:— viper.

661. אָפַף **'âphaph**, aw-faf´; a prim. root; to surround:— compass.

662. אָפַק **'âphaq**, aw-fak´; a prim. root; to contain, i.e. (reflex.) abstain:— force (oneself), restrain.

663. אֲפֵק **'Ăphêq**, af-ake´; or

אֲפִיק **'Ăphîyq**, af-eek´; from 662 (in the sense of strength); fortress; Aphek (or Aphik), the name of three places in Pal.:— Aphek, Aphik.

664. אֲפֵקָה **'Ăphêqâh**, af-ay-kaw´; fem. of 663; fortress; Aphekah, a place in Pal.:— Aphekah.

665. אֵפֶר **'êpher**, ay´-fer; from an unused root mean. to bestrew; ashes:— ashes.

666. אֲפֵר **'ăphêr**, af-ayr´; from the same as 665 (in the sense of covering); a turban:— ashes.

667. אֶפְרֹחַ **'ephrôach**, ef-ro´-akh; from 6524 (in the sense of bursting the shell); the brood of a bird:— young (one).

668. אַפִּרְיוֹן **'appiryôwn**, ap-pir-yone´; prob. of Eg. der.; a palanquin:— chariot.

669. אֶפְרַיִם **'Ephrayim**, ef-rah´-yim; dual of a masc. form of 672; double fruit; Ephrajim, a son of Joseph; also the tribe descended from him, and its territory:— Ephraim, Ephraimites.

670. אֲפָרְסַי **'Ăphâr°çay** (Chald.), af-aw-re-sah´ee; of for. or. (only in the plur.); an Apharesite or inhab. of an unknown region of Assyria:— Apharsite.

671. אֲפַרְסְכָי **'Ăpharç°kay** (Chald.), af-ar-sek-ah´ee; or

אֲפַרְסַתְכָי **'Ăpharçathkay** (Chald.), af-ar-sath-kah´ee; of for. or. (only in the plur.); an Apharsekite or Apharsathkite, an unknown Ass. tribe:— Apharsachites, Apharsathchites.

672. אֶפְרָת **'Ephrâth**, ef-rawth´; or

אֶפְרָתָה **'Ephrâthâh**, ef-raw´-thaw; from 6509; fruitfulness; Ephrath, another name for Bethlehem; once (Psa. 132:6) perh. for Ephraim; also of an Isr. woman:— Ephrath, Ephratah.

673. אֶפְרָתִי **'Ephrâthîy**, ef-rawth-ee´; patrial from 672; an Ephrathite or an Ephraimite:— Ephraimite, Ephrathite.

674. אַפְּתֹם **'app°thôm** (Chald.), ap-pe-thome´; of Pers. or.; revenue; others at the last:— revenue.

675. אֶצְבּוֹן **'Etsbôwn**, ets-bone´; or

אֶצְבֹּן **'Etsbôn**, ets-bone´; of uncert. der.; Etsbon, the name of two Isr.:— Ezbon.

676. אֶצְבַּע **'etsba'**, ets-bah´; from the same as 6648 (in the sense of grasping); something to seize with, i.e. a finger; by anal. a toe:— finger, toe.

677. אֶצְבַּע **'etsba'** (Chald.), ets-bah´; corresp. to 676:— finger, toe.

678. אָצִיל **'âtsîyl**, aw-tseel´; from 680 (in its second. sense of separation); an extremity (Isa. 41:9), also a noble:— chief man, noble.

679. אַצִּיל **'atstsîyl**, ats-tseel´; from 680 (in its primary sense of uniting); a joint of the hand (i.e. knuckle); also (according to some) a party-wall (Ezek. 41:8):— (arm) hole, great.

680. אָצַל **'âtsal**, aw-tsal´; a prim. root; prop. to join; used only as a denom. from 681; to separate; hence, to select, refuse, contract:— keep, reserve, straiten, take.

681. אֵצֶל **'êtsel**, ay´-tsel; from 680 (in the sense of joining); a side; (as a prep.) near:— at, (hard) by, (from) (beside), near (unto), toward, with. See also 1018.

682. אָצֵל **'Âtsêl**, aw-tsale´; from 680; noble; Atsel, the name of an Isr., and of a place in Pal.:— Azal, Azel.

683. אֲצַלְיָהוּ **'Ătsalyâhûw**, ats-al-yaw´-hoo; from 680 and 3050 prol.; Jah has reserved; Atsaljah, an Isr.:— Azaliah.

684. אֹצֶם **'Ôtsem**, o´-tsem; from an unused root prob. mean. to be strong; strength (i.e. strong); Otsem, the name of two Isr.:— Ozem.

685. אֶצְעָדָה **'ets'âdâh**, ets-aw-daw´; a

var. from 6807; prop. a *step-chain;* by anal. a *bracelet:*— bracelet, chain.

686. אֱצַר **'âtsar**, *aw-tsar';* a prim. root; to *store* up:— (lay up in) store, (make) treasure (-r).

687. אֵצֶר **'Etser**, *ay'-tser;* from 686; *treasure; Etser,* an Idumæan:— Ezer.

688. אֶקְדָּח **'eqdâch**, *ek-dawkh';* from 6916; *burning,* i.e. a *carbuncle* or other fiery gem:— carbuncle.

689. אַקּוֹ **'aqqôw**, *ak-ko';* prob. from 602; *slender,* i.e. the *ibex:*— wild goat.

690. אֲרָא **'Ârâ'**, *ar-aw';* prob. for 738; *lion; Ara,* an Isr.:— Ara.

691. אֶרְאֵל **'er'êl**, *er-ale';* prob. for 739; a *hero* (collect.):— valiant one.

692. אַרְאֵלִי **'Ar'êlîy**, *ar-ay-lee';* from 691; *heroic; Areli* (or an *Arelite,* collect.), an Isr. and his desc.:— Areli, Arelites.

693. אָרַב **'ârab**, *aw-rab';* a prim. root; to *lurk:*— (lie in) ambush (-ment), lay (lie in) wait.

694. אֲרָב **'Ârâb**, *ar-awb';* from 693; *ambush; Arab,* a place in Pal.:— Arab.

695. אֶרֶב **'ereb**, *eh'-reb;* from 693; *ambuscade:*— den, lie in wait.

696. אֹרֶב **'ôreb**, *o'-reb;* the same as 695:— wait.

אַרְבְּאֵל **'Arbê'l**. See 1009.

697. אַרְבֶּה **'arbeh**, *ar-beh';* from 7235; a *locust* (from its rapid *increase*):— grasshopper, locust.

698. אֳרֻבָּה **'orŏbâh**, *or-ob-aw';* fem. of 696 (only in the plur.); *ambuscades:*— spoils.

699. אֲרֻבָּה **'ârubbâh**, *ar-oob-baw';* fem. part. pass. of 693 (as if for *lurking*); a *lattice;* (by impl.) a *window, dove-cot* (because of the pigeon-holes), *chimney* (with its apertures for smoke), *sluice* (with openings for water):— chimney, window.

700. אֲרֻבּוֹה **'Ârubbôwth**, *ar-oob-both';* plur. of 699; *Arubboth,* a place in Pal.:— Aruboth.

701. אַרְבִּי **'Arbîy**, *ar-bee';* patrial from 694; an *Arbite* or native of Arab:— Arbite.

702. אַרְבַּע **'arba'**, *ar-bah';* masc.

אַרְבָּעָה **'arbâ'âh**, *ar-baw-aw';* from 7251; *four:*— four.

703. אַרְבַּע **'arba'** (Chald.), *ar-bah';* corresp. to 702:— four.

704. אַרְבַּע **'Arba'**, *ar-bah';* the same as 702; *Arba,* one of the Anakim:— Arba.

אַרְבָּעָה **'arbâ'âh**. See 702.

705. אַרְבָּעִים **'arbâ'îym**, *ar-baw-eem';* multiple of 702; *forty:*— forty.

706. אַרְבַּעְתַּיִם **'arba'tayim**, *ar-bah-tah'-yim;* dual of 702; *fourfold:*— fourfold.

707. אָרַג **'ârag**, *aw-rag';* a prim. root; to *plait* or *weave:*— weaver (-r).

708. אֶרֶג **'ereg**, *eh'-reg;* from 707; a *weaving;* a *braid;* also a *shuttle:*— beam, weaver's shuttle.

709. אַרְגֹּב **'Argôb**, *ar-gobe';* from the same as 7263; *stony; Argob,* a district of Pal.:— Argob.

710. אַרְגְּוָן **'argevân**, *arg-ev-awn';* a var. for 713; *purple:*— purple.

711. אַרְגְּוָן **'argevân** (Chald.), *arg-ev-awn';* corresp. to 710:— purple.

712. אַרְגָּז **'argâz**, *ar-gawz';* perh. from 7264 (in the sense of being *suspended*); a *box* (as a pannier):— coffer.

713. אַרְגָּמָן **'argâmân**, *ar-gaw-mawn';* of for. or.; *purple* (the color or the dyed stuff):— purple.

714. אַרְדְּ **'Ard**, *ard;* from an unused root prob. mean. to *wander; fugitive; Ard,* the name of two Isr.:— Ard.

715. אַרְדּוֹן **'Ardôwn**, *ar-dohn';* from the same as 714; *roaming; Ardon,* an Isr.:— Ardon.

716. אַרְדִּי **'Ardîy**, *ar-dee';* patron. from 714; an *Ardite* (collect.) or desc. of Ard:— Ardites.

717. אָרָה **'ârâh**, *aw-raw';* a prim. root; to *pluck:*— gather, pluck.

718. אֲרוּ **'ârûw** (Chald.), *ar-oo';* prob. akin to 431; *lo!:*— behold, lo.

719. אַרְוַד **'Arvad**, *ar-vad';* prob. from 7300; a refuge for the *roving; Arvad,* an island-city of Pal.:— Arvad.

720. אֲרוֹד **'Ârôwd**, *ar-ode';* an orth. var. of 719; *fugitive; Arod,* an Isr.:— Arod.

721. אֲרוֹדִי **'Ârvâdîy**, *ar-vaw-dee';* patrial from 719; an *Arvadite* or citizen of Arvad:— Arvadite.

722. אֲרוֹדִי **'Ârôwdîy**, *ar-o-dee';* patron. from 721; an *Arodite* or desc. of Arod:— Arodi, Arodites.

723. אֻרְוָה **'urvâh**, *oor-vaw';* or

אֲרָיָה **'ârâyâh**, *ar-aw-yah';* from 717 (in the sense of *feeding*); a *herding-place* for an animal:— stall.

724. אֲרוּכָה **'ârûwkâh**, *ar-oo-kaw';* or

אֲרֻכָה **'ârûkâh**, *ar-oo-kaw';* fem. pass. part. of 748 (in the sense of *restoring* to soundness); *wholeness* (lit. or fig.):— health, made up, perfected.

725. אֲרוּמָה **'Ârûwmâh**, *ar-oo-maw';* a var. of 7316; *height; Arumah,* a place in Pal.:— Arumah.

726. אֲרוֹמִי **'Ârôwmîy**, *ar-o-mee';* a clerical err. for 130; an *Edomite* (as in the marg.):— Syrian.

727. אֲרוֹן **'ârôwn**, *aw-rone';* or

אָרֹן **'ârôn**, *aw-rone';* from 717 (in the sense of *gathering*); a *box:*— ark, chest, coffin.

728. אֲרַוְנָה **'Ăravnâh**, *ar-av-naw';* or (by transp.)

אוֹרְנָה **'Ôwrnâh**, *ore-naw';* or

אֲרַנְיָה **'Arnîyah**, *ar-nee-yaw';* all by orth. var. for 771; *Aravnah* (or *Arnijah* or *Ornah*), a Jebusite:— Araunah.

729. אֶרֶז **'âraz**, *aw-raz';* a prim. root; to *be firm;* used only in the pass. part. as a denom. from 730; of *cedar:*— made of cedar.

730. אֶרֶז **'erez**, *eh-rez';* from 729; a *cedar* tree (from the tenacity of its roots):— cedar (tree).

731. אַרְזָה **'arzâh**, *ar-zaw';* fem. of 730; *cedar paneling:*— cedar work.

732. אָרַח **'ârach**, *aw-rakh';* a prim. root; to *travel:*— go, wayfaring (man).

733. אָרַח **'Ârach**, *aw-rakh';* from 732;

way-faring; *Arach,* the name of three Isr.:— Arah.

734. אֹרַח **'ôrach**, *o'-rakh;* from 732; a well-trodden *road* (lit. or fig.); also a *caravan:*— manner, path, race, rank, traveller, troop, [by-, high-] way.

735. אֹרַח **'ôrach** (Chald.), *o'-rakh;* corresp. to 734; a *road:*— way.

736. אֹרְחָה **'ôrechâh**, *o-rekh-aw';* fem. act. part. of 732; a *caravan:*— (travelling) company.

737. אֲרֻחָה **'ărûchâh**, *ar-oo-khaw';* fem. pass. part. of 732 (in the sense of *appointing*); a *ration* of food:— allowance, diet, dinner, victuals.

738. אֲרִי **'ărîy**, *ar-ee';* or (prol.)

אַרְיֵה **'aryêh**, *ar-yay';* from 717 (in the sense of *violence*); a *lion:*— (young) lion, + pierce [from the marg.].

739. אֲרִיאֵל **'ărîy'êl**, *ar-ee-ale';* or

אֲרִאֵל **'ărî'êl**, *ar-ee-ale';* from 738 and 410; *lion of God,* i.e. *heroic:*— lionlike men.

740. אֲרִיאֵל **'Ărî'êl**, *ar-ee-ale';* the same as 739; *Ariel,* a symb. name for Jerusalem, also the name of an Isr.:— Ariel.

741. אֲרִיאֵל **'ărî'êyl**, *ar-ee-ale';* either by transp. for 739 or, more prob. an orth. var. for 2025; the *altar* of the Temple:— altar.

742. אֲרִידַי **'Ărîyday**, *ar-ee-dah'-ee;* of Pers. or.; *Aridai,* a son of Haman:— Aridai.

743. אֲרִידָתָא **'Ărîydâthâ'**, *ar-ee-daw-thaw';* of Pers. or.; *Aridatha,* a son of Haman:— Aridatha.

אַרְיֵה **'aryêh**. See 738.

744. אַרְיֵה **'aryêh** (Chald.), *ar-yay';* corresp. to 738:— lion.

745. אַרְיֵה **'Aryêh**, *ar-yay';* the same as 738; *lion; Arjeh,* an Isr.:— Arieh.

אַרְיֵה **'ărâyâh**. See 723.

746. אַרְיוֹךְ **'Ăryôwk**, *ar-yoke';* of for. or.; *Arjok,* the name of two Babylonians:— Arioch.

747. אֲרִיסַי **'Ărîyçay**, *ar-ee-sah'-ee;* of Pers. or.; *Arisai,* a son of Haman:— Arisai.

748. אָרַךְ **'ârak**, *aw-rak';* a prim. root; to *be* (caus. *make*) *long* (lit. or fig.):— defer, draw out, lengthen, (be, become, make, pro-) long, + (out-, over-) live, tarry (long).

749. אֲרַךְ **'ărak** (Chald.), *ar-ak';* prop. corresp. to 748, but used only in the sense of *reaching* to a given point; to *suit:*— be meet.

750. אָרֵךְ **'ârêk**, *aw-rake';* from 748; *long:*— long [-suffering, -winged], patient, slow [to anger].

751. אֶרֶךְ **'Erek**, *eh'-rek;* from 748; *length; Erek,* a place in Bab.:— Erech.

752. אָרֹךְ **'ârôk**, *aw-roke';* from 748; *long:*— long.

753. אֹרֶךְ **'ôrek**, *o'rek';* from 748; *length:*— + for ever, length, long.

754. אַרְכָּא **'arkâ'** (Chald.), *ar-kaw';* or

אַרְכָה **'arkâh** (Chald.), *ar-kaw';* from 749; *length:*— lengthening, prolonged.

755. אַרְכֻּבָה **'arkûbâh** (Chald.), *ar-koo-baw´*; from an unused root corresp. to 7392 (in the sense of *bending* the knee); the *knee*:— knee.

אַרְכָה **'ărûkâh**. See 724.

756. אַרְכְוַי **'Ark⁰vay** (Chald.), *ar-kev-ah´ee*; patrial from 751; an *Arkevite* (collect.) or native of Erek:— Archevite.

757. אַרְכִּי **'Arkîy**, *ar-kee´*; patrial from another place (in Pal.) of similar name with 751; an *Arkite* or native of Erek:— Archi, Archite.

758. אֲרָם **'Arâm**, *arawm´*; from the same as 759; the *highland*; *Aram* or Syria, and its inhab.; also the name of a son of Shem, a grandson of Nahor, and of an Isr.:— Aram, Mesopotamia, Syria, Syrians.

759. אַרְמוֹן **'armôwn**, *ar-mone´*; from an unused root (mean. to be *elevated*); a *citadel* (from its *height*):— castle, palace. Comp. 2038.

760. אֲרַם צוֹבָה **'Aram Tsôwbâh**, *ar-am´ tso-baw´*; from 758 and 6678; *Aram of Tsoba* (or *Coele-Syria*):— Aram-zobah.

761. אֲרַמִּי **'Ărammîy**, *ar-am-mee´*; patrial from 758; an *Aramite* or Aramæan:— Syrian, Aramitess.

762. אֲרָמִית **'Ărâmîyth**, *ar-aw-meeth´*; fem. of 761; (only adv.) in *Aramæan*:— in the Syrian language (tongue), in Syriack.

763. אֲרַם נַהֲרַיִם **'Aram Nahărayim**, *ar-am´ nah-har-ah´-yim*; from 758 and the dual of 5104; *Aram of* (the) *two rivers* (Euphrates and Tigris) or *Mesopotamia*:— Aham-naharaim, Mesopotamia.

764. אַרְמֹנִי **'Armônîy**, *ar-mo-nee´*; from 759; *palatial*; *Armoni*, an Isr.:— Armoni.

765. אֲרָן **'Ărân**, *ar-awn´*; from 7442; *stridulous*; *Aran*, an Edomite:— Aran.

766. אֹרֶן **'ôren**, *o´-ren*; from the same as 765 (in the sense of *strength*); the *ash* tree (from its toughness):— ash.

767. אֹרֶן **'Ôren**, *o´-ren*; the same as 766; *Oren*, an Isr.:— Oren.

אָרֹן **'ârôn**. See 727.

768. אַרְנֶבֶת **'arnebeth**, *ar-neh´-beth*; of uncert. der.; the *hare*:— hare.

769. אַרְנוֹן **'Arnôwn**, *ar-nohn´*; or

אַרְנֹן **'Arnôn**, *ar-nohn´*; from 7442; a *brawling* stream; the *Arnon*, a river east of the Jordan; also its territory:— Arnon.

אַרְנִיָה **'Arnîyah**. See 728.

770. אַרְנָן **'Arnân**, *ar-nawn´*; prob. from the same as 769; *noisy*; *Arnan*, an Isr.:— Arnan.

771. אָרְנָן **'Ornân**, *or-nawn´*; prob. from 766; *strong*; *Ornan*, a Jebusite:— Ornan. See 728.

772. אֲרַע **'ăra'** (Chald.), *ar-ah´*; corresp. to 776; the *earth*; by impl. (fig.) *low*:— earth, interior.

773. אַרְעִית **'ar'îyth** (Chald.), *arh-eeth´*; fem. of 772; the *bottom*:— bottom.

774. אַרְפַּד **'Arpâd**, *ar-pawd´*; from 7502;

spread out; *Arpad*, a place in Syria:— Arpad, Arphad.

775. אַרְפַּכְשַׁד **'Arpakshad**, *ar-pak-shad´*; prob. of for. or.; *Arpakshad*, a son of Noah; also the region settled by him:— Arphaxad.

776. אֶרֶץ **'erets**, *eh´-rets*; from an unused root prob. mean. to be *firm*; the *earth* (at large, or partitively a *land*):— × common, country, earth, field, ground, land, × nations, way, + wilderness, world.

777. אַרְצָא **'artsâ'**, *ar-tsaw´*; from 776; *earthiness*; *Artsa*, an Isr.:— Arza.

778. אֲרַק **'ăraq** (Chald.), *ar-ak´*; by transm. for 772; the *earth*:— earth.

779. אָרַר **'ârar**, *aw-rar´*; a prim. root; to *execrate*:— × bitterly curse.

780. אֲרָרַט **'Ărârat**, *ar-aw-rat´*; of for. or.; *Ararat* (or rather Armenia):— Ararat, Armenia.

781. אָרַשׂ **'âras**, *aw-ras´*; a prim. root; to *engage* for matrimony:— betroth, espouse.

782. אֲרֶשֶׂת **'ăresheth**; from 781 (in the sense of *desiring* to possess); a *longing* for:— request.

783. אַרְתַּחְשַׁשְׂתָּא **'Artachshastâ'** (Chald.), *ar-takh-shas-taw´*; or

אַרְתַּחְשַׁשְׂתְּא **'Artachshast'** (Chald.), *ar-takh-shast´*; or by perm.

אַרְתַּחְשַׂשְׂתְּ **'Artachshaçt'** (Chald.), *ar-takh-shast´*; of for. or.; *Artachshasta* (or Artaxerxes), a title (rather than name) of several Pers. kings:— Artaxerxes.

784. אֵשׁ **'êsh**, *aysh*; a prim. word; *fire* (lit. or fig.):— burning, fiery, fire, flaming, hot.

785. אֵשׁ **'êsh** (Chald.), *aysh*; corresp. to 784:— flame.

786. אִשׁ **'ish**, *eesh*; ident. (in or. and formation) with 784; *entity*; used only adv., there *is* or *are*:— are there, none can. Comp. 3426.

787. אֹשׁ **'ôsh** (Chald.), *ohsh*; corresp. (by transp. and abb.) to 803; a *foundation*:— foundation.

788. אַשְׁבֵּל **'Ashbêl**, *ash-bale´*; prob. from the same as 7640; *flowing*; *Ashbel*, an Isr.:— Ashbel.

789. אַשְׁבֵּלִי **'Ashbêlîy**, *ash-bay-lee´*; patron. from 788; an *Ashbelite* (collect.) or desc. of Ashbel:— Ashbelites.

790. אֶשְׁבָּן **'Eshbân**, *esh-bawn´*; prob. from the same as 7644; *vigorous*; *Eshban*, an Idumæan:— Eshban.

791. אַשְׁבֵּעַ **'Ashbêa'**, *ash-bay´-ah*; from 7650; *adjurer*; *Asbeä*, an Isr.:— Ashbea.

792. אֶשְׁבַּעַל **'Eshba'al**, *esh-bah´-al*; from 376 and 1168; *man of Baal*; *Eshbaal* (or Ishbosheth), a son of King Saul:— Eshbaal.

793. אֶשֶׁד **'eshed**, *eh´-shed*; from an unused root mean. to *pour*; an *outpouring*:— stream.

794. אֲשֵׁדָה **'ăshêdâh**, *ash-ay-daw´*; fem. of 793; a *ravine*:— springs.

795. אַשְׁדּוֹד **'Ashdôwd**, *ash-dode´*; from 7703; *ravager*; *Ashdod*, a place in Pal.:— Ashdod.

796. אַשְׁדּוֹדִי **'Ashdôwdîy**, *ash-do-dee´*; patrial from 795; an *Ashdodite* (often collect.) or inhab. of Ashdod:— Ashdodites, of Ashdod.

797. אַשְׁדּוֹדִית **'Ashdôwdîyth**, *ash-do-deeth´*; fem. of 796; (only adv.) in the *language of Ashdod*:— in the speech of Ashdod.

798. אַשְׁדּוֹת הַפִּסְגָּה **'Ashdôwth hap-Piçgâh**, *ash-doth´ hap-pis-gaw´*; from the plur. of 794 and 6449 with the art. interposed; *ravines of the Pisgah*; *Ashdoth-Pisgah*, a place east of the Jordan:— Ashdoth-pisgah.

799. אֶשְׁדָּת **'eshdâth**, *esh-dawth´*; from 784 and 1881; a *fire-law*:— fiery law.

800. אֶשָּׁה **'eshshâh**, *esh-shaw´*; fem. of 784; *fire*:— fire.

801. אִשָּׁה **'ishshâh**, *ish-shaw´*; the same as 800, but used in a liturgical sense; prop. a *burnt-offering*; but occasionally of any *sacrifice*:— (offering, sacrifice), (made) by fire.

802. אִשָּׁה **'ishshâh**, *ish-shaw´*; fem. of 376 or 582; irreg. plur.

נָשִׁים **nâshîym**, *naw-sheem´*; a *woman* (used in the same wide sense as 582):— [adulterer]less, each, every, female, × many, + none, one, + together, wife, woman. [*Often unexpressed in English*.]

803. אֲשׁוּיָה° **'ăshûwyâh**, *ash-oo-yah´*; fem. pass. part. from an unused root mean. to *found*; *foundation*:— foundation.

804. אַשּׁוּר **'Ashshûwr**, *ash-shoor´*; or

אַשֻּׁר **'Ashshûr**, *ash-shoor´*; appar. from 833 (in the sense of *successful*); *Ashshur*, the second son of Shem; also his desc. and the country occupied by them (i.e. Assyria), its region and its empire:— Asshur, Assur, Assyria, Assyrians. See 838.

805. אַשּׁוּרִי **'Ashûwrîy**, *ash-oo-ree´*; or

אַשֻּׁרִי **'Ashshûwrîy**, *ash-shoo-ree´*; from a patrial word of the same form as 804; an *Ashurite* (collect.) or inhab. of Ashur, a district in Pal.:— Asshurim, Ashurites.

806. אַשְׁחוּר **'Ashchûwr**, *ash-khoor´*; prob. from 7835; *black*; *Ashchur*, an Isr.:— Ashur.

807. אֲשִׁימָא **'Ăshîymâ'**, *ash-ee-maw´*; of for. or.; *Ashima*, a deity of Hamath:— Ashima.

אֲשֵׁירָה **'ăshêyrâh**. See 842.

808. אָשִׁישׁ **'âshîysh**, *aw-sheesh´*; from the same as 784 (in the sense of *pressing* down firmly; comp. 803); a (ruined) *foundation*:— foundation.

809. אֲשִׁישָׁה **'ăshîyshâh**, *ash-ee-shaw´*; fem. of 808; something closely *pressed* together, i.e. a *cake* of raisins or other comfits:— flagon.

810. אֶשֶׁךְ **'eshek**, *eh´-shek*; from an unused root (prob. mean. to *bunch* together); a *testicle* (as a *lump*):— stone.

811. אֶשְׁכּוֹל **'eshkôwl**, *esh-kole´*; or

אֶשְׁכֹּל **'eshkôl**, *esh-kole´*; prob. prol. from 810; a *bunch of grapes* or other fruit:— cluster (of grapes).

812. אֶשְׁכֹּל **'Eshkôl**, *esh-kole´*; the same

as 811; *Eshcol*, the name of an Amorite, also of a valley in Pal.:— Eshcol.

813. אַשְׁכְּנַז **'Ashkᵉnaz**, *ash-ken-az´;* of for. or.; *Ashkenaz*, a Japhethite, also his desc.:— Ashkenaz.

814. אֶשְׁכָּר **'eshkâr**, *esh-kawr´;* for 7939; a *gratuity:*— gift, present.

815. אֵשֶׁל **'êshel**, *ay´-shel;* from a root of uncert. signif.; a *tamarisk* tree; by extens. a *grove* of any kind:— grove, tree.

816. אָשָׁם **'âsham**, *aw-sham´;* or

אָשֵׁם **'âshêm**, *aw-shame´;* a prim. root; to *be guilty;* by impl. to *be punished* or *perish:*— × certainly, be (-come, made) desolate, destroy, × greatly, be (-come, found, hold) guilty, offend (acknowledge offence), trespass.

817. אָשָׁם **'âshâm**, *aw-shawm´;* from 816; *guilt;* by impl. a *fault;* also a *sin-offering:*— guiltiness, (offering for) sin, trespass (offering).

818. אָשֵׁם **'âshêm**, *aw-shame´;* from 816; *guilty;* hence, *presenting a sin-offering:*— one which is faulty, guilty.

819. אַשְׁמָה **'ashmâh**, *ash-maw´;* fem. of 817; *guiltiness,* a *fault,* the *presentation of a sin-offering:*— offend, sin, (cause of) trespass (-ing, offering).

אַשְׁמוּרָה **'ashmûwrâh**. See 821.

820. אַשְׁמָן **'ashmân**, *ash-mawn´;* prob. from 8081; a *fat* field:— desolate place.

821. אַשְׁמֻרָה **'ashmurâh**, *ash-moo-raw´;* or

אַשְׁמוּרָה **'ashmûwrâh**, *ash-moo-raw´;* or

אַשְׁמֹרֶת **'ashmôreth**, *ash-mo´-reth;* fem. from 8104; a *night watch:*— watch.

822. אֶשְׁנָב **'eshnâb**, *esh-nawb´;* appar. from an unused root (prob. mean. to *leave small spaces between two things*); a latticed *window:*— casement, lattice.

823. אַשְׁנָה **'Ashnâh**, *ash-naw´;* prob. a var. for 3466; *Ashnah,* the name of two places in Pal.:— Ashnah.

824. אֶשְׁעָן **'Esh'ân**, *esh-awn´;* from 8172; *support; Eshan,* a place in Pal.:— Eshean.

825. אַשָּׁף **'ashshâph**, *ash-shawf´;* from an unused root (prob. mean. to *lisp,* i.e. *practice enchantment*); a *conjurer:*— astrologer.

826. אַשַּׁף **'ashshâph** (Chald.), *ash-shawf´;* corresp. to 825:— astrologer.

827. אַשְׁפָּה **'ashpâh**, *ash-paw´;* perh. (fem.) from the same as 825 (in the sense of *covering*); a *quiver* or arrow-case:— quiver.

828. אַשְׁפְּנַז **'Ashpᵉnaz**, *ash-pen-az´;* of for. or.; *Ashpenaz,* a Bab. eunuch:— Ashpenaz.

829. אֶשְׁפָּר **'eshpâr**, *esh-pawr´;* of uncert. der.; a measured *portion:*— good piece (of flesh).

830. אַשְׁפֹּת **'ashpôth**, *ash-pohth´;* or

אַשְׁפּוֹת **'ashpôwth**, *ash-pohth´;* (contr.)

שְׁפֹת **shᵉphôth**, *shef-ohth´;* plur. of a noun of the same form as 827, from

8192 (in the sense of *scraping*); a heap of *rubbish* or *filth:*— dung (hill).

831. אַשְׁקְלוֹן **'Ashqᵉlôwn**, *ash-kel-one´;* prob. from 8254 in the sense of *weighing-*place (i.e. *mart*); *Ashkelon,* a place in Pal.:— Ashkelon, Askalon.

832. אַשְׁקְלוֹנִי **'Eshqᵉlôwnîy**, *esh-kel-o-nee´;* patrial from 831; an *Ashkelonite* (collect.) or inhab. of Ashkelon:— Eshkalonites.

833. אָשַׁר **'âshar**, *aw-shar´;* or

אָשֵׁר **'âshêr**, *aw-share´;* a prim. root; to *be straight* (used in the widest sense, espec. to *be level, right, happy*); fig. to *go forward, be honest, prosper:*— (call, be) bless (-ed, happy), go, guide, lead, relieve.

834. אֲשֶׁר **'âsher**, *ash-er´;* a prim. rel. pron. (of every gender and number); *who, which, what, that;* also (as adv. and conjunc.) *when, where, how, because, in order that,* etc.:— × after, × alike, as (soon as), because, × every, for, + forasmuch, + from whence, + how (-soever), × if, (so) that ([thing] which, wherein), × though, + until, + whatsoever, when, where (+ -as, -in, -of, -on, -soever, -with), which, whilst, + whither (-soever), who (-m, -soever, -se). [As it is indeclinable, it is often accompanied by the personal pron. expletively, used to show the connection.]

835. אֶשֶׁר **'esher**, *eh´-sher;* from 833; *happiness;* only in masc. plur. constr. as interj., how *happy!:*— blessed, happy.

836. אָשֵׁר **'Ashêr**, *aw-share´;* from 833; *happy; Asher,* a son of Jacob, and the tribe descended from him, with its territory; also a place in Pal.:— Asher.

837. אֹשֶׁר **'ôsher**, *o´-sher;* from 833; *happiness:*— happy.

838. אָשֻׁר **'âshshûwr**, *aw-shoor´;* or

אַשֻׁר **'ashshûr**, *ash-shoor´;* from 833 in the sense of *going;* a *step:*— going, step.

839. אֲשֻׁר **'ăshûr**, *ash-oor´;* contr. for 8391; the *cedar* tree or some other light elastic wood:— Ashurite.

אַשְׁשׁוּר **'Ashshûr**. See 804, 838.

840. אֲשַׂרְאֵל **'Ăsar'êl**, *as-ar-ale´;* by orth. var. from 833 and 410; *right of God; Asarel,* an Isr.:— Asareel.

841. אֲשַׂרְאֵלָה **'Ăsar'êlâh**, *as-ar-ale´-aw;* from the same as 840; *right toward God; Asarelah,* an Isr.:— Asarelah. Comp. 3480.

842. אֲשֵׁרָה **'ăshêrâh**, *ash-ay-raw´;* or

אֲשֵׁירָה **'ăshêyrâh**, *ash-ay-raw´;* from 833; *happy; Asherah* (or Astarte) a Phœnician goddess; also an *image* of the same:— grove. Comp. 6253.

843. אֲשֵׁרִי **'Ashêrîy**, *aw-shay-ree´;* patron. from 836; an *Asherite* (collect.) or desc. of Asher:— Asherites.

844. אַשְׂרִיאֵל **'Asrîy'êl**, *as-ree-ale´;* an orth. var. for 840; *Asriel,* the name of two Isr.:— Ashriel, Asriel.

845. אַשְׂרִאֵלִי **'Asrî'êlîy**, *as-ree-ale-ee´;* patron. from 844; an *Asrielite* (collect.) or desc. of Asriel:— Asrielites.

846. אֻשַׁרְנָא **'ushsharnâ'** (Chald.), *oosh-*

ar-naw´; from a root corresp. to 833; a *wall* (from its uprightness):— wall.

847. אֶשְׁתָּאֹל **'Eshtâ'ôl**, *esh-taw-ole´;* or

אֶשְׁתָּאוֹל **'Eshtâ'ôwl**, *esh-taw-ole´;* prob. from 7592; *intreaty; Eshtaol,* a place in Pal.:— Eshtaol.

848. אֶשְׁתָּאֻלִי **'Eshtâ'ûlîy**, *esh-taw-oo-lee´;* patrial from 847; an *Eshtaolite* (collect.) or inhab. of Eshtaol:— Eshtaulites.

849. אֶשְׁתַּדּוּר **'eshtaddûwr** (Chald.), *esh-tad-dure´;* from 7712 (in a bad sense); *rebellion:*— sedition.

850. אֶשְׁתּוֹן **'Eshtôwn**, *esh-tone´;* prob. from the same as 7764; *restful; Eshton,* an Isr.:— Eshton.

851. אֶשְׁתְּמֹעַ **'Eshtᵉmôa**, *esh-tem-o´-ah;* or

אֶשְׁתְּמוֹעַ **'Eshtᵉmôwa'**, *esh-tem-o´-ah;* or

אֶשְׁתְּמֹה **'Eshtᵉmôh**, *esh-tem-o´;* from 8085 (in the sense of *obedience*); *Eshtemoa* or *Eshtemoh,* a place in Pal.:— Eshtemoa, Eshtemoh.

אָת° **'ath**. See 859.

852. אָת **'âth** (Chald.), *awth;* corresp. to 226; a *portent:*— sign.

853. אֵת **'êth**, *ayth;* appar. contr. from 226 in the demonstr. sense of *entity;* prop. *self* (but gen. used to point out more def. the obj. of a verb or prep., *even* or *namely*):— [as such unrepresented in English].

854. אֵת **'êth**, *ayth;* prob. from 579; prop. *nearness* (used only as a prep. or an adv.), *near;* hence, gen. *with, by, at, among,* etc.:— against, among, before, by, for, from, in (-to) (out) of, with. [Often with another prep. prefixed.]

855. אֵת **'êth**, *ayth;* of uncert. der.; a *hoe* or other digging implement:— coulter, plowshare.

אַתָּא **'âttâ**. See 859.

אָתָא **'âthâ'**. See 857.

856. אֶתְבַּעַל **'Ethba'al**, *eth-bah´-al;* from 854 and 1168; *with Baal; Ethbaal,* a Phœnician king:— Ethbaal.

857. אָתָה **'âthâh**, *aw-thaw´;* or

אָתָא **'âthâ'**, *aw-thaw´;* a prim. root [collat. to 225 contr.]; to *arrive:*— (be-, things to) come (upon), bring.

858. אֲתָה **'âthâh** (Chald.), *aw-thaw´;* or

אֲתָא **'âthâ'** (Chald.), *aw-thaw´;* corresp. to 857:— (be-) come, bring.

859. אַתָּה **'attâh**, *at-taw´;* or (short.);

אַתָּ **'attâ**, *at-taw´;* or

אָת° **'ath**, *ath;* fem. (irreg.) sometimes

אַתִּי **'attîy**, *at-tee´;* plur. masc.

אַתֶּם **'attem**, *at-tem´;* fem.

אַתֶּן **'atten**, *at-ten´;* or

אַתֵּנָה **'attênâh**, *at-tay´-naw;* or

אַתֵּנָּה **'attênnâh**, *at-tane´-naw;* a prim. pron. of the second pers.; *thou* and *thee,* or (plur.) *ye* and *you:*— thee, thou, ye, you.

860. אָתוֹן **'âthôwn**, *aw-thone´;* prob. from the same as 386 (in the sense of

patience); a female *ass* (from its docility):— (she) ass.

861. אָתוֹן **'attûwn** (Chald.), *at-toon'*; prob. from the corresp. to 784; prob. a *fire-place*, i.e. *furnace*:— furnace.

862. אַתּוּק **'attûwq**, *at-tooke'*; or

אַתִּיק **'attîyq**, *at-teek'*; from 5423 in the sense of *decreasing*; a *ledge* or offset in a building:— gallery.

863. אַתִּי **'attîy**. See 859.

אִתַּי **'Ittay**, *it-tah'ee*; or

אִיתַי **'Iythay**, *ee-thah'ee*; from 854; *near*; *Ittai* or *Ithai*, the name of a Gittite and of an Isr.:— Ithai, Ittai.

864. אֵתָם **'Êthâm**, *ay-thawm'*; of Eg. der.; *Etham*, a place in the Desert:— Etham.

אַתֶּם **'attem**. See 859.

865. אֶתְמוֹל **'ethmôwl**, *eth-mole'*; or

אִתְמוֹל **'ithmôwl**, *ith-mole'*; or

אֶתְמוּל **'ethmûwl**, *eth-mool'*; prob. from 853 or 854 and 4136; *heretofore*; def. *yesterday*:— + before (that) time, + heretofore, of late (old), + times past, yester[day].

אַתֶּן **'atten**. See 859.

866. אֶתְנָה **'ethnâh**, *eth-naw'*; from 8566; a *present* (as the price of harlotry):— reward.

אֶתְנָה **'attênâh** or

אֶתְנָה **'attênnâh**. See 859.

867. אֶתְנִי **'Ethnîy**, *eth-nee'*; perh. from 866; *munificence*; *Ethni*, an Isr.:— Ethni.

868. אֶתְנַן **'ethnan**, *eth-nan'*; the same as 866; a *gift* (as the price of harlotry or idolatry):— hire, reward.

869. אֶתְנַן **'Ethnan**, *eth-nan'*; the same as 868 in the sense of 867; *Ethnan*, an Isr.:— Ethnan.

870. אֲתַר **'âthar** (Chald.), *ath-ar'*; from a root corresp. to that of 871; a *place*; (adv.) *after*:— after, place.

871. אֲתָרִים **'Athârîym**, *ath-aw-reem'*; plur. from an unused root (prob. mean. to *step*); *places; Atharim*, a place near Pal.:— spies.

ב

872. בְּאָה **bᵉ'âh**, *bě-aw'*; from 935, an *entrance* to a building:— entry.

873. בְּאִישׁ **bi'ûwsh** (Chald.), *be-oosh'*; from 888; *wicked*:— bad.

874. בָּאַר **bâ'ar**, *baw-ar'*; a prim. root; to *dig*; by anal. to *engrave*; fig. to *explain*:— declare, (make) plain (-ly).

875. בְּאֵר **bᵉ'êr**, *bě-ayr'*; from 874; a *pit*; espec. a *well*:— pit, well.

876. בְּאֵר **Bᵉ'êr**, *bě-ayr'*; the same as 875; *Beër*, a place in the Desert, also one in Pal.:— Beer.

877. בֹּאר **bô'r**, *bore*; from 874; a *cistern*:— cistern.

878. בְּאֵרָא **Bᵉ'êrâ**, *bě-ay-raw'*; from 875; a *well; Beëra*, an Isr.:— Beera.

879. בְּאֵר אֵלִים **Bᵉ'êr 'Êlîym**, *bě-ayr' ay-leem'*; from 875 and the plur. of 410; *well of heroes; Beër-Elim*, a place in the Desert:— Beer-elim.

880. בְּאֵרָה **Bᵉ'êrâh**, *bě-ay-raw'*; the same as 878; *Beërah*, an Isr.:— Beerah.

881. בְּאֵרוֹת **Bᵉ'êrôwth**, *bě-ay-rohth'*; fem. plur. of 875; *wells; Beëroth*, a place in Pal.:— Beeroth.

882. בְּאֵרִי **Bᵉ'êrîy**, *bě-ay-ree'*; from 875; *fountained; Beëri*, the name of a Hittite and of an Isr.:— Beeri.

883. בְּאֵר לַחַי רֹאִי **Bᵉ'êr la-Chay Rô'îy**, *bě-ayr' lakh-ah'ee ro-ee'*; from 875 and 2416 (with pref.) and 7203; *well of a living* (One) *my seer; Beër-Lachai-Roï*, a place in the Desert:— Beer-lahai-roi.

884. בְּאֵר שֶׁבַע **Bᵉ'êr Sheba'**, *be-ayr' sheh'-bah*; from 875 and 7651 (in the sense of 7650); *well of an oath; Beër-Sheba*, a place in Pal.:— Beer-sheba.

885. בְּאֵרוֹת בְּנֵי־יַעֲקָן **Bᵉ'êrôth Bᵉnêy-Ya'ăqan**, *bě-ay-roth' be-nay' yah-a-kan'*; from the fem. plur. of 875, and the plur. contr. of 1121, and 3292; *wells of* (the) *sons of Jaakan; Beëroth-Bene-Jaakan*, a place in the Desert:— Beeroth of the children of Jaakan.

886. בְּאֵרֹתִי **Bᵉ'êrôthîy**, *bě-ay-ro-thee'*; patrial from 881; a *Beërothite* or inhab. of Beëroth:— Beerothite.

887. בָּאַשׁ **bâ'ash**, *baw-ash'*; a prim. root; to *smell* bad; fig. to *be offensive* mor.:— (make to) be abhorred (had in abomination, loathsome, odious), (cause a, make to) stink (-ing savour), × utterly.

888. בְּאֵשׁ **bᵉ'êsh** (Chald.), *bě-aysh'*; corresp. to 887:— displease.

889. בְּאֹשׁ **bᵉ'ôsh**, *bě-oshe'*; from 877; a *stench*:— stink.

890. בָּאְשָׁה **bo'shâh**, *bosh-aw'*; fem. of 889; *stink-weed* or any other noxious or useless plant:— cockle.

891. בְּאֻשִׁים **bᵉ'ushîym**, *bě-oo-sheem'*; plur. of 889; *poison-berries*:— wild grapes.

892. בָּבָה **bâbâh**, *baw-baw'*; fem. act. part. of an unused root mean. to *hollow* out; something *hollowed* (as a *gate*), i.e. the *pupil* of the eye:— apple [of the eye].

893. בֵּבַי **Bêbay**, *bay-bah'ee*; prob. of for. or.; *Bebai*, an Isr.:— Bebai.

894. בָּבֶל **Bâbel**, *baw-bel'*; from 1101; *confusion; Babel* (i.e. Babylon), incl. Babylonia and the Bab. empire:— Babel, Babylon.

895. בָּבֶל **Bâbel** (Chald.), *baw-bel'*; corresp. to 894:— Babylon.

896. בַּבְלִי **Bablîy** (Chald.), *bab-lee'*; patrial from 895; a *Babylonian*:— Babylonia.

897. בַּג **bag**, *bag*; a Pers. word; *food*:— spoil [from the marg. for 957.]

898. בָּגַד **bâgad**, *baw-gad'*; a prim. root; to *cover* (with a garment); fig. to *act covertly*; by impl. to *pillage*:— deal deceitfully (treacherously, unfaithfully), offend, transgress (-or), (depart), treacherous (dealer, -ly, man), unfaithful (-ly, man), × very [treacherously], vesture, wardrobe.

899. בֶּגֶד **beged**, *behg'-ed*; from 898; a *covering*, i.e. *clothing*; also *treachery* or *pillage*:— apparel, cloth (-es, ing), garment, lap, rag, raiment, robe, × very

900. בֹּגְדוֹת **bôgᵉdôwth**, *bohg-ed-ohth'*; fem. plur. act. part. of 898; *treacheries*:— treacherous.

901. בָּגוֹד **bâgôwd**, *baw-gode'*; from 898; *treacherous*:— treacherous.

902. בִּגְוַי **Bigvay**, *big-vah'ee*; prob. of for. or.; *Bigvai*, an Isr.:— Bigvai.

903. בִּגְתָא **Bigthâ'**, *big-thaw'*; of Pers. der.; *Bigtha*, a eunuch of Xerxes:— Bigtha.

904. בִּגְתָן **Bigthân**, *big-thawn'*; or

בִּגְתָנָא **Bigthânâ'**, *big-thaw'naw*; of similar der. to 903; *Bigthan* or *Bigthana*, a eunuch of Xerxes:— Bigthan, Bigthana.

905. בַּד **bad**, *bad*; from 909; prop. *separation*; by impl. a *part* of the body, *branch* of a tree, *bar* for carrying; fig. *chief* of a city; espec. (with prep. pref.) as adv., *apart, only, besides*:— alone, apart, bar, besides, branch, by self, of each añke, except, only, part, staff, strength.

906. בַּד **bad**, *bad*; perh. from 909 (in the sense of *divided* fibres); flaxen *thread* or yarn; hence, a *linen* garment:— linen.

907. בַּד **bad**, *bad*; from 908; a *brag* or *lie*; also a *liar*:— liar, lie.

908. בָּדָא **bâdâ'**, *baw-daw'*; a prim. root; (fig.) to *invent*:— devise, feign.

909. בָּדַד **bâdad**, *baw-dad'*; a prim. root; to *divide*, i.e. (reflex.) *be solitary*:— alone.

910. בָּדָד **bâdâd**, *baw-dawd'*; from 909; *separate*; adv. *separately*:— alone, desolate, only, solitary.

911. בְּדַד **Bᵉdad**, *bed-ad'*; from 909; *separation; Bedad*, an Edomite:— Bedad.

912. בְּדְיָה **Bêdᵉyâh**, *bay-dě-yaw'*; prob. short. form 5662; *servant of Jehovah; Bedejah*, an Isr.:— Bedeiah.

913. בְּדִיל **bᵉdîyl**, *bed-eel'*; from 914; *alloy* (because *removed* by smelting); by anal. *tin*:— + plummet, tin.

914. בָּדַל **bâdal**, *baw-dal'*; a prim. root; to *divide* (in var. senses lit. or fig., *separate, distinguish, differ, select,* etc.):— (make, put) difference, divide (asunder), (make) separate (self, -ation), sever (out), × utterly.

915. בָּדָל **bâdâl**, *baw-dawl'*; from 914; a *part*:— piece.

916. בְּדֹלַח **bᵉdôlach**, *bed-o'-lakh*; prob. from 914; something in *pieces*, i.e. *bdellium*, a (fragrant) gum (perh. *amber*); others a *pearl*:— bdellium.

917. בְּדָן **Bᵉdân**, *bed-awn'*; prob. short. for 5658; *servile; Bedan*, the name of two Isr.:— Bedan.

918. בָּדַק **bâdaq**, *baw-dak'*; a prim. root; to *gap* open; used only as a denom. from 919; to *mend* a breach:— repair.

919. בֶּדֶק **bedeq**, *beh'-dek*; from 918; a *gap* or *leak* (in a building or a ship):— breach, + calker.

920. בִּדְקַר **Bidqar**, *bid-car'*; prob. from 1856 with prep. pref.; *by stabbing*, i.e. *assassin; Bidkar*, an Isr.:— Bidkar.

921. בְּדַר **bᵉdar** (Chald.), *bed-ar'*; cor-

resp. (by transp.) to 6504; to *scatter:*— scatter.

922. בֹּהוּ **bôhûw**, *bo´-hoo;* from an unused root (mean. *to be empty*); a *vacuity,* i.e. (superficially) an undistinguishable *ruin:*— emptiness, void.

923. בַּהַט **bahaṭ**, *bah´-hat;* from an unused root (prob. mean. *to glisten*); white *marble* or perh. *alabaster:*— red [marble].

924. בְּהִילוּ **bᵉhîylûw** (Chald.), *bĕ-hee-loo´;* from 927; a *hurry;* only adv. *hastily:*— in haste.

925. בָּהִיר **bâhîyr**, *baw-here´;* from an unused root (mean. *to be bright*); *shining:*— bright.

926. בָּהַל **bâhal**, *baw-hal´;* a prim. root; to *tremble* inwardly (or *palpitate*), i.e. (fig.) *be* (caus. *make*) (suddenly) *alarmed* or *agitated;* by impl. to *hasten* anxiously:— be (make) affrighted (afraid, amazed, dismayed, rash), (be, get, make) haste (-n, -y, -ily) (give) speedy (-ily), thrust out, trouble, vex.

927. בְּהַל **bᵉhal** (Chald.), *bĕ-hal´;* corresp. to 926; to *terrify, hasten:*— in haste, trouble.

928. בֶּהָלָה **behâlâh**, *beh-haw-law´;* from 926; *panic, destruction:*— terror, trouble.

929. בְּהֵמָה **bᵉhêmâh**, *bĕ-hay-maw´;* from an unused root (prob. mean. *to be mute*); prop. a *dumb* beast; espec. any large quadruped or *animal* (often collect.):— beast, cattle.

930. בְּהֵמוֹת **bᵉhêmôwth**, *bĕ-hay-mōhth´;* in form a plur. of 929, but really a sing. of Eg. der.; a *water-ox,* i.e. the *hippopotamus* or Nile-*horse:*— Behemoth.

931. בֹּהֶן **bôhen**, *bo´-hen;* from an unused root appar. mean. *to be thick;* the *thumb* of the hand or *great toe* of the foot:— thumb, great toe.

932. בֹּהַן **Bôhan**, *bo´han;* an orth. var. of 931; *thumb, Bohan,* an Isr.:— Bohan.

933. בֹּהַק **bôhaq**, *bo´-hak;* from an unused root mean. *to be pale;* white *scurf:*— freckled spot.

934. בֹּהֶרֶת **bôhereth**, *bo-heh´-reth;* fem. act. part. of the same as 925; a *whitish* spot on the skin:— bright spot.

935. בּוֹא **bôw´**, *bo;* a prim. root; *to go* or *come* (in a wide variety of applications):— abide, apply, attain, × be, befall, + besiege, bring (forth, in, into, to pass), call, carry, × certainly, (cause, let, thing for) to come (against, in, out, upon, to pass), depart, × doubtless again, + eat, + employ, (cause to) enter (in, into, -tering, -trance, -try), be fallen, fetch, + follow, get, give, go (down, in, to war), grant, + have, × indeed, [in-]vade, lead, lift [up], mention, pull in, put, resort, run (down), send, set, × (well) stricken [in age], × surely, take (in), way.

בּוּב **bûwb**. See 892, 5014.

936. בּוּז **bûwz**, *booz;* a prim. root; to *disrespect:*— contemn, despise, × utterly.

937. בּוּז **bûwz**, *booz;* from 936; *disrespect:*— contempt (-uously), despised, shamed.

938. בּוּז **Bûwz**, *booz;* the same as 937;

Buz, the name of a son of Nahor, and of an Isr.:— Buz.

939. בּוּזָה **bûwzâh**, *boo-zaw´;* fem. pass. part. of 936; something *scorned;* an obj. of *contempt:*— despised.

940. בּוּזִי **Bûwziy**, *boo-zee´;* patron. from 938; a *Buzite* or desc. of Buz:— Buzite.

941. בּוּזִי **Bûwziy**, *boo-zee´;* the same as 940; *Buzi,* an Isr.:— Buzi.

942. בָּוַי **Bavvay**, *bav-vah´ee;* prob. of Pers. or.; *Bavvai,* an Isr.:— Bavai.

943. בּוּךְ **bûwk**, *book;* a prim. root; to *involve* (lit. or fig.):— be entangled, (perplexed).

944. בּוּל **bûwl**, *bool;* for 2981; *produce* (of the earth, etc.):— food, stock.

945. בּוּל **Bûwl**, *bool;* the same as 944 (in the sense of *rain*); *Bul,* the eighth Heb. month:— Bul.

בּוּם **bûwm**. See 1116.

946. בּוּנָה **Bûwnâh**, *boo-naw´;* from 995; *discretion; Bunah,* an Isr.:— Bunah.

בּוּנִי **Bûwniy**. See 1138.

947. בּוּס **bûwç**, *boos;* a prim. root; to *trample* (lit. or fig.):— loath, tread (down, under [foot]), be polluted.

948. בּוּץ **bûwts**, *boots;* from an unused root (of the same form) mean. to *bleach,* i.e. (intr.) *be white;* prob. *cotton* (of some sort):— fine (white) linen.

949. בּוֹצֵץ **Bôwtsêts**, *bo-tsates´;* from the same as 948; *shining; Botsets,* a rock near Michmash:— Bozez.

950. בּוּקָה **bûwqâh**, *boo-kaw´;* fem. pass. part. of an unused root (mean. to be *hollow*); *emptiness* (as adj.):— empty.

951. בּוֹקֵר **bôwkêr**, *bo-kare´;* prop. act. part. from 1239 as denom. from 1241; a *cattle-tender:*— herdman.

952. בּוּר **bûwr**, *boor;* a prim. root; to *bore,* i.e. (fig.) *examine:*— declare.

953. בּוֹר **bôwr**, *bore;* from 952 (in the sense of 877); a pit *hole* (espec. one used as a *cistern* or a *prison*):— cistern, dungeon, fountain, pit, well.

954. בּוּשׁ **bûwsh**, *boosh;* a prim. root; prop. to *pale,* i.e. by impl. to *be ashamed;* also (by impl.) to *be disappointed,* or *delayed:*— (be, make, bring to, cause, put to, with, a-) shamed (-d), be (put to) confounded (-fusion), become dry, delay, be long.

955. בּוּשָׁה **bûwshâh**, *boo-shaw´;* fem. part. pass. of 954; *shame:*— shame.

956. בּוּת **bûwth** (Chald.), *booth;* appar. denom. from 1005; to *lodge* over night:— pass the night.

957. בַּז **baz**, *baz;* from 962; *plunder:*— booty, prey, spoil (-ed).

958. בָּזָא **bâzâ´**, *baw-zaw´;* a prim. root; prob. to *cleave:*— spoil.

959. בָּזָה **bâzâh**, *baw-zaw´;* a prim. root; to *disesteem:*— despise, disdain, contemn (-ptible), + think to scorn, vile person.

960. בָּזֹה **bâzôh**, *baw-zo´;* from 959; *scorned:*— despise.

961. בִּזָּה **bizzâh**, *biz-zaw´;* fem. of 957; *booty:*— prey, spoil.

962. בָּזַז **bâzaz**, *baw-zaz´;* a prim. root;

to *plunder:*— catch, gather, (take) for a prey, rob (-ber), spoil, take (away, spoil), × utterly.

963. בִּזָּיוֹן **bizzâyôwn**, *biz-zaw-yone´;* from 959; *disesteem:*— contempt.

964. בּוֹזְיוֹתְיָה **bizyôwthᵉyâh**, *biz-yo-thĕ-yaw´;* from 959 and 3050; *contempts of Jah; Bizjothjah,* a place in Pal.:— Bizjothjah.

965. בָּזָק **bâzâq**, *baw-zawk´;* from an unused root mean. to *lighten;* a *flash* of lightning:— flash of lightning.

966. בֶּזֶק **Bezeq**, *beh´-zek;* from 965; *lightning; Bezek,* a place in Pal.:— Bezek.

967. בָּזַר **bâzar**, *baw-zar´;* a prim. root; to *disperse:*— scatter.

968. בִּזְתָא **Bizthâ´**, *biz-thaw´;* of Pers. or.; *Biztha,* a eunuch of Xerxes:— Biztha.

969. בָּחוֹן **bâchôwn**, *baw-khone´;* from 974; an *assayer* of metals:— tower.

970. בָּחוּר **bâchûwr**, *baw-khoor´;* or

בָּחֻר **bâchûr**, *baw-khoor´;* pass. part. of 977; prop. *selected,* i.e. a *youth* (often collect.):— (choice) young (man), chosen, × hole.

בְּחוּרוֹת **bᵉchûwrôwth**. See 979.

בַּחוּרִים **Bachûwrîym**. See 980.

971. בָּחִין **bachiyn**,° *bakh-een´;* another form of 975; a watch-*tower* of besiegers:— tower.

972. בָּחִיר **bâchîyr**, *baw-kheer´;* from 977; *select:*— choose, chosen one, elect.

973. בָּחַל **bâchal**, *baw-khal´;* a prim. root; to *loathe:*— abhor, get hastily [*from the marg. for* 926].

974. בָּחַן **bâchan**, *baw-khan´;* a prim. root; to *test* (espec. metals); gen. and fig. to *investigate:*— examine, prove, tempt, try (trial).

975. בַּחַן **bachan**, *bakh´-an;* from 974 (in the sense of keeping a *look-out*); a watch-*tower:*— tower.

976. בֹּחַן **bôchan**, *bo´-khan;* from 974; *trial:*— tried.

977. בָּחַר **bâchar**, *baw-khar´;* a prim. root; prop. to *try,* i.e. (by impl.) *select:*— acceptable, appoint, choose (choice), excellent, join, be rather, require.

בָּחֻר **bâchûr**. See 970.

978. בַּחֲרוּמִי **Bachărûwmîy**, *bakh-ar-oo-mee´;* patrial from 980 (by transp.); a *Bacharumite* or inhab. of Bachurim:— Baharumite.

979. בְּחֻרוֹת **bᵉchûrôwth**, *bekh-oo-rothe´;* or

בְּחוּרֹת **bᵉchûwrôth**, *bekh-oo-roth´;* fem. plur. of 970; also (masc. plur.)

בְּחֻרִים **bᵉchûrîym**, *bekh-oo-reem´;* youth (collect. and abstr.):— young men, youth.

980. בַּחֻרִים **Bachûrîym**, *bakh-oo-reem´;* or

בַּחוּרִים **Bachûwrîym**, *bakh-oo-reem´;* masc. plur. of 970; *young men; Bachurim,* a place in Pal.:— Bahurim.

981. בָּטָא **bâṭâ´**, *baw-taw´;* or

בָּטָה **bâṭâh**, *baw-taw´;* a prim. root;

to *babble;* hence, to *vociferate* angrily:— pronounce, speak (unadvisedly).

982. בְּטַח **bâṭach,** *baw-takh´;* a prim. root; prop. to *hie* for refuge [but not so *precipitately* as 2620]; fig. to *trust, be confident* or *sure:*— be bold (confident, secure, sure), careless (one, woman), put confidence, (make to) hope, (put, make to) trust.

983. בֶּטַח **beṭach,** *beh´takh;* from 982; prop. a place of *refuge;* abstr. *safety,* both the fact (*security*) and the feeling (*trust*); often (adv. with or without prep.) *safely:*— assurance, boldly, (without) care (-less), confidence, hope, safe (-ly, -ty), secure, surely.

984. בֶּטַח **Beṭach,** *beh´-takh; the same as* 983; *Betach,* a place in Syria:— Betah.

985. בִּטְחָה **biṭchâh,** *bit-khaw´;* fem. of 984; *trust:*— confidence.

986. בִּטָּחוֹן **biṭṭâchôwn,** *bit-taw-khone´;* from 982; *trust:*— confidence, hope.

987. בַּטֻּחוֹת **baṭṭûchôwth,** *bat-too-khôth´; fem. plur. from* 982; *security:*— secure.

988. בָּטֵל **bâṭêl,** *baw-tale´;* a prim. root; to *desist* from labor:— cease.

989. בְּטֵל **beṭêl** (Chald.), *bet-ale´;* corresp. to 988; to *stop:*— (cause, make to), cease, hinder.

990. בֶּטֶן **beṭen,** *beh´-ten;* from an unused root prob. mean. to *be hollow;* the *belly,* espec. the *womb;* also the *bosom* or *body* of anything:— belly, body, + as they be born, + within, womb.

991. בֶּטֶן **Beṭen,** *beh´-ten; the same as* 990; *Beten,* a place in Pal.:— Beten.

992. בֹּטֶן **bôṭen,** *bo´-ten;* from 990; (only in plur.) a *pistachio*-nut (from its form):— nut.

993. בְּטֹנִים **Beṭônîym,** *bet-o-neem´;* prob. plur. from 992; *hollows: Betonim,* a place in Pal.:— Betonim.

994. בִּי **bîy,** *bee;* perh. from 1158 (in the sense of *asking*); prop. a *request;* used only adv. (always with "my Lord") *Oh that!; with leave,* or *if it please:*— alas, O, oh.

995. בִּין **bîyn,** *bene;* a prim. root; to *separate* mentally (or *distinguish*), i.e.(gen.) *understand:*— attend, consider, be cunning, diligently, direct, discern, eloquent, feel, inform, instruct, have intelligence, know, look well to, mark, perceive, be prudent, regard, (can) skill (-full), teach, think, (cause, make to, get, give, have) understand (-ing), view, (deal) wise (-ly, man).

996. בֵּין **bêyn,** *bane* (sometimes in the plur. masc. or fem.); prop. the constr. contr. form of an otherwise unused noun from 995; a *distinction;* but used only as a prep. *between* (repeated before each noun, often with other particles); also as a conj., *either ... or:*— among, asunder, at, between (-twixt ... and), + from (the widest), × in, out of, whether (it be ... or), within.

997. בֵּין **bêyn** (Chald.), *bane;* corresp. to 996:— among, between.

998. בִּינָה **bîynâh,** *bee-naw´;* from 995; *understanding:*— knowledge, mean-

ing, × perfectly, understanding, wisdom.

999. בִּינָה **bîynâh** (Chald.), *bee-naw´;* corresp. to 998:— knowledge.

1000. בֵּיצָה **bêytsâh,** *bay-tsaw´;* from the same as 948; an *egg* (from its whiteness):— egg.

1001. בִּירָא **bîyrâ'** (Chald.), *bee-raw´;* corresp. to 1002; a *palace:*— palace.

1002. בִּירָה **bîyrâh,** *bee-raw´;* of for. or.; a *castle* or *palace:*— palace.

1003. בִּירָנִית **bîyrânîyth,** *bee-raw-neeth´;* from 1002; a *fortress:*— castle.

1004. בַּיִת **bayith,** *bah´-yith;* prob. from 1129 abb.; a *house* (in the greatest var. of applications, espec. *family,* etc.):— court, daughter, door, + dungeon, family, + forth of, × great as would contain, hangings, home[born], [winter]house (-hold), inside (-ward), palace, place, + prison, + steward, + tablet, temple, web, + within (-out).

1005. בַּיִת **bayith** (Chald.), *bah-yith;* corresp. to 1004:— house.

1006. בַּיִת **Bayith,** *bah´-yith;* the same as 1004; *Bajith,* a place in Pal.:— Bajith.

1007. בֵּית אָוֶן **Bêyth 'Âven,** *bayth aw´-ven;* from 1004 and 205; *house of vanity; Beth-Aven,* a place in Pal.:— Beth-aven.

1008. בֵּית־אֵל **Bêyth-'Êl,** *bayth-ale´;* from 1004 and 410; *house of God; Beth-El,* a place in Pal.:— Beth-el.

1009. בֵּית אַרְבֵּאל **Bêyth 'Arbê'l,** *bayth arbale´;* from 1004 and 695 and 410; *house of God's ambush; Beth-Arbel,* a place in Pal.:— Beth-Arbel.

1010. בֵּית בַּעַל מְעוֹן **Bêyth Ba'al Me'ôwn,** *bayth bah´-al mĕ-own´;* from 1004 and 1168 and 4583; *house of Baal of* (the) *habitation of* [appar. by transp.]; or (short.)

בֵּית מְעוֹן **Bêyth Me'ôwn,** *bayth mĕ-own´; house of habitation of* (Baal); *Beth-Baal-Meön,* a place in Pal.:— Beth-baal-meon. Comp. 1186 and 1194.

1011. בֵּית בִּרְאִי **Bêyth Bir'îy,** *bayth bir-ee´;* from 1004 and 1254; *house of a creative* one; *Beth-Biri,* a place in Pal.:— Beth-birei.

1012. בֵּית בָּרָה **Bêyth Bârâh,** *bayth baw-raw´;* prob. from 1004 and 5679; *house* (of the) *ford; Beth-Barah,* a place in Pal.:— Beth-barah.

1013. בֵּית־גָּדֵר **Bêyth-Gâdêr,** *bayth-gaw-dare´;* from 1004 and 1447; *house of* (the) *wall; Beth-Gader,* a place in Pal.:— Beth-gader.

1014. בֵּית גָּמוּל **Bêyth Gâmûwl,** *bayth gaw-mool´;* from 1004 and the pass. part. of 1576; *house of* (the) *weaned; Beth-Gamul,* a place E. of the Jordan:— Beth-gamul.

1015. בֵּית דִּבְלָתַיִם **Bêyth Diblâthayim,** *bayth dib-law-thah´-yim;* from 1004 and the dual of 1690; *house of* (the) *two figcakes; Beth-Diblathajim,* a place E. of the Jordan:— Beth-diblathaim.

1016. בֵּית־דָּגוֹן **Bêyth-Dâgôwn,** *bayth-daw-gohn´;* from 1004 and 1712; *house of Dagon; Beth-Dagon,* the name of two places in Pal.:— Beth-dagon.

1017. בֵּית אֵל **Bêyth hâ-'Êlîy,** *bayth haw-el-ee´;* patrial from 1008 with the art. interposed; a *Beth-elite,* or inhab. of Bethel:— Bethelite.

1018. בֵּית הָאֵצֶל **Bêyth hâ-'Êtsel,** *bayth haw-ay´-tsel;* from 1004 and 681 with the art. interposed; *house of the side; Beth-ha-Etsel,* a place in Pal.:— Beth-ezel.

1019. בֵּית הַגִּלְגָּל **Bêyth hag-Gilgâl,** *bayth hag-gil gawl´;* from 1004 and 1537 with the article interposed; *house of Gilgal* (or *rolling*); *Beth-hag-Gilgal,* a place in Pal.:— Beth-gilgal.

1020. בֵּית הַיְשִׁמוֹת **Bêyth ha-Yeshîymôwth,** *bayth hah-yesh-ee-môth´;* from 1004 and the plur. of 3451 with the art. interposed; *house of the deserts; Beth-ha-Jeshimoth,* a town E. of the Jordan:— Beth-jeshimoth.

1021. בֵּית הַכֶּרֶם **Bêyth hak-Kerem,** *bayth hak-keh´-rem;* from 1004 and 3754 with the art. interposed; *house of the vineyard; Beth-hak-Kerem,* a place in Pal.:— Beth-haccerem.

1022. בֵּית הַלַּחְמִי **Bêyth hal-Lachmîy,** *bayth hal-lakh-mee´;* patrial from 1035 with the art. ins.; a *Beth-lechemite,* or native of Bethlechem:— Bethlehemite.

1023. בֵּית הַמֶּרְחָק **Bêyth ham-Merchâq,** *bayth ham-mer-khawk´;* from 1004 and 4801 with the art. interposed; *house of the breadth; Beth-ham-Merchak,* a place in Pal.:— place that was far off.

1024. בֵּית הַמַּרְכָּבוֹת **Bêyth ham-Markâbôwth,** *bayth ham-mar-kaw-both´;* or (short.)

בֵּית מַרְכָּבוֹת **Bêyth Markâbôwth,** *bayth mar-kaw-both´;* from 1004 and the plur. of 4818 (with or without the art. interposed); *place of* (the) *chariots; Beth-ham-Markaboth* or *Beth-Markaboth,* a place in Pal.:— Beth-marcaboth.

1025. בֵּית הָעֵמֶק **Bêyth hâ-'Êmeq,** *bayth haw-ay´-mek;* from 1004 and 6010 with the art. interposed; *house of the valley; Beth-ha-Emek,* a place in Pal.:— Bethemek.

1026. בֵּית הָעֲרָבָה **Bêyth hâ-'Ărâbâh,** *bayth haw-ar-aw-baw´;* from 1004 and 6160 with the art. interposed; *house of the Desert; Beth-ha-Arabah,* a place in Pal.:— Beth-arabah.

1027. בֵּית הָרָם **Bêyth hâ-Râm,** *bayth haw-rawm´;* from 1004 and 7311 with the art. interposed; *house of the height; Beth-ha-Ram,* a place E. of the Jordan:— Beth-aram.

1028. בֵּית הָרָן **Bêyth hâ-Rân,** *bayth haw-rawn´;* prob. for 1027; *Beth-ha-Ran,* a place E. of the Jordan:— Beth-haran.

1029. בֵּית הַשִּׁטָּה **Bêyth hash-Shiṭṭâh,** *bayth hash-shit-taw´;* from 1004 and 7848 with the art. interposed; *house of the acacia; Beth-hash-Shittah,* a place in Pal.:— Beth-shittah.

1030. בֵּית הַשֶּׁמֶשׁ **Bêyth hash-Shimshîy,** *bayth hash-shim-shee´;* patrial from 1053 with the art. ins.; a *Beth-shimshite,* or inhab. of Bethshemesh:— Bethshemite.

1031. בֵּית חָגְלָה **Bêyth Choglâh,** *bayth chog-law´;* from 1004 and the same as

2295; *house of a partridge; Beth-Choglah*, a place in Pal.:— Beth-hoglah.

1032. בֵּית חוֹרוֹן **Bêyth Chôwrôwn**, *bayth kho-rone´*; from 1004 and 2356; *house of hollowness; Beth-Choron*, the name of two adjoining places in Pal.:— Beth-horon.

בֵּית חָנָן **Bêyth Chânân**. See 358.

1033. בֵּית כַּר **Bêyth Kar**, *bayth kar;* from 1004 and 3733; *house of pasture; Beth-Car*, a place in Pal.:— Beth-car.

1034. בֵּית לְבָאוֹת **Bêyth Lᵉbâ'ôwth**, *bayth leb-aw-ôth´;* from 1004 and the plural of 3833; *house of lionesses; Beth-Lebaoth*, a place in Pal.:— Beth-lebaoth. Comp. 3822.

1035. בֵּית לֶחֶם **Bêyth Lechem**, *bayth leh´-khem;* from 1004 and 3899; *house of bread; Beth-Lechem*, a place in Pal.:— Beth-lehem.

1036. בֵּית לְעַפְרָה **Bêyth lᵉ-'Aphrâh**, *bayth lĕ-af-raw´;* from 1004 and the fem. of 6083 (with prep. interposed); *house to* (i.e. *of*) *dust; Beth-le-Aphrah*, a place in Pal.:— house of Aphrah.

1037. בֵּית מִלֹּא **Bêyth Millôw'**, *bayth mil-lo´;* or

בֵּית מִלֹּא **Bêyth Millô'**, *bayth mil-lo´;* from 1004 and 4407; *house of* (the) *rampart; Beth-Millo*, the name of two citadels:— house of Millo.

1038. בֵּית מַעֲכָה **Bêyth Ma'ăkâh**, *bayth mah-ak-aw´;* from 1004 and 4601; *house of Maakah; Beth-Maakah*, a place in Pal.:— Beth-maachah.

1039. בֵּית נִמְרָה **Bêyth Nimrâh**, *bayth nim-raw´;* from 1004 and the fem. of 5246; *house of* (the) *leopard; Beth-Nimrah*, a place east of the Jordan:— Beth-nimrah. Comp. 5247.

1040. בֵּית עֵדֶן **Bêyth 'Êden**, *bayth ay´-den;* from 1004 and 5730; *house of pleasure; Beth-Eden*, a place in Syria:— Beth-eden.

1041. בֵּית עַזְמָוֶת **Bêyth 'Azmâveth**, *bayth az-maw´-veth;* from 1004 and 5820; *house of Azmaveth*, a place in Pal.:— Beth-az-maveth. Comp. 5820.

1042. בֵּית עֲנוֹת **Bêyth 'Ănôwth**, *bayth an-ôth´;* from 1004 and a plur. from 6030; *house of replies; Beth-Anoth*, a place in Pal.:— Beth-anoth.

1043. בֵּית עֲנָת **Bêyth 'Ănâth**, *bayth an-awth´;* an orth. var. for 1042; *Beth-Anath*, a place in Pal.:— Beth-anath.

1044. בֵּית עֵקֶד **Bêyth 'Êqed**, *bayth ay´-ked;* from 1004 and a der. of 6123; *house of* (the) *binding* (for sheep-shearing); *Beth-Eked*, a place in Pal.:— shearing house.

1045. בֵּית עַשְׁתָּרוֹת **Bêyth 'Ashtârôwth**, *bayth ash-taw-rôth´;* from 1004 and 6252; *house of Ashtoreths; Beth-Ashtaroth*, a place in Pal.:— house of Ashtaroth. Comp. 1203, 6252.

1046. בֵּית פֶּלֶט **Bêyth Peleṭ**, *bayth peh´-let;* from 1004 and 6412; *house of escape; Beth-Palet*, a place in Pal.:— Beth-palet.

1047. בֵּית פְּעוֹר **Bêyth Pᵉ'ôwr**, *bayth pĕ-ore´;* from 1004 and 6465; *house of Peor; Beth-Peor*, a place E. of the Jordan:— Beth-peor.

1048. בֵּית פַּצֵּץ **Bêyth Patstsêts**, *bayth pats-tsates´;* from 1004 and a der. from 6327; *house of dispersion; Beth-Patstsets*, a place in Pal.:— Beth-pazzez.

1049. בֵּית צוּר **Bêyth Tsûwr**, *bayth tsoor´;* from 1004 and 6697; *house of* (the) *rock; Beth-Tsur*, a place in Pal.:— Beth-zur.

1050. בֵּית רְחוֹב **Bêyth Rᵉchôwb**, *bayth rĕ-khobe´;* from 1004 and 7339; *house of* (the) *street; Beth-Rechob*, a place in Pal.:— Beth-rehob.

1051. בֵּית רָפָא **Bêyth Râphâ'**, *bayth raw-faw´;* from 1004 and 7497; *house of* (the) *giant; Beth-Rapha*, an Isr.:— Beth-rapha.

1052. בֵּית שְׁאָן **Bêyth Shᵉ'ân**, *bayth shĕ-awn´;* or

בֵּית שָׁן **Bêyth Shân**, *bayth shawn´;* from 1004 and 7599; *house of ease; Beth-Shean*, a place in Pal.:— Beth-shean, Beth-Shan.

1053. בֵּית שֶׁמֶשׁ **Bêyth Shemesh**, *bayth sheh´-mesh;* from 1004 and 8121; *house of* (the) *sun; Beth-Shemesh*, a place in Pal.:— Beth-shemesh.

1054. בֵּית תַּפּוּחַ **Bêyth Tappûwach**, *bayth tap-poo´-akh;* from 1004 and 8598; *house of* (the) *apple; Beth-Tappuach*, a place in Pal.:— Beth-tappuah.

1055. בִּיתָן **bîythân**, *bee-thawn´;* prob. from 1004; a *palace* (i.e. *large house*):— palace.

1056. בָּכָא **Bâkâ'**, *baw-kaw´;* from 1058, *weeping; Baca*, a valley in Pal.:— Baca.

1057. בָּכָא **bâkâ'**, *baw-kaw´;* the same as 1056; the *weeping* tree (some gum-distilling tree, perh. the *balsam*):— mulberry tree.

1058. בָּכָה **bâkâh**, *baw-kaw´;* a prim. root; to *weep;* gen. to *bemoan:*— × at all, bewail, complain, make lamentation, × more, mourn, × sore, × with tears, weep.

1059. בֶּכֶה **bekeh**, *beh´-keh;* from 1058; a *weeping:*— × sore.

1060. בְּכוֹר **bᵉkôwr**, *bek-ore´;* from 1069; *firstborn;* hence, *chief:*— eldest (son), firstborn (-ling).

1061. בִּכּוּר **bikkûwr**, *bik-koor´;* from 1069; the *first-fruits* of the crop:— first fruit (-ripe [fig.]), hasty fruit.

1062. בְּכוֹרָה **bᵉkôwrâh**, *bek-o-raw´;* or (short.)

בְּכֹרָה **bᵉkôrâh**, *bek-o-raw´;* fem. of 1060; the *firstling* of man or beast; abstr. *primogeniture:*— birthright, firstborn (-ling).

1063. בִּכּוּרָה **bikkûwrâh**, *bik-koo-raw´;* fem. of 1061; the *early* fig:— firstripe (fruit).

1064. בְּכוֹרַת **Bᵉkôwrath**, *bek-o-rath´;* fem. of 1062; *primogeniture; Bekorath*, an Isr.:— Bechorath.

1065. בְּכִי **bᵉkîy**, *bek-ee´;* from 1058; a *weeping;* by anal. a *dripping:*— overflowing, × sore, (continual) weeping, wept.

1066. בֹּכִים **Bôkîym**, *bo-keem´;* plur. act. part. of 1058; (with the art.) the *weepers; Bo-kim*, a place in Pal.:— Bochim.

1067. בְּכִירָה **bᵉkîyrâh**, *bek-ee-raw´;* fem. from 1069; the *eldest* daughter:— firstborn.

1068. בְּכִית **bᵉkîyth**, *bek-eeth´;* from 1058; a *weeping:*— mourning.

1069. בָּכַר **bâkar**, *baw-kar´;* a prim. root; prop. to *burst* the womb, i.e. (caus.) *bear* or *make early fruit* (of woman or tree); also (as denom. from 1061) to *give* the *birthright:*— make firstborn, be firstling, bring forth first child (new fruit).

1070. בֶּכֶר **beker**, *beh´-ker;* from 1069 (in the sense of *youth*); a young *camel:*— dromedary.

1071. בֶּכֶר **Beker**, *beh´-ker;* the same as 1070; *Beker*, the name of two Isr.:— Becher.

1072. בִּכְרָה **bikrâh**, *bik-raw´;* fem. of 1070; a young *she-camel:*— dromedary.

בְּכֹרָה **bᵉkôrâh**. See 1062.

1073. בַּכֻּרָה **bakkûrâh**, *bak-koo-raw´;* by orth. var. for 1063; a *first-ripe* fig:— firstripe.

1074. בֹּכְרוּ **Bôkᵉrûw**, *bo-ker-oo´;* from 1069; *first-born; Bokeru*, an Isr.:— Bocheru.

1075. בִּכְרִי **Bikrîy**, *bik-ree´;* from 1069; *youth-ful; Bikri*, an Isr.:— Bichri.

1076. בַּכְרִי **Bakrîy**, *bak-ree´;* patron. from 1071; a *Bakrite* (collect.) or desc. of Beker:— Bachrites.

1077. בַּל **bal**, *bal;* from 1086; prop. a *failure;* by impl. *nothing;* usually (adv.) *not* at all; also *lest:*— lest, neither, no, none (that ...), not (any), nothing.

1078. בֵּל **Bêl**, *bale;* by contr. for 1168; *Bel*, the Baal of the Babylonians:— Bel.

1079. בַּל **bâl** (Chald.), *bawl;* from 1080; prop. *anxiety*, i.e. (by impl.) the *heart* (as its seat):— heart.

1080. בְּלָא **bᵉlâ'** (Chald.), *bel-aw´;* corresp. to 1086 (but used only in a ment. sense); to *afflict:*— wear out.

1081. בַּלְאֲדָן **Bal'ădân**, *bal-ad-awn´;* from 1078 and 113 (contr.); *Bel* (is his) *lord; Baladan*, the name of a Bab. prince:— Baladan.

1082. בָּלַג **bâlag**, *baw-lag´;* a prim. root; to *break off* or *loose* (in a favorable or unfavorable sense), i.e. *desist* (from grief) or *invade* (with destruction):— comfort, (recover) strength (-en).

1083. בִּלְגָּה **Bilgâh**, *bil-gaw´;* from 1082; *desistance; Bilgah*, the name of two Isr.:— Bilgah.

1084. בִּלְגַּי **Bilgay**, *bil-gah-ee;* from 1082; *desistant; Bilgai*, an Isr.:— Bilgai.

1085. בִּלְדַּד **Bildad**, *bil-dad´;* of uncert. der.; *Bildad*, one of Job's friends:— Bildad.

1086. בָּלָה **bâlâh**, *baw-law´;* a prim. root; to *fail;* by impl. to *wear out, decay* (caus. *consume, spend*):— consume, enjoy long, become (make, wax) old, spend, waste.

1087. בָּלֶה **bâleh**, *baw-leh´;* from 1086; *worn out:*— old.

1088. בָּלָה **Bâlâh**, *baw-law´;* fem. of 1087; *failure; Balah*, a place in Pal.:— Balah.

1089. בָּלַהּ **bâlahh**, *baw-lah´;* a prim. root [rather by transp. for 926]; to *pal-*

pitate; hence, (caus.) to *terrify:—* trouble.

1090. בִּלְהָה **Bilhâh**, *bil-haw´;* from 1089; *timid; Bilhah*, the name of one of Jacob's concubines; also of a place in Pal.:— Bilhah.

1091. בִּלְהָה **ballâhâh**, *bal-law-haw´;* from 1089; *alarm;* hence, *destruction:—* terror, trouble.

1092. בִּלְהָן **Bilhân**, *bil-hawn´;* from 1089; *timid; Bilhan*, the name of an Edomite and of an Isr.:— Bilhan.

1093. בְּלוֹ **bᵉlôw** (Chald.), *bel-o´;* from a root corresp. to 1086; *excise* (on articles consumed):— tribute.

1094. בְּלוֹא **bᵉlôw'**, *bel-o´;* or (fully)

בְּלוֹי **bᵉlôwy**, *bel-o´-ee;* from 1086; (only in plur. constr.) *rags:—* old.

1095. בֵּלְטְשַׁאצַּר **Bêltᵉsha'tstsar**, *bale-tesh-ats-tsar´;* of for. der.; *Belteshatstsar*, the Bab. name of Daniel:— Belteshazzar.

1096. בֵּלְטְשַׁאצַּר **Bêltᵉsha'tstsar** (Chald.), *bale-tesh-ats-tsar´;* corresp. to 1095:— Belteshazzar.

1097. בְּלִי **bᵉlîy**, *bel-ee´;* from 1086; prop. *failure,* i.e. *nothing* or *destruction;* usually (with prep.) *without, not yet, because not, as long as,* etc.:— corruption, i⌊g⌋norant⌊ly⌋, for lack of, where no … is, so that no, none, not, un⌊awares⌋, without.

1098. בְּלִיל **bᵉlîyl**, *bel-eel´;* from 1101; *mixed,* i.e. (spec.) *feed* (for cattle):— corn, fodder, provender.

1099. בְּלִימָה **bᵉlîymâh**, *bel-ee-mah´;* from 1097 and 4100; (as indef.) *nothing whatever:—* nothing.

1100. בְּלִיַּעַל **bᵉlîya'al**, *bel-e-yah´-al;* from 1097 and 3276; *without profit, worthlessness;* by extens. *destruction, wickedness* (often in connection with 376, 802, 1121, etc.):— Belial, evil, naughty, ungodly (men), wicked.

1101. בָּלַל **bâlal**, *baw-lal´;* a prim. root; to *overflow* (spec. with oil); by impl. to *mix;* also (denom. from 1098) to *fodder:—* anoint, confound, × fade, mingle, mix (self), give provender, temper.

1102. בָּלַם **bâlam**, *baw-lam´;* a prim. root; to *muzzle:—* be held in.

1103. בָּלַס **bâlaç**, *baw-las´;* a prim. root; to *pinch* sycamore figs (a process necessary to ripen them):— gatherer.

1104. בָּלַע **bâla'**, *baw-lah´;* a prim. root; to *make away with* (spec. by *swallowing*); gen. to *destroy:—* cover, destroy, devour, eat up, be at end, spend up, swallow down (up).

1105. בֶּלַע **bela'**, *beh´-lah;* from 1104; a *gulp;* fig. *destruction:—* devouring, that which he hath swallowed up.

1106. בֶּלַע **Bela'**, *beh´-lah;* the same as 1105; *Bela*, the name of a place, also of an Edomite and of two Isr.:— Bela.

1107. בִּלְעֲדֵי **bil'ădêy**, *bil-ad-ay´;* or

בַּלְעֲדֵי **bal'ădêy**, *bal-ad-ay´;* constr. plur. from 1077 and 5703, not *till,* i.e. (as prep. or adv.) *except, without, besides:—* beside, not (in), save, without.

1108. בַּלְעִי **Bal'îy**, *bal-ee´;* patron. from

1106: a *Belaite* (collect.) or desc. of Bela:— Belaites.

1109. בִּלְעָם **Bil'âm**, *bil-awm´;* prob. from 1077 and 5971; *not* (of the) *people,* i.e. *foreigner; Bilam,* a Mesopotamian prophet; also a place in Pal.:— Balaam, Bileam.

1110. בָּלַק **bâlaq**, *baw-lak´;* a prim. root; to *annihilate:—* (make) waste.

1111. בָּלָק **Bâlâq**, *baw-lawk´;* from 1110; *waster; Balak,* a Moabitish king:— Balak.

1112. בֵּלְשַׁאצַּר **Bêlsha'tstsar**, *bale-shats-tsar´;* or

בֵּלְאשַׁצַּר **Bêl'shatstsar**, *bale-shats-tsar´;* of for. or. (comp. 1095); *Belshatstsar,* a Bab. king:— Belshazzar.

1113. בֵּלְשַׁאצַּר **Bêlsha'tstsar** (Chald.), *bale-shats-tsar´;* corresp. to 1112:— Belshazzar.

1114. בִּלְשָׁן **Bilshân**, *bil-shawn´;* of uncert. der.; *Bilshan,* an Isr.:— Bilshan.

1115. בִּלְתִּי **biltîy**, *bil-tee´;* constr. fem. of 1086 (equiv. to 1097); prop. a *failure* of, i.e. (used only as a neg. particle, usually with prep. pref.) *not, except, without, unless, besides, because not, until,* etc.:— because un⌊satiable⌋, beside, but, + continual, except, from, lest, neither, no more, none, not, nothing, save, that no, without.

1116. בָּמָה **bâmâh**, *baw-maw´;* from an unused root (mean. *to be high*); an *elevation:—* height, high place, wave.

1117. בָּמָה **Bâmâh**, *baw-maw´;* the same as 1116; *Bamah,* a place in Pal.:— Bamah. See also 1120.

1118. בִּמְהָל **Bimhâl**, *bim-hawl´;* prob. from 4107 with prep. pref.; *with pruning; Bimhal,* an Isr.:— Bimhal.

1119. בְּמוֹ **bᵉmôw**, *bem-o´;* prol. for prep. pref.; *in, with, by,* etc.:— for, in into, through.

1120. בָּמוֹת **Bâmôwth**, *baw-môth´;* plur. of 1116; *heights;* or (fully)

בָּמוֹת בַּעַל **Bâmôwth Ba'al**, *baw-môth´ bah´-al;* from the same and 1168; *heights of Baal; Bamoth* or *Bamoth-Baal,* a place E. of the Jordan:— Bamoth, Bamoth-baal.

1121. בֵּן **bên**, *bane;* from 1129; a *son* (as a *builder* of the family name), in the widest sense of (lit. and fig. relationship, incl. *grandson, subject, nation, quality* or *condition,* etc., ⌊like 1, 251, etc.⌋):— + afflicted, age, ⌊Ahoh-⌋ ⌊Ammon-⌋ ⌊Hachmon-⌋ ⌊Lev-⌋ite, ⌊anoint-⌋ed one, appointed to, (+) arrow, ⌊Assyr-⌋ ⌊Babylon-⌋ ⌊Egypt-⌋ ⌊Grec-⌋ian, one born, bough, branch, breed, + (young) bullock, + (young) calf, × came up in, child, colt, × common, × corn, daughter, × of first, + firstborn, foal, + very fruitful, + postage, × in, + kid, + lamb, (+) man, meet, + mighty, + nephew, old, (+) people, + rebel, + robber, × servant born, × soldier, son, + spark, + steward, + stranger, × surely, them of, + tumultuous one, + valiant ⌊-est⌋, whelp, worthy, young (one), youth.

1122. בֵּן **Bên**, *bane;* the same as 1121; *Ben,* an Isr.:— Ben.

1123. בֵּן **bên** (Chald.), *bane;* corresp. to 1121:— child, son, young.

1124. בְּנָא **bᵉnâ'** (Chald.), *ben-aw´;* or

בְּנָה **bᵉnâh** (Chald.), *ben-aw´;* corresp. to 1129; to *build:—* build, make.

1125. בֶּן־אֲבִינָדָב **Ben-'Âbîynâdâb**, *ben-ab-ee´-naw-dawb´;* from 1121 and 40; (the) *son of Abinadab; Ben-Abinadab,* an Isr.:— the son of Abinadab.

1126. בֶּן־אוֹנִי **Ben-'Ôwnîy**, *ben-o-nee´;* from 1121 and 205; *son of my sorrow; Ben-Oni,* the orig. name of Benjamin:— Ben-oni.

1127. בֶּן־גֶּבֶר **Ben-Geber**, *ben-gheh´-ber;* from 1121 and 1397; *son of* (the) *hero; Ben-Geber,* an Isr.:— the son of Geber.

1128. בֶּן־דֶּקֶר **Ben-Deqer**, *ben-deh´-ker;* from 1121 and a der. of 1856; *son of piercing* (or *of a lance*); *Ben-Deker,* an Isr.:— the son of Dekar.

1129. בָּנָה **bânâh**, *baw-naw´;* a prim. root; to *build* (lit. and fig.):— (begin to) build (-er), obtain children, make, repair, set (up), × surely.

1130. בֶּן־הֲדַד **Ben-Hădad**, *ben-had-ad´;* from 1121 and 1908; *son of Hadad; Ben-Hadad,* the name of several Syrian kings:— Ben-hadad.

1131. בִּנּוּי **Binnûwy**, *bin-noo´-ee;* from 1129; *built* up; *Binnui,* an Isr.:— Binnui.

1132. בֶּן־זוֹחֵת **Ben-Zôwchêth**, *ben-zo-khayth´;* from 1121 and 2105; *son of Zocheth; Ben-Zocheth,* an Isr.:— Ben-zoketh.

1133. בֶּן־חוּר **Ben-Chûwr**, *ben-khoor´;* from 1121 and 2354; *son of Chur; Ben-Chur,* an Isr.:— the son of Hur.

1134. בֶּן־חַיִל **Ben-Chayil**, *ben-khah´-yil;* from 1121 and 2428; *son of might; Ben-Chail,* an Isr.:— Ben-hail.

1135. בֶּן־חָנָן **Ben-Chânân**, *ben-khaw-nawn´;* from 1121 and 2605; *son of Chanan; Ben-Chanan,* an Isr.:— Ben-hanan.

1136. בֶּן־חֶסֶד **Ben-Cheçed**, *ben-kheh´-sed;* from 1121 and 2617; *son of kindness; Ben-Chesed,* an Isr.:— the son of Hesed.

1137. בָּנִי **Bâniy**, *baw-nee´;* from 1129; *built; Bani,* the name of five Isr.:— Bani.

1138. בֻּנִּי **Bunnîy**, *boon-nee´;* or (fuller)

בּוּנִי **Bûwnîy**, *boo-nee´;* from 1129; *built; Bunni* or *Buni,* an Isr.:— Bunni.

1139. בְּנֵי־בְרַק **Bᵉnêy-Bᵉraq**, *ben-ay´-ber-ak´;* from the plur. constr. of 1121 and 1300; *sons of lightning, Bene-berak,* a place in Pal.:— Bene-barak.

1140. בִּנְיָה **binyâh**, *bin-yaw´;* fem. from 1129; a *structure:—* building.

1141. בְּנָיָה **Bᵉnâyâh**, *ben-aw-yaw´;* or (prol.)

בְּנָיָהוּ **Bᵉnâyâhûw**, *ben-aw-yaw´-hoo;* from 1129 and 3050; *Jah has built; Benajah,* the name of twelve Isr.:— Benaiah.

1142. בְּנֵי יַעֲקָן **Bᵉnêy Ya'àqân**, *ben-ay´ yah-ak-awn´;* from the plur. of 1121 and 3292; *sons of Yaakan; Bene-Jaakan,* a place in the Desert:— Benejaakan.

1143. בֵּנַיִם **bênayim**, *bay-nah´-yim;* dual of 996; a *double interval,* i.e. the space between two armies:— + champion.

1144. בִּנְיָמִן **Binyâmîyn**, *bin-yaw-mene´;* from 1121 and 3225; *son of* (the) *right hand; Binjamin,* youngest son of Jacob; also the tribe descended from him, and its territory:— Benjamin.

1145. בֶּן־יְמִינִי **Ben-yᵉmîynîy**, *ben-yem-ee-nee´;* sometimes (with the art. ins.)

בֶּן־הַיְמִינִי **Ben-ha-yᵉmînîy**, *ben-hah-yem-ee-nee´;* with 376 ins. (1 Sam. 9:1)

בֶּן־אִישׁ יְמִינִי **Ben-'Îysh Yᵉmîynîy**, *ben-eesh´ yem-ee-nee´; son of a man of Jemini;* or short. (1 Sam. 9:4; Esth. 2:5)

אִישׁ יְמִינִי **'Îysh Yᵉmîynîy**, *eesh yem-ee-nee´; a man of Jemini,* or (1 Sam. 20:1) simply

יְמִינִי **Yᵉmîynîy**, *yem-ee-nee´; a Jeminite;* (plur.

בְּנֵי יְמִינִי **Bᵉnîy Yᵉmîynîy**, *ben-ay´ yem-ee-nee´;* patron. from 1144; a *Ben-jaminite,* or descendent of Benjamin:— Benjamite, of Benjamin.

1146. בִּנְיָן **binyân**, *bin-yawn´;* from 1129; an *edifice:*— building.

1147. בִּנְיָן **binyân** (Chald.), *bin-yawn´;* corresp. to 1146:— building.

1148. בְּנִינוּ **Bᵉnîynûw**, *ben-ee-noo´;* prob. from 1121 with pron. suff.; *our son; Beninu,* an Isr.:— Beninu.

1149. בְּנַס **bᵉnaç** (Chald.), *ben-as´;* of uncert. affin.; to *be enraged:*— be angry.

1150. בִּנְעָא **Bin'â'**, *bin-aw´;* or

בִּנְעָה **Bin'âh**, *bin-aw´;* of uncert. der.; *Bina* or *Binah,* an Isr.:— Binea, Bineah.

1151. בֶּן־עַמִּי **Ben-'Ammîy**, *ben-am-mee´;* from 1121 and 5971 with pron. suff.; *son of my people; Ben-Ammi,* a son of Lot:— Ben-ammi.

1152. בְּסוֹדְיָה **Bᵉçôwdᵉyâh**, *bes-o-deh-yaw´;* from 5475 and 3050 with prep. pref.; *in* (the) *counsel of Jehovah; Besodejah,* an Isr.:— Besodeiah.

1153. בֵּסַי **Bᵉçay**, *bes-ah´-ee;* from 947; *domineering; Besai,* one of the Nethinim:— Besai.

1154. בֶּסֶר **beçer**, *beh´-ser;* from an unused root mean. to *be sour;* an *immature* grape:— unripe grape.

1155. בֹּסֶר **bôçer**, *bo´ser;* from the same as 1154:— sour grape.

1156. בְּעָא **bᵉâ'** (Chald.), *beh-aw´;* or

בְּעָה **bᵉâh** (Chald.), *beh-aw´;* corresp. to 1158; to *seek* or *ask:*— ask, desire, make [petition], pray, request, seek.

1157. בְּעַד **bᵉad**, *beh-ad´;* from 5704 with prep. pref.; *in up to* or *over against;* gen. *at, beside, among, behind, for,* etc.:— about, at, by (means of), for, over, through, up (-on), within.

1158. בָּעָה **bâ'âh**, *baw-aw´;* a prim. root; to *gush* over, i.e. to *swell;* (fig.) to *desire* earnestly; by impl. to *ask:*— cause, inquire, seek up, swell out.

1159. בָּעוּ **bâ'ûw** (Chald.), *baw-oo´;* from 1156; a *request:*— petition.

1160. בְּעוֹר **Bᵉôwr**, *beh-ore´;* from 1197

(in the sense of *burning*); a *lamp; Beör,* the name of the father of an Edomitish king; also of that of Balaam:— Beor.

1161. בְּעוּתִים **bi'ûwthîym**, *be-oo-theme´;* masc. plur. from 1204; *alarms:*— terrors.

1162. בֹּעַז **Bô'az**, *bo´-az;* from an unused root of uncert. mean.; *Boaz,* the ancestor of David; also the name of a pillar in front of the temple:— Boaz.

1163. בָּעַט **bâ'aṭ**, *baw-at´;* a prim. root; to *trample* down, i.e. (fig.) *despise:*— kick.

1164. בְּעִי **bᵉîy**, *beh-ee´;* from 1158; a *prayer:*— grave.

1165. בְּעִיר **bᵉîyr**, *beh-ere´;* from 1197 (in the sense of *eating*); *cattle:*— beast, cattle.

1166. בָּעַל **bâ'al**, *baw-al´;* a prim. root; to *be master;* hence, (as denom. from 1167) to *marry:*— have dominion (over), be husband, marry (-ried, × wife).

1167. בַּעַל **ba'al**, *bah´-al;* from 1166; a *master;* hence, a *husband,* or (fig.) *owner* (often used with another noun in modifications of this latter sense):— + archer, + babbler, + bird, captain, chief man, + confederate, + have to do, + dreamer, those to whom it is due, + furious, those that are given to it, great, + hairy, he that hath it, have, + horseman, husband, lord, man, + married, master, person, + sworn, they of.

1168. בַּעַל **Ba'al**, *bah´-al;* the same as 1167; *Baal,* a Phœnician deity:— Baal, [plur.] Baalim.

1169. בְּעֵל **bᵉêl** (Chald.), *beh-ale´;* corresp. to 1167:— + chancellor.

1170. בַּעַל בְּרִית **Ba'al Bᵉrîyth**, *bah´-al ber-eeth´;* from 1168 and 1285; *Baal of* (the) *covenant; Baal-Berith,* a special deity of the Shechemites:— Baalberith.

1171. בַּעַל גָּד **Ba'al Gâd**, *bah´-al gawd;* from 1168 and 1409; *Baal of Fortune; Baal-Gad,* a place in Syria:— Baal-gad.

1172. בַּעֲלָה **ba'ălâh**, *bah-al-aw´;* fem. of 1167; a *mistress:*— that hath, mistress.

1173. בַּעֲלָה **Ba'ălâh**, *bah-al-aw´;* the same as 1172; *Baalah,* the name of three places in Pal.:— Baalah.

1174. בַּעַל חָמוֹן **Ba'al Hâmôwn**, *bah´-al haw-mone´;* from 1167 and 1995; *possessor of a multitude; Baal-Hamon,* a place in Pal.:— Baal-hamon.

1175. בְּעָלוֹת **Bᵉâlôwth**, *beh-aw-lōth´;* plur. of 1172; *mistresses; Beäloth,* a place in Pal.:— Bealoth, in Aloth [by mistake for a plur. from 5927 *with prep. pref.*].

1176. בַּעַל זְבוּב **Ba'al Zᵉbûwb**, *bah´-al zeb-oob´;* from 1168 and 2070; *Baal of* (the) *Fly; Baal-Zebub,* a special deity of the Ekronites:— Baal-zebub.

1177. בַּעַל חָנָן **Ba'al Chânân**, *bah´-al khaw-nawn´;* from 1167 and 2603; *possessor of grace; Baal-Chanan,* the name of an Edomite, also of an Isr.:— Baal-hanan.

1178. בַּעַל חָצוֹר **Ba'al Châtsôwr**, *bah´-al khaw-tsore´;* from 1167 and a modif. of 2691; *possessor of a village; Baal-Chatsor,* a place in Pal.:— Baal-hazor.

1179. בַּעַל חֶרְמוֹן **Ba'al Chermôwn**, *bah´-al kher-mone´;* from 1167 and 2768; *possessor of Hermon; Baal-Chermon,* a place in Pal.:— Baal-hermon.

1180. בַּעֲלִי **Ba'ălîy**, *bah-al-ee´;* from 1167 with pron. suff.; *my master; Baali,* a symb. name for Jehovah:— Baali.

1181. בַּעֲלֵי בָּמוֹת **Ba'ălêy Bâmôwth**, *bah-al-ay´ baw-mōth´;* from the plur. of 1168 and the plur. of 1116; *Baals of* (the) *heights; Baale-Bamoth,* a place E. of the Jordan:— lords of the high places.

1182. בַּעֶלְיָדָע **Bᵉelyâdâ'**, *beh-el-yaw-daw´;* from 1168 and 3045; *Baal has known; Beëljada,* an Isr.:— Beeliada.

1183. בַּעַלְיָה **Bᵉalyâh**, *beh-al-yaw´;* from 1167 and 3050; *Jah* (is) *master; Bealjah,* an Isr.:— Bealiah.

1184. בַּעֲלֵי יְהוּדָה **Ba'ălêy Yᵉhûwdâh**, *bah-al-ay´ yeh-hoo-daw´;* from the plural of 1167 and 3063; *masters of Judah; Baale-Jehudah,* a place in Pal.:— Baale of Judah.

1185. בַּעֲלִיס **Ba'ălîç**, *bah-al-ece´;* prob. from a der. of 5965 with prep. pref.; *in exultation; Baalis,* an Ammonitish king:— Baalis.

1186. בַּעַל מְעוֹן **Ba'al Mᵉôwn**, *bah-al meh-one´;* from 1168 and 4583; *Baal of* (the) *habitation* (of) [comp. 1010]; *Baal-Meön,* a place E. of the Jordan:— Baal-meon.

1187. בַּעַל פְּעוֹר **Ba'al Pᵉôwr**, *bah´-al peh-ore´;* from 1168 and 6465; *Baal of Peor; Baal-Peör,* a Moabitish deity:— Baal-peor.

1188. בַּעַל פְּרָצִים **Ba'al Pᵉrâtsîym**, *bah´-al per-aw-tseem´;* from 1167 and the plur. of 6556; *possessor of breaches; Baal-Peratsim,* a place in Pal.:— Baal-perazim.

1189. בַּעַל צְפוֹן **Ba'al Tsᵉphôwn**, *bah´-al tsef-one´;* from 1168 and 6828 (in the sense of *cold*) [according to others an Eg. form of *Typhon,* the destroyer]; *Baal of winter; Baal-Tsephon,* a place in Eqypt:— Baal-zephon.

1190. בַּעַל שָׁלִשָׁה **Ba'al Shâlishâh**, *bah´-al shaw-lee-shaw´;* from 1168 and 8031; *Baal of Shalishah, Baal-Shalishah,* a place in Pal.:— Baal-shalisha.

1191. בַּעֲלָת **Ba'ălâth**, *bah-al-awth´;* a modif. of 1172; *mistress-ship; Baalath,* a place in Pal.:— Baalath.

1192. בַּעֲלַת בְּאֵר **Ba'ălath Bᵉêr**, *bah-al-ath´ beh-ayr´;* from 1172 and 875; *mistress of a well; Baalath-Beër,* a place in Pal.:— Baalath-beer.

1193. בַּעַל תָּמָר **Ba'al Tâmâr**, *bah´-al taw-mawr´;* from 1167 and 8558; *possessor of* (the) *palm-tree; Baal-Tamar,* a place in Pal.:— Baal-tamar.

1194. בְּעֹן **Bᵉôn**, *beh-ohn´;* prob. a contr. of 1010; *Beön,* a place E. of the Jordan:— Beon.

1195. בַּעֲנָא **Ba'ănâ'**, *bah-an-aw´;* the same as 1196; *Baana,* the name of four Isr.:— Baana, Baanah.

1196. בַּעֲנָה **Ba'ănâh**, *bah-an-aw´;* from a der. of 6031 with prep. pref.; *in affliction; Baanah,* the name of four Isr.:— Baanah.

1197. בָּעַר **bâ'ar**, *baw-ar´;* a prim. root;

to *kindle*, i.e. *consume* (by fire or by eating); also (as denom. from 1198) to *be* (-*come*) *brutish*:— be brutish, bring (put, take) away, burn, (cause to) eat (up), feed, heat, kindle, set (lon fire), waste.

1198. בָּעַר **ba'ar**, *bah´-ar*; from 1197; prop. *food* (as *consumed*); i.e. (by exten.) of cattle *brutishness*; (concr.) *stupid*:— brutish (person), foolish.

1199. בַּעֲרָא **Bâ'ărâ'**, *bah-ar-aw´*; from 1198; *brutish*: *Baara*, an Isr. woman:— Baara.

1200. בְּעֵרָה **be'êrâh**, *bĕ-ay-raw´*; from 1197; a *burning*:— fire.

1201. בַּעְשָׁא **Ba'shâ'**, *bah-shaw´*; from an unused root mean. to *stink; offensiveness; Basha*, a king of Israel:— Baasha.

1202. בַּעֲשֵׂיָה **Ba'ăsêyâh**, *bah-as-ay-yaw´*; from 6213 and 3050 with a prep. pref.; *in* (the) *work of Jah; Baasejah*, an Isr.:— Baaseiah.

1203. בְּעֶשְׁתְּרָה **Be'esht°râh**, *beh-esh-ter-aw´*; from 6251 (as sing. of 6252) with prep. pref.; *with Ashtoreth; Beështerah*, a place E. of the Jordan:— Beeshterah.

1204. בָּעָת **bâ'ath**, *baw-ath´*; a prim. root; to *fear*:— affright, be (make) afraid, terrify, trouble.

1205. בְּעָתָה **be'âthâh**, *beh-aw-thaw´*; from 1204; *fear*:— trouble.

1206. בֹּץ **bôts**, *botse*; prob. the same as 948; *mud* (as *whitish* clay):— mire.

1207. בִּצָּה **bitstsâh**, *bits-tsaw´*; intens. from 1206; a *swamp*:— fen, mire (-ry place).

1208. בָּצוֹר **bâtsôwr**, *baw-tsore´*; from 1219; *inaccessible*, i.e. *lofty*:— vintage [by confusion with 1210].

1209. בְּצַי **Bêtsay**, *bay-tsah´-ee*; perh. the same as 1153; *Betsai*, the name of two Isr.:— Bezai.

1210. בָּצִיר **bâtsîyr**, *baw-tseer´*; from 1219; *clipped*, i.e. the *grape crop*:— vintage.

1211. בֶּצֶל **betsel**, *beh´-tsel*; from an unused root appar. mean. to *peel*; an *onion*:— onion.

1212. בְּצַלְאֵל **Betsal'êl**, *bets-al-ale´*; prob. from 6738 and 410 with prep. pref.; *in* (the) *shadow* (i.e. protection) *of God; Betsalel*, the name of two Isr.:— Bezaleel.

1213. בְּצָלוּת **Batslûwth**, *bats-looth´*; or

בְּצָלִית **Batslîyth**, *bats-leeth´*; from the same as 1211; a *peeling; Batsluth* or *Batslith*, an Isr.:— Bazlith, Bazluth.

1214. בָּצַע **bâtsa'**, *baw-tsah´*; a prim. root to *break off*, i.e. (usually) *plunder*; fig. to *finish*, or (intr.) *stop*:— (be) covet (-ous), cut (off), finish, fulfill, gain (greedily), get, be given to [covetousness], greedy, perform, be wounded.

1215. בֶּצַע **betsa'**, *beh´-tsah*; from 1214; *plunder*; by extens. *gain* (usually unjust):— covetousness, (dishonest) gain, lucre, profit.

1216. בָּצֵק **bâtsêq**, *baw-tsake´*; a prim. root; perh. to *swell* up, i.e. *blister*:— swell.

1217. בָּצֵק **bâtsêq**, *baw-tsake´*; from

1216; *dough* (as *swelling* by fermentation):— dough, flour.

1218. בָּצְקַת **Botsqath**, *bots-cath´*; from 1216; a *swell* of ground; *Botscath*, a place in Pal.:— Bozcath, Boskath.

1219. בָּצַר **bâtsar**, *baw-tsar´*; a prim. root; to *clip* off; spec. (as denom. from 1210) to *gather* grapes; also to *be isolated* (i.e. *inaccessible* by height or for fortification):— cut off, (de-) fenced, fortify, (grape) gather (-er), mighty things, restrain, strong, wall (up), withhold.

1220. בֶּצֶר **betser**, *beh´-tser*; from 1219; strictly a *clipping*, i.e. *gold* (as *dug* out):— gold defence.

1221. בֶּצֶר **Betser**, *beh´-tser*; the same as 1220, an *inaccessible* spot; *Betser*, a place in Pal.; also an Isr.:— Bezer.

1222. בְּצַר **betsar**, *bets-ar´*; another form for 1220; *gold*:— gold.

1223. בָּצְרָה **botsrâh**, *bots-raw´*; fem. from 1219; an *enclosure*, i.e. *sheepfold*:— Bozrah.

1224. בָּצְרָה **Botsrâh**; *bots-raw´*; the same as 1223; *Botsrah*, a place in Edom:— Bozrah.

1225. בִּצָּרוֹן **bitstsârôwn**, *bits-tsaw-rone´*; masc. intens. from 1219; a *fortress*:— stronghold.

1226. בַּצֹּרֶת **batstsôreth**, *bats-tso´-reth*; fem. intens. from 1219; *restraint* (of rain), i.e. *drought*:— dearth, drought.

1227. בַּקְבּוּק **Baqbûwq**, *bak-book´*; the same as 1228; *Bakbuk*, one of the Nethinim:— Bakbuk.

1228. בַּקְבֻּק **baqbûk**, *bak-book´*; from 1238; a *bottle* (from the gurgling in *emptying*):— bottle, cruse.

1229. בַּקְבֻּקְיָה **Baqbuqyâh**, *bak-book-yaw´*; from 1228 and 3050; *emptying* (i.e. *wasting*) *of Jah; Bakbukjah*, an Isr.:— Bakbukiah.

1230. בַּקְבַּקַּר **Baqbaqqar**, *bak-bak-kar´*; redupl. from 1239; *searcher; Bakbakkar*, an Isr.:— Bakbakkar.

1231. בֻּקִּי **Buqqîy**, *book-kee´*; from 1238; *wasteful; Bukki*, the name of two Isr.:— Bukki.

1232. בֻּקִּיָּה **Buqqîyâh**, *book-kee-yaw´*; from 1238 and 3050; *wasting of Jah; Bukkijah*, an Isr.:— Bukkiah.

1233. בְּקִיעַ **b°qîya'**, *bek-ee´-ah*; from 1234; a *fissure*:— breach, cleft.

1234. בָּקַע **bâqa'**, *baw-kah´*; a prim. root; to *cleave*; gen. to *rend, break, rip* or *open*— make a breach, break forth (into, out, in pieces, through, up), be ready to burst, cleave (asunder), cut out, divide, hatch, rend (asunder), rip up, tear, win.

1235. בֶּקַע **beqa'**, *beh´-kah*; from 1234; a *section* (half) of a shekel, i.e. a *beka* (a weight and a coin):— bekah, half a shekel.

1236. בִּקְעָא **biq'â'** (Chald.), *bik-aw´*; corresp. to 1237:— plain.

1237. בִּקְעָה **biq'âh**, *bik-aw´*; from 1234; prop. a *split*, i.e. a wide level *valley* between mountains:— plain, valley.

1238. בָּקַק **bâqaq**, *baw-kak´*; a prim. root; to *pour* out, i.e. to *empty*, fig. to *depopulate*; by anal. to *spread* out (as a

fruitful vine):— (make) empty (out), fail, × utterly, make void.

1239. בָּקַר **bâqar**, *baw-kar*; a prim. root; prop. to *plow*, or (gen.) *break forth*; (fig.) to *inspect, admire, care for, consider*:— (make) inquire (-ry), (make) search, seek out.

1240. בְּקַר **b°qar** (Chald.), *bek-ar´*; corresp. to 1239:— inquire, make search.

1241. בָּקָר **bâqâr**, *baw-kawr´*; from 1239; a *beeve* or animal of the ox kind of either gender (as used for *plowing*); collect. a *herd*:— beeve, bull (+ -ock), + calf, + cow, great [cattle], + heifer, herd, kine, ox.

1242. בֹּקֶר **bôçer**, *bo´-ker*; from 1239; prop. *dawn* (as the *break* of day); gen. *morning*:— (+) day, early, morning, morrow.

1243. בַּקָּרָה **baqqârâh**, *bak-kaw-raw´*; intens. from 1239; a *looking after*:— seek out.

1244. בִּקֹּרֶת **biqqoreth**, *bik-ko´-reth*; from 1239; prop. *examination*, i.e. (by impl.) *punishment*:— scourged.

1245. בָּקַשׁ **bâqash**, *baw-kash´*; a prim. root; to *search* out (by any method, spec. in worship or prayer); by impl. to *strive after*:— ask, beg, beseech, desire, enquire, get, make inquisition, procure, (make) request, require, seek (for).

1246. בַּקָּשָׁה **baqqâshâh**, *bak-kaw-shaw´*; from 1245; a *petition*:— request.

1247. בַּר **bar** (Chald.), *bar*; corresp. to 1121; a *son, grandson*, etc.:— × old, son.

1248. בַּר **bar**, *bar*; borrowed (as a title) from 1247; the *heir* (apparent to the throne):— son.

1249. בַּר **bar**, *bar*; from 1305 (in its various senses); *beloved*; also *pure, empty*:— choice, clean, clear, pure.

1250. בָּר **bâr**, *bawr*; or

בַּר **bar**, *bar*; from 1305 (in the sense of *winnowing*); *grain* of any kind (even while standing in the field); by extens. the open *country*:— corn, wheat.

1251. בַּר **bar** (Chald.), *bar*; corresp. to 1250; a *field*:— field.

1252. בֹּר **bôr**, *bore*; from 1305; *purity*:— cleanness, pureness.

1253. בֹּר **bôr**, *bore*; the same as 1252; vegetable *lye* (from its *cleansing*); used as a *soap* for washing, or a *flux* for metals:— × never so, purely.

1254. בָּרָא **bârâ'**, *baw-raw´*; a prim. root; (absolutely) to *create*; (qualified) to *cut down* (a wood), *select, feed* (as formative processes):— choose, create (creator), cut down, dispatch, do, make (fat).

1255. בְּרֹאדַךְ בַּלְאֲדָן **B°rô'dak Bal'ădân**, *ber-o-dak´ bal-ad-awn´*; a var. of 4757; *Berodach-Baladan*, a Bab. king:— Berodach-baladan.

בִּרְאִי **Bir'îy**. See 1011.

1256. בְּרָאיָה **B°râ'yâh**, *ber-aw-yaw´*; from 1254 and 3050; *Jah has created; Berajah*, an Isr.:— Beraiah.

1257. בַּרְבֻּר **barbûr**, *bar-boor´*; by redupl. from 1250; a *fowl* (as fattened on *grain*):— fowl.

1258. בָּרַד **bârad**, *baw-rad´*; a prim. root, to *hail*:— hail.

1259. בָּרָד **bârâd**, *baw-rawd´*; from 1258; *hail*:— hail (Istones]).

1260. בֶּרֶד **Bered**, *beh´red*; from 1258; *hail*; *Bered*, the name of a place south of Pal., also of an Isr.:— Bered.

1261. בָּרֹד **bârôd**, *baw-rode´*; from 1258; *spotted* (as if with *hail*):— grisled.

1262. בָּרָה **bârâh**, *baw-raw´*; a prim. root; to *select*; also (as denom. from 1250) to *feed*; also (as equiv. to 1305) to *render clear* (Eccl. 3:18):— choose, (cause to) eat, manifest, (give) meat.

1263. בָּרוּךְ **Bârûwk**, *baw-rook´*; pass. part. from 1288; *blessed*; *Baruk*, the name of three Isr.:— Baruch.

1264. בְּרוֹם **berôwm**, *ber-ome´*; prob. of for. or.; *damask* (stuff of variegated thread):— rich apparel.

1265. בְּרוֹשׁ **berôwsh**, *ber-ōsh´*; of uncert. der.; a *cypress* (?) tree; hence, a *lance* or a *musical* instrument (as made of that wood):— fir (tree).

1266. בְּרוֹת **berôwth**, *ber-ōth´*; a var. of 1265; the *cypress* (or some elastic tree):— fir.

1267. בָּרוּת **bârûwth**, *baw-rooth´*; from 1262; *food*:— meat.

1268. בֵּרוֹתָה **Bêrôwthâh**, *bay-ro-thaw´*; or

בֵּרֹתַי **Bêrôthay**, *bay-ro-tha´-ee*; prob. from 1266; *cypress* or *cypresslike*; *Berothah* or *Berothai*, a place north of Pal.:— Berothah, Berothai.

1269. בִּרְזוֹת° **Birzôwth**, *beer-zoth´*; prob. fem. plur. from an unused root (appar. mean. to *pierce*); *holes*; *Birzoth*, an Isr. Ifrom the marg.l.:— Birzavith [from the marg.].

1270. בַּרְזֶל **barzel**, *bar-zel´*; perh. from the root of 1269; *iron* (as *cutting*); by extens. an iron *implement*:— (ax) head, iron.

1271. בַּרְזִלַּי **Barzillay**, *bar-zil-lah´-ee*; from 1270; *iron*-hearted; *Barzillai*, the name of three Isr.:— Barzillai.

1272. בָּרַח **bârach**, *baw-rakh´*; a prim. root; to *bolt*, i.e. fig. to *flee* suddenly:— chase (away); drive away, fain, flee (away), put to flight, make haste, reach, run away, shoot.

1273. בַּרְחֻמִי **Barchûmîy**, *bar-khoo-mee´*; by transp. for 978; a *Barchumite*, or native of *Bachurim*:— Barhumite.

1274. בְּרִי **berîy**, *ber-ee´*; from 1262; *fat*:— fat.

1275. בֵּרִי **Bêrîy**, *bay-ree´*; prob. by contr. from 882; *Beri*, an Isr.:— Beri.

1276. בֵּרִי **Bêrîy**, *bay-ree´*; of uncert. der.; (only in the plur. and with the art.) the *Berites*, a place in Pal.:— Berites.

1277. בָּרִיא **bârîy´**, *baw-ree´*; from 1254 (in the sense of 1262); *fatted* or *plump*:— fat (Ifleshed], -ter), fed, firm, plenteous, rank.

1278. בְּרִיאָה **berîy´âh**, *ber-ee-aw´*; fem. from 1254; a *creation*, i.e. a *novelty*:— new thing.

1279. בִּרְיָה **biryâh**, *beer-yaw´*; fem. from 1262; *food*:— meat.

1280. בְּרִיחַ **berîyach**, *ber-ee´-akh*; from 1272; a *bolt*:— bar, fugitive.

1281. בָּרִיחַ **bârîyach**, *baw-ree´-akh*; or (short.)

בָּרִחַ **bârîach**, *baw-ree´-akh*; from 1272; a *fugitive*, i.e. the *serpent* (as *fleeing*), and the constellation by that name:— crooked, noble, piercing.

1282. בָּרִיחַ **Bârîyach**, *baw-ree´-akh*; the same as 1281; *Bariach*, an Isr.:— Bariah.

1283. בְּרִיעָה **Berîy´âh**, *ber-ee´-aw*; appar. from the fem. of 7451 with prep. pref.; *in trouble*; *Beriah*, the name of four Isr.:— Beriah.

1284. בְּרִיעִי **Berîy´îy**, *ber-ee-ee´*; patron. from 1283; a *Beriite* (collect.) or desc. of Beriah:— Beerites.

1285. בְּרִית **berîyth**, *ber-eeth´*; from 1262 (in the sense of *cutting* Ilike 1254]); a *compact* (because made by passing between *pieces* of flesh):— confederacy, Icon-Ifederl-atel, covenant, league.

1286. בְּרִית **Berîyth**, *ber-eeth´*; the same as 1285; *Berith*, a Shechemitish deity:— Berith.

1287. בֹּרִית **bôrîyth**, *bo-reeth´*; fem. of 1253; vegetable *alkali*:— sope.

1288. בָּרַךְ **bârak**, *baw-rak´*; a prim. root; to *kneel*; by impl. to *bless* God (as an act of adoration), and (vice-versa) man (as a benefit); also (by euphem.) to *curse* (God or the king, as treason):— × abundantly, × altogether, × at all, blaspheme, bless, congratulate, curse, × greatly, × indeed, kneel (down), praise, salute, × still, thank.

1289. בְּרַךְ **berak** (Chald.), *ber-ak´*; corresp. to 1288:— bless, kneel.

1290. בֶּרֶךְ **berek**, *beh´-rek*; from 1288; a *knee*:— knee.

1291. בֶּרֶךְ **berek** (Chald.), *beh´-rek*; corresp. to 1290:— knee.

1292. בָּרַכְאֵל **Bârak´êl**, *baw-rak-ale´*; from 1288 and 410, *God has blessed*; *Barakel*, the father of one of Job's friends:— Barachel.

1293. בְּרָכָה **berâkâh**, *ber-aw-kaw´*; from 1288; *benediction*; by impl. *prosperity*:— blessing, liberal, pool, present.

1294. בְּרָכָה **Berâkâh**, *ber-aw-kaw´*; the same as 1293; *Berakah*, the name of an Isr., and also of a valley in Pal.:— Berachah.

1295. בְּרֵכָה **berêkâh**, *ber-ay-kaw´*; from 1288; a *reservoir* (at which camels *kneel* as a resting-place):— (fish-) pool.

1296. בֶּרֶכְיָה **Berekyâh**, *beh-rek-yaw´*; or

בֶּרֶכְיָהוּ **Berekyâhûw**, *beh-rek-yaw´-hoo*; from 1290 and 3050; *knee* (i.e. *blessing*) of *Jah*; *Berekjah*, the name of six Isr.:— Berachiah, Berechiah.

1297. בְּרַם **beram** (Chald.), *ber-am´*; perh. from 7313 with prep. pref.; *prop. highly*, i.e. *surely*; but used adversatively, *however*:— but, nevertheless, yet.

1298. בֶּרַע **Bera´**, *beh´-rah*; of uncert. der.; *Bera*, a Sodomitish king:— Bera.

1299. בָּרַק **bâraq**, *baw-rak´*; a prim. root; to *lighten* (lightning):— cast forth.

1300. בָּרָק **bârâq**, *baw-rawk´*; from 1299; *lightning*; by anal. a *gleam*; concr. a *flashing* sword:— bright, glitter (-ing sword), lightning.

1301. בָּרָק **Bârâq**, *baw-rawk´*; the same as 1300; *Barak*, an Isr.:— Barak.

1302. בַּרְקוֹס **Barqôwç**, *bar-kose´*; of uncert. der.; *Barkos*, one of the Nethimim:— Barkos.

1303. בַּרְקָן **barqân**, *bar-kwan´*; from 1300; a *thorn* (perh. as burning *brightly*):— brier.

1304. בָּרֶקֶת **bâreqath**, *baw-reh´-keth*; or

בָּרְכַת **bârekath**, *baw-rek-ath´*; from 1300; a *gem* (as *flashing*), perh. the *emerald*:— carbuncle.

1305. בָּרַר **bârar**, *baw-rar´*; a prim. root; to *clarify* (i.e. *brighten*), *examine*, *select*:— make bright, choice, chosen, cleanse (be clean), clearly, polished, (shew self) pure (-ify), purge (out).

1306. בִּרְשַׁע **Birsha´**, *beer-shah´*; prob. from 7562 with a prep. pref.; *with wickedness*; *Birsha*, a king of Gomorrah:— Birsha.

1307. בֵּרֹתִי **Bêrôthîy**, *bay-ro-thee´*; patrial from 1268; a *Berothite*, or inhab. of Berothai:— Berothite.

1308. בְּשׂוֹר **Besôwr**, *bes-ore´*; from 1319; *cheerful*; *Besor*, a stream of Pal.:— Besor.

1309. בְּשׂוֹרָה **besôwrâh**, *bes-o-raw´*; or (short.)

בְּשֹׂרָה **besôrâh**, *bes-o-raw´*; fem. from 1319; glad *tidings*; by impl. *reward for good news*:— reward for tidings.

1310. בָּשַׁל **bâshal**, *baw-shal´*; a prim. root; prop. to *boil* up; hence, to *be done* in cooking; fig. to *ripen*:— bake, boil, bring forth, is ripe, roast, seethe, sod (be sodden).

1311. בָּשֵׁל **bâshêl**, *baw-shale´*; from 1310; *boiled*:— × at all, sodden.

1312. בִּשְׁלָם **Bishlâm**, *bish-lawm´*; of for. der.; *Bishlam*, a Pers.:— Bishlam.

1313. בָּשָׂם **bâsâm**, *baw-sawm´*; from an unused root mean. to *be fragrant*; Icomp. 5561l the *balsam* plant:— spice.

1314. בֶּשֶׂם **besem**, *beh´-sem*; or

בֹּשֶׂם **bôsem**, *bo´-sem*; from the same as 1313; *fragrance*; by impl. *spicery*; also the *balsam* plant:— smell, spice, sweet (odour).

1315. בָּשְׂמָה **Bosmath**, *bos-math´*; fem. of 1314 (the second form); *fragrance*; *Bosmath*, the name of a wife of Esau, and of a daughter of Solomon:— Bashemath, Basmath.

1316. בָּשָׁן **Bâshân**, *baw-shawn´*; of uncert. der.; *Bashan* (often with the art.), a region E. of the Jordan:— Bashan.

1317. בָּשְׁנָה **boshnâh**, *bosh-naw´*; fem. from 954; *shamefulness*:— shame.

1318. בָּשַׁס **bâshaç**, *baw-shas´*; a prim. root; to *trample* down:— tread.

1319. בָּשַׂר **bâsar**, *baw-sar´*; a prim. root; prop. to *be fresh*, i.e. *full* (rosy, (fig.) *cheerful*); to *announce* (glad news):— messenger, preach, publish, shew forth, (bear, bring, carry, preach, good, tell good) tidings.

1320. בָּשָׂר **bâsâr**, *baw-sawr´*; from 1319;

flesh (from its *freshness*); by extens. *body, person;* also (by euphem.) the *pudenda* of a man:— body, lfat, leanl flesh l-edl, kin, lman-l kind, + nakedness, self, skin.

1321. בְּסַר **b^esar** (Chald.), *bes-ar';* corresp. to 1320:— flesh.

בְּסֹרָה **b^esôrâh**. See 1309.

1322. בֹּשֶׁת **bôsheth**, *bo'-sheth;* from 954; *shame* (the feeling and the condition, as well as its cause); by impl. (spec.) an *idol:—* ashamed, confusion, + greatly, (put to) shame (-ful thing).

1323. בַּת **bath**, *bath;* from 1129 (as fem. of 1121); a *daughter* (used in the same wide sense as other terms of relationship, lit. and fig.):— apple lof the eyel, branch, company, daughter, × first, × old, + owl, town, village.

1324. בַּת **bath**, *bath;* prob. from the same as 1327; a *bath* or Heb. measure (as a means of *division*) of liquids:— bath.

1325. בַּת **bath** (Chald.), *bath;* corresp. to 1324:— bath.

1326. בָּתָה **bâthâh**, *baw-thaw';* prob. an orth. var. for 1327; *desolation:—* waste.

1327. בַּתָּה **battâh**, *bat-taw';* fem. from an unused root (mean. to *break* in pieces) *desolation:—* desolate.

1328. בְּתוּאֵל **B^ethûw'êl**, *beth-oo-ale';* appar. from the same as 1326 and 410; *destroyed of God; Bethuel,* the name of a nephew of Abraham, and of a place in Pal.:— Bethuel. Comp. 1329.

1329. בְּתוּל **B^ethûwl**, *beth-ool';* for 1328; *Bethul* (i.e. Bethuel), a place in Pal.:— Bethuel.

1330. בְּתוּלָה **b^ethûwlâh**, *beth-oo-law';* fem. pass. part. of an unused root mean. to *separate;* a *virgin* (from her *privacy*); sometimes (by continuation) a *bride;* also (fig.) a *city* or *state:—* maid, virgin.

1331. בְּתוּלִים **b^ethûwlîym**, *beth-oo-leem';* masc. plur. of the same as 1330; (collect. and abstr.) *virginity;* by impl. and concr. the *tokens* of it:— × maid, virginity.

1332. בִּתְיָה **Bithyâh**, *bith-yaw';* from 1323 and 3050; *daughter* (i.e. worshipper) *of Jah; Bithjah,* an Eg. woman:— Bithiah.

1333. בָּתַק **bâthaq**, *baw-thak';* a prim. root; to *cut* in pieces:— thrust through.

1334. בָּתַר **bâthar**, *baw-thar';* a prim. root, to *chop up:—* divide.

1335. בֶּתֶר **bether**, *beh'-ther;* from 1334; a *section:—* part, piece.

1336. בֶּתֶר **Bether**, *beh'-ther;* the same as 1335; *Bether,* a (craggy) place in Pal.:— Bether.

1337. בַּת רַבִּים **Bath Rabbîym**, *bath rab-beem';* from 1323 and a masc. plur. from 7227; the *daughter* (i.e. *city*) *of Rabbah:—* Bath-rabbim.

1338. בִּתְרוֹן **Bithrôwn**, *bith-rone';* from 1334; (with the art.) the *craggy* spot; *Bithron,* a place E. of the Jordan:— Bithron.

1339. בַּת־שֶׁבַע **Bath-Sheba'**, *bath-sheh'-bah;* from 1323 and 7651 (in the sense of

7650); *daughter of an oath; Bath-Sheba,* the mother of Solomon:— Bath-sheba.

1340. בַּת־שׁוּעַ **Bath-Shûwa'**, *bath-shoo'-ah;* from 1323 and 7771; *daughter of wealth; Bath-shua,* the same as 1339:— Bath-shua.

ג

1341. גֵּא **gê'**, *gay';* for 1343; *haughty:—* proud.

1342. גָּאָה **gâ'âh**, *gaw-aw';* a prim. root; to *mount* up; hence, in gen. to *rise,* (fig.) be *majestic:—* gloriously, grow up, increase, be risen, triumph.

1343. גֵּאֶה **gê'eh**, *gay-eh';* from 1342; *lofty;* fig. *arrogant:—* proud.

1344. גֵּאָה **gê'âh**, *gay-aw';* fem. from 1342; *arrogance:—* pride.

1345. גְּאוּאֵל **G^e'ûw'êl**, *gheh-oo-ale';* from 1342 and 410; *majesty of God; Geüel,* an Isr.:— Geuel.

1346. גַּאֲוָה **ga'ăvâh**, *gah-av-aw';* from 1342; *arrogance* or *majesty;* by impl. (concr.) *ornament:—* excellency, haughtiness, highness, pride, proudly, swelling.

1347. גָּאוֹן **gâ'ôwn**, *gaw-ohn';* from 1342; the same as 1346:— arrogancy, excellency (-lent), majesty, pomp, pride, proud, swelling.

1348. גֵּאוּת **gê'ûwth**, *gay-ooth';* from 1342; the same as 1346:— excellent things, lifting up, majesty, pride, proudly, raging.

1349. גַּאֲיוֹן **ga'ăyôwn**, *gah-äh-yone';* from 1342: *haughty:—* proud.

1350. גָּאַל **gâ'al**, *gaw-al';* a prim. root, to *redeem* (according to the Oriental law of kinship), i.e. to *be the next of kin* (and as such to *buy back* a relative's property, *marry* his widow, etc.):— × in any wise, × at all, avenger, deliver, (do, perform the part of near, next) kinsfolk (-man), purchase, ransom, redeem (-er), revenger.

1351. גָּאַל **gâ'al**, *gaw-al';* a prim. root, lrather ident. with 1350, through the idea of *freeing,* i.e. *repudiatingl;* to *soil* or (fig.) *desecrate:—* defile, pollute, stain.

1352. גֹּאֶל **gô'el**, *go'-el;* from 1351; *profanation:—* defile.

1353. גְּאֻלָּה **g^eullâh**, *gheh-ool-law';* fem. pass. part. of 1350; *redemption* (incl. the right and the object); by impl. *relationship:—* kindred, redeem, redemption, right.

1354. גַּב **gab**, *gab;* from an unused root mean. to *hollow* or *curve;* the *back* (as *rounded* lcomp. 1460 and 1479l; by anal. the *top* or *rim,* a *boss,* a *vault, arch* of eye, *bulwarks,* etc.:— back, body, boss, eminent (higher) place, leyel brows, nave, ring.

1355. גַּב **gab** (Chald.), *gab;* corresp. to 1354:— back.

1356. גֵּב **gêb**, *gabe;* from 1461; a *log* (as *cut* out); also *well* or *cistern* (as *dug*):— beam, ditch, pit.

1357. גֵּב **gêb**, *gabe;* prob. from 1461 lcomp. 1462l; a *locust* (from its *cutting*):— locust.

1358. גֹּב **gôb** (Chald.), *gobe;* from a root corresp. to 1461; a *pit* (for wild animals) (as *cut* out):— den.

1359. גֹּב **Gôb**, *gobe;* or (fully)

גוֹב **Gôwb**, *gobe;* from 1461; *pit; Gob,* a place in Pal.:— Gob.

1360. גֶּבֶא **gebe'**, *geh'-beh;* from an unused root mean. prob. to *collect;* a *reservoir;* by anal. a *marsh:—* marish, pit.

1361. גָּבַהּ **gâbahh**, *gaw-bah';* a prim. root; to *soar,* i.e. be *lofty;* fig. to be *haughty:—* exalt, be haughty, be (make) high (-er), lift up, mount up, be proud, raise up great height, upward.

1362. גָּבָהּ **gâbâhh**, *gaw-bawh';* from 1361; *lofty* (lit. or fig.):— high, proud.

1363. גֹּבַהּ **gôbahh**, *go'-bah;* from 1361; *elation, grandeur, arrogance:—* excellency, haughty, height, high, loftiness, pride.

1364. גָּבֹהַּ **gâbôahh**, *gaw-bo'-ah;* or (fully)

גָּבוֹהַּ **gâbôwahh**, *gaw-bo'-ah;* from 1361; *elevated* (or *elated*), *powerful, arrogant:—* haughty, height, high (-er), lofty, proud, × exceeding proudly.

1365. גַּבְהוּת **gabhûwth**, *gab-hooth';* from 1361; *pride:—* loftiness, lofty.

1366. גְּבוּל **g^ebûwl**, *gheb-ool';* or (short.)

גְּבֻל **g^ebûl**, *gheb-ool';* from 1379; prop. a *cord* (as *twisted*), i.e. (by impl.) a *boundary;* by extens. the *territory* inclosed:— border, bound, coast, × great, landmark, limit, quarter, space.

1367. גְּבוּלָה **g^ebûwlâh**, *gheb-oo-law';* or (short.)

גְּבֻלָה **g^ebûlâh**, *gheb-oo-law';* fem. of 1366; a *boundary, region:—* border, bound, coast, landmark, place.

1368. גִּבּוֹר **gibbôwr**, *ghib-bore';* or (short.)

גִּבֹּר **gibbôr**, *ghib-bore';* intens. from the same as 1397; *powerful;* by impl. *warrior, tyrant:—* champion, chief, × excel, giant, man, mighty (man, one), strong (man), valiant man.

1369. גְּבוּרָה **g^ebûwrâh**, *gheb-oo-raw';* fem. pass. part. from the same as 1368; *force* (lit. or fig.); by impl. *valor, victory:—* force, mastery, might, mighty (act, power), power, strength.

1370. גְּבוּרָה **g^ebûwrâh** (Chald.), *gheb-oo-raw';* corresp. to 1369; *power:—* might.

1371. גִּבֵּחַ **gibbêach**, *ghib-bay'-akh;* from an unused root mean. to *be high* (in the forehead); *bald* in the forehead:— forehead bald.

1372. גַּבַּחַת **gabbachath**, *gab-bakh'-ath;* from the same as 1371; *baldness* in the forehead; by anal. a *bare spot* on the right side of cloth:— bald forehead, × without.

1373. גַּבַּי **Gabbay**, *gab-bah'-ee;* from the same as 1354; *collective; Gabbai,* an Isr.:— Gabbai.

1374. גֵּבִים **Gêbîym**, *gay-beem';* plur. of 1356; *cisterns; Gebim,* a place in Pal.:— Gebim.

1375. גָּבִיעַ **g^ebîya'**, *gheb-ee'-ah;* from an unused root (mean. to *be convex*); a goblet; by anal. the *calyx* of a flower:— house, cup, pot.

1376. גְּבִיר **gᵉbîyr**, *gheb-eer´*; from 1396; a *master*:— lord.

1377. גְּבִירָה **gᵉbîyrâh**, *gheb-ee-raw´*; fem. of 1376; a *mistress*:— queen.

1378. גָּבִישׁ **gâbîysh**, *gaw-beesh´*; from an unused root (prob. mean. to *freeze*); *crystal* (from its resemblance to *ice*):— pearl.

1379. גָּבַל **gâbal**, *gaw-bal´*; a prim. root; prop. to *twist* as a rope; only (as a denom. from 1366) to *bound* (as by a line):— be border, set (bounds about).

1380. גְּבָל **Gᵉbal**, *gheb-al´*; from 1379 (in the sense of a *chain* of hills); a *mountain*; *Gebal*, a place in Phœnicia:— Gebal.

1381. גְּבָל **Gᵉbâl**, *gheb-awl´*; the same as 1380; *Gebal*, a region in Idumæa:— Gebal.

גְּבֻלָה **gᵉbûlâh**. See 1367.

1382. גִּבְלִי **Giblîy**, *ghib-lee´*; patrial from 1380; a *Gebalite*, or inhab. of Gebal:— Giblites, stone-squarer.

1383. גַּבְלוּת **gablûth**, *gab-looth´*; from 1379; a twisted *chain* or *lace*:— end.

1384. גִּבֵּן **gibbên**, *gib-bane´*; from an unused root mean. to *be arched* or *contracted; hunch-backed*:— crookbackt.

1385. גְּבִנָה **gᵉbînâh**, *gheb-ee-naw´*; fem. from the same as 1384; *curdled* milk:— cheese.

1386. גַּבְנֹן **gabnôn**, *gab-nohn´*; from the same as 1384; a *hump* or *peak* of hills:— high.

1387. גֶּבַע **Geba'**, *gheh´-bah*; from the same as 1375, a *hillock*; *Geba*, a place in Pal.:— Gaba, Geba, Gibeah.

1388. גִּבְעָא **Gib'â'**, *ghib-aw´*; by perm. for 1389; a *hill*; *Giba*, a place in Pal.:— Gibeah.

1389. גִּבְעָה **gib'âh**, *ghib-aw´*; fem. from the same as 1387; a *hillock*:— hill, little hill.

1390. גִּבְעָה **Gib'âh**, *ghib-aw´*; the same as 1389; *Gibah*, the name of three places in Pal.:— Gibeah, the hill.

1391. גִּבְעוֹן **Gib'ôwn**, *ghib-ohn´*; from the same as 1387; *hilly*; *Gibon*, a place in Pal.:— Gibeon.

1392. גִּבְעֹל **gib'ôl**, *ghib-ole´*; prol. from 1375; the *calyx* of a flower:— bolled.

1393. גִּבְעֹנִי **Gib'ôniy**, *ghib-o-nee´*; patrial from 1391; a *Gibonite*, or inhab. of Gibon:— Gibeonite.

1394. גִּבְעַת **Gib'ath**, *ghib-ath´*; from the same as 1375; *hilliness*; *Gibath*:— Gibeath.

1395. גִּבְעָתִי **Gib'âthîy**, *ghib-aw-thee´*; patrial from 1390; a *Gibathite*, or inhab. of Gibath:— Gibeathite.

1396. גָּבַר **gâbar**, *gaw-bar´*; a prim. root; to *be strong*; by impl. to *prevail, act insolently*:— exceed, confirm, be great, be mighty, prevail, put to more [strength], strengthen, be stronger, be valiant.

1397. גֶּבֶר **geber**, *gheh´-ber*; from 1396; prop. a *valiant* man or *warrior*; gen. a

person simply:— every one, man, × mighty.

1398. גֶּבֶר **Geber**, *gheh´-ber*; the same as 1397; *Geber*, the name of two Isr.:— Geber.

1399. גֶּבַר **gᵉbar**, *gheb-ar´*; from 1396; the same as 1397; a *person*:— man.

1400. גְּבַר **gᵉbar** (Chald.), *gheb-ar´*; corresp. to 1399:— certain, man.

1401. גִּבָּר **gibbâr** (Chald.), *ghib-bawr´*; intens. of 1400; *valiant*, or *warrior*:— mighty.

1402. גִּבָּר **Gibbâr**, *ghib-bawr´*; intens. of 1399; *Gibbar*, an Isr.:— Gibbar.

גְּבוּרָה **gᵉbûrâh**. See 1369.

1403. גַּבְרִיאֵל **Gabrîy'êl**, *gab-ree-ale´*; from 1397 and 410; *man of God*; *Gabriel*, an archangel:— Gabriel.

1404. גְּבֶרֶת **gᵉbereth**, *gheb-eh´-reth*; fem. of 1376; *mistress*:— lady, mistress.

1405. גִּבְּתוֹן **Gibbᵉthôwn**, *ghib-beth-one´*; intens. from 1389; a *hilly* spot; *Gibbethon*, a place in Pal.:— Gibbethon.

1406. גָּג **gâg**, *gawg*; prob. by redupl. from 1342; a *roof*; by anal. the *top* of an altar:— roof (of the house), (house) top (of the house).

1407. גַּד **gad**, *gad*; from 1413 (in the sense of *cutting*); *coriander* seed (from its furrows):— coriander.

1408. גַּד **Gad**, *gad*; a var. of 1409; *Fortune*, a Bab. deity:— that troop.

1409. גָּד **gâd**, *gawd*; from 1464 (in the sense of *distributing*); *fortune*:— troop.

1410. גָּד **Gâd**, *gawd*; from 1464; *Gad*, a son of Jacob, incl. his tribe and its territory; also a prophet:— Gad.

1411. גְּדָבָר **gᵉdâbâr** (Chald.), *ghed-aw-bawr´*; corresp. to 1489; a *treasurer*:— treasurer.

1412. גֻּדְגֹּדָה **Gudgôdâh**, *gud-go´-daw*; by redupl. from 1413 (in the sense of *cutting*) *cleft*; *Gudgodah*, a place in the Desert:— Gudgodah.

1413. גָּדַד **gâdad**, *gaw-dad´*; a prim. root [comp. 1464]; to *crowd*; also to *gash* (as if by *pressing* into):— assemble (selves by troops), gather (selves together, self in troops), cut selves.

1414. גְּדַד **gᵉdad** (Chald.), *ghed-ad´*; corresp. to 1413; to *cut* down:— hew down.

גְּדֻדָה **gᵉdûdâh**. See 1417.

1415. גָּדָה **gâdâh**, *gaw-daw´*; from an unused root (mean. to *cut* off); a *border* of a river (as *cut* into by the stream):— bank.

גֻּדָּה **Gaddâh**. See 2693.

1416. גְּדוּד **gᵉdûwd**, *ghed-ood´*; from 1413; a *crowd* (espec. of soldiers):— army, band (of men), company, troop (of robbers).

1417. גְּדוּד **gᵉdûwd**, *ghed-ood´*; or (fem.)

גְּדֻדָּה **gᵉdûddâh**, *ghed-ood-daw´*; from 1413; a *furrow* (as *cut*):— furrow.

1418. גְּדוּדָה **gᵉdûwdâh**, *ghed-oo-daw´*; fem. pass. part. of 1413; an *incision*:— cutting.

1419. גָּדוֹל **gâdôwl**, *gaw-dole´*; or (short.)

גָּדֹל **gâdôl**, *gaw-dole´*; from 1431;

great (in any sense); hence, *older*; also *insolent*:— + aloud, elder (-est), + exceeding (-ly), + far, (man of) great (man, matter, thing, -er, -ness), high, long, loud, mighty, more, much, noble. proud thing, × sore, (×) very.

1420. גְּדוּלָה **gᵉdûwlâh**, *ghed-oo-law´*; or (short.)

גְּדֻלָּה **gᵉdullâh**, *ghed-ool-law´*; or (less accurately)

גְּדוּלָּה **gᵉdûwllâh**, *ghed-ool-law´*; fem. of 1419; *greatness*; (concr.) *mighty acts*:— dignity, great things (-ness), majesty.

1421. גִּדּוּף **giddûwph**, *ghid-doof´*; or (short.)

גִּדֻּף **giddûph**, *ghid-doof´*; and (fem.)

גִּדּוּפָה **giddûwphâh**, *ghid-doo-faw´*; or

גִּדֻּפָה **giddûphâh**, *ghid-doo-faw´*; from 1422; *vilification*:— reproach, reviling.

1422. גְּדוּפָה **gᵉdûwphâh**, *ghed-oo-faw´*; fem. pass. part. of 1442; a *revilement*:— taunt.

גְּדוֹר **Gᵉdôwr**. See 1446.

1423. גְּדִי **gᵉdîy**, *ghed-ee´*; from the same as 1415; a young *goat* (from *browsing*):— kid.

1424. גָּדִי **Gâdîy**, *gaw-dee´*; from 1409; *fortunate*; *Gadi*, an Isr.:— Gadi.

1425. גָּדִי **Gâdîy**, *gaw-dee´*; patron. from 1410; a *Gadite* (collect.) or desc. of Gad:— Gadites, children of Gad.

1426. גַּדִּי **Gaddîy**, *gad-dee´*; intens. for 1424; *Gaddi*, an Isr.:— Gaddi.

1427. גַּדִּיאֵל **Gaddîy'êl**, *gad-dee-ale´*; from 1409 and 410; *fortune of God*; *Gaddiel*, an Isr.:— Gaddiel.

1428. גִּדְיָה **gidyâh**, *ghid-yaw´*; or

גִּדְיָה **gadyâh**, *gad-yaw´*; the same as 1415; a river *brink*:— bank.

1429. גְּדִיָּה **gᵉdîyâh**, *ghed-ee-yaw´*; fem. of 1423; a young female *goat*:— kid.

1430. גָּדִישׁ **gâdîysh**, *gaw-deesh´*; from an unused root (mean. to *heap* up); a *stack* of sheaves; by anal. a *tomb*:— shock (stack) (of corn), tomb.

1431. גָּדַל **gâdal**, *gaw-dal´*; a prim. root; prop. to *twist* [comp. 1434], i.e. to *be* (caus. *make*) *large* (in various senses, as in body, mind, estate or honor, also in pride):— advance, boast, bring up, exceed, excellent, be (-come, do, give, make, wax), great (-er, come to … estate, + things), grow (up), increase, lift up, magnify (-ifical), be much set by, nourish [up], pass, promote, proudly [spoken], tower.

1432. גָּדֵל **gâdêl**, *gaw-dale´*; from 1431; *large* (lit. or fig.):— great, grew.

1433. גֹּדֶל **gôdel**, *go´-del*; from 1431; *magnitude* (lit. or fig.):— greatness, stout (-ness).

1434. גְּדִל **gᵉdîl**, *ghed-eel´*; from 1431 (in the sense of *twisting*); *thread*, i.e. a *tassel* or *festoon*:— fringe, wreath.

1435. גִּדֵּל **Giddêl**, *ghid-dale´*; from 1431; *stout*; *Giddel*, the name of one of the

Nethinim, also of one of "Solomon's servants":— Giddel.

גָּדוֹל **gâdôl.** See 1419.

גְּדֻלָּה **gᵉdullâh.** See 1420.

1436. גְּדַלְיָה **Gᵉdalyâh,** ghed-al-yaw´; or (prol.)

גְּדַלְיָהוּ **Gᵉdalyâhûw,** ghed-al-yaw´-hoo; from 1431 and 3050; Jah has become great; Gedaljah, the name of five Isr.:— Gedaliah.

1437. גִּדַּלְתִּי **Giddaltiy,** ghid-dal´-tee; from 1431; I have made great; Giddalti, an Isr.:— Giddalti.

1438. גָּדַע **gâda´,** gaw-dah´; a prim. root; to fell a tree; gen. to destroy anything:— cut (asunder, in sunder, down, off), hew down.

1439. גִּדְעוֹן **Gid'ôwn,** ghid-ohn´; from 1438; feller (i.e. warrior); Gidon, an Isr.:— Gideon.

1440. גִּדְעֹם **Gid'ôm,** ghid-ohm´; from 1438; a cutting (i.e. desolation); Gidom, a place in Pal.:— Gidom.

1441. גִּדְעֹנִי **Gid'ôniy,** ghid-o-nee´; from 1438; warlike [comp. 1439]; Gidoni, an Isr.:— Gideoni.

1442. גָּדַף **gâdaph,** gaw-daf´; a prim. root; to hack (with words), i.e. revile:— blaspheme, reproach.

גִּדּוּף **giddûph,** and

גִּדֻּפָה **giddûphâh.** See 1421.

1443. גָּדַר **gâdar,** gaw-dar´; a prim. root; to wall in or around:— close up, fence up, hedge, inclose, make up [a wall], mason, repairer.

1444. גֶּדֶר **geder,** gheh´-der; from 1443; a circumvallation:— wall.

1445. גֶּדֶר **Geder,** gheh´-der; the same as 1444; Geder, a place in Pal.:— Geder.

1446. גְּדֹר **Gᵉdôr,** ghed-ore´; or (fully)

גְּדוֹר **Gᵉdôwr,** ghed-ore´; from 1443; inclosure; Gedor, a place in Pal.; also the name of three Isr.:— Gedor.

1447. גָּדֵר **gâdêr,** gaw-dare´; from 1443; a circumvallation; by impl. an inclosure:— fence, hedge, wall.

1448. גְּדֵרָה **gᵉdêrâh,** ghed-ay-raw´; fem. of 1447; inclosure (espec. for flocks):— [sheep-] cote (fold) hedge, wall.

1449. גְּדֵרָה **Gᵉdêrâh,** ghed-ay-raw´; the same as 1448; (with the art.) Gederah, a place in Pal.:— Gederah, hedges.

1450. גְּדֵרוֹת **Gᵉdêrôwth,** ghed-ay-rohth´; plur. of 1448; walls; Gederoth, a place in Pal.:— Gederoth.

1451. גְּדֵרִי **Gᵉdêriy,** ghed-ay-ree´; patrial from 1445; a Gederite, or inhab. of Geder:— Gederite.

1452. גְּדֵרָתִי **Gᵉdêrâthiy,** ghed-ay-raw-thee´; patrial from 1449; a Gederathite, or inhab. of Gederah:— Gederathite.

1453. גְּדֵרֹתַיִם **Gᵉdêrôthayim,** ghed-ay-ro-thah´-yim; dual of 1448; double wall; Gederothajim, a place in Pal.:— Gederothaim.

1454. גֵּה **gêh,** gay; prob. a clerical err. for 2088; this:— this.

1455. גָּהָה **gâhâh,** gaw-haw´; a prim. root; to remove (a bandage from a wound, i.e. heal it):— cure.

1456. גֵּהָה **gêhâh,** gay-haw´; from 1455; a cure:— medicine.

1457. גָּהַר **gâhar,** gaw-har´; a prim. root; to prostrate oneself:— cast self down, stretch self.

1458. גַּו **gav,** gav; another form for 1460; the back:— back.

1459. גַּו **gav** (Chald.), gav; corresp. to 1460; the middle:— midst, same, there-(where-) in.

1460. גֵּו **gêv,** gave; from 1342 [corresp. to 1354]; the back; by anal. the middle:— + among, back, body.

1461. גּוּב **gûwb,** goob; a prim. root; to dig:— husbandman.

1462. גּוֹב **gôwb,** gobe; from 1461; the locust (from its grubbing as a larvae):— grasshopper, × great.

1463. גּוֹג **Gôwg,** gohg; of uncert. der.; Gog, the name of an Isr., also of some northern nation:— Gog.

1464. גּוּד **gûwd,** goode; a prim. root [akin to 1413]; to crowd upon, i.e. attack:— invade, overcome.

1465. גֵּוָה **gêvâh,** gay-vaw´; fem. of 1460; the back, i.e. (by extens.) the person:— body.

1466. גֵּוָה **gêvâh,** gay-vaw´; the same as 1465; exaltation; (fig.) arrogance:— lifting up, pride.

1467. גֵּוָה **gêvâh** (Chald.), gay-vaw´; corresp. to 1466:— pride.

1468. גּוּז **gûwz,** gooz; a prim. root [comp. 1494]; prop. to shear off; but used only in the (fig.) sense of passing rapidly:— bring, cut off.

1469. גּוֹזָל **gôwzâl,** go-zawl´; or (short.)

גֹּזָל **gôzâl,** go-zawl´; from 1497; a nestling (as being comp. nude of feathers):— young (pigeon).

1470. גּוֹזָן **Gôwzân,** go-zawn´; prob. from 1468; a quarry (as a place of cutting stones); Gozan, a province of Assyria:— Gozan.

1471. גּוֹי **gôwy,** go´-ee; rarely (short.)

גֹּי **gôy,** go´-ee; appar. from the same root as 1465 (in the sense of massing); a foreign nation; hence, a Gentile; also (fig.) a troop of animals, or a flight of locusts:— Gentile, heathen, nation, people.

1472. גְּוִיָּה **gᵉviyâh,** ghev-ee-yaw´; prol. for 1465; a body, whether alive or dead:— (dead) body, carcase, corpse.

1473. גּוֹלָה **gôwlâh,** go-law´; or (short.)

גֹּלָה **gôlâh,** go-law´; act. part. fem. of 1540; exile; concr. and collect. exiles:— (carried away) captive (-ity), removing.

1474. גּוֹלָן **Gôwlân,** go-lawn´; from 1473; captive; Golan, a place E. of the Jordan:— Golan.

1475. גּוּמָּץ **gûwmmâts,** goom-mawts´; of uncert. der.; a pit:— pit.

1476. גּוּנִי **Gûwniy,** goo-nee´; prob. from 1598; protected; Guni, the name of two Isr.:— Guni.

1477. גּוּנִי **Gûwniy,** goo-nee´; patron. from 1476; a Gunite (collect. with art. pref.) or desc. of Guni:— Gunites.

1478. גָּוַע **gâva´,** gaw-vah´; a prim. root; to breathe out, i.e. (by impl.) expire:— die, be dead, give up the ghost, perish.

1479. גּוּף **gûwph,** goof; a prim. root; prop. to hollow or arch, i.e. (fig.) close; to shut:— shut.

1480. גּוּפָה **gûwphâh,** goo-faw´; from 1479; a corpse (as closed to sense):— body.

1481. גּוּר **gûwr,** goor; a prim. root; prop. to turn aside from the road (for a lodging or any other purpose), i.e. sojourn (as a guest); also to shrink, fear (as in a strange place); also to gather for hostility (as afraid):— abide, assemble, be afraid, dwell, fear, gather (together), inhabitant, remain, sojourn, stand in awe, (be) stranger, × surely.

1482. גּוּר **gûwr,** goor; or (short.)

גֻּר **gûr,** goor; perh. from 1481; a cub (as still abiding in the lair), espec. of the lion:— whelp, young one.

1483. גּוּר **Gûwr,** goor; the same as 1482; Gur, a place in Pal.:— Gur.

1484. גּוֹר **gôwr,** gore; or (fem.)

גֹּרָה **gôrâh,** go-raw´; a var. of 1482:— whelp.

1485. גּוּר־בַּעַל **Gûwr-Ba'al,** goor-bah´-al; from 1481 and 1168; dwelling of Baal; Gur-Baal, a place in Arabia:— Gur-baal.

1486. גּוֹרָל **gôwrâl,** go-rawl´; or (short.)

גֹּרָל **gôrâl,** go-ral´; from an unused root mean. to be rough (as stone); prop. a pebble, i.e. a lot (small stones being used for that purpose); fig. a portion or destiny (as if determined by lot):— lot.

1487. גּוּשׁ **gûwsh,** goosh; or rather (by perm.)

גִּישׁ° **gîysh,** gheesh; of uncert. der.; a mass of earth:— clod.

1488. גֵּז **gêz,** gaze; from 1494; a fleece (as shorn); also mown grass:— fleece, mowing, mown grass.

1489. גִּזְבָּר **gizbâr,** ghiz-bawr´; of for. der.; treasurer:— treasurer.

1490. גִּזְבָּר **gizbâr** (Chald.), ghiz-bawr´; corresp. to 1489:— treasurer.

1491. גָּזָה **gâzâh,** gaw-zaw´; a prim. root [akin to 1468]; to cut off, i.e. portion out:— take.

1492. גִּזָּה **gazzâh,** gaz-zaw´; fem. from 1494; a fleece:— fleece.

1493. גִּזוֹנִי **Gizôwniy,** ghee-zo-nee´; patrial from the unused name of a place appar. in Pal.; a Gizonite or inhab. of Gizoh:— Gizonite.

1494. גָּזַז **gâzaz,** gaw-zaz´; a prim. root [akin to 1468]; to cut off; spec. to shear a flock or shave the hair; fig. to destroy an enemy:— cut off (down), poll, shave, [sheep-] shear (-er).

1495. גָּזֵז **Gâzêz,** gaw-zaze´; from 1494; shearer; Gazez, the name of two Isr.:— Gazez.

1496. גָּזִית **gâzîyth,** gaw-zeeth´; from 1491; something cut, i.e. dressed stone:— hewed, hewn stone, wrought.

1497. גָּזַל **gâzal,** gaw-zal´; a prim. root; to pluck off; spec. to flay, strip or rob:— catch, consume, exercise [robbery], pluck (off), rob, spoil, take away (by force, violence), tear.

1498. גָּזֵל gâzêl, *gaw-zale'*; from 1497; *robbery*, or (concr.) *plunder*:— robbery, thing taken away by violence.

1499. גֶּזֶל gêzel, *ghe'-zel*; from 1497; *plunder*, i.e. *violence*:— violence, violent perverting.

גֹּזָל gôzâl. See 1469.

1500. גְּזֵלָה gᵉzêlâh, *ghez-ay-law'*; fem. of 1498 and mean. the same:— that (he had robbed) [which he took violently away], spoil, violence.

1501. גָּזָם gâzâm, *gaw-zawm'*; from an unused root mean. to *devour*; a kind of *locust*:— palmer-worm.

1502. גַּזָּם Gazzâm, *gaz-zawm'*; from the same as 1501; *devourer*; *Gazzam*, one of the Nethinim:— Gazzam.

1503. גֶּזַע geza', *geh'-zah*; from an unused root mean. to *cut* down (trees); the *trunk* or *stump* of a tree (as felled or as planted):— stem, stock.

1504. גָּזַר gâzar, *gaw-zar'*; a prim. root; to *cut* down or off; (fig.) to *destroy, divide, exclude*, or *decide*:— cut down (off), decree, divide, snatch.

1505. גְּזַר gᵉzar (Chald.), *ghez-ar'*; corresp. to 1504; to *quarry; determine*:— cut out, soothsayer.

1506. גֶּזֶר gezer, *gheh'-zer*; from 1504; something *cut* off; a *portion*:— part, piece.

1507. גֶּזֶר Gezer, *gheh'-zer*; the same as 1506; *Gezer*, a place in Pal.:— Gazer, Gezer.

1508. גִּזְרָה gizrâh, *ghiz-raw'*; fem. of 1506; the *figure* or person (as if *cut* out); also an *inclosure* (as *separated*):— polishing, separate place.

1509. גְּזֵרָה gᵉzêrâh, *ghez-ay-raw'*; from 1504; a *desert* (as *separated*):— not inhabited.

1510. גְּזֵרָה gᵉzêrâh (Chald.), *ghez-ay-raw'*; from 1505 (as 1504); a *decree*:— decree.

1511. גִּזְרִי Gizrîy (in the marg.), *ghiz-ree'*; patrial from 1507; a *Gezerite* (collect.) or inhab. of Gezer; but better (as in the text) by transp.

גִּרְזִי Girzîy, *gher-zee'*; patrial of 1630; a *Girzite* (collect.) or member of a native tribe in Pal.:— Gezrites.

גִּיחוֹן Gîchôwn. See 1521.

1512. גָּחוֹן gâchôwn, *gaw-khone'*; prob. from 1518; the external *abdomen, belly* (as the *source* of the fetus [comp. 1521]):— belly.

גֵּחֲזִי Gêchăzîy. See 1522.

גָּחֹל gâchol. See 1513.

1513. גֶּחֶל gechel, *geh'-khel*; or (fem.)

גַּחֶלֶת gacheleth, *gah-kheh'-leth*; from an unused root mean. to *glow* or *kindle*; an *ember*:— (burning) coal.

1514. גַּחַם Gacham, *gah'-kham*; from an unused root mean. to *burn; flame*; *Gacham*, a son of Nahor:— Gaham.

1515. גַּחַר Gachar, *gah'-khar*; from an unused root mean. to *hide; lurker*; *Gachar*, one of the Nethinim:— Gahar.

גֹּי gôy. See 1471.

1516. גַּיְא gay', *gah'-ee*; or (short.)

גַּי gay, *gah'-ee*; prob. (by transm.) from the same root as 1466 (abb.); a *gorge* (from its *lofty* sides; hence, narrow, but not a gully or winter-torrent):— valley.

1517. גִּיד gîyd, *gheed*; prob. from 1464; a *thong* (as *compressing*); by anal. a *tendon*:— sinew.

1518. גִּיחַ gîyach, *ghee'-akh*; or (short.)

גֹּחַ gôach, *go'-akh*; a prim. root; to *gush* forth (as water), gen. to *issue*:— break forth, labor to bring forth, come forth, draw up, take out.

1519. גִּיחַ gîyach (Chald.), *ghee'-akh*; or (short.)

גּוּחַ gûwach (Chald.), *goo'-akh*; corresp. to 1518; to *rush* forth:— strive.

1520. גִּיחַ Gîyach, *ghee'-akh*; from 1518; a *fountain; Giach*, a place in Pal.:— Giah.

1521. גִּיחוֹן Gîychôwn, *ghee-khone'*; or (short.)

גִּחוֹן Gichôwn, *ghee-khone'*; from 1518; *stream; Gichon*, a river of Paradise; also a valley (or pool) near Jerusalem:— Gihon.

1522. גֵּיחֲזִי Gêychăzîy, *gay-khah-zee'*; or

גֵּחֲזִי Gêchăzîy, *gay-khah-zee'*; appar. from 1516 and 2372; *valley of a visionary; Gechazi*, the servant of Elisha:— Gehazi.

1523. גִּיל gîyl, *gheel*; or (by perm.)

גּוּל gûwl, *gool*; a prim. root; prop. to *spin* round (under the influence of any violent emotion), i.e. usually *rejoice*, or (as *cringing*) *fear*:— be glad, joy, be joyful, rejoice.

1524. גִּיל gîyl, *gheel*; from 1523; a *revolution* (of time, i.e. an *age*); also *joy*:— × exceedingly, gladness, × greatly, joy, rejoice (-ing), sort.

1525. גִּילָה gîylâh, *ghee-law'*; or

גִּילַת gîylath, *ghee-lath'*; fem. of 1524; *joy*:— joy, rejoicing.

גִּילֹה Gîylôh. See 1542.

1526. גִּילֹנִי Gîylônîy, *ghee-lo-nee'*; patrial from 1542; a *Gilonite* or inhab. of Giloh:— Gilonite.

1527. גִּינַת Gîynath, *ghee-nath'*; of uncert. der.; *Ginath*, an Isr.:— Ginath.

1528. גִּיר gîyr (Chald.), *gheer*; corresp. to 1615; *lime*:— plaster.

גֵּיר gêyr. See 1616.

1529. גֵּישָׁן Gêyshân, *gay-shawn'*; from the same as 1487; *lumpish; Geshan*, an Isr.:— Geshan.

1530. גַּל gal, *gal*; from 1556; something *rolled*, i.e. a *heap* of stone or dung (plural *ruins*), by anal. a *spring* of water (plur. *waves*):— billow, heap, spring, wave.

1531. גֹּל gôl, *gole*; from 1556; a *cup* for oil (as *round*):— bowl.

גְּלָא gᵉlâ'. See 1541.

1532. גַּלָּב gallâb, *gal-lawb'*; from an unused root mean. to *shave*; a *barber*:— barber.

1533. גִּלְבֹּעַ Gilbôa', *ghil-bo'-ah*; from

1530 and 1158; *fountain of ebullition; Gilboa*, a mountain of Pal.:— Gilboa.

1534. גַּלְגַּל galgal, *gal-gal'*; by redupl. from 1556; a *wheel*; by anal. a *whirlwind*; also *dust* (as *whirled*):— heaven, rolling thing, wheel.

1535. גַּלְגַּל galgal (Chald.), *gal-gal'*; corresp. to 1534; a *wheel*:— wheel.

1536. גִּלְגָּל gilgâl, *ghil-gawl'*; a var. of 1534:— wheel.

1537. גִּלְגָּל Gilgâl, *ghil-gawl'*; the same as 1536 (with the art. as a prop. noun); *Gilgal*, the name of three places in Pal.:— Gilgal. See also 1019.

1538. גֻּלְגֹּלֶת gulgôleth, *gul-go'-leth*; by redupl. from 1556; a *skull* (as *round*); by impl. a *head* (in enumeration of persons):— head, every man, poll, skull.

1539. גֶּלֶד geled, *ghe'-led*; from an unused root prob. mean. to *polish*; the (human) *skin* (as *smooth*):— skin.

1540. גָּלָה gâlâh, *gaw-law'*; a prim. root; to *denude* (espec. in a disgraceful sense); by impl. to *exile* (captives being usually *stripped*), fig. to *reveal*:— + advertise, appear, bewray, bring, (carry, lead, go) captive (into captivity), depart, disclose, discover, exile, be gone, open, × plainly, publish, remove, reveal, × shamelessly, shew, × surely, tell, uncover.

1541. גְּלָה gᵉlâh (Chald.), *ghel-aw'*; or

גְּלָא gᵉlâ' (Chald.), *ghel-aw'*; corresp. to 1540:— bring over, carry away, reveal.

גּוֹלָה gôlâh. See 1473.

1542. גִּלֹה Gîlôh, *ghee-lo'*; or (fully)

גִּילֹה Gîylôh, *ghee-lo'*; from 1540; *open; Giloh*, a place in Pal.:— Giloh.

1543. גֻּלָּה gullâh, *gool-law'*; fem. from 1556; a *fountain, bowl* or *globe* (all as *round*):— bowl, pommel, spring.

1544. גִּלּוּל gillûwl, *ghil-lool'*; or (short.)

גִּלֻּל gillul, *ghil-lool'*; from 1556; prop. a *log* (as *round*); by impl. an *idol*:— idol.

1545. גְּלוֹם gᵉlôwm, *ghel-ome'*; from 1563; *clothing* (as *wrapped*):— clothes.

1546. גָּלוּת gâlûwth, *gaw-looth'*; fem. from 1540; *captivity*; concr. *exiles* (collect.):— (they that are carried away) captives (-ity).

1547. גָּלוּת gâlûwth (Chald.), *gaw-looth'*; corresp. to 1546:— captivity.

1548. גָּלַח gâlach, *gaw-lakh'*; a prim. root; prop. to *be bald*, i.e. (caus.) to *shave*; fig. to *lay waste*:— poll, shave (off).

1549. גִּלָּיוֹן gillâyôwn, *ghil-law-yone'*; or

גִּלְיוֹן gilyôwn, *ghil-yone'*; from 1540; a *tablet* for writing (as *bare*); by anal. a *mirror* (as a *plate*):— glass, roll.

1550. גָּלִיל gâlîyl, *gaw-leel'*; from 1556; a *valve* of a folding door (as *turning*); also a *ring* (as *round*):— folding, ring.

1551. גָּלִיל Gâlîyl, *gaw-leel'*; or (prol.)

גָּלִילָה Gâlîylâh, *gaw-lee-law'*; the same as 1550; a *circle* (with the art.); *Galil* (as a special *circuit*) in the North of Pal.:— Galilee.

1552. גְּלִילָה gᵉlîylâh, *ghel-ee-law'*; fem.

of 1550; a *circuit* or *region*:— border, coast, country.

1553. גְּלִילוֹת **Geliylôwth**, *ghel-ee-lowth'*; plur. of 1552; *circles*; *Geliloth*, a place in Pal.:— Geliloth.

1554. גָּלִּים **Gallîym**, *gal-leem'*; plur. of 1530; *springs*; *Gallim*, a place in Pal.:— Gallim.

1555. גָּלְיָת **Golyath**, *gol-yath'*; perh. from 1540; *exile*; *Goljath*, a Philistine:— Goliath.

1556. גָּלַל **gâlal**, *gaw-lal'*; a prim. root; to *roll* (lit. or fig.):— commit, remove, roll (away, down, together), run down, seek occasion, trust, wallow.

1557. גֵּל **gâlâl**, *gaw-lawl'*; from 1556; *dung* (as in *balls*):— dung.

1558. גָּלָל **gâlâl**, *gaw-lawl'*; from 1556; a *circumstance* (as *rolled* around); only used adv., on *account* of:— because of, for (sake).

1559. גָּלָל **Gâlâl**, *gaw-lawl'*; from 1556, in the sense of 1560; *great*; *Galal*, the name of two Isr.:— Galal.

1560. גְּלָל **gelâl** (Chald.), *ghel-awl'*; from a root corresp. to 1556; *weight* or *size* (as if *rolled*):— great.

1561. גֵּלֶל **gêlel**, *gay'-lel*; a var. of 1557; *dung* (plur. *balls* of dung):— dung.

1562. גִּלֲלַי **Gilălay**, *ghe-lal-ah'-ee*; from 1561; *dungy*; *Gilalai*, an Isr.:— Gilalai.

1563. גָּלַם **gâlam**, *gaw-lam'*; a prim. root; to *fold*:— wrap together.

1564. גֹּלֶם **gôlem**, *go'-lem*; from 1563; a *wrapped* (and unformed *mass*, i.e. as the *embryo*):— substance yet being unperfect.

1565. גַּלְמוּד **galmûwd**, *gal-mood'*; prob. by prol. from 1563; *sterile* (as *wrapped* up too hard); fig. *desolate*:— desolate, solitary.

1566. גָּלַע **gâla'**, *gaw-lah'*; a prim. root; to *be obstinate*:— (inter-) meddle (with).

1567. גַּלְעֵד **Gal'êd**, *gal-ade'*; from 1530 and 5707; *heap of testimony*; *Galed*, a memorial cairn E. of the Jordan:— Galeed.

1568. גִּלְעָד **Gil'âd**, *ghil-awd'*; prob. from 1567; *Gilad*, a region E. of the Jordan; also the name of three Isr.:— Gilead, Gileadite.

1569. גִּלְעָדִי **Gil'âdîy**, *ghil-aw-dee'*; patron. from 1568; a *Giladite* or desc. of Gilad:— Gileadite.

1570. גָּלַשׁ **gâlash**, *gaw-lash'*; a prim. root; prob. to *caper* (as a goat):— appear.

1571. גַּם **gam**, *gam*; by contr. from an unused root mean. to *gather*; prop. *assemblage*; used only adv. *also, even, yea, though*; often repeated as correl. *both ... and*:— again, alike, also, (so much) as (soon), both (so) ... and, but, either ... or, even, for all, (in) likewise (manner), moreover, nay ... neither, one, then (-refore), though, what, with, yea.

1572. גָּמָא **gâmâ'**, *gaw-maw'*; a prim. root (lit. or fig.) to *absorb*:— swallow, drink.

1573. גֹּמֶא **gôme'**, *go'-meh*; from 1572;

prop. an *absorbent*, i.e. the *bulrush* (from its *porosity*); spec. the *papyrus*:— (bul-) rush.

1574. גֹּמֶד **gômed**, *go'-med*; from an unused root appar. mean. to *grasp*; prop. a *span*:— cubit.

1575. גַּמָּד **Gammâd**, *gam-mawd'*; from the same as 1574; a *warrior* (as *grasping* weapons):— Gammadims.

1576. גְּמוּל **gemûwl**, *ghem-ool'*; from 1580; *treatment*, i.e. an *act* (of good or ill); by impl. *service* or *requital*:— + as hast served, benefit, desert, deserving, that which he hath given, recompense, reward.

1577. גָּמוּל **Gâmûwl**, *gaw-mool'*; pass. part. of 1580; *rewarded*; *Gamul*, an Isr.:— Gamul. See also 1014.

1578. גְּמוּלָה **gemûwlâh**, *ghem-oo-law'*; fem. of 1576; mean. the same:— deed, recompense, such a reward.

1579. גִּמְזוֹ **Gimzôw**, *ghim-zo'*; of uncert. der.; *Gimzo*, a place in Pal.:— Gimzo.

1580. גָּמַל **gâmal**, *gaw-mal'*; a prim. root; to *treat* a person (well or ill), i.e. *benefit* or *requite*; by impl. (of *toil*), to *ripen*, i.e. (spec.) to *wean*:— bestow on, deal bountifully, do (good), recompense, requite, reward, ripen, + serve, mean, yield.

1581. גָּמָל **gâmâl**, *gaw-mawl'*; appar. from 1580 (in the sense of *labor* or *burden-bearing*); a *camel*:— camel.

1582. גְּמַלִּי **Gemalliy**, *ghem-al-lee'*; prob. from 1581; *camel-driver*; *Gemalli*, an Isr.:— Gemalli.

1583. גַּמְלִיאֵל **Gamliy'êl**, *gam-lee-ale'*; from 1580 and 410; *reward of God*; *Gamliel*, an Isr.:— Gamaliel.

1584. גָּמַר **gâmar**, *gaw-mar'*; a prim. root; to *end* (in the sense of *completion* or *failure*):— cease, come to an end, fail, perfect, perform.

1585. גְּמַר **gemar** (Chald.), *ghem-ar'*; corresp. to 1584:— perfect.

1586. גֹּמֶר **Gômer**, *go'-mer*; from 1584; *completion*; *Gomer*, the name of a son of Japheth and of his desc.; also of a Hebrewess:— Gomer.

1587. גְּמַרְיָה **Gemaryâh**, *ghem-ar-yaw'*; or

גְּמַרְיָהוּ **Gemaryâhûw**, *ghem-ar-yaw'-hoo*; from 1584 and 3050; *Jah has perfected*; *Gemarjah*, the name of two Isr.:— Gemariah.

1588. גַּן **gan**, *gan*; from 1598; a *garden* (as *fenced*):— garden.

1589. גָּנַב **gânab**, *gaw-nab'*; a prim. root; to *thieve* (lit. or fig.); by impl. to *deceive*:— carry away, × indeed, secretly bring, steal (away), get by stealth.

1590. גַּנָּב **gannâb**, *gaw-nab'*; from 1589; a *stealer*:— thief.

1591. גְּנֵבָה **genêbâh**, *ghen-ay-baw'*; from 1589; *stealing*, i.e. (concr.) something *stolen*:— theft.

1592. גְּנֻבַת **Genûbath**, *ghen-oo-bath'*; from 1589; *theft*; *Genubath*, an Edomitish prince:— Genubath.

1593. גַּנָּה **gannâh**, *gan-naw'*; fem. of 1588; a *garden*:— garden.

1594. גִּנָּה **ginnâh**, *ghin-naw'*; another form for 1593:— garden.

1595. גֶּנֶז **genez**, *gheh'-nez*; from an unused root mean. to *store*; *treasure*; by impl. a *coffer*:— chest, treasury.

1596. גְּנַז **genaz** (Chald.), *ghen-az'*; corresp. to 1595; *treasure*:— treasure.

1597. גִּנְזַךְ **ginzak**, *ghin-zak'*; prol. from 1595; a *treasury*:— treasury.

1598. גָּנַן **gânan**, *gaw-nan'*; a prim. root; to *hedge* about, i.e. (gen.) *protect*:— defend.

1599. גִּנְּתוֹן **Ginnethôwn**, *ghin-neth-one'*; or

גִּנְּתוֹ **Ginnethôw**, *ghin-neth-o'*; from 1598; *gardener*; *Ginnethon* or *Ginnetho*, an Isr.:— Ginnetho, Ginnethon.

1600. גָּעָה **gâ'âh**, *gaw-aw'*; a prim. root; to *bellow* (as cattle):— low.

1601. גֹּעָה **Gô'âh**, *go-aw'*; fem. act. part. of 1600; *lowing*; *Goah*, a place near Jerusalem:— Goath.

1602. גָּעַל **gâ'al**, *gaw-al'*; a prim. root; to *detest*; by impl. to *reject*:— abhor, fail, lothe, vilely cast away.

1603. גַּעַל **Ga'al**, *gah'-al*; from 1602; *loathing*; *Gaal*, an Isr.:— Gaal.

1604. גֹּעַל **gô'al**, *go'-al*; from 1602; *abhorrence*:— loathing.

1605. גָּעַר **gâ'ar**, *gaw-ar'*; a prim. root; to *chide*:— corrupt, rebuke, reprove.

1606. גְּעָרָה **ge'ârâh**, *gheh-aw-raw'*; from 1605; a *chiding*:— rebuke (-ing), reproof.

1607. גָּעַשׁ **gâ'ash**, *gaw-ash'*; a prim. root to *agitate* violently:— move, shake, toss, trouble.

1608. גַּעַשׁ **Ga'ash**, *ga'-ash*; from 1607; a *quaking*; *Gaash*, a hill in Pal.:— Gaash.

1609. גַּעְתָּם **Ga'tâm**, *gah-tawm'*; of uncert. der.; *Gatam*, an Edomite:— Gatam.

1610. גַּף **gaph**, *gaf*; from an unused root mean. to *arch*; the *back*; by extens. the *body* or *self*:— + highest places, himself.

1611. גַּף **gaph** (Chald.), *gaf*; corresp. to 1610; a *wing*:— wing.

1612. גֶּפֶן **gephen**, *gheh'-fen*; from an unused root mean. to *bend*; a *vine* (as *twining*), espec. the grape:— vine, tree.

1613. גֹּפֶר **gôpher**, *go'-fer*; from an unused root, prob. mean. to *house in*; a kind of tree or wood (as used for *building*), appar. the *cypress*:— gopher.

1614. גָּפְרִית **gophrîyth**, *gof-reeth'*; prob. fem. of 1613; prop. *cypress-resin*; by anal. *sulphur* (as equally inflammable):— brimstone.

1615. גִּר **gîr**, *gheer*; perh. from 3564; *lime* (from being *burned* in a kiln):— chalk [-stone].

1616. גֵּר **gêr**, *gare*; or (fully)

גֵּיר **gêyr**, *gare*; from 1481; prop. a *guest*; by impl. a *foreigner*:— alien, sojourner, stranger.

גֻּר **gûr**. See 1482.

1617. גֵּרָא **Gêrâ'**, *gay-raw'*; perh. from 1626; a *grain*; *Gera*, the name of six Isr.:— Gera.

1618. גָּרָב **gârâb**, *gaw-rawb'*; from an unused root mean. to *scratch; scurf* (from *itching*):— scab, scurvy.

1619. גָּרָב **Gârêb**, *gaw-rabe'*; from the same as 1618; *scabby; Gareb*, the name of an Isr., also of a hill near Jerusalem:— Gareb.

1620. גַּרְגַּר **gargar**, *gar-gar'*; by redupl. from 1641; a *berry* (as if a pellet of *rumination*):— berry.

1621. גַּרְגְּרוֹת **gargᵉrôwth**, *gar-gher-owth'*; fem. plur. from 1641; the *throat* (as used in *rumination*):— neck.

1622. גִּרְגָּשִׁי **Girgâshiy**, *ghir-gaw-shee'*; patrial from an unused name [of uncert. der.]; a *Girgashite*, one of the native tribes of Canaan:— Girgashite, Girgasite.

1623. גָּרַד **gârad**, *gaw-rad'*; a prim. root; to *abrade*:— scrape.

1624. גָּרָה **gârâh**, *gaw-raw'*; a prim. root; prop. to *grate*, i.e. (fig.) to *anger*:— contend, meddle, stir up, strive.

1625. גֵּרָה **gêrâh**, *gay-raw'*; from 1641; the *cud* (as *scraping* the throat):— cud.

1626. גֵּרָה **gêrâh**, *gay-raw'*; from 1641 (as in 1625); prop. (like 1620) a *kernel* (round as if *scraped*), i.e. a *gerah* or small weight (and coin):— gerah.

גֹּרָה **gôrâh**. See 1484.

1627. גָּרוֹן **gârôwn**, *gaw-rone'*; or (short.) גָּרֹן **gârôn**, *gaw-rone'*; from 1641; the *throat* [comp. 1621] (as *roughened* by swallowing):— × aloud, mouth, neck, throat.

1628. גֵּרוּת **gêrûwth**, *gay-rooth'*; from 1481; a (temporary) *residence*:— habitation.

1629. גָּרַז **gâraz**, *gaw-raz'*; a prim. root; to *cut off*:— cut off.

1630. גְּרִזִים **Gᵉrîzîym**, *gher-ee-zeem'*; plur. of an unused noun from 1629 [comp. 1511], *cut up* (i.e. *rocky*); *Gerizim*, a mountain of Pal.:— Gerizim.

1631. גַּרְזֶן **garzen**, *gar-zen'*; from 1629; an *axe*: - ax.

1632. גָּרֹל **gârôl**, *gaw-role'*; from the same as 1486; *harsh*:— man of great [as in the marg. which reads 1419].

גֹּרָל **gôrâl**. See 1486.

1633. גָּרַם **gâram**, *gaw-ram'*; a prim. root; to *be spare* or *skeleton-like*; used only as a denom. from 1634; (caus.) to *bone*, i.e. *denude* (by extens. *crunch*) the bones:— gnaw the bones, break.

1634. גֶּרֶם **gerem**, *gheh'-rem*; from 1633; a *bone* (as the *skeleton* of the body); hence, *self*, i.e. (fig.) *very*:— bone, strong, top.

1635. גֶּרֶם **gerem** (Chald.), *gheh'-rem*; corresp. to 1634; a *bone*:— bone.

1636. גַּרְמִי **Garmîy**, *gar-mee'*; from 1634; *bony*, i.e. *strong*:— Garmite.

1637. גֹּרֶן **gôren**, *go'-ren*; from an unused root mean. to *smooth*; a threshing-*floor* (as made *even*); by anal. any open *area*:— (barn, corn, threshing-) floor, (threshing-, void) place.

גָּרֹן **gârôn**. See 1627.

1638. גָּרַס **gâraç**, *gaw-ras'*; a prim. root; to *crush*; also (intr. and fig.) to *dissolve*:— break.

1639. גָּרַע **gâra'**, *gaw-rah'*; a prim. root; to *scrape* off; by impl. to *shave, remove, lessen,* or *withhold*:— abate, clip, (di-) minish, do (take) away, keep back, restrain, make small, withdraw.

1640. גָּרַף **gâraph**, *gaw-raf'*; a prim. root; to *bear off* violently:— sweep away.

1641. גָּרַר **gârar**, *gaw-rar'*; a prim. root; to *drag off* roughly; by impl. to *bring up* the cud (i.e. *ruminate*); by anal. to *saw*:— catch, chew, × continuing, destroy, saw.

1642. גְּרָר **Gᵉrâr**, *gher-awr'*; prob. from 1641; a *rolling* country; *Gerar*, a Philistine city:— Gerar.

1643. גֶּרֶשׂ **geres**, *gheh'-res*; from an unused root mean. to *husk*; a *kernel* (collect.), i.e. *grain*:— beaten corn.

1644. גָּרַשׁ **gârash**, *gaw-rash'*; a prim. root; to *drive* out from a possession; espec. to *expatriate* or *divorce*:— cast up (out), divorced (woman), drive away (forth, out), expel, × surely put away, trouble, thrust out.

1645. גֶּרֶשׁ **geresh**, *gheh'-resh*; from 1644; *produce* (as if *expelled*):— put forth.

1646. גְּרֻשָׁה **gᵉrushâh**, *gher-oo-shaw'*; fem. pass. part. of 1644; (abstr.) *dispossession*:— exaction.

1647. גֵּרְשֹׁם **Gêrᵉshôm**, *gay-resh-ome'*; for 1648; *Gereshom*, the name of four Isr.:— Gershom.

1648. גֵּרְשׁוֹן **Gêrᵉshôwn**, *gay-resh-one'*; or גֵּרְשׁוֹם **Gêrᵉshôwm**, *gay-resh-ome'*; from 1644; a *refugee; Gereshon* or *Gereshom*, an Isr.:— Gershon, Gershom.

1649. גֵּרְשֻׁנִּי **Gêrᵉshunniy**, *gay-resh-oon-nee'*; patron. from 1648; a *Gereshonite* or desc. of Gereshon:— Gershonite, sons of Gershon.

1650. גְּשׁוּר **Gᵉshûwr**, *ghesh-oor'*; from an unused root (mean. to *join*); *bridge; Geshur*, a district of Syria:— Geshur, Geshurite.

1651. גְּשׁוּרִי **Gᵉshûwriy**, *ghe-shoo-ree'*; patrial from 1650; a *Geshurite* (also collect.) or inhab. of Geshur:— Geshuri, Geshurites.

1652. גָּשַׁם **gâsham**, *gaw-sham'*; a prim. root; to *shower* violently:— (cause to) rain.

1653. גֶּשֶׁם **geshem**, *gheh'-shem*; from 1652; a *shower*:— rain, shower.

1654. גֶּשֶׁם **Geshem**, *gheh'-shem*; or (prol.) גַּשְׁמוּ **Gashmûw**, *gash-moo'*; the same as 1653; *Geshem* or *Gashmu*, an Arabian:— Geshem, Gashmu.

1655. גֶּשֶׁם **geshem** (Chald.), *gheh'-shem*; appar. the same as 1653; used in a peculiar sense, the *body* (for the [fig.] idea of a *hard* rain):— body.

1656. גֹּשֶׁם **gôshem**, *go'-shem*; from 1652; equiv. to 1653:— rained upon.

גַּשְׁמוּ **Gashmûw**. See 1654.

1657. גֹּשֶׁן **Gôshen**, *go'-shen*; prob. of Eg.

or.; *Goshen*, the residence of the Isr. in Egypt; also a place in Pal.:— Goshen.

1658. גִּשְׁפָּא **Gishpâ'**, *ghish-paw'*; of uncert. der.; *Gispa*, an Isr.:— Gispa.

1659. גָּשַׁשׁ **gâshash**, *gaw-shash'*; a prim. root; appar. to *feel* about:— grope.

1660. גַּת **gath**, *gath*; prob. from 5059 (in the sense of *treading* out grapes); a wine-*press* (or vat for holding the grapes in pressing them):— (wine-) press (fat).

1661. גַּת **Gath**, *gath*; the same as 1660; *Gath*, a Philistine city:— Gath.

1662. גַּת־הַחֵפֶר **Gath-ha-Chêpher**, *gath-hah-khay'-fer*; or (abridged) גִּתָּה־חֵפֶר **Gittâh-Chêpher**, *ghit-taw-khay'-fer*; from 1660 and 2658 with the art. ins.; *wine-press of* (the) *well; Gath-Chepher*, a place in Pal.:— Gath-kephr, Gittah-kephr.

1663. גִּתִּי **Gittîy**, *ghit-tee'*; patrial from 1661; a *Gittite* or inhab. of Gath:— Gittite.

1664. גִּתַּיִם **Gittayim**, *ghit-tah'-yim*; dual of 1660; *double wine-press; Gittajim*, a place in Pal.:— Gittaim.

1665. גִּתִּית **Gittîyth**, *ghit-teeth'*; fem. of 1663; a *Gittite* harp:— Gittith.

1666. גֶּתֶר **Gether**, *gheh'-ther*; of uncert. der.; *Gether*, a son of Aram, and the region settled by him:— Gether.

1667. גַּת־רִמּוֹן **Gath-Rimmôwn**, *gath-rim-mone'*; from 1660 and 7416; *wine-press of* (the) *pomegranate; Gath-Rimmon*, a place in Pal.:— Gath-rimmon.

ד

1668. דָּא **dâ'** (Chald.), *daw*; corresp. to 2088; *this*:— one ... another, this.

1669. דָּאַב **dâ'ab**, *daw-ab'*; a prim. root; to *pine*:— mourn, sorrow (-ful).

1670. דְּאָבָה **dᵉ'âbâh**, *dĕh-aw-baw'*; from 1669; prop. *pining*; by anal. *fear*:— sorrow.

1671. דְּאָבוֹן **dᵉ'âbôwn**, *dĕh-aw-bone'*; from 1669; *pining*:— sorrow.

1672. דָּאַג **dâ'ag**, *daw-ag'*; a prim. root; *be anxious*:— be afraid (careful, sorry), sorrow, take thought.

1673. דֹּאֵג **Dô'êg**, *do-ayg'*; or (fully) דּוֹאֵג **Dôw'êg**, *do-ayg'*; act. part. of 1672; *anxious; Doëg*, an Edomite:— Doeg.

1674. דְּאָגָה **dᵉ'âgâh**, *dĕh-aw-gaw'*; from 1672; *anxiety*:— care (-fulness), fear, heaviness, sorrow.

1675. דָּאָה **dâ'âh**, *daw-aw'*; a prim. root; to *dart*, i.e. *fly* rapidly:— fly.

1676. דָּאָה **dâ'âh**, *daw-aw'*; from 1675; the *kite* (from its rapid *flight*):— vulture. See 7201.

1677. דֹּב **dôb**, *dobe*; or (fully) דּוֹב **dôwb**, *dobe*; from 1680; the *bear* (as slow):— bear.

1678. דֹּב **dôb** (Chald.), *dobe*; corresp. to 1677:— bear.

1679. דֹּבֶא **dôbe'**, *do'-beh*; from an unused root (comp. 1680) (prob. mean. to *be sluggish*, i.e. *restful*); *quiet*:— strength.

1680. דָּבַב **dâbab**, *daw-bab´*; a prim. root (comp. 1679); to *move* slowly, i.e. *glide*:— cause to speak.

1681. דִּבָּה **dibbâh**, *dib-baw´*; from 1680 (in the sense of *furtive* motion); *slander*:— defaming, evil report, infamy, slander.

1682. דְּבוֹרָה **dᵉbôwrâh**, *deb-o-raw´*; or (short.)

דְּבֹרָה **dᵉbôrâh**, *deb-o-raw´*; from 1696 (in the sense of *orderly* motion); the *bee* (from its *systematic* instincts):— bee.

1683. דְּבוֹרָה **Dᵉbôwrâh**, *deb-o-raw´*; or (short.)

דְּבֹרָה **Dᵉbôrâh**, *deb-o-raw´*; the same as 1682; *Deborah*, the name of two Hebrewesses:— Deborah.

1684. דְּבַח **dᵉbach** (Chald.), *deb-akh´*; corresp. to 2076; to *sacrifice* (an animal):— offer [sacrifice].

1685. דְּבַח **dᵉbach** (Chald.), *deb-akh´*; from 1684; a *sacrifice*:— sacrifice.

1686. דִּבְיוֹן **dibyôwn**, *dib-yone´*; in the marg. for the textual reading

חֲרֵיוֹן° **cheryôwn**, *kher-yone´*; both (in the plur. only and) of uncert. der.; prob. some cheap vegetable, perh. a bulbous root:— dove's dung.

1687. דְּבִיר **dᵉbîyr**, *deb-eer´*; or (short.)

דְּבִר **dᵉbir**, *deb-eer´*; from 1696 (appar. in the sense of *oracle*); the *shrine* or innermost part of the sanctuary:— oracle.

1688. דְּבִיר **Dᵉbîyr**, *deb-eer´*; or (short.)

דְּבִר **Dᵉbir** (Josh. 13:26 [but see 3810]), *deb-eer´*; the same as 1687; *Debir*, the name of an Amoritish king and of two places in Pal.:— Debir.

1689. דִּבְלָה **Diblâh**, *dib-law´*; prob. an orth. err. for 7247; *Diblah*, a place in Syria:— Diblath.

1690. דְּבֵלָה **dᵉbêlâh**, *deb-ay-law´*; from an unused root (akin to 2082) prob. mean. to *press* together; a *cake* of pressed figs:— cake (lump) of figs.

1691. דִּבְלַיִם **Diblayim**, *dib-lah´-yim*; dual from the masc. of 1690; *two cakes*; *Diblajim*, a symb. name:— Diblaim.

דִּבְלָתָיִם **Diblâthayim**. See 1015.

1692. דָּבַק **dâbaq**, *daw-bak´*; a prim. root; prop. to *impinge*, i.e. *cling* or *adhere*; fig. to *catch* by pursuit:— abide fast, cleave (fast together), follow close (hard after), be joined (together), keep (fast), overtake, pursue hard, stick, take.

1693. דְּבַק **dᵉbaq** (Chald.), *deb-ak´*; corresp. to 1692; to *stick* to:— cleave.

1694. דֶּבֶק **debeq**, *deh´-bek*; from 1692; a *joint*; by impl. *solder*:— joint, solder.

1695. דָּבֵק **dâbêq**, *daw-bake´*; from 1692; *adhering*:— cleave, joining, stick closer.

1696. דָּבַר **dâbar**, *daw-bar´*; a prim. root; perh. prop. to *arrange*; but used fig. (of words), to *speak*; rarely (in a destructive sense) to *subdue*:— answer, appoint, bid, command, commune, declare, destroy, give, name, promise, pronounce, rehearse, say, speak, be spokesman, subdue, talk,

teach, tell, think, use [entreaties], utter, × well, × work.

1697. דָּבָר **dâbâr**, *daw-baw´*; from 1696; a *word*; by impl. a *matter* (as *spoken of*) or *thing*; adv. a *cause*:— act, advice, affair, answer, × any such (thing), + because of, book, business, care, case, cause, certain rate, + chronicles, commandment, × commune (-ication), + concern [-ing], + confer, counsel, + dearth, decree, deed, × disease, due, duty, effect, + eloquent, errand, [evil favoured-] ness, + glory, + harm, hurt, + iniquity, + judgment, language, + lying, manner, matter, message, [no] thing, oracle, × ought, × parts, + pertaining, + please, portion, + power, promise, provision, purpose, question, rate, reason, report, request, × (as hast) said, sake, saying, sentence, + sign, + so, some [uncleanness], somewhat to say, + song, speech, × spoken, talk, task, + that, × there done, thing (concerning), thought, + thus, tidings, what [-soever], + wherewith, which, word, work.

1698. דֶּבֶר **deber**, *deh´-ber*; from 1696 (in the sense of *destroying*); a *pestilence*:— murrain, pestilence, plague.

1699. דֹּבֶר **dôber**, *do´-ber*; from 1696 (in its original sense); a *pasture* (from its *arrangement* of the flock):— fold, manner.

דְּבִר **dᵉbir** or

דְּבִר **Dᵉbir**. See 1687, 1688.

1699´. דִּבֵּר **dibbêr**, *dib-bare´*; for 1697:— word.

1700. דִּבְרָה **dibrâh**, *dib-raw´*; fem. of 1697; a *reason*, *suit* or *style*:— cause, end, estate, order, regard.

1701. דִּבְרָה **dibrâh** (Chald.), *dib-raw´*; corresp. to 1700:— intent, sake.

דִּבְרָה **dᵉbôrâh** or

דִּבְרָה **Dᵉbôrâh**. See 1682, 1683.

1702. דֹּבְרָה **dôbᵉrâh**, *do-ber-aw´*; fem. act. part. of 1696 in the sense of *driving* [comp. 1699]; a *raft*:— float.

1703. דַּבָּרָה **dabbârâh**, *dab-baw-raw´*; intens. from 1696; a *word*:— word.

1704. דִּבְרִי **Dibrîy**, *dib-ree´*; from 1697; *wordy*; *Dibri*, an Isr.:— Dibri.

1705. דָּבְרַת **Dâbᵉrath**, *daw-ber-ath´*; from 1697 (perh. in the sense of 1699); *Daberath*, a place in Pal.:— Dabareh, Daberath.

1706. דְּבַשׁ **dᵉbash**, *deb-ash´*; from an unused root mean. to *be gummy*; *honey* (from its *stickiness*); by anal. *syrup*:— honey [-comb].

1707. דַּבֶּשֶׁת **dabbesheth**, *dab-beh´-sheth*; intens. from the same as 1706; a *sticky mass*, i.e. the *hump* of a camel:— hunch [of a camel].

1708. דַּבֶּשֶׁת **Dabbesheth**, *dab-beh´-sheth*; the same as 1707; *Dabbesheth*, a place in Pal.:— Dabbesheth.

1709. דָּג **dâg**, *dawg*; or (fully)

דָּאג° **dâ'g** (Neh. 13:16), *dawg*; from 1711; a *fish* (as *prolific*); or perh. rather from 1672 (as *timid*); but still better from 1672 (in the sense of *squirming*, i.e. moving by the vibratory

action of the tail); a *fish* (often used collect.):— fish.

1710. דָּגָה **dâgâh**, *daw-gaw´*; fem. of 1709, and mean. the same:— fish.

1711. דָּגָה **dâgâh**, *daw-gaw´*; a prim. root; to *move rapidly*; used only as a denom. from 1709; to *spawn*, i.e. *become numerous*:— grow.

1712. דָּגוֹן **Dâgôwn**, *daw-gohn´*; from 1709; the *fish-god*; *Dagon*, a Philistine deity:— Dagon.

1713. דָּגַל **dâgal**, *daw-gal´*; a prim. root; to *flaunt*, i.e. *raise a flag*; fig. to *be conspicuous*:— (set up, with) banners, chiefest.

1714. דֶּגֶל **degel**, *deh´-gel*; from 1713; a *flag*:— banner, standard.

1715. דָּגָן **dâgân**, *daw-gawn´*; from 1711; prop. *increase*, i.e. *grain*:— corn ([floor]), wheat.

1716. דָּגַר **dâgar**, *daw-gar´*; a prim. root, to *brood* over eggs or young:— gather, sit.

1717. דַּד **dad**, *dad*; appar. from the same as 1730; the *breast* (as the seat of *love*, or from its shape):— breast, teat.

1718. דָּדָה **dâdâh**, *daw-daw´*; a doubtful root; to *walk gently*:— go (softly, with).

1719. דְּדָן **Dᵉdân**, *ded-awn´*; or (prol.)

דְּדָנֶה **Dᵉdâneh** (Ezek. 25:13), *deh-daw´-neh*; of uncert. der.; *Dedan*, the name of two Cushites and of their territory:— Dedan.

1720. דְּדָנִים **Dᵉdânîym**, *ded-aw-neem´*; plur. of 1719 (as patrial); *Dedanites*, the desc. or inhab. of Dedan:— Dedanim.

1721. דֹּדָנִים **Dôdânîym**, *do-daw-neem´*; or (by orth. err.)

רֹדָנִים **Rôdânîym** (1 Chron. 1:7), *ro-daw-neem´*; a plur. of uncert. der.; *Dodanites*, or desc. of a son of Javan:— Dodanim.

1722. דְּהַב **dᵉhab** (Chald.), *deh-hab´*; corresp. to 2091; *gold*:— gold (-en).

1723. דַּהֲוָא **Dahăvâ'** (Chald.), *dah-hav-aw´*; of uncert. der.; *Dahava*, a people colonized in Samaria:— Dehavites.

1724. דָּהַם **dâham**, *daw-ham´*; a prim. root (comp. 1740); to *be dumb*, i.e. (fig.) *dumb-founded*:— be astonished.

1725. דָּהַר **dâhar**, *daw-har´*; a prim. root; to *curvet* or move irregularly:— pause.

1726. דַּהֲהַר **dahăhar**, *dah-hah-har´*; by redupl. from 1725; a *gallop*:— pransing.

דּוֹאֵג **Dôw'êg**. See 1673.

1727. דּוּב **dûwb**, *doob*; a prim. root; to *mope*, i.e. (fig.) *pine*:— sorrow.

דּוֹב **dôwb**. See 1677.

1728. דַּוָּג **davvâg**, *dav-vawg´*; an orth. var. of 1709 as a denom. [1711]; a *fisherman*:— fisher.

1729. דּוּגָה **dûwgâh**, *doo-gaw´*; fem. from the same as 1728; prop. *fishery*, i.e. a *hook* for fishing:— fish [hook].

1730. דּוֹד **dôwd**, *dode*; or (short.)

דֹּד **dôd**, *dode*; from an unused root mean. prop. to *boil*, i.e. (fig.) to *love*; by impl. a *love-token, lover,* *friend*; spec. an *uncle*:— (well-) beloved, father's brother, love, uncle.

1731. דּוּד **dûwd**, *dood*; from the same as 1730; a *pot* (for *boiling*); also (by resemblance of shape) a *basket*:— basket, caldron, kettle, (seething) pot.

1732. דָּוִד **Dâvîd**, *daw-veed´*; rarely (fully)

דָּוִיד **Dâvîyd**, *daw-veed´*; from the same as 1730; *loving; David*, the youngest son of Jesse:— David.

1733. דּוֹדָה **dôwdâh**, *do-daw´*; fem. of 1730; an *aunt*:— aunt, father's sister, uncle's wife.

1734. דּוֹדוֹ **Dôwdôw**, *do-do´*; from 1730; *loving; Dodo*, the name of three Isr.:— Dodo.

1735. דּוֹדָוָהוּ **Dôwdâvâhûw**, *do-daw-vaw´-hoo*; from 1730 and 3050; *love of Jah; Dodavah*, an Isr.:— Dodavah.

1736. דּוּדַי **dûwday**, *doo-dah´-ee*; from 1731; a *boiler* or *basket*; also the *mandrake* (as *aphrodisiac*):— basket, mandrake.

1737. דּוֹדַי **Dôwday**, *do-dah´-ee*; formed like 1736; *amatory; Dodai*, an Isr.:— Dodai.

1738. דָּוָה **dâvâh**, *daw-vaw´*; a prim. root; to *be sick* (as if in menstruation):— infirmity.

1739. דָּוֶה **dâveh**, *daw-veh´*; from 1738; *sick* (espec. in menstruation):— faint, menstruous cloth, she that is sick, having sickness.

1740. דּוּחַ **dûwach**, *doo´-akh*; a prim. root; to *thrust* away; fig. to *cleanse*:— cast out, purge, wash.

1741. דְּוַי **dᵉvay**, *dev-ah´-ee*; from 1739; *sickness*; fig. *loathing*:— languishing, sorrowful.

1742. דַּוָּי **davvây**, *dav-voy´*; from 1739; *sick*; fig. *troubled*:— faint.

דָּוִיד **Dâvîyd**. See 1732.

1743. דּוּךְ **dûwk**, *dook*; a prim. root; to *bruise* in a mortar:— beat.

1744. דּוּכִיפַת **dûwkîyphath**, *doo-kee-fath´*; of uncert. der.; the *hoopoe* or else the *grouse*:— lapwing.

1745. דּוּמָה **dûwmâh**, *doo-maw´*; from an unused root mean. to be *dumb* (comp. 1820); *silence*; fig. *death*:— silence.

1746. דּוּמָה **Dûwmâh**, *doo-maw´*; the same as 1745; *Dumah*, a tribe and region of Arabia:— Dumah.

1747. דּוּמִיָּה **dûwmîyâh**, *doo-me-yaw´*; from 1820; *stillness*; adv. *silently*; abstr. *quiet, trust*:— silence, silent, waiteth.

1748. דּוּמָם **dûwmâm**, *doo-mawm´*; from 1826; *still*; adv. *silently*:— dumb, silent, quietly wait.

דּוּמֶשֶׂק° **Dûwmesheq**. See 1833.

1749. דּוֹנַג **dôwnag**, *do-nag´*; of uncert. der.; *wax*:— wax.

1750. דּוּץ **dûwts**, *doots*; a prim. root; to *leap*:— be turned.

1751. דּוּק **dûwq** (Chald.), *dook*; corresp. to 1854; to *crumble*:— be broken to pieces.

1752. דּוּר **dûwr**, *dure*; a prim. root;

prop. to *gyrate* (or move in a circle), i.e. to *remain*:— dwell.

1753. דּוּר **dûwr** (Chald.), *dure*; corresp. to 1752; to *reside*:— dwell.

1754. דּוּר **dûwr**, *dure*; from 1752; a *circle, ball* or *pile*:— ball, turn, round about.

1755. דּוֹר **dôwr**, *dore*; or (short.)

דֹּר **dôr**, *dore*; from 1752; prop. a *revolution* of time, i.e. an *age* or generation; also a *dwelling*:— age, × evermore, generation, [n-]lever, posterity.

1756. דּוֹר **Dôwr**, *dore* or (by perm.)

דֹּאר **Dô'r** (Josh. 17:11; 1 Kings 4:11), *dore*; from 1755; *dwelling; Dor*, a place in Pal.:— Dor.

1757. דּוּרָא **Dûwrâ'** (Chald.), *doo-raw´*; prob. from 1753; *circle* or *dwelling; Dura*, a place in Bab.:— Dura.

1758. דּוּשׁ **dûwsh**, *doosh*; or

דּוֹשׁ **dôwsh**, *dōsh*; or

דִּישׁ **dîysh**, *deesh*; a prim. root; to *trample* or *thresh*:— break, tear, thresh, tread out (down), at grass [Jer. 50:11, *by mistake for* 1877].

1759. דּוּשׁ **dûwsh** (Chald.), *doosh*; corresp. to 1758; to *trample*:— tread down.

1760. דָּחָה **dâchâh**, *daw-khaw´*; or

דָּחַח **dâchach** (Jer. 23:12), *daw-khakh´*; a prim. root; to *push* down:— chase, drive away (on), overthrow, outcast, × sore, thrust, totter.

1761. דַּחֲוָה **dachăvâh** (Chald.), *dakh-av-aw´*; from the equiv. of 1760; prob. a musical *instrument* (as being *struck*):— instrument of music.

1762. דְּחִי **dᵉchîy**, *deh-khee´*; from 1760; a *push*, i.e. (by impl.) a *fall*:— falling.

1763. דְּחַל **dᵉchal** (Chald.), *deh-khal´*; corresp. to 2119; to *slink*, i.e. (by impl.) to *fear*, or (caus.) be *formidable*:— make afraid, dreadful, fear, terrible.

1764. דֹּחַן **dôchan**, *do´-khan*; of uncert. der.; *millet*:— millet.

1765. דָּחַף **dâchaph**, *daw-khaf´*; a prim. root; to *urge*, i.e. *hasten*:— (be) haste(-ned), pressed on.

1766. דָּחַק **dâchaq**, *daw-khak´*; a prim. root; to *press*, i.e. *oppress*:— thrust, vex.

1767. דַּי **day**, *dahee*; of uncert. der.; *enough* (as noun or adv.), used chiefly with prep. in phrases:— able, according to, after (ability), among, as (oft as), (more than) enough, from, in, since, (much as is) sufficient (-ly), too much, very, when.

1768. דִּי **dîy** (Chald.), *dee*; appar. for 1668; *that*, used as rel., conjunc., and espec. (with prep.) in adv. phrases; also as prep. of:— × as, but, for (-asmuch +), + now, of, seeing, than, that, therefore, until, + what (-soever), when, which, whom, whose.

1769. דִּיבוֹן **Dîybôwn**, *dee-bome´*; or (short.)

דִּיבֹן **Dîybôn**, *dee-bone´*; from 1727; *pining; Dibon*, the name of three places in Pal.:— Dibon. [Also, *with* 1410 *added*, Dibon-gad.]

1770. דִּיג **dîyg**, *deeg*; denom. from 1709; to *fish*:— fish.

1771. דַּיָּג **dayâg**, *dah-yawg´*; from 1770; a *fisherman*:— fisher.

1772. דַּיָּה **dayâh**, *dah-yaw´*; intens. from 1675; a *falcon* (from its *rapid* flight):— vulture.

1773. דְּיוֹ **dᵉyôw**, *deh-yo´*; of uncert. der.; *ink*:— ink.

1774. דִּי זָהָב **Dîy zâhâb**, *dee zaw-hawb´*; as if from 1768 and 2091; *of gold; Dizahab*, a place in the Desert:— Dizahab.

1775. דִּימוֹן **Dîymôwn**, *dee-mone´*; perh. for 1769; *Dimon*, a place in Pal.:— Dimon.

1776. דִּימוֹנָה **Dîymôwnâh**, *dee-mo-naw´*; fem. of 1775; *Dimonah*, a place in Pal.:— Dimonah.

1777. דִּין **dîyn**, *deen*; or (Gen. 6:3)

דּוּן **dûwn**, *doon*; a prim. root [comp. 113]; to *rule*; by impl. to *judge* (as umpire); also to *strive* (as at law):— contend, execute (judgment), judge, minister judgment, plead (the cause), at strife, strive.

1778. דִּין **dîyn** (Chald.), *deen*; corresp. to 1777; to *judge*:— judge.

1779. דִּין **dîyn**, *deen*; or (Job 19:29)

דּוּן **dûwn**, *doon*; from 1777; *judgement* (the suit, justice, sentence or tribunal); by impl. also *strife*:— cause, judgement, plea, strife.

1780. דִּין **dîyn** (Chald.), *deen*; corresp. to 1779:— judgement.

1781. דַּיָּן **dayân**, *dah-yawn´*; from 1777; a *judge* or *advocate*:— judge.

1782. דַּיָּן **dayân** (Chald.), *dah-yawn´*; corresp. to 1781:— judge.

1783. דִּינָה **Dîynâh**, *dee-naw´*; fem. of 1779; *justice; Dinah*, the daughter of Jacob:— Dinah.

1784. דִּינַי **Dîynay** (Chald.), *dee-nah´-ee*; patrial from an uncert. prim.; a *Dinaite* or inhab. of some unknown Ass. province:— Dinaite.

דִּימְפַת **Dîyphath**. See 7384.

1785. דָּיֵק **dâyêq**, *daw-yake´*; from a root corresp. to 1751; a *battering-tower*:— fort.

1786. דַּיִשׁ **dayîsh**, *dah-yish´*; from 1758; *threshing*-time:— threshing.

1787. דִּישׁוֹן **Dîyshôwn**,

דִּישֹׁן **Dîyshôn**, or

דִּישֹׁן **Dishôn**, or

דִּשֹׁן **Dishôn**, *dee-shone´*; the same as 1788; *Dishon*, the name of two Edomites:— Dishon.

1788. דִּישֹׁן **dîyshôn**, *dee-shone´*; from 1758; the *leaper*, i.e. an *antelope*:— pygarg.

1789. דִּישָׁן **Dîyshân**, *dee-shawn´*; another form of 1787; *Dishan*, an Edomite:— Dishan, Dishon.

1790. דַּךְ **dak**, *dak*; from an unused root (comp. 1794); *crushed*, i.e. (fig.) *injured*:— afflicted, oppressed.

1791. דֵּךְ **dêk** (Chald.), *dake*; or

דָּךְ **dâk** (Chald.), *dawk*; prol. from 1668; *this*:— the same, this.

1792. דָּכָא **dâkâ'**, *daw-kaw´*; a prim. root (comp. 1794); to *crumble*; tran. to *bruise* (lit. or fig.):— beat to pieces, break (in pieces), bruise, contrite, crush, destroy, humble, oppress, smite.

1793. דִּכָּא **dakkâ'**, *dak-kaw'*; from 1792; *crushed* (lit. *powder*, or fig. *contrite*):— contrite, destruction.

1794. דָּכָה **dâkâh**, *daw-kaw'*; a prim. root (comp. 1790, 1792); to *collapse* (phys. or ment.):— break (sore), contrite, crouch.

1795. דַּכָּה **dakkâh**, *dak-kaw'*; from 1794 like 1793; *mutilated:*— + wounded.

1796. דְּכִי **dŏkiy**, *dok-ee'*; from 1794; a *dashing* of surf:— wave.

1797. דִּכֵּן **dikkên** (Chald.), *dik-kane'*; prol. from 1791; *this:*— same, that, this.

1798. דְּכַר **dᵉkar** (Chald.), *dek-ar'*; corresp. to 2145; prop. a *male*, i.e. of sheep:— ram.

1799. דִּכְרוֹן **dikrôwn** (Chald.), *dik-rone'*; or

דִּכְרֹן **dokrân**, *dok-rawn'* (Chald.); corresp. to 2146; a *register:*— record.

1800. דַּל **dal**, *dal*; from 1809; prop. *dangling*, i.e. (by impl.) *weak* or *thin:*— lean, needy, poor (man), weaker.

1801. דָּלַג **dâlag**, *daw-lag'*; a prim. root; to *spring:*— leap.

1802. דָּלָה **dâlâh**, *daw-law'*; a prim. root (comp. 1809); prop. to *dangle*, i.e. to *let down* a bucket (for *drawing* out water); fig. to *deliver:*— draw (out), × enough, lift up.

1803. דַּלָּה **dallâh**, *dal-law'*; from 1802; prop. something *dangling*, i.e. a loose *thread* or *hair*; fig. *indigent:*— hair, pining sickness, poor (-est sort).

1804. דָּלַח **dâlach**, *daw-lakh'*; a prim. root; to *roil* water:— trouble.

1805. דְּלִי **dᵉliy**, *del-ee'*; or

דֳּלִי **dŏliy**, *dol-ee'*; from 1802; a *pail* or *jar* (for *drawing* water):— bucket.

1806. דְּלָיָה **Dᵉlâyâh**, *del-aw-yaw'*; or (prol.)

דְּלָיָהוּ **Dᵉlâyâhûw**, *del-aw-yaw'-hoo*; from 1802 and 3050; *Jah has delivered*; *Delajah*, the name of five Isr.:— Dalaiah, Delaiah.

1807. דְּלִילָה **Dᵉliylâh**, *del-ee-law'*; from 1809; *languishing*; *Delilah*, a Philistine woman:— Delilah.

1808. דָּלִיָּה **dâliyâh**, *daw-lee-yaw'*; from 1802; something *dangling*, i.e. a *bough:*— branch.

1809. דָּלַל **dâlal**, *daw-lal'*; a prim. root (comp. 1802); to *slacken* or *be feeble*; fig. to *be oppressed:*— bring low, dry up, be emptied, be not equal, fail, be impoverished, be made thin.

1810. דִּלְעָן **Dil'ân**, *dil-awn'*; of uncert. der.; *Dilan*, a place in Pal.:— Dilean.

1811. דָּלַף **dâlaph**, *daw-laf'*; a prim. root; to *drip*; by impl. to *weep:*— drop through, melt, pour out.

1812. דֶּלֶף **deleph**, *deh'-lef*; from 1811; a *dripping:*— dropping.

1813. דַּלְפוֹן **Dalphôwn**, *dal-fone'*; from 1811; *dripping*; *Dalphon*, a son of Haman:— Dalphon.

1814. דָּלַק **dâlaq**, *daw-lak'*; a prim. root;

to *flame* (lit. or fig.):— burning, chase, inflame, kindle, persecute (-or), pursue hotly.

1815. דְּלַק **dᵉlaq** (Chald.), *del-ak'*; corresp. to 1814:— burn.

1816. דַּלֶּקֶת **dalleqeth**, *dal-lek'-keth*; from 1814; a *burning* fever:— inflammation.

1817. דֶּלֶת **deleth**, *deh'-leth*; from 1802; something *swinging*, i.e. the *valve* of a door:— door (two-leaved), gate, leaf, lid. [In Psa. 141:3, *dâl*, irreg.]

1818. דָּם **dâm**, *dawm*; from 1826 (comp. 119); *blood* (as that which when shed causes *death*) of man or an animal; by anal. the *juice* of the grape; fig. (espec. in the plur.) *bloodshed* (i.e. *drops* of blood):— blood (-y, -guiltiness, [-thirsty], + innocent.

1819. דָּמָה **dâmâh**, *daw-maw'*; a prim. root; to *compare*; by impl. to *resemble*, *liken*, *consider:*— compare, devise, (be) like (-n), mean, think, use similitudes.

1820. דָּמָה **dâmâh**, *daw-maw'*; a prim. root; to *be dumb* or *silent*; hence, to *fail* or *perish*; trans. to *destroy:*— cease, be cut down (off), destroy, be brought to silence, be undone, × utterly.

1821. דְּמָה **dᵉmâh** (Chald.), *dem-aw'*; corresp. to 1819; to *resemble:*— be like.

1822. דֻּמָּה **dummâh**, *doom-maw'*; from 1820; *desolation*; concr. *desolate:*— destroy.

1823. דְּמוּת **dᵉmûwth**, *dem-ooth'*; from 1819; *resemblance*; concr. *model*, *shape*; adv. *like:*— fashion, like (-ness, as), manner, similitude.

1824. דְּמִי **dᵉmiy**, *dem-ee'*; or

דֳּמִי **dŏmiy**, *dom-ee'*; from 1820; *quiet:*— cutting off, rest, silence.

1825. דִּמְיוֹן **dimyôwn**, *dim-yone'*; from 1819; *resemblance:*— × like.

1826. דָּמַם **dâmam**, *daw-mam'*; a prim. root [comp. 1724, 1820]; to *be dumb*; by impl. to *be astonished*, to *stop*; also to *perish:*— cease, be cut down (off), forbear, hold peace, quiet self, rest, be silent, keep (put to) silence, be (stand) still, tarry, wait.

1827. דְּמָמָה **dᵉmâmâh**, *dem-aw-maw'*; fem. from 1826; *quiet:*— calm, silence, still.

1828. דֹּמֶן **dômen**, *do'-men*; of uncert. der.; *manure:*— dung.

1829. דִּמְנָה **Dimnâh**, *dim-naw'*; fem. from the same as 1828; a *dung-heap*; *Dimnah*, a place in Pal.:— Dimnah.

1830. דָּמַע **dâma'**, *daw-mah'*; a prim. root; to *weep:*— × sore, weep.

1831. דֶּמַע **dema'**, *dah'-mah*; from 1830; a *tear*; fig. *juice:*— liquor.

1832. דִּמְעָה **dim'âh**, *dim-aw'*; fem. of 1831; *weeping:*— tears.

1833. דְּמֶשֶׁק **dᵉmesheq**, *dem-eh'-shek*; by orth. var. from 1834; *damask* (as a fabric of Damascus):— in Damascus.

1834. דַּמֶּשֶׂק **Dammeseq**, *dam-meh'-sek*; or

דּוּמֶשֶׂק° **Dûwmeseq**, *doo-meh'-sek*; or

דַּרְמֶשֶׂק **Darmeseq**, *dor-meh'-sek*;

of for. or.; *Damascus*, a city of Syria:— Damascus.

1835. דָּן **Dân**, *dawn*; from 1777; *judge*; *Dan*, one of the sons of Jacob; also the tribe descended from him, and its territory; likewise a place in Pal. colonized by them:— Dan.

1836. דֵּן **dên** (Chald.), *dane*; an orth. var. of 1791; *this:*— [afore-] time, + after this manner, here [-after], one ... another, such, there [-fore], these, this (matter), + thus, where [-fore], which.

דָנִיֵּאל **Dânî'êl**. See 1841.

1837. דַּנָּה **Dannâh**, *dan-naw'*; of uncert. der.; *Dannah*, a place in Pal.:— Dannah.

1838. דִּנְהָבָה **Dinhâbâh**, *din-haw-baw'*; of uncert. der.; *Dinhabah*, an Edomitish town:— Dinhaban.

1839. דָּנִי **Dâniy**, *daw-nee'*; patron. from 1835; a *Danite* (often collect.) or desc. (or inhab.) of Dan:— Danites, of Dan.

1840. דָּנִיֵּאל **Dânîyê'l**, *daw-nee-yale'*; in Ezek.

דָּנִאֵל **Dânî'êl**, *daw-nee-ale'*; from 1835 and 410; *judge of God*; *Daniel* or *Danijel*, the name of two Isr.:— Daniel.

1841. דָּנִיֵּאל **Dânîyê'l** (Chald.), *daw-nee-yale'*; corresp. to 1840; *Danijel*, the Heb. prophet:— Daniel.

1842. דָּן יַעַן **Dân Ya'an**, *dawn yah'-an*; from 1835 and (appar.) 3282; *judge of purpose*; *Dan-Jaan*, a place in Pal.:— Dan-jaan.

1843. דֵּעַ **dêa'**, *day'-ah*; from 3045; *knowledge:*— knowledge, opinion.

1844. דֵּעָה **dê'âh**, *day-aw'*; fem. of 1843; *knowledge:*— knowledge.

1845. דְּעוּאֵל **Dᵉ'ûw'êl**, *deh-oo-ale'*; from 3045 and 410; *known of God*; *Deüel*, an Isr.:— Deuel.

1846. דָּעַך **dâ'ak**, *daw-ak'*; a prim. root; to *be extinguished*; fig. to *expire* or *be dried up:*— be extinct, consumed, put out, quenched.

1847. דַּעַת **da'ath**, *dah'-ath*; from 3045; *knowledge:*— cunning, [ig-]norantly, know (-ledge), [un-] awares (wittingly).

1848. דֳּפִי **dŏphiy**, *dof-ee*; from an unused root (mean. to *push* over); a *stumbling-block:*— slanderest.

1849. דָּפַק **dâphaq**, *daw-fak'*; a prim. root; to *knock*; by anal. to *press* severely:— beat, knock, overdrive.

1850. דָּפְקָה **Dophqâh**, *dof-kaw'*; from 1849; a *knock*; *Dophkah*, a place in the Desert:— Dophkah.

1851. דַּק **daq**, *dak*; from 1854; *crushed*, i.e. (by impl.) *small* or *thin:*— dwarf, lean [-fleshed], very little thing, small, thin.

1852. דֹּק **dôq**, *doke*; from 1854; something *crumbling*, i.e. *fine* (as a *thin* cloth):— curtain.

1853. דִּקְלָה **Diqlâh**, *dik-law'*; of for. or.; *Diklah*, a region of Arabia:— Diklah.

1854. דָּקַק **dâqaq**, *daw-kak'*; a prim. root [comp. 1915]; to *crush* (or intr.) *crumble:*— beat in pieces (small), bruise, make dust, (into) × powder, (be, very) small, stamp (small).

1855. דְּקַק deqaq (Chald.), dek-ak´; corresp. to 1854; to crumble or (trans.) crush:— break to pieces.

1856. דָּקַר dâqar, daw-kar´; a prim. root; to stab; by anal. to starve; fig. to revile:— pierce, strike (thrust) through, wound.

1857. דֶּקֶר Deqer, deh´-ker; from 1856; a stab; Deker, an Isr.:— Dekar.

1858. דַּר dar, dar; appar. from the same as 1865; prop. a pearl (from its sheen as rapidly turned); by anal. pearl-stone, i.e. mother-of-pearl or alabaster:— × white.

1859. דָּר dâr (Chald.), dawr; corresp. to 1755; an age:— generation.

דּוֹר dôr. See 1755.

1860. דְּרָאוֹן derâ'ôwn, der-aw-one´; or

דֵּרָאוֹן derâ'ôwn, day-raw-one´; from an unused root (mean. to repulse); an obj. of aversion:— abhorring, contempt.

1861. דָּרְבוֹן dorbôwn, dor-bone´ [also dor-bawn´]; of uncert. der.; a goad:— goad.

1862. דַּרְדַּע Darda', dar-dah´; appar. from 1858 and 1843; pearl of knowledge; Darda, an Isr.:— Darda.

1863. דַּרְדַּר dardar, dar-dar´; of uncert. der.; a thorn:— thistle.

1864. דָּרוֹם dârôwm, daw-rome´; of uncert. der.; the south; poet. the south wind:— south.

1865. דְּרוֹר derôwr, der-ore´; from an unused root (mean. to move rapidly); freedom; hence, spontaneity of outflow, and so clear:— liberty, pure.

1866. דְּרוֹר derôwr, der-ore´; the same as 1865, applied to a bird; the swift, a kind of swallow:— swallow.

1867. דָּרְיָוֶשׁ Dâreyâvêsh, daw-reh-yaw-vaysh´; of Pers. or.; Darejavesh, a title (rather than name) of several Pers. kings:— Darius.

1868. דָּרְיָוֶשׁ Dâreyâvêsh (Chald.), daw-reh-yaw-vaysh´; corresp. to 1867:— Darius.

1869. דָּרַךְ dârak, daw-rak´; a prim. root; to tread; by impl. to walk; also to string a bow (by treading on it in bending):— archer, bend, come, draw, go (over), guide, lead (forth), thresh, tread (down), walk.

1870. דֶּרֶךְ derek, deh´-rek; from 1869; a road (as trodden); fig. a course of life or mode of action, often adv.:— along, away, because of, + by, conversation, custom, [east-] ward, journey, manner, passenger, through, toward, [high-] [path-] way [-side], whither [-soever].

1871. דַּרְכְּמוֹן darkemôwn, dar-kem-one´; of Pers. or.; a "drachma," or coin:— dram.

1872. דְּרַע dera' (Chald.), der-aw´; corresp. to 2220; an arm:— arm.

1873. דָּרַע Dâra', daw-rah´; prob. contr. from 1862; Dara, an Isr.:— Dara.

1874. דַּרְקוֹן Darqôwn, dar-kone´; of uncert. der.; Darkon, one of "Solomon's servants":— Darkon.

1875. דָּרַשׁ dârash, daw-rash´; a prim. root; prop. to tread or frequent; usually to follow (for pursuit or search); by impl. to seek or ask; spec. to worship:— ask, × at all, care for, × diligently, inquire, make inquisition, [necro-] mancer, question, require, search, seek [for, out], × surely.

1876. דָּשָׁא dâshâ', daw-shaw´; a prim. root; to sprout:— bring forth, spring.

1877. דֶּשֶׁא deshe', deh´-sheh; from 1876; a sprout; by anal. grass:— (tender) grass, green, (tender) herb.

1878. דָּשֵׁן dâshên, daw-shane´; a prim. root; to be fat; tran. to fatten (or regard as fat); spec. to anoint; fig. to satisfy; denom. (from 1880) to remove (fat) ashes (of sacrifices):— accept, anoint, take away the (receive) ashes (from), make (wax) fat.

1879. דָּשֵׁן dâshên, daw-shane´; from 1878; fat; fig. rich, fertile:— fat.

1880. דֶּשֶׁן deshen, deh´-shen; from 1878; the fat; abstr. fatness, i.e. (fig.) abundance; spec. the (fatty) ashes of sacrifices:— ashes, fatness.

1881. דָּת dâth, dawth; of uncert. (perh. for.) der.: a royal edict or statute:— commandment, commission, decree, law, manner.

1882. דָּת dâth (Chald.), dawth; corresp. to 1881:— decree, law.

1883. דֶּתֶא dethe' (Chald.), deh´-thay; corresp. to 1877:— tender grass.

1884. דְּתָבָר dethâbâr (Chald.), deth-aw-bawr´; of Pers. or.; mean. one skilled in law; a judge:— counsellor.

1885. דָּתָן Dâthân, daw-thawn´; of uncert. der.; Dathan, an Isr.:— Dathan.

1886. דֹּתָן Dôthân, do´-thawn; or (Chaldaizing dual)

דֹּתָיִן Dôthayin, do-thah´-yin; of uncert. der.; Dothan, a place in Pal.:— Dothan.

ה

1887. הֵא hê', hay; a prim. particle; lo!:— behold, lo.

1888. הֵא hê' (Chald.), hay; or

הָא hâ' (Chald.), haw; corresp. to 1887:— even, lo.

1889. הֶאָח he'âch, heh-awkh´; from 1887 and 253; aha!:— ah, aha, ha.

הָאֲרָרִי Hâ'rârîy. See 2043.

1890. הַבְהָב habhâb, hab-hawb´; by redupl. from 3051; gift (in sacrifice), i.e. holocaust:— offering.

1891. הָבַל hâbal, haw-bal´; a prim. root; to be vain in act, word, or expectation; spec. to lead astray:— be (become, make) vain.

1892. הֶבֶל hebel, heh´-bel; or (rarely in the abs.)

הֲבֵל hăbêl, hab-ale´; from 1891; emptiness or vanity; fig. something transitory and unsatisfactory; often used as an adv.:— × altogether, vain, vanity.

1893. הֶבֶל Hebel, heh´-bel; the same as 1892; Hebel, the son of Adam:— Abel.

1894. הֹבֶן hôben, ho´-ben; only in plur., from an unused root mean. to be hard; ebony:— ebony.

1895. הָבַר hâbar, haw-bar´; a prim. root of uncert. (perh. for.) der.; to be a horoscopist:— + (astro-)loger.

1896. הֵגֵא Hêgê', hay-gay´; or (by perm.)

הֵגַי Hêgay, hay-gah´-ee; prob. of Pers. or.; Hege or Hegai, a eunuch of Xerxes:— Hegai, Hege.

1897. הָגָה hâgâh, haw-gaw´; a prim. root [comp. 1901]; to murmur (in pleasure or anger); by impl. to ponder:— imagine, meditate, mourn, mutter, roar, × sore, speak, study, talk, utter.

1898. הָגָה hâgâh, haw-gaw´; a prim. root; to remove:— stay, take away.

1899. הֶגֶה hegeh, heh´-geh; from 1897; a muttering (in sighing, thought, or as thunder):— mourning, sound, tale.

1900. הָגוּת hâgûwth, haw-gooth´; from 1897; musing:— meditation.

1901. הָגִיג hâgîyg, haw-gheeg´; from an unused root akin to 1897; prop. a murmur, i.e. complaint:— meditation, musing.

1902. הִגָּיוֹן higgâyôwn, hig-gaw-yone´; intens. from 1897; a murmuring sound, i.e. a musical notation (prob. similar to the modern affettuoso to indicate solemnity of movement); by impl. a machination:— device, Higgaion, meditation, solemn sound.

1903. הָגִין hâgîyn, haw-gheen´; of uncert. der.; perh. suitable or turning:— directly.

1904. הָגָר Hâgâr, haw-gawr´; of uncert. (perhaps for.) der.; Hagar, the mother of Ishmael:— Hagar.

1905. הַגְרִי Hagrîy, hag-ree´; or (prol.)

הַגְרִיא Hagrîy', hag-ree´; perh. patron. from 1904; a Hagrite or member of a certain Arabian clan:— Hagarene, Hagarite, Haggeri.

1906. הֵד hêd, hade; for 1959; a shout:— sounding again.

1907. הַדָּבָר haddâbâr (Chald.), had-daw-bawr´; prob. of for. origin; a vizier:— counsellor.

1908. הֲדַד Hădad, had-ad´; prob. of for. or. [comp. 111]; Hadad, the name of an idol, and of several kings of Edom:— Hadad.

1909. הֲדַדְעֶזֶר Hădad'ezer, had-ad-eh´-zer; from 1908 and 5828; Hadad (is his) help; Hadadezer, a Syrian king:— Hadadezer. Comp. 1928.

1910. הֲדַדְרִמּוֹן Hădadrimmôwn, had-ad-rim-mone´; from 1908 and 7417; Hadad-Rimmon, a place in Pal.:— Hadad-rimmon.

1911. הָדָה hâdâh, haw-daw´; a prim. root [comp. 3034]; to stretch forth the hand:— put.

1912. הֹדוּ Hôdûw, ho´-doo; of for. or.; Hodu (i.e. Hindû-stan):— India.

1913. הֲדוֹרָם Hădôwrâm, had-o-rawm´; or

הֲדֹרָם Hădôrâm, had-o-rawm´; prob. of for. der.; Hadoram, a son of Joktan, and the tribe descended from him:— Hadoram.

1914. הִדַּי Hidday, hid-dah´-ee; of uncert. der.; Hiddai, an Isr.:— Hiddai.

1915. הָדַך **hâdak**, haw-dak´; a prim. root [comp. 1854]; to crush with the foot:— tread down.

1916. הֲדֹם **hădôm**, had-ome´; from an unused root mean. to stamp upon; a foot-stool:— [foot-] stool.

1917. הַדָּם **haddâm** (Chald.), had-dawm´; from a root corresp. to that of 1916; something stamped to pieces, i.e. a bit:— piece.

1918. הֲדַס **hădaç**, had-as´; of uncert. der.; the myrtle:— myrtle (tree).

1919. הֲדַסָּה **Hădaççâh**, had-as-saw´; fem. of 1918; Hadassah (or Esther):— Hadassah.

1920. הָדַף **hâdaph**, haw-daf´; a prim root; to push away or down:— cast away (out), drive, expel, thrust (away).

1921. הָדַר **hâdar**, haw-dar´; a prim. root; to swell up (lit. or fig., act. or pass.); by impl. to favor or honour, be high or proud:— countenance, crooked place, glorious, honour, put forth.

1922. הֲדַר **hădar** (Chald.), had-ar´; corresp. to 1921; to magnify (fig.):— glorify, honour.

1923. הֲדַר **hădar** (Chald.), had-ar´; from 1922; magnificence:— honour, majesty.

1924. הָדַר **Hâdar**, had-ar´; the same as 1926; Hadar, an Edomite:— Hadar.

1925. הֶדֶר **heder**, heh´-der; from 1921; honour; used (fig.) for the capital city (Jerusalem):— glory.

1926. הָדָר **hâdâr**, haw-dawr´; from 1921; magnificence, i.e. ornament or splendor:— beauty, comeliness, excellency, glorious, glory, goodly, honour, majesty.

1927. הֲדָרָה **hădârâh**, had-aw-raw´; fem. of 1926; decoration:— beauty, honour.

הֲדֹרָם **Hădôrâm**. See 1913.

1928. הֲדַרְעֶזֶר **Hădar'ezer**, had-ar-eh´-zer; from 1924 and 5828; Hadar (i.e. Hadad, 1908) is his help; Hadarezer (i.e. Hadadezer, 1909), a Syrian king:— Hadarezer.

1929. הָהּ **hâhh**, haw; a short. form of 162; ah! expressing grief:— woe worth.

1930. הוֹ **hôw**, ho; by perm. from 1929; oh!:— alas.

1931. הוּא **hûw'**, hoo; of which the fem. (beyond the Pentateuch) is

הִיא **hîy'**, he; a prim. word, the third pers. pron. sing., he (she or it); only expressed when emphat. or without a verb; also (intens.) self, or (espec. with the art.) the same; sometimes (as demonstr.) this or that; occasionally (instead of copula) as or are:— he, as for her, him (-self), it, the same, she (herself), such, that (… it), these, they, this, those, which (is), who.

1932. הוּא **hûw'** (Chald.), hoo; or (fem.)

הִיא **hîy'** (Chald.), he; corresp. to 1931:— × are, it, this.

1933. הָוָא **hâvâ'**, haw-vaw´; or

הָוָה **hâvâh**, haw-vaw´; a prim. root [comp. 183, 1961] supposed to mean prop. to breathe; to be (in the sense of existence):— be, × have.

1934. הֱוָא **hăvâ'** (Chald.), hav-aw´; or

הֲוָה **hăvâh** (Chald.), hav-aw´; corresp. to 1933; to exist; used in a great variety of applications (espec. in connection with other words):— be, become, + behold, + came (to pass), + cease, + cleave, + consider, + do, + give, + have, + judge, + keep, + labour, + mingle (self), + put, + see, + seek, + set, + slay, + take heed, tremble, + walk, + would.

1935. הוֹד **hôwd**, hode; from an unused root; grandeur (i.e. an imposing form and appearance):— beauty, comeliness, excellency, glorious, glory, goodly, honour, majesty.

1936. הוֹד **Hôwd**, hode; the same as 1935; Hod, an Isr.:— Hod.

1937. הוֹדְוָה **Hôwdᵉvâh**, ho-dev-aw´; a form of 1938; Hodevah (or Hodevjah), an Isr.:— Hodevah.

1938. הוֹדְיָה **Hôwdavyâh**, ho-dav-yaw´; from 1935 and 3050; majesty of Jah; Hodavjah, the name of three Isr.:— Hodaviah.

1939. הוֹדַוְיָהוּ **Howdayᵉvâhûw**, ho-dah-yeh-vaw´-hoo; a form of 1938; Hodajvah, an Isr.:— Hodaiah.

1940. הוֹדִיָּה **Hôwdîyâh**, ho-dee-yaw´; a form for the fem. of 3064; a Jewess:— Hodiah.

1941. הוֹדִיָּה **Hôwdîyâh**, ho-dee-yaw´; a form of 1938; Hodijah, the name of three Isr.:— Hodijah.

הֲוָה **hâvâh**. See 1933.

הֲוָה **hăvâh**. See 1934.

1942. הַוָּה **havvâh**, hav-vaw´; from 1933 (in the sense of eagerly coveting and rushing upon; by impl. of falling); desire; also ruin:— calamity, iniquity, mischief, mischievous (thing), naughtiness, naughty, noisome, perverse thing, substance, very wickedness.

1943. הֹוָה **hôvâh**, ho-vaw´; another form for 1942; ruin:— mischief.

1944. הוֹהָם **Hôwhâm**, ho-hawm´; of uncert. der.; Hoham, a Canaanitish king:— Hoham.

1945. הוֹי **hôwy**, hoh´-ee; a prol. form of 1930 [akin to 188]; oh!:— ah, alas, ho, O, woe.

1946. הוּך **hûwk** (Chald.), hook; corresp. to 1981; to go; caus. to bring:— bring again, come, go (up).

1947. הוֹלֵלָה **hôwlêlâh**, ho-lay-law´; fem. act. part. of 1984; folly:— madness.

1948. הוֹלֵלוּת **hôwlêlûwth**, ho-lay-looth´; from act. part. of 1984; folly:— madness.

1949. הוּם **hûwm**, hoom; a prim. root [comp. 2000]; to make an uproar, or agitate greatly:— destroy, move, make a noise, put, ring again.

1950. הוֹמָם **Hôwmâm**, ho-mawm´; from 2000; raging; Homam, an Edomitish chieftain:— Homam. Comp. 1967.

1951. הוּן **hûwn**, hoon; a prim. root; prop. to be naught, i.e. (fig.) to be (caus. act) light:— be ready.

1952. הוֹן **hôwn**, hone; from the same as 1951 in the sense of 202; wealth; by impl. enough:— enough, + for nought, riches, substance, wealth.

1953. הוֹשָׁמָע **Hôwshâmâ'**, ho-shaw-maw´; from 3068 and 8085; Jehovah has heard; Hoshama, an Isr.:— Hoshama.

1954. הוֹשֵׁעַ **Hôwshêa'**, ho-shay´-ah; from 3467; deliverer; Hosheä, the name of five Isr.:— Hosea, Hoshea, Oshea.

1955. הוֹשַׁעְיָה **Hôwshi'yâh**, ho-shee-yaw´; from 3467 and 3050; Jah has saved; Hoshajah, the name of two Isr.:— Hoshaiah.

1956. הוֹתִיר **Hôwthîyr**, ho-theer´; from 3498; he has caused to remain; Hothir, an Isr.:— Hothir.

1957. הָזָה **hâzâh**, haw-zaw´; a prim. root [comp. 2372]; to dream:— sleep.

1958. הִי **hîy**, he; for 5092; lamentation:— woe.

1959. הֵידָד **hêydâd**, hay-dawd´; from an unused root (mean. to shout); acclamation:— shout (-ing).

1960. הֻיְּדָה **huyᵉdâh**, hoo-yed-aw´; from the same as 1959; prop. an acclaim, i.e. a choir of singers:— thanksgiving.

1961. הָיָה **hâyâh**, haw-yaw´; a prim root [comp. 1933]; to exist, i.e. be or become, come to pass (always emphat., and not a mere copula or auxiliary):— beacon, × altogether, be (-come), accomplished, committed, like), break, cause, come (to pass), do, faint, fall, + follow, happen, × have, last, pertain, quit (one-) self, require, × use.

1962. הָיָה **hayâh**, hah-yaw´; another form for 1943; ruin:— calamity.

1963. הֵיך **hêyk**, hake; another form for 349; how?:— how.

1964. הֵיכָל **hêykâl**, hay-kawl´; prob. from 3201 (in the sense of capacity); a large public building, such as a palace or temple:— palace, temple.

1965. הֵיכַל **hêykal** (Chald.), hay-kal´; corresp. to 1964:— palace, temple.

1966. הֵילֵל **hêylêl**, hay-lale´; from 1984 (in the sense of brightness); the morning-star:— lucifer.

1967. הֵימָם **Hêymâm**, hay-mawm´; another form for 1950; Hemam, an Idumæan:— Hemam.

1968. הֵימָן **Hêymân**, hay-mawn´; prob. from 539; faithful; Heman, the name of at least two Isr.:— Heman.

1969. הִין **hîyn**, heen; prob. of Eg. or.; a hin or liquid measure:— hin.

1970. הָכַר **hâkar**, haw-kar´; a prim. root; appar. to injure:— make self strange.

1971. הַכָּרָה **hakkârâh**, hak-kaw-raw´; from 5234; respect, i.e. partiality:— shew.

הַל **hal**. See 1973.

1972. הָלָא **hâlâ'**, haw-law´; prob. denom. from 1973; to remove or be remote:— cast far off.

1973. הָלְאָה **hâlᵉâh**, haw-leh-aw´; from the prim. form of the art. [הַל hal]; to the distance, i.e. far away; also (of time) thus far:— back, beyond, (hence-) forward, hitherto, thenceforth, yonder.

1974. הִלּוּל **hillûwl,** *hil-lool´;* from 1984 (in the sense of *rejoicing*); a *celebration* of thanksgiving for harvest:— merry, praise.

1975. הַלָּז **hallâz,** *hal-lawz´;* from 1976; *this* or *that:*— side, that, this.

1976. הַלָּזֶה **hallâzeh,** *hal-law-zeh´;* from the art. [see 1973] and 2088; *this very:*— this.

1977. הַלָּזוּ **hallêzûw,** *hal-lay-zoo´;* another form of 1976; *that:*— this.

1978. הָלִיךְ **hâlîyk,** *haw-leek´;* from 1980; a *walk,* i.e. (by impl.) a *step:*— step.

1979. הֲלִיכָה **hălîykâh,** *hal-ee-kaw´;* fem. of 1978; a *walking;* by impl. a *procession* or *march,* a *caravan:*— company, going, walk, way.

1980. הָלַךְ **hâlak,** *haw-lak´;* akin to 3212; a prim. root; to *walk* (in a great variety of applications, lit. and fig.):— (all) along, apace, behave (self), come, (on) continually, be conversant, depart, + be eased, enter, exercise (self), + follow, forth, forward, get, go (about, abroad, along, away, forward, on, out, up and down), + greater, grow, be wont to haunt, lead, march, × more and more, move (self), needs, on, pass (away), be at the point, quite, run (along), + send, speedily, spread, still, surely, + tale-bearer, + travel (-ler), walk (abroad, on, to and fro, up and down, to places), wander, wax, [way-] faring man, × be weak, whirl.

1981. הֲלַךְ **hălak** (Chald.), *hal-ak´;* corresp. to 1980 [comp. 1946]; to *walk:*— walk.

1982. הֵלֶךְ **hêlek,** *hay´-lek;* from 1980; prop. a *journey,* i.e. (by impl.) a *wayfarer;* also a *flowing:*— × dropped, traveller.

1983. הֲלָךְ **hălâk** (Chald.), *hal-awk´;* from 1981; prop. a *journey,* i.e. (by impl.) *toll* on goods at a road:— custom.

1984. הָלַל **hâlal,** *haw-lal´;* a prim. root; to *be clear* (orig. of sound, but usually of color); to *shine;* hence, to *make a show,* to *boast;* and thus to *be* (clamorously) *foolish;* to *rave;* caus. to *celebrate;* also to *stultify:*— (make) boast (self), celebrate, commend, (deal, make), fool (-ish, -ly), glory, give [light], be (make, feign self) mad (against), give in marriage, [sing, be worthy of] praise, rage, renowned, shine.

1985. הִלֵּל **Hillêl,** *hil-layl´;* from 1984; *praising* (namely God); *Hillel,* an Isr.:— Hillel.

1986. הָלַם **hâlam,** *haw-lam´;* a prim. root; to *strike* down; by impl. to *hammer, stamp, conquer, disband:*— beat (down), break (down), overcome, smite (with the hammer).

1987. הֵלֶם **Hêlem,** *hay´-lem;* from 1986; *smiter; Helem,* the name of two Isr.:— Helem.

1988. הֲלֹם **hălôm,** *hal-ome´;* from the art. [see 1973]; *hither:*— here, hither (-[to]), thither.

1989. הַלְמוּת **halmûwth,** *hal-mooth´;* from 1986; a *hammer* (or *mallet*):— hammer.

1990. הָם **Hâm,** *hawm;* of uncert. der.; *Ham,* a region of Pal.:— Ham.

1991. הֵם **hêm,** *haym;* from 1993; *abundance,* i.e. *wealth:*— any of theirs.

1992. הֵם **hêm,** *haym;* or (prol.)

הֵמָּה **hêmmâh,** *haym´-maw;* masc. plur. from 1931; *they* (only used when emphat.):— it, like, × (how, so) many (soever, more as) they (be), (the) same, × so, × such, their, them, these, they, those, which, who, whom, withal, ye.

1993. הָמָה **hâmâh,** *haw-maw´;* a prim. root [comp. 1949]; to *make a loud sound* (like the English "hum"); by impl. to *be in great commotion* or *tumult,* to *rage, war, moan, clamor:*— clamorous, concourse, cry aloud, be disquieted, loud, mourn, be moved, make a noise, rage, roar, sound, be troubled, make in tumult, tumultuous, be in an uproar.

1994. הִמּוֹ **himmôw** (Chald.), *him-mo´;* or (prol.)

הִמּוֹן **himmôwn** (Chald.), *him-mone´;* corresp. to 1992; *they:*— × are, them, those.

1995. הָמוֹן **hâmôwn,** *haw-mone´;* or

הָמֹן **hâmôn** (Ezek. 5:7), *haw-mone´;* from 1993; a *noise, tumult, crowd;* also *disquietude, wealth:*— abundance, company, many, multitude, multiply, noise, riches, rumbling, sounding, store, tumult.

הַמֹּלֶכֶת **ham-môleketh.** See 4447.

1996. הֲמוֹן גּוֹג **Hămôwn Gôwg,** *ham-one´ gohg;* from 1995 and 1463; the *multitude of Gog;* the fanciful name of an emblematic place in Pal.:— Hamon-gog.

1997. הֲמוֹנָה **Hămôwnâh,** *ham-o-naw´;* fem. of 1995; *multitude; Hamonah,* the same as 1996:— Hamonah.

הֲמוּנֵךְ° **hămûwnêk.** See 2002.

1998. הֶמְיָה **hemyâh,** *hem-yaw´;* from 1993; *sound:*— noise.

1999. הֲמֻלָּה **hămullâh,** *ham-ool-law´;* or (too fully)

הֲמוּלָּה **hămûwllâh** (Jer. 11:16), *ham-ool-law´;* fem. pass. part. of an unused root mean. to *rush* (as rain with a windy roar); a *sound:*— speech, tumult.

הַמֶּלֶךְ **ham-melek.** See 4429.

2000. הָמַם **hâmam,** *haw-mam´;* a prim. root [comp. 1949, 1993]; prop. to *put in commotion;* by impl. to *disturb, drive, destroy:*— break, consume, crush, destroy, discomfit, trouble, vex.

הָמֹן **hâmôn.** See 1995.

2001. הָמָן **Hâmân,** *haw-mawn´;* of for. der.; *Haman,* a Pers. vizier:— Haman.

2002. הַמְנִיךְ **hamnîyk** (Chald.), *ham-neek´;* but the text is

הֲמוּנֵךְ° **hămûwnêk,** *ham-oo-nayk´;* of for. or.; a *necklace:*— chain.

2003. הָמָס **hâmâç,** *haw-mawce´;* from an unused root appar. mean. to *crackle;* a dry *twig* or *brushwood:*— melting.

2004. הֵן **hên,** *hane;* fem. plur. from 1931; *they* (only used when emphat.):— × in, such like, (with) them, thereby, therein, (more than) they, wherein, in which, whom, withal.

2005. הֵן **hên,** *hane;* a prim. particle; *lo!;* also (as expressing surprise) *if:*— behold, if, lo, though.

2006. הֵן **hên** (Chald.), *hane;* corresp. to 2005; *lo!* also *there* [-fore], [un-] *less, whether, but, if:*— (that) if, or, whether.

2007. הֵנָּה **hênnâh,** *hane´-naw;* prol. for 2004; *themselves* (often used emphat. for the copula, also in indirect relation):— × in, × such (and such things), their, (into) them, thence, therein, these, they (had), on this side, those, wherein.

2008. הֵנָּה **hênnâh,** *hane´-naw;* from 2004; *hither* or *thither* (but used both of place and time):— here, hither [-tol, now, on this (that) side, + since, this (that) way, thitherward, + thus far, to … fro, + yet.

2009. הִנֵּה **hinnêh,** *hin-nay´;* prol. for 2005; *lo!:*— behold, lo, see.

2010. הֲנָחָה **hănâchâh,** *han-aw-khaw´;* from 5117; *permission* of rest, i.e. *quiet:*— release.

2011. הִנֹּם **Hinnôm,** *hin-nome´;* prob. of for. or.; *Hinnom,* appar. a Jebusite:— Hinnom.

2012. הֵנַע **Hêna´,** *hay-nah´;* prob. of for. der.; *Hena,* a place appar. in Mesopotamia:— Hena.

2013. הָסָה **hâçâh,** *haw-saw´;* a prim. root; to *hush:*— hold peace (tongue), (keep) silence, be silent, still.

2014. הֲפֻגָה **hăphûgâh,** *haf-oo-gaw´;* from 6313; *relaxation:*— intermission.

2015. הָפַךְ **hâphak,** *haw-fak´;* a prim. root; to *turn* about or over; by impl. to *change, overturn, return, pervert:*— × become, change, come, be converted, give, make [a bed], overthrow (-turn), perverse, retire, tumble, turn (again, aside, back, to the contrary, every way).

2016. הֶפֶךְ **hephek,** *heh´-fek;* or

הֵפֶךְ **hêphek,** *hay´-fek;* from 2015; a *turn,* i.e. the *reverse:*— contrary.

2017. הֹפֶךְ **hôphek,** *ho´-fek;* from 2015; an *upset,* i.e. (abstr.) *perversity:*— turning of things upside down.

2018. הֲפֵכָה **hăphêkâh,** *haf-ay-kaw´;* fem. of 2016; *destruction:*— overthrow.

2019. הֲפַכְפַּךְ **hăphakpak,** *haf-ak-pak´;* by redupl. from 2015; *very perverse:*— froward.

2020. הַצָּלָה **hatstsâlâh,** *hats-tsaw-law´;* from 5337; *rescue:*— deliverance.

2021. הֹצֶן **hôtsen,** *ho´-tsen;* from an unused root appar. mean. to *be sharp* or *strong;* a *weapon* of war:— chariot.

2022. הַר **har,** *har;* a short. form of 2042; a *mountain* or *range* of hills (sometimes used fig.):— hill (country), mount (-ain), × promotion.

2023. הֹר **Hôr,** *hore;* another form of 2022; *mountain; Hor,* the name of a peak in Idumæa and of one in Syria:— Hor.

2024. הָרָא **Hârâ´,** *haw-raw´;* perh. from 2022; *mountainousness; Hara,* a region of Media:— Hara.

2025. הַראֵל **har'êl,** *har-ale´;* from 2022

and 410; *mount of God;* fig. the *altar* of burnt-offering:— altar. Comp. 739.

2026. הָרַג **hârag,** *haw-rag';* a prim. root; to *smite* with deadly intent:— destroy, out of hand, kill, murder (-er), put to [death], make [slaughter], slay (-er), × surely.

2027. הֶרֶג **hereg,** *heh'-reg;* from 2026; *slaughter:*— be slain, slaughter.

2028. הֲרֵגָה **hărêgâh,** *har-ay-gaw';* fem. of 2027; *slaughter:*— slaughter.

2029. הָרָה **hârâh,** *haw-raw';* a prim. root; to *be* (or *become) pregnant, conceive* (lit. or fig.):— been, be with child, conceive, progenitor.

2030. הָרֶה **hâreh,** *haw-reh';* or

הָרִי **hâriy** (Hos. 14:1), *haw-ree';* from 2029; *pregnant:*— (be, woman) with child, conceive, × great.

2031. הַרְהֹר **harhôr** (Chald.), *har-hor';* from a root corresp. to 2029; a mental *conception:*— thought.

2032. הֵרוֹן **hêrôwn,** *hay-rone';* or

הֵרָיוֹן **hêrâyôwn,** *hay-raw-yone';* from 2029; *pregnancy:*— conception.

2033. הֲרוֹרִי **Hărôwrîy,** *har-o-ree';* another form for 2043; a *Harorite* or mountaineer:— Harorite.

2034. הֲרִיסָה **hăriysâh,** *har-ee-saw';* from 2040; something *demolished:*— ruin.

2035. הֲרִיסוּת **hăriyçûwth,** *har-ee-sooth';* from 2040; *demolition:*— destruction.

2036. הֹרָם **Hôrâm,** *ho-rawm';* from an unused root (mean. to *tower* up); *high; Horam,* a Canaanitish king:— Horam.

2037. הָרֻם **Hârûm,** *haw-room';* pass. part. of the same as 2036; *high; Harum,* an Isr.:— Harum.

2038. הַרְמוֹן **harmôwn,** *har-mone';* from the same as 2036; a *castle* (from its height):— palace.

2039. הָרָן **Hârân,** *haw-rawn';* perh. from 2022; *mountaineer; Haran,* the name of two men:— Haran.

2040. הָרַס **hâraç,** *haw-ras';* a prim. root; to *pull* down or in pieces, *break, destroy:*— beat down, break (down, through), destroy, overthrow, pluck down, pull down, ruin, throw down, × utterly.

2041. הֶרֶס **hereç,** *heh'-res;* from 2040; *demolition:*— destruction.

2042. הָרָר **hârâr,** *haw-rawr';* from an unused root mean. to *loom* up; a *mountain:*— hill, mount (-ain).

2043. הֲרָרִי **Hărâriy,** *hah-raw-ree';* or

הָרָרִי **Hârâriy** (2 Sam. 23:11), *haw-raw-ree';* or

הָאָרָרִי **Hâ'râriy** (2 Sam. 23:34, last clause), *haw-raw-ree';* appar. from 2042; a *mountaineer:*— Hararite.

2044. הָשֵׁם **Hâshêm,** *haw-shame';* perh. from the same as 2828; *wealthy; Hashem,* an Isr.:— Hashem.

2045. הַשְׁמָעוּת **hâshmâ'ûwth,** *hashmaw-ooth';* from 8085; *announcement:*— to cause to hear.

2046. הִתּוּךְ **hittûwk,** *hit-took';* from 5413; a *melting:*— is melted.

2047. הֲתָךְ **Hăthâk,** *hath-awk';* prob. of for. or.; *Hathak,* a Pers. eunuch:— Hatach.

2048. הָתַל **hâthal,** *haw-thal';* a prim. root; to *deride;* by impl. to *cheat:*— deal deceitfully, deceive, mock.

2049. הָתֹל **hâthôl,** *haw-thole';* from 2048 (only in plur. collect.); a *derision:*— mocker.

2050. הָתַת **hâthath,** *haw-thath';* a prim. root; prop. to *break* in upon, i.e. to *assail:*— imagine mischief.

ו

2051. וְדָן **Vᵉdân,** *ved-awn';* perh. for 5730; *Vedan* (or Aden), a place in Arabia:— Dan also.

2052. וָהֵב **Vâhêb,** *vaw-habe';* of uncert. der.; *Vaheb,* a place in Moab:— what he did.

2053. וָו **vâv,** *vaw;* prob. a *hook* (the name of the sixth Heb. letter):— hook.

2054. וָזָר **vâzâr,** *vaw-zawr';* presumed to be from an unused root mean. to *bear* guilt; *crime:*— × strange.

2055. וַיְזָתָא **Vayᵉzâthâ',** *vah-yez-aw'-thaw;* of for. or.; *Vajezatha,* a son of Haman:— Vajezatha.

2056. וָלָד **vâlâd,** *vaw-lawd';* for 3206; a *boy:*— child.

2057. וַנְיָה **Vanyâh,** *van-yaw';* perh. for 6043; *Vanjah,* an Isr.:— Vaniah.

2058. וָפְסִי **Vophçiy,** *vof-see';* prob. from 3254; *additional; Vophsi,* an Isr.:— Vophsi.

2059. וַשְׁנִי **Vashniy,** *vash-nee';* prob. from 3461; *weak; Vashni,* an Isr.:— Vashni.

2060. וַשְׁתִּי **Vashtiy,** *vash-tee';* of Pers. or.; *Vashti,* the queen of Xerxes:— Vashti.

ז

2061. זְאֵב **zᵉ'êb,** *zeh-abe';* from an unused root mean. to *be yellow;* a *wolf:*— wolf.

2062. זְאֵב **Zᵉ'êb,** *zeh-abe';* the same as 2061; *Zeëb,* a Midianitish prince:— Zeeb.

2063. זֹאת **zô'th,** *zothe';* irreg. fem. of 2089; *this* (often used adv.):— hereby (-in, -with), it, likewise, the one (other, same), she, so (much), such (deed), that, therefore, these, this (thing), thus.

2064. זָבַד **zâbad,** *zaw-bad';* a prim. root; to *confer:*— endure.

2065. זֶבֶד **zebed,** *zeh'-bed;* from 2064; a *gift:*— dowry.

2066. זָבָד **Zâbâd,** *zaw-bawd';* from 2064; *giver; Zabad,* the name of seven Isr.:— Zabad.

2067. זַבְדִּי **Zabdiy,** *zab-dee';* from 2065; *giving; Zabdi,* the name of four Isr.:— Zabdi.

2068. זַבְדִּיאֵל **Zabdîy'êl,** *zab-dee-ale';* from 2065 and 410; *gift of God; Zabdiel,* the name of two Isr.:— Zabdiel.

2069. זְבַדְיָה **Zᵉbadyâh,** *zeb-ad-yaw';* or

זְבַדְיָהוּ **Zᵉbadyâhûw,** *zeb-ad-yaw'-hoo;* from 2064 and 3050; *Jah has given;*

Zebadjah, the name of nine Isr.:— Zebadiah.

2070. זְבוּב **zᵉbûwb,** *zeb-oob';* from an unused root (mean. to *flit*); a *fly* (espec. one of a stinging nature):— fly.

2071. זָבוּד **Zâbûwd,** *zaw-bood';* from 2064; *given; Zabud,* an Isr.:— Zabud.

2072. זַבּוּד **Zabbûwd,** *zab-bood';* a form of 2071; *given; Zabbud,* an Isr.:— Zabbud.

2073. זְבוּל **zᵉbûwl,** *ze-bool';* or

זְבֻל **zᵉbûl,** *zeb-ool';* from 2082; a *residence:*— dwell in, dwelling, habitation.

2074. זְבוּלוֹן **Zᵉbûwlûwn,** *zeb-oo-loon';* or

זְבֻלוֹן **Zᵉbûlûwn,** *zeb-oo-loon';* or

זְבֻלוּן **Zᵉbûwlûn,** *zeb-oo-loon';* from 2082; *habitation; Zebulon,* a son of Jacob; also his territory and tribe:— Zebulun.

2075. זְבוּלֹנִי **Zᵉbûwlônîy,** *zeb-oo-lo-nee';* patron. from 2074; a *Zebulonite* or desc. of Zebulun:— Zebulonite.

2076. זָבַח **zâbach,** *zaw-bakh';* a prim. root; to *slaughter* an animal (usually in sacrifice):— kill, offer, (do) sacrifice, slay.

2077. זֶבַח **zebach,** *zeh'-bakh;* from 2076; prop. a *slaughter,* i.e. the *flesh* of an animal; by impl. a *sacrifice* (the victim or the act):— offer (-ing), sacrifice.

2078. זֶבַח **Zebach,** *zeh'-bakh;* the same as 2077; *sacrifice; Zebach,* a Midianitish prince:— Zebah.

2079. זַבַּי **Zabbay,** *zab-bah'-ee;* prob. by orth. err. for 2140; *Zabbai* (or Zaccai), an Isr.:— Zabbai.

2080. זְבִידָה **Zᵉbîydâh,** *zeb-ee-daw';* fem. from 2064; *giving; Zebidah,* an Israelitess:— Zebudah.

2081. זְבִינָא **Zᵉbîynâ',** *zeb-ee-naw';* from an unused root (mean. to *purchase*); *gainfulness; Zebina,* an Isr.:— Zebina.

2082. זָבַל **zâbal,** *zaw-bal';* a prim. root; appar. prop. to *inclose,* i.e. to *reside:*— dwell with.

2083. זְבֻל **Zᵉbûl,** *zeb-ool';* the same as 2073; *dwelling; Zebul,* an Isr.:— Zebul. Comp. 2073.

זְבֻלוּן **Zᵉbûlûwn.** See 2074.

2084. זְבַן **zᵉban** (Chald.), *zeb-an';* corresp. to the root of 2081; to *acquire* by purchase:— gain.

2085. זָג **zâg,** *zawg;* from an unused root prob. mean. to *inclose;* the *skin* of a grape:— husk.

2086. זֵד **zêd,** *zade';* from 2102; *arrogant:*— presumptuous, proud.

2087. זָדוֹן **zâdôwn,** *zaw-done';* from 2102; *arrogance:*— presumptuously, pride, proud (man).

2088. זֶה **zeh,** *zeh;* a prim. word; the masc. demonstr. pron.; *this* or *that:*— he, × hence, × here, it (-self), × now, × of him, the one ... the other, × than the other, (× out of) the (self) same, such (an one) that, these, this (hath, man), on this side ... on that side, × thus, very, which. Comp. 2063, 2090, 2097, 2098.

2089. זֶה **zeh** (1 Sam. 17:34), zeh; by perm. for 7716; a *sheep*:— lamb.

2090. זֹה **zôh**, zo; for 2088; *this* or *that*:— as well as another, it, this, that, thus and thus.

2091. זָהָב **zâhâb**, zaw-hawb´; from an unused root mean. to *shimmer*; *gold*, fig. something *gold-colored* (i.e. *yellow*), as *oil*, a *clear sky*:— gold (-en), fair weather.

2092. זָהַם **zâham**, zaw-ham´; a prim. root; to *be rancid*, i.e. (tran.) to *loathe*:— abhor.

2093. זַהַם **Zaham**, zah´-ham; from 2092; *loathing*; *Zaham*, an Isr.:— Zaham.

2094. זָהַר **zâhar**, zaw-har´; a prim. root; to *gleam*; fig. to *enlighten* (by caution):— admonish, shine, teach, (give) warn (-ing).

2095. זְהַר **zᵉhar** (Chald.), zeh-har´; corresp. to 2094; (pass.) *be admonished*:— take heed.

2096. זֹהַר **zôhar**, zo´-har; from 2094; *brilliancy*:— brightness.

2097. זוֹ **zôw**, zo; for 2088; *this* or *that*:— that, this.

2098. זוּ **zûw**, zoo; for 2088; *this* or *that*:— that, this, × wherein, which, whom.

2099. זִו **Zîv**, zeev´; prob. from an unused root mean. to *be prominent*; prop. *brightness* [comp. 2122], i.e. (fig.) the month of *flowers*; *Ziv* (corresp. to Ijar or May):— Zif.

2100. זוּב **zûwb**, zoob; a prim. root; to *flow* freely (as water), i.e. (spec.) to *have a* (sexual) *flux*; fig. to *waste* away; also to *overflow*:— flow, gush out, have a (running) issue, pine away, run.

2101. זוֹב **zôwb**, zobe; from 2100; a seminal or menstrual *flux*:— issue.

2102. זוּד **zûwd**, zood; or (by perm.)

זִיד **zîyd**, zeed; a prim. root; to *seethe*; fig. to *be insolent*:— be proud, deal proudly, presume, (come) presumptuously, sod.

2103. זוּד **zûwd** (Chald.), zood; corresp. to 2102; to *be proud*:— in pride.

2104. זוּזִים **Zûwzîym**, zoo-zeem´; plur. prob. from the same as 2123; *prominent*; *Zuzites*, an aboriginal tribe of Pal.:— Zuzims.

2105. זוֹחֵת **Zôwchêth**, zo-khayth´; of uncert. or.; *Zocheth*, an Isr.:— Zoheth.

2106. זָוִית **zâvîyth**, zaw-veeth´; appar. from the same root as 2099 (in the sense of *prominence*); an *angle* (as projecting), i.e. (by impl.) a *corner-column* (or *anta*):— corner (stone).

2107. זוּל **zûwl**, zool; a prim. root [comp. 2151]; prob. to *shake* out, i.e. (by impl.) to *scatter* profusely; fig. to *treat lightly*:— lavish, despise.

2108. זוּלָה **zûwlâh**, zoo-law´; from 2107; prob. *scattering*, i.e. *removal*; used adv. *except*:— beside, but, only, save.

2109. זוּן **zûwn**, zoon; a prim. root; perh. prop. to *be plump*, i.e. (tran.) to *nourish*:— feed.

2110. זוּן **zûwn** (Chald.), zoon; corresp. to 2109:— feed.

2111. זוּעַ **zûwâ**', zoo´-ah; a prim. root; prop. to *shake* off, i.e. (fig.) to *agitate* (as with fear):— move, tremble, vex.

2112. זוּעַ **zûwa**' (Chald.), zoo´-ah; corresp. to 2111; to *shake* (with fear):— tremble.

2113. זְוָעָה **zᵉvâ**'**âh**, zev-aw-aw´; from 2111; *agitation*, *fear*:— be removed, trouble, vexation. Comp. 2189.

2114. זוּר **zûwr**, zoor; a prim. root; to *turn* aside (espec. for lodging); hence, to *be a foreign*, *strange*, *profane*; spec. (act. part.) to *commit adultery*:— (come from) another (man, place), fanner, go away, (e-) strange (-r, thing, woman).

2115. זוּר **zûwr**, zoor; a prim. root [comp. 6695]; to *press* together, *tighten*:— close, crush, thrust together.

2116. זוּרֶה **zûwreh**, zoo-reh´; from 2115; *trodden* on:— that which is crushed.

2117. זָזָא **Zâzâ**', zaw-zaw´; prob. from the root of 2123; *prominent*; *Zaza*, an Isr.:— Zaza.

2118. זָחַח **zâchach**, zaw-khakh´; a prim. root; to *shove* or *displace*:— loose.

2119. זָחַל **zâchal**, zaw-khal´; a prim. root; to *crawl*; by impl. to *fear*:— be afraid, serpent, worm.

2120. זֹחֶלֶת **Zôcheleth**, zo-kheh´-leth; fem. act. part. of 2119; *crawling* (i.e. *serpent*); *Zocheleth*, a boundary stone in Pal.:— Zoheleth.

2121. זֵידוֹן **zêydôwn**, zay-dohn´; from 2102; *boiling* of water, i.e. *wave*:— proud.

2122. זִיו **zîyv** (Chald.), zeev; corresp. to 2099; (fig.) *cheerfulness*:— brightness, countenance.

2123. זִיז **zîyz**, zeez; from an unused root appar. mean. to *be conspicuous*; *fulness* of the breast; also a moving *creature*:— abundance, wild beast.

2124. זִיזָא **Zîyzâ**', zee-zaw´; appar. from the same as 2123; *prominence*; *Ziza*, the name of two Isr.:— Ziza.

2125. זִיזָה **Zîyzâh**, zee-zaw´; another form for 2124; *Zizah*, an Isr.:— Zizah.

2126. זִינָא **Zîynâ**', zee-naw´; from 2109; well-*fed*; or perh. an orth. err. for 2124; *Zina*, an Isr.:— Zina.

2127. זִיעַ **Zîya**', zee´-ah; from 2111; *agitation*; *Zia*, an Isr.:— Zia.

2128. זִיף **Zîyph**, zeef; from the same as 2203; *flowing*; *Ziph*, the name of a place in Pal.; also of an Isr.:— Ziph.

2129. זִיפָה **Zîyphâh**, zee-faw´; fem. of 2128; a *flowing*; *Ziphah*, an Isr.:— Ziphah.

2130. זִיפִי **Zîyphîy**, zee-fee´; patrial from 2128; a *Ziphite* or inhab. of Ziph:— Ziphim, Ziphite.

2131. זִיקָה **zîyqâh** (Isa. 50:11), zee-kaw´ (fem.); and

זִק **zîq**, zeek; or

זֵק **zêq**, zake; from 2187; prop. what *leaps* forth, i.e. *flash* of fire, or a burning *arrow*; also (from the orig. sense of the root) a *bond*:— chain, fetter, firebrand, spark.

2132. זַיִת **zayith**, zay´-yith; prob. from an unused root [akin to 2099]; an *olive* (as yielding *illuminating* oil), the tree, the branch or the berry:— olive (tree, -yard), Olivet.

2133. זֵיתָן **Zêythân**, zay-thawn´; from 2132; *olive* grove; *Zethan*, an Isr.:— Zethan.

2134. זַךְ **zak**, zak; from 2141; *clear*:— clean, pure.

2135. זָכָה **zâkâh**, zaw-kaw´; a prim. root [comp. 2141]; to *be translucent*; fig. to *be innocent*:— be (make) clean, cleanse, be clear, count pure.

2136. זְכוּ **zᵉkûw** (Chald.), zaw-koo´; from a root corresp. to 2135; *purity*:— innocency.

2137. זְכוּכִית **zᵉkûwkîyth**, zek-oo-keeth´; from 2135; prop. *transparency*, i.e. *glass*:— crystal.

2138. זָכוּר **zâkûwr**, zaw-koor´; prop. pass. part. of 2142, but used for 2145; a *male* (of man or animals):— males, men-children.

2139. זַכּוּר **Zakkûwr**, zaw-koor´; from 2142; *mindful*; *Zakkur*, the name of seven Isr.:— Zaccur, Zacchur.

2140. זַכַּי **Zakkay**, zak-kah´-ee; from 2141; *pure*; *Zakkai*, an Isr.:— Zaccai.

2141. זָכַךְ **zâkak**, zaw-kak´; a prim. root [comp. 2135]; to *be transparent* or *clean* (phys. or mor.):— be (make) clean, be pure (-r).

2142. זָכַר **zâkar**, zaw-kar´; a prim. root; prop. to *mark* (so as to be recognized), i.e. to *remember*; by impl. to *mention*; also (as denom. from 2145) to *be male*:— × burn [incense], × earnestly, be male, (make) mention (of), be mindful, recount, record (-er), remember, make to be remembered, bring (call, come, keep, put) to (in) remembrance, × still, think on, × well.

2143. זֵכֶר **zêker**, zay´-ker; or

זֶכֶר **zeker**, zeh´-ker; from 2142; a *memento*, abstr. *recollection* (rarely if ever); by impl. *commemoration*:— memorial, memory, remembrance, scent.

2144. זֶכֶר **Zeker**, zeh´-ker; the same as 2143; *Zeker*, an Isr.:— Zeker.

2145. זָכָר **zâkâr**, zaw-kawr´; from 2142; prop. *remembered*, i.e. a *male* (of man or animals, as being the most noteworthy sex):— × him, male, man (child, -kind).

2146. זִכְרוֹן **zikrôwn**, zik-rone´; from 2142; a *memento* (or memorable thing, day or writing):— memorial, record.

2147. זִכְרִי **Zikrîy**, zik-ree´; from 2142; *memorable*; *Zicri*, the name of twelve Isr.:— Zichri.

2148. זְכַרְיָה **Zᵉkaryâh**, zek-ar-yaw´; or

זְכַרְיָהוּ **Zᵉkaryâhûw**, zek-ar-yaw´-hoo; from 2142 and 3050; *Jah has remembered*; *Zecarjah*, the name of twenty-nine Isr.:— Zachariah, Zechariah.

2149. זֻלּוּת **zullûwth**, zool-looth´; from 2151; prop. a *shaking*, i.e. perh. a *tempest*:— vilest.

2150. זַלְזַל **zalzal**, zal-zal´; by redupl. from 2151; *tremulous*, i.e. a *twig*:— sprig.

2151. זָלַל **zâlal**, zaw-lal´; a prim. root

[comp. 2107]; to *shake* (as in the wind), i.e. to *quake*; fig. to *be loose* morally, *worthless* or *prodigal*:— blow down, glutton, riotous (eater), vile.

2152. זַלְעָפָה **zal'âphâh**, *zal-aw-faw'*; or

זִלְעָפּף **zil'âphâph**, *zil-aw-faw'*; from 2196; a *glow* (of wind or anger); also a *famine* (as *consuming*):— horrible, horror, terrible.

2153. זִלְפָּה **Zilpâh**, *zil-paw'*; from an unused root appar. mean. to *trickle*, as myrrh; fragrant *dropping*; *Zilpah*, Leah's maid:— Zilpah.

2154. זִמָּה **zimmâh**, *zim-maw'*; or

זַמָּה **zammâh**, *zam-maw'*; from 2161; a *plan*, espec. a bad one:— heinous crime, lewd (-ly, -ness), mischief, purpose, thought, wicked (device, mind, -ness).

2155. זִמָּה **Zimmâh**, *zim-maw'*; the same as 2154; *Zimmah*, the name of two Isr.:— Zimmah.

2156. זְמוֹרָה **ze̱môwrâh**, *zem-o-raw'*; or

זְמֹרָה **ze̱môrâh**, *zem-o-raw'* (fem.); and

זְמֹר **ze̱môr**, *zem-ore'* (masc.); from 2168; a *twig* (as *pruned*):— vine, branch, slip.

2157. זַמְזֹם **Zamzôm**, *zam-zome'*; from 2161; *intriguing*; a Zamzumite, or native tribe of Pal.:— Zamzummim.

2158. זָמִיר **zâmîyr**, *zaw-meer'*; or

זָמִר **zâmîr**, *zaw-meer'*; and (fem.)

זְמִרָה **ze̱mîrâh**, *zem-ee-raw'*; from 2167; a *song* to be accompanied with instrumental music:— psalm (-ist), singing, song.

2159. זָמִיר **zâmîyr**, *zaw-meer'*; from 2168; a *twig* (as *pruned*):— branch.

2160. זְמִירָה **Ze̱mîyrâh**, *zem-ee-raw'*; fem. of 2158; *song*; *Zemirah*, an Isr.:— Zemira.

2161. זָמַם **zâmam**, *zaw-mam'*; a prim. root; to *plan*, usually in a bad sense:— consider, devise, imagine, plot, purpose, think (evil).

2162. זָמָם **zâmâm**, *zaw-mawm'*; from 2161; a *plot*:— wicked device.

2163. זָמַן **zâman**, *zaw-man'*; a prim. root; to *fix* (a time):— appoint.

2164. זְמַן **ze̱man** (Chald.), *zem-an'*; corresp. to 2163; to *agree* (on a time and place):— prepare.

2165. זְמָן **ze̱mân**, *zem-awn'*; from 2163; an *appointed* occasion:— season, time.

2166. זְמָן **ze̱mân** (Chald.), *zem-awn'*; from 2165; the same as 2165:— season, time.

2167. זָמַר **zâmar**, *zaw-mar'*; a prim. root [perh. ident. with 2168 through the idea of *striking* with the fingers]; prop. to *touch* the strings or parts of a musical instrument, i.e. *play* upon it; to make *music*, accompanied by the voice; hence, to *celebrate* in song and music:— give praise, sing forth praises, psalms.

2168. זָמַר **zâmar**, *zaw-mar'*; a prim. root [comp. 2167, 5568, 6785]; to *trim* (a vine):— prune.

2169. זֶמֶר **zemer**, *zeh'-mer*; appar. from

2167 or 2168; a *gazelle* (from its lightly *touching* the ground):— chamois.

2170. זְמָר **ze̱mâr** (Chald.), *zem-awr'*; from a root corresp. to 2167; instrumental *music*:— musick.

זָמִיר **zâmîr**. See 2158.

זְמֹר **ze̱môr**. See 2156.

2171. זַמָּר **zammâr** (Chald.), *zam-mawr'*; from the same as 2170; an instrumental *musician*:— singer.

2172. זִמְרָה **zimrâh**, *zim-raw'*; from 2167; a *musical* piece or *song* to be accompanied by an instrument:— melody, psalm.

2173. זִמְרָה **zimrâh**, *zim-raw'*; from 2168; *pruned* (i.e. *choice*) fruit:— best fruit.

זְמֹרָה **ze̱mîrâh**. See 2158.

זְמֹרָה **ze̱môrâh**. See 2156.

2174. זִמְרִי **Zimrîy**, *zim-ree'*; from 2167; *musical*; *Zimri*, the name of five Isr., and of an Arabian tribe:— Zimri.

2175. זִמְרָן **Zimrân**, *zim-rawn'*; from 2167; *musical*; *Zimran*, a son of Abraham by Keturah:— Zimran.

2176. זִמְרָת **zimrâth**, *zim-rawth'*; from 2167; instrumental *music*; by impl. *praise*:— song.

2177. זַן **zan**, *zan*; from 2109; prop. *nourished* (or fully *developed*), i.e. a *form* or *sort*:— divers kinds, × all manner of store.

2178. זַן **zan** (Chald.), *zan*; corresp. to 2177; *sort*:— kind.

2179. זָנַב **zânab**, *zaw-nab'*; a prim. root mean. to *wag*; used only as a denom. from 2180; to *curtail*, i.e. *cut* off the rear:— smite the hindmost.

2180. זָנָב **zânâb**, *zaw-nawb'*; from 2179 (in the orig. sense of *flapping*); the *tail* (lit. or fig.):— tail.

2181. זָנָה **zânâh**, *zaw-naw'*; a prim. root [highly-*fed* and therefore *wanton*]; to *commit adultery* (usually of the female, and less often of simple fornication, rarely of involuntary ravishment); fig. to *commit idolatry* (the Jewish people being regarded as the spouse of Jehovah):— (cause to) commit fornication, × continually, × great, (be an, play the) harlot, (cause to be, play the) whore, (commit, fall to) whoredom, (cause to) go a-whoring, whorish.

2182. זָנוֹחַ **Zânôwach**, *zaw-no'-akh*; from 2186; *rejected*; *Zanoach*, the name of two places in Pal.:— Zanoah.

2183. זָנוּן **zânûwn**, *zaw-noon'*; from 2181; *adultery*; fig. *idolatry*:— whoredom.

2184. זְנוּת **ze̱nûwth**, *zen-ooth'*; from 2181; *adultery*, i.e. (fig.) *infidelity*, *idolatry*:— whoredom.

2185. זֹנוֹת **zônôwth**, *zo-noth'*; regarded by some as if from 2109 or an unused root, and applied to military *equipments*; but evidently the fem. plur. act. part. of 2181; *harlots*:— armour.

2186. זָנַח **zânach**, *zaw-nakh'*; a prim. root mean. to *push aside*, i.e. *reject*, *forsake*, *fail*:— cast away (off), remove far away (off).

2187. זָנַק **zânaq**, *zaw-nak'*; a prim. root; prop. to *draw together* the feet (as an

animal about to dart upon its prey), i.e. to *spring* forward:— leap.

2188. זֵעָה **zê'âh**, *zay-aw'*; from 2111 (in the sense of 3154); *perspiration*:— sweat.

2189. זַעֲוָה **za'ăvâh**, *zah-av-aw'*; by transp. for 2113; *agitation*, *maltreatment*:— × removed, trouble.

2190. זַעֲוָן **Za'ăvân**, *zah-av-awn'*; from 2111; *disquiet*; *Zaavan*, an Idumæan:— Zaavan.

2191. זְעֵיר **ze̱'êyr**, *zeh-ayr'*; from an unused root [akin (by perm.) to 6819], mean. to *dwindle*; *small*:— little.

2192. זְעֵיר **ze̱'êyr** (Chald.), *zeh-ayr'*; corresp. to 2191:— little.

2193. זָעַךְ **zâ'ak**, *zaw-ak'*; a prim. root; to *extinguish*:— be extinct.

2194. זָעַם **zâ'am**, *zaw-am'*; a prim. root; prop. to *foam* at the mouth, i.e. to *be enraged*:— abhor, abominable, (be) angry, defy, (have) indignation.

2195. זַעַם **za'am**, *zah'-am*; from 2194; strictly *froth* at the mouth, i.e. (fig.) *fury* (espec. of God's displeasure with sin):— angry, indignation, rage.

2196. זָעַף **zâ'aph**, *zaw-af'*; a prim. root; prop. to *boil* up, i.e. (fig.) to *be peevish* or *angry*:— fret, sad, worse liking, be wroth.

2197. זַעַף **za'aph**, *zah'-af*; from 2196; *anger*:— indignation, rage (-ing), wrath.

2198. זָעֵף **zâ'êph**, *zaw-afe'*; from 2196; *angry*:— displeased.

2199. זָעַק **zâ'aq**, *zaw-ak'*; a prim. root; to *shriek* (from anguish or danger); by anal. (as a herald) to *announce* or *convene* publicly:— assemble, call (together), (make a) cry (out), come with such a company, gather (together), cause to be proclaimed.

2200. זְעִק **ze̱'îq** (Chald.), *zeh-eek'*; corresp. to 2199; to *make an outcry*:— cry.

2201. זַעַק **za'aq**, *zah'-ak*; and (fem.)

זְעָקָה **ze̱'âqâh**, *zeh-aw-kaw'*; from 2199; a *shriek* or *outcry*:— cry (-ing).

2202. זִפְרֹן **Ziphrôn**, *zi-frone'*; from an unused root (mean. to *be fragrant*); *Ziphron*, a place in Pal.:— Ziphron.

2203. זֶפֶת **zepheth**, *zeh'-feth*; from an unused root (mean. to *liquify*); *asphalt* (from its tendency to *soften* in the sun):— pitch.

זִק **zîq** or

זֵק **zêq**. See 2131.

2204. זָקֵן **zâqên**, *zaw-kane'*; a prim. root; to *be old*:— aged man, be (wax) old (man).

2205. זָקֵן **zâqên**, *zaw-kane'*; from 2204; *old*:— aged, ancient (man), elder (-est), old (man, men and ... women), senator.

2206. זָקָן **zâqân**, *zaw-kawn'*; from 2204; the *beard* (as indicating *age*):— beard.

2207. זֹקֶן **zôqen**, *zo'-ken*; from 2204; old *age*:— age.

2208. זָקוּן **zâqûn**, *zaw-koon'*; prop. pass. part. of 2204 (used only in the plur. as a noun); *old* age:— old age.

2209. זִקְנָה **ziqnâh**, *zik-naw'*; fem. of 2205; old *age*:— (old) age.

Hebrew

2210. זָקַף **zâqaph**, *zaw-kaf'*; a prim. root; to *lift*, i.e. (fig.) *comfort*:— raise (up).

2211. זְקַף **zᵉqaph** (Chald.), *zek-af'*; corresp. to 2210; to *hang*, i.e. *impale*:— set up.

2212. זָקַק **zâqaq**, *zaw-kak'*; a prim. root; to *strain*, (fig.) *extract, clarify*:— fine, pour down, purge, purify, refine.

2213. זֵר **zêr**, *zare*; from 2237 (in the sense of *scattering*); a *chaplet* (as *spread* around the top), i.e. (spec.) a border *moulding*:— crown.

2214. זָרָא **zârâ**, *zaw-raw'*; from 2114 (in the sense of *estrangement* lcomp. 2219l); *disgust*:— loathsome.

2215. זָרַב **zârab**, *zaw-rab'*; a prim. root; to *flow* away:— wax warm.

2216. זְרֻבָּבֶל **Zᵉrubbâbel**, *zer-oob-baw-bel'*; from 2215 and 894; *descended of* (i.e. from) *Babylon*, i.e. born there; *Zerubbabel*, an Isr.:— Zerubbabel.

2217. זְרֻבָּבֶל **Zᵉrubbâbel** (Chald.), *zer-oob-baw-bel'*; corresp. to 2216:— Zerubbabel.

2218. זֶרֶד **Zered**, *zeh'-red*; from an unused root mean. to *be exuberant* in growth; lined with *shrubbery*; *Zered*, a brook E. of the Dead Sea:— Zared, Zered.

2219. זָרָה **zârâh**, *zaw-raw'*; a prim. root lcomp. 2114l; to *toss* about; by impl. to *diffuse, winnow*:— cast away, compass, disperse, fan, scatter (away), spread, strew, winnow.

2220. זְרוֹעַ **zᵉrôwa'**, *zer-o'-ah*; or (short.) זְרֹעַ **zᵉrôa'**, *zer-o'-ah*; and (fem.) זְרוֹעָה **zᵉrôw'âh**, *zer-o-aw'*; or זְרֹעָה **zᵉrô'âh**, *zer-o-aw'*; from 2232; the *arm* (as *stretched* out), or (of animals) the *foreleg*; fig. *force*:— arm, + help, mighty, power, shoulder, strength.

2221. זֵרוּעַ **zêrûwa'**, *zay-roo'-ah*; from 2232; something *sown*, i.e. a *plant*:— sowing, thing that is sown.

2222. זַרְזִיף **zarzîyph**, *zar-zeef'*; by redupl. from an unused root mean. to *flow*; a *pouring rain*:— water.

זְרֹעָה **zᵉrôw'âh**. See 2220.

2223. זַרְזִיר **zarzîyr**, *zar-zeer'*; by redupl. from 2115; prop. tightly *girt*, i.e. prob. a *racer*, or some fleet animal (as being *slender* in the waist):— + greyhound.

2224. זָרַח **zârach**, *zaw-rakh'*; a prim. root; prop. to *irradiate* (or shoot forth beams), i.e. to *rise* (as the sun); spec. to *appear* (as a symptom of leprosy):— arise, rise (up), as soon as it is up.

2225. זֶרַח **zerach**, *zeh'-rakh*; from 2224; a *rising* of light:— rising.

2226. זֶרַח **Zerach**, *zeh'-rakh*; the same as 2225; *Zerach*, the name of three Isr., also of an Idumæan and an Ethiopian prince:— Zarah, Zerah.

2227. זַרְחִי **Zarchîy**, *zar-khee'*; patron. from 2226; a *Zarchite* or desc. of Zerach:— Zarchite.

2228. זְרַחְיָה **Zᵉrachyâh**, *zer-akh-yaw'*; from 2225 and 3050; *Jah has risen*; *Zerachjah*, the name of two Isr.:— Zerahiah.

2229. זָרַם **zâram**, *zaw-ram'*; a prim. root; to *gush* (as water):— carry away as with a flood, pour out.

2230. זֶרֶם **zerem**, *zeh'-rem*; from 2229; a *gush* of water:— flood, overflowing, shower, storm, tempest.

2231. זִרְמָה **zirmâh**, *zir-maw'*; fem. of 2230; a *gushing* of fluid (semen):— issue.

2232. זָרַע **zâra'**, *zaw-rah'*; a prim. root; to *sow*; fig. to *disseminate, plant, fructify*:— bear, conceive seed, set with, sow (-er), yield.

2233. זֶרַע **zera'**, *zeh'-rah*; from 2232; *seed*; fig. *fruit, plant, sowing-time, posterity*:— × carnally, child, fruitful, seed (-time), sowing-time.

2234. זְרַע **zᵉra'** (Chald.), *zer-ah'*; corresp. to 2233; *posterity*:— seed.

זְרֹעַ **zᵉrôa'**. See 2220.

2235. זֵרֹעַ **zêrôa'**, *zay-ro'-ah*; or זֵרָעֹן **zêrâ'ôn**, *zay-raw-ohn'*; from 2232; something *sown* (only in the plur.), i.e. a *vegetable* (as food):— pulse.

זְרֹעָה **zᵉrô'âh**. See 2220.

2236. זָרַק **zâraq**, *zaw-rak'*; a prim. root; to *sprinkle* (fluid or solid particles):— be here and there, scatter, sprinkle, strew.

2237. זָרַר **zârar**, *zaw-rar'*; a prim. root lcomp. 2114l; perh. to *diffuse*, i.e. (spec.) to *sneeze*:— sneeze.

2238. זֶרֶשׁ **Zeresh**, *zeh'-resh*; of Pers. or.; *Zeresh*, Haman's wife:— Zeresh.

2239. זֶרֶת **zereth**, *zeh'-reth*; from 2219; the *spread* of the fingers, i.e. a *span*:— span.

2240. זַתּוּא **Zattûw'**, *zat-too'*; of uncert. der.; *Zattu*, an Isr.:— Zattu.

2241. זֵתָם **Zêthâm**, *zay-thawm'*; appar. a var. for 2133; *Zetham*, an Isr.:— Zetham.

2242. זֵתַר **Zêthar**, *zay-thar'*; of Pers. or.; *Zethar*, a eunuch of Xerxes:— Zethar.

ח

2243. חֹב **chôb**, *khobe*; by contr. from 2245; prop. a *cherisher*, i.e. the *bosom*:— bosom.

2244. חָבָא **châbâ'**, *khaw-baw'*; a prim. root lcomp. 2245l; to *secrete*:— × held, hide (self), do secretly.

2245. חָבַב **châbab**, *khaw-bab'*; a prim. root lcomp. 2244, 2247l; prop. to *hide* (as in the bosom), i.e. to *cherish* (with affection):— love.

2246. חֹבָב **Chôbâb**, *kho-bawb'*; from 2245; *cherished*; *Chobab*, father-in-law of Moses:— Hobab.

2247. חָבָה **châbah**, *khaw-baw'*; a prim. root lcomp. 2245l; to *secrete*:— hide (self).

2248. חֲבוּלָה **chăbûwlâh** (Chald.), *khab-oo-law'*; from 2255; prop. *overthrown*, i.e. (morally) *crime*:— hurt.

2249. חָבוֹר **Châbôwr**, *khaw-bore'*; from 2266; *united*; *Chabor*, a river of Assyria:— Habor.

2250. חַבּוּרָה **chabbûwrâh**, *khab-boo-raw'*; or

חַבֻּרָה **chabbûrâh**, *khab-boo-raw'*; or

חֲבוּרָה **chăbûrâh**, *khab-oo-raw'*; from 2266; prop. *bound* (with stripes), i.e. a *weal* (or black-and-blue mark itself):— blueness, bruise, hurt, stripe, wound.

2251. חָבַט **châbaṭ**, *khaw-bat'*; a prim. root; to *knock* out or off:— beat (off, out), thresh.

2252. חֲבַיָּה **Chăbayâh**, *khab-ah-yaw'*; or

חֲבָיָה **Chăbâyâh**, *khab-aw-yaw'*; from 2247 and 3050; *Jah has hidden*; *Chabajah*, an Isr.:— Habaiah.

2253. חֶבְיוֹן **chebyôwn**, *kheb-yone'*; from 2247; a *concealment*:— hiding.

2254. חָבַל **châbal**, *khaw-bal'*; a prim. root; to *wind tightly* (as a rope), i.e. to *bind*; spec. by a *pledge*; fig. to *pervert, destroy*; also to *writhe* in pain (espec. of parturition):— × at all, band, bring forth, (deal) corrupt (-ly), destroy, offend, lay to (take a) pledge, spoil, travail, × very, withhold.

2255. חֲבַל **chăbal** (Chald.), *khab-al'*; corresp. to 2254; to *ruin*:— destroy, hurt.

2256. חֶבֶל **chebel**, *kheh'-bel*; or

חֵבֶל **chêbel**, *khay'-bel*; from 2254; a *rope* (as *twisted*); espec. a measuring *line*; by impl. a *district* or *inheritance* (as *measured*); or a *noose* (as of *cords*); fig. a *company* (as if *tied* together); also a *throe* (espec. of parturition); also *ruin*:— band, coast, company, cord, country, destruction, line, lot, pain, pang, portion, region, rope, snare, sorrow, tackling.

2257. חֲבַל **chăbal** (Chald.), *khab-al'*; from 2255; *harm* (personal or pecuniary):— damage, hurt.

2258. חֲבֹל **chăbôl**, *khab-ole'*; or (fem.)

חֲבֹלָה **chăbôlâh**, *khab-o-law'*; from 2254; a *pawn* (as security for debt):— pledge.

2259. חֹבֵל **chôbêl**, *kho-bale'*; act. part. from 2254 (in the sense of handling ropes); a *sailor*:— pilot, shipmaster.

2260. חִבֵּל **chibbêl**, *khib-bale'*; from 2254 (in the sense of furnished with ropes); a *mast*:— mast.

2261. חֲבַצֶּלֶת **chăbatstseleth**, *khab-ats-tseh'-leth*; of uncert. der.; prob. *meadow-saffron*:— rose.

2262. חֲבַצִּנְיָה **Chăbatstsanyâh**, *khab-ats-tsan-yaw'*; of uncert. der.; *Chabatstsanjah*, a Rechabite:— Habazaniah.

2263. חָבַק **châbaq**, *khaw-bak'*; a prim. root; to *clasp* (the hands or in embrace):— embrace, fold.

2264. חִבֻּק **chibbûq**, *khib-book'*; from 2263; a *clasping* of the hands (in idleness):— fold.

2265. חֲבַקּוּק **Chăbaqqûwq**, *khab-ak-kook'*; by redupl. from 2263; *embrace*; *Chabakkuk*, the prophet:— Habakkuk.

2266. חָבַר **châbar**, *khaw-bar'*; a prim. root; to *join* (lit. or fig.); spec. (by means of spells) to *fascinate*:— charm (-er), be compact, couple (together), have fellowship with, heap up, join (self, together), league.

2267. חֶבֶר **cheber**, *kheh´-ber*; from 2266; a *society*; also a *spell*:— + charmer (-ing), company, enchantment, × wide.

2268. חֶבֶר **Cheber**, *kheh´-ber*; the same as 2267; *community*; *Cheber*, the name of a Kenite and of three Isr.:— Heber.

2269. חֲבַר **chăbar** (Chald.), *khab-ar´*; from a root corresp. to 2266; an *associate*:— companion, fellow.

2270. חָבֵר **châbêr**, *khaw-bare´*; from 2266; an *associate*:— companion, fellow, knit together.

2271. חַבָּר **chabbâr**, *khab-bawr´*; from 2266; a *partner*:— companion.

2272. חֲבַרְבֻּרָה **chăbarbûrâh**, *khab-ar-boo-raw´*; by redupl. from 2266; a *streak* (like a *line*), as on the tiger:— spot.

2273. חַבְרָה **chabrâh** (Chald.), *khab-raw´*; fem. of 2269; an *associate*:— other.

2274. חֶבְרָה **chebrâh**, *kheb-raw´*; fem. of 2267; *association*:— company.

2275. חֶבְרוֹן **Chebrôwn**, *kheb-rone´*; from 2267; seat of *association*; *Chebron*, a place in Pal., also the name of two Isr.:— Hebron.

2276. חֶבְרוֹנִי **Chebrôwnîy**, *kheb-ro-nee´*; or

חֶבְרֹנִי **Chebrônîy**, *kheb-ro-nee´*; patron. from 2275; *Chebronite* (collect.), an inhab. of Chebron:— Hebronites.

2277. חֶבְרִי **Chebrîy**, *kheb-ree´*; patron. from 2268; a *Chebrite* (collect.) or desc. of Cheber:— Heberites.

2278. חֲבֶרֶת **chăbereth**, *khab-eh´-reth*; fem. of 2270; a *consort*:— companion.

2279. חֹבֶרֶת **chôbereth**, *kho-beh´-reth*; fem. act. part. of 2266; a *joint*:— which coupleth, coupling.

2280. חָבַשׁ **châbash**, *khaw-bash´*; a prim. root; to *wrap* firmly (espec. a turban, compress, or *saddle*); fig. to *stop*, to *rule*:— bind (up), gird about, govern, healer, put, saddle, wrap about.

2281. חָבֵת **châbêth**, *khaw-bayth´*; from an unused root prob. mean. to *cook* [comp. 4227]; something *fried*, prob. a griddle-*cake*:— pan.

2282. חַג **chag**, *khag*; or

חָג **châg**, *khawg*; from 2287; a *festival*, or a *victim* therefore:— (solemn) feast (day), sacrifice, solemnity.

2283. חָגָא **châgâ'**, *khaw-gaw´*; from an unused root mean. to *revolve* [comp. 2287]; prop. *vertigo*, i.e. (fig.) *fear*:— terror.

2284. חָגָב **châgâb**, *khaw-gawb´*; of uncert. der.; a *locust*:— locust.

2285. חָגָב **Châgâb**, *khaw-gawb´*; the same as 2284; *locust*; *Chagab*, one of the Nethinim:— Hagab.

2286. חֲגָבָא **Chăgâbâ'**, *khag-aw-baw´*; or

חֲגָבָה **Chăgâbâh**, *khag-aw-baw´*; fem. of 2285; *locust*; *Chagaba* or *Chagabah*, one of the Nethinim:— Hagaba, Hagabah.

2287. חָגַג **châgag**, *khaw-gag´*; a prim. root [comp. 2283, 2328]; prop. to *move* in a *circle*, i.e. (spec.) to *march* in a sacred procession, to *observe* a festival; by impl. to *be giddy*:— celebrate, dance, (keep, hold) a (solemn) feast (holiday), reel to and fro.

2288. חֲגָו **chăgâv**, *khag-awv´*; from an unused root mean. to *take refuge*; a *rift* in rocks:— cleft.

2289. חָגוֹר **châgôwr**, *khaw-gore´*; from 2296; *belted*:— girded with.

2290. חֲגוֹר **chăgôwr**, *khag-ore´*; or

חֲגֹר **chăgôr**, *khag-ore´*; and (fem.)

חֲגוֹרָה **chăgôwrâh**, *khag-o-raw´*; or

חֲגֹרָה **chăgôrâh**, *khag-o-raw´*; from 2296; a *belt* (for the waist):— apron, armour, gird (-le).

2291. חַגִּי **Chaggîy**, *khag-ghee´*; from 2287; *festive*, *Chaggi*, an Isr.; also (patron.) a *Chaggite*, or desc. of the same:— Haggi, Haggites.

2292. חַגַּי **Chaggay**, *khag-gah´-ee*; from 2282; *festive*; *Chaggai*, a Heb. prophet:— Haggai.

2293. חַגִּיָּה **Chaggîyâh**, *khag-ghee-yaw´*; from 2282 and 3050; *festival of Jah*; *Chaggijah*, an Isr.:— Haggiah.

2294. חַגִּית **Chaggîyîth**, *khag-gheeth´*; fem. of 2291; *festive*; *Chaggith*, a wife of David:— Haggith.

2295. חָגְלָה **Choglâh**, *khog-law´*; of uncert. der.; prob. a *partridge*; *Choglah*, an Israelitess:— Hoglah. See also 1031.

2296. חָגַר **châgar**, *khaw-gar´*; a prim. root; to *gird* on (as a belt, armor, etc.):— be able to put on, be afraid, appointed, gird, restrain, × on every side.

2297. חַד **chad**, *khad*; abridged from 259; *one*:— one.

2298. חַד **chad** (Chald.), *khad*; corresp. to 2297; as card. *one*; as art. *single*; as an ord. *first*; adv. *at once*:— a, first, one, together.

2299. חַד **chad**, *khad*; from 2300; *sharp*:— sharp.

2300. חָדַד **châdad**, *khaw-dad´*; a prim. root; to *be* (caus. *make*) *sharp* or (fig.) *severe*:— be fierce, sharpen.

2301. חֲדַד **Chădad**, *khad-ad´*; from 2300; *fierce*; *Chadad*, an Ishmaelite:— Hadad.

2302. חָדָה **châdâh**, *khaw-daw´*; a prim. root; to *rejoice*:— make glad, be joined, rejoice.

2303. חַדּוּד **chaddûwd**, *khad-dood´*; from 2300; a *point*:— sharp.

2304. חֶדְוָה **chedvâh**, *khed-vaw´*; from 2302; *rejoicing*:— gladness, joy.

2305. חֶדְוָה **chedvâh** (Chald.), *khed-vaw´*; corresp. to 2304:— joy.

2306. חֲדִי **chădîy** (Chald.), *khad-ee´*; corresp. to 2373; a *breast*:— breast.

2307. חָדִיד **Châdîyd**, *khaw-deed´*; from 2300; a *peak*; *Chadid*, a place in Pal.:— Hadid.

2308. חָדַל **châdal**, *khaw-dal´*; a prim. root; prop. to *be flabby*, i.e. (by impl.) *desist*; (fig.) *be lacking* or *idle*:— cease,

end, fail, forbear, forsake, leave (off), let alone, rest, be unoccupied, want.

2309. חֶדֶל **chedel**, *kheh´-del*; from 2308; *rest*, i.e. the state of the *dead*:— world.

2310. חָדֵל **châdêl**, *khaw-dale´*; from 2308; *vacant*, i.e. *ceasing* or *destitute*:— he that forbeareth, frail, rejected.

2311. חַדְלַי **Chadlay**, *khad-lah´-ee*; from 2309; *idle*; *Chadlai*, an Isr.:— Hadlai.

2312. חֵדֶק **chêdeq**, *khay´-dek*; from an unused root mean. to *sting*; a *prickly plant*:— brier, thorn.

2313. חִדֶּקֶל **Chiddeqel**, *khid-deh´-kel*; prob. of for.; the *Chiddekel* (or Tigris) river:— Hiddekel.

2314. חָדַר **châdar**, *khaw-dar´*; a prim. root; prop. to *inclose* (as a room), i.e. (by anal.) to *beset* (as in a siege):— enter a privy chamber.

2315. חֶדֶר **cheder**, *kheh´-der*; from 2314; an *apartment* (usually lit.):— [bed] inner) chamber, innermost (-ward) part, parlour, + south, × within.

2316. חֲדַר **Chădar**, *khad-ar´*; another form for 2315; *chamber*; *Chadar*, an Ishmaelite:— Hadar.

2317. חֲדָרֶךְ **Chadrâk**, *khad-rawk´*; of uncert. der.; *Chadrak*, a Syrian deity:— Hadrach.

2318. חָדַשׁ **châdash**, *khaw-dash´*; a prim. root; to *be new*; caus. to *rebuild*:— renew, repair.

2319. חָדָשׁ **châdâsh**, *khaw-dawsh´*; from 2318; *new*:— fresh, new thing.

2320. חֹדֶשׁ **chôdesh**, *kho´-desh*; from 2318; the *new moon*; by impl. a *month*:— month (-ly), new moon.

2321. חֹדֶשׁ **Chôdesh**, *kho´-desh*; the same as 2320; *Chodesh*, an Israelitess:— Hodesh.

2322. חֲדָשָׁה **Chădâshâh**, *khad-aw-shaw´*; fem. of 2319; *new*; *Chadashah*, a place in Pal.:— Hadashah.

2323. חֲדַת **chădath** (Chald.), *khad-ath´*; corresp. to 2319; *new*:— new.

2324. חֲוָא **chăvâ'** (Chald.), *khav-aw´*; corresp. to 2331; to *show*:— shew.

2325. חוּב **chûwb**, *khoob*; also

חָיַב **châyab**, *khaw-yab´*; a prim. root; prop. perh. to *tie*, i.e. (fig. and refl.) to *owe*, or (by impl.) to *forfeit*:— make endanger.

2326. חוֹב **chôwb**, *khobe*; from 2325; *debt*:— debtor.

2327. חוֹבָה **chôwbâh**, *kho-baw´*; fem. act. part. of 2247; *hiding* place; *Chobah*, a place in Syria:— Hobah.

2328. חוּג **chûwg**, *khoog*; a prim. root [comp. 2287]; to *describe* a *circle*:— compass.

2329. חוּג **chûwg**, *khoog*; from 2328; *circle*:— circle, circuit, compass.

2330. חוּד **chûwd**, *khood*; a prim. root; prop. to *tie* a knot, i.e. (fig.) to *propound* a riddle:— put forth.

2331. חָוָה **châvâh**, *khaw-vah´*; a prim. root; [comp. 2324, 2421]; prop. to *live*; by impl. (intens.) to *declare* or *show*:— show.

2332. חַוָּה **Chavvâh**, *khav-vaw´*; caus.

from 2331; *life-giver; Chavvah* (or Eve), the first woman:— Eve.

2333. חַוָּה **chavvâh**, *khav-vaw´*; prop. the same as 2332 (*life-giving*, i.e. *living-place*); by impl. an encampment or *village*:— (small) town.

2334. חַוֹּת יָעִיר **Chavvôwth Yâ´îyr**, *khav-vothe´yaw-eer´*; from the plural of 2333 and a modif. of 3265; *hamlets of Jair*, a region of Pal.:— [Bashan-] Havoth-jair.

2335. חוֹזַי **Chôwzay**, *kho-zah´-ee*; from 2374; *visionary; Chozai*, an Isr.:— the seers.

2336. חוֹחַ **chôwach**, *kho´-akh*; from an unused root appar. mean. to *pierce*; a *thorn*; by anal. a *ring* for the nose:— bramble, thistle, thorn.

2337. חֲוָח **châvâch**, *khaw-vawkh´*; perh. the same as 2336; a *dell* or *crevice* (as if *pierced* in the earth):— thicket.

2338. חוּט **chûwṭ** (Chald.), *khoot;* corresp. to the root of 2339, perhaps as a denom.; to *string* together, i.e. (fig.) to *repair:*— join.

2339. חוּט **chûwṭ**, *khoot;* from an unused root prob. mean. to *sew*; a *string*; by impl. a measuring *tape:*— cord, fillet, line, thread.

2340. חִוִּי **Chivvîy**, *khiv-vee´*; perh. from 2333; a *villager*; a *Chivvite*, one of the aboriginal tribes of Pal.:— Hivite.

2341. חֲוִילָה **Chăvîylâh**, *khav-ee-law´*; prob. from 2342; *circular; Chavilah*, the name of two or three eastern regions; also perh. of two men:— Havilah.

2342. חוּל **chûwl**, *khool;* or

חִיל **chîyl**, *kheel;* a prim. root; prop. to *twist* or *whirl* (in a circular or spiral manner), i.e. (spec.) to *dance*, to *writhe* in pain (espec. of parturition) or fear, (make) to *bring forth*, (make to) calve, dance, drive away, fall grievously (with pain), fear, form, great, grieve, (be) grievous, hope, look, make, be in pain, be much (sore) pained, rest, shake, shapen, (be) sorrow (-ful), stay, tarry, travail (with pain), tremble, trust, wait carefully (patiently), be wounded.

2343. חוּל **Chûwl**, *khool;* from 2342; a *circle; Chul*, a son of Aram; also the region settled by him:— Hul.

2344. חוֹל **chôwl**, *khole;* from 2342; *sand* (as *round* or whirling particles):— sand.

2345. חוּם **chûwm**, *khoom;* from an unused root mean. to *be warm*, i.e. (by impl.) *sunburnt* or *swarthy* (blackish):— brown.

2346. חוֹמָה **chôwmâh**, *kho-maw´;* fem. act. part. of an unused root appar. mean. to *join*; a *wall* of protection:— wall, walled.

2347. חוּס **chûwç**, *khoos;* a prim. root; prop. to *cover*, i.e. (fig.) to *compassionate:*— pity, regard, spare.

2348. חוֹף **chôwph**, *khofe;* from an unused root mean. to *cover*; a *cove* (as a *sheltered* bay):— coast [of the seal, haven, shore, [sea-] side.

2349. חוּפָם **Chûwphâm**, *khoo-fawm´;* from the same as 2348; *protection: Chupham*, an Isr.:— Hupham.

2350. חוּפָמִי **Chûwphâmîy**, *khoo-faw-mee´;* patron. from 2349; a *Chuphamite* or desc. of Chupham:— Huphamites.

2351. חוּץ **chûwts**, *khoots;* or (short.)

חֻץ **chûts**, *khoots;* (both forms fem. in the plur.) from an unused root mean. to *sever*; prop. *separate* by a wall, i.e. *outside, outdoors:*— abroad, field, forth, highway, more, out (-side, -ward), street, without.

חוֹק **chôwq**. See 2436.

חוּקֹק **Chûwqôq**. See 2712.

2352. חוּר **chûwr**, *khoor;* or (short.)

חֻר **chûr**, *khoor;* from an unused root prob. mean. to *bore*; the *crevice* of a serpent; the *cell* of a prison:— hole.

2353. חוּר **chûwr**, *khoor;* from 2357; *white* linen:— white.

2354. חוּר **Chûwr**, *khoor;* the same as 2353 or 2352; *Chur*, the name of four Isr. and one Midianite:— Hur.

2355. חוֹר **chôwr**, *khore;* the same as 2353; *white* linen:— network. Comp. 2715.

2356. חוֹר **chôwr**, *khore;* or (short.)

חֹר **chôr**, *khore;* the same as 2352; a *cavity, socket, den:*— cave, hole.

2357. חָוַר **châvar**, *khaw-var´;* a prim. root; to *blanch* (as with shame):— wax pale.

2358. חִוָּר **chivvâr** (Chald.), *khiv-vawr´;* from a root corresp. to 2357; *white:*— white.

חוֹרוֹן **Chôwrôwn**. See 1032.

חוֹרִי **chôwrîy**. See 2753.

2359. חוּרִי **Chûwrîy**, *khoo-ree´;* prob. from 2353; *linen*-worker; *Churi*, an Isr.:— Huri.

2360. חוּרַי **Chûwray**, *khoo-rah´ee;* prob. an orth. var. for 2359; *Churai*, an Isr.:— Hurai.

2361. חוּרָם **Chûwrâm**, *khoo-rawm´;* prob. from 2353; *whiteness*, i.e. noble; *Churam*, the name of an Isr. and two Syrians:— Huram. Comp. 2438.

2362. חַוְרָן **Chavrân**, *khav-rawn´;* appar. from 2357 (in the sense of 2352); *cavernous; Chavran*, a region E. of the Jordan:— Hauran.

2363. חוּשׁ **chûwsh**, *koosh;* a prim. root; to *hurry*; fig. to *be eager* with excitement or enjoyment:— (make) haste (-n), ready.

2364. חוּשָׁה **Chûwshâh**, *khoo-shaw´;* from 2363; *haste; Chushah*, an Isr.:— Hushah.

2365. חוּשַׁי **Chûwshay**, *khoo-shah´-ee;* from 2363; *hasty; Chushai*, an Isr.:— Hushai.

2366. חוּשִׁים **Chûwshîym**, *khoo-sheem´;* or

חֻשִׁים **Chûshîym**, *khoo-sheem´;* or

חֻשִׁם **Chûshîm**, *khoo-sheem´;* plur. from 2363; *hasters; Chushim*, the name of three Isr.:— Hushim.

2367. חוּשָׁם **Chûwshâm**, *khoo-shawm´;* or

חֻשָׁם **Chûshâm**, *khoo-shawm´;* from 2363; *hastily; Chusham*, an Idumæan:— Husham.

2368. חוֹתָם **chôwthâm**, *kho-thawm´;* or

חֹתָם **chôthâm**, *kho-thawm´;* from 2856; a *signature*-ring:— seal, signet.

2369. חוֹתָם **Chôwthâm**, *kho-thawm´;* the same as 2368; *seal; Chotham*, the name of two Isr.:— Hotham, Hothan.

2370. חֲזָא **chăzâ´** (Chald.), *khaz-aw´;* or

חֲזָה **chăzâh** (Chald.), *khaz-aw´;* corresp. to 2372; to *gaze* upon; ment. to *dream, be usual* (i.e. *seem*):— behold, have [a dream], see, be wont.

2371. חֲזָאֵל **Chăzâ´êl**, *khaz-aw-ale´;* or

חֲזָהאֵל **Chăzâh´êl**, *khaz-aw-ale´;* from 2372 and 410; *God has seen; Chazaël*, a king of Syria:— Hazael.

2372. חָזָה **châzâh**, *khaw-zaw´;* a prim. root; to *gaze* at; ment. to *perceive, contemplate* (with pleasure); spec. to *have a vision of:*— behold, look, prophesy, provide, see.

2373. חָזֶה **châzeh**, *khaw-zeh´;* from 2372; the *breast* (as most *seen* in front):— breast.

2374. חֹזֶה **chôzeh**, *kho-zeh´;* act. part. of 2372; a *beholder* in vision; also a *compact* (as *looked upon* with approval):— agreement, prophet, see that, seer, [star-] gazer.

חֲזָהאֵל **Chăzâh´êl**. See 2371.

2375. חֲזוֹ **Chăzow**, *khaz-o´;* from 2372; *seer; Chazo*, a nephew of Abraham:— Hazo.

2376. חֵזֶו **chêzev** (Chald.), *khay´-zev;* from 2370; a *sight:*— look, vision.

2377. חָזוֹן **châzôwn**, *khaw-zone´;* from 2372; a *sight* (ment.), i.e. a *dream, revelation,* or *oracle:*— vision.

2378. חָזוֹת **châzôwth**, *khaw-zooth´;* from 2372; a *revelation:*— vision.

2379. חֲזוֹת **chăzôwth** (Chald.), *khaz-oth´;* from 2370; a *view:*— sight.

2380. חָזוּת **châzûwth**, *khaw-zooth´;* from 2372; a *look;* hence, (fig.) striking *appearance, revelation,* or (by impl.) *compact:*— agreement, notable (one), vision.

2381. חֲזִיאֵל **Chăzîy´êl**, *khaz-ee-ale´;* from 2372 and 410; *seen of God; Chaziel*, a Levite:— Haziel.

2382. חֲזָיָה **Chăzâyâh**, *khaz-aw-yaw´;* from 2372 and 3050; *Jah has seen; Chazajah*, an Isr.:— Hazaiah.

2383. חֶזְיוֹן **Chezyôwn**, *khez-yone´;* from 2372; *vision; Chezjon*, a Syrian:— Hezion.

2384. חִזָּיוֹן **chizzâyôwn**, *khiz-zaw-yone´;* from 2372; a *revelation*, espec. by *dream:*— vision.

2385. חֲזִיז **chăzîyz**, *khaw-zeez´;* from an unused root mean. to *glare*; a *flash* of lightning:— bright cloud, lightning.

2386. חֲזִיר **chăzîyr**, *khaz-eer´;* from an unused root prob. mean. to *inclose*; a *hog* (perh. as *penned*):— boar, swine.

2387. חֵזִיר **Chêzîyr**, *khay-zeer´;* from the same as 2386; perh. *protected; Chezir*, the name of two Isr.:— Hezir.

2388. חָזַק **châzaq**, *khaw-zak´;* a prim. root; to *fasten* upon; hence, to *seize, be strong* (fig. *courageous*, caus. *strengthen, cure, help, repair, fortify*), *obstinate;* to *bind, restrain, conquer:*— aid, amend, × calker, catch, cleave, confirm, be constant, constrain, continue, be of good (take) courage (-ous, -ly), encourage (self), be established, fasten, force, fortify, make hard, harden, help, (lay) hold (fast), lean, maintain, play the man, mend, become (wax) mighty, prevail, be recovered, repair, retain, seize, be (wax) sore, strengthen (self), be stout, be (make, shew, wax) strong (-er), be sure, take (hold), be urgent, behave self valiantly, withstand.

2389. חָזָק **châzâq**, *khaw-zawk´;* from 2388; *strong* (usually in a bad sense, *hard, bold, violent):*— harder, hottest, + impudent, loud, mighty, sore, stiff [-hearted], strong (-er).

2390. חָזֵק **châzêq**, *khaw-zake´;* from 2388; *powerful:*— × wax louder, stronger.

2391. חֵזֶק **chêzeq**, *khay´-zek;* from 2388; *help:*— strength.

2392. חֹזֶק **chôzeq**, *kho´-zek;* from 2388; *power:*— strength.

2393. חֶזְקָה **chezqâh**, *khez-kaw´;* fem. of 2391; *prevailing power:*— strength (-en self), (was) strong.

2394. חׇזְקָה **chozqâh**, *khoz-kaw´;* fem. of 2392; *vehemence* (usually in a bad sense):— force, mightily, repair, sharply.

2395. חִזְקִי **Chizqîy**, *khiz-kee´;* from 2388; *strong;* Chizki, an Isr.:— Hezeki.

2396. חִזְקִיָּה **Chizqîyâh**, *khiz-kee-yaw´;* or

חִזְקִיָּהוּ **Chizqîyâhûw**, *khiz-kee-yaw´-hoo;* also

יְחִזְקִיָּה **Yᵉchizqîyâh**, *yekh-iz-kee-yaw´;* or

יְחִזְקִיָּהוּ **Yᵉchizqîyâhûw**, *yekh-iz-kee-yaw´-hoo;* from 2388 and 3050; *strengthened of Jah; Chizkijah,* a king of Judah, also the name of two other Isr.:— Hezekiah, Hizkiah, Hizkijah. Comp. 3169.

2397. חָח **châch**, *khawkh;* once (Ezek. 29:4)

יְחָח **chăchîy**, *khakh-ee´;* from the same as 2336; a *ring* for the nose (or lips):— bracelet, chain, hook.

יְחָחִי **châchîy**. See 2397.

2398. חָטָא **châtâ**, *khaw-taw´;* a prim. root; prop. to *miss;* hence, (fig. and gen.) to *sin;* by infer. to *forfeit, lack, expiate, repent,* (caus.) *lead astray, condemn:*— bear the blame, cleanse, commit [sin], by fault, harm he hath done, loss, miss, (make) offend (-er), offer for sin, purge, purify (self), make reconciliation, (cause, make) sin (-ful, -ness), trespass.

2399. חֵטְא **chêt´**, *khate;* from 2398; a *crime* or its *penalty:*— fault, × grievously, offence, (punishment of) sin.

2400. חַטָּא **chattâ´**, *khat-taw´;* intens. from 2398; a *criminal,* or one accounted *guilty:*— offender, sinful, sinner.

2401. חֲטָאָה **chătâ´âh**, *khat-aw-aw´;* fem. of 2399; an *offence,* or a *sacrifice* for it:— sin (offering), sinful.

2402. חַטָּאָה **chattâ´âh** (Chald.), *khat-taw-aw´;* corresp. to 2401; an *offence,* and the *penalty* or *sacrifice* for it:— sin (offering).

2403. חַטָּאָה **chattâ´âh**, *khat-taw-aw´;* or

חַטָּאת **chattâ´th**, *khat-tawth´;* from 2398; an *offence* (sometimes habitual *sinfulness*), and its penalty, occasion, sacrifice, or expiation; also (concr.) an *offender:*— punishment (of sin), purifying (-fication for sin), sin (-ner, offering).

2404. חָטַב **châtab**, *khaw-tab´;* a prim. root; to *chop* or *carve* wood:— cut down, hew (-er), polish.

2405. חֲטֻבָה **chătûbâh**, *khat-oo-baw´;* fem. pass. part. of 2404; prop. a *carving;* hence, a *tapestry* (as figured):— carved.

2406. חִטָּה **chittâh**, *khit-taw´;* of uncert. der.; *wheat,* whether the grain or the plant:— wheat (-en).

2407. חַטּוּשׁ **Chattûwsh**, *khat-toosh´;* from an unused root of uncert. signif.; *Chattush,* the name of four or five Isr.:— Hattush.

2408. חֲטִי **chătîy** (Chald.), *khat-ee´;* from a root corresp. to 2398; an *offence:*— sin.

2409. חַטָּיָא **chattâyâ´** (Chald.), *khat-taw-yaw´;* from the same as 2408; an *expiation:*— sin offering.

2410. חֲטִיטָא **Chătîyta´**, *khat-ee-taw´;* from an unused root appar. mean. to *dig* out; *explorer; Chatita,* a temple porter:— Hatita.

2411. חַטִּיל **Chattîyl**, *khat-teel´;* from an unused root appar. mean. to *wave; fluctuating; Chattil,* one of "Solomon's servants":— Hattil.

2412. חֲטִיפָא **Chătîyphâ´**, *khat-ee-faw´;* from 2414; *robber; Chatipha,* one of the Nethinim:— Hatipha.

2413. חָטַם **châtam**, *khaw-tam´;* a prim. root; to *stop:*— refrain.

2414. חָטַף **châtaph**, *khaw-taf´;* a prim. root; to *clutch;* hence, to *seize* as a prisoner:— catch.

2415. חֹטֶר **chôter**, *kho´-ter;* from an unused root of uncert. signif.; a *twig:*— rod.

2416. חַי **chay**, *khah´-ee;* from 2421; *alive;* hence, *raw* (flesh); *fresh* (plant, water, year), *strong;* also (as noun, espec. in the fem. sing. and masc. plur.) *life* (or living thing), whether lit. or fig.:— + age, alive, appetite, (wild) beast, company, congregation, life (-time), live (-ly), living (creature, thing), maintenance, + merry, multitude, + (be) old, quick, raw, running, springing, troop.

2417. חַי **chay** (Chald.), *khah´-ee;* from 2418; *alive;* also (as noun in plur.) *life:*— life, that liveth, living.

2418. חֲיָא **chăyâ´** (Chald.), *khah-yaw´;* or

חֲיָה **chăyâh** (Chald.), *khah-yaw´;* corresp. to 2421; to *live:*— live, keep alive.

2419. חִיאֵל **Chîy´êl**, *khee-ale´;* from 2416 and 410; *living of God; Chiel,* an Isr.:— Hiel.

2420. חִידָה **chîydâh**, *khee-daw´;* from 2330; a *puzzle,* hence, a *trick, conundrum,* sententious *maxim:*— dark saying (sentence, speech), hard question, proverb, riddle.

2421. חָיָה **châyâh**, *khaw-yaw´;* a prim. root [comp. 2331, 2421]; to *live,* whether lit. or fig.; caus. to *revive:*— keep (leave, make) alive, × certainly, give (promise) life, (let, suffer to) live, nourish up, preserve (alive), quicken, recover, repair, restore (to life), revive, (× God) save (alive, life, lives), × surely, be whole.

2422. חָיֶה **châyeh**, *khaw-yeh´;* from 2421; *vigorous:*— lively.

2423. חֵיוָא **chêyvâ´** (Chald.), *khay-vaw´;* from 2418; an *animal:*— beast.

2424. חַיּוּת **chayûwth**, *khah-yooth´;* from 2421; *life:*— × living.

2425. חָיַי **châyay**, *khaw-yah´-ee;* a prim. root [comp. 2421]; to *live;* caus. to *revive:*— live, save life.

2426. חֵיל **chêyl**, *khale;* or (short.)

חֵל **chêl**, *khale;* a collat. form of 2428; an *army;* also (by anal.) an *intrenchment:*— army, bulwark, host, + poor, rampart, trench, wall.

חִיל **chîyl**. See 2342.

2427. חִיל **chîyl**, *kheel;* and (fem.)

חִילָה **chîylâh**, *khee-law´;* from 2342; a *throe* (espec. of childbirth):— pain, pang, sorrow.

2428. חַיִל **chayil**, *khah´-yil;* from 2342; prob. a *force,* whether of men, means or other resources; an *army, wealth, virtue, valor, strength:*— able, activity, (+) army, band of men (soldiers), company, (great) forces, goods, host, might, power, riches, strength, strong, substance, train, (+) valiant (-ly), valour, virtuous (-ly), war, worthy (-ily).

2429. חַיִל **chayil** (Chald.), *khah´-yil;* corresp. to 2428; an *army,* or *strength:*— aloud, army, × most [mighty], power.

2430. חֵילָה **chêylâh**, *khay-law´;* fem. of 2428; an *intrenchment:*— bulwark.

2431. חֵילָם **Chêylâm**, *khay-lawm´;* or

חֵלָאם **Chêlâ´m**, *khay-lawm´;* from 2428; *fortress; Chelam,* a place E. of Pal.:— Helam.

2432. חִילֵן **Chîylên**, *khee-lane´;* from 2428; *fortress; Chilen,* a place in Pal.:— Hilen.

2433. חִין **chîyn**, *kheen;* another form for 2580; *beauty:*— comely.

2434. חַיִץ **chayits**, *khah´-yits;* another form for 2351; a *wall:*— wall.

2435. חִיצוֹן **chîytsôwn**, *khee-tsone´;* from 2434; prop. the (outer) *wall side;* hence, *exterior;* fig. *secular* (as opposed to sacred):— outer, outward, utter, without.

2436. חֵיק **chêyq**, *khake;* or

חֵק **chêq**, *khake;* and

חוֹק **chôwq**, *khoke;* from an unused root, appar. mean. to *inclose;* the *bosom* (lit. or fig.):— bosom, bottom, lap, midst, within.

2437. חִירָה **Chîyrâh**, *khee-raw´;* from

חָיב **châyab**. See 2325.

2357 in the sense of *splendor; Chirah*, an Adullamite:— Hirah.

2438. חִירָם **Chîyrâm**, *khee-rawm´;* or

חִירֹם **Chîyrôm**, *khee-rome´;* another form of 2361; *Chiram* or *Chirom*, the name of two Tyrians:— Hiram, Huram.

2439. חִישׁ **chîysh**, *kheesh;* another form of 2363; to *hurry:*— make haste.

2440. חִישׁ **chîysh**, *kheesh;* from 2439; prop. a *hurry;* hence, (adv.) *quickly:*— soon.

2441. חֵךְ **chêk**, *khake;* prob. from 2596 in the sense of *tasting;* prop. the *palate* or inside of the mouth; hence, the *mouth* itself (as the organ of speech, taste and kissing):— (roof of the) mouth, taste.

2442. חָכָה **châkâh**, *khaw-kaw´;* a prim. root [appar. akin to 2707 through the idea of *piercing*]; prop. to *adhere* to; hence, to *await:*— long, tarry, wait.

2443. חַכָּה **chakkâh**, *khak-kaw´;* prob. from 2442; a *hook* (as *adhering*):— angle, hook.

2444. חֲכִילָה **Chakîylâh**, *khak-ee-law´;* from the same as 2447; *dark; Chakilah*, a hill in Pal.:— Hachilah.

2445. חַכִּים **chakkîym** (Chald.), *khak-keem´;* from a root corresp. to 2449; *wise*, i.e. a *Magian:*— wise.

2446. חֲכַלְיָה **Chăkalyâh**, *khak-al-yaw´;* from the base of 2447 and 3050; *darkness* (of) *Jah; Chakaljah*, an Isr.:— Hachaliah.

2447. חַכְלִיל **chaklîyl**, *khak-leel´;* by redupl. from an unused root appar. mean. to *be dark; darkly flashing* (only of the eyes); in a good sense, *brilliant* (as stimulated by wine):— red.

2448. חַכְלִלוּת **chaklîlûwth**, *khak-lee-looth´;* from 2447; *flash* (of the eyes); in a bad sense, *blearedness:*— redness.

2449. חָכַם **châkam**, *khaw-kam´;* a prim. root, to *be wise* (in mind, word or act):— × exceeding, teach wisdom, be (make self, shew self) wise, deal (never so) wisely, make wiser.

2450. חָכָם **châkâm**, *khaw-kawm´;* from 2449; *wise*, (i.e. intelligent, skilful or artful):— cunning (man), subtil, ([un-])wise ([hearted], man).

2451. חָכְמָה **chokmâh**, *khok-maw´;* from 2449; *wisdom* (in a good sense):— skilful, wisdom, wisely, wit.

2452. חָכְמָה **chokmâh** (Chald.), *khok-maw´;* corresp. to 2451; *wisdom:*— wisdom.

2453. חַכְמוֹנִי **Chakmôwnîy**, *khak-mo-nee´;* from 2449; *skilful; Chakmoni*, an Isr.:— Hachmoni, Hachmonite.

2454. חָכְמוֹת **chokmôwth**, *khok-mōth´;* or

חַכְמוֹת **chakmôwth**, *khak-mōth´;* collat. forms of 2451; *wisdom:*— wisdom, every wise [woman].

חֵל **chêl**. See 2426.

2455. חֹל **chôl**, *khole;* from 2490; prop. *exposed;* hence, *profane:*— common, profane (place), unholy.

2456. חָלָא **châlâ'**, *khaw-law´;* a prim.

root [comp. 2470]; to *be sick:*— be diseased.

2457. חִלְאָה **chel'âh**, *khel-aw´;* from 2456; prop. *disease;* hence, *rust:*— scum.

2458. חֶלְאָה **Chel'âh**, *khel-aw´;* the same as 2457; *Chelah*, an Israelitess:— Helah.

2459. חֶלֶב **cheleb**, *kheh´-leb;* or

חֵלֶב **chêleb**, *khay´-leb;* from an unused root mean. to *be fat; fat*, whether lit. or fig.; hence, the *richest* or *choice* part:— × best, fat (-ness), × finest, grease, marrow.

2460. חֵלֶב **Chêleb**, *khay´-leb;* the same as 2459; *fatness; Cheleb*, an Isr.:— Heleb.

2461. חָלָב **châlâb**, *khaw-lawb´;* from the same as 2459; *milk* (as the *richness* of kine):— + cheese, milk, sucking.

2462. חֶלְבָּה **Chelbâh**, *khel-baw´;* fem. of 2459; *fertility; Chelbah*, a place in Pal.:— Helbah.

2463. חֶלְבּוֹן **Chelbôwn**, *khel-bone´;* from 2459; *fruitful; Chelbon*, a place in Syria:— Helbon.

2464. חֶלְבְּנָה **chelbᵉnâh**, *khel-ben-aw´;* from 2459; *galbanum*, an odorous gum (as if *fatty*):— galbanum.

2465. חֶלֶד **cheled**, *kheh´-led;* from an unused root appar. mean. to *glide* swiftly; *life* (as a *fleeting* portion of time); hence, the *world* (as *transient*):— age, short time, world.

2466. חֵלֶד **Chêled**, *khay´-led;* the same as 2465; *Cheled*, an Isr.:— Heled.

2467. חֹלֶד **chôled**, *kho´-led;* from the same as 2465; a *weasel* (from its *gliding* motion):— weasel.

2468. חֻלְדָּה **Chuldâh**, *khool-daw´;* fem. of 2467; *Chuldah*, an Israelitess:— Huldah.

2469. חֶלְדַּי **Chelday**, *khel-dah´-ee;* from 2466; *worldliness; Cheldai*, the name of two Isr.:— Heldai.

2470. חָלָה **châlâh**, *khaw-law´;* a prim. root [comp. 2342, 2470, 2490]; prop. to *be rubbed* or *worn;* hence, (fig.) to be *weak, sick, afflicted;* or (caus.) to *grieve, make sick;* also to *stroke* (in flattering), *entreat:*— beseech, (be) diseased, (put to) grief, be grieved, (be) grievous, infirmity, intreat, lay to, put to pain, × pray, make prayer, be (fall, make) sick, sore, be sorry, make suit (× supplication), woman in travail, be (become) weak, be wounded.

2471. חַלָּה **challâh**, *khal-law´;* from 2490; a *cake* (as usually *punctured*):— cake.

2472. חֲלוֹם **chălôwm**, *khal-ome´;* or (short.)

חֲלֹם **chălôm**, *khal-ome´;* from 2492; a *dream:*— dream (-er).

2473. חֹלוֹן **Chôlôwn**, *kho-lone´;* or (short.)

חֹלֹן **Chôlôn**, *kho-lone´;* prob. from 2344; *sandy; Cholon*, the name of two places in Pal.:— Holon.

2474. חַלּוֹן **challôwn**, *khal-lone´;* a *window* (as *perforated*):— window.

2475. חֲלוֹף **chălôwph**, *khal-ofe´;* from

2498; prop. *surviving;* by impl. (collect.) *orphans:*— × destruction.

2476. חֲלוּשָׁה **chălûwshâh**, *khal-oo-shaw´;* fem. pass. part. of 2522; *defeat:*— being overcome.

2477. חֲלַח **Chălach**, *khal-akh´;* prob. of for. or.; *Chalach*, a region of Assyria:— Halah.

2478. חַלְחוּל **Chalchûwl**, *khal-khool´;* by redupl. from 2342; *contorted; Chalchul*, a place in Pal.:— Halhul.

2479. חַלְחָלָה **chalchâlâh**, *khal-khaw-law´;* fem. from the same as 2478; *writhing* (in childbirth); by impl. *terror:*— (great, much) pain.

2480. חָלַט **châlaṭ**, *khaw-lat´;* a prim. root; to *snatch* at:— catch.

2481. חֲלִי **chălîy**, *khal-ee´;* from 2470; a *trinket* (as *polished*):— jewel, ornament.

2482. חֲלִי **Chălîy**, *khal-ee´;* the same as 2481; *Chali*, a place in Pal.:— Hali.

2483. חֳלִי **chŏlîy**, *khol-ee´;* from 2470; *malady, anxiety, calamity:*— disease, grief, (is) sick (-ness).

2484. חֶלְיָה **chelyâh**, *khel-yaw´;* fem. of 2481; a *trinket:*— jewel.

2485. חָלִיל **châlîyl**, *khaw-leel´;* from 2490; a *flute* (as *perforated*):— pipe.

2486. חָלִילָה **châlîylâh**, *khaw-lee´-law;* or

חָלִלָה **châlîlâh**, *khaw-lee´-law;* a directive from 2490; lit. *for a profaned* thing; used (interj.) *far be it!:*— be far, (× God) forbid.

2487. חֲלִיפָה **chălîyphâh**, *khal-ee-faw´;* from 2498; *alternation:*— change, course.

2488. חֲלִיצָה **chălîytsâh**, *khal-ee-tsaw´;* from 2503; *spoil:*— armour.

2489. חֵלְכָא **chêlᵉkâ'**, *khay-lek-aw´;* or

חֵלְכָה **chêlᵉkâh**, *khay-lek-aw´;* appar. from an unused root prob. mean. to *be dark* or (fig.) *unhappy;* a *wretch*, i.e. *unfortunate:*— poor.

2490. חָלַל **châlal**, *khaw-lal´;* a prim. root [comp. 2470]; prop. to *bore*, i.e. (by impl.) to *wound*, to *dissolve;* fig. to *profane* (a person, place or thing), to *break* (one's word), to *begin* (as if by an "opening wedge"); denom. (from 2485) to *play* (the flute):— begin (× men began), defile, × break, defile, × eat (as common things), × first, × gather the grape thereof, × take inheritance, pipe, player on instruments, pollute, (cast as) profane (self), prostitute, slay (slain), sorrow, stain, wound.

2491. חָלָל **châlâl**, *khaw-lawl´;* from 2490; *pierced* (espec. to death); fig. *polluted:*— kill, profane, slain (man), × slew, (deadly) wounded.

חָלִלָה **châlîlâh**. See 2486.

2492. חָלַם **châlam**, *khaw-lam´;* a prim. root; prop. to *bind* firmly, i.e. (by impl.) to *be* (caus. to *make*) *plump;* also (through the fig. sense of *dumbness*) to *dream:*— (cause to) dream (-er), be in good liking, recover.

2493. חֵלֶם **chêlem** (Chald.), *khay´-lem;* from a root corresp. to 2492; a *dream:*— dream.

2494. חֵלֶם **Chêlem**, *khay'lem;* from 2492; a *dream; Chelem*, an Isr.:— Helem. Comp. 2469.

2495. חֲלֻמָּה **challâmûwth**, *khal-law-mooth';* from 2492 (in the sense of *insipidity*); prob. *purslain:*— egg.

2496. חַלָּמִישׁ **challâmîysh**, *khal-law-meesh';* prob. from 2492 (in the sense of *hardness); flint:*— flint (-y), rock.

2497. חֵלוֹן **Chêlôn**, *khay-lone';* from 2428; *strong; Chelon*, an Isr.:— Helon.

2498. חָלַף **châlaph**, *khaw-laf';* a prim. root; prop. to *slide* by, i.e. (by impl.) to *hasten* away, *pass* on, *spring* up, *pierce* or *change:*— abolish, alter, change, cut off, go on forward, grow up, be over, pass (away, on, through), renew, sprout, strike through.

2499. חֲלַף **châlaph** (Chald.), *khal-af';* corresp. to 2498; to *pass* on (of time):— pass.

2500. חֵלֶף **chêleph**, *khay'-lef;* from 2498; prop. *exchange;* hence, (as prep.) *instead* of:— × for.

2501. חֵלֶף **Cheleph**, *kheh'-lef;* the same as 2500; *change; Cheleph*, a place in Pal.:— Heleph.

2502. חָלַץ **châlats**, *khaw-lats';* a prim. root; to *pull* off; hence, (intens.) to *strip*, (reflex.) to *depart;* by impl. to *deliver, equip* (for fight); *present, strengthen:*— arm (self), (go, ready) armed (× man, soldier), deliver, draw out, make fat, loose, (ready) prepared, put off, take away, withdraw self.

2503. חֶלֶץ **Chelets**, *kheh'-lets;* or

חֵלֶץ **Chêlets**, *khay'-lets;* from 2502; perh. *strength; Chelets*, the name of two Isr.:— Helez.

2504. חֲלָץ **châlâts**, *khaw-lawts';* from 2502 (in the sense of *strength*); only in the dual, the *loins* (as the seat of vigor):— loins, reins.

2505. חָלַק **châlaq**, *khaw-lak';* a prim. root; to *be smooth* (fig.); by impl. (as smooth stones were used for *lots*) to *apportion* or *separate:*— deal, distribute, divide, flatter, give, (have, im-) part (-ner), take away a portion, receive, separate self, (be) smooth (-er).

2506. חֵלֶק **chêleq**, *khay'-lek;* from 2505; prop. *smoothness* (of the tongue); also an *allotment:*— flattery, inheritance, part, × partake, portion.

2507. חֵלֶק **Chêleq**, *khay'-lek;* the same as 2506; *portion; Chelek*, an Isr.:— Helek.

2508. חֲלָק **châlâq** (Chald.), *khal-awk';* from a root corresp. to 2505; a *part:*— portion.

2509. חָלָק **châlâq**, *khaw-lawk';* from 2505; *smooth* (espec. of tongue):— flattering, smooth.

2510. חָלָק **Châlâq**, *khaw-lawk';* the same as 2509; *bare; Chalak*, a mountain of Idumaea:— Halak.

2511. חַלָּק **challâq**, *khal-lawk';* from 2505; *smooth:*— smooth.

2512. חַלֻּק **challûq**, *khal-look';* from 2505; *smooth:*— smooth.

2513. חֶלְקָה **chelqâh**, *khel-kaw';* fem. of 2506; prop. *smoothness;* fig. *flattery;*

also an *allotment:*— field, flattering (-ry), ground, parcel, part, piece of land [ground], plat, portion, slippery place, smooth (thing).

2514. חֲלַקָּה **châlaqqâh**, *khal-ak-kaw';* fem. from 2505; *flattery:*— flattery.

2515. חֲלֻקָּה **châluqqâh**, *khal-ook-kaw';* fem. of 2512; a *distribution:*— division.

2516. חֶלְקִי **Chelqîy**, *khel-kee';* patron. from 2507; a *Chelkite* or desc. of Chelek:— Helkites.

2517. חֶלְקַי **Chelqay**, *khel-kah'ee;* from 2505; *apportioned; Chelkai*, an Isr.:— Helkai.

2518. חִלְקִיָּה **Chilqîyâh**, *khil-kee-yaw';* or

חִלְקִיָּהוּ **Chilqîyâhûw**, *khil-kee-yaw'-hoo;* from 2506 and 3050; *portion* (of) *Jah; Chilhijah*, the name of eight Isr.:— Hilkiah.

2519. חֲלַקְלַקָּה **châlaqlaqqâh**, *khal-ak-lak-kaw';* by redupl. from 2505; prop. something *very smooth;* i.e. a *treacherous* spot; fig. *blandishment:*— flattery, slippery.

2520. חֶלְקָה **Chelqath**, *khel-kath';* a form of 2513; *smoothness; Chelkath*, a place in Pal.:— Helkath.

2521. חֶלְקַת הַצֻּרִים **Chelqath hats-Tsûrîym**, *khel-kath' hats-tsoo-reem';* from 2520 and the plur. of 6697, with the art. ins.; *smoothness of the rocks; Chelkath Hats-tsurim*, a place in Pal.:— Helkath-hazzurim.

2522. חָלַשׁ **châlash**, *khaw-lash';* a prim. root; to *prostrate;* by impl. to *overthrow, decay:*— discomfit, waste away, weaken.

2523. חַלָּשׁ **challâsh**, *khal-lawsh';* from 2522; *frail:*— weak.

2524. חָם **châm**, *khawm;* from the same as 2346; a *father-in-law* (as in *affinity*):— father in law.

2525. חָם **châm**, *khawm;* from 2552; *hot:*— hot, warm.

2526. חָם **Châm**, *khawm;* the same as 2525; *hot* (from the tropical habitat); *Cham*, a son of Noah; also (as a patron.) his desc. or their country:— Ham.

2527. חֹם **chôm**, *khome;* from 2552; *heat:*— heat, to be hot (warm).

2528. חֱמָא **chĕmâ'** (Chald.), *khem-aw';* or

חֱמָה **chămâh** (Chald.), *khem-aw';* corresp. to 2534; *anger:*— fury.

חֱמָא **chĕmâ'**. See 2534.

2529. חֶמְאָה **chem'âh**, *khem-aw';* or (short.)

חֵמָה **chêmâh**, *khay-maw';* from the same root as 2346; *curdled milk* or *cheese:*— butter.

2530. חָמַד **châmad**, *khaw-mad';* a prim. root; to *delight* in:— beauty, greatly beloved, covet, delectable thing, (× great) delight, desire, goodly, lust, (be) pleasant (thing), precious (thing).

2531. חֶמֶד **chemed**, *kheh'-med;* from 2530; *delight:*— desirable, pleasant.

2532. חֶמְדָּה **chemdâh**, *khem-daw';* fem. of 2531; *delight:*— desire, goodly, pleasant, precious.

2533. חֶמְדָּן **Chemdân**, *khem-dawn';* from 2531; *pleasant; Chemdan*, an Idumaean:— Hemdan.

2534. חֵמָה **chêmâh**, *khay-maw';* or (Dan. 11:44)

חֵמָא **chêmâ'**, *khay-maw';* from 3179; *heat;* fig. *anger, poison* (from its *fever*):— anger, bottles, hot displeasure, furious (-ly, -ry), heat, indignation, poison, rage, wrath (-ful). See 2529.

2535. חַמָּה **chammâh**, *kham-maw';* from 2525; *heat;* by impl. the *sun:*— heat, sun.

2536. חַמּוּאֵל **Chammûw'êl**, *kham-moo-ale';* from 2535 and 410; *anger of God; Chammuel*, an Isr.:— Hamuel.

2537. חֲמוּטַל **Chămûwṭal**, *kham-oo-tal';* or

חֲמִיטַל **Chămîyṭal**, *kham-ee-tal';* from 2524 and 2919; *father-in-law of dew; Chamutal* or *Chamital*, an Israelitess:— Hamutal.

2538. חָמוּל **Châmûwl**, *khaw-mool';* from 2550; *pitied; Chamul*, an Isr.:— Hamul.

2539. חָמוּלִי **Châmûwlîy**, *khaw-moo-lee';* patron. from 2538: a *Chamulite* (collect.) or desc. of Chamul:— Hamulites.

2540. חַמּוֹן **Chammôwn**, *kham-mone';* from 2552; *warm* spring; *Chammon*, the name of two places in Pal.:— Hammon.

2541. חָמוֹץ **châmôwts**, *khaw-motse';* from 2556; prop. *violent;* by impl. a *robber:*— oppressed.

2542. חַמּוּק **chammûwq**, *kham-mook';* from 2559; a *wrapping*, i.e. *drawers:*— joints.

2543. חֲמוֹר **chămôwr**, *kham-ore';* or (short.)

חֲמֹר **chămôr**, *kham-ore';* from 2560; a *male ass* (from its dun *red*):— (he) ass.

2544. חֲמוֹר **Chămôwr**, *kham-ore';* the same as 2543; *ass; Chamor*, a Canaanite:— Hamor.

2545. חֲמוֹת **chămôwth**, *kham-ōth';* or (short.)

חֲמֹת **chămôth**, *kham-ōth';* fem. of 2524; a *mother-in-law:*— mother in law.

2546. חֹמֶט **chômeṭ**, *kho'-met;* from an unused root prob. mean. to *lie low;* a *lizard* (as *creeping*):— snail.

2547. חֻמְטָה **Chumṭâh**, *khoom-taw';* fem. of 2546; *low; Chumtah*, a place in Pal.:— Humtah.

2548. חָמִיץ **châmîyts**, *khaw-meets';* from 2556; *seasoned*, i.e. *salt* provender:— clean.

2549. חֲמִישִׁי **chămîyshîy**, *kham-ee-shee';* or

חֲמִשִׁי **chamishshîy**, *kham-ish-shee';* ord. from 2568; *fifth;* also a *fifth:*— fifth (part).

2550. חָמַל **châmal**, *khaw-mal';* a prim. root; to *commiserate;* by impl. to *spare:*— have compassion, (have) pity, spare.

2551. חֶמְלָה **chemlâh**, *khem-law';* from 2550; *commiseration:*— merciful, pity.

2552. חָמַם **châmam**, *khaw-mam´*; a prim. root; to *be hot* (lit. or fig.):— enflame self, get (have) heat, be (wax) hot, (be, wax) warm (self, at).

2553. חַמָּן **chammân**, *kham-mawn´*; from 2535; a *sun-pillar*:— idol, image.

2554. חָמַס **châmaç**, *khaw-mas´*; a prim. root; to *be violent;* by impl. to *maltreat:*— make bare, shake off, violate, do violence, take away violently, wrong, imagine wrongfully.

2555. חָמָס **châmâç**, *khaw-mawce´;* from 2554; *violence;* by impl. *wrong;* by meton. unjust *gain:*— cruel (-ty), damage, false, injustice, × oppressor, unrighteous, violence (against, done), violent (dealing), wrong.

2556. חָמֵץ **châmêts**, *khaw-mates´;* a prim. root; to *be pungent;* i.e. in taste (*sour,* i.e. lit. *fermented,* or fig. *harsh*), in color (*dazzling*):— cruel (man), dyed, be grieved, leavened.

2557. חָמֵץ **châmêts**, *khaw-mates´;* from 2556; *ferment,* (fig.) *extortion:*— leaven, leavened (bread).

2558. חֹמֶץ **chômets**, *kho´-mets;* from 2556; *vinegar:*— vinegar.

2559. חָמַק **châmaq**, *khaw-mak´;* a prim. root; to *enwrap;* hence, to *depart* (i.e. turn about):— go about, withdraw self.

2560. חָמַר **châmar**, *khaw-mar´;* a prim. root; prop. to *boil* up; hence, to *ferment* (with scum); to *glow* (with redness); as denom. (from 2564) to *smear* with pitch:— daub, befoul, be red, trouble.

2561. חֶמֶר **chemer**, *kheh´-mer;* from 2560; *wine* (as *fermenting*):— × pure, red wine.

2562. חֲמַר **chămar** (Chald.), *kham-ar´;* corresp. to 2561; *wine:*— wine.

חֲמֹר **chămôr**. See 2543.

2563. חֹמֶר **chômer**, *kho´mer;* from 2560; prop. a *bubbling* up, i.e. of water, a *wave;* of earth, *mire* or *clay* (cement); also a *heap;* hence, a *chomer* or dry measure:— clay, heap, homer, mire, motion, mortar.

2564. חֵמָר **chêmâr**, *khay-mawr´;* from 2560; *bitumen* (as *rising* to the surface):— slime (-pit).

2565. חֲמֹרָה **chămôrâh**, *kham-o-raw´;* from 2560 [comp. 2563]; a *heap:*— heap.

2566. חַמְרָן **Chamrân**, *kham-rawn´;* from 2560; *red; Chamran,* an Idumæan:— Amran.

2567. חָמַשׁ **châmash**, *khaw-mash´;* a denom. from 2568; to *tax a fifth:*— take up the fifth part.

2568. חָמֵשׁ **châmêsh**, *khaw-maysh´;* masc.

חֲמִשָּׁה **chămishshâh**, *kham-ish-shaw´;* a prim. numeral; *five:*— fifteenl, fifth, five (× apiece).

2569. חֹמֶשׁ **chômesh**, *kho´-mesh;* from 2567; a *fifth* tax:— fifth part.

2570. חֹמֶשׁ **chômesh**, *kho´-mesh;* from an unused root prob. mean. to *be stout;* the *abdomen* (as *obese*):— fifth [rib].

2571. חָמֻשׁ **châmûsh**, *khaw-moosh´;* pass. part. of the same as 2570;

staunch, i.e. able-bodied *soldiers:*— armed (men), harnessed.

חֲמִשָּׁה **chămishshâh**. See 2568.

חֲמִשִּׁי **chămishshîy**. See 2549.

2572. חֲמִשִּׁים **chămishshîym**, *kham-ish-sheem´;* multiple of 2568; *fifty:*— fifty.

2573. חֵמֶת **chêmeth**, *khay´-meth;* from the same as 2346; a skin *bottle* (as *tied* up):— bottle.

2574. חֲמָת **Chămâth**, *kham-awth´;* from the same as 2346; *walled; Chamath,* a place in Syria:— Hamath, Hemath.

חֲמֹת **chămôth**. See 2545.

2575. חַמַּת **Chammath**, *kham-math´;* a var. for the first part of 2576; *hot springs; Chammath,* a place in Pal.:— Hammath.

2576. חַמֹּת דֹּאר **Chammôth Dô'r**, *kham-moth´ dore;* from the plur. of 2535 and 1756; *hot springs of Dor; Chammath-Dor,* a place in Pal.:— Hamath-Dor.

2577. חֲמָתִי **Chămâthîy**, *kham-aw-thee´;* patrial from 2574; a *Chamathite* or native of *Chamath:*— Hamathite.

2578. חֲמָת צוֹבָה **Chămath Tsôwbâh**, *kham-ath´ tso-baw´;* from 2574 and 6678; *Chamath of Tsobah; Chamath-Tsobah;* prob. the same as 2574:— Hamath-Zobah.

2579. חֲמָת רַבָּה **Chămath Rabbâh**, *kham-ath´ rab-baw´;* from 2574 and 7237; *Chamath of Rabbah; Chamath-Rabbah,* prob. the same as 2574.

2580. חֵן **chên**, *khane;* from 2603; *graciousness,* i.e. subj. (*kindness, favor*) or obj. (*beauty*):— favour, grace (-ious), pleasant, precious, [well-] favoured.

2581. חֵן **Chên**, *khane;* the same as 2580; *grace; Chen,* a fig. name for an Isr.:— Hen.

2582. חֵנָדָד **Chênâdâd**, *khay-naw-dawd´;* prob. from 2580 and 1908; *favor of Hadad; Chenadad,* an Isr.:— Henadad.

2583. חָנָה **chânâh**, *khaw-naw´;* a prim. root [comp. 2603]; prop. to *incline;* by impl. to *decline* (of the slanting rays of evening); spec. to *pitch* a tent; gen. to *encamp* (for abode or siege):— abide (in tents), camp, dwell, encamp, grow to an end, lie, pitch (tent), rest in tent.

2584. חַנָּה **Channâh**, *khan-naw´;* from 2603; *favored; Channah,* an Israelitess:— Hannah.

2585. חֲנוֹךְ **Chănôwk**, *khan-oke´;* from 2596; *initiated; Chanok,* an antediluvian patriarch:— Enoch.

2586. חָנוּן **Chânûwn**, *khaw-noon´;* from 2603; *favored; Chanun,* the name of an Ammonite and of two Isr.:— Hanun.

2587. חַנּוּן **channûwn**, *khan-noon´;* from 2603; *gracious:*— gracious.

2588. חָנוּת **chânûwth**, *khaw-nooth´;* from 2583; prop. a *vault* or *cell* (with an arch); by impl. a *prison:*— cabin.

2589. חַנּוֹת **channôwth**, *khan-nôth´;* from 2603 (in the sense of *prayer*); *supplication:*— be gracious, intreated.

2590. חָנַט **chânaṭ**, *khaw-nat´;* a prim. root; to *spice;* by impl. to *embalm;* also to *ripen:*— embalm, put forth.

2591. חִנְטָא **chinṭâ'** (Chald.), *khint-taw´;* corresp. to 2406; *wheat:*— wheat.

2592. חַנִּיאֵל **Channîy'êl**, *khan-nee-ale´;* from 2603 and 410; *favor of God; Channiel,* the name of two Isr.:— Hanniel.

2593. חָנִיךְ **chânîyk**, *kaw-neek´;* from 2596; *initiated;* i.e. *practiced:*— trained.

2594. חֲנִינָה **chănîynâh**, *khan-ee-naw´;* from 2603; *graciousness:*— favour.

2595. חֲנִית **chănîyth**, *khan-eeth´;* from 2583; a *lance* (for *thrusting,* like *pitching* a tent):— javelin, spear.

2596. חָנַךְ **chânak**, *khaw-nak´;* a prim. root; prop. to *narrow* (comp. 2614); fig. to *initiate* or *discipline:*— dedicate, train up.

2597. חֲנֻכָּא **chănukkâ'** (Chald.), *chan-ook-kaw´;* corresp. to 2598; *consecration:*— dedication.

2598. חֲנֻכָּה **chănukkâh**, *khan-ook-kaw´;* from 2596; *initiation,* i.e. *consecration:*— dedicating (-tion).

2599. חֲנֹכִי **Chănôkîy**, *khan-o-kee´;* patron. from 2585; a *Chanokite* (collect.) or desc. of Chanok:— Hanochites.

2600. חִנָּם **chinnâm**, *khin-nawm´;* from 2580; *gratis,* i.e. devoid of cost, reason or advantage:— without a cause (cost, wages), causeless, to cost nothing, free (-ly), innocent, for nothing (nought), in vain.

2601. חֲנַמְאֵל **Chănam'êl**, *khan-am-ale´;* prob. by orth. var. for 2606; *Chanamel,* an Isr.:— Hanameel.

2602. חֲנָמָל **chănâmâl**, *khan-aw-mawl´;* of uncert. der.; perh. the *aphis* or plant-louse:— frost.

2603. חָנַן **chânan**, *khaw-nan´;* a prim. root [comp. 2583]; prop. to *bend* or *stoop* in kindness to an inferior; to *favor, bestow;* caus. to *implore* (i.e. move to favor by petition):— beseech, × fair, (be, find, shew) favour (-able), be (deal, give, grant (gracious -ly), intreat, (be) merciful, have (shew) mercy (on, upon), have pity upon, pray, make supplication, × very.

2604. חֲנַן **chănan** (Chald.), *khan-an´;* corresp. to 2603; to *favor* or (caus.) to *entreat:*— shew mercy, make supplication.

2605. חָנָן **Chânân**, *khaw-nawn´;* from 2603; *favor; Chanan,* the name of seven Isr.:— Canan.

2606. חֲנַנְאֵל **Chănan'êl**, *khan-an-ale´;* from 2603 and 410; *God has favored; Chananel,* prob. an Isr., from whom a tower of Jerusalem was named:— Hananeel.

2607. חֲנָנִי **Chănânîy**, *khan-aw-nee´;* from 2603; *gracious; Chanani,* the name of six Isr.:— Hanani.

2608. חֲנַנְיָה **Chănanyâh**, *khan-an-yaw´;* or

חֲנַנְיָהוּ **Chănanyâhûw**, *khan-an-yaw´-hoo;* from 2603 and 3050; *Jah has favored; Chananjah,* the name of thirteen Isr.:— Hananiah.

2609. חָנֵס **Chânêç**, *khaw-nace´;* of Eg. der.; *Chanes,* a place in Egypt:— Hanes.

2610. חָנֵף **chânêph**, *khaw-nafe´;* a prim.

root; to *soil*, espec. in a mor. sense:— corrupt, defile, × greatly, pollute, profane.

2611. חָנֵף **chânêph**, *khaw-nafe´;* from 2610; *soiled* (i.e. with sin), *impious:*— hypocrite (-ical).

2612. חֹנֶף **chôneph**, *kho´-nef;* from 2610; *moral filth,* i.e. *wickedness:*— hypocrisy.

2613. חֲנֻפָּה **chănûphâh**, *khan-oo-faw´;* fem. from 2610; *impiety:*— profaneness.

2614. חָנַק **chânaq**, *khaw-nak´;* a prim. root [comp. 2596]; to *be narrow;* by impl. to *throttle,* or (reflex.) to *choke* oneself to death (by a rope):— hang self, strangle.

2615. חַנָּתֹן **Channâthôn**, *khan-naw-thone´;* prob. from 2603; *favored; Channathon,* a place in Pal.:— Hannathon.

2616. חָסַד **châçad**, *khaw-sad´;* a prim. root; prop. perh. to *bow* (the neck only [comp. 2603] in courtesy to an equal), i.e. to *be kind;* also (by euphem. [comp. 1288], but rarely) to *reprove:*— shew self merciful, put to shame.

2617. חֶסֶד **cheçed**, *kheh´-sed;* from 2616; *kindness;* by impl. (toward God) *piety;* rarely (by opposition) *reproof,* or (subj.) *beauty:*— favour, good deed (-liness, -ness), kindly, (loving-) kindness, merciful (kindness), mercy, pity, reproach, wicked thing.

2618. חֶסֶד **Cheçed**, *kheh´-sed;* the same as 2617: *favor; Chesed,* an Isr.:— Hesed.

2619. חֲסַדְיָה **Chăçadyâh**, *khas-ad-yaw´;* from 2617 and 3050; *Jah has favored; Chasadjâh,* an Isr.:— Hasadiah.

2620. חָסָה **châçâh**, *khaw-saw´;* a prim. root; to *flee* for protection [comp. 982]; fig. to *confide* in:— have hope, make refuge, (put) trust.

2621. חֹסָה **Chôçâh**, *kho-saw´;* from 2620; *hopeful; Chosah,* an Isr.; also a place in Pal.:— Hosah.

2622. חָסוּת **châçûwth**, *khaw-sooth´;* from 2620; *confidence:*— trust.

2623. חָסִיד **châçîyd**, *khaw-seed´;* from 2616; prop. *kind,* i.e. (relig.) *pious* (a saint):— godly (man), good, holy (one), merciful, saint, [un-] godly.

2624. חֲסִידָה **chăçîydâh**, *khas-ee-daw´;* fem. of 2623; the *kind* (maternal) bird, i.e. a *stork:*— × feather, stork.

2625. חָסִיל **chaçîyl**, *khaw-seel´;* from 2628; the *ravager,* i.e. a *locust:*— caterpillar.

2626. חָסִין **chăçîyn**, *khas-een´;* from 2630; prop. *firm,* i.e. (by impl.) *mighty:*— strong.

2627. חַסִּיר **chaççîyr** (Chald.), *khas-seer´;* from a root corresp. to 2637; *deficient:*— wanting.

2628. חָסַל **châçal**, *khaw-sal´;* a prim. root; to *eat off:*— consume.

2629. חָסַם **châçam**, *khaw-sam´;* a prim. root; to *muzzle;* by anal. to *stop* the nose:— muzzle, stop.

2630. חָסַן **châçan**, *khaw-san´;* a prim. root; prop. to (be) *compact;* by impl. to *hoard:*— lay up.

2631. חֲסַן **chăçan** (Chald.), *khas-an´;*

corresp. to 2630; to *hold* in occupancy:— possess.

2632. חֵסֶן **chêçen** (Chald.), *khay´-sen;* from 2631; *strength:*— power.

2633. חֹסֶן **chôçen**, *kho´-sen;* from 2630; *wealth:*— riches, strength, treasure.

2634. חָסֹן **châçôn**, *khaw-sone´;* from 2630; *powerful:*— strong.

2635. חֲסַף **chăçaph** (Chald.), *khas-af´;* from a root corresp. to that of 2636; a *clod:*— clay.

2636. חַסְפַּס **chaçpaç**, *khas-pas´;* redupl. from an unused root mean. appar. to *peel; a shred* or *scale:*— round thing.

2637. חָסֵר **châçêr**, *khaw-sare´;* a prim. root; to *lack;* by impl. to *fail, want, lessen:*— be abated, bereave, decrease, (cause to) fail, (have) lack, make lower, want.

2638. חָסֵר **châçêr**, *khaw-sare´;* from 2637; *lacking;* hence, *without:*— destitute, fail, lack, have need, void, want.

2639. חֶסֶר **cheçer**, *kheh´-ler;* from 2637; *lack;* hence, *destitution:*— poverty, want.

2640. חֹסֶר **chôçer**, *kho´-ser;* from 2637; *poverty:*— in want of.

2641. חַסְרָה **Chaçrâh**, *khas-raw´;* from 2637; *want; Chasrah,* an Isr.:— Hasrah.

2642. חֶסְרוֹן **cheçrôwn**, *khes-rone´;* from 2637; *deficiency:*— wanting.

2643. חַף **chaph**, *khaf;* from 2653 (in the mor. sense of *covered* from soil); *pure:*— innocent.

2644. חָפָא **châphâ'**, *khaw-faw´;* an orth. var. of 2645; prop. to *cover,* i.e. (in a sinister sense) to *act covertly:*— do secretly.

2645. חָפָה **châphâh**, *khaw-faw´;* a prim. root (comp. 2644, 2653); to *cover;* by impl. to *veil,* to *incase, protect:*— ceil, cover, overlay.

2646. חֻפָּה **chuppâh**, *khoop-paw´;* from 2645; a *canopy:*— chamber, closet, defence.

2647. חֻפָּה **Chuppâh**, *khoop-paw´;* the same as 2646; *Chuppah,* an Isr.:— Huppah.

2648. חָפַז **châphaz**, *khaw-faz´;* a prim. root; prop. to *start* up suddenly, i.e. (by impl.) to *hasten* away, to *fear:*— (make) haste (away), tremble.

2649. חִפָּזוֹן **chippâzôwn**, *khip-paw-zone´;* from 2648; *hasty flight:*— haste.

2650. חֻפִּים **Chuppîym**, *khoop-peem´;* plur. of 2646 [comp. 2349]; *Chuppim,* an Isr.:— Huppim.

2651. חֹפֶן **chôphen**, *kho-fen;* from an unused root of uncert. signif.; a *fist* (only in the dual):— fists, (both) hands, hand (-ful).

2652. חָפְנִי **Chophnîy**, *khof-nee´;* from 2651; perh. *pugilist; Chophni,* an Isr.:— Hophni.

2653. חָפַף **chôphaph**, *khof-faf´;* a prim. root (comp. 2645, 3182); to *cover* (in protection):— cover.

2654. חָפֵץ **châphêts**, *khaw-fates´;* a prim. root; prop. to *incline* to; by impl. (lit. but rarely) to *bend;* fig. to *be pleased* with, *desire:*— × any at all,

(have, take) delight, desire, favour, like, move, be (well) pleased, have pleasure, will, would.

2655. חָפֵץ **châphêts**, *khaw-fates´;* from 2654; *pleased* with:— delight in, desire, favour, please, have pleasure, whosoever would, willing, wish.

2656. חֵפֶץ **chêphets**, *khay´-fets;* from 2654; *pleasure;* hence, (abstr.) *desire;* concr. a *valuable* thing; hence, (by extens.) a *matter* (as something in mind):— acceptable, delight (-some), desire, things desired, matter, pleasant (-ure), purpose, willingly.

2657. חֶפְצִי בָהּ **Chephtsîy bâhh**, *kheftsee´-baw;* from 2656 with suffixes; *my delight* (is) *in her; Cheptsi-bah,* a fanciful name for Pal.:— Hephzi-bah.

2658. חָפַר **châphar**, *khaw-far´;* a prim. root; prop. to *pry* into; by impl. to *delve,* to *explore:*— dig, paw, search out, seek.

2659. חָפֵר **châphêr**, *khaw-fare´;* a prim. root [perhaps rath. the same as 2658 through the idea of *detection*]: to *blush;* fig. to *be ashamed, disappointed;* caus. to *shame, reproach:*— be ashamed, be confounded, be brought to confusion (unto shame), come (be put to) shame, bring reproach.

2660. חֵפֶר **Chêpher**, *khay´-fer;* from 2658 or 2659; a *pit* or *shame; Chepher,* a place in Pal.; also the name of three Isr.:— Hepher.

2661. חֲפֹר **chăphôr**, *khaf-ore´;* from 2658; a *hole;* only in connection with 6512, which ought rather to be joined as one word, thus

חֲפַרְפֵּרָה **chăpharpêrâh**, *khaf-ar-pay-raw´;* by redupl. from 2658; a *burrower,* i.e. prob. a *rat:*— + mole.

2662. חֶפְרִי **Chephrîy**, *khef-ree´;* patron. from 2660; a *Chephrite* (collect.) or desc. of *Chepher:*— Hepherites.

2663. חֲפָרַיִם **Chăphârayim**, *khaf-aw-rah´-yim;* dual of 2660; *double pit; Chapharajim,* a place in Pal.:— Haphraim.

חֲפַרְפֵּרָה **chăpharpêrâh.** See 2661.

2664. חָפַשׂ **châphas**, *khaw-fas´;* a prim. root; to *seek;* caus. to *conceal* oneself (i.e. let be sought), or *mask:*— change, (make) diligent (search), disguise self, hide, search (for, out).

2665. חֵפֶשׂ **chêphes**, *khay´-fes;* from 2664; something *covert,* i.e. a *trick:*— search.

2666. חָפַשׁ **châphash**, *khaw-fash´;* a prim. root; to *spread* loose; fig. to *manumit:*— be free.

2667. חֹפֶשׁ **chôphesh**, *kho´-fesh;* from 2666; something *spread* loosely, i.e. a *carpet:*— precious.

2668. חֻפְשָׁה **chuphshâh**, *khoof-shaw´;* from 2666; *liberty* (from slavery):— freedom.

2669. חָפְשׁוּת **chôphshûwth**, *khof-shooth´;* and

חָפְשִׁית **chophshîyth**, *khof-sheeth´;* from 2666; *prostration* by sickness (with 1004, a *hospital*):— several.

2670. חָפְשִׁי **chophshîy**, *khof-shee´;* from 2666; *exempt* (from bondage, tax or care):— free, liberty.

2671. חֵץ **chêts,** *khayts;* from 2686; prop. a *piercer,* i.e. an *arrow;* by impl. a *wound;* fig. (of God) thunder-*bolt;* (by interchange for 6086) the *shaft* of a spear:— + archer, arrow, dart, shaft, staff, wound.

חֵץ **chûts.** See 2351.

2672. חָצַב **châtsab,** *khaw-tsab´;* or

חָצֵב **châtsêb,** *khaw-tsabe´;* a prim. root; to *cut* or *carve* (wood), stone or other material); by impl. to *hew, split, square, quarry, engrave:*— cut, dig, divide, grave, hew (out, -er), make, mason.

2673. חָצָה **châtsâh,** *khaw-tsaw´;* a prim. root lcomp. 2686l); to *cut* or *split* in two; to *halve:*— divide, × live out half, reach to the midst. part.

2674. חָצוֹר **Châtsôwr,** *khaw-tsore´;* a collect. form of 2691; *village; Chatsor,* the name (thus simply) of two places in Pal. and of one in Arabia:— Hazor.

2675. חֲצוֹר חֲדַתָּה **Châtsôwr Chădattâh,** *khaw-tsore´ khad-at-taw´;* from 2674 and a Chaldaizing form of the fem. of 2319 lcomp. 2323l; *new Chatsor,* a place in Pal.:— Hazor, Hadattah las if two placesl.

2676. חָצוֹת **châtsôwth,** *khaw-tsoth´;* from 2673; the *middle* (of the night):— mid l-nightl.

2677. חֵצִי **chêtsîy,** *khay-tsee´;* from 2673; the *half* or *middle:*— half, middle, mid l-nightl, midst, part, two parts.

2678. חִצִּי **chitstsîy,** *khits-tsee´;* or

חֵצִי **chêtsîy,** *khay-tsee´;* prol. from 2671; an *arrow:*— arrow.

2679. חֲצִי הַמְּנֻחוֹת **Châtsîy ham-Menûchôwth,** *chat-tsee´ ham-men-oo-khoth´;* from 2677 and the plur. of 4496, with the art. interposed; *midst of the resting-places; Chatsi-ham-Menuchoth,* an Isr.:— half of the Manahethites.

2680. חֲצִי הַמְּנַחְתִּי **Châtsîy ham-Menachtîy,** *khat-see´ ham-men-akh-tee´;* patron. from 2679; a *Chatsi-ham-Menachtite* or desc. of Chatsi-ham-Menuchoth:— half of the Manahethites.

2681. חָצִיר **châtsîyr,** *khaw-tseer´;* a collat. form of 2691; a *court* or *abode:*— court.

2682. חָצִיר **châtsîyr,** *khaw-tseer´;* perh. orig. the same as 2681, from the *greenness* of a courtyard; *grass;* also a *leek* (collect.):— grass, hay, herb, leek.

2683. חֵצֶן **chêtsen,** *khay´-tsen;* from an unused root mean. to hold *firmly;* the *bosom* (as *comprised* between the arms):— bosom.

2684. חֹצֶן **chôtsen,** *kho´tsen;* a collat. form of 2683, and mean. the same:— arm, lap.

2685. חֲצַף **chătsaph** (Chald.), *khats-af´;* a prim. root; prop. to *shear* or cut close; fig. to *be severe:*— hasty, be urgent.

2686. חָצַץ **châtsats,** *khaw-tsats´;* a prim. root lcomp. 2673l; prop. to *chop* into, pierce or sever; hence, to *curtail,* to *distribute* (into ranks); as denom. from 2671, to *shoot* an arrow:— archer, × bands, cut off in the midst.

2687. חָצָץ **châtsâts,** *khaw-tsawts´;* from 2687; prop. something *cutting;* hence, *gravel* (as grit); also (like 2671) an *arrow:*— arrow, gravel (stone).

2688. חַצְצוֹן תָּמָר **Chatsetsôwn Tâmâr,** *khats-ets-one´ taw-mawr´;* or

חַצְצֹן תָּמָר **Chatsätsôn Tâmâr,** *khats-ats-one´ taw-mawr´;* from 2686 and 8558; *division* l i.e. perh. *rowl of* (the) *palm-tree; Chatsetson-tamar,* a place in Pal.:— Hazezon-tamar.

2689. חֲצֹצְרָה **châtsôtserâh,** *khats-o-tser-aw´;* by redupl. from 2690; a *trumpet* (from its *sundered* or quavering note):— trumpet (-er).

2690. חָצַר **châtsar,** *khaw-tsar´;* a prim. root; prop. to *surround* with a stockade, and thus *separate* from the open country; but used only in the redupl. form

חֲצֹצֵר **châtsôtsêr,** *khast-o-tsare´;* or (2 Chron. 5:12)

חֲצֹרֵר **châtsôrêr,** *khats-o-rare´;* as denom. from 2689; to *trumpet,* i.e. blow on that instrument:— blow, sound, trumpeter.

2691. חָצֵר **châtsêr,** *khaw-tsare´* (masc. and fem.); from 2690 in its orig. sense; a *yard* (as *inclosed* by a fence); also a *hamlet* (as similarly *surrounded* with walls):— court, tower, village.

2692. חֲצַר אַדָּר **Chătsar 'Addâr,** *khats-ar´ addawr´;* from 2691 and 146; (the) *village of Addar; Chatsar-Addar,* a place in Pal.:— Hazar-addar.

2693. חֲצַר גַּדָּה **Chătsar Gaddâh,** *khats-ar´ gad-daw´;* from 2691 and a fem. of 1408; (the) *village of* (female) *Fortune; Chatsar-Gaddah,* a place in Pal.:— Hazar-gaddah.

2694. חֲצַר הַתִּיכוֹן **Chătsar hat-Tîykôwn,** *khats-ar´ hat-tee-kone´;* from 2691 and 8484 with the art. interposed; *village of the middle; Chatsar-hat-Tikon,* a place in Pal.:— Hazar-hatticon.

2695. חֶצְרוֹ **Chetsrôw,** *khets-ro´;* by an orth. var. for 2696; *inclosure; Chetsro,* an Isr.:— Hezro, Hezrai.

2696. חֶצְרוֹן **Chetsrôwn,** *khets-rone´;* from 269l; *court-yard; Chetsron,* the name of a place in Pal.; also of two Isr.:— Hezron.

2697. חֶצְרוֹנִי **Chetsrôwnîy,** *khets-ro-nee´;* patron. from 2696; a *Chetsronite* or (collect.) desc. of Chetsron:— Hezronites.

2698. חֲצֵרוֹת **Chătsêrowth,** *khats-ay-roth´;* fem. plur. of 2691; *yards; Chatseroth,* a place in Pal.:— Hazeroth.

2699. חֲצֵרִים **Chătsêrîym,** *khats-ay-reem´;* plur. masc. of 2691; *yards; Chatserim,* a place in Pal.:— Hazerim.

2700. חֲצַרְמָוֶת **Chătsarmâveth,** *khats-ar-maw´-veth;* from 2691 and 4194; *village of death; Chatsarmaveth,* a place in Arabia:— Hazarmaveth.

2701. חֲצַר סוּסָה **Chătsar Çûwçâh,** *khats-ar´ soo-saw´;* from 2691 and 5484; *village of cavalry; Chatsar-Susah,* a place in Pal.:— Hazar-susah.

2702. חֲצַר סוּסִים **Chătsar Çûwçîym,** *khats-ar´ soo-seem´;* from 2691 and the

plur. of 5483; *village of horses; Chatsar-Susim,* a place in Pal.:— Hazar-susim.

2703. חֲצַר עֵינוֹן **Chătsar 'Êynôwn,** *khats-ar´ ay-nōne´;* from 2691 and a der. of 5869; *village of springs; Chatsar-Enon,* a place in Pal.:— Hazar-enon.

2704. חֲצַר עֵינָן **Chătsar 'Êynân,** *khats-ar´ ay-nawn´;* from 2691 and the same as 5881; *village of springs; Chatsar-Enan,* a place in Pal.:— Hazar-enan.

2705. חֲצַר שׁוּעָל **Chătsar Shûw'âl,** *khats-ar´ shoo-awl´;* from 2691 and 7776; *village of* (the) *fox; Chatsar-Shual,* a place in Pal.:— Hazar-shual.

חֵק **chêq.** See 2436.

2706. חֹק **chôq,** *khoke;* from 2710; an *enactment;* hence, an *appointment* (of time, space, quantity, labor or usage):— appointed, bound, commandment, convenient, custom, decree (-d), due, law, measure, × necessary, ordinance (-nary), portion, set time. statute, task.

2707. חָקָה **châqah,** *khaw-kaw´;* a prim. root; to *carve;* by impl. to *delineate;* also to *intrench:*— carved work, portrayed, set a print.

2708. חֻקָּה **chuqqâh,** *khook-kaw´;* fem. of 2706, and mean. substantially the same:— appointed, custom, manner, ordinance, site, statute.

2709. חֲקוּפָא **Chăqûwphâ',** *khak-oo-faw´;* from an unused root prob. mean. to *bend; crooked; Chakupha,* one of the Nethinim:— Hakupha.

2710. חָקַק **châqaq,** *khaw-kak´;* a prim. root; prop. to *hack,* i.e. *engrave* (Judg. 5:14, to *be a scribe* simply); by impl. to *enact* (laws being *cut* in stone or metal tablets in primitive times) or (gen.) *prescribe:*— appoint, decree, governor, grave, lawgiver, note, pourtray, print, set.

2711. חֵקֶק **chêqeq,** *khay´-kek;* from 2710; an *enactment,* a *resolution:*— decree, thought.

2712. חֻקֹּק **Chuqqôq,** *Khook-koke´;* or (fully)

חוּקֹק **Chûwqôq,** *khoo-koke´;* from 2710; *appointed; Chukkok* or *Chukok,* a place in Pal.:— Hukkok, Hukok.

2713. חָקַר **châqar,** *khaw-kar´;* a prim. root; prop. to *penetrate;* hence, to *examine* intimately:— find out, (make) search (out), seek (out), sound, try.

2714. חֵקֶר **chêqer,** *khay´-ker;* from 2713; *examination, enumeration, deliberation:*— finding out, number, lun-l search (-able, -ed, out, -ing).

2715. חֹר **chôr,** *khore;* or (fully)

חוֹר **chôwr,** *khore;* from 2787; prop. *white* or *pure* (from the *cleansing* or *shining* power of fire lcomp. 2751l; hence, (fig.) *noble* (in rank):— noble.

חוּר **chûr.** See 2352.

2716. חֱרֵא **chere',** *kheh´-reh;* from an unused (and vulgar) root prob. mean. to *evacuate* the bowels: *excrement:*— dung. Also

חֲרִי° **chărîy,** *khar-ee´.*

2717. חָרַב **chârab,** *khaw-rab´;* or

חֲרֵב **chârêb,** *khaw-rabe´;* a prim.

root; to *parch* (through drought) i.e. (by anal.) to *desolate, destroy, kill:*— decay, (be) desolate, destroy (-er), (be) dry (up), slay, × surely, (lay, lie, make) waste.

2718. חֲרַב **chărab** (Chald.), *khar-ab´*; a root corresp. to 2717; to *demolish:*— destroy.

2719. חֶרֶב **chereb**, *kheh´-reb*; from 2717; *drought;* also a *cutting* instrument (from its *destructive* effect), as a *knife, sword,* or other sharp implement:— axe, dagger, knife, mattock, sword, tool.

2720. חָרֵב **chârêb**, *khaw-rabe´*; from 2717; *parched* or *ruined:*— desolate, dry, waste.

2721. חֹרֶב **chôreb**, *kho´-reb*; a collat. form of 2719; *drought* or *desolation:*— desolation, drought, dry, heat, × utterly, waste.

2722. חֹרֵב **Chôrêb**, *kho-rabe´*; from 2717; *desolate*; *Choreb*, a (gen.) name for the Sinaitic mountains:— Horeb.

2723. חָרְבָּה **chorbâh**, *khor-baw´*; fem. of 2721; *prop. drought*, i.e. (by impl.) a *desolation:*— decayed place, desolate (place, -tion), destruction, (laid) waste (place).

2724. חָרָבָה **chârâbâh**, *khaw-raw-baw´*; fem. of 2720; a *desert:*— dry (ground, land).

2725. חֲרָבוֹן **chărâbôwn**, *khar-aw-bone´*; from 2717; *parching heat:*— drought.

2726. חַרְבוֹנָא **Charbôwnâ'**, *khar-bo-naw´*; or

חַרְבוֹנָה **Charbôwnâh**, *khar-bo-naw´*; of Pers. or.; *Charbona* or *Charbonah*, a eunuch of Xerxes:— Harbona, Harbonah.

2727. חָרַג **chârag**, *khaw-rag´*; a prim. root; prop. to *leap* suddenly, i.e. (by impl.) to *be dismayed:*— be afraid.

2728. חַרְגֹּל **chargôl**, *khar-gole´*; from 2727; the *leaping* insect, i.e. a *locust:*— beetle.

2729. חָרַד **chârad**, *khaw-rad´*; a prim. root; to *shudder* with terror; hence, to *fear*; also to *hasten* (with anxiety):— be (make) afraid, be careful, discomfit, fray (away), quake, tremble.

2730. חָרֵד **chârêd**, *khaw-rade´*; from 2729; *fearful*; also *reverential:*— afraid, trembling.

2731. חֲרָדָה **chărâdâh**, *khar-aw-daw´*; fem. of 2730; *fear, anxiety:*— care, × exceedingly, fear, quaking, trembling.

2732. חֲרָדָה **Chărâdâh**, *khar-aw-daw´*; the same as 2731; *Charadah*, a place in the Desert:— Haradah.

2733. חֲרֹדִי **Chărôdiy**, *khar-o-dee´*; patrial from a der. of 2729 [comp. 5878]; a *Charodite*, or inhab. of *Charod:*— Harodite.

2734. חָרָה **chârâh**, *khaw-raw´*; a prim. root [comp. 2787]; to *glow* or grow warm; fig. (usually) to *blaze* up, of anger, zeal, jealousy:— be angry, burn, be displeased, × earnestly, fret self, grieve, be (wax) hot, be incensed, kindle, × very, be wroth. See 8474.

2735. חֹר הַגִּדְגָּד **Chôr hag-Gidgâd**, *khore hag-ghid-gawd´*; from 2356 and a col-

lat. (masc.) form of 1412, with the art. interposed; *hole of the cleft; Chor-hag-Gidgad*, a place in the Desert:— Hor-hagidgad.

2736. חֲרַהְיָה **Charhăyâh**, *khar-hah-yaw´*; from 2734 and 3050; *fearing Jah*; *Charhajah*, an Isr.:— Harhaiah.

2737. חָרוּז **chârûwz**, *khaw-rooz´*; from an unused root mean. to *perforate*; prop. *pierced*, i.e. a *bead* of pearl, gems or jewels (as strung):— chain.

2738. חָרוּל **chârûwl**, *khaw-rool´*; or (short.)

חָרֻל **chârûl**, *khaw-rool´*; appar. a pass. part. of an unused root prob. mean. to *be prickly*; prop. *pointed*, i.e. a *bramble* or other thorny weed:— nettle.

חָרוֹן **chôrôwn**. See 1032, 2772.

2739. חֲרוּמַף **Chărûwmaph**, *khar-oo-maf´*; from pass. part. of 2763 and 639; *snub-nosed*; *Charumaph*, an Isr.:— Harumaph.

2740. חָרוֹן **chârôwn**, *khaw-rone´*; or (short.)

חָרֹן **chârôn**, *khaw-rone´*; from 2734; a *burning* of anger:— sore displeasure, fierce (-ness), fury, (fierce) wrath (-ful).

2741. חֲרוּפִי **Chărûwphiy**, *khar-oo-fee´*; a patrial from (prob.) a collat. form of 2756; a *Charuphite* or inhab. of Charuph (or Chariph):— Haruphite.

2742. חָרוּץ **chârûwts**, *khaw-roots´*; or

חָרֻץ **chârûts**, *khaw-roots´*; pass. part. of 2782; prop. *incised* or (act.) *incisive*; hence, (as noun masc. or fem.) a *trench* (as dug), *gold* (as mined), a *threshing-sledge* (having sharp teeth); (fig.) *determination*; also *eager:*— decision, diligent, (fine) gold, pointed things, sharp, threshing instrument, wall.

2743. חָרוּץ **Chârûwts**, *khaw-roots´*; the same as 2742; *earnest*; *Charuts*, an Isr.:— Haruz.

2744. חַרְחוּר **Charchûwr**, *khar-khoor´*; a fuller form of 2746; *inflammation*; *Charchur*, one of the Nethinim:— Harhur.

2745. חַרְחַס **Charchaṣ**, *khar-khas´*; from the same as 2775; perh. *shining*; *Charchas*, an Isr.:— Harhas.

2746. חַרְחֻר **charchûr**, *khar-khoor´*; from 2787; *fever* (as *hot*):— extreme burning.

2747. חֶרֶט **cheret**, *kheh´-ret*; from a prim. root mean. to *engrave*; a *chisel* or *graver*; also a *style* for writing:— graving tool, pen.

חָרִט **chârit**. See 2754.

2748. חַרְטֹם **chartôm**, *khar-tome´*; from the same as 2747; a *horoscopist* (as *drawing* magical lines or circles):— magician.

2749. חַרְטֹם **chartôm** (Chald.), *khar-tome´*; the same as 2748:— magician.

2750. חֳרִי **chŏriy**, *khor-ee´*; from 2734; a *burning* (i.e. intense) anger:— fierce, × great, heat.

חֳרִי° **chăriy**. See 2716.

2751. חֹרִי **chôriy**, *kho-ree´*; from the same as 2353; *white* bread:— white.

2752. חֹרִי **Chôriy**, *kho-ree´*; from 2356; *cave-dweller* or troglodyte; a *Chorite* or aboriginal Idumæan:— Horims, Horites.

2753. חֹרִי **Chôriy**, *kho-ree´*; or

חוֹרִי **Chôwriy**, *kho-ree´*; the same as 2752; *Chori*, the name of two men:— Hori.

2754. חָרִיט **chârîyt**, *khaw-reet´*; or

חָרִט **chârit**, *khaw-reet´*; from the same as 2747; prop. *cut* out (or *hollow*), i.e. (by impl.) a *pocket:*— bag, crisping pin.

2755. חֲרִי־יוֹנִים **chărêy-yôwnîym**, *khar-ay´-yo-neem´*; from the plur. of 2716 and the plur. of 3123; *excrements of doves* [or perh. rather the plur. of a single word

חֲרָאיוֹן **chârâ'yôwn**, *khar-aw-yone´*] of similar or uncert. deriv.], prob. a kind of *vegetable:*— doves' dung.

2756. חָרִיף **Chârîyph**, *khaw-reef´*; from 2778; *autumnal*; *Chariph*, the name of two Isr.:— Hariph.

2757. חָרִיץ **chârîyts**, *khaw-reets´*; or

חָרִץ **chârits**, *khaw-reets´*; from 2782; prop. *incisure* or (pass.) *incised* [comp. 2742]; hence, a *threshing-sledge* (with *sharp* teeth): also a *slice* (as cut):— + cheese, harrow.

2758. חָרִישׁ **chârîysh**, *khaw-reesh´*; from 2790; *plowing* or its season:— earing (time), ground.

2759. חֲרִישִׁי **chărîyshiy**, *khar-ee-shee´*; from 2790 in the sense of *silence; quiet*, i.e. *sultry* (as fem. noun, the *sirocco* or hot east wind):— vehement.

2760. חָרַךְ **chârak**, *khaw-rak´*; a prim. root; to *braid* (i.e. to *entangle* or snare) or *catch* (game) in a net:— roast.

2761. חֲרַךְ **chărak** (Chald.), *khar-ak´*; a root prob. allied to the equiv. of 2787; to *scorch:*— singe.

2762. חֶרֶךְ **cherek**, *kheh´-rek*; from 2760; prop. a *net*, i.e. (by anal.) *lattice:*— lattice.

חָרֻל **chârûl**. See 2738.

2763. חָרַם **charam**, *khaw-ram´*; a prim. root; to *seclude*; spec. (by a ban) to *devote* to relig. uses (espec. destruction); phys. and refl. to be *blunt* as to the nose:— make accursed, consecrate, (utterly) destroy, devote, forfeit, have a flat nose, utterly (slay, make away).

2764. חֵרֶם **chêrem**, *khay´-rem*; or (Zech. 14:11)

חֶרֶם **cherem**, *kheh´-rem*; from 2763; phys. (as *shutting in*) a *net* (either lit. or fig.); usually a *doomed* object; abstr. *extermination:*— (ac-) curse (-d, -d thing), dedicated thing, things which should have been utterly destroyed, (appointed to) utter destruction, devoted (thing), net.

2765. חֳרֵם **Chŏrêm**, *khor-ame´*; from 2763; *devoted*; *Chorem*, a place in Pal.:— Horem.

2766. חָרִם **Chârîm**, *khaw-reem´*; from

2763; *snub-nosed; Charim*, an Isr.:— Harim.

2767. חָרְמָה **Chormâh**, *khor-maw´;* from 2763; *devoted; Chormah*, a place in Pal.:— Hormah.

2768. חֶרְמוֹן **Chermôwn**, *kher-mone´;* from 2763; *abrupt; Chermon*, a mount of Pal.:— Hermon.

2769. חֶרְמוֹנִים **Chermôwnîym**, *kher-mo-neem´;* plur. of 2768; *Hermons*, i.e. its peaks:— the Hermonites.

2770. חֶרְמֵשׁ **chermêsh**, *kher-mashe´;* from 2763; a *sickle* (as *cutting*):— sickle.

2771. חָרָן **Chârân**, *kaw-rawn´;* from 2787; *parched; Charan*, the name of a man and also of a place:— Haran.

2772. חֹרֹנִי **Chôrônîy**, *kho-ro-nee´;* patrial from 2773; a *Choronite* or inhab. of Choronaim:— Horonite.

2773. חֹרֹנַיִם **Chôrônayim**, *kho-ro-nah´-yim;* dual of a der. from 2356; *double cave-town; Choronajim*, a place in Moab:— Horonaim.

2774. חַרְנֶפֶר **Charnepher**, *khar-neh´fer;* of uncert. der.; *Charnepher*, an Isr.:— Harnepher.

2775. חֶרֶס **chereç**, *kheh´-res;* or (with a directive enclitic)

חַרְסָה **charçâh**, *khar´-saw;* from an unused root mean. to *scrape;* the *itch;* also [perh. from the mediating idea of 2777] the *sun:*— itch, sun.

2776. חֶרֶס **Chereç**, *kheh´-res;* the same as 2775; *shining; Cheres*, a mountain in Pal.:— Heres.

2777. חַרְסוּת **charçûwth**, *khar-sooth´;* from 2775 (appar. in the sense of a red *tile* used for scraping); a *potsherd*, i.e. (by impl.) a *pottery;* the name of a gate at Jerusalem:— east.

2778. חָרַף **châraph**, *khaw-raf´;* a prim. root; to *pull off*, i.e. (by impl.) to *expose* (as by *stripping*); spec. to *betroth* (as if a surrender); fig. to carp at, i.e. *defame;* denom.ʲ(from 2779) to spend the *winter:*— betroth, blaspheme, defy, jeopard, rail, reproach, upbraid.

2779. חֹרֶף **chôreph**, *kho´-ref;* from 2778; prop. the *crop* gathered, i.e. (by impl.) the *autumn* (and winter) season; fig. *ripeness* of age:— cold, winter (l-house], youth.

2780. חָרֵף **Chârêph**, *khaw-rafe´;* from 2778; *reproachful; Chareph*, an Isr.:— Hareph.

2781. חֶרְפָּה **cherpâh**, *kher-paw´;* from 2778; *contumely*, *disgrace*, the *pudenda:*— rebuke, reproach (-fully), shame.

2782. חָרַץ **chârats**, *khaw-rats´;* a prim. root; prop. to *point* sharply, i.e. (lit.) to *wound;* fig. to be *alert*, to *decide:*— bestir self, decide, decree, determine, maim, move.

2783. חֲרַץ **charats** (Chald.), *khar-ats´;* from a root corresp. to 2782 in the sense of *vigor;* the *loin* (as the seat of strength):— loin.

חֶרְץ **chârûts**. See 2742.

2784. חַרְצֻבָּה **chartsubbâh**, *khar-tsoob-*

baw´; of uncert. der.; a *fetter;* fig. a *pain:*— band.

חָרֵץ **chârîts**. See 2757.

2785. חַרְצָן **chartsan**, *khar-tsan´;* from 2782; a *sour* grape (as *sharp* in taste):— kernel.

2786. חָרַק **châraq**, *khaw-rak´;* a prim. root; to *grate* the teeth:— gnash.

2787. חָרַר **chârar**, *khaw-rar´;* a prim. root; to *glow*, i.e. lit. (to *melt, burn, dry* up) or fig. (to *show* or *incite passion*):— be angry, burn, dry, kindle.

2788. חָרֵר **chârêr**, *khaw-rare´;* from 2787; *arid:*— parched place.

2789. חֶרֶשׂ **cheres**, *kheh´-res;* a collat. form mediating between 2775 and 2791; a piece of *pottery:*— earth (-en), (pot-) sherd, + stone.

2790. חָרַשׁ **chârash**, *khaw-rash´;* a prim. root; to *scratch*, i.e. (by impl.) to *engrave, plow;* hence, (from the use of tools) to *fabricate* (of any material); fig. to *devise* (in a bad sense); hence, (from the idea of secrecy) to *be silent*, to *let alone;* hence, (by impl.) to *be deaf* (as an accompaniment of dumbness):— × altogether, cease, conceal, be deaf, devise, ear, graven, imagine, leave off speaking, hold peace, plow (-er, man), be quiet, rest, practise secretly, keep silence, be silent, speak not a word, be still, hold tongue, worker.

2791. חֶרֶשׁ **cheresh**, *kheh´-resh;* from 2790; magical *craft;* also *silence:*— cunning, secretly.

2792. חֶרֶשׁ **Cheresh**, *kheh´-resh;* the same as 2791; *Cheresh*, a Levite:— Heresh.

2793. חֹרֶשׁ **chôresh**, *kho´-resh;* from 2790; a *forest* (perh. as furnishing the material for fabric):— bough, forest, shroud, wood.

2794. חֹרֵשׁ **chôrêsh**, *kho-rashe´;* act. part. of 2790; a *fabricator* or mechanic:— artificer.

2795. חֵרֵשׁ **chêrêsh**, *khay-rashe´;* from 2790; *deaf* (whether lit. or spir.):— deaf.

2796. חָרָשׁ **chârâsh**, *khaw-rawsh´;* from 2790; a *fabricator* or any material:— artificer, (+) carpenter, craftsman, engraver, maker, + mason, skilful, (+) smith, worker, workman, such as wrought.

2797. חַרְשָׁא **Charshâ’**, *khar-shaw´;* from 2792; *magician; Charsha*, one of the Nethinim:— Harsha.

2798. חֲרָשִׁים **Chărâshîym**, *khar-aw-sheem´;* plur. of 2796; *mechanics*, the name of a valley in Jerusalem:— Charashim, craftsmen.

2799. חֲרֹשֶׁת **chărôsheth**, *khar-o´-sheth;* from 2790; mechanical *work:*— carving, cutting.

2800. חֲרֹשֶׁת **Chărôsheth**, *khar-o´-sheth;* the same as 2799; *Charosheth*, a place in Pal.:— Harosheth.

2801. חָרַת **chârath**, *khaw-rath´;* a prim. root; to *engrave:*— graven.

2802. חֶרֶת **Chereth**, *kheh´-reth;* from 2801 [but equiv. to 2793]; *forest; Chereth*, a thicket in Pal.:— Hereth.

2803. חָשַׁב **châshab**, *khaw-shab´;* a

prim. root; prop. to *plait* or interpenetrate, i.e. (lit.) to *weave* or (gen.) to *fabricate;* fig. to *plot* or contrive (usually in a malicious sense); hence, (from the ment. effort) to *think, regard, value, compute:*— (make) account (of), conceive, consider, count, cunning (man, work, workman), devise, esteem, find out, forecast, hold, imagine, impute, invent, be like, mean, purpose, reckon (-ing be made), regard, think.

2804. חֲשַׁב **châshab** (Chald.), *khash-ab´;* corresp. to 2803; to *regard:*— repute.

2805. חֵשֶׁב **chêsheb**, *khay´-sheb;* from 2803; a *belt* or strap (as being interlaced):— curious girdle.

2806. חַשְׁבַּדָּנָה **Chashbaddânâh**, *khash-bad-daw´-naw;* from 2803 and 1777; *considerate judge; Chasbaddanah*, an Isr.:— Hasbadana.

2807. חֲשֻׁבָה **Chăshûbâh**, *khash-oo-baw´;* from 2803; *estimation; Cashubah*, an Isr.:— Hashubah.

2808. חֶשְׁבּוֹן **cheshbôwn**, *khesh-bone´;* from 2803; prop. *contrivance;* by impl. *intelligence:*— account, device, reason.

2809. חֶשְׁבּוֹן **Cheshbôwn**, *khesh-bone´;* the same as 2808; *Cheshbon*, a place E. of the Jordan:— Heshbon.

2810. חִשָּׁבוֹן **chishshâbôwn**, *khish-shaw-bone´;* from 2803; a *contrivance*, i.e. actual (a warlike *machine*) or ment. (a *machination*):— engine, invention.

2811. חֲשַׁבְיָה **Chăshabyâh**, *khash-ab-yaw´;* or

חֲשַׁבְיָהוּ **Chăshabyâhûw**, *khash-ab-yaw´-hoo;* from 2803 and 3050; *Jah has regarded; Chashabjah*, the name of nine Isr.:— Hashabiah.

2812. חֲשַׁבְנָה **Chăshabnâh**, *khash-ab-naw´;* fem. of 2808; *inventiveness; Chashnah*, an Isr.:— Hashabnah.

2813. חֲשַׁבְנְיָה **Chăshabnᵉyâh**, *khash-ab-neh-yaw´;* from 2808 and 3050; *thought of Jah; Chashabnejah*, the name of two Isr.:— Hashabniah.

2814. חָשָׁה **châshâh**, *khaw-shaw´;* a prim. root; to *hush* or keep quiet:— hold peace, keep silence, be silent, (be) still.

2815. חַשּׁוּב **Chashshûwb**, *khash-shoob´;* from 2803; *intelligent; Chashshub*, the name of two or three Isr.:— Hashub, Hasshub.

2816. חֲשׁוֹךְ **chăshôwk** (Chald.), *khash-oke´;* from a root corresp. to 2821; the *dark:*— darkness.

2817. חֲשׂוּפָא **Chăsûwphâ’**, *khas-oo-faw´;* or

חֲשֻׂפָא **Chăsûphâ’**, *khas-oo-faw´;* from 2834; *nakedness; Chasupha*, one of the Nethinim:— Hashupha, Hasupha.

חָשׂוּק **châshûwq**. See 2838.

2818. חֲשַׁח **chăshach** (Chald.), *khash-akh´;* a collat. root to one corresp. to 2363 in the sense of *readiness;* to be *necessary* (from the idea of *convenience*) or (tran.) to *need:*— careful, have need of.

2819. חַשְׁחוּת **chashchûwth**, *khash-khooth´;* from a root corresp. to 2818; *necessity:*— be needful.

חֲשֵׁיכָה **chăshêykăh.** See 2825.

חֻשִׁים **Chûshîym.** See 2366.

2820. חָשַׂךְ **châsak,** *khaw-sak´;* a prim. root; to *restrain* or (reflex.) *refrain;* by impl. to *refuse, spare, preserve;* also (by interch. with 2821) to *observe:*— assuage, × darken, forbear, hinder, hold back, keep (back), punish, refrain, reserve, spare, withhold.

2821. חָשַׁךְ **châshak,** *khaw-shak´;* a prim. root; to *be dark* (as *withholding* light); tran. to *darken:*— be black, be (make) dark, darken, cause darkness, be dim, hide.

2822. חֹשֶׁךְ **chôshek,** *kho-shek´;* from 2821; the *dark;* hence, (lit.) *darkness;* fig. *misery, destruction, death, ignorance, sorrow, wickedness:*— dark (-ness), night, obscurity.

2823. חָשֹׁךְ **châshôk,** *khaw-shoke´;* from 2821; *dark* (fig. i.e. *obscure*):— mean.

2824. חֶשְׁכָּה **cheshkâh,** *khesh-kaw´;* from 2821; *darkness:*— dark.

2825. חֲשֵׁכָה **chăshêkâh,** *khash-ay-kaw´;* or

חֲשֵׁיכָה **chăshêykâh,** *khash-ay-kaw´;* from 2821; *darkness;* fig. *misery:*— darkness.

2826. חָשַׁל **châshal,** *khaw-shal´;* a prim. root; to *make* (intrans. *be*) *unsteady,* i.e. *weak:*— feeble.

2827. חֲשַׁל **chăshal** (Chald.), *khash-al´;* a root corresp. to 2826; to *weaken,* i.e. *crush:*— subdue.

2828. חָשֻׁם **Châshûm,** *khaw-shoom´;* from the same as 2831; *enriched; Chashum,* the name of two or three Isr.:— Hashum.

חֻשָׁם **Chûshâm.** See 2367.

חֻשִׁם **Chûshîm.** See 2366.

2829. חֶשְׁמוֹן **Cheshmôwn,** *khesh-mone´;* the same as 2831; *opulent; Cheshmon,* a place in Pal.:— Heshmon.

2830. חַשְׁמַל **chashmal,** *khash-mal´;* of uncert. der.; prob. *bronze* or polished spectrum metal:— amber.

2831. חַשְׁמָן **chashmân,** *khash-man´;* from an unused root (prob. mean. *firm* or *capacious* in resources); appar. *wealthy:*— princes.

2832. חַשְׁמֹנָה **Chashmônâh,** *khash-mo-naw´;* fem. of 2831; *fertile; Chasmonah,* a place in the Desert:— Hashmonah.

2833. חֹשֶׁן **chôshen,** *kho´-shen;* from an unused root prob. mean. to *contain* or *sparkle;* perh. a *pocket* (as holding the Urim and Thummim), or *rich* (as containing gems), used only of the *gorget* of the high priest:— breastplate.

2834. חָשַׂף **châsaph,** *khaw-saf´;* a prim. root; to *strip off,* i.e. gen. to *make naked* (for exertion or in disgrace), to *drain* away or *bail* up (a liquid):— make bare, clean, discover, draw out, take, uncover.

2835. חָשִׂף **châsiph,** *khaw-seef´;* from 2834; prop. *drawn off,* i.e. *separated;* hence, a small *company* (as divided from the rest):— little flock.

2836. חָשַׁק **châshaq,** *khaw-shak´;* a prim. root; to *cling,* i.e. *join,* (fig.) to *love, delight* in; ellip. (or by interch. for 2820) to *deliver:*— have a delight, (have a) desire, fillet, long, set (in) love.

2837. חֵשֶׁק **chêsheq,** *khay´-shek;* from 2836; *delight:*— desire, pleasure.

2838. חָשֻׁק **châshûq,** *khaw-shook´;* or

חָשׁוּק **châshûwq,** *khaw-shook´;* pass. part. of 2836; *attached,* i.e. a fence-*rail* or rod connecting the posts or pillars:— fillet.

2839. חִשֻּׁק **chishshûq,** *khish-shook´;* from 2836; *conjoined,* i.e. a wheel-*spoke* or rod connecting the hub with the rim:— felloe.

2840. חִשֻּׁר **chishshûr,** *khish-shoor´;* from an unused root mean. to *bind* together; *combined,* i.e. the *nave* or hub of a wheel (as holding the spokes together):— spoke.

2841. חַשְׁרָה **chashrâh,** *khash-raw´;* from the same as 2840; prop. a *combination* or *gathering,* i.e. of watery *clouds:*— dark.

חֲשֻׁפָא **Chăsûphâ´.** See 2817.

2842. חָשַׁשׁ **châshash,** *khaw-shash´;* by var. for 7179; dry *grass:*— chaff.

2843. חֻשָׁתִי **Chûshâthîy,** *khoo-shaw-thee´;* patron. from 2364; a *Chushathite* or desc. of Chushah:— Hushathite.

2844. חַת **chath,** *khath;* from 2865; concr. *crushed;* also *afraid;* abstr. *terror:*— broken, dismayed, dread, fear.

2845. חֵת **Chêth,** *khayth;* from 2865; *terror; Cheth,* an aboriginal Canaanite:— Heth.

2846. חָתָה **châthâh,** *khaw-thaw´;* a prim. root; to *lay hold* of; espec. to *pick up* fire:— heap, take (away).

2847. חִתָּה **chittâh,** *khit-taw´;* from 2865; *fear:*— terror.

2848. חִתּוּל **chittûwl,** *khit-tool´;* from 2853; *swathed,* i.e. a *bandage:*— roller.

2849. חַתְחַת **chathchath,** *khath-khath´;* from 2844; *terror:*— fear.

2850. חִתִּי **Chittîy,** *khit-tee´;* patron. from 2845; a *Chittite,* or desc. of Cheth:— Hittite, Hittites.

2851. חִתִּית **chittîyth,** *khit-teeth´;* from 2865; *fear:*— terror.

2852. חָתַךְ **châthak,** *khaw-thak´;* a prim. root; prop. to *cut* off, i.e. (fig.) to *decree:*— determine.

2853. חָתַל **châthal,** *khaw-thal´;* a prim. root; to *swathe:*— × at all, swaddle.

2854. חֲתֻלָּה **chăthullâh,** *khath-ool-law´;* from 2853; a *swathing* cloth (fig.):— swaddling band.

2855. חֶתְלֹן **Chethlôn,** *kheth-lone´;* from 2853; *enswathed; Chethlon,* a place in Pal.:— Hethlon.

2856. חָתַם **châtham,** *khaw-tham´;* a prim. root; to *close* up; espec. to *seal:*— make an end, mark, seal (up), stop.

2857. חֲתַם **chătham** (Chald.), *khath-am´;* a root corresp. to 2856; to *seal:*— seal.

חֹתָם **chôthâm.** See 2368.

2858. חֹתֶמֶת **chôthemeth,** *kho-the-meth´;* fem. act. part. of 2856; a *seal:*— signet.

2859. חָתַן **châthan,** *khaw-than´;* a prim. root; to *give* (a daughter) *away* in marriage; hence, (gen.) to *contract affinity* by marriage:— join in affinity, father in law, make marriages, mother in law, son in law.

2860. חָתָן **châthân,** *khaw-thawn´;* from 2859; a *relative* by marriage (espec. through the bride); fig. a *circumcised* child (as a species of relig. espousal):— bridegroom, husband, son in law.

2861. חֲתֻנָּה **chăthunnâh,** *khath-oon-naw´;* from 2859; a *wedding:*— espousal.

2862. חָתַף **châthaph,** *khaw-thaf´;* a prim. root; to *clutch:*— take away.

2863. חֶתֶף **chetheph,** *kheh´-thef;* from 2862; prop. *rapine;* fig. *robbery:*— prey.

2864. חָתַר **châthar,** *khaw-thar´;* a prim. root; to *force* a passage, as by burglary; fig. with oars:— dig (through), row.

2865. חָתַת **châthath,** *khaw-thath´;* a prim. root; prop. to *prostrate;* hence, to *break* down, either (lit.) by violence, or (fig.) by confusion and fear:— abolish, affright, be (make) afraid, amaze, beat down, discourage, (cause to) dismay, go down, scare, terrify.

2866. חֲתַת **chătath,** *khath-ath´;* from 2865; *dismay:*— casting down.

2867. חֲתַת **Chătath,** *khath-ath´;* the same as 2866; *Chathath,* an Isr.:— Hathath.

ט

2868. טְאֵב **ţᵉʼêb** (Chald.), *teh-abe´;* a prim. root; to *rejoice:*— be glad.

2869. טָב **ţâb** (Chald.), *tawb;* from 2868; the same as 2896; *good:*— fine, good.

2870. טָבְאֵל **Ţâbᵉʼêl,** *taw-beh-ale´;* from 2895 and 410; *pleasing* (to) *God; Tabeël,* the name of a Syrian and of a Persian:— Tabeal, Tabeel.

2871. טָבוּל **ţâbûwl,** *taw-bool´;* pass. part. of 2881; prop. *dyed,* i.e. a *turban* (prob. as of *colored* stuff):— dyed attire.

2872. טַבּוּר **ţabbûwr,** *tab-boor´;* from an unused root mean. to *pile* up; prop. *accumulated;* i.e. (by impl.) a *summit:*— middle, midst.

2873. טָבַח **ţâbach,** *taw-bakh´;* a prim. root; to *slaughter* (animals or men):— kill, (make) slaughter, slay.

2874. טֶבַח **ţebach,** *teh´-bakh;* from 2873; prop. something *slaughtered;* hence, a *beast* (or *meat,* as butchered); abstr. *butchery* (or concr. a place of slaughter):— × beast, slaughter, × slay, × sore.

2875. טֶבַח **Ţebach,** *teh´-bakh;* the same as 2874; *massacre; Tebach,* the name of a Mesopotamian and of an Isr.:— Tebah.

2876. טַבָּח **ţabbâch,** *tab-bawkh´;* from 2873; prop. a *butcher;* hence, a *lifeguardsman* (because acting as an executioner); also a *cook* (as usually slaughtering the animal for food):— cook, guard.

2877. טַבָּח **ţabbâch** (Chald.), *tab-bawkh´;* the same as 2876; a *lifeguardsman:*— guard.

2878. טִבְחָה **ţibchâh,** *tib-khaw´;* fem. of 2874 and mean. the same:— flesh, slaughter.

2879. טַבָּחָה **ṭabbâchâh**, *tab-baw-khaw´*; fem. of 2876; a female *cook*:— cook.

2880. טִבְחָה **Ṭibchath**, *tib-khath´*; from 2878; *slaughter*; *Tibchath*, a place in Syria:— Tibhath.

2881. טָבַל **ṭâbal**, *taw-bal´*; a prim. root; to *dip*:— dip, plunge.

2882. טְבַלְיָהוּ **Ṭᵉbalyâhûw**, *teb-al-yaw´-hoo*; from 2881 and 3050; *Jah has dipped*; *Tebaljah*, an Isr.:— Tebaliah.

2883. טָבַע **ṭâba´**, *taw-bah´*; a prim. root; to *sink*:— drown, fasten, settle, sink.

2884. טַבָּעוֹת **Ṭabbâ'ôwth**, *tab-baw-othe´*; plur. of 2885; *rings*; *Tabbaoth*, one of the Nethinim:— Tabbaoth.

2885. טַבַּעַת **ṭabba'ath**, *tab-bah´-ath*; from 2883; prop. a *seal* (as *sunk* into the wax), i.e. *signet* (for sealing); hence, (gen.) a *ring* of any kind:— ring.

2886. טַבְרִמּוֹן **Ṭabrimmôwn**, *tab-rim-mone´*; from 2895 and 7417; *pleasing* (to) *Rimmon*; *Tabrimmon*, a Syrian:— Tabrimmon.

2887. טֵבֵת **Ṭêbeth**, *tay´-beth*; prob. of for. der.; *Tebeth*, the tenth Heb. month:— Tebeth.

2888. טַבַּת **Ṭabbath**, *tab-bath´*; of uncert. der.; *Tabbath*, a place E. of the Jordan:— Tabbath.

2889. טָהוֹר **ṭâhôwr**, *taw-hore´*; or

טָהֹר **ṭâhôr**, *taw-hore´*; from 2891; *pure* (in a physical, chemical, ceremonial or moral sense):— clean, fair, pure (-ness).

2890. טְהוֹר **ṭᵉhôwr**, *teh-hore´*; from 2891; *purity*:— pureness.

2891. טָהֵר **ṭâhêr**, *taw-hare´*; a prim. root; prop. to *be bright*; i.e. (by impl.) to *be pure* (phys. *sound*, *clear*, *unadulterated*; Levit. *uncontaminated*; mor. *innocent* or *holy*):— be (make, make self, pronounce) clean, cleanse (self), purge, purify (-ier, self).

2892. טֹהַר **ṭôhar**, *to´-har*; from 2891; lit. *brightness*; ceremonial *purification*:— clearness, glory, purifying.

2893. טָהֳרָה **ṭohŏrâh**, *toh-or-aw´*; fem. of 2892; ceremonial *purification*; moral *purity*:— × is cleansed, cleansing, purification (-fying).

2894. טוּא **ṭûw´**, *too*; a prim. root; to *sweep away*:— sweep.

2895. טוֹב **ṭowb**, *tobe*; a prim. root, to *be* (tran. *do* or *make*) *good* (or *well*) in the widest sense:— be (do) better, cheer, be (do, seem) good, (make) goodly, × please, (be, do, go, play) well.

2896. טוֹב **ṭôwb**, *tobe*; from 2895; *good* (as an adj.) in the widest sense; used likewise as a noun, both in the masc. and the fem., the sing. and the plur. (*good*, a *good* or *good thing*, a *good* man or woman; the *good*, *goods* or *good* things, *good* men or women), also as an adv. (*well*):— beautiful, best, better, bountiful, cheerful, at ease, × fair (word), (be in) favour, fine, glad, good (deed, -lier, -liest, -ly, -ness, -s), graciously, joyful, kindly, kindness, liketh (best), loving, merry, × most, pleasant, + pleaseth, pleasure, precious, prosperity, ready, sweet, wealth, welfare, (be) well (l-favoured]).

2897. טוֹב **Ṭôwb**, *tobe*; the same as 2896; *good*; *Tob*, a region appar. E. of the Jordan:— Tob.

2898. טוּב **ṭûwb**, *toob*; from 2895; *good* (as a noun), in the widest sense, espec. *goodness* (superl. concr. the *best*), *beauty*, *gladness*, *welfare*:— fair, gladness, good (-ness, thing, -s), joy, go well with.

2899. טוֹב אֲדֹנִיָּהוּ **Ṭôwb Ădônîyâhûw**, *tobe ado-nee-yaw´-hoo*; from 2896 and 138; *pleasing* (to) *Adonijah*; *Tob-Adonijah*, an Isr.:— Tob-adonijah.

2900. טוֹבִיָּה **Ṭôwbîyâh**, *to-bee-yaw´*; or

טוֹבִיָּהוּ **Ṭôwbîyâhûw**, *to-bee-yaw´-hoo*; from 2896 and 3050; *goodness of Jehovah*; *Tobijah*, the name of three Isr. and of one Samaritan:— Tobiah, Tobijah.

2901. טָוָה **ṭâvâh**, *taw-vaw´*; a prim. root; to *spin*:— spin.

2902. טוּחַ **ṭûwach**, *too´-akh*; a prim. root; to *smear*, espec. with lime:— daub, overlay, plaister, smut.

2903. טוֹפָפָה **ṭôwphâphâh**, *to-faw-faw´*; from an unused root mean. to *go around* or *bind*; a *fillet* for the forehead:— frontlet.

2904. טוּל **ṭûwl**, *tool*; a prim. root; to *pitch* over or *reel*; hence, (tran.) to *cast down* or *out*:— carry away, (utterly) cast (down, forth, out), send out.

2905. טוּר **ṭûwr**, *toor*; from an unused root mean. to *range* in a reg. manner; a *row*; hence, a *wall*:— row.

2906. טוּר **ṭûwr** (Chald.), *toor*; corresp. to 6697; a *rock* or hill:— mountain.

2907. טוּשׂ **ṭûws**, *toos*; a prim. root; to *pounce* as a bird of prey:— haste.

2908. טְוָת **ṭᵉvâth** (Chald.), *tev-awth´*; from a root corresp. to 2901; *hunger* (as *twisting*):— fasting.

2909. טָחָה **ṭâchâh**, *taw-khaw´*; a prim. root; to *stretch* a bow, as an *archer*:— [bow-] shot.

2910. טוּחָה **ṭûwchâh**, *too-khaw´*; from 2909 (or 2902) in the sense of *overlaying*; (in the plur. only) the *kidneys* (as being *covered*); hence, (fig.) the inmost *thought*:— inward parts.

2911. טְחוֹן **ṭᵉchôwn**, *tekh-one´*; from 2912; a hand *mill*; hence, a *millstone*:— to grind.

2912. טָחַן **ṭâchan**, *taw-khan´*; a prim. root; to *grind* meal; hence, to *be a concubine* (that being their employment):— grind (-er).

2913. טַחֲנָה **ṭachănâh**, *takh-an-aw´*; from 2912; a hand *mill*; hence, (fig.) *chewing*:— grinding.

2914. טְחֹר **ṭᵉchôr**, *tekh-ore´*; from an unused root mean. to *burn*; a *boil* or ulcer (from the inflammation), espec. a *tumor* in the anus or pudenda (the piles):— emerod.

2915. טִיחַ **ṭîyach**, *tee´akh*; from (the equiv. of) 2902; *mortar* or *plaster*:— daubing.

2916. טִיט **ṭîyṭ**, *teet*; from an unused root mean. appar. to *be sticky* [rather perh. a denom. from 2894, through the idea

of *dirt* to *be swept* away]; *mud* or *clay*; fig. *calamity*:— clay, dirt, mire.

2917. טִין **ṭîyn** (Chald.), *teen*; perh. by interchange, for a word corresp. to 2916; *clay*:— miry.

2918. טִירָה **ṭîyrâh**, *tee-raw´*; fem. of (an equiv. to) 2905; a *wall*; hence, a *fortress* or a *hamlet*:— (goodly) castle, habitation, palace, row.

2919. טַל **ṭal**, *tal*; from 2926; *dew* (as *covering* vegetation):— dew.

2920. טַל **ṭal** (Chald.), *tal*; the same as 2919:— dew.

2921. טָלָא **ṭâlâ´**, *taw-law´*; a prim. root; prop. to *cover* with pieces; i.e. (by impl.) to *spot* or *variegate* (as tapestry):— clouted, with divers colours, spotted.

2922. טְלָא **ṭᵉlâ´**, *tel-aw´*; appar. from 2921 in the (orig.) sense of *covering* (for protection); a *lamb* [comp. 2924]:— lamb.

2923. טְלָאִים **Ṭᵉlâ'îym**, *tel-aw-eem´*; from the plur. of 2922; *lambs*; *Telaim*, a place in Pal.:— Telaim.

2924. טָלֶה **ṭâleh**, *taw-leh´*; by var. for 2922; a *lamb*:— lamb.

2925. טַלְטֵלָה **ṭalṭêlâh**, *tal-tay-law´*; from 2904; *overthrow* or *rejection*:— captivity.

2926. טָלַל **ṭâlal**, *taw-lal´*; a prim. root; prop. to *strew* over, i.e. (by impl.) to *cover* in or *plate* (with beams):— cover.

2927. טְלַל **ṭᵉlal** (Chald.), *tel-al´*; corresp. to 2926; to *cover* with shade:— have a shadow.

2928. טֶלֶם **Ṭelem**, *teh´-lem*; from an unused root mean. to *break* up or treat violently; *oppression*; *Telem*, the name of a place in Idumæa, also of a temple doorkeeper:— Telem.

2929. טַלְמוֹן **Ṭalmôwn**, *tal-mone´*; from the same as 2728; *oppressive*; *Talmon*, a temple doorkeeper:— Talmon.

2930. טָמֵא **ṭâmê´**, *taw-may´*; a prim. root; to *be foul*, espec. in a cerem. or mor. sense (*contaminated*):— defile (self), pollute (self), be (make, make self, pronounce) unclean, × utterly.

2931. טָמֵא **ṭâmê´**, *taw-may´*; from 2930; *foul* in a relig. sense:— defiled, + infamous, polluted (-tion), unclean.

2932. טֻמְאָה **ṭum'âh**, *toom-aw´*; from 2930; relig. *impurity*:— filthiness, unclean (-ness).

2933. טָמָה **ṭâmâh**, *taw-maw´*; a collat. form of 2930; to *be impure* in a relig. sense:— be defiled, be reputed vile.

2934. טָמַן **ṭâman**, *taw-man´*; a prim. root; to *hide* (by *covering* over):— hide, lay privily, in secret.

2935. טֶנֶא **ṭene´**, *teh´-neh*; from an unused root prob. mean. to *weave*; a *basket* (of interlaced osiers):— basket.

2936. טָנַף **ṭânaph**, *taw-naf´*; a prim. root; to *soil*:— defile.

2937. טָעָה **ṭâ'âh**, *taw-aw´*; a prim. root; to *wander*; caus. to *lead astray*:— seduce.

2938. טָעַם **ṭâ'am**, *taw-am´*; a prim. root; to *taste*; fig. to *perceive*:— × but, perceive, taste.

2939. טְעַם ṭeʻam (Chald.), teh-am´; corresp. to 2938; to *taste*; caus. to *feed:*— make to eat, feed.

2940. טַעַם ṭaʻam, tah´-am; from 2938; prop. a *taste*, i.e. (fig.) *perception*; by impl. *intelligence*; tran. a *mandate:*— advice, behaviour, decree, discretion, judgment, reason, taste, understanding.

2941. טְעַם ṭaʻam (Chald.), tah´-am; from 2939; prop. a *taste*, i.e. (as in 2940) a judicial *sentence:*— account, × to be commanded, commandment, matter.

2942. טְעֵם ṭeʻêm (Chald.), teh-ame´; from 2939, and equiv. to 2941; prop. *flavor*; fig. *judgment* (both subj. and obj.); hence, *account* (both subj. and obj.):— + chancellor, + command, commandment, decree, + regard, taste, wisdom.

2943. טָעַן ṭâʻan, taw-an´; a prim. root; to *load* a beast:— lade.

2944. טָעַן ṭâʻan, taw-an´; a prim. root; to *stab:*— thrust through.

2945. טַף ṭaph, taf; from 2952 (perh. referring to the *tripping* gait of children); a *family* (mostly used collect. in the sing.):— (little) children (ones), families.

2946. טָפַח ṭâphach, taw-fakh´; a prim. root; to *flatten* out or *extend* (as a tent); fig. to *nurse* a child (as *promotive* of growth); or perh. a denom. from 2947, from *dandling* on the palms:— span, swaddle.

2947. טֶפַח ṭêphach, tay´-fakh; from 2946; a *spread* of the hand, i.e. a *palmbreadth* (not "span" of the fingers); arch. a *corbel* (as a supporting palm):— coping, hand-breadth.

2948. טֹפַח ṭôphach, to´-fakh; from 2946 (the same as 2947):— hand-breadth (broad).

2949. טִפֻּח ṭippûch, tip-pookh´; from 2946; *nursing:*— span long.

2950. טָפַל ṭâphal, taw-fal´; a prim. root; prop. to *stick* on as a patch; fig. to *impute* falsely:— forge (-r), sew up.

2951. טִפְסַר ṭiphçar, tif-sar´; of for. der.; a military *governor:*— captain.

2952. טָפַף ṭâphaph, taw-faf´; a prim. root; appar. to *trip* (with short steps) coquettishly:— mince.

2953. טְפַר ṭephar (Chald.), tef-ar´; from a root corresp. to 6852, and mean. the same as 6856; a finger-*nail*; also a *hoof* or *claw:*— nail.

2954. טָפַשׁ ṭâphash, taw-fash´; a prim. root; prop. appar. to *be thick*; fig. to be *stupid:*— be fat.

2955. טָפַת Ṭâphath, taw-fath´; prob. from 5197; a *dropping* (of ointment); *Taphath*, an Israelitess:— Taphath.

2956. טָרַד ṭârad, taw-rad´; a prim. root; to *drive* on; fig. to *follow* close:— continual.

2957. טְרַד ṭerad (Chald.), ter-ad´; corresp. to 2956; to *expel:*— drive.

2958. טְרוֹם ṭerôwm, ter-ome´; a var. of 2962; *not yet:*— before.

2959. טָרַח ṭârach, taw-rakh´; a prim. root; to *overburden:*— weary.

2960. טֹרַח ṭôrach, to´-rakh; from 2959; a *burden:*— cumbrance, trouble.

2961. טָרִי ṭârîy, taw-ree´; from an unused root appar. mean. to *be moist*; prop. *dripping*; hence, *fresh* (i.e. recently made such):— new, putrefying.

2962. טֶרֶם ṭerem, teh´-rem; from an unused root appar. mean. to *interrupt* or *suspend*; prop. *non-occurrence*; used adv. *not yet* or *before:*— before, ere, not yet.

2963. טָרַף ṭâraph, taw-raf´; a prim. root; to *pluck off* or *pull* to pieces; caus. to *supply* with food (as in morsels):— catch, × without doubt, feed, ravin, rend in pieces, × surely, tear (in pieces).

2964. טֶרֶף ṭereph, teh´-ref; from 2963; something *torn*, i.e. a fragment, e.g. a fresh leaf, *prey*, *food:*— leaf, meat, prey, spoil.

2965. טָרָף ṭârâph, taw-rawf´; from 2963; recently *torn* off, i.e. *fresh:*— pluckt off.

2966. טְרֵפָה ṭerêphâh, ter-ay-faw´; fem. (collect.) of 2964; *prey*, i.e. flocks devoured by animals:— ravin, (that which was) torn (of beasts, in pieces).

2967. טַרְפְּלַי Ṭarpelay (Chald.), tar-pel-ah´-ee; from a name of for. der.; a *Tarpelite* (collect.) or inhab. of Tarpel, a place in Assyria:— Tarpelites.

2968. יָאַב yâʼab, yaw-ab´; a prim. root; to *desire:*— long.

2969. יָאָה yâʼâh, yaw-aw´; a prim. root; to *be suitable:*— appertain.

יְאוֹר yeʼôwr. See 2975.

2970. יַאֲזַנְיָה Yaʼăzanyâh, yah-az-an-yaw´; or

יַאֲזַנְיָהוּ Yaʼăzanyâhûw, yah-az-an-yaw´-hoo; from 238 and 3050; *heard of Jah*; *Jaazanjah*, the name of four Isr.:— Jaazaniah. Comp. 3153.

2971. יָאִיר Yâʼîyr, yaw-ere´; from 215; *enlightener*; *Jair*, the name of four Isr.:— Jair.

2972. יָאִרִי Yâʼiriy, yaw-ee-ree´; patron. from 2971; a *Jaïrite* or desc. of Jair:— Jairite.

2973. יָאַל yâʼal, yaw-al´; a prim. root; prop. to *be slack*, i.e. (fig.) to *be foolish:*— dote, be (become, do) foolish (-ly).

2974. יָאַל yâʼal, yaw-al´; a prim. root [prob. rather the same as 2973 through the idea of mental *weakness*]; prop. to *yield*, espec. *assent*; hence, (pos.) to *undertake* as an act of volition:— assay, begin, be content, please, take upon, × willingly, would.

2975. יְאֹר yeʼôr, yeh-ore´; of Eg. or.; a *channel*, e.g. a fosse, canal, shaft; spec. the *Nile*, as the one river of Egypt, incl. its collat. trenches; also the *Tigris*, as the main river of Assyria:— brook, flood, river, stream.

2976. יָאַשׁ yâʼash, yaw-ash´; a prim. root; to *desist*, i.e. (fig.) to *despond:*— (cause to) despair, one that is desperate, be no hope.

2977. יֹאשִׁיָּה Yôʼshîyâh, yo-shee-yaw´; or

יֹאשִׁיָּהוּ Yôʼshîyâhûw, yo-she-yaw´-hoo; from the same root as 803 and 3050; *founded of Jah*; *Joshijah*, the name of two Isr.:— Josiah.

2978. יְאִתוֹן yeʼîthôwn, yeh-ee-thone´; from 857; an *entry:*— entrance.

2979. יְאָתְרַי Yeʼâthray, yeh-aw-ther-ah´ee; from the same as 871; *stepping*; *Jeätherai*, an Isr.:— Jeaterai.

2980. יָבַב yâbab´; a prim. root; to *bawl:*— cry out.

2981. יְבוּל yebûwl, yeb-ool´; from 2986; *produce*, i.e. a *crop* or (fig.) *wealth:*— fruit, increase.

2982. יְבוּס Yebûwç, yeb-oos´; from 947; *trodden*, i.e. threshing-place; *Jebus*, the aboriginal name of Jerusalem:— Jebus.

2983. יְבוּסִי Yebûwçiy, yeb-oo-see´; patrial from 2982; a *Jebusite* or inhab. of Jebus:— Jebusite (-s).

2984. יִבְחַר Yibchar, yib-khar´; from 977; *choice*; *Jibchar*, an Isr.:— Ibhar.

2985. יָבִין Yâbîyn, yaw-bene´; from 995; *intelligent*; *Jabin*, the name of two Canaanitish kings:— Jabin.

יָבֵשׁ Yâbêysh. See 3003.

2986. יָבַל yâbal, yaw-bal´; a prim. root; prop. to *flow*; caus. to *bring* (espec. with pomp):— bring (forth), carry, lead (forth).

2987. יְבַל yebal (Chald.), yeb-al´; corresp. to 2986; to *bring:*— bring, carry.

יוֹבֵל yôbêl. See 3104.

2988. יָבָל yâbâl, yaw-bawl´; from 2986; a *stream:*— [water-] course, stream.

2989. יָבָל Yâbâl, yaw-bawl´; the same as 2988; *Jabal*, an antediluvian:— Jabal.

יֹבֵל yôbêl. See 3104.

2990. יַבֵּל yabbêl, yab-bale´; from 2986; having *running* sores:— wen.

2991. יִבְלְעָם Yibleʻâm, yib-leh-awm´; from 1104 and 5971; *devouring people*; *Jibleäm*, a place in Pal.:— Ibleam.

2992. יָבַם yâbam, yaw-bam´; a prim. root of doubtful mean.; used only as a denom. from 2993; to *marry* a (deceased) brother's widow:— perform the duty of a husband's brother, marry.

2993. יָבָם yâbâm, yaw-bawm´; from (the orig. of) 2992; a *brother-in-law:*— husband's brother.

2994. יְבֵמֶת yebêmeth, yeb-ay´-meth; fem. part. of 2992; a *sister-in-law:*— brother's wife, sister in law.

2995. יַבְנְאֵל Yabnʼêl, yab-neh-ale´; from 1129 and 410; *built of God*; *Jabneël*, the name of two places in Pal.:— Jabneel.

2996. יַבְנֶה Yabneh, yab-neh´; from 1129; a *building*; *Jabneh*, a place in Pal.:— Jabneh.

2997. יִבְנְיָה Yibneyâh, yib-neh-yaw´; from 1129 and 3050; *built of Jah*; *Jibnejah*, an Isr.:— Ibneiah.

2998. יִבְנִיָּה Yibnîyâh, yib-nee-yaw´; from 1129 and 3050; *building of Jah*; *Jibnijah*, an Isr.:— Ibnijah.

2999. יַבֹּק Yabbôq, yab-boke´; prob.

from 1238; *pouring* forth; *Jabbok*, a river E. of the Jordan:— Jabbok.

3000. יְבֶרֶכְיָהוּ **Yᵉberekyâhûw**, *yeb-eh-rek-yaw´-hoo;* from 1288 and 3050: *blessed of Jah; Jeberekjah*, an Isr.:— Jeberechiah.

3001. בּוֹשׁ **yâbêsh**, *yaw-bashe´;* a prim. root; to *be ashamed, confused* or *disappointed;* also (as failing) to *dry* up (as water) or *wither* (as herbage):— be ashamed, clean, be confounded, (make) dry (up), (do) shame (-fully), × utterly, wither (away).

3002. בֵּשׁ **yâbêsh**, *yaw-bashe´;* from 3001; *dry:*— dried (away), dry.

3003. בֵּשׁ **Yâbêsh**, *yaw-bashe´;* the same as 3002 (also

בֵּישׁ **Yâbêysh**, *yaw-bashe´;* often with the addition of 1568, i.e. *Jabesh of Gilad); Jabesh*, the name of an Isr. and of a place in Pal.:— Jabesh (l-Gilead]).

3004. יַבָּשָׁה **yabbâshâh**, *yab-baw-shaw´;* from 3001; *dry ground:*— dry (ground, land).

3005. יִבְשָׂם **Yibsâm**, *yib-sawm´;* from the same as 1314; *fragrant; Jibsam*, an Isr.:— Jibsam.

3006. יַבֶּשֶׁת **yabbesheth**, *yab-beh´-sheth;* a var. of 3004; *dry ground:*— dry land.

3007. יַבֶּשֶׁת **yabbesheth** (Chald.), *yab-beh´-sheth;* corresp. to 3006; *dry* land:— earth.

3008. יִגְאָל **Yig'âl**, *yig-awl´;* from 1350; *avenger; Jigal*, the name of three Isr.:— Igal, Igeal.

3009. יָגַב **yâgab**, *yaw-gab´;* a prim. root; to *dig* or plow:— husbandman.

3010. יָגֵב **yâgêb**, *yaw-gabe´;* from 3009; a plowed *field:*— field.

3011. יָגְבְּהָה **Yogbᵉhâh**, *yog-beh-haw´;* fem. from 1361; *hillock; Jogbehah*, a place E. of the Jordan:— Jogbehah.

3012. יִגְדַּלְיָהוּ **Yigdalyâhûw**, *yig-dal-yaw´-hoo;* from 1431 and 3050; *magnified of Jah; Jigdaljah*, an Isr.:— Igdaliah.

3013. יָגָה **yâgâh**, *yaw-gaw´;* a prim. root; to *grieve:*— afflict, cause grief, grieve, sorrowful, vex.

3014. יָגָה **yâgâh**, *yaw-gaw´;* a prim. root [prob. rather the same as 3013 through the common idea of *dissatisfaction*]; to *push* away:— be removed.

3015. יָגוֹן **yâgôwn**, *yaw-gohn´;* from 3013; *affliction:*— grief, sorrow.

3016. יָגוֹר **yâgôwr**, *yaw-gore´;* from 3025; *fearful:*— afraid, fearest.

3017. יָגוּר **Yâgûwr**, *yaw-goor´;* prob. from 1481; a *lodging; Jagur*, a place in Pal.:— Jagur.

3018. יְגִיעַ **yᵉgîya'**, *yeg-ee´-ah;* from 3021; *toil;* hence, a *work, produce, property* (as the result of labor):— labour, work.

3019. יָגִיעַ **yâgîya'**, *yaw-ghee´-ah;* from 3021; *tired:*— weary.

3020. יָגְלִי **Yoglîy**, *yog-lee´;* from 1540; *exiled; Jogli*, an Isr.:— Jogli.

3021. יָגַע **yâga'**, *yaw-gah´;* a prim. root; prop. to *gasp;* hence, to *be exhausted*, to *tire*, to *toil:*— faint, (make) labour, (be) weary.

3022. יְגָע **yâgâ'**, *yaw-gaw´;* from 3021; *earnings* (as the product of toil):— that which he laboured for.

3023. יָגֵעַ **yâgêa'**, *yaw-gay´-ah;* from 3021; *tired;* hence, (tran.) *tiresome:*— full of labour, weary.

3024. יְגִעָה **yᵉgi'âh**, *yeg-ee-aw´;* fem. of 3019; *fatigue:*— weariness.

3025. יָגֹר **yâgôr**, *yaw-gore´;* a prim. root; to *fear:*— be afraid, fear.

3026. יְגַר שָׂהֲדוּתָא **Yᵉgar Sahădûwthâ'** (Chald.), *yegar´ sah-had-oo-thaw´;* from a word derived from an unused root (mean. to *gather*) and a der. of a root corresp. to 7717; *heap of the testimony; Jegar-Sahadutha*, a cairn E. of the Jordan:— Jegar-Sahadutha.

3027. יָד **yâd**, *yawd;* a prim. word; a *hand* (the *open* one [indicating *power, means, direction*, etc.], in distinction from 3709, the *closed* one); used (as noun, adv., etc.) in a great variety of applications, both lit. and fig., both prox. and remote [as follows]:— (+ be) able, × about, + armholes, at, axletree, because of, beside, border, × bounty, + broad, [broken-] handed, × by, charge, coast, + consecrate, + creditor, custody, debt, dominion, × enough, + fellowship, force, × from, hand [-staves, -y work], × he, himself, × in, labour, + large, ledge, [left-] handed, means, × mine, ministry, near, × of, × order, ordinance, × our, parts, pain, power, × presumptuously, service, side, sore, state, stay, draw with strength, stroke, + swear, terror, × thee, × by them, × themselves, × thine own, × thou, through, × throwing, + thumb, times, × to, × under, × us, × wait on, [way-] side, where, + wide, × with (him, me, you), work, + yield, × yourselves.

3028. יַד **yad** (Chald.), *yad;* corresp. to 3027:— hand, power.

3029. יְדָא **yᵉdâ'** (Chald.), *yed-aw´;* corresp. to 3034; to *praise:*— (give) thank (-s).

3030. יִדְאָלָה **Yid'âlâh**, *yid-al-aw´;* of uncert. der.; *Jidalah*, a place in Pal.:— Idalah.

3031. יִדְבָּשׁ **Yidbâsh**, *yid-bawsh´;* from the same as 1706; perh. *honeyed; Jidbash*, an Isr.:— Idbash.

3032. יָדַד **yâdad**, *yaw-dad´;* a prim. root; prop. to *handle* [comp. 3034], i.e. to *throw*, e.g. lots:— cast.

3033. יְדִדוּת **yᵉdîdûwth**, *yed-ee-dooth´;* from 3039; prop. *affection;* concr. a *darling* object:— dearly beloved.

3034. יָדָה **yâdâh**, *yaw-daw´;* a prim. root; used only as denom. from 3027; lit. to *use* (i.e. hold out) *the hand;* phys. to *throw* (a stone, an arrow) at or away; espec. to *revere* or *worship* (with extended hands); intens. to *bemoan* (by wringing the hands):— cast (out), (make) confess (-ion), praise, shoot, (give) thank (-ful, -s, -sgiving).

3035. יִדּוֹ **Yiddôw**, *yid-do´;* from 3034; *praised; Jiddo*, an Isr.:— Iddo.

3036. יָדוֹן **Yâdôwn**, *yaw-done´;* from 3034; *thankful; Jadon*, an Isr.:— Jadon.

3037. יַדּוּעַ **Yaddûwa'**, *yad-doo´-ah;*

from 3045; *knowing; Jadduä*, the name of two Isr.:— Jaddua.

3038. יְדוּתוּן **Yᵉdûwthûwn**, *yed-oo-thoon´;* or

יְדֻתוּן **Yᵉdûthûwn**, *yed-oo-thoon´;* or

יְדִיתוּן **Yᵉdîythûwn**, *yed-ee-thoon´;* prob. from 3034; *laudatory; Jeduthun*, an Isr.:— Jeduthun.

3039. יְדִיד **yᵉdîyd**, *yed-eed´;* from the same as 1730; *loved:*— amiable, (well-) beloved, loves.

3040. יְדִידָה **Yᵉdîydâh**, *yed-ee-daw´;* fem. of 3039; *beloved; Jedidah*, an Israelitess:— Jedidah.

3041. יְדִידְיָה **Yᵉdîydᵉyâh**, *yed-ee-deh-yaw´;* from 3039 and 3050; *beloved of Jah; Jedidejah*, a name of Solomon:— Jedidiah.

3042. יְדָיָה **Yᵉdâyâh**, *yed-aw-yaw´;* from 3034 and 3050; *praised of Jah; Jedajah*, the name of two Isr.:— Jedaiah.

3043. יְדִיעֲאֵל **Yᵉdîy'ă'êl**, *yed-ee-ah-ale´;* from 3045 and 410; *knowing God; Jediaël*, the name of three Isr.:— Jediael.

3044. יִדְלָף **Yidlâph**, *yid-lawf´;* from 1811; *tearful; Jidlaph*, a Mesopotamian:— Jidlaph.

3045. יָדַע **yâda'**, *yaw-dah´;* a prim. root; to *know* (prop. to ascertain by *seeing*); used in a great variety of senses, fig., lit., euphem. and infer. (incl. *observation, care, recognition;* and caus. *instruction, designation, punishment*, etc.) [as follow]:— acknowledge, acquaintance (-ted with), advise, answer, appoint, assuredly, be aware, [un-] awares, can [-not], certainly, for a certainty, comprehend, consider, × could they, cunning, declare, be diligent, (can, cause to) discern, discover, endued with, familiar friend, famous, feel, can have, be [ig-] norant, instruct, kinsfolk, kinsman, (cause to, let, make) know, (come to give, have, take) knowledge, have [knowledge], (be, make, make to be, make self) known, + be learned, + lie by man, mark, perceive, privy to, × prognosticator, regard, have respect, skilful, shew, can (man of) skill, be sure, of a surety, teach, (can) tell, understand, have [understanding], × will be, wist, wit, wot.

3046. יְדַע **yᵉda'** (Chald.), *yed-ah´;* corresp. to 3045:— certify, know, make known, teach.

3047. יָדָע **Yâdâ'**, *yaw-daw´;* from 3045; *knowing; Jada*, an Isr.:— Jada.

3048. יְדַעְיָה **Yᵉda'yâh**, *yed-ah-yaw´;* from 3045 and 3050; *Jah has known; Jedajah*, the name of two Isr.:— Jedaiah.

3049. יִדְּעֹנִי **yiddᵉ'ônîy**, *yid-deh-o-nee´;* from 3045; prop. a *knowing* one; spec. a *conjurer;* (by impl.) a *ghost:*— wizard.

3050. יָהּ **Yâhh**, *yaw;* contr. for 3068, and mean. the same; *Jah*, the sacred name:— Jah, the Lord, most vehement. Comp. names in "-iah," "-jah."

3051. יָהַב **yâhab**, *yaw-hab´;* a prim. root; to *give* (whether lit. or fig.); gen. to *put;* imper. (refl.) *come:*— ascribe, bring, come on, give, go, set, take.

3052. יְהַב y^ehab (Chald.), yeh-hab´; corresp. to 3051:— deliver, give, lay, + prolong, pay, yield.

3053. יְהָב y^ehâb, ye-hawb´; from 3051; prop. what is given (by Providence), i.e. a lot:— burden.

3054. יָהַד yâhad, yaw-had´; denom. from a form corresp. to 3061; to Judaize, i.e. become Jewish:— become Jews.

3055. יְהֻד Y^ehûd, yeh-hood´; a briefer form of one corresp. to 3061; Jehud, a place in Pal.:— Jehud.

3056. יֶהְדַי Yehday, yeh-dah´-ee; perh. from a form corresp. to 3061; Judaistic; Jehdai, an Isr.:— Jehdai.

3057. יְהֻדִיָּה Y^ehûdîyâh, yeh-hoo-dee-yaw´; fem. of 3064; Jehudijah, a Jewess:— Jehudijah.

3058. יֵהוּא Yêhûw´, yay-hoo´; from 3068 and 1931; Jehovah (is) He; Jehu, the name of five Isr.:— Jehu.

3059. יְהוֹאָחָז Y^ehôw´âchâz, yeh-ho-aw-khawz´; from 3068 and 270; Jehovah-seized; Jehoächaz, the name of three Isr.:— Jehoahaz. Comp. 3099.

3060. יְהוֹאָשׁ Y^ehôw´âsh, yeh-ho-awsh´; from 3068 and (perh.) 784; Jehovah-fired; Jehoäsh, the name of two Isr. kings:— Jehoash. Comp. 3101.

3061. יְהוּד Y^ehûwd (Chald.), yeh-hood´; contr. from a form corresp. to 3063; prop. Judah, hence, Judea:— Jewry, Judah, Judea.

3062. יְהוּדָאִי Y^ehûwdâ´îy (Chald.), yeh-hoo-daw-ee´; patrial from 3061; a Jehudaïte (or Judaïte), i.e. Jew:— Jew.

3063. יְהוּדָה Y^ehûwdâh, yeh-hoo-daw´; from 3034; celebrated; Jehudah (or Judah), the name of five Isr.; also of the tribe descended from the first, and of its territory:— Judah.

3064. יְהוּדִי Y^ehûwdîy, yeh-hoo-dee´; patron. from 3063; a Jehudite (i.e. Judaïte or Jew), or desc. of Jehudah (i.e. Judah):— Jew.

3065. יְהוּדִי Y^ehûwdîy, yeh-hoo-dee´; the same as 3064; Jehudi, an Isr.:— Jehudi.

3066. יְהוּדִית Y^ehûwdîyth, yeh-hoo-deeth´; fem. of 3064; the Jewish (used adv.) language:— in the Jews' language.

3067. יְהוּדִית Y^ehûwdîyth, yeh-ho-deeth´; the same as 3066; Jewess; Jehudith, a Canaanitess:— Judith.

3068. יְהֹוָה Y^ehôvâh, yeh-ho-vaw´; from 1961; (the) self-Existent or Eternal; Jehovah, Jewish national name of God:— Jehovah, the Lord. Comp. 3050, 3069.

3069. יְהֹוִה Y^ehôvih, yeh-ho-vee´; a var. of 3068 [used after 136, and pronounced by Jews as 430, in order to prevent the repetition of the same sound, since they elsewhere pronounce 3068 as 136]:— God.

3070. יְהֹוָה יִרְאֶה Y^ehôvâh Yir´eh, yeh-ho-vaw´ yir-eh´; from 3068 and 7200; Jehovah will see (to it); Jehovah-Jireh, a symb. name for Mt. Moriah:— Jehovah-jireh.

3071. יְהֹוָה נִסִּי Y^ehôvâh Niççîy, yeh-ho-vaw´ nis-see´; from 3068 and 5251 with the pron. suff.; Jehovah (is) my banner;

Jehovah-Nissi, a symb. name of an altar in the Desert:— Jehovah-nissi.

3072. יְהֹוָה צִדְקֵנוּ Y^ehôvâh Tsidqênûw, ye-ho-vaw´ tsid-kay´-noo; from 3068 and 6664 with pron. suff.; Jehovah (is) our right; Jehovah-Tsidkenu, a symb. epithet of the Messiah and of Jerusalem:— the Lord our righteousness.

3073. יְהֹוָה שָׁלוֹם Y^ehôvâh Shâlôwm, yeh-ho-vaw´ shaw-lome´; from 3068 and 7965; Jehovah (is) peace; Jehovah-Shalom, a symb. name of an altar in Pal.:— Jehovah-shalom.

3074. יְהֹוָה שָׁמָּה Y^ehôvâh Shâmmâh, yeh-ho-vaw´ shawm´-maw; from 3068 and 8033 with directive enclitic; Jehovah (is) thither; Jehovah-Shammah, a symbol. title of Jerusalem:— Jehovah-shammah.

3075. יְהוֹזָבָד Y^ehôwzâbâd, yeh-ho-zaw-bawd´; from 3068 and 2064; Jehovah-endowed; Jehozabad, the name of three Isr.:— Jehozabad. Comp. 3107.

3076. יְהוֹחָנָן Y^ehôwchânân, yeh-ho-khaw-nawn´; from 3068 and 2603; Jehovah-favored; Jehochanan, the name of eight Isr.:— Jehohanan, Johanan. Comp. 3110.

3077. יְהוֹיָדָע Y^ehôwyâdâ´, yeh-ho-yaw-daw´; from 3068 and 3045; Jehovah-known; Jehojada, the name of three Isr.:— Jehoiada. Comp. 3111.

3078. יְהוֹיָכִין Y^ehôwyâkîyn, yeh-ho-yaw-keen´; from 3068 and 3559; Jehovah will establish; Jehojakin, a Jewish king:— Jehoiachin. Comp. 3112.

3079. יְהוֹיָקִים Y^ehôwyâqîym, yeh-ho-yaw-keem´; from 3068 abb. and 6965; Jehovah will raise; Jehojakim, a Jewish king:— Jehoiakim. Comp. 3113.

3080. יְהוֹיָרִיב Y^ehôwyârîyb, yeh-ho-yaw-reeb´; from 3068 and 7378; Jehovah will contend; Jehojarib, the name of two Isr.:— Jehoiarib. Comp. 3114.

3081. יְהוּכַל Y^ehûwkal, yeh-hoo-kal´; from 3201; potent; Jehukal, an Isr.:— Jehucal. Comp. 3116.

3082. יְהוֹנָדָב Y^ehôwnâdâb, yeh-ho-naw-dawb´; from 3068 and 5068; Jehovah-largessed; Jehonadab, the name of an Isr. and of an Arab:— Jehonadab, Jonadab. Comp. 3122.

3083. יְהוֹנָתָן Y^ehôwnâthân, yeh-ho-naw-thawn´; from 3068 and 5414; Jehovah-given; Jehonathan, the name of four Isr.:— Jonathan. Comp. 3129.

3084. יְהוֹסֵף Y^ehôwçêph, yeh-ho-safe´; a fuller form of 3130; Jehoseph (i.e. Joseph), a son of Jacob:— Joseph.

3085. יְהוֹעַדָּה Y^ehôw´addâh, yeh-ho-ad-daw´; from 3068 and 5710; Jehovah-adorned; Jehoäddah, an Isr.:— Jehoada.

3086. יְהוֹעַדִּין Y^ehôw´addîyn, yeh-ho-ad-deen´; or

יְהוֹעַדָּן Y^ehôw´addân, yeh-ho-ad-dawn´; from 3068 and 5727; Jehovah-pleased; Jehoäddin or Jehoäddan, an Israelitess:— Jehoaddan.

3087. יְהוֹצָדָק Y^ehôwtsâdâq, yeh-ho-tsaw-dawk´; from 3068 and 6663; Jehovah-righted; Jehotsadak, an Isr.:— Jehozadek, Josedech. Comp. 3136.

3088. יְהוֹרָם Y^ehôwrâm, yeh-ho-rawm´; from 3068 and 7311; Jehovah-raised; Jehoram, the name of a Syrian and of three Isr.:— Jehoram, Joram. Comp. 3141.

3089. יְהוֹשֶׁבַע Y^ehôwsheba', yeh-ho-sheh´-bah; from 3068 and 7650; Jehovah-sworn; Jehosheba, an Israelitess:— Jehosheba. Comp. 3090.

3090. יְהוֹשַׁבְעַת Y^ehôwshab'ath, yeh-ho-shab-ath´; a form of 3089; Jehoshabath, an Israelitess:— Jehoshabeath.

3091. יְהוֹשׁוּעַ Y^ehôwshûw'a, yeh-ho-shoo´-ah; or

יְהוֹשֻׁעַ Y^ehôwshû'a, yeh-ho-shoo´-ah; from 3068 and 3467; Jehovah-saved; Jehoshuä (i.e. Joshua), the Jewish leader:— Jehoshua, Jehoshuah, Joshua. Comp. 1954, 3442.

3092. יְהוֹשָׁפָט Y^ehôwshâphât, yeh-ho-shaw-fawt´; from 3068 and 8199; Jehovah-judged; Jehoshaphat, the name of six Isr.; also of a valley near Jerusalem:— Jehoshaphat. Comp. 3146.

3093. יָהִיר yâhîyr, yaw-here´; prob. from the same as 2022; elated; hence, arrogant:— haughty, proud.

3094. יְהַלֶּלְאֵל Y^ehallel'êl, yeh-hal-lel-ale´; from 1984 and 410; praising God; Jehallel, the name of two Isr.:— Jehaleleel, Jehalelel.

3095. יַהֲלֹם yahălôm, yah-hal-ome´; from 1986 (in the sense of hardness); a precious stone, prob. onyx:— diamond.

3096. יַהַץ Yahats, yah´-hats; or

יַהְצָה Yahtsâh, yah´-tsaw; or (fem.)

יָהְצָה Yahtsâh, yah-tsaw´; from an unused root mean. to stamp; perh. threshing-floor; Jahats or Jahtsah, a place E. of the Jordan:— Jahaz, Jahazah, Jahzah.

3097. יוֹאָב Yôw´âb, yo-awb´; from 3068 and 1; Jehovah-fathered; Joäb, the name of three Isr.:— Joab.

3098. יוֹאָח Yôw´âch, yo-awkh´; from 3068 and 251; Jehovah-brothered; Joach, the name of four Isr.:— Joah.

3099. יוֹאָחָז Yôw´âchâz, yo-aw-khawz´; a form of 3059; Joächaz, the name of two Isr.:— Jehoahaz, Joahaz.

3100. יוֹאֵל Yôw´êl, yo-ale´; from 3068 and 410; Jehovah (is his) God; Joël, the name of twelve Isr.:— Joel.

3101. יוֹאָשׁ Yôw´âsh, yo-awsh´; or

יֹאָשׁ Yô´âsh (2 Chron. 24:1), yo-awsh´; a form of 3060; Joäsh, the name of six Isr.:— Joash.

3102. יוֹב Yôwb, yobe; perh. a form of 3103, but more prob. by err. transc. for 3437; Job, an Isr.:— Job.

3103. יוֹבָב Yôwbâb, yo-bawb´; from 2980; howler; Jobab, the name of two Isr. and of three foreigners:— Jobab.

3104. יוֹבֵל yôwbêl, yo-bale´; or

יֹבֵל yôbêl, yob-ale´; appar. from 2986; the blast of a horn (from its continuous sound); spec. the signal of the silver trumpets; hence, the instrument itself and the festival thus introduced:— jubile, ram's horn, trumpet.

3105. יוּבָל **yûwbal**, yoo-bal'; from 2986; a *stream*:— river.

3106. יוֹבָל **Yûwbâl**, yoo-bawl'; from 2986; *stream; Jubal*, an antediluvian:— Jubal.

3107. יוֹזָבָד **Yôwzâbâd'**, yo-zaw-bawd'; a form of 3075; *Jozabad*, the name of ten Isr.:— Josabad, Jozabad.

3108. יוֹזָכָר **Yôwzâkâr**, yo-zaw-kawr'; from 3068 and 2142; *Jehovah-remembered; Jozacar*, an Isr.:— Jozachar.

3109. יוֹחָא **Yôwchâ'**, yo-khaw'; prob. from 3068 and a var. of 2421; *Jehovah-revived; Jocha*, the name of two Isr.:— Joha.

3110. יוֹחָנָן **Yôwchânân**, yo-khaw-nawn'; a form of 3076; *Jochanan*, the name of nine Isr.:— Johanan.

יוּטָה **Yûwṭâh**. See 3194.

3111. יוֹיָדָע **Yôwyâdâ'**, yo-yaw-daw'; a form of 3077; *Jojada*, the name of two Isr.:— Jehoiada, Joiada.

3112. יוֹיָכִין **Yôwyâkîyn**, yo-yaw-keen'; a form of 3078; *Jojakin*, an Isr. king:— Jehoiachin.

3113. יוֹיָקִים **Yôwyâqîym**, yo-yaw-keem'; a form of 3079; *Jojakim*, an Isr.:— Joiakim. Comp. 3137.

3114. יוֹיָרִיב **Yôwyârîyb**, yo-yaw-reeb'; a form of 3080; *Jojarib*, the name of four Isr.:— Joiarib.

3115. יוֹכֶבֶד **Yôwkebed**, yo-keh'-bed; from 3068 contr. and 3513; *Jehovah-gloried; Jokebed*, the mother of Moses:— Jochebed.

3116. יוּכַל **Yûwkal**, yoo-kal'; a form of 3081; *Jukal*, an Isr.:— Jucal.

3117. יוֹם **yôwm**, yome; from an unused root mean. to *be hot*; a *day* (as the *warm* hours), whether lit. (from sunrise to sunset, or from one sunset to the next), or fig. (a space of time defined by an associated term), [often used adv.]:— age, + always, + chronicles, continually (-ance), daily, [(birth-]l, each, to) day, (now a, two) days (agone), + elder, × end, + evening, + (for) ever (-lasting, -more), × full, life, as (so) long as (... live), (even) now, + old, + outlived, + perpetually, presently, + remaineth, × required, season, × since, space, then, (process of) time, + as at other times, + in trouble, weather, (as) when, (a, the, within a) while (that), × whole (+ age), (full) year (-ly), + younger.

3118. יוֹם **yôwm** (Chald.), yome; corresp. to 3117; a *day*:— day (by day), time.

3119. יוֹמָם **yôwmâm**, yo-mawm'; from 3117; *daily*:— daily, (by, in the) day (-time).

3120. יָוָן **Yâvân**, yaw-vawn'; prob. from the same as 3196; *effervescing* (i.e. hot and active); *Javan*, the name of a son of Joktan, and of the race (*Ionians*, i.e. Greeks) descended from him, with their territory; also of a place in Arabia:— Javan.

3121. יָוֵן **yâvên**, yaw-ven'; from the same as 3196; prop. *dregs* (as *effervescing*);̓ hence, *mud*:— mire, miry.

3122. יוֹנָדָב **Yôwnâdâb**, yo-naw-dawb'; a form of 3082; *Jonadab*, the name of an Isr. and of a Rechabite:— Jonadab.

3123. יוֹנָה **yôwnâh**, yo-naw'; prob. from the same as 3196; a *dove* (appar. from the *warmth* of their mating):— dove, pigeon.

3124. יוֹנָה **Yôwnâh**, yo-naw'; the same as 3123; *Jonah*, an Isr.:— Jonah.

3125. יְוָנִי **Yevânîy**, yev-aw-nee'; patron. from 3121; a *Jevanite*, or desc. of Javan:— Grecian.

3126. יוֹנֵק **yôwnêq**, yo-nake'; act. part. of 3243; a *sucker*; hence, a *twig* (of a tree felled and sprouting):— tender plant.

3127. יוֹנֶקֶת **yôwneqeth**, yo-neh'-keth; fem. of 3126; a *sprout*:— (tender) branch, young twig.

3128. יוֹנַת אֵלֶם רְחֹקִים **Yôwnath 'êlem rechôqîym**, yo-nath' ay'-lem rekh-o-keem'; from 3123 and 482 and the plur. of 7350; *dove of* (the) *silence* (i.e. *dumb* Israel) *of* (i.e. *among*) *distances* (i.e. *strangers*); the title of a ditty (used for a name of its melody):— Jonath-elem-rechokim.

3129. יוֹנָתָן **Yôwnâthân**, yo-naw-thawn'; a form of 3083; *Jonathan*, the name of ten Isr.:— Jonathan.

3130. יוֹסֵף **Yôwçêph**, yo-safe'; future of 3254; *let him add* (or perh. simply act. part. *adding*); *Joseph*, the name of seven Isr.:— Joseph. Comp. 3084.

3131. יוֹסִפְיָה **Yôwçiphyâh**, yo-sif-yaw'; from act. part. of 3254 and 3050; *Jah* (is) *adding; Josiphjah*, an Isr.:— Josiphiah.

3132. יוֹעֵאלָה **Yôw'ê'lâh**, yo-ay-law'; perh. fem. act. part. of 3276; *furthermore; Joelah*, an Isr.:— Joelah.

3133. יוֹעֵד **Yôw'êd**, yo-ade'; appar. the act. part. of 3259; *appointer; Joed*, an Isr.:— Joed.

3134. יוֹעֶזֶר **Yôw'ezer**, yo-eh'-zer; from 3068 and 5828; *Jehovah* (is his) *help; Joezer*, an Isr.:— Joezer.

3135. יוֹעָשׁ **Yôw'âsh**, yo-awsh'; from 3068 and 5789; *Jehovah-hastened; Joash*, the name of two Isr.:— Joash.

3136. יוֹצָדָק **Yôwtsâdâq**, yo-tsaw-dawk'; a form of 3087; *Jotsadak*, an Isr.:— Jozadak.

3137. יוֹקִים **Yôwqîym**, yo-keem'; a form of 3113; *Jokim*, an Isr.:— Jokim.

3138. יוֹרֶה **yôwreh**, yo-reh'; act. part. of 3384; *sprinkling*; hence, a *sprinkling* (or autumnal showers):— first rain, former [rain].

3139. יוֹרָה **Yôwrâh**, yo-raw'; from 3384; *rainy; Jorah*, an Isr.:— Jorah.

3140. יוֹרַי **Yôwray**, yo-rah'-ee; from 3384; *rainy; Jorai*, an Isr.:— Jorai.

3141. יוֹרָם **Yôwrâm**, yo-rawm'; a form of 3088; *Joram*, the name of three Isr. and one Syrian:— Joram.

3142. יוּשַׁב חֶסֶד **Yûwshab Cheçed**, yoo-shab' kheh'-sed; from 7725 and 2617; *kindness will be returned; Jushab-Chesed*, an Isr.:— Jushab-hesed.

3143. יוֹשִׁבְיָה **Yôwshîbyâh**, yo-shib-yaw'; from 3427 and 3050; *Jehovah will cause to dwell; Josibjah*, an Isr.:— Josibiah.

3144. יוֹשָׁה **Yôwshâh**, yo-shaw'; prob. a form of 3145; *Joshah*, an Isr.:— Joshah.

3145. יוֹשַׁוְיָה **Yôwshavyâh**, yo-shav-yaw'; from 3068 and 7737; *Jehovah-set; Joshavjah*, an Isr.:— Joshaviah. Comp. 3144.

3146. יוֹשָׁפָט **Yôwshâphâṭ**, yo-shaw-fawt'; a form of 3092; *Joshaphat*, an Isr.:— Joshaphat.

3147. יוֹתָם **Yôwthâm**, yo-thawm'; from 3068 and 8535; *Jehovah* (is) *perfect; Jotham*, the name of three Isr.:— Jotham.

3148. יוֹתֵר **yôwthêr**, yo-thare'; act. part. of 3498; prop. *redundant*; hence, *over and above*, as adj., noun, adv. or conjunc. [as follows]:— better, more (-over), over, profit.

3149. יְזַואֵל° **Yezav'êl**, yez-av-ale'; from an unused root (mean. to *sprinkle*) and 410; *sprinkled of God; Jezavel*, an Isr.:— Jeziel [from the marg.].

3150. יִזִּיָּה **Yizziyâh**, yiz-zee-yaw'; from the same as the first part of 3149 and 3050; *sprinkled of Jah; Jizzijah*, an Isr.:— Jeziah.

3151. יָזִיז **Yâzîyz**, yaw-zeez'; from the same as 2123; *he will make prominent; Jaziz*, an Isr.:— Jaziz.

3152. יִזְלִיאָה **Yizlîy'âh**, yiz-lee-aw'; perh. from an unused root (mean. to *draw up*); *he will draw out; Jizliah*, an Isr.:— Jezliah.

3153. יְזַנְיָה **Yezanyâh**, yez-an-yaw'; or יְזַנְיָהוּ **Yezanyâhûw**, yez-an-yaw'-hoo; prob. for 2970; *Jezanjah*, an Isr.:— Jezaniah.

3154. יֶזַע **yeza'**, yeh'-zah; from an unused root mean. to *ooze; sweat*, i.e. (by impl.) a *sweating* dress:— any thing that causeth sweat.

3155. יִזְרָח **Yizrâch**, yiz-rawkh'; a var. for 250; a *Jizrach* (i.e. Ezrachite or Zarchite) or desc. of Zerach:— Izrahite.

3156. יִזְרַחְיָה **Yizrachyâh**, yiz-rakh-yaw'; from 2224 and 3050; *Jah will shine; Jizrachjah*, the name of two Isr.:— Izrahiah, Jezrahiah.

3157. יִזְרְעֵאל **Yizre'êl**, yiz-reh-ale'; from 2232 and 410; *God will sow; Jizreël*, the name of two places in Pal. and of two Isr.:— Jezreel.

3158. יִזְרְעֵאלִי **Yizre'êlîy**, yiz-reh-ay-lee'; patron. from 3157; a *Jizreëlite* or native of Jizreel:— Jezreelite.

3159. יִזְרְעֵאלִית **Yizre'êlîyth**, yiz-reh-ay-leeth'; fem. of 3158; a *Jezreëlitess*:— Jezreelitess.

3160. יְחֻבָּה **Yechubbâh**, yekh-oob-baw'; from 2247; *hidden; Jechubbah*, an Isr.:— Jehubbah.

3161. יָחַד **yâchad**, yaw-khad'; a prim. root; to *be* (or *become*) *one*:— join, unite.

3162. יַחַד **yachad**, yakh'-ad; from 3161; prop. a *unit*, i.e. (adv.) *unitedly*:— alike, at all (once), both, likewise, only, (al-) together, withal.

3163. יַחְדּוֹ **Yachdôw**, yakh-doe'; from 3162 with pron. suff.; *his unity*, i.e. (adv.) *together; Jachdo*, an Isr.:— Jahdo.

3164. יַחְדִּיאֵל **Yachdîy'êl**, *yakh-dee-ale'*; from 3162 and 410; *unity of God; Jachdiël*, an Isr.:— Jahdiel.

3165. יֶחְדִּיָּהוּ **Yechdîyâhûw**, *yekh-dee-yaw'-hoo*; from 3162 and 3050; *unity of Jah; Jechdijah*, the name of two Isr.:— Jehdeiah.

יַחְאֵל **Yᵉchav'êl**. See 3171.

3166. יַחֲזִיאֵל **Yachăzîy'êl**, *yakh-az-ee-ale'*; from 2372 and 410; *beheld of God; Jachaziël*, the name of five Isr.:— Jahaziel, Jahziel.

3167. יַחְזְיָה **Yachzᵉyâh**, *yakh-zeh-yaw'*; from 2372 and 3050; *Jah will behold; Jachzejah*, an Isr.:— Jahaziah.

3168. יְחֶזְקֵאל **Yᵉchezqê'l**, *yekh-ez-kale'*; from 2388 and 410; *God will strengthen; Jechezkel*, the name of two Isr.:— Ezekiel, Jehezekel.

3169. יְחִזְקִיָּה **Yᵉchizqîyâh**, *yekh-iz-kee-yaw'*; or

יְחִזְקִיָּהוּ **Yᵉchizqîyâhûw**, *yekh-iz-kee-yaw'-hoo*; from 3388 and 3050; *strengthened of Jah; Jechizkijah*, the name of five Isr.:— Hezekiah, Jehizkiah. Comp. 2396.

3170. יַחְזֵרָה **Yachzêrâh**, *yakh-zay-raw'*; from the same as 2386; perh. *protection; Jachzerah*, an Isr.:— Jahzerah.

3171. יְחִיאֵל **Yᵉchîy'êl**, *yekh-ee-ale'*; or (2 Chron. 29:14)

יְחַוּאֵל° **Yᵉchav'êl**, *yekh-av-ale'*; from 2421 and 410; *God will live; Jechiël* (or *Jechavel*), the name of eight Isr.:— Jehiel.

3172. יְחִיאֵלִי **Yᵉchîy'êlîy**, *yekh-ee-ay-lee'*; patron. from 3171; a *Jechiëlite* or desc. of Jechiel:— Jehieli.

3173. יָחִיד **yâchîyd**, *yaw-kheed'*; from 3161; prop. *united*, i.e. *sole*; by impl. *beloved*; also *lonely*; (fem.) the *life* (as not to be replaced):— darling, desolate, only (child, son), solitary.

3174. יְחִיָּה **Yᵉchîyâh**, *yekh-ee-yaw'*; from 2421 and 3050; *Jah will live; Jechijah*, an Isr.:— Jehiah.

3175. יָחִיל **yâchîyl**, *yaw-kheel'*; from 3176; *expectant*:— should hope.

3176. יָחַל **yâchal**, *yaw-chal'*; a prim. root; to *wait*; by impl. to *be patient*, *hope*:— (cause to, have, make to) hope, be pained, stay, tarry, trust, wait.

3177. יַחְלְאֵל **Yachlᵉ'êl**, *yakh-leh-ale'*; from 3176 and 410; *expectant of God; Jachleël*, an Isr.:— Jahleel.

3178. יַחְלְאֵלִי **Yachlᵉ'êlîy**, *yakh-leh-ay-lee'*; patron. from 3177; a *Jachleëlite* or desc. of Jachleel:— Jahleelites.

3179. יָחַם **yâcham**, *yaw-kham'*; a prim. root; prob. to *be hot*; fig. to *conceive*:— get heat, be hot, conceive, be warm.

3180. יַחְמוּר **yachmûwr**, *yakh-moor'*; from 2560; a kind of *deer* (from the color; comp. 2543):— fallow deer.

3181. יַחְמַי **Yachmay**, *yakh-mah'-ee*; prob. from 3179; *hot; Jachmai*, an Isr.:— Jahmai.

3182. יָחֵף **yâchêph**, *yaw-khafe'*; from an unused root mean. to *take off the shoes; unsandalled*:— barefoot, being unshod.

3183. יַחְצְאֵל **Yachtsᵉ'êl**, *yakh-tseh-ale'*;

from 2673 and 410; *God will allot; Jachtseël*, an Isr.:— Jahzeel. Comp. 3185.

3184. יַחְצְאֵלִי **Yachtsᵉ'êlîy**, *yakh-tseh-ay-lee'*; patron. from 3183; a *Jachtseëlite* (collect.) or desc. of Jachtseel:— Jahzeelites.

3185. יַחְצִיאֵל **Yachtsîy'êl**, *yakh-tsee-ale'*; from 2673 and 410; *allotted of God; Jachtsiël*, an Isr.:— Jahziel. Comp. 3183.

3186. יָחַר **yâchar**, *yaw-khar'*; a prim. root; to *delay*:— tarry longer.

3187. יָחַס **yâchas**, *yaw-khas'*; a prim. root; to *sprout*; used only as denom. from 3188; to *enroll* by pedigree:— (number after, number throughout the) genealogy (to be reckoned), be reckoned by genealogies.

3188. יַחַס **yachas**, *yakh'-as*; from 3187; a *pedigree* or family list (as *growing* spontaneously):— genealogy.

3189. יַחַת **Yachath**, *yakh'-ath*; from 3161; *unity; Jachath*, the name of four Isr.:— Jahath.

3190. יָטַב **yâṭab**, *yaw-tab'*; a prim. root; to *be* (caus.) *make well*, lit. (*sound, beautiful*) or fig. (*happy, successful, right*):— be accepted, amend, use aright, benefit, be (make) better, seem best, make cheerful, be comely, + be content, diligent (-ly), dress, earnestly, find favour, give, be glad, do (be, make) good (I-nessl), be (make) merry, please (+ well), shew more [kindness], skilfully, × very small, surely, make sweet, thoroughly, tire, trim, very, be (can, deal, entreat, go, have) well [said, seen].

3191. יְטַב **yᵉṭab** (Chald.), *yet-ab'*; corresp. to 3190:— seem good.

3192. יָטְבָה **Yoṭbâh**, *yot-baw'*; from 3190; *pleasantness; Jotbah*, a place in Pal.:— Jotbah.

3193. יָטְבָתָה **Yoṭbâthâh**, *yot-baw'-thaw*; from 3192; *Jotbathah*, a place in the Desert:— Jotbath, Jotbathah.

3194. יֻטָּה **Yuṭṭâh**, *yoo-taw'*; or

יוּטָה **Yûwṭâh**, *yoo-taw'*; from 5186; *extended; Juttah* (or *Jutah*), a place in Pal.:— Juttah.

3195. יְטוּר **Yᵉṭûwr**, *yet-oor'*; prob. from the same as 2905; *encircled* (i.e. *inclosed*); *Jetur*, a son of Ishmael:— Jetur.

3196. יַיִן **yayin**, *yah'-yin*; from an unused root mean. to *effervesce; wine* (as fermented); by impl. *intoxication*:— banqueting, wine, wine [-bibber].

3197. יַד **yak**, *yak*; by err. transc. for 3027; a *hand* or *side*:— [way-] side.

יָכוֹל **yâkôwl**. See 3201.

יְכָנְיָה **Yᵉkownᵉyâh**. See 3204.

3198. יָכַח **yâkach**, *yaw-kahh'*; a prim. root; to *be right* (i.e. *correct*); recip. to *argue*; caus. *decide, justify* or *convict*:— appoint, argue, chasten, convince, correct (-ion), daysman, dispute, judge, maintain, plead, reason (together), rebuke, reprove (-r), surely, in any wise.

יְכִילְיָה **Yᵉkîylᵉyâh**. See 3203.

3199. יָכִין **Yâkîyn**, *yaw-keen'*; from

3559; *he* (or *it*) *will establish; Jakin*, the name of three Isr. and of a temple pillar:— Jachin.

3200. יָכִינִי **Yâkîynîy**, *yaw-kee-nee'*; patron. from 3199; a *Jakinite* (collect.) or desc. of Jakin:— Jachinites.

3201. יָכֹל **yâkôl**, *yaw-kole'*; or (fuller)

יָכוֹל **yâkôwl**, *yaw-kole'*; a prim. root; to *be able*, lit. (*can, could*) or mor. (*may, might*):— be able, any at all (ways), attain, can (away with, [-not]), could, endure, might, overcome, have power, prevail, still, suffer.

3202. יְכֵל **yᵉkêl** (Chald.), *yek-ale'*; or

יְכִיל **yᵉkîyl** (Chald.), *yek-eel'*; corresp. to 3201:— be able, can, couldest, prevail.

3203. יְכָלְיָה **Yᵉkolyâh**, *yek-ol-yaw'*; and

יְכָלְיָהוּ **Yᵉkolyâhûw**, *yek-ol-yaw'-hoo*; or (2 Chron. 26:3)

יְכִילְיָה° **Yᵉkîylᵉyâh**, *yek-ee-leh-yaw'*; from 3201 and 3050; *Jah will enable; Jekoljah* or *Jekiljah*, an Israelitess:— Jecholiah, Jecoliah.

3204. יְכָנְיָה **Yᵉkonyâh**, *yek-on-yaw'*; and

יְכָנְיָהוּ **Yᵉkonyâhûw**, *yek-on-yaw'-hoo*; or (Jer. 27:20)

יְכוֹנְיָה° **Yᵉkôwnᵉyâh**, *yek-o-neh-yaw'*; from 3559 and 3050; *Jah will establish; Jekonjah*, a Jewish king:— Jeconiah. Comp. 3659.

3205. יָלַד **yâlad**, *yaw-lad'*; a prim. root; to *bear* young; caus. to *beget*; medically, to *act as midwife*; spec. to *show lineage*:— bear, beget, birth ([-day]), born, (make to) bring forth (children, young), bring up, calve, child, come, be delivered (of a child), time of delivery, gender, hatch, labour, (do the office of a) midwife, declare pedigrees, be the son of, (woman in, woman that) travail (-eth, -ing woman).

3206. יֶלֶד **yeled**, *yeh'-led*; from 3205; something *born*, i.e. a *lad* or *offspring*:— boy, child, fruit, son, young man (one).

3207. יַלְדָּה **yaldâh**, *yal-daw'*; fem. of 3206; a *lass*:— damsel, girl.

3208. יַלְדוּת **yaldûwth**, *yal-dooth'*; abstr. from 3206; *boyhood* (or *girlhood*):— childhood, youth.

3209. יִלּוֹד **yillôwd**, *yil-lode'*; pass. from 3205; *born*:— born.

3210. יָלוֹן **Yâlôwn**, *yaw-lone'*; from 3885; *lodging; Jalon*, an Isr.:— Jalon.

3211. יָלִיד **yâlîyd**, *yaw-leed'*; from 3205; *born*:— ([home-]) born, child, son.

3212. יָלַךְ **yâlak**, *yaw-lak'*; a prim. root [comp. 1980]; to *walk* (lit. or fig.); caus. to *carry* (in various senses):— × again, away, bear, bring, carry (away), come (away), depart, flow, + follow (-ing), get (away, hence, him), (cause to, make) go (away, ing, -ne, one's way, out), grow, lead (forth), let down, march, prosper, + pursue, cause to run, spread, take away ([-journey]), vanish, (cause to) walk (-ing), wax, × be weak.

3213. יָלַל **yâlal**, *yaw-lal'*; a prim. root; to *howl* (with a wailing tone) or *yell* (with a boisterous one):— (make to) howl, be howling.

3214. יְלֵל y^elêl, *yel-ale´*; from 3213; a *howl*:— howling.

3215. יְלָלָה y^elâlâh, *yel-aw-law´*; fem. of 3214; a *howling*:— howling.

3216. יְלַע yâla', *yaw-lah´*; a prim. root; to *blurt* or utter inconsiderately:— devour.

3217. יַלֶּפֶת yallepheth, *yal-leh´-feth;* from an unused root appar. mean. to *stick* or *scrape; scurf* or *tetter*:— scabbed.

3218. יֶלֶק yekeq, *yeh´-lek;* from an unused root mean. to *lick* up; a *devourer*; spec. the young *locust*:— cankerworm, caterpillar.

3219. יַלְקוּט yalqûwṭ, *yal-koot´;* from 3950; a travelling *pouch* (as if for gleanings):— scrip.

3220. יָם yâm, *yawm;* from an unused root mean. to *roar*; a *sea* (as breaking in *noisy* surf) or large body of water; spec. (with the art.), the *Mediterranean;* sometimes a large *river,* or an artificial *basin;* locally, the *west,* or (rarely) the *south*:— sea (×-faring man, [-shore], south, west (-ern, side, -ward).

3221. יָם yâm (Chald.), *yawm;* corresp. to 3220:— sea.

3222. יֵם yêm, *yame;* from the same as 3117; a *warm* spring:— mule.

3223. יְמוּאֵל Y^emûw'êl, *yem-oo-ale´;* from 3117 and 410; *day of God; Jemuel,* an Isr.:— Jemuel.

3224. יְמִימָה Y^emîymâh, *yem-ee-maw´;* perh. from the same as 3117; prop. *warm,* i.e. *affectionate;* hence, *dove* [comp. 3123]; *Jemimah,* one of Job's daughters:— Jemimah.

3225. יָמִין yâmîyn, *yaw-meen´;* from 3231; the *right* hand or side (leg, eye) of a person or other object (as the *stronger* and more dexterous); locally, the *south*:— + left-handed, right (hand, side), south.

3226. יָמִין Yâmîyn, *yaw-meen´;* the same as 3225; *Jamin,* the name of three Isr.:— Jamin. See also 1144.

3227. יְמִינִי y^emîyniy, *yem-ee-nee´;* for 3225; *right*:— (on the) right (hand).

3228. יְמִינִי Y^emîyniy, *yem-ee-nee´;* patron. from 3226; a *Jeminite* (collect.) or desc. of Jamin:— Jaminites. See also 1145.

3229. יִמְלָא Yimlâ', *yeem-law´;* or

יִמְלָה Yimlâh, *yim-law´;* from 4390; *full; Jimla* or *Jimlah,* an Isr.:— Imla, Imlah.

3230. יַמְלֵךְ Yamlêk, *yam-lake´;* from 4427; *he will make king; Jamlek,* an Isr.:— Jamlech.

3231. יָמַן yâman, *yaw-man´;* a prim. root; to be (phys.) *right* (i.e. firm); but used only as denom. from 3225 and tran. to *be right-handed* or *take the right-hand* side:— go (turn) to (on, use) the right hand.

3232. יִמְנָה Yimnâh, *yim-naw´;* from 3231; *prosperity* (as betokened by the *right* hand); *Jimnah,* the name of two Isr.; also (with the art.) of the *posterity* of one of them:— Imna, Imnah, Jimnah, Jimnites.

3233. יְמָנִי y^emânîy, *yem-aw-nee´;* from 3231; *right* (i.e. at the right hand):— (on the) right (hand).

3234. יִמְנָע Yimnâ', *yim-naw´;* from 4513; *he will restrain; Jimna,* an Isr.:— Imna.

3235. יָמַר yâmar, *yaw-mar´;* a prim. root; to *exchange;* by impl. to *change places*:— boast selves, change.

3236. יִמְרָה Yimrâh, *yim-raw´;* prob. from 3235; *interchange; Jimrah,* an Isr.:— Imrah.

3237. יָמַשׁ yâmash, *yaw-mash´;* a prim. root; to *touch*:— feel.

3238. יָנָה yânâh, *yaw-naw´;* a prim. root; to *rage* or *be violent;* by impl. to *suppress,* to *maltreat*:— destroy, (thrust out by) oppress (-ing, -ion, -or), proud, vex, do violence.

3239. יָנוֹחַ Yânôwach, *yaw-no´-akh;* or (with enclitic)

יָנוֹחָה Yânôwchâh, *yaw-no´-khaw;* from 3240; *quiet; Janoäch* or *Janochah,* a place in Pal.:— Janoah, Janohah.

יָנוּם Yânûm. See 3241.

3240. יַח yânach, *yaw-nakh´;* a prim. root; to *deposit;* by impl. to *allow to stay*:— bestow, cast down, lay (down, up), leave (off), let alone (remain), pacify, place, put, set (down), suffer, withdraw, withhold. (The Hiphil forms with the *dagesh* are here referred to, in accordance with the older grammarians; but if any distinction of the kind is to be made, these should rather be referred to 5117, and the others here.)

3241. יָנִים Yânîym, *yaw-neem´;* from 5123; *asleep; Janim,* a place in Pal.:— Janum [from the marg.].

3242. יְנִיקָה y^enîqâh, *yen-ee-kaw´;* from 3243; a *sucker* or sapling:— young twig.

3243. יָנַק yânaq, *yaw-nak´;* a prim. root; to *suck;* caus. to *give milk*:— milch, nurse (-ing mother), (give, make to) suck (-ing child, -ling).

3244. יַנְשׁוּף yanshûwph, *yan-shoof´;* or

יַנְשׁוֹף yanshôwph, *yan-shofe´;* appar. from 5398; an unclean (aquatic) bird; prob. the *heron* (perh. from its *blowing* cry, or because the *night*-heron is meant [comp. 5399]):— (great) owl.

3245. יָסַד yâçad, *yaw-sad´;* a prim. root; to *set* (lit. or fig.); intens. to *found;* refl. to *sit* down together, i.e. *settle, consult*:— appoint, take counsel, establish, (lay the, lay for a) found (-ation), instruct, lay, ordain, set, × sure.

3246. יְסֻד y^eçûd, *yes-ood´;* from 3245; a *foundation* (fig. i.e. *beginning*):— × began.

3247. יְסוֹד y^eçôwd, *yes-ode´;* from 3245; a *foundation* (lit. or fig.):— bottom, foundation, repairing.

3248. יְסוּדָה y^eçûwdâh, *yes-oo-daw´;* fem. of 3246; a *foundation*:— foundation.

3249. יָסוּר yâçûwr, *yaw-soor´;* from 5493; *departing*:— they that depart.

3250. יִסּוֹר yiççôwr, *yis-sore´;* from 3256; a *reprover*:— instruct.

3251. יָסַךְ yâçak, *yaw-sak´;* a prim. root; to *pour* (intr.):— be poured.

3252. יִסְכָּה Yiçkâh, *yis-kaw´;* from an unused root mean. to *watch; observant; Jiskah,* sister of Lot:— Iscah.

3253. יִסְמַכְיָהוּ Yiçmakyâhûw, *yis-mak-yaw-hoo´;* from 5564 and 3050; *Jah will sustain; Jismakjah,* an Isr.:— Ismachiah.

3254. יָסַף yâçaph, *yaw-saf´;* a prim. root; to *add* or *augment* (often adv. to *continue* to do a thing):— add, × again, × any more, × cease, × come more, + conceive again, continue, exceed, × further, × gather together, get more, give more-over, × henceforth, increase (more and more), join, × longer (bring, do, make, much, put), × (the, much, yet) more (and more), proceed (further), prolong, put, be [strong-] er, × yet, yield.

3255. יְסַף y^eçaph (Chald.), *yes-af´;* corresp. to 3254:— add.

3256. יָסַר yâçar, *yaw-sar´;* a prim. root; to *chastise,* lit. (with blows) or fig. (with words); hence, to *instruct*:— bind, chasten, chastise, correct, instruct, punish, reform, reprove, sore, teach.

3257. יָע yâ', *yaw;* from 3261; a *shovel*:— shovel.

3258. יַעְבֵּץ Ya'bêts, *yah-bates´;* from an unused root prob. mean. to *grieve; sorrowful; Jabets,* the name of an Isr., and also of a place in Pal.:— Jabez.

3259. יָעַד yâ'ad, *yaw-ad´;* a prim. root; to *fix* upon (by agreement or appointment); by impl. to *meet* (at a stated time), to *summon* (to trial), to *direct* (in a certain quarter or position), to *engage* (for marriage):— agree,(make an) appoint (-ment, a time), assemble (selves), betroth, gather (selves, together), meet (together), set (a time).

יַעְדּוֹ Y^edôw. See 3260.

3260. יֶעְדִּי Y^edîy, *yed-ee´;* from 3259; *appointed; Jedi,* an Isr.:— Iddo [from the marg.] See 3035.

3261. יָעָה yâ'âh, *yaw-aw´;* a prim. root; appar. to *brush* aside:— sweep away.

3262. יְעוּאֵל Y^eûw'êl, *yeh-oo-ale´;* from 3261 and 410; *carried away of God; Jeüel,* the name of four Isr.:— Jehiel, Jeiel, Jeuel. Comp. 3273.

3263. יְעוּץ Y^eûwts, *yeh-oots´;* from 5779; *counsellor; Jeüts,* an Isr.:— Jeuz.

3264. יָעוֹר yâ'ôwr, *yaw-ore´;* a var. of 3293; a *forest*:— wood.

3265. יָעוּר Yâ'ûwr, *yaw-oor´;* appar. pass. part. of the same as 3293; *wooded; Jaür,* an Isr.:— Jair [from the marg.].

3266. יְעוּשׁ Y^eûwsh, *yeh-oosh´;* from 5789; *hasty; Jeüsh,* the name of an Edomite and of four Isr.:— Jehush, Jeush. Comp. 3274.

3267. יָעַז yâ'az, *yaw-az´;* a prim. root; to *be bold* or *obstinate*:— fierce.

3268. יַעֲזִיאֵל Ya'ăzîy'êl, *yah-az-ee-ale´;* from 3267 and 410; *emboldened of God; Jaaziël,* an Isr.:— Jaaziel.

3269. יַעֲזִיָּהוּ Ya'ăzîyâhûw, *yah-az-ee-yaw´-hoo;* from 3267 and 3050; *emboldened of Jah; Jaazijah,* an Isr.:— Jaaziah.

3270. יַעֲזֵיר Ya'ăzêyr, *yah-az-ayr´;* or

Ya'zêr, *yah-zare'*; from 5826; *helpful*; *Jaazer* or *Jazer*, a place E. of the Jordan:— Jaazer, Jazer.

3271. יָעַט **yâ'aṭ**, *yaw-at'*; a prim. root; to *clothe*:— cover.

3272. יְעַט **yeʿaṭ** (Chald.), *yeh-at'*; corresp. to 3289; to *counsel*; refl. to *consult*:— counsellor, consult together.

3273. יְעִיאֵל **Yeʿîyʾêl**, *yeh-ee-ale'*; from 3261 and 410; *carried away of God*; *Jeïel*, the name of six Isr.:— Jeiel, Jehiel. Comp. 3262.

יָעִיר **Yâʿîyr**. See 3265.

3274. יְעִישׁ **Yeʿîysh**, *yeh-eesh'*; from 5789; *hasty*; *Jeïsh*, the name of an Edomite and of an Isr.:— Jeush [from the marg.]. Comp. 3266.

3275. יַעְכָּן **Ya'kân**, *yah-kawn'*; from the same as 5912; *troublesome*; *Jakan*, an Isr.:— Jachan.

3276. יָעַל **yâ'al**, *yaw-al'*; a prim. root; prop. to *ascend*; fig. to *be valuable* (obj. useful, subj. benefited):— × at all, set forward, can do good, (be, have) profit (-able).

3277. יָעֵל **yâ'êl**, *yaw-ale'*; from 3276; an *ibex* (as *climbing*):— wild goat.

3278. יָעֵל **Yâ'êl**, *yaw-ale'*; the same as 3277; *Jaël*, a Canaanite:— Jael.

3279. יַעְלָא **Ya'âlâʾ**, *yah-al-aw'*; or

יַעְלָה **Ya'âlâh**, *yah-al-aw'*; the same as 3280 or direct from 3276; *Jaala* or *Jaalah*, one of the Nethinim:— Jaala, Jaalah.

3280. יַעְלָה **ya'âlâh**, *yah-al-aw'*; fem. of 3277:— roe.

3281. יַעְלָם **Ya'lâm**, *yah-lawm'*; from 5956; *occult*; *Jalam*, an Edomite:— Jalam.

3282. יַעַן **ya'an**, *yah'-an*; from an unused root mean. to *pay attention*; prop. *heed*; by impl. *purpose* (sake or account); used adv. to indicate the *reason* or *cause*:— because (that), forasmuch (+ as), seeing then, + that, + whereas, + why.

3283. יָעֵן **yâ'ên**, *yaw-ane'*; from the same as 3282; the *ostrich* (prob. from its answering cry):— ostrich.

3284. יַעֲנָה **ya'ânâh**, *yah-an-aw'*; fem. of 3283, and mean. the same:— + owl.

3285. יַעֲנַי **Ya'ânay**, *yah-an-ah'ee*; from the same as 3283; *responsive*; *Jaanai*, an Isr.:— Jaanai.

3286. יָעַף **yâ'aph**, *yaw-af'*; a prim. root; to *tire* (as if from wearisome *flight*):— faint, cause to fly, (be) weary (self).

3287. יָעֵף **yâ'êph**, *yaw-afe'*; from 3286; *fatigued*; fig. *exhausted*:— faint, weary.

3288. יְעָף **yeʿâph**, *yaw-awf'*; from 3286; *fatigue* (adv. utterly *exhausted*):— swiftly.

3289. יָעַץ **yâ'ats**, *yaw-ats'*; a prim. root; to *advise*; refl. to *deliberate* or *resolve*:— advertise, take advice, advise (well), consult, (give, take) counsel (-lor), determine, devise, guide, purpose.

3290. יַעֲקֹב **Ya'âqôb**, *yah-ak-obe'*; from 6117; *heel*-catcher (i.e. supplanter); *Jaakob*, the Isr. patriarch:— Jacob.

3291. יַעֲקֹבָה **Ya'âqôbâh**, *yah-ak-o'-baw*; from 3290; *Jaakobah*, an Isr.:— Jaakobah.

3292. יַעֲקָן **Ya'âqân**, *yah-ak-awn'*; from the same as 6130; *Jaakan*, an Idumæan:— Jaakan. Comp. 1142.

3293. יַעַר **ya'ar**, *yah'-ar* from an unused root prob. mean. to *thicken* with verdure; a *copse* of bushes; hence, a *forest*; hence, *honey* in the *comb* (as hived in trees):— [honey-] comb, forest, wood.

3294. יַעְרָה **Ya'râh**, *yah-raw'*; a form of 3295; *Jarah*, an Isr.:— Jarah.

3295. יַעֲרָה **ya'ârâh**, *yah-ar-aw'*; fem. of 3293, and mean. the same:— [honey-] comb, forest.

3296. יַעֲרֵי אֹרְגִים **Ya'ârêy 'Orĕgîym**, *yah-ar-ay' o-reg-eem'*; from the plural of 3293 and the masc. plur. act. part. of 707; *woods of weavers*; *Jaare-Oregim*, an Isr.:— Jaare-oregim.

3297. יְעָרִים **Yĕ'ârîym**, *yeh-aw-reem'*; plur. of 3293; *forests*; *Jeärim*, a place in Pal.:— Jearim. Comp. 7157.

3298. יַעֲרֶשְׁיָה **Ya'âreshyâh**, *yah-ar-esh-yaw'*; from an unused root of uncert. signif. and 3050; *Jaareshjah*, an Isr.:— Jaresiah.

3299. יַעֲשׂוּ **Ya'âsûw**, *yah-as-oo'*; from 6213; *they will do*; *Jaasu*, an Isr.:— Jaasau.

3300. יַעֲשִׂיאֵל **Ya'âsîyʾêl**, *yah-as-ee-ale'*; from 6213 and 410; *made of God*; *Jaasiel*, an Isr.:— Jaasiel, Jasiel.

3301. יִפְדְיָה **Yiphdeʿyâh**, *yif-deh-yaw'*; from 6299 and 3050; *Jah will liberate*; *Jiphdejah*, an Isr.:— Iphedeiah.

3302. יָפָה **yâphâh**, *yaw-faw'*; a prim. root; prop. to *be bright*, i.e. (by impl.) *beautiful*:— be beautiful, be (make self) fair (-r), deck.

3303. יָפֶה **yâpheh**, *yaw-feh'*; from 3302; *beautiful* (lit. or fig.):— + beautiful, beauty, comely, fair (-est, one), + goodly, pleasant, well.

3304. יְפֵה־פִיָּה **yĕphêh-phîyâh**, *yef-eh' fee-yaw'*; from 3302 by redupl.; *very beautiful*:— very fair.

3305. יָפוֹ **Yâphôw**, *yaw-fo'*; or

יָפוֹא **Yâphôwʾ** (Ezra 3:7), *yaw-fo'*; from 3302; *beautiful*; *Japho*, a place in Pal.:— Japha, Joppa.

3306. יָפַח **yâphach**, *yaw-fakh'*; a prim. root; prop. to *breathe* hard, i.e. (by impl.) to *sigh*:— bewail self.

3307. יָפֵחַ **yâphêach**, *yaw-fay'-akh*; from 3306; prop. *puffing*, i.e. (fig.) *meditating*:— such as breathe out.

3308. יֳפִי **yŏphîy**, *yof-ee'*; from 3302; *beauty*:— beauty.

3309. יָפִיעַ **Yâphîya'**, *yaw-fee'-ah*; from 3313; *bright*; *Japhia*, the name of a Canaanite, an Isr., and a place in Pal.:— Japhia.

3310. יַפְלֵט **Yaphlêṭ**, *yaf-late'*; from 6403; *he will deliver*; *Japhlet*, an Isr.:— Japhlet.

3311. יַפְלֵטִי **Yaphlêṭiy**, *yaf-lay-tee'*; patron. from 3310; a *Japhletite* or desc. of Japhlet:— Japhleti.

3312. יְפֻנֶּה **Yĕphunneh**, *yef-oon-neh'*; from 6437; *he will be prepared*; *Jephun-*

neh, the name of two Isr.:— Jephunneh.

3313. יָפַע **yâpha'**, *yaw-fah'*; a prim. root; to *shine*:— be light, shew self, (cause to) shine (forth).

3314. יִפְעָה **yiph'âh**, *yif-aw'*; from 3313; *splendor* or (fig.) *beauty*:— brightness.

3315. יֶפֶת **Yepheth**, *yeh'-feth*; from 6601; *expansion*; *Jepheth*, a son of Noah; also his posterity:— Japheth.

3316. יִפְתָּח **Yiphtâch**, *yif-tawkh'*; from 6605; *he will open*; *Jiphtach*, an Isr.; also a place in Pal.:— Jephthah, Jiphtah.

3317. יִפְתַּח־אֵל **Yiphtach-ʾêl**, *yif-tach-ale'*; from 6605 and 410; *God will open*; *Jiphtach-el*, a place in Pal.:— Jiphthah-el.

3318. יָצָא **yâtsâ'**, *yaw-tsaw'*; a prim. root; to *go* (caus. *bring*) *out*, in a great variety of applications, lit. and fig., direct and proxim.:— × after, appear, × assuredly, bear out, × begotten, break out, bring forth (out, up), carry out, come (abroad, out, threat, without), + be condemned, depart (-ing, -ure), draw forth, in the end, escape, exact, fail, fall (out), fetch forth (out), get away (forth, hence, out), (able to, cause to, let) go abroad (forth, on, out), going out, grow, have forth (out), issue out, lay (lie) out, lead out, pluck out, proceed, pull out, put away, be risen, × scarce, send with commandment, shoot forth, spread, spring out, stand out, × still, × surely, take forth (out), at any time, × to [and fro], utter.

3319. יְצָא **yĕtsâʾ** (Chald.), *yets-aw'*; corresp. to 3318:— finish.

3320. יָצַב **yâtsab**, *yaw-tsab'*; a prim. root; to *place* (any thing so as to stay); refl. to *station*, *offer*, *continue*:— present selves, remaining, resort, set (selves), (be able to, can, with-) stand (fast, forth, -ing, still, up).

3321. יְצֵב **yĕtsêb** (Chald.), *yets-abe'*; corresp. to 3320; to *be firm*; hence, to *speak surely*:— truth.

3322. יָצַג **yâtsag**, *yaw-tsag'*; a prim. root; to *place* permanently:— establish, leave, make, present, put, set, stay.

3323. יִצְהָר **yitshâr**, *yits-hawr'*; from 6671; *oil* (as producing *light*); fig. *anointing*:— + anointed oil.

3324. יִצְהָר **Yitshâr**, *yits-hawr'*; the same as 3323; *Jitshar*, an Isr.:— Izhar.

3325. יִצְהָרִי **Yitshâriy**, *yits-haw-ree'*; patron. from 3324; a *Jitsharite* or desc. of Jitshar:— Izeharites, Izharites.

3326. יָצוּעַ **yâtsûwa'**, *yaw-tsoo'-ah*; pass. part. of 3331; *spread*, i.e. a *bed*; (arch.) an *extension*, i.e. *wing* or *lean-to* (a single story or collect.):— bed, chamber, couch.

3327. יִצְחָק **Yitschâq**, *yits-khawk'*; from 6711; *laughter* (i.e. *mockery*); *Jitschak* (or *Isaac*), son of Abraham:— Isaac. Comp. 3446.

3328. יִצְחָר **Yitschar**, *yits-khar'*; from the same as 6713; *he will shine*; *Jitschar*, an Isr.:— and Zehoar [from the marg.].

3329. יָצִיא **yâtsîy'**, *yaw-tsee'*; from 3318;

Hebrew

issue, i.e. offspring:— those that came forth.

3330. יַצִּיב **yatstsîyb** (Chald.), *yats-tseeb´*; from 3321; *fixed, sure*; concr. *certainty*:— certain (-ty), true, truth.

יָצִיעַ **yâtsîya**. See 3326.

3331. יָצַע **yâtsa'**, *yaw-tsah´*; a prim. root; to *strew* as a surface:— make [one's] bed, × lie, spread.

3332. יָצַק **yâtsaq**, *yaw-tsak´*; a prim. root; prop. to *pour* out (tran. or intr.); by impl. to *melt* or *cast* as metal; by extens. to *place* firmly, to *stiffen* or grow hard:— cast, cleave fast, be (as) firm, grow, be hard, lay out, molten, overflow, pour (out), run out, set down, stedfast.

3333. יְצֻקָה **yᵉtsûqâh**, *yets-oo-kaw´*; pass. part. fem. of 3332; *poured* out, i.e. *run* into a mould:— when it was cast.

3334. יָצַר **yâtsar**, *yaw-tsar´*; a prim. root; to *press* (intr.), i.e. *be narrow*; fig. *be in distress*:— be distressed, be narrow, be straitened (in straits), be vexed.

3335. יָצַר **yâtsar**, *yaw-tsar´*; prob. ident. with 3334 (through the *squeezing* into shape); ([comp. 3331]); to *mould* into a form; espec. as a *potter*; fig. to *determine* (i.e. form a resolution):— × earthen, fashion, form, frame, make (-r), potter, purpose.

3336. יֵצֶר **yêtser**, *yay´-tser*; from 3335; a *form*; fig. *conception* (i.e. *purpose*):— frame, thing framed, imagination, mind, work.

3337. יֵצֶר **Yêtser**, *yay-tser*; the same as 3336; *Jetser*, an Isr.:— Jezer.

3338. יָצֻר **yâtsûr**, *yaw-tsoor´*; pass. part. of 3335; *structure*, i.e. limb or part:— member.

3339. יִצְרִי **Yitsrîy**, *yits-ree´*; from 3335; *formative*; *Jitsri*, an Isr.:— Isri.

3340. יִצְרִי **Yitsrîy**, *yits-ree´*; patron. from 3337; a *Jitsrite* (collect.) or desc. of Jetser:— Jezerites.

3341. יָצַת **yâtsath**, *yaw-tsath´*; a prim. root; to *burn* or *set on fire*; fig. to *desolate*:— burn (up), be desolate, set (on) fire ([fire]), kindle.

3342. יֶקֶב **yeqeb**, *yeh´-keb*; from an unused root mean. to *excavate*; a *trough* (as dug out); spec. a wine-*vat* (whether the lower one, into which the juice drains; or the upper, in which the grapes are crushed):— fats, presses, press-fat, wine (-press).

3343. יְקַבְצְאֵל **Yᵉqabtsᵉ'êl**, *yek-ab-tseh-ale´*; from 6908 and 410; *God will gather*; *Jekabtseël*, a place in Pal.:— Jekabzeel. Comp. 6909.

3344. יָקַד **yâqad**, *yaw-kad´*; a prim. root; to *burn*:— (be) burn (-ing), × from the hearth, kindle.

3345. יְקַד **yᵉqad** (Chald.), *yek-ad´*; corresp. to 3344:— burning.

3346. יְקֵדָא **yᵉqêdâ'** (Chald.), *yek-ay-daw´*; from 3345; a *conflagration*:— burning.

3347. יָקְדְעָם **Yoqdᵉ'âm**, *yok-deh-awm´*; from 3344 and 5971; *burning of (the) people*; *Jokdeäm*, a place in Pal.:— Jokdeam.

3348. יָקֶה **Yâqeh**, *yaw-keh´*; from an unused root prob. mean. to *obey*; *obedient*; *Jakeh*, a symb. name (for Solomon):— Jakeh.

3349. יִקָּהָה **yiqqâhâh**, *yik-kaw-haw´*; from the same as 3348; *obedience*:— gathering, to obey.

3350. יְקוֹד **yᵉqôwd**, *yek-ode´*; from 3344; a *burning*:— burning.

3351. יְקוּם **yᵉqûwm**, *yek-oom´*; from 6965; prop. *standing* (extant), i.e. by impl. a *living thing*:— (living) substance.

3352. יָקוֹשׁ **yâqôwsh**, *yaw-koshe´*; from 3369; prop. *entangling*; hence, a *snarer*:— fowler.

3353. יָקוּשׁ **yâqûwsh**, *yaw-koosh´*; pass. part. of 3369; prop. *entangled*, i.e. by impl. (intr.) a *snare*, or (tran.) a *snarer*:— fowler, snare.

3354. יְקוּתִיאֵל **Yᵉqûwthîy'êl**, *yek-ooth-ee´-ale*; from the same as 3348 and 410; *obedience of God*; *Jekuthiël*, an Isr.:— Jekuthiel.

3355. יָקְטָן **Yoqtân**, *yok-tawn´*; from 6994; *he will be made little*; *Joktan*, an Arabian patriarch:— Joktan.

3356. יָקִים **Yâqîym**, *yaw-keem´*; from 6965; *he will raise*; *Jakim*, the name of two Isr.:— Jakim. Comp. 3079.

3357. יַקִּיר **yaqqîyr**, *yak-keer´*; from 3365; *precious*:— dear.

3358. יַקִּיר **yaqqîyr** (Chald.), *yak-keer´*; corresp. to 3357:— noble, rare.

3359. יְקַמְיָה **Yᵉqamyâh**, *yek-am-yaw´*; from 6965 and 3050; *Jah will rise*; *Jekamjah*, the name of two Isr.:— Jekamiah. Comp. 3079.

3360. יְקַמְעָם **Yᵉqam'âm**, *yek-am´-awm*; from 6965 and 5971; (the) *people will rise*; *Jekamam*, an Isr.:— Jekameam. Comp. 3079, 3361.

3361. יָקְמְעָם **Yoqmᵉ'âm**, *yok-meh-awm´*; from 6965 and 5971; (the) *people will be raised*; *Jokmeäm*, a place in Pal.:— Jokmeam. Comp. 3360, 3362.

3362. יָקְנְעָם **Yoqnᵉ'âm**, *yok-neh-awm´*; from 6969 and 5971; (the) *people will be lamented*; *Jokneäm*, a place in Pal.:— Jokneam.

3363. יָקַע **yâqa'**, *yaw-kah´*; a prim. root; prop. to *sever* oneself, i.e. (by impl.) to *be dislocated*; fig. to *abandon*; caus. to *impale* (and thus allow to drop to pieces by *rotting*):— be alienated, depart, hang (up), be out of joint.

3364. יָקַץ **yâqats**, *yaw-kats´*; a prim. root; to *awake* (intr.):— (be) awake (-d).

יָקַף **yâqaph**. See 5362.

3365. יָקַר **yâqar**, *yaw-kar´*; a prim. root; prop. to *be heavy*, i.e. (fig.) *valuable*; caus. to *make rare* (fig. to *inhibit*):— be (make) precious, be prized, be set by, withdraw.

3366. יְקָר **yᵉqâr**, *yek-awr´*; from 3365; *value*, i.e. (concr.) *wealth*; abstr. *costliness, dignity*:— honour, precious (things), price.

3367. יְקָר **yᵉqâr** (Chald.), *yek-awr´*; corresp. to 3366:— glory, honour.

3368. יָקָר **yâqâr**, *yaw-kawr´*; from 3365; *valuable* (obj. or subj.):— brightness,

clear, costly, excellent, fat, honourable women, precious, reputation.

3369. יָקֹשׁ **yâqôsh**, *yaw-koshe´*; a prim. root; to *ensnare* (lit. or fig.):— fowler (lay a) snare.

3370. יָקְשָׁן **Yoqshân**, *yok-shawn´*; from 3369; *insidious*; *Jokshan*, an Arabian patriarch:— Jokshan.

3371. יָקְתְאֵל **Yoqthᵉ'êl**, *yok-theh-ale´*; prob. from the same as 3348 and 410; *veneration of God* [comp. 3354]; *Joktheël*, the name of a place in Pal., and of one in Idumæa:— Joktheel.

יָרֵא **yârâ'**. See 3384.

3372. יָרֵא **yârê'**, *yaw-ray´*; a prim. root; to *fear*; mor. to *revere*; caus. to *frighten*:— affright, be (make) afraid, dread (-ful), (put in) fear (-ful, -fully, -ing), (be had in) reverence (-end), × see, terrible (act, -ness, thing).

3373. יָרֵא **yârê'**, *yaw-ray´*; from 3372; *fearing*; mor. *reverent*:— afraid, fear (-ful).

3374. יִרְאָה **yir'âh**, *yir-aw´*; fem. of 3373; *fear* (also used as infin.); mor. *reverence*:— × dreadful, × exceedingly, fear (-fulness).

3375. יִרְאוֹן **Yir'ôwn**, *yir-ohn´*; from 3372; *fearfulness*; *Jiron*, a place in Pal:— Iron.

3376. יִרְאִיָּיה **Yir'îyâyh**, *yir-ee-yaw´*; from 3373 and 3050; *fearful of Jah*; *Jirijah*, an Isr.:— Irijah.

3377. יָרֵב **Yârêb**, *yaw-rabe´*; from 7378; *he will contend*; *Jareb*, a symb. name for Assyria:— Jareb. Comp. 3402.

3378. יְרֻבַּעַל **Yᵉrubba'al**, *yer-oob-bah´-al*; from 7378 and 1168; *Baal will contend*; *Jerubbaal*, a symbol. name of Gideon:— Jerubbaal.

3379. יָרָבְעָם **Yârob'âm**, *yaw-rob-awm´*; from 7378 and 5971; (the) *people will contend*; *Jarobam*, the name of two Isr. kings:— Jeroboam.

3380. יְרֻבֶּשֶׁת **Yᵉrubbesheth**, *yer-oob-beh´-sheth*; from 7378 and 1322; *shame* (i.e. the idol) *will contend*; *Jerubbesheth*, a symbol. name for Gideon:— Jerubbesheth.

3381. יָרַד **yârad**, *yaw-rad´*; a prim. root; to *go downwards*; or conventionally to a lower region, as the shore, a boundary, the enemy, etc.; or fig. to *fall*); caus. to *bring down* (in all the above applications):— × abundantly, bring down, carry down, cast down, (cause to) come (-ing) down, fall (down), get down, go (-ing) down (-ward), hang down, × indeed, let down, light (down), put down (off, (cause to, let) run down, sink, subdue, take down.

3382. יֶרֶד **Yered**, *yeh´-red*; from 3381; a *descent*; *Jered*, the name of an antediluvian, and of an Isr.:— Jared.

3383. יַרְדֵּן **Yardên**, *yar-dane´*; from 3381; a *descender*; *Jarden*, the principal river of Pal.:— Jordan.

3384. יָרָה **yârâh**, *yaw-raw´*; or (2 Chron. 26:15)

יָרָא **yârâ'**, *yaw-raw´*; a prim. root; prop. to *flow* as water (i.e. to *rain*); tran. to *lay* or *throw* (espec. an arrow, i.e. to

shoot); fig. to *point* out (as if by *aiming*
the finger), to *teach*:— (+) archer, cast,
direct, inform, instruct, lay, shew,
shoot, teach (-er, -ing), through.

3385. יְרוּאֵל **Yᵉrûw'êl**, *yer-oo-ale'*; from
3384 and 410; *founded of God; Jeruel*, a
place in Pal.:— Jeruel.

3386. יְרוֹחַ **Yârôwach**, *yaw-ro'-akh*;
perh. denom. from 3394; (born at the)
new *moon; Jaroäch*, an Isr.:— Jaroah.

3387. יָרוֹק **yârôwq**, *yaw-roke'*; from
3417; *green*, i.e. an herb:— green thing.

3388. יְרוּשָׁא **Yᵉrûwshâ'**, *yer-oo-shaw'*; or

יְרוּשָׁה **Yᵉrûwshâh**, *yer-oo-shaw'*;
fem. pass. part. of 3423; *possessed;
Jerusha* or *Jerushah*, an Israelitess:—
Jerusha, Jerushah.

3389. יְרוּשָׁלַ͏ִם **Yᵉrûwshâlaim**, *yer-oo-
shaw-lah'-im*; rarely

יְרוּשָׁלַיִם **Yᵉrûwshâlayim**, *yer-oo-
shaw-lah'-yim*; a dual (in allusion to its
two main hills [the true pointing, at
least of the former reading, seems to
be that of 3390]); prob. from (the pass.
part. of) 3384 and 7999; *founded peaceful; Jerushalaïm* or *Jerushalem*, the
capital city of Pal.:— Jerusalem.

3390. יְרוּשָׁלֶם **Yᵉrûwshâlêm** (Chald.),
yer-oo-shaw-lame'; corresp. to 3389:—
Jerusalem.

3391. יֶרַח **yerach**, *yeh'-rakh*; from an
unused root of uncert. signif.; a *luna-
tion*, i.e. *month*:— month, moon.

3392. יֶרַח **Yerach**, *yeh'-rakh*; the same
as 3391; *Jerach*, an Arabian patriarch:— Jerah.

3393. יֶרַח **yᵉrach** (Chald.), *yeh-rakh'*;
corresp. to 3391; a *month*:— month.

3394. יֶרַח **yârêach**, *yaw-ray'-akh*; from
the same as 3391; the *moon*:— moon.

יְרֵחוֹ **Yᵉrêchôw**. See 3405.

3395. יְרֹחָם **Yᵉrôchâm**, *yer-o-khawm'*;
from 7355; *compassionate; Jerocham*,
the name of seven or eight Isr.:— Jeroham.

3396. יְרַחְמְאֵל **Yᵉrachmᵉ'êl**, *yer-akh-
meh-ale'*; from 7355 and 410; *God will
compassionate; Jerachmeël*, the name
of three Isr.:— Jerahmeel.

3397. יְרַחְמְאֵלִי **Yᵉrachmᵉêlîy**, *yer-akh-
meh-ay-lee'*; patron. from 3396; a *Jerachmeëlite* or desc. of Jerachmeel:—
Jerahmeelites.

3398. יַרְחָע **Yarchâ'**, *yar-khaw'*; prob. of
Eg. or.; *Jarcha*, an Eg.:— Jarha.

3399. יָרַט **yârat**, *yaw-rat'*; a prim. root;
to *precipitate* or *hurl* (rush) headlong;
(intr.) to *be rash*:— be perverse, turn
over.

3400. יְרִיאֵל **Yᵉrîy'êl**, *yer-ee-ale'*; from
3384 and 410; *thrown of God; Jeriël*, an
Isr.:— Jeriel. Comp. 3385.

3401. יָרִיב **yârîyb**, *yaw-rebe'*; from 7378;
lit. *he will contend*; prop. adj. *contentious*; used as noun, an *adversary*:—
that content (-eth), that strive.

3402. יָרִיב **Yârîyb**, *yaw-rebe'*; the same
as 3401; *Jarib*, the name of three Isr.:—
Jarib.

3403. יְרִיבַי **Yᵉrîybay**, *yer-eeb-ah'ee*;
from 3401; *contentious; Jeribai*, an
Isr.:— Jeribai.

3404. יְרִיָּה **Yᵉrîyâh**, *yer-ee-yaw'*; or

יְרִיָּהוּ **Yᵉrîyâhûw**, *yer-ee-yaw'-
hoo*; from 3384 and 3050; *Jah will throw;
Jerijah*, an Isr.:— Jeriah, Jerijah.

3405. יְרִיחוֹ **Yᵉrîychôw**, *yer-ee-kho'*; or

יְרֵחוֹ **Yᵉrêchôw**, *yer-ay-kho'*; or
var. (1 Kings 16:34)

יְרִיחֹה **Yᵉrîychôh**, *yer-ee-kho'*;
perh. from 3394; *its month*; or else from
7306; *fragrant; Jericho* or *Jerecho*, a
place in Pal.:— Jericho.

3406. יְרִימוֹת **Yᵉrîymôwth**, *yer-ee-
mohth'*; or

יְרִימוֹת **Yᵉrêymôwth**, *yer-ay-
mohth'*; or

יְרֵמוֹת **Yᵉrêmôwth**, *yer-ay-mohth'*;
fem. plur. from 7311; *elevations; Jerimoth* or *Jeremoth*, the name of twelve
Isr.:— Jeremoth, Jerimoth, and Ramoth [*from the marg.*].

3407. יְרִיעָה **yᵉrîy'âh**, *yer-ee-aw'*; from
3415; a *hanging* (as *tremulous*):— curtain.

3408. יְרִיעוֹת **Yᵉrîy'ôwth**, *yer-ee-ohth'*;
plur. of 3407; *curtains; Jerioth*, an Israelitess:— Jerioth.

3409. יָרֵךְ **yârêk**, *yaw-rake'*; from an unused root mean. to *be soft*; the *thigh*
(from its fleshy *softness*); by euphem.
the *generative parts*; fig. a *shank,
flank, side*:— × body, loins, shaft, side,
thigh.

3410. יַרְכָא **yarkâ'** (Chald.), *yar-kaw'*;
corresp. to 3411; a *thigh*:— thigh.

3411. יְרֵכָה **yᵉrêkâh**, *yer-ay-kaw'*; fem.
of 3409; prop. the *flank*; but used only
fig., the *rear* or *recess*:— border, coast,
part, quarter, side.

3412. יַרְמוּת **Yarmûwth**, *yar-mooth'*;
from 7311; *elevation; Jarmuth*, the
name of two places in Pal.:— Jarmuth.

יְרֵמוֹת **Yᵉrêmôwth**. See 3406.

3413. יְרֵמַי **Yᵉrêmay**, *yer-ay-mah'-ee*;
from 7311; *elevated; Jeremai*, an Isr.:—
Jeremai.

3414. יִרְמְיָה **Yirmᵉyâh**, *yir-meh-yaw'*; or

יִרְמְיָהוּ **Yirmᵉyâhûw**, *yir-meh-
yaw'-hoo*; from 7311 and 3050; *Jah will
rise; Jirmejah*, the name of eight or
nine Isr.:— Jeremiah.

3415. יָרַע **yâra'**, *yaw-rah'*; a prim. root;
prop. to *be broken* up (with any violent
action) i.e. (fig.) to *fear*:— be grievous
[only Isa. 15:4; the rest belong to 7489].

3416. יִרְפְּאֵל **Yirpᵉ'êl**, *yir-peh-ale'*; from
7495 and 410; *God will heal; Jirpeël*, a
place in Pal.:— Irpeel.

3417. יָרַק **yâraq**, *yaw-rak'*; a prim. root;
to *spit*:— × but, spit.

3418. יֶרֶק **yereq**, *yeh'-rek*; from 3417 (in
the sense of *vacuity* of color); prop. *pal-
lor*, i.e. hence, the yellowish *green* of
young and sickly vegetation; concr.
verdure, i.e. grass or vegetation:—
grass, green (thing).

3419. יָרָק **yârâq**, *yaw-rawk'*; from the
same as 3418; prop. *green*; concr. a
vegetable:— green, herbs.

יַרְקוֹן **Yarqôwn**. See 4313.

3420. יֵרָקוֹן **yêrâqôwn**, *yay-raw-kone'*;
from 3418; *paleness*, whether of per-

sons (from fright), or of plants (from
drought):— greenish, yellow.

3421. יָרְקְעָם **Yorqᵉ'âm**, *yor-keh-awm'*;
from 7324 and 5971; *people will be
poured forth; Jorkeäm*, a place in
Pal.:— Jorkeam.

3422. יְרַקְרַק **yᵉraqraq**, *yer-ak-rak'*;
from the same as 3418; *yellowishness*:— greenish, yellow.

3423. יָרַשׁ **yârash**, *yaw-rash'*; or

יָרֵשׁ **yârêsh**, *yaw-raysh'*; a prim.
root; to *occupy* (by *driving* out previous
tenants, and *possessing* in their place);
by impl. to *seize*, to *rob*, to *inherit*; also
to *expel*, to *impoverish*, to *ruin*:— cast
out, consume, destroy, disinherit, dispossess, drive (-ing) out, enjoy, expel, ×
without fail, (give to, leave for) inherit
(-ance, -or) + magistrate, be (make)
poor, come to poverty, (give to, make
to) possess, get (have) in (take) possession, seize upon, succeed, × utterly.

3424. יְרֵשָׁה **yᵉrêshâh**, *yer-ay-shaw'*;
from 3423; *occupancy*:— possession.

3425. יְרֻשָּׁה **yᵉrushâh**, *yer-oosh-shaw'*;
from 3423; something *occupied*; a *conquest*; also a *patrimony*:— heritage, inheritance, possession.

3426. יֵשׁ **yêsh**, *yaysh*; perh. from an unused root mean. to *stand* out, or *exist*;
entity; used adv. or as a copula for the
substantive verb (1961); there *is* or *are*
(or any other form of the verb to *be*, as
may suit the connection):— (there) are,
(he, it, shall, there, there may, there
shall, there should) be, thou do, had,
hast, (which) hath, (I, shalt, that) have,
(he, it, there) is, substance, it (there)
was, (there) were, ye will, thou wilt,
wouldest.

3427. יָשַׁב **yâshab**, *yaw-shab'*; a prim.
root; prop. to *sit* down (spec. as judgement in ambush, in quiet); by impl. to
dwell, to *remain*; caus. to *settle*, to
marry:— (make) to abide (-ing), continue, (cause to, make to) dwell (-ing),
ease self, endure, establish, × fail, habitation, haunt, (make to) inhabit (-ant),
make to keep [house], lurking, × marry
(-ing), (bring again to) place, remain,
return, seat, set (-tle), (down-) sit
(-down, still, -ting down, -ting [place],
-uate), take, tarry.

3428. יֶשֶׁבְאָב **Yesheb'âb**, *yeh-sheb-awb'*;
from 3427 and 1; *seat* of (his) *father;
Jeshebab*, an Isr.:— Jeshebeab.

3429. יֹשֵׁב בַּשֶּׁבֶת **Yôshêb bash-Shebeth**,
yo-shabe' bash-sheh'-beth; from the
act. part. of 3427 and 7674, with a prep.
and the art. interposed; *sitting in the
seat; Josheb-bash-Shebeth*, an Isr.:—
that sat in the seat.

3430. יִשְׁבּוֹ בְּנֹב **Yishbôw bᵉ-Nôb**, *yish-
bo' beh-nobe'*; from 3427 and 5011, with
a pron. suff. and a prep. interposed; *his
dwelling* (is) *in Nob; Jishbo-be-Nob*, a
Philistine:— Ishbi-benob [*from the
marg.*].

3431. יִשְׁבַּח **Yishbach**, *yish-bakh'*; from
7623; *he will praise; Jishbach*, an Isr.:—
Ishbah.

3432. יָשׁוּבִי **Yâshûbîy**, *yaw-shoo-bee'*;
patron. from 3437; a *Jashubite*, or desc.
of Jashub:— Jashubites.

3433. שֻׁבִי לֶחֶם **Yâshûbîy Lechem**, yaw-shoo-bee´ leh´-khem; from 7725 and 3899; *returner of bread; Jashubi-Lechem*, an Isr.:— Jashubi-lehem. [Prob. the text should be pointed

יֹשְׁבֵי לֶחֶם **Yôsh°bêy Lechem**, yo-sheh-bay´ leh´-khem, and rendered "(they were) inhab. of Lechem," i.e. of Bethlehem (by contr.). Comp. 3902].

3434. יָשָׁבְעָם **Yâshob'âm**, yaw-shob-awm´; from 7725 and 5971; *people will return; Jashobam*, the name of two or three Isr.:— Jashobeam.

3435. יִשְׁבָּק **Yishbâq**, yish-bawk´; from an unused root corresp. to 7662; *he will leave; Jishbak*, a son of Abraham:— Ishbak.

3436. יָשְׁבְקָשָׁה **Yoshb°qâshâh**, yosh-bek-aw-shaw´; from 3427 and 7186; a *hard seat; Joshbekashah*, an Isr.:— Josh-bekashah.

3437. יָשׁוּב **Yâshûwb**, yaw-shoob´; or

יָשִׁיב **Yâshîyb**, yaw-sheeb´; from 7725; *he will return; Jashub*, the name of two Isr.:— Jashub.

3438. יִשְׁוָה **Yishvâh**, yish-vaw´; from 7737; *he will level; Jishvah*, an Isr.:— Ishvah, Isvah.

3439. יְשׁוֹחָיָה **Y°shôwchâyâh**, yesh-o-khaw-yaw´; from the same as 3445 and 3050; *Jah will empty; Jeshochajah*, an Isr.:— Jeshoaiah.

3440. יִשְׁוִי **Yishvîy**, yish-vee´; from 7737; *level; Jishvi*, the name of two Isr.:— Ishuai, Ishvi, Isui, Jesui.

3441. יִשְׁוִי **Yishvîy**, yish-vee´; patron. from 3440; a *Jishvite* (collect.) or desc. of Jishvi:— Jesuites.

3442. יֵשׁוּעַ **Yêshûwa'**, yay-shoo´-ah; for 3091; *he will save; Jeshua*, the name of ten Isr., also of a place in Pal.:— Jeshua.

3443. יֵשׁוּעַ **Yêshûwa'** (Chald.), yay-shoo´-ah; corresp. to 3442:— Jeshua.

3444. יְשׁוּעָה **y°shûw'âh**, yesh-oo´-aw; fem. pass. part. of 3467; something *saved*, i.e. (abstr.) *deliverance;* hence, *aid, victory, prosperity:*— deliverance, health, help (-ing), salvation, save, saving (health), welfare.

3445. שַׁח **yeshach**, yeh´-shakh; from an unused root mean. to *gape* (as the empty stomach); *hunger:*— casting down.

3446. יִשְׂחָק **Yischâq**, yis-khawk´; from 7831; *he will laugh; Jischak*, the heir of Abraham:— Isaac. Comp. 3327.

3447. יָשַׁט **yâshat**, yaw-shat´; a prim. root; to *extend:*— hold out.

3448. יִשַׁי **Yîshay**, yee-shah´-ee; by Chald.

אִישַׁי **'Îyshay**, ee-shah´-ee; from the same as 3426; *extant; Jishai*, David's father:— Jesse.

יָשִׁיב **Yâshîyb**. See 3437.

3449. יִשְׁשִׁיָּה **Yishshîyâh**, yish-shee-yaw´; or

יִשְׁשִׁיָּהוּ **Yishshîyâhûw**, yish-shee-yaw´-hoo; from 5383 and 3050; *Jah will lend; Jishshijah*, the name of five Isr.:— Ishiah, Isshiah, Ishijah, Jesiah.

3450. יִשִׂמָאֵל **Y°sîymâ'êl**, yes-eem-aw-

ale´; from 7760 and 410; *God will place; Jesimaël*, an Isr.:— Jesimael.

3451. יְשִׁימָה **y°shîymâh**, yesh-ee-maw´; from 3456; *desolation:*— let death seize [from the marg.].

3452. יְשִׁימוֹן **y°shîymôwn**, yesh-ee-mone´; from 3456; a *desolation:*— desert, Jeshimon, solitary, wilderness.

יְשִׁימוֹת **y°shîymôwth**. See 1020, 3451.

3453. יָשִׁישׁ **yâshîysh**, yaw-sheesh´; from 3486; an *old* man:— (very) aged (man), ancient, very old.

3454. יְשִׁישַׁי **Y°shîyshay**, yesh-ee-shah´-ee; from 3453; *aged; Jeshishai*, an Isr.:— Jeshishai.

3455. יָשַׂם **yâsam**, yaw-sam´; a prim. root; to *place;* intr. to *be placed:*— be put (set).

3456. יָשַׁם **yâsham**, yaw-sham´; a prim. root; to *lie waste:*— be desolate.

3457. יִשְׁמָא **Yishmâ'**, yish-maw´; from 3456; *desolate; Jishma*, an Isr.:— Ishma.

3458. יִשְׁמָעֵאל **Yishmâ'ê'l**, yish-maw-ale´; from 8085 and 410; *God will hear; Jishmaël*, the name of Abraham's oldest son, and of five Isr.:— Ishmael.

3459. יִשְׁמָעֵאלִי **Yishmâ'ê'lîy**, yish-maw-ay-lee´; patron. from 3458; a *Jishmaëlite* or desc. of Jishmael:— Ishmaelite.

3460. יִשְׁמַעְיָה **Yishma'yâh**, yish-mah-yaw´; or

יִשְׁמַעְיָהוּ **Yishma'yâhûw**, yish-mah-yaw´-hoo; from 8085 and 3050; *Jah will hear; Jishmajah*, the name of two Isr.:— Ishmaiah.

3461. יִשְׁמְרַי **Yishm°ray**, yish-mer-ah´-ee; from 8104; *preservative; Jishmerai*, an Isr.:— Ishmerai.

3462. יָשֵׁן **yâshên**, yaw-shane´; a prim. root; prop. to *be slack* or *languid*, i.e. (by impl.) *sleep* (fig. to *die*); also to *grow old, stale* or *inveterate:*— old (store), remain long, (make to) sleep.

3463. יָשֵׁן **yâshên**, yaw-shane´; from 3462; *sleepy:*— asleep, (one out of) sleep (-eth, -ing), slept.

3464. יָשֵׁן **Yâshên**, yaw-shane´; the same as 3463; *Jashen*, an Isr.:— Jashen.

3465. יָשָׁן **yâshân**, yaw-shawn´; from 3462; *old:*— old.

3466. יְשָׁנָה **Y°shânâh**, yesh-aw-naw´; fem. of 3465; *Jeshanah*, a place in Pal.:— Jeshanah.

3467. יָשַׁע **yâsha'**, yaw-shah´; a prim. root; prop. to *be open, wide* or *free*, i.e. (by impl.) to *be safe;* caus. to *free* or *succor:*— × at all, avenging, defend, deliver (-er), help, preserve, rescue, be safe, bring (having) salvation, save (-iour), get victory.

3468. יֶשַׁע **yesha'**, yeh´-shah; or

יֵשַׁע **yêsha'**, yay´-shah; from 3467; *liberty, deliverance, prosperity:*— safety, salvation, saving.

3469. יִשְׁעִי **Yish'îy**, yish-ee´; from 3467; *saving; Jishi*, the name of four Isr.:— Ishi.

3470. יְשַׁעְיָה **Y°sha'yâh**, yesh-ah-yaw´; or

יְשַׁעְיָהוּ **Y°sha'yâhûw**, yesh-ah-yaw´-hoo; from 3467 and 3050; *Jah has saved; Jeshajah*, the name of seven Isr.:— Isaiah, Jesaiah, Jeshaiah.

3471. יָשְׁפֵה **yâsh°phêh**, yaw-shef-ay´; from an unused root mean. to *polish;* a gem supposed to be *jasper* (from the resemblance in name):— jasper.

3472. יִשְׁפָּה **Yishpâh**, yish-paw´; perh. from 8192; *he will scratch; Jishpah*, an Isr.:— Ispah.

3473. יִשְׁפָּן **Yishpân**, yish-pawn´; prob. from the same as 8227; *he will hide; Jishpan*, an Isr.:— Ishpan.

3474. יָשַׁר **yâshar**, yaw-shar´; a prim. root; to *be straight* or *even;* fig. to *be* (caus. to *make*) *right, pleasant, prosperous:*— direct, fit, seem good (meet), + please (will), be (esteem, go) right (on), bring (look, make, take the) straight (way), be upright (-ly).

3475. יֵשֶׁר **Yêsher**, yay´-sher; from 3474; *the right; Jesher*, an Isr.:— Jesher.

3476. יֹשֶׁר **yôsher**, yo´-sher; from 3474; *the right:*— equity, meet, right, upright (-ness).

3477. יָשָׁר **yâshâr**, yaw-shawr´; from 3474; *straight* (lit. or fig.):— convenient, equity, Jasher, just, meet (-est), + pleased well right (-eous), straight, (most) upright (-ly, -ness).

3478. יִשְׂרָאֵל **Yisrâ'êl**, yis-raw-ale´; from 8280 and 410; *he will rule* (as) *God; Jisraël*, a symb. name of Jacob; also (typ.) of his posterity:— Israel.

3479. יִשְׂרָאֵל **Yisrâ'êl** (Chald.), yis-raw-ale´; corresp. to 3478:— Israel.

3480. יְשַׂרְאֵלָה **Y°sar'êlâh**, yes-ar-ale´-aw; by var. from 3477 and 410 with directive enclitic; *right towards God; Jesarelah*, an Isr.:— Jesharelah. Comp. 841.

3481. יִשְׂרְאֵלִי **Yisr°'êlîy**, yis-reh-ay-lee´; patron. from 3478; a *Jisreëlite* or desc. of Jisrael:— of Israel, Israelite.

3482. יִשְׂרְאֵלִית **Yisr°'êlîyth**, yis-reh-ay-leeth´; fem. of 3481; a *Jisreëlitess* or female desc. of Jisrael:— Israelitish.

3483. יִשְׂרָה **yishrâh**, yish-raw´; fem. or 3477; *rectitude:*— uprightness.

3484. יְשֻׁרוּן **Y°shûrûwn**, yesh-oo-roon´; from 3474; *upright; Jeshurun*, a symbol. name for Israel:— Jeshurun.

3485. יִשָּׂשכָר **Yissâ°kâr**, yis-saw-kawr´; (strictly yis-saws-kawr´); from 5375 and 7939; *he will bring a reward; Jissaskar*, a son of Jacob:— Issachar.

3486. יָשֵׁשׁ **yâshêsh**, yaw-shaysh´; from an unused root mean. to *blanch;* gray-haired, i.e. an *aged* man:— stoop for age.

3487. יָת **yath** (Chald.), yath; corresp. to 853; a *sign of the object of a verb:*— + whom.

3488. יְתִב **y°thîb** (Chald.), yeth-eeb´; corresp. to 3427; to *sit* or *dwell:*— dwell, (be) set, sit.

3489. יָתֵד **yâthêd**, yaw-thade´; from an unused root mean. to *pin* through or *fast;* a *peg:*— nail, paddle, pin, stake.

3490. יָתוֹם **yâthôwm**, yaw-thome´; from an unused root mean. to *be lonely;* a bereaved person:— fatherless (child), orphan.

3491. יָתוּר **yâthûwr**, *yaw-thoor´*; pass. part. of 3498; prop. what is *left*, i.e. (by impl.) a *gleaning*:— range.

3492. יַתִּיר **Yattîyr**, *yat-teer´*; from 3498; redundant; *Jattir*, a place in Pal.:— Jattir.

3493. יַתִּיר **yattîyr** (Chald.), *yat-teer´*; corresp. to 3492; *preeminent*; adv. *very*:— exceeding (-ly), excellent.

3494. יִתְלָה **Yithlâh**, *yith-law´*; prob. from 8518; it *will hang*, i.e. *be high*; *Jithlah*, a place in Pal.:— Jethlah.

3495. יִתְמָה **Yithmâh**, *yith-maw´*; from the same as 3490; *orphanage*; *Jithmah*, an Isr.:— Ithmah.

3496. יַתְנִיאֵל **Yathnîy'êl**, *yath-nee-ale´*; from an unused root mean. to *endure*, and 410; *continued of God*; *Jathniël*, an Isr.:— Jathniel.

3497. יִתְנָן **Yithnân**, *yith-nawn´*; from the same as 8577; *extensive*; *Jithnan*, a place in Pal.:— Ithnan.

3498. יָתַר **yâthar**, *yaw-thar´*; a prim. root; to *jut* over or *exceed*; by impl. to *excel*; (intr.) to *remain* or *be left*; caus. to *leave, cause to abound, preserve*:— excel, leave (a remnant), left behind, too much, make plenteous, preserve, (be, let) remain (-der, -ing, -nant), reserve, residue, rest.

3499. יֶתֶר **yether**, *yeh´-ther*; from 3498; prop. an *overhanging*, i.e. (by impl.) an *excess, superiority, remainder*; also a small *rope* (as hanging free):— + abundant, cord, exceeding, excellency (-ent), what they leave, that hath left, plentifully , remnant, residue, rest, string, with.

3500. יֶתֶר **Yether**, *yeh´-ther*; the same as 3499; *Jether*, the name of five or six Isr. and of one Midianite:— Jether, Jethro. Comp. 3503.

3501. יִתְרָא **Yithrâ'**, *yith-raw´*; by var. for 3502; *Jithra*, an Isr. (or Ishmaelite):— Ithra.

3502. יִתְרָה **yithrâh**, *yith-raw´*; fem. of 3499; prop. *excellence*, i.e. (by impl.) *wealth*:— abundance, riches.

3503. יִתְרוֹ **Yithrôw**, *yith-ro´*; from 3499 with pron. suff.; *his excellence*; *Jethro*, Moses' father-in-law:— Jethro. Comp. 3500.

3504. יִתְרוֹן **yithrôwn**, *yith-rone´*; from 3498; *preeminence, gain*:— better, excellency (-leth), profit (-able).

3505. יִתְרִי **Yithrîy**, *yith-ree´*; patron. from 3500; a *Jithrite* or desc. of Jether:— Ithrite.

3506. יִתְרָן **Yithrân**, *yith-rawn´*; from 3498; *excellent*; *Jithran*, the name of an Edomite and of an Isr.:— Ithran.

3507. יִתְרְעָם **Yithre'âm**, *yith-reh-awm´*; from 3499 and 5971; *excellence of people*; *Jithreäm*, a son of David:— Ithream.

3508. יֹתֶרֶת **yôthereth**, *yo-theh´-reth*; fem. act. part. of 3498; the *lobe* or *flap* of the liver (as if redundant or outhanging):— caul.

3509. יְתֵת **Ye thêyth**, *yeh-thayth´*; of un-

cert. der.; *Jetheth*, an Edomite:— Jetheth.

כ

3510. כָּאַב **kâ'ab**, *kaw-ab´*; a prim. root; prop. to *feel pain*; by impl. to *grieve*; fig. to *spoil*:— grieving, mar, have pain, make sad (sore), (be) sorrowful.

3511. כְּאֵב **ke 'êb**, *keh-abe´*; from 3510; *suffering* (phys. or ment.), *adversity*:— grief, pain, sorrow.

3512. כָּאָה **kâ'âh**, *kaw-aw´*; a prim. root; to *despond*; caus. to *deject*:— broken, be grieved, make sad.

3513. כָּבַד **kâbad**, *kaw-bad´*; or

כָּבֵד **kâbêd**, *kaw-bade´*; a prim. root; to *be heavy*, i.e. in a bad sense (*burdensome, severe, dull*) or in a good sense (*numerous, rich, honorable*); caus. to *make weighty* (in the same two senses):— abounding with, more grievously afflict, boast, be chargeable, × be dim, glorify, be (make) glorious (things), glory, (very) great, be grievous, harden, be (make) heavy, be heavier, lay heavily, (bring to, come to, do, get, be had in) honour (self), (be) honourable (man) , lade, × more be laid, make self many, nobles, prevail, promote (to honour), be rich, be (go) sore, stop.

3514. כֹּבֶד **kôbed**, *ko´-bed*; from 3513; *weight, multitude, vehemence*:— grievousness, heavy, great number.

3515. כָּבֵד **kâbêd**, *kaw-bade´*; from 3513; *heavy*; fig. in a good sense (*numerous*) or in a bad sense (*severe, difficult, stupid*):— (so) great, grievous, hard (-ened), (too) heavy (-ier), laden, much, slow, sore, thick.

3516. כָּבֵד **kâbêd**, *kaw-bade´*; the same as 3515; the *liver* (as the *heaviest* of the viscera):— liver.

כָּבֹד **kâbôd**. See 3519.

3517. כְּבֵדֻת **ke bêdûth**, *keb-ay-dooth´*; fem. of 3515; *difficulty*:— × heavily.

3518. כָּבָה **kâbâh**, *kaw-baw´*; a prim. root; to *expire* or (caus.) to *extinguish* (fire, light, anger):— go (put) out, quench.

3519. כָּבוֹד **kâbôwd**, *kaw-bode´*; rarely

כָּבֹד **kâbôd**, *kaw-bode´*; from 3513; prop. *weight*, but only fig. in a good sense, *splendor* or *copiousness*:— glorious (-ly), glory, honour (-able).

3520. כְּבוּדָּה **ke bûwddâh**, *keb-ood-daw´*; irreg. fem. pass. part. of 3513; *weightiness*, i.e. *magnificence, wealth*:— carriage, all glorious, stately.

3521. כָּבוּל **Kâbûwl**, *kaw-bool´*; from the same as 3525 in the sense of *limitation*; *sterile*; *Cabul*, the name of two places in Pal.:— Cabul.

3522. כַּבּוֹן **Kabbôwn**, *kab-bone´*; from an unused root mean. to *heap* up; *hilly*; *Cabon*, a place in Pal.:— Cabbon.

3523. כְּבִיר **ke bîyr**, *keb-eer´*; from 3527 in the orig. sense of *plaiting*; a *matrass* (of intertwined materials):— pillow.

3524. כַּבִּיר **kabbîyr**, *kab-beer´*; from 3527; *vast*, whether in extent (fig. of power, *mighty*; of time, *aged*), or in

number, *many*:— + feeble, mighty, most, much, strong, valiant.

3525. כֶּבֶל **kebel**, *keh´-bel*; from an unused root mean. to *twine* or braid together; a *fetter*:— fetter.

3526. כָּבַס **kâbaç**, *kaw-bas´*; a prim. root; to *trample*; hence, to *wash* (prop. by stamping with the feet), whether lit. (incl. the *fulling* process) or fig.:— fuller, wash (-ing).

3527. כָּבַר **kâbar**, *kaw-bar´*; a prim. root; prop. to *plait* together, i.e. (fig.) to *augment* (espec. in number or quantity, to *accumulate*):— in abundance, multiply.

3528. כְּבָר **ke bâr**, *keb-awr´*; from 3527; prop. *extent* of time, i.e. a *great while*; hence, *long ago, formerly, hitherto*:— already, (seeing that which), now.

3529. כְּבָר **Ke bâr**, *keb-awr´*; the same as 3528; *length*; *Kebar*, a river of Mesopotamia:— Chebar. Comp. 2249.

3530. כִּבְרָה **kibrâh**, *kib-raw´*; fem. of 3528; prop. *length*, i.e. a *measure* (of uncert. dimension):— × little.

3531. כְּבָרָה **ke bârâh**, *keb-aw-raw´*; from 3527 in its orig. sense; a *sieve* (as netted):— sieve.

3532. כֶּבֶשׂ **kebes**, *keh-bes´*; from an unused root mean. to *dominate*; a *ram* (just old enough to *butt*):— lamb, sheep.

3533. כָּבַשׁ **kâbash**, *kaw-bash´*; a prim. root; to *tread* down; hence, neg. to *disregard*; pos. to *conquer, subjugate, violate*:— bring into bondage, force, keep under, subdue, bring into subjection.

3534. כֶּבֶשׁ **kebesh**, *keh´-besh*; from 3533; a *footstool* (as trodden upon):— footstool.

3535. כִּבְשָׂה **kibsâh**, *kib-saw´*; or

כַּבְשָׂה **kabsâh**, *kab-saw´*; fem. of 3532; a *ewe*:— (ewe) lamb.

3536. כִּבְשָׁן **kibshân**, *kib-shawn´*; from 3533; a smelting *furnace* (as *reducing* metals):— furnace.

3537. כַּד **kad**, *kad*; from an unused root mean. to *deepen*; prop. a *pail*; but gen. of earthenware; a *jar* for domestic purposes:— barrel, pitcher.

3538. כְּדַב **ke dab** (Chald.), *ked-ab´*; from a root corresp. to 3576; *false*:— lying.

3539. כַּדְכֹּד **kadkôd**, *kad-kobe´*; from the same as 3537 in the sense of *striking fire* from a metal forged; a *sparkling* gem, prob. the *ruby*:— agate.

3540. כְּדָרְלָעֹמֶר **Ke dorlâ'ômer**, *ked-or-law-o´-mer*; of for. or.; *Kedorlaomer*, an early Pers. king:— Chedorlaomer.

3541. כֹּה **kôh**, *ko*; from the pref. *k* and 1931; prop. *like this*, i.e. by impl. (of manner) *thus* (or so); also (of place) *here* (or hither); or (of time) *now*:— also, here, + hitherto, like, on the other side, so (and much), such, on that manner, (on) this (manner, side, way, way and that way), + mean while, yonder.

3542. כָּה **kâh** (Chald.), *kaw*; corresp. to 3541:— hitherto.

3543. כָּהָה **kâhâh**, *kaw-haw´*; a prim. root; to *be weak*, i.e. (fig.) to *despond* (caus. *rebuke*), or (of light, the eye) to *grow dull*:— darken, be dim, fail, faint, restrain, × utterly.

3544. כֵּהֶה **kêheh**, *kay-heh'*; from 3543; *feeble, obscure*:— somewhat dark, darkish, wax dim, heaviness, smoking.

3545. כֵּהָה **kêhâh**, *kay-haw'*; fem. of 3544; prop. a *weakening*; fig. *alleviation*, i.e. *cure*:— healing.

3546. כְּהַל **kᵉhal** (Chald.), *keh-hal'*; a root corresp. to 3201 and 3557; to be *able*:— be able, could.

3547. כָּהַן **kâhan**, *kaw-han'*; a prim. root, appar. mean. to *mediate* in relig. services; but used only as denom. from 3548; to *officiate* as a priest; fig. to *put on regalia*:— deck, be (do the office of a, execute the, minister in the) priest ('s office).

3548. כֹּהֵן **kôhên**, *ko-hane'*; act. part. of 3547; lit. one *officiating*, a *priest*; also (by courtesy) an *acting priest* (although a layman):— chief ruler, × own, priest, prince, principal officer.

3549. כָּהֵן **kâhên** (Chald.), *kaw-hane'*; corresp. to 3548:— priest.

3550. כְּהֻנָּה **kᵉhunnâh**, *keh-hoon-naw'*; from 3547; *priesthood*:— priesthood, priest's office.

3551. כַּו **kav** (Chald.), *kav*; from a root corresp. to 3854 in the sense of *piercing*; a *window* (as a perforation):— window.

3552. כּוּב **Kûwb**, *koob*; of for. der.; *Kub*, a country near Egypt:— Chub.

3553. כּוֹבַע **kôwba'**, *ko'-bah*; from an unused root mean. to be *high* or *rounded*; a *helmet* (as *arched*):— helmet. Comp. 6959.

3554. כָּוָה **kâvâh**, *kaw-vaw'*; a prim. root; prop. to *prick* or *penetrate*; hence, to *blister* (as smarting or eating into):— burn.

כּוּחַ **kôwach**. See 3581.

3555. כְּוִיָּה **kᵉvîyâh**, *kev-ee-yaw'*; from 3554; a *branding*:— burning.

3556. כּוֹכָב **kôwkâb**, *ko-kawb'*; prob. from the same as 3522 (in the sense of *rolling*) or 3554 (in the sense of *blazing*); a *star* (as *round* or as *shining*); fig. a *prince*:— star (l-gazer).

3557. כּוּל **kûwl**, *kool*; a prim. root; prop. to *keep in*; hence, to *measure*; fig. to *maintain* (in various senses):— (be able to, can) abide, bear, comprehend, contain, feed, forbearing, guide, hold (-ing in), nourish (-er), be present, make provision, receive, sustain, provide sustenance (victuals).

3558. כּוּמָז **kûwmâz**, *koo-mawz'*; from an unused root mean. to *store* away; a *jewel* (prob. gold beads):— tablet.

3559. כּוּן **kûwn**, *koon*; a prim. root; prop. to *be erect* (i.e. stand perpendicular); hence, (caus.) to *set up*, in a great variety of applications, whether lit. (*establish, fix, prepare, apply*), or fig. (*appoint, render sure, proper* or *prosperous*):— certain (-ty), confirm, direct, faithfulness, fashion, fasten, firm, be fitted, be fixed, frame, be meet, ordain, order, perfect, (make) preparation, prepare (self), provide, make provision, (be, make) ready, right, set

(aright, fast, forth), be stable , (e-) stablish, stand, tarry, × very deed.

3560. כּוּן **Kûwn**, *koon*; prob. from 3559; *established; Kun*, a place in Syria:— Chun.

3561. כַּוָּן **kavvân**, *kav-vawn'*; from 3559; something *prepared*, i.e. a sacrificial *wafer*:— cake.

3562. כּוֹנַנְיָהוּ **Kôwnanyâhûw**, *ko-nan-yaw'-hoo*; from 3559 and 3050; *Jah has sustained; Conanjah*, the name of two Isr.:— Conaniah, Cononiah. Comp. 3663.

3563. כּוֹס **kôwç**, *koce*; from an unused root mean. to *hold* together; a *cup* (as a container), often fig. a *lot* (as if a potion); also some unclean bird, prob. an *owl* (perh. from the cup-like cavity of its eye):— cup, (small) owl. Comp. 3599.

3564. כּוּר **kûwr**, *koor*; from an unused root mean. prop. to *dig* through; a *pot* or *furnace* (as if excavated):— furnace. Comp. 3600.

כּוּר **kôwr**. See 3733.

3565. כּוֹר עָשָׁן **Kôwr 'Âshân**, *kore aw-shawn'*; from 3564 and 6227; *furnace of smoke; Cor-Ashan*, a place in Pal.:— Chor-ashan.

3566. כּוֹרֶשׁ **Kôwresh**, *ko'-resh*; or (Ezra 1:1 last time), 2)

כֹּרֶשׁ **Kôresh**, *ko'-resh*; from the Pers.; *Koresh* (or *Cyrus*), the Pers. king:— Cyrus.

3567. כּוֹרֶשׁ **Kôwresh** (Chald.), *ko'-resh*; corresp. to 3566:— Cyrus.

3568. כּוּשׁ **Kûwsh**, *koosh*; prob. of for. or.; *Cush* (or *Ethiopia*), the name of a son of Ham, and of his territory; also of an Isr.:— Chush, Cush, Ethiopia.

3569. כּוּשִׁי **Kûwshîy**, *koo-shee'*; patron. from 3568; a *Cushite*, or desc. of Cush:— Cushi, Cushite, Ethiopian (-s).

3570. כּוּשִׁי **Kûwshîy**, *koo-shee'*; the same as 3569; *Cushi*, the name of two Isr.:— Cushi.

3571. כּוּשִׁית **Kûwshîyth**, *koo-sheeth'*; fem. of 3569; a *Cushite woman*:— Ethiopian.

3572. כּוּשָׁן **Kûwshân**, *koo-shawn'*; perh. from 3568; *Cushan*, a region of Arabia:— Cushan.

3573. כּוּשַׁן רִשְׁעָתַיִם **Kûwshan Rish'âthayim**, *koo-shan' rish-aw-thah'-yim*; appar. from 3572 and the dual of 7564; *Cushan of double wickedness; Cushan-Rishathajim*, a Mesopotamian king:— Chushan-rishathaim.

3574. כּוֹשָׁרָה **kôwshârâh**, *ko-shaw-raw'*; from 3787; *prosperity*; in plur. *freedom*:— × chain.

3575. כּוּת **Kûwth**, *kooth*; or (fem.)

כּוּתָה **Kûwthâh**, *koo-thaw'*; of for. or.; *Cuth* or *Cuthah*, a province of Assyria:— Cuth.

3576. כָּזַב **kâzab**, *kaw-zab'*; a prim. root; to *lie* (i.e. *deceive*), lit. or fig.:— fail, (be found a, make a) liar, lie, lying, be in vain.

3577. כָּזָב **kâzâb**, *kaw-zawb'*; from 3576; *falsehood*; lit. (*untruth*) or fig. (*idol*):— deceitful, false, leasing, + liar, lie, lying.

3578. כּוֹזְבָא **Kôzᵉbâ'**, *ko-zeb-aw'*; from 3576; *fallacious; Cozeba*, a place in Pal.:— Choseba.

3579. כָּזְבִּי **Kozbîy**, *koz-bee'*; from 3576; *false; Cozbi*, a Midianitess:— Cozbi.

3580. כָּזִיב **Kᵉzîyb**, *kez-eeb'*; from 3576; *falsified; Kezib*, a place in Pal.:— Chezib.

3581. כֹּחַ **kôach**, *ko'-akh*; or (Dan. 11:6)

כּוֹחַ **kôwach**, *ko'-akh*; from an unused root mean. to *be firm*; *vigor*, lit. (*force*, in a good or a bad sense) or fig. (*capacity, means, produce*); also (from its hardiness) a large *lizard*:— ability, able, chameleon, force, fruits, might, power (-ful), strength, substance, wealth.

3582. כָּחַד **kâchad**, *kaw-khad'*; a prim. root; to *secrete*, by act or word; hence, (intens.) to *destroy*:— conceal, cut down (off), desolate, hide.

3583. כָּחַל **kâchal**, *kaw-khal'*; a prim. root; to *paint* (with stibium):— paint.

3584. כָּחַשׁ **kâchash**, *kaw-khash'*; a prim. root; to *be untrue*, in word (to *lie, feign, disown*) or deed (to *disappoint, fail, cringe*):— deceive, deny, dissemble, fail, deal falsely, be found liars, (be-) lie, lying, submit selves.

3585. כַּחַשׁ **kachash**, *kakh'-ash*; from 3584; lit. a *failure* of flesh, i.e. *emaciation*; fig. *hypocrisy*:— leanness, lies, lying.

3586. כֶּחָשׁ **kechâsh**, *kekh-awsh'*; from 3584; *faithless*:— lying.

3587. כִּי **kîy**, *kee*; from 3554; a *brand* or *scar*:— burning.

3588. כִּי **kîy**, *kee*; a prim. particle [the full form of the prepositional prefix] indicating *causal* relations of all kinds, antecedent or consequent; (by impl.) very widely used as a rel. conjunc. or adv. [as below]; often largely modif. by other particles annexed:— and, + (forasmuch, inasmuch, where-) as, assured [-ly], + but, certainly, doubtless, + else, even, + except, for, how, (because, in, so, than) that, + nevertheless, now, rightly, seeing, since, surely, then, therefore, + (al-) + though, + till, truly, + until, when, whether, while, whom, yea, yet.

3589. כִּיד **kîyd**, *keed*; from a prim. root mean. to *strike*; a *crushing*; fig. *calamity*:— destruction.

3590. כִּידוֹד **kîydôwd**, *kee-dode'*; from the same as 3589 [comp. 3539]; prop. something *struck* off, i.e. a *spark* (as struck):— spark.

3591. כִּידוֹן **kîydôwn**, *kee-dohn'*; from the same as 3589; prop. something to *strike* with, i.e. a *dart* (perh. smaller than 2595):— lance, shield, spear, target.

3592. כִּידוֹן **Kîydôwn**, *kee-dohn'*; the same as 3591; *Kidon*, a place in Pal.:— Chidon.

3593. כִּידוֹר **kîydôwr**, *kee-dore'*; of uncert. der.; perh. *tumult*:— battle.

3594. כִּיּוּן **Kîyûwn**, *kee-yoon'*; from 3559; prop. a *statue*, i.e. idol; but used (by euphem.) for some heathen deity (perh. corresp. to Priapus or Baal-peor):— Chiun.

3595. כִּיֹּר **kîyôwr**, kee-yore´; or

כִּיֹר **kîyôr**, kee-yore´; from the same as 3564; prop. something *round* (as *excavated* or *bored*), i.e. a *chafing-dish* for coals or a *caldron* for cooking; hence, (from similarity of form) a *washbowl*; also (for the same reason) a *pulpit* or platform:— hearth, laver, pan, scaffold.

3596. כִּילַי **kîylay**, kee-lah´-ee; or

כֵּלַי **kêlay**, kay-lah´-ee; from 3557 in the sense of *withholding*; *niggardly*:— churl.

3597. כֵּילַף **kêylaph**, kay-laf´; from an unused root mean. to *clap* or strike with noise; a *club* or sledge-hammer:— hammer.

3598. כִּימָה **Kîymâh**, kee-maw´; from the same as 3558; a *cluster* of stars, i.e. the *Pleiades*:— Pleiades, seven stars.

3599. כִּיס **kîyç**, keece; a form for 3563; a *cup*; also a *bag* for money or weights:— bag, cup, purse.

3600. כִּיר **kîyr**, keer; a form for 3564 (only in the dual); a cooking *range* (consisting of two parallel stones, across which the boiler is set):— ranges for pots.

כִּיֹר **kîyôr**. See 3595.

3601. כִּישֹׁור **kîyshôwr**, kee-shore´; from 3787; lit. a *director*, i.e. the *spindle* or shank of a distaff (6418), by which it is twirled:— spindle.

3602. כָּכָה **kâkâh**, kaw´-kaw; from 3541; *just so*, referring to the previous or following context:— after that (this) manner, this matter, (even) so, in such a case, thus.

3603. כִּכָּר **kikkâr**, kik-kawr´; from 3769; a *circle*, i.e. (by impl.) a circumjacent *tract* or region, expec. the *Ghôr* or valley of the Jordan; also a (round) *loaf*; also a *talent* (or large [round] coin):— loaf, morsel, piece, plain, talent.

3604. כִּכָּר **kikkêr** (Chald.), kik-kare´; corresp. to 3603; a *talent*:— talent.

3605. כֹּל **kôl**, kole; or (Jer. 33:8)

כּוֹל **kôwl**, kole; from 3634; prop. the *whole*; hence, *all, any* or *every* (in the sing. only, but often in a plur. sense):— (in) all (manner, [ye]), altogether, any (manner), enough, every (one, place, thing), howsoever, as many as, [no-] thing, ought, whatsoever, (the) whole, whoso (-ever).

3606. כֹּל **kôl** (Chald.), kole; corresp. to 3605:— all, any, + (forasmuch) as, + be-(for this) cause, every, + no (manner, -ne), + there (where) -fore, + though, what (where, who) -soever, (the) whole.

3607. כָּלָא **kâlâ'**, kaw-law´; a prim. root; to *restrict*, by act (*hold* back or in) or word (*prohibit*):— finish, forbid, keep (back), refrain, restrain, retain, shut up, be stayed, withhold.

3608. כֶּלֶא **kele'**, keh´-leh; from 3607; a *prison*:— prison. Comp. 3628.

3609. כִּלְאָב **Kil'âb**, kil-awb´; appar. from 3607 and 1; *restraint of* (his) *father*; *Kilab*, an Isr.:— Chileab.

3610. כִּלְאַיִם **kil'ayim**, kil-ah´-yim; dual of 3608 in the orig. sense of *separation*; *two heterogeneities*:— divers seeds (-e kinds), mingled (seed).

3611. כֶּלֶב **keleb**, keh´-leb; from an unused root means. to *yelp*, or else to *attack*; a *dog*; hence, (by euphem.) a male *prostitute*:— dog.

3612. כָּלֵב **Kâlêb**, kaw-labe´; perh. a form of 3611, or else from the same root in the sense of *forcible*; *Caleb*, the name of three Isr.:— Caleb.

3613. כָּלֵב אֶפְרָתָה **Kâlêb 'Ephrâthâh**, kaw-labe´ ef-raw´-thaw; from 3612 and 672; *Caleb-Ephrathah*, a place in Egypt (if the text is correct):— Caleb-ephrathah.

3614. כָּלִבּוֹ **Kâlibbôw**, kaw-lib-bo´; prob. by err. transc. for

כָּלֵבִי **Kâlêbîy**, kaw-lay-bee´; patron. from 3612; a *Calebite* or desc. of Caleb:— of the house of Caleb.

3615. כָּלָה **kâlâh**, kaw-law´; a prim. root; to *end*, whether intr. (to *cease, be finished, perish*) or tran. (to *complete, prepare, consume*):— accomplish, cease, consume (away), determine, destroy (utterly), be (when ... end) done, (be an) end (of), expire, (cause to) fail, faint, finish, fulfil, × fully, × have, leave (off), long, bring to pass, wholly reap, make clean riddance, spend, quite take away, waste.

3616. כָּלֶה **kâleh**, kaw-leh´; from 3615; *pining*:— fail.

3617. כָּלָה **kâlâh**, kaw-law´; from 3615; a *completion*; adv. *completely*; also *destruction*:— altogether, (be, utterly) consume (-d), consummation (-ption), was determined, (full, utter) end, riddance.

3618. כַּלָּה **kallâh**, kal-law´; from 3634; a *bride* (as if *perfect*); hence, a *son's wife*:— bride, daughter-in-law, spouse.

כְּלוּא **kᵉlûw'**. See 3628.

3619. כְּלוּב **kᵉlûwb**, kel-oob´; from the same as 3611; a bird-*trap* (as furnished with a *clap*-stick or treadle to spring it); hence, a *basket* (as resembling a wicker cage):— basket, cage.

3620. כְּלוּב **Kᵉlûwb**, kel-oob´; the same as 3619; *Kelub*, the name of two Isr.:— Chelub.

3621. כְּלוּבַי **Kᵉlûwbay**, kel-oo-bay´-ee; a form of 3612; *Kelubai*, an Isr.:— Chelubai.

3622. כְּלוּהַי **Kᵉlûwhay**, kel-oo-hah´-ee; from 3615; *completed*; *Keluhai*, an Isr.:— Chelluh.

3623. כְּלוּלָה **kᵉlûwlâh**, kel-oo-law´; denom. pass. part. from 3618; *bridehood* (only in the plur.):— espousal.

3624. כֶּלַח **kelach**, keh´-lakh; from an unused root mean. to *be complete*; *maturity*:— full (old) age.

3625. כֶּלַח **Kelach**, keh´-lakh; the same as 3624; *Kelach*, a place in Assyria:— Calah.

3626. כָּל־חֹזֶה **Kol-Chôzeh**, kol-kho-zeh´; from 3605 and 2374; *every seer*; *Col-Chozeh*, an Isr.:— Col-hozeh.

3627. כְּלִי **kᵉlîy**, kel-ee´; from 3615; something *prepared*, i.e. any *appara-tus* (as an implement, utensil, dress, vessel or weapon):— armour ([-bearer]), artillery, bag, carriage, + furnish, furniture, instrument, jewel, that is made of, × one from another, that which pertaineth, pot, + psaltery, sack, stuff, thing, tool, vessel, ware, weapon, + whatsoever.

3628. כְּלִיא **kᵉlîy'**, kel-ee´; or

כְּלוּא **kᵉlûw'**, kel-oo´; from 3607 [comp. 3608]; a *prison*:— prison.

3629. כִּלְיָה **kilyâh**, kil-yaw´; fem. of 3627 (only in the plur.); a *kidney* (as an essential *organ*); fig. the *mind* (as the interior self):— kidneys, reins.

3630. כִּלְיוֹן **Kilyôwn**, kil-yone´; a form of 3631; *Kiljon*, an Isr.:— Chilion.

3631. כִּלָּיוֹן **killâyôwn**, kil-law-yone´; from 3615; *pining*, *destruction*:— consumption, failing.

3632. כָּלִיל **kâlîyl**, kaw-leel´; from 3634; *complete*; as noun, the *whole* (spec. a sacrifice *entirely consumed*); as adv. *fully*:— all, every whit, flame, perfect (-ion), utterly, whole burnt offering (sacrifice), wholly.

3633. כַּלְכֹּל **Kalkôl**, kal-kole´; from 3557; *sustenance*; *Calcol*, an Isr.:— Calcol, Chalcol.

3634. כָּלַל **kâlal**, kaw-lal´; a prim. root; to *complete*:— (make) perfect.

3635. כְּלַל **kᵉlal** (Chald.), kel-al´; corresp. to 3634; to *complete*:— finish, make (set) up.

3636. כְּלָל **Kᵉlâl**, kel-awl´; from 3634; *complete*; *Kelal*, an Isr.:— Chelal.

3637. כָּלַם **kâlam**, kaw-lawm´; a prim. root; prop. to *wound*; but only fig., to *taunt* or *insult*:— be (make) ashamed, blush, be confounded, be put to confusion, hurt, reproach, (do, put to) shame.

3638. כִּלְמָד **Kilmâd**, kil-mawd´; of for. der.; *Kilmad*, a place appar. in the Ass. empire:— Chilmad.

3639. כְּלִמָּה **kᵉlimmâh**, kel-im-maw´; from 3637; *disgrace*:— confusion, dishonour, reproach, shame.

3640. כְּלִמּוּת **kᵉlimmûwth**, kel-im-mooth´; from 3639; *disgrace*:— shame.

3641. כַּלְנֶה **Kalneh**, kal-neh´; or

כַּלְנֵה **Kalnêh**, kal-nay´; also

כַּלְנוֹ **Kalnôw**, kal-no´; of for. der.; *Calneh* or *Calno*, a place in the Ass. empire:— Calneh, Calno. Comp. 3656.

3642. כָּמַהּ **kâmahh**, kaw-mah´; a prim. root; to *pine* after:— long.

3643. כִּמְהָם **Kimhâm**, kim-hawm´; from 3642; *pining*; *Kimham*, an Isr.:— Chimham.

3644. כְּמוֹ **kᵉmôw**, kem-o´; or

כְּמוֹ **kâmôw**, kaw-mo´; a form of the pref. k, but used separately [comp. 3651]; *as, thus, so*:— according to, (such) as (it were, well as), in comp. of, like (as, to, unto), thus, when, worth.

3645. כְּמוֹשׁ **Kᵉmôwsh**, kem-oshe´; or (Jer. 48:7)

כְּמִישׁ **Kᵉmîysh**, kem-eesh´; from an unused root mean. to *subdue*; the *powerful; Kemosh,* the god of the Moabites:— Chemosh.

3646. כַּמֹּן **kammôn**, *kam-mone´*; from an unused root mean. to *store* up or *preserve;* "cummin" (from its use as a *condiment*):— cummin.

3647. כָּמַס **kâmaç**, *kaw-mas´*; a prim. root: to *store* away, i.e. (fig.) in the memory:— lay up in store.

3648. כָּמַר **kâmar**, *kaw-mar´*; a prim. root; prop. to *intertwine* or *contract,* i.e. (by impl.) to *shrivel* (as with heat); fig. to *be* deeply *affected* with passion (love or pity):— be black, be kindled, yearn.

3649. כָּמָר **kâmâr**, *kaw-mawr´*; from 3648; prop. an *ascetic* (as if *shrunk* with self-maceration), i.e. an idolatrous *priest* (only in plur.):— Chemarims (idolatrous) priests.

3650. כַּמְרִיר **kimrîyr**, *kim-reer´*; redupl. from 3648; *obscuration* (as if from *shrinkage* of light, i.e. an *eclipse* (only in plur.):— blackness.

3651. כֵּן **kên**, *kane*; from 3559; prop. *set upright;* hence, (fig. as adj.) *just;* but usually (as adv. or conjunc.) *rightly* or *so* (in various applications to manner, time and relation; often with other particles):— + after that (this, -ward, -wards), as ... as, + [for-] asmuch as yet, + be (for which) cause, + following, howbeit, in (the) like (manner, -wise), × the more, right, (even) so, state, straightway, such (thing), surely, + there (where-) fore, this, thus, true, well, × you.

3652. כֵּן **kên** (Chald.), *kane*; corresp. to 3651; *so:*— thus.

3653. כֵּן **kên**, *kane*; the same as 3651, used as a noun; a *stand,* i.e. pedestal or station:— base, estate, foot, office, place, well.

3654. כֵּן **kên**, *kane*; from 3661 in the sense of *fastening;* a *gnat* (from infixing its sting; used only in plur. [and irreg. in Exod. 8:17,18; Heb. 13:14]):— lice, × manner.

3655. כָּנָה **kânâh**, *kaw-naw´*; a prim. root; to *address* by an additional name; hence, to *eulogize:*— give flattering titles, surname (himself).

3656. כַּנֶּה **Kanneh**, *kan-neh´*; for 3641; *Canneh,* a place in Assyria:— Canneh.

3657. כַּנָּה **kannâh**, *kaw-naw´*; from 3661; a *plant* (as set):— × vineyard.

3658. כִּנּוֹר **kinnôwr**, *kin-nore´*; from a unused root mean. to *twang;* a *harp:*— harp.

3659. כָּנְיָהוּ **Konyâhûw**, *kon-yaw´-hoo;* for 3204; *Conjah,* an Isr. king:— Coniah.

3660. כְּנֵמָא **kᵉnêmâ'** (Chald.), *ken-ay-maw´;* corresp. to 3644; *so* or *thus:*— so, (in) this manner (sort), thus.

3661. כָּנַן **kânan**, *kaw-nan´*; a prim. root; to *set out,* i.e. *plant:*— × vineyard.

3662. כְּנָנִי **Kᵉnâníy**, *ken-aw-nee´;* from 3661; *planted; Kenani,* an Isr.:— Chenani.

3663. כְּנַנְיָה **Kᵉnanyâh**, *ken-an-yaw´;* or

כְּנַנְיָהוּ **Kᵉnanyâhûw**, *ken-an-yaw´-hoo;* from 3661 and 3050; *Jah has*

planted; Kenanjah, an Isr.:— Chenaniah.

3664. כָּנַס **kânaç**, *kaw-nas´*; a prim. root; to *collect;* hence, to *enfold:*— gather (together), heap up, wrap self.

3665. כָּנַע **kâna'**, *kaw-nah´*; a prim. root; prop. to *bend* the knee; hence, to *humiliate, vanquish:*— bring down (low), into subjection, under, humble (self), subdue.

3666. כִּנְעָה **kin'âh**, *kin-aw´;* from 3665 in the sense of *folding* [comp. 3664]; a *package:*— wares.

3667. כְּנַעַן **Kᵉna'an**, *ken-ah´-an;* from 3665; *humiliated; Kenaan,* a son of Ham; also the country inhabited by him:— Canaan, merchant, traffick.

3668. כְּנַעֲנָה **Kᵉna'ănâh**, *ken-ah-an-aw´;* fem. of 3667; *Kenaanah,* the name of two Isr.:— Chenaanah.

3669. כְּנַעֲנִי **Kᵉna'ăníy**, *ken-ah-an-ee´;* patrial from 3667; a *Kenaanite* or inhab. of Kenaan; by impl. a *pedlar* (the Canaanites standing for their neighbors thē Ishmaelites, who conducted mercantile caravans):— Canaanite, merchant, trafficker.

3670. כָּנַף **kânaph**, *kaw-naf´*; a prim. root; prop. to *project* laterally, i.e. prob. (refl.) to *withdraw:*— be removed.

3671. כָּנָף **kânâph**, *kaw-nawf´;* from 3670; an *edge* or *extremity;* spec. (of a bird or army) a *wing,* (of a garment or bed-clothing) a *flap,* (of the earth) a *quarter,* (of a building) a *pinnacle:*— + bird, border, corner, end, feather [-ed], × flying, + (one an-) other, overspreading, × quarters, skirt, × sort, uttermost part, wing ([-ed]).

3672. כִּנְּרוֹת **Kinnᵉrôwth**, *kin-ner-ôth´;* or

כִּנֶּרֶת **Kinnereth**, *kin-neh´-reth;* respectively plur. and sing. fem. from the same as 3658; perh. *harp*-shaped; *Kinneroth* or *Kinnereth,* a place in Pal.:— Chinnereth, Chinneroth, Cinneroth.

3673. כְּנַשׁ **kânash** (Chald.), *kaw-nash´;* corresp. to 3664; to *assemble:*— gather together.

3674. כְּנָת **kᵉnâth**, *ken-awth´;* from 3655; a *colleague* (as having the same title):— companion.

3675. כְּנָת **kᵉnâth** (Chald.), *ken-awth´;* corresp. to 3674:— companion.

3676. כֵּס **kêç**, *kace;* appar. a contr. for 3678, but prob. by err. transc. for 5251:— sworn.

3677. כֶּסֶא **keçe'**, *keh´-seh;* or

כֶּסֶה **keçeh**, *keh´-seh;* appar. from 3680; prop. *fulness* or the *full moon,* i.e. its festival:— (time) appointed.

3678. כִּסֵּא **kiççê'**, *kis-say´;* or

כִּסֵּה **kiççêh**, *kis-say´;* from 3680; prop. *covered,* i.e. a *throne* (as canopied):— seat, stool, throne.

3679. כַּסְדַּי **Kaçday**, *kas-dah´-ee;* for 3778:— Chaldean.

3680. כָּסָה **kâçâh**, *kaw-saw´;* a prim. root; prop. to *plump,* i.e. *fill up* hollows; by impl. to *cover* (for clothing or secrecy):— clad self, close, clothe, con-

ceal, cover (self), (flee to) hide, overwhelm. Comp. 3780.

כֶּסֶה **keçeh.** See 3677.

כִּסֵּה **kiççêh.** See 3678.

3681. כָּסוּי **kâçûwy**, *kaw-soo´-ee;* pass. part. of 3680; prop. *covered,* i.e. (as noun) a *covering:*— covering.

3682. כְּסוּת **kᵉçûwth**, *kes-ooth´;* from 3680; a *cover* (garment); fig. a *veiling:*— covering, raiment, vesture.

3683. כָּסַח **kâçach**, *kaw-sakh´;* a prim. root; to *cut off:*— cut down (up).

3684. כְּסִיל **kᵉçîyl**, *kes-eel´;* from 3688; prop. *fat,* i.e. (fig.) stupid or *silly:*— fool (-ish).

3685. כְּסִיל **Kᵉçîyl**, *kes-eel´;* the same as 3684; any notable *constellation;* spec. *Orion* (as if a *burly* one):— constellation, Orion.

3686. כְּסִיל **Kᵉçîyl**, *kes-eel´;* the same as 3684; *Kesil,* a place in Pal.:— Chesil.

3687. כְּסִילוּת **kᵉçîylûwth**, *kes-eel-ooth´;* from 3684; *silliness:*— foolish.

3688. כָּסַל **kâçal**, *kaw-sal´;* a prim. root; prop. to *be fat,* i.e. (fig.) *silly:*— be foolish.

3689. כֶּסֶל **keçel**, *keh´-sel;* from 3688; prop. *fatness,* i.e. by impl. (lit.) the *loin* (as the seat of the leaf *fat*) or (gen.) the *viscera;* also (fig.) *silliness* or (in a good sense) *trust:*— confidence, flank, folly, hope, loin.

3690. כִּסְלָה **kiçlâh**, *kis-law´;* fem. of 3689; in a good sense, *trust;* in a bad one, *silliness:*— confidence, folly.

3691. כִּסְלֵו **Kiçlêv**, *kis-lave´;* prob. of for. or.; *Kisleu,* the 9th Heb. month:— Chisleu.

3692. כִּסְלוֹן **Kiçlôwn**, *kis-lone´;* from 3688; *hopeful; Kislon,* an Isr.:— Chislon.

3693. כְּסָלוֹן **Kᵉçâlôwn**, *kes-aw-lone´;* from 3688; *fertile; Kesalon,* a place in Pal.:— Chesalon.

3694. כְּסֻלּוֹת **Kᵉçullôwth**, *kes-ool-lôth´;* fem. plur. of pass. part. of 3688; *fattened; Kesulloth,* a place in Pal.:— Chesulloth.

3695. כַּסְלֻחִים **Kaçlûchîym**, *kas-loo´-kheem;* a plur. prob. of for. der.; *Casluchim,* a people cognate to the Eg.:— Casluhim.

3696. כִּסְלֹת תָּבֹר **Kiçlôth Tâbôr**, *kis-lôth´ taw-bore´;* from the fem. plur. of 3689 and 8396; *flanks of Tabor; Kisloth-Tabor,* a place in Pal.:— Chisloth-tabor.

3697. כָּסַם **kâçam**, *kaw-sam´;* a prim. root; to *shear:*— × only, poll. Comp. 3765.

3698. כֻּסֶּמֶת **kuççemeth**, *koos-seh´-meth;* from 3697; *spelt* (from its bristliness as if just *shorn*):— fitches, rie.

3699. כָּסַס **kâçaç**, *kaw-sas´;* a prim. root; to *estimate:*— make count.

3700. כָּסַף **kâçaph**, *kaw-saf´;* a prim. root; prop. to *become pale,* i.e. (by impl.) to *pine* after; also to *fear:*— [have] desire, be greedy, long, sore.

3701. כֶּסֶף **keçeph**, *keh´-sef;* from 3700; *silver* (from its *pale* color); by impl. *money:*— money, price, silver (-ling).

3702. כְּסַף **kᵉçaph** (Chald.), kes-af´; corresp. to 3701:— money, silver.

3703. כָּסְפְיָא **Kâçiphyâ´**, kaw-sif-yaw´; perh. from 3701; silvery; Casiphja, a place in Bab.:— Casiphia.

3704. כֶּסֶת **keçeth**, keh´-seth; from 3680; a cushion or pillow (as covering a seat or bed):— pillow.

3705. כְּעַן **kᵉʿan** (Chald.), keh-an´; prob. from 3652; now:— now.

3706. כְּעֶנֶת **kᵉʿeneth** (Chald.), keh-eh´-neth; or

כְּעֶת **kᵉʿeth** (Chald.), keh-eth´; fem. of 3705; thus (only in the formula "and so forth"):— at such a time.

3707. כָּעַס **kâʿaç**, kaw-as´; a prim. root; to trouble; by impl. to grieve, rage, be indignant:— be angry, be grieved, take indignation, provoke (to anger, unto wrath), have sorrow, vex, be wroth.

3708. כַּעַס **kaʿaç**, kah´-as; or (in Job)

כַּעַשׂ **kaʿas**, kah´-as; from 3707; vexation:— anger, angry, grief, indignation, provocation, provoking, × sore, sorrow, spite, wrath.

כְּעֶת **kᵉʿeth**. See 3706.

3709. כַּף **kaph**, kaf; from 3721; the hollow hand or palm (so of the paw of an animal, of the sole, and even of the bowl of a dish or sling, the handle of a bolt, the leaves of a palm-tree); fig. power:— branch, + foot, hand (l-full, -dle, [-led]), hollow, middle, palm, paw, power, sole, spoon.

3710. כֵּף **kêph**, kafe; from 3721; a hollow rock:— rock.

3711. כָּפָה **kâphâh**, kaw-faw´; a prim. root; prop. to bend, i.e. (fig.) to tame or subdue:— pacify.

3712. כִּפָּה **kippâh**, kip-paw´; fem. of 3709; a leaf of a palm-tree:— branch.

3713. כְּפוֹר **kᵉphôwr**, kef-ore´; from 3722; prop. a cover, i.e. (by impl.) a tankard (or covered goblet); also white frost (as covering the ground):— bason, hoar (-y) frost.

3714. כָּפִיס **kâphîç**, kaw-fece´; from an unused root mean. to connect; a girder:— beam.

3715. כְּפִיר **kᵉphîyr**, kef-eer´; from 3722; a village (as covered in by walls); also a young lion (perh. as covered with a mane):— (young) lion, village. Comp. 3723.

3716. כְּפִירָה **Kᵉphîyrâh**, kef-ee-raw´; fem. of 3715; the village (always with the art.); Kephirah, a place in Pal.:— Chephirah.

3717. כָּפַל **kâphal**, kaw-fal´; a prim. root; to fold together; fig. to repeat:— double.

3718. כֶּפֶל **kephel**, keh´-fel; from 3717; a duplicate:— double.

3719. כָּפַן **kâphan**, kaw-fan´; a prim. root; to bend:— bend.

3720. כָּפָן **kâphân**, kaw-fawn´; from 3719; hunger (as making to stoop with emptiness and pain):— famine.

3721. כָּפַף **kâphaph**, kaw-faf´; a prim. root; to curve:— bow down (self).

3722. כָּפַר **kâphar**, kaw-far´; a prim.

---

root; to cover (spec. with bitumen); fig. to expiate or condone, to placate or cancel:— appease, make (an atonement, cleanse, disannul, forgive, be merciful, pacify, pardon, to pitch, purge (away), put off, (make) reconcile (-liation).

3723. כָּפָר **kâphâr**, kaw-fawr´; from 3722; a village (as protected by walls):— village. Comp. 3715.

3724. כֹּפֶר **kôpher**, ko´-fer; from 3722; prop. a cover, i.e. (lit.) a village (as covered in); (spec.) bitumen (as used for coating), and the henna plant (as used for dyeing); fig. a redemption-price:— bribe, camphire, pitch, ransom, satisfaction, sum of money, village.

3725. כִּפֻּר **kippûr**, kip-poor´; from 3722; expiation (only in plur.):— atonement.

3726. כְּפַר הָעַמֹּנִי **Kᵉphar hâ-ʿAmmôwnîy**, kef-ar´ haw-am-mo-nee´; from 3723 and 5984, with the art. interposed; village of the Ammonite; Kefar-ha-Ammoni, a place in Pal.:— Chefar-haamonai.

3727. כַּפֹּרֶת **kappôreth**, kap-po´-reth; from 3722; a lid (used only of the cover of the sacred Ark):— mercy seat.

3728. כָּפַשׁ **kâphash**, kaw-fash´; a prim. root; to tread down; fig. to humiliate:— cover.

3729. כְּפַת **kᵉphath** (Chald.), kef-ath´; a root of uncert. correspondence; to fetter:— bind.

3730. כַּפְתֹּר **kaphtôr**, kaf-tore´; or (Am. 9:1)

כַּפְתּוֹר **kaphtôwr**, kaf-tore´; prob. from an unused root mean. to encircle; a chaplet; but used only in an architectonic sense, i.e. the capital of a column, or a wreath-like button or disk on the candelabrum:— knop, (upper) lintel.

3731. כַּפְתֹּר **Kaphtôr**, kaf-tore´; or (Am. 9:7)

כַּפְתּוֹר **Kaphtôwr**, kaf-tore´; appar. the same as 3730; Caphtor (i.e. a wreath-shaped island), the orig. seat of the Philistines:— Caphtor.

3732. כַּפְתֹּרִי **Kaphtôrîy**, kaf-to-ree´; patrial from 3731; a Caphtorite (collect.) or native of Caphtor:— Caphthorim, Caphtorim (-s).

3733. כַּר **kar**, kar; from 3769 in the sense of plumpness; a ram (as full-grown and fat), incl. a battering-ram (as butting); hence, a meadow (as for sheep); also a pad or camel's saddle (as puffed out):— captain, furniture, lamb, (large) pasture, ram. See also 1033, 3746.

3734. כֹּר **kôr**, kore; from the same as 3564; prop. a deep round vessel, i.e. (spec.) a cor or measure for things dry:— cor, measure. Chald. the same.

3735. כָּרָא **kârâʾ** (Chald.), kaw-raw´; prob. corresp. to 3738 in the sense of piercing (fig.); to grieve:— be grieved.

3736. כַּרְבֵּל **karbêl**, kar-bale´; from the same as 3525; to gird or clothe:— clothed.

3737. כַּרְבְּלָא **karbᵉlâʾ** (Chald.), kar-bel-aw´; from a verb corresp. to that of 3736; a mantle:— hat.

3738. כָּרָה **kârâh**, kaw-raw´; a prim. root; prop. to dig; fig. to plot; gen. to bore or open:— dig, × make (a banquet), open.

3739. כָּרָה **kârâh**, kaw-raw´; usually assigned as a prim. root, but prob. only a special application of 3738 (through the common idea of planning impl. in a bargain); to purchase:— buy, prepare.

3740. כֵּרָה **kêrâh**, kay-raw´; from 3739; a purchase:— provision.

3741. כָּרָה **kârâh**, kaw-raw´; fem. of 3733; a meadow:— cottage.

3742. כְּרוּב **kᵉrûwb**, ker-oob´; of uncert. der.; a cherub or imaginary figure:— cherub, [plur.] cherubims.

3743. כְּרוּב **Kᵉrûwb**, ker-oob´; the same as 3742; Kerub, a place in Bab.:— Cherub.

3744. כָּרוֹז **kârôwz** (Chald.), kaw-roze´; from 3745; a herald:— herald.

3745. כְּרַז **kᵉraz** (Chald.), ker-az´; prob. of Gr. or. (κηρύσσω); to proclaim:— make a proclamation.

3746. כָּרִי **kârîy**, kaw-ree´; perh. an abridged plur. of 3733 in the sense of leader (of the flock); a life-guardsman:— captains, Cherethites [from the marg.].

3747. כְּרִית **Kᵉrîyth**, ker-eeth´; from 3772; a cut; Kerith, a brook of Pal.:— Cherith.

3748. כְּרִיתוּת **kᵉrîythûwth**, ker-ee-thooth´; from 3772; a cutting (of the matrimonial bond), i.e. divorce:— divorce (-ment).

3749. כַּרְכֹּב **karkôb**, kar-kobe´; expanded from the same as 3522; a rim or top margin:— compass.

3750. כַּרְכֹּם **karkôm**, kar-kome´; prob. of for. or.; the crocus:— saffron.

3751. כַּרְכְּמִישׁ **Karkᵉmîysh**, kar-kem-eesh´; of for. der.; Karkemish, a place in Syria:— Carchemish.

3752. כַּרְכַּס **Karkaç**, kar-kas´; of Pers. or.; Karkas, a eunuch of Xerxes:— Carcas.

3753. כַּרְכָּרָה **karkârâh**, kar-kaw-raw´; from 3769; a dromedary (from its rapid motion as if dancing):— swift beast.

3754. כֶּרֶם **kerem**, keh´-rem; from an unused root of uncert. mean.; a garden or vineyard:— vines, (increase of the) vineyard (-s), vintage. See also 1021.

3755. כֹּרֵם **kôrêm**, ko-rame´; act. part. of an imaginary denom. from 3754; a vinedresser:— vine dresser [as one or two words].

3756. כַּרְמִי **Karmîy**, kar-mee´; from 3754; gardener; Karmi, the name of three Isr.:— Carmi.

3757. כַּרְמִי **Karmîy**, kar-mee´; patron. from 3756; a Karmite or desc. of Karmi:— Carmites.

3758. כַּרְמִיל **karmîyl**, kar-mele´; prob. of for. or.; carmine, a deep red:— crimson.

3759. כַּרְמֶל **karmel**, kar-mel´; from 3754; a planted field (garden, orchard, vineyard or park); by impl. garden produce:— full (green) ears (of corn), fruit-ful field (place), plentiful (field).

3760. כַּרְמֶל **Karmel**, *kar-mel´*; the same as 3759; *Karmel*, the name of a hill and of a town in Pal.:— Carmel, fruitful (plentiful) field, (place).

3761. כַּרְמְלִי **Karmᵉlîy**, *kar-mel-ee´*; patron. from 3760; a *Karmelite* or inhab. of Karmel (the town):— Carmelite.

3762. כַּרְמְלִית **Karmᵉlîyth**, *kar-mel-eeth´*; fem. of 3761; a *Karmelitess* or female inhab. of Karmel:— Carmelitess.

3763. כְּרָן **Kᵉrân**, *ker-awn´*; of uncert. der.; *Keran*, an aboriginal Idumæan:— Cheran.

3764. כָּרְסָא **korçê´** (Chald.), *kor-say´*; corresp. to 3678; a *throne*:— throne.

3765. כִּרְסֵם **kirçêm**, *kir-same´*; from 3697; to *lay waste*:— waste.

3766. כָּרַע **kâra´**, *kaw-rah´*; a prim. root; to *bend* the knee; by impl. to *sink*, to *prostrate*:— bow (down, self), bring down (low), cast down, couch, fall, feeble, kneeling, sink, smite (stoop) down, subdue, × very.

3767. כָּרָע **kârâ´**, *kaw-raw´*; from 3766; the *leg* (from the knee to the ankle) of men or locusts (only in the dual):— leg.

3768. כַּרְפַּס **karpaç**, *kar-pas´*; of for. or.; *byssus* or fine vegetable wool:— green.

3769. כָּרַר **kârar**, *kaw-rar´*; a prim. root; to *dance* (i.e. *whirl*):— dance (-ing).

3770. כְּרֵשׂ **kᵉrês**, *ker-ace´*; by var. from 7164; the *paunch* or belly (as *swelling* out):— belly.

כֹּרֶשׁ **Kôresh**. See 3567.

3771. כַּרְשְׁנָא **Karshᵉnâ´**, *kar-shen-aw´*; of for. or.; *Karshena*, a courtier of Xerxes:— Carshena.

3772. כָּרַת **kârath**, *kaw-rath´*; a prim. root; to *cut* (off, down or asunder); by impl. to *destroy* or *consume*; spec. to *covenant* (i.e. make an alliance or bargain, orig. by cutting flesh and passing between the pieces):— be chewed, be con- [feder-] ate, covenant, cut (down, off), destroy, fail, feller, be freed, hew (down), make a league (covenant), × lose, perish, × utterly, × want.

3773. כָּרֻתָה **kârûthâh**, *kaw-rooth-aw´*; pass. part. fem. of 3772; something *cut*, i.e. a hewn *timber*:— beam.

3774. כְּרֵתִי **Kᵉrêthîy**, *ker-ay-thee´*; prob. from 3772 in the sense of *executioner*; a *Kerethite* or *life-guardsman* [comp. 2876] (only collect. in the sing. as plur.):— Cherethims, Cherethites.

3775. כֶּשֶׂב **keseb**, *keh´-seb*; appar. by transp. for 3532; a young *sheep*:— lamb, sheep.

3776. כִּשְׂבָּה **kisbâh**, *kis-baw´*; fem. of 3775; a young *ewe*:— lamb.

3777. כֶּשֶׂד **Kesed**, *keh´-sed*; from an unused root of uncert. mean.; *Kesed*, a relative of Abraham:— Chesed.

3778. כַּשְׂדִּי **Kasdîy**, *kas-dee´*; (occasionally with enclitic) כַּשְׂדִּימָה **Kasdîymâh**, *kas-dee´-maw*; toward (the) *Kasdites* (into Chaldea), patron. from 3777 (only in the plur.); a *Kasdite*, or desc. of Kesed; by impl. a *Chaldæan* (as if so descended);

also an *astrologer* (as if proverbial of that people:— Chaldeans, Chaldees, inhabitants of Chaldea.

3779. כַּשְׂדַּי **Kasday** (Chald.), *kas-dah´-ee*; corresp. to 3778; a *Chaldæan* or inhab. of Chaldæa; by impl. a *Magian* or professional astrologer:— Chaldean.

3780. כָּשָׂה **kâsâh**, *kaw-saw´*; a prim. root; to *grow fat* (i.e. *be covered* with flesh):— be covered. Comp. 3680.

3781. כַּשִּׂיל **kashshîyl**, *kash-sheel´*; from 3782; prop. a *feller*, i.e. an *axe*:— ax.

3782. כָּשַׁל **kâshal**, *kaw-shal´*; a prim. root; to *totter* or *waver* (through weakness of the legs, espec. the ankle); by impl. to *falter*, *stumble*, faint or fall:— bereave [from the marg.], cast down, be decayed, (cause to) fail, (cause, make to) fall (down, -ing), feeble, (the) ruin (-ed, of), (be) overthrown, (cause to) stumble, × utterly, be weak.

3783. כִּשָּׁלוֹן **kishshâlôwn**, *kish-shaw-lone´*; from 3782; prop. a *tottering*, i.e. *ruin*:— fall.

3784. כָּשַׁף **kâshaph**, *kaw-shaf´*; a prim. root; prop. to *whisper* a spell, i.e. to *inchant* or practise magic:— sorcerer, (use) witch (-craft).

3785. כֶּשֶׁף **kesheph**, *keh´-shef*; from 3784; *magic*:— sorcery, witchcraft.

3786. כַּשָּׁף **kashshâph**, *kash-shawf´*; from 3784; a *magician*:— sorcerer.

3787. כָּשֵׁר **kâshêr**, *kaw-share´*; a prim. root; prop. to *be straight* or *right*; by impl. to *be acceptable*; also to *succeed* or *prosper*:— direct, be right, prosper.

3788. כִּשְׁרוֹן **kishrôwn**, *kish-rone´*; from 3787; *success*, *advantage*:— equity, good, right.

3789. כָּתַב **kâthab**, *kaw-thab´*; a prim. root; to *grave*, by impl. to *write* (describe, inscribe, prescribe, subscribe):— describe, record, prescribe, subscribe, write (-ing, -ten).

3790. כְּתַב **kᵉthab** (Chald.), *keth-ab´*; corresp. to 3789:— write (-ten).

3791. כָּתָב **kâthâb**, *kaw-thawb´*; from 3789; something *written*, i.e. a *writing*, *record* or *book*:— register, scripture, writing.

3792. כְּתָב **kᵉthâb** (Chald.), *keth-awb´*; corresp. to 3791:— prescribing, writing (-ten).

3793. כְּתֹבֶת **kᵉthôbeth**, *keth-o´-beth*; from 3789; a *letter* or other *mark* branded on the skin:— × any [mark].

3794. כִּתִּי **Kittîy**, *kit-tee´* or כִּתִּיִּי **Kittîyîy**, *kit-tee-ee´*; patrial from an unused name denoting Cyprus (only in the plur.); a *Kittite* or Cypriote; hence, an *islander* in gen., i.e. the Greeks or Romans on the shores opposite Pal.:— Chittim, Kittim.

3795. כָּתִית **kâthîyth**, *kaw-theeth´*; from 3807; *beaten*, i.e. pure (oil):— beaten.

3796. כֹּתֶל **kôthel**, *ko´-thel*; from an unused root mean. to *compact*; a *wall* (as *gathering* inmates):— wall.

3797. כְּתַל **kᵉthal** (Chald.), *keth-al´*; corresp. to 3796:— wall.

3798. כִּתְלִישׁ **Kithlîysh**, *kith-leesh´*; from

3796 and 376; *wall of a man*; *Kithlish*, a place in Pal.:— Kithlish.

3799. כָּתַם **kâtham**, *kaw-tham´*; a prim. root; prop. to *carve* or *engrave*, i.e. (by impl.) to *inscribe* indelibly:— mark.

3800. כֶּתֶם **kethem**, *keh´-them*; from 3799; prop. something *carved* out, i.e. *ore*; hence, *gold* (pure as orig. mined):— (most) fine, (pure) gold (-en wedge).

3801. כְּתֹנֶת **kᵉthôneth**, *keth-o´-neth*; or כֻּתֹּנֶת **kuttôneth**, *koot-to´-neth*; from an unused root mean. to *cover* [comp. 3802]; a *shirt*:— coat, garment, robe.

3802. כָּתֵף **kâthêph**, *kaw-thafe´*; from an unused root mean. to *clothe*; the *shoulder* (proper, i.e. upper end of the arm; as being the spot where the garments hang); fig. *side-piece* or lateral projection of anything:— arm, corner, shoulder (-piece),side, undersetter.

3803. כָּתַר **kâthar**, *kaw-thar´*; a prim. root; to *enclose*; hence, (in a friendly sense) to *crown*, (in a hostile one) to *besiege*; also to *wait* (as restraining oneself):— beset round, compass about, be crowned, inclose round, suffer.

3804. כֶּתֶר **kether**, *keh´-ther*; from 3803; prop. a *circlet*, i.e. a *diadem*:— crown.

3805. כֹּתֶרֶת **kôthereth**, *ko-theh´-reth*; fem. act. part. of 3803; the *capital* of a column:— chapiter.

3806. כָּתַשׁ **kâthash**, *kaw-thash´*; a prim. root; to *butt* or *pound*:— bray.

3807. כָּתַת **kâthath**, *kaw-thath´*; a prim. root; to *bruise* or violently *strike*:— beat (down, to pieces), break in pieces, crushed, destroy, discomfit, smite, stamp.

ל

3808. לֹא **lô´**, *lo*; or לוֹא **lôw´**, *lo*; or לֹה **lôh** (Deut. 3:11), *lo*; a prim. particle; *not* (the simple or abs. negation); by impl. *no*; often used with other particles (as follows):— × before, + or else, ere, + except, ig[-norant], much, less, nay, neither, never, no ([-nel, -r, [-thing]), (× as though … , [can-], for) not (out of), of nought, otherwise, out of, + surely, + as truly as, + of a truth, + verily, for want, + whether, without.

3809. לָא **lâ´** (Chald.), *law*; or לָה **lâh** (Chald.) (Dan. 4:32), *law*; corresp. to 3808:— or even, neither, no (-ne, -r), ([can-]) not, as nothing, without.

לֻא **lû´**. See 3863.

3810. לֹא דְבַר **Lô´ Dᵉbar**, *lo deb-ar´*; or לוֹ דְבַר **Lôw Dᵉbar** (2 Sam. 9:4,5), *lo deb-ar´*; or לִדְבִר **Lidbîr** (Josh. 13:26), *lid-beer´*; [prob. rather לֹדְבַר **Lôdᵉbar**, *lo-deb-ar*]; from 3808 and 1699; *pastureless*; *Lo-Debar*, a place in Pal.:— Debir, Lo-debar.

3811. לָאָה **lâ'âh**, *law-aw´*; a prim. root; to *tire*; (fig.) to *be* (or *make*) disgusted:— faint, grieve, lothe, (be, make) weary (selves).

3812. לֵאָה **Lê'âh**, *lay-aw´*; from 3811; *weary; Leah*, a wife of Jacob:— Leah.

לְאוֹם **le'ôwm**. See 3816.

3813. לָאַט **lâ'aṭ**, *law-at´*; a prim. root; to *muffle:*— cover.

3814. לָאט **lâṭ**, *lawt*; from 3813 (or perh. for act. part. of 3874); prop. *muffled*, i.e. *silently:*— softly.

3815. לָאֵל **Lâ'êl**, *law-ale´*; from the prep. pref. and 410; (belonging) *to God; Laël*, an Isr.:— Lael.

3816. לְאֹם **le'ôm**, *leh-ome´* or

לְאוֹם **le'ôwm**, *leh-ome´*; from an unused root mean. to *gather*; a *community:*— nation, people.

3817. לְאֻמִּים **Le'ummîym**, *leh-oom-meem´*; plur. of 3816; *communities; Leümmim*, an Arabian:— Leummim.

3818. לֹא עַמִּי **Lô' 'Ammîy**, *lo am-mee´*; from 3808 and 5971 with pron. suff.; *not my people; Lo-Ammi*, the symbol. name of a son of Hosea:— Lo-ammi.

3819. לֹא רֻחָמָה **Lô' Rûchâmâh**, *lo roo-khaw-maw´*; from 3808 and 7355; *not pitied; Lo-Ruchamah*, the symbol. name of a son of Hosea:— Lo-ruhamah.

3820. לֵב **lêb**, *labe*; a form of 3824; the *heart*; also used (fig.) very widely for the feelings, the will and even the intellect; likewise for the *center* of anything:— + care for, comfortably, consent, × considered, courag[-eous], friend [-ly], [broken-], [hard-], [merry-], [stiff-], [stout-], double) heart (l-edl), × heed, × I, kindly, midst, mind (-ed), × regard (l-edl), × themselves, × unawares, understanding, × well, willingly, wisdom.

3821. לֵב **lêb** (Chald.), *labe*; corresp. to 3820:— heart.

3822. לְבָאוֹת **Lebâ'ôwth**, *leb-aw-ōth´*; plur. of 3833; *lionesses; Lebaoth*, a place in Pal.:— Lebaoth. See also 1034.

3823. לָבַב **lâbab**, *law-bab´*; a prim. root; prop. to *be enclosed* (as if with *fat*); by impl. (as denom. from 3824) to *unheart*, i.e. (in a good sense) *transport* (with love), or (in a bad sense) *stultify*; also (as denom. from 3834) to *make cakes:*— make cakes, ravish, be wise.

3824. לֵבָב **lêbâb**, *lay-bawb´*; from 3823; the *heart* (as the most interior organ); used also like 3820:— + bethink themselves, breast, comfortably, courage, ([faint], [tender-] heart [l-ed]), midst, mind, × unawares, understanding.

3825. לְבַב **lebab** (Chald.), *leb-ab´*; corresp. to 3824:— heart.

לְבִבָה **lebîbâh**. See 3834.

3826. לִבָּה **libbâh**, *lib-baw´*; fem. of 3820; the *heart:*— heart.

3827. לַבָּה **labbâh**, *lab-baw´*; for 3852; *flame:*— flame.

3828. לְבוֹנָה **lebôwnâh**, *leb-o-naw´*; or

לְבֹנָה **lebonâh**, *leb-o-naw´*; from 3836; *frankincense* (from its *whiteness* or perh. that of its *smoke*):— (frank-) incense.

3829. לְבֹנָה **Lebôwnâh**, *leb-o-naw´*; the

---

same as 3828; *Lebonah*, a place in Pal.:— Lebonah.

3830. לְבוּשׁ **lebûwsh**, *leb-oosh´*; or

לְבֻשׁ **lebûsh**, *leb-oosh´*; from 3847; a *garment* (lit. or fig.); by impl. (euphem.) a *wife:*— apparel, clothed with, clothing, garment, raiment, vestment, vesture.

3831. לְבוּשׁ **lebûwsh** (Chald.), *leb-oosh´*; corresp. to 3830:— garment.

3832. לְבַט **lâbaṭ**, *law-bat´*; a prim. root; to *overthrow*; intr. to *fall:*— fall.

לֻבִּי **Lubbîy**. See 3864.

3833. לָבִיא **lâbîy'**, *law-bee´*; or (Ezek. 19:2)

לְבִיָּא **lebîyâ'**, *leb-ee-yaw´*; irreg. masc. plur.

לְבָאִים **lebâ'îym**, *leb-aw-eem´*; irreg. fem. plur.

לְבָאוֹת **lebâ'ôwth**, *leb-aw-ōth´*; from an unused root mean. to *roar*; a *lion* (prop. a lioness as the fiercer [although not a *roarer*; comp. 738]):— (great, old, stout) lion, lioness, young [lion].

3834. לְבִיבָה **lâbîybâh**, *law-bee-baw´*; or rather

לְבִבָה **lebîbâh**, *leb-ee-baw´*; from 3823 in its orig. sense of *fatness* (or perh. of *folding*); a *cake* (either as *fried* or *turned*):— cake.

3835. לָבַן **lâban**, *law-ban´*; a prim. root; to *be* (or *become*) *white*; also (as denom. from 3843) to *make bricks:*— make brick, be (made, make) white (-r).

3836. לָבָן **lâbân**, *law-bawn´*; or (Gen. 49:12)

לָבֵן **lâbên**, *law-bane´*; from 3835; *white:*— white.

3837. לָבָן **Lâbân**, *law-bawn´*; the same as 3836; *Laban*, a Mesopotamian; also a place in the Desert:— Laban.

לַבֵּן **Labbên**. See 4192.

3838. לְבָנָא **Lebânâ'**, *leb-aw-naw´*; or

לְבָנָה **Lebânâh**, *leb-aw-naw´*; the same as 3842; *Lebana* or *Lebanah*, one of the Nethinim:— Lebana, Lebanah.

3839. לִבְנֶה **libneh**, *lib-neh´*; from 3835; some sort of *whitish* tree, perh. the *storax:*— poplar.

3840. לִבְנָה **libnâh**, *lib-naw´*; from 3835; prop. *whiteness*, i.e. (by impl.) *transparency:*— paved.

3841. לִבְנָה **Libnâh**, *lib-naw´*; the same as 3839; *Libnah*, a place in the Desert and one in Pal.:— Libnah.

3842. לְבָנָה **lebânâh**, *leb-aw-naw´*; from 3835; prop. (the) *white*, i.e. the *moon:*— moon. See also 3838.

3843. לְבֵנָה **lebênâh**, *leb-ay-naw´*; from 3835; a *brick* (from the *whiteness* of the clay):— (altar of) brick, tile.

לְבֹנָה **lebônâh**. See 3828.

3844. לְבָנוֹן **Lebânôwn**, *leb-aw-nohn´*; from 3825; (the) *white* mountain (from its *snow*); *Lebanon*, a mountain range in Pal.:— Lebanon.

3845. לִבְנִי **Libnîy**, *lib-nee´*; from 3835; *white; Libni*, an Isr.:— Libni.

3846. לִבְנִי **Libnîy**, *lib-nee´*; patron. from 3845; a *Libnite* or desc. of Libni (collect.):— Libnites.

3847. לָבַשׁ **lâbash**, *law-bash´*; or

לָבֵשׁ **lâbêsh**, *law-bashe´*; a prim. root; prop. *wrap* around, i.e. (by impl.) to *put on* a garment or *clothe* (oneself, or another), lit. or fig.:— (in) apparel, arm, array (self), clothe (self), come upon, put (on, upon), wear.

3848. לְבַשׁ **lebash** (Chald.), *leb-ash´*; corresp. to 3847:— clothe.

לְבוּשׁ **lebûsh**. See 3830.

3849. לֹג **lôg**, *lohg*; from an unused root appar. mean. to *deepen* or *hollow* [like 3537]; a *log* or measure for liquids:— log [of oil].

3850. לֹד **Lôd**, *lode*; from an unused root of uncert. signif.; *Lod*, a place in Pal.:— Lod.

לִדְבִר **Lidbîr**. See 3810.

3851. לַהַב **lahab**, *lah´-hab*; from an unused root mean. to *gleam*; a *flash*; fig. a sharply polished *blade* or *point* of a weapon:— blade, bright, flame, glittering.

3852. לֶהָבָה **lehâbâh**, *leh-aw-baw´*; or

לַהֶבֶת **lahebeth**, *lah-eh´-beth*; fem. of 3851, and mean. the same:— flame (-ming), head [of a spear].

3853. לְהָבִים **Lehâbîym**, *leh-haw-beem´*; plur. of 3851; *flames; Lehabim*, a son of Mizrain, and his desc.:— Lehabim.

3854. לַהַג **lahag**, *lah´-hag*; from an unused root mean. to *be eager*; intense mental *application:*— study.

3855. לַהַד **Lahad**, *lah´-had*; from an unused root mean. to *glow* [comp. 3851] or else to *be earnest* [comp. 3854]; *Lahad*, an Isr.:— Lahad.

3856. לָהַהּ **lâhahh**, *law-hah´*; a prim. root mean. prop. to *burn*, i.e. (by impl.) to *be rabid* (fig. *insane*); also (from the *exhaustion* of frenzy) to *languish:*— faint, mad.

3857. לָהַט **lâhaṭ**, *law-hat´*; a prim. root; prop. to *lick*, i.e. (by impl.) to *blaze:*— burn (up), set on fire, flaming, kindle.

3858. לַהַט **lahaṭ**, *lah´-hat*; from 3857; a *blaze*; also (from the idea of *enwrapping*) *magic* (as *covert*):— flaming, enchantment.

3859. לָהַם **lâham**, *law-ham´*; a prim. root; prop. to *burn* in, i.e. (fig.) to *rankle:*— wound.

3860. לָהֵן **lâhên**, *law-hane´*; from the pref. prep. mean. *to* or *for* and 2005; prop. *for if*; hence, *therefore:*— for them [by *mistake for prep. suff.*].

3861. לָהֵן **lâhên** (Chald.), *law-hane´*; corresp. to 3860; *therefore*; also *except:*— but, except, save, therefore, wherefore.

3862. לַהֲקָה **lahăqâh**, *lah-hak-aw´*; prob. from an unused root mean. to *gather*; an *assembly:*— company.

לוֹא **lôw'**. See 3808.

3863. לוּא **lûw'**, *loo*; or

לֻא **lu'**, *loo*; or

לוּ **lûw**, *loo*; a conditional particle; *if*; by impl. (interj. as a wish) *would* *that!*:— if (haply), peradventure, I pray thee, though, I would, would God (that).

3864. לוּבִי **Lûwbîy**, *loo-bee´*; or

לֻבִּי **Lubbîy** (Dan. 11:43) *loob-bee´*; patrial from a name prob. derived from an unused root mean. to *thirst*, i.e. a *dry* region; appar. a *Libyan* or inhab. of interior Africa (only in plur.):— Lubim (-s), Libyans.

3865. לוּד **Lûwd**, *lood*; prob. of for. der.; *Lud*, the name of two nations:— Lud, Lydia.

3866. לוּדִי **Lûwdîy**, *loo-dee´*; or

לוּדִי **Lûwdîyiy**, *loo-dee-ee´*; patrial from 3865; a *Ludite* or inhab. of Lud (only in plural):— Ludim, Lydians.

3867. לָוָה **lâvâh**, *law-vaw´*; a prim. root; prop. to *twine*, i.e. (by impl.) to *unite*, to *remain*; also to *borrow* (as a form of *obligation*) or (caus.) to *lend*:— abide with, borrow (-er), cleave, join (self), lend (-er).

3868. לוּז **lûwz**, *looz*; a prim. root; to *turn* aside [comp. 3867, 3874 and 3885], i.e. (lit.) to *depart*, (fig.) be *perverse*:— depart, froward, perverse (-ness).

3869. לוּז **lûwz**, *looz*; prob. of for. or.; some kind of *nut*-tree, perh. the *almond*:— hazel.

3870. לוּז **Lûwz**, *looz*; prob. from 3869 (as growing there); *Luz*, the name of two places in Pal.:— Luz.

3871. לוּחַ **lûwach**, *loo´-akh*; or

לֻחַ **lûach**, *loo´-akh*; from a prim. root; prob. mean. to *glisten*; a *tablet* (as *polished*), of stone, wood or metal:— board, plate, table.

3872. לוּחִית **Lûwchîyth**, *loo-kheeth´*; or

לֻחֹות **Lûchôwth** (Jer. 48:5), *loo-khoth´*; from the same as 3871; *floored*; *Luchith*, a place E. of the Jordan:— Luhith.

3873. לוֹחֵשׁ **Lôwchêsh**, *lo-khashe´*; act. part. of 3907; (the) *enchanter*; *Lochesh*, an Isr.:— Halloesh, Haloshesh [includ. the art.].

3874. לוּט **lûwṭ**, *loot*; a prim. root; to *wrap* up:— cast, wrap.

3875. לוֹט **lôwṭ**, *lote*; from 3874; a *veil*:— covering.

3876. לוֹט **Lôwṭ**, *lote*; the same as 3875; *Lot*, Abraham's nephew:— Lot.

3877. לוֹטָן **Lôwṭân**, *lo-tawn´*; from 3875; *covering*; *Lotan*, an Idumæan:— Lotan.

3878. לֵוִי **Lêvîy**, *lay-vee´*; from 3867; *attached*; *Levi*, a son of Jacob:— Levi. See also 3879, 3881.

3879. לֵוִי **Lêvîy** (Chald.), *lay-vee´*; corresp. to 3880:— Levite.

3880. לִוְיָה **livyâh**, *liv-yaw´*; from 3867; something *attached*, i.e. a *wreath*:— ornament.

3881. לֵוִי **Lêvîyiy**, *lay-vee´*; or

לֵוִי **Lêvîy**, *lay-vee´*; patron. from 3878; a *Levite* or desc. of Levi:— Levite.

3882. לִוְיָתָן **livyâthân**, *liv-yaw-thawn´*; from 3867; a *wreathed* animal, i.e. a *serpent* (espec. the *crocodile* or some other large sea-monster); fig. the con-

stellation of the *dragon*; also as a symbol of *Babylon*:— leviathan, mourning.

3883. לוּל **lûwl**, *lool*; from an unused root mean. to *fold* back; a *spiral* step:— winding stair. Comp. 3924.

3884. לוּלֵא **lûwlê**, *loo-lay´*; or

לוּלֵי **lûwlêy**, *loo lay´*; from 3863 and 3808; *if not*:— except, had not, if (... not), unless, were it not that.

3885. לוּן **lûwn**, *loon*; or

לִין **lîyn**, *leen*; a prim. root; to *stop* (usually over night); by impl. to *stay* permanently; hence, (in a bad sense) to *be obstinate* (espec. in words, to *complain*):— abide (all night), continue, dwell, endure, grudge, be left, lie all night, (cause to) lodge (all night, in, -ing, this night), (make to) murmur, remain, tarry (all night, that night).

3886. לוּעַ **lûwa´**, *loo´-ah*; a prim. root; to *gulp*; fig. to *be rash*:— swallow down (up).

3887. לוּץ **lûwts**, *loots*; a prim. root; prop. to *make mouths* at, i.e. to *scoff*; hence, (from the effort to pronounce a foreign language) to *interpret*, or (gen.) *intercede*:— ambassador, have in derision, interpreter, make a mock, mocker, scorn (-er, -ful), teacher.

3888. לוּשׁ **lûwsh**, *loosh*; a prim. root; to *knead*:— knead.

3889. לוּשׁ **Lûwsh**, *loosh*; from 3888; *kneading*; *Lush*, a place in Pal.:— Laish [from the marg.]. Comp. 3919.

3890. לְוָת **lᵉvâth** (Chald.), *lev-awth´*; from a root corresp. to 3867; prop. *adhesion*, i.e. (as prep.) *with*:— × thee.

לְוָחֹות **Lûchôwth**. See 3872.

לָז **lâz** and

לָזֶה **lâzeh**. See 1975 and 1976.

3891. לְזוּת **lᵉzûwth**, *lez-ooth´*; from 3868; *perverseness*:— perverse.

3892. לַח **lach**, *lakh*; from an unused root mean. to *be new*; *fresh*, i.e. *undried*:— green, moist.

3893. לֵחַ **lêach**, *lay´-akh*; from the same as 3892; *freshness*, i.e. *vigor*:— natural force.

לֻחַ **lùach**. See 3871.

3894. לָחוּם **lâchûwm**, *law-khoom´*; or

לָחֻם **lâchûm**, *law-khoom´*; pass. part. of 3898; prop. *eaten*, i.e. *food*; also *flesh*, i.e. *body*:— while ... is eating, flesh.

3895. לְחִי **lᵉchîy**, *lekh-ee´*; from an unused root mean. to *be soft*; the *cheek* (from its *fleshiness*); hence, the *jaw*-bone:— cheek (bone), jaw (bone).

3896. לֶחִי **Lechîy**, *lekh´-ee*; a form of 3895; *Lechi*, a place in Pal.:— Lehi. Comp. also 7437.

3897. לָחַךְ **lâchak**, *law-khak´*; a prim. root; to *lick*:— lick (up).

3898. לָחַם **lâcham**, *law-kham´*; a prim. root; to *feed* on; fig. to *consume*; by impl. to *battle* (as *destruction*):— devour, eat, × ever, fight (-ing), overcome, prevail, (make) war (-ring).

3899. לֶחֶם **lechem**, *lekh´-em*; from 3898; *food* (for man or beast), espec. *bread*, or *grain* (for making it):— [shew-]

bread, × eat, food, fruit, loaf, meat, victuals. See also 1036.

3900. לְחֶם **lᵉchem** (Chald.), *lekh-em´*; corresp. to 3899:— feast.

3901. לָחֶם **lâchem**, *law-khem´*; from 3898, *battle*:— war.

לָחֻם **lâchûm**. See 3894.

3902. לַחְמִי **Lachmîy**, *lakh-mee´*; from 3899; *foodful*; *Lachmi*, a Philis.: or rather prob. a brief form (or perh. err. transc.) for 1022:— Lahmi. See also 3433.

3903. לַחְמָס **Lachmâç**, *lakh-maws´*; prob. by err. transc. for

לַחְמָם° **Lachmâm**, *lakh-mawm´*; from 3899; *food-like*; *Lachmam* or *Lachmas*, a place in Pal.:— Lahmam.

3904. לֶחֱנָה **lᵉchênâh** (Chald.), *lekh-ay-naw´*; from an unused root of uncert. mean.; a *concubine*:— concubine.

3905. לָחַץ **lâchats**, *law-khats´*; a prim. root; prop. to *press*, i.e. (fig.) to *distress*:— afflict, crush, force, hold fast, oppress (-or), thrust self.

3906. לַחַץ **lachats**, *lakh´-ats*; from 3905; *distress*:— affliction, oppression.

3907. לָחַשׁ **lâchash**, *law-khash´*; a prim. root; to *whisper*; by impl. to *mumble* a spell (as a magician):— charmer, whisper (together).

3908. לַחַשׁ **lachash**, *lakh´-ash*; from 3907; prop. a *whisper*, i.e. by impl. (in a good sense) a private *prayer*, (in a bad one) an *incantation*; concr. an *amulet*:— charmed, earring, enchantment, orator, prayer.

3909. לָט **lâṭ**, *lawt*; a form of 3814 or else part. from 3874; prop. *covered*, i.e. *secret*; by impl. *incantation*; also *secrecy* or (adv.) *covertly*:— enchantment, privily, secretly, softly.

3910. לֹט **lôṭ**, *lote*; prob. from 3874; a gum (from its *sticky* nature), prob. *ladanum*:— myrrh.

3911. לְטָאָה **lᵉṭâ'âh**, *let-aw-aw´*; from an unused root mean. to *hide*; a kind of *lizard* (from its *covert* habits):— lizard.

3912. לְטוּשִׁם **Lᵉṭûwshîm**, *let-oo-sheem´*; masc. plur. of pass. part. of 3913; *hammered* (i.e. *oppressed*) ones; *Letushim*, an Arabian tribe:— Letushim.

3913. לָטַשׁ **lâṭash**, *law-tash´*; a prim. root; prop. to *hammer* out (an edge), i.e. to *sharpen*:— instructer, sharp (-en), whet.

3914. לֹיָה **lôyâh**, *lo-yaw´*; a form of 3880; a *wreath*:— addition.

3915. לַיִל **layil**, *lah´-yil*; or (Isa. 21:11)

לֵיל **lêyl**, *lale*; also

לַיְלָה **laylâh**, *lah´-yel-aw*; from the same as 3883; prop. a *twist* (away of the light), i.e. *night*; fig. *adversity*:— [mid-] night (season).

3916. לֵילְיָא **leylᵉyâ'** (Chald.), *lay-leh-yaw´*; corresp. to 3915:— night.

3917. לִילִית **lîylîyth**, *lee-leeth´*; from 3915; a *night* spectre:— screech owl.

3918. לַיִשׁ **layish**, *lah´-yish*; from 3888 in the sense of *crushing*; a lion (from his destructive *blows*):— (old) lion.

3919. לַיִשׁ **Layish**, *lah´-yish*; the same as

3918. Laïsh, the name of two places in Pal.:— Laish. Comp. 3889.

3920. לָכַד lâkad, law-kad´; a prim. root; to catch (in a net, trap or pit); gen. to capture or occupy; also to choose (by lot); fig. to cohere:— × at all, catch (self), be frozen, be holden, stick together, take.

3921. לֶכֶד leked, leh´ked; from 3920; something to capture with, i.e. a noose:— being taken.

3922. לְכָה Lêkâh, lay-kaw´; from 3212; a journey; Lekah, a place in Pal.:— Lecah.

3923. לָחִישׁ Lâchîysh, law-keesh´; from an unused root of uncert. mean.; Lakish, a place in Pal.:— Lachish.

3924. לֻלָאָה lûlâ'âh, loo-law-aw´; from the same as 3883; a loop:— loop.

3925. לָמַד lâmad, law-mad´; a prim. root; prop. to goad, i.e. (by impl.) to teach (the rod being an Oriental incentive):— [un-] accustomed, × diligently, expert, instruct, learn, skilful, teach (-er, ing).

לִמֻּד limmûd. See 3928.

3926. לְמוֹ lᵉmôw, lem-o´; a prol. and separable form of the pref. prep.; to or for:— at, for, to, upon.

3927. לְמוּאֵל Lᵉmûw'êl, lem-oo-ale´;

לְמוֹאֵל Lᵉmôw'êl, lem-o-ale´; from 3926 and 410; (belonging) to God; Lemuël or Lemoël, a symbol. name of Solomon:— Lemuel.

3928. לִמּוּד limmûwd, lim-mood´; or

לִמֻּד limmûd, lim-mood´; from 3925; instructed:— accustomed, disciple, learned, taught, used.

3929. לֶמֶךְ Lemek, leh´-mek; from an unused root of uncert. mean.; Lemek, the name of two antediluvian patriarchs:— Lamech.

3930. לֹעַ lôa', lo´ah; from 3886; the gullet:— throat.

3931. לָעַב lâ'ab, law-ab´; a prim. root; to deride:— mock.

3932. לָעַג lâ'ag, law-ag´; a prim. root; to deride; by impl. (as if imitating a foreigner) to speak unintelligibly:— have in derision, laugh (to scorn), mock (on), stammering.

3933. לַעַג la'ag, lah´-ag; from 3932; derision, scoffing:— derision, scorn (-ing).

3934. לָעֵג lâ'êg, law-ayg´; from 3932; a buffoon; also a foreigner:— mocker, stammering.

3935. לַעְדָּה La'dâh, lah-daw´; from an unused root of uncert. mean.; Ladah, an Isr.:— Laadah.

3936. לַעְדָּן La'dân, lah-dawn´; from the same as 3935; Ladan, the name of two Isr.:— Laadan.

3937. לָעַז lâ'az, law-az´; a prim. root; to speak in a foreign tongue:— strange language.

3938. לָעַט lâ'aṭ, law-at´; a prim. root; to swallow greedily; caus. to feed:— feed.

3939. לַעֲנָה la'ănâh, lah-an-aw´; from an unused root supposed to mean to curse; wormwood (regarded as poison-ous, and therefore accursed):— hemlock, wormwood.

3940. לַפִּיד lappîyd, lap-peed´; or

לַפִּד lappîd, lap-peed´; from an unused root prob. mean. to shine; a flambeau, lamp or flame:— (fire-) brand, (burning) lamp, lightning, torch.

3941. לַפִּידוֹת Lappîydôwth, lap-pee-dôth´; fem. plur. of 3940; Lappidoth, the husband of Deborah:— Lappidoth.

3942. לִפְנַי liphnay, lif-nah´ee; from the pref. prep. (to or for) and 6440; anterior:— before.

3943. לָפַת lâphath, law-fath´; a prim. root; prop. to bend, i.e. (by impl.) to clasp; also (refl.) to turn around or aside:— take hold, turn aside (self).

3944. לָצוֹן lâtsôwn, law-tsone´; from 3887; derision:— scornful (-ning).

3945. לָצַץ lâtsats, law-tsats´; a prim. root; to deride:— scorn.

3946. לַקּוּם Laqqûwm, lak-koom´; from an unused root thought to mean to stop up by a barricade; perh. fortification; Lakkum, a place in Pal.:— Lakum.

3947. לָקַח lâqach, law-kakh´; a prim. root; to take (in the widest variety of applications):— accept, bring, buy, carry away, drawn, fetch, get, infold, × many, mingle, place, receive (-ing), reserve, seize, send for, take (away, -ing, up), use, win.

3948. לֶקַח leqach, leh´-kakh; from 3947; prop. something received, i.e. (ment.) instruction (whether on the part of the teacher or hearer); also (in an act. and sinister sense) inveiglement:— doctrine, learning, fair speech.

3949. לִקְחִי Liqchîy, lik-khee´; from 3947; learned; Likchi, an Isr.:— Likhi.

3950. לָקַט lâqaṭ, law-kat´; a prim. root; prop. to pick up, i.e. (gen.) to gather; spec. to glean:— gather (up), glean.

3951. לֶקֶט leqeṭ, leh´-ket; from 3950; the gleaning:— gleaning.

3952. לָקַק lâqaq, law-kak´; a prim. root; to lick or lap:— lap, lick.

3953. לָקַשׁ lâqash, law-kash´; a prim. root; to gather the after crop:— gather.

3954. לֶקֶשׁ leqesh, leh´-kesh; from 3953; the after crop:— latter growth.

3955. לְשַׁד lᵉshad, lesh-ad´; from an unused root of uncert. mean.; appar. juice, i.e. (fig.) vigor; also a sweet or fat cake:— fresh, moisture.

3956. לָשׁוֹן lâshôwn, law-shone´; or

לָשֹׁן lâshôn, law-shone´; also (in plur.) fem.

לְשֹׁנָה lᵉshônâh, lesh-o-naw´; from 3960; the tongue (of man or animals), used lit. (as the instrument of licking, eating, or speech), and fig. (speech, an ingot, a fork of flame, a cove of water):— + babbler, bay, + evil speaker, language, talker, tongue, wedge.

3957. לִשְׁכָּה lishkâh, lish-kaw´; from an unused root of uncert. mean.; a room in a building (whether for storage, eating, or lodging):— chamber, parlour. Comp. 5393.

3958. לֶשֶׁם leshem, leh´-shem; from an unused root of uncert. mean.; a gem, perh. the jacinth:— ligure.

3959. לֶשֶׁם Leshem, leh´-shem; the same as 3958; Leshem, a place in Pal.:— Leshem.

3960. לָשַׁן lâshan, law-shan´; a prim. root; prop. to lick; but used only as a denom. from 3956; to wag the tongue, i.e. to calumniate:— accuse, slander.

3961. לִשָּׁן lishshân (Chald.), lish-shawn´; corresp. to 3956; speech, i.e. a nation:— language.

3962. לֶשַׁע Lesha', leh´-shah; from an unused root thought to mean to break through; a boiling spring; Lesha, a place prob. E. of the Jordan:— Lasha.

3963. לֶתֶךְ lethek, leh´-thek; from an unused root of uncert. mean.; a measure for things dry:— half homer.

מ

מ ma-, or

מָ mâ-. See 4100.

3964. מָא mâ' (Chald.), maw; corresp. to 4100; (as indef.) that:— + what.

3965. מַעֲבוּס ma'ăbûwç, mah-ab-ooce´; from 75; a granary:— storehouse.

3966. מְאֹד mᵉ'ôd, meh-ode´; from the same as 181; prop. vehemence, i.e. (with or without prep.) vehemently; by impl. wholly, speedily, etc. (often with other words as an intens. or superl.; espec. when repeated):— diligently, especially, exceeding (-ly), far, fast, good, great (-ly), × louder and louder, might (-ily, -y), (so) much, quickly, (so) sore, utterly, (+ much, sore), well.

3967. מֵאָה mê'âh, may-aw´; or

מֵאיָה mê'yâh, may-yaw´; prop. a prim. numeral; a hundred; also as a multiplicative and a fraction:— hundred (-fold], -th), + sixscore.

3968. מֵאָה Mê'âh, may-aw´; the same as 3967; Meäh, a tower in Jerusalem:— Meah.

3969. מְאָה mᵉ'âh (Chald.), meh-aw´; corresp. to 3967:— hundred.

3970. מַאֲוַי ma'ăvay, mah-av-ah´ee; from 183; a desire:— desire.

מוֹאל môw'l. See 4136.

3971. מאוּם m'ûwm, moom; usually

מוּם mûwm, moom; as if pass. part. from an unused root prob. mean. to stain; a blemish (phys. or mor.):— blemish, blot, spot.

3972. מְאוּמָה mᵉ'ûwmâh, meh-oo´-maw; appar. a form of 3971; prop. a speck or point, i.e. (by impl.) something; with neg. nothing:— fault, + no (-ught), ought, somewhat, any ([no-]) thing.

3973. מָאוֹס mâ'ôwç, maw-oce´; from 3988; refuse:— refuse.

3974. מָאוֹר mâ'ôwr, maw-ore´; or

מָאֹר mâ'ôr, maw-ore´; also (in plur.) fem.

מְאוֹרָה mᵉ'ôwrâh, meh-o-raw´; or

מְאֹרָה mᵉ'ôrâh, meh-o-raw´; from 215; prop. a luminous body or luminary, i.e. (abstr.) light (as an element); fig. brightness, i.e. cheerfulness; spec. a chandelier:— bright, light.

3975. מְאוּרָה **mᵉ'ûwrâh**, *meh-oo-raw'*; fem. pass. part. of 215; something *lighted*, i.e. an *aperture*; by impl. a *crevice* or *hole* (of a serpent):— den.

3976. מֹאזֵן **mô'zên**, *mo-zane'*; from 239; (only in the dual) a pair of *scales*:— balances.

3977. מֹאזֵן **mô'zên** (Chald.), *mo-zane'*; corresp. to 3976:— balances.

מֵאִיָּה **mê'yâh**. See 3967.

3978. מַאֲכָל **ma'ăkâl**, *mah-ak-awl'*; from 398; an *eatable* (includ. provender, flesh and fruit):— food, fruit, (bake-) meat (-s), victual.

3979. מַאֲכֶלֶת **ma'ăkeleth**, *mah-ak-eh'-leth*; from 398; something to *eat* with, i.e. a *knife*:— knife.

3980. מַאֲכֹלֶת **ma'ăkôleth**, *mah-ak-o'-leth*; from 398; something *eaten* (by fire), i.e. *fuel*:— fuel.

3981. מַאֲמָץ **ma'ămâts**, *mah-am-awts'*; from 553; *strength*, i.e. (plur.) *resources*:— force.

3982. מַאֲמָר **ma'ămar**, *mah-am-ar'*; from 559; something (authoritatively) *said*, i.e. an *edict*:— commandment, decree.

3983. מֵאמַר **mê'mar** (Chald.), *may-mar'*; corresp. to 3982:— appointment, word.

3984. מָאן **mâ'n** (Chald.), *mawn*; prob. from a root corresp. to 579 in the sense of an *inclosure* by sides; a *utensil*:— vessel.

3985. מָאֵן **mâ'ên**, *maw-ane'*; a prim. root; to *refuse*:— refuse, × utterly.

3986. מָאֵן **mâ'ên**, *maw-ane'*; from 3985; *unwilling*:— refuse.

3987. מֵאֵן **mê'ên**, *may-ane'*; from 3985; *refractory*:— refuse.

3988. מָאַס **mâ'aç**, *maw-as'*; a prim. root; to *spurn*; also (intr.) to *disappear*:— abhor, cast away (off), contemn, despise, disdain, (become) loathe (some), melt away, refuse, reject, reprobate, × utterly, vile person.

3989. מַאֲפֶה **mâ'ăpheh**, *mah-af-eh'*; from 644; something *baked*, i.e. a *batch*:— baken.

3990. מַאֲפֵל **ma'ăphêl**, *mah-af-ale'*; from the same as 651; something *opaque*:— darkness.

3991. ° מַאֲפֵלְיָה **ma'phêlᵉyâh**, *mah-af-ay-leh-yaw'*; prol. fem. of 3990; *opaqueness*:— darkness.

3992. מָאַר **mâ'ar**, *maw-ar'*; a prim. root; to *be bitter* or (caus.) to *embitter*, i.e. be *painful*:— fretting, picking.

מָאֹר **mâ'ôr**. See 3974.

3993. מַאֲרָב **ma'ărâb**, *mah-ar-awb'*; from 693; an *ambuscade*:— lie in ambush, ambushment, lurking place, lying in wait.

3994. מְאֵרָה **mᵉ'êrâh**, *meh-ay-raw'*; from 779; an *execration*:— curse.

מְאֹרָה **mᵉ'ôrâh**. See 3974.

3995. מִבְדָּלָה **mibdâlâh**, *mib-daw-law'*; from 914; a *separation*, i.e. (concr.) a *separate* place:— separate.

3996. מָבוֹא **mâbôw'**, *maw-bo'*; from 935; an *entrance* (the place or the act); spec. (with or without 8121) *sunset* or the

---

west; also (adv. with prep.) *towards*:— by which came, as cometh, in coming, as men enter into, entering, entrance into, entry, where goeth, going down, + westward. Comp. 4126.

3997. מְבוֹאָה **mᵉbôw'âh**, *meb-o-aw'*; fem. of 3996; a *haven*:— entry.

3998. מְבוּכָה **mᵉbûwkâh**, *meb-oo-kaw'*; from 943; *perplexity*:— perplexity.

3999. מַבּוּל **mabbûwl**, *mab-bool'*; from 2986 in the sense of *flowing*; a *deluge*:— flood.

4000. מָבוֹן **mâbôwn**, *maw-bone'*; from 995; *instructing*:— taught.

4001. מְבוּסָה **mᵉbûwçâh**, *meb-oo-saw'*; from 947; a *trampling*:— treading (trodden) down (under foot).

4002. מַבּוּעַ **mabbûwa'**, *mab-boo'-ah*; from 5042; a *fountain*:— fountain, spring.

4003. מְבוּקָה **mᵉbûwqâh**, *meb-oo-kaw'*; from the same as 950; *emptiness*:— void.

4004. מִבְחוֹר **mibchôwr**, *mib-khore'*; from 977; *select*, i.e. well fortified:— choice.

4005. מִבְחָר **mibchâr**, *mib-khawr'*; from 977; *select*, i.e. best:— choice (-st), chosen.

4006. מִבְחָר **Mibchâr**, *mib-khawr'*; the same as 4005; *Mibchar*, an Isr.:— Mibhar.

4007. מַבָּט **mabbâṭ**, *mab-bawt'*; or

מֶבָּט **mebbâṭ**, *meb-bawt'*; from 5027; something *expected*, i.e. (abstr.) *expectation*:— expectation.

4008. מִבְטָא **mibṭâ'**, *mib-taw'*; from 981; a rash *utterance* (hasty vow):— (that which ...) uttered (out of).

4009. מִבְטָח **mibṭâch**, *mib-tawkh'*; from 982; prop. a *refuge*, i.e. (obj.) *security*, or (subj.) *assurance*:— confidence, hope, sure, trust.

4010. מַבְלִיגִית **mabliygîyth**, *mab-leeg-eeth'*; from 1082; *desistance* (or rather *desolation*):— comfort self.

4011. מִבְנֶה **mibneh**, *mib-neh'*; from 1129; a *building*:— frame.

4012. מְבֻנַּי **Mᵉbunnay**, *meb-oon-hah'-ee*; from 1129; *built up*; *Mebunnai*, an Isr.:— Mebunnai.

4013. מִבְצָר **mibtsâr**, *mib-tsawr'*; also (in plur.) fem. (Dan. 11:15)

מִבְצָרָה **mibtsârâh**, *mib-tsaw-raw'*; from 1219; a *fortification*, *castle*, or *fortified* city; fig. a *defender*:— (de-, most) fenced, fortress, (most) strong (hold).

4014. מִבְצָר **Mibtsâr**, *mib-tsawr'*; the same as 4013; *Mibtsar*, an Idumæan:— Mibzar.

מִבְצָרָה **mibtsârâh**. See 4013.

4015. מִבְרָח **mibrâch**, *mib-rawkh'*; from 1272; a *refugee*:— fugitive.

4016. מָבוּשׁ **mâbûsh**, *maw-boosh'*; from 954; (plur.) the (male) *pudenda*:— secrets.

4017. מִבְשָׂם **Mibsâm**, *mib-sawm'*; from the same as 1314; *fragrant*; *Mibsam*, the name of an Ishmaelite and of an Isr.:— Mibsam.

4018. מִבְשֵׁלָה **mᵉbashshᵉlâh**, *meb-ash-shel-aw'*; from 1310; a *cooking hearth*:— boiling-place.

מָג **Mâg**. See 7248, 7249.

4019. מַגְבִּישׁ **Magbîysh**, *mag-beesh'*; from the same as 1378; *stiffening*; *Magbish*, an Isr., or a place in Pal.:— Magbish.

4020. מִגְבָּלָה **migbâlâh**, *mig-baw-law'*; from 1379; a *border*:— end.

4021. מִגְבָּעָה **migbâ'âh**, *mig-baw-aw'*; from the same as 1389; a *cap* (as hemispherical):— bonnet.

4022. מֶגֶד **meged**, *meh'-ghed*; from an unused root prob. mean. to *be eminent*; prop. a *distinguished* thing; hence, something *valuable*, as a product or fruit:— pleasant, precious fruit (thing).

4023. מְגִדּוֹן **Mᵉgiddôwn** (Zech. 12:11), *meg-id-dōne'*; or

מְגִדּוֹ **Mᵉgiddôw**, *meg-id-do'*; from 1413; *rendezvous*; *Megiddon* or *Megiddo*, a place in Pal.:— Megiddo, Megiddon.

4024. מִגְדּוֹל **Migdôwl**, *mig-dole'*; or

מִגְדֹּל **Migdôl**, *mig-dole'*; prob. of Eg. or.; *Migdol*, a place in Egypt:— Migdol, tower.

4025. מַגְדִּיאֵל **Magdîy'êl**, *mag-dee-ale'*; from 4022 and 410; *preciousness of God*; *Magdiël*, an Idumæan:— Magdiel.

4026. מִגְדָּל **migdâl**, *mig-dawl'*; also (in plur.) fem.

מִגְדָּלָה **migdâlâh**, *mig-daw-law'*; from 1431; a *tower* (from its size or height); by anal. a *rostrum*; fig. a (pyramidal) *bed* of flowers:— castle, flower, tower. Comp. the names following.

מִגְדֹּל **Migdôl**. See 4024.

מִגְדָּלָה **migdâlâh**. See 4026.

4027. מִגְדָּל־אֵל **Migdal-'Êl**, *mig-dal-ale'*; from 4026 and 410; *tower of God*; *Migdal-El*, a place in Pal.:— Migdal-el.

4028. מִגְדַּל־גָּד **Migdal-Gâd**, *migdal-gawd'*; from 4026 and 1408; *tower of Fortune*; *Migdal-Gad*, a place in Pal.:— Migdal-gad.

4029. מִגְדַּל־אֵדֶר **Migdal-'Êder**, *mig-dal'-ay-der*; from 4026 and 5739; *tower of a flock*; *Migdal-Eder*, a place in Pal.:— Migdal-eder, tower of the flock.

4030. מִגְדָּנָה **migdânâh**, *mig-daw-naw'*; from the same as 4022; *preciousness*, i.e. a *gem*:— precious thing, present.

4031. מָגוֹג **Mâgôwg**, *maw-gogue'*; from 1463; *Magog*, a son of Japheth; also a barbarous northern region:— Magog.

4032. מָגוֹר **mâgôwr**, *maw-gore'*; or (Lam. 2:22)

מָגוֹר **mâgûwr**, *maw-goor'*; from 1481 in the sense of *fearing*; a *fright* (obj. or subj.):— fear, terror. Comp. 4036.

4033. מָגוּר **mâgûwr**, *maw-goor'*; or

מָגֻר **mâgûr**, *maw-goor'*; from 1481 in the sense of *lodging*; a temporary *abode*; by extens. a permanent *residence*:— dwelling, pilgrimage, where sojourn, be a stranger. Comp. 4032.

4034. מְגוֹרָה **meʿgôwrâh**, *meg-o-raw´;* fem. of 4032; *affright:*— fear.

4035. מְגוּרָה **meʿgûwrâh**, *meg-oo-raw´;* fem. of 4032 or of 4033; a *fright;* also a *granary:*— barn, fear.

4036. מָגוֹר מִסָּבִיב **Mâgôwr miç-Çâbîyb**, *maw-gore´ mis-saw-beeb´;* from 4032 and 5439 with the prep. ins.; *affright from around; Magor-mis-Sabib*, a symbol. name of Pashur:— Magormissabib.

4037. מְגֵרָה **magzêrâh**, *mag-zay-raw´;* from 1504; a *cutting* implement, i.e. a *blade:*— axe.

4038. מַגָּל **maggâl**, *mag-gawl´;* from an unused root mean. to *reap;* a *sickle:*— sickle.

4039. מְגִלָּה **meʿgillâh**, *meg-il-law´;* from 1556; a *roll:*— roll, volume.

4040. מְגִלָּה **meʿgillâh** (Chald.), *meg-il-law´;* corresp. to 4039:— roll.

4041. מְגַמָּה **meʿgammâh**, *meg-am-maw´;* from the same as 1571; prop. *accumulation*, i.e. *impulse* or *direction:*— sup up.

4042. מָגַן **mâgan**, *maw-gan´;* a denom. from 4043; prop. to *shield; encompass* with; fig. to *rescue*, to *hand* safely *over* (i.e. *surrender):*— deliver.

4043. מָגֵן **mâgên**, *maw-gane´;* also (in plur.) fem.

מְגִנָּה **meʿginnâh**, *meg-in-naw´;* from 1598; a *shield* (i.e. the small one or *buckler)*; fig. a *protector;* also the scaly *hide* of the crocodile:— × armed, buckler, defence, ruler, + scale, shield.

4044. מְגִנָּה **meʿginnâh**, *meg-in-naw´;* from 4042; a *covering* (in a bad sense), i.e. *blindness* or obduracy:— sorrow. See also 4043.

4045. מִגְעֶרֶת **migʿereth**, *mig-eh´-reth;* from 1605; *reproof* (i.e. *curse):*— rebuke.

4046. מַגֵּפָה **maggêphâh**, *mag-gay-faw´;* from 5062; a *pestilence;* by anal. *defeat:*— (× be) plague (-d), slaughter, stroke.

4047. מַגְפִּיעָשׁ **Magpîyʿâsh**, *mag-pee-awsh´;* appar. from 1479 or 5062 and 6211; *exterminator of* (the) *moth; Magpiash*, an Isr.:— Magpiash.

4048. מָגַר **mâgar**, *maw-gar´;* a prim. root; to *yield up;* intens. to *precipitate:*— cast down, terror.

4049. מְגַר **meʿgar** (Chald.), *meg-ar´;* corresp. to 4048; to *overthrow:*— destroy.

4050. מְגֵרָה **meʿgêrâh**, *meg-ay-raw´;* from 1641; a *saw:*— axe, saw.

4051. מִגְרוֹן **Migrôwn**, *mig-rone´;* from 4048; *precipice; Migron*, a place in Pal.:— Migron.

4052. מִגְרָעָה **migrâʿâh**, *mig-raw-aw´;* from 1639; a *ledge* or offset:— narrowed rest.

4053. מִגְרָפָה **migrâphâh**, *mig-raw-faw´;* from 1640; something *thrown off* (by the spade), i.e. a *clod:*— clod.

4054. מִגְרָשׁ **migrâsh**, *mig-rawsh´;* also (in plur.) fem. (Ezek. 27:28)

מִגְרָשָׁה **migrâshâh**, *mig-raw-shaw´;* from 1644; a *suburb* (i.e. open country whither flocks are *driven)* for

pasture); hence, the *area* around a building, or the *margin* of the sea:— cast out, suburb.

4055. מַד **mad**, *mad;* or

מֵד **mêd**, *made;* from 4058; prop. *extent*, i.e. *height;* also a *measure;* by impl. a *vesture* (as measured); also a *carpet:*— armour, clothes, garment, judgment, measure, raiment, stature.

4056. מַדְבַּח **madbach** (Chald.), *madbakh´;* from 1684; a sacrificial *altar:*— altar.

4057. מִדְבָּר **midbâr**, *mid-bawr´;* from 1696 in the sense of *driving;* a *pasture* (i.e. open field, whither cattle are driven); by impl. a *desert;* also *speech* (incl. its organs):— desert, south, speech, wilderness.

4058. מָדַד **mâdad**, *maw-dad´;* a prim. root; prop. to *stretch;* by impl. to *measure* (as if by *stretching* a line); fig. to *be extended:*— measure, mete, stretch self.

4059. מִדַּד **middad**, *mid-dad´;* from 5074; *flight:*— be gone.

4060. מִדָּה **middâh**, *mid-daw´;* fem. of 4055; prop. *extension*, i.e. height or breadth; also a *measure* (incl. its standard); hence, a *portion* (as measured) or a *vestment;* spec. *tribute* (as measured):— garment, measure (-ing, meteyard, piece, size, (great) stature, tribute, wide.

4061. מִדָּה **middâh** (Chald.), *mid-daw´;* or

מִנְדָּה **mindâh** (Chald.), *min-daw´;* corresp. to 4060; *tribute* in money:— toll, tribute.

4062. מַדְהֵבָה **madhêbâh**, *mad-hay-baw´;* perh. from the equiv. of 1722; *goldmaking*, i.e. *exactness:*— golden city.

4063. מֶדֶו **medev**, *meh´-dev;* from an unused root mean. to *stretch;* prop. *extent*, i.e. *measure;* by impl. a *dress* (as measured):— garment.

4064. מַדְוֶה **madveh**, *mad-veh´;* from 1738; *sickness:*— disease.

4065. מַדּוּחַ **maddûwach**, *mad-doo´-akh;* from 5080; *seduction:*— cause of banishment.

4066. מָדוֹן **mâdôwn**, *maw-dohn´;* from 1777; a *contest* or quarrel:— brawling, contention (-ous), discord, strife. Comp. 4079, 4090.

4067. מָדוֹן **mâdôwn**, *maw-dohn´;* from the same as 4063; *extensiveness*, i.e. *height:*— stature.

4068. מָדוֹן **Mâdôwn**, *maw-dohn´;* the same as 4067; *Madon*, a place in Pal.:— Madon.

4069. מַדּוּעַ **maddûwaʿ**, *mad-doo´-ah;* or

מַדֻּעַ **madduaʿ**, *mad-doo´-ah;* from 4100 and the pass. part. of 3045; *what* (is) *known?;* i.e. (by impl.) (adv.) *why?:*— how, wherefore, why.

4070. מְדוֹר **meʿdôwr** (Chald.), *med-ore´;* or

מְדֹר **meʿdôr** (Chald.), *med-ore´;* or

מְדָר **meʿdâr** (Chald.), *med-awr´;* from 1753; a *dwelling:*— dwelling.

4071. מְדוּרָה **meʿdûwrâh**, *med-oo-raw´;* or

מְדֻרָה **meʿdûrâh**, *med-oo-raw´;* from 1752 in the sense of *accumulation;* a *pile* of fuel:— pile (for fire).

4072. מִדְחֶה **midcheh**, *mid-kheh´;* from 1760; *overthrow:*— ruin.

4073. מְדַחְפָה **meʿdachphâh**, *med-akh-faw´;* from 1765; a *push*, i.e. *ruin:*— overthrow.

4074. מָדַי **Mâday**, *maw-dah´-ee;* of for. der.; *Madai*, a country of central Asia:— Madai, Medes, Media.

4075. מָדַי **Mâday**, *maw-dah´-ee;* patrial from 4074; a *Madian* or native of Madai:— Mede.

4076. מָדַי **Mâday** (Chald.), *maw-dah´-ee;* corresp. to 4074:— Mede (-s).

4077. מָדַי **Mâday** (Chald.), *maw-dah´-ee;* corresp. to 4075:— Median.

4078. מַדַּי **madday**, *mad-dah´-ee;* from 4100 and 1767; *what* (is) *enough*, i.e. *sufficiently:*— sufficiently.

4079. מִדְיָן **midyân**, *mid-yawn´;* a var. for 4066:— brawling, contention (-ous).

4080. מִדְיָן **Midyân**, *mid-yawn´;* the same as 4079; *Midjan*, a son of Abraham; also his country and (collect.) his desc.:— Midian, Midianite.

4081. מִדִּין **Middîyn**, *mid-deen´;* a var. for 4080:— Middin.

4082. מְדִינָה **meʿdîynâh**, *med-ee-naw´;* from 1777; prop. a *judgeship*, i.e. *jurisdiction;* by impl. a *district* (as ruled by a judge); gen. a *region:*— (× every) province.

4083. מְדִינָה **meʿdîynâh** (Chald.), *med-ee-naw´;* corresp. to 4082:— province.

4084. מִדְיָנִי **Midyânîy**, *mid-yaw-nee´;* patron. or patrial from 4080; a *Midjanite* or descend. (native) of Midjan:— Midianite. Comp. 4092.

4085. מְדֹכָה **meʿdôkâh**, *med-o-kaw´;* from 1743; a *mortar:*— mortar.

4086. מַדְמֵן **Madmên**, *mad-mane´;* from the same as 1828; *dunghill; Madmen*, a place in Pal.:— Madmen.

4087. מַדְמֵנָה **madmênâh**, *mad-may-naw´;* fem. from the same as 1828; a *dunghill:*— dunghill.

4088. מַדְמֵנָה **Madmênâh**, *mad-may-naw´;* the same as 4087; *Madmenah*, a place in Pal.:— Madmenah.

4089. מַדְמַנָּה **Madmannâh**, *mad-man-naw´;* a var. for 4087; *Madmannah*, a place in Pal.:— Madmannah.

4090. מְדָן **meʿdân**, *med-awn´;* a form of 4066:— discord, strife.

4091. מְדָן **Meʿdân**, *med-awn´;* the same as 4090; *Medan*, a son of Abraham:— Medan.

4092. מְדָנִי **Meʿdânîy**, *med-aw-nee´;* a var. of 4084:— Midianite.

4093. מַדָּע **maddâʿ**, *mad-daw´;* or

מַדָּע **maddaʿ**, *mad-dah´;* from 3045; *intelligence* or *consciousness:*— knowledge, science, thought.

מֹדָע **môdâʿ**. See 4129.

מַדֻּעַ **madûaʿ**. See 4069.

4094. מִדְקָרָה **madqârâh**, *mad-kaw-raw'*; from 1856; a *wound*:— piercing.

מְדֹר **m'dôr**. See 4070.

4095. מִדְרֵגָה **madrêgâh**, *mad-ray-gaw'*; from an unused root mean. to *step*; prop. a *step*; by impl. a *steep* or inaccessible place:— stair, steep place.

מְדֻרָה **m'dûrâh**. See 4071.

4096. מִדְרָךְ **midrâk**, *mid-rawk'*; from 1869; a *treading*, i.e. a place for stepping on:— [foot-] breadth.

4097. מִדְרָשׁ **midrâsh**, *mid-rawsh'*; from 1875; prop. an *investigation*, i.e. (by impl.) a *treatise* or elaborate compilation:— story.

4098. מְדֻשָׁה **m'dushshâh**, *med-oosh-shaw'*; from 1758; a *threshing*, i.e. (concr. and fig.) *down-trodden* people:— threshing.

4099. מְדָתָא **M'dâthâ**, *med-aw-thaw'*; of Pers. or.; *Medatha*, the father of Haman:— Hammedatha [incl. the art.].

4100. מָה **mâh**, *maw*; or

מַה **mah**, *mah*; or

מָ **mâ**, *maw*; or

מַ **ma**, *mah*; also

מֶה **meh**, *meh*; a prim. particle; prop. interrog. *what?* (incl. *how? why? when?*); but also exclamation, *what!* (incl. *how!*), or indef. *what* (incl. *whatever*, and even rel. *that which*); often used with prefixes in various adv. or conjunc. senses:— how (long, oft, [-soever]), [no-] thing, what (end, good, purpose, thing), whereby ([-fore, -in, -to, -with], (for) why.

4101. מָה **mâh** (Chald.), *maw*; corresp. to 4100:— how great (mighty), that which, what (-soever) why.

4102. מָהַהּ **mâhahh**, *maw-hah'*; appar. a denom. from 4100; prop. to *question* or *hesitate*, i.e. (by impl.) to *be reluctant*:— delay, linger, stay selves, tarry.

4103. מְהוּמָה **m'hûwmâh**, *meh-hoo-maw'*; from 1949; *confusion* or *uproar*:— destruction, discomfiture, trouble, tumult, vexation, vexed.

4104. מְהוּמָן **M'hûwmân**, *meh-hoo-mawn'*; of Pers. or.; *Mehuman*, a eunuch of Xerxes:— Mehuman.

4105. מְהֵיטַבְאֵל **M'hêyṭab'êl**, *meh-hay-tab-ale'*; from 3190 (augmented) and 410; *bettered of God*; *Mehetabel*, the name of an Edomitish man and woman:— Mehetabeel, Mehetabel.

4106. מָהִיר **mâhîyr**, *maw-here'*; or

מָהִר **mâhir**, *maw-here'*; from 4116; *quick*; hence, *skilful*:— diligent, hasty, ready.

4107. מָהַל **mâhal**, *maw-hal'*; a prim. root; prop. to *cut down* or *reduce*, i.e. by impl. to *adulterate*:— mixed.

4108. מַהְלֵךְ **mahlêk**, *mah-lake'*; from 1980; a *walking* (plur. collect.), i.e. *access*:— place to walk.

4109. מַהֲלָךְ **mahălâk**, *mah-hal-awk'*; from 1980; a *walk*, i.e. a *passage* or a *distance*:— journey, walk.

4110. מַהֲלָל **mahălâl**, *mah-hal-awl'*; from 1984; *fame*:— praise.

4111. מַהֲלַלְאֵל **Mahălal'êl**, *mah-hal-al-*

ale'; from 4110 and 410; *praise of God*; *Mahalalel*, the name of an antediluvian patriarch and of an Isr.:— Mahalaleel.

4112. מַהֲלֻמָּה **mahălummâh**, *mah-hal-oom-maw'*; from 1986; a *blow*:— stripe, stroke.

4113. מַהֲמֹרָה **mahămôrâh**, *mah-ham-o-raw'*; from an unused root of uncert. mean.; perh. an *abyss*:— deep pit.

4114. מַהְפֵּכָה **mahpêkâh**, *mah-pay-kaw'*; from 2015; a *destruction*:— when ... overthrew, overthrow (-n).

4115. מַהְפֶּכֶת **mahpeketh**, *mah-peh'-keth*; from 2015; a *wrench*, i.e. the *stocks*:— prison, stocks.

4116. מָהַר **mâhar**, *maw-har'*; a prim. root; prop. to *be liquid* or *flow easily*, i.e. (by impl.); to *hurry* (in a good or a bad sense); often used (with another verb) adv. *promptly*:— be carried headlong, fearful, (cause to make, in, make) haste (-n, -ily), (be) hasty, (fetch, make ready) × quickly, rash, × shortly, (be so) × soon, make speed, × speedily, × straightway, × suddenly, swift.

4117. מָהַר **mâhar**, *maw-har'*; a prim. root (perh. rather the same as 4116 through the idea of *readiness* in assent); to *bargain* (for a wife), i.e. to *wed*:— endow, × surely.

4118. מַהֵר **mahêr**, *mah-hare'*; from 4116; prop. *hurrying*; hence, (adv.) *in a hurry*:— hasteth, hastily, at once, quickly, soon, speedily, suddenly.

מָהִיר **mâhîr**. See 4106.

4119. מֹהַר **môhar**, *mo'-har*; from 4117; a *price* (for a wife):— dowry.

4120. מְהֵרָה **m'hêrâh**, *meh-hay-raw'*; fem. of 4118; prop. a *hurry*; hence, (adv.) *promptly*:— hastily, quickly, shortly, soon, make (with) speed (-ily), swiftly.

4121. מַהֲרַי **Mahăray**, *mah-har-ah'-ee*; from 4116; *hasty*; *Maharai*, an Isr.:— Maharai.

4122. מַהֵר שָׁלָל חָשׁ בַּז **Mahêr Shâlâl Châsh Baz**, *mah-hare' shaw-lawl' khawsh baz*; from 4118 and 7998 and 2363 and 957; *hasting* (is he [the enemy] to the) *booty, swift* (to the) *prey*; *Maher-Shalal-Chash-Baz*; the symb. name of the son of Isaiah:— Maher-shalal-hash-baz.

4123. מַהֲתַלָּה **mahăthallâh**, *mah-hath-al-law'*; from 2048; a *delusion*:— deceit.

4124. מוֹאָב **Môw'âb**, *mo-awb*; from a prol. form of the prep. pref. *m-* and 1; *from* (her [the mother's]) *father*; *Moäb*, an incestuous son of Lot; also his territory and desc.:— Moab.

4125. מוֹאָבִי **Môw'âbîy**, *mo-aw-bee'*; fem.

מוֹאָבִיָּה **Môw'âbîyâh**, *mo-aw-bee-yaw'*; or

מוֹאָבִית **Môw'âbîyth**, *mo-aw-beeth'*; patron. from 4124; a *Moäbite* or *Moäbitess*, i.e. a desc. from Moab:— (woman) of Moab, Moabite (-ish, -ss).

מוֹאֵל **môw'l**. See 4136.

4126. מוֹבָא **môwbâ'**, *mo-baw'*; by transp. for 3996; an *entrance*:— coming.

4127. מוּג **mûwg**, *moog*; a prim. root; to *melt*, i.e. lit. (to *soften*, *flow down*, *disappear*), or fig. (to *fear*, *faint*):— consume, dissolve, (be) faint (-hearted), melt (away), make soft.

4128. מוּד **mûwd**, *mood*; a prim. root; to *shake*:— measure.

4129. מוֹדַע **môwda'**, *mo-dah'*; or rather

מֹדָע **môdâ'**; from 3045; an *acquaintance*:— kinswoman.

4130. מוֹדַעַת **môwda'ath**, *mo-dah'-ath*; from 3045; *acquaintance*:— kindred.

4131. מוֹט **môwṭ**, *mote*; a prim. root; to *waver*; by impl. to *slip, shake, fall*:— be carried, cast, be out of course, be fallen in decay, × exceedingly, fall (-ing down), be (re-) moved, be ready, shake, slide, slip.

4132. מוֹט **môwṭ**, *mote*; from 4131; a *wavering*, i.e. *fall*; by impl. a *pole* (as shaking); hence, a *yoke* (as essentially a bent pole):— bar, be moved, staff, yoke.

4133. מוֹטָה **môwṭâh**, *mo-taw'*; fem. of 4132; a *pole*; by impl. an ox-*bow*; hence, a *yoke* (either lit. or fig.):— bands, heavy, staves, yoke.

4134. מוּךְ **mûwk**, *mook*; a prim. root; to *become thin*, i.e. (fig.) *be impoverished*:— be (waxen) poor (-er).

4135. מוּל **mûwl**, *mool*; a prim. root; to *cut short*, i.e. *curtail* (spec. the prepuce, i.e. to *circumcise*); by impl. to *blunt*; fig. to *destroy*:— circumcise (-ing), selves), cut down (in pieces), destroy, × must needs.

4136. מוּל **mûwl**, *mool*; or

מוֹל **môwl** (Deut. 1:1), *mole*; or

מוֹאל **môw'l** (Neh. 12:38), *mole*; or

מֻל **mûl** (Num. 22:5), *mool*; from 4135; prop. *abrupt*, i.e. a *precipice*; by impl. the *front*; used only adv. (with prep. pref.) *opposite*:— (over) against, before, [fore-] front, from, [God-] ward, toward, with.

4137. מוֹלָדָה **Môwlâdâh**, *mo-law-daw'*; from 3205; *birth*; *Moladah*, a place in Pal.:— Moladah.

4138. מוֹלֶדֶת **môwledeth**, *mo-leh'-deth*; from 3205; *nativity* (plur. *birth-place*); by impl. *lineage, native country*; also *offspring, family*:— begotten, born, issue, kindred, native (-ity).

4139. מוּלָה **mûwlâh**, *moo-law'*; from 4135; *circumcision*:— circumcision.

4140. מוֹלִיד **Môwlîyd**, *mo-leed'*; from 3205; *genitor*; *Molid*, an Isr.:— Molid.

מוּם **muwm**. See 3971.

מוֹמֻכָן° **Môwmûkân**. See 4462.

4141. מוּסָב **mûwçâb**, *moo-sawb'*; from 5437; a *turn*, i.e. *circuit* (of a building):— winding about.

4142. מוּסַבָּה **mûwçabbâh**, *moo-sab-baw'*; or

מֻסַבָּה **mûçabbâh**, *moo-sab-baw'*; fem. of 4141; a *reversal*, i.e. the *backside* (of a gem), *fold* (of a double-leaved door), *transmutation* (of a name):— being changed, inclosed, be set, turning.

4143. מוּסָד **mûwçâd**, *moo-sawd'*; from 3245; a *foundation*:— foundation.

4144. מוֹצָד **môwçâd**, *mo-sawd´*; from 3245; a *foundation*:— foundation.

4145. מוּצָדָה **mûwçâdâh**, *moo-saw-daw´*; fem. of 4143; a *foundation*; fig. an *appointment*:— foundation, grounded. Comp. 4328.

4146. מוֹצָדָה **môwçâdâh**, *mo-saw-daw´*; or

מֹצָדָה **môçâdâh**, *mo-saw-daw´*; fem. of 4144; a *foundation*:— foundation.

4147. מוֹסֵר **môwçêr**, *mo-sare´*; also (in plur.) fem.

מוֹסֵרָה **môwçêrâh**, *mo-say-raw´*; or

מֹסְרָה **môçᵉrâh**, *mo-ser-aw´*; from 3256; prop. *chastisement*, i.e. (by impl.) a *halter*; fig. *restraint*:— band, bond.

4148. מוּסָר **mûwçâr**, *moo-sawr´*; from 3256; prop. *chastisement*; fig. *reproof*, *warning* or *instruction*; also *restraint*:— bond, chastening (I-eth), chastisement, check, correction, discipline, doctrine, instruction, rebuke.

4149. מֹסְרָה **Môwçêrâh**, *mo-say-raw´*; or (plur.)

מֹסְרוֹת **Môçᵉrôwth**, *mo-ser-othe´* fem. of 4147; *correction* or *corrections*; *Moserah* or *Moseroth*, a place in the Desert:— Mosera, Moseroth.

4150. מוֹעֵד **môw'êd**, *mo-ade´*; or

מֹעֵד **mô'êd**, *mo-ade´*; or (fem.)

מוֹעָדָה **môw'âdâh** (2 Chron. 8:13), *mo-aw-daw´*; from 3259; prop. an *appointment*, i.e. a fixed *time* or *season*; spec. a *festival*; conventionally a *year*; by impl. an *assembly* (as convened for a def. purpose); tech. the *congregation*; by extens. the *place of meeting*; also a *signal* (as appointed beforehand):— appointed (sign, time), (place of, solemn) assembly, congregation, (set, solemn) feast, (appointed, due) season, solemn (-ity), synagogue, (set) time (appointed).

4151. מוֹעָד **môw'âd**, *mo-awd´*; from 3259; prop. an *assembly* [as in 4150]; fig. a *troop*:— appointed time.

4152. מוּעָדָה **mûw'âdâh**, *moo-aw-daw´*; from 3259; an *appointed* place, i.e. *asylum*:— appointed.

4153. מוֹעַדְיָה **Môw'adyâh**, *mo-ad-yaw´*; from 4151 and 3050; *assembly of Jah*; *Moädjah*, an Isr.:— Moadiah. Comp. 4573.

4154. מוּעֶדֶת **mûw'edeth**, *moo-ay´-deth*; fem. pass. part. of 4571; prop. *made to slip*, i.e. *dislocated*:— out of joint.

4155. מוּעָף **mûw'âph**, *moo-awf´*; from 5774; prop. *covered*, i.e. *dark*; abstr. *obscurity*, i.e. *distress*:— dimness.

4156. מוֹעֵצָה **môw'êtsâh**, *mo-ay-tsaw´*; from 3289; a *purpose*:— counsel, device.

4157. מוּעָקָה **mûw'âqâh**, *moo-aw-kaw´*; from 5781; *pressure*, i.e. (fig.) *distress*:— affliction.

4158. מוֹפָעַת **Môwpha'ath** (Jer. 48:21), *mo-fah´-ath*; or

מֵיפַעַת **Mêyphaath**, *may-fah´-ath*; or

מֵפַעַת **Mêphaath**, *may-fah´-ath*; from 3313; *illuminative*; *Mophaath* or *Mephaath*, a place in Pal.:— Mephaath.

4159. מוֹפֵת **môwphêth**, *mo-faith´*; or

מֹפֵת **môphêth**, *mo-faith´*; from 3302 in the sense of *conspicuousness*; a *miracle*; by impl. a *token* or *omen*:— miracle, sign, wonder (-ed at).

4160. מוּץ **mûwts**, *moots*; a prim. root; to *press*, i.e. (fig.) to *oppress*:— extortioner.

4161. מוֹצָא **môwtsâ'**, *mo-tsaw´*; or

מֹצָא **môtsâ'**, *mo-tsaw´*; from 3318; a *going forth*, i.e. (the act) an *egress*, or (the place) an *exit*; hence, a *source* or *product*; spec. *dawn*, the *rising* of the sun (the *East*), *exportation*, *utterance*, a *gate*, a *fountain*, a *mine*, a *meadow* (as producing grass):— brought out, bud, that which came out, east, going forth, goings out, that which (thing that) is gone out, outgoing, proceeded out, spring, vein, [water-] course, [springs].

4162. מוֹצָא **Môwtsâ'**, *mo-tsaw´*; the same as 4161; *Motsa*, the name of two Isr.:— Moza.

4163. מוֹצָאָה **môwtsâ'âh**, *mo-tsaw-aw´*; fem. of 4161; a *family descent*; also a *sewer* [marg.; comp. 6675]:— draught house; going forth.

4164. מוּצָק **mûwtsaq**, *moo-tsak´*; or

מוּצָק **mûwtsâq**, *moo-tsawk´*; from 3332; *narrowness*; fig. *distress*:— anguish, is straitened, straitness.

4165. מוּצָק **mûwtsâq**, *moo-tsawk´*; from 5694; prop. *fusion*, i.e. lit. a *casting* (of metal); fig. a *mass* (of clay):— casting, hardness.

4166. מוּצָקָה **mûwtsâqâh**, *moo-tsaw-kaw´*; or

מֻצָקָה **mûtsâqâh**, *moo-tsaw-kaw´*; from 3332; prop. something *poured* out, i.e. a *casting* (of metal); by impl. a *tube* (as cast):— when it was cast, pipe.

4167. מוּק **mûwq**, *mook*; a prim. root; to *jeer*, i.e. (intens.) *blaspheme*:— be corrupt.

4168. מוֹקֵד **môwqêd**, *mo-kade´*; from 3344; a *fire* or *fuel*; abstr. a *conflagration*:— burning, hearth.

4169. מוֹקְדָה° **môwqᵉdâh**, *mo-ked-aw´*; fem. of 4168; *fuel*:— burning.

4170. מוֹקֵשׁ **môwqêsh**, *mo-kashe´*; or

מֹקֵשׁ **môqêsh**, *mo-kashe´*; from 3369 a *noose* (for catching animals) (lit. or fig.); by impl. a *hook* (for the nose):— be ensnared, gin, (is) snare (-d), trap.

4171. מוּר **mûwr**, *moor*; a prim. root; to *alter*; by impl. to *barter*, to *dispose of*:— × at all, (ex-) change, remove.

4172. מוֹרָא **môwrâ'**, *mo-raw´*; or

מֹרָא **môrâ'**, *mo-raw´*; or

מוֹרָה **môrâh** (Psa. 9:20), *mo-raw´*; from 3372; *fear*; by impl. a *fearful* thing or deed:— dread, (that ought to be) fear (-ed), terribleness, terror.

4173. מוֹרַג **môwrag**, *mo-rag´*; or

מֹרַג **môrag**, *mo-rag´*; from an unused root mean. to *triturate*; a *threshing sledge*:— threshing instrument.

4174. מוֹרָד **môwrâd**, *mo-rawd´*; from 3381; a *descent*; arch. an *ornamental appendage*, perh. a *festoon*:— going down, steep place, thin work.

4175. מוֹרֶה **môwreh**, *mo-reh´*; from 3384; an *archer*; also *teacher* or *teaching*; also the *early rain* [see 3138]:— (early) rain.

4176. מוֹרֶה **Môwreh**, *mo-reh´*; or

מֹרֶה **Môreh**, *mo-reh´*; the same as 4175; *Moreh*, a Canaanite; also a hill (perh. named from him):— Moreh.

4177. מוֹרָה **môwrâh**, *mo-raw´*; from 4171 in the sense of *shearing*; a *razor*:— razor.

4178. מוֹרָט **môwrât**, *mo-rawt´*; from 3399; *obstinate*, i.e. *independent*:— peeled.

4179. מוֹרִיָּה **Môwrîyâh**, *mo-ree-yaw´*; or

מֹרִיָּה **Môrîyâh**, *mo-ree-yaw´*; from 7200 and 3050; *seen of Jah*; *Morijah*, a hill in Pal.:— Moriah.

4180. מוֹרָשׁ **môwrâsh**, *mo-rawsh´*; from 3423; a *possession*; fig. *delight*:— possession, thought.

4181. מוֹרָשָׁה **môwrâshâh**, *mo-raw-shaw´*; fem. of 4180; a *possession*:— heritage, inheritance, possession.

4182. מוֹרֶשֶׁת גַּת **Môwresheth Gath**, *mo-reh´-sheth gath*; from 3423 and 1661; *possession of Gath*; *Moresheth-Gath*, a place in Pal.:— Moresheth-gath.

4183. מוֹרַשְׁתִּי **Mowrashtîy**, *mo-rash-tee´*; patrial from 4182; a *Morashtite* or inhab. of Moresheth-Gath:— Morashthite.

4184. מוּשׁ **mûwsh**, *moosh*; a prim. root; to *touch*:— feel, handle.

4185. מוּשׁ **mûwsh**, *moosh*; a prim. root [perh. rather the same as 4184 through the idea of receding by *contact*]; to *withdraw* (both lit. and fig., whether intr. or tran.):— cease, depart, go back, remove, take away.

4186. מוֹשָׁב **môwshâb**, *mo-shawb´*; or

מֹשָׁב **môshâb**, *mo-shawb´*; from 3427; a *seat*; fig. a *site*; abstr. a *session*; by extens. an *abode* (the place or the time); by impl. *population*:— assembly, dwell in, dwelling (-place), wherein (that) dwelt (in), inhabited place, seat, sitting, situation, sojourning.

4187. מוּשִׁי **Mûwshîy**, *moo-shee´*; or

מֻשִׁי **Mushshîy**, *mush-shee´*; from 4184; *sensitive*; *Mushi*, a Levite:— Mushi.

4188. מוּשִׁי **Mûwshîy**, *moo-shee´*; patron. from 4187; a *Mushite* (collect.) or desc. of Mushi:— Mushites.

4189. מוֹשְׁכָה **môwshᵉkâh**, *mo-shek-aw´*; act. part. fem. of 4900; something *drawing*, i.e. (fig.) a *cord*:— band.

4190. מוֹשָׁעָה **môwshâ'âh**, *mo-shaw-aw´*; from 3467; *deliverance*:— salvation.

4191. מוּת **mûwth**, *mooth*; a prim. root; to *die* (lit. or fig.); caus. to *kill*:— × at all, × crying, (be) dead (body, man, one), (put to, worthy of) death, destroy (-er), (cause to, be like to, must) die, kill, necro [-mancer], × must needs, slay, × surely, × very suddenly, × in [no] wise.

4192. מוּת **Mûwth** (Psa. 48:14), *mooth*; or

מת לבן **Mûwth lab-bên**, *mooth lab-bane´*; from 4191 and 1121 with the prep. and art. interposed; "*To die for the son*", prob. the title of a popular song:— death, Muthlabben.

4193. מות **môwth** (Chald.), *mohth;* corresp. to 4194; *death:*— death.

4194. מָות **mâveth**, *maw´-veth;* from 4191; *death* (nat. or violent); concr. the *dead*, their place or state (*hades*); fig. *pestilence, ruin:*— (be) dead (l-lyl), death, die (-d).

מת לבן **Mûwth lab-bên.** See 4192.

4195. מֹותָר **môwthar**, *mo-thar´*; from 3498; lit. *gain;* fig. *superiority:*— plenteousness, preeminence, profit.

4196. מִזְבֵּחַ **mizbêach**, *miz-bay´-akh;* from 2076; an *altar:*— altar.

4197. מֶזֶג **mezeg**, *meh´-zeg;* from an unused root mean. to *mingle* (water with wine); *tempered* wine:— liquor.

4198. מָזֶה **mâzeh**, *maw-zeh´;* from an unused root mean. to *suck* out; *exhausted:*— burnt.

4199. מִזָּה **Mizzâh**, *miz-zaw´;* prob. from an unused root mean. to *faint* with fear; *terror; Mizzah,* an Edomite:— Mizzah.

4200. מֶזֶו **mezev**, *meh´-zev;* prob. from an unused root mean. to *gather* in; a *granary:*— garner.

4201. מְזוּזָה **mᵉzûwzâh**, *mez-oo-zaw´;* or

מְזֻזָה **mᵉzûzâh**, *mez-oo-zaw´;* from the same as 2123; a *door-post* (as *prominent*):— (door, side) post.

4202. מָזֹון **mâzôwn**, *maw-zone´;* from 2109; *food:*— meat, victual.

4203. מָזֹון **mâzôwn** (Chald.), *mawzone´;* corresp. to 4202:— meat.

4204. מָזֹור **mâzôwr**, *maw-zore´;* from 2114 in the sense of *turning aside* from truth; *treachery,* i.e. a *plot:*— wound.

4205. מָזֹור **mâzôwr**, *maw-zore´;* or

מָזֹר **mâzôr**, *maw-zore´;* from 2115 in the sense of *binding* up; a *bandage,* i.e. remedy; hence, a *sore* (as needing a compress):— bound up, wound.

מְזֻזָה **mᵉzûzâh.** See 4201.

4206. מָזִיחַ **mâzîyach**, *maw-zee´-akh;* or

מֵזַח **mêzach**, *may-zakh´;* from 2118; a *belt* (as movable):— girdle, strength.

4207. מַזְלֵג **mazlêg**, *maz-layg´;* or (fem.)

מִזְלָגָה **mizlâgâh**, *miz-law-gaw´;* from an unused root mean. to *draw* up; a *fork:*— fleshhook.

4208. מַזָּלָה **mazzâlâh**, *maz-zaw-law´;* appar. from 5140 in the sense of *raining;* a *constellation,* i.e. Zodiacal sign (perh. as affecting the weather):— planet. Comp. 4216.

4209. מְזִמָּה **mᵉzimmâh**, *mez-im-maw´;* from 2161; a *plan,* usually evil (*machination*), sometimes good (*sagacity*):— (wicked) device, discretion, intent, witty invention, lewdness, mischievous (device), thought, wickedly.

4210. מִזְמֹור **mizmôwr**, *miz-more´;* from 2167; prop. instrumental *music;* by impl. a *poem* set to notes:— psalm.

4211. מַזְמֵרָה **mazmêrâh**, *maz-may-*

raw´; from 2168; a *pruning-knife:*— pruning-hook.

4212. מְזַמְּרָה **mᵉzammᵉrâh**, *mez-am-mer-aw´;* from 2168; a *tweezer* (only in the plur.):— snuffers.

4213. מִזְעָר **miz'âr**, *miz-awr´;* from the same as 2191; *fewness;* by impl. as superl. *diminutiveness:*— few, × very.

מָזֹר **mâzôr.** See 4205.

4214. מִזְרֶה **mizreh**, *miz-reh´;* from 2219; a winnowing *shovel* (as scattering the chaff):— fan.

4215. מְזָרֶה **mᵉzâreh**, *mez-aw-reh´;* appar. from 2219; prop. a *scatterer,* i.e. the north *wind* (as dispersing clouds; only in plur.):— north.

4216. מַזָּרָה **Mazzârâh**, *maz-zaw-raw´;* appar. from 5144 in the sense of *distinction;* some noted *constellation* (only in the plur.), perh. collect. the *zodiac:*— Mazzaroth. Comp. 4208.

4217. מִזְרָח **mizrâch**, *miz-rawkh´;* from 2224; *sunrise,* i.e. the *east:*— east (side, -ward), (sun-) rising (of the sun).

4218. מִזְרָע **mizrâ'**, *miz-raw´;* from 2232; a planted *field:*— thing sown.

4219. מִזְרָק **mîzrâq**, *miz-rawk´;* from 2236; a *bowl* (as if for sprinkling):— bason, bowl.

4220. מֵחַ **mêach**, *may´-akh;* from 4229 in the sense of *greasing; fat;* fig. *rich:*— fatling (one).

4221. מֹחַ **môach**, *mo´-akh;* from the same as 4220; *fat,* i.e. marrow:— marrow.

4222. מָחָא **mâchâ'**, *maw-khaw´;* a prim. root; to *rub* or *strike* the hands together (in exultation):— clap.

4223. מְחָא **mᵉchâ'** (Chald.), *mekh-aw´;* corresp. to 4222; to *strike* in pieces; also to *arrest;* spec. to *impale:*— hang, smite, stay.

4224. מַחֲבֵא **machăbê'**, *makh-ab-ay´;* or

מַחֲבֹא **machăbô'**, *makh-ab-o´;* from 2244; a *refuge:*— hiding (lurking) place.

4225. מַחְבֶּרֶה **machbereth**, *makh-beh´-reth;* from 2266; a *junction,* i.e. seam or sewed piece:— coupling.

4226. מְחַבְּרָה **mᵉchabbᵉrâh**, *mekh-ab-ber-aw´;* from 2266; a *joiner,* i.e. brace or cramp:— coupling, joining.

4227. מַחֲבַת **machăbath**, *makh-ab-ath´;* from the same as 2281; a *pan* for baking in:— pan.

4228. מַחֲגֹרֶת **machăgôreth**, *makh-ag-o´-reth;* from 2296; a *girdle:*— girding.

4229. מָחָה **mâchâh**, *maw-khaw´;* a prim. root; prop. to *stroke* or *rub;* by impl. to *erase;* also to *smooth* (as if with oil), i.e. *grease* or make fat; also to *touch,* i.e. reach to:— abolish, blot out, destroy, full of marrow, put out, reach unto, × utterly, wipe (away, out).

4230. מְחוּגָה **mᵉchûwgâh**, *mekk-oo-gaw´;* from 2328; an *instrument* for marking a circle, i.e. *compasses:*— compass.

4231. מָחֹוז **mâchôwz**, *maw-khoze´;* from an unused root mean. to *enclose;* a *harbor* (as *shut* in by the shore):— haven.

4232. מְחוּיָאֵל **Mᵉchûwyâ'êl**, *mekh-oo-yaw-ale´;* or

מְחִיָּאֵל **Mᵉchîyyâ'êl**, *mekh-ee-yaw-ale´;* from 4229 and 410; *smitten of God; Mechujael* or *Mechijael,* an antediluvian patriarch:— Mehujael.

4233. מַחֲוִים **Machăvîym**, *makh-av-eem´;* appar. a patrial, but from an unknown place (in the plur. only for a sing.); a *Machavite* or inhab. of some place named Machaveh:— Mahavite.

4234. מָחֹול **mâchôwl**, *maw-khole´;* from 2342; a (round) *dance:*— dance (-cing).

4235. מָחֹול **Mâchôwl**, *maw-khole´;* the same as 4234; *dancing; Machol,* an Isr.:— Mahol.

מְחֹולָה **mᵉchôwlâh.** See 65, 4246.

4236. מַחֲזֶה **machăzeh**, *makh-az-eh´;* from 2372; a *vision:*— vision.

4237. מֶחֱזָה **mechĕzâh**, *mekh-ez-aw´;* from 2372; a *window:*— light.

4238. מַחֲזִיאֹות **Machăzîy'ôwth**, *makh-az-ee-oth´;* fem. plur. from 2372; *visions; Machazioth,* an Isr.:— Mahazioth.

4239. מְחִי **mᵉchîy**, *mekh-ee´;* from 4229; a *stroke,* i.e. battering-*ram:*— engines.

4240. מְחִידָא **Mᵉchîydâ'**, *mek-ee-daw´;* from 2330; *junction; Mechida,* one of the Nethinim:— Mehida.

4241. מִחְיָה **michyâh**, *mikh-yaw´;* from 2421; *preservation of life;* hence, *sustenance;* also the live flesh, i.e. the *quick:*— preserve life, quick, recover selves, reviving, sustenance, victuals.

מְחִיָּאֵל **Mᵉchîyyâ'êl.** See 4232.

4242. מְחִיר **mᵉchîyr**, *mekk-eer´;* from an unused root mean. to *buy; price, payment, wages:*— gain, hire, price, sold, worth.

4243. מְחִיר **Mᵉchîyr**, *mekh-eer´;* the same as 4242; *price; Mechir,* an Isr.:— Mehir.

4244. מַחְלָה **Machlâh**, *makh-law´;* from 2470; *sickness; Machlah,* the name appar. of two Israelitesses:— Mahlah.

4245. מַחֲלֶה **machăleh**, *makh-al-eh´;* or (fem.)

מַחֲלָה **machălâh**, *makk-al-aw´;* from 2470; *sickness:*— disease, infirmity, sickness.

4246. מְחֹולָה **mᵉchôwlâh**, *mek-o-law´;* fem. of 4284; a *dance:*— company, dances (-cing).

4247. מְחִלָּה **mᵉchillâh**, *mekh-il-law´;* from 2490; a *cavern* (as if excavated):— cave.

4248. מַחְלֹון **Machlôwn**, *makh-lone´;* from 2470; *sick; Machlon,* an Isr.:— Mahlon.

4249. מַחְלִי **Machlîy**, *makh-lee´;* from 2470; *sick; Machli,* the name of two Isr.:— Mahli.

4250. מַחְלִי **Machlîy**, *makh-lee´;* patron. from 4249; a *Machlite* or (collect.) desc. of Machli:— Mahlites.

4251. מַחְלֻי **machlûy**, *makh-loo´-ee;* from 2470; a *disease:*— disease.

4252. מַחֲלָף **machălâph**, *makh-al-awf´;* from 2498; a (sacrificial) *knife* (as *gliding* through the flesh):— knife.

4253. מַחְלָפָה **machlâphâh**, *makh-law-*

faw´; from 2498; a *ringlet* of hair (as *gliding* over each other):— lock.

4254. מַחֲלָצָה **machălâtsâh**, *makh-al-aw-tsaw´*; from 2502; a *mantle* (as easily *drawn off*):— changeable suit of apparel, change of raiment.

4255. מַחְלְקָה **machlᵉqâh** (Chald.), *makh-lek-aw´*; corresp. to 4256; a *section* (of the Levites):— course.

4256. מַחֲלֹקֶת **machălôqeth**, *makh-al-o´-keth*; from 2505; a *section* (of Levites, people or soldiers):— company, course, division, portion. See also 5555.

4257. מַחֲלַת **Machălath**, *makh-al-ath´*; from 2470; *sickness*; *Machalath*, prob. the title (initial word) of a popular song:— Mahalath.

4258. מַחֲלַת **Machălath**, *makh-al-ath´*; the same as 4257; *sickness*; *Machalath*, the name of an Ishmaelitess and of an Israelitess:— Mahalath.

4259. מְחֹלָתִי **Mᵉchôlâthîy**, *mekh-o-law-thee´*; patrial from 65; a *Mecholathite* or inhab. of Abel-Mecholah:— Mecholathite.

4260. מַחֲמָאָה **machămâ'âh**, *makh-am-aw-aw´*; a denom. from 2529; something *buttery* (i.e. unctuous and pleasant), as (fig.) *flattery*:— × than butter.

4261. מַחְמָד **machmâd**, *makh-mawd´*; from 2530; *delightful*; hence, a *delight*, i.e. object of affection or desire:— beloved, desire, goodly, lovely, pleasant (thing).

4262. מַחְמֻד **machmûd**, *makh-mood´*; or

מַחְמוּד° **machmûwd**, *makh-mood´*; from 2530; *desired*; hence, a *valuable*:— pleasant thing.

4263. מַחְמָל **machmâl**, *makh-mawl´*; from 2550; prop. *sympathy*; (by paronomasia with 4261) *delight*:— pitieth.

4264. מַחֲנֶה **machăneh**, *makh-an-eh´*; from 2583; an *encampment* (of travellers or troops); hence, an *army*, whether lit. (of soldiers) or fig. (of dancers, angels, cattle, locusts, stars; or even the sacred courts):— army, band, battle, camp, company, drove, host, tents.

4265. מַחֲנֵה־דָן **Machănêh-Dân**, *makh-an-ay´-dawn*; from 4264 and 1835; *camp of Dan*; *Machaneh-Dan*, a place in Pal.:— Mahaneh-dan.

4266. מַחֲנַיִם **Machănayim**, *makh-an-ah´-yim*; dual of 4264; *double camp*; *Machanajim*, a place in Pal.:— Mahanaim.

4267. מַחֲנָק **machănaq**, *makh-an-ak´*; from 2614; *choking*:— strangling.

4268. מַחֲסֶה **machăçeh**, *makh-as-eh´*; or

מַחְסֶה **machçeh**, *makh-seh´*; from 2620; a *shelter* (lit. or fig.):— hope, (place of) refuge, shelter, trust.

4269. מַחְסֹם **machçôwm**, *makh-sohm´*; from 2629; a *muzzle*:— bridle.

4270. מַחְסוֹר **machçôwr**, *makh-sore´*; or

מַחְסֹר **machçôr**, *makh-sore´*; from 2637; *deficiency*; hence, *impoverishment*:— lack, need, penury, poor, poverty, want.

4271. מַחְסֵיָה **Machçêyâh**, *makh-say-yaw´*; from 4268 and 3050; *refuge of* (i.e.

in) *Jah*; *Machsejah*, an Isr.:— Maaseiah.

4272. מָחַץ **mâchats**, *maw-khats´*; a prim. root; to *dash* asunder; by impl. to *crush*, *smash* or violently *plunge*; fig. to *subdue* or *destroy*:— dip, pierce (through), smite (through), strike through, wound.

4273. מַחַץ **machats**, *makh´-ats*; from 4272; a *contusion*:— stroke.

4274. מַחְצֵב **machtsêb**, *makh-tsabe´*; from 2672; prop. a *hewing*; concr. a *quarry*:— hewed (-n).

4275. מֶחֱצָה **mechĕtsâh**, *mekh-ets-aw´*; from 2673; a *halving*:— half.

4276. מַחֲצִית **machătsîyth**, *makh-ats-eeth´*; from 2673; a *halving* or the *middle*:— half (so much), mid l-dayl.

4277. מָחַק **mâchaq**, *maw-khak´*; a prim. root; to *crush*:— smite off.

4278. מֶחְקָר **mechqâr**, *mekh-kawr´*; from 2713; prop. *scrutinized*, i.e. (by impl.) a *recess*:— deep place.

4279. מָחָר **mâchar**, *maw-khar´*; prob. from 309; prop. *deferred*, i.e. the *morrow*; usually (adv.) *tomorrow*; indef. *hereafter*:— time to come, tomorrow.

4280. מַחֲרָאָה **machără'âh**, *makh-ar-aw-aw´*; from the same as 2716; a *sink*:— draught house.

4281. מַחֲרֵשָׁה **machărêshâh**, *makh-ar-ay-shaw´*; from 2790; prob. a *pick-axe*:— mattock.

4282. מַחֲרֵשֶׁת **machăresheth**, *makh-ar-eh´-sheth*; from 2790; prob. a *hoe*:— share.

4283. מׇחֳרָת **mochŏrâth**, *mokh-or-awth´*; or

מׇחֳרָתָם **mochŏrâthâm** (1 Sam. 30:17), *mokh-or-aw-thawm´*; fem. from the same as 4279; the *morrow* or (adv.) *tomorrow*:— morrow, next day.

4284. מַחֲשָׁבָה **machăshâbâh**, *makh-ash-aw-baw´*; or

מַחֲשֶׁבֶת **machăshebeth**, *makh-ash-eh´-beth*; from 2803; a *contrivance*, i.e. (concr.) a *texture*, *machine*, or (abstr.) *intention*, *plan* (whether bad, a *plot*; or good, *advice*):— cunning (work), curious work, device (-sed), imagination, invented, means, purpose, thought.

4285. מַחְשָׁךְ **machshâk**, *makh-shawk´*; from 2821; *darkness*; concr. a *dark place*:— dark (-ness, place).

4286. מַחְסֹף **machsôph**, *makh-sofe´*; from 2834; a *peeling*:— made appear.

4287. מַחַת **Machath**, *makh´-ath*; prob. from 4229; *erasure*; *Machath*, the name of two Isr.:— Mahath.

4288. מְחִתָּה **mᵉchittâh**, *mekh-it-taw´*; from 2846; prop. a *dissolution*; concr. a *ruin*, or (abstr.) *consternation*:— destruction, dismaying, ruin, terror.

4289. מַחְתָּה **machtâh**, *makh-taw´*; the same as 4288 in the sense of *removal*; a *pan* for live coals:— censer, firepan, snuffdish.

4290. מַחְתֶּרֶת **machtereth**, *makh-teh´-reth*; from 2864; a *burglary*; fig. *unexpected examination*:— breaking up, secret search.

4291. מְטָא **mᵉtâ'** (Chald.), *met-aw´*; or

מְטָה **mᵉtâh** (Chald.) *met-aw´*; appar. corresp. to 4672 in the intr. sense of being found *present*; to *arrive*, *extend* or *happen*:— come, reach.

4292. מַטְאֲטֵא **mat'ăṭê'**, *mat-at-ay´*; appar. a denom. from 2916; a *broom* (as removing *dirt* [comp. Engl. "to dust", i.e. remove dust]):— besom.

4293. מַטְבֵּחַ **maṭbêach**, *mat-bay´-akh*; from 2873; *slaughter*:— slaughter.

4294. מַטֶּה **maṭṭeh**, *mat-teh´*; or (fem.)

מַטָּה **maṭṭâh**, *mat-taw´*; from 5186; a *branch* (as *extending*); fig. a *tribe*; also a *rod*, whether for chastising (fig. *correction*), ruling (a *sceptre*), throwing (a *lance*), or walking (a *staff*; fig. a *support* of life, e.g. bread):— rod, staff, tribe.

4295. מַטָּה **maṭṭâh**, *mat´-taw*; from 5786 with directive enclitic appended; *downward*, *below* or *beneath*; often adv. with or without prefixes:— beneath, down (-ward), less, very low, under (-neath).

4296. מִטָּה **miṭṭâh**, *mit-taw´*; from 5186; a *bed* (as *extended*) for sleeping or eating; by anal. a *sofa*, *litter* or *bier*:— bed (l-chamberl), bier.

4297. מַטֶּה **muṭṭeh**, *moot-teh´*; from 5186; a *stretching*, i.e. *distortion* (fig. *iniquity*):— perverseness.

4298. מֻטָּה **muṭṭâh**, *moot-taw´*; from 5186; *expansion*:— stretching out.

4299. מַטְוֶה **maṭveh**, *mat-veh´*; from 2901; something *spun*:— spun.

4300. מְטִיל **mᵉṭîyl**, *met-eel´*; from 2904 in the sense of *hammering* out; an iron *bar* (as *forged*):— bar.

4301. מַטְמוֹן **maṭmôwn**, *mat-mone´*; or

מַטְמֹן **maṭmôn**, *mat-mone´*; or

מַטְמֻן **maṭmûn**, *mat-moon´*; from 2934; a *secret* storehouse; hence, a *secreted* valuable (buried); gen. *money*:— hidden riches, (hid) treasure (-s).

4302. מַטָּע **maṭṭâ'**, *mat-taw´*; from 5193; something *planted*, i.e. the place (a *garden* or vineyard), or the thing (a *plant*, fig. of men); by impl. the act, *planting*:— plant (-ation, -ing).

4303. מַטְעַם **maṭ'am**, *mat-am´*; or (fem.)

מַטְעַמָּה **maṭ'ammâh**, *mat-am-maw´*; from 2938; a *delicacy*:— dainty (meat), savoury meat.

4304. מִטְפַּחַת **miṭpachath**, *mit-pakh´-ath*; from 2946; a wide *cloak* (for a woman):— vail, wimple.

4305. מָטַר **mâṭar**, *maw-tar´*; a prim. root; to *rain*:— (cause to) rain (upon).

4306. מָטָר **mâṭâr**, *maw-tawr´*; from 4305; *rain*:— rain.

4307. מַטָּרָא **maṭṭârâ'**, *mat-taw-raw´*; or

מַטָּרָה **maṭṭârâh**, *mat-taw-raw´*; from 5201; a *jail* (as a *guard*-house); also an *aim* (as being closely *watched*):— mark, prison.

4308. מָטְרֵד **Maṭrêd**, *mat-rade´*; from 2956; *propulsive*; *Matred*, an Edomitess:— Matred.

4309. מַטְרִי **Maṭrîy**, *mat-ree´*; from 4305; *rainy*; *Matri*, an Isr.:— Matri.

4310. מִי **mîy**, *me*; an interrog. pron. of

Hebrew

persons, as 4100 is of things, *who?* (occasionally, by a peculiar idiom, of things); also (indef.) *whoever; often* used in oblique constr. with pref. or suff.:— any (man), × he, × him, + O that! what, which, who (-m, -se, soever), + would to God.

4311. מֵידְבָא **Mêyd^ebâ'**, *may-deb-aw';* from 4325 and 1679; *water of quiet; Medeba*, a place in Pal.:— Medeba.

4312. מֵידָד **Mêydâd**, *may-dawd';* from 3032 in the sense of *loving; affectionate; Medad*, an Isr.:— Medad.

4313. מֵי הַיַּרְקוֹן **Mêy hay-Yarqôwn**, *may hah'-ee-yar-kone';* from 4325 and 3420 with the art. interposed; *water of the yellowness; Me-haj-Jarkon*, a place in Pal.:— Me-jarkon.

4314. מֵי זָהָב **Mêy Zâhâb**, *may zaw-hawb';* from 4325 and 2091, *water of gold; Me-Zahab*, an Edomite:— Mezahab.

4315. מֵיטָב **mêytâb**, *may-tawb';* from 3190; *the best part*:— best.

4316. מִיכָא **Mîykâ'**, *mee-kaw';* a var. for 4318; *Mica*, the name of two Isr.:— Micha.

4317. מִיכָאֵל **Mîykâ'êl**, *me-kaw-ale';* from 4310 and (the pref. der. from) 3588 and 410; *who* (is) *like God?; Mikael*, the name of an archangel and of nine Isr.:— Michael.

4318. מִיכָה **Mîykâh**, *mee-kaw';* an abbrev. of 4320; *Micah*, the name of seven Isr.:— Micah, Micaiah, Michah.

4319. מִיכָהוּ **Mîykâhûw**, *me-kaw'-hoo;* a contr. for 4321; *Mikehu*, an Isr. prophet:— Micaiah (2 Chron. 18:8).

4320. מִיכָיָה **Mîykâyâh**, *me-kaw-yaw';* from 4310 and (the pref. der. from) 3050; *who* (is) *like Jah?; Micajah*, the name of two Isr.:— Micah, Michaiah. Comp. 4318.

4321. מִיכָיְהוּ **Mîykây^ehûw**, *me-kaw-yeh-hoo';* or

מִכָיְהוּ **Mikây^ehûw** (Jer. 36:11), *me-kaw-yeh-hoo';* abbrev. for 4322; *Mikajah*, the name of three Isr.:— Micah, Micaiah, Michaiah.

4322. מִיכָיָהוּ **Mîykâyâhûw**, *me-kaw-yaw'-hoo;* for 4320; *Mikajah*, the name of an Isr. and an Israelitess:— Michaiah.

4323. מִיכָל **mîykâl**, *me-kawl';* from 3201; prop. a *container*, i.e. a *streamlet*:— brook.

4324. מִיכָל **Mîykâl**, *me-kawl';* appar. the same as 4323; *rivulet; Mikal*, Saul's daughter:— Michal.

4325. מַיִם **mayim**, *mah'-yim;* dual of a prim. noun (but used in a sing. sense); *water;* fig. *juice;* by euphem. *urine, semen*:— + piss, wasting, water (-ing, (-course, -flood, -spring)).

4326. מִיָמִן **Mîyâmin**, *me-yaw-meem';* a form for 4509; *Mijamin*, the name of three Isr.:— Miamin, Mijamin.

4327. מִין **mîyn**, *meen;* from an unused root mean. to *portion* out; a *sort*, i.e. *species*:— kind. Comp. 4480.

4328. מְיֻסָּדָה **m^eyuççâdâh**, *meh-yoos-saw-daw';* prop. fem. pass. part. of

3245; *something founded*, i.e. a *foundation*:— foundation.

4329. מֵיצָךְ **mêyçâk**, *may-sawk';* from 5526; a *portico* (as *covered*):— covert.

מֵיפְעָה **Mêypha'ath**. See 4158.

4330. מִיץ **mîyts**, *meets;* from 4160; *pressure*:— churning, forcing, wringing.

4331. מֵישָׁא **Mêyshâ'**, *may-shaw';* from 4185; *departure; Mesha*, a place in Arabia; also an Isr.:— Mesha.

4332. מֵישָׁאֵל **Mîyshâ'êl**, *mee-shaw-ale';* from 4310 and 410 with the abbrev. insep. rel. [see 834] interposed; *who* (is) *what God* (is)?; *Mishaël*, the name of three Isr.:— Mishael.

4333. מִישָׁאֵל **Mîyshâ'êl** (Chald.), *mee-shaw-ale';* corresp. to 4332; *Mishaël*, an Isr.:— Mishael.

4334. מִישׁוֹר **mîyshôwr**, *mee-shore';* or

מִישֹׁר **mîyshôr**, *mee-shore';* from 3474; a *level*, i.e. a *plain* (often used [with the art. pref.] as a prop. name of certain districts); fig. *concord;* also *straightness*, i.e. (fig.) *justice* (sometimes adv. *justly*):— equity, even place, plain, right (-eously), (made) straight, uprightness.

4335. מֵישַׁךְ **Mêyshak**, *may-shak';* borrowed from 4336; *Meshak*, an Isr.:— Meshak.

4336. מֵישַׁךְ **Mêyshak** (Chald.), *may-shak';* of for. or. and doubtful signif.; *Meshak*, the Bab. name of 4333:— Meshak.

4337. מֵישָׁע **Mêyshâ'**, *may-shah';* from 3467; *safety; Mesha*, an Isr.:— Mesha.

4338. מֵישַׁע **Mêysha'**, *may-shaw';* a var. for 4337; *safety; Mesha*, a Moabite:— Mesha.

4339. מֵישָׁר **mêyshâr**, *may-shawr';* from 3474; *evenness*, i.e. (fig.) *prosperity* or *concord;* also *straightness*, i.e. (fig.) *rectitude* (only in plur. with sing. sense; often adv.):— agreement, aright, that are equal, equity, (things that are) right (-eously, things), sweetly, upright (-ly, -ness).

4340. מֵיתָר **mêythâr**, *may-thar';* from 3498; a *cord* (of a tent) [comp. 3499] or the *string* (of a bow):— cord, string.

4341. מַכְאֹב **mak'ôb**, *mak-obe';* sometimes

מַכְאוֹב **mak'ôwb**, *mak-obe';* also (fem. Isa. 53:3)

מַכְאֹבָה **mak'ôbâh**, *mak-o-baw';* from 3510; *anguish* or (fig.) *affliction*:— grief, pain, sorrow.

4342. מַכְבִּיר **makbîyr**, *mak-beer';* tran. part. of 3527; *plenty*:— abundance.

4343. מַכְבְּנָא **Makbênâ'**, *mak-bay-naw';* from the same as 3522; *knoll; Macbena*, a place in Pal. settled by him:— Machbenah.

4344. מַכְבַּנַּי **Makbannay**, *mak-ban-nah'-ee;* patrial from 4343; a *Macbanite* or native of Macbena:— Machbanai.

4345. מַכְבֵּר **makbêr**, *mak-bare';* from 3527 in the sense of *covering* [comp. 3531]; a *grate*:— grate.

4346. מַכְבָּר **makbâr**, *mak-bawr';* from

3527 in the sense of *covering;* a *cloth* (as *netted* [comp. 4345]):— thick cloth.

4347. מַכָּה **makkâh**, *mak-kaw';* or (masc.)

מַכֶּה **makkeh**, *mak-keh';* (plur. only) from 5221; a *blow* (in 2 Chron. 2:10, of the flail); by impl. a *wound;* fig. *carnage*, also *pestilence*:— beaten, blow, plague, slaughter, smote, × sore, stripe, stroke, wound (l-edl).

4348. מִכְוָה **mikvâh**, *mik-vaw';* from 3554; a *burn*:— that burneth, burning.

4349. מָכוֹן **mâkôwn**, *maw-kone';* from 3559; prop. a *fixture*, i.e. a *basis;* gen. a *place*, espec. as an *abode*:— foundation, habitation, (dwelling-, settled) place.

4350. מְכוֹנָה **m^ekôwnâh**, *mek-o-naw';* or

מְכֹנָה **m^ekônâh**, *mek-o-naw';* fem. of 4349; a *pedestal*, also a *spot*:— base.

4351. מְכוּרָה **m^ekûwrâh**, *mek-oo-raw';* or

מְכֹרָה **m^ekôrâh**, *mek-o-raw';* from the same as 3564 in the sense of *digging; origin* (as if a mine):— birth, habitation, nativity.

4352. מָכִי **Mâkiy**, *maw-kee';* prob. from 4134; *pining; Maki*, an Isr.:— Machi.

4353. מָכִיר **Mâkîyr**, *maw-keer';* from 4376; *salesman; Makir*, an Isr.:— Machir.

4354. מָכִירִי **Mâkîyrîy**, *maw-kee-ree';* patron. from 4353; a *Makirite* or descend. of Makir:— of Machir.

4355. מָכַךְ **mâkak**, *maw-kak';* a prim. root; to *tumble* (in ruins); fig. to *perish*:— be brought low, decay.

4356. מִכְלָאָה **miklâ'âh**, *mik-law-aw';* or

מִכְלָה **miklâh**, *mik-law';* from 3607; a *pen* (for flocks):— (sheep-) fold. Comp. 4357.

4357. מִכְלָה **miklâh**, *mik-law';* from 3615; *completion* (in plur. concr. adv. *wholly*):— perfect. Comp. 4356.

4358. מִכְלוֹל **miklôwl**, *mik-lole';* from 3634; *perfection* (i.e. concr. adv. *splendidly*):— most gorgeously, all sorts.

4359. מִכְלָל **miklâl**, *mik-lawl';* from 3634; *perfection* (of beauty):— perfection.

4360. מִכְלֻל **miklûl**, *mik-lool';* from 3634; something *perfect*, i.e. a *splendid garment*:— all sorts.

4361. מַכֹּלֶת **makkôleth**, *mak-ko'-leth;* from 398; *nourishment*:— food.

4362. מִכְמָן **mikman**, *mik-man';* from the same as 3646 in the sense of *hiding; treasure* (as *hidden*):— treasure.

4363. מִכְמָס **Mikmâç** (Ezra 2:27; Neh. 7:31), *mik-maws';* or

מִכְמָשׁ **Mikmâsh**, *mik-mawsh';* or

מִכְמַשׁ **Mikmash** (Neh. 11:31), *mik-mash';* from 3647; *hidden; Mikmas* or *Mikmash*, a place in Pal.:— Mikmas, Mikmash.

4364. מַכְמָר **makmâr**, *mak-mawr';* or

מִכְמֹר **mikmôr**, *mik-more';* from 3648 in the sense of *blackening* by heat; a (hunter's) *net* (as *dark* from concealment):— net.

4365. מִכְמֶרֶת **mikmereth**, *mik-meh´-reth;* or

מִכְמֹרֶת **mikmôreth**, *mik-mo´-reth;* fem. of 4364; a (fisher's) *net:*— drag, net.

מִכְמָס **Mikmâsh**. See 4363.

4366. מִכְמְתָת **Mikmᵉthâth**, *mik-meth-awth´;* appar. from an unused root mean. to *hide; concealment; Mikmethath,* a place in Pal.:— Michmethath.

4367. מַכְנַדְבַי **Maknadbay**, *mak-nad-bah´-ee;* from 4100 and 5068 with a particle interposed; *what* (is) *like* (a) *liberal* (man)?; *Maknadbai,* an Isr.:— Machnadebai.

מְכֹנָה **mᵉkônâh**. See 4350.

4368. מְכֹנָה **Mᵉkônâh**, *mek-o-naw´;* the same as 4350; a *base; Mekonah,* a place in Pal.:— Mekonah.

4369. מְכֻנָה **mᵉkûnâh**, *mek-oo-naw´;* the same as 4350; a *spot:*— base.

4370. מִכְנָס **miknâç**, *mik-nawce´;* from 3647 in the sense of *hiding;* (only in dual) *drawers* (from *concealing* the private parts):— breeches.

4371. מֶכֶס **mekeç**, *meh´-kes;* prob. from an unused root mean. to *enumerate;* an *assessment* (as based upon a *census*):— tribute.

4372. מִכְסֶה **mikçeh**, *mik-seh´;* from 3680; a *covering,* i.e. weather-*boarding:*— covering.

4373. מִכְסָה **mikçâh**, *mik-saw´;* fem. of 4371; an *enumeration;* by impl. a *valuation:*— number, worth.

4374. מְכַסֶּה **mᵉkaççeh**, *mek-as-seh´;* from 3680; a *covering,* i.e. *garment;* spec. a *coverlet* (for a bed), an *awning* (from the sun); also the *omentum* (as covering the intestines):— clothing, to cover, that which covereth.

4375. מַכְפֵּלָה **Makpêlâh**, *mak-pay-law´;* from 3717; a *fold; Makpelah,* a place in Pal.:— Machpelah.

4376. מָכַר **mâkar**, *maw-kar´;* a prim. root; to *sell,* lit. (as merchandise, a daughter in marriage, into slavery), or fig. (to *surrender*):— × at all, sell (away, -er, self).

4377. מֶכֶר **meker**, *meh´-ker;* from 4376; *merchandise;* also *value:*— pay, price, ware.

4378. מַכָּר **makkâr**, *mak-kawr´;* from 5234; an *acquaintance:*— acquaintance.

4379. מִכְרֶה **mikreh**, *mik-reh´;* from 3738; a *pit* (for salt):— [salt-] pit.

4380. מְכֵרָה **mᵉkêrâh**, *mek-ay-raw´;* prob. from the same as 3564 in the sense of *stabbing;* a *sword:*— habitation.

מְכֹרָה **mᵉkôrâh**. See 4351.

4381. מִכְרִי **Mikrîy**, *mik-ree´;* from 4376; *salesman; Mikri,* an Isr.:— Michri.

4382. מְכֵרָתִי **Mᵉkêrâthîy**, *mek-ay-raw-thee´;* patrial from an unused name (the same as 4380) of a place in Pal.; a *Mekerathite,* or inhab. of Mekerah:— Mecherathite.

4383. מִכְשׁוֹל **mikshôwl**, *mik-shole´;* or

מִכְשֹׁל **mikshôl**, *mik-shole´;* masc.

from 3782; a *stumbling-block,* lit. or fig. (*obstacle, enticement* [spec. an idol, *scruple*):— caused to fall, offence, × [no-] thing offered, ruin, stumbling-block.

4384. מַכְשֵׁלָה **makshêlâh**, *mak-shay-law´;* fem. from 3782; a *stumbling-block,* but only fig. (*fall, enticement* [idol]):— ruin, stumbling-block.

4385. מִכְתָּב **miktâb**, *mik-tawb´;* from 3789; a thing *written,* the *characters,* or a *document* (letter, copy, edict, poem):— writing.

4386. מְכִתָּה **mᵉkittâh**, *mek-it-taw´;* from 3807; a *fracture:*— bursting.

4387. מִכְתָּם **Miktâm**, *mik-tawm´;* from 3799; an *engraving,* i.e. (techn.) a *poem:*— Michtam.

4388. מַכְתֵּשׁ **maktêsh**, *mak-taysh´;* from 3806; a *mortar;* by anal. a *socket* (of a tooth):— hollow place, mortar.

4389. מַכְתֵּשׁ **Maktêsh**, *mak-taysh´;* the same as 4388; *dell;* the *Maktesh,* a place in Jerusalem:— Maktesh.

מֻל **mûl**. See 4136.

4390. מָלֵא **mâlê´**, *maw-lay´;* or

מָלָא **mâlâ´** (Esth. 7:5), *maw-law´;* a prim. root, to *fill* or (intr.) *be full* of, in a wide application (lit. and fig.):— accomplish, confirm, + consecrate, be at an end, be expired, be fenced, fill, fulfil, (be, become, × draw, give in, go) full (-ly, -ly set, tale), [over-] flow, fulness, furnish, gather (selves, together), presume, replenish, satisfy, set, space, take a [hand-] full, + have wholly.

4391. מְלָא **mᵉlâ´** (Chald.), *mel-aw´;* corresp. to 4390; to *fill:*— fill, be full.

4392. מָלֵא **mâlê´**, *maw-lay´;* from 4390; *full* (lit. or fig.) or *filling* (lit.); also (concr.) *fulness;* adv. *fully:*— × she that was with child, fill (-ed, -ed with), full (-ly), multitude, as is worth.

4393. מְלֹא **mᵉlô´**, *mel-o´;* rarely

מְלוֹא **mᵉlôw´**, *mel-o´;* or

מְלוֹ **mᵉlôw** (Ezek. 41:8), *mel-o´;* from 4390; *fulness* (lit. or fig.):— × all along, × all that is (there-) in, fill, (× that whereof ... was) full, fulness, [hand-] full, multitude.

מְלֹא **Millô´**. See 4407.

4394. מִלֻּא **millû´**, *mil-loo´;* from 4390; a *fulfilling* (only in plur.), i.e. (lit.) a *setting* (of gems), or (tech.) *consecration* (also concr. a dedicatory *sacrifice*):— consecration, be set.

4395. מְלֵאָה **mᵉlê´âh**, *mel-ay-aw´;* fem. of 4392; something *fulfilled,* i.e. *abundance* (of produce):— (first of ripe) fruit, fulness.

4396. מִלֻּאָה **millû´âh**, *mil-loo-aw´;* fem. of 4394; a *filling,* i.e. *setting* (of gems):— inclosing, setting.

4397. מַלְאָךְ **mal'âk**, *mal-awk´;* from an unused root mean. to *despatch* as a *deputy;* a *messenger;* spec. of God, i.e. an *angel* (also a prophet, priest or teacher):— ambassador, angel, king, messenger.

4398. מַלְאַךְ **mal'ak** (Chald.), *mal-ak´;* corresp. to 4397; an *angel:*— angel.

4399. מְלָאכָה **mᵉlâ'kâh**, *mel-aw-kaw´;*

from the same as 4397; prop. *deputyship,* i.e. ministry; gen. *employment* (never servile) or work (abstr. or concr.); also *property* (as the result of *labor*):— business, + cattle, +industrious, occupation, (+ -pied), + officer, thing (made), use, (manner of) work ([-man], -manship).

4400. מַלְאֲכוּת **mal'äkûwth**, *mal-ak-ooth´;* from the same as 4397; a *message:*— message.

4401. מַלְאָכִי **Mal'âkîy**, *mal-aw-kee´;* from the same as 4397; *ministrative; Malaki,* a prophet:— Malachi.

4402. מִלֵּאת **millê'th**, *mil-layth´;* from 4390; *fulness* (as (concr.) a *plump* socket (of the eye):— × fitly.

4403. מַלְבּוּשׁ **malbûwsh**, *mal-boosh´;* or

מַלְבֻּשׁ **malbûsh**, *mal-boosh´;* from 3847; a *garment,* or (collect.) *clothing:*— apparel, raiment, vestment.

4404. מַלְבֵּן **malbên**, *mal-bane´;* from 3835 (denom.); a *brick-kiln:*— brick-kiln.

4405. מִלָּה **millâh**, *mil-law´;* from 4448 (plur. masc. as if from

מִלֶּה **milleh**, *mil-leh´;* a *word;* collect. a *discourse;* fig. a *topic:*— + answer, by-word, matter, any thing (what) to say, to speak (-ing), speak, talking, word.

4406. מִלָּה **millâh** (Chald.), *mil-law´;* corresp. to 4405; a *word, command, discourse,* or *subject:*— commandment, matter, thing, word.

מְלֹו **mᵉlôw**. See 4393.

מְלֹוא **mᵉlôw'**. See 4393.

4407. מִלּוֹא **millôw'**, *mil-lo´;* or

מִלֹּא **millô'** (2 Kings 12:20) *mil-lo´;* from 4390; a *rampart* (as *filled* in), i.e. the *citadel:*— Millo. See also 1037.

4408. מַלּוּחַ **mallûwach**, *mal-loo´-akh;* from 4414; *sea-purslain* (from its *saltness*):— mallows.

4409. מַלּוּךְ **Mallûwk**, *mal-luke´;* or

מַלּוּכִי **Mallûwkîy** (Neh. 12:14) *mal-loo-kee´;* from 4427; *regnant; Malluk,* the name of five Isr.:— Malluch, Melichu [from the marg.].

4410. מְלוּכָה **mᵉlûwkâh**, *mel-oo-kaw´;* fem. pass. part. of 4427; something *ruled,* i.e. a *realm:*— kingdom, king's, × royal.

4411. מָלוֹן **mâlôwn**, *maw-lone´;* from 3885; a *lodgment,* i.e. *caravanserai* or *encampment:*— inn, place where ... lodge, lodging (place).

4412. מְלוּנָה **mᵉlûwnâh**, *mel-oo-naw´;* fem. from 3885; a *hut,* a *hammock:*— cottage, lodge.

4413. מַלּוֹתִי **Mallôwthîy**, *mal-lo´-thee;* appar. from 4448; *I have talked* (i.e. *loquacious*); *Mallothi,* an Isr.:— Mallothi.

4414. מָלַח **mâlach**, *maw-lakh´;* a prim. root; prop. to *rub* to pieces or pulverize; intr. to *disappear* as dust; also (as denom. from 4417) to *salt* whether intern. (to *season* with salt) or extern. (to *rub* with salt):— × at all, salt, season, temper together, vanish away.

4415. מְלַח **mᵉlach** (Chald.), *mel-akh´;*

corresp. to 4414; to *eat* salt, i.e. (gen.) *subsist*:— + have maintenance.

4416. מְלַח **mᵉlach** (Chald.), *mel-akh´*; from 4415; *salt*:— + maintenance, salt.

4417. מֶלַח **melach**, *meh´-lakh*; from 4414; prop. *powder*, i.e. (spec.) *salt* (as easily pulverized and dissolved:— salt (l-pitl).

4418. מָלָח **mâlâch**, *maw-lawkh´*; from 4414 in its orig. sense; a *rag* or old garment:— rotten rag.

4419. מַלָּח **mallâch**, *mal-lawkh´*; from 4414 in its second. sense; a *sailor* (as following "the salt"):— mariner.

4420. מְלֵחָה **mᵉlêchâh**, *mel-ay-khaw´*; from 4414 (in its denom. sense); prop. *salted* (i.e. land [776 being understood]), i.e. a *desert*:— barren land (-ness), salt [land].

4421. מִלְחָמָה **milchâmâh**, *mil-khaw-maw´*; from 3898 (in the sense of *fighting*); a *battle* (i.e. the *engagement*); gen. *war* (i.e. *warfare*):— battle, fight (-ing), war (l-riorl).

4422. מָלַט **mâlaṭ**, *maw-lat´*; a prim. root; prop. to *be smooth*, i.e. (by impl.) to *escape* (as if by *slipperiness*); caus. to *release* or *rescue*; spec. to *bring forth* young, *emit* sparks:— deliver (self), escape, lay, leap out, let alone, let go, preserve, save, × speedily, × surely.

4423. מֶלֶט **meleṭ**, *meh´-let*; from 4422, *cement* (from its plastic *smoothness*):— clay.

4424. מְלַטְיָה **Mᵉlaṭyâh**, *mel-at-yaw´*; from 4423 and 3050; (whom) *Jah has delivered*; *Melatjah*, a Gibeonite:— Melatiah.

4425. מְלִילָה **mᵉlîylâh**, *mel-ee-law´*; from 4449 (in the sense of *cropping* [comp. 4135]); a *head* of grain (as *cut* off):— ear.

4426. מְלִיצָה **mᵉlîytsâh**, *mel-ee-tsaw´*; from 3887; an *aphorism*; also a *satire*:— interpretation, taunting.

4427. מָלַךְ **mâlak**, *maw-lak´*; a prim. root; to *reign*; incept. to *ascend the throne*; caus. to *induct* into royalty; hence, (by impl.) to *take counsel*:— consult, × indeed, be (make, set a, set up) king, be (make) queen, (begin to, make to) reign (-ing), rule, × surely.

4428. מֶלֶךְ **melek**, *meh´-lek*; from 4427; a *king*:— king, royal.

4429. מֶלֶךְ **Melek**, *meh´-lek*; the same as 4428; *king; Melek*, the name of two Isr.:— Melech, Hammelech [by incl. the art.].

4430. מֶלֶךְ **melek** (Chald.), *meh´-lek*; corresp. to 4428; a *king*:— king, royal.

4431. מְלַךְ **mᵉlak** (Chald.), *mel-ak´*; from a root corresp. to 4427 in the sense of *consultation; advice*:— counsel.

4432. מֹלֶךְ **Môlek**, *mo´-lek*; from 4427; *Molek* (i.e. king), the chief deity of the Ammonites:— Molech. Comp. 4445.

4433. מַלְכָּא **malkâ'** (Chald.), *mal-kaw´*; corresp. to 4436; a *queen*:— queen.

4434. מַלְכֹּדֶת **malkôdeth**, *mal-ko´-deth*; from 3920; a *snare*:— trap.

4435. מִלְכָּה **Milkâh**, *mil-kaw´*; a form of

4436; *queen; Milcah*, the name of a Hebrewss and of an Isr.:— Milcah.

4436. מַלְכָּה **malkâh**, *mal-kaw´*; fem. of 4428; a *queen*:— queen.

4437. מַלְכוּ **malkûw** (Chald.), *mal-koo´*; corresp. to 4438; *dominion* (abstr. or concr.):— kingdom, kingly, realm, reign.

4438. מַלְכוּה **malkûwth**, *mal-kooth´*; or מַלְכֻה **malkûth**, *mal-kooth´*; or (in plur.)

מַלְכֻיָה **malkûyâh**, *mal-koo-yâh´*; from 4427; a *rule*; concr. a *dominion*:— empire, kingdom, realm, reign, royal.

4439. מַלְכִּיאֵל **Malkîy'êl**, *mal-kee-ale´*; from 4428 and 410; *king of* (i.e. appointed by) *God; Malkiël*, an Isr.:— Malchiel.

4440. מַלְכִּיאֵלִי **Malkîy'êlîy**, *mal-kee-ay-lee´*; patron. from 4439; a *Malkiëlite* or desc. of Malkiel:— Malchielite.

4441. מַלְכִּיָה **Malkîyâh**, *mal-kee-yaw´*; or מַלְכִּיָהוּ **Malkîyâhûw** (Jer. 38:6), *mal-kee-yaw´-hoo*; from 4428 and 3050; *king of* (i.e. appointed by) *Jah; Malkijah*, the name of ten Isr.:— Malchiah, Malchijah.

4442. מַלְכִּי־צֶדֶק **Malkîy-Tsedeq**, *mal-kee-tseh´-dek*; from 4428 and 6664; *king of right; Malki-Tsedek*, an early king in Pal.:— Melchizedek.

4443. מַלְכִּירָם **Malkîyrâm**, *mal-kee-rawm´*; from 4428 and 7311; *king of a high one* (i.e. of exaltation); *Malkiram*, an Isr.:— Malchiram.

4444. מַלְכִּישׁוּעַ **Malkîyshùwa'**, *mal-kee-shoo´-ah*; from 4428 and 7769; *king of wealth; Malkishua*, an Isr.:— Malchishua.

4445. מַלְכָּם **Malkâm**, *mal-kawm´*; or מַלְכֹּם **Milkôwm**, *mil-kome´*; from 4428 for 4432; *Malcam* or *Milcom*, the national idol of the Ammonites:— Malcham, Milcom.

4446. מְלֶכֶת **mᵉleketh**, *mel-eh´-keth*; from 4427; a *queen*:— queen.

4447. מֹלֶכֶת **Môleketh**, *mo-leh´-keth*; fem. act. part. of 4427; *queen; Moleketh*, an Israelitess:— Hammoleketh [incl. the art.].

4448. מָלַל **mâlal**, *maw-lal´*; a prim. root; to *speak* (mostly poet.) or *say*:— say, speak, utter.

4449. מְלַל **mᵉlal** (Chald.), *mel-al´*; corresp. to 4448; to *speak*:— say, speak (-ing).

4450. מִלְלַי **Mîlalay**, *mee-lal-ah´-ee*; from 4448; *talkative; Milalai*, an Isr.:— Milalai.

4451. מַלְמָד **malmâd**, *mal-mawd´*; from 3925; a *goad* for oxen:— goad.

4452. מָלַץ **mâlats**, *maw-lats´*; a prim. root; to *be smooth*, i.e. (fig.) *pleasant*:— be sweet.

4453. מֶלְצָר **Meltsâr**, *mel-tsawr´*; of Pers. der.; the *butler* or other officer in the Bab. court:— Melzar.

4454. מָלַק **mâlaq**, *maw-lak´*; a prim. root; to *crack* a joint; by impl. to *wring* the neck of a fowl (without separating it):— wring off.

4455. מַלְקוֹחַ **malqôwach**, *mal-ko´-akh*; from 3947; tran. (in dual) the *jaws* (as taking food); intr. *spoil* [and captives] (as taken):— booty, jaws, prey.

4456. מַלְקוֹשׁ **malqôwsh**, *mal-koshe´*; from 3953; the spring *rain* (comp. 3954); fig. *eloquence*:— latter rain.

4457. מֶלְקָח **melqâch**, *mel-kawkh´*; or מַלְקָח **malqâch**, *mal-kawkh´*; from 3947; (only in dual) *tweezers*:— snuffers, tongs.

4458. מֶלְתְּחָה **meltâchâh**, *mel-taw-khaw´*; from an unused root mean. to *spread* out; a *wardrobe* (i.e. room where clothing is *spread*):— vestry.

4459. מַלְתָּעָה **maltâ'âh**, *mal-taw-aw´*; transp. for 4973; a *grinder*, i.e. back *tooth*:— great tooth.

4460. מַמְּגֻרָה **mammᵉgûrâh**, *mam-meg-oo-raw´*; from 4048 (in the sense of *depositing*); a *granary*:— barn.

4461. מֵמַד **mêmad**, *may-mad´*; from 4058; a *measure*:— measure.

4462. מְמוּכָן **Mᵉmûwkân**, *mem-oo-kawn´*; or (transp.)

מוֹמֻכָן° **Môwmûkân** (Esth. 1:16), *mo-moo-kawn´*; of Pers. der.; *Memucan* or *Momucan*, a Pers. satrap:— Memucan.

4463. מָמֹה **mâmôwth**, *maw-mothe´*; from 4191; a mortal *disease*; concr. a *corpse*:— death.

4464. מַמְזֵר **mamzêr**, *mam-zare´*; from an unused root mean. to *alienate*; a *mongrel*, i.e. born of a Jewish father and a heathen mother:— bastard.

4465. מִמְכָּר **mimkâr**, *mim-kawr´*; from 4376; *merchandise*; abstr. a *selling*:— × ought, (that which cometh of) sale, that which ... sold, ware.

4466. מִמְכֶּרֶת **mimkereth**, *mim-keh´-reth*; fem. of 4465; a *sale*:— + sold as.

4467. מַמְלָכָה **mamlâkâh**, *mam-law-kaw´*; from 4427; *dominion*, i.e. (abstr.) the estate (*rule*) or (concr.) the country (*realm*):— kingdom, king's, reign, royal.

4468. מַמְלָכוּה **mamlâkûwth**, *mam-law-kooth´*; a form of 4467 and equiv. to it:— kingdom, reign.

4469. מִמְסָךְ **mamçâk**, *mam-sawk´*; from 4537; *mixture*, i.e. (spec.) wine *mixed* (with water or spices):— drink-offering, mixed wine.

4470. מֶמֶר **memer**, *meh´-mer*; from an unused root mean. to *grieve*; *sorrow*:— bitterness.

4471. מַמְרֵא **Mamrê'**, *mam-ray´*; from 4754 (in the sense of *vigor*); *lusty; Mamre*, an Amorite:— Mamre.

4472. מַמְרֹר **mamrôr**, *mam-rore´*; from 4843; a *bitterness*, i.e. (fig.) calamity:— bitterness.

4473. מִמְשַׁח **mimshach**, *mim-shakh´*; from 4886, in the sense of *expansion*; *outspread* (i.e. with outstretched wings):— anointed.

4474. מִמְשָׁל **mimshâl**, *mim-shawl´*; from 4910; a *ruler* or (abstr.) *rule*:— dominion, that ruled.

4475. מֶמְשָׁלָה **memshâlâh**, *mem-shaw-law´*; fem. of 4474; *rule*; also (concr. in plur.) a *realm* or a *ruler*:— dominion, government, power, to rule.

4476. מִמְשָׁק **mimshâq**, *mim-shawk´*; from the same as 4943; a *possession*:— breeding.

4477. מַמְתַּק **mamtaq**, *mam-tak´*; from 4985; something *sweet* (lit. or fig.):— (most) sweet.

4478. מָן **mân**, *mawn*; from 4100; lit. a *whatness* (so to speak), i.e. *manna* (so called from the question about it):— manna.

4479. מָן **mân** (Chald.), *mawn*; from 4101; *who* or *what* (prop. interrog., hence, also indef. and rel.):— what, who (-msoever, + -so).

4480. מִן **min**, *min*; or

מִנֵּי **minnîy**, *min-nee´*; or

מִנֵּי **minnêy** (constr. plur.) *min-nay´*; (Isa. 30:11); for 4482; prop. a *part* of; hence, (prep.), *from* or *out of* in many senses (as follows):— above, after, among, at, because of, by (reason of), from (among), in, × neither, × nor, (out) of, over, since, × then, through, × whether, with.

4481. מִן **min** (Chald.), *min*; corresp. to 4480:— according, after, + because, + before, by, for, from, × him, × more than, (out) of, part, since, × these, to, upon, + when.

4482. מֵן **mên**, *mane*; from an unused root mean. to *apportion*; a *part*; hence, a musical *chord* (as parted into strings):— in [the same] (Psa. 68:23), stringed instrument (Psa. 150:4), whereby (Psa. 45:8 [defective plur.]).

4483. מְנָא **m⁴nâ'** (Chald.), *men-aw´*; or

מְנָה **m⁴nâh** (Chald.) *men-aw´*; corresp. to 4487; to *count, appoint*:— number, ordain, set.

4484. מְנֵא **menê'** (Chald.), *men-ay´*; pass. part. of 4483; *numbered*:— Mene.

4485. מַנְגִּינָה **mangîynâh**, *man-ghee-naw´*; from 5059; a *satire*:— music.

מִנְדָּה **mindâh**. See 4061.

4486. מַנְדַּע **manda'** (Chald.), *man-dah´*; corresp. to 4093; *wisdom* or *intelligence*:— knowledge, reason, understanding.

מְנָה **m⁴nâh**. See 4483.

4487. מָנָה **mânâh**, *maw-naw´*; a prim. root; prop. to *weigh* out; by impl. to *allot* or constitute officially; also to *enumerate* or enroll:— appoint, count, number, prepare, set, tell.

4488. מָנֶה **mâneh**, *maw-neh´*; from 4487; prop. a fixed *weight* or measured amount, i.e. (techn.) a *maneh* or mina:— maneh, pound.

4489. מֹנֶה **môneh**, *mo-neh´*; from 4487; prop. something *weighed* out, i.e. (fig.) a *portion* of time, i.e. an *instance*:— time.

4490. מָנָה **mânâh**, *maw-naw´*; from 4487; prop. something *weighed* out, i.e. (gen.) a *division*; spec. (of food) a *ration*; also a *lot*:— such things as belonged, part, portion.

4491. מִנְהָג **minhâg**, *min-hawg´*; from 5090; the *driving* (of a chariot):— driving.

4492. מִנְהָרָה **minhârâh**, *min-haw-raw´*; from 5102; prop. a *channel* or fissure, i.e. (by impl.) a *cavern*:— den.

4493. מָנוֹד **mânôwd**, *maw-node´*; from 5110 a *nodding* or *toss* (of the head in derision):— shaking.

4494. מָנוֹחַ **mânôwach**, *maw-no´-akh*; from 5117; *quiet*, i.e. (concr.) a *settled spot*, or (fig.) a *home*:— (place of) rest.

4495. מָנוֹחַ **Mânôwach**, *maw-no´-akh*; the same as 4494; *rest*; *Manoach*, an Isr.:— Manoah.

4496. מְנוּחָה **m⁴nûwchâh**, *men-oo-khaw´*; or

מְנֻחָה **m⁴nûchâh**, *men-oo-khaw´*; fem. of 4495; *repose* or (adv.) *peacefully*; fig. *consolation* (spec. *matrimony*); hence, (concr.) an *abode*:— comfortable, ease, quiet, rest (-ing place), still.

4497. מָנוֹן **mânôwn**, *maw-nohn´*; from 5125; a *continuator*, i.e. *heir*:— son.

4498. מָנוֹס **mânôwç**, *maw-noce´*; from 5127; a *retreat* (lit. or fig.); abstr. a *fleeing*:— × apace, escape, way to flee, flight, refuge.

4499. מְנוּסָה **m⁴nuwçâh**, *men-oo-saw´*; or

מְנֻסָה **m⁴nûçâh**, *men-oo-saw´*; fem. of 4498; *retreat*:— fleeing, flight.

4500. מָנוֹר **mânôwr**, *maw-nore´*; from 5214; a *yoke* (prop. for *plowing*), i.e. the *frame* of a loom:— beam.

4501. מְנוֹרָה **m⁴nôwrâh**, *men-o-raw´*; or

מְנֹרָה **m⁴nôrâh**, *men-o-raw´*; fem. of 4500 (in the orig. sense of 5216); a *chandelier*:— candlestick.

4502. מִנְּזָר **minn⁴zâr**, *min-ez-awr´*; from 5144; a *prince*:— crowned.

4503. מִנְחָה **minchâh**, *min-khaw´*; from an unused root mean. to *apportion*, i.e. *bestow*; a *donation*; euphem. *tribute*; spec. a *sacrificial offering* (usually bloodless and voluntary):— gift, oblation, (meat) offering, present, sacrifice.

4504. מִנְחָה **minchâh** (Chald.), *min-khaw´*; corresp. to 4503; a *sacrificial offering*:— oblation, meat offering.

מְנֻחָה **m⁴nûchâh**. See 4496.

מְנֻחוֹת **M⁴nûchôwth**. See 2679.

4505. מְנַחֵם **M⁴nachêm**, *men-akh-ame´*; from 5162; *comforter*; *Menachem*, an Isr.:— Menahem.

4506. מָנַחַת **Mânachath**, *maw-nakh´-ath*; from 5117; *rest*; *Manachath*, the name of an Edomite and of a place in Moab:— Manahath.

מְנַחְתִּי **M⁴nachtîy**. See 2680.

4507. מְנִי **M⁴nîy**, *men-ee´*; from 4487; the *Apportioner*, i.e. Fate (as an idol):— number.

מִנִּי **mînnîy**. See 4480, 4482.

4508. מִנִּי **Minnîy**, *min-nee´*; of for. der.; *Minni*, an Armenian province:— Minni.

מִנְיוֹת **m⁴nâyôwth**. See 4521.

4509. מִנְיָמִין **Minyâmîyn**, *min-yaw-meen´*; from 4480 and 3225; *from* (the) *right hand*; *Minjamin*, the name of two Isr.:— Miniamin. Comp. 4326.

4510. מִנְיָן **minyân** (Chald.), *min-yawn´*; from 4483; *enumeration*:— number.

4511. מִנִּית **Minnîyth**, *min-neeth´*; from the same as 4482; *enumeration*; *Minnith*, a place E. of the Jordan:— Minnith.

4512. מִנְלֶה **minleh**, *min-leh´*; from 5239; *completion*, i.e. (in produce) *wealth*:— perfection.

מְנֻחָה **m⁴nûçâh**. See 4499.

4513. מָנַע **mâna'**, *maw-nah´*; a prim. root; to *debar* (neg. or pos.) from benefit or injury:— deny, keep (back), refrain, restrain, withhold.

4514. מַנְעוּל **man'ûwl**, *man-ool´*; or

מַנְעֻל **man'ûl**, *man-ool´*; from 5274; a *bolt*:— lock.

4515. מַנְעָל **man'âl**, *man-awl´*; from 5274; a *bolt*:— shoe.

4516. מַנְעַם **man'am**, *man-am´*; from 5276; a *delicacy*:— dainty.

4517. מְנַעְנַע **m⁴na'na'**, *men-ah-ah´*; from 5128; a *sistrum* (so called from its *rattling* sound):— cornet.

4518. מְנַקִּית **m⁴naqqîyth**, *men-ak-keeth´*; from 5352; a *sacrificial basin* (for holding blood):— bowl.

מְנֹרָה **m⁴nôrâh**. See 4501.

4519. מְנַשֶּׁה **M⁴nashsheh**, *men-ash-sheh´*; from 5382; *causing to forget*; *Menashsheh*, a grandson of Jacob, also the tribe descended from him, and its territory:— Manasseh.

4520. מְנַשִּׁי **M⁴nashshîy**, *men-ash-shee´*; from 4519; a *Menashshite* or desc. of Menashsheh:— of Manasseh, Manassites.

4521. מְנָת **m⁴nâth**, *men-awth´*; from 4487; an *allotment* (by courtesy, law or providence):— portion.

4522. מַס **maç**, *mas*; or

מִס **miç**, *mees*; from 4549; prop. a *burden* (as causing to *faint*), i.e. a *tax* in the form of forced *labor*:— discomfited, levy, task [-master], tribute (-tary).

4523. מָס **mâç**, *mawce*; from 4549; *fainting*, i.e. (fig.) *disconsolate*:— is afflicted.

4524. מֵסַב **mêçab**, *may-sab´*; plur. masc.

מְסִבִּים **m⁴çibbîym**, *mes-ib-beem´*; or fem.

מְסִבּוֹת **m⁴çibbôwth**, *mes-ib-bohth´*; from 5437; a *divan* (as *enclosing* the room); abstr. (adv.) *around*:— that compass about, (place) round about, at table.

מֻסַבָּה **mûçabbâh**. See 4142.

4525. מַסְגֵּר **maçgêr**, *mas-gare´*; from 5462; a *fastener*, i.e. (of a person) a *smith*, (of a thing) a *prison*:— prison, smith.

4526. מִסְגֶּרֶת **miçgereth**, *mis-gheh´-reth*; from 5462; something *enclosing*, i.e. a *margin* (of a region, of a panel); concr. a *stronghold*:— border, close place, hole.

4527. מַסַּד **maççad**, *mas-sad´*; from 3245; a *foundation*:— foundation.

מֻסָדָה **môçâdâh**. See 4146.

4528. מִסְדְּרוֹן **miçd⁴rôwn**, *mis-der-ohn´*; from the same as 5468; a *colonnade* or *internal portico* (from its *rows* of pillars):— porch.

Hebrew

4529. מָצָה **mâçâh**, *maw-saw´*; a prim. root; to *dissolve:*— make to consume away, (make to) melt, water.

4530. מִצָּה **miççâh**, *mis-saw´*; from 4549 (in the sense of *flowing*); *abundance*, i.e. (adv.) *liberally:*— tribute.

4531. מַסָּה **maççâh**, *mas-saw´*; from 5254; a *testing*, of men (judicial) or of God (querulous):— temptation, trial.

4532. מַסָּה **Maççâh**, *mas-saw´*; the same as 4531; *Massah*, a place in the Desert:— Massah.

4533. מַסְוֶה **maçveh**, *mas-veh´*; appar. from an unused root mean. to *cover*; a *veil:*— vail.

4534. מְסוּכָה **me'çûwkâh**, *mes-oo-kaw´*; for 4881; a *hedge:*— thorn hedge.

4535. מַסָּח **maççâch**, *mas-sawkh´*; from 5255 in the sense of *staving* off; a *cordon*, (adv.) or (as a) military *barrier:*— broken down.

4536. מִסְחָר **miççhâr**, *mis-khawr´*; from 5503; *trade:*— traffic.

4537. מָסַךְ **mâçak**, *maw-sak´*; a prim. root; to *mix*, espec. wine (with spices):— mingle.

4538. מֶסֶךְ **meçek**, *meh´-sek*; from 4537; a *mixture*, i.e. of wine with spices:— mixture.

4539. מָסָךְ **mâçâk**, *maw-sawk´*; from 5526; a *cover*, i.e. *veil:*— covering, curtain, hanging.

4540. מְסֻכָּה **me'çukkâh**, *mes-ook-kaw´*; from 5526; a *covering*, i.e. garniture:— covering.

4541. מַסֵּכָה **maççêkâh**, *mas-say-kaw´*; from 5258; prop. a *pouring* over, i.e. *fusion* of metal (espec. a *cast* image); by impl. a *libation*, i.e. league; concr. a *coverlet* (as if *poured* out):— covering, molten (image), vail.

4542. מִסְכֵּן **miçkên**, *mis-kane´*; from 5531; *indigent:*— poor (man).

4543. מִסְכְּנָה **miçke'nâh**, *mis-ken-aw´*; by transp. from 3664; a *magazine:*— store (-house), treasure.

4544. מִסְכְּנֻת **miçkênûth**, *mis-kay-nooth´*; from 4542; *indigence:*— scarceness.

4545. מַסֶּכֶת **maççeketh**, *mas-seh´-keth*; from 5259 in the sense of *spreading* out; something *expanded*, i.e. the *warp* in a loom (as *stretched* out to receive the woof):— web.

4546. מְסִלָּה **me'çillâh**, *mes-il-law´*; from 5549; a *thoroughfare* (as turnpiked), lit. or fig.; spec. a *viaduct*, a *staircase:*— causeway, course, highway, path, terrace.

4547. מַסְלוּל **maçlûwl**, *mas-lool´*; from 5549; a *thoroughfare* (as turnpiked):— highway.

4548. מַסְמֵר **maçmêr**, *mas-mare´*; or

מִסְמֵר **miçmêr**, *mis-mare´*; also (fem.)

מַסְמְרָה **maçme'râh**, *mas-mer-aw´*; or

מִסְמְרָה **miçme'râh**, *mis-mer-aw´*; or even

מַשְׂמְרָה **masme'râh** (Eccles. 12:11),

mas-mer-aw´; from 5568; a *peg* (as *bristling* from the surface):— nail.

4549. מָסַס **mâçaç**, *maw-sas´*; a prim. root; to *liquefy*; fig. to *waste* (with disease), to *faint* (with fatigue, fear or grief):— discourage, faint, be loosed, melt (away), refuse, × utterly.

4550. מַסַּע **maçça'**, *mas-sah´*; from 5265; a *departure* (from *striking* the tents), i.e. march (not necessarily a single day's travel); by impl. a *station* (or point of *departure*):— journey (-ing).

4551. מַסָּע **maççâ'**, *mas-saw´*; from 5265 in the sense of *projecting*; a *missile* (spear or arrow); also a *quarry* (whence stones are, as it were, *ejected*):— before it was brought, dart.

4552. מִסְעָד **miç'âd**, *mis-awd´*; from 5582; a *balustrade* (for stairs):— pillar.

4553. מִסְפֵּד **miçpêd**, *mis-pade´*; from 5594; a *lamentation:*— lamentation, one mourneth, mourning, wailing.

4554. מִסְפּוֹא **miçpôw'**, *mis-po´*; from an unused root mean. to *collect; fodder:*— provender.

4555. מִסְפָּחָה **miçpâchâh**, *mis-paw-khaw´*; from 5596; a *veil* (as *spread* out):— kerchief.

4556. מִסְפַּחַת **miçpachath**, *mis-pakh´-ath*; from 5596; *scruf* (as *spreading* over the surface):— scab.

4557. מִסְפָּר **miçpâr**, *mis-pawr´*; from 5608; a *number*, def. (arithmetical) or indef. (large, *innumerable*; small, a *few*); also (abstr.) *narration:*— + abundance, account, × all, × few, [in-]finite, (certain) number (-ed), tale, telling, + time.

4558. מִסְפָּר **Miçpâr**, *mis-pawr´*; the same as 4557; *number*; *Mispar*, an Isr.:— Mizpar. Comp. 4559.

מֹסֵרוֹת **Môçe'rowth**. See 4149.

4559. מִסְפֶּרֶת **Miçpereth**, *mis-peh´-reth*; fem. of 4457; *enumeration*; *Mispereth*, an Isr.:— Mispereth. Comp. 4458.

4560. מָסַר **mâçar**, *maw-sar´*; a prim. root; to *sunder*, i.e. (tran.) *set apart*, or (reflex.) *apostatize:*— commit, deliver.

4561. מֹסָר **môçâr**, *mo-sawr´*; from 3256; *admonition:*— instruction.

4562. מָסֹרֶת **mâçôreth**, *maw-so´-reth*; from 631; a *band:*— bond.

4563. מִסְתּוֹר **miçtôwr**, *mis-tore´*; from 5641; a *refuge:*— covert.

4564. מַסְתֵּר **maçtêr**, *mas-tare´*; from 5641; prop. a *hider*, i.e. (abstr.) a hiding, i.e. *aversion:*— hid.

4565. מִסְתָּר **miçtâr**, *mis-tawr´*; from 5641; prop. a *concealer*, i.e. a *covert:*— secret (-ly, place).

מְעָא **me'â'**. See 4577.

4566. מַעְבָּד **ma'bâd**, *mah-bawd´*; from 5647; an *act:*— work.

4567. מַעְבָּד **ma'bâd** (Chald.), *mah-bawd´*; corresp. to 4566; an *act:*— work.

4568. מַעֲבֶה **ma'âbeh**, *mah-ab-eh´*; from 5666; prop. *compact* (part of soil), i.e. *loam:*— clay.

4569. מַעֲבָר **ma'âbâr**, *mah-ab-awr´*; or fem.

מַעֲבָרָה **ma'âbârâh**, *mah-ab-aw-*

raw´; from 5674; a *crossing*-place (of a river, a *ford*; of a mountain, a *pass*); abstr. a *transit*, i.e. (fig.) *overwhelming:*— ford, place where ... pass, passage.

4570. מַעְגָּל **ma'gâl**, *mah-gawl´*; or fem.

מַעְגָּלָה **ma'gâlâh**, *mah-gaw-law´*; from the same as 5696; a *track* (lit. or fig.); also a *rampart* (as *circular*):— going, path, trench, way (l-side l).

4571. מָעַד **mâ'ad**, *maw-ad´*; a prim. root; to *waver:*— make to shake, slide, slip.

מוֹעֵד **mô'êd**. See 4150.

4572. מַעֲדַי **Ma'âday**, *mah-ad-ah´-ee*; from 5710; *ornamental*; *Maadai*, an Isr.:— Maadai.

4573. מַעֲדְיָה **Ma'adyâh**, *mah-ad-yaw´*; from 5710 and 3050; *ornament of Jah*; *Maadjah*, an Isr.:— Maadiah. Comp. 4153.

4574. מַעֲדָן **ma'âdân**, *mah-ad-awn´*; or (fem.)

מַעֲדַנָּה **ma'âdannâh**, *mah-ad-an-naw´*; from 5727; a *delicacy* or (abstr.) *pleasure* (adv. *cheerfully*):— dainty, delicately, delight.

4575. מַעֲדַנָּה **ma'âdannâh**, *mah-ad-an-naw´*; by tran. from 6029; a *bond*, i.e. *group:*— influence.

4576. מַעְדֵּר **ma'dêr**, *mah-dare´*; from 5737; a (weeding) *hoe:*— mattock.

4577. מְעָה **me'âh** (Chald.), *meh-aw´*; or

מְעָא **me'â'** (Chald.), *meh-aw´*; corresp. to 4578; only in plur. the *bowels:*— belly.

4578. מֵעֶה **mê'âh**, *may-aw´*; from an unused root prob. mean. to *be soft*; used only in plur. the *intestines*, or (collect.) the *abdomen*, fig. *sympathy*; by impl. a *vest*; by extens. the *stomach*, the *uterus* (or of men, the seat of generation), the *heart* (fig.):— belly, bowels, × heart, womb.

4579. מֵעָה **mê'âh**, *may-aw´*; fem. of 4578; the *belly*, i.e. (fig.) interior:— gravel.

4580. מָעוֹג **mâ'ôwg**, *maw-ogue´*; from 5746; a *cake* of bread (with 3934 a *table-buffoon*, i.e. *parasite*):— cake, feast.

4581. מָעוֹז **mâ'ôwz**, *maw-oze´* (also

מָעוּז **mâ'ûwz**, *maw-ooz´*); or

מָעֹז **mâ'ôz**, *maw-oze´* (also

מָעֻז **mâ'uz**, *maw-ooz´*); from 5810; a *fortified* place; fig. a *defence:*— force, fort (-ress), rock, strength (-en), (× most) strong (hold).

4582. מָעוֹךְ **Mâ'owk**, *maw-oke´*; from 4600; *oppressed*; *Maok*, a Philistine:— Maoch.

4583. מָעוֹן **mâ'ôwn**, *maw-ohn´*; or

מָעִין **mâ'îyn** (1 Chron. 4:41), *maw-een´*; from the same as 5772; an *abode*, of God (the Tabernacle or the Temple), men (their home) or animals (their lair); hence, a *retreat* (asylum):— den, dwelling (l-l place), habitation.

4584. מָעוֹן **Mâ'ôwn**, *maw-ohn´*; the same as 4583; a *residence*; *Maon*, the name of an Isr. and of a place in Pal.:— Maon, Maonites. Comp. 1010, 4586.

4585. מְעוֹנָה **me'ôwnâh**, *meh-o-naw´*; or

4583. מְעֹנָה **meʻônâh**, meh-o-naw'; fem. of 4583, and mean. the same:— den, habitation, (dwelling) place, refuge.

4586. מְעוּנִי **Meʻûwnîy**, meh-oo-nee'; or

מְעִינִי **Meʻîynîy**, meh-ee-nee'; prob. patrial from 4584; a Meünite, or inhab. of Maon (only in plur.):— Mehunim (-s), Meunim.

4587. מְעוֹנֹתַי **Meʻôwnôthay**, meh-o-no-thah'-ee; plur. of 4585; habitative; Meonothai, an Isr.:— Meonothai.

4588. מָעוּף **mâʻûwph**, maw-off'; from 5774 in the sense of covering with shade [comp. 4155]; darkness:— dimness.

4589. מָעוֹר **mâʻôwr**, maw-ore'; from 5783; nakedness, i.e. (in plur.) the pudenda:— nakedness.

מָעוֹז **mâʻôz**. See 4581.

מָעוּז **mâʻûz**. See 4581.

4590. מַעַזְיָה **Maʻazyâh**, mah-az-yaw'; or

מַעַזְיָהוּ **Maʻazyâhûw**, mah-az-yaw'-hoo; prob. from 5756 (in the sense of protection) and 3050; rescue of Jah; Maazjah, the name of two Isr.:— Maaziah.

4591. מָעַט **mâʻaṭ**, maw-at'; a prim. root; prop. to pare off, i.e. lessen; intr. to be (or caus. to make) small or few (or fig. ineffective):— suffer to decrease, diminish, (be, x borrow a, give, make) few (in number, -ness), gather least (little), be (seem) little, (x give the) less, be minished, bring to nothing.

4592. מְעַט **meʻaṭ**, meh-at'; or

מְעָט **meʻâṭ**, meh-awt'; from 4591; a little or few (often adv. or compar.):— almost, (some, very) few (-er, -est), lightly, little (while), (very) small (matter, thing), some, soon, x very.

4593. מָעֹט **mâʻôṭ**, maw-ote'; pass. adj. of 4591; thinned (as to the edge), i.e. sharp:— wrapped up.

4594. מַעֲטֶה **maʻăṭeh**, mah-at-eh'; from 5844; a vestment:— garment.

4595. מַעֲטָפָה **maʻăṭâphâh**, mah-at-aw-faw'; from 5848; a cloak:— mantle.

4596. מְעִי **meʻîy**, meh-ee'; from 5753; a pile of rubbish (as contorted), i.e. a ruin (comp. 5856):— heap.

4597. מָעַי **Mâʻay**, maw-ah'-ee; prob. from 4578; sympathetic; Maai, an Isr.:— Maai.

4598. מְעִיל **meʻîyl**, meh-eel'; from 4603 in the sense of covering; a robe (i.e. upper and outer garment):— cloke, coat, mantle, robe.

מֵעִים **mêʻîym**. See 4578.

מְעִין **meʻîyn** (Chald.). See 4577.

4599. מַעְיָן **maʻyân**, mah-yawn'; or

מַעְיְנוֹ **maʻyᵉnôw** (Psa. 114:8) mah-yen-o'; or (fem.)

מַעְיָנָה **maʻyânâh**, mah-yaw-naw'; from 5869 (as a denom. in the sense of a spring); a fountain (also collect.), fig. a source (of satisfaction):— fountain, spring, well.

מְעִינִי **Meʻîynîy**. See 4586.

4600. מָעַךְ **mâʻak**, maw-ak'; a prim. root; to press, i.e. to pierce, emasculate, handle:— bruised, stuck, be pressed.

4601. מַעֲכָה **Maʻăkâh**, mah-ak-aw'; or

מַעֲכָת **Maʻăkâth** (Josh. 13:13), mah-ak-awth'; from 4600; depression; Maakah (or Maakath), the name of a place in Syria, also of a Mesopotamian, of three Isr., and of four Israelitesses and one Syrian woman:— Maachah, Maachathites. See also 1038.

4602. מַעֲכָתִי **Maʻăkâthîy**, mah-ak-aw-thee'; patrial from 4601; a Maakathite, or inhab. of Maakah:— Maachathite.

4603. מָעַל **mâʻal**, maw-al'; a prim. root; prop. to cover up; used only fig. to act covertly, i.e. treacherously:— transgress, (commit, do a) trespass (-ing).

4604. מַעַל **maʻal**, mah'-al; from 4603; treachery, i.e. sin:— falsehood, grievously, sore, transgression, trespass, x very.

4605. מַעַל **maʻal**, mah'al; from 5927; prop. the upper part, used only adv. with pref. upward, above, overhead, from the top, etc.:— above, exceeding (-ly), forward, on (x very) high, over, up (-on, -ward), very.

מַעַל **mêʻal**. See 5921.

4606. מֵעָל **mêʻal** (Chald.), may-awl'; from 5954; (only in plur. as sing.) the setting (of the sun):— going down.

4607. מֹעַל **môʻal**, mo'-al; from 5927; a raising (of the hands):— lifting up.

4608. מַעֲלֶה **maʻăleh**, mah-al-eh'; from 5927; an elevation, i.e. (concr.) acclivity or platform; abstr. (the relation or state) a rise or (fig.) priority:— ascent, before, chiefest, cliff, that goeth up, going up, hill, mounting up, stairs.

4609. מַעֲלָה **maʻălâh**, mah-al-aw'; fem. of 4608; elevation, i.e. the act (lit. a journey to a higher place, fig. a thought arising), or (concr.) the condition (lit. a step or grade-mark, fig. a superiority of station); spec. a climactic progression (in certain Psalms):— things that come up, (high) degree, deal, go up, stair, step, story.

4610. מַעֲלֵה עַקְרַבִּים **Maʻăleh ʻAqrabbîym**, mah-al-ay' ak-rab-beem'; from 4608 and (the plur. of) 6137; Steep of Scorpions, a place in the Desert:— Maalehaccrabim, the ascent (going up) of Akrabbim.

4611. מַעֲלָל **maʻălâl**, mah-al-awl'; from 5953; an act (good or bad):— doing, endeavour, invention, work.

4612. מַעֲמָד **maʻămâd**, mah-am-awd'; from 5975; (fig.) a position:— attendance, office, place, state.

4613. מָעֳמָד **moʻŏmâd**, moh-om-awd'; from 5975; lit. a foothold:— standing.

4614. מַעֲמָסָה **maʻămâçâh**, mah-am-aw-saw'; from 6006; burdensomeness:— burdensome.

4615. מַעֲמָק **maʻămâq**, mah-am-awk'; from 6009; a deep:— deep, depth.

4616. מַעַן **maʻan**, mah'-an; from 6030; prop. heed, i.e. purpose; used only adv. on account of (as a motive or an aim), teleologically in order that:— because of, to the end (intent) that, for (to, ... 's sake), + lest, that, to.

4617. מַעֲנֶה **maʻăneh**, mah-an-eh'; from

6030; a reply (favorable or contradictory):— answer, x himself.

4618. מַעֲנָה **maʻănâh**, mah-an-aw'; from 6031, in the sense of depression or tilling; a furrow:— + acre, furrow.

מְעֹנָה **meʻônâh**. See 4585.

4619. מַעַץ **Maʻats**, mah'-ats; from 6095; closure; Maats, an Isr.:— Maaz.

4620. מַעֲצֵבָה **maʻătsêbâh**, mah-ats-ay-baw'; from 6087; anguish:— sorrow.

4621. מַעֲצָד **maʻătsâd**, mah-ats-awd'; from an unused root mean. to hew; an axe:— ax, tongs.

4622. מַעְצוֹר **maʻtsôwr**, mah-tsore'; from 6113; obj. a hindrance:— restraint.

4623. מַעְצָר **maʻtsâr**, mah-tsawr'; from 6113; subj. control:— rule.

4624. מַעֲקֶה **maʻăqeh**, mah-ak-eh'; from an unused root mean. to repress; a parapet:— battlement.

4625. מַעֲקָשׁ **maʻăqâsh**, mah-ak-awsh'; from 6140; a crook (in a road):— crooked thing.

4626. מַעַר **maʻar**, mah'-ar; from 6168; a nude place, i.e. (lit.) the pudenda, or (fig.) a vacant space:— nakedness, proportion.

4627. מַעֲרָב **maʻărâb**, mah-ar-awb'; from 6148, in the sense of trading; traffic; by impl. mercantile goods:— market, merchandise.

4628. מַעֲרָב **maʻărâb**, mah-ar-awb'; or (fem.)

מַעֲרָבָה **maʻărâbâh**, mah-ar-aw-baw'; from 6150, in the sense of shading; the west (as a region of the evening sun):— west.

4629. מַעֲרֶה **maʻăreh**, mah-ar-eh'; from 6168; a nude place, i.e. a common:— meadows.

4630. מַעֲרָה **maʻărâh**, mah-ar-aw'; fem. of 4629; an open spot:— army [from the marg.].

4631. מְעָרָה **meʻârâh**, meh-aw-raw'; from 5783; a cavern (as dark):— cave, den, hole.

4632. מְעָרָה **Meʻârâh**, meh-aw-raw'; the same as 4631; cave; Meärah, a place in Pal.:— Mearah.

4633. מַעֲרָךְ **maʻărâk**, mah-ar-awk'; from 6186; an arrangement, i.e. (fig.) mental disposition:— preparation.

4634. מַעֲרָכָה **maʻărâkâh**, mah-ar-aw-kaw'; fem. of 4633; an arrangement; concr. a pile; spec. a military array:— army, fight, be set in order, ordered place, rank, row.

4635. מַעֲרֶכֶת **maʻăreketh**, mah-ar-eh'-keth; from 6186; an arrangement, i.e. (concr.) a pile (of loaves):— row, shewbread.

4636. מַעֲרֹם **maʻărôm**, mah-ar-ome'; from 6191, in the sense of stripping; bare:— naked.

4637. מַעֲרָצָה **maʻărâtsâh**, mah-ar-aw-tsaw'; from 6206; violence:— terror.

4638. מַעֲרָת **Maʻărâth**, mah-ar-awth'; a form of 4630; waste; Maarath, a place in Pal.:— Maarath.

4639. מַעֲשֶׂה **maʻaseh**, mah-as-eh'; from 6213; an action (good or bad); gen. a *transaction;* abstr. *activity;* by impl. a *product* (spec. a *poem*) or (gen.) *property*:— act, art, + bakemeat, business, deed, do (-ing), labour, thing made, ware of making, occupation, thing offered, operation, possession, × well, (lhandy-, needle-, net-l) work (ing, -manship), wrought.

4640. מַעַשׂ **Ma'say**, *mah-as-ah´ee;* from 6213; *operative; Maasai,* an Isr.:— Maasiai.

4641. מַעֲשֵׂיָה **Ma'âsêyâh**, *mah-as-ay-yaw´;* or

מַעֲשֵׂיָהוּ **Ma'âsêyâhûw**, *mah-as-ay-yaw´-hoo;* from 4639 and 3050; *work of Jah; Maasejah,* the name of sixteen Isr.:— Maaseiah.

4642. מַעֲשַׁקָּה **ma'âshaqqâh**, *mah-ash-ak-kaw´;* from 6231; *oppression:*— oppression, × oppressor.

4643. מַעֲשֵׂר **ma'âsêr**, *mah-as-ayr´;* or

מַעֲשַׂר **ma'âsar**, *mah-as-ar´;* and (in plur.) fem.

מַעֲשְׂרָה **ma'asrâh**, *mah-as-raw´;* from 6240; a *tenth;* espec. a *tithe:*— tenth (part), tithe (-ing).

4644. מֹף **Môph**, *mofe;* of Eg. or.; *Moph,* the capital of Lower Egypt:— Memphis. Comp. 5297.

מְפִבֹשֶׁת **M^ephîbôsheth**. See 4648.

4645. מִפְגָּע **miphgâ'**, *mif-gaw´;* from 6293; an *object of attack:*— mark.

4646. מַפָּח **mappâch**, *map-pawkh´;* from 5301; a *breathing out* (of life), i.e. expiring:— giving up.

4647. מַפֻּחַ **mappûach**, *map-poo´-akh;* from 5301; the *bellows* (i.e. *blower*) of a forge:— bellows.

4648. מְפִיבֹשֶׁת **M^ephîybôsheth**, *mef-ee-bo´-sheth;* or

מְפִבֹשֶׁת **M^ephîbôsheth**, *mef-ee-bo´-sheth;* prob. from 6284 and 1322; *dispeller of shame* (i.e. of Baal); *Mephibosheth,* the name of two Isr.:— Mephibosheth.

4649. מֻפִּים **Muppîym**, *moop-peem´;* a plur. appar. from 5130; *wavings; Muppim,* an Isr.:— Muppim. Comp. 8206.

4650. מֵפִיץ **mêphîyts**, *may-feets´;* from 6327; a *breaker,* i.e. mallet:— maul.

4651. מַפָּל **mappâl**, *map-pawl´;* from 5307; a *falling* off, i.e. chaff; also something *pendulous,* i.e. a flap:— flake, refuse.

4652. מִפְלָאָה **miphlâ'âh**, *mif-law-aw´;* from 6381; a *miracle:*— wondrous work.

4653. מִפְלַגָּה **miphlaggâh**, *mif-lag-gaw´;* from 6385; a *classification:*— division.

4654. מַפָּלָה **mappâlâh**, *map-paw-law´;* or

מַפֵּלָה **mappêlâh**, *map-pay-law´;* from 5307; something *fallen,* i.e. a *ruin:*— ruin (-ous).

4655. מִפְלָט **miphlât**, *mif-lawt´;* from 6403; an *escape:*— escape.

4656. מִפְלֶצֶת **miphletseth**, *mif-leh´-tseth;* from 6426; a *terror,* i.e. an idol:— idol.

4657. מִפְלָשׂ **miphlâs**, *mif-lawce´;* from

an unused root mean. to *balance;* a *poising:*— balancing.

4658. מַפֶּלֶת **mappeleth**, *map-peh´-leth;* from 5307; *fall,* i.e. *decadence;* concr. a *ruin;* spec. a *carcase:*— carcase, fall, ruin.

4659. מִפְעָל **miph'âl**, *mif-awl´;* or (fem.)

מִפְעָלָה **miph'âlâh**, *mif-aw-law´;* from 6466; a *performance:*— work.

4660. מַפָּץ **mappâts**, *map-pawts´;* from 5310; a *smiting* to pieces:— slaughter.

4661. מַפֵּץ **mappêts**, *map-pates´;* from 5310; a *smiter,* i.e. a war *club:*— battle ax.

4662. מִפְקָד **miphqâd**, *mif-kawd´;* from 6485; an *appointment,* i.e. *mandate;* concr. a designated *spot;* spec. a *census:*— appointed place, commandment, number.

4663. מִפְקָד **Miphqâd**, *mif-kawd´;* the same as 4662; *assignment; Miphkad,* the name of a gate in Jerusalem:— Miphkad.

4664. מִפְרָץ **miphrâts**, *mif-rawts´;* from 6555; a *break* (in the shore), i.e. a *haven:*— breach.

4665. מִפְרֶקֶת **miphreketh**, *mif-reh´-keth;* from 6561; prop. a *fracture,* i.e. *joint* (*vertebra*) of the neck:— neck.

4666. מִפְרָשׂ **miphrâs**, *mif-rawce´;* from 6566; an *expansion:*— that which ... spreadest forth, spreading.

4667. מִפְשָׂעָה **miphsâ'âh**, *mif-saw-aw´;* from 6585; a *stride,* i.e. (by euphem.) the *crotch:*— buttocks.

מֹפֵת **môphêth**. See 4159.

4668. מַפְתֵּחַ **maphtêach**, *maf-tay´-akh;* from 6605; an *opener,* i.e. a *key:*— key.

4669. מִפְתָּח **miphtâch**, *mif-tawkh´;* from 6605; an *aperture,* i.e. (fig.) *utterance:*— opening.

4670. מִפְתָּן **miphtân**, *mif-tawn´;* from the same as 6620; a *stretcher,* i.e. a *sill:*— threshold.

4671. מֹץ **môts**, *motes;* or

מוֹץ **môwts** (Zeph. 2:2), *motes;* from 4160; *chaff* (as *pressed* out, i.e. *winnowed* or [rather] *threshed* loose):— chaff.

4672. מָצָא **mâtsâ'**, *maw-tsaw´;* a prim. root; prop. to *come forth to,* i.e. *appear* or *exist;* tran. to *attain,* i.e. *find* or *acquire;* fig. to *occur, meet* or *be present:*— + be able, befall, being, catch, × certainly, (cause to) come (on to, to, to hand), deliver, be enough (cause to) find (-ing, occasion, out), get (hold upon), × have (here), be here, hit, be left, light (up-) on, meet (with), × occasion serve, (be) present, ready, speed, suffice, take hold on.

מֹצָא **môtsâ'**. See 4161.

4673. מַצָּב **matstsâb**, *mats-tsawb´;* from 5324; a fixed *spot;* fig. an *office,* a military *post:*— garrison, station, place where ... stood.

4674. מֻצָּב **mutstsâb**, *moots-tsawb´;* from 5324; a *station,* i.e. military *post:*— mount.

4675. מַצָּבָה **matstsâbâh**, *mats-tsaw-baw´;* or

מִצָּבָה **mitstsâbâh**, *mits-tsaw-baw´;* fem. of 4673; a military *guard:*— army, garrison.

4676. מַצֵּבָה **matstsêbâh**, *mats-tsay-baw´;* fem. (caus.) part. of 5324; something *stationed,* i.e. a *column* or (memorial *stone*); by anal. an *idol:*— garrison, (standing) image, pillar.

4677. מְצֹבָיָה **M^etsôbâyâh**, *mets-o-baw-yaw´;* appar. from 4672 and 3050; *found of Jah; Metsobajah,* a place in Pal.:— Mesobaite.

4678. מַצֶּבֶת **matstsebeth**, *mats-tseh´-beth;* from 5324; something *stationary,* i.e. a monumental *stone;* also the *stock* of a tree:— pillar, substance.

4679. מְצַד **m^etsad**, *mets-ad´;* or

מְצָד **m^etsâd**, *mets-awd´;* or (fem.)

מְצָדָה **m^etsâdâh**, *mets-aw-daw´;* from 6679; a *fastness* (as a *covert* of ambush):— castle, fort, (strong) hold, munition.

מְצֻדָה **m^etsûdâh**. See 4686.

4680. מָצָה **mâtsâh**, *maw-tsaw´;* a prim. root; to *suck* out; by impl. to *drain,* to *squeeze* out:— suck, wring (out).

4681. מֹצָה **Môtsâh**, *mo-tsaw´;* act. part. fem. of 4680; *drained; Motsah,* a place in Pal.:— Mozah.

4682. מַצָּה **matstsâh**, *mats-tsaw´;* from 4711 in the sense of *greedily* devouring for sweetness; prop. *sweetness;* concr. *sweet* (i.e. not soured or bittered with yeast); spec. an *unfermented cake* or loaf, or (ellip.) the festival of *Passover* (because no leaven was then used):— unleavened (bread, cake), without leaven.

4683. מַצָּה **matstsâh**, *mats-tsaw´;* from 5327; a *quarrel:*— contention, debate, strife.

4684. מַצְהָלָה **matshâlâh**, *mats-haw-law´;* from 6670; a *whinnying* (through impatience for battle or lust):— neighing.

4685. מָצֹד **mâtsôwd**, *maw-tsode´;* or (fem.)

מְצוֹדָה **m^etsôwdâh**, *mets-o-daw´;* or

מְצֹדָה **m^etsôdâh**, *mets-o-daw´;* from 6679; a *net* (for *capturing* animals or fishes); also (by interch. for 4679) a *fastness* or (besieging) *tower:*— bulwark, hold, munition, net, snare.

4686. מָצוּד **mâtsûwd**, *maw-tsood´;* or (fem.)

מְצוּדָה **m^etsûwdâh**, *mets-oo-daw´;* or

מְצֻדָה **m^etsûdâh**, *mets-oo-daw´;* for 4685; a *net,* or (abstr.) *capture;* also a *fastness:*— castle, defence, fort (-ress), (strong) hold, be hunted, net, snare, strong place.

4687. מִצְוָה **mitsvâh**, *mits-vaw´;* from 6680; a *command,* whether human or divine (collect. the *Law*):— (which was) commanded (-ment), law, ordinance, precept.

4688. מְצוֹלָה **m^etsôwlâh**, *mets-o-law´;* or

מְצֹלָה **m^etsôlâh**, *mets-o-law´;* also

מְצוּלָה **m^etsûwlâh**, *mets-oo-law´;* or

מְצֻלָה **mᵉtsûlâh**, *mets-oo-law´*; from the same as 6683; a *deep* place (of water or mud):— bottom, deep, depth.

4689. מָצוֹק **mâtsôwq**, *maw-tsoke´*; from 6693; a *narrow* place, i.e. (abstr. and fig.) *confinement* or *disability*:— anguish, distress, straitness.

4690. מָצוּק **mâtsûwq**, *maw-tsook´*; or

מָצֻק **mâtsûq**, *maw-tsook´*; from 6693; something *narrow*, i.e. a *column* or *hill*top:— pillar, situate.

4691. מְצוּקָה **mᵉtsûwqâh**, *mets-oo-kaw´*; or

מְצֻקָה **mᵉtsûqâh**, *mets-oo-kaw´*; fem. of 4690; *narrowness*, i.e. (fig.) *trouble*:— anguish, distress.

4692. מָצוֹר **mâtsôwr**, *maw-tsore´*; or

מָצוּר **mâtsûwr**, *maw-tsoor´*; from 6696; something *hemming* in, i.e. (obj.) a *mound* (of besiegers), (abstr.) a *siege*, (fig.) *distress*; or (subj.) a *fastness*:— besieged, bulwark, defence, fenced, fortress, siege, strong (hold), tower.

4693. מָצוֹד **mâtsôwr**, *maw-tsore´*; the same as 4692 in the sense of a *limit*; *Egypt* (as the *border* of Pal.):— besieged places, defence, fortified.

4694. מְצוּרָה **mᵉtsûwrâh**, *mets-oo-raw´*; or

מְצֻרָה **mᵉtsûrâh**, *mets-oo-raw´*; fem. of 4692; a *hemming* in, i.e. (obj.) a *mound* (of siege), or (subj.) a *rampart* (of protection), (abstr.) *fortification*:— fenced (city), fort, munition, strong hold.

4695. מַצּוּת **matstsûwth**, *mats-tsooth´*; from 5327; a *quarrel*:— that contended.

4696. מֵצַח **mêtsach**, *may´-tsakh*; from an unused root mean. to *be clear*, i.e. *conspicuous*; the *forehead* (as open and *prominent*):— brow, forehead, + impudent.

4697. מִצְחָה **mitschâh**, *mits-khaw´*; from the same as 4696; a *shin-piece* of armor (as *prominent*), only plur.:— greaves.

מְצֹלָה **mᵉtsôlâh**. See 4688.

מְצֻלָה **mᵉtsûlâh**. See 4688.

4698. מְצִלָּה **mᵉtsillâh**, *mets-il-law´*; from 6750; a *tinkler*, i.e. a *bell*:— bell.

4699. מְצֻלָּה **mᵉtsullâh**, *mets-ool-law´*; from 6751; *shade*:— bottom.

4700. מְצֵלָה **mᵉtsêleth**, *mets-ay´-leth*; from 6750; (only dual) double *tinklers*, i.e. cymbals:— cymbals.

4701. מִצְנֶפֶת **mitsnepheth**, *mits-neh´-feth*; from 6801; a *tiara*, i.e. official *turban* (of a king or high priest):— diadem, mitre.

4702. מַצָּע **matstsâ'**, *mats-tsaw´*; from 3331; a *couch*:— bed.

4703. מִצְעָד **mits'âd**, *mits-awd´*; from 6805; a *step*; fig. *companionship*:— going, step.

4704. מִצְעִירָה **mitstsᵉˆîyrâh**, *mits-tseh-ee-raw´*; fem. of 4705; prop. *littleness*; concr. *diminutive*:— little.

4705. מִצְעָר **mits'âr**, *mits-awr´*; from 6819; *petty* (in size or number); adv. a *short* (time):— little one (while), small.

4706. מִצְעָר **Mits'âr**, *mits-awr´*; the same

as 4705; *Mitsar*, a peak of Lebanon:— Mizar.

4707. מִצְפֶּה **mitspeh**, *mits-peh´*; from 6822; an *observatory*, espec. for military purposes:— watch tower.

4708. מִצְפֶּה **Mitspeh**, *mits-peh´*; the same as 4707; *Mitspeh*, the name of five places in Pal.:— Mizpeh, watch tower. Comp. 4709.

4709. מִצְפָּה **Mitspah**, *mits-paw´*; fem. of 4708; *Mitspah*, the name of two places in Pal.:— Mitspah. [This seems rather to be only an orthographic var. of 4708 when "in pause".]

4710. מִצְפֻּן **mitspûn**, *mits-poon´*; from 6845; a *secret* (place or thing, perh. *treasure*):— hidden thing.

4711. מָצַץ **mâtsats**, *maw-tsats´*; a prim. root; to *suck*:— milk.

מוּצָקָה **mûtsâqâh**. See 4166.

4712. מֵצַר **mêtsar**, *may-tsar´*; from 6896; something *tight*, i.e. (fig.) *trouble*:— distress, pain, strait.

מָצֻק **mâtsûq**. See 4690.

מְצֻקָה **mᵉtsûqâh**. See 4691.

מְצֻרָה **mᵉtsûrâh**. See 4694.

4713. מִצְרִי **Mitsrîy**, *mits-ree´*; from 4714; a *Mitsrite*, or inhab. of Mitsrajim:— Egyptian, of Egypt.

4714. מִצְרַיִם **Mitsrayim**, *mits-rah´-yim*; dual of 4693; *Mitsrajim*, i.e. Upper and Lower Egypt:— Egypt, Egyptians, Mizraim.

4715. מִצְרֵף **mitsrêph**, *mits-rafe´*; from 6884; a *crucible*:— fining pot.

4716. מַק **maq**, *mak*; from 4743; prop. a *melting*, i.e. *putridity*:— rottenness, stink.

4717. מַקָּבָה **maqqâbâh**, *mak-kaw-baw´*; from 5344; prop. a *perforatrix*, i.e. a *hammer* (as *piercing*):— hammer.

4718. מַקֶּבֶת **maqqebeth**, *mak-keh´-beth*; from 5344; prop. a *perforator*, i.e. a *hammer* (as *piercing*); also (intr.) a *perforation*, i.e. a *quarry*:— hammer, hole.

4719. מַקֵּדָה **Maqqêdâh**, *mak-kay-daw´*; from the same as 5348 in the denom. sense of *herding* (comp. 5349); *fold*; *Makkedah*, a place in Pal.:— Makkedah.

4720. מִקְדָּשׁ **miqdâsh**, *mik-dawsh´*; or

מִקְּדָּשׁ **miqqᵉdâsh** (Exod. 15:17), *mik-ked-awsh´*; from 6942; a *consecrated* thing or place, espec. a *palace*, *sanctuary* (whether of Jehovah or of idols) or *asylum*:— chapel, hallowed part, holy place, sanctuary.

4721. מַקְהֵל **maqhêl**, *mak-hale´*; or (fem.)

מַקְהֵלָה **maqhêlâh**, *mak-hay-law´*; from 6950; an *assembly*:— congregation.

4722. מַקְהֵלֹת **Maqhêlôth**, *mak-hay-loth´*; plur. of 4721 (fem.); *assemblies*; *Makheloth*, a place in the Desert:— Makheloth.

4723. מִקְוֶה **miqveh**, *mik-veh´*; or

מִקְוֵה **miqvêh** (1 Kings 10:28) *mik-vay´*; or

מִקְוֵא° **miqvê'** (2 Chron. 1:16), *mik-*

vay´; from 6960; something *waited* for, i.e. *confidence* (obj. or subj.); also a *collection*, i.e. (of water) a *pond*, or (of men and horses) a *caravan* or *drove*:— abiding, gathering together, hope, linen yarn, plenty [of water], pool.

4724. מִקְוָה **miqvâh**, *mik-vaw´*; fem. of 4723; a *collection*, i.e. (of water) a *reservoir*:— ditch.

4725. מָקוֹם **mâqôwm**, *maw-kome´*; or

מָקֹם **mâqôm**, *maw-kome´*; also (fem.)

מְקוֹמָה **mᵉqôwmâh**, *mek-o-mah´*; or

מְקֹמָה **mᵉqômâh**, *mek-o-mah´*; from 6965; prop. a *standing*, i.e. a *spot*; but used widely of a *locality* (gen. or spec.); also (fig.) of a *condition* (of body or mind):— country, × home, × open, place, room, space, × whither [-soever].

4726. מָקוֹר **mâqôwr**, *maw-kore´*; or

מָקֹר **mâqôr**, *maw-kore´*; from 6979; prop. something *dug*, i.e. a (gen.) *source* (of water, even when naturally flowing; also of tears, blood [by euphem. of the female *pudenda*]; fig. of happiness, wisdom, progeny):— fountain, issue, spring, well (-spring).

4727. מִקָּח **miqqâch**, *mik-kawkh´*; from 3947; *reception*:— taking.

4728. מַקָּחָה **maqqâchâh**, *mak-kaw-khaw´*; from 3947; something *received*, i.e. *merchandise* (purchased):— ware.

4729. מִקְטָר **miqtâr**, *mik-tawr´*; from 6999; something to *fume* (incense) on, i.e. a *hearth* place:— to burn ... upon.

מְקַטְּרָה **mᵉqattᵉrâh**. See 6999.

4730. מִקְטֶרֶת **miqtereth**, *mik-teh´-reth*; fem. of 4729; something to *fume* (incense) in, i.e. a *coal-pan*:— censer.

4731. מַקֵּל **maqqêl**, *mak-kale*; or (fem.)

מַקְּלָה **maqqᵉlâh**, *mak-kel-aw´*; from an unused root mean. appar. to *germinate*; a *shoot*, i.e. *stick* (with leaves on, or for walking, striking, guiding, divining):— rod, [hand-] staff.

4732. מִקְלוֹת **Miqlôwth**, *mik-lohth´*; (or perh. *mik-kel-ohth*); plur. of (fem.) 4731; *rods*; *Mikloth*, a place in the Desert:— Mikloth.

4733. מִקְלָט **miqlât**, *mik-lawt´*; from 7038 in the sense of *taking* in; an *asylum* (as a *receptacle*):— refuge.

4734. מִקְלַעַת **miqla'ath**, *mik-lah´-ath*; from 7049; a *sculpture* (prob. in bas-relief):— carved (figure), carving, graving.

מָקֹם **mâqôm**. See 4725.

מְקֹמָה **mᵉqômâh**. See 4725.

4735. מִקְנֶה **miqneh**, *mik-neh´*; from 7069; something *bought*, i.e. *property*, but only live *stock*; abstr. *acquisition*:— cattle, flock, herd, possession, purchase, substance.

4736. מִקְנָה **miqnâh**, *mik-naw´*; fem. of 4735; a *buying*, i.e. *acquisition*; concr. a piece of *property* (land or living); also the *sum* paid:— (he that is) bought, possession, piece, purchase.

4737. מִקְנֵיָהוּ **Miqnêyâhûw**, *mik-nay-*

yaw'-hoo; from 4735 and 3050; *possession of Jah; Miknejah,* an Isr.:— Mikneiah.

4738. מִקְסָם **miqçâm,** *mik-sawm';* from 7080; an *augury:*— divination.

4739. מָקֵץ **Mâqats,** *maw-kats';* from 7112; *end; Makats,* a place in Pal.:— Makaz.

4740. מַקְצוֹעַ **maqtsôwa',** *mak-tso'-ah;* or

מַקְצֹעַ **maqtsôa',** *mak-tso'-ah;* or (fem.)

מַקְצֹעָה **maqtsô'âh,** *mak-tso-aw';* from 7106 in the denom. sense of *bending;* an *angle* or recess:— corner, turning.

4741. מַקְצֻעָה **maqtsû'âh,** *mak-tsoo-aw';* from 7106; a *scraper,* i.e. a carving *chisel:*— plane.

4742. מְקֻצְעָה **mᵉquts'âh,** *mek-oots-aw';* from 7106 in the denom. sense of *bending;* an *angle:*— corner.

4743. מָקַק **mâqaq,** *maw-kak';* a prim. root; to *melt;* fig. to *flow, dwindle, vanish:*— consume away, be corrupt, dissolve, pine away.

מָקוֹר **mâqôr.** See 4726.

4744. מִקְרָא **miqrâ',** *mik-raw';* from 7121; something *called* out, i.e. a public *meeting* (the act, the persons, or the place); also a *rehearsal:*— assembly, calling, convocation, reading.

4745. מִקְרֶה **miqreh,** *mik-reh';* from 7136; something *met* with, i.e. an *accident* or *fortune:*— something befallen, befalleth, chance, event, hap (-peneth).

4746. מְקָרֶה **mᵉqâreh,** *mek-aw-reh';* from 7136; prop. something *meeting,* i.e. a *frame* (of timbers):— building.

4747. מְקֵרָה **mᵉqêrâh,** *mek-ay-raw';* from the same as 7119; a *cooling* off:— × summer.

מוֹקֵשׁ **môqêsh.** See 4170.

4748. מִקְשֶׁה **miqsheh,** *mik-sheh';* from 7185 in the sense of *knotting* up round and hard; something *turned* (rounded), i.e. a *curl* (of tresses):— × well [set] hair.

4749. מִקְשָׁה **miqshâh,** *mik-shaw';* fem. of 4748; *rounded* work, i.e. moulded by *hammering* (repoussé):— beaten (out of one piece, work), upright, whole piece.

4750. מִקְשָׁה **miqshâh,** *mik-shaw';* denom. from 7180; lit. a *cucumbered* field, i.e. a *cucumber* patch:— garden of cucumbers.

4751. מַר **mar,** *mar;* or (fem.)

מָרָה **mârâh,** *maw-raw';* from 4843; *bitter* (lit. or fig.); also (as noun) *bitterness,* or (adv.) *bitterly:*— + angry, bitter (-ly, -ness), chafed, discontented, × great, heavy.

4752. מַר **mar,** *mar;* from 4843 in its orig. sense of *distillation;* a *drop:*— drop.

4753. מֹר **môr,** *mor;* or

מוֹר **môwr,** *more;* from 4843; *myrrh* (as *distilling* in drops, and also as *bitter*):— myrrh.

4754. מָרָא **mârâ',** *maw-raw';* a prim. root; to *rebel;* hence, (through the idea

of *maltreating*) to *whip,* i.e. *lash* (self with wings, as the ostrich in running):— be filthy, lift up self.

4755. מָרָא **Mârâ',** *maw-raw';* for 4751 fem.; *bitter; Mara,* a symbol. name of Naomi:— Mara.

4756. מָרֵא **mârê'** (Chald.), *maw-ray';* from a root corresp. to 4754 in the sense of *domineering;* a *master:*— lord, Lord.

מֹרָא **môrâ'.** See 4172.

4757. מְראֹדַך בַּלְאָדָן **Mᵉrô'dak Bal'âdân,** *mer-o-dak' bal-aw-dawn';* of for. der.; *Merodak'-Baladan,* a Bab. king:— Merodach-baladan. Comp. 4781.

4758. מַרְאֶה **mar'eh,** *mar-eh';* from 7200; a *view* (the act of seeing); also an *appearance* (the thing seen), whether (real) a *shape* (espec. if handsome, *comeliness;* often plur. the *looks*), or (ment.) a *vision:*— × apparently, appearance (-reth), × as soon as beautiful (-ly), countenance, fair, favoured, form, goodly, to look (up) on (to), look [-eth], pattern, to see, seem, sight, visage, vision.

4759. מַרְאָה **mar'âh,** *mar-aw';* fem. of 4758; a *vision;* also (caus.) a *mirror:*— looking glass, vision.

4760. מֻרְאָה **mur'âh,** *moor-aw';* appar. fem. pass. caus. part. of 7200; something *conspicuous,* i.e. the *craw* of a bird (from its *prominence*):— crop.

מִרְאוֹן **Mᵉr'ôwn.** See 8112.

4761. מַרְאָשָׁה **mar'âshâh,** *mar-aw-shaw';* denom. from 7218; prop. *headship,* i.e. (plur. for collect.) *dominion:*— principality.

4762. מַרְאֵשָׁה **Mar'êshâh,** *mar-ay-shaw';* or

מָרֵשָׁה **Marêshâh,** *mar-ay-shaw';* formed like 4761; *summit; Mareshah,* the name of two Isr. and of a place in Pal.:— Mareshah.

4763. מְרַאֲשָׁה **mᵉra'äshâh,** *mer-ah-ash-aw';* formed like 4761; prop. a *headpiece,* i.e. (plur. for adv.) *at* (or *as*) the *head-rest* (or pillow):— bolster, head, pillow. Comp. 4772.

4764. מֵרָב **Mêrâb,** *may-rawb';* from 7231; *increase; Merab,* a daughter of Saul:— Merab.

4765. מַרְבַד **marbad,** *mar-bad';* from 7234; a *coverlet:*— covering of tapestry.

4766. מַרְבֶּה **marbeh,** *mar-beh';* from 7235; prop. *increasing;* as noun, *greatness,* or (adv.) *greatly:*— great, increase.

4767. מִרְבָּה **mirbâh,** *meer-baw';* from 7235; *abundance,* i.e. a great quantity:— much.

4768. מַרְבִּית **marbîyth,** *mar-beeth';* from 7235; a *multitude;* also *offspring;* spec. *interest* (on capital):— greatest part, greatness, increase, multitude.

4769. מַרְבֵּץ **marbêts,** *mar-bates';* from 7257; a *reclining* place, i.e. *fold* (for flocks):— couching place, place to lie down.

4770. מַרְבֵּק **marbêq,** *mar-bake';* from an unused root mean. to *tie* up; a *stall* (for cattle):— × fat (-ted), stall.

מֹרַג **môrag.** See 4173.

4771. מַרְגּוֹעַ **margôwa',** *mar-go'-ah;* from 7280; a *resting* place:— rest.

4772. מַרְגְּלָה **margᵉlâh,** *mar-ghel-aw';* denom. from 7272; (plur. for collect.) a *footpiece,* i.e. (adv.) *at the foot,* or (direct.) the *foot* itself:— feet. Comp. 4763.

4773. מַרְגֵּמָה **margêmâh,** *mar-gay-maw';* from 7275; a *stone*-heap:— sling.

4774. מַרְגֵּעָה **margê'âh,** *mar-gay-aw';* from 7280; *rest:*— refreshing.

4775. מָרַד **mârad,** *maw-rad';* a prim. root; to *rebel:*— rebel (-lious).

4776. מְרַד **mᵉrad** (Chald.), *mer-ad';* from a root corresp. to 4775; *rebellion:*— rebellion.

4777. מֶרֶד **mered,** *meh'-red;* from 4775; *rebellion:*— rebellion.

4778. מֶרֶד **Mered,** *meh'-red;* the same as 4777; *Mered,* an Isr.:— Mered.

4779. מָרָד **mârâd** (Chald.), *maw-rawd';* from the same as 4776; *rebellious:*— rebellious.

4780. מַרְדּוּת **mardûwth,** *mar-dooth';* from 4775; *rebelliousness:*— × rebellious.

4781. מְרֹדָך **Mᵉrôdâk,** *mer-o-dawk';* of for. der.; *Merodak,* a Bab. idol:— Merodach. Comp. 4757.

4782. מָרְדְּכַי **Mordᵉkay,** *mor-dek-ah'-ee;* of for. der.; *Mordecai,* an Isr.:— Mordecai.

4783. מֻרְדָּף **murdâph,** *moor-dawf';* from 7291; *persecuted:*— persecuted.

4784. מָרָה **mârâh,** *maw-raw';* a prim. root; to *be* (caus. *make*) *bitter* (or unpleasant); (fig.) to *rebel* (or resist; caus. to *provoke*):— bitter, change, be disobedient, disobey, grievously, provocation, provoke (-ing), (be) rebel (against, -lious).

4785. מָרָה **Mârâh,** *maw-raw';* the same as 4751 fem.; *bitter; Marah,* a place in the Desert:— Marah.

מֹרֶה **Môreh.** See 4175.

4786. מֹרָה **môrâh,** *mo-raw';* from 4843; *bitterness,* i.e. (fig.) *trouble:*— grief.

4787. מָרָּה **morrâh,** *mor-raw';* a form of 4786; *trouble:*— bitterness.

4788. מָרוּד **mârûwd,** *maw-rood';* from 7300 in the sense of *maltreatment;* an *outcast;* (abstr.) *destitution:*— cast out, misery.

4789. מֵרוֹז **Mêrôwz,** *may-roze';* of uncert. der.; *Meroz,* a place in Pal.:— Meroz.

4790. מְרוֹחַ **mᵉrôwach,** *mer-o-akh';* from 4799; *bruised,* i.e. *emasculated:*— broken.

4791. מָרוֹם **mârôwm,** *maw-rome';* from 7311; *altitude,* i.e. concr. (an *elevated place*), abstr. (*elevation,* fig. (*elation*), or adv. (*aloft*):— (far) above, dignity, haughty, height, (most, on) high (one, place), loftily, upward.

4792. מֵרוֹם **Mêrôwm,** *may-rome';* formed like 4791; *height; Merom,* a lake in Pal.:— Merom.

4793. מֵרוֹץ **mêrôwts,** *may-rotes';* from 7323; a *run* (the trial of speed):— race.

4794. מְרוּצָה **mᵉrûwtsâh**, *mer-oo-tsaw'*; or

מְרֻצָה **mᵉrûtsâh**, *mer-oo-tsaw'*; fem. of 4793; a *race* (the act), whether the manner or the progress:— course, running. Comp. 4835.

4795. מָרוּק **mârûwq**, *maw-rook'*; from 4838; prop. *rubbed*; but used abstr. a *rubbing* (with perfumery):— purification.

מְרוֹר **mᵉrôwr**. See 4844.

מְרוֹרָה **mᵉrôwrâh**. See 4846.

4796. מָרוֹה **Mârôwth**, *maw-rohth'*; plur. of 4751 fem.; *bitter* springs; *Maroth*, a place in Pal.:— Maroth.

4797. מִרְזַח **mirzach**, *meer-zakh'*; from an unused root mean. to *scream*; a *cry*, i.e. (of joy), a *revel*:— banquet.

4798. מַרְזֵחַ **marzêach**, *mar-zay'-akh*; formed like 4797; a *cry*, i.e. (of grief) a *lamentation*:— mourning.

4799. מָרַח **mârach**, *maw-rakh'*; a prim. root; prop. to *soften* by rubbing or pressure; hence, (medicinally) to *apply* as an emollient:— lay for a plaister.

4800. מֶרְחָב **merchâb**, *mer-khawb'*; from 7337; *enlargement*, either lit. (an *open space*, usually in a good sense), or fig. (*liberty*):— breadth, large place (room).

4801. מֶרְחָק **merchâq**, *mer-khawk'*; from 7368; *remoteness*, i.e. (concr.) a *distant* place; often (adv.) *from afar*:— (a-, dwell in, very) far (country, off). See also 1023.

4802. מַרְחֶשֶׁת **marchesheth**, *mar-kheh'-sheth*; from 7370; a *stew-pan*:— fryingpan.

4803. מָרַט **mâraṭ**, *maw-rat'*; a prim. root; to *polish*; by impl. to *make bald* (the head), to *gall* (the shoulder); also, to *sharpen*:— bright, furbish, (have his) hair (be) fallen off, peeled, pluck off (hair).

4804. מְרַט **mᵉraṭ** (Chald.), *mer-at'*; corresp. to 4803; to *pull* off:— be plucked.

4805. מְרִי **mᵉrîy**, *mer-ee'*; from 4784; *bitterness*, i.e. (fig.) *rebellion*; concr. *bitter*, or *rebellious*:— bitter, (most) rebel (-lion, -lious).

4806. מְרִיא **mᵉrîy'**, *mer-ee'*; from 4754 in the sense of *grossness*, through the idea of *domineering* (comp. 4756); *stall-fed*; often (as noun) a *beeve*:— fat (fed) beast (cattle, -ling).

4807. מְרִיב בַּעַל **Mᵉrîyb Ba'al**, *mer-eeb' bah'-al*; from 7378 and 1168; *quarreller of Baal*; *Merib-Baal*, an epithet of Gideon:— Merib-baal. Comp. 4810.

4808. מְרִיבָה **mᵉrîybâh**, *mer-ee-baw'*; from 7378; *quarrel*:— provocation, strife.

4809. מְרִיבָה **Mᵉrîybâh**, *mer-ee-baw'*; the same as 4808; *Meribah*, the name of two places in the Desert:— Meribah.

4810. מְרִי בַעַל **Mᵉrîy Ba'al**, *mer-ee' bah'-al*; from 4805 and 1168; *rebellion of* (i.e. *against*) *Baal*; *Meri-Baal*, an epithet of Gideon:— Meri-baal. Comp. 4807.

4811. מְרָיָה **Mᵉrâyâh**, *mer-aw-yaw'*; from 4784; *rebellion*; *Merajah*, an Isr.:— Meraiah. Comp. 3236.

מֹרִיָּה **Môrîyâh**. See 4179.

4812. מְרָיוֹת **Mᵉrâyôwth**, *mer-aw-yohth'*; plur. of 4811; *rebellious*; *Merajoth*, the name of two Isr.:— Meraioth.

4813. מִרְיָם **Miryâm**, *meer-yawm'*; from 4805; *rebelliously*; *Mirjam*, the name of two Israelitesses:— Miriam.

4814. מְרִירוּת **mᵉrîyrûwth**, *mer-ee-rooth'*; from 4843; *bitterness*, i.e. (fig.) *grief*:— bitterness.

4815. מְרִירִי **mᵉrîyrîy**, *mer-ee-ree'*; from 4843; *bitter*, i.e. *poisonous*:— bitter.

4816. מֹרֶךְ **môrek**, *mo'-rek*; perh. from 7401; *softness*, i.e. (fig.) *fear*:— faintness.

4817. מֶרְכָּב **merkâb**, *mer-kawb'*; from 7392; a *chariot*; also a *seat* (in a vehicle):— chariot, covering, saddle.

4818. מֶרְכָּבָה **merkâbâh**, *mer-kaw-baw'*; fem. of 4817; a *chariot*:— chariot. See also 1024.

4819. מַרְכֹּלֶת **markôleth**, *mar-ko'-leth*; from 7402; a *mart*:— merchandise.

4820. מִרְמָה **mirmâh**, *meer-maw'*; from 7411 in the sense of *deceiving*; *fraud*:— craft, deceit (-ful, -fully), false, feigned, guile, subtilly, treachery.

4821. מִרְמָה **Mirmâh**, *meer-maw'*; the same as 4820; *Mirmah*, an Isr.:— Mirma.

4822. מְרֵמוֹת **Mᵉrêmôwth**, *mer-ay-mohth'*; plur. from 7311; *heights*; *Meremoth*, the name of two Isr.:— Meremoth.

4823. מִרְמָס **mirmâç**, *meer-mawce'*; from 7429; *abasement* (the act or the thing):— tread (down)-ing, (to be) trodden (down) under foot.

4824. מְרֹנֹתִי **Mêrônôthîy**, *may-ro-no-thee'*; patrial from an unused noun; a *Meronothite*, or inhab. of some (otherwise unknown) *Meronoth*:— Meronothite.

4825. מֶרֶס **Mereç**, *meh'-res*; of for. der.; *Meres*, a Pers.:— Meres.

4826. מַרְסְנָא **Marçᵉnâ'**, *mar-sen-aw'*; of for. der.; *Marsena*, a Pers.:— Marsena.

4827. מֵרַע **mêra'**, *may-rah'*; from 7489; used as (abstr.) noun, *wickedness*:— do mischief.

4828. מֵרֵעַ **mêrêa'**, *may-ray'-ah*; from 7462 in the sense of *companionship*; a *friend*:— companion, friend.

4829. מִרְעֶה **mir'eh**, *meer-eh'*; from 7462 in the sense of *feeding*; *pasture* (the place or the act); also the *haunt* of wild animals:— feeding place, pasture.

4830. מִרְעִית **mir'îyth**, *meer-eeth'*; from 7462 in the sense of *feeding*; *pasturage*; concr. a *flock*:— flock, pasture.

4831. מַרְעָלָה **Mar'âlâh**, *mar-al-aw'*; from 7477; perh. *earthquake*; *Maralah*, a place in Pal.:— Maralah.

4832. מַרְפֵּא **marpê'**, *mar-pay'*; from 7495; prop. *curative*, i.e. lit. (concr.) a *medicine*, or (abstr.) a *cure*; fig. (concr.) *deliverance*, or (abstr.) *placidity*:— ((in-)) cure (-able), healing (-lth), remedy, sound, wholesome, yielding.

4833. מִרְפָּשׂ **mirpâs**, *meer-paws'*; from 7515; *muddled* water:— that which ... have fouled.

4834. מָרַץ **mârats**, *maw-rats'*; a prim. root; prop. to *press*, i.e. (fig.) to be *pungent* or *vehement*; to *irritate*:— embolden, be forcible, grievous, sore.

4835. מְרֻצָה **mᵉrûtsâh**, *mer-oo-tsaw'*; from 7533; *oppression*:— violence. See also 4794.

4836. מַרְצֵעַ **martsêa'**, *mar-tsay'-ah*; from 7527; an *awl*:— aul.

4837. מַרְצֶפֶת **martsepheth**, *mar-tseh'-feth*; from 7528; a *pavement*:— pavement.

4838. מָרַק **mâraq**, *maw-rak'*; a prim. root; to *polish*; by impl. to *sharpen*; also to *rinse*:— bright, furbish, scour.

4839. מָרָק **mârâq**, *maw-rawk'*; from 4838; *soup* (as if a *rinsing*):— broth. See also 6564.

4840. מֶרְקָח **merqâch**, *mer-kawkh'*; from 7543; a *spicy* herb:— × sweet.

4841. מֶרְקָחָה **merqâchâh**, *mer-kaw-khaw'*; fem. of 4840; abstr. a *seasoning* (with spicery); concr. an *unguent-kettle* (for preparing spiced oil):— pot of ointment, × well.

4842. מִרְקַחַת **mirqachath**, *meer-kakh'-ath*; from 7543; an *aromatic unguent*; also an *unguent-pot*:— prepared by the apothecaries' art, compound, ointment.

4843. מָרַר **mârar**, *maw-rar'*; a prim. root; prop. to *trickle* [see 4752]; but used only as a denom. from 4751; to be (caus. *make*) *bitter* (lit. or fig.):— (be, be in, deal, have, make) bitter (-ly, -ness), be moved with choler, (be, have sorely, it) grieved (-eth), provoke, vex.

4844. מְרֹר **mᵉrôr**, *mer-ore'*; or

מְרוֹר **mᵉrôwr**, *mer-ore'*; from 4843; a *bitter* herb:— bitter (-ness).

4845. מְרֵרָה **mᵉrêrâh**, *mer-ay-raw'*; from 4843; *bile* (from its bitterness):— gall.

4846. מְרֹרָה **mᵉrôrâh**, *mer-o-raw'*; or

מְרוֹרָה **mᵉrôwrâh**, *mer-o-raw'*; from 4843; prop. *bitterness*; concr. a *bitter thing*; spec. *bile*; also *venom* (of a serpent):— bitter (thing), gall.

4847. מְרָרִי **Mᵉrârîy**, *mer-aw-ree'*; from 4843; *bitter*; *Merari*, an Isr.:— Merari. See also 4848.

4848. מְרָרִי **Mᵉrârîy**, *mer-aw-ree'*; from 4847; a *Merarite* (collect.), or desc. of Merari:— Merarites.

מָרֵשָׁה **Mârêshâh**. See 4762.

4849. מִרְשַׁעַת **mirsha'ath**, *meer-shah'-ath*; from 7561; a female *wicked doer*:— wicked woman.

4850. מְרָתַיִם **Mᵉrâthayim**, *mer-aw-thah'-yim*; dual of 4751 fem.; *double bitterness*; *Merathajim*, an epithet of Bab.:— Merathaim.

4851. מַשׁ **Mash**, *mash*; of for. der.; *Mash*, a son of Aram, and the people desc. from him:— Mash.

4852. מֵשָׁא **Mêshâ'**, *may-shaw'*; of for. der.; *Mesha*, a place in Arabia:— Mesha.

4853. מַשָּׂא **massâ'**, *mas-saw'*; from 5375; a *burden*; spec. *tribute*, or (abstr.) *porterage*; fig. an *utterance*, chiefly a *doom*, espec. *singing*; ment. *desire*:—

burden, carry away, prophecy, × they set, song, tribute.

4854. מַשָּׂא **Massâ'**, *mas-saw'*; the same as 4853; *burden; Massa*, a son of Ishmael:— Massa.

4855. מַשָּׁא **mashshâ'**, *mash-shaw'*; from 5383; a *loan;* by impl. *interest* on a debt:— exaction, usury.

4856. מַשּׂוֹ **massô'**, *mas-so'*; from 5375; *partiality* (as a *lifting* up):— respect.

4857. מַשְׁאָב **mash'âb**, *mash-awb'*; from 7579; a *trough* for cattle to drink from:— place of drawing water.

4858. מַשָּׂאָה **massâ'âh**, *mas-saw-aw'*; from 5375; a *conflagration* (from the *rising* of smoke):— burden.

4859. מַשָּׁאָה **mashshâ'âh**, *mash-shaw-aw'*; fem. of 4855; a *loan:*— × any [-thing], debt.

מַשָּׁאָה **mashshû'âh**. See 4876.

4860. מַשָּׁאוֹן **mashshâ'ôwn**, *mash-shaw-ohn'*; from 5377; *dissimulation:*— deceit.

4861. מִשְׁאָל **Mish'âl**, *mish-awl'*; from 7592; *request; Mishal*, a place in Pal.:— Mishal, Misheal. Comp. 4913.

4862. מִשְׁאָלָה **mish'âlâh**, *mish-aw-law'*; from 7592; a *request:*— desire, petition.

4863. מִשְׁאֶרֶת **mish'ereth**, *mish-eh'-reth;* from 7604 in the orig. sense of *swelling;* a *kneading-trough* (in which the dough *rises*):— kneading trough, store.

4864. מַשְׂאֵת **mas'êth**, *mas-ayth';* from 5375; prop. (abstr.) a *raising* (as of the hands in prayer), or *rising* (of flame); fig. an *utterance;* concr. a *beacon* (as *raised*); a *present* (as taken), *mess,* or *tribute;* fig. a *reproach* (as a burden):— burden, collection, sign of fire, (great) flame, gift, lifting up, mess, oblation, reward.

מוֹשָׁב **môshâb**. See 4186.

מְשֻׁבָה **meshûbâh**. See 4878.

4865. מִשְׁבְּצָה **mishbetsâh**, *mish-bets-aw';* from 7660; a *brocade;* by anal. a (reticulated) *setting* of a gem:— ouch, wrought.

4866. מִשְׁבֵּר **mishbêr**, *mish-bare';* from 7665; the *orifice* of the womb (from which the fetus *breaks* forth):— birth, breaking forth.

4867. מִשְׁבָּר **mishbâr**, *mish-bawr';* from 7665; a *breaker* (of the sea):— billow, wave.

4868. מִשְׁבָּת **mishbâth**, *mish-bawth';* from 7673; *cessation,* i.e. destruction:— sabbath.

4869. מִשְׂגָּב **misgâb**, *mis-gawb';* from 7682; prop. a *cliff* (or other *lofty* or *inaccessible* place); abstr. *altitude;* fig. a *refuge:*— defence, high fort (tower), refuge.

4869'. מִשְׂגָּב **misgâb**, *mis-gawb'; Misgab,* a place in Moab:— Misgab.

4870. מִשְׁגֶּה **mishgeh**, *mish-gay';* from 7686; an *error:*— oversight.

4871. מָשָׁה **mâshâh**, *maw-shaw';* a prim. root; to *pull* out (lit. or fig.):— draw (out).

4872. מֹשֶׁה **Môsheh**, *mo-sheh';* from 4871; *drawing* out (of the water), i.e. *rescued; Mosheh,* the Isr. lawgiver:— Moses.

4873. מֹשֶׁה **Môsheh** (Chald.), *mo-sheh';* corresp. to 4872:— Moses.

4874. מַשֶּׁה **mashsheh**, *mash-sheh';* from 5383; a *debt:*— + creditor.

4875. מְשׁוֹאָה **meshôw'âh**, *meh-o-aw';* or

מְשֹׁאָה **meshô'âh**, *mesh-o-aw';* from the same as 7722; (a) *ruin,* abstr. (the act) or concr. (the wreck):— desolation, waste.

4876. מַשּׁוּאָה **mashshûw'âh**, *mash-shoo-aw';* or

מַשֻּׁאָה **mashshû'âh**, *mash-shoo-aw';* for 4875; *ruin:*— desolation, destruction.

4877. מְשׁוֹבָב **Meshôwbâb**, *mesh-o-bawb';* from 7725; *returned; Meshobab,* an Isr.:— Meshobab.

4878. מְשׁוּבָה **meshûwbâh**, *mesh-oo-baw';* or

מְשֻׁבָה **meshûbâh**, *mesh-oo-baw';* from 7725; *apostasy:*— backsliding, turning away.

4879. מְשׁוּגָה **meshûwgâh**, *mesh-oo-gaw';* from an unused root mean. to *stray; mistake:*— error.

4880. מָשׁוֹט **mâshôwṭ**, *maw-shote';* or

מִשּׁוֹט **mishshôwṭ**, *mish-shote';* from 7751; an *oar:*— oar.

4881. מְשׂוּכָה **mesûwkâh**, *mes-oo-kaw';* or

מְשׂוּכָה **mesûkâh**, *mes-oo-kaw';* from 7753; a *hedge:*— hedge.

4882. מְשׁוּסָה **meshûçâh**, *mesh-oo-saw';* from an unused root mean. to *plunder; spoilation:*— spoil.

4883. מַשּׂוֹר **massôwr**, *mas-sore';* from an unused root mean. to *rasp;* a *saw:*— saw.

4884. מְשׂוּרָה **mesûwrâh**, *mes-oo-raw';* from an unused root mean. appar. to *divide;* a *measure* (for liquids):— measure.

4885. מָשׂוֹשׂ **mâsôws**, *maw-soce';* from 7797; *delight,* concr. (the cause or object) or abstr. (the feeling):— joy, mirth, rejoice.

4886. מָשַׁח **mâshach**, *maw-shakh';* a prim. root; to *rub* with oil, i.e. to *anoint;* by impl. to *consecrate;* also to *paint:*— anoint, paint.

4887. מְשַׁח **meshach** (Chald.), *mesh-akh';* from a root corresp. to 4886; *oil:*— oil.

4888. מִשְׁחָה **mishchâh**, *meesh-khaw';* or

מָשְׁחָה **moshchâh**, *mosh-khaw';* from 4886; *unction* (the act); by impl. a consecratory *gift:*— (to be) anointed (-ing), ointment.

4889. מַשְׁחִית **mashchîyth**, *mash-kheeth';* from 7843; *destructive,* i.e. (as noun) *destruction,* lit. (spec. a *snare*) or fig. (*corruption*):— corruption, (to) destroy (-ing), destruction, trap, × utterly.

4890. מִשְׂחָק **mischâq**, *mis-khawk';* from 7831; a *laughing-stock:*— scorn.

4891. מִשְׁחָר **mishchâr**, *mish-khawr';* from 7836 in the sense of day *breaking; dawn:*— morning.

4892. מַשְׁחֵת **mashchêth**, *mash-khayth';* for 4889; *destruction:*— destroying.

4893. מִשְׁחָת **mishchâth**, *mish-khawth';* or

מָשְׁחָת **moshchâth**, *mosh-khawth';* from 7843; *disfigurement:*— corruption, marred.

4894. מִשְׁטוֹחַ **mishṭôwach**, *mish-to'-akh;* or

מִשְׁטַח **mishṭach**, *mish-takh';* from 7849; a *spreading*-place:— (to) spread (forth, -ing, upon).

4895. מַשְׂטֵמָה **masṭêmâh**, *mas-tay-maw';* from the same as 7850; *enmity:*— hatred.

4896. מִשְׁטָר **mishṭâr**, *mish-tawr';* from 7860; *jurisdiction:*— dominion.

4897. מֶשִׁי **meshîy**, *meh'-shee;* from 4871; *silk* (as *drawn* from the cocoon):— silk.

מֻשִׁי **Mushîy**. See 4187.

4898. מְשֵׁיזַבְאֵל **Meshêyzab'êl**, *mesh-ay-zab-ale';* from an equiv. to 7804 and 410; *delivered of God; Meshezabel,* an Isr.:— Meshezabeel.

4899. מָשִׁיחַ **mâshîyach**, *maw-shee'-akh;* from 4886; *anointed;* usually a *consecrated* person (as a king, priest, or saint); spec. the *Messiah:*— anointed, Messiah.

4900. מָשַׁךְ **mâshak**, *maw-shak';* a prim. root; to *draw,* used in a great variety of applications (incl. to *sow,* to *sound,* to *prolong,* to *develop,* to *march,* to *remove,* to *delay,* to *be tall.* etc.):— draw (along, out), continue, defer, extend, forbear, × give, handle, make (pro-, sound) long, × sow, scatter, stretch out.

4901. מֶשֶׁךְ **meshek**, *meh'shek;* from 4900; a *sowing;* also a *possession:*— precious, price.

4902. מֶשֶׁךְ **Meshek**, *meh'-shek;* the same in form as 4901, but prob. of for. der.; *Meshek,* a son of Japheth, and the people desc. from him:— Mesech, Meshech.

4903. מִשְׁכַּב **mishkab** (Chald.), *mishkab';* corresp. to 4904; a *bed:*— bed.

4904. מִשְׁכָּב **mishkâb**, *mish-kawb';* from 7901; a *bed* (fig. a *bier*); abstr. *sleep;* by euphem. carnal *intercourse:*— bed ([-chamber]), couch, lieth (lying) with.

מְשׂוּכָה **mesûkâh**. See 4881.

4905. מַשְׂכִּיל **maskîyl**, *mas-keel';* from 7919; *instructive,* i.e. a *didactic* poem:— Maschil.

מַשְׂכִּים **mashkîym**. See 7925.

4906. מַשְׂכִּית **maskîyth**, *mas-keeth';* from the same as 7906; a *figure* (carved on stone, the wall, or any object); fig. *imagination:*— conceit, image (-ry), picture, × wish.

4907. מִשְׁכַּן **mishkan** (Chald.), *mishkan';* corresp. to 4908; *residence:*— habitation.

4908. מִשְׁכָּן **mishkân**, *mish-kawn';* from 7931; a *residence* (incl. a shepherd's *hut,* the *lair* of animals, fig. the *grave;* also the *Temple*); spec. the *Tabernacle* (prop. its wooden *walls*):— dwelleth, dwelling (place), habitation, tabernacle, tent.

4909. מַשְׂכֹּרֶת **maskôreth**, *mas-koh´-reth*; from 7936; *wages* or a *reward*:— reward, wages.

4910. מָשַׁל **mâshal**, *maw-shal´*; a prim. root; to *rule*:— (have, make to have) dominion, governor, × indeed, reign, (bear, cause to, have) rule (-ing, -r), have power.

4911. מָשַׁל **mâshal**, *maw-shal´*; denom. from 4912; to *liken*, i.e. (tran.) to use fig. language (an allegory, adage, song or the like); intr. to *resemble*:— be (-come) like, compare, use (as a) proverb, speak (in proverbs), utter.

4912. מָשָׁל **mâshâl**, *maw-shawl´*; appar. from 4910 in some orig. sense of *superiority* in mental action; prop. a pithy *maxim*, usually of metaph. nature; hence, a *simile* (as an adage, poem, discourse):— byword, like, parable, proverb.

4913. מָשָׁל **Mâshâl**, *maw-shawl´*; for 4861; *Mashal*, a place in Pal.:— Mashal.

4914. מְשֹׁל **mᵉshôl**, *mesh-ol´*; from 4911; a *satire*:— byword.

4915. מֹשֶׁל **môshel**, *mo´-shel*; (1) from 4910; *empire*; (2) from 4911; a *parallel*:— dominion, like.

מִשְׁלוֹשׁ **mishlôwsh**. See 7969.

4916. מִשְׁלוֹחַ **mishlôwach**, *mish-lo´-akh*; or

מִשְׁלֹחַ **mishlôach**, *mish-lo´-akh*; also

מִשְׁלָח **mishlâch**, *mish-lawkh´*; from 7971; a *sending* out, i.e. (abstr.) *presentation* (favorable), or *seizure* (unfavorable); also (concr.) a place of *dismissal*, or a *business* to be discharged:— to lay, to put, sending (forth), to set.

4917. מִשְׁלַחַת **mishlachath**, *mish-lakh´-ath*; fem. of 4916; a *mission*, i.e. (abstr.) and favorable) *release*, or (concr. and unfavorable) an *army*:— discharge, sending.

4918. מְשֻׁלָּם **Mᵉshullâm**, *mesh-ool-lawm´*; from 7999; *allied*; *Meshullam*, the name of seventeen Isr.:— Meshullam.

4919. מְשֻׁלֵּמוֹת **Mᵉshillêmôwth**, *mesh-il-lay-mohth´*; plur. from 7999; *reconciliations*; *Meshillemoth*, an Isr.:— Meshillemoth. Comp. 4921.

4920. מְשֶׁלֶמְיָה **Mᵉshelemyâh**, *mesh-eh-lem-yaw´*; or

מְשֶׁלֶמְיָהוּ **Mᵉshelemyâhûw**, *mesh-eh-lem-yaw´-hoo*; from 7999 and 3050; *ally of Jah*; *Meshelemjah*, an Isr.:— Meshelemiah.

4921. מְשִׁלֵּמִית **Mᵉshillêmîyth**, *mesh-il-lay-meeth´*; from 7999; *reconciliation*; *Meshillemith*, an Isr.:— Meshillemith. Comp. 4919.

4922. מְשֻׁלֶּמֶת **Mᵉshullemeth**, *mesh-ool-leh´-meth*; fem. of 4918; *Meshullemeth*, an Israelitess:— Meshullemeth.

4923. מְשַׁמָּה **mᵉshammâh**, *mesh-am-maw´*; from 8074; a *waste* or *amazement*:— astonishment, desolate.

4924. מַשְׁמָן **mashmân**, *mash-mawn´*; from 8080; *fat*, i.e. (lit. and abstr.) *fatness*; but usually (fig. and concr.) a *rich* dish, a *fertile* field, a *robust* man:— fat (one, -ness, -test, -test place).

4925. מִשְׁמַנָּה **Mishmannâh**, *mish-man-naw´*; from 8080; *fatness*; *Mashmannah*, an Isr.:— Mishmannah.

4926. מִשְׁמָע **mishmâ´**, *mish-maw´*; from 8085; a *report*:— hearing.

4927. מִשְׁמָע **Mishmâ´**, *mish-maw´*; the same as 4926; *Mishma*, the name of a son of Ishmael, and of an Isr.:— Mishma.

4928. מִשְׁמַעַת **mishma'ath**, *mish-mah´-ath*; fem. of 4926; *audience*, i.e. the royal *court*; also *obedience*, i.e. (concr.) a *subject*:— bidding, guard, obey.

4929. מִשְׁמָר **mishmâr**, *mish-mawr´*; from 8104; a *guard* (the man, the post, or the *prison*); fig. a *deposit*; also (as observed) a *usage* (abstr.), or an *example* (concr.):— diligence, guard, office, prison, ward, watch.

4930. מַשְׂמְרָה **masmᵉrâh**, *mas-mer-aw´*; for 4548 fem.; a *peg*:— nail.

4931. מִשְׁמֶרֶת **mishmereth**, *mish-meh´-reth*; fem. of 4929; *watch*, i.e. the act (custody) or (concr.) the *sentry*, the *post*; obj. *preservation*, or (concr.) *safe*; fig. *observance*, i.e. (abstr.) *duty*, or (obj.) a *usage* or *party*:— charge, keep, to be kept, office, ordinance, safeguard, ward, watch.

4932. מִשְׁנֶה **mishneh**, *mish-neh´*; from 8138; prop. a *repetition*, i.e. a *duplicate* (copy of a document), or a *double* (in amount); by impl. a *second* (in order, rank, age, quality or location):— college, copy, double, fatlings, next, second (order), twice as much.

4933. מְשִׁסָּה **mᵉshiççâh**, *mesh-is-saw´*; from 8155; *plunder*:— booty, spoil.

4934. מִשְׁעוֹל **mish'ôwl**, *mish-ole´*; from the same as 8168; a *hollow*, i.e. a narrow passage:— path.

4935. מִשְׁעִי **mish'îy**, *mish-ee´*; prob. from 8159; *inspection*:— to supple.

4936. מִשְׁעָם **Mish'âm**, *mish-awm´*; appar. from 8159; *inspection*; *Misham*, an Isr.:— Misham.

4937. מִשְׁעֵן **mish'ên**, *mish-ane´*; or

מִשְׁעָן **mish'ân**, *mish-awn´*; from 8172; a *support* (concr.), i.e. (fig.) a *protector* or *sustenance*:— stay.

4938. מִשְׁעֵנָה **mish'ênâh**, *mish-ay-naw´*; or

מִשְׁעֶנֶת **mish'eneth**, *mish-eh´-neth*; fem. of 4937; *support* (abstr.), i.e. (fig.) *sustenance* or (concr.) a *walking-stick*:— staff.

4939. מִשְׂפָּח **mispâch**, *mis-pawkh´*; from 5596; *slaughter*:— oppression.

4940. מִשְׁפָּחָה **mishpâchâh**, *mish-paw-khaw´*; from 8192 [comp. 8198]; a *family*, i.e. circle of relatives; fig. a *class* (of persons), a *species* (of animals) or *sort* (of things); by extens. a *tribe* or *people*:— family, kind (-red).

4941. מִשְׁפָּט **mishpât**, *mish-pawt´*; from 8199; prop. a *verdict* (favorable or unfavorable) pronounced judicially, espec. a *sentence* or formal decree (human or [participant's] divine *law*, indiv. or collect.), incl. the act, the place, the suit, the crime, and the penalty; abstr. *justice*, incl. a participant's *right* or *privilege* (statutory or customary), or even a *style*:— + adversary, ceremony, charge, × crime, custom, desert, determination, discretion, disposing, due, fashion, form, to be judged, judgment, just (-ice, -ly), (manner of) law (-ful), manner, measure, (due) order, ordinance, right, sentence, usest, × worthy, + wrong.

4942. מִשְׁפָּת **mishpâth**, *mish-pawth´*; from 8192; a *stall* for cattle (only dual):— burden, sheepfold.

4943. מֶשֶׁק **mesheq**, *meh´-shek*; from an unused root mean. to *hold*; *possession*:— + steward.

4944. מַשָּׁק **mashshâq**, *mash-shawk´*; from 8264; a *traversing*, i.e. rapid *motion*:— running to and fro.

4945. מַשְׁקֶה **mashqeh**, *mash-keh´*; from 8248; prop. *causing to drink*, i.e. a *butler*; by impl. (intr.), *drink* (itself); fig. a *well-watered* region:— butler (-ship), cupbearer, drink (-ing), fat pasture, watered.

4946. מַשְׁקוֹל **mishqôwl**, *mish-kole´*; from 8254; *weight*:— weight.

4947. מַשְׁקוֹף **mashqôwph**, *mash-kofe´*; from 8259 in its orig. sense of *overhanging*; a *lintel*:— lintel.

4948. מִשְׁקָל **mishqâl**, *mish-kawl´*; from 8254; *weight* (numerically estimated); hence, *weighing* (the act):— (full) weight.

4949. מִשְׁקֶלֶת **mishqeleth**, *mish-keh´-leth*; or

מִשְׁקֹלֶת **mishqôleth**, *mish-ko´-leth*; fem. of 4948 or 4947; a *weight*, i.e. a *plummet* (with line attached):— plummet.

4950. מִשְׁקָע **mishqâ´**, *mish-kaw´*; from 8257; a *settling* place (of water), i.e. a pond:— deep.

4951. מִשְׂרָה **misrâh**, *mis-raw´*; from 8280; *empire*:— government.

4952. מִשְׁרָה **mishrâh**, *mish-raw´*; from 8281 in the sense of *loosening*; *maceration*, i.e. steeped *juice*:— liquor.

4953. מַשְׁרוֹקִי **mashrôwqîy** (Chald.), *mash-ro-kee´*; from a root corresp. to 8319; a (musical) *pipe* (from its *whistling* sound):— flute.

4954. מִשְׁרָעִי **Mishrâ'îy**, *mish-raw-ee´*; patrial from an unused noun from an unused root; prob. mean. to *stretch* out; *extension*; a *Mishraite*, or inhab. (collect.) of Mishra:— Mishraites.

4955. מִשְׂרָפָה **misrâphâh**, *mis-raw-faw´*; from 8313; *combustion*, i.e. *cremation* (of a corpse), or *calcination* (of lime):— burning.

4956. מִשְׂרְפוֹת מַיִם **Misrᵉphôwth Mayim**, *mis-ref-ohth´ mah´-yim*; from the plur. of 4955 and 4325; *burnings of water*; *Misrephoth-Majim*, a place in Pal.:— Misrephoth-mayim.

4957. מַשְׂרֵקָה **Masrêqâh**, *mas-ray-kaw´*; a form for 7796 used denom.; *vineyard*; *Masrekah*, a place in Idumæa:— Masrekah.

4958. מַשְׂרֵת **masrêth**, *mas-rayth´*; appar. from an unused root mean. to *perforate*, i.e. hollow out; a *pan*:— pan.

4959. מָשַׁשׁ **mâshash**, *maw-shash´*; a prim. root; to *feel* of; by impl. to *grope*:— feel, grope, search.

4960. מִשְׁתֶּה **mishteh**, *mish-teh´*; from 8354; *drink*, by impl. *drinking* (the act); also (by impl.) a *banquet* or (gen.) feast:— banquet, drank, drink, feast (I-ed), -ing).

4961. מִשְׁתֶּה **mishteh** (Chald.), *mish-teh´*; corresp. to 4960; a *banquet:*— banquet.

4962. מַת **math**, *math;* from the same as 4970; prop. an *adult* (as of full length); by impl. a *man* (only in the plur.):— + few, × friends, men, persons, × small.

4963. מַתְבֵּן **mathbên**, *math-bane´*; denom. from 8401; *straw* in the heap:— straw.

4964. מֶתֶג **metheg**, *meh-theg;* from an unused root mean. to *curb;* a *bit:*— bit, bridle.

4965. מֶתֶג הָאַמָּה **Metheg hâ-'Ammâh**, *meh´-theg haw-am-maw´;* from 4964 and 520 with the art. interposed; *bit of the metropolis; Metheg-ha-Ammah*, an epithet of Gath:— Metheg-ammah.

4966. מָתוֹק **mâthôwq**, *maw-thoke´;* or

מָתוּק **mâthûwq**, *maw-thook´;* from 4985; *sweet:*— sweet (-er, -ness).

4967. מְתוּשָׁאֵל **Mᵉthûwshâ'êl**, *meth-oo-shaw-ale´;* from 4962 and 410, with the rel. interposed; *man who* (is) *of God; Methushaël*, an antediluvian patriarch:— Methusael.

4968. מְתוּשֶׁלַח **Mᵉthûwshelach**, *meth-oo-sheh´-lakh;* from 4962 and 7973; *man of a dart; Methushelach*, an antediluvian patriarch:— Methuselah.

4969. מָתַח **mâthach**, *maw-thakh´;* a prim. root; to *stretch* out:— spread out.

4970. מָתַי **mâthay**, *maw-thah´ee;* from an unused root mean. to *extend;* prop. *extent* (of time); but used only adv. (espec. with other particles pref.), *when* (either rel. or interrog.):— long, when.

מְתִים **mᵉthîym**. See 4962.

4971. מַתְכֹּנֶת **mathkôneth**, *math-ko´-neth;* or

מַתְכֻּנֶת **mathkûneth**, *math-koo´-neth;* from 8505 in the transferred sense of *measuring; proportion* (in size, number or ingredients):— composition, measure, state, tale.

4972. מַתְלָאָה **mattᵉlâ'âh**, *mat-tel-aw-aw´;* from 4100 and 8513; *what a trouble!:*— what a weariness.

4973. מְתַלְּעָה **mᵉthalleᵃâh**, *meth-al-leh-aw´;* contr. from 3216; prop. a *biter*, i.e. a *tooth:*— cheek (jaw) tooth, jaw.

4974. מְתֹם **mᵉthôm**, *meth-ohm´;* from 8552; *wholesomeness;* also (adv.) *completely:*— men [by reading 4962], soundness.

מְתֶן **Methen**. See 4981.

4975. מֹתֶן **môthen**, *mo´-then;* from an unused root mean. to *be slender;* prop. the *waist* or small of the back; only in plur. the *loins:*— + greyhound, loins, side.

4976. מַתָּן **mattân**, *mat-tawn´;* from 5414; a *present:*— gift, to give, reward.

4977. מַתָּן **Mattân**, *mat-tawn´;* the same

as 4976; *Mattan*, the name of a priest of Baal, and of an Isr.:— Mattan.

4978. מַתְּנָא **mattᵉnâ'** (Chald.), *mat-ten-aw´;* corresp. to 4979:— gift.

4979. מַתָּנָה **mâttânâh**, *mat-taw-naw´;* fem. of 4976; a *present;* spec. (in a good sense), a sacrificial *offering*, (in a bad sense) a *bribe:*— gift.

4980. מַתָּנָה **Mattânâh**, *mat-taw-naw´;* the same as 4979; *Mattanah*, a place in the Desert:— Mattanah.

4981. מִתְנִי **Mithnîy**, *mith-nee´;* prob. patrial from an unused noun mean. *slenderness;* a *Mithnite*, or inhab. of Methen:— Mithnite.

4982. מַתְּנַי **Mattᵉnay**, *mat-ten-ah´ee;* from 4976; *liberal; Mattenai*, the name of three Isr.:— Mattenai.

4983. מַתַּנְיָה **Mattanyâh**, *mat-tan-yaw´;* or

מַתַּנְיָהוּ **Mattanyâhûw**, *mat-tan-yaw´-hoo;* from 4976 and 3050; *gift of Jah; Mattanjah*, the name of ten Isr.:— Mattaniah.

מָתְנַיִם **mothnayim**. See 4975.

4984. מִתְנַשֵּׂא **mithnassê'**, *mith-nas-say´;* from 5375; (used as abstr.) supreme *exaltation:*— exalted.

4985. מָתַק **mâthaq**, *maw-thak´;* a prim. root; to *suck*, by impl. to *relish*, or (intr.) *be sweet:*— be (made, × take) sweet.

4986. מֶתֶק **metheq**, *meh´-thek;* from 4985; fig. *pleasantness* (of discourse):— sweetness.

4987. מֹתֶק **môtheq**, *mo´-thek;* from 4985; *sweetness:*— sweetness.

4988. מָתָק **mâthâq**, *maw-thawk´;* from 4985; a *dainty*, i.e. (gen.) *food:*— feed sweetly.

4989. מִתְקָה **Mithqâh**, *mith-kaw´;* fem. of 4987; *sweetness; Mithkah*, a place in the Desert:— Mithcah.

4990. מִתְרְדָת **Mithrᵉdâth**, *mith-red-awth´;* of Pers. or.; *Mithredath*, the name of two Pers.:— Mithredath.

4991. מַתָּת **mattâth**, *mat-tawth´;* fem. of 4976 abb.; a *present:*— gift.

4992. מַתַּתָּה **Mattattâh**, *mat-tat-taw´;* for 4993; *gift of Jah; Mattattah*, an Isr.:— Mattathah.

4993. מַתִּתְיָה **Mattithyâh**, *mat-tith-yaw´;* or

מַתִּתְיָהוּ **Mattithyâhûw**, *mat-tith-yaw´-hoo;* from 4991 and 3050; *gift of Jah; Mattithjah*, the name of four Isr.:— Mattithiah.

נ

4994. נָא **nâ'**, *naw;* a prim. particle of incitement and entreaty, which may usually be rendered *I pray, now* or *then;* added mostly to verbs (in the imperative or future), or to interj., occasionally to an adv. or conjunc.:— I beseech (pray) thee (you), go to, now, oh.

4995. נָא **nâ'**, *naw;* appar. from 5106 in the sense of *harshness* from refusal; prop. *tough*, i.e. *uncooked* (flesh):— raw.

4996. נֹא **Nô'**, *no;* of Eg. or.; *No* (i.e.

Thebes), the capital of Upper Egypt:— No. Comp. 528.

4997. נֹאד **nô'd**, *node;* or

נֹאוד **nô'wd**, *node;* also (fem.)

נֹאדָה **nô'dâh**, *no-daw´;* from an unused root of uncert. signif.; a (skin or leather) *bag* (for fluids):— bottle.

נְאֹדְרִי **nᵉ'dârîy**. See 142.

4998. נָאָה **nâ'âh**, *naw-aw´;* a prim. root; prop. to *be at home*, i.e. (by impl.) to be *pleasant* (or *suitable*), i.e. *beautiful:*— be beautiful, become, be comely.

4999. נָאָה **nâ'âh**, *naw-aw´;* from 4998; a *home;* fig. a *pasture:*— habitation, house, pasture, pleasant place.

5000. נָאוֶה **nâ'veh**, *naw-veh´;* from 4998 or 5116; *suitable*, or *beautiful:*— becometh, comely, seemly.

5001. נָאַם **nâ'am**, *naw-am´;* a prim. root; prop. to *whisper*, i.e. (by impl.) to *utter* as an oracle:— say.

5002. נְאֻם **nᵉ'ûm**, *neh-oom´;* from 5001; an *oracle:*— (hath) said, saith.

5003. נָאַף **nâ'aph**, *naw-af´;* a prim. root; to *commit adultery;* fig. to *apostatize:*— adulterer (-ess), commit (-ing) adultery, woman that breaketh wedlock.

5004. נִאֻף **ni'ûph**, *nee-oof´;* from 5003; *adultery:*— adultery.

5005. נַאֲפוּף **na'ăphûwph**, *nah-af-oof´;* from 5003; *adultery:*— adultery.

5006. נָאַץ **nâ'ats**, *naw-ats´;* a prim. root; to *scorn;* or (Eccles. 12:5) by interchange for 5132, to *bloom:*— abhor, (give occasion to) blaspheme, contemn, despise, flourish, × great, provoke.

5007. נְאָצָה **nᵉ'âtsâh**, *neh-aw-tsaw´;* or

נֶאָצָה **ne'âtsâh**, *neh-aw-tsaw´;* from 5006; *scorn:*— blasphemy.

5008. נָאַק **nâ'aq**, *naw-ak´;* a prim. root; to *groan:*— groan.

5009. נְאָקָה **nᵉ'âqâh**, *neh-aw-kaw´;* from 5008; a *groan:*— groaning.

5010. נָאַר **nâ'ar**, *naw-ar´;* a prim. root; to *reject:*— abhor, make void.

5011. נֹב **Nôb**, *nobe;* the same as 5108; *fruit; Nob*, a place in Pal.:— Nob.

5012. נָבָא **nâbâ'**, *naw-baw´;* a prim. root; to *prophesy*, i.e. speak (or sing) by inspiration (in prediction or simple discourse):— prophesy (-ing), make self a prophet.

5013. נְבָא **nᵉbâ'** (Chald.), *neb-aw´;* corresp. to 5012:— prophesy.

5014. נָבַב **nâbab**, *naw-bab´;* a prim. root; to *pierce;* to *be hollow*, or (fig.) *foolish:*— hollow, vain.

5015. נְבוֹ **Nᵉbôw**, *neb-o´;* prob. of for. der.; *Nebo*, the name of a Bab. deity, also of a mountain in Moab, and of a place in Pal.:— Nebo.

5016. נְבוּאָה **nᵉbûw'âh**, *neb-oo-aw´;* from 5012; a *prediction* (spoken or written):— prophecy.

5017. נְבוּאָה **nᵉbûw'âh** (Chald.), *neb-oo-aw´;* corresp. to 5016; inspired *teaching:*— prophesying.

5018. נְבוּזַראֲדָן **Nᵉbûwzar'ădân**, *neb-oo-*

zar-ad-awn´; of for. or.; *Nebuzaradan*, a Bab. general:— Nebuzaradan.

5019. נְבוּכַדְרֶאצַּר **Nᵉbûwkadne'tstsar**, *neb-oo-kad-nets-tsar´*; or

נְבֻכַדְרֶאצַּר **Nᵉbûwkadne'tstsar** (2 Kings 24:1, 10), *neb-oo-kad-nets-tsar´*; or

נְבוּכַדְנֶצַּר **Nᵉbûwkadnetstsar** (Esth. 2:6; Dan. 1:18), *neb-oo-kad-nets-tsar´*; or

נְבוּכַדְרֶאצַּר **Nᵉbûwkadre'tstsar**, *neb-oo-kad-rets-tsar´*; or

נְבוּכַדְרֶאצּוֹר° **Nᵉbûwkadre'tstsôwr** (Ezra 2:1; Jer. 49:28), *neb-oo-kad-rets-tsore´*; or for. der.; *Nebukadnetstsar* (or *-retstsar*, or *-retstsor*), king of Bab.:— Nebuchadnezzar, Nebuchadrezzar.

5020. נְבוּכַדְנֶצַּר **Nᵉbûwkadnetstsar** (Chald.), *neb-oo-kad-nets-tsar´*; corresp. to 5019:— Nebuchadnezzar.

5021. נְבוּשַׁזְבָּן **Nᵉbûwshazbân**, *neb-oo-shaz-bawn´*; of for. der.; *Nebushazban*, Nebuchadnezzar's chief eunuch:— Nebushazban.

5022. נְבוֹ **Nâbôwth**, *naw-both´*; fem. plur. from the same as 5011; *fruits*; *Naboth*, an Isr.:— Naboth.

5023. נְבִזְבָּה **nᵉbizbâh** (Chald.), *neb-iz-baw´*; of uncert. der.; a *largess*:— reward.

5024. נָבַח **nâbach**, *naw-bakh´*; a prim. root; to *bark* (as a dog):— bark.

5025. נֹבַח **Nôbach**, *no´-bach*; from 5024; a *bark*; *Nobach*, the name of an Isr., and of a place E. of the Jordan:— Nobah.

5026. נִבְחַז **Nibchaz**, *nib-khaz´*; of for. or.; *Nibchaz*, a deity of the Avites:— Nibhaz.

5027. נָבַט **nâbaṭ**, *naw-bat´*; a prim. root; to *scan*, i.e. look intently at; by impl. to *regard* with pleasure, favor or care:— (cause to) behold, consider, look (down), regard, have respect, see.

5028. נְבָט **Nᵉbâṭ**, *neb-awt´*; from 5027; *regard*; *Nebat*, the father of Jeroboam I:— Nebat.

5029. נְבִיא **nᵉbîy** (Chald.), *neb-ee´*; corresp. to 5030; a *prophet*:— prophet.

5030. נָבִיא **nâbîy'**, *naw-bee´*; from 5012; a *prophet* or (gen.) *inspired* man:— prophecy, that prophesy, prophet.

5031. נְבִיאָה **nᵉbîy'âh**, *neb-ee-yaw´*; fem. of 5030; a *prophetess* or (gen.) *inspired* woman; by impl. a *poetess*; by association a *prophet's wife*:— prophetess.

5032. נְבָיוֹת **Nᵉbâyôwth**, *neb-aw-yoth´*; or

נְבָיֹת **Nᵉbâyôth**, *neb-aw-yoth´*; fem. plur. from 5107; *fruitfulnesses*; *Nebajoth*, a son of Ismael, and the country settled by him:— Nebaioth, Nebajoth.

5033. נֵבֶךְ **nêbek**, *nay´-bek*; from an unused root mean. to *burst* forth; a *fountain*:— spring.

5034. נָבֵל **nâbêl**, *naw-bale´*; a prim. root; to *wilt*; gen. to *fall away, fail, faint*; fig. to *be foolish* or (mor.) *wicked*; caus. to *despise, disgrace*:— disgrace, dishonour, lightly esteem, fade (away, -ing), fall (down, -ling, off), do foolishly,

come to nought, × surely, make vile, wither.

5035. נֶבֶל **nebel**, *neh´-bel*; or

נֵבֶל **nêbel**, *nay´-bel*; from 5034; a skin-*bag* for liquids (from collapsing when empty); hence, a *vase* (as similar in shape when full); also a *lyre* (as having a body of like form):— bottle, pitcher, psaltery, vessel, viol.

5036. נָבָל **nâbâl**, *naw-bawl´*; from 5034; *stupid*; *wicked* (espec. *impious*):— fool (-ish, -ish man, -ish woman), vile person.

5037. נָבָל **Nâbâl**, *naw-bawl´*; the same as 5036; *dolt*; *Nabal*, an Isr.:— Nabal.

5038. נְבֵלָה **nᵉbêlâh**, *neb-ay-law´*; from 5034; a *flabby* thing, i.e. a *carcase* or *carrion* (human or bestial, often collect.); fig. an *idol*:— (dead) body, (dead) carcase, dead of itself, which died, (beast) that (which) dieth of itself.

5039. נְבָלָה **nᵉbâlâh**, *neb-aw-law´*; fem. of 5036; *foolishness*, i.e. (mor.) *wickedness*; concr. a *crime*; by extens. *punishment*:— folly, vile, villany.

5040. נַבְלוּת **nablûwth**, *nab-looth´*; from 5036; prop. *disgrace*, i.e. the (female) *pudenda*:— lewdness.

5041. נְבַלָּט **Nᵉballâṭ**, *neb-al-lawt´*; appar. from 5036 and 3909; *foolish secrecy*; *Neballat*, a place in Pal.:— Neballat.

5042. נָבַע **nâba'**, *naw-bah´*; a prim. root; to *gush* forth; fig. to *utter* (good or bad words); spec. to *emit* (a foul odor):— belch out, flowing, pour out, send forth, utter (abundantly).

5043. נֶבְרְשָׁא **nebrᵉshâ'** (Chald.), *neb-reh-shaw´*; from an unused root mean. to *shine*; a *light*; plur. (collect.) a *chandelier*:— candlestick.

5044. נִבְשָׁן **Nibshân**, *nib-shawn´*; of uncert. der.; *Nibshan*, a place in Pal.:— Nibshan.

5045. נֶגֶב **negeb**, *neh´-gheb*; from an unused root mean. to *be parched*; the *south* (from its drought); spec. the *Negeb* or southern district of Judah, occasionally, *Egypt* (as south to Pal.):— south (country, side, -ward).

5046. נָגַד **nâgad**, *naw-gad´*; a prim. root; prop. to *front*, i.e. stand boldly out opposite; by impl. (caus.), to *manifest*; fig. to *announce* (always by word of mouth to one present); spec. to *expose, predict, explain, praise*:— bewray, × certainly, certify, declare (-ing), denounce, expound, × fully, messenger, plainly, profess, rehearse, report, shew (forth), speak, × surely, tell, utter.

5047. נְגַד **nᵉgad** (Chald.), *neg-ad´*; corresp. to 5046; to *flow* (through the idea of *clearing* the way):— issue.

5048. נֶגֶד **neged**, *neh´-ghed*; from 5046; a *front*, i.e. part opposite; spec. a *counterpart*, or *mate*; usually (adv., espec. with prep.) *over against* or *before*:— about, (over) against, × aloof, × far (off), × from, over, presence, × other side, sight, × to view.

5049. נֶגֶד **neged** (Chald.), *neh´-ghed*; corresp. to 5048; *opposite*:— toward.

5050. נָגַהּ **nâgahh**, *naw-gäh´*; a prim.

root; to *glitter*; caus. to *illuminate*:— (en-) lighten, (cause to) shine.

5051. נֹגַהּ **nôgahh**, *no´-gäh*; from 5050; *brilliancy* (lit. or fig.):— bright (-ness), light, (clear) shining.

5052. נֹגַהּ **Nôgahh**, *no´-gäh*; the same as 5051; *Nogah*, a son of David:— Nogah.

5053. נֹגַהּ **nôgahh** (Chald.), *no´-gäh*; corresp. to 5051; *dawn*:— morning.

5054. נְגֹהָה **nᵉgôhâh**, *neg-o-haw´*; fem. of 5051; *splendor*:— brightness.

5055. נָגַח **nâgach**, *naw-gakh´*; a prim. root; to *but* with the horns; fig. to *war* against:— gore, push (down, -ing).

5056. נַגָּח **naggâch**, *nag-gawkh´*; from 5055; *butting*, i.e. *vicious*:— used (wont) to push.

5057. נָגִיד **nâgîyd**, *naw-gheed´*; or

נָגִד **nâgid**, *naw-gheed´*; from 5046; a *commander* (as occupying the *front*), civil, military or religious; gen. (abstr. plur.), *honorable* themes:— captain, chief, excellent thing, (chief) governor, leader, noble, prince, (chief) ruler.

5058. נְגִינָה **nᵉgîynâh**, *neg-ee-naw´*; or

נְגִינַת **nᵉgîynath** (Psa. 61:title), *neg-ee-nath´*; from 5059; prop. instrumental *music*; by impl. a stringed *instrument*; by extens. a *poem* set to music; spec. an *epigram*:— stringed instrument, musick, Neginoth [plur.], song.

5059. נָגַן **nâgan**, *naw-gan´*; a prim. root; prop. to *thrum*, i.e. *beat* a tune with the fingers; expec. to *play* on a stringed instrument; hence, (gen.), to *make music*:— player on instruments, sing to the stringed instruments, melody, ministrel, play (-er, -ing).

5060. נָגַע **nâga'**, *naw-gah´*; a prim. root; prop. to *touch*, i.e. *lay the hand upon* (for any purpose; euphem. to *lie with* a woman); by impl. to *reach* (fig. to *arrive, acquire*); violently, to *strike* (punish, defeat, destroy, etc.):— beat, (× be able to) bring (down), cast, come (nigh), draw near (nigh), get up, happen, join, near, plague, reach (up), smite, strike, touch.

5061. נֶגַע **nega'**, *neh´-gah*; from 5060; a *blow* (fig. *infliction*); also (by impl.) a *spot* (concr. a *leprous* person or dress):— plague, sore, stricken, stripe, stroke, wound.

5062. נָגַף **nâgaph**, *naw-gaf´*; a prim. root; to *push, gore, defeat, stub* (the toe), *inflict* (a disease):— beat, dash, hurt, plague, slay, smite (down), strike, stumble, × surely, put to the worse.

5063. נֶגֶף **negeph**, *neh´-ghef*; from 5062; a *trip* (of the foot); fig. an *infliction* (of disease):— plague, stumbling.

5064. נָגַר **nâgar**, *naw-gar´*; a prim. root; to *flow*; fig. to *stretch* out; caus. to *pour* out or down; fig. to *deliver* over:— fall, flow away, pour down (out), run, shed, spilt, trickle down.

5065. נָגַשׂ **nâgas**, *naw-gas´*; a prim. root; to *drive* (an animal, a workman, a debtor, an army); by impl. to *tax, harass, tyrannize*:— distress, driver, exact (-or), oppress (-or), × raiser of taxes, taskmaster.

Hebrew

5066. נָגַשׁ **nâgash,** *naw-gash´;* a prim. root; to *be* or *come* (caus. *bring*) *near* (for any purpose); euphem. to *lie with* a woman; as an enemy, to *attack;* relig. to *worship;* caus. to *present;* fig. to *adduce* an argument; by reversal, to *stand back:*— (make to) approach (nigh), bring (forth, hither, near), (cause to) come (hither, near, nigh), give place, go hard (up), (be, draw, go) near (nigh), offer, overtake, present, put, stand.

5067. נֵד **nêd,** *nade;* from 5110 in the sense of *piling* up; a *mound,* i.e. *wave:*— heap.

5068. נָדַב **nâdab,** *naw-dab´;* a prim. root; to *impel;* hence, to *volunteer* (as a soldier), to *present* spontaneously:— offer freely, be (give, make, offer self) willing (-ly).

5069. נְדַב **nᵉdab** (Chald.), *ned-ab´;* corresp. to 5068; *be* (or *give*) *liberal* (-ly):— (be minded of ... own) freewill (offering), offer freely (willingly).

5070. נָדָב **Nâdâb,** *naw-dawb´;* from 5068; *liberal; Nadab,* the name of four Isr.:— Nadab.

5071. נְדָבָה **nᵉdâbâh,** *ned-aw-baw´;* from 5068; prop. (abstr.) *spontaneity,* or (adj.) *spontaneous;* also (concr.) a *spontaneous* or (by infer., in plur.) *abundant* gift:— free (-will) offering, freely, plentiful, voluntary (-ily, offering), willing (-ly, offering).

5072. נְדַבְיָה **Nᵉdabyâh,** *ned-ab-yaw´;* from 5068 and 3050; *largess of Jah; Nedabjah,* an Isr.:— Nedabiah.

5073. נִדְבָּךְ **nidbâk** (Chald.), *nid-bawk´;* from a root mean. to *stick;* a *layer* (of building materials):— row.

5074. נָדַד **nâdad,** *naw-dad´;* a prim. root; prop. to *wave* to and fro (rarely to *flap* up and down); fig. to *rove, flee,* or (caus.) to *drive* away:— chase (away), × could not, depart, flee (× apace, away), (re-) move, thrust away, wander (abroad, -er, -ing).

5075. נְדַד **nᵉdad** (Chald.), *ned-ad´;* corresp. to 5074; to *depart:*— go from.

5076. נָדֻד **nâdûd,** *naw-dood´;* pass. part. of 5074; prop. *tossed;* abstr. a *rolling* (on the bed):— tossing to and fro.

5077. נָדָה **nâdâh,** *naw-daw´;* or

נָדָא **nâdâ'** (2 Kings 17:21), *naw-daw´;* a prim. root; prop. to *toss;* fig. to *exclude,* i.e. *banish, postpone, prohibit:*— cast out, drive, put far away.

5078. נֵדֶה **nêdeh,** *nay´-deh;* from 5077 in the sense of freely *flinging* money; a *bounty* (for prostitution):— gifts.

5079. נִדָּה **niddâh,** *nid-daw´;* from 5074; prop. *rejection;* by impl. *impurity,* espec. pers. (menstruation) or mor. (idolatry, incest):— × far, filthiness, × flowers, menstruous (woman), put apart, × removed (woman), separation, set apart, unclean (-ness, thing, with filthiness).

5080. נָדַח **nâdach,** *naw-dakh´;* a prim. root; to *push* off; used in a great variety of applications, lit. and fig. (to *expel,* mislead, strike, inflict, etc.):— banish, bring, cast down (out), chase, compel, draw away, drive (away, out, quite),

fetch a stroke, force, go away, outcast, thrust away (out), withdraw.

5081. נָדִיב **nâdîyb,** *naw-deeb´;* from 5068; prop. *voluntary,* i.e. generous; hence, *magnanimous;* as noun, a *grandee* (sometimes a *tyrant*):— free, liberal (things), noble, prince, willing (lhearted).

5082. נְדִיבָה **nᵉdîybâh,** *ned-ee-baw´;* fem. of 5081; prop. *nobility,* i.e. *reputation:*— soul.

5083. נָדָן **nâdân,** *naw-dawn´;* prob. from an unused root mean. to *give;* a *present* (for prostitution):— gift.

5084. נָדָן **nâdân,** *naw-dawn´;* of uncert. der.; a *sheath* (of a sword):— sheath.

5085. נִדְנֶה **nidneh** (Chald.), *nid-neh´;* from the same as 5084; a *sheath;* fig. the *body* (as the receptacle of the soul):— body.

5086. נָדַף **nâdaph,** *naw-daf´;* a prim. root; to *shove* asunder, i.e. *disperse:*— drive (away, tossed to and fro), thrust down, shaken, tossed to and fro.

5087. נָדַר **nâdar,** *naw-dar´;* a prim. root; to *promise* (pos., to do or give something to God):— (make a) vow.

5088. נֶדֶר **neder,** *neh´-der;* or

נֵדֶר **nêder,** *nay´-der;* from 5087; a *promise* (to God); also (concr.) a thing *promised:*— vow (l-edl).

5089. נֹהַּ **nôahh,** *no´-ah;* from an unused root mean. to *lament; lamentation:*— wailing.

5090. נָהַג **nâhag,** *naw-hag´;* a prim. root; to *drive* forth (a person, an animal or chariot), i.e. *lead, carry away;* refl. to *proceed* (impel or guide oneself); also (from the *panting* induced by effort), to *sigh:*— acquaint, bring (away), carry away, drive (away), lead (away, forth), (be) guide, lead (away, forth).

5091. נָהָה **nâhâh,** *naw-haw´;* a prim. root; to *groan,* i.e. *bewail;* hence, (through the idea of *crying* aloud), to *assemble* (as if on proclamation):— lament, wail.

5092. נְהִי **nᵉhîy,** *neh-hee´;* from 5091; an *elegy:*— lamentation, wailing.

5093. נִהְיָה **nihyâh,** *nih-yaw´;* fem. of 5092; *lamentation:*— doleful.

5094. נְהִיר **nᵉhîyr** (Chald.), *neh-heere´;* or

נְהִירוּ **nehîyrû** (Chald.), *neh-hee-roo´;* from the same as 5105; *illumination,* i.e. (fig.) *wisdom:*— light.

5095. נָהַל **nâhal,** *naw-hal´;* a prim. root; prop. to run with a *sparkle,* i.e. *flow;* hence, (tran.), to *conduct,* and (by infer.) to *protect, sustain:*— carry, feed, guide, lead (gently, on).

5096. נַהֲלָל **Nahălâl,** *näh-hal-awl´;* or

נַהֲלֹל **Nahălôl,** *näh-hal-ole´;* the same as 5097; *Nahalal* or *Nahalol,* a place in Pal.:— Nahalal, Nahallal, Nahalol.

5097. נַהֲלֹל **nahălôl,** *näh-hal-ole´;* from 5095; *pasture:*— bush.

5098. נָהַם **nâham,** *naw-ham´;* a prim. root; to *growl:*— mourn, roar (-ing).

5099. נַהַם **naham,** *näh´-ham;* from 5098; a *snarl:*— roaring.

5100. נְהָמָה **nᵉhâmâh,** *neh-haw-maw´;* fem. of 5099; *snarling:*— disquietness, roaring.

5101. נָהַק **nâhaq,** *naw-hak´;* a prim. root; to *bray* (as an ass), *scream* (from hunger):— bray.

5102. נָהַר **nâhar,** *naw-har´;* a prim. root; to *sparkle,* i.e. (fig.) *be cheerful;* hence, (from the *sheen* of a running stream) to *flow,* i.e. (fig.) *assemble:*— flow (together), be lightened.

5103. נְהַר **nᵉhar** (Chald.), *neh-har´;* from a root corresp. to 5102; a *river,* espec. the Euphrates:— river, stream.

5104. נָהָר **nâhâr,** *naw-hawr´;* from 5102; a *stream* (incl. the *sea;* expec. the Nile, Euphrates, etc.); fig. *prosperity:*— flood, river.

5105. נְהָרָה **nᵉhârâh,** *neh-haw-raw´;* from 5102 in its orig. sense; *daylight:*— light.

5106. נוּא **nûw',** *noo;* a prim. root; to *refuse, forbid, dissuade,* or *neutralize:*— break, disallow, discourage, make of none effect.

5107. נוּב **nûwb,** *noob;* a prim. root; to *germinate,* i.e. (fig.) to (caus. *make*) *flourish;* also (of words), to *utter:*— bring forth (fruit), make cheerful, increase.

5108. נוֹב **nôwb,** *nobe;* or

נִיב **nêyb,** *nabe;* from 5107; *produce,* lit. or fig.:— fruit.

5109. נוֹבַי **Nôwbay,** *no-bah´ee;* from 5108; *fruitful; Nobai,* an Isr.:— Nebai lfrom the marg.l.

5110. נוּד **nûwd,** *nood;* a prim. root; to *nod,* i.e. *waver;* fig. to *wander, flee, disappear;* also (from *shaking* the head in sympathy), to *console, deplore,* or (from *tossing* the head in scorn) *taunt:*— bemoan, flee, get, mourn, make to move, take pity, remove, shake, skip for joy, be sorry, vagabond, way, wandering.

5111. נוּד **nûwd** (Chald.), *nood;* corresp. to 5116; to *flee:*— get away.

5112. נוֹד **nôwd,** *node* lonly defect.

נֹד **nôd,** *node*l; from 5110; *exile:*— wandering.

5113. נוֹד **Nôwd,** *node;* the same as 5112; *vagrancy; Nod,* the land of Cain:— Nod.

5114. נוֹדָב **Nôwdâb,** *no-dawb´;* from 5068; *noble; Nodab,* an Arab tribe:— Nodab.

5115. נָוָה **nâvâh,** *naw-vaw´;* a prim. root; to *rest* (as at home); caus. (through the impl. idea of *beauty* lcomp. 5116l), to *celebrate* (with praises):— keep at home, prepare an habitation.

5116. נָוֶה **nâveh,** *naw-veh´;* or (fem.)

נָוָה **nâvâh,** *naw-vaw´;* from 5115; (adj.) *at home;* hence, (by impl. of satisfaction) *lovely;* also (noun) a *home,* of God (temple); men (residence), flocks (pasture), or wild animals (*den*):— comely, dwelling (place), fold, habitation, pleasant place, sheepcote, stable, tarried.

5117. נוּחַ **nûwach,** *noo-akh´;* a prim. root; to *rest,* i.e. *settle* down; used in a great variety of applications, lit. and fig., intr., tran. and caus. (to *dwell, stay, let fall, place, let alone, withdraw, give comfort*, etc.):— cease, be confederate, lay, let down, (be) quiet, remain, (cause to, be at, give, have, make to) rest, set down. Comp. 3241.

5118. נוּחַ **nûwach**, noo'-akh; or

נוֹחַ **nôwach**, no'-akh; from 5117; *quiet*:— rest (-ed, -ing place).

5119. נוֹחָה **Nôwchâh**, no-chaw'; fem. of 5118; *quietude; Nochah*, an Isr.:— Nohah.

5120. נוּט **nûwṭ**, noot; to *quake*:— be moved.

5121. נָיוֹת° **Nâvîyth**, naw-veeth'; from 5115; *residence; Navith*, a place in Pal.:— Naioth [from the marg.].

5122. נְוָלוּ **nᵉvâlûw** (Chald.), nev-aw-loo'; or

נְוָלִי **nᵉvâlîy** (Chald.), nev-aw-lee'; from an unused root prob. mean. to *be foul; a sink*:— dunghill.

5123. נוּם **nûwm**, noom; a prim. root; to *slumber* (from drowsiness):— sleep, slumber.

5124. נוּמָה **nûwmâh**, noo-maw'; from 5123; *sleepiness*:— drowsiness.

5125. נוּן **nûwn**, noon; a prim. root; to *resprout*, i.e. propagate by shoots; fig., to *be perpetual*:— be continued.

5126. נוּן **Nûwn**, noon; or

נוֹן **Nôwn** (1 Chron. 7:27), nohn; from 5125; *perpetuity, Nun* or *Non*, the father of Joshua:— Non, Nun.

5127. נוּס **nûwç**, noos; a prim. root; to *flit*, i.e. *vanish* away (subside, escape; caus. chase, impel, deliver):— × abate, away, be displayed, (make to) flee (away, -ing), put to flight, × hide, lift up a standard.

5128. נוּעַ **nûwaʻ**, noo'-ah; a prim. root; to *waver*, in a great variety of applications, lit. and fig. (as subjoined):— continually, fugitive, × make, to [go] up and down, be gone away, (be) move (-able, -d), be promoted, reel, remove, scatter, set, shake, sift, stagger, to and fro, be vagabond, wag, (make) wander (up and down).

5129. נוֹעַדְיָה **Nôwʻadyâh**, no-ad-yaw'; from 3259 and 3050; *convened of Jah; Noadjah*, the name of an Isr., and a false prophetess:— Noadiah.

5130. נוּף **nûwph**, noof; a prim. root; to *quiver* (i.e. *vibrate* up and down, or *rock* to and fro); used in a great variety of applications (incl. *sprinkling, beckoning, rubbing, bastinadoing, sawing, waving*, etc.):— lift up, move, offer, perfume, send, shake, sift, strike, wave.

5131. נוֹף **nôwph**, nofe; from 5130; *elevation*:— situation. Comp. 5297.

5132. נוּץ **nûwts**, noots; a prim. root; prop. to *flash*; hence, to *blossom* (from the brilliancy of color); also, to *fly away* (from the quickness of motion):— flee away, bud (forth).

5133. נוֹצָה **nôwtsâh**, no-tsaw'; or

נֹצָה **nôtsâh**, no-tsaw'; fem. act. part. of 5327 in the sense of *flying*; a

pinion (or wing feather); often (collect.) *plumage*:— feather (-s), ostrich.

5134. נוּק **nûwq**, nook; a prim. root; to *suckle*:— nurse.

5135. נוּר **nûwr** (Chald.), noor; from an unused root (corresp. to that of 5216) mean. to *shine; fire*:— fiery, fire.

5136. נוּשׁ **nûwsh**, noosh; a prim. root; to *be sick*, i.e. (fig.) *distressed*:— be full of heaviness.

5137. נָזָה **nâzâh**, naw-zaw'; a prim. root; to *spirt*, i.e. *besprinkle* (espec. in expiation):— sprinkle.

5138. נָזִיד **nâzîyd**, naw-zeed'; from 2102; something *boiled*, i.e. *soup*:— pottage.

5139. נָזִיר **nâzîyr**, naw-zeer'; or

נָזִר **nâzir**, naw-zeer'; from 5144; *separate*, i.e. consecrated (as *prince*, a *Nazirite*); hence, (fig. from the latter) an *unpruned* vine (like an unshorn Nazirite):— Nazarite [by a false alliteration with Nazareth], separate (-d), vine undressed.

5140. נָזַל **nâzal**, naw-zal'; a prim. root; to *drip*, or *shed* by trickling:— distil, drop, flood, (cause to) flow (-ing), gush out, melt, pour (down), running water, stream.

5141. נֶזֶם **nezem**, neh'-zem; from an unused root of uncert. mean.; a *nosering*:— earring, jewel.

5142. נְזַק **nᵉzaq** (Chald.), nez-ak'; corresp. to the root of 5143; to *suffer* (caus. *inflict*) *loss*:— have (en-) damage, hurt (-ful).

5143. נֵזֶק **nêzeq**, nay'zek; from an unused root mean. to *injure; loss*:— damage.

5144. נָזַר **nâzar**, naw-zar'; a prim. root; to *hold aloof*, i.e. (intr.) *abstain* (from food and drink, from impurity, and even from divine worship [i.e. *apostatize*]); spec. to *set apart* (to sacred purposes), i.e. *devote*:— consecrate, separate (-ing, self).

5145. נֶזֶר **nezer**, neh'-zer; or

נֵזֶר **nêzer**, nay'-zer; from 5144; prop. something *set apart*, i.e. (abstr.) *dedication* (of a priest or Nazirite); hence, (concr.) unshorn *locks*; also (by impl.) a *chaplet* (espec. of royalty):— consecration, crown, hair, separation.

5146. נֹחַ **Nôach**, no'-akh; the same as 5118; *rest; Noach*, the patriarch of the flood:— Noah.

5147. נַחְבִּי **Nachbîy**, nakh-bee'; from 2247; *occult; Nachbi*, an Isr.:— Nakbi.

5148. נָחָה **nâchâh**, naw-khaw'; a prim. root; to *guide*; by impl. to *transport* (into exile, or as colonists):— bestow, bring, govern, guide, lead (forth), put, straiten.

5149. נְחוּם **Nᵉchûwm**, neh-khoom'; from 5162; *comforted; Nechum*, an Isr.:— Nehum.

5150. נִחוּם **nichûwm**, nee-khoom'; or

נִחֻם **nichûm**, nee-khoom'; from 5162; prop. *consoled*; abstr. *solace*:— comfort (-able), repenting.

5151. נַחוּם **Nachûwm**, nakh-oom'; from 5162; *comfortable; Nachum*, an Isr. prophet:— Nahum.

5152. נָחוֹר **Nâchôwr**, naw-khore'; from the same as 5170; *snorer; Nachor*, the name of the grandfather and a brother of Abraham:— Nahor.

5153. נָחוּשׁ **nâchûwsh**, naw-khoosh'; appar. pass. part. of 5172 (perh. in the sense of *ringing*, i.e. bell-metal; or from the *red* color of the throat of a serpent [5175, as denom.] when hissing); *coppery*, i.e. (fig.) *hard*:— of brass.

5154. נְחוּשָׁה **nᵉchûwshâh**, nekh-oo-shaw'; or

נְחֻשָׁה **nᵉchûshâh**, nekh-oo-shaw'; fem. of 5153; *copper*:— brass, steel. Comp. 5176.

5155. נְחִילָה **Nᵉchîylâh**, nekh-ee-law'; prob. denom. from 2485; a *flute*:— [plur.] Nehiloth.

5156. נְחִיר **nᵉchîyr**, nekh-eer'; from the same as 5170; a *nostril*:— [dual] nostrils.

5157. נָחַל **nâchal**, naw-khal'; a prim. root; to *inherit* (as a [fig.] mode of descent), or (gen.) to *occupy*; caus. to *bequeath*, or (gen.) *distribute, instate*:— divide, have (inheritance), take as an heritage, (cause to, give to, make to) inherit, (distribute for, divide [for, for an, by], give for, have, leave for, take [for]) inheritance, (have in, cause to, be made to) possess (-ion).

5158. נַחַל **nachal**, nakh'-al; or (fem.)

נַחְלָה **nachlâh** (Psa. 124:4), nakh'-law; or

נַחֲלָה **nachălâh** (Ezek. 47:19; 48:28), nakh-al-aw'; from 5157 in its orig. sense; a *stream*, espec. a winter *torrent*; (by impl.) a (narrow) *valley* (in which a brook runs); also a *shaft* (of a mine):— brook, flood, river, stream, valley.

5159. נַחֲלָה **nachălâh**, nakh-al-aw'; from 5157 (in its usual sense); prop. something *inherited*, i.e. (abstr.) *occupancy*, or (concr.) an *heirloom*; gen. an *estate, patrimony* or *portion*:— heritage, to inherit, inheritance, possession. Comp. 5158.

5160. נַחֲלִיאֵל **Nachălîyʼêl**, nakh-al-ee-ale'; from 5158 and 410; *valley of God; Nachaliël*, a place in the Desert:— Nahaliel.

5161. נְחֵלָמִי **Nechĕlâmîy**, nekh-el-aw-mee'; appar. a patron. from an unused name (appar. pass. part. of 2492); *dreamed*; a *Nechelamite*, or desc. of Nechlam:— Nehelamite.

5162. נָחַם **nâcham**, naw-kham'; a prim. root; prop. to *sigh*, i.e. *breathe* strongly; by impl. to *be sorry*, i.e. (in a favorable sense) to *pity, console* or (refl.) *rue*; or (unfavorably) to *avenge* (oneself):— comfort (self), ease [one's self], repent (-er, -ing, self).

5163. נַחַם **Nacham**, nakh'-am; from 5162; *consolation; Nacham*, an Isr.:— Naham.

5164. נֹחַם **nôcham**, no'-kham; from 5162; *ruefulness*, i.e. *desistance*:— repentance.

5165. נֶחָמָה **nechâmâh**, nekh-aw-maw'; from 5162; *consolation*:— comfort.

5166. נְחֶמְיָה **Nᵉchemyâh**, nekh-em-yaw';

from 5162 and 3050; *consolation of Jah;* *Nechemjah,* the name of three Isr.:— Nehemiah.

5167. נַחֲמָנִי **Nachămânîy,** *nakh-am-aw-nee´;* from 5162; *consolatory; Nachamani,* an Isr.:— Nahamani.

5168. נַחְנוּ **nachnûw,** *nakh-noo´;* for 587; *we:*— we.

5169. נָחַץ **nâchats,** *naw-khats´;* a prim. root; to *be urgent:*— require haste.

5170. נַחַר **nachar,** *nakh´-ar;* and (fem.)

נַחֲרָה **nachărâh,** *nakh-ar-aw´;* from an unused root mean. to *snort* or *snore;* a *snorting:*— nostrils, snorting.

5171. נַחֲרַי **Nachăray,** *nakh-ar-ah´-ee;* or

נַחְרַי **Nachray,** *nakh-rah´-ee;* from the same as 5170; *snorer; Nacharai* or *Nachrai,* an Isr.:— Naharai, Nahari.

5172. נָחַשׁ **nâchash,** *naw-khash´;* a prim. root; prop. to *hiss,* i.e. *whisper* a (magic) spell; gen. to *prognosticate:*— × certainly, divine, enchanter, (use) × enchantment, learn by experience, × indeed, diligently observe.

5173. נַחַשׁ **nachash,** *nakh´-ash;* from 5172; an *incantation* or *augury:*— enchantment.

5174. נְחָשׁ **n^echâsh** (Chald.), *nekh-awsh´;* corresp. to 5154; *copper:*— brass.

5175. נָחָשׁ **nâchâsh,** *naw-khawsh´;* from 5172; a *snake* (from its *hiss*):— serpent.

5176. נָחָשׁ **Nâchâsh,** *naw-khawsh´;* the same as 5175; *Nachash,* the name of two persons appar. non-Isr.:— Nahash.

נְחֻשָׁה **n^echûshâh.** See 5154.

5177. נַחְשׁוֹן **Nachshôwn,** *nakh-shone´;* from 5172; *enchanter; Nachshon,* an Isr.:— Naashon, Nahshon.

5178. נְחֹשֶׁת **n^echôsheth,** *nekh-o´-sheth;* for 5154; *copper,* hence, something made of that metal, i.e. *coin,* a *fetter;* fig. *base* (as compared with gold or silver):— brasen, brass, chain, copper, fetter (of brass), filthiness, steel.

5179. נְחֻשְׁתָּא **N^echushtâ´,** *nekh-oosh-taw´;* from 5178; *copper; Nechushta,* an Israelitess:— Nehushta.

5180. נְחֻשְׁתָּן **N^echushtân,** *nekh-oosh-tawn´;* from 5178; something made of *copper,* i.e. the copper *serpent* of the Desert:— Nehushtan.

5181. נָחַת **nâchath,** *naw-khath´;* a prim. root; to *sink,* i.e. *descend;* caus., to *press* or *lead* down:— be broken, (cause to) come down, enter, go down, press sore, settle, stick fast.

5182. נְחַת **n^echath** (Chald.), *nekh-ath´;* corresp. to 5181; to *descend;* caus., to *bring away, deposit, depose:*— carry, come down, depose, lay up, place.

5183. נַחַת **nachath,** *nakh´-ath;* from 5182; a *descent,* i.e. imposition, unfavorable (*punishment*) or favorable (*food*); also (intr.; perh. from 5117), *restfulness:*— lighting down, quiet (-ness), to rest, be set on.

5184. נַחַת **Nachath,** *nakh´-ath;* the same as 5183; *quiet; Nachath,* the name of an Edomite and of two Isr.:— Nahath.

5185. נָחֵת **nâchêth,** *naw-khayth´;* from 5181; *descending:*— come down.

5186. נָטָה **nâṭâh,** *naw-taw´;* a prim. root; to *stretch* or spread out; by impl. to *bend* away (incl. mor. deflection); used in a great variety of application (as follows):— + afternoon, apply, bow (down, -ing), carry aside, decline, deliver, extend, go down, be gone, incline, intend, lay, let down, offer, outstretched, overthrown, pervert, pitch, prolong, put away, shew, spread (out), stretch (forth, out), take (aside), turn (aside, away), wrest, cause to yield.

5187. נָטִיל **n^eṭîyl,** *net-eel´;* from 5190; *laden:*— that bear.

5188. נְטִיפָה **n^eṭîyphâh,** *net-ee-faw´;* from 5197; a *pendant* for the ears (espec. of pearls):— chain, collar.

5189. נְטִישָׁה **n^eṭîyshâh,** *net-ee-shaw´;* from 5203; a *tendril* (as an offshoot):— battlement, branch, plant.

5190. נָטַל **nâṭal,** *naw-tal´;* a prim. root; to *lift;* by impl. to *impose:*— bear, offer, take up.

5191. נְטַל **n^eṭal** (Chald.), *net-al´;* corresp. to 5190; to *raise:*— take up.

5192. נֵטֶל **nêṭel,** *nay´-tel;* from 5190; a *burden:*— weighty.

5193. נָטַע **nâṭa´,** *naw-tah´;* a prim. root; prop. to *strike* in, i.e. *fix;* spec. to *plant* (lit. or fig.):— fastened, plant (-er).

5194. נֶטַע **neṭa´,** *neh´-tah;* from 5193; a *plant;* collect. a *plantation;* abstr. a *planting:*— plant.

5195. נָטִיעַ **nâṭîya´,** *naw-tee´-ah;* from 5193; a *plant:*— plant.

5196. נְטָעִים **N^eṭâ´îym,** *net-aw-eem´;* plur. of 5194; *Netaim,* a place in Pal.:— plants.

5197. נָטַף **nâṭaph,** *naw-taf´;* a prim. root; to *ooze,* i.e. *distil* gradually; by impl. to *fall in drops;* fig. to *speak* by inspiration:— drop (-ping), prophesy (-et).

5198. נָטָף **nâṭâph,** *naw-tawf´;* from 5197; a *drop;* spec., an aromatic *gum* (prob. *stacte*):— drop, stacte.

5199. נְטֹפָה **N^eṭôphâh,** *net-o-faw´;* from 5197; *distillation; Netophah,* a place in Pal.:— Netophah.

5200. נְטֹפָתִי **N^eṭôphâthîy,** *net-o-faw-thee´;* patron. from 5199; a *Neto-phathite,* or inhab. of Netophah:— Netophathite.

5201. נָטַר **nâṭar,** *naw-tar´;* a prim. root; to *guard;* fig., to *cherish* (anger):— bear grudge, keep (-er), reserve.

5202. נְטַר **n^eṭar** (Chald.), *net-ar´;* corresp. to 5201; to *retain:*— keep.

5203. נָטַשׁ **nâṭash,** *naw-tash´;* a prim. root; prop. to *pound,* i.e. *smite;* by impl. (as if beating out, and thus expanding) to *disperse;* also, to *thrust* off, down, out or upon (incl. *reject, let alone, permit, remit,* etc.):— cast off, drawn, let fall, forsake, join (battle), leave (off), lie still, loose, spread (self) abroad, stretch out, suffer.

5204. נִי **nîy,** *nee;* a doubtful word; appar. from 5091; *lamentation:*— wailing.

5205. נִיד **nîyd,** *need;* from 5110; *motion* (of the lips in speech):— moving.

5206. נִידָה **nîydâh,** *nee-daw´;* fem. of 5205; *removal,* i.e. exile:— removed.

5207. נִיחוֹחַ **nîchôwach,** *nee-kho´-akh;* or

נִיחֹחַ **nîychôach,** *nee-kho´-akh;* from 5117; prop. *restful,* i.e. *pleasant;* abstr. *delight:*— sweet (odour).

5208. נִיחוֹחַ **nîychôwach** (Chald.), *nee-kho´-akh;* or (short.)

נִיחֹחַ **nîychôach** (Chald.), *nee-kho´-akh;* corresp. to 5207; *pleasure:*— sweet odour (savour).

5209. נִין **nîyn,** *neen;* from 5125; *progeny:*— son.

5210. נִינְוֵה **Nîynev̂êh,** *nee-nev-ay´;* of for. or.; *Nineveh,* the capital of Assyria:— Nineveh.

5211. נִיס **nîyç,** *neece;* from 5127; *fugitive:*— that fleeth.

5212. נִיסָן **Nîyçân,** *nee-sawn´;* prob. of for. or.; *Nisan,* the first month of the Jewish sacred year:— Nisan.

5213. נִיצֹוֹת **nîytsôwts,** *nee-tsots´;* from 5340; a *spark:*— spark.

5214. נִיר **nîyr,** *neer;* a root prob. ident. with that of 5216, through the idea of the *gleam* of a fresh furrow; to *till* the soil:— break up.

5215. נִיר **nîyr,** *neer;* or

נִר **nir,** *neer;* from 5214; prop. *plowing,* i.e. (concr.) freshly *plowed land:*— fallow ground, ploughing, tillage.

5216. נִיר **nîyr,** *neer* or

נִר **nir,** *neer;* also

נֵיר **nêyr,** *nare;* or

נֵר **nêr,** *nare;* or (fem.)

נֵרָה **nêrâh,** *nay-raw´;* from a prim. root [see 5214] prop. mean. to *glisten;* a *lamp* (i.e. the burner) or *light* (lit. or fig.):— candle, lamp, light.

5217. נָכָא **nâkâ´,** *naw-kaw´;* a prim. root; to *smite,* i.e. *drive* away:— be viler.

5218. נָכֵא **nâkê´,** *naw-kay´;* or

נָכָא **nâkâ´,** *naw-kaw´;* from 5217; *smitten,* i.e. (fig.) *afflicted:*— broken, stricken, wounded.

5219. נְכֹאת **n^ekô´th,** *nek-ohth´;* from 5218; prop. a *smiting,* i.e. (concr.) an aromatic *gum* [perh. *styrax*] (as powdered):— spicery (-ces).

5220. נֶכֶד **neked,** *neh´-ked;* from an unused root mean. to *propagate; offspring:*— nephew, son's son.

5221. נָכָה **nâkâh,** *naw-kaw´;* a prim. root; to *strike* (lightly or severely, lit. or fig.):— beat, cast forth, clap, give [wounds], × go forward, × indeed, kill, make [slaughter], murderer, punish, slaughter, slay (-er, -ing), smite (-r, -ing), strike, be stricken, (give) stripes, × surely, wound.

5222. נֵכֶה **nêkeh,** *nay-keh´;* from 5221; a *smiter,* i.e. (fig.) *traducer:*— abject.

5223. נָכֶה **nâkeh,** *naw-keh´; smitten,* i.e. (lit.) *maimed,* or (fig.) *dejected:*— contrite, lame.

5224. נְכֹו **N^ekôw,** *nek-o´;* prob. of Eg. or.;

Neko, an Eg. king:— Necho. Comp. 6549.

5225. נָכוֹן **Nâkôwn**, *naw-kone´*; from 3559; *prepared*; *Nakon*, prob. an Isr.:— Nachon.

5226. נֵכַח **nêkach**, *nay´-kakh*; from an unused root mean. to *be straightforward*; prop. the *fore* part; used adv., *opposite*:— before, over against.

5227. נֹכַח **nôkach**, *no´-kakh*; from the same as 5226; prop., the *front* part; used adv. (espec. with prep.), *opposite, in front of, forward, in behalf of*:— (over) against, before, direct [-ly], for, right (on).

5228. נָכֹחַ **nâkôach**, *naw-ko´-akh*; from the same as 5226; *straightforward*, i.e. (fig.), *equitable, correct*, or (abstr.), *integrity*:— plain, right, uprightness.

5229. נְכֹחָה **nᵉkôchâh**, *nek-o-khaw´*; fem. of 5228; prop. *straightforwardness*, i.e. (fig.) *integrity*, or (concr.) a *truth*:— equity, right (thing), uprightness.

5230. נָכַל **nâkal**, *naw-kal´*; a prim. root; to *defraud*, i.e. *act treacherously*:— beguile, conspire, deceiver, deal subtilly.

5231. נֵכֶל **nêkel**, *nay´-kel*; from 5230; *deceit*:— wile.

5232. נְכַס **nᵉkaç** (Chald.), *nek-as´*; corresp. to 5233:— goods.

5233. נֵכֶס **nekeç**, *neh´-kes*; from an unused root mean. to *accumulate*; *treasure*:— riches, wealth.

5234. נָכַר **nâkar**, *naw-kar´*; a prim. root; prop. to *scrutinize*, i.e. look intently at; hence (with *recognition* impl.), to *acknowledge, be acquainted with, care for, respect, revere*, or (with *suspicion* impl.), to *disregard, ignore, be strange toward, reject, resign, dissimulate* (as if ignorant or disowning):— acknowledge, x could, deliver, discern, dissemble, estrange, feign self to be another, know, take knowledge (notice), perceive, regard, (have) respect, behave (make) self strange (-ly).

5235. נֶכֶר **neker**, *neh´-ker*; or

נֹכֶר **nôker**, *no´-ker*; from 5234; something *strange*, i.e. unexpected *calamity*:— strange.

5236. נֵכָר **nêkâr**, *nay-kawr´*; from 5234; *foreign*, or (concr.) a *foreigner*, or (abstr.) *heathendom*:— alien, strange (+ -er).

5237. נָכְרִי **nokrîy**, *nok-ree´*; from 5235 (second form); *strange*, in a variety of degrees and applications (*foreign, non-relative, adulterous, different, wonderful*):— alien, foreigner, outlandish, strange (-r, woman).

5238. נְכֹת **nᵉkôth**, *nek-ôth´*; prob. for 5219; *spicery*, i.e. (gen.) *valuables*:— precious things.

5239. נָלָה **nâlâh**, *naw-law´*; appar. a prim. root; to *complete*:— make an end.

5240. נְמִבְזֶה **nᵉmibzeh**, *nem-ib-zeh´*; from 959. *despised*:— vile.

5241. נְמוּאֵל **Nᵉmûw'êl**, *nem-oo-ale´*; appar. for 3223; *Nemuel*, the name of two Isr.:— Nemuel.

5242. נְמוּאֵלִי **Nᵉmûw'êlîy**, *nem-oo-ay-*

lee´; from 5241; a *Nemuelite*, or desc. of *Nemuel*:— Nemuelite.

5243. נָמַל **nâmal**, *naw-mal´*; a prim. root; to *become clipped* or (spec.) *circumcised*:— (branch to) be cut down (off), circumcise.

5244. נְמָלָה **nᵉmâlâh**, *nem-aw-law´*; fem. from 5243; an *ant* (prob. from its almost *bisected* form):— ant.

5245. נְמַר **nᵉmar** (Chald.), *nem-ar´*; corresp. to 5246:— leopard.

5246. נָמֵר **nâmêr**, *naw-mare´*; from an unused root mean. prop. to *filtrate*, i.e. *be limpid* [comp 5247 and 5249]; and thus to *spot* or *stain* as if by dripping; a *leopard* (from its stripes):— leopard.

נִמְרֹד **Nimrôd**. See 5248.

5247. נִמְרָה **Nimrâh**, *nim-raw´*; from the same as 5246; *clear* water; *Nimrah*, a place E. of the Jordan:— Nimrah. See also 1039, 5249.

5248. נִמְרוֹד **Nimrôwd**, *nim-rode´*; or

נִמְרֹד **Nimrôd**, *nim-rode´*; prob. of for. or.; *Nimrod*, a son of Cush:— Nimrod.

5249. נִמְרִים **Nimrîym**, *nim-reem´*; plur. of a masc. corresp. to 5247; *clear* waters; *Nimrim*, a place E. of the Jordan:— Nimrim. Comp. 1039.

5250. נִמְשִׁי **Nimshîy**, *nim-shee´*; prob. from 4871; *extricated*; *Nimshi*, the (grand-) father of Jehu:— Nimshi.

5251. נֵס **nêç**, *nace*; from 5264; a *flag*; also a *sail*; by impl. a *flagstaff*; gen. a *signal*; fig. a *token*:— banner, pole, sail, (en-) sign, standard.

5252. נְסִבָּה **nᵉçibbâh**, *nes-ib-baw´*; fem. pass. part. of 5437; prop. an *environment*, i.e. *circumstance* or *turn* of affairs:— cause.

5253. נָסַג **nâçag**, *naw-sag´*; a prim. root; to *retreat*:— departing away, remove, take (hold), turn away.

נֶסָה **nᵉçâh**. See 5375.

5254. נָסָה **nâçâh**, *naw-saw´*; a prim. root; to *test*; by impl. to *attempt*:— adventure, assay, prove, tempt, try.

5255. נָסַח **nâçach**, *naw-sakh´*; a prim. root; to *tear* away:— destroy, pluck, root.

5256. נְסַח **nᵉçach** (Chald.), *nes-akh´*; corresp. to 5255:— pull down.

5257. נְסִיךְ **nᵉçîyk**, *nes-eek´*; from 5258; prop. something *poured* out, i.e. a *libation*; also a molten image; by impl. a *prince* (as *anointed*):— drink offering, duke, prince (-ipal).

5258. נָסַךְ **nâçak**, *naw-sak´*; a prim. root; to *pour* out, espec. a libation, or to *cast* (metal); by anal. to *anoint* a king:— cover, melt, offer, (cause to) pour (out), set (up).

5259. נָסַךְ **nâçak**, *naw-sak´*; a prim. root [prob. ident. with 5258 through the idea of fusion]; to *interweave*, i.e. (fig.) to *overspread*:— that is spread.

5260. נְסַךְ **nᵉçak** (Chald.), *nes-ak´*; corresp. to 5258; to *pour* out a libation:— offer.

5261. נְסַךְ **nᵉçak** (Chald.), *nes-ak´*; corresp. to 5262; a *libation*:— drink offering.

5262. נֶסֶךְ **neçek**, *neh´-sek*; or

נֵסֶךְ **nêçek**, *nay´-sek*; from 5258; a *libation*; also a *cast idol*:— cover, drink offering, molten image.

נִסְמָן **niçmân**. See 5567.

5263. נָסַס **nâçaç**, *naw-sas´*; a prim. root; to *wane*, i.e. *be sick*:— faint.

5264. נָסַס **nâçaç**, *naw-sas´*; a prim. root; to *gleam* from afar, i.e. to *be conspicuous* as a signal; or rather perh. a denom. from 5251 land ident. with 5263, through the idea of a flag as *fluttering* in the windl; to *raise a beacon*:— lift up as an ensign.

5265. נָסַע **nâça'**, *naw-sah´*; a prim. root; prop. to *pull* up, espec. the tent-pins, i.e. *start* on a journey:— cause to blow, bring, get, (make to) go (away, forth, forward, onward, out), (take) journey, march, remove, set aside (forward), x still, be on his (go their) way.

5266. נָסַק **nâçaq**, *naw-sak´*; a prim. root; to *go up*:— ascend.

5267. נְסַק **nᵉçaq** (Chald.), *nes-ak´*; corresp. to 5266:— take up.

5268. נִסְרֹךְ **Niçrôk**, *nis-roke´*; of for. or.; *Nisrok*, a Bab. idol:— Nisroch.

5269. נֵעָה **Nê'âh**, *nay-aw´*; from 5128; *motion*; *Neäh*, a place in Pal.:— Neah.

5270. נֹעָה **Nô'âh**, *no-aw´*; from 5128; *movement*; *Noah*, an Israelitess:— Noah.

5271. נָעוּר **nâ'ûwr**, *naw-oor´*; or

נָעֻר **nâ'ûr**, *naw-oor´*; and (fem.)

נְעֻרָה **nᵉ'ûrâh**, *neh-oo-raw´*; prop. pass. part. from 5288 as denom.; (only in plur. collect. or emphat.) *youth*, the state (*juvenility*) or the persons (*young* people):— childhood, youth.

5272. נְעִיאֵל **Nᵉîy'êl**, *neh-ee-ale´*; from 5128 and 410; *moved of God*; *Neiel*, a place in Pal.:— Neiel.

5273. נָעִים **nâ'îym**, *naw-eem´*; from 5276; *delightful* (obj. or subj., lit. or fig.):— pleasant (-ure), sweet.

5274. נָעַל **nâ'al**, *naw-al´*; a prim. root; prop. to *fasten* up, i.e. with a bar or cord; hence, (denom. from 5275), to *sandal*, i.e. furnish with slippers:— bolt, inclose, lock, shoe, shut up.

5275. נַעַל **na'al**, *nah´-al*; or (fem.)

נַעֲלָה **na'âlâh**, *nah-al-aw´*; from 5274; prop. a sandal *tongue*; by extens. a *sandal* or slipper (sometimes as a symbol of occupancy, a refusal to marry, or of something valueless):— dryshod, (pair of) shoe [-latchet], -s).

5276. נָעֵם **nâ'êm**, *naw-ame´*; a prim. root; to *be agreeable* (lit. or fig.):— pass in beauty, be delight, be pleasant, be sweet.

5277. נַעַם **Na'am**, *nah´-am*; from 5276; *pleasure*; *Naam*, an Isr.:— Naam.

5278. נֹעַם **no'am**, *no´-am*; from 5276; *agreeableness*, i.e. *delight, suitableness, splendor* or *grace*:— beauty, pleasant (-ness).

5279. נַעֲמָה **Na'âmâh**, *nah-am-aw´*; fem. of 5277; *pleasantness*; *Naamah*, the name of an antediluvian woman, of an Ammonitess, and of a place in Pal.:— Naamah.

5280. נַעֲמִי **Na'âmîy**, *nah-am-ee´*; patron. from 5283; a *Naamanite*, or desc. of Naaman (collect.):— Naamites.

5281. נָעֳמִי **No'ŏmîy**, *no-ŏm-ee´*; from 5278; *pleasant*; *Noomi*, an Israelitess:— Naomi.

5282. נַעֲמָן **na'âmân**, *nah-am-awn´*; from 5276; *pleasantness* (plur. as concr.):— pleasant.

5283. נַעֲמָן **Na'âmân**, *nah-am-awn´*; the same as 5282; *Naaman*, the name of an Isr. and of a Damascene:— Naaman.

5284. נַעֲמָתִי **Na'ămâthîy**, *nah-am-aw-thee´*; patrial from a place corresp. in name (but not ident.) with 5279; a *Naamathite*, or inhab. of Naamah:— Naamathite.

5285. נַעֲצוּץ **na'ătsûwts**, *nah-ats-oots´*; from an unused root mean. to *prick*; prob. a *brier*; by impl. a *thicket* of thorny bushes:— thorn.

5286. נָעַר **nâ'ar**, *naw-ar´*; a prim. root; to *growl*:— yell.

5287. נָעַר **nâ'ar**, *naw-ar´*; a prim. root [prob. ident. with 5286, through the idea of the *rustling* of mane, which usually accompanies the lion's roar]; to *tumble* about:— shake (off, out, self), overthrow, toss up and down.

5288. נַעַר **na'ar**, *nah´-ar*; from 5287; (concr.) a *boy* (as act.), from the age of infancy to adolescence; by impl. a *servant*; also (by interch. of sex), a *girl* (of similar latitude in age):— babe, boy, child, damsel [from the marg.], lad, servant, young (man).

5289. נַעַר **na'ar**, *nah´-ar*; from 5287 in its der. sense of *tossing* about; a *wanderer*:— young one.

5290. נֹעַר **nô'ar**, *no´-ar*; from 5287; (abstr.) *boyhood* [comp. 5288]:— child, youth.

נָעוּר **nâ'ûr**. See 5271.

5291. נַעֲרָה **na'ărâh**, *nah-ar-aw´*; fem. of 5288; a *girl* (from infancy to adolescence):— damsel, maid (-en), young (woman).

5292. נַעֲרָה **Na'ărâh**, *nah-ar-aw´*; the same as 5291; *Naarah*, the name of an Israelitess, and of a place in Pal.:— Naarah, Naarath.

נְעֻרָה **n**e**'ûrâh**. See 5271.

5293. נַעֲרַי **Na'ăray**, *nah-ar-ah´-ee*; from 5288; *youthful; Naarai*, an Isr.:— Naarai.

5294. נְעַרְיָה **N**e**'aryâh**, *neh-ar-yaw´*; from 5288 and 3050; *servant of Jah; Nearjah*, the name of two Isr.:— Neariah.

5295. נַעֲרָן **Na'ărân**, *nah-ar-awn´*; from 5288; *juvenile; Naaran*, a place in Pal.:— Naaran.

5296. נְעֹרֶת **n**e**'ôreth**, *neh-o´-reth*; from 5287; something *shaken* out, i.e. *tow* (as the refuse of flax):— tow.

נַעֲרָתָה **Na'ărâthâh**. See 5292.

5297. נֹף **Nôph**, *nofe*; a var. of 4644; *Noph*, the capital of Upper Egypt:— Noph.

5298. נֶפֶג **Nepheg**, *neh´-feg*; from an unused root prob. mean. to *spring* forth; a

sprout; Nepheg, the name of two Isr.:— Nepheg.

5299. נָפָה **nâphâh**, *naw-faw´*; from 5130 in the sense of *lifting*; a *height*; also a *sieve*:— border, coast, region, sieve.

5300. נְפוּשְׁסִים **N**e**phûwsh**e**çîym**, *nef-oo-shes-eem´*; for 5304; *Nephushesim*, a Temple-servant:— Nephisesim [from the marg.].

5301. נָפַח **nâphach**, *naw-fakh´*; a prim. root; to *puff*, in various applications (lit., to *inflate, blow* hard, *scatter, kindle, expire;* fig., to *disesteem*):— blow, breath, give up, cause to lose [life], seething, snuff.

5302. נֹפַח **Nôphach**, *no´-fakh*; from 5301; a *gust; Nophach*, a place in Moab:— Nophah.

5303. נְפִיל **n**e**phîyl**, *nef-eel´*; or

נְפִל **n**e**phîl**, *nef-eel´*; from 5307; prop., a *feller*, i.e. a *bully* or *tyrant*:— giant.

5304. נְפִיסִים **N**e**phîyçîym**, *nef-ee-seem´*; plur. from an unused root mean. to *scatter; expansions; Nephisim*, a Temple-servant:— Nephusim [from the marg.].

5305. נָפִישׁ **Nâphîysh**, *naw-feesh´*; from 5314; *refreshed; Naphish*, a son of Ishmael, and his posterity:— Naphish.

5306. נֹפֶךְ **nôphek**, *no´-fek*; from an unused root mean. to *glisten; shining;* a gem, prob. the *garnet:*— emerald.

5307. נָפַל **nâphal**, *naw-fal´*; a prim. root; to *fall*, in a great variety of applications (intr. or caus., lit. or fig.):— be accepted, cast (down, self, [lots], out), cease, die, divide (by lot), (let) fail, (cause to, let, make, ready to) fall (away, down, -en, -ing), fell (-ing), fugitive, have [inheritance], inferior, be judged [by mistake for 6419], lay (along), (cause to) lie down, light (down), be (× hast) lost, lying, overthrow, overwhelm, perish, present (-ed, -ing), (make to) rot, slay, smite out, × surely, throw down.

5308. נְפַל **n**e**phal** (Chald.), *nef-al´*; corresp. to 5307:— fall (down), have occasion.

5309. נֶפֶל **nephel**, *neh´-fel*; or

נֵפֶל **nêphel**, *nay´-fel*; from 5307; something *fallen*, i.e. an *abortion:*— untimely birth.

נְפִל **n**e**phîl**. See 5303.

5310. נָפַץ **nâphats**, *naw-fats´*; a prim. root; to *dash* to pieces, or *scatter:*— be beaten in sunder, break (in pieces), broken, dash (in pieces), cause to be discharged, dispersed, be overspread, scatter.

5311. נֶפֶץ **nephets**, *neh´-fets*; from 5310; a *storm* (as dispersing):— scattering.

5312. נְפַק **n**e**phaq** (Chald.), *nef-ak´*; a prim. root; to *issue*; caus. to *bring out:*— come (go, take) forth (out).

5313. נִפְקָא **niphqâ'** (Chald.), *nif-kaw´*; from 5312; an *outgo*, i.e. *expense:*— expense.

5314. נָפַשׁ **nâphash**, *naw-fash´*; a prim. root; to *breathe*; pass., to be *breathed* upon, i.e. (fig.) *refreshed* (as if by a current of air):— (be) refresh selves (-ed).

5315. נֶפֶשׁ **nephesh**, *neh´-fesh;* from 5314; prop. a *breathing* creature, i.e. *animal* of (abstr.) *vitality;* used very widely in a lit., accommodated or fig. sense (bodily or ment.):— any, appetite, beast, body, breath, creature, × dead (-ly), desire, × [dis-] contented, × fish, ghost, + greedy, he, heart (-y), (hath, × jeopardy of) life (× in jeopardy), lust, man, me, mind, mortally, one, own, person, pleasure, (her-, him-, my-, thy-) self, them (your)-selves, + slay, soul, + tablet, they, thing, (× she) will, × would have it.

5316. נֶפֶת **nepheth**, *neh´-feth;* for 5299; a *height:*— country.

5317. נֹפֶת **nôpheth**, *no´-feth;* from 5130 in the sense of *shaking* to pieces; a *dripping*, i.e. of *honey* (from the comb):— honeycomb.

5318. נַפְתּוֹחַ **Nephtôwach**, *nef-to´-akh;* from 6605; *opened*, i.e. a *spring; Nephtoach*, a place in Pal.:— Neptoah.

5319. נַפְתּוּל **naphtûwl**, *naf-tool´;* from 6617; prop. *wrestled;* but used (in the plur.) tran., a *struggle:*— wrestling.

5320. נַפְתֻּחִים **Naphtûchîym**, *naf-too-kheem´;* plur. of for. or., *Naphtuchim*, an Eg. tribe:— Naptuhim.

5321. נַפְתָּלִי **Naphtâlîy**, *naf-taw-lee´;* from 6617; *my wrestling; Naphtali*, a son of Jacob, with the tribe desc. from him, and its territory:— Naphtali.

5322. נֵץ **nêts**, *nayts;* from 5340; a *flower* (from its *brilliancy*); also a *hawk* (from it *flashing* speed):— blossom, hawk.

5323. נָצָא **nâtsâ'**, *naw-tsaw´;* a prim. root; to *go away:*— flee.

5324. נָצַב **nâtsab**, *naw-tsab´;* a prim. root; to *station*, in various applications (lit. or fig.):— appointed, deputy, erect, establish, × Huzzah [by mistake for a proper name], lay, officer, pillar, present, rear up, set (over, up), settle, sharpen, stablish, (make to) stand (-ing, still, up, upright), best state.

נְצִיב **n**e**tsîb**. See 5333.

5325. נִצָּב **nitstsâb**, *nits-tsawb´;* pass. part. of 5324; *fixed*, i.e. a *handle:*— haft.

5326. נִצְבָּה **nitsbâh** (Chald.), *nits-baw´;* from a root corresp. to 5324; *fixedness*, i.e. *firmness:*— strength.

5327. נָצָה **nâtsâh**, *naw-tsaw´;* a prim. root; prop. to *go forth*, i.e. (by impl.) to be *expelled*, and (consequently) *desolate;* caus. to *lay waste*; also (spec.), to *quarrel:*— be laid waste, ruinous, strive (together).

נֹצָה **nôtsâh**. See 5133.

5328. נִצָּה **nitstsâh**, *nits-tsaw´;* fem. of 5322; a *blossom:*— flower.

נְצוּרָה **n**e**tsûwrâh**. See 5341.

5329. נָצַח **nâtsach**, *naw-tsakh´;* a prim. root; prop. to *glitter* from afar, i.e. to be *eminent* (as a superintendent, espec. of the Temple services and its music); also (as denom. from 5331), to be *permanent:*— excel, chief musician (singer), oversee (-r), set forward.

5330. נְצַח **n**e**tsach** (Chald.), *nets-akh´;* corresp. to 5329; to *become chief:*— be preferred.

5331. נֶצַח **netsach**, *neh´-tsakh;* or

נֶצַח **nêtsach**, *nay´-tsakh;* from 5329; prop. a *goal*, i.e. the bright object at a distance travelled toward; hence, (fig.) *splendor*, or (subj.) *truthfulness*, or (obj.) *confidence;* but usually (adv.), *continually* (i.e. to the most distant point of view):— alway (-s) constantly, end, (+ n-) ever (more), perpetual, strength, victory.

5332. נֶצַח **nêtsach**, *nay´-tsakh;* prob. ident. with 5331, through the idea of *brilliancy* of color; *juice* of the grape (as blood red):— blood, strength.

5333. נְצִיב **nᵉtsîyb**, *nets-eeb´;* or

נְצִב **nᵉtsîb**, *nets-eeb´;* something *stationary*, i.e. a *prefect*, a military *post*, a *statue:*— garrison, officer, pillar.

5334. נְצִיב **Nᵉtsîyb**, *nets-eeb´;* the same as 5333; *station; Netsib*, a place in Pal.:— Nezib.

5335. נְצִיחַ **Nᵉtsîyach**, *nets-ee´-akh;* from 5329; *conspicuous; Netsiach*, a Temple-servant:— Neziah.

5336. נָצִיר **nâtsîyr**,° *naw-tsere´;* from 5341; prop. *conservative;* but used pass., *delivered:*— preserved.

5337. נָצַל **nâtsal**, *naw-tsal´;* a prim. root; to *snatch* away, whether in a good or a bad sense:— × at all, defend, deliver (self), escape, × without fail, part, pluck, preserve, recover, rescue, rid, save, spoil, strip, × surely, take (out).

5338. נְצַל **nᵉtsal** (Chald.), *nets-al´;* corresp. to 5337; to *extricate:*— deliver, rescue.

5339. נִצָּן **nitstsân**, *nits-tsawn´;* from 5322; a *blossom:*— flower.

5340. נָצַץ **nâtsats**, *naw-tsats´;* a prim. root; to *glare*, i.e. *be bright-*colored:— sparkle.

5341. נָצַר **nâtsar**, *naw-tsar´;* a prim. root; to *guard*, in a good sense (to *protect, maintain, obey*, etc.) or a bad one (to *conceal*, etc.):— besieged, hidden thing, keep (-er, -ing), monument, observe, preserve (-r), subtil, watcher (-man).

5342. נֵצֶר **nêtser**, *nay´-tser;* from 5341 in the sense of *greenness* as a striking color; a *shoot;* fig. a *descendant:*— branch.

5343. נְקֵא **nᵉqê'** (Chald.), *nek-ay´;* from a root corresp. to 5352; *clean:*— pure.

5344. נָקַב **nâqab**, *naw-kab´;* a prim. root; to *puncture*, lit. (to *perforate*, with more or less violence) or fig. (to *specify, designate, libel*):— appoint, blaspheme, bore, curse, express, with holes, name, pierce, strike through.

5345. נֶקֶב **neqeb**, *neh´keb;* a *bezel* (for a gem):— pipe.

5346. נֶקֶב **Neqeb**, *neh´-keb;* the same as 5345; *dell; Nekeb*, a place in Pal.:— Nekeb.

5347. נְקֵבָה **nᵉqêbâh**, *nek-ay-baw´;* from 5344; *female* (from the sexual form):— female.

5348. נָקֹד **nâqôd**, *naw-kode´;* from an unused root mean. to *mark* (by *puncturing* or *branding*); *spotted:*— speckled.

5349. נֹקֵד **nôqêd**, *no-kade´;* act. part.

from the same as 5348; a *spotter* (of sheep or cattle), i.e. the owner or tender (who thus marks them):— herdman, sheepmaster.

5350. נִקֻּד **niqqud**, *nik-kood´;* from the same as 5348; a *crumb* (as *broken* to spots); also a *biscuit* (as *pricked*):— cracknel, mouldy.

5351. נְקֻדָּה **nᵉquddâh**, *nek-ood-daw´;* fem. of 5348; a *boss:*— stud.

5352. נָקָה **nâqâh**, *naw-kaw´;* a prim. root; to *be* (or *make*) *clean* (lit. or fig.); by impl. (in an adverse sense) to *be bare*, i.e. *extirpated:*— acquit × at all, × altogether, be blameless, cleanse, (be) clear (-ing), cut off, be desolate, be free, be (hold) guiltless, be (hold) innocent, × by no means, be quit, be (leave) unpunished, × utterly, × wholly.

5353. נְקוֹדָא **Nᵉqôwdâ'**, *nek-o-daw´;* fem. of 5348 (in the fig. sense of *marked*); *distinction; Nekoda*, a Temple-servant:— Nekoda.

5354. נָקַט **nâqat**, *naw-kat´;* a prim. root; to *loathe:*— weary.

5355. נָקִי **nâqîy**, *naw-kee´;* or

נָקִיא **nâqîy'** (Joel 4:19; Jonah 1:14), *naw-kee´;* from 5352; *innocent:*— blameless, clean, clear, exempted, free, guiltless, innocent, quit.

5356. נִקָּיוֹן **niqqâyôwn**, *nik-kaw-yone´;* or

נִקָּיֹן **niqqâyôn**, *nik-kaw-yone´;* from 5352; *cleanness* (lit. or fig.):— cleanness, innocency.

5357. נָקִיק **nâqîyq**, *naw-keek´;* from an unused root mean. to *bore;* a *cleft:*— hole.

5358. נָקַם **nâqam**, *naw-kam´;* a prim. root; to *grudge*, i.e. *avenge* or *punish:*— avenge (-r, self), punish, revenge (self), × surely, take vengeance.

5359. נָקָם **nâqâm**, *naw-kawm´;* from 5358; *revenge:*— + avenged, quarrel, vengeance.

5360. נְקָמָה **nᵉqâmâh**, *nek-aw-maw´;* fem. of 5359; *avengement*, whether the act or the passion:— + avenge, revenge (-ing), vengeance.

5361. נָקַע **nâqa'**, *naw-kah´;* a prim. root; to *feel aversion:*— be alienated.

5362. נָקַף **nâqaph**, *naw-kaf´;* a prim. root; to *strike* with more or less violence (*beat, fell, corrode*); by impl. (of attack) to *knock together*, i.e. *surround* or *circulate:*— compass (about, -ing), cut down, destroy, go round (about), inclose, round.

5363. נֹקֶף **nôqeph**, *no´-kef;* from 5362; a *threshing* (of olives):— shaking.

5364. נִקְפָּה **niqpâh**, *nik-paw´;* from 5362; prob. a *rope* (as *encircling*):— rent.

5365. נָקַר **nâqar**, *naw-kar´;* a prim. root; to *bore* (*penetrate, quarry*):— dig, pick out, pierce, put (thrust) out.

5366. נְקָרָה **nᵉqârâh**, *nek-aw-raw´;* from 5365, a *fissure:*— cleft, clift.

5367. נָקַשׁ **nâqash**, *naw-kash´;* a prim. root; to *entrap* (with a noose), lit. or fig.:— catch, (lay a) snare.

5368. נְקַשׁ **nᵉqash** (Chald.), *nek-ash´;*

corresp. to 5367; but used in the sense of 5362; to *knock:*— smote.

נֵר **nêr**,

נִר **nîr**. See 5215, 5216.

5369. נֵר **Nêr**, *nare;* the same as 5216; *lamp; Ner*, an Isr.:— Ner.

5370. נֵרְגַל **Nêrgal**, *nare-gal´;* of for. or.; *Nergal*, a Cuthite deity:— Nergal.

5371. נֵרְגַל שַׁרְאֶצֶר **Nêrgal Shar'etser**, *nare-gal´ shar-eh´-tser;* from 5370 and 8272; *Nergal-Sharetser*, the name of two Bab.:— Nergal-sharezer.

5372. נִרְגָּן **nirgân**, *neer-gawn´;* from an unused root mean. to *roll* to pieces; a *slanderer:*— talebearer, whisperer.

5373. נֵרְדְּ **nêrd**, *nayrd;* of for. or.; *nard*, an aromatic:— spikenard.

נֵרָה **nêrâh**. See 5216.

5374. נֵרִיָּה **Nêrîyâh**, *nay-ree-yaw´;* or

נֵרִיָּהוּ **Nêrîyâhûw**, *nay-ree-yaw´-hoo;* from 5216 and 3050; *light of Jah; Nerijah*, an Isr.:— Neriah.

5375. נָשָׂא **nâsâ'**, *naw-saw´;* or

נָסָה **nâçâh** (Psa. 4:6 [7]) *naw-saw´;* a prim. root; to *lift*, in a great variety of applications, lit. and fig., absol. and rel. (as follows):— accept, advance, arise, (able to, [armour], suffer to) bear (-er, up), bring (forth), burn, carry (away), cast, contain, desire, ease, exact, exalt (self), extol, fetch, forgive, furnish, further, give, go on, help, high, hold up, honorable (+ man), lade, lay, lift (self) up, lofty, marry, magnify, × needs, obtain, pardon, raise (up), receive, regard, respect, set (up), spare, stir up, + swear, take (away, up), × utterly, wear, yield.

5376. נְשָׂא **nᵉsâ'** (Chald.), *nes-aw´;* corresp. to 5375:— carry away, make insurrection, take.

5377. נָשָׁא **nâshâ'**, *naw-shaw´;* a prim. root; to *lead astray*, i.e. (ment.) to *delude*, or (mor.) to *seduce:*— beguile, deceive, × greatly, × utterly.

5378. נָשָׁא **nâshâ'**, *naw-shaw´;* a prim. root [perh. ident. with 5377, through the idea of *imposition*]; to *lend* on interest; by impl. to *dun* for debt:— × debt, exact, giver of usury.

נָשִׂיא **nâsî'**. See 5387.

נְשׂוּאָה **nᵉsû'âh**. See 5385.

5379. נִשֵּׂאת **nissê'th**, *nis-sayth´;* pass. part. fem. of 5375; something *taken*, i.e. a *present:*— gift.

5380. נָשַׁב **nâshab**, *naw-shab´;* a prim. root; to *blow;* by impl. to *disperse:*— (cause to) blow, drive away.

5381. נָשַׂג **nâsag**, *naw-sag´;* a prim. root; to *reach* (lit. or fig.):— ability, be able, attain (unto), (be able to, can) get, lay at, put, reach, remove, wax rich, × surely, (over-) take (hold of, on, upon).

5382. נָשָׁה **nâshâh**, *naw-shaw´;* a prim. root; to *forget;* fig. to *neglect;* caus. to *remit, remove:*— forget, deprive, exact.

5383. נָשָׁה **nâshâh**, *naw-shaw´;* a prim. root [rather ident. with 5382, in the sense of 5378]; to *lend* or (by reciprocity) *borrow* on security or interest:— creditor, exact, extortioner, lend, usurer, lend on (taker of) usury.

Hebrew

5384. נָשֶׁה **nâsheh**, *naw-sheh´*; from 5382, in the sense of *failure*; *rheumatic* or *crippled* (from the incident to Jacob):— which shrank.

5385. נְשׂוּאָה **nᵉsûw'âh**, *nes-oo-aw´*; or rather,

נְשֻׂאָה **nᵉsû'âh**, *nes-oo-aw´*; fem.. pass. part. of 5375; something *borne*, i.e. a *load:*— carriage.

5386. נְשִׁי **nᵉshîy**, *nesh-ee´*; from 5383; a *debt:*— debt.

5387. נְשִׂיא **nâsîy'**, *naw-see´*; or

נָשִׂא **nâsi'**, *naw-see´*; from 5375; prop. an *exalted* one, i.e. a *king* or *sheik*; also a rising *mist:*— captain, chief, cloud, governor, prince, ruler, vapour.

5388. נְשִׁיָּה **nᵉshîyâh**, *nesh-ee-yaw´*; from 5382; *oblivion:*— forgetfulness.

נָשִׁים **nâshîym**. See 802.

5389. נָשִׁין **nâshîyn** (Chald.), *naw-sheen´*; irreg. plur. fem. of 606:— women.

5390. נְשִׁיקָה **nᵉshîyqâh**, *nesh-ee-kaw´*; from 5401; a *kiss:*— kiss.

5391. נָשַׁךְ **nâshak**, *naw-shak´*; a prim. root; to *strike* with a sting (as a serpent); fig. to *oppress* with interest on a loan:— bite, lend upon usury.

5392. נֶשֶׁךְ **neshek**, *neh´-shek*; from 5391; *interest* on a debt:— usury.

5393. נִשְׁכָּה **nishkâh**, *nish-kaw´*; for 3957; a *cell:*— chamber.

5394. נָשַׁל **nâshal**, *naw-shal´*; a prim. root; to *pluck* off, i.e. *divest, eject,* or *drop:*— cast (out), drive, loose, put off (out), slip.

5395. נָשַׁם **nâsham**, *naw-sham´*; a prim. root; prop. to *blow* away, i.e. *destroy:*— destroy.

5396. נִשְׁמָא **nishmâ'** (Chald.), *nish-maw´*; corresp. to 5397; vital *breath:*— breath.

5397. נְשָׁמָה **nᵉshâmâh**, *nesh-aw-maw´*; from 5395; a *puff,* i.e. *wind,* angry or vital *breath,* divine *inspiration, intellect,* or (concr.) an *animal:*— blast, (that) breath (-eth), inspiration, soul, spirit.

5398. נָשַׁף **nâshaph**, *naw-shaf´*; a prim. root; to *breeze,* i.e. *blow* up fresh (as the wind):— blow.

5399. נֶשֶׁף **nesheph**, *neh´-shef*; from 5398; prop. a *breeze,* i.e. (by impl.) *dusk* (when the evening breeze prevails):— dark, dawning of the day (morning), night, twilight.

5400. נָשַׂק **nâsaq**, *naw-sak´*; a prim. root; to *catch* fire:— burn, kindle.

5401. נָשַׁק **nâshaq**, *naw-shak´*; a prim. root [ident. with 5400, through the idea of *fastening* up; comp. 2388, 2836]; to *kiss,* lit. or fig. (*touch*); also (as a mode of *attachment*), to *equip* with weapons:— armed (men), rule, kiss, that touched.

5402. נֶשֶׁק **nesheq**, *neh´-shek*; or

נֵשֶׁק **nêsheq**, *nay´-shek*; from 5401; military *equipment,* i.e. (collect.) *arms* (offensive or defensive), or (concr.) an *arsenal:*— armed men, armour (-y), battle, harness, weapon.

5403. נְשַׁר **nᵉshar** (Chald.), *nesh-ar´*; corresp. to 5404; an *eagle:*— eagle.

5404. נֶשֶׁר **nesher**, *neh´-sher*; from an unused root mean. to *lacerate*; the *eagle* (or other large bird of prey):— eagle.

5405. נָשַׁת **nâshath**, *naw-shath´*; a prim. root; prop. to *eliminate,* i.e. (intr.) to *dry* up:— fail.

נְתִיבָה **nᵉthîbâh**. See 5410.

5406. נִשְׁתְּוָן **nisht°vân**, *nish-tev-awn´*; prob. of Pers. or.; an *epistle:*— letter.

5407. נִשְׁתְּוָן **nisht°vân** (Chald.), *nish-tev-awn´*; corresp. to 5406:— letter.

נָתוּן **Nâthûwn**. See 5411.

5408. נָתַח **nâthach**, *naw-thakh´*; a prim. root; to *dismember:*— cut (in pieces), divide, hew in pieces.

5409. נֵתַח **nêthach**, *nay´-thakh*; from 5408; a *fragment:*— part, piece.

5410. נָתִיב **nâthîyb**, *naw-theeb´*; or (fem.)

נְתִיבָה **nᵉthîybâh**, *neth-ee-baw´*; or

נְתִבָה **nᵉthibâh** (Jer. 6:16), *neth-ee-baw´*; from an unused root mean. to *tramp*; a (beaten) *track:*— path (l-wayl), × travel l-lerl, way.

5411. נָתִין **Nâthîyn**, *naw-theen´*; or

נָתוּן **Nâthûwn** (Ezra 8:17), *naw-thoon´* (the proper form, as pass. part.), from 5414; one *given,* i.e. (in the plur. only) the *Nethinim,* or Temple-servants (as *given* to that duty):— Nethinims.

5412. נְתִין **Nᵉthîyn** (Chald.), *netheen´*; corresp. to 5411:— Nethinims.

5413. נָתַךְ **nâthak**, *naw-thak´*; a prim. root; to *flow* forth (lit. or fig.); by impl. to *liquefy:*— drop, gather (together), melt, pour (forth, out).

5414. נָתַן **nâthan**, *naw-than´*; a prim. root; to *give,* used with greatest latitude of application (*put, make,* etc.):— add, apply, appoint, ascribe, assign, × avenge, × be (healed), bestow, bring (forth, hither), cast, cause, charge, come, commit, consider, count, + cry, deliver (up), direct, distribute, do, × doubtless, × without fail, fasten, frame, × get, give (forth, over, up), grant, hang (up), × have, × indeed, lay (unto charge, up), (give) leave, lend, let (out), + lie, lift up, make, + O that, occupy, offer, ordain, pay, perform, place, pour, print, × pull, put (forth), recompense, render, requite, restore, send (out), set (forth), shew, shoot forth (up), + sing, + slander, strike, lsub-l mit, suffer, × surely, × take, thrust, trade, turn, utter, + weep, × willingly, + withdraw, + would (to) God, yield.

5415. נְתַן **nᵉthan** (Chald.), *neth-an´*; corresp. to 5414; *give:*— bestow, give, pay.

5416. נָתָן **Nâthân**, *naw-thawn´*; from 5414; *given*; *Nathan,* the name of five Isr.:— Nathan.

5417. נְתַנְאֵל **Nᵉthan'êl**, *neth-an-ale´*; from 5414 and 410; *given of God*; *Nethanel,* the name of ten Isr.:— Nethaneel.

5418. נְתַנְיָה **Nᵉthanyâh**, *neth-an-yaw´*; or

נְתַנְיָהוּ **Nᵉthanyâhûw**, *neth-an-*

yaw´-hoo; from 5414 and 3050; *given of Jah*; *Nethanjah,* the name of four Isr.:— Nethaniah.

5419. נְתַן־מֶלֶךְ **Nᵉthan-Melek**, *neth-an´ meh´-lek*; from 5414 and 4428; *given of* (the) *king*; *Nethan-Melek,* an Isr.:— Nathan-melech.

5420. נָתַס **nâthaç**, *naw-thas´*; a prim. root; to *tear* up:— mar.

5421. נָתַע **nâtha'**, *naw-thah´*; for 5422; to *tear* out:— break.

5422. נָתַץ **nâthats**, *naw-thats´*; a prim. root; to *tear* down:— beat down, break down (out), cast down, destroy, overthrow, pull down, throw down.

5423. נָתַק **nâthaq**, *naw-thak´*; a prim. root; to *tear* off:— break (off), burst, draw (away), lift up, pluck (away, off), pull (out), root out.

5424. נֶתֶק **netheq**, *neh´-thek*; from 5423; *scurf:*— (dry) scall.

5425. נָתַר **nâthar**, *naw-thar´*; a prim. root; to *jump,* i.e. *be violently agitated*; caus., to *terrify, shake* off, *untie:*— drive asunder, leap, (let) loose, × make, move, undo.

5426. נְתַר **nᵉthar** (Chald.), *neth-ar´*; corresp. to 5425:— shake off.

5427. נֶתֶר **nether**, *neh´-ther*; from 5425; mineral *potash* (so called from *effervescing* with acid):— nitre.

5428. נָתַשׁ **nâthash**, *naw-thash´*; a prim. root; to *tear* away:— destroy, forsake, pluck (out, up, by the roots), pull up, root out (up), × utterly.

ס

5429. סְאָה **ç°'âh**, *seh-aw´*; from an unused root mean. to *define*; a *seah,* or certain measure (as *determinative*) for grain:— measure.

5430. סְאוֹן **ç°'ôwn**, *seh-own´*; from 5431; perh. a military *boot* (as a protection from *mud*:— battle.

5431. סָאַן **çâ'an**, *saw-an´*; a prim. root; to *be miry*; used only as denom. from 5430; to *shoe,* i.e. (act. part.) a *soldier* shod:— warrior.

5432. סַאסְּאָה **ça'ç°'âh**, *sah-seh-aw´*; for 5429; *measurement,* i.e. *moderation:*— measure.

5433. סָבָא **çâbâ'**, *saw-baw´*; a prim. root; to *quaff* to satiety, i.e. *become tipsy:*— drunkard, fill self, Sabean, lwine-lbibber.

5434. סְבָא **Ç°bâ'**, *seb-aw´*; of for. or.; *Seba,* a son of Cush, and the country settled by him:— Seba.

5435. סֹבֶא **çôbe'**, *so´-beh*; from 5433; *potation,* concr. (*wine*), or abstr. (*carousal*):— drink, drunken, wine.

5436. סְבָאִי **Ç°bâ'îy**, *seb-aw-ee´*; patrial from 5434; a *Sebaite,* or inhab. of Seba:— Sabean.

5437. סָבַב **çâbab**, *saw-bab´*; a prim. root; to *revolve, surround,* or *border*; used in various applications, lit. and fig. (as follows):— bring, cast, fetch, lead, make, walk, × whirl, × round about, be about on every side, apply, avoid, beset (about), besiege, bring again, carry (about), change, cause to come about, × circuit, (fetch a) compass (about, round), drive, environ, × on every side, beset (close, come, compass, go, stand) round about, inclose, remove, return, set, sit down, turn (self) (about, aside, away, back).

5438. סִבָּה çibbâh, sib-baw´; from 5437; a (providential) turn (of affairs):— cause.

5439. סָבִיב çâbîyb, saw-beeb´; or (fem.)

סְבִיבָה çᵉbîybâh, seb-ee-baw´; from 5437; (as noun) a circle, neighbour, or environs; but chiefly (as adv., with or without prep.) around:— (place, round) about, circuit, compass, on every side.

5440. סָבַךְ çâbak, saw-bak´; a prim. root; to entwine:— fold together, wrap.

5441. סֹבֶךְ çôbek, so´-bek; from 5440; a copse:— thicket.

5442. סְבָךְ çᵉbâk, seb-awk´; from 5440, a copse:— thick (-et).

5443. סַבְּכָא çabbᵉkâ' (Chald.), sab-bek-aw´; or

סַבְּכָא sabbᵉkâ' (Chald.), sab-bek-aw´; from a root corresp. to 5440; a lyre:— sackbut.

5444. סִבְּכַי Çibbᵉkay, sib-bek-ah´-ee; from 5440; copse-like; Sibbecai, an Isr.:— Sibbecai, Sibbechai.

5445. סָבַל çâbal, saw-bal´; a prim. root; to carry (lit. or fig.), or (refl.) be burdensome; spec. to be gravid:— bear, be a burden, carry, strong to labour.

5446. סְבַל çᵉbal (Chald.), seb-al´; corresp. to 5445; to erect:— strongly laid.

5447. סֵבֶל çêbel, say´-bel; from 5445; a load (lit. or fig.):— burden, charge.

5448. סֹבֶל çôbel, so´-bel; (only in the form

סֻבָּל çubbâl, soob-bawl´); from 5445; a load (fig.):— burden.

5449. סַבָּל çabbâl, sab-bawl´; from 5445; a porter:— (to bear, bearer of) burden (-s).

5450. סְבָלָה çᵉbâlâh, seb-aw-law´; from 5447; porterage:— burden.

5451. סִבֹּלֶת Çibbôleth, sib-bo´-leth; for 7641; an ear of grain:— Sibboleth.

5452. סְבַר çᵉbar (Chald.), seb-ar´; a prim. root; to bear in mind, i.e. hope:— think.

5453. סִבְרַיִם Çibrayim, sib-rah´-yim; dual from a root corresp. to 5452; double hope; Sibrajim, a place in Syria:— Sibraim.

5454. סַבְתָּא Çabtâ', sab-taw´; or

סַבְתָּה Çabtâh, sab-taw´; prob. of for. der.; Sabta or Sabtah, the name of a son of Cush, and the country occupied by his posterity:— Sabta, Sabtah.

5455. סַבְתְּכָא Çabtᵉkâ', sab-tek-aw´; prob. of for. der.; Sabteca, the name of a son of Cush, and the region settled by him:— Sabtecha, Sabtechah.

5456. סָגַד çâgad, saw-gad´; a prim. root; to prostrate oneself (in homage):— fall down.

5457. סְגִד çᵉgid (Chald.), seg-eed´; corresp. to 5456:— worship.

5458. סְגוֹר çᵉgôwr, seg-ore´; from 5462; prop. shut up, i.e. the breast (as inclos-

ing the heart); also gold (as gen. shut up safely):— caul, gold.

5459. סְגֻלָּה çᵉgullâh, seg-ool-law´; fem. pass. part. of an unused root mean. to shut up; wealth (as closely shut up):— jewel, peculiar (treasure), proper good, special.

5460. סְגַן çᵉgan (Chald.), seg-an´; corresp. to 5461:— governor.

5461. סָגָן çâgân, saw-gawn´; from an unused root mean. to superintend; a præfect of a province:— prince, ruler.

5462. סָגַר çâgar, saw-gar´; a prim. root; to shut up; fig. to surrender:— close up, deliver (up), give over (up), inclose, × pure, repair, shut (in, self, out, up, up together), stop, × straitly.

5463. סְגַר çᵉgar (Chald.), seg-ar´; corresp. to 5462:— shut up.

5464. סַגְרִיד çagrîyd, sag-reed´; prob. from 5462 in the sense of sweeping away; a pouring rain:— very rainy.

5465. סַד çad, sad; from an unused root mean. to estop; the stocks:— stocks.

5466. סָדִין çâdîyn, saw-deen´; from an unused root mean. to envelop; a wrapper, i.e. shirt:— fine linen, sheet.

5467. סְדֹם Çᵉdôm, sed-ome´; from an unused root mean. to scorch; burnt (i.e. volcanic or bituminous) district; Sedom, a place near the Dead Sea:— Sodom.

5468. סֶדֶר çeder, seh´-der; from an unused root mean. to arrange; order:— order.

5469. סֹהַר çahar, sah´-har; from an unused root mean. to be round; roundness:— round.

5470. סֹהַר çôhar, so´-har; from the same as 5469; a dungeon (as surrounded by walls):— prison.

5471. סוֹא Çôw', so; of for. der.; So, an Eg. king:— So.

5472. סוּג çûwg, soog; a prim. root; prop. to flinch, i.e. (by impl.) to go back, lit. (to retreat) or fig. (to apostatize):— backslider, drive, go back, turn (away, back).

5473. סוּג çûwg, soog; a prim. root [prob. rather ident. with 5472 through the idea of shrinking from a hedge; comp. 7735]; to hem in, i.e. bind:— set about.

סוּג çûwg. See 5509.

5474. סוּגַר çûwgar, soo-gar´; from 5462; an inclosure, i.e. cage (for an animal):— ward.

5475. סוֹד çôwd, sode; from 3245; a session, i.e. company of persons (in close deliberation); by impl. intimacy, consultation, a secret:— assembly, counsel, inward, secret (counsel).

5476. סוֹדִי Çôwdîy, so-dee´; from 5475; a confidant; Sodi, an Isr.:— Sodi.

5477. סוּחַ Çûwach, soo´-akh; from an unused root mean. to wipe away; sweeping; Suach, an Isr.:— Suah.

5478. סוּחָה çûwchâh, soo-khaw´; from the same as 5477; something swept away, i.e. filth:— torn.

סוּט çûwṭ. See 7750.

5479. סוֹטַי Çôwṭay, so-tah´-ee; from

7750; roving; Sotai, one of the Nethinim:— Sotai.

5480. סוּךְ çûwk, sook; a prim. root; prop. to smear over (with oil), i.e. anoint:— anoint (self), × at all.

סוּלֵלָה çôwlᵉlâh. See 5550.

5481. סוּמְפּוֹנְיָה çûwmpôwnᵉyâh (Chald.), soom-po-neh-yaw´; or

סוּמְפֹּנְיָה çûwmpônᵉyâh (Chald.), soom-po-neh-yaw´; or

סִיפֹנְיָא° çîyphônᵉyâ' (Dan. 3:10) (Chald.), see-fo-neh-yaw´; of Gr. or. (συμφωνία); a bagpipe (with a double pipe):— dulcimer.

5482. סְוֵנֵה Çᵉvênêh, sev-ay-nay´ [rather to be written

סְוֵנָה Çᵉvênâh, sev-ay´-naw; for

סְוֵן Çᵉvên, sev-ane´; i.e. to Seven]; of Eg. der.; Seven, a place in Upper Egypt:— Syene.

5483. סוּס çûwç, soos; or

סֻס çûç, soos; from an unused root mean. to skip (prop. for joy); a horse (as leaping); also a swallow (from its rapid flight):— crane, horse (I-back, -hoof). Comp. 6571.

5484. סוּסָה çûwçâh, soo-saw´; fem. of 5483; a mare:— company of horses.

5485. סוּסִי Çûwçîy, soo-see´; from 5483; horse-like; Susi, an Isr.:— Susi.

5486. סוּף çûwph, soof; a prim. root; to snatch away, i.e. terminate:— consume, have an end, perish, × be utterly.

5487. סוּף çûwph (Chald.), soof; corresp. to 5486; to come to an end:— consume, fulfil.

5488. סוּף çûwph, soof; prob. of Eg. or.; a reed, espec. the papyrus:— flag, Red [sea], weed. Comp. 5489.

5489. סוּף Çûwph, soof; for 5488 (by ellip. of 3220); the Reed (Sea):— Red Sea.

5490. סוֹף çôwph, sofe; from 5486; a termination:— conclusion, end, hinder part.

5491. סוֹף çôwph (Chald.), sofe; corresp. to 5490:— end.

5492. סוּפָה çûwphâh, soo-faw´; from 5486; a hurricane:— storm, tempest, whirlwind, Red sea.

5493. סוּר çûwr, soor; or

שׂוּר sûwr (Hosea 9:12), soor; a prim. root; to turn off (lit. or fig.):— be [-head], bring, call back, decline, depart, eschew, get [you], go (aside), × grievous, lay away (by), leave undone, be past, pluck away, put (away, down), rebel, remove (to and fro), revolt, × be sour, take (away, off), turn (aside, away, in), withdraw, be without.

5494. סוּר çûwr, soor; prob. pass. part. of 5493; turned off, i.e. deteriorated:— degenerate.

5495. סוּר Çûwr, soor; the same as 5494; Sur, a gate of the Temple:— Sur.

5496. סוּת çûwth, sooth; perh. denom. from 7898; prop. to prick, i.e. (fig.) stimulate; by impl. to seduce:— entice, move, persuade, provoke, remove, set on, stir up, take away.

5497. סוּת çûwth, sooth; prob. from the

same root as 4533; *covering*, i.e. *clothing:*— clothes.

5498. סָחַב **çâchab**, *saw-khab'*; a prim. root; to *trail* along:— draw (out), tear.

5499. סְחָבָה **çᵉchâbâh**, *seh-khaw-baw'*; from 5498; a *rag:*— cast clout.

5500. סָחָה **çâchâh**, *saw-khaw'*; a prim. root; to *sweep* away:— scrape.

5501. סְחִי **çᵉchîy**, *seh-khee'*; from 5500; *refuse* (as *swept* off):— offscouring.

5502. סָחַף **çâchaph**, *saw-khaf'*; a prim. root; to *scrape* off:— sweep (away).

5503. סָחַר **çâchar**, *saw-khar'*; a prim. root; to *travel* round (spec. as a *pedlar*); intens. to *palpitate:*— go about, merchant (-man), occupy with, pant, trade, traffick.

5504. סַחַר **çachar**, *sakh´-ar*; from 5503; *profit* (from trade):— merchandise.

5505. סָחַר **çâchar**, *saw-khar'*; from 5503; an *emporium;* abstr. *profit* (from trade):— mart, merchandise.

5506. סְחֹרָה **çᵉchôrâh**, *sekh-o-raw'*; from 5503; *traffic:*— merchandise.

5507. סֹחֵרָה **çôchêrâh**, *so-khay-raw'*; prop. act. part. fem. of 5503; something *surrounding* the person, i.e. a *shield:*— buckler.

5508. סֹחֵרֶת **çôchereth**, *so-kheh´-reth*; similar to 5507; prob. a (black) *tile* (or *tessara*) for laying borders with:— black marble.

סֵט **çêṭ**. See 7750.

5509. סִיג **çîyg**, *seeg;* or

סוּג° **çûwg** (Ezek. 22:18), *soog;* from 5472 in the sense of *refuse; scoria:*— dross.

5510. סִיוָן **Çîyvân**, *see-vawn';* prob. of Pers. or.; *Sivan*, the third Heb. month:— Sivan.

5511. סִיחוֹן **Çîychôwn**, *see-khone';* or

סִיחֹן **Çîychôn**, *see-khone';* from the same as 5477; *tempestuous; Sichon*, an Amoritish king:— Sihon.

5512. סִין **Çîyn**, *seen;* of uncert. der.; *Sin*, the name of an Eg. town and (prob.) desert adjoining:— Sin.

5513. סִינִי **Çîynîy**, *see-nee';* from an otherwise unknown name of a man; a *Sinite*, or desc. of one of the sons of Canaan:— Sinite.

5514. סִינַי **Çîynay**, *see-nah´-ee;* of uncert. der.; *Sinai*, a mountain of Arabia:— Sinai.

5515. סִינִים **Çîynîym**, *see-neem';* plur. of an otherwise unknown name; *Sinim*, a distant Oriental region:— Sinim.

5516. סִיסְרָא **Çîyçᵉrâ'**, *see-ser-aw';* of uncert. der.; *Sisera*, the name of a Canaanitish king and of one of the Nethinim:— Sisera.

5517. סִיעָא **Çîy'â'**, *see-ah';* or

סִיעֲהָא **Çîy'ăhâ'**, *see-ah-haw';* from an unused root mean. to *converse; congregation; Sia*, or *Siaha*, one of the Nethinim:— Sia, Siaha.

סִיפֹנְיָא° **çîyphᵉnᵉyâ'**. See 5481.

5518. סִיר **çîyr**, *seer;* or (fem.)

סִירָה **çîyrâh**, *see-raw';* or

סִרָה **çîrâh** (Jer. 52:18), *see-raw';* from a prim. root mean. to *boil* up; a *pot;* also a *thorn* (as springing up rapidly); by impl. a *hook:*— caldron, fishhook, pan, (lwash-l) pot, thorn.

5519. סָךְ **çâk**, *sawk;* from 5526; prop. a *thicket* of men, i.e. a *crowd:*— multitude.

5520. סֹךְ **çôk**, *soke;* from 5526; a *hut* (as of *entwined* boughs); also a *lair:*— covert, den, pavilion, tabernacle.

5521. סֻכָּה **çukkâh**, *sook-kaw';* fem of 5520; a *hut* or *lair:*— booth, cottage, covert, pavilion, tabernacle, tent.

5522. סִכּוּת **çikkûwth**, *sik-kooth';* fem. of 5519; an (idolatrous) *booth:*— tabernacle.

5523. סֻכּוֹת **Çukkôwth**, *sook-kohth';* or

סֻכֹּת **Çukkôth**, *sook-kohth';* plur. of 5521; *booths; Succoth*, the name of a place in Egypt and of three in Pal.:— Succoth.

5524. סֻכּוֹת בְּנוֹת **Çukkôwth Bᵉnôwth**, *sook-kohth´ ben-ohth';* from 5523 and the (irreg.) plur. of 1323; *booths of* (the) *daughters; brothels*, i.e. idolatrous *tents* for impure purposes:— Succothbenoth.

5525. סֻכִּי **Çukkîy**, *sook-kee';* patrial from an unknown name (perh. 5520); a *Sukkite*, or inhab. of some place near Egypt (i.e. *hut-dwellers*):— Sukkiims.

5526. סָכַךְ **çâkak**, *saw-kak';* or

שָׂכַךְ **sâkak** (Exod. 33:22), *saw-kak';* a prim. root; prop. to *entwine* as a screen; by impl. to *fence* in, *cover* over, (fig.) *protect:*— cover, defence, defend, hedge in, join together, set, shut up.

5527. סְכָכָה **Çᵉkâkâh**, *sek-aw-kaw';* from 5526; *inclosure; Secacah*, a place in Pal.:— Secacah.

5528. סָכַל **çâkal**, *saw-kal';* for 3688; to *be silly:*— do (make, play the, turn into) fool (-ish, -ishly, -ishness).

5529. סֶכֶל **çekel**, *seh´-kel;* from 5528; *silliness;* concr. and collect. *dolts:*— folly.

5530. סָכָל **çâkâl**, *saw-kawl';* from 5528; *silly:*— fool (-ish), sottish.

5531. סִכְלוּת **çiklûwth**, *sik-looth';* or

שִׂכְלוּת **siklûwth** (Eccl. 1:17) *siklooth';* from 5528; *silliness:*— folly, foolishness.

5532. סָכַן **çâkan**, *saw-kan';* a prim. root; to *be familiar* with; by impl. to *minister* to, *be serviceable* to, *be customary:*— acquaint (self), be advantage, × ever, (be, lun-l) profit (-able), treasurer, be wont.

5533. סָכַן **çâkan**, *saw-kan';* prob. a denom. from 7915; prop. to *cut*, i.e. *damage;* also to *grow* (caus. *make*) *poor:*— endanger, impoverish.

5534. סָכַר **çâkar**, *saw-kar';* a prim. root; to *shut* up; by impl. to *surrender:*— stop, give over. See also 5462, 7936.

5535. סָכַת **çâkath**, *saw-kath';* a prim. root; to *be silent;* by impl. to *observe* quietly:— take heed.

סֻכּוֹת **Çukkôth**. See 5523.

5536. סַל **çal**, *sal;* from 5549; prop. a willow *twig* (as *pendulous*), i.e. an *osier;*

but only as woven into a *basket:*— basket.

5537. סָלָא **çâlâ'**, *saw-law';* a prim. root; to *suspend* in a balance, i.e. *weigh:*— compare.

5538. סִלָּא **Çillâ'**, *sil-law';* from 5549; an *embankment; Silla*, a place in Jerusalem:— Silla.

5539. סָלַד **çâlad**, *saw-lad';* a prim. root; prob. to *leap* (with joy), i.e. *exult:*— harden self.

5540. סֶלֶד **Çeled**, *seh´-led;* from 5539; *exultation; Seled*, an Isr.:— Seled.

5541. סָלָה **çâlâh**, *saw-law';* a prim. root; to *hang* up, i.e. *weigh*, or (fig.) *contemn:*— tread down (under foot), value.

5542. סֶלָה **Çelâh**, *seh´-law;* from 5541; *suspension* (of music), i.e. *pause:*— Selah.

5543. סַלּוּ **Çallûw**, *sal-loo';* or

סַלּוּא **Çallûw'**, *sal-loo';* or

סָלוּא **Çâlûw**, *sal-loo';* or

סַלַּי **Çallay**, *sal-lah´-ee;* from 5541; *weighed; Sallu* or *Sallai*, the name of two Isr.:— Sallai, Sallu, Salu.

5544. סִלּוֹן **çillôwn**, *sil-lone';* or

סַלּוֹן **çallôwn**, *sal-lone';* from 5541; a *prickle* (as if *pendulous*):— brier, thorn.

5545. סָלַח **çâlach**, *saw-lakh';* a prim. root; to *forgive:*— forgive, pardon, spare.

5546. סַלָּח **çallâch**, *saw-lawkh';* from 5545; *placable:*— ready to forgive.

סַלַּי **Çallay**. See 5543.

5547. סְלִיחָה **çᵉlîychâh**, *sel-ee-khaw';* from 5545; *pardon:*— forgiveness, pardon.

5548. סַלְכָה **Çalkâh**, *sal-kaw';* from an unused root mean. to *walk; walking; Salcah*, a place E. of the Jordan:— Salcah, Salchah.

5549. סָלַל **çâlal**, *saw-lal';* a prim. root; to *mound* up (espec. a turnpike); fig. to *exalt;* refl. to *oppose* (as by a dam):— cast up, exalt (self), extol, make plain, raise up.

5550. סֹלְלָה **çôlᵉlâh**, *so-lel-aw';* or

סוֹלְלָה **çôwlᵉlâh**, *so-lel-aw';* act. part. fem. of 5549, but used pass.; a military *mound*, i.e. *rampart* of besiegers:— bank, mount.

5551. סֻלָּם **çullâm**, *sool-lawm';* from 5549; a *stair-case:*— ladder.

5552. סַלְסִלָּה **çalçillâh**, *sal-sil-law';* from 5541; a *twig* (as *pendulous*):— basket.

5553. סֶלַע **çela'**, *seh´-lah;* from an unused root mean. to be *lofty;* a craggy *rock*, lit. or fig. (a *fortress*):— (ragged) rock, stone (-ny), strong hold.

5554. סֶלַע **Çela'**, *seh´-lah;* the same as 5553; *Sela*, the rock-city of Idumaea:— rock, Sela (-h).

5555. סֶלַע הַמַּחְלְקוֹת **Çela' hammachlᵉqôwth**, *seh´-lah ham-makh-lek-ôth';* from 5553 and the plur. of 4256 with the art. interposed; *rock of the divisions; Sela-ham-Machlekoth*, a place in Pal.:— Sela-hammalekoth.

5556. סָלְעָם **çol'âm**, *sol-awm';* appar.

from the same as 5553 in the sense of *crushing* as with a rock, i.e. consuming; a kind of *locust* (from its *destructiveness*):— bald locust.

5557. קלף çâlaph, *saw-laf´*; a prim. root; prop. to *wrench*, i.e. (fig.) to *subvert*:— overthrow, pervert.

5558. קלף çeleph, *seh´-lef*; from 5557; *distortion*, i.e. (fig.) *viciousness*:— perverseness.

5559. סלק çᵉliq (Chald.), *sel-eek´*; a prim. root; to *ascend*:— come (up).

5560. סלת çôleth, *so´-leth*; from an unused root mean. to *strip*; *flour* (as *chipped* off):— (fine) flour, meal.

5561. סם çam, *sam*; from an unused root mean. to *smell* sweet; an *aroma*:— sweet (spice).

5562. סמגר נבו Çamgar Nᵉbôw, *sam-gar´ neb-o´*; of for. or.; *Samgar-Nebo*, a Bab. general:— Samgar-nebo.

5563. סמדר çᵉmâdar, *sem-aw-dar´*; of uncert. der.; a vine *blossom*; used also adv. *abloom*:— tender grape.

5564. סמך çâmak, *saw-mak´*; a prim. root; to *prop* (lit. or fig.); refl. to *lean* upon or *take hold* of (in a favorable or unfavorable sense):— bear up, establish, (up-) hold, lay, lean. lie hard, put, rest self, set self, stand fast, stay (self), sustain.

5565. סמכיהו Çᵉmakyâhûw, *sem-ak-yaw´-hoo*; from 5564 and 3050; *supported of Jah*; *Semakjah*, an Isr.:— Semachiah.

5566. סמל çemel, *seh´-mel*; or

סמל çêmel, *say´-mel*; from an unused root mean. to *resemble*; a *likeness*:— figure, idol, image.

5567. סמן çâman, *saw-man´*; a prim. root; to *designate*:— appointed.

5568. סמר çâmar, *saw-mar´*; a prim. root; to *be erect*, i.e. *bristle* as hair:— stand up, tremble.

5569. סמר çâmâr, *saw-mar´*; from 5568; *bristling*, i.e. *shaggy*:— rough.

5570. סנאה Çᵉnâ'âh, *sen-aw-aw´*; from an unused root mean. to *prick*; *thorny*; *Senaah*, a place in Pal.:— Senaah, Hassenaah [with the art.].

סנאה çᵉnû'âh. See 5574.

5571. סנבלט Çanballaṭ, *san-bal-lat´*; of for. or.; *Sanballat*, a Pers. satrap of Samaria:— Sanballat.

5572. סנה çᵉneh, *sen-eh´*; from an unused root mean. to *prick*; a *bramble*:— bush.

5573. סנה Çeneh, *seh-neh´*; the same as 5572; *thorn*; *Seneh*, a crag in Pal.:— Seneh.

סנה Çannâh. See 7158.

5574. סנואה Çᵉnûw'âh, *sen-oo-aw´*; or

סנאה Çᵉnû'âh, *sen-oo-aw´* from the same as 5570; *pointed*; (used with the art. as a proper name) *Senuah*, the name of two Isr.:— Hasenuah [incl. the art.], Senuah.

5575. סנור çanvêr, *san-vare´*; of uncert. der.; (in plur.) *blindness*:— blindness.

5576. סנחריב Çanchêrîyb, *san-khay-*

reeb´; of for. or.; *Sancherib*, an Ass. king:— Sennacherib.

5577. סנסן çançîn, *san-seen´*; from an unused root mean. to *be pointed*; a *twig* (as *tapering*):— bough.

5578. סנסנה Çançannâh, *san-san-naw´*; fem. of a form of 5577; a *bough*; *Sansannah*, a place in Pal.:— Sansannah.

5579. סנפיר çᵉnappîyr, *sen-ap-peer´*; of uncert. der.; a *fin* (collect.):— fins.

5580. סס çâç, *sawce*; from the same as 5483; a *moth* (from the *agility* of the fly):— moth.

סס çûç. See 5483.

5581. ססמי Çiçmay, *sis-mah´-ee*; of uncert. der.; *Sismai*, an Isr.:— Sisamai.

5582. סעד çâ'ad, *saw-ad´*; a prim. root; to *support* (mostly fig.):— comfort, establish, hold up, refresh ṣelf, strengthen, be upholden.

5583. סעד çᵉ'ad (Chald.), *seh-ad´*; corresp. to 5582; to *aid*:— helping.

5584. סעה çâ'âh, *saw-aw´*; a prim. root; to *rush*:— storm.

5585. סעיף çâ'îyph, *saw-eef´*; from 5586; a *fissure* (of rocks); also a *bough* (as *subdivided*):— (outmost) branch, clift, top.

5586. סעף çâ'aph, *saw-af´*; a prim. root; prop. to *divide* up; but used only as denom. from 5585, to *disbranch* (a tree):— top.

5587. סעף çâ'îph, *saw-eef´* or

סעף çâ'îph, *saw-eef´*; from 5586; *divided* (in mind), i.e. (abstr.) a *sentiment*:— opinion.

5588. סעף çê'êph, *say-afe´*; from 5586; *divided* (in mind), i.e. (concr.) a *skeptic*:— thought.

5589. סעפה çᵉ'appâh, *seh-ap-paw´*; fem. of 5585; a *twig*:— bough, branch. Comp. 5634.

5590. סער çâ'ar, *saw-ar´*; a prim. root; to *rush* upon; by impl. to *toss* (tran. or intr., lit. or fig.):— be (toss with) tempest (-uous), be sore troubled, come out as a (drive with, scatter with a) whirlwind.

5591. סער ça'ar, *sah´-ar*; or (fem.)

סערה çᵉ'ârâh, *seh-aw-raw´*; from 5590; a *hurricane*:— storm (-y), tempest, whirlwind.

5592. סף çaph, *saf*; from 5605, in its orig. sense of *containing*; a *vestibule* (as a *limit*); also a *dish* (for holding blood or wine):— bason, bowl, cup, door (post), gate, post, threshold.

5593. סף Çaph, *saf*; the same as 5592; *Saph*, a Philistine:— Saph. Comp. 5598.

5594. ספד çâphad, *saw-fad´*; a prim. root; prop. to *tear* the hair and *beat* the breasts (as Orientals do in grief); gen. to *lament*; by impl. to *wail*:— lament, mourn (-er), waiḷ.

5595. ספה çâphâh, *saw-faw´*; a prim. root; prop. to *scrape* (lit. to *shave*; but usually fig.) together (i.e. to *accumulate* or *increase*) or away (i.e. to *scatter*, *remove*, or *ruin*; intr. to *perish*):— add, augment, consume, destroy, heap, join, perish, put.

5596. ספח çâphach, *saw-fakh´*; or

ספח çâphach (Isa. 3:17) *saw-fakh´*; a prim. root; prop. to *scrape* out, but in certain peculiar senses (of *removal* or *association*):— abiding, gather together, cleave, smite with the scab.

5597. ספחת çappachath, *sap-pakh´-ath*; from 5596; the *mange* (as making the hair fall off):— scab.

5598. ספי Çippay, *sip-pah´-ee*; from 5592; *bason-like*; *Sippai*, a Philistine:— Sippai. Comp. 5593.

5599. ספיח çâphîyach, *saw-fee´-akh*; from 5596; something (spontaneously) *falling* off, i.e. a *self-sown* crop; fig. a *freshet*:— (such) things as (which) grow (of themselves), which groweth of its own accord (itself).

5600. ספינה çᵉphîynâh, *sef-ee-naw´*; from 5603; a (sea-going) *vessel* (as *ceiled* with a deck):— ship.

5601. ספיר çappîyr, *sap-peer´*; from 5608; a *gem* (perh. as used for *scratching* other substances), prob. the *sapphire*:— sapphire.

5602. ספל çêphel, *say´-fel*; from an unused root mean. to *depress*; a *basin* (as *deepened* out):— bowl, dish.

5603. ספן çâphan, *saw-fan´*; a prim. root; to *hide* by covering; spec. to *roof* (pass. part. as noun, a *roof*) or *paneling*; fig. to *reserve*:— cieled, cover, seated.

5604. ספן çippun, *sip-poon´*; from 5603; a *wainscot*:— cieling.

5605. ספף çâphaph, *saw-faf´*; a prim. root; prop. to *snatch* away, i.e. *terminate*; but used only as denom. from 5592 (in the sense of a *vestibule*), to *wait at* (the) *threshold*:— be a doorkeeper.

5606. ספק çâphaq, *saw-fak´*; or

שפק çâphaq (1 Kings 20:10; Job 27:23; Isa. 2:6), *saw-fak´*; a prim. root; to *clap* the hands (in token of compact, derision, grief, indignation, or punishment); by impl. of satisfaction, to *be enough*; by impl. of excess, to *vomit*:— clap, smite, strike, suffice, wallow.

5607. ספק çêpheq, *say´-fek*; or

שפק sepheq (Job 20:22; 36:18) *seh´-fek*; from 5606; *chastisement*; also *satiety*:— stroke, sufficiency.

5608. ספר çâphar, *saw-far´*; a prim. root; prop. to *score* with a mark as a tally or record, i.e. (by impl.) to *inscribe*, and also to *enumerate*; intens. to *recount*, i.e. *celebrate*:— commune, (ac-) count; declare, number, + penknife, reckon, scribe, shew forth, speak, talk, tell (out), writer.

5609. ספר çᵉphar (Chald.), *sef-ar´*; from a root corresp. to 5608; a *book*:— book, roll.

5610. ספר çᵉphâr, *sef-awr´*; from 5608; a *census*:— numbering.

5611. ספר Çᵉphâr, *sef-awr´*; the same as 5610; *Sephar*, a place in Arabia:— Sephar.

5612. ספר çêpher, *say´-fer*; or (fem.)

ספרה çiphrâh, *sif-raw´*; from 5608; prop. *writing* (the art or a document); by impl. a *book*:— bill, book, evidence, × learn [-ed] (-ing), letter, register, scroll.

5613. כְּפָר **çâphêr** (Chald.), *saw-fare´*; from the same as 5609; a *scribe* (secular or sacred):— scribe.

5614. סְפָרַד **Ç⁰phârâd**, *sef-aw-rawd´*; of for. der.; *Sepharad*, a region of Assyria:— Sepharad.

סִפְרָה **çiphrâh**. See 5612.

5615. סְפֹרָה **ç⁰phôrâh**, *sef-o-raw´*; from 5608; a *numeration*:— number.

5616. סְפַרְוִי **Ç⁰pharvîy**, *sef-ar-vee´*; patrial from 5617; a *Sepharvite* or inhab. of Sepharvaim:— Sepharvite.

5617. סְפַרְוַיִם **Ç⁰pharvayim** (dual), *sef-ar-vah´-yim*; or

סְפָרִים **Ç⁰phârîym** (plur.), *sef-aw-reem´*; of for. der.; *Sepharvajim* or *Sepharim*, a place in Assyria:— Sepharvaim.

5618. סֹפֶרֶת **Çôphereth**, *so-feh´-reth*; fem. act. part. of 5608; a *scribe* (prop. female); *Sophereth*, a temple servant:— Sophereth.

5619. סָקַל **çâqal**, *saw-kal´*; a prim. root; prop. to *be weighty*; but used only in the sense of *lapidation* or its contrary (as if a delapidation):— (cast, gather out, throw) stone (-s), × surely.

5620. סַר **çar**, *sar*; from 5637 contr.; *peevish*:— heavy, sad.

5621. סָרָב **çârâb**, *saw-rawb´*; from an unused root mean. to *sting*; a thistle:— brier.

5622. סַרְבָּל **çarbal** (Chald.), *sar-bal´*; of uncert. der.; a *cloak*:— coat.

5623. סַרְגוֹן **Çargôwn**, *sar-gōne´*; of for. der.; *Sargon*, an Ass. king:— Sargon.

5624. סֶרֶד **Çered**, *seh´-red*; from a prim. root mean. to *tremble*; *trembling*; *Sered*, an Isr.:— Sered.

5625. סַרְדִּי **Çardîy**, *sar-dee´*; patron. from 5624; a *Seredite* (collect.) or desc. of Sered:— Sardites.

5626. סִרָה **Çirâh**, *see-raw´*; from 5493; *departure*; *Sirah*, a cistern so-called:— Sirah. See also 5518.

5627. סָרָה **çârâh**, *saw-raw´*; from 5493; *apostasy, crime*; fig. *remission*:— × continual, rebellion, revolt [(-ed)], turn away, wrong.

5628. סָרַח **çârach**, *saw-rakh´*; a prim. root; to *extend* (even to *excess*):— exceeding, hand, spread, stretch self, banish.

5629. סֶרַח **çerach**, *seh´-rakh*; from 5628; a *redundancy*:— remnant.

5630. סִרְיֹן **çiyrôn**, *sir-yone´*; for 8302; a coat of *mail*:— brigandine.

5631. סָרִיס **çârîyç**, *saw-reece´*; or

סָרִס **çârîç**, *saw-reece´*; from an unused root mean. to *castrate*; a *eunuch*; by impl. *valet* (espec. of the female apartments), and thus, a *minister* of state:— chamberlain, eunuch, officer. Comp. 7249.

5632. סָרֵךְ **çârêk** (Chald.), *saw-rake´*; of for. or.; an *emir*:— president.

5633. סֶרֶן **çeren**, *seh´-ren*; from an un-

used root of uncert. mean.; an *axle*; fig. a *peer*:— lord, plate.

5634. שַׂרְעַפָּה **çar'appâh**, *sar-ap-paw´*; for 5589; a *twig*:— bough.

5635. שָׂרַף **çâraph**, *saw-raf´*; a prim. root; to *cremate*, i.e. to *be* (near) *of kin* (such being privileged to kindle the pyre):— burn.

5636. שַׂרְפָּד **çarpâd**, *sar-pawd´*; from 5635; a *nettle* (as stinging like a *burn*):— brier.

5637. שָׂרַר **çârar**, *saw-rar´*; a prim. root; to *turn* away, i.e. (mor.) be *refractory*:— × away, backsliding, rebellious, revolter (-ing), slide back, stubborn, withdrew.

5638. סְתָו **ç⁰thâv**, *seth-awv´*; from an unused root mean. to *hide*; *winter* (as the dark season):— winter.

5639. סְתוּר **Ç⁰thûwr**, *seth-oor´*; from 5641; *hidden*; *Sethur*, an Isr.:— Sethur.

5640. סָתַם **çâtham**, *saw-tham´*; or

שָׂתַם **sâtham** (Num. 24:15), *saw-tham´*; a prim. root; to *stop* up; by impl. to *repair*; fig. to *keep secret*:— closed up, hidden, secret, shut out (up), stop.

5641. סָתַר **çâthar**, *saw-thar´*; a prim. root; to *hide* (by covering), lit. or fig.:— be absent, keep close, conceal, hide (self), (keep) secret, × surely.

5642. סְתַר **ç⁰thar** (Chald.), *seth-ar´*; corresp. to 5641; to *conceal*; fig. to *demolish*:— destroy, secret thing.

5643. סֵתֶר **çêther**, *say´-ther*; or (fem.)

סִתְרָה **çithrâh** (Deut. 32:38), *sith-raw´*; from 5641; a *cover* (in a good or a bad, a lit. or a fig. sense):— backbiting, covering, covert, × disguise [-th], hiding place, privily, protection, secret (-ly, place).

5644. סִתְרִי **Çithrîy**, *sith-ree´*; from 5643; *protective*; *Sithri*, an Isr.:— Zithri.

ע

5645. עָב **'âb**, *awb* (masc. and fem.); from 5743; prop. an *envelope*, i.e. *darkness* (or *density*, 2 Chron. 4:17); spec. a (scud) *cloud*; also a *copse*:— clay, (thick) cloud, × thick, thicket. Comp. 5672.

5646. עָב **'âb**, *awb*; or

עֹב **'ôb**, *obe*; from an unused root mean. to *cover*; prop. equiv. to 5645; but used only as an arch. term, an *architrave* (as *shading* the pillars):— thick (beam, plant).

5647. עָבַד **'âbad**, *aw-bad´*; a prim. root; to *work* (in any sense); by impl. to *serve, till*, (caus.) *enslave*, etc.:— × be, keep in bondage, be, bondmen, bond-service, compel, do, dress, ear, execute, + husbandman, keep, labour (-ing man, bring to pass, (cause to, make to) serve (-ing, self), (be, become) servant (-s), do (use) service, till (-er), transgress [from marg.], (set a) work, be wrought, worshipper.

5648. עֲבַד **'ăbad** (Chald.), *ab-bad´*; corresp. to 5647; to *do, make, prepare, keep*, etc.:— × cut, do, execute, go on, make, move, work.

5649. עֲבַד **'ăbad** (Chald.), *ab-bad´*; from 5648; a *servant*:— servant.

5650. עֶבֶד **'ebed**, *eh´-bed*; from 5647; a *servant*:— × bondage, bondman, [bond-] servant, (man-) servant.

5651. עֶבֶד **'Ebed**, *eh´-bed*; the same as 5650; *Ebed*, the name of two Isr.:— Ebed.

5652. עֲבָד **'ăbâd**, *ab-awd´*; from 5647; a *deed*:— work.

5653. עַבְדָּא **'Abdâ'**, *ab-daw´*; from 5647; *work*; *Abda*, the name of two Isr.:— Abda.

5654. עֹבֵד אֱדוֹם **'Ôbêd 'Ĕdôwm**, *o-bade´ ed-ome´*; from the act. part. of 5647 and 123; *worker of Edom*; *Obed-Edom*, the name of five Isr.:— Obed-edom.

5655. עַבְדְּאֵל **'Abd⁰'êl**, *ab-deh-ale´*; from 5647 and 410; *serving God*; *Abdeel*, an Isr.:— Abdeel. Comp. 5661.

5656. עֲבֹדָה **'ăbôdâh**, *ab-o-daw´*; or

עֲבוֹדָה **'ăbôwdâh**, *ab-o-daw´*; from 5647; *work* of any kind:— act, bondage. + bondservant, effect, labour, ministering (-try), office, service (-ile, -itude), tillage, use, work, × wrought.

5657. עֲבֻדָּה **'ăbuddâh**, *ab-ood-daw´*; pass. part. of 5647; something *wrought*, i.e. (concr.) *service*:— household, store of servants.

5658. עַבְדּוֹן **'Abdôwn**, *ab-dohn´*; from 5647; *servitude*; *Abdon*, the name of a place in Pal. and of four Isr.:— Abdon. Comp. 5683.

5659. עַבְדוּת **'abdûwth**, *ab-dooth´*; from 5647; *servitude*:— bondage.

5660. עַבְדִּי **'Abdîy**, *ab-dee´*; from 5647; *serviceable*; *Abdi*, the name of two Isr.:— Abdi.

5661. עַבְדִּיאֵל **'Abdîy'êl**, *ab-dee-ale´*; from 5650 and 410; *servant of God*; *Abdiel*, an Isr.:— Abdiel. Comp. 5655.

5662. עֹבַדְיָה **'Ôbadyâh**, *o-bad-yaw´*; or

עֹבַדְיָהוּ **'Ôbadyâhûw**, *o-bad-yaw´-hoo*; act. part. of 5647 and 3050; *serving Jah*; *Obadjah*, the name of thirteen Isr.:— Obadiah.

5663. עֶבֶד מֶלֶךְ **'Ebed Melek**, *eh´-bed meh´-lek*; from 5650 and 4428; *servant of a king*; *Ebed-Melek*, a eunuch of Zedekeah:— Ebed-melech.

5664. עֶבֶד נְגוֹ **'Ăbêd N⁰gôw**, *ab-ade´ neg-o´*; the same as 5665; *Abed-Nego*, the Bab. name of one of Daniel's companions:— Abed-nego.

5665. עֲבֵד נְגוֹא **'Ăbêd N⁰gôw** (Chald.), *ab-ade´ neg-o´*; of for. or.; *Abed-Nego*, the name of Azariah:— Abed-nego.

5666. עָבָה **'âbâh**, *aw-baw´*; a prim. root; to *be dense*:— be (grow) thick (-er).

5667. עֲבוֹט **'ăbôwṭ**, *ab-ote´*; or

עֲבֹט **'ăbôṭ**, *ab-ote´*; from 5670; a *pawn*:— pledge.

5668. עָבוּר **'âbûwr**, *aw-boor´*; or

עָבֻר **'âbur**, *aw-boor´*; pass. part. of 5674; prop. *crossed*, i.e. (abstr.) *transit*; used only adv. on *account* of, in *order* that:— because of, for (... 's sake), (intent) that, to.

5669. עָבוּר **'âbûwr**, *aw-boor´*; the same

as 5668; *passed*, i.e. *kept* over; used only of *stored* grain:— old corn.

5670. עָבַט **'âbaṭ**, *aw-bat'*; a prim. root; to *pawn;* caus. to *lend* (on security); fig. to *entangle:*— borrow, break [ranks], fetch [a pledge], lend, × surely.

5671. עֲבָטִיט **'abṭîyṭ**, *ab-teet'*; from 5670; something *pledged*, i.e. (collect.) *pawned* goods:— thick clay [by *a false etym.*].

5672. עֲבִי **'ăbîy**, *ab-ee'*; or

עֳבִי **'ŏbîy**, *ob-ee'*; from 5666; *density*, i.e. *depth* or *width:*— thick (-ness). Comp. 5645.

5673. עֲבִידָה **'ăbîydâh** (Chald.), *ab-ee-daw'*; from 5648; *labor* or *business:*— affairs, service, work.

5674. עָבַר **'âbar**, *aw-bar'*; a prim. root; to *cross* over; used very widely of any *transition* (lit. or fig.; tran., intr., intens., or caus.); spec. to *cover* (in copulation):— alienate, alter, × at all, beyond, bring (over, through), carry over, (over-) come (on, over), conduct (over), convey over, current, deliver, do away, enter, escape, fail, gender, get over, (make) go (away, beyond, by, forth, his way, in, on, over, through), have away (more), lay, meddle, overrun, make partition, (cause to, give, make to, over) pass (-age, along, away, beyond, by, -enger, on, out, over, through), (cause to, make) + proclaim (-amation), perish, provoke to anger, put away, rage, + raiser of taxes, remove, send over, set apart, + shave, cause to (make) sound, × speedily, × sweet smelling, take (away), (make to) transgress (-or), translate, turn away, [way-] faring man, be wrath.

5675. עֲבַר **'ăbar** (Chald.), *ab-ar'*; corresp. to 5676:— beyond, this side.

5676. עֵבֶר **'êber**, *ay'-ber*; from 5674; prop. a region *across;* but used only adv. (with or without a prep.) on the *opposite* side (espec. of the Jordan; usually mean. the *east*):— × against, beyond, by, × from, over, passage, quarter, (other, this) side, straight.

5677. עֵבֶר **'Êber**, *ay'-ber*; the same as 5676; *Eber*, the name of two patriarchs and four Isr.:— Eber, Heber.

5678. עֶבְרָה **'ebrâh**, *eb-raw'*; fem. of 5676; an *outburst* of passion:— anger, rage, wrath.

5679. עֲבָרָה **'ăbârâh**, *ab-aw-raw'*; from 5674; a *crossing*-place:— ferry, plain [*from the marg.*].

5680. עִבְרִי **'Ibrîy**, *ib-ree'*; patron. from 5677; an *Eberite* (i.e. Hebrew) or desc. of Eber:— Hebrew (-ess, woman).

5681. עִבְרִי **'Ibrîy**, *ib-ree'*; the same as 5680; *Ibri*, an Isr.:— Ibri.

5682. עֲבָרִים **'Ăbârîym**, *ab-aw-reem'*; plur. of 5676; regions *beyond; Abarim*, a place in Pal.:— Abarim, passages.

5683. עֶבְרֹן **'Ebrôn**, *eb-rone'*; from 5676; *transitional; Ebron*, a place in Pal.:— Hebron. [*Perh. a clerical err. for* 5658.]

5684. עֶבְרֹנָה **'Ebrônâh**, *eb-raw-naw'*; fem. of 5683; *Ebronah*, a place in the Desert:— Ebronah.

5685. עָבַשׁ **'âbash**, *aw-bash'*; a prim. root; to *dry* up:— be rotten.

5686. עָבַת **'âbath**, *aw-bath'*; a prim. root; to *interlace*, i.e. (fig.) to *pervert:*— wrap up.

5687. עָבֹת **'âbôth**, *aw-both'*; or

עֲבוֹת **'ăbôwth**, *aw-both'*; from 5686; *intwined*, i.e. *dense:*— thick.

5688. עֲבֹת **'ăbôth**, *ab-oth'*; or

עֲבוֹת **'ăbôwth**, *ab-oth'*; or (fem.)

עֲבֹתָה **'ăbôthâh**, *ab-oth-aw'*; the same as 5687; something *intwined*, i.e. a *string, wreath* or *foliage:*— band, cord, rope, thick bough (branch), wreathen (chain).

5689. עָגַב **'âgab**, *aw-gab'*; a prim. root; to *breathe* after, i.e. to *love* (sensually):— dote, lover.

5690. עֶגֶב **'egeb**, *eh'-gheb*; from 5689; *love* (concr.), i.e. *amative* words:— much love, very lovely.

5691. עֲגָבָה **'ăgâbâh**, *ag-aw-baw'*; from 5689; *love* (abstr.), i.e. *amorousness:*— inordinate love.

5692. עֻגָּה **'uggâh**, *oog-gaw'*; from 5746; an *ash-cake* (as *round*):— cake (upon the hearth).

5693. עָגוֹל **'âgôwl**. See 5696.

5693. עָגוּר **'âgûwr**, *aw-goor'*; pass. part. [but with act. sense] of an unused root mean. to *twitter;* prob. the *swallow:*— swallow.

5694. עָגִיל **'âgîyl**, *aw-gheel'*; from the same as 5696; something *round*, i.e. a *ring* (for the ears):— earring.

5695. עֵגֶל **'êgel**, *ay-ghel'*; from the same as 5696; a (male) *calf* (as *frisking* round), espec. one nearly grown (i.e. a *steer*):— bullock, calf.

5696. עָגֹל **'âgôl**, *aw-gole'*; or

עָגוֹל **'âgôwl**, *aw-gole'*; from an unused root mean. to *revolve, circular:*— round.

5697. עֶגְלָה **'eglâh**, *eg-law'*; fem. of 5695; a (female) *calf*, espec. one nearly grown (i.e. a *heifer*):— calf, cow, heifer.

5698. עֶגְלָה **'Eglâh**, *eg-law'*; the same as 5697; *Eglah*, a wife of David:— Eglah.

5699. עֲגָלָה **'ăgâlâh**, *ag-aw-law'*; from the same as 5696; something *revolving*, i.e. a wheeled *vehicle:*— cart, chariot, wagon.

5700. עֶגְלוֹן **'Eglôwn**, *eg-lawn'*; from 5695; *vituline; Eglon*, the name of a place in Pal. and of a Moabitish king:— Eglon.

5701. עָגַם **'âgam**, *aw-gam'*; a prim. root; to *be sad:*— grieve.

5702. עָגַן **'âgan**, *aw-gan'*; a prim. root; to *debar*, i.e. from marriage:— stay.

5703. עַד **'ad**, *ad;* from 5710; prop. a (peremptory) *terminus*, i.e. (by impl.) *duration*, in the sense of *advance* or *perpetuity* (substantially as a noun, either with or without a prep.):— eternity, ever (-lasting, -more), old, perpetually, + world without end.

5704. עַד **'ad**, *ad;* prop. the same as 5703 (used as a prep., adv. or conjunc.; espec. with a prep.); *as far* (or *long*, or *much*) *as*, whether of space (*even unto*)

or time (*during, while, until*) or degree (*equally with*):— against, and, as, at, before, by (that), even (to), for (-asmuch as), [hither-] to, + how long, into, as long (much) as, (so) that, till, toward, until, when, while, (+ as) yet.

5705. עַד **'ad** (Chald.), *ad;* corresp. to 5704:— × and, at, for, [hither-] to, on, till, (un-) to, until, within.

5706. עַד **'ad**, *ad;* the same as 5703 in the sense of the *aim* of an attack; *booty:*— prey.

5707. עֵד **'êd**, *ayd;* contr. from 5749 ; concr. a *witness;* abstr. *testimony;* spec. a *recorder*, i.e. *prince:*— witness.

5708. עֵד **'êd**, *ayd;* from an unused root mean. to *set* a period [comp. 5710, 5749]; the *menstrual* flux (as periodical); by impl. (in plur.) *soiling:*— filthy.

5709. עֹד **'ôd**. See 5750.

5709. עֲדָא **'ădâ** (Chald.), *ad-aw'*; or

עֲדָה **'ădâh** (Chald.), *ad-aw'*; corresp. to 5710:— alter, depart, pass (away), remove, take (away).

5710. עֹדֵד **'Ôdêd**. See 5752.

5710. עָדָה **'âdâh**, *aw-daw'*; a prim. root; to *advance*, i.e. *pass* on or *continue;* caus. to *remove;* spec. to *bedeck* (i.e. bring an ornament upon):— adorn, deck (self), pass by, take away.

5711. עָדָה **'Âdâh**, *aw-daw'*; from 5710; *ornament; Adah*, the name of two women:— Adah.

5712. עֵדָה **'êdâh**, *ay-daw'*; fem. of 5707 in the orig. sense of *fixture;* a stated *assemblage* (spec. a *concourse*, or gen. a *family* or *crowd*):— assembly, company, congregation, multitude, people, swarm. Comp. 5713.

5713. עֵדָה **'êdâh**, *ay-daw'*; fem. of 5707 in its techn. sense; *testimony:*— testimony, witness. Comp. 5712.

5714. עִדּוֹ **'Iddôw**, *id-do'*; or

עִדּוֹא **'Iddôw'**, *id-do'*; or

עִדִּיא° **'Iddîy'**, *id-dee'*; from 5710; *timely; Iddo* (or *Iddi*), the name of five Isr.:— Iddo. Comp. 3035, 3260.

5715. עֵדוּת **'êdûwth**, *ay-dooth'*; fem. of 5707; *testimony:*— testimony, witness.

5716. עֲדִי **'ădîy**, *ad-ee'*; from 5710 in the sense of *trappings; finery;* gen. an *outfit;* spec. a *headstall:*— × excellent, mouth, ornament.

5717. עֲדִיאֵל **'Ădîy'êl**, *ad-ee-ale'*; from 5716 and 410; *ornament of God; Adiel*, the name of three Isr.:— Adiel.

5718. עֲדָיָה **'Ădâyâh**, *ad-aw-yaw'*; or

עֲדָיָהוּ **'Ădâyâhûw**, *ad-aw-yaw'-hoo;* from 5710 and 3050; *Jah has adorned; Adajah*, the name of eight Isr.:— Adaiah.

5719. עָדִין **'âdîyn**, *aw-deen'*; from 5727; *voluptuous:*— given to pleasures.

5720. עָדִין **'Âdîyn**, *aw-deen'*; the same as 5719; *Adin*, the name of two Isr.:— Adin.

5721. עֲדִינָא **'Ădîynâ'**, *ad-ee-naw'*; from 5719; *effeminacy; Adina*, an Isr.:— Adina.

5722. עֲדִינוֹ **'ădîynôw**, *ad-ee-no'*; prob.

from 5719 in the orig. sense of *slender* (i.e. a *spear*); *his spear*:— Adino.

5723. עֲדִיתָיִם **'Ădîythayim**, *ad-ee-thah´-yim*; dual of a fem. of 5706; *double prey*; *Adithajim*, a place in Pal.:— Adithaim.

5724. עַדְלַי **'Adlay**, *ad-lah´-ee*; prob. from an unused root of uncert. mean.; *Adlai*, an Isr.:— Adlai.

5725. עֲדֻלָּם **'Ădullâm**, *ad-ool-lawm´*; prob. from the pass. part. of the same as 5724; *Adullam*, a place in Pal.:— Adullam.

5726. עֲדֻלָּמִי **'Ădullâmîy**, *ad-ool-law-mee´*; patrial from 5725; an *Adullamite* or native of Adullam:— Adullamite.

5727. עָדַן **'âdan**, *aw-dan´*; a prim. root; to *be soft* or *pleasant*; fig. and refl. to *live voluptuously*:— delight self.

5728. עֶדֶן **'âden**, *ad-en´*; or

עֲדֶנָּה **'ădennâh**, *ad-en´-naw*; from 5704 and 2004; *till now*:— yet.

5729. עֶדֶן **'Eden**, *eh´-den*; from 5727; *pleasure*; *Eden*, a place in Mesopotamia:— Eden.

5730. עֵדֶן **'êden**, *ay´-den*; or (fem.)

עֶדְנָה **'ednâh**, *ed-naw´*; from 5727; *pleasure*:— delicate, delight, pleasure. See also 1040.

5731. עֵדֶן **'Êden**, *ay´-den*; the same as 5730 (masc.); *Eden*, the region of Adam's home:— Eden.

5732. עִדָּן **'iddân** (Chald.), *id-dawn´*; from a root corresp. to that of 5708; a set *time*; tech. a *year*:— time.

5733. עַדְנָא **'Adnâ'**, *ad-naw´* from 5727; *pleasure*; *Adna*, the name of two Isr.:— Adna.

5734. עַדְנָה **'Adnâh**, *ad-naw´*; from 5727; *pleasure*; *Adnah*, the name of two Isr.:— Adnah.

5735. עֲדְעָדָה **'Ăd'âdâh**, *ad-aw-daw´*; from 5712; *festival*; *Adadah*, a place in Pal.:— Adadah.

5736. עָדַף **'âdaph**, *aw-daf´*; a prim. root; to *be* (caus. *have*) *redundant*:— be more, odd number, be (have) over (and above), overplus, remain.

5737. עָדַר **'âdar**, *aw-dar´*; a prim. root; to *arrange*, as a battle, a vineyard (to *hoe*); hence, to *muster* and so to *miss* (or *find wanting*):— dig, fail, keep (rank), lack.

5738. עֶדֶר **'Eder**, *eh´-der*; from 5737; an *arrangement* (i.e. drove); *Eder*, an Isr.:— Ader.

5739. עֵדֶר **'êder**, *ay´-der*; from 5737; an *arrangement*, i.e. *muster* (of animals):— drove, flock, herd.

5740. עֵדֶר **'Êder**, *ay´-der*; the same as 5739; *Eder*, the name of an Isr. and of two places in Pal.:— Edar, Eder.

5741. עַדְרִיאֵל **'Adrîy'êl**, *ad-ree-ale´*; from 5739 and 410; *flock of God*; *Adriel*, an Isr.:— Adriel.

5742. עָדָשׁ **'âdâsh**, *aw-dawsh´*; from an unused root of uncert. mean.; a *lentil*:— lentile.

עַוָּא **'Avvâ'**. See 5755.

5743. עוּב **'ûwb**, *oob*; a prim. root; to *be dense* or *dark*, i.e. to *becloud*:— cover with a cloud.

5744. עוֹבֵד **'Ôwbêd**, *o-bade´*; act. part. of 5647; *serving*; *Obed*, the name of five Isr.:— Obed.

5745. עוֹבָל **'Ôwbâl**, *o-bawl´*; of for. der.; *Obal*, a son of Joktan:— Obal.

5746. עוּג **'ûwg**, *oog*; a prim. root; prop. to *gyrate*; but used only as a denom. from 5692, to *bake* (round cakes on the hearth):— bake.

5747. עוֹג **'Ôwg**, *ogue*; prob. from 5746; *round*; *Og*, a king of Bashan:— Og.

5748. עוּגָב **'ûwgâb**, *oo-gawb´*; or

עֻגָּב **'uggâb**, *oog-gawb´*; from 5689 in the orig. sense of *breathing*; a reed-instrument of music:— organ.

5749. עוּד **'ûwd**, *ood*; a prim. root; to *duplicate* or *repeat*; by impl. to *protest*, *testify* (as by reiteration); intens. to *encompass*, *restore* (as a sort of redupl.):— admonish, charge, earnestly, lift up, protest, call (take) to record, relieve, rob, solemnly, stand upright, testify, give warning, (bear, call to, give, take to) witness.

5750. עוֹד **'ôwd**, *ode*; or

עֹד **'ôd**, *ode*; from 5749; prop. *iteration* or *continuance*; used only adv. (with or without prep.), *again, repeatedly, still, more*:— again, × all life long, at all, besides, but, else, further (-more), henceforth, (any) longer, (any) more (-over), × once, since, (be) still, when, (good, the) while (having being), (as, because, whether, while) yet (within).

5751. עוֹד **'ôwd** (Chald.), *ode*; corresp. to 5750:— while.

5752. עוֹדֵד **'Ôwdêd**, *o-dade´*; or

עֹדֵד **'Ôdêd**, *o-dade´*; from 5749; *reiteration*; *Oded*, the name of two Isr.:— Oded.

5753. עָוָה **'âvâh**, *aw-vaw´*; a prim. root; to *crook*, lit. or fig. (as follows):— do amiss, bow down, make crooked, commit iniquity, pervert, (do) perverse (-ly), trouble, × turn, do wickedly, do wrong.

5754. עַוָּה **'avvâh**, *av-vaw´*; intens. from 5753 abb.; *overthrow*:— × overturn.

5755. עִוָּה **'Ivvâh**, *iv-vaw´*; or

עַוָּא **'Avvâ'** (2 Kings 17: 24) *av-vaw´*; for 5754; *Ivvah* or *Avva*, a region of Assyria:— Ava, Ivah.

עָוֹן **'âvôwn**. See 5771.

5756. עוּז **'ûwz**, *ooz*; a prim. root; to *be strong*; caus. to *strengthen*, i.e. (fig.) to *save* (by flight):— gather (self, self to flee), retire.

5757. עַוִּי **'Avvîy**, *av-vee´*; patrial from 5755; an *Avvite* or native of Avvah (only plur.):— Avims, Avites.

5758. עִוְיָא **'ivyâ'** (Chald.), *iv-yaw´*; from a root corresp. to 5753; *perverseness*:— iniquity.

5759. עֲוִיל **'ăvîyl**, *av-eel´*; from 5764; a *babe*:— young child, little one.

5760. עֲוִיל **'ăvîyl**, *av-eel´*; from 5765; *perverse* (morally):— ungodly.

5761. עַוִּים **'Avvîym**, *av-veem´*; plur. of 5757; *Avvim* (as inhabited by Avvites), a place in Pal. (with the art. pref.):— Avim.

5762. עֲוִית **'Ăvîyth**, *av-veeth´*; or |perh.

עֲיּוֹת **'Ayôwth**, *ah-yōth´*, as if plur. of 5857|

עֲיּוּת °**'Ayûwth**, *ah-yōth´*; from 5753; *ruin*; *Avvith* (or *Avvoth*), a place in Pal.:— Avith.

5763. עוּל **'ûwl**, *ool*; a prim. root; to *suckle*, i.e. *give milk*:— milch, (ewe great) with young.

5764. עוּל **'ûwl**, *ool*; from 5763; a *babe*:— sucking child, infant.

5765. עֲוַל **'âval**, *aw-val´*; a prim. root; to *distort* (morally):— deal unjustly, unrighteous.

עוֹל **'ôwl**. See 5923.

5766. עֶוֶל **'evel**, *eh´-vel*; or

עָוֶל **'âvel**, *aw´-vel*; and (fem.)

עַוְלָה **'avlâh**, *av-law´*; or

עוֹלָה **'ôwlâh**, *o-law´*; or

עֹלָה **'ôlâh**, *o-law´*; from 5765; (moral) *evil*:— iniquity, perverseness, unjust (-ly), unrighteousness (-ly), wicked (-ness).

5767. עַוָּל **'avvâl**, *av-vawl´*; intens. from 5765; *evil* (morally):— unjust, unrighteous, wicked.

עוֹלָה **'ôwlâh**. See 5930.

5768. עוֹלֵל **'ôwlêl**, *o-lale´*; or

עֹלָל **'ôlâl**, *o-lawl´*; from 5763; a *suckling*:— babe, (young) child, infant, little one.

5769. עוֹלָם **'ôwlâm**, *o-lawm´*; or

עֹלָם **'ôlâm**, *o-lawm´*; from 5956; prop. *concealed*, i.e. the *vanishing* point; gen. time *out of mind* (past or future), i.e. (practically) *eternity*; freq. adv. (espec. with prep. pref.) *always*:— alway (-s), ancient (time), any more, continuance, eternal, (for, |n-|) ever (-lasting, -more, of old), lasting, long (time), (of) old (time), perpetual, at any time, (beginning of the) world (+ without end). Comp. 5331, 5703.

5770. עָוַן °**'âvan**, *aw-van´*; denom. from 5869; to *watch* (with jealousy):— eye.

5771. עָוֹן **'âvôn**, *aw-vone´*; or

עָווֹן **'âvôwn** (2 Kings 7:9; Psa. 51:5 |7|), *aw-vone´*; from 5753; *perversity*, i.e. (moral) *evil*:— fault, iniquity, mischief, punishment (of iniquity), sin.

5772. עוֹנָה **'ôwnâh**, *o-naw´*; from an unused root appar. mean. to *dwell* together; sexual (*cohabitation*):— duty of marriage.

5773. עֲוְעֶה **'av'eh**, *av-eh´*; from 5753; *perversity*:— × perverse.

5774. עוּף **'ûwph**, *oof*; a prim. root; to *cover* (with wings or obscurity); hence, (as denom. from 5775) to *fly*; also (by impl. of dimness) to *faint* (from the darkness of swooning):— brandish, be (wax) faint, flee away, fly (away), × set, shine forth, weary.

5775. עוֹף **'ôwph**, *ofe*; from 5774; a *bird* (as covered with feathers, or rather as covering with wings), often collect.:— bird, that flieth, flying, fowl.

5776. עוֹף **'ôwph** (Chald.), *ofe*; corresp. to 5775:— fowl.

5777. עוֹפֶרֶת **'ôwphereth**, *o-feh´-reth*; or

עֹפֶרֶת **'ôphereth,** *o-feh´-reth;* fem. part. act. of 6080; *lead* (from its *dusty* color):— lead.

5778. עוֹפָי° **'Ôwphay,** *o-fah´-ee;* from 5775; *birdlike; Ephai,* an Isr.:— Ephai [from marg.].

5779. עוץ **'ûwts,** *oots;* a prim. root; to *consult:*— take advice [counsell together].

5780. עוּץ **'Ûwts,** *oots;* appar. from 5779; *consultation; Uts,* a son of Aram, also a Seirite, and the regions settled by them.:— Uz.

5781. עוּק **'ûwq,** *ook;* a prim. root; to *pack:*— be pressed.

5782. עוּר **'ûwr,** *oor;* a prim. root [rather ident. with 5783 through the idea of *opening* the eyes]; to *wake* (lit. or fig.):— (a-) wake (-n, up), lift up (self), × master, raise (up), stir up (self).

5783. עוּר **'ûwr,** *oor;* a prim. root; to (be) *bare:*— be made naked.

5784. עוּר **'ûwr** (Chald.), *oor; chaff* (as the *naked* husk):— chaff.

5785. עוֹר **'ôwr,** *ore;* from 5783; *skin* (as *naked);* by impl. *hide, leather:*— hide, leather, skin.

5786. עָוַר **'âvar,** *aw-var´;* a prim. root [rather denom. from 5785 through the idea of a *film* over the eyes]; to *blind:*— blind, put out. See also 5895.

5787. עִוֵּר **'ivvêr,** *iv-vare´;* intens. from 5786; *blind* (lit. or fig.):— blind (men, people).

עוֹרֵב **'ôwrêb.** See 6159.

5788. עִוָּרוֹן **'ivvârôwn,** *iv-vaw-rone´;* and (fem.)

עַוֶּרֶת **'avvereth,** *av-veh´-reth;* from 5787; *blindness:*— blind (-ness).

5789. עוּשׁ **'ûwsh,** *oosh;* a prim. root; to *hasten:*— assemble self.

5790. עוּת **'ûwth,** *ooth;* for 5789; to *hasten,* i.e. *succor:*— speak in season.

5791. עָוַת **'âvath,** *aw-vath´;* a prim. root; to *wrest:*— bow self, (make) crooked, falsifying, overthrow, deal perversely, pervert, subvert, turn upside down.

5792. עַוָּתָה **'avvâthâh,** *av-vaw-thaw´;* from 5791; *oppression:*— wrong.

5793. עוּתַי **'Ûwthay,** *oo-thah´-ee;* from 5790; *succoring; Uthai,* the name of two Isr.:— Uthai.

5794. עַז **'az,** *az;* from 5810; *strong, vehement, harsh:*— fierce, + greedy, mighty, power, roughly, strong.

5795. עֵז **'êz,** *aze;* from 5810; a she-*goat* (as *strong),* but masc. in plur. (which also is used ellipt. for *goat's hair):*— (she) goat, kid.

5796. עֵז **'êz** (Chald.), *aze;* corresp. to 5795:— goat.

5797. עֹז **'ôz,** *oze;* or (fully)

עוֹז **'ôwz,** *oze;* from 5810; *strength* in various applications *(force, security, majesty, praise):*— boldness, loud, might, power, strength, strong.

5798. עֻזָּא **'Uzzâ',** *ooz-zaw´;* or

עֻזָּה **'Uzzâh,** *ooz-zaw´;* fem. of 5797; *strength; Uzza* or *Uzzah,* the name of five Isr.:— Uzza, Uzzah.

5799. עֲזָאזֵל **'ăzâ'zêl,** *az-aw-zale´;* from 5795 and 235; *goat of departure;* the *scapegoat:*— scapegoat.

5800. עָזַב **'âzab,** *aw-zab´;* a prim. root; to *loosen,* i.e. *relinquish, permit,* etc.:— commit self, fail, forsake, fortify, help, leave (destitute, off), refuse, × surely.

5801. עִזָּבוֹן **'izzâbôwn,** *iz-zaw-bone´;* from 5800 in the sense of *letting go* (for a price, i.e. *selling); trade,* i.e. the place *(mart)* or the payment *(revenue):*— fair, ware.

5802. עַזְבּוּק **'Azbûwq,** *az-book´;* from 5794 and the root of 950; *stern depopulator; Azbuk,* an Isr.:— Azbuk.

5803. עַזְגָּד **'Azgâd,** *az-gawd´;* from 5794 and 1409; *stern troop; Azgad,* an Isr.:— Azgad.

5804. עַזָּה **'Azzâh,** *az-zaw´;* fem. of 5794; *strong; Azzah,* a place in Pal.:— Azzah, Gaza.

5805. עֲזוּבָה **'ăzûwbâh,** *az-oo-baw´;* fem. pass. part. of 5800; *desertion* (of inhabitants):— forsaking.

5806. עֲזוּבָה **'Ăzûwbâh,** *az-oo-baw´;* the same as 5805; *Azubah,* the name of two Israelitesses:— Azubah.

5807. עֱזוּז **'ĕzûwz,** *ez-ooz´;* from 5810; *forcibleness:*— might, strength.

5808. עִזּוּז **'izzûwz,** *iz-zooz´;* from 5810; *forcible;* collect. and concr. an *army:*— power, strong.

5809. עַזּוּר **'Azzûwr,** *az-zoor´;* or

עַזּוּר **'Azzûr,** *az-zoor´;* from 5826; *helpful; Azzur,* the name of three Isr.:— Azur, Azzur.

5810. עָזַז **'âzaz,** *aw-zaz´;* a prim. root; to *be stout* (lit. or fig.):— harden, impudent, prevail, strengthen (self), be strong.

5811. עָזָז **'Âzâz,** *aw-zawz´;* from 5810; *strong; Azaz,* an Isr.:— Azaz.

5812. עֲזַזְיָהוּ **'Ăzazyâhûw,** *az-az-yaw´-hoo;* from 5810 and 3050; *Jah has strengthened; Azazjah,* the name of three Isr.:— Azaziah.

5813. עֻזִּי **'Uzzîy,** *ooz-zee´;* from 5810; *forceful; Uzzi,* the name of six Isr.:— Uzzi.

5814. עֻזִּיָּא **'Uzzîyâ',** *ooz-zee-yaw´;* perh. for 5818; *Uzzija,* an Isr.:— Uzzia.

5815. עֲזִיאֵל **'Ăzîy'êl,** *az-ee-ale´;* from 5756 and 410; *strengthened of God; Aziël,* an Isr.:— Aziel. Comp. 3268.

5816. עֻזִּיאֵל **'Uzzîy'êl,** *ooz-zee-ale´;* from 5797 and 410; *strength of God; Uzziël,* the name of six Isr.:— Uzziel.

5817. עָזִּיאֵלִי **'Ozzîy'êlîy,** *oz-zee-ay-lee´;* patron. from 5816; an *Uzziëlite* (collect.) or desc. of Uzziel:— Uzzielites.

5818. עֻזִּיָּה **'Uzzîyâh,** *ooz-zee-yaw´;* or

עֻזִּיָּהוּ **'Uzzîyâhûw,** *ooz-zee-yaw´-hoo;* from 5797 and 3050; *strength of Jah; Uzzijah,* the name of five Isr.:— Uzziah.

5819. עֲזִיזָא **'Ăzîyzâ',** *az-ee-zaw´;* from 5756; *strengthfulness; Aziza,* an Isr.:— Aziza.

5820. עַזְמָוֶת **'Azmâveth,** *az-maw´-veth;* from 5794 and 4194; *strong* (one) *of death; Azmaveth,* the name of three

Isr. and of a place in Pal.:— Azmaveth. See also 1041.

5821. עַזָּן **'Azzân,** *az-zawn´;* from 5794; *strong one; Azzan,* an Isr.:— Azzan.

5822. עָזְנִיָּה **'oznîyâh,** *oz-nee-yaw´;* prob. fem. of 5797; prob. the *sea-eagle* (from its *strength):*— ospray.

5823. עָזַק **'âzaq,** *aw-zak´;* a prim. root; to *grub* over:— fence about.

5824. עִזְקָא **'izqâ'** (Chald.), *iz-kaw´;* from a root corresp. to 5823; a *signet*-ring (as engraved):— signet.

5825. עֲזֵקָה **'Ăzêqâh,** *az-ay-kaw´;* from 5823; *tilled; Azekah,* a place in Pal.:— Azekah.

5826. עָזַר **'âzar,** *aw-zar´;* a prim. root; to *surround,* i.e. *protect* or *aid:*— help, succour.

5827. עֶזֶר **'Ezer,** *eh´-zer;* from 5826; *help; Ezer,* the name of two Isr.:— Ezer. Comp. 5829.

5828. עֵזֶר **'êzer,** *ay´-zer;* from 5826; *aid:*— help.

5829. עֵזֶר **'Êzer,** *ay´-zer;* the same as 5828; *Ezer,* the name of four Isr.:— Ezer. Comp. 5827.

עַזּוּר **'Azzûr.** See 5809.

5830. עֶזְרָא **'Ezrâ',** *ez-raw´;* a var. of 5833; *Ezra,* an Isr.:— Ezra.

5831. עֶזְרָא **'Ezrâ'** (Chald.), *ez-raw´;* corresp. to 5830; *Ezra,* an Isr.:— Ezra.

5832. עֲזַרְאֵל **'Ăzar'êl,** *az-ar-ale´;* from 5826 and 410; *God has helped; Azarel,* the name of five Isr.:— Azarael, Azareel.

5833. עֶזְרָה **'ezrâh,** *ez-raw´;* or

עֶזְרָת **'ezrâth** (Psa. 60:11 [13]; 108:12 [13]), *ez-rawth´;* fem. of 5828; *aid:*— help (-ed, -er).

5834. עֶזְרָה **'Ezrâh,** *ez-raw´;* the same as 5833; *Ezrah,* an Isr.:— Ezrah.

5835. עֲזָרָה **'ăzârâh,** *az-aw-raw´;* from 5826 in its orig. mean. of *surrounding;* an *inclosure;* also a *border:*— court, settle.

5836. עֶזְרִי **'Ezrîy,** *ez-ree´;* from 5828; *helpful; Ezri,* an Isr.:— Ezri.

5837. עֲזְרִיאֵל **'Azrîy'êl,** *az-ree-ale´;* from 5828 and 410; *help of God; Azriël,* the name of three Isr.:— Azriel.

5838. עֲזַרְיָה **'Ăzaryâh,** *az-ar-yaw´;* or

עֲזַרְיָהוּ **'Ăzaryâhûw,** *az-ar-yaw´-hoo;* from 5826 and 3050; *Jah has helped; Azarjah,* the name of nineteen Isr.:— Azariah.

5839. עֲזַרְיָה **'Ăzaryâh** (Chald.), *az-ar-yaw´;* corresp. to 5838; *Azarjah,* one of Daniel's companions:— Azariah.

5840. עַזְרִיקָם **'Azrîyqâm,** *az-ree-kawm´;* from 5828 and act. part. of 6965; *help of an enemy; Azrikam,* the name of four Isr.:— Azrikam.

5841. עַזָּתִי **'Azzâthîy,** *az-zaw-thee´;* patrial from 5804; an *Azzathite* or inhab. of Azzah:— Gazathite, Gazite.

5842. עֵט **'êṭ,** *ate;* from 5860 (contr.) in the sense of *swooping,* i.e. *side-long stroke;* a *stylus* or marking stick:— pen.

5843. עֵטָא **'êṭâ'** (Chald.), *ay-taw´*; from 3272; *prudence*:— counsel.

5844. עָטָה **'âṭâh**, *aw-taw´*; a prim. root; to *wrap*, i.e. *cover, veil, clothe*, or *roll*:— array self, be clad, (put a) cover (-ing, self), fill, put on, × surely, turn aside.

5845. עֲטִין **'ăṭîyn**, *at-een´*; from an unused root mean. appar. to *contain*; a *receptacle* (for milk, i.e. *pail*; fig. *breast*):— breast.

5846. עֲטִישָׁה **'ăṭîyshâh**, *at-ee-shaw´*; from an unused root mean. to *sneeze*; *sneezing*:— sneezing.

5847. עֲטַלֵּף **'ăṭallêph**, *at-al-lafe´*; of uncert. der.; a *bat*:— bat.

5848. עָטַף **'âṭaph**, *aw-taf´*; a prim. root; to *clothe* (whether tran. or reflex.); hence, (from the idea of *darkness*) to *languish*:— cover (over), fail, faint, feebler, hide self, be overwhelmed, swoon.

5849. עָטַר **'âṭar**, *aw-tar´*; a prim. root; to *encircle* (for attack or protection); espec. to *crown* (lit. or fig.):— compass, crown.

5850. עֲטָרָה **'ăṭârâh**, *at-aw-raw´*; from 5849; a *crown*:— crown.

5851. עֲטָרָה **'Ăṭârâh**, *at-aw-raw´*; the same as 5850; *Atarah*, an Israelitess:— Atarah.

5852. עֲטָרוֹת **'Ăṭârôwth**, *at-aw-rôth´*; or

עֲטָרֹת **'Ăṭârôth**, *at-aw-rôth´*; plur. of 5850; *Ataroth*, the name (thus simply) of two places in Pal.:— Ataroth.

5853. עֲטְרוֹת אַדָּר **'Aṭrôwth 'Addâr**, *at-rôth´ ad-dawr´*; from the same as 5852 and 146; *crowns of Addar; Atroth-Addar*, a place in Pal.:— Ataroth-adar (-addar).

5854. עֲטְרוֹת בֵּית יוֹאָב **'Aṭrôwth Bêyth Yôw'âb**, *at-rôth´ bayth yo-awb´*; from the same as 5852 and 1004 and 3097; *crowns of* (the) *house of Joāb; Atroth-beth-Joāb*, a place in Pal.:— Ataroth, the house of Joab.

5855. עֲטְרוֹת שׁוֹפָן **'Aṭrôwth Shôwphân**, *at-rôth´ sho-fawn´*; from the same as 5852 and a name otherwise unused [being from the same as 8226] mean. *hidden; crowns of Shophan; Atroth-Shophan*, a place in Pal.:— Atroth, Shophan [as if two places].

5856. עִי **'îy**, *ee*; from 5753; a *ruin* (as if overturned):— heap.

5857. עַי **'Ay**, *ah´ee*; or (fem.)

עַיָּא **'Ayâ'** (Neh. 11:31), *ah-yaw´*; or

עַיָּת **'Ayâth** (Isa. 10:28), *ah-yawth´*; for 5856; *Ai, Aja* or *Ajath*, a place in Pal.:— Ai, Aija, Aijath, Hai.

5858. עֵיבָל **'Êybâl**, *ay-bawl´*; perh. from an unused root mean. to *be bald; bare; Ebal*, a mountain of Pal.:— Ebal.

עַיָּה **'Ayâh**. See 5857.

5859. עִיּוֹן **'Iyôwn**, *ee-yone´*; from 5856; *ruin; Ijon*, a place in Pal.:— Ijon.

5860. עִיט **'îyṭ**, *eet*; a prim. root; to *swoop* down upon (lit. or fig.):— fly, rail.

5861. עַיִט **'ayiṭ**, *ah´-yit*; from 5860; a *hawk* or other bird of prey:— bird, fowl, ravenous (bird).

5862. עֵיטָם **'Êyṭâm**, *ay-tawm´*; from

5861; *hawk-ground; Etam*, a place in Pal.:— Etam.

5863. עִיֵּי הָעֲבָרִים **'Iyêy hâ-'Ăbârîym**, *ee-yay´ haw-ab-aw-reem´*; from the plur. of 5856 and the plur. of the act. part. of 5674 with the art. interposed; *ruins of the passers; Ije-ha-Abarim*, a place near Pal.:— Ije-abarim.

5864. עִיִּים **'Iyîym**, *ee-yeem´*; plur. of 5856; *ruins; Ijim*, a place in the Desert:— Iim.

5865. עֵילוֹם **'êylôwm**, *ay-lome´*; for 5769:— ever.

5866. עִילַי **'Îylay**, *ee-lah´-ee*; from 5927; *elevated; Ilai*, an Isr.:— Ilai.

5867. עֵילָם **'Êylâm**, *ay-lawm´*; or

עוֹלָם° **'Ôwlâm** (Ezra 10:2; Jer. 49:36), *o-lawm´*; prob. from 5956; *hidden*, i.e. *distant; Elam*, a son of Shem, and his desc., with their country; also of six Isr.:— Elam.

5868. עֲיָם **'ăyâm**, *ah-yawm´*; of doubtful or. and authenticity; prob. mean. *strength*:— mighty.

5869. עַיִן **'ayin**, *ah´-yin*; prob. a prim. word; an *eye* (lit. or fig.); by anal. a *fountain* (as the *eye* of the landscape):— affliction, outward appearance, + before, + think best, colour, conceit, + be content, countenance, + displease, eye (l-browl, l-dl, -sight), face, + favour, fountain, furrow [from the marg.], × him, + humble, knowledge, look, (+ well), × me, open (-ly), + (not) please, presence, + regard, resemblance, sight, × thee, × them, + think, × us, well, × you (-rselves).

5870. עַיִן **'ayin** (Chald.), *ah´-yin*; corresp. to 5869; an *eye*:— eye.

5871. עַיִן **'Ayin**, *ah´-yin*; the same as 5869; *fountain; Ajin*, the name (thus simply) of two places in Pal.:— Ain.

5872. עֵין גֶּדִי **'Êyn Gedîy**, *ane geh´-dee*; from 5869 and 1423; *fountain of a kid; En-Gedi*, a place in Pal.:— En-gedi.

5873. עֵין גַּנִּים **'Êyn Gannîym**, *ane gan-neem´*; from 5869 and the plur. of 1588; *fountain of gardens; En-Gannim*, a place in Pal.:— En-gannim.

5874. עֵין־דּאר **'Êyn-Dô'r**, *ane-dore´*; or

עֵין דּוֹר **'Êyn Dôwr**, *ane dore´*; or

עֵין־דּר **'Êyn-Dôr**, *ane-dore´*; from 5869 and 1755; *fountain of dwelling; En-Dor*, a place in Pal.:— En-dor.

5875. עֵין הַקּוֹרֵא **'Êyn haq-Qôwrê'**, *ane-hak-ko-ray´*; from 5869 and the act. part. of 7121; *fountain of One calling; En-hak-Kore*, a place near Pal.:— En-hakhore.

עֵינוֹן **'Êynôwn**. See 2703.

5876. עֵין חַדָּה **'Êyn Chaddâh**, *ane khad-daw´*; from 5869 and the fem. of a der. from 2300; *fountain of sharpness; En-Chaddah*, a place in Pal.:— En-haddah.

5877. עֵין חָצוֹר **'Êyn Châtsôwr**, *ane khaw-tsore´*; from 5869 and the same as 2674; *fountain of a village; En-Chatsor*, a place in Pal.:— En-hazor.

5878. עֵין חֲרֹד **'Êyn Chărôd**, *ane khar-ode´*; from 5869 and a der. of 2729; *foun-

tain of trembling; En-Charod*, a place in Pal.:— well of Harod.

5879. עֵינַיִם **'Êynayim**, *ay-nah´-yim*; or

עֵינָם **'Êynâm**, *ay-nawm´*; dual of 5869; *double fountain; Enajim* or *Enam*, a place in Pal.:— Enaim, openly (Genesis 38:21).

5880. עֵין מִשְׁפָּט **'Êyn Mishpâṭ**, *ane mish-pawt´*; from 5869 and 4941; *fountain of judgment; En-Mishpat*, a place near Pal.:— En-mishpat.

5881. עֵינָן **'Êynân**, *ay-nawn´*; from 5869; *having eyes; Enan*, an Isr.:— Enan. Comp. 2704.

5882. עֵין עֶגְלַיִם **'Êyn 'Eglayim**, *ane eg-lah´-yim*; from 5869 and the dual of 5695; *fountain of two calves; En-Egla-jim*, a place in Pal.:— En-eglaim.

5883. עֵין רֹגֵל **'Êyn Rôgêl**, *ane ro-gale´*; from 5869 and the act. part. of 7270; *fountain of a traveller; En-Rogel*, a place near Jerusalem:— En-rogel.

5884. עֵין רִמּוֹן **'Êyn Rimmôwn**, *ane rim-mone´*; from 5869 and 7416; *fountain of a pomegranate; En-Rimmon*, a place in Pal.:— En-rimmon.

5885. עֵין שֶׁמֶס **'Êyn Shemesh**, *ane sheh´-mesh*; from 5869 and 8121; *fountain of* (the) *sun; En-Shemesh*, a place in Pal.:— En-shemesh.

5886. עֵין הַנִּים **'Êyn Tannîym**, *ane tan-neem´*; from 5869 and the plur. of 8565; *fountain of jackals; En-Tannim*, a pool near Jerusalem:— dragon well.

5887. עֵין תַּפּוּחַ **'Êyn Tappûwach**, *ane tap-poo´-akh*; from 5869 and 8598; *fountain of an apple tree; En-Tap-puäch*, a place in Pal.:— En-tappuah.

5888. עָיֵף **'âyêph**, *aw-yafe´*; a prim. root; to *languish*:— be wearied.

5889. עָיֵף **'âyêph**, *aw-yafe´*; from 5888; *languid*:— faint, thirsty, weary.

5890. עֵיפָה **'êyphâh**, *ay-faw´*; fem. from 5774; *obscurity* (as if from *covering*):— darkness.

5891. עֵיפָה **'Êyphâh**, *ay-faw´*; the same as 5890; *Ephah*, the name of a son of Midian, and of the region settled by him; also of an Isr. and of an Israelitess:— Ephah.

5892. עִיר **'îyr**, *eer*; or (in the plur.)

עָר **'âr**, *awr*; or

עָיַר **'âyar** (Judg. 10:4), *aw-yar´*; from 5782 a *city* (a place guarded by *waking* or a watch) in the widest sense (even of a mere *encampment* or *post*):— Ai [from marg.], city, court [from marg.], town.

5893. עִיר **'Îyr**, *eer*; the same as 5892; *Ir*, an Isr.:— Ir.

5894. עִיר **'îyr** (Chald.), *eer*; from a root corresp. to 5782; a *watcher*, i.e. an *angel* (as guardian):— watcher.

5895. עַיִר **'ayir**, *ah´-yeer*; from 5782 in the sense of *raising* (i.e. *bearing* a burden); prop. a young *ass* (as just broken to a load); hence, an ass-*colt*:— (ass) colt, foal, young ass.

5896. עִירָא **'Îyrâ'**, *ee-raw´*; from 5782; *wakefulness; Ira*, the name of three Isr.:— Ira.

5897. עִירָד **'Îyrâd**, *ee-rawd´*; from the

same as 6166; *fugitive; Irad*, an antediluvian:— Irad.

5898. עִיר הַמֶּלַח **'Îyr ham-Melach**, *eer ham-meh´-lakh*; from 5892 and 4417 with the art. of substance interp.; *city of* (the) *salt; Ir-ham-Melach*, a place near Pal.:— the city of salt.

5899. עִיר הַתְּמָרִים **'Îyr hat-Tᵉmârîym**, *eer hat-tem-aw-reem´*; from 5892 and the plur. of 8558 with the art. interpolated; *city of the palmtrees; Ir-hat-Temarim*, a place in Pal.:— the city of palmtrees.

5900. עִירוּ **'Îyrûw**, *ee-roo´*; from 5892; a *citizen; Iru*, an Isr.:— Iru.

5901. עִירִי **'Îyrîy**, *ee-ree´*; from 5892; *urbane; Iri*, an Isr.:— Iri.

5902. עִירָם **'Îyrâm**, *ee-rawm´*; from 5892; *city-wise; Iram*, an Idumæan:— Iram.

5903. עֵירֹם **'êyrôm**, *ay-rome´*; or

עֵרֹם **'êrôm**, *ay-rome´*; from 6191; *nudity:*— naked (-ness).

5904. עִיר נָחָשׁ **'Îyr Nâchâsh**, *eer naw-khawsh´*; from 5892 and 5175; *city of a serpent; Ir-Nachash*, a place in Pal.:— Ir-nahash.

5905. עִיר שֶׁמֶשׁ **'Îyr Shemesh**, *eer sheh´-mesh*; from 5892 and 8121; *city of* (the) *sun; Ir-Shemesh*, a place in Pal.:— Ir-shemesh.

5906. עַיִשׁ **'Ayish**, *ah´-yish*; or

עָשׁ **'Âsh**, *awsh*; from 5789; the constellation of the Great *Bear* (perh. from its *migration* through the heavens):— Arcturus.

5907. עַיָּה **'Ayâth**. See 5857.

5907. עַכְבּוֹר **'Akbôwr**, *ak-bore´*; prob. for 5909; *Akbor*, the name of an Idumæan and two Isr.:— Achbor.

5908. עַכָּבִישׁ **'akkâbîysh**, *ak-kaw-beesh´*; prob. from an unused root in the lit. sense of *entangling*; a *spider* (as *weaving* a network):— spider.

5909. עַכְבָּר **'akbâr**, *ak-bawr´*; prob. from the same as 5908 in the second. sense of *attacking*; a *mouse* (as *nibbling*):— mouse.

5910. עַכּוֹ **'Akkôw**, *ak-ko´*; appar. from an unused root mean. to *hem* in; *Akko* (from its situation on a bay):— Accho.

5911. עָכוֹר **'Âkôwr**, *aw-lore´*; from 5916; *troubled; Akor*, the name of a place in Pal.:— Achor.

5912. עָכָן **'Âkân**, *aw-kawn´*; from an unused root mean. to *trouble; troublesome; Akan*, an Isr.:— Achan. Comp. 5917.

5913. עָכַס **'âkaç**, *aw-kas´*; a prim. root; prop. to *tie*, spec. with fetters; but used only as denom. from 5914; to *put on anklets*:— make a tinkling ornament.

5914. עֶכֶס **'ekeç**, *eh´-kes*; from 5913; a *fetter*; hence, an *anklet*:— stocks, tinkling ornament.

5915. עַכְסָה **'Akçâh**, *ak-saw´*; fem. of 5914; *anklet; Aksah*, an Israelitess:— Achsah.

5916. עָכַר **'âkar**, *aw-kar´*; a prim. root; prop. to *roil* water; fig. to *disturb* or *afflict*:— trouble, stir.

5917. עָכָר **'Âkâr**, *aw-kawr´*; from 5916;

troublesome; Akar, an Isr.:— Achar. Comp. 5912.

5918. עָכְרָן **'Okrân**, *ok-rawn´*; from 5916; *muddler; Okran*, an Isr.:— Ocran.

5919. עַכְשׁוּב **'akshûwb**, *ak-shoob´*; prob. from an unused root mean. to *coil*; an *asp* (from lurking *coiled* up):— adder.

5920. עַל **'al**, *al*; from 5927; prop. the *top*; spec. the *Highest* (i.e. *God*); also (adv.) *aloft, to Jehovah*:— above, high, Most High.

5921. עַל **'al**, *al*; prop. the same as 5920 used as a prep. (in the sing. or plur. often with pref., or as conjunc. with a particle following); *above, over, upon*, or *against* (yet always in this last relation with a downward aspect) in a great variety of applications (as follow):— above, according to (-ly), after, (as) against, among, and, × as, at, because of, beside (the rest of), between, beyond the time, × both and, by (reason of), × had the charge of, concerning for, in (that), (forth, out) of, (from) (off), (up-) on, over, than, through (-out), to, touching, × with.

5922. עַל **'al** (Chald.), *al*; corresp. to 5921:— about, against, concerning, for, [there-]fore, from, in, × more, of, (there-, up-) on, (in-) to, + why with.

5923. עֹל **'ôl**, *ole*; or

עוֹל **'ôwl**, *ole*; from 5953; a *yoke* (as *imposed* on the neck), lit. or fig.:— yoke.

5924. עֵלָּא **'êllâ** (Chald.), *ale-law´*; from 5922; *above:*— over.

5925. עֻלָּא **'Ullâ**, *ool-law´*; fem. of 5923; *burden; Ulla*, an Isr.:— Ulla.

5926. עִלֵּג **'illêg**, *il-layg´*; from an unused root mean. to *stutter*; *stuttering:*— stammerer.

5927. עָלָה **'âlâh**, *aw-law´*; a prim. root; to *ascend*, intr. (*be high*) or act. (*mount*); used in a great variety of senses, primary and second., lit. and fig. (as follow):— arise (up), (cause to) ascend up, at once, break [the day] (up), bring (up), (cause to) burn, carry up, cast up, + shew, climb (up), (cause to, make to) come (up), cut off, dawn, depart, exalt, excel, fall, fetch up, get up, (make to) go (away, up); grow (over), increase, lay, leap, levy, lift (self) up, light, [make] up, × mention, mount up, offer, make to pay, + perfect, prefer, put (on), raise, recover, restore, (make to) rise (up), scale, set (up), shoot forth (up), (begin to) spring (up), stir up, take away (up), work.

5928. עֲלָה **'âlâh** (Chald.), *al-aw´*; corresp. to 5930; a *holocaust:*— burnt offering.

5929. עָלֶה **'âleh**, *aw-leh´*; from 5927; a *leaf* (as *coming up* on a tree); collect. *foliage:*— branch, leaf.

5930. עֹלָה **'ôlâh**, *o-law´*; or

עוֹלָה **'ôwlâh**, *o-law´*; fem. act. part. of 5927; a *step* or (collect. *stairs*, as *ascending*); usually a *holocaust* (as *going up* in smoke):— ascent, burnt offering (sacrifice), go up to. See also 5766.

5931. עִלָּה **'illâh** (Chald.), *il-law´*; fem. from a root corresp. to 5927; a *pretext* (as *arising* artificially):— occasion.

5932. עַלְוָה **'alvâh**, *al-vaw´*; for 5766; *moral perverseness:*— iniquity.

5933. עַלְוָה **'Alvâh**, *al-vaw´*; or

עַלְיָה° **'Alyâh**, *al-yaw´*; the same as 5932; *Alvah* or *Aljah*, an Idumæan:— Aliah, Alvah.

5934. עָלוּם **'âlûwm**, *aw-loom´*; pass. part. of 5956 in the denom. sense of 5958; (only in plur. as abstr.) *adolescence*; fig. *vigor:*— youth.

5935. עַלְוָן **'Alvân**, *al-vawn´*; or

עַלְיָן **'Alyân**, *al-yawn´*; from 5927; *lofty; Alvan* or *Aljan*, an Idumæan:— Alian, Alvan.

5936. עֲלוּקָה **'ălûwqâh**, *al-oo-kaw´*; fem. pass. part. of an unused root mean. to *suck*; the *leech:*— horse-leech.

5937. עָלַז **'âlaz**, *aw-laz´*; a prim. root; to *jump* for joy, i.e. *exult:*— be joyful, rejoice, triumph.

5938. עָלֵז **'âlêz**, *aw-laze´*; from 5937; *exultant:*— that rejoiceth.

5939. עֲלָטָה **'ălâṭâh**, *al-aw-taw´*; fem. from an unused root mean. to *cover*; *dusk:*— dark, twilight.

5940. עֱלִי **'ĕlîy**, *el-ee´*; from 5927; a *pestle* (as *lifted*):— pestle.

5941. עֵלִי **'Êlîy**, *ay-lee´*; from 5927; *lofty; Eli*, an Isr. high-priest:— Eli.

5942. עִלִּי **'illîy**, *il-lee´*; from 5927; *high*; i.e. comparative:— upper.

5943. עִלַּי **'illay** (Chald.), *il-lah´-ee*; corresp. to 5942; *supreme* (i.e. *God*):— (most) high.

עַלְיָה° **'Alyâh**. See 5933.

5944. עֲלִיָּה **'ălîyâh**, *al-ee-yaw´*; fem. from 5927; something *lofty*, i.e. a *stairway*; also a *second-story* room (or even one on the roof); fig. the *sky*:— ascent, (upper) chamber, going up, loft, parlour.

5945. עֶלְיוֹן **'elyôwn**, *el-yone´*; from 5927; an *elevation*, i.e. (adj.) *lofty* (comp.); as title, the *Supreme:*— (Most, on) high (-er, -est), upper (-most).

5946. עֶלְיוֹן **'elyôwn** (Chald.), *el-yone´*; corresp. to 5945; the *Supreme:*— Most high.

5947. עַלִּיז **'allîyz**, *al-leez´*; from 5937; *exultant:*— joyous, (that) rejoice (-ing).

5948. עֲלִיל **'ălîyl**, *al-eel´*; from 5953 in the sense of *completing*; prob. a *crucible* (as *working* over the metal):— furnace.

5949. עֲלִילָה **'ălîylâh**, *al-ee-law´*; or

עֲלִלָה **'ălîlâh**, *al-ee-law´*; from 5953 in the sense of *effecting*; an *exploit* (of God), or a *performance* (of man, often in a bad sense); by impl. an *opportunity:*— act (-ion), deed, doing, invention, occasion, work.

5950. עֲלִילִיָּה **'ălîylîyâh**, *al-ee-lee-yaw´*; for 5949; (miraculous) *execution:*— work.

עַלְיָן **'Alyân**. See 5935.

5951. עֲלִיצוּת **'ălîytsûwth**, *al-ee-tsooth´*; from 5970; *exultation:*— rejoicing.

5952. עִלִּית **'allîyth** (Chald.), *al-leeth´*; from 5927; a *second-story* room:— chamber. Comp. 5944.

Hebrew

5953. עָלַל 'âlal, aw-lal'; a prim. root; to effect thoroughly; spec. to glean (also fig.); by impl. (in a bad sense) to overdo, i.e. maltreat, be saucy to, pain, impose (also lit.):— abuse, affect, × child, defile, do, glean, mock, practise, thoroughly, work (wonderfully).

5954. עֲלַל 'âlal (Chald.), al-al'; corresp. to 5953 (in the sense of thrusting oneself in), to enter; caus. to introduce:— bring in, come in, go in.

עֹלָל 'ôlâl. See 5768.

עֲלִילָה 'ălîlâh. See 5949.

5955. עֹלֵלָה 'ôlêlâh, o-lay-law'; fem. act. part. of 5953; only in plur. gleanings; by extens. gleaning-time:— (gleaning) (of the) grapes, grapegleanings.

5956. עָלַם 'âlam, aw-lam'; a prim. root; to veil from sight, i.e. conceal (lit. or fig.):— × any ways, blind, dissembler, hide (self), secret (thing).

5957. עֲלַם 'âlam (Chald.), aw-lam'; corresp. to 5769; remote time, i.e. the future or past indefinitely; often adv. forever:— for (ln-l) ever (lasting), old.

5958. עֶלֶם 'elem, eh'-lem; from 5956; prop. something kept out of sight [comp. 5959], i.e. a lad:— young man, stripling.

עוֹלָם 'ôlâm. See 5769.

5959. עַלְמָה 'almâh, al-maw'; fem. of 5958; a lass (as veiled or private):— damsel, maid, virgin.

5960. עַלְמוֹן 'Almôwn, al-mone'; from 5956; hidden; Almon, a place in Pal.:— Almon. See also 5963.

5961. עֲלָמוֹת 'Ălâmôwth, al-aw-môth'; plur. of 5959; prop. girls, i.e. the soprano or female voice, perh. falsetto:— Alamoth.

עֲלָמוֹת 'almûwth. See 4192.

5962. עַלְמִי 'Almîy (Chald.), al-mee'; patrial from a name corresp. to 5867 contr.; an Elamite or inhab. of Elam:— Elamite.

5963. עַלְמוֹן דִּבְלָתָיְמָה 'Almôn Diblâthâyᵉmâh, al-mone' dib-law-thaw'-yem-aw; from the same as 5960 and the dual of 1690 [comp. 1015] with enclitic of direction; Almon toward Diblathajim; Almon-Diblathajemah, a place in Moab:— Almon-dilathaim.

5964. עָלֶמֶת 'Alemeth, aw-leh'-meth; from 5956; a covering; Alemeth, the name of a place in Pal. and of two Isr.:— Alameth, Alemeth.

5965. עָלַס 'âlaç, aw-las'; a prim. root; to leap for joy, i.e. exult, wave joyously:— × peacock, rejoice, solace self.

5966. עָלַע 'âla', aw-lah'; a prim root; to sip up:— suck up.

5967. עֲלַע 'âla' (Chald.), al-ah'; corresp. to 6763; a rib:— rib.

5968. עָלַף 'âlaph, aw-laf'; a prim. root; to veil or cover; fig. to be languid:— faint, overlaid, wrap self.

5969. עֻלְפֶּה 'ulpeh, ool-peh'; from 5968; an envelope, i.e. (fig.) mourning:— fainted.

5970. עָלַץ 'âlats, aw-lats'; a prim. root; to jump for joy, i.e. exult:— be joyful, rejoice, triumph.

5971. עַם 'am, am; from 6004; a people (as a congregated unit); spec. a tribe (as those of Israel); hence, (collect.) troops or attendants; fig. a flock:— folk, men, nation, people.

5972. עַם 'am (Chald.), am; corresp. to 5971:— people.

5973. עִם 'îm, eem; from 6004; adv. or prep., with (i.e. in conjunction with), in varied applications; spec. equally with, often with prep. pref. (and then usually unrepresented in English):— accompanying, against, and, as (× long as), before, beside, by (reason of), for all, from (among, between), in, like, more than, of, (un-) to, with (-al).

5974. עִם 'îm (Chald.), eem; corresp. to 5973:— by, from, like, to (-ward), with.

5975. עָמַד 'âmad, aw-mad'; a prim. root; to stand, in various relations (lit. and fig., intr. and tran.):— abide (behind), appoint, arise, cease, confirm, continue, dwell, be employed, endure, establish, leave, make, ordain, be [over], place, (be) present (self), raise up, remain, repair, + serve, set (forth, over, -tle, up), (make to, make to be at a, with-) stand (by, fast, firm, still, up), (be at a) stay (up), tarry.

5976. עָמַד 'âmad, aw-mad'; for 4571; to shake:— be at a stand.

5977. עֹמֶד 'ômed, o'-med; from 5975; a spot (as being fixed):— place, (+ where) stood, upright.

5978. עִמָּד 'immâd, im-mawd'; prol. for 5973; along with:— against, by, from, in, + me, + mine, of, + that I take, unto, upon, with (-in.)

עַמּוּד 'ammûd. See 5982.

5979. עֶמְדָּה 'emdâh, em-daw'; from 5975; a station, i.e. domicile:— standing.

5980. עֻמָּה 'ummâh, oom-maw'; from 6004; conjunction, i.e. society; mostly adv. or prep. (with prep. pref.), near, beside, along with:— (over) against, at, beside, hard by, in points.

5981. עֻמָּה 'Ummâh, oom-maw'; the same as 5980; association; Ummah, a place in Pal.:— Ummah.

5982. עַמּוּד 'ammûwd, am-mood'; or

עַמֻּד 'ammûd, am-mood'; from 5975; a column (as standing); also a stand, i.e. platform:— × apiece, pillar.

5983. עַמּוֹן 'Ammôwn, am-mone'; from 5971; tribal, i.e. inbred; Ammon, a son of Lot; also his posterity and their country:— Ammon, Ammonites.

5984. עַמּוֹנִי 'Ammôwnîy, am-mo-nee'; patron. from 5983; an Ammonite or (adj.) Ammonitish:— Ammonite (-s).

5985. עַמּוֹנִית 'Ammôwnîyth, am-mo-neeth'; fem. of 5984; an Ammonitess:— Ammonite (-ss).

5986. עָמוֹס 'Âmôwç, aw-moce'; from 6006; burdensome; Amos, an Isr. prophet:— Amos.

5987. עָמוֹק 'Âmôwq, aw-moke'; from 6009; deep; Amok, an Isr.:— Amok.

5988. עַמִּיאֵל 'Ammîy'êl, am-mee-ale'; from 5971 and 410; people of God; Ammiel, the name of three or four Isr.:— Ammiel.

5989. עַמִּיהוּד 'Ammîyhûwd, am-mee-hood'; from 5971 and 1935; people of splendor; Ammihud, the name of three Isr.:— Ammihud.

5990. עַמִּיזָבָד 'Ammîyzâbâd, am-mee-zaw-bawd'; from 5971 and 2064; people of endowment; Ammizabad, an Isr.:— Ammizabad.

5991. °עַמִּיחוּר 'Ammîychûwr, am-mee-khoor'; from 5971 and 2353; people of nobility; Ammichur, a Syrian prince:— Ammihud [from the marg.].

5992. עַמִּינָדָב 'Ammîynâdâb, am-mee-naw-dawb'; from 5971 and 5068; people of liberality; Amminadab, the name of four Isr.:— Amminadab.

5993. עַמִּי נָדִיב 'Ammîy Nâdîyb, am-mee' naw-deeb'; from 5971 and 5081; my people (is) liberal; Ammi-Nadib, prob. an Isr.:— Amminadib.

5994. עֲמִיק 'ămîyq (Chald.), am-eek'; corresp. to 6012; profound, i.e. unsearchable:— deep.

5995. עָמִיר 'âmîyr, aw-meer'; from 6014; a bunch of grain:— handful, sheaf.

5996. עַמִּישַׁדַּי 'Ammîyshadday, am-mee-shad-dah'ee; from 5971 and 7706; people of (the) Almighty; Ammishaddai, an Isr.:— Ammishaddai.

5997. עָמִית 'âmîyth, aw-meeth'; from a prim. root mean. to associate; companionship; hence, (concr.) a comrade or kindred man:— another, fellow, neighbour.

5998. עָמַל 'âmal, aw-mal'; a prim. root; to toil, i.e. work severely and with irksomeness:— [take] labour (in).

5999. עָמָל 'âmâl, aw-mawl'; from 5998; toil, i.e. wearing effort; hence, worry, wheth. of body or mind:— grievance (-vousness), iniquity, labour, mischief, miserable (-sery), pain (-ful), perverseness, sorrow, toil, travail, trouble, wearisome, wickedness.

6000. עָמָל 'Âmâl, aw-mawl'; the same as 5999; Amal, an Isr.:— Amal.

6001. עָמֵל 'âmêl, aw-male'; from 5998; toiling; concr. a laborer; fig. sorrowful:— that laboureth, that is a misery, had taken [labour], wicked, workman.

6002. עֲמָלֵק 'Ămâlêq, am-aw-lake'; prob. of for. or.; Amalek, a desc. of Esau; also his posterity and their country:— Amalek.

6003. עֲמָלֵקִי 'Ămâlêqîy, am-aw-lay-kee'; patron. from 6002; an Amalekite (or collect. the Amalekites) or desc. of Amalek:— Amalekite (-s).

6004. עָמַם 'âmam, aw-mam'; a prim. root; to associate; by impl. to overshadow (by huddling together):— become dim, hide.

6005. עִמָּנוּאֵל 'Immânûw'êl, im-maw-noo-ale'; from 5973 and 410 with a pron. suff. ins.; with us (is) God; Immanuel, a typical name of Isaiah's son:— Immanuel.

6006. עָמַס 'âmaç, aw-mas'; or

עָמַשׂ 'âmas, aw-mas'; a prim. root; to load, i.e. impose a burden (or fig. infliction):— be borne, (heavy) burden (self), lade, load, put.

6007. עֲמַסְיָה 'Ămaçyâh, am-as-yaw';

from 6006 and 3050; *Jah has loaded;*
Amasjah, an Isr.:— Amasiah.

6008. עַמְעָד **'Am'âd,** *am-awd´;* from 5971
and 5703; *people of time; Amad,* a place
in Pal.:— Amad.

6009. עָמַק **'âmaq,** *aw-mak´;* a prim.
root; to *be* (caus. *make*) *deep* (lit. or
fig.):— (be, have, make, seek) deep
(-ly), depth, be profound.

6010. עֵמֶק **'êmeq,** *ay´-mek;* from 6009; a
vale (i.e. broad *depression*):— dale,
vale, valley [often *used as a part of
proper names*]. See also 1025.

6011. עֹמֶק **'ômeq,** *o´-mek;* from 6009;
depth:— depth.

6012. עָמֵק **'âmêq,** *aw-make´;* from 6009;
deep (lit. or fig.):— deeper, depth,
strange.

6013. עָמֹק **'âmôq,** *aw-moke´;* from 6009;
deep (lit. or fig.):— (× exceeding) deep
(thing).

6014. עָמַר **'âmar,** *aw-mar´;* a prim. root;
prop. appar. to *heap;* fig. to *chastise* (as
if *piling* blows); spec. (as denom. from
6016) to *gather* grain:— bind sheaves,
make merchandise of.

6015. עֲמַר **'âmar** (Chald.), *am-ar´;* corresp. to 6785; *wool:*— wool.

6016. עֹמֶר **'ômer,** *o´-mer;* from 6014;
prop. a *heap,* i.e. a *sheaf;* also an *omer,*
as a dry measure:— omer, sheaf.

6017. עֲמֹרָה **'Ămôrâh,** *am-o-raw´;* from
6014; a (ruined) *heap; Amorah,* a place
in Pal.:— Gomorrah.

6018. עָמְרִי **'Omrîy,** *om-ree´;* from 6014;
heaping; Omri, an Isr.:— Omri.

6019. עַמְרָם **'Amrâm,** *am-rawm´;* prob.
from 5971 and 7311; *high people; Amram,* the name of two Isr.:— Amram.

6020. עַמְרָמִי **'Amrâmîy,** *am-raw-mee´;*
patron. from 6019; an *Amramite* or
desc. of Amram:— Amramite.

עֲמָס **'âmas.** See 6006.

6021. עֲמָסָא **'Ămâsâ,** *am-aw-saw´;* from
6006; *burden; Amasa,* the name of two
Isr.:— Amasa.

6022. עֲמָשַׂי **'Ămâsay,** *am-aw-sah´-ee;*
from 6006; *burdensome; Amasai,* the
name of three Isr.:— Amasai.

6023. עֲמַשְׂכַּי **'Ămashçay,** *am-ash-sah´-
ee;* prob. from 6006; *burdensome;
Amashsay,* an Isr.:— Amashai.

6024. עֵנָב **'Ănâb,** *an-awb´;* from the
same as 6025; *fruit; Anab,* a place in
Pal.:— Anab.

6025. עֵנָב **'ênâb,** *ay-nawb´;* from an unused root prob. mean. to *bear* fruit; a
grape:— (ripe) grape, wine.

6026. עָנַג **'ânag,** *aw-nag´;* a prim. root;
to *be soft* or *pliable,* i.e. (fig.) *effeminate*
or *luxurious:*— delicate (-ness), (have)
delight (self), sport self.

6027. עֹנֶג **'ôneg,** *o´-neg;* from 6026; *luxury:*— delight, pleasant.

6028. עָנֹג **'ânôg,** *aw-nogue´;* from 6026;
luxurious:— delicate.

6029. עָנַד **'ânad,** *aw-nad´;* a prim. root;
to *lace* fast:— bind, tie.

6030. עָנָה **'ânâh,** *aw-naw´;* a prim. root;
prop. to *eye* or (gen.) to *heed,* i.e. *pay
attention;* by impl. to *respond;* by ex-

tens. to *begin* to speak; spec. to *sing,
shout, testify, announce:*— give account, afflict [by *mistake for* 6031],
(cause to, give) answer, bring low [by
mistake for 6031], cry, hear, Leannoth,
lift up, say, × scholar, (give a) shout,
sing (together by course), speak, testify, utter, (bear) witness. See also 1042,
1043.

6031. עָנָה **'ânâh,** *aw-naw´;* a prim. root
[possibly rather ident. with 6030
through the idea of *looking* down or
browbeating]; to *depress* lit. or fig.,
tran. or intr. (in various applications,
as follows):— abase self, afflict (-ion,
self), answer [by *mistake for* 6030],
chasten self, deal hardly with, defile,
exercise, force, gentleness, humble
(self), hurt, ravish, sing [by *mistake for*
6030], speak [by *mistake for* 6030], submit self, weaken, × in any wise.

6032. עֲנָה **'ănâh** (Chald.), *an-aw´;* corresp. to 6030:— answer, speak.

6033. עֲנָה **'ănâh** (Chald.), *an-aw´;* corresp. to 6031:— poor.

6034. עֲנָה **'Ănâh,** *an-aw´;* prob. from
6030; an *answer; Anah,* the name of two
Edomites and one Edomitess:— Anah.

6035. עָנָו **'ânâv,** *aw-nawv´;* or [by inter-
mixture with 6041]

עָנָיו **'ânâyv,** *aw-nawv´;* from 6031;
depressed (fig.), in mind (*gentle*) or circumstances (*needy,* espec. *saintly*):—
humble, lowly, meek, poor. Comp.
6041.

6036. עָנוּב **'Ănûwb,** *aw-noob´;* pass.
part. from the same as 6025; *borne* (as
fruit); *Anub,* an Isr.:— Anub.

6037. עַנְוָה **'anvâh,** *an-vaw´;* fem. of 6035;
mildness (royal); also (concr.) *oppressed:*— gentleness, meekness.

6038. עֲנָוָה **'ănâvâh,** *an-aw-vaw´;* from
6035; *condescension,* human and subj.
(*modesty*), or divine and obj. (*clemency*):— gentleness, humility, meekness.

6039. עֱנוּת **'ĕnûwth,** *en-ooth´;* from 6031;
affliction:— affliction.

6040. עֳנִי **'ŏnîy,** *on-ee´;* from 6031; *depression,* i.e. misery:— afflicted (-ion),
trouble.

6041. עָנִי **'ânîy,** *aw-nee´;* from 6031; *depressed,* in mind or circumstances
[practically the same as 6035, although
the marg. constantly disputes this,
making 6035 subj. and 6041 obj.]:— afflicted, humble, lowly, needy, poor.

6042. עֻנִּי **'Unnîy,** *oon-nee´;* from 6031;
afflicted; Unni, the name of two Isr.:—
Unni.

6043. עֲנָיָה **'Ănâyâh,** *an-aw-yaw´;* from
6030; *Jah has answered; Anajah,* the
name of two Isr.:— Anaiah.

עָנָיו **'ânâyv** See 6035.

6044. עָנִים **'Ănîym,** *an-neem´;* for plur.
of 5869; *fountains; Anim,* a place in
Pal.:— Anim.

6045. עִנְיָן **'inyân,** *in-yawn´;* from 6031;
ado, i.e. (gen.) *employment* or (spec.)
an *affair:*— business, travail.

6046. עָנֵם **'Ănêm,** *aw-name´;* from the
dual of 5869; *two fountains; Anem,* a
place in Pal.:— Anem.

6047. עֲנָמִם **'Ănâmîm,** *an-aw-meem´;* as
if plur. of some Eg. word; *Anamim,* a
son of Mizraim and his desc., with their
country:— Anamim.

6048. עֲנַמֶּלֶךְ **'Ănammelek,** *an-am-
meh´-lek;* of for. or.; *Anammelek,* an
Ass. deity:— Anammelech.

6049. עָנַן **'ânan,** *aw-nan´;* a prim. root;
to *cover;* used only as a denom. from
6051, to *cloud* over; fig. to *act covertly,*
i.e. practise magic:— × bring, enchanter, Meonenim, observe (-r of)
times, soothsayer, sorcerer.

6050. עֲנַן **'ănan** (Chald.), *an-an´;* corresp. to 6051:— cloud.

6051. עָנָן **'ânân,** *aw-nawn´;* from 6049; a
cloud (as *covering* the sky), i.e. the *nimbus* or thunder-cloud:— cloud (-y).

6052. עָנָן **'Ânân,** *aw-nawn´;* the same as
6051; *cloud; Anan,* an Isr.:— Anan.

6053. עֲנָנָה **'ănânâh,** *an-aw-naw´;* fem. of
6051; *cloudiness:*— cloud.

6054. עֲנָנִי **'Ănânîy,** *an-aw-nee´;* from
6051; *cloudy; Anani,* an Isr.:— Anani.

6055. עֲנַנְיָה **'Ănanyâh,** *an-an-yaw´;* from
6049 and 3050; *Jah has covered; Anan-
jah,* the name of an Isr. and of a place
in Pal.:— Ananiah.

6056. עֲנַף **'ănaph** (Chald.), *an-af´;* or

עֶנֶף **'eneph** (Chald.), *eh´-nef;* corresp. to 6057:— bough, branch.

6057. עָנָף **'ânâph,** *aw-nawf´;* from an
unused root mean. to *cover;* a *twig* (as
covering the limbs):— bough, branch.

6058. עָנֵף **'ânêph,** *aw-nafe´;* from the
same as 6057; *branching:*— full of
branches.

6059. עָנַק **'ânaq,** *aw-nak´;* a prim. root;
prop. to *choke;* used only as denom.
from 6060, to *collar,* i.e. adorn with a
necklace; fig. to *fit out* with supplies:—
compass about as a chain, furnish, liberally.

6060. עֲנָק **'ânâq,** *aw-nawk´;* from 6059; a
necklace (as if *strangling*):— chain.

6061. עֲנָק **'Ânâq,** *aw-nawk´;* the same
as 6060; *Anak,* a Canaanite:— Anak.

6062. עֲנָקִי **'Ănâqîy,** *an-aw-kee´;* patron.
from 6061; an *Anakite* or desc. of
Anak:— Anakim.

6063. עָנֵר **'Ânêr,** *aw-nare´;* prob. for
5288; *Aner,* a Amorite, also a place in
Pal.:— Aner.

6064. עָנַשׁ **'ânash,** *aw-nash´;* a prim.
root; prop. to *urge;* by impl. to *inflict* a
penalty, spec. to *fine:*— amerce, condemn, punish, × surely.

6065. עֲנַשׁ **'ănash** (Chald.), *an-ash´;* corresp. to 6066; a *mulct:*— confiscation.

6066. עֹנֶשׁ **'ônesh,** *o´-nesh;* from 6064; a
fine:— punishment, tribute.

עֵנֶת **'eneth** See 3706.

6067. עֲנָת **'Ănâth,** *an-awth´;* from 6030;
answer; Anath, an Isr.:— Anath.

6068. עֲנָתוֹת **'Ănâthôwth,** *an-aw-thôth´;*
plur. of 6067; *Anathoth,* the name of
two Isr., also of a place in Pal.:—
Anathoth.

6069. עַנְתֹתִי **'Anthôthîy,** *an-tho-thee´;* or

עַנְּתוֹתִי **'Ann^ethôwthîy,** *an-ne-tho-
thee´;* patrial from 6068; a *Antothite* or

inhab. of Anathoth:— of Anathoth, Anethothite, Anetothite, Antothite.

6070. עֲנְתוֹתִיָּה **'Anthôthîyâh**, *an-tho-thee-yaw´*; from the same as 6068 and 3050; *answers of Jah; Anthothijah*, an Isr.:— Antothijah.

6071. עָסִיס **'âçîyç**, *aw-sees´*; from 6072; *must* or fresh grape-juice (as just *trodden* out):— juice, new (sweet) wine.

6072. עָסַס **'âçaç**, *aw-sas´*; a prim. root; to *squeeze* out juice; fig. to *trample*:— tread down.

6073. עֲפֶא **'ôphe'**, *of-eh´*; from an unused root mean. to *cover*; a *bough* (as covering the tree):— branch.

6074. עֳפִי **'ôphîy** (Chald.), *of-ee´*; corresp. to 6073; a *twig*; bough, i.e. (collect.) *foliage*:— leaves.

6075. עָפַל **'âphal**, *aw-fal´*; a prim. root; to *swell*; fig. *be elated*:— be lifted up, presume.

6076. עֹפֶל **'ôphel**, *o´-fel*; from 6075; a *tumor*; also a *mound*, i.e. *fortress*:— emerod, fort, strong hold, tower.

6077. עֹפֶל **'Ôphel**, *o´-fel*; the same as 6076; *Ophel*, a ridge in Jerusalem:— Ophel.

6078. עָפְנִי **'Ophnîy**, *of-nee´*; from an unused noun [denoting a place in Pal.; from an unused root of uncert. mean.]; an *Ophnite* (collect.) or inhab. of Ophen:— Ophni.

6079. עַפְעַף **'aph'aph**, *af-af´*; from 5774; an *eyelash* (as *fluttering*); fig. morning *ray*:— dawning, eye-lid.

6080. עָפַר **'âphar**, *aw-far´*; a prim. root: mean. either to *be gray* or perh. rather to *pulverize*; used only as denom. from 6083; to *be dust*:— cast [dust].

6081. עֵפֶר **'Êpher**, *ay´-fer*; prob. a var. of 6082; *gazelle; Epher*, the name of an Arabian and of two Isr.:— Epher.

6082. עֹפֶר **'ôpher**, *o´-fer*; from 6080; a *fawn* (from the *dusty* color):— young roe [hart].

6083. עָפָר **'âphâr**, *aw-fawr´*; from 6080; *dust* (as *powdered* or *gray*); hence, *clay, earth, mud*:— ashes, dust, earth, ground, morter, powder, rubbish.

עָפְרָה **'Aphrâh**. See 1036.

6084. עָפְרָה **'Ophrâh**, *of-raw´*; fem. of 6082; *female fawn; Ophrah*, the name of an Isr. and of two places in Pal.:— Ophrah.

6085. עֶפְרוֹן **'Ephrôwn**, *ef-rone´*; from the same as 6081; *fawn-like; Ephron*, the name of a Canaanite and of two places in Pal.:— Ephron, Ephrain [from the marg.].

עָפְרָה **'ôphereth**. See 5777.

6086. עֵץ **'êts**, *ates*; from 6095; a *tree* (from its *firmness*); hence, *wood* (plur. *sticks*):— + carpenter, gallows, helve, + pine, plank, staff, stalk, stick, stock, timber, tree, wood.

6087. עָצַב **'âtsab**, *aw-tsab´*; a prim. root; prop. to *carve*, i.e. *fabricate* or *fashion*; hence, (in a bad sense) to *worry, pain* or *anger*:— displease, grieve, hurt, make, be sorry, vex, worship, wrest.

6088. עֲצַב **'ătsab** (Chald.), *ats-ab´*; corresp. to 6087; to *afflict*:— lamentable.

6089. עֶצֶב **'etseb**, *eh´-tseb*; from 6087; an earthen *vessel*; usually (painful) *toil*; also a *pang* (whether of body or mind):— grievous, idol, labor, sorrow.

6090. עֹצֶב **'ôtseb**, *o´-tseb*; a var. of 6089; an *idol* (as fashioned); also *pain* (bodily or mental):— idol, sorrow, × wicked.

6091. עָצָב **'âtsâb**, *aw-tsawb´*; from 6087; an (idolatrous) *image*:— idol, image.

6092. עָצֵב **'âtsêb**, *aw-tsabe´*; from 6087; a (hired) *workman*:— labour.

6093. עִצָּבוֹן **'itstsâbôwn**, *its-tsaw-bone´*; from 6087; *worrisomeness*, i.e. *labor* or *pain*:— sorrow, toil.

6094. עַצֶּבֶת **'atstsebeth**, *ats-tseh´-beth*; from 6087; an *idol*; also a *pain* or *wound*:— sorrow, wound.

6095. עָצָה **'âtsâh**, *aw-tsaw´*; a prim. root; prop. to *fasten* (or make firm), i.e. to *close* (the eyes):— shut.

6096. עָצֶה **'âtseh**, *aw-tseh´*; from 6095; the *spine* (as giving *firmness* to the body):— backbone.

6097. עֵצָה **'êtsâh**, *ay-tsaw´*; fem. of 6086; *timber*:— trees.

6098. עֵצָה **'êtsâh**, *ay-tsaw´*; from 3289; *advice*; by impl. *plan*; also *prudence*:— advice, advisement, counsel ([-lor]), purpose.

6099. עָצוּם **'âtsûwm**, *aw-tsoom´*; or

עָצֻם **'âtsûm**, *aw-tsoom´*; pass. part. of 6105; *powerful* (spec. a *paw*); by impl. *numerous*:— + feeble, great, mighty, must, strong.

6100. עֶצְיוֹן גֶּבֶר **'Etsyôwn** (short.

עֶצְיֹן **'Etsyôn) Geber**, *ets-yone´ gheh´ber*; from 6096 and 1397; *backbone-like of a man; Etsjon-Geber*, a place on the Red Sea:— Ezion-gaber, Ezion-geber.

6101. עָצַל **'âtsal**, *aw-tsal´*; a prim. root; to *lean* idly, i.e. to *be indolent* or *slack*:— be slothful.

6102. עָצֵל **'âtsêl**, *aw-tsale´*; from 6101; *indolent*:— slothful, sluggard.

6103. עַצְלָה **'atslâh**, *ats-law´*; fem. of 6102; (as abstr.) *indolence*:— slothfulness.

6104. עַצְלוּת **'atslûwth**, *ats-looth´*; from 6101; *indolence*:— idleness.

6105. עָצַם **'âtsam**, *aw-tsam´*; a prim. root; to *bind* fast, i.e. *close* (the eyes); intr. to *be* (caus. *make*) *powerful* or *numerous*; denom. (from 6106) to *crunch* the bones:— break the bones, close, be great, be increased, be (wax) mighty (-ier), be more, shut, be (-come, make) strong (-er).

6106. עֶצֶם **'etsem**, *eh´tsem*; from 6105; a *bone* (as *strong*); by extens. the *body*; fig. the *substance*, i.e. (as pron.) *self-same*:— body, bone, × life, (self-) same, strength, × very.

6107. עֶצֶם **'Etsem**, *eh´-tsem*; the same as 6106; *bone; Etsem*, a place in Pal.:— Azem, Ezem.

6108. עֹצֶם **'ôtsem**, *o´-tsem*; from 6105; *power*; hence, *body*:— might, strong, substance.

עָצֻם **'âtsûm**. See 6099.

6109. עָצְמָה **'otsmâh**, *ots-maw´*; fem. of

6108; *powerfulness*; by extens. *numerousness*:— abundance, strength.

6110. עַצֻמָה **'atstsûmâh**, *ats-tsoo-maw´*; fem. of 6099; a *bulwark*, i.e. (fig.) *argument*:— strong.

6111. עַצְמוֹן **'Atsmôwn**, *ats-mone´*; or

עַצְמֹן **'Atsmôn**, *ats-mone´*; from 6107; *bone-like; Atsmon*, a place near Pal.:— Azmon.

6112. עֶצֶן **'Êtsen**, *ay´-tsen*; from an unused root mean. to *be sharp* or *strong*; a *spear*:— Eznite [from the marg.].

6113. עָצַר **'âtsar**, *aw-tsar´*; a prim. root; to *inclose*; by anal. to *hold back*; also to *maintain, rule, assemble*:— × be able, close up, detain, fast, keep (self close, still), prevail, recover, refrain, × reign, restrain, retain, shut (up), slack, stay, stop, withhold (self).

6114. עֶצֶר **'etser**, *eh´-tser*; from 6113; *restraint*:— + magistrate.

6115. עֹצֶר **'ôtser**, *o´-tser*; from 6113; *closure*; also *constraint*:— × barren, oppression, × prison.

6116. עֲצָרָה **'ătsârâh**, *ats-aw-raw´*; or

עֲצֶרֶת **'ătsereth**, *ats-eh´-reth*; from 6113; an *assembly*, espec. on a *festival* or *holiday*:— (solemn) assembly (meeting).

6117. עָקַב **'âqab**, *aw-kab´*; a prim. root; prop. to *swell* out or up; used only as denom. from 6119, to *seize by the heel*; fig. to *circumvent* (as if *tripping* up the heels); also to *restrain* (as if holding by the heel):— take by the heel, stay, supplant, × utterly.

6118. עֵקֶב **'êqeb**, *ay´-keb*; from 6117 in the sense of 6119; a *heel*, i.e. (fig.) the *last* of anything (used adv. *for ever*); also *result*, i.e. *compensation*; and so (adv. with prep. or rel.) on *account* of:— × because, by, end, for, if, reward.

6119. עָקֵב **'âqêb**, *aw-kabe´*; or (fem.)

עִקְּבָה **'iqqᵉbâh**, *ik-keb-aw´*; from 6117; a *heel* (as *protuberant*); hence, a *track*; fig. the *rear* (of an army):— heel, [horse-] hoof, last, lier in wait [by mistake for 6120], (foot-) step.

6120. עָקֵב **'âqêb**, *aw-kabe´*; from 6117 in its denom. sense; a *lier in wait*:— heel [by mistake for 6119].

6121. עָקֹב **'âqôb**, *aw-kobe´*; from 6117; in the orig. sense, a *knoll* (as *swelling* up); in the denom. sense (tran.) *fraudulent* or (intr.) *tracked*:— crooked, deceitful, polluted.

6122. עָקְבָה **'oqbâh**, *ok-baw´*; fem. of an unused form from 6117 mean. a *trick; trickery*:— subtilty.

6123. עָקַד **'âqad**, *aw-kad´*; a prim. root; to *tie* with thongs:— bind.

עֶקֶד **'Êqed**. See 1044.

6124. עָקֹד **'âqôd**, *aw-kode´*; from 6123; *striped* (with *bands*):— ring straked.

6125. עָקָה **'âqâh**, *aw-kaw´*; from 5781; *constraint*:— oppression.

6126. עַקּוּב **'Aqqûwb**, *ak-koob´*; from 6117; *insidious; Akkub*, the name of five Isr.:— Akkub.

6127. עָקַל **'âqal**, *aw-kal´*; a prim. root; to *wrest*:— wrong.

6128. עֲקַלְקַל **'âqalqal**, ak-al-kal'; from 6127; *winding*:— by [-way], crooked way.

6129. עֲקַלָּתוֹן **'âqallâthôwn**, ak-al-law-thone'; from 6127; *tortuous*:— crooked.

6130. עָקָן **'Âqân**, aw-kawn'; from an unused root mean. to *twist*; *tortuous*; *Akan*, an Idumæan:— Akan. Comp. 3292.

6131. עָקַר **'âqar**, aw-kar'; a prim. root; to *pluck* up (espec. by the roots); spec. to *hamstring*; fig. to *exterminate*:— dig down, hough, pluck up, root up.

6132. עֲקַר **'äqar** (Chald.), ak-ar'; corresp. to 6131:— pluck up by the roots.

6133. עֵקֶר **'êqer**, ay'-ker; from 6131; fig. a *transplanted* person, i.e. naturalized citizen:— stock.

6134. עֵקֶר **'Êqer**, ay'-ker; the same as 6133; *Eker*, an Isr.:— Eker.

6135. עָקָר **'âqâr**, aw-kawr'; from 6131; *sterile* (as if *extirpated* in the generative organs):— (× male or female) barren (woman).

6136. עִקַּר **'iqqar** (Chald.), ik-kar'; from 6132; a *stock*:— stump.

6137. עַקְרָב **'aqrâb**, ak-rawb'; of uncert. der.; a *scorpion*; fig. a *scourge* or knotted whip:— scorpion.

6138. עֶקְרוֹן **'Eqrôwn**, ek-rone'; from 6131; *eradication*; *Ekron*, a place in Pal.:— Ekron.

6139. עֶקְרוֹנִי **'Eqrôwnîy**, ek-ro-nee'; or

עֶקְרֹנִי **'Eqrônîy**, ek-ro-nee'; patrial from 6138; an *Ekronite* or inhab. of Ekron:— Ekronite.

6140. עָקַשׁ **'âqash**, aw-kash'; a prim. root; to *knot* or *distort*; fig. to *pervert* (act or declare perverse):— make crooked, (prove, that is) perverse (-rt).

6141. עִקֵּשׁ **'iqqêsh**, ik-kashe'; from 6140; *distorted*; hence, *false*:— crooked, froward, perverse.

6142. עִקֵּשׁ **'Iqqêsh**, ik-kashe'; the same as 6141; *perverse*; *Ikkesh*, an Isr.:— Ikkesh.

6143. עִקְּשׁוּת **'iqq°shûwth**, ik-kesh-ooth'; from 6141; *perversity*:— × froward.

עָר **'âr**. See 5892.

6144. עָר **'Âr**, awr; the same as 5892; a *city*; *Ar*, a place in Moab:— Ar.

6145. עָר **'âr**, awr; from 5782; a *foe* (as *watchful* for mischief):— enemy.

6146. עָר **'âr** (Chald.), awr; corresp. to 6145:— enemy.

6147. עֵר **'Êr**, ayr; from 5782; *watchful*; *Er*, the name of two Isr.:— Er.

6148. עָרַב **'ârab**, aw-rab'; a prim. root; to *braid*, i.e. *intermix*; tech. to *traffic* (as if by barter); also to *give* or *be security* (as a kind of exchange):— engage, (inter-) meddle (with), mingle (self), mortgage, occupy, give pledges, be (-come, put in) surety, undertake.

6149. עָרֵב **'ârêb**, aw-rabe' a prim. root [rather ident. with 6148 through the idea of close *association*]; to *be agreeable*:— be pleasant (-ing), take pleasure in, be sweet.

6150. עָרַב **'ârab**, aw-rab'; a prim. root [rather ident. with 6148 through the idea of *covering* with a texture]; to *grow dusky* at sundown:— be darkened, (toward) evening.

6151. עֲרַב **'ärab** (Chald.), ar-ab'; corresp. to 6148; to *commingle*:— mingle (self), mix.

6152. עֲרָב **'Ärâb**, ar-awb' or

עֲרָב **'Ärâb**, ar-ab'; from 6150 in the fig. sense of *sterility*; *Arab* (i.e. *Arabia*), a country E. of Pal.:— Arabia.

6153. עֶרֶב **'ereb**, eh'-reb; from 6150; *dusk*:— + day, even (-ing, tide), night.

6154. עֵרֶב **'êreb**, ay'-reb; or

עֵרֶב **'ereb** (1 Kings 10:15), (with the art. pref.), eh'-reb; from 6148; the *web* (or transverse threads of cloth); also a *mixture*, (or mongrel race):— Arabia, mingled people, mixed (multitude), woof.

6155. עָרָב **'ârâb**, aw-rawb'; from 6148; a *willow* (from the use of osiers as wattles):— willow.

6156. עָרֵב **'ârêb**, aw-rabe'; from 6149; *pleasant*:— sweet.

6157. עָרֹב **'ârôb**, aw-robe'; from 6148; a *mosquito* (from its *swarming*):— divers sorts of flies, swarm.

6158. עֹרֵב **'ôrêb**, o-rabe'; or

עוֹרֵב **'ôwrêb**, o-rabe'; from 6150; a *raven* (from its *dusky* hue):— raven.

6159. עֹרֵב **'Ôrêb**, o-rabe'; or

עוֹרֵב **'Ôwrêb**, o-rabe'; the same as 6158; *Oreb*, the name of a Midianite and of a cliff near the Jordan:— Oreb.

6160. עֲרָבָה **'ärâbâh**, ar-aw-baw'; from 6150 (in the sense of *sterility*); a *desert*; espec. (with the art. pref.) the (gen.) sterile valley of the Jordan and its continuation to the Red Sea:— Arabah, champaign, desert, evening, heaven, plain, wilderness. See also 1026.

6161. עֲרֻבָּה **'ärubbâh**, ar-oob-baw'; fem. pass. part. of 6148 in the sense of a *bargain* or *exchange*; something given as *security*, i.e. (lit.) a *token* (of safety) or (metaph.) a *bondsman*:— pledge, surety.

6162. עֲרָבוֹן **'ärâbôwn**, ar-aw-bone'; from 6148 (in the sense of *exchange*); a *pawn* (given as security):— pledge.

6163. עֲרָבִי **'Ärâbîy**, ar-aw-bee'; or

עַרְבִי **'Arbîy**, ar-bee'; patrial from 6152; an *Arabian* or inhab. of Arab (i.e. Arabia):— Arabian.

6164. עַרְבָתִי **'Arbâthîy**, ar-baw-thee'; patrial from 1026; an *Arbathite* or inhab. of (Beth-) Arabah:— Arbahite.

6165. עָרַג **'ârag**, aw-rag'; a prim. root; to *long* for:— cry, pant.

6166. עֲרָד **'Ärâd**, aw-awd'; from an unused root mean. to *sequester* itself; *fugitive*; *Arad*, the name of a place near Pal., also of a Canaanite and an Isr.:— Arad.

6167. עֲרָד **'äräd** (Chald.), ar-awd'; corresp. to 6171; an *onager*:— wild ass.

6168. עָרָה **'ârâh**, aw-raw'; a prim. root; to *be* (caus. *make*) *bare*; hence, to *empty*, *pour* out, *demolish*:— leave destitute, discover, empty, make naked, pour (out), rase, spread self, uncover.

6169. עָרָה **'ârâh**, aw-raw'; fem. from 6168; a *naked* (i.e. level) plot:— paper reed.

6170. עֲרוּגָה **'ärûwgâh**, ar-oo-gaw'; or

עֲרֻגָה **'ärûgâh**, ar-oo-gaw'; fem. pass. part. of 6165; something *piled* up (as if [fig.] *raised* by mental aspiration), i.e. a *parterre*:— bed, furrow.

6171. עָרוֹד **'ârôwd**, aw-rode'; from the same as 6166; an *onager* (from his *lonesome* habits):— wild ass.

6172. עֶרְוָה **'ervâh**, er-vaw'; from 6168; *nudity*, lit. (espec. the *pudenda*) or fig. (*disgrace, blemish*):— nakedness, shame, unclean (-ness).

6173. עַרְוָה **'arvâh** (Chald.), ar-vaw'; corresp. to 6172; *nakedness*, i.e. (fig.) *impoverishment*:— dishonour.

6174. עָרוֹם **'ârôwm**, aw-rome'; or

עָרֹם **'ârôm**, aw-rome'; from 6191 (in its orig. sense); *nude*, either partially or totally:— naked.

6175. עָרוּם **'ârûwm**, aw-room'; pass. part. of 6191; *cunning* (usually in a bad sense):— crafty, prudent, subtil.

6176. עֲרוֹעֵר **'ärôw'êr**, ar-o-ayr'; or

עַרְעָר **'ar'âr**, ar-awr'; from 6209 redupl.; a *juniper* (from its *nudity* of situation):— heath.

6177. עֲרוֹעֵר **'Ärôw'êr**, ar-o-ayr'; or

עַרְעֵר **'Arô'êr**, ar-o-ayr'; or

עַרְעוֹר **'Ar'ôwr**, ar-ore'; the same as 6176; *nudity* of situation; *Aroër*, the name of three places in or near Pal.:— Aroer.

6178. עָרוּץ **'ârûwts**, aw-roots'; pass. part. of 6206; *feared*, i.e. (concr.) a *horrible* place or *chasm*:— cliffs.

6179. עֵרִי **'Êrîy**, ay-ree'; from 5782; *watchful*; *Eri*, an Isr.:— Eri.

6180. עֵרִי **'Êrîy**, ay-ree'; patron. of 6179; a *Erite* (collect.) or desc. of Eri:— Erites.

6181. עֶרְיָה **'eryâh**, er-yaw'; for 6172; *nudity*:— bare, naked, × quite.

6182. עֲרִיסָה **'ärîçâh**, ar-ee-saw'; from an unused root mean. to *comminute*; *meal*:— dough.

6183. עָרִיף **'ârîph**, aw-reef'; from 6201; the *sky* (as *drooping* at the horizon):— heaven.

6184. עָרִיץ **'ârîts**, aw-reets'; from 6206; *fearful*, i.e. *powerful* or *tyrannical*:— mighty, oppressor, in great power, strong, terrible, violent.

6185. עֲרִירִי **'ärîyrîy**, ar-e-ree'; from 6209; *bare*, i.e. destitute (of children):— childless.

6186. עָרַךְ **'ârak**, aw-rak'; a prim. root; to set in a *row*, i.e. *arrange*, put in *order* (in a very wide variety of applications):— put (set) (the battle, self) in array, compare, direct, equal, esteem, estimate, expert [in war], furnish, handle, join [battle], ordain, (lay, put, reckon up, set) (in) order, prepare, tax, value.

6187. עֵרֶךְ **'êrek**, eh'rek; from 6186; a *pile, equipment, estimate*:— equal, estimation, (things that are set in) order, price, proportion, × set at, suit, taxation, × valuest.

Hebrew

6188. עָרֵל **'ârêl**, *aw-rale´*; a prim. root; prop. to *strip;* but used only as denom. from 6189; to *expose* or *remove* the *preputre,* whether lit. (to *go naked*) or fig. (to *refrain* from using):— count uncircumcised, foreskin to be uncovered.

6189. עָרֵל **'ârêl**, *aw-rale´*; from 6188; prop. *exposed,* i.e. projecting loose (as to the prepuce); used only tech. *uncircumcised* (i.e. still having the prepuce uncurtailed):— uncircumcised (person).

6190. עָרְלָה **'orlâh**, *or-law´*; fem. of 6189; the *prepuce:*— foreskin, + uncircumcised.

6191. עָרַם **'âram**, *aw-ram´*; a prim. root; prop. to *be* (or *make*) *bare;* but used only in the der. sense (through the idea perh. of *smoothness*) to be *cunning* (usually in a bad sense):— × very, beware, take crafty [counsel], be prudent, deal subtilly.

6192. עָרַם **'âram**, *aw-ram´* a prim. root; to *pile* up:— gather together.

6193. עֹרֶם **'ôrem**, *o´-rem;* from 6191; a *stratagem:*— craftiness.

    עָרֹם **'Êrôm**. See 5903.

    עָרֹם **'ârôm**. See 6174.

6194. עָרֵם **'ârêm** (Jer. 50:26), *aw-rame´;* or (fem.)

    עֲרֵמָה **'ârêmâh**, *ar-ay-maw´;* from 6192; a *heap;* spec. a *sheaf:*— heap (of corn), sheaf.

6195. עָרְמָה **'ormâh**, *or-maw´;* fem. of 6193; *trickery;* or (in a good sense) *discretion:*— guile, prudence, subtilty, wilily, wisdom.

    עֲרֵמָה **'ârêmâh**. See 6194.

6196. עַרְמוֹן **'armôwn**, *ar-mone´;* prob. from 6191; the *plane* tree (from its *smooth* and shed bark):— chestnut tree.

6197. עֵרָן **'Êrân**, *ay-rawn´;* prob. from 5782; *watchful; Eran,* an Isr.:— Eran.

6198. עֵרָנִי **'Êrâniy**, *ay-raw-nee´;* patron. from 6197; an *Eranite* or desc. (collect.) of Eran:— Eranites.

    עֲרֹעוֹר **'Ar'ôwr**. See 6177.

6199. עַרְעָר **'ar'âr**, *ar-awr´;* from 6209; *naked,* i.e. (fig.) *poor:*— destitute. See also 6176.

    עֲרֹעֵר **'Arô'êr**. See 6177.

6200. עֲרֹעֵרִי **'Arô'êriy**, *ar-o-ay-ree´;* patron. from 6177; an *Aroërite* or inhab. of Aroër:— Aroerite.

6201. עָרַף **'âraph**, *aw-raf´;* a prim. root; to *droop;* hence, to *drip:*— drop (down).

6202. עָרַף **'âraph**, *aw-raf´;* a prim. root [rather ident. with 6201 through the idea of *sloping*], prop. to *bend* downward; but used only as a denom. from 6203, to *break the neck;* hence, (fig.) to *destroy:*— that is beheaded, break down, break (cut off, strike off) neck.

6203. עֹרֶף **'ôreph**, *o-ref´;* from 6202; the *nape* or back of the neck (as *declining*); hence, the *back* generally (whether lit. or fig.):— back [stiff-] neck ([-ed).

6204. עָרְפָּה **'Orpâh**, *or-paw´;* fem. of 6203; *mane; Orpah,* a Moabitess:— Orpah.

6205. עֲרָפֶל **'âráphel**, *ar-aw-fel´;* prob. from 6201; *gloom* (as of a *lowering* sky):— (gross, thick) dark (cloud, -ness).

6206. עָרַץ **'ârats**, *aw-rats´;* a prim. root; to *awe* or (intr.) to *dread;* hence, to *harass:*— be affrighted (afraid, dread, feared, terrified), break, dread, fear, oppress, prevail, shake terribly.

6207. עָרַק **'âraq**, *aw-rak´;* a prim. root; to *gnaw,* i.e. (fig.) *eat* (by hyperbole); also (part.) a *pain:*— fleeing, sinew.

6208. עַרְקִי **'Arqiy**, *ar-kee´;* patrial from an unused name mean. a *tush;* an *Arkite* or inhab. of Erek:— Arkite.

6209. עָרַר **'ârar**, *aw-rar´;* a prim. root; to *bare;* fig. to *demolish:*— make bare, break, raise up [perh. *by clerical err.* for **razel**, × utterly.

6210. עֶרֶשׂ **'eres**, *eh´res;* from an unused root mean. perh. to *arch;* a *couch* (prop. with a *canopy*):— bed (-stead), couch.

6211. עָשׁ **'âsh**, *awsh;* from 6244; a *moth:*— moth. See also 5906.

6211'. עֲשַׂב **'ăsab** (Chald.), *as-ab´;* 6212:— grass.

6212. עֵשֶׂב **'eseb**, *eh´seb;* from an unused root mean. to *glisten* (or *be green*); *grass* (or any *tender shoot*):— grass, herb.

6213. עָשָׂה **'âsâh**, *aw-saw´;* a prim. root; to *do* or *make,* in the broadest sense and widest application (as follows):— accomplish, advance, appoint, apt, be at, become, bear, bestow, bring forth, bruise, be busy, × certainly, have the charge of, commit, deal (with), deck, + displease, do, (ready) dress (-ed), (put in) execute (-ion), exercise, fashion, + feast, [fight-]ling man, + finish, fit, fly, follow, fulfil, furnish, gather, get, go about, govern, grant, great, + hinder, hold ([a feast]), × indeed, + be industrious, + journey, keep, labour, maintain, make, be meet, observe, be occupied, offer, + officer, pare, bring (come) to pass, perform, practise, prepare, procure, provide, put, requite, × sacrifice, serve, set, shew, × sin, spend, × surely, take, × throughly, trim, × very, + vex, be [warr-] ior, work (-man), yield, use.

6214. עֲשָׂהאֵל **'Äsâh'êl**, *as-aw-ale´;* from 6213 and 410; *God has made; Asahel,* the name of four Isr.:— Asahel.

6215. עֵשָׂו **'Êsâv**, *ay-sawv´;* appar. a form of the pass. part. of 6213 in the orig. sense of *handling; rough* (i.e. sensibly *felt*); *Esau,* a son of Isaac, incl. his posterity:— Esau.

6216. עָשׁוֹק **'âshôwq**, *aw-shoke´;* from 6231; *oppressive* (as noun, a *tyrant*):— oppressor.

6217. עָשׁוּק **'âshûwq**, *aw-shook´;* or

    עָשֻׁק **'âshûq**, *aw-shook´;* pass. part. of 6231; used in plur. masc. as abstr. *tyranny:*— oppressed (-ion). [Doubtful.]

6218. עָשׂוֹר **'âsôwr**, *aw-sore´;* or

    עָשֹׂר **'âsôr**, *aw-sore´;* from 6235; *ten;* by abbrev. ten *strings,* and so a *decachord:*— (instrument of) ten (strings, -th).

6219. עָשׁוֹת **'âshôwth**, *aw-shôth´;* from 6245; *shining,* i.e. *polished:*— bright.

6220. עָשְׁוָת **'Ashvâth**, *ash-vawth´;* for 6219; *bright; Ashvath,* an Isr.:— Ashvath.

6221. עֲשִׂיאֵל **'Äsiy'êl**, *as-ee-ale´;* from 6213 and 410; *made of God; Asiël,* an Isr.:— Asiel.

6222. עֲשָׂיָה **'Äsâyâh**, *aw-saw-yaw´;* from 6213 and 3050; *Jah has made; Asajah,* the name of three or four Isr.:— Asaiah.

6223. עָשִׁיר **'âshîyr**, *aw-sheer´;* from 6238; *rich,* whether lit. or fig. (*noble*):— rich (man).

6224. עֲשִׂירִי **'ăsîyriy**, *as-ee-ree´;* from 6235; *tenth;* by abb. *tenth month* or (fem.) *part:*— tenth (part).

6225. עָשַׁן **'âshan**, *aw-shan´;* a prim. root; to *smoke,* whether lit. or fig.:— be angry, (be on a) smoke.

6226. עָשֵׁן **'âshên**, *aw-shane´;* from 6225; *smoky:*— smoking.

6227. עָשָׁן **'âshân**, *aw-shawn´;* from 6225; *smoke,* lit. or fig. (*vapor, dust, anger*):— smoke (-ing).

6228. עָשָׁן **'Âshân**, *aw-shawn´;* the same as 6227; *Ashan,* a place in Pal.:— Ashan.

6229. עָשַׂק **'âsaq**, *aw-sak´;* a prim. root (ident. with 6231); to *press upon,* i.e. *quarrel:*— strive with.

6230. עֵשֶׂק **'Êseq**, *ay´sek;* from 6229; *strife:*— Esek.

6231. עָשַׁק **'âshaq**, *aw-shak´;* a prim. root (comp. 6229); to *press upon,* i.e. *oppress, defraud, violate, overflow:*— get deceitfully, deceive, defraud, drink up, (use) oppress ([-ion], -or), do violence (wrong).

6232. עֵשֶׁק **'Êsheq**, *ay-shek´;* from 6231; *oppression; Eshek,* an Isr.:— Eshek.

6233. עֹשֶׁק **'ôsheq**, *o´-shek;* from 6231; *injury, fraud,* (subj.) *distress,* (concr.) *unjust gain:*— cruelly, extortion, oppression, thing [deceitfully gotten].

    עָשֻׁק **'âshûq**. See 6217.

6234. עָשְׁקָה **'oshqâh**, *osh-kaw´;* fem. of 6233; *anguish:*— oppressed.

6235. עֶשֶׂר **'eser**, *eh´ser;* masc.

    עֲשָׂרָה **'ăsârâh**, *as-aw-raw´;* from 6237; *ten* (as an *accumulation* to the extent of the digits):— ten, [fif-, seven-] teen.

6236. עֲשַׂר **'ăsar** (Chald.), *as-ar´;* masc.

    עֶשְׂרָה **'ăsrâh** (Chald.), *as-raw´;* corresp. to 6235; *ten:*— ten, + twelve.

6237. עָשַׂר **'âsar**, *aw-sar´;* a prim. root (ident. with 6238); to *accumulate;* but used only as denom. from 6235; to *tithe,* i.e. *take* or *give a tenth:*— × surely, give (take) the tenth, (have, take) tithe (-ing, -s), × truly.

6238. עָשַׁר **'âshar**, *aw-shar´;* a prim. root; prop. to *accumulate;* chiefly (spec.) to *grow* (caus. *make*) *rich:*— be (-come, en-, make, make self, wax) rich, make [1 Kings 22:48 *marg.*]. See 6240.

6239. עֹשֶׁר **'ôsher**, *o´-sher;* from 6238; *wealth:*— × far [richer], riches.

6240. עָשָׂר **'âsâr**, aw-sawr'; for 6235; *ten* (only in combination), i.e. *teen;* also (ord.) *-teenth:*— [eigh-, fif-, four-, nine-, seven-, six-, thir-lteen (-th), + eleven (-th), + sixscore thousand, + twelve (-th).

עָשֹׂר **'âsôr.** See 6218.

6241. עִשָּׂרוֹן **'issârôwn**, is-saw-rone'; or

עִשָּׂרֹן **'issârôn**, is-saw-rone'; from 6235; (fractional) a *tenth* part:— tenth deal.

6242. עֶשְׂרִים **'esrîym**, es-reem'; from 6235; *twenty;* also (ord.) *twentieth:*— [six-] score, twenty (-ieth).

6243. עֶשְׂרִין **'esrîyn** (Chald.), es-reen'; corresp. to 6242:— twenty.

6244. עָשֵׁשׁ **'âshêsh**, aw-shaysh'; a prim. root; prob. to *shrink*, i.e. *fail:*— be consumed.

6245. עָשַׁת **'âshath**, aw-shath'; a prim. root; prob. to *be sleek*, i.e. *glossy;* hence, (through the idea of *polishing*) to *excogitate* (as if *forming* in the mind):— shine, think.

6246. עֲשִׁת **'ăshith** (Chald.), ash-eeth'; corresp. to 6245; to *purpose:*— think.

6247. עֶשֶׁת **'esheth**, eh'-sheth; from 6245; a *fabric:*— bright.

6248. עַשְׁתוּת° **'ashtûwth**, ash-tooth'; from 6245; *cogitation:*— thought.

6249. עַשְׁתֵּי **'ashtêy**, ash-tay'; appar. masc. plur. constr. of 6247 in the sense of an *afterthought* (used only in connection with 6240 in lieu of 259) *eleven* or (ord.) *eleventh:*— + eleven (-th).

6250. עֶשְׁתֹּנָה **'eshtônâh**, esh-to-naw'; from 6245; *thinking:*— thought.

6251. עַשְׁתְּרָה **'asht°râh**, ash-ter-aw'; prob. from 6238; *increase:*— flock.

6252. עַשְׁתָּרוֹת **'Ashtârôwth**, ash-taw-rôth'; or

עַשְׁתָּרֹת **'Ashtârôth**, ash-taw-rôth'; plur. of 6251; *Ashtaroth*, the name of a Sidonian deity, and of a place E. of the Jordan:— Ashtaroth, Astaroth. See also 1045, 6253, 6255.

6253. עַשְׁתֹּרֶת **'Ashtôreth**, ash-to'reth; prob. for 6251; *Ashtoreth*, the Phœnician goddess of love (and *increase*):— Ashtoreth.

6254. עַשְׁתְּרָתִי **'Asht°râthîy**, ash-ter-aw-thee'; patrial from 6255; an *Ashterathite* or inhab. of Ashtaroth:— Ashterathite.

6255. עַשְׁתְּרֹת קַרְנַיִם **'Asht°rôth Qarnayim**, ash-ter-ôth' kar-nah'-yim; from 6252 and the dual of 7161; *Ashtaroth* of (the) *double horns* (a symbol of the deity), *Ashteroth-Karnaïm*, a place E. of the Jordan:— Ashteroth Karnaim.

6256. עֵת **'êth**, ayth; from 5703; *time*, espec. (adv. with prep.) *now, when*, etc.:— + after, [al-]ways, × certain, + continually, + evening, long, (due) season, so [long] as, [even-, evening-, noon-] tide, ([meal-], what) time, when.

6257. עָתַד **'âthad**, aw-thad'; a prim. root; to *prepare:*— make fit, be ready to become.

עָתֻד **'attûd.** See 6260.

6258. עַתָּה **'attâh**, at-taw'; from 6256; at *this time*, whether adv., conjunc. or expletive:— henceforth, now, straightway, this time, whereas.

6259. עָתוּד **'âthûwd**, aw-thood'; pass. part. of 6257; *prepared:*— ready.

6260. עַתּוּד **'attûwd**, at-tood'; or

עַתֻּד **'attûd**, at-tood'; from 6257; *prepared*, i.e. *full grown;* spoken only (in plur.) of *he-goats*, or (fig.) *leaders* of the people:— chief one, (he) goat, ram.

6261. עִתִּי **'ittîy**, it-tee'; from 6256; *timely:*— fit.

6262. עַתַּי **'Attay**, at-tah'ee; for 6261; *Attai*, the name of three Isr.:— Attai.

6263. עֲתִיד **'ăthîyd** (Chald.), ath-eed'; corresp. to 6264; *prepared:*— ready.

6264. עָתִיד **'âthîyd**, aw-theed'; from 6257; *prepared;* by impl. *skilful;* fem. plur. the *future;* also *treasure:*— things that shall come, ready, treasures.

6265. עֲתָיָה **'Athâyâh**, ath-aw-yaw'; from 5790 and 3050; *Jah has helped; Athajah*, an Isr.:— Athaiah.

6266. עָתִיק **'âthîyq**, aw-theek'; from 6275; prop. *antique*, i.e. *venerable* or *splendid:*— durable.

6267. עַתִּיק **'attîyq**, at-teek'; from 6275; *removed*, i.e. *weaned;* also *antique:*— ancient, drawn.

6268. עַתִּיק **'attîyq** (Chald.), at-teek'; corresp. to 6267; *venerable:*— ancient.

6269. עֲתָךְ **'Athâk**, ath-awk'; from an unused root mean. to *sojourn; lodging; Athak*, a place in Pal.:— Athach.

6270. עַתְלַי **'Athlay**, ath-lah'ee; from an unused root mean. to *compress; constringent; Athlai*, an Isr.:— Athlai.

6271. עֲתַלְיָה **'Athalyâh**, ath-al-yaw'; or

עֲתַלְיָהוּ **'Athalyâhûw**, ath-al-yaw'-hoo; from the same as 6270 and 3050; *Jah has constrained; Athaliah*, the name of an Israelitess and two Isr.:— Athaliah.

6272. עָתַם **'âtham**, aw-tham'; a prim. root; prob. to *glow*, i.e. (fig.) *be desolated:*— be darkened.

6273. עָתְנִי **'Otnîy**, oth-nee'; from an unused root mean. to *force; forcible; Othni*, an Isr.:— Othni.

6274. עָתְנִיאֵל **'Othnîy'êl**, oth-nee-ale'; from the same as 6273 and 410; *force of God; Othnïël*, an Isr.:— Othniel.

6275. עָתַק **'âthaq**, aw-thak'; a prim. root; to *remove* (intr. or tran.) fig. to *grow old;* spec. to *transcribe:*— copy out, leave off, become (wax) old, remove.

6276. עָתֵק **'âthêq**, aw-thake'; from 6275; *antique*, i.e. *valued:*— durable.

6277. עָתָק **'âthâq**, aw-thawk'; from 6275 in the sense of *license; impudent:*— arrogancy, grievous (hard) things, stiff.

6278. עֵת קָצִין **'Êth Qâtsîyn**, ayth kaw-tseen'; from 6256 and 7011; *time of a judge; Eth-Katsin*, a place in Pal.:— Ittah-kazin [by incl. directive encliticl.

6279. עָתַר **'âthar**, aw-thar'; a prim. root [rather denom. from 6281]; to *burn incense* in worship, i.e. *intercede* (recip. *listen* to prayer):— intreat, (make) pray (-er).

6280. עָתַר **'âthar**, aw-thar'; a prim. root; to *be* (caus. *make*) *abundant:*— deceitful, multiply.

6281. עֶתֶר **'Ether**, eh'ther; from 6280; *abundance; Ether*, a place in Pal.:— Ether.

6282. עָתָר **'âthâr**, aw-thawr'; from 6280; *incense* (as increasing to a *volume* of smoke); hence, (from 6279) a *worshipper:*— suppliant, thick.

6283. עֲתֶרֶת **'ăthereth**, ath-eh'-reth; from 6280; *copiousness:*— abundance.

פ

פֹּא **pô'.** See 6311.

6284. פָּאָה **pâ'âh**, paw-aw'; a prim. root; to *puff*, i.e. *blow away:*— scatter into corners.

6285. פֵּאָה **pê'âh**, pay-aw'; fem. of 6311; prop. *mouth* in a fig. sense, i.e. *direction, region, extremity:*— corner, end, quarter, side.

6286. פָּאַר **pâ'ar**, paw-ar'; a prim. root; to *gleam*, i.e. (caus.) *embellish;* fig. to *boast;* also to *explain* (i.e. make clear) oneself; denom. from 6288, to *shake* a tree:— beautify, boast self, go over the boughs, glorify (self), glory, vaunt self.

6287. פְּאֵר **p°'êr**, peh-ayr'; from 6286; an *embellishment*, i.e. fancy *head-dress:*— beauty, bonnet, goodly, ornament, tire.

6288. פְּאֹרָה **p°'ôrâh**, peh-o-raw'; or

פֹּרָאה **pôrâ'h**, po-raw'; or

פֻּרָאה **pu'râh**, poo-raw'; from 6286; prop. *ornamentation*, i.e. (plur.) *foliage* (incl. the limbs) as *bright* green:— bough, branch, sprig.

6289. פָּארוּר **pâ'rûwr**, paw-roor'; from 6286; prop. *illuminated*, i.e. a *glow;* as noun, a *flush* (of anxiety):— blackness.

6290. פָּארָן **Pâ'rân**, paw-rawn'; from 6286; *ornamental; Paran*, a desert of Arabia:— Paran.

6291. פַּג **pag**, pag; from an unused root mean. to *be torpid*, i.e. *crude; an unripe* fig:— green fig.

6292. פִּגּוּל **piggûwl**, pig-gool'; or

פִּגֻּל **piggûl**, pig-gool'; from an unused root mean. to *stink;* prop. *fetid*, i.e. (fig.) *unclean* (ceremonially):— abominable (-tion, thing).

6293. פָּגַע **pâga'**, paw-gah'; a prim. root; to *impinge*, by accident or violence, or (fig.) by importunity:— come (betwixt), cause to entreat, fall (upon), make intercession, intercessor, intreat, lay, light [upon], meet (together), pray, reach, run.

6294. פֶּגַע **pega'**, peh'-gah; from 6293; *impact* (casual):— chance, occurrent.

6295. פַּגְעִיאֵל **Pag'îy'êl**, pag-ee-ale'; from 6294 and 410; *accident of God; Pagiël*, an Isr.:— Pagiel.

6296. פָּגַר **pâgar**, paw-gar'; a prim. root; to *relax*, i.e. *become exhausted:*— be faint.

6297. פֶּגֶר **peger**, peh'gher; from 6296; a *carcase* (as *limp*), whether of man or beast; fig. an idolatrous *image:*— carcase (carcass), corpse, dead body.

6298. פָּגַשׁ **pâgash**, paw-gash'; a prim.

root; to *come in contact with*, whether by accident or violence; fig. to *concur*:— meet (with, together).

6299. פָּדָה **pâdâh**, *paw-daw´*; a prim. root; to *sever*, i.e. ransom; gen. to *release, preserve*:— × at all, deliver, × by any means, ransom, (that are to be, let be) redeem (-ed), rescue, × surely.

6300. פְּדַהְאֵל **Pᵉdah´êl**, *ped-ah-ale´*; from 6299 and 410; *God has ransomed; Pedahel*, an Isr.:— Pedahel.

6301. פְּדָהצוּר **Pᵉdâhtsûwr**, *ped-aw-tsoor´*; from 6299 and 6697; a *rock* (i.e. God) *has ransomed; Pedahtsur*, an Isr.:— Pedahzur.

6302. פָּדוּי **pâdûwy**, *paw-doo´-ee*; pass. part. of 6299; *ransomed* (and so occurring under 6299); as abstr. (in plur. masc.) a *ransom*:— (that are) to be (that were) redeemed.

6303. פָּדוֹן **Pâdôwn**, *paw-done´*; from 6299; *ransom; Padon*, one of the Nethinim:— Padon.

6304. פְּדוּת **pᵉdûwth**, *ped-ooth´*; or

פְּדֻת **pᵉdûth**, *ped-ooth´*; from 6929; *distinction*; also *deliverance*:— division, redeem, redemption.

6305. פְּדָיָה **Pᵉdâyâh**, *ped-aw-yaw´*; or

פְּדָיָהוּ **Pᵉdâyâhûw**, *ped-aw-yaw´-hoo*; from 6299 and 3050; *Jah has ransomed; Pedajah*, the name of six Isr.:— Pedaiah.

6306. פִּדְיוֹם **pidyôwm**, *pid-yome´*; or

פִּדְיֹם **pidyôm**, *pid-yome´*; also

פִּדְיוֹן **pidyôwn**, *pid-yone´*; or

פִּדְיֹן **pidyôn**, *pid-yone´*; from 6299; a *ransom*:— ransom, that were redeemed, redemption.

6307. פַּדָּן **Paddân**, *pad-dawn´*; from an unused root mean. to *extend*; a *plateau*; or

פַּדַּן אֲרָם **Paddan 'Ărâm**, *pad-dan´ ar-awm´*; from the same and 758; the *table-land of Aram; Paddan* or *Paddan-Aram*, a region of Syria:— Padan, Padan-aram.

6308. פָּדַע **pâda'**, *paw-dah´*; a prim. root; to *retrieve*:— deliver.

6309. פֶּדֶר **peder**, *peh´der*; from an unused root mean. to *be greasy; suet*:— fat.

פְּדֻת **pᵉdûth**. See 6304.

6310. פֶּה **peh**, *peh*; from 6284; the *mouth* (as the means of *blowing*), whether lit. or fig. (particularly *speech*); spec. *edge, portion* or *side*; adv. (with prep.) *according to*:— accord (-ing as, -ing to), after, appointment, assent, collar, command (-ment), × eat, edge, end, entry, + file, hole, × in, mind, mouth, part, portion, × (should) say (-ing), sentence, skirt, sound, speech, × spoken, talk, tenor, × to, + two-edged, wish, word.

6311. פֹּה **pôh**, *po*; or

פֹּא **pô'** (Job 38:11), *po*; or

פּוֹ **pôw**, *po*; prob. from a prim. inseparable particle פּ **p** (of demonstr. force) and 1931; *this place* (French *ici*), i.e. *here* or *hence*:— here, hither, the one (other, this, that) side.

פּוֹא **pôw'**. See 375.

6312. פּוּאָה **Pûw'âh**, *poo-aw´* or

פֻּוָּה **Puvvâh**, *poov-vaw´*; from 6284; a *blast; Puâh* or *Puvvah*, the name of two Isr.:— Phuvah, Pua, Puah.

6313. פּוּג **pûwg**, *poog*; a prim. root; to *be sluggish*:— cease, be feeble, faint, be slacked.

6314. פּוּגָה **pûwgâh**, *poo-gaw´*; from 6313; *intermission*:— rest.

פֻּוָּה **Puvvâh**. See 6312.

6315. פּוּחַ **pûwach**, *poo´akh*; a prim. root; to *puff*, i.e. blow with the breath or air; hence, to *fan* (as a breeze), to *utter*, to *kindle* (a fire), to *scoff*:— blow (upon), break, puff, bring into a snare, speak, utter.

6316. פּוּט **Pûwṭ**, *poot*; of for. or.; *Put*, a son of Ham, also the name of his desc. or their region, and of a Pers. tribe:— Phut, Put.

6317. פּוּטִיאֵל **Pûwṭîy'êl**, *poo-tee-ale´*; from an unused root (prob. mean. to *disparage*) and 410; *contempt of God; Putiël*, an Isr.:— Putiel.

6318. פּוֹטִיפַר **Pôwṭîyphar**, *po-tee-far´*; of Eg. der.; *Potiphar*, an Eg.:— Potiphar.

6319. פּוֹטִי פֶרַע **Pôwṭîy Phera'**, *po-tee feh´-rah*; of Eg. der.; *Poti-Phera*, an Eg.:— Poti-pherah.

6320. פּוּךְ **pûwk**, *pook*; from an unused root mean. to *paint; dye* (spec. *stibium* for the eyes):— fair colours, glistering, paint [-ed] (-ing).

6321. פּוֹל **pôwl**, *pole*; from an unused root mean. to *be thick*; a *bean* (as *plump*):— beans.

6322. פּוּל **Pûwl**, *pool*; of for. or.; *Pul*, the name of an Ass. king and of an Ethiopian tribe:— Pul.

6323. פּוּן **pûwn**, *poon*; a prim. root mean. to *turn*, i.e. *be perplexed*:— be distracted.

6324. פּוּנִי **Pûwnîy**, *poo-nee´*; patron. from an unused name mean. a *turn*; a *Punite* (collect.) or desc. of an unknown *Pun*:— Punites.

6325. פּוּנֹן **Pûwnôn**, *poo-none´*; from 6323; *perplexity; Punon*, a place in the Desert:— Punon.

6326. פּוּעָה **Pûw'âh**, *poo-aw´*; from an unused root mean. to *glitter; brilliancy; Puäh*, an Israelitess:— Puah.

6327. פּוּץ **pûwts**, *poots*; a prim. root; to *dash* in pieces, lit. or fig. (espec. to *disperse*):— break (dash, shake) in (to) pieces, cast (abroad), disperse (selves), drive, retire, scatter (abroad), spread abroad.

6328. פּוּק **pûwq**, *pook*; a prim. root; to *waver*:— stumble, move.

6329. פּוּק **pûwq**, *pook*; a prim. root [rather ident. with 6328 through the idea of *dropping* out; comp. 5312]; to *issue*, i.e. *furnish*; caus. to *secure*; fig. to *succeed*:— afford, draw out, further, get, obtain.

6330. פּוּקָה **pûwqâh**, *poo-kaw´*; from 6328; a *stumbling-block*:— grief.

6331. פּוּר **pûwr**, *poor*; a prim. root; to *crush*:— break, bring to nought, × utterly take.

6332. פּוּר **Pûwr**, *poor*; also (plur.)

פּוּרִים **Pûwrîym**, *poo-reem´*; or

פֻּרִים **Pûrîym**, *poo-reem´*; from 6331; a *lot* (as by means of a *broken* piece):— Pur, Purim.

6333. פּוּרָה **pûwrâh**, *poo-raw´*; from 6331; a *wine-press* (as *crushing* the grapes):— winepress.

פּוּרִים **Pûwrîym**. See 6332.

6334. פּוֹרָתָא **Pôwrâthâ'**, *po-raw-thaw´*; of Pers. or.; *Poratha*, a son of Haman:— Poratha.

6335. פּוּשׁ **pûwsh**, *poosh*; a prim. root; to *spread*; fig. *act proudly*:— grow up, be grown fat, spread selves, be scattered.

6336. פּוּתִי **Pûwthîy**, *poo-thee´*; patron. from an unused name mean. a *hinge*; a *Puthite* (collect.) or desc. of an unknown *Puth*:— Puhites [as if from 6312].

6337. פָּז **pâz**, *pawz*; from 6338; *pure* (gold); hence, *gold* itself (as *refined*):— fine (pure) gold.

6338. פָּזַז **pâzaz**, *paw-zaz´*; a prim. root; to *refine* (gold):— best [gold].

6339. פָּזַז **pâzaz**, *paw-zaz´*; a prim. root [rather ident. with 6338]; to *solidify* (as if by *refining*); also to *spring* (as if *separating* the limbs):— leap, be made strong.

6340. פָּזַר **pâzar**, *paw-zar´*; a prim. root; to *scatter*, whether in enmity or bounty:— disperse, scatter (abroad).

6341. פַּח **pach**, *pakh*; from 6351; a (metallic) *sheet* (as *pounded* thin); also a spring *net* (as spread out like a *lamina*):— gin, (thin) plate, snare.

6342. פָּחַד **pâchad**, *paw-khad´*; a prim. root; to *be startled* (by a sudden alarm); hence, to *fear* in general:— be afraid, stand in awe, (be in) fear, make to shake.

6343. פַּחַד **pachad**, *pakh´-ad*; from 6342; a (sudden) *alarm* (prop. the object feared, by impl. the feeling):— dread (-ful), fear, (thing) great [fear, -ly feared], terror.

6344. פַּחַד **pachad**, *pakh´-ad*; the same as 6343; a *testicle* (as a cause of *shame* akin to fear):— stone.

6345. פַּחְדָּה **pachdâh**, *pakh-daw´*; fem. of 6343; *alarm* (i.e. *awe*):— fear.

6346. פֶּחָה **pechâh**, *peh-khaw´*; of for. or.; a *prefect* (of a city or small district):— captain, deputy, governor.

6347. פֶּחָה **pechâh** (Chald.), *peh-khaw´*; corresp. to 6346:— captain, governor.

6348. פָּחַז **pâchaz**, *paw-khaz´*; a prim. root; to *bubble* up or *froth* (as boiling water), i.e. (fig.) to *be unimportant*:— light.

6349. פַּחַז **pachaz**, *pakh´-az*; from 6348; *ebullition*, i.e. froth (fig. lust):— unstable.

6350. פַּחֲזוּת **pachăzûwth**, *pakh-az-ooth´*; from 6348; *frivolity*:— lightness.

6351. פָּחַח **pâchach**, *paw-khakh´*; a prim. root; to *batter* out; but used only as denom. from 6341, to *spread a net*:— be snared.

6352. פֶּחָם **pechâm**, *peh-khawm´*; perh.

from an unused root prob. mean. to *be black*; a *coal*, whether charred or live:— coals.

6353. פֶּחָר **pechâr** (Chald.), *peh-khawr´*; from an unused root prob. mean. to *fashion*; a *potter*:— potter.

6354. פַּחַת **pachath**, *pakh´-ath*; prob. from an unused root appar. mean. to *dig*; a *pit*, espec. for catching animals:— hole, pit, snare.

6355. פַּחַת מוֹאָב **Pachath Môw´âb**, *pakh´-ath mo-awb´*; from 6354 and 4124; *pit of Moâb*; *Pachath-Moâb*, an Isr.:— Pahath-moab.

6356. פְּחֶתֶת **pᵉchetheth**, *pekh-eh´-theth*; from the same as 6354; a *hole* (by mildew in a garment):— fret inward.

6357. פִּטְדָה **piṭdâh**, *pit-daw´*; of for. der.; a *gem*, prob. the *topaz*:— topaz.

6358. פָּטוּר **pâṭûwr**, *paw-toor´*; pass. part. of 6362; *opened*, i.e. (as noun) a *bud*:— open.

6359. פָּטִיר **pâṭîyr**, *paw-teer´*; from 6362; *open*, i.e. *unoccupied*:— free.

6360. פַּטִּישׁ **paṭṭîysh**, *pat-teesh´*; intens. from an unused root mean. to *pound*; a *hammer*:— hammer.

6361. פַּטִּישׁ **paṭṭîysh** (Chald.), *pat-teesh´*; from a root corresp. to that of 6360; a *gown* (as if *hammered* out wide):— hose.

6362. פָּטַר **pâṭar**, *paw-tar´*; a prim. root; to *cleave* or burst through, i.e. (caus.) to *emit*, whether lit. or fig. (*gape*):— dismiss, free, let (shoot) out, slip away.

6363. פֶּטֶר **peṭer**, *peh´-ter*; or

פִּטְרָה **piṭrâh**, *pit-raw´*; from 6362; a *fissure*, i.e. (concr.) *firstling* (as *opening* the matrix):— firstling, openeth, such as open.

6364. פִּי־בֶסֶת **Pîy-Beçeth**, *pee beh´-seth*; of Eg. or.; *Pi-Beseth*, a place in Egypt:— Pi-beseth.

6365. פִּיד **pîyd**, *peed*; from an unused root prob. mean. to *pierce*; (fig.) *misfortune*:— destruction, ruin.

6366. פֵּיָה **pêyâh**, *pay-aw´*; or

פִּיָּה **pîyâh**, *pee-yaw´*; fem. of 6310; an *edge*:— (two-) edge (-d).

6367. פִּי הַחִירֹת **Piy ha-Chîrôth**, *pee hah-khee-rôth´*; from 6310 and the fem. plur. of a noun (from the same root as 2356), with the art. interpolated; *mouth of the gorges*; *Pi-ha-Chiroth*, a place in Egypt:— Pi-hahiroth. [In Num. 14:19 without Pi-.]

6368. פִּיחַ **pîyach**, *pee´-akh*; from 6315; a *powder* (as easily *puffed* away), i.e. *ashes* or *dust*:— ashes.

6369. פִּיכֹל **Pîykôl**, *pee-kole´*; appar. from 6310 and 3605; *mouth of all*; *Picol*, a Philistine:— Phichol.

6370. פִּילֶגֶשׁ **pîylegesh**, *pee-leh´-ghesh*; or

פִּלֶגֶשׁ **pîlegesh**, *pee-leh´-ghesh*; of uncert. der.; a *concubine*; also (masc.) a *paramour*:— concubine, paramour.

6371. פִּימָה **pîymâh**, *pee-maw´*; prob. from an unused root mean. to *be plump*; *obesity*:— collops.

6372. פִּינְחָס **Pîynᵉchâç**, *pee-nekh-aws´*; appar. from 6310 and a var. of 5175; *mouth of a serpent*; *Pinechas*, the name of three Isr.:— Phinehas.

6373. פִּינֹן **Pîynôn**, *pee-none´*; prob. the same as 6325; *Pinon*, an Idumæan:— Pinon.

6374. פִּיפִיָּה **pîyphîyâh**, *pee-fee-yaw´*; for 6366; an *edge* or *tooth*:— tooth, × two-edged.

6375. פִּיק **pîyq**, *peek*; from 6329; a *tottering*:— smite together.

6376. פִּישׁוֹן **Pîyshôwn**, *pee-shone´*; from 6335; *dispersive*; *Pishon*, a river of Eden:— Pison.

6377. פִּיתוֹן **Pîythôwn**, *pee-thone´*; prob. from the same as 6596; *expansive*; *Pithon*, an Isr.:— Pithon.

6378. פַּךְ **pak**, *pak*; from 6379; a *flask* (from which a liquid may *flow*):— box, vial.

6379. פָּכָה **pâkâh**, *paw-kaw´*; a prim. root; to *pour*:— run out.

6380. פֹּכֶרֶת צְבָיִם **Pôkereth Tsᵉbâyîm**, *po-keh´-reth tseb-aw-yeem´*; from the act. part. (of the same form as the first word) fem. of an unused root (mean. to *entrap*) and plur. of 6643; *trap of gazelles*; *Pokereth-Tsebajim*, one of the "servants of Solomon":— Pochereth of Zebaim.

6381. פָּלָא **pâlâ´**, *paw-law´*; a prim. root; prop. perh. to *separate*, i.e. *distinguish* (lit. or fig.); by impl. to be (caus. *make*) *great, difficult, wonderful*:— accomplish, (arise ... too, be too) hard, hidden, things too high, (be, do, do a, shew) marvelous (-ly, -els, things, work), miracles, perform, separate, make singular, (be, great, make) wonderful (-ers, -ly, things, works), wondrous (things, works, -ly).

6382. פֶּלֶא **pele´**, *peh´-leh*; from 6381; a *miracle*:— marvellous thing, wonder (-ful, -fully).

6383. פִּלְאִי **pil´îy**, *pil-ee´*; or

פָּלִיא **pâlîy´**, *paw-lee´*; from 6381; *remarkable*:— secret, wonderful.

6384. פַּלֻּאִי **Pallu´îy**, *pal-loo-ee´*; patron. from 6396; a *Palluïte* (collect.) or desc. of Pallu:— Palluites.

פְּלָאיָה **Pᵉlâ´yâh**. See 6411.

פִּלְאֶצֶר **Pil´eçer**. See 8407.

6385. פָּלַג **pâlag**, *paw-lag´*; a prim. root; to *split* (lit. or fig.):— divide.

6386. פְּלַג **pᵉlag** (Chald.), *pel-ag´*; corresp. to 6385:— divided.

6387. פְּלַג **pᵉlag** (Chald.), *pel-ag´*; from 6386; a *half*:— dividing.

6388. פֶּלֶג **peleg**, *peh´-leg*; from 6385; a *rill* (i.e. small *channel* of water, as in irrigation):— river, stream.

6389. פֶּלֶג **Peleg**, *peh´-leg*; the same as 6388; *earthquake*; *Peleg*, a son of Shem:— Peleg.

6390. פְּלַגָּה **pᵉlaggâh**, *pel-ag-gaw´*; from 6385; a *runlet*, i.e. *gully*:— division, river.

6391. פְּלֻגָּה **pᵉluggâh**, *pel-oog-gaw´*; from 6385; a *section*:— division.

6392. פְּלֻגָּה **pᵉluggâh** (Chald.), *pel-oog-gaw´*; corresp. to 6391:— division.

פִּלֶגֶשׁ **pîlegesh**. See 6370.

6393. פְּלֵדָה **pᵉlâdâh**, *pel-aw-daw´*; from an unused root mean. to *divide*; a *cleaver*, i.e. iron *armature* (of a chariot):— torch.

6394. פִּלְדָּשׁ **Pildâsh**, *pil-dawsh´*; of uncert. der.; *Pildash*, a relative of Abraham:— Pildash.

6395. פָּלָה **pâlâh**, *paw-law´*; a prim. root; to *distinguish* (lit. or fig.):— put a difference, show marvellous, separate, set apart, sever, make wonderfully.

6396. פַּלּוּא **Pallûw´**, *pal-loo´*; from 6395; *distinguished*; *Pallu*, an Isr.:— Pallu, Phallu.

6397. פְּלוֹנִי **Pᵉlôwnîy**, *pel-o-nee´*; patron. from an unused name (from 6395) mean. *separate*; a *Pelonite* or inhab. of an unknown Palon:— Pelonite.

6398. פָּלַח **pâlach**, *paw-lakh´*; a prim. root; to *slice*, i.e. *break* open or *pierce*:— bring forth, cleave, cut, shred, strike through.

6399. פְּלַח **pᵉlach** (Chald.), *pel-akh´*; corresp. to 6398; to *serve* or worship:— minister, serve.

6400. פֶּלַח **pelach**, *peh´-lakh*; from 6398; a *slice*:— piece.

6401. פִּלְחָא **Pilchâ´**, *pil-khaw´*; from 6400; *slicing*; *Pilcha*, an Isr.:— Pilcha.

6402. פׇּלְחָן **polchân** (Chald.), *pol-khawn´*; from 6399; *worship*:— service.

6403. פָּלַט **pâlaṭ**, *paw-laṭ´*; a prim. root; to *slip* out, i.e. *escape*; caus. to *deliver*:— calve, carry away safe, deliver, (cause to) escape.

6404. פֶּלֶט **Peleṭ**, *peh´-leṭ*; from 6403; *escape*; *Pelet*, the name of two Isr.:— Pelet. See also 1046.

פָּלֵט **pâlêṭ**. See 6412.

6405. פַּלֵּט **palлêṭ**, *pal-late´*; from 6403; *escape*:— deliverance, escape.

פְּלֵטָה **pᵉlêṭâh**. See 6413.

6406. פַּלְטִי **Palṭîy**, *pal-tee´*; from 6403; *delivered*; *Palti*, the name of two Isr.:— Palti, Phalti.

6407. פַּלְטִי **Palṭîy**, *pal-tee´*; patron. from 6406; a *Paltite* or desc. of Palti:— Paltite.

6408. פִּלְטַי **Pilṭay**, *pil-tah´-ee*; for 6407; *Piltai*, an Isr.:— Piltai.

6409. פַּלְטִיאֵל **Palṭîy´êl**, *pal-tee-ale´*; from the same as 6404 and 410; *deliverance of God*; *Paltiël*, the name of two Isr.:— Paltiel, Phaltiel.

6410. פְּלַטְיָה **Pᵉlaṭyâh**, *pel-at-yaw´*; or

פְּלַטְיָהוּ **Pᵉlaṭyâhûw**, *pel-at-yaw´-hoo*; from 6403 and 3050; *Jah has delivered*; *Pelatjah*, the name of four Isr.:— Pelatiah.

פָּלִיא **pâlîy´**. See 6383.

6411. פְּלָיָה **Pᵉlâyâh**, *pel-aw-yaw´*; or

פְּלָאיָה **Pᵉlâ´yâh**, *pel-aw-yaw´*; from 6381 and 3050; *Jah has distinguished*; *Pelajah*, the name of three Isr.:— Pelaiah.

6412. פָּלִיט **pâlîyṭ**, *paw-leet´*; or

פָּלֵיט **pâlêyṭ**, *paw-late´*; or

פָּלֵט **pâlêṭ**, *paw-late´*; from 6403; a

6413. פְּלֵיטָה **pᵉlêyṭâh**, pel-ay-taw´; or

פְּלֵטָה **pᵉlêṭâh**, pel-ay-taw´; fem. of 6412; *deliverance;* concr. an *escaped* portion:— deliverance, (that is) escape (-d), remnant.

6414. פָּלִיל **pâlîyl**, paw-leel´; from 6419; a *magistrate:*— judge.

6415. פְּלִילָה **pᵉlîylâh**, pel-ee-law´; fem. of 6414; *justice:*— judgment.

6416. פְּלִילִי **pᵉlîylîy**, pel-ee-lee´; from 6414; *judicial:*— judge.

6417. פְּלִילִיָּה **pᵉlîylîyâh**, pel-ee-lee-yaw´; fem. of 6416; *judicature:*— judgment.

6418. פֶּלֶךְ **pelek**, peh´-lek; from an unused root mean. to *be round;* a *circuit* (i.e. *district*); also a *spindle* (as *whirled*); hence, a *crutch:*— (di-) staff, part.

6419. פָּלַל **pâlal**, paw-lal´; a prim. root; to *judge* (officially or mentally); by extens. to *intercede, pray:*— intreat, judge (-ment), (make) pray (-er, -ing), make supplication.

6420. פָּלָל **Pâlâl**, paw-lawl´; from 6419; *judge; Palal,* an Isr.:— Palal.

6421. פְּלַלְיָה **Pᵉlalyâh**, pel-al-yaw´; from 6419 and 3050; *Jah has judged; Pelaljah,* an Isr.:— Pelaliah.

6422. פַּלְמוֹנִי **palmôwnîy**, pal-mo-nee´; prob. for 6423; a *certain* one, i.e. *so-and-so:*— certain.

פַּלְנֶאֶצֶר **Pilnᵉʼeçer.** See 8407.

6423. פְּלֹנִי **pᵉlônîy**, pel-o-nee´; from 6395; *such* a one, i.e. a specified *person:*— such.

פַּלְנֶצֶר **Pilneçer.** See 8407.

6424. פָּלַס **pâlaç**, paw-las´; a prim. root; prop. to *roll* flat, i.e. *prepare* (a road); also to *revolve,* i.e. *weigh* (mentally):— make, ponder, weigh.

6425. פֶּלֶס **peleç**, peh´-les; from 6424; a *balance:*— scales, weight.

פַּלְצֶר **Pᵉleçer.** See 8407.

6426. פָּלַץ **pâlats**, paw-lats´; a prim. root; prop. perh. to *rend,* i.e. (by impl.) to *quiver:*— tremble.

6427. פַּלָּצוּת **pallâtsûwth**, pal-law-tsooth´; from 6426; *affright:*— fearfulness, horror, trembling.

6428. פָּלַשׁ **pâlash**, paw-lash´; a prim. root; to *roll* (in dust):— roll (wallow) self.

6429. פְּלֶשֶׁת **Pᵉlesheth**, pel-eh´-sheth; from 6428; *rolling,* i.e. *migratory; Pelesheth,* a region of Syria:— Palestina, Palestine, Philistia, Philistines.

6430. פְּלִשְׁתִּי **Pᵉlishtîy**, pel-ish-tee´; patrial from 6429; a *Pelishtite* or inhab. of Pelesheth:— Philistine.

6431. פֶּלֶת **Peleth**, peh´-leth; from an unused root mean. to *flee; swiftness; Pe-leth,* the name of two Isr.:— Peleth.

6432. פְּלֵתִי **pᵉlêthîy**, pel-ay-thee´; from the same form as 6431; a *courier* (collect.) or official *messenger:*— Pelethites.

6433. פֻּם **pûm** (Chald.), poom; prob. for 6310; the *mouth* (lit. or fig.):— mouth.

6434. פֵּן **pên**, pane; from an unused

root mean. to *turn;* an *angle* (of a street or wall):— corner.

6435. פֵּן **pên**, pane; from 6437; prop. *removal;* used only (in the constr.) adv. as conjunc. *lest:*— (lest) (peradventure), that ... not.

6436. פַּנַּג **Pannag**, pan-nag´; of uncert. der.; prob. *pastry:*— Pannag.

6437. פָּנָה **pânâh**, paw-naw´; a prim. root; to *turn;* by impl. to *face,* i.e. *appear, look,* etc.:— appear, at (even-) tide, behold, cast out, come on, × corner, dawning, empty, go away, lie, look, mark, pass away, prepare, regard, (have) respect (to), (re-) turn (aside, away, back, face, self), × right [early].

פָּנֶה **pâneh.** See 6440.

6438. פִּנָּה **pinnâh**, pin-naw´; fem. of 6434; an *angle;* by impl. a *pinnacle;* fig. a *chieftain:*— bulwark, chief, corner, stay, tower.

6439. פְּנוּאֵל **Pᵉnûw'êl**, pen-oo-ale´; or (more prop.)

פְּנִיאֵל **Pᵉnîy'êl**, pen-ee-ale´; from 6437 and 410; *face of God; Penuël* or *Peniël,* a place E. of Jordan; also (as Penuel) the name of two Isr.:— Peniel, Penuel.

פְּנִי **pânîy.** See 6443.

6440. פָּנִים **pânîym**, paw-neem´; plur. (but always as sing.) of an unused noun

פָּנֶה **pâneh**, paw-neh´; from 6437l; the *face* (as the part that *turns*); used in a great variety of applications (lit. and fig.); also (with prep. pref.) as a prep. (*before,* etc.):— + accept, a-(be-)fore (-time), against, + anger, × as (long as), at, + battle, + because (of), + beseech, countenance, edge, + employ, endure, + enquire, face, favour, fear of, for, forefront (-part), form (-er time, -ward), from, front, heaviness, × him (-self), + honourable, + impudent, + in, it, look [-ethl (-s), × me, + meet, × more than, mouth, of, off, (off) old (time), × on, open, + out of, over against, the partial, person, + please, presence, propect, was purposed, by reason, of, + regard, right forth, + serve, × shewbread, sight, state, straight, + street, × thee, × them (-selves), through (+ -out), till, time (-s) past, (un-) to (-ward), + upon, upside (+ down), with (-in, + -stand), × ye, × you.

6441. פְּנִימָה **pᵉnîymâh**, pen-ee´-maw; from 6440 with directive enclitic; *faceward,* i.e. *indoors:*— (with-) in (-ner part, -ward).

6442. פְּנִימִי **pᵉnîymîy**, pen-ee-mee´; from 6440; *interior:*— (with-) in (-ner, -ward).

6443. פָּנִין **pânîyn**, paw-neen´; or

פָּנִי **pânîy**, paw-nee´; from the same as 6434; prob. a *pearl* (as *round*):— ruby.

6444. פְּנִנָּה **Pᵉninnâh**, pen-in-naw´; prob. fem. from 6443 contr.; *Peninnah,* an Israelitess:— Peninnah.

6445. פָּנַק **pânaq**, paw-nak´; a prim. root; to *enervate:*— bring up.

6446. פַּס **paç**, pas; from 6461; prop. the *palm* (of the hand) or *sole* (of the foot) [comp. 6447]; by impl. (plur.) a *long and sleeved* tunic (perh. simply a *wide* one;

from the orig. sense of the root, i.e. of *many breadths*):— (divers) colours.

6447. פַּס **paç** (Chald.), pas; from a root corresp. to 6461; the *palm* (of the hand), as being *spread* out):— part.

6448. פָּסַג **pâçag**, paw-sag´; a prim. root; to *cut up,* i.e. (fig.) *contemplate:*— consider.

6449. פִּסְגָּה **Piçgâh**, pis-gaw´; from 6448; a *cleft; Pisgah,* a mountain E. of Jordan:— Pisgah.

6450. פַּס דַּמִּים **Paç Dammîym**, pas dam-meem´; from 6446 and the plur. of 1818; *palm* (i.e. *dell*) *of bloodshed; Pas-Dam-mim,* a place in Pal.:— Pas-dammim. Comp. 658.

6451. פִּסָּה **piççâh**, pis-saw´; from 6461; *expansion,* i.e. *abundance:*— handful.

6452. פָּסַח **pâçach**, paw-sakh´; a prim. root; to *hop,* i.e. (fig.) *skip* over (or *spare*); by impl. to *hesitate;* also (lit.) to *limp,* to *dance:*— halt, become lame, leap, pass over.

6453. פֶּסַח **Peçach**, peh´-sakh; from 6452; a *pretermission,* i.e. *exemption;* used only tech. of the Jewish *Passover* (the festival or the victim):— passover (offering).

6454. פָּסֵחַ **Pâçêach**, paw-say´-akh; from 6452; *limping; Paseäch,* the name of two Isr.:— Paseah, Phaseah.

6455. פִּסֵּחַ **piççêach**, pis-say´-akh; from 6452; *lame:*— lame.

6456. פְּסִיל **pᵉçîyl**, pes-eel´; from 6458; an *idol:*— carved (graven) image, quarry.

6457. פָּסַךְ **Pâçak**, paw-sak´; from an unused root mean. to *divide; divider; Pasak,* an Isr.:— Pasach.

6458. פָּסַל **pâçal**, paw-sal´; a prim. root; to *carve,* whether wood or stone:— grave, hew.

6459. פֶּסֶל **peçel**, peh´-sel; from 6458; an *idol:*— carved (graven) image.

6460. פְּסַנְטֵרִין **pᵉçantêrîyn** (Chald.), pes-an-tay-reen´; or

פְּסַנְתֵרִין **pᵉçantêrîyn**, pes-an-tay-reen´; a transliteration of the Gr. ψαλτήριον psaltēriŏn; a *lyre:*— psaltery.

6461. פָּסַס **paçaç**, paw-sas´; a prim. root; prob. to *disperse,* i.e. (intr.) *disappear:*— cease.

6462. פִּסְפָּה **Piçpâh**, pis-paw´; perh. from 6461; *dispersion; Pispah,* an Isr.:— Pispah.

6463. פָּעָה **pâʻâh**, paw-aw´; a prim. root; to *scream:*— cry.

6464. פָּעוּ **Pâʻûw**, paw-oo´; or

פָּעִי **Pâʻîy**, paw-ee´; from 6463; *screaming; Paü* or *Paï,* a place in Edom:— Pai, Pau.

6465. פְּעוֹר **Pᵉʻôwr**, peh-ore´; from 6473; a *gap; Peör,* a mountain E. of Jordan; also (for 1187) a deity worshipped there:— Peor. See also 1047.

פָּעִי **Pâʻîy.** See 6464.

6466. פָּעַל **pâʻal**, paw-al´; a prim. root; to *do* or *make* (systematically and habitually), espec. to *practise:*— commit, [evil-] do (-er), make (-r), ordain, work (-er), wrought.

6467. פֹּעַל **pôʻal**, po´-al; from 6466; an

act or *work* (concr.):— act, deed, do, getting, maker, work.

6468. פְּעֻלָּה **pᵉ'ullâh**, *peh-ool-law´*; fem. pass. part. of 6466; (abstr.) *work:*— labour, reward, wages, work.

6469. פְּעֻלָּתִי **Pᵉ'ull'thay**, *peh-ool-leh-thah´-ee*; from 6468; *laborious*; *Peüllethai*, an Isr.:— Peulthai.

6470. פָּעַם **pâ'am**, *paw-am´*; a prim. root; to *tap*, i.e. *beat regularly*; hence, (gen.) to *impel* or *agitate:*— move, trouble.

6471. פַּעַם **pa'am**, *pah´-am*; or (fem.)

פַּעֲמָה **pa'âmâh**, *pah-am-aw´*; from 6470; a *stroke*, lit. or fig. (in various applications, as follow):— anvil, corner, foot (-step), going, [hundred-]fold, × now, (this) + once, order, rank, step, + thrice, (often-), second, (this, two) time (-s), twice, wheel.

6472. פַּעֲמֹן **pa'âmôn**, *pah-am-one´*; from 6471; a *bell* (as *struck*):— bell.

6473. פָּעַר **pâ'ar**, *paw-ar´*; a prim. root; to *yawn*, i.e. *open* wide (lit. or fig.):— gape, open (wide).

6474. פְּעֹרַי **Pa'âray**, *pah-ar-ah´-ee*; from 6473; *yawning*; *Paarai*, an Isr.:— Paarai.

6475. פָּצָה **pâtsâh**, *paw-tsaw´*; a prim. root; to *rend*, i.e. *open* (espec. the mouth):— deliver, gape, open, rid, utter.

6476. פָּצַח **pâtsach**, *paw-tsakh´*; a prim. root; to *break* out (in joyful sound):— break (forth, forth into joy), make a loud noise.

6477. פְּצִירָה **pᵉtsîyrâh**, *pets-ee-raw´*; from 6484; *bluntness:*— + file.

6478. פָּצַל **pâtsal**, *paw-tsal´*; a prim. root; to *peel:*— pill.

6479. פְּצָלָה **pᵉtsâlâh**, *pets-aw-law´*; from 6478; a *peeling:*— strake.

6480. פָּצַם **pâtsam**, *paw-tsam´*; a prim. root; to *rend* (by earthquake):— break.

6481. פָּצַע **pâtsa'**, *paw-tsah´*; a prim. root; to *split*, i.e. *wound:*— wound.

6482. פֶּצַע **petsa'**, *peh´-tsah*; from 6481; a *wound:*— wound (-ing).

פְּצִין **Patstsets**. See 1048.

6483. פִּצֵּץ **Pitstsêts**, *pits-tsates´*; from an unused root mean. to *dissever*; *dispersive*; *Pitstsets*, a priest:— Apses [incl. the art.].

6484. פָּצַר **pâtsar**, *paw-tsar´*; a prim. root; to *peck* at, i.e. (fig.) *stun* or *dull:*— press, urge, stubbornness.

6485. פָּקַד **pâqad**, *paw-kad´*; a prim. root; to *visit* (with friendly or hostile intent); by anal. to *oversee*, *muster*, *charge*, *care for*, *miss*, *deposit*, etc.:— appoint, × at all, avenge, bestow, (appoint to have the, give a) charge, commit, count, deliver to keep, be empty, enjoin, go see, hurt, do judgment, lack, lay up, look, make, × by any means, miss, number, officer, (make) overseer, have (the) oversight, punish, reckon, (call to) remember (-brance), set (over), sum, × surely, visit, want.

פִּקֻּד **piqqûd**. See 6490.

6486. פְּקֻדָּה **pᵉquddâh**, *pek-ood-daw´*; fem. pass. part. of 6485; *visitation* (in

many senses, chiefly official):— account, (that have the) charge, custody, that which ... laid up, numbers, office (-r), ordering, oversight, + prison, reckoning, visitation.

6487. פִּקָּדוֹן **piqqâdôwn**, *pik-kaw-done´*; from 6485; a *deposit:*— that which was delivered (to keep), store.

6488. פְּקִדֻת **pᵉqidûth**, *pek-ee-dooth´*; from 6496; *supervision:*— ward.

6489. פְּקוֹד **Pᵉqôwd**, *pek-ode´*; from 6485; *punishment*; *Pekod*, a symbol. name for Bab.:— Pekod.

6490. פִּקּוּד **piqqûwd**, *pik-kood´*; or

פִּקֻּד **piqqûd**, *pik-kood´*; from 6485; prop. *appointed*, i.e. a *mandate* (of God; plur. only, collect. for the *Law*):— commandment, precept, statute.

6491. פָּקַח **pâqach**, *paw-kakh´*; a prim. root; to *open* (the senses, espec. the eyes); fig. to *be observant:*— open.

6492. פֶּקַח **Peqach**, *peh´-kakh*; from 6491; *watch*; *Pekach*, an Isr. king:— Pekah.

6493. פִּקֵּחַ **piqqêach**, *pik-kay´-akh*; from 6491; *clear-sighted*; fig. *intelligent:*— seeing, wise.

6494. פְּקַחְיָה **Pᵉqachyâh**, *pek-akh-yaw´*; from 6491 and 3050; *Jah has observed*; *Pekachjah*, an Isr. king:— Pekahiah.

6495. פְּקַח־קוֹחַ **pᵉqach-qôwach**, *pek-akh-ko´-akh*; from 6491 redoubled; *opening* (of a dungeon), i.e. *jail-delivery* (fig. *salvation* from sin):— opening of the prison.

6496. פָּקִיד **pâqîyd**, *paw-keed´*; from 6485; a *superintendent* (civil, military, or religious):— which had the charge, governor, office, overseer, [that] was set.

6497. פֶּקַע **peqa'**, *peh´-kah*; from an unused root mean. to *burst*; only used as an arch. term of an ornament similar to 6498, a *semi-globe:*— knop.

6498. פַּקֻּעָה **paqqu'âh**, *pak-koo-aw´*; from the same as 6497; the *wild cucumber* (from *splitting* open to shed its seeds):— gourd.

6499. פַּר **par**, *par*; or

פָּר **pâr**, *pawr*; from 6565; a *bullock* (appar. as *breaking* forth in wild strength, or perh. as *dividing* the hoof):— (+ young) bull (-ock), calf, ox.

6500. פָּרָא **pârâ'**, *paw-raw´*; a prim. root; to *bear fruit:*— be fruitful.

6501. פֶּרֶא **pere'**, *peh´-reh*; or

פֶּרֶה **pereh** (Jer. 2:24), *peh´-reh*; from 6500 in the second. sense of *running* wild; the *onager:*— wild (ass).

פֹּרָאה **pôrâ'h**. See 6288.

6502. פִּרְאָם **Pir'âm**, *pir-awm´*; from 6501; *wildly*; *Piram*, a Canaanite:— Piram.

6503. פַּרְבָּר **Parbâr**, *par-bawr´*; or

פַּרְוָר **Parvâr**, *par-vawr´*; of for. or.; *Parbar* or *Parvar*, a quarter of Jerusalem:— Parbar, suburb.

6504. פָּרַד **pârad**, *paw-rad´*; a prim. root; to *break* through, i.e. *spread* or *separate* (oneself):— disperse, divide,

be out of joint, part, scatter (abroad), separate (self), sever self, stretch, sunder.

6505. פֶּרֶד **pered**, *peh´-red*; from 6504; a *mule* (perh. from his *lonely* habits):— mule.

6506. פִּרְדָּה **pirdâh**, *pir-daw´*; fem. of 6505; a *she-mule:*— mule.

6507. פְּרֻדָה **pᵉrudâh**, *per-oo-daw´*; fem. pass. part. of 6504; something *separated*, i.e. a *kernel:*— seed.

6508. פַּרְדֵּס **pardêç**, *par-dace´*; of for. or.; a *park:*— forest, orchard.

6509. פָּרָה **pârâh**, *paw-raw´*; a prim. root; to *bear fruit* (lit. or fig.):— bear, bring forth· (fruit), (be, cause to be, make) fruitful, grow, increase.

6510. פָּרָה **pârâh**, *paw-raw´*; fem. of 6499; a *heifer:*— cow, heifer, kine.

6511. פָּרָה **Pârâh**, *paw-raw´*; the same as 6510; *Parah*, a place in Pal.:— Parah.

פָּרָה **pereh**. See 6501.

6512. פֵּרָה **pêrâh**, *pay-raw´*; from 6331; a *hole* (as *broken*, i.e. *dug*):— + mole. Comp. 2661.

6513. פּוּרָה **Pûrâh**, *poo-raw´*; for 6288; *foliage*; *Purah*, an Isr.:— Phurah.

6514. פְּרוּדָא **Pᵉrûwdâ'**, *per-oo-daw´*; or

פְּרִידָא **Pᵉrîydâ'**, *per-ee-daw´*; from 6504; *dispersion*; *Peruda* or *Perida*, one of "Solomon's servants":— Perida, Peruda.

פְּרוֹזִי **pᵉrôwzîy**. See 6521.

6515. פָּרוּחַ **Pârûwach**, *paw-roo´-akh*; pass. part. of 6524; *blossomed*; *Paruäch*, an Isr.:— Paruah.

6516. פַּרְוַיִם **Parvayim**, *par-vah´-yim*; of for. or.; *Parvajim*, an Oriental region:— Parvaim.

6517. פָּרוּר **pârûwr**, *paw-roor´*; pass. part. of 6565 in the sense of *spreading* out [comp. 6524]; a *skillet* (as *flat* or *deep*):— pan, pot.

פַּרְוָר **Parvâr**. See 6503.

6518. פָּרָז **pârâz**, *paw-rawz´*; from an unused root mean. to *separate*, i.e. *decide*; a *chieftain:*— village.

6519. פְּרָזָה **pᵉrâzâh**, *per-aw-zaw´*; from the same as 6518; an *open* country:— (unwalled) town (without walls), unwalled village.

6520. פְּרָזוֹן **pᵉrâzôwn**, *per-aw-zone´*; from the same as 6518; *magistracy*, i.e. *leadership* (also concr. *chieftains*):— village.

6521. פְּרָזִי **pᵉrâzîy**, *per-aw-zee´*; or

פְּרוֹזִי **pᵉrôwzîy**, *per-o-zee´*; from 6519; a *rustic:*— village.

6522. פְּרִזִּי **Pᵉrizzîy**, *per-iz-zee´*; for 6521; inhab. *of the open country*; a *Perizzite*, one of the Canaanitish tribes:— Perizzite.

6523. פַּרְזֶל **parzel** (Chald.), *par-zel´*; corresp. to 1270; *iron:*— iron.

6524. פָּרַח **pârach**, *paw-rakh´*; a prim. root; to *break* forth as a bud, i.e. *bloom*; gen. to *spread*; spec. to *fly* (as extending the wings); fig. to *flourish:*— × abroad, × abundantly, blossom, break forth (out), bud, flourish, make fly, grow, spread, spring (up).

6525. פֶּרַח **perach**, *peh´-rakh;* from 6524; a *calyx* (nat. or artif.); gen. *bloom:*— blossom, bud, flower.

6526. פִּרְחַח **pirchach**, *pir-khakh´;* from 6524; *progeny*, i.e. a *brood:*— youth.

6527. פָּרַט **pârat**, *paw-rat´;* a prim. root; to *scatter* words, i.e. *prate* (or *hum*):— chant.

6528. פֶּרֶט **peret**, *peh´-ret;* from 6527; a *stray* or *single* berry:— grape.

6529. פְּרִי **periy**, *per-ee´;* from 6509; *fruit* (lit. or fig.):— bough, (lfirst-l) fruit (l-full), reward.

פְּרִידָא **Periydâ'**. See 6514.

פּוּרִים **Pûriym**. See 6332.

6530. פָּרִיץ **periyts**, *per-eets´;* from 6555; *violent*, i.e. a *tyrant:*— destroyer, ravenous, robber.

6531. פֶּרֶךְ **perek**, *peh´-rek;* from an unused root mean. to *break apart; fracture*, i.e. *severity:*— cruelty, rigour.

6532. פֹּרֶכֶת **pôreketh**, *po-reh´-keth;* fem. act. part. of the same as 6531; a *separatrix*, i.e. (the sacred) *screen:*— vail.

6533. פָּרַם **pâram**, *paw-ram´;* a prim. root; to *tear:*— rend.

6534. פַּרְמַשְׁתָּא **Parmashtâ'**, *par-mash-taw´;* of Pers. or.; *Parmashta*, a son of Haman:— Parmasta.

6535. פַּרְנַךְ **Parnak**, *par-nak´;* of uncert. der.; *Parnak*, an Isr.:— Parnach.

6536. פָּרַס **pâraç**, *paw-ras´;* a prim. root; to *break* in pieces, i.e. (usually without violence) to *split, distribute:*— deal, divide, have hoofs, part, tear.

6537. פְּרַס **peraç** (Chald.), *per-as´;* corresp. to 6536; to *split* up:— divide, lU-l pharsin.

6538. פֶּרֶס **pereç**, *peh´-res;* from 6536; a *claw;* also a kind of *eagle:*— claw, ossifrage.

6539. פָּרָס **Pârâç**, *paw-ras´;* of for. or.; *Paras* (i.e. *Persia*), an E. country, incl. its inhab.:— Persia, Persians.

6540. פָּרַס **Pârâç** (Chald.), *paw-ras´;* corresp. to 6539:— Persia, Persians.

6541. פַּרְסָה **parçâh**, *par-saw´;* fem. of 6538; a *claw* or split *hoof:*— claw, lcloven-l footed, hoof.

6542. פַּרְסִי **Parçiy**, *par-see´;* patrial from 6539; a *Parsite* (i.e. *Persian*), or inhab. of Peres:— Persian.

6543. פַּרְסִי **Parçiy** (Chald.), *par-see´;* corresp. to 6542:— Persian.

6544. פָּרַע **pâra'**, *paw-rah´;* a prim. root; to *loosen;* by impl. to *expose, dismiss;* fig. *absolve, begin:*— avenge, avoid, bare, go back, let, (make) naked, set at nought, perish, refuse, uncover.

6545. פֶּרַע **pera'**, *peh´-rah;* from 6544; the *hair* (as *dishevelled*):— locks.

6546. פִּרְעָה **par'âh**, *par-aw´;* fem. of 6545 (in the sense of *beginning*); *leadership* (plur. concr. *leaders*):— + avenging, revenge.

6547. פַּרְעֹה **Par'ôh**, *par-o´;* of Eg. der.; *Paroh*, a gen. title of Eg. kings:— Pharaoh.

6548. פַּרְעֹה חָפְרַע **Par'ôh Chophra'**, *par-o´ khof-rah´;* of Eg. der.; *Paroh-Chophra*, an Eg. king:— Pharaoh-hophra.

6549. פַּרְעֹה נְכֹה **Par'ôh Nekôh**, *par-o´ nek-o´;* or

פַּרְעֹה נְכוֹ **Par'ôh Nekôw**, *par-o´ nek-o´;* of Eg. der.; *Paroh-Nekoh* (or *-Neko*), an Eg. king:— Pharaoh-necho, Pharaoh-nechoh.

6550. פַּרְעֹשׁ **par'ôsh**, *par-oshe´;* prob. from 6544 and 6211; a *flea* (as the isolated insect):— flea.

6551. פַּרְעֹשׁ **Par'ôsh**, *par-oshe´;* the same as 6550; *Parosh*, the name of our Isr.:— Parosh, Pharosh.

6552. פִּרְעָתוֹן **Pir'âthôwn**, *pir-aw-thone´;* from 6546; *chieftaincy; Pirathon*, a place in Pal.:— Pirathon.

6553. פִּרְעָתֹנִי **Pir'âthôwniy**, *pir-aw-tho-nee´;* or

פִּרְעָתֹנִי **Pir'âthôniy**, *pir-aw-tho-nee´;* patrial from 6552; a *Pirathonite* or inhab. of Pirathon:— Pirathonite.

6554. פַּרְפַּר **Parpar**, *par-par´;* prob. from 6565 in the sense of *rushing; rapid; Parpar*, a river of Syria:— Pharpar.

6555. פָּרַץ **pârats**, *paw-rats´;* a prim. root; to *break* out (in many applications, dir. and indirect, lit. and fig.):— × abroad, (make a) breach, break (away, down, -er, forth, in, up), burst out, come (spread) abroad, compel, disperse, grow, increase, open, press, scatter, urge.

6556. פֶּרֶץ **perets**, *peh´-rets;* from 6555; a *break* (lit. or fig.):— breach, breaking forth (in), × forth, gap.

6557. פֶּרֶץ **Perets**, *peh´-rets;* the same as 6556; *Perets*, the name of two Isr.:— Perez, Pharez.

6558. פַּרְצִי **Partsiy**, *par-tsee´;* patron. from 6557; a *Partsite* (collect.) or desc. of Perets:— Pharzites.

6559. פְּרָצִים **Perâtsiym**, *per-aw-tseem´;* plur. of 6556; *breaks; Peratsim*, a mountain in Pal.:— Perazim.

6560. פֶּרֶץ עֻזָּא **Perets 'Uzzâ'**, *peh´-rets ooz-zaw´;* from 6556 and 5798; *break of Uzza; Perets-Uzza*, a place in Pal.:— Perez-uzza.

6561. פָּרַק **pâraq**, *paw-rak´;* a prim. root; to *break off* or *crunch;* fig. to *deliver:*— break (off), deliver, redeem, rend (in pieces), tear in pieces.

6562. פְּרַק **peraq** (Chald.), *per-ak´;* corresp. to 6561; to *discontinue:*— break off.

6563. פֶּרֶק **pereq**, *peh´-rek;* from 6561; *rapine;* also a *fork* (in roads):— crossway, robbery.

6564. פָּרָק **pârâq**, *paw-rawk´;* from 6561; *soup* (as full of *crumbed* meat):— broth. See also 4832.

6565. פָּרַר **pârar**, *paw-rar´;* a prim. root; to *break* up (usually fig., i.e. to *violate, frustrate):*— × any ways, break (asunder), cast off, cause to cease, × clean, defeat, disannul, disappoint, dissolve, divide, make of none effect, fail, frustrate, bring (come) to nought, × utterly, make void.

6566. פָּרַשׂ **pâras**, *paw-ras´;* a prim. root; to *break* apart, *disperse*, etc.:— break,

chop in pieces, lay open, scatter, spread (abroad, forth, selves, out), stretch (forth, out).

6567. פָּרַשׁ **pârash**, *paw-rash´;* a prim. root; to *separate*, lit. (to *disperse*) or fig. (to *specify*); also (by impl.) to *wound:*— scatter, declare, distinctly, shew, sting.

6568. פְּרַשׁ **perash** (Chald.), *per-ash´;* corresp. to 6567; to *specify:*— distinctly.

6569. פֶּרֶשׁ **peresh**, *peh´-resh;* from 6567; *excrement* (as *eliminated*):— dung.

6570. פֶּרֶשׁ **Peresh**, *peh´-resh;* the same as 6569; *Peresh*, an Isr.:— Peresh.

6571. פָּרָשׁ **pârâsh**, *paw-rawsh´;* from 6567; a *steed* (as *stretched* out to a vehicle, not single nor for mounting lcomp. 5483l); also (by impl.) a *driver* (in a chariot), i.e. (collect.) *cavalry:*— horseman.

6572. פַּרְשֶׁגֶן **parshegen**, *par-sheh´-ghen;* or

פַּתְשֶׁגֶן **pathshegen**, *path-sheh´-gen;* of for. or.; a *transcript:*— copy.

6573. פַּרְשֶׁגֶן **parshegen** (Chald.), *par-sheh´-ghen;* corresp. to 6572:— copy.

6574. פַּרְשְׁדֹן **parshedôn**, *par-shed-one´;* perh. by compounding 6567 and 6504 (in the sense of *straddling*) lcomp. 6576l; the *crotch* (or *anus*):— dirt.

6575. פָּרָשָׁה **pârâshâh**, *paw-raw-shaw´;* from 6567; *exposition:*— declaration, sum.

6576. פַּרְשֵׁז **parshêz**, *par-shaze´;* a root appar. formed by compounding 6567 and that of 6518 lcomp. 6574l; to *expand:*— spread.

6577. פַּרְשַׁנְדָּתָא **Parshandâthâ'**, *par-shan-daw-thaw´;* of Pers. or.; *Parshandatha*, a son of Haman:— Parshandatha.

6578. פְּרָת **Perâth**, *per-awth´;* from an unused root mean. to *break* forth; *rushing; Perath* (i.e. *Euphrates*), a river of the East:— Euphrates.

פֹּרָת **pôrâth**. See 6509.

6579. פַּרְתַּם **partam**, *par-tam´;* of Pers. or.; a *grandee:*— (most) noble, prince.

6580. פַּשׁ **pash**, *pash;* prob. from an unused root mean. to *disintegrate; stupidity* (as a result of *grossness* or of *degeneracy*):— extremity.

6581. פָּשָׂה **pâsâh**, *paw-saw´;* a prim. root; to *spread:*— spread.

6582. פָּשַׁח **pâshach**, *paw-shakh´;* a prim. root; to *tear* in pieces:— pull in pieces.

6583. פַּשְׁחוּר **Pashchûwr**, *pash-khoor´;* prob. from 6582; *liberation; Pashchur*, the name of four Isr.:— Pashur.

6584. פָּשַׁט **pâshat**, *paw-shat´;* a prim. root; to *spread* out (i.e. *deploy* in hostile array); by anal. to *strip* (i.e. *unclothe, plunder, flay*, etc.):— fall upon, flay, invade, make an invasion, pull off, put off, make a road, run upon, rush, set, spoil, spread selves (abroad), strip (off, self).

6585. פָּשַׂע **pâsa'**, *paw-sah´;* a prim. root; to *stride* (from *spreading* the legs), i.e. *rush* upon:— go.

6586. פָּשַׁע **pâsha'**, *paw-shah´;* a prim. root lrather ident. with 6585 through the idea of *expansion*l; to *break* away (from just authority), i.e. *trespass, apostatize, quarrel:*— offend, rebel, revolt, transgress (-ion, -or).

6587. פָּשַׂע **pesa'**, *peh'-sah;* from 6585; a *stride:*— step.

6588. פֶּשַׁע **pesha'**, *peh'-shah;* from 6586; a *revolt* (national, moral, or religious):— rebellion, sin, transgression, trespass.

6589. פָּשַׂק **pâsaq**, *paw-sak';* a prim. root; to *dispart* (the feet or lips), i.e. *become licentious:*— open (wide).

6590. פְּשַׁר **pᵉshar** (Chald.), *pesh-ar';* corresp. to 6622; to *interpret:*— make [interpretations], interpreting.

6591. פְּשַׁר **pᵉshar** (Chald.), *pesh-ar';* from 6590; an *interpretation:*— interpretation.

6592. פֵּשֶׁר **pêsher**, *pay'-sher;* corresp. to 6591:— interpretation.

6593. פִּשְׁתֶּה **pishteh**, *pish-teh';* from the same as 6580 as in the sense of *comminuting; linen* (i.e. the thread, as *carded*):— flax, linen.

6594. פִּשְׁתָּה **pishtâh**, *pish-taw';* fem. of 6593; *flax;* by impl. a *wick:*— flax, tow.

6595. פַּת **path**, *path;* from 6626; a *bit:*— meat, morsel, piece.

6596. פֹּת **pôth**, *pohth;* or

פֹּתָה **pothâh** (Ezek. 13:19), *po-thaw';* from an unused root mean. to *open;* a *hole,* i.e. *hinge* or the female *pudenda:*— hinge, secret part.

פְּתָאִי **pᵉthâ'îy**. See 6612.

6597. פִּתְאוֹם **pith'ôwm**, *pith-ome';* or

פִּתְאֹם **pith'ôm**, *pith-ome';* from 6621; *instantly:*— straightway, sudden (-ly).

6598. פַּתְבַּג **pathbag**, *pathbag';* of Pers. or.; a *dainty:*— portion (provision) of meat.

6599. פִּתְגָּם **pithgâm**, *pith-gawm';* of Pers. or.; a (judicial) *sentence:*— decree, sentence.

6600. פִּתְגָּם **pithgâm** (Chald.), *pithgawm';* corresp. to 6599; a *word, answer, letter* or *decree:*— answer, letter, matter, word.

6601. פָּתָה **pâthâh**, *paw-thaw';* a prim. root; to *open,* i.e. *be* (caus. *make*) *roomy;* usually fig. (in a mental or moral sense) to *be* (caus. *make*) *simple* or (in a sinister way) *delude:*— allure, deceive, enlarge, entice, flatter, persuade, silly (one).

6602. פְּתוּאֵל **Pᵉthûw'êl**, *peth-oo-ale';* from 6601 and 410; *enlarged of God; Pethuël,* an Isr.:— Pethuel.

6603. פִּתּוּחַ **pittûwach**, *pit-too'-akh;* or

פִּתֻּחַ **pittûach**, *pit-too'-akh;* pass. part. of 6605; *sculpture* (in low or high relief or even intaglio):— carved (work) (are, en-) grave (-ing, -n).

6604. פְּתוֹר **Pᵉthôwr**, *peth-ore';* of for. or.; *Pethor,* a place in Mesopotamia:— Pethor.

6605. פָּתַח **pâthach**, *paw-thakh';* a prim. root; to *open wide* (lit. or fig.); spec. to *loosen, begin, plow, carve:*— appear, break forth, draw (out), let go free, (en-) grave (-n), loose (self), (be, be set)

open (-ing), put off, ungird, unstop, have vent.

6606. פְּתַח **pᵉthach** (Chald.), *peth-akh';* corresp. to 6605; to *open:*— open.

6607. פֶּתַח **pethach**, *peh'-thakh;* from 6605; an *opening* (lit.), i.e. *door* (*gate*) or *entrance* way:— door, entering (in), entrance (-ry), gate, opening, place.

6608. פֵּתַח **pêthach**, *pay'-thakh;* from 6605; *opening* (fig.) i.e. *disclosure:*— entrance.

פְּתוּחַ **pâthûach**. See 6603.

6609. פְּתִחָה **pᵉthîchâh**, *peth-ee-khaw';* from 6605; something *opened,* i.e. a *drawn sword:*— drawn sword.

6610. פִּתְחוֹן **pithchôwn**, *pith-khone';* from 6605; *opening* (the act):— open (-ing).

6611. פְּתַחְיָה **Pᵉthachyâh**, *peth-akh-yaw';* from 6605 and 3050; *Jah has opened; Pethachjah,* the name of four Isr.:— Pethahiah.

6612. פְּתִי **pᵉthîy**, *peth-ee';* or

פֶּתִי **pethîy**, *peh'-thee;* or

פְּתָאִי **pᵉthâ'îy**, *peth-aw-ee';* from 6601; *silly* (i.e. *seducible*):— foolish, simple (-icity, one).

6613. פְּתַי **pᵉthay** (Chald.), *peth-ah'-ee;* from a root corresp. to 6601; *open,* i.e. (as noun) *width:*— breadth.

6614. פְּתִיגִיל **pᵉthîygîyl**, *peth-eeg-eel';* of uncert. der.; prob. a figured *mantle* for holidays:— stomacher.

6615. פְּתַיְוּת **Pᵉthayûwth**, *peth-ah-yooth';* from 6612; *silliness* (i.e. *seducibility*):— simple.

6616. פָּתִיל **pâthîyl**, *paw-theel';* from 6617; *twine:*— bound, bracelet, lace, line, ribband, thread, wire.

6617. פָּתַל **pâthal**, *paw-thal';* a prim. root; to *twine,* i.e. (lit.) to *struggle* or (fig.) be (morally) *tortuous:*— (shew self) froward, shew self unsavoury, wrestle.

6618. פְּתַלְתֹּל **pᵉthaltôl**, *peth-al-tole';* from 6617; *tortuous* (i.e. *crafty*):— crooked.

6619. פִּתֹם **Pîthôm**, *pee-thome';* of Eg. der.; *Pithom,* a place in Egypt:— Pithom.

6620. פֶּתֶן **pethen**, *peh'-then;* from an unused root mean. to *twist;* an *asp* (from its *contortions*):— adder.

6621. פֶּתַע **petha'**, *peh'-thah;* from an unused root mean. to *open* (the eyes); a *wink,* i.e. *moment* [comp. 6597] (used only [with or without prep.] adv. *quickly* or *unexpectedly*):— at an instant, suddenly, × very.

6622. פָּתַר **pâthar**, *paw-thar';* a prim. root; to *open up,* i.e. (fig.) *interpret* (a dream):— interpret (-ation, -er).

6623. פִּתְרוֹן **pithrôwn**, *pith-rone';* or

פִּתְרֹן **pithrôn**, *pith-rone';* from 6622; *interpretation* (of a dream):— interpretation.

6624. פַּתְרוֹס **Pathrôwç**, *path-roce';* of Eg. der.; *Pathros,* a part of Egypt:— Pathros.

6625. פַּתְרֻסִי **Pathrûçîy**, *path-roo-see';*

patrial from 6624; a *Pathrusite,* or inhab. of Pathros:— Pathrusim.

פַּתְשֶׁגֶן **pathshegen**. See 6572.

6626. פָּתַת **pâthath**, *paw-thath';* a prim. root; to *open,* i.e. *break:*— part.

צ

6627. צֵאָה **tsâ'âh**, *tsaw-aw';* from 3318; *issue,* i.e. (human) *excrement:*— that (which) cometh from [her].

צֹאָה **tsô'âh**. See 6675.

צֵאוֹן **tsᵉ'ôwn**. See 6629.

6628. צֶאֱל **tse'el**, *tseh'-el;* from an unused root mean. to *be slender;* the lotus tree:— shady tree.

6629. צֹאן **tsô'n**, *tsone;* or

צֵאוֹן **tsᵉ'ôwn** (Psa. 144:13) *tseh-one';* from an unused root mean. to *migrate;* a collect. name for a *flock* (of sheep or goats); also fig. (of men):— (small) cattle, flock (+ -s), lamb (+ -s), sheep [(-cote, -fold, -shearer, -herds]).

6630. צַאֲנָן **Tsa'ănân**, *tsah-an-awn';* from the same as 6629 used denom.; *sheep pasture; Zaanan,* a place in Pal.:— Zaanan.

6631. צֶאֱצָא **tse'ĕtsâ'**, *tseh-ets-aw';* from 3318; *issue,* i.e. *produce, children:*— that which cometh forth (out), offspring.

6632. צָב **tsâb**, *tsawb;* from an unused root mean. to *establish;* a *palanquin* or *canopy* (as a *fixture*); also a species of *lizard* (prob. as clinging *fast*):— covered, litter, tortoise.

6633. צָבָא **tsâbâ'**, *tsaw-baw';* a prim. root; to *mass* (an army or servants):— assemble, fight, perform, muster, wait upon, war.

6634. צְבָא **tsᵉbâ'** (Chald.), *tseb-aw';* corresp. to 6633 in the fig. sense of *summoning* one's wishes; to *please:*— will, would.

6635. צָבָא **tsâbâ'**, *tsaw-baw';* or (fem.)

צְבָאָה **tsᵉbâ'âh**, *tseb-aw-aw';* from 6633; a *mass* of persons (or fig. things), espec. reg. organized for war (an *army*); by impl. a *campaign,* lit. or fig. (spec. *hardship, worship*):— appointed time, (+) army, (+) battle, company, host, service, soldiers, waiting upon, war (-fare).

6636. צְבֹאִים **Tsᵉbô'iym**, *tseb-o-eem';* or

צְבִיִּים **Tsᵉbîyîym**, *tseb-ee-yeem';* or

צְבִיִּם **Tsᵉbîyîm**, *tseb-ee-yeem';* plur. of 6643; *gazelles; Tseboïm* or *Tsebijim,* a place in Pal.:— Zeboiim, Zeboim.

6637. צֹבֵבָה **Tsôbêbâh**, *tso-bay-baw';* fem. act. part. of the same as 6632; the *canopier* (with the art.); *Tsobebah,* an Israelitess:— Zobebah.

6638. צָבָה **tsâbâh**, *tsaw-baw';* a prim. root; to *amass,* i.e. *grow turgid;* spec. to *array* an army against:— fight, swell.

6639. צָבֶה **tsâbeh**, *tsaw-beh';* from 6638; *turgid:*— swell.

צֹבָה **Tsôbâh**. See 6678.

6640. צְבוּ **tsᵉbûw** (Chald.), *tseb-oo';*

Hebrew

from 6634; prop. *will;* concr. an *affair* (as a matter of *determination*):— purpose.

6641. צָבוּעַ **tsâbûwa'**, *tsaw-boo´-ah;* pass. part. of the same as 6648; *dyed* (in stripes), i.e. the *hyena:*— speckled.

6642. צָבַט **tsâbaṭ**, *tsaw-bat´;* a prim. root; to *grasp,* i.e. *hand* out:— reach.

6643. צְבִי **tsᵉbîy**, *tseb-ee´;* from 6638 in the sense of *prominence; splendor* (as *conspicuous*); also a *gazelle* (as *beautiful*):— beautiful (-ty), glorious (-ry), goodly, pleasant, roe (-buck).

6644. צִבְיָא **Tsibyâʼ**, *tsib-yaw´;* for 6645; *Tsibja,* an Isr.:— Zibia.

6645. צִבְיָה **Tsibyâh**, *tsib-yaw´;* for 6646; *Tsibjah,* an Israelitess:— Zibiah.

6646. צְבִיָּה **tsᵉbîyâh**, *tseb-ee-yaw´;* fem. of 6643; a *female* gazelle:— roe.

צְבֹיִים **Tsᵉbîyîym**. See 6636.

צְבֹיִם **Tsᵉbâyîm**. See 6380.

6647. צְבַע **tsᵉba'** (Chald.), *tseb-ah´;* a root corresp. to that of 6648; to *dip:*— wet.

6648. צֶבַע **tseba'**, *tseh´-bah;* from an unused root mean. to *dip* (into coloring fluid); a *dye:*— divers, colours.

6649. צִבְעוֹן **Tsibʻôwn**, *tsib-one´;* from the same as 6648; *variegated; Tsibon,* an Idumæan:— Zibeon.

6650. צְבֹעִים **Tsᵉbôʻîym**, *tseb-o-eem´;* plur. of 6641; *hyenas; Tseboïm,* a place in Pal.:— Zeboim.

6651. צָבַר **tsâbar**, *tsaw-bar´;* a prim. root; to *aggregate:*— gather (together), heap (up), lay up.

6652. צִבֻּר **tsibbûr**, *tsib-boor´;* from 6551; a *pile:*— heap.

6653. צֶבֶת **tsebeth**, *tseh´-beth;* from an unused root appar. mean. to *grip;* a *lock* of stalks:— handful.

6654. צַד **tsad**, *tsad;* contr. from an unused root mean. to *sidle* off; a *side;* fig. an *adversary:*— (be-) side.

6655. צַד **tsad** (Chald.), *tsad;* corresp. to 6654; used adv. (with prep.) at or upon the *side* of:— against, concerning.

6656. צְדָא **tsᵉdâ'** (Chald.), *tsed-aw´;* from an unused root corresp! to 6658 in the sense of *intentness;* a (sinister) *design:*— true.

6657. צְדָד **Tsᵉdâd**, *tsed-awd´;* from the same as 6654; a *siding; Tsedad,* a place near Pal.:— Zedad.

6658. צָדָה **tsâdâh**, *tsaw-daw´;* a prim. root; to *chase;* by impl. to *desolate:*— destroy, hunt, lie in wait.

צָדָה **tsêdâh**. See 6720.

6659. צָדוֹק **Tsâdôwq**, *tsaw-doke´;* from 6663; *just; Tsadok,* the name of eight or nine Isr.:— Zadok.

6660. צְדִיָּה **tsᵉdîyâh**, *tsed-ee-yaw´;* from 6658; *design* [comp. 6656]:— lying in wait.

6661. צִדִּים **Tsiddîym**, *tsid-deem´;* plur. of 6654; *sides; Tsiddim* (with the art.), a place in Pal.:— Ziddim.

6662. צַדִּיק **tsaddîyq**, *tsad-deek´;* from 6663; *just:*— just, lawful, righteous (man).

צִדֹּנִי° **Tsîdônîy**. See 6722.

6663. צָדַק **tsâdaq**, *tsaw-dak´;* a prim. root; to *be* (caus. *make*) *right* (in a moral or forensic sense):— cleanse, clear self, (be, do) just (-ice, -ify, -ify self), (be, turn to) righteous (-ness).

6664. צֶדֶק **tsedeq**, *tseh´-dek;* from 6663; the *right* (nat., mor. or legal); also (abstr.) *equity* or (fig.) *prosperity:*— × even, (× that which is altogether) just (-ice), (lun-l) right (-eous) (cause, -ly, -ness).

6665. צִדְקָה **tsidqâh** (Chald.), *tsid-kaw´;* corresp. to 6666; *beneficence:*— righteousness.

6666. צְדָקָה **tsᵉdâqâh**, *tsed-aw-kaw´;* from 6663; *rightness* (abstr.), subj. (*rectitude*), obj. (*justice*), mor. (*virtue*) or fig. (*prosperity*):— justice, moderately, right (-eous) (act, -ly, -ness).

6667. צִדְקִיָּה **Tsidqîyâh**, *tsid-kee-yaw´;* or

צִדְקִיָּהוּ **Tsidqîyâhûw**, *tsid-kee-yaw´-hoo;* from 6664 and 3050; *right of Jah; Tsidkijah,* the name of six Isr.:— Zedekiah, Zidkijah.

6668. צָהַב **tsâhab**, *tsaw-hab´;* a prim. root; to *glitter,* i.e. *be golden* in color:— × fine.

6669. צָהֹב **tsâhôb**, *tsaw-obe´;* from 6668; *golden* in color:— yellow.

6670. צָהַל **tsâhal**, *tsaw-hal´;* a prim. root; to *gleam,* i.e. (fig.) *be cheerful;* by transf. to *sound* clear (of various animal or human expressions):— bellow, cry aloud (out), lift up, neigh, rejoice, make to shine, shout.

6671. צָהַר **tsâhar**, *tsaw-har´;* a prim. root; to *glisten;* used only as denom. from 3323, to *press* out oil:— make oil.

6672. צֹהַר **tsôhar**, *tso´-har;* from 6671; a *light* (i.e. *window*): dual *double light,* i.e. *noon:*— midday, noon (-day, -tide), window.

6673. צַו **tsav**, *tsav;* or

צָו **tsâv**, *tsawv;* from 6680; an *injunction:*— commandment, precept.

6674. צוֹא **tsôw'**, *tso;* or

צֹא **tsô'**, *tso;* from an unused root mean. to *issue; soiled* (as if *excrementitious*):— filthy.

6675. צוֹאָה **tsôwʼâh**, *tso-aw´;* or

צֹאָה **tsôʼâh**, *tso-aw´;* fem. of 6674; *excrement;* gen. *dirt;* fig. *pollution:*— dung, filth (-iness). [Marg. for 2716.]

6676. צַוָּאר **tsavvâʼr** (Chald.), *tsav-var´;* corresp. to 6677:— neck.

6677. צַוָּאר **tsavvâʼr**, *tsav-vawr´;* or

צַוָּר **tsavvâr** (Neh. 3:5), *tsav-vawr´;* or

צַוָּרֹן **tsavvârôn** (Cant. 4:9), *tsav-vaw-rone´;* or (fem.)

צַוָּארָה **tsavvâ'râh** (Mic. 2:3) *tsav-vaw-raw´;* intens. from 6696 in the sense of *binding;* the back of the *neck* (as that on which burdens are *bound*):— neck.

6678. צוֹבָא **Tsôwbâ'**, *tso-baw´;* or

צוֹבָה **Tsôwbâh**, *tso-baw´;* or

צֹבָה **Tsôbâh**, *tso-baw´;* from an unused root mean. to *station; a station; Zoba* or *Zobah,* a region of Syria:— Zoba, Zobah.

6679. צוּד **tsûwd**, *tsood;* a prim. root; to *lie* alongside (i.e. in wait); by impl. to *catch* an animal (fig. men); (denom. from 6718) to *victual* (for a journey):— chase, hunt, sore, take (provision).

6680. צָוָה **tsâvâh**, *tsaw-vaw´;* a prim. root; (intens.) to *constitute, enjoin:*— appoint, (for-) bid, (give a) charge, (give a, give in, send with) command (-er, -ment), send a messenger, put, (set) in order.

6681. צָוַח **tsâvach**, *tsaw-vakh´;* a prim. root; to *screech* (exultingly):— shout.

6682. צְוָחָה **tsᵉvâchâh**, *tsev-aw-khaw´;* from 6681; a *screech* (of anguish):— cry (-ing).

6683. צוּלָה **tsûwlâh**, *tsoo-law´;* from an unused root mean. to *sink; an abyss* (of the sea):— deep.

6684. צוּם **tsûwm**, *tsoom;* a prim. root; to *cover* over (the mouth), i.e. to *fast:*— × at all, fast.

6685. צוֹם **tsôwm**, *tsome;* or

צֹם **tsôm**, *tsome;* from 6684; a *fast:*— fast (-ing).

6686. צוּעָר **Tsûw'âr**, *tsoo-awr´;* from 6819; *small; Tsuär,* an Isr.:— Zuar.

6687. צוּף **tsûwph**, *tsoof;* a prim. root; to *overflow:*— (make to over-) flow, swim.

6688. צוּף **tsûwph**, *tsoof;* from 6687; *comb* of honey (from *dripping*):— honeycomb.

6689. צוּף **Tsûwph**, *tsoof;* or

צוֹפַי° **Tsôwphay**, *tso-fah´-ee;* or

צִיף **Tsîyph**, *tseef;* from 6688; *honey-comb; Tsuph* or *Tsophai* or *Tsiph,* the name of an Isr. and of a place in Pal.:— Zophai, Zuph.

6690. צוֹפַח **Tsôwphach**, *tso-fakh´;* from an unused root mean. to *expand, breadth; Tsophach,* an Isr.:— Zophah.

צוֹפַי **Tsôwphay**. See 6689.

6691. צוֹפַר **Tsôwphar**, *tso-far´;* from 6852; *departing; Tsophar,* a friend of Job:— Zophar.

6692. צוּץ **tsûwts**, *tsoots;* a prim. root; to *twinkle,* i.e. *glance;* by anal. to *blossom* (fig. *flourish*):— bloom, blossom, flourish, shew self.

6693. צוּק **tsûwq**, *tsook;* a prim. root; to *compress,* i.e. (fig.) *oppress, distress:*— constrain, distress, lie sore, (op-) press (-or), straiten.

6694. צוּק **tsûwq**, *tsook;* a prim. root [rather ident. with 6693 through the idea of *narrowness* (of orifice)]; to *pour* out, i.e. (fig.) *smelt, utter:*— be molten, pour.

6695. צוֹק **tsôwq**, *tsoke;* or (fem.)

6695... צוּקָה **tsûwqâh**, *tsoo-kaw´;* from 6693; a *strait,* i.e. (fig.) *distress:*— anguish, × troublous.

6696. צוּר **tsûwr**, *tsoor;* a prim. root; to *cramp,* i.e. *confine* (in many applications, lit. and fig., formative or hostile):— adversary, assault, beset, besiege, bind (up), cast, distress, fashion, fortify, inclose, lay siege, put up in bags.

6697. צוּר **tsûwr**, *tsoor;* or

צֻר **tsûr**, *tsoor;* from 6696; prop. a *cliff* (or sharp rock, as *compressed*); gen. a *rock* or *boulder;* fig. a *refuge;* also an *edge* (as *precipitous*):— edge, × (mighty) God (one), rock, × sharp, stone, × strength, × strong. See also 1049.

6698. צוּר **Tsûwr**, *tsoor;* the same as 6697; *rock; Tsur*, the name of a Midianite and of an Isr.:— Zur.

צוּר **Tsôwr**. See 6865.

צֻוָּר **tsavvâr**. See 6677.

6699. צוּרָה **tsûwrâh**, *tsoo-raw;* fem. of 6697; a *rock* (Job 28:10); also a *form* (as if *pressed* out):— form, rock.

צֻוָּרֹן **tsavvârôn**. See 6677.

6700. צוּרִיאֵל **Tsûwriy'êl**, *tsoo-ree-ale;* from 6697 and 410; *rock of God; Tsuriël*, an Isr.:— Zuriel.

6701. צוּרִישַׁדַּי **Tsûwrîyshadday**, *tsoo-ree-shad-dah´-ee;* from 6697 and 7706; *rock of* (the) *Almighty; Tsurishaddai*, an Isr.:— Zurishaddai.

6702. צוּת **tsûwth**, *tsooth;* a prim. root; to *blaze:*— burn.

6703. צַח **tsach**, *tsakh;* from 6705; *dazzling*, i.e. *sunny, bright*, (fig.) *evident:*— clear, dry, plainly, white.

צַחָא **Tsichâ'**. See 6727.

6704. צִחֶה **tsîcheh**, *tsee-kheh;* from an unused root mean. to *glow; parched:*— dried up.

6705. צָחַח **tsâchach**, *tsaw-khakh;* a prim. root; to *glare*, i.e. *be dazzling* white:— be whiter.

6706. צְחִיחַ **tsechîyach**, *tsekh-ee´-akh;* from 6705; *glaring*, i.e. *exposed* to the bright sun:— higher place, top.

6707. צְחִיחָה **tsechîychâh**, *tsekh-ee-khaw´;* fem. of 6706; a *parched* region, i.e. the *desert:*— dry land.

6708. צְחִיחִי° **tsechîychîy**, *tsekh-ee-khee´;* from 6706; *bare* spot, i.e. in the *glaring* sun:— higher place.

6709. צַחֲנָה **tsachănâh**, *tsakh-an-aw´;* from an unused root mean. to *putrefy; stench:*— ill savour.

6710. צַחְצָחָה **tsachtsâchâh**, *tsakh-tsaw-khaw´;* from 6705; a *dry* place, i.e. *desert:*— drought.

6711. צָחַק **tsâchaq**, *tsaw-khak´;* a prim. root; to *laugh* outright (in merriment or scorn); by impl. to *sport:*— laugh, mock, play, make sport.

6712. צְחֹק **tsechôq**, *tsekh-oke´;* from 6711; *laughter* (in pleasure or derision):— laugh (-ed to scorn).

6713. צַחַר **tsachar**, *tsakh´-ar;* from an unused root mean. to *dazzle; sheen*, i.e. *whiteness:*— white.

6714. צֹחַר **Tsôchar**, *tso´-khar;* from the same as 6713; *whiteness; Tsochar*, the name of a Hittite and of an Isr.:— Zohar. Comp. 3328.

6715. צָחֹר **tsâchôr**, *tsaw-khore´;* from the same as 6713; *white:*— white.

6716. צִי **tsîy**, *tsee;* from 6680; a *ship* (as a *fixture*):— ship.

6717. צִיבָא **Tsîybâ'**, *tsee-baw´;* from the

same as 6678; *station; Tsiba*, an Isr.:— Ziba.

6718. צַיִד **tsayid**, *tsah´-yid;* from a form of 6679 and mean. the same; the *chase;* also *game* (thus taken); (gen.) *lunch* (espec. for a journey):— × catcheth, food, × hunter, (that which he took in) hunting, venison, victuals.

6719. צַיָּד **tsayâd**, *tsah´-yawd;* from the same as 6718; a *huntsman:*— hunter.

6720. צֵידָה **tsêydâh**, *tsay-daw´;* or

צֵדָה **tsêdâh**, *tsay-daw´;* fem. of 6718; *food:*— meat, provision, venison, victuals.

6721. צִידוֹן **Tsîydôwn**, *tsee-done´;* or

צִידֹן **Tsîydôn**, *tsee-done´;* from 6679 in the sense of *catching* fish; *fishery; Tsidon*, the name of a son of Canaan, and of a place in Pal.:— Sidon, Zidon.

6722. צִידֹנִי **Tsîydônîy**, *tsee-do-nee´;* patrial from 6721; a *Tsidonian* or inhab. of Tsidon:— Sidonian, of Sidon, Zidonian.

6723. צִיָּה **tsîyâh**, *tsee-yaw´;* from an unused root mean. to *parch; aridity;* concr. a *desert:*— barren, drought, dry (land, place), solitary place, wilderness.

6724. צִיּוֹן **tsîyôwn**, *tsee-yone´;* from the same as 6723; a *desert:*— dry place.

6725. צִיּוּן **tsîyûwn**, *tsee-yoon´;* from the same as 6723 in the sense of *conspicuousness* [comp. 5329]; a *monumental* or *guiding pillar:*— sign, title, waymark.

6726. צִיּוֹן **Tsîyôwn**, *tsee-yone´;* the same (reg.) as 6725; *Tsijon* (as a permanent *capital*), a mountain of Jerusalem:— Zion.

6727. צִיחָא **Tsîychâ'**, *tsee-khaw´;* or

צָחָא **Tsichâ'**, *tsee-khaw´;* as if fem. of 6704; *drought; Tsicha*, the name of two Nethinim:— Ziha.

6728. צִיִּי **tsîyîy**, *tsee-ee´;* from the same as 6723; a *desert-dweller*, i.e. *nomad* or wild *beast:*— wild beast of the desert, that dwell in (inhabiting) the wilderness.

6729. צִינֹק **tsîynôq**, *tsee-noke´;* from an unused root mean. to *confine;* the *pillory:*— stocks.

6730. צִיֹּר **Tsîy'ôr**, *tsee-ore´;* from 6819; *small; Tsior*, a place in Pal.:— Zior.

6731. צִיץ° **Tsîyph**. See 6689.

6731. צִיץ **tsîyts**, *tseets;* or

צִץ **tsits**, *tseets;* from 6692; prop. *glistening*, i.e. a *burnished plate;* also a *flower* (as *bright* colored); a *wing* (as *gleaming* in the air):— blossom, flower, plate, wing.

6732. צִיץ **Tsîyts**, *tseets;* the same as 6731; *bloom; Tsits*, a place in Pal.:— Ziz.

6733. צִיצָה **tsîytsâh**, *tsee-tsaw´;* fem. of 6731; a *flower:*— flower.

6734. צִיצִת **tsîytsîth**, *tsee-tseeth´;* fem. of 6731; a *floral* or *wing*-like projection, i.e. a *fore-lock* of hair, a *tassel:*— fringe, lock.

צִיקְלַג° **Tsîyqelag**. See 6860.

6735. צִיר **tsîyr**, *tseer;* from 6696; a *hinge* (as *pressed* in turning); also a *throe* (as a physical or mental *pressure*); also a

herald or errand-doer (as *constrained* by the principal):— ambassador, hinge, messenger, pain, pang, sorrow. Comp. 6736.

6736. צִיר **tsîyr**, *tseer;* the same as 6735; a *form* (of beauty; as if *pressed* out, i.e. *carved*); hence, an (idolatrous) *image:*— beauty, idol.

6737. צָיַר **tsâyar**, *tsaw-yar´;* a denom. from 6735 in the sense of *ambassador;* to *make an errand*, i.e. *betake* oneself:— make as if ... had been ambassador.

6738. צֵל **tsêl**, *tsale;* from 6751; *shade*, whether lit. or fig.:— defence, shade (-ow).

6739. צְלָא **tselâ'** (Chald.), *tsel-aw´;* prob. corresp. to 6760 in the sense of *bowing; pray:*— pray.

6740. צָלָה **tsâlâh**, *tsaw-law´;* a prim. root; to *roast:*— roast.

6741. צִלָּה **Tsillâh**, *tsil-law´;* fem. of 6738; *Tsillah*, an antediluvian woman:— Zillah.

6742. צְלוּל° **tselûwl**, *tsel-ool´;* from 6749 in the sense of *rolling;* a (round or flattened) *cake:*— cake.

6743. צָלַח **tsâlach**, *tsaw-lakh´;* or

צָלֵחַ **tsâlêach**, *tsaw-lay´-akh;* a prim. root; to *push* forward, in various senses (lit. or fig., tran. or intr.):— break out, come (mightily), go over, be good, be meet, be profitable, (cause to, effect, make to, send) prosper (-ity, -ous, -ously).

6744. צְלַח **tselach** (Chald.), *tsel-akh´;* corresp. to 6743; to *advance* (tran. or intr.):— promote, prosper.

6745. צֵלָחָה **tsêlâchâh**, *tsay-law-khaw´;* from 6743; something *protracted* or flattened out, i.e. a *platter:*— pan.

6746. צְלֹחִית **tselôchîyth**, *tsel-o-kheeth´;* from 6743; something *prolonged* or tall, i.e. a *vial* or salt-*cellar:*— cruse.

6747. צַלַּחַת **tsallachath**, *tsal-lakh´-ath;* from 6743; something *advanced* or deep, i.e. a *bowl;* fig. the *bosom:*— bosom, dish.

6748. צָלִי **tsâlîy**, *tsaw-lee´;* pass. part. of 6740; *roasted:*— roast.

6749. צָלַל **tsâlal**, *tsaw-lal´;* a prim. root; prop. to *tumble* down, i.e. *settle* by a waving motion:— sink. Comp. 6750, 6751.

6750. צָלַל **tsâlal**, *tsaw-lal´;* a prim. root [rather ident. with 6749 through the idea of *vibration*]; to *tinkle*, i.e. *rattle* together (as the ears in *reddening* with shame, or the teeth in *chattering* with fear):— quiver, tingle.

6751. צָלַל **tsâlal**, *tsaw-lal´;* a prim. root [rather ident. with 6749 through the idea of *hovering* over (comp. 6754)]; to *shade*, as twilight or an opaque object:— begin to be dark, shadowing.

6752. צֵלֶל **tsêlel**, *tsay´-lel;* from 6751; *shade:*— shadow.

6753. צְלֶלְפּוֹנִי **Tselelpôwnîy**, *tsel-el-po-nee´;* from 6752 and the act. part. of 6437; *shade-facing; Tselelponi*, an Israelitess:— Hazelelponi [incl. the art.].

6754. צֶלֶם **tselem**, *tseh´-lem;* from an

unused root mean. to *shade;* a *phantom,* i.e. (fig.) *illusion, resemblance;* hence, a representative *figure,* espec. an *idol:*— image, vain shew.

6755. צֶלֶם **tselem** (Chald.), *tseh´-lem;* or

צְלֵם **tsᵉlem** (Chald.), *tsel-em´;* corresp. to 6754; an idolatrous *figure:*— form, image.

6756. צַלְמוֹן **Tsalmôwn,** *tsal-mone´;* from 6754; *shady; Tsalmon,* the name of a place in Pal. and of an Isr.:— Zalmon.

6757. צַלְמָוֶת **tsalmâveth,** *tsal-maw´-veth;* from 6738 and 4194; *shade of death,* i.e. the *grave* (fig. *calamity*):— shadow of death.

6758. צַלְמֹנָה **Tsalmônâh,** *tsal-mo-naw´;* fem. of 6757; *shadiness; Tsalmonah,* a place in the Desert:— Zalmonah.

6759. צַלְמֻנָּע **Tsalmunnâ´,** *tsal-moon-naw´;* from 6738 and 4513; *shade has been denied; Tsalmunna,* a Midianite:— Zalmunna.

6760. צָלַע **tsâla´,** *tsaw-lah´;* a prim. root: prob. to *curve;* used only as denom. from 6763, to *limp* (as if *one-sided*):— halt.

6761. צֶלַע **tsela´,** *tseh´-lah;* from 6760; a *limping* or *fall* (fig.):— adversity, halt (-ing).

6762. צֶלַע **Tsela´,** *tseh´-lah;* the same as 6761; *Tsela,* a place in Pal.:— Zelah.

6763. צֵלָע **tsêlâ´,** *tsay-law´;* or (fem.)

צַלְעָה **tsal'âh,** *tsal-aw´;* from 6760; a *rib* (as *curved*), lit. (of the body) or fig. (of a door, i.e. *leaf*); hence, a *side,* lit. (of a person) or fig. (of an object or the sky, i.e. *quarter*); arch. a (espec. floor or ceiling) *timber* or *plank* (single or collect., i.e. a *flooring*):— beam, board, chamber, corner, leaf, plank, rib, side (chamber).

6764. צָלָף **Tsâlâph,** *tsaw-lawf´;* from an unused root of unknown mean.; *Tsalaph,* an Isr.:— Zalaph.

6765. צְלָפְחָד **Tsᵉlophchâd,** *tsel-of´-chawd´;* from the same as 6764 and 259; *Tselophchad,* an Isr.:— Zelophehad.

6766. צֶלְצַח **Tseltsach,** *tsel-tsakh´;* from 6738 and 6703; *clear shade; Tseltsach,* a place in Pal.:— Zelzah.

6767. צְלָצַל **tsᵉlâtsal,** *tsel-aw-tsal´;* from 6750 redupl.; a *clatter,* i.e. (abstr.) *whirring* (of wings); (concr.) a *cricket;* also a *harpoon* (as *rattling*), a *cymbal* (as *clanging*):— cymbal, locust, shadowing, spear.

6768. צֶלֶק **Tseleq,** *tseh´-lek;* from an unused root mean. to *split; fissure; Tselek,* an Isr.:— Zelek.

6769. צִלְּתַי **Tsillᵉthay,** *tsil-leth-ah´-ee;* from the fem. of 6738; *shady;* the name of two Isr.:— Zilthai.

6770. צָמֵא **tsâmê´,** *tsaw-may´;* a prim. root; to *thirst* (lit. or fig.):— (be a-, suffer) thirst (-y).

6771. צָמֵא **tsâmê´,** *tsaw-may´;* from 6770; *thirsty* (lit. or fig.):— (that) thirst (-eth, -y).

6772. צָמָא **tsâmâ´,** *tsaw-maw´;* from 6770; *thirst* (lit. or fig.):— thirst (-y).

6773. צִמְאָה **tsim'âh,** *tsim-aw´;* fem. of

6772; *thirst* (fig. of *libidinousnes*):— thirst.

6774. צִמָּאוֹן **tsimmâ'ôwn,** *tsim-maw-one´;* from 6771; a *thirsty* place, i.e. *desert:*— drought, dry ground, thirsty land.

6775. צָמַד **tsâmad,** *tsaw-mad´;* a prim. root; to *link,* i.e. *gird;* fig. to *serve,* (mentally) *contrive:*— fasten, frame, join (self).

6776. צֶמֶד **tsemed,** *tseh´-med;* a *yoke* or *team* (i.e. *pair*); hence, an *acre* (i.e. day's task for a yoke of cattle to plow):— acre, couple, × together, two [asses], yoke (of oxen).

6777. צַמָּה **tsammâh,** *tsam-maw´;* from an unused root mean. to *fasten on;* a *veil:*— locks.

6778. צַמּוּק **tsammûwq,** *tsam-mook´;* from 6784; a cake of *dried grapes:*— bunch (cluster) of raisins.

6779. צָמַח **tsâmach,** *tsaw-makh´;* a prim. root; to *sprout* (tran. or intr., lit. or fig.):— bear, bring forth, (cause to, make to) bud (forth), (cause to, make to) grow (again, up), (cause to) spring (forth, up).

6780. צֶמַח **tsemach,** *tseh´-makh;* from 6779; a *sprout* (usually concr.), lit. or fig.:— branch, bud, that which (where) grew (upon), spring (-ing).

6781. צָמִיד **tsâmiyd,** *tsaw-meed´;* or

צָמִד **tsâmid,** *tsaw-meed´;* from 6775; a *bracelet* or *arm-clasp;* gen. a *lid:*— bracelet, covering.

6782. צַמִּים **tsammiym,** *tsam-meem´;* from the same as 6777; a *noose* (as *fastening*); fig. *destruction:*— robber.

6783. צְמִיתֻת **tsᵉmiythûth,** *tsem-ee-thooth´;* or

צְמִתֻת **tsᵉmithûth,** *tsem-ee-thooth´;* from 6789; *excision,* i.e. *destruction;* used only (adv.) with pref. to *extinction,* i.e. *perpetually:*— ever.

6784. צָמַק **tsâmaq,** *tsaw-mak´;* a prim. root; to *dry up:*— dry.

6785. צֶמֶר **tsemer,** *tseh´-mer;* from an unused root prob. mean. to *be shaggy; wool:*— wool (-len).

6786. צְמָרִי **Tsᵉmâriy,** *tsem-aw-ree´;* patrial from an unused name of a place in Pal.; a *Tsemarite* or branch of the Canaanites:— Zemarite.

6787. צְמָרַיִם **Tsᵉmârayim,** *tsem-aw-rah´-yim;* dual of 6785; *double fleece; Tsemarajim,* a place in Pal.:— Zemaraim.

6788. צַמֶּרֶת **tsammereth,** *tsam-meh´-reth;* from the same as 6785; *fleeciness,* i.e. *foliage:*— highest branch, top.

6789. צָמַת **tsâmath,** *tsaw-math´;* a prim. root; to *extirpate* (lit. or fig.):— consume, cut off, destroy, vanish.

6783. צְמִתֻת **tsᵉmithûth.** See 6783.

6790. צִן **Tsin,** *tseen;* from an unused root mean. to *prick;* a *crag; Tsin,* a part of the Desert:— Zin.

6791. צֵן **tsên,** *tsane;* from an unused root mean. to *be prickly;* a *thorn;* hence, a cactus-*hedge:*— thorn.

6792. צֹנֵא **tsônê´,** *tso-nay´;* or

צֹנֶה **tsôneh,** *tso-neh´;* for 6629; a *flock:*— sheep.

6793. צִנָּה **tsinnâh,** *tsin-naw´;* fem. of 6791; a *hook* (as *pointed*); also a (large) *shield* (as if *guarding* by *prickliness*); also *cold* (as *piercing*):— buckler, cold, hook, shield, target.

6794. צִנּוּר **tsinnûwr,** *tsin-noor´;* from an unused root perh. mean. to *be hollow;* a *culvert:*— gutter, water-spout.

6795. צָנַח **tsânach,** *tsaw-nakh´;* a prim. root; to *alight;* (tran.) to *cause to descend,* i.e. *drive* down:— fasten, light [from off].

6796. צָנִין **tsâniyn,** *tsaw-neen´;* or

צָנִן **tsânin,** *tsaw-neen´;* from the same as 6791; a *thorn:*— thorn.

6797. צָנִיף **tsâniyph,** *tsaw-neef´;* or

צָנוֹף **tsânôwph,** *tsaw-nofe´;* or (fem.)

צְנִיפָה **tsânîyphâh,** *tsaw-nee-faw´;* from 6801; a *head-dress* (i.e. *piece* of cloth *wrapped* around):— diadem, hood, mitre.

6798. צָנַם **tsânam,** *tsaw-nam´;* a prim. root; to *blast* or *shrink:*— withered.

6799. צְנָן **Tsᵉnân,** *tsen-awn´;* prob. for 6630; *Tsenan,* a place near Pal.:— Zenan.

6796. צָנִן **tsânin.** See 6796.

6800. צָנַע **tsâna´,** *tsaw-nah´;* a prim. root; to *humiliate:*— humbly, lowly.

6801. צָנַף **tsânaph,** *tsaw-naf´;* a prim. root; to *wrap,* i.e. *roll* or *dress:*— be attired, × surely, violently turn.

6802. צְנֵפָה **tsᵉnêphâh,** *tsen-ay-faw´;* from 6801; a *ball:*— × toss.

6803. צִנְצֶנֶת **tsintseneth,** *tsin-tseh´-neth;* from the same as 6791; a *vase* (prob. a vial *tapering* at the top):— pot.

6804. צַנְתָּרָה **tsantârâh,** *tsan-taw-raw´;* prob. from the same as 6794; a *tube:*— pipe.

6805. צָעַד **tsâ'ad,** *tsaw-ad´;* a prim. root; to *pace,* i.e. *step* regularly; (upward) to *mount;* (along) to *march;* (down and caus.) to *hurl:*— bring, go, march (through), run over.

6806. צַעַד **tsa'ad,** *tsah´-ad;* from 6804; a *pace* or regular *step:*— pace. step.

6807. צְעָדָה **tsᵉ'âdâh,** *tseh-aw-daw´;* fem. of 6806; a *march;* (concr.) an (ornamental) *ankle-chain:*— going, ornament of the legs.

6808. צָעָה **tsâ'âh,** *tsaw-aw´;* a prim. root; to *tip* over (for the purpose of *spilling* or *pouring* out), i.e. (fig.) *depopulate;* by impl. to *imprison* or *conquer;* (refl.) to *lie down* (for coitus, sexual intercourse):— captive exile, travelling, (cause to) wander (-er).

6809. צָעִיף **tsâ'îyph,** *tsaw-eef´;* from an unused root mean. to *wrap* over; a *veil:*— vail.

6810. צָעִיר **tsâ'îyr,** *tsaw-eer´;* or

צָעוֹר **tsâ'ôwr,** *tsaw-ore´;* from 6819; *little,* (in number) *few;* (in age) *young,* (in value) *ignoble:*— least, little (one), small (one), + young (-er, -est).

6811. צָעִיר **Tsâ'îyr,** *tsaw-eer´;* the same

as 6810; *Tsaïr*, a place in Idumæa:— Zair.

6812. צְעִירָה **tseˑîyrâh**, *tseh-ee-raw´*; fem. of 6810; *smallness* (of age), i.e. *juvenility*:— youth.

6813. צָעַן **tsâ'an**, *tsaw-an´*; a prim. root; to *load* up (beasts), i.e. to *migrate*:— be taken down.

6814. צֹעַן **Tsô'an**, *tso´-an*; of Eg. der.; *Tsoän*, a place in Egypt:— Zoan.

6815. צַעֲנִים **Tsa'ănannîym**, *tsah-an-an-neem´*; or (dual)

צַעֲנַיִם° **Tsa'ănayim**, *tsah-an-ah´-yim*; plur. from 6813; *removals*; *Tsaanannim* or *Tsaanajim*, a place in Pal.:— Zaannannim, Zaanaim.

6816. צַעְצֻעַ **tsa'tsûa'**, *tsah-tsoo´-ah*; from an unused root mean. to *bestrew* with carvings; *sculpture*:— image [work].

6817. צָעַק **tsâ'aq**, *tsaw-ak´*; a prim. root; to *shriek*; (by impl.) to *proclaim* (an assembly):— × at all, call together, cry (out), gather (selves) (together).

6818. צְעָקָה **tsa'äqâh**, *tsah-ak-aw´*; from 6817; a *shriek*:— cry (-ing).

6819. צָעַר **tsâ'ar**, *tsaw-ar´*; a prim. root; to *be small*, i.e. (fig.) *ignoble*:— be brought low, little one, be small.

6820. צֹעַר **Tsô'ar**, *tso´ar*; from 6819; *little*; *Tsoär*, a place E. of the Jordan:— Zoar.

6821. צָפַד **tsâphad**, *tsaw-fad´*; a prim. root; to *adhere*:— cleave.

6822. צָפָה **tsâphâh**, *tsaw-faw´*; a prim. root; prop. to *lean* forward, i.e. to *peer* into the distance; by impl. to *observe*, *await*:— behold, espy, look up (well), wait for, (keep the) watch (-man).

6823. צָפָה **tsâphâh**, *tsaw-faw´*; a prim. root [prob. rather ident. with 6822 through the idea of *expansion* in outlook, transferring to act]; to *sheet* over (espec. with metal):— cover, overlay.

6824. צָפָה **tsâphâh**, *tsaw-faw´*; from 6823; an *inundation* (as *covering*):— × swimmest.

6825. צְפוֹ **Tseˑphôw**, *tsef-o´*; or

צְפִי **Tseˑphiy**, *tsef-ee´*; from 6822; *observant*; *Tsepho* or *Tsephi*, an Idumæan:— Zephi, Zepho.

6826. צִפּוּי **tsippûwy**, *tsip-poo´-ee*; from 6823; *encasement* (with metal):— covering, overlaying.

6827. צְפוֹן **Tseˑphôwn**, *tsef-one´*; prob. for 6837; *Tsephon*, an Isr.:— Zephon.

6828. צָפוֹן **tsâphôwn**, *tsaw-fone´*; or

צָפֹן **tsâphôn**, *tsaw-fone´*; from 6845; prop. *hidden*, i.e. *dark*; used only of the *north* as a quarter (*gloomy* and *unknown*):— north (-ern, side, -ward, wind).

6829. צָפוֹן **Tsâphôwn**, *tsaw-fone´*; the same as 6828; *boreal*; *Tsaphon*, a place in Pal.:— Zaphon.

6830. צְפוֹנִי **tseˑphôwnîy**, *tsef-o-nee´*; from 6828; *northern*:— northern.

6831. צְפוֹנִי **Tseˑphôwnîy**, *tsef-o-nee´*; patron. from 6827; a *Tsephonite*, or (collect.) desc. of Tsephon:— Zephonites.

6832. צְפוּעַ° **tseˑphûwa'**, *tsef-oo´-ah*; from

the same as 6848; *excrement* (as *protruded*):— dung.

6833. צִפּוֹר **tsippôwr**, *tsip-pore´*; or

צִפֹּר **tsippôr**, *tsip-pore´*; from 6852; a little *bird* (as *hopping*):— bird, fowl, sparrow.

6834. צִפּוֹר **Tsippôwr**, *tsip-pore´*; the same as 6833; *Tsippor*, a Moabite:— Zippor.

6835. צַפַּחַת **tsappachath**, *tsap-pakh´-ath*; from an unused root mean. to *expand*; a *saucer* (as *flat*):— cruse.

6836. צְפִיָּה **tseˑphîyâh**, *tsef-ee-yaw´*; from 6822; *watchfulness*:— watching.

6837. צִפְיוֹן **Tsiphyôwn**, *tsif-yone´*; from 6822; *watch*-tower; *Tsiphjon*, an Isr.:— Ziphion. Comp. 6827.

6838. צַפִּיחִת **tsappîychith**, *tsap-pee-kheeth´*; from the same as 6835; a flat thin *cake*:— wafer.

6839. צֹפִים **Tsôphîym**, *tso-feem´*; plur. of act. part. of 6822; *watchers*; *Tsophim*, a place E. of the Jordan:— Zophim.

6840. צָפִין° **tsâphîyn**, *tsaw-feen´*; from 6845; a *treasure* (as *hidden*):— hid.

6841. צְפִיר **tseˑphîyr** (Chald.), *tsef-eer´*; corresp. to 6842; a he-*goat*:— he [goat].

6842. צָפִיר **tsâphîyr**, *tsaw-feer´*; from 6852; a male *goat* (as *prancing*):— (he) goat.

6843. צְפִירָה **tseˑphîyrâh**, *tsef-ee-raw´*; fem. formed like 6842; a *crown* (as encircling the head); also a *turn* of affairs (i.e. *mishap*):— diadem, morning.

6844. צָפִית **tsâphîyth**, *tsaw-feeth´*; from 6822; a *sentry*:— watchtower.

6845. צָפַן **tsâphan**, *tsaw-fan´*; a prim. root; to *hide* (by *covering* over); by impl. to *hoard* or *reserve*; fig. to *deny*; spec. (favorably) to *protect*, (unfavorably) to *lurk*:— esteem, hide (-den one, self), lay up, lurk (be set) privily, (keep) secret (-ly, place).

צָפֹן **tsâphôn**. See 6828.

6846. צְפַנְיָה **Tseˑphanyâh**, *tsef-an-yaw´*; or

צְפַנְיָהוּ **Tseˑphanyâhûw**, *tsef-an-yaw´-hoo*; from 6845 and 3050; *Jah has secreted*; *Tsephanjah*, the name of four Isr.:— Zephaniah.

6847. צָפְנַת פַּעְנֵחַ **Tsophnath Pa'nêach**, *tsof-nath´ pah-nay´-akh*; of Eg. der.; *Tsophnath-Paneäch*, Joseph's Eg. name:— Zaphnath-paaneah.

6848. צֶפַע **tsepha'**, *tseh´-fah*; or

צִפְעֹנִי **tsiph'ônîy**, *tsif-o-nee´*; from an unused root mean. to *extrude*; a *viper* (as *thrusting* out the tongue, i.e. *hissing*):— adder, cockatrice.

6849. צְפִעָה **tseˑphî'âh**, *tsef-ee-aw´*; fem. from the same as 6848; an *outcast* thing:— issue.

צִפְעֹנִי **tsiph'ônîy**. See 6848.

6850. צָפַף **tsâphaph**, *tsaw-faf´*; a prim. root; to *coo* or *chirp* (as a bird):— chatter, peep, whisper.

6851. צַפְצָפָה **tsaphtsâphâh**, *tsaf-tsaw-faw´*; from 6687; a *willow* (as growing in *overflowed* places):— willow tree.

6852. צָפַר **tsâphar**, *tsaw-far´*; a prim.

root; to *skip* about, i.e. *return*:— depart early.

6853. צְפַר **tseˑphar** (Chald.), *tsef-ar´*; corresp. to 6833; a *bird*:— bird.

צִפֹּר **tsippôr**. See 6833.

6854. צְפַרְדֵּעַ **tseˑphardêa'**, *tsef-ar-day´-ah*; from 6852 and a word elsewhere unused mean. a *swamp*; a *marshleaper*, i.e. *frog*:— frog.

6855. צִפֹּרָה **Tsippôrâh**, *tsip-po-raw´*; fem. of 6833; *bird*; *Tsipporah*, Moses' wife:— Zipporah.

6856. צִפֹּרֶן **tsippôren**, *tsip-po´-ren*; from 6852 (in the denom. sense [from 6833] of *scratching*); prop. a *claw*, i.e. (human) *nail*; also the *point* of a style (or pen, tipped with adamant):— nail, point.

6857. צְפַת **Tseˑphath**, *tsef-ath´*; from 6822; *watch*-tower; *Tsephath*, a place in Pal.:— Zephath.

6858. צֶפֶת **tsepheth**, *tseh´-feth*; from an unused root mean. to *encircle*; a *capital* of a column:— chapiter.

6859. צְפָתָה **Tseˑphâthâh**, *tsef-aw´-thaw*; the same as 6857; *Tsephathah*, a place in Pal.:— Zephathah.

צִיץ **tsîts**. See 6732.

6860. צִקְלַג **Tsiqlâg**, *tsik-lag´*; or

צִיקְלַג **Tsîyqeˑlag** (1 Chron. 12:1, 20), *tsee-kel-ag´*; of uncert. der.: *Tsiklag* or *Tsikelag*, a place in Pal.:— Ziklag.

6861. צִקְלֹן **tsiqlôn**, *tsik-lone´*; from an unused root mean. to *wind*; a *sack* (as *tied* at the mouth):— husk.

6862. צַר **tsar**, *tsar*; or

צָר **tsâr**, *tsawr*; from 6887; *narrow*; (as a noun) a *tight* place (usually fig., i.e. *trouble*); also a *pebble* (as in 6864); (tran.) an *opponent* (as *crowding*):— adversary, afflicted (-tion), anguish, close, distress, enemy, flint, foe, narrow, small, sorrow, strait, tribulation, trouble.

6863. צֵר **Tsêr**, *tsare*; from 6887; *rock*; *Tser*, a place in Pal.:— Zer.

6864. צֹר **tsôr**, *tsore*; from 6696; a *stone* (as if *pressed* hard or to a point); (by impl. of use) a *knife*:— flint, sharp stone.

6865. צֹר **Tsôr**, *tsore*; or

צוֹר **Tsôwr**, *tsore*; the same as 6864; a *rock*; *Tsor*, a place in Pal.:— Tyre, Tyrus.

צוּר **tsûr**. See 6697.

6866. צָרַב **tsârab**, *tsaw-rab´*; a prim. root; to *burn*:— burn.

6867. צָרֶבֶת **tsârebeth**, *tsaw-reh´-beth*; from 6686; *conflagration* (of fire or disease):— burning, inflammation.

6868. צְרֵדָה **Tseˑrêdâh**, *tser-ay-daw´*; or

צְרֵדָתָה **Tseˑrêdâthâh**, *tser-ay-daw´-thaw*; appar. from an unused root mean. to *pierce*; *puncture*; *Tseredah*, a place in Pal.:— Zereda, Zeredathah.

6869. צָרָה **tsârâh**, *tsaw-raw´*; fem. of 6862; *tightness* (i.e. fig. *trouble*); tran. a female *rival*:— adversary, adversity, affliction, anguish, distress, tribulation, trouble.

6870. צְרוּיָה Tseꞏrûwyâh, *tser-oo-yaw´*; fem. pass. part. from the same as 6875; *wounded*; *Tserujah*, an Israelitess:— Zeruiah.

6871. צְרוּעָה Tseꞏrûw'âh, *tser-oo-aw´*; fem. pass. part. of 6879; *leprous*; *Tseruäh*, an Israelitess:— Zeruah.

6872. צְרוֹר tseꞏrôwr, *tser-ore´*; or (short.)

צְרֹר tseꞏrôr, *tser-ore´*; from 6887; a *parcel* (as *packed* up); also a *kernel* or *particle* (as if a *package*):— bag, × bendeth, bundle, least grain, small stone.

6873. צָרַח tsârach, *tsaw-rakh´*; a prim. root; to be *clear* (in tone, i.e. *shrill*), i.e. to *whoop*:— cry, roar.

6874. צְרִי Tseꞏrîy, *tser-ee´*; the same as 6875; *Tseri*, an Isr.:— Zeri. Comp. 3340.

6875. צְרִי tseꞏrîy, *tser-ee´*; or

צֳרִי tsŏrîy, *tsor-ee´*; from an unused root mean. to *crack* [as by pressure], hence, to *leak*; *distillation*, i.e. *balsam*:— balm.

6876. צֹרִי Tsôrîy, *tso-ree´*; patrial from 6865; a *Tsorite* or inhab. of Tsor (i.e. *Syrian*):— (man) of Tyre.

6877. צְרִיחַ tseꞏrîyach, *tser-ee´-akh*; from 6873 in the sense of *clearness* of vision; a *citadel*:— high place, hold.

6878. צֹרֶךְ tsôrek, *tso´-rek*; from an unused root mean. to *need*; *need*:— need.

6879. צָרַע tsâra', *tsaw-rah´*; a prim. root; to *scourge*, i.e. (intr. and fig.) to be *stricken with leprosy*:— leper, leprous.

6880. צִרְעָה tsir'âh, *tsir-aw´*; from 6879; a *wasp* (as *stinging*):— hornet.

6881. צָרְעָה Tsor'âh, *tsor-aw´*; appar. another form for 6880; *Tsorah*, a place in Pal.:— Zareah, Zorah, Zoreah.

6882. צָרְעִי Tsor'îy, *tsor-ee´*; or

צָרְעָתִי Tsor'âthîy, *tsor-aw-thee´*; patrial from 6881; a *Tsorite* or *Tsorathite*, i.e. inhab. of Tsorah:— Zorites, Zareathites, Zorathites.

6883. צָרַעַת tsâra'ath, *tsaw-rah´-ath*; from 6879; *leprosy*:— leprosy.

6884. צָרַף tsâraph, *tsaw-raf´*; a prim. root; to *fuse* (metal), i.e. *refine* (lit. or fig.):— cast, (re-) fine (-er), founder, goldsmith, melt, pure, purge away, try.

6885. צֹרְפִי Tsôrꞏphîy, *tso-ref-ee´*; from 6884; *refiner*; *Tsorephi* (with the art.), an Isr.:— goldsmith's.

6886. צָרְפַת Tsârꞏphath, *tsaq-ref-ath´*; from 6884; *refinement*; *Tsarephath*, a place in Pal.:— Zarephath.

6887. צָרַר tsârar, *tsaw-rar´*; a prim. root; to *cramp*, lit. or fig., tran. or intr. (as follows):— adversary, (be in) afflict (-ion), beseige, bind (up), (be in, bring) distress, enemy, narrower, oppress, pangs, shut up, be in a strait (trouble), vex.

6888. צְרֵרָה Tsꞏrêrâh, *tser-ay-raw´*; appar. by err. transc. for 6868; *Tsererah* for *Tseredah*:— Zererath.

6889. צֶרֶת Tsereth, *tseh´-reth*; perh. from 6671; *splendor*; *Tsereth*, an Isr.:— Zereth.

6890. צֶרֶת הַשַּׁחַר Tsereth hash-Shachar,

tseh´-reth hash-shakh´-ar; from the same as 6889 and 7837 with the art. interposed; *splendor of the dawn*; *Tsereth-hash-Shachar*, a place in Pal.:— Zareth-shahar.

6891. צָרְתָן Tsârꞏthân, *tsaw-reth-awn´*; perh. for 6868; *Tsarethan*, a place in Pal.:— Zarthan.

ק

6892. קֵא qê', *kay*; or

קִיא qîy', *kee*; from 6958; *vomit*:— vomit.

6893. קָאַת qâ'ath, *kaw-ath´*; from 6958; prob. the *pelican* (from *vomiting*):— cormorant.

6894. קַב qab, *kab*; from 6895; a *hollow*, i.e. vessel used as a (dry) *measure*:— cab.

6895. קָבַב qâbab, *kaw-bab´*; a prim. root; to *scoop* out, i.e. (fig.) to *malign* or *execrate* (i.e. *stab* with words):— × at all, curse.

6896. קֵבָה qêbâh, *kay-baw´*; from 6895; the *paunch* (as a *cavity*) or first stomach of ruminants:— maw.

6897. קֹבָה qôbâh, *ko´-baw*; from 6895; the *abdomen* (as a cavity):— belly.

6898. קֻבָּה qubbâh, *koob-baw´*; from 6895; a *pavilion* (as a domed *cavity*):— tent.

6899. קִבּוּץ qibbûwts, *kib-boots´*; from 6908; a *throng*:— company.

6900. קְבוּרָה qeꞏbûwrâh, *keb-oo-raw´*; or

קְבֻרָה qeꞏbûrâh, *keb-oo-raw´*; fem. pass. part. of 6912; *sepulture*; (concr.) a *sepulchre*:— burial, burying place, grave, sepulchre.

6901. קָבַל qâbal, *kaw-bal´*; a prim. root; to *admit*, i.e. *take* (lit. or fig.):— choose, (take) hold, receive, (under-) take.

6902. קְבַל qeꞏbal (Chald.), *keb-al´*; corresp. to 6901; to *acquire*:— receive, take.

6903. קְבֵל qeꞏbêl (Chald.), *keb-ale´*; or

קֳבֵל qŏbêl (Chald.), *kob-ale´*; (corresp. to 6905); (adv.) *in front of*; usually (with other particles) *on account of, so as, since, hence*:— + according to, + as, + because, before, + for this cause, + forasmuch as, + by this means, over against, by reason of, + that, + therefore, + though, + wherefore.

6904. קֹבֶל qôbel, *ko´-bel*; from 6901 in the sense of *confronting* (as standing *opposite* in order to receive); a *battering-ram*:— war.

6905. קָבָל qâbâl, *kaw-bawl´*; from 6901 in the sense of *opposite* [see 6904]; the *presence*, i.e. (adv.) *in front of*:— before.

6906. קָבַע qâba', *kaw-bah´*; a prim. root; to *cover*, i.e. (fig.) *defraud*:— rob, spoil.

6907. קֻבַּעַת qubba'ath, *koob-bah´-ath*; from 6906; a *goblet* (as deep like a *cover*):— dregs.

6908. קָבַץ qâbats, *kaw-bats´*; a prim. root; to *grasp*, i.e. *collect*:— assemble (selves), gather (bring) (together, selves together, up), heap, resort, × surely, take up.

6909. קַבְצְאֵל Qabtseꞏ'êl, *kab-tseh-ale´*; from 6908 and 410; *God has gathered*; *Kabtseël*, a place in Pal.:— Kabzeel. Comp. 3343.

6910. קְבֻצָה qeꞏbûtsâh, *keb-oo-tsaw´*; fem. pass. part. of 6908; a *hoard*:— × gather.

6911. קִבְצַיִם Qibtsayim, *kib-tsah´-yim*; dual from 6908; a *double heap*; *Kibtsajim*, a place in Pal.:— Kibzaim.

6912. קָבַר qâbar, *kaw-bar´*; a prim. root; to *inter*:— × in any wise, bury (-ier).

6913. קֶבֶר qeber, *keh´-ber*; or (fem.)

קִבְרָה qibrâh, *kib-raw´*; from 6912; a *sepulchre*:— burying place, grave, sepulchre.

קְבוּרָה qeꞏbûrâh. See 6900.

6914. קִבְרוֹת הַתַּאֲוָה Qibrôwth hatTa'ăvâh, *kib-rôth´ hat-tah-av-aw´*; from the fem. plur. of 6913 and 8378 with the art. interposed; *graves of the longing*; *Kibroth-hat-Taavh*, a place in the Desert:— Kibroth-hattaavah.

6915. קָדַד qâdad, *kaw-dad´*; a prim. root; to *shrivel* up, i.e. *contract* or *bend* the body (or neck) in deference:— bow (down) (the) head, stoop.

6916. קִדָּה qiddâh, *kid-daw´*; from 6915; *cassia* bark (as in *shrivelled* rolls):— cassia.

6917. קָדוּם qâdûwm, *kaw-doom´*; pass. part. of 6923; a *pristine* hero:— ancient.

6918. קָדוֹשׁ qâdôwsh, *kaw-doshe´*; or

קָדֹשׁ qâdôsh, *kaw-doshe´*; from 6942; *sacred* (cerem. or mor.); (as noun) *God* (by eminence), an *angel*, a *saint*, a *sanctuary*:— holy (One), saint.

6919. קָדַח qâdach, *kaw-dakh´*; a prim. root; to *inflame*:— burn, kindle.

6920. קַדַּחַת qaddachath, *kad-dakh´-ath*; from 6919; *inflammation*, i.e. febrile disease:— burning ague, fever.

6921. קָדִים qâdîym, *kaw-deem´*; or

קָדִם qâdim, *kaw-deem´*; from 6923; the *fore* or front part; hence, (by orientation) the *East* (often adv. *eastward*, for brevity the *east wind*):— east (-ward, wind).

6922. קַדִּישׁ qaddîysh (Chald.), *kad-deesh´*; corresp. to 6918:— holy (One), saint.

6923. קָדַם qâdam, *kaw-dam´*; a prim. root; to *project* (one self), i.e. *precede*; hence, to *anticipate, hasten, meet* (usually for help):— come (go, [flee]) before, + disappoint, meet, prevent.

6924. קֶדֶם qedem, *keh´-dem*; or

קֵדְמָה qêdmâh, *kayd´-maw*; from 6923; the *front*, of place (absolutely, the *fore part*, rel. the *East*) or time (*antiquity*); often used adv. (*before, anciently, eastward*):— aforetime, ancient (time), before, east (end, part, side, -ward), eternal, × ever (-lasting), forward, old, past. Comp. 6926.

6925. קֳדָם qŏdâm (Chald.), *kod-awm´*; or

קְדָם qeꞏdâm (Chald.) (Dan. 7:13), *ked-awm´*; corresp. to 6924; *before*:— before, × from, × I (thought), × me, + of, × it pleased, presence.

קָדִים **qâdîm**. See 6921.

6926. קִדְמָה **qidmâh**, *kid-maw'*; fem. of 6924; the *forward* part (or rel.) *East* (often adv. *on* (the) *east* or *in front*):— east (-ward).

6927. קְדְמָה **qadmâh**, *kad-maw'*; from 6923; *priority* (in time); also used adv. (*before*):— afore, antiquity, former (old) estate.

6928. קַדְמָה **qadmâh** (Chald.), *kad-maw'*; corresp. to 6927; *former* time:— afore [-time], ago.

קֵדְמָה **qêdmâh**. See 6924.

6929. קֵדְמָה **Qêdᵉmâh**, *kayd'-maw*; from 6923; *precedence*; *Kedemah*, a son of Ishmael:— Kedemah.

6930. קַדְמוֹן **qadmôwn**, *kad-mone'*; from 6923; *eastern*:— east.

6931. קַדְמוֹנִי **qadmôwnîy**, *kad-mo-nee'*; or

קַדְמֹנִי **qadmônîy**, *kad-mo-nee'*; from 6930; (of time) *anterior* or (of place) *oriental*:— ancient, they that went before, east, (thing of) old.

6932. קְדֵמוֹת **Qᵉdêmôwth**, *ked-ay-mothe'*; from 6923; *beginnings*; *Kedemoth*, a place in eastern Pal.:— Kedemoth.

6933. קַדְמַי **qadmay** (Chald.), *kad-mah'-ee*; from a root corresp. to 6923; *first*:— first.

6934. קַדְמִיאֵל **Qadmîy'êl**, *kad-mee-ale'*; from 6924 and 410; *presence of God*; *Kadmiël*, the name of three Isr.:— Kadmiel.

קַדְמֹנִי **qadmônîy**. See 6931.

6935. קַדְמֹנִי **Qadmônîy**, *kad-mo-nee'*; the same as 6931; *ancient*, i.e. aboriginal; *Kadmonite* (collect.), the name of a tribe in Pal.:— Kadmonites.

6936. קָדְקֹד **qodqôd**, *kod-kode'*; from 6915; the *crown* of the head (as the part most *bowed*):— crown (of the head), pate, scalp, top of the head.

6937. קָדַר **qâdar**, *kaw-dar'*; a prim. root; to *be ashy*, i.e. *dark*-colored; by impl. to *mourn* (in sackcloth or sordid garments):— be black (-ish), be (make) dark (-en), × heavily, (cause to) mourn.

6938. קֵדָר **Qêdâr**, *kay-dawr'*; from 6937; *dusky* (of the skin or the tent); *Kedar*, a son of Ishmael; also (collect.) *bedawin* (as his desc. or representatives):— Kedar.

6939. קִדְרוֹן **Qidrôwn**, *kid-rone'*; from 6937; *dusky* place; *Kidron*, a brook near Jerusalem:— Kidron.

6940. קַדְרוּת **qadrûwth**, *kad-rooth'*; from 6937; *duskiness*:— blackness.

6941. קְדֹרַנִּית **qᵉdôrannîyth**, *ked-o-ran-neeth'*; adv. from 6937; *blackish ones* (i.e. *in sackcloth*); used adv. in *mourning* weeds:— mournfully.

6942. קָדַשׁ **qâdash**, *kaw-dash'*; a prim. root; to *be* (caus. *make, pronounce* or *observe* as) *clean* (cerem. or mor.):— appoint, bid, consecrate, dedicate, defile, hallow, (be, keep) holy (-er, place), keep, prepare, proclaim, purify, sanctify (-ied one, self), × wholly.

6943. קֶדֶשׁ **Qedesh**, *keh'-desh*; from 6942; a *sanctum*; *Kedesh*, the name of four places in Pal.:— Kedesh.

6944. קֹדֶשׁ **qôdesh**, *ko'-desh*; from 6942; a *sacred* place or thing; rarely abstr. *sanctity*:— consecrated (thing), dedicated (thing), hallowed (thing), holiness, (× most) holy (× day, portion, thing), saint, sanctuary.

6945. קָדֵשׁ **qâdêsh**, *kaw-dashe'*; from 6942; a (quasi) *sacred* person, i.e. (tech.) a (male) *devotee* (by prostitution) to licentious idolatry:— sodomite, unclean.

6946. קָדֵשׁ **Qâdêsh**, *kaw-dashe'*; the same as 6945; *sanctuary*; *Kadesh*, a place in the Desert:— Kadesh. Comp. 6947.

קָדֹשׁ **qâdôsh**. See 6918.

6947. קָדֵשׁ בַּרְנֵעַ **Qâdêsh Barnêa'**, *kaw-dashe' bar-nay'-ah*; from the same as 6946 and an otherwise unused word (appar. compounded of a correspondent to 1251 and a der. of 5128) mean. *desert of a fugitive*; *Kadesh of* (the) *Wilderness of Wandering*; *Kadesh-Barneä*, a place in the Desert:— Kadesh-barnea.

6948. קְדֵשָׁה **qᵉdêshâh**, *ked-ay-shaw'*; fem. of 6945; a female *devotee* (i.e. *prostitute*):— harlot, whore.

6949. קָהָה **qâhâh**, *kaw-haw'*; a prim. root; to *be dull*:— be set on edge, be blunt.

6950. קָהַל **qâhal**, *kaw-hal'*; a prim. root; to *convoke*:— assemble (selves) (together), gather (selves) (together).

6951. קָהָל **qâhâl**, *kaw-hawl'*; from 6950; *assemblage* (usually concr.):— assembly, company, congregation, multitude.

6952. קְהִלָּה **qᵉhillâh**, *keh-hil-law'*; from 6950; an *assemblage*:— assembly, congregation.

6953. קֹהֶלֶת **qôheleth**, *ko-heh'-leth*; fem. of act. part. from 6950; a (female) *assembler* (i.e. *lecturer*); abstr. *preaching* (used as a "nom de plume", *Koheleth*):— preacher.

6954. קְהֵלָתָה **Qᵉhêlâthâh**, *keh-hay-law'-thaw*; from 6950; *convocation*; *Kehelathah*, a place in the Desert:— Kehelathah.

6955. קְהָת **Qᵉhâth**, *keh-hawth'*; from an unused root mean. to *ally oneself*; *allied*; *Kehath*, an Isr.:— Kohath.

6956. קְהָתִי **Qôhâthîy**, *ko-haw-thee'*; patron. from 6955; a *Kohathite* (collect.) or desc. of Kehath:— Kohathites.

6957. קַו **qav**, *kav*; or

קָו **qâv**, *kawv*; from 6960 [comp. 6961]; a *cord* (as *connecting*), espec. for measuring; fig. a *rule*; also a *rim*, a musical *string* or *accord*:— line. Comp. 6978.

6958. קוֹא **qôw'**, *ko*; or

קָיָה **qâyâh** (Jer. 25:27), *kaw-yaw'*; a prim. root; to *vomit*:— spue (out), vomit (out, up, up again).

6959. קוֹבַע **qôwba'**, *ko'-bah or ko-bah'*; a form collat. to 3553; a *helmet*:— helmet.

6960. קָוָה **qâvâh**, *kaw-vaw'*; a prim.

root; to *bind together* (perh. by *twisting*), i.e. *collect*; (fig.) to *expect*:— gather (together), look, patiently, tarry, wait (for, on, upon).

6961. קָוֶה **qâveh**, *kaw-veh'*; from 6960; a (measuring) *cord* (as if for *binding*):— line.

קוֹחַ **qôwach**. See 6495.

6962. קוּט **qûwṭ**, *koot*; a prim. root; prop. to *cut off*, i.e. (fig.) *detest*:— be grieved, loathe self.

6963. קוֹל **qôwl**, *kole*; or

קֹל **qôl**, *kole*; from an unused root mean. to *call* aloud; a *voice* or *sound*:— + aloud, bleating, crackling, cry (+ out), fame, lightness, lowing, noise, + hold peace, [pro-] claim, proclamation, + sing, sound, + spark, thunder (-ing), voice, + yell.

6964. קוֹלָיָה **Qôwlâyâh**, *ko-law-yaw'*; from 6963 and 3050; *voice of Jah*; *Kolajah*, the name of two Isr.:— Kolaiah.

6965. קוּם **qûwm**, *koom*; a prim. root; to *rise* (in various applications, lit., fig., intens. and caus.):— abide, accomplish, × be clearer, confirm, continue, decree, × be dim, endure, × enemy, enjoin, get up, make good, help, hold, (help to) lift up (again), make, × but newly, ordain, perform, pitch, raise (up), rear (up), remain, (a-) rise (up) (again, against), rouse up, set (up), (e-) stablish, (make to) stand (up), stir up, strengthen, succeed, (as-, make) sure (-ly), (be) up (-hold, -rising).

6966. קוּם **qûwm** (Chald.), *koom*; corresp. to 6965:— appoint, establish, make, raise up self, (a-) rise (up), (make to) stand, set (up).

6967. קוֹמָה **qôwmâh**, *ko-maw'*; from 6965; *height*:— × along, height, high, stature, tall.

6968. קוֹמְמִיּוּת **qôwmᵉmîyûwth**, *ko-mem-ee-yooth'*; from 6965; *elevation*, i.e. (adv.) *erectly* (fig.):— upright.

6969. קוּן **qûwn**, *koon*; a prim. root; to *strike* a musical note, i.e. *chant* or *wail* (at a funeral):— lament, mourning woman.

6970. קוֹעַ **Qôwa'**, *ko'-ah*; prob. from 6972 in the orig. sense of *cutting* off; *curtailment*; *Koä*, a region of Bab.:— Koa.

6971. קוֹף **qôwph**, *kofe*; or

קֹף **qôph**, *kofe*; prob. of for. or.; a *monkey*:— ape.

6972. קוּץ **qûwts**, *koots*; a prim. root; to *clip* off; used only as denom. from 7019; to *spend the harvest* season:— summer.

6973. קוּץ **qûwts**, *koots*; a prim. root [rather ident. with 6972 through the idea of *severing* oneself from (comp. 6962)]; to *be* (caus. *make*) *disgusted* or *anxious*:— abhor, be distressed, be grieved, loathe, vex, be weary.

6974. קוּץ **qûwts**, *koots*; a prim. root [rather ident. with 6972 through the idea of *abruptness* in starting up from sleep (comp. 3364)]; to *awake* (lit. or fig.):— arise, (be) (a-) wake, watch.

6975. קוֹץ **qôwts**, *kotse*; or

קֹץ **qôts**, *kotse;* from 6972 (in the sense of *pricking*); a *thorn:*— thorn.

6976. קוֹץ **Qôwts**, *kotse;* the same as 6975; *Kots*, the name of two Isr.:— Koz, Hakkoz [*incl. the art.*].

6977. קְוֻצָּה **qᵉvutstsâh**, *kev-oots-tsaw´;* fem. pass. part. of 6972 in its orig. sense; a *forelock* (as *shorn*):— lock.

6978. קַו־קַו **qav-qav**, *kav-kav´;* from 6957 (in the sense of a *fastening*); *stalwart:*— × meted out.

6979. קוּר **qûwr**, *koor;* a prim. root; to *trench;* by impl. to *throw forth;* also (denom. from 7023) to *wall up*, whether lit. (to *build* a wall) or fig. (to *estop*):— break down, cast out, destroy, dig.

6980. קוּר **qûwr**, *koor;* from 6979; (only plur.) *trenches*, i.e. a *web* (as if so formed):— web.

6981. קוֹרֵא **Qôwrê'**, *ko-ray´;* or

קֹרֵא **Qôrê'** (1 Chron. 26:1), *ko-ray´;* act. part. of 7121; *crier; Korè*, the name of two Isr.:— Kore.

6982. קוֹרָה **qôwrâh**, *ko-raw´;* or

קֹרָה **qôrâh**, *ko-raw´;* from 6979; a *rafter* (forming *trenches* as it were); by impl. a *roof:*— beam, roof.

6983. קוֹשׁ **qôwsh**, *koshe;* a prim. root; to *bend;* used only as denom. for 3369, to *set a trap:*— lay a snare.

6984. קוּשָׁיָהוּ **Qûwshâyâhûw**, *koo-shaw-yaw´-hoo;* from the pass. part. of 6983 and 3050; *entrapped of Jah; Kushajah*, an Isr.:— Kushaiah.

6985. קַט **qaṭ**, *kat;* from 6990 in the sense of *abbreviation;* a *little*, i.e. (adv.) *merely:*— very.

6986. קֶטֶב **qeṭeb**, *keh´-teb;* from an unused root mean. to *cut off; ruin:*— destroying, destruction.

6987. קֹטֶב **qôṭeb**, *ko´-teb;* from the same as 6986; *extermination:*— destruction.

6988. קְטוֹרָה **qᵉṭôwrâh**, *ket-o-raw´;* from 6999; *perfume:*— incense.

6989. קְטוּרָה **Qᵉṭûwrâh**, *ket-oo-raw´;* fem. pass. part. of 6999; *perfumed; Keturah*, a wife of Abraham:— Keturah.

6990. קָטַט **qâṭaṭ**, *kaw-tat´;* a prim. root; to *clip* off, i.e. (fig.) *destroy:*— be cut off.

6991. קָטַל **qâṭal**, *kaw-tal´;* a prim. root; prop. to *cut* off, i.e. (fig.) *put to death:*— kill, slay.

6992. קְטַל **qᵉṭal** (Chald.), *ket-al´;* corresp. to 6991; to *kill:*— slay.

6993. קֶטֶל **qeṭel**, *keh´-tel;* from 6991; a violent *death:*— slaughter.

6994. קָטֹן **qâṭôn**, *kaw-tone´;* a prim. root [rather denom. from 6996]; to *diminish*, i.e. *be* (caus. *make*) *diminutive* or (fig.) *of no account:*— be a (make) small (thing), be not worthy.

6995. קֹטֶן **qôṭen**, *ko´-ten;* from 6994; a *pettiness*, i.e. the *little finger:*— little finger.

6996. קָטָן **qâṭân**, *kaw-tawn´;* or

קָטֹן **qâṭôn**, *kaw-tone´;* from 6962; *abbreviated*, i.e. *diminutive*, lit. (in quantity, size or number) or fig. (in age or importance):— least, less (-er), little

(one), small (-est, one, quantity, thing), young (-er, -est).

6997. קָטָן **Qâṭân**, *kaw-tawn´;* the same as 6996; *small; Katan*, an Isr.:— Hakkatan [*incl. the art.*].

6998. קָטַף **qâṭaph**, *kaw-taf´;* a prim. root; to *strip* off:— crop off, cut down (up), pluck.

6999. קָטַר **qâṭar**, *kaw-tar´;* a prim. root [rather ident. with 7000 through the idea of fumigation in a *close* place and perh. thus *driving* out the occupants]; to *smoke*, i.e. turn into fragrance by fire (espec. as an act of worship):— burn (incense, sacrifice) (upon), (altar for) incense, kindle, offer (incense, a sacrifice).

7000. קָטַר **qâṭar**, *kaw-tar´;* a prim. root; to *inclose:*— join.

7001. קְטַר **qᵉṭar** (Chald.), *ket-ar´;* from a root corresp. to 7000; a *knot* (as *tied* up), i.e. (fig.) a *riddle;* also a *vertebra* (as if a knot):— doubt, joint.

7002. קִטֵּר **qiṭṭêr**, *kit-tare´;* from 6999; *perfume:*— perfume.

7003. קִטְרוֹן **Qiṭrôwn**, *kit-rone´;* from 6999; *fumigative; Kitron*, a place in Pal.:— Kitron.

7004. קְטֹרֶת **qᵉṭôreth**, *ket-o´-reth;* from 6999; a *fumigation:*— (sweet) incense, perfume.

7005. קַטָּת **Qaṭṭâth**, *kat-tawth´;* from 6996; *littleness; Kattath*, a place in Pal.:— Kattath.

7006. קָיָה **qâyâh**, *kaw-yaw´;* a prim. root; to *vomit:*— spue.

7007. קַיִט **qâyiṭ** (Chald.), *kah´-yit;* corresp. to 7019; *harvest:*— summer.

7008. קִיטוֹר **qîyṭôwr**, *kee-tore´;* or

קִיטֹר **qîyṭôr**, *kee-tore´;* from 6999; a *fume*, i.e. *cloud:*— smoke, vapour.

7009. קִים **qîym**, *keem;* from 6965; an *opponent* (as *rising* against one), i.e. (collect.) enemies:— substance.

7010. קְיָם **qᵉyâm** (Chald.), *keh-yawm´;* from 6966; an *edict* (as *arising* in law):— decree, statute.

7011. קַיָּם **qayâm** (Chald.), *kah-yawm´;* from 6966; *permanent* (as *rising* firmly):— stedfast, sure.

7012. קִימָה **qîymâh**, *kee-maw´;* from 6965; an *arising:*— rising up.

קִימוֹשׁ **Qîymôwsh**. See 7057.

7013. קַיִן **qayin**, *kah´-yin;* from 6969 in the orig. sense of *fixity;* a *lance* (as *striking fast*):— spear.

7014. קַיִן **Qayin**, *kah´-yin;* the same as 7013 (with a play upon the affinity to 7069); *Kajin*, the name of the first child, also of a place in Pal., and of an Oriental tribe:— Cain, Kenite (-s).

7015. קִינָה **qîynâh**, *kee-naw´;* from 6969; a *dirge* (as accompanied by *beating* the breasts or on instruments):— lamentation.

7016. קִינָה **Qîynâh**, *kee-naw´;* the same as 7015; *Kinah*, a place in Pal.:— Kinah.

7017. קֵינִי **Qêynîy**, *kay-nee´;* or

קִינִי **Qîynîy** (1 Chron. 2:55) *kee-nee´;* patron. from 7014; a *Kenite* or member of the tribe of Kajin:— Kenite.

7018. קֵינָן **Qêynân**, *kay-nawn´;* from the same as 7064; *fixed; Kenan*, an antediluvian:— Cainan, Kenan.

7019. קַיִץ **qayits**, *kah´-yits;* from 6972; *harvest* (as the *crop*), whether the product (grain or fruit) or the (dry) season:— summer (fruit, house).

7020. קִיצוֹן **qîytsôwn**, *kee-tsone´;* from 6972; *terminal:*— out(utter-) most.

7021. קִיקָיוֹן **qîyqâyôwn**, *kee-kaw-yone´;* perh. from 7006; the *gourd* (as *nauseous*):— gourd.

7022. קִיקָלוֹן **qîyqâlôwn**, *kee-kaw-lone´;* from 7036; intense *disgrace:*— shameful spewing.

7023. קִיר **qîyr**, *keer;* or

קִר **qîr** (Isa. 22:5), *keer;* or (fem.)

קִירָה **qîyrâh**, *kee-raw´;* from 6979; a *wall* (as built in a *trench*):— + mason, side, town, × very, wall.

7024. קִיר **Qîyr**, *keer;* the same as 7023; *fortress; Kir*, a place in Ass.; also one in Moab:— Kir. Comp. 7025.

7025. קִיר חֶרֶשׂ **Qîyr Cheres**, *keer kheh´-res;* or (fem. of the latter word)

קִיר חֲרֶשֶׂת **Qîyr Chăreseth**, *keer khar-eh´-seth;* from 7023 and 2789; *fortress of earthenware; Kir-Cheres* or *Kir-Chareseth*, a place in Moab:— Kirharaseth, Kir-hareseth, Kir-haresh, Kir-heres.

7026. קֵירֹס **Qêyrôç**, *kay-roce´;* or

קֵרֹס **Qêrôç**, *kay-roce´;* from the same as 7166; *ankled; Keros*, one of the Nethinim:— Keros.

7027. קִישׁ **Qîysh**, *keesh;* from 6983; a *bow; Kish*, the name of five Isr.:— Kish.

7028. קִישׁוֹן **Qîyshôwn**, *kee-shone´;* from 6983; *winding; Kishon*, a river of Pal.:— Kishon, Kison.

7029. קִישִׁי **Qîyshîy**, *kee-shee´;* from 6983; *bowed; Kishi*, an Isr.:— Kishi.

7030. קִיתָרֹס **qîythârôç** (Chald.), *kee-thaw-roce´;* of Gr. or. (κίθαρις); a *lyre:*— harp.

7031. קַל **qal**, *kal;* contr. from 7043; *light;* (by impl.) *rapid* (also adv.):— light, swift (-ly).

7032. קָל **qâl** (Chald.), *kawl;* corresp. to 6963; *sound, voice.*

קֹל **qôl**. See 6963.

7033. קָלָה **qâlâh**, *kaw-law´;* a prim. root [rather ident. with 7034 through the idea of *shrinkage* by heat]; to *toast*, i.e. *scorch* partially or slowly:— dried, loathsome, parch, roast.

7034. קָלָה **qâlâh**, *kaw-law´;* a prim. root; to *be light* (as impl. in *rapid* motion), but fig. only (*be* [caus. *hold*] *in contempt*):— base, contemn, despise, lightly esteem, set light, seem vile.

7035. קָלַהּ **qâlahh**, *kaw-lah´;* for 6950; to *assemble:*— gather together.

7036. קָלוֹן **qâlôwn**, *kaw-lone´;* from 7034; *disgrace;* (by impl.) the *pudenda:*— confusion, dishonour, ignominy, reproach, shame.

7037. קַלַּחַת **qallachath**, *kal-lakh´-ath;* appar. but a form for 6747; a *kettle:*— caldron.

7038. קָלַט **qâlaṭ**, *kaw-lat'*; a prim. root; to *maim*:— lacking in his parts.

7039. קָלִי **qâlîy**, *kaw-lee'*; or

קָלִא **qâlîy'**, *kaw-lee'*; from 7033; *roasted* ears of grain:— parched corn.

7040. קַלַּי **Qallay**, *kal-lah'-ee*; from 7043; *frivolous*; *Kallai*, an Isr.:— Kallai.

7041. קְלָיָה **Qêlâyâh**, *kay-law-yaw'*; from 7034; *insignificance*; *Kelajah*, an Isr.:— Kelaiah.

7042. קְלִיטָא **Qᵉlîyṭâ'**, *kel-ee-taw'*; from 7038; *maiming*; *Kelita*, the name of three Isr.:— Kelita.

7043. קָלַל **qâlal**, *kaw-lal'*; a prim. root; to *be* (caus. *make*) *light*, lit. (*swift*, *small*, *sharp*, etc.) or fig. (*easy*, *trifling*, *vile*, etc.):— abate, make bright, bring into contempt, (ac-) curse, despise, (be) ease (-y, -ier), (be a, make, make somewhat, move, seem a, set) light (-en, -er, -ly, -ly afflict, -ly esteem, thing), × slight [-ly], be swift (-er), (be, be more, make, re-) vile, whet.

7044. קָלָל **qâlâl**, *kaw-lawl'*; from 7043; *brightened* (as if *sharpened*):— burnished, polished.

7045. קְלָלָה **qᵉlâlâh**, *kel-aw-law'*; from 7043; *vilification*:— (ac-) curse (-d, -ing).

7046. קָלַס **qâlaç**, *kaw-las'*; a prim. root; to *disparage*, i.e. ridicule:— mock, scoff, scorn.

7047. קֶלֶס **qeleç**, *keh'-les*; from 7046; a *laughing-stock*:— derision.

7048. קַלָּסָה **qallâçâh**, *kal-law-saw'*; intens. from 7046; *ridicule*:— mocking.

7049. קָלַע **qâla'**, *kaw-lah'*; a prim. root; to *sling*; also to *carve* (as if a *circular* motion, or into *light* forms):— carve, sling (out).

7050. קֶלַע **qela'**, *keh'-lah*; from 7049; a *sling*; also a (door) *screen* (as if *slung* across), or the *valve* (of the door) itself:— hanging, leaf, sling.

7051. קַלָּע **qallâ'**, *kal-law'*; intens. from 7049; a *slinger*:— slinger.

7052. קְלֹקֵל **qᵉlôqêl**, *kel-o-kale'*; from 7043; *insubstantial*:— light.

7053. קִלְּשׁוֹן **qillᵉshôwn**, *kil-lesh-one'*; from an unused root mean. to *prick*; a *prong*, i.e. hay-fork:— fork.

7054. קָמָה **qâmâh**, *kaw-maw'*; fem. of act. part. of 6965; something that *rises*, i.e. a *stalk* of grain:— (standing) corn, grown up, stalk.

7055. קְמוּאֵל **Qᵉmûw'êl**, *kem-oo-ale'*; from 6965 and 410; *raised of God*; *Kemuël*, the name of a rel. of Abraham, and of two Isr.:— Kemuel.

7056. קָמוֹן **Qâmôwn**, *kaw-mone'*; from 6965; an *elevation*; *Kamon*, a place E. of the Jordan:— Camon.

7057. קִמּוֹשׁ **qimmôwsh**, *kim-moshe'*; or

קִימוֹשׁ **qîymôwsh**, *kee-moshe'*; from an unused root mean. to *sting*; a *prickly* plant:— nettle. Comp. 7063.

7058. קֶמַח **qemach**, *keh'-makh*; from an unused root prob. mean. to *grind*; *flour*:— flour, meal.

7059. קָמַט **qâmaṭ**, *kaw-mat'*; a prim. root; to *pluck*, i.e. *destroy*:— cut down, fill with wrinkles.

7060. קָמַל **qâmal**, *kaw-mal'*; a prim. root; to *wither*:— hew down, wither.

7061. קָמַץ **qâmats**, *kaw-mats'*; a prim. root; to *grasp* with the hand:— take an handful.

7062. קֹמֶץ **qômets**, *ko'mets*; from 7061; a *grasp*, i.e. *handful*:— handful.

7063. קִמָּשׁוֹן **qimmâshôwn**, *kim-maw-shone'*; from the same as 7057; a *prickly* plant:— thorn.

7064. קֵן **qên**, *kane*; contr. from 7077; a *nest* (as *fixed*), sometimes incl. the *nestlings*; fig. a *chamber* or *dwelling*:— nest, room.

7065. קָנָא **qânâ'**, *kaw-naw'*; a prim. root; to *be* (caus. *make*) *zealous*, i.e. (in a bad sense) *jealous* or *envious*:— (be) envy (-ious), be (move to, provoke to) jealous (-y), × very, (be) zeal (-ous).

7066. קְנָא **qᵉnâ'** (Chald.), *ken-aw'*; corresp. to 7069; to *purchase*:— buy.

7067. קַנָּא **qannâ'**, *kan-naw'*; from 7065; *jealous*:— jealous. Comp. 7072.

7068. קִנְאָה **qin'âh**, *kin-aw'*; from 7065; *jealousy* or *envy*:— envy (-ied), jealousy, × sake, zeal.

7069. קָנָה **qânâh**, *kaw-naw'*; a prim. root; to *erect*, i.e. *create*; by extens. to *procure*, espec. by purchase (caus. *sell*); by impl. to *own*:— attain, buy (-er), teach to keep cattle, get, provoke to jealousy, possess (-or), purchase, recover, redeem, × surely, × verily.

7070. קָנֶה **qâneh**, *kaw-neh'*; from 7069; a *reed* (as *erect*); by resemblance a *rod* (espec. for measuring), *shaft*, *tube*, *stem*, the *radius* (of the arm), *beam* (of a steelyard):— balance, bone, branch, calamus, cane, reed, × spearman, stalk.

7071. קָנָה **Qânâh**, *kaw-naw'*; fem. of 7070; *reediness*; *Kanah*, the name of a stream and of a place in Pal.:— Kanah.

7072. קַנּוֹא **qannôw'**, *kan-no'*; for 7067; *jealous* or *angry*:— jealous.

7073. קְנַז **Qᵉnaz**, *ken-az'*; prob. from an unused root mean. to *hunt*; *hunter*; *Kenaz*, the name of an Edomite and of two Isr.:— Kenaz.

7074. קְנִזִּי **Qᵉnizzîy**, *ken-iz-zee'*; patron. from 7073, a *Kenizzite* or desc. of Kenaz:— Kenezite, Kenizzites.

7075. קִנְיָן **qinyân**, *kin-yawn'*; from 7069; *creation*, i.e. (concr.) *creatures*; also *acquisition*, *purchase*, *wealth*:— getting, goods, × with money, riches, substance.

7076. קִנָּמוֹן **qinnâmôwn**, *kin-naw-mone'*; from an unused root (mean. to *erect*); *cinnamon* bark (as in *upright* rolls):— cinnamon.

7077. קָנַן **qânan**, *kaw-nan'*; a prim. root; to *erect*; but used only as denom. from 7064; to *nestle*, i.e. *build* or *occupy* as a nest:— make ... nest.

7078. קֶנֶץ **qenets**, *keh'-nets*; from an unused root mean. to *wrench*; *perversion*:— end.

7079. קְנָת **Qᵉnâth**, *ken-awth'*; from 7069; *possession*; *Kenath*, a place E. of the Jordan:— Kenath.

7080. קָסַם **qâçam**, *kaw-sam'*; a prim. root; prop. to *distribute*, i.e. *determine* by lot or magical scroll; by impl. to *divine*:— divine (-r, -ation), prudent, soothsayer, use [divination].

7081. קֶסֶם **qeçem**, *keh'-sem*; from 7080; a *lot*; also *divination* (incl. its *fee*), *oracle*:— (reward of) divination, divine sentence, witchcraft.

7082. קָסַס **qâçaç**, *kaw-sas'*; a prim. root; to *lop off*:— cut off.

7083. קֶסֶת **qeçeth**, *keh'-seth*; from the same as 3563 (or as 7185); prop. a *cup*, i.e. an *ink-stand*:— inkhorn.

7084. קְעִילָה **Qᵉʿîylâh**, *keh-ee-law'*; perh. from 7049 in the sense of *inclosing*; *citadel*; *Keïlah*, a place in Pal.:— Keilah.

7085. קַעֲקַע **qaʿăqa'**, *kah-ak-ah'*; from the same as 6970; an *incision* or gash:— + mark.

7086. קְעָרָה **qᵉʿârâh**, *keh-aw-raw'*; prob. from 7167; a *bowl* (as *cut* out hollow):— charger, dish.

קֹף **qôph**. See 6971.

7087. קָפָא **qâphâ'**, *kaw-faw'*; a prim. root; to *shrink*, i.e. *thicken* (as unracked wine, curdled milk, clouded sky, frozen water):— congeal, curdle, dark°, settle.

7088. קָפַד **qâphad**, *kaw-fad'*; a prim. root; to *contract*, i.e. *roll together*:— cut off.

7089. קְפָדָה **qᵉphâdâh**, *kef-aw-daw'*; from 7088; *shrinking*, i.e. *terror*:— destruction.

7090. קִפּוֹד **qippôwd**, *kip-pode'*; or

קִפֹּד **qippôd**, *kip-pode'*; from 7088; a species of *bird*, perh. the *bittern* (from its *contracted* form):— bittern.

7091. קִפּוֹז **qippôwz**, *kip-poze'*; from an unused root mean. to *contract*, i.e. *spring* forward; an *arrow-snake* (as *darting* on its prey):— great owl.

7092. קָפַץ **qâphats**, *kaw-fats'*; a prim. root; to *draw together*, i.e. *close*; by impl. to *leap* (by *contracting* the limbs); spec. to *die* (from *gathering* up the feet):— shut (up), skip, stop, take out of the way.

7093. קֵץ **qêts**, *kates*; contr. from 7112; an *extremity*; adv. (with prep. pref.) *after*:— + after, (utmost) border, end, [in-] finite, × process.

קֹץ **qôts**. See 6975.

7094. קָצַב **qâtsab**, *kaw-tsab'*; a prim. root; to *clip*, or (gen.) *chop*:— cut down, shorn.

7095. קֶצֶב **qetseb**, *keh'-tseb*; from 7094; *shape* (as if *cut* out); *base* (as if there *cut* off):— bottom, size.

7096. קָצָה **qâtsâh**, *kaw-tsaw'*; a prim. root; to *cut off*; (fig.) to *destroy*; (partially) to *scrape* off:— cut off, cut short, scrape (off).

7097. קָצֶה **qâtseh**, *kaw-tseh'*; or (neg. only)

קֵצֶה **qêtseh**, *kay'-tseh*; from 7096; an *extremity* (used in a great variety of applications and idioms; comp. 7093):— × after, border, brim, brink, edge, end, [in-] finite, frontier, outmost coast, quarter, shore, (out-) side, × some, ut(-ter-) most (part).

7098. קָצָה **qâtsâh**, kaw-tsaw´; fem. of 7097; a *termination* (used like 7097):— coast, corner, (selv-) edge, lowest, (uttermost) part.

7099. קֶצֶו **qetsev**, keh´-tsev; and (fem.)

קִצְוָה **qitsvâh**, kits-vaw´; from 7096; a *limit* (used like 7097, but with less variety):— end, edge, uttermost part.

7100. קֶצַח **qetsach**, keh´-tsakh; from an unused root appar. mean. to *incise; fennel-flower* (from its *pungency*):— fitches.

7101. קָצִין **qâtsîyn**, kaw-tseen´; from 7096 in the sense of *determining*; a *magistrate* (as *deciding*) or other *leader*:— captain, guide, prince, ruler. Comp. 6278.

7102. קְצִיעָה **qᵉtsîy'âh**, kets-ee-aw´; from 7106; *cassia* (as *peeled*; plur. the *bark*):— cassia.

7103. קְצִיעָה **Qᵉtsîy'âh**, kets-ee-aw´; the same as 7102; *Ketsiah*, a daughter of Job:— Kezia.

7104. קְצִיץ **Qᵉtsîyts**, kets-eets´; from 7112; *abrupt*; *Keziz*, a valley in Pal.:— Keziz.

7105. קָצִיר **qâtsîyr**, kaw-tseer´; from 7114; *severed*, i.e. *harvest* (as *reaped*); the crop, the time, the reaper, or fig.; also a *limb* (of a tree, or simply *foliage*):— bough, branch, harvest (man).

7106. קָצַע **qâtsa'**, kaw-tsah´; a prim. root; to *strip off*, i.e. (partially) *scrape*; by impl. to *segregate* (as an angle):— cause to scrape, corner.

7107. קָצַף **qâtsaph**, kaw-tsaf´; a prim. root; to *crack off*, i.e. (fig.) *burst out* in rage:— (be) anger (-ry), displease, fret self, (provoke to) wrath (come), be wroth.

7108. קְצַף **qᵉtsaph** (Chald.), kets-af´; corresp. to 7107; to *become enraged*:— be furious.

7109. קְצַף **qᵉtsaph** (Chald.), kets-af´; from 7108; *rage*:— wrath.

7110. קֶצֶף **qetseph**, keh´-tsef; from 7107; a *splinter* (as chipped off); fig. *rage* or *strife*:— foam, indignation, × sore, wrath.

7111. קְצָפָה **qᵉtsâphâh**, kets-aw-faw´; from 7107; a *fragment*:— bark (-ed).

7112. קָצַץ **qâtsats**, kaw-tsats´; a prim. root; to *chop off* (lit. or fig.):— cut (asunder, in pieces, in sunder, off), × utmost.

7113. קְצַץ **qᵉtsats** (Chald.), kets-ats´; corresp. to 7112:— cut off.

7114. קָצַר **qâtsar**, kaw-tsar´; a prim. root; to *dock off*, i.e. *curtail* (tran. or intr., lit. or fig.); espec. to *harvest* (grass or grain):— × at all, cut down, much discouraged, grieve, harvestman, lothe, mourn, reap (-er), (be, wax) short (-en, -er), straiten, trouble, vex.

7115. קֹצֶר **qôtser**, ko´-tser; from 7114; *shortness* (of spirit), i.e. *impatience*:— anguish.

7116. קָצֵר **qâtsêr**, kaw-tsare´; from 7114; *short* (whether in size, number,

life, strength or temper):— few, hasty, small, soon.

7117. קְצָת **qᵉtsâth**, kets-awth´; from 7096; a *termination* (lit. or fig.); also (by impl.) a *portion*; adv. (with prep. pref.) *after*:— end, part, × some.

7118. קְצָת **qᵉtsâth** (Chald.), kets-awth´; corresp. to 7117:— end, partly.

7119. קַר **qar**, kar; contr. from an unused root mean. to *chill*; *cool*; fig. *quiet*:— cold, excellent [from the marg.].

קִר **qîr**. See 7023.

7120. קֹר **qôr**, kore; from the same as 7119; *cold*:— cold.

7121. קָרָא **qârâ'**, kaw-raw´; a prim. root [rather ident. with 7122 through the idea of *accosting* a person met]; to *call* out to (i.e. prop. *address* by name, but used in a wide variety of applications):— bewray [self], that are bidden, call (for, forth, self, upon), cry (unto), (be) famous, guest, invite, mention, (give) name, preach, (make) proclaim (-ation), pronounce, publish, read, renowned, say.

7122. קָרָא **qârâ'**, kaw-raw´; a prim. root; to *encounter*, whether accidentally or in a hostile manner:— befall, (by) chance, (cause to) come (upon), fall out, happen, meet.

7123. קְרָא **qᵉrâ'** (Chald.), ker-aw´; corresp. to 7121:— call, cry, read.

7124. קֹרֵא **qôrê'**, ko-ray´; prop. act. part. of 7121; a *caller*, i.e. *partridge* (from its *cry*):— partridge. See also 6981.

7125. קִרְאָה **qîr'âh**, keer-aw´; from 7122; an *encountering*, accidental, friendly or hostile (also adv. *opposite*):— × against (he come), help, meet, seek, × to, × in the way.

7126. קָרַב **qârab**, kaw-rab´; a prim. root; to *approach* (caus. *bring near*) for whatever purpose:— (cause to) approach, (cause to) bring (forth, near), (cause to) come (near, nigh), (cause to) draw near (nigh), go (near), be at hand, join, be near, offer, present, produce, make ready, stand, take.

7127. קְרֵב **qᵉrêb** (Chald.), ker-abe´; corresp. to 7126:— approach, come (near, nigh), draw near.

7128. קְרָב **qᵉrâb**, ker-awb´; from 7126; hostile *encounter*:— battle, war.

7129. קְרָב **qᵉrâb** (Chald.), ker-awb´; corresp. to 7128:— war.

7130. קֶרֶב **qereb**, keh´-reb; from 7126; prop. the *nearest* part, i.e. the *center*, whether lit., fig. or adv. (espec. with prep.):— × among, × before, bowels, × unto charge, + eat (up), × heart, × him, × in, inward (× -ly, part, -s, thought), midst, + out of, purtenance, × therein, × through, × within self.

7131. קָרֵב **qârêb**, kaw-rabe´; from 7126; *near*:— approach, come (near, nigh), draw near.

קָרֹב **qârôb**. See 7138.

7132. קְרָבָה **qᵉrâbâh**, ker-aw-baw´; from 7126; *approach*:— approaching, draw near.

7133. קָרְבָּן **qorbân**, kor-bawn´; or

קֻרְבָּן **qurbân**, koor-bawn´; from 7126; something *brought near* the altar, i.e. a sacrificial *present*:— oblation, that is offered, offering.

7134. קַרְדֹּם **qardôm**, kar-dome´; perh. from 6923 in the sense of *striking* upon; an *axe*:— ax.

7135. קָרָה **qârâh**, kaw-raw´; fem. of 7119; *coolness*:— cold.

7136. קָרָה **qârâh**, kaw-raw´; a prim. root; to *light upon* (chiefly by accident); caus. to *bring about*; spec. to *impose* timbers (for roof or floor):— appoint, lay (make) beams, befall, bring, come (to pass unto), floor, [hap] was, happen (unto), meet, send good speed.

7137. קָרֶה **qâreh**, kaw-reh´; from 7136; an (unfortunate) *occurrence*, i.e. some accidental (ceremonial) *disqualification*:— uncleanness that chanceth.

קֹרָה **qôrâh**. See 6982.

7138. קָרוֹב **qârôwb**, kaw-robe´; or

קָרֹב **qârôb**, kaw-robe´; from 7126; *near* (in place, kindred or time):— allied, approach, at hand, + any of kin, kinsfolk (-sman), (that is) near (of kin), neighbour, (that is) next, (them that come) nigh (at hand), more ready, short (-ly).

7139. קָרַח **qârach**, kaw-rakh´; a prim. root; to *depilate*:— make (self) bald.

7140. קֶרַח **qerach**, keh´-rakh; or

קֹרַח **qôrach**, ko´-rakh; from 7139; *ice* (as if bald, i.e. *smooth*); hence, *hail*; by resemblance, rock *crystal*:— crystal, frost, ice.

7141. קֹרַח **Qôrach**, ko´rakh; from 7139; *ice*; *Korach*, the name of two Edomites and three Isr.:— Korah.

7142. קֵרֵחַ **qêrêach**, kay-ray´-akh; from 7139; *bald* (on the back of the head):— bald (head).

7143. קָרֵחַ **Qârêach**, kaw-ray´-akh; from 7139; *bald*; *Kareäch*, an Isr.:— Careah, Kareah.

7144. קָרְחָה **qorchâh**, kor-khaw´; or

קָרְחָא **qorchâ'** (Ezek. 27:31), kor-khaw´; from 7139; *baldness*:— bald (-ness), × utterly.

7145. קָרְחִי **Qorchîy**, kor-khee´; patron. from 7141; a *Korachite* (collect.) or desc. of Korach:— Korahite, Korathite, sons of Kore, Korhite.

7146. קָרַחַת **qârachath**, kaw-rakh´-ath; from 7139; a *bald* spot (on the back of the head); fig. a *threadbare* spot (on the back side of the cloth):— bald head, bare within.

7147. קְרִי **qᵉrîy**, ker-ee´; from 7136; *hostile encounter*:— contrary.

7148. קָרִיא **qârîy'**, kaw-ree´; from 7121; *called*, i.e. *select*:— famous, renowned.

7149. קִרְיָא **qiryâ'** (Chald.), keer-yaw´; or

קִרְיָה **qiryâh** (Chald.), keer-yaw´; corresp. to 7151:— city.

7150. קְרִיאָה **qᵉrîy'âh**, ker-ee-aw´; from 7121; a *proclamation*:— preaching.

7151. קִרְיָה **qiryâh**, kir-yaw´; from 7136 in the sense of *flooring*, i.e. *building*; a *city*:— city.

7152. קְרִיֹּת **Qᵉrîyôwth**, ker-ee-yoth´;

plur. of 7151; *buildings; Kerioth,* the name of two places in Pal.:— Kerioth, Kirioth.

7153. קִרְיַת עַרְבַּע **Qiryath 'Arba',** *keer-yath' ar-bah';* or (with the art. interposed)

קִרְיַת הָאַרְבַּע **Qiryath hâ-'Arba'** (Neh. 11:25), *keer-yath' haw-ar-bah';* from 7151 and 704 or 702; *city of Arba,* or *city of the four* (giants); *Kirjath-Arba* or *Kirjath-ha-Arba,* a place in Pal.:— Kirjath-arba.

7154. קִרְיַת בַּעַל **Qiryath Ba'al,** *keer-yath' bah'-al;* from 7151 and 1168; *city of Baal; Kirjath-Baal,* a place in Pal.:— Kirjath-baal.

7155. קִרְיַת חֻצוֹת **Qiryath Chûtsôwth,** *keer-yath' khoo-tsôth';* from 7151 and the fem. plur. of 2351; *city of streets; Kirjath-Chutsoth,* a place in Moab:— Kirjath-huzoth.

7156. קִרְיָתַיִם **Qiryâthayim,** *keer-yaw-thah'-yim;* dual of 7151; *double city; Kirjathaïm,* the name of two places in Pal.:— Kiriathaim, Kirjathaim.

7157. קִרְיַת יְעָרִים **Qiryath Yeʿârîym,** *keer-yath' yeh-aw-reem';* or (Jer. 26:20) with the art. interposed; or (Josh. 18:28) simply the former part of the word; or

קִרְיַת עָרִים **Qiryath 'Ârîym,** *keer-yath' aw-reem';* from 7151 and the plur. of 3293 or 5892; *city of forests,* or *city of towns; Kirjath-Jeärim* or *Kirjath-Arim,* a place in Pal.:— Kirjath-jearim, Kirjath-arim.

7158. קִרְיַת סַנָּה **Qiryath Çannâh,** *keer-yath' san-naw';* or

קִרְיַת סֵפֶר **Qiryath Çépher,** *keer-yath' say-fer;* from 7151 and a simpler fem. from the same as 5577, or (for the latter name) 5612; *city of branches,* or *of a book; Kirjath-Sannah* or *Kirjath-Sepher,* a place in Pal.:— Kirjath-sannah, Kirjath-sepher.

7159. קָרַם **qâram,** *kaw-ram';* a prim. root; to *cover:*— cover.

7160. קָרַן **qâran,** *kaw-ran';* a prim. root; to *push* or gore; used only as denom. from 7161, to *shoot out horns;* fig. *rays:*— have horns, shine.

7161. קֶרֶן **qeren,** *keh'-ren;* from 7160; a *horn* (as *projecting*); by impl. a *flask, cornet;* by resembl. an elephant's *tooth* (i.e. *ivory*), a *corner* (of the altar), a *peak* (of a mountain), a *ray* (of light); fig. *power:*— × hill, horn.

7162. קֶרֶן **qeren** (Chald.), *keh'-ren;* corresp. to 7161; a *horn* (lit. or for sound):— horn, cornet.

7163. קֶרֶן הַפּוּךְ **Qeren Hap-pûwk,** *keh'-ren hap-pook';* from 7161 and 6320; *horn of cosmetic; Keren-hap-Puk,* one of Job's daughters:— Keren-happuch.

7164. קָרַס **qâraç,** *kaw-ras';* a prim. root; prop. to *protrude;* used only as denom. from 7165 (for alliteration with 7167), to *hunch,* i.e. be hump-backed:— stoop.

7165. קֶרֶס **qereç,** *keh'-res;* from 7164; a *knob* or belaying-pin (from its swelling form):— tache.

קְרֹץ **Qêrôç.** See 7026.

7166. קַרְסֹל **qarçôl,** *kar-sole';* from 7164;

an *ankle* (as a *protuberance* or joint):— foot.

7167. קָרַע **qâra',** *kaw-rah';* a prim. root; to *rend,* lit. or fig. (*revile, paint* the eyes, as if enlarging them):— cut out, rend, × surely, tear.

7168. קֶרַע **qera',** *keh'-rah;* from 7167; a *rag:*— piece, rag.

7169. קָרַץ **qârats,** *kaw-rats';* a prim. root; to *pinch,* i.e. (partially) to *bite* the lips, *blink* the eyes (as a gesture of malice), or (fully) to *squeeze* off (a piece of clay in order to *mould* a vessel from it):— form, move, wink.

7170. קְרַץ **qerats** (Chald.), *ker-ats';* corresp. to 7171 in the sense of a *bit* (to "eat the *morsels* of" any one, i.e. *chew* him up [fig.] by *slander*):— + accuse.

7171. קֶרֶץ **qerets,** *keh'-rets;* from 7169; *extirpation* (as if by *constriction*):— destruction.

7172. קַרְקַע **qarqa',** *kar-kah';* from 7167; *floor* (as if a pavement of pieces or *tesseræ*), of a building or the sea:— bottom, (× one side of the) floor.

7173. קַרְקַע **Qarqa',** *kar-kah';* the same as 7172; *ground-floor; Karka* (with the art. pref.), a place in Pal.:— Karkaa.

7174. קַרְקֹר **Qarqôr,** *kar-kore';* from 6979; *foundation; Karkor,* a place E. of the Jordan:— Karkor.

7175. קֶרֶשׁ **qeresh,** *keh'-resh;* from an unused root mean. to *split* off; a *slab* or *plank;* by impl. a *deck* of a ship:— bench, board.

7176. קֶרֶת **qereth,** *keh'-reth;* from 7136 in the sense of building; a *city:*— city.

7177. קַרְתָּה **Qartâh,** *kar-taw';* from 7176; *city; Kartah,* a place in Pal.:— Kartah.

7178. קַרְתָּן **Qartân,** *kar-tawn';* from 7176; *city-plot; Kartan,* a place in Pal.:— Kartan.

7179. קַשׁ **qash,** *kash;* from 7197; *straw* (as *dry*):— stubble.

7180. קִשֻּׁא **qishshû',** *kish-shoo';* from an unused root (mean. to *be hard*); a *cucumber* (from the difficulty of *digestion*):— cucumber.

7181. קָשַׁב **qâshab,** *kaw-shab';* a prim. root; to *prick up* the ears, i.e. *hearken:*— attend, (cause to) hear (-ken), give heed, incline, mark (well), regard.

7182. קֶשֶׁב **qesheb,** *keh'-sheb;* from 7181; a *hearkening:*— × diligently, hearing, much heed, that regarded.

7183. קַשָּׁב **qashshâb,** *kash-shawb';* or

קַשֻּׁב **qashshûb,** *kash-shoob';* from 7181; *hearkening:*— attent(-ive).

7184. קָשָׂה **qâsâh,** *kaw-saw';*

קַשְׂוָה **qasvâh,** *kas-vaw';* from an unused root mean. to *be round;* a *jug* (from its shape):— cover, cup.

7185. קָשָׁה **qâshâh,** *kaw-shaw';* a prim. root; prop. to *be dense,* i.e. *tough* or *severe* (in various applications):— be cruel, be fiercer, make grievous, be (ask al, be in, have, seem, would) hard (-en, [labour], -ly, thing), be sore, (be, make) stiff (-en, [-necked]).

7186. קָשֶׁה **qâsheh,** *kaw-sheh';* from

7185; *severe* (in various applications):— churlish, cruel, grievous, hard ([-hearted], thing), heavy, + impudent, obstinate, prevailed, rough (-ly), sore, sorrowful, stiff ([-necked]), stubborn, + in trouble.

7187. קְשׁוֹט **qeshôwṭ** (Chald.), *kesh-ote';* or

קְשֹׁט **qeshôṭ** (Chald.), *kesh-ote';* corresp. to 7189; *fidelity:*— truth.

7188. קָשַׁח **qâshach,** *kaw-shakh';* a prim. root; to *be* (caus. *make*) *unfeeling:*— harden.

7189. קֹשֶׁט **qôsheṭ,** *ko'-sheṭ;* or

קֹשְׁט **qôshṭ,** *kösht;* from an unused root mean. to *balance; equity* (as evenly *weighed*), i.e. *reality:*— certainty, truth.

קֹשְׁט **qôshôṭ.** See 7187.

7190. קְשִׁי **qeshiy,** *kesh-ee';* from 7185; *obstinacy:*— stubbornness.

7191. קִשְׁיוֹן **Qishyôwn,** *kish-yone';* from 7190; *hard ground; Kishjon,* a place in Pal.:— Kishion, Keshon.

7192. קְשִׂיטָה **qesîyṭâh,** *kes-ee-taw';* from an unused root (prob. mean. to *weigh* out); an *ingot* (as def. *estimated* and stamped for a coin):— piece of money (silver).

7193. קַשְׂקֶשֶׂת **qasqeseth,** *kas-keh'-seth;* by redupl. from an unused root mean. to *shale* off as bark; a *scale* (of a fish); hence, a coat of *mail* (as composed of or covered with jointed *plates* of metal):— mail, scale.

7194. קָשַׁר **qâshar,** *kaw-shar';* a prim. root: to *tie,* phys. (*gird, confine, compact*) or ment. (in *love, league*):— bind (up), (make a) conspire (-acy, -ator), join together, knit, stronger, work [treason].

7195. קֶשֶׁר **qesher,** *keh'-sher;* from 7194; an (unlawful) *alliance:*— confederacy, conspiracy, treason.

7196. קִשֻּׁר **qishshûr,** *kish-shoor';* from 7194; an (ornamental) *girdle* (for women):— attire, headband.

7197. קָשַׁשׁ **qâshash,** *kaw-shash';* a prim. root; to *become sapless* through drought; used only as denom. from 7179; to *forage* for straw, stubble or wood; fig. to *assemble:*— gather (selves) (together).

7198. קֶשֶׁת **qesheth,** *keh'-sheth;* from 7185 in the orig. sense (of 6983) of *bending;* a *bow,* for *shooting* (hence, fig. *strength*) or the *iris:*— × arch (-er), + arrow, bow ([-man, -shot]).

7199. קַשָּׁת **qashshâth,** *kash-shawth';* intens. (as denom.) from 7198; a *bowman:*— × archer.

ר

7200. רָאָה **râ'âh,** *raw-aw';* a prim. root; to *see,* lit. or fig. (in numerous applications, dir. and impl., tran., intr. and caus.):— advise self, appear, approve, behold, × certainly, consider, discern, (make to) enjoy, have experience, gaze, take heed, × indeed, × joyfully, lo, look (on, one another, one on another, one upon another, out, up, upon), mark, meet, × be near, perceive, present, provide, regard, (have) respect, (fore-, cause to, let) see (-r, -m, one another), shew (self), × sight of others, (e-) spy, stare, × surely, × think, view, visions.

7201. רָאָה râ'âh, raw-aw'; from 7200; a bird of prey (prob. the vulture, from its sharp sight):— glede. Comp. 1676.

7202. רָאֶה râ'eh, raw-eh'; from 7200; seeing, i.e. experiencing:— see.

7203. רֹאֶה rô'eh, ro-eh'; act. part. of 7200; a seer (as often rendered); but also (abstr.) a vision:— vision.

7204. רֹאֶה Rô'êh, ro-ay'; for 7203; prophet; Roëh, an Isr.:— Haroeh [incl. the art.].

7205. רְאוּבֵן Re'ûwbên, reh-oo-bane'; from the imper. of 7200 and 1121; see ye a son; Reüben, a son of Jacob:— Reuben.

7206. רְאוּבֵנִי Re'ûwbênîy, reh-oob-ay-nee'; patron. from 7205; a Reübenite or desc. of Reüben:— children of Reuben, Reubenites.

7207. רַאֲוָה ra'ăvâh, rah-av-aw'; from 7200; sight, i.e. satisfaction:— behold.

7208. רְאוּמָה Re'ûwmâh, reh-oo-maw'; fem. pass. part. of 7213; raised; Reümah, a Syrian woman:— Reumah.

7209. רְאִי re'îy, reh-ee'; from 7200; a mirror (as seen):— looking glass.

7210. רֳאִי rŏ'îy, ro-ee'; from 7200; sight, whether abstr. (vision) or concr. (a spectacle):— gazingstock, look to, (that) see (-th).

7211. רְאָיָה Re'âyâh, reh-aw-yaw'; from 7200 and 3050; Jah has seen; Reäjah, the name of three Isr.:— Reaia, Reaiah.

7212. רְאִיּת° re'îyth, reh-eeth'; from 7200; sight:— beholding.

7213. רָאַם râ'am, raw-am'; a prim. root; to rise:— be lifted up.

7214. רְאֵם re'êm, reh-ame'; or

רְאֵים re'êym, reh-ame'; or

רֵים rêym, rame; or

רֵם rêm, rame; from 7213; a wild bull (from its conspicuousness):— unicorn.

7215. רָאמָה râ'mâh, raw-maw'; from 7213; something high in value, i.e. perh. coral:— coral.

7216. רָאמוֹת Râ'môwth, raw-môth'; or

רָאמֹת Râmôth, raw-môth'; plur. of 7215; heights; Ramoth, the name of two places in Pal.:— Ramoth.

7217. רֵאשׁ rê'sh (Chald.), raysh; corresp. to 7218; the head; fig. the sum:— chief, head, sum.

7218. רֹאשׁ rô'sh, roshe; from an unused root appar. mean. to shake; the head (as most easily shaken), whether lit. or fig. (in many applications, of place, time, rank, etc.):— band, beginning, captain, chapiter, chief (-est place, man, things), company, end, × every [man], excellent, first, forefront, ([be-]) head, height, (on) high (-est part, [priest]), × lead, × poor, principal, ruler, sum, top.

7219. רֹאשׁ rô'sh, roshe; or

רוֹשׁ rôwsh (Deut. 32:32), roshe;

appar. the same as 7218; a poisonous plant, prob. the poppy (from its conspicuous head); gen. poison (even of serpents):— gall, hemlock, poison, venom.

7220. רֹאשׁ Rô'sh, roshe; prob. the same as 7218; Rosh, the name of an Isr. and of a for. nation:— Rosh.

רֵאשׁ rê'sh. See 7389.

7221. רִאשָׁה rî'shâh, ree-shaw'; from the same as 7218; a beginning:— beginning.

7222. רֹאשָׁה rô'shâh, ro-shaw'; fem. of 7218; the head:— head [-stone].

7223. רִאשׁוֹן rî'shôwn, ree-shone'; or

רִאשֹׁן rî'shôn, ree-shone'; from 7221; first, in place, time or rank (as adj. or noun):— ancestor, (that were) before (-time), beginning, eldest, first, fore [-father] (-most), former (thing), of old time, past.

7224. רִאשֹׁנִי rî'shônîy, ree-sho-nee'; from 7223; first:— first.

7225. רֵאשִׁית rê'shîyth, ray-sheeth'; from the same as 7218; the first, in place, time, order or rank (spec. a firstfruit):— beginning, chief (-est), first (-fruits, part, time), principal thing.

7226. רַאֲשֹׁת ra'ăshôth, rah-ash-ōth'; from 7218; a pillow (being for the head):— bolster.

7227. רַב rab, rab; by contr. from 7231; abundant (in quantity, size, age, number, rank, quality):— (in) abound (-undance, -ant, -antly), captain, elder, enough, exceedingly, full, great (-ly, man, one), increase, long (enough, [time], (do, have) many (-ifold, things, a time), ([ship-]) master, mighty, more, (too, very) much, multiply (-tude), officer, often [-times], plenteous, populous, prince, process [of time], suffice (-ient).

7228. רַב rab, rab; by contr. from 7232; an archer [or perh. the same as 7227]:— archer.

7229. רַב rab (Chald.), rab; corresp. to 7227:— captain, chief, great, lord, master, stout.

רִיב rîb. See 7378.

7230. רֹב rôb, robe; from 7231; abundance (in any respect):— abundance (-antly), all, × common [sort], excellent, great (-ly, ness, number), huge, be increased, long, many, more in number, most, much, multitude, plenty (-ifully), × very [age].

7231. רָבַב râbab, raw-bab'; a prim. root; prop. to cast together [comp. 7241], i.e. increase, espec. in number; also as denom. from 7233) to multiply by the myriad:— increase, be many (-ifold), be more, multiply, ten thousands.

7232. רָבַב râbab, raw-bab'; a prim root [rather ident. with 7231 through the idea of projection]; to shoot an arrow:— shoot.

7233. רְבָבָה re'bâbâh, reb-aw-baw'; from 7231; abundance (in number), i.e. (spec.) a myriad (whether def. or indef.):— many, million, × multiply, ten thousand.

7234. רָבַד râbad, raw-bad'; a prim. root; to spread:— deck.

7235. רָבָה râbâh, raw-baw'; a prim. root; to increase (in whatever respect):— [bring in] abundance (× -antly), + archer [by mistake for 7232], be in authority, bring up, × continue, enlarge, excel, exceeding (-ly), be full of, (be, make) great (-er, -ly, × -ness), grow up, heap, increase, be long, (be, give, have, make, use) many (a time), (any, be, give, give the, have) more (in number), (ask, be, be so, gather, over, take, yield) much (greater, more), (make to) multiply, nourish, plenty (-eous), × process [of time], sore, store, thoroughly, very.

7236. רְבָה re'bâh (Chald.), reb-aw'; corresp. to 7235:— make a great man, grow.

7237. רַבָּה Rabbâh, rab-baw'; fem. of 7227; great; Rabbah, the name of two places in Pal., East and West:— Rabbah, Rabbath.

7238. רְבוּ re'bûw (Chald.), reb-oo'; from a root corresp. to 7235; increase (of dignity):— greatness, majesty.

7239. רִבּוֹ ribbôw, rib-bo'; from 7231; or

רִבּוֹא ribbôw', rib-bo'; from 7231; a myriad, i.e. indef. large number:— great things, ten [eight]-een, [for]-ty, + sixscore, + threescore, × twenty, [twen]-ty] thousand.

7240. רִבּוֹ ribbôw (Chald.), rib-bo'; corresp. to 7239:— × ten thousand times ten thousand.

7241. רָבִיב râbîyb, raw-beeb'; from 7231; a rain (as an accumulation of drops):— shower.

7242. רָבִיד râbîyd, raw-beed'; from 7234; a collar (as spread around the neck):— chain.

7243. רְבִיעִי re'bîy'îy, reb-ee-ee'; or

רְבִעִי re'bî'îy, reb-ee-ee'; from 7251; fourth; also (fractionally) a fourth:— foursquare, fourth (part).

7244. רְבִיעִי re'bîy'ay (Chald.), reb-ee-ah'-ee; corresp. to 7243:— fourth.

7245. רַבִּית Rabbîyth, rab-beeth'; from 7231; multitude; Rabbith, a place in Pal.:— Rabbith.

7246. רָבַךְ râbak, raw-bak'; a prim. root; to soak (bread in oil):— baken, (that which is) fried.

7247. רִבְלָה Riblâh, rib-law'; from an unused root mean. to be fruitful; fertile; Riblah, a place in Syria:— Riblah.

7248. רַב־מָג Rab-Mâg, rab-mawg'; from 7227 and a for. word for a Magian; chief Magian; Rab-Mag, a Bab. official:— Rab-mag.

7249. רַב־סָרִיס Rab-Çârîyç, rab-saw-reece'; from 7227 and a for. word for a eunuch; chief chamberlain; Rab-Saris, a Bab. official:— Rab-saris.

7250. רָבַע râba', raw-bah'; a prim. root; to squat or lie out flat, i.e. (spec.) in copulation:— let gender, lie down.

7251. רָבַע râba', raw-bah'; a prim. root [rather ident. with 7250 through the idea of sprawling "at all fours" (or possibly the reverse is the order of deriv.); comp. 702]; prop. to be four (sided):—

used only as denom. of 7253; to be quadrate:— (four-) square (-d).

7252. רֶבַע **reba'**, reh´-bah; from 7250; prostration (for sleep):— lying down.

7253. רֶבַע **reba'**, reh´-bah; from 7251; a fourth (part or side):— fourth part, side, square.

7254. רֶבַע **Reba'**, reh´-bah; the same as 7253; Reba, a Midianite:— Reba.

7255. רֹבַע **rôba'**, ro´-bah; from 7251; a quarter:— fourth part.

7256. רִבֵּעַ **ribbêa'**, rib-bay´-ah; from 7251; a desc. of the fourth generation, i.e. great great grandchild:— fourth.

רְבִיעִי **r^ebiy'îy.** See 7243.

7257. רָבַץ **râbats**, raw-bats´; a prim. root; to crouch (on all four legs folded, like a recumbent animal); by impl. to recline, repose, brood, lurk, imbed:— crouch (down), fall down, make a fold, lay, (cause to, make to) lie (down), make to rest, sit.

7258. רֵבֶץ **rebets**, reh´-bets; from 7257; a couch or place of repose:— where each lay, lie down in, resting place.

7259. רִבְקָה **Ribqâh**, rib-kaw´; from an unused root prob. mean. to clog by tying up the fetlock; fettering (by beauty); Ribkah, the wife of Isaac:— Rebekah.

7260. רַבְרַב **rabrab** (Chald.), rab-rab´; from 7229; huge (in size); domineering (in character):— (very) great (things).

7261. רַבְרְבָן **rabr^ebân** (Chald.), rab-reb-awn´; from 7260; a magnate:— lord, prince.

7262. רַבְשָׁקֵה **Rabshâqêh**, rab-shaw-kay´; from 7227 and 8248; chief butler; Rabshakeh, a Bab. official:— Rabshakeh.

7263. רֶגֶב **regeb**, reh´-gheb; from an unused root mean. to pile together; a lump of clay:— clod.

7264. רָגַז **râgaz**, raw-gaz´; a prim. root; to quiver (with any violent emotion, espec. anger or fear):— be afraid, stand in awe, disquiet, fall out, fret, move, provoke, quake, rage, shake, tremble, trouble, be wroth.

7265. רְגַז **r^egaz** (Chald.), reg-az´; corresp. to 7264:— provoke unto wrath.

7266. רְגַז **r^egaz** (Chald.), reg-az´; from 7265; violent anger:— rage.

7267. רֹגֶז **rôgez**, ro´-ghez; from 7264; commotion, restlessness (of a horse), crash (of thunder), disquiet, anger:— fear, noise, rage, trouble (-ing), wrath.

7268. רַגָּז **raggâz**, rag-gawz´; intens. from 7264; timid:— trembling.

7269. רָגְזָה **rogzâh**, rog-zaw´; fem. of 7267; trepidation:— trembling.

7270. רָגַל **râgal**, raw-gal´; a prim. root; to walk along; but only in spec. applications, to reconnoiter, to be a tale-bearer (i.e. slander); also (as denom. from 7272) to lead about:— backbite, search, slander, (e-) spy (out), teach to go, view.

7271. רְגַל **r^egal** (Chald.), reg-al´; corresp. to 7272:— foot.

7272. רֶגֶל **regel**, reh´-gel; from 7270; a foot (as used in walking); by impl. a step; by euphem. the pudenda:— × be

able to endure, × according as, × after, × coming, × follow, (broken-l) foot ([-ed, -stooll), × great toe, × haunt, × journey, leg, + piss, + possession, time.

7273. רַגְלִי **raglîy**, rag-lee´; from 7272; a footman (soldier):— (on) foot (-man).

7274. רֹגְלִים **Rôg^elîym**, ro-gel-eem´; plur. of act. part. of 7270; fullers (as tramping the cloth in washing); Rogelim, a place E. of the Jordan:— Rogelim.

7275. רָגַם **râgam**, raw-gam´; a prim. root [comp. 7263, 7321, 7551]; to cast together (stones), i.e. to lapidate:— × certainly, stone.

7276. רֶגֶם **Regem**, reh´-gem; from 7275; stone-heap; Regem, an Isr.:— Regem.

7277. רִגְמָה **rigmâh**, rig-maw´; fem. of the same as 7276; a pile (of stones), i.e. (fig.) a throng:— council.

7278. רֶגֶם מֶלֶךְ **Regem Melek**, reh´-gem meh´-lek; from 7276 and 4428; king's heap; Regem-Melek, an Isr.:— Regem-melech.

7279. רָגַן **râgan**, raw-gan´; a prim. root; to grumble, i.e. rebel:— murmur.

7280. רָגַע **râga'**, raw-gah´; a prim. root; prop. to toss violently and suddenly (the sea with waves, the skin with boils); fig. (in a favorable manner) to settle, i.e. quiet; spec. to wink (from the motion of the eye-lids):— break, divide, find ease, be a moment, (cause, give, make to) rest, make suddenly.

7281. רֶגַע **rega'**, reh´-gah; from 7280. a wink (of the eyes), i.e. a very short space of time:— instant, moment, space, suddenly.

7282. רָגֵעַ **râgêa'**, raw-gay´-ah; from 7280; restful, i.e. peaceable:— that are quiet.

7283. רָגַשׁ **râgash**, raw-gash´; a prim. root; to be tumultuous:— rage.

7284. רְגַשׁ **r^egash** (Chald.), reg-ash´; corresp. to 7283; to gather tumultuously:— assemble (together).

7285. רֶגֶשׁ **regesh**, reh´-ghesh; or (fem.)

רִגְשָׁה **rigshâh**, rig-shaw´; from 7283; a tumultuous crowd:— company, insurrection.

7286. רָדַד **râdad**, raw-dad´; a prim. root; to tread in pieces, i.e. (fig.) to conquer, or (spec.) to overlay:— spend, spread, subdue.

7287. רָדָה **râdâh**, raw-daw´; a prim. root; to tread down, i.e. subjugate; spec. to crumble off:— (come to, make to) have dominion, prevail against, reign, (bear, make to) rule (-r, over), take.

7288. רַדַּי **Radday**, rad-dah´-ee; intens. from 7287; domineering; Raddai, an Isr.:— Raddai.

7289. רָדִיד **râdîyd**, raw-deed´; from 7286 in the sense of spreading; a veil (as expanded):— vail, veil.

7290. רָדַם **râdam**, raw-dam´; a prim. root; to stun, i.e. stupefy (with sleep or death):— (be fast a-, be in a deep, cast into a dead, that) sleep (-er, -eth).

7291. רָדַף **râdaph**, raw-daf´; a prim. root; to run after (usually with hostile intent; fig. [of timel gone by):— chase,

put to flight,.follow (after, on), hunt, (be under) persecute (-ion, -or), pursue (-r).

7292. רָהַב **râhab**, raw-hab´; a prim. root; to urge severely, i.e. (fig.) importune, embolden, capture, act insolently:— overcome, behave self proudly, make sure, strengthen.

7293. רַהַב **rahab**, rah´-hab; from 7292, bluster (-er):— proud, strength.

7294. רַהַב **Rahab**, rah´-hab; the same as 7293; Rahab (i.e. boaster), an epithet of Egypt:— Rahab.

7295. רָהָב **râhâb**, raw-hawb´; from 7292; insolent:— proud.

7296. רֹהָב **rôhâb**, ro´-hab; from 7292; pride:— strength.

7297. רָהָה **râhâh**, raw-haw´; a prim. root; to fear:— be afraid.

7298. רַהַט **rahat**, rah´-hat; from an unused root appar. mean. to hollow out, a channel or watering-box; by resemblance a ringlet of hair (as forming parallel lines):— gallery, gutter, trough.

7299. רֵו **rêv** (Chald.), rave; from a root corresp. to 7200; aspect:— form.

רוּב **rûwb.** See 7378.

7300. רוּד **rûwd**, rood; a prim. root; to tramp about, i.e. ramble (free or disconsolate):— have the dominion, be lord, mourn, rule.

7301. רָוָה **râvâh**, raw-vaw´; a prim. root; to slake the thirst (occasionally of other appetites):— bathe, make drunk, (take the) fill, satiate, (abundantly) satisfy, soak, water (abundantly).

7302. רָוֶה **râveh**, raw-veh´; from 7301; sated (with drink):— drunkenness, watered.

7303. רוֹהֲגָה **Rôwhăgâh**, ro-hag-aw´; from an unused root prob. mean. to cry out; outcry; Rohagah, an Isr.:— Rohgah.

7304. רָוַח **râvach**, raw-vakh´; a prim. root [rather ident. with 7306]; prop. to breathe freely, i.e. revive; by impl. to have ample room:— be refreshed, large.

7305. רֶוַח **revach**, reh´-vakh; from 7304; room, lit. (an interval) or fig. (deliverance):— enlargement, space.

7306. רוּחַ **rûwach**, roo-akh´; a prim. root; prop. to blow, i.e. breathe; only (lit.) to smell or (by impl.) perceive (fig. to anticipate, enjoy):— accept, smell, × touch, make of quick understanding.

7307. רוּחַ **rûwach**, roo´-akh; from 7306; wind; by resemblance breath, i.e. a sensible (or even violent) exhalation; fig. life, anger, unsubstantiality; by extens. a region of the sky; by resemblance spirit, but only of a rational being (incl. its expression and functions):— air, anger, blast, breath, × cool, courage, mind, × quarter, × side, spirit (I-uall), tempest, × vain, ([whirl-]) wind (-y).

7308. רוּחַ **rûwach** (Chald.), roo´-akh; corresp. to 7307:— mind, spirit, wind.

7309. רְוָחָה **r^evâchâh**, rev-aw-khaw´; fem. of 7305; relief:— breathing, respite.

Hebrew

7310. רְוָיָה **r^evâyâh**, *rev-aw-yaw´*; from 7301; *satisfaction*:— runneth over, wealthy.

7311. רוּם **rûwm**, *room*; a prim. root; to *be high*; act. to *rise* or *raise* (in various applications, lit. or fig.):— bring up, exalt (self), extol, give, go up, haughty, heave (up), (be, lift up on, make on, set up on, too) high (-er, one), hold up, levy, lift (-er) up, (be) lofty, (× a-) loud, mount up, offer (up), + presumptuously, (be) promote (-ion), proud, set up, tall (-er), take (away, off, up), breed worms.

7312. רֻם **rûwm**, *room*; or

רֻם **rûm**, *room*; from 7311; (lit.) *elevation* or (fig.) *elation*:— haughtiness, height, × high.

7313. רוּם **rûwm** (Chald.), *room*; corresp. to 7311; (fig. only):— extol, lift up (self), set up.

7314. רוּם **rûwm** (Chald.), *room*; from 7313; (lit.) *altitude*:— height.

7315. רוֹם **rôwm**, *rome*; from 7311; *elevation*, i.e. (adv.) *aloft*:— on high.

7316. רוּמָה **Rûwmâh**, *roo-maw´*; from 7311; *height*; *Rumah*, a place in Pal.:— Rumah.

7317. רוּמָה **rôwmâh**, *ro-maw´*; fem. of 7315; *elation*, i.e. (adv.) *proudly*:— haughtily.

7318. רוּמָם **rôwmâm**, *ro-mawm´*; from 7426; *exaltation*, i.e. (fig. and spec.) *praise*:— be extolled.

7319. רוֹמְמָה **rôwm^emâh**, *ro-mem-aw´*; fem. act. part. of 7426; *exaltation*, i.e. *praise*:— high.

7320. רוֹמַמְתִּי עֶזֶר **Rôwmamtiy 'Ezer** (or

לְמַמְתִּי **Rômamtiy**), *ro-mam´-tee eh´-zer*; from 7311 and 5828; *I have raised* up a *help*; *Romamti-Ezer*, an Isr.:— Romamti-ezer.

7321. רוּעַ **rûwa'**, *roo-ah´*; a prim. root; to *mar* (espec. by breaking); fig. to *split* the ears (with sound), i.e. *shout* (for alarm or joy):— blow an alarm, cry (alarm, aloud, out), destroy, make a joyful noise, smart, shout (for joy), sound an alarm, triumph.

7322. רוּף **rûwph**, *roof*; a prim. root; prop. to *triturate* (in a mortar), i.e. (fig.) to *agitate* (by concussion):— tremble.

7323. רוּץ **rûwts**, *roots*; a prim. root; to *run* (for whatever reason, espec. to *rush*):— break down, divide speedily, footman, guard, bring hastily, (make) run (away, through), post, stretch out.

7324. רוּק **rûwq**, *rook*; a prim. root; to *pour* out (lit. or fig.), i.e. *empty*:— × arm, cast out, draw (out), (make) empty, pour forth (out).

7325. רוּר **rûwr**, *roor*; a prim. root; to *slaver* (with spittle), i.e. (by anal.) to *emit* a fluid (ulcerous or natural):— run.

7326. רוּשׁ **rûwsh**, *roosh*; a prim. root; to *be destitute*:— lack, needy, (make self) poor (man).

רוֹשׁ **rôwsh**. See 7219.

7327. רוּת **Rûwth**, *rooth*; prob. for 7468; *friend*; *Ruth*, a Moabitess:— Ruth.

7328. רָז **râz** (Chald.), *rawz*; from an un-

used root prob. mean. to *attenuate*, i.e. (fig.) *hide*; a *mystery*:— secret.

7329. רָזָה **râzâh**, *raw-zaw´*; a prim. root; to *emaciate*, i.e. *make* (become) *thin* (lit. or fig.):— famish, wax lean.

7330. רָזֶה **râzeh**, *raw-zeh´*; from 7329; *thin*:— lean.

7331. רְזוֹן **R^ezôwn**, *rez-one´*; from 7336; *prince*; *Rezon*, a Syrian:— Rezon.

7332. רָזוֹן **râzôwn**, *raw-zone´*; from 7329; *thinness*:— leanness, × scant.

7333. רָזוֹן **râzôwn**, *raw-zone´*; from 7336; a *dignitary*:— prince.

7334. רָזִי **râziy**, *raw-zee´*; from 7329; *thinness*:— leanness.

7335. רָזַם **râzam**, *raw-zam´*; a prim. root; to *twinkle* the eye (in mockery):— wink.

7336. רָזַן **râzan**, *raw-zan´*; a prim. root; prob. to *be heavy*, i.e. (fig.) *honorable*:— prince, ruler.

7337. רָחַב **râchab**, *raw-khab´*; a prim. root; to *broaden* (intr. or tran., lit. or fig.):— be an en- (make) large (-ing), make room, make (open) wide.

7338. רַחַב **rachab**, *rakh´-ab*; from 7337; a *width*:— breadth, broad place.

7339. רְחֹב **r^echôb**, *rekh-obe´*; or

רְחוֹב **r^echôwb**, *rekh-obe´*; from 7337; a *width*, i.e. (concr.) *avenue* or *area*:— broad place (way), street. See also 1050.

7340. רְחֹב **R^echôb**, *rekh-obe´*; or

רְחוֹב **R^echôwb**, *rekh-obe´*; the same as 7339; *Rechob*, the name of a place in Syria, also of a Syrian and an Isr.:— Rehob.

7341. רֹחַב **rôchab**, *ro´-khab*; from 7337; *width* (lit. or fig.):— breadth, broad, largeness, thickness, wideness.

7342. רָחָב **râchâb**, *raw-khawb´*; from 7337; *roomy*, in any (or every) direction, lit. or fig.:— broad, large, at liberty, proud, wide.

7343. רָחָב **Râchâb**, *raw-khawb´*; the same as 7342; *proud*; *Rachab*, a Canaanitess:— Rahab.

7344. רְחֹבוֹת **R^echôbôwth**, *rekh-o-both´*; or

רְחֹבֹת **R^echôbôth**, *rekh-o-both´*; plur. of 7339; *streets*; *Rechoboth*, a place in Assyria and one in Pal.:— Rehoboth.

7345. רְחַבְיָה **R^echabyâh**, *rekh-ab-yaw´*; or

רְחַבְיָהוּ **R^echabyâhûw**, *rek-ab-yaw´-hoo*; from 7337 and 3050; *Jah has enlarged*; *Rechabjah*, an Isr.:— Rehabiah.

7346. רְחַבְעָם **R^echab'âm**, *rekh-ab-awm´*; from 7337 and 5971; a *people has enlarged*; *Rechabam*, an Isr. king:— Rehoboam.

רְחֹבֹת **R^echôbôth**. See 7344.

7347. רֵחֶה **rêcheh**, *ray-kheh´*; from an unused root mean. to *pulverize*; a *millstone*:— mill (stone).

רְחוֹב **R^echôwb**. See 7339, 7340.

7348. רְחוּם **R^echûwm**, *rekh-oom´*; a

form of 7349; *Rechum*, the name of a Pers. and of three Isr.:— Rehum.

7349. רַחוּם **rachûwm**, *rakh-oom´*; from 7355; *compassionate*:— full of compassion, merciful.

7350. רָחוֹק **râchôwq**, *raw-khoke´*; or

רָחֹק **râchôq**, *raw-khoke´*; from 7368; *remote*, lit. or fig., of place or time; spec. *precious*; often used adv. (with prep.):— (a-) far (abroad, off), long ago, of old, space, great while to come.

7351. רְחִיט **r^echîyṭ**, *rekh-eet´*; from the same as 7298; a *panel* (as resembling a *trough*):— rafter.

7352. רַחִיק **rachîyq** (Chald.), *rakh-eek´*; corresp. to 7350:— far.

7353. רָחֵל **râchêl**, *raw-kale´*; from an unused root mean. to *journey*; a *ewe* [the *females* being the predominant element of a flock] (as a good *traveller*):— ewe, sheep.

7354. רָחֵל **Râchêl**, *raw-khale´*; the same as 7353; *Rachel*, a wife of Jacob:— Rachel.

7355. רָחַם **râcham**, *raw-kham´*; a prim. root; to *fondle*; by impl. to *love*, espec. to *compassionate*:— have compassion (on, upon), love, (find, have, obtain, shew) mercy (-iful, on, upon), (have) pity, Ruhamah, × surely.

7356. רַחַם **racham**, *rakh´-am*; from 7355; *compassion* (in the plur.); by extens. the *womb* (as *cherishing* the fetus); by impl. a *maiden*:— bowels, compassion, damsel, tender love, (great, tender) mercy, pity, womb.

7357. רַחַם **Racham**, *rakh´-am*; the same as 7356; *pity*; *Racham*, an Isr.:— Raham.

7358. רֶחֶם **rechem**, *rekh´-em*; from 7355; the *womb* [comp. 7356]:— matrix, womb.

7359. רְחֵם **r^echêm** (Chald.), *rekh-ame´*; corresp. to 7356; (plur.) *pity*:— mercy.

7360. רָחָם **râchâm**, *raw-khawm´*; or (fem.)

רָחָמָה **râchâmâh**, *raw-khaw-maw´*; from 7355; a kind of *vulture* (supposed to be *tender* toward its young):— gier-eagle.

7361. רַחֲמָה **rachămâh**, *rakh-am-aw´*; fem. of 7356; a *maiden*:— damsel.

7362. רַחְמָנִי **rachmâniy**, *rakh-maw-nee´*; from 7355; *compassionate*:— pitiful.

7363. רָחַף **râchaph**, *raw-khaf´*; a prim. root; to *brood*; by impl. to *be relaxed*:— flutter, move, shake.

7364. רָחַץ **râchats**, *raw-khats´*; a prim. root; to *lave* (the whole or a part of a thing):— bathe (self), wash (self).

7365. רְחַץ **r^echats** (Chald.), *rekh-ats´*; corresp. to 7364 [prob. through the accessory idea of *ministering* as a servant at the bath]; to *attend* upon:— trust.

7366. רַחַץ **rachats**, *rakh´-ats*; from 7364; a *bath*:— wash [-pot].

7367. רַחְצָה **rachtsâh**, *rakh-tsaw´*; fem. of 7366; a *bathing* place:— washing.

7368. רָחַק **râchaq**, *raw-khak´*; a prim. root; to *widen* (in any direction), i.e.

(intr.) *recede* or (tran.) *remove* (lit. or fig., of place or relation):— (a-, be, cast, drive, get, go, keep [self], put, remove, be too, [wander], withdraw) far (away, off), loose, × refrain, very, (be) a good way (off).

7369. רָחֵק **râchêq**, *raw-khake´;* from 7368; *remote:*— that are far.

רָחֹק **râchôq**. See 7350.

7370. רָחַשׁ **râchash**, *raw-khash´;* a prim. root; to *gush:*— indite.

7371. רַחַת **rachath**, *rakh´-ath;* from 7306; a *winnowing*-fork (as *blowing* the chaff away):— shovel.

7372. רָטַב **râṭab**, *raw-tab´;* a prim. root; to *be moist:*— be wet.

7373. רָטֹב **râṭôb**, *raw-tobe´;* from 7372; *moist* (with sap):— green.

7374. רֶטֶט **reṭeṭ**, *reh´-tet;* from an unused root mean. to *tremble; terror:*— fear.

7375. רֻטֲפַשׁ **rûwṭăphash**, *roo-taf-ash´;* a root compounded from 7373 and 2954; to *be rejuvenated:*— be fresh.

7376. רָטַשׁ **râṭash**, *raw-tash´;* a prim. root; to *dash* down:— dash (in pieces).

7377. רִי **rîy**, *ree;* from 7301; *irrigation,* i.e. a *shower:*— watering.

7378. רִיב **rîyb**, *reeb;* or

רוּב° **rûwb**, *roob;* a prim. root; prop. to *toss,* i.e. *grapple;* mostly fig. to *wrangle,* i.e. *hold a controversy;* (by impl.) to *defend:*— adversary, chide, complain, contend, debate, × ever, × lay wait, plead, rebuke, strive, × thoroughly.

7379. רִיב **rîyb**, *reeb;* or

רִב **rîb**, *reeb;* from 7378; a *contest* (personal or legal):— + adversary, cause, chiding, contend (-tion), controversy, multitude [from the marg.], pleading, strife, strive (-ing), suit.

7380. רִיבַי **Rîybay**, *ree-bah´-ee;* from 7378; *contentious; Ribai,* an Isr.:— Ribai.

7381. רֵיחַ **rêyach**, *ray´-akh;* from 7306; *odor* (as if *blown*):— savour, scent, smell.

7382. רֵיחַ **rêyach** (Chald.), *ray-akh;* corresp. to 7381:— smell.

רֵם **rêym**. See 7214.

רֵעַ **rêya'**. See 7453.

7383. רִיפָה **rîyphâh**, *ree-faw´;* or

רִפָה **riphâh**, *ree-faw´;* from 7322; (only plur.), *grits* (as *pounded*):— ground corn, wheat.

7384. רִיפַת **Rîyphath**, *ree-fath´;* or (prob. by orth. err.)

דִּיפַת **Dîyphath**, *dee-fath´;* of for. or.; *Riphath,* a grandson of Japheth and his desc.:— Riphath.

7385. רִיק **rîyq**, *reek;* from 7324; *emptiness;* fig. a *worthless* thing; adv. *in vain:*— empty, to no purpose, (in) vain (thing), vanity.

7386. רֵיק **rêyq**, *rake;* or (short.)

רֵק **rêq**, *rake;* from 7324; *empty;* fig. *worthless:*— emptied (-ty), vain (fellow, man).

7387. רֵיקָם **rêyqâm**, *ray-kawm´;* from

7386; *emptily;* fig. (obj.) *ineffectually,* (subj.) *undeservedly:*— without cause, empty, in vain, void.

7388. רִיר **rîyr**, *reer;* from 7325; *saliva;* by resemblance *broth:*— spittle, white [of an egg].

7389. רֵישׁ **rêysh**, *raysh;* or

רֵאשׁ **rê'sh**, *raysh;* or

רִישׁ **rîysh**, *reesh;* from 7326; *poverty:*— poverty.

7390. רַךְ **rak**, *rak;* from 7401; *tender* (lit. or fig.); by impl. *weak:*— faint [-hearted], soft, tender ([-hearted], one), weak.

7391. רֹךְ **rôk**, *roke;* from 7401; *softness* (fig.):— tenderness.

7392. רָכַב **râkab**, *raw-kab´;* a prim. root; to *ride* (on an animal or in a vehicle); caus. to *place upon* (for riding or gen.), to *despatch:*— bring (on [horse-] back), carry, get [oneself] up, on [horse-] back, put, (cause to, make to) ride (in a chariot, on, -r), set.

7393. רֶכֶב **rekeb**, *reh´-keb;* from 7392; a *vehicle;* by impl. a *team;* by extens. *cavalry;* by anal. a *rider,* i.e. the upper millstone:— chariot, (upper) millstone, multitude [from the marg.], wagon.

7394. רֵכָב **Rêkâb**, *ray-kawb´;* from 7392; *rider; Rekab,* the name of two Arabs and of two Isr.:— Rechab.

7395. רַכָּב **rakkâb**, *rak-kawb´;* from 7392; a *charioteer:*— chariot man, driver of a chariot, horseman.

7396. רִכְבָּה **rikbâh**, *rik-baw´;* fem. of 7393; a *chariot* (collect.):— chariots.

7397. רֵכָה **Rêkâh**, *ray-kaw´;* prob. fem. from 7401; *softness; Rekah,* a place in Pal.:— Rechah.

7398. רְכוּב **rᵉkûwb**, *rek-oob´;* from pass. part. of 7392; a *vehicle* (as *ridden* on):— chariot.

7399. רְכוּשׁ **rᵉkûwsh**, *rek-oosh´;* or

רְכֻשׁ **rᵉkûsh**, *rek-oosh´;* from pass. part. of 7408; *property* (as *gathered*):— good, riches, substance.

7400. רָכִיל **râkîyl**, *raw-keel´;* from 7402 a *scandal-monger* (as *travelling* about):— slander, carry tales, talebearer.

7401. רָכַךְ **râkak**, *raw-kak´;* a prim. root; to *soften* (intr. or tran.), used fig.:— (be) faint ([-hearted]), mollify, (be, make) soft (-er), be tender.

7402. רָכַל **râkal**, *raw-kal´;* a prim. root; to *travel* for trading:— (spice) merchant.

7403. רָכָל **Râkâl**, *raw-kawl´;* from 7402; *merchant; Rakal,* a place in Pal.:— Rachal.

7404. רְכֻלָּה **rᵉkullâh**, *rek-ool-law´;* fem. pass. part. of 7402; *trade* (as *peddled*):— merchandise, traffic.

7405. רָכַס **râkaç**, *raw-kas´;* a prim. root; to *tie:*— bind.

7406. רֶכֶס **rekeç**, *reh´-kes;* from 7405; a mountain *ridge* (as of *tied* summits):— rough place.

7407. רֹכֶס **rôkeç**, *ro´-kes;* from 7405; a *snare* (as of *tied* meshes):— pride.

7408. רָכַשׁ **râkash**, *raw-kash´;* a prim. root; to *lay up,* i.e. *collect:*— gather, get.

7409. רֶכֶשׁ **rekesh**, *reh´-kesh;* from 7408; a *relay* of animals on a post-route (as *stored* up for that purpose); by impl. a *courser:*— dromedary, mule, swift beast.

רְכֻשׁ **rᵉkûsh**. See 7399.

רֵם **rêm**. See 7214.

7410. רָם **Râm**, *rawm;* act. part. of 7311; *high; Ram,* the name of an Arabian and of an Isr.:— Ram. See also 1027.

רֻם **rûm**. See 7311.

7411. רָמָה **râmâh**, *raw-maw´;* a prim. root; to *hurl;* spec. to *shoot;* fig. to *delude* or *betray* (as if causing to fall):— beguile, betray, [bow-] man, carry, deceive, throw.

7412. רְמָה **rᵉmâh** (Chald.), *rem-aw´;* corresp. to 7411; to *throw, set,* (fig.) *assess:*— cast (down), impose.

7413. רָמָה **râmâh**, *raw-maw´;* fem. act. part. of 7311; a *height* (as a seat of idolatry):— high place.

7414. רָמָה **Râmâh**, *raw-maw´;* the same as 7413; *Ramah,* the name of four places in Pal.:— Ramah.

7415. רִמָּה **rimmâh**, *rim-maw´;* from 7426 in the sense of *breeding* [comp. 7311]; a *maggot* (as rapidly *bred*), lit. or fig.:— worm.

7416. רִמּוֹן **rimmôwn**, *rim-mone´;* or

רִמֹּן **rimmôn**, *rim-mone´;* from 7426; a *pomegranate,* the tree (from its *upright* growth) or the fruit (also an artificial ornament):— pomegranate.

7417. רִמּוֹן **Rimmôwn**, *rim-mone´;* or (short.)

רִמֹּן **Rimmôn**, *rim-mone´;* or

רִמּוֹנוֹ **Rimmôwnô** (1 Chron. 6:62 [77]), *rim-mo-no´;* the same as 7416; *Rimmon,* the name of a Syrian deity, also of five places in Pal.:— Remmon, Rimmon. The addition "-methoar" (Josh. 19:13) is

הַמְּתֹאָר **ham-mᵉthô'âr**, *ham-meth-o-awr´;* pass. part. of 8388 with the art.; *the* (one) *marked off,* i.e. *which pertains;* mistaken for part of the name.

רָמוֹת **Râmôwth**. See 7418, 7433.

7418. רָמוֹת־נֶגֶב **Râmôwth-Negeb**, *raw-môth-neh´-gheb;* or

רָמַת נֶגֶב **Râmath Negeb**, *raw-math neh´-gheb;* from the plur. or constr. form of 7413 and 5045; *heights* (or *height*) of (the) *South; Ramoth-Negeb* or *Ramath-Negeb,* a place in Pal.:— south Ramoth, Ramath of the south.

7419. רָמוּת **râmûwth**, *raw-mooth´;* from 7311; a *heap* (of carcases):— height.

7420. רֹמַח **rômach**, *ro´-makh;* from an unused root mean. to *hurl;* a *lance* (as *thrown*); espec. the iron *point:*— buckler, javelin, lancet, spear.

7421. רַמִּי **rammîy**, *ram-mee´;* for 761; a *Ramite,* i.e. Aramæan:— Syrian.

7422. רַמְיָה **Ramyâh**, *ram-yaw´;* from 7311 and 3050; *Jah has raised; Ramjah,* an Isr.:— Ramiah.

7423. רְמִיָּה **rᵉmîyâh**, *rem-ee-yaw´*; from 7411; *remissness*, *treachery*:— deceit (-ful, -fully), false, guile, idle, slack, slothful.

7424. רַמָּךְ **rammâk**, *ram-mawk´*; of for. or.; a brood *mare*:— dromedary.

7425. רְמַלְיָהוּ **Rᵉmalyâhûw**, *rem-al-yaw´-hoo*; from an unused root and 3050 (perh. mean. to *deck*); *Jah has bedecked*; *Remaljah*, an Isr.:— Remaliah.

7426. רָמַם **râmam**, *raw-mam´*; a prim. root; to *rise* (lit. or fig.):— exalt, get [oneself] up, lift up (self), mount up.

7427. רֹמֵמֻת **rômêmûth**, *ro-may-mooth´*; from the act. part. of 7426; *exaltation*:— lifting up of self.

רִמֹּן **rimmôn**. See 7416.

7428. רִמֹּן פֶּרֶץ **Rimmôn Perets**, *rim-mone´ peh´-rets*; from 7416 and 6556; *pomegranate of* (the) *breach*; *Rimmon-Perets*, a place in the Desert:— Rimmon-parez.

7429. רָמַס **râmaç**, *raw-mas´*; a prim. root; to *tread* upon (as a potter, in walking or abusively):— oppressor, stamp upon, trample (under feet), tread (down, upon).

7430. רָמַשׂ **râmas**, *raw-mas´*; a prim. root; prop. to *glide* swiftly, i.e. to *crawl* or *move* with short steps; by anal. to *swarm*:— creep, move.

7431. רֶמֶשׂ **remes**, *reh´-mes*; from 7430; a *reptile* or any other rapidly moving animal:— that creepeth, creeping (moving) thing.

7432. רֶמֶת **Remeth**, *reh´-meth*; from 7411; *height*; *Remeth*, a place in Pal.:— Remeth.

7433. רָמֹת **Râmôwth** (or רָמוֹת **Râmôth**) גִּלְעָד **Râmôth Gil'âd** (2 Chron. 22:5), *raw-moth´ gil-awd´*; from the plur. of 7413 and 1568; *heights of Gilad*; *Ramoth-Gilad*, a place E. of the Jordan:— Ramoth-gilead, Ramoth in Gilead. See also 7216.

7434. רָמַת הַמִּצְפֶּה **Râmath ham-Mitspeh**, *raw-math´ ham-mits-peh´*; from 7413 and 4707 with the art. interpolated; *height of the watch-*tower; *Ramath-ham-Mitspeh*, a place in Pal.:— Ramath-mizpeh.

7435. רָמָתִי **Râmâthîy**, *raw-maw-thee´*; patron. of 7414; a *Ramathite* or inhab. of Ramah:— Ramathite.

7436. רָמָתַיִם צוֹפִים **Râmâthayim Tsôwphîym**, *raw-maw-thah´-yim tso-feem´*; from the dual of 7413 and the plur. of the act. part. of 6822; *double height of watchers*; *Ramathajim-Tsophim*, a place in Pal.:— Ramathaim-zophim.

7437. רָמַת לְחִי **Râmath Lechîy**, *raw-math lekh´-ee*; from 7413 and 3895; *height of* (a) *jaw-bone*; *Ramath-Lechi*, a place in Pal.:— Ramath-lehi.

רָן **Rân**. See 1028.

7438. רֹן **rôn**, *rone*; from 7442; a *shout* (of deliverance):— song.

7439. רָנָה **rânâh**, *raw-naw´*; a prim. root; to *whiz*:— rattle.

7440. רִנָּה **rinnâh**, *rin-naw´*; from 7442; prop. a *creaking* (or shrill sound), i.e. *shout* (of joy or grief):— cry, gladness,

joy, proclamation, rejoicing, shouting, sing (-ing), triumph.

7441. רִנָּה **Rinnâh**, *rin-naw´*; the same as 7440; *Rinnah*, an Isr.:— Rinnah.

7442. רָנַן **rânan**, *raw-nan´*; a prim. root; prop. to *creak* (or emit a stridulous sound), i.e. to *shout* (usually for joy):— aloud for joy, cry out, be joyful (greatly), make to rejoice, (cause to) shout (for joy), (cause to) sing (aloud, for joy, out), triumph.

7443. רֶנֶן **renen**, *reh´-nen*; from 7442; an *ostrich* (from its *wail*):— × goodly.

7444. רַנֵּן **rannên**, *ran-nane´*; intens. from 7442; *shouting* (for joy):— singing.

7445. רְנָנָה **rᵉnânâh**, *ren-aw-naw´*; from 7442; a *shout* (for joy):— joyful (voice), singing, triumphing.

7446. רִסָּה **Riççâh**, *ris-saw´*; from 7450; a *ruin* (as *dripping* to pieces); *Rissah*, a place in the Desert:— Rissah.

7447. רָסִיס **râçîyç**, *raw-sees´*; from 7450; prop. *dripping* to pieces, i.e. a *ruin*; also a dew-*drop*:— breach, drop.

7448. רֶסֶן **reçen**, *reh´-sen*; from an unused root mean. to *curb*; a *halter* (as *restraining*); by impl. the *jaw*:— bridle.

7449. רֶסֶן **Reçen**, *reh´-sen*; the same as 7448; *Resen*, a place in Ass.:— Resen.

7450. רָסַס **râçaç**, *raw-sas´*; a prim. root; to *comminute*; used only as denom. from 7447, to *moisten* (with drops):— temper.

7451. רַע **ra'**, *rah*; from 7489; *bad* or (as noun) *evil* (nat. or mor.):— adversity, affliction, bad, calamity, + displease (-ure), distress, evil (-favouredness), man, thing), + exceedingly, × great, grief (-vous), harm, heavy, hurt (-ful), ill (favoured), + mark, mischief (-vous), misery, naught (-ty), noisome, + not please, sad (-ly), sore, sorrow, trouble, vex, wicked (-ly, -ness, one), worse (-st), wretchedness, wrong. [Incl. fem.

רָעָה **râ'âh**; as adj. or noun.]

7452. רֵעַ **rêa'**, *ray-ah´*; from 7321; a *crash* (of thunder), *noise* (of war), *shout* (of joy):— × aloud, noise, shouted.

7453. רֵעַ **rêa'**, *ray-ah´*; or

רֵעַ **rêya'**, *ray´-ah´*; from 7462; an *associate* (more or less close):— brother, companion, fellow, friend, husband, lover, neighbour, × (an-) other.

7454. רֵעַ **rêa'**, *ray-ah´*; from 7462; a *thought* (as *association* of ideas):— thought.

7455. רֹעַ **rôa'**, *ro-ah´*; from 7489; *badness* (as *marring*), phys. or mor.:— × be so bad, badness, (× be so) evil, naughtiness, sadness, sorrow, wickedness.

7456. רָעֵב **râ'êb**, *raw-abe´*; a prim. root; to *hunger*:— (suffer to) famish, (be, have, suffer, suffer to) hunger (-ry).

7457. רָעֵב **râ'êb**, *raw-abe´*; from 7456; *hungry* (more or less intensely):— hunger bitten, hungry.

7458. רָעָב **râ'âb**, *raw-awb´*; from 7456; *hunger* (more or less extensive):— dearth, famine, + famished, hunger.

7459. רְעָבוֹן **rᵉâbôwn**, *reh-aw-bone´*; from 7456; *famine*:— famine.

7460. רָעַד **râ'ad**, *raw-ad´*; a prim. root: to *shudder* (more or less violently):— tremble.

7461. רַעַד **ra'ad**, *rah´-ad*; or (fem.)

רְעָדָה **rᵉâdâh**, *reh-aw-daw´*; from 7460; a *shudder*:— trembling.

7462. רָעָה **râ'âh**, *raw-aw´*; a prim. root; to *tend* a flock; i.e. *pasture* it; intr. to *graze* (lit. or fig.); gen. to *rule*; by extens. to *associate* with (as a friend):— × break, companion, keep company with, devour, eat up, evil entreat, feed, use as a friend, make friendship with, herdman, keep [sheep] (-er), pastor, + shearing house, shepherd, wander, waste.

7463. רֵעֶה **rê'eh**, *ray-eh´*; from 7462; a (male) *companion*:— friend.

7464. רֵעָה **rê'âh**, *ray-aw´*; fem. of 7453; a female *associate*:— companion, fellow.

7465. רֹעָה **rô'âh**, *ro-aw´*; for 7455; *breakage*:— broken, utterly.

7466. רְעוּ **Rᵉûw**, *reh-oo´*; for 7471 in the sense of 7453; *friend*; *Reü*, a postdiluvian patriarch:— Reu.

7467. רְעוּאֵל **Rᵉûw'êl**, *reh-oo-ale´*; from the same as 7466 and 410; *friend of God*; *Reüel*, the name of Moses' father-in-law, also of an Edomite and an Isr.:— Raguel, Reuel.

7468. רְעוּת **rᵉûwth**, *reh-ooth´*; from 7462 in the sense of 7453; a female *associate*; gen. an *additional* one:— + another, mate, neighbour.

7469. רְעוּת **rᵉûwth**, *reh-ooth´*; prob. from 7462; a *feeding* upon, i.e. *grasping* after:— vexation.

7470. רְעוּת **rᵉûwth** (Chald.), *reh-ooth´*; corresp. to 7469; *desire*:— pleasure, will.

7471. רְעִי **rᵉîy**, *reh-ee´*; from 7462; *pasture*:— pasture.

7472. רֵעִי **Rê'îy**, *ray-ee´*; from 7453; *social*; *Reï*, an Isr.:— Rei.

7473. רֹעִי **rô'îy**, *ro-ee´*; from act. part. of 7462; *pastoral*; as noun, a *shepherd*:— shepherd.

7474. רַעְיָה **ra'yâh**, *rah-yaw´*; fem. of 7453; a female *associate*:— fellow, love.

7475. רַעְיוֹן **ra'yôwn**, *rah-yone´*; from 7462 in the sense of 7469; *desire*:— vexation.

7476. רַעְיוֹן **ra'yôwn** (Chald.), *rah-yone´*; corresp. to 7475; a *grasp*, i.e. (fig.) mental *conception*:— cogitation, thought.

7477. רָעַל **râ'al**, *raw-al´*; a prim. root; to *reel*, i.e. (fig.) to *brandish*:— terribly shake.

7478. רַעַל **ra'al**, *rah´-al*; from 7477; a *reeling* (from intoxication):— trembling.

7479. רַעֲלָה **ra'ălâh**, *rah-al-aw´*; fem. of 7478; a long *veil* (as *fluttering*):— muffler.

7480. רְעֵלָיָה **Rᵉêlâyâh**, *reh-ay-law-yaw´*; from 7477 and 3050; *made to tremble* (i.e. *fearful*) *of Jah*; *Reëlajah*, an Isr.:— Reeliah.

7481. רָעַם **râ'am**, *raw-am´*; a prim. root; to *tumble*, i.e. *be* violently *agitated*; spec. to *crash* (of thunder); fig. to *irri-*

tate (with anger):— make to fret, roar, thunder, trouble.

7482. רַעַם **ra'am**, *rah'am;* from 7481; a *peal* of thunder:— thunder.

7483. רַעְמָה **ra'mâh**, *rah-maw';* fem. of 7482; the *mane* of a horse (as *quivering* in the wind):— thunder.

7484. רַעְמָה **Ra'mâh**, *rah-maw';* the same as 7483; *Ramah*, the name of a grandson of Ham, and of a place (perh. founded by him):— Raamah.

7485. רַעַמְיָה **Ra'amyâh**, *rah-am-yaw';* from 7481 and 3050; *Jah has shaken; Raamjah*, an Isr.:— Raamiah.

7486. רַעְמְסֵס **Ra'mᵉçêç**, *rah-mes-ace';* or

רַעַמְסֵס **Ra'amçêç**, *rah-am-sace';* of Eg. or.; *Rameses* or *Raamses*, a place in Egypt:— Raamses, Rameses.

7487. רַעֲנַן **ra'anan** (Chald.), *rah-aw-nan';* corresp. to 7488; *green*, i.e. (fig.) *prosperous:*— flourishing.

7488. רַעֲנַן **ra'ănân**, *rah-an-awn';* from an unused root mean. to *be green; verdant;* by anal. *new;* fig. *prosperous:*— green, flourishing.

7489. רָעַע **râ'a'**, *raw-ah';* a prim. root; prop. to *spoil* (lit. by *breaking* to pieces); fig. to *make* (or *be*) *good for nothing*, i.e. *bad* (physically, socially or morally):— afflict, associate selves [by *mistake* for 7462], break (down, in pieces), + displease, (be, bring, do) evil (doer, entreat, man), show self friendly [by *mistake* for 7462], do harm, (do) hurt, (behave self, deal) ill, × indeed, do mischief, punish, still, vex, (do) wicked (doer, -ly), be (deal, do) worse.

7490. רְעַע **rᵉ'a'** (Chald.), *reh-ah';* corresp. to 7489:— break, bruise.

7491. רָעַף **râ'aph**, *raw-af';* a prim. root; to *drip:*— distil, drop (down).

7492. רָעַץ **râ'ats**, *raw-ats';* a prim. root; to *break* in pieces; fig. *harass:*— dash in pieces, vex.

7493. רָעַשׁ **râ'ash**, *raw-ash;* a prim. root; to *undulate* (as the earth, the sky, etc.); also a field of grain), partic. through fear; spec. to *spring* (as a locust):— make afraid, (re-) move, quake, (make to) shake, (make to) tremble.

7494. רַעַשׁ **ra'ash**, *rah'-ash;* from 7493; *vibration, bounding, uproar:*— commotion, confused noise, earthquake, fierceness, quaking, rattling, rushing, shaking.

7495. רָפָא **râphâ'**, *raw-faw';* or

רָפָה **râphâh**, *raw-faw';* a prim. root; prop. to *mend* (by stitching), i.e. (fig.) to *cure:*— cure, (cause to) heal, physician, repair, × thoroughly, make whole. See 7503.

7496. רְפָא **râphâ'**, *raw-faw';* from 7495 in the sense of 7503; prop. *lax*, i.e. (fig.) a *ghost* (as *dead*; in plur. only):— dead, deceased.

7497. רָפָא **râphâ'**, *raw-faw';* or

רָפָה **râphâh**, *raw-faw';* from 7495 in the sense of *invigorating;* a *giant:*— giant, Rapha, Rephaim (-s). See also 1051.

7498. רָפָא **Râphâ'**, *raw-faw';* or

רָפָה **Râphâh**, *raw-faw';* prob. the

same as 7497; *giant; Rapha* or *Raphah*, the name of two Isr.:— Rapha.

7499. רְפֻאָה **rᵉphu'âh**, *ref-oo-aw';* fem. pass. part. of 7495; a *medicament:*— heal [-ed], medicine.

7500. רִפְאוּת **riph'ûwth**, *rif-ooth';* from 7495; a *cure:*— health.

7501. רְפָאֵל **Rᵉphâ'êl**, *ref-aw-ale';* from 7495 and 410; *God has cured; Rephaël*, an Isr.:— Rephael.

7502. רָפַד **râphad**, *raw-fad';* a prim. root; to *spread* (a bed); by impl. to *refresh:*— comfort, make [a bed], spread.

7503. רָפָה **râphâh**, *raw-faw';* a prim. root; to *slacken* (in many applications, lit. or fig.):— abate, cease, consume, draw [toward evening], fail, (be) faint, be (wax) feeble, forsake, idle, leave, let alone (go, down), (be) slack, stay, be still, be slothful, (be) weak (-en). See 7495.

7504. רָפֶה **râpheh**, *raw-feh';* from 7503; *slack* (in body or mind):— weak.

רָפָה **râphâh**, **Râphâh**. See 7497, 7498.

רִפָה **riphâh**. See 7383.

7505. רָפוּא **Râphûw'**, *raw-foo';* pass. part. of 7495; *cured; Raphu*, an Isr.:— Raphu.

7506. רֶפַח **Rephach**, *reh'-fakh;* from an unused root appar. mean. to *sustain; support; Rephach*, an Isr.:— Rephah.

7507. רְפִידָה **rᵉphîydâh**, *ref-ee-daw';* from 7502; a *railing* (as *spread* along):— bottom.

7508. רְפִידִים **Rᵉphîydîym**, *ref-ee-deem';* plur. of the masc. of the same as 7507; *ballusters; Rephidim*, a place in the Desert:— Rephidim.

7509. רְפָיָה **Rᵉphâyâh**, *ref-aw-yaw';* from 7495 and 3050; *Jah has cured; Rephajah*, the name of five Isr.:— Rephaiah.

7510. רִפְיוֹן **riphyôwn**, *rif-yone';* from 7503; *slackness:*— feebleness.

7511. רָפַס **râphaç**, *raw-fas';* a prim. root; to *trample*, i.e. *prostrate:*— humble self, submit self.

7512. רְפַס **rᵉphaç** (Chald.), *ref-as';* corresp. to 7511:— stamp.

7513. רַפְסֹדָה **raphçôdâh**, *raf-so-daw';* from 7511; a *raft* (as *flat* on the water):— flote.

7514. רָפַק **râphaq**, *raw-fak';* a prim. root; to *recline:*— lean.

7515. רָפַשׂ **râphas**, *raw-fas';* a prim. root; to *trample*, i.e. *roil* water:— foul, trouble.

7516. רֶפֶשׁ **rephesh**, *reh'-fesh;* from 7515; *mud* (as *roiled*):— mire.

7517. רֶפֶת **repheth**, *reh'-feth;* prob. from 7503; a *stall* for cattle (from their *resting* there):— stall.

7518. רַץ **rats**, *rats;* contr. from 7533; a *fragment:*— piece.

7519. רָצָא **râtsâ'**, *raw-tsaw';* a prim. root; to *run;* also to *delight* in:— accept, run.

7520. רָצַד **râtsad**, *raw-tsad';* a prim. root; prob. to *look askant*, i.e. (fig.) *be jealous:*— leap.

7521. רָצָה **râtsâh**, *raw-tsaw';* a prim. root; to *be pleased with;* spec. to *satisfy* a debt:— (be) accept (-able), accomplish, set affection, approve, consent with, delight (self), enjoy, (be, have a) favour (-able), like, observe, pardon, (be, have, take) please (-ure), reconcile self.

7522. רָצוֹן **râtsôwn**, *raw-tsone';* or

רָצֹן **râtsôn**, *raw-tsone';* from 7521; *delight* (espec. as shown):— (be) acceptable (-ance, -ed), delight, desire, favour, (good) pleasure, (own, self, voluntary) will, as ... (what) would.

7523. רָצַח **râtsach**, *raw-tsakh';* a prim. root; prop. to *dash* in pieces, i.e. *kill* (a human being), espec. to *murder:*— put to death, kill, (man-) slay (-er), murder (-er).

7524. רֶצַח **retsach**, *reh-tsakh;* from 7523; a *crushing;* spec. a *murder*-cry:— slaughter, sword.

7525. רִצְיָא **Ritsyâ'**, *rits-yaw';* from 7521; *delight; Ritsjah*, an Isr.:— Rezia.

7526. רְצִין **Rᵉtsîyn**, *rets-een';* prob. for 7522; *Retsin*, the name of a Syrian and of an Isr.:— Rezin.

7527. רָצַע **râtsa'**, *raw-tsah';* a prim. root; to *pierce:*— bore.

7528. רָצַף **râtsaph**, *raw-tsaf;* a denom. from 7529; to *tessellate*, i.e. embroider (as if with bright stones):— pave.

7529. רֶצֶף **retseph**, *reh'-tsef;* for 7565; a red-hot *stone* (for baking):— coal.

7530. רֶצֶף **Retseph**, *reh'-tsef;* the same as 7529; *Retseph*, a place in Ass.:— Rezeph.

7531. רִצְפָה **ritspâh**, *rits-paw';* fem. of 7529; a hot *stone;* also a tessellated *pavement:*— live coal, pavement.

7532. רִצְפָה **Ritspâh**, *rits-paw';* the same as 7531; *Ritspah*, an Israelitess:— Rizpah.

7533. רָצַץ **râtsats**, *raw-tsats';* a prim. root; to *crack* in pieces, lit. or fig.:— break, bruise, crush, discourage, oppress, struggle together.

7534. רַק **raq**, *rak;* from 7556 in its orig. sense; *emaciated* (as if *flattened* out):— lean ([-fleshed]), thin.

7535. רַק **raq**, *rak;* the same as 7534 as a noun; prop. *leanness*, i.e. (fig.) *limitation;* only adv. *merely*, or conjunc. *although:*— but, even, except, howbeit, howsoever, at the least, nevertheless, nothing but, notwithstanding, only, save, so [that], surely, yet (so), in any wise.

7536. רֹק **rôq**, *roke;* from 7556; *spittle:*— spit (-ting, -tle).

7537. רָקַב **râqab**, *raw-kab';* a prim. root; to *decay* (as by worm-eating):— rot.

7538. רָקָב **râqâb**, *raw-kawb';* from 7537; *decay* (by *caries*):— rottenness (thing).

7539. רִקָּבוֹן **riqqâbôwn**, *rik-kaw-bone';* from 7538; *decay* (by *caries*):— rotten.

7540. רָקַד **râqad**, *raw-kad';* a prim. root; prop. to *stamp*, i.e. to *spring* about (wildly or for joy):— dance, jump, leap, skip.

7541. רַקָּה **raqqâh**, *rak-kaw'*; fem. of 7534; prop. *thinness*, i.e. the *side* of the head:— temple.

7542. רַקּוֹן **Raqqôwn**, *rak-kone'*; from 7534; *thinness; Rakkon*, a place in Pal.:— Rakkon.

7543. רָקַח **râqach**, *raw-kakh'*; a prim. root; to *perfume*:— apothecary, compound, make [ointment], prepare, spice.

7544. רֶקַח **reqach**, *reh'-kakh*; from 7543; prop. *perfumery*, i.e. (by impl.) *spicery* (for flavor):— spiced.

7545. רֹקַח **rôqach**, *ro'-kakh*; from 7542; an *aromatic*:— confection, ointment.

7546. רַקָּח **raqqâch**, *rak-kawkh'*; from 7543; a male *perfumer*:— apothecary.

7547. רַקֻּחַ **raqqûach**, *rak-koo'-akh*; from 7543; a *scented* substance:— perfume.

7548. רַקָּחָה **raqqâchâh**, *rak-kaw-khaw'*; fem. of 7547; a female *perfumer*:— confectioner.

7549. רָקִיעַ **râqîya'**, *raw-kee'-ah*; from 7554; prop. an *expanse*, i.e. the *firmament* or (appar.) visible arch of the sky:— firmament.

7550. רָקִיק **râqîyq**, *raw-keek'*; from 7556 in its orig. sense; a thin *cake*:— cake, wafer.

7551. רָקַם **râqam**, *raw-kam'*; a prim. root; to *variegate* color, i.e. *embroider*; by impl. to *fabricate*:— embroiderer, needlework, curiously work.

7552. רֶקֶם **Reqem**, *reh'-kem*; from 7551; *versi-color; Rekem*, the name of a place in Pal., also of a Midianite and an Isr.:— Rekem.

7553. רִקְמָה **riqmâh**, *rik-maw'*; from 7551; *variegation* of color; spec. *embroidery*:— broidered (work), divers colours, (raiment of) needlework (on both sides).

7554. רָקַע **râqa'**, *raw-kah'*; a prim. root; to *pound* the earth (as a sign of passion); by anal. to *expand* (by hammering); by impl. to *overlay* (with thin sheets of metal):— beat, make broad, spread abroad (forth, over, out, into plates), stamp, stretch.

7555. רִקֻּעַ **riqqûa'**, *rik-koo'-ah*; from 7554; *beaten* out, i.e. a (metallic) *plate*:— broad.

7556. רָקַק **râqaq**, *raw-kak'*; a prim. root; to *spit*:— spit.

7557. רַקַּת **Raqqath**, *rak-kath'*; from 7556 in its orig. sense of *diffusing*; a *beach* (as *expanded* shingle); *Rakkath*, a place in Pal.:— Rakkath.

7558. רִשְׁיוֹן **rîshyôwn**, *rish-yone'*; from an unused root mean. to *have leave*; a *permit*:— grant.

7559. רָשַׁם **râsham**, *raw-sham'*; a prim. root; to *record*:— note.

7560. רְשַׁם **rᵉsham** (Chald.), *resh-am'*; corresp. to 7559:— sign, write.

7561. רָשַׁע **râsha'**, *raw-shah'*; a prim. root; to *be* (caus. *do* or *declare*) *wrong*; by impl. to *disturb, violate*:— condemn, make trouble, vex, be (commit, deal, depart, do) wicked (-ly, -ness).

7562. רֶשַׁע **resha'**, *reh'-shah*; from 7561;

a *wrong* (espec. moral):— iniquity, wicked (-ness).

7563. רָשָׁע **râshâ'**, *raw-shaw'*; from 7561; morally *wrong*; concr. an (actively) *bad person*:— + condemned, guilty, ungodly, wicked (man), that did wrong.

7564. רִשְׁעָה **rish'âh**, *rish-aw'*; fem. of 7562; *wrong* (espec. moral):— fault, wickedly (-ness).

7565. רֶשֶׁף **resheph**, *reh'-shef*; from 8313; a live *coal*; by anal. *lightning*; fig. an *arrow*, (as *flashing* through the air); spec. *fever*:— arrow, (burning) coal, burning heat, + spark, hot thunderbolt.

7566. רֶשֶׁף **Resheph**, *reh'-shef*; the same as 7565; *Resheph*, an Isr.:— Resheph.

7567. רָשַׁשׁ **râshash**, *raw-shash'*; a prim. root; to *demolish*:— impoverish.

7568. רֶשֶׁת **resheth**, *reh'-sheth*; from 3423; a *net* (as *catching* animals):— net [-work].

7569. רַתּוֹק **rattôwq**, *rat-toke'*; from 7576; a *chain*:— chain.

7570. רָתַח **râthach**, *raw-thakh'*; a prim. root; to *boil*:— boil.

7571. רֶתַח **rethach**, *reh'-thakh*; from 7570; a *boiling*:— × [boil] well.

7572. רַתִּיקָה° **rattîyqâh**, *rat-tee-kaw'*; from 7576; a *chain*:— chain.

7573. רָתַם **râtham**, *raw-tham'*; a prim. root; to *yoke* up (to the pole of a vehicle):— bind.

7574. רֶתֶם **rethem**, *reh'-them*; or

רֹתֶם **rôthem**, *ro'-them*; from 7573; the Spanish *broom* (from its pole-like stems):— juniper (tree).

7575. רִתְמָה **Rithmâh**, *rith-maw'*; fem. of 7574; *Rithmah*, a place in the Desert:— Rithmah.

7576. רָתַק **râthaq**, *raw-thak'*; a prim. root; to *fasten*:— bind.

7577. רְתֻקָה **rᵉthûqâh**, *reth-oo-kaw'*; fem. pass. part. of 7576; something *fastened*, i.e. a *chain*:— chain.

7578. רְתֵת **rᵉthéth**, *reth-ayth'*; for 7374; *terror*:— trembling.

ש

7579. שָׁאַב **shâ'ab**, *sahw-ab'*; a prim. root; to *bale* up water:— (woman to) draw (-er, water).

7580. שָׁאַג **shâ'ag**, *shaw-ag'*; a prim. root; to *rumble* or *moan*:— × mightily, roar.

7581. שְׁאָגָה **shᵉ'âgâh**, *sheh-aw-gaw'*; from 7580; a *rumbling* or *moan*:— roaring.

7582. שָׁאָה **shâ'âh**, *shaw-aw'*; a prim. root; to *rush*; by impl. to *desolate*:— be desolate, (make a) rush (-ing), (lay) waste.

7583. שָׁאָה **shâ'âh**, *shaw-aw'*; a prim. root [rather ident. with 7582 through the idea of *whirling* to giddiness]; to *stun*, i.e. (intr.) *be astonished*:— wonder.

7584. שַׁאֲוָה **sha'ăvâh**, *shah-av-aw'*; from 7582; a *tempest* (as *rushing*):— desolation.

7585. שְׁאוֹל **shᵉ'ôwl**, *sheh-ole'*; or

שְׁאֹל **shᵉ'ôl**, *sheh-ole'*; from 7592; *hades* or the world of the dead (as if a subterranean *retreat*), incl. its accessories and inmates:— grave, hell, pit.

7586. שָׁאוּל **Shâ'ûwl**, *shaw-ool'*; pass. part. of 7592; *asked; Shaül*, the name of an Edomite and two Isr.:— Saul, Shaul.

7587. שָׁאוּלִי **Shâ'ûwlîy**, *shaw-oo-lee'*; patron. from 7856; a *Shaülite* or desc. of Shaül:— Shaulites.

7588. שָׁאוֹן **shâ'ôwn**, *shaw-one'*; from 7582; *uproar* (as of *rushing*); by impl. *destruction*:— × horrible, noise, pomp, rushing, tumult (×uous).

7589. שְׁאָט **shᵉ'ât**, *sheh-awt'*; from an unused root mean. to *push* aside; *contempt*:— despite (-ful).

7590. שָׁאט **shâ't**, *shawt*; for act. part. of 7750 [comp. 7589]; one *contemning*:— that (which) despise (-d).

7591. שְׁאִיָּה **shᵉ'îyâh**, *sheh-ee-yaw'*; from 7582; *desolation*:— destruction.

7592. שָׁאַל **shâ'al**, *shaw-al'*; or

שָׁאֵל **shâ'êl**, *shaw-ale'*; a prim. root; to *inquire*; by impl. to *request*; by extens. to *demand*:— ask (counsel, on), beg, borrow, lay to charge, consult, demand, desire, × earnestly, enquire, + greet, obtain leave, lend, pray, request, require, + salute, × straitly, × surely, wish.

7593. שְׁאֵל **shᵉ'êl** (Chald.), *sheh-ale'*; corresp. to 7592:— ask, demand, require.

7594. שְׁאָל **Shᵉ'âl**, *sheh-awl'*; from 7592; *request; Sheäl*, an Isr.:— Sheal.

שְׁאֹל **shᵉ'ôl**. See 7585.

7595. שְׁאֵלָא **shᵉ'êlâ'** (Chald.), *sheh-ay-law'*; from 7593; prop. a *question* (at law), i.e. judicial *decision* or *mandate*:— demand.

7596. שְׁאֵלָה **shᵉ'êlâh**, *sheh-ay-law'*; or

שֵׁלָה **shêlâh** (1 Sam. 1:17), *shay-law'*; from 7592; a *petition*; by impl. a *loan*:— loan, petition, request.

7597. שְׁאַלְתִּיאֵל **Shᵉ'altîy'êl**, *sheh-al-tee-ale'*; or

שַׁלְתִּיאֵל **Shaltîy'êl**, *shal-tee-ale'*; from 7592 and 410; *I have asked God; Sheältiel*, an Isr.:— Shalthiel, Shealtiel.

7598. שְׁאַלְתִּיאֵל **Shᵉ'altîy'êl** (Chald.), *sheh-al-tee-ale'*; corresp. to 7597:— Shealtiel.

7599. שָׁאַן **shâ'an**, *shaw-an'*; a prim. root; to *loll*, i.e. *be peaceful*:— be at ease, be quiet, rest. See also 1052.

7600. שַׁאֲנָן **sha'ănân**, *shah-an-awn'*; from 7599; *secure*; in a bad sense, *haughty*:— that is at ease, quiet, tumult. Comp. 7946.

7601. שָׁאַס° **shâ'aç**, *shaw-as'*; a prim. root; to *plunder*:— spoil.

7602. שָׁאַף **shâ'aph**, *shaw-af'*; a prim. root; to *inhale* eagerly; fig. to *covet*; by impl. to *be angry*; also to *hasten*:— desire (earnestly), devour, haste, pant, snuff up, swallow up.

7603. שְׂאֹר **sᵉ'ôr**, *seh-ore'*; from 7604; *barm* or *yeast-cake* (as *swelling* by fermentation):— leaven.

7604. שָׁאַר **shâ'ar**, *shaw-ar'*; a prim.

root; prop. to *swell* up, i.e. *be* (caus. *make*) *redundant*:— leave, (be) left, let, remain, remnant, reserve, the rest.

7605. שְׁאָר **sheʼâr**, *sheh-awr´*; from 7604; a *remainder*:— × other, remnant, residue, rest.

7606. שְׁאָר **sheʼâr** (Chald.), *sheh-awr´*; corresp. to 7605:— × whatsoever more, residue, rest.

7607. שְׁאֵר **sheʼêr**, *sheh-ayr´*; from 7604; *flesh* (as *swelling* out), as living or for food; gen. *food* of any kind; fig. *kindred* by blood:— body, flesh, food, (near) kin (-sman, -swoman), near (nigh) [of kin].

7608. שַׁאֲרָה **shaʼărâh**, *shah-ar-aw´*; fem. of 7607; *female kindred* by blood:— near kinswomen.

7609. שֶׁאֱרָה **Sheʼĕrâh**, *sheh-er-aw´*; the same as 7608; *Sheërah*, an Israelitess:— Sherah.

7610. שְׁאָר יָשׁוּב **Sheʼâr Yâshûwb**, *sheh-awr´ yaw-shoob´*; from 7605 and 7725; a *remnant will return*; *Sheär-Jashub*, the symbol. name of one of Isaiah's sons:— Shear-jashub.

7611. שְׁאֵרִית **sheʼêrîyth**, *sheh-ay-reeth´*; from 7604; a *remainder* or residual (surviving, final) portion:— that had escaped, be left, posterity, remain (-der), remnant, residue, rest.

7612. שֵׁאת **shêʼth**, *shayth*; from 7582: *devastation*:— desolation.

7613. שְׂאֵת **seʼêth**, *seh-ayth´*; from 5375; an *elevation* or leprous scab; fig. *elation* or cheerfulness; *exaltation* in rank or character:— be accepted, dignity, excellency, highness, raise up self, rising.

7614. שְׁבָא **Shebâʼ**, *sheb-aw´*; of for. or.; *Sheba*, the name of three early progenitors of tribes and of an Ethiopian district:— Sheba, Sabeans.

7615. שְׁבָאִי **Shebâʼîy**, *sheb-aw-ee´*; patron. from 7614; a *Shebaïte* or desc. of Sheba:— Sabean.

7616. שָׁבָב **shâbâb**, *shaw-bawb´*; from an unused root mean. to *break* up; a *fragment*, i.e. *ruin*:— broken in pieces.

7617. שָׁבָה **shâbâh**, *shaw-baw´*; a prim. root; to *transport* into captivity:— (bring away, carry, carry away, lead, lead away, take) captive (-s), drive (take) away.

7618. שְׁבוּ **shebûw**, *sheb-oo´*; from an unused root (prob. ident. with that of 7617 through the idea of *subdivision* into flashes or streamers [comp. 7632] mean. to *flame*; a *gem* (from its sparkle), prob. the *agate*:— agate.

7619. שְׁבוּאֵל **Shebûwʼêl**, *sheb-oo-ale´*; or

שׁוּבָאֵל **Shûwbâʼêl**, *shoo-baw-ale´*; from 7617 (abbrev.) or 7725 and 410; *captive* (or *returned*) *of God*; *Shebuël* or *Shubaël*, the name of two Isr.:— Shebuel, Shubael.

7620. שָׁבוּעַ **shâbûwaʻ**, *shaw-boo´-ah*; or

שָׁבֻעַ **shâbuaʻ**, *shaw-boo´-ah*; also (fem.)

שְׁבֻעָה **shebuʻâh**, *sheb-oo-aw´*; prop. pass. part. of 7650 as a denom. of 7651; lit. *sevened*, i.e. a *week* (spec. of years):— seven, week.

7621. שְׁבוּעָה **shebûwʻâh**, *sheb-oo-aw´*; fem. pass. part. of 7650; prop. something *sworn*, i.e. an *oath*:— curse, oath, × sworn.

7622. שְׁבוּת **shebûwth**, *sheb-ooth´*; or

שְׁבִית **shebîyth**, *sheb-eeth´*; from 7617; *exile*, concr. *prisoners*; fig. a *former state* of prosperity:— captive (-ity).

7623. שָׁבַח **shâbach**, *shaw-bakh´*; a prim. root; prop. to *address* in a loud tone, i.e. (spec.) *loud*; fig. to *pacify* (as if by words):— commend, glory, keep in, praise, still, triumph.

7624. שְׁבַח **shebach** (Chald.), *sheb-akh´*; corresp. to 7623; to *adulate*, i.e. *adore*:— praise.

7625. שְׁבַט **shebaṭ** (Chald.), *sheb-at´*; corresp. to 7626; a *clan*:— tribe.

7626. שֵׁבֶט **shêbeṭ**, *shay-bet*; from an unused root prob. mean. to *branch* off; a *scion*, i.e. (lit.) a *stick* (for punishing, writing, fighting, ruling, walking, etc.) or (fig.) a *clan*:— × correction, dart, rod, sceptre, staff, tribe.

7627. שְׁבָט **Shebâṭ**, *sheb-awt´*; of for. or.; *Shebat*, a Jewish month:— Sebat.

7628. שְׁבִי **shebîy**, *sheb-ee´*; from 7618; *exiled*; *captured*; as noun, *exile* (abstr. or concr. and collect.); by extens. *booty*:— captive (-ity), prisoners, × take away, that was taken.

7629. שֹׁבִי **Shôbîy**, *sho-bee´*; from 7617; *captor*; *Shobi*, an Ammonite:— Shobi.

7630. שֹׁבָי **Shôbây**, *sho-bah´-ee*; for 7629; *Shobai*, an Isr.:— Shobai.

7631. שְׁבִיב **shebîyb** (Chald.), *seb-eeb´*; corresp. to 7632:— flame.

7632. שָׁבִיב **shâbîyb**, *shaw-beeb´*; from the same as 7616; *flame* (as *split* into tongues):— spark.

7633. שִׁבְיָה **shibyâh**, *shib-yaw´*; fem. of 7628; *exile* (abstr. or concr. and collect.):— captives (-ity).

7634. שָׁבְיָה **Shobyâh**, *shob-yaw´*; fem. of the same as 7629; *captivation*; *Shobjah*, an Isr.:— Shachia [from the marg.].

7635. שָׁבִיל **shâbîyl**, *shaw-beel´*; from the same as 7640; a *track* or passageway (as if *flowing* along):— path.

7636. שָׁבִיס **shâbîyç**, *shaw-beece´*; from an unused root mean. to *interweave*; a *netting* for the hair:— caul.

7637. שְׁבִיעִי **shebîyʻîy**, *sheb-ee-ee´*; or

שְׁבִעִי **shebiʻîy**, *sheb-ee-ee´*; ord. from 7657; *seventh*:— seventh (time).

שְׁבִית **shebîyth**. See 7622.

7638. שָׂבָךְ **sâbâk**, *saw-bawk´*; from an unused root mean. to *intwine*; a *netting* (ornament to the capital of a column):— net.

שְׂבָכָא **sabbekâʼ**. See 5443.

7639. שְׂבָכָה **sebâkâh**, *seb-aw-kaw´*; fem. of 7638; a *net-work*, i.e (in hunting) a *snare*, (in arch.) a *ballustrade*; also a *reticulated* ornament to a pillar:— checker, lattice, network, snare, wreath (-enwork).

7640. שֹׁבֶל **shôbel**, *show´-bel*; from an unused root mean. to *flow*; a *lady's train* (as *trailing* after her):— leg.

7641. שִׁבֹּל **shibbôl**, *shib-bole´*; or (fem.)

שִׁבֹּלֶת **shibbôleth**, *shib-bo´-leth*; from the same as 7640; a *stream* (as *flowing*); also an *ear* of grain (as *growing* out); by anal. a *branch*:— branch, channel, ear (of corn), ([water-]) flood, Shibboleth. Comp. 5451.

7642. שַׁבְלוּל **shablûwl**, *shab-lool´*; from the same as 7640; a *snail* (as if *floating* in its own slime):— snail.

שִׁבֹּלֶת **shibbôleth**. See 7641.

7643. שְׂבָם **Sebâm**, *seb-awm´*; or (fem.)

שִׂבְמָה **Sibmâh**, *sib-maw´*; prob. from 1313; *spice*; *Sebam* or *Sibmah*, a place in Moab:— Shebam, Shibmah, Sibmah.

7644. שֶׁבְנָא **Shebnâʼ**, *sheb-naw´*; or

שֶׁבְנָה **Shebnâh**, *sheb-naw´*; from an unused root mean. to *grow*; *growth*; *Shebna* or *Shebnah*, an Isr.:— Shebna, Shebnah.

7645. שְׁבַנְיָה **Shebanyâh**, *sheb-an-yaw´*; or

שְׁבַנְיָהוּ **Shebanyâhûw**, *sheb-an-yaw´-hoo*; from the same as 7644 and 3050; *Jah has grown* (i.e. *prospered*); *Shebanjah*, the name of three or four Isr.:— Shebaniah.

7646. שָׂבַע **sâbaʻ**, *saw-bah´*; or

שָׂבֵעַ **sâbêaʻ**, *saw-bay´-ah*; a prim. root; to *sate*, i.e. *fill* to satisfaction (lit. or fig.):— have enough, fill (full, self, with), be (to the) full (of), have plenty of, be satiate, satisfy (with), suffice, be weary of.

7647. שָׂבָע **sâbâʻ**, *saw-baw´*; from 7646; *copiousness*:— abundance, plenteous (-ness, -ly).

7648. שֹׂבַע **sôbaʻ**, *so´-bah*; from 7646; *satisfaction* (of food or [fig.] joy):— fill, full (-ness), satisfying, be satisfied.

7649. שָׂבֵעַ **sâbêaʻ**, *saw-bay´-ah*; from 7646; *satiated* (in a pleasant or disagreeable sense):— full (of), satisfied (with).

7650. שָׁבַע **shâbaʻ**, *shaw-bah´*; a prim. root; prop. to *be complete*, but used only as a denom. from 7651; to *seven* oneself, i.e. *swear* (as if by repeating a declaration *seven times*):— adjure, charge (by an oath, with an oath), feed to the full [by mistake for 7646], take an oath, × straitly, (cause to, make to) swear.

7651. שֶׁבַע **sheba'**, *sheh´-bah*; or (masc.)

שִׁבְעָה **shib'âh**, *shib-aw´*; from 7650; a prim. cardinal number; *seven* (as the sacred *full* one); also (adv.) *seven times*; by impl. a *week*; by extens. an *indefinite* number:— (+ by) seven [-fold], -s, [-teen,teenth], -th, times). Comp. 7658.

7652. שֶׁבַע **Sheba'**, *sheh´-bah*; the same as 7651; *seven*; *Sheba*, the name of a place in Pal., and of two Isr.:— Sheba.

שָׁבֻעַ **shâbûa'**. See 7620.

7653. שִׂבְעָה **sib'âh**, *sib-aw´*; fem. of 7647; *satiety*:— fulness.

7654. שָׂבְעָה **sob'âh**, *sob-aw´*; fem. of 7648; *satiety*:— (to have) enough, × till ... be full, [un-] satiable, satisfy, × sufficiently.

שִׁבְעָה **shib'âh**. See 7651.

Hebrew

7655. שִׁבְעָה **shib'âh** (Chald.), *shib-aw´;* corresp. to 7651:— seven (times).

7656. שִׁבְעָה **Shib'âh,** *shib-aw´;* masc. of 7651; *seven (-th); Shebah,* a well in Pal.:— Shebah.

שְׁבוּעָה **shᵉbû'âh.** See 7620.

שְׁבִיעִי **shᵉbîy'îy.** See 7637.

7657. שִׁבְעִים **shib'îym,** *shib-eem´;* multiple of 7651; *seventy,* three-score and ten (+ -teen).

7658. שִׁבְעָנָה **shib'ânâh,** *shib-aw-naw´;* prol. for the masc. of 7651; *seven:*— seven.

7659. שִׁבְעָתַיִם **shib'âthayim,** *shib-aw-thah´-yim;* dual (adv.) of 7651; *seven-times:*— seven (-fold, times).

7660. שָׁבַץ **shâbats,** *shaw-bats´;* a prim. root; to *interweave* (colored) threads in squares; by impl. (*of reticulation*) to *inchase* gems in gold:— embroider, set.

7661. שָׁבָץ **shâbâts,** *shaw-bawts´;* from 7660; *intanglement,* i.e. (fig.) *perplexity:*— anguish.

7662. שְׁבַק **shᵉbaq** (Chald.), *sheb-ak´;* corresp. to the root of 7733; to *quit,* i.e. *allow to remain:*— leave, let alone.

7663. שָׂבַר **sâbar,** *saw-bar´;* err.

שָׂבַר **shâbar** (Neh. 2:13, 15), *shaw-bar´;* a prim. root; to *scrutinize;* by impl. (of *watching*) to *expect* (with hope and patience):— hope, tarry, view, wait.

7664. שֵׂבֶר **sêber,** *say´-ber;* from 7663; *expectation:*— hope.

7665. שָׁבַר **shâbar,** *shaw-bar´;* a prim. root; to *burst* (lit. or fig.):— break (down, off, in pieces, up), broken (I-hearted), bring to the birth, crush, destroy, hurt, quench, × quite, tear, view [by *mistake* for 7663].

7666. שָׁבַר **shâbar,** *shaw-bar´;* denom. from 7668; to *deal* in grain:— buy, sell.

7667. שֶׁבֶר **sheber,** *sheh´-ber;* or

שֶׁבֶר **shêber,** *shay´-ber;* from 7665; a *fracture,* fig. *ruin;* spec. a *solution* (of a dream):— affliction, breach, breaking, broken [-footed, -handed], bruise, crashing, destruction, hurt, interpretation, vexation.

7668. שֶׁבֶר **sheber,** *sheh´-ber;* the same as 7667; *grain* (as if *broken* into kernels):— corn, victuals.

7669. שֶׁבֶר **Sheber,** *sheh´-ber;* the same as 7667; *Sheber,* an Isr.:— Sheber.

7670. שִׁבְרוֹן **shibrôwn,** *shib-rone´;* from 7665; *rupture,* i.e. a *pang;* fig. *ruin:*— breaking, destruction.

7671. שְׁבָרִים **Shᵉbârîym,** *sheb-aw-reem´;* plur. of 7667; *ruins; Shebarim,* a place in Pal.:— Shebarim.

7672. שְׁבַשׁ **shᵉbash** (Chald.), *sheb-ash´;* corresp. to 7660; to *intangle,* i.e. *perplex:*— be astonished.

7673. שָׁבַת **shâbath,** *shaw-bath´;* a prim. root; to *repose,* i.e. *desist* from exertion; used in many impl. relations (caus., fig. or spec.):— (cause to, let, make to) cease, celebrate, cause (make) to fail, keep (sabbath), suffer to be lacking, leave, put away (down), (make to) rest, rid, still, take away.

7674. שֶׁבֶת **shebeth,** *sheh´-beth;* from

7673; *rest, interruption, cessation:*— cease, sit still, loss of time.

7675. שֶׁבֶת **shebeth,** *sheh´-beth;* infin. of 3427; prop. *session;* but used also concr. an *abode* or *locality:*— place, seat. Comp. 3429.

7676. שַׁבָּת **shabbâth,** *shab-bawth´;* intens. from 7673; *intermission,* i.e (spec.) the *Sabbath:*— (+ every) sabbath.

7677. שַׁבָּתוֹן **shabbâthôwn,** *shab-baw-thone´;* from 7676; a *sabbatism* or special *holiday:*— rest, sabbath.

7678. שַׁבְּתַי **Shabbᵉthay,** *shab-beth-ah´-ee;* from 7676; *restful; Shabbethai,* the name of three Isr.:— Shabbethai.

7679. שָׂגָא **sâgâ',** *saw-gaw´;* a prim. root; to *grow,* i.e. (caus.) to *enlarge,* (fig.) *laud:*— increase, magnify.

7680. שְׂגָא **sᵉgâ'** (Chald.), *seg-aw´;* corresp. to 7679; to *increase:*— grow, be multiplied.

7681. שָׁגֵא **Shâgê',** *shaw-gay´;* prob. from 7686; *erring; Shage,* an Isr.:— Shage.

7682. שָׂגַב **sâgab,** *saw-gab´;* a prim. root; to *be* (caus. *make*) *lofty,* espec. *inaccessible;* by impl. *safe, strong;* used lit. and fig.:— defend, exalt, be excellent, (be, set on) high, lofty, be safe, set up (on high), be too strong.

7683. שָׁגַג **shâgag,** *shaw-gag´;* a prim. root; to *stray,* i.e. (fig.) *sin* (with more or less apology):— × also for that, deceived, err, go astray, sin ignorantly.

7684. שְׁגָגָה **shᵉgâgâh,** *sheg-aw-gaw´;* from 7683; a *mistake* or inadvertent *transgression:*— error, ignorance, at unawares, unwittingly.

7685. שָׂגָה **sâgâh,** *saw-gaw´;* a prim. root; to *enlarge* (espec. upward, also fig.):— grow (up), increase.

7686. שָׁגָה **shâgâh,** *shaw-gaw´;* a prim. root; to *stray* (caus. *mislead*), usually (fig.) to *mistake,* espec. (mor.) to *transgress;* by extens. (through the idea of intoxication) to *reel,* (fig.) *be enraptured:*— (cause to) go astray, deceive, err, be ravished, sin through ignorance, (let, make to) wander.

7687. שְׂגוּב **Sᵉgûwb,** *seg-oob´;* from 7682; *aloft; Segub,* the name of two Isr.:— Segub.

7688. שָׁגַח **shâgach,** *shaw-gakh´;* a prim. root; to *peep,* i.e. *glance* sharply at:— look (narrowly).

7689. שַׂגִּיא **saggîy',** *sag-ghee´;* from 7679; (superl.) *mighty:*— excellent, great.

7690. שַׂגִּיא **saggîy'** (Chald.), *sag-ghee´;* corresp. to 7689; *large* (in size, quantity or number, also adv.):— exceeding, great (-ly); many, much, sore, very.

7691. שְׁגִיאָה **shᵉgîy'âh,** *sheg-ee-aw´;* from 7686; a moral *mistake:*— error.

7692. שִׁגָּיוֹן **Shiggâyôwn,** *shig-gaw-yone´;* or

שִׁגָּיֹנָה **Shiggâyônâh,** *shig-gaw-yo-naw´;* from 7686; prop. *aberration,* i.e. (tech.) a *dithyramb* or rambling poem:— Shiggaion, Shigionoth.

7693. שָׁגַל **shâgal,** *shaw-gal´;* a prim. root; to *copulate* with:— lie with, ravish.

7694. שֵׁגָל **shêgâl,** *shay-gawl´;* from 7693; a *queen* (from cohabitation):— queen.

7695. שֵׁגָל **shêgâl** (Chald.), *shay-gawl´;* corresp. to 7694; a (legitimate) *queen:*— wife.

7696. שָׁגַע **shâga',** *shaw-gah´;* a prim. root; to *rave* through insanity:— (be, play the) mad (man).

7697. שִׁגָּעוֹן **shiggâ'ôwn,** *shig-gaw-yone´;* from 7696; *craziness:*— furiously, madness.

7698. שֶׁגֶר **sheger,** *sheh´-ger;* from an unused root prob. mean. to *eject;* the *fetus* (as finally *expelled*):— that cometh of, increase.

7699. שַׁד **shad,** *shad;* or

שֹׁד **shôd,** *shode;* prob. from 7736 (in its orig. sense) contr.; the *breast* of a woman or animal (as *bulging*):— breast, pap, teat.

7700. שֵׁד **shêd,** *shade;* from 7736; a *demon* (as *malignant*):— devil.

7701. שֹׁד **shôd,** *shode;* or

שׁוֹד **shôwd** (Job 5:21), *shode;* from 7736; *violence, ravage:*— desolation, destruction, oppression, robbery, spoil (-ed, -er, -ing), wasting.

7702. שָׂדַד **sâdad,** *saw-dad´;* a prim. root; to *abrade,* i.e. *harrow* a field:— break clods, harrow.

7703. שָׁדַד **shâdad,** *shaw-dad´;* a prim. root; prop. to *be burly,* i.e. (fig.) *powerful* (pass. *impregnable*); by impl. to *ravage:*— dead, destroy (-er), oppress, robber, spoil (-er), × utterly, (lay) waste.

7704. שָׂדֶה **sâdeh,** *saw-deh´;* or

שָׂדַי **sâday,** *saw-dah´-ee;* from an unused root mean. to *spread* out; a *field* (as *flat*):— country, field, ground, land, soil, × wild.

7705. שִׁדָּה **shiddâh,** *shid-dah´;* from 7703; a *wife* (as *mistress* of the house):— × all sorts, musical instrument.

7706. שַׁדַּי **Shadday,** *shad-dah´-ee;* from 7703; the *Almighty:*— Almighty.

7707. שְׁדֵיאוּר **Shᵉdêy'ûwr,** *shed-ay-oor´;* from the same as 7704 and 217; *spreader of light; Shedejur,* an Isr.:— Shedeur.

7708. שִׁדִּים **Siddîym,** *sid-deem´;* plur. from the same as 7704; *flats; Siddim,* a valley in Pal.:— Siddim.

7709. שְׁדֵמָה **shᵉdêmâh,** *shed-ay-maw´;* appar. from 7704; a cultivated *field:*— blasted, field.

7710. שָׁדַף **shâdaph,** *shaw-daf´;* a prim. root; to *scorch:*— blast.

7711. שְׁדֵפָה **shᵉdêphâh,** *shed-ay-faw´;* or

שִׁדָּפוֹן **shiddâphôwn,** *shid-daw-fone´;* from 7710; *blight:*— blasted (-ing).

7712. שְׁדַר **shᵉdar** (Chald.), *shed-ar´;* a prim. root; to *endeavor:*— labour.

7713. שְׂדֵרָה **sᵉdêrâh,** *sed-ay-raw´;* from an unused root mean. to *regulate;* a *row,* i.e. *rank* (of soldiers), *story* (of rooms):— board, range.

7714. שַׁדְרַךְ **Shadrak,** *shad-rak´;* prob. of for. or.; *Shadrak,* the Bab. name of one of Daniel's companions:— Shadrach.

7715. שַׁדְרַךְ **Shadrak** (Chald.), *shadrak*; the same as 7714:— Shadrach.

7716. שֶׂה **seh**, *seh*; or

שֵׂי **sêy**, *say*; prob. from 7582 through the idea of *pushing* out to graze; a member of a flock, i.e. a *sheep* or *goat*:— (lesser, small) cattle, ewe, goat, lamb, sheep. Comp. 2089.

7717. שָׂהֵד **sâhêd**, *saw-hade'*; from an unused root mean. to *testify*; a *witness*:— record.

7718. שֹׁהַם **shôham**, *sho'-ham*; from an unused root prob. mean. to *blanch*; a gem, prob. the *beryl* (from its *pale green* color):— onyx.

7719. שֹׁהַם **Shôham**, *sho'-ham*; the same as 7718; *Shoham*, an Isr.:— Shoham.

7720. שַׂהֲרֹן **sahărôn**, *sah-har-one'*; from the same as 5469; a round *pendant* for the neck:— ornament, round tire like the moon.

שָׂו **shav**. See 7723.

7721. שׂוֹא **sôw'**, *so*; from an unused root (akin to 5375 and 7722) mean. to *rise*; a *rising*:— arise.

7722. שׁוֹא **shôw'**, *sho*; or (fem.)

שׁוֹאָה **shôw'âh**, *sho-aw'*; or

שֹׁאָה **shô'âh**; from an unused root mean. to *rush* over; a *tempest*; by impl. *devastation*:— desolate (-ion), destroy, destruction, storm, wasteness.

7723. שָׁוְא **shâv'**, *shawv*; or

שָׁו **shav**, *shav*; from the same as 7722 in the sense of *desolating*; *evil* (as *destructive*, lit. (*ruin*) or mor. (espec. *guile*); fig. *idolatry* (as false, subj.), *uselessness* (as deceptive, obj.; also adv. in *vain*):— false (-ly), lie, lying, vain, vanity.

7724. שְׁוָא **Shevâ'**, *shev-aw'*; from the same as 7723; *false*; *Sheva*, an Isr.:— Sheva.

7725. שׁוּב **shûwb**, *shoob*; a prim. root; to *turn* back (hence, away) tran. or intr., lit. or fig. (not necessarily with the idea of *return* to the starting point); gen. to *retreat*; often adv. *again*:— ([break, build, circumcise, dig, do anything, do evil, feed, lay down, lie down, lodge, make, rejoice, send, take, weep]) × again, (cause to) answer (+ again), × in any case (wise), × at all, averse, bring (again, back, home again), call [to mind], carry again (back), cease, × certainly, come again (back), × consider, + continually, convert, deliver (again), + deny, draw back, fetch home again, × fro, get [oneself] (back) again, × give (again), go again (back, home), [go] out, hinder, let, [see] more, × needs, be past, × pay, pervert, pull in again, put (again, up again), recall, recompense, recover, refresh, relieve, render (again), requite, rescue, restore, retrieve, (cause to, make to) return, reverse, reward, + say nay, send back, set again, slide back, still, × surely, take back (off), (cause to) turn (again, self again, away, back, back again, backward, from, off), withdraw.

שׂוּבָאֵל **Shûwbâ'êl**. See 7619.

7726. שׁוֹבָב **shôwbâb**, *sho-bawb'*; from 7725; *apostate*, i.e. *idolatrous*:— backsliding, frowardly, turn away [from marg.].

7727. שׁוֹבָב **Shôwbâb**, *sho-bawb'*; the same as 7726; *rebellious*; *Shobab*, the name of two Isr.:— Shobab.

7728. שׁוֹבֵב **shôwbêb**, *sho-babe'*; from 7725; *apostate*, i.e. *heathenish* or (actually) *heathen*:— backsliding.

7729. שׁוּבָה **shûwbâh**, *shoo-baw'*; from 7725; a *return*:- - returning.

7730. שׂוֹבֶךְ **sôwbek**, *so'-bek*; for 5441; a *thicket*, i.e. interlaced branches:— thick boughs.

7731. שׁוֹבָק **Shôwbâk**, *sho-bawk'*; perh. for 7730; *Shobak*, a Syrian:— Shobach.

7732. שׁוֹבָל **Shôwbâl**, *sho-bawl'*; from the same as 7640; *overflowing*; *Shobal*, the name of an Edomite and two Isr.:— Shobal.

7733. שׁוֹבֵק **Shôwbêq**, *sho-bake'*; act. part. from a prim. root mean. to *leave* (comp. 7662); *forsaking*; *Shobek*, an Isr.:— Shobek.

7734. שׂוּג **sûwg**, *soog*; a prim. root; to *retreat*:— turn back.

7735. שׂוּג **sûwg**, *soog*; a prim. root; to *hedge* in:— make to grow.

7736. שׁוּד **shûwd**, *shood*; a prim. root; prop. to *swell* up, i.e. fig. (by impl. of *insolence*) to *devastate*:— waste.

שׁוֹד **shôwd**. See 7699, 7701.

7737. שָׁוָה **shâvâh**, *shaw-vaw'*; a prim. root; prop. to *level*, i.e. *equalize*; fig. to *resemble*; by impl. to *adjust* (i.e. *counterbalance*, *be suitable*, *compose*, *place*, *yield*, etc.):— avail, behave, bring forth, compare, countervail, (be, make) equal, lay, be (make, a-) like, make plain, profit, reckon.

7738. שָׁוָה **shâvâh**, *shaw-vaw'*; a prim. root; to *destroy*:— × substance [from the marg.].

7739. שְׁוָה **shevâh** (Chald.), *shev-aw'*; corresp. to 7737; to *resemble*:— make like.

7740. שָׁוֵה **Shâvêh**, *shaw-vay'*; from 7737; *plain*; *Shaveh*, a place in Pal.:— Shaveh.

7741. שָׁוֵה קִרְיָתַיִם **Shâvêh Qiryâthayim**, *shaw-vay' kir-yaw-thah'-yim*; from the same as 7740 and the dual of 7151; *plain of a double city*; *Shaveh-Kirjathajim*, a place E. of the Jordan:— Shaveh Kiriathaim.

7742. שׂוּחַ **sûwach**, *soo-akh'*; a prim. root; to *muse* pensively:— meditate.

7743. שׁוּחַ **shûwach**, *shoo-akh'*; a prim. root; to *sink*, lit. or fig.:— bow down, incline, humble.

7744. שׁוּחַ **Shûwach**, *shoo'-akh*; from 7743; *dell*; *Shuach*, a son of Abraham:— Shuah.

7745. שׁוּחָה **shûwchâh**, *shoo-khaw'*; from 7743; a *chasm*:— ditch, pit.

7746. שׁוּחָה **Shûwchâh**, *shoo-khaw'*; the same as 7745; *Shuchah*, an Isr.:— Shuah.

7747. שׁוּחִי **Shuchîy**, *shoo-khee'*; patron.

from 7744; a *Shuchite* or desc. of Shuach:— Shuhite.

7748. שׁוּחָם **Shûwchâm**, *shoo-khawm'*; from 7743; *humbly*; *Shucham*, an Isr.:— Shuham.

7749. שׁוּחָמִי **Shûwchâmîy**, *shoo-khaw-mee'*; patron. from 7748; a *Shuchamite* (collect.):— Shuhamites.

7750. שׂוּט **sûwṭ**, *soot*; or (by perm.)

סוּט **çûwṭ**, *soot*; a prim. root; to *detrude*, i.e. (intr. and fig.) *become derelict* (wrongly practise; namely, idolatry):— turn aside to.

7751. שׁוּט **shûwṭ**, *shoot*; a prim. root; prop. to *push* forth; (but used only fig.) to *lash*, i.e. (the sea with oars) to *row*; by impl. to *travel*:— go (about, through, to and fro), mariner, rower, run to and fro.

7752. שׁוֹט **shôwṭ**, *shote*; from 7751; a *lash* (lit. or fig.):— scourge, whip.

7753. שׂוּךְ **sûwk**, *sook*; a prim. root; to *entwine*, i.e. *shut* in (for formation, protection or restraint):— fence, (make an) hedge (up).

7754. שׂוֹךְ **sôwk**, *soke*; or (fem.)

שׂוֹכָה **sôwkâh**, *so-kaw'*; from 7753; a *branch* (as *interleaved*):— bough.

7755. שׂוֹכֹה **Sôwkôh**, *so-ko'*; or

שֹׂכֹה **Sôkôh**, *so-ko'*; or

שׂוֹכוֹ **Sôwkôw**, *so-ko'*; from 7753; *Sokoh* or *Soko*, the name of two places in Pal.:— Shocho, Shochoh, Sochoh, Soco, Socoh.

7756. שׂוּכָתִי **Sûwkâthîy**, *soo-kaw-thee'*; prob. patron. from a name corresp. to 7754 (fem.); a *Sukathite* or desc. of an unknown Isr. named Sukah:— Suchathite.

7757. שׁוּל **shûwl**, *shool*; from an unused root mean. to *hang* down; a *skirt*; by impl. a bottom *edge*:— hem, skirt, train.

7758. שׁוֹלָל **shôwlâl**, *sho-lawl'*; or

שֵׁילָל **shêylâl** (Mic. 1:8), *shaylawl'*; from 7997; *nude* (espec. barefoot); by impl. *captive*:— spoiled, stripped.

7759. שׁוּלַמִּית **Shûwlammîyth**, *shoo-lammeeth'*; from 7999; *peaceful* (with the art. always pref., making it a pet name); the *Shulammith*, an epithet of Solomon's queen:— Shulamite.

7760. שׂוּם **sûwm**, *soom*; or

שִׂים **sîym**, *seem*; a prim. root; to *put* (used in a great variety of applications, lit., fig., infer. and ellip.):— × any wise, appoint, bring, call [a name], care, cast in, change, charge, commit, consider, convey, determine, + disguise, dispose, do, get, give, heap up, hold, impute, lay (down, up), leave, look, make (out), mark, + name, × on, ordain, order, + paint, place, preserve, purpose, put (on), + regard, rehearse, reward, (cause to) set (on, up), shew, + stedfastly, take, × tell, + tread down, ([over-]) turn, × wholly, work.

7761. שׂוּם **sûwm** (Chald.), *soom*; corresp. to 7760:— + command, give, lay, make, + name, + regard, set.

7762. שׁוּם **shûwm**, *shoom*; from an unused root mean. to *exhale; garlic* (from its rank *odor*):— garlic.

7763. שֹׁמֵר **Shôwmêr**, *sho-mare´*; or

שֹׁמֵר **Shômêr**, *sho-mare´*; act. part. of 8104; *keeper; Shomer*, the name of two Isr.:— Shomer.

7764. שׁוּנִי **Shûwnîy**, *shoo-nee´*; from an unused root mean. to *rest; quiet; Shuni*, an Isr.:— Shuni.

7765. שׁוּנִי **Shûwnîy**, *shoo-nee´*; patron. from 7764; a *Shunite* (collect.) or desc. of Shuni:— Shunites.

7766. שׁוּנֵם **Shûwnêm**, *shoo-name´*; prob. from the same as 7764; *quietly; Shunem*, a place in Pal:— Shunem.

7767. שׁוּנַמִּית **Shûwnammîyth**, *shoo-nam-meeth´*; patrial from 7766; a *Shunammitess*, or female inhab. of Shunem:— Shunamite.

7768. שָׁוַע **shâva´**, *shaw-vah´*; a prim. root; prop. to *be free;* but used only caus. and refl. to *halloo* (for help, i.e. *freedom* from some trouble):— cry (aloud, out), shout.

7769. שׁוּעַ **shûwa´**, *shoo´-ah*; from 7768; a *halloo:*— cry, riches.

7770. שׁוּעַ **Shûwa´**, *shoo´-ah*; the same as 7769; *Shuä*, a Canaanite:— Shua, Shuah.

7771. שׁוֹעַ **shôwa´**, *sho´-ah*; from 7768 in the orig. sense of *freedom;* a *noble*, i.e. *liberal, opulent;* also (as noun in the der. sense) a *halloo:*— bountiful, crying, rich.

7772. שֹׁעַ **Shôwa´**, *sho´-ah*; the same as 7771; *rich; Shoä*, an Oriental people:— Shoa.

7773. שֶׁוַע **sheva´**, *sheh´-vah*; from 7768; a *halloo:*— cry.

7774. שׁוּעָא **Shûw'â´**, *shoo-aw´*; from 7768; *wealth; Shuä*, an Israelitess:— Shua.

7775. שַׁוְעָה **shav'âh**, *shav-aw´*; fem. of 7773; a *hallooing:*— crying.

7776. שׁוּעָל **shûw'âl**, *shoo-awl´*; or

שֻׁעָל **shû'âl**, *shoo-awl´*; from the same as 8168; a *jackal* (as a *burrower*):— fox.

7777. שׁוּעָל **Shûw'âl**, *shoo-awl´*; the same as 7776; *Shuäl*, the name of an Isr. and of a place in Pal.:— Shual.

7778. שׁוֹעֵר **shôw'êr**, *sho-are´*; or

שֹׁעֵר **shô'êr**, *sho-are´*; act. part. of 8176 (as denom. from 8179); a *janitor:*— doorkeeper, porter.

7779. שׁוּף **shûwph**, *shoof;* a prim. root; prop. to *gape*, i.e. *snap* at; fig. to *overwhelm:*— break, bruise, cover.

7780. שׁוֹפָךְ **Shôwphâk**, *sho-fawk´*; from 8210; *poured; Shophak*, a Syrian:— Shophach.

7781. שׁוּפָמִי **Shûwphâmîy**, *shoo-faw-mee´*; patron. from 8197; a *Shuphamite* (collect.) or desc. of Shephupham:— Shuphamite.

שׁוֹפָן **Shôwphân**. See 5855.

7782. שׁוֹפָר **shôwphâr**, *sho-far´*; or

שֹׁפָר **shôphâr**, *sho-far´*; from 8231 in the orig. sense of *incising*; a *cornet* (as giving a *clear* sound) or curved horn:— cornet, trumpet.

7783. שׁוּק **shûwq**, *shook*; a prim. root; to *run* after or over, i.e. *overflow:*— overflow, water.

7784. שׁוּק **shûwq**, *shook;* from 7783; a *street* (as *run* over):— street.

7785. שׁוֹק **shôwq**, *shoke;* from 7783; the (lower) *leg* (as a *runner*):— hip, leg, shoulder, thigh.

7786. שׂוּר **sûwr**, *soor*; a prim. root; prop. to *vanquish;* by impl. to *rule* (caus. *crown*):— make princes, have power, reign. See 5493.

7787. שׂוּר **sûwr**, *soor*; a prim. root [rather ident. with 7786 through the idea of *reducing* to pieces; comp. 4883]; to *saw:*— cut.

7788. שׂוּר **shûwr**, *shoor*; a prim. root; prop. to *turn*, i.e. *travel* about (as a harlot or a merchant):— go, sing. See also 7891.

7789. שׂוּר **shûwr**, *shoor*; a prim. root [rather ident. with 7788 through the idea of *going round* for inspection]; to *spy* out, i.e. (gen.) *survey*, (for evil) *lurk for*, (for good) *care for:*— behold, lay wait, look, observe, perceive, regard, see.

7790. שׂוּר **shûwr**, *shoor;* from 7889; a *foe* (as *lying in wait*):— enemy.

7791. שׂוּר **shûwr**, *shoor;* from 7788; a *wall* (as *going about*):— wall.

7792. שׂוּר **shûwr** (Chald.), *shoor;* corresp. to 7791:— wall.

7793. שׂוּר **Shûwr**, *shoor*; the same as 7791; *Shur*, a region of the Desert:— Shur.

7794. שׂוֹר **shôwr**, *shore;* from 7788; a *bullock* (as a *traveller*):— bull (-ock), cow, ox, wall [by mistake for 7791].

7795. שׂוֹרָה **sôwrâh**, *so-raw´;* from 7786 in the prim. sense of 5493; prop. a *ring,* i.e. (by anal.) a *row* (adv.):— principal.

שׂוֹרֵק **sôwrêq**. See 8321.

7796. שׂוֹרֵק **Sôwrêq**, *so-rake´;* the same as 8321; a *vine; Sorek*, a valley in Pal.:— Sorek.

7797. שׂוּשׂ **sûws**, *soos;* or

שׂישׂ **sîys**, *sece;* a prim. root; to *be bright*, i.e. *cheerful:*— be glad, × greatly, joy, make mirth, rejoice.

7798. שַׁוְשָׁא **Shavshâ´**, *shav-shaw´;* from 7797; *joyful; Shavsha*, an Isr.:— Shavsha.

7799. שׁוּשַׁן **shûwshan**, *shoo-shan´;* or

שׁוֹשָׁן **shôwshân**, *sho-shawn´;* or

שֹׁשָׁן **shôshân**, *sho-shawn´;* and (fem.)

שׁוֹשַׁנָּה **shôwshannâh**, *sho-shan-naw´;* from 7797; a *lily* (from its *whiteness*), as a flower or arch. ornament; also a (straight) *trumpet* (from the *tubular* shape):— lily, Shoshannim.

7800. שׁוּשַׁן **Shûwshan**, *shoo-shan´;* the same as 7799; *Shushan*, a place in Pers.:— Shushan.

7801. שׁוּשַׁנְכִי **Shûwshankîy** (Chald.), *shoo-shan-kee´;* of for. or.; a *Shushankite* (collect.) or inhab. of some unknown place in Ass.:— Susanchites.

7802. שׁוּשַׁן עֵדוּת **Shûwshan 'Êdûwth**, *shoo-shan´ ay-dooth´;* or (plur. of former)

שׁוֹשַׁנִּים עֵדוּת **Shôwshannîym 'Êdûwth**, *sho-shan-neem´ ay-dooth´;* from 7799 and 5715; *lily* (or *trumpet*) *of assemblage; Shushan-Eduth* or *Shoshannim-Eduth*, the title of a popular song:— Shoshannim-Eduth, Shushan-eduth.

שׁוּשַׁק **Shûwshaq**. See 7895.

7803. שׁוּתֶלַח **Shûwthelach**, *shoo-theh´-lakh;* prob. from 7582 and the same as 8520; *crash of breakage; Shuthelach*, the name of two Isr.:— Shuthelah.

7804. שְׁזַב **shᵉzab** (Chald.), *shez-ab´;* corresp. to 5800; to *leave*, i.e. (caus.) *free:*— deliver.

7805. שָׁזַף **shâzaph**, *shaw-zaf´;* a prim. root; to *tan* (by sun-burning); fig. (as if by a piercing ray) to *scan:*— look up, see.

7806. שָׁזַר **shâzar**, *shaw-zar´;* a prim. root; to *twist* (a thread of straw):— twine.

7807. שַׁח **shach**, *shakh;* from 7817; *sunk*, i.e. *downcast:*— + humble.

7808. שֵׂחַ **sêach**, *say´-akh;* for 7879; *communion*, i.e. (refl.) *meditation:*— thought.

7809. שָׁחַד **shâchad**, *shaw-khad´;* a prim. root; to *donate*, i.e. *bribe:*— hire, give a reward.

7810. שַׁחַד **shachad**, *shakh´-ad;* from 7809; a *donation* (venal or redemptive):— bribe (-ry), gift, present, reward.

7811. שָׂחָה **sâchâh**, *saw-khaw´;* a prim. root; to *swim;* caus. to *inundate:*— (make to) swim.

7812. שָׁחָה **shâchâh**, *shaw-khaw´;* a prim. root; to *depress*, i.e. *prostrate* (espec. refl. in homage to royalty or God):— bow (self) down, crouch, fall down (flat), humbly beseech, do (make) obeisance, do reverence, make to stoop, worship.

7813. שָׂחוּ **sâchûw**, *saw´-khoo;* from 7811; a *pond* (for *swimming*):— to swim in.

7814. שְׂחוֹק **sᵉchôwq**, *sekh-oke´;* or

שְׂחֹק **sᵉchôq**, *sekh-oke´;* from 7832; *laughter* (in merriment or defiance):— derision, laughter (-ed to scorn, -ing), mocked, sport.

7815. שְׁחוֹר **shᵉchôwr**, *shekh-ore´;* from 7835; *dinginess*, i.e. perh. *soot:*— coal.

שִׁחוֹר **shichôwr**. See 7883.

שָׁחוֹר **shâchôwr**. See 7838.

7816. שְׁחוּת **shᵉchûwth**, *shekh-ooth´;* from 7812; *pit:*— pit.

7817. שָׁחַח **shâchach**, *shaw-khakh´;* a prim. root; to *sink* or *depress* (refl. or caus.):— bend, bow (down), bring (cast) down, couch, humble self, be (bring) low, stoop.

7818. שָׂחַט **sâchaṭ**, *saw-khat´;* a prim. root; to *tread* out, i.e. *squeeze* (grapes):— press.

7819. שָׁחַט **shâchaṭ**, *shaw-khat´;* a prim. root; to *slaughter* (in sacrifice or massacre):— kill, offer, shoot out, slay, slaughter.

7820. שָׁחַט **shâchaṭ**, *shaw-khat´*; a prim. root [rather ident. with 7819 through the idea of *striking*]; to *hammer* out:— beat.

7821. שְׁחִיטָה **sheʻchîyṭâh**, *shekh-ee-taw´*; from 7819; *slaughter*:— killing.

7822. שְׁחִין **sheʻchîyn**, *shekh-een´*; from an unused root prob. mean. to *burn*; *inflammation*, i.e. an *ulcer*;— boil, botch.

7823. שָׁחִיס **shâchîyç**, *shaw-khece´*; or סָחִיש **çâchîysh**, *saw-kheesh´*; from an unused root appar. mean. to *sprout*; *after-growth*:— (that) which springeth of the same.

7824. שָׁחִיף **shâchîyph**, *shaw-kheef´*; from the same as 7828; a *board* (as *chipped* thin):— cieled with.

7825. שְׁחִית **sheʻchîyth**, *shekh-eeth´*; from 7812; a *pit-*fall (lit. or fig.):— destruction, pit.

7826. שַׁחַל **shachal**, *shakh´-al*; from an unused root prob. mean. to *roar*; a *lion* (from his characteristic *roar*):— (fierce) lion.

7827. שְׁחֶלֶת **sheʻchêleth**, *shekh-ay´-leth*; appar. from the same as 7826 through some obscure idea, perh. that of *peeling* off by concussion of sound; a *scale* or shell, i.e. the aromatic *mussel*:— onycha.

7828. שַׁחַף **shachaph**, *shakh´-af*; from an unused root mean. to *peel*, i.e. *emaciate*; the *gull* (as *thin*):— cuckoo.

7829. שַׁחֶפֶת **shachepheth**, *shakh-eh´-feth*; from the same as 7828; *emaciation*:— consumption.

7830. שַׁחַץ **shachats**, *shakh´-ats*; from an unused root appar. mean. to *strut*; *haughtiness* (as evinced by the attitude):— × lion, pride.

7831. שַׁחֲצוֹם **Shachatsôwm**, *shakh-ats-ome´*; from the same as 7830; *proudly*; *Shachatsom*, a place in Pal.:— Shahazimah [from the marg.].

7832. שָׂחַק **sâchaq**, *saw-khak´*; a prim. root; to *laugh* (in pleasure or detraction); by impl. to *play*:— deride, have in derision, laugh, make merry, mock (-er), play, rejoice, (laugh to) scorn, be in (make) sport.

7833. שָׁחַק **shâchaq**, *shaw-khak´*; a prim. root; to *comminate* (by trituration or attrition):— beat, wear.

7834. שַׁחַק **shachaq**, *shakh´-ak*; from 7833; a *powder* (as *beaten* small): by anal. a thin *vapor*; by extens. the *firmament*:— cloud, small dust, heaven, sky.

שְׁחֹק **sheʻchôq**. See 7814.

7835. שָׁחַר **shâchar**, *shaw-khar´*; a prim. root [rather ident. with 7836 through the idea of the *duskiness* of early dawn]; to *be dim* or dark (in color):— be black.

7836. שָׁחַר **shâchar**, *shaw-khar´*; a prim. root; prop. to *dawn*, i.e. (fig.) *be* (up) *early* at any task (with the impl. of earnestness); by extens. to *search* for (with painstaking):— [do something] betimes, enquire early, rise (seek) betimes, seek (diligently) early, in the morning.

7837. שַׁחַר **shachar**, *shakh´-ar*; from

7836; *dawn* (lit., fig. or adv.):— day (-spring), early, light, morning, whence riseth.

שִׁחֹר **Shîchôr**. See 7883.

7838. שָׁחֹר **shâchôr**, *shaw-khore´*; or שָׁחוֹר **shâchôwr**, *shaw-khore´*; from 7835; prop. *dusky*, but also (absol.) *jetty*:— black.

7839. שַׁחֲרוּת **shachărûwth**, *shakh-arooth´*; from 7836; a *dawning*, i.e. (fig.) *juvenescence*:— youth.

7840. שְׁחַרְחֹרֶת **sheʻcharchôreth**, *shekh-ar-kho´-reth*; from 7835; *swarthy*:— black.

7841. שְׁחַרְיָה **Sheʻcharyâh**, *shekh-ar-yaw´*; from 7836 and 3050; *Jah has sought*; *Shecharjah*, an Isr.:— Shehariah.

7842. שַׁחֲרַיִם **Shachărayim**, *shakh-arah´-yim*; dual of 7837; *double dawn*; *Shacharajim*, an Isr.:— Shaharaim.

7843. שָׁחַת **shâchath**, *shaw-khath´*; a prim. root; to *decay*, i.e. (caus.) *ruin* (lit. or fig.):— batter, cast off, corrupt (-er, thing), destroy (-er, -uction), lose, mar, perish, spill, spoiler, × utterly, waste (-r).

7844. שְׁחַת **sheʻchath** (Chald.), *shekhath´*; corresp. to 7843:— corrupt, fault.

7845. שַׁחַת **shachath**, *shakh´-ath*; from 7743; a *pit* (espec. as a trap); fig. *destruction*:— corruption, destruction, ditch, grave, pit.

7846. שֵׂט **sêṭ**, *sayte*; or שֵׂט **çêṭ**, *sayt*; from 7750; a *departure* from right, i.e. *sin*:— revolter, that turn aside.

7847. שָׂטָה **sâṭâh**, *saw-taw´*; a prim. root; to *deviate* from duty:— decline, go aside, turn.

7848. שִׁטָּה **shiṭṭâh**, *shit-taw´*; fem. of der. [only in the plur.] שִׁטִּים **shiṭṭîym**, *shit-teem´*; mean. the *sticks* of wood] from the same as 7850; the *acacia* (from its *scourging* thorns):— shittah, shittim. See also 1029.

7849. שָׁטַח **shâṭach**, *shaw-takh´*; a prim. root; to *expand*:— all abroad, enlarge, spread, stretch out.

7850. שֹׁטֵט **shôṭêṭ**, *sho-tate´*; act. part. of an otherwise unused root mean. (prop. to *pierce*; but only as a denom. from 7752) to *flog*; a *goad*:— scourge.

7851. שִׁטִּים **Shiṭṭîym**, *shit-teem´*; the same as the plur. of 7848; *acacia* trees; *Shittim*, a place E. of the Jordan:— Shittim.

7852. שָׂטַם **sâṭam**, *saw-tam´*; a prim. root; prop. to *lurk* for, i.e. *persecute*:— hate, oppose self against.

7853. שָׂטַן **sâṭan**, *saw-tan´*; a prim. root; to *attack*, (fig.) *accuse*:— (be an) adversary, resist.

7854. שָׂטָן **sâṭân**, *saw-tawn´*; from 7853; an *opponent*; espec. (with the art. pref.) *Satan*, the arch-enemy of good:— adversary, Satan, withstand.

7855. שִׂטְנָה **siṭnâh**, *sit-naw´*; from 7853; *opposition* (by letter):— accusation.

7856. שִׂטְנָה **Siṭnâh**, *sit-naw´*; the same as

7855; *Sitnah*, the name of a well in Pal.:— Sitnah.

7857. שָׁטַף **shâṭaph**, *shaw-taf´*; a prim. root; to *gush*; by impl. to *inundate*, *cleanse*; by anal. to *gallop*, *conquer*:— drown, (over-) flow (-whelm), rinse, run, rush, (throughly) wash (away).

7858. שֶׁטֶף **sheṭeph**, *sheh´-tef*; or שֵׁטֶף **shêṭeph**, *shay´-tef*; from 7857; a *deluge* (lit. or fig.):— flood, outrageous, overflowing.

7859. שְׁטַר **seʻṭar** (Chald.), *set-ar´*; of uncert. der.; a *side*:— side.

7860. שֹׁטֵר **shôṭêr**, *sho-tare´*; act. part. of an otherwise unused root prob. mean. to *write*; prop. a *scribe*, i.e. (by anal. or impl.) an official *superintendent* or *magistrate*:— officer, overseer, ruler.

7861. שִׁטְרַי° **Shiṭray**, *shit-rah´-ee*; from the same as 7860; *magisterial*; *Shitrai*, an Isr.:— Shitrai.

7862. שַׁי **shay**, *shah-ee*; prob. from 7737; a *gift* (as *available*):— present.

7863. שִׂיא **sîy´**, *see*; from the same as 7721 by perm.; *elevation*:— excellency.

7864. שְׁיָא° **Sheʻyâ´**, *sheh-yaw´*; for 7724; *Sheja*, an Isr.:— Sheva [from the marg.].

7865. שִׂיאֹן **Sîy´ôn**, *see-ohn´*; from 7863; *peak*; *Sion*, the summit of Mt. Hermon:— Sion.

7866. שִׁאיוֹן **Shî´yôwn**, *shee-ohn´*; from the same as 7722; *ruin*; *Shijon*, a place in Pal.:— Shihon.

7867. שִׂיב **sîyb**, *seeb*; a prim. root; prop. to *become aged*, i.e. (by impl.) to *grow gray*:— (be) grayheaded.

7868. שִׂיב **sîyb** (Chald.), *seeb*; corresp. to 7867:— elder.

7869. שֵׂיב **sêyb**, *sabe*; from 7867; old *age*:— age.

7870. שִׁיבָה **shîybâh**, *shee-baw´*; by perm. from 7725; a *return* (of property):— captivity.

7871. שִׁיבָה **shîybâh**, *shee-baw´*; from 3427; *residence*:— while ... lay.

7872. שֵׂיבָה **sêybâh**, *say-baw´*; fem. of 7869; old *age*:— (be) gray (grey hoar,-y) hairs (head,-ed), old age.

7873. שִׂיג **sîyg**, *seeg*; from 7734; a *withdrawal* (into a private place):— pursuing.

7874. שִׂיד **sîyd**, *seed*; a prim. root prob. mean. to *boil* up (comp. 7736); used only as denom. from 7875; to *plaster*:— plaister.

7875. שִׂיד **sîyd**, *seed*; from 7874; *lime* (as *boiling* when slacked):— lime, plaister.

7876. שָׁיָה **shâyâh**, *shaw-yaw´*; a prim. root; to *keep* in memory:— be unmindful. [Render Deut. 32:18, "A Rock bore thee, *thou must recollect*; and (yet) thou hast forgotten," etc.]

7877. שִׁיזָא **Shîyzâ´**, *shee-zaw´*; of unknown der.; *Shiza*, an Isr.:— Shiza.

7878. שִׂיח **sîyach**, *see´-akh*; a prim. root; to *ponder*, i.e. (by impl.) *converse* (with oneself, and hence, aloud) or (tran.) *utter*:— commune, complain, declare, meditate, muse, pray, speak, talk (with).

Hebrew

7879. שִׂיחַ **sîyach**, *see´-akh;* from 7878; a *contemplation;* by impl. an *utterance:*— babbling, communication, complaint, meditation, prayer, talk.

7880. שִׂיחַ **sîyach**, *see´-akh;* from 7878; a *shoot* (as if *uttered* or *put forth*), i.e. (gen.) *shrubbery:*— bush, plant, shrub.

7881. שִׂיחָה **sîychâh**, *see-khaw´;* fem. of 7879; *reflection;* by extens. *devotion:*— meditation, prayer.

7882. שִׂיחָה **shîychâh**, *shee-khaw´;* for 7745; a *pit*-fall:— pit.

7883. שִׂיחוֹר **Shîychôwr**, *shee-khore´;* or

שִׁחוֹר **Shichôwr**, *shee-khore´;* or

שִׁחֹר **Shîchôr**, *shee-khore´;* prob. from 7835; *dark,* i.e. *turbid; Shichor,* a stream of Egypt:— Shihor, Sihor.

7884. שִׁיחוֹר לִבְנָת **Shîychôwr Libnâth**, *shee-khore´ lib-nawth´;* from the same as 7883 and 3835; *darkish whiteness; Shichor-Libnath,* a stream of Pal.:— Shihor-libnath.

7885. שַׁיִט **shayiṭ**, *shay´-yit;* from 7751; an *oar;* also (comp. 7752) a *scourge°* (fig.):— oar, scourge.

7886. שִׁילֹה **Shîylôh**, *shee-lo´;* from 7951; *tranquil; Shiloh,* an epithet of the Messiah:— Shiloh.

7887. שִׁילֹה **Shîylôh**, *shee-lo´;* or

שִׁלֹה **Shilôh**, *shee-lo´;* or

שִׁילוֹ **Shîylôw**, *shee-lo´;* or

שִׁלוֹ **Shilôw**, *shee-lo´;* from the same as 7886; *Shiloh,* a place in Pal.:— Shiloh.

7888. שִׁילוֹנִי **Shiylôwnîy**, *shee-lo-nee´;* or

שִׁילֹנִי **Shîylônîy**, *shee-lo-nee´;* or

שִׁלֹנִי **Shîlônîy**, *shee-lo-nee´;* from 7887; a *Shilonite* or inhab. of Shiloh:— Shilonite.

7889. שִׁילָל **shêylâl**. See 7758.

7889. שִׁימוֹן **Shîymôwn**, *shee-mone´;* appar. for 3452; *desert; Shimon,* an Isr.:— Shimon.

7890. שַׁיִן **shayin**, *shah´-yin;* from an unused root mean. to *urinate; urine:*— piss.

7891. שִׁיר **shîyr**, *sheer;* or (the orig. form)

שׁוּר **shûwr** (1 Sam. 18:6), *shoor;* a prim. root [rather ident. with 7788 through the idea of *strolling* minstrelsy]; to *sing:*— behold [by mistake for 7789], sing (-er, -ing man, -ing woman).

7892. שִׁיר **shîyr**, *sheer;* or fem.

שִׁירָה **shîyrâh**, *shee-raw´;* from 7891; a *song;* abstr. *singing:*— musical (-ick), × sing (-er, -ing), song.

שִׂיס **sîys**. See 7797.

7893. שַׁיִשׁ **shayish**, *shah´-yish;* from an unused root mean. to *bleach,* i.e. *whiten; white,* i.e. *marble:*— marble. See 8336.

7894. שִׁישָׁא **Shîyshâ'**, *shee-shaw´;* from the same as 7893; *whiteness; Shisha,* an Isr.:— Shisha.

7895. שִׁישַׁק **Shîyshaq**, *shee-shak´;* or

שׁוּשַׁק **Shûwshaq**, *shoo-shak´;* of Eg. der.; *Shishak,* an Eg. king:— Shishak.

7896. שִׁית **shîyth**, *sheeth;* a prim. root; to *place* (in a very wide application):— apply, appoint, array, bring, consider, lay (up), let alone, × look, make, mark, put (on), + regard, set, shew, be stayed, × take.

7897. שִׁית **shîyth**, *sheeth;* from 7896; a *dress* (as *put* on):— attire.

7898. שַׁיִת **shayith**, *shah´-yith;* from 7896; *scrub* or *trash,* i.e. wild *growth* of weeds or briers (as if *put* on the field):— thorns.

7899. שֵׂךְ **sêk**, *sake;* from 7753 in the sense of 7753; a *brier* (as of a hedge):— prick.

7900. שֹׂךְ **sôk**, *soke;* from 5526 in the sense of 7753; a *booth* (as *interlaced*):— tabernacle.

7901. שָׁכַב **shâkab**, *shaw-kab´;* a prim. root; to *lie* down (for rest, sexual connection, decease or any other purpose):— × at all, cast down, [(lover-)] lay (self) (down), (make to) lie (down, down to sleep, still, with), lodge, ravish, take rest, sleep, stay.

7902. שְׁכָבָה **sheꞌkâbâh**, *shek-aw-baw´;* from 7901; a *lying* down (of dew, or for the sexual act):— × carnally, copulation, × lay, seed.

7903. שְׁכֹבֶת **sheꞌkôbeth**, *shek-o´-beth;* from 7901; a (sexual) *lying* with:— × lie.

7904. שָׁכָה **shâkâh**, *shaw-kaw´;* a prim. root; to *roam* (through lust):— in the morning [by mistake for 7925].

7905. שֻׂכָּה **sukkâh**, *sook-kaw´;* fem. of 7900 in the sense of 7899; a *dart* (as pointed like a *thorn*):— barbed iron.

7906. שֵׂכוּ **Sêkûw**, *say´-koo;* from an unused root appar. mean. to *surmount;* an *observatory* (with the art.); *Seku,* a place in Pal.:— Sechu.

7907. שֶׂכְוִי **sekvîy**, *sek-vee´;* from the same as 7906; *observant,* i.e. (concr.) the *mind:*— heart.

7908. שְׁכוֹל **sheꞌkôwl**, *shek-ole´;* infin. of 7921; *bereavement:*— loss of children, spoiling.

7909. שַׁכּוּל **shakkuwl**, *shak-kool´;* or

שַׁכֻּל **shakkul**, *shak-kool´;* from 7921; *bereaved:*— barren, bereaved (robbed) of children (whelps).

7910. שִׁכּוֹר **shikkôwr**, *shik-kore´;* or

שִׁכֹּר **shikkôr**, *shik-kore´;* from 7937; *intoxicated,* as a state or a habit:— drunk (-ard, -en, -en man).

7911. שָׁכַח **shâkach**, *shaw-kakh´;* or

שָׁכֵחַ **shâkêach**, *shaw-kay´-akh;* a prim. root; to *mislay,* i.e. to *be oblivious of,* from want of memory or attention:— × at all, (cause to) forget.

7912. שְׁכַח **sheꞌkach** (Chald.), *shek-akh´;* corresp. to 7911 through the idea of disclosure of a *covered* or *forgotten* thing; to *discover* (lit. or fig.):— find.

7913. שָׁכֵחַ **shâkêach**, *shaw-kay´-akh;* from 7911; *oblivious:*— forget.

7914. שְׂכִיָּה **seꞌkîyâh**, *sek-ee-yaw´;* fem. from the same as 7906; a *conspicuous object:*— picture.

7915. שַׂכִּין **sakkîyn**, *sak-keen´;* intens. perh. from the same as 7906 in the sense of 7753; a *knife* (as *pointed* or *edged*):— knife.

7916. שָׂכִיר **sâkîyr**, *saw-keer´;* from 7936; a man *at wages* by the day or year:— hired (man, servant), hireling.

7917. שְׂכִירָה **seꞌkîyrâh**, *sek-ee-raw´;* fem. of 7916; a *hiring:*— that is hired.

7918. שָׁכַךְ **shâkak**, *shaw-kak´;* a prim. root; to *weave* (i.e. *lay*) a trap; fig. (through the idea of *secreting*) to *allay* (passions; phys. *abate* a flood):— appease, assuage, make to cease, pacify, set.

7919. שָׂכַל **sâkal**, *saw-kal´;* a prim. root; to *be* (caus. *make* or *act*) *circumspect* and hence, *intelligent:*— consider, expert, instruct, prosper, (deal) prudent (-ly), (give) skill (-ful), have good success, teach, (have, make to) understand (-ing), wisdom, (be, behave self, consider, make) wise (-ly), guide wittingly.

7920. שְׂכַל **seꞌkal** (Chald.), *sek-al´;* corresp. to 7919:— consider.

7921. שָׁכֹל **shâkôl**, *shaw-kole´;* a prim. root; prop. to *miscarry,* i.e. *suffer abortion;* by anal. to *bereave* (lit. or fig.):— bereave (of children), barren, cast calf (fruit, young), be (make) childless, deprive, destroy, × expect, lose children, miscarry, rob of children, spoil.

7922. שֶׂכֶל **sekel**, *seh´-kel;* or

שֵׂכֶל **sêkel**, *say´-kel;* from 7919; *intelligence;* by impl. *success:*— discretion, knowledge, policy, prudence, sense, understanding, wisdom, wise.

שַׁכֻּל **shakkûl**. See 7909.

שִׂכְלוּת **siklûwth**. See 5531.

7923. שִׁכֻּלִים **shikkulîym**, *shik-koo-leem´;* plur. from 7921; *childlessness* (by continued bereavements):— to have after loss of others.

7924. שָׂכְלְתָנוּ **soklethânûw** (Chald.), *sok-leth-aw-noo´;* from 7920; *intelligence:*— understanding.

7925. שָׁכַם **shâkam**, *shaw-kam´;* a prim. root; prop. to *incline* (the shoulder to a burden); but used only as denom. from 7926; lit. to *load up* (on the back of man or beast), i.e. to *start early* in the morning:— (arise, be up, get [oneself] up, rise up) early (betimes), morning.

7926. שְׁכֶם **sheꞌkem**, *shek-em´;* from 7925; the *neck* (between the shoulders) as the place of burdens; fig. the *spur* of a hill:— back, × consent, portion, shoulder.

7927. שְׁכֶם **Sheꞌkem**, *shek-em´;* the same as 7926; *ridge; Shekem,* a place in Pal.:— Shechem.

7928. שֶׁכֶם **Shekem**, *sheh´-kem;* for 7926; *Shekem,* the name of a Hivite and two Isr.:— Shechem.

7929. שִׁכְמָה **shikmâh**, *shik-maw´;* fem. of 7926; the *shoulder*-bone:— shoulder blade.

7930. שִׁכְמִי **Shikmîy**, *shik-mee´;* patron. from 7928; a *Shikmite* (collect.), or desc. of Shekem:— Shichemites.

7931. שָׁכַן **shâkan**, *shaw-kan´;* a prim. root [appar. akin (by transm.) to 7901 through the idea of *lodging;* comp. 5531, 7925]; to *reside* or permanently stay (lit. or fig.):— abide, continue, (cause to, make to) dwell (-er), have habitation, inhabit, lay, place, (cause to) remain, rest, set (up).

7932. שְׁכַן **shᵉkan** (Chald.), shek-an´; corresp. to 7931:— cause to dwell, have habitation.

7933. שֶׁכֶן **sheken**, sheh´-ken; from 7931; a *residence*:— habitation.

7934. שָׁכֵן **shâkên**, shaw-kane´; from 7931; a *resident*; by extens. a fellow-citizen:— inhabitant, neighbour, nigh.

7935. שְׁכַנְיָה **Shᵉkanyâh**, shek-an-yaw´; or (prol.)

שְׁכַנְיָהוּ **Shᵉkanyâhûw**, shek-an-yaw´-hoo; from 7931 and 3050; *Jah has dwelt*; *Shekanjah*, the name of nine Isr.:— Shecaniah, Shechaniah.

7936. שָׂכַר **sâkar**, saw-kar´; or (by perm.)

שָׂכַר **çâkar** (Ezra 4:5), saw-kar´; a prim. root [appar. akin (by prosthesis) to 3739 through the idea of temporary *purchase*; comp. 7937]; to *hire*:— earn wages, hire (out self), reward, × surely.

7937. שָׁכַר **shâkar**, shaw-kar´; a prim. root; to *become tipsy*; in a qualified sense, to *satiate* with a stimulating drink or (fig.) influence:— (be filled with) drink (abundantly), (be, make) drunk (-en), be merry. [Superlative of 8248.]

7938. שֶׁכֶר **seker**, seh´-ker; from 7936; *wages*:— reward, sluices.

7939. שָׂכָר **sâkâr**, saw-kawr´; from 7936; *payment* of contract; concr. *salary, fare, maintenance*; by impl. *compensation, benefit*:— hire, price, reward [-ed], wages, worth.

7940. שָׂכָר **Sâkar**, saw-kar´; the same as 7939; *recompense*; *Sakar*, the name of two Isr.:— Sacar.

7941. שֵׁכָר **shêkâr**, shay-kawr´; from 7937; an *intoxicant*, i.e. intensely alcoholic *liquor*:— strong drink, + drunkard, strong wine.

שִׁכּוֹר **shikkôr**. See 7910.

7942. שִׁכְּרוֹן **Shikkᵉrôwn**, shik-ker-one´; for 7943; *drunkenness*, *Shikkeron*, a place in Pal.:— Shicron.

7943. שִׁכָּרוֹן **shikkârôwn**, shik-kaw-rone´; from 7937; *intoxication*:— (be) drunken (-ness).

7944. שַׁל **shal**, shal; from 7952 abbrev.; a *fault*:— error.

7945. שֶׁל **shel**, shel; for the rel. 834; used with prep. pref., and often followed by some pron. aff.; on *account* of, *whatso*ever, *which*soever:— cause, sake.

7946. שַׁלְאֲנָן **shal'ănân**, shal-an-awn´; for 7600; *tranquil*:— being at ease.

7947. שָׁלַב **shâlab**, shaw-lab´; a prim. root; to *space off*; intens. (evenly) to *make equidistant*:— equally distant, set in order.

7948. שָׁלָב **shâlâb**, shaw-lawb´; from 7947; a *spacer* or raised *interval*, i.e. the *stile* in a frame or panel:— ledge.

7949. שָׁלַג **shâlag**, shaw-lag´; a prim. root; prop. mean. to *be white*; used only as denom. from 7950; to *be snow-white*

(with the linen clothing of the slain):— be as snow.

7950. שֶׁלֶג **sheleg**, sheh´-leg; from 7949; *snow* (prob. from its *whiteness*):— snow (-y).

7951. שָׁלָה **shâlâh**, shaw-law´; or

שָׁלָו **shâlav** (Job 3:26), shaw-lav´; a prim. root; to *be tranquil*, i.e. *secure* or *successful*:— be happy, prosper, be in safety.

7952. שָׁלָה **shâlâh**, shaw-law´; a prim. root [prob. rather ident. with 7953 through the idea of *educing*]; to *mislead*:— deceive, be negligent.

7953. שָׁלָה **shâlâh**, shaw-law´; a prim. root [rather cognate (by contr.) to the base of 5394, 7997 and their congeners through the idea of *extracting*]; to *draw* out or off, i.e. *remove* (the soul by death):— take away.

7954. שְׁלָה **shᵉlâh** (Chald.), shel-aw´; corresp. to 7951; to *be secure*:— at rest.

שִׁלֹה **Shîlôh**. See 7887.

7955. שָׁלָה **shâlâh** (Chald.), shaw-law´; from a root corresp. to 7952; a *wrong*:— thing amiss.

שֵׁלָה **shêlâh**. See 7596.

7956. שֵׁלָה **Shêlâh**, shay-law´; the same as 7596 (short.); *request*; *Shelah*, the name of a postdiluvian patriarch and of an Isr.:— Shelah.

7957. שַׁלְהֶבֶת **shalhebeth**, shal-heh´-beth; from the same as 3851 with sibilant pref.; a *flare* of fire:— (flaming) flame.

שָׁלָו **shâlav**. See 7951.

7958. שְׂלָו **sᵉlâv**, sel-awv´; or

שְׂלָיו **sᵉlâyv**, sel-awv´; by orth. var. from 7951 through the idea of *sluggishness*; the *quail* collect. (as *slow* in flight from its weight):— quails.

7959. שֶׁלֶו **shelev**, sheh´-lev; from 7951; *security*:— prosperity.

שִׁלוֹ **Shîlôw**. See 7887.

7960. שָׁלוּ **shâlûw** (Chald.), shaw-loo´; or

שָׁלוּת **shâlûwth** (Chald.), shaw-looth´; from the same as 7955; a *fault*:— error, × fail, thing amiss.

7961. שָׁלֵו **shâlêv**, shaw-lave´; or

שָׁלֵיו **shâlêyv**, shaw-lave´; fem.

שְׁלֵוָה **shᵉlêvâh**, shel-ay-vaw´; from 7951; *tranquil*; (in a bad sense) *careless*; abstr. *security*:— (being) at ease, peaceable, (in) prosper (-ity), quiet (-ness), wealthy.

7962. שַׁלְוָה **shalvâh**, shal-vaw´; from 7951; *security* (genuine or false):— abundance, peace (-ably), prosperity, quietness.

7963. שְׁלֵוָה **shᵉlêvâh** (Chald.), shel-ay-vaw´; corresp. to 7962; *safety*:— tranquillity. See also 7961.

7964. שִׁלּוּחַ **shillûwach**, shil-loo´-akh; or

שִׁלֻּחַ **shillûach**, shil-loo´-akh; from 7971; (only in plur.) a *dismissal*, i.e. (of a wife) *divorce* (espec. the document); also (of a daughter) *dower*:— presents, have sent back.

7965. שָׁלוֹם **shâlôwm**, shaw-lome´; or

שָׁלֹם **shâlôm**, shaw-lome´; from 7999; *safe*, i.e. (fig.) *well, happy, friendly*; also (abstr.) *welfare*, i.e. *health, prosperity, peace*:— × do, familiar, × fare, favour, + friend, × great, (good) health, (× perfect, such as be at) peace (-able, -ably), prosper (-ity, -ous), rest, safe (-ty), salute, welfare, (× all is, be) well, × wholly.

7966. שִׁלֻּם **shillûwm**, shil-loom´; or

שִׁלֻּם **shillûm**, shil-loom´; from 7999; a *requital*, i.e. (secure) *retribution*, (venal) a *fee*:— recompense, reward.

7967. שַׁלּוּם **Shallûwm**, shal-loom´; or (short.)

שַׁלֻּם **Shallûm**, shal-loom´; the same as 7966; *Shallum*, the name of fourteen Isr.:— Shallum.

שְׁלוֹמִית **Shᵉlôwmîyth**. See 8019.

7968. שַׁלּוּן **Shallûwn**, shal-loon´; prob. for 7967; *Shallun*, an Isr.:— Shallum.

7969. שָׁלוֹשׁ **shâlôwsh**, shaw-loshe´; or

שָׁלֹשׁ **shâlôsh**, shaw-loshe´; masc.

שְׁלוֹשָׁה **shᵉlôwshâh**, shel-o-shaw´; or

שְׁלֹשָׁה **shᵉlôshâh**, shel-o-shaw´; a prim. number; *three*; occasionally (ord.) *third*, or (multipl.) *thrice*:— + fork, + often [-times], third, thir[-teen, -teenth], three, + thrice. Comp. 7991.

7970. שְׁלוֹשִׁים **shᵉlôwshîym**, shel-o-sheem´; or

שְׁלֹשִׁים **shᵉlôshîym**, shel-o-sheem´; multiple of 7969; *thirty*; or (ord.) *thirtieth*:— thirty, thirtieth. Comp. 7991.

שָׁלוּת **shâlûwth**. See 7960.

7971. שָׁלַח **shâlach**, shaw-lakh´; a prim. root; to *send away*, for, or out (in a great variety of applications):— × any wise, appoint, bring (on the way), cast (away, out), conduct, × earnestly, forsake, give (up), grow long, lay, leave, let depart (down, go, loose), push away, put (away, forth, in, out), reach forth, send (away, forth, out), set, shoot (forth, out), sow, spread, stretch forth (out).

7972. שְׁלַח **shᵉlach** (Chald.), shel-akh´; corresp. to 7971:— put, send.

7973. שֶׁלַח **shelach**, sheh´-lakh; from 7971; a *missile* of attack, i.e. *spear*; also (fig.) a *shoot* of growth; i.e. *branch*:— dart, plant, × put off, sword, weapon.

7974. שֶׁלַח **Shelach**, sheh´-lakh; the same as 7973; *Shelach*, a postdiluvian patriarch:— Salah, Shelah. Comp. 7975.

7975. שִׁלֹחַ **Shilôach**, shee-lo´-akh; or (in imitation of 7974)

שֶׁלַח **Shelach** (Neh. 3:15), sheh´-lakh; from 7971; *rill*; *Shiloäch*, a fountain of Jerusalem:— Shiloah, Siloah.

שִׁלֹּחַ **shillûach**. See 7964.

7976. שִׁלֻּחָה **shilluchâh**, shil-loo-khaw´; fem. of 7964; a *shoot*:— branch.

7977. שִׁלְחִי **Shilchîy**, shil-khee´; from 7973; *missive*, i.e. *armed*; *Shilchi*, an Isr.:— Shilhi.

7978. שִׁלְחִים **Shilchîym**, shil-kheem´;

plur. of 7973; *javelins* or *sprouts; Shilchim*, a place in Pal.:— Shilhim.

7979. שֻׁלְחָן **shulchân**, *shool-khawn´;* from 7971; a *table* (as *spread* out); by impl. a *meal:*— table.

7980. שָׁלַט **shâlaṭ**, *shaw-lat´;* a prim. root; to *dominate*, i.e. *govern;* by impl. to *permit:*— (bear, have) rule, have dominion, give (have) power.

7981. שְׁלֵט **sh⁰lêṭ** (Chald.), *shel-ate´;* corresp. to 7980:— have the mastery, have power, bear rule, be (make) ruler.

7982. שֶׁלֶט **sheleṭ**, *sheh´-let;* from 7980; prob. a *shield* (as *controlling*, i.e. protecting the person):— shield.

7983. שִׁלְטוֹן **shilṭôwn**, *shil-tone´;* from 7980; a *potentate:*— power.

7984. שִׁלְטוֹן **shilṭôwn** (Chald.), *shiltone´;* or

שִׁלְטֹן **shilṭôn**, *shil-tone´;* corresp. to 7983:— ruler.

7985. שָׁלְטָן **sholṭân** (Chald.), *shol-tawn´;* from 7981; *empire* (abstr. or concr.):— dominion.

7986. שַׁלֶּטֶת **shalleṭeth**, *shal-leh´-teth;* fem. from 7980; a *vixen:*— imperious.

7987. שֶׁלִי **sh⁰lîy**, *shel-ee´;* from 7951; *privacy:*— + quietly.

7988. שִׁלְיָה **shilyâh**, *shil-yaw´;* fem. from 7953; a *fetus* or *babe* (as *extruded* in birth):— young one.

שָׁלִיו **s⁰lâyv**. See 7958.

שָׁלֵיו **shalêyv**. See 7961.

7989. שַׁלִּיט **shalliyṭ**, *shal-leet´;* from 7980; *potent;* concr. a *prince* or *warrior:*— governor, mighty, that hath power, ruler.

7990. שַׁלִּיט **shalliyṭ** (Chald.), *shal-leet´;* corresp. to 7989; *mighty;* abstr. *permission;* concr. a *premier:*— captain, be lawful, rule (-r).

7991. שָׁלִישׁ **shâlîysh**, *shaw-leesh´;* or

שָׁלוֹשׁ° **shâlôwsh** (1 Chron. 11:11; 12:18), *shaw-loshe´;* or

שָׁלֹשׁ° **shâlôsh** (2 Sam. 23:13), *shaw-loshe´;* from 7969; a *triple*, i.e. (as a musical instrument) a *triangle* (or perh. rather *three*-stringed lute); also (as an indef. great quantity) a *threefold* measure (perh. a *treble* ephah); also (as an officer) a general of the *third* rank (upward, i.e. the highest):— captain, instrument of musick, (great) lord, (great) measure, prince, three [from marg.].

7992. שְׁלִישִׁי **sh⁰lîyshîy**, *shel-ee-shee´;* ord. from 7969; *third;* fem. a *third* (part); by extens. a *third* (day, year or time); spec. a *third*-story cell):— third (part, rank, time), three (years old).

7993. שָׁלַךְ **shâlak**, *shaw-lak;* a prim. root; to *throw* out, down or away (lit. or fig.):— adventure, cast (away, down, forth, off, out), hurl, pluck, throw.

7994. שָׁלָךְ **shâlâk**, *shaw-lawk´;* from 7993; *bird of prey*, usually thought to be the *pelican* (from *casting* itself into the sea):— cormorant.

7995. שַׁלֶּכֶת **shalleketh**, *shal-leh´-keth;* from 7993; a *felling* (of trees):— when cast.

7996. שַׁלֶּכֶת **Shalleketh**, *shal-leh´-keth;* the same as 7995; *Shalleketh*, a gate in Jerusalem:— Shalleketh.

7997. שָׁלַל **shâlal**, *shaw-lal´;* a prim. root; to *drop* or *strip;* by impl. to *plunder:*— let fall, make self a prey, × of purpose, (make a, [take]) spoil.

7998. שָׁלָל **shâlâl**, *shaw-lawl´;* from 7997; *booty:*— prey, spoil.

7999. שָׁלַם **shâlam**, *shaw-lam´;* a prim. root; to *be safe* (in mind, body or estate); fig. to *be* (caus. *make*) *completed;* by impl. to *be friendly;* by extens. to *reciprocate* (in various applications):— make amends, (make an) end, finish, full, give again, make good, (re-) pay (again), (make) (to) (be at) peace (-able), that is perfect, perform, (make) prosper (-ous), recompense, render, requite, make restitution, restore, reward, × surely.

8000. שְׁלַם **sh⁰lam** (Chald.), *shel-am´;* corresp. to 7999; to *complete*, to *restore:*— deliver, finish.

8001. שְׁלָם **sh⁰lâm** (Chald.), *shel-awm´;* corresp. to 7965; *prosperity:*— peace.

8002. שֶׁלֶם **shelem**, *sheh´-lem;* from 7999; prop. *requital*, i.e. a (voluntary) sacrifice in *thanks:*— peace offering.

8003. שָׁלֵם **shâlêm**, *shaw-lame´;* from 7999; *complete* (lit. or fig.); espec. *friendly:*— full, just, made ready, peaceable, perfect (-ed), quiet, Shalem [by mistake for a name], whole.

8004. שָׁלֵם **Shâlêm**, *shaw-lame´;* the same as 8003; *peaceful; Shalem*, an early name of Jerusalem:— Salem.

שָׁלֹם **shâlôm**. See 7965.

8005. שִׁלֵּם **shillêm**, *shil-lame´;* from 7999; *requital:*— recompense.

8006. שִׁלֵּם **Shillêm**, *shil-lame´;* the same as 8005; *Shillem*, an Isr.:— Shillem.

שִׁלֻּם **shillûm**. See 7966.

שַׁלֻּם **Shallûm**. See 7967.

8007. שַׁלְמָא **Salmâ'**, *sal-maw´;* prob. for 8008; *clothing; Salma*, the name of two Isr.:— Salma.

8008. שַׂלְמָה **salmâh**, *sal-maw´;* transp. for 8071; a *dress:*— clothes, garment, raiment.

8009. שַׂלְמָה **Salmâh**, *sal-maw´;* the same as 8008; *clothing; Salmah*, an Isr.:— Salmon. Comp. 8012.

8010. שְׁלֹמֹה **Sh⁰lômôh**, *shel-o-mo´;* from 7965; *peaceful; Shelomah*, David's successor:— Solomon.

8011. שִׁלֻּמָה **shillumâh**, *shil-loo-maw´;* fem. of 7966; *retribution:*— recompense.

8012. שַׂלְמוֹן **Salmôwn**, *sal-mone´;* from 8008; *investiture; Salmon*, an Isr.:— Salmon. Comp. 8009.

8013. שְׁלֹמוֹת **Sh⁰lômôwth**, *shel-o-moth´;* fem. plur. of 7965; *pacifications; Shelomoth*, the name of two Isr.:— Shelomith [from the marg.], Shelomoth. Comp. 8019.

8014. שַׂלְמַי **Salmay**, *sal-mah´-ee;* from 8008; *clothed; Salmai*, an Isr.:— Shalmai.

8015. שְׁלֹמִי **Sh⁰lômîy**, *shel-o-mee´;* from

7965; *peaceable; Shelomi*, an Isr.:— Shelomi.

8016. שִׁלֵּמִי **Shillêmîy**, *shil-lay-mee´;* patron. from 8006; a *Shilemite* (collect.) or desc. of Shillem:— Shillemites.

8017. שְׁלֻמִיאֵל **Sh⁰lûmîy'êl**, *shel-oo-mee-ale´;* from 7965 and 410; *peace of God; Shelumiel*, an Isr.:— Shelumiel.

8018. שֶׁלֶמְיָה **Shelemyâh**, *shel-em-yaw´;* or

שֶׁלֶמְיָהוּ **Shelemyâhuw**, *shel-em-yaw´-hoo;* from 8002 and 3050; *thankoffering of Jah; Shelemjah*, the name of nine Isr.:— Shelemiah.

8019. שְׁלֹמִית **Sh⁰lômîyth**, *shel-o-meeth´;* or

שְׁלוֹמִית **Sh⁰lôwmiyth** (Ezra 8:10), *shel-o-meeth´;* from 7965; *peaceableness; Shelomith*, the name of five Isr. and three Israelitesses:— Shelomith.

8020. שַׁלְמַן **Shalman**, *shal-man´;* of for. der.; *Shalman*, a king appar. of Assyria:— Shalman. Comp. 8022.

8021. שַׁלְמֹן **shalmôn**, *shal-mone´;* from 7999; a *bribe:*— reward.

8022. שַׁלְמַנְאֶסֶר **Shalman'eçer**, *shalman-eh´-ser;* of for. der.; *Shalmaneser*, an Ass. king:— Shalmaneser. Comp 8020.

8023. שִׁלֹנִי **Shîlônîy**, *shee-lo-nee´;* the same as 7888; *Shiloni*, an Isr.:— Shiloni.

8024. שֵׁלָנִי **Shêlânîy**, *shay-law-nee´;* from 7956; a *Shelanite* (collect.), or desc. of Shelah:— Shelanites.

8025. שָׁלַף **shâlaph**, *saw-laf´;* a prim. root; to *pull* out, up or off:— draw (off), grow up, pluck off.

8026. שֶׁלֶף **Sheleph**, *sheh´-lef;* from 8025; *extract; Sheleph*, a son of Jokthan:— Sheleph.

8027. שָׁלַשׁ **shâlash**, *shaw-lash´;* a prim. root perh. orig. to *intensify*, i.e. *treble;* but appar. used only as denom. from 7969, to *be* (caus. *make*) *triplicate* (by restoration, in portions, strands, days or years):— do the third time, (divide into, stay) three (days, -fold, parts, years old).

8028. שֶׁלֶשׁ **Shelesh**, *sheh´-lesh;* from 8027; *triplet; Shelesh*, an Isr.:— Shelesh.

שָׁלֹשׁ **shâlôsh**. See 7969.

8029. שִׁלֵּשׁ **shillêsh**, *shil-laysh´;* from 8027; a *desc.* of the *third* degree, i.e. *great grandchild:*— third [generation].

8030. שִׁלְשָׁה **Shilshâh**, *shil-shaw´;* fem. from the same as 8028; *triplication; Shilshah*, an Isr.:— Shilshah.

8031. שָׁלִשָׁה **Shâlishâh**, *shaw-lee-shaw´;* fem. from 8027; *trebled* land; *Shalishah*, a place in Pal.:— Shalisha.

שָׁלִשָׁה **shâlishâh**. See 7969.

8032. שִׁלְשׁוֹם **shilshôwm**, *shil-shome´;* or

שִׁלְשֹׁם **shilshôm**, *shil-shome´;* from the same as 8028; *trebly*, i.e. (in time) *day before yesterday:*— + before (that time, -time), excellent things [from the marg.], + heretofore, three days, + time past.

שְׁלֹשִׁים **sh⁰lôshîym**. See 7970.

שַׁלְתִּיאֵל **Shaltîy'êl**. See 7597.

8033. שָׁם **shâm**, *shawm*; a prim. parti-cle [rather from the rel. 834]; *there* (transferring to time) *then*; often *thither*, or *thence*:— in it, + thence, there (-in, + of, + out), + thither, + whither.

8034. שֵׁם **shêm**, *shame*; a prim. word [perh. rather from 7760 through the idea of def. and conspicuous *position*; comp. 8064]; an *appellation*, as a mark or memorial of individuality; by impl. *honor, authority, character*:— + base, [in-] fame [-ous], named (-d), renown, report.

8035. שֵׁם **Shêm**, *shame*; the same as 8034; *name; Shem*, a son of Noah (often includ. his posterity):— Sem, Shem.

8036. שֻׁם **shum** (Chald.), *shoom*; cor-resp. to 8034:— name.

8037. שַׁמָּא **Shammâ'**, *sham-maw'*; from 8074; *desolation; Shamma*, an Isr.:— Shamma.

8038. שְׁמְאֵבֶר **Shem'êber**, *shem-ay'-ber*; appar. from 8034 and 83; *name of pin-ion*, i.e. *illustrious; Shemeber*, a king of Zeboim:— Shemeber.

8039. שִׁמְאָה **Shim'âh**, *shim-aw'*; perh. for 8093; *Shimah*, an Isr.:— Shimah. Comp. 8043.

8040. שְׂמֹאול **s^emô'wl**, *sem-ole'*; or

שְׂמֹאל **s^emô'l**, *sem-ole'*; a prim. word [rather perh. from the same as 8071 (by insertion of א) through the idea of *wrapping* up]; prop. *dark* (as *enveloped*), i.e. the *north*; hence (by orientation), the *left* hand:— left (hand, side).

8041. שָׂמָאל **sâma'l**, *saw-mal'*; a prim. root [rather denom. from 8040]; to use the *left* hand or pass in that direc-tion):— (go, turn) (on the, to the) left.

8042. שְׂמָאלִי **s^emâ'lîy**, *sem-aw-lee'*; from 8040; situated on the *left* side:— left.

8043. שִׁמְאָם **Shim'âm**, *shim-awm'*; for 8039 [comp. 38]; *Shimam*, an Isr.:— Shimeam.

8044. שַׁמְגַּר **Shamgar**, *sham-gar'*; of un-cert. der.; *Shamgar*, an Isr. judge:— Shamgar.

8045. שָׁמַד **shâmad**, *shaw-mad'*; a prim. root; to *desolate*:— destroy (-uction), bring to nought, overthrow, perish, pluck down, × utterly.

8046. שְׁמַד **sh^emad** (Chald.), *shem-ad'*; corresp. to 8045:— consume.

שָׁמֶה **shâmeh**. See 8064.

8047. שַׁמָּה **shammâh**, *sham-maw'*; from 8074; *ruin*; by impl. *consternation*:— astonishment, desolate (-ion), waste, wonderful thing.

8048. שַׁמָּה **Shammâh**, *sham-maw'*; the same as 8047; *Shammah*, the name of an Edomite and four Isr.:— Shammah.

8049. שַׁמְהוּת **Shamhûwth**, *sham-hooth'*; for 8048; *desolation; Shamhuth*, an Isr.:— Shamhuth.

8050. שְׁמוּאֵל **Sh^emûw'êl**, *sehm-oo-ale'*; from the pass. part. of 8085 and 410; *heard of God; Shemuel*, the name of three Isr.:— Samuel, Shemuel.

שְׁמוּנֶה **sh^emôwneh**. See 8083.

שְׁמוּנָה **sh^emôwnâh**. See 8083.

שְׁמוֹנִים **sh^emôwnîym**. See 8084.

8051. שַׁמּוּעַ **Shammûwa'**, *sham-moo'-ah*; from 8074; *renowned; Shammua*, the name of four Isr.:— Shammua, Shammuah.

8052. שְׁמוּעָה **sh^emûw'âh**, *sehm-oo-aw'*; fem. pass. part. of 8074; *something heard*, i.e. an *announcement*:— bruit, doctrine, fame, mentioned, news, re-port, rumor, tidings.

8053. שָׁמוּר **Shâmûwr**, *shaw-moor'*; pass. part. of 8103; *observed; Shamur*, an Isr.:— Shamir [from the marg.].

8054. שַׁמּוֹת **Shammôwth**, *sham-môth'*; plur. of 8047; *ruins; Shammoth*, an Isr.:— Shamoth.

8055. שָׂמַח **sâmach**, *saw-makh'*; a prim. root; prob. to *brighten* up, i.e. (fig.) *be* (caus. *make*) *blithe* or *gleesome*:— cheer up, be (make) glad, (have, make) joy (-ful), be (make) merry, (cause to, make to) rejoice, × very.

8056. שָׂמֵחַ **sâmêach**, *saw-may'-akh*; from 8055; *blithe* or *gleeful*:— (be) glad, joyful, (making) merry [-hearted], -ily), rejoice (-ing).

8057. שִׂמְחָה **simchâh**, *sim-khaw'*; from 8056; *blithesomeness* or *glee*, (relig. or festival):— × exceeding (-ly), gladness, joy (-fulness), mirth, pleasure, rejoice (-ing).

8058. שָׁמַט **shâmaṭ**, *shaw-mat'*; a prim. root; to *fling* down; incipiently to *jostle*; fig. to *let alone, desist, remit*:— discon-tinue, overthrow, release, let rest, shake, stumble, throw down.

8059. שְׁמִטָּה **sh^emiṭṭâh**, *shem-it-taw'*; from 8058; *remission* (of debt) or *sus-pension* of labor):— release.

8060. שַׁמַּי **Shammay**, *sham-mah'-ee*; from 8073; *destructive; Shammai*, the name of three Isr.:— Shammai.

8061. שְׁמִידָע **Sh^emîydâ'**, *shem-ee-daw'*; appar. from 8034 and 3045; *name of knowing; Shemida*, an Isr.:— Shemida, Shemidah.

8062. שְׁמִידָעִי **Sh^emîydâ'îy**, *shem-ee-daw-ee'*; patron. from 8061; a *Shemi-daite* (collect.) or desc. of Shemida:— Shemidaites.

8063. שְׂמִיכָה **s^emîykâh**, *sem-ee-kaw'*; from 5564; a *rug* (as *sustaining* the Ori-ental sitter):— mantle.

8064. שָׁמַיִם **shâmayim**, *shaw-mah'-yim*; dual of an unused sing.

שָׁמֶה **shâmeh**, *shaw-meh'*; from an unused root mean. to *be lofty*; the *sky* (as *aloft*; the dual perh. alluding to the visible arch in which the clouds move, as well as to the higher ether where the celestial bodies revolve):— air, × astrologer, heaven (-s).

8065. שָׁמַיִן **shâmayin** (Chald.), *shaw-mah'-yin*; corresp. to 8064:— heaven.

8066. שְׁמִינִי **sh^emîynîy**, *shem-ee-nee'*; from 8083; *eight*:— eight.

8067. שְׁמִינִית **sh^emîynîyth**, *shem-ee-neeth'*; fem. of 8066; prob. an *eight*-stringed lyre:— Sheminith.

8068. שָׁמִיר **shâmîyr**, *shaw-meer'*; from 8104 in the orig. sense of *pricking*; a *thorn*; also (from its *keenness* for scratching) a gem, prob. the *dia-mond*:— adamant (stone), brier, dia-mond.

8069. שָׁמִיר **Shâmîyr**, *shaw-meer'*; the same as 8068; *Shamir*, the name of two places in Pal.:— Shamir. Comp. 8053.

8070. שְׁמִירָמוֹת **Sh^emîyrâmôwth**, *shem-ee-raw-môth'*; or

שְׂמָרִימוֹת **Sh^emârîymôwth**, *shem-aw-ree-môth'*; prob. from 8034 and plur. of 7413; *name of heights; Shemi-ramoth*, the name of two Isr.:— Shemi-ramoth.

8071. שִׂמְלָה **simlâh**, *sim-law'*; perh. by perm. for the fem. of 5566 (through the idea of a *cover* assuming the shape of the object beneath); a *dress*, espec. a *mantle*:— apparel, cloth (-es, -ing), garment, raiment. Comp. 8008.

8072. שַׂמְלָה **Samlâh**, *sam-law'*; prob. for the same as 8071; *Samlah*, an Edomite:— Samlah.

8073. שַׂמְלַי **Shamlay**, *sham-lah'-ee*; for 8014; *Shamlai*, one of the Nethinim:— Shalmai [from the marg.].

8074. שָׁמֵם **shâmêm**, *shaw-mame'*; a prim. root; to *stun* (or intr. *grow numb*), i.e. *devastate* or (fig.) *stupefy* (both usu-ally in a pass. sense):— make amazed, be astonied, (be an) astonish (-ment), (be, bring into, unto, lay, lie, make) desolate (-ion, places), be destitute, destroy (self), (lay, lie, make) waste, wonder.

8075. שְׁמַם **sh^emam** (Chald.), *shem-am'*; corresp. to 8074:— be astonied.

8076. שָׁמֵם **shâmêm**, *shaw-mame'*; from 8074; *ruined*:— desolate.

8077. שְׁמָמָה **sh^emâmâh**, *shem-aw-maw'*; or

שִׁמָמָה **shîmâmâh**, *shee-mam-aw'*; fem. of 8076; *devastation*; fig. *astonishment*:— (laid, × most) desolate (-ion), waste.

8078. שִׁמָּמוֹן **shimmâmôwn**, *shim-maw-mone'*; from 8074; *stupefaction*:— astonishment.

8079. שְׂמָמִית **s^emâmîyth**, *sem-aw-meeth'*; prob. from 8074 (in the sense of *poisoning*); a *lizard* (from the supersti-tion of its *noxiousness*):— spider.

8080. שָׁמַן **shâman**, *shaw-man'*; a prim. root; to *shine*, i.e. (by anal.) *be* (caus. *make*) *oily* or *gross*:— become (make, wax) fat.

8081. שֶׁמֶן **shemen**, *sheh'-men*; from 8080; *grease*, espec. *liquid* (as from the olive, often perfumed); fig. *richness*:— anointing, × fat (things), × fruitful, oil ([-ed]), ointment, olive, + pine.

8082. שָׁמֵן **shâmên**, *shaw-mane'*; from 8080; *greasy*, i.e. *gross*; fig. *rich*:— fat, lusty, plenteous.

8083. שְׁמֹנֶה **sh^emôneh**, *shem-o-neh'*; or

שְׁמוֹנֶה **sh^emôwneh**, *shem-o-neh'*; fem.

שְׁמֹנָה **sh^emônâh**, *shem-o-naw'*; or

שְׁמוֹנָה **sh^emôwnâh**, *shem-o-naw'*; appar. from 8082 through the idea of *plumpness*; a cardinal number, *eight* (as if a *surplus* above the "perfect" seven); also (as ord.) *eighth*:— eight ([-een, -eenth]), eighth.

8084. שְׁמֹנִים **shᵉmônîym**, *shem-o-neem´*; or

שְׁמוֹנִים **shᵉmôwnîym**, *shem-o-neem´*; mult. from 8083; *eighty*, also *eightieth*:— eighty (-ieth), fourscore.

8085. שָׁמַע **shâma'**, *shaw-mah´*; a prim. root; to *hear* intelligently (often with impl. of attention, obedience, etc.; caus. to *tell*, etc.):— × attentively, call (gather) together, × carefully, × certainly, consent, consider, be content, declare, × diligently, discern, give ear, (cause to, let, make to) hear (-ken, tell), × indeed, listen, make (a) noise, (be) obedient, obey, perceive, (make a) proclaim (-ation), publish, regard, report, shew (forth), (make a) sound, × surely, tell, understand, whosoever [heareth], witness.

8086. שְׁמַע **shᵉma'** (Chald.), *shem-ah´*; corresp. to 8085:— hear, obey.

8087. שֶׁמַע **Shema'**, *sheh´-mah*; for the same as 8088; *Shema*, the name of a place in Pal. and of four Isr.:— Shema.

8088. שֵׁמַע **shêma'**, *shay´-mah*; from 8085; something *heard*, i.e. a *sound*, *rumor*, *announcement*; abstr. *audience*:— bruit, fame, hear (-ing), loud, report, speech, tidings.

8089. שֹׁמַע **shoma'**, *sho´-mah*; from 8085; a *report*:— fame.

8090. שֶׁמָע **Shᵉmâ'**, *shem-aw´*; for 8087; *Shema*, a place in Pal.:— Shema.

8091. שָׁמָע **Shâmâ'**, *shaw-maw´*; from 8085; *obedient*; *Shama*, an Isr.:— Shama.

8092. שִׁמְעָא **Shim'â'**, *shim-aw´*; for 8093; *Shima*, the name of four Isr.:— Shimea, Shimei, Shamma.

8093. שִׁמְעָה **Shim'âh**, *shim-aw´*; fem. of 8088; *annunciation*; *Shimah*, an Isr.:— Shimeah.

8094. שְׁמָעָה **Shᵉmâ'âh**, *shem-aw-aw´*; for 8093; *Shemaah*, an Isr.:— Shemaah.

8095. שִׁמְעוֹן **Shim'ôwn**, *shim-ône´*; from 8085; *hearing*; *Shimon*, one of Jacob's sons, also the tribe desc. from him:— Simeon.

8096. שִׁמְעִי **Shim'iy**, *shim-ee´*; from 8088; *famous*; *Shimi*, the name of twenty Isr.:— Shimeah [from the marg.], Shimei, Shimhi, Shimi.

8097. שִׁמְעִי **Shim'iy**, *shim-ee´*; patron. from 8096; a *Shimite* (collect.) or desc. of Shimi:— of Shimi, Shimites.

8098. שְׁמַעְיָה **Shᵉma'yâh**, *shem-aw-yaw´*; or

שְׁמַעְיָהוּ **Shᵉma'yâhûw**, *shem-aw-yaw´-hoo*; from 8085 and 3050; *Jah has heard*; *Shemajah*, the name of twenty-five Isr.:— Shemaiah.

8099. שִׁמְעֹנִי **Shim'ôniy**, *shim-o-nee´*; patron. from 8095; a *Shimonite* (collect.) or desc. of Shimon:— tribe of Simeon, Simeonites.

8100. שִׁמְעָת **Shim'âth**, *shim-awth´*; fem. of 8088; *annunciation*; *Shimath*, an Ammonitess:— Shimath.

8101. שִׁמְעָתִי **Shim'âthiy**, *shim-aw-thee´*; patron. from 8093; a *Shimathite* (collect.) or desc. of Shimah:— Shimeathites.

8102. שֶׁמֶץ **shemets**, *sheh´-mets*; from an unused root mean. to *emit* a sound; an *inkling*:— a little.

8103. שִׁמְצָה **shimtsâh**, *shim-tsaw´*; fem. of 8102; *scornful whispering* (of hostile spectators):— shame.

8104. שָׁמַר **shâmar**, *shaw-mar´*; a prim. root; prop. to *hedge* about (as with thorns), i.e. *guard*; gen. to *protect*, *attend to*, etc.:— beware, be circumspect, take heed (to self), keep (-er, self), mark, look narrowly, observe, preserve, regard, reserve, save (self), sure, (that lay) wait (for), watch (-man).

8105. שֶׁמֶר **shemer**, *sheh´-mer*; from 8104; something *preserved*, i.e. the *settlings* (plur. only) of wine:— dregs, (wines on the) lees.

8106. שֶׁמֶר **Shemer**, *sheh´-mer*; the same as 8105; *Shemer*, the name of three Isr.:— Shamer, Shemer.

8107. שִׁמֻּר **shimmûr**, *shim-moor´*; from 8104; an *observance*:— × be (much) observed.

שֹׁמֵר **Shômêr**. See 7763.

8108. שָׁמְרָה **shomrâh**, *shom-raw´*; fem. of an unused noun from 8104 mean. a *guard*; *watchfulness*:— watch.

8109. שְׁמֻרָה **shᵉmûrâh**, *shem-oo-raw´*; fem. of pass. part. of 8104; something *guarded*, i.e. an *eye-lid*:— waking.

8110. שִׁמְרוֹן **Shimrôwn**, *shim-rone´*; from 8105 in its orig. sense; *guardianship*; *Shimron*, the name of an Isr. and of a place in Pal.:— Shimron.

8111. שֹׁמְרוֹן **Shômᵉrown**, *sho-mer-ône´*; from the act. part. of 8104; *watch-station*; *Shomeron*, a place in Pal.:— Samaria.

8112. שִׁמְרוֹן מְראוֹן **Shimrôwn Mᵉr'ôwn**, *shim-rone´ mer-one´*; from 8110 and a der. of 4754; *guard of lashing*; *Shimron-Meron*, a place in Pal.:— Shimron-meron.

8113. שִׁמְרִי **Shimriy**, *shim-ree´*; from 8105 in its orig. sense; *watchful*; *Shimri*, the name of four Isr.:— Shimri.

8114. שְׁמַרְיָה **Shᵉmaryâh**, *shem-ar-yaw´*; or

שְׁמַרְיָהוּ **Shᵉmaryâhûw**, *shem-ar-yaw´-hoo*; from 8104 and 3050; *Jah has guarded*; *Shemarjah*, the name of four Isr.:— Shamariah, Shemariah.

שְׂמָרִימוֹת **Shᵉmâriymôwth**. See 8070.

8115. שָׁמְרַיִן **Shomrayin** (Chald.), *shom-rah´-yin*; corresp. to 8111; *Shomrain*, a place in Pal.:— Samaria.

8116. שִׁמְרִית **Shimrîyth**, *shim-reeth´*; fem. of 8113; *female guard*; *Shimrith*, a Moabitess:— Shimrith.

8117. שִׁמְרֹנִי **Shimrôniy**, *shim-ro-nee´*; patron. from 8110; a *Shimronite* (collect.) or desc. of Shimron:— Shimronites.

8118. שֹׁמְרֹנִי **Shômᵉrôniy**, *sho-mer-o-nee´*; patrial from 8111; a *Shomeronite* (collect.) or inhab. of Shomeron:— Samaritans.

8119. שִׁמְרָת **Shimrâth**, *shim-rawth´*; from 8104; *guardship*; *Shimrath*, an Isr.:— Shimrath.

8120. שְׁמַשׁ **shᵉmash** (Chald.), *shem-ash´*; corresp. to the root of 8121 through the idea of *activity* impl. in day-light; to *serve*:— minister.

8121. שֶׁמֶשׁ **shemesh**, *sheh´-mesh*; from an unused root mean. to *be brilliant*; the *sun*; by impl. the *east*; fig. a *ray*, i.e. (arch.) a notched *battlement*:— + east side (-ward), sun (rising), + west (-ward), window. See also 1053.

8122. שֶׁמֶשׁ **shemesh** (Chald.), *sheh´-mesh*; corresp. to 8121; the *sun*:— sun.

8123. שִׁמְשׁוֹן **Shimshôwn**, *shim-shone´*; from 8121; *sunlight*; *Shimshon*, an Isr.:— Samson.

שִׁמְשַׁי **Shimshîy**. See 1030.

8124. שִׁמְשַׁי **Shimshay** (Chald.), *shim-shah´-ee*; from 8122; *sunny*; *Shimshai*, a Samaritan:— Shimshai.

8125. שַׁמְשְׁרַי **Shamshᵉray**, *sham-sher-ah´-ee*; appar. from 8121; *sunlike*; *Shamsherai*, an Isr.:— Shamsherai.

8126. שׁוּמָתִי **Shûmâthîy**, *shoo-maw-thee´*; patron. from an unused name from 7762 prob. mean. *garlic*-smell; a *Shumathite* (collect.) or desc. of Shumah:— Shumathites.

8127. שֵׁן **shên**, *shane*; from 8150; a *tooth* (as *sharp*); spec. (for 8143) *ivory*; fig. a *cliff*:— crag, × forefront, ivory, × sharp, tooth.

8128. שֵׁן **shên** (Chald.), *shane*; corresp. to 8127; a *tooth*:— tooth.

8129. שֵׁן **Shên**, *shane*; the same as 8127; *crag*; *Shen*, a place in Pal.:— Shen.

8130. שָׂנֵא **sânê'**, *saw-nay´*; a prim. root; to *hate* (personally):— enemy, foe, (be) hate (-ful, -r), odious, × utterly.

8131. שְׂנֵא **sᵉnê'** (Chald.), *sen-ay´*; corresp. to 8130:— hate.

8132. שָׁנָא **shânâ'**, *shaw-naw´*; a prim. root; to *alter*:— change.

8133. שְׁנָא **shᵉnâ'** (Chald.), *shen-aw´*; corresp. to 8132:— alter, change, (be) diverse.

שְׂנֵא **sᵉnê'**. See 8142.

8134. שִׁנְאָב **Shin'âb**, *shin-awb´*; prob. from 8132 and 1; a *father has turned*; *Shinab*, a Canaanite:— Shinab.

8135. שִׂנְאָה **sin'âh**, *sin-aw´*; from 8130; *hate*:— + exceedingly, hate (-ful, -red).

8136. שִׁנְאָן **shin'ân**, *shin-awn´*; from 8132; *change*, i.e. *repetition*:— × angels.

8137. שֶׁנְאַצַּר **Shen'atstsar**, *shen-ats-tsar´*; appar. of Bab. or.; *Shenatstsar*, an Isr.:— Senazar.

8138. שָׁנָה **shânâh**, *shaw-naw´*; a prim. root; to *fold*, i.e. *duplicate* (lit. or fig.); by impl. to *transmute* (tran. or intr.):— do (speak, strike) again, alter, double, (be given to) change, disguise, (be) diverse, pervert, prefer, repeat, return, do the second time.

8139. שְׁנָה **shᵉnâh** (Chald.), *shen-aw´*; corresp. to 8142:— sleep.

8140. שְׁנָה **shᵉnâh** (Chald.), *shen-aw´*; corresp. to 8141:— year.

8141. שָׁנֶה **shâneh** (in plur. only), *shaw-neh´*; or (fem.)

שָׁנָה **shânâh**, *shaw-naw´*; from

8138; a *year* (as a *revolution* of time):— + whole age, × long, + old, year (× -ly).

8142. שְׁנָה **shênâh**, *shay-naw´;* or

שְׁנָא **shênâ'** (Psa. 127:2), *shay-naw´;* from 3462; *sleep:*— sleep.

8143. שֶׁנְהַבִּים **shenhabbîym**, *shen-hab-beem´;* from 8127 and the plur. appar. of a for. word; prob. *tooth of elephants,* i.e. *ivory tusk:*— ivory.

8144. שָׁנִי **shânîy**, *shaw-nee´;* of uncert. der.; *crimson,* prop. the insect or its color, also stuff dyed with it:— crimson, scarlet (thread).

8145. שֵׁנִי **shênîy**, *shay-nee´;* from 8138; prop. *double,* i.e. *second;* also adv. *again:*— again, either [of them], (an-)other, second (time).

8146. שָׂנִיא **sânîy'**, *saw-nee´;* from 8130; *hated:*— hated.

8147. שְׁנַיִם **shᵉnayim**, *shen-ah´-yim;* dual of 8145; fem.

שְׁתַּיִם **shᵉttayim**, *shet-tah´-yim;* *two;* also (as ord.) *twofold:*— both, couple, double, second, twain, + twelfth, + twelve, + twenty (sixscore) thousand, twice, two.

8148. שְׁנִינָה **shᵉnîynâh**, *shen-ee-naw´;* from 8150; *something pointed,* i.e. a *gibe:*— byword, taunt.

8149. שְׂנִיר **Shᵉnîyr**, *shen-eer´;* or

שְׂנִיר **Sᵉnîyr**, *sen-eer´;* from an unused root mean. to *be pointed; peak, Shenir* or *Senir,* a summit of Lebanon:— Senir, Shenir.

8150. שָׁנַן **shânan**, *shaw-nan´;* a prim. root; to *point* (tran. or intr.); intens. to *pierce;* fig. to *inculcate:*— prick, sharp (-en), teach diligently, whet.

8151. שָׁנַס **shânaç**, *shaw-nas´;* a prim. root; to *compress* (with a belt):— gird up.

8152. שִׁנְעָר **Shin'âr**, *shin-awr´;* prob. of for. der.; *Shinar,* a plain in Bab.:— Shinar.

8153. שְׁנָת **shᵉnâth**, *shen-awth´;* from 3462; *sleep:*— sleep.

8154. שָׁסָה **shâçâh**, *shaw-saw´;* or

שָׂסָה **shâsâh** (Isa. 10:13), *shaw-saw´;* a prim. root; to *plunder:*— destroyer, rob, spoil (-er).

8155. שָׁסַס **shâçaç**, *shaw-sas´;* a prim. root; to *plunder:*— rifle, spoil.

8156. שָׁסַע **shâça'**, *shaw-sah´;* a prim. root; to *split* or *tear;* fig. to *upbraid:*— cleave, (be) cloven [-footed], rend, stay.

8157. שֶׁסַע **sheça'**, *sheh´-sah;* from 8156; a *fissure:*— cleft, clovenfooted.

8158. שָׁסַף **shâçaph**, *shaw-saf´;* a prim. root; to *cut in pieces,* i.e. *slaughter:*— hew in pieces.

8159. שָׁעָה **shâ'âh**, *shaw-aw´;* a prim. root; to *gaze* at or about (prop. for help); by impl. to *inspect, consider, compassionate, be nonplussed* (as looking around in amazement) or *bewildered:*— depart, be dim, be dismayed, look (away), regard, have respect, spare, turn.

8160. שָׁעָה **shâ'âh** (Chald.), *shaw-aw´;*

from a root corresp. to 8159; prop. a *look,* i.e. a *moment:*— hour.

שְׁעוֹר **sᵉ'ôwr**. See 8184.

שְׁעוֹרָה **sᵉ'ôwrâh**. See 8184.

8161. שַׁעֲטָה **sha'ăṭâh**, *shah´-at-aw;* fem. from an unused root mean. to *stamp;* a *clatter* (of hoofs):— stamping.

8162. שַׁעַטְנֵז **sha'aṭnêz**, *shah-at-naze´;* prob. of for. der.; *linsey-woolsey,* i.e. cloth of linen and wool carded and spun together:— garment of divers sorts, linen and woollen.

8163. שָׂעִיר **sâ'îyr**, *saw-eer´;* or

שָׂעִר **sâ'ir**, *saw-eer´;* from 8175; *shaggy;* as noun, a *he-goat;* by anal. a *faun:*— devil, goat, hairy, kid, rough, satyr.

8164. שָׂעִיר **sâ'îyr**, *saw-eer´;* formed the same as 8163; a *shower* (as *tempestuous*):— small rain.

8165. שֵׂעִיר **Sê'îyr**, *say-eer´;* formed like 8163; *rough; Seir,* a mountain of Idumaea and its aboriginal occupants, also one in Pal.:— Seir.

8166. שְׂעִירָה **sᵉ'îyrâh**, *seh-ee-raw´;* fem. of 8163; a *she-goat:*— kid.

8167. שְׂעִירָה **Sᵉ'îyrâh**, *seh-ee-raw´;* formed as 8166; *roughness; Seirah,* a place in Pal.:— Seirath.

8168. שֹׁעַל **shô'al**, *sho´-al;* from an unused root mean. to *hollow* out; the *palm;* by extens. a *handful:*— handful, hollow of the hand.

שֻׁעַל **shu'âl**. See 7776.

8169. שַׁעַלְבִים **Sha'albîym**, *shah-al-beem´;* or

שַׁעֲלַבִּין **Sha'ălabbîyn**, *shah-al-ab-been´;* plur. from 7776; *fox-holes; Shaalbim* or *Shaalabbin,* a place in Pal.:— Shaalabbin, Shaalbim.

8170. שַׁעַלְבֹנִי **Sha'albôniy**, *shah-al-bo-nee´;* patrial from 8169; a *Shaalbonite* or inhab. of Shaalbin:— Shaalbonite.

8171. שַׁעֲלִים **Sha'ălîym**, *shah-al-eem´;* plur. of 7776; *foxes; Shaalim,* a place in Pal.:— Shalim.

8172. שָׁעַן **shâ'an**, *shaw-an´;* a prim. root; to *support* one's self:— lean, lie, rely, rest (on, self), stay.

8173. שָׁעַע **shâ'a'**, *shaw-ah´;* a prim. root; (in a good acceptation) to *look upon* (with complacency), i.e. *fondle, please* or *amuse* (self); (in a bad one) to *look about* (in dismay), i.e. *stare:*— cry (out) [by confusion with 7768], dandle, delight (self), play, shut.

שַׁעַף **sâ'iph**. See 5587.

8174. שַׁעַף **Sha'aph**, *shah´-af;* from 5586; *fluctuation; Shaaph,* the name of two Isr.:— Shaaph.

8175. שָׂעַר **sâ'ar**, *saw-ar´;* a prim. root; to *storm;* by impl. to *shiver,* i.e. *fear:*— be (horribly) afraid, fear, hurl as a storm, be tempestuous, come like (take away as with) a whirlwind.

8176. שָׁעַר **shâ'ar**, *shaw-ar´;* a prim. root; to *split* or *open,* but only as denom. from 8179) to *act as gatekeeper* (see 7778): (fig.) to *estimate:*— think.

8177. שְׂעַר **sᵉ'ar** (Chald.), *seh-ar´;* corresp. to 8181; *hair:*— hair.

8178. שַׂעַר **sa'ar**, *sah´-ar;* from 8175; a *tempest;* also a *terror:*— affrighted, × horribly, × sore, storm. See 8181.

8179. שַׁעַר **sha'ar**, *shah´-ar;* from 8176 in its orig. sense; an *opening,* i.e. *door* or *gate:*— city, door, gate, port (× -er).

8180. שַׁעַר **sha'ar**, *shah´-ar;* from 8176; a *measure* (as a *section*):— [hundred-] fold.

שָׂעִיר **sâ'îr**. See 8163.

8181. שֵׂעָר **sê'âr**, *say-awr´;* or

שַׂעַר **sa'ar** (Isa. 7:20), *sah´-ar;* from 8175 in the sense of *dishevelling; hair* (as if *tossed* or *bristling*):— hair (-y), × rough.

שֹׁעֵר **shô'êr**. See 7778.

8182. שֹׁעָר **shô'âr**, *sho-awr´;* from 8176; *harsh* or *horrid,* i.e. *offensive:*— vile.

8183. שְׂעָרָה **sᵉ'ârâh**, *seh-aw-raw´;* fem. of 8178; a *hurricane:*— storm, tempest.

8184. שְׂעֹרָה **sᵉ'ôrâh**, *seh-o-raw´;* or

שְׂעוֹרָה **sᵉ'ôwrâh**, *seh-o-raw´* (fem. mean. the *plant*); and (masc. mean. the *grain*); also

שְׂעֹר **sᵉ'ôr**, *seh-ore´;* or

שְׂעוֹר **sᵉ'ôwr**, *seh-ore´;* from 8175 in the sense of *roughness; barley* (as *villose*):— barley.

8185. שַׂעֲרָה **sa'ărâh**, *sah-ar-aw´;* fem. of 8181; *hairiness:*— hair.

8186. שַׁעֲרוּרָה **sha'ărûwrâh**, *shah-ar-oo-raw´;* or

שַׁעֲרִירִיָּה° **sha'ărîyrîyâh**, *shah-ar-ee-ree-yaw´;* or

שַׁעֲרֻרִת **sha'ărûrith**, *shah-ar-oo-reeth´;* fem. from 8176 in the sense of 8175; *something fearful:*— horrible thing.

8187. שְׁעַרְיָה **Shᵉ'aryâh**, *sheh-ar-yaw´;* from 8176 and 3050; *Jah has stormed; Shearjah,* an Isr.:— Sheariah.

8188. שְׂעֹרִים **Sᵉ'ôrîym**, *seh-o-reem´;* masc. plur. of 8184; *barley grains; Seorim,* an Isr.:— Seorim.

8189. שַׁעֲרַיִם **Sha'ărayim**, *shah-ar-ah´-yim;* dual of 8179; *double gates; Shaarajim,* a place in Pal.:— Shaaraim.

שַׁעֲרִירִיָּה **sha'ărîyrîyâh**. See 8186.

שַׁעֲרֻרִת **sha'ărûrith**. See 8186.

8190. שַׁעֲשְׁגַּז **Sha'ashgaz**, *shah-ash-gaz´;* of Pers. der.; *Shaashgaz,* a eunuch of Xerxes:— Shaashgaz.

8191. שַׁעֲשֻׁעַ **sha'shûa'**, *shah-shoo´-ah;* from 8173; *enjoyment:*— delight, pleasure.

8192. שָׁפָה **shâphâh**, *shaw-faw´;* a prim. root; to *abrade,* i.e. *bare:*— high, stick out.

8193. שָׂפָה **sâphâh**, *saw-faw´;* or (in dual and plur.)

שֶׂפֶת **sepheth**, *sef-eth´;* prob. from 5595 or 8192 through the idea of *termination* (comp. 5490); the *lip* (as a nat. boundary); by impl. *language;* by anal. a *margin* (of a vessel, water, cloth, etc.):— band, bank, binding, border, brim, brink, edge, language, lip, prating, ([sea-] shore, side, speech, talk, [vain] words.

8194. שָׁפָה **shâphâh**, shaw-faw'; from 8192 in the sense of *clarifying*; a *cheese* (as *strained* from the whey):— cheese.

8195. שְׁפוֹ **Sh⁰phôw**, shef-o'; or

שְׁפִי **Sh⁰phîy**, shef-ee'; from 8192; *baldness* [comp. 8205]; *Shepho* or *Shephi*, an Idumaean:— Shephi, Shepho.

8196. שְׁפוֹט **sh⁰phôwṭ**, shef-ote'; or

שְׁפוּט **sh⁰phûwṭ**, shef-oot'; from 8199; a judicial *sentence*, i.e. *punishment*:— judgment.

8197. שְׁפוּפָם **Sh⁰phûwphâm**, shef-oo-fawm'; or

שְׁפוּפָן **Sh⁰phûwphân**, shef-oo-fawn'; from the same as 8207; *serpentlike*; *Shephupham* or *Shephuphan*, an Isr.:— Shephupham, Shupham.

8198. שִׁפְחָה **shiphchâh**, shif-khaw'; fem. from an unused root mean. to *spread out* (as a *family*; see 4940); a *female slave* (as a member of the household):— (bond-, hand-) maid (-en, -servant), wench, bondwoman, womanservant.

8199. שָׁפַט **shâphaṭ**, shaw-fat'; a prim. root; to *judge*, i.e. pronounce *sentence* (for or against); by impl. to *vindicate* or *punish*; by extens. to *govern*; pass. to *litigate* (lit. or fig.):— + avenge, × that condemn, contend, defend, execute (judgment), (be a) judge (-ment), × needs, plead, reason, rule.

8200. שְׁפַט **sh⁰phaṭ** (Chald.), shef-at'; corresp. to 8199; to *judge*:— magistrate.

8201. שֶׁפֶט **shepheṭ**, sheh'-fet; from 8199; a *sentence*, i.e. *infliction*:— judgment.

8202. שָׁפָט **Shâphâṭ**, shaw-fawt'; from 8199; *judge*; *Shaphat*, the name of four Isr.:— Shaphat.

8203. שְׁפַטְיָה **Sh⁰phaṭyâh**, shef-at-yaw'; or

שְׁפַטְיָהוּ **Sh⁰phaṭyâhûw**, shef-at-yaw'-hoo; from 8199 and 3050; *Jah has judged*; *Shephatjah*, the name of ten Isr.:— Shephatiah.

8204. שִׁפְטָן **Shiphṭân**, shif-tawn'; from 8199; *judge-like*; *Shiphtan*, an Isr.:— Shiphtan.

8205. שְׁפִי **sh⁰phîy**, shef-ee'; from 8192; *bareness*; concr. a *bare* hill or plain:— high place, stick out.

8206. שֻׁפִּים **Shuppîym**, shoop-peem'; plur. of an unused noun from the same as 8207 and mean. the same; *serpents*; *Shuppim*, an Isr.:— Shuppim.

8207. שְׁפִיפֹן **sh⁰phîyphôn**, shef-ee-fone'; from an unused root mean. the same as 7779; a kind of *serpent* (as *snapping*), prob. the *cerastes* or horned adder:— adder.

8208. שָׁפִיר **Shâphîyr**, shaf-eer'; from 8231; *beautiful*; *Shaphir*, a place in Pal.:— Saphir.

8209. שַׁפִּיר **sappîyr** (Chald.), shap-peer'; intens. of a form corresp. to 8208; *beautiful*:— fair.

8210. שָׁפַךְ **shâphak**, shaw-fak'; a prim. root; to *spill* forth (blood, a libation, liquid metal; or even a solid, i.e. to *mound* up); also (fig.) to *expend* (life, soul, complaint, money, etc.); intens. to *sprawl* out:— cast (up), gush out, pour (out), shed (-der, out), slip.

8211. שֶׁפֶךְ **shephek**, sheh'-fek; from 8210; an *emptying* place, e.g. an ash-heap:— are poured out.

8212. שָׁפְכָה **shophkâh**, shof-kaw'; fem. of a der. from 8210; a *pipe* (for *pouring* forth, e.g. wine), i.e. the *penis*:— privy member.

8213. שָׁפֵל **shâphêl**, shaw-fale'; a prim. root; to *depress* or *sink* (expec. fig. to *humiliate*, intr. or tran.):— abase, bring (cast, put) down, debase, humble (self), be (bring, lay, make, put) low (-er).

8214. שְׁפַל **sh⁰phal** (Chald.), shef-al'; corresp. to 8213:— abase, humble, put down, subdue.

8215. שְׁפַל **sh⁰phal** (Chald.), shef-al'; from 8214; *low*:— basest.

8216. שֵׁפֶל **shêphel**, shay'-fel; from 8213; an *humble* rank:— low estate (place).

8217. שָׁפָל **shâphâl**, shaw-fawl'; from 8213; *depressed*, lit. or fig.:— base (-st), humble, low (-er, -ly).

8218. שִׁפְלָה **shiphlâh**, shif-law'; fem. of 8216; *depression*:— low place.

8219. שְׁפֵלָה **sh⁰phêlâh**, shef-ay-law'; from 8213; *Lowland*, i.e. (with the art.) the maritime slope of Pal.:— low country, (low) plain, vale (-ley).

8220. שִׁפְלוּת **shiphlûwth**, shif-looth'; from 8213; *remissness*:— idleness.

8221. שְׁפָם **Sh⁰phâm**, shef-awm'; prob. from 8192; *bare* spot; *Shepham*, a place in or near Pal.:— Shepham.

8222. שָׂפָם **sâphâm**, saw-fawm'; from 8193; the *beard* (as a *lip-piece*):— beard, (upper) lip.

8223. שָׁפָם **Shâphâm**, shaw-fawm'; formed like 8221; *baldly*; *Shapham*, an Isr.:— Shapham.

8224. שִׂפְמוֹת **Siphmôwth**, sif-môth'; fem. plur. of 8221; *Siphmoth*, a place in Pal.:— Siphmoth.

8225. שִׁפְמִי **Shiphmîy**, shif-mee'; patrial from 8221; a *Shiphmite* or inhab. of Shepham:— Shiphmite.

8226. שָׂפַן **sâphan**, saw-fan'; a prim. root; to *conceal* (as a valuable):— treasure.

8227. שָׁפָן **shâphân**, shaw-fawn'; from 8226; a species of *rock-rabbit* (from its *hiding*), i.e. prob. the *hyrax*:— coney.

8228. שֶׁפַע **shepha'**, sheh'-fah; from an unused root mean. to *abound*; *resources*:— abundance.

8229. שִׁפְעָה **shiph'âh**, shif-aw'; fem. of 8228; *copiousness*:— abundance, company, multitude.

8230. שִׁפְעִי **Shiph'îy**, shif-ee'; from 8228; *copious*; *Shiphi*, an Isr.:— Shiphi.

שָׂפַק **sâphaq**. See 5606.

8231. שָׁפַר **shâphar**, shaw-far'; a prim. root; to *glisten*, i.e. (fig.) be (caus. *make*) *fair*:— × goodly.

8232. שְׁפַר **sh⁰phar** (Chald.), shef-ar'; corresp. to 8231; to *be beautiful*:— be acceptable, please, + think good.

8233. שֶׁפֶר **shepher**, sheh'-fer; from 8231; *beauty*:— × goodly.

8234. שֶׁפֶר **Shepher**, sheh'-fer; the same as 8233; *Shepher*, a place in the Desert:— Shapper.

שׁוֹפָר **shôphâr**. See 7782.

8235. שִׁפְרָה **shiphrâh**, shif-raw'; from 8231; *brightness*:— garnish.

8236. שִׁפְרָה **Shiphrâh**, shif-raw'; the same as 8235; *Shiphrah*, an Israelitess:— Shiphrah.

8237. שַׁפְרוּר **shaphrûwr**, shaf-roor'; from 8231; *splendid*, i.e. a *tapestry* or *canopy*:— royal pavilion.

8238. שְׁפַרְפַר **sh⁰pharphar** (Chald.), shef-ar-far'; from 8231; the *dawn* (as *brilliant* with aurora):— × very early in the morning.

8239. שָׁפַת **shâphath**, shaw-fath'; a prim. root; to *locate*, i.e. (gen.) *hang* on or (fig.) *establish, reduce*:— bring, ordain, set on.

8240. שָׁפָת **shâphâth**, shaw-fawth'; from 8239; a (double) *stall* (for cattle); also a (two-pronged) *hook* (for flaying animals on):— hook, pot.

8241. שֶׁצֶף **shetseph**, sheh'-tsef; from 7857 (for alliteration with 7110); an *outburst* (of anger):— little.

8242. שַׂק **saq**, sak; from 8264; prop. a *mesh* (as allowing a liquid to *run* through), i.e. coarse loose cloth or *sacking* (used in mourning and for bagging); hence, a *bag* (for grain, etc.):— sack (-cloth, -clothes).

8243. שָׁק **shâq** (Chald.), shawk; corresp. to 7785; the *leg*:— leg.

8244. שָׂקַד **sâqad**, saw-kad'; a prim. root; to *fasten*:— bind.

8245. שָׁקַד **shâqad**, shaw-kad'; a prim. root; to *be alert*, i.e. *sleepless*; hence, to *be on the lookout* (whether for good or ill):— hasten, remain, wake, watch (for).

8246. שָׁקַד **shâqad**, shaw-kad'; a denom. from 8247; to *be* (intens. *make*) *almond-shaped*:— make like (unto, after the fashion of) almonds.

8247. שָׁקֵד **shâqêd**, shaw-kade'; from 8245; the *almond* (tree or nut; as being the *earliest* in bloom):— almond (tree).

8248. שָׁקָה **shâqâh**, shaw-kaw'; a prim. root; to *quaff*, i.e. (caus.) to *irrigate* or *furnish a potion* to:— cause to (give, give to, let, make to) drink, drown, moisten, water. See 7937, 8354.

8249. שִׁקֻּו **shiqqûv**, shik-koov'; from 8248; (plur. collect.) a *draught*:— drink.

8250. שִׁקּוּי **shiqqûwy**, shik-koo'-ee; from 8248; a *beverage*; *moisture*, i.e. (fig.) *refreshment*:— drink, marrow.

8251. שִׁקּוּץ **shiqqûwts**, shik-koots'; or

שִׁקֻּץ **shiqquts**, shik-koots'; from 8262; *disgusting*, i.e. *filthy*; espec. *idolatrous* or (concr.) an *idol*:— abominable filth (idol, -ation), detestable (thing).

8252. שָׁקַט **shâqaṭ**, shaw-kat'; a prim. root; to *repose* (usually fig.):— appease, idleness, (at, be at, be in, give) quiet (-ness), (be at, be in, give, have, take) rest, settle, be still.

8253. שֶׁקֶט **sheqeṭ**, *sheh´-keṭ*; from 8252; *tranquillity:*— quietness.

8254. שָׁקַל **shâqal**, *shaw-kal´*; a prim. root; to *suspend* or *poise* (espec. in trade):— pay, receive (-r), spend, × throughly, weigh.

8255. שֶׁקֶל **sheqel**, *sheh´-kel*; from 8254; prob. a *weight*; used as a commercial standard:— shekel.

8256. שָׁקָם **shâqâm**, *shaw-kawm´*; or (fem.)

שִׁקְמָה **shiqmâh**, *shik-maw´*; of uncert. der.; a *sycamore* (usually the tree):— sycamore (fruit, tree).

8257. שָׁקַע **shâqa'**, *shaw-kah´*; (abb. o Am. 8:8); a prim. root; to *subside;* by impl. to *be overflowed, cease;* caus. to *abate, subdue:*— make deep, let down, drown, quench, sink.

8258. שְׁקַעְרוּרָה **sheqa'rûwrâh**, *shek-ah-roo-raw´*; from 8257; a *depression:*— hollow strake.

8259. שָׁקַף **shâqaph**, *shaw-kaf´*; a prim. root; prop. to *lean out* (of a window), i.e. (by impl.) *peep* or *gaze* (pass. *be a spectacle*):— appear, look (down, forth, out).

8260. שֶׁקֶף **sheqeph**, *sheh´-kef*; from 8259; a *loophole* (for *looking out*), to admit light and air:— window.

8261. שָׁקֻף **shâquph**, *shaw-koof´*; pass. part. of 8259; an *embrasure* or opening [comp. 8260] with bevelled jam:— light, window.

8262. שָׁקַץ **shâqats**, *shaw-kats´*; a prim. root; to *be filthy,* i.e. (intens.) to *loathe, pollute:*— abhor, make abominable, have in abomination, detest, × utterly.

8263. שֶׁקֶץ **sheqets**, *sheh´-kets*; from 8262; *filth,* i.e. (fig. and spec.) an *idolatrous* object:— abominable (-tion).

שִׁקֻּץ **shiqquts**. See 8251.

8264. שָׁקַק **shâqaq**, *shaw-kak´*; a prim. root; to *course* (like a beast of prey); by impl. to *seek* greedily:— have appetite, justle one against another, long, range, run (to and fro).

8265. שָׂקַר **sâqar**, *saw-kar´*; a prim. root; to *ogle,* i.e. *blink* coquettishly:— wanton.

8266. שָׁקַר **shâqar**, *shaw-kar´*; a prim. root; to *cheat,* i.e. *be untrue* (usually in words):— fail, deal falsely, lie.

8267. שֶׁקֶר **sheqer**, *sheh´-ker*; from 8266; an *untruth;* by impl. a *sham* (often adv.):— without a cause, deceit (-ful), false (-hood, -ly), feignedly, liar, + lie, lying, vain (thing), wrongfully.

8268. שֹׁקֶת **shôqeth**, *sho´-keth*; from 8248; a *trough* (for *watering*):— trough.

8269. שַׂר **sar**, *sar*; from 8323; a *head* person (of any rank or class):— captain (that had rule), chief (captain), general, governor, keeper, lord, (l-task-l) master, prince (-ipal), ruler, steward.

8270. שֹׁר **shôr**, *shore*; from 8324; a *string* (as *twisted* [comp. 8306]), i.e. (spec.) the umbilical cord (also fig. as the centre of strength):— navel.

8271. שְׁרֵא **sherê'** (Chald.), *sher-ay´*; a root corresp. to that of 8293; to *free, separate;* fig. to *unravel, commence;* by

impl. (of unloading beasts) to *reside:*— begin, dissolve, dwell, loose.

8272. שַׁרְאֶצֶר **Shar'etser**, *shar-eh´-tser;* of for. der.; *Sharetser,* the name of an Ass. and an Isr.:— Sharezer.

8273. שָׁרָב **shârâb**, *shaw-rawb´;* from an unused root mean. to *glare;* quivering *glow* (of the air), expec. the *mirage:*— heat, parched ground.

8274. שֵׁרֵבְיָה **Shêrêbyâh**, *shay-rayb-yaw´;* from 8273 and 3050; *Jah has brought heat; Sherebjah,* the name of two Isr.:— Sherebiah.

8275. שַׁרְבִיט **sharbîyṭ**, *shar-beet´;* for 7626; a *rod* of empire:— sceptre.

8276. שָׂרַג **sârag**, *saw-rag´;* a prim. root; to *intwine:*— wrap together, wreath.

8277. שָׂרַד **sârad**, *saw-rad´;* a prim. root; prop. to *puncture* [comp. 8279], i.e. (fig. through the idea of *slipping* out) to *escape* or survive:— remain.

8278. שְׂרָד **serâd**, *ser-awd´;* from 8277; *stitching* (as *pierced* with a needle):— service.

8279. שֶׂרֶד **sered**, *seh´-red;* from 8277; a (carpenter's) *scribing-awl* (for *pricking* or scratching measurements):— line.

8280. שָׂרָה **sârâh**, *saw-raw´;* a prim. root; to *prevail:*— have power (as a prince).

8281. שָׁרָה **shârâh**, *shaw-raw´;* a prim. root; to *free:*— direct.

8282. שָׂרָה **sârâh**, *saw-raw´;* fem. of 8269; a *mistress,* i.e. *female noble:*— lady, princess, queen.

8283. שָׂרָה **Sârâh**, *saw-raw´;* the same as 8282; *Sarah,* Abraham's wife:— Sarah.

8284. שָׂרָה **shârâh**, *shaw-raw´;* prob. fem. of 7791; a *fortification* (lit. or fig.):— sing [by mistake for 7891], wall.

8285. שֵׁרָה **shêrâh**, *shay-raw´;* from 8324 in its orig. sense of *pressing;* a *wristband* (as *compact* or *clasping*):— bracelet.

8286. שְׂרוּג **Serûwg**, *ser-oog´;* from 8276; *tendril; Serug,* a postdiluvian patriarch:— Serug.

8287. שָׁרוּחֶן **Shârûwchen**, *shaw-roo-khen´;* prob. from 8281 (in the sense of *dwelling* [comp. 8271] and 2580; *abode of pleasure; Sharuchen,* a place in Pal.:— Sharuhen.

8288. שְׂרוֹךְ **serôwk**, *ser-oke´;* from 8308; a *thong* (as *laced* or *tied*):— (shoe-) latchet.

8289. שָׁרוֹן **Shârôwn**, *shaw-rone´;* prob. abridged from 3474; *plain; Sharon,* the name of a place in Pal.:— Lasharon, Sharon.

8290. שָׁרוֹנִי **Shârôwnîy**, *shaw-ro-nee´;* patrial from 8289; a *Sharonite* or inhab. of Sharon:— Sharonite.

8291. שָׂרוּק **sarûwq**, *sar-ook´;* pass. part. from the same as 8321; a *grapevine:*— principal plant. See 8320, 8321.

8292. שְׁרוּקָה **sherûwqâh**, *sher-oo-kaw´;* or (by perm.)

שְׁרִיקָה **sherîyqâh**, *sher-ee-kaw´;* fem. pass. part. of 8319; a *whistling* (in scorn); by anal. a *piping:*— bleating, hissing.

8293. שֵׁרוּת **shêrûwth**, *shay-rooth´;* from 8281 abb.; *freedom:*— remnant.

8294. שֶׂרַח **Serach**, *seh´-rakh;* by perm. for 5629; *superfluity; Serach,* an Israelitess:— Sarah, Serah.

8295. שָׂרַט **sâraṭ**, *saw-rat´;* a prim. root; to *gash:*— cut in pieces, make [cuttings] pieces.

8296. שֶׂרֶט **sereṭ**, *seh´-ret;* and

שָׂרֶטֶת **sâreṭeth**, *saw-reh´-teth;* from 8295; an *incision:*— cutting.

8297. שָׂרַי **Sâray**, *saw-rah´-ee;* from 8269; *dominative; Sarai,* the wife of Abraham:— Sarai.

8298. שָׂרַי **Shâray**, *shaw-rah´-ee;* prob. from 8324; *hostile; Sharay,* an Isr.:— Sharai.

8299. שָׂרִיג **sârîyg**, *saw-reeg´;* from 8276; a *tendril* (as *intwining*):— branch.

8300. שָׂרִיד **sârîyd**, *saw-reed´;* from 8277; a *survivor:*— × alive, left, remain (-ing), remnant, rest.

8301. שָׂרִיד **Sârîyd**, *saw-reed´;* the same as 8300; *Sarid,* a place in Pal.:— Sarid.

8302. שִׁרְיוֹן **shiryôwn**, *shir-yone´;* or

שִׁרְיֹן **shiryôn**, *shir-yone´;* and

שִׁרְיָן **shiryân**, *shir-yawn´;* also (fem.)

שִׁרְיָה **shiryâh**, *shir-yaw´;* and

שִׁרְיֹנָה **shiryônâh**, *shir-yo-naw´;* from 8281 in the orig. sense of *turning;* a *corslet* (as if *twisted*):— breastplate, coat of mail, habergeon, harness. See 5630.

8303. שִׁרְיוֹן **Shiryôwn**, *shir-yone´;* and

שִׂרְיֹן **Siryôn**, *sir-yone´;* the same as 8304 (i.e. *sheeted* with snow); *Shirjon* or *Sirjon,* a peak of the Lebanon:— Sirion.

8304. שְׂרָיָה **Serâyâh**, *ser-aw-yaw´;* or

שְׂרָיָהוּ **Serâyâhûw**, *ser-aw-yaw´-hoo;* from 8280 and 3050; *Jah has prevailed; Serajah,* the name of nine Isr.:— Seraiah.

8305. שְׂרִיקָה **serîyqâh**, *ser-ee-kaw´;* from the same as 8321 in the orig. sense of *piercing; hetchelling* (or combing flax), i.e. (concr.) *tow* (by extens. *linen* cloth):— fine.

8306. שָׂרִיר **shârîyr**, *shaw-reer´;* from 8324 in the orig. sense as in 8270 (comp. 8326); a *cord,* i.e. (by anal.) *sinew:*— navel.

8307. שְׂרִירוּת **sherîyrûwth**, *sher-ee-rooth´;* from 8324 in the sense of *twisted,* i.e. *firm; obstinacy:*— imagination, lust.

8308. שָׂרַךְ **sârak**, *saw-rak´;* a prim. root; to *interlace:*— traverse.

8309. שְׂרֵמָה **sherêmâh**, *sher-ay-maw´;* prob. by an orth. err. for 7709; a *common:*— field.

8310. שַׂרְסְכִים **Sarṣekîym**, *sar-seh-keem´;* of for. der.; *Sarsekim,* a Bab. general:— Sarsechim.

8311. שָׂרַע **sâra'**, *saw-rah´;* a prim. root; to *prolong,* i.e. (reflex.) *be deformed* by excess of members:— stretch out self, (have any) superfluous thing.

8312. שְׂרַף **sar'aph**, *sar-af´*; for 5587; *cogitation*:— thought.

8313. שָׂרַף **sâraph**, *saw-raf´*; a prim. root; to *be* (caus. *set) on fire*:— (cause to, make a) burn (I-ingI, up) kindle, × utterly.

8314. שָׂרָף **sârâph**, *saw-rawf´*; from 8313; *burning*, i.e. (fig.) *poisonous* (serpent); spec. a *saraph* or symb. creature (from their copper color):— fiery (serpent), seraph.

8315. שָׂרָף **Sâraph**, *saw-raf´*; the same as 8314; *Saraph*, an Isr.:— Saraph.

8316. שְׂרֵפָה **sᵉrêphâh**, *ser-ay-faw´*; from 8313; *cremation*:— burning.

8317. שָׂרַץ **shârats**, *shaw-rats´*; a prim. root; to *wriggle*, i.e. (by impl.) *swarm* or *abound*:— breed (bring forth, increase) abundantly (in abundance), creep, move.

8318. שֶׁרֶץ **sherets**, *sheh´-rets*; from 8317; a *swarm*, i.e. active mass of minute animals:— creep (-ing thing), move (-ing creature).

8319. שָׁרַק **shâraq**, *shaw-rak´*; a prim. root; prop. to *be shrill*, i.e. to whistle or *hiss* (as a call or in scorn):— hiss.

8320. שָׂרֻק **sâruq**, *saw-rook´*; from 8319; *bright red* (as *piercing* to the sight), i.e. *bay*:— speckled. See 8291.

8321. שֹׂרֵק **sôrêq**, *so-rake´*; or

שׂוֹרֵק **sôwrêq**, *so-rake´*; and (fem.)

שֹׂרֵקָה **sôrêqâh**, *so-ray-kaw´*; from 8319 in the sense of *redness* (comp. 8320); a *vine* stock (prop. one yielding *purple* grapes, the richest variety):— choice (-st, noble) wine. Comp. 8291.

8322. שְׂרֵקָה **sᵉrêqâh**, *sher-ay-kaw´*; from 8319; a *derision*:— hissing.

8323. שָׂרַר **sârar**, *saw-rar´*; a prim. root; to *have* (tran. *exercise*; refl. *get*) *dominion*:— × altogether, make self a prince, (bear) rule.

8324. שָׂרַר **shârar**, *shaw-rar´*; a prim. root; to *be hostile* (only act. part. an *opponent*):— enemy.

8325. שָׂרָר **Shârâr**, *shaw-rawr´*; from 8324; *hostile; Sharar*, an Isr.:— Sharar.

8326. שֹׁרֶר **shôrer**, *sho´-rer*; from 8324 in the sense of *twisting* (comp. 8270); the umbilical *cord*, i.e. (by extens.) a *bodice*:— navel.

8327. שָׁרַשׁ **shârash**, *shaw-rash´*; a prim. root; to *root*, i.e. strike into the soil, or (by impl.) to *pluck from* it:— (take, cause to take) root (out).

8328. שֶׁרֶשׁ **sheresh**, *sheh´-resh*; from 8327; a *root* (lit. or fig.):— bottom, deep, heel, root.

8329. שֶׁרֶשׁ **Sheresh**, *sheh´-resh*; the same as 8328; *Sheresh*, an Isr.:— Sharesh.

8330. שֹׁרֶשׁ **shôresh** (Chald.), *sho´-resh*; corresp. to 8328:— root.

8331. שַׁרְשָׁה **sharshâh**, *shar-shaw´*; from 8327; a *chain* (as *rooted*, i.e. *linked*):— chain. Comp. 8333.

8332. שְׁרֹשׁוּ **shᵉrôshûw** (Chald.), *sher-o-shoo´*; from a root corresp. to 8327; *eradication*, i.e. (fig.) *exile*:— banishment.

8333. שַׁרְשְׁרָה **sharshᵉrâh**, *shar-sher-aw´*; from 8327 Icomp. 8331I; a *chain*; (arch.) prob. a *garland*:— chain.

8334. שָׁרַת **shârath**, *shaw-rath´*; a prim. root; to *attend* as a menial or worshiper; fig. to *contribute to*:— minister (unto), (do) serve (-ant, -ice, -itor), wait on.

8335. שָׁרֵת **shârêth**, *shaw-rayth´*; infin. of 8334; *service* (in the Temple):— minister (-ry).

8336. שֵׁשׁ **shêsh**, *shaysh*; or (for alliteration with 4897)

שְׁשִׁי **shᵉshiy**, *shesh-ee´*; for 7893; *bleached* stuff, i.e. *white* linen or (by anal.) *marble*:— × blue, fine (Itwinedl) linen, marble, silk.

8337. שֵׁשׁ **shêsh**, *shaysh*; masc.

שִׁשָּׁה **shishshâh**, *shish-shaw´*; a prim. number; *six* (as an overplus Isee 7797I beyond five or the fingers of the hand); as ord. *sixth*:— six (I-teen, -teenthI), sixth.

8338. שָׁושָׁו **shâwshâw**, *shaw-shaw´*; a prim. root; appar. to *annihilate*:— leave but the sixth part Iby confusion with 8341I.

8339. שֵׁשְׁבַּצַּר **Shêshbatstsar**, *shaysh-bats-tsar´*; of for. der.; *Sheshbatstsar*, Zerubbabel's Pers. name:— Sheshbazzar.

8340. שֵׁשְׁבַּצַּר **Shêshbatstsar** (Chald.), *shaysh-bats-tsar´*; corresp. to 8339:— Sheshbazzar.

שָׁסָה **shâsâh**. See 8154.

8341. שָׁשָׁה **shâshâh**, *shaw-shaw´*; a denom. from 8337; to *sixth* or divide into sixths:— give the sixth part.

8342. שָׂשׂוֹן **sâsôwn**, *saw-sone´*; or

שָׂשֹׂן **sâsôn**, *saw-sone´*; from 7797; *cheerfulness*; spec. *welcome*:— gladness, joy, mirth, rejoicing.

8343. שָׁשַׁי **Shâshay**, *shaw-shah´-ee*; perh. from 8336; *whitish; Shashai*, an Isr.:— Shashai.

8344. שֵׁשַׁי **Shêshay**, *shay-shah´-ee*; prob. for 8343; *Sheshai*, a Canaanite:— Sheshai.

8345. שִׁשִּׁי **shishshiy**, *shish-shee´*; from 8337; *sixth*, ord. or (fem.) fractional:— sixth (part).

8346. שִׁשִּׁים **shishshîym**, *shish-sheem´*; multiple of 8337; *sixty:—* sixty, three score.

8347. שֵׁשַׁך **Shêshak**, *shay-shak´*; of for. der.; *Sheshak*, a symbol. name of Bab.:— Sheshach.

8348. שֵׁשָׁן **Shêshân**, *shay-shawn´*; perh. for 7799; *lily; Sheshan*, an Isr.:— Sheshan.

שׁוֹשָׁן **Shôshân**. See 7799.

8349. שָׁשַׁק **Shâshaq**, *shaw-shak´*; prob. from the base of 7785; *pedestrian; Shashak*, an Isr.:— Shashak.

8350. שָׁשַׁר **shâshar**, *shaw-shar´*; perh. from the base of 8324 in the sense of that of 8320; *red ochre* (from its *piercing* color):— vermillion.

8351. שֵׁת **shêth** (Num. 24:17), *shayth*; from 7582; *tumult*:— Sheth.

8352. שֵׁת **Shêth**, *shayth*; from 7896; *put*, i.e. *substituted; Sheth*, third son of Adam:— Seth, Sheth.

8353. שֵׁת **shêth** (Chald.), *shayth*; or

שִׁת **shith** (Chald.), *sheeth*; corresp. to 8337:— six (-th).

8354. שָׁתָה **shâthâh**, *shaw-thaw´*; a prim. root; to *imbibe* (lit. or fig.):— × assuredly, banquet, × certainly, drink (-er, -ing), drunk (× -ard), surely. IProp. *intens. of* 8248.I

8355. שְׁתָה **shᵉthâh** (Chald.), *sheth-aw´*; corresp. to 8354:— drink.

8356. שָׁתָה **shâthâh**, *shaw-thaw´*; from 7896; a *basis*, i.e. (fig.) political or moral *support*:— foundation, purpose.

8357. שֵׁתָה **shêthâh**, *shay-thaw´*; from 7896; the *seat* (of the person):— buttock.

8358. שְׁתִי **shᵉthiy**, *sheth-ee´*; from 8354; *intoxication*:— drunkenness.

8359. שְׁתִי **shᵉthiy**, *sheth-ee´*; from 7896; a *fixture*, i.e. the *warp* in weaving:— warp.

8360. שְׁתִיָּה **shᵉthiyâh**, *sheth-ee-yaw´*; fem. of 8358; *potation*:— drinking.

8361. שִׁתִּין **shittîyn** (Chald.), *shit-teen´*; corresp. to 8346 Icomp. 8353I; *sixty:—* threescore.

8362. שָׁתַל **shâthal**, *shaw-thal´*; a prim. root; to *transplant*:— plant.

8363. שְׁתִיל **shᵉthîyl**, *sheth-eel´*; from 8362; a *sprig* (as if *transplanted*), i.e. *sucker*:— plant.

8364. שֻׁתַלְחִי **Shûthalchiy**, *shoo-thal-kee´*; patron. from 7803; a *Shuthalchite* (collect.) or desc. of Shuthelach:— Shuthalhites.

שָׂתַם **sâtham**. See 5640.

8365. שָׂתַם **shâtham**, *shaw-tham´*; a prim. root; to *unveil* (fig.):— be open.

8366. שָׁתַן **shâthan**, *shaw-than´*; a prim. root; (caus.) to *make water*, i.e. *urinate*:— piss.

8367. שָׁתַק **shâthaq**, *shaw-thak´*; a prim. root; to *subside*:— be calm, cease, be quiet.

8368. שָׂתַר **sâthar**, *saw-thar´*; a prim. root; to *break* out (as an eruption):— have in Ione'sI secret parts.

8369. שֵׁתָר **Shêthâr**, *shay-thawr´*; of for. der.; *Shethar*, a Pers. satrap:— Shethar.

8370. שְׁתַר בּוֹזְנַי **Shᵉthar Bôwzᵉnay**, *sheth-ar´ bo-zen-ah´-ee*; of for. der.; *Shethar-Bozenai*, a Pers. officer:— Shethar-boznai.

8371. שָׁתַת **shâthath**, *shaw-thath´*; a prim. root; to *place*, i.e. *array*; reflex. to *lie*:— be laid, set.

ת

8372. תָּא **tâ'**, *taw*; and (fem.)

תָּאָה **tâ'âh** (Ezek. 40:12), *taw-aw´*; from (the base of) 8376; a *room* (as *circumscribed*):— (little) chamber.

8373. תָּאַב **tâ'ab**, *taw-ab´*; a prim. root; to *desire*:— long.

8374. תָּאַב **tâ'ab**, *taw-ab´*; a prim. root Iprob. rather ident. with 8373 through the idea of *puffing* disdainfully at; comp. 340]; to *loathe* (mor.):— abhor.

8375. תַּאֲבָה **ta'ăbâh**, *tah-ab-aw´*; from 8374 [comp. 15]; *desire*:— longing.

8376. תָּאָה **tâ'âh**, *taw-aw´*; a prim. root; to *mark* off, i.e. (intens.) *designate*:— point out.

8377. תְּאוֹ **te'ôw**, *teh-o´*; and

תּוֹא **tôw'** (the orig. form), *toh*; from 8376; a species of *antelope* (prob. from the white *stripe* on the cheek):— wild bull (ox).

8378. תַּאֲוָה **ta'ăvâh**, *tah-av-aw´*; from 183 (abb.); a *longing*; by impl. a *delight* (subj. *satisfaction*, obj. a *charm*):— dainty, desire, × exceedingly, × greedily, lust (ing), pleasant. See also 6914.

8379. תַּאֲוָה **ta'ăvâh**, *tah-av-aw´*; from 8376; a *limit*, i.e. *full extent*:— utmost bound.

8380. תְּאוֹם **tâ'ôwm**, *taw-ome´*; or

תְּאֹם **tâ'ôm**, *taw-ome´*; from 8382; a *twin* (in plur. only), lit. or fig.:— twins.

8381. תַּאֲלָה **ta'ălâh**, *tah-al-aw´*; from 422; an *imprecation*:— curse.

8382. תָּאַם **tâ'am**, *taw-am´*; a prim. root; to *be complete*; but used only as denom. from 8380, to *be* (caus. *make*) *twinned*, i.e. (fig.) *duplicate* or (arch.) *jointed*:— coupled (together), bear twins.

תְּאֹם **tâ'ôm**. See 8380.

8383. תְּאֻן **te'ûn**, *teh-oon´*; from 205; *naughtiness*, i.e. *toil*:— lie.

8384. תְּאֵן **te'ên**, *teh-ane´*; or (in the sing., fem.)

תְּאֵנָה **te'ênâh**, *teh-ay-naw´*; perh. of for. der.; the *fig* (tree or fruit):— fig (tree).

8385. תַּאֲנָה **ta'ănâh**, *tah-an-aw´*; or

תֹאֲנָה **tô'ănâh**, *to-an-aw´*; from 579; an *opportunity* or (subj.) *purpose*:— occasion.

8386. תַּאֲנִיָּה **ta'ănîyâh**, *tah-an-ee-yaw´*; from 578; *lamentation*:— heaviness, mourning.

8387. תַּאֲנַת שִׁלֹה **Ta'ănath Shîlôh**, *tah-an-ath´ shee-lo´*; from 8385 and 7887; *approach of Shiloh*; *Taanath-Shiloh*, a place in Pal.:— Taanath-shiloh.

8388. תָּאַר **tâ'ar**, *taw-ar´*; a prim. root; to *delineate*; reflex. to *extend*:— be drawn, mark out, [Rimmon-] methoar [by union with 7417].

8389. תֹּאַר **tô'ar**, *to´-ar*; from 8388; *outline*, i.e. *figure* or *appearance*:— + beautiful, × comely, countenance, + fair, × favoured, form, × goodly, × resemble, visage.

8390. תַּאֲרֵעַ **Ta'ărêa**, *tah-ar-ay´-ah*; perh. from 772; *Taarea*, an Isr.:— Tarea. See 8475.

8391. תְּאַשּׁוּר **te'ashshûwr**, *teh-ash-shoor´*; from 833; a species of *cedar* (from its *erectness*):— box (tree).

8392. תֵּבָה **têbâh**, *tay-baw´*; perh. of for. der.; a *box*:— ark.

8393. תְּבוּאָה **te'bûw'âh**, *teb-oo-aw´*; from 935; *income*, i.e. *produce* (lit. or fig.):— fruit, gain, increase, revenue.

8394. תָּבוּן **tâbûwn**, *taw-boon´*; and (fem.)

תְּבוּנָה **te'bûwnâh**, *teb-oo-naw´*; or

תּוֹבֻנָה° **tôwbûnâh**, *to-boo-naw´*; from 995; *intelligence*; by impl. an *argument*; by extens. *caprice*:— discretion, reason, skilfulness, understanding, wisdom.

8395. תְּבוּסָה **te'bûwçâh**, *teb-oo-saw´*; from 947; a *treading down*, i.e. *ruin*:— destruction.

8396. תָּבוֹר **Tâbôwr**, *taw-bore´*; from a root corresp. to 8406; *broken region*; *Tabor*, a mountain in Pal., also a city adjacent:— Tabor.

8397. תֶּבֶל **tebel**, *teh´-bel*; appar. from 1101; *mixture*, i.e. *unnatural* bestiality:— confusion.

8398. תֵּבֵל **têbêl**, *tay-bale´*; from 2986; the *earth* (as *moist* and therefore inhabited); by extens. the *globe*; by impl. its *inhabitants*; spec. a partic. *land*, as Babylonia, Pal.:— habitable part, world.

תֻּבַל **Tûbal**. See 8422.

8399. תַּבְלִית **tablîyth**, *tab-leeth´*; from 1086; *consumption*:— destruction.

8400. תְּבַלֻּל **te'ballûl**, *teb-al-lool´*; from 1101 in the orig. sense of *flowing*:— a cataract (in the eye):— blemish.

8401. תֶּבֶן **teben**, *teh´-ben*; prob. from 1129; prop. *material*, i.e. (spec.) refuse *haum* or stalks of grain (as *chopped* in threshing and used *for fodder):— chaff, straw, stubble.

8402. תִּבְנִי **Tibniy**, *tib-nee´*; from 8401; *strawy*; *Tibni*, an Isr.:— Tibni.

8403. תַּבְנִית **tabnîyth**, *tab-neeth´*; from 1129; *structure*; by impl. a *model*, *resemblance*:— figure, form, likeness, pattern, similitude.

8404. תַּבְעֵרָה **Tab'êrâh**, *tab-ay-raw´*; from 1197; *burning*; *Taberah*, a place in the Desert:— Taberah.

8405. תֵּבֵץ **Têbêts**, *tay-bates´*; from the same as 948; *whiteness*; *Tebets*, a place in Pal.:— Thebez.

8406. תְּבַר **te'bar** (Chald.), *teb-ar´*; corresp. to 7665; to *be fragile* (fig.):— broken.

8407. תִּגְלַת פִּלְאֶסֶר **Tiglath Pil'eçer**, *tig-lath´ pil-eh´-ser*; or

תִּגְלַת פְּלֶסֶר **Tiglath Peleçer**, *tig-lath pel-eh´-ser*; or

תִּלְגַּת פִּלְנְאֶסֶר **Tilgath Pilne'eçer**, *til-gath´ pil-neh-eh´-ser*; or

תִּלְגַּת פִּלְנֶסֶר **Tilgath Pilneçer**, *til-gath´ pil-neh´-ser*; of for. der.; *Tiglath-Pileser* or *Tilgath-pilneser*, an Ass. king:— Tiglath-pileser, Tilgath-pilneser.

8408. תַּגְמוּל **tagmûwl**, *tag-mool´*; from 1580; a *bestowment*:— benefit.

8409. תִּגְרָה **tigrâh**, *tig-raw´*; from 1624; *strife*, i.e. *infliction*:— blow.

תֹּגַרְמָה **Tôgarmâh**. See 8425.

8410. תִּדְהָר **tidhâr**, *tid-hawr´*; appar. from 1725; *enduring*; a species of hardwood or *lasting* tree (perh. *oak*):— pine (tree).

8411. תְּדִירָא **te'dîyrâ'** (Chald.), *ted-ee-*

raw´; from 1753 in the orig. sense of *enduring*; *permanence*, i.e. (adv.) *constantly*:— continually.

8412. תַּדְמֹר **Tadmôr**, *tad-more´*; or

תַּמֹּר° **Tammôr** (1 Kings 9:18), *tam-more´*; appar. from 8558; *palm*-city; *Tadmor*, a place near Pal.:— Tadmor.

8413. תִּדְעָל **Tid'âl**, *tid-awl´*; perh. from 1763; *fearfulness*; *Tidal*, a Canaanite:— Tidal.

8414. תֹּהוּ **tôhûw**, *to´-hoo*; from an unused root mean. to lie *waste*; a *desolation* (of surface), i.e. *desert*; fig. a *worthless* thing; adv. in *vain*:— confusion, empty place, without form, nothing, (thing of) nought, vain, vanity, waste, wilderness.

8415. תְּהוֹם **te'hôwm**, *teh-home´*; or

תְּהֹם **te'hôm**, *teh-home´*; (usually fem.) from 1949; an *abyss* (as a *surging* mass of water), espec. the *deep* (the main sea or the subterranean *water-supply*):— deep (place), depth.

8416. תְּהִלָּה **te'hillâh**, *teh-hil-law´*; from 1984; *laudation*; spec. (concr.) a *hymn*:— praise.

8417. תָּהֳלָה **tohŏlâh**, *to-hol-aw´*; fem. of an unused noun (appar. from 1984) mean. *bluster*; *braggadocio*, i.e. (by impl.) *fatuity*:— folly.

8418. תַּהֲלֻכָה **tahălûkâh**, *tah-hal-oo-kaw´*; from 1980; a *procession*:— × went.

תְּהֹם **te'hôm**. See 8415.

8419. תַּהְפֻּכָה **tahpûkâh**, *tah-poo-kaw´*; from 2015; a *perversity* or *fraud*:— (very) froward (-ness, thing), perverse thing.

8420. תָּו **tâv**, *tawv*; from 8427; a *mark*; by impl. a *signature*:— desire, mark.

8421. תּוּב **tûwb** (Chald.), *toob*; corresp. to 7725, to *come back*; spec. (tran. and ellip.) to *reply*:— answer, restore, return (an answer).

8422. תּוּבַל **Tûwbal**, *too-bal´*; or

תֻּבַל **Tûbal**, *too-bal´*; prob. of for. der.; *Tubal*, a postdiluvian patriarch and his posterity:— Tubal.

8423. תּוּבַל קַיִן **Tûwbal Qayin**, *too-bal´ kah´-yin*; appar. from 2986 (comp. 2981) and 7014; *offspring of Cain*; *Tubal-Kajin*, an antediluvian patriarch:— Tubalcain.

תּוֹבֻנָה° **tôwbûnâh**. See 8394.

8424. תּוּגָה **tûwgâh**, *too-gaw´*; from 3013; *depression* (of spirits); concr. a *grief*:— heaviness, sorrow.

8425. תּוֹגַרְמָה **Tôwgarmâh**, *to-gar-maw´*; or

תֹּגַרְמָה **Tôgarmâh**, *to-gar-maw´*; prob. of for. der.; *Togarmah*, a son of Gomer and his posterity:— Togarmah.

8426. תּוֹדָה **tôwdâh**, *to-daw´*; from 3034; prop. an *extension* of the hand, i.e. (by impl.) *avowal*, or (usually) *adoration*; spec. a *choir* of worshippers:— confession, (sacrifice of) praise, thanks (-giving, offering).

8427. תָּוָה **tâvâh**, *taw-vaw´*; a prim. root; to *mark* out, i.e. (prim.) *scratch* or (def.) *imprint*:— scrabble, set [a mark].

8428. תָּוָה **tâvâh**, *taw-vaw´*; a prim. root

lor perh. ident. with 8427 through a similar idea from *scraping to pieces*]; to *grieve*:— limit [by confusion with 8427].

8429. תְּוַהּ **tᵉvahh** (Chald.), *tev-ah´;* corresp. to 8539 or perh. to 7582 through the idea of *sweeping to ruin* [comp. 8428]; to *amaze*, i.e. (reflex. by impl.) *take alarm*:— be astonied.

8430. תּוֹחַ **Tôwach**, *to´-akh;* from an unused root mean. to *depress; humble; Toach*, an Isr.:— Toah.

8431. תּוֹחֶלֶת **tôwcheleth**, *to-kheh´-leth;* from 3176; *expectation*:— hope.

תּוֹךְ **tôwk**. See 8496.

8432. תָּוֶךְ **tâvek**, *taw´-vek;* from an unused root mean. to *sever;* a *bisection*, i.e. (by impl.) the *centre*:— among (-st), × between, half, × (there-, where-) in (-to), middle, mid [-night], midst (among), × out (of), × through, × with (-in).

8433. תּוֹכֵחָה **tôwkêchâh**, *to-kay-khaw´;* and

תּוֹכַחַת **tôwkachath**, *to-kakh´-ath;* from 3198; *chastisement;* fig. (by words) *correction, refutation, proof* (even in defence):— argument, × chastened, correction, reasoning, rebuke, reproof, × be (often) reproved.

תּוֹכִּי **tûwkkîy**. See 8500.

8434. תּוֹלָד **Tôwlâd**, *to-lawd´;* from 3205; *posterity; Tolad*, a place in Pal.:— Tolad. Comp. 513.

8435. תּוֹלֵדָה **tôwlᵉdâh**, *to-led-aw´;* or

תֹּלְדָה **tôlᵉdâh**, *to-led-aw´;* from 3205; (plur. only) *descent*, i.e. *family;* (fig.) *history*:— birth, generations.

8436. תּוּלוֹן° **Tûwlôn**, *too-lone´;* from 8524; *suspension; Tulon*, an Isr.:— Tilon [from the marg.].

8437. תּוֹלָל **tôwlâl**, *to-lawl´;* from 3213; *causing to howl*, i.e. an *oppressor*:— that wasted.

8438. תּוֹלָע **tôwlâ'**, *to-law´;* and (fem.)

תּוֹלֵעָה **tôwlê'âh**, *to-lay-aw´;* or

תּוֹלַעַת **tôwla'ath**, *to-lah´-ath;* or

תֹּלַעַת **tôla'ath**, *to-lah´-ath;* from 3216; a *maggot* (as *voracious*); spec. (often with ellip. of 8144) the crimson-*grub*, but used only (in this connection) of the color from it, and cloths dyed therewith:— crimson, scarlet, worm.

8439. תּוֹלָע **Tôwlâ'**, *to-law´;* the same as 8438; *worm; Tola*, the name of two Isr.:— Tola.

8440. תּוֹלָעִי **Tôwlâ'îy**, *to-law-ee´;* patron. from 8439; a *Tolaite* (collect.) or desc. of Tola:— Tolaites.

8441. תּוֹעֵבָה **tôw'êbâh**, *to-ay-baw´;* or

תֹּעֵבָה **tô'êbâh**, *to-ay-baw´;* fem. act. part. of 8581; prop. something *disgusting* (mor.), i.e. (as noun) an *abhorrence;* espec. *idolatry* or (concr.) an *idol*:— abominable (custom, thing), abomination.

8442. תּוֹעָה **tôw'âh**, *to-aw´;* fem. act. part. of 8582; *mistake*, i.e. (mor.) *impiety*, or (political) *injury*:— error, hinder.

8443. תּוֹעָפָה **tôw'âphâh**, *to-aw-faw´;*

from 3286; (only in plur. collect.) *weariness*, i.e. (by impl.) *toil* (*treasure* so obtained) or *speed*:— plenty, strength.

8444. תּוֹצָאָה **tôwtsâ'âh**, *to-tsaw-aw´;* or

תֹּצָאָה **tôtsâ'âh**, *to-tsaw-aw´;* from 3318; (only in plur. collect.) *exit*, i.e. (geographical) *boundary*, or (fig.) *deliverance*, (act.) *source*:— border (-s), going (-s) forth (out), issues, outgoings.

8445. תּוֹקַהַת **Tôwqahath**, *to-kah´-ath;* from the same as 3349; *obedience; Tokahath*, an Isr.:— Tikvath [by correction for 8616].

8446. תּוּר **tûwr**, *toor;* a prim. root; to *meander* (caus. *guide*) about, espec. for trade or reconnoitring:— chap [-man], sent to descry, be excellent, merchant [-man], search (out), seek, (e-) spy (out).

8447. תּוֹר **tôwr**, *tore;* or

תֹּר **tôr**, *tore;* from 8446; a *succession*, i.e. a *string* or (abstr.) *order*:— border, row, turn.

8448. תּוֹר **tôwr**, *tore;* prob. the same as 8447; a *manner* (as a sort of *turn*):— estate.

8449. תּוֹר **tôwr**, *tore;* or

תֹּר **tôr**, *tore;* prob. the same as 8447; a *ring*-dove, often (fig.) as a term of endearment:— (turtle) dove.

8450. תּוֹר **tôwr** (Chald.), *tore;* corresp. (by perm.) to 7794; a *bull*:— bullock, ox.

8451. תּוֹרָה **tôwrâh**, *to-raw´;* or

תֹּרָה **tôrâh**, *to-raw´;* from 3384; a *precept* or *statute*, espec. the Decalogue or Pentateuch:— law.

8452. תּוֹרָה **tôwrâh**, *to-raw´;* prob. fem. of 8448; a *custom*:— manner.

8453. תּוֹשָׁב **tôwshâb**, *to-shawb´;* or

תֹּשָׁב **tôshâb** (1 Kings 17:1), *to-shawb´;* from 3427; a *dweller* (but not outlandish [5237]); espec. (as distinguished from a native citizen [act. part. of 3427] and a temporary inmate [1616] or mere lodger [3885]) *resident alien*:— foreigner, inhabitant, sojourner, stranger.

8454. תּוּשִׁיָּה **tûwshîyâh**, *too-shee-yaw´;* or

תֻּשִׁיָּה **tûshîyâh**, *too-shee-yaw´;* from an unused root prob. mean. to *substantiate; support* or (by impl.) *ability*, i.e. (direct) *help*, (in purpose) an *undertaking*, (intellectual) *understanding*:— enterprise, that which (thing as it) is, substance, (sound) wisdom, working.

8455. תּוֹתָח **tôwthâch**, *to-thawkh´;* from an unused root mean. to *smite;* a *club*:— darts.

8456. תָּזַז **tâzaz**, *taw-zaz´;* a prim. root; to *lop off*:— cut down.

8457. תַּזְנוּת **taznûwth**, *taz-nooth´;* or

תַּזְנֻת **taznûth**, *taz-nooth´;* from 2181; *harlotry*, i.e. (fig.) *idolatry*:— fornication, whoredom.

8458. תַּחְבֻּלָה **tachbûlâh**, *takh-boo-law´;* or

תַּחְבּוּלָה **tachbûwlâh**, *takh-boo-law´;* from 2254 as denom. from 2256; (only in plur.) prop. *steerage* (as a management of *ropes*), i.e. (fig.) *guidance* or

(by impl.) a *plan*:— good advice, (wise) counsels.

8459. תֹּחוּ **Tôchûw**, *to´-khoo;* from an unused root mean. to *depress; abasement; Tochu*, an Isr.:— Tohu.

8460. תְּחוֹת **tᵉchôwth** (Chald.), *tekh-ôth´;* or

תְּחֹת **tᵉchôth** (Chald.), *tekh-ôth´;* corresp. to 8478; *beneath*:— under.

8461. תַּחְכְּמֹנִי **Tachkᵉmônîy**, *takh-kem-o-nee´;* prob. for 2453; *sagacious; Tachkemoni*, an Isr.:— Tachmonite.

8462. תְּחִלָּה **tᵉchillâh**, *tekh-il-law´;* from 2490 in the sense of *opening;* a *commencement;* rel. *original* (adv. -ly):— begin (-ning), first (time).

8463. תַּחֲלוּא **tachălûw'**, *takh-al-oo´;* or

תַּחֲלֻא **tachălû'**, *takh-al-oo´;* from 2456; a *malady*:— disease, × grievous, (that are) sick (-ness).

8464. תַּחְמָס **tachmâç**, *takh-mawce´;* from 2554; a species of unclean bird (from its *violence*), perh. an *owl*:— night hawk.

8465. תַּחַן **Tachan**, *takh´-an;* prob. from 2583; *station; Tachan*, the name of two Isr.:— Tahan.

8466. תַּחֲנָה **tachănâh**, *takh-an-aw´;* from 2583; (only plur. collect.) an *encampment*:— camp.

8467. תְּחִנָּה **tᵉchinnâh**, *tekh-in-naw´;* from 2603; *graciousness;* caus. *entreaty*:— favour, grace, supplication.

8468. תְּחִנָּה **Tᵉchinnâh**, *tekh-in-naw´;* the same as 8467; *Techinnah*, an Isr.:— Tehinnah.

8469. תַּחֲנוּן **tachănûwn**, *takh-an-oon´;* or (fem.)

תַּחֲנוּנָה **tachănûwnâh**, *takh-an-oo-naw´;* from 2603; earnest *prayer*:— intreaty, supplication.

8470. תַּחֲנִי **Tachănîy**, *takh-an-ee´;* patron. from 8465; a *Tachanite* (collect.) or desc. of Tachan:— Tahanites.

8471. תַּחְפַּנְחֵס **Tachpanchêç**, *takh-pan-khace´;* or

תְּחַפְנְחֵס **Tᵉchaphnᵉchêç** (Ezek. 30:18), *tekh-af-nekh-ace´;* or

תַּחְפְּנֵס° **Tachpᵉnêç** (Jer. 2:16), *takh-pen-ace´;* of Eg. der.;— *Tachpanches, Techaphneches* or *Tachpenes*, a place in Egypt:— Tahapanes, Tahpanhes, Tehaphnehes.

8472. תַּחְפְּנֵיס **Tachpᵉnêyç**, *takh-pen-ace´;* of Eg. der.: *Tachpenes*, an Eg. woman:— Tahpenes.

8473. תַּחֲרָא **tachără'**, *takh-ar-aw´;* from 2734 in the orig. sense of 2352 or 2353; a linen *corslet* (as *white* or *hollow*):— habergeon.

8474. תַּחֲרָה **tachârâh**, *takh-aw-raw´;* a factitious root from 2734 through the idea of the *heat* of jealousy; to *vie* with a rival:— close, contend.

8475. תַּחְרֵעַ **Tachrêa'**, *takh-ray´-ah;* for 8390; *Tachrea*, an Isr.:— Tahrea.

8476. תַּחַשׁ **tachash**, *takh´-ash;* prob. of for. der.; a (clean) animal with fur, prob. a species of *antelope*:— badger.

8477. תַּחַשׁ **Tachash**, *takh´-ash;* the

same as 8476; *Tachash*, a rel. of Abraham:— Thahash.

8478. תַּחַת **tachath**, *takh´-ath;* from the same as 8430; the *bottom* (as *depressed*); only adv. *below* (often with prep. pref. *underneath*), in *lieu of,* etc.:— as, beneath, × flat, in (-stead), (same) place (where … is), room, for … sake, stead of, under, × unto, × when … was mine, whereas, [where-] fore, with.

8479. תְּחוֹת **tachath** (Chald.), *takh´-ath;* corresp. to 8478:— under.

8480. תַּחַת **Tachath**, *takh´-ath;* the same as 8478; *Tachath*, the name of a place in the Desert, also of three Isr.:— Tahath.

תְּחֹת **t^echôth**. See 8460.

8481. תַּחְתּוֹן **tachtôwn**, *takh-tone´;* or

תַּחְתֹּן **tachtôn**, *takh-tone´;* from 8478; *bottommost:*— lower (-est), nether (-most).

8482. תַּחְתִּי **tachtîy**, *takh-tee´;* from 8478; *lowermost;* as noun (fem. plur.) the *depths* (fig. a *pit,* the *womb*):— low (parts, -er, -er parts, -est), nether (part).

8483. תַּחְתִּים חָדְשִׁי **Tachtîym Chodshîy**, *takh-teem´ khod-shee´;* appar. from the plur. masc. of 8482 or 8478 and 2320; *lower* (ones) *monthly; Tachtim-Chodshi*, a place in Pal.:— Tahtim-hodshi.

8484. תִּיכוֹן **tîykôwn**, *tee-kone´;* or

תִּיכֹן **tîykôn**, *tee-kone´;* from 8432; *central:*— middle (-most), midst.

8485. תֵּימָא **Têymâ´**, *tay-maw´;* or

תֵּמָא **Têmâ´**, *tay-maw´;* prob. of for. der.; *Tema,* a son of Ishmael, and the region settled by him:— Tema.

8486. תֵּימָן **têymân**, *tay-mawn´;* or

תֵּמָן **têmân**, *tay-mawn´;* denom. from 3225; the *south* (as being on the *right* hand of a person facing the east):— south (side, -ward, wind).

8487. תֵּימָן **Têymân**, *tay-mawn´;* or

תֵּמָן **Têmân**, *tay-mawn´;* the same as 8486; *Teman,* the name of two Edomites, and of the region and desc. of one of them:— south, Teman.

8488. תֵּימְנִי **Têym^enîy**, *tay-men-ee´;* prob. for 8489; *Temeni,* an Isr.:— Temeni.

8489. תֵּימָנִי **Têymânîy**, *tay-maw-nee´;* patron. from 8487; a *Temanite* or desc. of Teman:— Temani, Temanite.

8490. תִּימָרָה **tîymârâh**, *tee-maw-raw´;* or

תִּמָרָה **tîmârâh**, *tee-maw-raw´;* from the same as 8558; a *column,* i.e. *cloud:*— pillar.

8491. תִּיצִי **Tîytsîy**, *tee-tsee´;* patrial or patron. from an unused noun of uncert. mean.; a *Titsite* or desc. or inhab. of an unknown Tits:— Tizite.

8492. תִּירוֹשׁ **tîyrôwsh**, *tee-roshe´;* or

תִּירֹשׁ **tîyrôsh**, *tee-roshe´;* from 3423 in the sense of *expulsion; must* or fresh grape-juice (as just *squeezed* out); by impl. (rarely) *fermented wine:*— (new, sweet) wine.

8493. תִּירְיָא **Tîyr^eyâ´**, *tee-reh-yaw´;* prob. from 3372; *fearful, Tirja,* an Isr.:— Tiria.

8494. תִּירָס **Tîyrâç**, *tee-rawce´;* prob. of for. der.; *Tiras,* a son of Japheth:— Tiras.

תִּירָס **tîyrôsh**. See 8492.

8495. תַּיִשׁ **tayish**, *tah´-yeesh;* from an unused root mean. to *butt;* a *buck* or he-goat (as given to *butting*):— he goat.

8496. תּוֹךְ **tôk**, *toke;* or

תּוֹךְ **tôwk** (Psa. 72:14), *toke;* from the same base as 8432 (in the sense of *cutting* to pieces); *oppression:*— deceit, fraud.

8497. תָּכָה **tâkâh**, *taw-kaw´;* a prim. root; to *strew,* i.e. *encamp:*— sit down.

8498. תְּכוּנָה **t^ekûwnâh**, *tek-oo-naw´;* fem. pass. part. of 8505; *adjustment,* i.e. *structure;* by impl. *equipage:*— fashion, store.

8499. תְּכוּנָה **t^ekûwnâh**, *tek-oo-naw´;* from 3559; or prob. ident. with 8498; something *arranged* or *fixed,* i.e. a *place:*— seat.

8500. תֻּכִּי **tukkîy**, *took-kee´;* or

תּוּכִּי **tûwkkîy**, *took-kee´;* prob. of for. der.; some imported creature, prob. a *peacock:*— peacock.

8501. תָּכָךְ **tâkâk**, *taw-kawk´;* from an unused root mean. to *dissever,* i.e. *crush:*— deceitful.

8502. תִּכְלָה **tiklâh**, *tik-law´;* from 3615; *completeness:*— perfection.

8503. תַּכְלִית **takliyth**, *tak-leeth´;* from 3615; *completion;* by impl. an *extremity:*— end, perfect (-ion).

8504. תְּכֵלֶת **t^ekêleth**, *tek-ay´-leth;* prob. for 7827; the cerulean *mussel,* i.e. the color (*violet*) obtained therefrom or stuff dyed therewith:— blue.

8505. תָּכַן **tâkan**, *taw-kan´;* a prim. root; to *balance,* i.e. *measure* out (by weight or dimension); fig. to *arrange, equalize,* through the idea of *levelling* (ment. *estimate, test*):— bear up, direct, be ([un-]) equal, mete, ponder, tell, weigh.

8506. תֹּכֶן **tôken**, *to´-ken;* from 8505; a *fixed quantity:*— measure, tale.

8507. תֹּכֶן **Tôken**, *to´-ken;* the same as 8506; *Token,* a place in Pal.:— Tochen.

8508. תָּכְנִית **toknîyth**, *tok-neeth´;* from 8506; *admeasurement,* i.e. *consummation:*— pattern, sum.

8509. תַּכְרִיךְ **takrîyk**, *tak-reek´;* appar. from an unused root mean. to *encompass;* a *wrapper* or robe:— garment.

8510. תֵּל **têl**, *tale;* by contr. from 8524; a *mound:*— heap, × strength.

8511. תָּלָא **tâlâ´**, *taw-law´;* a prim. root; to *suspend;* fig. (through *hesitation*) to be *uncertain;* by impl. (of mental *dependence*) to *habituate:*— be bent, hang (in doubt).

8512. תֵּל אָבִיב **Têl 'Âbîyb**, *tale aw-beeb´;* from 8510 and 24; *mound of green growth; Tel-Abib,* a place in Chaldaea:— Tel-abib.

8513. תְּלָאָה **t^elâ'âh**, *tel-aw-aw´;* from 3811; *distress:*— travail, travel, trouble.

8514. תַּלְאוּבָה **tal'ûwbâh**, *tal-oo-baw´;* from 3851; *desiccation:*— great drought.

8515. תְּלַאשָּׂר **T^ela'ssar**, *tel-as-sar´;* or

8516. תְּלַשַּׂר **T^elassar**, *tel-as-sar´;* of for. der.; *Telassar,* a region of Assyria:— Telassar.

8516. תַּלְבֹּשֶׁת **talbôsheth**, *tal-bo´-sheth;* from 3847; a *garment:*— clothing.

8517. תְּלַג **t^elag** (Chald.), *tel-ag´;* corresp. to 7950; *snow:*— snow.

תִּלְגַת **Tilgath**. See 8407.

תֹּלְדָה **tôl^edâh**. See 8435.

8518. תָּלָה **tâlâh**, *taw-law´;* a prim. root; to *suspend* (espec. to *gibbet*):— hang (up).

8519. תְּלוּנָה **t^elûwnâh**, *tel-oo-naw´;* or

תְּלֻנָּה **t^elunnâh**, *tel-oon-naw´;* from 3885 in the sense of *obstinacy;* a *grumbling:*— murmuring.

8520. תֶּלַח **Telach**, *teh´-lakh;* prob. from an unused root mean. to *dissever; breach; Telach,* an Isr.:— Telah.

8521. תֵּל חַרְשָׁא **Têl Charshâ´**, *tale kharshaw´;* from 8510 and the fem. of 2798; *mound of workmanship; Tel-Charsha,* a place in Bab.:— Tel-haresha, Tel-harsa.

8522. תְּלִי **t^elîy**, *tel-ee´;* prob. from 8518; a *quiver* (as *slung*):— quiver.

8523. תְּלִיתַי **t^elîythay** (Chald.), *tel-ee-thah´-ee;* or

תַּלְתִי **taltîy**, *tal-tee´;* ord. from 8532; *third:*— third.

8524. תָּלַל **tâlal**, *taw-lal´;* a prim. root; to *pile* up, i.e. *elevate:*— eminent. Comp. 2048.

8525. תֶּלֶם **telem**, *teh´-lem;* from an unused root mean. to *accumulate;* a *bank* or *terrace:*— furrow, ridge.

8526. תַּלְמַי **Talmay**, *tal-mah´-ee;* from 8525; *ridged; Talmai,* the name of a Canaanite and a Syrian:— Talmai.

8527. תַּלְמִיד **talmîyd**, *tal-meed´;* from 3925; a *pupil:*— scholar.

8528. תֵּל מֶלַח **Têl Melach**, *tale meh´-lakh;* from 8510 and 4417; *mound of salt; Tel-Melach,* a place in Bab.:— Tel-melah.

8529. תְּלֻנָּה **t^elunnâh**. See 8519.

8529. תָּלַע **tâla'**, *taw-law´;* a denom. from 8438; to *crimson,* i.e. *dye* that color:— × scarlet.

תּוֹלַעַת **tôla'ath**. See 8438.

8530. תַּלְפִּיָּה **talpîyâh**, *tal-pee-yaw´;* fem. from an unused root mean. to *tower;* something *tall,* i.e. (plur. collect.) *slenderness:*— armoury.

תְּלַשַּׂר **T^elassar**. See 8515.

8531. תְּלָה **t^elath** (Chald.), *tel-ath´;* from 8532; a *tertiary* rank:— third.

8532. תְּלָת **t^elâth** (Chald.), *tel-awth´;* masc.

תְּלָתָה **t^elâthâh** (Chald.), *tel-aw-thaw´;* or

תְּלָתָא **t^elâthâ´** (Chald.), *tel-aw-thaw´;* corresp. to 7969; *three* or *third:*— third, three.

תַּלְתִי **taltiy**. See 8523.

8533. תְּלָתִין **t^elâthîyn** (Chald.), *tel-aw-theen´;* mult. of 8532; *ten times three:*— thirty.

8534. תַּלְתַּל **taltal**, *tal-tal´;* by redupl.

from 8524 through the idea of *vibration;* a trailing *bough* (as *pendulous*):— bushy.

8535. תָּם **tâm**, *tawm;* from 8552; *complete;* usually (mor.) *pious;* spec. *gentle, dear:*— coupled together, perfect, plain, undefiled, upright.

8536. תָּם **tâm** (Chald.), *tawm;* corresp. to 8033; *there:*— × thence, there, × where.

8537. תֹּם **tôm**, *tome;* from 8552; *completeness;* fig. *prosperity;* usually (mor.) *innocence:*— full, integrity, perfect (-ion), simplicity, upright (-ly, -ness), at a venture. See 8550.

תֻּמָּא **Têmâ'**. See 8485.

8538. תֻּמָּה **tummâh**, *toom-maw´;* fem. of 8537; *innocence:*— integrity.

8539. תָּמַהּ **tâmahh**, *taw-mah´;* a prim. root; to *be in consternation:*— be amazed, be astonished, marvel (-lously), wonder.

8540. תְּמַהּ **tᵉmahh** (Chald.), *tem-ah´;* from a root corresp. to 8539; a *miracle:*— wonder.

8541. תִּמָּהוֹן **timmâhôwn**, *tim-maw-hone´;* from 8539; *consternation:*— astonishment.

8542. תַּמּוּז **Tammûwz**, *tam-mooz´;* of uncert. der.; *Tammuz,* a Phoenician deity:— Tammuz.

8543. תְּמוֹל **tᵉmôwl**, *tem-ole´;* or

תְּמֹל **tᵉmôl**, *tem-ole´;* prob. for 865; prop. *ago,* i.e. a (short or long) *time since;* espec. *yesterday,* or (with 8032) *day before yesterday:*— + before (-time), + these [three] days, + heretofore, + time past, yesterday.

8544. תְּמוּנָה **tᵉmûwnâh**, *tem-oo-naw´;* or

תְּמֻנָה **tᵉmûnâh**, *tem-oo-naw´;* from 4327; *something portioned* (i.e. *fashioned*) out, as a *shape,* i.e. (indef.) *phantom,* or (spec.) *embodiment,* or (fig.) *manifestation* (of favor):— image, likeness, similitude.

8545. תְּמוּרָה **tᵉmûwrâh**, *tem-oo-raw´;* from 4171; *barter, compensation:*— (ex-) change (-ing), recompense, restitution.

8546. תְּמוּתָה **tᵉmûwthâh**, *tem-oo-thaw´;* from 4191; *execution* (as a doom):— death, die.

8547. תֶּמַח **Temach**, *teh´-makh;* of uncert. der.; *Temach,* one of the Nethinim:— Tamah, Thamah.

8548. תָּמִיד **tâmîyd**, *taw-meed´;* from an unused root mean. to *stretch;* prop. *continuance* (as indef. *extension*); but used only (attributively as adj.) *constant* (or adv. *constantly*); ellipt. the *regular* (daily) sacrifice:— alway (-s), continual (employment, -ly), daily, ([n-]) ever (-more), perpetual.

8549. תָּמִים **tâmîym**, *taw-meem´;* from 8552; *entire* (lit., fig. or mor.); also (as noun) *integrity, truth:*— without blemish, complete, full, perfect, sincerely (-ity), sound, without spot, undefiled, upright (-ly), whole.

8550. תֻּמִּים **Tummîym**, *toom-meem´;* plur. of 8537; *perfections,* i.e. (tech.) one of the epithets of the objects in the

high-priest's breastplate as an emblem of *complete* Truth:— Thummim.

8551. תָּמַךְ **tâmak**, *taw-mak´;* a prim. root; to *sustain;* by impl. to *obtain, keep fast;* fig. to *help, follow close:*— (take, up-) hold (up), maintain, retain, stay (up).

תְּמֹל **tᵉmôl**. See 8543.

8552. תָּמַם **tâmam**, *taw-mam´;* a prim. root; to *complete,* in a good or a bad sense, lit. or fig., tran. or intr. (as follows):— accomplish, cease, be clean [pass-] ed, consume, have done, (come to an, have an, make an) end, fail, come to the full, be all gone, × be all here, be (make) perfect, be spent, sum, be (shew self) upright, be wasted, whole.

תֵּימָן **têmân**, *Têmân.* See 8486, 8487.

8553. תִּמְנָה **Timnâh**, *tim-naw´;* from 4487; a *portion* assigned; *Timnah,* the name of two places in Pal.:— Timnah, Timnath, Thimnathah.

תְּמֻנָה **tᵉmûnâh**. See 8544.

8554. תִּמְנִי **Timnîy**, *tim-nee´;* patrial from 8553; a *Timnite* or inhab. of Timnah:— Timnite.

8555. תִּמְנָע **Timnâ'**, *tim-naw´;* from 4513; *restraint; Timna,* the name of two Edomites:— Timna, Timnah.

8556. תִּמְנַת חֶרֶס **Timnath Chereç**, *timnath kheh´-res;* or

תִּמְנַת סֶרַח **Timnath Çerach**, *timnath seh´-rakh;* from 8553 and 2775; *portion of* (the) *sun; Timnath-Cheres,* a place in Pal.:— Timnath-heres, Timnath-serah.

8557. תֶּמֶס **temeç**, *teh´-mes;* from 4529; *liquefaction,* i.e. *disappearance:*— melt.

8558. תָּמָר **tâmâr**, *taw-mawr´;* from an unused root mean. to *be erect;* a *palm* tree:— palm (tree).

8559. תָּמָר **Tâmâr**, *taw-mawr´;* the same as 8558; *Tamar,* the name of three women and a place:— Tamar.

8560. תֹּמֶר **tômer**, *to´-mer;* from the same root as 8558; a *palm trunk:*— palm tree.

8561. תִּמֹּר **timmôr** (plur. only), *tim-more´;* or (fem.)

תִּמֹּרָה **timmôrâh** (sing. and plur.), *tim-mo-raw´;* from the same root as 8558; (arch.) a *palm*-like pilaster (i.e. *umbellate*):— palm tree.

תַּמֹּר **Tammôr**. See 8412.

תִּמֹּרָה **timôrâh**. See 8490.

8562. תַּמְרוּק **tamrûwq**, *tam-rook´;* or

תַּמְרֻק **tamrûq**, *tam-rook´;* or

תַּמְרִיק° **tamrîyq**, *tam-reek´;* from 4838; prop. a *scouring,* i.e. *soap* or *perfumery* for the bath; fig. a *detergent:*— × cleanse, (thing for) purification (-fying).

8563. תַּמְרוּר **tamrûwr**, *tam-roor´;* from 4843; *bitterness* (plur. as collect.):— × most bitter (-ly).

תַּמְרֻק **tamrûq** and

תַּמְרִיק **tamrîyq**. See 8562.

8564. תַּמְרוּר **tamrûwr**, *tam-roor´;* from the same root as 8558; an *erection,* i.e.

pillar (prob. for a guide-board):— high heap.

8565. תַּן **tan**, *tan;* from an unused root prob. mean. to *elongate;* a *monster* (as preternaturally formed), i.e. a *sea-serpent* (or other huge marine animal); also a *jackal* (or other hideous land animal):— dragon, whale. Comp. 8577.

8566. תָּנָה **tânâh**, *taw-naw´;* a prim. root; to *present* (a mercenary inducement), i.e. *bargain* with (a harlot):— hire.

8567. תָּנָה **tânâh**, *taw-naw´;* a prim. root [rather ident. with 8566 through the idea of *attributing* honor]; to *ascribe* (praise), i.e. *celebrate, commemorate:*— lament, rehearse.

8568. תַּנָּה **tannâh**, *tan-naw´;* prob. fem. of 8565; a female *jackal:*— dragon.

8569. תְּנוּאָה **tᵉnûw'âh**, *ten-oo-aw´;* from 5106; *alienation;* by impl. *enmity:*— breach of promise, occasion.

8570. תְּנוּבָה **tᵉnûwbâh**, *ten-oo-baw´;* from 5107; *produce:*— fruit, increase.

8571. תְּנוּךְ **tᵉnûwk**, *ten-ook´;* perh. from the same as 594 through the idea of *protraction;* a *pinnacle,* i.e. *extremity:*— tip.

8572. תְּנוּמָה **tᵉnûwmâh**, *ten-oo-maw´;* from 5123; *drowsiness,* i.e. *sleep:*— slumber (-ing).

8573. תְּנוּפָה **tᵉnûwphâh**, *ten-oo-faw´;* from 5130; a *brandishing* (in threat); by impl. *tumult;* spec. the official *undulation* of sacrificial offerings:— offering, shaking, wave (offering).

8574. תַּנּוּר **tannûwr**, *tan-noor´;* from 5216; a *fire-pot:*— furnace, oven.

8575. תַּנְחוּם **tanchûwm**, *tan-khoom´;* or

תַּנְחֻם **tanchûm**, *tan-khoom´;* and (fem.)

תַּנְחוּמָה **tanchûwmâh**, *tan-khoomaw´;* from 5162; *compassion, solace:*— comfort, consolation.

8576. תַּנְחֻמֶת **Tanchûmeth**, *tan-khoo´meth;* for 8575 (fem.); *Tanchumeth,* an Isr.:— Tanhumeth.

8577. תַּנִּין **tannîyn**, *tan-neen´;* or

תַּנִּים **tannîym** (Ezek. 29:3), *tanneem´;* intens. from the same as 8565; a marine or land *monster,* i.e. *sea-serpent* or *jackal:*— dragon, sea-monster, serpent, whale.

8578. תִּנְיָן **tinyân** (Chald.), *tin-yawn´;* corresp. to 8147; *second:*— second.

8579. תִּנְיָנוּת **tinyânûwth** (Chald.), *tinyaw-nooth´;* from 8578; a *second time:*— again.

8580. תַּנְשֶׁמֶת **tanshemeth**, *tan-sheh´meth;* from 5395; prop. a hard *breather,* i.e. the name of two unclean creatures, a lizard and a bird (both perh. from changing color through their *irascibility*), prob. the *tree-toad* and the *waterhen:*— mole, swan.

8581. תָּעַב **tâ'ab**, *taw-ab´;* a prim. root; to *loathe,* i.e. (mor.) *detest:*— (make to be) abhor (-red), (be, commit more, do) abominable (-y), × utterly.

תּוֹעֵבָה **tô'êbâh**. See 8441.

8582. תָּעָה **tâ'âh**, *taw-aw´;* a prim. root; to *vacillate,* i.e. *reel* or *stray* (lit. or fig.); also caus. of both:— (cause to) go astray, deceive, dissemble, (cause to, make to) err, pant, seduce, (make to) stagger, (cause to) wander, be out of the way.

8583. תּוֹעוּ **Tô'ûw**, to´-oo; or

תּוֹעִי **Tô'îy**, to´-ee; from 8582; error, Tou or Toi, a Syrian king:— Toi, Tou.

8584. תְּעוּדָה **tᵉ'ûwdâh**, teh-oo-daw´; from 5749; attestation, i.e. a precept, usage:— testimony.

8585. תְּעָלָה **tᵉ'âlâh**, teh-aw-law´; from 5927; a channel (into which water is raised for irrigation); also a bandage or plaster (as placed upon a wound):— conduit, cured, healing, little river, trench, watercourse.

8586. תַּעֲלוּל **ta'ălûwl**, tah-al-ool´; from 5953; caprice (as a fit coming on), i.e. vexation; concr. a tyrant:— babe, delusion.

8587. תַּעֲלֻמָה **ta'ălummâh**, tah-al-oom-maw´; from 5956; a secret:— thing that is hid, secret.

8588. תַּעֲנֻג **ta'ănûwg**, tah-an-oog´; or

תַּעֲנֻג **ta'ănûg**, tah-an-oog´; and

(fem.) תַּעֲנֻגָה **ta'ănûgâh**, tah-ah-oog-aw´; from 6026; luxury:— delicate, delight, pleasant.

8589. תַּעֲנִית **ta'ănîyth**, tah-an-eeth´; from 6031; affliction (of self), i.e. fasting:— heaviness.

8590. תַּעֲנָךְ **Ta'ănâk**, tah-an-awk´; or

תַּעְנַךְ **Ta'nâk**, tah-nawk´; of uncert. der.; Taanak or Tanak, a place in Pal.:— Taanach, Tanach.

8591. תָּעַע **tâ'a'**, taw-ah´; a prim. root; to cheat; by anal. to maltreat:— deceive, misuse.

8592. תַּעֲצֻמָה **ta'ătsûmâh**, tah-ats-oo-maw´; from 6105; might (plur. collect.):— power.

8593. תַּעַר **ta'ar**, tah´-ar; from 6168; a knife or razor (as making bare): also a scabbard (as being bare, i.e. empty):— [pen-] knife, rasor, scabbard, shave, sheath.

8594. תַּעֲרֻבָה **ta'ărûbâh**, tah-ar-oo-baw´; from 6148; suretyship, i.e. (concr.) a pledge:— + hostage.

8595. תַּעְתֻּעַ **ta'tûa'**, tah-too´-ah; from 8591; a fraud:— error.

8596. תֹּף **tôph**, tofe; from 8608 contr.; a tambourine:— tabret, timbrel.

8597. תִּפְאָרָה **tiph'ârâh**, tif-aw-raw´; or

תִּפְאֶרֶת **tiph'ereth**, tif-eh´-reth; from 6286; ornament (abstr. or concr., lit. or fig.):— beauty (-iful), bravery, comely, fair, glory (-ious), honour, majesty.

8598. תַּפּוּחַ **tappûwach**, tap-poo´-akh; from 5301; an apple (from its fragrance), i.e. the fruit or the tree (prob. includ. others of the pome order, as the quince, the orange, etc.):— apple (tree). See also 1054.

8599. תַּפּוּחַ **Tappûwach**, tap-poo´-akh; the same as 8598; Tappuach, the name of two places in Pal., also of an Isr.:— Tappuah.

8600. תְּפוֹצָה **tᵉphôwtsâh**, tef-o-tsaw´; from 6327; a dispersal:— dispersion.

8601. תֻּפִין **tûphîyn**, too-feen´; from 644; cookery, i.e. (concr.) a cake:— baked piece.

8602. תָּפֵל **tâphêl**, taw-fale´; from an unused root mean. to smear; plaster (as gummy) or slime; (fig.) frivolity:— foolish things, unsavoury, untempered.

8603. תֹּפֶל **Tôphel**, to´-fel; from the same as 8602; quagmire; Tophel, a place near the Desert:— Tophel.

8604. תִּפְלָה **tiphlâh**, tif-law´; from the same as 8602; frivolity:— folly, foolishly.

8605. תְּפִלָּה **tᵉphillâh**, tef-il-law´; from 6419; intercession, supplication; by impl. a hymn:— prayer.

8606. תִּפְלֶצֶת **tiphletseth**, tif-leh´-tseth; from 6426; fearfulness:— terrible.

8607. תִּפְסַח **Tiphçach**, tif-sakh´; from 6452; ford; Tiphsach, a place in Mesopotamia:— Tipsah.

8608. תָּפַף **tâphaph**, taw-faf´; a prim. root; to drum, i.e. play (as) on the tambourine:— taber, play with timbrels.

8609. תָּפַר **tâphar**, taw-far´; a prim. root; to sew:— (women that) sew (together).

8610. תָּפַס **tâphas**, taw-fas´; a prim. root; to manipulate, i.e. seize; chiefly to capture, wield; spec. to overlay; fig. to use unwarrantably:— catch, handle, (lay, take) hold (on, over), stop, × surely, surprise, take.

8611. תֹּפֶת **tôpheth**, to´-feth; from the base of 8608; a smiting, i.e. (fig.) contempt:— tabret.

8612. תֹּפֶת **Tôpheth**, to´-feth; the same as 8611; Topheth, a place near Jerusalem:— Tophet, Topheth.

8613. תָּפְתֶּה **Tophteh**, tof-teh´; prob. a form of 8612; Tophteh, a place of cremation:— Tophet.

8614. תִּפְתַּי **tiphtay** (Chald.), tif-tah´-ee; perh. from 8199; judicial, i.e. a lawyer:— sheriff.

תּוֹצָאָה **tôtsâ'âh**. See 8444.

8615. תִּקְוָה **tiqvâh**, tik-vaw´; from 6960; lit. a cord (as an attachment [comp. 6961]); fig. expectancy:— expectation ([-ted]), hope, live, thing that I long for.

8616. תִּקְוָה **Tiqvâh**, tik-vaw´; the same as 8615; Tikvah, the name of two Isr.:— Tikvah.

8617. תְּקוּמָה **tᵉqûwmâh**, tek-oo-maw´; from 6965; resistfulness:— power to stand.

8618. תְּקוֹמֵם **tᵉqôwmêm**, tek-o-mame´; from 6965; an opponent:— rise up against.

8619. תָּקוֹעַ **tâqôwa'**, taw-ko´-ah; from 8628 (in the musical sense); a trumpet:— trumpet.

8620. תְּקוֹעַ **Tᵉqôwa'**, tek-o´-ah; a form of 8619; Tekoa, a place in Pal.:— Tekoa, Tekoah.

8621. תְּקוֹעִי **Tᵉqôw'îy**, tek-o-ee´; or

תְּקֹעִי **Tᵉqô'îy**, tek-o-ee´; patron. from 8620; a Tekoite or inhab. of Tekoah:— Tekoite.

8622. תְּקוּפָה **tᵉqûwphâh**, tek-oo-faw´; or

תְּקֻפָה **tᵉqûphâh**, tek-oo-faw´; from 5362; a revolution, i.e. (of the sun) course, (of time) lapse:— circuit, come about, end.

8623. תַּקִּיף **taqqîyph**, tak-keef´; from 8630; powerful:— mightier.

8624. תַּקִּיף **taqqîyph** (Chald.), tak-keef´; corresp. to 8623:— mighty, strong.

8625. תְּקַל **tᵉqal** (Chald.), tek-al´; corresp. to 8254; to balance:— Tekel, be weighed.

8626. תָּקַן **tâqan**, taw-kan´; a prim. root; to equalize, i.e. straighten (intr. or tran.); fig. to compose:— set in order, make straight.

8627. תְּקַן **tᵉqan** (Chald.), tek-an´; corresp. to 8626; to straighten up, i.e. confirm:— establish.

8628. תָּקַע **tâqa'**, taw-kah´; a prim. root; to clatter, i.e. slap (the hands together), clang (an instrument); by anal. to drive (a nail or tent-pin, a dart, etc.); by impl. to become bondsman (by hand-clasping):— blow ([a trumpet]), cast, clap, fasten, pitch [tent], smite, sound, strike, × suretyship, thrust.

8629. תֶּקַע **têqa'**, tay-kah´; from 8628; a blast of a trumpet:— sound.

תְּקֹעַ **Tᵉqô'îy**. See 8621.

8630. תָּקַף **tâqaph**, taw-kaf´; a prim. root; to overpower:— prevail (against).

8631. תְּקֵף **tᵉqêph** (Chald.), tek-afe´; corresp. to 8630; to become (caus. make) mighty or (fig.) obstinate:— make firm, harden, be (-come) strong.

8632. תְּקֹף **tᵉqôph** (Chald.), tek-ofe´; corresp. to 8633; power:— might, strength.

8633. תֹּקֶף **tôqeph**, to´-kef; from 8630; might or (fig.) positiveness:— authority, power, strength.

תְּקֻפָה **tᵉqûphâh**. See 8622.

תּוֹר **tôr**. See 8447, 8449.

8634. תַּרְאֵלָה **Tar'âlâh**, tar-al-aw´; prob. for 8653; a reeling; Taralah, a place in Pal.:— Taralah.

8635. תַּרְבּוּת **tarbûwth**, tar-booth´; from 7235; multiplication, i.e. progeny:— increase.

8636. תַּרְבִּית **tarbîyth**, tar-beeth´; from 7235; multiplication, i.e. percentage or bonus in addition to principal:— increase, unjust gain.

8637. תִּרְגַּל **tirgal**, teer-gal´; a denom. from 7270; to cause to walk:— teach to go.

8638. תִּרְגַּם **tirgam**, teer-gam´; a denom. from 7275 in the sense of throwing over; to transfer, i.e. translate:— interpret.

תּוֹרָה **tôrâh**. See 8451.

8639. תַּרְדֵּמָה **tardêmâh**, tar-day-maw´; from 7290; a lethargy or (by impl.) trance:— deep sleep.

8640. תִּרְהָקָה **Tirhâqâh**, teer-haw´-kaw; of for. der.; Tirhakah, a king of Kush:— Tirhakah.

8641. תְּרוּמָה **tᵉrûwmâh**, ter-oo-maw´; or

תְּרֻמָה **tᵉrûmâh** (Deut. 12:11), ter-oo-maw´; from 7311; a present (as offered up), espec. in sacrifice or as *tribute:*— gift, heave offering ([shoulder]), oblation, offered (-ing).

8642. תְּרוּמִיָּה **tᵉrûwmîyâh**, *ter-oo-mee-yaw´;* formed as 8641; a sacrificial *offering:*— oblation.

8643. תְּרוּעָה **tᵉrûw'âh**, *ter-oo-aw´;* from 7321; *clamor,* i.e. *acclamation* of joy or a *battle-cry;* espec. *clangor* of trumpets, as an *alarum:*— alarm, blow (-ing) (of, the) (trumpets), joy, jubile, loud noise, rejoicing, shout (-ing), (high, joyful) sound (-ing).

8644. תְּרוּפָה **tᵉrûwphâh**, *ter-oo-faw´;* from 7322 in the sense of its congener 7495; a *remedy:*— medicine.

8645. תִּרְזָה **tirzâh**, *teer-zaw´;* prob. from 7329; a species of tree (appar. from its *slenderness*), perh. the *cypress:*— cypress.

8646. תֶּרַח **Terach**, *teh´-rakh;* of uncert. der.; *Terach,* the father of Abraham; also a place in the Desert:— Tarah, Terah.

8647. תִּרְחֲנָה **Tirchânâh**, *teer-khan-aw´;* of uncert. der.; *Tirchanah,* an Isr.:— Tirhanah.

8648. תְּרֵין **tᵉrêyn** (Chald.), *ter-ane´;* fem.

תַּרְתֵּין **tartêyn**, *tar-tane´;* corresp. to 8147; *two:*— second, + twelve, two.

8649. תָּרְמָה **tormâh**, *tor-maw´;* and

תַּרְמוּת° **tarmûwth**, *tar-mooth´;* or

תַּרְמִית **tarmîyth**, *tar-meeth´;* from 7411; *fraud:*— deceit (-ful), privily.

תְּרוּמָה **tᵉrûmâh**. See 8641.

8650. תֹּרֶן **tôren**, *to´-ren;* prob. for 766; a *pole* (as a mast or flag-staff):— beacon, mast.

8651. תְּרַע **tᵉra'** (Chald.), *ter-ah´;* corresp. to 8179; a *door;* by impl. a *palace:*— gate mouth.

8652. תְּרָע **târâ'** (Chald.), *taw-raw´;* from 8651; a *doorkeeper:*— porter.

8653. תַּרְעֵלָה **tar'êlâh**, *tar-ay-law´;* from 7477; *reeling:*— astonishment, trembling.

8654. תִּרְעָתִי **Tir'âthîy**, *teer-aw-thee´;* patrial from an unused name mean. *gate;* a *Tirathite* or inhab. of an unknown Tirah:— Tirathite.

8655. תְּרָפִים **tᵉrâphîym**, *ter-aw-feme´;* plur. perh. from 7495; a *healer; Teraphim* (sing. or plur.) a family idol:— idols (-atry), images, teraphim.

8656. תִּרְצָה **Tirtsâh**, *teer-tsaw´;* from 7521; *delightsomeness; Tirtsah,* a place in Pal.; also an Israelitess:— Tirzah.

8657. תֶּרֶשׁ **Teresh**, *teh´-resh;* of for. der.; *Teresh,* a eunuch of Xerxes:— Teresh.

8658. תַּרְשִׁישׁ **tarshîysh**, *tar-sheesh´;* prob. of for. der. [comp. 8659]; a gem, perh. the *topaz:*— beryl.

8659. תַּרְשִׁישׁ **Tarshîysh**, *tar-sheesh´;* prob. the same as 8658 (as the region of the stone, or the reverse); *Tarshish,* a place on the Mediterranean, hence, the epithet of a *merchant* vessel (as if for or from that port); also the name of a Pers. and of an Isr.:— Tarshish, Tharshish.

8660. תִּרְשָׁתָא **Tirshâthâ'**, *teer-shaw-thaw´;* of for. der.; the title of a Pers. deputy or *governor:*— Tirshatha.

תַּרְתֵּין **tartêyn**. See 8648.

8661. תַּרְתָּן **Tartân**, *tar-tawn´;* of for. der.; *Tartan,* an Ass.:— Tartan.

8662. תַּרְתָּק **Tartâq**, *tar-tawk´;* of for. der.; *Tartak,* a deity of the Avvites:— Tartak.

8663. תְּשֻׁאָה **tᵉshû'âh**, *tesh-oo-aw´;* from 7722; a *crashing* or loud *clamor:*— crying, noise, shouting, stir.

תּוֹשָׁב **tôshâb**. See 8453.

8664. תִּשְׁבִּי **Tishbîy**, *tish-bee´;* patrial from an unused name mean. *recourse;* a *Tishbite* or inhab. of Tishbeh (in Gilead):— Tishbite.

8665. תַּשְׁבֵּץ **tashbêts**, *tash-bates´;* from 7660; *checkered* stuff (as *reticulated*):— broidered.

8666. תְּשׁוּבָה **tᵉshûwbâh**, *tesh-oo-baw´;* or

תְּשֻׁבָה **tᵉshûbâh**, *tesh-oo-baw´;* from 7725; a *recurrence* (of time or place); a *reply* (as *returned*):— answer, be expired, return.

8667. תְּשׂוּמֶת **tᵉsûwmeth**, *tes-oo-meth´;* from 7760; a *deposit,* i.e. *pledging:*— + fellowship.

8668. תְּשׁוּעָה **tᵉshûw'âh**, *tesh-oo-aw´;* or

תְּשֻׁעָה **tᵉshû'âh**, *tesh-oo-aw´;* from 7768 in the sense of 3467; *rescue* (lit. or fig., pers., national or spir.):— deliverance, help, safety, salvation, victory.

8669. תְּשׁוּקָה **tᵉshûwqâh**, *tesh-oo-kaw´;* from 7783 in the orig. sense of *stretching* out after; a *longing:*— desire.

8670. תְּשׁוּרָה **tᵉshûwrâh**, *tesh-oo-raw´;* from 7788 in the sense of *arrival;* a *gift:*— present.

תַּשְׁחֵת **tashchêth**. See 516.

תּוּשִׁיָּה **tûshîyâh**. See 8454.

8671. תְּשִׁיעִי **tᵉshîy'îy**, *tesh-ee-ee´;* ord. from 8672; *ninth:*— ninth.

תְּשֻׁעָה **tᵉshû'âh**. See 8668.

8672. תֵּשַׁע **têsha'**, *tay´-shah;* or (masc.)

תִּשְׁעָה **tish'âh**, *tish-aw´;* perh. from 8159 through the idea of a *turn* to the next or full number ten; *nine* or (ord.) *ninth:*— nine (+ -teen, + -teenth, -th).

8673. תִּשְׁעִים **tish'îym**, *tish-eem´;* multiple from 8672; *ninety:*— ninety.

8674. תַּתְּנַי **Tattᵉnay**, *tat-ten-ah´-ee;* of for. der.; *Tattenai,* a Pers.:— Tatnai.

New Strong's™
Concise Dictionary
of the Words in the
Greek Testament

with their Renderings in the
King James Version

Read this first!

How to Use the Greek Dictionary

For many people Strong's unique system of numbers continues to be *the* bridge between the original languages of the Bible and the English of the *King James Version* (AV). In order to enhance the strategic importance of *Strong's Greek Dictionary* for Bible students, it has been significantly improved in this brand-new, up-to-date edition. It is now completely re-typeset with modern, larger typefaces that are kind to the eye, and all known errors in the original typesetting have been corrected, bringing this pivotal work to a new level of usefulness and accuracy.

1. What the Dictionary Is

Strong's Greek Dictionary is a fully integrated companion to the main concordance. Its compact entries contain a wealth of information about the words of the Bible in their original language. You can enrich your study of the Bible enormously if you will invest the time to understand the various elements included in each entry and their significance. The example that follows identifies many of these entry elements; and the following sections on the transliteration, abbreviations, and special symbols used offer fuller explanations. While no dictionary designed for readers who do not know biblical Hebrew can explain all that a faithful student of the language would know, this *Dictionary* gives the serious student of the English Bible the basic information needed to pursue infinitely deeper and broader studies of God's Word. Vast amounts of biblical insight can be gained by using this *Concordance* alone or in conjunction with other time-proven biblical reference works, such as Thomas Nelson's *Vine's Complete Expository Dictionary of Old and New Testament Words* and *Nelson's New Illustrated Bible Dictionary*.

2. Using the Dictionary with the Main Concordance

To use this *Dictionary*, locate the number given next to the biblical reference for any particular entry in the main concordance. For example, under "EARNEST," you find *Strong's* number *728* next to the first Bible reference, "Eph. 1:14." Since Ephesians is in the New Testament (and since this numeral is set in italic type [and not regular type], you know that it refers to the *Greek Dictionary*. You may view that enlarged entry, here, or on page 13 in this *Dictionary*. The enlarged example that follows, together with the following sections of explanation, identify the kinds of information such entries provide.

3. Using the Dictionary to Do Word Studies

Careful Bible students do word studies, and *The New Strong's™ Exhaustive Concordance* with this revised, newly-typeset *Greek Dictionary*, offers unique assistance. Consider the word "love" as found the King James Bible. By skimming the main concordance, you find these numbers for Greek words that the King James Bible translates with the English word "love": *25, 5368, 26, 5360, 5362, 5363, 5361*. Now for any one Bible reference in this entry there is only one Greek word cited, and you may be interested only in establishing the precise meaning for just that word in that occurrence. If so, it will be very helpful for your to observe that same Greek word in *each* of its occurrences in the Bible. In that way, you develop an idea of its possible range of meanings, and you help clarify what it probably meant precisely in the specific Bible reference you are studying.

But don't overlook exploring each Greek word translated as "love." You may wish to take notes as you look up each occurrence of the word that goes with *25*, and then each occurrence of the word that goes with *26*, and so forth. This method gives you an excellent basis for understanding all that the New Testament signifies with the King James Version's word "love."

Now see the *Dictionary* entry *25* itself, and notice that after the symbol :— all the words and word prefixes and suffixes are listed. These show you that this one Greek word, *agapao*, is translated into a few similar words in the King James Bible: beloved, love, loved. This list tells you the range of uses of the one Greek word in the King James Bible. This information can help you distinguish between the nuances of meaning found where this and the other Greek words are translated by these same words and similar ones in the King James Bible.

These three ways of using the *Dictionary* in conjunction with the main concordance show you only a sampling of the many ways *The New Strong's™ Exhaustive Concordance* can enrich your study of the Bible. And they show you why it is important that you take the time to become familiar with each feature in the *Dictionary* as illustrated in the example on the following page.

An Example
from the
Greek New Testament Dictionary

Strong's number in *italics*, corresponding to the numbers at the ends of the context lines in the main concordance.

An unnumbered cross-reference entry.

The word as it appears in the original Greek spelling.

Where appropriate, important discussion of multiple uses and functions of the word.

The Greek word represented in English letters in **bold** type (the transliteration).

Strong's syllable-by-syllable pronunciation in *italics*, with the emphasized syllable marked by the accent.

When the Greek word relates to a Hebrew or Aramaic word from the Old Testament, the Strong's numbers is encased in square brackets [...].

Brief English definitions (shown by italics).

ἀπέπω **apĕpō**. See 550.

728. ἀῤῥαβών **arrhabōn**, *ar-hrab-ohn´*; of Heb. or. [6162]; a *pledge*, i.e. part of the purchase-money or property given in advance as *security* for the rest:— earnest.

3360. μέχρι **mĕchri** *mekh´-ree;* or

→ μεχρίς **mĕchris** *mekh-ris´;* from 3372; *as far as*, i.e. *up to* a certain point (as a prep. of extent [denoting the *terminus*, whereas *891* refers espec. to the *space* of time or place intervening] or a conjunc.):— till, (un-) to, until.

3361. μή **mē** *may;* a primary particle of qualified *negation* (whereas 3756 expresses an absolute denial); (adv.) *not*, (conjunc.) *lest;* also (as an interrog. implying a *neg.* answer [whereas 3756 expects an *affirmative* one]) *whether:*— any, but (that) × forbear, + God forbid, + lack, lest, neither, never, no (× wise in), none, nor, [can-] not, nothing, that not, un [-taken], without. Often used in compounds in substantially the same relations. See also *3362, 3363, 3364, 3372, 3373, 3375, 3378.*

See "Special Symbols."

Italic Strong's numbers refer to related Greek words in this Dictionary.

After the long dash (—), there is a complete, alphabetical listing of all ways this Greek word is translated in the KJV. (See also "Special Symbols").

Improved, consistent abbreviations. All abbreviations occur with their full spelling in the list of abbreviations.

Note that Greek spelling variations are conveniently indented for easy comparison.

Plan of the Greek Dictionary

1. All the original words are presented in their alphabetical order (according to Greek). They are numbered for easy matching between this Dictionary and the main part of the Concordance. Many reference books also use these same numbers which were originally created by Dr. Strong.

2. Immediately after each word, the exact equivalent of each sound (phoneme) is given in English characters, according to the transliteration system given below.

3. Next follows the precise pronunciation with the proper stress mark.

4. Then comes the etymology, root meaning, and common uses of the word, along with any other important related details.

5. In the case of proper names, the normal English spelling is given, accompanied by a few words of explanation.

6. Finally, after the colon and the dash (:—), all the different ways that the word appears in the Authorized Version (KJV) are listed in alphabetical order. When the Greek word appears in English as a phrase, the main word of the phrase is used to alphabetize it.

By looking up these words in the main concordance and by noting the passages which display the same number in the right-hand column, the reader also possesses a complete *Greek New Testament Concordance*, expressed in the words of the Authorized Version.

Transliteration and Pronunciation of the Greek

The following shows how the Greek words are transliterated into English in this Dictionary.

1. The *Alphabet* is as follows:

No.	Form upper	lower	Name	Transliteration and Pronunciation
1.	A	α	Alpha (*al´-fah*)	a, as in *Arm* or *mAn* [1]
2.	B	β	Bēta (*bay´-tah*)	b
3.	Γ	γ	Gamma (*gam´-mah*)	g, as in *Guard* [2]
4.	Δ	δ	Dĕlta (*del´-tah*)	d
5.	E	ε	Ĕpsilŏn (*ep´-see-lon*)	ĕ, as in *mEt*
6.	Z	ζ	Zēta (*dzay´-tah*)	z, as in *aDZe* [3]
7.	H	η	Ēta (*ay´-tah*)	ē, as in *thEy*
8.	Θ	θ	Thēta (*thay´-tah*)	th, as in *THin* [4]
9.	I	ι	Iota (*ee-o´-tah*)	i, as in *machIne* [5]
10.	K	κ	Kappa (*kap´-pah*)	k
11.	Λ	λ	Lambda (*lamb´-dah*)	l
12.	M	μ	Mu (*moo*)	m
13.	N	ν	Nu (*noo*)	n
14.	Ξ	ξ	Xi (*ksee*)	x = ks
15.	O	ο	Omikrŏn (*om´-e-cron*)	ŏ, as in *not*
16.	Π	π	Pi (*pee or pai*)	p
17.	P	ρ	Rhō (*hro*)	r
18.	Σ	σ, final ς	Sigma (*sig´-mah*)	s sharp
19.	T	τ	Tau (*tŏw*)	t, as in *Tree* [6]
20.	Υ	υ	Upsilŏn (*u´-pse-lon*)	u, as in *fUll*
21.	Φ	φ	Phi (*fee or fai*)	ph = f
22.	X	χ	Chi (*khee or khai*)	German ch [7]
23.	Ψ	ψ	Psi (*psee or psai*)	ps
24.	Ω	ω	Omĕga (*o´-meg-ah*)	ō, as in *no*

[1] a, when *final*, or before a final ρ or followed by any *other* consonant, is sounded like a in *Arm*; elsewhere like a in *mAn*.
[2] γ, when followed by γ, k, c, or ξ is sounded like *ng* in *kiNG*.
[3] ζ is always sounded like *dz*.
[4] θ never has the guttural sound, like *th* in *THis*.

[5] ι has the sound of *ee* when it ends an *accented* syllable; in other situations a more obscure sound, like *i* in *amIable* or *Imbecile*.
[6] τ never has an s-sound, like *t* in *naTion*.
[7] From the difficulty of producing the true sound of χ, it is generally sounded like *k*.

2. The mark ', placed over the *initial* vowel of a word, is called the *Rough Breathing*, and is equivalent to the English *h*, by which we have accordingly represented it. Its *absence* over an initial vowel is indicated by the mark ', called the *Smooth Breathing*, which is silent, and is therefore not represented in our method of transliteration. [8]

3. The following are the Greek *diphthongs*, properly so called: [9]

Form	Transliteration and Pronunciation
αι	**ai** (*ah´ee*) [ă + ē]
ει	**ei**, as in *hEIght*
οι	**oi**, as in *OIl*
υι	**we**, as in *sWEet*
αυ	**ow**, as in *nOW*
ευ	**eu**, as in *fEUd*
ου	**ou**, as in *thrOUgh*

4. The *accent* (stress of voice) falls on the syllable where it is written. [10] It occurs in three forms: the *acute* ('), which is the only true accent; the *grave* (`) which is its substitute; and the *circumflex* (ˆ), which is the union of the two. The acute may stand on any one of the last *three* syllables, and in case it occurs on the final syllable, before another word in the same sentence, it is written as a grave. The grave is understood (but never written as such) on every other syllable. The circumflex is written on any syllable (necessarily the last syllable or next to the last syllable of a word) formed by the contraction of two syllables, of which the *first* would properly have the acute accent.

5. The following *punctuation* marks are used: the comma (,), the semicolon (·), the colon or period (.), the question mark (;), and by some editors, also the exclamation mark, parentheses, and quotation marks.

Special Symbols

+ (*addition*) denotes a rendering in the A.V. of one or more Greek words in connection with the one under consideration. For example, in Rev. 17:17, No. 1106, γνώμη (**gnōmē**) is translated as a verb ("to agree"), when it is actually a noun and part of a Greek idiom that is literally translated "to do one mind."

× (*multiplication*) denotes a rendering in the A.V. that results from an idiom peculiar to the Greek. For example, in Heb. 12:21, the whole Greek phrase in which ἔντρομος, **ĕntrŏmŏs** (1790) appears is a way of expressing great anxiety. The same idiom is used about Moses in Acts 7:32.

( ) (*parentheses*), in the renderings from the A.V., denote a word or syllable which is sometimes given in connection with the principal word to which it is attached. In Mark 15:39 there are two Greek prepositions (1537 and 1727) which are used together ("over against"). One English preposition, "opposite," communicates the same idea.

[ ] (*brackets*), in the rendering from the A.V., denote the inclusion of an additional word in the Greek. For example, No. 2596 κατά (**kata**) is translated "daily" in Luke 19:47, along with No. 2250 ἡμέρα (**hēmĕra**). So, two Greek words were translated by one English word.

Italics, at the end of a rendering from the A.V., denote an explanation of the variations from the usual form.

Note

Because of some changes in the numbering system (while the original work was in progress) no Greek words are cited for 2717 or 3203-3302. These numbers were dropped altogether. This will not cause any problems in *Strong's* numbering system. **No Greek words have been left out.** Because so many other reference works use this numbering system, it has **not** been revised. If it were revised, much confusion would certainly result.

---

[8] These signs are placed over the *second* vowel of a *diphthong*. The same is true of the accents.

The *Rough* Breathing always belongs to an initial υ.

The *Rough* Breathing is always used with ρ, when it begins a word. If this letter is doubled in the middle of a word, the first ρ takes the Smooth Breathing mark and the second ρ takes the Rough Breathing mark.

Since these signs cannot conveniently be written above the first letter of a word, when it is a *capital*, they are placed *before* it in such cases. This observation applies also to the *accents*. The aspiration *always* begins the syllable.

Occasionally, in consequence of a contraction (*crasis*), the Smooth Breathing is made to stand in the middle of a word, and is then called *Coro´nis*.

[9] The above are combinations of two *short* vowels, and are pronounced like their respective elements, but in more rapid succession than otherwise. Thus, αι is midway between *i* in h*I*gh, and *ay* in s*AY*.

Besides these, there are what are called *improper* diphthongs, in which the former is a *long* vowel. In these,

ᾳ sounds like	α
ῃ "	η
ῳ "	ω
ηυ "	η + υ
ωυ "	ω + υ

the second vowel, when it is ι, is written *under* the first vowel (unless it is a capital), and is *silent*; when it is υ, it is sounded separately. When the initial vowel is a capital, the ι is placed after it, but it does not take a breathing mark or any accent.

The sign ¨ is called *diær;esis*. It is placed over the *second* of two vowels, indicating that they do *not* form a diphthong.

[10] Every word (except a few monosyllables, called *Aton´ics*) must have one accent; several small words (called *Enclit´ics*) put their accent (always as an acute) on the last syllable of the preceding word (in addition to its own accent, which still has the principal stress), where this is possible.

Abbreviations

abb. = abbreviated
  abbreviation
abstr. = abstract
  abstractly
act. = active (voice)
  actively
acc. = accusative (case) [1]
adj. = adjective
  adjectively
adv. = adverb
  adverbial
  adverbially
aff. = affix [2]
  affixed
affin. = affinity
alt. = alternate
  alternately
anal. = analogy
appar. = apparent
  apparently
arch. = architecture
  architectural
  architecturally
art. = article [3]
artif. = artificial
  artificially
Ass. = Assyrian
A.V. = Authorized Version
  (King James Version)
Bab. = Babylon
  Babylonia
  Babylonian
caus. = causative [4]
  causatively
cerem. = ceremony
  ceremonial
  ceremonially
Chald. = Chaldee (Aramaic)
  Chaldaism
  (Aramaism)
Chr. = Christian
collat. = collateral
  collaterally
collect. = collective
  collectively
comp. = compare [5]
  comparison
  comparative
  comparatively
concr. = concrete
  concretely
conjec. = conjecture
  conjectural
  conjecturally
conjug. = conjugation [6]
  conjugational
  conjugationally
conjunc. = conjunction
  conjunctional
  conjunctionally
constr. = construct [7]
  construction
  constructive
  constructively

contr. = contracted [8]
  contraction
correl. = correlated
  correlation
  correlative
  correlatively
corresp. = corresponding
  correspondingly
dat. = dative (case) [9]
def. = definite [10]
  definitely
demonstr. = demonstrative[11]
denom. = denominative [12]
  denominatively
der. = derived
  derivation
  derivative
  derivatively
desc. = descended
  descendant
  descendants
dimin. = diminutive [13]
dir. = direct
  directly
E. = East
  Eastern
eccl. = ecclesiastical
  ecclesiastically
e.g. = for example
Eg. = Egypt
  Egyptian
  Egyptians
ellip. = ellipsis [14]
  elliptical
  elliptically
emphat. = emphatic
  emphatically
equiv. = equivalent
  equivalently
err. = error
  erroneous
  erroneously
espec. = especially
etym. = etymology [15]
  etymological
  etymologically
euphem. = euphemism [16]
  euphemistic
  euphemistically
euphon. = euphonious [17]
  euphonically
extens. = extension [18]
  extensive
extern. = external
  externally
fem. = feminine (gender)
fig. = figurative
  figuratively
for. = foreign
  foreigner
freq. = frequentative
  frequentatively
fut. = future

gen. = general
  generally
  generic
  generical
  generically
Gr. = Greek
  Graecism
gut. = guttural [19]
Heb. = Hebrew
  Hebraism
i.e. = that is
ident. = identical
  identically
immed. = immediate
  immediately
imper. = imperative [20]
  imperatively
imperf. = imperfect [21]
impers. = impersonal
  impersonally
impl. = implied
  impliedly
  implication
incept. = inceptive [22]
  inceptively
incl. = including
  inclusive
  inclusively
indef. = indefinite
  indefinitely
ind. = indicative [23]
  indicatively
indiv. = individual
  individually
infer. = inference
  inferential
  inferentially
infin. = infinitive
inhab. = inhabitant
  inhabitants
ins. = inserted
intens. = intensive
  intensively
interch. = interchangeable
intern. = internal
  internally
interj. = interjection [24]
  interjectional
  interjectionally
interrog. = interrogative [25]
  interrogatively
intr. = intransitive [26]
  intransitively
invol. = involuntary
  involuntarily
irreg. = irregular
  irregularly
Isr. = Israelite
  Israelites
  Israelitish
Lat. = Latin
Levit. = Levitical
  Levitically

lit. = literal
  literally
marg. = margin
  marginal reading
masc. = masculine (gender)
mean. = meaning
ment. = mental
  mentally
metaph. = metaphorical
  metaphorically
mid. = middle (voice) [27]
modif. = modified
  modification
mor. = moral
  morally
mult. = multiplicative [28]
nat. = natural
  naturally
neg. = negative
  negatively
neut. = neuter (gender)
obj. = object
  objective
  objectively
obs. = obsolete
ord. = ordinal [29]
or. = origin
orig. = original
  originally
orth. = orthography [30]
  orthographical
  orthographically
Pal. = Palestine
part. = participle
pass. = passive (voice)
  passively
patron. = patronymic [31]
  patronymical
  patronymically
perh. = perhaps
perm. = permutation [32] (of
  adjacent letters)
pers. = person
  personal
  personally
Pers. = Persia
  Persian
  Persians
phys. = physical
  physically
plur. = plural
poet. = poetry
  poetical
  poetically
pos. = positive
  positively
pref. = prefix
  prefixed
prep. = preposition
  prepositional
  prepositionally
prim. = primitive
prob. = probable
  probably

prol. = prolonged [33]
  prolongation
pron. = pronoun
  pronominal
  pronominally
prop. = properly
prox. = proximate
  proximately
recip. = reciprocal
  reciprocally
redupl. = reduplicated [34]
  reduplication
refl. = reflexive [35]
  reflexively
reg. = regular
rel. = relative
  relatively
relig. = religion
  religious
  religiously
Rom. = Roman
second. = secondary
  secondarily
signif. = signification
  signifying
short. = shorter
  shortened
sing. = singular
spec. = specific
  specifically
streng. = strengthening
subdiv. = subdivision
  subdivisional
  subdivisionally
subj. = subjectively
  subjective
  subject
substit. = substituted
suff. = suffix
superl. = superlative [36]
  superlatively
symb. = symbolic
  symbolical
  symbolically
tech. = technical
  technically
term. = termination
tran. = transitive [37]
  transitively
transc. = transcription
transm. = transmutation [38]
transp. = transposed [39]
  transposition
typ. = typical
  typically
uncert. = uncertain
  uncertainly
var. = various
  variation
voc. = vocative (case) [40]
vol. = voluntary
  voluntarily

---

[1] often indicating the direct object of an action verb

[2] part of a word which, when attached to the beginning of the word is called a prefix; if attaching within a word, an infix; and if at the end, a suffix

[3] "the" is the definite article; "a" and "an" are indefinite articles

[4] expressing or denoting causation

[5] the comparative of an adjective or adverb expresses a greater degree of an attribute, e.g. "higher"; "more slowly"

[6] a systematic array of various verbal forms

[7] the condition in Hebrew and Aramaic when two adjacent nouns are combined semantically as follows, e.g."sword" + "king" = "(the) sword of (the) king" or "(the) king's sword". These languages tend to throw the stress of the entire noun phrase toward the end of the whole expression.

[8] a shortened form of a word. It is made by omitting or combining some elements or by reducing vowels or syllables, e.g. "is not" becomes "isn't".

[9] often the indirect object of an action verb

[10] the definite article ("the")

[11] demonstrative pronouns which point (show), e.g. "this," "that"

[12] derived from a noun

[13] a grammatical form which expresses smallness and/or endearment

[14] a construction which leaves out understood words

[15] the historical origin of a word

[16] the use of a pleasant, polite, or harmless-sounding word or phrase to hide harsh, rude, or infamous truths, e.g. "to pass away" = "to die"

[17] a linguistic mechanism to make pronunciation easier, e.g. "an" before "hour" instead of "a"

[18] when a general term can denote an entire class of things

[19] speech sounds which are produced deep in the throat

[20] the mood which expresses a command

[21] used of a tense which expresses a continuous but unfinished action or state

[22] used of a verbal aspect which denotes the beginning of an action

[23] used of the mood which expresses a verbal action as actually occurring (not hypothetical)

[24] an exclamation which expresses emotion

[25] indicating a question

[26] referring to verbs which do not govern direct objects

[27] reflexive

[28] capable of multiplying or tending to multiply

[29] This shows the position or the order within a series, e.g. "second"; the corresponding cardinal number is "two".

[30] the written system of spelling in a given language

[31] a name derived from that of a paternal ancestor, often created by an affix in various languages

[32] a rearrangement

[33] lengthening a pronunciation

[34] the repetition of a letter or syllable to form a new, inflected word

[35] denoting an action by the subject upon itself

[36] expressing the highest degree of comparison of the quality indicated by an adjective or an adverb, e.g. "highest"; "most timely"

[37] expressing an action directed toward a person or a thing (the direct object)

[38] the change of one grammatical element to another

[39] switching word order

[40] an inflection which is used when one is addressing a person or a thing directly, e.g. "John, come here!"

A

N. B.—The numbers *not in italics* refer to the words in the *Hebrew Dictionary*. Significations within quotation marks are derivative representatives of the Greek.

1. A **A**, *al´-fah;* of Heb. or.; the first letter of the alphabet; fig. only (from its use as a numeral) the *first:*— Alpha. Often used (usually ἄν **an**, before a vowel) also in composition (as a contr. from *427*) in the sense of *privation;* so in many words beginning with this letter; occasionally in the sense of *union* (as a contr. of *260*).

2. Ἀαρών **Aarōn**, *ah-ar-ohn´;* of Heb. or. [*175*]; *Aaron*, the brother of Moses:— Aaron.

3. Ἀβαδδών **Abaddōn**, *ab-ad-dōhn´;* of Heb. or. [*11*]; a destroying *angel:*— Abaddon.

4. ἀβαρής **abarēs**, *ab-ar-ace´;* from *1* (as a neg. particle) and *922; weightless,* i.e. (fig.) *not burdensome:*— from being burdensome.

5. Ἀββᾶ **Abba**, *ab-bah´;* of Chald. or. [*2*]; *father* (as a voc.):— Abba.

6. Ἄβελ **Abĕl**, *ab´-el;* of Heb. or. [*1893*]; *Abel*, the son of Adam:— Abel.

7. Ἀβιά **Abia**, *ab-ee-ah´;* of Heb. or. [*29*]; *Abijah*, the name of two Isr.:— Abia.

8. Ἀβιάθαρ **Abiathar**, *ab-ee-ath´-ar;* of Heb. or. [*54*]; *Abiathar*, an Isr.:— Abiathar.

9. Ἀβιληνή **Abilēnē**, *ab-ee-lay-nay´;* of for. or. [comp. *58*]; *Abilene*, a region of Syria:— Abilene.

10. Ἀβιούδ **Abiŏud**, *ab-ee-ood´;* of Heb. or. [*31*]; *Abihud*, an Isr.:— Abiud.

11. Ἀβραάμ **Abraam**, *ab-rah-am´;* of Heb. or. [*85*]; *Abraham*, the Heb. patriarch:— Abraham. [In Acts 7:16 the text should prob. read *Jacob.*]

12. ἄβυσσος **abussŏs**, *ab´-us-sos;* from *1* (as a neg. particle) and a var. of *1037; depthless,* i.e. (spec.) (infernal) "abyss":— deep, (bottomless) pit.

13. Ἄγαβος **Agabŏs**, *Ag´-ab-os;* of Heb. or. [comp. *2285*]; *Agabus*, an Isr.:— Agabus.

14. ἀγαθοεργέω **agathŏĕrgĕō**, *ag-ath-o-er-gheh´-o;* from *18* and *2041;* to *work good:*— do good.

15. ἀγαθοποιέω **agathŏpŏiĕō**, *ag-ath-op-oy-eh´-o;* from *17;* to *be a well-doer* (as a favor or a duty):— (when) do good (well).

16. ἀγαθοποιΐα **agathŏpŏiïa**, *ag-ath-op-oy-ee´-ah;* from *17; well-doing,* i.e. *virtue:*— well-doing.

17. ἀγαθοποιός **agathŏpŏiŏs**, *ag-ath-op-oy-os´;* from *18* and *4160;* a *well-doer,* i.e. *virtuous:*— them that do well.

18. ἀγαθός **agathŏs**, *ag-ath-os´;* a prim. word; "*good*" (in any sense, often as noun):— benefit, good (-s, things), well. Comp. *2570.*

19. ἀγαθωσύνη **agathōsunē**, *ag-ath-o-soo´-nay;* from *18; goodness,* i.e. *virtue* or *beneficence:*— goodness.

20. ἀγαλλίασις **agalliasis**, *ag-al-lee´-as-is;* from *21; exultation;* spec. *welcome:*— gladness, (exceeding) joy.

21. ἀγαλλιάω **agalliaō**, *ag-al-lee-ah´-o;* from ἄγαν **agan** (*much*) and *242;* prop. to *jump for joy,* i.e. *exult:*— be (exceeding) glad, with exceeding joy, rejoice (greatly).

22. ἄγαμος **agamŏs**, *ag´-am-os;* from *1* (as a neg. particle) and *1062; unmarried:*— unmarried.

23. ἀγανακτέω **aganaktĕō**, *ag-an-ak-teh´-o;* from ἄγαν **agan** (*much*) and ἄχθος **achthŏs** (*grief;* akin to the base of *43*); to *be greatly afflicted,* i.e. (fig.) *indignant:*— be much (sore) displeased, have (be moved with, with) indignation.

24. ἀγανάκτησις **aganaktēsis**, *ag-an-ak´-tay-sis;* from *23; indignation:*— indignation.

25. ἀγαπάω **agapaō**, *ag-ap-ah´-o;* perh. from ἄγαν **agan** (*much*) [or comp. *5689*]; to *love* (in a social or moral sense):— (be-) love (-ed). Comp. *5368.*

26. ἀγάπη **agapē**, *ag-ah´-pay;* from *25; love,* i.e. *affection* or *benevolence;* spec. (plur.) a *love-feast:*— (feast of) charity ([-ably]), dear, love.

27. ἀγαπητός **agapētŏs**, *ag-ap-ay-tos´;* from *25; beloved:*— (dearly, well) beloved, dear.

28. Ἄγαρ **Agar**, *ag´-ar;* of Heb. or. [*1904*]; *Hagar*, the concubine of Abraham:— Hagar.

29. ἀγγαρεύω **aggarĕuō**, *ang-ar-yew´-o;* of for. or. [comp. *104*]; prop. to *be a courier,* i.e. (by impl.) to *press* into public service:— compel (to go).

30. ἀγγεῖον **aggĕiŏn**, *ang-eye´-on;* from ἄγγος **aggŏs** (a *pail,* perh. as *bent;* comp. the base of *43*); a *receptacle:*— vessel.

31. ἀγγελία **aggĕlia**, *ang-el-ee´-ah;* from *32;* an *announcement,* i.e. (by impl.) *precept:*— message.

32. ἄγγελος **aggĕlŏs**, *ang´-el-os;* from ἀγγέλλω **aggĕllō** [prob. der. from *71;* comp. *34*] (to *bring tidings*); a *messenger;* esp. an "*angel*"; by impl. a *pastor:*— angel, messenger.

33. ἄγε **agĕ**, *ag´-eh;* imper. of *71;* prop. *lead,* i.e. *come* on:— go to.

34. ἀγέλη **agĕlē**, *ag-el´-ay;* from *71* [comp. *32*]; a *drove:*— herd.

35. ἀγενεαλόγητος **agĕnĕalŏgētŏs**, *ag-en-eh-al-og´-ay-tos;* from *1* (as neg. particle) and *1075; unregistered* as to *birth:*— without descent.

36. ἀγενής **agĕnēs**, *ag-en-ace´;* from *1* (as neg. particle) and *1085; properly, without kin,* i.e. (of unknown descent, and by impl.) *ignoble:*— base things.

37. ἁγιάζω **hagiazō**, *hag-ee-ad´-zo;* from *40;* to *make holy,* i.e. (cer.) *purify*

or *consecrate;* (mentally) to *venerate:*— hallow, be holy, sanctify.

38. ἁγιασμός **hagiasmŏs**, *hag-ee-as-mos´;* from *37;* prop. *purification,* i.e. (the state) *purity;* concr. (by Heb.) a *purifier:*— holiness, sanctification.

39. ἅγιον **hagiŏn**, *hag´-ee-on;* neut. of *40;* a *sacred* thing (i.e. spot):— holiest (of all), holy place, sanctuary.

40. ἅγιος **hagiŏs**, *hag´-ee-os;* from ἅγος **hagŏs** (an *awful* thing) [comp. *53,* *2282*]; *sacred* (phys. *pure,* mor. *blameless* or *religious,* cer. *consecrated*):— (most) holy (one, thing), saint.

41. ἁγιότης **hagiŏtēs**, *hag-ee-ot´-ace;* from *40; sanctity* (i.e. prop. the state):— holiness.

42. ἁγιωσύνη **hagiōsunē**, *hag-ee-o-soo´-nay;* from *40; sacredness* (i.e. prop. the quality):— holiness.

43. ἀγκάλη **agkalē**, *ang-kal´-ay;* from ἄγκος **agkŏs** (a *bend,* "ache"); an *arm* (as *curved*):— arm.

44. ἄγκιστρον **agkistrŏn**, *ang´-kis-tron;* from the same as *43;* a *hook* (as *bent*):— hook.

45. ἄγκυρα **agkura**, *ang´-koo-rah;* from the same as *43;* an "*anchor*" (as *crooked*):— anchor.

46. ἄγναφος **agnaphŏs**, *ag´-naf-os;* from *1* (as a neg. particle) and the same as *1102;* prop. *unfulled,* i.e. (by impl.) *new* (cloth):— new.

47. ἁγνεία **hagnĕia**, *hag-ni´-ah;* from *53; cleanliness* (the quality), i.e. (spec.) *chastity:*— purity.

48. ἁγνίζω **hagnizō**, *hag-nid´-zo;* from *53;* to *make clean,* i.e. (fig.) *sanctify* (cer. or mor.):— purify (self).

49. ἁγνισμός **hagnismŏs**, *hag-nis-mos´;* from *48;* a *cleansing* (the act), i.e. (cer.) *lustration:*— purification.

50. ἀγνοέω **agnŏĕō**, *ag-no-eh´-o;* from *1* (as a neg. particle) and *3539; not to know* (through lack of information or intelligence); by impl. to *ignore* (through disinclination):— (be) ignorant (-ly), not know, not understand, unknown.

51. ἀγνόημα **agnŏēma**, *ag-no´-ay-mah;* from *50;* a thing *ignored,* i.e. *shortcoming:*— error.

52. ἄγνοια **agnŏia**, *ag´-noy-ah;* from *50; ignorance* (prop. the quality):— ignorance.

53. ἁγνός **hagnŏs**, *hag-nos´;* from the same as *40;* prop. *clean,* i.e. (fig.) *innocent, modest, perfect:*— chaste, clean, pure.

54. ἁγνότης **hagnŏtēs**, *hag-not´-ace;* from *53; cleanness* (the state), i.e. (fig.) *blamelessness:*— pureness.

55. ἁγνῶς **hagnōs**, *hag-noce´;* adv. from *53; purely,* i.e. *honestly:*— sincerely.

56. ἀγνωσία **agnōsia**, *ag-no-see´-ah;* from *1* (as neg. particle) and *1108; ignorance* (prop. the state):— ignorance, not the knowledge.

57. ἄγνωστος **agnōstŏs**, *ag´-noce-tos´*; from *1* (as neg. particle) and *1110*; *unknown:*— unknown.

58. ἀγορά **agŏra**, *ag-or-ah´*; from ἀγείρω **agĕirō** (to *gather*; prob. akin to *1453*); prop. the *town-square* (as a place of public resort); by impl. a *market* or *thoroughfare:*— market (-place), street.

59. ἀγοράζω **agŏrazō**, *ag-or-ad´-zo*; from *58*; prop. to *go to market*, i.e. (by impl.) to *purchase*; spec. to *redeem:*— buy, redeem.

60. ἀγοραῖος **agŏraiŏs**, *ag-or-ah´-yos*; from *58*; *relating to the market-place*, i.e. *forensic* (times); by impl. *vulgar:*— baser sort, low.

61. ἄγρα **agra**, *ag´-rah*; from *71*; (abstr.) a *catching* (of fish); also (concr.) a *haul* (of fish):— draught.

62. ἀγράμματος **agrammatŏs**, *ag-ram-mat-os*; from *1* (as neg. particle) and *1121*; *unlettered*, i.e. *illiterate:*— unlearned.

63. ἀγραυλέω **agraulĕō**, *ag-row-leh´-o*: from *68* and *832* (in the sense of *833*); to *camp out:*— abide in the field.

64. ἀγρεύω **agrĕuō**, *ag-rew´-o*; from *61*; to *hunt*, i.e. (fig.) to *entrap:*— catch.

65. ἀγριέλαιος **agriĕlaiŏs**, *ag-ree-el´-ah-yos*; from *66* and *1636*; an *oleaster:*— olive tree (which is) wild.

66. ἄγριος **agriŏs**, *ag´-ree-os*; from *68*; *wild* (as pertaining to the *country*), lit. (*natural*) or fig. (*fierce*):— wild, raging.

67. Ἀγρίππας **Agrippas**, *ag-rip´-pas*; appar. from *66* and *2462*; *wild-horse tamer*; *Agrippas*, one of the Herods:— Agrippa.

68. ἀγρός **agrŏs**, *ag-ros´*; from *71*; a *field* (as a *drive* for cattle); gen. the *country*; spec. a *farm*, i.e. *hamlet:*— country, farm, piece of ground, land.

69. ἀγρυπνέω **agrupnĕō**, *ag-roop-neh´-o*; ultimately from *1* (as neg. particle) and *5258*; to *be sleepless*, i.e. *keep awake:*— watch.

70. ἀγρυπνία **agrupnia**, *ag-roop-nee´-ah*; from *69*; *sleeplessness*, i.e. a *keeping awake:*— watch.

71. ἄγω **agō**, *ag´-o*; a prim. verb; prop. to *lead*; by impl. to *bring*, *drive*, (refl.) *go*, (spec.) *pass* (time), or (fig.) *induce:*— be, bring (forth), carry, (let) go, keep, lead away, be open.

72. ἀγωγή **agōgē**, *ag-o-gay´*; redupl. from *71*; a *bringing* up, i.e. *mode of living:*— manner of life.

73. ἀγών **agōn**, *ag-one´*; from *71*; prop. a place of *assembly* (as if *led*), i.e. (by impl.) a *contest* (held there); fig. an *effort* or *anxiety:*— conflict, contention, fight, race.

74. ἀγωνία **agōnia**, *ag-o-nee´-ah*; from *73*; a *struggle* (prop. the state), i.e. (fig.) *anguish:*— agony.

75. ἀγωνίζομαι **agōnizŏmai**, *ag-o-nid´-zom-ahee*; from *73*; to *struggle*, lit. (to *compete* for a prize), fig. (to *contend* with an adversary), or gen. (to *endeavor* to accomplish something):— fight, labor fervently, strive.

76. Ἀδάμ **Adam**, *ad-am´*; of Heb. or. [121]; *Adam*, the first man; typ. (of Jesus) *man* (as his representative):— Adam.

77. ἀδάπανος **adapanŏs**, *ad-ap´-an-os*; from *1* (as neg. particle); and *1160*; *costless*, i.e. *gratuitous:*— without expense.

78. Ἀδδί **Addi**, *ad-dee´*; prob. of Heb. or. [comp. 5716]; *Addi*, an Isr.:— Addi.

79. ἀδελφή **adelphē**, *ad-el-fay´*; fem of *80*; a *sister* (nat. or eccl.):— sister.

80. ἀδελφός **adelphŏs**, *ad-el-fos´*; from *1* (as a connective particle) and δελφύς **delphus** (the *womb*); a *brother* (lit. or fig.) near or remote [much like 1]:— brother.

81. ἀδελφότης **adelphŏtēs**, *ad-el-fot´-ace*; from *80*; *brotherhood* (prop. the feeling of *brotherliness*), i.e. the (Chr.) *fraternity:*— brethren, brotherhood.

82. ἄδηλος **adēlŏs**, *ad´-ay-los*; from *1* (as a neg. particle) and *1212*; *hidden*, fig. *indistinct:*— appear not, uncertain.

83. ἀδηλότης **adēlŏtēs**, *ad-ay-lot´-ace*; from *82*; *uncertainty:*— × uncertain.

84. ἀδήλως **adēlōs**, *ad-ay´-loce*; adv. from *82*; *uncertainly:*— uncertainly.

85. ἀδημονέω **adēmŏnĕō**, *ad-ay-mon-eh´-o*; from a der. of ἀδέω **adeo** (to be *sated* to loathing); to *be in distress* (of mind):— be full of heaviness, be very heavy.

86. ᾅδης **haidēs**, *hah´-dace*; from *1* (as neg. particle) and *1492*; prop. *unseen*, i.e. "*Hades*" or the place (state) of departed souls:— grave, hell.

87. ἀδιάκριτος **adiakritŏs**, *ad-ee-ak´-ree-tos*; from *1* (as a neg. particle) and a der. of *1252*; prop. *undistinguished*, i.e. (act.) *impartial:*— without partiality.

88. ἀδιάλειπτος **adialĕiptŏs**, *ad-ee-al´-ipe-tos*; from *1* (as a neg. particle) and a der. of a compound of *1223* and *3007*; *unintermitted*, i.e. *permanent:*— without ceasing, continual.

89. ἀδιαλείπτως **adialĕiptōs**, *ad-ee-al-ipe´-toce*; adv. from *88*; *uninteruptedly*, i.e. *without omission* (on an appropriate occasion):— without ceasing.

90. ἀδιαφθορία **adiaphthŏria**, *ad-ee-af-thor-ee´-ah*; from a der. of a compound of *1* (as a neg. particle) and a der. of *1311*; *incorruptibleness*, i.e. (fig.) *purity* (of doctrine):— uncorruptness.

91. ἀδικέω **adikĕō**, *ad-ee-keh´-o*; from *94*; to *be unjust*, i.e. (act.) *do wrong* (mor., socially or phys.):— hurt, injure, be an offender, be unjust, (do, suffer, take) wrong.

92. ἀδίκημα **adikēma**, *ad-eek´-ay-mah*; from *91*; a *wrong* done:— evil doing, iniquity, matter of wrong.

93. ἀδικία **adikia**, *ad-ee-kee´-ah*; from *94*; (legal) *injustice* (prop. the quality, by impl. the act); mor. *wrongfulness* (of character, life or act):— iniquity, unjust, unrighteousness, wrong.

94. ἄδικος **adikŏs**, *ad´-ee-kos*; from *1* (as a neg. particle) and *1349*; *unjust*; by extens. *wicked*; by impl. *treacherous*; spec. *heathen:*— unjust, unrighteous.

95. ἀδίκως **adikōs**, *ad-ee´-koce*; adv. from *94*; *unjustly:*— wrongfully.

96. ἀδόκιμος **adŏkimŏs**, *ad-ok´-ee-mos*; from *1* (as a neg. particle) and *1384*; *unapproved*, i.e. *rejected*; by impl. *worthless* (lit. or mor.):— castaway, rejected, reprobate.

97. ἄδολος **adŏlŏs**, *ad´-ol-os*; from *1* (as a neg. particle) and *1388*; *undeceitful*, i.e. (fig.) *unadulterated:*— sincere.

98. Ἀδραμυττηνός **Adramuttēnŏs**, *ad-ram-oot-tay-nos´*; from Ἀδραμύττειον **Adramuttĕiŏn** (a place in Asia Minor); *Adramyttene* or belonging to Adramyttium:— of Adramyttium.

99. Ἀδρίας **Adrias**, *ad-ree´-as*; from Ἀδρία **Adria** (a place near its shore); the *Adriatic* sea (incl. the Ionian):— Adria.

100. ἀδρότης **hadrŏtēs**, *had-rot´-ace*; from ἁδρός **hadrŏs** (stout); *plumpness*, i.e. (fig.) *liberality:*— abundance.

101. ἀδυνατέω **adunatĕō**, *ad-oo-nat-eh´-o*; from *102*; to be *unable*, i.e. (pass.) *impossible:*— be impossible.

102. ἀδύνατος **adunatŏs**, *ad-oo´-nat-os*; from *1* (as a neg. particle) and *1415*; *unable*, i.e. *weak* (lit. or fig.); pass. *impossible:*— could not do, impossible, impotent, not possible, weak.

103. ᾄδω **aidō**, *ad´-o´* a prim. verb; to *sing:*— sing.

104. ἀεί **aĕi**, *ah-eye´*; from an obs. prim. noun (appar. mean. continued *duration*); "*ever*," by qualification *regularly*; by impl. *earnestly:*— always, ever.

105. ἀετός **aĕtŏs**, *ah-et-os´*; from the same as *109*; an *eagle* (from its *wind*-like flight):— eagle.

106. ἄζυμος **azumŏs**, *ad´-zoo-mos*; from *1* (as a neg. particle) and *2219*; *unleavened*, i.e. (fig.) *uncorrupted*; (in the neut. plur.) spec. (by impl.) (the *Passover* week:— unleavened (bread).

107. Ἀζώρ **Azōr**, *ad-zore´*; of Heb. or. [comp. 5809]; *Azor*, an Isr.:— Azor.

108. Ἄζωτος **Azōtŏs**, *ad´-zo-tos*; of Heb. or. [795]; *Azotus* (i.e. Ashdod), a place in Pal.:— Azotus.

109. ἀήρ **aēr**, *ah-ayr´*; from ἄημι **aēmi** (to *breathe* unconsciously, i.e. *respire*; by anal. to *blow*); "*air*" (as naturally *circumambient*):— air. Comp. 5594.

ἀθά **atha**. See *3134*.

110. ἀθανασία **athanasia**, *ath-an-as-ee´-ah*; from a compound of *1* (as a neg. particle) and *2288*; *deathlessness:*— immortality.

111. ἀθέμιτος **athĕmitŏs**, *ath-em´-ee-tos*; from *1* (as a neg. particle) and a der. of θέμις **thĕmis** (*statute*; from the base of *5087*); *illegal*; by impl. *flagitious:*— abominable, unlawful thing.

112. ἄθεος **athĕŏs**, *ath´-eh-os*; from *1* (as a neg. particle) and *2316*; *godless:*— without God.

113. ἄθεσμος **athĕsmŏs**, *ath´-es-mos*; from *1* (as a neg. particle) and a der. of *5087* (in the sense of *enacting*); *lawless*, i.e. (by impl.) *criminal:*— wicked.

114. ἀθετέω **athĕtĕō**, *ath-et-eh´-o*; from a compound of *1* (as a neg. particle)

and a der. of *5087;* to *set aside,* i.e. (by impl.) to *disesteem, neutralize* or *violate:*— cast off, despise, disannul, frustrate, bring to nought, reject.

115. ἀθέτησις **athĕtēsis,** *ath-et´-ay-sis;* from *114; cancellation* (lit. or fig.):— disannulling, put away.

116. Ἀθῆναι **Athēnai,** *ath-ay-nahee;* plur. of Ἀθήνη **Athēnē** (the goddess of wisdom, who was reputed to have founded the city); *Athenæ,* the capitol of Greece:— Athens.

117. Ἀθηναῖος **Athēnaiŏs,** *ath-ay-nah´-yos;* from *116;* an *Athenæan* or inhab. of Athenæ:— Athenian.

118. ἀθλέω **athlĕō,** *ath-leh´-o;* from ἆθλος **athlŏs** (a *contest* in the public lists); to *contend* in the competitive games:— strive.

119. ἄθλησις **athlēsis,** *ath´-lay-sis;* from *118;* a *struggle* (fig.):— fight.

120. ἀθυμέω **athumĕō,** *ath-oo-meh´-o;* from a comp. of *1* (as a neg. particle) and *2372;* to *be spiritless,* i.e. *disheartened:*— be dismayed.

121. ἄθωος **athŏŏs,** *ath´-o-os;* from *1* (as a neg. particle) and prob. a der. of *5087* (mean. a *penalty*); *not guilty:*— innocent.

122. αἴγειος **aigĕiŏs,** *ah´-ee-ghi-os;* from αἴξ **aix** (a *goat*); belonging to a *goat:*— goat.

123. αἰγιαλός **aigialŏs,** *ahee-ghee-al-os´;* from ἀΐσσω **aïssō** (to *rush*) and *251* (in the sense of the *sea;* a *beach* (on which the *waves dash*):— shore.

124. Αἰγύπτιος **Aiguptiŏs,** *ahee-goop´-tee-os;* from *125;* an *Ægyptian* or inhab. of Ægyptus:— Egyptian.

125. Αἴγυπτος **Aiguptŏs,** *ah´-ee-goop-tos;* of uncert. der.;— *Ægyptus,* the land of the Nile:— Egypt.

126. ἀΐδιος **aïdiŏs,** *ah-id´-ee-os;* from *104; everduring* (forward and backward, or forward only):— eternal, everlasting.

127. αἰδώς **aidōs,** *ahee-doce´;* perh. from *1* (as a neg. particle) and *1492* (through the idea of *downcast* eyes); *bashfulness,* i.e. (toward men), *modesty* or (toward God) *awe:*— reverence, shamefacedness.

128. Αἰθίοψ **Aithiŏps,** *ahee-thee´-ops;* from αἴθω **aithō** (to *scorch*) and ὤψ **ŏps** (the *face,* from *3700;* an *Æthiopian* (as a *blackamoor*):— Ethiopian.

129. αἷμα **haima,** *hah´-ee-mah;* of uncert. der.; *blood,* lit. (of men or animals), fig. (the *juice* of grapes) or spec. (the atoning *blood* of Christ); by impl. *bloodshed,* also *kindred:*— blood.

130. αἱματεκχυσία **haimatĕkchusia,** *hahee-mat-ek-khoo-see´-ah;* from *129* and a der. of *1632;* an *effusion of blood:*— shedding of blood.

131. αἱμορρέω **haimŏrrhĕō,** *hahee-mor-hreh´-o;* from *129* and *4482;* to *flow blood,* i.e. *have a hemorrhage:*— diseased with an issue of blood.

132. Αἰνέας **Ainĕas,** *ahee-neh´-as;* of uncert. der.;— *Ænĕas,* an Isr.:— Æneas.

133. αἴνεσις **ainēsis,** *ah´-ee-nes-is;* from *134;* a *praising* (the act), i.e. (spec.) a *thank* (-offering):— praise.

134. αἰνέω **ainĕō,** *ahee-neh´-o;* from *136;* to *praise* (God):— praise.

135. αἴνιγμα **ainigma,** *ah´-ee-nig-ma;* from a der. of *136* (in its prim. sense); an *obscure* saying ("enigma"), i.e. (abstr.) *obscureness:*— × darkly.

136. αἶνος **ainŏs,** *ah´-ee-nos;* appar. a prim. word; prop. a *story,* but used in the sense of *1868; praise* (of God):— praise.

137. Αἰνών **Ainōn,** *ahee-nohn´;* of Heb. or. [a der. of *5869, place of springs*]; *Ænon,* a place in Pal.:— Ænon.

138. αἱρέομαι **hairĕŏmai,** *hahee-reh´-om-ahee;* prob. akin to *142;* to *take for oneself,* i.e. to *prefer:*— choose. Some of the forms are borrowed from a cognate ἕλλομαι **hellŏmai** *hel´-lom-ahee;* which is otherwise obsolete.

139. αἵρεσις **hairĕsis,** *hah´-ee-res-is;* from *138;* prop. a *choice,* i.e. (spec.) a *party* or (abstr.) *disunion:*— heresy [which is the Gr. word itself], sect.

140. αἱρετίζω **hairĕtizō,** *hahee-ret-id´-zo;* from a der. of *138;* to *make a choice:*— choose.

141. αἱρετικός **hairĕtikŏs,** *hahee-ret-ee-kos´;* from the same as *140;* a *schismatic:*— heretic [the Gr. word itself].

142. αἴρω **airō,** *ah´-ee-ro;* a prim. verb; to *lift;* by impl. to *take up* or *away;* fig. to *raise* (the voice), *keep in suspense* (the mind), spec. to *sail* away (i.e. *weigh anchor*); by Heb. [comp. *5375*] to *expiate* sin:— away with, bear (up), carry, lift up, loose, make to doubt, put away, remove, take (away, up).

143. αἰσθάνομαι **aisthanŏmai,** *aheesthan´-om-ahee;* of uncert. der.; to *apprehend* (prop. by the senses):— perceive.

144. αἴσθησις **aisthēsis,** *ah´-ee-sthay-sis;* from *143; perception,* i.e. (fig.) *discernment:*— judgment.

145. αἰσθητήριον **aisthētēriŏn,** *aheesthay-tay´-ree-on;* from a der. of *143;* prop. an *organ of perception,* i.e. (fig.) *judgment:*— senses.

146. αἰσχροκερδής **aischrŏkĕrdēs,** *ahee-skhrok-er-dace´;* from *150* and κέρδος **kerdos** (*gain*); *sordid:*— given to (greedy of) filthy lucre.

147. αἰσχροκερδῶς **aischrŏkĕrdōs,** *ahee-skhrok-er-doce´;* adv. from *146; sordidly:*— for filthy lucre's sake.

148. αἰσχρολογία **aischrŏlŏgia,** *ahee-skhrol-og-ee´-ah;* from *150* and *3056; vile conversation:*— filthy communication.

149. αἰσχρόν **aischrŏn,** *ahee-skhron´;* neut. of *150;* a *shameful* thing, i.e. *indecorum:*— shame.

150. αἰσχρός **aischrŏs,** *ahee-skhros´;* from the same as *153; shameful,* i.e. *base* (spec. *venal*):— filthy.

151. αἰσχρότης **aischrŏtēs,** *aheeskhrot´-ace;* from *150; shamefulness,* i.e. *obscenity:*— filthiness.

152. αἰσχύνη **aischunē,** *ahee-skhoo´-nay;* from *153; shame* or *disgrace* (abstr. or concr.):— dishonesty, shame.

153. αἰσχύνομαι **aischunŏmai,** *aheeskhoo´-nom-ahee;* from αἶσχος **aischŏs** (*disfigurement,* i.e. *disgrace*); to *feel shame* (for oneself):— be ashamed.

154. αἰτέω **aitĕō,** *ahee-teh´-o;* of uncert. der.; to *ask* (in gen.):— ask, beg, call for, crave, desire, require. Comp. *4441.*

155. αἴτημα **aitēma,** *ah´-ee-tay-mah;* from *154;* a *thing asked* or (abstr.) an *asking:*— petition, request, required.

156. αἰτία **aitia,** *ahee-tee´-a;* from the same as *154;* a *cause* (as if *asked* for), i.e. (logical) *reason* (motive, matter), (legal) *crime* (alleged or proved):— accusation, case, cause, crime, fault, [wh-lerel-forel.

157. αἰτίαμα **aitiama,** *ahee-tee´-am-ah;* from a der. of *156;* a *thing charged:*— complaint.

158. αἴτιον **aitiŏn,** *ah´-ee-tee-on;* neut. of *159;* a *reason* or *crime* [like *156*]:— cause, fault.

159. αἴτιος **aitiŏs,** *ah´-ee-tee-os;* from the same as *154; causative,* i.e. (concr.) a *causer:*— author.

160. αἰφνίδιος **aiphnidiŏs,** *aheef-nid´-ee-os;* from a comp. of *1* (as a neg. particle) and *5316* [comp. *1810*] (mean. *non-apparent*); *unexpected,* i.e. (adv.) *suddenly:*— sudden, unawares.

161. αἰχμαλωσία **aichmalōsia,** *aheekhmal-o-see´-ah;* from *164; captivity:*— captivity.

162. αἰχμαλωτεύω **aichmalōtĕuō,** *aheekh-mal-o-tew´-o;* from *164;* to *capture* [like *163*]:— lead captive.

163. αἰχμαλωτίζω **aichmalŏtizō,** *aheekh-mal-o-tid´-zo;* from *164;* to *make captive:*— lead away captive, bring into captivity.

164. αἰχμαλωτός **aichmalōtŏs,** *aheekhmal-o-tos´;* from αἰχμή **aichmē** (a *spear*) and a der. of the same as *259;* prop. a *prisoner of war,* i.e. (gen.) a *captive:*— captive.

165. αἰών **aiōn,** *ahee-ohn´;* from the same as *104;* prop. an *age;* by extens. *perpetuity* (also past); by impl. the *world;* spec. (Jewish) a Messianic period (present or future):— age, course, eternal, (for) ever (-more), [n-lever, (beginning of the, while the) world (began, without end). Comp. *5550.*

166. αἰώνιος **aiōniŏs,** *ahee-o´-nee-os;* from *165; perpetual* (also used of past time, or past and future as well):— eternal, for ever, everlasting, world (began).

167. ἀκαθαρσία **akatharsia,** *ak-ath-ar-see´-ah;* from *169; impurity* (the quality), phys. or mor.:— uncleanness.

168. ἀκαθάρτης **akathartēs,** *ak-ath-ar´-tace;* from *169; impurity* (the state), mor.:— filthiness.

169. ἀκάθαρτος **akathartŏs,** *ak-ath´-ar-tos;* from *1* (as a neg. particle) and a presumed der. of *2508* (mean. *cleansed*); *impure* (cer., mor. [*lewd*] or spec. [*demonic*]):— foul, unclean.

170. ἀκαιρέομαι **akairĕŏmai,** *ak-ahee-reh´-om-ahee;* from a comp. of *1* (as a neg. particle) and *2540* (mean. *unseasonable*); to *be inopportune* (for one-

Greek

self), i.e. to *fail of a proper occasion*:— lack opportunity.

171. ἀκαίρως **akairōs**, *ak-ah´-ee-roce*; adv. from the same as *170; inopportunely*:— out of season.

172. ἄκακος **akakŏs**, *ak´-ak-os*; from *1* (as a neg. particle) and *2556; not bad*, i.e. (obj.) *innocent* or (subj.) *unsuspecting*:— harmless, simple.

173. ἄκανθα **akantha**, *ak´-an-thah*; prob. from the same as *188*; a *thorn*:— thorn.

174. ἀκάνθινος **akanthinŏs**, *ak-an´-thee-nos*; from *173*; *thorny*:— of thorns.

175. ἄκαρπος **akarpŏs**, *ak´-ar-pos*; from *1* (as a neg. particle) and *2590*; *barren* (lit. or fig.):— without fruit, unfruitful.

176. ἀκατάγνωστος **akatagnōstŏs**, *ak-at-ag´-noce-tos*; from *1* (as a neg. particle) and a der. of *2607*; *unblamable*:— that cannot be condemned.

177. ἀκατακάλυπτος **akatakaluptŏs**, *ak-at-ak-al´-oop-tos*; from *1* (as a neg. particle) and a der. of a comp. of *2596* and *2572*; *unveiled*:— uncovered.

178. ἀκατάκριτος **akatakritŏs**, *ak-at-ak´-ree-tos*; from *1* (as a neg. particle) and a der. of *2632*; *without* (legal) *trial*:— uncondemned.

179. ἀκατάλυτος **akatalutŏs**, *ak-at-al´-oo-tos*; from *1* (as a neg. particle) and a der. of *2647*; *indissoluble*, i.e. (fig.) *permanent*:— endless.

180. ἀκατάπαυστος **akatapaustŏs**, *ak-at-ap´-ow-stos*; from *1* (as a neg. particle) and a der. of *2664*; *unrefraining*:— that cannot cease.

181. ἀκαταστασία **akatastasia**, *ak-at-as-tah-see´-ah*; from *182*; *instability*, i.e. *disorder*:— commotion, confusion, tumult.

182. ἀκατάστατος **akatastatŏs**, *ak-at-as´-tat-os*; from *1* (as a neg. particle) and a der. of *2525*; *inconstant*:— unstable.

183. ἀκατάσχετος **akataschĕtŏs**, *ak-at-as´-khet-os*; from *1* (as a neg. particle) and a der. of *2722*; *unrestrainable*:— unruly.

184. Ἀκελδαμά **Akeldama**, *ak-el-dam-ah´*; of Chald. or. [mean. *field of blood*; corresp. to 2506 and 1818]; *Akeldama*, a place near Jerusalem:— Aceldama.

185. ἀκέραιος **akĕraiŏs**, *ak-er´-ah-yos*; from *1* (as a neg. particle) and a presumed der. of *2767*; *unmixed*, i.e. (fig.) *innocent*:— harmless, simple.

186. ἀκλινής **aklinēs**, *ak-lee-nace´*; from *1* (as a neg. particle) and *2827*; *not leaning*, i.e. (fig.) *firm*:— without wavering.

187. ἀκμάζω **akmazō**, *ak-mad´-zo*; from the same as *188*; to *make a point*, i.e. (fig.) *mature*:— be fully ripe.

188. ἀκμήν **akmēn**, *ak-mane´*; acc. of a noun ("*acme*") akin to ἀκή **akē** (a *point*) and mean. the same; adv. *just now*, i.e. *still*:— yet.

189. ἀκοή **akŏē**, *ak-o-ay´*; from *191*; *hearing* (the act, the sense or the thing heard):— audience, ear, fame, which ye heard, hearing, preached, report, rumor.

190. ἀκολουθέω **akŏlŏuthĕō**, *ak-ol-oo-theh´-o*; from *1* (as a particle of union) and κέλευθος **kĕlĕuthŏs** (a *road*); prop. to *be in the same way with*, i.e. to *accompany* (spec. as a disciple):— follow, reach.

191. ἀκούω **akŏuō**, *ak-oo´-o*; a prim. verb; to *hear* (in various senses):— give (in the) audience (of), come (to the ears), ([shall]) hear (-er, -ken), be noised, be reported, understand.

192. ἀκρασία **akrasia**, *ak-ras-ee´-a*; from *193*; *want of self-restraint*:— excess, incontinency.

193. ἀκράτης **akratēs**, *ak-rat´-ace*; from *1* (as a neg. particle) and *2904*; *powerless*, i.e. *without self-control*:— incontinent.

194. ἄκρατος **akratŏs**, *ak´-rat-os*; from *1* (as a neg. particle) and a presumed der. of *2767*; *undiluted*:— without mixture.

195. ἀκρίβεια **akribĕia**, *ak-ree´-bi-ah*; from the same as *196*; *exactness*:— perfect manner.

196. ἀκριβέστατος **akribĕstatŏs**, *ak-ree-bes´-ta-tos*; superlative of ἀκρίβης **akribēs** (a der. of the same as *206*); *most exact*:— most straitest.

197. ἀκριβέστερον **akribĕstĕrŏn**, *ak-ree-bes´-ter-on*; neut. of the comparative of the same as *196*; (adv.) *more exactly*:— more perfect (-ly).

198. ἀκριβόω **akribŏō**, *ak-ree-bŏ´-o*; from the same as *196*; to *be exact*, i.e. *ascertain*:— enquire diligently.

199. ἀκριβῶς **akribōs**, *ak-ree-boce´*; adv. from the same as *196*; *exactly*:— circumspectly, diligently, perfect (-ly).

200. ἀκρίς **akris**, *ak-rece´*; appar. from the same as *206*; a *locust* (as *pointed*, or as *lightning* on the *top* of vegetation):— locust.

201. ἀκροατήριον **akrŏatēriŏn**, *ak-rŏ-at-ay´-ree-on*; from *202*; an *audience-room*:— place of hearing.

202. ἀκροατής **akrŏatēs**, *ak-rŏ-at-ace´*; from ἀκροάομαι **akrŏaŏmai** (to *listen*; appar. an intens. of *191*); a *hearer* (merely):— hearer.

203. ἀκροβυστία **akrŏbustia**, *ak-rob-oos-tee´-ah*; from *206* and prob. a modified form of πόσθη **pŏsthē** (the *penis* or male sexual organ); the *prepuce*; by impl. an *uncircumcised* (i.e. *gentile*, fig. *unregenerate*) state or person:— not circumcised, uncircumcised [with 2192], uncircumcision.

204. ἀκρογωνιαῖος **akrŏgōniaiŏs**, *ak-rog-o-nee-ah´-yos*; from *206* and *1137*; belonging to the extreme *corner*:— chief corner.

205. ἀκροθίνιον **akrŏthiniŏn**, *ak-roth-in´-ee-on*; from *206* and θίς **this** (a *heap*); prop. (in the plur.) the *top of the heap*, i.e. (by impl.) *best of the booty*:— spoils.

206. ἄκρον **akrŏn**, *ak´-ron*; neut. of an adj. prob. akin to the base of *188*; the *extremity*:— one end ... other, tip, top, uttermost part.

207. Ἀκύλας **Akulas**, *ak-oo´-las*; prob. for Lat. *aquila* (an *eagle*); *Akulas*, an Isr.:— Aquila.

208. ἀκυρόω **akurŏō**, *ak-oo-rŏ´-o*; from *1* (as a neg. particle) and *2964*; to *invalidate*:— disannul, make of none effect.

209. ἀκωλύτως **akōlutōs**, *ak-o-loo´-toce*; adv. from a compound of *1* (as a neg. particle) and a der. of *2967*; in an *unhindered manner*, i.e. *freely*:— no man forbidding him.

210. ἄκων **akōn**, *ak´-ohn*; from *1* (as a neg. particle) and *1635*; *unwilling*:— against the will.

211. ἀλάβαστρον **alabastrŏn**, *al-ab´-as-tron*; neut. of ἀλάβαστρος **alabastrŏs** (of uncert. der.), the name of a stone; prop. an "*alabaster*" box, i.e. (by extens.) a perfume *vase* (of any material):— (alabaster) box.

212. ἀλαζονεία **alazŏnĕia**, *al-ad-zon-i´-a*; from *213*; *braggadocio*, i.e. (by impl.) *self-confidence*:— boasting, pride.

213. ἀλαζών **alazōn**, *al-ad-zone´*; from ἄλη **alē** (*vagrancy*); *braggart*:— boaster.

214. ἀλαλάζω **alalazō**, *al-al-ad´-zo*; from ἀλαλή **alalē** (a *shout*, "*halloo*"); to *vociferate*, i.e. (by impl.) to *wail*; fig. to *clang*:— tinkle, wail.

215. ἀλάλητος **alalētŏs**, *al-al´-ay-tos*; from *1* (as a neg. particle) and a der. of *2980*; *unspeakable*:— unutterable, which cannot be uttered.

216. ἄλαλος **alalŏs**, *al´-al-os*; from *1* (as a neg. particle) and *2980*; *mute*:— dumb.

217. ἅλας **halas**, *hal´-as*; from *251*; *salt*; fig. *prudence*:— salt.

218. ἀλείφω **alĕiphō**, *al-i´-fo*; from *1* (as particle of union) and the base of *3045*; to *oil* (with perfume):— anoint.

219. ἀλεκτοροφωνία **alektŏrŏphōnia**, *al-ek-tor-of-o-nee´-ah*; from *220* and *5456*; *cock-crow*, i.e. the third night-watch:— cockcrowing.

220. ἀλέκτωρ **alĕktōr**, *al-ek´-tore*; from ἀλέκω **alĕkō** (to *ward* off); a *cock* or male fowl:— cock.

221. Ἀλεξανδρεύς **Alĕxandrĕus**, *al-ex-and-reuce´*; from Ἀλεξάνδρεια **Alĕxandrĕia** (the city so called); an *Alexandreian* or inhab. of Alexandria:— of Alexandria, Alexandrian.

222. Ἀλεξανδρίνος **Alĕxandrinŏs**, *al-ex-an-dree´-nos*; from the same as *221*; *Alexandrine*, or belonging to Alexandria:— of Alexandria.

223. Ἀλέξανδρος **Alĕxandrŏs**, *al-ex´-an-dros*; from the same as (the first part of) *220* and *435*; *man-defender*; *Alexander*, the name of three Isr. and one other man:— Alexander.

224. ἄλευρον **alĕurŏn**, *al´-yoo-ron*; from ἀλέω **alĕō** (to *grind*); *flour*:— meal.

225. ἀλήθεια **alēthĕia**, *al-ay´-thi-a*; from *227*; *truth*:— true, × truly, truth, verity.

226. ἀληθεύω **alēthĕuō**, *al-ayth-yoo´-o*; from *227*; to *be true* (in doctrine and profession):— speak (tell) the truth.

227. ἀληθής **alēthēs**, *al-ay-thace´*; from *1* (as a neg. particle) and *2990*; *true* (as *not concealing*):— true, truly, truth.

228. ἀληθινός **alēthinŏs**, *al-ay-thee-nos´*; from *227*; *truthful*:— true.

229. ἀλήθω **alēthō**, *al-ay´-tho*; from the same as 224; to *grind*:— grind.

230. ἀληθῶς **alēthōs**, *al-ay-thoce´*; adv. from 227; *truly*:— indeed, surely, of a surety, truly, of a (in) truth, verily, very.

231. ἁλιεύς **haliĕus**, *hal-ee-yoos´*; from 251; a *sailor* (as engaged on the *salt* water), i.e. (by impl.) a *fisher*:— fisher (-man).

232. ἁλιεύω **haliĕuō**, *hal-ee-yoo´-o*; from 231; to *be a fisher*, i.e. (by impl.) to *fish*:— go a-fishing.

233. ἁλίζω **halizō**, *hal-id´-zo*; from 251; to *salt*:— salt.

234. ἀλίσγεμα **alisgĕma**, *al-is´-ghem-ah*; from ἀλισγέω **alisgĕō** (to *soil*); (cer.) *defilement*:— pollution.

235. ἀλλά **alla**, *al-lah´*; neut. plur. of 243; prop. *other* things, i.e. (adv.) *contrariwise* (in many relations):— and, but (even), howbeit, indeed, nay, nevertheless, no, notwithstanding, save, therefore, yea, yet.

236. ἀλλάσσω **allassō**, *al-las´-so*; from 243; to *make different*:— change.

237. ἀλλαχόθεν **allachŏthĕn**, *al-lakh-oth´-en*; from 243; *from elsewhere*:— some other way.

238. ἀλληγορέω **allēgŏrĕō**, *al-lay-gor-eh´-o*; from 243 and ἀγορέω **agŏrĕō** (to *harangue* [comp. 58]); to *allegorize*:— be an allegory [the Gr. word itself].

239. ἀλληλουϊα **allēlŏuïa**, *al-lay-loo´-ee-ah*; of Heb. or. [imper. of 1984 and 3050]; *praise ye Jah!*, an adoring exclamation:— alleluiah.

240. ἀλλήλων **allēlōn**, *al-lay´-lone*; Gen. plur. from 243 redupl.; *one another*:— each other, mutual, one another, (the other), (them-, your-) selves, (selves) together [sometimes with 3326 or 4314].

241. ἀλλογενής **allŏgĕnēs**, *al-log-en-ace´*; from 243 and 1085; *foreign*, i.e. not a Jew:— stranger.

242. ἅλλομαι **hallŏmai**, *hal´-lom-ahee*; mid. voice of appar. a prim. verb; to *jump*; fig. to *gush*:— leap, spring up.

243. ἄλλος **allŏs**, *al´-los*; a prim. word; "*else*," i.e. *different* (in many applications):— more, one (another), (an-, some an-) other (-s, -wise).

244. ἀλλοτριεπίσκοπος **allotriĕpiskŏpŏs**, *al-lot-ree-ep-is´-kop-os*; from 245 and 1985; *overseeing others´* affairs, i.e. a *meddler* (spec. in Gentile customs):— busybody in other men's matters.

245. ἀλλότριος **allŏtriŏs**, *al-lot´-ree-os*; from 243; *another's*, i.e. not one's own; by extens. *foreign, not akin, hostile*:— alien, (an-) other (man's, men's), strange (-r).

246. ἀλλόφυλος **allŏphulŏs**, *al-lof´-oo-los*; from 243 and 5443; *for.*, i.e. (spec.) *Gentile*:— one of another nation.

247. ἄλλως **allōs**, *al´-loce*; adv. from 243; *differently*:— otherwise.

248. ἀλοάω **alŏaō**, *al-o-ah´-o*; from the same as 257; to *tread* out grain:— thresh, tread out the corn.

249. ἄλογος **alŏgŏs**, *al´-og-os*; from 1 (as a neg. particle) and 3056; *irrational*:— brute, unreasonable.

250. ἀλοή **alŏē**, *al-o-ay´*; of for. or. [comp. 174]; *aloes* (the gum):— aloes.

251. ἅλς **hals**, *halce*; a prim. word; "*salt*":— salt.

252. ἁλυκός **halukŏs**, *hal-oo-kos´*; from 251; *briny*:— salt.

253. ἀλυπότερος **alupŏtĕrŏs**, *al-oo-pot´-er-os*; comparative of a comp. of 1 (as a neg. particle) and 3077; *more without grief*:— less sorrowful.

254. ἅλυσις **halusis**, *hal´-oo-sis*; of uncert. der.; a *fetter* or *manacle*:— bonds, chain.

255. ἀλυσιτελής **alusitĕlēs**, *al-oo-sit-el-ace´*; from 1 (as a neg. particle) and the base of 3081; *gainless*, i.e. (by impl.) *pernicious*:— unprofitable.

256. Ἀλφαῖος **Alphaiŏs**, *al-fah´-yos*; of Heb. or. [comp. 2501]; *Alphæus*, an Isr.:— Alpheus.

257. ἅλων **halōn**, *hal´-ohn*; prob. from the base of 1507; a threshing-*floor* (as *rolled* hard), i.e. (fig.) the *grain* (and chaff, as just threshed):— floor.

258. ἀλώπηξ **alōpēx**, *al-o´-pakes*; of uncert. der.; a *fox*, i.e. (fig.) a *cunning* person:— fox.

259. ἅλωσις **halōsis**, *hal´-o-sis*; from a collat. form of 138; *capture*:— be taken.

260. ἅμα **hama**, *ham´-ah*; a prim. particle; prop. *at the "same" time*, but freely used as a prep. or adv. denoting close association:— also, and, together, with (-al).

261. ἀμαθής **amathēs**, *am-ath-ace´*; from 1 (as a neg. particle) and 3129; *ignorant*:— unlearned.

262. ἀμαράντινος **amarantinŏs**, *am-ar-an´-tee-nos*; from 263; "*amaranthine*", i.e. (by impl.) *fadeless*:— that fadeth not away.

263. ἀμάραντος **amarantŏs**, *am-ar´-an-tos*; from 1 (as a neg. particle) and a presumed der. of 3133; *unfading*, i.e. (by impl.) *perpetual*:— that fadeth not away.

264. ἁμαρτάνω **hamartanō**, *ham-ar-tan´-o*; perh. from 1 (as a neg. particle) and the base of 3313; prop. to *miss the mark* (and so *not share* in the prize), i.e. (fig.) to *err*, esp. (mor.) to *sin*:— for your faults, offend, sin, trespass.

265. ἁμάρτημα **hamartēma**, *ham-ar´-tay-mah*; from 264; a *sin* (prop. concr.):— sin.

266. ἁμαρτία **hamartia**, *ham-ar-tee´-ah*; from 264; *sin* (prop. abstr.):— offence, sin (-ful).

267. ἀμάρτυρος **amarturŏs**, *am-ar´-too-ros*; from 1 (as a neg. particle) and a form of 3144; *unattested*:— without witness.

268. ἁμαρτωλός **hamartōlŏs**, *ham-ar-to-los´*; from 264; *sinful*, i.e. a *sinner*:— sinful, sinner.

269. ἄμαχος **amachŏs**, *am´-akh-os*; from 1 (as a neg. particle) and 3163; *peaceable*:— not a brawler.

270. ἀμάω **amaō**, *am-ah´-o*; from 260; prop. to *collect*, i.e. (by impl.) *reap*:— reap down.

271. ἀμέθυστος **amĕthustŏs**, *am-eth-*

oos-tos; from 1 (as a neg. particle) and a der. of 3184; the "*amethyst*" (supposed to *prevent intoxication*):— amethyst.

272. ἀμελέω **amĕlĕō**, *am-el-eh´-o*; from 1 (as a neg. particle) and 3199; to *be careless* of:— make light of, neglect, be negligent, not regard.

273. ἄμεμπτος **amĕmptŏs**, *am´-emp-tos*; from 1 (as a neg. particle) and a der. of 3201; *irreproachable*:— blameless, faultless, unblamable.

274. ἀμέμπτως **amĕmptōs**, *am-emp´-toce*; adv. from 273; *faultlessly*:— blameless, unblamably.

275. ἀμέριμνος **amĕrimnŏs**, *am-er´-im-nos*; from 1 (as a neg. particle) and 3308; *not anxious*:— without care (-fulness), secure.

276. ἀμετάθετος **amĕtathĕtŏs**, *am-et-ath´-et-os*; from 1 (as a neg. particle) and a der. of 3346; *unchangeable*, or (neut. as abstr.) *unchangeability*:— immutable (-ility).

277. ἀμετακίνητος **amĕtakinētŏs**, *am-et-ak-in´-ay-tos*; from 1 (as a neg. particle) and a der. of 3334; *immovable*:— unmovable.

278. ἀμεταμέλητος **amĕtamĕlētŏs**, *am-et-am-el´-ay-tos*; from 1 (as a neg. particle) and a presumed der. of 3338; *irrevocable*:— without repentance, not to be repented of.

279. ἀμετανόητος **amĕtanŏētŏs**, *am-et-an-o´-ay-tos*; from 1 (as a neg. particle) and a presumed der. of 3340; *unrepentant*:— impenitent.

280. ἄμετρος **amĕtrŏs**, *am´-et-ros*; from 1 (as a neg. particle) and 3358; *immoderate*:— (thing) without measure.

281. ἀμήν **amēn**, *am-ane´*; of Heb. or. [543]; prop. *firm*, i.e. (fig.) *trustworthy*; adv. *surely* (often as interj. *so be it*):— amen, verily.

282. ἀμήτωρ **amētōr**, *am-ay´-tore*; from 1 (as a neg. particle) and 3384; *motherless*, i.e. *of unknown maternity*:— without mother.

283. ἀμίαντος **amiantŏs**, *am-ee´-an-tos*; from 1 (as a neg. particle) and a der. of 3392; *unsoiled*, i.e. (fig.) *pure*:— undefiled.

284. Ἀμιναδάβ **Aminadab**, *am-ee-nad-ab´*; of Heb. or. [5992]; *Aminadab*, an Isr.:— Aminadab.

285. ἄμμος **ammŏs**, *am´-mos*; perh. from 260; *sand* (as *heaped* on the beach):— sand.

286. ἀμνός **amnŏs**, *am-nos´*; appar a prim. word; a *lamb*:— lamb.

287. ἀμοιβή **amŏibē**, *am-oy-bay´*; from ἀμείβω **amĕibō** (to *exchange*); *requital*:— requite.

288. ἄμπελος **ampĕlŏs**, *am´-pel-os*; prob. from the base of 297 and that of 257; a *vine* (as *coiling* about a support):— vine.

289. ἀμπελουργός **ampĕlŏurgŏs**, *am-pel-oor-gos´*; from 288 and 2041; a *vine-worker*, i.e. *pruner*:— vine-dresser.

290. ἀμπελών **ampĕlōn**, *am-pel-ohn´*; from 288; a *vineyard*:— vineyard.

291. Ἀμπλίας **Amplias**, *am-plee´-as*; contr. for Lat. *ampliatus* (enlarged); *Amplias*, a Rom. Chr.:— Amplias.

292. ἀμύνομαι **amunŏmai**, *am-oo´-nom-ahee*; mid. voice of a prim. verb; to *ward off* (for oneself), i.e. *protect*:— defend.

293. ἀμφίβληστρον **amphiblēstrŏn**, *am-feeb´-lace-tron*; from a comp. of the base of 297 and 906; a (fishing) *net* (as *thrown about* the fish):— net.

294. ἀμφιέννυμι **amphiĕnnumi**, *am-fee-en´-noo-mee*; from the base of 297 and ἕννυμι **hĕnnumi** (to *invest*); to *enrobe*:— clothe.

295. Ἀμφίπολις **Amphipŏlis**, *am-fip´-ol-is*; from the base of 297 and 4172; a *city surrounded* by a river; *Amphipolis*, a place in Macedonia:— Amphipolis.

296. ἄμφοδον **amphŏdŏn**, *am´-fod-on*; from the base of 297 and 3598; a *fork* in the road:— where two ways meet.

297. ἀμφότερος **amphŏtĕrŏs**, *am-fot´-er-os*; comp. of ἀμφί **amphi** (*around*); (in plur.) *both*:— both.

298. ἀμώμητος **amōmētŏs**, *am-o´-may-tos*; from *1* (as a neg. particle) and a der. of 3469; *unblameable*:— blameless.

299. ἄμωμος **amōmŏs**, *am´-o-mos*; from *1* (as a neg. particle) and 3470; *unblemished* (lit. or fig.):— without blame (blemish, fault, spot), faultless, unblameable.

300. Ἀμών **Amōn**, *am-one´*; of Heb. or. [526]; *Amon*, an Isr.:— Amon.

301. Ἀμώς **Amōs**, *am-oce´*; of Heb. or. [531]; *Amos*, an Isr.:— Amos.

302. ἄν **an**, *an*; a prim. particle, denoting a *supposition, wish, possibility* or *uncertainty*:— [what-, where-, wither-, who-] soever. Usually unexpressed except by the subjunctive or potential mood. Also contr. for *1437*.

303. ἀνά **ana**, *an-ah´*; a prim. prep. and adv.; prop. *up*; but (by extens.) used (distributively) *severally*, or (locally) *at* (etc.):— and, apiece, by, each, every (man), in, through. In compounds (as a prefix) it often means (by impl.) *repetition, intensity, reversal*, etc.

304. ἀναβαθμός **anabathmŏs**, *an-ab-ath-mos´*; from 305 [comp. 898]; a *stairway*:— stairs.

305. ἀναβαίνω **anabainō**, *an-ab-ah´-ee-no*; from 303 and the base of 939; to *go up* (lit. or fig.):— arise, ascend (up), climb (go, grow, rise, spring) up, come (up).

306. ἀναβάλλομαι **anaballŏmai**, *an-ab-al´-lom-ahee*; mid. voice from 303 and 906; to *put off* (for oneself):— defer.

307. ἀναβιβάζω **anabibazō**, *an-ab-ee-bad´-zo*; from 303 and a der. of the base of 939; to *cause to go up*, i.e. *haul* (a net):— draw.

308. ἀναβλέπω **anablepō**, *an-ab-lep´-o*; from 303 and 991; to *look up*; by impl. to *recover sight*:— look (up), see, receive sight.

309. ἀνάβλεψις **anablĕpsis**, *an-ab´-lep-sis*; from 308; *restoration of sight*:— recovery of sight.

310. ἀναβοάω **anabŏaō**, *an-ab-o-ah´-o*; from 303 and 994; to *halloo*:— cry (aloud, out).

311. ἀναβολή **anabŏlē**, *an-ab-ol-ay´*; from 306; a *putting off*:— delay.

312. ἀναγγέλλω **anaggĕllō**, *an-ang-el´-lo*; from 303 and the base of 32; to *announce* (in detail):— declare, rehearse, report, show, speak, tell.

313. ἀναγεννάω **anagĕnnaō**, *an-ag-en-nah´-o*; from 303 and 1080; to *beget* or (by extens.) *bear* (again):— beget, (bear) × (again).

314. ἀναγινώσκω **anaginŏskō**, *an-ag-in-oce´-ko*; from 303 and 1097; to *know again*, i.e. (by extens.) to *read*:— read.

315. ἀναγκάζω **anagkazō**, *an-ang-kad´-zo*; from 318; to *necessitate*:— compel, constrain.

316. ἀναγκαῖος **anagkaiŏs**, *an-ang-kah´-yos*; from 318; *necessary*; by impl. *close* (of kin):— near, necessary, necessity, needful.

317. ἀναγκαστῶς **anagkastŏs**, *an-ang-kas-toce´*; adv. from a der. of 315; *compulsorily*:— by constraint.

318. ἀναγκή **anagkē**, *an-ang-kay´*; from 303 and the base of 43; *constraint* (lit. or fig.); by impl. *distress*:— distress, must needs, (of) necessity (-sary), needeth, needful.

319. ἀναγνωρίζομαι **anagnōrizŏmai**, *an-ag-no-rid´-zom-ahee*; mid. voice from 303 and 1107; to *make* (oneself) *known*:— be made known.

320. ἀνάγνωσις **anagnōsis**, *an-ag´-no-sis*; from 314; (the act of) *reading*:— reading.

321. ἀνάγω **anagō**, *an-ag´-o*; from 303 and 71; to *lead up*; by extens. to *bring out*; spec. to *sail away*:— bring (again), forth, up again), depart, launch (forth), lead (up), loose, offer, sail, set forth, take up.

322. ἀναδείκνυμι **anadĕiknumi**, *an-ad-ike´-noo-mee*; from 303 and 1166; to *exhibit*, i.e. (by impl.) to *indicate, appoint*:— appoint, shew.

323. ἀνάδειξις **anadĕixis**, *an-ad´-ike-sis*; from 322; (the act of) *exhibition*:— shewing.

324. ἀναδέχομαι **anadĕchŏmai**, *an-ad-ekh´-om-ahee*; from 303 and 1209; to *entertain* (as a guest):— receive.

325. ἀναδίδωμι **anadidōmi**, *an-ad-eed´-om-ee*; from 303 and 1325; to *hand over*:— deliver.

326. ἀναζάω **anazaō**, *an-ad-zah´-o* from 303 and 2198; to *recover life* (lit. or fig.):— (be a-) live again, revive.

327. ἀναζητέω **anazētĕō**, *an-ad-zay-teh´-o*; from 303 and 2212; to *search out*:— seek.

328. ἀναζώννυμι **anazōnnumi**, *an-ad-zone´-noo-mee*; from 303 and 2224; to *gird afresh*:— gird up.

329. ἀναζωπυρέω **anazōpurĕō**, *an-ad-zo-poor-eh´-o*; from 303 and a comp. of the base of 2226 and 4442; to *re-enkindle*:— stir up.

330. ἀναθάλλω **anathallō**, *an-ath-al´-lo*;

from 303 and θάλλω **thallō** (to *flourish*); to *revive*:— flourish again.

331. ἀνάθεμα **anathĕma**, *an-ath´-em-ah*; from 394; a (religious) *ban* or (concr.) *excommunicated* (thing or person):— accursed, anathema, curse, × great.

332. ἀναθεματίζω **anathĕmatizō**, *an-ath-em-at-id´-zo*; from 331; to *declare* or *vow* under penalty of execration:— (bind under a) curse, bind with an oath.

333. ἀναθεωρέω **anathĕōrĕō**, *an-ath-eh-o-reh´-o*; from 303 and 2334; to *look again* (i.e. *attentively*) at (lit. or fig.):— behold, consider.

334. ἀνάθημα **anathĕma**, *an-ath´-ay-mah*; from 394 (like 331, but in a good sense]; a *votive offering*:— gift.

335. ἀναίδεια **anaidĕia**, *an-ah´-ee-die-ah´*; from a comp. of *1* (as a neg. particle [comp. 427]) and 127; *impudence*, i.e. (by impl.) *importunity*:— importunity.

336. ἀναίρεσις **anairĕsis**, *an-ah´-ee-res-is*; from 337; (the act of) *killing*:— death.

337. ἀναιρέω **anairĕō**, *an-ahee-reh´-o*; from 303 and (the act. of) 138; to *take up*, i.e. *adopt*; by impl. to *take away* (violently), i.e. *abolish, murder*:— put to death, kill, slay, take away, take up.

338. ἀναίτιος **anaitiŏs**, *an-ah´-ee-tee-os*; from *1* (as a neg. particle) and 159 (in the sense of 156); *innocent*:— blameless, guiltless.

339. ἀνακαθίζω **anakathizō**, *an-ak-ath-id´-zo*; from 303 and 2523; prop. to *set up*, i.e. (refl.) to *sit up*:— sit up.

340. ἀνακαινίζω **anakainizō**, *an-ak-ahee-nid´-zo*; from 303 and a der. of 2537; to *restore*:— renew.

341. ἀνακαινόω **anakainŏō**, *an-ak-ahee-nŏ´-o*; from 303 and a der. of 2537; to *renovate*:— renew.

342. ἀνακαίνωσις **anakainōsis**, *an-ak-ah´-ee-no-sis*; from 341; *renovation*:— renewing.

343. ἀνακαλύπτω **anakaluptō**, *an-ak-al-oop´-to*; from 303 (in the sense of *reversal*) and 2572; to *unveil*:— open, (un-l)taken away.

344. ἀνακάμπτω **anakamptō**, *an-ak-amp´-to*; from 303 and 2578; to *turn back*:— (re-) turn.

345. ἀνάκειμαι **anakĕimai**, *an-ak-i´-mahee*; from 303 and 2749; to *recline* (as a corpse or at a meal):— guest, lean, lie, sit (down, at meat), at the table.

346. ἀνακεφαλαίομαι **anakĕphalaiŏmai**, *an-ak-ef-al-ah´-ee-om-ahee*; from 303 and 2775 (in its or. sense); to *sum up*:— briefly comprehend, gather together in one.

347. ἀνακλίνω **anaklinō**, *an-ak-lee´-no*; from 303 and 2827; to *lean back*:— lay, (make) sit down.

348. ἀνακόπτω **anakŏptō**, *an-ak-op´-to*; from 303 and 2875; to *beat back*, i.e. *check*:— hinder.

349. ἀνακράζω **anakrazō**, *an-ak-rad´-zo*; from 303 and 2896; to *scream up* (aloud):— cry out.

350. ἀνακρίνω **anakrinō**, *an-ak-ree´-no*;

from *303* and *2919;* prop. to *scrutinize,* i.e. (by impl.) *investigate, interrogate, determine:*— ask, question, discern, examine, judge, search.

351. ἀνάκρισις **anakrisis,** *an-ak´-ree-sis;* from *350;* a (judicial) *investigation:*— examination.

352. ἀνακύπτω **anakuptō,** *an-ak-oop´-to;* from *303* (in the sense of *reversal*) and *2955;* to *unbend,* i.e. *rise;* fig. be *elated:*— lift up, look up.

353. ἀναλαμβάνω **analambanō,** *an-al-am-ban´-o;* from *303* and *2983;* to *take up:*— receive up, take (in, unto, up).

354. ἀνάληψις **analēpsis,** *an-al´-aip-sis;* from *353; ascension:*— taking up.

355. ἀναλίσκω **analiskō,** *an-al-is´-ko;* from *303* and a form of the alt. of *138;* prop. to *use up,* i.e. *destroy:*— consume.

356. ἀναλογία **analŏgia,** *an-al-og-ee´-ah;* from a comp. of *303* and *3056; proportion:*— proportion.

357. ἀναλογίζομαι **analŏgizŏmai,** *an-al-og-id´-zom-ahee;* mid. voice from *356;* to *estimate,* i.e. (fig.) *contemplate:*— consider.

358. ἄναλος **analŏs,** *an´-al-os;* from *1* (as a neg. particle) and *251; saltless,* i.e. *insipid:*— × lose saltness.

359. ἀνάλυσις **analusis,** *an-al´-oo-sis;* from *360; departure:*— departure.

360. ἀναλύω **analuō,** *an-al-oo´-o;* from *303* and *3089;* to *break up,* i.e. *depart* (lit. or fig.):— depart, return.

361. ἀναμάρτητος **anamartētŏs,** *an-am-ar´-tay-tos;* from *1* (as a neg. particle) and a presumed der. of *264; sinless:*— that is without sin.

362. ἀναμένω **anamĕnō,** *an-am-en´-o;* from *303* and *3306;* to *await:*— wait for.

363. ἀναμιμνήσκω **anamimnēskō,** *an-am-im-nace´-ko;* from *303* and *3403;* to *remind;* (refl.) to *recollect:*— call to mind, (bring to, call to, put in), remember (-brance).

364. ἀνάμνησις **anamnēsis,** *an-am´-nay-sis;* from *363; recollection:*— remembrance (again).

365. ἀνανεόω **ananĕŏō,** *an-an-neh-o´-o;* from *303* and a der. of *3501;* to *renovate,* i.e. *reform:*— renew.

366. ἀνανήφω **ananēphō,** *an-an-ay´-fo;* from *303* and *3525;* to become *sober again,* i.e. (fig.) *regain* (one's) *senses:*— recover self.

367. Ἀνανίας **Ananias,** *an-an-ee´-as;* of Heb. or. [2608]; *Ananias,* the name of three Isr.:— Ananias.

368. ἀναντίρρητος **anantirrhētŏs,** *an-an-tir´-hray-tos;* from *1* (as a neg. particle) and a presumed der. of a comp. of *473* and *4483; indisputable:*— cannot be spoken against.

369. ἀναντιρρήτως **anantirrhētōs,** *an-an-tir-hray´-toce;* adv. from *368;* promptly:*— without gainsaying.

370. ἀνάξιος **anaxiŏs,** *an-ax´-ee-os;* from *1* (as a neg. particle) and *514; unfit:*— unworthy.

371. ἀναξίως **anaxiōs,** *an-ax-ee´-oce;* adv. from *370; irreverently:*— unworthily.

372. ἀνάπαυσις **anapausis,** *an-ap´-ŏw-sis;* from *373; intermission;* by impl. *recreation:*— rest.

373. ἀναπαύω **anapauō,** *an-ap-ow´-o;* from *303* and *3973;* (refl.) to *repose* (lit. or fig. [be *exempt*], *remain*); by impl. to *refresh:*— take ease, refresh, (give, take) rest.

374. ἀναπείθω **anapĕithō,** *an-ap-i´-tho;* from *303* and *3982;* to *incite:*— persuade.

375. ἀναπέμπω **anapĕmpō,** *an-ap-em´-po;* from *303* and *3992;* to *send up* or *back:*— send (again).

376. ἀνάπηρος **anapērŏs,** *an-ap´-ay-ros);* from *303* (in the sense of *intensity*) and πήρος **pērŏs** (*maimed*); *crippled:*— maimed.

377. ἀναπίπτω **anapiptō,** *an-ap-ip´-to;* from *303* and *4098;* to *fall back,* i.e. *lie down, lean back:*— lean, sit down (to meat).

378. ἀναπληρόω **anaplērŏō,** *an-ap-lay-rŏ´-o;* from *303* and *4137;* to *complete;* by impl. to *occupy, supply;* fig. to *accomplish* (by coincidence or obedience):— fill up, fulfill, occupy, supply.

379. ἀναπολόγητος **anapŏlŏgētŏs,** *an-ap-ol-og´-ay-tos;* from *1* (as a neg. particle) and a presumed der. of *626; indefensible:*— without excuse, inexcuseable.

380. ἀναπτύσσω **anaptussō,** *an-aptoos´-so;* from *303* (in the sense of *reversal*) and *4428;* to *unroll* (a scroll or volume):— open.

381. ἀνάπτω **anaptō,** *an-ap´-to;* from *303* and *681;* to *enkindle:*— kindle, light.

382. ἀναρίθμητος **anarithmētŏs,** *an-arith´-may-tos;* from *1* (as a neg. particle) and a der. of *705; unnumbered,* i.e. *without number:*— innumerable.

383. ἀνασείω **anasĕiō,** *an-as-i´-o;* from *303* and *4579;* fig. to *excite:*— move, stir up.

384. ἀνασκευάζω **anaskĕuazō,** *an-askyoo-ad´-zo;* from *303* (in the sense of *reversal*) and a der. of *4632;* prop. to *pack up* (baggage), i.e. (by impl. and fig.) to *upset:*— subvert.

385. ἀνασπάω **anaspaō,** *an-as-pah´-o;* from *303* and *4685;* to *take up* or *extricate:*— draw up, pull out.

386. ἀνάστασις **anastasis,** *an-as´-tas-is;* from *450;* a *standing up* again, i.e. (lit.) a *resurrection* from death (individual, gen. or by impl. [its author]), or (fig.) a (moral) *recovery* (of spiritual truth):— raised to life again, resurrection, rise from the dead, that should rise, rising again.

387. ἀναστατόω **anastatŏō,** *an-as-tatŏ´-o;* from a der. of *450* (in the sense of *removal*); prop. to *drive out* of home, i.e. (by impl.) to *disturb* (lit. or fig.):— trouble, turn upside down, make an uproar.

388. ἀνασταυρόω **anastaurŏō,** *an-astŏw-rŏ´-o;* from *303* and *4717;* to *recrucify* (fig.):— crucify afresh.

389. ἀναστενάζω **anastĕnazō,** *an-as-*

ten-ad´-zo; from *303* and *4727;* to *sigh deeply:*— sigh deeply.

390. ἀναστρέφω **anastrĕphō,** *an-astref´-o;* from *303* and *4762;* to *overturn;* also to *return;* by impl. to *busy* oneself, i.e. *remain, live:*— abide, behave self, have conversation, live, overthrow, pass, return, be used.

391. ἀναστροφή **anastrŏphē,** *an-as-trof-ay´;* from *390; behavior:*— conversation.

392. ἀνατάσσομαι **anatassŏmai,** *an-at-as´-som-ahee;* from *303* and the mid. voice of *5021;* to *arrange:*— set in order.

393. ἀνατέλλω **anatĕllō,** *an-at-el´-lo;* from *303* and the base of *5056;* to (*cause* to) *arise:*— (a-, make to) rise, at the rising of, spring (up), be up.

394. ἀνατίθεμαι **anatithĕmai,** *an-atith´-em-ahee;* from *303* and the mid. voice of *5087;* to *set forth* (for oneself), i.e. *propound:*— communicate, declare.

395. ἀνατολή **anatŏlē,** *an-at-ol-ay´;* from *393;* a *rising* of light, i.e. *dawn* (fig.); by impl. the *east* (also in plur.):— dayspring, east, rising.

396. ἀνατρέπω **anatrĕpō,** *an-at-rep´-o;* from *303* and the base of *5157;* to *overturn* (fig.):— overthrow, subvert.

397. ἀνατρέφω **anatrĕphō,** *an-at-ref´-o;* from *303* and *5142;* to *rear* (phys. or ment.):— bring up, nourish (up).

398. ἀναφαίνω **anaphainō,** *an-af-ah´-ee-no;* from *303* and *5316;* to *show,* i.e. (refl.) *appear,* or (pass.) to *have pointed out:*— (should) appear, discover.

399. ἀναφέρω **anaphĕrō,** *an-af-er´-o;* from *303* and *5342;* to *take up* (lit. or fig.):— bear, bring (carry, lead) up, offer (up).

400. ἀναφωνέω **anaphōnĕō,** *an-af-o-neh´-o;* from *303* and *5455;* to *exclaim:*— speak out.

401. ἀνάχυσις **anachusis,** *an-akh´-oo-sis;* from a comp. of *303* and χέω **chĕō** (to *pour*); prop. *effusion,* i.e. (fig.) *license:*— excess.

402. ἀναχωρέω **anachōrĕō,** *an-akh-o-reh´-o;* from *303* and *5562;* to *retire:*— depart, give place, go (turn) aside, withdraw self.

403. ἀνάψυξις **anapsuxis,** *an-aps´-ook-sis;* from *404;* prop. a *recovery of breath,* i.e. (fig.) *revival:*— revival.

404. ἀναψύχω **anapsuchō,** *an-aps-oo´-kho;* from *303* and *5594;* prop. to *cool off,* i.e. (fig.) *relieve:*— refresh.

405. ἀνδραποδιστής **andrapŏdistēs,** *an-drap-od-is-tace´;* from a der. of a comp. of *435* and *4228;* an *enslaver* (as bringing *men* to his *feet*):— menstealer.

406. Ἀνδρέας **Andrĕas,** *an-dreh´-as;* from *435; manly; Andreas,* an Isr.:— Andrew.

407. ἀνδρίζομαι **andrizŏmai,** *an-drid´-zom-ahee;* mid. voice from *435;* to *act manly:*— quit like men.

408. Ἀνδρόνικος **Andrŏnikŏs,** *an-dron´-ee-kos;* from *435* and *3534; man of victory; Andronicos,* an Isr.:— Adronicus.

409. ἀνδροφόνος **andrŏphŏnŏs,** *an-drof-*

Greek

on´-os; from 435 and 5408; a murderer:— manslayer.

410. ἀνέγκλητος **anĕgklētŏs**, an-eng´-klay-tos; from 1 (as a neg. particle) and a der. of 1458; unaccused, i.e. (by impl.) irreproachable:— blameless.

411. ἀνεκδιήγητος **anĕkdiēgētŏs**, an-ek-dee-ay´-gay-tos; from 1 (as a neg. particle) and a presumed der. of 1555; not expounded in full, i.e. indescribable:— unspeakable.

412. ἀνεκλάλητος **anĕklalētŏs**, an-ek-lal´-ay-tos; from 1 (as a neg. particle) and a presumed der. of 1583; not spoken out, i.e. (by impl.) unutterable:— unspeakable.

413. ἀνέκλειπτος **anĕklĕiptŏs**, an-ek´-lipe-tos; from 1 (as a neg. particle) and a presumed der. of 1587; not left out, i.e. (by impl.) inexhaustible:— that faileth not.

414. ἀνεκτότερος **anĕktŏtĕrŏs**, an-ek-tot´-er-os; comp. of a der. of 430; more endurable:— more tolerable.

415. ἀνελεήμων **anĕlĕēmōn**, an-eleh-ay´-mone; from 1 (as a neg. particle) and 1655; merciless:— unmerciful.

416. ἀνεμίζω **anemizō**, an-em-id´-zo; from 417; to toss with the wind:— drive with the wind.

417. ἄνεμος **anĕmŏs**, an´-em-os; from the base of 109; wind; (plur.) by impl. (the four) quarters (of the earth):— wind.

418. ἀνένδεκτος **anĕndĕktŏs**, an-en´-dek-tos; from 1 (as a neg. particle) and a der. of the same as 1735; unadmitted, i.e. (by impl.) not supposable:— impossible.

419. ἀνεξερεύνητος **anĕxĕrĕunētŏs**, an-ex-er-yoo´-nay-tos; from 1 (as a neg. particle) and a presumed der. of 1830; not searched out, i.e. (by impl.) inscrutable:— unsearchable.

420. ἀνεξίκακος **anĕxikakŏs**, an-ex-ik´-ak-os; from 430 and 2556; enduring of ill, i.e. forbearing:— patient.

421. ἀνεξιχνίαστος **anĕxichniastŏs**, an-ex-ikh-nee´-as-tos; from 1 (as a neg. particle) and a presumed der. of a comp. of 1537 and a der. of 2487; not tracked out, i.e. (by impl.) untraceable:— past finding out; unsearchable.

422. ἀνεπαίσχυντος **anĕpaischuntŏs**, an-ep-ah´-ee-skhoon-tos; from 1 (as a neg. particle) and a presumed der. of a comp. of 1909 and 153; not ashamed, i.e. (by impl.) irreprehensible:— that needeth not to be ashamed.

423. ἀνεπίληπτος **anĕpilēptŏs**, an-ep-eel´-ape-tos; from 1 (as a neg. particle) and a der. of 1949; not arrested, i.e. (by impl.) inculpable:— blameless, unrebukeable.

424. ἀνέρχομαι **anĕrchŏmai**, an-erkh´-om-ahee; from 303 and 2064; to ascend:— go up.

425. ἄνεσις **anĕsis**, an´-es-is; from 447; relaxation or (fig.) relief:— eased, liberty, rest.

426. ἀνετάζω **anĕtazō**, an-et-ad´-zo; from 303 and ἐτάζω ĕtazō (to test); to

investigate (judicially):— (should have) examine (-d).

427. ἄνευ **anĕu**, an´-yoo; a prim. particle; without:— without. Comp. 1.

428. ἀνεύθετος **anĕuthĕtŏs**, an-yoo´-the-tos; from 1 (as a neg. particle) and 2111; not well set, i.e. inconvenient:— not commodious.

429. ἀνευρίσκω **anĕuriskō**, an-yoo-ris´-ko; from 303 and 2147; to find out:— find.

430. ἀνέχομαι **anĕchŏmai**, an-ekh´-om-ahee; mid. voice from 303 and 2192; to hold oneself up against, i.e. (fig.) put up with:— bear with, endure, forbear, suffer.

431. ἀνέψιος **anĕpsiŏs**, an-eps´-ee-os; from 1 (as a particle of union) and an obs. νέπος nĕpŏs (a brood); prop. akin, i.e. (spec.) a cousin:— sister's son.

432. ἄνηθον **anēthŏn**, an´-ay-thon; prob. of for. or.; dill:— anise.

433. ἀνήκω **anēkō**, an-ay´-ko; from 303 and 2240; to attain to, i.e. (fig.) be proper:— convenient, be fit.

434. ἀνήμερος **anēmĕrŏs**, an-ay´-mer-os; from 1 (as a neg. particle) and ἥμερος hēmĕrŏs (lame); savage:— fierce.

435. ἀνήρ **anēr**, an-ayr´; a prim. word [comp. 444]; a man (prop. as an indiv. male):— fellow, husband, man, sir.

436. ἀνθίστημι **anthistēmi**, anth-is´-tay-mee; from 473 and 2476; to stand against, i.e. oppose:— resist, withstand.

437. ἀνθομολογέομαι **anthŏmŏlŏgĕomai**, anth-om-ol-og-eh´-om-ahee; from 473 and the mid. voice of 3670; to confess in turn, i.e. respond in praise:— give thanks.

438. ἄνθος **anthŏs**, anth´-os; a prim. word; a blossom:— flower.

439. ἀνθρακιά **anthrakia**, anth-rak-ee-ah´; from 440; a bed of burning coals:— fire of coals.

440. ἄνθραξ **anthrax**, anth´-rax; of uncert. der.; a live coal:— coal of fire.

441. ἀνθρωπάρεσκος **anthrōparĕskŏs**, anth-ro-par´-es-kos; from 444 and 700; man-courting, i.e. fawning:— menpleaser.

442. ἀνθρώπινος **anthrōpinŏs**, anth-ro´-pee-nos; from 444; human:— human, common to man, man [-kind], [man-] kind, men's, after the manner of men.

443. ἀνθρωποκτόνος **anthrōpŏktŏnŏs**, anth-ro-pok-ton´-os; from 444 and κτείνω ktĕinō (to kill); a manslayer:— murderer. Comp. 5406.

444. ἄνθρωπος **anthrōpŏs**, anth´-ro-pos; from 435 and ὤψ ōps (the countenance; from 3700); man-faced, i.e. a human being:— certain, man.

445. ἀνθυπατεύω **anthupatĕuō**, anth-oo-pat-yoo´-o; from 446; to act as a proconsul:— be the deputy.

446. ἀνθύπατος **anthupatŏs**, anth-oo´-pat-os; from 473 and a superl. of 5228; instead of the highest officer, i.e. (spec.) a Roman proconsul:— deputy.

447. ἀνίημι **aniēmi**, an-ee´-ay-mee;

from 303 and ἵημι hiēmi (to send); to let up, i.e. (lit.) slacken or (fig.) desert, desist from:— forbear, leave, loose.

448. ἀνίλεως **anilĕōs**, an-ee´-leh-oce; from 1 (as a neg. particle) and 2436; inexorable:— without mercy.

449. ἄνιπτος **aniptŏs**, an´-ip-tos; from 1 (as a neg. particle) and a presumed der. of 3538; without ablution:— unwashen.

450. ἀνίστημι **anistēmi**, an-is´-tay-mee; from 303 and 2476; to stand up (lit. or fig., trans. or intr.):— arise, lift up, raise up (again), rise (again), stand up (-right).

451. Ἄννα **Anna**, an´-nah; of Heb. or. [2584]; Anna, an Israelitess:— Anna.

452. Ἄννας **Annas**, an´-nas; of Heb. or. [2608]; Annas (i.e. 367), an Isr.:— Annas.

453. ἀνόητος **anŏētŏs**, an-o´-ay-tos; from 1 (as a neg. particle) and a der. of 3539; unintelligent; by impl. sensual:— fool (-ish), unwise.

454. ἄνοια **anŏia**, an´-oy-ah; from a comp. of 1 (as a neg. particle) and 3563; stupidity; by impl. rage:— folly, madness.

455. ἀνοίγω **anŏigō**, an-oy´-go; from 303 and οἴγω ŏigō (to open); to open up (lit. or fig., in various applications):— open.

456. ἀνοικοδομέω **anŏikŏdŏmĕō**, an-oy-kod-om-eh´-o; from 303 and 3618; to rebuild:— build again.

457. ἄνοιξις **anŏixis**, an´-oix-is; from 455; opening (throat):— × open.

458. ἀνομία **anŏmia**, an-om-ee´-ah; from 459; illegality, i.e. violation of law or (gen.) wickedness:— iniquity, × transgress (-ion of) the law, unrighteousness.

459. ἄνομος **anŏmŏs**, an´-om-os; from 1 (as a neg. particle) and 3551; lawless, i.e. (neg.) not subject to (the Jewish) law; (by impl. a Gentile), or (pos.) wicked:— without law, lawless, transgressor, unlawful, wicked.

460. ἀνόμως **anŏmōs**, an-om´-oce; adv. from 459; lawlessly, i.e. (spec.) not amenable to (the Jewish) law:— without law.

461. ἀνορθόω **anŏrthŏō**, an-orth-ŏ´-o; from 303 and a der. of the base of 3717; to straighten up:— lift (set) up, make straight.

462. ἀνόσιος **anŏsiŏs**, an-os´-ee-os; from 1 (as a neg. particle) and 3741; wicked:— unholy.

463. ἀνοχή **anŏchē**, an-okh-ay´; from 430; self-restraint, i.e. tolerance:— forbearance.

464. ἀνταγωνίζομαι **antagōnizŏmai**, an-tag-o-nid´-zom-ahee; from 473 and 75; to struggle against (fig.) ["antagonize"]:— strive against.

465. ἀντάλλαγμα **antallagma**, an-tal´-lag-mah; from a comp. of 473 and 236; an equivalent or ransom:— in exchange.

466. ἀνταναπληρόω **antanaplērŏō**, an-tan-ap-lay-rŏ´-o; from 473 and 378; to supplement:— fill up.

467. ἀνταποδίδωμι **antapŏdidōmi**, an-

tap-od-ee´-do-mee; from 473 and 591; to requite (good or evil):— recompense, render, repay.

468. ἀνταπόδομα **antapŏdŏma**, *an-tap-od´-om-ah;* from 467; a requital (prop. the thing):— recompense.

469. ἀνταπόδοσις **antapŏdŏsis**, *an-tap-od´-os-is;* from 467; requital (prop. the act):— reward.

470. ἀνταποκρίνομαι **antapŏkrinŏmai**, *an-tap-ok-ree´-nom-ahee;* from 473 and 611; to contradict or dispute:— answer again, reply against.

471. ἀντέπω **antĕpō**, *an-tep´-o;* from 473 and 2036; to refute or deny:— gainsay, say against.

472. ἀντέχομαι **antĕchŏmai**, *an-tekh´-om-ahee;* from 473 and the mid. voice of 2192; to hold oneself opposite to, i.e. (by impl.) adhere to; by extens. to care for:— hold fast, hold to, support.

473. ἀντί **anti**, *an-tee´;* a prim. particle; opposite, i.e. instead or because of (rarely in addition to):— for, in the room of. Often used in composition to denote contrast, requital, substitution, correspondence, etc.

474. ἀντιβάλλω **antiballō**, *an-tee-bal´-lo;* from 473 and 906; to bandy:— have.

475. ἀντιδιατίθεμαι **antidiatithĕmai**, *an-tee-dee-at-eeth´-em-ahee;* from 473 and 1303; to set oneself opposite, i.e. be disputatious:— that oppose themselves.

476. ἀντίδικος **antidikŏs**, *an-tid´-ee-kos;* from 473 and 1349; an opponent (in a lawsuit); spec. Satan (as the arch-enemy):— adversary.

477. ἀντίθεσις **antithĕsis**, *an-tith´-es-is;* from a comp. of 473 and 5087; opposition, i.e. a conflict (of theories):— opposition.

478. ἀντικαθίστημι **antikathistĕmi**, *an-tee-kath-is´-tay-mee;* from 473 and 2525; to set down (troops) against, i.e. withstand:— resist.

479. ἀντικαλέω **antikalĕō**, *an-tee-kal-eh´-o;* from 473 and 2564; to invite in return:— bid again.

480. ἀντίκειμαι **antikĕimai**, *an-tik´-i-mahee;* from 473 and 2749; to lie opposite, i.e. be adverse (fig. repugnant) to:— adversary, be contrary, oppose.

481. ἀντικρύ **antikru**, *an-tee-kroo´;* prol. from 473; opposite:— over against.

482. ἀντιλαμβάνομαι **antilambanŏmai**, *an-tee-lam-ban´-om-ahee;* from 473 and the mid. voice of 2983; to take hold of in turn, i.e. succor; also to participate:— help, partaker, support.

483. ἀντιλέγω **antilĕgō**, *an-til´-eg-o;* from 473 and 3004; to dispute, refuse:— answer again, contradict, deny, gainsay (-er), speak against.

484. ἀντίληψις **antilĕpsis**, *an-til´-ape-sis;* from 482; relief:— help.

485. ἀντιλογία **antilŏgia**, *an-tee-log-ee´-ah;* from a der. of 483; dispute, disobedience:— contradiction, gainsaying, strife.

486. ἀντιλοιδορέω **antilŏidŏrĕō**, *an-tee-loy-dor-eh´-o;* from 473 and 3058; to rail in reply:— revile again.

487. ἀντίλυτρον **antilutrŏn**, *an-til´-oo-tron;* from 473 and 3083; a redemption-price:— ransom.

488. ἀντιμετρέω **antimĕtrĕō**, *an-tee-met-reh´-o;* from 473 and 3354; to mete in return:— measure again.

489. ἀντιμισθία **antimisthia**, *an-tee-mis-thee´-ah;* from a comp. of 473 and 3408; requital, correspondence:— recompense.

490. Ἀντιόχεια **Antiŏchĕia**, *an-tee-okh´-i-ah;* from Ἀντίοχος **Antiŏchus** (a Syrian king); Antiochia, a place in Syria:— Antioch.

491. Ἀντιοχεύς **Antiŏchĕus**, *an-tee-okh-yoos´;* from 490; an Antiochian or inhab. of Antiochia:— of Antioch.

492. ἀντιπαρέρχομαι **antiparĕrchŏmai**, *an-tee-par-er´-khom-ahee;* from 473 and 3928; to go along opposite:— pass by on the other side.

493. Ἀντίπας **Antipas**, *an-tee´-pas;* contr. for a comp. of 473 and a der. of 3962; Antipas, a Chr.:— Antipas.

494. Ἀντιπατρίς **Antipatris**, *an-tip-at-rece´;* from the same as 493; Antipatris, a place in Pal.:— Antipatris.

495. ἀντιπέραν **antipĕran**, *an-tee-per´-an;* from 473 and 4008; on the opposite side:— over against.

496. ἀντιπίπτω **antipiptō**, *an-tee-pip´-to;* from 473 and 4098 (incl. its alt.); to oppose:— resist.

497. ἀντιστρατεύομαι **antistratĕuŏmai**, *an-tee-strat-yoo´-om-ahee;* from 473 and 4754; (fig.) to attack, i.e. (by impl.) destroy:— war against.

498. ἀντιτάσσομαι **antitassŏmai**, *an-tee-tas´-som-ahee;* from 473 and the mid. voice of 5021; to range oneself against, i.e. oppose:— oppose themselves, resist.

499. ἀντίτυπον **antitupŏn**, *an-teet´-oo-pon;* neut. of a comp. of 473 and 5179; corresponding ["antitype"], i.e. a representative, counterpart:— (like) figure (whereunto).

500. ἀντίχριστος **antichristŏs**, *an-tee´-khris-tos;* from 473 and 5547; an opponent of the Messiah:— antichrist.

501. ἀντλέω **antlĕō**, *ant-leh-o;* from ἄντλος **antlŏs** (the hold of a ship); bale up (prop. bilge water), i.e. dip water (with a bucket, pitcher, etc.):— draw (out).

502. ἄντλημα **antlēma**, *ant´-lay-mah;* from 501; a baling-vessel:— thing to draw with.

503. ἀντοφθαλμέω **antŏphthalmĕō**, *ant-of-thal-meh´-o;* from a compound of 473 and 3788; to face:— bear up into.

504. ἄνυδρος **anudrŏs**, *an´-oo-dros;* from 1 (as a neg. particle) and 5204; waterless, i.e. dry:— dry, without water.

505. ἀνυπόκριτος **anupŏkritŏs**, *an-oo-pok´-ree-tos;* from 1 (as a neg. particle) and a presumed der. of 5271; undissembled, i.e. sincere:— without dissimulation (hypocrisy), unfeigned.

506. ἀνυπότακτος **anupŏtaktŏs**, *an-oo-pot´-ak-tos;* from 1 (as a neg. particle) and a presumed der. of 5293; unsub-

dued, i.e. insubordinate (in fact or temper):— disobedient, that is not put under, unruly.

507. ἄνω **anō**, *an´-o;* adv. from 473; upward or on the top:— above, brim, high, up.

508. ἀνώγεον **anōgĕŏn**, *an-ogue´-eh-on* (or, ἀνάγαιον *an-ag-ahee´-on;* from 507 and 1093; above the ground, i.e. (prop.) the second floor of a building; used for a dome or a balcony on the upper story:— upper room.

509. ἄνωθεν **anōthĕn**, *an´-o-then;* from 507; from above; by anal. from the first; by impl. anew:— from above, again, from the beginning (very first), the top.

510. ἀνωτερικός **anōtĕrikŏs**, *an-o-ter-ee-kos´;* from 511; superior, i.e. (locally) more remote:— upper.

511. ἀνώτερος **anōtĕrŏs**, *an-o´-ter-os;* comparative degree of 507; upper, i.e. (neut. as adv.) to a more conspicuous place, in a former part of the book:— above, higher.

512. ἀνωφελές **anōphĕlĕs**, *an-o-fel´-ace;* from 1 (as a neg. particle) and the base of 5624; useless or (neut.) inutility:— unprofitable (-ness).

513. ἀξίνη **axinē**, *ax-ee´-nay;* prob. from ἄγνυμι **agnumi** (to break; comp. 4486); an axe:— axe.

514. ἄξιος **axiŏs**, *ax´-ee-os;* prob. from 71; deserving, comparable or suitable (as if drawing praise):— due reward, meet, lun-l worthy.

515. ἀξιόω **axiŏō**, *ax-ee-ŏ´-o;* from 514; to deem entitled or fit:— desire, think good, count (think) worthy.

516. ἀξίως **axiōs**, *ax-ee´-oce;* adv. from 514; appropriately:— as becometh, after a godly sort, worthily (-thy).

517. ἀόρατος **aŏratŏs**, *ah-or´-at-os;* from 1 (as a neg. particle) and 3707; invisible:— invisible (thing).

518. ἀπαγγέλλω **apaggĕllō**, *ap-ang-el´-lo;* from 575 and the base of 32; to announce:— bring word (again), declare, report, shew (again), tell.

519. ἀπάγχομαι **apagchŏmai**, *ap-ang´-khom-ahee* from 575 and ἄγχω **agchō** (to choke; akin to the base of 43); to strangle oneself off (i.e. to death):— hang himself.

520. ἀπάγω **apagō**, *ap-ag´-o;* from 575 and 71; to take off (in various senses):— bring, carry away, lead (away), put to death, take away.

521. ἀπαίδευτος **apaidĕutŏs**, *ap-ah´-ee-dyoo-tos;* from 1 (as a neg. particle) and a der. of 3811; uninstructed, i.e. (fig.) stupid:— unlearned.

522. ἀπαίρω **apairō**, *ap-ah´-ee-ro;* from 575 and 142; to lift off, i.e. remove:— take (away).

523. ἀπαιτέω **apaitĕō**, *ap-ah´-ee-teh-o;* from 575 and 154; to demand back:— ask again, require.

524. ἀπαλγέω **apalgĕō**, *ap-alg-eh´-o;* from 575 and ἀλγέω **algĕō** (to smart); to grieve out, i.e. become apathetic:— be past feeling.

525. ἀπαλλάσσω **apallassō**, *ap-al-las´-so;* from 575 and 236; to change away,

i.e. *release*, (refl.) *remove:*— deliver, depart.

526. ἀπαλλοτριόω **apallŏtriŏŏ**, *ap-al-lot-ree-ŏ´-o*; from 575 and a der. of 245; to *estrange away*, i.e. (pass. and fig.) to *be non-participant:*— alienate, be alien.

527. ἁπαλός **hapalŏs**, *hap-al-os´*; of uncert. der.; *soft:*— tender.

528. ἀπαντάω **apantaŏ**, *ap-an-tah´-o*; from 575 and a der. of 473; to *meet away*, i.e. *encounter:*— meet.

529. ἀπάντησις **apantēsis**, *ap-an´-tay-sis*; from 528; a (friendly) *encounter:*— meet.

530. ἅπαξ **hapax**, *hap´-ax*; prob. from 537; *one* (or a *single*) *time* (numerically or conclusively):— once.

531. ἀπαράβατος **aparabatŏs**, *ap-ar-ab´-at-os*; from 1 (as a neg. particle) and a der. of 3845; *not passing away*, i.e. *untransferable* (perpetual):— unchangeable.

532. ἀπαρασκεύαστος **aparaskĕuastŏs**, *ap-ar-ask-yoo´-as-tos*; from 1 (as a neg. particle) and a der. of 3903; *unready:*— unprepared.

533. ἀπαρνέομαι **aparnĕŏmai**, *ap-ar-neh´-om-ahee*; from 575 and 720; to *deny utterly*, i.e. *disown, abstain:*— deny.

534. ἀπάρτι **aparti**, *ap-ar´-tee*; from 575 and 737; *from now*, i.e. *henceforth* (*already*):— from henceforth.

535. ἀπαρτισμός **apartismŏs**, *ap-ar-tis-mos´*; from a der. of 534; *completion:*— finishing.

536. ἀπαρχή **aparchē**, *ap-ar-khay´*; from a compound of 575 and 756; a *beginning* of sacrifice, i.e. the (Jewish) *first-fruit* (fig.):— first-fruits.

537. ἅπας **hapas**, *hap´-as*; from 1 (as a particle of union) and 3956; *absolutely all* or (sing.) *every* one:— all (things), every (one), whole.

538. ἀπατάω **apataŏ**, *ap-at-ah´-o*; of uncert. der.; to *cheat*, i.e. *delude:*— deceive.

539. ἀπάτη **apatē**, *ap-at´-ay*; from 538; *delusion:*— deceit (-ful,fulness), deceivableness (-ving).

540. ἀπάτωρ **apatōr**, *ap-at´-ore*; from 1 (as a neg. particle) and 3962; *fatherless*, i.e. *of unrecorded paternity:*— without father.

541. ἀπαύγασμα **apaugasma**, *ap-ŏw´-gas-mah*; from a compound of 575 and 826; an *off-flash*, i.e. *effulgence:*— brightness.

542. ἀπείδω **apĕidō**, *ap-i´-do*; from 575 and the same as 1492; to *see fully:*— see.

543. ἀπείθεια **apĕithĕia**, *ap-i´-thi-ah*; from 545; *disbelief* (obstinate and rebellious):— disobedience, unbelief.

544. ἀπειθέω **apĕithĕō**, *ap-i-theh´-o*; from 545; to *disbelieve* (wilfully and perversely):— not believe, disobedient, obey not, unbelieving.

545. ἀπειθής **apĕithēs**, *ap-i-thace´*; from 1 (as a neg. particle) and 3982; *unpersuadable*, i.e. *contumacious:*— disobedient.

546. ἀπειλέω **apĕilĕō**, *ap-i-leh´-o*; of uncert. der.; to *menace*; by impl. to *forbid:*— threaten.

547. ἀπειλή **apĕilē**, *ap-i-lay´*; from 546; a *menace:*— × straitly, threatening.

548. ἄπειμι **apĕimi**, *ap´-i-mee*; from 575 and 1510; to *be away:*— be absent. Comp. 549.

549. ἄπειμι **apĕimi**, *ap´-i-mee*; from 575 and εἶμι **ĕimi** (to go); to *go away:*— go. Comp. 548.

550. ἀπειπόμην **apĕipŏmēn**, *ap-i-pom´-ane*; refl. past of a compound of 575 and 2036; to *say off* for oneself, i.e. *disown:*— renounce.

551. ἀπείραστος **apĕirastŏs**, *ap-i´-ras-tos*; from 1 (as a neg. particle) and a presumed der. of 3987; *untried*, i.e. *not temptable:*— not to be tempted.

552. ἄπειρος **apĕirŏs**, *ap´-i-ros*; from 1 (as a neg. particle) and 3984; *inexperienced*, i.e. *ignorant:*— unskillful.

553. ἀπεκδέχομαι **apĕkdĕchŏmai**, *ap-ek-dekh´-om-ahee*; from 575 and 1551; to *expect fully:*— look (wait) for.

554. ἀπεκδύομαι **apĕkduŏmai**, *ap-ek-doo´-om-ahee*; mid. voice from 575 and 1562; to *divest wholly* oneself, or (for oneself) *despoil:*— put off, spoil.

555. ἀπέκδυσις **apĕkdusis**, *ap-ek´-doo-sis*; from 554; *divestment:*— putting off.

556. ἀπελαύνω **apĕlaunō**, *ap-el-ŏw´-no*; from 575 and 1643; to *dismiss:*— drive.

557. ἀπελεγμός **apĕlĕgmŏs**, *ap-el-eg-mos´*; from a compound of 575 and 1651; *refutation*, i.e. (by impl.) *contempt:*— nought.

558. ἀπελεύθερος **apĕlĕuthĕrŏs**, *ap-el-yoo´-ther-os*; from 575 and 1658; one *freed away*, i.e. a *freedman:*— freeman.

559. Ἀπελλῆς **Apĕllēs**, *ap-el-lace´*; of Lat. or.; *Apelles*, a Chr.:— Apelles.

560. ἀπελπίζω **apĕlpizō**, *ap-el-pid´-zo*; from 575 and 1679; to *hope out*, i.e. *fully expect:*— hope for again.

561. ἀπέναντι **apĕnanti**, *ap-en´-an-tee*; from 575 and 1725; *from in front*, i.e. *opposite, before* or *against:*— before, contrary, over against, in the presence of.

ἀπέπω **apĕpō**. See 550.

562. ἀπέραντος **apĕrantŏs**, *ap-er´-an-tos*; from 1 (as a neg. particle) and a second. der. of 4008; *unfinished*, i.e. (by impl.) *interminable:*— endless.

563. ἀπερισπάστως **apĕrispastōs**, *ap-er-is-pas-toce´*; adv. from a compound of 1 (as a neg. particle) and a presumed der. of 4049; *undistractedly*, i.e. *free from* (domestic) *solicitude:*— without distraction.

564. ἀπερίτμητος **apĕritmētŏs**, *ap-er-eet´-may-tos*; from 1 (as a neg. particle) and a presumed der. of 4059; *uncircumcised* (fig.):— uncircumcised.

565. ἀπέρχομαι **apĕrchŏmai**, *ap-erkh´-om-ahee*; from 575 and 2064; to *go off* (i.e. *depart*), *aside* (i.e. *apart*) or *behind* (i.e. *follow*), lit. or fig.:— come, depart, go (aside, away, back, out, ... ways), pass away, be past.

566. ἀπέχει **apĕchĕi**, *ap-ekh´-i*; third

pers. sing. pres. ind. act. of 568 used impers.; *it is sufficient:*— it is enough.

567. ἀπέχομαι **apĕchŏmai**, *ap-ekh´-om-ahee*; mid. voice (refl.) of 568; to *hold oneself off*, i.e. *refrain:*— abstain.

568. ἀπέχω **apĕchō**, *ap-ekh´-o*; from 575 and 2192; (act.) to *have out*, i.e. *receive in full*; (intr.) to *keep* (oneself) *away*, i.e. *be distant* (lit. or fig.):— be, have, receive.

569. ἀπιστέω **apistĕō**, *ap-is-teh´-o*; from 571; to *be unbelieving*, i.e. (trans.) *disbelieve*, or (by impl.) *disobey:*— believe not.

570. ἀπιστία **apistia**, *ap-is-tee´-ah*; from 571; *faithlessness*, i.e. (neg.) *disbelief* (*want* of Chr. faith), or (pos.) *unfaithfulness* (*disobedience*):— unbelief.

571. ἄπιστος **apistŏs**, *ap´-is-tos*; from 1 (as a neg. particle) and 4103; (act.) *disbelieving*, i.e. *without* Chr. *faith* (spec. a *heathen*); (pass.) *untrustworthy* (person), or *incredible* (thing):— that believeth not, faithless, incredible thing, infidel, unbeliever (-ing).

572. ἁπλότης **haplŏtēs**, *hap-lot´-ace*; from 573; *singleness*, i.e. (subj.) *sincerity* (*without dissimulation* or *self-seeking*), or (obj.) *generosity* (*copious bestowal*):— bountifulness, liberal (-ity), simplicity, singleness.

573. ἁπλοῦς **haplŏus**, *hap-looce´*; prob. from 1 (as a particle of union) and the base of 4120; prop. *folded together*, i.e. *single* (fig. *clear*):— single.

574. ἁπλῶς **haplōs**, *hap-loce´*; adv. from 573 (in the obj. sense of 572); *bountifully:*— liberally.

575. ἀπό **apŏ**, *apŏ´*; a primary particle; "*off*," i.e. *away* (from something near), in various senses (of place, time, or relation; lit. or fig.):— (× here-) after, ago, at, because of, before, by (the space of), for (-th), from, in, (out) of, off, (up-) on (-ce), since, with. In composition (as a prefix) it usually denotes *separation, departure, cessation, completion, reversal*, etc.

576. ἀποβαίνω **apŏbainō**, *ap-ob-ah´-ee-no*; from 575 and the base of 939; lit. to *disembark*; fig. to *eventuate:*— become, go out, turn.

577. ἀποβάλλω **apŏballō**, *ap-ob-al´-lo*; from 575 and 906; to *throw off*; fig. to *lose:*— cast away.

578. ἀποβλέπω **apŏblĕpō**, *ap-ob-lep´-o*; from 575 and 991; to *look away* from everything else, i.e. (fig.) intently *regard:*— have respect.

579. ἀπόβλητος **apŏblētŏs**, *ap-ob´-lay-tos*; from 577; *cast off*, i.e. (fig.) such as to *be rejected:*— be refused.

580. ἀποβολή **apŏbŏlē**, *ap-ob-ol-ay´*; from 577; *rejection*; fig. *loss:*— casting away, loss.

581. ἀπογενόμενος **apŏgĕnŏmĕnŏs**, *ap-og-en-om´-en-os*; past part. of a compound of 575 and 1096; *absent*, i.e. *deceased* (fig. *renounced*):— being dead.

582. ἀπογραφή **apŏgraphē**, *ap-og-raf-ay´*; from 583; an *enrollment*; by impl. an *assessment:*— taxing.

583. ἀπογράφω **apŏgraphō**, *ap-og-raf-*

o; from 575 and 1125; to write off (a copy or list), i.e. enroll:— tax, write.

584. ἀποδείκνυμι apŏdĕiknumi, ap-od-ike´-noo-mee; from 575 and 1166; to show off, i.e. exhibit; fig. to demonstrate, i.e. accredit:— (ap-) prove, set forth, shew.

585. ἀπόδειξις apŏdĕixis, ap-od´-ike-sis; from 584; manifestation:— demonstration.

586. ἀποδεκατόω apŏdĕkatŏō, ap-od-ek-at-ŏ´-o; from 575 and 1183; to tithe (as debtor or creditor):— (give, pay, take) tithe.

587. ἀπόδεκτος apŏdĕktŏs, ap-od´-ek-tos; from 588; accepted, i.e. agreeable:— acceptable.

588. ἀποδέχομαι apŏdĕchŏmai, ap-od-ekh´-om-ahee; from 575 and 1209; to take fully, i.e. welcome (persons), approve (things):— accept, receive (gladly).

589. ἀποδημέω apŏdēmĕō, ap-od-ay-meh´-o; from 590; to go abroad, i.e. visit a foreign land:— go (travel) into a far country, journey.

590. ἀπόδημος apŏdēmŏs, ap-od´-ay-mos; from 575 and 1218; absent from one's own people, i.e. a foreign traveller:— taking a far journey.

591. ἀποδίδωμι apŏdidōmi, ap-od-eed´-o-mee; from 575 and 1325; to give away, i.e. up, over, back, etc. (in various applications):— deliver (again), give (again), (re-) pay (-ment be made), perform, recompense, render, requite, restore, reward, sell, yield.

592. ἀποδιορίζω apŏdiŏrizō, ap-od-ee-or-id´-zo; from 575 and a compound of 1223 and 3724; to disjoin (by a boundary, fig. a party):— separate.

593. ἀποδοκιμάζω apŏdŏkimazō, ap-od-ok-ee-mad´-zo; from 575 and 1381; to disapprove, i.e. (by impl.) to repudiate:— disallow, reject.

594. ἀποδοχή apŏdŏchē, ap-od-okh-ay´; from 588; acceptance:— acceptation.

595. ἀπόθεσις apŏthĕsis, ap-oth´-es-is; from 659; a laying aside (lit. or fig.):— putting away (off).

596. ἀποθήκη apŏthēkē, ap-oth-ay´-kay; from 659; a repository, i.e. granary:— barn, garner.

597. ἀποθησαυρίζω apŏthēsaurizō, ap-oth-ay-sŏw-rid´-zo; from 575 and 2343; to treasure away:— lay up in store.

598. ἀποθλίβω apŏthlibō, ap-oth-lee´-bo; from 575 and 2346; to crowd (from every side):— press.

599. ἀποθνήσκω apŏthnēskō, ap-oth-nace´-ko; from 575 and 2348; to die off (lit. or fig.):— be dead, death, die, lie a-dying, be slain (x with).

600. ἀποκαθίστημι apŏkathistēmi, ap-ok-ath-is´-tay-mee; from 575 and 2525; to reconstitute (in health, home or organization):— restore (again).

601. ἀποκαλύπτω apŏkaluptō, ap-ok-al-oop´-to; from 575 and 2572; to take off the cover, i.e. disclose:— reveal.

602. ἀποκάλυψις apŏkalupsis, ap-ok-al´-oop-sis; from 601; disclosure:— ap-

pearing, coming, lighten, manifestation, be revealed, revelation.

603. ἀποκαραδοκία apŏkaradŏkia, ap-ok-ar-ad-ok-ee´-ah; from a compound of 575 and a comp. of κάρα kara (the head) and 1380 (in the sense of watching); intense anticipation:— earnest expectation.

604. ἀποκαταλλάσσω apŏkatallassō, ap-ok-at-al-las´-so; from 575 and 2644; to reconcile fully:— reconcile.

605. ἀποκατάστασις apŏkatastasis, ap-ok-at-as´-tas-is; from 600; reconstitution:— restitution.

606. ἀπόκειμαι apŏkĕimai, ap-ok´-i-mahee; from 575 and 2749; to be reserved; fig. to await:— be appointed, (be) laid up.

607. ἀποκεφαλίζω apŏkĕphalizō, ap-ok-ef-al-id´-zo; from 575 and 2776; to decapitate:— behead.

608. ἀποκλείω apŏklĕiō, ap-ok-li´-o; from 575 and 2808; to close fully:— shut up.

609. ἀποκόπτω apŏkŏptō, ap-ok-op´-to; from 575 and 2875; to amputate; refl. (by irony) to mutilate (the privy parts):— cut off. Comp. 2699.

610. ἀπόκριμα apŏkrima, ap-ok´-ree-mah; from 611 (in its orig. sense of judging); a judicial decision:— sentence.

611. ἀποκρίνομαι apŏkrinŏmai, ap-ok-ree´-nom-ahee; from 575 and κρίνω krinō) to conclude for oneself, i.e. (by impl.) to respond; by Heb. [comp. 6030] to begin to speak (where an address is expected):— answer.

612. ἀπόκρισις apŏkrisis, ap-ok´-ree-sis; from 611; a response:— answer.

613. ἀποκρύπτω apŏkruptō, ap-ok-roop´-to; from 575 and 2928; to conceal away (i.e. fully); fig. to keep secret:— hide.

614. ἀπόκρυφος apŏkruphŏs, ap-ok´-roo-fos; from 613; secret; by impl. treasured:— hid, kept secret.

615. ἀποκτείνω apŏktĕinō, ap-ok-ti´-no; from 575 and κτείνω ktĕinō (to slay); to kill outright; fig. to destroy:— put to death, kill, slay.

616. ἀποκυέω apŏkuĕō, ap-ok-oo-eh´-o; from 575 and the base of 2949; to breed forth, i.e. (by transf.) to generate (fig.):— beget, bring forth.

617. ἀποκυλίω apŏkuliō, ap-ok-oo-lee´-o; from 575 and 2947; to roll away:— roll away (back).

618. ἀπολαμβάνω apŏlambanō, ap-ol-am-ban´-o; from 575 and 2983; to receive (spec. in full, or as a host); also to take aside:— receive, take.

619. ἀπόλαυσις apŏlausis, ap-ol´-ow-sis; from a compound of 575 and λαύω lauō (to enjoy); full enjoyment:— enjoy (-ment).

620. ἀπολείπω apŏlĕipō, ap-ol-ipe´-o; from 575 and 3007; to leave behind (pass. remain); by impl. to forsake:— leave, remain.

621. ἀπολείχω apŏlĕichō, ap-ol-i´-kho; from 575 and λείχω lĕichō (to "lick"); to lick clean:— lick.

622. ἀπόλλυμι apŏllumi, ap-ol´-loo-mee; from 575 and the base of 3639; to destroy fully (refl. to perish, or lose), lit. or fig.:— destroy, die, lose, mar, perish.

623. Ἀπολλύων Apŏlluōn, ap-ol-loo´-ohn; act. part. of 622; a destroyer (i.e. Satan):— Apollyon.

624. Ἀπολλωνία Apŏllōnia, ap-ol-lo-nee´-ah; from the pagan deity Ἀπόλλων Apŏllōn (i.e. the sun; from 622); Apollonia, a place in Macedonia:— Apollonia.

625. Ἀπολλῶς Apŏllōs, ap-ol-loce´; prob. from the same as 624; Apollos, an Isr.:— Apollos.

626. ἀπολογέομαι apŏlŏgĕŏmai, ap-ol-og-eh´-om-ahee; mid. voice from a compound of 575 and 3056; to give an account (legal plea) of oneself, i.e. exculpate (self):— answer (for self), make defence, excuse (self), speak for self.

627. ἀπολογία apŏlŏgia, ap-ol-og-ee´-ah; from the same as 626; a plea ("apology"):— answer (for self), clearing of self, defence.

628. ἀπολούω apŏlŏuō, ap-ol-oo´-o; from 575 and 3068; to wash fully, i.e. (fig.) have remitted (refl.):— wash (away).

629. ἀπολύτρωσις apŏlutrōsis, ap-ol-oo´-tro-sis; from a compound of 575 and 3083; (the act) ransom in full, i.e. (fig.) riddance, or (spec.) Chr. salvation:— deliverance, redemption.

630. ἀπολύω apŏluō, ap-ol-oo´-o; from 575 and 3089; to free fully, i.e. (lit.) relieve, release, dismiss (refl. depart), or (fig.) let die, pardon or (spec.) divorce:— (let) depart, dismiss, divorce, forgive, let go, loose, put (send) away, release, set at liberty.

631. ἀπομάσσομαι apŏmassŏmai, ap-om-as´-som-ahee; mid. voice from 575 and μάσσω massō to squeeze, knead, smear); to scrape away:— wipe off.

632. ἀπονέμω apŏnĕmō, ap-on-em´-o; from 575 and the base of 3551; to apportion, i.e. bestow:— give.

633. ἀπονίπτω apŏniptō, ap-on-ip´-to; from 575 and 3538; to wash off (refl. one's own hands symb.):— wash.

634. ἀποπίπτω apŏpiptō, ap-op-ip´-to; from 575 and 4098; to fall off:— fall.

635. ἀποπλανάω apŏplanaō, ap-op-lan-ah´-o; from 575 and 4105; to lead astray (fig.); pass. to stray (from truth):— err, seduce.

636. ἀποπλέω apŏplĕō, ap-op-leh´-o; from 575 and 4126; to set sail:— sail away.

637. ἀποπλύνω apŏplunō, ap-op-loo´-no; from 575 and 4150; to rinse off:— wash.

638. ἀποπνίγω apŏpnigō, ap-op-nee´-go; from 575 and 4155; to stifle (by drowning or overgrowth):— choke.

639. ἀπορέω apŏrĕō, ap-or-eh´-o; from a compound of 1 (as a neg. particle) and the base of 4198; to have no way out, i.e. be at a loss (mentally):— (stand in) doubt, be perplexed.

640. ἀπορία apŏria, ap-or-ee´-a; from the same as 639; a (state of) quandary:— perplexity.

641. ἀπορρίπτω **apŏrrhiptō**, ap-or-hrip´-to; from 575 and 4496; to *hurl off*, i.e. *precipitate* (oneself):— cast.

642. ἀπορφανίζω **apŏrphanizō**, ap-or-fan-id´-zo; from 575 and a der. of 3737; to *bereave wholly*, i.e. (fig.) *separate* (from intercourse):— take.

643. ἀποσκευάζω **apŏskĕuazō**, ap-osk-yoo-ad´-zo; from 575 and a der. of 4632; to *pack up* (one's) *baggage*:— take up ... carriages.

644. ἀποσκίασμα **apŏskiasma**, ap-os-kee´-as-mah; from a compound of 575 and a der. of 4639; a *shading off*, i.e. *obscuration*:— shadow.

645. ἀποσπάω **apŏspaō**, ap-os-pah´-o; from 575 and 4685; to *drag forth*, i.e. (lit.) *unsheathe* (a sword), or rel. (with a degree of force impl.) *retire* (pers. or factiously):— (with-) draw (away), after we were gotten from.

646. ἀποστασία **apŏstasia**, ap-os-tas-ee´-ah; fem. of the same as 647; *defection* from truth (prop. the state) ["apostasy"]:— falling away, forsake.

647. ἀποστάσιον **apŏstasiŏn**, ap-os-tas´-ee-on; neut. of a (presumed) adj. from a der. of 868; prop. something *separative*, i.e. (spec.) *divorce*:— (writing of) divorcement.

648. ἀποστεγάζω **apŏstĕgazō**, ap-os-teg-ad´-zo; from 575 and a der. of 4721; to *unroof*:— uncover.

649. ἀποστέλλω **apŏstĕllō**, ap-os-tel´-lo; from 575 and 4724; *set apart*, i.e. (by impl.) to *send out* (prop. on a mission) lit. or fig.:— put in, send (away, forth, out), set (at liberty).

650. ἀποστερέω **apŏstĕrĕō**, ap-os-ter-eh´-o; from 575 and στερέω **stĕrĕō** (to *deprive*); to *despoil*:— defraud, destitute, kept back by fraud.

651. ἀποστολή **apŏstŏlē**, ap-os-tol-ay´; from 649; *commission*, i.e. (spec.) *apostolate*:— apostleship.

652. ἀπόστολος **apŏstŏlŏs**, ap-os´-tol-os; from 649; a *delegate*; spec. an *ambassador* of the Gospel; officially a *commissioner* of Christ ["apostle"] (with miraculous powers):— apostle, messenger, he that is sent.

653. ἀποστοματίζω **apŏstŏmatizō**, ap-os-tom-at-id´-zo; from 575 and a (presumed) der. of 4750; to *speak off-hand* (prop. *dictate*), i.e. to *catechize* (in an invidious manner):— provoke to speak.

654. ἀποστρέφω **apŏstrĕphō**, ap-os-tref´-o; from 575 and 4762; to *turn away* or *back* (lit. or fig.):— bring again, pervert, turn away (from).

655. ἀποστυγέω **apŏstugĕō**, ap-os-toog-eh´-o; from 575 and the base of 4767; to *detest* utterly:— abhor.

656. ἀποσυνάγωγος **apŏsunagōgŏs**, ap-os-oon-ag´-o-gos; from 575 and 4864; *excommunicated*:— (put) out of the synagogue (-s).

657. ἀποτάσσομαι **apŏtassŏmai**, ap-ot-as´-som-ahee; mid. voice from 575 and 5021; lit. to *say adieu* (by departing or dismissing); fig. to *renounce*:— bid farewell, forsake, take leave, send away.

658. ἀποτελέω **apŏtĕlĕō**, ap-ot-el-eh´-o; from 575 and 5055; to *complete entirely*, i.e. *consummate*:— finish.

659. ἀποτίθημι **apŏtithĕmi**, ap-ot-eeth´-ay-mee; from 575 and 5087; to *put away* (lit. or fig.):— cast off, lay apart (aside, down), put away (off).

660. ἀποτινάσσω **apŏtinassō**, ap-ot-in-as´-so; from 575 and τινάσσω **tinassō** (to *jostle*); to *brush off*:— shake off.

661. ἀποτίνω **apŏtinō**, ap-ot-ee´-no; from 575 and 5099; to *pay in full*:— repay.

662. ἀποτολμάω **apŏtŏlmaō**, ap-ot-ol-mah´-o; from 575 and 5111; to *venture* plainly:— be very bold.

663. ἀποτομία **apŏtŏmia**, ap-ot-om-ee´-ah; from the base of 664; (fig.) *decisiveness*, i.e. *rigor*:— severity.

664. ἀποτόμως **apŏtŏmōs**, ap-ot-om´-oce; adv. from a der. of a compound of 575 and τέμνω **tĕmnō** (to *cut*); *abruptly*, i.e. *peremptorily*:— sharply (-ness).

665. ἀποτρέπω **apŏtrĕpō**, ap-ot-rep´-o; from 575 and the base of 5157; to *deflect*, i.e. (refl.) *avoid*:— turn away.

666. ἀπουσία **apŏusia**, ap-oo-see´-ah; from the part. of 548; a *being away*:— absence.

667. ἀποφέρω **apŏhĕrō**, ap-of-er´-o; from 575 and 5342; to *bear off* (lit. or rel.):— bring, carry (away).

668. ἀποφεύγω **apŏhĕugō**, ap-of-yoo´-go; from 575 and 5343; (fig.) to *escape*:— escape.

669. ἀποφθέγγομαι **apŏphthĕggŏmai**, ap-of-theng´-om-ahee; from 575 and 5350; to *enunciate* plainly, i.e. *declare*:— say, speak forth, utterance.

670. ἀποφορτίζομαι **apŏphŏrtizŏmai**, ap-of-or-tid´-zom-ahee; from 575 and the mid. voice of 5412; to *unload*:— unlade.

671. ἀπόχρησις **apŏchrēsis**, ap-okh´-ray-sis; from a compound of 575 and 5530; the act of *using up*, i.e. *consumption*:— using.

672. ἀποχωρέω **apŏchōrĕō**, ap-okh-o-reh´-o; from 575 and 5562; to *go away*:— depart.

673. ἀποχωρίζω **apŏchōrizō**, ap-okh-o-rid´-zo; from 575 and 5563; to *rend apart*; refl. to *separate*:— depart (asunder).

674. ἀποψύχω **apŏpsuchō**, ap-ops-oo´-kho; from 575 and 5594; to *breathe out*, i.e. *faint*:— hearts failing.

675. Ἄππιος **'Appiŏs**, ap´-pee-os; of Lat. or.; (in the gen., i.e. possessive case) of *Appius*, the name of a Rom.:— Appii.

676. ἀπρόσιτος **aprŏsitŏs**, ap-ros´-ee-tos; from 1 (as a neg. particle) and a der. of a compound of 4314 and εἶμι **ĕimi** (to *go*); *inaccessible*:— which no man can approach.

677. ἀπρόσκοπος **aprŏskŏpŏs**, ap-ros´-kop-os; from 1 (as a neg. particle) and a presumed der. of 4350; act. *inoffensive*, i.e. *not leading into sin*; pass. *faultless*, i.e. *not led into sin*:— none (void of, without) offence.

678. ἀπροσωπολήπτως **aprŏsōpŏlēptōs**,

ap-ros-o-pol-ape´-toce; adv. from a compound of 1 (as a neg. particle) and a presumed der. of a presumed comp. of 4383 and 2983 [comp. 4381]; in a way *not accepting* the *person*, i.e. *impartially*:— without respect of persons.

679. ἄπταιστος **aptaistŏs**, ap-tah´-ee-stos; from 1 (as a neg. particle) and a der. of 4417; *not stumbling*, i.e. (fig.) *without sin*:— from falling.

680. ἅπτομαι **haptŏmai**, hap´-tom-ahee; refl. of 681; prop. to *attach* oneself to, i.e. to *touch* (in many impl. relations):— touch.

681. ἅπτω **haptō**, hap´-to; a primary verb; prop. to *fasten* to, i.e. (spec.) to *set* on fire:— kindle, light.

682. Ἀπφία **Apphia**, ap-fee´-a; prob. of for. or.; *Apphia*, a woman of Collosæ:— Apphia.

683. ἀπωθέομαι **apōthĕŏmai**, ap-o-theh´-om-ahee; or ἀπώθομαι **apōthŏmai**, ap-o´-thom-ahee; from 575 and the mid. voice of ὠθέω **ōthĕō** or ὤθω **ōthō** (to *shove*); to *push off*, fig. to *reject*:— cast away, put away (from), thrust away (from).

684. ἀπώλεια **apōlĕia**, ap-o´-li-a; from a presumed der. of 622; *ruin* or *loss* (phys. spiritual or eternal):— damnable (-nation), destruction, die, perdition, × perish, pernicious ways, waste.

685. ἀρά **ara**, ar-ah´; prob. from 142; prop. *prayer* (as *lifted* to Heaven), i.e. (by impl.) *imprecation*:— curse.

686. ἄρα **ara**, ar´-ah; prob. from 142 (through the idea of *drawing* a conclusion); a particle denoting an *inference* more or less decisive (as follows):— haply, (what) manner (of man), no doubt, perhaps, so be, then, therefore, truly, wherefore. Often used in connection with other particles, esp. 1065 or 3767 (after) or 1487 (before). Comp. also 687.

687. ἆρα **ara**, ar´-ah; a form of 686, denoting an *interrogation* to which a negative answer is presumed:— therefore.

688. Ἀραβία **Arabia**, ar-ab-ee´-ah; of Heb. or. [6152]; *Arabia*, a region of Asia:— Arabia.

ἄραγε **aragĕ**. See 686 and 1065.

689. Ἀράμ **Aram**, ar-am´; of Heb. or. [7410]; *Aram* (i.e. *Ram*), an Isr.:— Aram.

690. Ἄραψ **'Araps**, ar´-aps; from 688; an *Arab* or native of Arabia:— Arabian.

691. ἀργέω **argĕō**, arg-eh´-o; from 692; to *be idle*, i.e. (fig.) to *delay*:— linger.

692. ἀργός **argŏs**, ar-gos´; from 1 (as a neg. particle) and 2041; *inactive*, i.e. *unemployed*; (by impl.) *lazy, useless*:— barren, idle, slow.

693. ἀργύρεος **argurĕŏs**, ar-goo´-reh-os; from 696; made *of silver*:— (of) silver.

694. ἀργύριον **argurion**, ar-goo´-ree-on; neut. of a presumed der. of 696; *silvery*, i.e. (by impl.) *cash*; spec. a *silverling* (i.e. *drachma* or *shekel*):— money, (piece of) silver (piece).

695. ἀργυροκόπος **argurŏkŏpŏs**, ar-goo-

rok-op´-os; from 696 and 2875; a beater (i.e. worker) of silver:— silversmith.

696. ἀργυρος argurŏs, ar´-goo-ros; from ἀργός argŏs (shining); silver (the metal, in the articles or coin):— silver.

697. Ἄρειος Πάγος Arĕiŏs Pagŏs, ar´-i-os pag´-os; from Ἄρης Arēs (the name of the Greek deity of war) and a der. of 4078; rock of Ares, a place in Athens:— Areopagus, Mars' Hill.

698. Ἀρεοπαγίτης Arĕŏpagitēs, ar-eh-op-ag-ee´-tace; from 697; an Areopagite or member of the court held on Mars' Hill:— Areopagite.

699. ἀρέσκεια arĕskĕia, ar-es´-ki-ah; from a der. of 700; complaisance:— pleasing.

700. ἀρέσκω arĕskō, ar-es´-ko; prob. from 142 (through the idea of exciting emotion); to be agreeable (or by impl. to seek to be so):— please.

701. ἀρεστός arĕstŏs, ar-es-tos´; from 700; agreeable; by impl. fit:— (things that) please (-ing), reason.

702. Ἀρέτας Arĕtas, ar-et´-as; of for. or.; Aretas, an Arabian:— Aretas.

703. ἀρέτη arĕtē, ar-et´-ay; from the same as 730; prop. manliness (valor), i.e. excellence (intrinsic or attributed):— praise, virtue.

704. ἀρήν arēn, ar-ane´; perh. the same as 730; a lamb (as a male):— lamb.

705. ἀριθμέω arithmĕō, ar-ith-meh´-o; from 706; to enumerate or count:— number.

706. ἀριθμός arithmŏs, ar-ith-mos´; from 142; a number (as reckoned up):— number.

707. Ἀριμαθαία Arimathaia, ar-ee-math-ah´-ee-ah; of Heb. or. [7414]; Arimathæa (or Ramah), a place in Pal.:— Arimathæa.

708. Ἀρίσταρχος Aristarchŏs, ar-is´-tar-khos; from the same as 712 and 757; best ruling; Aristarchus, a Macedonian:— Aristarchus.

709. ἀριστάω aristaō, ar-is-tah´-o; from 712; to take the principle meal:— dine.

710. ἀριστερός aristĕrŏs, ar-is-ter-os´; appar. a comparative of the same as 712; the left hand (as second-best):— left [hand].

711. Ἀριστόβουλος Aristŏbŏulŏs, ar-is-tob´-oo-los; from the same as 712 and 1012; best counselling; Aristoboulus, a Chr.:— Aristobulus.

712. ἀριστον aristŏn, ar´-is-ton; appar. neut. of a superl. from the same as 730; the best meal [or breakfast; perh. from ἦρι ēri ("early")], i.e. luncheon:— dinner.

713. ἀρκετός arkĕtŏs, ar-ket-os´; from 714; satisfactory:— enough, suffice (-ient).

714. ἀρκέω arkĕō, ar-keh´-o; appar. a primary verb [but prob. akin to 142 through the idea of raising a barrier]; prop. to ward off, i.e. (by impl.) to avail (fig. be satisfactory):— be content, be enough, suffice, be sufficient.

715. ἀρκτος arktŏs, ark´-tos; prob. from

714; a bear (as obstructing by ferocity):— bear.

716. ἀρμα harma, har´-mah; prob. from 142 [perh. with 1 (as a particle of union) prefixed]; a chariot (as raised or fitted together [comp. 719]):— chariot.

717. Ἀρμαγεδδών Armagĕddŏn, ar-mag-ed-dohn´; of Heb. or. [2022 and 4023]; Armageddon (or Har-Meggiddon), a symbol. name:— Armageddon.

718. ἀρμόζω harmŏzō, har-mod´-zo; from 719; to joint, i.e. (fig.) to woo (refl. to betroth):— espouse.

719. ἀρμός harmŏs, har-mos´; from the same as 716; an articulation (of the body):— joint.

720. ἀρνέομαι arnĕŏmai, ar-neh´-om-ahee; perh. from 1 (as a neg. particle) and the mid. voice of 4483; to contradict, i.e. disavow, reject, abnegate:— deny, refuse.

721. ἀρνίον arniŏn, ar-nee´-on; dimin. from 704; a lambkin:— lamb.

722. ἀροτριόω arŏtriŏō, ar-ot-ree-o´-o; from 723; to plough:— plow.

723. ἀροτρον arŏtrŏn, ar´-ot-ron; from ἀρόω arŏō (to till); a plow:— plow.

724. ἀρπαγή harpagē, har-pag-ay´; from 726; pillage (prop. abstr.):— extortion, ravening, spoiling.

725. ἀρπαγμός harpagmŏs, har-pag-mos´; from 726; plunder (prop. concr.):— robbery.

726. ἀρπάζω harpazō, har-pad´-zo; from a der. of 138; to seize (in various applications):— catch (away, up), pluck, pull, take (by force).

727. ἀρπαξ harpax, har´-pax; from 726; rapacious:— extortion, ravening.

728. ἀρραβών arrhabōn, ar-hrab-ohn´; of Heb. or. [6162]; a pledge, i.e. part of the purchase-money or property given in advance as security for the rest:— earnest.

729. ἀρραφος arrhaphŏs, ar´-hraf-os; from 1 (as a neg. particle) and a presumed der. of the same as 4476; unsewed, i.e. of a single piece:— without seam.

730. ἀρρην arrhēn, ar´-hrane; or

ἀρσην arsēn, ar´-sane; prob. from 142; male (as stronger for lifting):— male, man.

731. ἀρρητος arrhētŏs, ar´-hray-tos; from 1 (as a neg. particle) and the same as 4490; unsaid, i.e. (by impl.) inexpressible:— unspeakable.

732. ἀρρωστος arrhōstŏs, ar´-hroce-tos; from 1 (as a neg. particle) and a presumed der. of 4517; infirm:— sick (folk, -ly).

733. ἀρσενοκοίτης arsĕnŏkŏitēs, ar-sen-ok-oy´-tace; from 730 and 2845; a sodomite:— abuser of (that defile) self with mankind.

734. Ἀρτεμάς Artĕmas, ar-tem-as´; contr. from a compound of 735 and 1435; gift of Artemis; Artemas (or Artemidorus), a Chr.:— Artemas.

735. Ἄρτεμις Artĕmis, ar´-tem-is; prob. from the same as 736; prompt; Artemis, the name of a Grecian god-

dess borrowed by the Asiatics for one of their deities:— Diana.

736. ἀρτέμων artĕmōn, ar-tem´-ohn; from a der. of 737; prop. something ready [or else more remotely from 142 (comp. 740); something hung up], i.e. (spec.) the topsail (rather foresail or jib) of a vessel:— mainsail.

737. ἀρτι arti, ar´-tee; adv. from a der. of 142 (comp. 740) through the idea of suspension; just now:— this day (hour), hence [-forth], here [-after], hither [-to], (even) now, (this) present.

738. ἀρτιγέννητος artigĕnnētŏs, ar-teeg-en´-nay-tos; from 737 and 1084; just born, i.e. (fig.) a young convert:— new born.

739. ἀρτιος artiŏs, ar´-tee-os; from 737; fresh, i.e. (by impl.) complete:— perfect.

740. ἀρτος artŏs, ar´-tos; from 142; bread (as raised) or a loaf:— (shew-) bread, loaf.

741. ἀρτύω artuō, ar-too´-o; from a presumed der. of 142; to prepare, i.e. spice (with stimulating condiments):— season.

742. Ἀρφαξάδ Arphaxad, ar-fax-ad´; of Heb. or. [775]; Arphaxad, a post-diluvian patriarch:— Arphaxad.

743. ἀρχάγγελος archaggĕlŏs, ar-khang´-el-os; from 757 and 32; a chief angel:— archangel.

744. ἀρχαῖος archaiŏs, ar-khah´-yos; from 746; original or primeval:— (them of) old (time).

745. Ἀρχέλαος Archĕlaŏs, ar-khel´-ah-os; from 757 and 2994; people-ruling; Archelaus, a Jewish king:— Archelaus.

746. ἀρχή archē, ar-khay´; from 756; (prop. abstr.) a commencement, or (concr.) chief (in various applications of order, time, place, or rank):— beginning, corner, (at the, the) first (estate), magistrate, power, principality, principle, rule.

747. ἀρχηγός archēgŏs, ar-khay-gos´; from 746 and 71; a chief leader:— author, captain, prince.

748. ἀρχιερατικός archiĕratikŏs, ar-khee-er-at-ee-kos´; from 746 and a der. of 2413; high-priestly:— of the high-priest.

749. ἀρχιερεύς archiĕrĕus, ar-khee-er-yuce´; from 746 and 2409; the high-priest (lit. of the Jews, typ. Christ); by extens. a chief priest:— chief (high) priest, chief of the priests.

750. ἀρχιποίμην archipŏimēn, ar-khee-poy´-mane; from 746 and 4166; a head shepherd:— chief shepherd.

751. Ἄρχιππος Archippŏs, ar´-khip-pos; from 746 and 2462; horse-ruler; Archippus, a Chr.:— Archippus.

752. ἀρχισυνάγωγος archisunagōgŏs, ar-khee-soon-ag´-o-gos; from 746 and 4864; director of the synagogue services:— (chief) ruler of the synagogue.

753. ἀρχιτέκτων architĕktōn, ar-khee-tek´-tone; from 746 and 5045; a chief constructor, i.e. "architect":— masterbuilder.

754. ἀρχιτελώνης architĕlōnēs, ar-khee-tel-o´-nace; from 746 and 5057; a

principle tax-gatherer:— chief among the publicans.

755. ἀρχιτρίκλινος **architriklinŏs**, *ar-khee-tree'-klee-nos;* from *746* and a compound of *5140* and *2827* (a *dinner-bed*, because composed of three couches); *director* of the *entertainment:*— governor (ruler) of the feast.

756. ἄρχομαι **archŏmai**, *ar'-khom-ahee;* mid. voice of *757* (through the impl. of *precedence*); to *commence* (in order of time):— (rehearse from the) begin (-ning).

757. ἄρχω **archō**, *ar'-kho;* a primary verb; to be *first* (in political rank or power):— reign (rule) over.

758. ἄρχων **archōn**, *ar'-khone;* pres. part. of *757;* a *first* (in rank or power):— chief (ruler), magistrate, prince, ruler.

759. ἄρωμα **"arŏma,"** *ar'-o-mah;* from *142* (in the sense of *sending* off scent); an *aromatic:*— (sweet) spice.

760. Ἀσά **Asa**, *as-ah';* of Heb. or. [609]; *Asa*, an Isr.:— Asa.

761. ἀσάλευτος **asalĕutŏs**, *as-al'-yoo-tos;* from *1* (as a neg. particle) and a der. of *4531; unshaken*, i.e. (by impl.) *immovable* (fig.):— which cannot be moved, unmovable.

762. ἀσβεστος **asbĕstŏs**, *as'-bes-tos;* from *1* (as a neg. particle) and a der. of *4570; not extinguished*, i.e. (by impl.) *perpetual:*— not to be quenched, unquenchable.

763. ἀσέβεια **asĕbĕia**, *as-eb'-i-ah;* from *765; impiety*, i.e. (by impl.) *wickedness:*— ungodly (-liness).

764. ἀσεβέω **asĕbĕō**, *as-eb-eh'-o;* from *765;* to *be* (by impl. *act*) *impious* or *wicked:*— commit (live, that after should live) ungodly.

765. ἀσεβής **asĕbēs**, *as-eb-ace';* from *1* (as a neg. particle) and a presumed der. of *4576; irreverent*, i.e. (by extens.) *impious* or *wicked:*— ungodly (man).

766. ἀσέλγεια **asĕlgĕia**, *as-elg'-i-a;* from a compound of *1* (as a neg. particle) and a presumed σελγής *sĕlgēs* (of uncert. der., but appar. mean. *continent*); *licentiousness* (sometimes incl. other vices):— filthy, lasciviousness, wantonness.

767. ἄσημος **asēmŏs**, *as'-ay-mos;* from *1* (as a neg. particle) and the base of *4591; unmarked*, i.e. (fig.) *ignoble:*— mean.

768. Ἀσήρ **Asēr**, *as-ayr';* of Heb. or. [836]; *Aser* (i.e. *Asher*), an Isr. tribe:— Aser.

769. ἀσθένεια **asthĕnĕia**, *as-then'-i-ah;* from *772; feebleness* (of body or mind); by impl. *malady;* mor. *frailty:*— disease, infirmity, sickness, weakness.

770. ἀσθενέω **asthĕnĕō**, *as-then-eh'-o;* from *772;* to *be feeble* (in any sense):— be diseased, impotent folk (man), (be) sick, (be, be made) weak.

771. ἀσθένημα **asthĕnēma**, *as-then'-ay-mah;* from *770;* a *scruple* of conscience:— infirmity.

772. ἀσθενής **asthĕnēs**, *as-then-ace';* from *1* (as a neg. particle) and the base of *4599; strengthless* (in various applications, lit., fig. and mor.):— more feeble, impotent, sick, without strength, weak (-er, -ness, thing).

773. Ἀσία **Asia**, *as-ee'-ah;* of uncert. der.; *Asia*, i.e. *Asia Minor*, or (usually) only its western shore:— Asia.

774. Ἀσιανός **Asianŏs**, *as-ee-an-os';* from *773;* an *Asian* (i.e. *Asiatic*) or an inhabitant of Asia:— of Asia.

775. Ἀσιάρχης **Asiarchēs**, *as-ee-ar'-khace;* from *773* and *746;* an *Asiarch* or president of the public festivities in a city of Asia Minor:— chief of Asia.

776. ἀσιτία **asitia**, *as-ee-tee'-ah;* from *777; fasting* (the state):— abstinence.

777. ἄσιτος **asitŏs**, *as'-ee-tos;* from *1* (as a neg. particle) and *4621; without* (taking) *food:*— fasting.

778. ἀσκέω **askĕō**, *as-keh'-o;* prob. from the same as *4632;* to *elaborate*, i.e. (fig.) *train* (by impl. *strive*):— exercise.

779. ἀσκός **askŏs**, *as-kos';* from the same as *778;* a leathern (or skin) *bag* used as a bottle:— bottle.

780. ἀσμένως **asmĕnōs**, *as-men'-oce;* adv. from a der. of the base of *2237; with pleasure:*— gladly.

781. ἄσοφος **asŏphŏs**, *as'-of-os;* from *1* (as a neg. particle) and *4680; unwise:*— fool.

782. ἀσπάζομαι **aspazŏmai**, *as-pad'-zom-ahee;* from *1* (as a particle of union) and a presumed form of *4685;* to *enfold* in the arms, i.e. (by impl.) to *salute*, (fig.) to *welcome:*— embrace, greet, salute, take leave.

783. ἀσπασμός **aspasmŏs**, *as-pas-mos';* from *782;* a *greeting* (in person or by letter):— greeting, salutation.

784. ἄσπιλος **aspilŏs**, *as'-pee-los;* from *1* (as a neg. particle) and *4695; unblemished* (phys. or mor.):— without spot, unspotted.

785. ἀσπίς **aspis**, *as-pece';* of uncert. der.; a *buckler* (or *round* shield); used of a serpent (as *coiling* itself), prob. the *"asp":*— asp.

786. ἄσπονδος **aspŏndŏs**, *as'-pon-dos;* from *1* (as a neg. particle) and a der. of *4689;* lit. *without libation* (which usually accompanied a treaty), i.e. (by impl.) *truceless:*— implacable, trucebreaker.

787. ἀσσάριον **assariŏn**, *as-sar'-ee-on;* of Lat. or.; an *assarius* or *as*, a Roman coin:— farthing.

788. ἄσσον **assŏn**, *as'-son;* neut. comparative of the base of *1451; more nearly*, i.e. *very near:*— nearly.

789. Ἄσσος **Assŏs**, *as'-sos;* prob. of for. or.; *Assus*, a city of Asia Minor:— Assos.

790. ἀστατέω **astatĕō**, *as-tat-eh'-o;* from *1* (as a neg. particle) and a der. of *2476;* to *be non-stationary*, i.e. (fig.) *homeless:*— have no certain dwelling-place.

791. ἀστεῖος **astĕiŏs**, *as-ti'-os;* from ἄστυ *astu* (a *city*); *urbane*, i.e. (by impl.) *handsome:*— fair.

792. ἀστήρ **astēr**, *as-tare';* prob. from the base of *4766;* a *star* (as *strown* over the sky), lit. or fig.:— star.

793. ἀστήρικτος **astēriktŏs**, *as-tay'-rik-tos;* from *1* (as a neg. particle) and a presumed der. of *4741; unfixed*, i.e. (fig.) *vacillating:*— unstable.

794. ἄστοργος **astŏrgŏs**, *as'-tor-gos;* from *1* (as a neg. particle) and a presumed der. of στέργω *stĕrgō* (to *cherish* affectionately); *hard-hearted* toward kindred:— without natural affection.

795. ἀστοχέω **astŏchĕō**, *as-tokh-eh'-o;* from a compound of *1* (as a neg. particle) and στοῖχος *stŏichŏs* (an *aim*); to *miss* the mark, i.e. (fig.) *deviate* from truth:— err, swerve.

796. ἀστραπή **astrapē**, *as-trap-ay';* from *797; lightning;* by anal. *glare:*— lightning, bright shining.

797. ἀστράπτω **astraptō**, *as-trap'-to;* prob. from *792;* to *flash* as lightning:— lighten, shine.

798. ἄστρον **astrŏn**, *as'-tron;* neut. from *792;* prop. a *constellation;* put for a single *star* (nat. or artif.):— star.

799. Ἀσύγκριτος **Asugkritŏs**, *as-oong'-kree-tos;* from *1* (as a neg. particle) and a der. of *4793; incomparable; Asyncritus*, a Chr.:— Asyncritus.

800. ἀσύμφωνος **asumphōnŏs**, *as-oom'-fo-nos;* from *1* (as a neg. particle) and *4859; inharmonious* (fig.):— agree not.

801. ἀσύνετος **asunĕtŏs**, *as-oon'-ay-tos;* from *1* (as a neg. particle) and *4908; unintelligent;* by impl. *wicked:*— foolish, without understanding.

802. ἀσύνθετος **asunthĕtŏs**, *as-oon'-thet-os;* from *1* (as a neg. particle) and a der. of *4934;* prop. *not agreed*, i.e. *treacherous* to compacts:— covenantbreaker.

803. ἀσφάλεια **asphalĕia**, *as-fal'-i-ah;* from *804; security* (lit. or fig.):— certainty, safety.

804. ἀσφαλής **asphalēs**, *as-fal-ace';* from *1* (as a neg. particle) and σφάλλω *sphallō* (to *"fail"*); *secure* (lit. or fig.):— certain (-ty), safe, sure.

805. ἀσφαλίζω **asphalizō**, *as-fal-id'-zo;* from *804;* to *render secure:*— make fast (sure).

806. ἀσφαλῶς **asphalōs**, *as-fal-oce';* adv. from *804; securely* (lit. or fig.):— assuredly, safely.

807. ἀσχημονέω **aschēmŏnĕō**, *as-kay-mon-eh'-o;* from *809;* to *be* (i.e. *act*) *unbecoming:*— behave self uncomely (unseemly).

808. ἀσχημοσύνη **aschēmŏsunē**, *as-kay-mos-oo'-nay;* from *809;* an *indecency;* by impl. the *pudenda:*— shame, that which is unseemly.

809. ἀσχήμων **aschēmōn**, *as-kay'-mone;* from *1* (as a neg. particle) and a presumed der. of *2192* (in the sense of its congener *4976*); prop. *shapeless*, i.e. (fig.) *inelegant:*— uncomely.

810. ἀσωτία **asōtia**, *as-o-tee'-ah;* from a compound of *1* (as a neg. particle) and a presumed der. of *4982;* prop. *unsavedness*, i.e. (by impl.) *profligacy:*— excess, riot.

811. ἀσώτως **asōtōs**, *as-o'-toce;* adv. from the same as *810; dissolutely:*— riotous.

812. ἀτακτέω **ataktĕō**, *at-ak-teh´-o*; from *813*; to *be* (i.e. *act*) *irregular*:— behave self disorderly.

813. ἄτακτος **ataktŏs**, *at´-ak-tos*; from *1* (as a neg. particle) and a der. of *5021*; *unarranged*, i.e. (by impl.) *insubordinate* (religiously):— unruly.

814. ἀτάκτως **ataktōs**, *at-ak´-toce*; adv. from *813*; *irregularly* (mor.):— disorderly.

815. ἄτεκνος **atĕknŏs**, *at´-ek-nos*; from *1* (as a neg. particle) and *5043*; *childless*:— childless, without children.

816. ἀτενίζω **atĕnizō**, *at-en-id´-zo*; from a compound of *1* (as a particle of union) and τείνω **tĕinō** (to *stretch*); to *gaze* intently:— behold earnestly (stedfastly), fasten (eyes), look (earnestly, stedfastly, up stedfastly), set eyes.

817. ἄτερ **atĕr**, *at´-er*; a particle prob. akin to *427*; *aloof*, i.e. *apart* from (lit. or fig.):— in the absence of, without.

818. ἀτιμάζω **atimazō**, *at-im-ad´-zo*; from *820*; to *render infamous*, i.e. (by impl.) *contemn* or *maltreat*:— despise, dishonour, suffer shame, entreat shamefully.

819. ἀτιμία **atimia**, *at-ee-mee´-ah*; from *820*; *infamy*, i.e. (subj.) comparative indignity, (obj.) *disgrace*:— dishonour, reproach, shame, vile.

820. ἄτιμος **atimŏs**, *at´-ee-mos*; from *1* (as a neg. particle) and *5092*; (neg.) *unhonoured* or (pos.) *dishonoured*:— despised, without honour, less honourable [comparative degree].

821. ἀτιμόω **atimŏō**, *at-ee-mŏ´-o*; from *820*; used like *818*, to *maltreat*:— handle shamefully.

822. ἀτμίς **atmis**, *at-mece´*; from the same as *109*; *mist*:— vapour.

823. ἄτομος **atŏmŏs**, *at´-om-os*; from *1* (as a neg. particle) and the base of *5114*; *uncut*, i.e. (by impl.) *indivisible* [an "atom" of time]:— moment.

824. ἄτοπος **atŏpŏs**, *at´-op-os*; from *1* (as a neg. particle) and *5117*; *out of place*, i.e. (fig.) *improper, injurious, wicked*:— amiss, harm, unreasonable.

825. Ἀττάλεια **Attalĕia**, *at-tal´-i-ah*; from Ἄτταλος **Attalŏs** (a king of Pergamus); *Attaleia*, a place in Pamphylia:— Attalia.

826. αὐγάζω **augazō**, *ŏw-gad´-zo*; from *827*; to *beam* forth (fig.):— shine.

827. αὐγή **augē**, *ŏwg´-ay*; of uncert. der.; a *ray* of light, i.e. (by impl.) *radiance, dawn*:— break of day.

828. Αὔγουστος **Augŏustŏs**, *ŏw´-goos-tos*; from Lat. ["august"]; *Augustus*, a title of the Rom. emperor:— Augustus.

829. αὐθάδης **authadēs**, *ŏw-thad´-ace*; from *846* and the base of *2237*; *self-pleasing*, i.e. *arrogant*:— self-willed.

830. αὐθαίρετος **authairĕtŏs**, *ŏw-thah´-ee-ret-os*; from *846* and the same as *140*; *self-chosen*, i.e. (by impl.) *voluntary*:— of own accord, willing of self.

831. αὐθεντέω **authĕntĕō**, *ŏw-then-teh´-o*; from a compound of *846* and an obs. ἕντης **hĕntēs** (a *worker*); to *act* of oneself, i.e. (fig.) *dominate*:— usurp authority over.

832. αὐλέω **aulĕō**, *ŏw-leh´-o*; from *836*; to play the *flute*:— pipe.

833. αὐλή **aulē**, *ŏw-lay´*; from the same as *109*; a *yard* (as open to the *wind*); by impl. a *mansion*:— court, ([sheep-]) fold, hall, palace.

834. αὐλητής **aulētēs**, *ŏw-lay-tace´*; from *832*; a *flute-player*:— minstrel, piper.

835. αὐλίζομαι **aulizŏmai**, *ŏw-lid´-zom-ahee*; mid. voice from *833*; to *pass the night* (prop. in the open air):— abide, lodge.

836. αὐλός **aulŏs**, *ŏw-los´*; from the same as *109*; a *flute* (as *blown*):— pipe.

837. αὐξάνω **auxanō**, *ŏwx-an´-o*; a prol. form of a primary verb; to *grow* ("*wax*"), i.e. *enlarge* (lit. or fig., act. or pass.):— grow (up), (give the) increase.

838. αὔξησις **auxēsis**, *ŏwx´-ay-sis*; from *837*; *growth*:— increase.

839. αὔριον **auriŏn**, *ŏw´-ree-on*; from a der. of the same as *109* (mean. a *breeze*, i.e. the morning *air*); prop. *fresh*, i.e. (adv. with ellipsis of *2250*) *to-morrow*:— (to-) morrow, next day.

840. αὐστηρός **austērŏs**, *ŏw-stay-ros´*; from a (presumed) der. of the same as *109* (mean. *blown*); *rough* (prop. as a *gale*), i.e. (fig.) *severe*:— austere.

841. αὐτάρκεια **autarkeia**, *ŏw-tar´-ki-ah*; from *842*; *self-satisfaction*, i.e. (abstr.) *contentedness*, or (concr.) a *competence*:— contentment, sufficiency.

842. αὐτάρκης **autarkēs**, *ŏw-tar´-kace*; from *846* and *714*; *self-complacent*, i.e. *contented*:— content.

843. αὐτοκατάκριτος **autŏkatakritŏs**, *ŏw-tok-at-ak´-ree-tos*; from *846* and a der. or *2632*; *self-condemned*:— condemned of self.

844. αὐτόματος **autŏmatŏs**, *ŏw-tom´-at-os*; from *846* and the same as *3155*; *self-moved* ["automatic"], i.e. *spontaneous*:— of own accord, of self.

845. αὐτόπτης **autŏptēs**, *ŏw-top´-tace*; from *846* and *3700*; *self-seeing*, i.e. an *eyewitness*:— eye-witness.

846. αὐτός **autŏs**, *ŏw-tos´*; from the particle αὖ **au** [perh. akin to the base of *109* through the idea of a *baffling* wind] (*backward*); the refl. pron. *self*, used (alone or in the comp. *1438*) of the third pers., and (with the proper pers. pron.) of the other persons:— her, it (-self), one, the other, (mine) own, said, ([self-], the) same, ([him-, my-, thy-]) self, [your-] selves, she, that, their (-s), them ([-selves]), there [-at, -by, -in, -into, -of, -on, -with], they, (these) things, this (man), those, together, very, which. Comp. *848*.

847. αὐτοῦ **autŏu**, *ŏw-too´*; gen. (i.e. possessive) of *846*, used as an adv. of location; prop. belonging to the *same* spot, i.e. *in this* (or *that*) *place*:— (t-) here.

848. αὑτοῦ **hautŏu**, *how-too´*; contr. for *1438*; *self* (in some oblique case or refl. relation):— her (own), (of) him (-self), his (own), of it, thee, their (own), them (-selves), they.

849. αὐτόχειρ **autŏchĕir**, *ŏw-tokh´-ire*; from *846* and *5495*; *self-handed*, i.e. doing *personally*:— with ... own hands.

850. αὐχμηρός **auchmērŏs**, *ŏwkh-may-ros´*; from αὐχμός **auchmŏs** [prob. from a base akin to that of *109*] (*dust*, as *dried* by wind); prop. *dirty*, i.e. (by impl.) *obscure*:— dark.

851. ἀφαιρέω **aphairĕō**, *af-ahee-reh´-o*; from *575* and *138*; to *remove* (lit. or fig.):— cut (smite) off, take away.

852. ἀφανής **aphanēs**, *af-an-ace´*; from *1* (as a neg. particle) and *5316*; *non-apparent*:— that is not manifest.

853. ἀφανίζω **aphanizō**, *af-an-id´-zo*; from *852*; to *render unapparent*, i.e. (act.) *consume* (*becloud*), or (pass.) *disappear* (*be destroyed*):— corrupt, disfigure, perish, vanish away.

854. ἀφανισμός **aphanismŏs**, *af-an-is-mos´*; from *853*; *disappearance*, i.e. (fig.) *abrogation*:— vanish away.

855. ἄφαντος **aphantŏs**, *af´-an-tŏs*; from *1* (as a neg. particle) and a der. of *5316*; *non-manifested*, i.e. *invisible*:— vanished out of sight.

856. ἀφεδρών **aphĕdrōn**, *af-ed-rone´*; from a compound of *575* and the base of *1476*; a place of *sitting apart*, i.e. a *privy*:— draught.

857. ἀφειδία **aphĕidia**, *af-i-dee´-ah*; from a compound of *1* (as a neg. particle) and *5339*; *unsparingness*, i.e. *austerity* (*asceticism*):— neglecting.

858. ἀφελότης **aphĕlŏtēs**, *af-el-ot´-ace*; from a compound of *1* (as a neg. particle) and φέλλος **phĕllŏs** (in the sense of a *stone* as *stubbing* the foot); *smoothness*, i.e. (fig.) *simplicity*:— singleness.

859. ἄφεσις **aphĕsis**, *af´-es-is*; from *863*; *freedom*; (fig.) *pardon*:— deliverance, forgiveness, liberty, remission.

860. ἁφή **haphē**, *haf-ay´*; from *680*; prob. a *ligament* (as *fastening*):— joint.

861. ἀφθαρσία **aphtharsia**, *af-thar-see´-ah*; from *862*; *incorruptibility*; gen. *unending existence*; (fig.) *genuineness*:— immortality, incorruption, sincerity.

862. ἄφθαρτος **aphthartŏs**, *af´-thar-tos*; from *1* (as a neg. particle) and a der. of *5351*; *undecaying* (in essence or continuance):— not (in-, un-) corruptible, immortal.

863. ἀφίημι **aphiēmi**, *af-ee´-ay-mee*; from *575* and ἵημι **hiēmi** (to *send*; an intens. form of εἶμι **ĕimi**, to *go*); to *send forth*, in various applications (as follow):— cry, forgive, forsake, lay aside, leave, let (alone, be, go, have), omit, put (send) away, remit, suffer, yield up.

864. ἀφικνέομαι **aphiknĕŏmai**, *af-ik-neh´-om-ahee*; from *575* and the base of *2425*; to *go* (i.e. *spread*) *forth* (by rumor):— come abroad.

865. ἀφιλάγαθος **aphilagathŏs**, *af-il-ag´-ath-os*; from *1* (as a neg. particle) and *5358*; *hostile to virtue*:— despiser of those that are good.

866. ἀφιλάργυρος **aphilargurŏs**, *af-il-ar´-goo-ros*; from *1* (as a neg. particle) and *5366*; *unavaricious*:— without covetousness, not greedy of filthy lucre.

867. ἄφιξις **aphixis**, *af´-ix-is*; from *864*;

prop. *arrival*, i.e. (by impl.) *departure*:— departing.

868. ἀφίστημι **aphistēmi**, *af-is´-tay-mee*; from 575 and 2476; to *remove*, i.e. (act.) *instigate* to revolt; usually (refl.) to *desist, desert*, etc.:— depart, draw (fall) away, refrain, withdraw self.

869. ἄφνω **aphnō**, *af´-no*; adv. from 852 (contr.); *unawares*, i.e. *unexpectedly:*— suddenly.

870. ἀφόβως **aphŏbōs**, *af-ob´-oce*; adv. from a compound of 1 (as a neg. particle) and 5401; *fearlessly:*— without fear.

871. ἀφομοιόω **aphŏmŏiŏō**, *af-om-oy-ŏ´-o*; from 575 and 3666; to *assimilate* closely:— make like.

872. ἀφοράω **aphŏraō**, *af-or-ah´-o*; from 575 and 3708; to *consider* attentively:— look.

873. ἀφορίζω **aphŏrizō**, *af-or-id´-zo*; from 575 and 3724; to *set off* by boundary, i.e. (fig.) *limit, exclude, appoint*, etc.:— divide, separate, sever.

874. ἀφορμή **aphŏrmē**, *af-or-may´*; from a compound of 575 and 3729; a *starting*-point, i.e. (fig.) an *opportunity:*— occasion.

875. ἀφρίζω **aphrizō**, *af-rid´-zo*; from 876; to *froth* at the mouth (in epilepsy):— foam.

876. ἀφρός **aphrŏs**, *af-ros´*; appar. a primary word; *froth*, i.e. *slaver:*— foaming.

877. ἀφροσύνη **aphrŏsunē**, *af-ros-oo´-nay*; from 878; *senselessness*, i.e. (euphem.) *egotism*; (mor.) *recklessness:*— folly, foolishly (-ness).

878. ἄφρων **aphrōn**, *af-rone*; from 1 (as a neg. particle) and 5424; prop. *mindless*, i.e. *stupid*, (by impl.) *ignorant*, (spec.) *egotistic*, (practically) *rash*, or (mor.) *unbelieving:*— fool (-ish), unwise.

879. ἀφυπνόω **aphupnŏō**, *af-oop-nŏ´-o*; from a compound of 575 and 5258; prop. to *become awake*, i.e. (by impl.) to *drop* (off) in slumber:— fall asleep.

880. ἄφωνος **aphōnŏs**, *af´-o-nos*; from 1 (as a neg. particle) and 5456; *voiceless*, i.e. *mute* (by nature or choice); fig. *unmeaning:*— dumb, without signification.

881. Ἀχάζ **Achaz**, *akh-adz´*; of Heb. or. [271]; *Achaz*, an Isr.:— Achaz.

882. Ἀχαΐα **Achaïa**, *ach-ah-ee´-ah*; of uncert. der.; *Achaia* (i.e. *Greece*), a country of Europe:— Achaia.

883. Ἀχαϊκός **Achaïkŏs**, *ach-ah-ee-kos´*; from 882; an *Achaïan; Achaïcus*, a Chr.:— Achaicus.

884. ἀχάριστος **acharistŏs**, *ach-ar´-is-tos*; from 1 (as a neg. particle) and a presumed der. of 5483; *thankless*, i.e. *ungrateful:*— unthankful.

885. Ἀχείμ **Achĕim** or Ἀχίμ **Achim**, *akh-ime´*; prob. of Heb. or. [comp. 3137]; *Achim*, an Isr.:— Achim.

886. ἀχειροποίητος **achĕirŏpŏiētŏs**, *akh-i-rop-oy´-ay-tos*; from 1 (as a neg. particle) and 5499; *unmanufactured*, i.e. *inartificial:*— made without (not made with) hands.

887. ἀχλύς **achlus**, *akh-looce´*; of un-cert. der.; *dimness* of sight, i.e. (prob.) a *cataract:*— mist.

888. ἀχρεῖος **achrĕiŏs**, *akh-ri´-os*; from 1 (as a neg. particle) and a der. of 5534 [comp. 5532]; *useless*, i.e. (euphem.) *unmeritorious:*— unprofitable.

889. ἀχρειόω **achrĕiŏō**, *akh-ri-ŏ´-o*; from 888; to *render useless*, i.e. *spoil:*— become unprofitable.

890. ἄχρηστος **achrēstŏs**, *akh´-race-tos*; from 1 (as a neg. particle) and 5543; *inefficient*, i.e. (by impl.) *detrimental:*— unprofitable.

891. ἄχρι **achri**, *akh´-ree*; or ἄχρις **achris**, *akh´-rece*; akin to 206 (through the idea of a *terminus*); (of time) *until* or (of place) *up to:*— as far as, for, in (-to), till, (even, un-) to, until, while. Comp. 3360.

892. ἄχυρον **achurŏn**, *akh´-oo-ron*; perh. remotely from χέω **chĕō** (to *shed* forth); *chaff* (as *diffusive*):— chaff.

893. ἀψευδής **apsĕudēs**, *aps-yoo-dace´*; from 1 (as a neg. particle) and 5579; *veracious:*— that cannot lie.

894. ἄψινθος **apsinthŏs**, *ap´-sin-thos*; of uncert. der.; *wormwood* (as a type of *bitterness*, i.e. [fig.] *calamity*):— wormwood.

895. ἄψυχος **apsuchŏs**, *ap´-soo-khos*; from 1 (as a neg. particle) and 5590; *lifeless*, i.e. *inanimate* (mechanical):— without life.

B

896. Βάαλ **Baal**, *bah´-al*; of Heb. or. [1168]; *Baal*, a Phœnician deity (used as a symbol of idolatry):— Baal.

897. Βαβυλών **Babulōn**, *bab-oo-lone´*; of Heb. or. [894]; *Babylon*, the capital of Chaldæa (lit. or fig. [as a type of tyranny]):— Babylon.

898. βαθμός **bathmŏs**, *bath-mos´*; from the same as 899; a *step*, i.e. (fig.) *grade* (of dignity):— degree.

899. βάθος **bathŏs**, *bath´-os*; from the same as 901; *profundity*, i.e. (by impl.) *extent*; (fig.) *mystery:*— deep (-ness), depth.

900. βαθύνω **bathunō**, *bath-oo´-no*; from 901; to *deepen:*— deep.

901. βαθύς **bathus**, *bath-oos´*; from the base of 939; *profound* (as *going down*), lit. or fig.:— deep, very early.

902. βαΐον **baïŏn**, *bah-ee-on´*; a diminutive of a der. prob. of the base of 939; a palm *twig* (as *going* out far):— branch.

903. Βαλαάμ **Balaam**, *bal-ah-am´*; of Heb. or. [1109]; *Balaam*, a Mesopotamian (symbolic of a false teacher):— Balaam.

904. Βαλάκ **Balak**, *bal-ak´*; of Heb. or. [1111]; *Balak*, a Moabite:— Balac.

905. βαλάντιον **balantiŏn**, *bal-an´-tee-on*; prob. remotely from 906 (as a *depository*); a *pouch* (for money):— bag, purse.

906. βάλλω **ballō**, *bal´-lo*; a primary verb; to *throw* (in various applications, more or less violent or intense):— arise, cast (out), × dung, lay, lie, pour,

put (up), send, strike, throw (down), thrust. Comp. 4496.

907. βαπτίζω **baptizō**, *bap-tid´-zo*; from a der. of 911; to *make overwhelmed* (i.e. *fully wet*); used only (in the N.T.) of ceremonial *ablution*, espec. (tech.) of the ordinance of Chr. *baptism:*— baptist, baptize, wash.

908. βάπτισμα **baptisma**, *bap´-tis-mah*; from 907; *baptism* (tech. or fig.):— baptism.

909. βαπτισμός **baptismŏs**, *bap-tis-mos´*; from 907; *ablution* (cerem. or Chr.):— baptism, washing.

910. Βαπτιστής **Baptistēs**, *bap-tis-tace´*; from 907; a *baptizer*, as an epithet of Christ's forerunner:— Baptist.

911. βάπτω **baptō**, *bap´-to*; a primary verb; to *overwhelm*, i.e. cover wholly with a fluid; in the N.T. only in a qualified or special sense, i.e. (lit.) to *moisten* (a part of one's person), or (by impl.) to *stain* (as with dye):— dip.

912. Βαραββᾶς **Barabbas**, *bar-ab-bas´*; of Chald. or. [1347 and 5]; *son of Abba*; *Bar-abbas*, an Isr.:— Barabbas.

913. Βαράκ **Barak**, *bar-ak´*; of Heb. or. [1301]; *Barak*, an Isr.:— Barak.

914. Βαραχίας **Barachias**, *bar-akh-ee´-as*; of Heb. or. [1296]; *Barachias* (i.e. *Berechijah*), an Isr.:— Barachias.

915. βάρβαρος **barbarŏs**, *bar´-bar-os*; of uncert. der.; a *foreigner* (i.e. *non-Greek*):— barbarian (-rous).

916. βαρέω **barĕō**, *bar-eh´-o*; from 926; to *weigh* down (fig.):— burden, charge, heavy, press.

917. βαρέως **barĕōs**, *bar-eh´-oce*; adv. from 926; *heavily* (fig.):— dull.

918. Βαρθολομαῖος **Barthŏlŏmaiŏs**, *bar-thol-om-ah´-yos*; of Chald. or. [1247 and 8526]; *son of Tolmai*; *Bar-tholomæus*, a Chr. apostle:— Bartholomeus.

919. Βαριησοῦς **Bariēsŏus**, *bar-ee-ay-sooce´*; of Chald. or. [1247 and 3091]; *son of Jesus* (or *Joshua*); *Bar-jesus*, an Isr.:— Barjesus.

920. Βαριωνᾶς **Bariōnas**, *bar-ee-oo-nas´*; of Chald. or. [1247 and 3124]; *son of Jonas* (or *Jonah*); *Bar-jonas*, an Isr.:— Bar-jona.

921. Βαρνάβας **Barnabas**, *bar-nab´-as*; of Chald. or. [1247 and 5029]; *son of Nabas* (i.e. *prophecy*); *Barnabas*, an Isr.:— Barnabas.

922. βάρος **barŏs**, *bar´-os*; prob. from the same as 939 (through the notion of *going* down; comp. 899); *weight*; in the N.T. only fig. a *load, abundance, authority:*— burden (-some), weight.

923. Βαρσαβᾶς **Barsabas**, *bar-sab-as´*; of Chald. or. [1247 and prob. 6634]; *son of Sabas* (or *Tsaba*); *Bar-sabas*, the name of two Isr.:— Barsabas.

924. Βαρτιμαῖος **Bartimaiŏs**, *bar-tim-ah´-yos*; of Chald. or. [1247 and 2931]; *son of Timæus* (or the *unclean*); *Bar-timæus*, an Isr.:— Bartimæus.

925. βαρύνω **barunō**, *bar-oo´-no*; from 926; to *burden* (fig.):— overcharge.

926. βαρύς **barus**, *bar-ooce´*; from the same as 922; *weighty*, i.e. (fig) *burden-*

some, grave:— grievous, heavy, weightier.

927. βαρύτιμος **barutimōs**, bar-oo´-tim-os; from 926 and 5092; highly valuable:— very precious.

928. βασανίζω **basanizō**, bas-an-id´-zo; from 931; to torture:— pain, toil, torment, toss, vex.

929. βασανισμός **basanismōs**, bas-an-is-mos´; from 928; torture:— torment.

930. βασανιστής **basanistēs**, bas-an-is-tace´; from 928; a torturer:— tormentor.

931. βάσανος **basanōs**, bas´-an-os; perh. remotely from the same as 939 (through the notion of going to the bottom); a touch-stone, i.e. (by anal.) torture:— torment.

932. βασιλεία **basilĕia**, bas-il-i´-ah; from 935; prop. royalty, i.e. (abstr.) rule, or (concr.) a realm (lit. or fig.):— kingdom, + reign.

933. βασίλειον **basilĕiŏn**, bas-il´-i-on; neut. of 934; a palace:— king's court.

934. βασίλειος **basilĕiŏs**, bas-il´-i-os; from 935; kingly (in nature):— royal.

935. βασιλεύς **basilĕus**, bas-il-yooce´; prob. from 939 (through the notion of a foundation of power); a sovereign (abstr., rel., or fig.):— king.

936. βασιλεύω **basilĕuō**, bas-il-yoo´-o; from 935; to rule (lit. or fig.):— king, reign.

937. βασιλικός **basilikŏs**, bas-il-ee-kos´; from 935; regal (in relation), i.e. (lit.) belonging to (or befitting) the sovereign (as land, dress, or a courtier), or (fig.) preeminent:— king's, nobleman, royal.

938. βασίλισσα **basilissa**, bas-il´-is-sah; fem. from 936; a queen:— queen.

939. βάσις **basis**, bas´-ece; from βαίνω bainō (to walk); a pace ("base"), i.e. (by impl.) the foot:— foot.

940. βασκαίνω **baskainō**, bas-kah´-ee-no; akin to 5335; to malign, i.e. (by extens.) to fascinate (by false representations):— bewitch.

941. βαστάζω **bastazō**, bas-tad´-zo; perh. remotely der. from the base of 939 (through the idea of removal); to lift, lit. or fig. (endure, declare, sustain, receive, etc.):— bear, carry, take up.

942. βάτος **batŏs**, bat´-os; of uncert. der.; a brier shrub:— bramble, bush.

943. βάτος **batŏs**, bat´-os; of Heb. or. [1324]; a bath, or measure for liquids:— measure.

944. βάτραχος **batrachŏs**, bat´-rakh-os; of uncert. der.; a frog:— frog.

945. βαττολογέω **battŏlŏgĕō**, bat-tol-og-eh´-o; from Βάττος Battŏs (a proverbial stammerer) and 3056; to stutter, i.e. (by impl.) to prate tediously:— use vain repetitions.

946. βδέλυγμα **bdĕlugma**, bdel´-oog-mah; from 948; a detestation, i.e. (spec.) idolatry:— abomination.

947. βδελυκτός **bdĕluktŏs**, bdel-ook-tos´; from 948; detestable, i.e. (spec.) idolatrous:— abominable.

948. βδελύσσω **bdĕlussō**, bdel-oos´-so; from a (presumed) der. of βδέω bdĕō (to

stink); to be disgusted, i.e. (by impl.) detest (esp. of idolatry):— abhor, abominable.

949. βέβαιος **bĕbaiŏs**, beb´-ah-yos; from the base of 939 (through the idea of basality); stable (lit. or fig.):— firm, of force, stedfast, sure.

950. βεβαιόω **bĕbaiŏō**, beb-ah-yŏ´-o; from 949; to stabilitate (fig.):— confirm, (e-) stablish.

951. βεβαίωσις **bĕbaiŏsis**, beb-ah´-yo-sis; from 950; stabiliment:— confirmation.

952. βέβηλος **bĕbēlŏs**, beb´-ay-los; from the base of 939 and βηλός bēlŏs (a threshold); accessible (as by crossing the door-way), i.e. (by impl. of Jewish notions) heathenish, wicked:— profane (person).

953. βεβηλόω **bĕbēlŏō**, beb-ay-lŏ´-o; from 952; to desecrate:— profane.

954. Βεελζεβούλ **Bĕĕlzĕbŏul**, beh-el-zeb-ool´; of Chald. or. [by parody on 1176]; dung-god; Beelzebul, a name of Satan:— Beelzebub.

955. Βελίαλ **Bĕlial**, bel-ee´-al; or Βελιάρ Beliar, bel-ee´-ar of Heb. or. [1100]; worthlessness; Belial, as an epithet of Satan:— Belial

956. βέλος **bĕlŏs**, bel´-os; from 906; a missile, i.e. spear or arrow:— dart.

957. βελτίον **bĕltiŏn**, bel-tee´-on; neut. of a comparative of a der. of 906 (used for the comparative of 18); better:— very well.

958. Βενιαμίν **Bĕniamin**, ben-ee-am-een´; of Heb. or. [1144]; Benjamin, an Isr.:— Benjamin.

959. Βερνίκη **Bĕrnikē**, ber-nee´-kay; from a provincial form of 5342 and 3529; victorious; Bernicè a member of the Herodian family:— Bernice.

960. Βέροια **Bĕrŏia**, ber´-oy-ah; perh. a provincial from a der. of 4008 [Peræa, i.e. the region beyond the coast-line]; Berœa, a place in Macedonia:— Berea.

961. Βεροιαῖος **Bĕrŏiaiŏs**, ber-oy-ah´-yos; from 960; a Berœœan or native of Beræa:— of Berea.

962. Βηθαβαρά **Bēthabara**, bay-thab-ar-ah´; of Heb. or. [1004 and 5679]; ferry-house; Bethabara (i.e. Bethabarah), a place on the Jordan:— Bethabara.

963. Βηθανία **Bēthania**, bay-than-ee´-ah; of Chald. or.; date-house; Beth-any, a place in Pal.:— Bethany.

964. Βηθεσδά **Bēthĕsda**, bay-thes-dah´; of Chald. or. [compound of 1004 and 2617]; house of kindness; Beth-esda, a pool in Jerusalem:— Bethesda.

965. Βηθλέεμ **Bēthlĕĕm**, bayth-leh-em´; of Heb. or. [1036]; Bethleem (i.e. Beth-lechem), a place in Pal.:— Bethlehem.

966. Βηθσαϊδά **Bēthsaïda**, bayth-sahee-dah´; of Chald. or. [compound of 1004 and 6719]; fishing-house; Bethsaïda, a place in Pal.:— Bethsaida.

967. Βηθφαγή **Bēthphagĕ**, bayth-fag-ay´; of Chald. or. [compound of 1004 and 6291]; fig-house; Beth-phagè, a place in Pal.:— Bethphage.

968. βῆμα **bēma**, bay´-ma; from the

base of 939; a step, i.e. foot-breath; by impl. a rostrum, i.e. a tribunal:— judgment-seat, set [foot] on, throne.

969. βήρυλλος **bĕrullŏs**, bay´-rool-los; of uncert. der.; a "beryl":— beryl.

970. βία **bia**, bee´-ah; prob. akin to 979 (through the idea of vital activity); force:— violence.

971. βιάζω **biazō**, bee-ad´-zo; from 970; to force, i.e. (refl.) to crowd oneself (into), or (pass.) to be seized:— press, suffer violence.

972. βίαιος **biaiŏs**, bee´-ah-yos; from 970; violent:— mighty.

973. βιαστής **biastēs**, bee-as-tace´; from 971; a forcer, i.e. (fig.) energetic:— violent.

974. βιβλιαρίδιον **bibliaridiŏn**, bib-lee-ar-id´-ee-on; a dimin. of 975; a booklet:— little book.

975. βιβλίον **bibliŏn**, bib-lee´-on; a dimin. of 976; a roll:— bill, book, scroll, writing.

976. βίβλος **biblŏs**, bib´-los; prop. the inner bark of the papyrus plant, i.e. (by impl.) a sheet or scroll of writing:— book.

977. βιβρώσκω **bibrŏskō**, bib-ro´-sko; a redupl. and prol. form of an obs. primary verb [perh. caus. of 1006]; to eat:— eat.

978. Βιθυνία **Bithunia**, bee-thoo-nee´-ah; of uncert. der.; Bithynia, a region of Asia:— Bithynia.

979. βίος **biŏs**, bee´-os; a primary word; life, i.e. (lit.) the present state of existence; by impl. the means of livelihood:— good, life, living.

980. βιόω **biŏō**, bee-ŏ´-o; from 979; to spend existence:— live.

981. βίωσις **biŏsis**, bee´-o-sis; from 980; living (prop. the act, by impl. the mode):— manner of life.

982. βιωτικός **biŏtikŏs**, bee-o-tee-kos´; from a der. of 980; relating to the present existence:— of (pertaining to, things that pertain to) this life.

983. βλαβερός **blabĕrŏs**, blab-er-os´; from 984; injurious:— hurtful.

984. βλάπτω **blaptō**, blap´-to; a primary verb; prop. to hinder, i.e. (by impl.) to injure:— hurt.

985. βλαστάνω **blastanō**, blas-tan´-o; from βλαστός blastŏs (a sprout); to germinate; by impl. to yield fruit:— bring forth, bud, spring (up).

986. Βλάστος **Blastŏs**, blas´-tos; perh. the same as the base of 985; Blastus, an officer of Herod Agrippa:— Blastus.

987. βλασφημέω **blasphēmĕō**, blas-fay-meh´-o; from 989; to vilify; spec. to speak impiously:— (speak) blaspheme (-er, -mously, my), defame, rail on, revile, speak evil.

988. βλασφημία **blasphēmia**, blas-fay-me´-ah; from 989; vilification (espec. against God):— blasphemy, evil speaking, railing.

989. βλάσφημος **blasphēmŏs**, blas´-fay-mos; from a der. of 984 and 5345; scurrilous, i.e. calumnious (against man),

or (spec.) *impious* (against God):—
blasphemer (-mous), railing.

990. βλέμμα **blemma**, *blem´-mah;* from
991; *vision* (prop. concr.; by impl.
abstr.):— seeing.

991. βλέπω **blĕpō**, *blep´-o;* a primary
verb; to *look* at (lit. or fig.):— behold,
beware, lie, look (on, to), perceive, regard, see, sight, take heed. Comp.
3700.

992. βλητέος **blētĕŏs**, *blay-teh´-os;* from
906; fit *to be cast* (i.e. *applied*):— must
be put.

993. Βοανεργές **Bŏanĕrgĕs**, *bŏ-an-erg-
es´;* of Chald. or. [1123 and 7266]; *sons of
commotion; Boänerges*, an epithet of
two of the Apostles:— Boanerges.

994. βοάω **bŏaō**, *bŏ-ah´-o;* appar. a prol.
form of a primary verb; to *halloo*, i.e.
shout (for help or in a tumultuous
way):— cry.

995. βοή **bŏē**, *bŏ-ay´;* from 994; a *halloo*,
i.e. *call* (for aid, etc.):— cry.

996. βοήθεια **bŏēthĕia**, *bŏ-ay´-thi-ah;*
from 998; *aid*; spec. a rope or chain for
frapping a vessel:— help.

997. βοηθέω **bŏēthĕō**, *bŏ-ay-theh´-o;*
from 998; to *aid* or *relieve*:— help, succour.

998. βοηθός **bŏēthŏs**, *bŏ-ay-thos´;* from
995 and θέω **thĕō** (to *run*); a *succorer*:—
helper.

999. βόθυνος **bŏthunŏs**, *both´-oo-nos;*
akin to 900; a *hole* (in the ground); spec.
a *cistern*:— ditch, pit.

1000. βολή **bŏlē**, *bol-ay´;* from 906; a
throw (as a measure of distance):—
cast.

1001. βολίζω **bŏlizō**, *bol-id´-zo;* from
1002; to *heave* the lead:— sound.

1002. βολίς **bŏlis**, *bol-ece´;* from 906; a
missile, i.e. *javelin*:— dart.

1003. Βοόζ **Bŏŏz**, *bŏ-oz´;* of Heb. or.
[1162]; Boöz (i.e. Boaz), an Isr.:— Booz.

1004. βόρβορος **bŏrbŏrŏs**, *bor´-bor-os;* of
uncert. der.; *mud*:— mire.

1005. βορρᾶς **borrhas**, *bor-hras´;* of uncert. der.; the *north* (prop. wind):—
north.

1006. βόσκω **bŏskō**, *bos´-ko;* a prol.
form of a primary verb [comp. 977,
1016]; to *pasture*; by extens. to, *fodder*;
refl. to *graze*:— feed, keep.

1007. Βοσόρ **Bŏsŏr**, *bos-or´;* of Heb. or.
[1160]; Bosor (i.e. Beör), a Moabite:—
Bosor.

1008. βοτάνη **bŏtanē**, *bot-an´-ay;* from
1006; *herbage* (as if for *grazing*):— herb.

1009. βότρυς **bŏtrus**, *bot´-rooce;* of uncert. der.; a *bunch* (of grapes):— (vine)
cluster (of the vine).

1010. βουλευτής **bŏulĕutēs**, *bool-yoo-
tace´;* from 1011; an *adviser*, i.e. (spec.)
a *councillor* or member of the Jewish
Sanhedrin:— counsellor.

1011. βουλεύω **bŏulĕuō**, *bool-yoo´-o;*
from 1012; to *advise*, i.e. (refl.) *deliberate*, or (by impl.) *resolve*:— consult,
take counsel, determine, be minded,
purpose.

1012. βουλή **bŏulē**, *boo-lay´;* from 1014;

---

volition, i.e. (obj.) *advice*, or (by impl.)
purpose:— + advise, counsel, will.

1013. βούλημα **bŏulēma**, *boo´-lay-mah;*
from 1014; a *resolve*:— purpose, will.

1014. βούλομαι **bŏulŏmai**, *boo´-lom-
ahee;* mid. voice of a primary verb.; to
"*will*," i.e. (refl.) *be willing*:— be disposed, minded, intend, list, (be, of own)
will (-ing). Comp. 2309.

1015. βουνός **bŏunŏs**, *boo-nos´;* prob. of
for. or.; a *hillock*:— hill.

1016. βοῦς **bŏus**, *booce;* prob. from the
base of 1006; an *ox* (as *grazing*), i.e. an
animal of that species ("beef"):— ox.

1017. βραβεῖον **brabĕiŏn**, *brab-i´-on;*
from βραβεύς **brabĕus** (an *umpire*; of
uncert. der.); an *award* (of arbitration),
i.e. (spec.) a *prize* in the public
games:— prize.

1018. βραβεύω **brabĕuō**, *brab-yoo´-o;*
from the same as 1017; to *arbitrate*, i.e.
(gen.) to *govern* (fig. *prevail*):— rule.

1019. βραδύνω **bradunō**, *brad-oo´-no;*
from 1021; to *delay*:— be slack, tarry.

1020. βραδυπλοέω **braduplŏĕō**, *brad-oo-
plŏ-eh´-o;* from 1021 and a prol. form of
4126; to *sail slowly*:— sail slowly.

1021. βραδύς **bradus**, *brad-ooce´;* of uncert. aff.; *slow*; fig. *dull*:— slow.

1022. βραδύτης **bradutēs**, *brad-oo´-
tace;* from 1021; *tardiness*:— slackness.

1023. βραχίων **brachiōn**, *brakh-ee´-
own;* prop. comp. of 1024, but appar. in
the sense of βράσσω **brassō** (to *wield*);
the *arm*, i.e. (fig.) *strength*:— arm.

1024. βραχύς **brachus**, *brakh-ooce´;* of
uncert. aff.; *short* (of time, place, quantity, or number):— few words, little
(space, while).

1025. βρέφος **brĕphŏs**, *bref´-os;* of uncert. affin.; an *infant* (prop. unborn) lit.
or fig.:— babe, (young) child, infant.

1026. βρέχω **brĕchō**, *brekh´-o;* a primary verb; to *moisten* (espec. by a
shower):— (send) rain, wash.

1027. βροντή **brŏntē**, *bron-tay´;* akin to
βρέμω **brĕmō** (to *roar*); *thunder*:— thunder (-ing).

1028. βροχή **brŏchē**, *brokh-ay´;* from
1026; *rain*:— rain.

1029. βρόχος **brŏchŏs**, *brokh´-os;* of uncert. der.; a *noose*:— snare.

1030. βρυγμός **brugmŏs**, *broog-mos´;*
from 1031; a *grating* (of the teeth):—
gnashing.

1031. βρύχω **bruchō**, *broo´-kho;* a primary verb; to *grate* the teeth (in pain or
rage):— gnash.

1032. βρύω **bruō**, *broo´-o;* a primary
verb; to *swell* out, i.e. (by impl.) to
gush:— send forth.

1033. βρῶμα **brōma**, *bro´-mah;* from the
base of 977; *food* (lit. or fig.), espec.
(cer.) articles allowed or forbidden by
the Jewish law:— meat, victuals.

1034. βρώσιμος **brōsimŏs**, *bro´-sim-os;*
from 1035; *eatable*:— meat.

1035. βρῶσις **brōsis**, *bro´-sis;* from the
base of 977; (abstr.) *eating* (lit. or fig.);
by extens. (concr.) *food* (lit. or fig.):—
eating, food, meat.

1036. βυθίζω **buthizō**, *boo-thid´-zo;*
from 1037; to *sink*; by impl. to *drown*:—
begin to sink, drown.

1037. βυθός **buthŏs**, *boo-thos´;* a var. of
899; *depth*, i.e. (by impl.) the *sea*:—
deep.

1038. βυρσεύς **bursĕus**, *boorce-yooce´;*
from βύρσα **bursa** (a *hide*); a *tanner*:—
tanner.

1039. βύσσινος **bussinŏs**, *boos´-see-nos;*
from 1040; made of *linen* (neut. a linen
cloth):— fine linen.

1040. βύσσος **bussŏs**, *boos´-sos;* of Heb.
or. [948]; white *linen*:— fine linen.

1041. βῶμος **bōmŏs**, *bo´-mos;* from the
base of 939; prop. a *stand*, i.e. (spec.) an
altar:— altar.

Γ

1042. γαββαθά **gabbatha**, *gab-bath-ah´;*
of Chald. or. [comp. 1355]; *the knoll;
gabbatha*, a vernacular term for the
Roman tribunal in Jerusalem:— Gabbatha.

1043. Γαβριήλ **Gabriēl**, *gab-ree-ale´;* of
Heb. or. [1403]; *Gabriel*, an archangel:— Gabriel.

1044. γάγγραινα **gaggraina**, *gang´-gra-
hee-nah;* from γραίνω **grainō** (to *gnaw*);
an *ulcer* ("gangrene"):— canker.

1045. Γάδ **Gad**, *gad;* of Heb. or. [1410];
Gad, a tribe of Isr.:— Gad.

1046. Γαδαρηνός **Gadarēnŏs**, *gad-ar-
ay-nos´;* from Γαδαρά (a town E. of the
Jordan); a *Gadarene* or inhab. of
Gadara:— Gadarene.

1047. γάζα **gaza**, *gad´-zah;* of for. or.; a
treasure:— treasure.

1048. Γάζα **Gaza**, *gad´-zah;* of Heb. or.
[5804]; *Gazah* (i.e. *Azzah*), a place in
Pal.:— Gaza.

1049. γαζοφυλάκιον **gazŏphulakiŏn**,
gad-zof-oo-lak´-ee-on; from 1047 and
5438; a *treasure-house*, i.e. a court in
the temple for the collection-boxes:—
treasury.

1050. Γάϊος **Gaïŏs**, *gah´-ee-os;* of Lat.
or.; *Gaïus* (i.e. *Caius*), a Chr.:— Gaius.

1051. γάλα **gala**, *gal´-ah;* of uncert. aff.;
milk (fig.):— milk.

1052. Γαλάτης **Galatēs**, *gal-at´-ace;*
from 1053; a *Galatian* or inhab. of Galatia:— Galatian.

1053. Γαλατία **Galatia**, *gal-at-ee´-ah;* of
for. or.; *Galatia*, a region of Asia:—
Galatia.

1054. Γαλατικός **Galatikŏs**, *gal-at-ee-
kos´;* from 1053; *Galatic* or relating to
Galatia:— of Galatia.

1055. γαλήνη **galēnē**, *gal-ay´-nay;* of
uncert. der.; *tranquillity*:— calm.

1056. Γαλιλαία **Galilaia**, *gal-il-ah´-yah;*
of Heb. or. [1551]; *Galilæa* (i.e. the *heathen circle*), a region of Pal.:— Galilee.

1057. Γαλιλαῖος **Galilaiŏs**, *gal-ee-lah´-
yos;* from 1056; *Galilæan* or belonging
to Galilæa:— Galilæan, of Galilee.

1058. Γαλλίων **Galliōn**, *gal-lee-own´;* of
Lat. or.; *Gallion* (i.e. *Gallio*), a Roman
officer:— Gallio.

1059. Γαμαλιήλ **Gamaliēl**, *gam-al-ee-*

ale'; of Heb. or. [1583]; *Gamaliel* (i.e. *Gamliel*), an Isr.:— Gamaliel.

1060. γαμέω **gamĕō**, *gam-eh´-o;* from 1062; to *wed* (of either sex):— marry (a wife).

1061. γαμίσκω **gamiskō**, *gam-is´-ko;* from 1062; to *espouse* (a daughter to a husband):— give in marriage.

1062. γάμος **gamŏs**, *gam´-os;* of uncert. aff.; *nuptials:*— marriage, wedding.

1063. γάρ **gar**, *gar;* a primary particle; prop. assigning a *reason* (used in argument, explanation or intensification; often with other particles):— and, as, because (that), but, even, for, indeed, no doubt, seeing, then, therefore, verily, what, why, yet.

1064. γαστήρ **gastĕr**, *gas-tare´;* of uncert. der.; the *stomach;* by anal. the *matrix;* fig. a *gourmand:*— belly, + with child, womb.

1065. γέ **gĕ**, *gheh;* a primary particle of *emphasis* or *qualification* (often used with other particles pref.):— and besides, doubtless, at least, yet.

1066. Γεδεών **Gĕdĕōn**, *ghed-eh-own´;* of Heb. or. [1439]; *Gedeon* (i.e. *Gidlelon*), an Isr.:— Gedeon (Gideon).

1067. γέεννα **gĕĕnna**, *gheh´-en-nah;* of Heb. or. [1516 and 2011]; *valley of* (the son of) *Hinnom;* ge-henna (or Ge-Hinnom), a valley of Jerusalem, used (fig.) as a name for the place (or state) of everlasting punishment:— hell.

1068. Γεθσημανῆ **Gĕthsēmanē**, *gheth-say-man-ay´;* of Chald. or. [comp. 1660 and 8081]; *oil-press; Gethsemane,* a garden near Jerusalem:— Gethsemane.

1069. γείτων **gĕitōn**, *ghi´-tone;* from 1093; a *neighbour* (as adjoining one's *ground*); by impl. a *friend:*— neighbour.

1070. γελάω **gĕlaō**, *ghel-ah´-o;* of uncert. aff.; to *laugh* (as a sign of joy or satisfaction):— laugh.

1071. γέλως **gĕlōs**, *ghel´-oce;* from 1070; *laughter* (as a mark of gratification):— laughter.

1072. γεμίζω **gĕmizō**, *ghem-id´-zo;* tran. from 1073; to *fill* entirely:— fill (be) full.

1073. γέμω **gĕmō**, *ghem´-o;* a primary verb; to *swell* out, i.e. be *full:*— be full.

1074. γενεά **gĕnĕa**, *ghen-eh-ah´;* from (a presumed der. of) 1085; a *generation;* by impl. an *age* (the period or the persons):— age, generation, nation, time.

1075. γενεαλογέω **gĕnĕalŏgĕō**, *ghen-eh-al-og-eh´-o;* from 1074 and 3056; to *reckon by generations,* i.e. *trace in genealogy:*— count by descent.

1076. γενεαλογία **gĕnĕalŏgia**, *ghen-eh-al-og-ee´-ah;* from the same as 1075; *tracing by generations,* i.e. "*genealogy*":— genealogy.

1077. γενέσια **gĕnĕsia**, *ghen-es´-ee-ah;* neut. plur. of a der. of 1078; *birthday ceremonies:*— birthday.

1078. γένεσις **genesis**, *ghen´-es-is;* from the same as 1074; *nativity;* fig. *nature* (-ral):— generation, nature (-ral).

1079. γενετή **gĕnĕtē**, *ghen-et-ay;* fem. of a presumed der. of the base of 1074; *birth:*— birth.

1080. γεννάω **gĕnnaō**, *ghen-nah´-o;* from a var. of 1085; to *procreate* (prop. of the father, but by extens. of the mother); fig. to *regenerate:*— bear, beget, be born, bring forth, conceive, be delivered of, gender, make, spring.

1081. γέννημα **gĕnnēma**, or γένημα **gĕnēma**, *ghen´-nay-mah;* from 1080; *offspring;* by anal. *produce* (lit. or fig.):— fruit, generation.

1082. Γεννησαρέτ **Gĕnnēsarĕt**, *ghennay-sar-et´;* of Heb. or. [comp. 3672]; *Gennesaret* (i.e. *Kinnereth*), a lake and plain in Pal.:— Gennesaret.

1083. γέννησις **gĕnnēsis**, *ghen´-nay-sis;* from 1080; *nativity:*— birth.

1084. γεννητός **gĕnnētŏs**, *ghen-naytos´;* from 1080; *born:*— they that are born.

1085. γένος **gĕnŏs**, *ghen´-os;* from 1096; "*kin*" (abstr. or concr., lit. or fig., indiv. or collect.):— born, country (-man), diversity, generation, kind (-red), nation, offspring, stock.

1086. Γεργεσηνός **Gĕrgĕsēnŏs**, *gherghes-ay-nos´;* of Heb. or. [1622]; a *Gergesene* (i.e. *Girgashite*) or one of the aborigines of Pal.:— Gergesene.

1087. γερουσία **gĕrŏusia**, *gher-oo-see´-ah;* from 1088; the *eldership,* i.e. (collect.) the Jewish *Sanhedrin:*— senate.

1088. γέρων **gĕrōn**, *gher´-own;* of uncert. aff. [comp. 1094]; *aged:*— old.

1089. γεύομαι **gĕuŏmai**, *ghyoo´-omahee;* a primary verb; to *taste;* by impl. to *eat;* fig. to *experience* (good or ill):— eat, taste.

1090. γεωργέω **gĕōrgĕō**, *gheh-or-gheh´-o;* from 1092; to *till* (the soil):— dress.

1091. γεώργιον **gĕōrgiŏn**, *gheh-ore´-ghee-on;* neut. of a (presumed) der. of 1092; *cultivable,* i.e. a *farm:*— husbandry.

1092. γεωργός **gĕōrgŏs**, *gheh-ore-gos´;* from 1093 and the base of 2041; a *land-worker,* i.e. *farmer:*— husbandman.

1093. γῆ **gē**, *ghay;* contr. from a primary word; *soil;* by extension a *region,* or the solid part or the whole of the *terrene* globe (incl. the occupants in each application):— country, earth (-ly), ground, land, world.

1094. γῆρας **gēras**, *ghay´-ras;* akin to 1088; *senility:*— old age.

1095. γηράσκω **gēraskō**, *ghay-ras´-ko;* from 1094; to *be senescent:*— be (wax) old.

1096. γίνομαι **ginŏmai**, *ghin´-om-ahee;* a prol. and mid. voice form of a primary verb; to *cause to be* ("*gen*"-erate), i.e. (refl.) to *become* (come into being), used with great latitude (lit., fig., intens., etc.):— arise, be assembled, be (-come, -fall, -have self), be brought (to pass), (be) come (to pass), continue, be divided, draw, be ended, fall, be finished, follow, be found, be fulfilled, + God forbid, grow, happen, have, be kept, be made, be married, be ordained to be, partake, pass, be performed, be published, require, seem,

be showed, × soon as it was, sound, be taken, be turned, use, wax, will, would, be wrought.

1097. γινώσκω **ginōskō**, *ghin-oce´-ko;* a prol. form of a primary verb; to "*know*" (absolutely) in a great variety of applications and with many impl. (as follow, with others not thus clearly expressed):— allow, be aware (of), feel, (have) know (-ledge), perceive, be resolved, can speak, be sure, understand.

1098. γλεῦκος **glĕukŏs**, *glyoo´-kos;* akin to 1099; *sweet* wine, i.e. (prop.) *must* (fresh juice), but used of the more saccharine (and therefore highly inebriating) fermented *wine:*— new wine.

1099. γλυκύς **glukus**, *gloo-koos´;* of uncert. aff.; *sweet* (i.e. not bitter nor salt):— sweet, fresh.

1100. γλῶσσα **glōssa**, *gloce-sah´;* of uncert. aff.; the *tongue;* by impl. a *language* (spec., one naturally unacquired):— tongue.

1101. γλωσσόκομον **glōssŏkŏmŏn**, *gloce-sok´-om-on;* from 1100 and the base of 2889; prop. a *case* (to keep mouthpieces of wind-instruments in) i.e. (by extens.) a *casket* or (spec.) *purse:*— bag.

1102. γναφεύς **gnaphĕus**, *gnaf-yuce´;* by var. for a der. from κνάπτω **knaptō** (to *tease* cloth); a cloth-*dresser:*— fuller.

1103. γνήσιος **gnēsiŏs**, *gnay´-see-os;* from the same as 1077; *legitimate* (of birth), i.e. *genuine:*— own, sincerity, true.

1104. γνησίως **gnēsiōs**, *gnay-see´-oce;* adv. from 1103; *genuinely,* i.e. *really:*— naturally.

1105. γνόφος **gnŏphŏs**, *gnof´-os;* akin to 3509; *gloom* (as of a storm):— blackness.

1106. γνώμη **gnōmē**, *gno´-may;* from 1097; *cognition,* i.e. (subj.) *opinion,* or (obj.) *resolve* (counsel, consent, etc.):— advice, + agree, judgment, mind, purpose, will.

1107. γνωρίζω **gnōrizō**, *gno-rid´-zo;* from a der. of 1097; to *make known;* subj. to *know:*— certify, declare, make known, give to understand, do to wit, wot.

1108. γνῶσις **gnōsis**, *gno´-sis;* from 1097; *knowing* (the act), i.e. (by impl.) *knowledge:*— knowledge, science.

1109. γνώστης **gnōstēs**, *gnoce´-tace;* from 1097; a *knower:*— expert.

1110. γνωστός **gnōstŏs**, *gnoce-tos´;* from 1097; *well-known:*— acquaintance, (which may be) known, notable.

1111. γογγύζω **gŏgguzō**, *gong-good´-zo;* of uncert. der.; to *grumble:*— murmur.

1112. γογγυσμός **gŏggusmŏs**, *gong-goos-mos´;* from 1111; a *grumbling:*— grudging, murmuring.

1113. γογγυστής **gŏggustēs**, *gong-goos-tace´;* from 1111; a *grumbler:*— murmurer.

1114. γόης **gŏēs**, *go´-ace;* from γοάω **gŏaō** (to *wail*); prop. a *wizard* (as *muttering* spells), i.e. (by impl.) an *imposter:*— seducer.

1115. Γολγοθᾶ **Golgŏtha**, *gol-goth-ah´;* of Chald. or. [comp. 1538]; *the skull;* Golgotha, a knoll near Jerusalem:— Golgotha.

1116. Γόμορρα **Gŏmŏrrha**, *gom´-or-hrhah;* of Heb. or. [6017]; Gomorrha (i.e. `Amorah), a place near the Dead Sea:— Gomorrha.

1117. γόμος **gŏmŏs**, *gom´-os;* from 1073; a *load* (as *filling*), i.e. (spec.) a *cargo*, or (by extens.) *wares:*— burden, merchandise.

1118. γονεύς **gŏnĕus**, *gon-yooce´;* from the base of 1096; a *parent:*— parent.

1119. γονύ **gŏnu**, *gon-oo´;* of uncert. aff.; the "*knee*":— knee (xl).

1120. γονυπετέω **gŏnupĕtĕō**, *gon-oo-pet-eh´-o;* from a compound of 1119 and the alt. of 4098; to *fall on the knee:*— bow the knee, kneel down.

1121. γράμμα **gramma**, *gram´-mah;* from 1125; a *writing*, i.e. a *letter, note, epistle, book*, etc.; plur. *learning:*— bill, learning, letter, scripture, writing, written.

1122. γραμματεύς **grammatĕus**, *grammat-yooce´;* from 1121; a *writer*, i.e. (professionally) *scribe* or *secretary:*— scribe, town-clerk.

1123. γραπτός **graptŏs**, *grap-tos´;* from 1125; *inscribed* (fig.):— written.

1124. γραφή **graphē**, *graf-ay´;* from 1125; a *document*, i.e. holy *Writ* (or its contents or a statement in it):— scripture.

1125. γράφω **graphō**, *graf´-o;* a primary verb; to "*grave*", espec. to *write;* fig. to *describe:*— describe, write (-ing, -ten).

1126. γραώδης **graōdēs**, *grah-o´-dace;* from γραύς **graus** (an *old woman*) and 1491; *crone-like*, i.e. *silly:*— old wives'.

1127. γρηγορεύω **grēgŏrĕuō**, *gray-gor-yoo´-o;* from 1453; to *keep awake*, i.e. *watch* (lit. or fig.):— be vigilant, wake, (be) watch (-ful).

1128. γυμνάζω **gumnazō**, *goom-nad´-zo;* from 1131; to *practise naked* (in the games), i.e. *train* (fig.):— exercise.

1129. γυμνασία **gumnasia**, *goom-nasee´-ah;* from 1128; *training*, i.e. (fig.) *asceticism:*— exercise.

1130. γυμνητεύω **gumnētĕuō**, *goomnayt-yoo´-o* or γυμνιτεύω **gumniteuo**, *goom-niyt-yoo´-o;* from a der. of 1131; to *strip*, i.e. (refl.) *go poorly clad:*— be naked.

1131. γυμνός **gumnŏs**, *goom-nos´;* of uncert. aff.; *nude* (absol. or rel., lit. or fig.):— naked.

1132. γυμνότης **gumnŏtēs**, *goom-not´-ace;* from 1131; *nudity* (absol. or comp.):— nakedness.

1133. γυναικάριον **gunaikariŏn**, *goo-nahee-kar´-ee-on;* a dimin. from 1135; a *little* (i.e. *foolish*) *woman:*— silly woman.

1134. γυναικεῖος **gunaikĕiŏs**, *goo-nahee-ki´-os;* from 1135; *feminine:*— wife.

1135. γυνή **gunē**, *goo-nay´;* prob. from the base of 1096; a *woman;* spec. a *wife:*— wife, woman.

1136. Γώγ **Gōg**, *gogue;* of Heb. or.

[1463]; *Gog*, a symb. name for some future Antichrist:— Gog.

1137. γωνία **gōnia**, *go-nee´-ah;* prob. akin to 1119; an *angle:*— corner, quarter.

Δ

1138. Δαβίδ **Dabid**, *dab-eed´;* of Heb. or. [1732]; *Dabid* (i.e. *David*), the Isr. king:— David.

1139. δαιμονίζομαι **daimŏnizŏmai**, *dahee-mon-id´-zom-ahee;* mid. voice from 1142; to *be exercised by a demon:*— have a (be vexed with, be possessed with) devil (-s).

1140. δαιμόνιον **daimŏniŏn**, *daheemon´-ee-on;* neut. of a der. of 1142; a *demonic being;* by extens. a *deity:*— devil, god.

1141. δαιμονιώδης **daimŏniōdēs**, *dahee-mon-ee-o´-dace;* from 1140 and 1142; *demon-like:*— devilish.

1142. δαίμων **daimōn**, *dah´-ee-mown;* from δαίω **daiō** (to *distribute* fortunes); a *demon* or supernatural spirit (of a bad nature):— devil.

1143. δάκνω **daknō**, *dak´-no;* a prol. form of a primary root; to *bite*, i.e. (fig.) *thwart:*— bite.

1144. δάκρυ **dakru**, *dak´-roo;* or δάκρυον **dakruŏn**, *dak´-roo-on;* of uncert. affin.; a *tear:*— tear.

1145. δακρύω **dakruō**, *dak-roo´-o;* from 1144; to *shed tears:*— weep. Comp. 2799.

1146. δακτύλιος **daktuliŏs**, *dak-too´-lee-os;* from 1147; a *finger*-ring:— ring.

1147. δάκτυλος **daktulŏs**, *dak´-too-los;* prob. from 1176; a *finger:*— finger.

1148. Δαλμανουθά **Dalmanŏutha**, *dalman-oo-thah´;* prob. of Chald. or.; *Dalmanütha*, a place in Pal.:— Dalmanutha.

1149. Δαλματία **Dalmatia**, *dal-mat-ee´-ah;* prob. of for. der.; *Dalmatia*, a region of Europe:— Dalmatia.

1150. δαμάζω **damazō**, *dam-ad´-zo;* a var. of an obs. primary of the same mean.; to *tame:*— tame.

1151. δάμαλις **damalis**, *dam´-al-is;* prob. from the base of 1150; a *heifer* (as *tame*):— heifer.

1152. Δάμαρις **Damaris**, *dam´-ar-is;* prob. from the base of 1150; perh. *gentle; Damaris*, an Athenian woman:— Damaris.

1153. Δαμασκηνός **Damaskēnŏs**, *damas-kay-nos´;* from 1154; a *Damascene* or inhab. of Damascus:— Damascene.

1154. Δαμασκός **Damaskŏs**, *dam-askos´;* of Heb. or. [1834]; *Damascus*, a city of Syria:— Damascus.

1155. δανείζω **danĕizō**, *dan-ayd´-zo;* or δανίζω **danizō**, *dan-ide´-zo* from 1156; to *loan* on interest; refl. to *borrow:*— borrow, lend.

1156. δάνειον **danĕiŏn**, *dan´-i-on;* from δάνος **danŏs** (a *gift*); prob. akin to the base of 1325; a *loan:*— debt.

1157. δανειστής **danĕistēs**, *dan-ice-tace´;* or

δανιστής **danistēs**, *dan-iys-tace´* from 1155; a *lender:*— creditor.

1158. Δανιήλ **Daniēl**, *dan-ee-ale´;* of Heb. or. [1840]; *Daniel*, an Isr.:— Daniel.

1159. δαπανάω **dapanaō**, *dap-an-ah´-o;* from 1160; to *expend*, i.e. (in a good sense) to *incur cost*, or (in a bad one) to *waste:*— be at charges, consume, spend.

1160. δαπάνη **dapanē**, *dap-an´-ay;* from δάπτω **daptō** (to *devour*); *expense* (as *consuming*):— cost.

1161. δέ **dĕ**, *deh;* a primary particle (adversative or continuative); *but, and,* etc.:— also, and, but, moreover, now [often unexpressed in English].

1162. δέησις **dĕēsis**, *deh´-ay-sis;* from 1189; a *petition:*— prayer, request, supplication.

1163. δεῖ **dĕi**, *die;* third pers. sing. act. present of 1210; also δέον **dĕŏn**, *deh-on´;* neut. act. part. of the same; both used impers.; *it is* (*was*, etc.) *necessary* (as *binding*):— behoved, be meet, must (needs), (be) need (-ful), ought, should.

1164. δεῖγμα **dĕigma**, *digh´-mah;* from the base of 1166; a *specimen* (as *shown*):— example.

1165. δειγματίζω **dĕigmatizō**, *dighmat-id´-zo;* from 1164; to *exhibit:*— make a shew.

1166. δεικνύω **dĕiknuō**, *dike-noo´-o;* a prol. form of an obs. primary of the same mean.; to *show* (lit. or fig.):— shew.

1167. δειλία **dĕilia**, *di-lee-ah;* from 1169; *timidity:*— fear.

1168. δειλιάω **dĕiliaō**, *di-lee-ah´-o;* from 1167; to *be timid:*— be afraid.

1169. δειλός **dĕilŏs**, *di-los´;* from δέος **dĕŏs** (*dread*); *timid*, i.e. (by impl.) *faithless:*— fearful.

1170. δεῖνα **dĕina**, *di´-nah;* prob. from the same as 1171 (through the idea of forgetting the name as *fearful*, i.e. *strange*); *so and so* (when the person is not specified):— such a man.

1171. δεινῶς **dĕinōs**, *di-noce´;* adv. from a der. of the same as 1169; *terribly*, i.e. *excessively:*— grievously, vehemently.

1172. δειπνέω **dĕipnĕō**, *dipe-neh´-o;* from 1173; to *dine*, i.e. take the principal (or evening) meal:— sup (x -er).

1173. δεῖπνον **dĕipnŏn**, *dipe´-non;* from the same as 1160; *dinner*, i.e. the chief meal (usually in the evening):— feast, supper.

1174. δεισιδαιμονέστερος **dĕisidaimŏnĕstĕrŏs**, *dice-ee-dahee-mon-es´-ter-os;* the comparative of a der. of the base of 1169 and 1142; *more religious* than others:— too superstitious.

1175. δεισιδαιμονία **dĕisidaimŏnia**, *dice-ee-dahee-mon-ee´-ah;* from the same as 1174; *relig.:*— superstition.

1176. δέκα **dĕka**, *dek´-ah;* a primary number; *ten:*— [eight-] een, ten.

1177. δεκαδύο **dĕkaduŏ**, *dek-ad-oo´-o;* from 1176 and 1417; *two and ten*, i.e. *twelve:*— twelve.

1178. δεκαπέντε **dĕkapĕntĕ**, *dek-ap-*

en´-teh; from 1176 and 4002; ten and five, i.e. fifteen:— fifteen.

1179. Δεκάπολις **Děkapŏlis**, dek-ap´-ol-is; from 1176 and 4172; the ten-city region; the Decapolis, a district in Syria:— Decapolis.

1180. δεκατέσσαρες **děkatěssarěs**, dek-at-es´-sar-es; from 1176 and 5064; ten and four, i.e. fourteen:— fourteen.

1181. δεκάτη **děkatě**, dek-at´-ay; fem. of 1182; a tenth, i.e. as a percentage or (tech.) tithe:— tenth (part), tithe.

1182. δέκατος **děkatŏs**, dek´-at-os; ordinal from 1176; tenth:— tenth.

1183. δεκατόω **děkatŏō**, dek-at-ŏ´-o; from 1181; to tithe, i.e. to give or take a tenth:— pay (receive) tithes.

1184. δεκτός **děktŏs**, dek-tos´; from 1209; approved; (fig.) propitious:— accepted (-table).

1185. δελεάζω **dělěazō**, del-eh-ad´-zo; from the base of 1388; to entrap, i.e. (fig.) delude:— allure, beguile, entice.

1186. δένδρον **děndrŏn**, den´-dron; prob. from δρύς drus (an oak); a tree:— tree.

1187. δεξιολάβος **děxiŏlabŏs**, dex-ee-ol-ab´-os; from 1188 and 2983; a guardsman (as if taking the right) or light-armed soldier:— spearman.

1188. δεξιός **děxiŏs**, dex-ee-os´; from 1209; the right side or (fem.) hand (as that which usually takes):— right (hand, side).

1189. δέομαι **děŏmai**, deh´-om-ahee; mid. voice of 1210; to beg (as binding oneself), i.e. petition:— beseech, pray (to), make request. Comp. 4441.

δεόν **děŏn**. See 1163.

1190. Δερβαῖος **Děrbaiŏs**, der-bah´-ee-os; from 1191; a Derbæan or inhab. of Derbe:— of Derbe.

1191. Δέρβη **Děrbě**, der-bay´; of for. or.; Derbě, a place in Asia Minor:— Derbe.

1192. δέρμα **děrma**, der´-mah; from 1194; a hide:— skin.

1193. δερμάτινος **děrmatinŏs**, der-mat´-ee-nos; from 1192; made of hide:— leathern, of a skin.

1194. δέρω **děrō**, der´-o; a primary verb; prop. to flay, i.e. (by impl.) to scourge, or (by anal.) to thrash:— beat, smite.

1195. δεσμεύω **děsměuō**, des-myoo´-o; from a (presumed) der. of 1196; to be a binder (captor), i.e. to enchain (a prisoner), to tie on (a load):— bind.

1196. δεσμέω **děsměō**, des-meh´-o; from 1199; to tie, i.e. shackle:— bind.

1197. δεσμή **děsmě**, des-may´; from 1196; a bundle:— bundle.

1198. δέσμιος **děsmiŏs**, des´-mee-os; from 1199; a captive (as bound):— in bonds, prisoner.

1199. δεσμόν **děsmŏn**, des-mon´; or

δεσμός **děsmŏs**, des-mos´; neut. and masc. respectively from 1210; a band, i.e. ligament (of the body) or shackle (of a prisoner); fig. an impediment or disability:— band, bond, chain, string.

1200. δεσμοφύλαξ **děsmŏphulax**, des-

mof-oo´-lax; from 1199 and 5441; a jailer (as guarding the prisoners):— jailor, keeper of the prison.

1201. δεσμωτήριον **děsmōtěriŏn**, des-mo-tay´-ree-on; from a der. of 1199 (equiv. to 1196); a place of bondage, i.e. a dungeon:— prison.

1202. δεσμώτης **děsmōtěs**, des-mo´-tace; from the same as 1201; (pass.) a captive:— prisoner.

1203. δεσπότης **děspŏtěs**, des-pot´-ace; perh. from 1210 and πόσις pŏsis (a husband); an absolute ruler ("despot"):— Lord, master.

1204. δεῦρο **děurŏ**, dyoo´-ro; of uncert. aff.; here; used also imperative hither!; and of time, hitherto:— come (hither), hither [-to].

1205. δεῦτε **děutě**, dyoo´-teh; from 1204 and an imper. form of εἶμι **ěimi** (to go); come hither!:— come, × follow.

1206. δευτεραῖος **děutěraiŏs**, dyoo-ter-ah´-yos; from 1208; secondary, i.e. (spec.) on the second day:— next day.

1207. δευτερόπρωτος **děutěrŏprōtŏs**, dyoo-ter-op´-ro-tos; from 1208 and 4413; second-first, i.e. (spec.) a designation of the Sabbath immediately after the Paschal week (being the second after Passover day, and the first of the seven Sabbaths intervening before Pentecost):— second ... after the first.

1208. δεύτερος **děutěrŏs**, dyoo´-ter-os; as the comp. of 1417; (ordinal) second (in time, place, or rank; also adv.):— afterward, again, second (-arily, time).

1209. δέχομαι **děchŏmai**, dekh´-om-ahee; mid. voice of a primary verb; to receive (in various applications, lit. or fig.):— accept, receive, take. Comp. 2983.

1210. δέω **děō**, deh´-o; a primary verb; to bind (in various applications, lit. or fig.):— bind, be in bonds, knit, tie, wind. See also 1163, 1189.

1211. δή **dě**, day; prob. akin to 1161; a particle of emphasis or explicitness; now, then, etc.:— also, and, doubtless, now, therefore.

1212. δῆλος **dělŏs**, day´-los; of uncert. der.; clear:— + bewray, certain, evident, manifest.

1213. δηλόω **dělŏō**, day-lŏ´-o; from 1212; to make plain (by words):— declare, shew, signify.

1214. Δημᾶς **Děmas**, day-mas´; prob. for 1216; Demas, a Chr.:— Demas.

1215. δημηγορέω **děmēgŏrěō**, day-may-gor-eh´-o; from a compound of 1218 and 58; to be a people-gatherer, i.e. to address a public assembly:— make an oration.

1216. Δημήτριος **Děmětriŏs**, day-may´-tree-os; from Δημήτηρ **Děmětěr** (Ceres); Demetrius, the name of an Ephesian and of a Chr.:— Demetrius.

1217. δημιουργός **děmiŏurgŏs**, day-me-oor-gos´; from 1218 and 2041; a worker for the people, i.e. mechanic (spoken of the Creator):— maker.

1218. δῆμος **děmŏs**, day´-mos; from 1210; the public (as bound together socially):— people.

1219. δημόσιος **děmŏsiŏs**, day-mos´ee-os; from 1218; public; (fem. sing. dat. case as adv.) in public:— common, openly, publickly.

1220. δηνάριον **děnariŏn**, day-nar´-ee-on; of Lat. or.; a denarius (or ten asses):— pence, penny [-worth].

1221. δήποτε **děpŏtě**, day´-pot-eh; from 1211 and 4218; a particle of generalization; indeed, at any time:— (what-) soever.

1222. δήπου **děpŏu**, day´-poo; from 1211 and 4225; a particle of asseveration; indeed doubtless:— verily.

1223. διά **dia**, dee-ah´; a primary prep. denoting the channel of an act; through (in very wide applications, local, causal, or occasional):— after, always, among, at, to avoid, because of (that), briefly, by, for (cause) ... fore, from, in, by occasion of, of, by reason of, for sake, that, thereby, therefore, × though, through (-out), to, wherefore, with (-in). In composition it retains the same general import.

Δία **Dia**. See 2203.

1224. διαβαίνω **diabainō**, dee-ab-ah´-ee-no; from 1223 and the base of 939; to cross:— come over, pass (through).

1225. διαβάλλω **diaballō**, dee-ab-al´-lo; from 1223 and 906; (fig.) to traduce:— accuse.

1226. διαβεβαιόομαι **diaběbaiŏŏmai**, dee-ab-eb-ahee-ŏ´-om-ahee; mid. voice of a compound of 1223 and 950; to confirm thoroughly (by words), i.e. asseverate:— affirm constantly.

1227. διαβλέπω **diablěpō**, dee-ab-lep´-o; from 1223 and 991; to look through, i.e. recover full vision:— see clearly.

1228. διάβολος **diabŏlŏs**, dee-ab´-ol-os; from 1225; a traducer; spec. Satan [comp. 7854]:— false accuser, devil, slanderer.

1229. διαγγέλλω **diaggěllō**, de-ang-gel´-lo; from 1223 and the base of 32; to herald thoroughly:— declare, preach, signify.

1230. διαγίνομαι **diaginŏmai**, dee-ag-in´-om-ahee; from 1223 and 1096; to elapse meanwhile:— × after, be past, be spent.

1231. διαγινώσκω **diaginōskō**, dee-ag-in-o´-sko; from 1223 and 1097; to know thoroughly, i.e. ascertain exactly:— (would) enquire, know the uttermost.

1232. διαγνωρίζω **diagnōrizō**, dee-ag-no-rid´-zo; from 1123 and 1107; to tell abroad:— make known.

1233. διάγνωσις **diagnōsis**, dee-ag´-no-sis; from 1231; (magisterial) examination ("diagnosis"):— hearing.

1234. διαγογγύζω **diagŏgguzō**, dee-ag-ong-good´-zo; from 1223 and 1111; to complain throughout a crowd:— murmur.

1235. διαγρηγορέω **diagrēgŏrěō**, dee-ag-ray-gor-eh´-o; from 1223 and 1127; to waken thoroughly:— be awake.

1236. διάγω **diagō**, dee-ag´-o; from 1223 and 71; to pass time or life:— lead life, living.

1237. διαδέχομαι **diaděchŏmai**, dee-ad-

ekh´-om-ahee; from 1223 and 1209; to *receive in turn,* i.e. (fig.) *succeed to:*— come after.

1238. διάδημα **diadēma,** *dee-ad´-ay-mah;* from a compound of 1223 and 1210; a *"diadem"* (as *bound about* the head):— crown. Comp. 4735.

1239. διαδίδωμι **diadidōmi,** *dee-ad-id´-o-mee;* from 1223 and 1325; to *give throughout* a crowd, i.e. *deal out;* also to *deliver over* (as to a successor):— (make) distribute (-ion), divide, give.

1240. διάδοχος **diadŏchŏs,** *dee-ad´-okh-os;* from 1237; a *successor* in office:— room.

1241. διαζώννυμι **diazōnnumi,** *dee-az-own´-noo-mee;* from 1223 and 2224; to *gird tightly:*— gird.

1242. διαθήκη **diathēkē,** *dee-ath-ay´-kay;* from 1303; prop. a *disposition,* i.e. (spec.) a *contract* (espec. a devisory *will*):— covenant, testament.

1243. διαίρεσις **diairĕsis,** *dee-ah´-ee-res-is;* from 1244; a *distinction* or (concr.) *variety:*— difference, diversity.

1244. διαιρέω **diairĕō,** *dee-ahee-reh´-o;* from 1223 and 138; to *separate,* i.e. *distribute:*— divide.

1245. διακαθαρίζω **diakatharizō,** *dee-ak-ath-ar-id´-zo;* from 1223 and 2511; to *cleanse perfectly,* i.e. (spec.) *winnow:*— thoroughly purge.

1246. διακατελέγχομαι **diakatĕlĕgchŏmai,** *dee-ak-at-el-eng´-khom-ahee;* mid. voice from 1223 and a compound of 2596 and 1651; to *prove downright,* i.e. *confute:*— convince.

1247. διακονέω **diakŏnĕō,** *dee-ak-on-eh´-o;* from 1249; to *be an attendant,* i.e. *wait upon* (menially or as a host, friend, or [fig.] teacher); techn. to *act as a Chr. deacon:*— (ad-) minister (unto), serve, use the office of a deacon.

1248. διακονία **diakŏnia,** *dee-ak-on-ee´-ah;* from 1249; *attendance* (as a servant, etc.); fig. (eleemosynary) *aid,* (official) *service* (espec. of the Chr. teacher, or techn. of the *diaconate*):— (ad-) minister (-ing, -tration, -try), office, relief, service (-ing).

1249. διάκονος **diakŏnŏs,** *dee-ak´-on-os;* prob. from an obs. διάκω *diakō* (to *run* on errands; comp. 1377); an *attendant,* i.e. (gen.) a *waiter* (at table or in other menial duties); spec. a Chr. *teacher* and *pastor* (tech. a *deacon* or *deaconess*):— deacon, minister, servant.

1250. διακόσιοι **diakŏsiŏi,** *dee-ak-os´-ee-oy;* from 1364 and 1540; *two hundred:*— two hundred.

1251. διακούομαι **diakŏuŏmai,** *dee-ak-oo´-om-ahee;* mid. voice from 1223 and 191; to *hear throughout,* i.e. *patiently listen* (to a prisoner's plea):— hear.

1252. διακρίνω **diakrinō,** *dee-ak-ree´-no;* from 1223 and 2919; to *separate thoroughly,* i.e. (lit. and refl.) to *withdraw* from, or (by impl.) *oppose;* fig. to *discriminate* (by impl. *decide*), or (refl.) *hesitate:*— contend, make (to) differ (-ence), discern, doubt, judge, be partial, stagger, waver.

1253. διάκρισις **diakrisis,** *dee-ak´-ree-sis;* from 1252; judicial *estimation:*— discern (-ing), disputation.

1254. διακωλύω **diakōluō,** *dee-ak-o-loo´-o;* from 1223 and 2967; to *hinder altogether,* i.e. *utterly prohibit:*— forbid.

1255. διαλαλέω **dialalĕō,** *dee-al-al-eh´-o;* from 1223 and 2980; to *talk throughout* a company, i.e. *converse* or (gen.) *publish:*— commune, noise abroad.

1256. διαλέγομαι **dialĕgŏmai,** *dee-al-eg´-om-ahee;* mid. voice from 1223 and 3004; to *say thoroughly,* i.e. *discuss* (in argument or exhortation):— dispute, preach (unto), reason (with), speak.

1257. διαλείπω **dialĕipō,** *dee-al-i´-po;* from 1223 and 3007; to *leave off in the middle,* i.e. *intermit:*— cease.

1258. διάλεκτος **dialĕktŏs,** *dee-al´-ek-tos;* from 1256; a (mode of) *discourse,* i.e. *"dialect":*— language, tongue.

1259. διαλλάσσω **diallassō,** *dee-al-las´-so;* from 1223 and 236; to *change thoroughly,* i.e. (ment.) to *conciliate:*— reconcile.

1260. διαλογίζομαι **dialŏgizŏmai,** *dee-al-og-id´-zom-ahee;* from 1223 and 3049; to *reckon thoroughly,* i.e. (gen.) to *deliberate* (by reflection or discussion):— cast in mind, consider, dispute, muse, reason, think.

1261. διαλογισμός **dialŏgismŏs,** *dee-al-og-is-mos´;* from 1260; *discussion,* i.e. (internal) *consideration* (by impl. *purpose*), or (external) *debate:*— dispute, doubtful (-ing), imagination, reasoning, thought.

1262. διαλύω **dialuō,** *dee-al-oo´-o;* from 1223 and 3089; to *dissolve utterly:*— scatter.

1263. διαμαρτύρομαι **diamarturŏmai,** *dee-am-ar-too´-rom-ahee;* from 1223 and 3140; to *attest* or *protest earnestly,* or (by impl.) *hortatively:*— charge, testify (unto), witness.

1264. διαμάχομαι **diamachŏmai,** *dee-am-akh´-om-ahee;* from 1223 and 3164; to *fight fiercely* (in altercation):— strive.

1265. διαμένω **diamĕnō,** *dee-am-en´-o;* from 1223 and 3306; to *stay constantly* (in being or relation):— continue, remain.

1266. διαμερίζω **diamĕrizō,** *dee-am-er-id´-zo;* from 1223 and 3307; to *partition thoroughly* (lit. in distribution, fig. in dissension):— cloven, divide, part.

1267. διαμερισμός **diamĕrismŏs,** *dee-am-er-is-mos´;* from 1266; *disunion* (of opinion and conduct):— division.

1268. διανέμω **dianĕmō,** *dee-an-em´-o;* from 1223 and the base of 3551; to *distribute,* i.e. (of information) to *disseminate:*— spread.

1269. διανεύω **dianĕuō,** *dee-an-yoo´-o;* from 1223 and 3506; to *nod* (or *express by signs*) *across* an intervening space:— beckon.

1270. διανόημα **dianŏēma,** *dee-an-o´-ay-mah;* from a compound of 1223 and 3539; something *thought through,* i.e. a *sentiment:*— thought.

1271. διάνοια **dianŏia,** *dee-an´-oy-ah;* from 1223 and 3563; *deep thought,* prop. the faculty (*mind* or its *disposition*), by impl. its exercise:— imagination, mind, understanding.

1272. διανοίγω **dianŏigō,** *dee-an-oy´-go;* from 1223 and 455; to *open thoroughly,* lit. (as a first-born) or fig. (to *expound*):— open.

1273. διανυκτερεύω **dianuktĕrĕuō,** *dee-an-ook-ter-yoo´-o;* from 1223 and a der. of 3571; to *sit up the whole night:*— continue all night.

1274. διανύω **dianuō,** *dee-an-oo´-o;* from 1223 and ἀνύω *anuō* (to *effect*); to *accomplish thoroughly:*— finish.

1275. διαπαντός **diapantŏs,** *dee-ap-an-tos´;* from 1223 and the genit. of 3956; *through all* the time, i.e. (adv.) *constantly:*— alway (-s), continually.

1276. διαπεράω **diapĕraō,** *dee-ap-er-ah´-o;* from 1223 and a der. of the base of 4008; to *cross entirely:*— go over, pass (over), sail over.

1277. διαπλέω **diaplĕō,** *dee-ap-leh´-o;* from 1223 and 4126; to *sail through:*— sail over.

1278. διαπονέω **diapŏnĕō,** *dee-ap-on-eh´-o;* from 1223 and a der. of 4192; to *toil through,* i.e. (pass.) *be worried:*— be grieved.

1279. διαπορεύομαι **diapŏrĕuŏmai,** *dee-ap-or-yoo´-om-ahee;* from 1223 and 4198; to *travel through:*— go through, journey in, pass by.

1280. διαπορέω **diapŏrĕō,** *dee-ap-or-eh´-o;* from 1223 and 639; to *be thoroughly nonplussed:*— (be in) doubt, be (much) perplexed.

1281. διαπραγματεύομαι **diapragmatĕuŏmai,** *dee-ap-rag-mat-yoo´-om-ahee;* from 1223 and 4231; to *thoroughly occupy oneself,* i.e. (tran. and by impl.) to *earn in business:*— gain by trading.

1282. διαπρίω **diapriō,** *dee-ap-ree´-o;* from 1223 and the base of 4249; to *saw asunder,* i.e. (fig.) to *exasperate:*— cut (to the heart).

1283. διαρπάζω **diarpazō,** *dee-ar-pad´-zo;* from 1223 and 726; to *seize asunder,* i.e. *plunder:*— spoil.

1284. διαρρήσσω **diarrhēssō,** *dee-ar-hrayce´-so;* from 1223 and 4486; to *tear asunder:*— break, rend.

1285. διασαφέω **diasaphĕō,** *dee-as-af-eh´-o;* from 1223 and σαφής **saphēs** (*clear*); to *clear thoroughly,* i.e. (fig.) *declare:*— tell unto.

1286. διασείω **diasĕiō,** *dee-as-i´-o;* from 1223 and 4579; to *shake thoroughly,* i.e. (fig.) to *intimidate:*— do violence to.

1287. διασκορπίζω **diaskŏrpizō,** *dee-as-kor-pid´-zo;* from 1223 and 4650; to *dissipate,* i.e. (gen.) to *rout* or *separate;* spec. to *winnow;* fig. to *squander:*— disperse, scatter (abroad), strew, waste.

1288. διασπάω **diaspaō,** *dee-as-pah´-o;* from 1223 and 4685; to *draw apart,* i.e. *sever* or *dismember:*— pluck asunder, pull in pieces.

1289. διασπείρω **diaspĕirō,** *dee-as-pi´-ro;* from 1223 and 4687; to *sow through-*

out, i.e. (fig.) *distribute* in foreign lands:— scatter abroad.

1290. διασπορά **diaspŏra**, *dee-as-por-ah´*; from *1289*; *dispersion*, i.e. (spec. and concr.) the (converted) Isr. *resident* in Gentile countries:— (which are) scattered (abroad).

1291. διαστέλλομαι **diastĕllŏmai**, *dee-as-tel´-lom-ahee*; mid. voice from *1223* and *4724*; to *set* (oneself) *apart* (fig. *distinguish*), i.e. (by impl.) to *enjoin:*— charge, that which was (give) commanded (-ment).

1292. διάστημα **diastēma**, *dee-as´-tay-mah*; from *1339*; an *interval:*— space.

1293. διαστολή **diastŏlē**, *dee-as-tol-ay´*; from *1291*; a *variation:*— difference, distinction.

1294. διαστρέφω **diastrĕphō**, *dee-as-tref´-o*; from *1223* and *4762*; to *distort*, i.e. (fig.) *misinterpret*, or (morally) *corrupt:*— perverse (-rt), turn away.

1295. διασώζω **diasōzō**, *dee-as-odze´-o*; from *1223* and *4982*; to *save thoroughly*, i.e. (by impl. or anal.) to *cure, preserve, rescue*, etc.:— bring safe, escape (safe), heal, make perfectly whole, save.

1296. διαταγή **diatagē**, *dee-at-ag-ay´*; from *1299*; *arrangement*, i.e. *institution:*— instrumentality.

1297. διάταγμα **diatagma**, *dee-at´-ag-mah*; from *1299*; an *arrangement*, i.e. (authoritative) *edict:*— commandment.

1298. διαταράσσω **diatarassō**, *dee-at-ar-as´-so*; from *1223* and *5015*; to *disturb wholly*, i.e. *agitate* (with alarm):— trouble.

1299. διατάσσω **diatassō**, *dee-at-as´-so*; from *1223* and *5021*; to *arrange thoroughly*, i.e. (spec.) *institute, prescribe*, etc.:— appoint, command, give, (set in) order, ordain.

1300. διατελέω **diatĕlĕō**, *dee-at-el-eh´-o*; from *1223* and *5055*; to *accomplish thoroughly*, i.e. (subj.) to *persist:*— continue.

1301. διατηρέω **diatērĕō**, *dee-at-ay-reh´-o*; from *1223* and *5083*; to *watch thoroughly*, i.e. (pos. and tran.) to *observe* strictly, or (neg. and refl.) to *avoid* wholly:— keep.

1302. διατί **diati**, *dee-at-ee´*; from *1223* and *5101*; *through what* cause?, i.e. *why?:*— wherefore, why.

1303. διατίθεμαι **diatithĕmai**, *dee-at-ith´-em-ahee*; mid. voice from *1223* and *5087*; to *put apart*, i.e. (fig.) *dispose* (by assignment, compact, or bequest):— appoint, make, testator.

1304. διατρίβω **diatribō**, *dee-at-ree´-bo*; from *1223* and the base of *5147*; to *wear through* (time), i.e. *remain:*— abide, be, continue, tarry.

1305. διατροφή **diatrŏphē**, *dee-at-rof-ay´*; from a compound of *1223* and *5142*; *nourishment:*— food.

1306. διαυγάζω **diaugazō**, *dee-ow-gad´-zo*; from *1223* and *826*; to *glimmer through):*— break (as day):— dawn.

1307. διαφανής **diaphanēs**, *dee-af-an-ace´*; from *1223* and *5316*; *appearing through*, i.e. "*diaphanous*":— transparent.

1308. διαφέρω **diaphĕrō**, *dee-af-er´-o*; from *1223* and *5342*; to *bear through*, i.e. (lit.) *transport*; usually to *bear apart*, i.e. (obj.) to *toss about* (fig. *report*); subj. to "*differ*," or (by impl.) *surpass:*— be better, carry, differ from, drive up and down, be (more) excellent, make matter, publish, be of more value.

1309. διαφεύγω **diaphĕugō**, *dee-af-yoo´-go*; from *1223* and *5343*; to *flee through*, i.e. *escape:*— escape.

1310. διαφημίζω **diaphēmizō**, *dee-af-ay-mid´-zo*; from *1223* and a der. of *5345*; to *report thoroughly*, i.e. *divulgate:*— blaze abroad, commonly report, spread abroad, fame.

1311. διαφθείρω **diaphthĕirō**, *dee-af-thi´-ro*; from *1225* and *5351*; to *rot thoroughly*, i.e. (by impl.) to *ruin* (pass. *decay* utterly, fig. *pervert*):— corrupt, destroy, perish.

1312. διαφθορά **diaphthŏra**, *dee-af-thor-ah´*; from *1311*; *decay:*— corruption.

1313. διάφορος **diaphŏrŏs**, *dee-af-or-os*; from *1308*; *varying*; also *surpassing:*— differing, divers, more excellent.

1314. διαφυλάσσω **diaphulassō**, *dee-af-oo-las´-so*; from *1223* and *5442*; to *guard thoroughly*, i.e. *protect:*— keep.

1315. διαχειρίζομαι **diachĕirizŏmai**, *dee-akh-i-rid´-zom-ahee*; from *1223* and a der. of *5495*; to *handle thoroughly*, i.e. *lay* violent *hands* upon:— kill, slay.

1316. διαχωρίζομαι **diachōrizŏmai**, *dee-akh-o-rid´-zom-ahee*; from *1223* and the mid. voice of *5563*; to *remove* (oneself) *wholly*, i.e. *retire:*— depart.

1317. διδακτικός **didaktikŏs**, *did-ak-tik-os´*; from *1318*; *instructive* ("didactic"):— apt to teach.

1318. διδακτός **didaktŏs**, *did-ak-tos´*; from *1321*; (subj.) *instructed*, or (obj.) *communicated* by teaching:— taught, which ... teacheth.

1319. διδασκαλία **didaskalia**, *did-as-kal-ee´-ah*; from *1320*; *instruction* (the function or the information):— doctrine, learning, teaching.

1320. διδάσκαλος **didaskalŏs**, *did-as´-kal-os*; from *1321*; an *instructor* (gen. or spec.):— doctor, master, teacher.

1321. διδάσκω **didaskō**, *did-as´-ko*; a prol. (caus.) form of a primary verb δάω **daō** (to *learn*); to *teach* (in the same broad application):— teach.

1322. διδαχή **didachē**, *did-akh-ay´*; from *1321*; *instruction* (the act or the matter):— doctrine, hath been taught.

1323. δίδραχμον **didrachmŏn**, *did´-rakh-mon*; from *1364* and *1406*; a *double drachma* (*didrachm*):— tribute.

1324. Δίδυμος **Didumŏs**, *did´-oo-mos*; prol. from *1364*; *double*, i.e. *twin*; Didymus, a Chr.:— Didymus.

1325. δίδωμι **didōmi**, *did´-o-mee*; a prol. form of a primary verb (which is used as an altern. in most of the tenses); to *give* (used in a very wide application, prop. or by impl., lit. or fig.; greatly modified by the connection):— adven-

ture, bestow, bring forth, commit, deliver (up), give, grant, hinder, make, minister, number, offer, have power, put, receive, set, shew, smite (+ with the hand), strike (+ with the palm of the hand), suffer, take, utter, yield.

1326. διεγείρω **diĕgĕirō**, *dee-eg-i´-ro*; from *1223* and *1453*; to *wake fully*; i.e. *arouse* (lit. or fig.):— arise, awake, raise, stir up.

1327. διέξοδος **diĕxŏdŏs**, *dee-ex´-od-os*; from *1223* and *1841*; an *outlet through*, i.e. prob. an open *square* (from which roads diverge):— highway.

1328. διερμηνευτής **diĕrmēnĕutēs**, *dee-er-main-yoo-tace´*; from *1329*; an *explainer:*— interpreter.

1329. διερμηνεύω **diĕrmēnĕuō**, *dee-er-main-yoo´-o*; from *1223* and *2059*; to *explain thoroughly*, by impl. to *translate:*— expound, interpret (-ation).

1330. διέρχομαι **diĕrchŏmai**, *dee-er´-khom-ahee*; from *1223* and *2064*; to *traverse* (lit.):— come, depart, go (about, abroad, everywhere, over, through, throughout), pass (by, over, through, throughout), pierce through, travel, walk through.

1331. διερωτάω **diĕrōtaō**, *dee-er-o-tah´-o*; from *1223* and *2065*; to *question throughout*, i.e. *ascertain* by interrogation:— make enquiry for.

1332. διετής **diĕtēs**, *dee-et-ace´*; from *1364* and *2094*; of *two years* (in age):— two years old.

1333. διετία **diĕtia**, *dee-et-ee-a´*; from *1332*; a space of *two years* (*biennium*):— two years.

1334. διηγέομαι **diēgĕŏmai**, *dee-ayg-eh´-om-ahee*; from *1223* and *2233*; to *relate fully:*— declare, shew, tell.

1335. διήγεσις **diēgĕsis**, *dee-ayg´-es-is*; or διήγησις **diēgēsis** *dee-ayg´-es-is*; from *1334*; a *recital:*— declaration.

1336. διηνεκές **diēnĕkĕs**, *dee-ay-nek-es´*; neut. of a compound of *1223* and a der. of an alt. of *5342*; *carried through*, i.e. (adv. with *1519* and *3588* pref.) *perpetually:*— + continually, for ever.

1337. διθάλασσος **dithalassŏs**, *dee-thal´-as-sos*; from *1364* and *2281*; having *two seas*, i.e. a *sound* with a double outlet:— where two seas meet.

1338. διϊκνέομαι **diïknĕŏmai**, *dee-ik-neh´-om-ahee*; from *1223* and the base of *2425*; to *reach through*, i.e. *penetrate:*— pierce.

1339. διΐστημι **diïstēmi**, *dee-is´-tay-mee*; from *1223* and *2476*; to *stand apart*, i.e. (refl.) to *remove, intervene:*— go further, be parted, after the space of.

1340. διϊσχυρίζομαι **diïschurizŏmai**, *dee-is-khoo-rid´-zom-ahee*; from *1223* and a der. of *2478*; to *stout* it *through*, i.e. *asseverate:*— confidently (constantly) affirm.

1341. δικαιοκρισία **dikaiŏkrisia**, *dik-ah-yok-ris-ee´-ah*; from *1342* and *2920*; a *just sentence:*— righteous judgment.

1342. δίκαιος **dikaiŏs**, *dik´-ah-yos*; from *1349*; *equitable* (in character or act); by impl. *innocent, holy* (absol. or rel.):— just, meet, right (-eous).

1343. δικαιοσύνη **dikaiŏsunē**, *dik-ah-yos-oo´-nay;* from 1342; *equity* (of character or act); spec. (Chr.) *justification:*— righteousness.

1344. δικαιόω **dikaiŏō**, *dik-ah-yŏ´-o;* from 1342; to *render* (i.e. *show* or *regard* as) *just* or *innocent:*— free, justify (-ier), be righteous.

1345. δικαίωμα **dikaiŏma**, *dik-ah´-yo-mah;* from 1344; an *equitable deed;* by impl. a *statute* or *decision:*— judgment, justification, ordinance, righteousness.

1346. δικαίως **dikaiŏs**, *dik-ah´-yoce;* adv. from 1342; *equitably:*— justly, (to) righteously (-ness).

1347. δικαίωσις **dikaiŏsis**, *dik-ah´-yo-sis;* from 1344; *acquittal* (for Christ's sake):— justification.

1348. δικαστής **dikastēs**, *dik-as-tace´;* from a der. of 1349; a *judger:*— judge.

1349. δίκη **dikē**, *dee´-kay;* prob. from 1166; *right* (as self-*evident*), i.e. *justice* (the principle, a decision, or its execution):— judgment, punish, vengeance.

1350. δίκτυον **diktuŏn**, *dik´-too-on;* prob. from a primary verb δίκω **dikō** (to *cast*); a *seine* (for fishing):— net.

1351. δίλογος **dilŏgŏs**, *dil´-og-os;* from 1364 and 3056; *equivocal*, i.e. telling a different story:— double-tongued.

1352. διό **diŏ**, *dee-ŏ´;* from 1223 and 3739; *through which* thing, i.e. *consequently:*— for which cause, therefore, wherefore.

1353. διοδεύω **diŏdĕuō**, *dee-od-yoo´-o;* from 1223 and 3593; to *travel through:*— go throughout, pass through.

1354. Διονύσιος **Diŏnusiŏs**, *dee-on-oo´-see-os;* from Διόνυσος **Diŏnusŏs** (*Bacchus*); *reveller; Dionysius*, an Athenian:— Dionysius.

1355. διόπερ **diŏpĕr**, *dee-op´-er;* from 1352 and 4007; *on which very account:*— wherefore.

1356. διοπετής **diŏpĕtēs**, *dee-op-et´-ace;* from the alt. of 2203 and the alt. of 4098; *sky-fallen* (i.e. an *aerolite*):— which fell down from Jupiter.

1357. διόρθωσις **diŏrthōsis**, *dee-or´-tho-sis;* from a compound of 1223 and a der. of 3717, mean. to *straighten thoroughly; rectification*, i.e. (spec.) the Messianic *restoration:*— reformation.

1358. διορύσσω **diŏrussō**, *dee-or-oos´-so;* from 1223 and 3736; to *penetrate burglariously:*— break through (up).

Διός **Diŏs**. See 2203.

1359. Διόσκουροι **Diŏskŏurŏi**, *dee-os´-koo-roy;* from the alt. of 2203 and a form of the base of 2877; *sons of Jupiter*, i.e. the twins *Dioscuri:*— Castor and Pollux.

1360. διότι **diŏti**, *dee-ot´-ee;* from 1223 and 3754; *on the very account that*, or *inasmuch as:*— because (that), for, therefore.

1361. Διοτρεφής **Diŏtrĕphēs**, *dee-ot-ref-ace´;* from the alt. of 2203 and 5142;

Jove-nourished; Diotrephes, an opponent of Christianity:— Diotrephes.

1362. διπλοῦς **diplŏus**, *dip-looce´;* or διπλόος **diploos**, *dip-loce´* from 1364 and (prob.) the base of 4119; *two-fold:*— double, two-fold more.

1363. διπλόω **diplŏō**, *dip-lŏ´-o;* from 1362; to *render two-fold:*— double.

1364. δίς **dis**, *dece;* adv. from 1417; *twice:*— again, twice.

Δίς **Dis**. See 2203.

1365. διστάζω **distazō**, *dis-tad´-zo;* from 1364; prop. to *duplicate*, i.e. (ment.) to *waver* (in opinion):— doubt.

1366. δίστομος **distŏmŏs**, *dis´-tom-os;* from 1364 and 4750; *double-edged:*— with two edges, two-edged.

1367. δισχίλιοι **dischiliŏi**, *dis-khil´-ee-oy;* from 1364 and 5507; *two thousand:*— two thousand.

1368. διυλίζω **diulizō**, *dee-oo-lid´-zo;* from 1223 and ὑλίζω **hulizō**, *hoo-lid´-zo* (to *filter*); to *strain out:*— strain at [prob. by misprint].

1369. διχάζω **dichazō**, *dee-khad´-zo;* from a der. of 1364; to *make apart*, i.e. *sunder* (fig. *alienate*):— set at variance.

1370. διχοστασία **dichŏstasia**, *dee-khos-tas-ee´-ah;* from a der. of 1364 and 4714; *disunion*, i.e. (fig.) *dissension:*— division, sedition.

1371. διχοτομέω **dichŏtŏmĕō**, *dee-khot-om-eh´-o;* from a compound of a der. of 1364 and a der. of τέμνω **tĕmnō** (to *cut*); to *bisect*, i.e. (by extens.) to *flog* severely:— cut asunder (in sunder).

1372. διψάω **dipsaō**, *dip-sah´-o;* from a var. of 1373; to *thirst* for (lit. or fig.):— (be, be a-) thirst (-y).

1373. δίψος **dipsŏs**, *dip´-sos;* of uncert. aff.; *thirst:*— thirst.

1374. δίψυχος **dipsuchŏs**, *dip´-soo-khos;* from 1364 and 5590; *two-spirited*, i.e. *vacillating* (in opinion or purpose):— double minded.

1375. διωγμός **diōgmŏs**, *dee-ogue-mos´;* from 1377; *persecution:*— persecution.

1376. διώκτης **diōktēs**, *dee-oke´-tace;* from 1377; a *persecutor:*— persecutor.

1377. διώκω **diōkō**, *dee-o´-ko;* a prol. (and caus.) form of a primary verb δίω **diō** (to *flee;* comp. the base of 1169 and 1249); to *pursue* (lit. or fig.); by impl. to *persecute:*— ensue, follow (after), given to, (suffer) persecute (-ion), press toward.

1378. δόγμα **dŏgma**, *dog´-mah;* from the base of 1380; a *law* (civil, cerem. or eccl.):— decree, ordinance.

1379. δογματίζω **dŏgmatizō**, *dog-mat-id´-zo;* from 1378; to *prescribe* by statute, i.e. (refl.) to *submit* to cer. *rule:*— be subject to ordinances.

1380. δοκέω **dŏkĕō**, *dok-eh´-o;* a prol. form of a primary verb δόκω **dŏkō**, *dok´-o* (used only in an alt. in certain tenses; comp. the base of 1166) of the same mean.; to *think;* by impl. to *seem* (truthfully or uncertainly):— be accounted, (of own) please (-ure), be of reputation, seem (good), suppose, think, trow.

1381. δοκιμάζω **dŏkimazō**, *dok-im-ad´-zo;* from 1384; to *test* (lit. or fig.); by impl. to *approve:*— allow, discern, examine, × like, (ap-) prove, try.

1382. δοκιμή **dŏkimē**, *dok-ee-may´;* from the same as 1384; *test* (abstr. or concr.); by impl. *trustiness:*— experience (-riment), proof, trial.

1383. δοκίμιον **dŏkimiŏn**, *dok-im´-ee-on;* neut. of a presumed der. of 1382; a *testing;* by impl. *trustworthiness:*— trial, trying.

1384. δόκιμος **dŏkimŏs**, *dok´-ee-mos;* from 1380; prop. *acceptable* (*current* after assayal), i.e. *approved:*— approved, tried.

1385. δοκός **dŏkŏs**, *dok-os´;* from 1209 (through the idea of *holding* up); a *stick* of timber:— beam.

δόκω **dŏkō**. See 1380.

1386. δόλιος **dŏliŏs**, *dol´-ee-os;* from 1388; *guileful:*— deceitful.

1387. δολιόω **dŏliŏō**, *dol-ee-ŏ´-o;* from 1386; to *be guileful:*— use deceit.

1388. δόλος **dŏlŏs**, *dol´-os;* from an obs. primary verb, δέλλω **dĕllō** (prob. mean. to *decoy;* comp. 1185); a *trick* (*bait*), i.e. (fig.) *wile:*— craft, deceit, guile, subtilty (subtlety).

1389. δολόω **dŏlŏō**, *dol-ŏ´-o;* from 1388; to *ensnare*, i.e. (fig.) *adulterate:*— handle deceitfully.

1390. δόμα **dŏma**, *dom-ah;* from the base of 1325; a *present:*— gift.

1391. δόξα **dŏxa**, *dox´-ah;* from the base of 1380; *glory* (as very *apparent*), in a wide application (lit. or fig., obj. or subj.):— dignity, glory (-ious), honour, praise, worship.

1392. δοξάζω **dŏxazō**, *dox-ad´-zo;* from 1391; to *render* (or *esteem*) *glorious* (in a wide application):— (make) glorify (-ious), full of (have) glory, honour, magnify.

1393. Δορκάς **Dŏrkas**, *dor-kas´;* gazelle; *Dorcas*, a Chr. woman:— Dorcas.

1394. δόσις **dŏsis**, *dos´-is;* from the base of 1325; a *giving;* by impl. (concr.) a *gift:*— gift, giving.

1395. δότης **dŏtēs**, *dot´-ace;* from the base of 1325; a *giver:*— giver.

1396. δουλαγωγέω **dŏulagōgĕō**, *doo-lag-ogue-eh´-o;* from a presumed compound of 1401 and 71; to *be a slave-driver*, i.e. to *enslave* (fig. *subdue*):— bring into subjection.

1397. δουλεία **dŏulĕia**, *doo-li´-ah;* from 1398; *slavery* (cerem. or fig.):— bondage.

1398. δουλεύω **dŏulĕuō**, *dool-yoo´-o;* from 1401; to *be a slave* to (lit. or fig., invol. or vol.):— be in bondage, (do) serve (-ice).

1399. δούλη **dŏulē**, *doo-lay;* fem. of 1401; a *female slave* (invol. or vol.):— handmaid (-en).

1400. δοῦλον **dŏulŏn**, *doo´-lon;* neut. of 1401; *subservient:*— servant.

1401. δοῦλος **dŏulŏs**, *doo´-los;* from 1210; a *slave* (lit. or fig., invol. or vol.; frequently, therefore in a qualified sense of *subjection* or *subserviency*):— bond (-man), servant.

1402. δουλόω **dŏulŏō**, *doo-lŏ´-o;* from *1401;* to *enslave* (lit. or fig.):— bring into (be under) bondage, × given, become (make) servant.

1403. δοχή **dŏchē**, *dokh-ay´;* from *1209;* a *reception,* i.e. convivial *entertainment:*— feast.

1404. δράκων **drakōn**, *drak´-own;* prob. from an alt. form of δέρκομαι **dĕrkŏmai** (to *look*); a fabulous kind of *serpent* (perh. as supposed to *fascinate*):— dragon.

1405. δράσσομαι **drassŏmai**, *dras´-som-ahee;* perh. akin to the base of *1404* (through the idea of *capturing*); to *grasp,* i.e. (fig.) *entrap:*— take.

1406. δραχμή **drachmē**, *drakh-may´;* from *1405;* a *drachma* or (silver) coin (as *handled*):— piece (of silver).

δρέμω **drĕmō**. See *5143.*

1407. δρέπανον **drĕpanŏn**, *drep´-an-on;* from δρέπω **drĕpō** (to *pluck*); a gathering *hook* (espec. for harvesting):— sickle.

1408. δρόμος **drŏmŏs**, *drom´-os;* from the alt. of *5143;* a *race,* i.e. (fig.) *career:*— course.

1409. Δρούσιλλα **Drŏusilla**, *droo´-sil-lah;* a fem. dimin. of *Drusus* (a Rom. name); *Drusilla,* a member of the Herodian family:— Drusilla.

δῦμι **dumi**. See *1416.*

1410. δύναμαι **dunamai**, *doo´-nam-ahee;* of uncert. aff.; to *be able* or *possible:*— be able, can (do, + -not), could, may, might, be possible, be of power.

1411. δύναμις **dunamis**, *doo´-nam-is;* from *1410; force* (lit. or fig.); spec. miraculous *power* (usually by impl. a *miracle* itself):— ability, abundance, meaning, might (-ily, -y, -y deed), (worker of) miracle (-s), power, strength, violence, mighty (wonderful) work.

1412. δυναμόω **dunamŏō**, *doo-nam-ŏ´-o;* from *1411;* to *enable:*— strengthen.

1413. δυνάστης **dunastēs**, *doo-nas´-tace;* from *1410;* a *ruler* or *officer:*— of great authority, mighty, potentate.

1414. δυνατέω **dunatĕō**, *doo-nat-eh´-o;* from *1415;* to *be efficient* (fig.):— be mighty.

1415. δυνατός **dunatŏs**, *doo-nat-os´;* from *1410; powerful* or *capable* (lit. or fig.); neut. *possible:*— able, could, (that is) mighty (man), possible, power, strong.

1416. δύνω **dunō**, *doo´-no;* or

δῦμι **dumi**, *doo´-mee;* prol. forms of an obsolete primary δύω **duō**, *doo´-o* (to *sink*); to *go* "*down*":— set.

1417. δύο **duō**, *doo´-ŏ;* a primary numeral; "*two*":— both, twain, two.

1418. δυσ- **dus-**, *doos;* a primary inseparable particle of uncert. der.; used only in composition as a pref.; *hard,* i.e. *with difficulty:*— + hard, + grievous, *etc.*

1419. δυσβάστακτος **dusbastaktŏs**, *doos-bas´-tak-tos;* from *1418* and a der.

of *941; oppressive:*— grievous to be borne.

1420. δυσεντερία **dusĕntĕria**, *doos-en-ter-ee´-ah;* from *1418* and a comp. of *1787* (mean. a *bowel*); a "*dysentery*":— bloody flux.

1421. δυσερμήνευτος **dusĕrmēnĕutŏs**, *doos-er-mane´-yoo-tos;* from *1418* and a presumed der. of *2059; difficult of explanation:*— hard to be uttered.

1422. δύσκολος **duskŏlŏs**, *doos´-kol-os;* from *1418* and κόλον **kŏlŏn** (*food*); prop. *fastidious about eating* (*peevish*), i.e. (gen.) *impracticable:*— hard.

1423. δυσκόλως **duskŏlōs**, *doos-kol´-oce;* adv. from *1422; impracticably:*— hardly.

1424. δυσμή **dusmē**, *doos-may´;* from *1416;* the sun-*set,* i.e. (by impl.) the *western* region:— west.

1425. δυσνόητος **dusnŏētŏs**, *doos-no´-ay-tos;* from *1418* and a der. of *3539; difficult of perception:*— hard to be understood.

1426. δυσφημία **dusphēmia**, *doos-fay-mee´-ah;* from a compound of *1418* and *5345; defamation:*— evil report.

δύω **duō**. See *1416.*

1427. δώδεκα **dōdĕka**, *do´-dek-ah;* from *1417* and *1176; two* and *ten,* i.e. a *dozen:*— twelve.

1428. δωδέκατος **dōdĕkatŏs**, *do-dek´-at-os;* from *1427; twelfth:*— twelfth.

1429. δωδεκάφυλον **dōdĕkaphulŏn**, *do-dek-af´-oo-lon;* from *1427* and *5443;* the *commonwealth* of Israel:— twelve tribes.

1430. δῶμα **dōma**, *do´-mah;* from δέμω **dĕmō** (to *build*); prop. an *edifice,* i.e. (spec.) a *roof:*— housetop.

1431. δωρεά **dōrĕa**, *do-reh-ah´;* from *1435;* a *gratuity:*— gift.

1432. δωρεάν **dōrĕan**, *do-reh-an´;* acc. of *1431* as adv.; *gratuitously* (lit. or fig.):— without a cause, freely, for naught, in vain.

1433. δωρέομαι **dōrĕŏmai**, *do-reh´-om-ahee;* mid. voice from *1435;* to *bestow gratuitously:*— give.

1434. δώρημα **dōrēma**, *do´-ray-mah;* from *1433;* a *bestowment:*— gift.

1435. δῶρον **dōrŏn**, *do´-ron;* a *present;* spec. a *sacrifice:*— gift, offering.

E

1436. ἔα **ĕa**, *eh´-ah;* appar. imper. of *1439;* prop. *let it be,* i.e. (as interj.) *aha!:*— let alone.

1437. ἐάν **ĕan**, *eh-an´;* from *1487* and *302;* a *conditional* particle; *in case* that, *provided,* etc.; often used in connection with other particles to denote *indefiniteness* or *uncertainty:*— before, but, except, (and) if, (if) so, (what-, whither-) soever, though, when (-soever), whether (or), to whom, [who-] so (-ever). See *3361.*

ἐάν μή **ĕan mē**. See *3361* and *3362.*

1438. ἑαυτοῦ **hĕautŏu**, *heh-ow-too´* (incl. all other cases); from a refl. pron. otherwise obs. and the gen. (dat. or

acc.) of *846; him-* (*her-, it-, them-,* also [in conjunction with the pers. pron. of the other persons] *my-, thy-, our-, your-*) *self* (*selves*), etc.:— alone, her (own, -self), (he) himself, his (own), itself, one (to) another, our (thine) own (-selves), + that she had, their (own, own selves), (of) them (-selves), they, thyself, you, your (own, own conceits, own selves, -selves).

1439. ἐάω **ĕaō**, *eh-ah´-o;* of uncert. aff.; to *let be,* i.e. *permit* or *leave* alone:— commit, leave, let (alone), suffer. See also *1436.*

1440. ἑβδομήκοντα **hĕbdŏmēkŏnta**, *heb-dom-ay´-kon-tah;* from *1442* and a modified form of *1176; seventy:*— seventy, three score and ten.

1441. ἑβδομηκοντάκις **hĕbdŏmēkŏntakis**, *heb-dom-ay-kon-tak-is;* multiple adv. from *1440; seventy times:*— seventy times.

1442. ἕβδομος **hĕbdŏmŏs**, *heb´-dom-os;* ord. from *2033; seventh:*— seventh.

1443. Ἐβέρ **Ĕbĕr**, *eb´-er;* of Heb. or. [5677]; *Eber,* a patriarch:— Eber.

1444. Ἑβραϊκός **Hĕbraïkŏs**, *heb-rah-ee-kos´;* from *1443; Hebraïc* or the *Jewish* language:— Hebrew (Aramaic).

1445. Ἑβραῖος **Hĕbraiŏs**, *heb-rah´-yos;* from *1443;* a *Hebrӕan* (i.e. Hebrew) or *Jew:*— Hebrew.

1446. Ἑβραΐς **Hĕbraïs**, *heb-rah-is´;* from *1443;* the *Hebraistic* (i.e. *Hebrew*) or *Jewish* (*Chaldee*) language:— Hebrew (Aramaic).

1447. Ἑβραϊστί **Hĕbraïsti**, *heb-rah-is-tee´;* adv. from *1446; Hebraistically* or in the Jewish (Chaldee) language:— in (the) Hebrew (tongue).

1448. ἐγγίζω **ĕggizō**, *eng-id´-zo;* from *1451;* to make *near,* i.e. (refl.) *approach:*— approach, be at hand, come (draw) near, be (come, draw) nigh.

1449. ἐγγράφω **ĕggraphō**, *eng-graf´-o;* from *1722* and *1125;* to "*engrave,*" i.e. *inscribe:*— write (in).

1450. ἔγγυος **ĕgguŏs**, *eng´-goo-os;* from *1722* and γυῖον **guiŏn** (a *limb*); *pledged* (as if *articulated* by a member), i.e. a *bondsman:*— surety.

1451. ἐγγύς **ĕggus**, *eng-goos´;* from a primary verb ἄγχω **agchō** (to *squeeze* or *throttle;* akin to the base of *43*); *near* (lit. or fig., of place or time):— from, at hand, near, nigh (at hand, unto), ready.

1452. ἐγγύτερον **ĕggutĕrŏn**, *eng-goo´-ter-on;* neut. of the comp. of *1451; nearer:*— nearer.

1453. ἐγείρω **ĕgeirō**, *eg-i´-ro;* prob. akin to the base of *58* (through the idea of *collecting* one's faculties); to *waken* (tran. or intr.), i.e. *rouse* (lit. from sleep, from sitting or lying, from disease, from death; or fig. from obscurity, inactivity, ruins, nonexistence):— awake, lift (up), raise (again, up), rear up, (a-) rise (again, up), stand, take up.

1454. ἔγερσις **ĕgĕrsis**, *eg´-er-sis;* from *1453;* a *resurgence* (from death):— resurrection.

1455. ἐγκάθετος **ĕgkathĕtŏs**, *eng-kath´-et-os;* from *1722* and a der. of *2524;*

subinduced, i.e. surreptitiously sub-orned as a lier-in-wait:— spy.

1456. ἐγκαίνια ĕgkainia, eng-kah´-ee-nee-ah; neut. plur. of a presumed compound from 1722 and 2537; innovatives, i.e. (spec.) renewal (of relig. services after the Antiochian interruption):— dedication.

1457. ἐγκαινίζω ĕgkainizō, eng-kahee-nid´-zo; from 1456; to renew, i.e. inaugurate:— consecrate, dedicate.

1458. ἐγκαλέω ĕgkaleō, eng-kal-eh´-o; from 1722 and 2564; to call in (as a debt or demand), i.e. bring to account (charge, criminate, etc.):— accuse, call in question, implead, lay to the charge.

1459. ἐγκαταλείπω ĕgkataleipō, eng-kat-al-i´-po; from 1722 and 2641; to leave behind in some place, i.e. (in a good sense) let remain over, or (in a bad sense) to desert:— forsake, leave.

1460. ἐγκατοικέω ĕgkatoikeō, eng-kat-oy-keh´-o; from 1722 and 2730; to settle down in a place, i.e. reside:— dwell among.

1461. ἐγκεντρίζω ĕgkĕntrizō, eng-kentrid´-zo; from 1722 and a der. of 2759; to prick in, i.e. ingraft:— graff in (-to).

1462. ἔγκλημα ĕgklēma, eng´-klay-mah; from 1458; an accusation, i.e. offence alleged:— crime laid against, laid to charge.

1463. ἐγκομβόομαι ĕgkombŏomai, eng-kom-bŏ´-om-ahee; mid. voice from 1722 and κομβόω kombŏō (to gird); to engirdle oneself (for labor), i.e. fig. (the apron being a badge of servitude) to wear (in token of mutual deference):— be clothed with.

1464. ἐγκοπή ĕgkŏpē, eng-kop-ay´; from 1465; a hindrance:— × hinder.

1465. ἐγκόπτω ĕgkŏptō, eng-kop´-to; from 1722 and 2875; to cut into, i.e. (fig.) impede, detain:— hinder, be tedious unto.

1466. ἐγκράτεια ĕgkratĕia, eng-krat´-i-ah; from 1468; self-control (espec. continence):— temperance.

1467. ἐγκρατεύομαι ĕgkratĕuŏmai, eng-krat-yoo´-om-ahee; mid. voice from 1468; to exercise self-restraint (in diet and chastity):— can ([-not]) contain, be temperate.

1468. ἐγκρατής ĕgkratēs, eng-krat-ace´; from 1722 and 2904; strong in a thing (masterful), i.e. (fig. and refl.) self-controlled (in appetite, etc.):— temperate.

1469. ἐγκρίνω ĕgkrinō, eng-kree´-no; from 1722 and 2919; to judge in, i.e. count among:— make of the number.

1470. ἐγκρύπτω ĕgkruptō, eng-kroop´-to; from 1722 and 2928; to conceal in, i.e. incorporate with:— hid in.

1471. ἔγκυος ĕgkuŏs, eng´-koo-os; from 1722 and the base of 2949; swelling inside, i.e. pregnant:— great with child.

1472. ἐγχρίω ĕgchriō, eng-khree´-o; from 1722 and 5548; to rub in (oil), i.e. besmear:— anoint.

1473. ἐγώ ĕgō, eg-o´; a primary pron. of the first pers. I (only expressed when emphatic):— I, me. For the other cases and the plur. see 1691, 1698, 1700, 2248, 2249, 2254, 2257, etc.

1474. ἐδαφίζω ĕdaphizō, ed-af-id´-zo; from 1475; to raze:— lay even with the ground.

1475. ἔδαφος ĕdaphŏs, ed´-af-os; from the base of 1476; a basis (bottom), i.e. the soil:— ground.

1476. ἑδραῖος hĕdraiŏs, hed-rah´-yos; from a der. of ἕζομαι hĕzŏmai (to sit); sedentary, i.e. (by impl.) immovable:— settled, stedfast.

1477. ἑδραίωμα hĕdraiōma, hed-rah´-yo-mah; from a der. of 1476; a support, i.e. (fig.) basis:— ground.

1478. Ἐζεκίας Ĕzĕkias, ed-zek-ee´-as; of Heb. or. [2396]; Ezekias (i.e. Hezekiah), an Isr.:— Ezekias.

1479. ἐθελοθρησκεία ĕthĕlŏthrēskĕia, eth-el-oth-race-ki´-ah; from 2309 and 2356; voluntary (arbitrary and unwarranted) piety, i.e. sanctimony:— will worship.

ἐθέλω ĕthĕlō. See 2309.

1480. ἐθίζω ĕthizō, eth-id´-zo; from 1485; to accustom, i.e. (neut. pass. part.) customary:— custom.

1481. ἐθνάρχης ĕthnarchēs, eth-nar´-khace; from 1484 and 746; the governor [not king] of a district:— ethnarch.

1482. ἐθνικός ĕthnikŏs, eth-nee-kos´; from 1484; national ("ethnic"), i.e. (spec.) a Gentile:— heathen (man).

1483. ἐθνικῶς ĕthnikōs, eth-nee-koce´; adv. from 1482; as a Gentile:— after the manner of Gentiles.

1484. ἔθνος ĕthnŏs, eth´-nos; prob. from 1486; a race (as of the same habit), i.e. a tribe; spec. a foreign (non-Jewish) one (usually by impl. pagan):— Gentile, heathen, nation, people.

1485. ἔθος ĕthŏs, eth´-os; from 1486; a usage (prescribed by habit or law):— custom, manner, be wont.

1486. ἔθω ĕthō, eth´-o; a primary verb; to be used (by habit or conventionality); neut. perfect part. usage:— be custom (manner, wont).

1487. εἰ ĕi, i; a primary particle of conditionality; if, whether, that, etc.:— forasmuch as, if, that, ([al-])though, whether. Often used in connection or composition with other particles, espec. as in 1489, 1490, 1499, 1508, 1509, 1512, 1513, 1536, 1537. See also 1437.

1488. εἶ ĕi, i; second pers. sing. present of 1510; thou art:— art, be.

1489. εἴγε ĕigĕ, i´-gheh; from 1487 and 1065; if indeed, seeing that, unless, (with neg.) otherwise:— if (so be that, yet).

1490. εἰ δὲ μή(γε) ĕi dĕ mē(gĕ) i deh may´-(gheh); from 1487, 1161, and 3361 (sometimes with 1065 added); but if not:— (or) else, if (not, otherwise), otherwise.

1491. εἶδος ĕidŏs, i´-dos; from 1492; a view, i.e. form (lit. or fig.):— appearance, fashion, shape, sight.

1492. εἴδω ĕidō, i´-do; a primary verb; used only in certain past tenses, the others being borrowed from the equiv.

3700 and 3708; prop. to see (lit. or fig.); by impl. (in the perf. only) to know:— be aware, behold, × can (+ not tell), consider, (have) know (-ledge), look (on), perceive, see, be sure, tell, understand, wish, wot. Comp. 3700.

1493. εἰδωλεῖον ĕidōlĕiŏn, i-do-li´-on; neut. of a presumed der. of 1497; an image-fane:— idol's temple.

1494. εἰδωλόθυτον ĕidōlŏthutŏn, i-do-loth´-oo-ton; neut. of a compound of 1497 and a presumed der. of 2380; an image-sacrifice, i.e. part of an idolatrous offering:— (meat, thing that is) offered (in sacrifice, sacrificed) to (unto) idols.

1495. εἰδωλολατρεία ĕidōlŏlatrĕia, i-do-lol-at-ri´-ah; from 1497 and 2999; image-worship (lit. or fig.):— idolatry.

1496. εἰδωλολάτρης ĕidōlŏlatrēs, i-do-lol-at´-race; from 1497 and the base of 3000; an image-(servant or) worshipper (lit. or fig.):— idolater.

1497. εἴδωλον ĕidōlŏn, i´-do-lon; from 1491; an image (i.e. for worship); by impl. a heathen god, or (plur.) the worship of such:— idol.

1498. εἴην ĕiēn, i´-ane; optative (i.e. English subjunctive) present of 1510 (incl. the other pers.); might (could, would, or should) be:— mean, + perish, should be, was, were.

1499. εἰ καί ĕi kai, i kahee; from 1487 and 2532; if also (or even):— if (that), though.

1500. εἰκῆ ĕikē, i-kay´; prob. from 1502 (through the idea of failure); idly, i.e. without reason (or effect):— without a cause, (in) vain (-ly).

1501. εἴκοσι ĕikŏsi, i´-kos-ee; of uncert. aff.; a score:— twenty.

1502. εἴκω ĕikō, i´-ko; appar. a primary verb; prop. to be weak, i.e. yield:— give place.

1503. εἴκω ĕikō, i´-ko; appar. a primary verb [perh. akin to 1502 through the idea of faintness as a copy]; to resemble:— be like.

1504. εἰκών ĕikōn, i-kone´; from 1503; a likeness, i.e. (lit.) statue, profile, or (fig.) representation, resemblance:— image.

1505. εἰλικρίνεια ĕilikrinĕia, i-lik-ree´-ni-ah; from 1506; clearness, i.e. (by impl.) purity (fig.):— sincerity.

1506. εἰλικρινής ĕilikrinēs, i-lik-ree-nace´; from εἵλη hĕilē (the sun's ray) and 2919; judged by sunlight, i.e. tested as genuine (fig.):— pure, sincere.

1507. εἰλίσσω hĕilissō, hi-lis´-so; a prol. form of a primary but defective verb εἴλω hĕilō (of the same mean.); to coil or wrap:— roll together. See also 1667.

1508. εἰ μή ĕi mē, i may; from 1487 and 3361; if not:— but, except (that), if not, more than, save (only) that, saving, till.

1509. εἰ μή τι ĕi mē ti, i may tee; from 1508 and the neut. of 5100; if not somewhat:— except.

1510. εἰμί ĕimi, i-mee´; the first pers. sing. present ind.; a prol. form of a primary and defective verb; I exist (used only when emphatic):— am, have been, × it is I, was. See also 1488, 1498, 1511,

Greek

2258, 2071, 2070, 2075, 2076, 2771, 2468, 5600, 5607.

1511. εἶναι **ĕinai**, *i´-nahee;* present infin. from *1510; to exist:*— am, are, come, is, × lust after, × please well, there is, to be, was.

εἵνεκεν **hĕinĕkĕn.** See *1752.*

1512. εἰ περ **ĕi pĕr,** *i per;* from *1487* and *4007; if perhaps:*— if so be (that), seeing, though.

1513. εἰ πως **ĕi pōs,** *i poce;* from *1487* and *4458; if somehow:*— if by any means.

1514. εἰρηνεύω **ĕirēnĕuō,** *i-rane-yoo´-o;* from *1515; to be (act) peaceful:*— be at (have, live in) peace, live peaceably.

1515. εἰρήνη **ĕirēnē,** *i-ray´-nay;* prob. from a primary verb εἴρω **ĕirō** (to *join*); *peace* (lit. or fig.); by impl. *prosperity:*— one, peace, quietness, rest, + set at one again.

1516. εἰρηνικός **ĕirēnikŏs,** *i-ray-nee-kos´;* from *1515; pacific;* by impl. *salutary:*— peaceable.

1517. εἰρηνοποιέω **ĕirēnŏpŏiĕō,** *i-ray-nop-oy-eh´-o;* from *1518; to be a peacemaker,* i.e. (fig.) to *harmonize:*— make peace.

1518. εἰρηνοποιός **ĕirēnŏpŏiŏs,** *i-ray-nop-oy-os´;* from *1515* and *4160; pacificatory,* i.e. (subj.) *peaceable:*— peacemaker.

εἴρω **ĕirō.** See *1515, 4483, 5346.*

1519. εἰς **ĕis,** *ice;* a primary prep.; *to* or *into* (indicating the point reached or entered), of place, time, or (fig.) purpose (result, etc.); also in adv. phrases:— [abundant-] ly, against, among, as, at, [back-] ward, before, by, concerning, + continual, + far more exceeding, for [intent, purpose], fore, + forth, in (among, at, unto, -so much that,to), to the intent that, + of one mind, + never, of, (up-) on, + perish, + set at one again, (so) that, therefore (-unto), throughout, till, to (be, the end, -ward), (here-) until (-to), ... ward, [where-] fore, with. Often used in composition with the same general import, but only with verbs (etc.) expressing motion (lit. or fig.).

1520. εἷς **hĕis,** *hice;* (incl. the neut. [etc.] ἕν **hĕn**); a primary numeral; *one:*— a (-n, -ny, certain), + abundantly, man, one (another), only, other, some. See also *1527, 3367, 3391, 3762.*

1521. εἰσάγω **ĕisagō,** *ice-ag´-o;* from *1519* and *71; to introduce* (lit. or fig.):— bring in (-to), (+ was to) lead into.

1522. εἰσακούω **ĕisakŏuō,** *ice-ak-oo´-o;* from *1519* and *191; to listen to:*— hear.

1523. εἰσδέχομαι **ĕisdĕchŏmai,** *ice-dekh´-om-ahee;* from *1519* and *1209; to take into* one's favor:— receive.

1524. εἴσειμι **ĕisĕimi,** *ice´-i-mee;* from *1519* and εἶμι **ĕimi** (to *go*); *to enter:*— enter (go) into.

1525. εἰσέρχομαι **ĕisĕrchŏmai,** *ice-er´-khom-ahee;* from *1519* and *2064; to enter* (lit. or fig.):— × arise, come (in, into), enter in (-to), go in (through).

1526. εἰσί **ĕisi,** *i-see´;* third pers. plur. present ind. of *1510;* they *are:*— agree, are, be, dure, × is, were.

1527. εἷς καθ᾽ εἷς **hĕis kath' hĕis,** *hice kath hice;* from *1520* repeated with *2596* inserted; *severally:*— one by one.

1528. εἰσκαλέω **ĕiskalĕō,** *ice-kal-eh´-o;* from *1519* and *2564; to invite* in:— call in.

1529. εἴσοδος **ĕisŏdŏs,** *ice´-od-os;* from *1519* and *3598; an entrance* (lit. or fig.):— coming, enter (-ing) in (to).

1530. εἰσπηδάω **ĕispēdaō,** *ice-pay-dah´-o;* from *1519* and πηδάω **pēdaō** (to *leap*); to *rush in:*— run (spring) in.

1531. εἰσπορεύομαι **ĕispŏrĕuŏmai,** *ice-por-yoo´-om-ahee;* from *1519* and *4198; to enter* (lit. or fig.):— come (enter) in, go into.

1532. εἰστρέχω **ĕistrĕchō,** *ice-trekh´-o;* from *1519* and *5143; to hasten inward:*— run in.

1533. εἰσφέρω **ĕisphĕrō,** *ice-fer´-o;* from *1519* and *5342; to carry inward* (lit. or fig.):— bring (in), lead into.

1534. εἶτα **ĕita,** *i´-tah;* of uncert. aff.; a particle of *succession* (in time or logical enumeration), *then, moreover:*— after that (-ward), furthermore, then. See also *1899.*

1535. εἴτε **ĕitĕ,** *i´-teh;* from *1487* and *5037; if too:*— if, or, whether.

1536. εἴ τις **ĕi tis,** *i tis;* from *1487* and *5100; if any:*— he that, if a (-ny) man ('s, thing, from any, ought), whether any, whosoever.

1537. ἐκ **ĕk,** *ek* or

ἐξ **ĕx,** *ex;* a primary prep. denoting *origin* (the point *whence* motion or action proceeds), *from, out* (of place, time, or cause; lit. or fig.; direct or remote):— after, among, × are, at, betwixt (-yond), by (the means of), exceedingly, (+ abundantly above), for (-th), from (among, forth, up), + grudgingly, heartily, × heavenly, × hereby, + very highly, in, ... ly, (because, by reason) of, off (from), on, out among (from, of), over, since, × thenceforth, through, × unto, × vehemently, with (-out). Often used in composition, with the same general import; often of completion.

1538. ἕκαστος **hĕkastŏs,** *hek´-as-tos;* as if a superl. of ἕκας **hĕkas** (*afar*); *each* or *every:*— any, both, each (one), every (man, one, woman), particularly.

1539. ἑκάστοτε **hĕkastŏtĕ,** *hek-as´-tot-eh;* as if from *1538* and *5119; at every time:*— always.

1540. ἑκατόν **hĕkatŏn,** *hek-at-on´;* of uncert. aff.; a *hundred:*— hundred.

1541. ἑκατονταέτης **hĕkatŏntaĕtēs,** *hek-at-on-tah-et´-ace;* from *1540* and *2094; centenarian:*— hundred years old.

1542. ἑκατονταπλασίων **hĕkatŏntaplasiōn,** *hek-at-on-ta-plah-see´-own;* from *1540* and a presumed der. of *4111; a hundred times:*— hundredfold.

1543. ἑκατοντάρχης **hĕkatŏntarchēs,** *hek-at-on-tar´-khace;* or

ἑκατόνταρχος **hĕkatŏntarchŏs,** *hek-at-on´-tar-khos;* from *1540* and 757; the *captain of one hundred men:*— centurion.

1544. ἐκβάλλω **ĕkballō,** *ek-bal´-lo;* from *1537* and *906; to eject* (lit. or fig.):— bring forth, cast (forth, out), drive (out), expel, leave, pluck (pull, take, thrust) out, put forth (out), send away (forth, out).

1545. ἔκβασις **ĕkbasis,** *ek´-bas-is;* from a compound of *1537* and the base of *939* (mean. to *go out*); an *exit* (lit. or fig.):— end, way to escape.

1546. ἐκβολή **ĕkbŏlē,** *ek-bol-ay´;* from *1544; ejection,* i.e. (spec.) a *throwing overboard* of the cargo:— + lighten the ship.

1547. ἐκγαμίζω **ĕkgamizō,** *ek-gam-id´-zo;* from *1537* and a form of *1061* [comp. *1548*]; to *marry off* a daughter:— give in marriage.

1548. ἐκγαμίσκω **ĕkgamiskō,** *ek-gam-is´-ko;* from *1537* and *1061;* the same as *1547:*— give in marriage.

1549. ἔκγονον **ĕkgŏnŏn,** *ek´-gon-on;* neut. of a der. of a compound of *1537* and *1096; a descendant,* i.e. (spec.) *grandchild:*— nephew.

1550. ἐκδαπανάω **ĕkdapanaō,** *ek-dap-an-ah´-o;* from *1537* and *1159; to expend* (wholly), i.e. (fig.) *exhaust:*— spend.

1551. ἐκδέχομαι **ĕkdĕchŏmai,** *ek-dekh´-om-ahee;* from *1537* and *1209;* to *accept from* some source, i.e. (by impl.) to *await:*— expect, look (tarry) for, wait (for).

1552. ἔκδηλος **ĕkdēlŏs,** *ek´-day-los;* from *1537* and *1212; wholly evident:*— manifest.

1553. ἐκδημέω **ĕkdēmĕō,** *ek-day-meh´-o;* from a compound of *1537* and *1218;* to *emigrate,* i.e. (fig.) *vacate* or *quit:*— be absent.

1554. ἐκδίδωμι **ĕkdidōmi,** *ek-did-o´-mee;* from *1537* and *1325; to give forth,* i.e. (spec.) to *lease:*— let forth (out).

1555. ἐκδιηγέομαι **ĕkdiēgĕŏmai,** *ek-dee-ayg-eh´-om-ahee;* from *1537* and a compound of *1223* and *2233;* to *narrate through wholly:*— declare.

1556. ἐκδικέω **ĕkdikĕō,** *ek-dik-eh´-o;* from *1558;* to *vindicate, retaliate, punish:*— (a-) venge.

1557. ἐκδίκησις **ĕkdikēsis,** *ek-dik´-ay-sis;* from *1556; vindication, retribution:*— (a-, re-) venge (-ance), punishment.

1558. ἔκδικος **ĕkdikŏs,** *ek´-dik-os;* from *1537* and *1349;* carrying *justice* out, i.e. a *punisher:*— a (re-) venger.

1559. ἐκδιώκω **ĕkdiōkō,** *ek-dee-o´-ko;* from *1537* and *1377;* to *pursue out,* i.e. *expel* or *persecute* implacably:— persecute.

1560. ἔκδοτος **ĕkdŏtŏs,** *ek´-dot-os;* from *1537* and a der. of *1325; given out* or *over,* i.e. *surrendered:*— delivered.

1561. ἐκδοχή **ĕkdŏchē,** *ek-dokh-ay´;* from *1551; expectation:*— looking for.

1562. ἐκδύω **ĕkduō,** *ek-doo´-o;* from *1537* and the base of *1416;* to cause to *sink out* of, i.e. (spec. as of clothing) to *divest:*— strip, take off from, unclothe.

1563. ἐκεῖ ĕkĕi, *ek-i´*; of uncert. aff.; *there;* by extens. *thither:*— there, thither (-ward), (to) yonder (place).

1564. ἐκεῖθεν ĕkĕithĕn, *ek-i´-then*; from 1563; *thence:*— from that place, (from) thence, there.

1565. ἐκεῖνος ĕkĕinŏs, *ek-i´-nos*; from 1563; *that* one (or [neut.] thing); often intensified by the art. prefixed:— he, it, the other (same), selfsame, that (same, very), × their, × them, they, this, those. See also 3778.

1566. ἐκεῖσε ĕkĕisĕ, *ek-i´-seh*; from 1563; *thither:*— there.

1567. ἐκζητέω ĕkzētĕō, *ek-zay-teh´-o*; from 1537 and 2212; to *search out,* i.e. (fig.) *investigate, crave, demand,* (by Heb.) *worship:*— en- (re-) quire, seek after (carefully, diligently).

1568. ἐκθαμβέω ĕkthambĕō, *ek-tham-beh´-o*; from 1569; to *astonish* utterly:— affright, greatly (sore) amaze.

1569. ἔκθαμβος ĕkthambŏs, *ek´-tham-bos*; from 1537 and 2285; *utterly astounded:*— greatly wondering.

1570. ἔκθετος ĕkthĕtŏs, *ek´-thet-os*; from 1537 and a der. of 5087; *put out,* i.e. *exposed* to perish:— cast out.

1571. ἐκκαθαίρω ĕkkathairō, *ek-kath-ah´-ee-ro*; from 1537 and 2508; to *cleanse thoroughly:*— purge (out).

1572. ἐκκαίω ĕkkaiō, *ek-kah´-yo*; from 1537 and 2545; to *inflame* deeply:— burn.

1573. ἐκκακέω ĕkkakĕō, *ek-kak-eh´-o* or ἐγκακέω egkakĕō *eng-kak-eh´-o*; from 1537 and 2556; to *be* (bad or) *weak,* i.e. (by impl.) to *fail* (in heart):— faint, be weary.

1574. ἐκκεντέω ĕkkĕntĕō, *ek-ken-teh´-o*; from 1537 and the base of 2759; to *transfix:*— pierce.

1575. ἐκκλάω ĕkklaō, *ek-klah´-o*; from 1537 and 2806; to *exscind:*— break off.

1576. ἐκκλείω ĕkklĕiō, *ek-kli´-o*; from 1537 and 2808; to *shut out* (lit. or fig.):— exclude.

1577. ἐκκλησία ĕkklēsia, *ek-klay-see´-ah*; from a compound of 1537 and a der. of 2564; a *calling* out, i.e. (concr.) a popular *meeting,* espec. a religious *congregation* (Jewish *synagogue,* or Chr. community of members on earth or saints in heaven or both):— assembly, church.

1578. ἐκκλίνω ĕkklinō, *ek-klee´-no*; from 1537 and 2827; to *deviate,* i.e. (absolutely) to *shun* (lit. or fig.), or (rel.) to *decline* (from piety):— avoid, eschew, go out of the way.

1579. ἐκκολυμβάω ĕkkŏlumbaō, *ek-kol-oom-bah´-o*; from 1537 and 2860; to *escape* by *swimming:*— swim out.

1580. ἐκκομίζω ĕkkŏmizō, *ek-kom-id´-zo*; from 1537 and 2865; to *bear forth* (to burial):— carry out.

1581. ἐκκόπτω ĕkkŏptō, *ek-kop´-to*; from 1537 and 2875; to *exscind;* fig. to *frustrate:*— cut down (off, out), hew down, hinder.

1582. ἐκκρέμαμαι ĕkkrĕmamai, *ek-krem´-am-ahee*; mid. voice from 1537 and 2910; to *hang upon* the lips of a speaker, i.e. *listen closely:*— be very attentive.

1583. ἐκλαλέω ĕklalĕō, *ek-lal-eh´-o*; from 1537 and 2980; to *divulge:*— tell.

1584. ἐκλάμπω ĕklampō, *ek-lam´-po*; from 1537 and 2989; to *be resplendent:*— shine forth.

1585. ἐκλανθάνομαι ĕklanthanŏmai, *ek-lan-than´-om-ahee*; mid. voice from 1537 and 2990; to *be* utterly *oblivious* of:— forget.

1586. ἐκλέγομαι ĕklĕgŏmai, *ek-leg´-om-ahee*; mid. voice from 1537 and 3004 (in its primary sense); to *select:*— make choice, choose (out), chosen.

1587. ἐκλείπω ĕklĕipō, *ek-li´-po*; from 1537 and 3007; to *omit,* i.e. (by impl.) *cease* (die):— fail.

1588. ἐκλεκτός ĕklĕktŏs, *ek-lek-tos´*; from 1586; *select;* by impl. *favorite:*— chosen, elect.

1589. ἐκλογή ĕklŏgē, *ek-log-ay´*; from 1586; (divine) *selection* (abstr. or concr.):— chosen, election.

1590. ἐκλύω ĕkluō, *ek-loo´-o*; from 1537 and 3089; to *relax* (lit. or fig.):— faint.

1591. ἐκμάσσω ĕkmassō, *ek-mas´-so*; from 1537 and the base of 3145; to *knead out,* i.e. (by anal.) to *wipe dry:*— wipe.

1592. ἐκμυκτερίζω ĕkmuktĕrizō, *ek-mook-ter-id´-zo*; from 1537 and 3456; to *sneer* outright at:— deride.

1593. ἐκνεύω ĕknĕuō, *ek-nyoo´-o*; from 1537 and 3506; (by anal.) to *slip off,* i.e. quietly *withdraw:*— convey self away.

1594. ἐκνήφω ĕknēphō, *ek-nay´-fo*; from 1537 and 3525; (fig.) to *rouse* (oneself) *out* of stupor:— awake.

1595. ἑκούσιον hĕkŏusiŏn, *hek-oo´-see-on*; neut. of a der. from 1635; *voluntariness:*— willingly.

1596. ἑκουσίως hĕkŏusiōs, *hek-oo-see´-oce*; adv. from the same as 1595; *voluntarily:*— wilfully, willingly.

1597. ἔκπαλαι ĕkpalai, *ek´-pal-ahee*; from 1537 and 3819; *long ago, for a long while:*— of a long time, of old.

1598. ἐκπειράζω ĕkpĕirazō, *ek-pi-rad´-zo*; from 1537 and 3985; to *test thoroughly:*— tempt.

1599. ἐκπέμπω ĕkpĕmpō, *ek-pem´-po*; from 1537 and 3992; to *despatch:*— send away (forth).

ἐκπερισσοῦ ĕkpĕrissŏu. See 1537 and 4053.

1600. ἐκπετάννυμι ĕkpĕtannumi, *ek-pet-an´-noo-mee*; from 1537 and a form of 4072; to *fly out,* i.e. (by anal.) to *extend:*— stretch forth.

1601. ἐκπίπτω ĕkpiptō, *ek-pip´-to*; from 1537 and 4098; to *drop away;* spec. *be driven out* of one's course; fig. to *lose, become inefficient:*— be cast, fail, fall (away, off), take none effect.

1602. ἐκπλέω ĕkplĕō, *ek-pleh´-o*; from 1537 and 4126; to *depart* by ship:— sail (away, thence).

1603. ἐκπληρόω ĕkplērŏō, *ek-play-rŏ´-o*; from 1537 and 4137; to *accomplish* entirely:— fulfill.

1604. ἐκπλήρωσις ĕkplērōsis, *ek-play´-ro-sis*; from 1603; *completion:*— accomplishment.

1605. ἐκπλήσσω ĕkplēssō, *ek-place´-so*; from 1537 and 4141; to *strike* with astonishment:— amaze, astonish.

1606. ἐκπνέω ĕkpnĕō, *ek-pneh´-o*; from 1537 and 4154; to *expire:*— give up the ghost.

1607. ἐκπορεύομαι ĕkpŏrĕuŏmai, *ek-por-yoo´-om-ahee*; from 1537 and 4198; to *depart, be discharged, proceed, project:*— come (forth, out of), depart, go (forth, out), issue, proceed (out of).

1608. ἐκπορνεύω ĕkpŏrnĕuō, *ek-porn-yoo´-o*; from 1537 and 4203; to *be utterly unchaste:*— give self over to fornication.

1609. ἐκπτύω ĕkptuō, *ek-ptoo´-o*; from 1537 and 4429; to *spit out,* i.e. (fig.) *spurn:*— reject.

1610. ἐκριζόω ĕkrizŏō, *ek-rid-zŏ´-o*; from 1537 and 4492; to *uproot:*— pluck up by the root, root up.

1611. ἔκστασις ĕkstasis, *ek´-stas-is*; from 1839; a *displacement* of the mind, i.e. *bewilderment,* "*ecstasy*":— + be amazed, amazement, astonishment, trance.

1612. ἐκστρέφω ĕkstrĕphō, *ek-stref´-o*; from 1537 and 4762; to *pervert* (fig.):— subvert.

1613. ἐκταράσσω ĕktarassō, *ek-tar-as´-so*; from 1537 and 5015; to *disturb wholly:*— exceedingly trouble.

1614. ἐκτείνω ĕktĕinō, *ek-ti´-no*; from 1537 and τείνω tĕinō (to *stretch*); to *extend:*— cast, put forth, stretch forth (out).

1615. ἐκτελέω ĕktĕlĕō, *ek-tel-eh´-o*; from 1537 and 5055; to *complete* fully:— finish.

1616. ἐκτένεια ĕktĕnĕia, *ek-ten-i´-ah*; from 1618; *intentness:*— × instantly.

1617. ἐκτενέστερον ĕktĕnĕstĕrŏn, *ek-ten-es´-ter-on*; neut. of the comparative of 1618; *more intently:*— more earnestly.

1618. ἐκτενής ĕktĕnēs, *ek-ten-ace´*; from 1614; *intent:*— without ceasing, fervent.

1619. ἐκτενῶς ĕktĕnōs, *ek-ten-oce´*; adv. from 1618; *intently:*— fervently.

1620. ἐκτίθημι ĕktithēmi, *ek-tith´-ay-mee*; from 1537 and 5087; to *expose;* fig. to *declare:*— cast out, expound.

1621. ἐκτινάσσω ĕktinassō, *ek-tin-as´-so*; from 1537 and τινάσσω tinassō (to *swing*); to *shake* violently:— shake (off).

1622. ἐκτός ĕktŏs, *ek-tos´*; from 1537; the *exterior;* fig. (as a prep.) *aside from, besides:*— but, except (-ed), other than, out of, outside, unless, without.

1623. ἕκτος hĕktŏs, *hek´-tos*; ordinal from 1803; *sixth:*— sixth.

1624. ἐκτρέπω ĕktrĕpō, *ek-trep´-o*; from 1537 and the base of 5157; to *deflect,* i.e. *turn away* (lit. or fig.):— avoid, turn (aside, out of the way).

1625. ἐκτρέφω ĕktrĕphō, *ek-tref´-o*; from 1537 and 5142; to *rear up* to ma-

Greek

turity, i.e. (gen.) to *cherish* or *train:*— bring up, nourish.

1626. ἔκτρωμα **ĕktrōma**, *ek´-tro-mah;* from a compound of *1537* and τιτρώσκω **titrōskō** (to *wound*); a *miscarriage* (*abortion*), i.e. (by anal.) *untimely birth:*— born out of due time.

1627. ἐκφέρω **ĕkphĕrō**, *ek-fer´-o;* from *1537* and *5342;* to *bear out* (lit. or fig.):— bear, bring forth, carry forth (out).

1628. ἐκφεύγω **ĕkphĕugō**, *ek-fyoo´-go;* from *1537* and *5343;* to *flee out:*— escape, flee.

1629. ἐκφοβέω **ĕkphŏbĕō**, *ek-fob-eh´-o;* from *1537* and *5399;* to *frighten utterly:*— terrify.

1630. ἔκφοβος **ĕkphŏbŏs**, *ek´-fob-os;* from *1537* and *5401; frightened* out of one's wits: sore afraid, exceedingly fear.

1631. ἐκφύω **ĕkphuō**, *ek-foo´-o;* from *1537* and *5453;* to *sprout up:*— put forth.

1632. ἐκχέω **ĕkchĕō**, *ek-kheh´-o;* or (by var.)

ἐκχύνω **ĕkchunō**, *ek-khoo´-no;* from *1537;* and χέω **chĕō** (to *pour*); to *pour forth;* fig. to *bestow:*— gush (pour) out, run greedily (out), shed (abroad, forth), spill.

1633. ἐκχωρέω **ĕkchōrĕō**, *ek-kho-reh´-o;* from *1537* and *5562;* to *depart:*— depart out.

1634. ἐκψύχω **ĕkpsuchō**, *ek-psoo´-kho;* from *1537* and *5594;* to *expire:*— give (yield) up the ghost.

1635. ἑκών **hĕkōn**, *hek-own´;* of uncert. aff.; *voluntary:*— willingly.

1636. ἐλαία **ĕlaia**, *el-ah´-yah;* fem. of a presumed der. from an obsolete primary; an *olive* (the tree or the fruit):— olive (berry, tree).

1637. ἔλαιον **ĕlaiŏn**, *el´-ah-yon;* neut. of the same as *1636;* olive *oil:*— oil.

1638. ἐλαιών **ĕlaiōn**, *el-ah-yone´;* from *1636;* an *olive-orchard,* i.e. (spec.) the *Mt. of Olives:*— Olivet.

1639. Ἐλαμίτης **Ĕlamitēs**, *el-am-ee´-tace;* of Heb. or. [5867]; an *Elamite* or Persian:— Elamite.

1640. ἐλάσσων **ĕlassōn**, *el-as´-sone;* or

ἐλάττων **ĕlattōn** *el-at-tone´;* comparative of *1646; smaller* (in size, quantity, age or quality):— less, under, worse, younger.

1641. ἐλαττονέω **ĕlattŏnĕō**, *el-at-ton-eh-o;* from *1640;* to *diminish,* i.e. *fall short:*— have lack.

1642. ἐλαττόω **ĕlattŏō**, *el-at-tŏ´-o;* from *1640;* to *lessen* (in rank or influence):— decrease, make lower.

1643. ἐλαύνω **ĕlaunō**, *el-ŏw´-no;* a prol. form of a primary verb (obsolete except in certain tenses as an altern. of this) of uncert. affin; to *push* (as wind, oars or demoniacal power):— carry, drive, row.

1644. ἐλαφρία **ĕlaphria**, *el-af-ree´-ah;* from *1645; levity* (fig.), i.e. *fickleness:*— lightness.

1645. ἐλαφρός **ĕlaphrŏs**, *el-af-ros´;* prob. akin to *1643* and the base of *1640; light,* i.e. *easy:*— light.

1646. ἐλάχιστος **ĕlachistŏs**, *el-akh´-is-tos;* superl. of ἐλαχυς **ĕlachus** (*short*); used as equiv. to *3398; least* (in size, amount, dignity, etc.):— least, very little (small), smallest.

1647. ἐλαχιστότερος **ĕlachistŏtĕrŏs**, *el-akh-is-tot´-er-os;* comparative of *1646; far less:*— less than the least.

1648. Ἐλεάζαρ **Ĕleazar**, *el-eh-ad´-zar;* of Heb. or. [499]; *Eleazar,* an Isr.:— Eleazar.

1649. ἔλεγξις **ĕlĕgxis**, *el´-eng-xis;* from *1651; refutation,* i.e. *reproof:*— rebuke.

1650. ἔλεγχος **ĕlĕgchŏs**, *el´-eng-khos;* from *1651; proof, conviction:*— evidence, reproof.

1651. ἐλέγχω **ĕlĕgchō**, *el-eng´-kho;* of uncert. aff.; to *confute, admonish:*— convict, convince, tell a fault, rebuke, reprove.

1652. ἐλεεινός **ĕlĕĕinŏs**, *el-eh-i-nos´;* from *1656; pitiable:*— miserable.

1653. ἐλεέω **ĕlĕĕō**, *el-eh-eh´-o;* from *1656;* to *compassionate* (by word or deed, spec., by divine grace):— have compassion (pity on), have (obtain, receive, shew) mercy (on).

1654. ἐλεημοσύνη **ĕlĕēmŏsunē**, *el-eh-ay-mos-oo´-nay;* from *1656; compassionateness,* i.e. (as exercised toward the poor) *beneficence,* or (concr.) a *benefaction:*— alms (-deeds).

1655. ἐλεήμων **ĕlĕēmōn**, *el-eh-ay´-mone;* from *1653; compassionate* (actively):— merciful.

1656. ἔλεος **ĕlĕŏs**, *el´-eh-os;* of uncert. aff.; *compassion* (human or divine, espec. active):— (+ tender) mercy.

1657. ἐλευθερία **ĕlĕuthĕria**, *el-yoo-ther-ee´-ah;* from *1658; freedom* (legitimate or licentious, chiefly mor. or cerem.):— liberty.

1658. ἐλεύθερος **ĕlĕuthĕrŏs**, *el-yoo´-ther-os;* prob. from the alt. of *2064; unrestrained* (to go at pleasure), i.e. (as a citizen) *not a slave* (whether *freeborn* or *manumitted*), or (gen.) *exempt* (from obligation or liability):— free (man, woman), at liberty.

1659. ἐλευθερόω **ĕlĕuthĕrŏō**, *el-yoo-ther-ŏ´-o;* from *1658;* to *liberate,* i.e. (fig.) to *exempt* (from mor., cerem. or mortal liability):— deliver, make free.

ἐλεύθω **ĕlĕuthō**. See *2064.*

1660. ἔλευσις **ĕlĕusis**, *el´-yoo-sis;* from the alt. of *2064;* an *advent:*— coming.

1661. ἐλεφάντινος **ĕlĕphantinŏs**, *el-ef-an´-tee-nos;* from ἔλεφας **ĕlĕphas** (an "*elephant*"); *elephantine,* i.e. (by impl.) composed of *ivory:*— of ivory.

1662. Ἐλιακείμ **Ĕliakĕim**, *el-ee-ak-ehm´* or Ἐλιακίμ **Ĕliakim** *el-ee-ak-ime´;* of Heb. or. [471]; *Eliakim,* an Isr.:— Eliakim.

1663. Ἐλιέζερ **Ĕliĕzĕr**, *el-ee-ed´-zer;* of Heb. or. [461]; *Eliezer,* an Isr.:— Eliezer.

1664. Ἐλιούδ **Ĕliŏud**, *el-ee-ood´;* of Heb. or. [410 and 1935]; *God of majesty; Eliud,* an Isr.:— Eliud.

1665. Ἐλισάβετ **Ĕlisabĕt**, *el-ee-sab´-et;* of Heb. or. [472]; *Elisabet,* an Israelitess:— Elisabeth.

1666. Ἐλισσαῖος **Ĕlissaiŏs**, *el-is-sah´-yos;* of Heb. or. [477]; *Elissæus,* an Isr.:— Elissæus.

1667. ἑλίσσω **hĕlissō**, *hel-is´-so;* a form of *1507;* to *coil* or *wrap:*— fold up.

1668. ἕλκος **hĕlkŏs**, *hel´-kos;* prob. from *1670;* an *ulcer* (as if drawn together):— sore.

1669. ἑλκόω **hĕlkŏō**, *hel-kŏ´-o;* from *1668;* to *cause to ulcerate,* i.e. (pass.) *be ulcerous:*— full of sores.

1670. ἑλκύω **hĕlkuō**, *hel-koo´-o;* or

ἕλκω **hĕlkō**, *hel´-ko;* prob. akin to *138;* to *drag* (lit. or fig.):— draw. Comp. *1667.*

1671. Ἑλλάς **Hĕllas**, *hel-las´;* of uncert. aff.; *Hellas* (or *Greece*), a country of Europe:— Greece.

1672. Ἕλλην **Hĕllēn**, *hel´-lane;* from *1671;* a *Hellen* (*Grecian*) or inhab. of Hellas; by extens. a *Greek-speaking* person, espec. a *non-Jew:*— Gentile, Greek.

1673. Ἑλληνικός **Hĕllēnikŏs**, *hel-lay-nee-kos´;* from *1672; Hellenic,* i.e. *Grecian* (in language):— Greek.

1674. Ἑλληνίς **Hĕllēnis**, *hel-lay-nis´;* fem. of *1672;* a *Grecian* (i.e. *non-Jewish*) *woman:*— Greek.

1675. Ἑλληνιστής **Hĕllēnistēs**, *hel-lay-nis-tace´;* from a der. of *1672;* a *Hellenist* or *Greek-speaking Jew:*— Grecian.

1676. Ἑλληνιστί **Hĕllēnisti**, *hel-lay-nis-tee´;* adv. from the same as *1675; Hellenistically,* i.e. in the Grecian language:— Greek.

1677. ἐλλογέω **ĕllŏgĕō**, *el-log-eh´-o;* from *1722* and *3056* (in the sense of account); to *reckon in,* i.e. *attribute:*— impute, put on account.

ἔλλομαι **hĕllŏmai**. See *138.*

1678. Ἐλμωδάμ **Ĕlmōdam**, *el-mo-dam´;* of Heb. or. [perh. for 486]; *Elmodam,* an Isr.:— Elmodam.

1679. ἐλπίζω **ĕlpizō**, *el-pid´-zo;* from *1680;* to *expect* or *confide:*— (have, thing) hope (-d) (for), trust.

1680. ἐλπίς **ĕlpis**, *el-pece´;* from a primary ἔλπω **ĕlpō** (to *anticipate,* usually with pleasure); *expectation* (abstr. or concr.) or *confidence:*— faith, hope.

1681. Ἐλύμας **Ĕlumas**, *el-oo´-mas;* of for. or.; *Elymas,* a wizard:— Elymas.

1682. ἐλοΐ **ĕlŏï**, *el-o-ee´;* of Chald. or. [426 with pron. suff.] *my God:*— Eloi.

1683. ἐμαυτοῦ **ĕmautŏu**, *em-ŏw-too´;* gen. compound of *1700* and *846; of myself* (so likewise the dat.

ἐμαυτῷ **ĕmautŏi**, *em-ow-to´;* and acc.

ἐμαυτόν **ĕmautŏn**, *em-ow-ton´:*— me, mine own (self), myself.

1684. ἐμβαίνω **ĕmbainō**, *em-ba´-hee-no;* from *1722* and the base of *939;* to *walk on,* i.e. *embark* (aboard a vessel), *reach* (a pool):— come (get) into, enter (into), go (up) into, step in, take ship.

1685. ἐμβάλλω **ĕmballō**, *em-bal´-lo;* from *1722* and *906;* to *throw on,* i.e. (fig.)

subject to (eternal punishment):— cast into.

1686. ἐμβάπτω **ĕmbaptō**, *em-bap´-to*; from 1722 and 911; to *whelm on*, i.e. *wet* (a part of the person, etc.) by contact with a fluid:— dip.

1687. ἐμβατεύω **ĕmbatĕuō**, *em-bat-yoo´-o*; from 1722 and a presumed der. of the base of 939; equiv. to 1684; to *intrude on* (fig.):— intrude into.

1688. ἐμβιβάζω **ĕmbibazō**, *em-bib-ad´-zo*; from 1722 and βιβάζω bibazō (to *mount*; caus. of 1684); to *place on*, i.e. *transfer* (aboard a vessel):— put in.

1689. ἐμβλέπω **ĕmblĕpō**, *em-blep´-o*; from 1722 and 991; to *look on*, i.e. (rel.) to *observe* fixedly, or (absolutely) to *discern* clearly:— behold, gaze up, look upon, (could) see.

1690. ἐμβριμάομαι **ĕmbrimaŏmai**, *em-brim-ah´-om-ahee*; from 1722 and βριμάομαι brimaŏmai (to *snort* with anger); to have *indignation on*, i.e. (tran.) to *blame*, (intr.) to *sigh* with chagrin, (spec.) to sternly *enjoin*:— straitly charge, groan, murmur against.

1691. ἐμέ **ĕmĕ**, *em-eh´*; a prol. form of 3165; *me*:— I, me, my (-self).

1692. ἐμέω **ĕmĕō**, *em-eh´-o*; of uncert. aff.; to *vomit*:— (will) spue.

1693. ἐμμαίνομαι **ĕmmainŏmai**, *em-mah´-ee-nom-ahee*; from 1722 and 3105; to *rave on*, i.e. *rage at*:— be mad against.

1694. Ἐμμανουήλ **Ĕmmanŏuēl**, *em-man-oo-ale´*; of Heb. or. [6005]; *God with us*; Emmanuel, a name of Christ:— Emmanuel.

1695. Ἐμμαούς **Ĕmmaŏus**, *em-mah-ooce´*; prob. of Heb. or. [comp. 3222]; *Emmaüs*, a place in Pal.:— Emmaus.

1696. ἐμμένω **ĕmmĕnō**, *em-men´-o*; from 1722 and 3306; to *stay in* the same place, i.e. (fig.) *persevere*:— continue.

1697. Ἐμμόρ **Ĕmmŏr**, *em-mor´*; of Heb. or. [2544]; *Emmor* (i.e. *Chamor*), a Canaanite:— Emmor.

1698. ἐμοί **ĕmŏi**, *em-oy´*; a prol. form of 3427; *to me*:— I, me, mine, my.

1699. ἐμός **ĕmŏs**, *em-os´*; from the oblique cases of 1473 (1698, 1700, 1691); *my*:— of me, mine (own), my.

1700. ἐμοῦ **ĕmŏu**, *em-oo´*; a prol. form of 3450; *of me*:— me, mine, my.

1701. ἐμπαιγμός **ĕmpaigmŏs**, *emp-aheeg-mos´*; from 1702; *derision*:— mocking.

1702. ἐμπαίζω **ĕmpaizō**, *emp-aheed´-zo*; from 1722 and 3815; to *jeer at*, i.e. *deride*:— mock.

1703. ἐμπαίκτης **ĕmpaiktēs**, *emp-aheek-tace´*; from 1702; a *derider*, i.e. (by impl.) a *false teacher*:— mocker, scoffer.

1704. ἐμπεριπατέω **ĕmpĕripatĕō**, *em-per-ee-pat-eh´-o*; from 1722 and 4043; to *perambulate on* a place, i.e. (fig.) to *be occupied among* persons:— walk in.

1705. ἐμπίπλημι **ĕmpiplēmi**, *em-pip´-lay-mee*; or

ἐμπλήθω **ĕmplēthō**, *em-play´-tho*; from 1722 and the base of 4118; to *fill in*

(up), i.e. (by impl.) to *satisfy* (lit. or fig.):— fill.

1706. ἐμπίπτω **ĕmpiptō**, *em-pip´-to*; from 1722 and 4098; to *fall on*, i.e. (lit.) to *be entrapped by*, or (fig.) *be over-whelmed with*:— fall among (into).

1707. ἐμπλέκω **ĕmplĕkō**, *em-plek´-o*; from 1722 and 4120; to *entwine*, i.e. (fig.) *involve* with:— entangle (in, self with).

ἐμπλήθω **ĕmplēthō**. See 1705.

1708. ἐμπλοκή **ĕmplŏkē**, *em-plok-ay´*; from 1707; elaborate *braiding* of the hair:— plaiting.

1709. ἐμπνέω **ĕmpnĕō**, *emp-neh´-o*; from 1722 and 4154; to *inhale*, i.e. (fig.) to *be animated by* (bent upon):— breathe.

1710. ἐμπορεύομαι **ĕmpŏrĕuŏmai**, *em-por-yoo´-om-ahee*; from 1722 and 4198; to *travel in* (a country as a pedlar), i.e. (by impl.) to *trade*:— buy and sell, make merchandise.

1711. ἐμπορία **ĕmpŏria**, *em-por-ee´-ah*; fem. from 1713; *traffic*:— merchandise.

1712. ἐμπόριον **ĕmpŏriŏn**, *em-por´-ee-on*; neut. from 1713; a *mart* ("*emporium*"):— merchandise.

1713. ἔμπορος **ĕmpŏrŏs**, *em´-por-os*; from 1722 and the base of 4198; a (wholesale) *tradesman*:— merchant.

1714. ἐμπρήθω **ĕmprēthō**, *em-pray-tho*; from 1722 and πρήθω prēthō (to *blow* a flame); to *enkindle*, i.e. *set on fire*:— burn up.

1715. ἔμπροσθεν **ĕmprŏsthĕn**, *em´-pros-then*; from 1722 and 4314; *in front of* (in place [lit. or fig.] or time):— against, at, before, (in presence, sight) of.

1716. ἐμπτύω **ĕmptuō**, *emp-too´-o*; from 1722 and 4429; to *spit at* or *on*:— spit (upon).

1717. ἐμφανής **ĕmphanēs**, *em-fan-ace´*; from a compound of 1722 and 5316; *apparent in* self:— manifest, openly.

1718. ἐμφανίζω **ĕmphanizō**, *em-fan-id´-zo*; from 1717; to *exhibit* (in person) or *disclose* (by words):— appear, declare (plainly), inform, (will) manifest, shew, signify.

1719. ἔμφοβος **ĕmphŏbŏs**, *em´-fob-os*; from 1722 and 5401; in *fear*, i.e. *alarmed*:— affrighted, afraid, tremble.

1720. ἐμφυσάω **ĕmphusaō**, *em-foo-sah´-o*; from 1722 and φυσάω phusaō (to *puff*) [comp. 5453]; to *blow at* or *on*:— breathe on.

1721. ἔμφυτος **ĕmphutŏs**, *em´-foo-tos*; from 1722 and a der. of 5453; *implanted* (fig.):— engrafted.

1722. ἐν **ĕn**, *en*; a primary prep. denoting (fixed) *position* (in place, time or state), and (by impl.) *instrumentality* (medially or constructively), i.e. a relation of *rest* (intermediate between 1519 and 1537); "*in*," *at*, (up-) *on*, *by*, etc.:— about, after, against, + almost, × altogether, among, × as, at, before, between, (here-) by (+ all means), for (…sake of), + give self wholly to, (here-) in (-to, wardly), × mightily, (because) of, (up-) on, [open-] ly, × outwardly, one, × quickly, × shortly, [speedi-] ly, × that, ×

there (-in, -on), through (-out), (un-) to (-ward), under, when, where (-with), while, with (-in). Often used in compounds, with substantially the same import; rarely with verbs of motion, and then not to indicate direction, except (elliptically) by a separate (and different) prep.

1723. ἐναγκαλίζομαι **ĕnagkalizŏmai**, *en-ang-kal-id´-zom-ahee*; from 1722 and a der. of 43; to *take in* one's arms, i.e. *embrace*:— take up in arms.

1724. ἐνάλιος **ĕnaliŏs**, *en-al´-ee-os*; from 1722 and 251; *in* the *sea*, i.e. *marine*:— thing in the sea.

1725. ἔναντι **ĕnanti**, *en´-an-tee*; from 1722 and 473; *in front* (i.e. fig. *presence*) *of*:— before.

1726. ἐναντίον **ĕnantiŏn**, *en-an-tee´-on*; neut. of 1727; (adv.) *in* the *presence* (view) *of*:— before, in the presence of.

1727. ἐναντίος **ĕnantiŏs**, *en-an-tee´-os*; from 1725; *opposite*; fig. *antagonistic*:— (over) against, contrary.

1728. ἐνάρχομαι **ĕnarchŏmai**, *en-ar´-khom-ahee*; from 1722 and 756; to *commence on*:— rule [by mistake for 757].

1729. ἐνδεής **ĕndĕēs**, *en-deh-ace´*; from a compound of 1722 and 1210 (in the sense of *lacking*); *deficient in*:— lacking.

1730. ἔνδειγμα **ĕndĕigma**, *en´-dighe-mah*; from 1731; an *indication* (concr.):— manifest token.

1731. ἐνδείκνυμι **ĕndĕiknumi**, *en-dike´-noo-mee*; from 1722 and 1166; to *indicate* (by word or act):— do, show (forth).

1732. ἔνδειξις **ĕndĕixis**, *en´-dike-sis*; from 1731; *indication* (abstr.):— declare, evident token, proof.

1733. ἔνδεκα **hĕndĕka**, *hen´-dek-ah*; from (the neut. of) 1520 and 1176; *one and ten*, i.e. *eleven*:— eleven.

1734. ἐνδέκατος **hĕndĕkatŏs**, *hen-dek´-at-os*; ord. from 1733; *eleventh*:— eleventh.

1735. ἐνδέχεται **ĕndĕchĕtai**, *en-dekh´-et-ahee*; third pers. sing. present of a compound of 1722 and 1209; (impers.) *it is accepted in*, i.e. *admitted* (possible):— can (+ not) be.

1736. ἐνδημέω **ĕndēmĕō**, *en-day-meh´-o*; from a compound of 1722 and 1218; to *be in* one's own *country*, i.e. *home* (fig.):— be at home.

1737. ἐνδιδύσκω **ĕndiduskō**, *en-did-oos´-ko*; a prol. form of 1746; to *invest* (with a garment):— clothe in, wear.

1738. ἔνδικος **ĕndikŏs**, *en´-dee-kos*; from 1722 and 1349; *in the right*, i.e. *equitable*:— just.

1739. ἐνδόμησις **ĕndŏmēsis**, *en-dom´-ay-sis*; from a compound of 1722 and a der. of the base of 1218; a *housing in* (*residence*), i.e. *structure*:— building.

1740. ἐνδοξάζω **ĕndŏxazō**, *en-dox-ad´-zo*; from 1741; to *glorify*:— glorify.

1741. ἔνδοξος **ĕndŏxŏs**, *en´-dox-os*; from 1722 and 1391; *in glory*, i.e. *splendid*, (fig.) *noble*:— glorious, gorgeous [-ly], honourable.

1742. ἔνδυμα **ĕnduma**, *en´-doo-mah*;

from *1746; apparel* (espec. the outer robe):— clothing, garment, raiment.

1743. ἐνδυναμόω **ĕndunamŏō**, *en-doo-nam-ŏ´-o;* from *1722* and *1412;* to *empower:*— enable, (increase in) strength (-en), be (make) strong.

1744. ἐνδύνω **ĕndunō**, *en-doo´-no;* from *1772* and *1416;* to *sink* (by impl. *wrap* [comp. *1746*]) *on,* i.e. (fig.) *sneak:*— creep.

1745. ἔνδυσις **ĕndusis**, *en´-doo-sis;* from *1746; investment* with clothing:— putting on.

1746. ἐνδύω **ĕnduō**, *en-doo´-o;* from *1722* and *1416* (in the sense of *sinking* into a garment); to *invest* with clothing (lit. or fig.):— array, clothe (with), endue, have (put) on.

ἐνέγκω **ĕnĕgkō**. See *5342*.

1747. ἐνέδρα **ĕnĕdra**, *en-ed´-rah;* fem. from *1722* and the base of *1476;* an *ambuscade,* i.e. (fig.) *murderous purpose:*— lay wait. See also *1749*.

1748. ἐνεδρεύω **ĕnĕdrĕuō**, *en-ed-ryoo´-o;* from *1747;* to *lurk,* i.e. (fig.) *plot* assassination:— lay wait for.

1749. ἔνεδρον **ĕnĕdrŏn**, *en´-ed-ron;* neut. of the same as *1747;* an *ambush,* i.e. (fig.) murderous *design:*— lying in wait.

1750. ἐνειλέω **ĕnĕilĕō**, *en-i-leh´-o;* from *1772* and the base of *1507;* to *enwrap:*— wrap in.

1751. ἔνειμι **ĕnĕimi**, *en´-i-mee;* from *1772* and *1510;* to *be within* (neut. part. plur.):— such things as ... have. See also *1762*.

1752. ἕνεκα **hĕnĕka**, *hen´-ek-ah;* or

ἕνεκεν **hĕnĕkĕn**, *hen´-ek-en;* or

εἵνεκεν **hĕinĕkĕn**, *hi´-nek-en;* of uncert. aff.; *on account of:*— because, for (cause, sake), (where-) fore, by reason of, that.

1753. ἐνέργεια **ĕnĕrgĕia**, *en-erg´-i-ah;* from *1756; efficiency* ("energy"):— operation, strong, (effectual) working.

1754. ἐνεργέω **ĕnĕrgĕō**, *en-erg-eh´-o;* from *1756;* to *be active, efficient:*— do, (be) effectual (fervent), be mighty in, shew forth self, work (effectually in).

1755. ἐνέργημα **ĕnĕrgēma**, *en-erg´-ay-mah;* from *1754;* an *effect:*— operation, working.

1756. ἐνεργής **ĕnĕrgēs**, *en-er-gace´;* from *1722* and *2041; active, operative:*— effectual, powerful.

1757. ἐνευλογέω **ĕnĕulŏgĕō**, *en-yoo-log-eh´-o;* from *1722* and *2127;* to *confer a benefit on:*— bless.

1758. ἐνέχω **ĕnĕchō**, *en-ekh´-o;* from *1722* and *2192;* to *hold in* or *upon,* i.e. *ensnare;* by impl. to *keep a grudge:*— entangle with, have a quarrel against, urge.

1759. ἐνθάδε **ĕnthadĕ**, *en-thad´-eh;* from a prol. form of *1722;* prop. *within,* i.e. (of place) *here, hither:*— (t-) here, hither.

1760. ἐνθυμέομαι **ĕnthumĕŏmai**, *en-thoo-meh´-om-ahee;* from a compound of *1722* and *2372;* to *be inspirited,* i.e. *ponder:*— think.

1761. ἐνθύμησις **ĕnthumēsis**, *en-thoo´-may-sis;* from *1760; deliberation:*— device, thought.

1762. ἔνι **ĕni**, *en´-ee;* contr. for the third pers. sing. pres. ind. of *1751;* impers. *there is* in or among:— be, (there) is.

1763. ἐνιαυτός **ĕniautŏs**, *en-ee-ŏw-tos´;* prol. from a primary ἔνος **ĕnŏs** (a *year*); a *year:*— year.

1764. ἐνίστημι **ĕnistēmi**, *en-is´-tay-mee;* from *1722* and *2476;* to *place on* hand, i.e. (refl.) *impend,* (part.) be *instant:*— come, be at hand, present.

1765. ἐνισχύω **ĕnischuō**, *en-is-khoo´-o;* from *1722* and *2480;* to *invigorate* (tran. or refl.):— strengthen.

1766. ἔννατος **ĕnnatŏs**, *en´-nat-os;* ord. from *1767; ninth:*— ninth.

1767. ἐννέα **ĕnnĕa**, *en-neh´-ah;* a primary number; *nine:*— nine.

1768. ἐννενηκονταεννέα **ĕnnĕnēkŏntaĕnnĕa**, *en-nen-ay-kon-tah-en-neh´-ah;* from a (tenth) multiple of *1767* and *1767* itself; *ninety-nine:*— ninety and nine.

1769. ἐννεός **ĕnnĕŏs**, *en-neh-os´;* from *1770; dumb* (as *making signs*), i.e. *silent* from astonishment:— speechless.

1770. ἐννεύω **ĕnnĕuō**, *en-nyoo´-o;* from *1722* and *3506;* to *nod at,* i.e. *beckon* or *communicate by gesture:*— make signs.

1771. ἔννοια **ĕnnŏia**, *en´-noy-ah;* from a compound of *1722* and *3563; thoughtfulness,* i.e. moral *understanding:*— intent, mind.

1772. ἔννομος **ĕnnŏmŏs**, *en´-nom-os;* from *1722* and *3551;* (subj.) *legal,* or (obj.) *subject* to:— lawful, under law.

1773. ἔννυχον **ĕnnuchŏn**, *en´-noo-khon;* neut. of a compound of *1722* and *3571;* (adv.) *by night:*— before day.

1774. ἐνοικέω **ĕnŏikĕō**, *en-oy-keh´-o;* from *1722* and *3611;* to *inhabit* (fig.):— dwell in.

1775. ἑνότης **hĕnŏtēs**, *hen-ot-ace´;* from *1520; oneness,* i.e. (fig.) *unanimity:*— unity.

1776. ἐνοχλέω **ĕnŏchlĕō**, *en-okh-leh´-o;* from *1722* and *3791;* to *crowd in,* i.e. (fig.) to *annoy:*— trouble.

1777. ἔνοχος **ĕnŏchŏs**, *en´-okh-os;* from *1758; liable* to (a condition, penalty or imputation):— in danger of, guilty of, subject to.

1778. ἔνταλμα **ĕntalma**, *en´-tal-mah;* from *1781;* an *injunction,* i.e. relig. *precept:*— commandment.

1779. ἐνταφιάζω **ĕntaphiazō**, *en-taf-ee-ad´-zo;* from a compound of *1722* and *5028;* to *inswathe* with cerements for interment:— bury.

1780. ἐνταφιασμός **ĕntaphiasmŏs**, *en-taf-ee-as-mos´;* from *1779; preparation* for interment:— burying.

1781. ἐντέλλομαι **ĕntĕllŏmai**, *en-tel´-lom-ahee;* from *1722* and the base of *5056;* to *enjoin:*— (give) charge, (give) command (-ments), injoin.

1782. ἐντεῦθεν **ĕntĕuthĕn**, *ent-yoo´-then;* from the same as *1759; hence* (lit.

or fig.); (repeated) on *both sides:*— (from) hence, on either side.

1783. ἔντευξις **ĕntĕuxis**, *ent´-yook-sis;* from *1793;* an *interview,* i.e. (spec.) *supplication:*— intercession, prayer.

1784. ἔντιμος **ĕntimŏs**, *en´-tee-mos;* from *1722* and *5092; valued* (fig.):— dear, more honourable, precious, in reputation.

1785. ἐντολή **ĕntŏlē**, *en-tol-ay´;* from *1781; injunction,* i.e. an authoritative *prescription:*— commandment, precept.

1786. ἐντόπιος **ĕntŏpiŏs**, *en-top´-ee-os;* from *1722* and *5117;* a *resident:*— of that place.

1787. ἐντός **ĕntŏs**, *en-tos´;* from *1722; inside* (adverb or noun):— within.

1788. ἐντρέπω **ĕntrĕpō**, *en-trep´-o;* from *1722* and the base of *5157;* to *invert,* i.e. (fig. and refl.) in a good sense, to *respect;* or in a bad one, to *confound:*— regard, (give) reverence, shame.

1789. ἐντρέφω **ĕntrĕphō**, *en-tref´-o;* from *1722* and *5142;* (fig.) to *educate:*— nourish up in.

1790. ἔντρομος **ĕntrŏmŏs**, *en´-trom-os;* from *1722* and *5156; terrified:*— × quake, × trembled.

1791. ἐντροπή **ĕntrŏpē**, *en-trop-ay´;* from *1788; confusion:*— shame.

1792. ἐντρυφάω **ĕntruphaō**, *en-troo-fah´-o;* from *1722* and *5171;* to *revel in:*— sporting selves.

1793. ἐντυγχάνω **ĕntugchanō**, *en-toong-khan´-o;* from *1722* and *5177;* to *chance upon,* i.e. (by impl.) *confer with;* by extens. to *entreat* (in favor or against):— deal with, make intercession.

1794. ἐντυλίσσω **ĕntulissō**, *en-too-lis´-so;* from *1722* and τυλίσσω **tulissō** (to *twist;* prob. akin to *1507*); to *entwine,* i.e. *wind up* in:— wrap in (together).

1795. ἐντυπόω **ĕntupŏō**, *en-too-pŏ´-o;* from *1722* and a der. of *5179;* to *enstamp,* i.e. *engrave:*— engrave.

1796. ἐνυβρίζω **ĕnubrizō**, *en-oo-brid´-zo;* from *1722* and *5195;* to *insult:*— do despite unto.

1797. ἐνυπνιάζομαι **ĕnupniazŏmai**, *en-oop-nee-ad´-zom-ahee;* mid. voice from *1798;* to *dream:*— dream (-er).

1798. ἐνύπνιον **ĕnupniŏn**, *en-oop´-nee-on;* from *1722* and *5258; something seen in sleep,* i.e. a *dream (vision in a* dream):— dream.

1799. ἐνώπιον **ĕnōpiŏn**, *en-o´-pee-on;* neut. of a compound of *1722* and a der. of *3700; in the face of* (lit. or fig.):— before, in the presence (sight) of, in.

1800. Ἐνώς **Ĕnōs**, *en-oce´;* of Heb. or. [583]; *Enos* (i.e. *Enosh*), a patriarch:— Enos.

1801. ἐνωτίζομαι **ĕnōtizŏmai**, *en-o-tid´-zom-ahee;* mid. voice from a compound of *1722* and *3775;* to *take in one's ear,* i.e. to *listen:*— hearken.

1802. Ἐνώχ **Ĕnŏch**, *en-oke´;* of Heb. or. [2585]; *Enoch* (i.e. *Chanok*), an antediluvian:— Enoch.

ἐξ **ĕx**. See *1537*.

1803. ἕξ **hĕx**, *hex*; a primary numeral; *six*:— six.

1804. ἐξαγγέλλω **ĕxaggĕllō**, *ex-ang-el´-lo*; from 1537 and the base of 32; to *publish*, i.e. *celebrate*:— shew forth.

1805. ἐξαγοράζω **ĕxagŏrazō**, *ex-ag-or-ad´-zo*; from 1537 and 59; to *buy up*, i.e. *ransom*; fig. to *rescue* from loss (*improve* opportunity):— redeem.

1806. ἐξάγω **ĕxagō**, *ex-ag´-o*; from 1537 and 71; to *lead forth*:— bring forth (out), fetch (lead) out.

1807. ἐξαιρέω **ĕxairĕō**, *ex-ahee-reh´-o*; from 1537 and 138; act. to *tear out*; mid. voice to *select*; fig. to *release*:— deliver, pluck out, rescue.

1808. ἐξαίρω **ĕxairō**, *ex-ah´-ee-ro*; from 1537 and 142; to *remove*:— put (take) away.

1809. ἐξαιτέομαι **ĕxaitĕōmai**, *ex-aheeteh´-om-ahee*; mid. voice from 1537 and 154; to *demand* (for trial):— desire.

1810. ἐξαίφνης **ĕxaiphnēs**, *ex-ah´-eefnace*; from 1537 and the base of 160; *of a sudden* (*unexpectedly*):— suddenly. Comp. 1819.

1811. ἐξακολουθέω **ĕxakŏlŏuthĕō**, *ex-ak-ol-oo-theh´-o*; from 1537 and 190; to *follow out*, i.e. (fig.) to *imitate*, *obey*, *yield to*:— follow.

1812. ἐξακόσιοι **hĕxakŏsiŏi**, *hex-ak-os´-ee-oy*; plur. ordinal from 1803 and 1540; *six hundred*:— six hundred.

1813. ἐξαλείφω **ĕxalĕiphō**, *ex-al-i´-fo*; from 1537 and 218; to *smear out*, i.e. *obliterate* (erase tears, fig. *pardon* sin):— blot out, wipe away.

1814. ἐξάλλομαι **ĕxallŏmai**, *ex-al´-lom-ahee*; from 1537 and 242; to *spring forth*:— leap up.

1815. ἐξανάστασις **ĕxanastasis**, *ex-anas´-tas-is*; from 1817; a *rising from* death:— resurrection.

1816. ἐξανατέλλω **ĕxanatĕllō**, *ex-an-at-el´-lo*; from 1537 and 393; to *start up out* of the ground, i.e. *germinate*:— spring up.

1817. ἐξανίστημι **ĕxanistēmi**, *ex-an-is´-tay-mee*; from 1537 and 450; obj. to *produce*, i.e. (fig.) *beget*; subj. to *arise*, i.e. (fig.) *object*:— raise (rise) up.

1818. ἐξαπατάω **ĕxapataō**, *ex-ap-at-ah´-o*; from 1537 and 538; to *seduce wholly*:— beguile, deceive.

1819. ἐξάπινα **ĕxapina**, *ex-ap´-ee-nah*; from 1537 and a der. of the same as 160; *of a sudden*, i.e. *unexpectedly*:— suddenly. Comp. 1810.

1820. ἐξαπορέομαι **ĕxapŏrĕōmai**, *ex-ap-or-eh´-om-ahee*; mid. voice from 1537 and 639; to *be utterly at a loss*, i.e. *despond*:— (in) despair.

1821. ἐξαποστέλλω **ĕxapŏstĕllō**, *ex-ap-os-tel´-lo*; from 1537 and 649; to *send away forth*, i.e. (on a mission) to *despatch*, or (peremptorily) to *dismiss*:— send (away, forth, out).

1822. ἐξαρτίζω **ĕxartizō**, *ex-ar-tid´-zo*; from 1537 and a der. of 739; to *finish out* (time); fig. to *equip fully* (a teacher):— accomplish, thoroughly furnish.

1823. ἐξαστράπτω **ĕxastraptō**, *ex-as-*

trap´-*to*; from 1537 and 797; to *lighten forth*, i.e. (fig.) to *be radiant* (of very white garments):— glistening.

1824. ἐξαυτῆς **ĕxautēs**, *ex-ow´-tace*; from 1537 and the gen. sing. fem. of 846 (5610 being understood); *from that hour*, i.e. *instantly*:— by and by, immediately, presently, straightway.

1825. ἐξεγείρω **ĕxĕgĕirō**, *ex-eg-i´-ro*; from 1537 and 1453; to *rouse fully*, i.e. (fig.) to *resuscitate* (from death), *release* (from infliction):— raise up.

1826. ἔξειμι **ĕxĕimi**, *ex´-i-mee*; from 1537 and εἶμι **ĕimi** (*to go*); to *issue*, i.e. *leave* (a place), *escape* (to the shore):— depart, get [to land], go out.

1827. ἐξελέγχω **ĕxĕlĕgchō**, *ex-el-eng´-kho*; from 1537 and 1651; to *convict fully*, i.e. (by impl.) to *punish*:— convince.

1828. ἐξέλκω **ĕxĕlkō**, *ex-el´-ko*; from 1537 and 1670; to *drag forth*, i.e. (fig.) to *entice* (to sin):— draw away.

1829. ἐξέραμα **ĕxĕrama**, *ex-er´-am-ah*; from a compound of 1537 and a presumed ἐράω **ĕraō** (to *spue*); *vomit*, i.e. *food disgorged*:— vomit.

1830. ἐξερευνάω **ĕxĕrĕunaō**, *ex-er-yoo-nah´-o*; from 1537 and 2045; to *explore* (fig.):— search diligently.

1831. ἐξέρχομαι **ĕxĕrchŏmai**, *ex-er´-khom-ahee*; from 1537 and 2064; to *issue* (lit. or fig.):— come (forth, out), depart (out of), escape, get out, go (abroad, away, forth, out, thence), proceed (forth), spread abroad.

1832. ἔξεστι **ĕxĕsti**, *ex´-es-tee* or ἔξεστιν **exestin**, *ex´-es-teen*; third pers. sing. pres. ind. of a compound of 1537 and 1510; so also

ἐξόν **ĕxŏn**, *ex-on´*; neut. pres. part. of the same (with or without some form of 1510 expressed); impers. *it is right* (through the fig. idea of *being out* in public):— be lawful, let, × may (-est).

1833. ἐξετάζω **ĕxĕtazō**, *ex-et-ad´-zo*; from 1537 and ἐτάζω **ĕtazō** (to *examine*); to *test thoroughly* (by questions), i.e. *ascertain* or *interrogate*:— ask, enquire, search.

1834. ἐξηγέομαι **ĕxēgĕŏmai**, *ex-ayg-eh´-om-ahee*; from 1537 and 2233; to *consider out* (aloud), i.e. *rehearse*, *unfold*:— declare, tell.

1835. ἐξήκοντα **hĕxēkŏnta**, *hex-ay´-kon-tah*; the tenth multiple of 1803; *sixty*:— sixty [-fold], threescore.

1836. ἑξῆς **hĕxēs**, *hex-ace´*; from 2192 (in the sense of *taking hold of*, i.e. *adjoining*); *successive*:— after, following, × morrow, next.

1837. ἐξηχέομαι **ĕxēchĕŏmai**, *ex-ay-kheh´-om-ahee*; mid. voice from 1537 and 2278; to "*echo*" *forth*, i.e. *resound* (be generally *reported*):— sound forth.

1838. ἕξις **hĕxis**, *hex´-is*; from 2192; *habit*, i.e. (by impl.) *practice*:— use.

1839. ἐξίστημι **ĕxistēmi**, *ex-is´-tay-mee*; from 1537 and 2476; to *put* (*stand*) *out of wits*, i.e. *astound*, or (refl.) *become astounded*, *insane*:— amaze, be (make) astonished, be beside self (selves), bewitch, wonder.

1840. ἐξισχύω **ĕxischuō**, *ex-is-khoo´-o*; from 1537 and 2480; to *have full strength*, i.e. *be entirely competent*:— be able.

1841. ἔξοδος **ĕxŏdŏs**, *ex´-od-os*; from 1537 and 3598; an *exit*, i.e. (fig.) *death*:— decease, departing.

1842. ἐξολοθρεύω **ĕxŏlŏthrĕuō**, *ex-ol-oth-ryoo´-o*; from 1537 and 3645; to *extirpate*:— destroy.

1843. ἐξομολογέω **ĕxŏmŏlŏgĕō**, *ex-om-ol-og-eh´-o*; from 1537 and 3670; to *acknowledge* or (by impl. of *assent*) *agree fully*:— confess, profess, promise.

ἐξόν **ĕxŏn**. See 1832.

1844. ἐξορκίζω **ĕxŏrkizō**, *ex-or-kid´-zo*; from 1537 and 3726; to *exact an oath*, i.e. *conjure*:— adjure.

1845. ἐξορκιστής **ĕxŏrkistēs**, *ex-or-kis-tace´*; from 1844; *one that binds by an oath* (or *spell*), i.e. (by impl.) an "*exorcist*" (*conjurer*):— exorcist.

1846. ἐξορύσσω **ĕxŏrussō**, *ex-or-oos´-so*; from 1537 and 3736; to *dig out*, i.e. (by extens.) to *extract* (an eye), *remove* (roofing):— break up, pluck out.

1847. ἐξουδενόω **ĕxŏudĕnŏō**, *ex-oo-den-ŏ´-o*; from 1537 and a der. of the neut. of 3762; to *make utterly nothing of*, i.e. *despise*:— set at nought. See also 1848.

1848. ἐξουθενέω **ĕxŏuthĕnĕō**, *ex-oo-then-eh´-o*; a var. of 1847 and mean. the same:— contemptible, despise, least esteemed, set at nought.

1849. ἐξουσία **ĕxŏusia**, *ex-oo-see´-ah*; from 1832 (in the sense of *ability*); *privilege*, i.e. (subj.) *force*, *capacity*, *competency*, *freedom*, or (obj.) *mastery* (concr. *magistrate*, *superhuman*, *potentate*, *token of control*), delegated *influence*:— authority, jurisdiction, liberty, power, right, strength.

1850. ἐξουσιάζω **ĕxŏusiazō**, *ex-oo-see-ad´-zo*; from 1849; to *control*:— exercise authority upon, bring under the (have) power of.

1851. ἐξοχή **ĕxŏchē**, *ex-okh-ay´*; from a compound of 1537 and 2192 (mean. to *stand out*); *prominence* (fig.):— principal.

1852. ἐξυπνίζω **ĕxupnizō**, *ex-oop-nid´-zo*; from 1853; to *waken*:— awake out of sleep.

1853. ἔξυπνος **ĕxupnŏs**, *ex´-oop-nos*; from 1537 and 5258; *awake*:— × out of sleep.

1854. ἔξω **ĕxō**, *ex´-o*; adv. from 1537; *out* (-*side*, *of doors*), lit. or fig.:— away, forth, (with-) out (of, -ward), strange.

1855. ἔξωθεν **ĕxōthĕn**, *ex´-o-then*; from 1854; *external* (-*ly*):— out (-side, -ward, -wardly), (from) without.

1856. ἐξωθέω **ĕxōthĕō**, *ex-o-theh´-o*; or

ἐξώθω **ĕxōthō**, *ex-o´-tho*; from 1537 and ὠθέω **ōthĕō** (to *push*); to *expel*; by impl. to *propel*:— drive out, thrust in.

1857. ἐξώτερος **ĕxōtĕrŏs**, *ex-o´-ter-os*; comp. of 1854; *exterior*:— outer.

1858. ἑορτάζω **hĕŏrtazō**, *heh-or-tad´-zo*; from 1859; to *observe a festival*:— keep the feast.

1859. ἑορτή **hĕŏrtē**, *heh-or-tay´*; of uncert. aff.; a *festival*:— feast, holyday.

1860. ἐπαγγελία **ĕpaggĕlia**, *ep-ang-el-ee´-ah*; from *1861*; an *announcement* (for information, assent or pledge; espec. a divine *assurance* of good):— message, promise.

1861. ἐπαγγέλλω **ĕpaggĕllō**, *ep-ang-el´-lo*; from *1909* and the base of *32*; to *announce upon* (refl.), i.e. (by impl.) to *engage* to do something, to *assert* something respecting oneself:— profess, (make) promise.

1862. ἐπάγγελμα **ĕpaggĕlma**, *ep-ang´-el-mah*; from *1861*; a *self-committal* (by *assurance* of conferring some good):— promise.

1863. ἐπάγω **ĕpagō**, *ep-ag´-o*; from *1909* and *71*; to *superinduce*, i.e. *inflict* (an evil), *charge* (a crime):— bring upon.

1864. ἐπαγωνίζομαι **ĕpagōnizŏmai**, *ep-ag-o-nid´-zom-ahee*; from *1909* and *75*; to *struggle for*:— earnestly contend for.

1865. ἐπαθροίζω **ĕpathrŏizō**, *ep-ath-roid´-zo*; from *1909* and ἀθροίζω **athrŏizō** (to *assemble*); to *accumulate*:— gather thick together.

1866. Ἐπαίνετος **Ĕpainĕtŏs**, *ep-a´-hee-net-os*; from *1867*; *praised*; *Epænetus*, a Chr.:— Epenetus.

1867. ἐπαινέω **ĕpainĕō**, *ep-ahee-neh´-o*; from *1909* and *134*; to *applaud*:— commend, laud, praise.

1868. ἔπαινος **ĕpainŏs**, *ep´-ahee-nos*; from *1909* and the base of *134*; *laudation*; concr. a *commendable* thing:— praise.

1869. ἐπαίρω **ĕpairō**, *ep-ahee´-ro*; from *1909* and *142*; to *raise up* (lit. or fig.):— exalt self, poise (lift, take) up.

1870. ἐπαισχύνομαι **ĕpaischunŏmai**, *ep-ahee-skhoo´-nom-ahee*; from *1909* and *153*; to *feel shame for* something:— be ashamed.

1871. ἐπαιτέω **ĕpaitĕō**, *ep-ahee-teh´-o*; from *1909* and *154*; to *ask for*:— beg.

1872. ἐπακολουθέω **ĕpakŏlŏuthĕō**, *ep-ak-ol-oo-theh´-o*; from *1909* and *190*; to *accompany*:— follow (after).

1873. ἐπακούω **ĕpakŏuō**, *ep-ak-oo´-o*; from *1909* and *191*; to *hearken* (favorably) *to*:— hear.

1874. ἐπακροάομαι **ĕpakrŏaŏmai**, *ep-ak-rŏ-ah´-om-ahee*; from *1909* and the base of *202*; to *listen* (intently) *to*:— hear.

1875. ἐπάν **ĕpan**, *ep-an´*; from *1909* and *302*; a particle of indef. contemporaneousness; *whenever, as soon as*:— when.

1876. ἐπάναγκες **ĕpanagkĕs**, *ep-an´-ang-kes*; neut. of a presumed compound of *1909* and *318*; (adv.) *on necessity*, i.e. *necessarily*:— necessary.

1877. ἐπανάγω **ĕpanagō**, *ep-an-ag´-o*; from *1909* and *321*; to *lead up* on, i.e. (tech.) to *put out* (to sea); (intr.) to *return*:— launch (thrust) out, return.

1878. ἐπαναμιμνήσκω **ĕpanamimnēskō**, *ep-an-ah-mim-nace´-ko*; from *1909* and *363*; to *remind upon*:— put in mind.

1879. ἐπαναπαύομαι **ĕpanapauŏmai**, *ep-an-ah-pŏw´-om-ahee*; mid. voice

from *1909* and *373*; to *settle on*; lit. (re-main) or fig. (rely):— rest in (upon).

1880. ἐπανέρχομαι **ĕpanĕrchōmai**, *ep-an-er´-khom-ahee*; from *1909* and *424*; to *come up on*, i.e. *return*:— come again, return.

1881. ἐπανίσταμαι **ĕpanistamai**, *ep-an-is´-tam-ahee*; mid. voice from *1909* and *450*; to *stand up* on, i.e. (fig.) to *attack*:— rise up against.

1882. ἐπανόρθωσις **ĕpanŏrthōsis**, *ep-an-or´-tho-sis*; from a compound of *1909* and *461*; a *straightening up again*, i.e. (fig.) *rectification* (*reformation*):— correction.

1883. ἐπάνω **ĕpanō**, *ep-an´-o*; from *1909* and *507*; *up above*, i.e. *over* or *on* (of place, amount, rank, etc.):— above, more than, (up-) on, over.

1884. ἐπαρκέω **ĕparkĕō**, *ep-ar-keh´-o*; from *1909* and *714*; to *avail for*, i.e. *help*:— relieve.

1885. ἐπαρχία **ĕparchia**, *ep-ar-khee´-ah* or ἐπαρχεία **ĕparchĕia**, *ep-ar-khi´-ah*; from a compound of *1909* and *757* (mean. a *governor* of a district, "eparch"); a special *region* of government, i.e. a Roman *præfecture*:— province.

1886. ἔπαυλις **ĕpaulis**, *ep´-ŏw-lis*; from *1909* and an equiv. of *833*; a *hut over* the head, i.e. a *dwelling*.

1887. ἐπαύριον **ĕpauriŏn**, *ep-ow´-ree-on*; from *1909* and *839*; occurring on the *succeeding* day, i.e. (*2250* being implied) *to-morrow*:— day following, morrow, next day (after).

1888. ἐπαυτοφώρῳ **ĕpautŏphōrŏi**, *ep-ow-tof-o´-ro*; from *1909* and *846* and (the dat. sing. of) a der. of φώρ **phōr** (a *thief*); *in theft itself*, i.e. (by anal.) *in actual crime*:— in the very act.

1889. Ἐπαφρᾶς **Ĕpaphras**, *ep-af-ras´*; contr. from *1891*; *Epaphras*, a Chr.:— Epaphras.

1890. ἐπαφρίζω **ĕpaphrizō**, *ep-af-rid´-zo*; from *1909* and *875*; to *foam upon*, i.e. (fig.) to *exhibit* (a vile passion):— foam out.

1891. Ἐπαφρόδιτος **Ĕpaphrŏditŏs**, *ep-af-rod´-ee-tos*; from *1909* (in the sense of *devoted* to) and Ἀφροδίτη **Aphrŏditē** (*Venus*); *Epaphroditus*, a Chr.:— Epaphroditus. Comp. *1889*.

1892. ἐπεγείρω **ĕpĕgĕirō**, *ep-eg-i´-ro*; from *1909* and *1453*; to *rouse upon*, i.e. (fig.) to *excite* against:— raise, stir up.

1893. ἐπεί **ĕpĕi**, *ep-i´*; from *1909* and *1487*; *thereupon*, i.e. *since* (of time or cause):— because, else, for that (then, -asmuch as), otherwise, seeing that, since, when.

1894. ἐπειδή **ĕpĕidē**, *ep-i-day´*; from *1893* and *1211*; *since now*, i.e. (of time) *when*, or (of cause) *whereas*:— after that, because, for (that, -asmuch as), seeing, since.

1895. ἐπειδήπερ **ĕpĕidēpĕr**, *ep-i-day´-per*; from *1894* and *4007*; *since indeed* (of cause):— forasmuch.

1896. ἐπεῖδον **ĕpĕidŏn**, *ep-i´-don*; and other moods and persons of the same tense; from *1909* and *1492*; to *regard*

(favorably or otherwise):— behold, look upon.

1897. ἐπείπερ **ĕpĕipĕr**, *ep-i´-per*; from *1893* and *4007*; *since indeed* (of cause):— seeing.

1898. ἐπεισαγωγή **ĕpĕisagōgē**, *ep-ice-ag-o-gay´*; from a compound of *1909* and *1521*; a *superintroduction*:— bringing in.

1899. ἔπειτα **ĕpĕita**, *ep´-i-tah*; from *1909* and *1534*; *thereafter*:— after that (-ward), then.

1900. ἐπέκεινα **ĕpĕkĕina**, *ep-ek´-i-nah*; from *1909* and (the acc. plur. neut. of) *1565*; *upon those* parts of, i.e. *on the further side of*:— beyond.

1901. ἐπεκτείνομαι **ĕpĕktĕinŏmai**, *ep-ek-ti´-nom-ahee*; mid. voice from *1909* and *1614*; to *stretch* (oneself) forward *upon*:— reach forth.

1902. ἐπενδύομαι **ĕpĕnduŏmai**, *ep-en-doo´-om-ahee*; mid. voice from *1909* and *1746*; to *invest upon* oneself:— be clothed upon.

1903. ἐπενδύτης **ĕpĕndutēs**, *ep-en-doo´-tace*; from *1902*; a *wrapper*, i.e. outer garment:— fisher's coat.

1904. ἐπέρχομαι **ĕpĕrchōmai**, *ep-er´-khom-ahee*; from *1909* and *2064*; to *supervene*, i.e. *arrive, occur, impend, attack*, (fig.) *influence*:— come (in, upon).

1905. ἐπερωτάω **ĕpĕrōtaō**, *ep-er-o-tah´-o*; from *1909* and *2065*; to *ask for*, i.e. *inquire, seek*:— ask (after, questions), demand, desire, question.

1906. ἐπερώτημα **ĕpĕrōtēma**, *ep-er-o´-tay-mah*; from *1905*; an *inquiry*:— answer.

1907. ἐπέχω **ĕpĕchō**, *ep-ekh´-o*; from *1909* and *2192*; to *hold upon*, i.e. (by impl.) to *retain*; (by extens.) to *detain*; (with impl. of *3563*) to *pay attention to*:— give (take) heed unto, hold forth, mark, stay.

1908. ἐπηρεάζω **ĕpērĕazō**, *ep-ay-reh-ad´-zo*; from a comp. of *1909* and (prob.) ἀρειά **arĕia** (*threats*); to *insult, slander*:— use despitefully, falsely accuse.

1909. ἐπί **ĕpi**, *ep-ee´*; a primary prep.; prop. mean. *superimposition* (of time, place, order, etc.), as a relation of *distribution* [with the gen.], i.e. *over, upon*, etc.; of *rest* (with the dat.) *at*, on, etc.; of *direction* (with the acc.) *toward, upon*, etc.:— about (the times), above, after, against, among, as long as (touching), at, beside, × have charge of, (be-, [where-]fore, in (a place, as much as, the time of, -to), (because) of, (up-) on (behalf of), over, (by, for) the space of, through (-out), (un-) to (-ward), with. In compounds it retains essentially the same import, *at, upon*, etc. (lit. or fig.).

1910. ἐπιβαίνω **ĕpibainō**, *ep-ee-bah´-ee-no*; from *1909* and the base of *939*; to *walk upon*, i.e. *mount, ascend, embark, arrive*:— come (into), enter into, go abroad, sit upon, take ship.

1911. ἐπιβάλλω **ĕpiballō**, *ep-ee-bal´-lo*; from *1909* and *906*; to *throw upon* (lit. or fig., tran. or refl.; usually with more or less force); spec. (with *1438* implied) to *reflect*; impers. to *belong to*:— beat into, cast (up-) on, fall, lay (on), put (unto), stretch forth, think on.

1912. ἐπιβαρέω **ĕpibarĕō**, *ep-ee-bar-eh´-o;* from *1909* and *916;* to *be heavy upon,* i.e. (pecuniarily) to *be expensive to;* fig. to *be severe toward:*— be chargeable to, overcharge.

1913. ἐπιβιβάζω **ĕpibibazō**, *ep-ee-bee-bad´-zo;* from *1909* and a redupl. deriv. of the base of *939* [comp. 307]; to *cause to mount* (an animal):— set on.

1914. ἐπιβλέπω **ĕpiblĕpō**, *ep-ee-blep´-o;* from *1909* and *991;* to *gaze at* (with favor, pity or partiality):— look upon, regard, have respect to.

1915. ἐπίβλημα **ĕpiblēma**, *ep-ib´-lay-mah;* from *1911;* a *patch:*— piece.

1916. ἐπιβοάω **ĕpibŏaō**, *ep-ee-bo-ah´-o;* from *1909* and *994;* to *exclaim against:*— cry.

1917. ἐπιβουλή **ĕpibŏulē**, *ep-ee-boo-lay´;* from a presumed compound of *1909* and *1014;* a *plan against* someone, i.e. a *plot:*— laying (lying) in wait.

1918. ἐπιγαμβρεύω **ĕpigambrĕuō**, *ep-ee-gam-bryoo´-o;* from *1909* and a der. of *1062;* to *form affinity with,* i.e. (spec.) in a levirate way:— marry.

1919. ἐπίγειος **ĕpigĕiŏs**, *ep-ig´-i-os;* from *1909* and *1093;* *worldly* (phys. or mor.):— earthly, in earth, terrestrial.

1920. ἐπιγίνομαι **ĕpiginŏmai**, *ep-ig-in´-om-ahee;* from *1909* and *1096;* to *arrive upon,* i.e. *spring up* (as a wind):— blow.

1921. ἐπιγινώσκω **ĕpiginōskō**, *ep-ig-in-oce´-ko;* from *1909* and *1097;* to *know upon* some mark, i.e. *recognize;* by impl. to *become fully acquainted with,* to *acknowledge:*— (ac-, have, take) know (-ledge, well), perceive.

1922. ἐπίγνωσις **ĕpignōsis**, *ep-ig´-no-sis;* from *1921;* *recognition,* i.e. (by impl.) full *discernment, acknowledgement:*— (ac-) knowledge (-ing, -ment).

1923. ἐπιγραφή **ĕpigraphē**, *ep-ig-raf-ay´;* from *1924;* an *inscription:*— superscription.

1924. ἐπιγράφω **ĕpigraphō**, *ep-ee-graf-o;* from *1909* and *1125;* to *inscribe* (phys. or ment.):— inscription, write in (over, thereon).

1925. ἐπιδείκνυμι **ĕpidĕiknumi**, *ep-ee-dike´-noo-mee;* from *1909* and *1166;* to *exhibit* (phys. or ment.):— shew.

1926. ἐπιδέχομαι **ĕpidĕchŏmai**, *ep-ee-dekh´-om-ahee;* from *1909* and *1209;* to *admit* (as a guest or [fig.] teacher):— receive.

1927. ἐπιδημέω **ĕpidēmĕō**, *ep-ee-day-meh´-o;* from a compound of *1909* and *1218;* to *make oneself at home,* i.e. (by extens.) to *reside* (in a foreign country):— [be] dwelling (which were) there, stranger.

1928. ἐπιδιατάσσομαι **ĕpidiatassŏmai**, *ep-ee-dee-ah-tas´-som-ahee;* mid. voice from *1909* and *1299;* to *appoint besides,* i.e. *supplement* (as a codicil):— add to.

1929. ἐπιδίδωμι **ĕpididōmi**, *ep-ee-did´-o-mee;* from *1909* and *1325;* to *give over* (by hand or surrender):— deliver unto, give, let (+ [her drive]), offer.

1930. ἐπιδιορθόω **ĕpidiŏrthŏō**, *ep-ee-dee-or-thŏ´-o;* from *1909* and a der. of *3717;* to *straighten further,* i.e. (fig.) *arrange additionally:*— set in order.

1931. ἐπιδύω **ĕpiduō**, *ep-ee-doo´-o;* from *1909* and *1416;* to *set fully* (as the sun):— go down.

1932. ἐπιείκεια **ĕpiĕikĕia**, *ep-ee-i´-ki-ah;* from *1933;* *suitableness,* i.e. (by impl.) *equity, mildness:*— clemency, gentleness.

1933. ἐπιεικής **ĕpiĕikēs**, *ep-ee-i-kace´;* from *1909* and *1503;* *appropriate,* i.e. (by impl.) *mild:*— gentle, moderation, patient.

1934. ἐπιζητέω **ĕpizētĕō**, *ep-eed-zay-teh´-o;* from *1909* and *2212;* to *search* (*inquire*) *for;* intens. to *demand,* to *crave:*— desire, enquire, seek (after, for).

1935. ἐπιθανάτιος **ĕpithanatiŏs**, *ep-ee-than-at´-ee-os;* from *1909* and *2288;* *doomed to death:*— appointed to death.

1936. ἐπίθεσις **ĕpithĕsis**, *ep-ith´-es-is;* from *2007;* an *imposition* (of hands officially):— laying (putting) on.

1937. ἐπιθυμέω **ĕpithumĕō**, *ep-ee-thoo-meh´-o;* from *1909* and *2372;* to *set the heart upon,* i.e. *long for* (rightfully or otherwise):— covet, desire, would fain, lust (after).

1938. ἐπιθυμητής **ĕpithumētēs**, *ep-ee-thoo-may-tace´;* from *1937;* a *craver:*— + lust after.

1939. ἐπιθυμία **ĕpithumia**, *ep-ee-thoo-mee´-ah;* from *1937;* a *longing* (espec. for what is forbidden):— concupiscence, desire, lust (after).

1940. ἐπικαθίζω **ĕpikathizō**, *ep-ee-kath-id´-zo;* from *1909* and *2523;* to *seat upon:*— set on.

1941. ἐπικαλέομαι **ĕpikalĕŏmai**, *ep-ee-kal-eh´-om-ahee;* mid. voice from *1909* and *2564;* to *entitle;* by impl. to *invoke* (for aid, worship, testimony, decision, etc.):— appeal (unto), call (on, upon), surname.

1942. ἐπικάλυμα **ĕpikaluma**, *ep-ee-kal´-oo-mah;* from *1943;* a *covering,* i.e. (fig.) *pretext:*— cloke.

1943. ἐπικαλύπτω **ĕpikaluptō**, *ep-ee-kal-oop´-to;* from *1909* and *2572;* to *conceal,* i.e. (fig.) *forgive:*— cover.

1944. ἐπικατάρατος **ĕpikataratŏs**, *ep-ee-kat-ar´-at-os;* from *1909* and a der. of *2672;* *imprecated,* i.e. *execrable:*— accursed.

1945. ἐπίκειμαι **ĕpikĕimai**, *ep-ik´-i-ma-hee;* from *1909* and *2749;* to *rest upon* (lit. or fig.):— impose, be instant, (be) laid (there-, up-) on, (when) lay (on), lie (on), press upon.

1946. Ἐπικούρειος **Ĕpikŏurĕiŏs**, *ep-ee-koo´-ri-os* or Ἐπικούριος **Ĕpikŏuriŏs**, *ep-ee-koo´-ree-os;* from Ἐπίκουρος **Ĕpikŏurŏs** [comp. *1947*] (a noted philosopher); an *Epicurean* or follower of Epicurus:— Epicurean.

1947. ἐπικουρία **ĕpikŏuria**, *ep-ee-koo-ree´-ah;* from a compound of *1909* and a (prol.) form of the base of *2877* (in the sense of *servant*); *assistance:*— help.

1948. ἐπικρίνω **ĕpikrinō**, *ep-ee-kree´-no;* from *1909* and *2919;* to *adjudge:*— give sentence.

1949. ἐπιλαμβάνομαι **ĕpilambanŏmai**, *ep-ee-lam-ban´-om-ahee;* mid. voice from *1909* and *2983;* to *seize* (for help, injury, attainment, or any other purpose; lit. or fig.):— catch, lay hold (up-) on, take (by, hold of, on).

1950. ἐπιλανθάνομαι **ĕpilanthanŏmai**, *ep-ee-lan-than´-om-ahee;* mid. voice from *1909* and *2990;* to *lose out* of mind; by impl. to *neglect:*— (be) forget (-ful of).

1951. ἐπιλέγομαι **ĕpilĕgŏmai**, *ep-ee-leg´-om-ahee;* mid. voice from *1909* and *3004;* to *surname, select:*— call, choose.

1952. ἐπιλείπω **ĕpilĕipō**, *ep-ee-li´-po;* from *1909* and *3007;* to *leave upon,* i.e. (fig.) to *be insufficient for:*— fail.

1953. ἐπιλησμονή **ĕpilēsmŏnē**, *ep-ee-lace-mon-ay´;* from a der. of *1950;* *negligence:*— × forgetful.

1954. ἐπίλοιπος **ĕpilŏipŏs**, *ep-il´-oy-pos;* from *1909* and *3062;* *left over,* i.e. *remaining:*— rest.

1955. ἐπίλυσις **ĕpilusis**, *ep-il´-oo-sis;* from *1956;* *explanation,* i.e. *application:*— interpretation.

1956. ἐπιλύω **ĕpiluō**, *ep-ee-loo´-o;* from *1909* and *3089;* to *solve further,* i.e. (fig.) to *explain, decide:*— determine, expound.

1957. ἐπιμαρτυρέω **ĕpimarturĕō**, *ep-ee-mar-too-reh´-o;* from *1909* and *3140;* to *attest further,* i.e. *corroborate:*— testify.

1958. ἐπιμέλεια **ĕpimĕlĕia**, *ep-ee-mel´-i-ah;* from *1959;* *carefulness,* i.e. *kind attention* (*hospitality*):— + refresh self.

1959. ἐπιμελέομαι **ĕpimĕlĕŏmai**, *ep-ee-mel-eh´-om-ahee;* mid. voice from *1909* and the same as *3199;* to *care for* (phys. or otherwise):— take care of.

1960. ἐπιμελῶς **ĕpimĕlōs**, *ep-ee-mel-oce´;* adv. from a der. of *1959;* *carefully:*— diligently.

1961. ἐπιμένω **ĕpimĕnō**, *ep-ee-men´-o;* from *1909* and *3306;* to *stay over,* i.e. *remain* (fig. *persevere*):— abide (in), continue (in), tarry.

1962. ἐπινεύω **ĕpinĕuō**, *ep-een-yoo´-o;* from *1909* and *3506;* to *nod at,* i.e. (by impl.) to *assent:*— consent.

1963. ἐπίνοια **ĕpinŏia**, *ep-in´-oy-ah;* from *1909* and *3563;* *attention* of the mind, i.e. (by impl.) *purpose:*— thought.

1964. ἐπιορκέω **ĕpiŏrkĕō**, *ep-ee-or-keh´-o;* from *1965;* to *commit perjury:*— forswear self.

1965. ἐπίορκος **ĕpiŏrkŏs**, *ep-ee´-or-kos;* from *1909* and *3727;* *on oath,* i.e. (falsely) a *forswearer:*— perjured person.

1966. ἐπιοῦσα **ĕpiŏusa**, *ep-ee-oo´-sah;* fem. sing. part. of a compound of *1909* and εἶμι **ĕimi** (to *go*); *supervening,* i.e. (*2250* or *3571* being expressed or implied) the *ensuing* day or night:— following, next.

1967. ἐπιούσιος **ĕpioŭsiŏs**, *ep-ee-oo´-see-os;* perh. from the same as *1966; tomorrow's;* but more prob. from *1909* and a der. of the pres. part. fem. of

1510; for subsistence, i.e. needful:— daily.

1968. ἐπιπίπτω **ĕpipiptō**, ep-ee-pip´-to; from 1909 and 4098; to embrace (with affection) or seize (with more or less violence; lit. or fig.):— fall into (on, upon) lie on, press upon.

1969. ἐπιπλήσσω **ĕpiplēssō**, ep-ee-place´-so; from 1909 and 4141; to chastise, i.e. (with words) to upbraid:— rebuke.

1970. ἐπιπνίγω **ĕpipnigō**, ep-ee-pnee´-go; from 1909 and 4155; to throttle upon, i.e. (fig.) overgrow:— choke.

1971. ἐπιποθέω **ĕpipŏthĕō**, ep-ee-poth-eh´-o; from 1909 and ποθέω **pŏthĕō** (to yearn); to dote upon, i.e. intensely crave possession (lawfully or wrongfully):— (earnestly) desire (greatly), (greatly) long (after), lust.

1972. ἐπιπόθησις **ĕpipŏthēsis**, ep-ee-poth´-ay-sis; from 1971; a longing for:— earnest (vehement) desire.

1973. ἐπιπόθητος **ĕpipŏthētŏs**, ep-ee-poth´-ay-tos; from 1909 and a der. of the latter part of 1971; yearned upon, i.e. greatly loved:— longed for.

1974. ἐπιποθία **ĕpipŏthia**, ep-ee-poth-ee´-ah; from 1971; intense longing:— great desire.

1975. ἐπιπορεύομαι **ĕpipŏrĕuŏmai**, ep-ee-por-yoo´-om-ahee; from 1909 and 4198; to journey further, i.e. travel on (reach):— come.

1976. ἐπιρράπτω **ĕpirrhaptō**, ep-ir-hrap´-to; from 1909 and the base of 4476; to stitch upon, i.e. fasten with the needle:— sew on.

1977. ἐπιρρίπτω **ĕpirrhiptō**, ep-ir-hrip´-to; from 1909 and 4496; to throw upon (lit. or fig.):— cast upon.

1978. ἐπίσημος **ĕpisēmŏs**, ep-is´-ay-mos; from 1909 and some form of the base of 4591; remarkable, i.e. (fig.) eminent:— notable, of note.

1979. ἐπισιτισμός **ĕpisitismŏs**, ep-ee-sit-is-mos´; from a compound of 1909 and a der. of 4621; a provisioning, i.e. (concr.) food:— victuals.

1980. ἐπισκέπτομαι **ĕpiskĕptŏmai**, ep-ee-skep´-tom-ahee; mid. voice from 1909 and the base of 4649; to inspect, i.e. (by impl.) to select; by extens. to go to see, relieve:— look out, visit.

1981. ἐπισκηνόω **ĕpiskēnŏō**, ep-ee-skay-nŏ´-o; from 1909 and 4637; to tent upon, i.e. (fig.) abide with:— rest upon.

1982. ἐπισκιάζω **ĕpiskiazō**, ep-ee-skee-ad´-zo; from 1909 and a der. of 4639; to cast a shade upon, i.e. (by anal.) to envelop in a haze of brilliancy; fig. to invest with preternatural influence:— overshadow.

1983. ἐπισκοπέω **ĕpiskŏpĕō**, ep-ee-skop-eh´-o; from 1909 and 4648; to oversee; by impl. to beware:— look diligently, take the oversight.

1984. ἐπισκοπή **ĕpiskŏpē**, ep-is-kop-ay´; from 1980; inspection (for relief); by impl. superintendence; spec., the Chr. "episcopate":— the office of a "bishop," bishoprick, visitation.

1985. ἐπίσκοπος **ĕpiskŏpŏs**, ep-is´-kop-

os; from 1909 and 4649 (in the sense of 1983); a superintendent, i.e. Chr. officer in general charge of a (or the) church (lit. or fig.):— bishop, overseer.

1986. ἐπισπάομαι **ĕpispaŏmai**, ep-ee-spah´-om-ahee; from 1909 and 4685; to draw over, i.e. (with 203 impl.) efface the mark of circumcision (by recovering with the foreskin):— become uncircumcised.

1987. ἐπίσταμαι **ĕpistamai**, ep-is´-tam-ahee; appar. a mid. voice of 2186 (with 3563 implied); to put the mind upon, i.e. comprehend, or be acquainted with:— know, understand.

1988. ἐπιστάτης **ĕpistatēs**, ep-is-tat´-ace; from 1909 and a presumed der. of 2476; an appointee over, i.e. commander (teacher):— master.

1989. ἐπιστέλλω **ĕpistĕllō**, ep-ee-stel´-lo; from 1909 and 4724; to enjoin (by writing), i.e. (gen.) to communicate by letter (for any purpose):— write (a letter, unto).

1990. ἐπιστήμων **ĕpistēmōn**, ep-ee-stay´-mone; from 1987; intelligent:— endued with knowledge.

1991. ἐπιστηρίζω **ĕpistērizō**, ep-ee-stay-rid´-zo; from 1909 and 4741; to support further, i.e. reestablish:— confirm, strengthen.

1992. ἐπιστολή **ĕpistŏlē**, ep-is-tol-ay´; from 1989; a written message:— "epistle," letter.

1993. ἐπιστομίζω **ĕpistŏmizō**, ep-ee-stom-id´-zo; from 1909 and 4750; to put something over the mouth, i.e. (fig.) to silence:— stop mouths.

1994. ἐπιστρέφω **ĕpistrĕphō**, ep-ee-stref´-o; from 1909 and 4762; to revert (lit., fig. or mor.):— come (go) again, convert, (re-) turn (about, again).

1995. ἐπιστροφή **ĕpistrŏphē**, ep-is-trof-ay´; from 1994; reversion, i.e. mor. revolution:— conversion.

1996. ἐπισυνάγω **ĕpisunagō**, ep-ee-soon-ag´-o; from 1909 and 4863; to collect upon the same place:— gather (together).

1997. ἐπισυναγωγή **ĕpisunagōgē**, ep-ee-soon-ag-o-gay´; from 1996; a complete collection; spec. a Chr. meeting (for worship):— assembling (gathering) together.

1998. ἐπισυντρέχω **ĕpisuntrĕchō**, ep-ee-soon-trekh´-o; from 1909 and 4936; to hasten together upon one place (or a particular occasion):— come running together.

1999. ἐπισύστασις **ĕpisustasis**, ep-ee-soo´-stas-is; from the mid. voice of a compound of 1909 and 4921; a conspiracy, i.e. concourse (riotous or friendly):— that which cometh upon, + raising up.

2000. ἐπισφαλής **ĕpisphalēs**, ep-ee-sfal-ace´; from a compound of 1909 and σφάλλω **sphallō** (to trip); fig. insecure:— dangerous.

2001. ἐπισχύω **ĕpischuō**, ep-is-khoo´-o; from 1909 and 2480; to avail further, i.e. (fig.) insist stoutly:— be the more fierce.

2002. ἐπισωρεύω **ĕpisōrĕuō**, ep-ee-so-ryoo´-o; from 1909 and 4987; to accumulate further, i.e. (fig.) seek additionally:— heap.

2003. ἐπιταγή **ĕpitagē**, ep-ee-tag-ay´; from 2004; an injunction or decree; by impl. authoritativeness:— authority, commandment.

2004. ἐπιτάσσω **ĕpitassō**, ep-ee-tas´-so; from 1909 and 5021; to arrange upon, i.e. order:— charge, command, injoin.

2005. ἐπιτελέω **ĕpitĕlĕō**, ep-ee-tel-eh´-o; from 1909 and 5055; to fulfill further (or completely), i.e. execute; by impl. to terminate, undergo:— accomplish, do, finish, (make) (perfect), perform (× -ance).

2006. ἐπιτήδειος **ĕpitēdĕiŏs**, ep-ee-tay´-di-os; from ἐπιτηδές **ĕpitēdĕs** (enough); serviceable, i.e. (by impl.) requisite:— things which are needful.

2007. ἐπιτίθημι **ĕpitithēmi**, ep-ee-tith´-ay-mee; from 1909 and 5087; to impose (in a friendly or hostile sense):— add unto, lade, lay upon, put (up) on, set on (up), + surname, × wound.

2008. ἐπιτιμάω **ĕpitimaō**, ep-ee-tee-mah´-o; from 1909 and 5091; to tax upon, i.e. censure or admonish; by impl. forbid:— (straitly) charge, rebuke.

2009. ἐπιτιμία **ĕpitimia**, ep-ee-tee-mee´-ah; from a compound of 1909 and 5092; prop. esteem, i.e. citizenship; used (in the sense of 2008) of a penalty:— punishment.

2010. ἐπιτρέπω **ĕpitrĕpō**, ep-ee-trep´-o; from 1909 and the base of 5157; to turn over (transfer), i.e. allow:— give leave (liberty, license), let, permit, suffer.

2011. ἐπιτροπή **ĕpitrŏpē**, ep-ee-trop-ay´; from 2010; permission, i.e. (by impl.) full power:— commission.

2012. ἐπίτροπος **ĕpitrŏpŏs**, ep-it´-rop-os; from 1909 and 5158 (in the sense of 2011); a commissioner, i.e. domestic manager, guardian:— steward, tutor.

2013. ἐπιτυγχάνω **ĕpitugchanō**, ep-ee-toong-khan´-o; from 1909 and 5177; to chance upon, i.e. (by impl.) to attain:— obtain.

2014. ἐπιφαίνω **ĕpiphainō**, ep-ee-fah´-ee-no; from 1909 and 5316; to shine upon, i.e. become (lit.) visible or (fig.) known:— appear, give light.

2015. ἐπιφάνεια **ĕpiphanĕia**, ep-if-an´-i-ah; from 2016; a manifestation, i.e. (spec.) the advent of Christ (past or future):— appearing, brightness.

2016. ἐπιφανής **ĕpiphanēs**, ep-if-an-ace´; from 2014; conspicuous, i.e. (fig.) memorable:— notable.

2017. ἐπιφαύω **ĕpiphauō**, ep-ee-fŏw´-o; a form of 2014; to illuminate (fig.):— give light.

2018. ἐπιφέρω **ĕpiphĕrō**, ep-ee-fer´-o; from 1909 and 5342; to bear upon (or further), i.e. adduce (pers. or judicially [accuse, inflict]), superinduce:— add, bring (against), take.

2019. ἐπιφωνέω **ĕpiphōnĕō**, ep-ee-fo-neh´-o; from 1909 and 5455; to call at something, i.e. *exclaim:*— cry (against), give a shout.

2020. ἐπιφώσκω **ĕpiphōskō**, *ep-ee-foce´-ko;* a form of *2017;* to begin to grow *light:*— begin to dawn, × draw on.

2021. ἐπιχειρέω **ĕpichĕirĕō**, *ep-ee-khi-reh´-o;* from *1909* and *5495;* to put the *hand upon,* i.e. *undertake:*— go about, take in hand (upon).

2022. ἐπιχέω **ĕpichĕō**, *ep-ee-kheh´-o;* from *1909* and χέω **chĕō** (to pour);—to *pour upon:*— pour in.

2023. ἐπιχορηγέω **ĕpichŏrēgĕō**, *ep-ee-khor-ayg-eh´-o;* from *1909* and *5524;* to *furnish besides,* i.e. fully *supply,* (fig.) *aid* or *contribute:*— add, minister (nourishment, unto).

2024. ἐπιχορηγία **ĕpichŏrēgia**, *ep-ee-khor-ayg-ee´-ah;* from *2023; contribution:*— supply.

2025. ἐπιχρίω **ĕpichriō**, *ep-ee-khree´-o;* from *1909* and *5548;* to *smear over:*— anoint.

2026. ἐποικοδομέω **ĕpŏikŏdŏmĕō**, *ep-oy-kod-om-eh´-o;* from *1909* and *3618;* to *build upon,* i.e. (fig.) to *rear up:*— build thereon (thereupon, on, upon).

2027. ἐποκέλλω **ĕpŏkĕllō**, *ep-ok-el´-lo;* from *1909* and ὀκέλλω **ŏkĕllō** (to *urge*); to *drive upon* the shore, i.e. to *beach* a vessel:— run aground.

2028. ἐπονομάζω **ĕpŏnŏmazō**, *ep-on-om-ad´-zo;* from *1909* and *3687;* to *name further,* i.e. *denominate:*— call.

2029. ἐποπτεύω **ĕpŏptĕuō**, *ep-opt-yoo´-o;* from *1909* and a der. of *3700;* to *inspect,* i.e. *watch:*— behold.

2030. ἐπόπτης **ĕpŏptēs**, *ep-op´-tace;* from *1909* and a presumed der. of *3700;* a *looker-on:*— eye-witness.

2031. ἔπος **ĕpŏs**, *ep´-os;* from *2036;* a *word:*— × say.

2032. ἐπουράνιος **ĕpŏuraniŏs**, *ep-oo-ran´-ee-os;* from *1909* and *3772; above* the *sky:*— celestial, (in) heaven (-ly), high.

2033. ἑπτά **hĕpta**, *hep-tah´;* a primary number; *seven:*— seven.

2034. ἑπτάκις **hĕptakis**, *hep-tak-is´;* adv. from *2033; seven times:*— seven times.

2035. ἑπτακισχίλιοι **hĕptakischiliŏi**, *hep-tak-is-khil´-ee-oy;* from *2034* and *5507; seven times a thousand:*— seven thousand.

2036. ἔπω **ĕpō**, *ep´-o;* a primary verb (used only in the def. past tense, the others being borrowed from *2046, 4483,* and *5346*); to *speak* or *say* (by word or writing):— answer, bid, bring word, call, command, grant, say (on), speak, tell. Comp. *3004.*

2037. Ἔραστος **Ĕrastŏs**, *er´-as-tos;* from ἐράω **ĕraō** (to *love*); *beloved; Erastus,* a Chr.:— Erastus.

ἐραυνάω **ĕraunaō**. See *2045.*

2038. ἐργάζομαι **ĕrgazŏmai**, *er-gad´-zom-ahee;* mid. voice from *2041;* to *toil* (as a task, occupation, etc.), (by impl.) *effect, be engaged in* or with, etc.:— commit, do, labor for, minister about, trade (by), work.

2039. ἐργασία **ĕrgasia**, *er-gas-ee´-ah;* from *2040; occupation;* by impl. *profit, pains:*— craft, diligence, gain, work.

2040. ἐργάτης **ĕrgatēs**, *er-gat´-ace;* from *2041;* a *toiler;* fig. a *teacher:*— labourer, worker (-men).

2041. ἔργον **ĕrgŏn**, *er´-gon;* from a primary (but obs.) ἔργω **ĕrgō** (to *work*); *toil* (as an effort or occupation); by impl. an *act:*— deed, doing, labour, work.

2042. ἐρεθίζω **ĕrĕthizō**, *er-eth-id´-zo;* from a presumed prol. form of *2054;* to *stimulate* (espec. to anger):— provoke.

2043. ἐρείδω **ĕrĕidō**, *er-i´-do;* of obscure aff.; to *prop,* i.e. (refl.) *get fast:*— stick fast.

2044. ἐρεύγομαι **ĕrĕugŏmai**, *er-yoog´-om-ahee;* of uncert. aff.; to *belch,* i.e. (fig.) to *speak out:*— utter.

2045. ἐρευνάω **ĕrĕunaō**, *er-yoo-nah´-o* or ἐραυνάω **ĕraunaō**, *er-ouw-nah´-o;* appar. from *2046* (through the idea of *inquiry*); to *seek,* i.e. (fig.) to *investigate:*— search.

2046. ἐρέω **ĕrĕō**, *er-eh´-o;* prob. a fuller form of *4483,* an alternate for *2036* in cert. tenses; to *utter,* i.e. *speak* or *say:*— call, say, speak (of), tell.

2047. ἐρημία **ĕrēmia**, *er-ay-mee´-ah;* from *2048; solitude* (concr.):— desert, wilderness.

2048. ἔρημος **ĕrēmŏs**, *er´-ay-mos;* of uncert. aff.; *lonesome,* i.e. (by impl.) *waste* (usually as a noun, *5561* being implied):— desert, desolate, solitary, wilderness.

2049. ἐρημόω **ĕrēmŏō**, *er-ay-mŏ´-o;* from *2048;* to *lay waste* (lit. or fig.):— (bring to, make) desolate (-ion), come to nought.

2050. ἐρήμωσις **ĕrēmōsis**, *er-ay´-mo-sis;* from *2049; despoliation:*— desolation.

2051. ἐρίζω **ĕrizō**, *er-id´-zo;* from *2054;* to *wrangle:*— strive.

2052. ἐριθεία **ĕrithĕia**, *er-ith-i´-ah;* perh. as the same as *2042;* prop. *intrigue,* i.e. (by impl.) *faction:*— contention (-ious), strife.

2053. ἔριον **ĕriŏn**, *er´-ee-on;* of obscure aff.; *wool:*— wool.

2054. ἔρις **ĕris**, *er´-is;* of uncert. aff.; a *quarrel,* i.e. (by impl.) *wrangling:*— contention, debate, strife, variance.

2055. ἐρίφιον **ĕriphiŏn**, *er-if´-ee-on;* from *2056;* a *kidling,* i.e. (gen.) *goat* (symbol. *wicked* person):— goat.

2056. ἔριφος **ĕriphŏs**, *er´-if-os;* perh. from the same as *2053* (through the idea of *hairiness*); a *kid* or (gen.) *goat:*— goat, kid.

2057. Ἑρμᾶς **Hĕrmas**, *her-mas´;* prob. from *2060; Hermas,* a Chr.:— Hermas.

2058. ἑρμηνεία **hĕrmēnĕia**, *her-may-ni´-ah;* from the same as *2059; translation:*— interpretation.

2059. ἑρμηνεύω **hĕrmēnĕuō**, *her-mayn-yoo´-o;* from a presumed der. of *2060* (as the god of language); to *translate:*— interpret.

2060. Ἑρμῆς **Hĕrmēs**, *her-mace´;* perh. from *2046; Hermes,* the name of the messenger of the Gr. deities; also of a Chr.:— Hermes, Mercury.

2061. Ἑρμογένης **Hĕrmŏgĕnēs**, *her-mog-en´-ace;* from *2060* and *1096; born* of *Hermes; Hermogenes,* an apostate Chr.:— Hermogenes.

2062. ἑρπετόν **hĕrpĕtŏn**, *her-pet-on´;* neut. of a der. of ἕρπω **hĕrpō** (to *creep*); a *reptile,* i.e. (by Heb. [comp. 7431]) a small *animal:*— creeping thing, serpent.

2063. ἐρυθρός **ĕruthrŏs**, *er-oo-thros´;* of uncert. aff.; *red,* i.e. (with *2281*) the *Red* Sea:— red.

2064. ἔρχομαι **ĕrchŏmai**, *er´-khom-ahee;* mid. voice of a primary verb (used only in the present and imperfect tenses, the others being supplied by a kindred [mid. voice]

ἐλεύθομαι **ĕlĕuthŏmai**, *el-yoo´-thom-ahee;* or [act.]

ἔλθω **ĕlthō**, *el´-tho;* which do not otherwise occur); to *come* or *go* (in a great variety of applications, lit. and fig.):— accompany, appear, bring, come, enter, fall out, go, grow, × light, × next, pass, resort, be set.

2065. ἐρωτάω **ĕrōtaō**, *er-o-tah´-o;* appar. from *2046* [comp. *2045*]; to *interrogate;* by impl. to *request:*— ask, beseech, desire, intreat, pray. Comp. *4441.*

2066. ἐσθής **ĕsthēs**, *es-thace´;* from ἕννυμι **hĕnnumi** (to *clothe*); *dress:*— apparel, clothing, raiment, robe.

2067. ἔσθησις **ĕsthēsis**, *es´-thay-sis;* from a der. of *2066; clothing* (concr.):— garment.

2068. ἐσθίω **ĕsthiō**, *es-thee´-o;* strengthened for a primary ἔδω **ĕdō** (to *eat*); used only in certain tenses, the rest being supplied by *5315;* to *eat* (usually lit.):— devour, eat, live.

2069. Ἐσλί **Ĕsli**, *es-lee´;* of Heb. or. [prob. for 454]; *Esli,* an Isr.:— Esli.

2070. ἐσμέν **ĕsmĕn**, *es-men´;* first pers. plur. ind. of *1510;* we *are:*— are, be, have our being, × have hope, + [the gospel] was [preached unto] us.

2071. ἔσομαι **ĕsŏmai**, *es´-om-ahee;* future of *1510; will be:*— shall (should) be (have), (shall) come (to pass), × may have, × fall, what would follow, × live long, × sojourn.

2072. ἔσοπτρον **ĕsŏptrŏn**, *es´-op-tron;* from *1519* and a presumed der. of *3700;* a *mirror* (for *looking into*):— glass. Comp. *2734.*

2073. ἑσπέρα **hĕspĕra**, *hes-per´-ah;* fem. of an adj. ἑσπερός **hĕspĕrŏs** (*evening*); the *eve* (*5610* being implied):— evening (-tide).

2074. Ἑσρώμ **Ĕsrōm**, *es-rome´;* of Heb. or. [2696]; *Esrom* (i.e. *Chetsron*), an Isr.:— Esrom.

2075. ἐστέ **ĕstĕ**, *es-teh´;* second pers. plur. pres. ind. of *1510;* ye *are:*— be, have been, belong.

2076. ἐστί **ĕsti**, *es-tee´;* third pers. sing. pres. ind. of *1510;* he (she or it) *is;* also (with neut. plur.) *they are:*— are, be (-long), call, × can [-not], come, consisteth, × dure for a while, + follow, ×

have, (that) is (to say), make, meaneth, × must needs, + profit, + remaineth, + wrestle.

2077. ἔστω **ĕstō**, *es´-to;* second pers. sing. pres. imper. of *1510; be* thou; also

ἔστωσαν **ĕstōsan**, *es´-to-san;* third pers. of the same; *let them be:*— be.

2078. ἔσχατος **ĕschatŏs**, *es´-khat-os;* a superl. prob. from *2192* (in the sense of *contiguity); farthest, final* (of place or time):— ends of, last, latter end, lowest, uttermost.

2079. ἐσχάτως **ĕschatōs**, *es-khat´-oce;* adv. from *2078; finally,* i.e. (with *2192) at the extremity* of life:— point of death.

2080. ἔσω **ĕsō**, *es´-o;* from *1519; inside* (as prep. or adj.):— (with-) in (-ner, -to, -ward).

2081. ἔσωθεν **ĕsōthĕn**, *es´-o-then;* from *2080; from inside;* also used as equiv. to *2080 (inside):*— inward (-ly), (from) within, without.

2082. ἐσώτερος **ĕsōtĕrŏs**, *es-o´-ter-os;* comparative of *2080; interior:*— inner, within.

2083. ἑταῖρος **hĕtairŏs**, *het-ah´-ee-ros;* from ἔτης **ĕtēs** (a *clansman); a comrade:*— fellow, friend.

2084. ἑτερόγλωσσος **hĕtĕrŏglōssŏs**, *heter-og´-loce-sos;* from *2087* and *1100; other-tongued,* i.e. a *foreigner:*— man of other tongue.

2085. ἑτεροδιδασκαλέω **hĕtĕrŏdidaskalĕō**, *het-er-od-id-as-kal-eh´-o;* from *2087* and *1320; to instruct differently:*— teach other doctrine (-wise).

2086. ἑτεροζυγέω **hĕtĕrŏzugĕō**, *het-er-od-zoog-eh´-o;* from a compound of *2087* and *2218; to yoke* up *differently,* i.e. (fig.) to *associate discordantly:*— unequally yoke together with.

2087. ἕτερος **hĕtĕrŏs**, *het´-er-os;* of uncert. aff.; (an-, the) *other* or *different:*— altered, else, next (day), one, (an-) other, some, strange.

2088. ἑτέρως **hĕtĕrōs**, *het-er´-oce;* adv. from *2087; differently:*— otherwise.

2089. ἔτι **ĕti**, *et´-ee;* perh. akin to *2094; "yet," still* (of time or degree):— after that, also, ever, (any) further, (t-) henceforth (more), hereafter, (any) longer, (any) more (-one), now, still, yet.

2090. ἑτοιμάζω **hĕtŏimazō**, *het-oymad´-zo;* from *2092; to prepare:*— prepare, provide, make ready. Comp. *2680*.

2091. ἑτοιμασία **hĕtŏimasia**, *het-oymas-ee´-ah;* from *2090; preparation:*— preparation.

2092. ἕτοιμος **hĕtŏimŏs**, *het´-oy-mos;* from an old noun ἔτεος **hĕtĕŏs** (*fitness); adjusted,* i.e. *ready:*— prepared, (made) ready (-iness, to our hand).

2093. ἑτοίμως **hĕtŏimōs**, *het-oy´-moce;* adv. from *2092; in readiness:*— ready.

2094. ἔτος **ĕtŏs**, *et´-os;* appar. a primary word; a *year:*— year.

2095. εὖ **ĕu**, *yoo;* neut. of a primary εὖς **ĕus** (*good);* (adv.) *well:*— good, well (done).

2096. Εὖα **Ĕua**, *yoo´-ah;* of Heb. or. [2332]; *Eua* (or *Eva,* i.e. *Chavvah),* the first woman:— Eve.

2097. εὐαγγελίζω **ĕuaggĕlizō**, *yoo-angghel-id´-zo;* from *2095* and *32;* to *announce good* news ("evangelize") espec. the gospel:— declare, bring (declare, show) glad (good) tidings, preach (the gospel).

2098. εὐαγγέλιον **ĕuaggĕliŏn**, *yoo-angghel´-ee-on;* from the same as *2097;* a *good message,* i.e. the *gospel:*— gospel.

2099. εὐαγγελιστής **ĕuaggĕlistēs**, *yooang-ghel-is-tace´;* from *2097;* a *preacher* of the gospel:— evangelist.

2100. εὐαρεστέω **ĕuarĕstĕō**, *yoo-ar-esteh´-o;* from *2101; to gratify entirely:*— please (well).

2101. εὐάρεστος **ĕuarĕstŏs**, *yoo-ar´-estos;* from *2095* and *701; fully agreeable:*— acceptable (-ted), wellpleasing.

2102. εὐαρέστως **ĕuarĕstōs**, *yoo-ar-es´-toce;* adv. from *2101; quite agreeably:*— acceptably, + please well.

2103. Εὔβουλος **Ĕubŏulŏs**, *yoo´-boo-los;* from *2095* and *1014; good-willer; Eubulus,* a Chr.:— Eubulus.

2104. εὐγένης **ĕugĕnēs**, *yoog-en´-ace;* from *2095* and *1096; well born,* i.e. (lit.) *high* in rank, or (fig.) *generous:*— more noble, nobleman.

2105. εὐδία **ĕudia**, *yoo-dee´-ah;* fem. from *2095* and the alternate of *2203* (as the god of the weather); a *clear sky,* i.e. *fine weather:*— fair weather.

2106. εὐδοκέω **ĕudŏkĕō**, *yoo-dok-eh´-o;* from *2095* and *1380; to think well* of, i.e. *approve* (an act); spec., to *approbate* (a person or thing):— think good, (be well) please (-d), be the good (have, take) pleasure, be willing.

2107. εὐδοκία **ĕudŏkia**, *yoo-dok-ee´-ah;* from a presumed compound of *2095* and the base of *1380; satisfaction,* i.e. (subj.) *delight,* or (obj.) *kindness, wish, purpose:*— desire, good pleasure (will), × seem good.

2108. εὐεργεσία **ĕuĕrgĕsia**, *yoo-erg-esee´-ah;* from *2110; beneficence* (gen. or spec.):— benefit, good deed done.

2109. εὐεργετέω **ĕuĕrgĕtĕō**, *yoo-erg-eteh´-o;* from *2110; to be philanthropic:*— do good.

2110. εὐεργέτης **ĕuĕrgĕtēs**, *yoo-erg-et´-ace;* from *2095* and the base of *2041;* a *worker* of good, i.e. (spec.) a *philanthropist:*— benefactor.

2111. εὔθετος **ĕuthĕtŏs**, *yoo´-thet-os;* from *2095* and a der. of *5087; well placed,* i.e. (fig.) *appropriate:*— fit, meet.

2112. εὐθέως **ĕuthĕōs**, *yoo-theh´-oce;* adv. from *2117; directly,* i.e. *at once* or *soon:*— anon, as soon as, forthwith, immediately, shortly, straightway.

2113. εὐθυδρομέω **ĕuthudrŏmĕō**, *yoothoo-drom-eh´-o;* from *2117* and *1408;* to *lay a straight course,* i.e. *sail direct:*— (come) with a straight course.

2114. εὐθυμέω **ĕuthumĕō**, *yoo-thoomeh´-o;* from *2115; to cheer up,* i.e. (intr.) *be cheerful;* neut. comparative

(adv.) *more cheerfully:*— be of good cheer (merry).

2115. εὔθυμος **ĕuthumŏs**, *yoo´-thoomos;* from *2095* and *2372;* in *fine spirits,* i.e. *cheerful:*— of good cheer, the more cheerfully.

2116. εὐθύνω **ĕuthunō**, *yoo-thoo´-no;* from *2117; to straighten* (level); tech. to *steer:*— governor, make straight.

2117. εὐθύς **ĕuthus**, *yoo-thoos´;* perh. from *2095* and *5087; straight,* i.e. (lit.) *level,* or (fig.) *true;* adv. (of time) *at once:*— anon, by and by, forthwith, immediately, straightway.

2118. εὐθύτης **ĕuthutēs**, *yoo-thoo´-tace;* from *2117; rectitude:*— righteousness.

2119. εὐκαιρέω **ĕukairĕō**, *yoo-kaheereh´-o;* from *2121; to have good time,* i.e. *opportunity* or *leisure:*— have leisure (convenient time), spend time.

2120. εὐκαιρία **ĕukairia**, *yoo-kaheeree´-ah;* from *2121;* a *favorable occasion:*— opportunity.

2121. εὔκαιρος **ĕukairŏs**, *yoo´-kaheeros;* from *2095* and *2540; well-timed,* i.e. *opportune:*— convenient, in time of need.

2122. εὐκαίρως **ĕukairōs**, *yoo-kah´-eeroce;* adv. from *2121; opportunely:*— conveniently, in season.

2123. εὐκοπώτερος **ĕukŏpōtĕrŏs**, *yookop-o´-ter-os;* comp. of a compound of *2095* and *2873; better for toil,* i.e. *more facile:*— easier.

2124. εὐλάβεια **ĕulabĕia**, *yoo-lab´-i-ah;* from *2126;* prop. *caution,* i.e. (religiously) *reverence* (piety); by impl. *dread* (concr.):— fear (-ed).

2125. εὐλαβέομαι **ĕulabĕŏmai**, *yoo-labeh´-om-ahee;* mid. voice from *2126;* to *be circumspect,* i.e. (by impl.) *to be apprehensive;* religiously *to reverence:*— (moved with) fear.

2126. εὐλαβής **ĕulabēs**, *yoo-lab-ace´;* from *2095* and *2983; taking well* (carefully), i.e. *circumspect* (religiously, *pious):*— devout.

2127. εὐλογέω **ĕulŏgĕō**, *yoo-log-eh´-o;* from a compound of *2095* and *3056;* to *speak well* of, i.e. (religiously) to *bless* (thank or invoke a benediction upon, prosper):— bless, praise.

2128. εὐλογητός **ĕulŏgētŏs**, *yoo-log-aytos´;* from *2127; adorable:*— blessed.

2129. εὐλογία **ĕulŏgia**, *yoo-log-ee´-ah;* from the same as *2127; fine speaking,* i.e. *elegance of language; commendation* ("eulogy"), i.e. (reverentially) *adoration;* religiously *benediction;* by impl. *consecration;* by extens. *benefit* or *largess:*— blessing (a matter of) bounty (× -tifully), fair speech.

2130. εὐμετάδοτος **ĕumĕtadŏtŏs**, *yoomet-ad´-ot-os;* from *2095* and a presumed der. of *3330; good at imparting,* i.e. *liberal:*— ready to distribute.

2131. Εὐνίκη **Ĕunikē**, *yoo-nee´-kay;* from *2095* and *3529; victorious; Eunice,* a Jewess:— Eunice.

2132. εὐνοέω **ĕunŏĕō**, *yoo-no-eh´-o;* from a compound of *2095* and *3563;* to *be well-minded,* i.e. *reconcile:*— agree.

2133. εὔνοια **ĕunŏia**, *yoo´-noy-ah;* from

the same as 2132; kindness; euphem. conjugal duty:— benevolence, good will.

2134. εὐνουχίζω ĕunŏuchizō, yoo-noo-khid´-zo; from 2135; to castrate (fig. live unmarried):— make ... eunuch.

2135. εὐνοῦχος ĕunŏuchŏs, yoo-noo´-khos; from εὐνή ĕunē (a bed) and 2192; a castrated person (such being employed in Oriental bed-chambers); by extens. an impotent or unmarried man; by impl. a chamberlain (state-officer):— eunuch.

2136. Εὐοδία Ĕuŏdia, yoo-od-ee´-ah; from the same as 2137; fine travelling; Euodia, a Chr. woman:— Euodias.

2137. εὐοδόω ĕuŏdŏō, yoo-od-ŏ´-o; from a compound of 2095 and 3598; to help on the road, i.e. (pass.) succeed in reaching; fig. to succeed in business affairs:— (have a) prosper (-ous journey).

2138. εὐπειθής ĕupĕithēs, yoo-pi-thace´; from 2095 and 3982; good for persuasion, i.e. (intr.) compliant:— easy to be intreated.

2139. εὐπερίστατος ĕupĕristatŏs, yoo-per-is´-tat-os; from 2095 and a der. of a presumed compound of 4012 and 2476; well standing around, i.e. (a competitor) thwarting (a racer) in every direction (fig. of sin in gen.):— which doth so easily beset.

2140. εὐποιΐα ĕupŏiïa, yoo-poy-ee´-ah; from a compound of 2095 and 4160; well-doing, i.e. beneficence:— to do good.

2141. εὐπορέω ĕupŏrĕō, yoo-por-eh´-o; from a compound of 2090 and the base of 4197; (intr.) to be good for passing through, i.e. (fig.) have pecuniary means:— ability.

2142. εὐπορία ĕupŏria, yoo-por-ee´-ah; from the same as 2141; pecuniary resources:— wealth.

2143. εὐπρέπεια ĕuprĕpĕia, yoo-prep´-i-ah; from a compound of 2095 and 4241; good suitableness, i.e. gracefulness:— grace.

2144. εὐπρόσδεκτος ĕuprŏsdĕktŏs, yoo-pros´-dek-tos; from 2095 and a der. of 4327; well-received, i.e. approved, favorable:— acceptable (-ted).

2145. εὐπρόσεδρος ĕuprŏsĕdrŏs, yoo-pros´-ed-ros; from 2095 and the same as 4332; sitting well toward, i.e. (fig.) assiduous (neut. diligent service):— × attend upon.

2146. εὐπροσωπέω ĕuprŏsōpĕō, yoo-pros-o-peh´-o; from a compound of 2095 and 4383; to be of good countenance, i.e. (fig.) to make a display:— make a fair show.

2147. εὑρίσκω hĕuriskō, hyoo-ris´-ko; a prol. form of a primary

εὕρω hĕurō, hyoo´-ro; which (together with another cognate form

εὑρέω hĕurĕō, hyoo-reh´-o) is used for it in all the tenses except the present and imperfect; to find (lit. or fig.):— find, get, obtain, perceive, see.

2148. Εὐροκλύδων Ĕurŏkludōn, yoo-rok-loo´-dohn; from Εὖρος Ĕurŏs (the east wind) and 2830; a storm from the East (or Southeast), i.e. (in modern phrase) a Levanter:— Euroklydon.

2149. εὐρύχωρος ĕuruchōrŏs, yoo-roo-kho-ros; from εὐρύς ĕurus (wide) and 5561; spacious:— broad.

2150. εὐσέβεια ĕusĕbĕia, yoo-seb´-i-ah; from 2152; piety; spec. the gospel scheme:— godliness, holiness.

2151. εὐσεβέω ĕusĕbĕō, yoo-seb-eh´-o; from 2152; to be pious, i.e. (toward God) to worship, or (toward parents) to respect (support):— show piety, worship.

2152. εὐσεβής ĕusĕbēs, yoo-seb-ace´; from 2095 and 4576; well-reverent, i.e. pious:— devout, godly.

2153. εὐσεβῶς ĕusĕbōs, yoo-seb-oce´; adv. from 2152; piously:— godly.

2154. εὔσημος ĕusēmŏs, yoo´-say-mos; from 2095 and the base of 4591; well indicated, i.e. (fig.) significant:— easy to be understood.

2155. εὔσπλαγχνος ĕusplagchnŏs, yoo´-splangkh-nos; from 2095 and 4698; well compassioned, i.e. sympathetic:— pitiful, tender-hearted.

2156. εὐσχημόνως ĕuschēmŏnōs, yoo-skhay-mon´-oce; adv. from 2158; decorously:— decently, honestly.

2157. εὐσχημοσύνη ĕuschēmŏsunē, yoo-skhay-mos-oo´-nay; from 2158; decorousness:— comeliness.

2158. εὐσχήμων ĕuschēmōn, yoo-skhay´-mone; from 2095 and 4976; well-formed, i.e. (fig.) decorous, noble (in rank):— comely, honourable.

2159. εὐτόνως ĕutŏnōs, yoo-ton´-oce; adv. from a compound of 2095 and a der. of τείνω tĕinō (to stretch); in a well-strung manner, i.e. (fig.) intensely (in a good sense, cogently; in a bad one, fiercely):— mightily, vehemently.

2160. εὐτραπελία ĕutrapĕlia, yoo-trap-el-ee´-ah; from a compound of 2095 and a der. of the base of 5157 (mean. well-turned, i.e. ready at repartee, jocose); witticism, i.e. (in a vulgar sense) ribaldry:— jesting.

2161. Εὔτυχος Ĕutuchŏs, yoo´-too-khos; from 2095 and a der. of 5177; well-fated, i.e. fortunate; Eutychus, a young man:— Eutychus.

2162. εὐφημία ĕuphēmia, yoo-fay-mee´-ah; from 2163; good language ("euphemy"), i.e. praise (repute):— good report.

2163. εὔφημος ĕuphēmŏs, yoo´-fay-mos; from 2095 and 5345; well spoken of, i.e. reputable:— of good report.

2164. εὐφορέω ĕuphŏrĕō, yoo-for-eh´-o; from 2095 and 5409; to bear well, i.e. be fertile:— bring forth abundantly.

2165. εὐφραίνω ĕuphrainō, yoo-frah´-ee-no; from 2095 and 5424; to put (mid. or pass. be) in a good frame of mind, i.e. rejoice:— fare, make glad, be (make) merry, rejoice.

2166. Εὐφράτης Ĕuphratēs, yoo-frat´-ace; of for. or. [comp. 6578]; Euphrates, a river of Asia:— Euphrates.

2167. εὐφροσύνη ĕuphrŏsunē, yoo-fros-oo´-nay; from the same as 2165; joyfulness:— gladness, joy.

2168. εὐχαριστέω ĕucharistĕō, yoo-khar-is-teh´-o; from 2170; to be grateful, i.e. (act.) to express gratitude (toward); spec. to say grace at a meal:— (give) thank (-ful, -s).

2169. εὐχαριστία ĕucharistia, yoo-khar-is-tee´-ah; from 2170; gratitude; act. grateful language (to God, as an act of worship):— thankfulness, (giving of) thanks (-giving).

2170. εὐχάριστος ĕucharistŏs, yoo-khar´-is-tos; from 2095 and a der. of 5483; well favored, i.e. (by impl.) grateful:— thankful.

2171. εὐχή ĕuchē, yoo-khay´; from 2172; prop. a wish, expressed as a petition to God, or in votive obligation:— prayer, vow.

2172. εὔχομαι ĕuchŏmai, yoo´-khom-ahee; mid. voice of a primary verb; to wish; by impl. to pray to God:— pray, will, wish.

2173. εὔχρηστος ĕuchrēstŏs, yoo´-khrays-tos; from 2095 and 5543; easily used, i.e. useful:— profitable, meet for use.

2174. εὐψυχέω ĕupsuchĕō, yoo-psoo-kheh´-o; from a compound of 2095 and 5590; to be in good spirits, i.e. feel encouraged:— be of good comfort.

2175. εὐωδία ĕuōdia, yoo-o-dee´-ah; from a compound of 2095 and a der. of 3605; good-scentedness, i.e. fragrance:— sweet savour (smell, -smelling).

2176. εὐώνυμος ĕuōnumŏs, yoo-o´-noo-mos; from 2095 and 3686; prop. well-named (good-omened), i.e. the left (which was the lucky side among the pagan Greeks); neut. as adv. at the left hand:— (on the) left.

2177. ἐφάλλομαι ĕphallŏmai, ef-al´-lom-ahee; from 1909 and 242; to spring upon:— leap on.

2178. ἐφάπαξ ĕphapax, ef-ap´-ax; from 1909 and 530; upon one occasion (only):— (at) once (for all).

2179. Ἐφέσινος Ĕphĕsinŏs, ef-es-ee´-nos; from 2181; Ephesine, or situated at Ephesus:— of Ephesus.

2180. Ἐφέσιος Ĕphĕsiŏs, ef-es´-ee-os; from 2181; an Ephesian or inhab. of Ephesus:— Ephesian, of Ephesus.

2181. Ἔφεσος Ĕphĕsŏs, ef´-es-os; prob. of for. or.; Ephesus, a city of Asia Minor:— Ephesus.

2182. ἐφευρέτης ĕphĕurĕtēs, ef-yoo-ret´-ace; from a compound of 1909 and 2147; a discoverer, i.e. contriver:— inventor.

2183. ἐφημερία ĕphēmĕria, ef-ay-mer-ee´-ah; from 2184; diurnality, i.e. (spec.) the quotidian rotation or class of the Jewish priests' service at the Temple, as distributed by families:— course.

2184. ἐφήμερος ĕphēmĕrŏs, ef-ay´-mer-os; from 1909 and 2250; for a day ("ephemeral"), i.e. diurnal:— daily.

2185. ἐφικνέομαι ĕphiknĕŏmai, ef-ik-neh´-om-ahee; from 1909 and a cognate of 2240; to arrive upon, i.e. extend to:— reach.

2186. ἐφίστημι ĕphistēmi, ef-is´-tay-mee; from 1909 and 2476; to *stand upon*, i.e. *be present* (in various applications, friendly or otherwise, usually lit.);—assault, come (in, to, unto, upon), be at hand (instant), present, stand (before, by, over).

2187. Ἐφραίμ **Ēphraïm**, *ef-rah-im´*; of Heb. or. [669 or better 6085]; *Ephraïm*, a place in Pal.:— Ephraim.

2188. ἐφφαθά **ēphphatha**, *ef-fath-ah´*; of Chald. or. [6606]; *be opened!*:— Ephphatha.

2189. ἔχθρα **ēchthra**, *ekh´-thrah*; fem. of 2190; *hostility*; by impl. a reason for *opposition*:— enmity, hatred.

2190. ἐχθρός **ēchthrŏs**, *ekh-thros´*; from a primary ἔχθω **ēchthō** (*to hate*); *hateful* (pass. *odious*, or act. *hostile*); usually as a noun, an *adversary* (espec. *Satan*):— enemy, foe.

2191. ἔχιδνα **ēchidna**, *ekh´-id-nah;* of uncert. or.; an *adder* or other poisonous snake (lit. or fig.):— viper.

2192. ἔχω **ēchō**, *ekh´-o;* incl. an alt. form

σχέω **schēō**, *skheh´-o;* used in certain tenses only); a primary verb; to *hold* (used in very various applications, lit. or fig., direct or remote; such as *possession; ability, contiguity, relation,* or *condition*):— be (able, × hold, possessed with), accompany, + begin to amend, can (+ -not), × conceive, count, diseased, do + eat, + enjoy, + fear, following, have, hold, keep, + lack, + go to law, lie, + must needs, + of necessity, + need, next, + recover, + reign, + rest, return, × sick, take for, + tremble, + uncircumcised, use.

2193. ἕως **hēŏs**, *heh´-oce;* of uncert. aff.; a conjunc., prep. and adv. of continuance, *until* (of time and place):— even (until, unto), (as) far (as), how long, (un-) til (-l), (hither-, un-, up) to, while (-s).

Z

2194. Ζαβουλών **Zabŏulōn**, *dzab-oolone´;* of Heb. or. [2074]; *Zabulon* (i.e. *Zebulon*), a region of Pal.:— Zabulon.

2195. Ζακχαῖος **Zakchaiŏs**, *dzak-chah´-ee-yos;* of Heb. or. [comp. 2140]; *Zacchæus*, an Isr.:— Zacchæus.

2196. Ζαρά **Zara**, *dzar-ah´;* of Heb. or. [2226]; *Zara*, (i.e. *Zerach*), an Isr.:— Zara.

2197. Ζαχαρίας **Zacharias**, *dzakh-aree´-as;* of Heb. or. [2148]; *Zacharias* (i.e. *Zechariah*), the name of two Isr.:— Zacharias.

2198. ζάω **zaō**, *dzah´-o;* a primary verb; to *live* (lit. or fig.):— life (-time), (a-) live (-ly), quick.

2199. Ζεβεδαῖος **Zĕbĕdaiŏs**, *dzeb-ed-ah´-yos;* of Heb. or. [comp. 2067]; *Zebedæus*, an Isr.:— Zebedee.

2200. ζεστός **zĕstŏs**, *dzes-tos´;* from 2204; *boiled*, i.e. (by impl.) *calid* (fig. *fervent*):— hot.

2201. ζεῦγος **zĕugŏs**, *dzyoo´-gos;* from the same as 2218; a *couple*, i.e. a *team* (of oxen yoked together) or *brace* (of birds tied together):— yoke, pair.

2202. ζευκτηρία **zĕuktēria**, *dzook-tay-ree´-ah;* fem. of a der. (at the second stage) from the same as 2218; a *fastening* (*tiller-rope*):— band.

2203. Ζεύς **Zĕus**, *dzyooce;* of uncert. aff.; in the oblique cases there is used instead of it a (prob. cognate) name

Δίς **Dis**, *deece*, which is otherwise obs.; *Zeus* or *Dis* (among the Latins *Jupiter* or *Jove*), the supreme deity of the Greeks:— Jupiter.

2204. ζέω **zĕō**, *dzeh´-o;* a primary verb; to *be hot* (*boil*, of liquids; or *glow*, of solids), i.e. (fig.) *be fervid* (*earnest*):—be fervent.

2205. ζῆλος **zēlŏs**, *dzay´-los;* from 2204; prop. *heat*, i.e. (fig.) "*zeal*" (in a favorable sense, *ardor;* in an unfavorable one, *jealousy*, as of a husband [fig. of God], or an enemy, *malice*):— emulation, envy (-ing), fervent mind, indignation, jealousy, zeal.

2206. ζηλόω **zēlŏō**, *dzay-lŏ´-o* or ζηλεύω **zēlĕuō** *dzay-loo´-o;* from 2205; to *have warmth* of feeling for or against:— affect, covet (earnestly), (have) desire, (move with) envy, be jealous over, (be) zealous (-ly affect).

2207. ζηλωτής **zēlōtēs**, *dzay-lo-tace´;* from 2206; a "*zealot*":— zealous.

2208. Ζηλωτής **Zēlōtēs**, *dzay-lo-tace´;* the same as 2208; a *Zealot*, i.e. (spec.) *partisan* for Jewish political independence:— Zelotes.

2209. ζημία **zēmia**, *dzay-mee´-ah;* prob. akin to the base of 1150 (through the idea of *violence*); *detriment*:— damage, loss.

2210. ζημιόω **zēmiŏō**, *dzay-mee-ŏ´-o;* from 2209; to *injure*, i.e. (refl. or pass.) to *experience detriment*:— be cast away, receive damage, lose, suffer loss.

2211. Ζηνᾶς **Zēnas**, *dzay-nas´;* prob. contr. from a poetic form of 2203 and 1435; *Jove-given; Zenas*, a Chr.:— Zenas.

2212. ζητέω **zētĕō**, *dzay-teh´-o;* of uncert. aff.; to *seek* (lit. or fig.); spec. (by Heb.) to *worship* (God), or (in a bad sense) to *plot* (against life):— be (go) about, desire, endeavour, enquire (for), require, (× will) seek (after, for, means). Comp. 4441.

2213. ζήτημα **zētēma**, *dzay´-tay-mah;* from 2212; a *search* (prop. concr.), i.e. (in words) a *debate*:— question.

2214. ζήτησις **zētēsis**, *dzay´-tay-sis;* from 2212; a *searching* (prop. the act), i.e. a *dispute* or its *theme*:— question.

2215. ζιζάνιον **zizaniŏn**, *dziz-an´-ee-on;* of uncert. or.; *darnel* or false grain:— tares.

2216. Ζοροβάβελ **Zŏrŏbabĕl**, *dzor-ob-ab´-el;* of Heb. or. [2216]; *Zorobabel* (i.e. *Zerubbabel*), an Isr.:— Zorobabel.

2217. ζόφος **zŏphŏs**, *dzof´-os;* akin to the base of 3509; *gloom* (as shrouding like a *cloud*):— blackness, darkness, mist.

2218. ζυγός **zugŏs**, *dzoo-gos´;* from the root of ζεύγνυμι **zĕugnumi** (to *join*, espec. by a "yoke"); a *coupling*, i.e. (fig.) *servitude* (a *law* or *obligation*); also

(lit.) the *beam* of the balance (as *connecting* the scales):— pair of balances, yoke.

2219. ζύμη **zumē**, *dzoo´-may;* prob. from 2204; *ferment* (as if *boiling* up):— leaven.

2220. ζυμόω **zumŏō**, *dzoo-mŏ´-o;* from 2219; to *cause to ferment*:— leaven.

2221. ζωγρέω **zōgrĕō**, *dzogue-reh´-o;* from the same as 2226 and 64; to *take alive* (*make a prisoner of war*), i.e. (fig.) to *capture* or *ensnare*:— take captive, catch.

2222. ζωή **zōē**, *dzo-ay´;* from 2198; *life* (lit. or fig.):— life (-time). Comp. 5590.

2223. ζώνη **zōnē**, *dzo´-nay;* prob. akin to the base of 2218; a *belt*; by impl. a *pocket*:— girdle, purse.

2224. ζώννυμι **zōnnumi**, *dzone´-noo-mi;* from 2223; to *bind about* (espec. with a belt):— gird.

2225. ζωογονέω **zōŏgŏnĕō**, *dzo-og-on-eh´-o;* from the same as 2226 and a der. of 1096; to *engender alive*, i.e. (by anal.) to *rescue* (pass. *be saved*) from death:— live, preserve.

2226. ζῶον **zōŏn**, *dzo´-on;* neut. of a der. of 2198; a *live* thing, i.e. an *animal*:— beast.

2227. ζωοποιέω **zōŏpŏiĕō**, *dzo-op-oy-eh´-o;* from the same as 2226 and 4160; to *(re-) vitalize* (lit. or fig.):— make alive, give life, quicken.

H

2228. ἤ **ē**, *ay;* a primary particle of distinction between two connected terms; disjunctive, *or;* comparative, *than*:— and, but (either), (n-) either, except it be, (n-) or (else), rather, save, than, that, what, yea. Often used in connection with other particles. Comp. especially 2235, 2260, 2273.

2229. ἦ **ē**, *ay;* an adv. of *confirmation;* perh. intens. of 2228; used only (in the N.T.) before 3303; *assuredly*:— surely.

ἤ **hē**. See 3588.

ᾗ **hē**. See 3739.

ᾖ **ēi**. See 5600.

2230. ἡγεμονεύω **hēgĕmŏnĕuō**, *hayg-em-on-yoo´-o;* from 2232; to *act as ruler*:— be governor.

2231. ἡγεμονία **hēgĕmŏnia**, *hayg-em-on-ee´-ah;* from 2232; *government*, i.e. (in time) official *term*:— reign.

2232. ἡγεμών **hēgĕmōn**, *hayg-em-ohn´;* from 2233; a *leader*, i.e. *chief* person (or fig. place) of a province:— governor, prince, ruler.

2233. ἡγέομαι **hēgĕŏmai**, *hayg-eh´-om-ahee;* mid. voice of a (presumed) strengthened form of 71; to *lead*, i.e. *command* (with official authority); fig. to *deem*, i.e. *consider*:— account, (be) chief, count, esteem, governor, judge, have the rule over, suppose, think.

2234. ἡδέως **hēdĕōs**, *hay-deh´-oce;* adv. from a der. of the base of 2237; *sweetly*, i.e. (fig.) *with pleasure*:— gladly.

2235. ἤδη **ēdē**, *ay´-day;* appar. from 2228 (or possibly 2229) and 1211; *even* *now:*— already, (even) now (already), by this time.

2236. ἥδιστα **hēdista**, *hay´-dis-tah;* neut. plur. of the superl. of the same as 2234; *with great pleasure:*— most (very) gladly.

2237. ἡδονή **hēdŏnē**, *hay-don-ay´;* from ἁνδάνω **handanō** (to *please*); sensual *delight;* by impl. *desire:*— lust, pleasure.

2238. ἡδύοσμον **hēduŏsmŏn**, *hay-doo´-os-mon;* neut. of the compound of the same as 2234 and 3744; a *sweet-scented* plant, i.e. *mint:*— mint.

2239. ἦθος **ēthŏs**, *ay´-thos;* a strengthened form of 1485; *usage,* i.e. (plur.) moral *habits:*— manners.

2240. ἥκω **hēkō**, *hay´-ko;* a primary verb; to *arrive,* i.e. *be present* (lit. or fig.):— come.

2241. ἠλί **ēli**, *ay-lee´* or ἐλοὶ **ĕloi** *ay-lo´-ee;* of Heb. or. [410 with pron. suff.]; *my God:*— Eli.

2242. Ἡλί **Hēli**, *hay-lee´;* of Heb. or. [5941]; *Heli* (i.e. *Eli*), an Isr.:— Heli.

2243. Ἡλίας **Hēlias**, *hay-lee´-as;* of Heb. or. [452]; *Helias* (i.e. *Elijah*), an Isr.:— Elias.

2244. ἡλικία **hēlikia**, *hay-lik-ee´-ah;* from the same as 2245; *maturity* (in years or size):— age, stature.

2245. ἡλίκος **hēlikŏs**, *hay-lee´-kos;* from ἧλιξ **hēlix** (a *comrade,* i.e. one of the same age); *as big as,* i.e. (interjectively) *how much:*— how (what) great.

2246. ἥλιος **hēliŏs**, *hay´-lee-os;* from ἕλη **hēlē** (a *ray;* perh. akin to the alt. of 138); the *sun;* by impl. *light:*— + east, sun.

2247. ἧλος **hēlŏs**, *hay´-los;* of uncert. aff.; a *stud,* i.e. *spike:*— nail.

2248. ἡμᾶς **hēmas**, *hay-mas´;* acc. plur. of 1473; *us:*— our, us, we.

2249. ἡμεῖς **hēmĕis**, *hay-mice´;* nom. plur. of 1473; *we* (only used when emphat.):— us, we (ourselves).

2250. ἡμέρα **hēmĕra**, *hay-mer´-ah;* fem. (with 5610 impl.) of a der. of ἧμαι **hēmai** (to *sit;* akin to the base of 1476) mean. *tame,* i.e. *gentle; day,* i.e. (lit.) the time space between dawn and dark, or the whole 24 hours (but several days were usually reckoned by the Jews as inclusive of the parts of both extremes); fig. a *period* (always defined more or less clearly by the context):— age, + alway, (mid-) day (by day, [-lyl), + for ever, judgment, (day) time, while, years.

2251. ἡμέτερος **hēmĕtĕrŏs**, *hay-met´-er-os;* from 2349; *our:*— our, your [by a different reading].

2252. ἤμην **ēmēn**, *ay´-mane;* a prol. form of 2358; *I was:*— be, was. [Sometimes unexpressed].

2253. ἡμιθανής **hēmithanēs**, *hay-mee-than-ace´;* from a presumed compound of the base of 2255 and 2348; *half dead,* i.e. *entirely exhausted:*— half dead.

2254. ἡμῖν **hēmin**, *hay-meen´;* dat. plur. of 1473; *to* (or *for, with, by*) *us:*— our, (for) us, we.

2255. ἥμισυ **hēmisu**, *hay´-mee-soo;*

neut. of a der. from an inseparable pref. akin to 260 (through the idea of *partition* involved in *connection*) and mean. *semi-;* (as noun) *half:*— half.

2256. ἡμιώριον **hēmiōriŏn**, *hay-mee-o´-ree-on;* from the base of 2255 and 5610; a *half-hour:*— half an hour.

2257. ἡμῶν **hēmōn**, *hay-mone´;* gen. plur. of 1473; *of* (or *from*) *us:*— our (company), us, we.

2258. ἦν **ēn**, *ane;* imperf. of 1510; *I* (*thou,* etc.) *was* (*wast* or *were*):— + agree, be, × have (+ charge of), hold, use, was (-t), were.

2259. ἡνίκα **hēnika**, *hay-nee´-kah;* of uncert. aff.; *at which time:*— when.

2260. ἤπερ **ēpĕr**, *ay´-per;* from 2228 and 4007; *than at all* (or *than perhaps, than indeed*):— than.

2261. ἤπιος **ēpiŏs**, *ay´-pee-os;* prob. from 2031; prop. *affable,* i.e. *mild* or *kind:*— gentle.

2262. Ἢρ **Ēr**, *ayr;* of Heb. or. [6147]; *Er,* an Isr.:— Er.

2263. ἤρεμος **ērĕmŏs**, *ay´-rem-os;* perh. by transposition from 2048 (through the idea of *stillness*); *tranquil:*— quiet.

2264. Ἡρώδης **Hērōdēs**, *hay-ro´-dace;* compound of ἤρως **hērōs** (a "*hero*") and 1491; *heroic; Herod,* the name of four Jewish kings:— Herod.

2265. Ἡρωδιανοί **Hērōdianŏi**, *hay-ro-dee-an-oy´;* plur. of a der. of 2264; *Herodians,* i.e. partisans of Herod:— Herodians.

2266. Ἡρωδιάς **Hērōdias**, *hay-ro-dee-as´;* from 2264; *Herodias,* a woman of the Herodian family:— Herodias.

2267. Ἡρωδίων **Hērōdiōn**, *hay-ro-dee´-ohn;* from 2264; *Herodion,* a Chr.:— Herodion.

2268. Ἡσαΐας **Hēsaïas**, *hay-sah-ee´-as;* of Heb. or. [3470]; *Hesaias* (i.e. *Jeshajah*), an Isr.:— Esaias.

2269. Ἡσαῦ **Ēsau**, *ay-sow´;* of Heb. or. [6215]; *Esau,* an Edomite:— Esau.

2270. ἡσυχάζω **hēsuchazō**, *hay-soo-khad´-zo;* from the same as 2272; to *keep still* (intr.), i.e. *refrain* from labor, meddlesomeness or speech:— cease, hold peace, be quiet, rest.

2271. ἡσυχία **hēsuchia**, *hay-soo-khee´-ah;* fem. of 2272; (as noun) *stillness,* i.e. *desistance* from bustle or language:— quietness, silence.

2272. ἡσύχιος **hēsuchiŏs**, *hay-soo-khee-os;* a prol. form of a compound prob. of a der. of the base of 1476 and perh. 2192; prop. *keeping* one's *seat* (*sedentary*), i.e. (by impl.) *still* (*undisturbed, undisturbing*):— peaceable, quiet.

2273. ἤτοι **ētŏi**, *ay´-toy;* from 2228 and 5104; *either indeed:*— whether.

2274. ἡττάω **hēttaō**, *hayt-tah´-o;* from the same as 2276; to *make worse,* i.e. *vanquish* (lit. or fig.); by impl. to *rate lower:*— be inferior, overcome.

2275. ἥττημα **hēttēma**, *hayt´-tay-mah;* from 2274; a *deterioration,* i.e. (obj.) *failure* or (subj.) *loss:*— diminishing, fault.

2276. ἥττον **hēttŏn**, *hate´-ton;* neut. of comp. of ἥκα **hēka** (*slightly*) used for that of 2556; *worse* (as noun); by impl. *less* (as adv.):— less, worse.

2277. ἤτω **ētō**, *ay´-to;* third pers. sing. imper. of 1510; *let him* (or *it*) *be:*— let ... be.

2278. ἠχέω **ēchĕō**, *ay-kheh´-o;* from 2279; to *make* a loud *noise,* i.e. *reverberate:*— roar, sound.

2279. ἦχος **ēchŏs**, *ay´-khos;* of uncert. aff.; a loud or confused *noise* ("*echo*"), i.e. *roar;* fig. a *rumor:*— fame, sound.

Θ

2280. Θαδδαῖος **Thaddaiŏs**, *thad-dah´-yos;* of uncert. or.; *Thaddæus,* one of the Apostles:— Thaddæus.

2281. θάλασσα **thalassa**, *thal´-as-sah;* prob. prol. from 251; the *sea* (gen. or spec.):— sea.

2282. θάλπω **thalpō**, *thal´-po;* prob. akin to θάλλω **thallō** (to *warm*); to *brood,* i.e. (fig.) to *foster:*— cherish.

2283. Θάμαρ **Thamar**, *tham´-ar;* of Heb. or. [8559]; *Thamar* (i.e. *Tamar*), an Israelitess:— Thamar.

2284. θαμβέω **thambĕō**, *tham-beh´-o;* from 2285; to *stupefy* (with surprise), i.e. *astound:*— amaze, astonish.

2285. θάμβος **thambŏs**, *tham´-bos;* akin to an obs. τάφω **taphō** (to *dumbfound*); *stupefaction* (by surprise), i.e. *astonishment:*— × amazed, + astonished, wonder.

2286. θανάσιμος **thanasimŏs**, *than-as´-ee-mos;* from 2288; *fatal,* i.e. *poisonous:*— deadly.

2287. θανατήφορος **thanatēphŏrŏs**, *than-at-ay´-for-os;* from (the fem. form of) 2288 and 5342; *death-bearing,* i.e. *fatal:*— deadly.

2288. θάνατος **thanatŏs**, *than´-at-os;* from 2348; (prop. an adj. used as a noun) *death* (lit. or fig.):— × deadly, (be...) death.

2289. θανατόω **thanatŏō**, *than-at-ŏ´-o;* from 2288; to *kill* (lit. or fig.):— become dead, (cause to be) put to death, kill, mortify.

θάνω **thanō**. See 2348.

2290. θάπτω **thaptō**, *thap´-to;* a primary verb; to *celebrate funeral rites,* i.e. *inter:*— bury.

2291. Θάρα **Thara**, *thar´-ah;* of Heb. or. [8646]; *Thara* (i.e. *Terach*), the father of Abraham:— Thara.

2292. θαρρέω **tharrhĕō**, *thar-hreh´-o;* another form for 2293; to *exercise courage:*— be bold, × boldly, have confidence, be confident. Comp. 5111.

2293. θαρσέω **tharsĕō**, *thar-seh´-o;* from 2294; to *have courage:*— be of good cheer (comfort). Comp. 2292.

2294. θάρσος **tharsŏs**, *thar´-sos;* akin (by transp.) to θράσος **thrasŏs** (*daring*); *boldness* (subj.):— courage.

2295. θαῦμα **thauma**, *thŏu´-mah;* appar. from a form of 2300; *wonder* (prop. concr.; but by impl. abstr.):— admiration.

2296. θαυμάζω **thaumazō**, *thŏu-mad´-*

zo; from 2295; to *wonder*; by impl. to *admire*:— admire, have in admiration, marvel, wonder.

2297. θαυμάσιος **thaumasiōs**, *thŏw-mas´-ee-os*; from 2295; *wondrous*, i.e. (neut. as noun) a *miracle*:— wonderful thing.

2298. θαυμαστός **thaumastŏs**, *thŏw-mas-tos´*; from 2296; *wondered* at, i.e. (by impl.) *wonderful*:— marvel (-lous).

2299. θεά **thĕa**, *theh-ah´*; fem. of 2316; a female *deity*:— goddess.

2300. θεάομαι **thĕaŏmai**, *theh-ah´-om-ahee*; a prol. form of a primary verb; to *look* closely at, i.e. (by impl.) *perceive* (lit. or fig.); by extens. to *visit*:— behold, look (upon), see. Comp. 3700.

2301. θεατρίζω **thĕatrizō**, *theh-at-rid´-zo*; from 2302; to *expose as a spectacle*:— make a gazing stock.

2302. θέατρον **thĕatrŏn**, *theh´-at-ron*; from 2300; a *place for public show* ("theatre"), i.e. general *audience-room*; by impl. a *show* itself (fig.):— spectacle, theatre.

2303. θεῖον **thĕiŏn**, *thi´-on*; prob. neut. of 2304 (in its orig. sense of *flashing*); *sulphur*:— brimstone.

2304. θεῖος **thĕiŏs**, *thi´-os*; from 2316; *godlike* (neut. as noun, *divinity*):— divine, godhead.

2305. θειότης **thĕiŏtēs**, *thi-ot´-ace*; from 2304; *divinity* (abstr.):— godhead.

2306. θειώδης **thĕiōdēs**, *thi-o´-dace*; from 2303 and 1491; *sulphur-like*, i.e. *sulphurous*:— brimstone.

θελέω **thĕlĕō**. See 2309.

2307. θέλημα **thĕlēma**, *thel´-ay-mah*; from the prol. form of 2309; a *determination* (prop. the thing), i.e. (act.) *choice* (spec. *purpose, decree*; abstr. *volition*) or (pass.) *inclination*:— desire, pleasure, will.

2308. θέλησις **thĕlēsis**, *thel´-ay-sis*; from 2309; *determination* (prop. the act), i.e. *option*:— will.

2309. θέλω **thĕlō**, *thel´-o*; or ἐθέλω **ĕthĕlō**, *eth-el´-o*; in certain tenses θελέω **thĕlĕō**, *thel-eh´-o*; and ἐθελέω **ĕthĕlĕō**, *eth-el-eh´-o*; which are otherwise obs.; appar. strengthened from the alt. form of 138; to *determine* (as an act. *option* from subj. impulse; whereas 1014 prop. denotes rather a pass. *acquiescence* in obj. considerations), i.e. *choose* or *prefer* (lit. or fig.); by impl. to *wish*, i.e. be *inclined* to (sometimes adv. *gladly*); impers. for the future tense, to *be about to*; by Heb. to *delight in*:— desire, be disposed (forward), intend, list, love, mean, please, have rather, (be) will (have, -ling, -ling [-ly]).

2310. θεμέλιος **thĕmĕliŏs**, *them-el´-ee-os*; from a der. of 5087; something *put down*, i.e. a *substruction* (of a building, etc.), (lit. or fig.):— foundation.

2311. θεμελιόω **thĕmĕliŏō**, *them-el-ee-ŏ´-o*; from 2310; to *lay a basis* for, i.e. (lit.) *erect*, or (fig.) *consolidate*:— (lay the) found (-ation), ground, settle.

2312. θεοδίδακτος **thĕŏdidaktŏs**, *theh-od-id´-ak-tos*; from 2316 and 1321; *divinely instructed*:— taught of God.

2312'. θεολόγος **thĕŏlŏgŏs**, *theh-ol-og´-os*; from 2316 and 3004; a "theologian":— divine.

2313. θεομαχέω **thĕŏmachĕō**, *theh-o-makh-eh´-o*; from 2314; to *resist deity*:— fight against God.

2314. θεόμαχος **thĕŏmachŏs**, *theh-om´-akh-os*; from 2316 and 3164; an *opponent of deity*:— to fight against God.

2315. θεόπνευστος **thĕŏpnĕustŏs**, *theh-op´-nyoo-stos*; from 2316 and a presumed der. of 4154; *divinely breathed in*:— given by inspiration of God.

2316. θεός **thĕŏs**, *theh´-os*; of uncert. aff.; a *deity*, espec. (with 3588) the supreme *Divinity*; fig. a *magistrate*; by Heb. *very*:— × exceeding, God, god [-ly, -ward].

2317. θεοσέβεια **thĕŏsĕbĕia**, *theh-os-eb´-i-ah*; from 2318; *devoutness*, i.e. *piety*:— godliness.

2318. θεοσεβής **thĕŏsĕbēs**, *theh-os-eb-ace´*; from 2316 and 4576; *reverent of God*, i.e. *pious*:— worshipper of God.

2319. θεοστυγής **thĕŏstugēs**, *theh-os-too-gace´*; from 2316 and the base of 4767; *hateful to God*, i.e. *impious*:— hater of God.

2320. θεότης **thĕŏtēs**, *theh-ot´-ace*; from 2316; *divinity* (abstr.):— godhead.

2321. Θεόφιλος **Thĕŏphilŏs**, *theh-of´-il-os*; from 2316 and 5384; *friend of God*; *Theophilus*, a Chr.:— Theophilus.

2322. θεραπεία **thĕrapĕia**, *ther-ap-i´-ah*; from 2323; *attendance* (spec. medical, i.e. *cure*); fig. and collec. *domestics*:— healing, household.

2323. θεραπεύω **thĕrapĕuō**, *ther-ap-yoo´-o*; from the same as 2324; to *wait upon* menially, i.e. (fig.) to *adore* (God), or (spec.) to *relieve* (of disease):— cure, heal, worship.

2324. θεράπων **thĕrapōn**, *ther-ap´-ohn*; appar. a part. from an otherwise obs. der. of the base of 2330; a menial *attendant* (as if *cherishing*):— servant.

2325. θερίζω **thĕrizō**, *ther-id´-zo*; from 2330 (in the sense of the *crop*); to *harvest*:— reap.

2326. θερισμός **thĕrismŏs**, *ther-is-mos´*; from 2325; *reaping*, i.e. the *crop*:— harvest.

2327. θεριστής **thĕristēs**, *ther-is-tace´*; from 2325; a *harvester*:— reaper.

2328. θερμαίνω **thĕrmainō**, *ther-mah´-ee-no*; from 2329; to *heat* (oneself):— (be) warm (-ed, self).

2329. θέρμη **thĕrmē**, *ther´-may*; from the base of 2330; *warmth*:— heat.

2330. θέρος **thĕrŏs**, *ther´-os*; from a primary θέρω **thĕrō** (to *heat*); prop. *heat*, i.e. *summer*:— summer.

2331. Θεσσαλονικεύς **Thĕssalŏnikĕus**, *thes-sal-on-ik-yoos´*; from 2332; a *Thessalonican*, i.e. inhab. of Thessalonice:— Thessalonian.

2332. Θεσσαλονίκη **Thĕssalŏnikē**, *thes-sal-on-ee´-kay*; from Θεσσαλός **thĕssalŏs** (a *Thessalian*) and 3529; *Thessalonice*, a place in Asia Minor:— Thessalonica.

2333. Θευδᾶς **Thĕudas**, *thyoo-das´*; of uncert. or.; *Theudas*, an Isr.:— Theudas.

θέω **thĕō**. See 5087.

2334. θεωρέω **thĕōrĕō**, *theh-o-reh´-o*; from a der. of 2300 (perh. by add. of 3708); to *be a spectator* of, i.e. *discern*, (lit., fig. [*experience*] or intens. [*acknowledge*]):— behold, consider, look on, perceive, see. Comp. 3700.

2335. θεωρία **thĕōria**, *theh-o-ree´-ah*; from the same as 2334; *spectatorship*, i.e. (concr.) a *spectacle*:— sight.

2336. θήκη **thēkē**, *thay´-kay*; from 5087; a *receptacle*, i.e. *scabbard*:— sheath.

2337. θηλάζω **thēlazō**, *thay-lad´-zo*; from θηλή **thēlē** (the *nipple*); to *suckle*, (by impl.) to *suck*:— (give) suck (-ling).

2338. θῆλυς **thēlus**, *thay´-loos*; from the same as 2337; *female*:— female, woman.

2339. θήρα **thēra**, *thay´-rah*; from θήρ **thēr** (a wild *animal*, as *game*); *hunting*, i.e. (fig.) *destruction*:— trap.

2340. θηρεύω **thērĕuō**, *thay-ryoo´-o*; from 2339; to *hunt* (an animal), i.e. (fig.) to *carp at*:— catch.

2341. θηριομαχέω **thēriŏmachĕō**, *thay-ree-om-akh-eh´-o*; from a compound of 2342 and 3164; to *be a beast-fighter* (in the gladiatorial show), i.e. (fig.) to *encounter* (furious men):— fight with wild beasts.

2342. θηρίον **thēriŏn**, *thay-ree´-on*; dimin. from the same as 2339; a *dangerous animal*:— (venomous, wild) beast.

2343. θησαυρίζω **thēsaurizō**, *thay-sŏw-rid´-zo*; from 2344; to *amass* or *reserve* (lit. or fig.):— lay up (treasure), (keep) in store, (heap) treasure (together, up).

2344. θησαυρός **thēsaurŏs**, *thay-sow-ros´*; from 5087; a *deposit*, i.e. *wealth* (lit. or fig.):— treasure.

2345. θιγγάνω **thigganō**, *thing-gan´-o*; a prol. form of an obs. primary θίγω **thigō** (to *finger*); to *manipulate*, i.e. *have to do with*; by impl. to *injure*:— handle, touch.

2346. θλίβω **thlibō**, *thlee-bo*; akin to the base of 5147; to *crowd* (lit. or fig.):— afflict, narrow, throng, suffer tribulation, trouble.

2347. θλίψις **thlipsis**, *thlip´-sis*; from 2346; *pressure* (lit. or fig.):— afflicted (-tion), anguish, burdened, persecution, tribulation, trouble.

2348. θνήσκω **thnēskō**, *thnay´-sko*; a strengthened form of a simpler primary θάνω **thanō**, *than´-o* (which is used for it only in certain tenses); to *die* (lit. or fig.):— be dead, die.

2349. θνητός **thnētŏs**, *thnay-tos´*; from 2348; *liable to die*:— mortal (-ity).

2350. θορυβέω **thŏrubĕō**, *thor-oo-beh´-o*; from 2351; to *be in tumult*, i.e. *disturb, clamor*:— make ado (a noise), trouble self, set on an uproar.

2351. θόρυβος **thŏrubŏs**, *thor´-oo-bos*; from the base of 2360; a *disturbance*:— tumult, uproar.

2352. θραύω **thrauō**, *thrŏw´-o*; a primary verb; to *crush*:— bruise. Comp. 4486.

2353. θρέμμα **thrĕmma**, *threm´-mah;* from *5142;* stock (as raised on a farm):— cattle.

2354. θρηνέω **thrēnĕō**, *thray-neh´-o;* from 2355; to *bewail:*— lament, mourn.

2355. θρῆνος **thrēnŏs**, *thray´-nos;* from the base of *2360; wailing:*— lamentation.

2356. θρησκεία **thrēskĕia**, *thrace-ki´-ah;* from a der. of *2357;* ceremonial *observance:*— religion, worshipping.

2357. θρῆσκος **thrēskŏs**, *thrace´-kos;* prob. from the base of *2360; ceremonious* in worship (as *demonstrative*), i.e. *pious:*— religious.

2358. θριαμβεύω **thriambĕuō**, *three-am-byoo´-o;* from a prol. compound of the base of *2360;* and a der. of *680* (mean. a *noisy iambus,* sung in honor of Bacchus); to *make an acclamatory procession,* i.e. (fig.) to *conquer* or (by Heb.) to *give victory:*— (cause) to triumph (over).

2359. θρίξ **thrix**, *threeks;* gen. τριχός **trichŏs**, etc.; of uncert. der.; *hair:*— hair. Comp. *2864.*

2360. θροέω **thrŏĕō**, *thrŏ-eh´-o;* from θρέομαι **thrĕomai** to *wail;* to *clamor,* i.e. (by impl.) to *frighten:*— trouble.

2361. θρόμβος **thrŏmbŏs**, *throm´-bos;* perh. from *5142* (in the sense of *thickening*); a *clot:*— great drop.

2362. θρόνος **thrŏnŏs**, *thron´-os;* from θράω **thraō** (to *sit*); a stately *seat* ("*throne*"); by impl. *power* or (concr.) a *potentate:*— seat, throne.

2363. Θυάτειρα **Thuatĕira**, *thoo-at´-i-rah;* of uncert. der.; *Thyatira,* a place in Asia Minor:— Thyatira.

2364. θυγάτηρ **thugatĕr**, *thoo-gat´-air;* appar. a primary word [comp. "daughter"]; a *female child,* or (by Heb.) *descendant* (or *inhabitant*):— daughter.

2365. θυγάτριον **thugatriŏn**, *thoo-gat´-ree-on;* from *2364;* a *daughterling:*— little (young) daughter.

2366. θύελλα **thuĕlla**, *thoo´-el-lah;* from *2380* (in the sense of *blowing*) a storm:— tempest.

2367. θύϊνος **thuïnŏs**, *thoo´-ee-nos;* from a der. of *2380* (in the sense of *blowing;* denoting a certain *fragrant* tree); made of *citron*-wood:— thyine.

2368. θυμίαμα **thumiama**, *thoo-mee´-am-ah;* from *2370;* an *aroma,* i.e. fragrant *powder* burnt in relig. service; by impl. the *burning* itself:— incense, odour.

2369. θυμιαστήριον **thumiastēriŏn**, *thoo-mee-as-tay´-ree-on;* or

θυμιατήριον **thumiatērion**, *thoo-mee-a-tay´-ree-on;* from a der. of *2370;* a *place of fumigation,* i.e. the *alter of incense* (in the Temple):— censer.

2370. θυμιάω **thumiaō**, *thoo-mee-ah´-o;* from a der. of *2380* (in the sense of *smoking*); to *fumigate,* i.e. *offer* aromatic *fumes:*— burn incense.

2371. θυμομαχέω **thumŏmachĕō**, *thoo-mom-akh-eh´-o;* from a presumed compound of *2372* and *3164;* to *be in a furious fight,* i.e. (fig.) to be *exasperated:*— be highly displeased.

2372. θυμός **thumŏs**, *thoo-mos´;* from *2380; passion* (as if *breathing* hard):— fierceness, indignation, wrath. Comp. *5590.*

2373. θυμόω **thumŏō**, *tho-mŏ´-o;* from *2372;* to *put in a passion,* i.e. *enrage:*— be wroth.

2374. θύρα **thura**, *thoo´-rah;* appar. a primary word [comp. "door"]; a *portal* or *entrance* (the opening or the closure, lit. or fig.):— door, gate.

2375. θυρεός **thurĕŏs**, *thoo-reh-os´;* from *2374;* a large *shield* (as doorshaped):— shield.

2376. θυρίς **thuris**, *thoo-rece´;* from *2374;* an *aperture,* i.e. *window:*— window.

2377. θυρωρός **thurōrŏs**, *thoo-ro-ros´;* from *2374* and οὖρος **ŏurŏs** (a *watcher*); a *gate-warden:*— that kept the door, porter.

2378. θυσία **thusia**, *thoo-see´-ah;* from *2380; sacrifice* (the act or the victim, lit. or fig.):— sacrifice.

2379. θυσιαστήριον **thusiastēriŏn**, *thoo-see-as-tay´-ree-on;* from a der. of *2378;* a *place of sacrifice,* i.e. an *altar* (spec. or gen., lit. or fig.):— altar.

2380. θύω **thuō**, *thoo´-o;* a primary verb; prop. to *rush* (*breathe* hard, *blow, smoke*), i.e. (by impl.) to *sacrifice* (prop. by fire, but gen.); by extens. to *immolate* (*slaughter* for any purpose):— kill, (do) sacrifice, slay.

2381. Θωμᾶς **Thōmas**, *tho-mas´;* of Chald. or. [comp. 8380]; *the twin; Thomas,* a Chr.:— Thomas.

2382. θώραξ **thōrax**, *tho´-rax;* of uncert. aff.; the *chest* ("*thorax*"), i.e. (by impl.) a *corslet:*— breast-plate.

I

2383. Ἰάειρος **Iaĕirŏs**, *ee-ah´-i-ros;* or

Ἰάϊρος **Iairŏs**, *ee-ahee´-ros;* of Heb. or. [2971]; *Jaïrus* (i.e. *Jair*), an Isr.:— Jairus.

2384. Ἰακώβ **Iakŏb**, *ee-ak-obe´;* of Heb. or. [3290]; *Jacob* (i.e. *Ja`akob*), the progenitor of the Isr.:— also an Isr.:— Jacob.

2385. Ἰάκωβος **Iakōbŏs**, *ee-ak´-o-bos;* the same as *2384* Græcized; *Jacobus,* the name of three Isr.:— James.

2386. ἴαμα **iama**, *ee´-am-ah;* from *2390;* a *cure* (the effect):— healing.

2387. Ἰαμβρῆς **Iambrēs**, *ee-am-brace´;* of Eg. or.; *Jambres,* an Eg.:— Jambres.

2388. Ἰαννά **Ianna**, *ee-an-nah´;* prob. of Heb. or. [comp. 3238]; *Janna,* an Isr.:— Janna.

2389. Ἰαννῆς **Iannēs**, *ee-an-nace´;* of Eg. or.; *Jannes,* an Eg.:— Jannes.

2390. ἰάομαι **iaŏmai**, *ee-ah´-om-ahee;* mid. voice of appar. a primary verb; to *cure* (lit. or fig.):— heal, make whole.

2391. Ἰάρεδ **Iarĕd**, *ee-ar´-ed* or

Ἰάρετ **Iaret**, *ee-ar´-et;* of Heb. or. [3382]; *Jared* (i.e. *Jered*), an antediluvian:— Jared.

2392. ἴασις **iasis**, *ee´-as-is;* from *2390; curing* (the act):— cure, heal (-ing).

2393. ἴασπις **iaspis**, *ee´-as-pis;* prob. of for. or. [see 3471]; "*jasper,*" a gem:— jasper.

2394. Ἰάσων **Iasōn**, *ee-as´-oan;* future act. part. masc. of *2390; about to cure; Jason,* a Chr.:— Jason.

2395. ἰατρός **iatrŏs**, *ee-at-ros´;* from *2390;* a *physician:*— physician.

2396. ἴδε **idĕ**, *id´-eh;* second pers. sing. imper. act. of *1492;* used as an interj. to denote *surprise; lo!:*— behold, lo, see.

2397. ἰδέα **idĕa**, *id-eh´-ah;* from *1492;* a *sight* [comp. fig. "idea"], i.e. *aspect:*— countenance.

2398. ἴδιος **idiŏs**, *id´-ee-os;* of uncert. aff.; *pertaining to self,* i.e. one's *own;* by impl. *private* or *separate:*— × his acquaintance, when they were alone, apart, aside, due, his (own, proper, several), home, (her, our, thine, your) own (business), private (-ly), proper, severally, their (own).

2399. ἰδιώτης **idiōtēs**, *id-ee-o´-tace;* from *2398;* a *private* person, i.e. (by impl.) an *ignoramus* (comp. "idiot"):— ignorant, rude, unlearned.

2400. ἰδού **idŏu**, *id-oo´;* second pers. sing. imper. mid. voice of *1492;* used as imper. *lo!:*— behold, lo, see.

2401. Ἰδουμαία **Idŏumaia**, *id-oo-mah´-yah;* of Heb. or. [123]; *Idumæa* (i.e. *Edom*), a region E. (and S.) of Pal.:— Idumaea.

2402. ἰδρώς **hidrōs**, *hid-roce´;* a strengthened form of a primary ἴδος **idŏs** (*sweat*); *perspiration:*— sweat.

2403. Ἰεζαβήλ **Iĕzabĕl**, *ee-ed-zab-ale´;* of Heb. or. [348]; *Jezabel* (i.e. *Jezebel*), a Tyrian woman (used as a synonym of a termagant or false teacher):— Jezabel.

2404. Ἱεράπολις **Hiĕrapŏlis**, *hee-er-ap´-ol-is;* from *2413* and *4172; holy city; Hierapolis,* a place in Asia Minor:— Hierapolis.

2405. ἱερατεία **hiĕratĕia**, *hee-er-at-i´-ah;* from *2407; priestliness,* i.e. the *sacerdotal function:*— office of the priesthood, priest's office.

2406. ἱεράτευμα **hiĕratĕuma**, *hee-er-at´-yoo-mah;* from *2407;* the *priestly fraternity,* i.e. *sacerdotal order* (fig.):— priesthood.

2407. ἱερατεύω **hiĕratĕuō**, *hee-er-at-yoo´-o;* prol. from *2409;* to *be a priest,* i.e. *perform his functions:*— execute the priest's office.

2408. Ἱερεμίας **Hiĕrĕmias**, *hee-er-em-ee´-as;* of Heb. or. [3414]; *Hieremias* (i.e. *Jermijah*), an Isr.:— Jeremiah.

2409. ἱερεύς **hiĕrĕus**, *hee-er-yooce´;* from *2413;* a *priest* (lit. or fig.):— (high) priest.

2410. Ἱεριχώ **Hiĕrichō**, *hee-er-ee-kho´;* of Heb. or. [3405]; *Jericho,* a place in Pal.:— Jericho.

2411. ἱερόν **hiĕrŏn**, *hee-er-on´;* neut. of *2413;* a *sacred* place, i.e. the entire precincts (whereas *3485* denotes the central *sanctuary* itself) of the *Temple* (at Jerusalem or elsewhere):— temple.

2412. ἱεροπρεπής **hiĕrŏprĕpēs**, *hee-er-op-rep-ace´;* from *2413* and the same as *4241; reverent:*— as becometh holiness.

2413. ἱερός hiĕrŏs, hee-er-os´; of uncert. aff.; sacred:— holy.

2414. Ἱεροσόλυμα Hiĕrŏsŏluma, hee-er-os-ol´-oo-mah; of Heb. or. [3389]; Hierosolyma (i.e. Jerushalaim), the capital of Pal.:— Jerusalem. Comp. 2419.

2415. Ἱεροσολυμίτης Hiĕrŏsŏlumitēs, hee-er-os-ol-oo-mee´-tace; from 2414; a Hierosolymite, i.e. inhab. of Hierosolyma:— of Jerusalem.

2416. ἱεροσυλέω hiĕrŏsuléō, hee-er-os-ool-eh´-o; from 2417; to be a temple-robber (fig.):— commit sacrilege.

2417. ἱερόσυλος hiĕrŏsulŏs, hee-er-os´-oo-los; from 2411 and 4813; a temple-despoiler:— robber of churches.

2418. ἱερουργέω hiĕrŏurgĕō, hee-er-oorg-eh´-o; from a compound of 2411 and the base of 2041; to be a temple-worker, i.e. officiate as a priest (fig.):— minister.

2419. Ἱερουσαλήμ Hiĕrŏusalēm, hee-er-oo-sal-ame´; of Heb. or. [3389]; Hierusalem (i.e. Jerushalem), the capital of Pal.:— Jerusalem. Comp. 2414.

2420. ἱερωσύνη hiĕrŏsunē, hee-er-o-soo´-nay; from 2413; sacredness, i.e. (by impl.) the priestly office:— priesthood.

2421. Ἰεσσαί Iĕssai, es-es-sah´-ee; of Heb. or. [3448]; Jessae (i.e. Jishai), an Isr.:— Jesse.

2422. Ἰεφθάε Iĕphthaĕ, ee-ef-thah´-eh; of Heb. or. [3316]; Jephthaë (i.e. Jiphtach), an Isr.:— Jephthah.

2423. Ἰεχονίας Iĕchŏnias, ee-ekh-on-ee´-as; of Heb. or. [3204]; Jechonias (i.e. Jekonjah), an Isr.:— Jechonias.

2424. Ἰησοῦς Iēsŏus, ee-ay-sooce´; of Heb. or. [3091]; Jesus (i.e. Jehoshua), the name of our Lord and two (three) other Isr.:— Jesus.

2425. ἱκανός hikanŏs, hik-an-os´; from ἵκω hikō ἵκανω hikanō or ἱκνέομαι hiknĕŏmai, akin to 2240] (to arrive); competent (as if coming in season), i.e. ample (in amount) or fit (in character):— able, + content, enough, good, great, large, long (while), many, meet, much, security, sore, sufficient, worthy.

2426. ἱκανότης hikanŏtēs, hik-an-ot´-ace; from 2425; ability:— sufficiency.

2427. ἱκανόω hikanŏō, hik-an-ŏ´-o; from 2425; to enable, i.e. qualify:— make able (meet).

2428. ἱκετηρία hikĕtēria, hik-et-ay-ree´-ah; from a der. of the base of 2425 (through the idea of approaching for a favor); intreaty:— supplication.

2429. ἱκμάς hikmas, hik-mas´; of uncert aff.; dampness:— moisture.

2430. Ἰκόνιον Ikŏniŏn, ee-kon´-ee-on; perh. from 1504; image-like; Iconium, a place in Asia Minor:— Iconium.

2431. ἱλαρός hilarŏs, hil-ar-os´; from the same as 2436; propitious or merry ("hilarious"), i.e. prompt or willing:— cheerful.

2432. ἱλαρότης hilarŏtēs, hil-ar-ot´-ace; from 2431; alacrity:— cheerfulness.

2433. ἱλάσκομαι hilaskŏmai, hil-as´-kom-ahee; mid. voice from the same as

2436; to conciliate, i.e. (tran.) to atone for (sin), or (intr.) be propitious:— be merciful, make reconciliation for.

2434. ἱλασμός hilasmŏs, hil-as-mos´; atonement, i.e. (concr.) an expiator:— propitiation.

2435. ἱλαστήριον hilastēriŏn, hil-as-tay´-ree-on; neut. of a der. of 2433; an expiatory (place or thing), i.e. (concr.) an atoning victim, or (spec.) the lid of the Ark (in the Temple):— mercyseat, propitiation.

2436. ἵλεως hilĕōs, hil´-eh-oce; perh. from the alt. form of 138; cheerful (as attractive), i.e. propitious; adv. (by Heb.) God be gracious!, i.e. (in averting some calamity) far be it:— be it far, merciful.

2437. Ἰλλυρικόν Illurikŏn, il-loo-ree-kon´; neut. of an adj. from a name of uncert. der.: (the) Illyrican (shore), i.e. (as a name itself) Illyricum, a region of Europe:— Illyricum.

2438. ἱμάς himas, hee-mas´; perh. from the same as 260; a strap, i.e. (spec.) the tie (of a sandal) or the lash (of a scourge):— latchet, thong.

2439. ἱματίζω himatizō, him-at-id´-zo; from 2440; to dress:— clothe.

2440. ἱμάτιον himatiŏn, him-at´-ee-on; neut. of a presumed der. of ἕννυμι ĕnnumi (to put on); a dress (inner or outer):— apparel, cloke, clothes, garment, raiment, robe, vesture.

2441. ἱματισμός himatismŏs, him-at-is-mos´; from 2439; clothing:— apparel (x -led); array, raiment, vesture.

2442. ἱμείρομαι himĕirŏmai, him-i´-rom-ahee; mid. voice from ἵμερος himĕrŏs (a yearning; of uncert. aff.); to long for:— be affectionately desirous.

2443. ἵνα hina, hin´-ah; prob. from the same as the former part of 1438 (through the demonstrative idea; comp. 3588); in order that (denoting the purpose or the result):— albeit, because, to the intent (that), lest, so as, (so) that, (for) to. Comp. 3363.

ἵνα μή hina mē. See 3363.

2444. ἱνατί hinati, hin-at-ee´; from 2443 and 5101; for what reason?, i.e. why?:— wherefore, why.

2445. Ἰόππη Iŏppē, ee-op´-pay; of Heb. or. [3305]; Joppe (i.e. Japho), a place in Pal.:— Joppa.

2446. Ἰορδάνης Iŏrdanēs, ee-or-dan´-ace; of Heb. or. [3383]; the Jordanes (i.e. Jarden), a river of Pal.:— Jordan.

2447. ἰός iŏs, ee-os´; perh. from εἶμι ĕimi (to go) or ἵημι hiĕmi (to send); rust (as if emitted by metals); also venom (as emitted by serpents):— poison, rust.

2448. Ἰουδά Iŏuda, ee-oo-dah´; of Heb. or. [3063 or perh. 3194]; Judah (i.e. Jehudah or Juttah), a part of (or place in) Pal.:— Judah.

2449. Ἰουδαία Iŏudaia, ee-oo-dah´-yah; fem. of 2453 (with 1093 impl.); the Judæan land (i.e. Judæa), a region of Pal.:— Judæa.

2450. Ἰουδαΐζω Iŏudaizō, ee-oo-dah-id´-zo; from 2453; to become a Judæan, i.e. "Judaize":— live as the Jews.

2451. Ἰουδαϊκός Iŏudaïkŏs, ee-oo-dah-ee-kos´; from 2453; Judaïc, i.e. resembling a Judæan:— Jewish.

2452. Ἰουδαϊκῶς Iŏudaïkōs, ee-oo-dah-ee-koce´; adv. from 2451; Judaïcally or in a manner resembling a Judæan:— as do the Jews.

2453. Ἰουδαῖος Iŏudaiŏs, ee-oo-dah´-yos; from 2448 (in the sense of 2455 as a country); Judæan, i.e. belonging to Jehudah:— Jew (-ess), of Judæa.

2454. Ἰουδαϊσμός Iŏudaismŏs, ee-oo-dah-is-mos´; from 2450; "Judaism", i.e. the Jewish faith and usages:— Jews' religion.

2455. Ἰουδάς Iŏudas, ee-oo-das´; of Heb. or. [3063]; Judas (i.e. Jehudah), the name of ten Isr.; also of the posterity of one of them and its region:— Juda (-h, -s); Jude.

2456. Ἰουλία Iŏulia, ee-oo-lee´-ah; fem. of the same as 2457; Julia, a Chr. woman:— Julia.

2457. Ἰούλιος Iŏuliŏs, ee-oo´-lee-os; of Lat. or.; Julius, a centurion:— Julius.

2458. Ἰουνίας Iŏunias, ee-oo-nee´-as; of Lat. or.; Junias, a Chr.:— Junias.

2459. Ἰοῦστος Iŏustŏs, ee-ooce´-tos; of Lat. or. ("just"); Justus, the name of three Chr.:— Justus.

2460. ἱππεύς hippĕus, hip-yooce´; from 2462; an equestrian, i.e. member of a cavalry corps:— horseman.

2461. ἱππικόν hippikŏn, hip-pee-kon´; neut. of a der. of 2462; the cavalry force:— horse (-men).

2462. ἵππος hippŏs, hip´-pos; of uncert. aff.; a horse:— horse.

2463. ἶρις iris, ee´-ris; perh. from 2046 (as a symbol of the female messenger of the pagan deities); a rainbow ("iris"):— rainbow.

2464. Ἰσαάκ Isaak, ee-sah-ak´; of Heb. or. [3327]; Isaac (i.e. Jitschak), the son of Abraham:— Isaac.

2465. ἰσάγγελος isaggĕlŏs, ee-sang´-el-los; from 2470 and 32; like an angel, i.e. angelic:— equal unto the angels.

2466. Ἰσαχάρ Isachar, ee-sakh-ar´; of Heb. or. [3485]; Isachar (i.e. Jissaskar), a son of Jacob (fig. his desc.):— Issachar.

2467. ἴστημι isēmi, is´-ay-mee; assumed by some as the base of cert. irreg. forms of 1492; to know:— know.

2468. ἴσθι isthi, is´-thee; second pers. imper. present of 1510; be thou:— + agree, be, × give thyself unto it.

2469. Ἰσκαριώτης Iskariōtēs, is-kar-ee-o´-tace; of Heb. or. [prob. 377 and 7149]; inhabitant of Kerioth; Iscariotes (i.e. Keriothite), an epithet of Judas the traitor:— Iscariot.

2470. ἴσος isŏs, ee´-sos; prob. from 1492 (through the idea of seeming); similar (in amount and kind):— + agree, as much, equal, like.

2471. ἰσότης isŏtēs, ee-sot´-ace; likeness (in condition or proportion); by impl. equity:— equal (-ity).

2472. ἰσότιμος isŏtimŏs, ee-sot´-ee-

mos; from 2470 and 5092; *of equal value* or *honor:*— like precious.

2473. ἰσόψυχος **isŏpsuchŏs,** *ee-sop´-soo-khos;* from 2470 and 5590; *of similar spirit:*— likeminded.

2474. Ἰσραήλ **Israēl,** *is-rah-ale´;* of Heb. or. [3478]; *Israel* (i.e. *Jisrael*), the adopted name of Jacob, incl. his desc. (lit. or fig.):— Israel.

2475. Ἰσραηλίτης **Israēlitēs,** *is-rah-ale-ee´-tace;* from 2474; an *"Israelite",* i.e. desc. of Israel (lit. or fig.):— Israelite.

2476. ἵστημι **histēmi,** *his´-tay-mee;* a prol. form of a primary στάω **staō,** *stah´-o* (of the same mean., and used for it in certain tenses); *to stand* (tran. or intr.), used in various applications (lit. or fig.):— abide, appoint, bring, continue, covenant, establish, hold up, lay, present, set (up), stanch, stand (by, forth, still, up). Comp. 5087.

2477. ἱστορέω **histŏrĕō,** *his-tor-eh´-o;* from a der. of 1492; *to be knowing* (*learned*), i.e. (by impl.) *to visit* for information (*interview*):— see.

2478. ἰσχυρός **ischurŏs,** *is-khoo-ros´;* from 2479; *forcible* (lit. or fig.):— boisterous, mighty (-ier), powerful, strong (-er, man), valiant.

2479. ἰσχύς **ischus,** *is-khoos´;* from a der. of ἴς **is** (*force;* comp. ἔσχον **ĕschŏn,** a form of 2192); *forcefulness* (lit. or fig.):— ability, might (-ily), power, strength.

2480. ἰσχύω **ischuō,** *is-khoo´-o;* from 2479; *to have* (or *exercise*) *force* (lit. or fig.):— be able, avail, can do (I-notI), could, be good, might, prevail, be of strength, be whole, + much work.

2481. ἴσως **isŏs,** *ee´-soce;* adv. from 2470; *likely,* i.e. *perhaps:*— it may be.

2482. Ἰταλία **Italia,** *ee-tal-ee´-ah;* prob. of for. or.; *Italia,* a region of Europe:— Italy.

2483. Ἰταλικός **Italikŏs,** *ee-tal-ee-kos´;* from 2482; *Italic,* i.e. belonging to Italia:— Italian.

2484. Ἰτουραία **Itŏuraia,** *ee-too-rah´-yah;* of Heb. or. [3195]; *Ituræa* (i.e. *Jetur*), a region of Pal.:— Ituræa.

2485. ἰχθύδιον **ichthudiŏn,** *ikh-thoo´-dee-on;* dimin. from 2486; a *petty fish:*— little (small) fish.

2486. ἰχθύς **ichthus,** *ikh-thoos´;* of uncert. aff.; a *fish:*— fish.

2487. ἴχνος **ichnŏs,** *ikh´-nos;* from ἱκνέομαι **iknĕŏmai** (to *arrive;* comp. 2240); a *track* (fig.):— step.

2488. Ἰωάθαμ **Iŏatham,** *ee-o-ath´-am;* of Heb. or. [3147]; *Joatham* (i.e. *Jotham*), an Isr.:— Joatham.

2489. Ἰωάννα **Iŏanna,** *ee-o-an´-nah;* fem. of the same as 2491; *Joanna,* a Chr.:— Joanna.

2490. Ἰωαννᾶς **Iŏannas,** *ee-o-an-nas´;* a form of 2491; *Joannas,* an Isr.:— Joannas.

2491. Ἰωάννης **Iŏannēs,** *ee-o-an´-nace;* of Heb. or. [3110]; *Joannes* (i.e. *Jochanan*), the name of four Isr.:— John.

2492. Ἰώβ **Iŏb,** *ee-obe´;* of Heb. or. [347]; *Job* (i.e. *Ijob*), a patriarch:— Job.

2493. Ἰωήλ **Iŏēl,** *ee-o-ale´;* of Heb. or. [3100]; *Joel,* an Isr.:— Joel.

2494. Ἰωνάν **Iŏnan,** *ee-o-nan´* or Ιωναμ **Iŏnam,** *ee-o-nam´;* prob. for 2491 or 2495; *Jonan,* an Isr.:— Jonan (Jonam).

2495. Ἰωνᾶς **Iŏnas,** *ee-o-nas´;* of Heb. or. [3124]; *Jonas* (i.e. *Jonah*), the name of two Isr.:— Jonas.

2496. Ἰωράμ **Iŏram,** *ee-o-ram´;* of Heb. or. [3141]; *Joram,* an Isr.:— Joram.

2497. Ἰωρείμ **Iŏrĕim,** *ee-o-rime´* or Ἰωρίμ **Iŏrim,** *ee-o-reem´;* perh. for 2496; *Jorim,* an Isr.:— Jorim.

2498. Ἰωσαφάτ **Iŏsaphat,** *ee-o-saf-at´;* of Heb. or. [3092]; *Josaphat* (i.e. *Jehoshaphat*), an Isr.:— Josaphat.

2499. Ἰωσή **Iŏsē,** *ee-o-say´;* gen. of 2500; *Jose,* an Isr.:— Jose.

2500. Ἰωσῆς **Iŏsēs,** *ee-o-sace´;* perh. for 2501; *Joses,* the name of two Isr.:— Joses. Comp. 2499.

2501. Ἰωσήφ **Iŏsēph,** *ee-o-safe´;* of Heb. or. [3130]; *Joseph,* the name of seven Isr.:— Joseph.

2502. Ἰωσίας **Iŏsias,** *ee-o-see´-as;* of Heb. or. [2977]; *Josias* (i.e. *Josiah*), an Isr.:— Josias.

2503. ἰῶτα **iŏta,** *ee-o´-tah;* of Heb. or. [the tenth letter of the Heb. alphabet]; *"iota,"* the name of the eighth letter of the Greek alphabet, put (fig.) for a very small part of anything:— jot.

Κ

2504. κἀγώ **kagō,** *kag-o´;* from 2532 and 1473 (so also the dat.

κἀμοί **kamŏi,** *kam-oy´;* and acc.

κἀμέ **kamĕ,** *kam-eh´; and* (or *also, even,* etc.) *I,* (*to*) *me:*— (and, even, even so, so) I (also, in like wise), both me, me also.

2505. καθά **katha,** *kath-ah´;* from 2596 and the neut. plur. of 3739; *according to which* things, i.e. *just as:*— as.

2506. καθαίρεσις **kathairĕsis,** *kath-ah´-ee-res-is;* from 2507; *demolition;* fig. *extinction:*— destruction, pulling down.

2507. καθαιρέω **kathairĕō,** *kath-ahee-reh´-o;* from 2596 and 138 (incl. its alt.); *to lower* (or *with violence*) *demolish* (lit. or fig.):— cast (pull, put, take) down, destroy.

2508. καθαίρω **kathairō,** *kath-ah´-ee-ro;* from 2513; *to cleanse,* i.e. (spec.) *to prune;* fig. *to expiate:*— purge.

2509. καθάπερ **kathapĕr,** *kath-ap´-er;* from 2505 and 4007; *exactly as:*— (even, as well) as.

2510. καθάπτω **kathaptō,** *kath-ap´-to;* from 2596 and 680; *to seize upon:*— fasten on.

2511. καθαρίζω **katharizō,** *kath-ar-id´-zo;* from 2513; *to cleanse* (lit. or fig.):— (make) clean (-se), purge, purify.

2512. καθαρισμός **katharismŏs,** *kath-ar-is-mos´;* from 2511; a *washing* off, i.e. (cer.) *ablution,* (mor.) *expiation:*— cleansing, + purge, purification (-fying).

2513. καθαρός **katharŏs,** *kath-ar-os´;* of

uncert. aff.; *clean* (lit. or fig.):— clean, clear, pure.

2514. καθαρότης **katharŏtēs,** *kath-ar-ot´-ace;* from 2513; *cleanness* (cer.):— purification.

2515. καθέδρα **kathĕdra,** *kath-ed´-rah;* from 2596 and the same as 1476; a *bench* (lit. or fig.):— seat.

2516. καθέζομαι **kathĕzŏmai,** *kath-ed´-zom-ahee;* from 2596 and the base of 1476; *to sit down:*— sit.

2517. καθεξῆς **kathĕxēs,** *kath-ex-ace´;* from 2596 and 1836; *thereafter,* i.e. *consecutively;* as a noun (by ellip. of noun) a *subsequent* person or time:— after (-ward), by (in) order.

2518. καθεύδω **kathĕudō,** *kath-yoo´-do;* from 2596 and εὕδω **hĕudō** (to *sleep*); *to lie down to rest,* i.e. (by impl.) *to fall asleep* (lit. or fig.):— (be a-) sleep.

2519. καθηγητής **kathēgĕtēs,** *kath-ayg-ay-tace´;* from a compound of 2596 and 2233; a *guide,* i.e. (fig.) a *teacher:*— master.

2520. καθήκω **kathēkō,** *kath-ay´-ko;* from 2596 and 2240; *to reach to,* i.e. (neut. of pres. act. part., fig. as adj.) *becoming:*— convenient, fit.

2521. κάθημαι **kathēmai,** *kath´-ay-mahee;* from 2596; and ἧμαι **hēmai** (to *sit;* akin to the base of 1476); *to sit down;* fig. *to remain, reside:*— dwell, sit (by, down).

2522. καθημερινός **kathēmĕrinŏs,** *kath-ay-mer-ee-nos´;* from 2596 and 2250; *quotidian:*— daily.

2523. καθίζω **kathizō,** *kath-id´-zo;* another (act.) form for 2516; *to seat down,* i.e. *set* (fig. *appoint*); intr. *to sit* (down); fig. *to settle* (*hover, dwell*):— continue, set, sit (down), tarry.

2524. καθίημι **kathiēmi,** *kath-ee´-ay-mee;* from 2596; and ἵημι **hiēmi** (to *send*); *to lower:*— let down.

2525. καθίστημι **kathistēmi,** *kath-is´-tay-mee;* from 2596 and 2476; *to place down* (permanently), i.e. (fig.) *to designate, constitute, convoy:*— appoint, be, conduct, make, ordain, set.

2526. καθό **kathŏ,** *kath-o´;* from 2596 and 3739; *according to which* thing, i.e. *precisely as, in proportion as:*— according to that, (inasmuch) as.

2526´. καθολικός **kathŏlikŏs,** *kath-ol-ee-kos´;* from 2527; *universal:*— general.

2527. καθόλου **kathŏlŏu,** *kath-ol´-oo;* from 2596 and 3650; *on the whole,* i.e. *entirely:*— at all.

2528. καθοπλίζω **kathŏplizō,** *kath-op-lid´-zo;* from 2596; and 3695; *to equip fully* with armor:— arm.

2529. καθοράω **kathŏraō,** *kath-or-ah´-o;* from 2596 and 3708; *to behold fully,* i.e. (fig.) *distinctly apprehend:*— clearly see.

2530. καθότι **kathŏti,** *kath-ot´-ee;* from 2596; and 3739 and 5100; *according to which certain* thing, i.e. *as far* (or *inasmuch*) *as:*— (according, forasmuch) as, because (that).

2531. καθώς **kathōs,** *kath-oce´;* from 2596 and 5613; *just* (or *inasmuch*) *as,* *that*:— according to, (according, even) as, how, when.

2532. καί **kai,** *kahee*; appar. a primary particle, having a *copulative* and sometimes also a *cumulative* force; *and, also, even, so, then, too,* etc.; often used in connection (or composition) with other particles or small words:— and, also, both, but, even, for, if, indeed, likewise, moreover, or, so, that, then, therefore, when, yet.

2533. Καϊάφας **Kaïaphas,** *kah-ee-af´-as*; of Chald. or.; *the dell; Caïaphas* (i.e. *Cajepha*), an Isr.:— Caiaphas.

2534. καίγε **kaige,** *kah´-ee-gheh*; from *2532* and *1065; and at least* (or *even, indeed*):— and, at least.

2535. Κάϊν **Kaïn,** *kah´-in*; of Heb. or. [7014]; *Caïn,* (i.e. *Cajin*), the son of Adam:— Cain.

2536. Καϊνάν **Kaïnan,** *kah-ee-nan´* or

Καϊνάμ **Kaïnam** *kah-ee-nam´*; of Heb. or. [7018]; *Caïnan* (i.e. *Kenan*), the name of two patriarchs:— Cainan (Cainam).

2537. καινός **kainŏs,** *kahee-nos´*; of uncert. aff.; *new* (espec. in *freshness;* while *3501* is prop. so with respect to *age*:— new.

2538. καινότης **kainŏtēs,** *kahee-not´-ace;* from *2537; renewal* (fig.):— newness.

2539. καίπερ **kaipĕr,** *kah´-ee-per;* from *2532* and *4007;* and *indeed,* i.e. *nevertheless* or *notwithstanding*:— and yet, although.

2540. καιρός **kairŏs,** *kahee-ros´;* of uncert. aff.; an *occasion,* i.e. *set* or *proper time*:— × always, opportunity, (convenient, due) season, (due, short, while) time, a while. Comp. *5550.*

2541. Καῖσαρ **Kaisar,** *kah´-ee-sar;* of Lat. or.; *Cæsar,* a title of the Rom. emperor:— Cæsar.

2542. Καισάρεια **Kaisarĕia,** *kahee-sar´-i-a;* from *2541; Cæsaria,* the name of two places in Pal.:— Cæsarea.

2543. καίτοι **kaitŏi,** *kah´-ee-toy;* from *2532* and *5104; and yet,* i.e. *nevertheless*:— although.

2544. καίτοιγε **kaitŏigĕ,** *kah´-ee-toyg-eh;* from *2543* and *1065; and yet indeed,* i.e. *although really*:— nevertheless, though.

2545. καίω **kaiō,** *kah´-yo;* appar. a primary verb; *to set on fire,* i.e. *kindle* or (by impl.) *consume*:— burn, light.

2546. κἀκεῖ **kakĕi,** *kak-i´;* from *2532* and *1563; likewise in that place*:— and there, there (thither) also.

2547. κἀκεῖθεν **kakĕithĕn,** *kak-i´-then;* from *2532* and *1564; likewise from that place* (or *time*):— and afterward (from) (thence), thence also.

2548. κἀκεῖνος **kakĕinŏs,** *kak-i´-nos;* from *2532* and *1565; likewise that* (or *those*):— and him (other, them), even he, him also, them (also), (and) they.

2549. κακία **kakia,** *kak-ee´-ah;* from *2556; badness,* i.e. (subj.) *depravity,* or (act.) *malignity,* or (pass.) *trouble*:— evil, malice (-iousness), naughtiness, wickedness.

2550. κακοήθεια **kakŏēthĕia,** *kak-ŏ-ay´-thi-ah;* from a compound of *2556* and *2239; bad character,* i.e. (spec.) *mischievousness*:— malignity.

2551. κακολογέω **kakŏlŏgĕō,** *kak-ol-og-eh´-o;* from a compound of *2556* and *3056; to revile*:— curse, speak evil of.

2552. κακοπάθεια **kakŏpathĕia,** *kak-op-ath´-i-ah;* from a compound of *2556* and *3806; hardship*:— suffering affliction.

2553. κακοπαθέω **kakŏpathĕō,** *kak-op-ath-eh´-o;* from the same as *2552;* to *undergo hardship*:— be afflicted, endure afflictions (hardness), suffer trouble.

2554. κακοποιέω **kakŏpŏiĕō,** *kak-op-oy-eh´-o;* from *2555;* to *be a bad-doer,* i.e. (obj.) to *injure,* or (gen.) to *sin*:— do (ing) evil.

2555. κακοποιός **kakŏpŏiŏs,** *kak-op-oy-os´;* from *2556* and *4160;* a *bad-doer;* (spec.) a *criminal*:— evil-doer, malefactor.

2556. κακός **kakŏs,** *kak-os´;* appar. a primary word; *worthless* (intrinsically, such; whereas *4190* prop. refers to *effects*), i.e. (subj.) *depraved,* or (obj.) *injurious*:— bad, evil, harm, ill, noisome, wicked.

2557. κακοῦργος **kakŏurgŏs,** *kak-oor´-gos;* from *2556* and the base of *2041;* a *wrong-doer,* i.e. *criminal*:— evil-doer, malefactor.

2558. κακουχέω **kakŏuchĕō,** *kak-oo-kheh´-o;* from a presumed compound of *2556* and *2192;* to *maltreat*:— which suffer adversity, torment.

2559. κακόω **kakŏō,** *kak-ŏ´-o;* from *2556;* to *injure;* fig. to *exasperate*:— make evil affected, entreat evil, harm, hurt, vex.

2560. κακῶς **kakŏs,** *kak-oce´;* from *2556; badly* (phys. or mor.):— amiss, diseased, evil, grievously, miserably, sick, sore.

2561. κάκωσις **kakōsis,** *kak´-o-sis;* from *2559; maltreatment*:— affliction.

2562. καλάμη **kalamē,** *kal-am´-ay;* fem. of *2563;* a *stalk* of grain, i.e. (collect.) *stubble*:— stubble.

2563. κάλαμος **kalamŏs,** *kal´-am-os;* or uncert. aff.; a *reed* (the plant or its stem, or that of a similar plant); by impl. a *pen*:— pen, reed.

2564. καλέω **kalĕō,** *kal-eh´-o;* akin to the base of *2753;* to *"call"* (prop. aloud, but used in a variety of applications, dir. or otherwise):— bid, call (forth), (whose, whose sur-) name (was [called]).

2565. καλλιέλαιος **kalliĕlaiŏs,** *kal-le-el´-ah-yos;* from the base of *2566* and *1636;* a *cultivated olive* tree, i.e. a *domesticated* or *improved* one:— good olive tree.

2566. κάλλιον **kalliŏn,** *kal-lee´-on;* neut. of the (irreg.) comp. of *2570;* (adv.) *better than many*:— very well.

2567. καλοδιδάσκαλος **kalŏdidaskalŏs,** *kal-od-id-as´-kal-os;* from *2570* and *1320;* a *teacher of the right*:— teacher of good things.

2568. Καλοὶ Λιμένες **Kalŏi Limĕnĕs,**

kal-oy´ lee-men´-es; plur. of *2570* and *3040; Good Harbors,* i.e. *Fairhaven,* a bay of Crete:— fair havens.

2569. καλοποιέω **kalŏpŏiĕō,** *kal-op-oy-eh´-o;* from *2570* and *4160;* to *do well,* i.e. live virtuously:— well doing.

2570. καλός **kalŏs,** *kal-os´;* of uncert. aff.; prop. *beautiful,* but chiefly (fig.) *good* (lit. or mor.), i.e. *valuable* or *virtuous* (for *appearance* or *use,* and thus distinguished from *18,* which is prop. *intrinsic*):— × better, fair, good (-ly), honest, meet, well, worthy.

2571. κάλυμα **kaluma,** *kal´-oo-mah;* from *2572;* a *cover,* i.e. *veil*:— vail.

2572. καλύπτω **kaluptō,** *kal-oop´-to;* akin to *2813* and *2928;* to *cover* up (lit. or fig.):— cover, hide.

2573. καλῶς **kalŏs,** *kal-oce´;* adv. from *2570; well* (usually mor.):— (in a) good (place), honestly, + recover, (full) well.

2574. κάμηλος **kamēlŏs,** *kam´-ay-los;* of Heb. or. [1581]; a *"camel"*:— camel.

2575. κάμινος **kaminŏs,** *kam´-ee-nos;* prob. from *2545;* a *furnace*:— furnace.

2576. καμμύω **kammuō,** *kam-moo´-o;* from a compound of *2596* and the base of *3466;* to *shut down,* i.e. *close* the eyes:— close.

2577. κάμνω **kamnō,** *kam´-no;* appar. a primary verb; prop. to *toil,* i.e. (by impl.) to *tire* (fig. *faint, sicken*):— faint, sick, be wearied.

2578. κάμπτω **kamptō,** *kamp´-to;* appar. a primary verb; to *bend*:— bow.

2579. κἄν **kan,** *kan;* from *2532* and *1437; and* (or *even*) *if*:— and (also) if (so much as), if but, at the least, though, yet.

2580. Κανᾶ **Kana,** *kan-ah´;* of Heb. or. [comp. 7071]; *Cana,* a place in Pal.:— Cana.

2581. Κανανίτης **Kananitēs,** *kan-an-ee´-tace;* of Chald. or. [comp. 7067]; *zealous; Cananitēs,* an epithet:— Canaanite [by mistake for a der. from 5477].

2582. Κανδάκη **Kandakē,** *kan-dak´-ay;* of for. or.; *Candacē,* an Eg. queen:— Candace.

2583. κανών **kanōn,** *kan-ohn´;* from κάνη **kanē** (a straight *reed,* i.e. *rod*); a *rule* ("canon"), i.e. (fig.) a *standard* (of faith and practice); by impl. a *boundary,* i.e. (fig.) a *sphere* (of activity):— line, rule.

2584. Καπερναούμ **Kapĕrnaŏum,** *kap-er-nah-oom´;* of Heb. or. [prob. 3723 and 5151]; *Capernaüm* (i.e. *Caphanachum*), a place in Pal.:— Capernaum.

2585. καπηλεύω **kapēlĕuō,** *kap-ale-yoo´-o;* from κάπηλος **kapēlŏs** (a *huckster*); to *retail,* i.e. (by impl.) to *adulterate* (fig.):— corrupt.

2586. καπνός **kapnŏs,** *kap-nos´;* of uncert. aff.; *smoke*:— smoke.

2587. Καππαδοκία **Kappadŏkia,** *kappad-ok-ee´-ah;* of for. or.; *Cappadocia,* a region of Asia Minor:— Cappadocia.

2588. καρδία **kardia,** *kar-dee´-ah;* prol. from a primary κάρ **kar** (Lat. *cor,* *"heart"*); the *heart,* i.e. (fig.) the *thoughts* or *feelings* (*mind*); also (by anal.) the *middle*:— (+ broken-) heart (-ed).

2589. καρδιογνώστης **kardiŏgnōstēs**, *kar-dee-og-noce´-tace*; from 2588 and 1097; a *heart-knower*:— which knowest the hearts.

2590. καρπός **karpŏs**, *kar-pos´*; prob. from the base of 726; *fruit* (as *plucked*), lit. or fig.:— fruit.

2591. Κάρπος **Karpŏs**, *kar´-pos*; perh. for 2590; *Carpus*, prob. a Chr.:— Carpus.

2592. καρποφορέω **karpŏphŏrĕō**, *kar-pof-or-eh´-o*; from 2593; to *be fertile* (lit. or fig.):— be (bear, bring forth) fruit (-ful).

2593. καρποφόρος **karpŏphŏrŏs**, *kar-pof-or´-os*; from 2590 and 5342; *fruit-bearing* (fig.):— fruitful.

2594. καρτερέω **kartĕrĕō**, *kar-ter-eh´-o*; from a der. of 2904 (transp.); to *be strong*, i.e. (fig.) *steadfast* (*patient*):— endure.

2595. κάρφος **karphŏs**, *kar´-fos*; from κάρφω **karphō** (to *wither*); a dry *twig* or *straw*:— mote.

2596. κατά **kata**, *kat-ah´*; a primary particle; (prep.) *down* (in place or time), in varied relations (according to the case [gen., dat. or acc.] with which it is joined):— about, according as (to), after, against, (when they were) × alone, among, and, × apart, (even, like) as (concerning, pertaining to touching), × aside, at, before, beyond, by, to the charge of, [charita-] bly, concerning, + covered, [dai-] ly, down, every, (+ far more) exceeding, × more excellent, for, from ... to, godly, in (-asmuch, divers, every, -to, respect of), ... by, after the manner of, + by any means, beyond (out of) measure, × mightily, more, × natural, of (up-) on (× part), out (of every), over against, (+ your) × own, + particularly, so, through (-oughout, oughout every), thus, (un-) to (-gether, -ward), × uttermost, where (-by), with. In composition it retains many of these applications, and frequently denotes *opposition, distribution,* or *intensity*.

2597. καταβαίνω **katabainō**, *kat-ab-ah´-ee-no*; from 2596 and the base of 939; to *descend* (lit. or fig.):— come (get, go, step) down, descend, fall (down).

2598. καταβάλλω **kataballō**, *kat-ab-al´-lo*; from 2596 and 906; to *throw down*:— cast down, descend, fall (down), lay.

2599. καταβαρέω **katabarĕō**, *kat-ab-ar-eh´-o*; from 2596 and 916; to *impose upon*:— burden.

2600. κατάβασις **katabasis**, *kat-ab´-as-is*; from 2597; a *declivity*:— descent.

2601. καταβιβάζω **katabibazō**, *kat-ab-ib-ad´-zo*; from 2596 and a der. of the base of 939; to *cause to go down*, i.e. *precipitate*:— bring (thrust) down.

2602. καταβολή **katabŏlē**, *kat-ab-ol-ay´*; from 2598; a *deposition*, i.e. *founding*; fig. *conception*:— conceive, foundation.

2603. καταβραβεύω **katabrabĕuō**, *kat-ab-rab-yoo´-o*; from 2596 and 1018 (in its orig. sense); to *award the price*

against, i.e. (fig.) to *defraud* (of salvation):— beguile of reward.

2604. καταγγελεύς **kataggĕlĕus**, *kat-ang-gel-yooce´*; from 2605; a *proclaimer*:— setter forth.

2605. καταγγέλλω **kataggĕllō**, *kat-ang-gel´-lo*; from 2596 and the base of 32; to *proclaim, promulgate*:— declare, preach, shew, speak of, teach.

2606. καταγελάω **katagĕlaō**, *kat-ag-el-ah´-o*; to *laugh down*, i.e. *deride*:— laugh to scorn.

2607. καταγινώσκω **kataginōskō**, *kat-ag-in-o´-sko*; from 2596 and 1097; to *note against*, i.e. *find fault with*:— blame, condemn.

2608. κατάγνυμι **katagnumi**, *kat-ag´-noo-mee*; from 2596 and the base of 4486; to *rend in pieces*, i.e. *crack apart*:— break.

2609. κατάγω **katagō**, *kat-ag´-o*; from 2596 and 71; to *lead down*; spec. to *moor a vessel*:— bring (down, forth), (bring to) land, touch.

2610. καταγωνίζομαι **katagōnizŏmai**, *kat-ag-o-nid´-zom-ahee*; from 2596 and 75; to *struggle against*, i.e. (by impl.) to *overcome*:— subdue.

2611. καταδέω **katadĕō**, *kat-ad-eh´-o*; from 2596 and 1210; to *tie down*, i.e. *bandage* (a wound):— bind up.

2612. κατάδηλος **katadēlŏs**, *kat-ad´-ay-los*; from 2596 intens. and 1212; *manifest*:— far more evident.

2613. καταδικάζω **katadikazō**, *kat-ad-ik-ad´-zo*; from 2596 and a der. of 1349; to *adjudge against*, i.e. *pronounce guilty*:— condemn.

2614. καταδιώκω **katadiōkō**, *kat-ad-ee-o´-ko*; from 2596 and 1377; to *hunt down*, i.e. *search for*:— follow after.

2615. καταδουλόω **katadŏulŏō**, *kat-ad-oo-lŏ´-o*; from 2596 and 1402; to *enslave utterly*:— bring into bondage.

2616. καταδυναστεύω **katadunastĕuō**, *kat-ad-oo-nas-tyoo´-o*; from 2596 and a der. of 1413; to *exercise dominion against*, i.e. *oppress*:— oppress.

2617. καταισχύνω **kataischunō**, *kat-ahee-skhoo´-no*; from 2596 and 153; to *shame down*, i.e. *disgrace* or (by impl.) *put to the blush*:— confound, dishonour, (be a-, make a-) shame (-d).

2618. κατακαίω **katakaiō**, *kat-ak-ah´-ee-o*; from 2596 and 2545; to *burn down* (to the ground), i.e. *consume wholly*:— burn (up, utterly).

2619. κατακαλύπτω **katakaluptō**, *kat-ak-al-oop´-to*; from 2596 and 2572; to *cover wholly*, i.e. *veil*:— cover, hide.

2620. κατακαυχάομαι **katakauchaŏmai**, *kat-ak-ŏw-khah´-om-ahee*; from 2596 and 2744; to *exult against* (i.e. *over*):— boast (against), glory, rejoice against.

2621. κατάκειμαι **katakĕimai**, *kat-ak´-i-mahee*; from 2596 and 2749; to *lie down*, i.e. (by impl.) *be sick*; spec. to *recline* at a meal:— keep, lie, sit at meat (down).

2622. κατακλάω **kataklaō**, *kat-ak-lah´-o*; from 2596 and 2806; to *break down*, i.e. *divide*:— break.

2623. κατακλείω **kataklĕiō**, *kat-ak-li´-o*; from 2596 and 2808; to *shut down* (in a dungeon), i.e. *incarcerate*:— shut up.

2624. κατακληροδοτέω **kataklērŏdŏtĕō**, *kat-ak-lay-rod-ot-eh´-o*; from 2596 and a der. of a compound of 2819 and 1325; to *be a giver of lots to each*, i.e. (by impl.) to *apportion an estate*:— divide by lot.

2625. κατακλίνω **kataklinō**, *kat-ak-lee´-no*; from 2596 and 2827; to *recline down*, i.e. (spec.) to *take a place* at table:— (make) sit down (at meat).

2626. κατακλύζω **katakluzō**, *kat-ak-lood´-zo*; from 2596 and the base of 2830; to *dash* (*wash*) *down*, i.e. (by impl.) to *deluge*:— overflow.

2627. κατακλυσμός **kataklusmŏs**, *kat-ak-looce-mos´*; from 2626; an *inundation*:— flood.

2628. κατακολουθέω **katakŏlŏuthĕō**, *kat-ak-ol-oo-theh´-o*; from 2596 and 190; to *accompany closely*:— follow (after).

2629. κατακόπτω **katakŏptō**, *kat-ak-op´-to*; from 2596 and 2875; to *chop down*, i.e. *mangle*:— cut.

2630. κατακρημνίζω **katakrēmnizō**, *kat-ak-rame-nid´-zo*; from 2596 and a der. of 2911; to *precipitate down*:— cast down headlong.

2631. κατάκριμα **katakrima**, *kat-ak´-ree-mah*; from 2632; an *adverse sentence* (the verdict):— condemnation.

2632. κατακρίνω **katakrinō**, *kat-ak-ree´-no*; from 2596 and 2919; to *judge against*, i.e. *sentence*:— condemn, damn.

2633. κατάκρισις **katakrisis**, *kat-ak´-ree-sis*; from 2632; *sentencing adversely* (the act):— condemn (-ation).

2634. κατακυριεύω **katakuriĕuō**, *kat-ak-oo-ree-yoo´-o*; from 2596 and 2961; to *lord against*, i.e. *control, subjugate*:— exercise dominion over (lordship), be lord over, overcome.

2635. καταλαλέω **katalalĕō**, *kat-al-al-eh´-o*; from 2637; to *be a traducer*, i.e. to *slander*:— speak against (evil of).

2636. καταλαλία **katalalia**, *kat-al-al-ee´-ah*; from 2637; *defamation*:— backbiting, evil speaking.

2637. κατάλαλος **katalalŏs**, *kat-al´-al-os*; from 2596 and the base of 2980; *talkative against*, i.e. a *slanderer*:— backbiter.

2638. καταλαμβάνω **katalambanō**, *kat-al-am-ban´-o*; from 2596 and 2983; to *take eagerly*, i.e. *seize, possess*, etc. (lit. or fig.):— apprehend, attain, come upon, comprehend, find, obtain, perceive, (over-) take.

2639. καταλέγω **katalĕgō**, *kat-al-eg´-o*; from 2596 and 3004 (in its orig. mean.); to *lay down*, i.e. (fig.) to *enrol*:— take into the number.

2640. κατάλειμμα **katalĕimma**, *kat-al´-ime-mah*; from 2641; a *remainder*, i.e. (by impl.) a *few*:— remnant.

2641. καταλείπω **katalĕipō**, *kat-al-i´-po*; from 2596 and 3007; to *leave down*, i.e. *behind*; by impl. to *abandon, have remaining*:— forsake, leave, reserve.

Greek

2642. καταλιθάζω **katalithazō**, *kat-al-ith-ad´-zo*; from 2596 and 3034; to *stone down*, i.e. to *death*:— stone.

2643. καταλλαγή **katallagē**, *kat-al-lag-ay´*; from 2644; *exchange* (fig. *adjustment*), i.e. *restoration* to (the divine) favor:— atonement, reconciliation (-ing).

2644. καταλλάσσω **katallassō**, *kat-al-las´-so*; from 2596 and 236; to *change mutually*, i.e. (fig.) to *compound* a difference:— reconcile.

2645. κατάλοιπος **kataloipŏs**, *kat-al´-oy-pos*; from 2596 and 3062; *left down* (*behind*), i.e. *remaining* (plur. the *rest*):— residue.

2646. κατάλυμα **kataluma**, *kat-al´-oo-mah*; from 2647; prop. a *dissolution* (breaking up of a journey), i.e. (by impl.) a *lodging-place*:— guestchamber, inn.

2647. καταλύω **kataluō**, *kat-al-oo´-o*; from 2596 and 3089; to *loosen down* (*disintegrate*), i.e. (by impl.) to *demolish* (lit. or fig.); spec. [comp. 2646] to *halt* for the night:— destroy, dissolve, be guest, lodge, come to nought, overthrow, throw down.

2648. καταμανθάνω **katamanthanō**, *kat-am-an-than´-o*; from 2596 and 3129; to *learn thoroughly*, i.e. (by impl.) to *note carefully*:— consider.

2649. καταμαρτυρέω **katamartureō**, *kat-am-ar-too-reh´-o*; from 2596 and 3140; to *testify against*:— witness against.

2650. καταμένω **katamĕnō**, *kat-am-en´-o*; from 2596 and 3306; to *stay fully*, i.e. *reside*:— abide.

2651. καταμόνας **katamŏnas**, *kat-am-on´-as*; from 2596 and acc. plur. fem. of 3441 (with 5561 impl.); *according to sole* places, i.e. (adv.) *separately*:— alone.

2652. κατανάθεμα **katanathĕma**, *kat-an-ath´-em-ah*; from 2596 (intens.) and 331; an *imprecation*:— curse.

2653. καταναθεματίζω **katanathĕmatizō**, *kat-an-ath-em-at-id´-zo*; from 2596 (intens.) and 332; to *imprecate*:— curse.

2654. καταναλίσκω **katanaliskō**, *kat-an-al-is´-ko*; from 2596 and 355; to *consume utterly*:— consume.

2655. καταναρκάω **katanarkaō**, *kat-an-ar-kah´-o*; from 2596 and ναρκάω **narkaō** (to *be numb*); to *grow utterly torpid*, i.e. (by impl.) *slothful* (fig. *expensive*):— be burdensome (chargeable).

2656. κατανεύω **katanĕuō**, *kat-an-yoo´-o*; from 2596 and 3506; to *nod down* (*toward*), i.e. (by anal.) to *make signs* to:— beckon.

2657. κατανοέω **katanŏĕō**, *kat-an-o-eh´-o*; from 2596 and 3539; to *observe fully*:— behold, consider, discover, perceive.

2658. καταντάω **katantaō**, *kat-an-tah´-o*; from 2596 and a der. of 473; to *meet against*, i.e. *arrive* at (lit. or fig.):— attain, come.

2659. κατάνυξις **katanuxis**, *kat-an´-oox-is*; from 2660; a *prickling* (sensa-

tion, as of the limbs *asleep*), i.e. (by impl. [perh. by some confusion with 3506 or even with 3571]) *stupor* (*lethargy*):— slumber.

2660. κατανύσσω **katanussō**, *kat-an-oos´-so*; from 2596 and 3572; to *pierce thoroughly*, i.e. (fig.) to *agitate* violently ("sting to the quick"):— prick.

2661. καταξιόω **kataxiŏō**, *kat-ax-ee-ŏ´-o*; from 2596 and 515; to *deem entirely deserving*:— (ac-) count worthy.

2662. καταπατέω **katapatĕō**, *kat-ap-at-eh´-o*; from 2596 and 3961; to *trample down*; fig. to *reject* with disdain:— trample, tread (down, underfoot).

2663. κατάπαυσις **katapausis**, *kat-ap´-ow-sis*; from 2664; *reposing down*, i.e. (by Heb.) *abode*:— rest.

2664. καταπαύω **katapauō**, *kat-ap-ŏw´-o*; from 2596 and 3973; to *settle down*, i.e. (lit.) to *colonize*, or (fig.) to (*cause* to) *desist*:— cease, (give) rest (-rain).

2665. καταπέτασμα **katapĕtasma**, *kat-ap-et´-as-mah*; from a compound of 2596 and a congener of 4072; something *spread thoroughly*, i.e. (spec.) the door *screen* (to the Most Holy Place) in the Jewish Temple:— vail.

2666. καταπίνω **katapinō**, *kat-ap-ee´-no*; from 2596 and 4095; to *drink down*, i.e. *gulp entire* (lit. or fig.):— devour, drown, swallow (up).

2667. καταπίπτω **katapiptō**, *kat-ap-ip´-to*; from 2596 and 4098; to *fall down*:— fall (down).

2668. καταπλέω **kataplĕō**, *kat-ap-leh´-o*; from 2596 and 4126; to *sail down* upon a place, i.e. to *land at*:— arrive.

2669. καταπονέω **kataponĕō**, *kat-ap-on-eh´-o*; from 2596 and a der. of 4192; to *labor down*, i.e. *wear with toil* (fig. *harass*):— oppress, vex.

2670. καταποντίζω **katapŏntizō**, *kat-ap-on-tid´-zo*; from 2596 and a der. of the same as 4195; to *plunge down*, i.e. *submerge*:— drown, sink.

2671. κατάρα **katara**, *kat-ar´-ah*; from 2596 (intens.) and 685; *imprecation*, *execration*:— curse (-d, ing).

2672. καταράομαι **kataraŏmai**, *kat-ar-ah´-om-ahee*; mid. voice from 2671; to *execrate*; by anal. to *doom*:— curse.

2673. καταργέω **katargĕō**, *kat-arg-eh´-o*; from 2596 and 691; to *be* (*render*) *entirely idle* (*useless*), lit. or fig.:— abolish, cease, cumber, deliver, destroy, do away, become (make) of no (none, without) effect, fail, loose, bring (come) to nought, put away (down), vanish away, make void.

2674. καταριθμέω **katarithmĕō**, *kat-ar-ith-meh´-o*; from 2596 and 705; to *reckon among*:— number with.

2675. καταρτίζω **katartizō**, *kat-ar-tid´-zo*; from 2596 and a der. of 739; to *complete thoroughly*, i.e. *repair* (lit. or fig.) or *adjust*:— fit, frame, mend, (make) perfect (-ly join together), prepare, restore.

2676. κατάρτισις **katartisis**, *kat-ar´-tis-is*; from 2675; *thorough equipment* (subj.):— perfection.

2677. καταρτισμός **katartismŏs**, *kat-ar-*

tis-mos´; from 2675; *complete furnishing* (obj.):— perfecting.

2678. κατασείω **katasĕiō**, *kat-as-i´-o*; from 2596 and 4579; to *sway downward*, i.e. *make a signal*:— beckon.

2679. κατασκάπτω **kataskaptō**, *kat-as-kap´-to*; from 2596 and 4626; to *undermine*, i.e. (by impl.) *destroy*:— dig down, ruin.

2680. κατασκευάζω **kataskĕuazō**, *kat-ask-yoo-ad´-zo*; from 2596 and a der. of 4632; to *prepare thoroughly* (prop. by extern. *equipment*; whereas 2090 refers rather to intern. *fitness*); by impl. to *construct*, *create*:— build, make, ordain, prepare.

2681. κατασκηνόω **kataskēnŏō**, *kat-as-kay-nŏ´-o*; from 2596 and 4637; to *camp down*, i.e. *haunt*; fig. to *remain*:— lodge, rest.

2682. κατασκήνωσις **kataskēnōsis**, *kat-as-kay´-no-sis*; from 2681; an *encamping*, i.e. (fig.) a *perch*:— nest.

2683. κατασκιάζω **kataskiazō**, *kat-as-kee-ad´-zo*; from 2596 and a der. of 4639; to *overshade*, i.e. *cover*:— shadow.

2684. κατασκοπέω **kataskŏpĕō**, *kat-as-kop-eh´-o*; from 2685; to *be a sentinel*, i.e. to *inspect* insidiously:— spy out.

2685. κατάσκοπος **kataskŏpŏs**, *kat-as´-kop-os*; from 2596 (intens.) and 4649 (in the sense of a *watcher*); a *reconnoiterer*:— spy.

2686. κατασοφίζομαι **katasŏphizŏmai**, *kat-as-of-id´-zom-ahee*; mid. voice from 2596 and 4679; to *be crafty against*, i.e. *circumvent*:— deal subtilly (subtly) with.

2687. καταστέλλω **katastĕllō**, *kat-as-tel´-lo*; from 2596 and 4724; to *put down*, i.e. *quell*:— appease, quiet.

2688. κατάστημα **katastēma**, *kat-as´-tay-mah*; from 2525; prop. a *position* or *condition*, i.e. (subj.) *demeanor*:— behaviour.

2689. καταστολή **katastŏlē**, *kat-as-tol-ay´*; from 2687; a *deposit*, i.e. (spec.) *costume*:— apparel.

2690. καταστρέφω **katastrĕphō**, *kat-as-tref´-o*; from 2596 and 4762; to *turn upside down*, i.e. *upset*:— overthrow.

2691. καταστρηνιάω **katastrēniaō**, *kat-as-tray-nee-ah´-o*; from 2596 and 4763; to *become voluptuous against*:— begin to wax wanton against.

2692. καταστροφή **katastrŏphē**, *kat-as-trof-ay´*; from 2690; an *overturn* ("*catastrophe*"), i.e. *demolition*; fig. *apostasy*:— overthrow, subverting.

2693. καταστρώννυμι **katastrōnnumi**, *kat-as-trone´-noo-mee*; from 2596 and 4766; to *strew down*, i.e. (by impl.) to *prostrate* (*slay*):— overthrow.

2694. κατασύρω **katasurō**, *kat-as-oo´-ro*; from 2596 and 4951; to *drag down*, i.e. *arrest* judicially:— hale.

2695. κατασφάττω **katasphattō**, *kat-as-fat´-to*; from 2596 and 4969; to *kill down*, i.e. *slaughter*:— slay.

2696. κατασφραγίζω **katasphragizō**, *kat-as-frag-id´-zo*; from 2596 and 4972; to *seal closely*:— seal.

2697. κατάσχεσις **kataschēsis**, *kat-as´-khes-is*; from 2722; a *holding down*, i.e. *occupancy:*— possession.

2698. κατατίθημι **katatithēmi**, *kat-at-ith´-ay-mee*; from 2596 and 5087; to *place down*, i.e. *deposit* (lit. or fig.):— do, lay, shew.

2699. κατατομή **katatŏmē**, *kat-at-om-ay´*; from a compound of 2596 and τέμνω **tĕmnō** (to *cut*); a *cutting down* (off), i.e. *mutilation* (ironically):— concision. Comp. 609.

2700. κατατοξεύω **katatŏxĕuō**, *kat-at-ox-yoo´-o*; from 2596 and a der. of 5115; to *shoot down* with an arrow or other missile:— thrust through.

2701. κατατρέχω **katatrĕchō**, *kat-at-rekh´-o*; from 2596 and 5143; to *run down*, i.e. *hasten* from a tower:— run down.

καταφάγω **kataphagō**. See 2719.

2702. καταφέρω **kataphĕrō**, *kat-af-er´-o*; from 2596 and 5342 (incl. its alt.); to *bear down*, i.e. (fig.) *overcome* (with drowsiness); spec. to *cast* a vote:— fall, give, sink down.

2703. καταφεύγω **kataphĕugō**, *kat-af-yoo´-go*; from 2596 and 5343; to *flee down* (away):— flee.

2704. καταφθείρω **kataphthĕirō**, *kat-af-thi´-ro*; from 2596 and 5351; to *spoil entirely*, i.e. (lit.) to *destroy*; or (fig.) to *deprave:*— corrupt, utterly perish.

2705. καταφιλέω **kataphilĕō**, *kat-af-ee-leh´-o*; from 2596 and 5368; to *kiss earnestly:*— kiss.

2706. καταφρονέω **kataphrŏnĕō**, *kat-af-ron-eh´-o*; from 2596 and 5426; to *think against*, i.e. *disesteem:*— despise.

2707. καταφροντής **kataphrŏntēs**, *kat-af-ron-tace´*; from 2706; a *contemner:*— despiser.

2708. καταχέω **katachĕō**, *kat-akh-eh´-o*; from 2596 and χέω **chĕō** (to *pour*); to *pour down* (out):— pour.

2709. καταχθόνιος **katachthŏniŏs**, *kat-akh-thon´-ee-os*; from 2596 and χθών **chthōn** (the *ground*); *subterranean*, i.e. *infernal* (belonging to the world of departed spirits):— under the earth.

2710. καταχράομαι **katachraŏmai**, *kat-akh-rah´-om-ahee*; from 2596 and 5530; to *overuse*, i.e. *misuse:*— abuse.

2711. καταψύχω **katapsuchō**, *kat-ap-soo´-kho*; from 2596 and 5594; to *cool down* (off), i.e. *refresh:*— cool.

2712. κατείδωλος **katĕidōlŏs**, *kat-i´-do-los*; from 2596 (intens.) and 1497; *utterly idolatrous:*— wholly given to idolatry.

κατελεύθω **katĕlĕuthō**. See 2718.

2713. κατέναντι **katĕnanti**, *kat-en-´an-tee*; from 2596 and 1725; *directly opposite:*— before, over against.

κατενέγκω **katĕnĕgkō**. See 2702.

2714. κατενώπιον **katĕnōpiŏn**, *kat-en-o´-pee-on*; from 2596 and 1799; *dir. in front of:*— before (the presence of), in the sight of.

2715. κατεξουσιάζω **katĕxŏusiazō**, *kat-ex-oo-see-ad´-zo*; from 2596 and 1850; to *have* (wield) *full privilege over:*— exercise authority.

2716. κατεργάζομαι **katĕrgazŏmai**, *kat-er-gad´-zom-ahee*; from 2596 and 2038; do *work fully*, i.e. *accomplish*; by impl. to *finish*, *fashion:*— cause, do (deed), perform, work (out).

2717. Because of some changes in the numbering system (while the original work was in progress) no Greek words were cited for 2717 or 3203-3302. These numbers were dropped altogether. This will not cause any problems in Strong's numbering system. No Greek words have been left out. Because so many other reference works use this numbering system, it has not been revised. If it were revised, much confusion would certainly result.

2718. κατέρχομαι **katĕrchŏmai**, *kat-er´-khom-ahee*; from 2596 and 2064 (incl. its alt.); to *come* (or *go*) *down* (lit. or fig.):— come (down), depart, descend, go down, land.

2719. κατεσθίω **katĕsthiō**, *kat-es-thee´-o*; from 2596 and 2068 (incl. its alt.); to *eat down*, i.e. *devour* (lit. or fig.):— devour.

2720. κατευθύνω **katĕuthunō**, *kat-yoo-thoo´-no*; from 2596 and 2116; to *straighten fully*, i.e. (fig.) *direct:*— guide, direct.

2721. κατεφίστημι **katĕphistēmi**, *kat-ef-is´-tay-mee*; from 2596 and 2186; to *stand over against*, i.e. *rush upon* (assault):— make insurrection against.

2722. κατέχω **katĕchō**, *kat-ekh´-o*; from 2596 and 2192; to *hold down* (fast), in various applications (lit. or fig.):— have, hold (fast), keep (in memory), let, × make toward, possess, retain, seize on, stay, take, withhold.

2723. κατηγορέω **katēgŏrĕō**, *kat-ay-gor-eh´-o*; from 2725; to *be a plaintiff*, i.e. to *charge* with some offence:— accuse, object.

2724. κατηγορία **katēgŏria**, *kat-ay-gor-ee´-ah*; from 2725; a *complaint* ("category"), i.e. criminal *charge:*— accusation (× -ed).

2725. κατήγορος **katēgŏrŏs**, *kat-ay´-gor-os*; from 2596 and 58; *against* one in the *assembly*, i.e. a *complainant* at law; spec. *Satan:*— accuser.

2726. κατήφεια **katēphĕia**, *kat-ay´-fi-ah*; from a compound of 2596 and perh. a der. of the base of 5316 (mean. *downcast* in look); *demureness*, i.e. (by impl.) *sadness:*— heaviness.

2727. κατηχέω **katēchĕō**, *kat-ay-kheh´-o*; from 2596 and 2279; to *sound down* into the ears, i.e. (by impl.) to *indoctrinate* ("catechize") or (gen.) to *apprise* of:— inform, instruct, teach.

2728. κατιόω **katiŏō**, *kat-ee-ŏ´-o*; from 2596 and a der. of 2447; to *rust down*, i.e. *corrode:*— canker.

2729. κατισχύω **katischuō**, *kat-is-khoo´-o*; from 2596 and 2480; to *overpower:*— prevail (against).

2730. κατοικέω **katŏikĕō**, *kat-oy-keh´-o*; from 2596 and 3611; to *house permanently*, i.e. *reside* (lit. or fig.):— dwell (-er), inhabitant (-ter).

2731. κατοίκησις **katŏikēsis**, *kat-oy´-kay-sis*; from 2730; *residence* (prop. the act; but by impl. concr. the mansion):— dwelling.

2732. κατοικητήριον **katŏikētēriŏn**, *kat-oy-kay-tay´-ree-on*; from a der. of 2730; a *dwelling-place:*— habitation.

2733. κατοικία **katŏikia**, *kat-oy-kee´-ah*; *residence* (prop. the condition; but by impl. the abode itself):— habitation.

2734. κατοπτρίζομαι **katŏptrizŏmai**, *kat-op-trid´-zom-ahee*; mid. voice from a compound of 2596 and a der. of 3700 (comp. 2072); to *mirror oneself*, i.e. to *see reflected* (fig.):— behold as in a glass.

2735. κατόρθωμα **katŏrthōma**, *kat-or´-tho-mah*; from a compound of 2596 and a der. of 3717 (comp. 1357); something *made fully upright*, i.e. (fig.) *rectification* (spec. good public *administration*):— very worthy deed.

2736. κάτω **katō**, *kat´-o*; also (comparative)

κατωτέρω **katŏtĕrō**, *kat-o-ter´-o*; (comp. 2737); adv. from 2596; *downwards:*— beneath, bottom, down, under.

2737. κατώτερος **katŏtĕrŏs**, *kat-o´-ter-os*; comparative from 2736; *inferior* (locally, of Hades):— lower.

2738. καῦμα **kauma**, *kŏw´-mah*; from 2545; prop. a *burn* (concr.), but used (abstr.) of a *glow:*— heat.

2739. καυματίζω **kaumatizō**, *kŏw-mat-id´-zo*; from 2738; to *burn:*— scorch.

2740. καῦσις **kausis**, *kŏw´-sis*; from 2545; *burning* (the act):— be burned.

2741. καυσόω **kausŏō**, *kŏw-sŏ´-o*; from 2740; to *set on fire:*— with fervent heat.

2742. καύσων **kausōn**, *kŏw´-sone*; from 2741; a *glare:*— (burning) heat.

2743. καυτηριάζω **kautēriazō**, *kŏw-tay-ree-ad´-zo* or

καυστηριάζω **kaustēriazō** *kŏws-tay-ree-ad´-zo*; from a der. of 2545; to *brand* ("cauterize"), i.e. (by impl.) to *render unsensitive* (fig.):— sear with a hot iron.

2744. καυχάομαι **kauchaŏmai**, *kŏw-khah´-om-ahee*; from some (obsolete) base akin to that of αὐχέω **auchĕō** (to *boast*) and 2172; to *vaunt* (in a good or a bad sense):— (make) boast, glory, joy, rejoice.

2745. καύχημα **kauchēma**, *kŏw´-khay-mah*; from 2744; a *boast* (prop. the obj.; by impl. the act) in a good or a bad sense:— boasting, (whereof) to glory (of), glorying, rejoice (-ing).

2746. καύχησις **kauchēsis**, *kŏw´-khay-sis*; from 2744; *boasting* (prop. the act; by impl. the obj.), in a good or a bad sense:— boasting, whereof I may glory, glorying, rejoicing.

2747. Κεγχρεαί **Kĕgchrĕai**, *keng-khreh-a´-hee*; prob. from κέγχρος **kĕgchrŏs** (*millet*); *Cenchreæ*, a port of Corinth:— Cenchrea.

2748. Κεδρών **Kĕdrōn**, *ked-rone´*; of Heb. or. [6939]; *Cedron* (i.e. *Kidron*), a brook near Jerusalem:— Cedron.

2749. κεῖμαι **kĕimai**, *ki´-mahee*; mid. voice of a primary verb; to *lie* outstretched (lit. or fig.):— be (appointed, laid up, made, set), lay, lie. Comp. 5087.

2750. κειρία kĕiria, ki-ree´-ah; of uncert. aff.; a swathe, i.e. winding-sheet:— graveclothes.

2751. κείρω kĕirō, ki´-ro; a primary verb; to shear:— shear (-er).

2752. κέλευμα kĕlĕuma, kel´-yoo-mah or

κέλευσμα kĕlĕusma, kel´-yoos-mah; from 2753; a cry of incitement:— shout.

2753. κελεύω kĕlĕuō, kel-yoo´-o; from a primary κέλλω kĕllō (to urge on); "hail;" to incite by word, i.e. order:— bid, (at, give) command (-ment).

2754. κενοδοξία kĕnŏdŏxia, ken-od-ox-ee´-ah; from 2755; empty glorying, i.e. self-conceit:— vain-glory.

2755. κενόδοξος kĕnŏdŏxŏs, ken-od´-ox-os; from 2756 and 1391; vainly glorifying, i.e. self-conceited:— desirous of vain-glory.

2756. κενός kĕnŏs, ken-os´; appar. a primary word; empty (lit. or fig.):— empty, (in) vain.

2757. κενοφωνία kĕnŏphōnia, ken-of-o-nee´-ah; from a presumed compound of 2756 and 5456; empty sounding, i.e. fruitless discussion:— vain.

2758. κενόω kĕnŏō, ken-ŏ´-o; from 2756; to make empty, i.e. (fig.) to abase, neutralize, falsify:— make (of none effect, of no reputation, void), be in vain.

2759. κέντρον kĕntrŏn, ken´-tron; from κεντέω kĕntĕō (to prick); a point ("centre"), i.e. a sting (fig. poison) or goad (fig. divine impulse):— prick, sting.

2760. κεντυρίων kĕnturiōn, ken-too-ree´-ohn; of Lat. or.; a centurion, i.e. captain of one hundred soldiers:— centurion.

2761. κενῶς kĕnōs, ken-oce´; adv. from 2756; vainly, i.e. to no purpose:— in vain.

2762. κεραία kĕraia, ker-ah´-yah; fem. of a presumed der. of the base of 2768; something horn-like, i.e. (spec.) the apex of a Heb. letter (fig. the least particle):— tittle.

2763. κεραμεύς kĕramĕus, ker-am-yooce´; from 2766; a potter:— potter.

2764. κεραμικός kĕramikŏs, ker-am-ik-os´; from 2766; made of clay, i.e. earthen:— of a potter.

2765. κεράμιον kĕramiŏn, ker-am´-ee-on; neut. of a presumed der. of 2766; an earthenware vessel, i.e. jar:— pitcher.

2766. κέραμος kĕramŏs, ker´-am-os; prob. from the base of 2767 (through the idea of mixing clay and water); earthenware, i.e. a tile (by anal. a thin roof or awning):— tiling.

2767. κεράννυμι kĕrannumi, ker-an´-noo-mee; a prol. form of a more primary κεράω kĕraō, ker-ah´-o (which is used in certain tenses); to mingle, i.e. (by impl.) to pour out (for drinking):— fill, pour out. Comp. 3396.

2768. κέρας kĕras, ker´-as; from a primary κάρ kar (the hair of the head); a horn (lit. or fig.):— horn.

2769. κεράτιον kĕratiŏn, ker-at´-ee-on; neut. of a presumed der. of 2768; something horned, i.e. (spec.) the pod of the carob-tree:— husk.

κεράω kĕraō. See 2767.

2770. κερδαίνω kĕrdainō, ker-dah´-ee-no; from 2771; to gain (lit. or fig.):— (get) gain, win.

2771. κέρδος kĕrdŏs, ker´-dos; of uncert. aff.; gain (pecuniary or gen.):— gain, lucre.

2772. κέρμα kĕrma, ker´-mah; from 2751; a clipping (bit), i.e. (spec.) a coin:— money.

2773. κερματιστής kĕrmatistēs, ker-mat-is-tace´; from a der. of 2772; a handler of coins, i.e. money-broker:— changer of money.

2774. κεφάλαιον kĕphalaiŏn, kef-al´-ah-yon; neut. of a der. of 2776; a principal thing, i.e. main point; spec. an amount (of money):— sum.

2775. κεφαλαιόω kĕphalaiŏō, kef-al-ahee-ŏ´-o; from the same as 2774; (spec.) to strike on the head:— wound in the head.

2776. κεφαλή kĕphalē, kef-al-ay´; prob. from the primary κάπτω kaptō (in the sense of seizing); the head (as the part most readily taken hold of), lit. or fig.:— head.

2777. κεφαλίς kĕphalis, kef-al-is´; from 2776; prop. a knob, i.e. (by impl.) a roll (by extens. from the end of a stick on which the MS. was rolled):— volume.

2778. κῆνσος kēnsŏs, kane´-sos; of Lat. or.; prop. an enrollment ("census"), i.e. (by impl.) a tax:— tribute.

2779. κῆπος kēpŏs, kay´-pos; of uncert. aff.; a garden:— garden.

2780. κηπουρός kēpŏurŏs, kay-poo-ros´; from 2779 and οὖρος ŏurŏs (a warden); a garden-keeper, i.e. gardener:— gardener.

2781. κηρίον kēriŏn, kay-ree´-on; dimin. from κηός kēŏs (wax); a cell for honey, i.e. (collect.) the comb:— [honey-] comb.

2782. κήρυγμα kērugma, kay´-roog-mah; from 2784; a proclamation (espec. of the gospel; by impl. the gospel itself):— preaching.

2783. κῆρυξ kērux, kay´-roox; from 2784; a herald, i.e. of divine truth (espec. of the gospel):— preacher.

2784. κηρύσσω kērussō, kay-roos´-so; of uncert. aff.; to herald (as a public crier), espec. divine truth (the gospel):— preacher (-er), proclaim, publish.

2785. κῆτος kētŏs, kay´-tos; prob. from the base of 5490; a huge fish (as gaping for prey):— whale.

2786. Κηφᾶς Kēphas, kay-fas´; of Chald. or. [comp. 3710]; the Rock; Cephas (i.e. Kepha), a surname of Peter:— Cephas.

2787. κιβωτός kibōtŏs, kib-o-tos´; of uncert. der.; a box, i.e. the sacred ark and that of Noah:— ark.

2788. κιθάρα kithara, kith-ar´-ah; of uncert. aff.; a lyre:— harp.

2789. κιθαρίζω kitharizō, kith-ar-id´-zo; from 2788; to play on a lyre:— harp.

2790. κιθαρῳδός kitharōidŏs, kith-ar-o´-dos; from 2788 and a der. of the same as 5603; a lyre-singer (-player), i.e. harpist:— harper.

2791. Κιλικία Kilikia, kil-ik-ee´-ah; prob. of for. or.; Cilicia, a region of Asia Minor:— Cilicia.

2792. κινάμωμον kinamōmŏn, kin-am´-o-mon; of for. or. [comp. 7076]; cinnamon:— cinnamon.

2793. κινδυνεύω kindunĕuō, kin-doon-yoo´-o; from 2794; to undergo peril:— be in danger, be (stand) in jeopardy.

2794. κίνδυνος kindunŏs, kin´-doo-nos; of uncert. der.; danger:— peril.

2795. κινέω kinĕō, kin-eh´-o; from κίω kiō (poetic for εἶμι ĕimi, to go); to stir (tran.), lit. or fig.:— (re-) move (-r), way.

2796. κίνησις kinēsis, kin´-ay-sis; from 2795; a stirring:— moving.

2797. Κίς Kis, kis; of Heb. or. [7027]; Cis (i.e. Kish), an Isr.:— Cis.

κίχρημι kichrēmi. See 5531.

2798. κλάδος kladŏs, klad´-os; from 2806; a twig or bough (as if broken off):— branch.

2799. κλαίω klaiō, klah´-yo; of uncert. aff.; to sob, i.e. wail aloud (whereas 1145 is rather to cry silently):— bewail, weep.

2800. κλάσις klasis, klas´-is; from 2806; fracture (the act):— breaking.

2801. κλάσμα klasma, klas´-mah; from 2806; a piece (bit):— broken, fragment.

2802. Κλαύδη Klaudē, klŏw´-day or

Καύδη Kaudē, kŏw´-day; of uncert. der.; Claude, an island near Crete:— Clauda (Cauda).

2803. Κλαυδία Klaudia, klŏw-dee´-ah; fem. of 2804; Claudia, a Chr. woman:— Claudia.

2804. Κλαύδιος Klaudiŏs, klŏw´-dee-os; of Lat. or.; Claudius, the name of two Romans:— Claudius.

2805. κλαυθμός klauthmŏs, klŏwth-mos´; from 2799; lamentation:— wailing, weeping, × wept.

2806. κλάω klaō, klah´-o; a primary verb; to break (spec. of bread):— break.

2807. κλείς klĕis, klice; from 2808; a key (as shutting a lock), lit. or fig.:— key.

2808. κλείω klĕiō, kli´-o; a primary verb; to close (lit. or fig.):— shut (up).

2809. κλέμμα klĕmma, klem´-mah; from 2813; stealing (prop. the thing stolen, but used of the act):— theft.

2810. Κλεόπας Klĕŏpas, kleh-op´-as; prob. contr. from Κλεόπατρος Klĕŏpatrŏs (compound of 2811 and 3962); Cleopas, a Chr.:— Cleopas.

2811. κλέος klĕŏs, kleh´-os; from a short. form of 2564; renown (as if being called):— glory.

2812. κλέπτης klĕptēs, klep´-tace; from 2813; a stealer (lit. or fig.):— thief. Comp. 3027.

2813. κλέπτω klĕptō, klep´-to; a primary verb; to filch:— steal.

Greek

2814. κλῆμα **klēma,** *klay´-mah;* from 2806; a *limb* or *shoot* (as if *broken* off):— branch.

2815. Κλήμης **Klēmēs,** *klay´-mace;* of Lat. or.; *merciful; Clemes* (i.e. *Clemens*), a Chr.:— Clement.

2816. κληρονομέω **klērŏnŏmĕō,** *klay-ron-om-eh´-o;* from 2818; to *be* an *heir* to (lit. or fig.):— be heir, (obtain by) inherit (-ance).

2817. κληρονομία **klērŏnŏmia,** *klay-ron-om-ee´-ah;* from 2818; *heirship,* i.e. (concr.) a *patrimony* or (gen.) a *possession.*— inheritance.

2818. κληρονόμος **klērŏnŏmŏs,** *klay-ron-om´-os;* from 2819 and the base of 3551 (in its orig. sense of *partitioning,* i.e. [refl.] *getting* by apportionment); a *sharer* by *lot,* i.e. *inheritor* (lit. or fig.); by impl. a *possessor.*— heir.

2819. κλῆρος **klērŏs,** *klay´-ros;* prob. from 2806 (through the idea of using *bits* of wood, etc., for the purpose); a *die* (for drawing chances); by impl. a *portion* (as if so secured); by extens. an *acquisition* (espec. a *patrimony,* fig.):— heritage, inheritance, lot, part.

2820. κληρόω **klērŏō,** *klay-rŏ´-o;* from 2819; to *allot,* i.e. (fig.) to *assign* (a privilege):— obtain an inheritance.

2821. κλῆσις **klēsis,** *klay´-sis;* from a shorter form of 2564; an *invitation* (fig.):— calling.

2822. κλητός **klētŏs,** *klay-tos´;* from the same as 2821; *invited,* i.e. *appointed,* or (spec.) a *saint:*— called.

2823. κλίβανος **klibanŏs,** *klib´-an-os;* of uncert. der.; an earthen *pot* used for baking in:— oven.

2824. κλίμα **klima,** *klee´-mah;* from 2827; a *slope,* i.e. (spec.) a "*clime*" or *tract* of country:— part, region.

2825. κλίνη **klinē,** *klee´-nay;* from 2827; a *couch* for sleep, sickness, sitting or eating):— bed, table.

2826. κλινίδιον **klinidiŏn,** *kleen-eed´-ee-on;* neut. of a presumed der. of 2825; a *pallet* or *little couch:*— bed.

2827. κλίνω **klinō,** *klee´-no;* a primary verb; to *slant* or *slope,* i.e. *incline* or *recline* (lit. or fig.):— bow (down), be far spent, lay, turn to flight, wear away.

2828. κλισία **klisia,** *klee-see´-ah;* from a der. of 2827; prop. *reclination,* i.e. (concr. and spec.) a *party* at a meal:— company.

2829. κλοπή **klŏpē,** *klop-ay´;* from 2813; *stealing.*— theft.

2830. κλύδων **kludōn,** *kloo´-dohn;* from κλύζω **kluzo** (to *billow* or *dash* over); a *surge* of the sea (lit. or fig.):— raging, wave.

2831. κλυδωνίζομαι **kludōnizŏmai,** *kloo-do-nid´-zom-ahee;* mid. voice from 2830; to *surge,* i.e. (fig.) to *fluctuate:*— toss to and fro.

2832. Κλωπᾶς **Klōpas,** *klo-pas´;* of Chald. or. (corresp. to 256); *Clopas,* an Isr.:— Cleopas.

2833. κνήθω **knēthō,** *knay´-tho;* from a primary κνάω **knaō** (to *scrape*); to *scratch,* i.e. (by impl.) to *tickle:*— × itching.

2834. Κνίδος **Knidŏs,** *knee´-dos;* prob. of for. or.; *Cnidus,* a place in Asia Minor:— Cnidus.

2835. κοδράντης **kŏdrantēs,** *kod-ran´-tace;* of Lat. or.; a *quadrans,* i.e. the fourth part of an as:— farthing.

2836. κοιλία **kŏilia,** *koy-lee´-ah;* from κοῖλος **kŏilŏs** ("*hollow*"); a *cavity,* i.e. (spec.) the *abdomen;* by impl. the *matrix;* fig. the *heart:*— belly, womb.

2837. κοιμάω **kŏimaō,** *koy-mah´-o;* from 2749; to *put to sleep,* i.e. (pass. or refl.) to *slumber;* fig. to *decease:*— (be a-, fall a-, fall on) sleep, be dead.

2838. κοίμησις **kŏimēsis,** *koy´-may-sis;* from 2837; *sleeping,* i.e. (by impl.) *repose:*— taking of rest.

2839. κοινός **kŏinŏs,** *koy-nos´;* prob. from 4862; *common,* i.e. (lit.) shared by all or several, or (cer.) *profane:*— common, defiled, unclean, unholy.

2840. κοινόω **kŏinŏō,** *koy-nŏ´-o;* from 2839; to *make* (or *consider*) *profane* (ceremon.):— call common, defile, pollute, unclean.

2841. κοινωνέω **kŏinōnĕō,** *koy-no-neh´-o;* from 2844; to *share* with others (obj. or subj.):— communicate, distribute, be partaker.

2842. κοινωνία **kŏinōnia,** *koy-nohn-ee´-ah;* from 2844; *partnership,* i.e. (lit.) *participation,* or (social) *intercourse,* or (pecuniary) *benefaction:*— (to) communicate (-ation), communion, (contri-) distribution, fellowship.

2843. κοινωνικός **kŏinōnikŏs,** *koy-no-nee-kos´;* from 2844; *communicative,* i.e. (pecuniarily) *liberal:*— willing to communicate.

2844. κοινωνός **kŏinōnŏs,** *koy-no-nos´;* from 2839; a *sharer,* i.e. *associate:*— companion, × fellowship, partaker, partner.

2845. κοίτη **kŏitē,** *koy´-tay;* from 2749; a *couch;* by extens. *cohabitation;* by impl. the male *sperm:*— bed, chambering, × conceive.

2846. κοιτών **kŏitōn,** *koy-tone´;* from 2845; a *bedroom:*— + chamberlain.

2847. κόκκινος **kŏkkinŏs,** *kok´-kee-nos;* from 2848 (from the *kernel*-shape of the insect); *crimson*-colored:— scarlet (colour, coloured).

2848. κόκκος **kŏkkŏs,** *kok´-kos;* appar. a primary word; a *kernel* of seed:— corn, grain.

2849. κολάζω **kŏlazō,** *kol-ad´-zo;* from κόλος **kŏlos** (*dwarf*); prop. to *curtail,* i.e. (fig.) to *chastise* (or *reserve* for infliction):— punish.

2850. κολακεία **kŏlakĕia,** *kol-ak-i´-ah;* from a der. of κόλαξ **kŏlax** (a *fawner*); *flattery:*— × flattering.

2851. κόλασις **kŏlasis,** *kol´-as-is;* from 2849; penal *infliction:*— punishment, torment.

2852. κολαφίζω **kŏlaphizō,** *kol-af-id´-zo;* from a der. of the base of 2849; to *rap* with the fist:— buffet.

2853. κολλάω **kŏllaō,** *kol-lah´-o;* from κόλλα **kŏlla** ("*glue*"); to *glue,* i.e. (pass. or refl.) to *stick* (fig.):— cleave, join (self), keep company.

2854. κολλούριον **kŏllŏuriŏn,** *kol-loo´-ree-on;* neut. of a presumed der. of κολλύρα **kŏllura** (a *cake;* prob akin to the base of 2853); prop. a *poultice* (as made of or in the form of *crackers*), i.e. (by anal.) a *plaster:*— eyesalve.

2855. κολλυβιστής **kŏllubistēs,** *kol-loo-bis-tace´;* from a presumed der. of κόλλυβος **kŏllubŏs** (a small *coin;* prob. akin to 2854); a *coin-dealer:*— (money-) changer.

2856. κολοβόω **kŏlŏbŏō,** *kol-ob-ŏ´-o;* from a der. of the base of 2849; to *dock,* i.e. (fig.) *abridge:*— shorten.

2857. Κολοσσαί **Kŏlŏssai,** *kol-os-sah´-ee;* appar. fem. plur. of κολοσσός **kŏlŏssŏs** ("*colossal*"); *Colossæ,* a place in Asia Minor:— Colosse.

2858. Κολοσσαεύς **Kŏlŏssaĕus,** *kol-os-sayoos´;* from 2857; a *Colossæan,* (i.e. inhab. of Colossæ:— Colossian.

2859. κόλπος **kŏlpŏs,** *kol´-pos;* appar. a primary word; the *bosom;* by anal. a *bay:*— bosom, creek.

2860. κολυμβάω **kŏlumbaō,** *kol-oom-bah´-o;* from κόλυμβος **kŏlumbŏs** (a *diver*); to *plunge* into water:— swim.

2861. κολυμβήθρα **kŏlumbēthra,** *kol-oom-bay´-thrah;* from 2860; a *diving-place,* i.e. *pond* for bathing (or swimming):— pool.

2862. κολωνία **kŏlōnia,** *kol-o-nee´-ah;* of Lat. or.; a Rom. "*colony*" for veterans:— colony.

2863. κομάω **kŏmaō,** *kom-ah´-o;* from 2864; to *wear tresses* of hair:— have long hair.

2864. κόμη **kŏmē,** *kom´-ay;* appar. from the same as 2865; the *hair* of the head (*locks,* as *ornamental,* and thus differing from 2359; which prop. denotes merely the *scalp*):— hair.

2865. κομίζω **kŏmizō,** *kom-id´-zo;* from a primary κομέω **kŏmĕō** (to *tend,* i.e. take care of); prop. to *provide* for, i.e. (by impl.) to *carry* off (as if from harm; generally *obtain*):— bring, receive.

2866. κομψότερον **kŏmpsŏtĕrŏn,** *kompsot´-er-on;* neut. comparative of a der. of the base of 2865 (mean. prop. *well dressed,* i.e. *nice*); fig. *convalescent:*— + began to amend.

2867. κονιάω **kŏniaō,** *kon-ee-ah´-o;* from κονία **kŏnia** (*dust;* by anal. *lime*) to *whitewash:*— whiten.

2868. κονιορτός **kŏniŏrtŏs,** *kon-ee-or-tos´;* from the base of 2867 and ὄρνυμι **ŏrnumi** (to "*rouse*"); *pulverulence* (as *blown* about):— dust.

2869. κοπάζω **kŏpazō,** *kop-ad´-zo;* from 2873; to *tire,* i.e. (fig.) to *relax:*— cease.

2870. κοπετός **kŏpĕtŏs,** *kop-et-os´;* from 2875; *mourning* (prop. by *beating* the breast):— lamentation.

2871. κοπή **kŏpē,** *kop-ay´;* from 2875; *cutting,* i.e. *carnage:*— slaughter.

2872. κοπιάω **kŏpiaō,** *kop-ee-ah´-o;* from a der. of 2873; to *feel fatigue;* by impl. to *work hard:*— (bestow) labour, toil, be wearied.

2873. κόπος **kŏpŏs,** *kop´-os;* from 2875; a *cut,* i.e. (by anal.) *toil* (as *reducing* the strength), lit. or fig.; by impl. *pains:*— labour, + trouble, weariness.

2874. κοπρία **kŏpria**, *kop-ree´-ah;* from κόπρος **kŏprŏs** (*ordure;* perh. akin to 2875); *manure:*— dung (-hill).

2875. κόπτω **kŏptō**, *kop´-to;* a primary verb; to "*chop;*" spec. to *beat* the breast in grief:— cut down, lament, mourn, (be-) wail. Comp. the base of 5114.

2876. κόραξ **kŏrax**, *kor´-ax;* perh. from 2880; a *crow* (from its *voracity*):— raven.

2877. κοράσιον **kŏrasiŏn**, *kor-as´-ee-on;* neut. of a presumed der. of κόρη **kŏrē** (a *maiden*); a (little) *girl:*— damsel, maid.

2878. κορβᾶν **kŏrban**, *kor-ban´;* and

κορβανᾶς **kŏrbanas**, *kor-ban-as´;* of Heb. and Chald. or. respectively [7133]; a votive *offering* and *the offering;* a *consecrated present* (to the Temple fund); by extens. (the latter term) the *Treasury* itself, i.e. the room where the contribution boxes stood:— Corban, treasury.

2879. Κορέ **Kŏrĕ´**, *kor-eh´;* of Heb. or. [7141]; *Corē* (i.e. *Korach*), an Isr.:— Core.

2880. κορέννυμι **kŏrĕnnumi**, *kor-en´-noo-mee;* a primary verb; to *cram*, i.e. *glut* or *sate:*— eat enough, full.

2881. Κορίνθιος **Kŏrinthiŏs**, *kor-in´-thee-os;* from 2882; a *Corinthian*, i.e. inhab. of Corinth:— Corinthian.

2882. Κόρινθος **Kŏrinthŏs**, *kor´-in-thos;* of uncert. der.; *Corinthus*, a city of Greece:— Corinth.

2883. Κορνήλιος **Kŏrnēliŏs**, *kor-nay´-lee-os;* of Lat. or.; *Cornelius*, a Rom.:— Cornelius.

2884. κόρος **kŏrŏs**, *kor´-os;* of Heb. or. [3734]; a *cor*, i.e. a spec. measure:— measure.

2885. κοσμέω **kŏsmĕō**, *kos-meh´-o;* from 2889; to *put in* proper *order*, i.e. *decorate* (lit. or fig.); spec. to *snuff* (a wick):— adorn, garnish, trim.

2886. κοσμικός **kŏsmikŏs**, *kos-mee-kos´;* from 2889 (in its second. sense); *terrene* ("*cosmic*"), lit. (*mundane*) or fig. (*corrupt*):— worldly.

2887. κόσμιος **kŏsmiŏs**, *kos´-mee-os;* from 2889 (in its primary sense); *orderly*, i.e. *decorous:*— of good behaviour, modest.

2888. κοσμοκράτωρ **kŏsmŏkratŏr**, *kos-mok-rat´-ore;* from 2889 and 2902; a *world-ruler*, an epithet of Satan:— ruler.

2889. κόσμος **kŏsmŏs**, *kos´-mos;* prob. from the base of 2865; orderly *arrangement*, i.e. *decoration;* by impl. the *world* (in a wide or narrow sense incl. its inhab., lit. or fig. [mor.]):— adorning, world.

2890. Κούαρτος **Kŏuartŏs**, *koo´-ar-tos;* of Lat. or. (*fourth*); *Quartus*, a Chr.:— Quartus.

2891. κοῦμι **kŏumi**, *koo´-mee* or κουμ **koum**, *koom´;* of Chald. origin [6966]; *cumi* (i.e. *rise!*):— cumi.

2892. κουστωδία **kŏustŏdia**, *koos-to-dee´-ah;* of Lat. or.; "*custody*," i.e. a Rom. *sentry:*— watch.

2893. κουφίζω **kŏuphizō**, *koo-fid´-zo;* from κοῦφος **kŏuphŏs** (*light* in weight); to *unload:*— lighten.

2894. κόφινος **kŏphinŏs**, *kof´-ee-nos;* of uncert. der.; a (small) *basket:*— basket.

2895. κράββατος **krabbatŏs**, *krab´-bat-os;* prob. of for. or.; a *mattress:*— bed.

2896. κράζω **krazō**, *krad´-zo;* a primary verb; prop. to "*croak*" (as a raven) or *scream*, i.e. (gen.) to *call* aloud (*shriek, exclaim, intreat*):— cry (out).

2897. κραιπάλη **kraipalē**, *krahee-pal´-ay;* prob. from the same as 726; prop. a *headache* (as a *seizure* of pain) from drunkenness, i.e. (by impl.) a *debauch* (by anal. a *glut*):— surfeiting.

2898. κρανίον **kraniŏn**, *kran-ee´-on;* dimin. of a der. of the base of 2768; a *skull* ("*cranium*"):— Calvary, skull.

2899. κράσπεδον **kraspĕdŏn**, *kras´-pedon;* of uncert. der.; a *margin*, i.e. (spec.) a *fringe* or *tassel:*— border, hem.

2900. κραταιός **krataiŏs**, *krat-ah-yos´;* from 2904; *powerful:*— mighty.

2901. κραταιόω **krataiŏō**, *krat-ah-yŏ´-o;* from 2900; to *empower*, i.e. (pass.) *increase in vigor:*— be strengthened, be (wax) strong.

2902. κρατέω **kratĕō**, *krat-eh´-o;* from 2904; to *use strength*, i.e. *seize* or *retain* (lit. or fig.):— hold (by, fast), keep, lay hand (hold) on, obtain, retain, take (by).

2903. κράτιστος **kratistŏs**, *krat´-is-tos;* superl. of a der. of 2904; *strongest*, i.e. (in dignity) *very honorable:*— most excellent (noble).

2904. κράτος **kratŏs**, *krat´-os;* perh. a primary word; *vigor* ["*great*"] (lit. or fig.):— dominion, might [-ily], power, strength.

2905. κραυγάζω **kraugazō**, *krŏw-gad´-zo;* from 2906; to *clamor:*— cry out.

2906. κραυγή **kraugē**, *krŏw-gay´;* from 2896; an *outcry* (in notification, tumult or grief):— clamour, cry (-ing).

2907. κρέας **krĕas**, *kreh´-as;* perh. a primary word; (butcher's) *meat:*— flesh.

2908. κρεῖσσον **krĕissŏn**, *krice´-son;* neut. of an alt. form of 2909; (as noun) *better*, i.e. *greater advantage:*— better.

2909. κρείττων **krĕittōn**, *krite´-tohn;* comparative of a der. of 2904; *stronger*, i.e. (fig.) *better*, i.e. *nobler:*— best, better.

2910. κρεμάννυμι **krĕmannumi**, *kreman´-noo-mee;* a prol. form of a primary verb; to *hang:*— hang.

2911. κρημνός **krēmnŏs**, *krame-nos´;* from 2910; *overhanging*, i.e. a *precipice:*— steep place.

2912. Κρής **Krēs**, *krace;* from 2914; a *Cretan*, i.e. inhab. of Crete:— Crete, Cretian.

2913. Κρήσκης **Krēskēs**, *krace´-kace;* of Lat. or.; *growing; Cresces* (i.e. *Crescens*), a Chr.:— Crescens.

2914. Κρήτη **Krētē**, *kray´-tay;* of uncert. der.; *Cretē*, an island in the Mediterranean:— Crete.

2915. κριθή **krithē**, *kree-thay´;* of uncert. der.; *barley:*— barley.

2916. κρίθινος **krithinŏs**, *kree´-thee-nos;* from 2915; consisting of *barley:*— barley.

2917. κρίμα **krima**, *kree´-mah;* from 2919; a *decision* (the function or the effect, for or against ["*crime*"]):— avenge, condemned, condemnation, damnation, + go to law, judgment.

2918. κρίνον **krinŏn**, *kree´-non;* perh. a prim word; a *lily:*— lily.

2919. κρίνω **krinō**, *kree´-no;* prop. to *distinguish*, i.e. *decide* (mentally or judicially); by impl. to *try, condemn, punish:*— avenge, conclude, condemn, damn, decree, determine, esteem, judge, go to (sue at the) law, ordain, call in question, sentence to, think.

2920. κρίσις **krisis**, *kree´-sis;* decision (subj. or obj., for or against); by extens. a *tribunal;* by impl. *justice* (spec. divine *law*):— accusation, condemnation, damnation, judgment.

2921. Κρίσπος **Krispŏs**, *kris´-pos;* of Lat. or.; "*crisp*"; *Crispus*, a Corinthian:— Crispus.

2922. κριτήριον **kritēriŏn**, *kree-tay´-ree-on;* neut. of a presumed der. of 2923; a *rule* of judging ("*criterion*"), i.e. (by impl.) a *tribunal:*— to judge, judgment (seat).

2923. κριτής **kritēs**, *kree-tace´;* from 2919; a *judge* (gen. or spec.):— judge.

2924. κριτικός **kritikŏs**, *krit-ee-kos´;* from 2923; *decisive* ("*critical*"), i.e. *discriminative:*— discerner.

2925. κρούω **krŏuō**, *kroo´-o;* appar. a primary verb; to *rap:*— knock.

2926. κρυπτή **kruptē**, *kroop-tay´;* fem. of 2927; a *hidden* place, i.e. *cellar* ("*crypt*"):— secret.

2927. κρυπτός **kruptŏs**, *kroop-tos´;* from 2928; *concealed*, i.e. *private:*— hid (-den), inward [-ly], secret.

2928. κρύπτω **kruptō**, *kroop´-to;* a primary verb; to *conceal* (prop. by *covering*):— hide (self), keep secret, secret [-ly].

2929. κρυσταλλίζω **krustallizō**, *kroostal-lid´-zo;* from 2930; to *make* (i.e. intr. *resemble*) *ice* ("*crystallize*"):— be clear as crystal.

2930. κρύσταλλος **krustallŏs**, *kroos´-tallos;* from a der. of κρύος **kruos** (*frost*); *ice*, i.e. (by anal.) rock "*crystal*":— crystal.

2931. κρυφῆ **kruphē**, *kroo-fay´;* adv. from 2928; *privately:*— in secret.

2932. κτάομαι **ktaŏmai**, *ktah´-omahee;* a primary verb; to *get*, i.e. *acquire* (by any means; *own*):— obtain, possess, provide, purchase.

2933. κτῆμα **ktēma**, *ktay´-mah;* from 2932; an *acquirement*, i.e. *estate:*— possession.

2934. κτῆνος **ktēnŏs**, *ktay´-nos;* from 2932; *property*, i.e. (spec.) a *domestic animal:*— beast.

Greek

2935. κτήτωρ **ktētōr**, *ktay´-tore;* from 2932; an *owner:*— possessor.

2936. κτίζω **ktizō**, *ktid´-zo;* prob. akin to 2932 (through the idea of *proprietorship* of the *manufacturer*); to *fabricate*, i.e. *found* (*form* orig.):— create, Creator, make.

2937. κτίσις **ktisis**, *ktis´-is;* from 2936; orig. *formation* (prop. the act; by impl. the thing, lit. or fig.):— building, creation, creature, ordinance.

2938. κτίσμα **ktisma**, *ktis´-mah;* from 2936; an orig. *formation* (concr.), i.e. *product* (created thing):— creature.

2939. κτιστής **ktistēs**, *ktis-tace´;* from 2936; a *founder*, i.e. *God* (as author of all things):— Creator.

2940. κυβεία **kubĕia**, *koo-bi´-ah;* from κύβος kubŏs (a "*cube*," i.e. *die* for playing); *gambling*, i.e. (fig.) *artifice* or *fraud:*— sleight.

2941. κυβέρνησις **kubĕrnēsis**, *koo-ber´-nay-sis;* from κυβερνάω kubĕrnaō (of Lat. or., to *steer*); *pilotage*, i.e. (fig.) *directorship* (in the church):— government.

2942. κυβερνήτης **kubĕrnētēs**, *koo-ber-nay´-tace;* from the same as 2941; *helmsman*, i.e. (by impl.) *captain:*— (ship) master.

2943. κυκλόθεν **kuklŏthĕn**, *koo-kloth´-en;* adv. from the same as 2945; *from the circle*, i.e. *all around:*— (round) about.

κυκλός **kuklŏs**. See 2945.

2944. κυκλόω **kuklŏō**, *koo-klŏ´-o;* from the same as 2945; to *encircle*, i.e. *surround:*— compass (about), come (stand) round about.

2945. κύκλῳ **kuklŏi**, *koo´-klo;* as if dat. of κύκλος kuklŏs (a *ring*, "*cycle*"; akin to 2947); i.e. *in a circle* (by impl. of 1722), i.e. (adv.) *all around:*— round about.

2946. κύλισμα **kulisma**, *koo´-lis-mah;* from 2947; a *wallow* (the effect of *rolling*), i.e. *filth:*— wallowing.

2947. κυλιόω **kuliŏō**, *koo-lee-ŏ´-o;* from the base of 2949 (through the idea of *circularity*; comp. 2945, 1507); to *roll* about:— wallow.

2948. κυλλός **kullŏs**, *kool-los´;* from the same as 2947; *rocking* about, i.e. *crippled* (*maimed*, in feet or hands):— maimed.

2949. κῦμα **kuma**, *koo´-mah;* from κύω kuŏ (to *swell* [with young], i.e. *bend, curve*); a *billow* (as *bursting* or *toppling*):— wave.

2950. κύμβαλον **kumbalŏn**, *koom´-bal-on;* from a der. of the base of 2949; a "*cymbal*" (as *hollow*):— cymbal.

2951. κύμινον **kuminŏn**, *koo´-min-on;* of for. or. [comp. 3646]; *dill* or *fennel* ("cummin"):— cummin.

2952. κυνάριον **kunariŏn**, *koo-nar´-ee-on;* neut. of a presumed der. of 2965; a *puppy:*— dog.

2953. Κύπριος **Kupriŏs**, *koo´-pree-os;* from 2954; a *Cyprian* (*Cypriot*), i.e. inhab. of Cyprus:— of Cyprus.

2954. Κύπρος **Kuprŏs**, *koo´-pros;* of un-

cert. or.; *Cyprus*, an island in the Mediterranean:— Cyprus.

2955. κύπτω **kuptō**, *koop´-to;* prob. from the base of 2949; to *bend* forward:— stoop (down).

2956. Κυρηναῖος **Kurēnaiŏs**, *koo-ray-nah´-yos;* from 2957; i.e. *Cyrenæan*, i.e. inhab. of Cyrene:— of Cyrene, Cyrenian.

2957. Κυρήνη **Kurēnē**, *koo-ray´-nay;* of uncert. der.; *Cyrenē*, a region of Africa:— Cyrene.

2958. Κυρήνιος **Kurēniŏs**, *koo-ray´-nee-os;* of Lat. or.; *Cyrenius* (i.e. *Quirinus*), a Rom.:— Cyrenius.

2959. Κυρία **Kuria**, *koo-ree´-ah;* fem. of 2962; *Cyria*, a Chr. woman:— lady.

2960. κυριακός **kuriakŏs**, *koo-ree-ak-os´;* from 2962; *belonging to the Lord* (Jehovah or Jesus):— Lord's.

2961. κυριεύω **kuriĕuō**, *koo-ree-yoo´-o;* from 2962; to *rule:*— have dominion over, lord, be lord of, exercise lordship over.

2962. κύριος **kuriŏs**, *koo´-ree-os;* from κῦρος kurŏs (*supremacy*); *supreme* in authority, i.e. (as noun) *controller;* by impl. *Mr.* (as a respectful title):— God, Lord, master, Sir.

2963. κυριότης **kuriŏtēs**, *koo-ree-ot´-ace;* from 2962; *mastery*, i.e. (concr. and collect.) *rulers:*— dominion, government.

2964. κυρόω **kurŏō**, *koo-rŏ´-o;* from the same as 2962; to *make authoritative*, i.e. *ratify:*— confirm.

2965. κύων **kuōn**, *koo´-ohn;* a primary word; a *dog* ["*hound*"] (lit. or fig.):— dog.

2966. κῶλον **kōlŏn**, *ko´-lon;* from the base of 2849; a *limb* of the body (as if *lopped*):— carcase (carcass).

2967. κωλύω **kōluō**, *ko-loo´-o;* from the base of 2849; to *estop*, i.e. *prevent* (by word or act):— forbid, hinder, keep from, let, not suffer, withstand.

2968. κώμη **kōmē**, *ko´-may;* from 2749; a *hamlet* (as if *laid* down):— town, village.

2969. κωμόπολις **kōmŏpŏlis**, *ko-mop´-ol-is;* from 2968 and 4172; an unwalled *city:*— town.

2970. κῶμος **kōmŏs**, *ko´-mos;* from 2749; a *carousal* (as if *letting loose*):— revelling, rioting.

2971. κώνωψ **kōnōps**, *ko´-nopes;* appar. a der. of the base of 2759 and a der. of 3700; a *mosquito* (from its *stinging proboscis*):— gnat.

2972. Κῶς **Kōs**, *koce;* of uncert. or.; *Cos*, an island in the Mediterranean:— Cos.

2973. Κωσάμ **Kōsam**, *ko-sam´;* of Heb. or. [comp. 7081]; *Cosam* (i.e. *Kosam*) an Isr.:— Cosam.

2974. κωφός **kōphŏs**, *ko-fos´;* from 2875; *blunted*, i.e. (fig.) of hearing (*deaf*) or speech (*dumb*):— deaf, dumb, speechless.

Λ

2975. λαγχάνω **lagchanō**, *lang-khan´-o;*

a prol. form of a primary verb, which is only used as an alt. in certain tenses; to *lot*, i.e. *determine* (by impl. *receive*) espec. by lot:— his lot be, cast lots, obtain.

2976. Λάζαρος **Lazarŏs**, *lad´-zar-os;* prob. of Heb. or. [499]; *Lazarus* (i.e. *Elazar*), the name of two Isr. (one imaginary):— Lazarus.

2977. λάθρα **lathra**, *lath´-rah;* adv. from 2990; *privately:*— privily, secretly.

2978. λαῖλαψ **lailaps**, *lah´-ee-laps;* of uncert. der.; a *whirlwind* (*squall*):— storm, tempest.

2979. λακτίζω **laktizō**, *lak-tid´-zo;* from adv. λάξ lax (*heelwise*); to *recalcitrate:*— kick.

2980. λαλέω **laleō**, *lal-eh´-o;* a prol. form of an otherwise obs. verb; to *talk*, i.e. *utter* words:— preach, say, speak (after), talk, tell, utter. Comp. 3004.

2981. λαλιά **lalia**, *lal-ee-ah´;* from 2980; *talk:*— saying, speech.

2982. λαμά **lama**, *lam-ah´;* or

λαμμά **lamma**, *lam-mah´;* or

λεμά **lĕma**, *leh-mah´;* of Heb. or. [4100 with prep. pref.]; *lama* (i.e. *why*):— lama.

2983. λαμβάνω **lambanō**, *lam-ban´-o;* a prol. form of a primary verb, which is use only as an alt. in certain tenses; to *take* (in very many applications, lit. and fig. [properly obj. or act., to *get hold* of; whereas 1209 is rather subj. or pass., to *have offered* to one; while 138 is more violent, to *seize* or *remove*]):— accept, + be amazed, assay, attain, bring, × when I call, catch, come on (× unto), + forget, have, hold, obtain, receive (× after), take (away, up).

2984. Λάμεχ **Lamĕch**, *lam´-ekh;* of Heb. or. [3929]; *Lamech* (i.e. *Lemek*), a patriarch:— Lamech.

λαμμά **lamma**. See 2982.

2985. λαμπάς **lampas**, *lam-pas´;* from 2989; a "*lamp*" or *flambeau:*— lamp, light, torch.

2986. λαμπρός **lamprŏs**, *lam-pros´;* from the same as 2985; *radiant;* by anal. *limpid;* fig. *magnificent* or *sumptuous* (in appearance):— bright, clear, gay, goodly, gorgeous, white.

2987. λαμπρότης **lamprŏtēs**, *lam-prot´-ace;* from 2986; *brilliancy:*— brightness.

2988. λαμπρῶς **lamprōs**, *lam-proce´;* adv. from 2986; *brilliantly*, i.e. fig. *luxuriously:*— sumptuously.

2989. λάμπω **lampō**, *lam´-po;* a primary verb; to *radiate* brilliancy (lit. or fig.):— give light, shine.

2990. λανθάνω **lanthanō**, *lan-than´-o;* a prol. form of a primary verb, which is used only an alt. in certain tenses; to *lie hid* (lit. or fig.); often used adv. *unwittingly:*— be hid, be ignorate of, unawares.

2991. λαξευτός **laxĕutŏs**, *lax-yoo-tos´;* from a compound of λᾶς las (a *stone*) and the base of 3584 (in its orig. sense of *scraping*); *rock-quarried:*— hewn in stone.

2992. λαός **laŏs**, *lah-os´;* appar. a primary word; a *people* (in general; thus differing from *1218*, which denotes one's *own* populace):— people.

2993. Λαοδίκεια Laŏdikĕia, *lah-od-ik´-i-ah;* from a compound of *2992* and *1349; Laodicia*, a place in Asia Minor:— Laodicea.

2994. Λαοδικεύς Laŏdikĕus, *lah-od-ik-yooce´;* from *2993;* a *Laodicean*, i.e. inhab. of Laodicia:— Laodicean.

2995. λάρυγξ larugx, *lar´-oongks;* of uncert. der.; the *throat* ("*larynx*"):— throat.

2996. Λασαία Lasaia, *las-ah´-yah;* of uncert. or.; *Lasæa*, a place in Crete:— Lasea.

2997. λάσχω laschō, *las´-kho;* a strengthened form of a primary verb, which only occurs in this and another prol. form as alt. in certain tenses; to *crack* open (from a fall):— burst asunder.

2998. λατομέω latŏmĕō, *lat-om-eh´-o;* from the same as the first part of *2991* and the base of *5114;* to *quarry*:— hew.

2999. λατρεία latrĕia, *lat-ri´-ah;* from *3000; ministration* of God, i.e. *worship*:— (divine) service.

3000. λατρεύω latrĕuō, *lat-ryoo´-o;* from λάτρις latris (a hired *menial*); to *minister* (to God), i.e. *render*, relig. *homage*:— serve, do the service, worship (-per).

3001. λάχανον lachanŏn, *lakh´-an-on;* from λαχαίνω lachainō (to *dig*); a *vegetable*:— herb.

3002. Λεββαῖος Lĕbbaiŏs, *leb-bah´-yos;* of uncert. or.; *Lebbæus*, a Chr.:— Lebbæus.

3003. λεγεών lĕgĕōn, *leg-eh-ohn´* or

λεγιών lĕgiōn, *leg-ee-ohn´;* of Lat. or.; a "*legion*," i.e. Rom. *regiment* (fig.):— legion.

3004. λέγω lĕgō, *leg´-o;* a primary verb; prop. to "*lay*" forth, i.e. (fig.) *relate* (in words [usually of systematic or set *discourse;* whereas *2036* and *5346* generally refer to an *individual* expression or speech respectively; while *4483* is prop. to *break silence* merely, and *2980* means an *extended* or random haranguel); by impl. to *mean:*— ask, bid, boast, call, describe, give out, name, put forth, say (-ing, on), shew, speak, tell, utter.

3005. λεῖμμα lĕimma, *lime´-mah;* from *3007;* a *remainder:*— remnant.

3006. λεῖος lĕiŏs, *li´-os;* appar. a primary word; *smooth*, i.e. "*level*":— smooth.

3007. λείπω lĕipō, *li´-po;* a primary verb; to *leave*, i.e. (intr. or pass.) to *fail* or *be absent:*— be destitute (wanting), lack.

3008. λειτουργέω lĕitŏurgĕō, *li-toorg-eh´-o;* from *3011;* to be a *public servant*, i.e. (by anal.) to *perform* relig. or charitable *functions* (*worship, obey, relieve*):— minister.

3009. λειτουργία lĕitŏurgia, *li-toorg-ee´-ah;* from *3008; public function* (as priest ["liturgy"] or almsgiver):— ministration (-try), service.

3010. λειτουργικός lĕitŏurgikŏs, *li-toorg-ik-os´;* from the same as *3008; functional publicly* ("liturgic"); i.e. *beneficent:*— ministering.

3011. λειτουργός lĕitŏurgŏs, *li-toorg-os´;* from a der. of *2992* and *2041;* a *public servant*, i.e. a *functionary* in the Temple or Gospel, or (gen.) a *worshipper* (of God) or *benefactor* (of man):— minister (-ed).

3012. λέντιον lĕntiŏn, *len´-tee-on;* of Lat. or.; a "*linen*" cloth, i.e. *apron:*— towel.

3013. λεπίς lĕpis, *lep-is´;* from λέπω lĕpō (to *peel*); a *flake:*— scale.

3014. λέπρα lĕpra, *lep´-rah;* from the same as *3013; scaliness,* i.e. "*leprosy*":— leprosy.

3015. λεπρός lĕprŏs, *lep-ros´;* from the same as *3014; scaly,* i.e. *leprous* (a *leper*):— leper.

3016. λεπτόν lĕptŏn, *lep-ton´;* neut. of a der. of the same as *3013;* something *scaled* (*light*), i.e. a small *coin:*— mite.

3017. Λευΐ Lĕuï, *lyoo-ee´;* of Heb. or. [3878]; *Levi*, the name of three Isr.:— Levi. Comp. *3018.*

3018. Λευΐς Lĕuïs, *lyoo-is´;* a form of *3017; Lewis* (i.e. *Levi*), a Chr.:— Levi.

3019. Λευΐτης Lĕuïtēs, *lyoo-ee´-tace;* from *3017;* a *Levite*, i.e. desc. of Levi:— Levite.

3020. Λευϊτικός Lĕuïtikŏs, *lyoo-it-ee-kos´;* from *3019; Levitic,* i.e. relating to the Levites:— Levitical.

3021. λευκαίνω lĕukainō, *lyoo-kah´-ee-no;* from *3022;* to *whiten:*— make white, whiten.

3022. λευκός lĕukŏs, *lyoo-kos´;* from λύκη lukē, ("*light*"); *white:*— white.

3023. λεών lĕōn, *leh-ohn´;* a primary word; a "*lion*":— lion.

3024. λήθη lēthē, *lay´-thay;* from *2990; forgetfulness:*— + forget.

3025. ληνός lēnŏs, *lay-nos´;* appar. a primary word; a *trough,* i.e. wine-*vat:*— winepress.

3026. λῆρος lērŏs, *lay´-ros;* appar. a primary word; *twaddle,* i.e. an *incredible* story:— idle tale.

3027. ληστης lēistēs, *lace-tace´;* from λήϊζομαι leizomai (to *plunder*); a *brigand:*— robber, thief.

3028. λῆμψις lēmpsis, *lemp´-sis;* from *2983; receipt* (the act):— receiving.

3029. λίαν lian, *lee-an;* of uncert. aff.; *much* (adv.):— exceeding, great (-ly), sore, very (+ chiefest).

3030. λίβανος libanŏs, *lib´-an-os;* of for. or. [3828]; the *incense*-tree, i.e. (by impl.) *incense* itself:— frankincense.

3031. λιβανωτός libanōtŏs, *lib-an-o-tos´;* from *3030; frankincense,* i.e. (by extens.) a *censer* for burning it:— censer.

3032. Λιβερτίνος Libĕrtinŏs, *lib-er-tee´-nos;* of Lat. or.; a Rom. *freedman:*— Libertine.

3033. Λιβύη Libuē, *lib-oo´-ay;* prob. from *3047; Libye,* a region of Africa:— Libya.

3034. λιθάζω lithazō, *lith-ad´-zo;* from *3037;* to *lapidate:*— stone.

3035. λίθινος lithinŏs, *lith-ee´-nos;* from *3037; stony,* i.e. made of *stone:*— of stone.

3036. λιθοβολέω lithŏbŏlĕō, *lith-ob-ol-eh´-o;* from a compound of *3037* and *906;* to *throw stones,* i.e. *lapidate:*— stone, cast stones.

3037. λίθος lithŏs, *lee´-thos;* appar. a primary word; a *stone* (lit. or fig.):— (mill-, stumbling-) stone.

3038. λιθόστρωτος lithŏstrōtŏs, *lith-os´-tro-tos;* from *3037* and a der. of *4766; stone-strewed,* i.e. a tessellated *mosaic* on which the Rom. tribunal was placed:— Pavement.

3039. λικμάω likmaō, *lik-mah´-o;* from λικμός likmŏs, the equiv. of λίκνον liknŏn (a winnowing *fan* or basket); to *winnow,* i.e. (by anal.) to *triturate:*— grind to powder.

3040. λιμήν limēn, *lee-mane´;* appar. a primary word; a *harbor:*— haven. Comp. *2568.*

3041. λίμνη limnē, *lim´-nay;* prob. from *3040* (through the idea of nearness of shore); a *pond* (large or small):— lake.

3042. λιμός limŏs, *lee-mos´;* prob. from *3007* (through the idea of *destitution*); a *scarcity* of food:— dearth, famine, hunger.

3043. λίνον linŏn, *lee´-non;* prob. a primary word; *flax,* i.e. (by impl.) "*linen*":— linen.

3044. Λῖνος Linŏs, *lee´-nos;* perh. from *3043; Linus,* a Chr.:— Linus.

3045. λιπαρός liparŏs, *lip-ar-os´;* from λίπος lipŏs (*grease*); *fat,* i.e. (fig.) *sumptuous:*— dainty.

3046. λίτρα litra, *lee´-trah;* of Lat. or. (*libra*); a *pound* in weight:— pound.

3047. λίψ lips, *leeps;* prob. from λείβω lĕibō (to *pour* a "libation"); the *south* (-west) wind (as bringing rain, i.e. (by extens.) the *south* quarter):— southwest.

3048. λογία lŏgia, *log-ee´-ah* or

λογεία lŏgĕia, *log-i´-ah;* from *3056* (in the commercial sense); a *contribution:*— collection, gathering.

3049. λογίζομαι lŏgizŏmai, *log-id´-zom-ahee;* mid. voice from *3056;* to *take an inventory,* i.e. *estimate* (lit. or fig.):— conclude, (ac-) count (of), + despise, esteem, impute, lay, number, reason, reckon, suppose, think (on).

3050. λογικός lŏgikŏs, *log-ik-os´;* from *3056; rational* ("*logical*"):— reasonable, of the word.

3051. λόγιον lŏgiŏn, *log´-ee-on;* neut. of *3052;* an *utterance* (of God):— oracle.

3052. λόγιος lŏgiŏs, *log´-ee-os;* from *3056; fluent,* i.e. an *orator:*— eloquent.

3053. λογισμός lŏgismŏs, *log-is-mos´;* from *3049; computation,* i.e. (fig.) *reasoning* (*conscience, conceit*):— imagination, thought.

3054. λογομαχέω lŏgŏmachĕō, *log-om-akh-eh´-o;* from a compound of *3056* and *3164;* to be *disputatious* (on trifles):— strive about words.

3055. λογομαχία **lŏgŏmachia**, *log-om-akh-ee´-ah*; from the same as *3054*; disputation about trifles (*"logomachy"*):— strife of words.

3056. λόγος **lŏgŏs**, *log´-os*; from *3004*; something *said* (incl. the *thought*); by impl. a *topic* (subject of discourse), also *reasoning* (the mental faculty) or *motive*; by extens. a *computation*; spec. (with the art. in John) the Divine *Expression* (i.e. *Christ*):— account, cause, communication, × concerning, doctrine, fame, × have to do, intent, matter, mouth, preaching, question, reason, + reckon, remove, say (-ing), shew, × speaker, speech, talk, thing, + none of these things move me, tidings, treatise, utterance, word, work.

3057. λόγχη **lŏgchē**, *long´-khay*; perh. a primary word; a *"lance"*:— spear.

3058. λοιδορέω **lŏidŏrĕō**, *loy-dor-eh´-o*; from *3060*; to *reproach*, i.e. *vilify*:— revile.

3059. λοιδορία **lŏidŏria**, *loy-dor-ee´-ah*; from *3060*; *slander* or *vituperation*:— railing, reproach [-fully].

3060. λοίδορος **lŏidŏrŏs**, *loy´-dor-os*; from λοιδός **lŏidŏs** (*mischief*); *abusive*, i.e. a *blackguard*:— railer, reviler.

3061. λοιμός **lŏimŏs**, *loy´-mos*; of uncert. aff.; a *plague* (lit. the *disease*, or fig. a *pest*):— pestilence (-t).

3062. λοιποί **lŏipŏi**, *loy-poy´*; masc. plur. of a der. of *3007*; *remaining* ones:— other, which remain, remnant, residue, rest.

3063. λοιπόν **lŏipŏn**, *loy-pon´*; neut. sing. of the same as *3062*; something *remaining* (adv.):— besides, finally, furthermore, (from) henceforth, moreover, now, + it remaineth, then.

3064. λοιποῦ **lŏipŏu**, *loy-poo´*; gen. sing. of the same as *3062*; *remaining* time:— from henceforth.

3065. Λουκᾶς **Lŏukas**, *loo-kas´*; contr. from Lat. *Lucanus*; *Lucas*, a Chr.:— Lucas, Luke.

3066. Λούκιος **Lŏukiŏs**, *loo´-kee-os*; of Lat. or.; *illuminative*; *Lucius*, a Chr.:— Lucius.

3067. λουτρόν **lŏutrŏn**, *loo-tron´*; from *3068*; a *bath*, i.e. (fig.), *baptism*:— washing.

3068. λούω **lŏuō**, *loo´-o*; a primary verb; to *bathe* (the *whole* person; whereas *3538* means to wet a *part* only, and *4150* to wash, cleanse *garments* exclusively):— wash.

3069. Λύδδα **Ludda**, *lud´-dah*; of Heb. or. [3850]; *Lydda* (i.e. *Lod*), a place in Pal.:— Lydda.

3070. Λυδία **Ludia**, *loo-dee´-ah*; prop. fem. of Λύδιος **Ludiŏs** [of for. or.] (a *Lydian*, in Asia Minor); *Lydia*, a Chr. woman:— Lydia.

3071. Λυκαονία **Lukaŏnia**, *loo-kah-on-ee´-ah*; perh. remotely from *3074*; *Lycaonia*, a region of Asia Minor:— Lycaonia.

3072. Λυκαονιστί **Lukaŏnisti**, *loo-kah-on-is-tee´*; adv. from a der. of *3071*; *Lycaonistically*, i.e. in the language of the Lycaonians:— in the speech of Lycaonia.

3073. Λυκία **Lukia**, *loo-kee´-ah*; prob. remotely from *3074*; *Lycia*, a province of Asia Minor:— Lycia.

3074. λύκος **lukŏs**, *loo´-kos*; perh. akin to the base of *3022* (from the *whitish* hair); a *wolf*:— wolf.

3075. λυμαίνομαι **lumainŏmai**, *loo-mah´-ee-nom-ahee*; mid. voice from a prob. der. of *3089* (mean. *filth*); prop. to *soil*, i.e. (fig.) *insult* (*maltreat*):— make havock of.

3076. λυπέω **lupĕō**, *loo-peh´-o*; from *3077*; to *distress*; refl. or pass. to be *sad*:— cause grief, grieve, be in heaviness, (be) sorrow (-ful), be (make) sorry.

3077. λύπη **lupē**, *loo´-pay*; appar. a primary word; *sadness*:— grief, grievous, + grudgingly, heaviness, sorrow.

3078. Λυσανίας **Lusanias**, *loo-san-ee´-as*; from *3080* and ἀνία **ania** (*trouble*); *grief-dispelling*; *Lysanias*, a governor of Abilene:— Lysanias.

3079. Λυσίας **Lusias**, *loo-see´-as*; of uncert. aff.; *Lysias*, a Rom.:— Lysias.

3080. λύσις **lusis**, *loo´-sis*; from *3089*; a *loosening*, i.e. (spec.) *divorce*:— to be loosed.

3081. λυσιτελεῖ **lusitĕlĕi**, *loo-sit-el-i´*; third pers. sing. pres. ind. act. of a der. of a compound of *3080* and *5056*; impers. it *answers the purpose*, i.e. is advantageous:— it is better.

3082. Λύστρα **Lustra**, *loos´-trah*; of uncert. or.; *Lystra*, a place in Asia Minor:— Lystra.

3083. λύτρον **lutrŏn**, *loo´-tron*; from *3089*; something to *loosen* with, i.e. a redemption *price* (fig. *atonement*):— ransom.

3084. λυτρόω **lutrŏō**, *loo-trŏ´-o*; from *3083*; to *ransom* (lit. or fig.):— redeem.

3085. λύτρωσις **lutrōsis**, *loo´-tro-sis*; from *3084*; a *ransoming* (fig.):— + redeemed, redemption.

3086. λυτρωτής **lutrōtēs**, *loo-tro-tace´*; from *3084*; a *redeemer* (fig.):— deliverer.

3087. λυχνία **luchnia**, *lookh-nee´-ah*; from *3088*; a *lamp-stand* (lit. or fig.):— candlestick.

3088. λύχνος **luchnŏs**, *lookh´-nos*; from the base of *3022*; a portable *lamp* or other *illuminator* (lit. or fig.):— candle, light.

3089. λύω **luō**, *loo´-o*; a primary verb; to *"loosen"* (lit. or fig.):— break (up), destroy, dissolve, (un-) loose, melt, put off. Comp. *4486*.

3090. Λωΐς **Lōïs**, *lo-ece´*; of uncert. or.; *Loïs*, a Chr. woman:— Lois.

3091. Λώτ **Lōt**, *lote*; of Heb. or. [3876]; *Lot*, a patriarch:— Lot.

M

3092. Μααθ **Maath**, *mah-ath´*; prob. of Heb. or.; *Maath*, an Isr.:— Maath.

3093. Μαγδαλά **Magdala**, *mag-dal-ah´*; of Chald. or. [comp. 4026]; *the tower*; *Magdala* (i.e. *Migdala*), a place in Pal.:— Magdala.

3094. Μαγδαληνή **Magdalēnē**, *mag-dal-ay-nay*; fem. of a der. of *3093*; a female *Magdalene*, i.e. inhab. of Magdala:— Magdalene.

3095. μαγεία **magĕia**, *mag-i´-ah*; from *3096*; *"magic"*:— sorcery.

3096. μαγεύω **magĕuō**, *mag-yoo´-o*; from *3097*; to *practice magic*:— use sorcery.

3097. μάγος **magŏs**, *mag´-os*; of for. or. [7248]; a *Magian*, i.e. Oriental *scientist*; by impl. a *magician*:— sorcerer, wise man.

3098. Μαγώγ **Magōg**, *mag-ogue´*; of Heb. or. [4031]; *Magog*, a for. nation, i.e. (fig.) an Antichristian party:— Magog.

3099. Μαδιάν **Madian**, *mad-ee-on´* or

Μαδιάμ **Madiam**, *mad-ee-on´*; of Heb. origin [4080]; *Madian* (i.e. *Midian*), a region of Arabia:— Madian.

3100. μαθητεύω **mathētĕuō**, *math-ayt-yoo´-o*; from *3101*; intr. to *become a pupil*; tran. to *disciple*, i.e. enroll as scholar:— be disciple, instruct, teach.

3101. μαθητής **mathētēs**, *math-ay-tes´*; from *3129*; a *learner*, i.e. *pupil*:— disciple.

3102. μαθήτρια **mathētria**, *math-ay´-tree-ah*; fem. from *3101*; a female *pupil*:— disciple.

3103. Μαθουσάλα **Mathŏusala**, *math-oo-sal´-ah*; of Heb. or. [4968]; *Mathusala* (i.e. *Methushelach*), an antediluvian:— Mathusala.

3104. Μαϊνάν **Maïnan**, *mahee-nan´*; prob. of Heb. or.; *Maïnan*, an Isr.:— Mainan.

3105. μαίνομαι **mainŏmai**, *mah´-ee-nom-ahee*; mid. voice from a primary μάω **maō** (to *long* for; through the idea of insensate *craving*); to *rave* as a *"maniac"*:— be beside self (mad).

3106. μακαρίζω **makarizō**, *mak-ar-id´-zo*; from *3107*; to *beatify*, i.e. *pronounce* (or *esteem*) *fortunate*:— call blessed, count happy.

3107. μακάριος **makariŏs**, *mak-ar´-ee-os*; a prol. form of the poet. μάκαρ **makar** (mean. the same); supremely *blest*; by extens. *fortunate*, *well off*:— blessed, happy (× -ier).

3108. μακαρισμός **makarismŏs**, *mak-ar-is-mos´*; from *3106*; *beatification*, i.e. *attribution of good fortune*:— blessedness.

3109. Μακεδονία **Makĕdŏnia**, *mak-ed-on-ee´-ah*; from *3110*; *Macedonia*, a region of Greece:— Macedonia.

3110. Μακεδών **Makĕdōn**, *mak-ed´-ohn*; of uncert. der.; a *Macedon* (*Macedonian*), i.e. inhab. of Macedonia:— of Macedonia, Macedonian.

3111. μάκελλον **makĕllŏn**, *mak´-el-lon*; of Lat. or. [macellum]; a *butcher's stall*, *meat market* or *provision-shop*:— shambles.

3112. μακράν **makran**, *mak-ran´*; fem. acc. sing. of *3117* (*3598* being impl.); at a *distance* (lit. or fig.):— (a-) far (off), good (great) way off.

3113. μακρόθεν **makrŏthĕn**, *mak-roth´-*

en; adv. from *3117; from a distance* or *afar:*— afar off, from far.

3114. μακροθυμέω **makrŏthumĕō,** *mak-roth-oo-meh´-o;* from the same as *3116;* to *be long-spirited,* i.e. (obj.) *forbearing* or (subj.) *patient:*— bear (suffer) long, be longsuffering, have (long) patience, be patient, patiently endure.

3115. μακροθυμία **makrŏthumia,** *mak-roth-oo-mee´-ah;* from the same as *3116; longanimity,* i.e. (obj.) *forbearance* or (subj.) *fortitude:*— longsuffering, patience.

3116. μακροθυμώς **makrŏthumōs,** *mak-roth-oo-moce´;* adv. of a compound of *3117* and *2372; with long (enduring) temper,* i.e. *leniently:*— patiently.

3117. μακρός **makrŏs,** *mak-ros´;* from *3372; long* (in place [distant] or time [neut. plur.]):— far, long.

3118. μακροχρόνιος **makrŏchrŏniŏs,** *mak-rokh-ron´-ee-os;* from *3117* and *5550; long-timed,* i.e. *long-lived:*— live long.

3119. μαλακία **malakia,** *mal-ak-ee´-ah;* from *3120; softness,* i.e. *enervation (debility):*— disease.

3120. μαλακός **malakŏs,** *mal-ak-os´;* of uncert. aff.; *soft,* i.e. *fine* (clothing); fig. a *catamite:*— effeminate, soft.

3121. Μαλελεήλ **Malĕlĕēl,** *mal-el-eh-ale´;* of Heb. or. [4111]; *Maleleël* (i.e. *Mahalalel*), an antediluvian:— Maleleel.

3122. μάλιστα **malista,** *mal´-is-tah;* neut. plur. of the superl. of an appar. primary adv. μάλα **mala** *(very);* (adv.) *most* (in the greatest degree) or *particularly:*— chiefly, most of all, (e-) specially.

3123. μᾶλλον **mallŏn,** *mal´-lon;* neut. of the comparative of the same as *3122;* (adv.) *more* (in a greater degree) or *rather:*— + better, x far, (the) more (and more), (so) much (the more), rather.

3124. Μάλχος **Malchŏs,** *mal´-khos;* of Heb. or. [4429]; *Malchus,* an Isr.:— Malchus.

3125. μάμμη **mammĕ,** *mam´-may;* of nat. or. ["mammy"]; a *grandmother:*— grandmother.

3126. μαμμωνᾶς **mammōnas** *mam-mo-nas´,* or

μαμωνᾶς **mamōnas** *mam-o-nas´;* of Chald. or. (*confidence,* i.e. *wealth,* personified); *mammonas,* i.e. *avarice* (deified):— mammon.

3127. Μαναήν **Manaēn,** *man-ah-ane´;* of uncert. or.; *Manaën,* a Chr.:— Manaen.

3128. Μανασσῆς **Manassēs,** *man-as-sace´;* of Heb. or. [4519]; *Mannasses* (i.e. *Menashsheh*), an Isr.:— Manasses.

3129. μανθάνω **manthanō,** *man-than´-o;* prol. from a primary verb, another form of which, μαθέω **mathĕō,** is used as an alt. in cert. tenses; to *learn* (in any way):— learn, understand.

3130. μανία **mania,** *man-ee´-ah;* from *3105; craziness:*— [+ make] x mad.

3131. μάννα **manna,** *man´-nah;* of Heb. or. [4478]; *manna* (i.e. *man*), an edible gum:— manna.

3132. μαντεύομαι **mantĕuŏmai,** *mant-yoo´-om-ahee;* from a der. of *3105* (mean. a *prophet,* as supposed to *rave* through *inspiration*); to *divine,* i.e. *utter spells* (under pretense of foretelling:— by soothsaying.

3133. μαραίνω **marainō,** *mar-ah´-ee-no;* of uncert. aff.; to *extinguish* (as fire), i.e. (fig. and pass.) to *pass away:*— fade away.

3134. μαρὰν ἀθά **maran atha,** *mar-an´ ath-ah´;* of Chald. or. (mean. *our Lord has come*); *maranatha,* i.e. an exclamation of the approaching *divine judgment:*— Maran-atha.

3135. μαργαρίτης **margaritēs,** *mar-gar-ee´-tace;* from μάργαρος **margarŏs** (a *pearl-oyster*); a *pearl:*— pearl.

3136. Μάρθα **Martha,** *mar´-thah;* prob. of Chald. or. (mean. *mistress*); *Martha,* a Chr. woman:— Martha.

3137. Μαρία **Maria,** *mar-ee´-ah;* or

Μαριάμ **Mariam,** *mar-ee-am´;* Heb. or. [4813]; *Maria* or *Mariam* (i.e. *Mirjam*), the name of six Chr. females:— Mary.

3138. Μάρκος **Markŏs,** *mar´-kos;* of Lat. or.; *Marcus,* a Chr.:— Marcus, Mark.

3139. μάρμαρος **marmarŏs,** *mar´-mar-os;* from μαρμαίρω **marmairō,** (to *glisten*); *marble* (as sparkling *white*):— marble.

μάρτυρ **martur.** See *3144.*

3140. μαρτυρέω **marturĕō,** *mar-too-reh´-o;* from *3144;* to *be a witness,* i.e. *testify* (lit. or fig.):— charge, give [evidence], bear record, have (obtain, of) good (honest) report, be well reported of, testify, give (have) testimony, (be, bear, give, obtain) witness.

3141. μαρτυρία **marturia,** *mar-too-ree´-ah;* from *3144; evidence* given (judicially or gen.):— record, report, testimony, witness.

3142. μαρτύριον **marturiŏn,** *mar-too-ree-on;* neut. of a presumed der. of *3144; something evidential,* i.e. (gen.) *evidence* given or (spec.) the *Decalogue* (in the sacred Tabernacle):— to be testified, testimony, witness.

3143. μαρτύρομαι **marturŏmai,** *mar-too´-rom-ahee;* mid. voice from *3144;* to *be adduced* as a *witness,* i.e. (fig.) to *obtest* (in affirmation or exhortation):— take to record, testify.

3144. μάρτυς **martus,** *mar´-toos;* of uncert. aff.; a *witness* (lit. [judicially] or fig. [gen.]); by anal. a *"martyr":*— martyr, record, witness.

3145. μασσάομαι **massaŏmai,** *mas-sah´-om-ahee;* from a primary μάσσω **massō** (to *handle* or *squeeze*); to *chew:*— gnaw.

3146. μαστιγόω **mastigŏō,** *mas-tig-ŏ´-o;* from *3148;* to *flog* (lit. or fig.):— scourge.

3147. μαστίζω **mastizō,** *mas-tid´-zo;* from *3149;* to *whip* (lit.):— scourge.

3148. μάστιξ **mastix,** *mas´-tix;* prob. from the base of *3145* (through the idea of *contact*); a *whip* (lit. the Rom. *flagellum* for criminals; fig. a *disease*):— plague, scourging.

3149. μαστός **mastŏs,** *mas-tos´;* from

the base of *3145;* a (prop. female) *breast* (as if *kneaded* up):— pap.

3150. ματαιολογία **mataiŏlŏgia,** *mat-ah-yol-og-ee´-ah;* from *3151; random talk,* i.e. *babble:*— vain jangling.

3151. ματαιολόγος **mataiŏlŏgŏs,** *mat-ah-yol-og´-os;* from *3152* and *3004;* an *idle* (i.e. *senseless* or *mischievous*) *talker,* i.e. a *wrangler:*— vain talker.

3152. μάταιος **mataiŏs,** *mat´-ah-yos;* from the base of *3155; empty,* i.e. (lit.) *profitless,* or (spec.) an *idol:*— vain, vanity.

3153. ματαιότης **mataiŏtēs,** *mat-ah-yot´-ace;* from *3152; inutility;* fig. *transientness;* mor. *depravity:*— vanity.

3154. ματαιόω **mataiŏō,** *mat-ah-yŏ´-o;* from *3152;* to *render* (pass. *become*) *foolish,* i.e. (mor.) *wicked* or (spec.) *idolatrous:*— become vain.

3155. μάτην **matēn,** *mat´-ane;* accus. of a der. of the base of *3145* (through the idea of tentative *manipulation,* i.e. unsuccessful *search,* or else of *punishment*); *folly,* i.e. (adv.) to *no purpose:*— in vain.

3156. Ματθαῖος **Matthaiŏs,** *mat-thah´-yos;* or

Μαθθαῖος **Maththaiŏs,** *math-thah´-yos;* a short. form of *3161; Matthæus* (i.e. *Matthitjah*), an Isr. and a Chr.:— Matthew.

3157. Ματθάν **Matthan,** *mat-than´;* of Heb. or. [4977]; *Matthan* (i.e. *Mattan*), an Isr.:— Matthan.

3158. Ματθάτ **Matthat,** *mat-that´;* or

Μαθθάτ **Maththat,** *math-that´;* prob. a short. form of *3161; Matthat* (i.e. *Mattithjah*), the name of two Isr.:— Mathat.

3159. Ματθίας **Matthias** *mat-thee´-as,* or Μαθθίας **Maththias,** *math-thee´-as;* appar. a short. form of *3161; Matthias* (i.e. *Mattithjah*), an Isr.:— Matthias.

3160. Ματταθά **Mattatha,** *mat-tath-ah´;* prob. a short. form of *3161* [comp. 4992]; *Mattatha* (i.e. *Mattithjah*), an Isr.:— Mattatha.

3161. Ματταθίας **Mattathias,** *mat-tath-ee´-as;* of Heb. or. [4993]; *Mattathias* (i.e. *Mattithjah*), an Isr. and a Chr.:— Mattathias.

3162. μάχαιρα **machaira,** *makh´-ahee-rah;* prob. fem. of a presumed der. of *3163;* a *knife,* i.e. *dirk;* fig. *war,* judicial *punishment:*— sword.

3163. μάχη **machē,** *makh´-ay;* from *3164;* a *battle,* i.e. (fig.) *controversy:*— fighting, strive, striving.

3164. μάχομαι **machŏmai,** *makh´-om-ahee;* mid. voice of an appar. primary verb; to *war,* i.e. (fig.) to *quarrel, dispute:*— fight, strive.

3165. μέ **mĕ,** *meh;* a short. (and prob. orig.) form of *1691; me:*— I, me, my.

3166. μεγαλαυχέω **mĕgalauchĕō,** *meg-al-ow-kheh´-o;* from a compound of *3173* and αὐχέω **auchĕō,** (to *boast;* akin to *837* and *2744);* to *talk big,* i.e. *be grandiloquent* (arrogant, egotistic):— boast great things.

3167. μεγαλεῖος **mĕgalĕiŏs,** *meg-al-i´-*

os; from 3173; magnificent, i.e. (neut, plur. as noun) a conspicuous favor, or (subj.) perfection:— great things, wonderful works.

3168. μεγαλειότης měgalěiŏtēs, meg-al-i-ot´-ace; from 3167; superbness, i.e. glory or splendor:— magnificence, majesty, mighty power.

3169. μεγαλοπρεπής měgalŏprěpēs, meg-al-op-rep-ace´; from 3173 and 4241; befitting greatness or magnificence (majestic):— excellent.

3170. μεγαλύνω měgalunō, meg-al-oo´-no; from 3173; to make (or declare) great, i.e. increase or (fig.) extol:— enlarge, magnify, shew great.

3171. μεγάλως měgalōs, meg-al´-oce; adv. from 3173; much:— greatly.

3172. μεγαλωσύνη měgalōsunē, meg-al-o-soo´-nay; from 3173; greatness, i.e. (fig.) divinity (often God himself):— majesty.

3173. μέγας měgas, meg´-as; [incl. the prol. forms, fem.

μεγάλη měgalē, plur.

μεγάλοι měgalŏi, etc.; comp. also 3176, 3187]; big (lit. or fig. in a very wide application):— (+ fear) exceedingly, great (-est), high, large, loud, mighty, + (be) sore (afraid), strong, × to years.

3174. μέγεθος měgěthŏs, meg´-eth-os; from 3173; magnitude (fig.):— greatness.

3175. μεγιστάνες měgistaněs, meg-is-tan´-es; plur. from 3176; grandees:— great men, lords.

3176. μέγιστος měgistŏs, meg´-is-tos; superl. of 3173; greatest or very great:— exceeding great.

3177. μεθερμηνεύω měthěrmēněuō, meth-er-mane-yoo´-o; from 3326 and 2059; to explain over, i.e. translate:— (by) interpret (-ation).

3178. μέθη měthē, meth´-ay; appar. a primary word; an intoxicant, i.e. (by impl.) intoxication:— drunkenness.

3179. μεθίστημι měthistēmi, meth-is´-tay-mee; or (1 Cor. 13:2)

μεθιστάνω měthistanō, meth-is-tan´-o; from 3326 and 2476; to transfer, i.e. carry away, depose or (fig.) exchange, seduce:— put out, remove, translate, turn away.

3180. μεθοδεία měthŏděia, meth-od-i´-ah; from a compound of 3326 and 3593 [comp. "method"]; travelling over, i.e. travesty (trickery):— wile, lie in wait.

3181. μεθόριος měthŏriŏs, meth-or´-ee-os; from 3326 and 3725; bounded alongside, i.e. contiguous (neut. plur. as noun, frontier):— border.

3182. μεθύσκω měthuskō, meth-oos´-ko; a prol. (tran.) form of 3184; to intoxicate:— be drunk (-en).

3183. μέθυσος měthusŏs, meth´-oo-sos; from 3184; tipsy, i.e. (as noun) a sot:— drunkard.

3184. μεθύω měthuō, meth-oo´-o; from another form of 3178; to drink to intoxication, i.e. get drunk:— drink well, make (be) drunk (-en).

3185. μεῖζον měizŏn, mide´-zon; neut.

of 3187; (adv.) in greater degree:— the more.

3186. μειζότερος měizŏtěrŏs, mide-zot´-er-os; continued comparative of 3187; still larger (fig.):— greater.

3187. μείζων měizōn, mide´-zone; irreg. comparative of 3173; larger (lit. or fig. spec. in age):— elder, greater (-est), more.

3188. μέλαν mělan, mel´-an; neut. of 3189 as noun; ink:— ink.

3189. μέλας mělas, mel´-as; appar. a primary word; black:— black.

3190. Μελεᾶς Mělěas, mel-eh-as´; of uncert. or.; Meleas, an Isr.:— Meleas.

μέλει mělěi. See 3199.

3191. μελετάω mělětaō, mel-et-ah´-o; from a presumed der. of 3199; to take care of, i.e. (by impl.) revolve in the mind:— imagine, (pre-) meditate.

3192. μέλι měli, mel´-ee; appar. a primary word; honey:— honey.

3193. μελίσσιος mělissiŏs, mel-is´-see-os; from 3192; relating to honey, i.e. bee (comb):— honeycomb.

3194. Μελίτη Mělitē, mel-ee´-tay; of uncert. or.; Melita, an island in the Mediterranean:— Melita.

3195. μέλλω měllō, mel´-lo; a strengthened form of 3199 (through the idea of expectation); to intend, i.e. be about to be, do, or suffer something (of persons or things, espec. events; in the sense of purpose, duty, necessity, probability, possibility, or hesitation):— about, after that, be (almost), (that which is, things, + which was for) to come, intend, was to (be), mean, mind, be at the point, (be) ready, + return, shall (begin), (which, that) should (after, afterwards, hereafter) tarry, which was for, will, would, be yet.

3196. μέλος mělŏs, mel´-os; of uncert. aff.; a limb or part of the body:— member.

3197. Μελχί Mělchi, mel-khee´; of Heb. or [4428 with pron. suffix my king]; Melchi (i.e. Malki), the name of two Isr.:— Melchi.

3198. Μελχισεδέκ Mělchiseděk, mel-khis-ed-ek´; of Heb. or. [4442]; Melchisedek (i.e. Malkitsedek), a patriarch:— Melchisedec.

3199. μέλω mělō, mel´-o; a primary verb; to be of interest to, i.e. to concern (only third pers. sing. pres. ind. used impers. it matters):— (take) care.

3200. μεμβράνα měmbrana, mem-bran´-ah; of Lat. or. ("membrane"); a (written) sheep-skin:— parchment.

3201. μέμφομαι měmphŏmai, mem´-fom-ahee; mid. voice of an appar. primary verb; to blame:— find fault.

3202. μεμψίμοιρος měmpsimŏirŏs, mem-psim´-oy-ros; from a presumed der. of 3201 and μοῖρα mŏira (fate; akin to the base of 3313); blaming fate, i.e. querulous (discontented):— complainer.

3203–3302. Because of some changes in the numbering system (while the original work was in progress) no Greek words were cited for 2717 or

3203–3302. These numbers were dropped altogether. This will not cause any problems in Strong's numbering system. No Greek words have been left out. Because so many other reference works use this numbering system, it has not been revised. If it were revised, much confusion would certainly result.

3303. μέν měn, men; a primary particle; prop. ind. of affirmation or concession (in fact); usually followed by a contrasted clause with 1161 (this one, the former, etc):— even, indeed, so, some, truly, verily. Often compounded with other particles in an intens. or asseverative sense.

3304. μενοῦνγε měnŏungě, men-oon´-geh or

μενοῦν měnŏun, men-oon´ or

μενοῦν γε měnŏun ge men-oon´geh; from 3203 and 3767 and 1065; so then at least:— nay but, yea doubtless (rather, verily).

3305. μέντοι měntŏi, men´-toy; from 3303 and 5104; indeed though, i.e. however:— also, but, howbeit, nevertheless, yet.

3306. μένω měnō, men´-o; a primary verb; to stay (in a given place, state, relation or expectancy):— abide, continue, dwell, endure, be present, remain, stand, tarry (for), × thine own.

3307. μερίζω měrizō, mer-id´-zo; from 3313; to part, i.e. (lit.) to apportion, bestow, share, or (fig.) to disunite, differ:— deal, be difference between, distribute, divide, give part.

3308. μέριμνα měrimna, mer´-im-nah; from 3307 (through the idea of distraction); solicitude:— care.

3309. μεριμνάω měrimnaō, mer-im-nah´-o; from 3308; to be anxious about:— (be, have) care (-ful), take thought.

3310. μερίς měris, mer-ece´; fem. of 3313; a portion, i.e. province, share or (abstr.) participation:— part (× -akers).

3311. μερισμός měrismŏs, mer-is-mos´; from 3307; a separation or distribution:— dividing asunder, gift.

3312. μεριστής měristēs, mer-is-tace´; from 3307; an apportioner (administrator):— divider.

3313. μέρος měrŏs, mer´-os; from an obs. but more primary form of μείρομαι měirŏmai (to get as a section or allotment); a division or share (lit. or fig. in a wide application):— behalf, coast, course, craft, particular (+ -ly), part (+ -ly), piece, portion, respect, side, some sort (-what).

3314. μεσημβρία měsēmbria, mes-ame-bree´-ah; from 3319 and 2250; midday; by impl. the south:— noon, south.

3315. μεσιτεύω měsitěuō, mes-it-yoo´-o; from 3316; to interpose (as arbiter), i.e (by impl.) to ratify (as surety):— confirm.

3316. μεσίτης měsitēs, mes-ee´-tace; from 3319; a go-between, i.e. (simply) an internunciator, or (by impl.) a reconciler (intercessor):— mediator.

3317. μεσονύκτιον **mĕsŏnuktiŏn**, *mes-on-ook´-tee-on*; neut. of compound of 3319 and 3571; *midnight* (espec. as a watch):— midnight.

3318. Μεσοποταμία **Mĕsŏpŏtamia**, *mes-op-ot-am-ee´-ah*; from 3319 and 4215; *Mesopotamia* (as lying between the Euphrates and the Tigris; comp. 763), a region of Asia:— Mesopotamia.

3319. μέσος **mĕsŏs**, *mes´-os*; from 3326; *middle* (as an adj. or [neut.] noun):— among, × before them, between, + forth, mid [-day,night], midst, way.

3320. μεσότοιχον **mĕsŏtŏichŏn**, *mes-ot´-oy-khon*; from 3319 and 5109; a *partition* (fig.):— middle wall.

3321. μεσουράνημα **mĕsŏuranēma**, *mes-oo-ran´-ay-mah*; from a presumed compound of 3319 and 3772; *mid-sky*:— midst of heaven.

3322. μεσόω **mĕsŏō**, *mes-ŏ´-o*; from 3319; to *form* the *middle*, i.e. (in point of time), to *be half-way* over:— be about the midst.

3323. Μεσσίας **Mĕssias**, *mes-see´-as*; of Heb. or. [4899]; the *Messias* (i.e. *Mashiach*), or Christ:— Messias.

3324. μεστός **mĕstŏs**, *mes-tos´*; of uncert. der.; *replete* (lit. or fig.):— full.

3325. μεστόω **mĕstŏō**, *mes-tŏ´-o*; from 3324; to *replenish*, i.e. (by impl.) to *intoxicate*:— fill.

3326. μετά **mĕta**, *met-ah´*; a primary prep. (often used adv.); prop. denoting *accompaniment*; "*amid*" (local or causal); modif. variously according to the case (gen. *association*, or acc. *succession*) with which it is joined; occupying an intermediate position between 575 or 1537 and 1519 or 4314; less intimate than 1722 and less close than 4862):— after (-ward), × that he again, against, among, × and, + follow, hence, hereafter, in, of, (up-) on, + our, × and setting, since, (un-) to, + together, when, with (+ -out). Often used in composition, in substantially the same relations of *participation* or *proximity*, and *transfer* or *sequence*.

3327. μεταβαίνω **mĕtabainō**, *met-ab-ah´-ee-no*; from 3326 and the base of 939; to *change place*:— depart, go, pass, remove.

3328. μεταβάλλω **mĕtaballō**, *met-ab-al´-lo*; from 3326 and 906; to *throw over*, i.e. (mid. voice fig.) to *turn about* in opinion:— change mind.

3329. μετάγω **mĕtagō**, *met-ag´-o*; from 3326 and 71; to *lead over*, i.e. *transfer* (*direct*):— turn about.

3330. μεταδίδωμι **mĕtadidōmi**, *met-ad-id´-o-mee*; from 3326 and 1325; to *give over*, i.e. *share*:— give, impart.

3331. μετάθεσις **mĕtathĕsis**, *met-ath´-es-is*; from 3346; *transp.*, i.e. *transferral* (to heaven), *disestablishment* (of a law):— change, removing, translation.

3332. μεταίρω **mĕtairō**, *met-ah´-ee-ro*; from 3326 and 142; to *betake* oneself, i.e. *remove* (locally):— depart.

3333. μετακαλέω **mĕtakalĕō**, *met-ak-al-eh´-o*; from 3326 and 2564; to *call elsewhere*, i.e. *summon*:— call (for, hither).

3334. μετακινέω **mĕtakinĕō**, *met-ak-ee-neh´-o*; from 3326 and 2795; to *stir* to a place *elsewhere*, i.e. *remove* (fig.):— move away.

3335. μεταλαμβάνω **mĕtalambanō**, *met-al-am-ban´-o*; from 3326 and 2983; to *participate*; generally to *accept* (and use):— eat, have, be partaker, receive, take.

3336. μετάληψις **mĕtalēmpsis**, *met-al´-ampe-sis*; from 3335; *participation*:— taking.

3337. μεταλλάσσω **mĕtallassō**, *met-allas´-so*; from 3326 and 236; to *exchange*:— change.

3338. μεταμέλλομαι **mĕtamĕllŏmai**, *met-am-el´-lom-ahee*; from 3326 and the mid. voice of 3199; to *care afterwards*, i.e. *regret*:— repent (self).

3339. μεταμορφόω **mĕtamŏrphŏō**, *met-am-or-fŏ´-o*; from 3326 and 3445; to *transform* (lit. or fig. "metamorphose"):— change, transfigure, transform.

3340. μετανοέω **mĕtanŏĕō**, *met-an-ŏeh´-o*; from 3326 and 3539; to *think differently* or *afterwards*, i.e. *reconsider* (mor. *feel compunction*):— repent.

3341. μετάνοια **mĕtanŏia**, *met-an´-oyah*; from 3340; (subj.) *compunction* (for guilt, incl. *reformation*); by impl. *reversal* of [another's] *decision*):— repentance.

3342. μεταξύ **mĕtaxu**, *met-ax-oo´*; from 3326 and a form of 4862; *betwixt* (of place or pers.); (of time) as adj. *intervening*, or (by impl.) *adjoining*:— between, mean while, next.

3343. μεταπέμπω **mĕtapĕmpō**, *met-apemp´-o*; from 3326 and 3992; to *send* from *elsewhere*, i.e. (mid. voice) to *summon* or *invite*:— call (send) for.

3344. μεταστρέφω **mĕtastrĕphō**, *met-as-tref´-o*; from 3326 and 4762; to *turn across*, i.e. *transmute* or (fig.) *corrupt*:— pervert, turn.

3345. μετασχηματίζω **mĕtaschēmatizō**, *met-askh-ay-mat-id´-zo*; from 3326 and a der. of 4976; to *transfigure* or *disguise*; fig. to *apply* (by accommodation):— transfer, transform (self).

3346. μετατίθημι **mĕtatithēmi**, *met-atith´-ay-mee*; from 3326 and 5087; to *transfer*, i.e. (lit.) *transport*, (by impl.) *exchange* (refl.) *change sides*, or (fig.) *pervert*:— carry over, change, remove, translate, turn.

3347. μετέπειτα **mĕtĕpĕita**, *met-ep´-itah*; from 3326 and 1899; *thereafter*:— afterward.

3348. μετέχω **mĕtĕchō**, *met-ekh´-o*; from 3326 and 2192; to *share* or *participate*; by impl. *belong* to, *eat* (or *drink*):— be partaker, pertain, take part, use.

3349. μετεωρίζω **mĕtĕōrizō**, *met-eh-o-rid´-zo*; from a compound of 3326 and a collat. form of 142 or perh. rather 109 (comp. "meteor"); to *raise* in *mid-air*, i.e. (fig.) *suspend* (pass. *fluctuate* or *be anxious*):— be of doubtful mind.

3350. μετοικεσία **mĕtŏikĕsia**, *met-oy-kes-ee´-ah*; from a der. of a compound of 3326 and 3624; a *change of abode*, i.e.

(spec.) *expatriation*:— × brought, carried (-ying) away (in-) to.

3351. μετοικίζω **mĕtŏikizō**, *met-oy-kid´-zo*; from the same as 3350; to *transfer* as a *settler* or *captive*, i.e *colonize* or *exile*:— carry away, remove into.

3352. μετοχή **mĕtŏchē**, *met-okh-ay´*; from 3348; *participation*, i.e. *intercourse*:— fellowship.

3353. μέτοχος **mĕtŏchŏs**, *met´-okh-os*; from 3348; *participant*, i.e. (as noun) a *sharer*; by impl. an *associate*:— fellow, partaker, partner.

3354. μετρέω **mĕtrĕō**, *met-reh´-o*; from 3358; to *measure* (i.e. ascertain in size by a fixed standard); by impl. to *admeasure* (i.e. allot by rule); fig. to *estimate*:— measure, mete.

3355. μετρητής **mĕtrētēs**, *met-raytace´*; from 3354; a *measurer*, i.e. (spec.) a certain standard *measure* of capacity for liquids:— firkin.

3356. μετριοπαθέω **mĕtriŏpathĕō**, *met-ree-op-ath-eh´-o*; from a compound of the base of 3357 and 3806; to *be moderate in passion*, i.e. *gentle* (to *treat indulgently*):— have compassion.

3357. μετρίως **mĕtriōs**, *met-ree´-oce*; adv. from a der. of 3358; *moderately*, i.e. *slightly*:— a little.

3358. μέτρον **mĕtrŏn**, *met´-ron*; an appar. primary word; a *measure* ("metre"), lit. or fig.; by impl. a limited *portion* (*degree*):— measure.

3359. μέτωπον **mĕtōpŏn**, *met´-o-pon* ; from 3326 and ὤψ **ōps** (the *face*); the *forehead* (as *opposite*, the *countenance*):— forehead.

3360. μέχρι **mĕchri** *mekh´-ree*; or

μεχρίς **mĕchris**, *mekh-ris´*; from 3372; *as far as*, i.e. *up to* a certain point (as a prep. of extent [denoting the *terminus*, whereas 891 refers espec. to the *space* of time or place intervening] or a conjuc.):— till, (un-) to, until.

3361. μή **mē**, *may*; a primary particle of qualified *negation* (whereas 3756 expresses an absolute denial); (adv.) *not*, (conjunc.) *lest*; also (as an interrog. implying a *neg.* answer [whereas 3756 expects an *affirmative* one] *whether*:— any, but (that), × forbear, + God forbid, + lack, lest, neither, never, no (× wise in), none, nor, [can-] not, nothing, that not, un [-taken], without. Often used in compounds in substantially the same relations. See also 3362, 3363, 3364, 3372, 3373, 3375, 3378.

3362. ἐὰν μή **ĕan mē**, *eh-an´ may*; i.e. 1437 and 3361; *if not*, i.e. *unless*:— × before, but, except, if, no, (if, + whosoever) not.

3363. ἵνα μή **hina mē** *hin´-ah may*; i.e. 2443 and 3361; *in order* (or *so*) *that not*:— albeit not, lest, that, no (-t, [-thing]).

3364. οὐ μή **ŏu mē**, *oo may*; i.e. 3756 and 3361; a double neg. streng. the denial; *not at all*:— any more, at all, by any (no) means, neither, never, no (at all), in no case (wise), nor ever, not (at all, in any wise). Comp. 3378.

3365. μηδαμῶς **mēdamŏs**, *may-dam-*

oce´; adv. from a compound of 3361 and ἀμός **amŏs** (*somebody*); *by no means:*— not so.

3366. μηδέ **mēdĕ**, *may-deh´*; from 3361 and 1161; *but not, not even;* in a continued negation, *nor:*— neither, nor (yet), (no) not (once, so much as).

3367. μηδείς **mēdĕis**, *may-dice´*; incl. the irreg. fem. μηδεμία **mēdĕmia** *may-dem-ee´-ah;* and the neut. μηδέν **mēdĕn**, *may-den´;* from 3361 and 1520; *not even one* (man, woman, thing):— any (man, thing), no (man), none, not (at all, any man, a whit), nothing, + without delay.

3368. μηδέποτε **mēdĕpŏtĕ**, *may-dep´-ot-eh;* from 3366 and 4218; *not even ever:*— never.

3369. μηδέπω **mēdĕpō**, *may-dep´-o;* from 3366 and 4452; *not even yet:*— not yet.

3370. Μῆδος **Mēdŏs**, *may´-dos;* of for. or. [comp. 4074]; a *Median*, or inhab. of *Media*:— Mede.

3371. μηκέτι **mēkĕti**, *may-ket´-ee;* from 3361 and 2089; *no further:*— any longer, (not) henceforth, hereafter, no henceforward (longer, more, soon), not any more.

3372. μῆκος **mēkŏs**, *may´-kos;* prob. akin to 3173; *length* (lit. or fig.) length.

3373. μηκύνω **mēkunō**, *may-koo´-no;* from 3372; to *lengthen,* i.e. (mid. voice) to *enlarge:*— grow up.

3374. μηλωτή **mēlōtē**, *may-lo-tay´;* from μῆλον **mēlŏn**, (a *sheep*); a *sheep-skin:*— sheepskin.

3375. μήν **mēn**, *mane;* a stronger form of 3303; a particle of affirmation (only with 2229); *assuredly:*— + surely.

3376. μήν **mēn**, *mane;* a primary word; a *month:*— month.

3377. μηνύω **mēnuō**, *may-noo´-o;* prob. from the same base as 3145 and 3415 (i.e. μάω **maō**, to *strive*); to *disclose* (through the idea of ment. *effort* and thus calling to *mind*), i.e. *report, declare, intimate:*— shew, tell.

3378. μὴ οὐκ **mē ŏuk**, *may ook;* i.e. 3361 and 3756; as interrog. and neg. *is it not that?:*— neither (followed by *no*), + never, not. Comp. 3364.

3379. μήποτε **mēpŏtĕ**, *may´-pot-eh;* or

μή ποτε **mē pŏtĕ**, *may pot´-eh;* from 3361 and 4218; *not ever;* also *if* (or *lest*) *ever* (or *perhaps*):— if peradventure, lest (at any time, haply), not at all, whether or not.

3380. μήπω **mēpō**, *may´-po;* from 3361 and 4452; *not yet:*— not yet.

3381. μήπως **mēpōs**, *may´-poce;* or

μή πως **mē pōs**, *may poce;* from 3361 and 4458; *lest somehow:*— lest (by any means, by some means, haply, perhaps).

3382. μηρός **mērŏs**, *may-ros´;* perh. a primary word; a *thigh:*— thigh.

3383. μήτε **mētĕ**, *may´-teh;* from 3361 and 5037; *not too,* i.e. (in continued negation) *neither* or *nor;* also, *not even:*— neither, (n-) or, so as much.

3384. μήτηρ **mētēr**, *may´-tare;* appar. a

primary word; a *"mother"* (lit. or fig., immed. or remote):— mother.

3385. μήτι **mēti**, *may´-tee;* from 3361 and the neut. of 5100; *whether at all:*— not [*the particle usually not expressed, except by the form of the question*].

3386. μήτιγε **mētigĕ**, *may´-tig-eh;* from 3385 and 1065; *not at all then,* i.e. *not to say* (*the rather still*):— how much more.

3387. μήτις **mētis**, *may´-tis;* or

μή τις **mē tis** *may tis;* from 3361 and 5100; *whether any:*— any [*sometimes unexpressed except by the simple interrogative form of the sentence*].

3388. μήτρα **mētra**, *may´-trah;* from 3384; the *matrix:*— womb.

3389. μητραλῴας **mētralōias**, *may-tral-o´-as* or

μετρολῴας **mētrolōias**, *may-trol-o´-as;* from 3384 and the base of 257; a *mother-thresher,* i.e. *matricide:*— murderer of mothers.

3390. μητρόπολις **mētrŏpŏlis**, *may-trop´-ol-is;* from 3384 and 4172; a *mother city,* i.e. *"metropolis"*:— chiefest city.

3391. μία **mia**, *mee´-ah;* irreg. fem. of 1520; *one* or *first:*— a (certain), + agree, first, one, × other.

3392. μιαίνω **miainō**, *me-ah´-ee-no;* perh. a primary verb; to *sully* or *taint,* i.e. *contaminate* (cer. or mor.):— defile.

3393. μίασμα **miasma**, *mee´-as-mah;* from 3392 (*"miasma"*); (mor.) *foulness* (prop. the effect):— pollution.

3394. μιασμός **miasmŏs**, *mee-as-mos´;* from 3392; (mor.) *contamination* (prop.the act):— uncleanness.

3395. μίγμα **migma**, *mig´-mah;* from 3396; a *compound:*— mixture.

3396. μίγνυμι **mignumi**, *mig´-noo-mee;* a primary verb; to *mix:*— mingle.

3397. μικρόν **mikrŏn**, *mik-ron´;* masc. or neut. sing. of 3398 (as noun); a *small space* of *time* or *degree:*— a (little) (while).

3398. μικρός **mikrŏs**, *mik-ros´;* incl. the comp.

μικρότερος **mikrŏtĕrŏs**, *mik-rot´-er-os;* appar. a primary word; *small* (in size, quantity, number or (fig.) dignity):— least, less, little, small.

3399. Μίλητος **Milētŏs**, *mil´-ay-tos;* of uncert. or.; *Miletus,* a city of Asia Minor:— Miletus.

3400. μίλιον **miliŏn**, *mil´-ee-on;* of Lat. or.; a *thousand* paces, i.e. a *"mile"*:— mile.

3401. μιμέομαι **mimĕŏmai**, *mim-eh´-om-ahee;* mid. voice from μῖμος **mimŏs** (a *"mimic"*); to *imitate:*— follow.

3402. μιμητής **mimētēs**, *mim-ay-tace´;* from 3401; an *imitator:*— follower.

3403. μιμνήσκω **mimnēskō**, *mim-nace´-ko;* a prol. form of 3415 (from which some of the tenses are borrowed); to *remind,* i.e. (mid. voice) to *recall to mind:*— be mindful, remember.

3404. μισέω **misĕō**, *mis-eh´-o;* from a primary μῖσος **misŏs** (*hatred*); to *detest*

(espec. to *persecute*); by extens. to *love less:*— hate (-ful).

3405. μισθαποδοσία **misthapŏdŏsia**, *mis-thap-od-os-ee´-ah;* from 3406; *requital* (good or bad):— recompence of reward.

3406. μισθαποδότης **misthapŏdŏtēs**, *mis-thap-od-ot´-ace;* from 3409 and 591; a *renumerator:*— rewarder.

3407. μίσθιος **misthiŏs**, *mis´-thee-os;* from 3408; a *wage-earner:*— hired servant.

3408. μισθός **misthŏs**, *mis-thos´;* appar. a primary word; *pay* for services (lit. or fig.), good or bad:— hire, reward, wages.

3409. μισθόω **misthŏō**, *mis-thŏ´-o;* from 3408; to *let* out for wages, i.e. (mid. voice) to *hire:*— hire.

3410. μίσθωμα **misthōma**, *mis´-thomah;* from 3409; a *rented* building:— hired house.

3411. μισθωτός **misthōtŏs**, *mis-tho-tos´;* from 3409; a *wage-worker* (good or bad):— hired servant, hireling.

3412. Μιτυλήνη **Mitulēnē**, *mit-oo-lay´-nay;* for μυτιλήνη **mutilēnē**, (*abounding in shell-fish*); *Mitylene* (or *Mytilene*), a town on the island of Lesbos:— Mitylene.

3413. Μιχαήλ **Michaēl**, *mikh-ah-ale´;* of Heb. or. [4317]; *Michaël,* an archangel:— Michael.

3414. μνᾶ **mna**, *mnah;* of Lat. or.; a *mna* (i.e. *mina*), a certain *weight:*— pound.

3415. μνάομαι **mnaŏmai**, *mnah´-om-ahee;* mid. voice of a der. of 3306 or perh. of the base of 3145 (through the idea of *fixture* in the mind or of mental *grasp*); to *bear in mind,* i.e. *recollect;* by impl. to *reward* or *punish:*— be mindful, remember, come (have) in remembrance. Comp. 3403.

3416. Μνάσων **Mnasōn**, *mnah´-sohn;* of uncert. or.; *Mnason,* a Chr.:— Mnason.

3417. μνεία **mnĕia**, *mni´-ah;* from 3415 or 3403; *recollection;* by impl. *recital:*— mention, remembrance.

3418. μνῆμα **mnēma**, *mnay´-mah;* from 3415; a *memorial,* i.e. sepulchral *monument* (*burial-place*):— grave, sepulchre, tomb.

3419. μνημεῖον **mnēmĕiŏn**, *mnay-mi´-on;* from 3420; a *remembrance,* i.e. *cenotaph* (*place of interment*):— grave, sepulchre, tomb.

3420. μνήμη **mnēmē**, *mnay´-may;* from 3403; *memory:*— remembrance.

3421. μνημονεύω **mnēmŏnĕuō**, *mnay-mon-yoo´-o;* from a der. of 3420; to *exercise memory,* i.e. *recollect;* by impl. to *punish;* also to *rehearse:*— make mention; be mindful, remember.

3422. μνημόσυνον **mnēmŏsunŏn**, *mnay-mos´-oo-non;* from 3421; a *reminder* (*memorandum*), i.e. *record:*— memorial.

3423. μνηστεύω **mnēstĕuō**, *mnace-tyoo´-o;* from a der. of 3415; to *give a souvenir* (engagement present), i.e. *betroth:*— espouse.

3424. μογιλάλος **mŏgilalŏs**, *mog-il-al´-*

os; from 3425 and 2980; hardly talking, i.e. dumb (tongue-tied):— having an impediment in his speech.

3425. μόγις mŏgis, mog´-is; adv. from a primary μόγος mŏgŏs, (toil); with difficulty:— hardly.

3426. μόδιος mŏdiŏs, mod´-ee-os; of Lat. or.; a modius, i.e. certain measure for things dry (the quantity or the utensil):— bushel.

3427. μοί mŏi, moy; the simpler form of 1698; to me:— I, me, mine, my.

3428. μοιχαλίς mŏichalis, moy-khal-is´; a prol. form of the fem. of 3432; an adulteress (lit. or fig.):— adulteress (-ous, -y).

3429. μοιχάω mŏichaō, moy-khah´-o; from 3432; (mid. voice) to commit adultery:— commit adultery.

3430. μοιχεία mŏichĕia, moy-khi´-ah; from 3431; adultery:— adultery.

3431. μοιχεύω mŏichĕuō, moy-khyoo´-o; from 3432; to commit adultery:— commit adultery.

3432. μοιχός mŏichŏs, moy-khos´; perh. a primary word; a (male) paramour; fig. apostate:— adulterer.

3433. μόλις mŏlis, mol´-is; prob. by var. for 3425; with difficulty:— hardly, scarce (-ly), + with much work.

3434. Μολόχ Mŏlŏch, mol-okh´; of Heb. or. [4432]; Moloch (i.e. Molek), an idol:— Moloch.

3435. μολύνω mŏlunō, mol-oo´-no; prob. from 3189; to soil (fig.):— defile.

3436. μολυσμός mŏlusmŏs, mol-oos-mos´; from 3435; a stain; i.e. (fig.) immorality:— filthiness.

3437. μομφή mŏmphē, mom-fay´; from 3201; blame, i.e. (by impl.) a fault:— quarrel.

3438. μονή mŏnē, mon-ay´; from 3306; a staying, i.e. residence (the act or the place):— abode, mansion.

3439. μονογενής mŏnŏgĕnēs, mon-og-en-ace´; from 3441 and 1096; only-born, i.e. sole:— only (begotten, child).

3440. μόνον mŏnŏn, mon´-on; neut. of 3441 as adv.; merely:— alone, but, only.

3441. μόνος mŏnŏs, mon´-os; prob. from 3306; remaining, i.e. sole or single; by impl. mere:— alone, only, by themselves.

3442. μονόφθαλμος mŏnŏphthalmŏs, mon-of´-thal-mos; from 3441 and 3788; one-eyed:— with one eye.

3443. μονόω mŏnŏō, mon-ŏ´-o; from 3441; to isolate, i.e. bereave:— be desolate.

3444. μορφή mŏrphē, mor-fay´; perh. from the base of 3313 (through the idea of adjustment of parts); shape; fig. nature:— form.

3445. μορφόω mŏrphŏō, mor-fŏ´-o; from the same as 3444; to fashion (fig.):— form.

3446. μόρφωσις mŏrphōsis, mor´-fo-sis; from 3445; formation, i.e. (by impl.) appearance (semblance or [concr.] formula):— form.

3447. μοσχοποιέω mŏschŏpŏiĕō, mos-

khop-oy-eh´-o; from 3448 and 4160; to fabricate the image of a bullock:— make a calf.

3448. μόσχος mŏschŏs, mos´-khos; prob. strengthened for ὄσχος ŏschŏs (a shoot); a young bullock:— calf.

3449. μόχθος mŏchthŏs, mokh´-thos; from the base of 3425; toil, i.e. (by impl.) sadness:— painfulness, travail.

3450. μοῦ mŏu, moo; the simpler form of 1700; of me:— I, me, mine (own), my.

3451. μουσικός mŏusikŏs, moo-sik-os´; from Μοῦσα Mŏusa, (a Muse); "musical", i.e. (as noun) a minstrel:— musician.

3452. μυελός muĕlŏs, moo-el-os´; perh. a primary word; the marrow:— marrow.

3453. μυέω muĕō, moo-eh´-o; from the base of 3466; to initiate, i.e. (by impl.) to teach:— instruct.

3454. μῦθος muthŏs, moo´-thos; perh. from the same as 3453 (through the idea of tuition); a tale, i.e. fiction ("myth"):— fable.

3455. μυκάομαι mukaŏmai, moo-kah´-om-ahee; from a presumed der. of μύζω muzō (to "moo"); to bellow (roar):— roar.

3456. μυκτηρίζω muktērizō, mook-tay-rid´-zo; from a der. of the base of 3455 (mean. snout, as that whence lowing proceeds); to make mouths at, i.e. ridicule:— mock.

3457. μυλικός mulikŏs, moo-lee-kos´; from 3458; belonging to a mill:— mill [-stone].

3458. μύλος mulŏs, moo´-los; prob. ultimately from the base of 3433 (through the idea of hardship); a "mill", i.e. (by impl.) a grinder (millstone):— millstone.

3459. μύλων mulōn, moo´-lone; from 3458; a mill-house:— mill.

3460. Μύρα Mura, moo´-rah; of uncert. der.; Myra, a place in Asia Minor:— Myra.

3461. μυριάς murias, moo-ree´-as; from 3463; a ten-thousand; by extens. a "myriad" or indef. number:— ten thousand.

3462. μυρίζω murizō, moo-rid´-zo; from 3464; to apply (perfumed) unguent to:— anoint.

3463. μύριοι muriŏi, moo´-ree-oi; plur. of an appar. primary word (prop. mean. very many); ten thousand; by extens. innumerably many:— ten thousand.

3464. μύρον murŏn, moo´-ron; prob. of for. or. [comp. 4753, 4666]; "myrrh", i.e. (by impl.) perfumed oil:— ointment.

3465. Μυσία Musia, moo-see´-ah; of uncert. or.; Mysia, a region of Asia Minor:— Mysia.

3466. μυστήριον mustēriŏn, moos-tay´-ree-on; from a der. of μύω muō (to shut the mouth); a secret or "mystery" (through the idea of silence imposed by initiation into relig. rites):— mystery.

3467. μυωπάζω muōpazō, moo-ope-ad´-zo; from a compound of the base of

3466 and ὤψ ōps (the face; from 3700); to shut the eyes, i.e. blink (see indistinctly):— cannot see far off.

3468. μώλωψ mōlōps, mo´-lopes; from μῶλος mōlŏs, ("moil;" prob. akin to the base of 3433) and prob. ὤψ ōps, (the face; from 3700); a mole ("black eye") or blow-mark:— stripe.

3469. μωμάομαι mōmaŏmai, mo-mah´-om-ahee; from 3470; to carp at, i.e. censure (discredit):— blame.

3470. μῶμος mōmŏs, mo´-mos; perh. from 3201; a flaw or blot, i.e. (fig.) disgraceful person:— blemish.

3471. μωραίνω mōrainō, mo-rah´-ee-no; from 3474; to become insipid; fig. to make (pass. act) as a simpleton:— become fool, make foolish, lose savour.

3472. μωρία mōria, mo-ree´-ah; from 3474; silliness, i.e. absurdity:— foolishness.

3473. μωρολογία mōrŏlŏgia, mo-rol-og-ee´-ah; from a compound of 3474 and 3004; silly talk, i.e. buffoonery:— foolish talking.

3474. μωρός mōrŏs, mo-ros´; prob. from the base of 3466; dull or stupid (as if shut up), i.e. heedless, (mor.) blockhead, (appar.) absurd:— fool (-ish, × -ishness).

3475. Μωσεύς Mōsĕus, moce-yoos´; or

Μωσῆς Mōsēs, mo-sace´; or

Μωϋσῆς Mōüsēs, mo-oo-sace´; of Heb. or.; [4872]; Moseus, Moses, or Moüses (i.e. Mosheh), the Heb. lawgiver:— Moses.

N

3476. Ναασσών Naassōn, nah-as-sone´; of Heb. or. [5177]; Naasson (i.e. Nachshon), an Isr.:— Naasson.

3477. Ναγγαί Naggai, nang-gah´-ee; prob. of Heb. or. [comp. 5052]; Nangæ (i.e. perh. Nogach), an Isr.:— Nagge.

3478. Ναζαρέθ Nazarĕth, nad-zar-eth´; or

Ναζαρέτ Nazarĕt, nad-zar-et´; of uncert. der.; Nazareth or Nazaret, a place in Pal.:— Nazareth.

3479. Ναζαρηνός Nazarēnŏs, nad-zar-ay-nos´; from 3478; a Nazarene, i.e. inhab. of Nazareth:— of Nazareth.

3480. Ναζωραῖος Nazōraiŏs, nad-zo-rah´-yos; from 3478; a Nazoræan, i.e. inhab. of Nazareth; by extens. a Christian:— Nazarene, of Nazareth.

3481. Ναθάν Nathan, nath-an´; or

Ναθάμ Natham, nath-am´; of Heb. or. [5416]; Nathan, an Isr.:— Nathan (father).

3482. Ναθαναήλ Nathanaēl, nath-an-ah-ale´; of Heb. or. [5417]; Nathanaël (i.e. Nathanel), an Isr. and Chr.:— Nathanael.

3483. ναί nai, nahee; a primary particle of strong affirmation; yes:— even so, surely, truth, verily, yea, yes.

3484. Ναΐν Naïn, nah-in´; prob. of Heb. or. [comp. 4999]; Naïn, a place in Pal.:— Nain.

3485. ναός naŏs, nah-os´; from a primary ναίω naiō (to *dwell*); a *fane, shrine, temple*:— shrine, temple. Comp 2411.

3486. Ναούμ **Naŏum**, *nah-oom´*; of Heb. or. [5151]; *Naüm* (i.e. *Nachum*), an Isr.:— Naum.

3487. νάρδος **nardŏs**, *nar´dos*; of for. or. [comp. 5373]; "*nard*":— [spike-] nard.

3488. Νάρκισσος **Narkissŏs**, *nar´-kis-sos*; a flower of the same name, from νάρκη **narkē** (*stupefaction*, as a "narcotic"); *Narcissus*, a Rom.:— Narcissus.

3489. ναυαγέω **nauagĕō**, *now-ag-eh´-o*; from a compound of 3491 and 71; to *be shipwrecked* (*stranded*, "navigate"), lit. or fig.:— make (suffer) shipwreck.

3490. ναύκληρος **nauklērŏs**, *now´-klay-ros*; from 3491 and 2819 ("clerk"); a *captain*:— owner of a ship.

3491. ναῦς **naus**, *nŏwce*; from νάω **naō** or νέω **nĕō** (to *float*); a *boat* (of any size):— ship.

3492. ναύτης **nautēs**, *now´-tace*; from 3491; a *boatman*, i.e. *seaman*:— sailor, shipman.

3493. Ναχώρ **Nachōr**, *nakh-ore´*; of Heb. or. [5152]; *Nachor*, the grandfather of Abraham:— Nachor.

3494. νεανίας **nĕanias**, *neh-an-ee´-as*; from a der. of 3501; a *youth* (up to about forty years):— young man.

3495. νεανίσκος **nĕaniskŏs**, *neh-an-is´-kos*; from the same as 3494; a *youth* (under forty):— young man.

3496. Νεάπολις **Nĕapŏlis**, *neh-ap´-ol-is*; from 3501 and 4172; *new town*; *Neäpolis*, a place in Macedonia:— Neapolis.

3497. Νεεμάν **Nĕĕman**, *neh-eh-man´* or

Ναιμάν **Naïman**, *nah-ee-man´*; of Heb. or. [5283]; *Neëman* (i.e. *Naaman*), a Syrian:— Naaman.

3498. νεκρός **nĕkrŏs**, *nek-ros´*; from an appar. primary νέκυς **nĕkus** (a *corpse*); *dead* (lit. or fig.; also as noun):— dead.

3499. νεκρόω **nĕkrŏō**, *nek-rŏ´-o*; from 3498; to *deaden*, i.e. (fig.) to *subdue*:— be dead, mortify.

3500. νέκρωσις **nĕkrōsis**, *nek´-ro-sis*; from 3499; *decease*; fig. *impotency*:— deadness, dying.

3501. νέος **nĕŏs**, *neh´-os*; incl. the comparative νεώτερος **nĕŏtĕrŏs**, *neh-o´-ter-os*; a primary word; "*new*", i.e. (of persons) *youthful*, or (of things) *fresh*; fig. *regenerate*:— new, young.

3502. νεοσσός **nĕŏssŏs**, *neh-os-sos´* or

νοσσός **nossŏs**, *nos-sos´*; from 3501; a *youngling* (*nestling*):— young.

3503. νεότης **nĕŏtēs**, *neh-ot´-ace*; from 3501; *newness*, i.e. *youthfulness*:— youth.

3504. νεόφυτος **nĕŏphutŏs** *neh-of´-oo-tos*; from 3501 and a der. of 5453; *newly planted*, i.e. (fig.) a *young convert* ("*neophyte*"):— novice.

3505. Νέρων **Nĕrōn**, *ner´-ohn*; of Lat. or.; *Neron* (i.e. *Nero*), a Rom. emperor:— Nero.

3506. νεύω **nĕuō**, *nyoo´-o*; appar. a primary verb; to "*nod*," i.e. (by anal.) *signal*:— beckon.

3507. νεφέλη **nĕphĕlē**, *nef-el´-ay*; from

3509; prop. *cloudiness*, i.e. (concr.) a *cloud*:— cloud.

3508. Νεφθαλείμ **Nĕphthalĕim**, *nef-thal-ime´*; of Heb. or. [5321]; *Nephthaleim* (i.e. *Naphthali*), a tribe in Pal.:— Nephthalim.

3509. νέφος **nĕphŏs**, *nef´-os*; appar. a primary word; a *cloud*:— cloud.

3510. νεφρός **nĕphrŏs**, *nef-ros´*; of uncert. aff.; a *kidney* (plur.), i.e. (fig.) the inmost *mind*:— reins.

3511. νεωκόρος **nĕōkŏrŏs**, *neh-o-kor´-os*; from a form of 3485 and κορέω **kŏrĕō** (to *sweep*); a *temple-servant*, i.e. (by impl.) a *votary*:— worshipper.

3512. νεωτερικός **nĕōtĕrikŏs**, *neh-o-ter´-ik-os*; from the comparative of 3501; *appertaining to younger* persons, i.e. *juvenile*:— youthful.

νεώτερος **nĕōtĕrŏs**. See 3501.

3513. νή **nē**, *nay*; prob. an intens. form of 3483; a particle of attestation (accompanied by the obj. invoked or appealed to in confirmation); *as sure as*:— I protest by.

3514. νήθω **nēthō**, *nay´-tho*; from νέω **nĕō** (of like mean.); to *spin*:— spin.

3515. νηπιάζω **nēpiazō**, *nay-pee-ad´-zo*; from 3516; to *act as a babe*, i.e. (fig.) *innocently*:— be a child.

3516. νήπιος **nēpiŏs**, *nay´-pee-os*; from an obs. particle νη- **nē-** (implying *negation*) and 2031; *not speaking*, i.e. an *infant* (*minor*); fig. a *simple-minded* person, an *immature* Christian:— babe, child (+ -ish).

3517. Νηρεύς **Nērĕus**, *nare-yoos´*; appar. from a der. of the base of 3491 (mean. *wet*); *Nereus*, a Chr.:— Nereus.

3518. Νηρί **Nēri**, *nay-ree´*; of Heb. or. [5374]; *Neri* (i.e. *Nerijah*), an Isr.:— Neri.

3519. νησίον **nēsiŏn**, *nay-see´-on*; dimin. of 3520; an *islet*:— island.

3520. νῆσος **nēsŏs**, *nay´-sos*; prob. from the base of 3491; an *island*:— island, isle.

3521. νηστεία **nēstĕia**, *nace-ti´-ah*; from 3522; *abstinence* (from lack of food, or vol. and relig.); spec. the *fast* of the Day of Atonement:— fast (-ing.).

3522. νηστεύω **nēstĕuō**, *nace-tyoo´-o*; from 3523; to *abstain* from food (relig.):— fast.

3523. νῆστις **nēstis**, *nace´-tis*; from the insep. neg. particle νη- **nē-**, (*not*) and 2068; *not eating*, i.e. *abstinent* from food (relig.):— fasting.

3524. νηφάλεος **nēphalĕŏs**, *nay-fal´-eh-os*; or

νηφάλιος **nēphaliŏs**, *nay-fal´-ee-os*; from 3525; *sober*, i.e. (fig.) *circumspect*:— sober, vigilant.

3525. νήφω **nēphō**, *nay´-fo*; of uncert. aff.: to *abstain* from wine (*keep sober*), i.e. (fig.) *be discreet*:— be sober, watch.

3526. Νίγερ **Nigĕr**, *neeg´-er*; of Lat. or.; *black*; *Niger*, a Chr.:— Niger.

3527. Νικάνωρ **Nikanōr**, *nik-an´-ore*; prob. from 3528; *victorious*; *Nicanor*, a Chr.:— Nicanor.

3528. νικάω **nikaō**, *nik-ah´-o*; from

3529; to *subdue* (lit. or fig.):— conquer, overcome, prevail, get the victory.

3529. νίκη **nikē**, *nee´-kay*; appar. a primary word; *conquest* (abstr.), i.e. (fig.) the *means of success*:— victory.

3530. Νικόδημος **Nikŏdēmŏs**, *nik-od´-ay-mos*; from 3534 and 1218; *victorious among his people*; *Nicodemus*, an Isr.:— Nicodemus.

3531. Νικολαΐτης **Nikŏlaïtēs**, *nik-ol-ah-ee´-tace*; from 3532; a *Nicolaïte*, i.e. adherent of *Nicolaüs*:— Nicolaitane.

3532. Νικόλαος **Nikŏlaŏs**, *nik-ol´-ah-os*; from 3534 and 2992; *victorious over the people*; *Nicolaüs*, a heretic:— Nicolaus.

3533. Νικόπολις **Nikŏpŏlis**, *nik-op´-ol-is*; from 3534 and 4172; *victorious city*; *Nicopolis*, a place in Macedonia:— Nicopolis.

3534. νῖκος **nikŏs**, *nee´-kos*; from 3529; a *conquest* (concr.), i.e. (by impl.) *triumph*:— victory.

3535. Νινευΐ **Ninĕuï**, *nin-yoo-ee´*; of Heb. or. [5210]; *Nineui* (i.e. *Nineveh*), the capital of Assyria:— Nineve.

3536. Νινευΐτης **Ninĕuïtēs**, *nin-yoo-ee´-tace*; from 3535; a *Ninevite*, i.e. inhab. of Nineveh:— of Nineve, Ninevite.

3537. νιπτήρ **niptēr**, *nip-tare´*; from 3538; a *ewer*:— bason.

3538. νίπτω **niptō**, *nip´-to*; to *cleanse* (espec. the hands or the feet or the face); cerem. to *perform ablution*:— wash. Comp. 3068.

3539. νοιέω **nŏiĕō**, *noy-eh´-o*; from 3563

νοέω **nŏĕō** *no-eh´-o*; to *exercise the mind*, (*observe*), i.e. (fig.) to *comprehend, heed*:— consider, perceive, think, understand.

3540. νόημα **nŏēma**, *nŏ´-ay-mah*; from 3539; a *perception*, i.e. *purpose*, or (by impl.) the *intellect, disposition*, itself:— device, mind, thought.

3541. νόθος **nŏthŏs**, *noth´-os*; of uncert. aff.; a *spurious* or *illegitimate* son:— bastard.

3542. νομή **nŏmē**, *nom-ay´*; fem. from the same as 3551; *pasture*, i.e. (the act) *feeding* (fig. *spreading* of a gangrene), or (the food) *pasturage*:— × eat, pasture.

3543. νομίζω **nŏmizō**, *nom-id´-zo*; from 3551; prop. to *do by law* (*usage*), i.e. to *accustom* (pass. *be usual*); by extens. to *deem* or *regard*:— suppose, thing, be wont.

3544. νομικός **nŏmikŏs**, *nom-ik-os´*; from 3551; *according* (or *pertaining*) *to law*, i.e. *legal* (cer.); as noun, an *expert in* the (Mosaic) *law*:— about the law, lawyer.

3545. νομίμως **nŏmimōs**, *nom-im´-oce*; adv. from a der. of 3551; *legitimately* (spec. *agreeably* to the rules of the lists):— lawfully.

3546. νόμισμα **nŏmisma**, *nom´-is-mah*; from 3543; *what is reckoned* as of value (after the Lat. *numisma*), i.e. *current coin*:— money.

3547. νομοδιδάσκαλος **nŏmŏdidaskalŏs**, *nom-od-id-as´-kal-os*; from 3551 and 1320; an *expounder of* the (Jewish) *law*, i.e. a *Rabbi*:— doctor (teacher) of the law.

3548. νομοθεσία **nŏmŏthĕsia**, *nom-oth-es-ee´-ah;* from 3550; *legislation* (spec. the *institution* of the Mosaic *code*):— giving of the law.

3549. νομοθετέω **nŏmŏthĕtĕō**, *nom-oth-et-eh´-o;* from 3550; to *legislate*, i.e. (pass.) to *have* (the Mosaic) *enactments* injoined, *be sanctioned* (by them):— establish, receive the law.

3550. νομοθέτης **nŏmŏthĕtēs**, *nom-oth-et´-ace;* from 3551 and a der. of 5087; a *legislator*:— lawgiver.

3551. νόμος **nŏmŏs**, *nom´-os;* from a primary νέμω **nĕmō**, (to *parcel* out, espec. *food* or *grazing* to animals); *law* (through the idea of prescriptive *usage*), gen. (*regulation*), spec. (of Moses [incl. the volume]; also of the Gospel), or fig. (a *principle*):— law.

3552. νοσέω **nŏsĕō**, *nos-eh´-o;* from 3554; to *be sick*, i.e. (by impl. of a diseased appetite) to *hanker* after (fig. to *harp* upon):— dote.

3553. νόσημα **nŏsēma**, *nos´-ay-ma;* from 3552; an *ailment*:— disease.

3554. νόσος **nŏsŏs**, *nos´-os;* of uncert. aff.; a *malady* (rarely fig. of mor. *disability*):— disease, infirmity, sickness.

3555. νοσσιά **nŏssia**, *nos-see-ah´;* from 3502; a *brood* (of chickens):— brood.

3556. νοσσίον **nŏssiŏn**, *nos-see´-on;* dimin. of 3502; a *birdling*:— chicken.

3557. νοσσφίζομαι **nŏsphizŏmai**, *nos-fid´-zom-ahee;* mid. voice from νοσφί **nŏsphi** (*apart* or *clandestinely*); to *sequestrate*, for oneself, i.e. *embezzle*:— keep back, purloin.

3558. νότος **nŏtŏs**, *not´-os;* of uncert. aff.; the *south* (*-west*) *wind;* by extens. the *southern quarter* itself:— south (wind).

3559. νουθεσία **nŏuthĕsia**, *noo-thes-ee´-ah;* from 3563 and a der. of 5087; calling *attention* to, i.e. (by impl.) mild *rebuke* or *warning*:— admonition.

3560. νουθετέω **nŏuthĕtĕō**, *noo-thet-eh´-o;* from the same as 3559; to *put in mind*, i.e. (by impl.) to *caution* or *reprove* gently:— admonish, warn.

3561. νουμηνία **nŏumēnia**, *noo-may-nee´-ah;* fem. of a compound of 3501 and 3376 (as noun by impl. of 2250); the festival of *new moon*:— new moon.

3562. νουνεχῶς **nŏunĕchōs**, *noon-ekh-oce´;* adv. from a comp. of the acc. of 3563 and 2192; in a *mind-having* way, i.e. *prudently*:— discreetly.

3563. νοῦς **nŏus**, *nooce;* prob. from the base of 1097; the *intellect*, i.e. *mind* (divine or human; in thought, feeling, or will); by impl. *meaning*:— mind, understanding. Comp. 5590.

3564. Νυμφᾶς **Numphas**, *noom-fas´;* prob. contr. for a compound of 3565 and 1435; *nymph-given* (i.e. *-born*); *Nymphas*, a Chr.:— Nymphas.

3565. νύμφη **numphē**, *noom-fay´;* from a primary but obs. verb νύπτω **nuptō**, (to *veil* as a bride; comp. Lat. "*nupto*," to *marry*); a young *married* woman (as

veiled), incl. a *betrothed* girl; by impl. a *son's wife*:— bride, daughter in law.

3566. νυμφίος **numphiŏs**, *noom-fee´-os;* from 3565; a *bride-groom* (lit. or fig.):— bridegroom.

3567. νυμφών **numphōn**, *noom-fohn´;* from 3565; the *bridal* room:— bridechamber.

3568. νῦν **nun**, *noon;* a primary particle of present time; "*now*" (as adv. of date, a transition or emphasis); also as noun or adj. *present* or *immediate*:— henceforth, + hereafter, of late, soon, present, this (time). See also 3569, 3570.

3569. τανῦν **tanun**, *tan-oon´;* or

τὰ νῦν **ta nun** *tah noon;* from neut. plur. of 3588 and 3568; *the* things *now*, i.e. (adv.) *at present*:— (but) now.

3570. νυνί **nuni**, *noo-nee´;* a prol. form of 3568 for emphasis; *just now*:— now.

3571. νύξ **nux**, *noox;* a primary word; "*night*" (lit. or fig.):— (mid-) night.

3572. νύσσω **nussō**, *noos´-so;* appar. a primary word; to *prick* ("*nudge*"):— pierce.

3573. νυστάζω **nustazō**, *noos-tad´-zo;* from a presumed der. of 3506; to *nod*, i.e. (by impl.) to *fall asleep;* fig. to *delay*:— slumber.

3574. νυχθήμερον **nuchthēmĕrŏn** *nookh-thay´-mer-on;* from 3571 and 2250; a *day-and-night*, i.e. full *day* of twenty-four hours:— night and day.

3575. Νῶε **Nŏĕ**, *no´-eh;* of Heb. or. [5146]; *Noë*, (i.e. *Noäch*), a patriarch:— Noe.

3576. νωθρός **nōthrŏs**, *no-thros´;* from a der. of 3541; *sluggish*, i.e. (lit.) *lazy*, or (fig.) *stupid*:— dull, slothful.

3577. νῶτος **nōtŏs**, *no´-tos;* of uncert. aff.; the *back*:— back.

Ξ

3578. ξενία **xĕnia**, *xen-ee-ah;* from 3581; *hospitality*, i.e. (by impl.) a *place of entertainment*:— lodging.

3579. ξενίζω **xĕnizō**, *xen-id´-zo;* from 3581; to *be a host* (pass. a *guest*); by impl. be (*make, appear*) *strange*:— entertain, lodge, (think it) strange.

3580. ξενοδοχέω **xĕnŏdŏchĕō**, *xen-od-okh-eh´-o;* from a compound of 3581 and 1209; to *be hospitable*:— lodge strangers.

3581. ξένος **xĕnŏs**, *xen´-os;* appar. a primary word; *for.* (lit. *alien*, or fig. *novel*); by impl. a *guest* or (vice-versa) *entertainer*:— host, strange (-r).

3582. ξέστης **xĕstēs**, *xes´-tace;* as if from ξέω **xĕō**, (prop. to *smooth;* by impl. [of *friction*] to *boil* or *heat*); a *vessel* (as *fashioned* or for *cooking*) [or perh. by corruption from the Lat. *sextarius*, the *sixth* of a modius, i.e. about a *pint*], i.e. (spec.) a *measure* for liquids or solids, (by anal. a *pitcher*):— pot.

3583. ξηραίνω **xērainō**, *xay-rah´-ee-no;* from 3584; to *desiccate;* by impl. to *shrivel*, to *mature*:— dry up, pine away, be ripe, wither (away).

3584. ξηρός **xērŏs**, *xay-ros´;* from the base of 3582 (through the idea of

scorching); *arid;* by impl. *shrunken*, *earth* (as opposed to water):— dry land, withered.

3585. ξύλινος **xulinŏs**, *xoo´-lin-os;* from 3586; *wooden*:— of wood.

3586. ξύλον **xulŏn**, *xoo´-lon;* from another form of the base of 3582; *timber* (as fuel or material); by impl. a *stick*, *club* or *tree* or other wooden art. or substance:— staff, stocks, tree, wood.

3587. ξυράω **xuraō**, *xoo-rah´-o;* from a der. of the same as 3586 (mean. a *razor*); to *shave* or "*shear*" the hair:— shave.

O

3588. ὁ **hŏ**, *hŏ;* incl. the fem.

ἡ **hē**, *hay;* and the neut.

τό **tŏ**, *tŏ;* in all their inflections; the def. art.; *the* (sometimes to be supplied, at others omitted, in English idiom):— the, this, that, one, he, she, it, etc.

ὁ **hŏ**. See 3739.

3589. ὀγδοήκοντα **ŏgdŏĕkŏnta**, *og-do-ay´-kon-tah;* from 3590; *ten times eight*:— fourscore.

3590. ὄγδοος **ŏgdŏŏs**, *og´-dŏ-os;* from 3638; the *eighth*:— eighth.

3591. ὄγκος **ŏgkŏs**, *ong´-kos;* prob. from the same as 43; a *mass* (as *bending* or *bulging* by its load), i.e. *burden* (*hindrance*):— weight.

3592. ὅδε **hŏdĕ**, *hod´-eh;* incl. the fem.

ἥδε **hēdĕ**, *hay´-deh;* and the neut.

τόδε **tŏdĕ**, *tod´-e;* from 3588 and 1161; the *same*, i.e. *this* or *that* one (plur. *these* or *those*); often used as pers. pron.:— he, she, such, these, thus.

3593. ὁδεύω **hŏdĕuō**, *hod-yoo´-o;* from 3598; to *travel*:— journey.

3594. ὁδηγέω **hŏdēgĕō**, *hod-ayg-eh´-o;* from 3595; to *show the way* (lit. or fig. [teach]):— guide, lead.

3595. ὁδηγός **hŏdēgŏs**, *hod-ayg-os´;* from 3598 and 2233; a *conductor* (lit. or fig. [teacher]):— guide, leader.

3596. ὁδοιπορέω **hŏdŏipŏrĕō**, *hod-oy-por-eh´-o;* from a compound of 3598 and 4198; to *be a wayfarer*, i.e. *travel*:— go on a journey.

3597. ὁδοιπορία **hŏdŏipŏria**, *hod-oy-por-ee´-ah;* from the same as 3596; *travel*:— journey (-ing).

3598. ὁδός **hŏdŏs**, *hod-os´;* appar. a primary word; a *road;* by impl. a *progress* (the route, act or distance); fig. a *mode* or *means*:— journey, (high-) way.

3599. ὀδούς **ŏdŏus**, *od-ooce;* perh. from the base of 2068; a "*tooth*":— tooth.

3600. ὀδυνάω **ŏdunaō**, *od-oo-nah´-o;* from 3601; to *grieve*:— sorrow, torment.

3601. ὀδύνη **ŏdunē**, *od-oo´-nay;* from 1416; *grief* (as *dejecting*):— sorrow.

3602. ὀδυρμός **ŏdurmŏs**, *od-oor-mos´;* from a der. of the base of 1416; *moaning*, i.e. *lamentation*:— mourning.

3603. ὅ ἐστι **hŏ esti**, *hŏ es-tee´* or

ὅ ἐστιν **hŏ estin**, *hŏ es-teen´;* from

the neut. of 3739 and the third pers. sing. pres. ind. of 1510; *which is:*— called, which is (make), i.e. (to say).

3604. Ὀζίας **Ŏzias**, od-zee´-as; of Heb. or. [5818]; *Ozias* (i.e. *Uzzijah*), an Isr.:— Ozias.

3605. ὄζω **ŏzō**, od´-zo; a primary verb (in a strengthened form); to *scent* (usually an ill "odor"): stink.

3606. ὅθεν **hŏthĕn**, hoth´-en; from 3739 with the directive enclitic of source; *from which* place or source or cause (adv. or conjunc.):— from thence, (from) whence, where (-by, -fore, -upon).

3607. ὀθόνη **ŏthŏnē**, oth-on´-ay; of uncert. aff.; a *linen* cloth, i.e. (espec.) a *sail*:— sheet.

3608. ὀθόνιον **ŏthŏniŏn**, oth-on´-ee-on; neut. of a presumed der. of 3607; a linen *bandage*:— linen clothes.

3609. οἰκεῖος **ŏikĕiŏs**, oy-ki´-os; from 3624; *domestic*, i.e. (as noun), a *relative*, *adherent*:— (those) of the (his own) house (-hold).

3610. οἰκέτης **ŏikĕtēs**, oy-ket´-ace; from 3611; a fellow *resident*, i.e. menial *domestic*:— (household) servant.

3611. οἰκέω **ŏikĕō**, oy-keh´-o; from 3624; to *occupy a house*, i.e. *reside* (fig. *inhabit, remain, inhere*); by impl. to *cohabit*:— dwell. See also 3625.

3612. οἴκημα **ŏikēma**, oy´-kay-mah; from 3611; a *tenement*, i.e. (spec.) a *jail*:— prison.

3613. οἰκητήριον **ŏikētēriŏn**, oy-kay-tay´-ree-on; neut. of a presumed der. of 3611 (equiv. to 3612); a *residence* (lit. or fig.):— habitation, house.

3614. οἰκία **ŏikia**, oy-kee´-ah; from 3624; prop. *residence* (abstr.), but usually (concr.) an *abode* (lit. or fig.); by impl. a *family* (espec. *domestics*):— home, house (-hold).

3615. οἰκιακός **ŏikiakŏs**, oy-kee-ak-os´; from 3614; *familiar*, i.e. (as noun) *relatives*:— they (them) of (his own) household.

3616. οἰκοδεσποτέω **ŏikŏdĕspŏtĕō**, oy-kod-es-pot-eh´-o; from 3617; to *be* the *head of* (i.e. *rule*) a *family*:— guide the house.

3617. οἰκοδεσπότης **ŏikŏdĕspŏtēs**, oy-kod-es-pot´-ace; from 3624 and 1203; the *head of a family*:— goodman (of the house), householder, master of the house.

3618. οἰκοδομέω **ŏikŏdŏmĕō**, oy-kod-om-eh´-o; from the same as 3619; to *be* a *house-builder*, i.e. *construct* or (fig.) *confirm*:— (be in) build (-er, -ing, up), edify, embolden.

3619. οἰκοδομή **ŏikŏdŏmē**, oy-kod-om-ay´; fem. (abstr.) of a compound of 3624 and the base of 1430; *architecture*, i.e. (concr.) a *structure*; fig. *confirmation*:— building, edify (-ication, ing).

3620. οἰκοδομία **ŏikŏdŏmia**, oy-kod-om-ee´-ah; from the same as 3619; *confirmation*:— edifying.

3621. οἰκονομέω **ŏikŏnŏmĕō**, oy-kon-om-eh´-o; from 3623; to *manage* (a house, i.e. an estate):— be steward.

3622. οἰκονομία **ŏikŏnŏmia**, oy-kon-om-ee´-ah; from 3623; *administration* (of a household or estate); spec. a (relig.) "*economy*":— dispensation, stewardship.

3623. οἰκονόμος **ŏikŏnŏmŏs**, oy-kon-om´-os; from 3624 and the base of 3551; a *house-distributor* (i.e. *manager*), or *overseer*, i.e. an employee in that capacity; by extens. a fiscal *agent* (*treasurer*); fig. a *preacher* (of the Gospel):— chamberlain, governor, steward.

3624. οἶκος **ŏikŏs**, oy´-kos; of uncert. aff.; a *dwelling* (more or less extens., lit. or fig.); by impl. a *family* (more or less related, lit. or fig.):— home, house (-hold), temple.

3625. οἰκουμένη **ŏikŏumĕnē**, oy-kou-men´-ay; fem. part. pres. pass. of 3611 (as noun, by impl. of 1093); *land*, i.e. the (terrene part of the) *globe*; spec. the Rom. *empire*:— earth, world.

3626. οἰκουρός **ŏikŏurŏs**, oy-koo-ros´ or

οἰκουργός **ŏikŏurgŏs**, oy-koor-gos´; from 3624 and οὖρος **ŏurŏs** (a *guard*; be "ware"); a *stayer at home*, i.e. *domestically inclined* (a "good housekeeper"):— keeper at home.

3627. οἰκτείρω **ŏiktĕirō**, oyk-ti´-ro; also (in certain tenses) prol.

οἰκτερέω **ŏiktĕrĕō**, oyk-ter-eh´-o; from οἶκτος **ŏiktŏs**, (*pity*); to *exercise pity*:— have compassion on.

3628. οἰκτιρμός **ŏiktirmŏs**, oyk-tir-mos´; from 3627; *pity*:— mercy.

3629. οἰκτίρμων **ŏiktirmōn**, oyk-tir´-mone; from 3627; *compassionate*:— merciful, of tender mercy.

οἶμαι **ŏimai**. See 3633.

3630. οἰνοπότης **ŏinŏpŏtēs**, oy-nop-ot´-ace; from 3631 and a der. of the alt. of 4095; a *tippler*:— winebibber.

3631. οἶνος **ŏinŏs**, oy´-nos; a primary word (or perh. of Heb. origin [3196]); "*wine*" (lit. or fig.):— wine.

3632. οἰνοφλυγία **ŏinŏphlugia**, oy-nof-loog-ee´-ah; from 3631 and a form of the base of 5397; an *overflow* (or surplus) of *wine*, i.e. *vinolency* (*drunkenness*):— excess of wine.

3633. οἴομαι **ŏiŏmai**, oy´-om-ahee; or (shorter)

οἶμαι **ŏimai**, oy´-mahee; mid. voice appar. from 3634; to *make like* (oneself), i.e. *imagine* (be of the opinion):— suppose, think.

3634. οἷος **hŏiŏs**, hoy´-os; prob. akin to 3588, 3739, and 3745; *such* or *what sort* of (as a correl. or exclamation); espec. the neut. (adv.) with neg. not *so*:— so (as), such as, what (manner of), which.

οἴω **ŏiō**. See 5342.

3635. ὀκνέω **ŏknĕō**, ok-neh´-o; from ὄκνος **ŏknŏs**, (*hesitation*); to *be slow* (fig. *loath*):— delay.

3636. ὀκνηρός **ŏknērŏs**, ok-nay-ros´; from 3635; *tardy*, i.e. *indolent*; (fig.) *irksome*:— grievous, slothful.

3637. ὀκταήμερος **ŏktaēmĕrŏs**, ok-tah-ay´-mer-os; from 3638 and 2250; an *eight-day* old person or act:— the eighth day.

3638. ὀκτώ **ŏktō**, ok-to´; a primary numeral; "*eight*":— eight.

3639. ὄλεθρος **ŏlĕthrŏs**, ol´-eth-ros; from a primary ὄλλυμι **ŏllumi** (to *destroy*; a prol. form); *ruin*, i.e. *death*, *punishment*:— destruction.

3640. ὀλιγόπιστος **ŏligŏpistŏs**, ol-ig-op´-is-tos; from 3641 and 4102; *incredulous*, i.e. *lacking confidence* (in Christ):— of little faith.

3641. ὀλίγος **ŏligŏs**, ol-ee´-gos; of uncert. aff.; *puny* (in extent, degree, number, duration or value); espec. neut. (adv.) *somewhat*:— + almost, brief [-ly], few, (a) little, + long, a season, short, small, a while.

3642. ὀλιγόψυχος **ŏligŏpsuchŏs**, ol-ig-op´-soo-khos; from 3641 and 6590; *little-spirited*, i.e. *faint-hearted*:— feebleminded.

3643. ὀλιγωρέω **ŏligōrĕō**, ol-ig-o-reh´-o; from a compound of 3641 and ὤρα **ōra** ("*care*"); to *have little regard*, for, i.e. to *disesteem*:— despise.

3644. ὀλοθρευτής **ŏlŏthrĕutēs**, ol-oth-ryoo-tace´; from 3645; a *ruiner*, i.e. (spec.) a venomous *serpent*:— destroyer.

3645. ὀλοθρεύω **ŏlŏthrĕuō**, ol-oth-ryoo´-o; from 3639; to *spoil*, i.e. *slay*:— destroy.

3646. ὁλοκαύτωμα **hŏlŏkautōma**, hol-ok-ŏw´-to-mah; from a der. of a compound of 3650 and a der. of 2545; a *wholly-consumed* sacrifice ("holocaust"):— (whole) burnt offering.

3647. ὁλοκληρία **hŏlŏklēria**, hol-ok-lay-ree´-ah; from 3648; *integrity*, i.e. phys. *wholeness*:— perfect soundness.

3648. ὁλόκληρος **hŏlŏklērŏs**, hol´-ok´-lay-ros; from 3650 and 2819; *complete* in every *part*, i.e. perfectly *sound* (in body):— entire, whole.

3649. ὀλολύζω **ŏlŏluzō**, ol-ol-ood´-zo; a redupl. primary verb; to "*howl*" or "*halloo*", i.e. *shriek*:— howl.

3650. ὅλος **hŏlŏs**, hol´-os; a primary word; "*whole*" or "*all*", i.e. *complete* (in extent, amount, time or degree), espec. (neut.) as noun or adv.:— all, altogether, every whit, + throughout, whole.

3651. ὁλοτελής **hŏlŏtĕlēs**, hol-ot-el-ace´; from 3650 and 5056; *complete* to the *end*, i.e. *absolutely perfect*:— wholly.

3652. Ὀλυμπᾶς **Ŏlumpas**, ol-oom-pas´; prob. a contr. from Ὀλυμπιόδωρος **Ŏlumpiŏdōrŏs**, (*Olympian-bestowed*), i.e. *heaven-descended*); *Olympas*, a Chr.:— Olympas.

3653. ὄλυνθος **ŏlunthŏs**, ol´-oon-thos; of uncert. der.; an *unripe* (because out of season) *fig*:— untimely fig.

3654. ὅλως **hŏlōs**, hol-oce; adv. from 3650; *completely*, i.e. *altogether*; (by anal.) *everywhere*; (neg.) not *by any means*:— at all, commonly, utterly.

3655. ὄμβρος **ŏmbrŏs**, om´-bros; of uncert. aff.; a thunder *storm*:— shower.

3656. ὁμιλέω **hŏmilĕō**, hom-il-eh´-o; from 3658; to *be in company* with, i.e.

(by impl.) to *converse:*— commune, talk.

3657. ὁμιλία **hŏmilia**, *hom-il-ee´-ah;* from 3658; *companionship* ("homily"), i.e. (by impl.) *intercourse:*— communication.

3658. ὅμιλος **hŏmilŏs**, *hom´-il-os;* from the base of 3674 and a der. of the alt. of 138 (mean. a *crowd*); *association together,* i.e. a *multitude:*— company.

3659. ὄμμα **ŏmma**, *om´-mah;* from 3700; a *sight,* i.e. (by impl.) the *eye:*— eye.

3660. ὀμνύω **ŏmnuō**, *om-noo´-o;* a prol. form of a primary but obsolete ὄμω **ŏmō**, for which another prol. form ὀμόω **ŏmŏō** *om-ŏ´-o*) is used in certain tenses; to *swear,* i.e. *take* (or *declare on) oath:*— swear.

3661. ὁμοθυμαδόν **hŏmŏthumadŏn**, *hom-oth-oo-mad-on´;* adv. from a compound of the base of 3674 and 2372; *unanimously:*— with one accord (mind).

3662. ὁμοιάζω **hŏmŏiazō**, *hom-oy-ad´-zo;* from 3664; to *resemble:*— agree.

3663. ὁμοιοπαθής **hŏmŏiŏpathēs**, *hom-oy-op-ath-ace´;* from 3664 and the alt. of 3958; *similarly affected:*— of (subject to) like passions.

3664. ὅμοιος **hŏmŏiŏs**, *hom´-oy-os;* from the base of 3674; *similar* (in appearance or character):— like, + manner.

3665. ὁμοιότης **hŏmŏiŏtēs**, *hom-oy-ot´-ace;* from 3664; *resemblance:*— like as, similitude.

3666. ὁμοιόω **hŏmŏiŏō**, *hom-oy-ŏ´-o;* from 3664; to *assimilate,* i.e. *compare;* pass. to *become similar:*— be (make) like, (in the) liken (-ess), resemble.

3667. ὁμοίωμα **hŏmŏiōma**, *hom-oy´-o-mah;* from 3666; a *form;* abstr. *resemblance:*— made like to, likeness, shape, similitude.

3668. ὁμοίως **hŏmŏiōs**, *hom-oy´-oce;* adv. from 3664; *similarly:*— likewise, so.

3669. ὁμοίωσις **hŏmŏiōsis**, *hom-oy´-o-sis;* from 3666; *assimilation,* i.e. *resemblance:*— similitude.

3670. ὁμολογέω **hŏmŏlŏgĕō**, *hom-ol-og-eh´-o;* from a compound of the base of 3674 and 3056; to *assent,* i.e. *covenant, acknowledge:*— con (pro-) fess, confession is made, give thanks, promise.

3671. ὁμολογία **hŏmŏlŏgia**, *hom-ol-og-ee´-ah;* from the same as 3670; *acknowledgment:*— con- (pro-) fession, professed.

3672. ὁμολογουμένως **hŏmŏlŏgŏumĕnōs**, *hom-ol-og-ŏw-men´-oce;* adv. of pres. pass. part. of 3670; *confessedly:*— without controversy.

3673. ὁμότεχνος **hŏmŏtĕchnŏs**, *hom-ot´-ekh-nos;* from the base of 3674 and 5078; a *fellow-artificer:*— of the same craft.

3674. ὁμοῦ **hŏmŏu**, *hom-oo´;* gen. of ὁμός **hŏmŏs**, (the *same;* akin to 260) as adv.; *at the same* place or time:— together.

3675. ὁμόφρων **hŏmŏphrŏn**, *hom-of´-*

rone; from the base of 3674 and 5424; *like-minded,* i.e. *harmonious:*— of one mind.

ὁμόω **ŏmŏō**. See 3660.

3676. ὅμως **hŏmōs**, *hom´-oce;* adv. from the base of 3674; *at the same* time, i.e. (conjunc.) *notwithstanding, yet still:*— and even, nevertheless, though but.

3677. ὄναρ **ŏnar**, *on´-ar;* of uncert. der.; a *dream:*— dream.

3678. ὀνάριον **ŏnariŏn**, *on-ar´-ee-on;* neut. of a presumed der. of 3688; a *little ass:*— young ass.

ὀνάω **ŏnaō**. See 3685.

3679. ὀνειδίζω **ŏnĕidizō**, *on-i-did´-zo;* from 3681; to *defame,* i.e. *rail at, chide, taunt:*— cast in teeth, (suffer) reproach, revile, upbraid.

3680. ὀνειδισμός **ŏnĕidismŏs**, *on-i-dis-mos´;* from 3679; *contumely:*— reproach.

3681. ὄνειδος **ŏnĕidŏs**, *on´-i-dos;* prob. akin to the base of 3686; *notoriety,* i.e. a *taunt* (*disgrace*):— reproach.

3682. Ὀνήσιμος **Ŏnēsimŏs**, *on-ay´-sim-os;* from 3685; *profitable; Onesimus,* a Chr.:— Onesimus.

3683. Ὀνησίφορος **Ŏnēsiphŏrŏs**, *on-ay-sif´-or-os;* from a der. of 3685 and 5411; *profit-bearer; Onesiphorus,* a Chr.:— Onesiphorus.

3684. ὀνικός **ŏnikŏs**, *on-ik-os´;* from 3688; *belonging to an ass,* i.e. *large* (so as to be turned by an ass):— millstone.

3685. ὀνίνημι **ŏninēmi**, *on-in´-ay-mee;* a prol. form of an appar. primary verb (ὄνομαι **ŏnŏmai**, to *slur*); for which another prol. form (ὀνάω **ŏnaō**) is used as an alt. in some tenses (unless indeed it be ident. with the base of 3686 through the idea of *notoriety*); to *gratify,* i.e. (mid. voice) to *derive pleasure* or *advantage* from:— have joy.

3686. ὄνομα **ŏnŏma**, *on´-om-ah;* from a presumed der. of the base of 1097 (comp. 3685); a "*name*" (lit. or fig.) [*authority, character*]:— called, (+ sur-) name (-d).

3687. ὀνομάζω **ŏnŏmazō**, *on-om-ad´-zo;* from 3686; to *name,* i.e. *assign an appellation;* by extens. to *utter, mention, profess:*— call, name.

3688. ὄνος **ŏnŏs**, *on´-os;* appar. a primary word; a *donkey:*— an ass.

3689. ὄντως **ŏntōs**, *on´-toce;* adv. of the oblique cases of 5607; *really:*— certainly, clean, indeed, of a truth, verily.

3690. ὄξος **ŏxŏs**, *ox-os;* from 3691; *vinegar,* i.e. *sour wine:*— vinegar.

3691. ὀξύς **ŏxus**, *ox-oos´;* prob. akin to the base of 188 ["*acid*"]; *keen;* by anal. *rapid:*— sharp, swift.

3692. ὀπή **ŏpē**, *op-ay´;* prob. from 3700; a *hole* (as if for light), i.e. *cavern;* by anal. a *spring* (of water):— cave, place.

3693. ὄπισθεν **ŏpisthĕn**, *op´-is-then;* from ὄπις **ŏpis**, (*regard;* from 3700) with enclitic of source; *from the rear* (as a secure aspect), i.e. *at the back* (adv. and prep. of place or time):— after, backside, behind.

3694. ὀπίσω **ŏpisō**, *op-is´-o;* from the

same as 3693 with enclitic of direction; *to the back,* i.e. *aback* (as adv. or prep. of time or place; or as noun):— after, back (-ward), (+ get) behind, + follow.

3695. ὁπλίζω **hŏplizō**, *hop-lid´-zo;* from 3696; to *equip* (with weapons [mid. voice and fig.]):— arm self.

3696. ὅπλον **hŏplŏn**, *hop´-lon;* prob. from a primary ἔπω **hĕpō** (to be *busy* about); an *implement,* or *utensil* or *tool* (lit. or fig., espec. offensive for war):— armour, instrument, weapon.

3697. ὁποῖος **hŏpŏiŏs**, *hop-oy´-os;* from 3739 and 4169; of *what* kind *that,* i.e. *how* (*as*) *great* (*excellent*) (spec. as an indef. correl. to the antecedent def. 5108 of quality):— what manner (sort) of, such as whatsoever.

3698. ὁπότε **hŏpŏtĕ**, *hop-ot´-eh;* from 3739 and 4218; *what* (-ever) *then,* i.e. (of time) *as soon as:*— when.

3699. ὅπου **hŏpŏu**, *hop´-oo;* from 3739 and 4225; *what* (-ever) *where,* i.e. *at* whichever spot:— in what place, where (-as, -soever), whither (+ soever).

3700. ὀπτάνομαι **ŏptanŏmai**, *op-tan´-om-ahee;* a (mid. voice) prol. form of the primary (mid. voice)

ὄπτομαι **ŏptŏmai**, *op´-tom-ahee;* which is used for it in certain tenses; and both as alternate of 3708; to *gaze* (i.e. with wide-open eyes, as at something remarkable; and thus differing from 991, which denotes simply *voluntary* observation; and from 1492, which expresses merely mechanical, passive or casual vision; while 2300, and still more emphatically its intensive 2334, signifies an earnest but more continued *inspection;* and 4648 a watching *from a distance*):— appear, look, see, shew self.

3701. ὀπτασία **ŏptasia**, *op-tas-ee´-ah;* from a presumed der. of 3700; *visuality,* i.e. (concr.) an *apparition:*— vision.

ὄπτομαι **ŏptŏmai**. See 3700.

3702. ὀπτός **ŏptŏs**, *op-tos´;* from an obs. verb akin to ἔπω **hĕpsō** (to "*steep*"); *cooked,* i.e. *roasted:*— broiled.

3703. ὀπώρα **ŏpōra**, *op-o´-rah;* appar. from the base of 3796 and 5610; prop. *even-tide* of the (summer) season (*dogdays*), i.e. (by impl.) *ripe fruit:*— fruit.

3704. ὅπως **hŏpōs**, *hop´-oce;* from 3739 and 4459; *what* (-ever) *how,* i.e. in the *manner that* (as adv. or conjunc. of coincidence, intentional or actual):— because, how, (so) that, to, when.

3705. ὅραμα **hŏrama**, *hor´-am-ah;* from 3708; *something gazed at,* i.e. a *spectacle* (espec. supernatural):— sight, vision.

3706. ὅρασις **hŏrasis**, *hor´-as-is;* from 3708; the act of *gazing,* i.e. (external) an *aspect* or (intern.) an inspired *appearance:*— sight, vision.

3707. ὁρατός **hŏratŏs**, *hor-at-os´;* from 3708; *gazed at,* i.e. (by impl.) *capable of being seen:*— visible.

3708. ὁράω **hŏraō**, *hor-ah´-o;* prop. to *stare* at [comp. 3700], i.e. (by impl.) to *discern* clearly (phys. or ment.); by extens. to *attend* to; by Heb. to *experi-*

ence; pass. to *appear:*— behold, perceive, see, take heed.

3709. ὀργή **örgē**, *or-gay´;* from *3713;* prop. *desire* (as a *reaching* forth or *excitement* of the mind), i.e. (by anal.) violent *passion* (*ire,* or [justifiable] *abhorrence*); by impl. *punishment:*— anger, indignation, vengeance, wrath.

3710. ὀργίζω **örgizō**, *or-gid´-zo;* from *3709;* to *provoke* or *enrage,* i.e. (pass.) *become exasperated:*— be angry (wroth).

3711. ὀργίλος **örgilös**, *org-ee´-los;* from *3709; irascible:*— soon angry.

3712. ὀργυιά **örguia**, *org-wee-ah´;* from *3713;* a *stretch* of the arms, i.e. a *fathom:*— fathom.

3713. ὀρέγομαι **öregŏmai**, *or-eg´-om-ahee;* mid. voice of appar. a prol. form of an obs. primary [comp. *3735*]; to *stretch* oneself, i.e. *reach* out after (*long* for):— covet after, desire.

3714. ὀρεινός **öreinŏs**, *or-i-nos;* from *3735; mountainous,* i.e. (fem. by impl. of *5561*) the *Highlands* (of Judæa):— hill country.

3715. ὄρεξις **örexis**, *or´-ex-is;* from *3713; excitement* of the mind, i.e. *longing* after:— lust.

3716. ὀρθοποδέω **örthŏpŏdĕō**, *or-thop-od-eh´-o;* from a compound of *3717* and *4228;* to *be straight-footed,* i.e. (fig.) to *go directly* forward:— walk uprightly.

3717. ὀρθός **örthŏs**, *or-thos´;* prob. from the base of *3735; right* (as *rising,* i.e. (perpendicularly) *erect* (fig. *honest*), or (horizontally) *level* or *direct:*— straight, upright.

3718. ὀρθοτομέω **örthŏtŏmĕō**, *or-thot-om-eh´-o;* from a compound of *3717* and the base of *5114,* to *make a straight cut,* i.e. (fig.) to *dissect* (*expound*) *correctly* (the divine message):— rightly divide.

3719. ὀρθρίζω **örthrizō**, *or-thrid´-zo;* from *3722;* to *use* the *dawn,* i.e. (by impl.) to *repair betimes:*— come early in the morning.

3720. ὀρθρινός **örthrinŏs**, *or-thrin-os´;* from *3722; relating to* the *dawn,* i.e. *matutinal* (as an epithet of Venus, espec. brilliant in the early day):— morning.

3721. ὄρθριος **örthriŏs**, *or´-three-os;* from *3722; in* the *dawn,* i.e. up at *daybreak:*— early.

3722. ὄρθρος **örthrŏs**, *or´-thros;* from the same as *3735; dawn* (as *sun-rise, rising* of light); by extens. *morn:*— early in the morning.

3723. ὀρθῶς **örthŏs**, *or-thoce´;* adv. from *3717; in* a *straight* manner, i.e. (fig.) *correctly* (also mor.):— plain, right (-ly).

3724. ὁρίζω **hŏrizō**, *hor-id´-zo;* from *3725;* to *mark* out or *bound* ("horizon"), i.e. (fig.) to *appoint, decree, specify:*— declare, determine, limit, ordain.

3725. ὅριον **hŏriŏn**, *hor´-ee-on;* neut. of a der. of an appar. primary ὅρος **hŏrŏs** (a *bound* or *limit*); a *boundary*-line, i.e. (by impl.) a *frontier* (*region*):— border, coast.

3726. ὁρκίζω **hŏrkizō**, *hor-kid´-zo;* from

3727; to *put on oath,* i.e. *make swear;* by anal. to solemnly *enjoin:*— adjure, charge.

3727. ὅρκος **hŏrkŏs**, *hor´-kos;* from ἕρκος **hĕrkŏs**, (a *fence;* perh. akin to *3725*); a *limit,* i.e. (sacred) *restraint* (spec. an *oath*):— oath.

3728. ὁρκωμοσία **hŏrkōmŏsia**, *hor-ko-mos-ee´ah;* from a compound of *3727* and a der. of *3660; asseveration on oath:*— oath.

3729. ὁρμάω **hŏrmaō**, *hor-mah´-o;* from *3730;* to *start, spur* or *urge* on, i.e. (refl.) to *dash* or *plunge:*— run (violently), rush.

3730. ὁρμή **hŏrmē**, *hor-may´;* of uncert. aff.; a violent *impulse,* i.e. *onset:*— assault.

3731. ὅρμημα **hŏrmēma**, *hor´-may-mah;* from *3730;* an *attack,* i.e. (abstr.) *precipitancy:*— violence.

3732. ὄρνεον **örnĕŏn**, *or´-neh-on;* neut. of a presumed der. of *3733;* a *birdling:*— bird, fowl.

3733. ὄρνις **örnis**, *or´-nis;* prob. from a prol. form of the base of *3735;* a *bird* (as *rising* in the air), i.e. (spec.) a *hen* (or female domestic fowl):— hen.

3734. ὁροθεσία **hŏrŏthĕsia**, *hor-oth-es-ee´-ah;* from a compound of the base of *3725* and a der. of *5087;* a *limit-placing,* i.e. (concr.) *boundary-line:*— bound.

3735. ὄρος **örŏs**, *or´-os;* prob. from an obs. ὄρω **örō** (to *rise* or "*rear;*" perh. akin to *142;* comp. *3733*); a *mountain* (as *lifting* itself above the plain):— hill, mount (-ain).

3736. ὀρύσσω **örussō**, *or-oos´-so;* appar. a primary verb; to "*burrow*" in the ground, i.e. *dig:*— dig.

3737. ὀρφανός **örphanŏs**, *or-fan-os´;* of uncert. aff.; *bereaved* ("*orphan*"), i.e. *parentless:*— comfortless, fatherless.

3738. ὀρχέομαι **örchĕŏmai**, *or-kheh´-om-ahee;* mid. voice from ὄρχος **örchŏs** (a *row* or *ring*); to *dance,* (from the *ranklike* or *regular* motion):— dance.

3739. ὅς **hŏs**, *hos;* incl. fem.

ἥ **hē**, *hay;* and neut.

ὅ **hŏ** *hŏ´;* prob. a primary word (or perh. a form of the art. *3588*); the rel. (sometimes demonstr.) pron., *who, which, what, that:*— one, (an-, the) other, some, that, what, which, who (-m, -se), etc. See also *3757.*

3740. ὁσάκις **hŏsakis**, *hos-ak´-is;* multiple adv. from *3739; how* (i.e. with *302, so*) *many times* as:— as oft (-en) as.

3741. ὅσιος **hŏsiŏs**, *hos´-ee-os;* of uncert. aff.; prop. *right* (by intrinsic or divine character; thus distinguished from *1342,* which refers rather to *human* statutes and relations; from *2413,* which denotes formal *consecration;* and from *40,* which relates to *purity* from defilement), i.e. *hallowed* (*pious, sacred, sure*):— holy, mercy, shalt be.

3742. ὁσιότης **hŏsiŏtēs**, *hos-ee-ot´-ace;* from *3741; piety:*— holiness.

3743. ὁσίως **hŏsiōs**, *hos-ee-oce´;* adv. from *3741; piously:*— holily.

3744. ὀσμή **ösmē**, *os-may´;* from *3605; fragrance* (lit. or fig.):— odour, savour.

3745. ὅσος **hŏsŏs**, *hos´-os;* by redupl. from *3739; as* (*much, great, long,* etc.) *as:*— all (that), as (long, many, much) (as), how great (many, much), [in-] as-much as, so many as, that (ever), the more, those things, what (great, -soever), wheresoever, wherewithsoever, which, × while, who (-soever).

3746. ὅσπερ **hŏspĕr**, *hos´-per;* from *3739* and *4007; who especially:*— whomsoever.

3747. ὀστέον **östĕŏn**, *os-teh´-on;* or contr.

ὀστοῦν **östŏun**, *os-toon´;* of uncert. aff.; a *bone:*— bone.

3748. ὅστις **hŏstis**, *hos´-tis;* incl. the fem.

ἥτις **hētis**, *hay´-tis;* and the neut.

ὅ,τι **hŏ,ti**, *hot´-ee;* from *3739* and *5100; which some,* i.e. *any that;* also (def.) *which same:*— × and (they), (such) as, (they) that, in that they, what (-soever), whereas ye, (they) which, who (-soever). Comp. *3754.*

3749. ὀστράκινος **östrakinŏs**, *os-tra´-kin-os;* from ὄστρακον **östrakŏn**, ["oyster"] (a *tile,* i.e. *terra cotta*); *earthenware,* i.e. *clayey;* by impl. *frail:*— of earth, earthen.

3750. ὄσφρησις **ösphrēsis**, *os´-fray-sis;* from a der. of *3605; smell* (the sense):— smelling.

3751. ὀσφύς **ösphus**, *os-foos´;* of uncert. aff.; the *loin* (extern.), i.e. the *hip;* intern. (by extens.) *procreative power:*— loin.

3752. ὅταν **hŏtan**, *hot´-an;* from *3753* and *302; whenever* (implying *hypothesis* or more or less *uncertainty*); also caus. (conjunc.) *inasmuch as:*— as long (soon) as, that, + till, when (-soever), while.

3753. ὅτε **hŏtĕ**, *hot´-eh;* from *3739* and *5037;* at *which* (thing) too, i.e. *when:*— after (that), as soon as, that, when, while.

ὅ, τε **hŏ, tĕ**, *hŏ´,t´-eh;* also fem.

ἥ, τε **hē, tĕ**, *hay´-teh;* and neut.

τό, τε **tŏ, tĕ**, *tot´-eh;* simply the art. *3588* followed by *5037;* so written (in some editions) to distinguish them from *3752* and *5119.*

3754. ὅτι **hŏti**, *hot´-ee;* neut. of *3748* as conjunc.; demonst. *that* (sometimes redundant); caus. *because:*— as concerning that, as though, because (that), for (that), how (that), (in) that, though, why.

3755. ὅτου **hŏtŏu**, *hot´-oo;* for the gen. of *3748* (as adverb); during *which same* time, i.e. *whilst:*— whiles.

3756. οὐ **ŏu**, *oo;* also (before a vowel)

οὐκ **ŏuk**, *ook;* and (before an aspirate)

οὐχ **ŏuch**, *ookh;* a primary word; the absolute neg. [comp. *3361*] adv.; *no* or *not:*— + long, nay, neither, never, no (× man), none, [can-] not, + nothing, + special, un (-worthy], when, + without, + yet but. See also *3364, 3372.*

3757. οὗ **hŏu**, *hoo;* gen. of *3739* as adv.; at *which* place, i.e. *where:*— where (-in), whither (I-soever).

3758. οὐά **ŏua**, *oo-ah´;* a primary exclamation of surprise; *"ah":*— ah.

3759. οὐαί **ŏuai**, *oo-ah´-ee;* a primary exclamation of grief; *"woe":*— alas, woe.

3760. οὐδαμῶς **ŏudamŏs**, *oo-dam-oce´;* adv. from (the fem.) of *3762; by no means:*— not.

3761. οὐδέ **ŏudĕ**, *oo-deh´;* from *3756* and *1161; not however*, i.e. *neither, nor, not even:*— neither (indeed), never, no (more, nor, not), nor (yet), (also, even, then) not (even, so much as), + nothing, so much as.

3762. οὐδείς **ŏudĕis**, *oo-dice´;* incl. fem.

οὐδεμία **ŏudĕmia**, *oo-dem-ee´-ah;* and neut.

οὐδέν **ŏudĕn**, *oo-den´;* from *3761* and *1520; not even one* (man, woman or thing), i.e. *none, nobody, nothing:*— any (man), aught, man, neither any (thing), never (man), no (man), none (+ of these things), not (any, at all, -thing), nought.

3763. οὐδέποτε **ŏudĕpŏtĕ**, *oo-dep´-ot-eh;* from *3761* and *4218; not even at any time*, i.e. *never at all:*— neither at any time, never, nothing at any time.

3764. οὐδέπω **ŏudĕpō**, *oo-dep´-o;* from *3761* and *4452; not even yet:*— as yet not, never before (yet), (not) yet.

3765. οὐκέτι **ŏukĕti**, *ook-et´-ee;* also (separately)

οὐκ ἔτι **ŏuk ĕti**, *ook et´-ee;* from *3756* and *2089; not yet, no longer:*— after that (not), (not) any more, henceforth (hereafter) not, no longer (more), not as yet (now), now no more (not), yet (not).

3766. οὐκοῦν **ŏukŏun**, *ook-oon´;* from *3756* and *3767;* is it *not therefore* that, i.e. (affirmatively) *hence* or *so:*— then.

3767. οὖν **ŏun**, *oon;* appar. a primary word; (adv.) *certainly,* or (conjunc.) *accordingly:*— and (so, truly), but, now (then), so (likewise then), then, therefore, verily, wherefore.

3768. οὔπω **ŏupō**, *oo´-po;* from *3756* and *4452; not yet:*— hitherto not, (no ...) as yet, not yet.

3769. οὐρά **ŏura**, *oo-rah´;* appar. a primary word; a *tail:*— tail.

3770. οὐράνιος **ŏuraniŏs**, *oo-ran´-ee-os;* from *3772; celestial,* i.e. *belonging to* or *coming from the sky:*— heavenly.

3771. οὐρανόθεν **ŏuranŏthĕn**, *oo-ran-oth´-en;* from *3772* and the enclitic of source; *from the sky:*— from heaven.

3772. οὐρανός **ŏuranŏs**, *oo-ran-os´;* perh. from the same as *3735* (through the idea of *elevation*); the *sky;* by extens. *heaven* (as the abode of God); by impl. *happiness, power, eternity;* spec. the *Gospel* (Christianity):— air, heaven (I-lyl), sky.

3773. οὐρβανός **Ŏurbanŏs**, *oor-ban-os´;* of Lat. or.; *Urbanus* (*of the city,* "*urbane*"), a Chr.:— Urbanus.

3774. Οὐρίας **Ŏurias**, *oo-ree´-as;* of Heb.

or. [223]; *Urias* (i.e. *Urijah*), a Hittite:— Urias.

3775. οὖς **ŏus**, *ooce;* appar. a primary word; the *ear* (phys. or ment.):— ear.

3776. οὐσία **ŏusia**, *oo-see´-ah;* from the fem. of *5607; substance,* i.e. *property* (possessions):— goods, substance.

3777. οὔτε **ŏutĕ**, *oo´-teh;* from *3756* and *5037; not too,* i.e. *neither* or *nor;* by anal. *not even:*— neither, none, nor (yet), (no, yet) not, nothing.

3778. οὗτος **hŏutŏs**, *hoo´-tos;* incl. nom. masc. plur.

οὗτοι **hŏutŏi**, *hoo´-toy;* nom. fem. sing.

αὕτη **hautē**, *hŏw´-tay;* and nom. fem. plur.

αὗται **hautai**, *hŏw´-tahee;* from the art. *3588* and *846; the he* (*she* or it), i.e. *this* or *that* (often with art. repeated):— he (it was that), hereof, it, she, such as, the same, these, they, this (man, same, woman), which, who.

3779. οὕτω **hŏutō**, *hoo´-to;* or (before a vowel)

οὕτως **hŏutŏs**, *hoo´-toce;* adv. from *3778; in this way* (referring to what precedes or follows):— after that, after (in) this manner, as, even (so), for all that, like (-wise), no more, on this fashion (-wise), so (in like manner), thus, what.

3780. οὐχί **ŏuchi**, *oo-khee´;* intens. of *3756; not indeed:*— nay, not.

3781. ὀφειλέτης **ŏphĕilĕtēs**, *of-i-let´-ace;* from *3784;* an *ower,* i.e. person *indebted;* fig. a *delinquent;* mor. a *transgressor* (against God):— debtor, which owed, sinner.

3782. ὀφειλή **ŏphĕilē**, *of-i-lay´;* from *3784; indebtedness,* i.e. (concr.) a *sum owed;* fig. *obligation,* i.e. (conjugal) *duty:*— debt, due.

3783. ὀφείλημα **ŏphĕilēma**, *of-i´-lay-mah;* from (the alt. of) *3784; something owed,* i.e. (fig.) a *due;* mor. a *fault:*— debt.

3784. ὀφείλω **ŏphĕilō**, *of-i´-lo;* or (in certain tenses) its prol. form

ὀφειλέω **ŏphĕilĕō**, *of-i-leh´-o;* prob. from the base of *3786* (through the idea of *accruing*); to *owe* (pecuniarily); fig. to *be under obligation* (*ought, must, should*); mor. to *fail* in duty:— behove, be bound, (be) debt (-or), (be) due (-ty), be guilty (indebted), (must) need (-s), ought, owe, should. See also *3785.*

3785. ὄφελον **ŏphĕlŏn**, *of´-el-on;* first pers. sing. of a past tense of *3784; I ought* (*wish*), i.e. (interj.) *oh that!:*— would (to God.)

3786. ὄφελος **ŏphĕlŏs**, *of´-el-os;* from ὀφέλλω **ŏphĕllō**, (to *heap* up, i.e. *accumulate* or *benefit*); *gain:*— advantageth, profit.

3787. ὀφθαλμοδουλεία **ŏphthalmŏdŏulĕia**, *of-thal-mod-oo-li´-ah;* from *3788* and *1397; sight-labor,* i.e. that needs watching (remissness):— eye-service.

3788. ὀφθαλμός **ŏphthalmŏs**, *of-thal-mos´;* from *3700;* the *eye* (lit. or fig.); by

impl. *vision;* fig. *envy* (from the jealous side-glance):— eye, sight.

3789. ὄφις **ŏphis**, *of´-is;* prob. from *3700* (through the idea of *sharpness* of vision); a *snake,* fig. (as a type of sly cunning) an artful *malicious* person, espec. *Satan:*— serpent.

3790. ὀφρύς **ŏphrus**, *of-roos´;* perh. from *3700* (through the idea of the shading or proximity to the organ of *vision*); the eye-"*brow*" or *forehead,* i.e. (fig.) the *brink* of a precipice:— brow.

3791. ὀχλέω **ŏchlĕō**, *okh-leh´-o;* from *3793;* to *mob,* i.e. (by impl.) to *harass:*— vex.

3792. ὀχλοποιέω **ŏchlŏpŏiĕō**, *okh-lop-oy-eh´-o;* from *3793* and *4160;* to *make a crowd,* i.e. *raise a* public *disturbance:*— gather a company.

3793. ὄχλος **ŏchlŏs**, *okh´los;* from a der. of *2192* (mean. a *vehicle*); a *throng* (as *borne* along); by impl. the *rabble;* by extens. a *class* of people; fig. a *riot:*— company, multitude, number (of people), people, press.

3794. ὀχύρωμα **ŏchurōma**, *okh-oo´-ro-mah;* from a remote der. of *2192* (mean. to *fortify,* through the idea of *holding safely*); a *castle* (fig. *argument*):— stronghold.

3795. ὀψάριον **ŏpsariŏn**, *op-sar´-ee-on;* neut. of a presumed der. of the base of *3702; a relish* to other food (as if cooked *sauce*), i.e. (spec.) *fish* (presumably salted and dried as a condiment):— fish.

3796. ὀψέ **ŏpsĕ**, *op-seh´;* from the same as *3694* (through the idea of *backwardness*); (adv.) *late* in the day; by extens. *after the close* of the day:— (at) even, in the end.

3797. ὄψιμος **ŏpsimŏs**, *op´-sim-os;* from *3796; later,* i.e. *vernal* (*showering*):— latter.

3798. ὄψιος **ŏpsiŏs**, *op´-see-os;* from *3796; late;* fem. (as noun) *afternoon* (early eve) or *nightfall* (later eve):— even (-ing, I-tidel).

3799. ὄψις **ŏpsis**, *op´-sis;* from *3700; prop. sight* (the act), i.e. (by impl) the *visage,* an extern. *show:*— appearance, countenance, face.

3800. ὀψώνιον **ŏpsōniŏn**, *op-so´-nee-on;* neut. of a presumed der. of the same as *3795; rations* for a soldier, i.e. (by extens.) his *stipend* or *pay:*— wages.

3801. ὁ ὢν καί ὁ ἦν καί ὁ ἐρχόμενος **hŏ ōn kai hŏ ēn kai hŏ ĕrchŏmĕnŏs**, *hŏ own kahee hŏ ane kahee hŏ er-khom´-en-os;* a phrase combining *3588* with the pres. part. and imperf. of *1510* and the pres. part. of *2064* by means of *2532; the one being and the one that was and the one coming,* i.e. *the Eternal,* as a divine epithet of Christ:— which art (is, was), and (which) wast (is, was), and art (is) to come (shalt be).

Π

3802. παγιδεύω **pagidĕuō**, *pag-id-yoo´-o;* from *3803;* to *ensnare* (fig.):— entangle.

3803. παγίς **pagis**, *pag-ece´;* from *4078;* a *trap* (as *fastened* by a noose or notch);

fig. a *trick* or *statagem* (*temptation*):— snare.

Πάγος **Pagŏs**. See *697*.

3804. πάθημα **pathēma**, *path´-ay-mah;* from a presumed der. of *3806;* something *undergone*, i.e. *hardship* or *pain;* subj. an *emotion* or *influence:*— affection, affliction, motion, suffering.

3805. παθητός **pathētŏs**, *path-ay-tos´;* from the same as *3804; liable* (i.e. *doomed*) to experience *pain:*— suffer.

3806. πάθος **pathŏs**, *path´-os;* from the alt. of *3958;* prop. *suffering* ("*pathos*"), i.e. (subj.) a *passion* (espec. *concupiscence*):— (inordinate) affection, lust.

πάθω **pathō**. See *3958*.

3807. παιδαγωγός **paidagōgŏs**, *paheedag-o-gos´;* from *3816* and a redupl. form of *71;* a *boy-leader*, i.e. a servant whose office it was to take the children to school; (by impl. [fig.] a *tutor* ["*pædagogue*"]):— instructor, schoolmaster.

3808. παιδάριον **paidariŏn**, *pahee-dar´-ee-on;* neut. of a presumed der. of *3816;* a *little boy:*— child, lad.

3809. παιδεία **paidĕia**, *pahee-di´-ah;* from *3811; tutorage*, i.e. *education* or *training;* by impl. disciplinary *correction:*— chastening, chastisement, instruction, nurture.

3810. παιδευτής **paidĕutēs**, *paheedyoo-tace´;* from *3811;* a *trainer*, i.e. *teacher* or (by impl.) *discipliner:*— which corrected, instructor.

3811. παιδεύω **paidĕuō**, *pahee-dyoo´-o;* from *3816;* to *train* up a child, i.e. *educate*, or (by impl.) *discipline* (by punishment):— chasten (-ise), instruct, learn, teach.

3812. παιδιόθεν **paidiŏthĕn**, *pahee-dee-oth´-en;* adv. (of *source*) from *3813; from infancy:*— of a child.

3813. παιδίον **paidiŏn**, *pahee-dee´-on;* neut. dimin. of *3816;* a *childling* (of either sex), i.e. (prop.) an *infant*, or (by extens.) a half-grown *boy* or girl; fig. an *immature* Chr.:— (little, young) child, damsel.

3814. παιδίσκη **paidiskē**, *pahee-dis´-kay;* fem. dimin. of *3816;* a *girl*, i.e. (spec.) a *female slave* or *servant:*— bondmaid (-woman), damsel, maid (-en).

3815. παίζω **paizō**, *paheed´-zo;* from *3816;* to *sport* (as a boy):— play.

3816. παῖς **pais**, *paheece;* perh. from *3817;* a *boy* (as often *beaten* with impunity), or (by anal.) a *girl*, and (gen.) a *child;* spec. a *slave* or *servant* (espec. a *minister* to a king; and by eminence to God):— child, maid (-en), (man) servant, son, young man.

3817. παίω **paiō**, *pah´-yo;* a primary verb; to *hit* (as if by a single blow and less violently than *5180);* spec. to *sting* (as a scorpion):— smite, strike.

3818. Πακατιανή **Pakatianē**, *pak-at-ee-an-ay´;* fem. of an adj. of uncert. der.; *Pacatianian*, a section of Phrygia:— Pacatiana.

3819. πάλαι **palai**, *pal´-ahee;* prob. another form for *3825* (through the idea of *retrocession*); (adv.) *formerly*, or (by

rel.) *sometime since;* (ellip. as adj.) *ancient:*— any while, a great while ago, (of) old, in time past.

3820. παλαιός **palaiŏs**, *pal-ah-yos´;* from *3819; antique*, i.e. *not recent, worn out:*— old.

3821. παλαιότης **palaiŏtēs**, *pal-ah-yot´-ace;* from *3820; antiquatedness:*— oldness.

3822. παλαιόω **palaiŏō**, *pal-ah-yŏ´-o;* from *3820;* to *make* (pass. *become*) *worn out*, or *declare* obs.:— decay, make (wax) old.

3823. πάλη **palē**, *pal´-ay;* from πάλλω **pallō**, (to *vibrate;* another form for *906); wrestling:*— + wrestle.

3824. παλιγγενεσία **paliggĕnĕsia**, *pal-ing-ghen-es-ee´-ah;* from *3825* and *1078;* (spiritual) *rebirth* (the state or the act), i.e. (fig.) spiritual *renovation;* spec. Messianic *restoration:*— regeneration.

3825. πάλιν **palin**, *pal´-in;* prob. from the same as *3823* (through the idea of *oscillatory* repetition); (adv.) *anew*, i.e. (of place) *back*, (of time) *once more*, or (conjunc.) *furthermore* or *on the other hand:*— again.

3826. παμπληθεί **pamplēthĕi**, *pamplay-thi´;* dat. (adv.) of a compound of *3956* and *4128; in full multitude*, i.e. *concertedly* or *simultaneously:*— all at once.

3827. πάμπολυς **pampŏlus**, *pam-pol-ooce;* from *3956* and *4183; full many*, i.e. *immense:*— very great.

3828. Παμφυλία **Pamphulia**, *pam-foolee´-ah;* from a compound of *3956* and *5443; every-tribal*, i.e. *heterogeneous* (*5561* being impl.); *Pamphylia*, a region of Asia Minor:— Pamphylia.

3829. πανδοχεῖον **pandŏchĕiŏn**, *pandokh-i´-on;* neut. of a presumed compound of *3956* and a der. of *1209; all-receptive*, i.e. a public *lodging*-place (*caravanserai* or *khan*):— inn.

3830. πανδοχεύς **pandŏchĕus**, *pandokh-yoos´;* from the same as *3829;* an *innkeeper* (*warden of a caravanserai*):— host.

3831. πανήγυρις **panēguris**, *pan-ay´-goo-ris;* from *3956* and a der. of *58;* a *mass-meeting*, i.e. (fig.) *universal companionship:*— gen. assembly.

3832. πανοικί **panŏiki**, *pan-oy-kee´* or

πανοικεί **panŏikei**, *pan-oy-ki´* adv. from *3956* and *3624; with the whole family:*— with all his house.

3833. πανοπλία **panŏplia**, *pan-op-lee´-ah;* from a compound of *3956* and *3696; full armor* ("*panoply*"):— all (whole) armour.

3834. πανουργία **panŏurgia**, *pan-oorgee´-ah;* from *3835; adroitness*, i.e. (in a bad sense) *trickery* or *sophistry:*— (cunning) craftiness, subtilty (subtlety).

3835. πανοῦργος **panŏurgŏs**, *pan-oor-gos;* from *3956* and *2041; all-working*, i.e. *adroit* (*shrewd*):— crafty.

3836. πανταχόθεν **pantachŏthĕn**, *pan-takh-oth´-en;* adv. (of *source*) from *3837; from all* directions:— from every quarter.

3837. πανταχοῦ **pantachŏu**, *pan-takhoo´;* gen. (as adv. of *place*) of a presumed der. of *3956; universally:*— in all places, everywhere.

3838. παντελής **pantĕlēs**, *pan-tel-ace´;* from *3956* and *5056; full-ended*, i.e. *entire* (neut. as noun, *completion*):— + in [no] wise, uttermost.

3839. πάντη **pantē**, *pan´-tay;* adv. (of *manner*) from *3956; wholly:*— always.

3840. παντόθεν **pantŏthĕn**, *pan-toth´-en;* adv. (of *source*) from *3956; from* (i.e. *on*) *all* sides:— on every side, round about.

3841. παντοκράτωρ **pantŏkratōr**, *pan-tok-rat´-ore;* from *3956* and *2904;* the *all-ruling*, i.e. *God* (as absolute and universal *sovereign*):— Almighty, Omnipotent.

3842. πάντοτε **pantŏtĕ**, *pan´-tot-eh;* from *3956* and *3753; every when*, i.e. *at all* times:— alway (-s), ever (-more).

3843. πάντως **pantŏs**, *pan´-toce;* adv. from *3956; entirely;* spec. *at all events*, (with neg. following) *in no event:*— by all means, altogether, at all, needs, no doubt, in [no] wise, surely.

3844. παρά **para**, *par-ah´;* a primary prep.; prop. *near;* i.e. (with gen.) *from beside* (lit. or fig.), (with dat.) *at* (or *in*) the *vicinity* of (object or subject), (with acc.) to the *proximity* with (local [espec. *beyond* or *opposed* to] or causal [on *account* of]:— above, against, among, at, before, by, contrary to, × friend, from, + give [such things as they], + that [she] had, × his, in, more than, nigh unto, (out) of, past, save, side ... by, in the sight of, then, [there-] fore, with. In compounds it retains the same variety of application.

3845. παραβαίνω **parabainō**, *par-ab-ah´-ee-no;* from *3844* and the base of *939;* to *go contrary* to, i.e. *violate* a command:— (by) transgress (-ion).

3846. παραβάλλω **paraballō**, *par-ab-al´-lo;* from *3844* and *906;* to *throw alongside*, i.e. (refl.) to *reach* a place, or (fig.) to *liken:*— arrive, compare.

3847. παράβασις **parabasis**, *par-ab´-asis;* from *3845; violation:*— breaking, transgression.

3848. παραβάτης **parabatēs**, *par-ab-at´-ace;* from *3845;* a *violator:*— breaker, transgress (-or).

3849. παραβιάζομαι **parabiazŏmai**, *par-ab-ee-ad´-zom-ahee;* from *3844* and the mid. voice of *971;* to *force contrary* to (nature), i.e. *compel* (by entreaty):— constrain.

3850. παραβολή **parabŏlē**, *par-ab-ol-ay´;* from *3846;* a *similitude* ("*parable*"), i.e. (symbol.) *fictitious narrative* (of common life conveying a mor.), *apothegm* or *adage:*— comparison, figure, parable, proverb.

3851. παραβουλεύομαι **parabŏulĕuŏmai**, *par-ab-ool-yoo´-om-ahee* or

παραβολεύομαι **parabŏlĕuŏmai**, *par-ab-ol-yoo´-om-ahee* from *3844* and the mid. voice of *1011;* to *misconsult*, i.e. *disregard:*— not (to) regard (-ing).

3852. παραγγελία **paraggĕlia**, *par-ang-*

gel-ee´-ah; from 3853; a mandate:— charge, command.

3853. παραγγέλλω **paraggĕllō**, par-ang-gel´-lo; from 3844 and the base of 32; to transmit a message, i.e. (by impl.) to enjoin:— (give in) charge, (give) command (-ment), declare.

3854. παραγίνομαι **paraginŏmai**, par-ag-in´-om-ahee; from 3844 and 1096; to become near, i.e. approach (have arrived); by impl. to appear publicly:— come, go, be present.

3855. παράγω **paragō**, par-ag´-o; from 3844 and 71; to lead near, i.e. (refl. or intr.) to go along or away:— depart, pass (away, by, forth).

3856. παραδειγματίζω **paradĕigmatizō**, par-ad-igue-mat-id´-zo; from 3844 and 1165; to show alongside (the public), i.e. expose to infamy:— make a public example, put to an open shame.

3857. παράδεισος **paradĕisŏs**, par-ad´-i-sos; of Oriental or. [comp. 6508]; a park, i.e. (spec.) an Eden (place of future happiness, "paradise"):— paradise.

3858. παραδέχομαι **paradĕchŏmai**, par-ad-ekh´-om-ahee; from 3844 and 1209; to accept near, i.e. admit or (by impl.) delight in:— receive.

3859. παραδιατριβή **paradiatribē**, par-ad-ee-at-ree-bay´; from a compound of 3844 and 1304; misemployment, i.e. meddlesomeness:— perverse disputing.

3860. παραδίδωμι **paradidōmi**, par-ad-id´-o-mee; from 3844 and 1325; to surrender, i.e yield up, intrust, transmit:— betray, bring forth, cast, commit, deliver (up), give (over, up), hazard, put in prison, recommend.

3861. παράδοξος **paradŏxŏs**, par-ad´-ox-os; from 3844 and 1391 (in the sense of seeming); contrary to expectation, i.e. extraordinary ("paradox"):— strange.

3862. παράδοσις **paradŏsis**, par-ad´-os-is; from 3860; transmission, i.e. (concr.) a precept; spec. the Jewish traditional law:— ordinance, tradition.

3863. παραζηλόω **parazēlŏō**, par-ad-zay-lŏ´-o; from 3844 and 2206; to stimulate alongside, i.e. excite to rivalry:— provoke to emulation (jealousy).

3864. παραθαλάσσιος **parathalassiŏs**, par-ath-al-as´-see-os; from 3844 and 2281; along the sea, i.e. maritime (lacustrine):— upon the sea coast.

3865. παραθεωρέω **parathĕōrĕō**, par-ath-eh-o-reh´-o; from 3844 and 2334; to overlook or disregard:— neglect.

3866. παραθήκη **parathēkē**, par-ath-ay´-kay; from 3908; a deposit, i.e. (fig.) trust:— committed unto.

3867. παραινέω **parainĕō**, par-ahee-neh´-o; from 3844 and 134; to mispraise, i.e. recommend or advise (a different course):— admonish, exhort.

3868. παραιτέομαι **paraitĕŏmai**, par-ahee-teh´-om-ahee; from 3844 and the mid. voice of 154; to beg off, i.e. deprecate, decline, shun:— avoid, (make) excuse, intreat, refuse, reject.

3869. παρακαθίζω **parakathizō**, par-ak-ath-id´-zo; from 3844 and 2523; to sit down near:— sit.

3870. παρακαλέω **parakalĕō**, par-ak-al-eh´-o; from 3844 and 2564; to call near, i.e. invite, invoke (by imploration, hortation or consolation):— beseech, call for, (be of good) comfort, desire, (give) exhort (-ation), intreat, pray.

3871. παρακαλύπτω **parakaluptō**, par-ak-al-oop´-to; from 3844 and 2572; to cover alongside, i.e. veil (fig.):— hide.

3872. παρακαταθήκη **parakatathēkē**, par-ak-at-ath-ay´-kay; from a compound of 3844 and 2698; something put down alongside, i.e. a deposit (sacred trust):— that (thing) which is committed (un-) to (trust).

3873. παράκειμαι **parakĕimai**, par-ak´-i-mahee; from 3844 and 2749; to lie near, i.e. be at hand (fig. be prompt or easy):— be present.

3874. παράκλησις **paraklēsis**, par-ak´-lay-sis; from 3870; imploration, hortation, solace:— comfort, consolation, exhortation, intreaty.

3875. παράκλητος **paraklētŏs**, par-ak´-lay-tos; an intercessor, consoler:— advocate, comforter.

3876. παρακοή **parakŏē**, par-ak-ŏ-ay´; from 3878; inattention, i.e. (by impl.) disobedience:— disobedience.

3877. παρακολουθέω **parakŏlŏuthĕō**, par-ak-ol-oo-theh´-o; from 3844 and 190; to follow near, i.e. (fig.) attend (as a result), trace out, conform to:— attain, follow, fully know, have understanding.

3878. παρακούω **parakŏuō**, par-ak-oo´-o; from 3844 and 191; to mishear, i.e. (by impl.) to disobey:— neglect to hear.

3879. παρακύπτω **parakuptō**, par-ak-oop´-to; from 3844 and 2955; to bend beside, i.e. lean over (so as to peer within):— look (into), stoop down.

3880. παραλαμβάνω **paralambanō**, par-al-am-ban´-o; from 3844 and 2983; to receive near, i.e. associate with oneself (in any familiar or intimate act or relation); by anal. to assume an office; fig. to learn:— receive, take (unto, with).

3881. παραλέγομαι **paralĕgŏmai**, par-al-eg´-om-ahee; from 3844 and the mid. voice of 3004 (in its orig. sense); (spec.) to lay one's course near, i.e. sail past:— pass, sail by.

3882. παράλιος **paraliŏs**, par-al´-ee-os; from 3844 and 251; beside the salt (sea), i.e. maritime:— sea coast.

3883. παραλλαγή **parallagē**, par-al-lag-ay´; from a compound of 3844 and 236; transmutation (of phase or orbit), i.e. (fig.) fickleness:— variableness.

3884. παραλογίζομαι **paralŏgizŏmai**, par-al-og-id´-zom-ahee; from 3844 and 3049; to misreckon, i.e. delude:— beguile, deceive.

3885. παραλυτικός **paralutikŏs**, par-al-oo-tee-kos´; from a der. of 3886; as if dissolved, i.e. "paralytic":— that had (sick of) the palsy.

3886. παραλύω **paraluō**, par-al-oo´-o; from 3844 and 3089; to loosen beside, i.e. relax (perf. pass. part. paralyzed or enfeebled):— feeble, sick of the (taken with) palsy.

3887. παραμένω **paramĕnō**, par-am-en´-o; from 3844 and 3306; to stay near, i.e. remain (lit. tarry; or fig. be permanent, persevere):— abide, continue.

3888. παραμυθέομαι **paramuthĕŏmai**, par-am-oo-theh´-om-ahee; from 3844 and the mid. voice of a der. of 3454; to relate near, i.e. (by impl.) encourage, console:— comfort.

3889. παραμυθία **paramuthia**, par-am-oo-thee´-ah; from 3888; consolation (prop. abstr.):— comfort.

3890. παραμύθιον **paramuthiŏn**, par-am-oo´-thee-on; neut. of 3889; consolation (prop. concr.):— comfort.

3891. παρανομέω **paranŏmĕō**, par-an-om-eh´-o; from a compound of 3844 and 3551; to be opposed to law, i.e. to transgress:— contrary to law.

3892. παρανομία **paranŏmia**, par-an-om-ee´-ah; from the same as 3891; transgression:— iniquity.

3893. παραπικραίνω **parapikrainō**, par-ap-ik-rah´-ee-no; from 3844 and 4087; to embitter alongside, i.e. (fig.) to exasperate:— provoke.

3894. παραπικρασμός **parapikrasmŏs**, par-ap-ik-ras-mos´; from 3893; irritation:— provocation.

3895. παραπίπτω **parapiptō**, par-ap-ip´-to; from 3844 and 4098; to fall aside, i.e. (fig.) to apostatize:— fall away.

3896. παραπλέω **paraplĕō**, par-ap-leh´-o; from 3844 and 4126; to sail near:— sail by.

3897. παραπλήσιον **paraplēsiŏn**, par-ap-lay-see-on; neut. of a compound of 3844 and the base of 4139 (as adv.); close by, i.e. (fig.) almost:— nigh unto.

3898. παραπλησίως **paraplēsiŏs**, par-ap-lay-see´-oce; adv. from the same as 3897; in a manner near by, i.e. (fig.) similarly:— likewise.

3899. παραπορεύομαι **parapŏrĕuŏmai**, par-ap-or-yoo´-om-ahee; from 3844 and 4198; to travel near:— go, pass (by).

3900. παράπτωμα **paraptōma**, par-ap´-to-mah; from 3895; a side-slip (lapse or deviation), i.e. (unintentional) error or (willful) transgression:— fall, fault, offence, sin, trespass.

3901. παραρρέω **pararrhuĕō**, par-ar-hroo-eh´-o; from 3844 and the alternate of 4482; to flow by, i.e. (fig.) carelessly pass (miss):— let slip.

3902. παράσημος **parasēmŏs**, par-as´-ay-mos; from 3844 and the base of 4591; side-marked, i.e. labelled (with a badge [figure-head] of a ship):— sign.

3903. παρασκευάζω **paraskĕuazō**, par-ask-yoo-ad´-zo; from 3844 and a der. of 4632; to furnish aside, i.e. get ready:— prepare self, be (make) ready.

3904. παρασκευή **paraskĕuē**, par-ask-yoo-ay´; as if from 3903; readiness:— preparation.

3905. παρατείνω **paratĕinō**, par-at-i´-no; from 3844 and τείνω **tĕinō** (to stretch); to extend along, i.e. prolong (in point of time):— continue.

3906. παρατηρέω **paratēreō**, par-at-ay-reh´-o; from 3844 and 5083; to inspect alongside, i.e. note insidiously or scrupulously:— observe, watch.

3907. παρατήρησις **paratērēsis**, par-at-ay´-ray-sis; from 3906; inspection, i.e. ocular evidence:— observation.

3908. παρατίθημι **paratithēmi**, par-at-ith´-ay-mee; from 3844 and 5087; to place alongside, i.e. present (food, truth); by impl. to deposit (as a trust or for protection):— allege, commend, commit (the keeping of), put forth, set before.

3909. παρατυγχάνω **paratugchanō**, par-at-oong-khan´-o; from 3844 and 5177; to chance near, i.e. fall in with:— meet with.

3910. παραυτίκα **parautika**, par-ŏw-tee´-kah; from 3844 and a der. of 846; at the very instant, i.e. momentary:— but for a moment.

3911. παραφέρω **paraphĕrō**, par-af-er´-o; from 3844 and 5342 (incl. its alt. forms); to bear along or aside, i.e. carry off (lit. or fig.); by impl. to avert:— remove, take away.

3912. παραφρονέω **paraphrŏnĕō**, par-af-ron-eh´-o; from 3844 and 5426; to misthink, i.e. be insane (silly):— as a fool.

3913. παραφρονία **paraphrŏnia**, par-af-ron-ee´-ah; from 3912; insanity, i.e. foolhardiness:— madness.

3914. παραχειμάζω **parachĕimazō**, par-akh-i-mad´-zo; from 3844 and 5492; to winter near, i.e. stay with over the rainy season:— winter.

3915. παραχειμασία **parachĕimasia**, par-akh-i-mas-ee´-ah; from 3914; a wintering over:— winter in.

3916. παραχρῆμα **parachrēma**, par-akh-ray´-mah; from 3844 and 5536 (in its orig. sense); at the thing itself, i.e. instantly:— forthwith, immediately, presently, straightway, soon.

3917. πάρδαλις **pardalis**, par´-dal-is; fem. of πάρδος **pardŏs** (a panther); a leopard:— leopard.

3918. πάρειμι **parĕimi**, par´-i-mee; from 3844 and 1510 (incl. its various forms); to be near, i.e. at hand; neut. pres. part. (sing.) time being, or (plural) property:— come, × have, be here, + lack, (be here) present.

3919. παρεισάγω **parĕisagō**, par-ice-ag´-o; from 3844 and 1521; to lead in aside, i.e. introduce surreptitiously:— privily bring in.

3920. παρείσακτος **parĕisaktŏs**, par-ice´-ak-tos; from 3919; smuggled in:— unawares brought in.

3921. παρεισδύνω **parĕisdunō**, par-ice-doo´-no; from 3844 and a compound of 1519 and 1416; to settle in alongside, i.e. lodge stealthily:— creep in unawares.

3922. παρεισέρχομαι **parĕisĕrchŏmai**, par-ice-er´-khom-ahee; from 3844 and 1525; to come in alongside, i.e. supervene additionally or stealthily:— come in privily, enter.

3923. παρεισφέρω **parĕisphĕrō**, par-ice-fer´-o; from 3844 and 1533; to bear in alongside, i.e. introduce simultaneously:— give.

3924. παρεκτός **parĕktŏs**, par-ek-tos´; from 3844 and 1622; near outside, i.e. besides:— except, saving, without.

3925. παρεμβολή **parĕmbŏlē**, par-em-bol-ay´; from a compound of 3844 and 1685; a throwing in beside (juxtaposition), i.e. (spec.) battle-array, encampment or barracks (tower Antonia):— army, camp, castle.

3926. παρενοχλέω **parĕnŏchlĕō**, par-en-okh-leh´-o; from 3844 and 1776; to harass further, i.e. annoy:— trouble.

3927. παρεπίδημος **parepidēmŏs**, par-ep-id´-ay-mos; from 3844 and the base of 1927; an alien alongside, i.e. a resident foreigner:— pilgrim, stranger.

3928. παρέρχομαι **parĕrchŏmai**, par-er´-khom-ahee; from 3844 and 2064; to come near or aside, i.e. to approach (arrive), go by (or away), (fig.) perish or neglect, (caus.) avert:— come (forth), go, pass (away, by, over), past, transgress.

3929. πάρεσις **parēsis**, par´-es-is; from 2935; prætermission, i.e. toleration:— remission.

3930. παρέχω **parĕchō**, par-ekh´-o; from 3844 and 2192; to hold near, i.e. present, afford, exhibit, furnish occasion:— bring, do, give, keep, minister, offer, shew, + trouble.

3931. παρηγορία **parēgŏria**, par-ay-gor-ee´-ah; from a compound of 3844 and a der. of 58 (mean. to harangue an assembly); an address alongside, i.e. (spec.) consolation:— comfort.

3932. παρθενία **parthĕnia**, par-then-ee´-ah; from 3933; maidenhood:— virginity.

3933. παρθένος **parthĕnŏs**, par-then´-os; of unknown or.; a maiden; by impl. an unmarried daughter:— virgin.

3934. Πάρθος **Parthŏs**, par´-thos; prob. of for. or.; a Parthian, i.e. inhab. of Parthia:— Parthian.

3935. παρίημι **pariēmi**, par-ee´-ay-mi; from 3844 and ἵημι hiēmi, (to send); to let by, i.e. relax:— hang down.

3936. παρίστημι **paristēmi**, par-is´-tay-mee; or prol.

παριστάνω **paristanō** par-is-tan´-o; from 3844, and 2476; to stand beside, i.e. (tran.) to exhibit, proffer, (spec.) recommend, (fig.) substantiate; or (intr.) to be at hand (or ready), aid:— assist, bring before, command, commend, give presently, present, prove, provide, shew, stand (before, by, here, up, with), yield.

3937. Παρμενᾶς **Parmĕnas**, par-men-as´; prob. by contr. for Παρμενίδης Parmĕnidēs (a der. of a compound of 3844 and 3306); constant; Parmenas, a Chr.:— Parmenas.

3938. πάροδος **parŏdŏs**, par´-od-os; from 3844 and 3598; a by-road, i.e. (act.) a route:— way.

3939. παροικέω **parŏikĕō**, par-oy-keh´-o; from 3844 and 3611; to dwell near, i.e. reside as a foreigner:— sojourn in, be a stranger.

3940. παροικία **parŏikia**, par-oy-kee´-ah; from 3941; foreign residence:— sojourning, × as strangers.

3941. πάροικος **parŏikŏs**, par´-oy-kos; from 3844 and 3624; having a home near, i.e. (as noun) a by-dweller (alien resident):— foreigner, sojourn, stranger.

3942. παροιμία **parŏimia**, par-oy-mee´-ah; from a compound of 3844 and perh. a der. of 3633; appar. a state alongside of supposition, i.e. (concr.) an adage; spec. an enigmatical or fictitious illustration:— parable, proverb.

3943. πάροινος **parŏinŏs**, par´-oy-nos; from 3844 and 3631; staying near wine, i.e. tippling (a toper):— given to wine.

3944. παροίχομαι **parŏichŏmai**, par-oy-khom-ahee; from 3844 and οἴχομαι ŏichŏmai (to depart); to escape along, i.e. be gone:— past.

3945. παρομοιάζω **parŏmŏiazō**, par-om-oy-ad´-zo; from 3946; to resemble:— be like unto.

3946. παρόμοιος **parŏmŏiŏs**, par-om´-oy-os; from 3844 and 3664; alike nearly, i.e. similar:— like.

3947. παροξύνω **parŏxunō**, par-ox-oo´-no; from 3844 and a der. of 3691; to sharpen alongside, i.e. (fig.) to exasperate:— easily provoke, stir.

3948. παροξυσμός **parŏxusmŏs**, par-ox-oos-mos´; from 3947 ("paroxysm"); incitement (to good), or dispute (in anger):— contention, provoke unto.

3949. παροργίζω **parŏrgizō**, par-org-id´-zo; from 3844 and 3710; to anger alongside, i.e. enrage:— anger, provoke to wrath.

3950. παροργισμός **parŏrgismŏs**, par-org-is-mos´; from 3949; rage:— wrath.

3951. παροτρύνω **parŏtrunō**, par-ot-roo´-no; from 3844 and ὀτρύνω ŏtrunō (to spur); to urge along, i.e. stimulate (to hostility):— stir up.

3952. παρουσία **parŏusia**, par-oo-see´-ah; from the present part. of 3918; a being near, i.e. advent (often, return; spec. of Christ to punish Jerusalem, or finally the wicked); (by impl.) phys. aspect:— coming, presence.

3953. παροψίς **parŏpsis**, par-op-sis´; from 3844 and the base of 3795; a side-dish (the receptacle):— platter.

3954. παρρησία **parrhēsia**, par-rhay-see´-ah; from 3956 and a der. of 4483; all out-spokenness, i.e. frankness, bluntness, publicity; by impl. assurance:— bold (× -ly, -ness, -ness of speech), confidence, × freely, × openly, × plainly (-ness).

3955. παρρησιάζομαι **parrhēsiazŏmai**, par-hray-see-ad´-zom-ahee; mid. voice from 3954; to be frank in utterance, or confident in spirit and demeanor:— be (wax) bold, (preach, speak) boldly.

3956. πᾶς **pas**, pas; incl. all the forms of declension; appar. a primary word; all, any, every, the whole:— all (manner of, means), alway (-s), any (one), × daily, + ever, every (one, way), as many as, + no (-thing), × thoroughly, whatsoever, whole, whosoever.

3957. πάσχα **pascha**, *pas´-khah;* of Chald. or. [comp. 6453]; the *Passover* (the meal, the day, the festival or the special sacrifices connected with it):— Easter, Passover.

3958. πάσχω **paschō**, *pas´-kho;* incl. the forms

πάθω (**pathō**, *path´-o*) and

πένθω (**pĕnthō**, *pen´-tho*), used only in certain tenses for it; appar. a primary verb; to *experience* a sensation or impression (usually painful):— feel, passion, suffer, vex.

3959. Πάταρα **Patara**, *pat´-ar-ah;* prob. of for. or.; *Patara*, a place in Asia Minor:— Patara.

3960. πατάσσω **patassō**, *pat-as´-so;* prob. prol. from *3817;* to *knock* (gently or with a weapon or fatally):— smite, strike. Comp. *5180.*

3961. πατέω **patĕō**, *pat-eh´-o;* from a der. prob. of *3817* (mean. a "*path*"); to *trample* (lit. or fig.):— tread (down, under foot).

3962. πατήρ **patēr**, *pat-ayr´;* appar. a primary word; a "*father*" (lit. or fig., near or more remote):— father, parent.

3963. Πάτμος **Patmos**, *pat´-mos;* of uncert. der.; *Patmos*, an islet in the Mediterranean:— Patmos.

3964. πατραλῴας **patralōas**, *pat-ral-o´-as* πατρολῴας **patrŏlōas**, *pat-rol-o´-as;* from *3962* and the same as the latter part of *3389;* a *parricide:*— murderer of fathers.

3965. πατριά **patria**, *pat-ree-ah´;* as if fem. of a der. of *3962;* paternal *descent*, i.e. (concr.) a *group* of families or a whole *race* (*nation*):— family, kindred, lineage.

3966. πατριάρχης **patriarchēs**, *pat-ree-arkh´-ace;* from *3965* and *757;* a *progenitor* ("patriarch"):— patriarch.

3967. πατρικός **patrikŏs**, *pat-ree-kos;* from *3962; paternal*, i.e. *ancestral:*— of fathers.

3968. πατρίς **patris**, *pat-rece´;* from *3962;* a *father-land*, i.e. *native town;* (fig.) heavenly *home:*— (own) country.

3969. Πατρόβας **Patrŏbas**, *pat-rob´-as;* perh. contr. for Πατρόβιος **Patrŏbiŏs** (a compound of *3962* and *979); father's life; Patrobas*, a Chr.:— Patrobas.

3970. πατροπαράδοτος **patrŏparadŏtŏs**, *pat-rop-ar-ad´-ot-os;* from *3962* and a der. of *3860* (in the sense of *handing over* or *down); traditionary:*— received by tradition from fathers.

3971. πατρῷος **patrōŏs**, *pat-ro´-os;* from *3962; paternal*, i.e. *hereditary:*— of fathers.

3972. Παῦλος **Paulŏs**, *pŏw´-los;* of Lat. or.; (*little;* but remotely from a der. of *3973*, mean. the same); *Paulus*, the name of a Rom. and of an apostle:— Paul, Paulus.

3973. παύω **pauō**, *pŏw´-o;* a primary verb ("*pause*"); to *stop* (tran. or intr.), i.e. *restrain, quit, desist, come to an end:*— cease, leave, refrain.

3974. Πάφος **Paphŏs**, *paf´-os;* of uncert.

der.; *Paphus*, a place in Cyprus:— Paphos.

3975. παχύνω **pachunō**, *pakh-oo´-no;* from a der. of *4078* (mean. *thick*); to *thicken*, i.e. (by impl.) to *fatten* (fig. *stupefy* or *render callous*):— wax gross.

3976. πέδη **pĕdē**, *ped´-ay;* ultimately from *4228;* a *shackle* for the feet:— fetter.

3977. πεδινός **pĕdinŏs**, *ped-ee-nos´;* from a der. of *4228* (mean. the *ground*); *level* (as easy for the *feet*):— plain.

3978. πεζεύω **pĕzĕuō**, *ped-zyoo´-o;* from the same as *3979;* to *foot* a journey, i.e. *travel* by land:— go afoot.

3979. πεζῇ **pĕzēi**, *ped-zay´;* dat. fem. of a der. of *4228* (as adv.); *foot-wise*, i.e. by *walking:*— a- (on) foot.

3980. πειθαρχέω **pĕitharchĕō**, *pitharkh-eh´-o;* from a compound of *3982* and *757;* to *be persuaded* by a *ruler*, i.e. (gen.) to *submit* to authority; by anal. to *conform* to advice:— hearken, obey (magistrates).

3981. πειθός **pĕithŏs**, *pi-thos´;* from *3982; persuasive:*— enticing.

3982. πείθω **pĕithō**, *pi´-tho;* a primary verb; to *convince* (by argument, true or false); by anal. to *pacify* or *conciliate* (by other fair means); refl. or pass. to *assent* (to evidence or authority), to *rely* (by inward certainty):— agree, assure, believe, have confidence, be (wax) confident, make friend, obey, persuade, trust, yield.

3983. πεινάω **pĕinaō**, *pi-nah´-o;* from the same as *3993* (through the idea of pinching *toil;* "*pine*"); to *famish* (absol. or comp.); fig. to *crave:*— be an hungered.

3984. πεῖρα **pĕira**, *pi´-rah;* from the base of *4008* (through the idea of *piercing*); a *test*, i.e. *attempt, experience:*— assaying, trial.

3985. πειράζω **pĕirazō**, *pi-rad´-zo;* from *3984;* to *test* (obj.), i.e. *endeavor, scrutinize, entice, discipline:*— assay, examine, go about, prove, tempt (-er), try.

3986. πειρασμός **pĕirasmŏs**, *pi-rasmos´;* from *3985;* a *putting* to *proof* (by experiment [of good], *experience* [of evil], solicitation, discipline or provocation); by impl. *adversity:*— temptation, × try.

3987. πειράω **pĕiraō**, *pi-rah´-o;* from *3984;* to *test* (subj.), i.e. (refl.) to *attempt:*— assay.

3988. πεισμονή **pĕismŏnē**, *pice-mon-ay´;* from a presumed der. of *3982; persuadableness*, i.e. *credulity:*— persuasion.

3989. πέλαγος **pĕlagŏs**, *pel´-ag-os;* of uncert. aff.; deep or open *sea*, i.e. the *main:*— depth, sea.

3990. πελεκίζω **pĕlĕkizō**, *pel-ek-id´-zo;* from a der. of *4141* (mean. an *axe*); to *chop* off (the head), i.e. *truncate:*— behead.

3991. πέμπτος **pĕmptŏs**, *pemp´-tos;* from *4002; fifth:*— fifth.

3992. πέμπω **pĕmpō**, *pem´-po;* appar. a primary verb; to *dispatch* (from the subj. view or point of *departure*,

whereas ἵημι **hiēmi** [as a stronger form of εἶμι **ĕimi**] refers rather to the obj. point or *terminus ad quem*, and *4724* denotes prop. the *orderly* motion involved), espec. on a temporary errand; also to *transmit, bestow*, or *wield:*— send, thrust in.

3993. πένης **pĕnēs**, *pen´-ace;* from a primary πένω **pĕnō**, (to *toil* for daily subsistence); *starving*, i.e. *indigent:*— poor. Comp. *4434.*

3994. πενθερά **pĕnthĕra**, *pen-ther-ah´;* fem. of *3995;* a *wife's* mother:— mother in law, wife's mother.

3995. πενθερός **pĕnthĕrŏs**, *pen-ther-os´;* of uncert. aff.; a *wife's father:*— father in law.

3996. πενθέω **pĕnthĕō**, *pen-theh´-o;* from *3997;* to *grieve* (the feeling or the act):— mourn, (be-) wail.

3997. πένθος **pĕnthŏs**, *pen´-thos;* strengthened from the alt. of *3958; grief:*— mourning, sorrow.

3998. πενιχρός **pĕnichrŏs**, *pen-ikh-ros´;* prol. from the base of *3993; necessitous:*— poor.

3999. πεντάκις **pĕntakis**, *pen-tak-ece´;* mult. adv. from *4002; five times:*— five times.

4000. πεντακισχίλιοι **pĕntakischiliŏi**, *pen-tak-is-khil´-ee-oy;* from *3999* and *5507; five times a thousand:*— five thousand.

4001. πεντακόσιοι **pĕntakŏsiŏi**, *pen-tak-os´-ee-oy;* from *4002* and *1540; five hundred:*— five hundred.

4002. πέντε **pĕntĕ**, *pen´-teh;* a primary number; "*five*":— five.

4003. πεντεκαιδέκατος **pĕntĕkaidĕkatŏs**, *pen-tek-ahee-dek´-at-os;* from *4002* and *2532* and *1182; five and tenth:*— fifteenth.

4004. πεντήκοντα **pĕntēkŏnta**, *pentay´-kon-tah;* mult. of *4002; fifty:*— fifty.

4005. πεντηκοστή **pĕntēkŏstē**, *pen-taykos-tay´;* fem. of the ord. of *4004; fiftieth* (2250 being impl.) from Passover, i.e. the festival of "*Pentecost*":— Pentecost.

4006. πεποίθησις **pĕpŏithēsis**, *pep-oy´-thay-sis;* from the perfect of the alt. of *3958; reliance:*— confidence, trust.

4007. περ **per**, *per;* from the base of *4008;* an enclitic particle significant of *abundance* (*thoroughness*), i.e. *emphasis; much, very* or *ever:*— [whom-] soever.

4008. πέραν **pĕran**, *per´-an;* appar. acc. of an obs. der. of πείρω **pĕirō**, (to "*pierce*"); *through* (as adv. or prep.), i.e. *across:*— beyond, farther (other) side, over.

4009. πέρας **pĕras**, *per´-as;* from the same as *4008;* an *extremity:*— end, (utter-) most part.

4010. Πέργαμος **Pĕrgamŏs**, *per´-gamos;* from *4444; fortified; Pergamus*, a place in Asia Minor:— Pergamos.

4011. Πέργη **Pĕrgē**, *perg´-ay;* prob. from the same as *4010;* a *tower; Perga*, a place in Asia Minor:— Perga.

4012. περί **pĕri**, *per-ee´;* from the base of *4008;* prop. *through* (all over), i.e.

around; fig. *with respect to;* used in various applications, of place, cause or time (with the gen. denoting the *subject* or *occasion* or *superlative* point; with the acc. the *locality, circuit, matter, circumstance* or general *period):*— (there-) about, above, against, at, on behalf of, × and his company, which concern, (as) concerning, for, × how it will go with, ([there-, where-]) of, on, over, pertaining (to), for sake, × (e-) state, (as) touching, [where-] by (in), with. In composition it retains substantially the same meaning of circuit (*around*), excess (*beyond*), or completeness (*through*).

4013. περιάγω **pĕriagō**, *per-ee-ag´-o;* from *4012* and *71;* to *take around* (as a companion); refl. to *walk around:*— compass, go (round) about, lead about.

4014. περιαιρέω **pĕriairĕō**, *per-ee-ahee-reh´-o;* from *4012* and *138* (incl. its alt.); to *remove* all *around,* i.e. *unveil, cast off* (anchor); fig. to *expiate:*— take away (up).

4015. περιαστράπτω **pĕriastraptō**, *per-ee-as-trap´-to;* from *4012* and *797;* to *flash* all *around,* i.e. *to envelop in light:*— shine round (about).

4016. περιβάλλω **pĕriballō**, *per-ee-bal´-lo;* from *4012* and *906;* to *throw* all *around,* i.e. *invest* (with a palisade or with clothing):— array, cast about, clothe (-d me), put on.

4017. περιβλέπω **pĕriblĕpō**, *per-ee-blep´-o;* from *4012* and *991;* to *look* all *around:*— look (round) about (on).

4018. περιβόλαιον **pĕribŏlaiŏn**, *per-ib-ol´-ah-yon;* neut. of a presumed der. of *4016;* something *thrown around* one, i.e. a *mantle, veil:*— covering, vesture.

4019. περιδέω **pĕridĕō**, *per-ee-deh´-o;* from *4012* and *1210;* to *bind around* one, i.e. *enwrap:*— bind about.

περιδρέμω **pĕridrĕmō.** See *4063.*

περιέλλω **pĕriĕllō.** See *4014.*

περιέλθω **pĕriĕlthō.** See *4022.*

4020. περιεργάζομαι **pĕriĕrgazŏmai**, *per-ee-er-gad´-zom-ahee;* from *4012* and *2038;* to *work* all *around,* i.e. *bustle about* (*meddle*):— be a busybody.

4021. περίεργος **pĕriĕrgŏs**, *per-ee-er´-gos;* from *4012* and *2041; working* all *around,* i.e. *officious* (*meddlesome,* neut. plur. *magic*):— busybody, curious arts.

4022. περιέρχομαι **pĕriĕrchŏmai**, *per-ee-er´-khom-ahee;* from *4012* and *2064* (incl. its alt.); to *come* all *around,* i.e. *stroll, vacillate, veer:*— fetch a compass, vagabond, wandering about.

4023. περιέχω **pĕriĕchō**, *per-ee-ekh´-o;* from *4012* and *2192;* to *hold* all *around,* i.e. *include, clasp* (fig.):— + astonished, contain, after [this manner].

4024. περιζώννυμι **pĕrizōnnumi**, *per-id-zone´-noo-mee;* from *4012* and *2224;* to *gird* all *around,* i.e. (middle or passive voice) to *fasten on one's belt* (lit. or fig.):— gird (about, self).

4025. περίθεσις **pĕrithĕsis**, *per-ith´-es-is;* from *4060;* a *putting* all *around,* i.e. *decorating* oneself with:— wearing.

4026. περιΐστημι **pĕriistĕmi**, *per-ee-is´-tay-mee;* from *4012* and *2476;* to *stand* all *around,* i.e. (near) to *be a bystander,* or (aloof) to *keep away* from:— avoid, shun, stand by (round about).

4027. περικάθαρμα **pĕrikatharma**, *per-ee-kath´-ar-mah;* from a compound of *4012* and *2508;* something *cleaned off* all *around,* i.e. *refuse* (fig.):— filth.

4028. περικαλύπτω **pĕrikaluptō**, *per-ee-kal-oop´-to;* from *4012* and *2572;* to *cover* all *around,* i.e. *entirely* (the face, a surface):— blindfold, cover, overlay.

4029. περίκειμαι **pĕrikĕimai**, *per-ik´-i-mahee;* from *4012* and *2749;* to *lie* all *around,* i.e. *enclose, encircle, hamper* (lit. or fig.):— be bound (compassed) with, hang about.

4030. περικεφαλαία **pĕrikĕphalaia**, *per-ee-kef-al-ah´-yah;* fem. of a compound of *4012* and *2776; encirclement* of the *head,* i.e. a *helmet:*— helmet.

4031. περικρατής **pĕrikratēs**, *per-ee-krat-ace´;* from *4012* and *2904; strong* all *around,* i.e. a *master* (*manager*):— + come by.

4032. περικρύπτω **pĕrikruptō**, *per-ee-kroop´-to;* from *4012* and *2928;* to *conceal* all *around,* i.e. *entirely:*— hide.

4033. περικυκλόω **pĕrikuklŏō**, *per-ee-koo-klŏ´-o;* from *4012* and *2944;* to *encircle* all *around,* i.e. *blockade completely:*— compass round.

4034. περιλάμπω **pĕrilampō**, *per-ee-lam´-po;* from *4012* and *2989;* to *illuminate* all *around,* i.e. *invest with a halo:*— shine round about.

4035. περιλείπω **pĕrilĕipō**, *per-ee-li´-po;* from *4012* and *3007;* to *leave* all *around,* i.e. (pass.) *survive:*— remain.

4036. περίλυπος **pĕrilupŏs**, *per-il´-oo-pos;* from *4012* and *3077; grieved* all *around,* i.e. *intensely sad:*— exceeding (very) sorry (-owful).

4037. περιμένω **pĕrimĕnō**, *per-ee-men´-o;* from *4012* and *3306;* to *stay around,* i.e. *await:*— wait for.

4038. πέριξ **pĕrix**, *per´-ix;* adv. from *4012;* all *around,* i.e. (as an adj.) *circumjacent:*— round about.

4039. περιοικέω **pĕriŏikĕō**, *per-ee-oy-keh´-o;* from *4012* and *3611;* to *reside around,* i.e. *be a neighbor:*— dwell round about.

4040. περίοικος **pĕriŏikŏs**, *per-ee´-oy-kos;* from *4012* and *3624; housed around,* i.e. *neighboring* (ellip. used as a noun):— neighbour.

4041. περιούσιος **pĕriŏusiŏs**, *per-ee-oo´-see-os;* from the pres. part. fem. of a compound of *4012* and *1510; being beyond* usual, i.e. *special* (one's own):— peculiar.

4042. περιοχή **pĕriŏchē**, *per-ee-okh-ay´;* from *4023;* a *being held around,* i.e. (concr.) a *passage* (of Scripture, as *circumscribed*):— place.

4043. περιπατέω **pĕripatĕō**, *per-ee-pat-eh´-o;* from *4012* and *3961;* to *tread* all *around,* i.e. *walk at large* (espec. as proof of ability); fig. to *live, deport oneself, follow* (as a companion or vo-

tary):— go, be occupied with, walk (about).

4044. περιπείρω **pĕripĕirō**, *per-ee-pi´-ro;* from *4012* and the base of *4008;* to *penetrate entirely,* i.e. *transfix* (fig.):— pierce through.

4045. περιπίπτω **pĕripiptō**, *per-ee-pip´-to;* from *4012* and *4098;* to *fall into* something i.e. all *around,* i.e. *light among* or *upon, be surrounded with:*— fall among (into).

4046. περιποιέομαι **pĕripŏiĕŏmai**, *per-ee-poy-eh´-om-ahee;* mid. voice from *4012* and *4160;* to *make around oneself,* i.e. *acquire* (*buy*):— purchase.

4047. περιποίησις **pĕripŏiēsis**, *per-ee-poy´-ay-sis;* from *4046; acquisition* (the act or the thing); by extens. *preservation:*— obtain (-ing), peculiar, purchased, possession, saving.

4048. περιρρήγνυμι **pĕrirrhēgnumi**, *per-ir-hrayg´-noo-mee;* from *4012* and *4486;* to *tear* all *around,* i.e. *completely away:*— rend off.

4049. περισπάω **pĕrispaō**, *per-ee-spah´-o;* from *4012* and *4685;* to *drag* all *around,* i.e. (fig.) to *distract* (with care):— cumber.

4050. περισσεία **pĕrissĕia**, *per-is-si´-ah;* from *4052; surplusage,* i.e. *superabundance:*— abundance (-ant, [-ly]), superfluity.

4051. περίσσευμα **pĕrissĕuma**, *per-is´-syoo-mah;* from *4052;* a *surplus,* or *superabundance:*— abundance, that was left, over and above.

4052. περισσεύω **pĕrissĕuō**, *per-is-syoo´-o;* from *4053;* to *superabound* (in quantity or quality), *be in excess, be superfluous;* also (tran.) to *cause to superabound* or *excel:*— (make, more) abound, (have, have more) abundance (be more) abundant, be the better, enough and to spare, exceed, excel, increase, be left, redound, remain (over and above).

4053. περισσός **pĕrissŏs**, *per-is-sos´;* from *4012* (in the sense of *beyond*); *superabundant* (in quantity) or *superior* (in quality); by impl. *excessive;* adv. (with *1537*) *violently;* neut. (as noun) *preeminence:*— exceeding abundantly above, more abundantly, advantage, exceedingly, very highly, beyond measure, more, superfluous, vehement [-ly].

4054. περισσότερον **pĕrissŏtĕrŏn**, *per-is-sot´-er-on;* neut. of *4055* (as adv.); in a *more superabundant* way:— more abundantly, a great deal, far more.

4055. περισσότερος **pĕrissŏtĕrŏs**, *per-is-sot´-er-os;* comp. of *4053; more superabundant* (in number, degree or character):— more abundant, greater (much) more, overmuch.

4056. περισσοτέρως **pĕrissŏtĕrōs**, *per-is-sot´-er-oce;* adv. from *4055; more superabundantly:*— more abundant (-ly), × the more earnest, (more) exceedingly, more frequent, much more, the rather.

4057. περισσῶς **pĕrissōs**, *per-is-soce´;* adv. from *4053; superabundantly:*— exceedingly, out of measure, the more.

4058. περιστερά **pĕristĕra**, *per-is-ter-ah´*; of uncert. der.; a *pigeon:*— dove, pigeon.

4059. περιτέμνω **pĕritĕmnō**, *per-ee-tem´-no;* from *4012* and the base of *5114;* to *cut around*, i.e. (spec.) to *circumcise:*— circumcise.

4060. περιτίθημι **pĕritithēmi**, *per-ee-tith´-ay-mee;* from *4012* and *5087;* to *place around;* by impl. to *present:*— bestow upon, hedge round about, put about (on, upon), set about.

4061. περιτομή **pĕritŏmē**, *per-it-om-ay´;* from *4059;* *circumcision* (the rite, the condition or the people, lit. or fig.):— × circumcised, circumcision.

4062. περιτρέπω **pĕritrĕpō**, *per-ee-trep´-o;* from *4012* and the base of *5157;* to *turn around*, i.e. (ment.) to *craze:*— + make mad.

4063. περιτρέχω **pĕritrĕchō**, *per-ee-trekh´-o;* from *4012* and *5143* (incl. its alt.); to *run around*, i.e. *traverse:*— run through.

4064. περιφέρω **pĕriphĕrō**, *per-ee-fer´-o;* from *4012* and *5342;* to *convey around*, i.e. *transport hither and thither:*— bear (carry) about.

4065. περιφρονέω **pĕriphrŏnĕō**, *per-ee-fron-eh´-o;* from *4012* and *5426;* to *think beyond*, i.e. *depreciate* (contemn):— despise.

4066. περίχωρος **pĕrichōrŏs**, *per-ikh´-o-ros;* from *4012* and *5561;* *around* the *region*, i.e. *circumjacent* (as noun, with *1093* impl. *vicinity*):— country (round) about, region (that lieth) round about.

4067. περίψωμα **pĕripsōma**, *per-ip´-so-mah* or

περίψημα **pĕripsēma**, *per-ip´-say-mah;* from a compound of *4012* and ψάω *psaō* (to *rub*); something *brushed* all *around*, i.e. *off-scrapings* (fig. *scum*):— offscouring.

4068. περπερεύομαι **pĕrpĕrĕuŏmai**, *per-per-yoo´-om-ahee;* mid. voice from πέρπερος *pĕrpĕrŏs* (*braggart;* perh. by redupl. of the base of *4008*); to *boast:*— vaunt itself.

4069. Περσίς **Pĕrsis**, *per-sece´;* a *Pers.* woman; *Persis*, a Chr. female:— Persis.

4070. πέρυσι **pĕrusi**, *per´-oo-si;* adv. from *4009;* the *by-gone*, i.e. (as noun) *last year:*— + a year ago.

πετάομαι **pĕtaŏmai**. See *4072.*

4071. πετεινόν **pĕtĕinŏn**, *pet-i-non´;* neut. of a der. of *4072;* a *flying* animal, i.e. *bird:*— bird, fowl.

4072. πέτομαι **pĕtŏmai**, *pet´-om-ahee;* or prol.

πετάομαι **pĕtaŏmai**, *pet-ah´-om-ahee;* or contr. πτάομαι **ptaŏmai**, *ptah´-om-ahee;* mid. voice of a primary verb; to *fly:*— fly (-ing).

4073. πέτρα **pĕtra**, *pet´-ra;* fem. of the same as *4074;* a (mass of) *rock* (lit. or fig.):— rock.

4074. Πέτρος **Pĕtrŏs**, *pet´-ros;* appar. a primary word; a (piece of) *rock* (larger than *3037*); as a name, *Petrus*, an apostle:— Peter, rock. Comp. *2786.*

4075. πετρώδης **pĕtrōdēs**, *pet-ro´-dace;*

from *4073* and *1491;* *rock-like*, i.e. *rocky:*— stony.

4076. πήγανον **pēganŏn**, *pay´-gan-on;* from *4078;* *rue* (from its *thick* or *fleshy* leaves):— rue.

4077. πηγή **pēgē**, *pay-gay´;* prob. from *4078* (through the idea of *gushing* plumply); a *fount* (lit. or fig.), i.e. *source* or *supply* (of water, blood, enjoyment) (not necessarily the orig. spring):— fountain, well.

4078. πήγνυμι **pēgnumi**, *payg´-noo-mee;* a prol. form of a primary verb (which in its simpler form occurs only as an alt. in certain tenses); to *fix* ("peg"), i.e. (spec.) to *set up* (a tent):— pitch.

4079. πηδάλιον **pēdaliŏn**, *pay-dal´-ee-on;* neut. of a (presumed) der. of πηδόν *pēdŏn* (the *blade* of an oar; from the same as *3976*); a "*pedal*," i.e. *helm:*— rudder.

4080. πηλίκος **pēlikŏs**, *pay-lee´-kos;* a quantitative form (the fem.) of the base of *4225;* *how much* (as an indef.), i.e. in *size* or (fig.) *dignity:*— how great (large).

4081. πηλός **pēlŏs**, *pay-los´;* perh. a primary word; *clay:*— clay.

4082. πήρα **pēra**, *pay´-rah;* of uncert. aff.; a *wallet* or leather *pouch* for food:— scrip.

4083. πῆχυς **pēchus**, *pay´-khoos;* of uncert. aff.; the *fore-arm*, i.e. (as a measure) a *cubit:*— cubit.

4084. πιάζω **piazō**, *pee-ad´-zo;* prob. another form of *971;* to *squeeze*, i.e. *seize* (gently by the hand [press], or officially [arrest], or in hunting [capture]):— apprehend, catch, lay hand on, take. Comp. *4085.*

4085. πιέζω **piĕzō**, *pee-ed´-zo;* another form for *4084;* to *pack:*— press down.

4086. πιθανολογία **pithanŏlŏgia**, *pith-an-ol-og-ee´-ah;* from a compound of a der. of *3982* and *3056;* *persuasive language:*— enticing words.

4087. πικραίνω **pikrainō**, *pik-rah´-ee-no;* from *4089;* to *embitter* (lit. or fig.):— be (make) bitter.

4088. πικρία **pikria**, *pik-ree´-ah;* from *4089;* *acridity* (espec. *poison*), lit. or fig.:— bitterness.

4089. πικρός **pikrŏs**, *pik-ros´;* perh. from *4078* (through the idea of *piercing*); *sharp* (*pungent*), i.e. *acrid* (lit. or fig.):— bitter.

4090. πικρῶς **pikrōs**, *pik-roce´;* adv. from *4089;* *bitterly*, i.e. (fig.) *violently:*— bitterly.

4091. Πιλάτος **Pilatŏs**, *pil-at´-os;* of Lat. or.; *close-pressed*, i.e. *firm; Pilatus*, a Rom.:— Pilate.

πίμπλημι **pimplēmi**. See *4130.*

4092. πίμπρημι **pimprēmi**, *pim´-pray-mee;* a redupl. and prol. form of a primary

πρέω **prĕō**, *preh´-o;* which occurs only as an alt. in certain tenses); to *fire*, i.e. *burn* (fig. and pass. *become inflamed* with fever):— be (× should have) swollen.

4093. πινακίδιον **pinakidiŏn**, *pin-ak-id´-ee-on;* dimin. of *4094;* a *tablet* (for writing on):— writing table.

4094. πίναξ **pinax**, *pin´-ax;* appar. a form of *4109;* a *plate:*— charger, platter.

4095. πίνω **pinō**, *pee´-no;* a prol. form of

πίω **piō**, *pee´-o;* which (together with another form πόω *pŏō*, *pŏ´-o;* occurs only as an alt. in certain tenses): to *imbibe* (lit. or fig.):— drink.

4096. πιότης **piŏtēs**, *pee-ot´-ace;* from πίων *piōn*, (*fat;* perh. akin to the alt. of *4095* through the idea of *repletion*); *plumpness*, i.e. (by impl.) *richness* (*oiliness*):— fatness.

4097. πιπράσκω **pipraskō**, *pip-ras´-ko;* a redupl. and prol. form of

πράω **praō**, *prah´-o;* (which occurs only as an alt. in certain tenses); contr. from περάω **pĕraō** (to *traverse;* from the base of *4008*), i.e. (by *travelling*), i.e. *dispose* of as merchandise or into slavery (lit. or fig.):— sell.

4098. πίπτω **piptō**, *pip´-to;* a redupl. and contr. form of πέτω **pĕtō**, *pet´-o;* (which occurs only as an alt. in certain tenses); prob. akin to *4072* through the idea of *alighting;* to *fall* (lit. or fig.):— fail, fall (down), light on.

4099. Πισιδία **Pisidia**, *pis-id-ee´-ah;* prob. of for. or.; *Pisidia*, a region of Asia Minor:— Pisidia.

4100. πιστεύω **pistĕuō**, *pist-yoo´-o;* from *4102;* to *have faith* (in, upon, or with respect to, a person or thing), i.e. *credit;* by impl. to *entrust* (espec. one's spiritual well-being to Christ):— believe (-r), commit (to trust), put in trust with.

4101. πιστικός **pistikŏs**, *pis-tik-os´;* from *4102; trustworthy*, i.e. *genuine* (*unadulterated*):— spike-[nard].

4102. πίστις **pistis**, *pis´-tis;* from *3982; persuasion*, i.e. *credence;* mor. *conviction* (of *relig.* truth, or the truthfulness of God or a relig. teacher), espec. *reliance* upon Christ for salvation; abstr. *constancy* in such profession; by extension, the system of religious (Gospel) *truth* itself:— assurance, belief, believe, faith, fidelity.

4103. πιστός **pistŏs**, *pis-tos´;* from *3982;* obj. *trustworthy;* subj. *trustful:*— believe (-ing, -r), faithful (-ly), sure, true.

4104. πιστόω **pistŏō**, *pis-tŏ´-o;* from *4103;* to *assure:*— assure of.

4105. πλανάω **planaō**, *plan-ah´-o;* from *4106;* to (prop. *cause* to) *roam* (from safety, truth, or virtue):— go astray, deceive, err, seduce, wander, be out of the way.

4106. πλάνη **planē**, *plan´-ay;* fem. of *4108* (as abstr.); obj. *fraudulence;* subj. a *straying* from orthodoxy or piety:— deceit, to deceive, delusion, error.

4107. πλανήτης **planētēs**, *plan-ay´-tace;* from *4108;* a *rover* ("planet"), i.e. (fig.) an *erratic* teacher:— wandering.

4108. πλάνος **planŏs**, *plan´-os;* of uncert. aff.; *roving* (as a *tramp*), i.e. (by impl.) an *impostor* or *misleader:*— deceiver, seducing.

4109. πλάξ **plax**, *plax;* from *4111;* a *moulding-board,* i.e. *flat* surface ("*plate*", or *tablet,* lit. or fig.):— table.

4110. πλάσμα **plasma,** *plas´-mah;* from *4111;* something *moulded:*— thing formed.

4111. πλάσσω **plassō,** *plas´-so;* a primary verb; to *mould,* i.e. *shape* or *fabricate:*— form.

4112. πλαστός **plastŏs,** *plas-tos´;* from *4111; moulded,* i.e. (by impl.) *artificial* or (fig.) *fictitious (false)*:— feigned.

4113. πλατεῖα **platĕia,** *plat-i´-ah;* fem. of *4116;* a *wide* "*plat*" or "*place*", i.e. open *square:*— street.

4114. πλάτος **platŏs,** *plat´-os;* from *4116; width:*— breadth.

4115. πλατύνω **platunō,** *plat-oo´-no;* from *4116;* to *widen* (lit. or fig.):— make broad, enlarge.

4116. πλατύς **platus,** *plat-oos´;* from *4111;* spread out "*flat*" ("plot"), i.e. *broad:*— wide.

4117. πλέγμα **plĕgma,** *pleg´-mah;* from *4120;* a *plait* (of hair):— broidered hair.

πλεῖον **plĕiŏn.** See *4119.*

4118. πλεῖστος **plĕistŏs,** *plice´-tos;* irreg. superl. of *4183;* the *largest number* or *very large:*— very great, most.

4119. πλείων **plĕiōn,** *pli-own;* neut.

πλεῖον **plĕiŏn,** *pli´-on;* or

πλέον **plĕŏn,** *pleh´-on;* comparative of *4183; more* in quantity, number, or quality; also (in plur.) the *major portion:*— × above, + exceed, more excellent, further, (very) great (-er), long (-er), (very) many, greater (more) part, + yet but.

4120. πλέκω **plĕkō,** *plek´-o;* a primary word; to *twine* or *braid:*— plait.

πλέον **plĕŏn.** See *4119.*

4121. πλεονάζω **plĕŏnazō,** *pleh-on-ad´-zo;* from *4119;* to *do, make* or *be more,* i.e. *increase* (tran. or intr.); by extens. to *superabound:*— abound, abundant, make to increase, have over.

4122. πλεονεκτέω **plĕŏnektĕō,** *pleh-on-ek-teh´-o;* from *4123;* to *be covetous,* i.e. (by impl.) to *over-reach:*— get an advantage, defraud, make a gain.

4123. πλεονέκτης **plĕŏnĕktēs,** *pleh-on-ek´-tace;* from *4119* and *2192; holding (desiring) more,* i.e. *eager for gain (avaricious,* hence, a *defrauder*):— covetous.

4124. πλεονεξία **plĕŏnĕxia,** *pleh-on-ex-ee´-ah;* from *4123; avarice,* i.e. (by impl.) *fraudulency, extortion:*— covetous (-ness) practices, greediness.

4125. πλευρά **plĕura,** *plyoo-rah´;* of uncert. aff.; a *rib,* i.e. (by extens.) *side:*— side.

4126. πλέω **plĕō,** *pleh´-o;* another form for

πλεύω **plĕuō,** *plyoo´-o;* which is used as an alt. in certain tenses; prob. a form of *4150* (through the idea of *plunging* through the water); to *pass in* a vessel:— sail. See also *4130.*

4127. πληγή **plēgē,** *play-gay´;* from *4141;* a *stroke;* by impl. a *wound;* fig. a *calamity:*— plague, stripe, wound (-ed).

4128. πλῆθος **plēthŏs,** *play´-thos;* from *4130;* a *fulness,* i.e. a *large number, throng, populace:*— bundle, company, multitude.

4129. πληθύνω **plēthunō,** *play-thoo´-no;* from another form of *4128;* to *increase* (tran. or intr.):— abound, multiply.

4130. πλήθω **plēthō,** *play´-tho;* a prol. form of a primary πλέω **plĕō,** *pleh´-o* (which appears only as an alt. in certain tenses and in the redupl. form πίμπλημι **pimplēmi**); to "*fill*" (lit. or fig. *imbue, influence, supply*]; spec. to *fulfil* (time):— accomplish, full (...come), furnish.

4131. πλήκτης **plēktēs,** *plake´-tace;* from *4141;* a *smiter,* i.e. *pugnacious (quarrelsome)*:— striker.

4132. πλημμύρα **plēmmura,** *plame-moo´-rah;* prol. from *4130; flood-tide,* i.e. (by anal.) a *freshet:*— flood.

4133. πλήν **plēn,** *plane;* from *4119; moreover* (*besides*), i.e. *albeit, save that, rather, yet:*— but (rather), except, nevertheless, notwithstanding, save, than.

4134. πλήρης **plērēs,** *play´-race;* from *4130; replete,* or *covered* over; by anal. *complete:*— full.

4135. πληροφορέω **plērŏphŏrĕō,** *play-rof-or-eh´-o;* from *4134* and *5409;* to *carry out fully* (in evidence), i.e. *completely assure* (or *convince*), *entirely accomplish:*— most surely believe, fully know (persuade), make full proof of.

4136. πληροφορία **plērŏphŏria,** *play-rof-or-ee-ah´;* from *4135; entire confidence:*— (full) assurance.

4137. πληρόω **plērŏō,** *play-rŏ´-o;* from *4134;* to *make replete,* i.e. (lit.) to *cram* (a net), *level* up (a hollow), or (fig.) to *furnish* (or *imbue, diffuse, influence*), *satisfy, execute* (an office), *finish* (a period or task), *verify* (or *coincide* with a prediction), etc.:— accomplish, × after, (be) complete, end, expire, fill (up), fulfil, (be, make) full (come), fully preach, perfect, supply.

4138. πλήρωμα **plērōma,** *play´-ro-mah;* from *4137; repletion* or *completion,* i.e. (subj.) what *fills* (as contents, supplement, copiousness, multitude), or (obj.) what is *filled* (as container, performance, period):— which is put in to fill up, piece that filled up, fulfilling, full, fulness.

4139. πλησίον **plēsiŏn,** *play-see´-on;* neut. of a der. of πέλας **pĕlas** (near); (adv.) *close* by; as noun, a *neighbor,* i.e. *fellow* (as man, countryman, Chr. or friend):— near, neighbour.

4140. πλησμονή **plēsmŏnē,** *place-mon-ay´;* from a presumed der. of *4130;* a *filling* up, i.e. (fig.) *gratification:*— satisfying.

4141. πλήσσω **plēssō,** *place´-so;* appar. another form of *4111* (through the idea of *flattening* out); to *pound,* i.e. (fig.) to *inflict* with (calamity):— smite. Comp. *5180.*

4142. πλοιάριον **plŏiariŏn,** *ploy-ar´-ee-on;* neut. of a presumed der. of *4143;* a *boat:*— boat, little (small) ship.

4143. πλοῖον **plŏiŏn,** *ploy´-on;* from *4126;* a *sailer,* i.e. *vessel:*— ship (-ping).

4144. πλόος **plŏŏs,** *plŏ´-os;* from *4126;* a *sail,* i.e. *navigation:*— course, sailing, voyage.

4145. πλούσιος **plŏusiŏs,** *ploo´-see-os;* from *4149; wealthy;* fig. *abounding* with:— rich.

4146. πλουσίως **plŏusiōs,** *ploo-see´-oce;* adv. from *4145; copiously:*— abundantly, richly.

4147. πλουτέω **plŏutĕō,** *ploo-teh´-o;* from *4148;* to *be* (or *become*) *wealthy* (lit. or fig.):— be increased with goods, (be made, wax) rich.

4148. πλουτίζω **plŏutizō,** *ploo-tid´-zo;* from *4149;* to *make wealthy* (fig.):— en (make) rich.

4149. πλοῦτος **plŏutŏs,** *ploo´-tos;* from the base of *4130; wealth* (as *fulness*), i.e. (lit.) *money, possessions,* or (fig.) *abundance, richness,* (spec.) *valuable bestowment:*— riches.

4150. πλύνω **plunō,** *ploo´-no;* a prol. form of an obs. πλύω **pluō,** (to "*flow*"); to "*plunge,*" i.e. *launder* clothing:— wash. Comp. *3068, 3538.*

4151. πνεῦμα **pnĕuma,** *pnyoo´-mah;* from *4154;* a *current* of air, i.e. *breath* (*blast*) or a *breeze;* by anal. or fig. a *spirit,* i.e. (human) the rational *soul,* (by impl.) *vital principle,* ment. *disposition,* etc., or (superhuman) an *angel, demon,* or (divine) *God,* Christ's *spirit,* the Holy *Spirit:*— ghost, life, spirit (-ual, -ually), mind. Comp. *5590.*

4152. πνευματικός **pnĕumatikŏs,** *pnyoo-mat-ik-os´;* from *4151; non-carnal,* i.e. (humanly) *ethereal* (as opposed to gross), or (demoniacally) a *spirit* (concr.), or (divinely) *supernatural, regenerate, religious:*— spiritual. Comp. *5591.*

4153. πνευματικῶς **pnĕumatikōs,** *pnyoo-mat-ik-oce´;* adv. from *4152; non-physical,* i.e. *divinely, figuratively:*— spiritually.

4154. πνέω **pnĕō,** *pneh´-o;* a primary word; to *breathe* hard, i.e. *breeze:*— blow. Comp. *5594.*

4155. πνίγω **pnigō,** *pnee´-go;* strengthened from *4154;* to *wheeze,* i.e. (cause. by impl.) to *throttle* or *strangle* (*drown*):— choke, take by the throat.

4156. πνικτός **pniktŏs,** *pnik-tos´;* from *4155; throttled,* i.e. (neut. concr.) an animal *choked* to death (*not bled*):— strangled.

4157. πνοή **pnŏē,** *pno-ay´;* from *4154; respiration,* a *breeze;*— breath, wind.

4158. ποδήρης **pŏdērēs,** *pod-ay´-race;* from *4228* and another element of uncert. aff.; a *dress* (*2066* impl.) *reaching* the *ankles:*— garment down to the foot.

4159. πόθεν **pŏthĕn,** *poth´-en;* from the base of *4213* with enclitic adverb of origin; *from which* (as interr.) or *what* (as rel.) place, state, source or cause:— whence.

4160. ποιέω **pŏiĕō,** *poy-eh´-o;* appar. a

prol. form of an obs. primary; to *make* or *do* (in a very wide application, more or less dir.):— abide, + agree, appoint, × avenge, + band together, be, bear, + bewray, bring (forth), cast out, cause, commit, + content, continue, deal, + without any delay, (would) do (-ing), execute, exercise, fulfil, gain, give, have, hold, × journeying, keep, + lay wait, + lighten the ship, make, × mean, + none of these things move me, observe, ordain, perform, provide, + have purged, purpose, put, + raising up, × secure, shew, × shoot out, spend, take, tarry, + transgress the law, work, yield. Comp. *4238*.

4161. ποίημα **pŏiēma**, *poy´-ay-mah;* from *4160;* a *product,* i.e. *fabric* (lit. or fig.):— thing that is made, workmanship.

4162. ποίησις **pŏiēsis**, *poy´-ay-sis;* from *4160; action,* i.e. *performance* (of the law):— deed.

4163. ποιητής **pŏiētēs**, *poy-ay-tace´;* from *4160;* a *performer;* spec. a "*poet*":— doer, poet.

4164. ποικίλος **pŏikilŏs**, *poy-kee´-los;* of uncert. der.; *motley,* i.e. *various* in character:— divers, manifold.

4165. ποιμαίνω **pŏimainō**, *poy-mah´-ee-no;* from *4166;* to *tend* as a shepherd (or fig. *superviser*):— feed (cattle), rule.

4166. ποιμήν **pŏimēn**, *poy-mane´;* of uncert. aff.; a *shepherd* (lit. or fig.):— shepherd, pastor.

4167. ποίμνη **pŏimnē**, *poym´-nay;* contr. from *4165;* a *flock* (lit. or fig.):— flock, fold.

4168. ποίμνιον **pŏimniŏn**, *poym´-nee-on;* neut. of a presumed der. of *4167;* a *flock,* i.e. (fig.) *group* (of believers):— flock.

4169. ποῖος **pŏiŏs**, *poy´-os;* from the base of *4226* and *3634;* individualizing interr. (of character) *what* sort of, or (of number) *which* one:— what (manner of), which.

4170. πολεμέω **pŏlĕmĕō**, *pol-em-eh´-o;* from *4171;* to *be* (engaged) in *warfare,* i.e. to *battle* (lit. or fig.):— fight, (make) war.

4171. πόλεμος **pŏlĕmŏs**, *pol´-em-os;* from πέλομαι **pĕlŏmai**, (to *bustle*); *warfare* (lit. or fig.; a single encounter or a series):— battle, fight, war.

4172. πόλις **pŏlis**, *pol´-is;* prob. from the same as *4171,* or perh. from *4183;* a *town* (prop. with walls, of greater or less size):— city.

4173. πολιτάρχης **pŏlitarchēs**, *pol-it-ar´-khace;* from *4172* and *757;* a *town-officer,* i.e. *magistrate:*— ruler of the city.

4174. πολιτεία **pŏlitĕia**, *pol-ee-ti´-ah;* from *4177* ("polity"); *citizenship;* concr. a *commu:ity:*— commonwealth, freedom.

4175. πολίτευμα **pŏlitĕuma**, *pol-it´-yoo-mah;* from *4176;* a *community,* i.e. (abstr.) *citizenship* (fig.):— conversation.

4176. πολιτεύομαι **pŏlitĕuŏmai**, *pol-it-yoo´-om-ahee;* mid. voice of a der. of

4177; to *behave* as a citizen (fig.):— let conversation be, live.

4177. πολίτης **pŏlitēs**, *pol-ee´-tace;* from *4172;* a *townsman:*— citizen.

4178. πολλάκις **pŏllakis**, *pol-lak´-is;* mult. adv. from *4183; many times,* i.e. *frequently:*— oft (-en, -entimes, -times).

4179. πολλαπλασίων **pŏllaplasiōn**, *pol-lap-las-ee´-ohn;* from *4183* and prob. a der. of *4120; manifold,* i.e. (neut. as noun) *very much more:*— manifold more.

4180. πολυλογία **pŏlulŏgia**, *pol-oo-log-ee´-ah;* from a compound of *4183* and *3056; loquacity,* i.e. *prolixity:*— much speaking.

4181. πολυμέρως **pŏlumĕrōs**, *pol-oo-mer´-oce;* adv. from a compound of *4183* and *3313; in many portions,* i.e. *variously* as to time and agency (*piece-meal*):— at sundry times.

4182. πολυποίκιλος **pŏlupŏikilŏs**, *pol-oo-poy´-kil-os;* from *4183* and *4164; much variegated,* i.e. *multifarious:*— manifold.

4183. πολύς **pŏlus**, *pol-oos´;* incl. the forms from the alt. πολλός **pŏllŏs;** (sing.) *much* (in any respect) or (plural) *many;* neut. (sing.) as adv. *largely;* neut. (plural) as adv. or noun *often, mostly, largely:*— abundant, + altogether, common, + far (passed, spent), (+ be of a) great (age, deal, -ly, while), long, many, much, oft (-en [-times]), plenteous, sore, straitly. Comp. *4118, 4119.*

4184. πολύσπλαγχνος **pŏlusplagchnŏs**, *pol-oo´-splankh-nos;* from *4183* and *4698* (fig.); *extremely compassionate:*— very pitiful.

4185. πολυτελής **pŏlutĕlēs**, *pol-oo-tel-ace´;* from *4183* and *5056; extremely expensive:*— costly, very precious, of great price.

4186. πολύτιμος **pŏlutimŏs**, *pol-oot´-ee-mos;* from *4183* and *5092; extremely valuable:*— very costly, of great price.

4187. πολυτρόπως **pŏlutrŏpōs**, *pol-oot-rop´-oce;* adv. from a compound of *4183* and *5158; in many ways,* i.e. *variously* as to method or form:— in divers manners.

4188. πόμα **pŏma**, *pom´-ah;* from the alt. of *4095;* a *beverage:*— drink.

4189. πονηρία **pŏnēria**, *pon-ay-ree´-ah;* from *4190; depravity,* i.e. (spec.) *malice;* plur. (concr.) *plots, sins:*— iniquity, wickedness.

4190. πονηρός **pŏnērŏs**, *pon-ay-ros´;* from a der. of *4192; hurtful,* i.e. *evil* (prop. in effect or influence, and thus differing from *2556,* which refers rather to *essential* character, as well as from *4550,* which indicates *degeneracy* from original virtue); fig. *calamitous;* also (pass.) *ill,* i.e. *diseased;* but espec. (mor.) *culpable,* i.e. *derelict, vicious, facinorous;* neut. (sing.) *mischief, malice,* or (plural) *guilt;* masc. (sing.) the *devil,* or (plural) *sinners:*— bad, evil, grievous, harm, lewd, malicious, wicked (-ness). See also *4191.*

4191. πονηρότερος **pŏnērŏtĕrŏs**, *pon-ay-rot´-er-os;* comp. of *4190; more evil:*— more wicked.

4192. πόνος **pŏnŏs**, *pon´-os;* from the base of *3993; toil,* i.e. (by impl.) *anguish:*— pain.

4193. Ποντικός **Pŏntikŏs**, *pon-tik-os´;* from *4195;* a *Pontican,* i.e. native of Pontus:— born in Pontus.

4194. Πόντιος **Pŏntiŏs**, *pon´-tee-os;* of Lat. or.; appar. *bridged; Pontius,* a Rom.:— Pontius.

4195. Πόντος **Pŏntŏs**, *pon´-tos;* a *sea; Pontus,* a region of Asia Minor:— Pontus.

4196. Πόπλιος **Pŏpliŏs**, *pop´-lee-os;* of Lat. or.; appar. "*popular*"; *Poplius* (i.e. *Publius*), a Rom.:— Publius.

4197. πορεία **pŏreia**, *por-i´-ah;* from *4198; travel* (by land); fig. (plural) *proceedings,* i.e. *career:*— journey [-ing], ways.

4198. πορεύομαι **pŏreuŏmai**, *por-yoo´-om-ahee;* mid. voice from a der. of the same as *3984;* to *traverse,* i.e. *travel* (lit. or fig.; espec. to *remove* [fig. *die*], *live,* etc.):—depart, go (away, forth, one's way, up), (make a, take a) journey, walk.

4199. πορθέω **pŏrthĕō**, *por-theh´-o;* prol. from πέρθω **pērthō**, (to *sack*); to *ravage* (fig.):— destroy, waste.

4200. πορισμός **pŏrismŏs**, *por-is-mos´;* from a der. of πόρος **pŏrŏs** (a *way,* i.e. *means*); *furnishing,* (*procuring*), i.e. (by impl.) *money-getting* (*acquisition*):— gain.

4201. Πόρκιος **Pŏrkiŏs**, *por´-kee-os;* of Lat. or.; appar. *swinish; Porcius,* a Rom.:— Porcius.

4202. πορνεία **pŏrneia**, *por-ni´-ah;* from *4203; harlotry* (incl. *adultery* and *incest*); fig. *idolatry:*— fornication.

4203. πορνεύω **pŏrneuō**, *porn-yoo´-o;* from *4204;* to *act* the *harlot,* i.e. (lit.) *indulge* unlawful *lust* (of either sex), or (fig.) *practice idolatry:*— commit (fornication).

4204. πόρνη **pŏrnē**, *por´-nay;* fem. of *4205;* a *strumpet;* fig. an *idolater:*— harlot, whore.

4205. πόρνος **pŏrnŏs**, *por´-nos;* from πέρνημι **pērnēmi**, (to *sell;* akin to the base of *4097*); a (male) *prostitute* (as *venal*), i.e. (by anal.) a *debauchee* (*libertine*):— fornicator, whoremonger.

4206. πόρρω **pŏrrhō**, *por´-rho;* adv. from *4253; forwards,* i.e. *at a distance:*— far, a great way off. See also *4207.*

4207. πόρρωθεν **pŏrrhōthĕn**, *por´-rho-then;* from *4206* with adv. enclitic of source; *from far,* or (by impl.) *at a distance,* i.e. *distantly:*— afar off.

4208. πορρωτέρω **pŏrrhōtĕrō**, *por-rho-ter´-o;* adv. comparative of *4206; further,* i.e. a *greater distance:*— farther.

4209. πορφύρα **pŏrphura**, *por-foo´-rah;* of Lat. or.; the "*purple*" mussel, i.e. (by impl.) the *red-blue* color itself, and finally a garment dyed with it:— purple.

4210. πορφυροῦς **pŏrphurŏus**, *por-foo-rooce´;* from *4209; purpureal,* i.e. *bluish red:*— purple.

4211. πορφυρόπωλις **pŏrphurŏpŏlis**, *por-foo-rop´-o-lis;* fem. of a compound of *4209* and *4453;* a *female trader in purple* cloth:— seller of purple.

4212. ποσάκις **pŏsakis**, *pos-ak´-is;* mult. from *4214; how many times:—* how oft (-en).

4213. πόσις **pŏsis**, *pos´-is;* from the alt. of *4095;* a *drinking* (the act), i.e. (concr.) a *draught:—* drink.

4214. πόσος **pŏsŏs**, *pos´-os;* from an obs. πός **pŏs**, (*who, what*) and *3739;* interr. pron. (of amount) *how much* (*large, long* or [plural] *many*):— how great (long, many), what.

4215. ποταμός **pŏtamŏs**, *pot-am-os´;* prob. from a der. of the alt. of *4095* (comp. *4224*); a *current, brook* or *freshet* (as *drinkable*), i.e. *running water:—* flood, river, stream, water.

4216. ποταμοφόρητος **pŏtamŏphŏrētŏs**, *pot-am-of-or´-ay-tos;* from *4215* and a der. of *5409; river-borne,* i.e. *overwhelmed by a stream:—* carried away of the flood.

4217. ποταπός **pŏtapŏs**, *pot-ap-os´;* appar. from *4219* and the base of *4226;* interrog. *whatever,* i.e. of *what possible* sort:— what (manner of).

4218. ποτέ **pŏtĕ**, *pot-eh´;* from the base of *4225* and *5037;* indef. adv., at *some time, ever:—* afore-(any, some-) time (-s), at length (the last), (+ n-) ever, in the old time, in time past, once, when.

4219. πότε **pŏtĕ**, *pot´-eh;* from the base of *4226* and *5037;* interr. adv., at *what time:—* + how long, when.

4220. πότερον **pŏtĕrŏn**, *pot´-er-on;* neut. of a comparative of the base of *4226;* interr. as adv., *which* (of two), i.e. *is it* this or that:— whether.

4221. ποτήριον **pŏtērion**, *pot-ay´-ree-on;* neut. of a der. of the alt. of *4095;* a *drinking-vessel;* by extens. the contents thereof, i.e. a *cupful* (*draught*); fig. a *lot* or *fate:—* cup.

4222. ποτίζω **pŏtizō**, *pot-id´-zo;* from a der. of the alt. of *4095;* to *furnish drink, irrigate:—* give (make) to drink, feed, water.

4223. Ποτίολοι **Pŏtiŏlŏi**, *pot-ee´-ol-oy;* of Lat. or.; *little wells,* i.e. *mineral springs; Potioli* (i.e. *Puteoli*), a place in Italy:— Puteoli.

4224. πότος **pŏtŏs**, *pot´-os;* from the alt. of *4095;* a *drinking-bout* or *carousal:—* banqueting.

4225. πού **pŏu**, *poo;* gen. of an indef. pron. πός **pŏs** (*some*) otherwise obs. (comp. *4214*); as adv. of place, *somewhere,* i.e. *nearly:—* about, a certain place.

4226. ποῦ **pŏu**, *poo;* gen. of an interr. pron. πός **pŏs**, (*what*) otherwise obs. (perh. the same as *4225* used with the rising slide of inquiry); as adv. of place; *at* (by impl. to) *what* locality:— where, whither.

4227. Πούδης **Pŏudēs**, *poo´-dace;* of Lat. or.; *modest; Pudes* (i.e. *Pudens*), a Chr.:— Pudens.

4228. πούς **pŏus**, *pooce;* a primary word; a "*foot*" (fig. or lit.):— foot (-stool).

4229. πρᾶγμα **pragma**, *prag´-mah;* from *4238;* a *deed;* by impl. an *affair;* by ex-

tens. an *object* (material):— business, matter, thing, work.

4230. πραγματεία **pragmatĕia**, *prag-mat-i´-ah;* from *4231;* a *transaction,* i.e. negotiation:— affair.

4231. πραγματεύομαι **pragmatĕuŏmai**, *prag-mat-yoo´-om-ahee;* from *4229;* to *busy oneself* with, i.e. to *trade:—* occupy.

4232. πραιτώριον **praitōriŏn**, *prahee-to´-ree-on;* of Lat. or.; the *prætorium* or governor's *court-room* (sometimes incl. the whole *edifice* and *camp*):— (common, judgment) hall (of judgment), palace, prætorium.

4233. πράκτωρ **praktōr**, *prak´-tor;* from a der. of *4238;* a *practiser,* i.e. (spec.) an official *collector:—* officer.

4234. πρᾶξις **praxis**, *prax´-is;* from *4238; practice,* i.e. (concr.) an *act;* by extens. a *function:—* deed, office, work.

4235. πρᾷος **praiŏs**, *prah´-os;* a form of *4239,* used in certain parts; *gentle,* i.e. *humble:—* meek.

4236. πραότης **praiŏtēs**, *prah-ot´-ace;* from *4235; gentleness,* by impl. *humility:—* meekness.

4237. πρασιά **prasia**, *pras-ee-ah´;* perh. from *4854;* πράσον **prasŏn** (a *leek,* and so an *onion-patch*); a *garden plot,* i.e. (by impl. of reg. *beds*) a *row* (repeated in plur. by Heb., to indicate an arrangement):— in ranks.

4238. πράσσω **prassō**, *pras´-so;* a primary verb; to "*practice*", i.e. *perform repeatedly* or *habitually* (thus differing from *4160,* which prop. refers to a *single* act); by impl. to *execute, accomplish,* etc.; spec. to *collect* (dues), *fare* (personally):— commit, deeds, do, exact, keep, require, use arts.

4239. πραΰς **praÿs**, *prah-ooce´;* appar. a primary word; *mild,* i.e. (by impl.) *humble:—* meek. See also *4235.*

4240. πραΰτης **praÿtēs**, *prah-oo´-tace;* from *4239; mildness,* i.e. (by impl.) *humility:—* meekness.

4241. πρέπω **prĕpō**, *prep´-o;* appar. a primary verb; to *tower* up (*be conspicuous*), i.e. (by impl.) to be *suitable* or *proper* (third pers. sing. pres. ind., often used impers., it is *fit* or *right*):— become, comely.

4242. πρεσβεία **prĕsbĕia**, *pres-bi´-ah;* from *4243; seniority* (*eldership*), i.e. (by impl.) an *embassy* (concr. *ambassadors*):— ambassage, message.

4243. πρεσβεύω **prĕsbĕuō**, *pres-byoo´-o;* from the base of *4245;* to be a *senior,* i.e. (by impl.) *act as a representative* (fig. *preacher*):— be an ambassador.

4244. πρεσβυτέριον **prĕsbutēriŏn**, *pres-boo-ter´-ee-on;* neut. of a presumed der. of *4245;* the *order of elders,* i.e. (spec.) Isr. *Sanhedrin* or Chr. "*presbytery*":— (estate of) elder (-s), presbytery.

4245. πρεσβύτερος **prĕsbutĕrŏs**, *pres-boo´-ter-os;* comparative of πρέσβυς **prĕsbus** (*elderly*); *older;* as noun, a *senior;* spec. an Isr. *Sanhedrist* (also fig. member of the celestial council) or Chr. "*presbyter*":— elder (-est), old.

4246. πρεσβύτης **prĕsbutēs**, *pres-boo´-tace;* from the same as *4245;* an *old man:—* aged (man), old man.

4247. πρεσβῦτις **prĕsbutis**, *pres-boo´-tis;* fem. of *4246;* an *old woman:—* aged woman.

πρήθω **prēthō**. See *4092.*

4248. πρηνής **prēnēs**, *pray-nace´;* from *4253; leaning* (*falling*) *forward* ("*prone*"), i.e. *head foremost:—* headlong.

4249. πρίζω **prizō**, *prid´-zo;* a strengthened form of a primary πρίω **priō**, (to *saw*); to *saw* in two:— saw asunder.

4250. πρίν **prin**, *prin;* adv. from *4253; prior, sooner:—* before (that), ere.

4251. Πρίσκα **Priska**, *pris´-kah;* of Lat. or.; fem. of *Priscus, ancient; Priska,* a Chr. woman:— Prisca. See also *4252.*

4252. Πρίσκιλλα **Priskilla**, *pris´-kil-lah;* dimin. of *4251; Priscilla* (i.e. *little Prisca*), a Chr. woman:— Priscilla.

4253. πρό **prŏ**, *prŏ;* a primary prep.; "*fore*", i.e. *in front of, prior* (fig. *superior*) *to:—* above, ago, before, or ever. In composition it retains the same significations.

4254. προάγω **prŏagō**, *prŏ-ag´-o;* from *4253* and *71;* to *lead forward* (magisterially); intr. to *precede* (in place or time [part. *previous*]):— bring (forth, out), go before.

4255. προαιρέομαι **prŏairĕŏmai**, *prŏ-ahee-reh´-om-ahee;* from *4253* and *138;* to *choose* for oneself *before* another thing (*prefer*), i.e. (by impl.) to *propose* (*intend*):— purpose.

4256. προαιτιάομαι **prŏaitiaŏmai**, *prŏ-ahee-tee-ah´-om-ahee;* from *4253* and a der. of *156;* to *accuse already,* i.e. *previously charge:—* prove before.

4257. προακούω **prŏakŏuō**, *prŏ-ak-oo´-o;* from *4253* and *191;* to *hear already,* i.e. *anticipate:—* hear before.

4258. προαμαρτάνω **prŏamartanō**, *prŏ-am-ar-tan´-o;* from *4253* and *264;* to *sin previously* (to conversion):— sin already, heretofore sin.

4259. προαύλιον **prŏauliŏn**, *prŏ-ŏw´-lee-on;* neut. of a presumed compound of *4253* and *833;* a *forecourt,* i.e. *vestibule* (*alley-way*):— porch.

4260. προβαίνω **prŏbainō**, *prob-ah´-ee-no;* from *4253* and the base of *939;* to *walk forward,* i.e. *advance* (lit. or in years):— + be of a great age, go farther (on), be well stricken.

4261. προβάλλω **prŏballō**, *prob-al´-lo;* from *4253* and *906;* to *throw forward,* i.e. *push to the front, germinate:—* put forward, shoot forth.

4262. προβατικός **prŏbatikŏs**, *prob-at-ik-os´;* from *4263; relating to sheep,* i.e. (a *gate*) through which they were led into Jerusalem:— sheep (market).

4263. πρόβατον **prŏbatŏn**, *prob´-at-on;* prob. neut. of a presumed der. of *4260; something that walks forward* (a *quadruped*), i.e. (spec.) a *sheep* (lit. or fig.):— sheep (l-fold).

4264. προβιβάζω **prŏbibazō**, *prob-ib-ad´-zo;* from *4253* and a redupl. form of *971;* to *force forward,* i.e. *bring to the* *front, instigate:*— draw, before instruct.

4265. προβλέπω **prŏblĕpō**, *prob-lep´-o*; from 4253 and 991; to *look* out *before-hand*, i.e. *furnish in advance:*— provide.

4266. προγίνομαι **prŏginŏmai**, *prog-in´-om-ahee*; from 4253 and 1096; to *be already*, i.e. *have previously transpired:*— be past.

4267. προγινώσκω **prŏginōskō**, *prog-in-oce´-ko*; from 4253 and 1097; to *know beforehand*, i.e. *foresee:*— foreknow (ordain), know (before).

4268. πρόγνωσις **prŏgnōsis**, *prog´-no-sis*; from 4267; *forethought:*— foreknowledge.

4269. πρόγονος **prŏgŏnŏs**, *prog´-on-os*; from 4266; an *ancestor*, (*grand-*) *parent:*— forefather, parent.

4270. προγράφω **prŏgraphō**, *prog-raf´-o*; from 4253 and 1125; to *write previously*; fig. to *announce*, *prescribe:*— before ordain, evidently set forth, write (afore, aforetime).

4271. πρόδηλος **prŏdēlŏs**, *prod´-ay-los*; from 4253 and 1212; *plain before* all men, i.e. *obvious:*— evident, manifest (open) beforehand.

4272. προδίδωμι **prŏdidōmi**, *prod-id´-o-mee*; from 4253 and 1325; to *give before* the other party has given:— first give.

4273. προδότης **prŏdŏtēs**, *prod-ot´-ace*; from 4272 (in the sense of *giving forward* into another's [the enemy's] hands); a *surrender:*— betrayer, traitor.

προδρέμω **prŏdrĕmō**. See 4390.

4274. πρόδρομος **prŏdrŏmŏs**, *prod´-rom-os*; from the alt. of 4390; a *runner ahead*, i.e. *scout* (fig. *precursor*):— forerunner.

4275. προείδω **prŏĕidō**, *pro-i´-do*; from 4253 and 1492; *foresee:*— foresee, saw before.

προειρέω **prŏĕirĕō**. See 4280.

4276. προελπίζω **prŏĕlpizō**, *prŏ-el-pid´-zo*; from 4253 and 1679; to *hope in advance* of other confirmation:— first trust.

4277. προέπω **prŏĕpō**, *prŏ-ep´-o*; from 4253 and 2036; to *say already*, to *predict:*— forewarn, say (speak, tell) before. Comp. 4280.

4278. προενάρχομαι **prŏĕnarchŏmai**, *prŏ-en-ar´-khom-ahee*; from 4253 and 1728; to *commence already:*— begin (before).

4279. προεπαγγέλλομαι **prŏĕpaggĕllŏmai**, *prŏ-ep-ang-ghel´-lom-ahee*; mid. voice from 4253 and 1861; to *promise of old:*— promise before.

4280. προερέω **prŏĕrĕō**, *prŏ-er-eh´-o*; from 4253 and 2046; used as alt. of 4277; to *say already*, *predict:*— foretell, say (speak, tell) before.

4281. προέρχομαι **prŏĕrchŏmai**, *prŏ-er´-khom-ahee*; from 4253 and 2064 (incl. its alt.); to *go onward, precede* (in place or time):— go before (farther, forward), outgo, pass on.

4282. προετοιμάζω **prŏĕtŏimazō**, *pro-*

et-oy-mad´-zo; from 4253 and 2090; to *fit up in advance* (lit. or fig.):— ordain before, prepare afore.

4283. προευαγγελίζομαι **prŏĕuaggĕlizŏmai**, *prŏ-yoo-ang-ghel-id´-zom-ahee*; mid. voice from 4253 and 2097; to *announce* glad news *in advance:*— preach before the gospel.

4284. προέχομαι **prŏĕchŏmai**, *prŏ-ekh-om-ahee*; mid. voice from 4253 and 2192; to *hold* oneself *before* others, i.e. (fig.) to *excel:*— be better.

4285. προηγέομαι **prŏēgĕŏmai**, *prŏ-ay-geh´-om-ahee*; from 4253 and 2233; to *lead the way* for others, i.e. *show deference:*— prefer.

4286. πρόθεσις **prŏthĕsis**, *proth´-es-is*; from 4388; a *setting forth*, i.e. (fig.) *proposal* (intention); spec. the *show*-bread (in the Temple) as *exposed* before God:— purpose, shew [-bread].

4287. προθέσμιος **prŏthĕsmiŏs**, *proth-es´-mee-os*; from 4253 and a der. of 5087; *fixed beforehand*, i.e. (fem. with 2250 implied) a *designated* day:— time appointed.

4288. προθυμία **prŏthumia**, *proth-oo-mee´-ah*; from 4289; *predisposition*, i.e. *alacrity:*— forwardness of mind, readiness (of mind), ready (willing) mind.

4289. πρόθυμος **prŏthumŏs**, *proth´-oo-mos*; from 4253 and 2372; *forward* in *spirit*, i.e. *predisposed*; neut. (as noun) *alacrity:*— ready, willing.

4290. προθύμως **prŏthumōs**, *proth-oo´-moce*; adv. from 4289; *with alacrity:*— willingly.

4291. προΐστημι **prŏistēmi**, *prŏ-is´-tay-mee*; from 4253 and 2476; to *stand before*, i.e. (in rank) to *preside*, or (by impl.) to *practice:*— maintain, be over, rule.

4292. προκαλέομαι **prŏkalĕŏmai**, *prok-al-eh´-om-ahee*; mid. voice from 4253 and 2564; to *call forth to oneself* (*challenge*), i.e. (by impl.) to *irritate:*— provoke.

4293. προκαταγγέλλω **prŏkataggĕllō**, *prok-at-ang-ghel´-lo*; from 4253 and 2605; to *announce beforehand*, i.e. *predict, promise:*— foretell, have notice, (shew) before.

4294. προκαταρτίζω **prŏkatartizō**, *prok-at-ar-tid´-zo*; from 4253 and 2675; to *prepare in advance:*— make up beforehand.

4295. πρόκειμαι **prŏkĕimai**, *prok´-i-ma-hee*; from 4253 and 2749; to *lie before* the view, i.e. (fig.) to *be present* (to the mind), to *stand forth* (as an example or reward):— be first, set before (forth).

4296. προκηρύσσω **prŏkērussō**, *prok-ay-rooce´-so*; from 4253 and 2784; to *herald* (i.e. *proclaim*) *in advance:*— before (first) preach.

4297. προκοπή **prŏkŏpē**, *prok-op-ay´*; from 4298; *progress*, i.e. *advancement* (subj. or obj.):— furtherance, profit.

4298. προκόπτω **prŏkŏptō**, *prok-op´-to*; from 4253 and 2875; to *drive forward* (as if by beating), i.e. (fig. and intr.) to *advance* (in amount, to *grow*; in time, to *be well along*):— increase, proceed, profit, be far spent, wax.

4299. πρόκριμα **prŏkrima**, *prok´-ree-mah*; from a compound of 4253 and 2919; a *prejudgment* (*prejudice*), i.e. *prepossession:*— prefer one before another.

4300. προκυρόω **prŏkurŏō**, *prok-oo-rŏ´-o*; from 4253 and 2964; to *ratify previously:*— confirm before.

4301. προλαμβάνω **prŏlambanō**, *prol-am-ban´-o*; from 4253 and 2983; to *take in advance*, i.e. (lit.) *eat before* others have an opportunity; (fig.) to *anticipate, surprise:*— come aforehand, overtake, take before.

4302. προλέγω **prŏlĕgō**, *prol-eg´-o*; from 4253 and 3004; to *say beforehand*, i.e. *predict, forewarn:*— foretell, tell before.

4303. προμαρτύρομαι **prŏmarturŏmai**, *prom-ar-too´-rom-ahee*; from 4253 and 3143; to *be a witness in advance*, i.e. *predict:*— testify beforehand.

4304. προμελετάω **prŏmĕlĕtaō**, *prom-el-et-ah´-o*; from 4253 and 3191; to *premeditate:*— meditate before.

4305. προμεριμνάω **prŏmĕrimnaō**, *prom-er-im-nah´-o*; from 4253 and 3309; to *care* (anxiously) *in advance:*— take thought beforehand.

4306. προνοέω **prŏnŏĕō**, *pron-ŏ-eh´-o*; from 4253 and 3539; to *consider in advance*, i.e. *look* out for *beforehand* (act. by way of *maintenance* for others; mid. voice by way of *circumspection* for oneself):— provide (for).

4307. πρόνοια **prŏnŏia**, *pron´-oy-ah*; from 4306; *forethought*, i.e. provident *care* or *supply:*— providence, provision.

4308. προοράω **prŏŏraō**, *prŏ-or-ah´-o*; from 4253 and 3708; to *behold in advance*, i.e. (act.) to *notice* (another) *previously*, or (mid. voice) to *keep in* (one's own) *view:*— foresee, see before.

4309. προορίζω **prŏŏrizō**, *prŏ-or-id´-zo*; from 4253 and 3724; to *limit in advance*, i.e. (fig.) *predetermine:*— determine before, ordain, predestinate.

4310. προπάσχω **prŏpaschō**, *prop-as´-kho*; from 4253 and 3958; to *undergo* hardship *previously:*— suffer before.

4311. προπέμπω **prŏpĕmpō**, *prop-em´-po*; from 4253 and 3992; to *send forward*, i.e. *escort* or *aid* in travel:— accompany, bring (forward) on journey (way), conduct forth.

4312. προπετής **prŏpĕtēs**, *prop-et-ace´*; from a compound of 4253 and 4098; *falling forward*, i.e. *headlong* (fig. *precipitate*):— heady, rash [-ly].

4313. προπορεύομαι **prŏpŏrĕuŏmai**, *prop-or-yoo´-om-ahee*; from 4253 and 4198; to *precede* (as guide or herald):— go before.

4314. πρός **prŏs**, *pros*; a strengthened form of 4253; a prep. of direction; *forward to*, i.e. *toward* (with the gen. *the side of*, i.e. *pertaining to*; with the dat. *by the side of*, i.e. *near to*; usually with the acc., the place, time, occasion, or respect, which is the *destination* of the relation, i.e. *whither* or *for* which it is predicated):— about, according to, against, among, at, because of, before, between, ((where-)) by, for, × at thy house, in, for intent, nigh unto, of, which pertain to, that, to (the end that), + together, to ((you)) -ward, unto, with (-in). In composition it denotes essentially the same applications, namely, motion *toward*, accession *to*, or nearness *at*.

4315. προσάββατον prŏsabbatŏn, *pros-ab´-bat-on*; from 4253 and 4521; a *foresabbath*, i.e. the *Sabbath-eve*:— day before the sabbath. Comp. 3904.

4316. προσαγορεύω prŏsagŏreuō, *pros-ag-or-yoo´-o*; from 4314 and a der. of 58 (mean to *harangue*); to *address*, i.e. salute by *name*:— call.

4317. προσάγω prŏsagō, *pros-ag´-o*; from 4314 and 71; to *lead toward*, i.e. (tran.) to *conduct near* (*summon, present*), or (intr.) to *approach*:— bring, draw near.

4318. προσαγωγή prŏsagōgē, *pros-agogue-ay´*; from 4317 (comp. 72); *admission*:— access.

4319. προσαιτέω prŏsaiteō, *pros-aheeteh´-o*; from 4314 and 154; to *ask repeatedly* (*importune*), i.e. *solicit*:— beg.

4320. προσαναβαίνω prŏsanabainō, *pros-an-ab-ah´-ee-no*; from 4314 and 305; to *ascend farther*, i.e. *be promoted* (*take an upper (more honorable) seat*):— go up.

4321. προσαναλίσκω prŏsanaliskō, *pros-an-al-is´-ko*; from 4314 and 355; to *expend further*:— spend.

4322. προσαναπληρόω prŏsanaplērŏō, *pros-an-ap-lay-ro´-o*; from 4314 and 378; to *fill up further*, i.e. *furnish fully*:— supply.

4323. προσανατίθημι prŏsanatithēmi, *pros-an-at-ith´-ay-mee*; from 4314 and 394; to *lay up in addition*, i.e. (mid. voice and fig.) to *impart* or (by impl.) to *consult*:— in conference add, confer.

4324. προσαπειλέω prŏsapeileō, *pros-ap-i-leh´-o*; from 4314 and 546; to *menace additionally*:— threaten further.

4325. προσδαπανάω prŏsdapanaō, *pros-dap-an-ah´-o*; from 4314 and 1159; to *expend additionally*:— spend more.

4326. προσδέομαι prŏsdĕŏmai, *pros-deh´-om-ahee*; from 4314 and 1189; to *require additionally*, i.e. *want further*:— need.

4327. προσδέχομαι prŏsdĕchŏmai, *pros-dekh´-om-ahee*; from 4314 and 1209; to *admit* (to intercourse, hospitality, credence, or (fig.) endurance); by impl. to *await* (with confidence or patience):— accept, allow, look (wait) for, take.

4328. προσδοκάω prŏsdŏkaō, *pros-dok-ah´-o*; from 4314 and δοκεύω dŏkĕuō (to watch); to *anticipate* (in thought, hope or fear); by impl. to *await*:— (be in) expect (-ation), look (for), when looked, tarry, wait for.

4329. προσδοκία prŏsdŏkia, *pros-dok-ee´-ah*; from 4328; *apprehension* (of evil); by impl. *infliction* anticipated:— expectation, looking after.

προσδρέμω prŏsdrĕmō. See 4370.

4330. προσεάω prŏsĕaō, *pros-eh-ah´-o*;

from 4314 and 1439; to *permit further progress*:— suffer.

4331. προσεγγίζω prŏsĕggizō, *pros-eng-ghid´-zo*; from 4314 and 1448; to *approach near*:— come nigh.

4332. προσεδρεύω prŏsĕdrĕuō, *pros-edryoo´-o*; from a compound of 4314 and the base of 1476; to *sit near*, i.e. *attend as a servant*:— wait at.

4333. προσεργάζομαι prŏsĕrgazŏmai, *pros-er-gad´-zom-ahee*; from 4314 and 2038; to *work additionally*, i.e. (by impl.) *acquire besides*:— gain.

4334. προσέρχομαι prŏsĕrchŏmai, *pros-er´-khom-ahee*; from 4314 and 2064 (incl. its alt.); to *approach*, i.e. (lit.) *come near, visit*, or (fig.) *worship, assent to*:— (as soon as he) come (unto), come thereunto, consent, draw near, go (near, to, unto).

4335. προσευχή prŏsĕuchē, *pros-yookhay´*; from 4336; *prayer* (*worship*); by impl. an *oratory* (*chapel*):— × pray earnestly, prayer.

4336. προσεύχομαι prŏsĕuchŏmai, *pros-yoo´-khom-ahee*; from 4314 and 2172; to *pray* to God, i.e. *supplicate, worship*:— pray (× earnestly, for), make prayer.

4337. προσέχω prŏsĕchō, *pros-ekh´-o*; from 4314 and 2192; (fig.) to *hold the mind* (3563 impl.) *toward*, i.e. *pay attention to, be cautious about, apply oneself to, adhere to*:— (give) attend (-ance, -ance at, -ance to, unto), beware, be given to, give (take) heed (to, unto); have regard.

4338. προσηλόω prŏsēlŏō, *pros-ay-lŏ´-o*; from 4314 and a der. of 2247; to *peg to*, i.e. *spike fast*:— nail to.

4339. προσήλυτος prŏsēlutŏs, *pros-ay´-loo-tos*; from the alt. of 4334; an *arriver* from a for. region, i.e. (spec.) an *acceder* (*convert*) to Judaism ("*proselyte*"):— proselyte.

4340. πρόσκαιρος prŏskairŏs, *pros´-kahee-ros*; from 4314 and 2540; for the *occasion only*, i.e. *temporary*:— dur-(eth) for awhile, endure for a time, for a season, temporal.

4341. προσκαλέομαι prŏskalĕŏmai, *pros-kal-eh´-om-ahee*; mid. voice from 4314 and 2564; to *call toward oneself*, i.e. *summon, invite*:— call (for, to, unto).

4342. προσκαρτερέω prŏskartĕreō, *pros-kar-ter-eh´-o*; from 4314 and 2594; to *be earnest toward*, i.e. (to a thing) to *persevere, be constantly diligent*, or (in a place) to *attend* assiduously all the exercises, or (to a person) to *adhere closely to* (as a servitor):— attend (give self) continually (upon), continue (in, instant in, with), wait on (continually).

4343. προσκαρτέρησις prŏskartĕrēsis, *pros-kar-ter´-ay-sis*; from 4342; *persistency*:— perseverance.

4344. προσκεφάλαιον prŏskĕphalaiŏn, *pros-kef-al´-ahee-on*; neut. of a presumed compound of 4314 and 2776; something for the *head*, i.e. a *cushion*:— pillow.

4345. προσκληρόω prŏsklērŏō, *prosklay-rŏ´-o*; from 4314 and 2820; to *give a*

common *lot to*, i.e. (fig.) to *associate with*:— consort with.

4346. πρόσκλισις prŏsklisis, *pros´-klisis*; from a compound of 4314 and 2827; a *leaning toward*, i.e. (fig.) *proclivity* (*favoritism*):— partiality.

4347. προσκολλάω prŏskŏllaō, *pros-kollah´-o*; from 4314 and 2853; to *glue to*, i.e. (fig.) to *adhere*:— cleave, join (self).

4348. πρόσκομμα prŏskŏmma, *pros´-kom-mah*; from 4350; a *stub*, i.e. (fig.) *occasion of apostasy*:— offence, stumbling (-block, (-stone)).

4349. προσκοπή prŏskŏpē, *pros-kopay´*; from 4350; a *stumbling*, i.e. (fig. and concr.) *occasion of sin*:— offence.

4350. προσκόπτω prŏskŏptō, *pros-kop´-to*; from 4314 and 2875; to *strike at*, i.e. *surge against* (as water); spec. to *stub on*, i.e. *trip up* (lit. or fig.):— beat upon, dash, stumble (at).

4351. προσκυλίω prŏskuliō, *pros-koolee´-o*; from 4314 and 2947; to *roll toward*, i.e. *block against*:— roll (to).

4352. προσκυνέω prŏskunĕō, *pros-kooneh´-o*; from 4314 and a probable der. of 2965 (mean. to *kiss*, like a dog *licking* his master's hand); to *fawn* or *crouch to*, i.e. (lit. or fig.) *prostrate* oneself in homage (do *reverence to, adore*):— worship.

4353. προσκυνητής prŏskunētēs, *proskoo-nay-tace´*; from 4352; an *adorer*:— worshipper.

4354. προσλαλέω prŏslalĕō, *pros-laleh´-o*; from 4314 and 2980; to *talk to*, i.e. *converse with*:— speak to (with).

4355. προσλαμβάνω prŏslambanō, *proslam-ban´-o*; from 4314 and 2983; to *take to oneself*, i.e. *use* (food), *lead* (aside), *admit* (to friendship or hospitality):— receive, take (unto).

4356. πρόσληψις prŏslēpsis, *pros´-lapesis*; from 4355; *admission*:— receiving.

4357. προσμένω prŏsmĕnō, *pros-men´-o*; from 4314 and 3306; to *stay further*, i.e. *remain* in a place, with a person; fig. to *adhere to, persevere in*:— abide still, be with, cleave unto, continue in (with).

4358. προσορμίζω prŏsŏrmizō, *pros-ormid´-zo*; from 4314 and a der. of the same as 3730 (mean. to *tie* (anchor) or *lull*); to *moor to*, i.e. (by impl.) *land at*:— draw to the shore.

4359. προσοφείλω prŏsŏpheilō, *pros-of-i´-lo*; from 4314 and 3784; to *be indebted additionally*:— over besides.

4360. προσοχθίζω prŏsŏchthizō, *prosokh-thid´-zo*; from 4314 and a form of όχθέω ŏchthĕō (to *be vexed* with something irksome); to *feel indignant at*:— be grieved with.

4361. πρόσπεινος prŏspĕinŏs, *pros´-pinos*; from 4314 and the same as 3983; *hungering further*, i.e. *intensely hungry*:— very hungry.

4362. προσπήγνυμι prŏspēgnumi, *prospayg´-noo-mee*; from 4314 and 4078; to *fasten to*, i.e. (spec.) to *impale* (on a cross):— crucify.

4363. προσπίπτω prŏspiptō, *pros-pip´-to*; from 4314 and 4098; to *fall toward*, i.e. (gently) *prostrate* oneself (in supplication or homage), or (violently) to *rush* upon (in storm):— beat upon, fall (down) at (before).

4364. προσποιέομαι **prŏspŏiĕŏmai**, *pros-poy-eh´-om-ahee*; mid. voice from *4314* and *4160*; to *do forward for oneself*, i.e. *pretend* (as if about to do a thing):— make as though.

4365. προσπορεύομαι **prŏspŏrĕuŏmai**, *pros-por-yoo´-om-ahee*; from *4314* and *4198*; to *journey toward*, i.e. *approach* [not the same as *4313*]:— go before.

4366. προσρήγνυμι **prŏsrēgnumi**, *pros-rayg´-noo-mee*; from *4314* and *4486*; to *tear toward*, i.e. *burst upon* (as a tempest or flood):— beat vehemently against (upon).

4367. προστάσσω **prŏstassō**, *pros-tas´-so*; from *4314* and *5021*; to *arrange toward*, i.e. (fig.) *enjoin*:— bid, command.

4368. προστάτις **prŏstatis**, *pros-tat´-is*; fem. of a der. of *4291*; a *patroness*, i.e. *assistant*:— succourer.

4369. προστίθημι **prŏstithēmi**, *pros-tith´-ay-mee*; from *4314* and *5087*; to *place additionally*, i.e. *lay beside*, *annex*, *repeat*:— add, again, give more, increase, lay unto, proceed further, speak to any more.

4370. προστρέχω **prŏstrĕchō**, *pros-trekh´-o*; from *4314* and *5143* (incl. its alt.); to *run toward*, i.e. *hasten* to meet or join:— run (thither to, to).

4371. προσφάγιον **prŏsphagiŏn**, *pros-fag´-ee-on*; neut. of a presumed der. of a compound of *4314* and *5315*; something *eaten in addition* to bread, i.e. a *relish* (spec. *fish*; comp. *3795*):— meat.

4372. πρόσφατος **prŏsphatŏs**, *pros´-fat-os*; from *4253* and a der. of *4969*; *previously* (*recently*) *slain* (*fresh*), i.e. (fig.) *lately made*:— new.

4373. προσφάτως **prŏsphatōs**, *pros-fat´-oce*; adv. from *4372*; *recently*:— lately.

4374. προσφέρω **prŏsphĕrō**, *pros-fer´-o*; from *4314* and *5342* (incl. its alt.); to *bear toward*, i.e. *lead* to, *tender* (espec. to God), *treat*:— bring (to, unto), deal with, do, offer (unto, up), present unto, put to.

4375. προσφιλής **prŏsphilēs**, *pros-fee-lace´*; from a presumed compound of *4314* and *5368*; *friendly toward*, i.e. *acceptable*:— lovely.

4376. προσφορά **prŏsphŏra**, *pros-for-ah´*; from *4374*; *presentation*; concr. an *oblation* (bloodless) or *sacrifice*:— offering (up).

4377. προσφωνέω **prŏsphōnĕō**, *pros-fo-neh´-o*; from *4314* and *5455*; to *sound toward*, i.e. *address*, *exclaim*, *summon*:— call unto, speak (un-) to.

4378. πρόσχυσις **prŏschusis**, *pros´-khoo-sis*; from a comp. of *4314* and χέω **chĕō** (to *pour*); a *shedding forth*, i.e. *affusion*:— sprinkling.

4379. προσψαύω **prŏspsauō**, *pros-psow´-o*; from *4314* and ψαύω psauō (to *touch*); to *impinge*, i.e. *lay a finger on* (in order to relieve):— touch.

4380. προσωπολημπτέω **prŏsōpŏlēptĕō**, *pros-o-pol-ape-teh´-o*; from *4381*; to

favor an individual, i.e. *show partiality*:— have respect to persons.

4381. προσωπολήπτης **prŏsōpŏlēptēs**, *pros-o-pol-ape´-tace*; from *4383* and *2983*; an *accepter of a face* (individual), i.e. (spec.) one *exhibiting partiality*:— respecter of persons.

4382. προσωποληψία **prŏsōpŏlēpsia**, *pros-o-pol-ape-see´-ah*; from *4381*; *partiality*, i.e. *favoritism*:— respect of persons.

4383. πρόσωπον **prŏsōpŏn**, *pros´-o-pon*; from *4314* and ὤψ **ōps** (the *visage*, from *3700*); the *front*, (as being *toward* view), i.e. the *countenance*, *aspect*, *appearance*, *surface*; by impl. *presence*, *person*:— (outward) appearance, × before, countenance, face, fashion, (men's) person, presence.

4384. προτάσσω **prŏtassō**, *prot-as´-so*; from *4253* and *5021*; to *pre-arrange*, i.e. *prescribe*:— before appoint.

4385. προτείνω **prŏtĕinō**, *prot-i´-no*; from *4253* and τείνω **tĕinō** (to *stretch*); to *protend*, i.e. *tie prostrate* (for scourging):— bind.

4386. πρότερον **prŏtĕrŏn**, *prot´-er-on*; neut. of *4387* as adv. (with or without the art.); *previously*:— before, (at the) first, former.

4387. πρότερος **prŏtĕrŏs**, *prot´-er-os*; comp. of *4253*; *prior or previous*:— former.

4388. προτίθεμαι **prŏtithĕmai**, *prot-ith´-em-ahee*; mid. voice from *4253* and *5087*; to *place before*, i.e. (for oneself) to *exhibit*; (to oneself) to *propose* (determine):— purpose, set forth.

4389. προτρέπομαι **prŏtrĕpŏmai**, *prot-rep´-om-ahee*; mid. voice from *4253* and the base of *5157*; to *turn forward* for oneself, i.e. *encourage*:— exhort.

4390. προτρέχω **prŏtrĕchō**, *prot-rekh´-o*; from *4253* and *5143* (incl. its alt.); to *run forward*, i.e. *outstrip*, *precede*:— outrun, run before.

4391. προϋπάρχω **prŏüparchō**, *prŏ-oop-ar´-kho*; from *4253* and *5225*; to *exist before*, i.e. (adv.) to *be or do something previously*:— + be before (-time).

4392. πρόφασις **prŏphasis**, *prof´-as-is*; from a compound of *4253* and *5316*; an *outward showing*, i.e. *pretext*:— cloke, colour, pretence, show.

4393. προφέρω **prŏphĕrō**, *prof-er´-o*; from *4253* and *5342*; to *bear forward*, i.e. *produce*:— bring forth.

4394. προφητεία **prŏphētĕia**, *prof-ay-ti´-ah*; from *4396* ("prophecy"); *prediction* (scriptural or other):— prophecy, prophesying.

4395. προφητεύω **prŏphētĕuō**, *prof-ate-yoo´-o*; from *4396*; to *foretell* events, *divine*, *speak* under *inspiration*, exercise the prophetic office:— prophesy.

4396. προφήτης **prŏphētēs**, *prof-ay´-tace*; from a compound of *4253* and *5346*; a *foreteller* ("prophet"); by anal. an *inspired speaker*; by extens. a *poet*:— prophet.

4397. προφητικός **prŏphētikŏs**, *prof-ay-tik-os´*; from *4396*; *pertaining to a fore-*

teller ("prophetic"):— of prophecy, of the prophets.

4398. προφῆτις **prŏphētis**, *prof-ay´-tis*; fem. of *4396*; a *female foreteller* or an *inspired woman*:— prophetess.

4399. προφθάνω **prŏphthanō**, *prof-than´-o*; from *4253* and *5348*; to *get an earlier start of*, i.e. *anticipate*:— prevent.

4400. προχειρίζομαι **prŏchĕirizŏmai**, *prokh-i-rid´-zom-ahee*; mid. voice from *4253* and a der. of *5495*; to *handle* for oneself *in advance*, i.e. (fig.) to *purpose*:— choose, make.

4401. προχειροτονέω **prŏchĕirŏtŏnĕō**, *prokh-i-rot-on-eh´-o*; from *4253* and *5500*; to *elect in advance*:— choose before.

4402. Πρόχορος **Prŏchŏrŏs**, *prokh´-or-os*; from *4253* and *5525*; *before the dance*; *Prochorus*, a Chr.:— Prochorus.

4403. πρύμνα **prumna**, *proom´-nah*; fem. of πρυμνύς **prumnus** (hindmost); the *stern* of a ship:— hinder part, stern.

4404. πρωΐ **prōï**, *pro-ee´*; adv. from *4253*; at *dawn*; by impl. the *day-break watch*:— early (in the morning), (in the) morning.

4405. πρωΐα **prōïa**, *pro-ee´-ah*; fem. of a der. of *4404* as noun; *day-dawn*:— early, morning.

4406. πρώϊμος **prōïmŏs**, *pro´-ee-mos*; from *4404*; *dawning*, i.e. (by anal.) *autumnal* (showering, the first of the rainy season):— early.

4407. πρωϊνός **prōïnŏs**, *pro-ee-nos´*; from *4404*; pertaining to the *dawn*, i.e. *matutinal*:— morning.

4408. πρώρα **prōra**, *pro´-ra*; fem. of a presumed der. of *4253* as noun; the *prow*, i.e. *forward part* of a vessel:— forepart (-ship).

4409. πρωτεύω **prōtĕuō**, *prote-yoo´-o*; from *4413*; to *be first* (in rank or influence):— have the preeminence.

4410. πρωτοκαθεδρία **prōtŏkathĕdria**, *pro-tok-ath-ed-ree´-ah*; from *4413* and *2515*; a *sitting first* (in the front row), i.e. *preeminence* in council:— chief (highest, uppermost) seat.

4411. πρωτοκλισία **prōtŏklisia**, *pro-tok-lis-ee´-ah*; from *4413* and *2828*; a *reclining first* (in the place of honor) at the dinner-bed, i.e. *preeminence* at meals:— chief (highest, uppermost) room.

4412. πρῶτον **prōtŏn**, *pro´-ton*; neut. of *4413* as adv. (with or without *3588*); *firstly* (in time, place, order, or importance):— before, at the beginning, chiefly (at, at the) first (of all).

4413. πρῶτος **prōtŏs**, *pro´-tos*; contr. superl. of *4253*; *foremost* (in time, place, order or importance):— before, beginning, best, chief (-est), first (of all), former.

4414. πρωτοστάτης **prōtŏstatēs**, *pro-tos-tat´-ace*; from *4413* and *2476*; one *standing first* in the ranks, i.e. a *captain* (champion):— ringleader.

4415. πρωτοτόκια **prōtŏtŏkia**, *pro-tot-ok´-ee-ah*; from *4416*; *primogeniture* (as a privilege):— birthright.

4416. πρωτοτόκος **prōtŏtŏkŏs**, pro-tot-ok´-os; from 4413 and the alt. of 5088; first-born (usually as noun, lit. or fig.):— firstbegotten (-born).

4417. πταίω **ptaiō**, ptah´-yo; a form of 4098; to trip, i.e. (fig.) to err, sin, fail (of salvation):— fall, offend, stumble.

4418. πτέρνα **ptĕrna**, pter´-nah; of uncert. der.; the heel (fig.):— heel.

4419. πτερύγιον **ptĕrugiŏn**, pter-oog-ee-on; neut. of a presumed der. of 4420; a winglet, i.e. (fig.) extremity (top corner):— pinnacle.

4420. πτέρυξ **ptĕrux**, pter´-oox; from a der. of 4072 (mean. a feather); a wing:— wing.

4421. πτηνόν **ptēnŏn**, ptay-non´; contr. for 4071; a bird:— bird.

4422. πτοέω **ptŏĕō**, ptŏ-eh´-o; prob. akin to the alt. of 4098 (through the idea of causing to fall) or to 4072 (through that of causing to fly away); to scare:— frighten.

4423. πτόησις **ptŏēsis**, ptŏ´-ay-sis; from 4422; alarm:— amazement.

4424. Πτολεμαΐς **Ptŏlĕmaïs**, ptol-em-ah-is´; from Πτολεμαῖος **Ptŏlĕmaiŏs** (Ptolemy, after whom it was named); Ptolemais, a place in Pal.:— Ptolemais.

4425. πτύον **ptuŏn**, ptoo´-on; from 4429; a winnowing-fork (as scattering like spittle):— fan.

4426. πτύρω **pturō**, ptoo´-ro; from a presumed der. of 4429 (and thus akin to 4422); to frighten:— terrify.

4427. πτύσμα **ptusma**, ptoos´-mah; from 4429; saliva:— spittle.

4428. πτύσσω **ptussō**, ptoos´-so; prob. akin to πετάννυμι **pĕtannumi**, (to spread; and thus appar. allied to 4072 through the idea of expansion, and to 4429 through that of flattening; comp. 3961); to fold, i.e. furl a scroll:— close.

4429. πτύω **ptuō**, ptoo´-o; a primary verb (comp. 4428); to spit:— spit.

4430. πτῶμα **ptōma**, pto´-mah; from the alt. of 4098; a ruin, i.e. (spec.) lifeless body (corpse, carrion):— dead body, carcase, corpse.

4431. πτῶσις **ptōsis**, pto´-sis; from the alt. of 4098; a crash, i.e. downfall (lit. or fig.):— fall.

4432. πτωχεία **ptōchĕia**, pto-khi´-ah; from 4433; beggary, i.e. indigence (lit. or fig.):— poverty.

4433. πτωχεύω **ptōchĕuō**, pto-khyoo´-o; from 4434; to be a beggar, i.e. (by impl.) to become indigent (fig.):— become poor.

4434. πτωχός **ptōchŏs**, pto-khos´; from πτώσσω **ptōssō**, to crouch; akin to 4422 and the alt. of 4098; a beggar (as cringing), i.e. pauper (strictly denoting absolute or public mendicancy, although also used in a qualified or relative sense; whereas 3993 prop. means only straitened circumstances in private), lit. (often used as a noun) or fig. (distressed):— beggar (-ly), poor.

4435. πυγμή **pugmē**, poog-may´; from a primary πύξ **pux** (the fist, as a weapon); the clenched hand, i.e. (only in dat. as

adverb) with the fist (hard scrubbing):— oft.

4436. Πύθων **Puthōn**, poo´-thone; from Πυθώ **Puthō** (the name of the region where Delphi, the seat of the famous oracle, was located); a Python, i.e. (by anal. with the supposed diviner there) inspiration (soothsaying):— divination.

4437. πυκνός **puknŏs**, pook-nos´; from the same as 4635; clasped (thick), i.e. (fig.) frequent; neut. plur. (as adv.) frequently:— often (-er).

4438. πυκτέω **puktĕō**, pook-teh´-o; from a der. of the same as 4435; to box (with the fist), i.e. contend (as a boxer) at the games (fig.):— fight.

4439. πύλη **pulē**, poo´-lay; appar. a primary word; a gate, i.e. the leaf or wing of a folding entrance (lit. or fig.):— gate.

4440. πυλών **pulōn**, poo-lone´; from 4439; a gate-way, door-way of a building or city; by impl. a portal or vestibule:— gate, porch.

4441. πυνθάνομαι **punthanŏmai**, poon-than´-om-ahee; mid. voice prol. from a primary πύθω **puthō** (which occurs only as an alt. in certain tenses); to question, i.e. ascertain by inquiry (as a matter of information merely; and thus differing from 2065, which prop. means a request as a favor; and from 154, which is strictly a demand for something due; as well as from 2212, which implies a search for something hidden; and from 1189, which involves the idea of urgent need); by impl. to learn (by casual intelligence):— ask, demand, enquire, understand.

4442. πῦρ **pur**, poor; a primary word; "fire" (lit. or fig., spec. lightning):— fiery, fire.

4443. πυρά **pura**, poo-rah´; from 4442; a fire (concr.):— fire.

4444. πύργος **purgŏs**, poor´-gos; appar. a primary word ("burgh"); a tower or castle:— tower.

4445. πυρέσσω **purĕssō**, poo-res´-so; from 4443; to be on fire, i.e. (spec.) to have a fever:— be sick of a fever.

4446. πυρετός **purĕtŏs**, poo-ret-os´; from 4445; inflamed, i.e. (by impl.) feverish (as noun, fever):— fever.

4447. πύρινος **purinŏs**, poo´-ree-nos; from 4443; fiery, i.e. (by impl.) flaming:— of fire.

4448. πυρόω **purŏō**, poo-rŏ´-o; from 4442; to kindle, i.e. (pass.) to be ignited, glow (lit.), be refined (by impl.), or (fig.) to be inflamed (with anger, grief, lust):— burn, fiery, be on fire, try.

4449. πυρράζω **purrhazō**, poor-hrad´-zo; from 4450; to redden (intr.):— be red.

4450. πυρρός **purrhŏs**, poor-hros´; from 4442; fire-like, i.e. (spec.) flame-colored:— red.

4451. πύρωσις **purōsis**, poo´-ro-sis; from 4448; ignition, i.e. (spec.) smelting (fig. conflagration, calamity as a test):— burning, trial.

4452. -πω **-pō**, po; another form of the base of 4458; an enclitic particle of indefiniteness; yet, even; used only in

composition. See 3369, 3380, 3764, 3768, 4455.

4453. πωλέω **pōlĕō**, po-leh´-o; prob. ultimately from πέλομαι **pĕlŏmai** (to be busy, to trade); to barter (as a pedlar), i.e. to sell:— sell, whatever is sold.

4454. πῶλος **pōlŏs**, po´-los; appar. a primary word; a "foal" or "filly", i.e. (spec.) a young ass:— colt.

4455. πώποτε **pōpŏtĕ**, po´-pot-e; from 4452 and 4218; at any time, i.e. (with neg. particle) at no time:— at any time, + never (... to any man), + yet, never man.

4456. πωρόω **pōrŏō**, po-rŏ´-o; appar. from πῶρος **pōrŏs**, (a kind of stone); to petrify, i.e. (fig.) to indurate (render stupid or callous):— blind, harden.

4457. πώρωσις **pōrōsis**, po´-ro-sis; from 4456; stupidity or callousness:— blindness, hardness.

4458. -πώς **-pōs**, poce; adv. from the base of 4225; an enclitic particle of indefiniteness of manner; somehow or anyhow; used only in composition:— haply, by any (some) means, perhaps. See 1513, 3381. Comp. 4459.

4459. πῶς **pōs**, poce; adv. from the base of 4226; an interr. particle of manner; in what way? (sometimes the question is indirect, how?); also as exclamation, how much!:— how, after (by) what manner (means), that. [Occasionally unexpressed in English].

P

4460. Ῥαάβ **Rhaab**, hrah-ab´; of Heb. or. [7343]; Raab (i.e. Rachab), a Canaanitess:— Rahab. See also 4477.

4461. ῥαββί **rhabbi**, hrab-bee´; of Heb. or. [7227 with pron. suff.]; my master, i.e Rabbi, as an official title of honor:— Master, Rabbi.

4462. ῥαββονί **rhabbŏni**, hrab-bon-ee´; or

ῥαββουνί **rhabbŏuni**, hrab-boo-nee´; of Chald. or.; corresp. to 4461:— Lord, Rabboni.

4463. ῥαβδίζω **rhabdizō**, hrab-did´-zo; from 4464; to strike with a stick, i.e. bastinado:— beat (with rods).

4464. ῥάβδος **rhabdŏs**, hrab´-dos; from the base of 4474; a stick or wand (as a cudgel, a cane or a baton of royalty):— rod, sceptre, staff.

4465. ῥαβδοῦχος **rhabdŏuchŏs**, hrab-doo´-khos; from 4464 and 2192; a rod-(the Lat. fasces) holder, i.e. a Rom. lictor (constable or executioner):— serjeant.

4466. Ῥαγαύ **Rhagau**, hrag-ow´; of Heb. or. [7466]; Ragaü (i.e. Reu), a patriarch:— Ragau.

4467. ῥᾳδιούργημα **rhaidiŏurgēma**, hrad-ee-oorg´-ay-mah; from a comp. of ῥᾴδιος **rhaidiŏs** (easy, i.e. reckless) and 2041; easy-going behavior, i.e. (by extens.) a crime:— lewdness.

4468. ῥᾳδιουργία **rhaidiŏurgia**, hrad-ee-oorg-ee´-a; from the same as 4467; recklessness, i.e. (by extens.) malignity:— mischief.

4469. ῥακά **rhaka**, hrak-ah´; of Chald.

or. [comp. 7386]; O empty one, i.e. thou worthless (as a term of utter vilification):— Raca.

4470. ῥάκος rhakòs, rhak´-os; from 4486; a "rag", i.e. piece of cloth:— cloth.

4471. Ῥαμᾶ Rhama, hram-ah´; of Heb. or. [7414]; Rama (i.e. Ramah), a place in Pal.:— Rama.

4472. ῥαντίζω rhantizō, hran-tid´-zo; from a der. of ῥαίνω rhainō (to sprinkle); to render besprinkled, i.e. asperse (cerem. or fig.):— sprinkle.

4473. ῥαντισμός rhantismòs, hran-tis-mos´; from 4472; aspersion (cerem. or fig.):— sprinkling.

4474. ῥαπίζω rhapizō, hrap-id´-zo; from a. der. of a primary ῥέπω rhĕpō (to let fall, "rap"); to slap:— smite (with the palm of the hand). Comp. 5180.

4475. ῥάπισμα rhapisma, hrap´-is-mah; from 4474; a slap:— (+ strike with the) palm of the hand, smite with the hand.

4476. ῥαφίς rhaphis, hraf-ece´; from a primary ῥάπτω rhaptō (to sew; perh. rather akin to the base of 4474 through the idea of puncturing); a needle:— needle.

4477. Ῥαχάβ Rhachab, hrakh-ab´; from the same as 4460; Rachab, a Canaanitess:— Rachab.

4478. Ῥαχήλ Rhachēl, hrakh-ale´; of Heb. or. [7354]; Rachel, the wife of Jacob:— Rachel.

4479. Ῥεβέκκα Rhĕbĕkka, hreb-bek´-kah; of Heb. or. [7259]; Rebecca (i.e. Ribkah), the wife of Isaac:— Rebecca.

4480. ῥέδα rhĕda, hred´-ah; of Lat. or.; a rheda, i.e. four-wheeled carriage (wagon for riding):— chariot.

4481. Ῥεμφάν Rhĕmphan, hrem-fan´or

Ῥαιφάν Rhaiphan, hrahee-fan´; by incorrect transliteration for a word of Heb. of [3594]; Remphan (i.e. Kijun), an Eg. idol:—Remphan.

4482. ῥέω rhĕō, hreh´-o; a primary verb; for some tenses of which a prol. form

ῥεύω rhĕuō, hryoo´-o is used; to flow ("run"; as water):— flow.

4483. ῥέω rhĕō, hreh´-o; for certain tenses of which a prol. form

ἐρέω ĕrĕō, er-eh´-o; is used; and both as alt. for 2036; perh. akin (or ident.) with 4482 (through the idea of pouring forth); to utter, i.e. speak or say:— command, make, say, speak (of). Comp. 3004.

4484. Ῥήγιον Rhēgiòn, hrayg´-ee-on; of Lat. or.; Rhegium, a place in Italy:— Rhegium.

4485. ῥῆγμα rhēgma, hrayg´-mah; from 4486; something torn, i.e. a fragment (by impl. and abstr. a fall):— ruin.

4486. ῥήγνυμι rhēgnumi, hrayg´-noo-mee; or

ῥήσσω rhēssō, hrace´-so; both prol. forms of ῥήκω rhēkō (which appears only in certain forms, and is itself prob. a strengthened form of ἄγνυμι agnumi, [see in 2608]); to "break", "wreck" or "crack", i.e. (espec.) to sunder (by separation of the parts;

2608 being its intensive [with the prep. in composition], and 2352 a shattering to minute fragments; but not a reduction to the constituent particles, like 3089) or disrupt, lacerate; by impl. to convulse (with spasms); fig. to give vent to joyful emotions:— break (forth), burst, rend, tear.

4487. ῥῆμα rhēma, hray´-mah; from 4483; an utterance (indiv., collect. or spec.); by impl. a matter or topic (espec. of narration, command or dispute); with a neg. naught whatever:— + evil, + nothing, saying, word.

4488. Ῥησά Rhēsa, hray-sah´; prob. of Heb. or. [appar. for 7509]; Resa (i.e. Rephajah), an Isr.:— Rhesa.

4489. ῥήτωρ rhētōr, hray´-tore; from 4483; a speaker, i.e. (by impl.) a forensic advocate:— orator.

4490. ῥητῶς rhētōs, hray-toce´; adv. from a der. of 4483; out-spokenly, i.e. distinctly:— expressly.

4491. ῥίζα rhiza, hrid´-zah; appar. a primary word; a "root" (lit. or fig.):— root.

4492. ῥιζόω rhizòō, hrid-zŏ´-o; from 4491; to root (fig. become stable):— root.

4493. ῥιπή rhipē, hree-pay´; from 4496; a jerk (of the eye, i.e. [by anal.] an instant):— twinkling.

4494. ῥιπίζω rhipizō, hrip-id´-zo; from a der. of 4496 (mean. a fan or bellows); to breeze up, i.e. (by anal.) to agitate (into waves):— toss.

4495. ῥιπτέω rhiptĕō, hrip-teh´-o; from a der. of 4496; to toss up:— cast off.

4496. ῥίπτω rhiptō, hrip´-to; a primary verb (perh. rather akin to the base of 4474, through the idea of sudden motion); to fling (prop. with a quick toss, thus differing from 906, which denotes a deliberate hurl; and from τείνω tĕinō, [see in 1614], which indicates an extended projection); by qualification, to deposit (as if a load); by extens. to disperse:— cast (down, out), scatter abroad, throw.

4497. Ῥοβοάμ Rhŏbŏam, hrob-ŏ-am´; of Heb. or. [7346]; Roboäm (i.e. Rechabam), an Isr.:— Roboam.

4498. Ῥόδη Rhŏdē, hrod´-ay; prob. for ῥοδῆ rhŏdē, (a rose); Rodë, a servant girl:— Rhoda.

4499. Ῥόδος Rhŏdŏs, hrod´-os; prob. from ῥόδον rhŏdŏn, (a rose); Rhodus, an island of the Mediterranean:— Rhodes.

4500. ῥοιζηδόν rhŏizēdŏn, hroyd-zay-don´; adv. from a der. of ῥοῖζος rhŏizŏs (a whir); whizzingly, i.e. with a crash:— with a great noise.

4501. ῥομφαία rhŏmphaia, hrom-fah´-yah; prob. of for. or.; a sabre, i.e. a long and broad cutlass (any weapon of the kind, lit. or fig.):— sword.

4502. Ῥουβήν Rhŏubēn, hroo-bane´; of Heb. or. [7205]; Ruben (i.e. Reuben), an Isr.:— Reuben.

4503. Ῥούθ Rhŏuth, hrooth; of Heb. or. [7327]; Ruth, a Moabitess:— Ruth.

4504. Ῥοῦφος Rhŏuphŏs, hroo´-fos; of Lat. or.; red; Rufus, a Chr.:— Rufus.

4505. ῥύμη rhumē, hroo´-may; prol. from 4506 in its orig. sense; an alley or avenue (as crowded):— lane, street.

4506. ῥύομαι rhuŏmai, hroo´-om-ahee; mid. voice of an obs. verb, akin to 4482 (through the idea of a current; comp. 4511); to rush or draw (for oneself), i.e. rescue:— deliver (-er).

4507. ῥυπαρία rhuparia, hroo-par-ee´-ah; from 4508; dirtiness (mor.):— turpitude.

4508. ῥυπαρός rhuparòs, hroo-par-os´; from 4509; dirty, i.e. (rel.) cheap or shabby; mor. wicked:— vile.

4509. ῥύπος rhupŏs, hroo´-pos; of uncert. aff.; dirt, i.e. (mor.) depravity:— filth.

4510. ῥυπόω rhupŏō, hroo-pŏ´-o; from 4509; to soil, i.e. (intr.) to become dirty (mor.):— be filthy.

4511. ῥύσις rhusis, hroo´-sis; from 4506 in the sense of its congener 4482; a flux (of blood):— issue.

4512. ῥυτίς rhutis, hroo-tece´; from 4506; a fold (as drawing together), i.e. a wrinkle (espec. on the face):— wrinkle.

4513. Ῥωμαϊκός Rhōmaïkòs, hro-mah-ee-kos´; from 4514; Romaïc, i.e. Lat.:— Latin.

4514. Ῥωμαῖος Rhōmaiŏs, hro-mah´-yos; from 4516; Romæan, i.e. Roman (as noun):— Roman, of Rome.

4515. Ῥωμαϊστί Rhōmaïsti, hro-mah-is-tee´; adv. from a presumed der. of 4516; Romaïstically, i.e. in the Latin language:— Latin.

4516. Ῥώμη Rhōmē, hro´-may; from the base of 4517; strength; Roma, the capital of Italy:— Rome.

4517. ῥώννυμι rhōnnumi, hrone´-noo-mee; prol. from ῥώομαι rhŏōmai (to dart; prob. akin to 4506); to strengthen, i.e. (impers. pass.) have health (as a parting exclamation, good-bye):— farewell.

Σ

4518. σαβαχθανί sabachthani, sab-akh-than-ee´; of Chald. or. [7662 with pron. suff.]; thou hast left me; sabachthani (i.e. shebakthani), a cry of distress:— sabachthani.

4519. σαβαώθ sabaōth, sab-ah-owth´; of Heb. or. [6635 in fem. plur.]; armies; sabaoth (i.e. tsebaoth), a military epithet of God:— sabaoth.

4520. σαββατισμός sabbatismòs, sab-bat-is-mos´; from a der. of 4521; a "sabbatism," i.e. (fig.) the repose of Christianity (as a type of heaven):— rest.

4521. σάββατον sabbaton, sab´-bat-on; of Heb. or. [7676]; the Sabbath (i.e. Shabbath), or day of weekly repose from secular avocations (also the observance or institution itself); by extens. a se´nnight, i.e. the interval between two Sabbaths; likewise the plural in all the above applications:— sabbath (day), week.

4522. σαγήνη sagēnē, sag-ay´-nay; from a der. of σάττω sattō (to equip) mean. furniture, espec. a pack-saddle (which in the E. is merely a bag of *netted* rope); a "*seine*" for fishing:— net.

4523. Σαδδουκαῖος **Saddŏukaiŏs**, *saddoo-kah´-yos*; prob. from *4524*; a *Sadducæan* (i.e. *Tsadokian*), or follower of a certain heretical Isr.:— Sadducee.

4524. Σαδώκ **Sadōk**, *sad-oke´*; of Heb. or. [6659]; *Sadoc* (i.e. *Tsadok*), an Isr.:— Sadoc.

4525. σαίνω **sainō**, *sah´-ee-no*; akin to *4579*; to *wag* (as a dog its tail fawningly), i.e. (gen.) to *shake* (fig. *disturb*):— move.

4526. σάκκος **sakkŏs**, *sak´-kos*; of Heb. or. [8242]; "*sack*"-*cloth*, i.e. *mohair* (the material or garments made of it, worn as a sign of grief):— sackcloth.

4527. Σαλά **Sala**, *sal-ah´*; of Heb. or. [7974]; *Sala* (i.e. *Shelach*), a patriarch:— Sala.

4528. Σαλαθιήλ **Salathiēl**, *sal-ath-ee-ale´*; of Heb. or. [7597]; *Salathiël* (i.e. *Sheältiël*), an Isr.:— Salathiel.

4529. Σαλαμίς **Salamis**, *sal-am-ece´*; prob. from *4535* (from the *surge* on the shore); *Salamis*, a place in Cyprus:— Salamis.

4530. Σαλείμ **Salĕim**, *sal-ime´*; prob. from the same as *4531*; *Salim*, a place in Pal.:— Salim.

4531. σαλεύω **salĕuō**, *sal-yoo´-o*; from *4535*; to *waver*, i.e. *agitate, rock, topple* or (by impl.) *destroy*; fig. to *disturb, incite*:— move, shake (together), which can [-not] be shaken, stir up.

4532. Σαλήμ **Salēm**, *sal-ame´*; of Heb. or. [8004]; *Salem* (i.e. *Shalem*), a place in Pal.:— Salem.

4533. Σαλμών **Salmōn**, *sal-mone´*; of Heb. or. [8012]; *Salmon*, an Isr.:— Salmon.

4534. Σαλμώνη **Salmōnē**, *sal-mo´-nay*; perh. of similar or. to *4529*; *Salmone*, a place in Crete:— Salmone.

4535. σάλος **salŏs**, *sal´-os*; prob. from the base of *4525*; a *vibration*, i.e. (spec.) *billow*:— wave.

4536. σάλπιγξ **salpigx**, *sal´-pinx*; perh. from *4535* (through the idea of *quavering* or *reverberation*); a *trumpet*:— trump (-et).

4537. σαλπίζω **salpizō**, *sal-pid´-zo*; from *4536*; to *trumpet*, i.e. *sound a blast* (lit. or fig.):— (which are yet to) sound (a trumpet).

4538. σαλπιστής **salpistēs**, *sal-pis-tace´*; from *4537*; a *trumpeter*:— trumpeter.

4539. Σαλώμη **Salōmē**, *sal-o´-may*; prob. of Heb. or. [fem. from 7965]; *Salome* (i.e. *Shelomah*), an Israelitess:— Salome.

4540. Σαμάρεια **Samarĕia**, *sam-ar´-i-ah*; of Heb. or. [8111]; *Samaria* (i.e. *Shomeron*), a city and region of Pal.:— Samaria.

4541. Σαμαρείτης **Samarĕitēs**, *sam-ar-i´-tace* or

Σαμαρίτης **Samaritēs**, *sam-ar-ee´-tace*; from *4540*; a *Samarite*, i.e. inhab. of Samaria:— Samaritan.

4542. Σαμαρεῖτις **Samarĕitis**, *sam-ar-i´-tis* or

Σαμαριτῖς **Samaritis**, *sam-ar-ee´-tis* fem. of *4541*; a *Samaritess*, i.e. woman of Samaria:— of Samaria.

4543. Σαμοθράκη **Samŏthraįkē**, *sam-oth-rak´-ay*; from *4544* and Θράκη **Thraįkē** (*Thrace*); *Samo-thracè* (*Samos of Thrace*), an island in the Mediterranean:— Samothracia.

4544. Σάμος **Samŏs**, *sam´-os*; of uncert. aff.; *Samus*, an island of the Mediterranean:— Samos.

4545. Σαμουήλ **Samŏuēl**, *sam-oo-ale´*; of Heb. or. [8050]; *Samuel* (i.e. *Shemuel*), an Isr.:— Samuel.

4546. Σαμψών **Sampsōn**, *samp-sone´*; of Heb. or. [8123]; *Sampson* (i.e. *Shimshon*), an Isr.:— Samson.

4547. σανδάλιον **sandaliŏn**, *san-dal´-ee-on*; neut. of a der. of σάνδαλον **sandalŏn** (a "*sandal*"; of uncert. or.); a *slipper* or *sole-pad*:— sandal.

4548. σανίς **sanis**, *san-ece´*; of uncert. aff.; a *plank*:— board.

4549. Σαούλ **Saŏul**, *sah-ool´*; of Heb. or. [7586]; *Saül* (i.e. *Shaül*), the Jewish name of *Paul*:— Saul. Comp. *4569*.

4550. σαπρός **saprŏs**, *sap-ros´*; from *4595*; *rotten*, i.e. *worthless* (lit. or mor.):— bad, corrupt. Comp. *4190*.

4551. Σαπφείρη **Sapphĕirē**, *sap-fi´-ray*; fem. of *4552*; *Sapphirē*, an Israelitess:— Sapphira.

4552. σάπφειρος **sapphĕirŏs**, *sap´-fi-ros*; of Heb. or. [5601]; a "*sapphire*" or *lapis-lazuli* gem:— sapphire.

4553. σαργάνη **sarganē**, *sar-gan´-ay*; appar. of Heb. or. [8276]; a *basket* (as *interwoven* or *wicker*-work:— basket.

4554. Σάρδεις **Sardĕis**, *sar´-dice*; plur. of uncert. der.; *Sardis*, a place in Asia Minor:— Sardis.

4555. σάρδινος **sardinŏs**, *sar´-dee-nos*; from the same as *4556*; *sardine* (3037 being impl.), i.e. a gem, so called:— sardine.

4556. σάρδιος **sardiŏs**, *sar´-dee-os*; prop. an adj. from an uncert. base; *sardian* (3037 being impl.), i.e. (as noun) the gem so called:— sardius.

4557. σαρδόνυξ **sardŏnux**, *sar-don´-oox*; from the base of *4556* and ὄνυξ **ŏnux** (the *nail* of a finger; hence, the "*onyx*" stone); a "*sardonyx*", i.e. the gem so called:— sardonyx.

4558. Σάρεπτα **Sarĕpta**, *sar´-ep-tah*; of Heb. or. [6886]; *Sarepta* (i.e. *Tsarephath*), a place in Pal.:— Sarepta.

4559. σαρκικός **sarkikŏs**, *sar-kee-kos´*; from *4561*; *pertaining to flesh*, i.e. (by extens.) *bodily, temporal*, or (by impl.) *animal, unregenerate*:— carnal, fleshly.

4560. σάρκινος **sarkinŏs**, *sar´-kee-nos*; from *4561*; *similar to flesh*, i.e. (by anal.) *soft*:— fleshly.

4561. σάρξ **sarx**, *sarx*; prob. from the base of *4563*; *flesh* (as *stripped* of the skin), i.e. (strictly) the *meat* of an animal (as food), or (by extens.) the *body* (as opposed to the soul [or spirit], or as

the symbol of what is external, or as the means of kindred), or (by impl.) *human nature* (with its frailties [phys. or mor.] and passions), or (spec.) a *human being* (as such):— carnal (-ly, + -ly minded), flesh (l-lyl).

4562. Σαρούχ **Sarŏuch** *sa-rooch´*, or

Σερούχ **Sĕrŏuch**, *seh-rooch´*; of Heb. or. [8286]; *Saruch* (i.e. *Serug*), a patriarch:— Saruch.

4563. σαρόω **sarŏō**, *sar-ŏ´-o*; from a der. of σαίρω **sairō** (to *brush* off; akin to *4951*); mean. a *broom*; to *sweep*:— sweep.

4564. Σάρρα **Sarrha**, *sar´-hrah*; of Heb. or. [8283]; *Sarra* (i.e. *Sarah*), the wife of Abraham:— Sara, Sarah.

4565. Σάρων **Sarōn**, *sar´-one*; of Heb. or. [8289]; *Saron* (i.e. *Sharon*), a district of Pal.:— Saron.

4566. Σατάν **Satan**, *sat-an´*; of Heb. or. [7854]; *Satan*, i.e. the *devil*:— Satan. Comp. *4567*.

4567. Σατανᾶς **Satanas**, *sat-an-as´*; of Chald. or. corresp. to *4566* (with the def. aff.); *the accuser*, i.e. the *devil*:— Satan.

4568. σάτον **satŏn**, *sat´-on*; of Heb. or. [5429]; a certain *measure* for things dry:— measure.

4569. Σαῦλος **Saulŏs**, *sŏw´-los*; of Heb. or., the same as *4549*; *Saulus* (i.e. *Shaül*), the Jewish name of *Paul*:— Saul.

σαυτοῦ **sautŏu**. etc. See *4572*.

4570. σβέννυμι **sbĕnnumi**, *sben´-noo-mee*; a prol. form of an appar. primary verb; to *extinguish* (lit. or fig.):— go out, quench.

4571. σέ **sĕ**, *seh*; acc. sing. of *4771*; *thee*:— thee, thou, × thy house.

4572. σεαυτοῦ **sĕautŏu**, *seh-ŏw-too´*; gen. from *4571* and *846*; also dat. of the same,

σεαυτῷ **sĕautōį**, *seh-ŏw-to´*; and acc.

σεαυτόν **sĕautŏn**, *seh-ŏw-ton´*; likewise contr.

σαυτοῦ **sautŏu**, *sŏw-too´*;

σαυτῷ **sautōį**, *sŏw-to´*; and

σαυτόν **sautŏn**, *sŏw-ton´*; respectively; *of (with, to) thyself*:— thee, thine own self, (thou) thy (-self).

4573. σεβάζομαι **sĕbazŏmai**, *seb-ad´-zom-ahee*; mid. voice from a der. of *4576*; to *venerate*, i.e. *adore*:— worship.

4574. σέβασμα **sĕbasma**, *seb´-as-mah*; from *4573*; something *adored*, i.e. an *object of worship* (god, altar, etc):— devotion, that is worshipped.

4575. σεβαστός **sĕbastŏs**, *seb-as-tos´*; from *4573*; *venerable* (*august*), i.e. (as noun) a title of the Rom. *Emperor*, or (as adj.) *imperial*:— Augustus (-').

4576. σέβομαι **sĕbŏmai**, *seb´-om-ahee*; mid. voice of an appar. primary verb; to *revere*, i.e. *adore*:— devout, religious, worship.

4577. σειρά **sĕira**, *si-rah´*; prob. from *4951* through its congener εἴρω **ĕirō** (to

Greek

fasten; akin to *138);* a *chain,* (as *binding* or *drawing):*— chain.

4578. σεισμός **sĕismŏs,** *sice-mos´;* from *4579;* a *commotion,* i.e. (of the air) a *gale,* (of the ground) an *earthquake:*— earthquake, tempest.

4579. σείω **sĕiō,** *si´-o;* appar. a primary verb; to *rock* (*vibrate,* prop. sideways or to and fro), i.e. (gen.) to *agitate* (in any direction; cause to *tremble);* fig. to throw into a *tremor* (of fear or concern):— move, quake, shake.

4580. Σεκοῦνδος **Sĕkŏundŏs,** *sek-oon´-dos;* of Lat. or.; *"second"; Secundus,* a Chr.:— Secundus.

4581. Σελεύκεια **Sĕlĕukĕia,** *sel-yook´-i-ah;* from Σέλευκος **Sĕleukŏs,** (*Seleucus,* a Syrian king); *Seleuceia,* a place in Syria:— Seleucia.

4582. σελήνη **sĕlēnē,** *sel-ay´-nay;* from σέλας **sĕlas,** (*brilliancy;* prob. akin to the alt. of *138,* through the idea of *attractiveness*); the *moon:*— moon.

4583. σεληνιάζομαι **sĕlēniazŏmai,** *sel-ay-nee-ad´-zom-ahee;* middle or passive voice from a presumed der. of *4582;* to *be moon-struck,* i.e. *crazy:*— be a lunatic.

4584. Σεμεΐ **Sĕmĕï,** *sem-eh-ee´* or

Σεμεΐν **Sĕmĕïn,** *sem-eh-een´* of Heb. or. [8096]; *Semeï* (i.e. *Shimi*), an Isr.:— Semei (Semein).

4585. σεμίδαλις **sĕmidalis,** *sem-id´-al-is;* prob. of for. origin; fine wheaten *flour:*— fine flour.

4586. σεμνός **sĕmnŏs,** *sem-nos´;* from *4576; venerable,* i.e. *honorable:*— grave, honest.

4587. σεμνότης **sĕmnŏtēs,** *sem-not´-ace;* from *4586; venerableness,* i.e. *probity:*— gravity, honesty.

4588. Σέργιος **Sĕrgiŏs,** *serg´-ee-os;* of Lat. or.; *Sergius,* a Rom.:— Sergius.

4589. Σήθ **Sēth,** *sayth;* of Heb. or. [8352]; *Seth* (i.e. *Sheth*), a patriarch:— Seth.

4590. Σήμ **Sēm,** *same;* of Heb. or. [8035]; *Sem* (i.e. *Shem*), a patriarch:— Sem.

4591. σημαίνω **sēmainō,** *say-mah´-ee-no;* from σῆμα **sēma,** (a *mark;* of uncert. der.); to *indicate:*— signify.

4592. σημεῖον **sēmĕïŏn,** *say-mi´-on;* neut. of a presumed der. of the base of *4591;* an *indication,* espec. cerem. or supernat.:— miracle, sign, token, wonder.

4593. σημειόω **sēmĕïŏō,** *say-mi-ŏ´-o;* from *4592;* to *distinguish,* i.e. *mark* (for avoidance):— note.

4594. σήμερον **sēmĕrŏn,** *say´-mer-on;* neut. (as adv.) of a presumed compound of the art. *3588* (τ changed to σ) and *2250;* on *the* (i.e. *this*) day (or *night* current or just passed); gen. *now* (i.e. at *present, hitherto*):— this (to-) day.

4595. σήπω **sēpō,** *say´-po;* appar. a primary verb; to *putrefy,* i.e. (fig.) *perish:*— be corrupted.

4596. σηρικός **sērikŏs,** *say-ree-kos´*

σιρικός **sirikŏs,** *see-ree-kos´;* from Σήρ **Sēr,** (an Indian tribe from whom *silk* was procured; hence, the name of the *silk-worm*); *Seric,* i.e.

silken (neut. as noun, a *silky* fabric):— silk.

4597. σής **sēs,** *sace;* appar. of Heb. or. [5580]; a *moth:*— moth.

4598. σητόβρωτος **sētŏbrōtŏs,** *say-tob´-ro-tos;* from *4597* and a der. of *977; moth-eaten:*— motheaten.

4599. σθενόω **sthĕnŏō,** *sthen-ŏ´-o;* from σθένος **sthĕnŏs,** (bodily *vigor;* prob. akin to the base of *2476*); to *strengthen,* i.e. (fig.) *confirm* (in spiritual knowledge and power):— strengthen.

4600. σιαγών **siagōn,** *see-ag-one´;* of uncert. der.; the *jaw-bone,* i.e. (by impl.) the *cheek* or side of the face:— cheek.

4601. σιγάω **sigaō,** *see-gah´-o;* from *4602;* to *keep silent* (tran. or intr.):— keep close (secret, silence), hold peace.

4602. σιγή **sigē,** *see-gay´;* appar. from σίζω **sizō** (to *hiss,* i.e. *hist* or *hush*); *silence:*— silence. Comp. *4623.*

4603. σιδήρεος **sidērĕŏs,** *sid-ay´-reh-os;* from *4604;* made of *iron:*— (of) iron.

4604. σίδηρος **sidērŏs,** *sid´-ay-ros;* of uncert. der.; *iron:*— iron.

4605. Σιδών **Sidōn,** *sid-one´;* of Heb. or. [6721]; *Sidon* (i.e. *Tsidon*), a place in Pal.:— Sidon.

4606. Σιδώνιος **Sidōniŏs,** *sid-o´-nee-os;* from *4605;* a *Sidonian,* i.e. inhab. of Sidon:— of Sidon.

4607. σικάριος **sikariŏs,** *sik-ar´-ee-os;* of Lat. or.; a *dagger-man* or *assassin;* a *freebooter* (Jewish *fanatic* outlawed by the Romans):— murderer. Comp. *5406.*

4608. σίκερα **sikĕra,** *sik´-er-ah;* of Heb. or. [7941]; an *intoxicant,* i.e. intensely fermented *liquor:*— strong drink.

4609. Σίλας **Silas,** *see´-las;* contr. for *4610; Silas,* a Chr.:— Silas.

4610. Σιλουανός **Silŏuanŏs,** *sil-oo-an-os´;* of Lat. or.; *"silvan;" Silvanus,* a Chr.:— Silvanus. Comp. *4609.*

4611. Σιλωάμ **Silŏam,** *sil-o-am´;* of Heb. or. [7975]; *Siloäm* (i.e. *Shiloäch*), a pool of Jerusalem:— Siloam.

4612. σιμικίνθιον **simikinthiŏn,** *sim-ee-kin´-thee-on;* of Lat. or.; a *semicinctium* or *half-girding,* i.e. narrow covering (*apron*):— apron.

4613. Σίμων **Simōn,** *see´-mone;* of Heb. or. [8095]; *Simon* (i.e. *Shimon*), the name of nine Isr.:— Simon. Comp. *4826.*

4614. Σινᾶ **Sina,** *see-nah´;* of Heb. or. [5514]; *Sina* (i.e. *Sinai*), a mountain in Arabia:— Sina.

4615. σίναπι **sinapi,** *sin´-ap-ee;* perh. from σίνομαι **sinŏmai** (to *hurt,* i.e. *sting*); *mustard* (the plant):— mustard.

4616. σινδών **sindōn,** *sin-done´;* of uncert. (perh. for.) or.; *byssos,* i.e. bleached *linen* (the cloth or a garment of it):— (fine) linen (cloth).

4617. σινιάζω **siniazō,** *sin-ee-ad´-zo;* from σινίον **siniŏn,** (a *sieve*); to *riddle* (fig.):— sift.

σῖτα **sita.** See *4621.*

4618. σιτευτός **sitĕutŏs,** *sit-yoo-tos´;*

from a der. of *4621; grain-fed,* i.e. *fattened:*— fatted.

4619. σιτιστός **sitistŏs,** *sit-is-tos´;* from a der. of *4621; grained,* i.e. *fatted:*— fatling.

4620. σιτόμετρον **sitŏmĕtrŏn,** *sit-om´-et-ron;* from *4621* and *3358;* a *grain-measure,* i.e. (by impl.) *ration* (*allowance* of food):— portion of meat.

4621. σῖτος **sitŏs,** *see´-tos;* plur. irreg. neut.

σῖτα **sita,** *see´-tah;* of uncert. der.; *grain,* espec. *wheat:*— corn, wheat.

4622. Σιών **Siōn,** *see-own´;* of Heb. or. [6726]; *Sion* (i.e. *Tsijon*), a hill of Jerusalem; fig. the *Church* (militant or triumphant):— Sion.

4623. σιωπάω **siōpaō,** *see-o-pah´-o;* from σιωπή **siōpē,** (*silence,* i.e. a *hush;* prop. *muteness,* i.e. *involuntary* stillness, or *inability* to speak; and thus differing from *4602,* which is rather a voluntary *refusal* or *indisposition* to speak, although the terms are often used synonymously); to *be dumb* (but not *deaf* also, like *2974* prop.); fig. to *be calm* (as *quiet* water):— dumb, (hold) peace.

4624. σκανδαλίζω **skandalizō,** *skan-dal-id´-zo* ("scandalize"); from *4625;* to *entrap,* i.e. *trip* up (fig. *stumble* [tran.] or *entice* to sin, apostasy or displeasure):— (make to) offend.

4625. σκάνδαλον **skandalŏn,** *skan´-dal-on* ("scandal"); prob. from a der. of *2578;* a *trap-stick* (*bent* sapling), i.e. *snare* (fig. *cause* of displeasure or sin):— occasion to fall (of stumbling), offence, thing that offends, stumblingblock.

4626. σκάπτω **skaptō,** *skap´-to;* appar. a primary verb; to *dig:*— dig.

4627. σκάφη **skaphē,** *skaf´-ay;* a *"skiff"* (as if *dug* out), or *yawl* (carried aboard a large vessel for landing):— boat.

4628. σκέλος **skĕlŏs,** *skel´-os;* appar. from σκέλλω **skĕllō,** (to *parch;* through the idea of *leanness*); the *leg* (as *lank*):— leg.

4629. σκέπασμα **skĕpasma,** *skep´-as-mah;* from a der. of σκέπας **skĕpas** (a *covering;* perh. akin to the base of *4649,* through the idea of *noticeableness*); *clothing:*— raiment.

4630. Σκευᾶς **Skĕuas,** *skyoo-as´;* appar. of Lat. or.; *left-handed; Scevas* (i.e. *Scævus*), an Isr.:— Sceva.

4631. σκευή **skĕuē,** *skyoo-ay´;* from *4632; furniture,* i.e. spare *tackle:*— tackling.

4632. σκεῦος **skĕuŏs,** *skyoo´-os;* of uncert. aff.; a *vessel, implement, equipment* or *apparatus* (lit. or fig. [spec. a *wife* as contributing to the usefulness of the husband]):— goods, sail, stuff, vessel.

4633. σκηνή **skēnē,** *skay-nay´;* appar. akin to *4632* and *4639;* a *tent* or cloth hut (lit. or fig.):— habitation, tabernacle.

4634. σκηνοπηγία **skēnŏpēgia,** *skay-nop-ayg-ee´-ah;* from *4636* and *4078;*

the *Festival of Tabernacles* (so called from the custom of erecting booths for temporary homes):— tabernacles.

4635. σκηνοποιός **skēnŏpŏiŏs**, *skay-nop-oy-os´*; from *4633* and *4160*; a *manufacturer of tents:*— tent-maker.

4636. σκῆνος **skēnŏs**, *skay´-nos*; from *4633*; a *hut* or temporary residence, i.e. (fig.) the human *body* (as the abode of the spirit):— tabernacle.

4637. σκηνόω **skēnŏō**, *skay-nŏ´-o*; from *4636*; to *tent* or *encamp*, i.e. (fig.) to *occupy* (as a mansion) or (spec.) to *reside* (as God did in the Tabernacle of old, a symbol of protection and communion):— dwell.

4638. σκήνωμα **skēnōma**, *skay´-no-mah*; from *4637*; an *encampment*, i.e. (fig.) the *Temple* (as God's residence), the *body* (as a tenement for the soul):— tabernacle.

4639. σκία **skia**, *skee´-ah*; appar. a primary word; "*shade*" or a shadow (lit. or fig. [darkness of *error* or an *adumbration*]):— shadow.

4640. σκιρτάω **skirtaō**, *skeer-tah´-o*; akin to σκαίρω **skairŏ**, (to *skip*); to *jump*, i.e. sympathetically *move* (as the *quickening* of a fetus):— leap (for joy).

4641. σκληροκαρδία **sklērŏkardia**, *sklay-rok-ar-dee´-ah*; fem. of a compound of *4642* and *2588*; *hard-heartedness*, i.e. (spec.) *destitution of* (spiritual) *perception:*— hardness of heart.

4642. σκληρός **sklērŏs**, *sklay-ros´*; from the base of *4628*; *dry*, i.e. *hard* or *tough* (fig. *harsh, severe*):— fierce, hard.

4643. σκληρότης **sklērŏtēs**, *sklay-rot´-ace*; from *4642*; *callousness*, i.e. (fig.) *stubbornness:*— hardness.

4644. σκληροτράχηλος **sklērŏtrachēlŏs**, *sklay-rot-rakh´-ay-los*; from *4642* and *5137*; *hardnaped*, i.e. (fig.) *obstinate:*— stiffnecked.

4645. σκληρύνω **sklērunō**, *sklay-roo´-no*; from *4642*; to *indurate*, i.e. (fig.) *render stubborn:*— harden.

4646. σκολιός **skŏliŏs**, *skol-ee-os´*; from the base of *4628*; *warped*, i.e. *winding*; fig. *perverse:*— crooked, froward, untoward.

4647. σκόλοψ **skŏlŏps**, *skol´-ops*; perh. from the base of *4628* and *3700*; *withered* at the *front*, i.e. a *point* or *prickle* (fig. a bodily *annoyance* or *disability*):— thorn.

4648. σκοπέω **skŏpĕō**, *skop-eh´-o*; from *4649*; to *take aim* at (*spy*), i.e. (fig.) *regard:*— consider, take heed, look at (on), mark. Comp. *3700*.

4649. σκοπός **skŏpŏs**, *skop-os´* ("scope"); from σκέπτομαι **skĕptŏmai** (to *peer* about ["skeptic"]; perh. akin to *4626* through the idea of *concealment*; comp. *4629*); a *watch* (*sentry* or *scout*), i.e. (by impl.) a *goal:*— mark.

4650. σκορπίζω **skŏrpizō**, *skor-pid´-zo*; appar. from the same as *4651* (through the idea of *penetrating*); to *dissipate*, i.e. (fig.) *put to flight, waste, be liberal:*— disperse abroad, scatter (abroad).

4651. σκορπίος **skŏrpiŏs**, *skor-pee´-os*;

prob. from an obs. σκέρπω **skĕrpō** (perh. strengthened from the base of *4649*, and mean. to *pierce*); a "*scorpion*" (from its *sting*):— scorpion.

4652. σκοτεινός **skŏtĕinŏs**, *skot-i-nos´*; from *4655*; *opaque*, i.e. (fig.) *benighted:*— dark, full of darkness.

4653. σκοτία **skŏtia**, *skot-ee´-ah*; from *4655*; *dimness, obscurity* (lit. or fig.):— dark (-ness).

4654. σκοτίζω **skŏtizō**, *skot-id-zo*; from *4655*; to *obscure* (lit. or fig.):— darken.

4655. σκότος **skŏtŏs**, *skot´-os*; from the base of *4639*; *shadiness*, i.e. *obscurity* (lit. or fig.):— darkness.

4656. σκοτόω **skŏtŏō**, *skot-ŏ´-o*; from *4655*; to *obscure* or *blind* (lit. or fig.):— be full of darkness.

4657. σκύβαλον **skubalŏn**, *skoo´-bal-on*; neut. of **a** presumed der. of *1519* and *2965* and *906*; what is *thrown to* the *dogs*, i.e. *refuse* (*ordure*):— dung.

4658. Σκύθης **Skuthēs**, *skoo´-thace*; prob. of for. or.; a *Scythene* or *Scythian*, i.e. (by impl.) a *savage:*— Scythian.

4659. σκυθρωπός **skuthrōpŏs**, *skoo-thro-pos´*; from σκυθρός **skuthrŏs**, (*sullen*) and a der. of *3700*; *angry-visaged*, i.e. *gloomy* or affecting a *mournful* appearance:— of a sad countenance.

4660. σκύλλω **skullō**, *skool´-lo*; appar. a primary verb; to *flay*, i.e. (fig.) to *harass:*— trouble (self).

4661. σκῦλον **skulŏn**, *skoo´-lon*; neut. from *4660*; something *stripped* (as a hide), i.e. *booty:*— spoil.

4662. σκωληκόβρωτος **skōlēkŏbrōtŏs**, *sko-lay-kob´-ro-tos*; from *4663* and a der. of *977*; *worm-eaten*, i.e. *diseased with maggots:*— eaten of worms.

4663. σκώληξ **skōlēx**, *sko´-lakes*; of uncert. der.; a *grub, maggot* or *earth-worm:*— worm.

4664. σμαράγδινος **smaragdinŏs**, *smar-ag´-dee-nos*; from *4665*; consisting of *emerald:*— emerald.

4665. σμάραγδος **smaragdŏs**, *smar´-ag-dos*; of uncert. der.; the *emerald* or green gem so called:— emerald.

4666. σμύρνα **smurna**, *smoor´-nah*; appar. strengthened for *3464*; *myrrh:*— myrrh.

4667. Σμύρνα **Smurna**, *smoor´-nah*; the same as *4666*; *Smyrna*, a place in Asia Minor:— Smyrna.

4668. Σμυρναῖος **Smurnaiŏs**, *smoor-nah´-yos*; from *4667*; a *Smyrnæan:*— in Smyrna.

4669. σμυρνίζω **smurnizō**, *smoor-nid´-zo*; from *4667*; to *tincture with myrrh*, i.e. *embitter* (as a narcotic):— mingle with myrrh.

4670. Σόδομα **Sŏdŏma**, *sod´-om-ah*; plur. of Heb. or. [5467]; *Sodoma* (i.e. *Sedom*), a place in Pal.:— Sodom.

4671. σοί **sŏi**, *soy*; dat. of *4771*; to *thee:*— thee, thine own, thou, thy.

4672. Σολομών or Σολομῶν **Sŏlŏmōn**, *sol-om-one´*; of Heb. or. [8010]; *Solomon* (i.e. *Shelomoh*), the son of David:— Solomon.

4673. σορός **sŏrŏs**, *sor-os´*; prob. akin to

the base of *4987*; a *funereal receptacle* (*urn, coffin*), i.e. (by anal.) a *bier:*— bier.

4674. σός **sŏs**, *sos*; from *4771*; *thine:*— thine (own), thy (friend).

4675. σοῦ **sŏu**, *soo*; gen. of *4771*; of *thee, thy:*— × home, thee, thine (own), thou, thy.

4676. σουδάριον **sŏudariŏn**, *soo-dar´-ee-on*; of Lat. or.; a *sudarium* (*sweat-cloth*), i.e. *towel* (for wiping the perspiration from the face, or binding the face of a corpse):— handkerchief, napkin.

4677. Σουσάννα **Sŏusanna**, *soo-san´-nah*; of Heb. or. [7799 fem.]; *lily*; *Susannah* (i.e. *Shoshannah*), an Israelitess:— Susanna.

4678. σοφία **sŏphia**, *sof-ee´-ah*; from *4680*; *wisdom* (higher or lower, worldly or spiritual):— wisdom.

4679. σοφίζω **sŏphizō**, *sof-id´-zo*; from *4680*; to *render wise*; in a sinister acceptation, to *form* "*sophisms*", i.e. *continue plausible error:*— cunningly devised, make wise.

4680. σοφός **sŏphŏs**, *sof-os´*; akin to σαφής **saphēs**, (*clear*); *wise* (in a most gen. application):— wise. Comp. *5429*.

4681. Σπανία **Spania**, *span-ee´-ah*; prob. of for. or.; *Spania*, a region of Europe:— Spain.

4682. σπαράσσω **sparassō**, *spar-as´-so*; prol. from σπαίρω **spairŏ** (to *gasp*; appar. strengthened from *4685*, through the idea of *spasmodic* contraction); to *mangle*, i.e. *convulse* with epilepsy:— rend, tear.

4683. σπαργανόω **sparganŏō**, *spar-gan-ŏ´-o*; from σπάργανον **sparganŏn**, (a *strip*; from a der. of the base of *4682* mean. to *strap* or *wrap* with strips); to *swathe* (an infant after the Oriental custom):— wrap in swaddling clothes.

4684. σπαταλάω **spatalaō**, *spat-al-ah´-o*; from σπατάλη **spatalē**, (*luxury*); to *be voluptuous:*— live in pleasure, be wanton.

4685. σπάω **spaō**, *spah´-o*; a primary verb; to *draw:*— draw (out).

4686. σπεῖρα **spĕira**, *spi´-rah*; of immed. Lat. or., but ultimately a der. of *138* in the sense of its cognate *1507*; a *coil* (*spira*, "*spire*"), i.e. (fig.) a *mass* of men (a Rom. military *cohort*; also [by anal.] a *squad* of Levitical janitors):— band.

4687. σπείρω **spĕirō**, *spi´-ro*; prob. strengthened from *4685* (through the idea of *extending*); to *scatter*, i.e. *sow* (lit. or fig.):— sow (-er), receive seed.

4688. σπεκουλάτωρ **spĕkŏulatōr**, *spek-oo-lat´-ore*; of Lat. or.; a *speculator*, i.e. military *scout* (*spy* or [by extens.] *life-guardsman*):— executioner.

4689. σπένδω **spĕndō**, *spen´-do*; appar. a primary verb; to *pour* out as a libation, i.e. (fig.) to *devote* (one's life or blood, as a sacrifice) ("*spend*"):— (be ready to) be offered.

4690. σπέρμα **spĕrma**, *sper´-mah*; from *4687*; something *sown*, i.e. *seed* (incl. the male "*sperm*"); by impl. *offspring*;

spec. a *remnant* (fig. as if kept over for planting):— issue, seed.

4691. σπερμολόγος **spĕrmŏlŏgŏs**, *sper-mol-og´-os*; from 4690 and 3004; a *seed-picker* (as the crow), i.e. (fig.) a *sponger*, *loafer* (spec. a *gossip* or *trifler* in talk):— babbler.

4692. σπεύδω **spĕudō**, *spyoo´-do*; prob. strengthened from 4228; to "*speed*" ("study"), i.e. *urge* on (diligently or earnestly); by impl. to *await* eagerly:— (make, with) haste unto.

4693. σπήλαιον **spēlaiŏn**, *spay´-lah-yon*; neut. of a presumed der. of σπέος **spĕŏs** (a *grotto*); a *cavern*; by impl. a *hiding-place* or *resort*:— cave, den.

4694. σπιλάς **spilas**, *spee-las´*; of uncert. der.; a *ledge* or *reef* of rock in the sea:— spot [by confusion with 4696].

4695. σπιλόω **spilŏō**, *spee-lŏ´-o*; from 4696; to *stain* or *soil* (lit. or fig.):— defile, spot.

4696. σπίλος **spilŏs**, *spee´-los*; of uncert. der.; a *stain* or *blemish*, i.e. (fig.) *defect*, *disgrace*:— spot.

4697. σπλαγχνίζομαι **splagchnizŏmai**, *splangkh-nid´-zom-ahee*; mid. voice from 4698; to have the *bowels* yearn, i.e. (fig.) *feel sympathy*, to *pity*:— have (be moved with) compassion.

4698. σπλάγχνον **splagchnŏn**, *splangkh´-non*; prob. strengthened from σπλήν **splēn** (the "*spleen*"); an *intestine*, (plural); fig. *pity* or *sympathy*:— bowels, inward affection, + tender mercy.

4699. σπόγγος **spŏggŏs**, *spong´-gos*; perh. of for. or.; a "*sponge*":— spunge.

4700. σποδός **spŏdŏs**, *spod-os´*; of uncert. der.; *ashes*:— ashes.

4701. σπορά **spŏra**, *spor-ah´*; from 4687; a *sowing*, i.e. (by impl.) *parentage*:— seed.

4702. σπόριμος **spŏrimŏs**, *spor´-ee-mos*; from 4703; *sown*, i.e. (neut. plur.) a planted *field*:— corn (-field).

4703. σπόρος **spŏrŏs**, *spor´-os*; from 4687; a *scattering* (of seed), i.e. (concr.) *seed* (as sown):— seed (x sown).

4704. σπουδάζω **spŏudazō**, *spoo-dad´-zo*; from 4710; to *use speed*, i.e. to *make effort, be prompt* or *earnest*:— do (give) diligence, be diligent (forward), endeavour, labour, study.

4705. σπουδαῖος **spŏudaiŏs**, *spoo-dah´-yos*; from 4710; *prompt, energetic, earnest*:— diligent.

4706. σπουδαιότερον **spŏudaiŏtĕrŏn**, *spoo-dah-yot´-er-on*; neut. of 4707 as adv.; *more earnestly* than others, i.e. very *promptly*:— very diligently.

4707. σπουδαιότερος **spŏudaiŏtĕrŏs**, *spoo-dah-yot´-er-os*; comparative of 4705; *more prompt, more earnest*:— more diligent (forward).

4708. σπουδαιοτέρως **spŏudaiŏtĕrōs**, *spoo-dah-yot-er´-oce*; adv. from 4707; *more speedily*, i.e. *sooner* than otherwise:— more carefully.

4709. σπουδαίως **spŏudaiōs**, *spoo-dah´-yoce*; adv. from 4705; *earnestly, promptly*:— diligently, instantly.

4710. σπουδή **spŏudē**, *spoo-day´*; from 4692; "*speed*", i.e. (by impl.) *despatch, eagerness, earnestness*:— business, (earnest) care (-fulness), diligence, forwardness, haste.

4711. σπυρίς **spuris**, *spoo-rece´*; from 4687 (as *woven*); a *hamper* or *lunch-receptacle*:— basket.

4712. στάδιον **stadiŏn**, *stad´-ee-on*; or masc. (in plur.) στάδιος **stadiŏs**, *stad´-ee-os*; from the base of 2476, (as *fixed*); a *stade* or certain measure of distance; by impl. a *stadium* or *race-course*:— furlong, race.

4713. στάμνος **stamnŏs**, *stam´-nos*; from the base of 2476 (as *stationary*); a *jar* or earthen *tank*:— pot.

4714. στάσις **stasis**, *stas´-is*; from the base of 2476; a *standing* (prop. the act), i.e. (by anal.) *position* (*existence*); by impl. a popular *uprising*; fig. *controversy*:— dissension, insurrection, × standing, uproar.

4715. στατήρ **statēr**, *stat-air´*; from the base of 2746; a *stander* (*standard* of value), i.e. (spec.) a *stater* or certain coin:— piece of money.

4716. σταυρός **staurŏs**, *stŏw-ros´*; from the base of 2476; a *stake* or *post* (as *set* upright), i.e. (spec.) a *pole* or *cross* (as an instrument of capital punishment); fig. *exposure to death*, i.e. *self-denial*; by impl. the *atonement* of Christ:— cross.

4717. σταυρόω **staurŏō**, *stŏw-rŏ´-o*; from 4716; to *impale* on the cross; fig. to *extinguish* (*subdue*) passion or selfishness:— crucify.

4718. σταφυλή **staphulē**, *staf-oo-lay´*; prob. from the base of 4735; a *cluster* of grapes (as if *intertwined*):— grapes.

4719. στάχυς **stachus**, *stakh´-oos*; from the base of 2476; a *head* of grain (as *standing* out from the stalk):— ear (of corn).

4720. Στάχυς **Stachus**, *stakh´-oos*; the same as 4719; *Stachys*, a Chr.:— Stachys.

4721. στέγη **stĕgē**, *steg´-ay*; strengthened from a primary τέγος **tĕgŏs** a "*thatch*" or "*deck*" of a building); a *roof*:— roof.

4722. στέγω **stĕgō**, *steg´-o*; from 4721; to *roof* over, i.e. (fig.) to *cover* with silence (*endure* patiently):— (for-) bear, suffer.

4723. στείρος **stĕirŏs**, *sti´-ros*; a contr. from 4731 (as *stiff* and *unnatural*); "*sterile*":— barren.

4724. στέλλω **stĕllō**, *stel´-lo*; prob. strengthened from the base of 2476; prop. to *set fast* ("*stall*"), i.e. (fig.) to *repress* (refl. *abstain* from associating with):— avoid, withdraw self.

4725. στέμμα **stĕmma**, *stem´-mah*; from the base of 4735; a *wreath* for show:— garland.

4726. στεναγμός **stĕnagmŏs**, *sten-ag-mos´*; from 4727; a *sigh*:— groaning.

4727. στενάζω **stĕnazō**, *sten-ad´-zo*; from 4728; to *make* (intr. *be*) *in straits*, i.e. (by impl.) to *sigh, murmur, pray* inaudibly:— with grief, groan, grudge, sigh.

4728. στενός **stĕnŏs**, *sten-os´*; prob. from the base of 2476; *narrow* (from obstacles *standing* close about):— strait.

4729. στενοχωρέω **stĕnŏchōrĕō**, *sten-okh-o-reh´-o*; from the same as 4730; to *hem* in closely, i.e. (fig.) *cramp*:— distress, straiten.

4730. στενοχωρία **stĕnŏchōria**, *sten-okh-o-ree´-ah*; from a compound of 4728 and 5561; *narrowness of room*, i.e. (fig.) *calamity*:— anguish, distress.

4731. στερεός **stĕrĕŏs**, *ster-eh-os´*; from 2476; *stiff*, i.e. *solid, stable* (lit. or fig.):— stedfast, strong, sure.

4732. στερεόω **stĕrĕŏō**, *ster-eh-ŏ´-o*; from 4731; to *solidify*, i.e. *confirm* (lit. or fig.):— establish, receive strength, make strong.

4733. στερέωμα **stĕrĕōma**, *ster-eh´-o-mah*; from 4732; something *established*, i.e. (abstr.) *confirmation* (*stability*):— stedfastness.

4734. Στεφανᾶς **Stĕphanas**, *stef-an-as´*; prob. contr. for στεφανωτός **stĕphanōtŏs** (*crowned*; from 4737); *Stephanas*, a Chr.:— Stephanas.

4735. στέφανος **stĕphanŏs**, *stef´-an-os*; from an appar. primary στέφω **stĕphō** (to *twine* or *wreathe*); a *chaplet*, (as a badge of royalty, a prize in the public games or a symbol of honor gen.; but more conspicuous and elaborate than the simple *fillet*, 1238), lit. or fig.:— crown.

4736. Στέφανος **Stĕphanŏs**, *stef´-an-os*; the same as 4735; *Stephanus*, a Chr.:— Stephen.

4737. στεφανόω **stephanŏō**, *stef-an-ŏ´-o*; from 4735; to *adorn* with an honorary *wreath* (lit. or fig.):— crown.

4738. στῆθος **stēthŏs**, *stay´-thos*; from 2476 (as *standing* prominently); the (entire extern.) *bosom*, i.e. *chest*:— breast.

4739. στήκω **stēkō**, *stay´-ko*; from the perfect tense of 2476; to *be stationary*, i.e. (fig.) to *persevere*:— stand (fast).

4740. στηριγμός **stērigmŏs**, *stay-rig-mos´*; from 4741; *stability* (fig.):— stedfastness.

4741. στηρίζω **stērizō**, *stay-rid´-zo*; from a presumed der. of 2476 (like 4731); to *set fast*, i.e. (lit.) to *turn resolutely* in a certain direction, or (fig.) to *confirm*:— fix, (e-) stablish, stedfastly set, strengthen.

4742. στίγμα **stigma**, *stig´-mah*; from a primary στίζω **stizō** (to "*stick*", i.e. *prick*); a *mark* incised or punched (for recognition of ownership), i.e. (fig.) *scar* of service:— mark.

4743. στιγμή **stigmē**, *stig-may´*; fem. of 4742; a *point* of time, i.e. an *instant*:— moment.

4744. στίλβω **stilbō**, *stil´-bo*; appar. a primary verb; to *gleam*, i.e. *flash* intensely:— shining.

4745. στοά **stŏa**, *stŏ-ah´*; prob. from 2476; a *colonnade* or interior *piazza*:— porch.

4746. στοιβάς **stŏibas**, *stoy-bas´* or στιβάς **stibas**, *stee-bas´*; from a primary στείβω stěibō (to "*step*" or "*stamp*"); a *spread* (as if *tramped* flat) of loose materials for a couch, i.e. (by impl.) a *bough* of a tree so employed:— branch.

4747. στοιχεῖον stŏichēiŏn, *stoy-khi'-on*; neut. of a presumed der. of the base of 4748; something *orderly* in arrangement, i.e. (by impl.) a *serial* (*basal, fundamental, initial*) constituent (lit.), proposition (fig.):— element, principle, rudiment.

4748. στοιχέω stŏichěō, *stoy-kheh'-o*; from a der. of στείχω stěichō (to *range* in regular line); to *march*, in (military) rank (*keep step*), i.e. (fig.) to *conform* to virtue and piety:— walk (orderly).

4749. στολή stŏlē, *stol-ay'*; from 4724; *equipment*, i.e. (spec.) a "*stole*" or long-fitting *gown* (as a mark of dignity):— long clothing (garment), (long) robe.

4750. στόμα stŏma, *stom'-a*; prob. strengthened from a presumed der. of the base of 5114; the *mouth* (as if a *gash* in the face); by impl. *language* (and its relations); fig. an *opening* (in the earth); spec. the *front* or *edge* (of a weapon):— edge, face, mouth.

4751. στόμαχος stŏmachŏs, *stom'-akh-os*; from 4750; an *orifice* (the *gullet*), i.e. (spec.) the "*stomach*":— stomach.

4752. στρατεία stratěia, *strat-i'-ah*; from 4754; military *service*, i.e. (fig.) the apostolic *career* (as one of hardship and danger):— warfare.

4753. στράτευμα stratěuma, *strat'-yoo-mah*; from 4754; an *armament*, i.e. (by impl.) a body of *troops* (more or less extensive or systematic):— army, soldier, man of war.

4754. στρατεύομαι stratěuŏmai, *strat-yoo'-om-ahee*; mid. voice from the base of 4756; to *serve* in a military campaign; fig. to *execute the apostolate* (with its arduous duties and functions), to *contend* with carnal inclinations:— soldier, (go to) war (-fare).

4755. στρατηγός stratēgŏs, *strat-ay-gos'*; from the base of 4756 and 71 or 2233; a *general*, i.e. (by impl. or anal.) a (military) *governor* (*prætor*), the chief (*præfect*) of the (Levitical) temple-wardens:— captain, magistrate.

4756. στρατία stratia, *strat-ee'-ah*; fem. of a der. of στρατός stratŏs, (an *army*; from the base of 4766, as encamped); *camp-likeness*, i.e. an *army*, i.e. (fig.) the *angels*, the celestial *luminaries*:— host.

4757. στρατιώτης stratiōtēs, *strat-ee-o'-tace*; from a presumed der. of the same as 4756; a *camper-out*, i.e. a (common) *warrior* (lit. or fig.):— soldier.

4758. στρατολογέω stratŏlŏgěō, *strat-ol-og-eh'-o*; from a compound of the base of 4756 and 3004 (in its orig. sense); to *gather* (or *select*) as a *warrior*, i.e. *enlist* in the army:— choose to be a soldier.

4759. στρατοπεδάρχης stratŏpědarchēs, *strat-op-ed-ar'-khace*; from 4760 and 757; a *ruler of an army*, i.e. (spec.) a *Prætorian præfect*:— captain of the guard.

4760. στρατόπεδον stratŏpědŏn, *strat-op'-ed-on*; from the base of 4756 and the same as 3977; a *camping-ground*, i.e. (by impl.) a body of *troops*:— army.

4761. στρεβλόω strěblŏō, *streb-lŏ'-o*; from a der. of 4762; to *wrench*, i.e. (spec.) to *torture* (by the rack), but only fig. to *pervert*:— wrest.

4762. στρέφω strěphō, *stref'-o*; strengthened from the base of 5157; to *twist*, i.e. *turn* quite around or *reverse* (lit. or fig.):— convert, turn (again, back again, self, self about).

4763. στρηνιάω strēniaō, *stray-nee-ah'-o*; from a presumed der. of 4764; to *be luxurious*:— live deliciously.

4764. στρῆνος strēnŏs, *stray'-nos*; akin to 4731; a "*straining*", "*strenuousness*" or "*strength*", i.e. (fig.) *luxury* (*voluptuousness*):— delicacy.

4765. στρουθίον strŏuthiŏn, *stroo-thee'-on*; dimin. of στρουθός strŏuthŏs (a *sparrow*); a *little sparrow*:— sparrow.

4766. στρώννυμι strōnnumi, *strone'-noo-mee*; or simpler

στρωννύω strōnnuō, *strone-noo'-o*; prol. from a still simpler

στρόω strŏō, *strŏ'-o* (used only as an alt. in certain tenses; prob. akin to 4731 through the idea of *positing*); to "*strew*", i.e. *spread* (as a carpet or couch):— make bed, furnish, spread, strew.

4767. στυγνητός stugnētŏs, *stoog-nay-tos'*; from a der. of an obs. appar. primary στύγω stugō (to *hate*); *hated*, i.e. *odious*:— hateful.

4768. στυγνάζω stugnazō, *stoog-nad'-zo*; from the same as 4767; to *render gloomy*, i.e. (by impl.) *glower* (be *overcast* with clouds, or *sombreness* of speech):— lower, be sad.

4769. στύλος stulŏs, *stoo'-los*; from στύω stuō (to *stiffen*; prop. akin to the base of 2476); a *post* ("*style*"), i.e. (fig.) *support*:— pillar.

4770. Στωϊκός Stōïkŏs, *sto-ik-os'*; from 4745; a "*Stoic*" (as occupying a particular porch in Athens), i.e. adherent of a certain philosophy:— Stoick.

4771. σύ su, *soo*; the pers. pron. of the second pers. sing.; *thou*:— thou. See also 4571, 4671, 4675; and for the plur. 5209, 5210, 5213, 5216.

4772. συγγένεια suggěněia, *soong-ghen'-i-ah*; from 4773; *relationship*, i.e. (concr.) *relatives*:— kindred.

4773. συγγενής suggěnēs, *soong-ghen-ace'*; from 4862 and 1085; a *relative* (by blood); by extens. a fellow *countryman*:— cousin, kin (-sfolk, -sman).

4774. συγγνώμη suggnōmē, *soong-gno'-may*; from a compound of 4862 and 1097; *fellow knowledge*, i.e. *concession*:— permission.

4775. συγκάθημαι sugkathēmai, *soong-kath'-ay-mahee*; from 4862 and 2521; to *seat oneself* in company *with*:— sit with.

4776. συγκαθίζω sugkathizō, *soong-kath-id'-zo*; from 4862 and 2523; to *give* (or *take*) *a seat* in company *with*:— (make) sit (down) together.

4777. συγκακοπαθέω sugkakŏpathěō, *soong-kak-op-ath-eh'-o*; from 4862 and 2553; to *suffer hardship* in company *with*:— be partaker of afflictions.

4778. συγκακουχέω sugkakŏuchěō, *soong-kak-oo-kheh'-o*; from 4862 and 2558; to *maltreat* in company *with*, i.e. (pass.) *endure persecution together*:— suffer affliction with.

4779. συγκαλέω sugkalěō, *soong-kal-eh'-o*; from 4862 and 2564; to *convoke*:— call together.

4780. συγκαλύπτω sugkaluptō, *soong-kal-oop'-to*; from 4862 and 2572; to *conceal altogether*:— cover.

4781. συγκάμπτω sugkamptō, *soong-kamp'-to*; from 4862 and 2578; to *bend together*, i.e. (fig.) to *afflict*:— bow down.

4782. συγκαταβαίνω sugkatabainō, *soong-kat-ab-ah'-ee-no*; from 4862 and 2597; to *descend* in company *with*:— go down with.

4783. συγκατάθεσις sugkatathěsis, *soong-kat-ath'-es-is*; from 4784; a *deposition* (of sentiment) in company *with*, i.e. (fig.) *accord* with:— agreement.

4784. συγκατατίθεμαι sugkatatithěmai, *soong-kat-at-ith'-em-ahee*; mid. from 4862 and 2698; to *deposit* (one's vote or opinion) in company *with*, i.e. (fig.) to *accord* with:— consent.

4785. συγκαταψηφίζω sugkatapsěphizō, *soong-kat-aps-ay-fid'-zo*; from 4862 and a compound of 2596 and 5585; to *count down* in company *with*, i.e. *enroll among*:— number with.

4786. συγκεράννυμι sugkěrannumi, *soong-ker-an'-noo-mee*; from 4862 and 2767; to *commingle*, i.e. (fig.) to *combine* or *assimilate*:— mix with, temper together.

4787. συγκινέω sugkiněō, *soong-kin-eh'-o*; from 4682 and 2795; to *move together*, i.e. (spec.) to *excite* as a mass (to sedition):— stir up.

4788. συγκλείω sugklěiō, *soong-kli'-o*; from 4862 and 2808; to *shut together*, i.e. *include* or (fig.) *embrace* in a common subjection to:— conclude, inclose, shut up.

4789. συγκληρονόμος sugklērŏnŏmŏs, *soong-klay-ron-om'-os*; from 4862 and 2818; a *co-heir*, i.e. (by anal.) *participant in common*:— fellow (joint-)heir, heir together, heir with.

4790. συγκοινωνέω sugkŏinōněō, *soong-koy-no-neh'-o*; from 4862 and 2841; to *share* in company *with*, i.e. *co-participate* in:— communicate (have fellowship) with, be partaker of.

4791. συγκοινωνός sugkŏinōnŏs, *soong-koy-no-nos'*; from 4862 and 2844; a *co-participant*:— companion, partake (-r, -r with).

4792. συγκομίζω sugkŏmizō, *soong-kom-id'-zo*; from 4862 and 2865; to *convey together*, i.e. *collect* or *bear* away in company *with* others:— carry.

4793. συγκρίνω sugkrinō, *soong-kree'-no*; from 4862 and 2919; to *judge* of one thing in connection *with* another, i.e. *combine* (spiritual ideas with appropriate expressions) or *collate* (one person with another by way of contrast or resemblance):— compare among (with).

4794. συγκύπτω **sugkuptō**, *soong-koop´-to;* from 4862 and 2955; to *stoop altogether,* i.e. *be completely overcome* by:— bow together.

4795. συγκυρία **sugkuria**, *soong-koo-ree´-ah;* from a compound of 4862 and κυρέω **kurĕō**, (to *light* or *happen;* from the base of 2962); *concurrence,* i.e. *accident:*— chance.

4796. συγχαίρω **sugchairō**, *soong-khah´-ee-ro;* from 4862 and 5463; to *sympathize in gladness, congratulate:*— rejoice in (with).

4797. συγχέω **sugchĕō**, *soong-kheh´-o;* or

συγχύνω **sugchunō**, *soong-khoo´-no;* from 4862 and χέω **chĕō** (to *pour*) or its alt.; to *commingle,* promiscuously, i.e. (fig.) to *throw* (an assembly) *into disorder,* to *perplex* (the mind):— confound, confuse, stir up, be in an uproar.

4798. συγχράομαι **sugchraŏmai**, *soong-khrah´-om-ahee;* from 4862 and 5530; to *use jointly,* i.e. (by impl.) to *hold intercourse in common:*— have dealings with.

4799. σύγχυσις **sugchusis**, *soong-khoo-sis;* from 4797; *commixture,* i.e. (fig.) riotous *disturbance:*— confusion.

4800. συζάω **suzaō**, *sood-zah´-o;* from 4862 and 2198; to *continue to live* in common *with,* i.e. *co-survive* (lit. or fig.):— live with.

4801. συζεύγνυμι **suzĕugnumi**, *sood-zyoog´-noo-mee;* from 4862 and the base of 2201; to *yoke together,* i.e. (fig.) *conjoin* (in marriage):— join together.

4802. συζητέω **suzētĕō**, *sood-zay-teh´-o;* from 4862 and 2212; to *investigate jointly,* i.e. *discuss, controvert, cavil:*— dispute (with), enquire, question (with), reason (together).

4803. συζήτησις **suzētēsis**, *sood-zay´-tay-sis;* from 4802; *mutual questioning,* i.e. *discussion:*— disputation (-ting), reasoning.

4804. συζητητής **suzētētēs**, *sood-zay-tay-tace´;* from 4802; a *disputant,* i.e. *sophist:*— disputer.

4805. σύζυγος **suzugŏs**, *sood´-zoo-gos;* from 4801; *co-yoked,* i.e. (fig.) as noun, a *colleague;* prob. rather as a proper name; *Syzygus,* a Chr.:— yokefellow.

4806. συζωοποιέω **suzōŏpŏiĕō**, *sood-zo-op-oy-eh´-o;* from 4862 and 2227; to *re-animate conjointly* with (fig.):— quicken together with.

4807. συκάμινος **sukaminŏs**, *soo-kam´-ee-nos;* of Heb. or. [8256] in imitation of 4809; a *sycamore-fig tree:*— sycamine tree.

4808. συκῆ **sukē**, *soo-kay´;* from 4810; a *fig-tree:*— fig tree.

4809. συκομωραία **sukŏmōraia**, *soo-kom-o-rah´-yah;* from 4810 and μόρον **mŏron** (the *mulberry*); the "*sycamore*"-fig tree:— sycamore tree. Comp. 4807.

4810. σῦκον **sukŏn**, *soo´-kon;* appar. a primary word; a *fig:*— fig.

4811. συκοφαντέω **sukŏphantĕō**, *soo-kof-an-teh´-o;* from a compound of 4810 and a der. of 5316; to *be a fig-informer* (reporter of the law forbidding the exportation of figs from Greece), "*sycophant*", i.e. (gen. and by extens.) to *defraud* (*exact* unlawfully, *extort*):— accuse falsely, take by false accusation.

4812. συλαγωγέω **sulagōgĕō**, *soo-lag-ogue-eh´-o;* from the base of 4813 and (the redupl. form of) 71; to *lead away* as booty, i.e. (fig.) *seduce:*— spoil.

4813. συλάω **sulaō**, *soo-lah´-o;* from a der. of σύλλω **sullō** (to *strip;* prob. akin to 138; comp. 4661); to *despoil:*— rob.

4814. συλλαλέω **sullalĕō**, *sool-lal-eh´-o;* from 4862 and 2980; to *talk together,* i.e. *converse:*— commune (confer, talk) with, speak among.

4815. συλλαμβάνω **sullambanō**, *sool-lam-ban´-o;* from 4862 and 2983; to *clasp,* i.e. *seize* (*arrest, capture*); spec. to *conceive* (lit. or fig.); by impl. to *aid:*— catch, conceive, help, take.

4816. συλλέγω **sullĕgō**, *sool-leg´-o;* from 4862 and 3004 in its orig. sense; to *collect:*— gather (together, up).

4817. συλλογίζομαι **sullŏgizŏmai**, *sool-log-id´-zom-ahee;* from 4862 and 3049; to *reckon together* (with oneself), i.e. *deliberate:*— reason with.

4818. συλλυπέω **sullupĕō**, *sool-loop-eh´-o;* from 4862 and 3076; to *afflict jointly,* i.e. (pass.) *sorrow at* (on account of) someone:— be grieved.

4819. συμβαίνω **sumbainō**, *soom-bah´-ee-no;* from 4862 and the base of 939; to *walk* (fig. *transpire*) *together,* i.e. *concur* (*take place*):— be (-fall), happen (unto).

4820. συμβάλλω **sumballō**, *soom-bal´-lo;* from 4862 and 906; to *combine,* i.e. (in speaking) to *converse, consult, dispute,* (mentally) to *consider,* (by impl.) to *aid,* (personally) to *join, attack:*— confer, encounter, help, make, meet with, ponder.

4821. συμβασιλεύω **sumbasilĕuō**, *soom-bas-il-yoo´-o;* from 4862 and 936; to *be co-regent* (fig.):— reign with.

4822. συμβιβάζω **sumbibazō**, *soom-bib-ad´-zo;* from 4862 and βιβάζω **bibazō** (to *force;* caus. [by redupl.] of the base of 939; to *drive together,* i.e. *unite* (in association or affection), (mentally) to *infer, show, teach:*— compact, assuredly gather, intrust, knit together, prove.

4823. συμβουλεύω **sumbŏulĕuō**, *soom-bool-yoo´-o;* from 4862 and 1011; to *give* (or *take*) *advice jointly,* i.e. *recommend, deliberate* or *determine:*— consult, (give, take) counsel (together).

4824. συμβούλιον **sumbŏuliŏn**, *soom-boo´-lee-on;* neut. of a presumed der. of 4825; *advisement;* spec. a *deliberative body,* i.e. the provincial *assessors* or *lay-court:*— consultation, counsel, council.

4825. σύμβουλος **sumbŏulŏs**, *soom´-boo-los;* from 4862 and 1012; a *consultor,* i.e. *adviser:*— counsellor.

4826. Συμεών **Sumĕōn**, *soom-eh-one´;* from the same as 4613; *Symeon* (i.e.

Shimon), the name of five Isr.:— Simeon, Simon.

4827. συμμαθητής **summathētēs**, *soom-math-ay-tace´;* from a compound of 4862 and 3129; a *co-learner* (of Christianity):— fellowdisciple.

4828. συμμαρτυρέω **summarturĕō**, *soom-mar-too-reh´-o;* from 4862 and 3140; to *testify jointly,* i.e. *corroborate* by (concurrent) evidence:— testify unto, (also) bear witness (with).

4829. συμμερίζομαι **summĕrizŏmai**, *soom-mer-id´-zom-ahee;* mid. voice from 4862 and 3307; to *share jointly,* i.e. *participate* in:— be partaker with.

4830. συμμέτοχος **summĕtŏchŏs**, *soom-met´-okh-os;* from 4862 and 3353; a *co-participant:*— partaker.

4831. συμμιμητής **summimētēs**, *soom-mim-ay-tace´;* from a presumed compound of 4862 and 3401; a *co-imitator,* i.e. *fellow votary:*— follower together.

4832. συμμορφός **summŏrphŏs**, *soom-mor-fos´;* from 4862 and 3444; *jointly formed,* i.e. (fig.) *similar:*— conformed to, fashioned like unto.

4833. συμμορφόω **summŏrphŏō**, *soom-mor-fŏ´-o;* from 4832; to *render like,* i.e. (fig.) to *assimilate:*— make conformable unto.

4834. συμπαθέω **sumpathĕō**, *soom-path-eh´-o;* from 4835; to *feel* "*sympathy*" with, i.e. (by impl.) to *commiserate:*— have compassion, be touched with a feeling of.

4835. συμπαθής **sumpathēs**, *soom-path-ace´;* from 4841; *having a fellow-feeling* ("*sympathetic*"), i.e. (by impl.) *mutually commiserative:*— having compassion one of another.

4836. συμπαραγίνομαι **sumparagin-ŏmai**, *soom-par-ag-in´-om-ahee;* from 4862 and 3854; to *be present together,* i.e. to *convene;* by impl. to *appear in aid:*— come together, stand with.

4837. συμπαρακαλέω **sumparakalĕō**, *soom-par-ak-al-eh´-o;* from 4862 and 3870; to *console jointly:*— comfort together.

4838. συμπαραλαμβάνω **sumparalambanō**, *soom-par-al-am-ban´-o;* from 4862 and 3880; to *take along in company:*— take with.

4839. συμπαραμένω **sumparamĕnō**, *soom-par-am-en´-o;* from 4862 and 3887; to *remain in company,* i.e. *still live:*— continue with.

4840. συμπάρειμι **sumparĕimi**, *soom-par´-i-mee;* from 4862 and 3918; to *be at hand together,* i.e. *now present:*— be here present with.

4841. συμπάσχω **sumpaschō**, *soom-pas´-kho;* from 4862 and 3958 (incl. its alt.); to *experience pain jointly* or of the *same kind* (spec. *persecution;* to "*sympathize*"):— suffer with.

4842. συμπέμπω **sumpĕmpō**, *soom-pem´-po;* from 4862 and 3992; to *dispatch in company:*— send with.

4843. συμπεριλαμβάνω **sumpĕrilambanō**, *soom-per-ee-lam-ban´-o;* from 4862 and a compound of 4012 and 2983; to *take by enclosing altogether,* i.e. *ear-*

nestly throw the arms about one:— embrace.

4844. συμπίνω **sumpinō**, *soom-pee´-no;* from *4862* and *4095;* to partake a beverage in company:— drink with.

4845. συμπληρόω **sumplĕrŏō**, *soomplay-rŏ´-o;* from *4862* and *4137;* to implenish completely, i.e. (of space) to swamp (a boat), or (of time) to accomplish (pass. be complete):— (fully) come, fill up.

4846. συμπνίγω **sumpnigō**, *soom-pnee´-go;* from *4862* and *4155;* to strangle completely, i.e. (lit.) to drown, or (fig.) to crowd:— choke, throng.

4847. συμπολίτης **sumpŏlitēs**, *soompol-ee´-tace;* from *4862* and *4177;* a native of the same town, i.e. (fig.) co-religionist (fellow-Christian):— fellow-citizen.

4848. συμπορεύομαι **sumpŏrĕuŏmai**, *soom-por-yoo´-om-ahee;* from *4862* and *4198;* to journey together; by impl. to assemble:— go with, resort.

4849. συμπόσιον **sumpŏsiŏn**, *soom-pos´-ee-on;* neut. of a der. of the alt. of *4844;* a drinking-party ("symposium"), i.e. (by extens.) a room of guests:— company.

4850. συμπρεσβύτερος **sumprĕsbutĕrŏs**, *soom-pres-boo´-ter-os;* from *4862* and *4245;* a co-presbyter:— presbyter, also an elder.

συμφάγω **sumphagō**. See *4906.*

4851. συμφέρω **sumphĕrō**, *soom-fer´-o;* from *4862* and *5342* (incl. its alt.); to bear together (contribute), i.e. (lit.) to collect, or (fig.) to conduce; espec. (neut. part. as a noun) advantage:— be better for, bring together, be expedient (for), be good, (be) profit (-able for).

4852. σύμφημι **sumphēmi**, *soom´-fay-mee;* from *4862* and *5346;* to say jointly, i.e. assent to:— consent unto.

4853. συμφυλέτης **sumphulētēs**, *soom-foo-let´-ace;* from *4862* and a der. of *5443;* a co-tribesman, i.e. native of the same country:— countryman.

4854. σύμφυτος **sumphutŏs**, *soom´-footos;* from *4862* and a der. of *5453;* grown along with (connate), i.e. (fig.) closely united to:— planted together.

4855. συμφύω **sumphuō**, *soom-foo´-o;* from *4862* and *5453;* pass. to grow jointly:— spring up with.

4856. συμφωνέω **sumphōnĕō**, *soom-foneh´-o;* from *4859;* to be harmonious, i.e. (fig.) to accord (be suitable, concur) or stipulate (by compact):— agree (together, with).

4857. συμφώνησις **sumphōnēsis**, *soomfo´-nay-sis;* from *4856;* accordance:— concord.

4858. συμφωνία **sumphōnia**, *soom-fonee´-ah;* from *4859;* unison of sound ("symphony"), i.e. a concert of instruments (harmonious note):— music.

4859. σύμφωνος **sumphōnŏs**, *soom´-fonos;* from *4862* and *5456;* sounding together (alike), i.e. (fig.) accordant (neut. as noun, agreement):— consent.

4860. συμψηφίζω **sumpsēphizō**, *soom-*

psay-fid´-zo; from *4862* and *5585;* to compute jointly:— reckon.

4861. σύμψυχος **sumpsuchŏs**, *soom´-psoo-khos;* from *4862* and *5590;* co-spirited, i.e. similar in sentiment:— likeminded.

4862. σύν **sun**, *soon;* a primary prep. denoting union; with or together (but much closer than *3326* or *3844*), i.e. by association, companionship, process, resemblance, possession, instrumentality, addition, etc.:— beside, with. [In composition, it has similar applications, including completeness.]

4863. συνάγω **sunagō**, *soon-ag´-o;* from *4862* and *71;* to lead together, i.e. collect or convene; spec. to entertain (hospitably):— + accompany, assemble (selves, together), bestow, come together, gather (selves together, up, together), lead into, resort, take in.

4864. συναγωγή **sunagōgē**, *soon-ag-o-gay´;* from (the redupl. form of) *4863;* an assemblage of persons; spec. a Jewish "synagogue" (the meeting or the place); by anal. a Christian church:— assembly, congregation, synagogue.

4865. συναγωνίζομαι **sunagōnizŏmai**, *soon-ag-o-nid´-zom-ahee;* from *4862* and *75;* to struggle in company with, i.e. (fig.) to be a partner (assistant):— strive together with.

4866. συναθλέω **sunathlĕō**, *soon-athleh´-o;* from *4862* and *118;* to wrestle in company with, i.e. (fig.) to seek jointly:— labour with, strive together for.

4867. συναθροίζω **sunathrŏizō**, *soonath-royd´-zo;* from *4862* and ἀθροίζω **athrŏizō** (to hoard); to convene:— call (gather) together.

4868. συναίρω **sunairō**, *soon-ah´-ee-ro;* from *4862* and *142;* to make up together, i.e. (fig.) to compute (an account):— reckon, take.

4869. συναιχμάλωτος **sunaichmalōtŏs**, *soon-aheekh-mal´-o-tos;* from *4862* and *164;* a co-captive:— fellowprisoner.

4870. συνακολουθέω **sunakŏlŏuthĕō**, *soon-ak-ol-oo-theh´-o;* from *4862* and *190;* to accompany:— follow.

4871. συναλίζω **sunalizō**, *soon-al-id´-zo;* from *4862* and ἁλίζω **halizō** (to throng); to accumulate, i.e. convene:— assemble together.

4872. συναναβαίνω **sunanabainō**, *soon-an-ab-ah´-ee-no;* from *4862* and *305;* to ascend in company with:— come up with.

4873. συνανάκειμαι **sunanakĕimai**, *soon-an-ak´-i-mahee;* from *4862* and *345;* to recline in company with (at a meal):— sit (down, at the table, together) with (at meat).

4874. συναναμίγνυμι **sunanamignumi**, *soon-an-am-ig´-noo-mee;* from *4862* and a compound of *303* and *3396;* to mix up together, i.e. (fig.) associate with:— (have, keep) company (with).

4875. συναναπαύομαι **sunanapauŏmai**, *soon-an-ap-ŏw´-om-ahee;* mid. voice from *4862* and *373;* to recruit oneself in company with:— refresh with.

4876. συναντάω **sunantaō**, *soon-an-*

tah´-o; from *4862* and a der. of *473;* to meet with; fig. to occur:— befall, meet.

4877. συνάντησις **sunantēsis**, *soon-an´-tay-sis;* from *4876;* a meeting with:— meet.

4878. συναντιλαμβάνομαι **sunantilambanŏmai**, *soon-an-tee-lam-ban´-omahee;* from *4862* and *482;* to take hold of opposite together, i.e. co-operate (assist):— help.

4879. συναπάγω **sunapagō**, *soon-apag´-o;* from *4862* and *520;* to take off together, i.e. transport with (seduce, pass. yield):— carry (lead) away with, condescend.

4880. συναποθνήσκω **sunapŏthnēskō**, *soon-ap-oth-nace´-ko;* from *4862* and *599;* to decease (lit.) in company with, or (fig.) similarly to:— be dead (die) with.

4881. συναπόλλυμι **sunapŏllumi**, *soon-ap-ol´-loo-mee;* from *4862* and *622;* to destroy (middle or passive voice be slain) in company with:— perish with.

4882. συναποστέλλω **sunapŏstĕllō**, *soon-ap-os-tel´-lo;* from *4862* and *649;* to despatch (on an errand) in company with:— send with.

4883. συναρμολογέω **sunarmŏlŏgĕō**, *soon-ar-mol-og-eh´-o;* from *4862* and a der. of a compound of *719* and *3004* (in its orig. sense of laying); to render close-jointed together, i.e. organize compactly:— be fitly framed (joined) together.

4884. συναρπάζω **sunarpazō**, *soon-arpad´-zo;* from *4862* and *726;* to snatch together, i.e. seize:— catch.

4885. συναυξάνω **sunauxanō**, *soon-ŏwx-an´-o;* from *4862* and *837;* to increase (grow up) together:— grow together.

4886. σύνδεσμος **sundĕsmŏs**, *soon´-des-mos;* from *4862* and *1199;* a joint tie, i.e. ligament, (fig.) uniting principle, control:— band, bond.

4887. συνδέω **sundĕō**, *soon-deh´-o;* from *4862* and *1210;* to bind with, i.e. (pass.) be a fellow-prisoner (fig.):— be bound with.

4888. συνδοξάζω **sundŏxazō**, *soon-doxad´-zo;* from *4862* and *1392;* to exalt to dignity in company (i.e. similarly) with:— glorify together.

4889. σύνδουλος **sundŏulŏs**, *soon´-doolos;* from *4862* and *1401;* a co-slave, i.e. servitor or ministrant of the same master (human or divine):— fellowservant.

συνδρέμω **sundrĕmō**. See *4936.*

4890. συνδρομή **sundrŏmē**, *soon-dromay´;* from (the alt. of) *4936;* a running together, i.e. (riotous) concourse:— run together.

4891. συνεγείρω **sunĕgĕirō**, *soon-eg-i´-ro;* from *4862* and *1453;* to rouse (from death) in company with, i.e. (fig.) to revivify (spiritually) in resemblance to:— raise up together, rise with.

4892. συνέδριον **sunĕdriŏn**, *soon-ed´-ree-on;* neut. of a presumed der. of a compound of *4862* and the base of *1476;* a joint session, i.e. (spec.) the Jewish Sanhedrin; by anal. a subordinate tribunal:— council.

4893. συνείδησις **suneidēsis,** *soon-i´-day-sis;* from a prol. form of *4894; co-perception,* i.e. moral *consciousness:—* conscience.

4894. συνείδω **suneidō,** *soon-i´-do;* from *4862* and *1492;* to *see completely;* used (like its primary) only in two past tenses, respectively mean. to *understand* or *become aware,* and to *be conscious* or (clandestinely) *informed of:—* consider, know, be privy, be ware of.

4895. σύνειμι **suneimi,** *soon´-i-mee;* from *4862* and *1510* (incl. its various inflections); to *be in company with,* i.e. *present* at the time:— be with.

4896. σύνειμι **suneimi,** *soon´-i-mee;* from *4862* and εἶμι **eimi** (to *go*); to *assemble:—* gather together.

4897. συνεισέρχομαι **suneiserchomai,** *soon-ice-er´-khom-ahee;* from *4862* and *1525;* to *enter* in company *with:—* go in with, go with into.

4898. συνέκδημος **sunekdēmos,** *soon-ek´-day-mos;* from *4862* and the base of *1553;* a *co-absentee* from home, i.e. *fellow-traveller:—* companion in travel, travel with.

4899. συνεκλεκτός **suneklektos,** *soon-ek-lek-tos´;* from a compound of *4862* and *1586; chosen* in company *with,* i.e. *co-elect* (*fellow Christian*):— elected together with.

4900. συνελαύνω **sunelaunō,** *soon-el-ow´-no;* from *4862* and *1643;* to *drive together,* i.e. (fig.) *exhort* (to reconciliation):— + set at one again.

4901. συνεπιμαρτυρέω **sunepimartureō,** *soon-ep-ee-mar-too-reh´-o;* from *4862* and *1957;* to *testify further jointly,* i.e. *unite in adding evidence:—* also bear witness.

4902. συνέπομαι **sunepomai,** *soon-ep´-om-ahee;* mid. voice from *4862* and a primary ἕπω **hepō** (to *follow*); to *attend* (*travel*) in company *with:—* accompany.

4903. συνεργέω **sunergeō,** *soon-erg-eh´-o;* from *4904;* to *be a fellow-worker,* i.e. *co-operate:—* help (work) with, work (-er) together.

4904. συνεργός **sunergos,** *soon-er-gos´;* from a presumed compound of *4862* and the base of *2041;* a *co-laborer,* i.e. *coadjutor:—* companion in labour, (fellow-) helper (-labourer, -worker), labourer together with, workfellow.

4905. συνέρχομαι **sunerchomai,** *soon-er´-khom-ahee;* from *4862* and *2064;* to *convene, depart* in company *with, associate* with, or (spec.) *cohabit* (conjugally):— accompany, assemble (with), come (together), come (company, go) with, resort.

4906. συνεσθίω **sunesthiō,** *soon-es-thee´-o;* from *4862* and *2068* (incl. its alt.); to *take food* in company *with:—* eat with.

4907. σύνεσις **sunesis,** *soon´-es-is;* from *4920;* a mental *putting together,* i.e. *intelligence* or (concr.) the *intellect:—* knowledge, understanding.

4908. συνετός **sunetos,** *soon-et´-os;* from *4920;* mentally *put* (or *putting*) *together,* i.e. *sagacious:—* prudent. Comp. *5429.*

4909. συνευδοκέω **suneudokeō,** *soon-yoo-dok-eh´-o;* from *4862* and *2106;* to *think well of in common,* i.e. *assent* to, feel gratified *with:—* allow, assent, be pleased, have pleasure.

4910. συνευωχέω **suneuōcheō,** *soon-yoo-o-kheh´-o;* from *4862* and a der. of a presumed compound of *2095* and a der. of *2192* (mean. to *be in good condition,* i.e. (by impl.) to *fare well,* or *feast*); to *entertain* sumptuously in company *with,* i.e. (middle or passive voice) to *revel together:—* feast with.

4911. συνεφίστημι **sunephistēmi,** *soon-ef-is´-tay-mee;* from *4862* and *2186;* to *stand up together,* i.e. to *resist* (or *assault*) jointly:— rise up together.

4912. συνέχω **sunechō,** *soon-ekh´-o;* from *4862* and *2192;* to *hold together,* i.e. to *compress* (the ears, with a crowd or siege) or *arrest* (a prisoner); fig. to *compel, perplex, afflict, preoccupy:—* constrain, hold, keep in, press, lie sick of, stop, be in a strait, straiten, be taken with, throng.

4913. συνήδομαι **sunēdomai,** *soon-ay´-dom-ahee;* mid. voice from *4862* and the base of *2237;* to *rejoice in with* oneself, i.e. *feel satisfaction concerning:—* delight.

4914. συνήθεια **sunētheia,** *soon-ay´-thi-ah;* from a compound of *4862* and *2239; mutual habituation,* i.e. *usage:—* custom.

4915. συνηλικιώτης **sunēlikiōtēs,** *soon-ay-lik-ee-o´-tace;* from *4862* and a der. of *2244;* a *co-aged* person, i.e. *alike* in years:— equal.

4916. συνθάπτω **sunthaptō,** *soon-thap´-to;* from *4862* and *2290;* to *inter* in company *with,* i.e. (fig.) to *assimilate* spiritually (to Christ by a sepulture as to sin):— bury with.

4917. συνθλάω **sunthlaō,** *soon-thlah´-o;* from *4862* and θλάω **thlaō** (to *crush*); to *dash together,* i.e. *shatter:—* break.

4918. συνθλίβω **sunthlibō,** *soon-thlee´-bo;* from *4862* and *2346;* to *compress,* i.e. *crowd* on all sides:— throng.

4919. συνθρύπτω **sunthruptō,** *soon-throop´-to;* from *4862* and θρύπτω **thruptō** (to *crumble*); to *crush together,* i.e. (fig.) to *dispirit:—* break.

4920. συνίημι **suniēmi,** *soon-ee´-ay-mee;* from *4862* and ἵημι **hiēmi** (to *send*); to *put together,* i.e. (mentally) to *comprehend;* by impl. to *act piously:—* consider, understand, be wise.

4921. συνιστάω **sunistaō,** *soon-is-tah´-o;* or (strengthened)

συνιστάνω **sunistanō,** *soon-is-tan´-o;* or

συνίστημι **sunistēmi,** *soon-is´-tay-mee;* from *4862* and *2476* (incl. its collat. forms); to *set together,* i.e. (by impl.) to *introduce* (favorably), or (fig.) to *exhibit;* intr. to *stand near,* or (fig.) to *constitute:—* approve, commend, consist, make, stand (with).

4922. συνοδεύω **sunodeuō,** *soon-od-yoo´-o;* from *4862* and *3593;* to *travel* in company *with:—* journey with.

4923. συνοδία **sunodia,** *soon-od-ee´-ah;* from a compound of *4862* and *3598* ("*synod*"); *companionship* on a journey, i.e. (by impl.) a *caravan:—* company.

4924. συνοικέω **sunoikeō,** *soon-oy-keh´-o;* from *4862* and *3611;* to *reside together* (as a family):— dwell together.

4925. συνοικοδομέω **sunoikodomeō,** *soon-oy-kod-om-eh´-o;* from *4862* and *3618;* to *construct,* i.e. (pass.) to *compose* (in company with other Christians, fig.):— build together.

4926. συνομιλέω **sunomileō,** *soon-om-il-eh´-o;* from *4862* and *3656;* to *converse* mutually:— talk with.

4927. συνομορέω **sunomoreō,** *soon-om-or-eh´-o;* from *4862* and a der. of a compound of the base of *3674* and the base of *3725;* to *border together,* i.e. *adjoin:—* join hard.

4928. συνοχή **sunochē,** *soon-okh-ay´;* from *4912; restraint,* i.e. (fig.) *anxiety:—* anguish, distress.

4929. συντάσσω **suntassō,** *soon-tas-so;* from *4862* and *5021;* to *arrange jointly,* i.e. (fig.) to *direct:—* appoint.

4930. συντέλεια **sunteleia,** *soon-tel´-i-ah;* from *4931; entire completion,* i.e. *consummation* (of a dispensation):— end.

4931. συντελέω **sunteleō,** *soon-tel-eh´-o;* from *4862* and *5055;* to *complete entirely;* gen. to *execute* (lit. or fig.):— end, finish, fulfil, make.

4932. συντέμνω **suntemnō,** *soon-tem´-no;* from *4862* and the base of *5114;* to *contract* by cutting, i.e. (fig.) *do concisely* (*speedily*):— (cut) short.

4933. συντηρέω **suntēreō,** *soon-tay-reh´-o;* from *4862* and *5083;* to *keep closely together,* i.e. (by impl.) to *conserve* (from ruin); ment. to *remember* (and *obey*):— keep, observe, preserve.

4934. συντίθεμαι **suntithemai,** *soon-tith´-em-ahee;* mid. voice from *4862* and *5087;* to *place jointly,* i.e. (fig.) to *consent* (*bargain, stipulate*), *concur:—* agree, assent, covenant.

4935. συντόμως **suntomōs,** *soon-tom´-oce;* adv. from a der. of *4932; concisely* (*briefly*):— a few words.

4936. συντρέχω **suntrechō,** *soon-trekh´-o;* from *4862* and *5143* (incl. its alt.); to *rush together* (hastily *assemble*) or *headlong* (fig.):— run (together, with).

4937. συντρίβω **suntribō,** *soon-tree´-bo;* from *4862* and the base of *5147;* to *crush completely,* i.e. to *shatter* (lit. or fig.):— break (in pieces), broken to shivers (+-hearted), bruise.

4938. σύντριμμα **suntrimma,** *soon-trim´-mah;* from *4937; concussion* or utter *fracture* (prop. concr.), i.e. *complete ruin:—* destruction.

4939. σύντροφος **suntrophos,** *soon´-trof-os;* from *4862* and *5162* (in a pass. sense); a *fellow-nursling,* i.e. *comrade:—* brought up with.

4940. συντυγχάνω **suntugchanō,** *soon-toong-khan´-o;* from *4862* and *5177;* to *chance together,* i.e. *meet* with (*reach*):— come at.

4941. Συντύχη **Suntuchē**, *soon-too´-khay*; from *4940*; an *accident*; *Syntyche*, a Chr. female:— Syntyche.

4942. συνυποκρίνομαι **sunupŏkrinŏmai**, *soon-oo-pok-rin´-om-ahee*; from *4862* and *5271*; to *act hypocritically* in concert *with*:— dissemble with.

4943. συνυπουργέω **sunupŏurgĕō**, *soon-oop-oorg-eh´-o*; from *4862* and a der. of a compound of *5259* and the base of *2041*; to *be a co-auxiliary*, i.e. *assist*:— help together.

4944. συνωδίνω **sunōdinō**, *soon-o-dee´-no*; from *4862* and *5605*; to *have* (parturition) *pangs* in company (concert, simultaneously) *with*, i.e. (fig.) to *sympathize* (in expectation of relief from suffering):— travail in pain together.

4945. συνωμοσία **sunōmŏsia**, *soon-o-mos-ee´-ah*; from a compound of *4862* and *3660*; a *swearing together*, i.e. (by impl.) a *plot*:— conspiracy.

4946. Συράκουσαι **Surakŏusai**, *soo-rak´-oo-sahee*; plur. of uncert. der.; *Syracuse*, the capital of Sicily:— Syracuse.

4947. Συρία **Suria**, *soo-ree´-ah*; prob. of Heb. or. [6865]; *Syria* (i.e. *Tsyria* or *Tyre*), a region of Asia:— Syria.

4948. Σύρος **Surŏs**, *soo´-ros*; from the same as *4947*; a *Syran* (i.e. prob. *Tyrian*), a native of Syria:— Syrian.

4949. Συροφοίνισσα **Surŏphŏinissa**, *soo-rof-oy´-nis-sah*; fem. of a compound of *4948* and the same as *5403*; a *Syro-phœnician* woman, i.e. a female native of Phœnicia in Syria:— Syrophenician.

4950. σύρτις **surtis**, *soor´-tis*; from *4951*; a *shoal* (from the sand *drawn* thither by the waves), i.e. the *Syrtis* Major or great bay on the N. coast of Africa:— quicksands.

4951. σύρω **surō**, *soo´-ro*; prob. akin to *138*; to *trail*:— drag, draw, hale.

4952. συσπαράσσω **susparassō**, *soos-par-as´-so*; from *4862* and *4682*; to *rend completely*, i.e. (by anal.) to *convulse* violently:— throw down.

4953. σύσσημον **sussēmŏn**, *soos´-say-mon*; neut. of a compound of *4862* and the base of *4591*; a *sign in common*, i.e. preconcerted *signal*:— token.

4954. σύσσωμος **sussōmŏs**, *soos´-so-mos*; from *4862* and *4983*; *of a joint body*, i.e. (fig.) a *fellow-member* of the Chr. community:— of the same body.

4955. συστασιαστής **sustasiastēs**, *soos-tas-ee-as-tace´*; from a compound of *4862* and a der. of *4714*; a *fellow-insurgent*:— make insurrection with.

4956. συστατικός **sustatikŏs**, *soos-tat-ee-kos´*; from a der. of *4921*; *introductory*, i.e. *recommendatory*:— of commendation.

4957. συσταυρόω **sustaurŏō**, *soos-tow-rŏ´-o*; from *4862* and *4717*; to *impale in company with* (lit. or fig.):— crucify with.

4958. συστέλλω **sustĕllō**, *soos-tel´-lo*; from *4862* and *4724*; to *send* (*draw*) together, i.e. *enwrap* (*enshroud* a corpse

for burial), *contract* (an interval):— short, wind up.

4959. συστενάζω **sustĕnazō**, *soos-ten-ad´-zo*; from *4862* and *4727*; to *moan jointly*, i.e. (fig.) *experience a common calamity*:— groan together.

4960. συστοιχέω **sustŏichĕō**, *soos-toy-kheh´-o*; from *4862* and *4748*; to *file together* (as soldiers in ranks), i.e. (fig.) to *correspond to*:— answer to.

4961. συστρατιώτης **sustratiōtēs**, *soos-trat-ee-o´-tace*; from *4862* and *4757*; a *co-campaigner*, i.e. (fig.) an *associate* in Chr. toil:— fellowsoldier.

4962. συστρέφω **sustrĕphō**, *soos-tref´-o*; from *4862* and *4762*; to *twist together*, i.e. *collect* (a bundle, a crowd):— gather.

4963. συστροφή **sustrŏphē**, *soos-trof-ay´*; from *4962*; a *twisting together*, i.e. (fig.) a *secret coalition*, riotous *crowd*:— + band together, concourse.

4964. συσχηματίζω **suschēmatizō**, *soos-khay-mat-id´-zo*; from *4862* and a der. of *4976*; to *fashion alike*, i.e. *conform to* the same pattern (fig.):— conform to, fashion self according to.

4965. Συχάρ **Suchar**, *soo-khar´*; of Heb. or. [7941]; *Sychar* (i.e. *Shekar*), a place in Pal.:— Sychar.

4966. Συχέμ **Suchĕm**, *soo-khem´*; of Heb. or. [7927]; *Sychem* (i.e. *Shekem*), the name of a Canaanite and of a place in Pal.:— Sychem.

4967. σφαγή **sphagē**, *sfag-ay´*; from *4969*; *butchery* (of animals for food or sacrifice, or [fig.] of men [destruction]):— slaughter.

4968. σφάγιον **sphagiŏn**, *sfag´-ee-on*; neut. of a der. of *4967*; a *victim* (in sacrifice):— slain beast.

4969. σφάζω **sphazō**, *sfad´-zo*; a primary verb; to *butcher* (espec. an animal for food or in sacrifice) or (gen.) to *slaughter*, or (spec.) to *maim* (violently):— kill, slay, wound.

4970. σφόδρα **sphŏdra**, *sfod´-rah*; neut. plur. of σφοδρός **sphŏdrŏs**, (*violent*; of uncert. der.) as adv.; *vehemently*, i.e. in a *high degree, much*:— exceeding (-ly), greatly, sore, very.

4971. σφοδρῶς **sphŏdrōs**, *sfod-roce´*; adv. from the same as *4970*; *very much*:— exceedingly.

4972. σφραγίζω **sphragizō**, *sfrag-id´-zo*; from *4973*; to *stamp* (with a signet or private mark) for security or preservation (lit. or fig.); by impl. to *keep secret*, to *attest*:— (set a, set to) seal up, stop.

4973. σφραγίς **sphragis**, *sfrag-ece´*; prob. strengthened from *5420*; a *signet* (as *fencing* in or protecting from misappropriation); by impl. the *stamp* impressed (as a mark of privacy, or genuineness), lit. or fig.:— seal.

4974. σφυρόν **sphurŏn**, *sfoo-ron´*; neut. of a presumed der. prob. of the same as σφαῖρα **sphaira** (a *ball*, "sphere;" compare the fem. σφῦρα **sphura**, a *hammer*); the *ankle* (as *globular*):— ancle bone.

4975. σχεδόν **schĕdŏn**, *skhed-on´*; neut.

of a presumed der. of the alt. of *2192* as adv.; *nigh*, i.e. *nearly*:— almost.

σχέω **schĕō**. See *2192*.

4976. σχῆμα **schēma**, *skhay´-mah*; from the alt. of *2192*; a *figure* (as a *mode* or *circumstance*), i.e. (by impl.) extern. *condition*:— fashion.

4977. σχίζω **schizō**, *skhid´-zo*; appar. a primary verb; to *split* or *sever* (lit. or fig.):— break, divide, open, rend, make a rent.

4978. σχίσμα **schisma**, *skhis´-mah*; from *4977*; a *split* or *gap* ("*schism*"), lit. or fig.:— division, rent, schism.

4979. σχοινίον **schŏiniŏn**, *skhoy-nee´-on*; dimin. of σχοῖνος **schŏinŏs** (a *rush* or *flag*-plant; of uncert. der.); a *rushlet*, i.e. *grass-withe* or *tie* (gen.):— small cord, rope.

4980. σχολάζω **schŏlazō**, *skhol-ad´-zo*; from *4981*; to *take a holiday*, i.e. *be at leisure* for (by impl. *devote oneself wholly to*); fig. to *be vacant* (of a house):— empty, give self.

4981. σχολή **schŏlē**, *skhol-ay´*; prob. fem. of a presumed der. of the alt. of *2192*; prop. *loitering* (as a *withholding* of oneself from work) or *leisure*, i.e. (by impl.) a "*school*" (as *vacation* from phys. employment):— school.

4982. σώζω **sōzō**, *sode´-zo*; from a primary σῶς **sōs** (contr. for obs. σάος **saŏs**, "*safe*"); to *save*, i.e. *deliver* or *protect* (lit. or fig.):— heal, preserve, save (self), do well, be (make) whole.

4983. σῶμα **sōma**, *so´-mah*; from *4982*; the *body* (as a *sound* whole), used in a very wide application, lit. or fig.:— bodily, body, slave.

4984. σωματικός **sōmatikŏs**, *so-mat-ee-kos´*; from *4983*; *corporeal* or *physical*:— bodily.

4985. σωματικῶς **sōmatikōs**, *so-mat-ee-koce´*; adv. from *4984*; *corporeally* or *physically*:— bodily.

4986. Σώπατρος **Sōpatrŏs**, *so´-pat-ros*; from the base of *4982* and *3962*; *of a safe father*; *Sopatrus*, a Chr.:— Sopater. Comp. *4989*.

4987. σωρεύω **sōrĕuō**, *sore-yoo´-o*; from another form of *4673*; to *pile* up (lit. or fig.):— heap, load.

4988. Σωσθένης **Sōsthĕnēs**, *soce-then´-ace*; from the base of *4982* and that of *4599*; *of safe strength*; *Sosthenes*, a Chr.:— Sosthenes.

4989. Σωσίπατρος **Sōsipatrŏs**, *so-sip-at-ros*; prol. for *4986*; *Sosipatrus*, a Chr.:— Sosipater.

4990. σωτήρ **sōtēr**, *so-tare´*; from *4982*; a *deliverer*, i.e. God or Christ:— saviour.

4991. σωτηρία **sōtēria**, *so-tay-ree´-ah*; fem. of a der. of *4990* as (prop. abstr.) noun; *rescue* or *safety* (phys. or mor.):— deliver, health, salvation, save, saving.

4992. σωτήριον **sōtēriŏn**, *so-tay´-ree-on*; neut. of the same as *4991* as (prop. concr.) noun; *defender* or (by impl.) *defence*:— salvation.

4993. σωφρονέω **sōphrŏnĕō**, *so-fron-eh´-o*; from *4998*; to *be of sound mind*, i.e. *sane*, (fig.) *moderate*:— be in right mind, be sober (minded), soberly.

4994. σωφρονίζω **sōphrŏnizō**, so-fron-id´-zo; from *4998*; to *make of sound mind*, i.e. (fig.) to *discipline* or *correct*:— teach to be sober.

4995. σωφρονισμός **sōphrŏnismŏs**, so-fron-is-mos´; from *4994*; *discipline*, i.e. *self-control*:— sound mind.

4996. σωφρόνως **sōphrŏnōs**, so-fron´-oce; adv. from *4998*; *with sound mind*, i.e. *moderately*:— soberly.

4997. σωφροσύνη **sōphrŏsunē**, so-fros-oo´-nay; from *4998*; *soundness of mind*, i.e. (lit.) *sanity* or (fig.) *self-control*:— soberness, sobriety.

4998. σώφρων **sōphrŏn**, so´-frone; from the base of *4982* and that of *5424*; *safe* (*sound*) *in mind*, i.e. *self-controlled* (*moderate* as to opinion or passion):— discreet, sober, temperate.

T

τά **ta**. See *3588*.

4999. Ταβέρναι **Tabĕrnai**, tab-er´-nahee or

Ταβερνῶν **Tabĕrnōn**, tab-er-non´; plur. of Lat. or.; *huts* or *wooden-walled buildings*; *Tabernæ*:— taverns.

5000. Ταβιθά **Tabitha**, tab-ee-thah´; of Chald. or. [comp. 6646]; *the gazelle*; *Tabitha* (i.e. *Tabjetha*), a Chr. female:— Tabitha.

5001. τάγμα **tagma**, tag´-mah; from *5021*; something orderly in *arrangement* (a *troop*), i.e. (fig.) a *series* or *succession*:— order.

5002. τακτός **taktŏs**, tak-tos´; from *5021*; *arranged*, i.e. *appointed* or *stated*:— set.

5003. ταλαιπωρέω **talaipōrĕō**, tal-ahee-po-reh´-o; from *5005*; to *be wretched*, i.e. *realize* one's own *misery*:— be afflicted.

5004. ταλαιπωρία **talaipōria**, tal-ahee-po-ree´-ah; from *5005*; *wretchedness*, i.e. *calamity*:— misery.

5005. ταλαίπωρος **talaipōrŏs**, tal-ah´-ee-po-ros; from the base of *5007* and a der. of the base of *3984*; *enduring trial*, i.e. *miserable*:— wretched.

5006. ταλαντιαῖος **talantiaiŏs**, tal-an-tee-ah´-yos; from *5007*; *talent-like* in weight:— weight of a talent.

5007. τάλαντον **talantŏn**, tal´-an-ton; neut. of a presumed der. of the orig. form of τλάω **tlaō** (to *bear*; equiv. to *5342*); a *balance* (as *supporting weights*), i.e. (by impl.) a certain *weight* (and thence a *coin* or rather *sum* of money) or "*talent*":— talent.

5008. ταλιθά **talitha**, tal-ee-thah´; of Chald. or. [comp. 2924]; *the fresh*, i.e. *young girl*; *talitha* (O *maiden*):— talitha.

5009. ταμεῖον **tamĕiŏn**, tam-i´-on; neut. contr. of a presumed der. of ταμίας **tamias** (a *dispenser* or *distributor*; akin to τέμνω **tĕmnō**, to *cut*); a *dispensary* or *magazine*, i.e. a chamber on the ground-floor or interior of an Oriental house (gen. used for *storage* or *privacy*, a spot for retirement):— secret chamber, closet, storehouse.

τανυν **tanun**. See *3568*.

5010. τάξις **taxis**, tax´-is; from *5021*; reg. *arrangement*, i.e. (in time) fixed *succession* (of rank or character), official *dignity*:— order.

5011. ταπεινός **tapĕinŏs**, tap-i-nos´; of uncert. der.; *depressed*, i.e. (fig.) *humiliated* (in circumstances or disposition):— base, cast down, humble, of low degree (estate), lowly.

5012. ταπεινοφροσύνη **tapĕinŏphrŏsunē**, tap-i-nof-ros-oo´-nay; from a compound of *5011* and the base of *5424*; *humiliation of mind*, i.e. *modesty*:— humbleness of mind, humility (of mind, loneliness (of mind).

5013. ταπεινόω **tapĕinŏō**, tap-i-nŏ´-o; from *5011*; to *depress*; fig. to *humiliate* (in condition or heart):— abase, bring low, humble (self).

5014. ταπείνωσις **tapĕinōsis**, tap-i´-no-sis; from *5013*; *depression* (in rank or feeling):— humiliation, be made low, low estate, vile.

5015. ταράσσω **tarassō**, tar-as´-so; of uncert. aff.; to *stir* or *agitate* (roil water):— trouble.

5016. ταραχή **tarachē**, tar-akh-ay´; fem. from *5015*; *disturbance*, i.e. (of water) *roiling*, or (of a mob) *sedition*:— trouble (-ing).

5017. τάραχος **tarachŏs**, tar´-akh-os; masc. from *5015*; a *disturbance*, i.e. (popular) *tumult*:— stir.

5018. Ταρσεύς **Tarsĕus**, tar-syoos´; from *5019*; a *Tarsean*, i.e. native of Tarsus:— of Tarsus.

5019. Ταρσός **Tarsŏs**, tar-sos´; perh. the same as ταρσός **tarsŏs** (a *flat* basket); *Tarsus*, a place in Asia Minor:— Tarsus.

5020. ταρταρόω **tartarŏō**, tar-tar-ŏ´-o; from Τάρταρος **Tartarŏs**, (the deepest *abyss* of Hades); to *incarcerate* in eternal torment:— cast down to hell.

5021. τάσσω **tassō**, tas´-so; a prol. form of a primary verb (which latter appears only in certain tenses); to *arrange* in an orderly manner, i.e. *assign* or *dispose* (to a certain position or lot):— addict, appoint, determine, ordain, set.

5022. ταῦρος **taurŏs**, tow´-ros; appar. a primary word [comp. 8450, "*steer*"]; a *bullock*:— bull, ox.

5023. ταῦτα **tauta**, tŏw´-tah; nominative or acc. neut. plur. of *3778; these things*:— + afterward, follow, + hereafter, × him, the same, so, such, that, then, these, they, this, those, thus.

5024. ταὐτά **tauta**, tŏw-tah´; neut. plur. of *3588* and *846* as adv.; in *the same* way:— even thus, (manner) like, so.

5025. ταύταις **tautais**, tŏw´-taheece; and

ταύτας **tautas**, tŏw´-tas; dat. and acc. fem. plur. respectively of *3778*; (*to* or *with* or *by*, etc.) *these*:— hence, that, then, these, those.

5026. ταύτῃ **tautĕi**, tŏw´-tay; and

ταύτην **tautēn**, tŏw´-tane; and

ταύτης **tautēs**, tŏw´-tace; dat., acc., and gen. respectively of the fem. sing. of *3778*; (*toward* or *of*) *this*:— her,

+ hereof, it, that, + thereby, the (same), this (same).

5027. ταφή **taphē**, taf-ay´; fem. from *2290*; *burial* (the act):— × bury.

5028. τάφος **taphŏs**, taf´-os; masc. from *2290*; a *grave* (the place of interment):— sepulchre, tomb.

5029. τάχα **tacha**, takh´-ah; as if neut. plur. of *5036* (adv.); *shortly*, i.e. (fig.) *possibly*:— peradventure (-haps).

5030. ταχέως **tachĕōs**, takh-eh´-oce; adv. from *5036; briefly*, i.e. (in time) *speedily*, or (in manner) *rapidly*:— hastily, quickly, shortly, soon, suddenly.

5031. ταχινός **tachinŏs**, takh-ee-nos´; from *5034; curt*, i.e. *impending*:— shortly, swift.

5032. τάχιον **tachiŏn**, takh´-ee-on; neut. sing. of the comp. of *5036* (as adv.); *more swiftly*, i.e. (in manner) *more rapidly*, or (in time) *more speedily*:— out [run], quickly, shortly, sooner.

5033. τάχιστα **tachista**, takh´-is-tah; neut. plur. of the superl. of *5036* (as adv.); *most quickly*, i.e. (with *5613* pref.) *as soon* as possible:— + with all speed.

5034. τάχος **tachŏs**, takh´-os; from the same as *5036*; a *brief* space (of time), i.e. (with *1722* pref.) in *haste*:— + quickly, + shortly, + speedily.

5035. ταχύ **tachu**, takh-oo´; neut. sing. of *5036* (as adv.); *shortly*, i.e. *without delay, soon*, or (by surprise) *suddenly*, or (by impl. of ease) *readily*:— lightly, quickly.

5036. ταχύς **tachus**, takh-oos´; of uncert. aff.; *fleet*, i.e. (fig.) *prompt* or *ready*:— swift.

5037. τε **tĕ**, teh; a primary particle (enclitic) of connection or addition; *both* or *also* (prop. as correl. of *2532*):— also, and, both, even, then, whether. Often used in comp., usually as the latter part.

5038. τεῖχος **tĕichŏs**, ti´-khos; akin to the base of *5088*; a *wall* (as *formative* of a house):— wall.

5039. τεκμήριον **tĕkmēriŏn**, tek-may´-ree-on; neut. of a presumed der. of τεκμάρ **tĕkmar** (a *goal* or fixed *limit*); a *token*, (as *defining* a fact), i.e. *criterion* of certainty:— infallible proof.

5040. τεκνίον **tĕkniŏn**, tek-nee´-on; dimin. of *5043*; an *infant*, i.e. (plur. fig.) *darlings* (Chr. *converts*):— little children.

5041. τεκνογονέω **tĕknŏgŏnĕō**, tek-nog-on-eh´-o; from a compound of *5043* and the base of *1096*; to *be a child-bearer*, i.e. *parent* (*mother*):— bear children.

5042. τεκνογονία **tĕknŏgŏnia**, tek-nog-on-ee´-ah; from the same as *5041*; *childbirth* (*parentage*), i.e. (by impl.) *maternity* (the performance of *maternal duties*):— childbearing.

5043. τέκνον **tĕknŏn**, tek´-non; from the base of *5098*; a *child* (as *produced*):— child, daughter, son.

5044. τεκνοτροφέω **tĕknŏtrŏphĕō**, tek-not-rof-eh´-o; from a compound of *5043* and *5142*; to *be a child-rearer*, i.e. *fulfil* the duties of a *female parent:*— bring up children.

5045. τέκτων **tĕktōn**, *tek´-tone;* from the base of *5098;* an *artificer* (as *producer* of fabrics), i.e. (spec.) a *craftsman* in wood:— carpenter.

5046. τέλειος **tĕlĕiŏs**, *tel´-i-os;* from *5056; complete* (in various applications of labor, growth, ment. and mor. character, etc.); neut. (as noun, with *3588*) *completeness:*— of full age, man, perfect.

5047. τελειότης **tĕlĕiŏtēs**, *tel-i-ot´-ace;* from *5046;* (the state) *completeness* (ment. or mor.):— perfection (-ness).

5048. τελειόω **tĕlĕiŏō**, *tel-i-ŏ´-o;* from *5046;* to *complete,* i.e. (lit.) *accomplish,* or (fig.) *consummate* (in character):— consecrate, finish, fulfil, make) perfect.

5049. τελείως **tĕlĕiŏs**, *tel-i´-oce;* adv. from *5046; completely,* i.e. (of hope) *without wavering:*— to the end.

5050. τελείωσις **tĕlĕiōsis**, *tel-i´-o-sis;* from *5448;* (the act) *completion,* i.e. (of prophecy) *verification,* or (of expiation) *absolution:*— perfection, performance.

5051. τελειωτής **tĕlĕiōtēs**, *tel-i-o-tace´;* from *5048;* a *completer,* i.e. *consummater:*— finisher.

5052. τελεσφορέω **tĕlĕsphŏrĕō**, *tel-es-for-eh´-o;* from a compound of *5056* and *5342;* to *be a bearer to completion* (maturity), i.e. to *ripen* fruit (fig.):— bring fruit to perfection.

5053. τελευτάω **tĕlĕutaō**, *tel-yoo-tah´-o;* from a presumed der. of *5055;* to *finish* life (by impl. of *979),* i.e. *expire* (*demise*):— be dead, decease, die.

5054. τελευτή **tĕlĕutē**, *tel-yoo-tay´;* from *5053; decease:*— death.

5055. τελέω **tĕlĕō**, *tel-eh´-o;* from *5056;* to *end,* i.e. *complete, execute, conclude, discharge* (a debt):— accomplish, make an end, expire, fill up, finish, go over, pay, perform.

5056. τέλος **tĕlŏs**, *tel´-os;* from a primary τέλλω **tĕllō**, (to *set out* for a def. point or *goal*); prop. the point aimed at as a *limit,* i.e. (by impl.) the *conclusion* of an act or state (*termination* [lit., fig. or indef.], *result* [immed., ultimate or prophetic], *purpose*); spec. an *impost* or *levy* (as *paid*):— + continual, custom, end (-ing), finally, uttermost. Comp. *5411.*

5057. τελώνης **tĕlōnēs**, *tel-o´-nace;* from *5056* and *5608;* a *tax-farmer,* i.e. *collector* of public *revenue:*— publican.

5058. τελώνιον **tĕlōniŏn**, *tel-o´-nee-on;* neut. of a presumed der. of *5057;* a *tax-gatherer's* place of business:— receipt of custom.

5059. τέρας **tĕras**, *ter´-as;* of uncert. aff.; a *prodigy* or omen:— wonder.

5060. Τέρτιος **Tĕrtiŏs**, *ter´-tee-os;* of Lat. or.; *third; Tertius,* a Chr.:— Tertius.

5061. Τέρτυλλος **Tĕrtullŏs**, *ter´-tool-los;* of uncert. der.; *Tertullus,* a Rom.:— Tertullus.

τέσσαρα **tĕssara**. See *5064.*

5062. τεσσαράκοντα **tĕssarakŏnta**, *tes-sar-ak´-on-tah;* the decade of *5064; forty:*— forty.

5063. τεσσαρακονταετής **tĕssarakŏntaĕtēs**, *tes-sar-ak-on-tah-et-ace´;* from *5062* and *2094; of forty years* of age:— (+ full, of) forty years (old).

5064. τέσσαρες **tĕssarĕs**, *tes´-sar-es;* neut.

τέσσαρα **tĕssara**, *tes´-sar-ah;* a plur. number; *four:*— four.

5065. τεσσαρεσκαιδέκατος **tĕssarĕskaidĕkatŏs**, *tes-sar-es-kahee-dek´-at-os;* from *5064* and *2532* and *1182; fourteenth:*— fourteenth.

5066. τεταρταῖος **tĕtartaiŏs**, *tet-ar-tah´-yos;* from *5064;* pertaining to the *fourth* day:— four days.

5067. τέταρτος **tĕtartŏs**, *tet´-ar-tos;* ord. from *5064; fourth:*— four (-th).

5068. τετράγωνος **tĕtragōnŏs**, *tet-rag´-o-nos;* from *5064* and *1137; four-cornered,* i.e. *square:*— foursquare.

5069. τετράδιον **tĕtradiŏn**, *tet-rad´-ee-on;* neut. of a presumed der. of τέτρας **tĕtras** (a *tetrad;* from *5064*); a *quaternion,* or squad (picket) of four Rom. soldiers:— quaternion.

5070. τετρακισχίλιοι **tĕtrakischiliŏi**, *tet-rak-is-khil´-ee-oy;* from the mult. adv. of *5064* and *5507; four times a thousand:*— four thousand.

5071. τετρακόσιοι **tĕtrakŏsiŏi**, *tet-rak-os´-ee-oy;* neut. τετρακόσια **tĕtrakŏsia**, *tet-rak-os´-ee-ah;* plur. from *5064* and *1540; four hundred:*— four hundred.

5072. τετράμηνον **tĕtramēnŏn**, *tet-ram´-ay-non;* neut. of a compound of *5064* and *3376;* a *four months'* space:— four months.

5073. τετραπλόος **tĕtraplŏŏs**, *tet-rap-lŏ´-os;* from *5064* and a der. of the base of *4118; quadruple:*— fourfold.

5074. τετράπους **tĕtrapŏus**, *tet-rap´-ooce;* from *5064* and *4228;* a *quadruped:*— fourfooted beast.

5075. τετραρχέω **tĕtrarchĕō**, *tet-rar-kheh´-o;* from *5076;* to *be a tetrarch:*— (be) tetrarch.

5076. τετράρχης **tĕtrarchēs**, *tet-rar´-khace;* from *5064* and *757;* the *ruler of* a *fourth* part of a country ("*tetrarch*"):— tetrarch.

τεύχω **tĕuchō**. See *5177.*

5077. τεφρόω **tĕphrŏō**, *tef-rŏ´-o;* from τέφρα **tephra** (*ashes*); to *incinerate,* i.e. *consume:*— turn to ashes.

5078. τέχνη **tĕchnē**, *tekh´-nay;* from the base of *5088; art* (as *productive*), i.e. (spec.) a *trade,* or (gen.) *skill:*— art, craft, occupation.

5079. τεχνίτης **tĕchnitēs**, *tekh-nee´-tace;* from *5078;* an *artisan;* fig. a *founder* (*Creator*):— builder, craftsman.

5080. τήκω **tēkō**, *tay´-ko;* appar. a primary verb; to *liquefy:*— melt.

5081. τηλαυγῶς **tēlaugōs**, *tay-lŏw-goce´;* adv. from a compound of a der. of *5056* and *827;* in a *far-shining* manner, i.e. *plainly:*— clearly.

5082. τηλικοῦτος **tēlikŏutŏs**, *tay-lik-oo´-tos;* fem.

τηλικαύτη **tēlikautē**, *tay-lik-ŏw´-tay;* from a compound of *3588* with *2245* and *3778; such as this,* i.e. (in [fig.] magnitude) *so vast:*— so great, so mighty.

5083. τηρέω **tērĕō**, *tay-reh´-o;* from τερός **tĕrŏs**, (a *watch;* perh. akin to *2334*); to *guard* (from *loss* or *injury,* prop. by keeping *the eye* upon; and thus differing from *5442,* which is prop. to *prevent escaping;* and from *2892,* which implies a *fortress* or full military lines of apparatus), i.e. to *note* (a prophecy; fig. to *fulfil* a command); by impl. to *detain* (in custody; fig. to *maintain*); by extens. to *withhold* (for personal ends; fig. to *keep unmarried*):— hold fast, keep (-er), (pre-, re-) serve, watch.

5084. τήρησις **tērēsis**, *tay´-ray-sis;* from *5083;* a *watching,* i.e. (fig.) *observance,* or (concr.) a *prison:*— hold.

τῇ **tēi**, τήν **tēn**, τῆς **tēs**. See *3588.*

5085. Τιβεριάς **Tibĕrias**, *tib-er-ee-as´;* from *5086; Tiberias,* the name of a town and a lake in Pal.:— Tiberias.

5086. Τιβέριος **Tibĕriŏs**, *tib-er´-ee-os;* of Lat. or.; prob. *pertaining to the river Tiberis* or *Tiber; Tiberius,* a Rom. emperor:— Tiberius.

5087. τίθημι **tithēmi**, *tith´-ay-mee;* a prol. form of a primary

θέω **thĕō**, *theh´-o* (which is used only as alt. in certain tenses); to *place* (in the widest application, lit. and fig.; prop. in a pass. or horizontal posture, and thus different from *2476,* which prop. denotes an upright and active position, while *2749* is prop. refl. and utterly prostrate):— + advise, appoint, bow, commit, conceive, give, × kneel down, lay (aside, down, up), make, ordain, purpose, put, set (forth), settle, sink down.

5088. τίκτω **tiktō**, *tik´-to;* a strengthened form of a primary τέκω **tekō**, *tek´-o* (which is used only as alt. in certain tenses); to *produce* (from seed, as a mother, a plant, the earth, etc.), lit. or fig.:— bear, be born, bring forth, be delivered, be in travail.

5089. τίλλω **tillō**, *til´-lo;* perh. akin to the alt. of *138,* and thus to *4951;* to *pull* off:— pluck.

5090. Τίμαιος **Timaiŏs**, *tim´-ah-yos;* prob. of Chald. or. [comp. 2931]; *Timæus* (i.e. *Timay*), an Isr.:— Timæus.

5091. τιμάω **timaō**, *tim-ah´-o;* from *5093;* to *prize,* i.e. *fix a valuation* upon; by impl. to *revere:*— honour, value.

5092. τιμή **timē**, *tee-may´;* from *5099;* a *value,* i.e. *money* paid, or (concr. and collect.) *valuables;* by anal. *esteem* (espec. of the highest degree), or the *dignity* itself:— honour, precious, price, some.

5093. τίμιος **timiŏs**, *tim´-ee-os;* including the comparative

τιμιώτερος **timiŏtĕrŏs**, *tim-ee-o´-ter-os;* and the superlative

τιμιώτατος **timiŏtatŏs**, *tim-ee-o´-tat-os;* from *5092; valuable,* i.e. (obj.) *costly,* or (subj.) *honored, esteemed,* or (fig.) *beloved:*— dear, honourable, (more, most) precious, had in reputation.

5094. τιμιότης **timiŏtēs**, *tim-ee-ot´-ace;* from 5093; *expensiveness,* i.e. (by impl.) *magnificence:*— costliness.

5095. Τιμόθεος **Timŏthĕŏs**, *tee-moth´-eh-os;* from 5092 and 2316; *dear to God; Timotheus,* a Chr.:— Timotheus, Timothy.

5096. Τίμων **Timōn**, *tee´-mone;* from 5092; *valuable; Timon,* a Chr.:— Timon.

5097. τιμωρέω **timōrĕō**, *tim-o-reh´-o;* from a comp. of 5092 and οὖρος (a *guard*); prop. to *protect,* one's *honor,* i.e. to *avenge* (*inflict a penalty*):— punish.

5098. τιμωρία **timōria**, *tee-mo-ree´-ah;* from 5097; *vindication,* i.e. (by impl.) a *penalty:*— punishment.

5099. τίνω **tinō**, *tee´-no;* strengthened for a primary

τίω **tiō**, *tee´-o* (which is only used as an alt. in certain tenses); to *pay* a price, i.e. as a *penalty:*— be punished with.

5100. τὶς **tis**, *tis;* an enclit. indef. pron.; *some* or *any* person or object:— a (kind of), any (man, thing, thing at all), certain (thing), divers, he (every) man, one (× thing), ought, + partly, some (man, body, -thing, -what), (+ that no-) thing, what (-soever), × wherewith, whom [-soever], whose ([-soever]).

5101. τίς **tis**, *tis;* prob. emphat. of 5100; an interrog. pron., *who, which* or *what* (in direct or indirect · questions):— every man, how (much), + no (-ne, thing), what (manner, thing), where ([-by, -fore, -of, -unto, -with, -withall]), whether, which, who (-m, -se), why.

5102. τίτλος **titlŏs**, *tit´-los;* of Lat. or.: a *titulus* or "*title*" (*placard*):— title.

5103. Τίτος **Titŏs**, *tee´-tos;* of Lat. or. but uncert. signif.; *Titus,* a Chr.:— Titus.

τίω **tiō**. See 5099.

τό **tŏ**. See 3588.

5104. τοί **tŏi**, *toy;* prob. for the dat. of 3588; an enclit. particle of *asseveration* by way of contrast; *in sooth:*— [used only with other particles in comp. as 2544, 3305, 5105, 5106, etc.].

5105. τοιγαροῦν **tŏigarŏun**, *toy-gar-oon´;* from 5104 and 1063 and 3767; *truly for then,* i.e. *consequently:*— there-(where-) fore.

τοίγε **tŏigĕ**. See 2544.

5106. τοίνυν **tŏinun**, *toy´-noon;* from 5104 and 3568; *truly now,* i.e. *accordingly:* —then, therefore.

5107. τοιόσδε **tŏiŏsdĕ**, *toy-os´-deh;* (incl. the other inflections); from a der. of 5104 and 1161; *such-like then,* i.e. *so great:*— such.

5108. τοιοῦτος **tŏiŏutŏs**, *toy-oo´-tos;* (incl. the other inflections); from 5104 and 3778; *truly this,* i.e. *of this sort* (to denote character or individuality):— like, such (an one).

5109. τοῖχος **tŏichŏs**, *toy´-khos;* another form of 5038; a *wall:*— wall.

5110. τόκος **tŏkŏs**, *tok´-os;* from the

base of 5088; *interest* on money loaned (as a *produce*):— usury.

5111. τολμάω **tŏlmaŏ**, *tol-mah´-o;* from τόλμα **tŏlma**, (*boldness*; prob. itself from the base of 5056 through the idea of *extreme* conduct); to *venture* (obj. or in *act*; while 2292 is rather subj. or in *feeling*); by impl. to be *courageous:*— be bold, boldly, dare, durst.

5112. τολμηρότερον **tŏlmērŏtĕrŏn**, *tol-may-rot´-er-on;* neut. of the comparative of a der. of the base of 5111 (as adv.); *more daringly,* i.e. *with greater confidence* than otherwise:— the more boldly.

5113. τολμητής **tŏlmētēs**, *tol-may-tace´;* from 5111; a *daring* (*audacious*) man:— presumptuous.

5114. τομώτερος **tŏmōtĕrŏs**, *tom-o´-ter-os;* comparative of a der. of the primary τέμνω **tĕmnō** (to *cut;* more comprehensive or decisive than 2875, as if by a *single* stroke; whereas that implies repeated blows, like *hacking*); *more keen:*— sharper.

5115. τόξον **tŏxŏn**, *tox´-on;* from the base of 5088; a *bow* (appar. as the simplest fabric):— bow.

5116. τοπάζιον **tŏpaziŏn**, *top-ad´-zee-on;* neut. of a presumed der. (alt.) of τόπαζος **tŏpazŏs** (a "*topaz*"; of uncert. or.); a gem, prob. the *chrysolite:*— topaz.

5117. τόπος **tŏpŏs**, *top´-os;* appar. a primary word; a *spot* (gen. in *space,* but limited by occupancy; whereas 5561 is a larger but part. *locality*), i.e. *location* (as a position, home, tract, etc.); fig. *condition, opportunity;* spec. a *scabbard:*— coast, licence, place, × plain, quarter, + rock, room, where.

5118. τοσοῦτος **tŏsŏutŏs**, *tos-oo´-tos;* from τόσος **tŏsŏs**, (*so much;* appar. from 3588 and 3739) and 3778 (including its variations); so *vast as this,* i.e. *such* (in quantity, amount, number or space):— as large, so great (long, many, much), these many.

5119. τότε **tŏtĕ**, *tot´-eh;* from (the neut. of) 3588 and 3753; *the when,* i.e. *at the time* that (of the past or future, also in consecution):— that time, then.

5120. τοῦ **tŏu**, *too;* prop. the gen. of 3588; sometimes used for 5127; *of this person:*— his.

5121. τοὐναντίον **tŏunantiŏn**, *too-nan-tee´-on;* contr. for the neut. of 3588 and 1726; *on the contrary:*— contrariwise.

5122. τοὔνομα **tŏunŏma**, *too´-no-mah;* contr. for the neut. of 3588 and 3686; *the name* (is):— named.

5123. τουτέστι **tŏutĕsti**, *toot-es´-tee;* contr. for 5124 and 2076; *that is:*— that is (to say).

5124. τοῦτο **tŏutŏ**, *too´-tŏ;* neut. sing. nom. or acc. of 3778; *that* thing:— here [-unto], it, partly, self [-same], so, that (intent), the same, there [-fore, -unto], this, thus, where [-fore].

5125. τούτοις **tŏutŏis**, *too´-toice;* dat. plur. masc. or neut. of 3778; *to* (for, in, *with* or *by*) these (persons or things):— such, them, there [-in, -with], these, this, those.

5126. τοῦτον **tŏutŏn**, *too´-ton;* acc. sing. masc. of 3778; *this* (person, as obj. of verb or prep.):— him, the same, that, this.

5127. τούτου **tŏutŏu**, *too´-too;* gen. sing. masc. or neut. of 3778; *of* (from or concerning) *this* (person or thing):— here [-by], him, it, + such manner of, that, thence [-forth], thereabout, this, thus.

5128. τούτους **tŏutŏus**, *too´-tooce;* acc. plur. masc. of 3778; *these* (persons, as obj. of verb or prep.):— such, them, these, this.

5129. τούτῳ **tŏutŏi**, *too´-to;* dat. sing. masc. or neut. of 3778; *to* (in, *with* or *by*) *this* (person or thing):— here [-by, -in], him, one, the same, there [-in], this.

5130. τούτων **tŏutōn**, *too´-tone;* gen. plur. masc. or neut. of 3778; *of* (from or concerning) *these* (persons or things):— such, their, these (things), they, this sort, those.

5131. τράγος **tragŏs**, *trag´-os;* from the base of 5176; a *he-goat* (as a *gnawer*):— goat.

5132. τράπεζα **trapĕza**, *trap´-ed-zah;* prob. contr. from 5064 and 3979; a *table* or *stool* (as being *four-legged*), usually for food (fig. a *meal*); also a *counter* for money (fig. a broker's *office* for loans at interest):— bank, meat, table.

5133. τραπεζίτης **trapĕzitēs**, *trap-ed-zee´-tace;* from 5132; a *money-broker* or *banker:* —exchanger.

5134. τραῦμα **trauma**, *trŏw´-mah;* from the base of τιτρώσκω **titrŏskō**, (to *wound;* akin to the base of 2352, 5147, 5149, etc.); a *wound:*— wound.

5135. τραυματίζω **traumatizŏ**, *trŏw-mat-id´-zo;* from 5134; to *inflict a wound:*— wound.

5136. τραχηλίζω **trachēlizŏ**, *trakh-ay-lid´-zo;* from 5137; to *seize* by the *throat* or *neck,* i.e. to *expose* the *gullet* of a victim for killing (gen. to *lay bare*):— opened.

5137. τράχηλος **trachēlŏs**, *trakh´-ay-los;* prob. from 5143 (through the idea of *mobility*); the *throat* (*neck*), i.e. (fig.) *life:*— neck.

5138. τραχύς **trachus**, *trakh-oos´;* perh. strengthened from the base of 4486 (as if *jagged* by rents); *uneven, rocky* (*reefy*):— rock, rough.

5139. Τραχωνῖτις **Trachōnitis**, *trakh-o-nee´-tis;* from a der. of 5138; *rough* district; *Trachonitis,* a region of Syria:— Trachonitis.

5140. τρεῖς **trĕis**, *trice;* neut.

τρία **tria**, *tree´-ah;* or

τριῶν **triōn**, *tree-on´;* a primary (plural) number; "*three*":— three.

5141. τρέμω **trĕmō**, *trem´-o;* strengthened from a primary τρέω **trĕō** (to "*dread*," "*terrify*"); to "*tremble*" or *fear:*— be afraid, trembling.

5142. τρέφω **trĕphō**, *tref´-o;* a primary verb (prop. θρέφω **thrĕphō**; but perhaps strengthened from the base of 5157 through the idea of *convolution*); prop. to *stiffen,* i.e. *fatten* (by impl. to *cherish* [with food, etc.], *pamper, rear*):— bring up, feed, nourish.

5143. τρέχω **trĕchō**, *trekh´-o;* appar. a primary verb (prop. θρέχω **thrĕchō**; comp. 2359); which uses δρέμω **drĕmō**, *drem´-o* (the base of *1408*) as alt. in certain tenses; to *run* or *walk hastily* (lit. or fig.):— have course, run.

5144. τριάκοντα **triakŏnta**, *tree-ak´-on-tah;* the decade of *5140; thirty:*— thirty.

5145. τριακόσιοι **triakŏsiŏi**, *tree-ak-os´-ee-oy;* plur. from *5140* and *1540; three hundred:*— three hundred.

5146. τρίβολος **tribŏlŏs**, *trib´-ol-os;* from *5140* and *956;* prop. a *crow-foot* (*three-pronged* obstruction in war), i.e. (by anal.) a *thorny* plant (*caltrop*):— brier, thistle.

5147. τρίβος **tribŏs**, *tree´-bos;* from τρίβω **tribō** (to *"rub"*; akin to τείρω **tĕirō**, τρύω **truō**, and the base of *5131, 5134*); a *rut*, or worn *track:*— path.

5148. τριετία **triĕtia**, *tree-et-ee´-ah;* from a compound of *5140* and *2094;* a *three years' period* (*triennium*):— space of three years.

5149. τρίζω **trizō**, *trid´-zo;* appar. a primary verb; to *creak* (*squeak*), i.e. (by anal.) to *grate* the teeth (in frenzy):— gnash.

5150. τρίμηνον **trimēnŏn**, *trim´-ay-non;* neut. of a compound of *5140* and *3376* as noun; a *three months'* space:— three months.

5151. τρίς **tris**, *trece;* adv. from *5140; three times:*— three times, thrice.

5152. τρίστεγον **tristĕgŏn**, *tris´-teg-on;* neut. of a compound of *5140* and *4721* as noun; a *third roof* (*story*):— third loft.

5153. τρισχίλιοι **trischiliŏi**, *tris-khil´-ee-oy;* from *5151* and *5507; three times a thousand:*— three thousand.

5154. τρίτος **tritŏs**, *tree´-tos;* ord. from *5140; third;* neut. (as noun) a *third part*, or (as adv.) a (or the) *third* time, *thirdly:*— third (-ly).

τρίχες **trichĕs**, etc. See 2359.

5155. τρίχινος **trichinŏs**, *trikh´-ee-nos;* from *2359; hairy*, i.e. made of *hair* (*mohair*):— of hair.

5156. τρόμος **trŏmŏs**, *trom´-os;* from *5141;* a *"trembling"*, i.e. quaking with *fear:* —+ tremble (-ing).

5157. τροπή **trŏpē**, *trop-ay´;* from an appar. primary τρέπω **trĕpō**, to *turn*); a *turn* ("trope"), i.e. *revolution* (fig. *variation*):— turning.

5158. τρόπος **trŏpŏs**, *trop´-os;* from the same as *5157;* a *turn*, i.e. (by impl.) *mode* or *style* (espec. with prep. or rel. pref. as adv. *like*); fig. *deportment* or *character:*— (even) as, conversation, [+ likel manner, (+ by any) means, way.

5159. τροποφορέω **trŏpŏphŏrĕō**, *trop-of-or-eh´-o;* from *5158* and *5409;* to *endure* one's *habits:*— suffer the manners.

5160. τροφή **trŏphē**, *trof-ay´;* from *5142; nourishment* (lit. or fig.); by impl. *rations* (*wages*):— food, meat.

5161. Τρόφιμος **Trŏphimŏs**, *trof´-ee-mos;* from *5160; nutritive; Trophimus*, a Chr.:— Trophimus.

5162. τροφός **trŏphŏs**, *trof-os´;* from *5142;* a *nourisher*, i.e. *nurse:*— nurse.

5163. τροχιά **trŏchia**, *trokh-ee-ah´;* from *5164;* a *track* (as a wheel-*rut*), i.e. (fig.) a *course* of conduct:— path.

5164. τροχός **trŏchŏs**, *trokh-os´;* from *5143;* a *wheel* (as a *runner*), i.e. (fig.) a *circuit* of phys. effects:— course.

5165. τρύβλιον **trubliŏn**, *troob´-lee-on;* neut. of a presumed der. of uncert. aff.; a *bowl:*— dish.

5166. τρυγάω **trugaō**, *troo-gah´-o;* from a der. of τρύγω **trugō** (to *dry*) mean. ripe *fruit* (as if *dry*); to *collect* the vintage:— gather.

5167. τρυγών **trugōn**, *troo-gone´;* from τρύζω **truzō** (to *murmur;* akin to *5149*, but denoting a *duller* sound); a *turtle-dove* (as *cooing*):— turtle-dove.

5168. τρυμαλιά **trumalia**, *troo-mal-ee-ah´;* from a der. of τρύω **truō** (to *wear*, away; akin to the base of *5134, 5147* and *5176*); an *orifice*, i.e. needle's *eye:*— eye. Comp. *5169.*

5169. τρύπημα **trupēma**, *troo´-pay-mah;* from a der. of the base of *5168;* an *aperture*, i.e. a needle's *eye:*— eye.

5170. Τρύφαινα **Truphaina**, *troo´-fahee-nah;* from *5172; luxurious; Tryphæna*, a Chr. woman:— Tryphena.

5171. τρυφάω **truphaō**, *troo-fah´-o;* from *5172;* to *indulge in luxury:*— live in pleasure.

5172. τρυφή **truphē**, *troo-fay´;* from θρύπτω **thruptō** (to *break*, up or [fig.] *enfeeble*, espec. the mind and body by *indulgence*); *effeminacy*, i.e. *luxury* or *debauchery:*— delicately, riot.

5173. Τρυφῶσα **Truphōsa**, *troo-fo´-sah;* from *5172; luxuriating; Tryphosa*, a Chr. female:— Tryphosa.

5174. Τρωάς **Trōas**, *tro-as´;* from Τρός **Trōs** (a *Trojan*); the *Troad* (or plain of Troy), i.e. *Troas*, a place in Asia Minor:— Troas.

5175. Τρωγύλλιον **Trōgulliŏn**, *tro-gool´-lee-on;* of uncert. der.; *Trogyllium*, a place in Asia Minor:— Trogyllium.

5176. τρώγω **trōgō**, *tro´-go;* probably strengthened from a collateral form of the base of *5134* and *5147* through the idea of *corrosion* or *wear;* or perh. rather of a base of *5167* and *5149* through the idea of a *crunching* sound; to *gnaw* or *chew*, i.e. (gen.) to *eat:*— eat.

5177. τυγχάνω **tugchanō**, *toong-khan´-o;* prob. for an obs. τύχω **tuchō** (for which the mid. voice of another alt. τεύχω **tĕuchō** [to *make ready* or *bring to pass*] is used in certain tenses; akin to the base of *5088* through the idea of *effecting;* prop. to *affect;* or (spec.) to *hit* or *light upon* (as a mark to be reached), i.e. (tran.) to *attain* or *secure* an object or end, or (intr.) to *happen* (as if *meeting* with); but in the latter application only impers. (with *1487*), i.e. *perchance;* or (pres. part.) as adj. *usual* (as if commonly *met with*, with *3756*, *extraordinary*), neut. (as adv.) *perhaps;* or (with another verb) as adv. by *accident* (*as it were*):— be, chance, enjoy, little, obtain, × refresh ... self, + special. Comp. *5180.*

5178. τυμπανίζω **tumpanizō**, *toom-pan-id´-zo;* from a der. of *5180* (mean. a drum, "*tympanum*"); to stretch on an instrument of *torture* resembling a drum, and thus *beat* to death:— torture.

5179. τύπος **tupŏs**, *too´-pos;* from *5180;* a *die* (as *struck*), i.e. (by impl.) a *stamp* or *scar;* by anal. a *shape*, i.e. a *statue*, (fig.) *style* or *resemblance;* spec. a *sampler* (*"type"*), i.e. a *model* (for imitation) or *instance* (for warning):— en- (ex-) ample, fashion, figure, form, manner, pattern, print.

5180. τύπτω **tuptō**, *toop´-to;* a primary verb (in a strengthened form); to "*thump*", i.e. *cudgel* or *pummel* (prop. with a stick or *bastinado*), but in any case by *repeated* blows; thus differing from *3817* and *3960*, which denote a [usually single] blow with the hand or any instrument, or *4141* with the fist [or a *hammer*], or *4474* with the *palm;* as well as from *5177*, an *accidental* collision); by impl. to *punish;* fig. to *offend* (the conscience):— beat, smite, strike, wound.

5181. Τύραννος **Turannŏs**, *too´-ran-nos;* a provincial form of the der. of the base of *2962;* a *"tyrant"; Tyrannus*, an Ephesian:— Tyrannus.

5182. τυρβάζω **turbazō**, *toor-bad´-zo;* from τύρβη **turbē**, (Lat. *turba*, a *crowd;* akin to *2351*); to *make "turbid"*, i.e. *disturb:*— trouble.

5183. Τύριος **Turiŏs**, *too´-ree-os;* from *5184;* a *Tyrian*, i.e. inhab. of Tyrus:— of Tyre.

5184. Τύρος **Turŏs**, *too´-ros;* of Heb. or. [6865]: *Tyrus* (i.e. *Tsor*), a place in Pal.:— Tyre.

5185. τυφλός **tuphlŏs**, *toof-los´;* from *5187; opaque* (as if *smoky*), i.e. (by anal.) *blind* (phys. or ment.):— blind.

5186. τυφλόω **tuphlŏō**, *toof-lŏ´-o;* from *5185;* to *make blind*, i.e. (fig.) to *obscure:*— blind.

5187. τυφόω **tuphŏō**, *toof-ŏ´-o;* from a der. of *5188;* to *envelop* with *smoke*, i.e. (fig.) to *inflate* with self-conceit:— high-minded, be lifted up with pride, be proud.

5188. τύφω **tuphō**, *too´-fo;* appar. a primary verb; to make a *smoke*, i.e. slowly *consume* without flame:— smoke.

5189. τυφωνικός **tuphōnikŏs**, *too-fo-nee-kos´;* from a der. of *5188; stormy* (as if *smoky*):— tempestuous.

5190. Τυχικός **Tuchikŏs**, *too-khee-kos´;* from a der. of *5177; fortuitous*, i.e. *fortunate; Tychicus*, a Chr.:— Tychicus.

Υ

5191. ὑακίνθινος **huakinthinŏs**, *hoo-ak-in´-thee-nos;* from *5192;* "*hyacinthine*" or "*jacinthine*", i.e. deep *blue:*— jacinth.

5192. ὑάκινθος **huakinthŏs**, *hoo-ak´-in-thos;* of uncert. der.; the "*hyacinth*" or "*jacinth*", i.e. some gem of a deep *blue* color, prob. the *zirkon:*— jacinth.

5193. ὑάλινος **hualinŏs**, *hoo-al´-ee-nos;* from *5194; glassy*, i.e. *transparent:*— of glass.

5194. ὕαλος **hualŏs**, *hoo´-al-os;* perh.

from the same as 5205 (as being transparent like *rain*); *glass*:— glass.

5195. ὑβρίζω **hubrizō**, *hoo-brid´-zo*; from *5196*; to *exercise violence*, i.e. *abuse*:— use despitefully, reproach, entreat shamefully (spitefully).

5196. ὕβρις **hubris**, *hoo´-bris*; from *5228*; *insolence* (as *over*-bearing), i.e. *insult, injury*:— harm, hurt, reproach.

5197. ὑβριστής **hubristēs**, *hoo-bris-tace´*; from *5195*; an *insulter*, i.e. *maltreater*:— despiteful, injurious.

5198. ὑγιαίνω **hugiainō**, *hoog-ee-ah´-ee-no*; from *5199*; to *have sound health*, i.e. *be well* (in body); fig. to be *uncorrupt* (*true* in doctrine):— be in health, (be safe and) sound, (be) whole (-some).

5199. ὑγιής **hugiēs**, *hoog-ee-ace´*; from the base of *837*; *healthy*, i.e. *well* (in body); fig. *true* (in doctrine):— sound, whole.

5200. ὑγρός **hugrŏs**, *hoo-gros´*; from the base of *5205*; *wet* (as if with *rain*), i.e. (by impl.) *sappy* (*fresh*):— green.

5201. ὑδρία **hudria**, *hoo-dree-ah´*; from *5204*; a *water-jar*, i.e. *receptacle* for family supply:— water-pot.

5202. ὑδροποτέω **hudrŏpŏtĕō**, *hoo-drop-ot-eh´-o*; from a compound of *5204* and a der. of *4095*; to *be a water-drinker*, i.e. to *abstain from vinous beverages*:— drink water.

5203. ὑδρωπικός **hudrōpikŏs**, *hoo-dro-pik-os´*; from a compound of *5204* and a der. of *3700* (as if *looking watery*); to be *"dropsical"*:— have the dropsy.

5204. ὕδωρ **hudōr**, *hoo´-dore*; gen.,

ὕδατος **hudatŏs**, *hoo´-dat-os*, etc.; from the base of *5205*; *water* (as if *rainy*) lit. or fig.:— water.

5205. ὑετός **huĕtŏs**, *hoo-et-os´*; from a primary ὕω **huō**, (to *rain*); *rain*, espec. a *shower*:— rain.

5206. υἱοθεσία **huiŏthĕsia**, *hwee-oth-es-ee´-ah*; from a presumed compound of *5207* and a der. of *5087*; the *placing as a son*, i.e. *adoption* (fig. Chr. *sonship* in respect to God):— adoption (of children, of sons).

5207. υἱός **huiŏs**, *hwee-os´*; appar. a primary word; a *"son"* (sometimes of animals), used very widely of immed. remote or fig. kinship:— child, foal, son.

5208. ὕλη **hulē**, *hoo´-lay*; perh. akin to *3586*; a *forest*, i.e. (by impl.) *fuel*:— matter.

5209. ὑμᾶς **humas**, *hoo-mas´*; acc. of *5210*; *you* (as the obj. of a verb or prep.):— ye, you (+ -ward), your (+ own).

5210. ὑμεῖς **humĕis**, *hoo-mice´*; irreg. plur. of *4771*; *you* (as subj. of verb):— ye (yourselves), you.

5211. Ὑμεναῖος **Humĕnaiŏs**, *hoo-men-ah´-yos*; from Ὑμήν **Humēn**, (the god of *weddings*); *"hymenæeal"*; *Hymenæus*, an opponent of Christianity:— Hymenæus.

5212. ὑμέτερος **humĕtĕrŏs**, *hoo-met´-er-os*; from *5210*; *yours*, i.e. *pertaining to you*:— your (own).

5213. ὑμῖν **humin**, *hoo-min´*; irreg. dat.

of *5210*; *to* (*with* or *by*) *you*:— ye, you, your (-selves).

5214. ὑμνέω **humnĕō**, *hoom-neh´-o*; from *5215*; to *hymn*, i.e. sing a relig. ode; by impl. to *celebrate* (God) in song:— sing a hymn (praise unto).

5215. ὕμνος **humnŏs**, *hoom´-nos*; appar. from a simpler (obs.) form of ὕδέω **hudĕō**, (to *celebrate*; prob. akin to *103*; comp. *5667*); a *"hymn"* or relig. ode (one of the Psalms):— hymn.

5216. ὑμῶν **humōn**, *hoo-mone´*; gen. of *5210*; of (*from* or *concerning*) *you*:— ye, you, your (own, -selves).

5217. ὑπάγω **hupagō**, *hoop-ag´-o*; from *5259* and *71*; to *lead* (oneself) *under*, i.e. *withdraw* or *retire* (as if *sinking* out of sight), lit. or fig.:— depart, get hence, go (a-) way.

5218. ὑπακοή **hupakŏē**, *hoop-ak-ŏ-ay´*; from *5219*; *attentive hearkening*, i.e. (by impl.) *compliance* or *submission*:— obedience, (make) obedient, obey (-ing).

5219. ὑπακούω **hupakŏuō**, *hoop-ak-oo´-o*; from *5259* and *191*; to *hear under* (as a *subordinate*), i.e. to *listen attentively*; by impl. to *heed* or *conform* to a command or authority:— hearken, be obedient to, obey.

5220. ὕπανδρος **hupandrŏs**, *hoop´-an-dros*; from *5259* and *435*; in subjection *under* a man, i.e. a *married* woman:— which hath an husband.

5221. ὑπαντάω **hupantaō**, *hoop-an-tah´-o*; from *5259* and a der. of *473*; to *go opposite* (*meet*) *under* (*quietly*), i.e. to *encounter, fall in with*:— (go to) meet.

5222. ὑπάντησις **hupantēsis**, *hoop-an´-tay-sis*; from *5221*; an *encounter* or *concurrence* (with *1519* for infin. in order to *fall in with*):— meeting.

5223. ὕπαρξις **huparxis**, *hoop´-arx-is*; from *5225*; *existency* or *proprietorship*, i.e. (concr.) *property, wealth*:— goods, substance.

5224. ὑπάρχοντα **huparchŏnta**, *hoop-ar´-khon-tah*; neut. plur. of pres. part. act. of *5225* as noun; *things extant* or *in hand*, i.e. *property* or *possessions*:— goods, that which one has, things which (one) possesseth, substance, that hast.

5225. ὑπάρχω **huparchō**, *hoop-ar´-kho*; from *5259* and *756*; to *begin under* (*quietly*), i.e. *come into existence* (be *present* or *at hand*); expletively, to *exist* (as copula or subordinate to an adj., part., adv. or prep., or as auxil. to principal verb):— after, behave, live.

5226. ὑπείκω **hupeikō**, *hoop-i´-ko*; from *5259* and εἴκω **eikō** (to *yield*, be *"weak"*); to *surrender*:— submit self.

5227. ὑπεναντίος **hupĕnantiŏs**, *hoop-en-an-tee´-os*; from *5259* and *1727*; *under* (*covertly*) *contrary to*, i.e. *opposed* or (as noun) an *opponent*:— adversary, against.

5228. ὑπέρ **hupĕr**, *hoop-er´*; a primary prep.; *"over"*, i.e. (with the gen.) of place, *above, beyond, across*, or causal, *for* the sake of, *instead, regarding*; with the acc. *superior to*, more *than*:— (+ exceeding, abundantly) above, in (on)

behalf of, beyond, by, + very chiefest, concerning, exceeding (above, -ly), for, + very highly, more (than), of, over, on the part of, for sake of, in stead, than, to (-ward), very. [In composition, it retains many of the above applications.]

5229. ὑπεραίρομαι **hupĕrairŏmai**, *hoop-er-ah´-ee-rom-ahee*; mid. voice from *5228* and *142*; to *raise* oneself *over*, i.e. (fig.) to *become haughty*:— exalt self, be exalted above measure.

5230. ὑπέρακμος **hupĕrakmŏs**, *hoop-er´-ak-mos*; from *5228* and the base of *188*; *beyond* the *"acme"*, i.e. fig. (of a daughter) *past* the *bloom* (*prime*) of youth:— + pass the flower of (her) age.

5231. ὑπεράνω **hupĕranō**, *hoop-er-an´-o*; from *5228* and *507*; *above upward*, i.e. *greatly higher* (in place or rank):— far above, over.

5232. ὑπεραυξάνω **hupĕrauxanō**, *hoop-er-öwx-an´-o*; from *5228* and *837*; to *increase above* ordinary degree:— grow exceedingly.

5233. ὑπερβαίνω **hupĕrbainō**, *hoop-er-bah´-ee-no*; from *5228* and the base of *939*; to *transcend*, i.e. (fig.) to *overreach*:— go beyond.

5234. ὑπερβαλλόντως **hupĕrballŏntōs**, *hoop-er-bal-lon´-toce*; adv. from pres. part. act. of *5235*; *excessively*:— beyond measure.

5235. ὑπερβάλλω **hupĕrballō**, *hoop-er-bal´-lo*; from *5228* and *906*; to *throw beyond* the usual mark, i.e. (fig.) to *surpass* (only act. part. *supereminent*):— exceeding, excel, pass.

5236. ὑπερβολή **hupĕrbŏlē**, *hoop-er-bol-ay´*; from *5235*; a *throwing beyond* others, i.e. (fig.) *supereminence*; adv. (with *1519* or *2596*) *pre-eminently*:— abundance, (far more) exceeding, excellency, more excellent, beyond (out of) measure.

5237. ὑπερείδω **hupĕrĕidō**, *hoop-er-i´-do*; from *5228* and *1492*; to *overlook*, i.e. *not punish*:— wink at.

5238. ὑπερέκεινα **hupĕrĕkĕina**, *hoop-er-ek´-i-nah*; from *5228* and the neut. plur. of *1565*; *above those* parts, i.e. *still farther*:— beyond.

5239. ὑπερεκτείνω **hupĕrĕktĕinō**, *hoop-er-ek-ti´-no*; from *5228* and *1614*; to *extend inordinately*:— stretch beyond.

5240. ὑπερεκχύνω **hupĕrĕkchunō**, *hoop-er-ek-khoo´-no*; from *5228* and the alt. form of *1632*; to *pour out over*, i.e. (pass.) to *overflow*:— run over.

ὑπερεκπερισσοῦ **hupĕrĕkpĕrissŏu**. See *5228* and *1537* and *4053*.

5241. ὑπερεντυγχάνω **hupĕrĕntugchanō**, *hoop-er-en-toong-khan´-o*; from *5228* and *1793*; to *intercede in behalf of*:— make intercession for.

5242. ὑπερέχω **hupĕrĕchō**, *hoop-er-ekh´-o*; from *5228* and *2192*; to *hold* oneself *above*, i.e. (fig.) to *excel*; part. (as adj. or neut. as noun) *superior, superiority*:— better, excellency, higher, pass, supreme.

5243. ὑπερηφανία **hupĕrēphania**, *hoop-er-ay-fan-ee´-ah*; from *5244*; *haughtiness*:— pride.

5244. ὑπερήφανος **hupĕrēphanŏs**, hoop-er-ay'-fan-os; from 5228 and 5316; appearing above others (conspicuous), i.e. (fig.) haughty:— proud.

ὑπερλίαν **hupĕrlian**. See 5228 and 3029.

5245. ὑπερνικάω **hupĕrnikaō**, hoop-er-nik-ah'-o; from 5228 and 3528; to vanquish beyond, i.e. gain a decisive victory:— more than conquer.

5246. ὑπέρογκος **hupĕrŏgkŏs**, hoop-er'-ong-kos; from 5228 and 3591; bulging over, i.e. (fig.) insolent:— great swelling.

5247. ὑπεροχή **hupĕrŏchē**, hoop-er-okh-ay'; from 5242; prominence, i.e. (fig.) superiority (in rank or character):— authority, excellency.

5248. ὑπερπερισσεύω **hupĕrpĕrissĕuŏ**, hoop-er-per-is-syoo'-o; from 5228 and 4052; to super-abound:— abound much more, exceeding.

5249. ὑπερπερισσῶς **hupĕrpĕrissōs**, hoop-er-per-is-soce'; from 5228 and 4057; superabundantly, i.e. exceedingly:— beyond measure.

5250. ὑπερπλεονάζω **hupĕrplĕŏnazō**, hoop-er-pleh-on-ad'-zo; from 5228 and 4121; to superabound:— be exceeding abundant.

5251. ὑπερυψόω **hupĕrupsŏō**, hoop-er-oop-so'-o; from 5228 and 5312; to elevate above others, i.e. raise to the highest position:— highly exalt.

5252. ὑπερφρονέω **hupĕrphrŏnĕō**, hoop-er-fron-eh'-o; from 5228 and 5426; to esteem oneself overmuch, i.e. be vain or arrogant:— think more highly.

5253. ὑπερῷον **hupĕrǫ̆ŏn**, hoop-er-o'-on; neut. of a der. of 5228; a higher part of the house, i.e. apartment in the third story:— upper chamber (room).

5254. ὑπέχω **hupĕchō**, hoop-ekh'-o; from 5259 and 2192; to hold oneself under, i.e. endure with patience:— suffer.

5255. ὑπήκοος **hupēkŏŏs**, hoop-ay'-ko-os; from 5219; attentively listening, i.e. (by impl.) submissive:— obedient.

5256. ὑπηρετέω **hupērĕtĕō**, hoop-ay-ret-eh'-o; from 5257; to be a subordinate, i.e. (by impl.) subserve:— minister (unto), serve.

5257. ὑπηρέτης **hupērĕtēs**, hoop-ay-ret'-ace; from 5259 and a der. of ἐρέσσω ĕressō (to row); an under-oarsman, i.e. (gen.) subordinate (assistant, sexton, constable):— minister, officer, servant.

5258. ὕπνος **hupnŏs**, hoop'-nos; from an obs. primary (perh. akin to 5259 through the idea of subsilience); sleep, i.e. (fig.) spiritual torpor:— sleep.

5259. ὑπό **hupŏ**, hoop-ŏ'; a primary prep.; under, i.e. (with the gen.) of place (beneath), or with verbs (the agency or means, through); (with the acc.) of place (whither [underneath] or where [below] or time (when [at]):— among, by, from, in, of, under, with. [In composition, it retains the same general applications, espec. of inferior position or condition, and spec. covertly or moderately.]

5260. ὑποβάλλω **hupŏballō**, hoop-ob-al'-lo; from 5259 and 906; to throw in stealthily, i.e. introduce by collusion:— suborn.

5261. ὑπογραμμός **hupŏgrammŏs**, hoop-og-ram-mos'; from a compound of 5259 and 1125; an underwriting, i.e. copy for imitation (fig.):— example.

5262. ὑπόδειγμα **hupŏdĕigma**, hoop-od'-igue-mah; from 5263; an exhibit for imitation or warning (fig. specimen, adumbration):— en- (ex-) ample, pattern.

5263. ὑποδείκνυμι **hupŏdĕiknumi**, hoop-od-ike'-noo-mee; from 5259 and 1166; to exhibit under the eyes, i.e. (fig.) to exemplify (instruct, admonish):— show, (fore-) warn.

5264. ὑποδέχομαι **hupŏdĕchŏmai**, hoop-od-ekh'-om-ahee; from 5259 and 1209; to admit under one's roof, i.e. entertain hospitably:— receive.

5265. ὑποδέω **hupŏdĕō**, hoop-od-eh'-o; from 5259 and 1210; to bind under one's feet, i.e. put on shoes or sandals:— bind on, (be) shod.

5266. ὑπόδημα **hupŏdēma**, hoop-od'-ay-mah; from 5265; something bound under the feet, i.e. a shoe or sandal:— shoe.

5267. ὑπόδικος **hupŏdikŏs**, hoop-od'-ee-kos; from 5259 and 1349; under sentence, i.e. (by impl.) condemned:— guilty.

5268. ὑποζύγιον **hupŏzugiŏn**, hoop-od-zoog'-ee-on; neut. of a compound of 5259 and 2218; an animal under the yoke (draught-beast), i.e. (spec.) a donkey:— ass.

5269. ὑποζώννυμι **hupŏzōnnumi**, hoop-od-zone'-noo-mee; from 5259 and 2224; to gird under, i.e. frap (a vessel with cables across the keel, sides and deck):— undergirt.

5270. ὑποκάτω **hupŏkatō**, hoop-ok-at'-o; from 5259 and 2736; down under, i.e. beneath:— under.

5271. ὑποκρίνομαι **hupŏkrinŏmai**, hoop-ok-rin'-om-ahee; mid. voice from 5259 and 2919; to decide (speak or act) under a false part, i.e. (fig.) dissemble (pretend):— feign.

5272. ὑπόκρισις **hupŏkrisis**, hoop-ok'-ree-sis; from 5271; acting under a feigned part, i.e. (fig.) deceit ("hypocrisy"):— condemnation, dissimulation, hypocrisy.

5273. ὑποκριτής **hupŏkritēs**, hoop-ok-ree-tace'; from 5271; an actor under an assumed character (stage-player), i.e. (fig.) a dissembler ("hypocrite"):— hypocrite.

5274. ὑπολαμβάνω **hupŏlambanō**, hoop-ol-am-ban'-o; from 5259 and 2983; to take from below, i.e. carry upward; fig. to take up, i.e. continue a discourse or topic; ment. to assume (presume):— answer, receive, suppose.

5275. ὑπολείπω **hupŏlĕipō**, hoop-ol-i'-po; from 5295 and 3007; to leave under (behind), i.e. (pass.) to remain (survive):— be left.

5276. ὑπολήνιον **hupŏlēniŏn**, hoop-ol-ay'-nee-on; neut. of a presumed compound of 5259 and 3025; vessel or receptacle under the press, i.e. lower winevat:— winefat.

5277. ὑπολιμπάνω **hupŏlimpanō**, hoop-ol-im-pan'-o; a prol. form for 5275; to leave behind, i.e. bequeath:— leave.

5278. ὑπομένω **hupŏmĕnō**, hoop-omen'-o; from 5259 and 3306; to stay under (behind), i.e. remain; fig. to undergo, i.e. bear (trials), have fortitude, persevere:— abide, endure, (take) patient (-ly), suffer, tarry behind.

5279. ὑπομιμνήσκω **hupŏmimnēskō**, hoop-om-im-nace'-ko; from 5259 and 3403; to remind quietly, i.e. suggest to the (mid. voice, one's own) memory:— put in mind, remember, bring to (put in) remembrance.

5280. ὑπόμνησις **hupŏmnēsis**, hoop-om'-nay-sis; from 5279; a reminding or (refl.) recollection:— remembrance.

5281. ὑπομονή **hupŏmŏnē**, hoop-om-on-ay'; from 5278; cheerful (or hopeful) endurance, constancy:— enduring, patience, patient continuance (waiting).

5282. ὑπονοέω **hupŏnŏĕō**, hoop-on-ŏ-eh'-o; from 5259 and 3539; to think under (privately), i.e. to surmise or conjec.:— think, suppose, deem.

5283. ὑπόνοια **hupŏnŏia**, hoop-on'-oy-ah; from 5282; suspicion:— surmising.

5284. ὑποπλέω **hupŏplĕō**, hoop-op-leh'-o; from 5259 and 4126; to sail under the lee of:— sail under.

5285. ὑποπνέω **hupŏpnĕō**, hoop-op-neh'-o; from 5259 and 4154; to breathe gently, i.e. breeze:— blow softly.

5286. ὑποπόδιον **hupŏpŏdiŏn**, hoop-op-od'-ee-on; neut. of a compound of 5259 and 4228; something under the feet, i.e. a foot-rest (fig.):— footstool.

5287. ὑπόστασις **hupŏstasis**, hoop-os'-tas-is; from a compound of 5259 and 2476; a setting under (support), i.e. (fig.) concr. essence, or abstr. assurance (obj. or subj.):— confidence, confident, person, substance.

5288. ὑποστέλλω **hupŏstĕllō**, hoop-os-tel'-lo; from 5259 and 4724; to withhold under (out of sight), i.e. (refl.) to cower or shrink, (fig.) to conceal (reserve):— draw (keep) back, shun, withdraw.

5289. ὑποστολή **hupŏstŏlē**, hoop-os-tol-ay'; from 5288; shrinkage (timidity), i.e. (by impl.) apostasy:— draw back.

5290. ὑποστρέφω **hupŏstrĕphō**, hoop-os-tref'-o; from 5259 and 4762; to turn under (behind), i.e. to return (lit. or fig.):— come again, return (again, back again), turn back (again).

5291. ὑποστρώννυμι **hupŏstrōnnumi**, hoop-os-trone'-noo-mee; from 5259 and 4766; to strew underneath (the feet as a carpet):— spread.

5292. ὑποταγή **hupŏtagē**, hoop-ot-ag-ay'; from 5293; subordination:— subjection.

5293. ὑποτάσσω **hupŏtassō**, hoop-ot-as'-so; from 5259 and 5021; to subordinate; refl. to obey:— be under obedience (obedient), put under, subdue unto, (be, make) subj. (to, unto), be (put) in subjection (to, under), submit self unto.

5294. ὑποτίθημι **hupŏtíthēmi**, *hoop-ot-ith´-ay-mee;* from 5259 and 5087; to *place underneath,* i.e. (fig.) to *hazard,* (refl.) to *suggest:*— lay down, put in remembrance.

5295. ὑποτρέχω **hupŏtrĕchō**, *hoop-ot-rekh´-o;* from 5259 and 5143 (incl. its alt.); to *run under,* i.e. (spec.) to *sail past:*— run under.

5296. ὑποτύπωσις **hupŏtupōsis**, *hoop-ot-oop´-o-sis;* from a compound of 5259 and a der. of 5179; *typification under (after),* i.e. (concr.) a *sketch* (fig.) for *imitation:*— form, pattern.

5297. ὑποφέρω **hupŏphĕrō**, *hoop-of-er´-o;* from 5259 and 5342; to *bear* from *underneath,* i.e. (fig.) to *undergo* hardship:— bear, endure.

5298. ὑποχωρέω **hupŏchōrĕō**, *hoop-okh-o-reh´-o;* from 5259 and 5562; to *vacate down,* i.e. *retire* i.e. *retire* quietly:— go aside, withdraw self.

5299. ὑπωπιάζω **hupōpiazō**, *hoop-o-pee-ad´-zo;* from a compound of 5259 and a der. of 3700; to *hit under the eye* (*buffet* or *disable* an antagonist as a pugilist), i.e. (fig.) to *tease* or *annoy* (into compliance), *subdue* (one's passions):— keep under, weary.

5300. ὗς **hus**, *hoos;* appar. a primary word; a *hog* ("*swine*"):— sow.

5301. ὕσσωπος **hussōpŏs**, *hoos´-so-pos;* of for. or. [231]; "*hyssop*":— hyssop.

5302. ὑστερέω **hustĕrĕō**, *hoos-ter-eh´-o;* from 5306; to *be later,* i.e. (by impl.) to *be inferior;* gen. to *fall short* (be *deficient*):— come behind (short), be destitute, fail, lack, suffer need, (be in) want, be the worse.

5303. ὑστέρημα **hustĕrēma**, *hoos-ter´-ay-mah;* from 5302; a *deficit;* spec. *poverty:*— that which is behind, (that which was) lack (-ing), penury, want.

5304. ὑστέρησις **hustĕrēsis**, *hoos-ter´-ay-sis* from 5302; a *falling short,* i.e. (spec.) *penury:*— want.

5305. ὕστερον **hustĕrŏn**, *hoos´-ter-on;* neut. of 5306 as adv.; *more lately,* i.e. *eventually:*— afterward, (at the) last (of all).

5306. ὕστερος **hustĕrŏs**, *hoos´-ter-os;* comparative from 5259 (in the sense of *behind*); *later:*— latter.

5307. ὑφαντός **huphantŏs**, *hoo-fan-tos´;* from ὑφαίνω **huphainō**, to *weave; woven,* i.e. (perh.) *knitted:*— woven.

5308. ὑψηλός **hupsēlŏs**, *hoop-say-los´;* from 5311; *lofty* (in place or character):— high (-er, -ly) (esteemed).

5309. ὑψηλοφρονέω **hupsēlŏphrŏnĕō**, *hoop-say-lo-fron-eh´-o;* from a compound of 5308 and 5424; to *be lofty in mind,* i.e. *arrogant:*— be highminded.

5310. ὕψιστος **hupsistŏs**, *hoop´-sis-tos;* superl. from the base of 5311; *highest,* i.e. (masc. sing.) the *Supreme* (God), or (neut. plur.) the *heavens:*— most high, highest.

5311. ὕψος **hupsŏs**, *hoop´-sos;* from a der. of 5228; *elevation,* i.e. (abstr.) *altitude,* (spec.) the *sky,* or (fig.) *dignity:*— be exalted, height, (on) high.

5312. ὑψόω **hupsŏō**, *hoop-sŏ´-o;* from 5311; to *elevate* (lit. or fig.):— exalt, lift up.

5313. ὕψωμα **hupsōma**, *hoop´-so-mah;* from 5312; an *elevated* place or thing, i.e. (abstr.) *altitude,* or (by impl.) a *barrier* (fig.):— height, high thing.

Φ

5314. φάγος **phagŏs**, *fag´-os;* from 5315; a *glutton:*— gluttonous.

5315. φάγω **phagō**, *fag´-o;* a primary verb (used as an alt. of 2068 in certain tenses); to *eat* (lit. or fig.):— eat, meat.

φαιλόνης **phailŏnēs**, *fahee-lohn´-ace;* an *alt.* spelling of 5341 which see; found only in 2 Tim. 4:13.

5316. φαίνω **phainō**, *fah´-ee-no;* prol. for the base of 5457; to *lighten* (*shine*), i.e. *show* (tran. or intr., lit. or fig.):— appear, seem, be seen, shine, × think.

5317. Φάλεκ **Phalĕk**, *fal´-ek;* of Heb. or. [6389]; *Phalek* (i.e. *Peleg*), a patriarch:— Phalec.

5318. φανερός **phanĕrŏs**, *fan-er-os´;* from 5316; *shining,* i.e. *apparent* (lit. or fig.); neut. (as adv.) *publicly, extern.:*— abroad, + appear, known, manifest, open [+ -ly], outward (l+ly]).

5319. φανερόω **phanĕrŏō**, *fan-er-ŏ´-o;* from 5318; to *render apparent* (lit. or fig.):— appear, manifestly declare, (make) manifest (forth), shew (self).

5320. φανερῶς **phanĕrōs**, *fan-er-oce´;* adv. from 5318; *plainly,* i.e. *clearly* or *publicly:*— evidently, openly.

5321. φανέρωσις **phanĕrōsis**, *fan-er´-o-sis;* from 5319; *exhibition,* i.e. (fig.) *expression,* (by extens.) a *bestowment:*— manifestation.

5322. φανός **phanŏs**, *fan-os´;* from 5316; a *lightener,* i.e. *light; lantern:*— lantern.

5323. Φανουήλ **Phanŏuēl**, *fan-oo-ale´;* of Heb. or. [6439]; *Phanuël* (i.e. *Penuël*), an Isr.:— Phanuel.

5324. φαντάζω **phantazō**, *fan-tad´-zo;* from a der. of 5316; to *make apparent* i.e. (pass.) to *appear* (neut. part. as noun, a *spectacle*):— sight.

5325. φαντασία **phantasia**, *fan-tas-ee´-ah;* from a der. of 5324; (prop. abstr.) a (vain) *show* ("fantasy"):— pomp.

5326. φάντασμα **phantasma**, *fan´-tas-mah;* from 5324; (prop. concr.) a (mere) *show* ("phantasm"), i.e. *spectre:*— spirit.

5327. φάραγξ **pharagx**, *far´-anx;* prop. streng. from the base of 4008 or rather of 4486; a *gap* or *chasm,* i.e. *ravine* (*winter-torrent*):— valley.

5328. Φαραώ **Pharaō**, *far-ah-o´;* of for. or. [6547]; *Pharaō* (i.e. *Pharoh*), an Eg. king:— Pharaoh.

5329. Φαρές **Pharĕs**, *far-es´;* of Heb. or. [6557]; *Phares* (i.e. *Perets*), an Isr.:— Phares.

5330. Φαρισαῖος **Pharisaiŏs**, *far-is-ah´-yos;* of Heb. or. [comp. 6567]; a *separatist,* i.e. exclusively *relig.;* a *Pharisæan,* i.e. Jewish sectary:— Pharisee.

5331. φαρμακεία **pharmakĕia**, *far-mak-i´-ah;* from 5332; *medication* ("pharmacy"), i.e. (by extens.) *magic* (lit. or fig.):— sorcery, witchcraft.

5332. φαρμακεύς **pharmakĕus**, *far-mak-yoos´;* from φάρμακον **pharmakŏn**, (a *drug,* i.e. spell-giving *potion*); a *druggist* ("pharmacist") or *poisoner,* i.e. (by extens.) a *magician:*— sorcerer.

5333. φαρμακός **pharmakŏs**, *far-mak-os´;* the same as 5332:— sorcerer.

5334. φάσις **phasis**, *fas´-is;* from 5346 (not the same as "phase", which is from 5316); a *saying,* i.e. *report:*— tidings.

5335. φάσκω **phaskō**, *fas´-ko;* prol. from the same as 5346; to *assert:*— affirm, profess, say.

5336. φάτνη **phatnē**, *fat´-nay;* from πατέομαι **patĕŏmai** (to *eat*); a *crib* (for fodder):— manger, stall.

5337. φαῦλος **phaulŏs**, *fŏw´-los;* appar. a primary word; "*foul*" or "*flawy*", i.e. (fig.) *wicked:*— evil.

5338. φέγγος **phĕggŏs**, *feng´-gos;* prob. akin to the base of 5457 [comp. 5350]; *brilliancy:*— light.

5339. φείδομαι **phĕidŏmai**, *fī´-dom-ahee;* of uncert. aff.; to *be chary* of, i.e. (subj.) to *abstain* or (obj.) to *treat leniently:*— forbear, spare.

5340. φειδομένως **phĕidŏmĕnōs**, *fī-dom-en´-oce;* adv. from part. of 5339; *abstemiously,* i.e. *stingily:*— sparingly.

5341. φελόνης **phĕlŏnēs**, *fel-on´-ace* or

φαιλόνης **phailŏnēs**, *fayl-on´-ace;* by transp. for a der. prob. of 5316 (as *showing* outside the other garments); a *mantle* (*surtout*):— cloke.

5342. φέρω **phĕrō**, *fer´-o;* a primary verb (for which other and appar. not cognate ones are used in certain tenses only; namely,

οἴω **ŏiō**, *oy´-o;* and

ἐνέγκω **ĕnĕgkō**, *en-eng´-ko;* to "*bear*" or *carry* (in a very wide application, lit. and fig. as follows):— be, bear, bring (forth), carry, come, + let her drive, be driven, endure, go on, lay, lead, move, reach, rushing, uphold.

5343. φεύγω **phĕugō**, *fyoo´-go;* appar. a primary verb; to *run away* (lit. or fig.); by impl. to *shun;* by anal. to *vanish:*— escape, flee (away).

5344. Φῆλιξ **Phēlix**, *fay´-lix;* of Lat. or.; *happy; Phelix* (i.e. *Felix*), a Rom.:— Felix.

5345. φήμη **phēmē**, *fay´-may;* from 5346; a *saying,* i.e. *rumor* ("fame"):— fame.

5346. φημί **phēmi**, *fay-mee´;* prop. the same as the base of 5457 and 5316; to *show* or *make known* one's thoughts, i.e. *speak* or *say:*— affirm, say. Comp. 3004.

5347. Φῆστος **Phēstŏs**, *face´-tos;* of Lat. der.; *festal; Phestus* (i.e. *Festus*), a Rom.:— Festus.

5348. φθάνω **phthanō**, *fthan´-o;* appar. a primary verb; to *be beforehand,* i.e. *anticipate* or *precede;* by extens. to *have arrived* at:— (already) attain, come, prevent.

5349. φθαρτός **phthartŏs**, *fthar-tos´;*

from 5351; *decayed*, i.e. (by impl.) *perishable*:— corruptible.

5350. φθέγγομαι **phthĕggŏmai**, *fthengʹ-gom-ahee*; prob. akin to 5338 and thus to 5346; to *utter* a clear sound, i.e. (gen.) to *proclaim*:— speak.

5351. φθείρω **phthĕirō**, *fthiʹ-ro*; probably strengthened from φθίω **phthiō** (to *pine* or *waste*); prop. to *shrivel*, (or *wither*, i.e. to *spoil* (by any process) or (gen.) to *ruin* (espec. fig., by mor. influences, to *deprave*):— corrupt (self), defile, destroy.

5352. φθινοπωρινός **phthinŏpōrinŏs**, *fthin-op-o-ree-nosʹ*; from der. of φθίνω **phthinō** (to *wane*; akin to the base of 5351) and 3703 (mean. *late autumn*); *autumnal* (as *stripped* of leaves):— whose fruit withereth.

5353. φθόγγος **phthŏggŏs**, *fthongʹ-gos*; from 5350; *utterance*, i.e. a *musical* note (vocal or instrumental):— sound.

5354. φθονέω **phthŏnĕō**, *fthon-ehʹ-o*; from 5355; to *be jealous* of:— envy.

5355. φθόνος **phthŏnŏs**, *fthonʹ-os*; prob. akin to the base of 5351; *ill-will* (as *detraction*), i.e. *jealousy* (*spite*):— envy.

5356. φθορά **phthŏra**, *fthor-ahʹ*; from 5351; *decay*, i.e. *ruin* (spontaneous or inflicted, lit. or fig.):— corruption. destroy, perish.

5357. φιάλη **phialē**, *fee-alʹ-ay*; of uncert. aff.; a broad shallow *cup* ("phial"):— vial.

5358. φιλάγαθος **philagathŏs**, *fil-agʹ-ath-os*; from 5384 and 18; *fond to good*, i.e. a *promoter of virtue*:— love of good men.

5359. Φιλαδέλφεια **Philadĕlphĕia**, *fil-ad-elʹ-fee-ah*; from Φιλάδελφος **Philadĕlphŏs** (the same as 5361), a king of Pergamos; *Philadelphia*, a place in Asia Minor:— Philadelphia.

5360. φιλαδελφία **philadĕlphia**, *fil-ad-el-feeʹ-ah*; from 5361; *fraternal affection*:— brotherly love (kindness), love of the brethren.

5361. φιλάδελφος **philadĕlphŏs**, *fil-adʹ-el-fos*; from 5384 and 80; *fond of brethren*, i.e. *fraternal*:— love as brethren.

5362. φίλανδρος **philandrŏs**, *filʹ-an-dros*; from 5384 and 435; *fond of man*, i.e. *affectionate* as a wife:— love their husbands.

5363. φιλανθρωπία **philanthrōpia**, *fil-an-thro-peeʹ-ah*; from the same as 5364; *fondness of mankind*, i.e. *benevolence* ("philanthropy"):— kindness, love toward man.

5364. φιλανθρώπως **philanthrōpōs**, *fil-an-throʹ-poce*; adv. from a compound of 5384 and 444; *fondly to man* ("philanthropically"), i.e. *humanely*:— courteously.

5365. φιλαργυρία **philarguria**, *fil-ar-goo-reeʹ-ah*; from 5366; *avarice*:— love of money.

5366. φιλάργυρος **philargurŏs**, *fil-arʹ-goo-ros*; from 5384 and 696; *fond of silver* (*money*), i.e. *avaricious*:— covetous.

5367. φίλαυτος **philautŏs**, *filʹ-ŏw-tos*; from 5384 and 846; *fond of self*, i.e. *selfish*:— lover of own self.

5368. φιλέω **philĕō**, *fil-ehʹ-o*; from 5384; to *be a friend to* (*fond of* (an indiv. or an obj.)), i.e. *have affection* for (denoting *personal* attachment, as a matter of sentiment or feeling; while 25 is wider, embracing espec. the judgment and the *deliberate* assent of the will as a matter of principle, duty and propriety: the two thus stand related very much as 2309 and 1014, or as 2372 and 3563 respectively; the former being chiefly of the *heart* and the latter of the *head*; spec. to *kiss* (as a mark of tenderness):— kiss, love.

5369. φιλήδονος **philēdŏnŏs**, *fil-ayʹ-don-os*; from 5384 and 2237; *fond of pleasure*, i.e. *voluptuous*:— lover of pleasure.

5370. φίλημα **philēma**, *filʹ-ay-mah*; from 5368; a *kiss*:— kiss.

5371. Φιλήμων **Philēmōn**, *fil-ayʹ-mone*; from 5368; *friendly*; *Philemon*, a Chr.:— Philemon.

5372. Φιλητός **Philētŏs**, *fil-ay-tosʹ*; from 5368; *amiable*; *Philetus*, an opposer of Christianity:— Philetus.

5373. φιλία **philia**, *fil-eeʹ-ah*; from 5384; *fondness*:— friendship.

5374. Φιλιππήσιος **Philippēsiŏs**, *fil-ip-pay-ʹsee-os*; from 5375; a *Philippesian* (*Philippian*), i.e. native of Philippi:— Philippian.

5375. Φίλιπποι **Philippŏi**, *filʹ-ip-poy*; plur. of 5376; *Philippi*, a place in Macedonia:— Philippi.

5376. Φίλιππος **Philippŏs**, *filʹ-ip-pos*; from 5384 and 2462; *fond of horses*; *Philippus*, the name of four Isr.:— Philip.

5377. φιλόθεος **philŏthĕŏs**, *fil-othʹ-eh-os*; from 5384 and 2316; *fond of God*, i.e. *pious*:— lover of God.

5378. Φιλόλογος **Philŏlŏgŏs**, *fil-olʹ-og-os*; from 5384 and 3056; *fond of words*, i.e. *talkative* (*argumentative*, *learned*, "philological"); *Philologus*, a Chr.:— Philologus.

5379. φιλονεικία **philŏnĕikia**, *fil-on-i-keeʹ-ah*; from 5380; *quarrelsomeness*, i.e. a *dispute*:— strife.

5380. φιλόνεικος **philŏnĕikŏs**, *fil-onʹ-i-kos*; from 5384 and νεῖκος **nĕikŏs** (a *quarrel*; prob. akin to 3534) *fond of strife*, i.e. *disputatious*:— contentious.

5381. φιλονεξία **philŏnĕxia**, *fil-on-ex-eeʹ-ah*; from 5382; *hospitableness*:— entertain strangers, hospitality.

5382. φιλόξενος **philŏxĕnŏs**, *fil-oxʹ-en-os*; from 5384 and 3581; *fond of guests*, i.e. *hospitable*:— given to (lover of, use) hospitality.

5383. φιλοπρωτεύω **philŏprōtĕuō**, *fil-op-rote-yooʹ-o*; from a compound of 5384 and 4413; to *be fond of being first*, i.e. *ambitious* of distinction:— love to have the preeminence.

5384. φίλος **philŏs**, *feeʹ-los*; prop. *dear*, i.e. a *friend*; act. *fond*, i.e. *friendly* (still as a noun, an *associate*, *neighbor*, etc.):— friend.

5385. φιλοσοφία **philŏsŏphia**, *fil-os-of-eeʹ-ah*; from 5386; "philosophy", i.e. (spec.) Jewish *sophistry*:— philosophy.

5386. φιλόσοφος **philŏsŏphŏs**, *fil-os-ʹof-os*; from 5384 and 4680; *fond of wise things*, i.e. a "philosopher":— philosopher.

5387. φιλόστοργος **philŏstŏrgŏs**, *fil-os-ʹtor-gos*; from 5384 and στοργή **stŏrgē** (*cherishing* one's kindred, espec. parents or children); *fond of natural relatives*, i.e. *fraternal* toward fellow Chr.:— kindly affectioned.

5388. φιλότεκνος **philŏtĕknŏs**, *fil-otʹ-ek-nos*; from 5384 and 5043; *fond of one's children*, i.e. *maternal*:— love their children.

5389. φιλοτιμέομαι **philŏtimĕŏmai**, *fil-ot-im-ehʹ-om-ahee*; mid. voice from a compound of 5384 and 5092; to *be fond of honor*, i.e. *emulous* (*eager* or *earnest* to do something):— labour, strive, study.

5390. φιλοφρόνως **philŏphrŏnōs**, *fil-of-ronʹ-oce*; adv. from 5391; *with friendliness of mind*, i.e. *kindly*:— courteously.

5391. φιλόφρων **philŏphrōn**, *fil-ofʹ-rone*; from 5384 and 5424; *friendly of mind*, i.e. *kind*:— courteous.

5392. φιμόω **phimŏō**, *fee-mŏʹ-o*; from φιμός **phimŏs**, (a *muzzle*); to *muzzle*:— muzzle.

5393. Φλέγων **Phlĕgōn**, *flegʹ-one*; act. part. of the base of 5395; *blazing*; *Phlegon*, a Chr.:— Phlegon.

5394. φλογίζω **phlŏgizō**, *flog-idʹ-zo*; from 5395; to *cause a blaze*, i.e. *ignite* (fig. to *inflame* with passion):— set on fire.

5395. φλόξ **phlŏx**, *flox*; from a primary φλέγω **phlĕgō**, (to "flash" or "flame"); a *blaze*:— flame (-ing).

5396. φλυαρέω **phluarĕō**, *floo-ar-ehʹ-o*; from 5397; to *be a babbler* or *trifler*, i.e. (by impl.) to *berate* idly or mischievously:— prate against.

5397. φλύαρος **phluarŏs**, *flooʹ-ar-os*; from φλύω **phluō**, (to *bubble*); a *garrulous* person, i.e. *prater*:— tattler.

5398. φοβερός **phŏbĕrŏs**, *fob-er-osʹ*; from 5401; *frightful*, i.e. (obj.) *formidable*:— fearful, terrible.

5399. φοβέω **phŏbĕō**, *fob-ehʹ-o*; from 5401; to *frighten*, i.e. (pass.) to *be alarmed*; by anal. to *be in awe* of, i.e. *revere*:— be (+ sore) afraid, fear (exceedingly), reverence.

5400. φόβητρον **phŏbētrŏn**, *fobʹ-ay-tron*; neut. of a der. of 5399; a *frightening* thing, i.e. *terrific* portent:— fearful sight.

5401. φόβος **phŏbŏs**, *fobʹ-os*; from a primary φέβομαι **phĕbŏmai** (to *be put in fear*); *alarm*, or *fright*:— be afraid, + exceedingly, fear, terror.

5402. Φοίβη **Phŏibē**, *foyʹ-bay*; fem. of φοῖβος **phŏibŏs**, (*bright*; prob. akin to the base of 5457); *Phœbe*, a Chr. woman:— Phebe.

5403. Φοινίκη **Phŏinikē**, *foy-neeʹ-kay*; from 5404; *palm*-country; *Phœnice* (or *Phœnicia*), a region of Pal.:— Phenice, Phenicia.

5404. φοῖνιξ **phŏinix**, *foyʹ-nix*; of uncert. der.; a *palm*-tree:— palm (tree).

5405. Φοῖνιξ **Phŏinix**, *foyʹ-nix*; prob. the

same as 5404; *Phœnix*, a place in Crete:— Phenice.

5406. φονεύς **phŏnĕus**, *fon-yooce´*; from 5408; a *murderer* (always of *criminal* [or at least *intentional*] homicide; which 443 does not necessarily imply; while 4607 is a special term for a *public* bandit):— murderer.

5407. φονεύω **phŏnĕuō**, *fon-yoo´-o*; from 5406; to *be a murderer* (of):— kill, do murder, slay.

5408. φόνος **phŏnŏs**, *fon´-os*; from an obs. primary φένω **phĕnō** (to *slay*); *murder*:— murder, + be slain with, slaughter.

5409. φορέω **phŏrĕō**, *for-eh´-o*; from 5411; to *have a burden*, i.e. (by anal.) to *wear* as clothing or a constant accompaniment:— bear, wear.

5410. Φόρον **Phŏrŏn**, *for´-on*; of Lat. or.; a *forum* or market-place; only in comparison with 675; a *station* on the Appian road:— forum.

5411. φόρος **phŏrŏs**, *for´-os*; from 5342; a *load* (as *borne*), i.e. (fig.) a *tax* (prop. an indiv. *assessment* on persons or property; whereas 5056 is usually a gen. *toll* on goods or travel):— tribute.

5412. φορτίζω **phŏrtizō**, *for-tid´-zo*; from 5414; to *load* up (prop. as a vessel or animal), i.e. (fig.) to *overburden* with cerem. (or spiritual anxiety):— lade, be heavy laden.

5413. φορτίον **phŏrtiŏn**, *for-tee´-on*; dimin. of 5414; an *invoice* (as part of *freight*), i.e. (fig.) a *task* or *service*:— burden.

5414. φόρτος **phŏrtŏs**, *for´-tos*; from 5342; something *carried*, i.e. the *cargo* of a ship:— lading.

5415. Φορτουνάτος **Phŏrtŏunatŏs**, *for-too-nat´-os*; of Lat. or.; "*fortunate,*" *Fortunatus*, a Chr.:— Fortunatus.

5416. φραγέλλιον **phragĕlliŏn**, *frag-el´-le-on*; neut. of a der. from the base of 5417; a *whip*, i.e. Rom. *lash* as a public punishment:— scourge.

5417. φραγελλόω **phragĕllŏō**, *frag-el-lŏ´-o*; from a presumed equiv. of the Lat. *flagellum*; to *whip*, i.e. *lash* as a public punishment:— scourge.

5418. φραγμός **phragmŏs**, *frag-mos´*; from 5420; a *fence*, or inclosing *barrier* (lit. or fig.):— hedge (+ round about), partition.

5419. φράζω **phrazō**, *frad´-zo*; prob. akin to 5420 through the idea of *defining*; to *indicate* (by word or act), i.e. (spec.) to *expound*:— declare.

5420. φράσσω **phrassō**, *fras´-so*; appar. a streng. form of the base of 5424; to *fence* or inclose, i.e. (spec.) to *block* up (fig. to *silence*):— stop.

5421. φρέαρ **phrĕar**, *freh´-ar*; of uncert. der.; a *hole* in the ground (dug for obtaining or holding water or other purposes), i.e. a *cistern* or *well*; fig. an *abyss* (as a *prison*):— well, pit.

5422. φρεναπατάω **phrĕnapataō**, *fren-ap-at-ah´-o*; from 5423; to *be a mind-misleader*, i.e. *delude*:— deceive.

5423. φρεναπάτης **phrĕnapatēs**, *fren-*

ap-at´-ace; from 5424 and 539; a *mind-misleader*, i.e. *seducer*:— deceiver.

5424. φρήν **phrēn**, *frane*; prob. from an obs. φράω **phraō** (to *rein* in or *curb*; comp. 5420); the *midrif* (as a *partition* of the body), i.e. (fig. and by impl. of sympathy) the *feelings* (or sensitive nature; by extens. [also in the plur.] the *mind* or cognitive faculties):— understanding.

5425. φρίσσω **phrissō**, *fris´-so*; appar. a primary verb; to "*bristle*" or chill, i.e. *shudder* (*fear*):— tremble.

5426. φρονέω **phrŏnĕō**, *fron-eh´-o*; from 5424; to *exercise the mind*, i.e. *entertain* or *have a sentiment* or *opinion*; by impl. to *be* (mentally) *disposed* (more or less earnestly in a certain direction); intens. to *interest oneself* in (with concern or obedience):— set the affection on, (be) care (-ful), (be like-, + be of one, + be of the same, + let this) mind (-ed), regard, savour, think.

5427. φρόνημα **phrŏnēma**, *fron´-ay-mah*; from 5426; (mental) *inclination* or *purpose*: —(be, + be carnally, + be spiritually) mind (-ed).

5428. φρόνησις **phrŏnēsis**, *fron´-ay-sis*; from 5426; mental *action* or *activity*, i.e. intellectual or mor. *insight*:— prudence, wisdom.

5429. φρόνιμος **phrŏnimŏs**, *fron´-ee-mos*; from 5424; *thoughtful*, i.e. *sagacious* or *discreet* (implying a *cautious* character; while 4680 denotes *practical* skill or acumen; and 4908 indicates rather *intelligence* or mental acquirement); in a bad sense *conceited* (also in the comparative):— wise (-r).

5430. φρονίμως **phrŏnimōs**, *fron-im´-oce*; adv. from 5429; *prudently*:— wisely.

5431. φροντίζω **phrŏntizō**, *fron-tid´-zo*; from a der. of 5424; to *exercise thought*, i.e. *be anxious*:— be careful.

5432. φρουρέω **phrŏurĕō**, *froo-reh´-o*; from a compound of 4253 and 3708; to *be a watcher in advance*, i.e. to *mount guard* as a sentinel (*post spies* at gates); fig. to *hem in, protect*:— keep (with a garrison). Comp. 5083.

5433. φρυάσσω **phruassō**, *froo-as´-so*; akin to 1032, 1031; to *snort* (as a spirited horse), i.e. (fig.) to *make a tumult*:— rage.

5434. φρύγανον **phruganŏn**, *froo´-gan-on*; neut. of a presumed der. of φρύγω **phrugō** (to *roast* or *parch*; akin to the base of 5395); something *desiccated*, i.e. a dry *twig*:— stick.

5435. Φρυγία **Phrugia**, *froog-ee-ah´*; prob. of for. or.; *Phrygia*, a region of Asia Minor:— Phrygia.

5436. Φύγελλος **Phugĕllŏs**, *foog´-el-los*; prob. from 5343; *fugitive*; *Phygellus*, an apostate Chr.:— Phygellus.

5437. φυγή **phugē**, *foog-ay´*; from 5343; a *fleeing*, i.e. *escape*:— flight.

5438. φυλακή **phulakē**, *foo-lak-ay´*; from 5442; a *guarding* or (concr. *guard*), the act, the person; fig. the place, the condition, or (spec.) the time (as a division of day or night), lit. or

fig.:— cage, hold, (im-) prison (-ment), ward, watch.

5439. φυλακίζω **phulakizō**, *foo-lak-id´-zo*; from 5441; to *incarcerate*:— imprison.

5440. φυλακτήριον **phulaktēriŏn**, *foo-lak-tay´-ree-on*; neut. of a der. of 5442; a *guard-case*, i.e. "*phylactery*" for wearing slips of Scripture texts:— phylactery.

5441. φύλαξ **phulax**, *foo´-lax*; from 5442; a *watcher* or *sentry*:— keeper.

5442. φυλάσσω **phulassō**, *foo-las´-so*; prob. from 5443 through the idea of *isolation*; to *watch*, i.e. *be on guard* (lit. or fig.); by impl. to *preserve, obey, avoid*:— beware, keep (self), observe, save. Comp. 5083.

5443. φυλή **phulē**, *foo-lay´*; from 5453 (comp. 5444); an *offshoot*, i.e. *race* or *clan*:— kindred, tribe.

5444. φύλλον **phullŏn**, *fool´-lon*; from the same as 5443; a *sprout*, i.e. *leaf*:— leaf.

5445. φύραμα **phurama**, *foo´-ram-ah*; from a prol. form of φύρω **phurō** (to *mix* a liquid with a solid; perh. akin to 5453 through the idea of *swelling* in bulk), mean to *knead*; a *mass* of dough:— lump.

5446. φυσικός **phusikŏs**, *foo-see-kos´*; from 5449; "*physical*", i.e. (by impl.) *instinctive*:— natural. Comp. 5591.

5447. φυσικῶς **phusikōs**, *foo-see-koce´*; adv. from 5446; "*physically*", i.e. (by impl.) *instinctively*:— naturally.

5448. φυσιόω **phusiŏō**, *foo-see-ŏ´-o*; from 5449 in the primary sense of *blowing*; to *inflate*, i.e. (fig.) *make proud* (*haughty*):— puff up.

5449. φύσις **phusis**, *foo´-sis*; from 5453; *growth* (by *germination* or *expansion*), i.e. (by impl.) natural *production* (lineal *descent*); by extens. a *genus* or *sort*; fig. native *disposition, constitution* or *usage*:— ([man-]) kind, nature ([-all]).

5450. φυσίωσις **phusiōsis**, *foo-see´-o-sis*; from 5448; *inflation*, i.e. (fig.) *haughtiness*:— swelling.

5451. φυτεία **phutĕia**, *foo-ti´-ah*; from 5452; *trans-planting*, i.e. (concr.) a *shrub* or *vegetable*:— plant.

5452. φυτεύω **phutĕuō**, *foot-yoo´-o*; from a der. of 5453; to *set out* in the earth, i.e. *implant*; fig. to *instil* doctrine:— plant.

5453. φύω **phuō**, *foo´-o*; a primary verb; prob. orig. to "*puff*" or blow, i.e. to *swell* up; but only used in the impl. sense, to *germinate* or *grow* (*sprout, produce*), lit. or fig.:— spring (up).

5454. φωλεός **phōlĕŏs**, *fo-leh-os´*; of uncert. der.; a *burrow* or *lurking-place*:— hole.

5455. φωνέω **phōnĕō**, *fo-neh´-o*; from 5456; to emit a *sound* (animal, human or instrumental); by impl. to *address* in words or by name, also in imitation:— call (for), crow, cry.

5456. φωνή **phōnē**, *fo-nay´*; prob. akin to 5316 through the idea of *disclosure*; a *tone* (articulate, bestial or artif.); by impl. an *address* (for any purpose), *saying* or *language:*— noise, sound, voice.

5457. φῶς **phōs**, *foce;* from an obs. φάω **phaō** (to *shine*, or make *manifest*, espec. by *rays;* comp. *5316, 5346); luminousness* (in the widest application, nat. or artif., abstr. or concr., lit. or fig.):— fire, light.

5458. φωστήρ **phōstēr**, *foce-tare´;* from *5457;* an *illuminator*, i.e. (concr.) a *luminary*, or (abstr.) *brilliancy:*— light.

5459. φωσφόρος **phōsphŏrŏs**, *foce-for´-os;* from *5457* and *5342; light-bearing* ("phosphorus"), i.e. (spec.) the *morning-star* (fig.):— day star.

5460. φωτεινός **phōtĕinŏs**, *fo-ti-nos´;* from *5457; lustrous*, i.e. *transparent* or *well-illuminated* (fig.):— bright, full of light.

5461. φωτίζω **phōtizō**, *fo-tid´-zo;* from *5457;* to *shed rays*, i.e. to *shine* or (tran.) to *brighten* up (lit. or fig.):— enlighten, illuminate, (bring to, give) light, make to see.

5462. φωτισμός **phōtismŏs**, *fo-tis-mos´;* from *5461; illumination* (fig.):— light.

X

5463. χαίρω **chairō**, *khah´-ee-ro;* a primary verb; to be "*cheer*"*ful*, i.e. calmly *happy* or well-off; impers. espec. as salutation (on meeting or parting), *be well:*— farewell, be glad, God speed, greeting, hall, joy (- fully), rejoice.

5464. χάλαζα **chalaza**, *khal´-ad-zah;* prob. from *5465; hail:*— hail.

5465. χαλάω **chalaō**, *khal-ah´-o;* from the base of *5490;* to *lower* (as into a *void*):— let down, strike.

5466. Χαλδαῖος **Chaldaiŏs**, *khal-dah´-yos;* prob. of Heb. or. [3778]; a *Chaldæan* (i.e. *Kasdi*), or native or the region of the lower Euphrates:— Chaldæan.

5467. χαλεπός **chalĕpŏs**, *khal-ep-os´;* perh. from *5465* through the idea of *reducing* the strength; *difficult*, i.e. *dangerous*, or (by impl.) *furious:*— fierce, perilous.

5468. χαλιναγωγέω **chalinagōgĕō**, *khal-in-ag-ogue-eh´-o;* from a compound of *5469* and the redupl. form of *71;* to *be a bit-leader*, i.e. to *curb* (fig.):— bridle.

5469. χαλινός **chalinŏs**, *khal-ee-nos´;* from *5465;* a *curb* or *head-stall* (as *curbing* the spirit):— bit, bridle.

5470. χάλκεος **chalkĕŏs**, *khal´-keh-os;* from *5475; coppery:*— brass.

5471. χαλκεύς **chalkĕus**, *khalk-yooce´;* from *5475;* a *copper-worker* or *brazier:*— coppersmith.

5472. χαλκηδών **chalkēdōn**, *khal-kay-dohn´;* from *5475* and perh. *1491; copper-like*, i.e. "*chalcedony*":— chalcedony.

5473. χαλκίον **chalkiŏn**, *khal-kee-on;* dimin. from *5475;* a *copper dish:*— brazen vessel.

5474. χαλκολίβανον **chalkŏlibanŏn**, *khal-kol-ib´-an-on;* neut. of a compound of *5475* and *3030* (in the impl. mean of *whiteness* or *brilliancy); burnished copper*, an alloy of copper (or

gold) and silver having a brilliant lustre:— fine brass.

5475. χαλκός **chalkŏs**, *khal-kos´;* perh. from *5465* through the idea of *hollowing* out as a vessel (this metal being chiefly used for that purpose); *copper* (the substance, or some implement or coin made of it):— brass, money.

5476. χαμαί **chamai**, *kham-ah´-ee;* adv. perh. from the base of *5490* through the idea of a *fissure* in the soil; *earthward*, i.e. *prostrate:*— on (to) the ground.

5477. Χαναάν **Chanaan**, *khan-ah´-an;* of Heb. or. [3667]; *Chanaan* (i.e. *Kenaan*), the early name of Pal.:— Chanaan.

5478. Χαναναῖος **Chanaanaiŏs**, *khan-ah-an-ah´-yos;* from *5477;* a *Chanaanæan* (i.e. *Kenaanite*), or native of Gentile Pal.:— of Canaan.

5479. χαρά **chara**, *khar-ah´;* from *5463; cheerfulness*, i.e. calm *delight:*— gladness, × greatly, (× be exceeding) joy (-ful, -fully,fulness, -ous).

5480. χάραγμα **charagma**, *khar´-agmah;* from the same as *5482;* a *scratch* or *etching*, i.e. *stamp* (as a *badge* of servitude), or *sculptured* figure (*statue*):— graven, mark.

5481. χαρακτήρ **charaktēr**, *khar-aktare´;* from the same as *5482;* a *graver* (the tool or the person), i.e. (by impl.) *engraving* (["*character*"], the *figure* stamped, i.e. an exact *copy* or [fig.] *representation*):— express image.

5482. χάραξ **charax**, *khar´-ax;* from χαράσσω **charassō** (to *sharpen*, to a point; akin to *1125* through the idea of *scratching*); a *stake*, i.e. (by impl.) a *palisade* or *rampart* (military *mound* for circumvallation in a siege):— trench.

5483. χαρίζομαι **charizŏmai**, *khar-id´-zom-ahee;* mid. voice from *5485;* to grant as a *favor*, i.e. gratuitously, in kindness, pardon or rescue:— deliver, (frankly) forgive, (freely) give, grant.

5484. χάριν **charin**, *khar´-in;* acc. of *5485* as prep.; through *favor of*, i.e. *on account of:*— be- (for) cause of, for sake of, + ... fore, × reproachfully.

5485. χάρις **charis**, *khar´-ece;* from *5463; graciousness* (as *gratifying*), of manner or act (abstr. or concr.; lit., fig., or spiritual; espec. the divine influence upon the heart, and its reflection in the life; incl. *gratitude*):— acceptable, benefit, favour, gift, grace (-ious), joy, liberality, pleasure, thank (-s, worthy).

5486. χάρισμα **charisma**, *khar´-is-mah;* from *5483;* a (divine) *gratuity*, i.e. *deliverance* (from danger or passion); (spec.) a (spiritual) *endowment*, i.e. (subj.) relig. *qualification*, or (obj.) miraculous *faculty:*— (free) gift.

5487. χαριτόω **charitŏō**, *khar-ee-tŏ´-o;* from *5485;* to *grace*, i.e. indue with special *honor:*— make accepted, be highly favoured.

5488. Χαρράν **Charrhan**, *khar-hran´;* of Heb. or. [2771]; *Charrhan* (i.e. *Charan*), a place in Mesopotamia:— Charran.

5489. χάρτης **chartēs**, *khar´-tace;* from the same as *5482;* a *sheet* ("chart") of

writing-material (as to be *scribbled* over):— paper.

5490. χάσμα **chasma**, *khas´-mah;* from a form of an obs. primary χάω **chaō**, to "gape" or "yawn"); a "*chasm*" or *vacancy* (impassable *interval*):— gulf.

5491. χεῖλος **cheilŏs**, *khi´-los;* from a form of the same as *5490;* a *lip* (as a *pouring* place); fig. a *margin* (of water):— lip, shore.

5492. χειμάζω **cheimazō**, *khi-mad´-zo;* from the same as *5494;* to *storm*, i.e. (pass.) to *labor under a gale:*— be tossed with tempest.

5493. χείμαρρος **cheimarrhŏs**, *khi´-mar-hros;* from the base of *5494* and *4482;* a *storm-runlet*, i.e. *winter-torrent:*— brook.

5494. χειμών **cheimōn**, *khi-mone´;* from a der. of χέω **chĕō**, (to *pour*; akin to the base of *5490* through the idea of a *channel*), mean. a *storm* (as *pouring* rain); by impl. the *rainy* season, i.e. *winter:*— tempest, foul weather, winter.

5495. χείρ **cheir**, *khire;* perh. from the base of *5494* in the sense of its congener the base of *5490* (through the idea of *hollowness* for grasping); the *hand* (lit. or fig. [power]; espec. [by Heb.] a *means* or *instrument*):— hand.

5496. χειραγωγέω **cheiragōgĕō**, *khi-rag-ogue-eh´-o;* from *5497;* to be a *hand-leader*, i.e. to *guide* (a blind person):— lead by the hand.

5497. χειραγωγός **cheiragōgŏs**, *khi-rag-o-gos´;* from *5495* and a redupl. form of *71;* a *hand-leader*, i.e. personal *conductor* (of a blind person):— some to lead by the hand.

5498. χειρόγραφον **cheirŏgraphŏn**, *khi-rog´-raf-on;* neut. of a compound of *5495* and *1125;* something *hand-written* ("*chirograph*"), i.e. a *manuscript* (spec. a legal *document* or *bond* [fig.]):— handwriting.

5499. χειροποίητος **cheirŏpŏiētŏs**, *khi-rop-oy´-ay-tos;* from *5495* and a der. of *4160; manufactured*, i.e. of *human construction:*— made by (make with) hands.

5500. χειροτονέω **cheirŏtŏnĕō**, *khi-rot-on-eh´-o;* from a comp. of *5495* and τείνω **tĕinō** (to *stretch*); to be a *hand-reacher*, or *voter* (by raising the hand), i.e. (gen.) to *select* or *appoint:*— choose, ordain.

5501. χείρων **cheirōn**, *khi´-rone;* irreg. comp. of *2556;* from an obs. equiv. χέρης **chĕrēs** (of uncert. der.); *more evil* or *aggravated* (phys., ment. or mor.):— sorer, worse.

5502. χερουβίμ **chĕrŏubim**, *kher-oo-beem´;* plur. of Heb. or. [3742]; "*cherubim*" (i.e. *cherubs* or *kerubim*):— cherubims.

5503. χήρα **chēra**, *khay´-rah;* fem. of a presumed der. appar. from the base of *5490* through the idea of *deficiency;* a *widow* (as *lacking* a husband), lit. or fig.:— widow.

5504. χθές **chthĕs**, *khthes;* of uncert. der.; "*yesterday*"; by extens. *in time past* or *hitherto:*— yesterday.

5505. χιλιάς **chilias**, *khil-ee-as´*; from 5507; one *thousand* ("*chiliad*"):— thousand.

5506. χιλίαρχος **chiliarchŏs**, *khil-ee´-ar-khos*; from 5507 and 757; the *commander of a thousand* soldiers ("*chiliarch*"), i.e. *colonel*:— (chief, high) captain.

5507. χίλιοι **chiliŏi**, *khil´-ee-oy*; plur. of uncert. aff.; a *thousand*:— thousand.

5508. Χίος **Chiŏs**, *khee´-os*; of uncert. der.; *Chios*, an island in the Mediterranean:— Chios.

5509. χιτών **chitōn**, *khee-tone´*; of for. or. [3801]; a *tunic* or *shirt*:— clothes, coat, garment.

5510. χιών **chiōn**, *khee-one´*; perh. akin to the base of 5490 (5465) or 5494 (as *descending* or *empty*); *snow*:— snow.

5511. χλαμύς **chlamus**, *khlam-ooce´*; of uncert. der.; a military *cloak*:— robe.

5512. χλευάζω **chlĕuazō**, *khlyoo-ad´-zo*; from a der. prob. of 5491; to *throw out the lip*, i.e. *jeer* at:— mock.

5513. χλιαρός **chliarŏs**, *khlee-ar-os´*; from χλίω chliō, (to *warm*); *tepid*:— lukewarm.

5514. Χλόη **Chlŏē**, *khlŏ´-ay*; fem. of appar. a primary word; "*green*"; *Chlŏē*, a Chr. female:— Chloe.

5515. χλωρός **chlōrŏs**, *khlo-ros´*; from the same as 5514; *greenish*, i.e. *verdant*, *dun-colored*:— green, pale.

5516. χξϛ **chi xi stigma**, *khee xee stig´-ma*; the 22nd, 14th and an obs. letter (4742 as a *cross*) of the Greek alphabet (intermediate between the 5th and 6th), used as numbers; denoting respectively 600, 60 and 6; 666 as a numeral:— six hundred threescore and six.

5517. χοϊκός **chŏïkŏs**, *khŏ-ik-os´*; from 5522; *dusty* or *dirty* (*soil*-like), i.e. (by impl.) *terrene*:— earthy.

5518. χοῖνιξ **chŏinix**, *khoy´-nix*; of uncertain der.; a *chœnix* or certain dry measure:— measure.

5519. χοῖρος **chŏirŏs**, *khoy´-ros*; of uncert. der.; a *hog*:— swine.

5520. χολάω **chŏlaō**, *khol-ah´-o*; from 5521; to *be bilious*, i.e. (by impl.) *irritable* (*enraged*, "*choleric*"):— be angry.

5521. χολή **chŏlē**, *khol-ay´*; fem. of an equiv. perh. akin to the same as 5514 (from the *greenish* hue); "*gall*" or *bile*, i.e. (by anal.) *poison* or an *anodyne* (wormwood, poppy, etc.):— gall.

5522. χόος **chŏŏs**, *khŏ´-os*; from the base of 5494; a *heap* (as *poured* out), i.e. *rubbish*; loose *dirt*:— dust.

5523. Χοραζίν **Chŏrazin**, *khor-ad-zin´*; of uncert. der.; *Chorazin*, a place in Pal.:— Chorazin.

5524. χορηγέω **chŏrēgĕō**, *khor-ayg-eh´-o*; from a compound of 5525 and 71; to be a *dance-leader*, i.e. (gen.) to *furnish*:— give, minister.

5525. χορός **chŏrŏs**, *khor-os´*; of uncert. der.; a *ring*, i.e. round *dance* ("*choir*"):— dancing.

5526. χορτάζω **chŏrtazō**, *khor-tad´-zo*; from 5528; to *fodder*, i.e. (gen.) to *gorge* (*supply food* in abundance):— feed, fill, satisfy.

5527. χόρτασμα **chŏrtasma**, *khor´-tas-mah*; from 5526; *forage*, i.e. *food*:— sustenance.

5528. χόρτος **chŏrtŏs**, *khor´-tos*; appar. a primary word; a "*court*" or "*garden*", i.e. (by impl. of *pasture*) *herbage* or *vegetation*:— blade, grass, hay.

5529. Χουζᾶς **Chŏuzas**, *khood-zas´*; of uncert. or.: *Chuzas*, an officer of Herod:— Chuza.

5530. χράομαι **chraŏmai**, *khrah´-om-ahee*; mid. voice of a primary verb (perh. rather from 5495, to *handle*); to *furnish* what is needed; (give an *oracle*, "*graze*" [touch slightly], *light* upon, etc.), i.e. (by impl.) to *employ* or (by extens.) to *act toward* one in a given manner:— entreat, use. Comp. 5531; 5534.

5531. χράω **chraō**, *khrah´-o*; prob. the same as the base of 5530; to *loan*:— lend.

5532. χρεία **chrĕia**, *khri´-ah*; from the base of 5530 or 5534; *employment*, i.e. an *affair*; also (by impl.) *occasion*, *demand*, *requirement* or *destitution*:— business, lack, necessary (-ity), need (-ful), use, want.

5533. χρεωφειλέτης **chrĕōphĕilĕtēs**, *khreh-o-fi-let´-ace*; from a der. of 5531 and 3781; a *loan-ower*, i.e. *indebted* person:— debtor.

5534. χρή **chrē**, *khray*; third pers. sing. of the same as 5530 or 5531 used impers.; it *needs* (*must* or *should*) be:— ought.

5535. χρῄζω **chrēizō**, *khrade´-zo*; from 5532; to *make* (i.e. *have*) *necessity*, i.e. *be in want of*:— (have) need.

5536. χρῆμα **chrēma**, *khray´-mah*; something *useful* or *needed*, i.e. *wealth*, *price*:— money, riches.

5537. χρηματίζω **chrēmatizō**, *khray-mat-id´-zo*; from 5536; to *utter an oracle* (comp. the orig. sense of 5530), i.e. *divinely intimate*; by impl. (comp. the *secular sense* of 5532) to constitute a *firm* for business, i.e. (gen.) *bear* as a *title*:— be called, be admonished (warned) of God, reveal, speak.

5538. χρηματισμός **chrēmatismŏs**, *khray-mat-is-mos´*; from 5537; a *divine response* or *revelation*:— answer of God.

5539. χρήσιμος **chrēsimŏs**, *khray´-see-mos*; from 5540; *serviceable*:— profit.

5540. χρῆσις **chrēsis**, *khray´-sis*; from 5530; *employment*, i.e. (spec.) sexual *intercourse* (as an *occupation* of the body):— use.

5541. χρηστεύομαι **chrēstĕuŏmai**, *khraste-yoo´-om-ahee*; mid. voice from 5543; to *show oneself useful*, i.e. *act benevolently*:— be kind.

5542. χρηστολογία **chrēstŏlŏgia**, *khrase-tol-og-ee´-ah*; from a compound of 5543 and 3004; *fair speech*, i.e. *plausibility*:— good words.

5543. χρηστός **chrēstŏs**, *khrase-tos´*; from 5530; *employed*, i.e. (by impl.) *use-ful* (in manner or morals):— better, easy, good (-ness), gracious, kind.

5544. χρηστότης **chrēstŏtēs**, *khray-stot´-ace*; from 5543; *usefulness*, i.e. mor. *excellence* (in character or demeanor):— gentleness, good (-ness), kindness.

5545. χρίσμα **chrisma**, *khris´-mah*; from 5548; an *unguent* or *smearing*, i.e. (fig.) the spec. *endowment* ("chrism") of the Holy Spirit:— anointing, unction.

5546. Χριστιανός **Christianŏs**, *khris-tee-an-os´*; from 5547; a *Christian*, i.e. *follower* of Christ:— Christian.

5547. Χριστός **Christŏs**, *khris-tos´*; from 5548; *anointed*, i.e. the *Messiah*, an epithet of Jesus:— Christ.

5548. χρίω **chriō**, *khree´-o*; prob. akin to 5530 through the idea of *contact*; to *smear* or *rub* with oil, i.e. (by impl.) to *consecrate* to an office or relig. service:— anoint.

5549. χρονίζω **chrŏnizō**, *khron-id´-zo*; from 5550; to *take time*, i.e. *linger*:— delay, tarry.

5550. χρόνος **chrŏnŏs**, *khron´-os*; of uncert. der.; a space of *time* (in gen., and thus prop. distinguished from 2540, which designates a *fixed* or special occasion; and from 165, which denotes a particular *period*) or *interval*; by extens. an indiv. *opportunity*; by impl. *delay*:— + years old, season, space, (× often-) time (-s), (a) while.

5551. χρονοτριβέω **chrŏnŏtribĕō**, *khron-ot-rib-eh´-o*; from a presumed compound of 5550 and the base of 5147; to be a *time-wearer*, i.e. to *procrastinate* (*linger*):— spend time.

5552. χρύσεος **chrusĕŏs**, *khroo´-seh-os*; from 5557; made of *gold*:— of gold, golden.

5553. χρυσίον **chrusiŏn**, *khroo-see´-on*; dimin. of 5557; a *golden* article, i.e. gold *plating*, *ornament*, or *coin*:— gold.

5554. χρυσοδακτύλιος **chrusŏdaktuliŏs**, *khroo-sod-ak-too´-lee-os*; from 5557 and 1146; *gold-ringed*, i.e. *wearing* a golden finger-ring or similar *jewelry*:— with a gold ring.

5555. χρυσόλιθος **chrusŏlithŏs**, *khroo-sol´-ee-thos*; from 5557 and 3037; *gold-stone*, i.e. a *yellow gem* ("chrysolite"):— chrysolite.

5556. χρυσόπρασος **chrusŏprasŏs**, *khroo-sop´-ras-os*; from 5557 and πράσον prason (a *leek*); a *greenish-yellow* gem ("chrysoprase"):— chrysoprase.

5557. χρυσός **chrusŏs**, *khroo-sos´*; perh. from the base of 5530 (through the idea of the *utility* of the metal); *gold*; by extens. a *golden* article, as an ornament or coin:— gold.

5558. χρυσόω **chrusŏō**, *khroo-sŏ´-o*; from 5557; to *gild*, i.e. *bespangle* with golden ornaments:— deck.

5559. χρώς **chrōs**, *khroce*; prob. akin to the base of 5530 through the idea of *handling*; the *body* (prop. its *surface* or *skin*):— body.

5560. χωλός **chōlŏs**, *kho-los´*; appar. a

primary word; "*halt*," i.e. *limping:*— cripple, halt, lame.

5561. χώρα **chōra**, *kho´-rah;* fem. of a der. of the base of *5490* through the idea of *empty* expanse; *room,* i.e. a space of *territory* (more or less extens.; often incl. its inhab.):— coast, county, fields, ground, land, region. Comp. *5117.*

5562. χωρέω **chōrĕō**, *kho-reh´-o;* from *5561;* to *be* in (*give*) space, i.e. (intr.) to *pass, enter,* or (tran.) to *hold, admit* (lit. or fig.):— come, contain, go; have place, (can, be room to) receive.

5563. χωρίζω **chōrizō**, *kho-rid´-zo;* from *5561;* to *place room* between, i.e. *part;* refl. to *go away:*— depart, put asunder, separate.

5564. χωρίον **chōriŏn**, *kho-ree´-on;* dimin. of *5561;* a *spot* or *plot* of ground:— field, land, parcel of ground, place, possession.

5565. χωρίς **chōris**, *kho-rece´;* adv. from *5561;* at a *space,* i.e. *separately* or *apart* from (often as prep.):— beside, by itself, without.

5566. χῶρος **chōrŏs**, *kho´-ros;* of Lat. or.; the *north-west* wind:— north west.

Ψ

5567. ψάλλω **psallō**, *psal´-lo;* probably strengthened from ψάω **psaō**, (to *rub* or *touch* the surface; comp. *5597*); to *twitch* or *twang,* i.e. to *play* on a stringed instrument (*celebrate* the divine worship *with music* and accompanying odes):— make melody, sing (psalms).

5568. ψαλμός **psalmŏs**, *psal-mos´;* from *5567;* a set piece of *music,* i.e. a sacred *ode* (accompanied with the voice, harp or other instrument; a "*psalm*"); collect. the book of the *Psalms:*— psalm. Comp. *5603.*

5569. ψευδάδελφος **psĕudadĕlphŏs**, *psyoo-dad´-el-fos;* from *5571* and *80;* a *spurious brother,* i.e. *pretended associate:*— false brethren.

5570. ψευδαπόστολος **psĕudapŏstŏlŏs**, *psyoo-dap-os´-tol-os;* from *5571* and *652;* a *spurious apostle,* i.e. *pretended preacher:*— false teacher.

5571. ψευδής **psĕudēs**, *psyoo-dace´;* from *5574;* *untrue,* i.e. *erroneous, deceitful, wicked:*— false, liar.

5572. ψευδοδιδάσκαλος **psĕudŏdidaskalŏs**, *psyoo-dod-id-as´-kal-os;* from *5571* and *1320;* a *spurious teacher,* i.e. *propagator* of erroneous Chr. *doctrine:*— false teacher.

5573. ψευδολόγος **psĕudŏlŏgŏs**, *psyoo-dol-og´-os;* from *5571* and *3004; mendacious,* i.e. *promulgating erroneous* Chr. *doctrine:*— speaking lies.

5574. ψεύδομαι **psĕudŏmai**, *psyoo-dom-ahee;* mid. voice of an appar. primary verb; to *utter an untruth* or attempt to *deceive* by falsehood:— falsely, lie.

5575. ψευδομάρτυρ **psĕudŏmartur**, *psyoo-dom-ar´-toor;* from *5571* and a kindred form of *3144;* a *spurious witness,* i.e. *bearer of untrue testimony:*— false witness.

5576. ψευδομαρτυρέω **psĕudŏmarturĕō**, *psyoo-dom-ar-too-reh´-o;* from *5575;* to be an *untrue testifier,* i.e. offer *falsehood in evidence:*— be a false witness.

5577. ψευδομαρτυρία **psĕudŏmarturia**, *psyoo-dom-ar-too-ree´-ah;* from *5575; untrue testimony:*— false witness.

5578. ψευδοπροφήτης **psĕudŏprŏphētēs**, *psyoo-dop-rof-ay´-tace;* from *5571* and *4396;* a *spurious prophet,* i.e. *pretended* foreteller or relig. *impostor:*— false prophet.

5579. ψεῦδος **psĕudŏs**, *psyoo´-dos;* from *5574;* a *falsehood:*— lie, lying.

5580. ψευδόχριστος **psĕudŏchristŏs**, *psyoo-dokh´-ris-tos;* from *5571* and *5547;* a *spurious Messiah:*— false Christ.

5581. ψευδώνυμος **psĕudōnumŏs**, *psyoo-do´-noo-mos;* from *5571* and *3686; untruly named:*— falsely so called.

5582. ψεῦσμα **psĕusma**, *psyoos´-mah;* from *5574;* a *fabrication,* i.e. *falsehood:*— lie.

5583. ψεύστης **psĕustēs**, *psyoos-tace´;* from *5574;* a *falsifier:*— liar.

5584. ψηλαφάω **psēlaphaō**, *psay-laf-ah´-o;* from the base of *5567* (comp. *5586*); to *manipulate,* i.e. *verify* by contact; fig. to *search for:*— feel after, handle, touch.

5585. ψηφίζω **psēphizō**, *psay-fid´-zo;* from *5586;* to *use pebbles* in enumeration, i.e. (gen.) to *compute:*— count.

5586. ψῆφος **psēphŏs**, *psay´-fos;* from the same as *5584;* a *pebble* (as worn smooth by *handling*), i.e. (by impl. of use as a *counter* or *ballot*) a *verdict* (of acquittal) or *ticket* (of admission); a *vote:*— stone, voice.

5587. ψιθυρισμός **psithurismŏs**, *psith-oo-ris-mos´;* from a der. of ψίθος **psithŏs** (a *whisper;* by impl. a *slander;* prob. akin to *5574*); *whispering,* i.e. secret *detraction:*— whispering.

5588. ψιθυριστής **psithuristēs**, *psith-oo-ris-tace´;* from the same as *5587;* a secret *calumniator:*— whisperer.

5589. ψιχίον **psichiŏn**, *psikh-ee´-on;* dimin. from a der. of the base of *5567* (mean. a *crumb*); a *little bit* or *morsel:*— crumb.

5590. ψυχή **psuchē**, *psoo-khay´;* from *5594; breath,* i.e. (by impl.) *spirit,* abstr. or concr. (the *animal* sentient principle only; thus distinguished on the one hand from *4151,* which is the rational and immortal *soul;* and on the other from *2222,* which is mere *vitality,* even of plants: these terms thus exactly correspond respectively to the Heb. *5315, 7307* and *2416*):— heart (+ -ily), life, mind, soul, + us, + you.

5591. ψυχικός **psuchikŏs**, *psoo-khee-kos´;* from *5590; sensitive,* i.e. *animate* (in distinction on the one hand from *4152,* which is the higher or *renovated* nature; and on the other from *5446,* which is the lower or *bestial* nature):— natural, sensual.

5592. ψύχος **psuchŏs**, *psoo´-khos;* from *5594*; *coldness:*— cold.

5593. ψυχρός **psuchrŏs**, *psoo-chros´;* from *5592; chilly* (lit. or fig.):— cold.

5594. ψύχω **psuchō**, *psoo´-kho;* a primary verb; to *breathe* (voluntarily but *gently,* thus differing on the one hand from *4154,* which denotes prop. a *forcible* respiration; and on the other from the base of *109,* which refers prop. to an inanimate *breeze*), i.e. (by impl. of reduction of temperature by evaporation) to *chill* (fig.):— wax cold.

5595. ψωμίζω **psōmizō**, *pso-mid´-zo;* from the base of *5596;* to *supply* with *bits,* i.e. (gen.) to *nourish:*— (bestow to) feed.

5596. ψωμίον **psōmiŏn**, *pso-mee´-on;* dimin. from a der. of the base of *5597;* a *crumb* or *morsel* (as if *rubbed off*), i.e. a *mouthful:*— sop.

5597. ψώχω **psōchō**, *pso´-kho;* prol. from the same base as *5567;* to *triturate,* i.e. (by anal.) to *rub* out (kernels from husks with the fingers or hand):— rub.

Ω

5598. Ω **Ō**, i.e. ὤμεγα **ōmĕga**, *o´-meg-ah;* the last letter of the Greek alphabet, i.e. (fig.) the *finality:*— Omega.

5599. ὦ **ō**, *o;* a primary interj.; as a sign of the voc. *O;* as a note of exclamation, *oh:*— O.

5600. ὦ **ō**, *o;* incl. the oblique forms, as well as ἦς **ēs**, *ace;* ἦ **ē**, *ay;* etc.; the subjunctive of *1510;* (*may, might, can, could, would, should, must,* etc.; also with *1487* and its comp., as well as with other particles) *be:*— + appear, are, (may, might, should) be, × have, is, + pass the flower of her age, should stand, were.

5601. Ὠβήδ **Obēd**, *o-bade´*

or Ἰωβήδ **Iōbēd**, *yo-bade´;* of Heb. or. [5744]; *Obed,* an Isr.:— Obed.

5602. ὧδε **hōdĕ**, *ho´-deh;* from an adv. form of *3592; in this* same spot, i.e. *here* or *hither:*— here, hither, (in) this place, there.

5603. ᾠδή **ōdē**, *o-day´;* from *103;* a *chant* or "*ode*" (the gen. term for any words sung; while *5215* denotes espec. a *relig.* metrical composition, and *5568* still more spec. a *Heb.* cantillation):— song.

5604. ὠδίν **ōdin**, *o-deen´;* akin to *3601;* a *pang* or *throe,* espec. of childbirth:— pain, sorrow, travail.

5605. ὠδίνω **ōdinō**, *o-dee´-no;* from *5604;* to *experience* the *pains* of parturition (lit. or fig.):— travail in (birth).

5606. ὦμος **ōmŏs**, *o´-mos;* perh. from the alt. of *5342;* the *shoulder* (as that on which burdens are *borne*):— shoulder.

5607. ὤν **ōn**, *oan;* incl. the fem.

οὖσα **ousa**, *oo´-sah;* and the neut.

ὄν **ŏn**, *on;* pres. part. of *1510; being:*— be, come, have.

5608. ὠνέομαι **ōnĕŏmai**, *o-neh´-om-ahee;* mid. voice from an appar. primary ὦνος **ōnŏs** (a *sum* or *price*); to *purchase,* (synonymous with the earlier *4092*):— buy.